# ANNOTATED COMPA..... LEGISLATION

# ANNOTATED COMPANIES LEGISLATION

## Third Edition

*Edited by*

PROFESSOR JOHN BIRDS

*Consultant Editors*

NIGEL BOARDMAN
SIR ROBERT HILDYARD
ROBERT MILES QC

*Contributors*

PROFESSOR JOHN BIRDS, NIGEL BOARDMAN, HERMANN BOEDDINGHAUS,
GEORGE BOMPAS QC, JOHN BRETTLER, OLIVER BROOMFIELD,
SARAH CARTER, ROBERT COOMBES, JONATHAN COTTON,
REBECCA COUSIN, JONATHAN CROW QC, DR JOHN DE LACY,
ANDREW DE MESTRE, PROFESSOR ALAN DIGNAM, SEAN GERAGHTY,
ROBERT GODDARD, PETER GRIFFITHS, CHRIS HALE, CHRISTOPHER HARRISON,
RICHARD HILL, ELEANOR HOLLAND, ADAM HOLLIMAN, DONALD LILLY,
PROFESSOR JOHN LOWRY, PROFESSOR IAIN MACNEIL, ANNA MARKHAM,
CHARLES MARQUAND, MIKE METCALF, PROFESSOR DAVID MILMAN,
TIRAN NERESSIAN, RICHARD O'BRIEN, ALEX OWEN, TOLEK PETCH,
JAN PUTNIS, DR ARAD REISBERG, CHRISTOPHER RILEY, IAN SHAWYER,
SHARIG ASIM SHIVJI, RICHARD SMITH, ALASTAIR TOMSON,
AND RACHEL WOODBURN

## OXFORD

UNIVERSITY PRESS

# OXFORD
## UNIVERSITY PRESS

Great Clarendon Street, Oxford, OX2 6DP,
United Kingdom

Oxford University Press is a department of the University of Oxford.
It furthers the University's objective of excellence in research, scholarship,
and education by publishing worldwide. Oxford is a registered trade mark of
Oxford University Press in the UK and in certain other countries

First Edition published in 2010

Third Edition published in 2013

Impression: 1

British Library Cataloguing in Publication Data

Data available

ISBN 978-0-19-967769-6

Printed in Italy on acid-free paper by L.E.G.O. S.p.A.

# FOREWORD TO THE FIRST EDITION

When the Companies Act 2006 came into force, I said in the foreword to the first edition of *Annotated Companies Acts*, that it should be welcomed as an authoritative and clear book on the new company law legislation which was to be unreservedly welcomed as being very much in the public interest. After four years that remains my view, and the four reasons which I gave it remain as valid now as they did then.

Those four reasons, which underlined the considerable expertise and enormous amount of work required to produce such a book, were as follows. First, the 2006 Act is concerned with a very important and technical area of the law, affecting most businesses, irrespective of size or complexity. Second, the Act is currently the longest statute on the books, with an unprecedented 47 Parts and 1,300 sections. Third, the Act is the product of over eight years' review and consultation, especially through the work of the Company Law Review launched by the Secretary of State for Trade and Industry in March 1998. Fourth, the Act consolidates almost all the statutory provisions on company law, as well as introducing some major, even revolutionary, changes, perhaps most importantly those relating to directors' duties in sections 170 to 178 and section 417, and changes to, and codification of, the rights of shareholders in sections 146 to 153, sections 260 to 269, and sections 324 to 340.

The 2006 Act is a very bulky 1,600 pages containing an amalgam of (a) unchanged provisions, on many of which there is often a welter of case law (not always consistent or easy to understand); (b) revised provisions, which often involve some subtle but important departures from the past; and (c) entirely novel provisions, many of which are controversial and bear the hallmarks of legislative compromise. The need for expert and user-friendly guidance on all these types of provision, and on other company law legislation, is acute and self-evident.

As I said in my 2006 foreword, it seemed to me that the first edition of this book met this need admirably. The format was sensible, in that it followed the sections of the 2006 Act, which itself is logically structured, and this minimized the risk of confusion for the reader. The style was as clear and engaging as the rather technical topic permitted. The effect of each legislative provision was explained as simply as possible, any similarities with, or differences from, a statutory predecessor were mentioned, and any significant relevant authorities were identified, and their effect simply summarized. Above all, the contents struck me as being as full and authoritative as one would expect from the large and impressive list of contributors, who are all highly renowned and experienced in this field. Very wisely, they included academics, accountants, solicitors, and barristers, so that the topic was covered from the perspective of the four main professions, who were primarily concerned with all aspects of company law.

The publishers have now decided that *Annotated Companies Acts* should be converted from the original looseleaf format into a paperback publication entitled *Annotated Companies Legislation*. It seems to me that this new edition retains all the benefits of the first edition which I described in my original foreword. In addition, the new edition has the advantage of including detailed section-by-section commentary and legislation from the looseleaf version in a portable format. The new and fully updated version of the text retains the excellent group of contributors who produced the original looseleaf edition.

As in the case of the original looseleaf edition, I would like to congratulate all the contributors for their impressive work, and I have no hesitation in recommending this book to anyone who needs clear and authoritative guidance or assistance on the law relating to companies in the United Kingdom, which has been so substantially overhauled in the Companies Act 2006.

David Neuberger

# PREFACE TO THIRD EDITION

In the past year there have been a number of changes to statutory company law and case law developments, the principal ones of which are mentioned below, but the wholly new feature of this edition is the inclusion of the provisions on prospectuses (and commentary thereon) from the Financial Services and Markets Act 2000. In this respect we have anticipated the changes made by the Financial Services Act 2012. The parts of the commentary on the companies legislation where reference is made to the 2000 Act also contain indications of the changes to be made when the 2012 Act is commenced in 2013. In contrast, it seemed a little premature to refer to the changes in the Enterprise and Regulatory Reform Bill 2012 to the provisions on the remuneration of directors in the Companies Act 2006; assuming that this Bill becomes an Act, the changes will still not be effective as quickly as those made by the Financial Services Act.

Legislative changes that have been taken into this edition include those made by the Companies and Limited Liability Partnerships (Accounts and Audit Exemptions and Change in Accounting Framework) Regulations 2012 and the Registrar of Companies (Fees) (Companies, Overseas Companies and Limited Liability Partnerships) Regulations 2012. There is reference to the anticipated changes concerning the registration of charges and to possible changes that might materialize from the Government's 'Red Tape Challenge' and the European Commission's review of the Takeovers Directive.

There has been a steady stream of case law covering, among others, sections in Parts 11 (derivative claims), 13 (resolutions and meetings) and 30 (unfair prejudice), and new cases referred to include *Templeton Insurance Ltd v Motorcare Warranties Ltd, Parry v Bartlett, Hughes v Weiss, Langley Ward Ltd v Trevor, Kleanthous v Paphitis, Schofield v Schofield, Re Uniq plc, Wheeler v Ross, Smith v Butler, Re Halcrow Holdings Ltd, Fulham FC v Richards, Re Coroin Ltd, Sikorski v Sikorski* and *Maidment v Attwood*.

The key aims of the book, namely to provide an accurate, authoritative and portable guide to the companies legislation, remain as identified in the preface to the first edition, which is reproduced below. Thanks again are due to all the contributors (especially those new to the team) and the staff at Oxford University Press for maintaining the quality of the book.

John Birds
October 2012

# PREFACE TO SECOND EDITION

This second edition incorporates legislative changes to the Companies Act 2006 and key new secondary legislation, together with updated commentary reflecting case law and other relevant developments. It is up to date to July 2011.

The most important statutory developments, which incidentally have added further to the length and complexity of the 2006 Act, are to be found in Parts 27 (Company Mergers and Divisions) and 42 (Statutory Auditors) reflecting the changes to the Act that implement EU changes). The publication of the UK Corporate Governance Code has required changes in Parts 10 and 15, in particular. Notable case law developments (including *Re Paycheck Services 3 Ltd, Revenue and Customs Commissioners v Holland, R (on the application of People & Planet) v HM Treasury* and *Sinclair Investments (UK) Ltd v Versailles Trading Finance Ltd*) are covered in Part 10, and Part 30 (the unfair prejudice remedy) also is updated to reflect recent case law. The developing jurisprudence of the Company Names Tribunal is covered in Part 5.

The key aims of the book, namely to provide an accurate, authoritative and portable guide to the companies legislation, remain as stated in the preface to the first edition, which is reproduced above. Thanks again are due to the contributors and the staff at Oxford University Press for maintaining the extremely high quality of the work.

John Birds
November 2011

# PREFACE TO FIRST EDITION

The looseleaf predecessor to this work was originally conceived when it became clear, in 2005, that the Government would introduce a very important Bill amending the Companies Act 1985 and the legislation itself amending that Act. As is now well-known, that Bill turned into a consolidation of virtually the whole of the legislation governing companies and it is fair to say that the Companies Act 2006 is the ultimate product of the most far-reaching review of company law since the registered company form was first made available in 1844.

Once virtually the whole Act was completely implemented by 1 October 2009, it seemed sensible to produce an annotated version in one portable volume that can be fully updated annually. Of course, the Act by itself, notwithstanding that it was the largest single piece of legislation ever enacted by the UK Parliament, does not tell the full story. It has been amended since enactment, both to correct some drafting errors and in order to implement the changes that have been needed, often in order to comply with European requirements, but also to reflect changing commercial considerations. It has also been supplemented by an extremely large volume of secondary legislation fleshing out a number of provisions of the Act where the detail is sparse. It is a notable feature of the 2006 Act that it leaves much more detail to secondary legislation than earlier Companies Acts. The relevant Orders and Regulations are reproduced in this work and cross-referred to as appropriate in the annotations. One of the most important practical pieces of secondary legislation, that containing the model forms of Articles of Association, is fully annotated and we retain full coverage of Table A to both the 1948 and 1985 Companies Acts, as there seems little doubt that many companies will continue to have articles incorporating or based on those Tables.

It was more than 10 years from the start of the review of company law in 1998 (under the title Modern Company Law for a Competitive Economy) to final implementation. Whether the end product really meets some of the key aims of the review, which were repeatedly emphasized by Government, may be open to some doubt. There is certainly some deregulation, especially so far as private companies are concerned, and there are clear attempts to enhance shareholder engagement in larger companies. But whether the deregulatory measures mean a great deal to many smaller companies is perhaps doubtful and it is not at all clear that many shareholders in larger companies actually want greater involvement. More fundamentally, whether another key aim, namely that of simplification, can really be said to have resulted is even more doubtful. While it is certainly true that the 2006 Act is drafted in a much clearer manner than the Acts it replaces or will replace, the very size and complexity already mentioned militate strongly against the achievement of this aim.

As yet there has been relatively little case law exploring the Parts of the Act that were really new. Of these Parts, perhaps the most controversial, when the legislation was going through Parliament, were the provisions in Part 10 stating in statutory form the duties of company directors and those in Part 11 putting the derivative claim on a statutory basis. Fears that these would lead to problems and open the floodgates to unmeritorious claims by minority shareholders have, so far at least, proved unfounded.

The production of this work has involved a massive effort by a team of dedicated contributors from the profession and academia and, especially, by the colleagues at Oxford University Press who have had to work to incredibly tight deadlines. Thanks are due to all these people, as well as to the consultant editors, whose wise counsel, based on unparalleled experience and expertise, has proved invaluable.

John Birds

# CONTENTS

## 1 GENERAL INTRODUCTORY PROVISIONS

## 2 COMPANY FORMATION

## 3 A COMPANY'S CONSTITUTION

### CHAPTER 1 INTRODUCTORY

### CHAPTER 2 ARTICLES OF ASSOCIATION

CHAPTER 4 TRANSACTIONS WITH DIRECTORS REQUIRING
APPROVAL OF MEMBERS

*Service contracts*

*Substantial property transactions*

*Loans, quasi-loans and credit transactions*

*Payments for loss of office*

*Supplementary*

## 11 DERIVATIVE CLAIMS AND PROCEEDINGS BY MEMBERS

### CHAPTER 1 DERIVATIVE CLAIMS IN ENGLAND AND WALES OR NORTHERN IRELAND

### CHAPTER 2 DERIVATIVE PROCEEDINGS IN SCOTLAND

## 12 COMPANY SECRETARIES

*Private companies*

*Public companies*

*Provisions applying to private companies with a secretary and to public companies*

## 13 RESOLUTIONS AND MEETINGS

### CHAPTER 1 GENERAL PROVISIONS ABOUT RESOLUTIONS

### CHAPTER 4 PUBLIC COMPANIES [AND TRADED COMPANIES]: ADDITIONAL REQUIREMENTS FOR AGMs

### CHAPTER 5 ADDITIONAL REQUIREMENTS FOR QUOTED COMPANIES [AND TRADED COMPANIES]

*Website publication of poll results*

CHAPTER 10 FILING OF ACCOUNTS AND REPORTS

*Duty to file accounts and reports*

*Filing obligations of different descriptions of company*

*Requirements where abbreviated accounts delivered*

*Failure to file accounts and reports*

CHAPTER 11 REVISION OF DEFECTIVE ACCOUNTS AND REPORTS

*Voluntary revision*

*Secretary of State's notice*

*Application to court*

*Power of authorised person to require documents etc*

CHAPTER 12 SUPPLEMENTARY PROVISIONS

*Liability for false or misleading statements in reports*

*Accounting and reporting standards*

*Companies qualifying as medium-sized*

# 16  AUDIT

### CHAPTER 1   REQUIREMENT FOR AUDITED ACCOUNTS

*Requirement for audited accounts*

*Exemption from audit: small companies*

*Exemption from audit: dormant companies*

*Companies subject to public sector audit*

*General power of amendment by regulations*

### CHAPTER 2   APPOINTMENT OF AUDITORS

*Private companies*

*Public companies*

*General provisions*

CHAPTER 5 QUOTED COMPANIES: RIGHT OF MEMBERS
TO RAISE AUDIT CONCERNS AT ACCOUNTS MEETING

CHAPTER 6 AUDITORS' LIABILITY

*Voidness of provisions protecting auditors from liability*

*Indemnity for costs of defending proceedings*

*Liability limitation agreements*

## 17   A COMPANY'S SHARE CAPITAL

CHAPTER 1 SHARES AND SHARE CAPITAL OF A COMPANY

*Shares*

*Share capital*

CHAPTER 2 ALLOTMENT OF SHARES: GENERAL PROVISIONS

*Power of directors to allot shares*

*Prohibition of commissions, discounts and allowances*

*Registration of allotment*

*Return of allotment*

CHAPTER 9 CLASSES OF SHARE AND CLASS RIGHTS

CHAPTER 10 REDUCTION OF SHARE CAPITAL

## 20 PRIVATE AND PUBLIC COMPANIES

CHAPTER 1 PROHIBITION OF PUBLIC OFFERS
BY PRIVATE COMPANIES

### Introduction

CHAPTER 2 MINIMUM SHARE CAPITAL
REQUIREMENT FOR PUBLIC COMPANIES

## 21 CERTIFICATION AND TRANSFER OF SECURITIES

CHAPTER 1 CERTIFICATION AND TRANSFER OF SECURITIES: GENERAL

### Share certificates

### Issue of certificates etc on allotment

### Transfer of securities

### Issue of certificates etc on transfer

### Issue of certificates etc on allotment or transfer to financial institution

### Share warrants

### Supplementary provisions

CHAPTER 2 EVIDENCING AND TRANSFER OF TITLE
TO SECURITIES WITHOUT WRITTEN INSTRUMENT

## 22 INFORMATION ABOUT INTERESTS
## IN A COMPANY'S SHARES

## 23 DISTRIBUTIONS

### CHAPTER 1 RESTRICTIONS ON WHEN DISTRIBUTIONS MAY BE MADE

#### *Introductory*

#### *General rules*

#### *Distributions by investment companies*

### CHAPTER 2 JUSTIFICATION OF DISTRIBUTION BY REFERENCE TO ACCOUNTS

#### *Justification of distribution by reference to accounts*

#### *Requirements applicable in relation to relevant accounts*

#### *Application of provisions to successive distributions etc*

### CHAPTER 3 SUPPLEMENTARY PROVISIONS

#### *Accounting matters*

#### *Distributions in kind*

*Consequences of unlawful distribution*

*Other matters*

## 24  A COMPANY'S ANNUAL RETURN

## 25  COMPANY CHARGES

### CHAPTER 1 COMPANIES REGISTERED IN ENGLAND AND WALES OR IN NORTHERN IRELAND

*Requirement to register company charges*

*Special rules about debentures*

*Charges in other jurisdictions*

*Orders charging land: Northern Ireland*

*The register of charges*

*Avoidance of certain charges*

## 27  MERGERS AND DIVISIONS OF PUBLIC COMPANIES

## Companies Act 1985

### PART XIV INVESTIGATION OF COMPANIES AND THEIR AFFAIRS; REQUISITION OF DOCUMENTS

#### Appointment and functions of inspectors

#### Powers of Secretary of State to give directions to inspectors

#### Resignation, removal and replacement of inspectors

#### Power to obtain information from former inspectors etc

#### Requisition and seizure of books and papers

### PART XV ORDERS IMPOSING RESTRICTIONS ON SHARES (SECTIONS 210, 216, 445)

## 40  COMPANY DIRECTORS: FOREIGN DISQUALIFICATION ETC

### *Introductory*

### *Power to disqualify*

### *Power to make persons liable for company's debts*

### *Power to require statements to be sent to the registrar of companies*

## 41  BUSINESS NAMES
### CHAPTER 1 RESTRICTED OR PROHIBITED NAMES

### *Introductory*

### *Sensitive words or expressions*

### *Misleading names*

### *Supplementary*

### CHAPTER 2 DISCLOSURE REQUIRED IN CASE OF INDIVIDUAL OR PARTNERSHIP

### *Introductory*

Chapter 6 Supplementary and General

# 52 STATUTORY INSTRUMENTS

## Financial Services and Markets Act 2000

### 53 INTRODUCTORY NOTE
#### PART VI OFFICIAL LISTING

*Compensation for false or misleading statements etc*

*Penalties*

*Competition*

*Miscellaneous*

*Interpretative provisions*

# EDITORIAL TEAM

## Editorial board

### Professor John Birds (General Editor)

Emeritus Professor in the School of Law, University of Manchester and Honorary Professor in the School of Law, University of Sheffield. He was previously Professor of Commercial Law at the Universities of Manchester and Sheffield (and Head of Department of Law at the latter). He has published many books, articles, and book chapters on company law, including *Boyle & Birds; Company Law Edn 8* (Jordans, 2011), and is editor of twelve chapters of *Gore-Browne on Companies* (Jordans). John Birds has also written books and edited chapters on insurance law, and held editorial positions in leading company and commercial law journals. He is a Fellow of the Royal Society of Arts, was a member of the Law Panel for the Research Assessment Exercise 2001, and a member of the Law Sub-Panel for the 2008 Exercise. In 2003–04 he was President of the Society of Legal Scholars.

### Nigel Boardman (Consultant Editor)

A partner at Slaughter and May since 1982, he has a broad practice including domestic and international corporate finance, mergers and acquisitions, joint ventures, IPOs, demergers, private acquisitions and disposals, private equity, public takeovers, issues of compliance and corporate governance and insolvency, restructurings, and investigations. He is a contributor to the *Prospectus for the Public Offering of Securities in Europe* and *The European Company*.

### Malcolm Davis-White QC (Consultant Editor in respect of Chapter 10)

Called to the Bar in 1984 and took silk in 2003. He was Junior Counsel to the Crown (Chancery) (The Attorney General's A Panel) between 1994 and 2003. His practice is mainly in the fields of company law, insolvency, financial services, regulatory work, and commercial disputes. Malcolm Davis-White has co-authored *Directors' Disqualification & Insolvency Restrictions 3rd Edn* (Sweet and Maxwell, 2010) and *Kerr & Hunter on Receivers and Administrators 19th Edn* (Sweet & Maxwell, 2010) He is a contributor to the companies volumes of *Atkin's Court Forms* (Butterworths). He has been Chairman of the Chancery Bar Association since 2010 and is a Bencher of Lincoln's Inn.

### Sir Robert Hildyard (Consultant Editor)

One of Her Majesty's Justices of the High Court Judge, Chancery Division. Previously a barrister at 4 Stone Buildings, specializing in company and commercial law. Called to the Bar in 1977, he was junior counsel to the Crown (Chancery) from 1992 until taking silk in 1994. He was a member of the Financial Reporting Review Panel from 2002 to 2008, Attorney General to the Duchy of Lancaster from 2006 to 2011, and is a Bencher of Lincoln's Inn. He was a member of the Company Law Review Working Group advising the Department of Trade and Industry on the review of company law which led to the Companies Act 2006.

### Robert Miles QC (Consultant Editor)

Called to the Bar in 1987 and took silk in 2002. A barrister at 4 Stone Buildings, he is acknowledged as a leading company, insolvency, and commercial practitioner, and has been instructed in many of the leading corporate cases over the past two decades. Many of his cases involve cross-border elements, and he has also appeared as counsel before foreign courts and international arbitration.

# Contributors

*Barrister contributors (4 Stone Buildings)*

### Hermann Boeddinghaus (Contributed to Chapter 10)

Called to the Bar in 1996 as a Kennedy Scholar of Lincoln's Inn. He specializes in commercial litigation and advisory work, with a particular emphasis on all aspects of company law.

### George Bompas QC (Contributed to Chapters 17 and 18)

George Bompas QC has many years' experience in company law. He is the Head of Chambers at 4 Stone Buildings. He was called to the Bar in 1975 and took silk in 1994. He has been called to the Bar of the BVI and, for specific cases, the Bar of Trinidad and Tobago. He is a Deputy High Court Judge and a Bencher of Lincoln's Inn.

### Jonathan Brettler (Contributed to Chapter 10)

Called to the Bar in 1988, specializing in company law (litigation, advisory, schemes of arrangement), insolvency law, directors' disqualification proceedings, oil & gas joint ventures, and asset recovery. He is a member of the Chancery Bar Association, the Commercial Bar Association, and has been called to the Bar of the Isle of Man in specific cases.

### Jonathan Crow QC (Contributed to Chapter 35)

Specialized in company/commercial litigation as a junior (1981–98). As First Treasury Counsel, Chancery (1998–2006), his practice broadened to include all aspects of public law, especially human rights and freedom of information. Since taking silk in 2006, he has combined these two elements to develop a cross-over practice embracing both company/commercial litigation and public law. He is also a Deputy High Court Judge, Attorney General to HRH the Prince of Wales, a Court of Appeal Judge in Guernsey and Jersey, and a Bencher of Lincoln's Inn.

### Andrew de Mestre (Contributed to Chapters 12, 13, 37, and 48)

Specialist in commercial, company, and insolvency law with particular emphasis on civil fraud, asset recovery, proceedings under the Insolvency Act 1986, directors' duties, unfair prejudice petitions, and other shareholder disputes. He was called to the Bar in 1998.

### Peter Griffiths (Contributed to Chapter 35)

Called to the Bar in 1977. He specializes in company law, particularly shareholder disputes, and has advised on cases in Ghana, the Isle of Man, Malaysia, and Cyprus. He is a contributor to various publications, including *Atkin's Court Forms* (Butterworths), *Encyclopaedia of Forms & Precedents* (Butterworths) and *Butterworths Practical Insolvency*.

### Christopher Harrison (Contributed to Chapters 11, 13, and 30)

In practice since 1990, his work is largely City-based, in the areas of company and commercial law, and covers both advisory work and litigation. He has been a member of the Attorney General's panel of barristers acting for the government in company and insolvency matters and has acted as an inspector on an insider-dealing inquiry. Christopher Harrison's work frequently has an international element and he has worked with lawyers in several jurisdictions, including the US, Luxembourg, Saudi Arabia, and the Cayman Islands.

### Richard Hill (Contributed to Chapters 13 and 44)

Called to the Bar in 1993, Richard specializes in company law, corporate insolvency, and commercial disputes. He is on the Attorney General's A Panel for government instructions.

### Adam Holliman (Contributed to Chapters 17, 18, and 35)

Specialist in litigation and giving advice in the fields of company law, corporate fraud, insolvency, shareholder disputes, and commercial litigation. He was called to the Bar in 2005.

### Charles Marquand (Contributed to Chapter 20)

Called to the Bar in 1987, practising in company law and financial services law. He was previously a legal adviser at HM Treasury, where he advised in those areas.

### Tiran Nersessian (Contributed to Chapter 35)

Called to the Bar in 2002, he specializes in advice and litigation in the fields of company law, insolvency, corporate fraud, and public law. He has been on the Attorney General's Panel for government instructions since 2006 and is a contributor to *Atkin's Court Forms on 'Companies' (Volume 8)* (Butterworths).

**Sharif Asim Shivji (Contributed to Chapter 35)**

Specialist in company, insolvency, and financial services law. Prior to coming to the Bar, Sharif worked as a derivatives trader in London and Hong Kong. Following his call to the Bar in 2001, he has acted in matters involving many different aspects of the Companies Act 1985 and the Company Directors Disqualification Act 1986; from financial assistance to shareholder disputes. He is a contributor to *Atkin's Court Forms on 'Companies–Insolvency'* (Butterworths) and to *Tolley's Insolvency Law and Practice*.

**Alastair Tomson (Contributed to Chapter 10)**

Alastair Tomson has a litigation-focused practice encompassing disputes relating to companies, insolvency (both personal and corporate), civil fraud, asset recovery and financial services. He also gives advice in these areas. Alastair's practice has an international flavour, and he has worked for clients in Continental Europe, Africa, and offshore jurisdictions.

## *Practitioner and academic contributors*

**Professor John Birds (Contributed to Chapters 1, 8, 9, 17, 18, and 21)**

See profile above.

**Nigel Boardman (Contributed to Chapter 10)**

See profile above.

**Jonathan Cotton (Contributed to Chapter 26)**

Dispute Resolution Partner at Slaughter and May, he advises on a broad range of commercial disputes in litigation and arbitration for the firm's clients and his practice includes schemes of arrangement and other Companies Court proceedings.

**Rebecca Cousin (Contributed to Chapter 10)**

A corporate partner at Slaughter and May, her corporate and corporate finance practice consists principally of advising on domestic and international corporate finance and M&A transactions, including public takeovers, private acquisitions and disposals, joint ventures, equity issues, and restructurings. Rebecca Cousin also advises generally on day-to-day company law and corporate governance matters.

**Dr John de Lacy (Contributed to Chapters 19 and 25)**

Senior Lecturer in Law at Sheffield University. He has provided advice and opinions, as well as lecturing and writing extensively on company law matters.

**Professor Alan Dignam (Contributed to Chapters 8, 22, and 48)**

Professor of Corporate law at the School of Law, Queen Mary, University of London. He has written widely in domestic and international law journals on company and commercial law matters, and is the co-author with Professor John Lowry of *Company Law* (Oxford University Press, 2006) and with David Allen of *Company Law and the Human Rights Act* (Butterworths, 2000). Alan Digman is an advisor to Amnesty International's Business Group on their corporate accountability campaign, the Convenor of the Company Law section of the Society of Legal Scholars, and a member of the International Advisory Committee to the South African Department of Trade and Industry Company Law Review.

**Sean Geraghty (Contributed to Chapter 27)**

A partner in Dechert's Corporate and Securities Group. He has acted for major UK and overseas-based corporate clients and financial institutions on substantial transactions, including public takeovers, mergers and acquisitions, IPOs, share offerings, joint ventures and general corporate matters. Sean Geraghty is a regular speaker at conferences on corporate law and corporate finance issues.

**Robert Goddard (Contributed to Chapters 4 and 14)**

A senior lecturer in law at Aston University, Robert has degrees in accountancy and law and publishes widely in academic and professional journals on company law and taxation matters. He teaches company law, corporate governance, taxation, capital markets law and financial regulation.

**Chris Hale (Contributed to Chapters 5, 6, and 7)**

A partner at Travers Smith and head of the firm's Corporate Department, for the past 16 years he has specialized in UK and international buyout work, acting for both institutional investors and management teams on investments and divestments, as well as private equity-backed companies on mergers and acquisitions and other corporate matters. Chris Hale writes and lectures regularly on company law and private equity in particular.

**Professor David Kershaw (Contributed to Chapters 15, 16, 24, and 42)**

Professor in the Law Department at the London School of Economics and Political Science, where he teaches the law of business associations, corporate governance, and mergers and acquisitions. A Senior Researcher in the LSE's Financial Markets Group, he qualified as a Solicitor with Herbert Smith and has practised corporate law with Wolf Theiss & Partners, Vienna and Shearman & Sterling in New York and London. David researches in the areas of corporate governance, accounting regulation, and takeover regulation.

**Professor John Lowry (Contributed to Chapter 10)**

Joined the Faculty of Laws at University College London in 2004, having moved from the Centre for Commercial Law Studies at Queen Mary London. He has written widely in domestic and international journals on directors' fiduciary obligations, shareholder remedies and insurance law. John Lowry is a contributing editor to *Gore-Browne on Companies* (Jordans), Company Law section editor for the *Journal of Business Law*, and Case Review editor for *International Corporate Rescue*. Current research interests include directors' fiduciary obligations, shareholder remedies and the duty of good faith in insurance law.

**Professor Iain MacNeil (Contributed to Chapters 11, 17, 21, 23, 25, 49, and 50)**

Alexander Stone Professor of Commercial Law at the University of Glasgow. His teaching and research interests are primarily in the fields of company law, financial markets and related aspects of contract law. Before entering the academic world he worked for eight years as an investment analyst in the City of London. Iain has published widely on corporate governance and financial regulation.

**Mike Metcalf (Contributed to Chapters 15 and 16)**

Chartered Accountant and Partner in KPMG LLP, he joined KPMG in 1987 and since 1994 has worked in the firm's Department of Professional Practice, where he covers a range of technical accounting issues and associated company law matters. During 2000–2002 Mike was seconded to the Department of Trade and Industry, where he worked on the accounting and capital maintenance aspects of the Company Law Review. He chairs the Company Law Committee of the Institute of Chartered Accountants in England and Wales and is a member of the joint committee of that Institute and of the Institute of Chartered Accountants of Scotland that is responsible for guidance on the accounting determination of realized profits.

**Professor David Milman (Contributed to Chapters 11, 29, 30, 31, 32, 34, 36–39, 44, and 48)**

Professor of Law at Lancaster University Centre for Law and Business, appointed a Fellow of the Royal Society of Arts in 1996, and an Honorary Member of the Insolvency Lawyers Association, whose Academic Advisory Group he chairs. David Milman has interests in corporate Law and insolvency Law. He is Joint General Editor of *Insolvency Intelligence* and Consultant Editor of *Sweet and Maxwell's Company Law Newsletter*.

**Richard O'Brien (Contributed to Chapter 27)**

Assistant Solicitor in Dechert's Corporate and Securities Group, he has acted for clients on a range of mergers and acquisitions, corporate reorganizations, private equity investments, joint ventures, and general corporate and securities matters for both listed and private companies.

**Alex Owen (Contributed to Chapters 15 and 16)**

Chartered Accountant and Senior Manager at KPMG LLP, he joined KPMG in 1999 after qualifying at a smaller firm of chartered accountants. He has worked in the firm's Audit Practice, in the Property Sector; and he has worked in the firm's Department of Professional Practice since 2004, advising on technical accounting issues and associated company law matters.

**Tolek Petch (Contributed to Chapters 28 and 48)**

Qualified at Slaughter and May in 1995. From 1996 to 1999 he taught competition law at Oxford University and from 1997–99 was a tutor at Wadham College, Oxford. In 1999 he returned to private practice, where he advises on financial regulation, e-commerce, insolvency, private international law, and banking law. His clients include banks, securities dealers, firms involved in clearing and settlement, and a wide range of other financial institutions. He has published in the fields of financial law, competition law, and private international law.

**Jan Putnis (Contributed to Chapter 28)**

Solicitor and partner at Slaughter and May, his corporate and commercial work comprises a broad range of advice on acquisitions and disposals, joint ventures and reorganizations for financial institutions and corporate clients, principally with a cross-border emphasis and often focussing on complex regulatory matters which affect and determine the structure of international transactions. Jan Putnis also acts for a broad range of financial institutions generally on regulatory matters and investigations.

### Dr Arad Reisberg (Contributed to Chapters 10, 20, and 33)

Reader in Corporate and Financial Law and Vice Dean For Research at the Faculty of Laws, University College London. He is also the Director of the UCL Centre for Commercial Law and Co-Director of the UCL Centre for Law and Economics. He is an Academic Member of ECGI (European Corporate Governance Institute), a co-editor of *Pettet's Company Law*, sits on the Editorial Boards of the Journal *International Corporate Rescue* and the *Journal of Corporate Ownership and Control*, and is author of the first book providing a detailed and theoretical explanation of the law governing derivative actions: *Derivative Actions and Corporate Governance* (Oxford University Press, 2007).

### Christopher Riley (Contributed to Chapters 2, 3, and 51)

Qualified as a solicitor in 1985 and worked in the corporate law department of a medium-sized commercial practice before returning to academic life. A reader in company law at Durham University since 2002, his main teaching areas include company law, and UK and comparative corporate governance, subjects on which he has written and lectured widely, both in the UK and abroad. Recent research has included a study into the governance of chartered corporations, funded by the British Academy, and a forthcoming monograph on the governance of not-for-profit companies.

### Ian Shawyer (Contributed to Chapter 51)

Partner in Travers Smith's Corporate Department since 2007, he advises on a wide range of general corporate matters but, in particular, specializes in UK and international private equity (acting for management, institutional investors and investee companies) and general mergers and acquisitions.

### Rachel Woodburn (Contributed to Chapters 5, 6, and 7)

Head of Professional Support at Travers Smith, having previously been a Partner in the Company Department, specializing in private mergers and acquisitions and private equity transactions. As Head of Professional Support she now coordinates the knowhow and training requirements across the firm, as well as continuing to keep the Company Department and its clients up to date on company law matters.

# TABLE OF CASES

# TABLE OF STATUTES

# TABLE OF STATUTORY INSTRUMENTS

# COMPANIES ACT 2006
## TABLE OF ORIGINS

*Notes*

1. This table shows the origin of the company law provisions of the Companies Act 2006 by reference to the enactments in force on the date that Act received Royal Assent (subject to the note to the origins for Part 28). The Act received Royal Assent on 8 November 2006. Where an enactment had been amended before that date, the reference is to the text at that date; the table does not show the source of such amendments.

2. The origin of a provision of the Companies Act 2006 in the Companies (Northern Ireland) Order 1986 is acknowledged where it makes significantly different provision in relation to Northern Ireland than in relation to England and Wales or, as the case may be, Great Britain.

3. In the table—

'1985' means the Companies Act 1985 (c 6);
'IA 1986' means the Insolvency Act 1986 (c 45);
'1986' means the Companies (Northern Ireland) Order 1986 (SI 1096/1032 (NI 6));
'ICTA' means the Income and Corporation Taxes Act 1988 (c 1);
'1989' means the Companies Act 1989 (c 40).

4. The entry 'drafting' indicates a new provision of a mechanical or editorial nature — for example, a provision defining an expression to avoid repetition or indicating where other relevant provisions are to be found.

5. A reference followed by '(changed)' means that the provision referred to has been re-enacted with one or more changes. In general, a change is noted only in the primary context affected and not in every provision where a consequential change results. The table does not show changes in the maximum penalties for offences.

6. The entry 'new' indicates a provision which has no predecessor in the repealed legislation or which is fundamentally different from its predecessor.

7. The entries in the table are intended only as a general indication of what has changed and what is new. They should not be read as expressing any view as to the application or otherwise of any provision relating to enactments repealed and re-enacted.

| Section of 2006 Act | Origin |
| --- | --- |
| PART 1  GENERAL INTRODUCTORY PROVISIONS | |
| 1(1) | 1985 s 735(1)(a) and (b) |
| (2) and (3) | drafting |
| 2(1) and (2) | 1985 s 744 (changed) |
| 3(1) to (4) | 1985 s 1(2) |
| 4(1) and (2) | 1985 s 1(3) |
| (3) | 1985 s 1(3), 1986 art 12(3) |
| (4) | drafting |
| 5(1) | 1985 s 1(4) |
| (2) | 1984 s 1(4), 1986 art 12(4) |
| (3) | 1985 s 15(2) |
| 6(1) and (2) | drafting |
| PART 2 COMPANY FORMATION | |
| 7(1) and (2) | 1985 s 1(1) (changed) |
| 8(1) | new |
| (2) | 1985 s 3(1) |
| 9(1) | 1985 s 10(1) (changed) |
| (2) | 1985 s 2(1)(a) and (b), (2) and (3) (changed) |
| (3) | 1985 s 10(4) |
| (4) | new |
| (5) | 1985 s 10(1) and (6) |
| (6) | 1985 s 10(1) |

| Section of 2006 Act | Origin |
| --- | --- |
| 10(1) to (5) | new |
| 11(1) | drafting |
| (2) | new |
| (3) | 1985 s 2(4) (changed) |
| 12(1) | 1985 s 10(2) (changed) |
| (2) | new |
| (3), first sentence | 1985 s 10(3) |
| (3), second sentence | new |
| 13(1) and (2) | 1985 s 12(3) and (3A) (changed) |
| 14 | 1985 s 12(1) and (2) |
| 15(1) | 1985 s 13(1) |
| (2) | new |
| (3) | 1985 s 13(2) |
| (4) | 1985 s 13(7)(a) |
| 16(1) | drafting |
| (2) | 1985 s 13(3) (changed) |
| (3) | 1984 s 13(4) |
| (4) | new |
| (5) | new |
| (6) | 1985 s 13(5) |
| PART 3 A COMPANY'S CONSTITUTION | |
| **Chapter 1  Introductory** | |
| 17 | new |

| Section of 2006 Act | Origin |
|---|---|
| **Chapter 2  Articles of association** | |
| 18(1) | new |
| (2) | 1985 s 7(1) (changed) |
| (3) | 1985 s 7(3) (changed) |
| (4) | 1985 s 744 |
| 19(1) to (3) | 1985 s 8(1) and (4) (changed) |
| (4) | 1985 s 8(3) |
| (5) | 1985 s 8(5) |
| 20(1) and (2) | 1985 s 8(2) (changed) |
| 21(1) | 1985 s 9(1) |
| (2) and (3) | drafting |
| 22(1) to (3) | new |
| 23(1) and (2) | new |
| 24(1) to (4) | new |
| 25(1) | 1985 s 16(1) |
| (2) | 1985 s 16(2) |
| 26(1) | 1985 s 18(2) (changed) |
| (2) | new |
| (3) and (4) | 1985 s 18(3) and Sch 24 |
| 27(1) to (5) | new |
| 28(1) to (3) | new |
| **Chapter 3  Resolutions and agreements affecting a company's constitution** | |
| 29(1) | 1985 s 380(4) (changed) |
| (2) | 1985 s 380(4A) |
| 30(1) | 1985 s 380(1) |
| (2) and (3) | 1985 s 380(5) and Sch 24 |
| (4) | 1985 s 380(7) |
| **Chapter 4  Miscellaneous and supplementary provisions** | |
| 31(1) to (5) | new |
| 32(1) | 1985 s 19(1) (changed) |
| (2) | new |
| (3) and (4) | 1985 s 19(2) (changed) and Sch 24 |
| 33(1) | 1985 s 14(1) (changed) |
| (2) | 1985 s 14(2) (changed) |
| 34(1) | drafting |
| (2) | 1985 s 18(1) (changed) |
| (3) | 1985 s 18(2) (changed) |
| (4) | new |
| (5) and (6) | 1985 s 18(3) and Sch 24 |
| 35(1) to (5) | new |
| 36(1) and (2) | 1985 s 380(2) (changed) |
| (3) and (4) | 1985 s 380(6) (changed) and Sch 24 |
| (5) | 1985 s 380(7) |
| 37 | 1985 s 15(1) |
| 38 | Companies (Single Member Private Limited Companies) Regulations 1992 (SI 1992/1699) (changed) |
| **PART 4 A COMPANY'S CAPACITY AND RELATED MATTERS** | |
| 39(1) | 1985 s 35(1) (changed) |
| (2) | 1985 s 35(4) |
| 40(1) | 1985 s 35A(1) |
| (2) | 1985 s 35A(2) and 35B |
| (3) | 1985 s 35A(3) |
| (4) | 1985 s 35A(4) |
| (5) | 1985 s 35A(5) |
| (6) | 1985 s 35A(6) |
| 41(1) | 1985 s 322A(1) and (4) |
| (2) | 1985 s 322A(1) and (2) |

| Section of 2006 Act | Origin |
|---|---|
| (3) | 1985 s 322A(3) |
| (4) | 1985 s 322A(5) |
| (5) | 1985 s 322A(6) |
| (6) | 1985 s 322A(7) |
| (7) | 1985 s 322A(8) |
| 42(1) | Charities Act 1993 s 65(1) |
| (2) | Charities Act 1993 s 65(2) |
| (3) | Charities Act 1993 s 65(3) |
| (4) | Charities Act 1993 s 65(4) |
| (5) | drafting |
| 43(1) and (2) | 1985 s 36 |
| 44(1) | 1985 s 36A(1) to (3) |
| (2)(a), (3) and (4) | 1985 s 36A(4) |
| (2)(b) | new |
| (5) | 1985 s 36A(6) (changed) |
| (6) | 1985 s 36A(4A) |
| (7) | 1985 s 36A(8) |
| (8) | 1985 s 36A(7) |
| 45(1) | 1985 s 36A(3) |
| (2) | 1985 s 350(1) |
| (3) | 1985 s 350(1) (changed) |
| (4) and (5) | 1985 s 350(2) and Sch 24 |
| (6) | drafting |
| 46(1) | 1985 s 36AA(1) |
| (2) | 1985 s 36AA(2) |
| 47(1) | 1985 s 38(1) (changed) and (3) |
| (2) | 1985 s 38(2) (changed) |
| 48(1) | Requirements of Writing (Scotland) Act 1995 (c 7) s 15(3) |
| (2) | 1985 s 36B(1) |
| (3) | 1985 s 36B(2) |
| 49(1) | 1985 s 39(1) (changed) |
| (2) | 1985 s 39(1) |
| (3) | 1985 s 39(2) and (2A) |
| (4) | 1985 s 39(3) |
| (5) | 1985 s 39(4) |
| (6) | 1985 s 39(5) |
| 50(1) and (2) | 1985 s 40(1) |
| 51(1) | 1985 s 36C(1) |
| (2) | 1985 s 36C(2) |
| 52 | 1985 s 37 |
| **PART 5 A COMPANY'S NAME** | |
| **Chapter 1  General requirements** | |
| 53 | 1985 s 26(1)(d) and (e) |
| 54(1) to (3) | 1985 s 26(2)(a) and second sentence (changed) |
| 55(1) | 1985 s 26(2)(b) and 29(1)(a) |
| (2) | 1985 s 29(6) |
| 56(1) | 1985 s 29(1)(b) (changed) |
| (2) | 1985 s 29(2) |
| (3) and (4) | 1985 s 29(3) (changed) |
| (5) | drafting |
| 57(1) to (5) | new |
| **Chapter 2  Indications of company type or legal form** | |
| 58(1) | 1985 s 25(1) and 27(4)(b) |

| Section of 2006 Act | Origin |
|---|---|
| (2) | 1985 s 25(1) and 27(4)(d) |
| (3) | drafting |
| 59(1) | 1985 s 25(2) (opening words) and 27(4)(a) |
| (2) | 1985 s 25(2)(b) and 27(4)(c) |
| (3) | 1985 s 25(2)(a) |
| (4) | drafting |
| 60(1)(a) and (b) | new |
| (1)(c) | drafting |
| (2) | 1985 s 30(5B) |
| (3) | 1985 s 30(4) |
| (4) | new |
| 61(1) | 1985 s 30(2), 1986 art 40(2) |
| (2) to (4) | 1985 s 30(2) and (3) (changed) |
| 62(1) to (3) | 1985 s 30(2) and (3) (changed) |
| 63(1) | 1985 s 31(1) |
| (2) and (3) | 1985 s 31(5) and Sch 24 |
| (4) and (5) | new |
| 64(1) to (3) | 1985 s 31(2) first sentence |
| (4) | 1985 s 31(2) second sentence (changed) |
| (5) and (6) | 1985 s 31(6) and Sch 24 |
| (7) | 1985 s 31(3) |
| 65(1) to (5) | 1985 s 26(1)(a), (b), (bb) and (bbb) (changed) |

**Chapter 3 Similarity to other names**

| Section of 2006 Act | Origin |
|---|---|
| 66(1) | 1985 s 26(1)(c) |
| (2) and (3) | 1985 s 26(3) (changed) |
| (4) to (6) | new |
| 67(1) | 1985 s 28(2) |
| (2) to (6) | new |
| 68(1) | drafting |
| (2) | 1985 s 28(2) full out |
| (3) | 1985 s 28(4) |
| (4) | 1985 s 28(2) full out and (4) |
| (5) and (6) | 1985 s 28(5) and Sch 24 |
| 69(1) to (7) | new |
| 70(1) to (6) | new |
| 71(1) to (4) | new |
| 72(1) and (2) | new |
| 73(1) to (6) | new |
| 74(1) to (5) | new |

**Chapter 4 Other powers of the Secretary of State**

| Section of 2006 Act | Origin |
|---|---|
| 75(1) and (2) | 1985 s 28(3) |
| (3) | 1985 s 28(4) |
| (4) | 1985 s 28(3) |
| (5) and (6) | 1985 s 28(5) and Sch 24 |
| 76(1) | 1985 s 32(1) |
| (2) | new |
| (3) | 1985 s 32(2) |
| (4) and (5) | 1985 s 32(3) |
| (6) and (7) | 1985 s 32(4) (changed) and Sch 24 |

**Chapter 5 Change of name**

| Section of 2006 Act | Origin |
|---|---|
| 77(1)(a) | 1985 s 28(1) |
| 1(b) | new |
| (2) | drafting |
| 78(1) to (3) | new |

| Section of 2006 Act | Origin |
|---|---|
| 79(1) and (2) | new |
| 80(1) and (2) | 1985 s 28(6) and 32(5) (changed) |
| (3) | 1985 s 28(6) and 32(5) |
| 81(1) | 1985 s 28(6) and 32(5) |
| (2) and (3) | 1985 s 28(7) and 32(6) |

**Chapter 6 Trading disclosures**

| Section of 2006 Act | Origin |
|---|---|
| 82(1) and (2) | 1985 ss 348(1), 349(1), 351(1) and (2), Business Names Act 1985 s 4(1) (changed) |
| (3) to (5) | new |
| 83(1) and (2) | Business Names Act 1985 s 5(1) |
| (3) | Business Names Act 1985 s 5(2) |
| 84(1) and (2) | 1985 ss 348(2), 349(2) and (3), 351(5), Business Names Act 1985 s 7 (changed) |
| (3) | new |
| 85(1) and (2) | new |

**PART 6 A COMPANY'S REGISTERED OFFFIICE**

| Section of 2006 Act | Origin |
|---|---|
| 86 | 1985 s 287(1) |
| 87(1) | 1985 s 287(3) |
| (2) | 1985 s 287(4) |
| (3) | 1985 s 287(5) |
| (4) | 1985 s 287(6) |
| 88(1) | drafting |
| (2) | 1985 s 2(2) |
| (3) and (4) | new |

**PART 7 RE-REGISTRATION AS A MEANS OF ALTERING A COMPANY'S STATUS**

| Section of 2006 Act | Origin |
|---|---|
| 89 | drafting |
| 90(1) | 1985 s 43(1) (changed) |
| (2) | 1985 s 43(1); drafting |
| (3) | 1985 s 43(2) |
| (4) | 1985 s 48(1) and (2) |
| 91(1) | 1985 s 45(1) to (4) |
| (2) | 1985 s 45(5), 1986 art 55(5) |
| (3) | 1985 s 45(6) |
| (4) | 1985 s 45(7) |
| (5) | 1985 s 47(3) (changed) |
| 92(1) | 1985 s 43(3)(b) and (c), (4) |
| (2) | 1985 s 43(e)(ii) |
| (3) and (4) | 1985 s 46(2) and (3) |
| (5) and (6) | 1985 s 46(4) |
| 93(1) | 1985 s 44(1) |
| (2) | 1985 s 44(2), drafting |
| (3) to (5) | 1985 s 44(4) and (5) |
| (6) | 1985 s 44(6) and (7)(b) |
| (7) | 1985 s 44(2) and (7)(a) |
| 94(1) | new |
| (2) | 1985 s 43(3)(a) to (d) |
| (3) | 1985 s 43(e)(i) |
| (4) | 1984 s 47(2) |
| 95(1) to (3) | new |
| 96(1) and (2) | 1985 s 47(1) |
| (3) | new |
| (4) and (5) | 1985 s 47(4) and (5) |
| 97(1) | 1985 s 53(1) (changed) |
| (2) | new |
| (3) | 1985 s 53(2) |

| Section of 2006 Act | Origin |
|---|---|
| 236(1) | 1985 s 309C(1) (changed) |
| (2) and (3) | 1985 s 309C(2) |
| (4) and (5) | 1985 s 309C(3) |
| 237(1) | 1985 s 309C(4) and (5) |
| (2) | 1985 s 309C(5), s 318(1) |
| (3) | 1985 s 309C(5), s 318(2) and (3) (changed) |
| (4) | new |
| (5) | 1985 s 309C(5), s 318(4) |
| (6) | 1985 s 309C(5), s 318(8) (changed). |
| (7) | 1985 s 309C(5), s 318(8), Sch 24 |
| (8) | 1985 s 309C(5), s 318(10) |
| (9) | new |
| 238(1) | 1985 s 309C(5), s 318(7) |
| (2) | new |
| (3) | 1985 s 309C(5), s 318(8) (changed) |
| (4) | 1985 s 309C(5), 1985 s 318(8), Sch 24 |
| (5) | 1985 s 309C(5), s 318(9) (changed) |
| 239(1) to (7) | new |

**Chapter 8 Directors' residential addresses: protection from disclosure**

| | |
|---|---|
| 240(1) to (3) | new |
| 241(1) and (2) | new |
| 242(1) to (3) | new |
| 243(1) to (8) | new |
| 244(1) to (4) | new |
| 245(1) to (6) | new |
| 246(1) to (7) | new |

**Chapter 9 Supplementary provisions**

| | |
|---|---|
| 247(1) | 1985 s 719(1) |
| (2) | 1985 s 719(2) (changed) |
| (3) | new |
| (4) | 1985 s 719(3) |
| (5) | 1985 s 719(3) (changed) |
| (6) | 1985 s 719(3) |
| (7) | 1985 s 719(4) (changed) |
| 248(1) | 1985 s 382(1) |
| (2) | new |
| (3) | 1985 s 382(5) (changed) |
| (4) | 1985 s 382(5), Sch 24 |
| 249(1) | 1985 s 382(2) |
| (2) | 1985 s 382(4) |
| 250 | 1985 s 741(1) |
| 251(1) and (2) | 1985 s 741(2) |
| (3) | 1985 s 741(3) |
| 252(1) | 1985 s 346(1) |
| (2) | 1985 s 346(2) and (3) (changed) |
| (3) | 1985 s 346(2) |
| 253(1) | drafting |
| (2) | 1985 s 346(2) and (3) (changed) |
| (3) | new |
| 254(1) | 1985 s 346(1) |
| (2) | 1985 s 346(4) |
| (3) | 1985 s 346(7) |
| (4) | 1985 s 346(8) |
| (5) | 1985 s 346(4) |
| (6) | 1985 s 346(6) |
| 255(1) | 1985 s 346(1) |

| Section of 2006 Act | Origin |
|---|---|
| (2) | 1985 s 346(5) |
| (3) | 1985 s 346(7) |
| (4) | 1985 s 346(8) |
| (5) | 1985 s 346(5) |
| (6) | 1985 s 346(6) |
| 256 | new |
| 257(1) and (2) | new |
| 258(1) | 1985 s 345(1) |
| (2) | 1985 s 345(2) |
| (3) | 1985 s 345(3) |
| 259 | 1985 s 347 |

**PART 11 DERIVATIVE CLAIMS AND PROCEEDINGS BY MEMBERS**

**Chapter 1 Derivative claims in England and Wales or Northern Ireland**

| | |
|---|---|
| 260(1) to (5) | new |
| 261(1) to (4) | new |
| 262(1) to (5) | new |
| 263(1) to (7) | new |
| 264(1) to (5) | new |

**Chapter 2 Derivative proceedings in Scotland**

| | |
|---|---|
| 265(1) to (7) | new |
| 266(1) to (5) | new |
| 267(1) to (5) | new |
| 268(1) to (6) | new |
| 269(1) to (5) | new |

**PART 12 COMPANY SECRETARIES**

| | |
|---|---|
| 270(1) and (2) | new |
| (3) | 1985 s 283(3) (changed) |
| 271 | 1985 s 283(1) (changed) |
| 272(1) to (7) | new |
| 273(1) and (2) | 1985 s 286(1) (changed) |
| (3) | 1985 s 286(2) |
| 274 | 1985 s 283(3) (changed) |
| 275(1) to (3) | 1985 s 288(1) (changed) |
| (4) | new |
| (5) | 1985 s 288(3) |
| (6) | 1985 s 288(4) and (6) |
| (7) | 1985 s 288(4), Sch 24 |
| (8) | 1985 s 288(5) |
| 276(1) and (2) | 1985 s 288(2) |
| (3) | 1985 s 288(4) and (6) (changed) |
| (4) | 1985 s 288(4), Sch 24 |
| 277(1) | 1985 s 290(1)(a) (changed) |
| (2) | 1985 s 289(2)(a), s 290(3) |
| (3) | new |
| (4) | 1985 s 289(2)(b), s 290(3) (changed) |
| (5) | new |
| 278(1) | 1985 s 290(1)(b) (changed) |
| (2) | 1985 s 290(2) |
| 279(1) and (2) | new |
| 280 | 1985 s 284 |

**PART 13 RESOLUTIONS AND MEETINGS**

**Chapter 1 General provisions about resolutions**

| | |
|---|---|
| 281(1) to (4) | new |
| 282(1) to (5) | new |
| 283(1) | 1985 s 378(1) and (2) (changed) |
| (2) and (3) | new |

| Section of 2006 Act | Origin | Section of 2006 Act | Origin |
|---|---|---|---|
| (4) | 1985 s 378(1) and (2) (changed) | (5) and (6) | 1985 s 369(4) (changed) |
| | | (7) | drafting |
| (5) | 1985 s 378(1), (2) and (5) (changed) | 308 | 1985 s 369(4A), (4B) (changed) |
| (6) | 1985 s 378(2) (changed) | 309(1) | 1985 s 369(4B) |
| 284(1) | 1985 s 370(6) | (2) | 1985 s 369(4C) (changed) |
| (2) | Table A, para 54 (changed) | (3) | 1985 s 369(4B)(d) |
| (3) | 1985 s 370(6), Table A, para 54 (changed) | 310(1) | 1985 s 370(2), Table A, para 38 (changed) |
| (4) | 1985 s 370(1), Table A, para 54 | (2) | Table A, para 38 (changed) |
| 285(1) to (3) | new | (3) | new |
| 286(1) to (3) | Table A, para 55 | (4) | 1985 s 370(1), Table A para 38 |
| 287 | new | 311(1) and (2) | Table A, para 38 |
| | | 312(1) | 1985 s 379(1) |
| **Chapter 2 Written resolutions** | | (2) | 1985 s 379(2) |
| 288(1) | new | (3) | 1985 s 379(2) (changed) |
| (2) | 1985 s 381A(7), Sch 15A, para 1 | (4) | 1985 s 379(3) |
| (3) | new | 313(1) and (2) | 1985 Table A, para 39 (changed) |
| (4) | 1985 s 381A(1) (changed) | 314(1) | 1985 s 376(1)(b) |
| (5) | 1985 s 381A(4) | (2) and (3) | 1985 s 376(2) (changed) |
| 289(1) | 1985 s 381A(1) (changed) | (4) | 1985 s 376(1), s 377(1)(a) (changed) |
| (2) | new | 315(1) | 1985 s 376(3) and (5) |
| 290 | new | (2) | 1985 s 376(1) |
| 291(1) to (7) | new | (3) | 1985 s 376(7) |
| 292(1) to (6) | new | (4) | 1985 s 376(7), Sch 24 |
| 293(1) to (7) | new | 316(1) | new |
| 294(1) and (2) | new | (2) | 1985 s 376(1), s 377(1)(b) (changed) |
| 295(1) and (2) | new | 317(1) | 1985 s 377(3) (changed) |
| 296(1) | 1985 s 381A(2) (changed) | (2) | 1985 s 377(3) |
| (2) to (4) | new | 318(1) | 1985 s 370A |
| 297(1) and (2) | new | (2) | 1985 s 370(1) and (4) (changed) |
| 298(1) and (2) | new | (3) | 1985 s 370A (changed) |
| 299(1) and (2) | new | 319(1) | 1985 s 370(5) |
| 300 | 1985 s 381C(1) | (2) | 1985 s 370(1) |
| | | 320(1) | 1985 s 378(4), Table A, para 47 |
| **Chapter 3 Resolutions at meetings** | | | |
| 301 | 1985 s 378(6) (changed) | (2) | Table A, para 47 |
| 302 | Table A, para 37 | (3) | 1985 s 378(4), Table A, paras 47 and 48 (changed) |
| 303(1) | 1985 s 368(1) | | |
| (2) | 1985 s 368(1), (2) and (2A) | 321(1) | 1985 s 373(1)(a) |
| (3) | 1985 s 368(2) (changed) | (2) | 1985 s 373(1)(b) (changed) |
| (4) | 1985 s 368(3) (changed) | 322 | 1985 s 374 |
| (5) | new | 323(1) | 1985 s 375(1)(a) |
| (6) | 1985 s 368(3) (changed) | (2) and (3) | 1985 s 375(2) (changed) |
| 304(1) | 1985 s 368(4) and (8) | (4) | new |
| (2) and (3) | new | 324(1) | 1985 s 372(1) (changed) |
| (4) | 1985 s 368(7) | (2) | 1985 s 372(2)(b) (changed) |
| 305(1) | 1985 s 368(4) | 325(1) | 1985 s 372(3) (changed) |
| (2) | new | (2) | new |
| (3) | 1985 s 368(4) | (3) | 1985 s 372(4) |
| (4) | 1985 s 368(5) | (4) | 1985 s 372(4), Sch 24 |
| (5) | new | 326(1) and (2) | 1985 s 372(6) |
| (6) and (7) | 1985 s 368(6) | (3) | 1985 s 372(6) (changed) |
| 306(1) and (2) | 1985 s 371(1) | (4) | 1985 s 372(6), Sch 24 |
| (3) and (4) | 1985 s 371(2) | 327(1) | 1985 s 372(5) |
| (5) | 1985 s 371(3) | (2) | 1985 s 372(5) (changed) |
| 307(1) | new | (3) | new |
| (2) | 1985 s 369(1) and (2) (changed) | 328(1) and (2) | new |
| (3) | 1985 s 369(1) and (2) | | |
| (4) | 1985 s 369(3) (changed) | | |

| Section of 2006 Act | Origin |
|---|---|
| 329(1) | 1985 s 373(2) |
| (2) | 1985 s 373(2) (changed) |
| 330(1) to (7) | Table A, para 63 (changed) |
| 331 | new |
| 332 | 1985 s 381 |
| 333(1) to (4) | new |
| 334(1) to (3) | 1985 s 125(6) (changed) |
| (4) | 1985 s 125(6)(a) |
| (5) | new |
| (6) | 1985 s 125(6)(b) |
| (7) | 1985 s 125(7) and (8) |
| 335(1) to (6) | new |

**Chapter 4 Public companies: additional requirements for AGMs**

| | |
|---|---|
| 336(1) | 1985 s 366(1) (changed) |
| (2) | new |
| (3) | 1985 s 366(4) (changed) |
| (4) | 1985 s 366(4), Sch 24 |
| 337(1) | 1985 s 366(1) |
| (2) | 1985 s 369(3)(a) |
| 338(1) | 1985 s 376(1)(b) |
| (2) | new |
| (3) | 1985 s 376(2) (changed) |
| (4) | 1985 s 376(1), s 377(1)(a) and (2) (changed) |
| 339(1) | 1985 s 376(3) and (5) |
| (2) | 1985 s 376(1) |
| (3) | 1985 s 376(6) |
| (4) | 1985 s 376(7) |
| (5) | 1985 s 376(7), Sch 24 |
| 340(1) | new |
| (2) | 1985 s 376(1), s 377(1)(b) (changed) |

**Chapter 5 Additional requirements for quoted companies**

| | |
|---|---|
| 341(1) to (6) | new |
| 342(1) to (4) | new |
| 343(1) to (6) | new |
| 344(1) to (4) | new |
| 345(1) to (6) | new |
| 346(1) to (5) | new |
| 347(1) to (4) | new |
| 348(1) to (4) | new |
| 349(1) to (5) | new |
| 350(1) to (5) | new |
| 351(1) to (5) | new |
| 352(1) and (2) | new |
| 353(1) to (5) | new |
| 354(1) to (4) | new |

**Chapter 6 Records of resolutions and meetings**

| | |
|---|---|
| 355(1) | 1985 s 382(1), s 382A(1) (changed) |
| (2) | new |
| (3) | 1985 s 382(5) (changed) |
| (4) | 1985 s 382(5), Sch 24 |
| 356(1) | drafting |
| (2) and (3) | 1985 s 382A(2) |
| (4) | 1985 s 382(2) |
| (5) | 1985 s 382(4) |
| 357(1) and (2) | 1985 s 382B(1) |
| (3) | 1985 s 382B(2) |
| (4) | 1985 s 382B(2), Sch 24 |
| (5) | 1985 s 382B(3) |
| 358(1) | 1985 s 383(1) (changed) |
| (2) | new |

| Section of 2006 Act | Origin |
|---|---|
| (3) | 1985 s 383(1) |
| (4) | 1985 s 383(3) (changed) |
| (5) | 1985 s 383(4) (changed) |
| (6) | 1985 s 383(4), Sch 24 |
| (7) | 1985 s 383(5) |
| 359 | new |

**Chapter 7 Supplementary provisions**

| | |
|---|---|
| 360(1) and (2) | new |
| 361 | new |

**PART 14 CONTROL OF POLITICAL DONATIONS AND EXPENDITURE**

| | |
|---|---|
| 362 | 1985 s 347A(1) (changed) |
| 363(1) | 1985 s 347A(6), (7)(a) and (9) |
| (2) | 1985 s 347A(6)(b) and (7)(b) and (c) (changed) |
| (3) | new |
| (4) | drafting |
| 364(1) | drafting |
| (2) | 1985 s 347A(4) |
| (3) | new |
| (4) | new |
| 365(1) | 1985 s 347A(5) (changed) |
| (2) | new |
| 366(1) | 1985 s 347C(1) (changed) |
| (2) | 1985 s 347C(1), 347D(1), (2) and (3) (changed) |
| (3) | 1985 s 347D(3) (changed) |
| (4) | new |
| (5) | 1985 s 347A(10), s 347C(1), s 347D(2) and (3) |
| (6) | 1985 s 347C(6), s 347D(9) |
| 367(1) and (2) | new |
| (3) | 1985 s 347C(2), s 347D(4) (changed) |
| (4) | new |
| (5) | 1985 s 347C(4), s 347D(6) |
| (6) | 1985 s 347C(2), s 347D(4) (changed) |
| (7) | new |
| 368(1) | 1985 s 347C(3)(b), s 347D(5) |
| (2) | 1985 s 347C(3), s 347D(5) |
| 369(1) | 1985 s 347F(1) |
| (2) | 1985 s 347F(2), (3) and (4) |
| (3) | 1985 s 347F(2) and (6) (changed) |
| (4) | new |
| (5) | 1985 s 347F(3) |
| (6) | 1985 s 347F(5) |
| 370(1) | 1985 s 347I(1) (changed) |
| (2) | 1985 s 347I(1) |
| (3) | 1985 s 54(2), s 347I(2) (changed) |
| (4) | 1985 s 347I(3) |
| (5) | new |
| 371(1) | 1985 s 347I(3) |

| Section of 2006 Act | Origin |
|---|---|
| (4) and (5) | 1985 s 233(5) (changed), Sch 24 |
| **Chapter 5  Directors' report** | |
| 415(1) | 1985 s 234(1) |
| (2) and (3) | 1985 s 234(2) and (3) |
| (4) and (5) | 1985 s 234(5), Sch 24 |
| 416(1) | 1985 s 234ZZA(1)(a) and (b) |
| (2) | 1985 s 234ZZA(2) |
| (3) | 1985 ss 234ZZA(1)(c), 246(4)(a) |
| (4) | 1985 s 234ZZA(3) and (4) (changed) |
| 417(1) | 1985 ss 234(1)(a), 246(4)(a) |
| (2) | new |
| (3) and (4) | 1985 s 234ZZB(1) and (2) |
| (5) | new |
| (6) | 1985 s 234ZZB(3) and (5) |
| (7) | 1985 s 246A(2A) |
| (8) | 1985 s 234ZZB(4) |
| (9) | 1985 s 234ZZB(6) |
| (10) and (11) | new |
| 418(1) | 1985 s 234ZA(1) |
| (2) | 1985 ss 234(1)(b), 234ZA(2) |
| (3) and (4) | 1985 s 234ZA(3) and (4) |
| (5) and (6) | 1985 s 234ZA(6), Sch 24 |
| 419(1) | 1985 s 234A(1) |
| (2) | 1985 s 246(8)(b) |
| (3) and (4) | 1985 ss 234(5), 234A(4) (changed), Sch 24 |

**Chapter 6  Quoted companies: directors' remuneration report**

| | |
|---|---|
| 420(1) | 1985 s 421(1) |
| (2) | 1985 s 234B(3) and (4) (changed) |
| (3) | 1985 s 234B(3), Sch 24 |
| 421(1) and (2) | 1985 s 234B(1) and (2) (changed) |
| (3) | 1985 s 234B(5) and (6) |
| (4) | 1985 s 234B(6), Sch 24 |
| 422(1) | 1985 s 234C(1) |
| (2) and (3) | 1985 s 234C(4) (changed), Sch 24 |

**Chapter 7  Publication of accounts and reports**

| | |
|---|---|
| 423(1) | 1985 s 238(1) and (1A) |
| (2) and (3) | new |
| (4) | 1985 s 238(3) |
| (5) | 1985 s 238(6) |
| (6) | drafting |
| 424(1) to (3) | 1985 s 238(1) (changed) |
| (4) | 1985 s 238(4) (changed) |
| (5) | new |
| (6) | drafting |
| 425(1) and (2) | 1985 s 238(5), Sch 24 |
| 426(1) | 1985 s 251(1) |
| (2) and (3) | 1985 s 251(2) |
| (4) | drafting |
| (5) | new |
| (6) | 1985 s 251(5) |
| 427(1) | 1985 s 251(1) 'summary financial statement' |
| (2) | 1985 s 251(3) |

| Section of 2006 Act | Origin |
|---|---|
| (3) | 1985 s 251(3A) |
| (4) | 1985 s 251(4) |
| (5) | new |
| (6) | 1985 s 251(5) |
| 428(1) | 1985 s 251(1) 'summary financial statement' |
| (2) | 1985 s 251(3) |
| (3) | 1985 s 251(3A) |
| (4) | 1985 s 251(4) |
| (5) | new |
| (6) | 1985 s 251(5) |
| 429(1) and (2) | 1985 s 251(6), Sch 24 |
| 430(1) to (7) | new |
| 431(1) and (2) | 1985 s 239(1) and (2) |
| (3) and (4) | 1985 s 239(3), Sch 24 |
| 432(1) and (2) | 1985 s 239(1) and (2) |
| (3) and (4) | 1985 s 239(3), Sch 24 |
| 433(1) to (3) | 1985 ss 233(3), 234A(2) and 234C(2) |
| (4) and (5) | 1985 ss 233(6)(a), 234A(4)(a) and 234C(4)(a), Sch 24 |
| 434(1) | 1985 s 240(1) (changed) |
| (2) | 1985 s 240(2) (changed) |
| (3) | 1985 s 240(5) |
| (4) and (5) | 1985 s 240(6), Sch 24 |
| (6) | 1985 s 251(7) |
| 435(1) and (2) | 1985 s 240(3) (changed) |
| (3) | 1985 s 240(5) (changed) |
| (4) | new |
| (5) and (6) | 1985 s 240(6), Sch 24 |
| (7) | 1985 s 251(7) |
| 436(1) and (2) | 1985 ss 233(3), 234A(2), 234C(2), 240(4) (changed) |

**Chapter 8 Public companies: laying of accounts and reports before general meeting**

| | |
|---|---|
| 437(1) | 1985 s 241(1) (changed) |
| (2) | 1985 s 241(2) |
| (3) | drafting |
| 438(1) to (3) | 1985 s 241(2) to (4) |
| (4) | 1985 s 241(2), Sch 24 |

**Chapter 9 Quoted companies: members' approval of directors' remuneration report**

| | |
|---|---|
| 439(1) | 1985 s 241A(1) and (3) |
| (2) | 1985 s 241A(4) |
| (3) | 1985 s 241A(5) and (7) |
| (4) | 1985 s 241A(6) |
| (5) | 1985 s 241A(8) |
| (6) | 1985 s 241A(2) and (12) |
| 440(1) | 1985 s 241A(9) |
| (2) and (3) | 1985 s 241A(10) and (11) |
| (4) | 1985 s 241A(9) and (10), Sch 24 |
| (5) | 1985 s 241A(2) and (12) |

**Chapter 10 Filing of accounts and reports**

| | |
|---|---|
| 441(1) | 1985 s 242(1) |
| (2) | drafting |
| 442(1) | drafting |
| (2) and (3) | 1985 s 244(1) and (2) (changed) |
| (4) and (5) | 1985 s 244(4) and (5) |
| (6) | new |
| (7) | 1985 s 244(6) |
| 443(1) to (5) | new |

| Section of 2006 Act | Origin |
|---|---|
| (2) and (3) | 1985 s 249B(4) |
| (4) | 1985 s 249B(5) |
| 476(1) to (3) | 1985 s 249B(2) |
| 477(1) | 1985 s 249A(1) |
| (2) | 1985 s 249A(3) |
| (3) | 1985 s 249A(6) |
| (4) | 1985 s 249A(3)(a) and (7) |
| (5) | drafting |
| 478 | 1985 s 249B(1)(a) to (e) |
| 479(1) to (3) | 1985 s 249B(1)(f) and (1A) to (1C) |
| (4) | drafting |
| (5) and (6) | 1985 s 249B(1)(C) |
| 480(1) and (2) | 1985 s 249AA(1) and (2) |
| (3) | drafting |
| 481 | 1985 s 249AA(3) |
| 482(1) to (4) | new |
| 483(1) to (5) | new |
| 484(1) | 1985 s 257(1) |
| 484(2) | 1985 s 257(4)(c) |
| 484(3) | 1985 s 257(2)(b) and (d) |
| 484(4) | 1985 s 257(3) |

**Chapter 2 Appointment of auditors**

| Section of 2006 Act | Origin |
|---|---|
| 485(1) | 1985 s 384(1) |
| (2) to (5) | new |
| 486(1) and (2) | 1985 s 387(1) and (2) |
| (3) and (4) | 1985 s 387(2), Sch 24 |
| 487(1) to (4) | new |
| 488(1) to (3) | new |
| 489(1) | 1985 s 384(1) (changed) |
| (2) | 1985 ss 384(2), 385(2) |
| (3) | 1985 ss 385(3), 388(1) (changed) |
| (4) | 1985 s 385(2) and (4) (changed) |
| (5) | drafting |
| 490(1) and (2) | 1985 s 387(1) and (2) |
| (3) and (4) | 1985 s 387(2), Sch 24 |
| 491(1) | 1985 s 385(2) (changed) |
| (2) | drafting |
| 492(1) | 1985 s 390A(1) |
| (2) and (3) | 1985 s 390A(2) |
| (4) and (5) | 1985 s 390A(4) and (5) |
| 493(1) to (4) | new |
| 494(1) | 1985 s 390B(1), (8) |
| (2) to (4) | 1985 s 390B(2) to (4) |
| (5) | 1985 s 390B(5)(a) |
| (6) | 1985 s 390B(9) |

**Chapter 3 Functions of auditor**

| Section of 2006 Act | Origin |
|---|---|
| 495(1) | 1985 s 235(1); drafting |
| (2) | 1985 s 235(1A) |
| (3) | 1985 s 235(1B), (2) |
| (4) | 1985 s 235(2A) |
| 496 | 1985 s 235(3) |
| 497(1) and (2) | 1985 s 235(4) and (5) |
| 498(1) to (4) | 1985 s 237(1) to (4) |
| (5) | 1985 s 237(4A) |
| 499(1) and (2) | 1985 s 389A(1) and (2) |
| (3) | 1985 s 389A(6) |
| (4) | 1985 s 389A(7) |
| 500(1) to (3) | 1985 s 389A(3) to (5) |
| (4) | 1985 s 389A(6) |
| (5) | 1985 s 389A(7) |
| 501(1) | 1985 s 389B(1) |
| (2) | 1985 s 389B(1), Sch 24 |

| Section of 2006 Act | Origin |
|---|---|
| (3) | 1985 s 389B(2), (3) (changed) |
| (4) | 1985 s 389B(4) |
| (5) | 1985 s 389B(4), Sch 24 |
| (6) | 1985 s 389B(5) |
| 502(1) | 1985 s 390(2) |
| (2) | 1985 s 390(1) |
| (3) | 1985 s 390(3) |
| 503(1) and (2) | 1985 s 236(1) |
| (3) | new |
| 504(1) to (4) | new |
| 505(1) and (2) | 1985 s 236(2) (changed) |
| (3) and (4) | 1985 s 236(4), Sch 24 |
| 506(1) and (2) | new |
| 507(1) to (4) | new |
| 508(1) to (4) | new |
| 509(1) to (4) | new |

**Chapter 4 Removal, resignation, etc of auditors**

| Section of 2006 Act | Origin |
|---|---|
| 510(1) and (2) | 1985 s 391(1); drafting |
| (3) | 1985 s 391(3) |
| (4) | drafting |
| 511(1) | 1985 s 391A(1)(a) |
| (2) to (6) | 1985 s 391A(2) to (6) |
| 512(1) | 1985 s 391(2) |
| (2) and (3) | 1985 s 391(2), Sch 24 |
| 513(1) and (2) | 1985 s 391(4) |
| 514(1) to (8) | new |
| 515(1) | 1985 s 391A(1)(b) |
| (2) | 1985 s 391A(1) opening words (changed) |
| (3) to (7) | 1985 s 391A(2) to (6) |
| 516(1) and (2) | 1985 s 392(1) |
| (3) | 1985 s 392(2) |
| 517(1) | 1985 s 392(3) |
| (2) and (3) | 1985 s 392(3), Sch 24 |
| 518(1) to (4) | 1985 s 392A(1) to (4) |
| (5) | 1985 s 392A(5) |
| (6) and (7) | 1985 s 392A(5), Sch 24 |
| (8) to (10) | 1985 s 392A(6) to (8) |
| 519(1) to (3) | 1985 s 394(1) (changed) |
| (4) | 1985 s 394(2) (changed) |
| (5) and (6) | 1985 s 394A(1) and (2) |
| (7) | 1985 s 394(1), Sch 24 |
| 520(1) | drafting |
| (2) and (3) | 1985 s 394(3) and (4) |
| (4) | 1985 s 394(6) |
| (5) | 1985 s 394(7) (changed) |
| (6) | 1985 s 394A(4) |
| (7) | new |
| (8) | 1985 s 394A(4), Sch 24 (changed) |
| 521(1) | 1985 s 394(5) |
| (2) | 1985 s 394(7) |
| (3) and (4) | 1985 s 394A(1) and (2) |
| (5) | 1985 s 394A(1), Sch 24 |
| 522(1) to (8) | new |
| 523(1) to (6) | new |
| 524(1) to 4) | new |
| 525(1) to (3) | new |
| 526 | 1985 s 388(2) |

**Chapter 5 Quoted companies: right of members to raise audit concerns at accounts meeting**

| Section of 2006 Act | Origin |
|---|---|
| 527(1) to (6) | new |
| 528(1) to (5) | new |
| 529(1) to (4) | new |

| Section of 2006 Act | Origin |
| --- | --- |
| (4) | 1985 s 84(4) |
| (5) | 1985 s 84(4) and (5) |
| (6) | 1985 s 84(6) |
| 579(1) and (2) | 1985 s 85(1) |
| (3) | 1985 s 85(2) |
| (4) | 1985 s 85(3) |

**Chapter 5 Payment for shares**

| | |
| --- | --- |
| 580(1) | 1985 s 100(1) |
| (2) | 1985 s 100(2) |
| 581 | 1985 s 119 |
| 582(1) | 1985 s 99(1) |
| (2) | 1985 s 99(4) |
| (3) | 1985 s 99(1) |
| 583(1) | drafting |
| (2) to (3)(d) | 1985 s 738(2) |
| (3)(e) and (4) | new |
| (4) | new |
| (5) | 1985 s 738(3) |
| (6) | 1985 s 738(4) |
| (7) | new |
| 584 | 1985 s 106 |
| 585(1) | 1985 s 99(2) |
| (2) | 1985 s 99(3) |
| (3) | 1985 s 99(5) |
| 586(1) | 1985 s 101(1) |
| (2) | 1985 s 101(2) |
| (3) | 1985 s 101(3) and (4) |
| (4) | 1985 s 101(5) |
| 587(1) | 1985 s 102(1) |
| (2) | 1985 s 102(2) |
| (3) | 1985 s 102(3) and (4) |
| (4) | 1985 s 102(5) and (6) |
| (5) | 1985 s 102(7) |
| 588(1) | 1985 s 112(1) and (5)(a) |
| (2) | 1985 s 112(3) |
| (3) | 1985 s 112(4) |
| (4) | 1985 s 112(5)(b) |
| 589(1) and (2) | 1985 s 113(1) |
| (3) | 1985 s 113(2) and (3) (changed) |
| (4) | 1985 s 113(4) |
| (5) | 1985 s 113(5) |
| (6) | 1985 s 113(6) and (7) |
| 590(1) | 1985 s 114 |
| (2) | 1985 s 114. Sch 24 |
| 591(1) and (2) | 1985 s 115(1) |
| 592(1) and (2) | 1985 s 107 |

**Chapter 6 Public companies: independent valuation of non-cash consideration**

| | |
| --- | --- |
| 593(1) | 1985 s 103(1) |
| (2) | 1985 s 103(2) |
| (3) | 1985 s 103(6) |
| (4) | drafting |
| 594(1) to (3) | 1985 s 103(3) |
| (4) and (5) | 1985 s 103(4) |
| (6) | 1985 s 103(7) |
| 595(1) and (2) | 1985 s 103(5) |
| (3) | 1985 s 103(7)(b) |
| 596(1) | drafting |
| (2) | 1985 s 108(4) |
| (3) | 1985 s 108(6) |
| (4) and (5) | 1985 s 108(7) |
| 597(1) and (2) | 1985 s 111(1) |
| (3) and (4) | 1985 s 111(3), Sch 24 |
| (5) and (6) | 1985 ss 88(6), 111(3) |
| 598(1) | 1985 s 104(1) |
| (2) | 1985 s 104(2) |

| Section of 2006 Act | Origin |
| --- | --- |
| (3) | drafting |
| (4) | 1985 s 104(6)(a) |
| (5) | 1985 s 104(6)(b) |
| 599(1) | 1985 s 104(4)(a), (b) and (d) |
| (2) | 1985 s 104(5)(a) |
| (3) | 1985 s 104(4)(d) |
| (4) | 1985 s 104(5)(b) |
| 600(1) | drafting |
| (2) | 1985 s 109(2)(a) and (b) |
| (3) | 1985 s 108(6)(a), (b) and (c), 109(2)(c) and (d) |
| (4) and (5) | 1985 s 109(3) |
| 601(1) and (2) | 1985 s 104(4)(c) and (d) |
| (3) | 1985 s 104(4)(c) (changed) |
| 602(1) | 1985 s 111(2) |
| (2) and (3) | 1984 s 111(4), Sch 24 |
| 603 | 1985 s 104(3) |
| 604(1) | 1985 s 105(1) |
| (2) | 1985 s 105(2) |
| (3) | 1985 s 105(3) |
| 605(1) | 1985 s 112(1) |
| (2) | 1985 s 112(2) |
| (3) | 1985 s 112(3) |
| (4) | 1985 s 112(4) |
| 606(1) | 1985 s 113(1) |
| (2) | 1985 s 113(2) and (3) (changed) |
| (3) | 1985 s 113(4) |
| (4) | 1985 s 113(5) |
| (5) | 1986 s 113(6) and (7) |
| (6) | 1986 s 113(8) |
| 607(1) | drafting |
| (2) | 1985 s 114 |
| (3) | 1985 s 114, Sch 24 |
| 608(1) and (2) | 1985 s 115(1) |
| 609(1) and (2) | 1985 s 107 |

**Chapter 7 Share premiums**

| | |
| --- | --- |
| 610(1) | 1985 s 130(1) |
| (2) and (3) | 1985 s 130(2) (changed) |
| (4) | 1985 s 130(3) |
| (5) and (6) | 1985 s 130(4) |
| 611(1) | 1985 s 132(1) |
| (2) | 1985 s 132(2) |
| (3) | 1985 s 132(3) |
| (4) | 1985 s 132(4) |
| (5) | 1985 s 132(5) |
| 612(1) | 1985 s 131(1) |
| (2) | 1985 s 131(2) |
| (3) | 1985 s 131(3) |
| (4) | 1985 s 131(1), 132(8) |
| 613(1) | drafting |
| (2) and (3) | 1985 s 131(4) |
| (4) | 1985 s 131(5) |
| (5) | 1985 s 131(6) |
| 614(1) | 1985 s 134(1) |
| (2) | 1985 s 134(3) |
| 615 | 1985 s 133(1) |
| 616(1) | 1985 s 131(7), 133(4) |
| (2) | 1985 s 133(2) |
| (3) | 1985 s 133(3) |

**Chapter 8 Alteration of share capital**

| | |
| --- | --- |
| 617(1) | 1985 s 121(1) (changed) |

| Section of 2006 Act | Origin |
|---|---|
| (5) | 1985 s 122(2), Sch 24 |
| 664(1) and (2) | 1985 s 147(2) (changed) |
| (3) | new |
| (4) | 1985 s 147(3) (changed) |
| (5) and (6) | new |
| 665(1) and (2) | 1985 s 147(4) |
| (3) | new |
| (4) | 1985 s 147(4)(a) (changed) |
| (5) | 1985 s 147(4)(b) |
| 666(1) and (2) | 1985 s 149(1) |
| 667(1) and (2) | 1985 s 149(2) |
| (3) | 1985 s 149(2), Sch 24 |
| 668(1) and (2) | 1985 s 148(1) |
| (3) | 1985 s 148(2) |
| 669(1) and (2) | 1985 s 148(4) |
| 670(1) | 1985 s 150(1) |
| (2) | 1985 s 150(2) |
| (3) | 1985 s 150(3) |
| (4) | 1985 s 150(4) |
| 671 | 1985 s 145(3), s 146(1), s 148(3) |
| 672(1) | 1985 Sch 2 para 1(1) |
| (2) | 1985 Sch 2 para 1(2) |
| (3) | 1985 Sch 2 para 1(3) |
| (4) | 1985 Sch 2 para 1(4) |
| (5) | 1985 Sch 2 para 2(3) |
| (6) | 1985 Sch 2 para 2(4) |
| 673(1) | 1985 Sch 2 para 3(1)(a) and (2) |
| (2) | 1985 Sch 2 para 3(1)(b) and (2)(a) |
| 674 | 1985 Sch 2 para 4(1) and (3) |
| 675(1) and (2) | 1985 Sch 2 para 5(1) and (2) |
| 676 | 1985 Sch 2 para 5(1) and (3) |

**Chapter 2 Financial assistance for purchase of own shares**

| Section of 2006 Act | Origin |
|---|---|
| 677(1) | 1985 s 152(1)(a) |
| (2) and (3) | 1985 s 152(2) |
| 678(1) | 1985 s 151(1) (changed) |
| (2) | 1985 s 153(1) |
| (3) | 1985 s 151(2) (changed) |
| (4) | 1985 s 153(2) |
| (5) | drafting |
| 679(1) | 1985 s 151(1) (changed) |
| (2) | 1985 s 153(1) (changed) |
| (3) | 1985 s 151(2) (changed) |
| (4) | 1985 s 153(2) (changed) |
| (5) | drafting |
| 680(1) | 1985 s 151(3) |
| (2) | 1985 s 151(3), Sch 24 |
| 681(1) and (2) | 1985 s 153(3) |
| 682(1) | 1985 s 153(4), s 154(1) |
| (2) | 1985 s 153(4) |
| (3) and (4) | 1985 s 154(2) |
| (5) | 1985 s 153(5) |
| 683(1) | 1985 s 152(1)(b) and (c) |
| (2) | 1985 s 152(3) |

**Chapter 3 Redeemable shares**

| Section of 2006 Act | Origin |
|---|---|
| 684(1) | 1985 s 159(1) (changed) |
| (2) | new |
| (3) | 1985 s 159(1) (changed) |
| (4) | 1985 s 159(2) |

| Section of 2006 Act | Origin |
|---|---|
| 685(1) to (4) | new |
| 686(1) to (3) | 1985 s 159(3) (changed) |
| 687(1) to (3) | 1985 s 160(1) |
| (4) and (5) | 1985 s 160(2) |
| (6) | 1985 s 160(1) |
| 688 | 1985 s 160(4) (changed) |
| 689(1) | 1985 s 122(1)(e) |
| (2) and (3) | new |
| (4) | 1985 s 122(2) |
| (5) | 1985 s 122(2), Sch 24 |

**Chapter 4 Purchase of own shares**

| Section of 2006 Act | Origin |
|---|---|
| 690(1) | 1985 s 162(1) (changed) |
| (2) | 1985 s 162(3) |
| 691(1) and (2) | 1985 s 159(3), s 162(2) |
| 692(1) and (2) | 1985 s 160(1), s 162(2) |
| (3) and (4) | 1985 s 160(2), s 162(2) |
| (5) | 1985 s 160(1), s 162(2) |
| 693(1) | 1985 s 164(1), s 166(1) |
| (2) | 1985 s 163(1) |
| (3) | 1985 s 163(2) |
| (4) | 1985 s 163(3) |
| (5) | 1985 s 163(4) and (5) |
| 694(1) | 1985 s 164(1) |
| (2) | 1985 s 164(2), s 165(2) (changed) |
| (3) | 1985 s 165(1) |
| (4) | 1985 s 164(3), 165(2) |
| (5) | 1985 s 164(4), 165(2) |
| (6) | drafting |
| 695(1) | 1985 s 164(5), 165(2) |
| (2) | 1985 Sch 15A para 5(1) and (2) |
| (3) and (4) | 1985 s 164(5), s 165(2) |
| 696(1) | 1985 s 164(6), s 165(2) |
| (2) | 1985 s 164(6), s 165(2), Sch 15A, para 5(3) and (4) |
| (3) to (5) | 1985 s 164(6), s 165(2) |
| 697(1) and (2) | 1985 s 164(7) |
| (3) | 1985 s 164(3) and (7) |
| (4) | 1985 s 164(4) and (7) |
| (5) | drafting |
| 698(1) | 1985 s 164(5) and (7) |
| (2) | 1985 Sch 15A, para 5(1) and (2) |
| (3) and (4) | 1985 s 164(5) and (7) |
| 699(1) | 1985 s 164(6) and (7) |
| (2) | 1985 s 164(6) and (7), Sch 15A para 5(3) |
| (3) to (6) | 1985 s 164(6) and (7) |
| 700(1) and (2) | 1985 s 167(2) |
| (3) | 1985 s 164(3) and (7), s 167(2) |
| (4) | 1985 s 164(4) and (7), s 167(2) |
| (5) | 1985 s 164(5), (6) and (7), s 167(2) |
| 701(1) | 1985 s 166(1) |
| (2) | 1985 s 166(2) |
| (3) | 1985 s 166(3)(a) and (b) |
| (4) | 1985 s 166(4) |
| (5) | 1985 s 166(3)(c) and (4) |
| (6) | 1985 s 166(5) |
| (7) | 1985 s 166(6) |
| (8) | 1985 s 166(7) |
| 702(1) to (4) | 1985 s 169(4) (changed) |
| (5) | new |

| Section of 2006 Act | Origin |
|---|---|
| (2) | 1985 s 204(2), s 212(5) |
| (3) | 1985 s 204(3), s 212(5) |
| (4) | 1985 s 204(4), s 212(5) |
| (5) | 1985 s 204(5), s 212(5) |
| (6) | 1985 s 204(6), s 212(5) |
| 825(1) | 1985 s 205(1), s 212(5) |
| (2) | 1985 s 205(2), s 212(5) |
| (3) | 1985 s 205(3), s 212(5) |
| (4) | 1985 s 205(4), s 212(5) |
| 826(1) | 1985 s 211(9), s 213(3), s 215(4) |
| (2) | 1985 s 215(4) |
| 827 | 1985 s 220(2) (changed) |
| 828(1) and (2) | 1985 s 210A(1) |
| (3) | 1985 s 210A(5) |

PART 23 DISTRIBUTIONS

**Chapter 1 Restrictions on when distributions may be made**

| | |
|---|---|
| 829(1) and (2) | 1985 s 263(2) |
| 830(1) | 1985 s 263(1) |
| (2) and (3) | 1985 s 263(3) |
| 831(1) | 1985 s 264(1) |
| (2) and (3) | 1985 s 264(2) |
| (4) | 1985 s 264(3) |
| (5) | 1985 s 264(4) |
| (6) | 1985 s 264(1) |
| 832(1) to (3) | 1985 s 265(1) |
| (4) | 1985 s 265(2) |
| (5) | 1985 s 265(4) and (6) |
| (6) | 1985 s 265(4A) and (5) |
| (7) | 1985 s 265(3) |
| 833(1) | 1985 s 266(1) |
| (2) | 1985 s 266(2) |
| (3) | 1985 s 266(2A) |
| (4) and (5) | 1985 s 266(3) |
| 834(1) | 1985 s 266(2)(b) |
| (2) | 1985 s 266(4), ICTA s 842(1A) |
| (3) | 1985 s 266(4), ICTA s 842(2) |
| (4) | 1985 s 266(4), ICTA s 842(3) |
| (5) | 1985 s 266(4), ICTA s 838, s 842(1A) and (4) |
| 835(1) | 1985 s 267(1) |
| (2) | 1985 s 267(2)(b) |

**Chapter 2 Justification of distribution by reference to accounts**

| | |
|---|---|
| 836(1) | 1985 s 270(1) and (2) |
| (2) | 1985 s 270(3) and (4) |
| (3) and (4) | 1985 s 270(5) |
| 837(1) | 1985 s 270(3) |
| (2) | 1985 s 271(2) |
| (3) | 1985 s 271(3) |
| (4) | 1985 s 271(3) and (4) |
| (5) | 1985 s 271(5) |
| 838(1) | 1985 s 270(4) |
| (2) | 1985 s 272(1) |
| (3) | 1985 s 272(2) |
| (4) and (5) | 1985 s 272(3) |
| (6) | 1985 s 272(4) and (5) |
| 839(1) | 1985 s 270(4) |
| (2) | 1985 s 273(1) |
| (3) | 1985 s 273(2) |
| (4) | 1985 s 272(3), s 273(3) |
| (5) | 1985 s 273(4) |

| Section of 2006 Act | Origin |
|---|---|
| (6) | 1985 s 273(4) and (5) |
| (7) | 1985 s 273(6) and (7) |
| 840(1) | 1985 s 274(1) and (2) |
| (2) | 1985 s 274(2) |
| (3) | 1985 s 274(3) ('financial assistance') |
| (4) | 1985 s 154(2)(a), s 274(3) ('net assets' and 'net liabilities') |
| (5) | 1985 s 154(2)(b), s 274(3) ('net liabilities') |

**Chapter 3 Supplementary provisions**

| | |
|---|---|
| 841(1) and (2) | 1985 s 275(1) |
| (3) | 1985 s 275(1A) |
| (4) | 1985 s 275(4), (5) and (6) |
| (5) | 1985 s 275(2) |
| 842 | 1985 s 275(3) |
| 843(1) | 1985 s 268(1) |
| (2) | 1985 s 268(1)(a) |
| (3) | 1985 s 268(2)(aa), (a) |
| (4) | 1985 s 268(1)(b), (2)(b) |
| (5) | 1985 s 268(1) |
| (6) | 1985 s 268(3)(a) |
| (7) | 1985 s 268(3)(b) and (4) |
| 844(1) | 1985 s 269(1) |
| (2) and (3) | 1985 s 269(2) |
| 845(1) to (5) | new |
| 846(1) and (2) | 1985 s 276 (changed) |
| 847(1) and (2) | 1985 s 277(1) |
| (3) and (4) | 1985 s 277(2) |
| 848(1) | 1985 s 278 |
| (2) | 1985 s 278, 1986 art 286 |
| 849 | 1985 s 263(4) |
| 850(1) and (2) | 1985 s 263(5) |
| (3) | 1985 s 263(5), 1986 art 271(5) |
| 851(1) | 1985 s 281 (changed) |
| (2) and (3) | new |
| 852 | 1985 s 281 |
| 853(1) | 1985 s 280(1) |
| (2) | 1985 s 280(3) |
| (3) | 1985 s 280(2) |
| (4) and (5) | 1985 s 262(3), s 742(2) |
| (6) | 1985 s 262(1), s 742(1) |

PART 24 A COMPANY'S ANNUAL RETURN

| | |
|---|---|
| 854(1) and (2) | 1985 s 363(1) |
| (3) | 1985 s 363(2) (changed) |
| 855(1) | 1985 s 364(1) (changed) |
| (2) | 1985 s 364(2) |
| (3) | 1985 s 364(3) |
| 856(1) | 1985 s 364A(1) |
| (2) | 1985 s 364A(2) and (3) (changed) |
| (3) | 1985 s 364A(4) (changed) |
| (4) | 1985 s 364A(5) |
| (5) | 1985 s 364A(6) |
| (6) | 1985 s 364A(8) |
| 857(1) and (2) | 1985 s 365(1) |
| (3) | 1985 s 365(2) |
| 858(1) | 1985 s 363(3) and (4) (changed) |
| (2) | 1985 s 363(3) and (4), Sch 24 |
| (3) | 1985 s 363(3) |
| (4) | 1985 s 363(4) |

| Section of 2006 Act | Origin |
|---|---|
| (5) | new |
| 859 | 1985 s 365(3) |

**PART 25 COMPANY CHARGES**

**Chapter 1 Companies registered in England and Wales or in Northern Ireland**

| Section of 2006 Act | Origin |
|---|---|
| 860(1) | 1985 ss 395(1), 399(1) |
| (2) | 1985 s 399(1) |
| (3) | 1985 s 399(2) |
| (4) to (6) | 1985 s 399(3), Sch 24 (changed) |
| (7) | 1985 s 396(1) |
| 861(1) | 1985 s 396(3) |
| (2) | 1985 s 396(1)(d) |
| (3) | 1985 s 396(2) |
| (4) | 1985 s 396(3A) |
| (5) | 1985 ss 395(1) ('company'), 396(4) ('charge'), 400(1) ('company') |
| 862(1) | 1985 s 400(1) |
| (2) and (3) | 1985 s 400(2) |
| (4) and (5) | 1985 s 400(4), Sch 24 (changed) |
| 863(1) to (4) | 1985 s 397(1) |
| (5) | 1985 s 399(1) to (3) |
| 864(1) | 1985 s 397(2) |
| (2) | 1985 s 397(3) |
| (3) | 1985 s 397(2) |
| 865(1) | 1985 s 402(1) |
| (2) | 1985 s 402(2) |
| (3) and (4) | 1985 s 402(3), Sch 24 |
| 866(1) | 1985 s 398(1) |
| (2) | 1985 s 398(3) |
| 867(1) and (2) | 1985 s 398(4) |
| 868(1) and (2) | 1986 art 408(1) |
| (3) | 1986 art 408(2) |
| (4) | 1986 art 408(3) |
| (5) | drafting |
| 869(1) | 1985 s 401(1) (opening words) |
| (2) | 1985 s 401(1)(a) |
| (3) | 1986 art 409(2)(b) |
| (4) | 1985 s 401(1)(b) |
| (5) and (6) | 1985 s 401(2) |
| (7) | 1985 s 401(3) |
| 870(1) | 1985 ss 395(1), 398(2) |
| (2) | 1985 s 400(2) and (3) |
| (3) | 1985 s 397(1) |
| 871(1) | 1985 s 405(1) |
| (2) | 1985 s 405(2) |
| (3) | 1985 s 405(1) and (2) |
| (4) and (5) | 1985 s 405(4), Sch 24 |
| 872(1) and (2) | 1985 s 403(1) (changed) |
| (3) | 1985 s 403(2) |
| 873(1) | 1985 s 404(1) |
| (2) | 1985 s 404(2) |
| 874(1) and (2) | 1985 s 395(1) |
| (3) | 1985 s 395(2) |
| 875(1) | 1985 s 406(1), 1986 art 414(1) |
| (2) | 1985 s 406(2) |
| 876(1) | 1985 s 407(1) |
| (2) | 1985 s 407(2) |
| (3) and (4) | 1985 s 407(3), Sch 24 |
| 877(1) | 1985 s 408(1) |

| Section of 2006 Act | Origin |
|---|---|
| (2) | 1985 ss 406(1), 407(1), 408(1) (changed) |
| (3) | new |
| (4) | 1985 s 408(1) and (2) (changed) |
| (5) and (6) | 1985 s 408(3), Sch 24 (changed) |
| (7) | 1985 s 408(4) |

**Chapter 2 Companies registered in Scotland**

| Section of 2006 Act | Origin |
|---|---|
| 878(1) | 1985 ss 410(2), 415(1) |
| (2) | 1985 s 415(1) |
| (3) | 1985 s 415(2) |
| (4) to (6) | 1985 s 415(3), Sch 24 (changed) |
| (7) | 1985 s 410(4) |
| 879(1) | 1985 s 410(4)(a) |
| (2) | 1985 s 413(1) |
| (3) | 1985 s 410(4)(a) |
| (4) | 1985 s 412 |
| (5) | 1985 s 410(5) |
| (6) | 1985 s 410(5) ('company') |
| 880(1) and (2) | 1985 s 416(1) |
| (3) and (4) | 1985 s 416(3), Sch 24 (changed) |
| 881(1) | 1985 s 414(1) |
| (2) and (3) | 1985 s 414(2) |
| 882(1) to (4) | 1985 s 413(2) |
| (5) | 1985 s 415(1) to (3) |
| 883(1) to (3) | 1985 s 413(3) |
| 884 | 1985 s 411(2) |
| 885(1) | 1985 s 417(1) |
| (2) | 1985 s 417(2) |
| (3) | 1985 s 417(3) |
| (4) | 1985 s 418(1) and (2)(b) |
| (5) | 1985 s 418(2)(a) and (c) |
| (6) | 1985 s 417(4) |
| 886(1) | 1985 ss 410(2), 411(1) |
| (2) | 1985 s 416(1) and (2) |
| (3) | 1985 s 413(2) |
| 887(1) | 1985 s 419(1) (changed) |
| (2) | 1985 s 419(1B)(a) and (c), (3) (changed) |
| (3) | 1985 s 419(1) |
| (4) | 1985 s 419(2) |
| (5) | 1985 s 419(4) |
| 888(1) and (2) | 1985 s 420 |
| 889(1) | 1985 s 410(2) |
| (2) | 1985 s 410(3) |
| 890(1) | 1985 s 421(1) |
| (2) | 1985 s 421(2) |
| 891(1) | 1985 s 422(1) |
| (2) | 1985 s 422(2) |
| (3) and (4) | 1985 s 422(3), Sch 24 |
| 892(1) | 1985 s 423(1) |
| (2) | 1985 ss 421(1), 422(1), 423(1) (changed) |
| (3) | new |
| (4) | 1985 s 423(1) and (2) (changed) |
| (5) and (6) | 1985 s 423(3), Sch 24 (changed) |
| (7) | 1985 s 423(4) |

**Chapter 3 Powers of the Secretary of State**

| Section of 2006 Act | Origin |
|---|---|
| 893(1) to (9) | new |
| 894(1) and (2) | new |

| Section of 2006 Act | Origin |
|---|---|
| 926(1) and (2) | 1985 Sch 15B para 3(e) |
| (3) | 1985 Sch 15B para 6(1) |
| (4) | 1985 Sch 15B para 3 opening words |
| 927(1) | 1985 Sch 15B para 3(b) |
| (2) | 1985 Sch 15B para 3(c) |
| (3) | 1985 Sch 15B para 3 opening words |
| 928 | 1985 Sch 15B para 3(f) |
| 929(1) | 1985 Sch 15B para 8(1) |
| (2) | 1985 Sch 15B para 8(2) |
| 930 | 1985 Sch 15B para 7 |
| 931(1) | 1985 Sch 15B para 13(1) |
| (2) | 1985 Sch 15B para 13(2) |
| (3) | 1985 Sch 15B paras 12(5)(a), 13(3)(a) |
| (4) | 1985 Sch 15B para 13(3)(b) |
| (5) | 1985 Sch 15B paras 12(5)(c), 13(3)(a) |
| (6) | 1985 Sch 15B para 13(3)(c) |
| 932(1) | 1985 Sch 15B para 10(1) |
| (2) to (4) | 1985 Sch 15B para 10(2) |
| (5) | 1985 Sch 15B para 10(2) opening words |
| 933(1) to (3) | 1985 Sch 15B para 11(1) and (2) |
| 934(1) | 1985 Sch 15B para 11(1) and (3) |
| (2) | 1985 Sch 15B para 11(4)(a) and (b) |
| (3) | 1985 Sch 15B para 11(4)(c) |
| (4) | 1985 Sch 15B para 11(4)(d) |

**Chapter 4 Supplementary provisions**

| Section of 2006 Act | Origin |
|---|---|
| 935(1) | 1985 Sch 15B para 5(4) (changed) |
| (2) | 1985 Sch 15B para 5(6) |
| 936(1) to (4) | new |
| 937(1) to (6) | new |
| 938(1) and (2) | 1985 s 427A(3) |
| 939(1) | 1985 Sch 15B para 9(1) and (2) |
| (2) | 1985 Sch 15B para 9(2) |
| (3) and (4) | 1985 Sch 15B para 9(3) |
| (5) | 1985 Sch 15B para 9(4) |
| 940(1) | 1985 Sch 15B para 15(1) |
| (2) | 1985 Sch 15B para 15(2) |
| (3) | 1985 Sch 15B para 15(1) |
| 941 | 1985 ss 427(6), 427A(8) |

**PART 28 TAKEOVERS ETC**

[Note: The Takeovers Directive (Interim Implementation) Regulations 2006 (SI 2006/1183) are based on the provisions of this Part So although the regulations came into force on 20 May 2006 and so before the date of Royal Assent to the Companies Act 2006, they are not cited as origins for those provisions]

**Chapter 1 The Takeover Panel**

| Section of 2006 Act | Origin |
|---|---|
| 942(1) to (3) | new |
| 943(1) to (9) | new |
| 944(1) to (7) | new |
| 945(1) and (2) | new |
| 946 | new |

| Section of 2006 Act | Origin |
|---|---|
| 947(1) to (10) | new |
| 948(1) to (9) | new |
| 949(1) to (3) | new |
| 950(1) and (2) | new |
| 951(1) to (5) | new |
| 952(1) to (8) | new |
| 953(1) to (9) | new |
| 954(1) and (2) | new |
| 955(1) to (4) | new |
| 956(1) to (3) | new |
| 957(1) and (2) | new |
| 958(1) to (8) | new |
| 959 | new |
| 960 | new |
| 961(1) to (3) | new |
| 962(1) and (2) | new |
| 963(1) and (2) | new |
| 964(1) to (6) | new |
| 965 | new |

**Chapter 2 Impediments to takeovers**

| Section of 2006 Act | Origin |
|---|---|
| 966(1) to (8) | new |
| 967(1) to (7) | new |
| 968(1) to (8) | new |
| 969(1) to (3) | new |
| 970(1) to (4) | new |
| 971(1) and (2) | new |
| 972(1) to (4) | new |
| 973 | new |

**Chapter 3 'Squeeze-out' and 'sell-out'**

| Section of 2006 Act | Origin |
|---|---|
| 974(1) to (3) | 1985 s 428(1), drafting |
| (4) and (5) | 1985 s 428(2) |
| (6) | 1985 s 428(2A) |
| (7) | 1985 s 428(7) |
| 975(1) and (2) | 1985 s 428(5) (changed) |
| (3) | 1985 s 428(6) (changed) |
| (4) | 1985 s 430E(1) |
| 976(1) | 1985 s 428(3) |
| (2) | new |
| (3) | 1985 s 428(4) |
| 977(1) | 1985 s 429(8) (changed) |
| (2) | 1985 s 430E(1) (changed) |
| (3) | drafting |
| 978(1) to (3) | new |
| 979(1) and (2) | 1985 s 429(1) (changed) |
| (3) and (4) | 1985 s 429(2) (changed) |
| (5) to (7) | new |
| (8) | 1985 s 429(8) (changed) |
| (9) | 1985 ss 429(8), 430E(2) (changed) |
| (10) | 1985 s 429(8) (changed) |
| 980(1) | 1985 s 429(4) |
| (2) | 1985 s 429(3) (changed) |
| (3) | new |
| (4) | 1985 s 429(4) |
| (5) | 1985 s 429(5) |
| (6) | 1985 s 429(6) |
| (7) | 1985 s 429(7) |
| (8) | 1985 s 429(6), Sch 24 |
| 981(1) | 1985 s 430(1) |
| (2) | 1985 s 430(2) |
| (3) | 1985 s 430(3) |
| (4) | 1985 s 430(4) |
| (5) | 1985 s 430(4) (changed) |
| (6) | 1985 s 430(5) and (8) |
| (7) | 1985 s 430(6) |
| (8) | 1985 s 430(7) |
| (9) | 1985 s 430(9), drafting |

| Section of 2006 Act | Origin |
|---|---|
| 982(1) | drafting |
| (2) and (3) | 1985 s 430(10) |
| (4) and (5) | 1985 s 430(11) |
| (6) | 1985 s 430(12) |
| (7) | 1985 s 430(13) |
| (8) | 1985 s 430(14) |
| (9) | 1985 s 430(15) |
| 983(1) | 1985 s 430A(1), (1A) |
| (2) and (3) | 1985 s 430A(1) (changed) |
| (4) | 1985 s 430A(2) (changed) |
| (5) | 1985 s 430A(2A) |
| (6) and (7) | new |
| (8) | 1985 s 430E(3) |
| 984(1) | 1985 s 430A(1) |
| (2) | 1985 s 430A(4) (changed) |
| (3) | 1985 s 430A(3) |
| (4) | 1985 s 430A(5) |
| (5) | 1985 s 430A(6) |
| (6) | 1985 s 430A(7) |
| (7) | 1985 s 430A(6), Sch 24 |
| 985(1) | 1985 s 430B(1) |
| (2) | 1985 s 430B(2) |
| (3) | 1985 s 430B(3) |
| (4) | 1985 s 430B(4) |
| (5) | 1985 s 430B(4) (changed) |
| 986(1) | 1985 s 430C(1) |
| (2) | 1985 s 430C(1), (2) |
| (3) | 1985 s 430C(3) |
| (4) | new |
| (5) | 1985 s 430C(4) |
| (6) to (8) | new |
| (9) and (10) | 1985 s 430C(5) |
| 987(1) | 1985 s 430D(1) |
| (2) and (3) | 1985 s 430D(2) (changed) |
| (4) | 1985 s 430D(4) (changed) |
| (5) and (6) | 1985 s 430D(3) |
| (7) | 1985 s 430D(4) |
| (8) | 1985 s 430D(5) |
| (9) | 1985 s 430D(6) |
| (10) | 1985 s 430D(7) |
| 988(1) | 1985 s 430E(4) and (8) |
| (2) | 1985 s 430E(5) |
| (3) | 1985 s 430E(6) and (7) |
| (4) | 1985 ss 204(2)(a), 430E(4)(d) |
| (5) | 1985 ss 204(6), 430E(7) |
| (6) | 1985 s 204(3) |
| (7) | 1985 ss 204(5), 430E(7) |
| 989(1) | 1985 s 430F(1) |
| (2) | 1985 s 430F(2) |
| 990(1) to (3) | new |
| 991(1) | 1985 s 428(8) ('the company' and 'the offeror'), new ('date of the offer', 'non-voting shares', 'voting rights' and 'voting shares') |
| (2) | new |

**Chapter 4 Amendments to Part 7 of the Companies Act 1985**

| | |
|---|---|
| 992(1) to (6) | new (amends 1985 Pt 7) |

| Section of 2006 Act | Origin |
|---|---|
| **PART 29 FRAUDULENT TRADING** | |
| 993(1) to (3) | 1985 s 458, Sch 24 |
| **PART 30 PROTECTION OF MEMBERS AGAINST UNFAIR PREJUDICE** | |
| 994(1) | 1985 s 459(1) |
| (2) | 1985 s 459(2) |
| (3) | 1985 s 459(3) |
| 995(1) | 1985 s 460(1A) |
| (2) and (3) | 1985 s 460(1) |
| (4) | 1985 s 460(2) |
| 996(1) | 1985 s 461(1) |
| (2) | 1985 s 461(2) and (3) |
| 997 | 1985 s 461(6) |
| 998(1) to (4) | 1985 s 461(5) |
| 999(1) to (5) | new |
| **PART 31 DISSOLUTION AND RESTORATION TO THE REGISTER** | |
| **Chapter 1 Striking off** | |
| 1000(1) | 1985 s 652(1) |
| (2) | 1985 s 652(2) |
| (3) | 1985 s 652(3) |
| (4) to (6) | 1985 s 652(5) |
| (7) | 1985 s 652(6) |
| 1001(1) | 1985 s 652(4) |
| (2) to (4) | 1985 s 652(5) |
| (5) | 1985 s 652(6) |
| 1002(1) to (3) | 1985 s 652(7) |
| 1003(1) | 1985 s 652A(1) (changed) |
| (2) | 1985 s 652A(2) (changed) |
| (3) | 1985 s 652A(3) |
| (4) | 1985 s 652A(4) |
| (5) | 1985 s 652A(5) |
| (6) | 1985 s 652A(6) and (7) |
| 1004(1) | 1985 s 652B(1) |
| (2) | 1985 s 652B(2) |
| (3) | 1985 s 652B(9) |
| (4) | 1985 s 652D(5)(c) |
| (5) | 1985 s 652E(1) |
| (6) | 1985 s 652E(3) |
| (7) | 1985 s 652E(1), Sch 24 |
| 1005(1) | 1985 s 652B(3) |
| (2) | 1985 s 652B(4) |
| (3) | 1985 s 652B(5) |
| (4) | 1985 s 652E(1) |
| (5) | 1985 s 652E(3) |
| (6) | 1985 s 652E(1), Sch 24 |
| 1006(1) | 1985 ss 652B(6), 652D(5)(c) |
| (2) | 1985 s 652B(7) |
| (3) | 1985 s 652B(8) |
| (4) | 1985 s 652E(1) and (2) |
| (5) | 1985 s 652E(4) |
| (6) | 1985 s 652E(1), Sch 24 |
| (7) | 1985 s 652E(2), Sch 24 |
| 1007(1) | 1985 s 652C(1) |
| (2) | 1985 ss 652C(2), 652D(5)(c) |
| (3) | 1985 s 652C(3) |
| (4) | 1985 s 652E(1) and (2) |
| (5) | 1985 s 652E(5) |
| (6) | 1985 s 652E(1), Sch 24 |
| (7) | 1985 s 652E(2), Sch 24 |
| 1008(1) and (2) | 1985 s 652D(1) |
| (3) | 1985 s 652D(2) and (3) |

| Section of 2006 Act | Origin | Section of 2006 Act | Origin |
|---|---|---|---|
| (4) | 1985 s 652D(4) | 1031(1) to (4) | new |
| 1009(1) | 1985 s 652C(4) | 1032(1) to (5) | new |
| (2) | 1985 s 652C(5) | 1033(1) to (7) | new |
| (3) | 1985 s 652C(7) | 1034(1) | 1985 s 655(1) |
| (4) | 1985 ss 652C(6), 652D(5)(c) | (2) | 1985 s 655(2) |
| | | (3) | new |
| (5) | 1985 s 652E(1) | (4) | 1985 s 655(3) |
| (6) | 1985 s 652E(5) | (5) | 1985 s 655(4) |
| (7) | 1985 s 652E(1), Sch 24 | (6) | drafting |
| 1010 | 1985 s 652D(6) | | |
| 1011 | 1985 s 652D(8) | | |

**PART 32 COMPANY INVESTIGATIONS: AMENDMENTS**

**Chapter 2 Property of dissolved company**

| Section of 2006 Act | Origin | Section of 2006 Act | Origin |
|---|---|---|---|
| 1012(1) | 1985 s 654(1) | 1035(1) to (5) | new (inserts 1985 ss 446A and 446B; amends 1985 ss 431, 432, 437 and 442) |
| (2) | 1985 s 654(2) | | |
| 1013(1) | 1985 s 656(1) | 1036 | new (inserts 1985 ss 446C and 446D) |
| (2) | 1985 s 656(2) (changed) | | |
| (3) to (5) | 1985 s 656(3) (changed) | 1037(1) to (3) | new (inserts 1985 s 446E; amends 1985 ss 451A and 452) |
| (6) and (7) | 1985 s 656(5) | | |
| (8) | 1985 s 656(6) | 1038(1) and (2) | new (amends 1985 ss 434 and 447) |
| 1014(1) | 1985 s 657(1) | | |
| (2) | drafting | 1039 | new (amends Company Directors Disqualification Act 1986 s 8) |
| 1015(1) and (2) | 1985 s 657(2), IA 1986 s 178(4) | | |
| 1016(1) | 1985 s 657(2), IA 1986 s 179(1) | | |

**PART 33 UK COMPANIES NOT FORMED UNDER THE COMPANIES LEGISLATION**

**Chapter 1 Companies not formed under companies legislation but authorised to register**

| Section of 2006 Act | Origin | Section of 2006 Act | Origin |
|---|---|---|---|
| (2) | 1985 s 657(2), IA 1986 s 179(2) | 1040(1) | 1985 s 680(1)(a) and (b), (1A) and (2) |
| (3) | drafting | (2) and (3) | 1985 s 680(1) (closing words) |
| 1017(1) | 1985 s 657(2), 1A 1986 s 181(2) and (3) | (4) | 1985 s 680(3) and (4) |
| (2) | 1985 s 657(2), 1A 1986 s 181(3) | (5) | 1985 s 680(5) |
| (3) | 1985 s 657(2), 1A 1986 s 181(4) | (6) | 1985 s 680(1) (closing words) |
| (4) | 1985 s 657(2), 1A 1986 s 181(3) | 1041(1) | 1985 s 683(1) |
| (5) | 1985 s 657(2), 1A 1986 s 181(6) | (2) | 1985 s 683(2) |
| 1018(1) | 1985 s 657(2), 1A 1986 s 182(1) | 1042(1) to (3) | new |

**Chapter 2 Unregistered companies**

| Section of 2006 Act | Origin | Section of 2006 Act | Origin |
|---|---|---|---|
| (2) | 1985 s 657(2), 1A 1986 s 182(2) | 1043(1) | 1985 s 718(1) and (2) |
| (3) | 1985 s 657(2), 1A 1986 s 182(4) | (2) | 1985 s 718(3) (changed) |
| (4) and (5) | 1985 s 657(2), 1A 1986 s 182(3) | (3) | 1985 s 718(1) (changed) |
| | | (4) | 1985 s 718(5) |
| 1019 | 1985 s 657(2), 1A 1986 s 180(1) and (2) | (5) | 1985 s 718(1) and (3) |
| | | (6) | 1985 s 718(6) |
| 1020(1) and (2) | 1985 s 657(4) | | |
| 1021(1) and (2) | 1985 s 657(5) | | |

**PART 34 OVERSEAS COMPANIES**

| Section of 2006 Act | Origin | Section of 2006 Act | Origin |
|---|---|---|---|
| (3) | 1985 s 657(6) | | |
| 1022(1) | 1985 Sch 20 para 5 | 1044 | 1985 s 744 ('overseas company') (changed) |
| (2) | 1985 Sch 20 para 6 | 1045(1) and (2) | 1989 s 130(6) |
| (3) | 1985 Sch 20 para 7 | 1046(1) to (8) | new |
| (4) and (5) | 1985 Sch 20 para 8 | 1047(1) to (6) | new |
| (6) | 1985 Sch 20 para 9 | 1048(1) and (2) | 1985 s 694(4) (changed) |
| 1023(1) | 1985 s 658(1), IA s 180(1) | (3) to (5) | 1985 s 694(5) |
| (2) | 1985 s 658(1), IA s 180(2) | 1049(1) to (4) | new |
| (3) | 1985 s 658(2) | 1050(1) to (6) | new |

**Chapter 3 Restoration to the register**

| Section of 2006 Act | Origin | Section of 2006 Act | Origin |
|---|---|---|---|
| 1024(1) to (4) | new | 1051(1) to (5) | new |
| 1025(1) to (6) | new | 1052(1) to (6) | new |
| 1026(1) to (3) | new | 1053(1) to (6) | new |
| 1027(1) to (4) | new | 1054(1) to (4) | new |
| 1028(1) to (4) | new | 1055 | new |
| 1029(1) and (2) | new | 1056 | new |
| 1030(1) to (6) | new | 1057(1) to (3) | new |

| Section of 2006 Act | Origin |
|---|---|
| 1058(1) to (4) | new |
| 1059 | 1985 s 695A(4) |

PART 35 THE REGISTRAR OF COMPANIES

| Section of 2006 Act | Origin |
|---|---|
| 1060(1) and (2) | 1985 s 704(2) |
| (3) | 1985 s 744 ('the registrar of companies' and 'the registrar') |
| (4) | drafting |
| 1061(1) to (3) | drafting |
| 1062 | 1985 s 704(4) (changed) |
| 1063(1) to (3) | 1985 s 708(1) (changed) |
| (4) | 1985 s 708(2) and (3) (changed) |
| (5) | 1985 s 708(5) (changed) |
| (6) | 1985 s 708(4) |
| (7) | new |
| 1064(1) to (3) | 1985 s 711(1)(a) (changed) |
| 1065 | 1985 s 710 |
| 1066(1) to (3) | 1985 s 705(1) to (3) |
| (4) and (5) | 1985 s 705(4) |
| (6) | 1985 s 705(5)(za) |
| 1067(1) | 1985 s 705A(1) and (2) (changed) |
| (2) | 1985 s 705A(3) |
| (3) | 1985 s 705A(4) |
| (4) and (5) | 1985 s 705A(5) |
| 1068(1) to (7) | new |
| 1069(1) to (3) | new |
| 1070(1) to (3) | new |
| 1071(1) and (2) | new |
| 1072(1) and (2) | new |
| 1073(1) to (6) | new |
| 1074(1) to (5) | new |
| 1075(1) to (7) | new |
| 1076(1) to (4) | new |
| 1077(1) | 1985 s 711(1) opening words |
| (2) and (3) | new |
| 1078(1) | drafting |
| (2) and (3) | 1985 s 711(1) (changed) |
| (4) | new |
| (5) and (6) | new |
| 1079(1) to (3) | 1985 s 42(1) |
| (4) | 1985 s 711(2) (changed) |
| 1080(1) and (2) | drafting |
| (3) | new |
| (4) | 1985 s 707A(1) |
| (5) | new |
| 1081(1) to (7) | new |
| 1082(1) to (5) | new |
| 1083(1) | 1985 s 707A(2) (changed) |
| (2) and (3) | new |
| 1084(1) to (3) | 1985 s 707A(3) (changed) |
| (4) | 1985 s 707A(4) |
| (5) | 1985 s 707A(3) |
| 1085(1) | 1985 s 709(1) opening words |
| (2) | 1985 s 709(2) (changed) |
| (3) | drafting |
| 1086(1) | 1985 s 709(1)(a) and (b) |
| (2) | new |
| (3) | drafting |
| 1087(1) to (3) | new |
| 1088(1) to (6) | new |

| Section of 2006 Act | Origin |
|---|---|
| 1089(1) and (2) | new |
| 1090(1) to (4) | new |
| 1091(1) and (2) | new |
| (3) | 1985 s 709(3) |
| (4) | new |
| (5) | 1985 s 709(4) |
| 1092(1) and (2) | 1985 s 709(5) |
| 1093(1) to (4) | new |
| 1094(1) to (5) | new |
| 1095(1) to (6) | new |
| 1096(1) to (6) | new |
| 1097(1) to (5) | new |
| 1098(1) and (2) | new |
| 1099(1) to (3) | 1985 s 714(1) (changed) |
| (4) and (5) | 1985 s 714(2) |
| 1100 | 1985 s 709(1) opening words |
| 1101(1) and (2) | new |
| 1102(1) to (4) | new |
| 1103(1) and (2) | new |
| 1104(1) and (2) | 1985 s 710B(1) to (3) |
| (3) | 1985 s 710B(4) |
| (4) | 1985 s 710B(5) |
| (5) | drafting |
| 1105(1) to (3) | new |
| 1106(1) to (6) | new |
| 1107(1) | drafting |
| 1107(2) and (3) | new |
| 1108(1) to (3) | new |
| 1109(1) and (2) | new |
| 1110(1) to (3) | new |
| 1111(1) to (3) | new |
| 1112(1) and (2) | new |
| 1113(1) to (3) | 1985 s 713(1) |
| (4) and (5) | 1985 s 713(2) and (3) |
| 1114(1) | 1985 s 715A(1) 'document', (2) |
| (2) | new |
| 1115(1) | new |
| (2) | 1985 s 710A(2) |
| 1116(1) to (6) | new |
| 1117(1) to (3) | new |
| 1118 | drafting |
| 1119(1) and (2) | 1985 s 704(7) and (8) |
| (3) | new |
| 1120 | new |

PART 36 OFFENCES UNDER THE COMPANIES ACTS

| Section of 2006 Act | Origin |
|---|---|
| 1121(1) | 1985 s 730(5) |
| (2) | 1985 s 744 'officer' |
| (3) | 1985 s 730(5) (changed) |
| 1122(1) to (3) | new |
| 1123(1) to (4) | new |
| 1124 and Sch 3 | new (amend 1985 Act) |
| 1125(1) | drafting |
| (2) | 1985 s 730(4) |
| 1126(1) | 1985 s 732(1) |
| (2) | 1985 s 732(2) (changed) |
| (3) | 1986 art 680(2) (changed) |
| 1127(1) and (2) | 1985 s 731(1) |
| 1128(1) | 1985 s 731(2) |
| (2) | 1985 s 731(3) |
| (3) | 1986 art 679(2) |
| (4) | 1985 s 731(4), 1986 art 679(3) |
| 1129 | 1985 s 732(3) (changed) |
| 1130(1) | 1985 s 734(1) (changed) |

# COMPANIES ACT 2006
# TABLE OF DESTINATIONS

*Notes*

1. The table identifies the provisions of the Companies Act 1985 (c 6) that are repealed and re-enacted (with or without changes) by the Companies Act 2006 and identifies the corresponding provisions in that Act.

2. The table is based on the table of origins. So it only shows a provision of the Companies Act 2006 as a destination of a provision of the Companies Act 1985 if the latter is cited in that table as an origin for the new provision.

3. A repealed provision of the Companies Act 1985 may not be listed in this table because the provision is spent or it is otherwise unnecessary to re-enact it, because the new provision is fundamentally different from the existing provision or because as a matter of policy it has been decided to repeal the existing provision without replacing it.

4. There is no entry for Schedule 24 to the Companies Act 1985 (punishment of offences) in the table. This is cited in the Table of Origins as the origin for a large number of provisions in the Companies Act 2006.

5. A section at the end of the table identifies the substantive provisions of the Companies Act 1989 (c 40) that are repealed and re-enacted by the Companies Act 2006.

## COMPANIES ACT 1985

| Provision of Companies Act 1985 | Destination in Companies Act 2006 |
|---|---|
| **s 1 Mode of forming incorporated company** | |
| (1) | s 7(1) and (2) (changed) |
| (2) | s 3(1) to (4) |
| (3) | s 4(1) to (3) |
| (4) | s 5(1) and (2) |
| **s 2 Requirements with respect to memorandum** | |
| (1) | s 9(2) |
| (2) | ss 9(2), 88(2) |
| (3) | s 9(2) (changed) |
| (4) | s 11(3) (changed) |
| **s 3 Forms of memorandum** | |
| (1) | s 8(2) |
| **s 7 Articles prescribing regulations for companies** | |
| (1) | s 18(2) (changed) |
| (3) | s 18(3) (changed) |
| **s 8 Tables A, C, D and E** | |
| (1) | s 19(1) to (3) (changed) |
| (2) | s 20(1) and (2) (changed) |
| (3) | s 19(4) |
| (4) | s 19(1) to (3) (changed) |
| (5) | s 19(5) |
| **s 9 Alteration of articles by special resolution** | |
| (1) and (2) | s 21(1) |
| **s 10 Documents to be sent to registrar** | |
| (1) | s 9(1), (5) and (6) (changed) |
| (2) | s 12(1) (changed) |
| (3) | s 12(3) |
| (4) | s 9(3) |
| (6) | s 9(5) |
| **s 12 Duty of registrar** | |
| (1) and (2) | s 14 |

| Provision of Companies Act 1985 | Destination in Companies Act 2006 |
|---|---|
| (3) and (3A) | s 13(1) and (2) (changed) |
| **s 13 Effect of registration** | |
| (1) | s 15(1) |
| (2) | s 15(3) |
| (3) | s 16(2) (changed) |
| (4) | s 16(3) |
| (5) | s 16(6) |
| (7) | s 15(4) |
| **s 14 Effect of memorandum and articles** | |
| (1) | s 33(1) (changed) |
| (2) | s 33(2) (changed) |
| **s 15 Memorandum and articles of company limited by guarantee** | |
| (1) | s 37 |
| (2) | s 5(3) |
| **s 16 Effect of alteration on company's members** | |
| (1) | s 25(1) |
| (2) | s 25(2) |
| **s 18 Amendments of memorandum or articles to be registered** | |
| (1) | s 34(2) (changed) |
| (2) | ss 26(1), 34(3) (changed) |
| (3) | ss 26(3) and (4), 34(5) and (6) |
| **s 19 Copies of memorandum and articles to be given to members** | |
| (1) | s 32(1) (changed) |
| (2) | s 32(3) and (4) (changed) |
| **s 22 Definition of 'member'** | |
| (1) | s 112(1) (changed) |
| (2) | s 112(2) |
| **s 23 Membership of holding company** | |
| (1) | s 136(1) |

| Provision of Companies Act 1985 | Destination in Companies Act 2006 |
|---|---|
| **s 118 The authorised minimum** | |
| (1) | ss 763(1), 764(1) (changed) |
| (2) | s 764(3) |
| (3) | s 764(4) |
| **s 119 Provision for different amounts to be paid on shares** | |
| | s 581 |
| **s 121 Alteration of share capital (limited companies)** | |
| (1) | s 617(1) (changed) |
| (2) | ss 617(2) and (3), 618(1), 620(1) (changed) |
| (3) | s 618(2) |
| (4) | ss 618(3), 620(2) (changed) |
| **s 122 Notice to registrar of alteration** | |
| (1) | ss 619(1) to (3), 621(1), 663(1), 689(1) (changed) |
| (2) | ss 619(4) and (5), 621(4) and (5), 663(4) and (5), 689(4) and (5) |
| **s 125 Variation of class rights** | |
| (1) | s 630(1) |
| (2) | s 632 to (4) (changed) |
| (6) | s 334(1) to (4) and (6) (changed) |
| (7) | ss 334(7), 630(5) |
| (8) | s 630(6) |
| **s 126 Saving for court's powers under other provisions** | |
| | s 630 |
| **s 127 Shareholders' right to object to variation** | |
| (1) | s 633(1) |
| (2) | s 633(2) and (3) |
| (2A) | s 633(2) |
| (3) | s 633(4) |
| (4) | s 633(5) |
| (5) | s 635(1) to (3) |
| (6) | s 633(6) |
| **s 128 Registration of particulars of special rights** | |
| (1) | s 556(1) to (3) (changed) |
| (2) | ss 556(1) and (4), 629(2) |
| (3) | s 637(1) (changed) |
| (4) | s 636(1) (changed) |
| (5) | ss 557(1) and (2), 636(2) and (3), 637(2) and (3) (changed) |
| **s 129 Registration of newly created class rights** | |
| (1) | s 638(1) (changed) |
| (2) | s 640(1) (changed) |
| (3) | s 639(1) (changed) |
| (4) | ss 638(2) and (3), 639(2) and (3), 640(2) and (3) |
| **s 130 Application of share premiums** | |
| (1) | s 610(1) |
| (2) | s 610(2) and (2) (changed) |
| (3) | s 610(4) |
| (4) | s 610(5) and (6) |
| **s 131 Merger relief** | |
| (1) | s 612(1) and (4) |
| (2) | s 612(2) |
| (3) | s 612(3) |
| (4) | s 613(2) and (3) |
| (5) | s 613(4) |
| (6) | s 613(5) |
| (7) | s 616(1) |
| **s 132 Relief in respect of group reconstructions** | |
| (1) | s 611(1) |
| (2) | s 611(2) |
| (3) | s 611(3) |
| (4) | s 611(4) |
| (5) | s 611(5) |
| (8) | s 612(4) |
| **s 133 Provisions supplementing ss 131, 132** | |
| (1) | s 615 |
| (2) | s 616(2) |
| (3) | s 616(3) |
| (4) | s 616(1) |
| **s 134 Provision for extending or restricting relief from s 130** | |
| (1) | s 614(1) |
| (3) | s 614(2) |
| **s 135 Special resolution for reduction of share capital** | |
| (1) | s 641(1) to (3) (changed) |
| (2) | s 641(4) |
| **s 136 Application to court for order of confirmation** | |
| (1) | s 645(1) |
| (2) | ss 645(2) and (4), 646(4) |
| (3) | s 646(1) |
| (4) | s 646(2) and (3) |
| (5) | s 646(4) and (5) |
| (6) | s 645(2) and (3) |
| **s 137 Court order confirming reduction** | |
| (1) | s 648(1) and (2) |
| (2) | s 648(3) and (4) |
| (3) | s 648(4) |
| **s 138 Registration of order and minute of reduction** | |
| (1) | s 649(1) (changed) |
| (2) | s 649(3) (changed) |
| (3) | s 649(4) (changed) |
| (4) | s 649(5) and (6) (changed) |
| **s 139 Public company reducing capital below authorised minimum** | |
| (1) | s 650(1) |
| (2) | s 650(2) |
| (3) | s 651(1) and (2) |
| (4) | s 651(3) (changed) |
| (5) | s 651(4), (6) and (7) |
| **s 140 Liability of members on reduced shares** | |
| (1) | s 652(1) (changed) |
| (2) | s 653(1) |
| (3) | s 653(2) |
| (4) | s 653(3) |
| (5) | s 653(3) |
| **s 141 Penalty for concealing name of creditor, etc** | |
| | s 647(1), (2) (changed) |
| **s 142 Duty of directors on serious loss of capital** | |
| (1) | s 656(1) to (3) |
| (2) | s 656(4) and (5) (changed) |
| (3) | s 656(6) |

| Provision of Companies Act 1985 | Destination in Companies Act 2006 |
|---|---|
| (5) | ss 694(1), (3) and (4), 698(1), (3) and (4), 700(5) |
| (6) | ss 696(1) to (5), 699(1) to (6), 700(5) (changed) |
| (7) | ss 697(1) to (4), 698(1), (3) and (4), 699(1) to (6), 700(3) to (5) |

**s 165 Authority for contingent purchase contract**

| | |
|---|---|
| (1) | s 694(3) |
| (2) | ss 694(2), (4) and (5), 695(1), (3) and (5), 696(1) to (5) |

**s 166 Authority for market purchase**

| | |
|---|---|
| (1) | ss 693(1), 701(1) |
| (2) | s 701(2) |
| (3) | s 701(3) and (5) |
| (4) | s 701(4) and (5) |
| (5) | s 701(6) |
| (6) | s 701(7) |
| (7) | s 701(8) |

**s 167 Assignment or release of company's right to purchase own shares**

| | |
|---|---|
| (1) | s 704 |
| (2) | s 700(1) to (5) |

**s 168 Payments apart from purchase price to be made out of distributable profits**

| | |
|---|---|
| (1) | s 705(1) |
| (2) | s 705(2) |

**s 169 Disclosure by company of purchase of own shares**

| | |
|---|---|
| (1) | ss 707(1) to (3), 708(1) (changed) |
| (1A) | ss 707(1) to (3), 708(1) (changed) |
| (1B) | ss 707(1) to (3), 708(1) (changed) |
| (2) | s 707(4) |
| (3) | s 707(5) |
| (4) | s 702(1) to (4) (changed) |
| (5) | s 702(6) |
| (6) | ss 707(6) and (7), 708(4) and (5) |
| (7) | s 703(1) and (2) (changed) |
| (8) | s 703(3) |
| (9) | s 702(7) |

**s 169A Disclosure by company of cancellation or disposal of treasury shares**

| | |
|---|---|
| (1) | ss 728(1), 730(1) |
| (2) | ss 728(2), 730(2) |
| (3) | ss 728(3), 730(3) |
| (4) | ss 728(4) and (5), 730(6) and (7) |

**s 170 The capital redemption reserve**

| | |
|---|---|
| (1) | s 733(1), (2) and (4) |
| (2) and (3) | s 733(3) |
| (4) | s 733(5) and (6) |

**s 171 Power of private companies to redeem or purchase own shares out of capital**

| | |
|---|---|
| (1) | s 709(1) (changed) |
| (2) | s 709(2) |
| (3) | s 710(1) and (2) |
| (4) | s 734(2) |

| Provision of Companies Act 1985 | Destination in Companies Act 2006 |
|---|---|
| (5) | s 734(3) |
| (6) | s 734(4) |

**s 172 Availability of profits for purposes of s 171**

| | |
|---|---|
| (1) | s 711(1) and (2) |
| (2) | s 712(2) |
| (3) | s 712(6) |
| (4) | s 712(3) |
| (5) | s 712(4) |
| (6) | s 712(7) |

**s 173 Conditions for payment out of capital**

| | |
|---|---|
| (1) | s 713(1) and (2) |
| (2) | s 716(1) |
| (3) | s 714(1) to (3) |
| (4) | s 714(4) (changed) |
| (5) | s 714(5) and (6) (changed) |
| (6) | s 715(1) and (2) |

**s 174 Procedure for special resolution under s 173**

| | |
|---|---|
| (1) | ss 716(2), 723(1) |
| (2) | s 717(3) |
| (3) | s 717(4) |
| (4) | s 718(2) and (3) (changed) |
| (5) | s 717(5) |

**s 175 Publicity for proposed payment out of capital**

| | |
|---|---|
| (1) | s 719(1) |
| (2) | s 719(2) |
| (3) | s 719(3) |
| (4) | ss 719(4), 720(1) |
| (5) | s 719(4) |
| (6) | s 720(1), (2) and (4) (changed) |
| (7) | s 720(5) and (6) |
| (8) | s 720(7) |

**s 176 Objections by company's members or creditors**

| | |
|---|---|
| (1) | s 721(1) and (2) |
| (2) | s 721(2) |
| (3) | s 722(2) and (3) |
| (4) | s 722(4) and (5) |

**s 177 Powers of court on application under s 176**

| | |
|---|---|
| (1) | s 721(3) |
| (2) | s 721(4) and (5) |
| (3) | s 721(6) |
| (4) | s 721(7) |

**s 178 Effect of company's failure to redeem or purchase**

| | |
|---|---|
| (1) | s 735(1) |
| (2) | s 735(2) |
| (3) | s 735(2) and (3) |
| (4) | s 735(4) |
| (5) | s 735(5) |
| (6) | s 735(6) |

**s 181 Definitions for Chapter VII**

| | |
|---|---|
| | s 736 |

**s 182 Nature, transfer and numbering of shares**

| | |
|---|---|
| (1) | ss 541, 544(1) and (2) |
| (2) | s 543(1) and (2) |

**s 183 Transfer and registration**

| | |
|---|---|
| (1) | s 770(1) |
| (2) | s 770(2) |
| (3) | s 773 |
| (4) | s 772 |

| Provision of Companies Act 1985 | Destination in Companies Act 2006 | Provision of Companies Act 1985 | Destination in Companies Act 2006 |
|---|---|---|---|
| **s 275 Treatment of assets in the relevant accounts** | | (1) | ss 277(1), 278(1) (changed) |
| (1) | s 841(1) and (2) | (2) | s 278(2) |
| (1A) | s 841(3) | (3) | s 277(2) and (4) |
| (2) | s 841(5) | **s 292 Appointment of directors to be voted on individually** | |
| (3) | s 842 | | |
| (4) to (6) | s 841(4) | (1) | s 160(1) |
| **s 276 Distributions in kind** | | (2) | s 160(2) |
| | s 846(1) and (2) (changed) | (3) | s 160(3) |
| | | (4) | s 160(4) |
| **s 277 Consequences of unlawful distribution** | | **s 303 Resolution to remove director** | |
| (1) | s 847(1) and (2) | (1) | s 168(1) (changed) |
| (2) | s 847(3) and (4) | (2) | s 168(2) |
| **s 278 Saving for provision in articles operative before Act of 1980** | | (3) | s 168(3) |
| | | (4) | s 168(4) |
| | s 848(1) and (2) | (5) | s 168(5) |
| **s 280 Definitions for Part VIII** | | **s 304 Director's right to protest removal** | |
| (1) | s 853(1) | (1) | s 169(1) and (2) |
| (2) | s 853(2) | (2) | s 169(3) |
| (3) | s 853(3) | (3) | s 169(4) |
| **s 281 Saving for other restraints on distribution** | | (4) | s 169(5) |
| | ss 851, 852 (changed) | (5) | s 169(6) |
| **s 282 Directors** | | **s 309 Directors to have regard to interests of employees** | |
| (1) | s 154(2) (changed) | | |
| (3) | s 154(1) | (1) | s 172(1) |
| **s 283 Secretary** | | **s 309A Provisions protecting directors from liability** | |
| (1) | s 271 (changed) | | |
| (3) | ss 270(3), 274 (changed) | (1) | s 232(1) and (2) |
| **s 284 Acts done by person in dual capacity** | | (2) | s 232(1) |
| | s 280 | (3) | s 232(2) |
| **s 285 Validity of acts of directors** | | (4) | s 234(1) |
| | s 161(1) and (2) (changed) | (5) | s 233 |
| | | (6) | s 232(3) |
| **s 286 Qualifications of company secretaries** | | **s 309B Qualifying third party indemnity provisions** | |
| (1) | s 273(1) and (2) (changed) | (1) and (2) | s 234(2) |
| | | (3) | s 234(3) |
| (2) | s 273(3) | (4) | s 234(3) and (6) |
| **s 287 Registered office** | | (5) | s 234(4) |
| (1) | s 86 | (6) and (7) | s 234(5) |
| (3) | s 87(1) | **s 309C Disclosure of qualifying third party indemnity provisions** | |
| (4) | s 87(2) | | |
| (5) | s 87(3) | (1) | s 236(1) (changed) |
| (6) | s 87(4) | (2) | s 236(2) and (3) |
| **s 288 Register of directors and secretaries** | | (3) | s 236(4) and (5) (changed) |
| (1) | ss 162(1) to (3), 275(1) to (3) (changed) | (4) | s 237(1) |
| (2) | ss 167(1) and (2), 276(1) and (2) | (5) | ss 237(1) to (3) and (5) to (8), 238(1) and (3) to (5) |
| (3) | ss 162(5), 275(5) | **s 310 Provisions protecting auditors from liability** | |
| (4) | ss 162(6) and (7), 167(4) and (5), 275(6) and (7), 276(3) and (4) | (1) | s 532(1) and (3) (changed) |
| (5) | ss 162(8), 275(8) | (2) | s 532(2) |
| (6) | s 162(6), 167(4), 275(6), 276(3) | (3) | s 533 |
| **s 289 Particulars of directors to be registered under s 288** | | **s 312 Payment to director for loss of office, etc** | |
| | | | s 215(1), 217(1) and (3) (changed) |
| (1) | ss 163(1), 164 (changed) | **s 313 Company approval for property transfer** | |
| (2) | ss 163(2) and (4), 277(2) and (4) (changed) | (1) | ss 215(1), 218(1) and (3) (changed) |
| **s 290 Particulars of secretaries to be registered under s 288** | | (2) | s 222(2) |
| | | **s 314 Director's duty of disclosure on takeover, etc** | |
| | | (1) | ss 215(1), 219(1) (changed) |

| Provision of Companies Act 1985 | Destination in Companies Act 2006 |
| --- | --- |
| **s 315 Consequences of non-compliance with s 314** | |
| (1) | ss 219(1) and (2), 222(3) (changed) |
| (3) | s 219(5) |
| **s 316 Provisions supplementing ss 312 to 315** | |
| (1) | ss 218(5), 219(7) |
| (2) | s 216(1) and (2) (changed) |
| (3) | s 220(1) |
| **s 317 Directors to disclose interest in contracts** | |
| (1) | s 182(1) (changed) |
| (2) | s 182(2) (changed) |
| (3) | s 185(1) and (2) (changed) |
| (4) | s 185(4) |
| (5) | s 185(1) (changed) |
| (7) | s 183(1) and (2) |
| (8) | s 187(1) to (4) |
| **s 318 Director's service contracts to be open to inspection** | |
| (1) | ss 228(1), 237(2) |
| (2) and (3) | ss 228(2), 237(3) (changed) |
| (4) | ss 228(4), 237(5) |
| (6) | s 230 |
| (7) | ss 229(1), 238(1) |
| (8) | ss 228(5) and (6), 229(3) and (4), 237(6) and (7), 238(3) and (4) (changed) |
| (9) | ss 229(5), 238(5) (changed) |
| (10) | ss 228(7), 237(8) |
| **s 319 Director's contract of employment for more than 5 years** | |
| (1) | s 188(1) and (3) (changed) |
| (2) | s 188(4) (changed) |
| (3) | s 188(2) (changed) |
| (4) | s 188(6) |
| (5) | s 188(5) |
| (6) | s 189 |
| (7) | ss 188(7), 223(1) |
| **s 320 Substantial property transactions involving directors, etc** | |
| (1) | s 190(1) and (2) (changed) |
| (2) | s 191(1) to (5) (changed) |
| (3) | s 223(1) |
| **s 321 Exceptions from s 320** | |
| (1) | s 190(4) |
| (2) | s 192, 193(1) and (2) (changed) |
| (3) | s 192 |
| (4) | s 194(1) and (2) |
| **s 322 Liabilities arising from contravention of s 320** | |
| (1) | s 195(1) and (2) |
| (2) | ss 195(2) and 196 |
| (3) | s 195(1), (3) and (4) |
| (4) | s 195(3), (5) and (8) |
| (5) | s 195(6) |
| (6) | s 195(7) |
| **s 322A Invalidity of certain transactions involving directors, etc** | |

| Provision of Companies Act 1985 | Destination in Companies Act 2006 |
| --- | --- |
| (1) | s 41(1) and (2) |
| (2) | s 41(2) |
| (3) | s 41(3) |
| (4) | s 41(1) |
| (5) | s 41(4) |
| (6) | s 41(5) |
| (7) | s 41(6) |
| (8) | s 41(7) |
| **s 322B Contracts with sole members who are directors** | |
| (1) | s 231(1) and (2) (changed) |
| (2) | s 231(1) |
| (3) | s 231(5) |
| (4) | s 231(3) and (4) (changed) |
| (5) | s 231(7) |
| (6) | s 231(6) |
| **s 325 Register of directors' interests notified under s 324** | |
| (5) | s 809(2) and (3) |
| **s 330 General restriction on loans etc to directors and persons connected with them** | |
| (2) | s 197(1) (changed) |
| (3) | ss 198(1) and (2) (changed), 200(1) and (2) |
| (4) | s 201(1) and (2) (changed) |
| (5) | s 223(1) |
| (6) | s 203(1) and (6) (changed) |
| (7) | s 203(1) (changed) |
| **s 331 Definitions for ss 330 ff** | |
| (3) | s 199(1) |
| (4) | s 199(2) and (3) |
| (6) | ss 198(1), 200(1), 201(1) |
| (7) | s 202(1) |
| (8) | s 202(3) |
| (9) | ss 202(2), 212 |
| (10) | s 202(3) |
| **s 333 Inter-company loans in same group** | |
| | s 208(1) (changed) |
| **s 334 Loans of small amounts** | |
| | s 207(1) (changed) |
| **s 335 Minor and business transactions** | |
| (1) | s 207(2) (changed) |
| (2) | s 207(3) |
| **s 336 Transactions at behest of holding company** | |
| | 208(1) and (2) (changed) |
| **s 337 Funding of director's expenditure on duty to company** | |
| (1) and (2) | s 204(1) (changed) |
| (3) | s 204(2) (changed) |
| **s 337A Funding of director's expenditure on defending proceedings** | |
| (1) | s 205(1) (changed) |
| (2) | s 205(5) |
| (3) | s 205(1) (changed) |
| (4) | s 205(2) |
| (5) | s 205(3) |
| (6) | s 205(4) |
| **s 338 Loan or quasi-loan by money-lending company** | |

| Provision of Companies Act 1985 | Destination in Companies Act 2006 |
|---|---|
| (3) | s 1013(3) to (5) (changed) |
| (5) | s 1013(6) and (7) |
| (6) | s 1013(8) |
| **s 657 Effect of Crown disclaimer under s 656** | |
| (1) | s 1014(1) |
| (2) | ss 1015(1) and (2), 1016(1) and (2), 1017(1) to (5), 1018(1) to (5), 1019 |
| (4) | s 1020(1) and (2) |
| (5) | s 1021(1) and (2) |
| (6) | s 1021(3) |
| **s 658 Liability for rentcharge on company's land after dissolution** | |
| (1) | s 1023(1) and (2) |
| (2) | s 1023(3) |
| **s 680 Companies capable of being registered under this Chapter** | |
| (1)(a) and (b) | s 1040(1) |
| (1) (closing words) | s 1040(2), (3) and (6) |
| (1A) | s 1040(1) |
| (2) | s 1040(1) |
| (3) | s 1040(4) |
| (4) | s 1040(4) |
| (5) | s 1040(5) |
| **s 683 Definition of 'joint stock company'** | |
| (1) | s 1041(1) |
| (2) | s 1041(2) |
| **s 694 Regulation of oversea companies in respect of their names** | |
| (4) | s 1048(1) and (2) (changed) |
| (5) | s 1048(3) to (5) |
| **s 695 Service of documents on overseas company** | |
| (1) and (2) | s 1139(2) (changed) |
| **s 695A Registrar to whom documents to be delivered: companies to which section 690A applies** | |
| (4) | s 1059 |
| **s 699A Credit and financial institutions to which the Bank Branches Directive (89/117/EEC) applies** | |
| (3) ('financial institution') | s 1173(1) |
| **s 704 Registration offices** | |
| (2) | s 1060(1) and (2) |
| (4) | s 1062 (changed) |
| (7) and (8) | s 1119(1) and (2) |
| **s 705 Companies' registered numbers** | |
| (1) to (3) | s 1066(1) to (3) |
| (4) | s 1066(4) and (5) |
| (5)(za) | s 1066(6) |
| **s 705A Registration of branches of overseas companies** | |
| (1) | s 1067(1) (changed) |
| (2) | s 1067(1) |
| (3) | s 1067(2) |
| (4) | s 1067(3) |
| (5) | s 1067(4) and (5) |
| **s 707A The keeping of company records by the registrar** | |
| (1) | s 1080(4) |
| (2) | s 1083(1) (changed) |

| Provision of Companies Act 1985 | Destination in Companies Act 2006 |
|---|---|
| (3) | s 1084(1) to (3) (changed) and (5) |
| (4) | s 1084(4) |
| **s 708 Fees payable to registrar** | |
| (1) | s 1063(1) to (3) (changed) |
| (2) and (3) | s 1063(4) (changed) |
| (4) | s 1063(6) |
| (5) | s 1063(5) (changed) |
| **s 709 Inspection, &c. of records kept by the registrar** | |
| (1) opening words | s 1085(1) and s 1100 |
| (1)(a) and (b) | s 1086(1) |
| (2) | s 1085(2) (changed) |
| (3) | s 1091(3) |
| (4) | s 1091(5) |
| (5) | s 1092(1) and (2) |
| **s 710 Certificate of incorporation** | |
| | s 1065 |
| **s 710A Provision and authentication by registrar of documents in non-legible form** | |
| (2) | s 1115(2) |
| **s 710B Documents relating to Welsh companies** | |
| (1) to (3) | s 1104(1) and (2) |
| (4) | s 1104(3) |
| (5) | s 1104(4) |
| **s 711 Public notice by registrar of receipt and issue of certain documents** | |
| (1) | ss 1064(1) to (3), 1077(1) to (3), 1078(2) and (3) (changed) |
| (2) | s 1079(4) (changed) |
| **s 713 Enforcement of company's duty to make returns** | |
| (1) | s 1113(1) to (3) |
| (2) and (3) | s 1113(4) and (5) |
| **s 714 Registrar's index of company and corporate names** | |
| (1) | s 1099(1) to (3) (changed) |
| (2) | s 1099(4) and (5) |
| **s 715A Interpretation** | |
| (1) ('document') and (2) | s 1114(1) |
| **s 718 Unregistered companies** | |
| (1) | s 1043(1), (3) and (5) (changed) |
| (2) | s 1043(1) |
| (3) | s 1043(2) and (5) (changed) |
| (5) | s 1043(4) |
| (6) | s 1043(6) |
| **s 719 Power of company to provide for employees on cessation or transfer of business** | |
| (1) | s 247(1) |
| (2) | s 247(2) (changed) |
| (3) | s 247(4) to (6) (changed) |
| (4) | s 247(7) (changed) |
| **s 721 Production and inspection of books where offence suspected** | |
| (1) | s 1132(1) and (2) |
| (2) to (4) | s 1132(3) to (5) |
| **s 722 Form of company registers, etc** | |

# COMPANIES ACT 1989

1. Section 130(6) of the Companies Act 1989 (power by regulations to apply provisions relating to company contracts and execution of documents by companies to overseas companies) is re-enacted in section 1045 of the Companies Act 2006.

2. Section 207 of the Companies Act 1989 (transfer of securities) is re-enacted in sections 783, 784(3), 785 and 788 of the Companies Act 2006.

# COMPANIES ACT 2006
## TABLE OF COMMENCEMENT DATES

The following table is intended to provide guidance on the commencement timetable for the Companies Act 2006. It cannot however provide a definitive guide: you may therefore also wish to refer to the relevant commencement order.

Provisions relating to accounts and reports were generally commenced for financial years beginning on or after the relevant date (eg Schedule 3 to the Third Commencement Order provides that 'Section 417 of the Companies Act 2006 (contents of directors' report: business review) applies to directors' reports for the financial years beginning on or after 1 October 2007').

The commencement of powers to make orders or regulations by statutory instrument does not necessarily mean that the Government intends to use the powers as part of its implementation of the Act.

Some provisions (eg definitions) were progressively brought into force for the purposes of each tranche of provisions commenced, and have been finally commenced completely from 1 October 2009.

Following the final commencement on 1 October 2009, five provisions will not have been commenced. These are:

- Section 22(2)
- Section 327 (2)(c)
- Section 330 (6)(c)
- Section 1175 as it applies in Northern Ireland
- Part 2 of Schedule 9

---

1 General introductory provisions (1–6)
        1 October 2009
   Section 2: 6 April 2007

---

2 Company formation (7–16)   1 October 2009

---

3 A company's constitution 1 October 2009 (17–38)
   Sections 29 & 30: 1 October 2007

---

4 A company's capacity and related matters (39–52)
        1 October 2009
   Section 44: 6 April 2008

---

5 A company's name (53–85)   1 October 2009
   Sections 69 to 74: 1 October 2008
   Sections 82 to 85: 1 October 2008

---

6 A company's registered office (86–88)
        1 October 2009

---

7 Re-registration as a means of altering a company's status (89–111)
        1 October 2009

---

8 A company's members (112–144) 1 October 2009

   Sections 116 to 119: 1 October 2007
   Sections 121 & 128: 6 April 2008

---

9 Exercise of members' rights (145–153)
        1 October 2007

---

10 A company's directors (154–259) 1 October 2007

   Sections 155 to 159: 1 October 2008
   Sections 162 to 167: 1 October 2009
   Sections 175 to 177: 1 October 2008

   Sections 180(1), (2)(in part), & 4(b), and 181(2) & (3): 1 October 2008
   Sections 182 to 187: 1 October 2008
   Sections 240 to 247: 1 October 2009

---

11 Derivative claims and proceedings by members (260–269)
        1 October 2007

---

12 Company secretaries (270–280)   6 April 2008
   Section 270(3)(b)(ii): 1 October 2009
   Sections 275 to 279: 1 October 2009

---

13 Resolutions and meetings (281–361)
        1 October 2007
   Sections 308 & 309: 20 January 2007

   Section 333: 20 January 2007
   Sections 327(2)(c) & 330(6)(c) are not being commenced.

---

14 Control of political donations and expenditure (362–379)   1 October 2007

   Provisions relating to independent election candidates: 1 October 2008

   Part 14 comes into force in Northern Ireland on 1 November 2007, except for provisions relating to independent election candidates.

---

15 Accounts and reports (380–474)   6 April 2008
   Section 417: 1 October 2007
   Section 463: 20 January 2007 for reports and statements first sent to members and others after that date.

---

16 Audit (475–539)   6 April 2008
   Sections 485 to 488: 1 October 2007

---

17 A company's share capital (540–657)
        1 October 2009
   Section 544: 6 April 2008
   Sections 641(1)(a) & (2)–(6), 642–644,; 652(1) and (3) & 654: 1 October 2008

---

18 Acquisition by limited company of its own shares (658–737)   1 October 2009

   Repeal of the restrictions under the Companies Act 1985 on financial assistance for acquisition of shares in private companies including the "Whitewash" procedure: 1 October 2008

---

19 Debentures (738–754)   6 April 2008

# 1

# GENERAL INTRODUCTORY PROVISIONS

## Companies Act 2006

### PART 1
### GENERAL INTRODUCTORY PROVISIONS
#### Companies and Companies Acts

## 1 Companies

(1) In the Companies Acts, unless the context otherwise requires—       **1.1.01**
'company' means a company formed and registered under this Act, that is—
  (a) a company so formed and registered after the commencement of this Part, or
  (b) a company that immediately before the commencement of this Part—
    (i) was formed and registered under the Companies Act 1985 (c. 6) or the Companies (Northern Ireland) Order 1986 (S.I. 1986/1032 (N.I. 6)), or
    (ii) was an existing company for the purposes of that Act or that Order, (which is to be treated on commencement as if formed and registered under this Act),
    (iii) was an existing company for the purposes of that Act or that Order, (which is to be treated on commencement as if formed and registered under this Act).
(2) Certain provisions of the Companies Acts apply to—
  (a) companies registered, but not formed, under this Act (see Chapter 1 of Part 33), and
  (b) bodies incorporated in the United Kingdom but not registered under this Act (see Chapter 2 of that Part).
(3) For provisions applying to companies incorporated outside the United Kingdom, see Part 34 (overseas companies).

COMMENCEMENT DATE 1 October 2009[1]

This section defines the 'companies' to which the legislation applies. The 'Companies Acts' are defined    **1.1.02** in section 2. In previous Companies Acts the definition appeared towards the end of the statute,[2] but it does seem more helpful to commence the legislation in this way. The wording of the section does not exactly follow that of its predecessors, which applied the new legislation to what were defined as 'existing companies', that is companies registered under a previous Act. The drafting here refers to companies existing at the time of the 1985 Act or its Northern Irish equivalent as well as companies formed and registered under that legislation, but it deems them on commencement of Part 1 of this Act to be treated as if formed and registered under it. This form of drafting was no doubt adopted to facilitate the application of this Act to the many companies that will have been formed before commencement.[3] In this regard, a general savings provision[4] expressly provides that nothing in the Act affects the registration or reregistration of a company under the former Companies Acts or the

---

[1] Companies Act 2006 (Commencement No 8, Transitional Provisions and Savings) Order 2008, SI 2008/2860, art 3(a).
[2] Eg s 735 in the 1985 Act.
[3] Note that the 'former Companies Acts' are defined in s 1171 to include all the Acts since the Joint Stock Companies Act 1856, although this definition is not needed for the purposes of s 1. It is referred to in s 4 and is made use of in transitional provisions and savings, for example in the text immediately following.
[4] Companies Act 2006 (Commencement No 8, Transitional Provisions and Savings) Order 2008, SI 2008/2860, Sch 2, para 1(1).

continued existence of a company by virtue of such registration or reregistration. For the first time, a Companies Act passed by the UK Parliament includes companies registered in Northern Ireland.[5]

**1.1.03**    The reference in subsection (1)(a) to a company formed and registered after the commencement of Part 1 is to be read as a reference to a company formed and registered on an application received by the registrar on or after 1 October 2009.[6] The reference in subsection (1)(b)(i) to a company formed and registered under the 1985 Act or 1986 Order immediately before the commencement of Part 1 includes a company formed and registered on an application received by the registrar and meeting the requirements as to registration before 1 October 2009.[7]

**1.1.04**    Subsection (2)(a) refers to joint stock companies (see further section 1040 and the commentary thereto) and subsection (2)(b) to unregistered companies (see further section 1043 and the commentary thereto). As is made clear by subsection (3), the provisions applying to overseas companies are in Part 34.

### 2  The Companies Acts

**1.2.01**        (1)  In this Act 'the Companies Acts' means—
            (a)  the company law provisions of this Act,
            (b)  Part 2 of the Companies (Audit, Investigations and Community Enterprise) Act 2004 (c. 27) (community interest companies), and
            (c)  the provisions of the Companies Act 1985 (c. 6) and the Companies Consolidation (Consequential Provisions) Act 1985 (c. 9) that remain in force.
        (2)  The company law provisions of this Act are—
            (a)  the provisions of Parts 1 to 39 of this Act, and
            (b)  the provisions of Parts 45 to 47 of this Act so far as they apply for the purposes of those Parts.

COMMENCEMENT DATE  6 April 2007[8]

**1.2.02**    When the Bill that became this Act was going through Parliament, the government bowed to pressure and took the opportunity to make the Act not just a reforming measure, but also a virtually complete restatement of the statutory law applicable to registered and other companies. In the result, a few sections of the Companies Act 1985 remain on the statute book,[9] as well as a number of provisions of the Companies Act 1989 and Part 2 of the Companies (Audit, Investigations and Community Enterprise) Act 2004 regarding community interest companies.[10] Apart from the special provisions relating to community interest companies, the surviving provisions are almost exclusively concerned with the powers of inspection vested in the Secretary of State.[11]

**1.2.03**    It was thus necessary to define in section 2(1) the 'Companies Acts' as including the surviving provisions of these other Acts as well as the company law provisions of this Act. Note that Parts 40 to 44 of this Act are not within the meaning of the company law provisions.

### *Types of company*

### 3  Limited and unlimited companies

**1.3.01**        (1)  A company is a 'limited company' if the liability of its members is limited by its constitution. It may be limited by shares or limited by guarantee.
        (2)  If their liability is limited to the amount, if any, unpaid on the shares held by them, the company is 'limited by shares'.
        (3)  If their liability is limited to such amount as the members undertake to contribute to the assets of the company in the event of its being wound up, the company is 'limited by guarantee'.

---

[5]  See s 1299, discussed in Chapter 47.
[6]  Companies Act 2006 (Commencement No 8, Transitional Provisions and Savings) Order 2008, SI 2008/2860, Sch 2, para 2(6)(a).
[7]  Companies Act 2006 (Commencement No 8, Transitional Provisions and Savings) Order 2008, SI 2008/2860, Sch 2, para 2(6)(b).
[8]  Companies Act 2006 (Commencement No 2, Consequential Amendments, Transitional Provisions and Savings) Order 2007, SI 2007/1093, art 2.
[9]  Schedule 16 contains the repeals. Note that this does not repeal any of the Companies Consolidation (Consequential Provisions) Act 1985, but this was effected, with effect from 1 October 2009, by the Companies Act 2006 (Commencement No 8, Transitional Provisions and Savings) Order 2008, SI 2008/2860, Sch 1.
[10]  See s 6.
[11]  See Chapter 32. These will probably be consolidated separately at some time.

(4)  If there is no limit on the liability of its members, the company is an 'unlimited company'.

COMMENCEMENT DATE 1 October 2009[12]

This section provides for the same types of company as did section 1(2) of the Companies Act 1985,   **1.3.02**
namely companies limited by shares, companies limited by guarantee and unlimited companies. The
only substantive change is the removal of the requirement for limits on the liability of members to be
stated in the memorandum of association, because the importance of that document has been
substantially reduced.[13] Instead the limit must be in the constitution, defined in section 17,[14] but which
essentially for this purpose means the articles of association.

## 4  Private and public companies

(1)  A 'private company' is any company that is not a public company.   **1.4.01**
(2)  A 'public company' is a company limited by shares or limited by guarantee and having a share
     capital—
     (a)  whose certificate of incorporation states that it is a public company, and
     (b)  in relation to which the requirements of this Act, or the former Companies Acts, as to
          registration or re-registration as a public company have been complied with on or after the
          relevant date.
(3)  For the purposes of subsection (2)(b) the relevant date is—
     (a)  in relation to registration or re-registration in Great Britain, 22nd December 1980;
     (b)  in relation to registration or re-registration in Northern Ireland, 1st July 1983.
(4)  For the two major differences between private and public companies, see Part 20.

COMMENCEMENT DATE 1 October 2009[15]

This section re-enacts the legal distinction between private and public companies that was formerly in   **1.4.02**
section 1(3) of the Companies Act 1985, although the order is recast so that the private company
appears clearly as the default type of company. The two major differences referred to in section 4(4) as
covered in Part 20 are that a private company may not offer its shares to the public and a public
company must have a minimum allotted share capital of £50,000 or the euro equivalent.[16] It is the latter
requirement that dictates the special requirements for registration or re-registration referred to in
subsection (2)(b). The former Companies Acts referred to in subsection (2)(b) are defined in section 1171.

A company can be a public company only if it has a share capital and, since the dates in 1980 or 1983   **1.4.03**
in subsection (3),[17] it has not been possible to form a guarantee company with a share capital, so that
only such guarantee companies, if any, that were registered before then can be public companies.

This Act does not contain any provisions relating to 'old public companies', that is public companies   **1.4.04**
existing before the modern system of classification was introduced by the Companies Act 1980. The
relevant provisions were previously in the Companies Consolidation (Consequential Provisions) Act
1985. They have been re-enacted, in the event of there being any such companies still in existence, in
article 12 of and Schedule 3 to the Companies Act 2006 (Consequential Amendments, Transitional
Provisions and Savings) Order 2009.[18]

## 5  Companies limited by guarantee and having share capital

(1)  A company cannot be formed as, or become, a company limited by guarantee with a share   **1.5.01**
     capital.
(2)  Provision to this effect has been in force—
     (a)  in Great Britain since 22nd December 1980, and
     (b)  in Northern Ireland since 1st July 1983.

---

[12] Companies Act 2006 (Commencement No 8, Transitional Provisions and Savings) Order 2008, SI 2008/
2860, art 3(a).
[13] See Chapter 2.
[14] See Chapter 3.
[15] Companies Act 2006 (Commencement No 8, Transitional Provisions and Savings) Order 2008, SI 2008/
2860, art 3(a).
[16] As to these, see Chapter 20.
[17] Depending on whether the company is registered in Great Britain or Northern Ireland; see s 5.
[18] SI 2009/1941.

(3) Any provision in the constitution of a company limited by guarantee that purports to divide the company's undertaking into shares or interests is a provision for a share capital.
This applies whether or not the nominal value or number of the shares or interests is specified by the provision.

COMMENCEMENT DATE 1 October 2009[19]

**1.5.02**  Section 5(1) and (2) replaces section 1(4) of the Companies Act 1985 and the corresponding provision in the Northern Irish legislation. The section thus ensures that it has not been possible to form a company limited by guarantee with a share capital since the dates in subsection (2). The effect of subsection (3), which was previously in section 15(2) of the Companies Act 1985, is that a company that purports to be a guarantee company, but which provides in its constitution for the division of the company's undertaking into shares or interests, is treated as a company limited by shares. For this purpose, it is not necessary that each share or interest has a nominal value or number, which would otherwise be required by section 10.

### 6 Community interest companies

**1.6.01**  (1) In accordance with Part 2 of the Companies (Audit, Investigations and Community Enterprise) Act 2004 (c. 27)—
  (a) a company limited by shares or a company limited by guarantee and not having a share capital may be formed as or become a community interest company, and
  (b) a company limited by guarantee and having a share capital may become a community interest company.

(2) The other provisions of the Companies Acts have effect subject to that Part.

COMMENCEMENT DATE 1 October 2009[20]

**1.6.02**  Rather than enacting any specific requirements, this section acts as a signpost to Part 2 of the 2004 Act, which created the concept of the community interest company and which was not included in the general consolidation under this Act. A community interest company is a company formed, for use by social enterprises, in the same way as other limited companies, but with additional formal and regulatory requirements under Part 2 of the 2004 Act. By subsection (2), the general provisions of the Companies Acts have effect subject to Part 2 of the 2004 Act.

**1.6.03**  It should be noted that, as well as companies limited by shares or limited by guarantee having the option to form as or become community interest companies, any surviving guarantee companies with a share capital, that is those existing before section 5 or its predecessors came into force, may become such companies.

---

[19] Companies Act 2006 (Commencement No 8, Transitional Provisions and Savings) Order 2008, SI 2008/2860, art 3(a).
[20] Companies Act 2006 (Commencement No 8, Transitional Provisions and Savings) Order 2008, SI 2008/2860, art 3(a).

# COMPANY FORMATION

## Companies Act 2006

### PART 2
### COMPANY FORMATION

#### General

### 7 Method of forming company

(1) A company is formed under this Act by one or more persons—     **2.7.01**
    (a) subscribing their names to a memorandum of association (see section 8), and
    (b) complying with the requirements of this Act as to registration (see sections 9 to 13).
(2) A company may not be so formed for an unlawful purpose.

COMMENCEMENT DATE 1 October 2009[1]

This section replaced section 1 of the Companies Act 1985. It is the enabling provision that allows one **2.7.02** or more persons to form a company. It includes, by reference, the various procedural requirements for incorporation that are now to be found in Part 2. In contrast to section 1 of the Companies Act 1985, section 7 enables a single person to form *either* a private *or* a public company. As a result, section 24 of the Companies Act 1985, which imposed personal liability on a single member of a public company in certain circumstances, is repealed (but note the requirement, under section 123 of the Act, to record in the company's register of members the fact that the company has only one member). By subsection (1)(a), incorporators are (still) required to register a memorandum of association. However, under section 8 the content and role of memoranda are substantially reduced (compared to memoranda submitted upon the incorporation of companies under the Companies Act 1985).

Sections 7 to 16 of the Act apply to applications for registration that are received by the registrar of **2.7.03** companies on or after 1 October 2009.[2] The Companies Act 2006 (Commencement No 8, Transitional Provisions and Savings) Order 2008, SI 2008/2860, Schedule 2 contains various saving provisions to deal with the application of Parts 2 (and 3) of the Act to companies formed under earlier Companies Acts. Note that to be formed under CA 1985, the application for registration must be received by the registrar, and the requirements as to registration must be met, before 1 October 2009.

Subsection (2) repeats the rule, previously found in section 1(1) of the Companies Act 1985 that a **2.7.04** company cannot be formed for an 'unlawful purpose'. (Note also the provision in section 10(3) of the Trade Union and Labour Relations (Consolidation) Act 1992 prohibiting a trade union from registering as a company.) The Act gives no further indication of what may constitute an unlawful purpose, and the rule has generated only a narrow vein of case-law. In *R v Registrar of Joint Stock Companies,*

---

[1] Companies Act 2006 (Commencement No 8, Transitional Provisions and Savings) Order 2008, SI 2008/2860, art 3.
[2] Companies Act 2006 (Commencement No 8, Transitional Provisions and Savings) Order 2008, SI 2008/2860, Sch 2, para 2(1).

*ex p More*[3] the registrar refused to register a company whose main object was selling, in Britain, tickets in an Irish lottery. His reason for so doing was that the sale of such tickets was at that time an offence in England. The Court of Appeal upheld this refusal. Greater difficulty arises in relation to objects that are not criminal, but go against prevailing public policy. In *R v Registrar of Companies, ex p Attorney-General*,[4] it was held that a company formed to carry on the business of prostitution was improperly registered, notwithstanding that prostitution itself is not a criminal offence. The learned judge emphasized that whilst carrying on the trade of prostitution may not itself be a criminal offence, contracts for prostitution are illegal because the purpose of such contracts is sexually immoral and therefore against public policy.

**2.7.05**   To say that a company may not be formed for an unlawful purpose begs the question of how the company's purpose or purposes are to be established. In the cases cited above, each company's objects clause conveniently made clear the dominant purpose for which the company was being formed (and which was then found to be unlawful). Similarly, in *Bowman v Secular Society*[5] the House of Lords, when faced with a memorandum containing a long list of objects, some of which were 'not affected by any taint of illegality', nevertheless held the company's first object to be 'governing' and the remainder merely 'subsidiary'. It is uncertain, however, how the law should be applied to a company that either has a 'general commercial company' objects clause (as defined in section 3A of the Companies Act 1985), or else is in due course formed under the Companies Act 2006 and chooses not to restrict its objects (pursuant to section 31 of the Act).[6] In such cases, it would seem that the challenge to the lawfulness of the company's purpose will have to be brought after the company has been incorporated, and will be based on a factual claim about the activities in which the company is actually engaged and which will then be taken as evidence of its purpose. This, however, raises a further difficulty. If the registrar allows a company to be registered, and only at some later date is it alleged that the company's purpose is unlawful, challenging the registration at that stage faces the additional hurdle of the supposed 'conclusive nature' of a company's certificate of incorporation: see the commentary to section 15(4). (By contrast, if the registrar concludes, *ex ante*, that a company is being formed for an unlawful purpose, she can simply refuse to register it, although that decision can be challenged by the promoters, by way of proceedings for judicial review; see for example *R v Registrar of Joint Stock Companies ex p More*[7] and *R v Registrar of Companies ex p Bowen*.[8] )

### 8   Memorandum of association

**2.8.01**        (1)  A memorandum of association is a memorandum stating that the subscribers—
                       (a)  wish to form a company under this Act, and
                       (b)  agree to become members of the company and, in the case of a company that is to have a share capital, to take at least one share each.
                  (2)  The memorandum must be in the prescribed form and must be authenticated by each subscriber.

         COMMENCEMENT DATE 1 October 2009[9]

**2.8.02**   Section 8 deals with the content of the memorandum of association to which incorporators must subscribe. Subsection (2) specifies that the memorandum must be in the prescribed form, which varies depending upon whether or not the company has a share capital.[10] It is clear that the content (and thus the function) of the memorandum is now much reduced compared to its predecessors under earlier Companies Acts (compare sections 2 and 3 of the Companies Act 1985). The memorandum evidences the fact that the subscribers wish to form a company, and (for companies with a share capital) that each agrees to take at least one share in the company. However, beyond that it no longer states the jurisdiction of the company's registered office, or (for companies limited by guarantee) the terms of the members' guarantee. This information is instead to be found in the supporting documents that must be submitted to the registrar on incorporation (see sections 9 and 11). Likewise, companies with a share capital are no longer required to have an 'authorised' share capital and so no statement of this

---

  [3]  [1931] 2KB 197.
  [4]  [1991] BCLC 476.
  [5]  [1917] AC 406.
  [6]  See the commentary to s 31 below on the significance of a company choosing not to restrict its objects.
  [7]  [1931] 2 KB 197.
  [8]  [1914] 3 KB 1161.
  [9]  Companies Act 2006 (Commencement No 8, Transitional Provisions and Savings) Order 2008, SI 2008/2860, art 3.
  [10]  See the Companies (Registration) Regulations 2008, SI 2008/3014, reg 2. A pro forma memorandum is available from Companies House at: ⟨http://www.companieshouse.gov.uk/forms/generalForms/pro_forma_of_ca_2006_memorandum_for_a_company_with_a_share_capital.pdf⟩.

is to appear in the memorandum.[11] Such companies are required to produce a 'statement of capital and initial shareholdings', but this too is to be recorded in a document outside of the memorandum. Similarly, the memorandum no longer contains an objects clause. Insofar as the company wishes to restrict its objects, such a restriction must be placed in the company's articles of association (see section 31). This is intended to ensure that the 'internal' rules regarding the running of the company appear together in one document, namely the articles.

The memorandum represents a 'snapshot' of the intention of the subscribers at the moment of their **2.8.03** incorporation of the company. Given that, it should no longer be necessary for the memorandum to be amended and, indeed, the Act makes no provision for this to be done (on the meanings of, and differences between, the terms 'altered' and 'amended' within the Act, see section 21 below). The objects clause, insofar as companies have one, will be located in the company's articles and will be capable of being amended accordingly. There is no requirement for a company formed before these provisions come into force to amend its memorandum to bring it into line with these 'new style' memoranda. Instead, terms in its memorandum that will, henceforth, no longer be found in memoranda are to be treated as if they were in the company's articles (see section 28).

The subscribers to the memorandum need not be domiciled in Great Britain: see *Re General Company* **2.8.04** *for Promotion of Land Credit*.[12] It has been held that a minor can be a subscriber, on the grounds that a contract of subscription entered into by a minor would be only voidable, not void: see *Re Laxon & Co (No 2)*.[13] However, in *Seymour v Royal Naval School*,[14] an infant was precluded from membership of a corporation on the grounds that, on the proper construction of the legislation creating the corporation, the legislature neither contemplated, nor intended, that infants could be members. By analogy, it might be said that wherever, on a true construction of the company's purposes, membership of the company by a minor is inconsistent with those purposes, then a minor cannot be a member.

Section 8 stipulates that a memorandum must include a statement that the subscribers agree to become **2.8.05** members. That of itself does not mean that those named as subscribers really have so agreed. However, section 112 of the Act declares that 'the subscribers are deemed to have agreed to become members of the company', precluding challenges to the company's validity on the ground that those named as members never agreed to become such.

The memorandum must also be 'authenticated' by each subscriber. This requirement of authentication **2.8.06** replaces the provision in section 2(6) of the Companies Act 1985, which required the memorandum to be signed by the subscriber(s) in the presence of a witness who was then required to attest the signature (although that requirement had already been amended by the Companies Act 1985 (Electronic Communications) Order 2000[15] to deal with the case of electronic formations). Section 1068 confers upon the registrar the authority to impose requirements with regard to, *inter alia*, the authentication of documents submitted to her: see in particular subsection (3).

### *Requirements for registration*

## 9  Registration documents

(1) The memorandum of association must be delivered to the registrar together with an application **2.9.01** for registration of the company, the documents required by this section and a statement of compliance.

(2) The application for registration must state—
   (a) the company's proposed name,
   (b) whether the company's registered office is to be situated in England and Wales (or in Wales), in Scotland or in Northern Ireland,
   (c) whether the liability of the members of the company is to be limited, and if so whether it is to be limited by shares or by guarantee, and
   (d) whether the company is to be a private or a public company.

(3) If the application is delivered by a person as agent for the subscribers to the memorandum of association, it must state his name and address.

(4) The application must contain—
   (a) in the case of a company that is to have a share capital, a statement of capital and initial shareholdings (see section 10);

---

[11] For the position with regard to existing statements of authorized share capital, see the commentary to section 10, below.
[12] (1870) 5 Ch App 464.
[13] [1892] 3 Ch 555.
[14] [1910] 1 Ch 806.
[15] SI 2000/3373.

(b)  in the case of a company that is to be limited by guarantee, a statement of guarantee (see section 11);

(c)  a statement of the company's proposed officers (see section 12).

(5)  The application must also contain—

(a)  a statement of the intended address of the company's registered office; and

(b)  a copy of any proposed articles of association (to the extent that these are not supplied by the default application of model articles: see section 20).

(6)  The application must be delivered—

(a)  to the registrar of companies for England and Wales, if the registered office of the company is to be situated in England and Wales (or in Wales);

(b)  to the registrar of companies for Scotland, if the registered office of the company is to be situated in Scotland;

(c)  to the registrar of companies for Northern Ireland, if the registered office of the company is to be situated in Northern Ireland.

COMMENCEMENT DATE 1 October 2009[16]

**2.9.02**   Section 9 replaces section 10 of the Companies Act 1985. It lists the documents that must be submitted to the registrar upon incorporation of a company.[17] Further information and guidance on the different methods of submitting the necessary incorporation documents are available from Companies House, at <http://www.companieshouse.gov.uk/infoAndGuide/companyRegistration.shtml>. The documents that must be submitted include an 'application for registration'[18] which contains much of the information that, for a company incorporated under the Companies Act 1985 or its predecessors, was found in the company's memorandum. It must include the company's intended name, whether the liability of the members is to be limited (and, if so, whether by shares or by guarantee), and whether the company is to be private or public. In addition, it must also state the country in which its registered office is to be *situated*. This obligation is over and above that in subsection (5) which requires the actual address of the registered office to be stated. The *situation* of the company's registered office determines both with which registrar the company is to be registered (whether the registrar for England and Wales, for Scotland, or for Northern Ireland) as well as the country which will have jurisdiction over it in respect of those matters for which jurisdiction depends upon the place of incorporation. So far as the application of company law itself is concerned, the issue of jurisdiction has become less important, given that the Companies Acts apply to each of the aforementioned jurisdictions (see section 1284 for the extension of the Companies Acts to Northern Ireland). However, there remain some differences between these jurisdictions in relation to other bodies of law, for example the law relating to insolvency or the granting of charges by companies.

**2.9.03**   As noted, the situation (meaning 'jurisdiction') of the company's registered office is different from the actual address of that office. The requirement to have a registered office is found in section 86 of the Act. Section 1139 allows for the service of documents on companies registered under the Companies Acts by leaving them at, or sending them by post to, the company's registered office. A company that declares its registered office to be situated in 'England and Wales' can move the actual address of its registered office from one in England to an address in Wales, and vice versa. However, a company that states that its registered office is to be situated in Wales cannot do so (but see section 88 of the Act on the right of such a company to change the statement of where its registered office is to be situated). On the right of a Welsh company to draw up, and deliver to the registrar, documents in Welsh, see section 1104. The jurisdiction of the company's registered office will also appear on the company's certificate of incorporation, thereby disclosing that fact to the public (see section 15).

**2.9.04**   The application must also be accompanied by a statement of the company's proposed officers. In addition, for companies with a share capital there must be a statement of capital and initial shareholdings and, for companies limited by guarantee, there must be a statement of the terms of the guarantee. Insofar as the company is not seeking to rely wholly on the 'model articles' supplied by the Secretary of State (see sections 18–20 below), the application must also contain a copy of the company's proposed articles. Finally, the application must also be accompanied by payment of the registration fee. Section 1063 empowers the Secretary of State to make regulations setting the fees payable to the Registrar of Companies. The current fees (which vary according to the method of incorporation) are set out in The

---

[16]  Companies Act 2006 (Commencement No 8, Transitional Provisions and Savings) Order 2008, SI 2008/2860, art 3.

[17]  For guidance generally on the incorporation process, see the Companies House information sheet at: ⟨http://www.companieshouse.gov.uk/about/gbhtml/gp1.shtml#ch1⟩.

[18]  This is available online as Form IN01 at: ⟨http://www.companieshouse.gov.uk/forms/generalForms/IN01_application_to_register_a_company.pdf⟩.

Registrar of Companies (Fees) (Companies, Overseas Companies and Limited Liability Partnerships) (Amendment) Regulations 2011.[19]

## 10   Statement of capital and initial shareholdings

(1)  The statement of capital and initial shareholdings required to be delivered in the case of a       **2.10.01**
company that is to have a share capital must comply with this section.

(2)  It must state—

    (a)  the total number of shares of the company to be taken on formation by the subscribers to the memorandum of association,

    (b)  the aggregate nominal value of those shares,

    (c)  for each class of shares—

        (i)   prescribed particulars of the rights attached to the shares,

        (ii)  the total number of shares of that class, and

        (iii) the aggregate nominal value of shares of that class, and

    (d)  the amount to be paid up and the amount (if any) to be unpaid on each share (whether on account of the nominal value of the share or by way of premium).

(3)  It must contain such information as may be prescribed for the purpose of identifying the subscribers to the memorandum of association.

(4)  It must state, with respect to each subscriber to the memorandum—

    (a)  the number, nominal value (of each share) and class of shares to be taken by him on formation, and

    (b)  the amount to be paid up and the amount (if any) to be unpaid on each share (whether on account of the nominal value of the share or by way of premium).

(5)  Where a subscriber to the memorandum is to take shares of more than one class, the information required under subsection (4)(a) is required for each class.

COMMENCEMENT DATE  1 October 2009[20]

This section replaces the provision of the Companies Act 1985 (section 2(5)) that required a company       **2.10.02**
having a share capital to spell out in its memorandum details of its authorized, and subscribed for, capital. In accordance with the recommendations of the Modern Company Law Review, the requirement for registered companies to have an authorized share capital has been abolished.[21] Instead, the subscribers must now include with their application for registration a statement of the company's capital, and of their initial shareholdings. Subsection (2) sets out the details that are required with regard to the total amount of capital being subscribed for on formation. This again constitutes a snapshot of the company's actual share capital at that moment in time. Subsection (2)(c) requires additional information to be supplied where different classes of shares are being subscribed for. That information is:[22] particulars of voting rights (including rights that arise only in certain circumstances); rights to participate in a distribution (either as respects dividend or as respects capital (including on a winding-up)); and whether the shares are to be redeemed or are liable to be redeemed at the option of the company or the shareholder. Section 10 does not itself set out what details, with regards to the subscribers, must be included in the statement, but instead provides for those details to be 'prescribed'. Regulations have now been enacted prescribing that the statements of capital and of initial shareholdings must contain the name and address of each subscriber to the memorandum.[23]

Whereas subsection (2) deals with the total amount of share capital being subscribed for upon       **2.10.03**
incorporation, subsection (4) deals with the individual amount each subscriber is taking. The information required here includes the number, nominal value and class of shares each subscriber takes, together with the amount paid up and the amount left unpaid. It is this latter amount that sets the limit to what the member may be required to contribute to the company as a member (section 74(2)(d) of the Insolvency Act 1986).

There are a number of other provisions within the Companies Act 2006 which require companies to       **2.10.04**
prepare and file statements of capital.[24] Following a consultation exercise launched in 2009, the

---

[19]  SI 2011/309.

[20]  Companies Act 2006 (Commencement No 8, Transitional Provisions and Savings) Order 2008, SI 2008/2860, art 3.

[21]  Note, however, that any provision in a company's memorandum specifying the company's authorized share capital that was in force immediately before 1 October 2009 is deemed to be a provision in the company's articles. Such a provision continues to operate as a limit on the maximum amount of shares that may be allotted by the company, and is alterable by ordinary resolution; see Companies Act 2006 (Commencement No 8, Transitional Provisions and Savings) Order 2008, SI 2008/2860, sch 2, para 42.

[22]  Companies (Shares and Share Capital) Order 2009, SI 2009/388. art 2(3).

[23]  Companies (Registration) Regulations 2008, SI 2008/3014, reg 3.

[24]  See eg sections 108, 555 and 856.

Government indicated in May 2011 that it intends to bring forward, 'as soon as a suitable legislative vehicle is available', proposals to simplify the financial information requirements for all companies.[25] However, those changes will *not* apply to the statement of capital and shareholdings required on formation.

## 11  Statement of guarantee

**2.11.01**
(1) The statement of guarantee required to be delivered in the case of a company that is to be limited by guarantee must comply with this section.

(2) It must contain such information as may be prescribed for the purpose of identifying the subscribers to the memorandum of association.

(3) It must state that each member undertakes that, if the company is wound up while he is a member, or within one year after he ceases to be a member, he will contribute to the assets of the company such amount as may be required for—

   (a) payment of the debts and liabilities of the company contracted before he ceases to be a member,

   (b) payment of the costs, charges and expenses of winding up, and

   (c) adjustment of the rights of the contributories among themselves, not exceeding a specified amount.

COMMENCEMENT DATE 1 October 2009[26]

**2.11.02**   Section 11 replaces section 2(4) of the Companies Act 1985. It deals with the statement of guarantee that must be given by members of a company that is to be limited by guarantee. The guarantee constitutes the amount each member undertakes to contribute to the assets of the company in the event of its being wound up, and which thus sets the maximum amount that can be required of him as a member (see section 74(3) of the Insolvency Act 1986). However, this amount is in addition to any other monies the member may be required to pay to the company as, say, a subscription fee, or a fee for services rendered by the company to the member.

**2.11.03**   The section sets out the conditions with which such companies' guarantees must comply. It specifies that the member remains liable to make his guaranteed contribution to the assets of the company if it is wound up whilst he is, or within one year of his ceasing to be, a member of the company. The guarantee relates to the company's own debts (but only those incurred during his membership of the company) as well as the costs of the winding up and the costs of adjusting the rights of the contributories *inter se*. The amount of members' guarantee must also be stated, although the Act does not say how much, or how little, that guarantee must be. It seems to be generally assumed that there is nothing to prevent different members entering into guarantees for different amounts, and for different members' entitlement to participate in profits varying to reflect the differences in the amounts they guarantee (see also section 37 below).

**2.11.04**   Previously, the terms of the members' guarantee were included within the memorandum of the company, and it has been held that there was no power to alter that provision in the memorandum: see *Hennessy v National Agricultural and Industrial Development Association*.[27] This must remain the position now that the guarantee is to appear in the section 11 statement. Although the statutory rules relating to the members' guarantee may seem more prescriptive than those relating to the company's share capital, those rules are rendered somewhat toothless by the section's failure to spell out any minimum amount of the guarantee, together with guarantee companies' own practice of setting that amount at an entirely nominal level.

**2.11.05**   The aggregate amount guaranteed by the members does not form part of the company's capital, and cannot be charged by the company: see *Re Pyle Works*[28] and also *Re Irish Club Co.*[29] in which Buckley J said that it would be 'a melancholy thing' if that were not the law 'for in that case there would be no use in having reserve capital'. Finally, section 11, like section 10, does not itself set out the details of the subscribers that must be included in the statement, but instead allows those details to be 'prescribed' by the Secretary of State. Regulations have now been enacted requiring that the statement of guarantee contain the name and address of each subscriber to the memorandum.[30]

[25] See ⟨http://www.bis.gov.uk/Consultations/companies-act-2006-statements-of-capital-consultation⟩.

[26] Companies Act 2006 (Commencement No 8, Transitional Provisions and Savings) Order 2008, SI 2008/ 2860, art 3.

[27] (1974) IR 159.

[28] (1890) 44 Ch D 544, 574.

[29] [1906] WN 127.

[30] Companies (Registration) Regulations 2008, SI 2008/3014, reg 4.

## 12   Statement of proposed officers

(1) The statement of the company's proposed officers required to be delivered to the registrar must contain the required particulars of—                                         **2.12.01**
  (a) the person who is, or persons who are, to be the first director or directors of the company;
  (b) in the case of a company that is to be a private company, any person who is (or any persons who are) to be the first secretary (or joint secretaries) of the company;
  (c) in the case of a company that is to be a public company, the person who is (or the persons who are) to be the first secretary (or joint secretaries) of the company.
(2) The required particulars are the particulars that will be required to be stated—
  (a) in the case of a director, in the company's register of directors and register of directors' residential addresses (see sections 162 to 166);
  (b) in the case of a secretary, in the company's register of secretaries (see sections 277 to 279).
(3) The statement must also contain a consent by each of the persons named as a director, as secretary or as one of joint secretaries, to act in the relevant capacity.
  If all the partners in a firm are to be joint secretaries, consent may be given by one partner on behalf of all of them.

COMMENCEMENT DATE  1 October 2009[31]

Section 12 replaces (parts of) section 10 of the Companies Act 1985. It deals with the information that must be supplied with the application for registration with regard to the company's officers. Section 12(1) identifies those officers of the company for whom this information must be provided. Note that for other provisions of the Act, a wider definition of company officers is used (see, for example, section 26 (liability of officers in default for failure to register amended articles)).     **2.12.02**

Under section 12, the company officers in respect of whom the required information must be supplied include its first director(s), and the first secretary (or joint secretaries) of the company. Public companies continue to be required to have a secretary, and the prescribed information must accordingly be supplied for such person (or persons in the case of joint secretaries). Private companies are no longer required to have a secretary. However, where they *choose* to do so, then the prescribed information must be supplied in relation to such person(s).     **2.12.03**

Subsection (2) spells out—by reference—the information that must be supplied in relation to the individuals described above, namely the information that must be stated in the relevant registers for directors and secretaries. The reference, in the case of directors, to the 'register of directors' and 'the register of directors' residential addresses' reflects the changes introduced in the Act to permit *all* directors to keep their residential addresses secret; see Chapter 8 of Part 10. Finally, subsection (3) requires the statement to include a consent to act by those named in it.     **2.12.04**

## 13   Statement of compliance

(1) The statement of compliance required to be delivered to the registrar is a statement that the requirements of this Act as to registration have been complied with.     **2.13.01**
(2) The registrar may accept the statement of compliance as sufficient evidence of compliance.

COMMENCEMENT DATE  1 October 2009[32]

This section repeats the requirement, previously found in section 12(3) of the Companies Act 1985, that an application for registration must include a statement of compliance with the 'registration requirements' of the Act. Under the Companies Act 1985, the application for registration had to be accompanied by a statutory declaration that those requirements had been complied with, albeit with a relaxation for registrations submitted by 'electronic means' (introduced by the Companies Act 1985 (Electronic Communications) Order 2000).[33] Section 13 now simplifies matters somewhat by no longer insisting on a statutory declaration in *any* circumstances. The section does not specify what form the statement must take, thereby permitting the form to be sent either on paper or electronically. The registrar will be able to use her power under section 1068 to specify rules about the form the statement must take.Section 1112 renders the making of a false statement to the registrar a criminal offence.     **2.13.02**

Subsection (2) permits the registrar to accept the compliance statement as evidence that the registration requirements have been complied with. It does not, however, require the registrar to do so. It     **2.13.03**

---

[31] Companies Act 2006 (Commencement No 8, Transitional Provisions and Savings) Order 2008, SI 2008/2860, art 3.
[32] Companies Act 2006 (Commencement No 8, Transitional Provisions and Savings) Order 2008, SI 2008/2860, art 3.
[33] SI 2000/3373.

provides a protection for registrars who have failed to notice errors in the application, rather than a ground for incorporators to prevent registrars looking behind their statements of compliance.

### *Registration and its effect*

### 14  Registration

**2.14.01**     If the registrar is satisfied that the requirements of this Act as to registration are complied with, he shall register the documents delivered to him.

COMMENCEMENT DATE 1 October 2009[34]

**2.14.02**  Section 14 replaces section 12(1) of the Companies Act 1985. It obliges the registrar to register the incorporation documents submitted to him, provided that he is satisfied that the Act's requirements as to registration have been complied with. If the registrar refuses to do so, then that refusal can be challenged by an application for judicial review, and an order of *mandamus* sought against the registrar: see, for example, *R v Registrar of Joint Stock Companies, ex p More*[35] (registrar's refusal to register upheld) and *R v Registrar of Companies, ex p Bowen*[36] (order granted).

### 15  Issue of certificate of incorporation

**2.15.01**     (1)  On the registration of a company, the registrar of companies shall give a certificate that the company is incorporated.
         (2)  The certificate must state—
              (a)  the name and registered number of the company,
              (b)  the date of its incorporation,
              (c)  whether it is a limited or unlimited company, and if it is limited whether it is limited by shares or limited by guarantee,
              (d)  whether it is a private or a public company, and
              (e)  whether the company's registered office is situated in England and Wales (or in Wales), in Scotland or in Northern Ireland.
         (3)  The certificate must be signed by the registrar or authenticated by the registrar's official seal.
         (4)  The certificate is conclusive evidence that the requirements of this Act as to registration have been complied with and that the company is duly registered under this Act.

COMMENCEMENT DATE 1 October 2009[37]

**2.15.02**  Section 15 replaces (certain parts of) section 13 of the Companies Act 1985. It deals with the content, and the legal status, of a certificate of incorporation. Subsection (1) requires the registrar to issue such a certificate upon the registration of a company, whilst subsection (2) spells out what the content of the certificate must be. Besides the name, registered number, and date of incorporation, the certificate must also identify what type of company has been formed. Thus, it must show whether it is limited or unlimited (and, if limited, whether by shares or by guarantee), and whether it is public or private. There is no requirement to show whether the company is a 'community interest company' (see section 6 on community interest companies). In a change from the position under the Companies Act 1985, the certificate must now also show in which jurisdiction the company has its registered office. Previously, it was the practice of the registrar to include this information on the certificate, although there was no statutory requirement on her to do so.

**2.15.03**  By subsection (3), the certificate is to be signed or authenticated by the registrar. Where an application to register a company is made, and accepted, online, the certificate of incorporation is attached, as a PDF file, to the email which is sent by Companies House to the applicant and which confirms that the application for registration has been accepted.

**2.15.04**  Subsection (4) repeats the provision previously found in section 13(7) of the Companies Act 1985 that the certificate 'is conclusive evidence' of the matters stated in the subsection. The intention behind the subsection is to avoid challenges to the validity of companies based on alleged defects in the registration process, including the alleged unlawfulness of the company's purpose. Those dealing with a company need to be able to trust that it has been properly incorporated. However, the effect of this subsection (4), which has a long and somewhat fraught history, is rather more limited than it may appear, on its face, to be. For one, the provision does not mean that the purposes of a company, once the company is

---

[34]  Companies Act 2006 (Commencement No 8, Transitional Provisions and Savings) Order 2008, SI 2008/2860, art 3.
[35]  [1931] 2KB 197.
[36]  [1914] 3 KB 1161.
[37]  Companies Act 2006 (Commencement No 8, Transitional Provisions and Savings) Order 2008, SI 2008/2860, art 3.

registered, must be taken to be lawful. It only means, at most, that any unlawfulness in those purposes cannot be a ground for challenging the validity of the company (see eg Lord Finlay LC in *Bowman v Secular Society*: 'What the Legislature was dealing with was the validity of the incorporation, and it is for the purpose of incorporation, and for this purpose only, that the certificate is made conclusive'[38] ). Thus, even if the certificate of incorporation cannot be challenged on the ground of the unlawfulness of the company's objects, still directors might be in breach of the criminal law, or in breach of their duties to the company, if they act in pursuit of such objects.

Further, it has also been held that (the predecessor to) section 15(4) does not bind the Crown. In   **2.15.05**
*Bowman v Secular Society Ltd*, Lord Parker of Waddington declared '[i]t should be observed that neither s 1 of the Companies Act, 1900 nor the corresponding section of the Companies (Consolidation) Act, 1908, is so expressed as to bind the Crown, and the Attorney-General, on behalf of the Crown, could institute proceedings by way of *certiorari* to cancel a registration which the registrar in affected discharge of his quasi-judicial duties had improperly or erroneously allowed'.[39] It was on this basis that the court granted the Attorney-General an order of *certiorari* to quash the registration of a company set up to carry on the trade of prostitution in *R v Registrar of Companies ex p Attorney General*.[40]

Moreover, it appeared for a short while as if *private* actors—say creditors, or members —might also be   **2.15.06**
able to challenge the conclusiveness of certificates issued by the registrar, by bringing actions for *judicial review* of the registrar's decision (to issue a certificate). In *R v Registrar of Companies ex p Esal (Commodities) Ltd*.[41] the judge at first instance allowed a creditor bank to challenge, by way of proceedings for judicial review, a certificate issued by the registrar confirming the registration of a charge created by a company. Such a certificate was, by virtue of section 98(2) of the Companies Act 1985 (and echoing section 15), 'conclusive evidence that the requirements of this Part of this Act as to registration have been complied with'. On appeal, however, the Court of Appeal ruled that whilst a creditor bank would indeed have *locus standi* (at least once winding-up proceedings had been commenced against a company) to seek a judicial review of the registrar's decision to issue such a certificate, nevertheless the conclusive nature of the certificate precluded the Court, notwithstanding that the proceedings were proceedings for judicial review, from considering evidence adduced to show that the requirements as to registration had not been complied with.

Where the court does, exceptionally, grant an order quashing the registration of a company, it is   **2.15.07**
unclear what precise legal consequences follow from that. In *R v Registrar of Companies ex p Attorney General*,[42] for example, there was not, so far as one can tell from the case report, a great deal of corporate property whose ownership would become problematic with the demise of the company, nor were there outstanding liabilities that might, potentially, have to be reassigned. Nevertheless, the absence of a developed law on the nullity of UK companies might well cause difficulties were a certificate to be quashed in the case of a company with substantial property, or substantial ongoing rights and obligations.

## 16   Effect of registration

    (1)  The registration of a company has the following effects as from the date of incorporation.   **2.16.01**
    (2)  The subscribers to the memorandum, together with such other persons as may from time to time become members of the company, are a body corporate by the name stated in the certificate of incorporation.
    (3)  That body corporate is capable of exercising all the functions of an incorporated company.
    (4)  The status and registered office of the company are as stated in, or in connection with, the application for registration.
    (5)  In the case of a company having a share capital, the subscribers to the memorandum become holders of the shares specified in the statement of capital and initial shareholdings.
    (6)  The persons named in the statement of proposed officers—
        (a)  as director, or
        (b)  as secretary or joint secretary of the company, are deemed to have been appointed to that office.

COMMENCEMENT DATE 1 October 2009[43]

---

[38]  [1917] AC 406, 421.
[39]  [1917] AC 406, 439–440.
[40]  [1991] BCLC 476.
[41]  [1986] 2 WLR 177.
[42]  [1991] BCLC 476.
[43]  Companies Act 2006 (Commencement No 8, Transitional Provisions and Savings) Order 2008, SI 2008/2860, art 3.

**2.16.02**  Section 16 replaces (parts of) section 13 of the Companies Act 1985. It declares, somewhat tersely, the effects of the registration of a company. The fundamental consequence is that the subscribers (and subsequent members of the company) become 'a body corporate' which, by subsection (3), is declared to be 'capable of exercising all the functions of an incorporated company'. It is this legal personality enjoyed by the body corporate, separate and distinct from its members, that represents the most fundamental consequence of the company's incorporation. Being a legal person, the company is able to enter into contracts with others, and thus to incur liabilities separate from those of its members. Indeed, it can do so even when it is contracting with its own members.[44] The company is able to own property in its own name, separate from that of its members. Members own their shares in the company, but not the property of the company itself.[45] Likewise, the company is capable of both suing, and being sued, in its own name. It also enjoys 'perpetual succession'. Once registered, it survives the death of its members or directors, ending only when its own separate existence is terminated, say by being wound up. Understandably, the full consequences of a company's separate legal personality have been worked out mostly through those cases which have sought to challenge the separateness of the company from its members or directors, by seeking to 'pierce the veil of incorporation'. To summarize a great deal of jurisprudence in a very short space, UK courts have been slow to allow this veil to be lifted, although it remains difficult to identify, from those exceptional cases where the veil is lifted, a clear and coherent body of principles governing such judicial intervention. The courts' reluctance can be seen in the (in)famous case of *Salomon v Salomon & Co*,[46] in which the House of Lords refused to lift the veil in what was, in substance, a 'one-man' company, thereby paving the way for the proliferation of small businesses using the corporate form. And this judicial reluctance continues in the steady trickle of cases that have emerged involving corporate groups. In *Adams v Cape Industries plc*[47] the Court of Appeal took the opportunity to restate and clarify the law, but in so doing heavily circumscribed the situations in which the veil might be lifted. In particular, their Lordships accepted that to do so might be appropriate where there was fraud, or where a company was being used as a 'façade' to hide the true facts of a situation. However, the court rejected any general policy of piercing the veil between the members of a group of companies that formed a 'single economic entity', unless, say, the construction of a statute or of a contractual document required the veil to be pierced. The court emphasized that UK company law permits groups to use different companies in order to assign liabilities to different parts of the group. This approach was followed in the recent case of *Linsen International Ltd v Humpuss Sea Transport Pte Ltd*.[48] On the other hand, this reluctance to pierce the veil has itself been circumvented through actions in tort against parent companies. In *Chandler v Cape plc*,[49] an employee of a wholly owned subsidiary of Cape plc successfully sued Cape, as a joint tortfeasor, for injuries sustained in the course of his employment. The Court of Appeal identified the circumstances in which a parent company might owe a duty of care towards the employees of its subsidiary. Those circumstances included where the business of the parent and subsidiary were the same, the parent had superior knowledge of health and safety matters within the industry, and the parent knew, or ought to have foreseen, that the employee or subsidiary would rely on the parent's superior knowledge.

**2.16.03**  The consequences which follow from registration begin 'as from the date of incorporation'. It has been held that this means that a company is deemed incorporated from the first moment of that day; see *Jubilee Cotton Mills v Lewis*.[50] Nevertheless, promoters need to bear in mind the rules relating to transactions entered into before the date of incorporation. For the position in relation to such 'pre-incorporation contracts' see section 51. The provisions of subsections (4) to (6) kick-start the life of the company by providing that those identified in the memorandum as subscribers become the first members of the company, whilst those named as director or as secretary are deemed appointed to those offices.

---

[44]  *Lee v Lee's Air Farming Ltd* [1961] AC 12.
[45]  *Macaura v Northern Assurance Co Ltd* [1925] AC 619.
[46]  [1897] AC 22.
[47]  [1990] BCLC 479.
[48]  [2011] EWHC 2339 (Comm).
[49]  [2012] 3 All ER 640.
[50]  [1924] AC 958 (HL).

# 3

# A COMPANY'S CONSTITUTION

---

# Companies Act 2006

## PART 3
## A COMPANY'S CONSTITUTION

## CHAPTER 1
## INTRODUCTORY

### 17 A company's constitution

Unless the context otherwise requires, references in the Companies Acts to a company's constitution include—     **3.17.01**

    (a) the company's articles, and

    (b) any resolutions and agreements to which Chapter 3 applies (see section 29).

    COMMENCEMENT DATE 1 October 2009[1]

The Companies Act 1985 made occasional reference to a company's constitution (say under section 35A of that Act) but did not provide any general definition thereof. The Companies Act 2006 contains more references to the company's constitution, and also now provides this general definition. The     **3.17.02**

---

[1] Companies Act 2006 (Commencement No 8, Transitional Provisions and Savings) Order 2008, SI 2008/2860, art 3. The Companies Act 2006 (Commencement No 3, etc) Order 2007, SI 2007/2194, art 2(3) had already commenced s 17, with effect from 1 October 2007, for the limited purposes of the provisions specified in art 2(1) of that Order. Note also that the transitional adaptation in Sch 1, para 1 to that Order is repealed by art 6(1) of the Companies Act 2006 (Commencement No 8, Transitional Provisions and Savings) Order 2008, SI2008/2860.

definition does not include the company's memorandum, reflecting the reduced role that document now plays (see section 8). It does, however, include not merely the articles but also all those 'resolutions and agreements' which are listed in section 29. The section 17 definition is non-exhaustive. Some provisions of the Act (for example, section 257) provide their own account of additional provisions that are deemed to be included within the constitution. The 'Companies Acts' are defined in section 2 of the Act.

CHAPTER 2
ARTICLES OF ASSOCIATION

*General*

### 18  Articles of association

**3.18.01**
(1)  A company must have articles of association prescribing regulations for the company.
(2)  Unless it is a company to which model articles apply by virtue of section 20 (default application of model articles in case of limited company), it must register articles of association.
(3)  Articles of association registered by a company must—
    (a)  be contained in a single document, and
    (b)  be divided into paragraphs numbered consecutively.
(4)  References in the Companies Acts to a company's 'articles' are to its articles of association.

COMMENCEMENT DATE 1 October 2009[2]

**3.18.02**  Section 18 replaces, with modifications, section 7 of the Companies Act 1985. By subsection (1), all companies must *have* articles. Subsection (2) also requires all companies to *register* articles. However, this latter obligation does not apply where the company is of a description for which the Secretary of State has used her power under section 19 of the Act to prescribe a model set of articles. In such a case, if the company chooses not to register articles of its own, then the model articles will apply 'by default'. Note that pursuant to the power under section 19, the Secretary of State has now prescribed model articles for private companies limited by shares, private companies limited by guarantee and public companies.[3] Accordingly, for companies of each of those descriptions, it is no longer necessary to register articles. (By comparison, under the Companies Act 1985, it was only the model articles prescribed for companies limited by shares (so-called 'Table A') that became 'default' articles, which thus applied unless excluded by the company and obviated the need for the company to register articles of its own.) Note that where a company does choose to rely in whole, or in part, on regulations from the relevant model, it is not required to *set out* the content of those regulations in its own articles (see section 26(2)).

**3.18.03**  A company cannot include, within its articles, anything that is contrary to the mandatory provisions of the Companies Acts. That begs the question, of course, as to which provisions are mandatory. In earlier Companies Acts, it was unclear which provisions were to be regarded as such. Some provisions (for example section 303 of the Companies Act 1985) expressly declared that they applied notwithstanding anything to the contrary in the company's articles. Other provisions expressly declared that they applied subject to contrary provision in the articles, while others were simply silent as to their status. Under the Companies Act 2006, however, there appears to be a presumption that a provision in the Act is mandatory, and overrides a contrary provision in the articles, unless it expressly permits the articles to exclude or modify it. So, some provisions still expressly declare that they are 'defaults' that permit the members to make alternative provision in the articles.[4] At least some provisions that previously expressly stated that they applied notwithstanding contrary provision in the articles no longer do so.[5] Nevertheless, the argument that all the provisions of the Act can now be *presumed* to be mandatory unless they expressly state otherwise is undercut by a number of provisions which still take the trouble to declare expressly that they override any contrary provision in the articles.[6]

---

[2] Companies Act 2006 (Commencement No 8, Transitional Provisions and Savings) Order 2008, SI 2008/2860, art 3. By Sch 2, para 3(1) to that Order, s 18 does not apply to a company where the application to register that company is received by the registrar of companies (and the requirements as to registration are met) before 1 October 2009.
[3] See the Companies (Model Articles) Regulations 2008, SI 2008/3229; see Chapter 51 for the model articles and commentary thereon.
[4] See s 31 (statement of company's objects), s 318 (quorum at meetings), s 319 (chairman at meetings), and so on.
[5] See eg s 168 of the Act, which replaces s 303 of the Companies Act 1985.
[6] See eg s 321 (right to demand a poll) and s 327 (notice required of appointment of proxy).

### 19  Power of Secretary of State to prescribe model articles

(1) The Secretary of State may by regulations prescribe model articles of association for companies.   **3.19.01**
(2) Different model articles may be prescribed for different descriptions of company.
(3) A company may adopt all or any of the provisions of model articles.
(4) Any amendment of model articles by regulations under this section does not affect a company registered before the amendment takes effect.
   'Amendment' here includes addition, alteration or repeal.
(5) Regulations under this section are subject to negative resolution procedure.

COMMENCEMENT DATE 1 October 2009[7]

Section 19 enables the Secretary of State to prescribe different model articles for different types of   **3.19.02**
company. Under this power, model articles have now been prescribed for private companies limited by shares, private companies limited by guarantee and public companies.[8]

Subsection (3) makes clear that companies may, but are not required to, adopt the model articles pre-   **3.19.03**
scribed for a company of their description, and that they are free to adopt them in whole or in part. By subsection (4), a company is not affected by amendments made by regulations under section 19 to the model articles that occur after the company's registration. Companies (and their advisers) need to bear this in mind both in ascertaining the terms of their articles at any point in time, and in deciding whether or not to update their own articles in response to changes to the prescribed model. It should be stressed that subsection (4) applies only to amendments made by regulations *under this section*. Where amendments to a model set of articles are effected by some other enactment, then it would be a question of interpretation as to whether such amendments affect a company registered before the amendment takes effect.[9]

In *Fell v Derby Leather Co Ltd*[10] the court held that the Interpretation Act 1889 (now the Interpretation   **3.19.04**
Act 1978) applied both to the interpretation of Table A, since this had legislative force, and also to the 'special articles' that the company had itself adopted alongside Table A. The court so held on the ground that to do otherwise would lead to different interpretative practices in relation to what was a single document. It may be doubted, therefore, whether the same would apply where a company had wholly excluded Table A.

### 20  Default application of model articles

(1) On the formation of a limited company—   **3.20.01**
   (a) if articles are not registered, or
   (b) if articles are registered, in so far as they do not exclude or modify the relevant model articles,
   the relevant model articles (so far as applicable) form part of the company's articles in the same manner and to the same extent as if articles in the form of those articles had been duly registered.
(2) The 'relevant model articles' means the model articles prescribed for a company of that description as in force at the date on which the company is registered.

COMMENCEMENT DATE 1 October 2009[11]

Section 20 replaces section 8(2) of the Companies Act 1985. It deals with the status of the different sets   **3.20.02**
of articles that may be prescribed, under section 19, for different types of (limited) company. Those articles are to apply, by default, to the type of company to which they are addressed (say the private company limited by shares, or the private company limited by guarantee, etc.), to the extent that such companies choose not to exclude them. Subsection (2) specifies that the model regulations that apply in default are those in force at the date on which the company is registered. In fact, the application form used by Companies House to register a company still requires the incorporators to specify whether

---

[7] Companies Act 2006 (Commencement No 8, Transitional Provisions and Savings) Order 2008, SI 2008/2860, art 3. By Sch 2, para 3(1) to that Order, s 19 does not apply to a company where the application to register that company is received by the registrar of companies (and the requirements as to registration are met) before 1 October 2009.

[8] See the Companies (Model Articles) Regulations 2008, SI 2008/3229; see Chapter 51 for the model articles and commentary thereon.

[9] See also the discussion in Chapter 51.

[10] [1931] 2 Ch 252.

[11] Companies Act 2006 (Commencement No 8, Transitional Provisions and Savings) Order 2008, SI 2008/2860, art 3. By Sch 2, para 3(1) to that Order, s 20 does not apply to a company where the application to register that company is received by the registrar of companies (and the requirements as to registration are met) before 1 October 2009.

they wish to take the model articles or to register their own bespoke articles instead.[12] If incorporators fail to register their own bespoke articles and fail positively to opt for the model articles, then it seems that Companies House usually returns the application rather than applying the relevant model by default.

**3.20.03**  As noted, the model articles apply insofar as they are not excluded or modified by the company's own registered articles (subsection (1)(b)). This could be the source of some uncertainty. If a company does not directly state that some provision in the relevant model articles, identified by number, is not to apply, then it will become a question of interpretation whether that provision is in fact excluded or modified by the company's own regulations. In *Stothers v William Steward (Holdings) Ltd* Peter Gibson LJ declared that '[t]he articles, including the regulations of Table A incorporated into the articles, must be construed together and effect given, so far as possible, to every provision; it is only if the express articles are inconsistent with the incorporated regulations of Table A that the former will override the latter'.[13]

## *Alteration of articles*

### 21  Amendment of articles

**3.21.01**      (1)  A company may amend its articles by special resolution.
         (2)  In the case of a company that is a charity, this is subject to—
             (a)  in England and Wales, section 64 of the Charities Act 1993 (c. 10);
             (b)  in Northern Ireland, Article 9 of the Charities (Northern Ireland) Order 1987 (S.I. 1987/2048 (N.I. 19)).
         (3)  In the case of a company that is registered in the Scottish Charity Register, this is subject to—
             (a)  section 112 of the Companies Act 1989 (c. 40), and
             (b)  section 16 of the Charities and Trustee Investment (Scotland) Act 2005 (asp 10).

      COMMENCEMENT DATE 1 October 2009[14]

**3.21.02**  Sections 21 to 27 of the Act are listed under the sub-heading of 'alteration' of the company's articles. Some of these sections, however, deal with what are termed therein 'amendments' to the articles. The intended distinction between 'amendment' and 'alteration' was explained, during the Bill's passage through Parliament, as follows: '... a company's articles can be changed either by changing the text or by means of some free-standing overriding provision. We think that "amendment" is the normal way of describing textual changes, and that it is by textual changes that companies normally change their articles, whereas legislation and courts are more likely to adopt free-standing overriding provisions. Since "alteration" naturally has a broader range of meaning, encompassing both textual changes and overriding provisions, the Bill should generally refer to amendments when it is dealing with changes made by the company's members and to alterations when it is dealing with changes made by legislation or external agencies.'[15] This usage of amendment and alteration is generally followed in the Act, but not invariably so. Thus, section 19(4) refers to 'amendment by regulations' (issued by the Secretary of State).

**3.21.03**  Section 21 itself replaces section 9 of the Companies Act 1985. It deals with amendments of articles (by companies themselves). It permits such amendment by a special resolution. That is the usual way in which amendments to the articles are made. However, there is a line of authority[16] holding that the informed and *unanimous* consent of all shareholders with a right to vote is as effective as would be a resolution passed at a shareholders' meeting.[17] It was held in *Cane v Jones*[18] that this 'unanimous consent' principle extends to amendments to the articles. Moreover, it was held in *Ho Tung v Man On Insurance Company Limited* that articles which had never been formally adopted by special resolution

---

    [12] See sec. A7 of Form IN01, 'Application to register a company', available from Companies House at: ⟨http://www.companieshouse.gov.uk/forms/generalForms/IN01_application_to_register_a_company.pdf⟩.
    [13] [1994] 2 BCLC 266, 273(a).
    [14] Companies Act 2006 (Commencement No 8, Transitional Provisions and Savings) Order 2008, SI 2008/2860, art 3. In relation to provisions in the articles of existing (or 'transitional') companies that were not themselves alterable, see para 3.21.11 below.
    [15] Rt Hon Margaret Hodge, *Official Report, House of Commons*, 20 June 2006 Standing Committee D, cols 50–51.
    [16] See eg *In re Express Engineering Works Ltd* [1920] Ch 466; *Parker and Cooper Ltd v Reading* [1926] Ch 975; *In re Duomatic Ltd* [1969] 2 Ch 365.
    [17] Indeed, it seems unnecessary for any meeting of shareholders to have taken place, and the consent of the shareholders might be given at different times or in different places; see *Parker and Cooper Ltd v Reading* [1926] Ch 975.
    [18] [1981] 1 All ER 533.

of the shareholders, but which they had acquiesced in by a long course of dealing, were to be regarded as the valid and operative articles of the company.[19]

Historically, the courts have not looked kindly on attempts to *exclude* a company's power (exercisable   **3.21.04**
by its shareholders) to amend its articles; see section 22 below. However, the courts have imposed their own—albeit limited—control on the power of the majority to amend the articles. The courts will overturn amendments that are not passed '*bona fide* for the benefit of the company as a whole'.[20] It seems clearly settled now[21] that this formulation constitutes one rule, not two.[22] Thus, the test is *not* whether the amendment was *both* passed *bona fide* and was, objectively, for the benefit of the company. Rather, the question is whether the majority shareholder(s) honestly believed the amendment was for the benefit of the company. Thus, courts should defer heavily to the views of the majority of the shareholders themselves, rather than imposing their own view on the merits of the amendment under the guise of the 'reasonable man'. This approach was confirmed in the recent case of *Citco Banking Corp NV v Pusser's Ltd*,[23] where Lord Hoffmann also emphasized that it should apply whether the proposed amendment operated to the disadvantage of some shareholders or, equally, where it operated to the advantage of others.[24]

Although this subjective approach inevitably makes judicial intervention less likely, if the court finds   **3.21.05**
that there was *no reasonable ground* on which a shareholder could have believed that the amendment was for the benefit of the company, then it might still set aside the amendment. Such a clear absence of corporate benefit might be taken to establish either that the members were not acting *bona fide*, or that they did not turn their minds to the right issues in addressing the question of corporate benefit.[25] Moreover, even where a particular amendment of the articles might, objectively, be seen as for the benefit of the company, it might still be struck down if it were in fact motivated by a malicious desire to harm the minority.[26]

Thus, notwithstanding that the test here is essentially a unified, and subjective, one it remains   **3.21.06**
important to ascertain what might constitute a benefit for the company. The courts have, however, struggled to deal with this question. Sometimes the court has treated the company as a separate commercial entity, with interests of its own over and above those of individual members.[27] However, even if the 'reification' of the company that this approach requires is accepted, the problem remains that many amendments to the articles involve changes to the rights of the members *inter se* which are of little relevance to the company as a separate commercial entity. That the 'company as a commercial entity test' will sometimes prove unhelpful was acknowledged by the Australian High Court in *Peters American Delicacy Co Ltd v Heath*,[28] by the UK's Court of Appeal in *Greenhalgh v Arderne Cinemas Ltd*,[29] and by the Privy Council in *Citco Banking Corp NV v Pusser's Ltd*.[30] In *Greenhalgh*, Lord Evershed MR stated that 'the phrase, "the company as a whole" does not (at any rate in such a case as the present) mean the company as a commercial entity, distinct from the corporators; it means the corporators as a general body'.[31] The difficulty in this formulation, however, is that it treats as a 'general body' a group of shareholders which is factionalized around the consequences, and thus the merits, of the amendment in question.[32] Nor does Lord Evershed's further explanation of this test avoid this problem. '[T]he case may be taken', he continued, 'of an individual hypothetical member and it may be asked whether what is proposed is, in the honest opinion of those who voted in its favour, for that person's benefit.' In those cases where the amendment gives a benefit to some, at the expense of others,

---

[19] [1902] AC 232.
[20] The burden of proof lies upon the shareholder challenging the amendment: *Citco Banking Corp NV v Pusser's Ltd* [2007] BCC 205, 211.
[21] But see the discussion at para 3.21.08 below.
[22] See *Shuttleworth v Cox Bros & Co* [1927] 2 KB 9; *Greenhalgh v Arderne Cinemas Ltd* [1951] Ch 286.
[23] [2007] BCC 205
[24] [2007] BCC 205, 210.
[25] See Scrutton LJ in *Shuttleworth v Cox Bros & Co* [1927] 2 KB 9.
[26] See *Sidebottom v Kershaw, Leese & Co* [1920] 1 Ch 154.
[27] See eg *Allen v Gold Reefs of West Africa Ltd* [1900] 1 Ch 656; *Sidebottom v Kershaw, Leese & Co Ltd* [1920] 1 Ch 154.
[28] (1939) 61 CLR 457.
[29] [1951] Ch 286.
[30] [2007] BCC 205.
[31] [2007] BCC 205, 291.
[32] See also *Redwood Master Fund Ltd v TD Bank Europe Ltd* [2006] 1 BCLC 149, a case involving alteration of an agreement for a syndicated loan, rather than alteration of articles of association, but in which Rimer J felt that a test of what was in the interests of the 'lenders as a whole' was inappropriate where there were conflicts of interest between the three lenders.

however, the question will immediately arise whether the hypothetical member is to be taken as belonging to the favoured, or disfavoured, group.

**3.21.07**  His Lordship did suggest yet another formulation of the test, in terms of whether the amendment 'discriminated between the majority and the minority shareholders, so as to give the former an advantage of which the latter were deprived'.[33] Yet, given that most amendments that are subsequently litigated will, in their real world operation, be discriminatory in this (rather weak) sense, the test seems to provide little guidance as to which amendments will be struck down. Indeed, in *Greenhalgh* itself, the court found that the amendment was not discriminatory, notwithstanding that it clearly benefited the majority faction and disadvantaged the minority shareholder. In *Citco Banking Corp NV v Pusser's Ltd*, Lord Hoffmann acknowledged that '[s]ome commentators have not found this approach entirely illuminating',[34] but declined to suggest any alternative. As already noted, however, it was accepted that an amendment might be judged lawful notwithstanding that it benefits some shareholders, or harms others. Indeed, *Citco* also reiterated that shareholders who stand to gain from an amendment are not for that reason precluded from voting on the alteration; there is no requirement of 'disinterested approval', nor are shareholders required to forego all thought of personal gain when they vote on such amendments.[35]

**3.21.08**  Although the test applied in reviewing alterations is, as argued above, best now viewed as a subjective one, it is worth observing that in some first instance decisions (dealing with alterations that sought to permit the *expropriation* of a member's shares) the courts did, in fact, take a more robust line, striking out alterations where, *in the view of the court*, there was no evidence of a benefit to the company.[36] The reasoning in these cases has been criticized in some of the more recent decisions discussed above, but they have not been formally overruled. In that regard, it might be noted that the High Court of Australia, in *Gambotto v WCP Ltd*,[37] held that a power of expropriation conferred by an alteration to the articles would be validly exercisable only if for a proper purpose and if its exercise will not operate oppressively in relation to minority shareholders. Not only did the court envisage an objective approach here (with the court, not the shareholders, applying these tests of fairness and oppression), but the tests themselves seemed relatively demanding. So, whilst saving the company from 'significant detriment or harm' might constitute a proper purpose, merely advancing 'the interests of the company as a legal and commercial entity or those of the majority, albeit the great majority, of corporators' would not.[38] It is unclear whether the UK courts would now take a similarly robust line in cases involving expropriation, although in *Citco Banking Corporation NV v Pusser's Limited* (a case not itself involving expropriation), the Privy Council agreed with the Australian High Court that the '*Gambotto* rule' had 'no support in English Authority'.[39]

**3.21.09**  Note that a member wishing to challenge an alteration of the articles might also petition the courts (under section 994) alleging that the affairs of the company have been conducted in a way that is 'unfairly prejudicial' to the interests of the member.

**3.21.10**  Subsections (2) and (3) deal with a further, but more limited, restriction on the power of companies to amend their articles. The restriction applies only to companies that are charities in England and Wales, or in Northern Ireland, or are registered in the Scottish Charity Register. For those in England and Wales, or Northern Ireland, the consent of the Charity Commission is required for certain amendments to such a company's articles. For those registered in the Scottish Charity Register, certain amendments are prohibited (under section 112 of the Companies Act 1989), or require the consent of the 'Office of the Scottish Charity Regulator' (under section 16 of the Charities and Trustee Investment (Scotland) Act 2005).

**3.21.11**  Finally, note that section 21 must also be read as subject to three further restrictions. The first is the restriction on amendment of articles in section 63 (companies that are exempt from the use of, and do not use, 'limited' as part of the company's name). The second arises where a company has a 'provision for entrenchment' in its articles.[40] The third restriction is found in Sch 2, para 4(1) to the Companies

---

[33]  *Greenhalgh v Arderne Cinemas Ltd* [1951] Ch 286, 291.

[34]  [2007] BCC 205, 211.

[35]  [2007] BCC 205, 213. Compare the process for ratifying breaches of duty under s 239 of Companies Act 2006.

[36]  See eg *Brown v British Abrasive Wheel Co* [1919] 1 Ch 290; *Dafen Tinplate Co v Llanelly Steel Co* [1920] 2 Ch 124.

[37]  (1995) 182 CLR 432.

[38]  (1995) 182 CLR 432, 445–456.

[39]  [2007] UKPC 13. For a similar view on the status of *Gambotto* in English law, as well as an acknowledgement that English law on this issue is itself less than clear, see *Constable v Executive Connections Ltd* [2002] 2 BCLC 638, 646–653.

[40]  See s 22 below.

Act 2006 (Commencement No 8, Transitional Provisions and Savings) Order 2008, SI 2008/2860. This provides that the power in section 21 to amend the articles does not apply to any provision of a company's articles that was not itself capable of being amended either (a) immediately before 1 October 2009, in the case of an 'existing company' or (b) at the date of the company's registration (or reregistration), in the case of a 'transitional company'. A 'provision of the company's articles' includes (by Schedule 2, paragraph 4(3)) any provision of the company's memorandum that is deemed, by virtue of section 28 of the Act, to be a provision of the company's articles. An 'existing company' is one that is formed and registered before 1 October 2009. A 'transitional company' is one which is formed and registered, or reregistered, on or after 1 October 2009, but is done so under the Companies Act 1985 (because the application to register (or reregister) is received by the registrar of companies, and all the requirements as to registration (or reregistration) are met, before 1 October 2009.[41]

## 22   Entrenched provisions of the articles

(1)  A company's articles may contain provision ('provision for entrenchment') to the effect that      **3.22.01**
specified provisions of the articles may be amended or repealed only if conditions are met, or procedures are complied with, that are more restrictive than those applicable in the case of a special resolution.

(2)  Provision for entrenchment may only be made—
   (a)  in the company's articles on formation, or
   (b)  by an amendment of the company's articles agreed to by all the members of the company.

(3)  Provision for entrenchment does not prevent amendment of the company's articles—
   (a)  by agreement of all the members of the company, or
   (b)  by order of a court or other authority having power to alter the company's articles.

(4)  Nothing in this section affects any power of a court or other authority to alter a company's articles.

COMMENCEMENT DATE For subsections (1) and (3)–(4): 1 October 2009[42]

For subsection (2): to be announced[43]

Historically, efforts to entrench the whole, or part, of a company's articles have been constrained by the      **3.22.02**
courts. In *Allen v Gold Reefs of West Africa Ltd* Lord Lindley MR declared that 'the company is empowered by the statute to alter the regulations contained in its articles from time to time by special resolutions … and any regulation or article purporting to deprive the company of this power is invalid on the ground that it is contrary to the statute'.[44] Further, in *Punt v Symons & Co Ltd*[45] it was held that this restriction (on a company contracting itself out of its right to alter the articles) applied not only to provisions inserted in the articles themselves, but also to provisions in 'extrinsic' contracts with third parties.

This restriction does not, however, preclude shareholders themselves from entering into agreements      **3.22.03**
*inter se* regarding the exercise of their voting rights, say by requiring shareholders to vote against any resolution to alter the articles: see *Russell v Northern Bank Development Corporation Ltd*.[46] Nevertheless, so long as the agreement remains one that operates only between the signatory shareholders, it will not bind other shareholders who are not a party to it, including, say, new members joining the company post-agreement. A provision inserted in the company's articles, by contrast, or a promise made by the company itself not to alter its articles, *would* effectively bind future members (by taking away their ability to amend the articles).

It was possible to get around this difficulty of binding future members by placing some regulation that      **3.22.04**
the current member(s) wished to entrench in the company's *memorandum*, rather than in its articles. Although provisions placed in the memorandum that *could have been* put in the articles were *prima facie* also susceptible to alteration by special resolution (under section 17 of the Companies Act 1985), that was only a 'default rule' that did not apply where the memorandum *also* prohibited (or made

---

[41]  Companies Act 2006 (Commencement No 8, Transitional Provisions and Savings) Order 2008, SI 2008/2860, art 2.

[42]  Companies Act 2006 (Commencement No 8, Transitional Provisions and Savings) Order 2008, SI 2008/2860, art 3.

[43]  Companies Act 2006 and Limited Liability Partnerships (Transitional Pprovisions and Savings) (Amendment) Regulations 2009, SI 2009/2476, reg 2. The delay in the commencement of subs (2) is to enable the Government to address the possible difficulty that provision might cause to the creation or amendment of class rights.

[44]  [1900] 1 Ch 656, 671.

[45]  [1903] 2 Ch 506.

[46]  [1992] 3 All ER 161.

express provision for) alteration of the regulation.[47] However, this mechanism was, like the use of voting agreements, somewhat cumbersome and, in any case, is no longer available given the reduced function that will, henceforth, be played by a company's memorandum. Provisions that were entrenched in the memoranda of companies before the entry into force of Part 3 of the Act are deemed to be provisions in those companies' articles of association.[48]

**3.22.05**    The Company Law Review (CLR) recommended that members should be able to entrench regulations in the articles, and section 22 tries to enable them to do so. The section does not overturn the decisions cited above (that rendered invalid regulations or articles depriving the company of the power to alter its articles). Rather, it seems to provide a specific exemption from the application of those decisions, namely in relation to articles that amount to 'provisions for entrenchment'. To gain this exemption, the article will have to fall within the definition of such a provision. If it does *not*, then presumably the article will still be invalid, in virtue of the decisions noted above.

**3.22.06**    To qualify as such a provision, the article may restrict either the amendment *or* the repeal of other articles. It must also relate to 'specified provisions' of the company's articles. It is unclear whether this condition merely requires that all the articles to which the provision applies must be specifically, ie expressly, identified, or whether it excludes a provision that purports to apply to *all* the articles. Further, under section 22(1), a provision for entrenchment must be one that states that specified provisions in the articles may be amended or repealed *only if conditions are met, or procedures are complied with, that are more restrictive than those applicable in the case of a special resolution.* A provision for entrenchment, therefore, is one that demands more than a mere special resolution in order to amend, or repeal, specified articles. (On the requirements, now, for the passing of a special resolution, see section 283.) These 'more restrictive conditions' could include, for example, ones requiring a larger proportion of votes cast than the 75 per cent necessary for the passing of a special resolution, or a longer notice period than that which is now required.

**3.22.07**    Perhaps the most obvious and straightforward example of a provision for entrenchment might be thought to be one that simply declares, bluntly, that specified provisions in the articles 'cannot be amended or repealed'. Yet there is arguably some doubt about whether this will actually qualify as a 'provision for entrenchment'. The original definition of a provision for entrenchment in the Bill did indeed include,[49] *inter alia*, an article stating that specified provisions of the articles 'could not be altered or repealed'. However, this part of the definition of a provision for entrenchment was deleted as the Bill was amended in Committee Stage in the Commons. The reason given for this deletion was connected to the introduction of what is now section 22(3)(a). Section 22(3)(a) allows the members of a company, by unanimity, to amend *any* article, notwithstanding that the company has a provision for entrenchment in its articles. Since, by virtue of section 22(3)(a), there can no longer be an 'absolute' entrenching provision (since such a provision can always be overcome, provided all the current members agree), it was said to be inappropriate to include, within the definition of a provision for entrenchment, a provision declaring that specified articles 'could not be altered or repealed'. However, the reasoning here seems flawed. The intention in the legislation—to allow the current members, by unanimity, to change the constitution as they see fit—is achieved by the 'over-ride' provision of section 22(3)(a). With that in place, it does not matter how 'absolute' the members express their entrenching provision to be. However, the danger now is that a provision for entrenchment that *does* bluntly state that some articles 'cannot be altered or repealed' will be held to fall outside the definition of a provision for entrenchment and will, in consequence, not enjoy the limited validity that section 22 seeks to confer on entrenching provisions (ie that they are effective until amended by unanimity). This seems an unnecessary trap for those wishing to draft entrenchment provisions, especially given that it is the most 'straightforward' wording of such a provision that might be held to be ineffective. Moreover, it is a trap that may catch those who included an entrenchment provision as part of their company's memorandum long before the Act was passed and, of course, in ignorance of the precise wording of section 22.

---

[47]  It is unclear whether the informed and unanimous assent of all shareholders would have been sufficient to overcome such a prohibition on the alteration of a provision in the memorandum. Note, eg, that in *Re Duomatic*, Buckley J expressed the 'unanimous consent' principle in the following (more limited) terms: 'where it can be shown that all shareholders who have a right to attend and vote at a general meeting of the company assent to some matter which a general meeting of the company could carry into effect, that assent is as binding as a resolution in general meeting would be' [1969] 2 Ch 365, 369. Thus, unanimous consent would be as good as, but no better than, a resolution, yet a resolution would not be sufficient in the face of a prohibition on amendment. Note also that were the unanimous consent principle at common law sufficient to overcome a prohibition on alteration, then s 22(3) of the Act (discussed below) would have been unnecessary.

[48]  See s 28 and, for the continuing effectiveness of those provisions, see Sch 2, para 4(1) to the Companies Act 2006 (Commencement No 8, Transitional Provisions and Savings) Order 2008, SI 2008/2860, discussed at para 3.21.11 above.

[49]  See cl 22(1)(a).

Such an existing provision is deemed, under section 28, to form part of the company's articles of association, but otherwise the provisions of Part 3 apply to it.

Subsection (2) places a further restriction on the validity of entrenching provisions, namely that they must form part either of the company's articles on formation, or of an amendment to the articles agreed to by all members of the company. There are two points here. The first is the requirement that *all* the members agree to the provision. The second is about *where* the provision must be found, namely in the articles—either in their original form, or in an amendment thereto. This ties in with the definition of a provision for entrenchment in section 22(1), which defines such a provision as one found *in* a company's articles. This would, however, seem to exclude agreements entered into *outside* of the articles—for example in an agreement between all the members (either with, or without, the company) that did not purport to operate as an amendment to the articles. (It is, of course, not the case that any agreement to entrench articles must *inevitably* constitute an amendment to the articles. Companies' articles do not typically include an express provision that they are alterable by special resolution; that provision is found in (section 21 of) the Act itself). An agreement outside of the articles, then, does not appear to qualify as a 'provision for entrenchment', and does not benefit from the validity that section 22 confers on such a provision. Where the agreement is merely one between the shareholders, this is hardly a problem, since such agreements are not invalid in any case, and thus do not need section 22 to 'save' them. Where, however, the company is a party to an agreement outside of the articles, then the promise *by the company* not to amend (specified) articles would be unenforceable (*Russell v Northern Bank Development Corporation Ltd*[50] ) and, not being a provision for entrenchment in the articles, would not be saved by section 22. The point for those drafting would seem to be that, if the company (and, through the company, future shareholders) are to be bound by such provisions, then they should be located in the articles, rather than in agreements outside of the articles.   **3.22.08**

Note again that section 22(3)(a) allows any provision for entrenchment to be overridden by a unanimous agreement amongst the shareholders. (The section does not state that such an agreement need be in writing.) There was rather protracted debate, both in the Lords and in the Commons, over whether it is desirable to limit the power of entrenchment provisions in this way. Those critical of the limitation introduced by section 22(3)(a) noted, for example, that it might sometimes be desirable for shareholders *irrevocably* to give up their right to amend the articles. They might wish to do so where they want to avoid, in the future, any pressure being brought to bear upon them by other members desiring to overturn a provision for entrenchment. Further, prior to 1 October 2009, members *could* effectively achieve an irrevocable entrenchment of provisions, by including such an entrenchment in the memorandum and specifying that the provision could not be amended. The Act, by the inclusion of section 22(3), effectively deprives shareholders of the possibility of introducing, after 1 October 2009, such an irrevocable entrenchment.[51]   **3.22.09**

Finally, note that section 22(3)(b) and (4) ensures that a provision for entrenchment remains subject to any overriding power of the court or other authority to alter the articles.   **3.22.10**

## 23   Notice to registrar of existence of restriction on amendment of articles

(1)  Where a company's articles—   **3.23.01**
  (a)  on formation contain provision for entrenchment,
  (b)  are amended so as to include such provision, or
  (c)  are altered by order of a court or other authority so as to restrict or exclude the power of the company to amend its articles,
the company must give notice of that fact to the registrar.
(2)  Where a company's articles—
  (a)  are amended so as to remove provision for entrenchment, or
  (b)  are altered by order of a court or other authority—
    (i)   so as to remove such provision, or

---

[50]  [1992] 3 All ER 161.
[51]  Moreover, note that irrevocably entrenched provisions created before 1 October (for 'existing companies'), or at the date of the company's registration (or re-registration) (for 'transitional companies'), continue to be irrevocable even by unanimity, since s 22(3)(a) does not apply to such provisions: see Sch 2, para 4(2) to the Companies Act 2006 (Commencement No 8, Transitional Provisions and Savings) Order 2008, SI 2008/2860. On the meaning of 'existing' and 'transitional' companies in that Order, see para 3.21.11 above.

(ii) so as to remove any other restriction on, or any exclusion of, the power of the company
to amend its articles,
the company must give notice of that fact to the registrar.

COMMENCEMENT DATE 1 October 2009[52]

**3.23.02** Section 23 imposes two different requirements of notification to the registrar. Subsection (1) requires
notification to the registrar that a company has a provision for entrenchment—whether such a
provision exists on formation, or is subsequently introduced into the articles (either by their amendment by the members or by an alteration imposed by a court or other authority).

**3.23.03** Subsection (2) deals with the removal, rather than the existence, of a provision for entrenchment.
Where the members amend the articles so as to remove a provision for entrenchment, the company
must notify the registrar of that fact. It seems unlikely that this obligation will be satisfied by the
company merely sending the registrar a copy of the amended articles, as required by section 26 (see
below). Further, note that by section 24, such notification must be accompanied by 'a statement of
compliance', ie a statement that the removal of the entrenched provision has been made in accordance
with the articles. By section 23(2)(b) the requirement of notification is extended to situations where a
provision for entrenchment is removed by order of a court or other authority. Indeed, for good
measure, section 23(2)(b)(ii) extends this notification requirement to cover the removal of *any other*
restriction on, or any exclusion of, the power of the company to amend its articles (provided this
removal is effected through an alteration to the company's articles by a court or other authority). Thus,
if a company's articles contain a restriction on their amendment that was, say, introduced by the court
under section 996 (following proceedings under section 994: protection of the members against unfair
prejudice), the subsequent removal of that provision by the court will also require notification to the
registrar.

**3.23.04** No penalty is specified for breach of this provision.

## 24 Statement of compliance where amendment of articles restricted

**3.24.01**
(1) This section applies where a company's articles are subject—
    (a) to provision for entrenchment, or
    (b) to an order of a court or other authority restricting or excluding the company's power to
        amend the articles.
(2) If the company—
    (a) amends its articles, and
    (b) is required to send to the registrar a document making or evidencing the amendment, the
        company must deliver with that document a statement of compliance.
(3) The statement of compliance required is a statement certifying that the amendment has been
    made in accordance with the company's articles and, where relevant, any applicable order of a
    court or other authority.
(4) The registrar may rely on the statement of compliance as sufficient evidence of the matters stated
    in it.

COMMENCEMENT DATE 1 October 2009[53]

**3.24.02** This section applies to a company that has a provision for entrenchment (or is otherwise restricted
from amending its articles as a result of an order of a court or other authority).[54] Any amendment to the
articles must (provided that the amendment itself must be notified to the registrar) be certified by the
company as having been made in accordance with the provision for entrenchment (or in accordance
with the order of the court or other authority). Note that such a statement of compliance is required not
just in relation to amendments to the provision for entrenchment itself, nor even just to those other
'specified articles' that might be covered by the provision for entrenchment (or by the order of the court
or other authority). Rather, once the articles contain a provision for entrenchment (or are subject to an
order of a court or other authority), then every amendment to the articles also triggers an obligation

---

[52] Companies Act 2006 (Commencement No 8, Transitional Provisions and Savings) Order 2008, SI 2008/
2860, art 3. The requirement of notification to the registrar does not apply to a 'transitional' company: see Sch 2,
para 5 to the Order. On the meaning of 'transitional' company, see para 3.21.11 above.
[53] Companies Act 2006 (Commencement No 8, Transitional Provisions and Savings) Order 2008, SI 2008/
2860, art 3.
[54] It would not appear that the restriction on amendment of articles found in s 63 of the Act (companies that
are exempt from the use of, and do not use, 'limited' as part of the company's name) constitutes a restriction 'as
a result of an order of a court or other authority'. Accordingly, companies subject to a restriction on the
amendment of their articles under s 63 would not appear to be required to file a 'statement of compliance' where
the company's articles are amended.

to submit a compliance notice. This is an ongoing burden that ought to be borne in mind when a decision is taken to include an entrenchment provision in the articles (although, again, the section specifies no penalty for a failure to submit a compliance notice).

The interplay between section 24(3) and section 22(3) seems unclear. As noted above, under section **3.24.03** 22(3) all the members can agree to amend the company's articles notwithstanding a provision for entrenchment. In such a case, it is not immediately obvious that the members can certify that they have 'amended in accordance with the articles'. Rather, they have amended contrary to the articles but in accordance with a statutory provision. To say that they have amended in accordance with the articles, one would, presumably, need to argue that the articles, and in particular the provision for entrenchment, must itself be read as qualified by section 22(3).

## 25   Effect of alteration of articles on company's members

(1) A member of a company is not bound by an alteration to its articles after the date on which he **3.25.01** became a member, if and so far as the alteration—

   (a) requires him to take or subscribe for more shares than the number held by him at the date on which the alteration is made, or

   (b) in any way increases his liability as at that date to contribute to the company's share capital or otherwise to pay money to the company.

(2) Subsection (1) does not apply in a case where the member agrees in writing, either before or after the alteration is made, to be bound by the alteration.

COMMENCEMENT DATE 1 October 2009[55]

Section 25 replaces section 16 of the Companies Act 1985. It provides a further mechanism for **3.25.02** protecting a shareholder from the disadvantageous effects of an alteration to a company's articles to which he does not consent (over and above that provided by the requirement that any amendment to the articles should be *bona fide* for the benefit of the company). The member is not bound by any such alteration insofar as it requires him to take or subscribe for more shares, or increases his liability to contribute to the company's share capital or otherwise to pay money to the company. The protection does not apply where the member agrees, in writing, to be bound by the alteration. Such agreement can be given either before or after the alteration. Section 25 does not prevent a member entering into an agreement with a third party (including another member of the company) to acquire further shares in the company.

## 26   Registrar to be sent copy of amended articles

(1) Where a company amends its articles it must send to the registrar a copy of the articles as **3.26.01** amended not later than 15 days after the amendment takes effect.

(2) This section does not require a company to set out in its articles any provisions of model articles that—

   (a) are applied by the articles, or

   (b) apply by virtue of section 20 (default application of model articles).

(3) If a company fails to comply with this section an offence is committed by—

   (a) the company, and

   (b) every officer of the company who is in default.

(4) A person guilty of an offence under this section is liable on summary conviction to a fine not exceeding level 3 on the standard scale and, for continued contravention, a daily default fine not exceeding one-tenth of level 3 on the standard scale.

COMMENCEMENT DATE 1 October 2009[56]

This section replaces section 18 of the Companies Act 1985. It imposes a requirement on companies to **3.26.02** send the registrar copies of amended articles not later than 15 days after the amendment takes effect. Subsection (3) provides that failure to comply constitutes an offence both by the company, and by every officer of the company who is in default. Subsection (4) specifies the penalties for such offences.

Subsection (2) makes clear that the section does not require a company to *spell out* in its articles **3.26.03** provisions incorporated—either expressly, or by default—from the prescribed model articles. Nevertheless, where a company changes its articles so as to incorporate such provisions (say, by expressly adopting a provision from the model, or by removing an express exclusion of a model provision) that

---

[55] Companies Act 2006 (Commencement No 8, Transitional Provisions and Savings) Order 2008, SI 2008/ 2860, art 3.

[56] Companies Act 2006 (Commencement No 8, Transitional Provisions and Savings) Order 2008, SI 2008/ 2860, art 3. By Sch 2, para 6 to that Order, this applies to amendments taking effect on or after 1 October 2009, while those taking effect before 1 October 2009 remain subject to Companies Act 1985, s 18(2) and (3).

amendment would trigger the obligation to send the registrar a copy of the amended articles under section 26. In any case, although companies are not required to spell out provisions incorporated from the model, doing so will avoid the need to refer to two documents in discovering the terms of the company's articles. Note also that where a company was formed prior to 1 October 2009 and accordingly had an 'old style' memorandum which included a statement of the company's name, then by virtue of section 28 its articles are now deemed to include a statement of that name. However, a change of name does not require the company to send a copy of its articles to the Registrar of Companies.[57]

**3.26.04**    Subsection (3) imposes criminal liability on the company, and on every officer of the company who is in default, for a failure by the company to comply with this section. The company is 'strictly liable' for such a failure, whereas an officer is only liable where he is in default, ie where he 'authorises or permits, participates in, or fails to take all reasonable steps to prevent, the contravention': see section 1121(3).

### 27    Registrar's notice to comply in case of failure with respect to amended articles

**3.27.01**    (1)  If it appears to the registrar that a company has failed to comply with any enactment requiring it—
            (a)  to send to the registrar a document making or evidencing an alteration in the company's articles, or
            (b)  to send to the registrar a copy of the company's articles as amended,
        the registrar may give notice to the company requiring it to comply.
    (2)  The notice must—
            (a)  state the date on which it is issued, and
            (b)  require the company to comply within 28 days from that date.
    (3)  If the company complies with the notice within the specified time, no criminal proceedings may be brought in respect of the failure to comply with the enactment mentioned in subsection (1).
    (4)  If the company does not comply with the notice within the specified time, it is liable to a civil penalty of £200.
        This is in addition to any liability to criminal proceedings in respect of the failure mentioned in subsection (1).
    (5)  The penalty may be recovered by the registrar and is to be paid into the Consolidated Fund.

    COMMENCEMENT DATE  1 October 2009[58]

**3.27.02**    This section allows the registrar to apply greater pressure on companies to comply with certain registration requirement, ie those requiring a company to send to the registrar a document making, or evidencing, a change to the company's articles (such as under section 30), or to send to the registrar the articles as amended (such as under section 26). Where the registrar believes the company has failed to make such notification, on the terms set out in subsection (1), he may serve a further notice on the company requiring it to comply. The company is thus effectively given a second chance. If it complies with the registrar's notice, no criminal proceedings may then be brought in respect of the original failure. If the company fails to comply, however, it then becomes liable to a civil penalty of £200, in addition to any criminal liability in respect of the original failure. It would seem that a section 27 notice cannot be used by the registrar where the company has failed to send to the registrar a notice of compliance under section 24.

## *Supplementary*

### 28    Existing companies: provisions of memorandum treated as provisions of articles

**3.28.01**    (1)  Provisions that immediately before the commencement of this Part were contained in a company's memorandum but are not provisions of the kind mentioned in section 8 (provisions of new-style memorandum) are to be treated after the commencement of this Part as provisions of the company's articles.
    (2)  This applies not only to substantive provisions but also to provision for entrenchment (as defined in section 22).
    (3)  The provisions of this Part about provision for entrenchment apply to such provision as they apply to provision made on the company's formation, except that the duty under section 23(1)(a) to give notice to the registrar does not apply.

    COMMENCEMENT DATE  1 October 2009[59]

---

[57] Companies Act 2006 (Consequential Amendments, Transitional Provisions and Savings) Order 2009, SI 2009/1941, art 5.
[58] Companies Act 2006 (Commencement No 8, Transitional Provisions and Savings) Order 2008, SI 2008/2860, art 3.
[59] Companies Act 2006 (Commencement No 8, Transitional Provisions and Savings) Order 2008, SI 2008/2860, art 3. Note that s 28 applies to both 'existing' *and* 'transitional' companies: see further Sch 2, para 7(1) to that Order. For the meaning of 'existing' and 'transitional' companies, see para 3.21.11 above.

This section is intended to deal with some of the consequences of the reduction in the content of **3.28.02** company memoranda introduced by the Act. The memorandum of a company incorporated under earlier Companies Acts will contain provisions—say as to the company's objects—that would, if that company were now being formed under the Act, be found in the articles of association. Such provisions are to be treated as if they were part of the company's articles. As to the legal consequences of the company retaining an objects clause in its articles in this way, see the commentary to section 31 below. Because any such objects clause is now treated as if it were in the articles, it can be amended under section 21, in the same way as other provisions of the articles. In a change from the position under the Companies Act 1985,[60] there is now no statutory right for dissentient minority shareholders to apply to cancel the amendment.[61] However, the 'migration' of provisions from the memorandum into the articles does not make such provisions capable of being amended (under section 21) *if* they were *otherwise* not capable of being amended when they were part of the memorandum.[62] Nor is there any requirement on the company to notify the registrar of this 'deemed' alteration of its articles.[63]

Although a company that was formed prior to 1 October 2009 will also be deemed, under section 28, to **3.28.03** have a statement of its name in its articles, such a company will not be required to change its articles if it wishes to change its name, nor will a change of name require the company to send a copy of its articles to the Registrar of Companies.[64]

Subsections (2) and (3) move beyond substantive provisions and deal specifically with the case of an **3.28.04** 'entrenching provision' (as defined in section 22) that was previously put in a company's memorandum. First, such a provision is also to be treated as if it formed part of the company's articles, rather than of its memorandum. Second, the rules in this Part of the Act dealing with entrenchment provisions then apply to such provision in the same way as they apply to provisions adopted on the formation of a company (although there is no obligation to give the registrar notice of the provision, as there now is when such a provision is adopted on the formation of a company).

CHAPTER 3

RESOLUTIONS AND AGREEMENTS AFFECTING A
COMPANY'S CONSTITUTION

### 29  Resolutions and agreements affecting a company's constitution

(1) This Chapter applies to—                                                                                        **3.29.01**
    (a) any special resolution;
    (b) any resolution or agreement agreed to by all the members of a company that, if not so agreed to, would not have been effective for its purpose unless passed as a special resolution;
    (c) any resolution or agreement agreed to by all the members of a class of shareholders that, if not so agreed to, would not have been effective for its purpose unless passed by some particular majority or otherwise in some particular manner;
    (d) any resolution or agreement that effectively binds all members of a class of shareholders though not agreed to by all those members;
    (e) any other resolution or agreement to which this Chapter applies by virtue of any enactment.
(2) References in subsection (1) to a member of a company, or of a class of members of a company, do not include the company itself where it is such a member by virtue only of its holding shares as treasury shares.

COMMENCEMENT DATE 1 October 2007[65]

This section provides for special resolutions, and for other resolutions and agreements affecting a **3.29.02** company's constitution that are treated as similarly binding (for example, because unanimously agreed by members) though not passed as special resolutions. They are included, along with a company's

---

[60] See Companies Act 1985, s 5.

[61] Shareholders will still have the right, however, to argue, as with any other amendment to the articles, that it was not passed bona fide for the benefit of the company or that it constituted unfair prejudice under s 994 (see commentary to ss 21 and 994 respectively).

[62] See Sch 2, para 4(1) and (3) to the Companies Act 2006 (Commencement No 8, Transitional Provisions and Savings) Order 2008, SI 2008/2860.

[63] See Sch 2, para 8 to the Companies Act 2006 (Commencement No 8, Transitional Provisions and Savings) Order 2008, SI 2008/2860. See Sch 9, para 9 to that Order for how a company can comply with any obligation to send a person a copy of its articles where those articles are deemed to contain a provision previously found in its memorandum.

[64] Companies Act 2006 (Consequential Amendments, Transitional Provisions and Savings) Order 2009, SI 2009/ 1941, art 5.

[65] Companies Act 2006 (Commencement No 3, etc) Order 2007, SI 2007/2194, art 2(1).

articles, in the definition of a 'company's constitution' under section 17. And they are subject to the provisions of section 30 (copies of which must be forwarded to the registrar), section 32 (constitutional documents to be provided to members), and section 36 (documents to be incorporated in or accompany copies of the articles issued by company).

**3.29.03**    This class of agreements or resolutions includes, of course, special resolutions (see subsection (1)(a)). By section 29(1)(b), however, it is extended to some unanimous resolutions or agreements reached between all the shareholders, namely those which, had they not been unanimously agreed to, would have needed to be passed as special resolutions. This might include a resolution that was passed as an ordinary resolution, *nem con*, but which should have been passed as a special resolution. It would also include an agreement between all the shareholders that, say, amended the company's articles. Under *Cane v Jones*,[66] such agreements are effective to amend the articles, notwithstanding that no formal resolution is passed (see the commentary to section 21). It is worth stressing, however, that such agreements are caught only if they do something that would have required a special resolution between the shareholders. Thus, for example, an agreement made only between the members about how they will exercise their voting rights, which does not purport to amend the articles, would not need to have been passed as a special resolution and would therefore not be caught by this section.

**3.29.04**    Whereas the Companies Bill specified a longer list of resolutions and agreements under this section, subsection (1)(e) now includes many of these only by reference. Examples of resolutions to which this Chapter (3) applies by virtue of 'an enactment' include a resolution passed under section 551 (authority by company for directors to allot shares) and section 622 (resolution to redenominate share capital).

**3.29.05**    On 'Treasury Shares', see Chapter 6 of Part 18 of this Act.

### 30    Copies of resolutions or agreements to be forwarded to registrar

**3.30.01**
    (1)  A copy of every resolution or agreement to which this Chapter applies, or (in the case of a resolution or agreement that is not in writing) a written memorandum setting out its terms, must be forwarded to the registrar within 15 days after it is passed or made.
    (2)  If a company fails to comply with this section, an offence is committed by—
        (a)  the company, and
        (b)  every officer of it who is in default.
    (3)  A person guilty of an offence under this section is liable on summary conviction to a fine not exceeding level 3 on the standard scale and, for continued contravention, a daily default fine not exceeding one-tenth of level 3 on the standard scale.
    (4)  For the purposes of this section, a liquidator of the company is treated as an officer of it.

    COMMENCEMENT DATE 1 October 2007[67]

**3.30.02**    Section 30 replaces section 380 of the Companies Act 1985. It requires that copies of the resolutions and agreements listed in section 29 be sent to the registrar. The section imposes a time limit of 15 days for the submission of the relevant copies of resolutions or agreements to the registrar. Where the resolution or agreement is not in writing, a written memorandum must be sent. The sanction for a failure to comply with the section is a criminal one, and is imposed upon both the company itself, and every officer 'in default' (defined in section 1121(3)).

**3.30.03**    The company will not necessarily be a party to an agreement that requires registration under this section, and accordingly the company (and its officers) will not necessarily be aware of its existence. Nevertheless, the section imposes a strict liability upon the company (although, as noted, officers of the company are liable only if they are personally in default).

**3.30.04**    A failure to submit the resolution or agreement to the registrar, either on time or at all, does not, *under this particular section*, have any effect on the validity of that resolution or agreement. Thus, a person buying shares in the company, say, obtains no relief under this section if he discovers after his purchase the existence of any section 29 resolutions or agreements that materially affect his position within the company. Note, however, that other provisions of this Act may condition the effect of particular resolutions on the fact of registration. One such provision is section 31(2)(c), where amendment of a company's statement of objects (in its articles) must similarly be given to the registrar and registered by him, and where the amendment is not itself 'effective' until this has been done. Perhaps of most general application is section 1079. Put briefly, this section precludes the company from relying, as against other persons, on certain events (including, for example, amendments to the company's articles) unless that event had been 'officially notified' (or unless the other person actually knew of the event).

---

[66] [1981] 1 All ER 533.
[67] Companies Act 2006 (Commencement No 3, etc) Order 2007, SI 2007/2194, art 2(1).

## CHAPTER 4
## MISCELLANEOUS AND SUPPLEMENTARY PROVISIONS
### *Statement of company's objects*

### 31   Statement of company's objects

(1)   Unless a company's articles specifically restrict the objects of the company, its objects are       **3.31.01**
unrestricted.

(2)   Where a company amends its articles so as to add, remove or alter a statement of the company's
objects—

(a)   it must give notice to the registrar,

(b)   on receipt of the notice, the registrar shall register it, and

(c)   the amendment is not effective until entry of that notice on the register.

(3)   Any such amendment does not affect any rights or obligations of the company or render defective
any legal proceedings by or against it.

(4)   In the case of a company that is a charity, the provisions of this section have effect subject to—

(a)   in England and Wales, section 64 of the Charities Act 1993 (c. 10);

(b)   in Northern Ireland, Article 9 of the Charities (Northern Ireland) Order 1987 (S.I. 1987/2048
(N.I. 19)).

(5)   In the case of a company that is entered in the Scottish Charity Register, the provisions of this
section have effect subject to the provisions of the Charities and Trustee Investment (Scotland) Act
2005 (asp 10).

COMMENCEMENT DATE 1 October 2009[68]

Section 31 is substantially new. It constitutes a further nail in the coffin of the *ultra vires* doctrine in       **3.31.02**
relation to companies, although reports of the doctrine's death would still be a little premature. Under
the Companies Act 1985, companies were required to include a statement of their objects in the
company's memorandum. Companies could, however, declare their objects as being to 'carry on
business as a general commercial company'. If a company so declared, then its object was, under section
3A of the 1985 Act, deemed to include the carrying on of 'any trade or business whatsoever' and the
company was also deemed to have 'power to do all such things as are incidental or conducive to the
carrying on of any trade or business by it'. Section 31 carries this process (of facilitating companies'
adoption of very wide objects) two steps further. First, under section 3A of the Companies Act 1985,
there might have been some activities that would still have fallen outside 'the business of a general
commercial company'. Under section 31, by contrast, the company's objects can be entirely 'unrestricted'. Second, it makes this 'unrestricted objects clause' the default rule, rather than something the
company must expressly adopt. Unless the company's objects are 'specifically restricted' by its articles,
they are deemed to be unrestricted.

What of companies formed before section 31 comes into force? Such companies will have 'old style'       **3.31.03**
memoranda. These will include a clause that states, positively, the objects (and the associated powers)
that the company has.[69] Under section 28, this clause will be deemed to be contained in the company's
articles. The Government stated, in its consultation on transitional arrangements for existing companies, that '[i]n our view, this means that existing companies that do not want to change their objects do
not need to do anything to preserve the legal effect of their objects clauses. An objects clause drafted as
a list of things that the company is set up, or has the power, to do—which is what most existing
companies have—will, in future, be read as a restriction on what the company can do.'[70]

In deciding whether or not to retain, or to introduce, restrictions on a company's objects, the following       **3.31.04**
might be borne in mind. The consequences of such restrictions will still fall to be settled by the general
law on *ultra vires*, as applied to companies, and on the law dealing with shareholders' rights and
directors' duties. Briefly, the combined effect of sections 39 and 40 of the Companies Act 2006 mean
that a restriction on a company's capacity will be unlikely to have much effect 'externally', ie insofar as
relationships between the company and third parties are concerned. However, it may still have what
are sometimes termed 'internal' consequences. So, introducing (or retaining) a restriction on the
company's objects will constitute a limitation on the powers of directors. Directors who act beyond

---

[68]   Companies Act 2006 (Commencement No 8, Transitional Provisions and Savings) Order 2008, SI 2008/
2860, art 3.

[69]   This may, of course, simply be the object 'of carrying on business as a general commercial company'.

[70]   Department of Trade and Industry, *Paper seeking views on the application of the Companies Bill to existing
companies* (2006), para 13; available at ⟨http://www.dti.gov.uk/files/file33125.doc⟩.

their powers may thereby breach their duties to the company.[71] Similarly, a shareholder who discovers a prospective act that will be beyond the company's capacity may still[72] bring proceedings[73] to prevent such an act (although she must do so before any legal obligation has been incurred by the company).[74]

**3.31.05**    Given these internal consequences of restrictions on a company's capacity, the proper construction of a company's objects clause remains a matter of some (although admittedly diminished) significance. Even prior to the enactment of section 31, the courts had taken an increasingly liberal approach to the construction of objects clauses. So-called 'subjective objects clauses' were upheld,[75] and acting in pursuit of express powers was held to be within the capacity of the company, even if the power was not in fact being exercised to achieve a main object of the company.[76] It seems unlikely that the courts' construction of objects clauses will, or should, be any less permissive in the future. The courts' interpretative task will be somewhat strained, since it will be required to read a clause that was drafted as a positive statement of all the company can do, as if it were drafted as a negative account of what the company cannot do. In construing the extent of these negative restrictions, the courts should proceed as they do when interpreting other provisions in the articles, namely to give them 'reasonable business efficacy', discovering the meaning 'the instrument would convey to a reasonable person having all the background knowledge which would reasonably be available to the audience to whom it is addressed'.[77] This has tended to result in articles being read somewhat narrowly by the courts. However, construing narrowly the *restrictions* on the company's capacity would surely be appropriate, given that the default position is now 'unlimited capacity'. The audience to whom the articles are addressed—present and future shareholders—would reasonably know that an objects clause imported from the company's memorandum existed in all likelihood only because it was compulsory, and was drafted not to establish broad restrictions, but rather to make the company's capacity as extensive as possible. Likewise with regard to identifying the ancillary powers of the company. Although courts have *implied* into objects clauses powers to do things that are incidental to the objects of the company,[78] they should construe the articles as permitting a company the power to do all things, incidental or not, unless the company has expressly stated that its powers are to be limited to those which are incidental.

**3.31.06**    Section 31(2) deals with those situations where the company seeks to make any of the three specified changes to its articles, namely to add, or to remove, or to alter a statement of its objects. Several points deserve emphasis. First, as amendments to the company's articles (rather than to its memorandum), they will be governed by section 21 of the Act. There is now no specific 'right to object' to an amendment, passed under section 21, of a company's 'objects clause',[79] as there was previously under section 5 of the Companies Act 1985 (application by the court to cancel the alteration by holders of not less than 15 per cent in nominal value of the company's shares, etc). However shareholders will be able, by collectively adopting a 'provision for entrenchment' under section 22 of the Act, to give individual shareholders a veto over amendments to a company's objects clause. Moreover, resolutions to amend the articles in respect of the company's objects will also be subject to review on the grounds that such a resolution was not passed *bona fide* in the best interests of the company (see commentary to section 21), or was unfairly prejudicial to the interests of its members (see section 994).

**3.31.07**    Second, an amendment must be notified to the registrar, who must then register it. No time limit is specified for such notification, although the resolution itself, and the amended articles, must also both be sent to the registrar (under sections 30 and 26 respectively) within 15 days. Section 31(2)(c) declares the amendment to be 'ineffective' until the registrar has entered the notice of the amendment on the register. Thus, the company's objects are to be treated as having their pre-amendment content until the notice is entered on the register. The consequences of this would then turn upon the *ultra vires* doctrine, as applied to companies and sketched out briefly above. Thus, it is unlikely to matter

---

[71] In particular, she may breach her duty under Companies Act 2006, s 171.

[72] See Companies Act 2006, s 40(4).

[73] Such proceedings would be a personal action, to enforce the company's constitution, under Companies Act 2006, s 33.

[74] See s 40(4).

[75] See eg *Bell Houses Ltd v City Wall Properties Ltd* [1966] 2 QB 656, in which the company had the capacity, *inter alia*, to 'to carry on any other trade or business whatsoever which can, in the opinion of the board of directors, be advantageously carried on by the company in connection with or as ancillary to any of the above businesses or the general business of the company'.

[76] Or, indeed, even if the exercise of the power was not in pursuit of the purposes of the company, provided the power was one that *could be* exercised in pursuit of the company's main objects: see *Rolled Steel Products (Holdings) Ltd v British Steel Corporation* [1982] 3 All ER 1057.

[77] See *Attorney General of Belize v Belize Telecom Ltd* [2009] BCC 433, 437. See also the commentary to s 33 below.

[78] See eg *Attorney-General v Great Eastern Railway Co* (1880) 5 App Cas 473.

[79] Meaning, here, a provision that 'specifically restricts the objects of the company' under s 31 of the Act.

'externally', given section 39(1). 'Internally', on the other hand, things may again be rather different. Pending entry of the notice of amendment on the register, a member might still be able to seek injunctive relief against a proposed transaction that offends the company's pre-amended objects clause. However, this is surely rather academic, given that the directors can ensure that the amendment is indeed registered well before any hearing of the member's claim for relief. Perhaps more worrying for directors might be the possibility of their being found to be in breach of their duties if they cause the company, prior to entry of the notice of amendment on the register, to enter into a contract that is beyond the company's pre-amended objects clause. Even here, however, directors might be able to argue that the company has lost little as a result of any such breach of duty. Indeed, they might be able to show that waiting until the amendment had been registered would have lost the company the valuable transaction into which they entered. Further, it might also be argued that once the notice of amendment is registered, this then renders the amendment itself 'effective' from the date it was actually passed, not the date it was registered. Registration, in other words, would be a condition of, but would not determine the date of, effectiveness. The argument in favour of this interpretation would be one of commercial practicalities: companies, and their directors, need to be able to get on with business once the articles have been altered, and should not be forced to wait until the registrar has effected the registration. Against this, one might note that no date is specified for the registration to be completed; directors could then wait an eternity before registering, safe in the knowledge that when they eventually do so, the effectiveness of the amendment will be 'backdated' to the date of the amendment itself.

The foregoing presumes, implicitly, that amendments have only prospective effect. Section 31(3) tries,   **3.31.08**
it would seem, to make this the position in law. Whenever an amendment takes effect—whether on being passed, or on being registered—it does not affect any rights or obligations of the company or render defective any legal proceedings by or against the company. Thus, an action by the company against its directors for breach of duty, based on their exceeding their powers through causing the company to enter into a contract beyond the company's own capacity, would not be affected by a subsequent amendment to the company's 'objects clause'. However, again, the practical importance of this provision is reduced by the reduced significance of the *ultra vires* doctrine itself (in relation to companies).

Once again, so far as charitable companies are concerned the provisions of the section are made   **3.31.09**
expressly subject to the controls on the content of the objects clauses of such companies, found in the legislation referred to in subsection (4). See also the commentary to section 21 above.

### *Other provisions with respect to a company's constitution*

## 32   Constitutional documents to be provided to members

(1)  A company must, on request by any member, send to him the following documents—                  **3.32.01**
    (a)  an up-to-date copy of the company's articles;
    (b)  a copy of any resolution or agreement relating to the company to which Chapter 3 applies (resolutions and agreements affecting a company's constitution) and that is for the time being in force;
    (c)  a copy of any document required to be sent to the registrar under—
        (i)   section 34(2) (notice where company's constitution altered by enactment), or
        (ii)  section 35(2)(a) (notice where order of court or other authority alters company's constitution);
    (d)  a copy of any court order under section 899 (order sanctioning compromise or arrangement) or section 900 (order facilitating reconstruction or amalgamation);
    (e)  a copy of any court order under section 996 (protection of members against unfair prejudice: powers of the court) that alters the company's constitution;
    (f)  a copy of the company's current certificate of incorporation, and of any past certificates of incorporation;
    (g)  in the case of a company with a share capital, a current statement of capital;
    (h)  in the case of a company limited by guarantee, a copy of the statement of guarantee.
(2)  The statement of capital required by subsection (1)(g) is a statement of—
    (a)  the total number of shares of the company,
    (b)  the aggregate nominal value of those shares,
    (c)  for each class of shares—
        (i)   prescribed particulars of the rights attached to the shares,
        (ii)  the total number of shares of that class, and
        (iii) the aggregate nominal value of shares of that class, and
    (d)  the amount paid up and the amount (if any) unpaid on each share (whether on account of the nominal value of the share or by way of premium).
(3)  If a company makes default in complying with this section, an offence is committed by every officer of the company who is in default.

(4) A person guilty of an offence under this section is liable on summary conviction to a fine not exceeding level 3 on the standard scale.

COMMENCEMENT DATE 1 October 2009[80]

**3.32.02**    This section replaces (and extends) section 19 of the Companies Act 1985. It gives members the right to receive, from the company, copies of its constitutional documents. Such documents include its articles, those 'resolutions and agreements' referred to in section 29, as well as certain other constitutional materials, such as its certificate of incorporation and statements of the company's capital or, in the case of a guarantee company, of the terms of the members' guarantee. The statement of capital that is required is set out in subsection (2). It is an up-to-date statement, not the statement filed upon the company's registration. No time limit is imposed upon the company to comply with the member's request. Breach of the provision constitutes a criminal offence by any officer in default (although not by the company itself).

**3.32.03**    Section 32 varies the equivalent provision in the Companies Act 1985 by requiring the company to provide these constitutional documents without charge. This provides one reason for a member to request documents under this section, rather than applying to the registrar of companies, which would incur a fee. A second reason for the member so doing is the fact that, for most of the documents listed in section 32, up-to-date copies must be supplied by the company. By contrast, the file of documents held by the registrar may be less up to date. This may happen because the time limit for the company to send to the registrar the relevant document (for example, amended articles, pursuant to section 26) has not yet expired or, because although the company has sent the document, the registrar has not yet recorded it against the company.

### 33  Effect of company's constitution

**3.33.01**        (1) The provisions of a company's constitution bind the company and its members to the same extent as if there were covenants on the part of the company and of each member to observe those provisions.
            (2) Money payable by a member to the company under its constitution is a debt due from him to the company.
            In England and Wales and Northern Ireland it is of the nature of an ordinary contract debt.

COMMENCEMENT DATE 1 October 2009[81]

**3.33.02**    Section 33 replaces section 14 of the Companies Act 1985. It gives 'contractual effect' to the company's constitution. The new section makes clear that both the members *and* the company itself are to be regarded as having covenanted to observe the terms of the articles. This largely reflects the position that the courts eventually came to take on section 14 (see, for example, *Wood v Odessa Waterworks Co*)[82] but avoids any remaining uncertainty. The new wording also declares, in subsection (2), that money due to the company from a member is a debt. However, in contrast to the position under section 14, it is no longer to be regarded as a 'specialty debt' (for which there would be a longer limitation period).

**3.33.03**    So far as the proper construction of a company's articles of association is concerned,[83] it has been held that a company's articles are a commercial document, and should be construed as a whole[84] and so as to give them 'reasonable business efficacy': see *Holmes v Keyes*[85] and *Rayfield v Hands*.[86] In *Attorney General of Belize v Belize Telecom Ltd*[87] the Privy Council stressed that the courts' task is not to 'improve' the articles by adding provisions that would be fair, or reasonable. Rather, the overriding objective of the court in interpreting the terms of the articles was to ascertain 'the meaning which the instrument would convey to a reasonable person having all the background knowledge which would reasonably be available to the audience to whom the instrument is addressed'.[88] And whilst other rubrics, such as the 'reasonable business efficacy' test mentioned above, might be helpful to a court,

---

[80] Companies Act 2006 (Commencement No 8, Transitional Provisions and Savings) Order 2008, SI 2008/2860, art 3. By Sch 2, para 11 to that Order, s 32 applies where the request is received by the company on or after 1 October 2009. Otherwise, s 19 of the Companies Act 1985 continues to apply.

[81] Companies Act 2006 (Commencement No 8, Transitional Provisions and Savings) Order 2008, SI 2008/2860, art 3.

[82] (1889) 42 Ch D 636.

[83] In addition to the issues mentioned here, note also the interpretive consequences of a company adopting part of the model articles prescribed by the Secretary of State; see the commentary to ss 19 and 20.

[84] See *Cream Holdings Ltd v Davenport* [2009] BCC 183.

[85] [1959] Ch 199.

[86] [1960] Ch 1.

[87] [2009] BCC 433.

[88] [2009] BCC 433, 437.

these formulations should not take on 'a life of their own'. They merely directed the court to ascertaining what a reasonable person would understand the articles to mean.[89]

In ascertaining that meaning, such a person would of course have regard to the *other* (express) terms of **3.33.04** the articles, so that a term might be implied if it were necessary to give effect to the meaning captured by those express terms. In *Cream Holdings Ltd v Davenport*,[90] for example, the court implied a term that a member who was bound to transfer his shares in accordance with machinery in the articles could not unreasonably withold his consent to the appoinment of an accountant to value those shares. That was 'the minimum term' that needed to be implied to give business efficacy to the remainder of the articles.[91] What is less certain, however, is how far other background knowledge might be imputed to the reasonable person who is striving to understand the meaning of the articles. In *Bratton Seymour Service Co Ltd v Oxborough*,[92] the Court of Appeal refused to imply a term based on 'extrinsic evidence' about the circumstances in which the company was being set up, and the business scheme of which the company was a part. The Court reiterated the usual objection that this knowledge might be limited to some only of the members of the company. However, in *Belize* itself the Privy Council distinguished *Bratton* on its facts, and imputed to the reasonable person interpreting the company's articles such knowledge as 'anyone in Belize would have known' about the purpose behind the formation of the company (namely its role in securing the privatization of telecommunications in Belize).

The courts have also refused to rectify the articles where the registered document did not reflect the **3.33.05** terms actually agreed between the parties: see *Scott v Frank F Scott (London) Ltd*.[93] This judicial approach has been justified on the ground that the articles are a public document, and those dealing with the company (such as potential investors) ought to be entitled to assume that the articles are accurate. However, this argument clearly does not apply where the implication is a 'constructional exercise' based upon the wording of the articles themselves, and it has also been argued that this insistence upon enforcing the articles 'as is' sits uncomfortably with the developing body of case-law that allows members to enforce informal agreements to which all consented (see eg *Re Duomatic*),[94] including agreements which amend the terms of the articles (see *Cane v Jones*).[95]

So far as the terms of the section 33 contract itself are concerned, a number of further issues arise. First, **3.33.06** it might be noted that this contract covers not merely the company's articles, but rather its 'constitution'. That is defined in section 17 of the Act and includes, by virtue of section 29(1)(b) 'any resolution or agreement agreed to by all the members of a company that, if not so agreed to, would not have been effective for its purpose unless passed as a special resolution'. This would, clearly, include a '*Cane v Jones*' agreement, so that it might be said that section 33 puts the enforcement of these agreements on a statutory footing. In the Companies Bill, the clause that became section 33 required that provisions of the constitution were contractually binding only 'when registered', but this requirement has now been abandoned. Thus, in principle, 'section 29 resolutions' become binding on members even before their registration. Of course, this hardly matters as between those members who themselves passed the resolution. But for those who become members after the passing, but before the registration, of such resolutions, the position is more problematic. Although, as noted above,[96] section 1079 restricts *the company* from relying, as against members, on certain events (including amendments to the articles) before those events have been 'officially notified', this would not preclude members from so doing.

Secondly, it now seems that the contract can be enforced by one member directly against another, **3.33.07** without needing to sue the company. In *Welton v Saffery*,[97] Lord Herschell had (albeit in a dissenting judgement) opined that '[s]uch rights can only be enforced by or against a member through the company, or through the liquidator representing the company'.[98] However, in *Rayfield v Hands*[99]

---

[89] In *Stena Line Limited v Merchant Navy Ratings Pension Fund Trustees Ltd* [2011] EWCA Civ 543 the Court of Appeal chose to follow the *Belize* decision, 'even though it is a decision of the Privy Council since it is based on authorities from this jurisdiction' (para 44).
[90] [2011] EWCA 1287.
[91] For another example of such an exercise, see *Folkes Group plc v Alexander* [2002] 2 BCLC 254. See also the comments of Steyn LJ in *Bratton Seymour Service Co Ltd v Oxborough* [1992] BCLC 693 at 475–6 and of Lord Steyn in *Equitable Life Assurance Society v Hyman* [2002] 1 AC 408 at 458–9.
[92] [1992] BCLC 693.
[93] [1940] Ch 794.
[94] [1969] 2 Ch 365.
[95] [1981] 1 All ER 533.
[96] See discussion of s 30.
[97] [1897] AC 299.
[98] [1897] AC 299, 315.
[99] [1960] Ch 1.

Vaisey J was prepared to allow a member to sue another directly, although it is not clear how far he intended such direct actions to be restricted to 'partnership like' companies.[100]

**3.33.08**   A third issue concerns so-called 'third party rights' under the articles. The contract created by section 33 is exempted from section 1 of the Contracts (Rights of Third Parties) Act 1999. Thus, the provisions of the constitution will not, by virtue of section 33 alone, confer rights on parties other than the company or its members. (It may, however, still be possible for so-called 'extrinsic contracts', existing independently of section 33, to include provisions 'borrowed' from the company's constitution: see, for example, *Re New British Iron Company ex p Beckwith*.[101] Such a contract may itself be changed, however, by amendments to the articles that have been borrowed in this way; see *Swabey v Port Darwin Gold Mining Co*.)[102]

**3.33.09**   The greater uncertainty, however, relates to the ability of a person who *is* a member, but who seeks to enforce an article which confers rights on him in some capacity other than that of member, say as a director of, or solicitor to, the company. It was declared, in *Hickman v Kent or Romney Marsh Sheepbreeders' Association* that 'no right merely purporting to be given by an article to a person, whether a member or not, in a capacity other than that of a member, as, for instance, solicitor, promoter, director, can be enforced against the company'.[103] The same decision had already been reached in the earlier case of *Eley v Positive Government Security Life Assurance Co*,[104] in which the court refused to enforce an article that stipulated that one of the company's members was also to be its solicitor.[105] On this interpretation of the scope of section 33, regulations fall into two categories. Some confer rights on members in their capacity as members, such as the right to vote at shareholder meetings,[106] or the right to receive a lawfully declared dividend, and are clearly enforceable. Other regulations within the articles are, however, simply unenforceable under the section, since they seek to confer rights on members in some other capacity.

**3.33.10**   The cases do not, however, all support this restriction on the articles' enforceability. In *Quinn & Axtens Ltd v Salmon*,[107] the House of Lords allowed a member to enforce a term in the constitution which effectively gave that member a right of veto at board meetings (and thus, it would seem, a right enjoyed in his capacity as a director). Based upon this and other authorities,[108] it has been argued that, provided a member makes clear that she comes to court in her capacity as a member, she will have the right to insist that the company observes all the terms of the articles, even if that results in her, or other members, indirectly benefitting from the company's adherence to 'non-membership' regulations in the articles.[109] On this view, it is how the shareholder 'puts her case' in court, rather than any 'classification' of the particular article (as conferring a membership or a non-membership right) that determines whether the shareholder will succeed under section 33. Section 33 does nothing to resolve the uncertainty that these apparently conflicting lines of authority have created.

**3.33.11**   The fourth and final issue concerns the relationship between section 33 and the 'rule in *Foss v Harbottle*'.[110] An action under section 33 is a personal one, brought by an individual member to enforce the personal, contractual rights he claims to enjoy as a result of the statutory contract based upon the articles. It is this that makes the action so promising, since a member is able to bring it notwithstanding the views of his fellow members (who may disapprove of those proceedings precisely because they are responsible for the very conduct of which the would-be plaintiff member complains). Nevertheless, in some cases the courts have found the matter being complained of (such as, for example, a refusal, contrary to the articles, to hold a poll at a shareholders' meeting) to be merely an 'internal irregularity'. Any wrongdoing is thus construed as a harm done to the company itself, and any action to redress that wrong must, in accordance with the decision in *Foss v Harbottle*, be brought by the company. In this

---

[100]   See [1960] Ch 1, 9. The wording of s 33 is substantially the same as that in the Companies Acts with which these cases were concerned, namely s 16 of the Companies Act 1862 (in *Welton v Saffery*), and s 20 of the Companies Act 1948 (in *Rayfield v Hands*).

[101]   [1898] 1 Ch 324.

[102]   (1898) 1 Meg 385.

[103]   [1915] 1 Ch 881, 900.

[104]   (1876) 1 Ex D 88

[105]   See also the later Court of Appeal decision in *Beattie v E & F Beattie Ltd* [1938] Ch 708.

[106]   See *Pender v Lushington* (1877) 6 Ch 70.

[107]   [1909] AC 442.

[108]   See eg *Imperial Hydropathic v Hampson* (1882) 23 Ch 1; *Pulbrook v Richmond Consolidated Mining Co* (1878) 9 Ch 610; *Re Richmond Gate Property Co* [1965] 1 WLR 335.

[109]   This argument was advanced by Lord Wedderburn, 'The Rule in *Foss v Harbottle*' [1957] CLJ 194, 212. See also R Gregory, 'The Section 20 Contract' (1981) 44 MLR 526.

[110]   (1843) 2 Hare 461.

way, the wrongdoing becomes subject to majority rule, for the majority are then free either to condone, or to cause the company to sue in respect of, the alleged wrongdoing.

Not only is this approach to the section 33 contract restrictive for shareholders, but its effect is also **3.33.12** uncertain. It is unclear when wrongdoing will be held to constitute a breach of the contract based upon the articles, giving a shareholder a right to bring a personal action, and when that wrongdoing will be said to be a mere internal irregularity which the majority enjoys the right to condone. In practice, minority shareholders who are dissatisfied at the way the company's affairs are being conducted have, since the unfair prejudice remedy was first introduced in 1980,[111] tended to rely far more upon that remedy which largely side-steps these problems. It seems unlikely that the restatement of the contractual effect of the company's constitution will change that tendency.

## 34 Notice to registrar where company's constitution altered by enactment

(1) This section applies where a company's constitution is altered by an enactment, other than an **3.34.01** enactment amending the general law.
(2) The company must give notice of the alteration to the registrar, specifying the enactment, not later than 15 days after the enactment comes into force.
   In the case of a special enactment the notice must be accompanied by a copy of the enactment.
(3) If the enactment amends—
   (a) the company's articles, or
   (b) a resolution or agreement to which Chapter 3 applies (resolutions and agreements affecting a company's constitution),
   the notice must be accompanied by a copy of the company's articles, or the resolution or agreement in question, as amended.
(4) A 'special enactment' means an enactment that is not a public general enactment, and includes—
   (a) an Act for confirming a provisional order,
   (b) any provision of a public general Act in relation to the passing of which any of the standing orders of the House of Lords or the House of Commons relating to Private Business applied, or
   (c) any enactment to the extent that it is incorporated in or applied for the purposes of a special enactment.
(5) If a company fails to comply with this section an offence is committed by—
   (a) the company, and
   (b) every officer of the company who is in default.
(6) A person guilty of an offence under this section is liable on summary conviction to a fine not exceeding level 3 on the standard scale and, for continued contravention, a daily default fine not exceeding one-tenth of level 3 on the standard scale.

COMMENCEMENT DATE 1 October 2009[112]

Section 34 replaces section 18 of the Companies Act 1985. It extends the reporting requirements of **3.34.02** companies in respect of constitutional changes. Changes that are required to be notified under this section are those that arise as a result of certain 'enactments'. 'Enactments' is defined in section 1293. As the notes accompanying the Bill made clear, the Act seeks to draw a balance between 'maintaining transparency on the one hand and inundating the registrar and searchers with mountains of paper which will be of little practical use to them (and whose contents are generally available in any event) on the other'. Accordingly, section 34 requires enactments that change a company's constitution to be notified to the registrar, but not where these are enactments which 'amend the general law' (and which therefore are presumably widely available). Furthermore, amongst these notifiable enactments, it is only in relation to 'special enactments' (defined in subsection (4)) that the company is required to submit a copy of the enactment. Once again, a breach of the section constitutes an offence both by the company and by any officer in default.

The company is also required, under subsection (3), to send the registrar a copy of the part of its **3.34.03** constitution that is being altered. However, this applies only where the part of the constitution that is being altered is either the company's articles or one of the 'resolutions or agreements' listed in section 29. No provision is made for the situation where the part of the constitution that is being altered is not in writing. (Contrast section 30, where the company must send the registrar 'a written memorandum setting out the terms' of any such agreement or resolution that is not in writing.)

---

[111] As s 75 of CA 1980; see now ss 994–996 of the Act.
[112] Companies Act 2006 (Commencement No 8, Transitional Provisions and Savings) Order 2008, SI 2008/2860, art 3. By Sch 2, para 12 to that Order, s 34 applies where the enactment comes into force on or after 1 October 2009. Otherwise, s 18(1) and (3) of the Companies Act 1985 continues to apply.

**35  Notice to registrar where company's constitution altered by order**

**3.35.01**

(1) Where a company's constitution is altered by an order of a court or other authority, the company must give notice to the registrar of the alteration not later than 15 days after the alteration takes effect.

(2) The notice must be accompanied by—

(a) a copy of the order, and

(b) if the order amends—

(i) the company's articles, or

(ii) a resolution or agreement to which Chapter 3 applies (resolutions and agreements affecting the company's constitution),

a copy of the company's articles, or the resolution or agreement in question, as amended.

(3) If a company fails to comply with this section an offence is committed by—

(a) the company, and

(b) every officer of the company who is in default.

(4) A person guilty of an offence under this section is liable on summary conviction to a fine not exceeding level 3 on the standard scale and, for continued contravention, a daily default fine not exceeding one-tenth of level 3 on the standard scale.

(5) This section does not apply where provision is made by another enactment for the delivery to the registrar of a copy of the order in question.

COMMENCEMENT DATE 1 October 2009[113]

**3.35.02**   Section 35 is similar in form to section 34, also extending the reporting requirements of companies in respect of changes to their constitutions. Section 35 requires notification of constitutional changes effected by orders of the court, or of other authorities. It has been suggested that the Charity Commission would be an authority whose orders might amend the constitution of a company, triggering the requirement of notification under this section. Section 35, like section 34, requires the company to forward to the registrar a copy of the company's articles, or of a resolution or agreement, which is amended by the order. Again, no provision is made for how this obligation is to be applied where such an agreement or resolution is not in writing.

**36  Documents to be incorporated in or accompany copies of articles issued by company**

**3.36.01**

(1) Every copy of a company's articles issued by the company must be accompanied by—

(a) a copy of any resolution or agreement relating to the company to which Chapter 3 applies (resolutions and agreements affecting a company's constitution),

(b) where the company has been required to give notice to the registrar under section 34(2) (notice where company's constitution altered by enactment), a statement that the enactment in question alters the effect of the company's constitution,

(c) where the company's constitution is altered by a special enactment (see section 34(4)), a copy of the enactment, and

(d) a copy of any order required to be sent to the registrar under section 35(2)(a) (order of court or other authority altering company's constitution).

(2) This does not require the articles to be accompanied by a copy of a document or by a statement if—

(a) the effect of the resolution, agreement, enactment or order (as the case may be) on the company's constitution has been incorporated into the articles by amendment, or

(b) the resolution, agreement, enactment or order (as the case may be) is not for the time being in force.

(3) If the company fails to comply with this section, an offence is committed by every officer of the company who is in default.

(4) A person guilty of an offence under this section is liable on summary conviction to a fine not exceeding level 3 on the standard scale for each occasion on which copies are issued, or, as the case may be, requested.

(5) For the purposes of this section, a liquidator of the company is treated as an officer of it.

COMMENCEMENT DATE 1 October 2009[114]

**3.36.02**   Section 36 replaces parts of section 380 of the Companies Act 1985. It reinforces the obligation to register the resolutions or agreements listed under section 29 by also requiring those resolutions or agreements (as well as the other documents listed at section 36(1)(b) to (d)) to accompany copies of its

---

[113] Companies Act 2006 (Commencement No 8, Transitional Provisions and Savings) Order 2008, SI 2008/2860, art 3. By Sch 2, para 13 to that Order, s 35 applies in relation to orders made on or after 1 October 2009.

[114] Companies Act 2006 (Commencement No 8, Transitional Provisions and Savings) Order 2008, SI 2008/2860, art 3. By Sch 2, para 14 to that Order, s 36 applies to copies of a company's articles issued on or after 1 October 2009. Otherwise, s 380(2), (6) and (7) of the Companies Act 1985 continue to apply.

articles that are issued by a company. The title to the section has been transplanted from the comparable (but modified) provision of the Companies Bill, but is now a little misleading. There is no longer an obligation to *incorporate*, in the articles, any of the documents referred to. Rather, incorporation becomes an alternative to ensuring that copies of the documents accompany copies of the articles that the company issues (see section 26(2)(a)). Note also that under section 36(2)(b) the obligation subsists only so long as the resolution or agreement remains 'in force'. The obligation is to maintain an up-to-date record of the constitution, not a historical archive. Again, the failure to comply with this provision does not affect the effectiveness of the resolution or agreement itself. Under this section, only an officer 'in default'—and not the company itself—commits an offence where there is non-compliance with this section.

## *Supplementary provisions*

### 37  Right to participate in profits otherwise than as member void

In the case of a company limited by guarantee and not having a share capital any provision in the company's articles, or in any resolution of the company, purporting to give a person a right to participate in the divisible profits of the company otherwise than as a member is void.    **3.37.01**

  Commencement Date  1 October 2009[115]

Section 37 replaces section 15(1) of the Companies Act 1985. It deals with companies that are limited by guarantee, and do not have a share capital. (Under section 5, a company cannot be formed as, or become, a company limited by guarantee with a share capital. Such a provision has been in force since 22 December 1980 in Great Britain (and since 1 July 1983 in Northern Ireland) but there are extant guarantee companies with a share capital that pre-date that restriction.) Section 37 does not prevent guarantee companies either making, or distributing, their profits.[116] Rather the section deals with the basis on which such profits may lawfully be distributed. The section renders void provisions in a company's articles, or in any resolution of the company, which give a person the right to share in profits otherwise than as a member. Thus, articles/resolutions that give non-members a share of profits would be rendered void. So too would such provisions that seek to give, say, some members a greater share of profits according to the extra work they perform for the company, the extra goods they purchase from the company, and so on.    **3.37.02**

The section does not, however, seem to require an equality of treatment between members, and thus an equal division of profits between them. Moreover, the section renders void only provisions in a company's articles or in shareholder resolutions. It would not, therefore, appear to outlaw a provision in, say, a service contract with an employee of the company, or in a debenture with a creditor, entitling such a person to a share of the profits.    **3.37.03**

### 38  Application to single member companies of enactments and rules of law

Any enactment or rule of law applicable to companies formed by two or more persons or having two or more members applies with any necessary modification in relation to a company formed by one person or having only one person as a member.    **3.38.01**

  Commencement Date  1 October 2009[117]

The Act permits single member private and public companies (see section 7). Section 38 ensures that any single member company will be subject (with necessary modifications) to enactments or rules of law applicable to companies formed by two or more persons. It thus effectively extends the Companies (Single Member Private Limited Companies) Regulations 1992 (SI 1992/1699) (which dealt only with single member private companies).    **3.38.02**

---

[115] Companies Act 2006 (Commencement No 8, Transitional Provisions and Savings) Order 2008, SI 2008/2860, art 3.

[116] Community interest companies, by contrast, cannot distribute profits. Note also the conditions for exemption from the use of the word 'limited' in a company's name, under s 60.

[117] Companies Act 2006 (Commencement No 8, Transitional Provisions and Savings) Order 2008, SI 2008/2860, art 3.

# 4

# A COMPANY'S CAPACITY AND RELATED MATTERS

## Companies Act 2006

### PART 4
### A COMPANY'S CAPACITY AND RELATED MATTERS

The provisions in this Part address three related issues: (i) the question of the company's capacity to contract and the ability of third parties to hold the company to a transaction despite the existence of constitutional limitations on the authority to bind; (ii) the formalities required for company contracts; and (iii) the question of the enforceability of pre-incorporation contracts. The applicable legislation remains largely unaltered in terms of substance, with a couple of exceptions relating to corporate *ultra vires*, and the consequences of the Companies Act 2006, section 270 (abolishing the previous mandatory requirement that all private companies had a company secretary) in terms of the execution of deeds and documents by companies. However, the opportunity has been taken to re-order the presentation and, hence, the clarity of the legislative provisions.   **4.01**

### *Capacity of company and the powers of directors to bind it*

There are four provisions which deal with the 'capacity' question. The term capacity usually relates to the ability of the company to contract ('the *ultra vires*' question) whereas it is possible that the company may have the capacity to contract but the directors of the company purporting to make the contract on its behalf may exceed their powers under the constitution, eg by exceeding a restriction on their ability to borrow a particular sum without the prior approval of the general meeting. This involves a question of the authority of the directors to contract—and specifically their ability to bind the company when exceeding that authority. Section 39 addresses the capacity (*vires*) question, whereas section 40 is concerned with the authority question and its impact on those dealing with the company.[1] Of course, if the company lacks the capacity to contract then those who enter into the contract on the company's behalf will necessarily be exceeding their authority.   **4.02**

### 39  A company's capacity[a]

(1)  The validity of an act done by a company shall not be called into question on the ground of lack of capacity by reason of anything in the company's constitution.   **4.39.01**

(2)  This section has effect subject to section 42 (companies that are charities).

---

[1]  For a recent restatement of the importance of the distinction between capacity and authority see *Haugesund Kommune, Narvik Kommune v Depfa ACS Bank* [2010] EWCA Civ 579, [2011] 1 All ER 190.

AMENDMENTS AND NOTES

ᵃ This section applies without modification to unregistered companies by reg 3 of and Sch 1 to the Unregistered Companies Regulations 2009, SI 2009/2436 and by Sch 2 applies to acts of a company done on or after 1 October 2009.

COMMENCEMENT DATE 1 October 2009[2]

**4.39.02**   This section largely re-enacts the Companies Acts 1985, section 35(1) and (4), although the Companies Act 2006, section 39 now refers to limitations in the company's constitution rather than simply the memorandum (and therefore the company's objects clause). This is because the company's constitution is now contained in the articles of association, as extended by section 17(b) to include shareholder agreements and resolutions (as defined by section 29).

**4.39.03**   Section 39(1) provides that constitutional limitations cannot be relied upon to deny the validity of a corporate act. However, this is not the same as a statement that a company has unlimited capacity, which had been the proposal of the Company Law Review Steering Group (CLRSG).[3] The difficulty with the CLRSG proposal would have been to reconcile it with the requirement for a statement of objects for public companies contained in the Second Company Law Directive[4] and this no doubt explains the wording of the related section 31(1) which states that, unless the company's articles specifically restrict the objects of the company, those objects are unrestricted.[5]

**4.39.04**   It follows that where the company's objects are unrestricted, the company's capacity to contract cannot be denied for any purposes and, it seems, on the basis of the wording of section 39(1) that the same must be true where there is a restriction on capacity in the company's constitution.

**4.39.05**   Whereas the previous position restricted protection to outside purposes, ie capacity could not be denied against the third party or by the third party in favour of the company, section 39 contains no equivalent provisions to the previous Companies Act 1985, section 35(2) and (3),[6] whereby a member could bring an action to prevent prospective *ultra vires* (ie acts outside the company's capacity)[7] and, since directors had a duty to abide by limitations in the memorandum, a director's action exceeding this capacity could only be ratified by special resolution. Explanatory Note 123 to the Act states that these provisions are unnecessary either because the objects may be unrestricted or because, if they are restricted, the directors' powers are also restricted and the directors are also under a statutory duty to act in accordance with the company's constitution (section 171(a)). Nevertheless, unless all companies have unrestricted capacity, it is difficult to see why some attempt to recognize the internal significance of capacity has not been retained since it is inevitable that some contracts will be *ultra vires* a company with restricted objects.[8] The assumption appears to be that capacity and authority may amount to the same thing in practice so that actions which lack capacity will necessarily also amount to actions whereby the directors exceed their powers (section 40(4) and (5)) and that is sufficient to recognize that an objects clause may have some purpose.

**4.39.06**   Thus, at the root of the difficulties with section 39 is the perceived conflict between section 31, allowing a company to restrict its activities in the articles, and section 39, stating that nothing in the constitution can restrict the company from contracting—and this position extends to protection for contracting

---

[2] Companies Act 2006 (Commencement No 8, Transitional Provisions and Savings) Order 2008, SI 2008/2860, art 3. In respect of acts conducted by the company prior to 1 October 2009, see the transitional provisions in Sch 2, para 15.

[3] Company Law Review, *Company Formation and Capital Maintenance*, DTI, October 1999, para 2.35 ff and the Final Report, *Modern Company Law for a Competitive Economy*, DTI, June 2001, para 9.10. However, this proposal was not included in the White Paper, *Modernising Company Law*, July 2002, Cm 5553, at 2.2, which permitted an objects clause and declared that it would have only internal effect for directors and members.

[4] Second Council Directive (EC) 77/91 on company law [1977] OJ L26/1, as amended by [1992] OJ L347/64 and [2006] OJ L264/32.

[5] Such a position also reflects the objective of ensuring flexibility for companies who may consider it commercially convenient or have other reasons for wanting to restrict objects, eg community interest companies or joint venture companies (Comm, SCD, Third Sitting, 20 June 2006, col 82).

[6] However, in Standing Committee the Minister claimed that clause 39 was concerned solely with third party protection and erroneously considered that the protection would be available under this section only where that third party was acting in good faith; Comm SCD, Third Sitting, 20 June 2006, cols 91 and 92.

[7] It is likely that this provision had little practical effect since in larger companies shareholders would be unlikely to have notice of prospective *ultra vires* and the Companies Act (CA) 1985 provisions prevented such proceedings where a legal obligation had already arisen.

[8] *Company Law Reform*, DTI, March 2005, Cm 6456, clause A39 of the Draft Bill expressly stated (A39(3)) that where the objects were restricted this would have no effect on the validity of any act which fell outside the company's capacity, thereby suggesting that it was intended that there should be no consequences at all for failure to comply with capacity restrictions.

parties and the company. The conflict can be resolved if section 31 is seen as relating only to internal matters and section 39 as relating only to external matters (and whether a third party is affected by lack of capacity). However, any such distinction should be made clearer even if it is possible to claim that the internal remedies are retained by section 40.

In addition, the abolition of a constructive notice provision is now limited to the wording contained in   **4.39.07** section 40(2)(b)(i) that a person dealing with the company 'is not bound to enquire as to any limitation on the powers of the directors to bind the company or authorize others to do so'. This differs from the previous section 35B in failing to state explicitly that there is no duty to enquire as to whether the company has the capacity to make the contract; presumably because it would obviously make no difference to enforceability.[9]

Subsection (2) provides that where the company is a charity the capacity rules are modified in   **4.39.08** accordance with the provisions of section 42.

## 40  Power of directors to bind the company[a]

(1)  In favour of a person dealing with a company in good faith, the power of the directors to bind the   **4.40.01** company, or authorise others to do so, is deemed to be free of any limitation under the company's constitution.

(2)  For this purpose—
    (a)  a person 'deals with' a company if he is a party to any transaction or other act to which the company is a party,
    (b)  a person dealing with a company—
        (i)  is not bound to enquire as to any limitation on the powers of the directors to bind the company or authorise others to do so,
        (ii)  is presumed to have acted in good faith unless the contrary is proved, and
        (iii)  is not to be regarded as acting in bad faith by reason only of his knowing that an act is beyond the powers of the directors under the company's constitution.

(3)  The references above to limitations on the directors' powers under the company's constitution include limitations deriving—
    (a)  from a resolution of the company or of any class of shareholders, or
    (b)  from any agreement between the members of the company or of any class of shareholders.

(4)  This section does not affect any right of a member of the company to bring proceedings to restrain the doing of an action that is beyond the powers of the directors.
But no such proceedings lie in respect of an act to be done in fulfilment of a legal obligation arising from a previous act of the company.

(5)  This section does not affect any liability incurred by the directors, or any other person, by reason of the directors' exceeding their powers.

(6)  This section has effect subject to—
    section 41 (transactions with directors or their associates), and
    section 42 (companies that are charities).

AMENDMENTS AND NOTES

[a]  This section applies without modification to unregistered companies by reg 3 of and Sch 1 to the Unregistered Companies Regulations 2009, SI 2009/2436.

COMMENCEMENT DATE  1 October 2009[10]

This provision largely corresponds to the Companies Act 1985, sections 35A and 35B. Its broad effect   **4.40.02** is that a third party 'dealing with' a company (as defined in section 40(2)(a)) 'in good faith' (section 40(2)(b)(ii) and (iii)) need not concern itself with whether the directors of the company have the power to bind the company to the transaction or to authorize others to do so under the terms of the company's constitution. Section 40(1) no longer refers to 'the board' as a single organ but can now extend to 'directors' acting in committees. This accepts the practical reality that the board frequently delegates in this way and will extend the scope of direct application of section 40 whilst reducing the need for third parties to rely on agency principles[11] in order to hold the company to a transaction made by committee

---

[9]  This is stated explicitly in Explanatory Note 126 to the CA 2006.
[10]  Companies Act 2006 (Commencement No 8, Transitional Provisions and Savings) Order 2008, SI 2008/ 2860, art 3.
[11]  In this context agency principles could hold the company to the transaction based on either implied actual authority or ostensible authority. Actual authority is implied from the position of director and what a director would usually be authorized to do in the company, although no express actual authority has been given. Ostensible authority occurs where the board of directors or general meeting has represented that the person in question is a director and so possesses the authority that such a person would usually have; eg *Freeman & Lockyer v Buckhurst Park Properties (Mangal) Ltd* [1964] 2 QB 480: represented as acting as managing director and so had

or by individual directors. Section 250 of the Companies Act 2006 defines 'director' as including 'any person occupying the position of director, by whatever name called',[12] ie anyone who exercises 'real power within the company, particularly in relation to decision taking'.[13] In particular, it includes a *de facto* director, ie someone who has assumed the status and functions of a director although not *properly* appointed. Section 161(1) provides that 'the acts of a person acting as a director are valid notwithstanding that it is afterwards discovered (a) that there was a defect in his appointment'. Nevertheless, it seems clear that section 161 will be interpreted narrowly in accordance with the case-law interpreting its predecessor, the Companies Act 1985, section 285, so that there must have been an appointment (albeit defective), as opposed to no appointment at all.[14] It therefore follows that reliance on ostensible authority may still be required where a person has been represented as holding office as a director but has never been formally appointed.

**4.40.03**   The second part of section 40(1) states that the third party dealing with the company in good faith also need not be concerned with any limitations on the powers of the directors under the terms of the company's constitution to authorize others to bind the company. Section 40(3) provides an extended definition of constitutional limitations as including those deriving from shareholder resolutions and agreements. The combined effect of these provisions should be to reduce the need to rely on the rule in *Turquand*,[15] for example because, in favour of a third party dealing with the company in good faith, ostensible authority to bind the company cannot be denied simply on the basis that there is a conflicting provision in the company's constitution.

**4.40.04**   A person can be 'dealing with a company' although the transaction involves a gratuitous disposition since the transaction can include an 'act' (section 40(2)(a)(i) and note also *William Grant and Sons Ltd and others v Mercer Ltd*[16] ). However, in *EIC Services Ltd v Phipps*[17] the Court of Appeal held that a shareholder receiving bonus shares was not 'a person dealing with the company' within the previous section 35A. It appears that this conclusion was reached by relying on the terms of the First Directive on Company Law[18] which suggested that the intention was to protect 'third parties' and, in this context, that could not include the company or its members.

**4.40.05**   There is some presentational adjustment in section 40(2) when compared to the previous section 35A(2) of the 1985 Act, in particular, the order, but not the content, of the good faith provisions is reversed. The third party is presumed to have acted in good faith unless the contrary is proved and a third party will not act in bad faith simply because that party knows that an act is beyond the constitutional powers of the directors. This suggests that there must be real subjective dishonesty in order for the third party to act in bad faith and lose the section 40(1) protection. It seems that the third party would need to appreciate the significance of any such knowledge. *Ford v Polymer*[19] illustrates the difficulties associated with establishing bad faith. In an application for summary judgment, the court upheld the validity of a debenture under section 40 in circumstances where board meetings had not been validly convened in accordance with the company's articles of association and a shareholders agreement. One defect was the failure to give notice of the meeting to all those entitled to receive it. The third party knew that there were differences of opinion on the board and a dispute about whether proper notice had been given but the trial judge held that this was not sufficient to demonstrate bad faith.

**4.40.06**   It is clear that, unlike section 39, this section provides protection only for 'third parties', and only for external third parties (section 41). The constitutional limitations still apply internally so that section 40 does not affect the ability of a member to hold the company to the constitution under the terms of the section 33 membership contract by pre-emptive challenge. Further, by section 40(5) it is clear that neither does the section 40 protection for third parties prevent action against the directors in question

---

ostensible authority to bind the company. See further the discussion in J Birds and AJ Boyle et al, *Boyle & Birds' Company Law* (8th edn, Jordan Publishing, 2011), esp 6.13–6.24, and note, too, *Kelly v Fraser (Jamaicas)* [2012] UKPC 25.

   [12]   Previously CA 1985, s 741(1).
   [13]   Explanatory Notes to the Bill as introduced in the Commons, [260].
   [14]   *Morris v Kanssen* [1946] AC 459, *per* Lord Simonds at 471. This is reinforced by the reference to 'not properly appointed' in the definition of a *de facto* director given in the Explanatory Notes.
   [15]   *Royal British Bank v Turquand* (1856) 6 E & B 327 (the indoor management rule): third parties are entitled to assume that any internal management procedures have been complied with unless they know of any irregularity. In this last respect, s 40(1) may provide better protection because of the extended definition of 'good faith', ie even actual notice will not constitute bad faith.
   [16]   [2010] CSOH 52.
   [17]   [2004] EWCA Civ 1069, [2005] 1 WLR 1377.
   [18]   First Council Directive (EC) 68/151 on company law [1968] OJ L65/8, as amended by [2003] OJ L221/13.
   [19]   [2009] EWHC 945 (Ch), [2009] 2 BCLC 160.

for breach of authority in exceeding the constitutional limitations on their powers, although such acts are capable of ratification by ordinary resolution (section 239), and that fact alone *may* be capable of preventing a derivative claim under section 263(2) and (3) if ratification is likely and it *must* prevent such a claim where ratification has already occurred. In addition, subsection (6) makes it clear that the section 40 protection is removed in relation to insiders (section 41) and modified in relation to transactions with companies which are charities (section 42).

### 41  Constitutional limitations: transactions involving directors or their associates[a]

(1)  This section applies to a transaction if or to the extent that its validity depends on section 40 (power of directors deemed to be free of limitations under company's constitution in favour of person dealing with company in good faith).          **4.41.01**
Nothing in this section shall be read as excluding the operation of any other enactment or rule of law by virtue of which the transaction may be called in question or any liability to the company may arise.

(2)  Where—
   (a)  a company enters into such a transaction, and
   (b)  the parties to the transaction include—
      (i)   a director of the company or of its holding company, or
      (ii)  a person connected with any such director,
   the transaction is voidable at the instance of the company.

(3)  Whether or not it is avoided, any such party to the transaction as is mentioned in subsection (2)(b)(i) or (ii), and any director of the company who authorised the transaction, is liable—
   (a)  to account to the company for any gain he has made directly or indirectly by the transaction, and
   (b)  to indemnify the company for any loss or damage resulting from the transaction.

(4)  The transaction ceases to be voidable if—
   (a)  restitution of any money or other asset which was the subject-matter of the transaction is no longer possible, or
   (b)  the company is indemnified for any loss or damage resulting from the transaction, or
   (c)  rights acquired bona fide for value and without actual notice of the directors' exceeding their powers by a person who is not party to the transaction would be affected by the avoidance, or
   (d)  the transaction is affirmed by the company.

(5)  A person other than a director of the company is not liable under subsection (3) if he shows that at the time the transaction was entered into he did not know that the directors were exceeding their powers.

(6)  Nothing in the preceding provisions of this section affects the rights of any party to the transaction not within subsection (2)(b)(i) or (ii).
But the court may, on the application of the company or any such party, make an order affirming, severing or setting aside the transaction on such terms as appear to the court to be just.

(7)  In this section—
   (a)  'transaction' includes any act; and
   (b)  the reference to a person connected with a director has the same meaning as in Part 10 (company directors).

AMENDMENTS AND NOTES

[a]  This section applies without modification to unregistered companies by reg 3 of and Sch 1 to the Unregistered Companies Regulations 2009, SI 2009/2436.

COMMENCEMENT DATE  1 October 2009[20]

This section is equivalent in substance to section 322A of the Companies Act 1985 but is helpfully    **4.41.02** repositioned with the applicable authority provision to which it relates, ie section 40. Section 41 applies to 'insider' transactions which depend for their validity on section 40 (power of directors to bind the company), ie transactions between the company and a director of that company or of its holding company or any person connected with any such director (as defined in section 252, for example, members of the director's family, a partner of the director, or a company with which the director is connected). These transactions are in principle caught by the section 40 protection (*Smith v Henniker-Major & Co*)[21] but by section 41 this section 40 protection for third parties will not apply to such insider transactions which are made voidable by the company.

---

[20]  Companies Act 2006 (Commencement No 8, Transitional Provisions and Savings) Order 2008, SI 2008/2860, art 3.

[21]  [2002] EWCA Civ 762, [2002] 2 BCLC 655.

**4.41.03**    In any event, whether or not the transaction is avoided, the 'insider' or connected person, and any director who authorized such a transaction, is liable to account to the company for any direct or indirect gain from the transaction and to indemnify the company for any loss or damage it has incurred from the transaction (subsection (3)). However, a person other than a director will escape this subsection (3) liability if he or she is able to show that he or she did not know that the directors were exceeding their powers at the time the transaction was entered into.

**4.41.04**    Subsection (4) sets out the circumstances in which the transaction will cease to be voidable as including some of the usual bars to rescission, ie where restitution of any money or asset covered by the transaction is no longer possible, affirmation of the transaction by the company (ie ratification in accordance with section 239), or where the company is indemnified for loss or damage in respect of the transaction. Alternatively, rescission will be barred where it would impact on a *bona fide* subsequent purchaser for value who has no notice of the fact that the directors exceeded their powers. There is similar protection for other third parties who are not 'insiders' or connected persons since section 41(6) provides that section 41 does not affect the rights of such parties to the transaction. However, on the application of the company or any such external party to the transaction, the court may make an order affirming, severing or setting aside the transaction on such terms as appear to the court to be just.

**4.41.05**    Subsection (7)(a) states that transaction includes 'any act', thereby ensuring that the protection of the section extends to charitable gifts and any gratuitous distribution of assets. In addition, this subsection is neater than the equivalent previous provision, Companies Act 1985, section 322A(8), since there is no need, given the position of this provision, to explain what is meant by limitations under the company's constitution (defined in section 40(3)).

**4.41.06**    Finally, section 41(1) makes it clear that this ability to avoid a transaction as against an 'internal' contracting party is additional to the scope of any other rules of law or statutory provisions which may enable the transaction to be called into question or impose liability on directors.

### 42 Constitutional limitations: companies that are charities[a]

**4.42.01**
(1) Sections 39 and 40 (company's capacity and power of directors to bind company) do not apply to the acts of a company that is a charity except in favour of a person who—
   (a) does not know at the time the act is done that the company is a charity, or
   (b) gives full consideration in money or money's worth in relation to the act in question and does not know (as the case may be)—
      (i) that the act is not permitted by the company's constitution or,
      (ii) that the act is beyond the powers of the directors.
(2) Where a company that is a charity purports to transfer or grant an interest in property, the fact that (as the case may be)—
   (a) the act was not permitted by the company's constitution, or
   (b) the directors in connection with the act exceeded any limitation on their powers under the company's constitution,
does not affect the title of a person who subsequently acquires the property or any interest in it for full consideration without actual notice of any such circumstances affecting the validity of the company's act.
(3) In any proceedings arising out of subsection (1) or (2) the burden of proving—
   (a) that a person knew that the company was a charity, or
   (b) that a person knew that an act was not permitted by the company's constitution or was beyond the powers of the directors,
lies on the person asserting that fact.
(4) In the case of a company that is a charity the affirmation of a transaction to which section 41 applies (transactions with directors or their associates) is ineffective without the prior written consent of—
   (a) in England and Wales, the Charity Commission;
   (b) in Northern Ireland, the Department for Social Development.
(5) This section does not extend to Scotland (but see section 112 of the Companies Act 1989 (c. 40)).

AMENDMENTS AND NOTES

   [a] This section applies without modification to unregistered companies by reg 3 of and Sch 1 to the Unregistered Companies Regulations 2009, SI 2009/2436.

COMMENCEMENT DATE 1 October 2009[22]

**4.42.02**    This section replaces the Companies Act 1985, sections 35(4) and 35A(6) and reproduces the substance of the Charities Act 1993, section 65, qualifying the capacity provision and the provision dealing with

---

[22] Companies Act 2006 (Commencement No 8, Transitional Provisions and Savings) Order 2008, SI 2008/2860, art 3.

the power of directors to bind the company where the company in question is a charity. By subsection (1) (in the terms of the Charities Act 1993, section 65(1)) the third party protection in sections 39 and 40 will not apply if the company is a charity unless the person dealing with that company either does not know at the time the act is done that the company is a charity, or the company received full consideration for the act and the third party was unaware that the act was either beyond the company's capacity or beyond the powers of the directors. The burden of proof in respect of this knowledge requirement lies on the person asserting that the knowledge existed (subsection (3)).

However, there is protection for those who are not parties to the contract but subsequently acquire rights in property covered by that contract. Subsection (2) states that nothing in section 42 affects the rights of a subsequent purchaser for full consideration who has no actual notice of the circumstances affecting the validity of the original contract. In addition, there is protection where the transaction is with insiders or connected persons since any affirmation (presumably in relation to the directors exceeding their powers to bind the company) is ineffective unless the prior written consent of the Charity Commission (England and Wales) or Department of Social Development (Northern Ireland) has been obtained.    **4.42.03**

The previous reference to section 35(3) ratification (for lack of corporate capacity) has been removed as section 35(3) is not re-enacted in the 2006 Act. Therefore it appears that no ratification is required in respect of capacity questions, as opposed to instances where the directors exceed their powers, despite the fact that some such companies may choose to retain an objects clause. This seems to be because no action of any kind will follow from lack of capacity to contract.[23]    **4.42.04**

This section applies only to England, Wales, and Northern Ireland. However, corresponding provisions for charities registered in Scotland are contained in the Companies Act 1989, section 112(5). Note also, with regard to Scottish charitable incorporated organizations, the provisions regarding third parties in section 62 of the Charities and Trustee Investment (Scotland) Act 2005, asp 10.    **4.42.05**

## *Formalities of doing business under the law of England and Wales or Northern Ireland*

These provisions apply to the formal authority to execute documents, as opposed to the question of the substantive authority to actually enter into the contract or other transaction, dealt with in sections 39 to 42. Thus, where a document has been formally executed by the company, eg in accordance with the rules regarding signatures, the company cannot deny its formal validity[24] and will be bound by it.    **4.43.01**

### 43 Company contracts[a]

(1) Under the law of England and Wales or Northern Ireland a contract may be made—    **4.43.02**
    (a) by a company, by writing under its common seal, or
    (b) on behalf of a company, by a person acting under its authority, express or implied.
(2) Any formalities required by law in the case of a contract made by an individual also apply, unless a contrary intention appears, to a contract made by or on behalf of a company.

AMENDMENTS AND NOTES

[a] This section applies with modification to LLPs by reg 4 of the Limited Liability Partnerships (Application of Companies Act 2006) Regulations 2009, SI 2009/1804. It applies without modification to unregistered companies by reg 3 of and Sch 1 to the Unregistered Companies Regulations 2009, SI 2009/2436. It applies with modification to overseas companies by reg 4 of the Overseas Companies (Execution of Documents and Registration of Charges) Regulations 2009, SI 2009/1917.

COMMENCEMENT DATE 1 October 2009[25]

This section replaces the Companies Act 1985, section 36 (which had been inserted by the Companies Act 1989, section 130), whilst extending its application to Northern Ireland. There are two aspects to the provision.    **4.43.03**

Subsection (1) explains that a company contract can either be made in writing by the company under its common seal (see section 45(1)), or on behalf of the company by a person acting under its authority, express or implied. The question of authority to bind the company is determined by the principles of agency law (actual authority or ostensible authority). Where statute requires that the contract or other    **4.43.04**

---

[23] This is discussed in relation to s 39 above.
[24] *Duck v Tower Galvanizing Co* [1901] 2 KB 314.
[25] Companies Act 2006 (Commencement No 8, Transitional Provisions and Savings) Order 2008, SI 2008/2860, art 3.

document be executed, there are specific provisions to identify those officers who may execute a document on behalf of the company (see the Companies Act 2006, section 44(2)–(4)).

**4.43.05**   Subsection (2) explains that any formalities required by law where an individual contracts, also apply to a contract made by the company or on its behalf, unless a contrary intention appears, eg from a provision in the company's articles requiring additional formalities for particular transactions. Statutory formalities requirements include the fact that the conveyance of a legal estate in land must be made in the form of a deed,[26] and a contract involving a gratuitous promise must also be made in the form of a deed (see section 46 for execution of deeds by companies). Other contracts must be made in writing, eg dispositions of equitable interests in land must be made in writing,[27] distance selling contracts,[28] and bills of exchange and promissory notes must be in writing and signed.[29] Contracts of guarantee, as opposed to contracts of indemnity, are required to be evidenced in writing.[30]

**4.43.06**   For a contract where there are no such formality requirements, the fact that it is made in writing serves an evidentiary role only and is not a requirement for validity.

### 44 Execution of documents[a]

**4.44.01**
  (1) Under the law of England and Wales or Northern Ireland a document is executed by a company—
    (a) by the affixing of its common seal, or
    (b) by signature in accordance with the following provisions.
  (2) A document is validly executed by a company if it is signed on behalf of the company—
    (a) by two authorised signatories, or
    (b) by a director of the company in the presence of a witness who attests the signature.
  (3) The following are 'authorised signatories' for the purposes of subsection (2)—
    (a) every director of the company, and
    (b) in the case of a private company with a secretary or a public company, the secretary (or any joint secretary) of the company.
  (4) A document signed in accordance with subsection (2) and expressed, in whatever words, to be executed by the company has the same effect as if executed under the common seal of the company.
  (5) In favour of a purchaser a document is deemed to have been duly executed by a company if it purports to be signed in accordance with subsection (2).
    A 'purchaser' means a purchaser in good faith for valuable consideration and includes a lessee, mortgagee or other person who for valuable consideration acquires an interest in property.
  (6) Where a document is to be signed by a person on behalf of more than one company, it is not duly signed by that person for the purposes of this section unless he signs it separately in each capacity.
  (7) References in this section to a document being (or purporting to be) signed by a director or secretary are to be read, in a case where that office is held by a firm, as references to its being (or purporting to be) signed by an individual authorised by the firm to sign on its behalf.
  (8) This section applies to a document that is (or purports to be) executed by a company in the name of or on behalf of another person whether or not that person is also a company.

AMENDMENTS AND NOTES

[a] This section applies with modification to LLPs by reg 4 of the Limited Liability Partnerships (Application of Companies Act 2006) Regulations 2009, SI 2009/1804. It applies with modification to overseas companies by reg 4 of the Overseas Companies (Execution of Documents and Registration of Charges) Regulations 2009, SI 2009/1917. It applies without modification to unregistered companies by reg 3 of and Sch 1 to the Unregistered Companies Regulations 2009, SI 2009/2436 and by Sch 2 applies to the execution of documents on or after 1 October 2009.

COMMENCEMENT DATE 6 April 2008[31]

**4.44.02**   This provision substantially re-enacts section 36A of the Companies Act 1985 whilst extending its application to cover Northern Ireland and taking account of the fact that private companies are no

---

[26] Law of Property Act 1925, ss 52 and 54.
[27] Law of Property Act 1925, s 53(1)(c), and the Law of Property (Miscellaneous Provisions) Act 1989, s 2(1).
[28] Consumer Protection (Distance Selling) Regulations 2000, SI 2000/2334, as amended by SI 2005/689.
[29] Bills of Exchange Act 1882, ss 3(1) and 83(1); see also CA 2006, s 52.
[30] Statute of Frauds 1677, s 4: 'some memorandum or note thereof in writing' which has been signed by the party to be charged.
[31] Companies Act 2006 (Commencement No 5, Transitional Provisions and Savings) Order 2007, SI 2007/3495, art 2(5), Sch 4, para 9(1). This section will apply to the execution of documents by a company on or after 6 April 2008, and this includes instances where a document is signed by one authorized signatory before 6 April 2008 and by another on or after that date. Such a document is treated as executed on 6 April 2008. The Companies Act 1985, s 36A will continue to apply to documents executed before 6 April 2008.

longer required to have a company secretary.[32] The Bill as originally introduced into the Lords in November 2005 contained separate provisions detailing the execution requirements for private and public companies which excluded signature by a company secretary of a private company despite the fact that the relevant clause did not prohibit appointment and so implicitly accepted that such a company secretary might be appointed. During the progress of the Bill, the relevant parts of the clause were replaced with a single, and more general, system of 'authorised signatories' for all companies, including a requirement to maintain a register of such persons. However, the definition of 'authorised signatories' continued to exclude an automatic appointment of any company secretary of a private company and allowed the company to make additional individual appointments. Thus, although a private company's secretary could have been appointed as an 'authorised signatory', this would not necessarily have followed. The anomaly thus created was recognized in debate and the Bill was later amended[33] so as to provide a more streamlined provision for execution of company documents by signature. This allows for signature by two directors, by a director and a secretary, or, significantly, by a single director as long as that director's signature is duly attested. There is also no explicit need to include a clause relating to the authentication of company documents as a result of the ability to provide for this in a company's articles and the fact that the authentication 'has been overtaken by common law developments'.[34] In addition, section 44 is clear on the rules governing the execution of corporate documents. Accordingly, clause 48 of the original Bill (authentication of company documents) was also deleted.[35]

Thus, subsection (1) of section 44 provides that a document is executed by a company through the affixing of its common seal (see section 45) or by signature in accordance with the requirements of section 44. By subsection (4), signature in accordance with the requirements in subsection (2) has the same effect as if the document had been executed under the common seal. **4.44.03**

In its final form, subsection (2) sets out a simple set of requirements for valid signature for all types of companies. The document in question must be signed on the company's behalf by two 'authorised signatories' or by a single director in the presence of a witness who attests the signature. The ability of a single director to execute company documents is inserted for the first time into the companies' legislation, albeit with the protection of witness attestation of signature. **4.44.04**

Subsection (3) was included at the Report Stage in the Commons and defines 'authorised signatories' for the purposes of section 44(2)(a) (execution by two 'authorised signatories') as meaning every director and the company secretary (or joint secretary) of a public company, or a private company if a secretary has been appointed. This is clear and simple and avoids the complexities of possible additional appointments, varying positions between companies and the need to maintain a separate register for 'authorised signatories'. **4.44.05**

Article 81 of the Model Articles of Association for Public Companies[36] makes it clear that in the case of a public company where a common seal is affixed to a document, normally that document must also be signed by an authorized person in the presence of a witness who attests the signature (Article 81(3)). An authorized person in this context is any director, or any person whom the directors have authorized to sign such a document (Article 81(4)). This is an extension on the definition of authorized signatories for the purposes of section 44 of the Companies Act 2006. A similar article is contained in the Model Articles for Private Companies Limited by Shares,[37] which recognizes that the company secretary (if one has been appointed) is an authorized person. **4.44.06**

As noted in 4.44.03, the effect of subsection (4) is that signature in accordance with the requirements in subsection (2) has the same effect as if the document had been executed under the common seal. In *Williams v Redcard Ltd*[38] the Court of Appeal considered the significance of the words 'expressed, in whatever words, to be executed by the company' within subsection (4). The court held that these words did not require, in addition to the signatures of the 'authorised signatories', words spelling out that those signatures were by or on behalf of the company where the agreement defined the company as seller and the signatures appeared under the words 'Signed ... Seller'. **4.44.07**

---

[32] CA 2006, s 270.

[33] Commons Amendments at Report Stage, 11 Oct 2006, 723 and 724.

[34] DTI Implementation Briefing Paper (available at ⟨www.berr.gov.uk/files/file38805.doc⟩, last accessed 30 September 2012).

[35] Commons Amendments at Report Stage, 727. The corresponding provision of the CA 1985, s 41 is repealed with effect from 6 April 2007.

[36] Companies (Model Articles) Regulations 2008, SI 2008/3229, reg 4, Sch 3. These articles apply to companies formed on or after 1 October 2009 and can be found in Chapter 51.

[37] Companies (Model Articles) Regulations 2008, SI 2008/3229, reg 2, ch 1, art 49.

[38] [2011] EWCA Civ 466.

**4.44.08**   Subsections (5) to (8) reflect the previous provisions in the Companies Act 1985, section 36A(4A) to (7).[39]

**4.44.09**   Subsection (5) states that in favour of a 'purchaser' a document is deemed to have been duly executed by the company if it 'purports to be signed' in accordance with the requirements of subsection (2) (ie by two authorized signatories or by a single director whose signature has been witnessed and attested). The subsection defines 'purchaser' as a purchaser in good faith, eg lessee or mortgagee, who acquires an interest in property for valuable consideration. The word 'purports' is not defined; however, in *Lovett v Carson Country Homes Ltd*[40] it was held to be 'on its face a wide word which ... operates to refer to the impression a document conveys'.[41]

**4.44.10**   The use of the words 'purports to be signed' covers lack of authority to sign the document, eg if there has been a defect in appointment as a director or the appointee was not qualified to be appointed (see section 161). Thus, the section 44(5) protection means that the purchaser does not need to establish any actual or ostensible authority on the part of those attaching the signatures. The Law Commission took the view that this did not, however, enable such a 'purchaser' to hold the company to a forged signature by a director of the company.[42] The Law Commission relied on the decision in *Ruben v Great Fingall Consolidated,*[43] which denies legal effect to forged documents. On this view it therefore appears that the intention was that section 44(5) will apply in the case of genuine signatures by officers who lack authority to sign or where there is some defect in their appointment. However, in *Lovett v Carson Country Homes Ltd,*[44] section 44(5) protection was available in respect of a debenture bearing a director's signature forged by another director where the director committing the forgery had ostensible authority to warrant that the signatures were genuine.

**4.44.11**   The previous equivalent provision, Companies Act 1985, section 36A(6), referred to the old signature requirements, but was otherwise in identical terms. The previous irrebutable presumption that deeds were delivered on execution had already been removed by the Regulatory Reform (Execution of Deeds and Documents) Order 2005.[45]

**4.44.12**   Subsection (6) makes it clear that if a person is signing a document on behalf of more than one company, the document must be signed separately in each capacity if it is to satisfy the requirements of section 44 and be validly executed.[46]

**4.44.13**   Subsection (7) provides that references to the signature of a director or a secretary where that office is held by a firm, are references to the individual authorized by that firm to sign on its behalf.[47]

**4.44.14**   Subsection (8) makes it clear that this section can apply to documents executed by a company in the name of, or on behalf of, another person which can also be a company.[48]

**4.44.15**   In May 2009 the City of London Law Society Company Law Committee published guidance[49] on the execution of documents involving a 'virtual' signing or closing (eg where signature pages are sent by fax or email), the effectiveness of which, under English law, had been questioned by *obiter dicta* in *R (Mercury Tax Group and another) v HMRC.*[50] The Committee noted that such *dicta* could, by analogy, be applied to section 44, but nevertheless maintained, on the advice of leading counsel Mark Hapgood

---

[39] As inserted by the Regulatory Reform (Execution of Deeds and Documents) Order 2005, SI 2005/1906. See also Law Com Report, *The Execution of Deeds and Documents by or on behalf of Bodies Corporate*, Law Com No 253, Cm 4026, 1998.

[40] [2009] EWHC 1143 (Ch), [2009] 2 BCLC 196.

[41] *Per* Davis J, para 79.

[42] Law Com Report, *The Execution of Deeds and Documents by or on behalf of Bodies Corporate*, Law Com No 253, Cm 4026, 1998, paras 5.34–5.37.

[43] [1906] AC 439.

[44] [2009] EWHC 1143 (Ch), [2009] 2 BCLC 196.

[45] See art 5, and see CA 2006, s 46(2).

[46] Previously CA 1985, s 36A(4A), as inserted by the Regulatory Reform (Execution of Deeds and Documents) Order 2005, Sch 1, para 10.

[47] Previously CA 1985, s 36A(8), as inserted by the Regulatory Reform (Execution of Deeds and Documents) Order 2005, Sch 1, para 11.

[48] Previously CA 1985, s 36A(7), as inserted by the Regulatory Reform (Execution of Deeds and Documents) Order 2005, art 7(2).

[49] City of London Law Society: Company Law Committee and Financial Law Committee, *Guidance on Execution of Documents at a Virtual Signing or Closing*, May 2009 (available at ⟨http://www.citysolicitors.org.uk/ FileServer.aspx?oID=571&lID=0⟩, last accessed 30 September 2012).

[50] [2008] EWHC 2721 (Admin).

QC, that the authority of *Mercury* should be limited to its own facts. The Committee's guidance was subsequently included in a Law Society practice note.[51]

A good illustration of the issues that can arise under section 44 is provided by *Hilmi & Associates Ltd* **4.44.16** *v 20 Pembridge Villas Freehold Ltd*,[52] in which the Court of Appeal applied section 36A of the 1985 Act and held invalid a notice by a company to exercise the statutory right to acquire freehold property under the Leasehold Reform, Housing and Urban Development Act 1993. Note also *Bower Terrace Student Accommodation Ltd v Space Student Living Ltd* [2012] EWHC 2206 (Ch).

## 45  Common seal[a]

(1) A company may have a common seal, but need not have one. **4.45.01**

(2) A company which has a common seal shall have its name engraved in legible characters on the seal.

(3) If a company fails to comply with subsection (2) an offence is committed by—
    (a) the company, and
    (b) every officer of the company who is in default.

(4) An officer of a company, or a person acting on behalf of a company, commits an offence if he uses, or authorises the use of, a seal purporting to be a seal of the company on which its name is not engraved as required by subsection (2).

(5) A person guilty of an offence under this section is liable on summary conviction to a fine not exceeding level 3 on the standard scale.

(6) This section does not form part of the law of Scotland.

AMENDMENTS AND NOTES

[a] This section applies with modification to LLPs by reg 4 of the Limited Liability Partnerships (Application of Companies Act 2006) Regulations 2009, SI 2009/1804. Section 45(1) applies without modification to unregistered companies by reg 3 of and Sch 1 to the Unregistered Companies Regulations 2009, SI 2009/2436.

COMMENCEMENT DATE  1 October 2009[53]

This section applies to England, Wales, and Northern Ireland only. Execution of company documents **4.45.02** in Scotland is dealt with in section 48.

Section 45 re-enacts the Companies Act 1985, section 36A(3), permitting, but not requiring, a **4.45.03** company to have a common seal. Such seals are now rarer but if a company has a common seal it may make a contract by writing under its common seal (section 43(1)(a)). In addition, a common seal is a prerequisite to the ability to have an official seal (facsimile of the common seal) for use abroad (section 49) and an official seal for sealing securities (section 50).

Section 45 consolidates other related provisions concerning a company's common seal. Subsections (2) **4.45.04** to (5) contain the provisions previously contained in the Companies Act 1985, section 350.

Subsection (2) contains the requirement that if the company has a common seal it must have its name **4.45.05** engraved in legible characters on the seal, and if this requirement is not complied with then (subsection (3)) the company and every officer in default is guilty of an offence. Subsection (4) provides that an offence, punishable by a fine on summary conviction, is also committed by any officer or person acting on the company's behalf who uses or authorizes the use of a seal which does not comply with the subsection (2) mandatory requirement.

It is usual for the procedures governing the use of the common seal to be set out in the company's **4.45.06** articles of association and the Model Articles of Association for Public Companies and Private Companies Limited by Shares, Articles 81 and 49 respectively, contain such provisions, discussed in the commentary to section 44.[54] However, it may prove confusing since, although there is a clear definition of 'authorised signatories' for the purposes of the execution of documents within section 44(2) and (3), 'authorised persons' (as specified in the model articles for the purposes of authorizing the application of the common seal) may include persons authorized by the directors for this purpose alone and is therefore not limited to directors or the company secretary.

---

[51] Law Society, *Execution of documents by virtual means*, February 2010 (available at ⟨http://www.lawsociety.org.uk/advice/practice-notes/virtual-execution-of-documents/⟩, last accessed 30 September 2012).

[52] [2010] EWCA Civ 314.

[53] Companies Act 2006 (Commencement No 8, Transitional Provisions and Savings) Order 2008, SI 2008/2860, art 3.

[54] Companies (Model Articles) Regulations 2008, SI 2008/3229. The articles apply to companies formed on or after 1 October 2009 and can be found in Chapter 51.

### 46 Execution of deeds[a]

**4.46.01**
(1) A document is validly executed by a company as a deed for the purposes of section 1(2)(b) of the Law of Property (Miscellaneous Provisions) Act 1989 (c. 34) and for the purposes of the law of Northern Ireland if, and only if—
  (a) it is duly executed by the company, and
  (b) it is delivered as a deed.
(2) For the purposes of subsection (1)(b) a document is presumed to be delivered upon its being executed, unless a contrary intention is proved.

AMENDMENTS AND NOTES

[a] This section applies with modification to LLPs by reg 4 of the Limited Liability Partnerships (Application of Companies Act 2006) Regulations 2009. It applies without modification to unregistered companies by reg 3 of and Sch 1 to the Unregistered Companies Regulations 2009, SI 2009/2436. It applies with modification to overseas companies by reg 4 of the Overseas Companies (Execution of Documents and Registration of Charges) Regulations 2009, SI 2009/1917.

COMMENCEMENT DATE 1 October 2009[55]

**4.46.02** This section re-enacts section 36AA (inserted into the Companies Act 1985 by the Regulatory Reform (Execution of Deeds and Documents) Order 2005) and extends its application to Northern Ireland.

**4.46.03** To be validly executed as a deed for the purposes of the Law of Property (Miscellaneous Provisions) Act 1989, section 1(2)(b), and under the law of Northern Ireland, the company document must be both duly executed in accordance with the requirements of section 44 (ie in writing and under the common seal or in accordance with the signature requirements in section 44(2) and (3)), and the document must be delivered as a deed. However, in the case of a company this delivery is presumed on execution unless a contrary intention is proved (subsection (2)). Thus, section 46(2) makes it clear that the presumption of delivery on execution is rebuttable by evidence that the intention was for the company to sign a deed but hold it for later delivery, eg on the satisfaction of some outstanding condition.[56] In *Silver Queen Maritime Ltd v Persia Petroleum Services plc* [2010] EWHC 2867 (QB), the court confirmed that proving a contrary intention required an examination of the objective intention of the parties.

**4.46.04** *Obiter dicta* in *R (Mercury Tax Group and another) v HMRC*[57] suggest that section 1(3) of the Law of Property (Miscellaneous Provisions) Act 1989 requires a deed to be executed by an individual in its final version, thereby raising questions about the efficacy of 'virtual' signings and closings. The City of London Law Society Company Law Committee rejected this interpretation but nevertheless published guidance in May 2009 that noted the possibility that the approach in *Mercury* could, by analogy, be applied to sections 44 and 46 and which set out several options for dealing with virtual signings and closings.[58] This guidance was reproduced in a Law Society practice note published in February 2010.[59]

### 47 Execution of deeds or other documents by attorney[a]

**4.47.01**
(1) Under the law of England and Wales or Northern Ireland a company may, by instrument executed as a deed, empower a person, either generally or in respect of specified matters, as its attorney to execute deeds or other documents on its behalf.
(2) A deed or other document so executed, whether in the United Kingdom or elsewhere, has effect as if executed by the company.

AMENDMENTS AND NOTES

[a] This section applies with modification to LLPs by reg 4 of the Limited Liability Partnerships (Application of Companies Act 2006) Regulations 2009.

COMMENCEMENT DATE 1 October 2009[60]

---

[55] Companies Act 2006 (Commencement No 8, Transitional Provisions and Savings) Order 2008, SI 2008/2860, art 3.
[56] See the Regulatory Reform Order 2005, art 6.
[57] [2008] EWHC 2721 (Admin).
[58] City of London Law Society: Company Law Committee and Financial Law Committee, *Guidance on Execution of Documents at a Virtual Signing or Closing*, May 2009 (available at ⟨http://www.citysolicitors.org.uk/FileServer.aspx?oID=571&lID=0⟩, last accessed 30 September 2012).
[59] Law Society, *Execution of documents by virtual means*, February 2010 (available at ⟨http://www.lawsociety.org.uk/advice/practice-notes/virtual-execution-of-documents/⟩, last accessed 30 September 2012).
[60] Companies Act 2006 (Commencement No 8, Transitional Provisions and Savings) Order 2008, SI 2008/2860, art 3. In respect of instruments executed prior to 1 October 2009, see the transitional provisions in Sch 2, para 16.

This provision broadly reflects the Companies Act 1985, section 38, although recognizing that there **4.47.02**
can no longer be any requirement for the empowering instrument to be made under the company's
common seal since there is no requirement to have such a seal (section 45(1)) and a company without
one should not be denied the ability to appoint an attorney. Prior to the Report Stage in the Commons,
the clause had therefore required only that the empowering instrument should be made in writing by
the company. However, the significance of the appointment of an attorney to execute both 'deeds' and
'other documents' should require more than simple writing and this was therefore amended to require
the empowering appointment to be made by deed.[61] This also brings the formality requirements into
line with those applicable where an individual appoints an attorney.

The 2006 Act also extends the application of this provision to Northern Ireland. (It does not apply to a **4.47.03**
company incorporated in Scotland which may therefore authorize any person to execute a document
on its behalf under the general provision of the 1995 Requirements of Writing (Scotland) Act, ie no
requirement for a second director or witness.)

The Companies Act 1985, section 38, was limited to the execution by the attorney of deeds and to **4.47.04**
execution *outside* the UK. Neither restriction applies to section 47 which applies to the appointment of
an attorney to execute deeds and other documents and specifically extends the scope of application to
include the UK, as well as execution abroad. It therefore applies generally to powers of attorney to
execute documents.

Thus, section 47 provides that a company may empower a person as its attorney to execute deeds or **4.47.05**
other documents on its behalf by means of an empowering deed, so that any such deed or other
documents falling within the scope of the authority granted by this instrument, whether executed in
the UK or abroad, will have effect as if executed by the company.

The Reform Order of 2005[62] had earlier clarified section 7 of the Powers of Attorney Act 1971 by **4.47.06**
inserting section 7(1A) to make it clear that execution by an individual attorney on behalf of a
corporate donor would be effective, and consequential amendments were also made to the Law of
Property (Miscellaneous Provisions) Act 1989, section 1, to make it clear that a deed can be executed by
such an attorney on the company's behalf.

## Formalities of doing business under the law of Scotland

### 48 Execution of documents by companies[a]

   (1)  The following provisions form part of the law of Scotland only. **4.48.01**
   (2)  Notwithstanding the provisions of any enactment, a company need not have a company seal.
   (3)  For the purposes of any enactment—
      (a)  providing for a document to be executed by a company by affixing its common seal, or
      (b)  referring (in whatever terms) to a document so executed, a document signed or subscribed
         by or on behalf of the company in accordance with the provisions of the Requirements of
         Writing (Scotland) Act 1995 (c. 7) has effect as if so executed.

AMENDMENTS AND NOTES

  [a]  This section applies with modification to LLPs by reg 5 of the Limited Liability Partnerships
    (Application of Companies Act 2006) Regulations 2009, SI 2009/1804. It applies without modifi-
    cation to unregistered companies by reg 3 of and Sch 1 to the Unregistered Companies Regulations
    2009, SI 2009/2436. It applies with modification to overseas companies by reg 5 of the Overseas
    Companies (Execution of Documents and Registration of Charges) Regulations 2009, SI 2009/
    1917.

COMMENCEMENT DATE 1 October 2009[63]

This section re-enacts the Companies Act 1985, section 36B, although subsection (1) of section 48 is **4.48.02**
inserted to make it absolutely clear that this provision applies only to Scotland.

Section 48 makes it clear that a company need not have a seal and any references to requirements for **4.48.03**
the use of a common seal are satisfied in Scotland by a document signed or subscribed by or on behalf
of the company in accordance with the provisions of the Requirements of Writing (Scotland) Act 1995.
This version of the Companies Act 1985, section 36B, was substituted by the 1995 Scottish Act to
remedy some of the anomalies created by the attempt in the Companies Act 1989, section 130(3) to
align the laws of England and Scotland by dispensing with the need for a company seal.

---

[61]  Commons Amendments at Report Stage, 9 October 2006, 347.
[62]  Regulatory Reform Order 2005, art 6(5)–(8).
[63]  Companies Act 2006 (Commencement No 8, Transitional Provisions and Savings) Order 2008, SI 2008/
2860, art 3.

**4.48.04**   A document is generally regarded as subscribed by a company if it is signed on its behalf by a director, by its secretary, or by a person authorized to sign the document on its behalf (Requirements of Writing (Scotland) Act 1995, Schedule 2, paragraph 3(1)). Where the Act requires that the subscription must have been authenticated (section 3), in the case of a company this means either that the subscription must have been witnessed (and the witness must sign and provide their name and address) or the document must have been subscribed by two directors, or a director and secretary, or by two persons authorized to subscribe on the company's behalf (Schedule 2, paragraph 3(5)). However, there is no presumption that any such officer in fact holds the office in question or that the persons subscribing as authorized have in fact been so authorized.

## *Other matters*

### 49 Official seal for use abroad[a]

**4.49.01**   (1) A company that has a common seal may have an official seal for use outside the United Kingdom.
   (2) The official seal must be a facsimile of the company's common seal, with the addition on its face of the place or places where it is to be used.
   (3) The official seal when duly affixed to a document has the same effect as the company's common seal.
      This subsection does not extend to Scotland.
   (4) A company having an official seal for use outside the United Kingdom may—
      (a) by writing under its common seal, or
      (b) as respects Scotland, by writing subscribed in accordance with the Requirements of Writing (Scotland) Act 1995,
      authorise any person appointed for the purpose to affix the official seal to any deed or other document to which the company is party.
   (5) As between the company and a person dealing with such an agent, the agent's authority continues—
      (a) during the period mentioned in the instrument conferring the authority, or
      (b) if no period is mentioned, until notice of the revocation or termination of the agent's authority has been given to the person dealing with him.
   (6) The person affixing the official seal must certify in writing on the deed or other document to which the seal is affixed the date on which, and place at which, it is affixed.

AMENDMENTS AND NOTES

[a] This section applies with modification to LLPs by reg 6 of the Limited Liability Partnerships (Application of Companies Act 2006) Regulations 2009, SI 2009/1804.

COMMENCEMENT DATE 1 October 2009[64]

**4.49.02**   This provision applies to all of the UK, with the exception of subsection (3) which does not apply to Scotland. Instead, the formality requirements for Scotland are governed by the Requirements of Writing (Scotland) Act 1995.

**4.49.03**   Section 49 largely re-enacts the Companies Act 1985, section 39, with some adjustment to remove references to objects as permitting the conduct of business abroad. These references are now considered to be redundant since objects of companies are unrestricted unless specifically restricted by the company's articles (section 31(1)), and any such limitations that do exist cannot be relied upon by the company to deny the validity of a corporate act (section 39(1)). Accordingly, subsection (1) of section 49 simply provides that a company which has a common seal may have an official seal for use outside the UK. Any such official seal must be a facsimile of the common seal with the addition of the place or places where it is to be used (subsection (2)). In relation to England, Wales, and Northern Ireland (but not Scotland), affixing the official seal has the same effect as affixing the company's common seal to a document (subsection (3)).

**4.49.04**   The company may authorize, either by writing under its common seal (England, Wales, or Northern Ireland) or by writing subscribed to accord with the Requirements of Writing (Scotland) Act 1995 (Scotland), any person appointed for the purpose to affix the official seal to any deed or other document to which the company is a party (subsection (4)). (It follows that in relation to a Scottish company there is no sealing requirement.)

**4.49.05**   The authority of such an agent to bind the company in favour of the person dealing with that agent continues either for the period set out in the written instrument conferring the authority (subsection (4)), or, if no period is mentioned in that instrument, until the third party is given notice of termination or revocation of the agent's authority (subsection (5)).

---

[64] Companies Act 2006 (Commencement No 8, Transitional Provisions and Savings) Order 2008, SI 2008/2860, art 3.

The agent who affixes the official seal to a deed or document is required by subsection (6) to certify, in    **4.49.06**
writing on that deed or document, the date and place where the official seal is affixed. Other
requirements may be necessary if these are specified in the company's articles, eg Article 81(5) of the
Companies (Model Articles) Regulations 2008, regulation 4, Schedule 3, provides that the official seal
of a public company may be affixed to the document in question only if its use has been authorized by
a decision of the directors.[65] It follows that the authority of the affixing agent in section 49(5) would not
protect in the case of a public company if there is no such authority by the directors to use the official
seal in relation to this document or type of document.

## 50  Official seal for share certificates etc[a]

(1)  A company that has a common seal may have an official seal for use—    **4.50.01**
    (a)  for sealing securities issued by the company, or
    (b)  for sealing documents creating or evidencing securities so issued.
(2)  The official seal—
    (a)  must be a facsimile of the company's common seal, with the addition on its face of the word
       'Securities', and
    (b)  when duly affixed to the document has the same effect as the company's common seal.

AMENDMENTS AND NOTES

[a]  This section applies without modification to unregistered companies by reg 3 of and Sch 1 to the
Unregistered Companies Regulations 2009, SI 2009/2436.

COMMENCEMENT DATE  1 October 2009[66]

This provision re-enacts the Companies Act 1985, section 40(1). It enables a company having a    **4.50.02**
common seal to have an official (securities) seal (subsection (1)). This official seal must be a facsimile
of the company's common seal with the addition of the word 'Securities' (section 50(2)(a)) and when
affixed to the document it has the same effect as the company's common seal. A share certificate sealed
with the common seal or official (securities) seal is *prima facie* evidence of a member's title to the
specified shares (Companies Act 2006, section 768).

The Companies (Model Articles) Regulations 2008 for Public Companies,[67] provide in Article 81(6)    **4.50.03**
that the securities seal shall be applied by the company secretary or person so authorized by the
company secretary. There is no equivalent provision in the Model Articles for Private Companies
Limited by Shares.

The Requirements of Writing (Scotland) Act 1995 means that a Scottish company can subscribe such    **4.50.04**
documents in accordance with the general subscription requirements in that Act, ie without sealing.
Thus, a share certificate subscribed by the company in accordance with the 1995 Act is regarded, unless
the contrary is shown, as sufficient evidence of the member's entitlement to the securities (Companies
Act 2006, section 768(2)(b)).

## 51  Pre-incorporation contracts, deeds and obligations[a]

(1)  A contract that purports to be made by or on behalf of a company at a time when the company    **4.51.01**
    has not been formed has effect, subject to any agreement to the contrary, as one made with the
    person purporting to act for the company or as agent for it, and he is personally liable on the
    contract accordingly.
(2)  Subsection (1) applies—
    (a)  to the making of a deed under the law of England and Wales or Northern Ireland, and
    (b)  to the undertaking of an obligation under the law of Scotland,
as it applies to the making of a contract.

AMENDMENTS AND NOTES

[a]  This section applies with modification to LLPs by reg 7 of the Limited Liability Partnerships (Application of Companies Act 2006) Regulations 2009, SI 2009/1804. It applies without modification to
unregistered companies by reg 3 of and Sch 1 to the Unregistered Companies Regulations 2009, SI
2009/2436. It applies with modification to overseas companies by reg 6 of the Overseas Companies
(Execution of Documents and Registration of Charges) Regulations 2009, SI 2009/1917.

COMMENCEMENT DATE  1 October 2009[68]

---

[65]  Companies (Model Articles) Regulations 2008, SI 2008/3229. See Chapter 51.
[66]  Companies Act 2006 (Commencement No 8, Transitional Provisions and Savings) Order 2008, SI 2008/
2860, art 3.
[67]  Companies (Model Articles) Regulations 2008, SI 2008/3229, reg 4, Sch 3. These articles apply to companies
formed on or after 1 October 2009 and can be found in Chapter 51.
[68]  Companies Act 2006 (Commencement No 8, Transitional Provisions and Savings) Order 2008, SI 2008/
2860, art 3.

**4.51.02**   This provision is identical to, and it therefore re-enacts, the Companies Act 1985, section 36C.[69] Its effect is that a company is not bound by a contract or deed purportedly made on its behalf before the company existed unless the obligations are expressly or impliedly novated by the company once in existence, ie a new contract is entered into on the original terms. It must be clear that there is an intention to enter into a new contract and simply performing the pre-incorporation contract in the mistaken belief that it is binding is not sufficient.[70]

**4.51.03**   In the absence of novation, the contract is taken to be made with the person purporting to act for the company or as its agent and that person will be personally liable on the contract, in the absence of agreement to the contrary. However, although the agent will not be personally liable where there is 'agreement to the contrary', clear words are required to achieve such an exclusion. In *Phonogram Ltd v Lane*[71] Lord Denning MR interpreted this strictly so as to require 'express agreement that the man who is signing was not to be liable'. In the absence of such express agreement, there would be personal liability 'however he expresses his signature'. Therefore signing 'for and on behalf of' the company would not be sufficient to exclude the agent's personal liability.

**4.51.04**   Although the section does not deal with this issue, it has been held that the previous section 36C could be used by the agent in order to enforce a pre-incorporation contract whereby the 'company' had agreed to sell land to property developers. The majority of the Court of Appeal in *Braymist v Wise Finance Co Ltd*[72] held that a person who is personally liable for a contract is also able to enforce it, since otherwise it would be possible for the other party to escape from a possible bad bargain by pleading a technicality.[73] However, the doctrine of privity of contract will be relevant here since the party suffering the loss will be the previously non-existent company rather than the agent, and the agent will therefore need to secure substantial damages on behalf of that party. The possibility that property obtained by the agent under a pre-incorporation contract will be held on constructive trust for the company once it has been incorporated has also been acknowledged.[74]

**4.51.05**   On the basis of previous interpretation of the Companies Act 1985, section 36C, the Companies Act 2006, section 51 will not apply to a company which purports to contract while waiting for a new certificate of incorporation on a change of name.[75] It will apply only to a company contracting at a time when it has not been incorporated or 'formed'.

### 52  Bills of exchange and promissory notes[a]

**4.52.01**   A bill of exchange or promissory note is deemed to have been made, accepted or endorsed on behalf of a company if made, accepted or endorsed in the name of, or by or on behalf or on account of, the company by a person acting under its authority.

AMENDMENTS AND NOTES

   [a]  This section applies with modification to LLPs by reg 7 of the Limited Liability Partnerships (Application of Companies Act 2006) Regulations 2009, SI 2009/1804.

COMMENCEMENT DATE 1 October 2009[76]

---

[69]  Section 36C was inserted by the CA 1989 and replaced s 36(4), itself originally enacted as the European Communities Act 1972, s 9(2). The difficulties stem from the fact that the company cannot be a party to a contract at a time when the company does not exist and cannot subsequently ratify the contract since ratification operates with retrospective effect and can apply only where the principal had the capacity to make the contract when purportedly made on its behalf by the agent.

[70]  *Re Northumberland Avenue Hotel Co* (1886) 33 Ch D 16.

[71]  [1982] QB 938, 944.

[72]  [2002] EWCA Civ 127, [2002] Ch 273.

[73]  In debate at Committee Stage in the Commons it was argued that the legislation should address this issue specifically, particularly as there was some uncertainty concerning whether the right in question was created by the common law of contract, which would raise complex issues concerning the law of mistaken identity. However, the government's view was that, since no recommendation had been made on the matter by the Company Law Review, it was a matter best left to the common law; Comm, SCD, Third Sitting, 20 June 2006, cols 99–101.

[74]  *Hoppitt v Waterfield* [2010] EWHC 115 (QB).

[75]  *Oshkosh B'Gosh v Dan Marbel Inc* [1989] BCLC 507.

[76]  Companies Act 2006 (Commencement No 8, Transitional Provisions and Savings) Order 2008, SI 2008/2860, art 3.

This provision re-enacts the Companies Act 1985, section 37. It provides that when someone acting   **4.52.02**
under the company's authority makes, accepts, or endorses such an instrument in the company's name
or on its behalf, this is treated as if it had been done by the company.

A bill of exchange enables an enforceable right to money to be transferred from one person to another.   **4.52.03**
It is an unconditional order in writing addressed by the drawer to the drawee and signed by the drawer,
requiring the drawee to pay, on demand or at a fixed or determinable future time, a specified sum to or
to the order of the payee or to the bearer. If payable at a future time then the drawee will signify his
acceptance making him the party primarily liable on the bill. The bill may also be endorsed by the
endorser. Anyone signing will be liable on the bill of exchange. Section 52 makes it clear that if signed
with authority by one or more individuals on behalf of the company, whether that person is signing as
the drawer or on acceptance as drawee or as endorser, the company will be liable.

The Bills of Exchange Act 1882, section 26 states that if the person signs with their own signature and   **4.52.04**
indicates that they are signing in a representative capacity, they will not be personally liable but they
will be personally liable if they omit this.

The cheque is the best known bill of exchange although it is payable on demand and so need not be   **4.52.05**
accepted by the bank as drawee. Cheques are frequently non-transferable as a result of the use of the
words 'account payee' printed or written on the cheque. Company cheques are usually pre-printed
with the company's name as the drawer and the Companies Act 1985, section 349(4) had provided that
if the company's name did not appear in legible characters on the cheque anyone signing it would be
liable to a fine and personally liable on the cheque unless the company honoured it. The Companies Act
2006, sections 82 to 85 contain provisions specifying that the Secretary of State can make regulations
requiring the disclosure of the company name and the consequences of the failure to do so. The
Companies (Trading Disclosures) Regulations 2008, SI 2008/495, achieve this purpose. Regulation 6
requires the company's name to appear in various communications including bills of exchange and
cheques. Criminal liability may be imposed on both the company and every officer who is in default
(regulation 10). There is no equivalent provision to the Companies Act 1985, section 349(4) imposing
personal liability on officers in default. For the purposes of these provisions minor variations in name
are to be left out of account (section 85).

A promissory note is an unconditional promise in writing and signed by the maker, to pay a specified   **4.52.06**
sum of money to, or to the order of, a specified person or to the bearer. Promissory notes are not
presented for acceptance and the party primarily liable is the maker of the promissory note. Therefore,
if a company is the maker of the promissory note, the note will be that of the company if signed by a
person having authority to do so.

# 5

## A COMPANY'S NAME

## Companies Act 2006

### PART 5
### A COMPANY'S NAME

### CHAPTER 1
### GENERAL REQUIREMENTS

*Prohibited names*

### 53 Prohibited names

**5.53.01**    A company must not be registered under the Companies Acts by a name if, in the opinion of the Secretary of State—

(a) its use by the company would constitute an offence, or

(b) it is offensive.

COMMENCEMENT DATE 1 October 2009[1]

**5.53.02**    This section replaces section 26(1)(d) and (e) of the 1985 Act without substantive amendment.

**5.53.03**    Section 53(a): The use of certain words in a company name may constitute an offence under other legislation. The Companies House guidance on company incorporation and names[2] contains at Annex C a (non-exhaustive) list of words which fall into this category, the use of which may be prohibited under statute. For example, the words 'Olympic' and 'Olympics' are protected under the Olympic Symbol (Protection) Act 1995 (as amended by the London Olympic Games and Paralympic Games Act 2006). Section 216 of the Insolvency Act makes it an offence to use a company or business name of a company which has gone into insolvent liquidation within the previous five years, and it is a strict liability offence. The section 53(a) prohibition is also absolute so there is no scope for obtaining the consent of the Secretary of State or another regulatory body under the Act itself, although the provisions of the relevant statute prescribing the offence may offer some consent or safe harbour mechanism. The list at Appendix C to the Companies House guidance referred to above includes words which suggest a link with certain professions and the consent of the relevant professional body may sanction the use of the name. For example, the use of the words 'dentist' or 'dental surgeon' in a company name will be an offence under the Dentists Act 1984 unless the consent of the General Dental Council has been obtained. Similarly, the use of the word 'architect' may be permitted if the business of the company is controlled and managed by a person registered under the Architects Act 1997. The Companies House guidance suggests that a company wishing to use a name on the list should contact the relevant professional or regulatory body (if any) before seeking to register a name which may fall foul of this section and Companies House will require written support from that body before it will register the name.

**5.53.04**    Section 53(b): There is currently no guidance as such on what the Secretary of State[3] will consider to be offensive so whether a name will be rejected under this section will be a matter for common sense judgment. There have been few cases on this prohibition, but see *R v Registrar of Companies ex p A-G*,[4] which concerned an application for registration of a company name which suggested a link with prostitution. This case pre-dates the Act and was brought under the 1985 Act but as section 26(i)(e) of the 1985 Act was substantively the same as section 53(b) it is still relevant.

*Sensitive words and expressions*

### 54 Names suggesting connection with government or public authority

**5.54.01**    (1) The approval of the Secretary of State is required for a company to be registered under this Act by a name that would be likely to give the impression that the company is connected with—

(a) Her Majesty's Government, any part of the Scottish administration[, the Welsh Assembly Government][a] or Her Majesty's Government in Northern Ireland,

---

[1] Companies Act 2006 (Commencement No 8, Transitional Provisions and Savings) Order 2008, SI 2008/2860, art 3(e).

[2] This guidance (reference GP1) is available from the Companies House website at ⟨http://www.companieshouse.gov.uk⟩.

[3] The Secretary of State will usually act through the Registrar of Companies, as the body designated by the Secretary of State for these purposes.

[4] [1991] BCLC 476.

(b) a local authority, or

(c) any public authority specified for the purposes of this section by regulations made by the Secretary of State.

(2) For the purposes of this section—

'local authority' means—

(a) a local authority within the meaning of the Local Government Act 1972 (c. 70), the Common Council of the City of London or the Council of the Isles of Scilly,

(b) a council constituted under section 2 of the Local Government etc. (Scotland) Act 1994 (c. 39), or

(c) a district council in Northern Ireland;

'public authority' includes any person or body having functions of a public nature.

(3) Regulations under this section are subject to affirmative resolution procedure.

AMENDMENTS

[a] Amended by the Government of Wales Act 2006 (Consequential Modifications, Transitional Provisions and Saving) Order 2009, SI 2009/2958, art 1(2).

COMMENCEMENT DATE 1 October 2009[5]

This section replaces section 26(2)(a) of the 1985 Act. It prohibits the use of certain names suggesting a link with the Government or any devolved administration or local or public authority without the consent of the Secretary of State. **5.54.02**

Section 54(1)(a): As the Act applies to Northern Ireland incorporated companies (unlike the 1985 Act), the Northern Ireland administration is included, as is the Scottish administration and in both cases, their local government counterparts. **5.54.03**

Section 54(1)(c): The prohibition relating to names suggesting a connection with a 'public authority' is new under the Act. The expression 'public authority' is widely defined in subsection 54(2) to include any person or body with functions of a public nature. However, section 54 only covers public authorities specified in the Company, Limited Liability Partnership and Business Names (Public Authorities) Regulations 2009,[6] which came into force on 10 November 2009. The Schedule to those Regulations sets out a list of specified public authorities and the relevant government departments and other bodies whose views must be sought for the use of the relevant name. Even if the proposed name contains a reference to an agency or body which does not appear on the list prescribed under this section, it may be caught by the list of sensitive words and expressions in the Regulations prescribed by section 55, so both lists should be checked. **5.54.04**

Section 54(2): A local authority would include any county or district council, a London borough council, or the Greater London Assembly, or a parish or community council, or their Scottish or Northern Irish equivalents.[7] **5.54.05**

The consent of the Secretary of State, where required under the regulations, will be given by the Registrar of Companies, as the body designated by the Secretary of State for these purposes. The Companies House guidance on company names[8] contains (at Annex B) a complete list of names suggesting a connection with a public authority and the relevant body whose consent must be obtained. **5.54.06**

Note that the Company, Limited Liability Partnership and Business Names (Public Authorities) Regulations 2009 are included within the scope of the Government's Red Tape Challenge, a consultation on whether these and other regulations covering allowable names for companies carrying on business in the UK should be simplified, streamlined, replaced with a voluntary code or scrapped altogether. The outcome of the consultation is expected to be announced by December 2013 at the latest. **5.54.07**

## 55 Other sensitive words or expressions

(1) The approval of the Secretary of State is required for a company to be registered under this Act by a name that includes a word or expression for the time being specified in regulations made by the Secretary of State under this section. **5.55.01**

(2) Regulations under this section are subject to approval after being made.

COMMENCEMENT DATE 1 October 2009[9]

---

[5] Companies Act 2006 (Commencement No 8, Transitional Provisions and Savings) Order 2008, SI 2008/2860, art 3(e).

[6] SI 2009/2982.

[7] See Local Government Act 1972, s 270.

[8] This guidance (reference GP1) is available from the Companies House website at ⟨http://www.companieshouse.gov.uk⟩.

[9] Companies Act 2006 (Commencement No 8, Transitional Provisions and Savings) Order 2008, SI 2008/2860, art 3(e).

**5.55.02**   This section replaces sections 26(2)(b) and 29(1)(a) of the 1985 Act, and the regulations made under section 55(1) are the Company, Limited Liability Partnership and Business Names (Sensitive Words and Expressions) Regulations 2009,[10] which replace the Company and Business Names Regulations 1981 with effect from 1 October 2009. The Regulations set out a list of words and expressions, the use of which in a company name will require the prior consent of the Secretary of State (in practice, the Registrar of Companies) or another relevant authority designated by the Regulations. The prescribed words and expressions fall into three main categories:

- words implying national or international pre-eminence: for example, 'National', 'International', 'British', 'English', 'Scottish', 'Welsh', 'Irish' or 'United Kingdom', 'Britain', 'England', 'Scotland', 'Wales' or 'Northern Ireland';
- words implying business pre-eminence or representative or authoritative status: for example, 'Board', 'Authority', 'Association', or 'Society'; and
- words implying specific objects or functions: for example, 'Group', 'Holdings', 'Trust', 'Fund', 'Insurance', or 'Charity'.Note that the plural, possessive, and, where relevant, feminine forms of the specified words and expressions will also be caught by the Regulations (so, for example, 'Holdings' requires consent as 'Holding' is on the list in Schedule 1, Part 1 to the Regulations).

**5.55.03**   Schedule 1, Part 1 to the Company, Limited Liability Partnership and Business Names (Sensitive Words and Expressions) Regulations 2009 contains the list of specified words and expressions for the purposes of section 55 and also section 1194(1), which relates to business names. Schedule 1, Part 2 contains a much shorter list which applies only to company names under section 55 and not to business names under section 1194(1). Schedule 2 to the Regulations lists the government department or body whose 'view' must be sought before attempting to register the relevant name. Section 56 explains this requirement in more detail. In the case of a name containing a word or expression which is listed in Schedule 1 to the Regulations but which does not also appear in Schedule 2, there is no requirement for consent of any body other than Companies House itself, although applicants should refer to the Companies House guidance on incorporation and names (GP1) (see para 5.53.03 above) which provides an indication of the documentary or other evidence that should accompany the application to support the use of the prescribed word or expression in the company (or where relevant, business) name.

**5.55.04**   The Companies House guidance note on company names contains some useful indications as to the reason why a particular word or expression is sensitive, and furthermore sets out examples of what might be required by the registrar as evidence in support of an application to use a prescribed name. For example, the use of the word 'Group' usually requires evidence of a parent/subsidiary relationship involving at least two other British or overseas companies. Similarly, to use the word 'Holdings', a company must be a holding company as defined in section 1159 of the Act.[11] Note that if misleading information is given to the registrar in support of an application, or if an undertaking or assurance given to the registrar in support of an application is unfulfilled, the company may be directed to change its name under section 75 of the Act.

**5.55.05**   Note in particular that the use of the word 'trust' in a company name can be difficult. The Companies House guidance on company names[12] states that the name will normally only be permitted if the company is an artistic, educational, charitable, enterprise, family, investment, financial, pensions, staff, or unit trust and there are specific requirements for each category. Any category of trust outside this list will need to be specifically approved by Companies House.

**5.55.06**   A company with a name incorporating a word or expression prescribed for the first time by the regulations (ie which was not previously restricted under the Company and Business Names Regulations 1981) will be required to obtain approval for the use of the relevant word or expression only if and when it changes its name following the Company, Limited Liability Partnership and Business Names (Sensitive Words and Expressions) Regulations 2009[13] coming into force on 1 October 2009 and the new name contains a word or expression requiring approval for some reason under the Regulations. This is the case even if the name change is applied for in the context of a name swap, which has caused particular problems since the 2006 Act regime came into force. See para 5.66.06 et seq. for more details.

---

[10] SI 2009/2615.

[11] The words 'Group' and 'Holdings' now appear on the list of words which will be disregarded by the registrar in considering whether a name is the same as another already on the register—see para 5.66.03 for further details.

[12] This guidance (reference GP1) is available from the Companies House website at ⟨http://www.companieshouse.gov.uk⟩.

[13] SI 2009/2615.

## 56  Duty to seek comments of government department or other specified body

(1)  The Secretary of State may by regulations under—                                           5.56.01
    (a)  section 54 (name suggesting connection with government or public authority), or
    (b)  section 55 (other sensitive words or expressions),
require that, in connection with an application for the approval of the Secretary of State under that section, the applicant must seek the view of a specified Government department or other body.

(2)  Where such a requirement applies, the applicant must request the specified department or other body (in writing) to indicate whether (and if so why) it has any objections to the proposed name.

(3)  Where a request under this section is made in connection with an application for the registration of a company under this Act, the application must—
    (a)  include a statement that a request under this section has been made, and
    (b)  be accompanied by a copy of any response received.

(4)  Where a request under this section is made in connection with a change in a company's name, the notice of the change sent to the registrar must be accompanied by—
    (a)  a statement by a director or secretary of the company that a request under this section has been made, and
    (b)  a copy of any response received.

(5)  In this section 'specified' means specified in the regulations.

COMMENCEMENT DATE  1 October 2009[14]

This section replaces sections 26(2)(b), 29(2), 29(3), and 29(4) of the 1985 Act. It provides power for the   **5.56.02**
Secretary of State to specify either a government department other than the Department for Business, Innovation and Skills (BIS) or another body whose comments on a proposed name must be obtained before submitting the application to Companies House. The relevant government departments and other bodies are listed in the Schedule to the Company, Limited Liability Partnership and Business Names (Public Authorities) Regulations 2009,[15] and in Schedule 2 to the Company, Limited Liability Partnership and Business Names (Sensitive Words and Expressions) Regulations 2009.[16] For example, the use of a word in a company name implying a link with a particular profession may mean that the relevant professional body must be consulted before the name may be used. So, the General Dental Council must be consulted on the use of the word 'dental' in a company name. For fairly obvious reasons, the Home Office must be consulted on the use of the word 'royal' in a company name.

Section 56(2)–(4): In practical terms, the applicant should write to the relevant government department   **5.56.03**
or other specified body to seek approval for the relevant name before submitting the application for the name (either on an incorporation or a name change) to Companies House, and a copy of any response received from such department or body should accompany the application to Companies House. The complete lists of names requiring approval are also set out in Annexes A, B, and C of the Companies House guidance on company names.[17] Where relevant, the consent of the Secretary of State is usually given by the Registrar of Companies, as the body designated by the Secretary of State for these purposes. Note that there is no time limit for the grant of approval by the relevant department or body so where an application is time-critical in any way, the approval should be applied for as soon as possible. The FSA is the designated body for sensitive words and expressions related to financial services activities (e.g. 'fund' and 'insurance'), and the FSA's website has a list of FAQs on the process for obtaining its authorization for the use of any such words or expressions.

The Company, Limited Liability Partnership and Business Names (Public Authorities) Regulations   **5.56.04**
2009 and the Company, Limited Liability Partnership and Business Names (Sensitive Words and Expressions) Regulations 2009 are within the scope of the Government's Red Tape Challenge. This review may result in the Regulations relating to company names being simplified, streamlined, replaced with a voluntary code, or (although unlikely) scrapped altogether. The review is due for completion by December 2013.

---

[14]  Companies Act 2006 (Commencement No 8, Transitional Provisions and Savings) Order 2008, SI 2008/2860, art 3(e).

[15]  SI 2009/2982.

[16]  SI 2009/2615.

[17]  This guidance (reference GP1) is available from the Companies House website at ⟨http://www.companieshouse.gov.uk⟩.

*Permitted characters etc*

### 57  Permitted characters etc

**5.57.01**      (1)  The Secretary of State may make provision by regulations—

   (a)  as to the letters or other characters, signs or symbols (including accents and other diacritical marks) and punctuation that may be used in the name of a company registered under this Act and

   (b)  specifying a standard style or format for the name of a company for the purposes of registration.

   (2)  The regulations may prohibit the use of specified characters, signs or symbols when appearing in a specified position (in particular, at the beginning of a name).

   (3)  A company may not be registered under this Act by a name that consists of or includes anything that is not permitted in accordance with regulations under this section.

   (4)  Regulations under this section are subject to negative resolution procedure.

   (5)  In this section 'specified' means specified in the regulations.

   COMMENCEMENT DATE 1 October 2009[18]

**5.57.02**    From 1 October 2009, the regulations made under this section[19] specify which letters, symbols, signs and punctuation marks may be used in a company's registered name. As the UK is chosen as the place of incorporation for many overseas businesses, the Government foresees pressure to register companies with names in languages other than English, but under the regulations[20] the choice of characters is limited to those in the Roman alphabet (in upper case only), and the numbers 0–9 in Arabic numerals.

**5.57.03**    The regulations deal for the first time in legislation with a number of issues relating to company names which arose during the years preceeding the 2006 Act as modern business practice evolved. For example, Companies House had previously struggled with applications for registration of names incorporating non-alphanumeric symbols, for example '@'. Under the 1985 Act, 'and' and '&' were treated as the same but otherwise neither the 1985 Act nor the regulations made under that Act contained any rules or other guidance on the use of non-alphanumeric symbols. In addition to the prescribed letters and numerals, the regulations restrict the choice of characters to be used in a company's name to basic punctuation marks (eg full stop, comma, apostrophe, bracket, dash/ hyphen, etc), the common currency symbols (£, $, € and ¥), the symbol '&' and, except in the first three characters of a name, the symbols '*', '=', '#' and '%' and '+'. Following suggestions made by respondents to the Government's original consultation on these issues, the regulations permit the symbol '@' to be included at the start of the name.[21] The regulations also limit the length of a company name to 160 characters, excluding spaces.

**5.57.04**    *Hansard* records that during the House of Lords Grand Committee debate on this section,[22] the Government made it clear that any company incorporated under the 1985 Act or earlier statutes, whose name incorporates a symbol or other mark or is otherwise presented in a format which is regulated in some way by the regulations but which was previously unrestricted will be permitted to carry on using the name until such time as it voluntarily changes its name following the relevant sections of the Act coming into force. At that point, the company would either have to go through the requisite consent procedure under the regulations or change its name to one omitting a prohibited symbol. This is the case even if the name change is applied for in the context of the name swap, which has caused particular problems since the 2006 Act regime came into force. See para 5.66.06 et seq. for more details.

**5.57.05**    The Company and Business Names (Miscellaneous Provisions) Regulations 2009 are within the scope of the Government's Red Tape Challenge, which may result in the Regulations relating to company names being simplified, streamlined, replaced with a voluntary code, or (although unlikely) scrapped altogether. The review is due for completion by December 2013.

---

[18]  Companies Act 2006 (Commencement No 8, Transitional Provisions and Savings) Order 2008, SI 2008/ 2860, art 3(e).

[19]  Company and Business Names (Miscellaneous Provisions) Regulations 2009, SI 2009/1085.

[20]  Ibid, Sch 1.

[21]  DBERR response to consultation paper reference URN 07/666.

[22]  See *Hansard*, HL, vol 678, col GC50 (30 January 2006).

# CHAPTER 2
## INDICATIONS OF COMPANY TYPE OR LEGAL FORM

### *Required indications for limited companies*

### 58  Public limited companies

(1)  The name of a limited company that is a public company must end with 'public limited company' or 'p.l.c.'.

(2)  In the case of a Welsh company, its name may instead end with 'cwmni cyfyngedig cyhoeddus' or 'c.c.c.'.

(3)  This section does not apply to community interest companies (but see section 33(3) and (4) of the Companies (Audit, Investigations and Community Enterprise) Act 2004 (c. 27)).

COMMENCEMENT DATE  1 October 2009[23]

This section replaces section 25(1) of the 1985 Act and also section 27(4)(b) and (d) in its application to section 25(2) of the 1985 Act. It brings together in a single provision all the alternative indications of legal status that must be used by a public company in its registered name, ie 'public limited company' or the Welsh equivalent or the specified abbreviations.  **5.58.02**

Section 58(1)–(2): As under the 1985 Act, the only permitted abbreviation of 'public limited company' is 'p.l.c.' or the Welsh equivalent, not 'Plc', 'PLC' (with or without full stops) or technically even 'plc'. However, Companies House does in practice accept such variations. The Companies House guidance on names[24] explicitly states that 'plc' (without full stops) is acceptable, as does the FAQs section of the Companies House website, which contains an exhaustive list of permitted abbreviations for each of the various types of company, and which is designed to reduce the number of rejected applications.[25]  **5.58.03**

The name of the company is no longer required to be stated in the company's memorandum of association, which, under section 8 of the Act, is a simple 'snapshot' document recording the initial subscribers' wish to form a company, and is incapable of amendment. The company name provision in the memoranda of association of companies formed under the 1985 Act and earlier statutes will have been imported automatically into their articles by virtue of section 28 of the Act. Changes in legal status, eg upon re-registration under Part 7 of this Act, will not require a change to the company name set out in the memorandum as required under the 1985 Act. However, on the basis that the company name provisions will have been imported into the company's articles of association by virtue of the operation of section 28 of the Act, consequential alterations to such provisions will need to be made to the articles following any such re-registration, unless and until the relevant provision has been removed from the company's articles.  **5.58.04**

Section 58(3): Community interest companies which are public companies must end their name with 'community interest public limited company' or 'community interest p.l.c.'.  **5.58.05**

### 59  Private limited companies

(1)  The name of a limited company that is a private company must end with 'limited' or 'ltd.'.  **5.59.01**

(2)  In the case of a Welsh company, its name may instead end with 'cyfyngedig' or 'cyf.'.

(3)  Certain companies are exempt from this requirement (see section 60).

(4)  This section does not apply to community interest companies (but see section 33(1) and (2) of the Companies (Audit, Investigations and Community Enterprise) Act 2004).

COMMENCEMENT DATE  1 October 2009[26]

This section replaces section 25(2) of the 1985 Act and also section 27(4)(a) and (c) in their application to section 25(2). It brings together in a single provision all the alternative statutory indications of legal status that must be used by a private company as part of its registered name, ie 'limited' or the Welsh equivalent or the permitted abbreviations.  **5.59.02**

Section 59(1)–(2): Mirroring section 58, the only permitted abbreviation of 'limited' is 'ltd' and of 'cyfyngedig', 'cyf'.  **5.59.03**

---

[23]  Companies Act 2006 (Commencement No 8, Transitional Provisions and Savings) Order 2008, SI 2008/2860, art 3(e).

[24]  GP1.

[25]  See ⟨http://www.companieshouse.gov.uk/infoAndGuide/faq/companyNamePolicy.shtml⟩.

[26]  Companies Act 2006 (Commencement No 8, Transitional Provisions and Savings) Order 2008, SI 2008/2860, art 3(e).

9.031

63

...ain companies qualify for a complete exemption from the requirement for their
... or 'ltd', as provided in section 60, and there are separate rules for community
...ction 33(1) and (2) of the Companies (Audit, Investigations and Commu-

5.58.01

### ...nt as to use of 'limited'

...empt from section 59 (requirement to have name ending with 'limited' or
...e) if—

-y,
...pted from the requirement of that section by regulations made by the Secretary of
..., or
. meets the conditions specified in
...ontinuation of existing exemption: companies limited by shares), or
...2 (continuation of existing exemption: companies limited by guarantee).

(2) The registrar may refuse to register a private limited company by a name that does not include the word 'limited' (or a permitted alternative) unless a statement has been delivered to him that the company meets the conditions for exemption.

(3) The registrar may accept the statement as sufficient evidence of the matters stated in it.

(4) Regulations under this section are subject to negative resolution procedure.

COMMENCEMENT DATE 1 October 2009[28]

**5.60.02** This section replaces section 30 of the 1985 Act and exempts certain companies from the requirement for their names to end with the wording 'limited'.

**5.60.03** Section 60(1): There are four main categories of companies who may qualify for the exemption. They are:

(i) charities;
(ii) companies falling within the regulations made under section 60(1)(b);[29]
(iii) companies limited by shares which are exempt by virtue of a licence granted under section 19 of the Companies Act 1948;[30] and
(iv) companies limited by guarantee who benefited from the exemption under section 30 of the 1985 Act (or the Northern Ireland equivalent).[31]

The main purpose of these exemptions is to ensure that the commercial connotations of the word 'limited' are not conveyed to the public by means of the company name of such companies.

**5.60.04** Section 60(2): If a company wishes to register a name without the word 'limited' (or a permitted alternative) at the end, the application for the name must be accompanied by a statement made on behalf of the company that the company meets the conditions for exemption. Section 60(2) does not specify by whom the statement must be made, but in practice it will usually be made by one of the officers of the company. The conditions for exemption are set out, in the case of a company falling within section 60(1)(b), in the regulations made under that subsection,[32] and in the case of a company falling within section 60(1)(c), in either section 61 or section 62 as appropriate. Since 1 October 2009, the regulations made under section 60(1)(b)[33] have exempted future companies limited by guarantee (not just those falling under section 62 who benefited from the 1985 Act exemption). Prior to the Act coming into force the Government said that it would also exempt statutory regulators (such as the FSA) which are established as companies[34] but the regulations made under section 60(1)(b) do not deal with this.

**5.60.05** Section 60(3): This provision suggests that the registrar will not usually make his own enquiries as to the legitimacy of the statement made under section 60(2), although the use of the word 'may' in this section does leave open the possibility that he may seek supporting evidence.

---

[27] A community interest company which is a private company must end its name with 'community interest company' or 'c.i.c.' or one of the Welsh equivalents if the registered office is in Wales.

[28] Companies Act 2006 (Commencement No 8, Transitional Provisions and Savings) Order 2008, SI 2008/2860, art 3(e).

[29] Company and Business Names (Miscellaneous Provisions) Regulations 2009, SI 2009/1085.

[30] For further details, see notes to s 61.

[31] For further details, see notes to s 62.

[32] Company and Business Names (Miscellaneous Provisions) Regulations 2009, SI 2009/1085.

[33] Ibid.

[34] DBERR (now BIS) response to consultation paper reference URN 07/666.

If a company has ceased to be entitled to the relevant exemption for any reason, it may be the subject   **5.60.06**
of a direction under section 64 to change its name to one ending with the word 'limited' or a permitted
alternative.

The regulations made under section 60(1)(b)[35] also prohibit a company which is exempt from the   **5.60.07**
requirement to end its name with 'limited' from having a name concluding with another indication of
company type or legal form (eg 'PLC') as this would also be misleading.

## 61 Continuation of existing exemption: companies limited by shares

   (1)  This section applies to a private company limited by shares—   **5.61.01**
      (a)  that on 25th February 1982—
         (i)  was registered in Great Britain, and
        (ii)  had a name that, by virtue of a licence under section 19 of the Companies Act 1948 (c.
             38) (or corresponding earlier legislation), did not include the word 'limited' or any of the
             permitted alternatives, or
      (b)  that on 30th June 1983—
         (i)  was registered in Northern Ireland, and
        (ii)  had a name that, by virtue of a licence under section 19 of the Companies Act (Northern
             Ireland) 1960 (c. 22 (N.I.)) (or corresponding earlier legislation), did not include the word
             'limited' or any of the permitted alternatives.
   (2)  A company to which this section applies is exempt from section 60 (requirement to have name
      ending with 'limited' or permitted alternative) so long as—
      (a)  it continues to meet the following two conditions, and
      (b)  it does not change its name.
   (3)  The first condition is that the objects of the company are the promotion of commerce, art,
      science, education, religion, charity or any profession, and anything incidental or conducive to any
      of those objects.
   (4)  The second condition is that the company's articles—
      (a)  require its income to be applied in promoting its objects,
      (b)  prohibit the payment of dividends, or any return of capital, to its members, and
      (c)  require all the assets that would otherwise be available to its members generally to be
         transferred on its winding up either—
         (i)  to another body with objects similar to its own, or
        (ii)  to another body the objects of which are the promotion of charity and anything
             incidental or conducive thereto,
      (whether or not the body is a member of the company).

COMMENCEMENT DATE 1 October 2009[36]

This section, and section 62, together replace section 30(2) and (3) of the 1985 Act, and set out the   **5.61.02**
conditions to be met for a company limited by shares which was exempt under previous legislation
from using in its name the word 'limited' or a permitted alternative to continue to qualify for the
exemption under the Act.[37] The Act preserves the exemption for companies licensed under the
Companies Act 1948 notwithstanding that there were thought only to be around 21 such companies
which were still active when the Act was passed.[38]

Section 61(1): To qualify for the exemption under this section, the company must have obtained a   **5.61.03**
licence prior to 25 February 1982 under section 19 of the Companies Act 1948 (or before 30 June 1983
under the Companies Act (Northern Ireland) Order 1960, in the case of a Northern Irish company).
Those sections were designed to allow certain charitable and other companies formed for the purposes
of promoting commerce, art, science, religion, charity, or other non-profit-making companies to
dispense with the word 'limited' at the end of their name. In order to be licensed, a company had to be
registered in Great Britain and have objects restricted to the promotion of commerce, art, science,
education, religion, charity, or any profession and its articles had to preclude distributions of dividends
to its members and require its assets to be passed to a body with similar objects on a winding-up.

Section 61(2): This section provides that the conditions for a licence under the 1948 Act (and the   **5.61.04**
Northern Ireland equivalent) are now reflected in section 61(3) and (4), but notably with one new
requirement in section 61(4)(b) (see below). Note that if an exempt company changes its name, section

---

[35] The Company and Business Names (Miscellaneous Provisions) Regulations 2009, SI 2009/1085.
[36] Companies Act 2006 (Commencement No 8, Transitional Provisions and Savings) Order 2008, SI 2008/
2860, art 3(e).
[37] Companies limited by guarantee are dealt with under s 62.
[38] *Hansard*, HL, vol 678, col GC51 (30 January 2006).

61(2)(b) states that it will lose the benefit of the exemption upon changing its name, even if it otherwise continues to qualify for the exemption.

**5.61.05**   Section 61(4)(b): This section adds a new condition, that the company's articles must also prevent a distribution of capital. The Government explained during the debate on this section in the House of Lords Grand Committee[39] that the reason for this is the deregulation of capital distributions under the Act. Under the 1985 Act, companies had to have a power in their articles to return capital to shareholders, so a company licensed under the 1948 Act wishing to include such a power (which would be inconsistent with their exempt status) would require permission from the Secretary of State for the change (under section 31(1) and (2) of the 1985 Act), whereupon the company would lose its exemption under section 30 of that Act. As companies are now free under the Act to return capital to shareholders without an express power to do so in their articles, the addition of the condition relating to return of capital in section 61(4)(b) was necessary to ensure exempt companies do not act in a way which is inconsistent with their exempt status, ie by returning capital to shareholders.

### 62  Continuation of existing exemption: companies limited by guarantee

**5.62.01**   (1)  A private company limited by guarantee that immediately before the commencement of this Part—

(a)  was exempt by virtue of section 30 of the Companies Act 1985 (c. 6) or Article 40 of the Companies (Northern Ireland) Order 1986 (S.I. 1986/1032 (N.I. 6)) from the requirement to have a name including the word 'limited' or a permitted alternative, and

(b)  had a name that did not include the word 'limited' or any of the permitted alternatives,

is exempt from section 59 (requirement to have name ending with 'limited' or permitted alternative) so long as it continues to meet the following two conditions and does not change its name.

(2)  The first condition is that the objects of the company are the promotion of commerce, art, science, education, religion, charity or any profession, and anything incidental or conducive to any of those objects.

(3)  The second condition is that the company's articles—

(a)  require its income to be applied in promoting its objects,

(b)  prohibit the payment of dividends to its members, and

(c)  require all the assets that would otherwise be available to its members generally to be transferred on its winding up either—

(i)  to another body with objects similar to its own, or

(ii)  to another body the objects of which are the promotion of charity and anything incidental or conducive thereto,

(whether or not the body is a member of the company).

COMMENCEMENT DATE  1 October 2009[40]

**5.62.02**   In addition to companies licensed under the 1948 Act to dispense with the word 'limited', companies limited by guarantee were permitted under section 30 of the 1985 Act to do so. Section 62 preserves the exemption for such companies for so long as they continue to be non-profit-making and otherwise continue to meet the criteria set out in section 62(2) and (3), which are the same as those relating to a company licensed under the 1948 Act.

Companies limited by guarantee which are incorporated under the Act (which do not therefore fall within this section) appear to benefit from a similar exemption in the regulations made under section 60(1)(b) above and the criteria for obtaining the exemption are the same as those set out in section 62(2) and (3).

**5.62.03**   Section 62(1): Mirroring section 61(2)(b) for companies limited by shares, a company limited by guarantee will lose the benefit of the exemption if it changes its name.

**5.62.04**   Section 62(3)(b): Note that a company limited by guarantee does not also have to have a restriction in its articles on the return of capital to members, unlike a company limited by shares under section 62(4)(b), as it does not generally have share capital (it has not been possible to incorporate a company limited by guarantee with a share capital since 1980).

---

[39]  *Hansard*, HL, vol 678, col GC51 (30 January 2006).

[40]  Companies Act 2006 (Commencement No 8, Transitional Provisions and Savings) Order 2008, SI 2008/2860, art 3(e).

## 63 Exempt company: restriction on amendment of articles

(1) A private company— 5.63.01
   (a) that is exempt under section 61 or 62 from the requirement to use 'limited' (or a permitted alternative) as part of its name, and
   (b) whose name does not include 'limited' or any of the permitted alternatives,
   must not amend its articles so that it ceases to comply with the conditions for exemption under that section.
(2) If subsection (1) above is contravened an offence is committed by—
   (a) the company, and
   (b) every officer of the company who is in default.
   For this purpose a shadow director is treated as an officer of the company.
(3) A person guilty of an offence under this section is liable on summary conviction to a fine not exceeding level 5 on the standard scale and, for continued contravention, to a daily default fine not exceeding one-tenth of level 5 on the standard scale.
(4) Where immediately before the commencement of this section—
   (a) a company was exempt by virtue of section 30 of the Companies Act 1985 (c. 6) or Article 40 of the Companies (Northern Ireland) Order 1986 (S.I. 1986/1032 (N.I. 6)) from the requirement to have a name including the word 'limited' (or a permitted alternative), and
   (b) the company's memorandum or articles contained provision preventing an alteration of them without the approval of—
      (i) the Board of Trade or a Northern Ireland department (or any other department or Minister), or
      (ii) the Charity Commission
   that provision, and any condition of any such licence as is mentioned in section 61(1) (a)(ii) or (b)(ii) requiring such provision, shall cease to have effect.
   This does not apply if, or to the extent that, the provision is required by or under any other enactment.
(5) It is hereby declared that any such provision as is mentioned in subsection (4)(b) formerly contained in a company's memorandum was at all material times capable, with the appropriate approval, of being altered or removed under section 17 of the Companies Act 1985 or Article 28 of the Companies (Northern Ireland) Order 1986 (S.I. 1986/1032 (N.I. 6)) (or corresponding earlier enactments).

COMMENCEMENT DATE 1 October 2009[41]

This section replaces section 31(1) and (5) of the 1985 Act. It prohibits a company benefiting from an exemption under either the 1948 Act or the 1985 Act (or their Northern Irish equivalents) in relation to the use of the word 'limited' from changing its articles in such a way that it no longer meets the requirements for the exemption. 5.63.02

Section 63(2): This section makes it a criminal offence to change the company's articles in such a way, although no offence will be committed if at the same time, the company changes its name so as to include the word 'limited', thus voluntarily abandoning the exemption. Note that the offence is committed by the company and every officer in default,[42] and may also be committed by a shadow director who for these purposes will be treated as an officer of the company. 5.63.03

Section 63(3): The standard scale for fines for Companies Act offences is prescribed by section 37 of the Criminal Justice Act 1982. The expression 'daily default fine' is defined in section 1125. 5.63.04

Section 63(4)–(5): Previously under the 1985 Act, companies benefiting from an exemption under the 1948 Act (or its Northern Irish equivalent) were made to include a provision in their memorandum preventing an amendment to their memorandum or articles without the consent of the Secretary of State (or its predecessor, the Board of Trade). Section 63(4) and (5) removed this administrative burden. Under the new regime introduced by the Act, if a company appears to be taking advantage of the exemption when it is no longer entitled to do so, for example, having changed its articles so as to include provisions allowing a distribution of profits or a return of capital to shareholders, the company may be directed under section 64 to change its name to include the word 'limited' or a permitted alternative. 5.63.05

---

[41] Companies Act 2006 (Commencement No 8, Transitional Provisions and Savings) Order 2008, SI 2008/2860, art 3(e).
[42] See s 1121 for a definition of 'officer' in this context.

### 64 Power to direct change of name in case of company ceasing to be entitled to exemption

**5.64.01**

(1) If it appears to the Secretary of State that a company whose name does not include 'limited' or any of the permitted alternatives—

  (a) has ceased to be entitled to exemption under section 60(1)(a) or (b), or

  (b) in the case of a company within section 61 or 62 (which impose conditions as to the objects and articles of the company)—

    (i) has carried on any business other than the promotion of any of the objects mentioned in subsection (3) of section 61 or, as the case may be, subsection (2) of section 62, or

    (ii) has acted inconsistently with the provision required by subsection (4)(a) or (b) of section 61 or, as the case may be, subsection (3)(a) or (b) of section 62,

the Secretary of State may direct the company to change its name so that it ends with 'limited' or one of the permitted alternatives.

(2) The direction must be in writing and must specify the period within which the company is to change its name.

(3) A change of name in order to comply with a direction under this section may be made by resolution of the directors.

This is without prejudice to any other method of changing the company's name.

(4) Where a resolution of the directors is passed in accordance with subsection (3), the company must give notice to the registrar of the change.

Sections 80 and 81 apply as regards the registration and effect of the change.

(5) If the company fails to comply with a direction under this section an offence is committed by—

  (a) the company, and

  (b) every officer of the company who is in default.

(6) A person guilty of an offence under this section is liable on summary conviction to a fine not exceeding level 5 on the standard scale and, for continued contravention, to a daily default fine not exceeding one-tenth of level 5 on the standard scale.

(7) A company that has been directed to change its name under this section may not, without the approval of the Secretary of State, subsequently change its name so that it does not include 'limited' or one of the permitted alternatives.

This does not apply to a change of name on re-registration or on conversion to a community interest company.

COMMENCEMENT DATE 1 October 2009[43]

**5.64.02** This section replaces section 31(2)–(4) and (6) of the 1985 Act. It gives the Secretary of State power to withdraw a private company's exemption from the requirement for its name to conclude with the word 'limited' if it appears to the Secretary of State (note the subjective element) that the company no longer meets the criteria which applied when it was originally granted the exemption.

**5.64.03** Section 64(3): In a change from the corresponding 1985 Act provisions, section 64(3) allows the directors to effect the name change, rather than requiring a special resolution of the company's members. This ties in with the new name change provisions which were introduced in Chapter 5 of Part 5 of the Act.

**5.64.04** Section 64(4): Even if the name is changed by a resolution of the directors, the Registrar of Companies must be notified under this section. The same notification would have to be made upon any name change, even if effected by special resolution under section 78 of the Act.

**5.64.05** Section 64(5) and (6): See section 1124 for a definition of 'officer' in this context, and section 1125 for a definition of 'daily default fine'. The standard scale for fines for Companies Act offences is prescribed by section 37 of the Criminal Justice Act 1982.

**5.64.06** Section 64(7): If a company changes its constitution after having been directed to change its name under this section, so that it then meets the requirement for any relevant exemption, it would still have to get permission from the Secretary of State then to drop the word 'limited' (or a permitted alternative) from its name. Presumably, tying in with the provisions of sections 61(2)(b) and 62(1), if that company had subsequently changed its name (other than adding the word 'limited' (or a permitted alternative) to comply with a direction under this section), then it will not be able to re-apply for an exemption under sections 61 or 62. The restriction does not apply if the company changes its name on re-registration[44] or on conversion to a community interest company.[45]

---

[43] Companies Act 2006 (Commencement No 8, Transitional Provisions and Savings) Order 2008, SI 2008/2860, art 3(e).

[44] See s 90(3)(a) (re-registration of private company as public), s 97(3)(a) (re-registration of a public company as private), s 102(3) (re-registration of a private limited company as unlimited), s 105(4) (re- registration of an unlimited company as limited), and s 109(3) (re-registration of public company as private and unlimited).

[45] See ss 33 and 37(1)(c) of the Companies (Audit, Investigations and Community Enterprise) Act 2004.

*Inappropriate use of indications of company type or legal form*

## 65  Inappropriate use of indications of company type or legal form

(1)  The Secretary of State may make provision by regulations prohibiting the use in a company name     **5.65.01**
of specified words, expressions or other indications—

(a)  that are associated with a particular type of company or form of organisation, or

(b)  that are similar to words, expressions or other indications associated with a particular type of
company or form of organisation.

(2)  The regulations may prohibit the use of words, expressions or other indications—

(a)  in a specified part, or otherwise than in a specified part, of a company's name;

(b)  in conjunction with, or otherwise than in conjunction with, such other words, expressions or
indications as may be specified.

(3)  A company must not be registered under this Act by a name that consists of or includes anything
prohibited by regulations under this section.

(4)  In this section 'specified' means specified in the regulations.

(5)  Regulations under this section are subject to negative resolution procedure.

COMMENCEMENT DATE 1 October 2009[46]

This section replaces section 26(1)(a), (b), (bb), and (bbb) of the 1985 Act, and restricts the use of   **5.65.02**
various words, expressions, and abbreviations that indicate the legal status of the various types of
commercial entity, eg limited, plc, community interest company, open-ended investment company
etc. Since 1 October 2009, the regulations[47] made under this section have imposed restrictions on all
companies including, other than at the end of their company name, words indicating legal form or
status, such as 'public limited company', 'plc', or 'community interest company' (or the Welsh equivalents) and excludes the use of other inappropriate indicators of legal form entirely, such as 'limited
partnership', 'limited liability partnership', or 'open-ended investment company' (or the Welsh equivalents). Companies which are exempt from the requirement to have a name ending with 'limited' or a
permitted alternative, and unlimited companies, are specifically prohibited from using a company
name ending with another designation (eg 'plc'), which would give an incorrect or misleading
indication of the company's status. Public companies and other types of private company do not
require similar provisions since sections 58 and 59 respectively of the Act stipulate the inclusion of a
statutory indicator in their names. All types of company are restricted under the regulations in terms
of the use of words indicating legal form or status in their business name (rather than the registered,
company name) for the purposes of section 1197. The regulations also cover the use of specified words
or expressions which are confusingly similar to those indicating the legal status of a company or other
entity (section 65(1)(b)).

# CHAPTER 3
## SIMILARITY TO OTHER NAMES

*Similarity to other name on registrar's index*

## 66  Name not to be the same as another in the index

(1)  A company must not be registered under this Act by a name that is the same as another name     **5.66.01**
appearing in the registrar's index of company names.

(2)  The Secretary of State may make provision by regulations supplementing this section.

(3)  The regulations may make provision—

(a)  as to matters that are to be disregarded, and

(b)  as to words, expressions, signs or symbols that are, or are not, to be regarded as the same,
for the purposes of this section.

(4)  The regulations may provide—

(a)  that registration by a name that would otherwise be prohibited under this section is
permitted—

(i)  in specified circumstances, or

(ii)  with specified consent, and

(b)  that if those circumstances obtain or that consent is given at the time a company is registered
by a name, a subsequent change of circumstances or withdrawal of consent does not affect
the registration.

(5)  Regulations under this section are subject to negative resolution procedure.

---

[46] Companies Act 2006 (Commencement No 8, Transitional Provisions and Savings) Order 2008, SI 2008/
2860, art 3(e).

[47] Company and Business Names (Miscellaneous Provisions) Regulations 2009, SI 2009/1085.

(6) In this section 'specified' means specified in the regulations.

COMMENCEMENT DATE 1 October 2009[48]

**5.66.02** From 1 October 2009, section 66(2), together with the regulations made under it,[49] replace section 26(1)(c) and (3) of the 1985 Act. The regulations set out detailed rules as to (i) what is to be disregarded and (ii) which words, expressions, signs and symbols are to be taken as the same when comparing a proposed and an existing name. For example, punctuation and spacing, indications of status (eg limited or plc), the definite article (ie 'the') as the first word, and the addition of the word 'Company' or 'Co' at the end of the name will be disregarded. By way of illustration, according to the Companies House guidance on company names,[50] if a company is already registered under the name Hands Limited, the following would not be allowed: H and S Limited, H and S plc, H & S Limited or plc, H & S Company (or Co) Limited, or H & S and Co Limited. The addition of the letter 's' will also be disregarded in certain circumstances so the plural will not generally be sufficient to distinguish a name from another already on the register. In April 2010, Companies House introduced a search facility which is designed to return 'same as' matches with company names already on the Register, as defined in the regulations. The Company Name Availability Search is available as part of the Companies House WebCHeck service.

**5.66.03** The list of words, expressions, signs and symbols which are to be treated as the same for the purposes of this section is updated and expanded under the 2006 Act regulations as compared with the 1985 Act, making the regime more certain, if more restrictive. Under the 1985 Act regime, apart from restrictions based only on the word(s) indicating legal status (eg limited or plc), the type and case of the letters, punctuation and spacing, only 'and' and '&' were taken as the same under the 1985 Act itself (although the then Companies House guidance provided additional examples).[51] The regulations set out (in Schedule 3) a complete list of words or combinations of words in a name which will be disregarded by the registrar in determining whether a proposed company name is the same as another which is already on the index. The list now includes common domain name endings such as '.co.uk', '.com', '.org' and '.net' (with or without the full stop) as well as common group company distinctions such as 'group', 'holdings', 'imports', 'exports', 'UK' and 'GB'. So, adopting the example given in the Companies House guidance on names,[52] if 'Catering Limited' is already on the register, Companies House will, subject to compliance with the consent procedure described in para 5.66.05 below, reject 'Catering UK Limited', 'Catering International Limited' and even 'Catering Company (Services) Limited' (in the latter case presumably because 'Services' is deemed to be a word starved of meaning).

**5.66.04** Currency symbols (£, $, € and ¥) and their respective English word equivalents, '%' and 'percent', and the numbers 1 to 9 and the words 'one' to 'nine' will also be treated as the same, as will the symbol '@' and the word 'at'. Under the 1985 Act, Companies House could only consider names incorporating symbols under the 'too like' rules in section 28 of that Act.

**5.66.05** Since 1 October 2009, the regulations have also, for the first time, provided a mechanism for enabling the registration of a name which would otherwise be treated as the same as another already registered provided that other entity consents in writing to the registration.[53] However, the two companies must be part of the same group. This mechanism should prove useful in the context of a group reorganization and where a group company wishes to use one of the words or expressions on the 'disregarded' list in Schedule 3 to the regulations under this section (for example, the word 'group'). In these circumstances, the application for the new name should be accompanied by a letter of consent from the company already on the register which confirms that the other company is, or will be, part of the same group. The regulations provide expressly that a subsequent withdrawal of that consent will not affect the other company's registration. The consent procedure does not, however, apply to companies who are not in the same group.

**5.66.06** The regulations made under this section do not themselves deal with a situation where a company incorporated prior to 1 October 2009 has in its name a word or expression which was previously unregulated. However, the transitional provisions in the relevant Commencement Order provide that nothing in sections 54, 55, 57, 65, or 66 will affect the continued registration of a company by a name

---

[48] Companies Act 2006 (Commencement No 8, Transitional Provisions and Savings) Order 2008, SI 2008/2860, art 3(e).

[49] Company and Business Names (Miscellaneous Provisions) Regulations 2009, SI 2009/1085.

[50] Companies House guidance note reference GP1, available from the Companies House website at ⟨http://www.companieshouse.gov.uk⟩.

[51] See Companies Act 1985, s 26(3).

[52] GP1.

[53] SI 2009/1085, Part 2, art 8.

by which it was duly registered prior to 1 October 2009.[54] Consequently, such a company will only be subject to the operation of the provisions in this section if it changes its name following this section coming into force, and the new name contains a word or expression on the 'disregarded' list in Schedule 3 to the regulations made under this section, which would otherwise give it the same name as another company already on the register.

This should be borne in mind when contemplating a name swap in the context of a group reorgani-    **5.66.07** zation. As the name swap will involve a change of name for each of the companies involved, the name change may trigger the operation of the 'same as' provisions. Since the list of disregarded words and expressions is greatly expanded as compared with the equivalent list under the 1985 Act, where Company A and Company B were formed under the 1985 Act with names which were not then treated as the same, they might be so treated under the 2006 Act. For example, Catering Holdings Limited will be treated as the same as Catering Group Limited under the 2006 Act (but would not have been under the 1985 Act), so if these companies were to swap names, they would have to follow the consent procedure (provided they are to remain in the same group). The consent procedure only applies where companies are in the same corporate group. There is no facility for companies which are, or become (by virtue of a demerger for example) unconnected, to consent to the use of a 'same as' name.

The fact that a name swap, often carried out as part of a group reorganization, triggers the application    **5.66.08** of the new, more restrictive rules on 'same as' names and other sensitive words and expressions has caused considerable difficulties and associated costs to companies. For example, Company A and Company B are subsidiaries of Company X plc. Company X plc is carrying out a group reorganization and wishes Company A and Company B to swap names. The name swap triggers the application of the 'same as' rules under the 2006 Act, and it is discovered that, following the incorporation of Companies A and B, but prior to the new regime coming into effect, a third party incorporated a company with a name similar to that of Company A, thus preventing the name swap. Company X plc instead had to effect a costly business transfer (or perhaps offer to pay the third party to change its name unless it does so voluntarily). There is no mechanism for the third party in this situation to consent to the use of the 'same as' name by Company A, nor for the Registrar to exercise any discretion in respect of names which have been used for many years without giving rise to any confusion.

This difficulty has been raised by a number of respondents to the Government's ongoing consultation    **5.66.08A** on the rules on company names in the context of its Red Tape Challenge. The Red Tape Challenge asks respondents for views on whether the current rules should be preserved in their current form, or simplified, streamlined, or even replaced by a voluntary code or scrapped altogether. It remains to be seen whether the 'same as' rules are amended as a result of this review. The Government is due to report on the outcome of its consultation, and confirm which Regulations will be amended, simplified, or scrapped before December 2013.

There is a specific order to the matters to be disregarded when determining if two names are the same    **5.66.09** under the regulations. So, for example, if the registrar is considering the names 'H and S plc' and 'H&S.com Limited', the words 'plc' and 'Limited' would be disregarded first, then 'and' and '&', and finally '.com' (making the two names the same).

Even if a name passes the 'same as' test, it is also necessary to consider the 'too like' rules (see section    **5.66.10** 67), although note that the 'too like' rules only appear to permit the Secretary of State to direct a company to change its name after it has registered the name, not to refuse permission when it first seeks to register the name. Companies should also note that the registration of the name at Companies House offers no protection against:

(i)   another company trading under a business name which is substantively the same (ie without the word 'limited') as the company's registered name (although there may be scope for a passing-off action against the other company);
(ii)  the company itself being the subject of a passing-off action (if the company is proposing to operate a similar business to an existing company with a similar name); or
(iii) trade mark infringement,

so it is worth investigating whether any company on the register with a similar name carries on a similar business, and whether anyone has trade mark protection in respect of the name.

It is not possible to 'reserve' a name, something which has long been considered (see the Jenkins    **5.66.11** Committee Report)[55] but so far rejected. If a company has particularly important reasons for wishing to adopt a specific company name, it should be advised to do so as soon as possible, even before it has

---

[54]  Companies Act 2006 (Commencement No 8, Transitional Provisions and Savings) Order 2008, SI 2008/ 2860, Sch 2, para 17.
[55]  Cmnd 1749, para 450.

started trading. Note, however, the provisions of section 69 which are designed to prevent companies registering a name in which another company has goodwill, where this is done deliberately in order to extract money from that other company or otherwise prevent it from using the name.

**5.66.12** It is possible to swap names with another company, but it is usually advisable to notify Companies House in advance of what is proposed so that the two name change applications are not rejected under this section. As noted in paras 5.66.05 to 5.66.07 above, the consent procedures for group companies registering the same name as an existing company should assist in name swaps in a group reorganization context, but do not help where a third party is involved.

**5.66.13** Unlike the regime under section 28 of the 1985 Act, section 66 gives the Secretary of State power to refuse registration of a company name when it is first incorporated or subsequently seeks to change its name, rather than directing a company to change its name once it has already been registered. The 'after the fact' power is dealt with in section 67.

### 67 Power to direct change of name in case of similarity to existing name

**5.67.01**
(1) The Secretary of State may direct a company to change its name if it has been registered in a name that is the same as or, in the opinion of the Secretary of State, too like—
  (a) a name appearing at the time of the registration in the registrar's index of company names, or
  (b) a name that should have appeared in that index at that time.
(2) The Secretary of State may make provision by regulations supplementing this section.
(3) The regulations may make provision—
  (a) as to matters that are to be disregarded, and
  (b) as to words, expressions, signs or symbols that are, or are not, to be regarded as the same, for the purposes of this section.
(4) The regulations may provide—
  (a) that no direction is to be given under this section in respect of a name—
    (i) in specified circumstances, or
    (ii) if specified consent is given, and
  (b) that a subsequent change of circumstances or withdrawal of consent does not give rise to grounds for a direction under this section.
(5) Regulations under this section are subject to negative resolution procedure.
(6) In this section 'specified' means specified in the regulations.

COMMENCEMENT DATE 1 October 2009[56]

**5.67.02** This section replaces the 'same as' and 'too like' provisions of section 28(2) of the 1985 Act. The Government has not published regulations specifically referring to section 67, but the regulations made under section 66 (see above) contain a list of matters to be disregarded and of words, expressions, signs or symbols that are to be regarded as the same. These provisions are designed to enable the Secretary of State to direct a company to change its name if the name is the same as or too like a name already on the register.

**5.67.03** Whereas section 66 enables Companies House to reject a name as being the same as another name on the register when the company is first incorporated or changes its name, under this section a company could be required to change its name after it has been registered, if it is the same as another company's registered name. The last-registered company would be the one vulnerable to a direction under this section. For these purposes, the 'same as' rules set out in the regulations will apply in the same way as under section 66. An 'after the fact' direction under this section may also be made if a company name is too like another company name on the register. The 'too like' rule is designed to cover names which do not strictly fall within the 'same as' regime, but would still be likely to give rise to confusion, eg 'H & S Consultants Limited' and 'H & S Consulting Limited'. In this context, Companies House will usually perform only a visual comparison. Whilst Companies House will take account of phonetic similarities, it will disregard whether or not companies are in the same group or under common ownership, whether or not a company is trading or intending to trade, or of any intended trading names, or whether the two companies under consideration share any common activity or geographical location.

**5.67.04** Section 67(1)(b): A company may be the subject of a direction under this section if its name is the same as or too like the name of another company which was not actually on the register at the time but should have been, for example, as a result of a delay in the entry on the index of that other company's name. This ought to be a fairly rare occurrence as Companies House usually enters names on the register immediately, but such a delay sometimes arises, particularly in relation to the registration of a non-UK

---

[56] Companies Act 2006 (Commencement No 8, Transitional Provisions and Savings) Order 2008, SI 2008/2860, art 3(e).

company or because the name is registered under other legislation (eg the Industrial and Provident Societies Act 1965) and may not appear on the index immediately.

Section 67(4): Mirroring section 66(4), section 67(4) provides that where the regulations provide an exemption from this section in specified circumstances or where a specified consent is given, if those circumstances change or such consent is withdrawn, that will not automatically lead to a direction being made under this section. So, for example, if a group company withdraws its consent to the use of one of the words or expressions on the 'disregarded' list in the regulations under section 66, this should not of itself lead to a direction under this section. The regulations provide expressly that a withdrawal of such a consent would not affect the company's registration under the name which was the subject of the consent.   **5.67.05**

Note that subject to the passing-off and trade mark regimes, there is nothing to prevent a company trading under a name which might otherwise fall foul of sections 66 or 67.   **5.67.06**

## 68 Direction to change name: supplementary provisions

(1) The following provisions have effect in relation to a direction under section 67 (power to direct change of name in case of similarity to existing name).   **5.68.01**
(2) Any such direction—
   (a) must be given within twelve months of the company's registration by the name in question, and
   (b) must specify the period within which the company is to change its name.
(3) The Secretary of State may by a further direction extend that period.
   Any such direction must be given before the end of the period for the time being specified.
(4) A direction under section 67 or this section must be in writing.
(5) If a company fails to comply with the direction, an offence is committed by—
   (a) the company, and
   (b) every officer of the company who is in default.
   For this purpose a shadow director is treated as an officer of the company.
(6) A person guilty of an offence under this section is liable on summary conviction to a fine not exceeding level 3 on the standard scale and, for continued contravention, a daily default fine not exceeding one-tenth of level 3 on the standard scale.

COMMENCEMENT DATE 1 October 2009[57]

This section replaces section 28(4) and (5) of the 1985 Act.   **5.68.02**

Section 68(2)–(3): As with the 1985 Act regime, a company will only be vulnerable to a direction under section 68 during the first 12 months following registration of the name in question. The direction itself will specify the period within which the company must change its name and, under section 68(3), the deadline for changing the name may be extended further by a separate direction. The Company Law Review recommendation of a 15-month rather than a 12-month period during which the direction may be given[58] was not taken up when the Act was passed, to ensure that a company will not have to wait too long before it can be certain it will not be subject to a section 67 direction. In the House of Lords debate on this section,[59] the Government made clear that in considering whether or not to make a direction under section 67, the Registrar of Companies will not listen to representations made by any of the parties involved, but will make its judgment based on the rules set out in these sections and the relevant regulations, on the basis of a visual comparison between the names in question, applying a simple test of whether or not the public will be confused.   **5.68.03**

Section 68(4)–(5): See section 1124 for a definition of 'officer' in this context, and section 1125 for a definition of 'daily default fine'. The standard scale for fines for Companies Act offences is prescribed by section 37 of the Criminal Justice Act 1982.   **5.68.04**

### *Similarity to other name in which person has goodwill*

## 69 Objection to company's registered name

(1) A person ('the applicant') may object to a company's registered name on the ground—   **5.69.01**
   (a) that it is the same as a name associated with the applicant in which he has goodwill, or
   (b) that it is sufficiently similar to such a name that its use in the United Kingdom would be likely to mislead by suggesting a connection between the company and the applicant.

---

[57] Companies Act 2006 (Commencement No 8, Transitional Provisions and Savings) Order 2008, SI 2008/2860, art 3(e).
[58] See Company Law Review Final Report (para 11.50).
[59] See *Hansard*, HL, vol 678, col GC56 (30 January 2006).

(2)  The objection must be made by application to a company names adjudicator (see section 70).

(3)  The company concerned shall be the primary respondent to the application.

Any of its members or directors may be joined as respondents.

(4)  If the ground specified in subsection (1)(a) or (b) is established, it is for the respondents to show—

(a)  that the name was registered before the commencement of the activities on which the applicant relies to show goodwill; or

(b)  that the company—

(i)   is operating under the name, or

(ii)  is proposing to do so and has incurred substantial start-up costs in preparation, or

(iii) was formerly operating under the name and is now dormant; or

(c)  that the name was registered in the ordinary course of a company formation business and the company is available for sale to the applicant on the standard terms of that business; or

(d)  that the name was adopted in good faith; or

(e)  that the interests of the applicant are not adversely affected to any significant extent.

If none of those is shown, the objection shall be upheld.

(5)  If the facts mentioned in subsection (4)(a), (b) or (c) are established, the objection shall nevertheless be upheld if the applicant shows that the main purpose of the respondents (or any of them) in registering the name was to obtain money (or other consideration) from the applicant or prevent him from registering the name.

(6)  If the objection is not upheld under subsection (4) or (5), it shall be dismissed.

(7)  In this section 'goodwill' includes reputation of any description.

COMMENCEMENT DATE 1 October 2008[60]

**5.69.02**    This section, along with sections 70 to 74, were newly introduced in the Act to respond to the concern about opportunistic registration of company names, ie companies registered with names which are chosen with the principal intention of obtaining money from another company who has previously acquired goodwill in the name, or preventing that other company from using the name. The case of *Glaxo plc v Glaxo-Wellcome Limited*[61] is a good example of the sort of practice these sections were designed to prevent. In that case, which was brought under the 1985 Act, the defendants registered the name Glaxo-Wellcome Limited in anticipation of the merger between Glaxo and Wellcome. When the merged companies came to register the name of the new entity, they discovered the existence of the defendants' company, whereupon the defendants offered to change its name for a substantial sum of money. The court granted a mandatory injunction requiring the defendants to change the name of their company. There was nothing in the 1985 Act which specifically dealt with opportunistic registration and although the registrar could have used the section 28 procedure under the 1985 Act, in the circumstances the court would not insist on following that procedure since to do so would result in a delay in forcing the defendants to change the name of their company and such delay would prejudice the plaintiffs. The court recognized the potential for abuse of the system of registration company names under the 1985 Act regime, which resulted in the provisions now set out in sections 70 to 74 of the Act. More recently the merger of Boots and Alliance Unichem raised some interesting issues about the priority of applications for registration of a name. On the same day as these companies announced their intention to merge and operate under the name Alliance Boots, they attempted to register a new company with that name only to find that an individual had done so on the same day in an attempt to obtain payment for the release of the name to the merged entity. The merging companies filed their application at Companies House, London before the individual filed his application at Companies House, Cardiff, but as the Cardiff office processed the application more quickly, the London office rejected the merging companies' application. Whilst the new procedure may not prevent a repeat of this situation, it would at least provide some redress for the legitimate applicant. In the Alliance Boots example, the parties negotiated surrender of the name by the individual in return for payment of expenses.

**5.69.03**    The Company Names Tribunal issued its first decision under section 69 following an application by The Coca-Cola Company against the company Coke Cola Ltd.[62] Under the power conferred upon it under section 73(1), the Company Names Tribunal ordered the company Coke Cola Ltd to change its name within one month of the decision to a name that did not contravene the provisions of section 69. The Tribunal also determined that if Coke Cola Ltd failed to take this course of action, it would exercise its power under section 73(4) to change the company's name to a name of its choosing, and would give notice of this under section 73(5). Since then the Tribunal has issued a number of decisions. The majority have found in favour of the applicant and an order has been made for the respondent to

---

[60]  Companies Act 2006 (Commencement No 5 etc) Order 2007, SI 2007/3495, art 5.

[61]  [1996] FSR 388.

[62]  Decision O-318-08.

change the company name, but there have been some notable decisions in which the respondent's claim to the relevant name has been upheld, either because the applicant failed to establish goodwill in the relevant name (see 5.69.04 below), or because the respondent succeeded with one of the defences in section 69(4)–(5)(see 5.69.07 et seq. below).

Section 69(1): It is key to a successful action under section 69 that the applicant can establish that it has goodwill in the name (section 69(1)(a)) at the date of the application, or that the name in question is sufficiently similar to the applicant's company name that it would suggest a connection between them which would be misleading (section 69(1)(b)). The application by Miller Rosenfalck LLP in respect of the company name European Business Lawyers Limited[63] failed because Miller Rosenfalck had not established that the descriptor European Business Lawyers was distinctive to them and that they had goodwill in relation to the name. This was so notwithstanding that www.europeanbusinesslawyer-s.com had been used by them as a domain name and as part of their email address, but the Company Names Adjudicators found no clear evidence that the firm's clients placed any significance on the domain name. Section 69(7) provides that goodwill includes reputation of any description, and a number of the Company Names Tribunal decisions refer to the definition of goodwill in *IRC v Muller*,[64] drawing attention to the fact that 'reputation' may be wider than goodwill. Despite this, in the *Tektronix* case,[65] the application failed on the basis that the applicant, Tektronix Inc., a US-based company, had not established evidence of a reputation in the UK notwithstanding the existence of UK trade mark and company name registrations. It is not necessary to show that that the goodwill or reputation was established before the name was registered as this would mitigate against a successful application being brought where a company name was registered in anticipation of goodwill being generated.[66] **5.69.04**

The *IRC V Muller* definition of goodwill refers to 'locality'. In the recent Company Names Tribunal 'Nectar' case,[67] reference is made to the fact that for goodwill to exist in the UK, it is essential that a business has a 'reputation' in the UK, but goodwill or reputation in a jurisdiction may be established even if there is no business in that jurisdiction. **5.69.05**

There is no time limit during which an objection may be made, so a company will not be safe from an application under this section after a certain period of time has elapsed following registration (notwithstanding that the Company Law Review recommended a 12-month time limit).[68] **5.69.06**

Section 69(3): The primary respondent in the action will be the company itself, but under section 69(3) any of the company's members or directors may be joined as respondents in the action, so individuals will not be able to shelter behind a company. The Company Names Tribunal Practice Direction[69] deals with the approach to be taken where the company is also the subject of a striking-off application to Companies House. **5.69.07**

Section 69(4)–(5): This section sets out a number of primary defences available to the respondents to an action under section 69, which will raise a presumption that a name was adopted legitimately. Even if the respondents are able to rely on the defences set out in section 69(4)(a), (b), or (c), the objection may still be upheld under section 69(5) if the applicant can show that the name was registered in order to obtain money (or other consideration) from the applicant or prevent it from registering the name. However, the exceptions set out in section 69(4)(d) and (e) are absolute. During the consultation stages on the Act, the Confederation of British Industry (CBI)[70] was vehemently opposed to the defences in section 69(4), but the Government refused to water down or remove them, placing heavy reliance on section 69(5) in ensuring that registrations for an improper purpose are open to challenge. **5.69.08**

Section 69(4)(a): This defence would be available even if a dormant name is brought into use after the applicant has established goodwill in the relevant name. It does not require the respondent to have traded under the name before the applicant established goodwill in it, or to continue to operate under the name at the time the application is brought. However, if the applicant can show that the name was originally registered for an abusive purpose under section 69(5), the application should succeed. **5.69.09**

Section 69(4)(b)(ii): A company could take advantage of this defence by registering the offending name and merely preparing to trade, without actually trading, but once again, the respondent could fall back **5.69.10**

---

[63] ⟨http://www.ipogov.uk/cna/cna-practicenotice.htm⟩
[64] *IRC v Muller & Co's Margarine Ltd* [1901] AC 217.
[65] Decision 0/36/11.
[66] Decision 0/197/10 at para 34.
[67] Decision 0/282/12 at para 33.
[68] See Company Law Review Final Report (paragraph 11.50) and the discussion on this recommendation in the House of Lords Grand Committee in *Hansard*, HL, vol 678, cols 54–56 (30 January 2006).
[69] ⟨http://www.ipogov.uk/cna/cna-practicenotice.htm⟩.
[70] For a copy of the CBI's response, see ⟨http://www.cbi.org.uk/ndbs/positiondoc.nsf/⟩.

on section 69(5). The meaning of the word 'substantial' in the context of the start-up costs required to establish a defence under section 69(4)(b)(ii) was discussed in the House of Lords Grand Committee. The Government confirmed that whether or not start-up costs were 'substantial' would be determined having regard to all the circumstances of the case.[71]

**5.69.11**     Section 69(4)(b)(iii): It is also a defence for a company to establish that it was formerly operating under the name even if it is now dormant, subject again to the overriding test in section 69(5).

**5.69.12**     Section 69(4)(d): The application by Zurich Insurance Company in 2009[72] for an order that an unconnected company, Zurich Investments Limited, should drop the word 'Zurich' from its name provides a helpful insight into the meaning of 'good faith' for the purposes of section 69(4)(d). The Company Names Adjudicators commented that the issue of good faith turns on the respondent's motivation and knowledge when the company was registered under the offending name. In the Zurich case, the Adjudicators found no evidence of any intention to trade off the goodwill in the Zurich name, and that the adoption of the name was more coincidence than conspiracy, so they refused the application.

**5.69.13**     Sections 69(4)(e): The Zurich case[73] also provides a useful illustration of what will be required to establish a 'significant' adverse effect under section 69(4)(e). Whether or not an adverse effect is present will be judged by reference to the facts as at the use or potential use of the company name in the course of business, so the mere registration of the name in itself will not be sufficient. In that case even though the principal activities of the respondent company (mineral mining) were in an entirely different field from those of the applicant (insurance and financial services), the Company Names Adjudicators took the view that it was open to the respondent company to operate in any business area and there was therefore a risk that if it undertook poorly judged activities in the financial services field, it would significantly affect Zurich's reputation, so the defence under section 69(4)(e) was unavailable.

### 70 Company names adjudicators

**5.70.01**          (1) The Secretary of State shall appoint persons to be company names adjudicators.

                (2) The persons appointed must have such legal or other experience as, in the Secretary of State's opinion, makes them suitable for appointment.

                (3) An adjudicator—

                     (a) holds office in accordance with the terms of his appointment,

                     (b) is eligible for re-appointment when his term of office ends,

                     (c) may resign at any time by notice in writing given to the Secretary of State, and

                     (d) may be dismissed by the Secretary of State on the ground of incapacity or misconduct.

                (4) One of the adjudicators shall be appointed Chief Adjudicator.

                  He shall perform such functions as the Secretary of State may assign to him.

                (5) The other adjudicators shall undertake such duties as the Chief Adjudicator may determine.

                (6) The Secretary of State may—

                     (a) appoint staff for the adjudicators;

                     (b) pay remuneration and expenses to the adjudicators and their staff;

                     (c) defray other costs arising in relation to the performance by the adjudicators of their functions;

                     (d) compensate persons for ceasing to be adjudicators.

         COMMENCEMENT DATE 1 October 2008[74]

**5.70.02**     The company names adjudicators who are appointed to the Company Names Tribunal are, for the time being at least, trade mark adjudicators from the UK Intellectual Property Office (formerly known as the Patent Office) and adjudications take place at the UK Intellectual Property Office, which is based in Newport, South Wales, although hearings may also be held at the UK Intellectual Property Office in London or elsewhere via video conference. The detailed procedural rules under which adjudications take place are provided for under section 71. The adjudicators' decisions are subject to appeal through the courts, and the adjudicators will be ultimately accountable to the Secretary of State.

---

[71]   See *Hansard*, HL, vol 678, col GC59 (30 January 2006).
[72]   Decision 0/197/10.
[73]   Decision 0/197/10.
[74]   Companies Act 2006 (Commencement No 5 etc) Order 2007, SI 2007/3495, art 5.

## 71  Procedural rules

(1) The Secretary of State may make rules about proceedings before a company names adjudicator.    **5.71.01**
(2) The rules may, in particular, make provision—
    (a) as to how an application is to be made and the form and content of an application or other documents;
    (b) for fees to be charged;
    (c) about the service of documents and the consequences of failure to serve them;
    (d) as to the form and manner in which evidence is to be given;
    (e) for circumstances in which hearings are required and those in which they are not;
    (f) for cases to be heard by more than one adjudicator;
    (g) setting time limits for anything required to be done in connection with the proceedings (and allowing for such limits to be extended, even if they have expired);
    (h) enabling the adjudicator to strike out an application, or any defence, in whole or in part—
        (i) on the ground that it is vexatious, has no reasonable prospect of success or is otherwise misconceived, or
        (ii) for failure to comply with the requirements of the rules;
    (i) conferring power to order security for costs (in Scotland, caution for expenses);
    (j) as to how far proceedings are to be held in public;
    (k) requiring one party to bear the costs (in Scotland, expenses) of another and as to the taxing (or settling) the amount of such costs (or expenses).
(3) The rules may confer on the Chief Adjudicator power to determine any matter that could be the subject of provision in the rules.
(4) Rules under this section shall be made by statutory instrument which shall be subject to annulment in pursuance of a resolution of either House of Parliament.

COMMENCEMENT DATE 1 October 2008[75]

The rules made under section 71(1)[76] more or less follow section 71(2) in setting out the procedure for    **5.71.02** objecting to a company's registered name as well as the general powers of the adjudicator to regulate the proceedings and award costs. The rules do not specify the time periods applicable to actions brought in the Company Names Tribunal but the chief adjudicator has set standard time periods (which may be varied in any particular case as necessary) which are set out in the Company Names Tribunal Practice Direction, available on the Company Names Tribunal website.[77] There are also standard application and defence forms on the website. The standard fee for filing an application is currently £400,[78] not including the cost of employing lawyers or other advisers.

## 72  Decision of adjudicator to be made available to public

(1) A company names adjudicator must, within 90 days of determining an application under section    **5.72.01** 69, make his decision and his reasons for it available to the public.
(2) He may do so by means of a website or by such other means as appear to him to be appropriate.

COMMENCEMENT DATE 1 October 2008[79]

The decisions of the company names adjudicators are published on the website of the Company Names    **5.72.02** Tribunal[80] and whilst the majority of applications made since these provisions came into force in October 2008 have been successful (at the time of writing), there have been some cases where the Tribunal has found in favour of the respondent, either because the applicant failed to establish goodwill in the relevant name or because the respondent succeeded with one of the defences set out in section 69(4)–(5) (see 5.69.04–5.69.13 above).

## 73  Order requiring name to be changed

(1) If an application under section 69 is upheld, the adjudicators will make an order—    **5.73.01**
    (a) requiring the respondent company to change its name to one that is not an offending name, and
    (b) requiring all the respondents—
        (i) to take all such steps as are within their power to make, or facilitate the making, of that change, and

---

[75] Companies Act 2006 (Commencement No 5 etc) Order 2007, SI 2007/3495, art 5.
[76] Company Names Adjudicator Rules 2008, SI 2008/1738.
[77] ⟨http://www.ipo.gov.uk/cna/cna-practicenotice.htm⟩
[78] As at June 2011.
[79] Companies Act 2006 (Commencement No 5 etc) Order 2007, SI 2007/3495, art 5.
[80] ⟨http://www.ipo.gov.uk/cna/cna-decisions.htm⟩.

        (ii)  not to cause or permit any steps to be taken calculated to result in another company being registered with a name that is an offending name.

(2)  An 'offending name' means a name that, by reason of its similarity to the name associated with the applicant in which he claims goodwill, would be likely—

    (a)  to be the subject of a direction under section 67 (power of registrar to direct change of name), or

    (b)  to give rise to a further application under section 69.

(3)  The order must specify a date by which the respondent company's name is to be changed and may be enforced—

    (a)  in England and Wales or Northern Ireland, in the same way as an order of the High Court;

    (b)  in Scotland, in the same way as a decree of the Court of Session.

(4)  If the respondent company's name is not changed in accordance with the order by the specified date, the adjudicators may determine a new name for the company.

(5)  If the adjudicators determine a new name for the respondent company they must give notice of their determination—

    (a)  to the applicant,

    (b)  to the respondents, and

    (c)  to the registrar.

(6)  For the purposes of this section a company's name is changed when the change takes effect in accordance with section 81(1) (on the issue of the new certification of incorporation).

(7)  The adjudicators' decision will typically also award costs against the unsuccessful party.

COMMENCEMENT DATE 1 October 2008[81]

**5.73.02**    If an objection made under section 69 is upheld, the company names adjudicators will direct the company with the offending name to change its name and will set a deadline for compliance with the direction.

**5.73.03**    Section 73(1)(b): The respondents other than the company (for example, the directors and/or shareholders of the respondent company) may also be required under the terms of the direction to procure compliance with the direction, either by changing the name of the company by a board or shareholders' resolution, and not to register another company with the offending name.

**5.73.04**    Section 73(3): Note that a direction made by the company names adjudicators will be enforceable in the same way as an order of the High Court, or the Scottish equivalent.

**5.73.05**    Section 73(4)–(5): As an additional sanction, if the adjudicators' direction is not complied with, the adjudicators themselves will determine a new name for the company, notify the company, and issue the certificate of incorporation accordingly.

**5.73.06**    Even if the applicant and respondent companies are trading in entirely different fields of activity or at different levels in the same market, there is no scope for the adjudicator to make an order allowing the use of the offending name outside specific activities where its use would be likely to cause damage.

## 74 Appeal from adjudicator's decision

**5.74.01**    (1)  An appeal lies to the court from any decision of a company names adjudicator to uphold or dismiss an application under section 69.

(2)  Notice of appeal against a decision upholding an application must be given before the date specified in the adjudicator's order by which the respondent company's name is to be changed.

(3)  If notice of appeal is given against a decision upholding an application, the effect of the adjudicator's order is suspended.

(4)  If on appeal the court—

    (a)  affirms the decision of the adjudicator to uphold the application, or

    (b)  reverses the decision of the adjudicator to dismiss the application,

the court may (as the case may require) specify the date by which the adjudicator's order is to be complied with, remit the matter to the adjudicator or make any order that the adjudicator might have made.

(5)  If the court determines a new name for the company it must give notice of the determination—

    (a)  to the parties to the appeal, and

    (b)  to the registrar.

COMMENCEMENT DATE 1 October 2008[82]

**5.74.02**    If an order under section 73 is the subject of an appeal under section 74(1), the order will be suspended automatically under section 74(3). This suggests that until the appeal process is completed, the

---

[81]  Companies Act 2006 (Commencement No 5 etc) Order 2007, SI 2007/3495, art 5.
[82]  Companies Act 2006 (Commencement No 5 etc) Order 2007, SI 2007/3495, art 5.

respondents will be free to use the name that was previously the subject of the order. Whilst this might appear to be an incentive to companies not only to appeal, but to prolong any such appeal and continue trading under the offending name, the fact that a company has registered a particular name does not confer the right to trade under it, and the proper remedy for trading under the offending name would be a passing-off action.[83]

Assuming the respondent company intends to appeal, it is unlikely to have changed its name in compliance with the order under section 73, so in practice the applicant will not be able to register the name itself unless and until the respondent has complied with the order, pending the outcome of the appeal process, but could use or carry on using the name as a trading name. **5.74.03**

## CHAPTER 4
## OTHER POWERS OF THE SECRETARY OF STATE

### 75 Provision of misleading information etc

(1) If it appears to the Secretary of State— **5.75.01**
  (a) that misleading information has been given for the purposes of a company's registration by a particular name, or
  (b) that an undertaking or assurance has been given for that purpose and has not been fulfilled,
  the Secretary of State may direct the company to change its name.
(2) Any direction under this section—
  (a) must be given within five years of the company's registration by that name, and
  (b) must specify the period within which the company is to change its name.
(3) The Secretary of State may by a further direction extend the period within which the company is to change its name.
  Any such direction must be given before the end of the period for the time being specified.
(4) A direction under this section must be in writing.
(5) If a company fails to comply with a direction under this section, an offence is committed by—
  (a) the company, and
  (b) every officer of the company who is in default.
  For this purpose a shadow director is treated as an officer of the company.
(6) A person guilty of an offence under this section is liable on summary conviction to a fine not exceeding level 3 on the standard scale and, for continued contravention, a daily default fine not exceeding one-tenth of level 3 on the standard scale.

COMMENCEMENT DATE 1 October 2009[84]

This section replaces section 28(3) of the 1985 Act, and insofar as it related to that section, section 28(4)–(6), and enables the Secretary of State to direct a company to change its name within five years of the adoption of the name in two circumstances. **5.75.02**

Section 75(1)(a): First, where misleading information was given to the registrar when the name was adopted. For example, if a company wishes to adopt a name which incorporates one of the sensitive words or expressions prescribed by the regulations made under section 55,[85] Companies House will usually ask for evidence in support of the application which is sufficient to establish that the company fulfils whatever criteria are laid down for the use of the relevant word or expression. If a company wishes to use the word 'British' in its company name, for example, Companies House will usually require evidence that the company is British-owned and that the company is pre-eminent in its field. To show such pre-eminence, Companies House would expect evidence from an independent source such as a government department or a Trade Association. If any statement made or information provided in support of the company's application turns out to be false, the registrar may consider using the powers under section 75 to require the company to drop the word 'British' from its name. **5.75.03**

Section 75(1)(b): Alternatively, the powers under this section may be exercised if a company gives an undertaking or assurance to do something which would enable the company to satisfy the criteria for using a particular word or expression in its company name. For example, a company may seek to use the word 'Scotland' in its company name on the basis of an assurance that when the new name is adopted, the company's main place of business will be in Scotland, which would justify the use of the word 'Scotland' in its name. If it becomes apparent that the assurance was never fulfilled and the **5.75.04**

---

[83] See *Hansard*, HL, vol 378, cols 121–122 (1 February 2006).
[84] Companies Act 2006 (Commencement No 8, Transitional Provisions and Savings) Order 2008, SI 2008/2860, art 3(e).
[85] Company, Limited Liability Partnership and Business Names (Sensitive Words and Expressions) Regulations 2009, SI 2009/2615.

company's main place of business is in England, the use of the word 'Scotland' in its name would be misleading and the company would be vulnerable to a direction under section 75.

**5.75.05**  Section 28(6) and (7) of the 1985 Act, dealing with the issue of a new certificate of incorporation on change of name and the effect of the name change on any rights or obligations of the company arising prior to a name change, was not carried over into section 75, but these matters are dealt with in sections 80 and 81, which will apply to the application to change the company's name following a direction under this section 75.

**5.75.06**  Section 75(5)–(6): Failure to comply with a direction is a criminal offence for the company and its officers in default, and the offence may be committed by a shadow director, who for these purposes will be treated as an officer of the company.[86]

**5.75.07**  Note also the additional powers of the Secretary of State under section 76 to require a company to change its name if the name gives a misleading indication of its activities and is likely to result in harm to the public.

### 76 Misleading indication of activities

**5.76.01**
(1) If in the opinion of the Secretary of State the name by which a company is registered gives so misleading an indication of the nature of its activities as to be likely to cause harm to the public, the Secretary of State may direct the company to change its name.
(2) The direction must be in writing.
(3) The direction must be complied with within a period of six weeks from the date of the direction or such longer period as the Secretary of State may think fit to allow.
This does not apply if an application is duly made to the court under the following provisions.
(4) The company may apply to the court to set the direction aside.
The application must be made within the period of three weeks from the date of the direction.
(5) The court may set the direction aside or confirm it.
If the direction is confirmed, the court shall specify the period within which the direction is to be complied with.
(6) If a company fails to comply with a direction under this section, an offence is committed by—
(a) the company, and
(b) every officer of the company who is in default.
For this purpose a shadow director is treated as an officer of the company.
(7) A person guilty of an offence under this section is liable on summary conviction to a fine not exceeding level 3 on the standard scale and, for continued contravention, a daily default fine not exceeding one-tenth of level 3 on the standard scale.

COMMENCEMENT DATE 1 October 2009[87]

**5.76.02**  This section replaces section 32 of the 1985 Act. It enables the Secretary of State to direct a company to change its name, regardless of how long the company has had the name, if the name gives a misleading indication of the nature of the company's activities, and the public is likely to suffer harm as a result. It will not be a defence that no one has actually been misled or suffered harm as a result of the name. The likelihood of that happening may be sufficient, although evidence of persons being misled or not may be taken into account by the Secretary of State in deciding whether or not to make a section 76 direction.

**5.76.03**  The company must comply with the direction within six weeks, although it does have a right of appeal to the court if it disagrees with the direction. The appeal must be lodged within three weeks from the date of the direction, and the court then has an unfettered discretion to set aside or confirm the direction. If the court confirms the direction, the court will itself set a deadline for compliance.

**5.76.04**  In *Association of Certified Public Accountants of Britain v Secretary of State for Trade and Industry*[88] it was held that in an application under section 32 of the 1985 Act, the predecessor to section 76, the court must form its own view on the evidence presented to it of whether a breach of the section has occurred; it is not the function of the court to review the Secretary of State's decision as such.

**5.76.05**  Section 1198 of the Act contains a parallel provision relating to trading under a misleading name. In a letter to Opposition MPs during the Act's passage through Parliament, the Government confirmed that for an application under that section to succeed, the trader must be carrying on business under the

---

[86]  See s 1121 for a definition of 'officer' in this context. The standard scale for Companies Act offences is prescribed by s 37 of the Criminal Justice Act 1982. The expression 'daily default fine' is defined in s 1125.
[87]  Companies Act 2006 (Commencement No 8, Transitional Provisions and Savings) Order 2008, SI 2008/2860, art 3(e).
[88]  [1997] 2 BCLC 307.

misleading name; a degree of permanence is required, so an isolated transaction will not amount to carrying on business. It was also confirmed that the question about harm to the public falls to be assessed objectively: would a reasonable man or woman consider there is likely to be harm? Although these comments were addressed to section 1198, they may be relevant in the context of this section as the wording of the offence under section 1198(1) is almost identical to that in section 76.

# CHAPTER 5
## CHANGE OF NAME

## 77 Change of name

(1) A company may change its name—                                                                 **5.77.01**
   (a) by special resolution (see section 78), or
   (b) by other means provided for by the company's articles (see section 79).
(2) The name of a company may also be changed—
   (a) by resolution of the directors acting under section 64 (change of name to comply with direction of Secretary of State under that section); or
   (b) by order under section 73 (order of adjudicator following objection to company name).
   (c) on the determination of a new name by the court under section 74 (appeal against decision of company names adjudicator);
   (d) under section 1033 (company's name on restoration to the register).

COMMENCEMENT DATE 1 October 2009[89]

The Act added two additional means of effecting a name change beyond those already provided for in   **5.77.02**
the 1985 Act, and made provision for conditional name change resolutions for the first time. Section 77 replaces section 28(1) of the 1985 Act. The two new methods of effecting a name change are specified in sections 77(1)(b) and 79 (change of name by any means provided for in the company's articles) and 77(2)(b) (as a result of an order of the adjudicator following objection to a company name under section 73).

A change of name does not of itself alter the company's status unless it is done as part of a re-   **5.77.03**
registration under Part 7. Even then, if XYZ Limited becomes XYZ plc, it is not changing its name and the provisions of Chapter 5 of Part 5 will only apply if at the same time as re-registering, the company alters its name other than the indication of its status, eg XYZ Limited becomes XYZ Group plc.

The rules on sensitive words and expressions and the other provisions of Chapters 1 to 4 of Part 5 will   **5.77.04**
apply on a name change in the same way as they apply on incorporation. So, in addition to the filing requirements under Chapter 5, it is also necessary to comply with the consent and other requirements of Chapters 1 to 4 and provide whatever supporting information is required by Companies House for the new name (if any). Any company wishing to change its name to a name which gives rise to consent or other requirements under Parts 1 to 4 should therefore deal with those other requirements and prepare whatever will be necessary for the new name to be registered before the resolution is passed (or filed for registration).

As noted in relation to section 66 above, if two companies are contemplating a name swap, to avoid   **5.77.05**
their name change applications being rejected under the 'same as' rules, they should contact Companies House in advance and warn them about the name swap proposal. Companies House will usually require a letter in support of the two applications to explain what is envisaged. The fee payable on a change of name is currently £10 (£50 for a same-day name change). or if the requisite documents are delivered to the Registrar of Companies by electronic means, £8 and £30 respectively. For companies in the same group, the consent procedure set out in the regulations under section 66 should facilitate the name swap.[90]

On a name change, companies incorporated under the 1985 Act and other statutes should check   **5.77.06**
whether any word or expression used in their company name before the Act came into force which was not previously restricted has been added to the list of sensitive words and expressions in the Company, Limited Liability Partnership and Business Names (Sensitive Words and Expressions) Regulations 2009.[91] This is because the name change will trigger the obligation to obtain the requisite consents for any such word or expression; a company with a name incorporating a word or expression prescribed for the first time by the regulations (ie which was not previously restricted under the Company and

---

[89] Companies Act 2006 (Commencement No 8, Transitional Provisions and Savings) Order 2008, SI 2008/2860, art 3(e).
[90] See para 5.66.05 above.
[91] SI 2009/2615.

Business Names Regulations 1981) will be required to obtain approval for the use of the relevant word or expression only if and when it changes its name following the Regulations coming into force on 1 October 2009 and the new name contains a word or expression requiring approval for some reason under the Regulations.

**5.77.07**   Note also that companies incorporated under the 1985 Act which have not changed their memorandum following the Act coming into force will still have a company name clause in their memorandum. The new-style memorandum under section 8 of the Act does not have a company name clause and by virtue of section 28 of the Act, the company name provision of the memorandum will be deemed to have been incorporated automatically into the company's articles. The transitional provisions dealing with this[92] provide that there is no need for companies incorporated under the 1985 Act and earlier statutes to amend their articles to effect a name change or to file the articles at Companies House upon a name change, but when they change their name for the first time since the Act came into force, the name change resolution will cause the deemed statement of the old company name in the articles to cease to have effect when the name change takes effect. This will not affect substantive provisions about the company's name in the articles, for example, a provision which states that 'the company name shall always include the words 'XYZ', which will remain in place.

### 78  Change of name by special resolution

**5.78.01**     (1)  Where a change of name has been agreed to by a company by special resolution, the company must give notice to the registrar.
This is in addition to the obligation to forward a copy of the resolution to the registrar.
(2)  Where a change of name by special resolution is conditional on the occurrence of an event, the notice given to the registrar of the change must—
(a)  specify that the change is conditional, and
(b)  state whether the event has occurred.
(3)  If the notice states that the event has not occurred—
(a)  the registrar is not required to act under section 80 (registration and issue of new certificate of incorporation) until further notice,
(b)  when the event occurs, the company must give notice to the registrar stating that it has occurred, and
(c)  the registrar may rely on the statement as sufficient evidence of the matters stated in it.

COMMENCEMENT DATE 1 October 2009[93]

**5.78.02**   Alteration by special resolution was the traditional means by which a company would change its name under the 1985 Act. This section replaces section 28(1) of the 1985 Act with substantive amendment, introducing for the first time a procedure for conditional name changes.

**5.78.03**   Section 78(2): This section contemplates that the name change may be conditional on the happening of a specified event, commonly, for example, completion of a particular transaction involving the company. Section 78 sets out a two-stage notification process for conditional resolutions. Firstly, when the resolution is passed, the resolution must be filed with Companies House in the usual way under section 30. In addition, a notice must be filed at Companies House indicating whether the resolution is conditional or not. If it is not, it will be registered straight away and the certificate of incorporation on change of name will be issued.

**5.78.04**   Section 78(3): If the resolution is conditional, the notice must specify whether the event has occurred or not. If it has, and the notice specifies that it has (ie the condition was satisfied during the 15-day filing period prescribed by section 30 of the Act), the name change will be registered straight away and no further action is required. If the notice indicates that the condition has not been satisfied, then section 78(3)(b) requires a further notice to be filed as and when it is satisfied. There is no time limit for filing the second notice, but until it has been filed, the name change will not be effective. Until such time as the second notice has been filed, Companies House will not act on the resolution (section 78(3)(a)). Companies House will not expect any supporting evidence to demonstrate that the condition has been satisfied; the notice under section 78(3)(b) will suffice (section 78(3)(c)).

**5.78.05**   The conditional resolution procedure appears only to apply to a name change effected by special resolution, not by any other means under section 79. Equally, the two-tier filing process does not apply to any type of resolution other than a resolution to change the company's name (but see section 622 on redenomination of share capital).

---

[92] Companies Act 2006 (Consequential Amendments, Transitional Provisions and Savings) Order 2009, SI 2009/1941.
[93] Companies Act 2006 (Commencement No 8, Transitional Provisions and Savings) Order 2008, SI 2008/2860, art 3(e).

## 79 Change of name by means provided for in company's articles

(1) Where a change of a company's name has been made by other means provided for by its articles—   **5.79.01**
  (a) the company must give notice to the registrar, and
  (b) the notice must be accompanied by a statement that the change of name has been made by means provided for by the company's articles.
(2) The registrar may rely on the statement as sufficient evidence of the matters stated in it.

COMMENCEMENT DATE 1 October 2009[94]

This section was a new provision when the Act was passed, and supplements section 77(1)(b), providing that a company may change its name by any means provided for in its articles. So, it would be possible under this section to provide in the articles for a name change to be effected by an ordinary resolution of members, or for the consent of a specific shareholder or holders of a specific class of shares to be obtained, or even a simple board resolution. However, it seems that the name change must be effected by a special resolution if it is to be conditional, since this section 79 does not provide for the two-tier filing process for conditional resolutions.   **5.79.02**

Section 79(1): Whatever procedure is set out in the articles must be followed, and section 79(1) requires the company to provide Companies House with both a notice of the name change and a statement that the change has been made in accordance with the company's articles.   **5.79.03**

Section 79(2): This section provides that the registrar will rely on the integrity of the statement made that the resolution complies with the relevant provisions of the articles; the registrar will not make his own enquiries and there is no need for supporting evidence.   **5.79.04**

## 80 Change of name: registration and issue of new certificate of incorporation

(1) This section applies where the registrar receives notice of a change of a company's name.   **5.80.01**
(2) If the registrar is satisfied—
  (a) that the new name complies with the requirements of this Part, and
  (b) that the requirements of the Companies Acts, and any relevant requirements of the company's articles, with respect to a change of name are complied with,
  the registrar must enter the new name on the register in place of the former name.
(3) On the registration of the new name, the registrar must issue a certificate of incorporation altered to meet the circumstances of the case.

COMMENCEMENT DATE 1 October 2009[95]

This section, which partly replaces section 28(6) of the 1985 Act, provides for the procedures that the registrar must perform before a company's proposed new name is effective.   **5.80.02**

Section 80(2)(a): The registrar must be satisfied that the new name complies with the requirements of the whole of Part 5 before entering the new name on the register. This means that if the application for the new name gives rise to any other obligations under Part 5, for example, consent of the Secretary of State or another body under sections 55, 56, or 57, whether the name correctly indicates the company type or legal form under Chapter 2, or whether the company benefits from an exemption from the requirement to use the word 'limited' or its permitted alternatives, or whether the name falls within the 'same as' or 'too like' regimes in Chapter 3, then the registrar must be satisfied that those obligations have been complied with.   **5.80.03**

Section 80(2)(b): The registrar must also be satisfied that the requirements of the Companies Acts, and any relevant requirements of the company's articles with respect to the name change are complied with. The expression 'Companies Acts' is defined in section 2 of the Act to include, as well as the Act, the Companies (Audit, Investigations and Community Enterprise) Act 2004,[96] what remains of the 1985 Act and the Companies Consolidation (Consequential Provisions) Act 1985.[97]   **5.80.04**

---

[94] Companies Act 2006 (Commencement No 8, Transitional Provisions and Savings) Order 2008, SI 2008/2860, art 3(e).
[95] Companies Act 2006 (Commencement No 8, Transitional Provisions and Savings) Order 2008, SI 2008/2860, art 3(e).
[96] Section 33 of the Companies (Audit, Investigations and Community Enterprise) Act 2004 sets out provisions relating to the name of a Community Interest Company.
[97] There are provisions relating to 'old public companies' (ie those incorporated before 1980) in s 8 of the Companies Consolidation (Consequential Provisions) Act 1985. This Act was repealed with effect from 1 October 2009, but its provisions were re-enacted in regulations; see 1.4.04.

**5.80.05**   As regards the provisions in the articles relating to change of name, Companies House itself is unlikely to check the articles, but will rely on a statement made that the resolution complies with the relevant provisions under section 79(1)(b).

### 81 Change of name: effect

**5.81.01**       (1)  A change of a company's name has effect from the date on which the new certificate of incorporation is issued.
          (2)  The change does not affect any rights or obligations of the company or render defective any legal proceedings by or against it.
          (3)  Any legal proceedings that might have been continued or commenced against it by its former name may be continued or commenced against it by its new name.

COMMENCEMENT DATE  1 October 2009[98]

**5.81.02**   This section replaces section 28(6) in part and section 28(7) of the 1985 Act and provides that the new name will be effective as soon as the certificate of incorporation on change of name is issued. It also provides that the change of name does not affect the company's rights or obligations or legal proceedings by or against it in its previous name. As the company remains the same entity on a change of name, the company number and its legal personality will remain unaffected, and this is confirmed in section 81(2) and (3). Before effecting a name change, companies should consider the timing of the name change and make provision for new company stationery, etc. Although the name change will not be effective until the certificate on incorporation on change of name has been issued, in the case of *Lin Pac Containers (Scotland) v Kelly*[99] it was held that a contract entered into by a company in its new name after the special resolution had been passed but before the certificate of incorporation on change of name had been issued was nonetheless enforceable. In the case of *Osh Kosh B'Gosh Inc v Dan Marbel Inc Limited and another*,[100] due to 'inefficient professional advisers', the change of name was not registered for five years after the resolution had been passed. The argument that the company bearing the new name did not actually exist until the certificate of incorporation on change of name had been issued was rejected by the Court of Appeal, which upheld the principle now outlined in section 81(2) (although the court was looking at its predecessor sections).

## CHAPTER 6
## TRADING DISCLOSURES

### 82 Requirement to disclose company name etc

**5.82.01**       (1)  The Secretary of State may by regulations make provision requiring companies—
               (a)  to display specified information in specified locations,
               (b)  to state specified information in specified descriptions of document or communication, and
               (c)  to provide specified information on request to those they deal with in the course of their business.
          (2)  The regulations—
               (a)  must in every case require disclosure of the name of the company, and
               (b)  may make provision as to the manner in which any specified information is to be displayed, stated or provided.
          (3)  The regulations may provide that, for the purposes of any requirement to disclose a company's name, any variation between a word or words required to be part of the name and a permitted abbreviation of that word or those words (or vice versa) shall be disregarded.
          (4)  In this section 'specified' means specified in the regulations.
          (5)  Regulations under this section are subject to affirmative resolution procedure.

COMMENCEMENT DATE  1 October 2008[101]

**5.82.02**   This section replaces sections 348(1), 349(1), and 351(1) and (2) of the 1985 Act[102] and, insofar as it applies to companies as opposed to other entities, section 4(1) of the Business Names Act 1985. It provides power for the Secretary of State to make regulations requiring every company:

---

[98]  Companies Act 2006 (Commencement No 8, Transitional Provisions and Savings) Order 2008, SI 2008/2860, art 3(e).
[99]  1983 SLT 422.
[100]  [1988] 4 BCC 795.
[101]  Companies Act 2006 (Commencement No 5 etc) Order 2007, SI 2007/3495, art 5.
[102]  As amended by the Companies (Registrar, Languages and Trading Disclosures) Regulations 2006, (SI 2006/3428) with effect from 31 December 2006 implementing the requirements of the First Company Law Directive as it was itself amended by Directive (EC) 2003/58 [2003] OJ L221/13.

- to display a sign with its name and specified other information at specified locations;
- to include its name and specified other information in specified documents and communications; and
- to provide its name and specified other information to those who request it in the course of business (this was a new provision under the Act insofar as it applies to companies doing business under their registered names).

Under the Act, the detail of what must be displayed on which documents and in what form are set out in new regulations made under this section 82 and section 1051. Those regulations (the Companies (Trading Disclosures) Regulations 2008[103] reflect the modernization of the trading disclosures regime which took place in January 2007, whereby the original requirements under the 1985 Act for a company to include its name and other details on documents and other communications sent out by companies were amended to extend to documents sent out electronically such as by email and to a company's websites. **5.82.03**

Otherwise, the regulations largely follow the recommendations of the Company Law Review in modernizing the trading disclosures regime still further.[104] The regulations cover both company names and business names used by companies, whereas the business names provisions in Chapter 2 of Part 41 of the Act deal with disclosure of business names used by individuals and partnerships. Unregistered companies are not generally 'companies' for the purposes of the Act, by virtue of section 1(1) of the Act, although section 1(2)(b) provides that certain provisions may apply to unregistered companies pursuant to regulations made under section 1043. **5.82.04**

The regulations introduced under this section deal with various difficulties which arose under the 1985 Act. For example, under the 1985 Act, the requirement for a company to display its name outside every place in which its business is carried out was problematic for companies whose premises are, for example, a floor in a multi-occupancy skyscraper, or from websites or from the private addresses of the directors. Under the regulations, for multi-occupancy locations (six or more companies), the name must be displayed 'for at least fifteen continuous seconds at least once in every three minutes' (eg on an electronic/scrolling notice board). There is also an exemption for locations primarily used as living accommodation. Despite the attempt to modernize the regime in the 2006 Act, these provisions have attracted criticism from respondents to the Government's Red Tape Challenge, as being difficult to comply with in practice and serving no useful purpose. However, consumer protection and trading standards bodies are keen to preserve the rules as they stand. For more on the Red Tape Challenge see para 5.66.07. **5.82.05**

There are various other exemptions under the regulations, including, in respect of companies in liquidation, administration, or administrative receivership, where the relevant company's registered office or other business location is also a place of the business of the liquidator, administrator, or administrative receiver. **5.82.06**

It was not clear under the old regime whether the requirements for the companies name to appear in all its notices and official publications applied to advertisements. Although advertising is subject to self regulation via the Advertising Standards Authority, which requires advertisements to be decent, legal, and honest, there is no requirement for the advertiser to identify itself. This has not been dealt with in the regulations. However, it may be helpful to refer to the Government's pre-2006 Act consultation on the trading disclosures regime, in which it stated that 'We tend to the view that the Act's requirement for the company to disclose its name should not apply to advertisements which seek to raise awareness, e.g. those on hoardings and stickers, but that they should apply to any advertisement that is a direct attempt to persuade someone to enter into a contract. However this distinction may not be easy to define'. The reference to the 'Act' here was to the 1985 Act but the observation remains relevant since no change was made as regards advertisements in the 2006 Act. **5.82.07**

Under the 1985 Act regime, a company called ABC Limited would be allowed to trade under the name XYZ Limited provided it complied with its obligations to disclose its corporate name. However, the inclusion of the word 'limited' or its Welsh equivalent as part of a trading name that is completely different to the corporate name was potentially misleading. This has been addressed in the Company and Business Names (Miscellaneous Provisions) Regulations 2009, which prohibit a company from using a business name ending with the word 'limited' unless that is also its registered name. **5.82.08**

---

[103] SI 2008/495.
[104] Modern Company Law for a Competitive Economy: Trading Disclosures (available from ⟨http://www.dti.gov. uk/files/file23241.pdf⟩).

**5.82.09**    Section 82(3): The Government's power under section 82(3) to include a provision in the trading disclosures regulations (The Companies (Trading Disclosures) Regulations 2008 ) to allow companies to display an abbreviation of their registered name (e.g. 'Ltd' rather than 'Limited') has not been exercised. This is understood to have been an oversight but it has not yet been corrected.

**5.82.10**    The regulations retain the prohibition originally contained in section 305 of the 1985 Act on companies cherry picking which directors' names appear on company stationery. As before, the option will be to include all or none.

### 83 Civil consequences of failure to make required disclosure

**5.83.01**
    (1)   This section applies to any legal proceedings brought by a company to which section 82 applies (requirement to disclose company name etc) to enforce a right arising out of a contract made in the course of a business in respect of which the company was, at the time the contract was made, in breach of regulations under that section.

    (2)   The proceedings shall be dismissed if the defendant (in Scotland, the defender) to the proceedings shows—

       (a)   that he has a claim against the claimant (pursuer) arising out of the contract that he has been unable to pursue by reason of the latter's breach of the regulations, or

       (b)   that he has suffered some financial loss in connection with the contract by reason of the claimant's (pursuer's) breach of the regulations,

      unless the court before which the proceedings are brought is satisfied that it is just and equitable to permit the proceedings to continue.

    (3)   This section does not affect the right of any person to enforce such rights as he may have against another person in any proceedings brought by that person.

    COMMENCEMENT DATE 1 October 2008[105]

**5.83.02**    This section replaces section 349(4) of the 1985 Act, and insofar as it applied to companies, section 5 of the Business Names Act 1985, and provides for a new civil penalty for breach of section 82 and the regulations made thereunder.

**5.83.03**    Breach of sections 348 to 349 of the 1985 Act carried a criminal penalty for the company or any officer of the company or other person who signed, issued, or authorized the signature or issue of any contract or other document on the company's behalf, which did not comply with the relevant provisions. In addition, under the 1985 Act regime, such a person would also be exposed to personal liability under the relevant contract or document, which the Company Law Review said was unduly harsh,[106] particularly as there was no obligation on the other contracting party to prove that whatever loss it may have suffered resulted from the breach of the trading disclosure requirements rather than from another reason (eg the insolvency of the company). This element of personal liability is removed under the Act, although the company and any officer in default may still be liable to a fine under section 84. (See notes to section 84 on the definition of 'officer in default'.)

**5.83.04**    This section 83 replicates the civil sanction for breach of the requirements of the Business Names Act 1985, and applies it to a breach of the regulations made under sections 82 and 1051 which will cover both the requirements relating to disclosure of the corporate name and the business name. The removal of personal civil liability for the directors, officers, and other persons acting on behalf of a company in breach of its disclosure requirements may also reduce the potential for litigation under this section, since most of the cases on the corresponding provisions of the 1985 Act were under brought section 349(4) of that Act and concerned directors having signed cheques on behalf of their company where the company name was incorrectly stated or not stated in full (see for example *Banque de L'Indochine et de Suez SA v Euroseas Group Finance Co Limited and Others*[107] and *Durham Fancy Goods v Michael Jackson (Fancy Goods) and Another*[108] ). Section 82(3) now provides that abbreviations of the word 'limited or 'public limited company' will be acceptable for these purposes. Section 85 also provides that punctuation, accents, formatting, and upper or lower case will be disregarded in determining whether a company has complied with these provisions.

---

[105]   Companies Act 2006 (Commencement No 5 etc) Order 2007, SI 2007/3495, art 5.

[106]   See Modern Company Law for a Competitive Economy: Trading Disclosures (para 24). Available from ⟨http://www.dti.gov.uk/files/file23241.pdf⟩.

[107]   [1981] 3 All ER 198.

[108]   [1968] 2 All ER 987.

## 84  Criminal consequences of failure to make required disclosures

(1) Regulations under section 82 may provide—                                **5.84.01**

    (a) that where a company fails, without reasonable excuse, to comply with any specified requirement of regulations under that section an offence is committed by—

        (i) the company, and

        (ii) every officer of the company who is in default;

    (b) that a person guilty of such an offence is liable on summary conviction to a fine not exceeding level 3 on the standard scale and, in the case of continued contravention, to a daily default fine not exceeding one-tenth of level 3 on the standard scale.

(2) The regulations may provide that, for the purposes of any provision made under subsection (1), a shadow director of the company is to be treated as an officer of the company.

(3) In subsection (1)(a) 'specified' means specified in the regulations.

COMMENCEMENT DATE  1 October 2008[109]

This section replaces sections 348(2), 349(2) and (3), and 351(5) of the 1985 Act, and, insofar as it   **5.84.02**
applied to companies, part of section 7 of the Business Names Act 1985. It makes it an offence not to comply with the trading disclosure requirements set out in the regulations made under sections 82 and 1051. The regulations referred to in para 5.82.03 above (the Companies (Trading Disclosures) Regulations[110] ) set out the offence. The key change as compared with the 1985 Act is that the offence can only be committed by the company or an officer in default. (Under section 349(4) of the 1985 Act, it was also the case that a person signing a cheque, order or other such document on behalf of an officer of the company could also be liable to a fine if the company's name was not mentioned as required by that Act.) The 1985 Act did not define 'officer in default' as such although it did define 'officer', at section 744, to mean a director, secretary, or manager. Sections 1121 and 1122 of the Act set out a slightly extended definition of 'officer in default' and provisions governing their liability as such. In line with the 1985 Act definition of 'officer', 'officer in default' still includes a director, secretary, or 'manager'. The term 'manager' is not defined elsewhere in the Act (nor was it in the 1985 Act) and the *Hansard* report of the debate on this issue in the House of Lords[111] suggests that a manager will be someone with 'an appropriate degree of influence and seniority within the company and who has responsibility for the particular area in question'. The intention in not defining 'manager' was to take account of the wide variety of management structures, but without a definition as such, a degree of uncertainty will remain as to who will be a 'manager' for these purposes. The section 1121 definition of 'officer in default' then also goes on to include anyone who is treated as an officer for the purposes of the relevant section.

The standard scale for fines for Companies Act offences is prescribed by section 37 of the Criminal   **5.84.03**
Justice Act 1982. The expression 'daily default fine' is defined in section 1125.

## 85  Minor variations in form of name to be left out of account

(1) For the purposes of this Chapter, in considering a company's name no account is to be taken of—   **5.85.01**

    (a) whether upper or lower case characters (or a combination of the two) are used,

    (b) whether diacritical marks or punctuation are present or absent,

    (c) whether the name is in the same format or style as is specified under section 58(1)(b) for the purposes of registration,

    provided there is no real likelihood of names differing only in those respects being taken to be different names.

(2) This does not affect the operation of regulations under section 57(1)(a) permitting only specified characters, diacritical marks or punctuation.

COMMENCEMENT DATE  1 October 2008[112]

This is a new provision introduced under the Act, and permits minor variations between the registered   **5.85.02**
corporate name and the name used in complying with the trading disclosure requirements under this Chapter 6. However, the only permitted differences are those set out in section 85(1)(a)–(c), and the differences must not be so significant as to result in there being a risk of confusion as to whether it is in fact the same company. Under section 85(2), if the regulations to be made under section 57(1)(a) only permit certain characters, accents, or punctuation, those requirements will still prevail as regards the requirements relating to the registered corporate name.

[109] Companies Act 2006 (Commencement No 5 etc) Order 2007, SI 2007/3495, art 5.
[110] SI 2008/495.
[111] See *Hansard*, HL, vol 680, col GC69 (30 March 2006).
[112] Companies Act 2006 (Commencement No 5 etc) Order 2007, SI 2007/3495, art 5.

# 6

## A COMPANY'S REGISTERED OFFICE

## Companies Act 2006

### PART 6

### A COMPANY'S REGISTERED OFFICE

#### *General*

### 86  A company's registered office

A company must at all times have a registered office to which all communications and notices may be addressed.     **6.86.01**

COMMENCEMENT DATE 1 October 2009[1]

This section replaces section 287(1) of the 1985 Act without substantive amendment. As under section 287(1) of that Act, every company is required to have a registered office, which will be the company's address for service (see section 1139) and which will be used by the registrar for official communications. For these purposes, 'company' is defined in section 1(1) of the Act to include any public or private limited company, an unlimited company, a company limited by guarantee, or a Community Interest Company, and will include companies formed under the 1985 Act (and the Northern Ireland equivalent) and earlier statutes as well as the Act itself.     **6.86.02**

There is no registered office clause in the simplified memorandum of association now required in prescribed form under section 8 of the Act. Instead, as part of the initial registration process, section 9(2)(b) states that the company's application for registration must state whether the registered office is England and Wales, Wales, Scotland, or Northern Ireland, and section 9(5) requires a statement of the actual postal address of the first registered office. Subsequent changes to the registered office must be notified to the registrar under section 87 (see below). The location of the registered office when a company is first registered will determine the company's domicile and applicable law—see section 9(6). There are special requirements relating to Welsh companies—see section 88.     **6.86.03**

Note that it is impossible, should a company wish to do so, for a company to stipulate that its registered office will be situated in England (only). 'England and Wales' is the only relevant alternative for a company which intends to be registered, and to remain in, England, reflecting the fact that England and Wales is a single jurisdiction and, save for the limited exceptions for Welsh companies set out in the Act, company law applies equally across England and Wales.     **6.86.04**

The registered office must be a physical location. A PO Box number will not suffice, but it is not necessary for the registered office to be the same as the company's head office or for the company actually to carry on business from the registered office. Some company formation agents and professional advisers provide 'registered office services', ie acceptance of service of notices and other communications, although for the reasons referred to in the notes to section 87(1) below, this is not always advisable.     **6.86.05**

Section 351 of the 1985 Act, which required details of the registered office (along with other prescribed information) to be disclosed on all business letters and all of the forms of the company, was itself amended in December 2006 alongside sections 348 and 349 of the 1985 Act to provide that the relevant     **6.86.06**

---

[1] Companies Act 2006 (Commencement No 8, Transitional Provisions and Savings) Order 2008, SI 2008/2860, art 3(f).

details were to appear not only on physical documents but also on documents and communications sent out in electronic form (for example by email) and on the company's websites. The detailed requirements of sections 348, 349, and 351 are replaced by regulations brought in under sections 82 and 1051 of the Act, which came into force on 1 October 2008 (see para 5.82.03 above).

**6.86.07**   The Department of Business, Innovation and Skills (BIS) launched a consultation in November 2009 on the possibility of introducing a procedure for objecting to a registered office address as there is some evidence that companies are using the address of an unconnected business or private individual as their registered office address. The response to the consultation was generally supportive of the proposals but the changes would require primary legislation. BIS has stated that it will consider making the necessary changes should a suitable legislative vehicle become available, but it is not a priority.

### 87  Change of address of registered office

**6.87.01**   (1)  A company may change the address of its registered office by giving notice to the registrar.
   (2)  The change takes effect upon the notice being registered by the registrar, but until the end of the period of 14 days beginning with the date on which it is registered a person may validly serve any document on the company at the address previously registered.
   (3)  For the purposes of any duty of a company—
      (a)  to keep available for inspection at its registered office any register, index or other document, or
      (b)  to mention the address of its registered office in any document,
      a company that has given notice to the registrar of a change in the address of its registered office may act on the change as from such date, not more than 14 days after the notice is given, as it may determine.
   (4)  Where a company unavoidably ceases to perform at its registered office any such duty as is mentioned in subsection (3)(a) in circumstances in which it was not practicable to give prior notice to the registrar of a change in the address of its registered office, but—
      (a)  resumes performance of that duty at other premises as soon as practicable, and
      (b)  gives notice accordingly to the registrar of a change in the situation of its registered office within 14 days of doing so,
      it is not to be treated as having failed to comply with that duty.

   COMMENCEMENT DATE  1 October 2009[2]

**6.87.02**   This section replaces 287(3), (4), (5), and (6) of the 1985 Act, and retains the procedure for a change of registered office provided both the old and new addresses are within the same part of the UK, ie England and Wales, Scotland, Northern Ireland, or, in the case of a Welsh company (see section 88), Wales only. The inclusion here of the reference to Northern Ireland indicates that Northern Irish companies are, for the first time under the Act, covered by the same statute as companies incorporated in England and Wales, Wales, or Scotland. The Act also repeals the Companies Act 1985 (Northern Ireland) Order 1986 and related legislation which is replaced by relevant provisions of the Act (see Schedule 16 to the Act).

**6.87.03**   Section 87(1): This section requires notice to be given by the company itself (acting by a director or secretary who will sign the relevant form—Companies House form AD01). So, if a company changes its registered office and fails to notify the registrar of the change, mail will still be delivered to the old registered office. Once it becomes apparent to the new occupier that its predecessor has failed to notify the change, as a third party, the new occupier cannot formally notify the registrar of the change, even if it knows the new registered office address of the previous occupants. For this reason, some company formation agents and professional advisers may be reluctant to allow their address to be used as the registered office for a client, as their address will continue to be used for service even after they have lost touch with the client if the client changes its registered office without notifying the registrar.

**6.87.04**   If a company fails to notify the registrar of any change of registered office under this section, there is no criminal sanction as such, but there may be criminal sanctions for breach of other sections of the Act requiring registers and other documents to be available for inspection at the registered office (see, for example, sections 114 and 743 relating to the registers of members and debenture holders, both of which carry criminal penalties for breach). Also, Companies House will only ever use the registered office as notified to it for communications with the company. So, if a company fails to notify the change, reminders relating to filing the annual return, etc will be sent to the old registered office and the company could incur penalties for missing filing deadlines, and, in the worst case, the company could be struck off for failing to make the necessary returns to Companies House.

---

[2] Companies Act 2006 (Commencement No 8, Transitional Provisions and Savings) Order 2008, SI 2008/ 2860, art 3(f).

The registrar is obliged under section 1064 to publicize the change of a company's registered office in **6.87.05** the Gazette and/or by any other means prescribed in regulations to be made under section 1116 which have yet to be published.

Section 87(2): The change of registered office does not take effect until the new address is on the public **6.87.06** record, to ensure there cannot be any period during which the company does not have an effective service address. This subsection provides for a 14-day grace period during which both the old and the new registered office addresses will be effective for service of documents on the company. The company should therefore arrange for collection or forwarding of any notices or other correspondence delivered to the old registered office during this 14-day period.

Section 87(3): This subsection allows the company, during the same 14-day period, to make the **6.87.07** necessary alterations to its business letters, etc, if they have not already been made prior to the change of registered office, and to transfer documents required to be kept at the registered office under various provisions of the Act from the old to the new office. See, for example, sections 114 and 743 relating to the registers of members and debenture holders, section 358 (resolutions and meetings), section 892 (copies of charges), and section 228(2) (copies of directors' service contracts).[3]

Section 87(4): This subsection covers the possibility of an unplanned change in registered office, for **6.87.08** example, in the event of a fire. It allows the company a period of 14 days in the event of such an unplanned change in which to notify the registrar of the change of registered office. This grace period will also allow the company time to transfer the company's records and other documents to the new registered office without being in breach of section 87(3)(a) and the other provisions of the Act relating to inspection of registers and other documents at the registered office.[4]

Section 87 deals only with a change of registered office within the same domicile. Once a company is **6.87.09** registered in one domicile, it cannot redomicile simply by changing its registered office, either within the UK or internationally. So, a company which stated in its application for registration under section 9 of the Act that its registered office would be in 'England and Wales' must have a registered office in either England or Wales. In the case of *Re Baby Moon (UK) Limited*,[5] the court held that a company registered in England cannot have a registered office situated in Scotland. However, a company registered in 'England and Wales' could change its registered office from England to Wales or vice versa. A Welsh company (within the meaning set out in section 88) can now move its registered office to England, provided it has passed the necessary special resolution to amend the register under section 88(3) (see notes to section 88 below).

The Company Law Review recommended that the Act should contain a procedure facilitating redo- **6.87.10** miciliation of UK companies between jurisdictions in the UK.[6] A draft provision appeared in early versions of the Companies Bill but this proposal was dropped subsequently.

UK company law does not currently make any provision for companies to redomicile overseas, **6.87.11** although it is thought that it would be possible with a private Act of Parliament. This will be impracticable for most companies, although the Transas Group used this method to redomicile five subsidiary companies incorporated under the 1985 Act to the Republic of Ireland. A more realistic option for most companies would be either to form a separate company in the other jurisdiction and wind up the original company, or effect a takeover, either by way of offer or by scheme of arrangement, of another company in the chosen jurisdiction, or a simple share-for-share exchange under a private contract.

To the disappointment of those seeking a straightforward mechanism for the redomicilation of **6.87.12** companies within the EU, the case of *R v HM Treasury ex p Daily Mail*[7] confirmed that the freedom of movement provisions of the Treaty of Rome did not permit re-domiciliation of corporate entities within the EU, under the then-existing EU law framework. The *Daily Mail* decision came under scrutiny in the more recent Cartesio case,[8] in which a Hungarian Limited Partnership sought to transfer its HQ to Italy. The Advocate General opined in that case that *Daily Mail* was not good law and contrary to the freedom of establishment principles outlined in the *Centros* case, but in the end, the ECJ followed the *Daily Mail* decision in the *Cartesio* case, so the position remained unchanged. However, in March 2012, the European Commission launched a consultation on the future of European

---

[3] From 1 October 2009, the full list of documents required to be kept at the registered office is contained in the Companies (Company Records) Regulations 2008, SI 2008/3006.

[4] Eg those imposed by regulations made under s 82 (requirement to disclose company name, etc).

[5] [1985] PCC 103.

[6] See Modern Company Law: Final Report, paras 14.13–14.17.

[7] [1989] 1 All ER 328.

[8] *Cartesio Oktato es Szolgaltato bt* (Case C-210/06).

Company law which again raised the possibility of EU legislation to facilitate a cross-border transfer of registered office. This followed the Commission's decision in 2009 to shelve the proposed Fourteenth Company Law Directive which would have permitted the transfer of registered office between EU Member States.[9] The responses to the March 2012 consultation were overwhelmingly in favour of such a facility. The decision of the EC is still awaited. Meanwhile, European law does have provision for the transfer of domicile within the EU under Article 8 of the European Company Statute,[10] but this provision only applies to SEs (Societas Europaea). It would, therefore, be possible for a UK company to form an SE in order to move jurisdiction within the EU. In the UK, BIS (then the DTI) consulted on implementation of the proposed fourteenth Directive in March 2005 and concluded that (if it ever becomes a reality) there would be relatively little appetite for using the procedure among UK companies, particularly in view of the employee participation rules which apply in many other European jurisdictions.

## *Welsh companies*

### 88   Welsh companies

**6.88.01**   (1) In the Companies Acts a 'Welsh company' means a company as to which it is stated in the register that its registered office is to be situated in Wales.

(2) A company—
   (a) whose registered office is in Wales, and
   (b) as to which it is stated in the register that its registered office is to be situated in England and Wales, may by special resolution require the register to be amended so that it states that the company's registered office is to be situated in Wales.

(3) A company—
   (a) whose registered office is in Wales, and
   (b) as to which it is stated in the register that its registered office is to be situated in Wales,
may by special resolution require the register to be amended so that it states that the company's registered office is to be situated in England and Wales.

(4) Where a company passes a resolution under this section it must give notice to the registrar, who shall—
   (a) amend the register accordingly, and
   (b) issue a new certificate of incorporation altered to meet the circumstances of the case.

COMMENCEMENT DATE 1 October 2009[11]

**6.88.02**   This provision is new under the Act and provides a definition of a Welsh company, namely a company as to which it is stated in the register that its registered office is to be situated in Wales (rather than, for example, 'England and Wales'). Such a statement may be made in the original application for registration under section 9(2)(b) of the Act.

**6.88.03**   Section 88(2): In addition, a company may migrate from England to Wales as long as it was originally registered in England and Wales and passes a special resolution requiring the register to be amended so that it states that the company's registered office is to be situated in Wales only.

**6.88.04**   Section 88(3): This subsection (3) provides a mechanism whereby a company can cease to be a Welsh company (ie so that the register states that its registered office is to be situated in 'England and Wales' rather than Wales alone). This is a new procedure. Under the 1985 Act, a company incorporated in Wales with a statement in its memorandum that its registered office is to be situated in Wales was not permitted to change the registered office provision to permit a registered office anywhere in England or Wales.

**6.88.05**   Having become or having been incorporated as a Welsh company, the company may use the Welsh equivalent of 'limited' and 'public limited company' in its company name[12] and may deliver documents to the registrar in Welsh.[13] These exceptions reflect the requirements of the Welsh Language Act 1993.

**6.88.06**   Since the new-style memorandum of association under the Act does not contain a registered office provision, no change will be made to the memorandum when a company passes a special resolution under subsections (2) or (3), and so becomes or ceases to be a Welsh company.

---

[9]  See ⟨http://ec.europa.eu/internal_market/company/seat-transfer/index_en.htm⟩.

[10]  Council Regulation (EC) No 2157/2001 of 8 October 2001.

[11]  Companies Act 2006 (Commencement No 8, Transitional Provisions and Savings) Order 2008, SI 2008/2860, art 3(f).

[12]  See ss 58 and 59 of the Act.

[13]  See s 1104 of the Act.

Section 88(4): Upon passing a special resolution under this section, the company must notify Compa-    **6.88.07**
nies House using form AD05 and the registrar will issue a new certificate of incorporation to reflect the
company's new status. If the registered office *address* is also changed, form AD01 must also be
completed and filed at Companies House.

# 7

# RE-REGISTRATION AS A MEANS OF ALTERING A COMPANY'S STATUS

---

## Companies Act 2006

### PART 7

### RE-REGISTRATION AS A MEANS OF ALTERING A COMPANY'S STATUS

### *Introductory*

### 89 Alteration of status by re-registration

A company may by re-registration under this Part alter its status—                    **7.89.01**

(a)  from a private company to a public company (see sections 90 to 96);
(b)  from a public company to a private company (see sections 97 to 101);
(c)  from a private limited company to an unlimited company (see sections 102 to 104);
(d)  from an unlimited private company to a limited company (see sections 105 to 108);
(e)  from a public company to an unlimited private company (see sections 109 to 111).

COMMENCEMENT DATE 1 October 2009[1]

This section, which was a new section when the Act came into force, sets out the various ways provided    **7.89.02**
for in the Act by which a company may alter its status. The provisions of sections 43 to 55 of the
Companies Act 1985, which contained the previous provisions on re-registration and are replaced by
the provisions in Part 7, are largely replicated with one significant change. Under the 1985 Act regime

---

[1] Companies Act 2006 (Commencement No 8, Transitional Provisions and Savings) Order 2008, SI 2008/
2860, art 3(g).

it was not possible for a public company to re-register as an unlimited private company without first having to re-register as a private limited company. This is now possible under sections 109 to 111, implementing a recommendation of the Company Law Review.[2] However, the Company Law Review recommendation that the Act should also provide for a means of re-registering a company limited by guarantee as a company limited by shares and vice versa was not taken up. This remains the only conceivable conversion process which is not now provided for under the Act (apart from successive switches between limited and unlimited status, which are also restricted under this Part 7, as they were under the 1985 Act).

**7.89.03**   In an Australian case on the equivalent provisions under Australian law[3] the court held that there was no basis for implying a power to convert where there is no such power under statute, so it should be assumed that in the absence of an express power in the Act to convert from a company limited by shares to a company limited by guarantee and vice versa, it is not possible to do so without winding up and incorporating a new company.

**7.89.04**   The new mechanism for re-registering a public company as an unlimited private company requires the consent of all members and is, therefore, unlikely to be used very often, by listed companies at least, for whom a unanimous shareholder consent is impractical.

## Private company becoming public

### 90  Re-registration of private company as public

**7.90.01**   (1) A private company (whether limited or unlimited) may be re-registered as a public company limited by shares if—
    (a) a special resolution that it should be so re-registered is passed,
    (b) the conditions specified below are met, and
    (c) an application for re-registration is delivered to the registrar in accordance with section 94, together with—
        (i)  the other documents required by that section, and
        (ii) a statement of compliance.
(2) The conditions are—
    (a) that the company has a share capital;
    (b) that the requirements of section 91 are met as regards its share capital;
    (c) that the requirements of section 92 are met as regards its net assets;
    (d) if section 93 applies (recent allotment of shares for non-cash consideration), that the requirements of that section are met; and
    (e) that the company has not previously been re-registered as unlimited.
(3) The company must make such changes—
    (a) in its name, and
    (b) in its articles,
as are necessary in connection with its becoming a public company.
(4) If the company is unlimited it must also make such changes in its articles as are necessary in connection with its becoming a company limited by shares.

COMMENCEMENT DATE  1 October 2009[4]

**7.90.02**   This section replaces section 43(1)(a) and (2), and section 48 of the 1985 Act, and enables a private company to re-register as a public company provided certain conditions, set out in section 90(2) to (4), are met. The conditions are broadly similar to the conditions which applied to the 1985 Act re-registration regime, which in turn, reflected the procedure prescribed by the Second Company Law Directive[5] for incorporation of a public company. However, it remains the case under the Act that a public company incorporated as such must obtain a trading certificate, under section 761 (which replaced section 117 of the 1985 Act), whereas a company which becomes a public company by virtue of re-registration does not (see section 761(a)). This is because the conditions as to the company's share capital which are inherent in the trading certificate requirements must be satisfied as part of the re-registration process in any event. For this reason, under the 1985 Act regime, often a public company started out life as a private company and re-registered, to avoid the trading certificate requirements, rather than incorporating as a public company at the outset, and this is likely to continue under the Act.

---

  [2] See Company Law Review Final Report, para 11.16.
  [3] *Peter Grenfell Windsor v The National Mutual Life Association of Australasia Ltd* (1992) 7 ASCR 210, (1992) 106 ALR 282.
  [4] Companies Act 2006 (Commencement No 8, Transitional Provisions and Savings) Order 2008, SI 2008/2860, art 3(g).
  [5] 77/91/EEC.

Section 90(1): As under the 1985 Act, a private company (now defined in section 4(1) as a 'company' **7.90.03** which is not a 'public company'[6]) can re-register as a public company. For these purposes, 'company' includes a limited or unlimited company (for more on unlimited companies, see below), but does not include a company limited by guarantee by virtue of condition 90(2)(a), unless it is a company limited by guarantee with a share capital. Such companies are rare since it has not been possible to incorporate a company limited by guarantee with a share capital since the Companies Act 1980 came into force in December 1980.

Schedule 1 para 3 of the Companies Act 2006 (Consequential Amendments and Transitional Provi- **7.90.04** sions) Order 2011[7] provides that references in this section to a 'private company" include an 'old public company' (i.e. one incorporated before 22 December 1980), thus permitting such a company to re-register as a 2006 Act public company. The special resolution of the company required by section 90(1)(a) shall, in the case of an old public company, be read as a reference to a resolution of the directors, which must be filed at Companies House. Schedule 1 para 4 of that Order provides that an old public company may by special resolution decide not to be re-registered as a public company and, if no objection under section 98 is received to such special resolution, the company will be re-registered as a private company instead.

The special resolution required under section 90(1)(a) must comply with section 283 and must be filed **7.90.05** at Companies House within 15 days[8]. The resolution may be passed in writing under the requirements set out in Chapter 2 of Part 13 and under the new written resolution procedure under the Act, unanimity is no longer required. The 75 per cent majority required is the same as if the resolution were to be passed at a meeting. The special resolution will usually be filed at Companies House at the same time as the application for re-registration is submitted[9], but the application may be submitted later as there is no cut-off for filing the application once the resolution has been passed[10]. However, the balance sheet which accompanies the application must, under section 92(1)(a), be no more than seven months old when the application is submitted.

The statement of compliance required under section 90(1)(c)(ii) is, pursuant to section 94(3), a **7.90.06** statement that the requirements of Part 7 as to re-registration as a public company have been complied with. The statement replaces the 1985 Act requirement for a statutory declaration (in line with the rest of the Act which replaces statutory declarations generally with statements of compliance).

The statement of compliance (which is in standard form in the relevant Companies House form RR01) **7.90.07** must be made by a director, the secretary (if there is one), or by another person authorized under section 270 or 274 of the Act. As with all documents delivered to the registrar, it will be an offence under section 1112 to make a false statement of compliance.

Section 90(2)(e): This subsection retains the requirement previously contained in section 43(1) of the **7.90.08** 1985 Act that an unlimited company can only re-register as a public company if it was originally incorporated as an unlimited company, not if it was re-registered as an unlimited company previously. This limitation is designed to prevent companies switching between limited and unlimited status (perhaps to take temporary advantage of the fact that some capital maintenance and other restrictions do not apply to unlimited companies. For more on this, see notes to section 102 below).

Section 90(3)(a): Under section 58, the name of a public company must end with 'p.l.c.' or 'public **7.90.09** limited company'[11] or the Welsh equivalents for a Welsh company. A change of name which merely replaces 'limited' with 'p.l.c.' does not constitute a change of name for the purposes of Chapter 5 of Part 5. Any more substantive change to the name itself, other than to the indication of legal status, must comply with Chapter 5 of Part 5 and will require a special resolution under section 78 or whatever other procedure is required to be followed under section 79. If a special resolution is needed for a substantive change to the name, it could be wrapped up in a single resolution to re-register the company.

Section 90(3)(b): Few private companies' articles will be suitable for a public company, so most **7.90.10** companies will adopt new articles on re-registration as a public company. There are model articles for public companies,[12] but these will only apply if and to the extent specifically adopted by the company, and if the company's shares are to be listed following re-registration, bespoke articles will almost certainly be needed. If the company does not register any articles, the model articles will apply by

---

[6] But see para 7.90.04.
[7] SI 2011/1265.
[8] See ss 29–30.
[9] Under s 94.
[10] See s 94(2)(a).
[11] For further detail, see the notes to s 58.
[12] See s 19.

default under section 20. The adoption of new articles will also require a special resolution,[13] but the resolution could also form part of the re-registration resolution (along with any name change resolution which may be required (see notes to section 90(3)(a) above)). A copy of the new or amended articles must accompany the application for re-registration under section 94(2)(b).

**7.90.11**    Section 90(4): As noted in this subsection, if an unlimited company is re-registering as a public company limited by shares, not only will it need to alter its articles to make them better suited to its public company status, it will also have to reflect in its articles the move from unlimited to limited status. If the company previously had a share capital as an unlimited company, it may already have share capital provisions in its articles. However, unlimited companies often have provisions dealing with alterations of share capital which will be inappropriate for a public company limited by shares (see Table E[14] for example).

**7.90.12**    Note that there is no longer any requirement under the Act to alter the company's memorandum as part of the re-registration procedure. Under the Act,[15] the memorandum of association is merely a snapshot document prepared and filed upon incorporation. There is no share capital or name provision as was previously required under the 1985 Act, so no changes are necessary upon re-registration.

## 91  Requirements as to share capital

**7.91.01**
(1) The following requirements must be met at the time the special resolution is passed that the company should be re-registered as a public company—
  (a) the nominal value of the company's allotted share capital must be not less than the authorised minimum;
  (b) each of the company's allotted shares must be paid up at least as to one-quarter of the nominal value of that share and the whole of any premium on it;
  (c) if any shares in the company or any premium on them have been fully or partly paid up by an undertaking given by any person that he or another should do work or perform services (whether for the company or any other person), the undertaking must have been performed or otherwise discharged;
  (d) if shares have been allotted as fully or partly paid up as to their nominal value or any premium on them otherwise than in cash, and the consideration for the allotment consists of or includes an undertaking to the company (other than one to which paragraph (c) applies), then either—
    (i) the undertaking must have been performed or otherwise discharged, or
    (ii) there must be a contract between the company and some person pursuant to which the undertaking is to be performed within five years from the time the special resolution is passed.
(2) For the purpose of determining whether the requirements in subsection (1)(b), (c) and (d) are met, the following may be disregarded—
  (a) shares allotted—
    (i) before 22nd June 1982 in the case of a company then registered in Great Britain, or
    (ii) before 31st December 1984 in the case of a company then registered in Northern Ireland;
  (b) shares allotted in pursuance of an employees' share scheme by reason of which the company would, but for this subsection, be precluded under subsection (1)(b) (but not otherwise) from being re-registered as a public company.
(3) No more than one-tenth of the nominal value of the company's allotted share capital is to be disregarded under subsection (2)(a).
  For this purpose the allotted share capital is treated as not including shares disregarded under subsection (2)(b).
(4) Shares disregarded under subsection (2) are treated as not forming part of the allotted share capital for the purposes of subsection (1)(a).
(5) A company must not be re-registered as a public company if it appears to the registrar that—
  (a) the company has resolved to reduce its share capital,
  (b) the reduction—
    (i) is made under section 626 (reduction in connection with redenomination of share capital),
    (ii) is supported by a solvency statement in accordance with section 643, or
    (iii) has been confirmed by an order of the court under section 648, and

---

[13] See s 21.
[14] Companies (Tables A to F) Regulations 1985, SI 1985/805. The Government did not prescribe model articles for unlimited companies in the Companies (Model Articles) Regulations 2008, SI 2008/3229, pursuant to s 19 of the Act, on the basis that unlimited companies could easily adapt the model articles for public or private companies. Table E remains in force.
[15] See s 8.

(c)  the effect of the reduction is, or will be, that the nominal value of the company's allotted share capital is below the authorised minimum.

COMMENCEMENT DATE  1 October 2009[16]

This section replaces sections 45 and 47(3) of the 1985 Act, and sets out the share capital requirements    **7.91.02**
for a private company proposing to re-register as a public company. The requirements of this section are substantially the same as those set out in the corresponding provisions of the 1985 Act and, as noted in the commentary to section 90 above, reflect the share capital requirements for a company incorporating as a public company which are, in turn, derived from the Second Company Law Directive.[17]

Section 91(1)(a): The authorized minimum is set out in section 763 and is currently[18] £50,000, or the    **7.91.03**
euro equivalent as prescribed by Order from time to time. The Companies (Authorised Minimum) Regulations 2009,[19] which came into force on 1 October 2009, prescribe the euro equivalent at €57,100. Note that the share capital must meet the authorized minimum criterion when the special resolution is passed and not when the application is submitted, if later.

Section 91(1)(b): This subsection requires the share capital to be paid up as to at least a quarter,[20] in line    **7.91.04**
with the general requirements for public companies.

Section 91(1)(c): This subsection reflects the general prohibition on public company shares being paid    **7.91.05**
up as consideration for an undertaking to do work or perform services.[21]

Section 91(1)(d): This subsection reflects the general prohibition on long-term undertakings being    **7.91.06**
given as consideration for the allotment of public company shares.[22]

Section 91(2)–(4): In determining whether the conditions set out in section 91(1)(b) to (d) are met, it    **7.91.07**
is permissible to disregard up to one tenth of the nominal value of the allotted share capital, if any of those shares were allotted prior to 22 June 1982[23] or were allotted pursuant to an 'employees' share scheme'[24] and are not paid up as to a quarter, or the premium (if any) on which remains unpaid. However, any shares so disregarded will also be excluded from the calculation of the authorized minimum for the purposes of section 91(1)(a). These exclusions are the same as those previously contained in sections 45(5) and (6) of the 1985 Act.

Section 91(5): This subsection replaced section 47(3) of the 1985 Act, and updated that section to    **7.91.08**
reflect the two new mechanisms under the Act for the reduction of capital, ie a reduction by means of a solvency statement under section 643, in the case of a private company, or a reduction in connection with a re-denomination of shares under section 626. This subsection 91(5) mirrors the effect of section 650, which sets out the consequences of a public company reducing its capital below the authorized minimum.

## 92  Requirements as to net assets

(1)  A company applying to re-register as a public company must obtain—    **7.92.01**
  (a)  a balance sheet prepared as at a date not more than seven months before the date on which the application is delivered to the registrar,
  (b)  an unqualified report by the company's auditor on that balance sheet, and
  (c)  a written statement by the company's auditor that in his opinion at the balance sheet date the amount of the company's net assets was not less than the aggregate of its called-up share capital and undistributable reserves.
(2)  Between the balance sheet date and the date on which the application for re-registration is delivered to the registrar, there must be no change in the company's financial position that results in the amount of its net assets becoming less than the aggregate of its called-up share capital and undistributable reserves.
(3)  In subsection (1)(b) an 'unqualified report' means—
  (a)  if the balance sheet was prepared for a financial year of the company, a report stating without material qualification the auditor's opinion that the balance sheet has been properly prepared in accordance with the requirements of this Act;

---

[16]  Companies Act 2006 (Commencement No 8, Transitional Provisions and Savings) Order 2008, SI 2008/2860, art 3(g).
[17]  77/91/EEC.
[18]  As at June 2011.
[19]  SI 2009/2424, replacing SI 2008/729 under which the amount was €65,600.
[20]  See s 586.
[21]  See s 585.
[22]  See s 587.
[23]  Or 31 December 1984, for Northern Ireland incorporated companies.
[24]  Defined in s 1166.

(b) if the balance sheet was not prepared for a financial year of the company, a report stating without material qualification the auditor's opinion that the balance sheet has been properly prepared in accordance with the provisions of this Act which would have applied if it had been prepared for a financial year of the company.

(4) For the purposes of an auditor's report on a balance sheet that was not prepared for a financial year of the company, the provisions of this Act apply with such modifications as are necessary by reason of that fact.

(5) For the purposes of subsection (3) a qualification is material unless the auditor states in his report that the matter giving rise to the qualification is not material for the purpose of determining (by reference to the company's balance sheet) whether at the balance sheet date the amount of the company's net assets was not less than the aggregate of its called-up share capital and undistributable reserves.

(6) In this Part 'net assets' and 'undistributable reserves' have the same meaning as in section 831 (net asset restriction on distributions by public companies).

COMMENCEMENT DATE 1 October 2009[25]

**7.92.02** This section replaces section 43(3)(b) to (c) and (4) and section 46 of the 1985 Act, making no substantive changes to those provisions. In particular, the requirements as to net assets for a public company, which apply on re-registration, are unchanged as compared with the 1985 Act.

**7.92.03** Section 92(1)(a): The balance sheet can be the one prepared for the purposes of the most recent year-end audit, but if that balance sheet was prepared as at a date which is more than seven months before the date on which the application is to be delivered to the registrar, a new balance sheet will need to be prepared specifically for the re-registration (sections 92(3)(b) and (4) deal with the auditors' report on a balance sheet prepared otherwise than for the purposes of the year-end audit).

**7.92.04** Section 92(1)(b): The unqualified report is defined in section 92(3).

**7.92.05** Section 92(1)(c): As explained in section 92(6), the expressions 'net assets' and 'undistributable reserves' are as defined in section 831 (net asset restriction on distributions by public companies). The expression 'called-up share capital' is defined in section 547.

**7.92.06** Section 92(2): The auditors' report is not required to cover the position since the balance sheet date, but compliance with this section will be part of a statement of compliance made pursuant to section 90(1)(c) above.

**7.92.07** Section 92(3): Note that whether or not a qualification is 'material' is defined further in section 92(5).

### 93 Recent allotment of shares for non-cash consideration

**7.93.01**    (1) This section applies where—

(a) shares are allotted by the company in the period between the date as at which the balance sheet required by section 92 is prepared and the passing of the resolution that the company should re-register as a public company, and

(b) the shares are allotted as fully or partly paid up as to their nominal value or any premium on them otherwise than in cash.

(2) The registrar shall not entertain an application by the company for re-registration as a public company unless—

(a) the requirements of section 593(1)(a) and (b) have been complied with (independent valuation of non-cash consideration; valuer's report to company not more than six months before allotment), or

(b) the allotment is in connection with—

(i) a share exchange (see subsections (3) to (5) below), or

(ii) a proposed merger with another company (see subsection (6) below).

(3) An allotment is in connection with a share exchange if—

(a) the shares are allotted in connection with an arrangement under which the whole or part of the consideration for the shares allotted is provided by—

(i) the transfer to the company allotting the shares of shares (or shares of a particular class) in another company, or

(ii) the cancellation of shares (or shares of a particular class) in another company; and

(b) the allotment is open to all the holders of the shares of the other company in question (or, where the arrangement applies only to shares of a particular class, to all the holders of the company's shares of that class) to take part in the arrangement in connection with which the shares are allotted.

---

[25] Companies Act 2006 (Commencement No 8, Transitional Provisions and Savings) Order 2008, SI 2008/2860, art 3(g).

(4) In determining whether a person is a holder of shares for the purposes of subsection (3), there shall be disregarded—

   (a) shares held by, or by a nominee of, the company allotting the shares;

   (b) shares held by, or by a nominee of—

      (i) the holding company of the company allotting the shares,

      (ii) a subsidiary of the company allotting the shares, or

      (iii) a subsidiary of the holding company of the company allotting the shares.

(5) It is immaterial, for the purposes of deciding whether an allotment is in connection with a share exchange, whether or not the arrangement in connection with which the shares are allotted involves the issue to the company allotting the shares of shares (or shares of a particular class) in the other company.

(6) There is a proposed merger with another company if one of the companies concerned proposes to acquire all the assets and liabilities of the other in exchange for the issue of its shares or other securities to shareholders of the other (whether or not accompanied by a cash payment). 'Another company' includes any body corporate.

(7) For the purposes of this section—

   (a) the consideration for an allotment does not include any amount standing to the credit of any of the company's reserve accounts, or of its profit and loss account, that has been applied in paying up (to any extent) any of the shares allotted or any premium on those shares; and

   (b) 'arrangement' means any agreement, scheme or arrangement, including an arrangement sanctioned in accordance with—

      (i) Part 26 of this Act (arrangements and reconstructions), or

      (ii) section 110 of the Insolvency Act 1986 (c. 45) or Article 96 of the Insolvency (Northern Ireland) Order 1989 (S.I. 1989/2405 (N.I. 19)) (liquidator in winding up accepting shares as consideration for sale of company's property).

Commencement Date  1 October 2009[26]

This section replaces section 44 of the 1985 Act without substantive change. Where there has been an allotment of shares for non-cash consideration between the date of the balance sheet required under section 92 and the date of the resolution to re-register as a public company, the company must demonstrate that the consideration for the allotment has been valued in accordance with sections 598 to 602 (which replace sections 103 to 108 of the 1985 Act).  **7.93.02**

This provision (as with its predecessor, section 44 of the 1985 Act) is designed to prevent a company circumventing the requirements in section 593 for a valuation of non-cash consideration received for the allotment of shares in the company by allotting the shares whilst still a private company but shortly before the company re-registers as a public company. The valuation must have been carried out no more than six months prior to the allotment (section 93(2)(a)). However, the valuation requirements do not apply to shares allotted as part of a bonus or capitalization issue.[27]  **7.93.03**

Section 603 applies the valuation provisions in sections 598 to 602 in the context of a company re-registering (with necessary adaptations). Section 603(b) replicates the effect of section 116 of the 1985 Act, ie if the company allots shares for non-cash consideration between the date on which a resolution to re-register is passed under section 90 and the date of the actual re-registration (when the certificate is issued under section 96), the valuation requirements of sections 598 to 602 will still apply even though section 93(1) and (2) only appears to require the valuation for an allotment carried out between the balance sheet date and the date of the resolution.  **7.93.04**

Section 93(1)(b): For more on the meaning of 'allotted', see section 546(1)(b) and (2). Whether or not the consideration is deemed to be cash will be determined by section 583.  **7.93.05**

Section 93(2)(b)(i) and (ii): No valuation is required if the allotment is made in connection with a share-for-share exchange or merger. These provisions are substantively the same as the sections they replaced, section 44(5) to (7) of the 1985 Act, but have been reworded in an attempt to make the requirements clearer.  **7.93.06**

Section 93(3): 'Class of shares' is defined in section 629.  **7.93.07**

Section 93(5): To qualify as a share-for-share exchange for these purposes, it is not necessary for the shares to be issued directly to the company in question. The shares could be issued to another group company and would still qualify under these provisions.  **7.93.08**

---

[26] Companies Act 2006 (Commencement No 8, Transitional Provisions and Savings) Order 2008, SI 2008/2860, art 3(g).

[27] See s 93(7)(a).

**7.93.09**    Section 93(6): Note that 'another company' includes any body corporate.[28]

**7.93.10**    Section 93(7): Note the wide definition of 'arrangement' for these purposes. It encompasses not only a scheme of arrangement under section 110 of the Insolvency Act 1986, or Part 26 of the Act, but any other arrangement provided it satisfies the criteria set out in section 93(3) to (6).

### 94 Application and accompanying documents

**7.94.01**
(1) An application for re-registration as a public company must contain—
   (a) a statement of the company's proposed name on re-registration; and
   (b) a statement of the company's proposed secretary (see section 95).
(2) The application must be accompanied by—
   (a) a copy of the special resolution that the company should re-register as a public company (unless a copy has already been forwarded to the registrar under Chapter 3 of Part 3);
   (b) a copy of the company's articles as proposed to be amended;
   (c) a copy of the balance sheet and other documents referred to in section 92(1); and
   (d) if section 93 applies (recent allotment of shares for non-cash consideration), a copy of the valuation report (if any) under subsection (2)(a) of that section.
(3) The statement of compliance required to be delivered together with the application is a statement that the requirements of this Part as to re-registration as a public company have been complied with.
(4) The registrar may accept the statement of compliance as sufficient evidence that the company is entitled to be re-registered as a public company.

COMMENCEMENT DATE 1 October 2009[29]

**7.94.02**    This section replaces section 43(1)(b), (2)(a), (3)(a) and (e), and (3A) of the 1985 Act, and prescribes the contents of the application for re-registration.

**7.94.03**    Section 94(1)(a): As to the requirements for the proposed name on re-registration, see the notes to section 90(3)(a) above.

**7.94.04**    Section 94(1)(b): Private companies are no longer required to have a company secretary under the Act (see section 270), so one must be appointed upon re-registration. Note that even if the company has a secretary prior to re-registration, that person (or company or firm) must, upon re-registration, meet the eligibility requirements for a public company secretary if they are to continue in their post following re-registration.[30] If the incumbent secretary does not meet the requirements, the company will have to appoint a new secretary who has the requisite qualifications.

**7.94.05**    Section 94(2)(a): See notes to section 90(1).

**7.94.06**    Section 94(2)(b): See notes to section 90(3)(b).

**7.94.07**    Section 94(2)(c): See notes to section 92(1).

**7.94.08**    Section 94(2)(d): See notes to section 93. Under the Companies (Registrar of Companies and Applications for Striking Off) Regulations 2008, the valuation report may be drawn up and delivered to the registrar in a foreign language.

**7.94.09**    Section 94(3): See notes to section 90(1).

### 95 Statement of proposed secretary

**7.95.01**
(1) The statement of the company's proposed secretary must contain the required particulars of the person who is or the persons who are to be (or continue to be) the secretary or joint secretaries of the company.
(2) The required particulars are the particulars that will be required to be stated in the company's register of secretaries (see sections 277 to 279).
(3) The statement must also contain a consent by the person named as secretary, or each of the persons named as joint secretaries, to act in the relevant capacity.
   If all the partners in a firm are to be joint secretaries, consent may be given by one partner on behalf of all of them.

COMMENCEMENT DATE 1 October 2009[31]

---

[28]  The definition of 'body corporate' is contained in s 1173(1) and could include a foreign company.
[29]  Companies Act 2006 (Commencement No 8, Transitional Provisions and Savings) Order 2008, SI 2008/2860, art 3(g).
[30]  See s 273 for the qualification requirements.
[31]  Companies Act 2006 (Commencement No 8, Transitional Provisions and Savings) Order 2008, SI 2008/2860, art 3(g).

This was a new provision introduced under the Act, consequent upon the removal by the Act of the   **7.95.02**
requirement for private companies to have a company secretary. For more on this see the notes to
section 94(1)(b) above.

## 96  Issue of certificate of incorporation on re-registration

(1) If on an application for re-registration as a public company the registrar is satisfied that the   **7.96.01**
company is entitled to be so re-registered, the company shall be re-registered accordingly.
(2) The registrar must issue a certificate of incorporation altered to meet the circumstances of the
case.
(3) The certificate must state that it is issued on re-registration and the date on which it is issued.
(4) On the issue of the certificate—
(a) the company by virtue of the issue of the certificate becomes a public company,
(b) the changes in the company's name and articles take effect, and
(c) the person or persons named in the statement under section 95 (statement of proposed
secretary) as secretary or joint secretary of the company are deemed to have been appointed
to that office.
(5) The certificate is conclusive evidence that the requirements of this Act as to re-registration have
been complied with.

COMMENCEMENT DATE  1 October 2009[32]

This section replaces section 47 of the 1985 Act, and determines the date on which the re-registration   **7.96.02**
becomes effective, ie when the registrar issues the certificate of re-registration. As under the 1985 Act
regime, the registrar provides a facility for 'same-day' re-registration, where the certificate is issued on
the same day as the application is lodged at Companies House, for an additional fee.[33] Otherwise, there
is no time limit for the issue of the certificate, but it is usually turned around within approximately five
working days. Companies will need to prepare business stationery, etc, reflecting the change of name
and status in readiness for the issue of the certificate.

As under the 1985 Act regime, the certificate of incorporation on re-registration is conclusive evidence   **7.96.03**
that the company is a public company and the relevant requirements for a company re-registering as a
public company have been met.

As noted in relation to section 90(3)(a) above, a change in name which merely replaces 'limited' with   **7.96.04**
'p.l.c.' does not constitute a change of name for the purposes of Chapter 5 Part 5, but this sub-section
confirms when the changes to the company's stationery and branding should take effect, even if only to
reflect the change of status.

*Public company becoming private*

## 97  Re-registration of public company as private limited company

(1) A public company may be re-registered as a private limited company if—   **7.97.01**
(a) a special resolution that it should be so re-registered is passed,
(b) the conditions specified below are met, and
(c) an application for re-registration is delivered to the registrar in accordance with section 100,
together with—
(i) the other documents required by that section, and
(ii) a statement of compliance.
(2) The conditions are that—
(a) where no application under section 98 for cancellation of the resolution has been made—
(i) having regard to the number of members who consented to or voted in favour of the
resolution, no such application may be made, or
(ii) the period within which such an application could be made has expired, or
(b) where such an application has been made—
(i) the application has been withdrawn, or
(ii) an order has been made confirming the resolution and a copy of that order has been
delivered to the registrar.
(3) The company must make such changes—
(a) in its name, and
(b) in its articles,

---

[32] Companies Act 2006 (Commencement No 8, Transitional Provisions and Savings) Order 2008, SI 2008/
2860, art 3(g).
[33] The fee for a 'normal' re-registration is currently £20 and for a same-day re-registration it is currently £50
(as at October 2012).

as are necessary in connection with its becoming a private company limited by shares or, as the case may be, by guarantee.

COMMENCEMENT DATE 1 October 2009[34]

**7.97.02**    This section replaced section 53 of the 1985 Act and enables a public company to re-register as a private company limited by shares. For these purposes, the public company may have been a public company on incorporation or by subsequent re-registration (ie it is permissible to switch back and forth from public to private provided the relevant criteria are satisfied each time). Re-registration of a public company as a private limited company takes place most commonly in the context of a take-private transaction where a listed company is acquired by a private equity-backed private company and de-listed. As well as the cancellation of the listing, the company is also re-registered as a private company. Less commonly, re-registration may be compulsory if a public company's share capital falls below the authorized minimum.[35] Section 651 provides for an expedited procedure for re-registering as a private company with the sanction of the court but without the usual special resolution required under this section. A public company is also obliged to re-register as a private company if it cancels shares under section 662 and, as a result, its share capital falls below the authorized minimum.[36]

**7.97.03**    Section 97(1)(a): The special resolution required under this subsection must comply with section 283 and must be filed at Companies House within 15 days.[37] The written resolution procedure in Chapter 2 of Part 13 is not available to public companies. The special resolution will usually be filed at the same time as the application for re-registration under section 100.

**7.97.04**    Section 97(1)(c): See notes to section 90(1) on the statement of compliance. The relevant Companies House form is RR02.

**7.97.05**    Section 97(2)(a)(i): This is a new provision introduced by the Act, which enables the registrar to process an application under this section before the expiry of the 28-day period during which dissenting shareholders may lodge an objection. Under the 1985 Act, there was no express power enabling the registrar to issue a certificate of incorporation upon re-registration any earlier than 28 days after the resolution was passed. However, prior to the Act coming into force, it had become common practice for the registrar to accept written confirmation from the company's solicitors that the resolution had been passed either unanimously or by such a large majority that there would be an insufficient number of dissenting shareholders to mount an objection under what was section 54 of the 1985 Act (now section 98). Such a confirmation was usually sufficient to persuade the registrar to issue the certificate prior to the expiry of the 28-day objection period. This practice is now placed on a statutory footing by section 97(2)(a)(ii). Alternatively, the registrar will wait until either the 28-day period has expired[38] or any objection has been withdrawn[39] or the application has been overturned by a court order.[40]

**7.97.06**    Section 97(3)(a): Under section 59, the name of a private limited company must end with 'limited' or 'ltd.' or either of the Welsh equivalents, unless the company is exempt under section 60. A change of name which merely replaces 'plc' with 'limited' or one of the permitted equivalents does not constitute a change of name for the purposes of Chapter 5 of Part 5. Any more substantive change to the name itself other than the indication of legal status must comply with Chapter 5 of Part 5 and will require either a special resolution under section 78 or whatever other procedure is required under section 79 to be followed. If a special resolution is needed for a substantive name change, it could form part of the re-registration resolution.

**7.97.07**    Section 97(3)(b): A company re-registering as a private company has various options for its articles on becoming a private company. It could adopt one of the forms of the model articles prescribed under section 19 (see the Companies (Model Articles) Regulations 2008),[41] or it could adopt bespoke articles which may incorporate by reference some aspects of the model articles for either public or private companies, or it could adopt entirely separate bespoke articles, which will usually be the case if the company has private equity or other professional investors involved in it. If the company was previously listed, its existing articles would have had to comply with the Listing Rules so are unlikely to be appropriate for a private company. If the alterations to be made to the company's articles are

---

[34] Companies Act 2006 (Commencement No 8, Transitional Provisions and Savings) Order 2008, SI 2008/2860, art 3(g).
[35] As to the authorized minimum, see s 650.
[36] See ss 666 and 667.
[37] See ss 29–30.
[38] See s 97(2)(a)(ii).
[39] See s 97(2)(b)(i).
[40] See s 97(2)(b)(ii).
[41] SI 2008/3229.

substantial, it is usually easier to adopt a whole new set of articles rather than making piecemeal amendments. The alteration to the articles or adoption of new articles will require a special resolution, which could form part of the re-registration resolution required under section 97(1)(a). A copy of the new articles must be filed with the registrar under section 100.

If the company is to be a private company limited by guarantee, there are separate model articles **7.97.08** prescribed for guarantee companies under section 19(2).[42]

Note that there is no longer any requirement under the Act to alter the company's memorandum as **7.97.09** part of the re-registration procedure. Under the Act,[43] the memorandum of association is merely a snapshot document prepared and filed upon incorporation. There is no share capital or name provision as was previously required under the 1985 Act, so no changes are necessary upon re-registration.

## 98  Application to court to cancel resolution

(1) Where a special resolution by a public company to be re-registered as a private limited company **7.98.01** has been passed, an application to the court for the cancellation of the resolution may be made—
  (a) by the holders of not less in the aggregate than 5% in nominal value of the company's issued share capital or any class of the company's issued share capital (disregarding any shares held by the company as treasury shares);
  (b) if the company is not limited by shares, by not less than 5% of its members; or
  (c) by not less than 50 of the company's members;
but not by a person who has consented to or voted in favour of the resolution.
(2) The application must be made within 28 days after the passing of the resolution and may be made on behalf of the persons entitled to make it by such one or more of their number as they may appoint for the purpose.
(3) On the hearing of the application the court shall make an order either cancelling or confirming the resolution.
(4) The court may—
  (a) make that order on such terms and conditions as it thinks fit,
  (b) if it thinks fit adjourn the proceedings in order that an arrangement may be made to the satisfaction of the court for the purchase of the interests of dissentient members, and
  (c) give such directions, and make such orders, as it thinks expedient for facilitating or carrying into effect any such arrangement.
(5) The court's order may, if the court thinks fit—
  (a) provide for the purchase by the company of the shares of any of its members and for the reduction accordingly of the company's capital; and
  (b) make such alteration in the company's articles as may be required in consequence of that provision.
(6) The court's order may, if the court thinks fit, require the company not to make any, or any specified, amendments to its articles without the leave of the court.

COMMENCEMENT DATE 1 October 2009[44]

This section replaces section 54(1) to (3), (5) to (6), and (8) of the 1985 Act. As under the 1985 Act, **7.98.02** members who, in terms of their number or the percentage of shares they hold, exceed a certain threshold may apply to the court for the cancellation of a resolution to re-register the company as a private company. This is an important protection for shareholders, particularly if the company was previously listed, since as a result of becoming a private company, there will no longer be a liquid market for the company's shares and transferability of shares may be restricted. The Act does not require the company to give reasons for the re-registration,[45] although if the company is also cancelling its listing on the London Stock Exchange the de-listing will require shareholder approval and an explanatory circular to shareholders[46] under the FSA's Listing Rules, unless the de-listing is as a consequence of either a takeover offer which has received over 75 per cent acceptances or a takeover or restructuring effected by way of scheme of arrangement, in which case no shareholder approval is required.[47]

---

[42] See the Companies (Model Articles) Regulations 2008, SI 2008/3229.
[43] See s 8.
[44] Companies Act 2006 (Commencement No 8, Transitional Provisions and Savings) Order 2008, SI 2008/2860, art 3(g).
[45] See *Re a Company (No 005685 of 1998) ex p Schwarcz (No 2)* [1989] BCLC 427.
[46] See Listing Rule 5.2.5.
[47] See Listing Rules 5.2.10 and 5.2.12.

**7.98.03**    Section 98(1)(a): The expression 'issued share capital' is defined in section 546(1)(a) and (2). The expression 'class of shares' is defined in section 629 and for a definition of 'treasury shares', see section 724(5).

**7.98.04**    Section 98(2): Note that the application cannot be made by any person who has consented to or voted in favour of the resolution. Therefore, if a nominee holding shares for a number of different share-holders has voted for the resolution on behalf of some shareholders and against the resolution on behalf of others, it will be unable to participate in the application as it will be a 'person' who has consented to or voted in favour of the resolution.

**7.98.05**    Section 98(3): The court has a wide discretion as to the order it can make upon a successful application under section 98. The court may confirm or cancel the resolution or make such other order as it thinks fit. The provisions of sections 98(5) and 98(4)(b) contemplate a sale of the dissenter's shares, which is the most obvious solution where loss of liquidity and transferability is an important factor behind the application (although note that, if the re-registration followed a takeover, the dissenter will have the opportunity to sell or will have been compulsorily acquired in the course of the takeover).

**7.98.06**    Section 98(6): Without an order under this subsection, the company could subsequently alter its articles under section 21.

### 99  Notice to registrar of court application or order

**7.99.01**    (1)  On making an application under section 98 (application to court to cancel resolution) the applicants, or the person making the application on their behalf, must immediately give notice to the registrar.
This is without prejudice to any provision of rules of court as to service of notice of the application.
        (2)  On being served with notice of any such application, the company must immediately give notice to the registrar.
        (3)  Within 15 days of the making of the court's order on the application, or such longer period as the court may at any time direct, the company must deliver to the registrar a copy of the order.
        (4)  If a company fails to comply with subsection (2) or (3) an offence is committed by—
            (a)  the company, and
            (b)  every officer of the company who is in default.
        (5)  A person guilty of an offence under this section is liable on summary conviction to a fine not exceeding level 3 on the standard scale and, for continued contravention, a daily default fine not exceeding one-tenth of level 3 on the standard scale.
        COMMENCEMENT DATE 1 October 2009[48]

**7.99.02**    This section replaces section 54(4), (7), and (10) of the 1985 Act and ensures that the registrar is kept up to date with any court applications made under section 98. The applicants, under section 99(1), and the company, under section 99(2), must give notice to the registrar of the application and once the court order has been made, the company must deliver a copy to the registrar (section 99). This notification procedure ensures that the registrar is able to process the application for re-registration without delay if he is satisfied that no court application may be made (see notes to section 97 above).

**7.99.03**    Section 99(4): The expression 'officer in default' is defined in section 1121.

**7.99.04**    Section 99(5): The expression 'daily default fine' is defined in section 1125. The standard scale for Companies Act offences is prescribed by section 37 of the Criminal Justice Act 1982.

### 100  Application and accompanying documents

**7.100.01**    (1)  An application for re-registration as a private limited company must contain a statement of the company's proposed name on re-registration.
        (2)  The application must be accompanied by—
            (a)  a copy of the resolution that the company should re-register as a private limited company (unless a copy has already been forwarded to the registrar under Chapter 3 of Part 3); and
            (b)  a copy of the company's articles as proposed to be amended.
        (3)  The statement of compliance required to be delivered together with the application is a statement that the requirements of this Part as to re-registration as a private limited company have been complied with.

---

[48] Companies Act 2006 (Commencement No 8, Transitional Provisions and Savings) Order 2008, SI 2008/2860, art 3(g).

(4)  The registrar may accept the statement of compliance as sufficient evidence that the company is entitled to be re-registered as a private limited company.

COMMENCEMENT DATE  1 October 2009[49]

This section replaces section 53(1)(b) of the 1985 Act and prescribes the documents and information that must accompany the application for re-registration as a private company. The relevant Companies House form is RR02.                                                                                     **7.100.02**

Section 100(1): See the notes to section 97(3)(c) on the requirements for the company name upon re-registration as a private limited company.                                                            **7.100.03**

Section 100(2)(a): The resolution may already have been filed (but not acted upon by the registrar) if the application is made outside the 15-day filing period for the resolution under section 30.      **7.100.04**

Section 100(2)(b): See notes to section 97(3)(b) on the requirements in relation to the company's articles of association.                                                                               **7.100.05**

Section 100(3): Under the 1985 Act, no statutory declaration or an electronic equivalent was required in connection with an application for re-registration as a private company and there was, therefore, no potential liability for directors under the 1985 Act regime. Under this section 100, a statement of compliance is required, and the person or persons making it[50] will potentially incur personal liability for making a false statement of compliance.[51] However, the requirements for re-registration as a private company are less onerous than those relating to re-registration as a public company, so the scope for potential liability is reduced.                                                       **7.100.06**

## 101  Issue of certificate of incorporation on re-registration

(1)  If on an application for re-registration as a private limited company the registrar is satisfied that the company is entitled to be so re-registered, the company shall be re-registered accordingly.   **7.101.01**
(2)  The registrar must issue a certificate of incorporation altered to meet the circumstances of the case.
(3)  The certificate must state that it is issued on re-registration and the date on which it is issued.
(4)  On the issue of the certificate—
    (a)  the company by virtue of the issue of the certificate becomes a private limited company, and
    (b)  the changes in the company's name and articles take effect.
(5)  The certificate is conclusive evidence that the requirements of this Act as to re-registration have been complied with.

COMMENCEMENT DATE  1 October 2009[52]

This section replaces section 55 of the 1985 Act and provides that, upon the issue of a new certificate of incorporation as a private company upon re-registration, the company becomes a private limited company, and the name change and any amended or new articles will take effect.                      **7.101.02**

Section 101(1): The effect of section 100(4) is that the registrar is unlikely to make his own enquiries as to compliance with the relevant requirements, but will rely upon the statement of compliance.       **7.101.03**

Section 101(3)–(4): The effective date of re-registration is the date on which the certificate is issued.[53]   **7.101.04**

### *Private limited company becoming unlimited*

## 102  Re-registration of private limited company as unlimited

(1)  A private limited company may be re-registered as an unlimited company if—                         **7.102.01**
    (a)  all the members of the company have assented to its being so re-registered,
    (b)  the condition specified below is met, and
    (c)  an application for re-registration is delivered to the registrar in accordance with section 103, together with—
        (i)   the other documents required by that section, and
        (ii)  a statement of compliance.
(2)  The condition is that the company has not previously been re-registered as limited.

---

[49]  Companies Act 2006 (Commencement No 8, Transitional Provisions and Savings) Order 2008, SI 2008/2860, art 3(g).

[50]  See the standard form statement of compliance in Companies House form RR02 which envisages signature by a director, the secretary, or a person authorized under s 270 or 274 of the Act.

[51]  See s 1112, which makes it a criminal offence to deliver a false statement of compliance.

[52]  Companies Act 2006 (Commencement No 8, Transitional Provisions and Savings) Order 2008, SI 2008/2860, art 3(g).

[53]  See notes to s 96 on the effect of re-registration and on same-day re-registration.

(3) The company must make such changes in its name and its articles—
    (a) as are necessary in connection with its becoming an unlimited company; and
    (b) if it is to have a share capital, as are necessary in connection with its becoming an unlimited company having a share capital.

(4) For the purposes of this section—
    (a) a trustee in bankruptcy of a member of the company is entitled, to the exclusion of the member, to assent to the company's becoming unlimited; and
    (b) the personal representative of a deceased member of the company may assent on behalf of the deceased.

(5) In subsection (4)(a), 'a trustee in bankruptcy of a member of the company' includes—
    (a) a permanent trustee or an interim trustee (within the meaning of the Bankruptcy (Scotland) Act 1985 (c. 66)) on the sequestrated estate of a member of the company;
    (b) a trustee under a protected trustee deed (within the meaning of the Bankruptcy (Scotland) Act 1985) granted by a member of the company.

COMMENCEMENT DATE 1 October 2009[54]

**7.102.02**    This section replaces section 49(1), (2), and (9) of the 1985 Act and, as under those sections, permits a private company limited by shares or by guarantee to re-register as an unlimited private company provided certain conditions are met, the key one being that all of the members have consented. In practice, re-registration as an unlimited company may take place in order for the company to take advantage of the more flexible capital maintenance regime that applies to unlimited companies. For example, Part 17 Chapter 8 (Alteration of Share Capital), Part 17 Chapter 10 (Reduction of Capital), and Part 18 Chapter 1 (Purchase of Own Shares) apply only to limited companies. An additional or alternative reason for re-registration as an unlimited company may be to take advantage of the reduced filing requirements for the accounts of unlimited companies, which may be beneficial if secrecy is an issue in relation to the financial position of the company. For example, section 448 provides that unlimited companies are exempt from the obligation to file accounts with the registrar unless it is part of a group containing limited entities. (The section 448 exemption therefore really only applies to freestanding unlimited companies.) Sections 102(2) and 105(2) will prevent companies switching back and forward between limited and unlimited company status, avoiding companies taking temporary advantage of unlimited company status (for example, to effect a reduction of capital without the restrictions contained in Part 17 Chapter 10). So, once a company has been re-registered as unlimited (having been a limited company previously), it cannot revert to limited company status.

**7.102.03**    Section 102(1)(a): The key condition for re-registration as an unlimited company is the unanimous consent of all members, since on a winding-up, the liability of members would be unlimited[55] (even though a member cannot be sued in person by the company's creditors). Section 102(4) deals with the mechanism for obtaining the consent of deceased or bankrupt members (consent may be given on their behalf by the trustee in bankruptcy or personal representative, as the case may be). The Act does not prescribe a solution for dealing with dissenting shareholders, but in practice, as consent must be unanimous, a single dissenting shareholder can block a proposal to re-register a company as unlimited. A practical solution for dealing with a dissenting shareholder is for that person's shares to be acquired by the company (in compliance with Part 18 Chapter 1) or by one or more of the other shareholders. However, past members may still be liable to contribute to the company's assets if the company is wound up within the following 12 months.[56] The form of the assent must be in the form prescribed by the regulations made under section 103(2)(a) of the Companies (Registration) Regulations 2008.[57] The expression 'prescribed' is defined in section 1167.

**7.102.04**    Section 102(3)(a): The name of an unlimited company does not need to end with the word 'unlimited', but a limited company re-registering as an unlimited company must at least drop the word 'limited' from its name. Under the Company and Business Names (Miscellaneous Provisions) Regulations 2009[58] an unlimited company is specifically prohibited from ending its name with the word 'limited' or any other word which would give a misleading impression of the company's legal status. If any more substantive change is made to the name, the name change must comply with the requirements set out in Part 5 Chapter 5. As to the company's articles on re-registration as an unlimited company, the company will need to adopt articles consistent with unlimited company status. Section 21 requires a special resolution for any amendment to a company's articles of association or the adoption of new

---

[54] Companies Act 2006 (Commencement No 8, Transitional Provisions and Savings) Order 2008, SI 2008/2860, art 3(g).
[55] See Insolvency Act 1986, s 78(2).
[56] See ibid, s 74.
[57] See Schedule 3 of the Companies (Registration) Regulations 2008 – SI 2008/3014.
[58] SI 2009/1085, reg 6.

articles. Unlike section 50(2)(b) of the 1985 Act, this section does not contain any deeming provision in relation to the change in the articles taking effect, nor does section 104. In the absence of such a deeming provision, a special resolution will be required. As to the form of the articles, the Secretary of State has not prescribed model articles for unlimited companies under section 19. The model articles set out in Table E[59] used to be the most common form for unlimited companies and may continue to be used by some unlimited companies in the absence of a new model form under the Act, as Table E remains in force. However, the Government's rationale for not producing model articles for unlimited companies under the Act was that such companies could either adapt the model articles for public or private limited companies, or produce bespoke articles to suit their specialized nature, and this is what most unlimited companies are expected to do going forward. As noted in section 103(3)(b), it is possible to re-register as an unlimited company with or without a share capital, and the articles will reflect the existence or not of a share capital. It is also common in the articles of association of unlimited companies with a share capital (as in Table E) to provide for various alterations to be made to the share capital of the company by special resolution or other procedure, since these matters are not prescribed by the Act itself. The existence of a share capital does not prejudice the unlimited status of the company.

Section 102(5): For a definition of 'permanent trustee', see section 3 of the Bankruptcy (Scotland) Act **7.102.05** 1985. For a definition of 'interim trustee', see section 2 of the Bankruptcy (Scotland) Act 1985. For a definition of 'Protected Trustee Deed', see section 8 of Schedule 5 of the Bankruptcy (Scotland) Act 1985.

## 103 Application and accompanying documents

(1) An application for re-registration as an unlimited company must contain a statement of the **7.103.01** company's proposed name on re-registration.
(2) The application must be accompanied by—
  (a) the prescribed form of assent to the company's being registered as an unlimited company, authenticated by or on behalf of all the members of the company;
  (b) a copy of the company's articles as proposed to be amended.
(3) The statement of compliance required to be delivered together with the application is a statement that the requirements of this Part as to re-registration as an unlimited company have been complied with.
(4) The statement must contain a statement by the directors of the company—
  (a) that the persons by whom or on whose behalf the form of assent is authenticated constitute the whole membership of the company, and
  (b) if any of the members have not authenticated that form themselves, that the directors have taken all reasonable steps to satisfy themselves that each person who authenticated it on behalf of a member was lawfully empowered to do so.
(5) The registrar may accept the statement of compliance as sufficient evidence that the company is entitled to be re-registered as an unlimited company.

COMMENCEMENT DATE 1 October 2009[60]

This section replaces section 49(4) to (8)(a) of the 1985 Act and prescribes the contents of the **7.103.02** application for re-registration as an unlimited company and the documents and information that must accompany the application. The relevant Companies House form is RR05.

Section 103(1): See the notes on section 102(3)(a) on the requirements for the name of an unlimited **7.103.03** company.

Section 103(2)(a): Note that there is no resolution to re-register as an unlimited company as such under **7.103.04** this section. Instead, there must be a form of assent in the prescribed form, which is signed by all members. 'Prescribed' means prescribed by an order or regulations made by the Secretary of State.[61] The form of the assent is prescribed in the regulations made under this section (see Schedule 3 to the Companies (Registration) Regulations 2008[62] ). For the meaning of the word 'authenticated', see section 1146. The manner of authentication will depend on whether the form of assent is in hard copy or in electronic form. The authentication requirements as far as the registrar is concerned are dealt with in registrar's rules made under section 1117 of the Act.[63]

---

[59] See the Companies (Tables A to F) Regulations 1985, SI 1985/805.
[60] Companies Act 2006 (Commencement No 8, Transitional Provisions and Savings) Order 2008, SI 2008/2860, art 3(g).
[61] See s 1167.
[62] SI 2008/3014.
[63] See Volume 5 of the Registrar's Rules 2009, available from Companies House at ⟨http://www.companies-house.gov.uk/about/policyDocuments/registrarsRules.pdf⟩.

**7.103.05**   Section 103(3): The statement of compliance replaces the 1985 Act requirement for a statutory declaration (or its electronic equivalent). Section 103(4) prescribes the content of the statement (unlike some other statements of compliance required under other sections of the Act, where the content is not prescribed as such). The statement of compliance must be signed by all the directors of the company (see the relevant Companies House form RR05). Note that there is potential liability for those persons making the statement of compliance under section 1112, which makes it an offence to make a false statement. The contents of the statement of compliance under this section are broadly the same as those of a statutory declaration under the predecessor of this section, section 49(8) of the 1985 Act.

### 104  Issue of certificate of incorporation on re-registration

**7.104.01**   (1) If on an application for re-registration of a private limited company as an unlimited company the registrar is satisfied that the company is entitled to be so re-registered, the company shall be re-registered accordingly.
(2) The registrar must issue a certificate of incorporation altered to meet the circumstances of the case.
(3) The certificate must state that it is issued on re-registration and the date on which it is issued.
(4) On the issue of the certificate—
  (a) the company by virtue of the issue of the certificate becomes an unlimited company, and
  (b) the changes in the company's name and articles take effect.
(5) The certificate is conclusive evidence that the requirements of this Act as to re-registration have been complied with.

COMMENCEMENT DATE 1 October 2009[64]

**7.104.02**   This section replaces section 50 of the 1985 Act and will determine the effective date of re-registration. The new certificate of incorporation will state that it has been issued upon re-registration.

**7.104.03**   Section 104(1): Section 103(5) suggests that the registrar will not normally make enquiries as to compliance with the requirements for re-registration as an unlimited company. Instead, the registrar will rely upon the statement of compliance as evidence that the requirements have been met.

**7.104.04**   Section 104(4): The date on which the certificate of incorporation on re-registration is issued is the effective date of re-registration. As with other changes of status, this will also determine the effective date of the change of name and articles. See the notes to section 96 relating to the effect on re-registration and on same-day re-registration.

*Unlimited private company becoming limited*

### 105  Re-registration of unlimited company as limited

**7.105.01**   (1) An unlimited company may be re-registered as a private limited company if—
  (a) a special resolution that it should be so re-registered is passed,
  (b) the condition specified below is met, and
  (c) an application for re-registration is delivered to the registrar in accordance with section 106, together with—
    (i) the other documents required by that section, and
    (ii) a statement of compliance.
(2) The condition is that the company has not previously been re-registered as unlimited.
(3) The special resolution must state whether the company is to be limited by shares or by guarantee.
(4) The company must make such changes—
  (a) in its name, and
  (b) in its articles,
as are necessary in connection with its becoming a company limited by shares or, as the case may be, by guarantee.

COMMENCEMENT DATE 1 October 2009[65]

**7.105.02**   This section replaces section 51(1) to (3) and (6) of the 1985 Act. The requirements for re-registration of an unlimited company as limited are similar to the re-registration of a limited company as unlimited. In the case of re-registration to a company limited by shares, there is nothing requiring the unanimous consent of the members is not required. All that is needed is a special resolution, in view of the reduced exposure to risk for members in becoming limited. The special resolution must state whether the

---

[64] Companies Act 2006 (Commencement No 8, Transitional Provisions and Savings) Order 2008, SI 2008/2860, art 3(g).

[65] Companies Act 2006 (Commencement No 8, Transitional Provisions and Savings) Order 2008, SI 2008/2860, art 3(g).

company is to be limited by shares or by guarantee. In the case of re-registration to a company limited by guarantee, in addition to the special resolution, a statement of guarantee is required under section 106(3). Companies House originally interpreted section 106(3) to mean that every member had to sign up to the statement of guarantee, but the relevant Companies House form (RR06) has recently been amended so that it no longer requires the signature of every member. On the face of it, there is still an apparent contradiction between section 105(1)(a), which requires only a special resolution, and section 106(3), which requires a statement of guarantee in which each member gives the relevant undertaking, but in view of the new approach adopted by Companies House, it appears that a dissenting member can no longer block the re-registration provided the special resolution is passed.

Section 105(1): Note that re-registration under this section can only result in a private limited **7.105.03** company. If the company wishes to become a public company, it must first reregister as a private limited company under this section and then follow the procedure for re-registration as a public company set out in sections 90 to 96.

Section 105(2): As with section 102 (re-registration of a private limited company as unlimited), it is a **7.105.04** condition of re-registration that the company has not previously been re-registered as unlimited. As noted in connection with section 102, this is to prevent companies taking temporary advantage of unlimited company status.

Section 105(3): As indicated by this subsection, it is possible for an unlimited company upon re- **7.105.05** registration as a limited company to be limited by shares or by guarantee. If the company is to be limited by guarantee, it will have no share capital, since it has been impossible since December 1980[66] to incorporate or re-register a company as a company limited by guarantee with a share capital. Guarantee companies are commonly used by charitable or other non-trading organizations.

Section 105(4)(a): In the case of a company limited by shares, see the notes to section 97(3)(a) on the **7.105.06** name of a private limited company. (In the case of a guarantee company, the company may be exempted from the requirement to end the name with the word 'Limited' by the regulations made under section 60(1)(b).[67]) The section 62 exemption only applies to companies limited by guarantee in existence prior to the commencement of Part 5. Without the benefit of an exemption, the company must, upon re-registration as a private limited company, comply with the requirements of section 59. If more substantive changes are to be made to the name (other than to the indication of legal status), the company will need either a special resolution to change the name under section 78 or to follow whatever other procedure is required for a name change under section 79. If a special resolution is required, it could be part of the re-registration resolution required under section 105(1)(a).

Section 105(4)(b): In the case of a company limited by shares, see the notes to section 97(3)(b). In the **7.105.07** case of a guarantee company, such companies commonly use model articles, which under the Act are prescribed under section 19.[68] Prior to the commencement of the Act, guarantee companies had a statement of the guarantee in their memorandum of association. As the memorandum of association for companies incorporated under the Act is a simple snapshot document[69] containing no share capital clause or the equivalent for a guarantee company, a statement of guarantee will be made separately under section 106(3), which in turn reflects the requirements of section 11 for a company incorporated for the first time as a guarantee company.

## 106 Application and accompanying documents

    (1) An application for re-registration as a limited company must contain a statement of the **7.106.01** company's proposed name on re-registration.

    (2) The application must be accompanied by—
      (a) a copy of the resolution that the company should re-register as a private limited company (unless a copy has already been forwarded to the registrar under Chapter 3 of Part 3);
      (b) if the company is to be limited by guarantee, a statement of guarantee;
      (c) a copy of the company's articles as proposed to be amended.

    (3) The statement of guarantee required to be delivered in the case of a company that is to be limited by guarantee must state that each member undertakes that, if the company is wound up while he is a member, or within one year after he ceases to be a member, he will contribute to the assets of the company such amount as may be required for—
      (a) payment of the debts and liabilities of the company contracted before he ceases to be a member,

---

[66] See the Companies Act 1980.
[67] See the Company and Business Names (Miscellaneous Provisions) Regulations 2009, SI 2009/1085, reg 3.
[68] See the Companies (Model Articles) Regulations 2008, SI 2008/3229.
[69] See s 8.

(b) payment of the costs, charges and expenses of winding up, and

(c) adjustment of the rights of the contributories among themselves, not exceeding a specified amount.

(4) The statement of compliance required to be delivered together with the application is a statement that the requirements of this Part as to re-registration as a limited company have been complied with.

(5) The registrar may accept the statement of compliance as sufficient evidence that the company is entitled to be re-registered as a limited company.

COMMENCEMENT DATE 1 October 2009[70]

**7.106.02** This section replaces section 51(3), (4), and (5) of the 1985 Act and prescribes the contents of the application for re-registration as a limited company and the documents and information that must accompany the application. The application is in the form set out in Companies House form RR06.

**7.106.03** Section 106(1): See notes to section 105(4)(a) above.

**7.106.04** Section 106(2): See notes to section 100(2)(a) above.

**7.106.05** Section 106(2)(b): See notes to section 106(3) below.

**7.106.06** Section 106(2)(c): See notes to section 105(4)(b) above.

**7.106.07** Section 106(3): The statement of guarantee used (under the 1985 Act regime) to be part of the memorandum of association (as noted in connection with section 105(4)(b) above). This section replicates the effect of section 11 of the Act, which requires a separate statement of guarantee to be made when a company is first incorporated as a company limited by guarantee. The statement of guarantee forms part of the relevant Companies House form, RR06. See the notes to section 105 above on who must sign the statement of guarantee. The memorandum of association of a company incorporated or re-registered under the Act also no longer contains a share capital clause. Instead, under section 10, when a company limited by shares is first incorporated with a share capital, it must deliver a statement of capital to the registrar and the statement of capital will be the definitive statement of the company's share capital from time to time. Note that, subject to section 108, no statement of capital is required upon a company re-registering as a private company limited by shares.

**7.106.08** Section 106(4): The requirement for a statement of compliance replaced the 1985 Act requirement for a statutory declaration (or its electronic equivalent). The statement of compliance is part of the Companies House form RR06 and must be signed by a director, secretary, or person authorized under section 270 or 274 of the Act.

### 107 Issue of certificate of incorporation on re-registration

**7.107.01** (1) If on an application for re-registration of an unlimited company as a limited company the registrar is satisfied that the company is entitled to be so re-registered, the company shall be re-registered accordingly.

(2) The registrar must issue a certificate of incorporation altered to meet the circumstances of the case.

(3) The certificate must state that it is issued on re-registration and the date on which it is so issued.

(4) On the issue of the certificate—

(a) the company by virtue of the issue of the certificate becomes a limited company, and

(b) the changes in the company's name and articles take effect.

(5) The certificate is conclusive evidence that the requirements of this Act as to re-registration have been complied with.

COMMENCEMENT DATE 1 October 2009[71]

**7.107.02** This section replaces section 52 of the 1985 Act and provides for the issue of the certificate of incorporation on re-registration, whereupon the re-registration will become effective, as will the change of name and any alteration to the articles or adoption of new articles.

**7.107.03** Section 107(1): Section 106(5) suggests that the registrar will not make his own enquiries as to compliance with the relevant requirements for re-registration of an unlimited company as limited, but is likely to take the statement of compliance delivered under section 106 as conclusive evidence that the requirements have been met.

---

[70] Companies Act 2006 (Commencement No 8, Transitional Provisions and Savings) Order 2008, SI 2008/2860, art 3(g).

[71] Companies Act 2006 (Commencement No 8, Transitional Provisions and Savings) Order 2008, SI 2008/2860, art 3(g).

Section 107(4): The date of issue of the certificate will be the effective date of the re-registration, **7.107.04** including the date of the name change and the date on which the new articles come into effect. See the notes to section 96 relating to the effect of re-registration and on same-day re-registration.

## 108  Statement of capital required where company already has share capital

(1) A company which on re-registration under section 107 already has allotted share capital must **7.108.01** within 15 days after the re-registration deliver a statement of capital to the registrar.

(2) This does not apply if the information which would be included in the statement has already been sent to the registrar in—

　(a) a statement of capital and initial shareholdings (see section 10), or

　(b) a statement of capital contained in an annual return (see section 856(2)).

(3) The statement of capital must state with respect to the company's share capital on re-registration—

　(a) the total number of shares of the company,

　(b) the aggregate nominal value of those shares,

　(c) for each class of shares—

　　(i) prescribed particulars of the rights attached to the shares,

　　(ii) the total number of shares of that class, and

　　(iii) the aggregate nominal value of shares of that class, and

　(d) the amount paid up and the amount (if any) unpaid on each share (whether on account of the nominal value of the share or by way of premium).

(4) If default is made in complying this section, an offence is committed by—

　(a) the company, and

　(b) every officer of the company who is in default.

(5) A person guilty of an offence under this section is liable on summary conviction to a fine not exceeding level 3 on the standard scale and, for continued contravention, a daily default fine not exceeding one-tenth of level 3 on the standard scale.

COMMENCEMENT DATE 1 October 2009[72]

This is a new section introduced by the Act and is needed as a result of the abolition of the share capital **7.108.02** clause in the memorandum of association and the concept of authorized share capital for companies incorporated or re-registered under the Act. If the company re-registering was previously an unlimited company with a share capital, it will have been exempt from the requirement to file a return of allotments under section 555 of the Act, so if it has allotted shares since it was first incorporated or since its last annual return, there will be no way of ascertaining the company's share capital upon it becoming a private company limited by shares. In that case, it must deliver a statement of capital to the registrar within 15 days of re-registration. If, however, the company still has the share capital with which it was first incorporated as an unlimited company with a share capital, details of the share capital will already have been notified under section 10. Alternatively, it may have subsequently notified an alteration in its share capital by means of the annual return required under section 856. If the share capital is the same as previously notified under either section 10 and/or section 856, no statement of capital is required under this section.

Section 108(3): The requirements for the statement of capital are similar to those required by a private **7.108.03** company limited by shares on first registration. See section 10.

Section 108(4): The expression 'officer in default' is defined in section 1121. **7.108.04**

Section 108(5): The expression 'daily default fine' is defined in section 1125. The standard scale for **7.108.05** Companies Act offences is prescribed by section 37 of the Criminal Justice Act 1982.

## *Public company becoming private and unlimited*

## 109  Re-registration of public company as private and unlimited

(1) A public company limited by shares may be re-registered as an unlimited private company with a **7.109.01** share capital if—

　(a) all the members of the company have assented to its being so re-registered,

　(b) the condition specified below is met, and

　(c) an application for re-registration is delivered to the registrar in accordance with section 110, together with—

　　(i) the other documents required by that section, and

　　(ii) a statement of compliance.

---

[72] Companies Act 2006 (Commencement No 8, Transitional Provisions and Savings) Order 2008, SI 2008/2860, art 3(g).

(2) The condition is that the company has not previously been re-registered—
    (a) as limited, or
    (b) as unlimited.

(3) The company must make such changes—
    (a) in its name, and
    (b) in its articles, as are necessary in connection with its becoming an unlimited private company.

(4) For the purposes of this section—
    (a) a trustee in bankruptcy of a member of the company is entitled, to the exclusion of the member, to assent to the company's re-registration; and
    (b) the personal representative of a deceased member of the company may assent on behalf of the deceased.

(5) In subsection (4)(a), 'a trustee in bankruptcy of a member of the company' includes—
    (a) a permanent trustee or an interim trustee (within the meaning of the Bankruptcy (Scotland) Act 1985 (c. 66)) on the sequestrated estate of a member of the company;
    (b) a trustee under a protected trustee deed (within the meaning of the Bankruptcy (Scotland) Act 1985) granted by a member of the company.

Commencement Date 1 October 2009[73]

**7.109.02** This is a new section introduced by the Act and follows the recommendations of the Company Law Review[74] that a public company should be able to re-register as a private unlimited company with a share capital without first having to re-register as a private company limited by shares. As with a private company re-registering as an unlimited company, unanimous consent on the part of all shareholders is necessary in view of the additional risks involved in unlimited status.[75] The requirement for the individual assent of every member to the re-registration as an unlimited company will mean that such a change of status will be relatively rare, in view of the shareholder profile of many public companies.

**7.109.03** Otherwise, the requirements are identical to those applying to a private company re-registering as an unlimited company under section 102.

**7.109.04** Section 109(4): For a definition of 'permanent trustee' see section 3 of the Bankruptcy (Scotland) Act 1985. For a definition of 'interim trustee', see section 2 of the Bankruptcy (Scotland) Act 1985. For a definition of 'Protected Trustee Deed', see section 8 of Schedule 5 of the Bankruptcy (Scotland) Act 1985.

### 110 Application and accompanying documents

**7.110.01**
(1) An application for re-registration of a public company as an unlimited private company must contain a statement of the company's proposed name on re-registration.

(2) The application must be accompanied by—
    (a) the prescribed form of assent to the company's being registered as an unlimited company, authenticated by or on behalf of all the members of the company, and
    (b) a copy of the company's articles as proposed to be amended.

(3) The statement of compliance required to be delivered together with the application is a statement that the requirements of this Part as to re-registration as an unlimited private company have been complied with.

(4) The statement must contain a statement by the directors of the company—
    (a) that the persons by whom or on whose behalf the form of assent is authenticated constitute the whole membership of the company, and
    (b) if any of the members have not authenticated that form themselves, that the directors have taken all reasonable steps to satisfy themselves that each person who authenticated it on behalf of a member was lawfully empowered to do so.

(5) The registrar may accept the statement of compliance as sufficient evidence that the company is entitled to be re-registered as an unlimited private company.

Commencement Date 1 October 2009[76]

**7.110.02** This is also a new section introduced under the Act, which prescribes the contents of the application for re-registration from a public company to an unlimited private company and the documents and information that must accompany the application. The form of the assent is prescribed in the Companies (Registration) Regulations 2008 (see Schedule 4). The relevant Companies House form is

---

[73] Companies Act 2006 (Commencement No 8, Transitional Provisions and Savings) Order 2008, SI 2008/2860, art 3(g).

[74] See para 11.16 of the Company Law Review Final Report.

[75] See notes to s 102(1)(a).

[76] Companies Act 2006 (Commencement No 8, Transitional Provisions and Savings) Order 2008, SI 2008/2860, art 3(g).

RR07, and the statement of compliance must be signed by all the directors of the company. For further details, see section 103 relating to the application for re-registration of a private limited company as unlimited, whose provisions are the same (*mutatis mutandis*).

## 111  Issue of certificate of incorporation on re-registration

(1) If on an application for re-registration of a public company as an unlimited private company the registrar is satisfied that the company is entitled to be so re-registered, the company shall be re-registered accordingly.                    **7.111.01**

(2) The registrar must issue a certificate of incorporation altered to meet the circumstances of the case.

(3) The certificate must state that it is issued on re-registration and the date on which it is so issued.

(4) On the issue of the certificate—

   (a)  the company by virtue of the issue of the certificate becomes an unlimited private company, and

   (b)  the changes in the company's name and articles take effect.

(5) The certificate is conclusive evidence that the requirements of this Act as to re-registration have been complied with.

COMMENCEMENT DATE 1 October 2009[77]

This is also a new section introduced under the Act and provides that the registrar will issue the certificate of incorporation on re-registration of the public company as a private unlimited company when he is satisfied that the relevant requirements have been met. Section 110(5) suggests that the registrar will not make his own enquiries as to compliance with the relevant requirements, but instead will rely upon the statement of compliance delivered under section 110. See the notes to section 96 on the effect of re-registration and on same-day re-registration.                    **7.111.02**

---

[77] Companies Act 2006 (Commencement No 8, Transitional Provisions and Savings) Order 2008, SI 2008/2860, art 3(g).

# 8

# A COMPANY'S MEMBERS

## Companies Act 2006

## PART 8
### A COMPANY'S MEMBERS

## CHAPTER 1
### THE MEMBERS OF A COMPANY

### 112  The members of a company

8.112.01

(1)  The subscribers of a company's memorandum are deemed to have agreed to become members of the company, and on its registration become members and must be entered as such in its register of members.

(2) Every other person who agrees to become a member of a company, and whose name is entered in its register of members, is a member of the company.

COMMENCEMENT DATE 1 October 2009[1]

**8.112.02**   In defining who are the members of a company, this section reenacted and replaced section 22 of the Companies Act 1985[2] with only one minor modification in subsection (1). The words 'become members' have been added to make it clear in the statute that the subscribers to the memorandum become members of the company once it is registered, even if they are not entered in the register of members. The common law is to the same effect anyway, the cases[3] making it clear that, at least in the case of a company with a share capital, the subscribers are bound to take and pay for the shares written opposite their names,[4] and the directors have no power to relieve them of this responsibility.[5] They will, however, be relieved from liability if all the shares in the company are allotted to others.[6]

**8.112.03**   For any other person to become a member, two steps are required, namely their agreement and their entry on the register of members.[7] In most situations, agreement is likely to be constituted by some form of application for and allotment of shares, but it is clear that this degree of formality is not essential. In the leading modern decision in *Re Nuneaton Borough Association Football Club Ltd*,[8] the Court of Appeal held that it is sufficient if someone has consented to become a member and there does not have to be a binding contract between the company and him, confirming much earlier authorities to the same effect.[9]

**8.112.04**   However, section 112 is not conclusive in a case where the articles of the company impose an additional requirement for someone to be admitted to membership, such as the consent of the Council required in *POW Services Ltd v Clare*.[10] In practice this is likely to be significant only in cases of companies limited by guarantee, as in that case.

# CHAPTER 2
## REGISTER OF MEMBERS
### *General*

### 113 Register of members

**8.113.01**
(1) Every company must keep a register of its members.
(2) There must be entered in the register—
   (a) the names and addresses of the members,
   (b) the date on which each person was registered as a member, and
   (c) the date at which any person ceased to be a member.
(3) In the case of a company having a share capital, there must be entered in the register, with the names and addresses of the members, a statement of—
   (a) the shares held by each member, distinguishing each share—
      (i) by its number (so long as the share has a number), and
      (ii) where the company has more than one class of issued shares, by its class, and
   (b) the amount paid or agreed to be considered as paid on the shares of each member.
(4) If the company has converted any of its shares into stock, and given notice of the conversion to the registrar, the register of members must show the amount and class of stock held by each member instead of the amount of shares and the particulars relating to shares specified above.
(5) In the case of joint holders of shares or stock in a company, the company's register of members must state the names of each joint holder.
   In other respects joint holders are regarded for the purposes of this Chapter as a single member (so that the register must show a single address).

---

[1] Companies Act 2006 (Commencement No 8, Transitional Provisions and Savings) Order 2008, SI 2008/2860, art 3(h).
[2] Provisions in the earlier Companies Acts, all the way back to s 23 of the 1862 Act, were the same.
[3] See, eg *Drummond's Case* (1869) 4 Ch App 772.
[4] Although a subsequent application for an allotment of an equal or greater number of shares may be treated as satisfying an obligation under the memorandum: *Gilman's Case* (1886) 31 Ch D 420.
[5] *Re London and Provincial Consolidated Coal Co* (1877) 5 Ch D 525.
[6] See, eg *Evan's Case* (1867) 2 Ch App 427.
[7] Note, however, that if there is agreement, the register can be rectified to insert their name: see para 8.125.02.
[8] [1989] BCLC 454.
[9] *Re Railway Time Tables Publishing Co* (1889) 42 Ch D 98; *Re Disderi & Co* (1870) LR 11 Eq 242, 247; *Re James Pilkin & Co Ltd* (1916) 85 LJ Ch 318, 320.
[10] [1995] 2 BCLC 435.

(6)  In the case of a company that does not have a share capital but has more than one class of members, there must be entered in the register, with the names and addresses of the members, a statement of the class to which each member belongs.

(7)  If a company makes default in complying with this section an offence is committed by—

(a)  the company, and

(b)  every officer of the company who is in default.

(8)  A person guilty of an offence under this section is liable on summary conviction to a fine not exceeding level 3 on the standard scale and, for continued contravention, a daily default fine not exceeding one-tenth of level 3 on the standard scale.

COMMENCEMENT DATE 1 October 2009[11]

In imposing an obligation on every registered company to keep a register of its members and specifying what must be included, this section replaced section 352(1) to (5) of the 1985 Act.[12] The form of the register is governed by the general provision of the Act relating to the form of registers and other records, namely section 1135,[13] so that, among other things, it may be kept in electronic form. It should be noted that the requirement in subsection (2) of the entry of the date a person was registered as a member means the date they were formally admitted to membership, not the date when they agreed to become a member. As to the requirements for the numbering of shares, see section 543.[14] Note that the obligation under section 113 is disapplied where a company has uncertificated shares traded on CREST, but the equivalent obligation is imposed, with the same sanctions for default, under the Uncertificated Securities Regulations.[15]   **8.113.02**

The register of members is a public register for the purpose of the exclusive jurisdiction under the Civil Jurisdiction and Judgments Act 1982, incorporating the Brussels Convention on Jurisdiction and the Enforcement of Judgments.[16]   **8.113.03**

Subsection (5) regarding joint holders of shares or stock is an entirely new provision. Previously the question of how to treat joint holders was left entirely to the articles. Although now the Act requires that the names of all joint holders must be entered in the register, they are regarded for statutory purposes as a single member with only one address in the register. The Act now also provides that only the vote of the senior holder, that is the joint holder first named in the register, may vote, although this is subject to anything to the contrary in the articles.[17] Clearly the joint holders retain the right that they had at common law to determine the order in which their names are to be entered on the register.[18]   **8.113.04**

As to the provisions of subsection (3)(a)(ii) regarding the entry of the class of shares that must be noted in the register, there is a general provision, section 629,[19] defining shares as of one class if the rights attached to them are in all respects uniform.[20] Whether this is concerned only with conventional rights of classes as regards dividend, capital, or voting, or whether 'class' has the meaning that has been ascribed to it for the purpose of the variation of rights provisions, is considered elsewhere.[21]   **8.113.05**

It should be noted that the Act abolished the power of a company to convert shares into stock,[22] so that subsection (4) is now applicable only to stock existing before the Act came into force.   **8.113.06**

As to the meaning of officer in default, see section 1121.[23]   **8.113.07**

---

[11] Companies Act 2006 (Commencement No 8, Transitional Provisions and Savings) Order 2008, SI 2008/2860, art 3(h).

[12] And earlier provisions to the same effect.

[13] See para 37.1135.02.

[14] See para 17.543.02.

[15] SI 2001/3755; see paras 21.789.03 *et seq.*

[16] *Re Fagins Bookshop plc* [1992] BCLC 118, where the case arose under what is now s 125 concerning the rectification of the register; see para 8.125.03.

[17] Section 286; see para 13.286.02.

[18] *Re T H Saunders & Co* [1908] 1 Ch 415. See para 8.125.06 regarding rectification of the register for the benefit of joint holders and para 37.1144.19 regarding the provision about communications with joint holders in Sch 5.

[19] See generally para 17.629.02.

[20] Except that different rights to dividend in the 12 months following allotment do not make shares of a different class: s 629(2).

[21] See para 17.629.05.

[22] See para 17.620.02.

[23] See para 36.1121.02.

## 114 Register to be kept available for inspection

**8.114.01**
(1) A company's register of members must be kept available for inspection—
(a) at its registered office, or
(b) at a place specified in regulations under section 1136.
(2) A company must give notice to the registrar of the place where its register of members is kept available for inspection and of any change in that place.
(3) No such notice is required if the register has, at all times since it came into existence (or, in the case of a register in existence on the relevant date, at all times since then) been kept available for inspection at the company's registered office.
(4) The relevant date for the purposes of subsection (3) is—
(a) 1st July 1948 in the case of a company registered in Great Britain, and
(b) 1st April 1961 in the case of a company registered in Northern Ireland.
(5) If a company makes default for 14 days in complying with subsection (2), an offence is committed by—
(a) the company, and
(b) every officer of the company who is in default.
(6) A person guilty of an offence under this section is liable on summary conviction to a fine not exceeding level 3 on the standard scale and, for continued contravention, a daily default fine not exceeding one-tenth of level 3 on the standard scale.

COMMENCEMENT DATE 1 October 2009[24]

**8.114.02** This section replaced section 353 of the 1985 Act and in doing so made a notable change of emphasis. Instead of specifying the location of the register, it specifies where the register must be available for inspection,[25] so it is now irrelevant where the register is actually compiled and updated, which in any event, if the register is in web-based electronic form could be anywhere in the world! Inspection must be available at the company's registered office or at a place specified in regulations under section 1136;[26] in the latter case, the effect of subsections (2) and (3) is that notice of the place must be filed with the registrar. The regulations[27] require an alternative inspection location situated in the part of the United Kingdom where the company is registered. It must be the same place for all company registers.

**8.114.03** Failure to give such notice within 14 days attracts a criminal penalty on both the company and any officer in default. As to the meaning of officer in default, see section 1121.[28]

## 115 Index of members

**8.115.01**
(1) Every company having more than 50 members must keep an index of the names of the members of the company, unless the register of members is in such a form as to constitute in itself an index.
(2) The company must make any necessary alteration in the index within 14 days after the date on which any alteration is made in the register of members.
(3) The index must contain, in respect of each member, a sufficient indication to enable the account of that member in the register to be readily found.
(4) The index must be at all times kept available for inspection at the same place as the register of members.
(5) If default is made in complying with this section, an offence is committed by—
(a) the company, and
(b) every officer of the company who is in default.
(6) A person guilty of an offence under this section is liable on summary conviction to a fine not exceeding level 3 on the standard scale and, for continued contravention, a daily default fine not exceeding one-tenth of level 3 on the standard scale.

COMMENCEMENT DATE 1 October 2009[29]

**8.115.02** This section replaced section 354 of the 1985 Act with no real changes in meaning. The need for a continuing requirement to keep an index of the names of members was queried as the Bill that became the Act was debated in Parliament. However, as the index to the register of members may, like the register itself, be kept in electronic form,[30] it seems likely that in all companies with more than 50

---

[24] Companies Act 2006 (Commencement No 8, Transitional Provisions and Savings) Order 2008, SI 2008/2860, art 3(h).
[25] Rights of inspection are governed by s 116; see para 8.116.02.
[26] This is a general provision regarding the keeping of records; see para 37.1136.02.
[27] Companies (Company Records) Regulations 2008, SI 2008/3006.
[28] See para 36.1121.02.
[29] Companies Act 2006 (Commencement No 8, Transitional Provisions and Savings) Order 2008, SI 2008/2860, art 3(h).
[30] Section 1135; see para 37.1135.02.

members, to which the section applies, the index is an integral part of the electronic package used for the register. It is thus likely to be automatically updated when the register itself is updated. Failing that, the index must be updated within 14 days after the date on which any alteration is made in the register.

As is the case with the register itself under the previous section, rather than being kept at a location the index must now be kept available for inspection at the same place as the register itself. **8.115.03**

Failure to comply with the requirements of the section is an offence both by the company and by any officer in default. As to the meaning of officer in default, see section 1121.[31] **8.115.04**

### 116 Rights to inspect and require copies

(1) The register and the index of members' names must be open to the inspection— **8.116.01**
  (a) of any member of the company without charge, and
  (b) of any other person on payment of such fee as may be prescribed.
(2) Any person may require a copy of a company's register of members, or of any part of it, on payment of such fee as may be prescribed.
(3) A person seeking to exercise either of the rights conferred by this section must make a request to the company to that effect.
(4) The request must contain the following information—
  (a) in the case of an individual, his name and address;
  (b) in the case of an organisation, the name and address of an individual responsible for making the request on behalf of the organisation;
  (c) the purpose for which the information is to be used; and
  (d) whether the information will be disclosed to any other person, and if so—
    (i) where that person is an individual, his name and address,
    (ii) where that person is an organisation, the name and address of an individual responsible for receiving the information on its behalf, and
    (iii) the purpose for which the information is to be used by that person.

COMMENCEMENT DATE 1 October 2007[32]

The right of any person to inspect the register and obtain copies has long been a feature of the Companies legislation, but this and the following sections are very different from their predecessor, in particular section 356 of the 1985 Act. The provision in the original Company Law Reform Bill restricted the rights of inspection pursuant to recommendations of the Steering Group of the Company Law Review,[33] but, following concern about the activities of organizations targeting shareholders in drug companies, the rights were further restricted as the Bill went through Parliament. **8.116.02**

So, although subsections (1) and (2) retain the basic rights to inspect the register and have copies available to members without charge and to others on payment of the prescribed fee,[34] any person seeking to exercise these rights must make a request, which must contain the information specified in subsection (4). Apart from names and addresses, the key information required is the purpose for which the information will be used and whether it is to be disclosed to any other person. This links to the jurisdiction of the court under the following section. The criminal penalties for the supply of false information are contained in section 119 and are quite severe. **8.116.03**

### 117 Register of members: response to request for inspection or copy

(1) Where a company receives a request under section 116 (register of members: right to inspect and require copy), it must within five working days either— **8.117.01**
  (a) comply with the request, or
  (b) apply to the court.
(2) If it applies to the court it must notify the person making the request.
(3) If on an application under this section the court is satisfied that the inspection or copy is not sought for a proper purpose—
  (a) it shall direct the company not to comply with the request, and
  (b) it may further order that the company's costs (in Scotland, expenses) on the application be paid in whole or in part by the person who made the request, even if he is not a party to the application.

---

[31] See para 36.1121.02.
[32] Companies Act 2006 (Commencement No 3, etc) Order 2007, SI 2007/2194, art 2(1).
[33] See Final Report, para 44.
[34] The fee is prescribed by the Companies (Fees for Inspection and Copying of Company Records) Regulations 2007, SI 2007/2612.

(4) If the court makes such a direction and it appears to the court that the company is or may be subject to other requests made for a similar purpose (whether made by the same person or different persons), it may direct that the company is not to comply with any such request. The order must contain such provision as appears to the court appropriate to identify the requests to which it applies.

(5) If on an application under this section the court does not direct the company not to comply with the request, the company must comply with the request immediately upon the court giving its decision or, as the case may be, the proceedings being discontinued.

COMMENCEMENT DATE 1 October 2007[35]

**8.117.02**    In the predecessor to this group of sections, there was no reference to timing as regards a request to inspect the register and a copy had to be supplied within 10 days. Further, it was illegal for a company to refuse inspection or a copy. Now, under this section, a company must either accede to a request for inspection or a copy within five working days or apply to the court to seek an order that the inspection or copy is not sought for a proper purpose. If such an application fails or the proceedings are discontinued, the company must immediately comply with a request.

**8.117.03**    Giving the court jurisdiction in this way follows a recommendation of the Steering Group of the Company Law Review,[36] who, because of concerns about misuse of the right, considered that the use of information in the register should be restricted to purposes relevant to either the holding of interests recorded in the register, or the exercise of rights attached to them, and to other purposes approved by the company. This section does not specify the grounds in this way, leaving a great deal to the discretion of the court to decide what is or is not a proper purpose,[37] although this should be facilitated by the fact that an application under section 116 must identify the purpose.

**8.117.04**    However, it is thought that guidance may be sought from cases under the previous provision, section 356(8) of the 1985 Act, where an order was sought to compel inspection or the provision of a copy. The equivalent of that section is now contained in section 118(3).[38]

**8.117.05**    In the context of subsection (3) it is thought that a proper purpose would include the wish to communicate with members of the company.[39] It seems much more likely that an existing member would have a proper purpose for a request than someone who was not a member, although even a member's request might legitimately be refused if it could be shown that he was not acting in the interests of the company. An example of such a situation, which is the sort of case that appears to have been in the minds of the Steering Group and exercised Members of Parliament very much during the debates on the Bill, would be that of animal rights activists using a shareholding in a pharmaceutical company to try to get access to the register for the purpose of circulating other members about what they would see as the misuse of animals in drugs research. As long as the research was being conducted in accordance with legal guidelines, it would seem clearly contrary to the interests of the company to allow such a request.

**8.117.06**    Note that the court has power in making an order under this section to direct the company not to comply with other requests made for a similar purpose, but it is required to make appropriate provision in order to identify such requests.

## 118  Register of members: refusal of inspection or default in providing copy

**8.118.01**    (1) If an inspection required under section 116 (register of members: right to inspect and require copy) is refused or default is made in providing a copy required under that section, otherwise than in accordance with an order of the court, an offence is committed by—
(a) the company, and
(b) every officer of the company who is in default.

(2) A person guilty of an offence under this section is liable on summary conviction to a fine not exceeding level 3 on the standard scale and, for continued contravention, a daily default fine not exceeding one-tenth of level 3 on the standard scale.

---

[35] Companies Act (Commencement No 3, etc) Order 2007, SI 2007/2194, art 2(1); note the transitional adaptation in Sch 1, para 2 to the Order.

[36] Final Report, para 11.44.

[37] This issue was much debated in Parliament. Pending definitive case law, useful guidance has been provided by the Institute of Chartered Secretaries and Administrators: available at ⟨http://www.icsa.org.uk/assets/files/pdfs/Policy/PP2.pdf⟩.

[38] See para 8.118.02 below.

[39] See *Pelling v Families Need Fathers Ltd* [2002] 1 BCLC 645, which is discussed in the commentary to the next section.

(3) In the case of any such refusal or default the court may by order compel an immediate inspection or, as the case may be, direct that the copy required be sent to the person requesting it.

COMMENCEMENT DATE 1 October 2007[40]

This section provides the criminal penalties for a failure to permit inspection of the register of members or provide a copy, unless the court orders otherwise under the previous section 117. Subsection (3) reenacts section 356(8) of the 1985 Act. It is clear that, quite apart from the jurisdiction under section 117, the court has a discretion whether or not to compel inspection or the provision of a copy.[41] In *Pelling v Families Need Fathers Ltd,*[42] the Court of Appeal explained that there may be special circumstances that lead the court to refuse to make an order, such as where it would be pointless because the request has been complied with after the application was issued but before it was heard, or where the request was physically impossible to comply with because the register had been destroyed or lost. It was also held that there are circumstances where the court can make an order on qualified terms and in that way can cater both for the applicant's wish to gain access to the register for the purpose of legitimately communicating with members as well as the company's proper and understandable concerns about the detrimental effects of an unqualified order for the disclosure of the names and addresses of the members. **8.118.02**

### 119 Register of members: offences in connection with request for or disclosure of information

(1) It is an offence for a person knowingly or recklessly to make in a request under section 116 (register of members: right to inspect or require copy) a statement that is misleading, false or deceptive in a material particular. **8.119.01**
(2) It is an offence for a person in possession of information obtained by exercise of either of the rights conferred by that section—
   (a) to do anything that results in the information being disclosed to another person, or
   (b) to fail to do anything with the result that the information is disclosed to another person, knowing, or having reason to suspect, that person may use the information for a purpose that is not a proper purpose.
(3) A person guilty of an offence under this section is liable—
   (a) on conviction on indictment, to imprisonment for a term not exceeding two years or a fine (or both);
   (b) on summary conviction—
     (i) in England and Wales, to imprisonment for a term not exceeding twelve months or to a fine not exceeding the statutory maximum (or both);
     (ii) in Scotland or Northern Ireland, to imprisonment for a term not exceeding six months, or to a fine not exceeding the statutory maximum (or both).

COMMENCEMENT DATE 1 October 2007[43]

This section introduces new, and potentially severe, criminal penalties to reinforce the importance of giving accurate information in support of a request under section 116. There are two separate offences. First, under subsection (1), it is an offence knowingly or recklessly to make a false statement in a section 116 request. Secondly, under subsection (2) the mere disclosure of information obtained under that section or neglect that leads to disclosure to another person is also an offence if someone knows or has reason to suspect that that person may use the information for 'a purpose that is not a proper purpose'. **8.119.02**

As far as using information for a proper purpose is concerned, the same considerations will apply as under section 117, although in this situation it may well be the case that the original applicant specified a legitimate purpose in his application under section 116. **8.119.03**

### 120 Information as to state of register and index

(1) When a person inspects the register, or the company provides him with a copy of the register or any part of it, the company must inform him of the most recent date (if any) on which alterations were made to the register and there were no further alterations to be made. **8.120.01**
(2) When a person inspects the index of members' names, the company must inform him whether there is any alteration to the register that is not reflected in the index.

---

[40] Companies Act 2006 (Commencement No 3, etc) Order 2007, SI 2007/2194, art 2(1).
[41] *Armstrong v Sheppard & Short Ltd* [1959] 2 All ER 651, 656 *per* Lord Evershed MR; *Pelling v Families Need Fathers Ltd* [2002] 1 BCLC 645, 652–653; see also the Australian case of *O'Brien v Sporting Shooters Association of Australia (Victoria)* [1999] VR 251 on the similar provision in the Australian Corporations Law.
[42] [2002] 1 BCLC 645.
[43] Companies Act 2006 (Commencement No 3, etc) Order 2007, SI 2007/2194, art 2(1).

(3) If a company fails to provide the information required under subsection (1) or (2), an offence is committed by—
(a) the company, and
(b) every officer of the company who is in default.
(4) A person guilty of an offence under this section is liable on summary conviction to a fine not exceeding level 3 on the standard scale.

COMMENCEMENT DATE 1 October 2009[44]

**8.120.02** This provision, requiring a company to provide information as to the most recent alterations to the register of members or to the index, is wholly new to the 2006 Act, being based on a recommendation of the Steering Group of the Company Law Review, who thought that it was a sensible adjunct to the right to inspect and have copies of the register. There do not seem to be any difficulties of interpretation about this section. Note that it applies where someone inspects the register or index on or after 1 October 2009 or is provided on or after that date with a copy of the register or part of it whether the request to do so was made before, on, or after that date.[45]

**8.120.03** As to the meaning of officer in default, see section 1121.[46]

### 121 Removal of entries relating to former members

**8.121.01** An entry relating to a former member of the company may be removed from the register after the expiration of ten years from the date on which he ceased to be a member.

COMMENCEMENT DATE 6 April 2008[47]

**8.121.02** This provision about the removal of entries from the register was previously in section 352 (6) of the 1985 Act. However, the period after which deletion is allowed is now 10 years, rather than the 20 years under the former legislation, and this is so whenever the period of 10 years expired. However, a copy of any details included in the register immediately before 6 April 2008 and removed under the power conferred by this section must be retained by the company until 6 April 2008, or, if earlier, 20 years after the member concerned ceased to be a member.[48]

## *Special cases*

### 122 Share warrants

**8.122.01** (1) On the issue of a share warrant the company must—
(a) enter in the register of members—
(i) the fact of the issue of the warrant,
(ii) a statement of the shares included in the warrant, distinguishing each share by its number so long as the share has a number, and
(iii) the date of the issue of the warrant, and
(b) amend the register, if necessary, so that no person is named on the register as the holder of the shares specified in the warrant.
(2) Until the warrant is surrendered, the particulars specified in subsection (1)(a) are deemed to be those required by this Act to be entered in the register of members.
(3) The bearer of a share warrant may, if the articles of the company so provide, be deemed a member of the company within the meaning of this Act, either to the full extent or for any purposes defined in the articles.
(4) Subject to the company's articles, the bearer of a share warrant is entitled, on surrendering it for cancellation, to have his name entered as a member in the register of members.
(5) The company is responsible for any loss incurred by any person by reason of the company entering in the register the name of a bearer of a share warrant in respect of the shares specified in it without the warrant being surrendered and cancelled.
(6) On the surrender of a share warrant, the date of the surrender must be entered in the register.

COMMENCEMENT DATE 1 October 2009[49]

---

[44] Companies Act 2006 (Commencement No 8, Transitional Provisions and Savings) Order 2008, SI 2008/2860, art 3(h).
[45] Companies Act 2006 (Commencement No 8, Transitional Provisions and Savings) Order 2008, SI 2008/2860, Sch 2, para 23.
[46] See para 37.1121.02.
[47] Companies Act 2006 (Commencement No 5, Transitional Provisions and Savings) Order 2007, SI 2007/3495, art 2.
[48] Companies Act 2006 (Commencement No 5, Transitional Provisions and Savings) Order 2007, SI 2007/3495, Sch 4, para 2.
[49] Companies Act 2006 (Commencement No 8, Transitional Provisions and Savings) Order 2008, SI 2008/2860, art 3(h).

This section replaced section 355 of the 1985 Act with minor modifications to make it clear that shares **8.122.02** can be directly issued in bearer form, rather than having first to be issued as registered form and then converted to bearer form, and to remove any reference to directors' qualification shares, a concept that has been abolished.

The power to issue shares in bearer form, namely shares that are evidenced by warrant and transferable **8.122.03** by delivery, rather than by certificate, is in section 779.[50] Section 122 deals simply with how they are dealt with in the register of members, the crucial point being that the register simply records the details in subsection (1)(a) and does not name any person as holder of the shares, unless and until the warrant is surrendered, when the date of surrender must be entered in the register. As subsection (3) makes clear, the holder of a share warrant is a member of the company, and thus entitled to the rights that the Act gives to members, only if and to the extent that the articles so provide, but the holder of a warrant can, if the articles permit, surrender it and be entered as a registered member.[51]

If the company enters the name of the holder of a share warrant in the register without its being **8.122.04** surrendered and cancelled, it is liable under subsection (5) for any loss incurred by any person as a result. There appears to be no reported example of a claim made under this provision, but it is thought that loss might be incurred by the purchaser of bearer shares who discovers that the previous holder's name is on the register and incurs expense in having the entry removed.

## 123  Single member companies

(1) If a limited company is formed under this Act with only one member there shall be entered in the **8.123.01** company's register of members, with the name and address of the sole member, a statement that the company has only one member.
(2) If the number of members of a limited company falls to one, or if an unlimited company with only one member becomes a limited company on re-registration, there shall upon the occurrence of that event be entered in the company's register of members, with the name and address of the sole member—
  (a) a statement that the company has only one member, and
  (b) the date on which the company became a company having only one member.
(3) If the membership of a limited company increases from one to two or more members, there shall upon the occurrence of that event be entered in the company's register of members, with the name and address of the person who was formerly the sole member—
  (a) a statement that the company has ceased to have only one member, and
  (b) the date on which that event occurred.
(4) If a company makes default in complying with this section, an offence is committed by—
  (a) the company, and
  (b) every officer of the company who is in default.
(5) A person guilty of an offence under this section is liable on summary conviction to a fine not exceeding level 3 on the standard scale and, for continued contravention, a daily default fine not exceeding one-tenth of level 3 on the standard scale.

COMMENCEMENT DATE 1 October 2009[52]

This section replaces section 352A of the 1985 Act, which was inserted to comply with the requirements **8.123.02** of the Twelfth EC Company Law Directive.[53] The previous section was concerned with private companies only, but now that a public limited company can be formed with only one member,[54] this section simply makes reference to where a limited company has one member, or where an unlimited company with only one member converts to limited company form. In any of these cases, the statements and date listed in subsections (1) and (2) must be entered in the company's register of members. If a company ceases to have only one member, the statement and date in subsection (3) must be entered.

As to the meaning of officer in default, see section 1121.[55] **8.123.03**

---

[50] See para 21.779.02.
[51] Subsection (4).
[52] Companies Act 2006 (Commencement No 8, Transitional Provisions and Savings) Order 2008, SI 2008/ 2860, art 3(h).
[53] Directive (EC) 89/667 [1989] OJ L395/40.
[54] See s 7; para 2.7.02.
[55] See para 36.1121.02.

### 124 Company holding its own shares as treasury shares

**8.124.01**    (1) Where a company purchases its own shares in circumstances in which section 724 (treasury shares) applies—
 (a) the requirements of section 113 (register of members) need not be complied with if the company cancels all of the shares forthwith after the purchase, and
 (b) if the company does not cancel all of the shares forthwith after the purchase, any share that is so cancelled shall be disregarded for the purposes of that section.
 (2) Subject to subsection (1), where a company holds shares as treasury shares the company must be entered in the register as the member holding those shares.

COMMENCEMENT DATE 1 October 2009[56]

**8.124.02**    This section replaced section 352(3A) of the 1985 Act, which was inserted when companies purchasing their own shares were first allowed to hold them in treasury. As to these in general, see 18.724.02. In the normal situation when a company holds its own shares as treasury shares, it must be entered in the register as member,[57] but in respect of any shares that are cancelled after such a purchase, there is no requirement to comply with the requirements of section 113.

## *Supplementary*

### 125 Power of court to rectify register

**8.125.01**    (1) If—
 (a) the name of any person is, without sufficient cause, entered in or omitted from a company's register of members, or
 (b) default is made or unnecessary delay takes place in entering on the register the fact of any person having ceased to be a member,
 the person aggrieved, or any member of the company, or the company, may apply to the court for rectification of the register.
 (2) The court may either refuse the application or may order rectification of the register and payment by the company of any damages sustained by any party aggrieved.
 (3) On such an application the court may decide any question relating to the title of a person who is a party to the application to have his name entered in or omitted from the register, whether the question arises between members or alleged members, or between members or alleged members on the one hand and the company on the other hand, and generally may decide any question necessary or expedient to be decided for rectification of the register.
 (4) In the case of a company required by this Act to send a list of its members to the registrar of companies, the court, when making an order for rectification of the register, shall by its order direct notice of the rectification to be given to the registrar.

COMMENCEMENT DATE 1 October 2009[58]

**8.125.02**    This section, giving the court power to rectify the register of members,[59] replaced section 359 of the 1985 Act and is worded in an identical manner.[60] Although the court can award damages under subsection (2), this is only when there is a claim for rectification; an ordinary claim for damages must be brought by action.[61]

**8.125.03**    A large number of cases have considered the nature of the jurisdiction under section 125. It is a wide jurisdiction covering all situations where a name is wrongly on the register,[62] whether that is the fault of the company[63] or not,[64] but it is a discretionary jurisdiction and regard has to be had to the justice of

---

[56] Companies Act 2006 (Commencement No 8, Transitional Provisions and Savings) Order 2008, SI 2008/2860, art 3(h).

[57] See also s 724(4) (see para 18.724.03), which replicates subs (2).

[58] Companies Act 2006 (Commencement No 8, Transitional Provisions and Savings) Order 2008, SI 2008/2860, art 3(h).

[59] As to the possibility of the company recognizing a right to rectification and acting on that without an application to the court, see *Reese River Silver Mining Co* (1869) LR 4 HL 64, 74; *Re Poole Firebrick Co* (1875) 10 Ch App 157; *First National Reinsurance Co v Greenfield* [1921] 2 KB 260, 278–280; *Re Derham and Allen* [1946] Ch 31, 36.

[60] As to the power of the court to rectify the register after a winding-up order has been made, see s 148 of the Insolvency Act 1986.

[61] *Re Ottos Kopje Diamond Mines Ltd* [1893] 1 Ch 618.

[62] *Re Imperial Chemical Industries* [1936] 2 All ER 463.

[63] *Ward and Henry's Case* (1867) 2 Ch App 431; *Reese River Silver Mining Co v Smith* (1869) LR 4 HL 64, 57.

[64] *Ex p Shaw, Re Diamond Rock Boring Co Ltd* (1877) 2 QBD 463; *Re Fagins Bookshop plc* [1992] BCLC 118.

the case.[65] It has been held that, as the section provides for a summary remedy, it should be used only in straightforward and uncomplicated cases and that it is not appropriate to determine substantial issues of fact with only affidavit evidence.[66] So if, a dispute between two individuals as to which ought to be registered as a member of the company is a simple one, the court will decide it on a motion under section 125, but if it is complicated or there are issues concerning the rights of third parties, it has been held that the court will not act on a motion, but will allow the aggrieved person to pursue an action.[67] On the other hand it may now, in accordance with objectives of the Civil Procedure Rules 1998, be more appropriate that the case be actively managed than that it is struck out and the applicant forced to commence a new action.

When a motion is brought by a shareholder or transferee, the company is the proper respondent, not    **8.125.04**
the directors, unless they are added at their own request.[68] In an appropriate case the company can be ordered to disclose documents.[69] A typical situation where a motion may be brought by a shareholder is where he claims that he was induced to subscribe for shares by fraud or misrepresentation.[70] Here the same principles apply as would apply in a claim for rescission of the contract and the application must be made within a reasonable time and before the commencement of a winding up.[71] If there is no contract to take shares or the contract is void, rectification can be ordered even after a winding up[72] and delay does not bar the claim.[73] Other cases have been based on the company acting on a forged transfer[74] and wrongfully assuming that the member acted in breach of pre-emption provisions in the articles.[75] Rectification will be ordered when an allotment of shares has been made without authority.[76]

The company can itself apply to the court under the section, for example where a transferee of shares    **8.125.05**
has been wrongly removed from the register and the transferor restored.[77] In a situation where a transfer has not been registered because of unnecessary delay on the part of the company, the court can order rectification retrospectively if it matters, for example to validate dissent to a scheme of reconstruction.[78]

Joint holders of shares have the right to have the register rectified so that they can fairly and reasonably    **8.125.06**
exercise their powers as members. In *Burns v Siemens Brothers Dynamo Works*,[79] the register was rectified so that each holder appeared first in respect of some of their shares. This was important because of the then standard provision in articles allowing only the first-named holder to vote.[80]

## 126  Trusts not to be entered on register

No notice of any trust, expressed, implied or constructive, shall be entered on the register of members    **8.126.01**
of a company registered in England and Wales or Northern Ireland, or be receivable by the registrar.

COMMENCEMENT DATE  1 October 2009[81]

---

[65]  *Sichell's Case* (1868) LR 3 Ch App 119, 122; *Re Dronfield Silkstone Co* (1880) 17 Ch D 76, 97; see also the *dictum* of Lord Macnaghten in *Trevor v Whitworth* (1888) 12 AC 409, 440.

[66]  *Re Hoicrest Ltd, Keene v Martin* [2000] 1 BCLC 194.

[67]  *Ward and Henry's Case* (1867) 2 Ch App 431; *Ex p Shaw* (1877) 2 QBD 463; *Ex p Sargent* (1874) 17 Eq 273; *Re Greater Britain Products Development Corporation* (1924) 40 TLR 488.

[68]  *Re Copal Varnish Co* [1917] 2 Ch 349. Normally the directors will only be liable for costs in such a case (*Re Keith Prowse & Co* [1918] 1 Ch 487). In *Morgan v Morgan Insurance Brokers Ltd* [1993] BCC 145, an order for payment of costs was made against defendant directors where they admitted that they had no right to register the transfers in question.

[69]  *Cory v Cory* [1923] 1 Ch 90.

[70]  See *Ex p Ward* (1867) LR 3 Ex 180; *Ex p Kintrea* (1870) 4 Ch App 95; *Re London and Staffordshire Fire Insurance Co* (1883) 24 Ch D 14.

[71]  *Muir v City of Glasgow Bank* (1879) 4 App Cas 337; *Tennent v City of Glasgow Bank* (1879) 4 App Cas 615.

[72]  *Oakes v Turquand* (1867) LR 2 HL 325; *Alabaster's Case* (1868) 7 Eq 273; *Baillie's Case* [1898] 1 Ch 110.

[73]  *Gorrissen's Case* (1873) 8 Ch App 507; *Wynne's Case* (1873) 8 Ch App 1002; *Beck's Case* (1874) 9 Ch App 392; *Baillie's Case* [1898] 1 Ch 110. The order may operate retrospectively: *Barbor v Middleton* (1988) 4 BCC 681.

[74]  *Re Bahia and San Francisco Railway Co* (1868) LR 3 QB 584.

[75]  *Re Claygreen Ltd* [2005] EWHC 2032 (Ch).

[76]  *Avenue Road Developments Ltd v Reggiesco Ltd* [2012] EWHC 1625 (Ch).

[77]  *Re Indo-China Steam Navigation Co* [1917] 2 Ch 100; the objecting transferor was ordered to pay the costs of the company and the transferee.

[78]  *Re Sussex Brick Co* [1904] 1 Ch 598; see also *Nation's Case* (1866) 3 Eq 77; *Hill's Case* (1869) 4 Ch App 769n, where rectification was retrospective in order to relieve the transferor from liability as a contributory.

[79]  [1919] 1 Ch 225.

[80]  Although this is now governed by s 286 (see para 13.286.02), there seems no reason for the principle not to be applicable.

[81]  Companies Act 2006 (Commencement No 8, Transitional Provisions and Savings) Order 2008, SI 2008/2860, art 3(h).

**8.126.02**    This section replaced section 360 of the 1985 Act, the only change being the coverage of Northern Ireland.[82] Scottish companies may recognize trusts unless their articles provide otherwise.

**8.126.03**    The prohibition on entering notice of any trust extends to a lien that the company may claim to have over shares.[83] Conversely it follows from section 126 that the company cannot be under any liability for ignoring a notice of a trust, although the directors may be.[84] However, the principle enshrined in the section does not mean that the company can ignore equitable interests of which it has notice. For example, a lien which arises if a company advances money to a shareholder will not have priority over earlier charges of which it has notice.[85] Nor can it enforce a lien on shares vested in trustees if at the time of making the advance it knows that the shares are held in trust.[86] A company that knows that shares are being held for the benefit of creditors is justified in refusing to give effect to a subsequent transfer by the debtor to a purchaser for value.[87] A company is not concerned with whether trustees who are the registered shareholders are acting within their powers in dealing with the shares,[88] and can enforce its own rights against the shareholders irrespective of the rights of the beneficiaries,[89] unless it had notice of the trust before its rights arose. Priority in giving notice to the company does not affect the priority of two charges among themselves.[90]

### 127  Register to be evidence

**8.127.01**    The register of members is prima facie evidence of any matters which are by this Act directed or authorised to be inserted in it.

COMMENCEMENT DATE  1 October 2009[91]

**8.127.02**    This section reenacted section 361 of the 1985 Act and is self-explanatory, although it should be noted that, while the register is *prima facie* evidence, it is not conclusive evidence as to its contents. Thus it can be amended, either by the company to correct administrative errors or by the court on application under section 125.

### 128  Time limit for claims arising from entry in register

**8.128.01**    (1)  Liability incurred by a company—
    (a)  from the making or deletion of an entry in the register of members, or
    (b)  from a failure to make or delete any such entry,
    is not enforceable more than ten years after the date on which the entry was made or deleted or, as the case may be, the failure first occurred.
    (2)  This is without prejudice to any lesser period of limitation (and, in Scotland, to any rule that the obligation giving rise to the liability prescribes before the expiry of that period).

COMMENCEMENT DATE  6 April 2008[92]

**8.128.02**    The limitation period imposed by this section for claims arising from an entry or deletion of an entry in the register, or from a failure to make or delete an entry, was previously in section 352(7) of the 1985 Act. The important change is the reduction of the period to 10 years.[93] Note, however, that, as subsection (2) provides, there may be a lesser period of limitation or, in Scotland, prescription. This would be the case if, for example, an error was a breach of contract, in respect of which an action for breach is subject to a six-year limitation period (in England and Wales)[94] or a five-year prescription

---

[82]  For the application of the Act to Northern Ireland, see s 1 and Part 45.
[83]  *Re W Key & Son* [1902] 1 Ch 467.
[84]  *Société Générale de Paris v Tramways Union Co* (1884) 14 QBD 424 (affirmed sub nom *Société Générale de Paris v Walker* (1886) 11 App Cas 20), *Simpson v Molson's Bank* [1895] AC 270. Someone having equitable rights in shares should serve a notice under RSC Ord 50, rr 11–15 in order to obtain protection.
[85]  *Bradford Banking Co v Henry Briggs & Co* (1886) 12 AC 29; *Rearden v Provincial Bank of Ireland* [1896] 1 Ir R 532; *Binney v Ince Hall Coal Co* (1866) 35 LJ Ch 363.
[86]  *Mackereth v Wigan Coal and Iron Co* [1916] 2 Ch 293.
[87]  *Peat v Clayton* [1906] 1 Ch 649; *Roots v Williamson* (1888) 38 Ch D 485; *Moore v North-Western Bank* [1891] 2 Ch 599.
[88]  *Simpson v Molson's Bank* [1895] AC 270.
[89]  *London and Brazilian Bank v Brocklebank* (1882) 21 Ch D 302.
[90]  *Société Générale de Paris v Walker* (1886) 11 App Cas 20.
[91]  Companies Act 2006 (Commencement No 8, Transitional Provisions and Savings) Order 2008, SI 2008/2860, art 3(h).
[92]  Companies Act 2006 (Commencement No 5, Transitional Provisions and Savings) Order 2007, SI 2007/3495, art 2.
[93]  Under earlier Acts it was 20 years, but note the effect of the transitional provision described below.
[94]  Limitation Act 1980, s 5.

period (in Scotland),[95] although a claim for rectification under section 125 or an action for damages arising from a failure to enter someone in the register[96] is subject to the 10-year period prescribed by this section. The 10-year period applies to causes of action arising on or after 6 April 2008; as regards causes of action arising before then, the limitation period is 10 years from 6 April 2008 or 20 years, whichever expires first.[97]

# CHAPTER 3
## OVERSEAS BRANCH REGISTERS

Chapter 3 concerns the general regulation of overseas branch registers. Sections 129 to 135 were **8.129.01** originally contained in the early drafts of the Companies Act 2006 in a single section which simply referred to the power of a company to keep an overseas register under section 362 of and Schedule 14 to the 1985 Act, being unaffected by the Company Law Reform Bill 2005 as it then was. The section also contained a power to make future regulation relating to the registers, subject to a negative resolution procedure. However once the government decided to consolidate the companies legislation in the Companies Bill in the Summer of 2006 the provisions relating to Overseas Branch Registers in section 362 of and Schedule 14 to the 1985 Act were introduced into the Companies Bill as sections 129 to 135 largely restating and clarifying those same provisions.

## 129  Overseas branch registers

(1) A company having a share capital may, if it transacts business in a country or territory to which this **8.129.02** Chapter applies, cause to be kept there a branch register of members resident there (an 'overseas branch register').

(2) This Chapter applies to—
  (a) any part of Her Majesty's dominions outside the UK, the Channel Islands and the Isle of Man, and
  (b) the countries or territories listed below.

| | |
|---|---|
| Bangladesh | Malawi |
| Cyprus | Malaysia |
| Dominica | Malta |
| The Gambia | Nigeria |
| Ghana | Pakistan |
| Guyana | Seychelles |
| The Hong Kong Special Administrative | Sierra Leone |
| Region of the People's Republic of | Singapore |
| China | South Africa |
| India | Sri Lanka |
| Ireland | Swaziland |
| Kenya | Trinidad and Tobago |
| Kiribati | Uganda |
| Lesotho | Zimbabwe |

(3) The Secretary of State may make provision by regulations as to the circumstances in which a company is to be regarded as keeping a register in a particular country or territory.

(4) Regulations under this section are subject to negative resolution procedure.

(5) References—
  (a) in any Act or instrument (including, in particular, a company's articles) to a dominion register, or
  (b) in articles registered before 1st November 1929 to a colonial register,
  are to be read (unless the context otherwise requires) as a reference to an overseas branch register kept under this section.

COMMENCEMENT DATE 1 October 2009[98]

**8.129.03**

This section merges and to some extent clarifies the provisions previously contained in section 362 and Schedule 14 Part I of the 1985 Act. Those provisions themselves derived from the Dominion Registers

---

[95] Prescription and Limitation (Scotland) Act 1973, s 6.
[96] See *Re Ottos Kopje Diamond Mines* [1893] 1 Ch 618; *Tomkinson v Balkis Consolidated Co* [1893] AC 397.
[97] Companies Act 2006 (Commencement No 5, Transitional Provisions and Savings) Order 2007, SI 2007/3495, Sch 4, para 3.
[98] Companies Act 2006 (Commencement No 8, Transitional Provisions and Savings) Order 2008, SI 2008/2860, art 3(h).

required by section 119 of the 1948 Act. Section 362 stated: 'A company having a share capital whose objects comprise the transaction of business in any of the countries or territories specified in Part I of Schedule 14 to this Act may cause to be kept in any such country or territory in which it transacts business a branch register of members resident in that country or territory.' The dropping in section 129 of the requirement to have the objects state that the transaction of business in certain overseas countries or territories is part of its business is a welcome updating and clarifying of this provision. A company is now required simply to transact business in a specified country for the requirements of the section to apply. Having said that in *Bishop v Balkis Consolidated Co*[99] Lindley LJ suggested that keeping such a register would amount to transacting business.

**8.129.04**     Schedule 14 Part I of the 1985 Act specified the list of countries or territories to which section 362 applied. This list is repeated in section 129 with the only noteworthy change being that Northern Ireland and the Republic of Ireland are no longer listed separately but now seemingly consolidated as 'Ireland'. This creates a somewhat anomalous status for Northern Ireland with regard to overseas registers. Under the 1985 Act the text of section 362 and Schedule 14 confusingly refers to Great Britain (thus excluding Northern Ireland) at times and at others the UK (which includes Northern Ireland). It also lists Northern Ireland specifically as an overseas territory. This makes clear that for the purposes of the general obligation to keep an overseas register Northern Ireland is an overseas territory. Under section 129 the UK is preferred to Great Britain, thus including Northern Ireland. Northern Ireland has also been dropped from the list of overseas territories and countries. This either means that Northern Ireland is no longer considered an overseas country or territory, and thus no overseas register is needed, or Northern Ireland and the Republic of Ireland are both considered an overseas country or territory under the consolidation of both into 'Ireland' in the list. This is also problematic for section 133 below.

### 130  Notice of opening of overseas branch register

**8.130.01**     (1)  A company that begins to keep an overseas branch register must give notice to the registrar within 14 days of doing so, stating the country or territory in which the register is kept.

(2)  If default is made in complying with subsection (1), an offence is committed by—
   (a)  the company, and
   (b)  every officer of the company who is in default.

(3)  A person guilty of an offence under subsection (2) is liable on summary conviction to a fine not exceeding level 3 on the standard scale and, for continued contravention, a daily default fine not exceeding one-tenth of level 3 on the standard scale.

COMMENCEMENT DATE 1 October 2009[100]

**8.130.02**     Section 130 provides for notice to be given to the Registrar of Companies within 14 days of the opening of an overseas register. The notice must state what country or territory the register is kept in and failure to comply is an offence. This section restates Schedule 14 Part II(1) of the 1985 Act. The previous provision in Schedule 14 stated:

(1)  A company keeping an overseas branch register shall give to the registrar of companies notice in the prescribed form of the situation of the office where any overseas branch register is kept and of any change in its situation, and, if it is discontinued, of its discontinuance.

(2)  Any such notice shall be given within 14 days of the opening of the office or of the change or discontinuance, as the case may be.

(3)  If default is made in complying with this paragraph, the company and every officer of it who is in default is liable to a fine and, for continued contravention, to a daily default fine.

---

[99]  (1890) 25 QBD 512, CA.

[100]  Companies Act 2006 (Commencement No 8, Transitional Provisions and Savings) Order 2008, SI 2008/2860, art 3(h).

Section 130 does not change the substance of the obligation in the previous provision to notify the    **8.130.03**
register of the opening of a register, but uses a simpler drafting style and restates the fines consistent
with the new consolidated Act. The obligation to provide notification of discontinuance has also been
separated out and is now contained in section 135 below.

### 131 Keeping of overseas branch register

  (1) An overseas branch register is regarded as part of the company's register of members ('the main    **8.131.01**
      register').
  (2) The Secretary of State may make provision by regulations modifying any provision of Chapter 2
      (register of members) as it applies in relation to an overseas branch register.
  (3) Regulations under this section are subject to negative resolution procedure.
  (4) Subject to the provisions of this Act, a company may by its articles make such provision as it thinks
      fit as to the keeping of overseas branch registers.

COMMENCEMENT DATE 1 October 2009[101]

Section 131 provides that the overseas register is treated as if it were part of the main register as well as    **8.131.02**
miscellaneous provisions for further regulation, negative resolution procedure, and provision for
regulating the overseas register through the articles of association. Section 131(1) restates Schedule 14
Part II(2) of the 1985 Act in a simpler form but with no change of substance. Section 131(2) and (3) was
part of the original non-consolidated Company Law Reform Bill 2005 which was based on the various
recommendations of the Company Law Reform Steering Group.[102] All of Chapter 3, sections 129 to
135 were originally contained in a single section which simply referred to the power of a company to
keep an overseas register under section 362 of and Schedule 14 to the 1985 Act, being unaffected by the
Company Law Reform Bill 2005 as it then was. The section also contained a provision to make future
regulation relating to the registers, subject to a negative resolution procedure. Section 131(4) is an
almost exact restatement of the previous power of a company with regard to overseas branch registers
in Schedule 14 Part II(7) of the 1985 Act.

### 132 Register or duplicate to be kept available for inspection in UK

  (1) A company that keeps an overseas branch register must keep available for inspection—    **8.132.01**
      (a) the register, or
      (b) a duplicate of the register duly entered up from time to time,
      at the place in the United Kingdom where the company's main register is kept available for
      inspection.
  (2) Any such duplicate is treated for all purposes of this Act as part of the main register.
  (3) If default is made in complying with subsection (1), an offence is committed by—
      (a) the company, and
      (b) every officer of the company who is in default.
  (4) A person guilty of an offence under subsection (3) is liable on summary conviction to a fine not
      exceeding level 3 on the standard scale and, for continued contravention, a daily default fine not
      exceeding one-tenth of level 3 on the standard scale.

COMMENCEMENT DATE 1 October 2009[103]

Section 132 provides for the company to keep the overseas register or a duplicate of the overseas    **8.132.02**
register available for inspection. It restates Schedule 14 Part II(4) of the 1985 Act in a simpler form but
with no change of substance. It also restates the fines for non-compliance consistent with the new
consolidated Act.

### 133 Transactions in shares registered in overseas branch register

  (1) Shares registered in an overseas branch register must be distinguished from those registered in    **8.133.01**
      the main register.
  (2) No transaction with respect to shares registered in an overseas branch register may be registered
      in any other register.
  (3) An instrument of transfer of a share registered in an overseas branch register—
      (a) is regarded as a transfer of property situated outside the United Kingdom, and

---

[101] Companies Act 2006 (Commencement No 8, Transitional Provisions and Savings) Order 2008, SI
2008/2860, art 3(h).
  [102] See ⟨http://www.dti.gov.uk/bbf/co-act-2006/index.html⟩.
  [103] Companies Act 2006 (Commencement No 8, Transitional Provisions and Savings) Order 2008, SI
2008/2860, art 3(h).

(b)  unless executed in a part of the United Kingdom, is exempt from stamp duty.

COMMENCEMENT DATE 1 October 2009[104]

8.133.02  Section 133 provides that shares registered on an overseas register must be distinguished from those registered in the main register and that transactions regarding shares registered on an overseas register must not be registered anywhere else. Section 133(1) and (2) restates Schedule 14 Part II(5) of the 1985 Act with no change of substance. Section 133(3) restates Schedule 14 Part II(8) of the 1985 Act with only one significant change. Schedule 14 Part II(8) stated: 'An instrument of transfer of a share registered in an overseas branch register (other than such a register kept in Northern Ireland) is deemed a transfer of property situated outside the United Kingdom.' The restatement in section 133(3) drops the Northern Ireland exemption from the provision. However, as was noted above when considering section 129, the anomalous status of Northern Ireland as to whether it is covered by the overseas branch register provisions is further confused here. Thus if Northern Ireland is an overseas territory then a transfer of a share registered in an overseas branch register there would be oddly a transfer of property outside the UK but specifically not exempt from stamp duty. The framing of the section clearly contemplates this anomaly but is far from satisfactory.

### 134 Jurisdiction of local courts

8.134.01  (1)  A competent court in a country or territory where an overseas branch register is kept may exercise the same jurisdiction as is exercisable by a court in the United Kingdom—
  (a)  to rectify the register (see section 125), or
  (b)  in relation to a request for inspection or a copy of the register (see section 117).
(2)  The offences—
  (a)  of refusing inspection or failing to provide a copy of the register (see section 118), and
  (b)  of making a false, misleading or deceptive statement in a request for inspection or a copy (see section 119),
  may be prosecuted summarily before any tribunal having summary criminal jurisdiction in the country or territory where the register is kept.
(3)  This section extends only to those countries and territories to which paragraph 3 of Schedule 14 to the Companies Act 1985 (c. 6) (which made similar provision) extended immediately before the coming into force of this Chapter.

COMMENCEMENT DATE 1 October 2009[105]

8.134.02  Section 134 sets out the jurisdiction of a local court to deal with the overseas register. It restates and updates, by removing an inappropriate reference to the 1948 Act, Schedule 14 Part II(3) of the 1985 Act with no change of substance.

### 135 Discontinuance of overseas branch register

8.135.01  (1)  A company may discontinue an overseas branch register.
(2)  If it does so all the entries in that register must be transferred—
  (a)  to some other overseas branch register kept in the same country or territory, or
  (b)  to the main register.
(3)  The company must give notice to the registrar within 14 days of the discontinuance.
(4)  If default is made in complying with subsection (3), an offence is committed by—
  (a)  the company, and
  (b)  every officer of the company who is in default.
(5)  A person guilty of an offence under subsection (4) is liable on summary conviction to a fine not exceeding level 3 on the standard scale and, for continued contravention, a daily default fine not exceeding one-tenth of level 3 on the standard scale.

COMMENCEMENT DATE 1 October 2009[106]

8.135.02  Section 135 sets out the procedure for the discontinuance of an overseas register and the fines for non-compliance. Section 135(1) and (2) restates Schedule 14 Part II(6) of the 1985 Act with no change of substance. Section 135(3) to (5) restates Schedule 14 Part II (1) of the 1985 Act in a simpler form but with no change of substance. It also restates the fines consistent with the new consolidated Act.

---

[104] Companies Act 2006 (Commencement No 8, Transitional Provisions and Savings) Order 2008, SI 2008/2860, art 3(h).
[105] Companies Act 2006 (Commencement No 8, Transitional Provisions and Savings) Order 2008, SI 2008/2860, art 3(h).
[106] Companies Act 2006 (Commencement No 8, Transitional Provisions and Savings) Order 2008, SI 2008/2860, art 3(h).

# CHAPTER 4
## PROHIBITION ON SUBSIDIARY BEING MEMBER OF ITS HOLDING COMPANY

This chapter sets out the range of prohibitions and exceptions to a subsidiary being a member of its holding company. It largely restates section 23 of the 1985 Act and Part 1 of Schedule 2 without any change of substance.     **8.136.01**

### *General prohibtion*

### 136  Prohibition on subsidiary being a member of its holding company

(1) Except as provided by this Chapter—     **8.136.02**
    (a) a body corporate cannot be a member of a company that is its holding company, and
    (b) any allotment or transfer of shares in a company to its subsidiary is void.
(2) The exceptions are provided for in—
        section 138 (subsidiary acting as personal representative or trustee), and
        section 141 (subsidiary acting as authorised dealer in securities).

COMMENCEMENT DATE 1 October 2009[107]

Section 136 sets out the general prohibition on a company being a member of its holding company.     **8.136.03**
Section 136 restates the central prohibition previously contained in section 23 of the 1985 Act. The more detailed exceptions which were previously contained in section 23(3), (3A), (3B), (3BA), (3C), and (4)–(8) had become unwieldy as a result of constant amendments and so have been spread out within the various sections that make up Chapter 4 of the Companies Act 2006. Section 23 of the 1985 Act was introduced by the Companies Act 1989, section 129 to supplement the larger prohibition in section 143(1) of the 1985 Act which prohibited a company acquiring its own shares. This prohibition itself was based on the common law principle that companies cannot acquire their own shares: *Trevor v Whitworth*.[108] It does not apply to unincorporated bodies.

### 137  Shares acquired before prohibition became applicable

(1) Where a body corporate became a holder of shares in a company—     **8.137.01**
    (a) before the relevant date, or
    (b) on or after that date and before the commencement of this Chapter in circumstances in which the prohibition in section 23(1) of the Companies Act 1985 (c. 6) or Article 33(1) of the Companies (Northern Ireland) Order 1986 (S.I. 1986/1032 (N.I. 6)) (or any corresponding earlier enactment), as it then had effect, did not apply, or
    (c) on or after the commencement of this Chapter in circumstances in which the prohibition in section 136 did not apply,
    it may continue to be a member of the company.
(2) The relevant date for the purposes of subsection (1)(a) is—
    (a) 1st July 1948 in the case of a company registered in Great Britain, and
    (b) 1st April 1961 in the case of a company registered in Northern Ireland.
(3) So long as it is permitted to continue as a member of a company by virtue of this section, an allotment to it of fully paid shares in the company may be validly made by way of capitalisation of reserves of the company.
(4) But, so long as the prohibition in section 136 would (apart from this section) apply, it has no right to vote in respect of the shares mentioned in subsection (1) above, or any shares allotted as mentioned in subsection (2) above, on a written resolution or at meetings of the company or of any class of its members.

COMMENCEMENT DATE 1 October 2009[109]

Section 137 qualifies the general prohibition for certain historic shareholdings. Section 137 restates     **8.137.02**
and updates section 23(4) to (6) of the 1985 Act with no change of substance. It is in essence a saving provision for qualifying shares acquired before the date the prohibition originally came into force. The original need for a saving provision was because of changes to the definition of subsidiary in the 1948 and 1989 Acts which meant many companies held prohibited shares in companies newly classified as

---

[107] Companies Act 2006 (Commencement No 8, Transitional Provisions and Savings) Order 2008, SI 2008/2860, art 3(h).

[108] (1887) 12 App Ca 409.

[109] Companies Act 2006 (Commencement No 8, Transitional Provisions and Savings) Order 2008, SI 2008/2860, art 3(h).

subsidiaries. The provision allows the continued holding of the shares but not the voting of those shares: *Acatos & Hutcheson Plc v Watson*.[110] Section 137 is clearer than the original section 23 as to the cut off dates generally and the effect in Northern Ireland specifically. Section 137(4) is also more detailed than the previous prohibition in stating that written resolutions are covered by the voting prohibition.

## *Subsidiary acting as personal representative or trustee*

### 138 Subsidiary acting as personal representative or trustee

8.138.01
(1) The prohibition in section 136 (prohibition on subsidiary being a member of its holding company) does not apply where the subsidiary is concerned only—
   (a) as personal representative, or
   (b) as trustee,
   unless, in the latter case, the holding company or a subsidiary of it is beneficially interested under the trust.
(2) For the purpose of ascertaining whether the holding company or a subsidiary is so interested, there shall be disregarded—
   (a) any interest held only by way of security for the purposes of a transaction entered into by the holding company or subsidiary in the ordinary course of a business that includes the lending or money;
   (b) any interest within—
   section 139 (interests to be disregarded: residual interest under pension scheme or employees' share scheme), or
   section 140 (interests to be disregarded: employer's rights of recovery under pension scheme or employees' share scheme);
   (c) any rights that the company or subsidiary has in its capacity as trustee, including in particular—
      (i) any right to recover its expenses or be remunerated out of the trust property, and
      (ii) any right to be indemnified out of the trust property for any liability incurred by reason of any act or omission in the performance of its duties as trustee.

COMMENCEMENT DATE 1 October 2009[111]

8.138.02   Section 138 provides an exception to the general prohibition for personal representatives and trustee holdings where there is no beneficial interest under the trust. This was contained previously in section 23(2) of the 1985 Act and is reenacted here with no change of substance.

### 139 Interests to be disregarded: residual interest under pension scheme or employees' share scheme

8.139.01
(1) Where shares in a company are held on trust for the purposes of a pension scheme or employees' share scheme, there shall be disregarded for the purposes of section 138 any residual interest that has not vested in possession.
(2) A 'residual interest' means a right of the company or subsidiary ("the residual beneficiary") to receive any of the trust property in the event of—
   (a) all the liabilities arising under the scheme having been satisfied or provided for, or
   (b) the residual beneficiary ceasing to participate in the scheme, or
   (c) the trust property at any time exceeding what is necessary for satisfying the liabilities arising or expected to arise under the scheme.
(3) In subsection (2)—
   (a) the reference to a right includes a right dependent on the exercise of a discretion vested by the scheme in the trustee or another person, and
   (b) the reference to liabilities arising under a scheme includes liabilities that have resulted, or may result, from the exercise of any such discretion.
(4) For the purposes of this section a residual interest vests in possession—
   (a) in a case within subsection (2)(a), on the occurrence of the event mentioned there (whether or not the amount of the property receivable pursuant to the right is ascertained);
   (b) in a case within subsection (2)(b) or (c), when the residual beneficiary becomes entitled to require the trustee to transfer to him any of the property receivable pursuant to the right.
(5) In this section 'pension scheme' means a scheme for the provision of benefits consisting of or including relevant benefits for or in respect of employees or former employees.

---

[110] [1995] BCC 446.
[111] Companies Act 2006 (Commencement No 8, Transitional Provisions and Savings) Order 2008, SI 2008/2860, art 3(h).

(6)  In subsection (5)—

    (a)  'relevant benefits' here means any pension, lump sum, gratuity or other like benefit given or to be given on retirement or on death or in anticipation of retirement or, in connection with past service, after retirement or death; and

    (b)  'employee' shall be read as if a director of a company were employed by it.

COMMENCEMENT DATE  1 October 2009[112]

Section 139 provides an exception to the general prohibition that applies to residual interest under pension scheme or employees' share scheme. This was previously contained in Part 1(1) of Schedule 2 of the 1985 Act. Part I of Schedule 2 was itself a consolidating provision arising out of the Companies (Beneficial Interests) Act 1983 which was designed to remedy the situation where, as part of the running of a pension or employee share scheme, a company in its capacity as trustee comes to hold shares in a subsidiary company. As such it would technically have a beneficial interest which would fall under the section 23 general prohibition. Part I of Schedule 2 provided an exception to this prohibition which is reflected again in section 139. Section 139(5) is a restatement of the supplementary definitions provisions previous contained in Part I of Schedule 2(5). **8.139.02**

## 140  Interests to be disregarded: employer's rights of recovery under pension scheme or employees' share scheme

(1)  Where shares in a company are held on trust for the purposes of a pension scheme or employees' share scheme, there shall be disregarded for the purposes of section 138 any charge or lien on, or set-off against, any benefit or other right or interest under the scheme for the purpose of enabling the employer or former employer of a member of the scheme to obtain the discharge of a monetary obligation due to him from the member. **8.140.01**

(2)  In the case of a trust for the purposes of a pension scheme there shall also be disregarded any right to receive from the trustee of the scheme, or as trustee of the scheme to retain, an amount that can be recovered or retained, under section 61 of the Pension Schemes Act 1993 (c. 48) or section 57 of the Pension Schemes (Northern Ireland) Act 1993 (c. 49) (deduction of contributions equivalent premium from refund of scheme contributions) or otherwise, as reimbursement or partial reimbursement for any contributions equivalent premium paid in connection with the scheme under Part 3 of that Act.

(3)  In this section 'pension scheme' means a scheme for the provision of benefits consisting of or including relevant benefits for or in respect of employees or former employees.
'Relevant benefits' here means any pension, lump sum, gratuity or other like benefit given or to be given on retirement or on death or in anticipation of retirement or, in connection with past service, after retirement or death.

(4)  In this section 'employer' and 'employee' shall be read as if a director of a company were employed by it.

COMMENCEMENT DATE  1 October 2009[113]

Again as with section 139, section 140 provides an exception to the general prohibition that applies to a beneficial interest that might arise when running a pension scheme or employees' share scheme. This was previously contained in Part 1(3) of Schedule 2 of the 1985 Act with regard to rights of recovery. Part I of Schedule 2 was a consolidating provision arising out of the Companies (Beneficial Interests) Act 1983 which was designed to remedy the situation where as part of the running of a pension or employee share scheme a company in its capacity as trustee acquires a beneficial interest. Section 140 provides an exception to the general prohibition contained in section 136 specifically for rights of recovery which might amount to a beneficial interest. Again as with section 139, section 140(3) is a restatement of the supplementary definitions provisions previously contained in Part I of Schedule 2(5). **8.140.02**

## *Subsidiary acting as dealer in securities*

## 141  Subsidiary acting as authorised dealer in securities

(1)  The prohibition in section 136 (prohibition on subsidiary being a member of its holding company) does not apply where the shares are held by the subsidiary in the ordinary course of its business as an intermediary. **8.141.01**

---

[112] Companies Act 2006 (Commencement No 8, Transitional Provisions and Savings) Order 2008, SI 2008/2860, art 3(h).
[113] Companies Act 2006 (Commencement No 8, Transitional Provisions and Savings) Order 2008, SI 2008/2860, art 3(h).

(2) For this purpose a person is an intermediary if he—
    (a) carries on a bona fide business of dealing in securities,
    (b) is a member of or has access to a regulated market, and
    (c) does not carry on an excluded business.
(3) The following are excluded businesses—
    (a) a business that consists wholly or mainly in the making or managing of investments;
    (b) a business that consists wholly or mainly in, or is carried on wholly or mainly for the purposes of, providing services to persons who are connected with the person carrying on the business;
    (c) a business that consists in insurance business;
    (d) a business that consists in managing or acting as trustee in relation to a pension scheme, or that is carried on by the manager or trustee of such a scheme in connection with or for the purposes of the scheme;
    (e) a business that consists in operating or acting as trustee in relation to a collective investment scheme, or that is carried on by the operator or trustee of such a scheme in connection with and for the purposes of the scheme.
(4) For the purposes of this section—
    (a) the question whether a person is connected with another shall be determined in accordance with section 839 of the Income and Corporation Taxes Act 1988 (c. 1);
    (b) 'collective investment scheme' has the meaning given in section 235 of the Financial Services and Markets Act 2000 (c. 8);
    (c) 'insurance business' means business that consists in the effecting or carrying out of contracts of insurance;
    (d) 'securities' includes—
        (i) options,
        (ii) futures, and
        (iii) contracts for differences,
        and rights or interests in those investments;
    (e) 'trustee' and 'the operator' in relation to a collective investment scheme shall be construed in accordance with section 237(2) of the Financial Services and Markets Act 2000 (c. 8).
(5) Expressions used in this section that are also used in the provisions regulating activities under the Financial Services and Markets Act 2000 have the same meaning here as they do in those provisions.
    See section 22 of that Act, orders made under that section and Schedule 2 to that Act.

COMMENCEMENT DATE 1 October 2009[114]

**8.141.02**   Section 141 contains an exception to the general prohibition in section 136 where a subsidiary is holding shares while acting as authorized dealer in securities. This section is a restatement of the previous exception contained in section 23(3) to (3BA) of the 1985 Act. Those subsections were introduced by the Companies (Membership of Holding Company) (Dealers in Securities) Regulations 1997[115] in order to widen the ambit of the previous exception to ensure that subject to certain specified criteria a subsidiary holding shares in its holding company while acting as an authorized dealer in securities was not prohibited from doing so. Section 141 achieves this by simply restating in one section the previous provisions in section 23(3) to (3BA) of the 1985 Act.

### 142 Protection of third parties in other cases where subsidiary acting as dealer in securities

**8.142.01**   (1) This section applies where—
    (a) a subsidiary that is a dealer in securities has purportedly acquired shares in its holding company in contravention of the prohibition in section 136, and
    (b) a person acting in good faith has agreed, for value and without notice of the contravention, to acquire shares in the holding company—
        (i) from the subsidiary or
        (ii) from someone who has purportedly acquired the shares after their disposal by the subsidiary.
(2) A transfer to that person of the shares mentioned in subsection (1)(a) has the same effect as it would have had if their original acquisition by the subsidiary had not been in contravention of the prohibition.

COMMENCEMENT DATE 1 October 2009[116]

---

[114] Companies Act 2006 (Commencement No 8, Transitional Provisions and Savings) Order 2008, SI 2008/2860, art 3(h).

[115] SI 1997/2306.

[116] Companies Act 2006 (Commencement No 8, Transitional Provisions and Savings) Order 2008, SI 2008/2860, art 3(h).

Section 142 is a saving provision for transactions that arise as a result of a breach of the section 136    **8.142.02**
prohibition on a subsidiary holding shares in its holding company. This saving provision will protect
a third party acting in good faith, for value and without notice, who acquires the prohibited shares from
the subsidiary while the subsidiary is acting as a dealer in securities. The provision replicates the
previous protection contained in section 23(3c) of the 1985 Act which itself was introduced into the
1985 Act by the Companies (Membership of Holding Company) (Dealers in Securities) Regulations
1997.[117]

## *Supplementary*

### 143  Application of provisions to companies not limited by shares

In relation to a company other than a company limited by shares, the references in this Chapter to    **8.143.01**
shares shall be read as references to the interest of its members as such, whatever the form of that
interest.

COMMENCEMENT DATE  1 October 2009[118]

Section 143 provides for the application of provisions in this chapter to companies not limited by    **8.143.02**
shares. This section replicates the supplementary definition of shares as applied to companies not
limited by shares previously contained in section 23(8) of the 1985 Act.

### 144  Application of provisions to nominees

The provisions of this Chapter apply to a nominee acting on behalf of a subsidiary as to the subsidiary    **8.144.01**
itself.

COMMENCEMENT DATE  1 October 2009[119]

Section 144 provides for the application of this Chapter to nominees. This section replicates the    **8.144.02**
supplementary provision previously contained in section 23(7) of the 1985 Act applying the provisions
of this chapter to a nominee.

---

[117] SI 1997/2306.
[118] Companies Act 2006 (Commencement No 8, Transitional Provisions and Savings) Order 2008, SI
2008/2860, art 3(h).
[119] Companies Act 2006 (Commencement No 8, Transitional Provisions and Savings) Order 2008, SI
2008/2860, art 3(h).

# 9

# EXERCISE OF MEMBERS' RIGHTS

## Companies Act 2006

## PART 9
## EXERCISE OF MEMBERS' RIGHTS

This Part of the Act proved to be one of the most controversial during the parliamentary stages. There were no disagreements as to the basic purpose of it, namely to confer rights on persons who are beneficially interested in shares but not registered as members of a company. However, the original government proposals, which would have made compliance with the obligations in effect voluntary, were defeated in Grand Committee in the House of Lords, and replaced by compulsory requirements. The final provisions, which are extensive and contain a mix of voluntary provisions applying to all companies (sections 145, 152, and 153) and compulsory provisions applying to companies with shares admitted to trading on a regulated market (sections 146 to 151), were introduced in place of those inserted in the House of Lords at Standing Committee and Report stages in the House of Commons.   **9.01**

### *Effect of provisions in company's articles*

### 145  Effect of provisions of articles as to enjoyment or exercise of members' rights

(1) This section applies where provision is made by a company's articles enabling a member to   **9.145.01**
nominate another person or persons as entitled to enjoy or exercise all or any specified rights of
the member in relation to the company.

(2) So far as is necessary to give effect to that provision, anything required or authorized by any
provision of the Companies Acts to be done by or in relation to the member shall instead be done,
or (as the case may be) may instead be done, by or in relation to the nominated person (or each
of them) as if he were a member of the company.

(3) This applies, in particular, to the rights conferred by—
  (a)  sections 291 and 293 (right to be sent proposed written resolution);
  (b)  section 292 (right to require circulation of written resolution);
  (c)  section 303 (right to require directors to call general meeting);
  (d)  section 310 (right to notice of general meetings);
  (e)  section 314 (right to require circulation of a statement);
  [(ea) section 319A (right to ask question at meeting of traded company);][a]
  (f)  section 324 (right to appoint proxy to act at meeting);
  (g)  section 338 (right to require circulation of resolution for AGM of public company);
  [(ga) section 338A (traded companies: members' power to include matters in business dealt with
     at AGM);][b] and
  (h)  section 423 (right to be sent a copy of annual accounts and reports).

(4) This section and any such provision as is mentioned in subsection (1)—
  (a)  do not confer rights enforceable against the company by anyone other than the member, and

(b)  do not affect the requirements for an effective transfer or other disposition of the whole or part of a member's interest in the company.

AMENDMENTS

<sup>a</sup> Inserted by the Companies (Shareholders' Rights) Regulations 2009, SI 2009/1632, reg 12(2).

<sup>b</sup> Inserted by the Companies (Shareholders' Rights) Regulations 2009, SI 2009/1632, reg 17(2).

COMMENCEMENT DATE  1 OCTOBER 2007[1]

**9.145.02**  As indicated in the general note to this Part of the Act, this section introduced entirely new provisions into company law regarding the rights of persons who are the beneficial members, but who are not registered as members of the company. They are based on recommendations of the Steering Group of the Company Law Review.[2] The most typical, although by no means the only, situation where beneficial ownership is separate from legal title is where investors hold their shares through intermediaries, for example when shares in a quoted company are held through the CREST system,[3] or where shares are held via the mechanism of an Individual Savings Account. The intermediaries are registered as members and previously the beneficiaries had to reply on their arrangements with the intermediaries regarding both the obtaining of information from the company and the giving of instructions as to the exercise of voting rights.

**9.145.03**  This section applies to all companies, whether private or public, quoted or not, but there are additional detailed provisions in the following sections regarding quoted companies and some of the rights listed apply only as regards traded companies. Its operation is, however, voluntary, in the sense that a company's articles must contain provision enabling a member to nominate someone else to exercise membership rights before the section can apply. Previously such arrangements have been made without legal obligation by some quoted companies.

**9.145.04**  Section 145(2) is designed to ensure that all relevant references in the Companies Acts[4] to a 'member' should be read as if the reference was a reference to the nominated person, that is the beneficial owner. It seems from the wording of the subsection that the articles may provide either that the beneficial owner has appropriate rights instead of the member or in addition to the member. However, a beneficial owner will not have directly enforceable rights against the company, only rights against the registered member.[5] The latter remains the person entitled to enforce rights against the company under what is now section 33.[6]

**9.145.05**  Although subsection (3) details a number of statutory rights that are covered, it is clearly not an exhaustive list because it refers only to those rights 'in particular' and the wording of subsection (1) indicates that provision can be made that covers not just statutory rights. The only right of a member that cannot be included in a relevant provision in the articles is the right to transfer shares, because subsection (4)(b) provides that the section and any provision in the articles do not affect the requirements for an effective transfer or other disposition of the whole or part of a member's interest in the company.

## Information rights

### 146  Traded companies: nomination of persons to enjoy information rights

**9.146.01**  (1) This section applies to a company whose shares are admitted to trading on a regulated market.

(2) A member of such a company who holds shares on behalf of another person may nominate that person to enjoy information rights.

(3) 'Information rights' means—

(a) the right to receive a copy of all communications that the company sends to its members generally or to any class of its members that includes the person making the nomination, and

(b) the rights conferred by—

(i) section 431 or 432 (right to require copies of accounts and reports), and

(ii) section 1145 (right to require hard copy version of document or information provided in another form).

(4) The reference in subsection (3)(a) to communications that a company sends to its members generally includes the company's annual accounts and reports.

---

[1] Companies Act 2006 (Commencement No 3, etc) Order 2007, SI 2007/2194, art 2.
[2] *Final Report*, Chap 5.
[3] See para 21.785.02.
[4] These are defined in s 2.
[5] See subs (4)(a).
[6] See para 3.33.02.

For the application of section 426 (option to provide summary financial statement) in relation to a person nominated to enjoy information rights, see subsection (5) of that section.

(5) A company need not act on a nomination purporting to relate to certain information rights only.

COMMENCEMENT DATE 1 October 2007[7]

This section, which was wholly new, confers what are called 'information rights' on the beneficial owners of shares, but only in respect of a company whose shares are admitted to trading on a regulated market.[8] This covers listed shares but does not, among other things, include shares traded on the Alternative Investment Market. By subsection (2) a member of such a company who holds shares on behalf of another person may nominate that person to enjoy information rights, although a company need not act on a nomination purporting to relate to only certain of these rights (subsection (5)). **9.146.02**

Information rights are defined widely in subsection (3) as (a) the right to receive a copy of all communications that the company sends to its members generally or to any class of its members that includes the person making the nomination; (b) the right to require copies of accounts and reports;[9] and (c) the right to require a hard copy version of a document or information provided in another form.[10] The first sentence of subsection (4) seems designed to ensure that information rights extend to the annual accounts and reports and not just the specific rights in sections 431 and 432 to copies of those documents. The second sentence of that subsection inserts what is effectively a cross-reference to section 426(5) regarding summary financial statements in the context of information rights.[11] **9.146.03**

### 147 Information rights: form in which copies to be provided

(1) This section applies as regards the form in which copies are to be provided to a person nominated under section 146 (nomination of person to enjoy information rights). **9.147.01**

(2) If the person to be nominated wishes to receive hard copy communications, he must—
   (a) request the person making the nomination to notify the company of that fact, and
   (b) provide an address to which such copies may be sent.
   This must be done before the nomination is made.

(3) If having received such a request the person making the nomination—
   (a) notifies the company that the nominated person wishes to receive hard copy communications, and
   (b) provides the company with that address,
   the right of the nominated person is to receive hard copy communications accordingly.

(4) This is subject to the provisions of Parts 3 and 4 of Schedule 5 (communications by company) under which the company may take steps to enable it to communicate in electronic form or by means of a website.

(5) If no such notification is given (or no address is provided), the nominated person is taken to have agreed that documents or information may be sent or supplied to him by the company by means of a website.

(6) That agreement—
   (a) may be revoked by the nominated person, and
   (b) does not affect his right under section 1145 to require a hard copy version of a document or information provided in any other form.

COMMENCEMENT DATE 1 October 2007[12]

This section deals with the formalities regarding the information rights that are conferred by section 146. A person nominated under section 146 (referred to here as the 'nominee') has the right to choose the form in which he receives copies of documents or information, but if he wishes to receive it in hard copy, by subsection (2) he must, before the nomination is made, request the member to notify the company and provide an address to which the copies may be sent. If the member acts on this request by notifying the company and passing on the address, the nominee has the right to hard copy, as is made clear by subsection (3). However, this is subject to the general provisions on electronic communications by a company in Parts 3 and 4 of Schedule 5.[13] **9.147.02**

In the absence of notification or the provision of an address, the nominee is taken to have agreed that documents or information may be sent or supplied to him by means of a website, but this 'agreement' **9.147.03**

---

[7] Companies Act 2006 (Commencement No 3, etc) Order 2007, SI 2007/2194, art 2.

[8] 'Regulated market' is defined in s 1173 by reference to Directive (EC) 2004/39 [2004] OJ L145/1; see para 38.1173.01.

[9] Under ss 431 and 432; see paras 15.432.02 and 15.433.02.

[10] Under s 1145; see para 37.1145.02.

[11] See para 15.426.02.

[12] Companies Act 2006 (Commencement No 3, etc) Order 2007, SI 2007/2194, art 2.

[13] See para 37.1144.08.

may be revoked by the nominee and does not affect his right under section 1145[14] to require hard copy of a document or information; see subsections (5) and (6). The result of this appears to be that a nominee has the right to hard copy information, but if that is not exercised in time he will receive electronic copy generally, except that he still retains the section 1145 right to have a hard copy of a particular document.

### 148 Termination or suspension of nomination

**9.148.01**
(1) The following provisions have effect in relation to a nomination under section 146 (nomination of person to enjoy information rights).

(2) The nomination may be terminated at the request of the member or of the nominated person.

(3) The nomination ceases to have effect on the occurrence in relation to the member or the nominated person of any of the following—
  (a) in the case of an individual, death or bankruptcy;
  (b) in the case of a body corporate, dissolution or the making of an order for the winding up of the body otherwise than for the purposes of reconstruction.

(4) In subsection (3)—
  (a) the reference to bankruptcy includes—
    (i) the sequestration of a person's estate, and
    (ii) a person's estate being the subject of a protected trust deed (within the meaning of the Bankruptcy (Scotland) Act 1985 (c. 66)); and
  (b) the reference to the making of an order for winding up is to—
    (i) the making of such an order under the Insolvency Act 1986 (c. 45) or the Insolvency (Northern Ireland) Order 1989 (S.I. 1989/2405 (N.I. 19)), or
    (ii) any corresponding proceeding under the law of a country or territory outside the United Kingdom.

(5) The effect of any nominations made by a member is suspended at any time when there are more nominated persons than the member has shares in the company.

(6) Where—
  (a) the member holds different classes of shares with different information rights, and
  (b) there are more nominated persons than he has shares conferring a particular right,
  the effect of any nominations made by him is suspended to the extent that they confer that right.

(7) Where the company—
  (a) enquires of a nominated person whether he wishes to retain information rights, and
  (b) does not receive a response within the period of 28 days beginning with the date on which the company's enquiry was sent,
  the nomination ceases to have effect at the end of that period.
  Such an enquiry is not to be made of a person more than once in any twelve-month period.

(8) The termination or suspension of a nomination means that the company is not required to act on it.
  It does not prevent the company from continuing to do so, to such extent or for such period as it thinks fit.

COMMENCEMENT DATE 1 October 2007[15]

**9.148.02**  This section deals with the termination or suspension of a nomination under section 146, although if that happens in the circumstances described below, the company is not required to act on it and can do so to such extent or for such period as it thinks fit; see subsection (8). This is no doubt intended to cover a situation where a member's holdings in the company and the number of nominees for whom he is holding shares may fluctuate from time to time and the cost of suspension might outweigh the cost of suspending and recommencing rights.

**9.148.03**  Subject to this, by subsection (2), either the member or the nominee may terminate the nomination, and, under subsection (3), it automatically terminates if either dies or becomes bankrupt or, if a body corporate, is wound up other than for the purposes of a reconstruction.[16] In addition, under subsection (7), the company may enquire of a nominee whether he wishes to retain information rights and, if it does not receive a response within 28 days from sending the enquiry, the nomination ceases to have effect at the end of that period. However, it can make such an enquiry only once in any 12-month period.

**9.148.04**  The provisions on suspension, subsections (5) and (6), cover the situation where there are more nominees than the member has shares in the company or shares of a particular class, which could arise

---

[14] See para 37.1145.02.

[15] Companies Act 2006 (Commencement No 3, etc) Order 2007, SI 2007/2194, art 2.

[16] Bankruptcy includes sequestration and, in Scotland, an estate being the subject of a protected trust deed. Winding up includes any corresponding proceeding under a non-UK law: s 148(4).

in respect of shares held on the basis of, for example, an Individual Savings Account; here any nominations by the member are suspended.

## 149   Information as to possible rights in relation to voting

(1) This section applies where a company sends a copy of a notice of a meeting to a person nominated under section 146 (nomination of person to enjoy information rights).                           **9.149.01**

(2) The copy of the notice must be accompanied by a statement that—

   (a) he may have a right under an agreement between him and the member by whom he was nominated to be appointed, or to have someone else appointed, as a proxy for the meeting, and

   (b) if he has no such right or does not wish to exercise it, he may have a right under such an agreement to give instructions to the member as to the exercise of voting rights.

(3) Section 325 (notice of meeting to contain statement of member's rights in relation to appointment of proxy) does not apply to the copy, and the company must either—

   (a) omit the notice required by that section, or

   (b) include it but state that it does not apply to the nominated person.

COMMENCEMENT DATE  1 October 2007[17]

This specific provision concerns voting rights and is clearly designed to encourage participation by   **9.149.02**
nominees at company meetings, although its effectiveness will depend on agreements between them and the member who is registered in respect of the shares. Where a nominee receives a copy of a notice of a meeting from the company, it must be accompanied by a statement that he may have the right under an agreement between him and the member who nominated him to be appointed, or to have someone else appointed, as a proxy for the meeting or, if he has no such right or does not want to exercise it, he may have a right under such an agreement to give instructions to the member as to the exercise of voting rights: see subsection (2). In this situation, the statutorily required notice of proxy rights[18] must either be omitted from the copy or stated not to apply to the nominee: see subsection (3).

## 150   Information rights: status of rights

(1) This section has effect as regards the rights conferred by a nomination under section 146   **9.150.01**
(nomination of person to enjoy information rights).

(2) Enjoyment by the nominated person of the rights conferred by the nomination is enforceable against the company by the member as if they were rights conferred by the company's articles.

(3) Any enactment, and any provision of the company's articles, having effect in relation to communications with members has a corresponding effect (subject to any necessary adaptations) in relation to communications with the nominated person.

(4) In particular—

   (a) where under any enactment, or any provision of the company's articles, the members of a company entitled to receive a document or information are determined as at a date or time before it is sent or supplied, the company need not send or supply it to a nominated person—

     (i) whose nomination was received by the company after that date or time, or

     (ii) if that date or time falls in a period of suspension of his nomination; and

   (b) where under any enactment, or any provision of the company's articles, the right of a member to receive a document or information depends on the company having a current address for him, the same applies to any person nominated by him.

(5) The rights conferred by the nomination—

   (a) are in addition to the rights of the member himself, and

   (b) do not affect any rights exercisable by virtue of any such provision as is mentioned in section 145 (provisions of company's articles as to enjoyment or exercise of members' rights).

(6) A failure to give effect to the rights conferred by the nomination does not affect the validity of anything done by or on behalf of the company.

(7) References in this section to the rights conferred by the nomination are to—

   (a) the rights referred to in section 146(3) (information rights), and

   (b) where applicable, the rights conferred by section 147(3) (right to hard copy communications) and section 149 (information as to possible voting rights).

COMMENCEMENT DATE  1 October 2007[19]

The effect of this section is that the information rights granted by section 146 do not give a nominee   **9.150.02**
direct rights against the company. Rather, as regards information rights and, where applicable, the rights to hard copy communications and information as to possible voting rights, by this section the

---

[17] Companies Act 2006 (Commencement No 3, etc) Order 2007, SI 2007/2194, art 2.

[18] Under s 325; see para 13.325.02.

[19] Companies Act 2006 (Commencement No 3, etc) Order 2007, SI 2007/2194, art 2.

member can enforce them against the company as if they were rights conferred by the company's articles: see subsection (2).[20] These rights are in addition to the rights of the member himself and do not affect any rights exercisable by virtue of section 145 (subsection (5)), but, by subsection (6), failure to give effect to a nominee's rights does not affect the validity of anything done by the company. Any enactment or provision of the company's articles relating to communications with members has a corresponding effect in relation to communications with the nominee. This provision of subsection (3) is particularly directed at the circumstances mentioned in subsection (4), namely determining the date or time at which or the address to which information is to be sent or supplied. So a company that does not receive a nomination in time, or when nomination is suspended, or that does not have a current address, is excused from communicating with a nominee.

### 151 Information rights: power to amend

**9.151.01**
(1) The Secretary of State may by regulations amend the provisions of sections 146 to 150 (information rights) so as to—
   (a) extend or restrict the classes of companies to which section 146 applies,
   (b) make other provision as to the circumstances in which a nomination may be made under that section, or
   (c) extend or restrict the rights conferred by such a nomination.
(2) The regulations may make such consequential modifications of any other provisions of this Part, or of any other enactment, as appear to the Secretary of State to be necessary.
(3) Regulations under this section are subject to affirmative resolution procedure.

COMMENCEMENT DATE 1 October 2007[21]

**9.151.02**    This section, which is self-explanatory, confers extensive powers on the Secretary of State to amend sections 146 to 150 by statutory instrument subject to the affirmative resolution procedure. Such regulations may extend or restrict the rights given to nominees and extend or restrict the types of company in respect of which such rights may be given.

*Exercise of rights where shares held on behalf of others*

### 152 Exercise of rights where shares held on behalf of others: exercise in different ways

**9.152.01**
(1) Where a member holds shares in a company on behalf of more than one person—
   (a) rights attached to the shares, and
   (b) rights under any enactment exercisable by virtue of holding the shares,
   need not all be exercised, and if exercised, need not all be exercised in the same way.
(2) A member who exercises such rights but does not exercise all his rights, must inform the company to what extent he is exercising the rights.
(3) A member who exercises such rights in different ways must inform the company of the ways in which he is exercising them and to what extent they are exercised in each way.
(4) If a member exercises such rights without informing the company—
   (a) that he is not exercising all his rights, or
   (b) that he is exercising his rights in different ways,
   the company is entitled to assume that he is exercising all his rights and is exercising them in the same way.

COMMENCEMENT DATE 1 October 2007[22]

**9.152.02**    This section provides for the very common situation where a member holds shares on behalf of a number of different people. However, it should be noted that it is applicable to all companies, public or private, with or without shares that are traded on a regulated market, unlike the information rights that are conferred by the preceding sections. It will thus apply to, for example, a situation where shares are held by trustees or personal representatives for more than one beneficiary.

**9.152.03**    Subsection (1) states that the rights attached to the shares and the rights under any enactment that are exercisable by virtue of holding the shares need not all be exercised and need not all be exercised in the same way. It would seem, therefore, that this could override standard pre-emption provisions found in the articles of some private companies under which a member wishing to transfer shares must offer them to existing members. A right to take up such an offer vested in a member holding shares on behalf of more than one person need not be exercised in the same way in respect of all the shares so held.

---

[20] As to the enforcement of rights under the articles, see s 33 and the commentary thereto.
[21] Companies Act 2006 (Commencement No 3, etc) Order 2007, SI 2007/2194, art 2.
[22] Companies Act 2006 (Commencement No 3, etc) Order 2007, SI 2007/2194, art 2.

If a member does not exercise all his rights or exercises them in different ways, he must inform the  **9.152.04**
company either of the extent to which he is exercising the rights or of the different ways and to what
extent they are exercised in each way. The sanction for failure to inform the company is that, in the
absence of information to the contrary, the company is entitled to assume that a member is exercising
all his rights and doing so in the same way. This will protect the company from any claim by a nominee
that a member had not acted in accordance with his instructions.

### 153 Exercise of rights where shares held on behalf of others: members' requests

(1) This section applies for the purposes of—  **9.153.01**
    (a)  section 314 (power to require circulation of statement),
    (b)  section 338 (public companies: power to require circulation of resolution for AGM),
    [(ba) section 338A (traded companies: members' power to include matters in business dealt with
        at AGM);][a]
    (c)  section 342 (power to require independent report on poll), and
    (d)  section 527 (power to require website publication of audit concerns).
(2) A company is required to act under any of those sections if it receives a request in relation to which
    the following conditions are met—
    (a)  it is made by at least 100 persons;
    (b)  it is authenticated by all the persons making it;
    (c)  in the case of any of those persons who is not a member of the company, it is accompanied
       by a statement—
       (i)   of the full name and address of a person ('the member') who is a member of the
           company and holds shares on behalf of that person,
       (ii)  that the member is holding those shares on behalf of that person in the course of a
           business,
       (iii) of the number of shares in the company that the member holds on behalf of that
           person,
       (iv)  of the total amount paid up on those shares,
       (v)   that those shares are not held on behalf of anyone else or, if they are, that the other
           person or persons are not among the other persons making the request,
       (vi)  that some or all of those shares confer voting rights that are relevant for the purposes of
           making a request under the section in question, and
       (vii) that the person has the right to instruct the member how to exercise those rights;
    (d)  in the case of any of those persons who is a member of the company, it is accompanied by a
       statement—
       (i)   that he holds shares otherwise than on behalf of another person, or
       (ii)  that he holds shares on behalf of one or more other persons but those persons are not
           among the other persons making the request;
    (e)  it is accompanied by such evidence as the company may reasonably require of the matters
       mentioned in paragraph (c) and (d);
    (f)   the total amount of the sums paid up on—
       (i)   shares held as mentioned in paragraph (c), and
       (ii)  shares held as mentioned in paragraph (d),
           divided by the number of persons making the request, is not less than £100;
    (g)  the request complies with any other requirements of the section in question as to contents,
       timing and otherwise.

AMENDMENTS

  [a]  Inserted by the Companies (Shareholders' Rights) Regulations 2009, SI 2009/1632, reg 17(3).

COMMENCEMENT DATE  1 October 2007[23]

This section confers special rights over and above the information rights conferred by section 146 and,  **9.153.02**
like the immediately preceding section, *prima facie* applies to all companies limited by shares. However
only the right in subsection (1)(a), namely that under section 314 regarding the circulation of
statements to members,[24] can apply in respect of a private company, unless it is also a traded
company.[25] Of the other rights in that subsection, that in section 338 regarding the right of members of
a public company to require the circulation of a resolution at the annual general meeting,[26] can apply
to any public company, whereas those in section 342 regarding the power of members of a quoted
company to require an independent report on a poll[27] and section 527 regarding the power of members

---

[23]  Companies Act 2006 (Commencement No 3, etc) Order 2007, SI 2007/2194, art 2.
[24]  See para 13.314.02.
[25]  See the commentary to s 338A.
[26]  See para 13.338.02.
[27]  See para 13.324.02.

of a quoted company to require the website publication of concerns about the audit[28] obviously apply only to quoted companies.

**9.153.03**   All these rights are exercisable if, among other things, 100 members act together. In effect this section allows that number to include beneficial owners and not just members of the company. It is, however, subject to the conditions specified in subsection (2), as well as the individual requirements of the sections to which it applies.

**9.153.04**   The conditions in subsection (2) are, not entirely surprisingly, detailed. First, the request must be made by at least 100 persons and authenticated by all of them.[29] Secondly, as regards any of the 100 who are not members, it must be accompanied by a statement (a) of the full name and address of a person ('the member') who is a member of the company and holds shares on behalf of that person; (b) that the member is holding those shares on behalf of that person in the course of a business; (c) of the number of shares in the company that the member holds on behalf of that person, of the total amount paid up on those shares; (d) that those shares are not held on behalf of anyone else or, if they are, that the other person or persons are not among the other persons making the request; (e) that some or all of those shares confer voting rights that are relevant for the purposes of making a request under the section in question; and (f) that the person has the right to instruct the member how to exercise those rights. In addition the request must be accompanied by such evidence as the company may reasonably require of the above matters.

**9.153.05**   Thirdly, as regards members, it must be accompanied by a statement (a) that he holds shares otherwise than on behalf of another person, or (b) that he holds shares on behalf of one or more other persons but those persons are not among the other persons making the request. Finally, the total amount paid up on all the shares held by such members and non-members, divided by the number of persons making the request, must be not less than £100.

---

[28]  See para 16.527.02.
[29]  As to authenticated, see s 1146.

# 10

## A COMPANY'S DIRECTORS

# Companies Act 2006

## PART 10
## A COMPANY'S DIRECTORS

### CHAPTER 1
### APPOINTMENT AND REMOVAL OF DIRECTORS

Part IX of the Companies Act 1985,[1] which related to both directors and secretaries, has been repealed by the Companies Act 2006.[2] Chapter 1 of Part 10 of the Companies Act 2006 replaces the provisions of that part relating specifically to the appointment and removal of directors. The most significant changes are in: the new requirement that at least one of a company's directors should be a natural person (section 155); the abolition of the maximum age limit of 70 for directors and the introduction of a minimum age of 16 (sections 157 to 159); the introduction of a separate register for directors' residential addresses (sections 166 and 167).  **10.0.01**

### *Requirement to have directors*

### 154 Companies required to have directors

(1) A private company must have at least one director.  **10.154.01**
(2) A public company must have at least two directors.

COMMENCEMENT DATE 1 October 2007[3]

Section 154 replaced section 282 of the Companies Act 1985. It preserves the different requirements for private and public companies: a private company must have at least one director, and a public company at least two directors. However, section 154 abandons the distinction made in the Companies Acts 1929 to 1985 between public companies registered before and after 1 November 1929.  **10.154.02**

### 155 Companies required to have at least one director who is a natural person

(1) A company must have at least one director who is a natural person.  **10.155.01**
(2) This requirement is met if the office of director is held by a natural person as a corporation sole or otherwise by virtue of an office.

COMMENCEMENT DATE 1 October 2008.[4]

This provision, which had no antecedent in earlier companies legislation, reflects concerns that the flexibility of British company law in allowing the appointment of legal persons other than natural persons as directors of companies was being abused by those who wished to conceal the true identity of  **10.155.02**

---

[1] Sections 282–310.
[2] CA 2006, s 1295 and Sch 16.
[3] Companies Act 2006 (Commencement No 3, etc) Order 2007, SI 2007/2194, art 2.
[4] Companies Act 2006 (Commencement No 5 etc) Order 2007, SI 2007/3495, art 5(1)(c): For the transitional provisions see Sch 4, para 46.

those controlling companies.[5] Thus under subsection (1) a company must have at least one natural person as a director. Subsection (2) provides that a corporation sole[6] is a natural person for the purposes of subsection (1), as is a natural person who is appointed by virtue of their office.

## 156  Direction requiring company to make appointment

**10.156.01**

(1)  If it appears to the Secretary of State that a company is in breach of—
  section 154 (requirements as to number of directors), or
  section 155 (requirement to have at least one director who is a natural person),
the Secretary of State may give the company a direction under this section.

(2)  The direction must specify—
  (a)  the statutory requirement the company appears to be in breach of,
  (b)  what the company must do in order to comply with the direction, and
  (c)  the period within which it must do so.
That period must be not less than one month or more than three months after the date on which the direction is given.

(3)  The direction must also inform the company of the consequences of failing to comply.

(4)  Where the company is in breach of section 154 or 155 it must comply with the direction by—
  (a)  making the necessary appointment or appointments, and
  (b)  giving notice of them under section 167,
before the end of the period specified in the direction.

(5)  If the company has already made the necessary appointment or appointments (or so far as it has done so), it must comply with the direction by giving notice of them under section 167 before the end of the period specified in the direction.

(6)  If a company fails to comply with a direction under this section, an offence is committed by—
  (a)  the company, and
  (b)  every officer of the company who is in default.
For this purpose a shadow director is treated as an officer of the company.

(7)  A person guilty of an offence under this section is liable on summary conviction to a fine not exceeding level 5 on the standard scale and, for continued contravention, a daily default fine not exceeding one-tenth of level 5 on the standard scale.

COMMENCEMENT DATE 1 October 2008.[7]

**10.156.02**  This provision, new in the 2006 Act, enables enforcement of both the requirements under section 154 and under section 155 if it appears that a company has failed to comply. This power is intended to ensure the effectiveness of the general enforcement regime envisaged by the Companies Act (2006), in particular the 'officer in default framework'.[8]

**10.156.03**  If the Secretary of State gives the company a direction under his power in section 156(1) it must contain the information specified in section 156(2), and must require compliance within a period of not less than one month and not more than three months after the date of the direction. The direction must also inform the company of the consequences of non-compliance (subsection (3)). The relevant consequences of which a company is to be informed are that the company's failure to comply involves the commission of an offence by both the company and every officer in default, including a shadow director (subsection (6)); a person found guilty of an offence under section 156 is liable upon summary conviction to a fine and daily default fines (subsection (7)).

**10.156.04**  Subsection (4) provides that in order to comply with a direction issued when a company is in breach of sections 154 or 155 the company must make the required appointments (if they have not already been made), and notify the registrar of the appointments under section 167 before the end of the period specified in the notice. If the appointments have already been made at the time of the direction only notice to the registrar is required (subsection (5)).

## *Appointment*

## 157  Minimum age for appointment as director

**10.157.01**

(1)  A person may not be appointed a director of a company unless he has attained the age of 16 years.

(2)  This does not affect the validity of an appointment that is not to take effect until the person appointed attains that age.

---

[5]  White Paper, 'Company Law Reform', March 2005, 3.3, p 24.
[6]  For example the Archbishop of Canterbury or other clergy. A corporation sole is not a 'body corporate' or 'corporation' for the purposes of CA 2006: s 1173(1)(a).
[7]  Companies Act 2006 (Commencement No 5 etc) Order 2007, SI 2007/3495, art 5(1)(c).
[8]  White Paper, 'Company Law Reform', March 2005, s 4.6.

(3)  Where the office of director of a company is held by a corporation sole, or otherwise by virtue of another office, the appointment to that other office of a person who has not attained the age of 16 years is not effective also to make him a director of the company until he attains the age of 16 years.

(4)  An appointment made in contravention of this section is void.

(5)  Nothing in this section affects any liability of a person under any provision of the Companies Acts if he—

(a)  purports to act as director or

(b)  acts as a shadow director,

although he could not, by virtue of this section, be validly appointed as a director.

(6)  This section has effect subject to section 158 (power to provide for exceptions from minimum age requirement).

COMMENCEMENT DATE 1 October 2008.[9]

This provision, new in the 2006 Act, represents a significant policy change from the requirements of the Companies Act 1985. Under section 293 of the Companies Act 1985[10] a public company, or a private company which was the subsidiary of a public company, was not permitted to appoint a person aged 70 or older to become a director, and a director attaining that age whilst in office was required to vacate his office at the general meeting following his 70th birthday. This was subject to the company's articles providing otherwise, or the appointment or continuation in office being approved by the company in general meeting. The Companies Act 2006 does not contain any provisions stipulating an upper age limit for directors. Instead, the Companies Act 2006 introduces this prohibition on any person under the age of 16 years being a director of a company (subsection (1)). An appointment which is not due to take effect until a person attains the age of 16 is not invalidated by the prohibition (subsection (2)). If a person who has not attained the age of 16 is appointed to a corporation sole or another office holding the office of director of a company[11] such appointment is not also effective to make him a director of the company (subsection (3)). Although any appointment made in contravention of section 157 is void (subsection (4)) a person under the age of 16 will still be liable under any provision (criminal or civil) of the Companies Act 2006 if he purports so to act, or acts, as a shadow director even though he could not have been validly appointed as a director of the company (subsection (5)). The prohibition contained in section 157 is subject to the Secretary of State's power to make provisions under section 158.    **10.157.02**

## 158  Power to provide for exceptions from minimum age requirement

(1)  The Secretary of State may make provision by regulations for cases in which a person who has not attained the age of 16 years may be appointed a director of a company.    **10.158.01**

(2)  The regulations must specify the circumstances in which, and any conditions subject to which, the appointment may be made.

(3)  If the specified circumstances cease to obtain, or any specified conditions cease to be met, a person who was appointed by virtue of the regulations and who has not since attained the age of 16 years ceases to hold office.

(4)  The regulations may make different provision for different parts of the United Kingdom.
This is without prejudice to the general power to make different provision for different cases.

(5)  Regulations under this section are subject to negative resolution procedure.

COMMENCEMENT DATE 1 October 2008.[12]

Section 158 gives the Secretary of State power to make provision by regulations for cases in which persons under the age of 16 may be appointed as a director. The provisions made by such regulations may be different for the different parts of the UK. Regulations made by the Secretary of State under this section are subject to negative resolution procedure and can therefore be annulled pursuant to a resolution of either the House of Commons or the House of Lords.    **10.158.02**

## 159  Existing under-age directors

(1)  This section applies where—    **10.159.01**

(a)  a person appointed a director of a company before section 157 (minimum age for appointment as director) comes into force has not attained the age of 16 when that section comes into force, or

---

[9]  Companies Act 2006 (Commencement No 5 etc) Order 2007, SI 2007/3495, art 5(1)(c).
[10]  Repealed by CA 2006, s 1295 and Sch 16.
[11]  As envisaged by s 155(2) of CA 2006.
[12]  Companies Act 2006 (Commencement No 5 etc) Order 2007, SI 2007/3495, art 5(1)(c).

(b)   the office of director of a company is held by a corporation sole, or otherwise by virtue of
another office, and the person appointed to that other office has not attained the age of 16
years when that section comes into force,

and the case is not one excepted from that section by regulations under section 158.

(2)   That person ceases to be a director on section 157 coming into force.

(3)   The company must make the necessary consequential alteration in its register of directors but
need not give notice to the registrar of the change.

(4)   If it appears to the registrar (from other information) that a person has ceased by virtue of this
section to be a director of a company, the registrar shall note that fact on the register.

COMMENCEMENT DATE  1 October 2008.[13]

**10.159.02**   This section is a transitional provision which provides that, subject to regulations made under section
158, where a person has been appointed as a director and is under 16 years of age when section 157
comes into force, or where he has been appointed to a corporation sole or other office which holds the
office of director, he will cease to be a director of the company at that time. A company is thereafter
required to amend its register accordingly (subsection (3)), but is not required to give notice to the
registrar of companies as would ordinarily be required under section 167. However, the registrar is
required to amend the register of companies of his own motion if it appears to him from other
information[14] that a person has ceased to be a director by virtue of section 159.

### 160  Appointment of directors of public company to be voted on individually

**10.160.01**   (1)   At a general meeting of a public company a motion for the appointment of two or more persons
as directors of the company by a single resolution must not be made unless a resolution that it
should be so made has first been agreed to by the meeting without any vote being given against
it.

(2)   A resolution moved in contravention of this section is void, whether or not its being so moved was
objected to at the time.
But where a resolution so moved is passed, no provision for the automatic reappointment of
retiring directors in default of another appointment applies.

(3)   For the purposes of this section a motion for approving a person's appointment, or for nominating
a person for appointment, is treated as a motion for his appointment.

(4)   Nothing in this section applies to a resolution amending the company's articles.

COMMENCEMENT DATE  1 October 2007[15]

**10.160.02**   This section is substantially the same as section 292 of the Companies Act 1985 and introduces no new
provisions. It applies only to public companies, and only where directors are appointed by way of a
general meeting. The effect of the section where applicable is that the appointment of each proposed
director must be voted on individually unless a prior resolution has been passed unanimously
permitting a block resolution. The section is intended to ensure that members of a public company can
express disapproval at the appointment of an individual member without having to vote against the
appointment of the whole board. Any appointment made under a resolution moved in contravention
of this section is accordingly void.

### 161  Validity of acts of directors

**10.161.01**   (1)   The acts of a person acting as a director are valid notwithstanding that it is afterwards
discovered—
(a)   that there was a defect in his appointment;
(b)   that he was disqualified from holding office;
(c)   that he had ceased to hold office;
(d)   that he was not entitled to vote on the matter in question.

(2)   This applies even if the resolution for his appointment is void under section 160 (appointment of
directors of public company to be voted on individually).

COMMENCEMENT DATE  1 October 2007[16]

**10.161.02**   This section is substantially the same as section 285 of the Companies Act 1985. Subsections (1)(b) to
(1)(d) provide more detailed particulars than the former provision of a subsequently discovered defect
in qualification which is now expressly stated to include: having been disqualified from holding office;

[13]  Companies Act 2006 (Commencement No 5 etc) Order 2007, SI 2007/3495, art 5(1)(c).
[14]  Presumably the information envisaged is the details of date of birth provided to the registrar when the
appointment was originally notified to him under s 288 of CA 1985.
[15]  Companies Act 2006 (Commencement No 3, etc) Order 2007, SI 2007/2194, art 2.
[16]  Companies Act 2006 (Commencement No 3, etc) Order 2007, SI 2007/2194, art 2.

having ceased to hold office before the act in question; or not having been entitled to vote on the matter in question. As in the former provision, this section applies even if the resolution for appointment is void under section 160.

Article 92 of Table A extends the statutory validation of section 161.                                    **10.161.03**

The section operates to make good the acts of *de facto* directors where a *bona fide* oversight or slip has    **10.161.04**
resulted in them not being *de iure* directors at the time of the material acts.[17] A person seeking to rely
on the section must have acted in good faith,[18] and must not have known of the defect at the time of the
appointment.[19]

A distinction is to be drawn between an appointment which is defective and the situation in which    **10.161.05**
there has been no appointment at all. The section does not operate to validate acts of persons where no
act has been done purportedly appointing them at all,[20] or where the director has vacated office but has
continued to act.[21]

## Register of directors, etc

## 162  Register of directors

  (1)  Every company must keep a register of its directors.                                          **10.162.01**
  (2)  The register must contain the required particulars (see sections 163, 164 and 166) of each person
       who is a director of the company.
  (3)  The register must be kept available for inspection—
       (a)  at the company's registered office, or
       (b)  at a place specified in the regulations under section 1136.
  (4)  The company must give notice to the registrar—
       (a)  of the place at which the register is kept available for inspection, and
       (b)  of any change in that place,
       unless it has at all times been kept at the company's registered office.
  (5)  The register must be open to the inspection—
       (a)  of any member of the company without charge, and
       (b)  of any other person on payment of such fee as may be prescribed.
  (6)  If default is made in complying with subsection (1), (2) or (3) or if default is made for 14 days in
       complying with subsection (4), or if an inspection required under subsection (5) is refused, an
       offence is committed by—
       (a)  the company, and
       (b)  every officer of the company who is in default.
       For this purpose a shadow director is treated as an officer of the company.
  (7)  A person guilty of an offence under this section is liable on summary conviction to a fine not
       exceeding level 5 on the standard scale and, for continued contravention, a daily default fine not
       exceeding one-tenth of level 5 on the standard scale.
  (8)  In the case of a refusal of inspection of the register, the court may by order compel an immediate
       inspection of it.

COMMENCEMENT DATE  1 October 2009[22]

This section replaced section 288 of the Companies Act 1985 in respect of directors, although the    **10.162.02**
provisions relating to a company's[23] obligations to notify the registrar of changes[24] are now set out
separately in section 167.

The requirements of section 162 also apply to shadow directors by virtue of subsection (6).             **10.162.03**

---

  [17]  *British Asbestos Co Ltd v Boyd* [1903] 2 Ch 439, 444–445 *per* Farwell J.
  [18]  *Channel Collieries Trust Ltd v Dover, St Margaret's and Martin Mill Light Railway Co* [1914] 2 Ch 506, 512
*per* Lord Cozens-Hardy MR.
  [19]  Where the person concerned honestly believed the appointment to have been valid although was aware of
the facts which actually invalidated it he can still rely on the section: *British Asbestos Co Ltd v Boyd*.
  [20]  *Morris v Kanssen* [1946] AC 459, 471–472 *per* Lord Simonds; *MacCullum v Sneddon* [2011] CSOH 59.
  [21]  *Morris v Kanssen*; *Tyne Mutual Steamship Insurance Association v Brown* (1896) 74 LT 283.
  [22]  Companies Act 2006 (Commencement No 8, etc) Order 2008, SI 2008/2860, art 3(i). See also Sch 2 para 25.
  [23]  This section also applies in a modified form to unregistered companies: see Unregistered Companies
Regulations 2009, SI 2009/2436, reg 6. Sections 162–165 also apply to limited liability partnerships *mutatis
mutandis*: Limited Liability Partnerships (Application of Companies Act 2006) Regulations 2009, SI 2009/1804,
reg 18.
  [24]  CA 1985, s 288(2).

**10.162.04** Failure to keep a register at all, to keep the particulars required by sections 163, 164, and 166, to give the notice required to the registrar under subsection (4) within 14 days, or to allow the register to be inspected in compliance with this section is an offence.

**10.162.05** Section 162 does not repeat the provisions of the old section 288(5A) in relation to confidentiality of directors' residential addresses given the introduction of the register of directors' residential addresses under section 165.

**10.162.06** The Companies Act 2006, Part 37, sections 1135 to 1138 set out further provisions applying to company records,[25] including the required form.[26] Under sections 1136 and 1137 the Secretary of State has power to make provision by regulation as to where the register of directors should be kept available, and the obligations of the company to make the register available for inspection.[27] The power of the Secretary of State to make provisions by regulations for fees for the inspection of the register by persons who are not members of the company is provided for in section 1137(4) of the Companies Act 2006.

**10.162.07** The register of directors may be kept in hard copy or electronic form[28] provided that the information is adequately recorded for future reference. However, if the register is kept in electronic form it must be capable of being reproduced in hard copy form,[29] and where it is maintained other than in bound books adequate precautions must be taken to guard against falsification and to facilitate the discovery of any falsification.[30]

**10.162.08** The prescribed fee for the purposes of section 162(5)(b) is currently £3.50 'for each hour or part thereof during which the right of inspection is exercised'.[31]

### 163 Particulars of directors to be registered: individuals

**10.163.01** (1) A company's register of directors must contain the following particulars in the case of an individual—
    (a) name and any former name;
    (b) a service address;
    (c) the country or state (or part of the United Kingdom) in which he is usually resident;
    (d) nationality;
    (e) business occupation (if any);
    (f) date of birth.
(2) For the purposes of this section 'name' means a person's Christian name (or other forename) and surname, except that in the case of—
    (a) a peer, or
    (b) an individual usually known by a title,
    the title may be stated instead of his Christian name (or other forename) and surname or in addition to either or both of them.
(3) For the purposes of this section a 'former name' means a name by which the individual was formerly known for business purposes.
    Where a person is or was formerly known by more than one such name, each of them must be stated.
(4) It is not necessary for the register to contain particulars of a former name in the following cases—
    (a) in the case of a peer or an individual normally known by a British title, where the name is one by which the person was known previous to the adoption of or succession to the title;
    (b) in the case of any person, where the former name—
        (i) was changed or disused before the person attained the age of 16 years, or
        (ii) has been changed or disused for 20 years or more.
(5) A person's service address may be stated to be 'The company's registered office'.
COMMENCEMENT DATE 1 October 2009[32]

---

[25] The register of company directors is a 'company record' for the purpose of Part 37: s 1134(a).
[26] Section 1135 replacing CA 1985, s 722.
[27] Companies (Company Records) Regulations 2008, SI 2008/3006.
[28] Section 1135(1)(a).
[29] Section 1135(2).
[30] Section 1138(1)(a).
[31] Companies (Fees for Inspection of Company Records) Regulations 2008, SI 2008/3007, reg 2.
[32] Companies Act 2006 (Commencement No 8, etc) Order 2008, SI 2008/2860, art 3(i). See also Sch 2 paras 26–29.

This section repeats in large part section 289 of the Companies Act 1985. The main significant change is the requirement in subsection (1)(b) for a company's[33] register to provide a service address which, with section 165, replaces the confidentiality order regime under the Companies Act 1985[34] in respect of directors. There is no longer a requirement for information about current or previous directorships to be entered on the register.[35] Also new is the requirement in subsection (3) for a director to provide details of any former name only if he was known by it for business purposes.[36] However, the exception[37] which allowed a married woman to record only her married name has been repealed to the extent that she used that name for business purposes.[38] Subsection (4) retains the protection for former names of peers or others usually known by a British title where he was known by that name prior to the adoption of or succession to the title. Neither is a former name required to be recorded on the register if it ceased being used before the person attained the age of 16,[39] or has been changed or not been used for 20 years or more, even if used for business purposes. The provisions of section 163 also apply to managers of European Economic Interest Groupings.[40]

**10.163.02**

### 164 Particulars of directors to be registered: corporate directors and firms

A company's register of directors must contain the following particulars in the case of a body corporate, or a firm that is a legal person under the law by which it is governed—

**10.164.01**

(a) corporate or firm name;
(b) registered or principal office;
(c) in the case of an EEA company to which the First Company Law Directive applies, particulars of—
    (i) the register in which the company file mentioned in Article 3 of that Directive is kept (including details of the relevant state), and
    (ii) the registration number in that register;
(d) in any other case, particulars of—
    (i) the legal form of the company or firm and the law by which it is governed, and
    (ii) if applicable, the register in which it is entered (including details of the state) and its registration number in that register.

COMMENCEMENT DATE 1 October 2009[41]

Particulars of corporate directors and firms which are required to be registered have been placed in a separate section in this Act: subsections (a) and (b) repeat the provisions of section 289(1)(b) of the old Act in respect of the particulars or corporate directors and firms which must be kept on a company's[42] register; subsections (c) and (d) are new. Following the recommendation of the CLR[43] it is now a requirement for EEA companies to register details of the EEA state and register in which the company file is kept, and its registration number.[44] For foreign companies outside the EEA the legal form of the firm or company, governing law, details of the register, state and registration number are all required. The provisions of section 164 also apply to managers of European Economic Interest Groupings.[45]

**10.164.02**

### 165 Register of directors' residential addresses

(1) Every company must keep a register of directors' residential addresses.
(2) The register must state the usual residential address of each of the company's directors.
(3) If a director's usual residential address is the same as his service address (as stated in the company's register of directors), the register of directors' residential addresses need only contain an entry to that effect.

**10.165.01**

---

[33] Sections 162–165 apply to limited liability partnerships *mutatis mutandis*: Limited Liability Partnerships (Application of Companies Act 2006) Regulations 2009, SI 2009/1804, reg 18. Sections 162–167 apply to unregistered companies: Unregistered Companies Regulations 2009, SI 2009/2436, reg 6(1).
[34] CA 1985, ss 288(5A), 289(1A), 723B–F.
[35] As was required by CA 1985, s 289(1)(a)(vi).
[36] CA 1985, s 289(1)(a)(ii) did not qualify the requirement to provide details of a former name in such a way.
[37] CA 1985, s 289(2)(b)(iii).
[38] As recommended by the CLR (Final Report, para 11.38).
[39] The requirement under CA 1985, s 289(2)(b)(ii) was 18 years of age.
[40] European Economic Interest Grouping Regulations 1989/638 (as amended), reg 5.
[41] Companies Act 2006 (Commencement No 8, etc) Order 2008, SI 2008/2860, art 3(i). See also Sch 2 paras 26–29.
[42] Sections 162–165 apply to limited liability partnerships *mutatis mutandis*: Limited Liability Partnerships (Application of Companies Act 2006) Regulations 2009, SI 2009/1804, reg 18. Sections 162–167 apply to unregistered companies: Unregistered Companies Regulations 2009, SI 2009/2436, reg 6(1).
[43] Final Report, para 11.38.
[44] Article 3(1) of the First Company Law Directive provides that: 'In each Member State a file shall be opened in a central register, commercial register or companies register, for each of the companies registered therein'.
[45] European Economic Interest Grouping Regulations 1989/638 (as amended), reg 5.

This does not apply if his service address is stated to be 'The company's registered office'.

(4) If default is made in complying with this section, an offence is committed by—

(a) the company, and

(b) every officer of the company who is in default.

For this purpose a shadow director is treated as an officer of the company.

(5) A person guilty of an offence under this section is liable on summary conviction to a fine not exceeding level 5 on the standard scale and, for continued contravention, a daily default fine not exceeding one-tenth of level 5 on the standard scale.

(6) This section applies only to directors who are individuals, not where the director is a body corporate or a firm that is a legal person under the law by which it is governed.

COMMENCEMENT DATE 1 October 2009[46]

**10.165.02** This is one of the provisions replacing the confidentiality order regime of the Companies Act 1985. It reflects concerns that information about directors' home addresses was publicly available information under the old Act, and that such information was increasingly at risk of being used for improper purposes.[47] A company[48] must keep a separate register of its directors' residential addresses for the purposes of the provisions of Chapter 8 relating to disclosure and the permitted use of the protected information.[49] The effect of this section and the requirement for a service address to be contained in the register of directors is that a director can choose whether to place his residential address on the register of directors as his service address, or protect the confidentiality of his residential address by providing it only on the register of residential addresses. Failure properly to keep a register of directors' residential addresses is an offence, and under subsection (4) a shadow director is also liable for any default in complying with the section.

### 166 Particulars of directors to be registered: power to make regulations

**10.166.01** (1) The Secretary of State may make provision by regulations amending—

section 163 (particulars of directors to be registered: individuals),

section 164 (particulars of directors to be registered: corporate directors and firms), or

section 165 (register of directors' residential addresses), so as to add to or remove items from the particulars required to be contained in a company's register of directors or register of directors' residential addresses.

(2) Regulations under this section are subject to affirmative resolution procedure.

COMMENCEMENT DATE 1 October 2009[50]

**10.166.02** This has no antecedent in previous companies legislation and relates to both the particulars of directors to be registered on a company's[51] register and the register of directors' residential addresses. As any regulations proposed by the Secretary of State are subject to the affirmative resolution procedure (section 166(2)) both the House of Lords and the House of Commons must agree to the regulations, although have no amending power.

### 167 Duty to notify registrar of changes

**10.167.01** (1) A company must, within the period of 14 days from the occurrence of—

(a) a person becoming or ceasing to be a director, or

(b) the occurrence of any change in the particulars contained in its register of directors or its register of directors' residential addresses,

give notice to the registrar of the change and of the date on which it occurred.

(2) Notice of a person having become a director of the company must—

(a) contain a statement of the particulars of the new director that are required to be included in the company's register of directors and its register of directors' residential addresses, and

(b) be accompanied by a consent, by that person, to act in that capacity.

(3) Where—

(a) a company gives notice of a change of a director's service address as stated in the company's register of directors, and

---

[46] Companies Act 2006 (Commencement No 8, etc) Order 2008, SI 2008/2860, art 3(i). See also Sch 2 para 30.

[47] White Paper, March 2005, para 5.3.

[48] Sections 162–165 apply to limited liability partnerships *mutatis mutandis*: Limited Liability Partnerships (Application of Companies Act 2006) Regulations 2009, SI 2009/1804, reg 18. Sections 162–167 apply to unregistered companies: Unregistered Companies Regulations 2009, SI 2009/2436, reg 6(1).

[49] Sections 240–246.

[50] Companies Act 2006 (Commencement No 8, etc) Order 2008, SI 2008/2860, art 3(i). See also Sch 2 paras 26–29.

[51] Sections 162–167 apply to unregistered companies: Unregistered Companies Regulations 2009, SI 2009/2436, reg 6(1).

(b)   the notice is not accompanied by notice of any resulting change in the particulars contained in the company's register of directors' residential addresses, the notice must be accompanied by a statement that no such change is required.

(4)   If default is made in complying with this section, an offence is committed by—

(a)   the company, and

(b)   every officer of the company who is in default.

For this purpose a shadow director is treated as an officer of the company.

(5)   A person guilty of an offence under this section is liable on summary conviction to a fine not exceeding level 5 on the standard scale and, for continued contravention, a daily default fine not exceeding one-tenth of level 5 on the standard scale.

COMMENCEMENT DATE  1 October 2009[52]

Several changes were necessary to what was section 288(2) in the Companies Act 1985 because of the introduction of the requirement for a company[53] to maintain a register of directors' residential addresses.[54] Subsection (2) dispenses with the previous requirement for the necessary information to be provided in the prescribed form. Failure to comply with the section is an offence, and a shadow director is treated as an officer of the company for the purpose of liability for default.[55]   **10.167.02**

Section 167(1)(a) is disapplied in limited circumstances by s 46(12) of the Companies (Audit, Investigations and Community Enterprise) Act 2004.   **10.167.03**

## *Removal*

## 168   Resolution to remove director

(1)   A company may by ordinary resolution at a meeting remove a director before the expiration of his period of office, notwithstanding anything in any agreement between it and him.   **10.168.01**

(2)   Special notice is required of a resolution to remove a director under this section or to appoint somebody instead of a director so removed at the meeting at which he is removed.

(3)   A vacancy created by the removal of a director under this section, if not filled at the meeting at which he is removed, may be filled as a casual vacancy.

(4)   A person appointed director in place of a person removed under this section is treated, for the purpose of determining the time at which he or any other director is to retire, as if he had become director on the day on which the person in whose place he is appointed was last appointed a director.

(5)   This section is not to be taken—

(a)   as depriving a person removed under it of compensation or damages payable to him in respect of the termination of his appointment as director or of any appointment terminating with that as director, or

(b)   as derogating from any power to remove a director that may exist apart from this section.

COMMENCEMENT DATE  1 October 2007[56]

This section replaced section 303 of the Companies Act 1985. A director[57] may be removed by an ordinary resolution,[58] but the requirement that this should be in a meeting ensures the director's right to be heard.   **10.168.02**

Under subsection (1) a company has the power by ordinary resolution to remove a director from office before the end of his period in office and regardless of any contrary provision in any agreement[59] between the company and the director in question. A special notice is required in respect of a resolution under section 168 to remove a director or appoint somebody in the place of a director removed at that meeting (section 168(2)).   **10.168.03**

---

[52]   Companies Act 2006 (Commencement No 8, etc) Order 2008, SI 2008/2860, art 3(i). See also Sch 2 para 31.

[53]   Sections 162–167 apply to unregistered companies: Unregistered Companies Regulations 2009, SI 2009/2436, reg 6(1).

[54]   And the separation of the provisions relating to secretaries to a separate part: Part 12.

[55]   Under CA 1985, s 288(6) a shadow director was deemed to be both a director and an officer.

[56]   Companies Act 2006 (Commencement No 3, etc) Order 2007, SI 2007/2194, art 2.

[57]   A resolution can propose the dismissal of more than one director: *National Roads and Motorists' Association Ltd v Scandrett* [2002] NSWC 1123, 43 ACSR 401. But see Co L.N. 2010, 284, 1–4, for an alternative possible analysis.

[58]   A resolution passed upon a bare majority of votes: *Bushell v Faith* [1970] AC 1099, *per* Lord Upjohn at 1108 and Lord Donovan at 1110.

[59]   Section 303 of CA 1985 made specific reference to 'anything in its articles or in any agreement between it and him'. The draftsman omitted the explicit reference to a company's articles apparently on the basis that articles cannot exclude a statutory power and so mention of the articles was unnecessary.

**10.168.04** It appears that a resolution for the removal of a director cannot be adopted by unanimous agreement without a meeting because it would deny the director his right to protest against removal under section 169. For the same reason the procedure under Part 14 Chapter 2 for agreement to written resolutions cannot be used for the dismissal of a director under section 168.[60]

**10.168.05** The House of Lords has held that a provision in a company's articles for weighted voting rights in respect of a resolution to remove a director is valid.[61] By extension it would seem possible for members to agree in a unanimous shareholders' agreement not to use section 168 for the dismissal of directors.

**10.168.06** If the vacancy created by the removal of a director under this section is not filled at the meeting pursuant to a special resolution under section 168(2) it can be filled as a 'casual vacancy'.[62]

**10.168.07** Subsection (4) provides that the provisions for retirement by rotation in the articles[63] of the company are to apply to the person appointed in place of the dismissed director as if that replacement had been appointed at the same time as his predecessor.[64]

**10.168.08** A director dismissed under this section does not lose any entitlement to compensation or damages for the termination of his appointment, or the termination of any appointment connected with it, such as a contract of service (section 168(5)(a)). Thus if removal from office prevents that person from performing the remaining term of his contract as managing director,[65] for example, the company may be liable to compensate him.[66]

**10.168.09** Nothing in section 168 provides a derogation from any additional power to remove a director which may exist. A company's articles may therefore permit dismissal without the provisions of sections 168 or 169 being followed.[67]

### 169 Director's right to protest against removal

**10.169.01** (1) On receipt of notice of an intended resolution to remove a director under section 168, the company must forthwith send a copy of the notice to the director concerned.
(2) The director (whether or not a member of the company) is entitled to be heard on the resolution at the meeting.
(3) Where notice is given of an intended resolution to remove a director under that section, and the director concerned makes with respect to it representations in writing to the company (not exceeding a reasonable length) and requests their notification to members of the company, the company shall, unless the representations are received by it too late for it to do so—
  (a) in any notice of the resolution given to members of the company state the fact of the representations having been made; and
  (b) send a copy of the representations to every member of the company to whom notice of the meeting is sent (whether before or after receipt of the representations by the company).
(4) If a copy of the representations is not sent as required by subsection (3) because received too late or because of the company's default, the director may (without prejudice to his right to be heard orally) require that the representations shall be read out at the meeting.
(5) Copies of the representations need not be sent out and the representations need not be read out at the meeting if, on the application either of the company or of any other person who claims to be aggrieved, the court is satisfied that the rights conferred by this section are being abused.
(6) The court may order the company's costs (in Scotland, expenses) on an application under subsection (5) to be paid in whole or in part by the director, notwithstanding that he is not a party to the application.

---

[60] Section 288(2)(a).
[61] *Bushell v Faith* [1970] AC 1099, 1109 *per* Lord Upjohn in respect of CA 1948, s 184. Despite academic criticism of the outcome in that case the provision was re-enacted in CA 1985 and remains unaltered in the current Act. However, the issue will generally arise only in respect of small companies, and it is easier to justify the result of *Bushell v Faith* in the circumstances of a quasi partnership company.
[62] A vacancy occurring otherwise than by retirement by rotation: *Munster v Cammell Co* (1882) 21 Ch D 183, 187. See Table A Art 78 (appointment by the members) and Table A Art 79 (appointment by the directors).
[63] See Table A Art 73. Note that the Model Articles in the Companies (Model Articles) Regulations 2008, SI 2008/3229 significantly simplify the provisions of the CA 1985 Table A in this regard for private companies, abandoning the requirement that directors retire by rotation: see model article 17.
[64] Although this does not remove the requirement of Art 79 that a director appointed by the directors under that article must be confirmed in office by the members in the next general meeting.
[65] By virtue, for example, of Table A Art 84.
[66] *Southern Foundries (1926) Ltd v Shirlaw* [1940] AC 701; *Shindler v Northern Raincoat Co Ltd* [1960] 1 WLR 1038 both of which concerned unexpired fixed term contracts of 10 years.
[67] *Browne v Panga Pty Ltd* (1995) 120 FLR 34.

COMMENCEMENT DATE 1 October 2007[68]

This section is substantially the same as section 304 of the Companies Act 1985 and provides for a direc- **10.169.02**
tor who is the subject of a proposed resolution under section 168 to be given notice of the resolution and
entitles him to make representations at the meeting. The section provides a director whose removal is
sought with substantive protection and cannot be waived by a company's shareholders.[69]

A director may also make representations of reasonable length in writing to the company and request **10.169.03**
that they be sent to every member of the company receiving notice of the meeting (section 169(3)).
Upon such request and receipt of written representations, the company must advert in the notice to the
fact that representations have been made, unless it is too late to do so (section 169(3)(a)). The company
must then send the written representations to those members in advance of the meeting, again unless
it is too late to do so. This is so even if the notices of the meeting have already been sent to those
members (section 169(3)(b)).

If the written representations were not sent as required by section 169(3) on account of having been **10.169.04**
received too late, or by default of the company, the director is entitled to require that they be read out
orally in addition to his right to address the meeting orally (section 169(4)).

The only material change from the previous legislation is that a court need now only be satisfied that **10.169.05**
the rights conferred by this section are being abused in order to make an order under section 169(5)[70]
relieving the company of its obligations to send out the written representations or allow them to be read
out in the meeting.

If a company makes an application for relief under section 169(5) the court may order that the director **10.169.06**
in question pay the company's costs even though he may not be a party to the application.

# CHAPTER 2
## GENERAL DUTIES OF DIRECTORS

Part 10 of the Act introduces a new statutory code for directors that is intended to both restate and **10.0.02**
clarify the general common law duties owed by directors to their companies. Prior to the announcement of the Company Law Review in March 1998, the English and Scottish Law Commissions had
embarked upon an examination of directors' duties.[71] As part of this project, the case for restating
directors' duties in statute was examined. Arguments against codification were founded on loss of
flexibility, while those in favour saw advantages in terms of certainty and accessibility. The Law
Commissions concluded that the case for legislative restatement was convincing and that the issue of
inflexibility could be addressed by (i) ensuring the restatement was at a high level of generality by way
of a statement of principles; and (ii) providing that it was not exhaustive: ie while the restatement
would be a comprehensive and binding statement of the law, it would not prevent the courts
developing new general principles. The report was placed before the Company Law Review Steering
Group and it served to inform its approach towards restating the equitable and common law duties of
directors.[72] The Government's position on the issue was made clear in its 2005 White Paper,[73] which
states that companies work best where the respective roles and responsibilities of directors and
shareholders are clearly understood. It was noted that directors may not appreciate the full extent of
their duties under the law and that such obligations may be misunderstood by shareholders, in whose
interests the directors should be acting. As a means of making the relevant law 'consistent, certain,
accessible and comprehensible' the Government therefore supported a statutory restatement of
directors' duties.[74]

---

[68] Companies Act 2006 (Commencement No 3, etc) Order 2007, SI 2007/2194, art 2.
[69] *Bonham-Carter v Situ Ventures Ltd* [2012] EWHC 230 (Ch), in which judgment Richard Sheldon QC also
observed (without deciding the point) that a powerful argument could be made for contending that a failure to
comply with any of the requirements of s 169 would render any resolution purportedly passed under s 168
invalid.
[70] CA 1985, s 304(4) provided that a court had to be satisfied that the rights conferred were 'being abused to
secure needless publicity for defamatory matter'.
[71] See the joint report, *Company Directors: Regulating Conflicts of Interests* and *Formulating A Statement Of
Duties* (Nos 261 and 173, respectively) (London, The Stationery Office Ltd, 1999).
[72] See Chap 3 of the Company Law Review Steering Group's Final Report.
[73] *Company Law Reform* (Cm 6456) 16.
[74] In the Lords Grand Committee, 6 February 2006 (column 254), Lord Goldsmith stated that the purpose of
the restatement is 'to make what is expected of directors clearer and to make the law more accessible to them and
to others'.

**10.0.03**    As has been seen, the primary objective of the restatement is to provide greater clarity on the obligations of directors. It is designed to make the development of the law in this area more predictable but without hindering its development by the courts. Further, it is framed so as to correct what the Steering Group identified as defects in the present duties relating to the no-conflict rule. The general duties owed by a director to the company are set out in Part 10, sections 171 to 177 of the Act. The restatement is not an exhaustive code and not all of the duties of directors appear in Part 10 of the statute. For example, the duties relating to the preparation and delivery of accounts are found elsewhere in the Act (see, for example, sections 399 and 404 found in Chapter 2, Part 15 of the Act).[75]

**10.0.04**    It is noteworthy that the way in which the duties are framed results in an overlap between them. For example, where a director accepts a bribe from a third party, this will place him in breach of section 176 (duty not to accept benefits from third parties), the duty to avoid conflicts of interest (section 175), and, depending on the particular circumstances, also place him in breach of the duty to promote the success of the company (section 172). In this respect, it should be noted that section 179 makes it clear that the duties are *cumulative*. It is therefore necessary for directors to comply with every duty that, in any given situation, may trigger. As will be seen, this is subject to an exception found in section 175 (duty to avoid conflicts of interest) which is made subject to the disclosure requirements contained in sections 177 and 182.[76]

## Introductory

### 170 Scope and nature of general duties

**10.170.01**    (1)  The general duties specified in sections 171 to 177 are owed by a director of a company to the company.
(2)  A person who ceases to be a director continues to be subject—
   (a)  to the duty in section 175 (duty to avoid conflicts of interest) as regards the exploitation of any property, information or opportunity of which he became aware at a time when he was a director, and
   (b)  to the duty in section 176 (duty not to accept benefits from third parties) as regards things done or omitted by him before he ceased to be a director.
To that extent those duties apply to a former director as to a director, subject to any necessary adaptations.
(3)  The general duties are based on certain common law rules and equitable principles as they apply in relation to directors and have effect in place of those rules and principles as regards the duties owed to a company by a director.
(4)  The general duties shall be interpreted and applied in the same way as common law rules or equitable principles, and regard shall be had to the corresponding common law rules and equitable principles in interpreting and applying the general duties.
(5)  The general duties apply to shadow directors where, and to the extent that, the corresponding common law rules or equitable principles so apply.

COMMENCEMENT DATE 1 October 2007[77]

**10.170.02**    This section provides the starting point for considering the scope and nature of the new regime governing the general duties owed by directors to their companies.[78] Subsection (1) restates the common law position that the duties of directors are owed to the company.[79] It therefore follows that

---

[75] In the Lords Grand Committee, 6 February 2006 (column 249), Lord Goldsmith explained that: 'The statement of general duties … is not intended to be an exhaustive list of all the duties … The directors may owe a wide range of duties to their companies in addition to the general duties listed … including obligations under the Insolvency Act 1986.'
[76] See paras 10.177.01–10.182.08 below.
[77] Companies Act 2006 (Commencement No 3, etc) Order 2007, SI 2007/2194, art 2.
[78] It is noteworthy that in October 2008 the ICAEW published a new technical release: number 06/08, titled 'Guidance on directors' duties and responsibilities of a financial or accounting nature'. It is principally concerned with the main duties and responsibilities of a financial or accounting nature owed by directors to their company and its shareholders and others, but also includes an overview of more general duties and responsibilities. It sets out, where appropriate, what is considered to be good practice rather than what may be acceptable as the legal minimum required.
[79] See eg *Percival v Wright* [1902] 2 Ch 241. In *Multinational Gas and Petrochemical Co Ltd v Multinational Gas and Petrochemical Services Ltd* [1983] Ch 258, Dillon LJ explained, at 288, that: 'directors indeed stand in a fiduciary relationship to the company, as they are appointed to manage the affairs of the company and they owe fiduciary duties to the company though not to the creditors, present or future, or to individual shareholders.' But in special circumstances, directors may owe duties to individual shareholders: see, for example, *Peskin v Anderson* [2001] 1 BCLC 372, at [33][34], Mummery LJ. See also *Allen v Hyatt* (1914) 30 TLR 444. The position of a nominee director was considered in *Hawkes v Cuddy (No 2)* [2009] 2 BCLC 427. The Court of Appeal held that

the proper claimant in any action for breach is the company itself.[80] The term 'director' is defined in section 250 and the duties extend to both de facto directors and shadow directors by reason of subsection (5).[81] Subsection (2) restates the common law position that resignation is no defence to an action for breach of the no-conflict rule (see section 175 below) or to an action where a director has accepted a benefit from a third party (see section 176 below).[82] Responding to the point of contention that emerged during the Company Law Review Steering Group's consultation exercise as to whether or not the restatement should be exhaustive, subsection (3) seeks to put the matter beyond doubt in two ways. First, it states that the general duties are so drafted as to reflect the case law in which the equitable and common law duties governing the behaviour of directors was developed. Secondly, it states that the code replaces those principles. Thus, claims for breach of duty by a director will need to be aligned with one or more of the duties set out in the Act, except insofar as the statute preserves the common law duties which it does, for example, with respect to creditors' interests.[83] Subsection (3) is supplemented by subsection (4) which directs the courts to interpret and apply the codified duties having regard to the pre-existing case law. Taking subsections (3) and (4) together, considerable doubt remains over the extent to which the codified duties merely replicate or, indeed, replace the pre-existing duties.[84] Such uncertainty arises because the draftsmen use different phraseology to that found in the judicial formulations of the duties contained in the case law. This runs counter to the declared objectives of the Company Law Review Steering Group's recommendations in respect of directors' general duties.[85] The issue will need to be addressed as a matter of priority in future litigation. Further questions which will need to be addressed include the remedies for breach together with the issue of accessory liability.[86]

Subsection (5) makes it clear that where a common law rule or equitable principle applied to a shadow    **10.170.03**
director, the statutory duty replacing that common law rule or equitable principle will apply to the shadow director in place of that rule or principle. Conversely, where the rule or principle did not apply to a shadow director, the statutory duty replacing that rule or principle will not apply either.[87]

*The general duties*

### 171  Duty to act within powers

A director of a company must—    **10.171.01**

> (a)  act in accordance with the company's constitution, and
> (b)  only exercise powers for the purposes for which they are conferred.

COMMENCEMENT DATE  1 October 2007[88]

---

the fact that a director was nominated by a shareholder did not, of itself, impose any duty owed to his nominator by the director. A nominee director could take into account the interests of his nominator without being in breach of his duties to the company, provided that his decisions as a director were taken in what he *bona fide* considered to be in the best interests of the company.

[80]  One of the main ways in which the company can take legal action against a director (or, more usually, a former director) for breach of duty is through 'a derivative claim' brought by one or more shareholders to enforce a right which is vested not in himself or herself but in the company. For 'derivative claims' see Part 11 of the Act, ss 260–269, under para 11.260 below.

[81]  For the definition of the term 'shadow director', see s 251, considered below at para 10.170.03.

[82]  See eg *IDC v Cooley* [1972] 1 WLR 443; *Canadian Aero Service Ltd v O'Malley* (1973) 40 DLR (3d) 371; and *CMS Dolphin Ltd v Simonet* [2001] 2 BCLC 704.

[83]  See further s 172 and commentary at paras 10.172.06–10.172.08 below.

[84]  Eg, the duties of directors now enshrined in ss 175 and 176 are not the same as the common law rules or equitable principles applying to those duties. See paras 10.175.01–10.176.03 below.

[85]  See Chap 3 of the Company Law Review Steering Group's Final Report. See also s 170 and commentary at paras 10.170.01–10.170.02 above.

[86]  See further s 178 and commentary, paras 10.178.01–10.178.05 below.

[87]  In *Ultraframe (UK) Ltd v Fielding* [2005] EWHC 1638 the High Court clarified the meaning of the term 'shadow director' as defined in s 741(2) of CA 1985, now broadly reproduced in s 251 of the 2006 Act. S 251(1) provides that 'shadow director', in relation to a company, means a person in accordance with whose directions or instructions the directors of the company are accustomed to act. The judge stated that a governing majority of the board must be accustomed to act in accordance with the directions of the alleged shadow director. The court also considered the nature and scope of the duties of shadow directors. From the time that it can be established that a person is a shadow director, then he will be subject to certain statutory duties and prohibitions to the company (in this respect, recall that s 170(5), at para 10.170.05 above, states that the general duties apply to shadow directors where, and to the extent that, the corresponding common law rules or equitable principles so apply). Lewison J, applying *Paragon Finance plc v DB Thakerar & Co* [1999] 1 All ER 400 and *Dubai Aluminium Co Ltd v Salaam* [2002] UKHL 48, took the view that shadow directors would not usually owe fiduciary duties to a company given that they do not deal directly with corporate assets. However, a shadow director will be required to declare his interest in any contract with the company at a board meeting (see s 177 at paras 10.177.01–10.177.08 below) and obtain members' approval in relation to substantial property transactions (see s 190 at para 10.190.05 below).

[88]  Companies Act 2006 (Commencement No 3, etc) Order 2007, SI 2007/2194, art 2.

**10.171.02**    This section codifies the director's duty under which a director should exercise his powers in accordance with the terms on which they were granted (ie to comply with the company's constitution), and do so for a proper purpose (ie a purpose for which power was conferred).

**10.171.03**    For the purpose of paragraph (a) the company's constitution is defined in section 257 and includes the company's articles of association, decisions taken in accordance with the articles, and other decisions taken by the members, or a class of them, if they can be regarded as decisions of the company.[89] The importance of directors appreciating the purposes of the company as detailed in the constitution is critical if they are to fulfil the duty laid down by section 172 to promote its success.

**10.171.04**    The articles of association may increase the burden of the duties by, for example, requiring directors to obtain shareholder authorization for their remuneration packages. However, the articles may not dilute the duties except to the extent expressly provided for in the relevant provisions. In this regard, section 173 (duty to exercise independent judgment) provides that a director will not be in breach if he has acted in accordance with the constitution. As will be seen, section 175 (duty to avoid conflicts of interest) provides that a director will not be in breach where, subject to the constitution, the matter has been authorized by independent directors. Further, section 180 (consent, approval, or authorization by members) preserves the common law position whereby the company's members may authorize an act that would otherwise be a breach of duty.

**10.171.05**    Paragraph (b) of section 171 codifies the pre-existing proper purposes doctrine. In *Re Smith & Fawcett,*[90] Lord Greene MR stated that directors must not exercise their powers for any 'collateral purpose'. *Extrasure Travel Insurances Ltd v Scattergood,*[91] is a paradigm case. The directors had misused corporate assets for an improper purpose. The learned judge stated that it is not necessary for a claimant to prove that a director was dishonest, or that he knew he was pursuing a collateral purpose. He went on to lay down a four-part test for the determination of liability:

(i)   identify the power whose exercise is in question;
(ii)  identify the proper purpose for which that power was delegated to the directors;
(iii) identify the substantial purpose for which the power was in fact exercised; and
(iv)  decide whether that purpose was proper.

**10.171.06**    In a recent Court of Session decision in Scotland this provision was relied upon. Lord Glennie expressed the view that although there was no equivalent in the earlier Companies Acts, this section does 'little more than set out the pre-existing law on the subject'.[92] It will be interesting to see whether this interpretation is followed.

**10.171.07**    The proper purposes doctrine has come to the fore in relation to the authority of directors to issue shares.[93] If shares are allotted in exchange for cash where the company is in need of additional capital the duty will not be broken. But where directors issue shares in order to dilute the voting rights of an existing majority shareholder because he or she is blocking a resolution supporting, for example, a

---

[89] See below under s 257. On the question of whether informal shareholder assent will suffice to satisfy formalities laid down in the Act or in a company's constitution, see *Re Duomatic Ltd* [1969] 2 Ch 365; and *Euro Brokers Holdings Ltd v Monecor (London) Ltd* [2003] 1 BCLC 506.

[90] [1942] Ch 304, CA.

[91] [2003] 1 BCLC 598. See also *Selangor United Rubber Estates Ltd v Cradock (No 3)* [1968] 1 WLR 1555 where Ungoed-Thomas J, at 1578, explained the nature of the 'proper purposes' duty. He stressed that directors and trustees have this in common: 'that the property in their hands or under their control must be applied for the specified purposes of the company or the settlement; and to apply it otherwise is to misapply it in breach of the obligation to apply it to those purposes for the company or the settlement beneficiaries. So, even though the scope and operation of such obligation differs in the case of directors and strict settlement trustees, the nature of the obligation with regard to property in their hands or under their control is identical, namely, to apply it to specified purposes for others beneficially.' An unusual illustration of the proper purposes doctrine is afforded by *Criterion Properties plc v Stratford UK Properties LLC* [2004] UKHL 28, which concerned a 'poison pill' arrangement that was held by the Court of Appeal to amount to a gratuitous disposition of the company's assets. The House of Lords approached the issue on the basis of directors' authority, ie whether the directors had actual, apparent, or ostensible authority to sign the agreement. Since this could not be decided on the evidence available, the case was remitted for trial.

[92] *Re West Coast Capital (Lios) Ltd* [2008] CSOH 72, [21].

[93] Other examples include: approving transfers of shares (*Bennett's Case* (1867) 5 De GM&G 284); making calls on shares (*Galloway v Hallé Concerts Society* [1915] 2 Ch 233); and the forfeiture of shares (*Re Agriculturist Cattle Insurance Co, Stanhope's Case* (1866) 1 Ch App 161).

takeover bid, then the duty will be breached.[94] The Privy Council in *Howard Smith Ltd v Ampol Petroleum Ltd*,[95] subjected the duty to detailed scrutiny. The directors allotted shares to a company which had made a takeover bid. The effect of the share issue was to reduce the majority holding of two other shareholders, who had made a rival bid, from 55 per cent to 36 per cent. The two shareholders sought a declaration that the share allotment was invalid as being an improper exercise of power. It was held the directors had improperly exercised their powers on the basis that it is unconstitutional for directors to use their fiduciary powers over the shares in the company purely for the purpose of destroying an existing majority, or creating a new majority which did not previously exist, or otherwise interfering with that element of the company's constitution which is separate from and set against their powers. Lord Wilberforce stressed that the court must examine the substantial purpose for which a power is exercised, and must reach a conclusion as to whether that purpose was proper or not. However, the power to issue shares may be exercised for reasons other than the raising of capital provided 'those reasons relate to a purpose benefiting the company as a whole; as distinguished from a purpose, for example, of maintaining control of the company in the hands of the directors themselves or their friends'.[96] If a dispute arises as to the substantial or primary purpose of the exercise of power the court may look at the situation objectively in order to estimate how critical or pressing the objective or requirement asserted really was.[97]

It should be noted that sections 549 to 551 and 561 of the Act (replacing section 80 of the Companies    **10.171.08**
Act 1985) provide for the allotment of shares by directors. The new provisions (in line with the general approach advocated by the CLR) distinguish between private and public companies. As with the pre-existing statutory provisions, the principle that directors should only allot shares for the benefit of the company is, of course, implicit.

## 172  Duty to promote the success of the company

(1)  A director of a company must act in the way he considers, in good faith, would be most likely to    **10.172.01**
promote the success of the company for the benefit of its members as a whole, and in doing so have regard (amongst other matters) to—
(a)  the likely consequences of any decision in the long term,
(b)  the interests of the company's employees,[a]
(c)  the need to foster the company's business relationships with suppliers, customers and others,
(d)  the impact of the company's operations on the community and the environment,
(e)  the desirability of the company maintaining a reputation for high standards of business conduct, and
(f)  the need to act fairly as between members of the company.[98]
(2)  Where or to the extent that the purposes of the company consist of or include purposes other than the benefit of its members, subsection (1) has effect as if the reference to promoting the success of the company for the benefit of its members were to achieving those purposes.
(3)  The duty imposed by this section has effect subject to any enactment or rule of law requiring directors, in certain circumstances, to consider or act in the interests of creditors of the company.

AMENDMENTS AND NOTES

[a]  This provision replaces s 309 of CA 1985.

COMMENCEMENT DATE  1 October 2007[99]

The duty in this section to promote the success of the company enshrines in statute a reformed and    **10.172.02**
broader concept of shareholder value, labelled by the CLR the principle of 'enlightened shareholder value'.[100] This duty has two elements. First, a director must act in the way he or she considers, in good

---

[94]  *Hogg v Cramphorn* [1967] Ch 254. In *Piercy v S Mills & Co Ltd* [1920] 1 Ch 77 the court set aside a share issue on the basis that this was done 'simply and solely for the purpose of retaining control in the hands of the existing directors'.

[95]  [1974] AC 821.

[96]  *Harlowe's Nominees Pty Ltd v Woodside (Lake Entrance) Oil Co* (1968) CLR 483.

[97]  [1974] AC 821, 832G.

[98]  As seen above, para 10.170.01, this reflects the fundamental principle that directors' duties are owed to the company not to individual shareholders. But directors in their decision-making will be in breach of duty if they fail to consider whether a course of action will be fair as between different groups of shareholders: see, for example, *Hirsche v Sims* [1894] AC 654, PC. See also *Bennett's Case* (1867) 5 De GM&G 284 (approving transfers of shares). See generally J Lowry, 'Self-Dealing Directors Constructing A Regime of Accountability' [1997] *Northern Ireland Legal Quarterly* 211.

[99]  Companies Act 2006 (Commencement No 3, etc) Order 2007, SI 2007/2194, art 2.

[100]  The CLR considered whether to retain the traditional understanding that companies should be run for the benefit of shareholders. The CLR recognized the merits of a stakeholder approach but did not recommend its adoption. Instead, it proposed that the duty of loyalty should promote 'enlightened shareholder value'. See

faith, would be most likely to promote the success of the company for the benefit of its members as a whole. Secondly, in doing so, the director should have regard (amongst other matters) to the factors listed in subsection (1). This list is not exhaustive, but highlights areas of particular importance which reflect wider expectations of responsible business behaviour (see below).

**10.172.03**  It is trite law that because directors control the assets of the company they are, by analogy with the law of trusts, regarded as owing fiduciary duties in respect of those assets. It has been seen that section 170 restates the common law position that the duties of directors are owed to the company and not to the individual shareholders.[101] The over-arching fiduciary duty is that of good faith which the Steering Group referred to as the duty of loyalty.[102] In *Re Smith & Fawcett*,[103] Lord Greene MR said that directors should exercise their powers 'bona fide in what they consider—not what a court may consider—is in the best interests of the company'.[104] The meaning of the term 'company' in this context was construed by the courts as referring to present and future members,[105] and section 172 proceeds on the basis that it is owed to the 'members as a whole', subject to the requirement to take into consideration the interests of other constituencies. The court will not substitute its own view about which course of action the directors should have taken in place of the board's own judgment,[106] although this is subject to the overriding jurisdiction of the courts to assess objectively the conduct in question. As explained by Arden LJ in *Item Software (UK) Ltd v Fassihi*,[107] if a director embarks on a course of action without considering the interests of the company and there is no basis on which he or she could reasonably have come to the conclusion that it was in the interests of the company, the director will be in breach. In a recent Court of Session decision in Scotland Lord Glennie expressed the view that although there was no equivalent in the earlier Companies Acts, this section does 'little more than set out the pre-existing law on the subject'.[108] Similarly, Warren J observed recently that:

> The perhaps old-fashioned phrase acting 'bona fide in the interests of the company' is reflected in the statutory words acting 'in good faith in a way most likely to promote the success of the company for the benefit of its members as a whole'. They come to the same thing with the modern formulation giving a more readily understood definition of the scope of the duty.[109]

---

*Developing the Framework* (URN 00/656, Department of Trade and Industry (DTI), 2000), paras 2.19–2.22; *Completing the Structure* (URN 00/1335, DTI, 2000), para 3.5). According to this approach, directors, whilst ultimately required to promote shareholder interests, must take account of the factors affecting the company's relationships and performance. The CLR proposed to formulate the duty in such a way as to remind directors that shareholder value depends on successful management of the company's relationships with other stakeholders. This is now reflected in s 172.

[101]  *Percival v Wright* [1902] 2 Ch 241.

[102]  Couching this duty within the realms of fiduciary loyalty is evident from the language adopted by the judges. For example, in *Berryland Books Ltd v BK Books Ltd* [2009] EWHC 1877 (Ch), at [22], HHJ Hodge QC noted that '[a] director ... is subject to a fundamental duty of loyalty, which requires him to act in what he in good faith considers to be the best interests of his company.' See also the judgment of Arden LJ in *Item Software (UK) Ltd v Fassihi* [2005] 2 BCLC 91.

[103]  [1942] Ch 304. He went on to add that directors should not exercise their powers for any collateral purpose, see s 171 above.

[104]  [1942] Ch 304, 306.

[105]  See eg *Gaiman v Association for Mental Health* [1971] Ch 317, 330, Megarry J said 'I would accept the interests of both present and future members of the company as a whole, as being a helpful expression of a human equivalent'.

[106]  See *Howard Smith Ltd v Ampol Petroleum Ltd* [1974] AC 82, PC; and *Re Southern Counties Fresh Foods Ltd* [2008] EWHC 2810 (Ch). In *Dorchester Finance v Stebbing* [1989] BCLC 498, 501–502, Foster J stated [a] director must exercise any power vested in him as such, honestly, in good faith and in the interests of the company ...' Similarly, in *Regentcrest plc v Cohen* [2001] 2 BCLC 80, Jonathan Parker J, at 105, explained that the duty to act *bona fide* in the interests of a company is a subjective one: 'The question is not whether, viewed objectively by the court, the particular act or omission which is challenged was in fact in the interests of the company; still less is the question whether the court, had it been in the position of the director at the relevant time, might have acted differently. Rather, the question is whether the director honestly believed that his act or omission was in the interests of the company. The issue is as to the directors state of mind ...'. As seen above, para 10.171.05, in *Extrasure Travel Insurances Ltd v Scattergood* [2003] 1 BCLC 598, the directors of Extrasure had transferred company funds, some £200,000, to another company in the group, Citygate Insurance Brokers Ltd (the parent company), to enable it to pay a creditor who had been pressing for payment. It was held that the directors had acted without any honest belief that the transfer was in the interests of the transferor company. See also *Knight v Frost* [1999] 1 BCLC 364.

[107]  [2005] 2 BCLC 91. See J Lowry, 'The Duty of Loyalty of Company Directors: Bridging the Accountability Gap Through Efficient Disclosure' [2009] CLJ 607.

[108]  *Re West Coast Capital (Lios) Ltd* [2008] CSOH 72, [21].

[109]  *Cobden Investments Ltd v RWM Langport Ltd and others* [2008] EWHC 2810 (Ch) [52]. This statement should be read in conjunction with Warren J's observation in the following sentence that 'I do not intend to

As commented above, the factors listed in subsection (1) to be taken into account by directors in discharging this duty are designed to give content to the concept of 'enlightened shareholder value'[110] which, in the view of the Company Law Review Steering Group, 'is more likely to drive long-term company performance and maximize overall competitiveness and wealth and welfare for all'.[111] The phrase 'have regard to' was explained by Margaret Hodge, then Minister of State for Industry and the Regions:

> The words 'have regard to' mean 'think about'; they are absolutely not about just ticking boxes. If 'thinking about' leads to the conclusion, as we believe it will in many cases, that the proper course is to act positively to achieve the objects in the [provision], that will be what the director's duty is. In other words 'have regard to' means 'give proper consideration to'....[112]

It therefore seems that the legislative intention, at least, is that a director who completely disregards the specified factors listed in subsection (1) will be in breach of duty. It should be noted that in response to debates in the House of Lords as well as detailed engagement with interested parties, the Government made amendments to subsection (1) which it thought would put beyond doubt that the need to have regard to certain factors (including the interest of the employees and impact on the environment) is subject to the overriding duty to act in the way the director considers, in good faith, would be most likely to promote the success of the company for the benefit of its members as a whole. The list is *not exhaustive* but is indicative of the importance that the Steering Group paid to the wider expectations of responsible business behaviour.[113] The question of what will promote the success of the company is one for the director's good faith judgment.[114] In the Lords Grand Committee,[115] Lord Goldsmith summarized the scope of s 172 thus: 'it is for the directors, by reference to those things we are talking about—the objective of the company—to judge and form a good faith judgment about what is to be regarded as success for the members as a whole ... the duty is to promote the success for the benefit of the members as a whole—that is, for the members as a collective body—not only to benefit the majority shareholders, or any particular shareholder or section of shareholders, still less the interests of directors who might happen to be shareholders themselves.' The starting point is that 'it is essentially for the members of the company to define the objectives that they wish to achieve. Success means what the members collectively want the company to achieve'.[116] This aligns the duty with the position long taken by the courts that, as a general rule, their role is not to interfere in the internal management of companies. The orthodoxy here is that the management of companies is best left to the judgment of their directors, subject to the good faith requirement.[117] In this regard, the approach taken by Mr

---

consider whether, and if so how, the statutory duties differ from established common law and equitable duties in the present case, since the matters relied on by CIL to establish breach of duty nearly all pre-date the coming into effect of the Act': ibid.

[110] See para 10.172.02, n 1 above.

[111] White Paper, 2005, para 3.3: ⟨http://www.dti.gov.uk/bbf/co-act-2006/white-paper/page22800.html⟩.

[112] Hansard, HC, vol 450, col 789 (17 October 2006).

[113] The requirement for directors to take account of the interests of other stakeholders has been criticized on the basis that it will potentially increase liability for directors, create additional bureaucracy, and result in directors being too cautious in their decision making. See eg *The Telegraph*, 7 June 2006, 'Investors the true arbiters of social role'.

[114] This ensures that 'business decisions on...the strategy and tactics are for the directors, and not subject to decision by the courts, subject to good faith'. See the Explanatory Notes to the Act available at: ⟨http://www.dti.gov.uk/bbf/co-act-2006/index.html⟩ The Law Society raised a concern that this could raise the spectre of courts reviewing business decisions taken in good faith by subjecting such decisions to objective tests, with serious resulting implications for the management of companies by their directors. See, the Law Society's 'Proposed Amendments and Briefing for Parts 10 & 11' (issued 23 January 2006). On the scope of the duty of loyalty which includes the duty to disclose improper actions by the director to the company, see further the judgment of Arden LJ in *Item Software (UK) Ltd v Fassihi* [2005] 2 BCLC 91. See also *Midland Tool Ltd v Midland International Tooling Ltd* [2003] 2 BCLC 523; and *Lexi Holdings plc v Lugman* [2008] 2 BCLC 725.

[115] 6 February 2006 (column 256),

[116] Lord Goldsmith in the Lords Grand Committee, 6 February 2006 (cols 255–256). He then went further to explain: 'For a commercial company, success will usually mean long-term increase in value. For certain companies, such as charities and community interest companies, it will mean the attainment of the objectives for which the company has been established. But one can be more refined than that. A company's constitution and the decisions that a company makes can also go on to be more specific about what is the appropriate success model for the company. I have indicated that usually for a company it will be a long-term increase in value, but I can imagine commercial companies that would have a different objective as to their success. Success can ultimately be determined only on a company-by-company basis, and it is possible that it may change over time': ibid.

[117] This non-interventionist policy (the internal management rule) was explained by Lord Eldon LC in *Carlen v Drury* (1812) 1 Ves & B 154, who said: 'This Court is not required on every Occasion to take the Management

Justice Sales in *R (on the application of People & Planet) v HM Treasury*,[118] illustrates a modern manifestation of this non-interventionist policy. The case arose by way of an application for permission to bring judicial review proceedings. People & Planet objected to HM Treasury's policy in relation to the management of the Royal Bank of Scotland (RBS) by UK Financial Investments Ltd (UKFI), the company through which the Government owns RBS. The claimant argued that HM Treasury acted unlawfully in adopting the policy it promulgated relating to how UKFI should manage the investment in RBS. The policy it adopted calls for a commercial approach on the part of UKFI. The claimant objected to this on the basis that UKFI should be promoting a more interventionist approach as a major shareholder in RBS, and seek to persuade or require RBS to change its current commercial lending practices and adopt instead lending policies which did not support ventures or businesses which might be said to be harmful to the environment by reason of their carbon emissions or be said to be insufficiently respectful of human rights. One of the lines of attack made by the claimant was that there was a misdirection of law by HM Treasury as to the effect of s 172. The application was refused. The judge held that in evaluating the policy with reference to the Green Book (which set out guidance for decision-making in central government), officials correctly identified the proper way in which social and environmental considerations may be taken into account by the directors of RBS in the context of the duties of those directors under s 172. He noted that the question then was whether HM Treasury should have sought to go further, so as in effect to seek to impose its own policy in relation to combating climate change and promoting human rights on the board of RBS, contrary to the judgment of the directors:

> In my view, that clearly would have a tendency to come into conflict with, and hence would cut across, the duties of the RBS Board as set out in section 172(1). It would also have given rise to a real risk of litigation by minority shareholders seeking to complain that the value of their shares had been detrimentally affected by the Government seeking to impose its policy on RBS, as was identified in the background document which accompanied the Green Book assessment.[119]

Mr Justice Sales went on to state that decisions regarding the management of RBS will be matters for the judgment of the directors of RBS:

> The policy adopted by HM Treasury is that UKFI can properly seek to influence the Board of RBS to have regard to environmental and human rights considerations in accordance with the RBS Board's duty under s 172 ... It was a legitimate argument against going further than that that there would be a risk of trying to press the RBS Board beyond the limits of their own duties, and in my view that is all that has been said in paragraph 13(e) of the Green Book assessment, read in its proper context as one reason among others. In my view, on a fair reading of that document, it was not being said that there was an absolute legal bar to the introduction of a different policy, but rather that was a good reason for not pressing the RBS Board by means of a more interventionist policy for UKFI.[120]

In discharging this duty and, more particularly, in taking account of the factors listed in subsection (1), directors are bound to exercise reasonable care, skill, and diligence (see section 174 below). A director will, therefore, need to demonstrate that the interests listed informed his or her deliberations.[121] The reformulated core duty of loyalty contained in subsection (1) is bolstered by the requirement, introduced by section 417, for the directors' report (to be produced for each financial year of the company[122]) to contain a business review. Its purpose is stated in section 417(2) as being 'to inform members and help them assess how the directors have performed their duty under section 172'.

**10.172.05**    Subsection (2) applies to altruistic, or partly altruistic, companies such as charities and community interest companies. Any company may, however, have wider 'charitable' objectives that will take precedence over the narrower interests of its members. For companies with altruistic or partly altruistic purposes, directors must act in the way they consider, in good faith, is the best way to achieve such purposes.

**10.172.06**    Subsection (3) displaces the duty when the company is insolvent. The reference to any 'rule of law' appears to encompass the trend found in the modern case law to the effect that where the company is

---

of every Playhouse and Brewhouse in the Kingdom.' Indeed, Lord Greene MR in his formulation of the good faith duty in *Re Smith & Fawcett*, see para 10.172.03 above, paid particular emphasis to the point.

[118] [2009] EWHC 3020 (Admin), See, S F Copp, 'S 172 of the Companies Act 2006 fails people and planet' [2010] *Comp Law* 406.

[119] Ibid, [34].

[120] Ibid, at [35].

[121] Consideration of the factors will be an integral part of the duty to promote the success of the company for the benefit of its members as a whole. The [provision] makes it clear that a director is to have regard to the factors in fulfilling that duty. The decisions taken by a director and the weight given to the factors will continue to be a matter for his good faith judgment.' Margaret Hodge, Hansard, HC, vol 450, col 789 (17 October 2006).

[122] See s 415. See further, below.

insolvent, the interests of creditors supersede those of its members with the consequence that the focus of the duty changes accordingly. For example, in *West Mercia Safetywear Ltd v Dodd*,[123] the Court of Appeal cited, with approval, the view expressed by Street CJ in *Kinsela v Russell Kinsela Pty Ltd*,[124] that:

> where a company is insolvent the interests of the creditors intrude. They become prospectively entitled, through the mechanism of liquidation, to displace the power of the shareholders and directors to deal with the company's assets. It is in a practical sense their assets and not the shareholders' assets that, through the medium of the company, are under the management of the directors pending either liquidation, return to solvency, or the imposition of some alternative administration...[125]

The Court of Appeal in *West Mercia* held that shareholders do not have the power to absolve directors from a breach of duty to the creditors so as to bar the liquidator's claim.[126] Similarly, in *Colin Gwyer and Associates Ltd v London Wharf (Limehouse) Ltd*,[127] it was held that a resolution of the board of directors passed without proper consideration being given by certain directors to the interests of creditors would be open to challenge if the company had been insolvent at the date of the resolution. Leslie Kosmin QC, sitting as a deputy judge in the High Court, stated that:

> In relation to an insolvent company, the directors when considering the company's interests must have regard to the interests of the creditors. If they fail to do so, and therefore ignore the relevant question, the [*Charterbridge Corpn Ltd v Lloyds Bank Ltd* [1970] Ch 62] test can be applied with the modification that in considering the interests of the company the honest and intelligent director must have been capable of believing that the decision was for the benefit of the creditors. In my view the *Charterbridge Corporation* test is of general application.[128]

In *Nicholson v Permakraft (NZ) Ltd*,[129] Cooke J adopted a rather more open textured approach to that       **10.172.07**
seen in the cases above, or, indeed, to that taken by his brethren, Somers and Richardson JJ, by suggesting that directors are to have regard to the interests of creditors where the company is 'near-insolvent, or of doubtful solvency'. It is unclear whether the English courts would be prepared to follow such a widely framed duty. The drafting of subsection (3) is such as to leave the matter open to doubt and the Explanatory Notes to the Act state that it is intended to leave the law to develop in this area.[130] There is also a practical difficulty that arises, namely that of identifying when a company's finances are such as to render it of 'doubtful solvency'.

Subsection (3) also makes express reference to 'any enactment'. In this respect, it should be noted that       **10.172.08**
section 214 of the Insolvency Act 1986 provides that a liquidator of a company in insolvent liquidation can apply to the court to have a person who is or has been a director of the company declared personally liable to make such contribution to the company's assets as the court thinks proper for the benefit of the unsecured creditors. The liquidator must prove that the director in question allowed the company to continue to trade, at some time before the commencement of its winding up, when he knew or ought to have concluded that there was no reasonable prospect that the company would avoid going into insolvent liquidation.[131]

---

[123]  [1988] BCLC 250.
[124]  (1986) 10 ACLR 395. See also *Walker v Wimborne* (1976) 50 ALJR 446.
[125]  (1986) 10 ACLR 395, 401.
[126]  See also *Winkworth v Edward Baron Development Co Ltd* [1987] BCLC 193, in which Lord Templeman stated that directors owe a duty to the company and to its creditors to ensure that its affairs are properly administered and that its property is not dissipated. See further, *Yukong Line Ltd of Korea v Rendsburg Investment Corpn of Liberia (No 2)* [1998] 2 BCLC 385; *Re Pantone 485 Ltd* [2002] 1 BCLC 266; and *Whalley (Liquidator of MDA Investment Management Ltd) v Doney* [2004] 1 BCLC 217.
[127]  [2003] 2 BCLC 153.
[128]  Ibid [87]. Recently, in *Roberts v Frohlich* [2011] EWHC 257 (Ch), Norris J, citing this passage, held that if there is no reasonable prospect of the company avoiding an insolvent liquidation, the directors have a duty to minimize potential loss to the company's creditors.
[129]  [1985] 1 NZLR 242, 249.
[130]  Paragraph 332.
[131]  Section 214(2)(b) of the Insolvency Act 1986. See eg *Rubin v Gunner* [2004] EWHC 316. In *Re Continental Assurance Co of London plc* [2001] BPIR 733, Park J stressed that '[t]he continued trading—albeit wrongful—has to make the company's position worse, so that it has less money available to pay creditors, rather than leave the company's position at the same level'. See further, *Re DKG Contractors Ltd* [1990] BCC 903. On the drafting of subs (3) and its interrelationship with subs (1), Lord Mance, dissenting, in *Stone & Rolls Ltd v Moore Stephens* [2009] UKHL 39, [224], commented that: 'Section 172(1) of the Companies Act 2006 now states the duty, in terms expressly based on common law rules and equitable principles (see s 170(3)), as being to "act in the way he considers, in good faith, would be most likely to promote the success of the company for the benefit of its members as a whole"—a duty made expressly "subject to any enactment or rule of law requiring directors, in certain circumstances, to consider or act in the interests of creditors of the company" (see s 172(3))'.

### 173 Duty to exercise independent judgment

**10.173.01**
(1) A director of a company must exercise independent judgment.
(2) This duty is not infringed by his acting—
  (a) in accordance with an agreement duly entered into by the company that restricts the future exercise of discretion by its directors, or
  (b) in a way authorised by the company's constitution.

COMMENCEMENT DATE 1 October 2007[132]

**10.173.02** This section codifies the principle developed in the case law that directors must exercise their powers independently and not subordinate their powers to the control of others by, for example, contracting with a third party as to how a particular discretion conferred by the articles will be exercised.[133] The duty has come to the fore in relation to nominee directors: they cannot be the puppets of those who appoint them.[134] More generally, directors are not permitted to delegate their powers unless the company's constitution provides otherwise.[135] Where delegation is permitted, a director must exercise reasonable care and skill in deciding to whom to delegate particular functions. In *Re Westmid Packing Services Ltd*,[136] Lord Woolf explained that:

> A proper degree of delegation and division of responsibility is of course permissible, and often necessary, but total abrogation of responsibility is not. A board of directors must not permit one individual to dominate them and use them. ...[137]

**10.173.03** It is also noteworthy that it has been suggested that section 173 casts doubt on the extent to which directors can rely on other directors (for example, a managing director or a director with specialist expertise in relation to a matter requiring a decision of the board) or external advisers.[138] The law in this area is developing and it is unclear what the effect of this provision will be.[139] However, Lord Goldsmith, in the Lords Grand Committee, did explain that:

> The duty does not prevent a director from relying on the advice or work of others, but the final judgment must be his responsibility. He clearly cannot be expected to do everything himself. Indeed, in certain circumstances directors may be in breach of their duty if they fail to take appropriate advice—for example, legal advice. As with all advice, slavish reliance is not acceptable, and the obtaining of outside advice does not absolve directors from exercising their judgment on the basis of such advice.[140]

**10.173.04** Importantly, subsection (2)(a) reflects the position, developed in the case law, whereby the company may contract in such a way so as to fetter the future exercise of discretion by directors. Further, the company's constitution may also authorize such discretion to be fettered. Thus, where the board is able to establish, in accordance with section 172, that it was in the best interests of the company to enter into such an agreement with a third party, the duty will not be broken. For example, the directors may be able to point to some commercial benefit accruing to the company as a result of such an undertaking. In *Fulham Football Club Ltd v Cabra Estates plc*,[141] the Court of Appeal stated that:

> It is trite law that directors are under a duty to act *bona fide* in the interests of their company. However, it does not follow from that proposition that directors can never make a contract by which they bind

---

[132] Companies Act 2006 (Commencement No 3, etc) Order 2007, SI 2007/2194, art 2.

[133] *Kregor v Hollins* (1913) 109 LT 225. See also *Horn v Henry Faulder & Co Ltd* (1908) 99 LT 524. See further, *Clark v Workman* [1920] 1 IR 107, in which it was held improper for directors to undertake to a third party that they would 'look after' his interests. On the position of a nominee director, see *Scottish Co-operative Wholesale Society Ltd v Meyer* [1959] AC 324.

[134] *Scottish Co-operative Wholesale Society Ltd v Meyer* [1959] AC 324. See also *Re Neath Rugby Club Ltd* [2008] BCLC 527, at [26]–[27], HHJ Havelock-Allan QC (reversed in part by the Court of Appeal at [2008] BCC 125; the judge's reasoning set out in [26]–[27] was not in issue on appeal). See further para 10.173.06, below.

[135] Table A, art 72 (Companies (Tables A to F) Regulations 1985 (SI 1985/805) provides for the delegation of functions by directors. See also, the Companies (Model Articles) Regulations 2008 (SI 2008/3229) for private companies limited by shares (Sch 1) and public companies (Sch 3), arts 5, respectively.

[136] [1998] 2 BCLC 646, CA.

[137] Ibid, 653. See also, *Re Barings plc (No 5) Secretary of State for Trade and Industry v Baker (No 5)* [2000] 1 BCLC 523, CA, at 536.

[138] See the Law Society's 'Proposed Amendments and Briefing for Parts 10 & 11' (issued 23 January 2006) 11.

[139] See further, *Re Brian D Pierson (Contractors) Ltd* [2001] 1 BCLC 275, discussed at para 10.174.03 below.

[140] Lords Grand Committee, 6 February 2006 (col 282).

[141] [1992] BCC 863.

themselves to the future exercise of their powers in a particular manner, even though the contract taken as a whole is manifestly for the benefit of the company. Such a rule could well prevent companies from entering into contracts which were commercially beneficial to them.[142]

In this case the court drew a distinction between directors fettering their discretion, which is a clear breach of duty, and directors exercising their discretion in a manner which restricts their future conduct; which will not constitute a breach of duty. Difficult problems may arise, however, if the directors commit to a course of action which requires further exercise of discretion thereafter in order to implement the commitment. In particular, the problem typically arises in the context of takeover bids where the directors, in order to ensure what they consider a beneficial offer is put to shareholders, commit to recommend resolutions to approve it, but then subsequently a better offer is made by another suitor. There is, then, a conflict between the directors' past commitment and their continuing obligations. It has become a standard to include in such a context what is sometimes called a 'fiduciary out' which enables directors to comply with the fiduciary duties even if in consequence they feel obliged to recommend against the bid which they had previously committed to recommend. But a number of difficult points remain: it is not clear whether in making recommendations to their shareholders directors are acting in the discharge of fiduciary duty.[143] **10.173.05**

During the passage of the Bill through Parliament, the Solicitor General sought to explain the scope of subsection (2)(b): **10.173.06**

> Subsection (2)(b) will allow the status of the nominee director to be enshrined in the company's constitution so that the nominee is able to follow the instructions of the person who appointed him without breaching that duty. The extent to which that is possible under the existing law was unclear, but we have now made it clear. However, even where a nominee follows instructions, he must still comply with all his other duties—there may well be other duties—such as a duty to act broadly in the interests of the company.

The intent, therefore, is that the constitution can alleviate the duty laid down in subsection (1) for nominee directors, though they will continue to be subject to the other duties.

### 174 Duty to exercise reasonable care, skill and diligence

(1) A director of a company must exercise reasonable care, skill and diligence. **10.174.01**
(2) This means the care, skill and diligence that would be exercised by a reasonably diligent person with—
    (a) the general knowledge, skill and experience that may reasonably be expected of a person carrying out the functions carried out by the director in relation to the company, and
    (b) the general knowledge, skill and experience that the director has.

COMMENCEMENT DATE 1 October 2007[144]

This section places on a statutory footing the director's duty at common law to exercise reasonable care, skill, and diligence. The duty is not fiduciary in nature and is not enforceable as such.[145] It gives statutory effect to the modern judicial stance taken towards the determination of the standard of care expected of directors. In *Norman v Theodore Goddard*,[146] Hoffmann J, implicitly rejecting the subjective approach taken towards the assessment of directors conduct in the old case law,[147] accepted counsel's submission that the appropriate test was accurately laid down in section 214(4) of the Insolvency Act 1986. This defines negligent conduct for the purposes of holding directors liable for 'wrongful trading' in terms of: **10.174.02**

> the facts which a director of a company ought to know or ascertain, the conclusions which he ought to reach and the steps which he ought to take are those which would be known or ascertained, or reached or taken, by a reasonably diligent person having both (a) the general knowledge, skill and

---

[142] [1992] BCC 863, 875. Neil LJ endorsed the view of Kitto J in the Australian case *Thorby v Goldberg* (1964) 112 CLR 597, 605–606, who had stated that: 'There are many kinds of transaction in which the proper time for the exercise of the directors' discretion is the time of the negotiation of a contract and not the time at which the contract is to be performed … If at the former time they are *bona fide* of opinion that it is in the interests of the company that the transaction should be entered into and carried into effect I see no reason in law why they should not bind themselves to do whatever under the transaction is to be done by the board'.

[143] See further, *Rackam v Peek Foods Ltd* [1990] BCLC 895; *John Crowther Group Ltd v Carpets International plc* [1990] BCLC 460; and *Dawson International plc v Coats Paton plc* [1989] BCLC 233.

[144] Companies Act 2006 (Commencement No 3, etc) Order 2007, SI 2007/2194, art 2.

[145] See s 178(2), below.

[146] [1991] BCLC 1028.

[147] See eg *Re Cardiff Savings Bank: The Marquis of Bute's case* [1892] 2 Ch 100.

experience that may reasonably be expected of a person carrying out the same functions as are carried out by that director in relation to the company, and (b) the general knowledge, skill and experience that that director has.[148]

Section 174 is modelled on the wrongful trading provision and thus requires both an objective and subjective determination of the conduct in question.[149]

**10.174.03**   The issue of negligence in the context of company directors has come to the fore in relation to the delegation of powers.[150] The modern view is that inactivity on the part of directors is no longer acceptable so that short shrift is given to any contention to the effect that the director was unaware of a state of affairs because he had trusted others to manage the company.[151] In *Re Brian D Pierson (Contractors) Ltd*,[152] the court refused to countenance symbolic roles for directors. Hazel Williamson, QC, observed that:

> The office of director has certain minimum responsibilities and functions, which are not simply discharged by leaving all management functions, and consideration of the company's affairs to another director without question, even in the case of a family company ... One cannot be a 'sleeping' director; the function of 'directing' on its own requires some consideration of the company's affairs to be exercised.[153]

The introduction of a minimum age for directors by section 157 of the Act appears to reflect the same thinking.

**10.174.04**   Overall, there is a paucity of case law in which directors have been challenged for negligent mismanagement. This no doubt reflects the fact that at common law such an allegation could not form the basis of a derivative action (though negligence now falls within the scope of the derivative claim placed on a statutory footing by Part 11 of the 2006 Act—see Chapter 11 below). In addition, petitions brought under section 994 (the unfair prejudice remedy—see Chapter 30 below) routinely allege mismanagement. There is, however, a significant body of case law on negligent mismanagement by virtue of actions brought by the Secretary of State under the Company Directors Disqualification Act 1986, seeking disqualification on the ground of unfitness.[154] For example, in *Re Barings plc (No 5)*,[155] proceedings were brought seeking the disqualification of directors of the Barings Bank following the spectacular losses resulting from the unauthorized dealings of a trader, Nick Leeson, who was based in the bank's Singapore office. One of the issues in the case was what level of supervision should be expected of Mr Tuckey (T), the deputy chairman of the Barings Group, chairman of Barings Investment Bank, and chairman of the Barings Investment Bank Managing Committee. T had argued that in view of the size of the bank's operations his role was essentially reactive and that he was justified in trusting delegatees until matters came to his attention which required his response. However, it was held that in determining the period for disqualification, the guiding principle is that directors, collectively and individually, had a duty to acquire and maintain a sufficient knowledge of the company's business so as to enable them to discharge their responsibilities. The power to delegate did not absolve directors from the duty to supervise the way in which delegated functions are carried out. For the duty to be discharged it would appear that proactive monitoring of the operations of delegatees must be demonstrated. The courts will not countenance the argument that the director lacked sufficient time to undertake this task.[156] *Secretary of State for Trade and Industry v Thornbury*[157] concerned the non-payment of Crown debts. While it was accepted that the director in question, T, was unaware of the problems over the debts insofar as he did not have actual knowledge, the court accepted the Secretary of State's alternative argument that T ought to have known. He took no steps beyond speaking to his colleagues of ascertaining what the true financial position of the company was. He did not check to see whether the Crown debts, or even any debts, were being paid. His questions were of a

---

[148]  See also *Re D'Jan of London Ltd* [1993] BCC 646, in which Hoffmann LJ again adopted the same approach. See further, *Dorchester Finance Co Ltd v Stebbing* [1989] BCLC 498.

[149]  See s 214(4) of the Insolvency Act 1986.

[150]  Generally in proceedings brought by the Secretary of State under the Company Directors Disqualification Act 1986.

[151]  See eg *Re Landhurst Leasing plc* [1999] 1 BCLC 286.

[152]  [2001] 1 BCLC 275.

[153]  [2001] 1 BCLC 275, 278. See also *Re Westmid Packing Services Ltd, Secretary of State for Trade and Industry v Griffiths* [1998] 2 BCLC 646.

[154]  See s 6 of the 1986 Act.

[155]  [1999] 1 BCLC 433.

[156]  See, further, *Re Peppermint Park Ltd* [1998] BCC 23; *Re Park House Properties Ltd* [1997] 2 BCLC 530; *Re Landhurst Leasing plc* [1999] 1 BCLC 286; *Equitable Life Assurance Society v Ernst & Young* [2003] EWHC 112 (Ch); and *Lexi Holdings plc (in administration) v Luqman* [2009] 2 BCLC 1.

[157]  [2007] EWHC 3202 (Ch).

general nature merely seeking the verbal assurances of his fellow directors. While directors are entitled to rely on their colleagues, that did not mean they could abdicate all responsibility. T was guilty of a culpable failure to make enquiries, he allowed the company to trade to the detriment of the Crown, and was, therefore, unfit within the scope of section 6.

## 175  Duty to avoid conflicts of interest[158]

(1) A director of a company must avoid a situation in which he has, or can have, a direct or indirect interest that conflicts, or possibly may conflict, with the interests of the company.

(2) This applies in particular to the exploitation of any property, information or opportunity (and it is immaterial whether the company could take advantage of the property, information or opportunity).

(3) This duty does not apply to a conflict of interest arising in relation to a transaction or arrangement with the company.

(4) This duty is not infringed—
   (a) if the situation cannot reasonably be regarded as likely to give rise to a conflict of interest; or
   (b) if the matter has been authorised by the directors.

(5) Authorisation may be given by the directors—
   (a) where the company is a private company and nothing in the company's constitution invalidates such authorisation, by the matter being proposed to and authorised by the directors; or
   (b) where the company is a public company and its constitution includes provision enabling the directors to authorise the matter, by the matter being proposed to and authorised by them in accordance with the constitution.

(6) The authorisation is effective only if—
   (a) any requirement as to the quorum at the meeting at which the matter is considered is met without counting the director in question or any other interested director, and
   (b) the matter was agreed to without their voting or would have been agreed to if their votes had not been counted.

(7) Any reference in this section to a conflict of interest includes a conflict of interest and duty and a conflict of duties.

COMMENCEMENT DATE  1 October 2008.[159]

**10.175.01**

Section 175 replaces the equitable obligation to avoid conflicts of interest whereby directors are liable to account for any profit made personally in circumstances where their interests may conflict with their duty owed to the company.[160] Liability is avoided where the company gives its consent to the breach.[161] The substance of the rule is strict. This is reflected in the language of subsection (1) in that it is framed in terms of the possibility of conflict rather than actual conflicts of interest. This encompasses the significant body of case law spanning over a century or so upon which the provision is based.[162] The duty was stated by Lord Herschell in *Bray v Ford*:[163]

**10.175.02**

---

[158]  This section applies where the situation described in subs (1) arises on or after 1 October 2008. The law that applied before that date continues to apply to such a situation that arose before that date. See the Companies Act 2006 (Commencement No 5, Transitional Provisions and Savings) Order 2007, SI 2007/3495, Sch 4, para 47.

[159]  Companies Act 2006 (Commencement No 5, etc) Order 2007, SI 2007/3495, art 4.

[160]  In *Phipps v Boardman* [1967] 2 AC 46, Lord Upjohn explained, at 123, that: '[T]he fundamental rule of equity [is] that a person in a fiduciary capacity must not make a profit out of his trust which is part of the wider rule that a trustee must not place himself in a position where his duty and his interest may conflict.' See also *Chan v Zacharia* (1984) 154 CLR 178, in which Deane J, at 199, observed that the fiduciary in breach of the no-conflict duty: 'must account … for any benefit or gain which has been obtained or received in circumstances where a conflict or significant possibility of conflict existed between his fiduciary duty and his personal interest in the pursuit or possible receipt of such a benefit or gain.'

[161]  See eg Lord Russell's speech in *Regal (Hastings) Ltd v Gulliver* [1942] 1 All ER 378; [1967] 2 AC 134n. See now, s 180 at paras 10.180.01–10.180.06 below.

[162]  The leading case on this duty is *Boardman v Phipps* [1967] 2 AC 46, HL. The policy underlying the duty is based upon prophylaxis: see eg Lord Cranworth LC's speech in *Aberdeen Rly Co v Blaikie Bros* (1854) 1 Macq 461 who stated that no fiduciary 'shall be allowed to enter into engagements in which he has or can have a personal interest conflicting or which possibly may conflict with the interests of those whom he is bound to protect.' During the Grand Committee Stage, Lord Goldsmith noted that the words 'can have' in subs (1) constitute the common law. See, Official Report, 6/2/2006; col. GC287 (Lord Goldsmith). GC100, the Association of General Counsel and Company Secretaries of the FTSE100, has published a number of guidance documents on this section including identifying situations in which s 175 is likely to be breached and guidance for company secretaries when dealing with directors' conflicts of interest.

[163]  [1896] AC 44.

> It is an inflexible rule of a court of equity that a person in a fiduciary position ... is not, unless otherwise expressly provided, ... allowed to put himself in a position where his interest and duty conflict. It does not appear to me that this rule is ... founded upon principles of morality. I regard it rather as based on the consideration that, human nature being what it is, there is a danger, in such circumstances, of the person holding a fiduciary position being swayed by interest rather than by duty, and thus prejudicing those whom he was bound to protect.[164]

**10.175.03**   In modern times breach of the no-conflict rule has frequently come before the courts where directors have diverted into their own hands a business opportunity which was going to be vested in the company, rather than pursuing it with due diligence on its behalf.[165] This is reflected in the language of subsection (2) which makes it clear by expressly providing that the no-conflict duty encapsulated in subsection (1) applies to the exploitation of any 'any property, information or opportunity' by directors and, by way of reinforcing the strictness of the duty, subsection (2) goes on to encapsulate the equitable principle that 'it is immaterial whether the company could take advantage of the property, information or opportunity'. In a line of cases the courts have held that a business or corporate opportunity is to be regarded as an asset belonging to the company.[166] For example, in *Industrial Development Consultants Ltd v Cooley*,[167] the defendant, who was managing director of Industrial Development Consultants Ltd (IDC), a design and construction company, failed to obtain for the company a lucrative contract to undertake work for the Eastern Gas Board. The Gas Board subsequently approached Cooley indicating that they wished to deal with him personally and would not, in any case, contract with IDC. Cooley did not disclose the offer to the company, but promptly resigned his office so that he could take up the contract having deceived the company into thinking he was suffering from ill health. Roskill J held that he was accountable to the company for all of the profits he received under the contract. Information which came to Cooley while he was managing director and which was of concern to the claimants and relevant for the claimants to know, was information which it was his duty to pass on to the claimants. It was irrelevant to the issue of liability that Cooley had been approached in his personal capacity and that the Gas Board would not have contracted with IDC. Roskill J concluded that it seems to me plain that it was {Cooley's} duty once he got this information to pass it to his employers and not to guard it for his own personal purposes and profit. He put himself into the position when his duty and his interests conflicted.'[168] Further, if such a breach takes the form of a fraudulent expropriation of corporate assets, it cannot be whitewashed by obtaining the sanction of the company.[169] Subsection (3) excludes from the ambit of the duty conflicts arising in relation to transactions or arrangements with the company (these must be declared under sections 177 and 182).[170]

**10.175.04**   The precise scope of the duty has been subjected to considerable judicial scrutiny in cases where the allegation is that a director, having resigned his or her post (or in preparation for such resignation), has usurped a corporate asset, such as information or business opportunity, with the intention of exploiting it personally post-resignation.[171] We have seen that resignation will not immunize a director from

---

[164]   [1896] AC 44, 51–52.

[165]   A modern statement of the duty was given by Lawrence Collins J in *CMS Dolphin Ltd v Simonet* [2001] 2 BCLC 704, [96]: 'the underlying basis of the liability of a director who exploits after his resignation a maturing business opportunity of the company is that the opportunity is to be treated as if it were property of the company in relation to which the director had fiduciary duties. By seeking to exploit the opportunity after resignation he is appropriating for himself that property. He is just as accountable as a trustee who retires without properly accounting for trust property. In the case of the director he becomes a constructive trustee of the fruits of his abuse of the company's property, which he has acquired in circumstances where he knowingly had a conflict of interest, and exploited it by resigning from the company.' See also Peter Smith J in *Crown Dilmun v Sutton* [2004] 1 BCLC 468, 179, who said: 'Given my decision that Mr Sutton [the defendant] had no right to make any decision to take opportunities which came his way whilst he was a director of the claimants, the parties all agree that he came under a duty not to take opportunities which arose that might put him in conflict with his duties to the claimants. As a director of the claimants, he had a duty to exploit every opportunity that he became aware of for the benefit of the claimants. The only exception is if they permit him to take such opportunities after he has made full and frank disclosure and they have given full and informed consent.'

[166]   See *Cook v Deeks* [1916] 1 AC 554, PC. For more recent examples, see *Don King Productions Inc v Warren* [2000] BCC 263, CA; *Gencor ACP Ltd v Dalby* [2000] 2 BCLC 734; *Bhullar v Bhullar* [2003] 2 BCLC 241, CA; *Shepherds Investments Ltd v Andrew Walters* [2006] EWHC 836 (Ch); and *O'Donnell v Shanahan* [2009] 1 BCLC 328. Cf *Foster Bryant Surveying Ltd v Bryant* [2007] EWCA Civ 200.

[167]   [1972] 1 WLR 443.

[168]   Ibid, 453.

[169]   *Cook v Deeks* [1916] 1 AC 554, PC.

[170]   See paras 10.177.01–10.177.08 and 10.182.01–10.182.08 below.

[171]   See eg *Island Export Finance Ltd v Umunna* [1986] BCLC 460; *Balston Ltd v Headline Filters Ltd* [1990] FSR 385; *Framlington Group plc v Anderson* [1995] 1 BCLC 495; and *Foster Bryant Surveying Ltd v Bryant* [2007] EWCA Civ 200.

liability for breaches of duty.[172] The principle that can be distilled from the cases is that the general fiduciary duties do not prevent a director from forming the intention, while still a director, to set up a competing business after his or her directorship has ceased. Nor do the duties prevent directors taking preliminary steps to investigate or forward that intention provided they do not engage in any actual competitive activity while the directorship in question continues, provided, of course, any contract of service does not prohibit such activity.[173] Further, a director can utilize confidential information or 'know-how' acquired while working for the company after he or she departs but not 'trade secrets'.[174] Typical examples of trade secrets include company databases, customer lists, suppliers' agreements, and business and sales strategy.[175] The pragmatic approach adopted by the judges in such circumstances is carried forward by subsection (4)(a) which provides that the duty will not be broken if the 'situation cannot reasonably be regarded as likely to give rise to a conflict of interest'.[176]

In other words, subsection (4)(a) recognizes that unexpected situations can arise where a conflict exists, and directors will not be in breach because of that without more.[177]  **10.175.05**

Section 180(4) preserves the common law position whereby the members of the company may authorize conflicts that would otherwise contravene the no-conflict duty.[178] However, a major concern expressed by the Company Law Review was that the pre-existing case law 'fetters entrepreneurial and business start-up activity by existing directors so that 'the law should only prevent the exploitation of business opportunities where there is a clear case for doing so'.[179] Subsection (5) therefore implements the Steering Group's recommendation that prior authorization by independent directors will excuse a potential breach of the duty. The provision distinguishes between private and public companies. In the case of a private company such authorization may be given unless the company's constitution otherwise provides;[180] while in the case of a public company the directors will only be able to authorize such conflicts if its constitution so permits (subsection (5)(b)). It should be noted that subsection (5)(b) relates to subsection (4)(b) but not to subsection (4)(a).[181] Further, subsection (6) provides that board authorization is effective only if the conflicted directors have not participated in the taking of the decision or if the decision would have been valid even without the participation of the conflicted directors; the votes of the conflicted directors in favour of the decision will be ignored and the conflicted directors are not counted in the quorum.  **10.175.06**

Finally, subsection (7) makes it clear that any reference in this section to a conflict of interest includes also a conflict of interest and duty and a conflict of duties. This gives legislative effect to the equitable principle forbidding a fiduciary from placing himself in a position of conflict to another person unless both principals have given informed consent.[182] It settles the vexed issue of whether a director can hold  **10.175.07**

---

[172]  See s 170(2) at para 10.170.05 above.

[173]  *Coleman Taymar Ltd v Oakes* [2001] 2 BCLC 749; and *LC Services Ltd v Brown* [2003] EWHC 3024. In *Island Export Finance Ltd v Umunna* [1986] BCLC 460, 469, Hutchinson J said: 'It would … be surprising to find that directors alone, because of the fiduciary nature of their relationship with the company, were restrained from exploiting after they had ceased to be such any opportunity of which they had acquired knowledge while directors. Directors, no less than employees, acquire a general fund of knowledge and expertise in the course of their work, and it is plainly in the public interest that they should be free to exploit it in a new position.'

[174]  *Dranez Anstalt v Hayek* [2002] 1 BCLC 693, *per* Evans-Lombe J; *FSS Travel and Leisure Systems Ltd v Johnson* [1998] IRLR 382, *per* Mummery LJ.

[175]  See eg *Item Software (UK) Ltd v Fassihi* [2003] IRLR 769; and *Quarter Master UK Ltd v Pyke* [2005] 1 BCLC 245.

[176]  See eg Rix LJ's judgment in *Foster Bryant Surveying Ltd v Bryant* [2007] EWCA Civ 200.

[177]  See Official Report, 6/2/2006; col GC289 (Lord Goldsmith): 'Once you know that you are now in a situation of conflict, you will have to do something about it, but you are not in breach simply because it happened when, as is set out in subsection (4)(a), it could not, "reasonably be regarded as likely to give rise to" the conflict.'

[178]  See para 10.180.05 below.

[179]  *Completing the Structure*, para 3.26. The 2005 White Paper at ⟨http://www.dti.gov.uk/bbf/co-act-2006/white-paper.html⟩ at para 3.26, echoes this concern by stating that it is important that the duties do not impose impractical and onerous requirements which stifle entrepreneurial activity.

[180]  Chapter 3 of Pt 3 of the Companies Act 2006 (resolutions and agreements affecting a company's constitution) applies to any such resolution. For the purposes of 'section 30 of that Act (copies of resolutions to be forwarded to registrar) such a resolution passed before 1st October 2008 is treated as if passed on that date'. See the Companies Act 2006 (Commencement No 5, Transitional Provisions and Savings) Order 2007, SI 2007/3495, Sch 4, para 47.

[181]  Official Report, 6/2/2006; col GC289 (Lord Goldsmith).

[182]  See *Clark Boyce v Mouat* [1994] 1 AC 428. In *Bristol and West BS v Mothew* [1998] Ch 1, CA, Millett LJ explained, at 18, that: 'A fiduciary who acts for two principals with potentially conflicting interests without the informed consent of both is in breach of the obligation of undivided loyalty; he puts himself in a position where his duty to one principal may conflict with his duty to the other … This is sometimes described as "the double employment rule." Breach of the rule automatically constitutes a breach of fiduciary duty.'

a directorship with a competing company.[183] It is now clear that this situation falls within the general duty to avoid conflicts of interest contained in section 175.

**10.175.08** It is noteworthy that section 175 and section 176 (duty not to accept benefits from third parties, see below) describe the no-conflict rule and the related duty not to accept benefits from third parties, as 'duties'. This terminology addresses the issue arising in *Movitex v Bulfield*,[184] in which Vinelott J sought to reconcile section 310 of the Companies Act 1985, which prohibited a company including in its articles or in any contract with a director any provision which exempts him from liability in respect of a breach of duty, with Article 85 of Table A, which, subject to disclosure being made to the board, permitted a director to be a party to a conflict transaction. The judge reasoned, applying *dicta* in *Tito v Waddell*,[185] that the no-conflict rule was not a duty as such, but rather it should be viewed as a disability. On this basis, it did not fall within the language of section 310 of the 1985 Act and it was, therefore, open to the company to exclude the 'disability' in its articles. In line with the recommendations of the Company Law Review Steering Group to clarify the law, the extent to which the duties laid down by sections 175 to 176 can be modified are now set out in the Act itself (see subsections (5) and (6) above, and section 180 below).

### 176 Duty not to accept benefits from third parties

**10.176.01**
(1) A director of a company must not accept a benefit from a third party conferred by reason of—
    (a) his being a director, or
    (b) his doing (or not doing) anything as director.
(2) A 'third party' means a person other than the company, an associated body corporate or a person acting on behalf of the company or an associated body corporate.
(3) Benefits received by a director from a person by whom his services (as a director or otherwise) are provided to the company are not regarded as conferred by a third party.
(4) This duty is not infringed if the acceptance of the benefit cannot reasonably be regarded as likely to give rise to a conflict of interest.
(5) Any reference in this section to a conflict of interest includes a conflict of interest and duty and a conflict of duties.

COMMENCEMENT DATE 1 October 2008.[186]

**10.176.02** This section codifies the equitable rule prohibiting the exploitation of the position of director for personal benefit. There has been some debate over whether the no-conflict duty (see section 175 above) and the no-profit rule encompassed in this section are distinct. In *Boardman v Phipps*,[187] Lord Upjohn described the no-profit rule as being but a part of the wider no-conflict duty; and in *Bray v Ford*,[188] Lord Herschell took the view that there was only one rule.[189] However, in *Chan v Zacharia*,[190] Deane J thought that the two rules, while overlapping, are distinct. Accordingly, a transaction may be struck down on the basis that it involved a conflicted director irrespective of whether or not he profited from it.[191] The drafting of these two provisions mirrors this latter line of reasoning by splitting the duty into two separate parts. The classic judicial formulation of the duty now encompassed in this section was delivered by Lord Russell of Killowen in *Regal (Hastings) Ltd v Gulliver*:[192]

> The rule of equity which insists on those, who by use of a fiduciary position make a profit, being liable to account for that profit, in no way depends on fraud, or absence of *bona fides*; or upon such questions or considerations as whether profit would or should otherwise have gone to the plaintiff, or whether the profiteer was under a duty to obtain the source of the profit for the plaintiff, or whether

---

[183] See eg *London and Mashonaland Exploration Co Ltd v New Mashonaland Exploration Co Ltd* [1891] WN 165 and *Bell v Lever Bros Ltd* [1932] AC 161 which suggests that a director is free to direct a competing company unless prohibited by contract. Thus, in *In Plus Group Ltd v Pyke* [2002] 2 BCLC 201, the Court of Appeal held that there was no completely rigid rule that a director could not be involved in the business of another company which was in competition with a company of which he was a director, and they stressed that every situation was 'fact-specific'. Following the reasoning of Millett LJ in the *Mothew* decision, ibid, the general rule appears to be that directors are barred from acting for two companies with competing interests unless the informed consent of both companies, or the authorization of the directors as required by subsections (4)–(6), is obtained. See further the comments of Lord Goldsmith, Lords Grand Committee, 6 February 2006 (col 288).
[184] [1988] BCLC 104.
[185] [1977] 3 All ER 129, 247 (Megarry V-C).
[186] Companies Act 2006 (Commencement No 5, etc) Order 2007, SI 2007/3495, art 4.
[187] [1967] 2 AC 46.
[188] [1896] AC 44.
[189] This was also the view of Lord Cranworth LC in *Broughton v Broughton* (1855) 5 De G M and G 160.
[190] (1984) 154 CLR 178.
[191] *Movitex v Bulfield* [1988] BCLC 104.
[192] [1967] 2 AC 134n.

he took a risk or acted as he did for the benefit of the plaintiff, or whether the plaintiff has in fact been damaged or benefited by his action. The liability arises from the mere fact of a profit having, in the stated circumstances, been made.[193]

Subsection (1) thus prohibits a director accepting a personal benefit, including a bribe, from a third party which is conferred on him or her *qua* director. It applies only to benefits conferred because the director is a director of the company or because of something that the director does or does not do as director. The word 'benefit', for the purpose of this section, includes benefits of any description, including non-financial benefits.[194] As such this section overlaps with section 175 (duty to avoid conflicts of interest)[195] and, therefore, a breach will trigger both provisions. While section 175(5) provides for board authorization in respect of conflicts of interest, this is not the case with this particular duty. However, the company may authorize the acceptance of benefits by virtue of section 180(4).[196] Subsection (2) defines a 'third party' as a person other than the company or its holding company or its subsidiaries and thus subsection (3) provides that benefits provided by the company fall outside the prohibition. Subsection (4) adds the proviso that the duty is not infringed if the acceptance of a benefit from a third party cannot reasonably be regarded as likely to give rise to a conflict of interest.

Finally, subsection (5) makes it clear that any reference in this section to a conflict of interest includes also a conflict of interest and duty and a conflict of duties.     **10.176.03**

## 177 Duty to declare interest in proposed transaction or arrangement

(1) If a director of a company is in any way, directly or indirectly, interested in a proposed transaction     **10.177.01**
or arrangement with the company, he must declare the nature and extent of that interest to the other directors.
(2) The declaration may (but need not) be made—
  (a) at a meeting of the directors, or
  (b) by notice to the directors in accordance with—
    (i) section 184 (notice in writing),[a] or
    (ii) section 185 (general notice).[b]
(3) If a declaration of interest under this section proves to be, or becomes, inaccurate or incomplete, a further declaration must be made.
(4) Any declaration required by this section must be made before the company enters into the transaction or arrangement.
(5) This section does not require a declaration of an interest of which the director is not aware or where the director is not aware of the transaction or arrangement in question.
  For this purpose a director is treated as being aware of matters of which he ought reasonably to be aware.
(6) A director need not declare an interest—
  (a) if it cannot reasonably be regarded as likely to give rise to a conflict of interest;
  (b) if, or to the extent that, the other directors are already aware of it (and for this purpose the other directors are treated as aware of anything of which they ought reasonably to be aware); or
  (c) if, or to the extent that, it concerns terms of his service contract that have been or are to be considered—
    (i) by a meeting of the directors, or
    (ii) by a committee of the directors appointed for the purpose under the company's constitution.

AMENDMENTS AND NOTES

[a] See paras 10.184.01–10.184.04 below.

[b] See paras 10.185.01–10.185.04 below.

COMMENCEMENT DATE 1 October 2008[197]

This section replaces section 317(1) of the Companies Act 1985 which relaxed the equitable rule that     **10.177.02**
forbids directors having an interest in a transaction with the company where such interest has been

[193] [1967] 2 AC 134, 144. Lord Porter said (at 159), 'Directors, no doubt, are not trustees, but they occupy a fiduciary position towards the company whose board they form. Their liability in this respect does not depend upon breach of duty but upon the proposition that a director must not make a profit out of property acquired by reason of his relationship to the company of which he is director.'
[194] Official Report, 9/2/2006; col GC330 (Lord Goldsmith).
[195] See paras 10.175.01–10.175.08 above.
[196] See para 10.180.05 below.
[197] Companies Act 2006 (Commencement No 5 etc) Order 2007, SI 2007/3495, art 4.

authorized by the board.[198] Instead, subsection (1) now requires directors to disclose any interest, whether direct or indirect, in a *proposed* transaction or arrangement with the company, to the other directors.[199] Such disclosure must be made, according to subsection (4), *before* the company enters into the transaction. The provision does not lay down how such disclosure is to be made, although subsection (2) permits it to be done by written notice (see section 185 below), general notice (see section 185 below), or by making such disclosure at a meeting of directors. It is noteworthy that this section is deliberately intended to apply only to proposed transactions. Different consequences flow from not disclosing an interest in a proposed transaction and failing to disclose an interest in an existing transaction (see section 182 below).[200]

**10.177.03**   As noted above, this section replaces section 317(1) of the Companies Act 1985. Section 317 required a director, including a shadow director, who was in any way interested in a proposed (or subsisting) contract with the company to declare the nature of such interest to a meeting of the directors of the company. It is noteworthy that it has been held that breach of the statutory disclosure duty (under section 317 of the Companies Act 1985) may also trigger other liability. For example, in *JJ Harrison (Properties) Ltd v Harrison*,[201] the trial judge stressed that the defendant director's breach of the duty of disclosure also placed him in breach of the equitable obligation to act *bona fide* in the interests of the company which, as seen above,[202] is now encompassed in section 172. As explained by Lightman J in *Neptune (Vehicle Washing Equipment) Ltd v Fitzgerald*,[203] the policy underlying the disclosure duty is designed to secure three objectives:

> First, all the directors should know or be reminded of the interest; second, the making of the declaration should be the occasion for a statutory pause for thought about the existence of the conflict of interest and of the duty to prefer the interests of the company to their own; third, the disclosure … must be a distinct happening at the meeting…'[204]

**10.177.04**   Section 317 of the Companies Act 1985 was criticized as being too narrow because the extent of the directors' interest did not have to be disclosed, and too broad because all interests, however trivial, had to be disclosed.[205] The CLR, in line with the Law Commissions, therefore recommended that the extent of interests be disclosed as well, albeit only material interests. Subsection (1), in laying down the standard of disclosure, states that the declaration must give the 'nature and extent' of the interest to the other directors.[206] In discharging this duty it is, therefore, not enough for a director to merely state that he has an interest.[207] Further, under subsection (3), if having made a declaration of interest, the director becomes aware that the circumstances have changed, or for some other reason the earlier disclosure is no longer accurate or complete, he must make a further declaration.

**10.177.05**   While no *de minimis* financial threshold is laid down in this section, subsection (6)(a) does state that the interest in question must be such that it can reasonably be regarded as likely to give rise to a conflict of interest. In this respect, it should be noted that subsection (5) makes it clear that a declaration of an interest is not required of which the director is not aware, or where the director is not aware of the

---

[198] The articles of association generally permitted directors to be interested in transactions or arrangements with the company provided they disclosed the nature and extent of any such interest to the board; see, for example, Table A, reg 85, the Companies (Tables A to F) Regulations 1985. See *Guinness v Saunders* [1990] 2 AC 663, HL.

[199] As the Explanatory Notes to the Act (para 348) state, the members of the company may still impose requirements for shareholder approval in the articles of association.

[200] As Lord Goldsmith noted during the Grand Committee Stage, there 'is a difference in fact, in principle and in business sense because, if a company is told that a director has an interest in a proposed transaction, it can decide whether to enter into the transaction, on what terms and with what safeguards, whereas, if the transaction has already taken place, we are in a very different position'. See Official Report, 9/2/2006; col GC334.

[201] [2001] 1 BCLC 158. See also, *Neptune (Vehicle Washing Equipment) Ltd v Fitzgerald (No 2)* [1995] BCC 1000.

[202] See paras 10.172.01–10.172.08 above.

[203] [1995] 1 BCLC 352.

[204] [1995] 1 BCLC 352, 359.

[205] See the 7th edition of PL Davies, *Gower and Davies' Principles of Modern Company Law* (Sweet & Maxwell, London, 2003), 399.

[206] Table A, reg 85 laid down a materiality test. In essence, it stated that provided the director has disclosed to the board 'the nature and extent of any *material* interest of his', then the director may be a party to a conflict transaction with the company.

[207] In *New Zealand Netherlands Society Oranje Inc v Kuys* [1973] 1 WLR 1126, 1131, PC, Lord Wilberforce stated that: 'as a matter of law, … if an arrangement is to stand, whereby a particular transaction, which would otherwise come within a person's fiduciary duty, is to be exempted from it, there must be full and frank disclosure of all material facts'. In *Gwembe Valley Development Co Ltd v Koshy* [1998] 2 BCLC 613, it was held that the board must be given full and precise information.

transaction or arrangement in question. For this purpose a director is treated as being aware 'of matters of which he ought reasonably to be aware' (subsection (5)). It appears that the test to be applied to determine when a director is treated 'as being aware of matters of which he ought reasonably to be aware' is objective, that is, it must be judged objectively whether this is a matter of which the director ought to be reasonably aware.[208] This is not necessarily the same test as one would apply in deciding whether someone ought to be aware of his own interests in other transactions.[209] It appears that the word 'aware' means, or includes, that 'you ought to have been aware based on the following facts and matters'.[210] It should also be noted that there is some reciprocity here. There is similar wording in subsection (6)(b), where the state of knowledge or the awareness available to the other directors is tested in exactly the same way. It thus appears that it would not be appropriate to view subsection (5) in the abstract, but rather it should be looked at in conjunction with subsection (6).[211]

The Explanatory Notes to the Act state that a director need not be a party to the transaction for the disclosure duty to apply.[212] In this respect, the term 'directly or indirectly' used in subsection (1) is carried over from section 317(1) of the Companies Act 1985. It covers the interests of persons *connected* with the director. Although the language lacks precision, it seems directed towards ensuring that the interests of connected persons in contracts with the company may be such as to render a director 'indirectly' interested.[213]     **10.177.06**

Subsection (6)(b) and (c) is aimed at settling issues which generated some controversy in the pre-existing case law.[214] It should be noted that the statutory duty is to declare an interest to the other directors and no such disclosure is required where the company has only one director.[215] Thus, paragraph (b) makes it clear that there is no need to disclose matters that the other directors already know or ought reasonably to have known. Subsection (6)(c) relaxes the requirement of disclosure in relation to a director's interest in his service contract where it has been considered by a meeting of the directors or a committee appointed for such purpose, such as a remuneration committee.[216]     **10.177.07**

Conflicted directors are not precluded from participating in the decision-taking process relating to such transactions or arrangements with the company, unless the articles of association provide otherwise. Subject to some exceptions, under the model articles of association for both private companies limited by shares and for public companies, the directors must disregard the views of the interested director when taking a majority decision in relation to such transactions with the company.[217]     **10.177.08**

## Supplementary provisions

### 178  Civil consequences of breach of general duties

(1)  The consequences of breach (or threatened breach) of sections 171 to 177 are the same as would apply if the corresponding common law rule or equitable principle applied.     **10.178.01**

---

[208]  See Official Report, 9/2/2006; col GC334 (Lord Goldsmith).

[209]  Ibid.

[210]  Ibid (Lord Grabiner).

[211]  Ibid, cols GC334–GC335 (Lord Grabiner).

[212]  Paragraph 347.

[213]  A useful recent authority on the duty to disclose potential conflicts of interest is *Newgate Stud Co v Penfold* [2004] EWHC 2993 (Ch), [2008] 1 BCLC 46 where David Richards J undertook a thorough review of the minutiae of this disclosure obligation and in particular of the associated questions of dealings with spouses, other relatives and appropriate limitation periods.

[214]  In *Lee Panavision Ltd v Lee Lighting Ltd* [1992] BCLC 22, Dillon LJ took the view that a 'technical' failure to disclose an interest which was well known to all the directors should not invalidate the contract in question. This was followed in *Runciman v Walter Runciman plc* [1992] BCLC 1084 and *MacPherson v European Strategic Bureau Ltd* [1999] 2 BCLC 203, in which Ferris J concluded that '[n]o amount of formal disclosure by each other to the other would have increased the other's relevant knowledge'. On the other hand, in *Neptune (Vehicle Washing Equipment) Ltd v Fitzgerald* [1996] Ch 274, Lightman J held that strict compliance with the statutory disclosure requirement was necessary even in the case of companies with a sole director. Such a director should make the declaration to himself and record the declaration in the minutes.

[215]  Thus overruling Lightman J's conclusion on the issue in *Neptune (Vehicle Washing Equipment) Ltd v Fitzgerald*, [1996] Ch 274.

[216]  It is noteworthy that under CA 1985, s 317, the Court of Appeal held in *Guinness plc v Saunders* [1988] 2 All ER 940, that the duty of disclosure required disclosure to a duly convened and constituted board meeting, a function which could not be delegated to a sub-committee of the board. Fox LJ said that even if all the members of the board had known of a contract this would not validate payments made thereunder.

[217]  Companies (Model Articles) Regulations 2008, SI 2008/3229, art 14 in both sets of model articles.

(2)  The duties in those sections (with the exception of section 174 (duty to exercise reasonable care, skill and diligence)) are, accordingly, enforceable in the same way as any other fiduciary duty owed to a company by its directors.

COMMENCEMENT DATE 1 October 2007[218]

**10.178.02**  This section preserves the previous civil consequences of breach (or threatened breach)[219] of any of the general duties. Although an attempt was made to codify the remedies available for breach of directors' duties,[220] this proved to be a very difficult exercise and eventually it became 'too difficult to pursue'.[221]

**10.178.03**  Subsection (1) makes it clear that the remedies for breach of the general duties will be exactly the same as those that were available following a breach of the equitable principles and common law rules that the general duties replace. It remains to be seen how these remedies will interact with the general duties under the code, which introduce some new concepts and terminology.[222] In general, the remedies available to the company for breach of fiduciary duty are:[223] (i) damages or compensation where the company has suffered loss; (ii) restoration of the company's property;[224] (iii) an account of profits made by the director;[225] (iv) injunction or declaration;[226] and (v) rescission of a contract where the director failed to disclose an interest.[227] The consequences of a breach of the duty of care and skill may include the court awarding compensation or damages.[228] Although section 178 offers little guidance on the remedial consequences of a director's breach of fiduciary duty, the Court of Appeal in *Sinclair Investments (UK) Ltd v Versailles Trading Finance Ltd*[229] recently took the opportunity to consider in detail what relief is available. In what promises to be a landmark decision, the Master of the Rolls, delivering the leading judgment, held that a beneficiary of a fiduciary's duties has no proprietary interest in any money or asset acquired by the fiduciary in breach of his duties, 'unless the asset or money is or has been beneficially the property of the beneficiary or the trustee acquired the asset or money by taking advantage of an opportunity or right which was properly that of the beneiciary',[230] even if the fiduciary could not have acquired the asset had he not been a fiduciary. In holding that the appropriate remedy is an equitable account, the Court of Appeal expressly disapproved the decision of the Privy Council in *Attorney General for Hong Kong v Reid*,[231] preferring its own decision in *Lister & Co v Stubbs*.[232] Lord Neuberger MR added that if it is a matter of equitable policy that a fiduciary should not be allowed to profit from his breach of duties, that can be achieved by extending or adjusting the rules relating to equitable compensation rather than those relating to proprietary interests.[233]

---

218  Companies Act 2006 (Commencement No 3, etc) Order 2007, SI 2007/2194, art 2.

219  No guidance is given as to what might constitute a 'threatened' breach in this respect. For the consequences of breach of fiduciary duty in case the breach is threatened but has not yet occurred see para 10.178.03 below.

220  The CLR noted that a restatement of remedies for breach of directors' duties would break new ground, nonetheless, it provisionally considered that it would be of value if any new statutory statement of directors' duties were accompanied by a statement of the principal remedies as regards directors. See *Completing the Structure* (DTI, London, November 2000), paras 13.72–13.74.

221  See Official Report, 9/2/2006; col GC335 (Lord Goldsmith).

222  See ss 171–177 above. For example, the duties of directors now enshrined in ss 175 and 176 are not the same as the previous common law rules or equitable principles applying to those duties.

223  For a full discussion of the remedies, see S. Worthington, 'Corporate Governance: Remedying and Ratifying Directors' Breaches' [2000] *LQR* 638, at 659–674.

224  *Re Forest of Dean Coal Co* (1879) 10 Ch D 450; *JJ Harrison (Properties) Ltd v Harrison* [2002] 1 BCLC 162, CA.

225  This liability may arise either out of a contract between a director and the company (see e.g., *Imperial Mercantile Credit Association v Coleman* (1873) LR 6 HL 189) or as a result of some contract or arrangement between the director and a third person (see eg *Burland v Earle* [1902] AC 83).

226  In case the breach is threatened but has not yet occurred. An injunction may also be suitable where the breach has already occurred but is likely to continue or if some of its consequences can be avoided. See eg *Cranleigh Precision Engineering Ltd v Bryant* [1965] 1 WLR 1293.

227  See eg *Transvaal Lands Co v New Belgium (Transvaal) Land & Development Co* [1914] 2 Ch 488, CA.

228  See, for example, *Dorchester Finance Co v Stebbing* [1989] BCLC 498; and Re *D'Jan of London* [1994] 1 BCLC 561.

229  [2011] EWCA Civ 347.

230  Ibid, at [88].

231  [1994] 1 AC 324.

232  (1890) LR 45 Ch D 1. Lord Neuberger MR also noted that *Lister* had been followed in two recent Court of Appeal decisions, namely *Gwembe Valley Development Co Ltd v Koshy (No 3)* [2004] 1 BCLC 131 and *Halton International Inc v Guernoy* [2006] EWCA Civ 801. The reasoning in *Lister* is supported by numerous academic commentators including: RM Goode, 'Ownership and obligation in commercial transactions' [1997] *LQR* 433; and P Watts, 'Bribes and Constructive Trusts' [1994] *LQR* 178. See also P Birks, *Introduction to the Law of Restitution* (Oxford, OUP, 1989), pp 386–389.

233  [2011] EWCA Civ 347, at [90].

Subsection (2) provides that the statutory duties are to be regarded as fiduciary, with the exception of **10.178.04** the duty to exercise reasonable care, skill, and diligence (see section 174 above), which is *not* considered to be a fiduciary duty.[234] Thus, the duties are enforceable in the same way as any other fiduciary duty owed to a company by its directors.

Presumably the rules developed for establishing the liability of accessories (eg in the case of receipt of **10.178.05** property pursuant to a breach of fiduciary duty, or dishonest assistance of such a breach) will be applied notwithstanding that the breach may be of a duty which is now statutorily defined and imposed.

### 179  Cases within more than one of the general duties

Except as otherwise provided, more than one of the general duties may apply in any given case.    **10.179.01**

COMMENCEMENT DATE 1 October 2007[235]

The way in which the duties are framed results in an overlap between them. This section serves to **10.179.02** emphasize that the effect of the duties is cumulative. It is therefore necessary for directors to comply with every duty that, in any given situation, may trigger. For example, the duty to promote the success of the company (section 172) will not authorize the director to breach his duty to act within his powers (section 171), even if he considers that it would be most likely to promote the success of the company. Another example is where a director accepts a bribe from a third party, this will place him in breach of section 176 (duty not to accept benefits from third parties) and, depending on the particular circumstances, also place him in breach of the duty to promote the success of the company (section 172) and in breach of section 175 (duty to avoid conflicts of interest).

This section is subject to one exception which relates to the duty to avoid conflicts of interest (section **10.179.03** 175 above). This particular duty does not apply to a conflict of interest arising in relation to a transaction or arrangement with the company. In such cases the duty to declare interests in proposed transactions or arrangements (section 177 above) or the requirement to declare interests in existing transactions or arrangements (section 182 below) will apply instead. It should be noted that as well as complying with all the duties, the directors must continue to comply with all other applicable laws. The duties do not require or authorize a director to breach any other prohibition or requirement imposed on him by law.[236]

### 180  Consent, approval or authorisation by members

(1) In a case where—    **10.180.01**
    (a)  section 175 (duty to avoid conflicts of interest) is complied with by authorisation by the directors, or
    (b)  section 177 (duty to declare interest in proposed transaction or arrangement) is complied with,
    the transaction or arrangement is not liable to be set aside by virtue of any common law rule or equitable principle requiring the consent or approval of the members of the company.
    This is without prejudice to any enactment, or provision of the company's constitution, requiring such consent or approval.
(2)  ª The application of the general duties is not affected by the fact that the case also falls within Chapter 4 (transactions requiring approval of members), except that where that Chapter applies and—
    (a)  approval is given under that Chapter, or
    (b)  the matter is one as to which it is provided that approval is not needed,
    it is not necessary also to comply with section 175 (duty to avoid conflicts of interest) or section 176 (duty not to accept benefits from third parties).
(3)  Compliance with the general duties does not remove the need for approval under any applicable provision of Chapter 4 (transactions requiring approval of members).
(4)  The general duties—
    (a)  have effect subject to any rule of law enabling the company to give authority, specifically or generally, for anything to be done (or omitted) by the directors, or any of them, that would otherwise be a breach of duty, and
    (b)  where the company's articles contain provisions for dealing with conflicts of interest, are not infringed by anything done (or omitted) by the directors, or any of them, in accordance with those provisions.
(5)  Otherwise, the general duties have effect (except as otherwise provided or the context otherwise requires) notwithstanding any enactment or rule of law.

AMENDMENT AND NOTES

---

[234]  See eg *Bristol and West Building Society v Mothew* [1998] Ch 1, CA Millett LJ.
[235]  Companies Act 2006 (Commencement No 3, etc) Order 2007, SI 2007/2194, art 2.
[236]  Explanatory Notes to the Bill, para 296.

[a]The reference in this subsection to approval given under Ch 4 of Pt 10 of the Companies Act 2006 (transactions requiring approval of members) includes approval given by a resolution passed before 1 October 2007 that is effective by virtue of para 6(2), 7(2), 8(2) or 12(2) of Sch 3 to the Companies Act 2006 (Commencement No. 3, Consequential Amendments, Transitional Provisions and Savings) Order 2007. See the Companies Act 2006 (Commencement No 5, Transitional Provisions and Savings) Order 2007, SI 2007/3495, Sch 4, para 49.

COMMENCEMENT DATE 1 October 2007,[237] 1 October 2008 (subs (1)(2)(part) & (4)(b))[238]

**10.180.02**  This section preserves the common law position whereby the company's members may authorize an act that would otherwise be a breach of duty.[239] The section should be read in conjunction with section 239 (ratification of acts of directors, see below). However, it is an area where the statutory restatement of the general duties of directors have made some significant changes to the common law rules and equitable principles concerning conflicts of interest.[240] Lord Goldsmith explained the nature of the change in the following terms:[241]

> Section 161[[242]] permits director authorization of what would otherwise be impermissible conflicts of interest. Section 163[[243]] requires declarations of interest in proposed company transactions. In both those cases, the general duty no longer requires the consent of members.

> The common law rules or principles that refer to the failure to have had a conflict of interest approved by the members of a company under certain circumstances need to be set aside. If they are not, although the Act provided that it was all right for there to be an authorization, it might be suggested that the director should still be capable of being impeached by reference to this common law rule or principle. However, subsection (1) goes on to say: 'This is without prejudice to any enactment, or provision of the company's constitution, requiring such consent or approval'.

> Certainly, the company's constitution can reverse the change and can insist on certain steps being taken requiring the consent of the members in certain circumstances. In that event, that provision would have to be given effect to. That is the consequence of the change of approach—and therefore a change of approach to the appropriate consequence of there not being members' approval in particular cases because it would no longer be required.

**10.180.03**  Turning to the substance of section 180, the following should be noted. Under Chapter 4 of this Part, directors must sometimes obtain prior shareholder approval for the following types of transaction involving a director or, in some cases, a person connected to a director: long service contracts (sections 188 to 189 below); substantial property transactions (sections 190 to 196 below); loans, quasi loans and credit transactions (sections 197 to 214 below); and payments for loss of office (sections 215 to 222 below). Subsection (3) provides that compliance with the general duties does not remove the need for member approval of such transactions. Likewise, the general duties apply even if the transaction also falls within the provisions in Chapter 4.[244] So, for example, the directors should only approve a loan to a director if they consider that it would promote the success of the company (in line with section 172 above). This is so, even if the loan does not require the approval of members under Chapter 4 because it falls within a relevant exception, such as the exception for expenditure on company business in section 204 (see below).

**10.180.04**  However, subsection (2) provides that if the transaction falls within Chapter 4[245] and approval of the members is obtained to the transaction in accordance with that Chapter, or an exception applies, so that approval is not necessary under that Chapter, then the director does *not* need to comply with the duty to avoid conflicts of interest (section 175 above) or the duty not to accept benefits from third parties (section 176 above) in respect of that transaction. For example, a director would not be acting in breach of the duty to avoid conflicts of interests (section 175 above) if he failed to obtain authorization from the directors or the members for a loan from the company in respect of legal defence costs. All other applicable duties will still apply.[246]

[237] Companies Act 2006 (Commencement No 3, etc) Order 2007, SI 2007/2194, art 2.
[238] Companies Act 2006 (Commencement No 5 etc) Order 2007, SI 2007/3495, art 4.
[239] *Regal (Hastings) Ltd v Gulliver* [1942] 1 All ER 378, HL.
[240] See Official Report, 9/2/2006; col GC337 (Lord Goldsmith).
[241] Ibid.
[242] Now s 175.
[243] Now s 177.
[244] Because it is a long service contract, substantial property transaction, loan, quasi-loan, credit transaction, or payment for loss of office.
[245] Ie because it is a long service contract, substantial property transaction, loan, quasi-loan, credit transaction, or payment for loss of office.
[246] Explanatory Notes to the Bill, para 301.

Subsection (4) preserves the common law position on prior authorization of conduct that would **10.180.05**
otherwise be a breach of the duties.[247] Companies may, through their articles, go further than the
statutory duties by placing more onerous requirements on their directors (eg by requiring shareholder
authorization of the remuneration of the directors). Subsection (4) also makes it clear that the
company's articles may not dilute the general duties except to the extent this is explicitly permitted.[248]
The effect of subsection (4) appears to be that interested members can vote on a resolution to approve
a prospective breach of the statutory duties, but cannot do so to ratify a breach after the event (see
section 239 below).

Finally, subsection (5) provides that the general duties have effect notwithstanding any enactment or **10.180.06**
rule of law except where there is an express or implied exception to this rule. For example, section 247
provides that directors may make provision for employees on the cessation or transfer of a company's
business even if this would otherwise constitute a breach of the general duty to promote the success of
the company (see section 172 above).

### 181  Modification of provisions in relation to charitable companies

(1)  In their application to a company that is a charity, the provisions of this Chapter have effect subject   **10.181.01**
to this section.
(2)  Section 175 (duty to avoid conflicts of interest) has effect as if—
  (a)  for subsection (3) (which disapplies the duty to avoid conflicts of interest in the case of a
  transaction or arrangement with the company) there were substituted—

  '(3) This duty does not apply to a conflict of interest arising in relation to a transaction or
  arrangement with the company if or to the extent that the company's articles allow that duty to be
  so disapplied, which they may do only in relation to descriptions of transaction or arrangement
  specified in the company's articles.';
  (b)  for subsection (5) (which specifies how directors of a company may give authority under that
  section for a transaction or arrangement) there were substituted—

  '(5) Authorisation may be given by the directors where the company's constitution includes
  provision enabling them to authorise the matter, by the matter being proposed to and authorised
  by them in accordance with the constitution.'.
(3)  Section 180(2)(b) (which disapplies certain duties under this Chapter in relation to cases excepted
from requirement to obtain approval by members under Chapter 4) applies only if or to the extent
that the company's articles allow those duties to be so disapplied, which they may do only in
relation to descriptions of transaction or arrangement specified in the company's articles.
(4)  After section 26(5) of the Charities Act 1993 (c. 10) (power of Charity Commission to authorise
dealings with charity property etc) insert—
  '(5A) In the case of a charity that is a company, an order under this section may authorise an
  act notwithstanding that it involves the breach of a duty imposed on a director of the
  company under Chapter 2 of Part 10 of the Companies Act (2006) (general duties of
  directors).'
(5)  This section does not extend to Scotland.
COMMENCEMENT DATE 1 October 2007,[249] 1 October 2008 (subs (2) & (3))[250]

This section applies to charitable (altruistic) companies. It reverses certain relaxations made to the **10.181.02**
no-conflict rule as it applies to the directors of charitable companies in England, Wales, and Northern
Ireland.[251] Charitable companies will still be able to take advantage of the various relaxations, where
their constitutions allow it. That has the benefit of openness and transparency.[252]

Subsection (2)(a) replaces section 175(3) (duty to avoid conflicts of interest, see above) which excludes **10.181.03**
conflicts of interest arising out of transactions or arrangements with the company. The replacement
excludes such conflicts of interest from the duty only if or to the extent that the charitable company's
articles so allow. The articles must describe the transactions or arrangements, which are to be so
excluded from the duty.

---

[247] See the discussion of *Regal (Hastings) Ltd v Gulliver* at paras 10.176.02 and 10.180.02 above. Note in
particular the overlap between this provision and s 175(4), (5)(a), and (5)(b) and s 176. See also s 239 below
(ratification of acts of directors).
[248] Explanatory Notes to the Bill, para 315.
[249] Companies Act 2006 (Commencement No 3, etc) Order 2007, SI 2007/2194, art 2. Note the transitional
adaptation referred to in para 10.170.13, n 1b.
[250] Companies Act 2006 (Commencement No 5 etc) Order 2007, SI 2007/3495, art 4.
[251] CA 1989 made special provision regarding charitable companies, which are now contained in the Charities
Act 1993.
[252] See Official Report, 11/7/2006; col 628 (the Solicitor-General).

**10.181.04**    Subsection (2)(b) replaces section 175(5) (see above) which allows authorization for conflicts of interest to be given by the directors. The replacement only allows authorization to be given by the directors where the charitable company's constitution expressly allows them to do so.[253]

**10.181.05**    Subsection (3) restricts the application of section 180(2)(b) which disapplies sections 175 and 176 (see above) in relation to those matters excepted from the requirements for member approval under Chapter 4. Section 180(2)(b) is restricted so that it only applies if or to the extent that the charitable company's articles allow the duties in sections 175 and 176 to be disapplied. The articles must describe the transactions or arrangements which are to be so excluded from those duties.

**10.181.06**    Subsection (4) amends section 26(5) the Charities Act 1993 to give the Charity Commission the power to authorize acts that would otherwise be in breach of the general duties.[254] This is necessary to preserve the current power of the Charity Commissioners to do so, in the light of the statutory statement of the general duties.[255]

**10.181.07**    Finally, subsection (5) makes it clear that this section does not extend to Scotland, ie it applies to the directors of charitable companies in England, Wales, and Northern Ireland only.[256] Initially, this section did not extend to Northern Ireland as well. However, an amendment introduced during the Standing Committee stage changed that.[257]

# CHAPTER 3
## DECLARATION OF INTEREST IN EXISTING TRANSACTION OR ARRANGEMENT

**10.0.05**    This Chapter in part replaces section 317 of the Companies Act 1985. The changes in the law derive principally from the recommendations of the Company Law Review Steering Group's reports, following the recommendations of the Law Commission.[258] This Chapter requires a director to declare the nature and extent of any direct or indirect interest that he has in any transaction or arrangement entered into by the company. As will be seen, this Chapter differs from the old section 317 in a number of important respects. For example, there is now a new written procedure for the declarations of interest (see section 184 below). In addition, the way of expressing the law is much simpler and clearer than was the case under section 317 of the Companies Act 1985. For example, under section 182(5) a director is regarded as failing to make the declarations required by this section if he fails to declare something that he ought reasonably to have known. Another example is that whereas section 317(2) required the declaration to be made at the meeting of the directors at which the question of entering into the transaction is first taken into consideration (in a case of a proposed transaction), under section 182(4) the declaration now should be made as soon as is reasonably practicable.

### 182 Declaration of interest in existing transaction or arrangement[259]

**10.182.01**    (1) Where a director of a company is in any way, directly or indirectly, interested in a transaction or arrangement that has been entered into by the company, he must declare the nature and extent of the interest to the other directors in accordance with this section.

This section does not apply if or to the extent that the interest has been declared under section 177 (duty to declare interest in proposed transaction or arrangement).

(2) The declaration must be made—
(a) at a meeting of the directors, or
(b) by notice in writing (see section 184), or
(c) by general notice (see section 185).

(3) If a declaration of interest under this section proves to be, or becomes, inaccurate or incomplete, a further declaration must be made.

---

[253] In case the articles need to altered, s 64 of the Charities Act 1993 deals with alterations by a charitable company of its objects clause.

[254] Section 26 of the Charities Act 1993 deals with the power to authorize dealings with charity property etc.

[255] The Charity Commissioners functions and responsibilities are defined in s 1 of the Charities Act 1993.

[256] It should be noted that subject to s 100(3)–(6) of the Charities Act 1993 (Short title and extent), the Charities Act 1993 extends only to England and Wales.

[257] Amendment No 301 introduced on 11 July 2006. See Official Report, 11/7/2006; cols 627–628.

[258] The key recommendations by the CLR on s 317 can be found in *Developing the Framework* (DTI, London, March 2000) Annex C, paras 10–18 and *Completing the Structure* (DTI, London, November 2000), paras 4.11–4.16.

[259] This section applies in relation to transactions or arrangements entered into by a company on or after 1 October 2008. Section 317 of the 1985 Act or art 325 of the 1986 Order continues to apply in relation to transactions or arrangements entered into before that date. See the Companies Act 2006 (Commencement No 5, Transitional Provisions and Savings) Order 2007, SI 2007/3495, Sch 4, para 50.

(4)  Any declaration required by this section must be made as soon as is reasonably practicable. Failure to comply with this requirement does not affect the underlying duty to make the declaration.

(5)  This section does not require a declaration of an interest of which the director is not aware or where the director is not aware of the transaction or arrangement in question.

For this purpose a director is treated as being aware of matters of which he ought reasonably to be aware.

(6)  A director need not declare an interest under this section—

(a)  if it cannot reasonably be regarded as likely to give rise to a conflict of interest;

(b)  if, or to the extent that, the other directors are already aware of it (and for this purpose the other directors are treated as aware of anything of which they ought reasonably to be aware); or

(c)  if, or to the extent that, it concerns terms of his service contract that have been or are to be considered—

(i)  by a meeting of the directors, or

(ii)  by a committee of the directors appointed for the purpose under the company's constitution.

COMMENCEMENT DATE 1 October 2008[260]

As commented above, section 317 of the Companies Act 1985 is partly replaced.[261] Instead, this section **10.182.02** requires a director to declare the nature and extent of any direct or indirect interest that he has in any transaction or arrangement entered into by the company. It differs from the provisions of section 317 of the Companies Act 1985 in a number of important respects. It is considered next what should be declared, when the declaration should be made, and how the declaration should be made.

## What should be declared?

It appears directors are required to declare any interest, direct or indirect, that they have in an *existing* **10.182.03** transaction or arrangement entered into by the company.[262] This section only applies to transactions or arrangements already entered into by the company. Section 177 (duty to declare interests) applies in the case of proposed transactions or arrangements with the company. The director does not need to be a party to the transaction with the company in order for a declaration to be required under this section, for example, where the director's spouse enters into a transaction with the company that may (but need not necessarily) give rise to an indirect interest on the part of the director in that transaction. The declaration must be of the nature and extent of the director's direct or indirect interest.[263]

Subsection (1) makes it clear that if the director has declared his interest in accordance with section 177 **10.182.04** at the time the transaction was proposed, and before it was entered into by the company, the director does not need to repeat that declaration once the transaction becomes an existing transaction to which this section applies. Furthermore, a director need not declare any interest that cannot reasonably be regarded as likely to give rise to a conflict of interest; that the other directors already know about, or ought reasonably to know about; or that concerns the terms of his service contract, considered (or to be considered) by a meeting of directors or by the relevant committee of directors.[264]

---

[260]  Companies Act 2006 (Commencement No 5, etc) Order 2007, SI 2007/3495, art 4.

[261]  Section 317 of CA 1985 tried to ensure that although the articles may remove from the director the obligation to obtain shareholder approval in advance, the director is nevertheless obliged to inform his fellow directors about any potential conflicts of interest. However, the legal relationship between the articles and s 317 was far from clear. See PL Davies, *Gower and Davies' Principles of Modern Company Law* (7th edn, Sweet & Maxwell, London, 2003), 397.

[262]  Explanatory Notes to the Act, para 360. CA 1985, s 317(1) required a declaration at a meeting of directors of the nature of the director's interest where the director was interested in any way, directly or indirectly in a contract or proposed contract. Thus, the extent of the directors' interest did not need to be disclosed. At the same time, under s 317(1) all interests, no matter how trivial, needed to be disclosed. See, PL Davies, *Gower and Davies' Principles of Modern Company Law* (7th edn, Sweet & Maxwell, London, 2003), 399. In a decision under the previous provision, it was held that disclosure is not required of interests already known to the members of the board. See *Runciman v Walter Runciman plc* [1992] BCLC 1084.

[263]  Explanatory Notes to the Act, para 364. The CLR recommended that the nature of interests be disclosed as well, but only material interests. *Developing the Framework* (DTI, London, March 2000), para 3.89 and *Completing the Structure* (DTI, London, Nov 2000) para 4.11. The Law Commission concluded that it is not possible to define 'material interests' and instead settled for disclosure of all interests other than where there was no real risk of an actual conflict or where the rest of the board was aware of the nature and extent of the interest. See Law Commission Report, paras 8.20–8.33.

[264]  Explanatory Notes to the Act, paras 365–366.

**10.182.05**    Subsection (5) provides that a director is regarded as failing to make the declarations required by this section if he fails to declare something that he ought reasonably to have known.[265] However, it should be noted that the director is not otherwise expected by this section to declare things he does not know.[266]

### When should the declaration be made?

**10.182.06**    Subsection (4) provides that the declaration should be made as soon as is reasonably practicable. This is different from the previous legislation.[267] Subsection (4) also makes it clear that even if the declaration is not made as soon as it should have been, it must still be made. Subsection (3) adds that if after a declaration has been made the director's interest in the transaction or arrangement changes, or the director realizes that his interests were not as originally declared, the director must make another declaration of interest, correcting or updating the earlier one.

### How should the declaration be made?

**10.182.07**    Subsections (2) and (6) taken together provide that the declaration of interest must be made to the other directors using one of the following three methods: (i) at a meeting of the directors; or (ii) by notice in writing (in accordance with the requirements of section 184, see below); or (iii) by general notice (in accordance with the requirements of section 185, see below).

### 183 Offence of failure to declare interest[268]

**10.183.01**
     (1)   A director who fails to comply with the requirements of section 182 (declaration of interest in existing transaction or arrangement) commits an offence.
     (2)   A person guilty of an offence under this section is liable—
         (a)   on conviction on indictment, to a fine;
         (b)   on summary conviction, to a fine not exceeding the statutory maximum.

     COMMENCEMENT DATE 1 October 2008[269]

**10.183.02**    This section replaces section 317(7) of the Companies Act 1985, under which a director who failed to comply with the section (requiring disclosure of interest in contracts) was liable to a fine. The law is effectively restated, but it is done more expansively.

**10.183.03**    This section, which is self-explanatory, provides that a director who fails to comply with the requirements of section 182 (see above) commits an offence. On conviction on indictment the maximum liability is an unlimited fine. On summary conviction the fine must not exceed the statutory maximum (currently £5,000). It should be noted that this section does not affect the validity of the transaction or impose any other civil consequences for a failure to make the declarations of interest required by section 182.[270]

### 184 Declaration made by notice in writing[271]

**10.184.01**
     (1)   This section applies to a declaration of interest made by notice in writing.
     (2)   The director must send the notice to the other directors.
     (3)   The notice may be sent in hard copy form or, if the recipient has agreed to receive it in electronic form, in an agreed electronic form.
     (4)   The notice may be sent—
         (a)   by hand or by post, or

---

[265] Under CA 1985, s 317(1) all interests, no matter how trivial, needed to be disclosed.

[266] Explanatory Notes to the Act, para 367.

[267] Under CA 1985, s 317(2), in a case of a proposed transaction, the declaration was required to be made at the meeting of the directors at which the question of entering into the transaction is first taken into consideration or, if the director was not present at that meeting, at the next meeting held after he became so interested. In a case where the director became interested in a contract after it was made, s 317(2) required the declaration to be made at the first meeting of the directors held after he becomes so interested.

[268] This section applies in relation to transactions or arrangements entered into by a company on or after 1 October 2008. Section 317 of the 1985 Act or art 325 of the 1986 Order continues to apply in relation to transactions or arrangements entered into before that date. See the Companies Act 2006 (Commencement No 5, Transitional Provisions and Savings) Order 2007, SI 2007/3495, Sch 4, para 50.

[269] Companies Act 2006 (Commencement No 5, etc) Order 2007, SI 2007/3495, art 4.

[270] Explanatory Notes to the Act, para 370.

[271] This section applies in relation to transactions or arrangements entered into by a company on or after 1 October 2008. Section 317 of the 1985 Act or art 325 of the 1986 Order continues to apply in relation to transactions or arrangements entered into before that date. See the Companies Act 2006 (Commencement No 5, Transitional Provisions and Savings) Order 2007, SI 2007/3495, Sch 4, para 50.

    (b) if the recipient has agreed to receive it by electronic means, by agreed electronic means.

(5) Where a director declares an interest by notice in writing in accordance with this section—

    (a) the making of the declaration is deemed to form part of the proceedings at the next meeting of the directors after the notice is given, and

    (b) the provisions of section 248 (minutes of meetings of directors) apply as if the declaration had been made at that meeting.

COMMENCEMENT DATE 1 October 2008[272]

This is a new provision. It provides a new written procedure for the declarations of interest required by section 182 (see above).   **10.184.02**

Subsection (2) provides that a written notice declaring the nature and extent of the director's interest must be sent to all the other directors.[273] Subsections (3) and (4) make it clear that it is possible to send the declaration of interest in hard copy form or, if agreed, in electronic form.[274] Likewise, the declaration may be posted, delivered by hand or by electronic means. The inclusion of electronic means is part of the Government's overall objective to (a) produce significant cost savings; (b) enable companies and their shareholders to reap the great benefits of improved delivery of and access to information; and (c) provide for easier decision-making processes.[275]   **10.184.03**

Finally, subsection (5) provides that when a declaration of interest made by notice in writing is done, the notice is treated as forming part of the proceedings of the next meeting of the directors, and so should form part of the minutes of that meeting (see section 248 below).[276]   **10.184.04**

## 185 General notice treated as sufficient declaration[277]

(1) General notice in accordance with this section is a sufficient declaration of interest in relation to the matters to which it relates.   **10.185.01**

(2) General notice is notice given to the directors of a company to the effect that the director—

    (a) has an interest (as member, officer, employee or otherwise) in a specified body corporate or firm and is to be regarded as interested in any transaction or arrangement that may, after the date of the notice, be made with that body corporate or firm, or

    (b) is connected with a specified person (other than a body corporate or firm) and is to be regarded as interested in any transaction or arrangement that may, after the date of the notice, be made with that person.

(3) The notice must state the nature and extent of the director's interest in the body corporate or firm or, as the case may be, the nature of his connection with the person.

(4) General notice is not effective unless—

    (a) it is given at a meeting of the directors, or

    (b) the director takes reasonable steps to secure that it is brought up and read at the next meeting of the directors after it is given.

COMMENCEMENT DATE 1 October 2008[278]

---

[272] Companies Act 2006 (Commencement No 5, etc) Order 2007, SI 2007/3495, art 4.

[273] The Law Society parliamentary brief proposed an amendment to subs (2) to require a director who makes a declaration to send the notice not only to the other directors, but to the company secretary, if the company has one. The secretary should be aware of declarations, and a central record should be kept. However, the Government view was that informing a company secretary is insufficient and that the other directors need to know about any declaration of interest by a fellow director: 'We do not accept that it is particularly onerous to tell other directors of a declaration, because they will—particularly these days—be in contact with their office or place of business, and there will be a method of sending them a letter or other communication.' See Official Report, 11/7/2006; col 629 (the Solicitor-General).

[274] It is noteworthy that s 1168 (see below) defines electronic means as including faxes, e-mails or by any other means while in an electronic form (eg, sending a disk by post). However, as subs (3) makes it clear the recipient has to agree to receive it in electronic form. It follows, that 'some people may wish to receive the declaration by fax, in which case authorization may be given. If the recipient agrees that they will receive a declaration by fax, that is fine; if they do not, they should receive it in the proper form, and the director has an obligation to send it in a form that is easily readable. Indeed, these days, e-mail is probably an easier way of getting in contact with people than fax, but e-mails, too, have a habit of going astray.' See Official Report, 11/7/2006; col 630 (the Solicitor-General).

[275] See Official Report, 9/2/2006; col GC341 (Lord Goldsmith).

[276] Explanatory Notes to the Act, para 371.

[277] This section applies in relation to transactions or arrangements entered into by a company on or after 1 October 2008. Section 317 of the 1985 Act or art 325 of the 1986 Order continues to apply in relation to transactions or arrangements entered into before that date. See Pt 3 of the Companies Act 2006 (Commencement No 5, Transitional Provisions and Savings) Order 2007, SI 2007/3495, Sch 4, para 50.

[278] Companies Act 2006 (Commencement No 5, etc) Order 2007, SI 2007/3495, art 4.

**10.185.02**    This section replaces section 317(3) and (4) of the Companies Act 1985.[279] The section enables a director to give a general notice of his interests, thus providing an avenue which directors can take to protect themselves from breaching the statutory duty under section 182 (see above).

**10.185.03**    Subsection (2) provides that a general notice is a declaration that the director is interested in another body corporate or firm, or that the director is connected with another person. If the company enters into a contract with the body corporate, firm, or other person named in the general notice, the director does not need to declare any direct or indirect interest that he has in that contract arising as a result of his interest in the body corporate or firm named in the general notice or arising as a result of his connection to the person named in the general notice.[280]

**10.185.04**    Subsection (3) provides that in order to be effective, the general notice must state the nature and extent of the director's interest in the body corporate or firm (for example, sole shareholder of the company) or the nature of his connection with the person (for example, spouse or other connected person as defined in sections 252 to 253).[281] The requirement to disclose the extent of the interest implements a recommendation of the CLR.[282] It appears that if there are minor or immaterial omissions (rather than deliberate intention) in the general notice, the director would have succeeded in meeting the obligation to state the nature and extent of his interest in the body corporate. However, if there is a material mistake in the notice, the director may well have failed to state the nature and extent of his interest.[283]

### 186  Declaration of interest in case of company with sole director[284]

**10.186.01**
(1)  Where a declaration of interest under section 182 (duty to declare interest in existing transaction or arrangement) is required of a sole director of a company that is required to have more than one director—
   (a)  the declaration must be recorded in writing,
   (b)  the making of the declaration is deemed to form part of the proceedings at the next meeting of the directors after the notice is given, and
   (c)  the provisions of section 248 (minutes of meetings of directors) apply as if the declaration had been made at that meeting.
(2)  Nothing in this section affects the operation of section 231 (contract with sole member who is also a director: terms to be set out in writing or recorded in minutes).

COMMENCEMENT DATE 1 October 2008[285]

**10.186.02**    This is a new provision. It deals with the situation where a company has only one director but it is required to have more (eg because it is a public company). In the past, the courts have insisted that disclosure is required under section 317 of the Companies Act 1985, even in the case of a sole director.[286] The CLR recommended that this requirement should be disapplied in respect of a sole director.[287] The Act implements that recommendation, but only where the company legitimately has just one director.[288]

---

[279]  Which had an 'undoubted weakness'. See PL Davies, *Gower and Davies' Principles of Modern Company Law* (7th edn, Sweet & Maxwell, London, 2003), 400.

[280]  Explanatory Notes to the Act, para 372.

[281]  Explanatory Notes to the Act, para 373.

[282]  The CLR recommended that the nature of interests be disclosed as well, but only material interests. *Developing the Framework* (DTI, London, March 2000) para 3.89 and *Completing the Structure* (DTI, London, November 2000) para 4.11. See also discussion under s 183 at paras 10.183.01–10.183.03 above.

[283]  See Official Report, 9/2/2006; col GC342 (Lord Goldsmith).

[284]  This section applies in relation to transactions or arrangements entered into by a company on or after 1 October 2008. Section 317 of the 1985 Act or art 325 of the 1986 Order continues to apply in relation to transactions or arrangements entered into before that date. See the Companies Act 2006 (Commencement No 5, Transitional Provisions and Savings) Order 2007, SI 2007/3495, Sch 4, para 50.

[285]  Companies Act 2006 (Commencement No 5, etc) Order 2007, SI 2007/3495, art 4.

[286]  *Neptune (Vehicle Washing Equipment) Ltd v Fitzgerald* [1996] Ch 274 (Lightman J). In this case the court held that even if the secretary were not present, the director could make the declaration silently! In *Neptune (Vehicle Washing Equipment) Ltd v Fitzgerald (No 2)* [1995] BCC 1000, 1003 the court had some doubts about the correctness of Lightman J's approach; nonetheless, the case was reluctantly applied. See also *Movitex Ltd v Bulfield* [1988] BCLC 104. But see *MacPherson v European Strategic Bureau Ltd* (2000) The Times, 5 September 2000 revsd [2002] BCC 39, CA. It should be likewise noted that a board's knowledge in general terms that one of their members has engaged in a conflict-transaction will not amount to sufficient disclosure. The board has to be given full and precise information: see *Gwembe Valley Development Co Ltd v Koshy* [1998] 2 BCLC 613.

[287]  *Completing the Structure* (DTI, London, November 2000) paras 2.23–2.26. The Law Commission favoured disclosure either in a register of interests or in writing as part of board minutes. See Law Commission Report, paras 8.76–8.88. The creation of register of interests was subsequently rejected by the CLR on the grounds that it

Thus, subsection (1) provides that where a company has only one director it is not possible for the       **10.186.03**
director to declare his interests to the other directors, because, naturally, there are no other directors.[289]
Therefore, a sole director does not need to comply with section 182 (declaration of interest in existing
transaction or arrangement). However, subsection (1) also makes special provision where the company has only one director, when it should in fact have more than one director (for example, because
it is a public company). In such a case, the sole director must record in writing the nature and extent of
his interest in any transaction or arrangement that has been entered into by the company.[290] The
consequence is that there will be a record so that when another director comes along, as should be the
case, the position is clear and can be seen.

### 187  Declaration of interest in existing transaction by shadow director[291]

(1)  The provisions of this Chapter relating to the duty under section 182 (duty to declare interest in       **10.187.01**
     existing transaction or arrangement) apply to a shadow director as to a director, but with the
     following adaptations.
(2)  Subsection (2)(a) of that section (declaration at meeting of directors) does not apply.
(3)  In section 185 (general notice treated as sufficient declaration), subsection (4) (notice to be given
     at or brought up and read at meeting of directors) does not apply.
(4)  General notice by a shadow director is not effective unless given by notice in writing in accordance
     with section 184.

COMMENCEMENT DATE  1 October 2008[292]

This section replaces section 317(8) of the Companies Act 1985.[293] Like in the previous legislation, the       **10.187.02**
section extends the application of this Chapter to shadow directors, so that a shadow director[294] must
also declare the nature and extent of his interest in any transaction or arrangement that has been
entered into by the company, in accordance with section 182 (duty to declare interest in existing
transaction or arrangement, see above).

Subsections (3) and (4) provide that the declaration must be made by notice in writing (section 184, see       **10.187.03**
above) or by general notice (section 185, see above). The declaration is not made at a meeting of the
directors, as this is not appropriate in the case of a shadow director.[295] If the shadow director makes the
declaration by general notice, that notice must be given in accordance with the notice in writing
procedure set out in section 184. This means that a general notice given by a shadow director must
comply with both section 184 and the first three subsections of section 185.

It should be noted that otherwise, apart from section 186 (declaration of interest in case of company       **10.187.04**
with sole director), which is not relevant to a shadow director, all the other provisions of this chapter
apply to a shadow director, including the exemptions in section 182.[296]

---

would not substantially help to regulate conflicts of interests. See CLR, *Developing the Framework* (DTI, London,
March 2000) Annex C, para 14).

[288]  See Official Report, 9/2/2006; col GC343 (Lord Goldsmith).

[289]  Effectively, then, overturning *Neptune (Vehicle Washing Equipment Ltd v Fitzgerald* [1996] Ch 274. See
para 10.186.02 above.

[290]  Explanatory Notes to the Act, para 375.

[291]  This section applies in relation to transactions or arrangements entered into by a company on or after 1
October 2008. Section 317 of the 1985 Act or art 325 of the 1986 Order continues to apply in relation to
transactions or arrangements entered into before that date. See the Companies Act 2006 (Commencement No 5,
Transitional Provisions and Savings) Order 2007, SI 2007/3495, Sch 4, para 50.

[292]  Companies Act 2006 (Commencement No 5, etc) Order 2007, SI 2007/3495, art 4.

[293]  CA 1985, s 317(8) extended the application of s 317 to shadow directors and in that case disclosure was
made by notice in writing to the board.

[294]  For the meaning of a 'shadow director' see s 251 below.

[295]  Explanatory Notes to the Act, para 377.

[296]  Explanatory Notes to the Act, para 378.

CHAPTER 4

TRANSACTIONS WITH DIRECTORS REQUIRING
APPROVAL OF MEMBERS

*Service contracts*

### 188  Directors' long-term service contracts: requirement of members' approval

**10.188.01**    (1)  This section applies to provision under which the guaranteed term of a director's employment—
   (a)  with the company of which he is a director, or
   (b)  where he is the director of a holding company, within the group consisting of that company and its subsidiaries,
   is, or may be, longer than two years.
   (2)  A company may not agree to such provision unless it has been approved—
   (a)  by resolution of the members of the company, and
   (b)  in the case of a director of a holding company, by resolution of the members of that company.
   (3)  The guaranteed term of a director's employment is—
   (a)  the period (if any) during which the director's employment—
      (i)  is to continue, or may be continued otherwise than at the instance of the company (whether under the original agreement or under a new agreement entered into in pursuance of it), and
      (ii)  cannot be terminated by the company by notice, or can be so terminated only in specified circumstances, or
   (b)  in the case of employment terminable by the company by notice, the period of notice required to be given,
   or, in the case of employment having a period within paragraph (a) and a period within paragraph (b), the aggregate of those periods.
   (4)  If more than six months before the end of the guaranteed term of a director's employment the company enters into a further service contract (otherwise than in pursuance of a right conferred, by or under the original contract, on the other party to it), this section applies as if there were added to the guaranteed term of the new contract the unexpired period of the guaranteed term of the original contract.
   (5)  A resolution approving provision to which this section applies must not be passed unless a memorandum setting out the proposed contract incorporating the provision is made available to members—
   (a)  in the case of a written resolution, by being sent or submitted to every eligible member at or before the time at which the proposed resolution is sent or submitted to him;
   (b)  in the case of a resolution at a meeting, by being made available for inspection by members of the company both—
      (i)  at the company's registered office for not less than 15 days ending with the date of the meeting, and
      (ii)  at the meeting itself.
   (6)  No approval is required under this section on the part of the members of a body corporate that—
   (a)  is not a UK-registered company, or
   (b)  is a wholly-owned subsidiary of another body corporate.
   (7)  In this section 'employment' means any employment under a director's service contract.

   COMMENCEMENT DATE  1 October 2007[297]

**10.188.02**    A director[298] may not be guaranteed a service contract longer than two years without a resolution of the members.

**10.188.03**    This and the following section, like their predecessor section 319 of the Companies Act 1985, apply to all UK companies and are aimed at controlling the board's ability to commit the company to making termination payments to a director who is dismissed without notice or otherwise in breach[299] of his

---

[297] Companies Act 2006 (Commencement No 3, etc) Order 2007, SI 2007/2194, art 2. For transitional provisions, see SI 2007/2194, art 9, Sch 3, para 6. This section has been disapplied in respect of certain specified persons while Northern Rock, Bradford & Bingley and Deposits Management (Heritable) are wholly owned by the Treasury, pursuant to the Northern Rock plc Transfer Order 2008, SI 2008/432, art 17, Sch, para 2(g), the Bradford & Bingley plc Transfer of Securities and Property etc Order 2008, SI 2008/2546, art 13(1), Sch, para 2(g) and the Heritable Bank plc Transfer of Certain Rights and Liabilities Order 2008, SI 2008/2644, art 26, Sch 2, para 2(g), respectively.

[298] For the purposes of this and the following section a shadow director is treated as a director: s 223(1)(a).

[299] No guaranteed term can prevent summary determination of a service contract with cause. Most written service contracts provide for their determination by the company in specified circumstances, and implied terms

service contract (so-called 'golden parachute' provisions). Together with the rules governing the disclosure of directors' service contracts (sections 227 to 230)[300] and the declaration of personal interest to other directors (section 177)[301] they take a dual approach of full disclosure and partial approval to protecting members against the risk of directors awarding themselves service contracts with inappropriately generous terms.[302]

The principal change introduced in section 188 is that the length of any fixed-term contract or of any **10.188.04** fixed or rolling notice period (or, if applicable, the combined length of a fixed-term contract and a notice period) requiring member approval has been reduced from five years under the Companies Act 1985 to two years. The reduction from five years to two years was heralded as one of the important reforms in the 2006 Act (the size of termination payments having been the subject of much public controversy). The intention underlying the change was clearly to send a strong signal that contracts or notice periods with guaranteed terms of longer than two[303] years should be regarded as exceptional. Whether, however, this has in fact introduced significant changes to market practice remains to be seen: modern best practice in the case of larger companies (and certainly in the case of listed companies) already regards anything longer than a one-year guaranteed term as generally unaccept-able, while the tendency for there to be a community of ownership and management in the case of smaller private companies (combined with the possibility of informal approval)[304] may mean that greater shareholder power in such companies will have little practical impact.

In making this amendment Parliament opted to retain a simple and uniform approach. Thus despite **10.188.05** the debate initiated by the Law Commissions[305] and the CLR[306] about a permissible longer initial cut-off period for directors recruited from outside, the possibility of advance blanket approval by special resolution for an intermediate length of cut-off period, and the use of different cut-off periods for public and private companies, a single rule applies in all cases, though of course an additional layer of UK and overseas[307] corporate governance regulation applies in the case of listed companies (see below).

Strictly speaking section 188 remains the sole statutory exception to the principle that the board of **10.188.06** directors may (and under most companies' articles do) determine the terms on which directors are employed or appointed by the company or its subsidiaries. However, in addition to the statutory requirement under section 188, regard must also be had, in the case of quoted[308] companies, to the provisions in Part 15 dealing with the annual directors' remuneration report. This report, which must be approved by the board of directors, must specify certain details upon which directors are employed (or appointed[309] ).[310] Under section 439, the report must be circulated to members and a resolution put to the vote at the meeting before which the annual accounts for the financial year are to be laid

---

also operate both in the case of express and implied service contracts (including where there is no express term to the contrary as to termination on reasonable notice). S 188 does not regulate the length of notice that a company may be required to give, for example under the Employment Rights Act 1996, s 86.

[300] Supplemented in the case of listed companies by the Prospectus Rules, Listing Rules and other corporate governance requirements.

[301] This is now in most cases of only vestigial application in the context of directors' service contracts, in part because of the growing prevalence of remuneration committees: see s 177(6)(b) and (c).

[302] Those provisions do not exempt the directors from their duty to act bona fide in the best interests of the company and not for an improper purpose in agreeing the terms of any service contract: see, eg, *Wilton Group plc v Abrams and others* [1991] BCLC 315 at 322–323 (per Scott J).

[303] Suggestions from some quarters that the period should be reduced to as low as one year were offset by concerns about 'short-termism' and the need to strike a regulatory balance between rewarding poor performance and continuing to attract to British companies (and retain) the best executives.

[304] *Wright v Atlas Wright (Europe) Ltd*, see below, para 10.188.12, n 1.

[305] See *Company Directors: Regulating Conflicts of Interest and Formulating a Statement of Duties*, Cm 4436 (1999), paras 9.24–9.33.

[306] See the CLR's Final Report (26 July 2001), paras 6.12–6.14.

[307] Eg under the Sarbanes-Oxley Act of 2002 (for UK companies listed on any US stock exchange or having a parent company listed on any US stock exchange, or having 300 or more US shareholders).

[308] Note that under s 385(2) these include not only companies with equity share capital listed on the London Stock Exchange but also those whose equity share capital is officially listed in an EEA state or is admitted to dealing on the New York Stock Exchange or Nasdaq—the aim of this rather wide definition being to avoid introducing a competitive disadvantage in the case of the London Stock Exchange.

[309] Since the appointment of non-executive directors is also covered by the Regulations made under s 421(1). See below.

[310] See ss 420–422. Under CA 1985, those details were spelled out in Sch 7A, having been introduced by the Directors' Remuneration Report Regulations 2002 (SI 2002/1986). The Regulations under s 421 replace the provisions in Sch 7A, and also specify the extent to which the directors' remuneration report should be subject to audit. See 15.421.02 et seq.

approving the contents of the report. The members' vote is advisory only, in that no person's entitlement to remuneration is conditional upon such resolution being passed,[311] but in practice it clearly acts as an important check on directors' ability to set their own terms of employment and is persuasive as regards remuneration policy for future periods.[312]

**10.188.07**   For UK-listed companies incorporated in the UK, the Listing Rules require boards to report annually on details of service contracts with a notice period of longer than a year or with provisions for pre-determined compensation on termination which exceeds one year's salary and benefits in kind, giving the reasons for such a notice period.[313] For those incorporated overseas and having a premium listing, the Listing Rules require boards to report annually on details of the unexpired term of any directors' service contract of a director proposed for election or re-election at the forthcoming annual general meeting, and, if any director proposed for election or re-election does not have a directors' service contract, a statement to that effect.[314] The Listing Rules also require boards of listed companies of both kinds to report annually on how their company has applied the Main Principles set out in the UK Corporate Governance Code, in a manner that would enable shareholders to evaluate how the principles have been applied.[315] Furthermore, boards are required either to comply with all relevant provisions of the UK Corporate Governance Code, or identify those with which they have not complied and explain the reason for non-compliance.[316] Section D.1 of the UK Corporate Governance Code includes a statement of practice in the following terms: 'Notice or contract periods should be set at one year or less. If it is necessary to offer longer notice or contract periods to new directors recruited from outside, such periods should reduce to one year or less after the initial period.'[317]

**10.188.08**   Section 188 is directed only at provisions in directors' service contracts governing compensation for breach of employment by the company. Being removed from office in circumstances where there is no breach of any employment contract is not an event for which a director is entitled to be compensated as a matter of employment or company law. However, the board of directors on behalf of the company might choose to pay compensation for loss of office (or as consideration for or in connection with retirement from office) at or around the time of the director's departure from office, particularly where a takeover offer (or some other change of control) is anticipated. Such payments are subject to the restrictions set out in sections 215 and following.

**10.188.09**   Subsections (1) and (3): Although substantially reworded (notably by the introduction of the definition of a 'guaranteed term'),[318] section 188 is in most respects no more than a continuation of section 319 of the Companies Act 1985, with a shorter cut-off period before the requirement for members' approval under subsection (2) is engaged.

**10.188.10**   Subsection (2): Where the relevant service contract is between the director and a subsidiary of the company of which he is a director, resolutions are required both in the case of the company and its subsidiary.[319] It should be noted that although the approval required is an ordinary resolution[320] the company's articles may impose more stringent requirements.[321] Furthermore, where approval for a

---

[311] S 439(5).

[312] As has been shown by research produced by Deloittes (cited in col GC 345 of Hansard on 9 February 2006) in relation to the equivalent provisions in CA 1985 introduced by the Directors' Remuneration Report Regulations 2002 (SI 2002/1986).

[313] LR 9.8.6 R(7) and 9.8.8R(8).

[314] LR 9.8.7 R and 9.8.8 R (9).

[315] LR 9.8.6 R(5) and 9.8.7 R.

[316] LR 9.8.6 R(6) and 9.8.7 R.

[317] UK Corporate Governance Code D.1.5 (published by the Financial Reporting Council in June 2010 in respect of reporting periods commencing on or after 29 June 2010). Similar provisions applied in respect of earlier reporting periods, under the Combined Code on Corporate Governance. For all listed companies, regard should also be had to guidance issued by the Investment Protection Committees.

[318] The scope of the restriction is in certain respects more tightly defined than under the previous provision in s 319(1), and in particular puts beyond doubt the question whether the term of the contract and any rolling notice period are to be aggregated.

[319] Unless the subsidiary is wholly-owned, in which case only a resolution of the holding company is required: s 188(6)(b). This exception extends to any body corporate that is a wholly-owned subsidiary of another body corporate. The requirement for a resolution of the holding company is an anti-avoidance provision, aimed at preventing the employment of the director by the subsidiary on a guaranteed term exceeding two years with merely the approval of the holding company given as shareholder.

[320] S 281(3).

[321] Ibid. In addition to setting out requirements for member approval, the articles may themselves contain restrictions as to the terms on which directors may be employed or appointed. The company may not engage a director on terms that conflict with its articles: *Bluett v Stutchbury's Limited* [1908] 24 TLR 469. However, as the articles are a contract only between shareholders and the service contract a contract between the company and its

service contract is also required under another provision of Chapter 4 of this Part, the requirements of each applicable provision must be met.[322]

In the case of private companies, approval may be given by written resolution.[323]     **10.188.11**

Under section 319 of the Companies Act 1985 it was possible to override the requirements of formal   **10.188.12**
shareholder approval (and indeed the apparently mandatory terms of section 319(3) and (5)) of a term
or notice period exceeding five years by unanimous shareholder consent: *Wright v Atlas Wright
(Europe) Ltd*.[324] The reasoning behind the Court of Appeal's decision in that case was that the statutory
protection was aimed primarily at shareholders (as opposed to creditors), and accordingly, save in
exceptional cases, one would expect the common law position as a matter of principle to remain the
same in relation to the new provision,[325] assuming the company's articles allow it.

See further, in relation to charitable companies in England and Wales, section 201 of the Charities Act   **10.188.13**
2011, which provides that any member approval under section 188 is ineffective without the prior
written consent of the Charity Commission for England and Wales.

Subsection (4) is an anti-avoidance provision. Where a director is employed under an agreement with   **10.188.14**
a guaranteed term[326] and, more than six months before the end of the original agreement, the
company[327] enters into a further service contract with that director, the unexpired part of the
guaranteed term of the original agreement must be added to the guaranteed term of the fresh
agreement in calculating the guaranteed term of that agreement for the purposes of this section. This
does not, however, apply where the fresh agreement is entered into pursuant to a right conferred by or
under the original agreement on the other party to it (though that may of course have the effect of
bringing the original agreement within the approval requirement under the section).[328]

Subsection (5) provides that a memorandum setting out certain particulars about the transaction   **10.188.15**
requiring approval of the members must be made available to the members if their approval is to be
valid. If the approval is to be given by way of written resolution, the memorandum must be sent to the
members able to vote on the written resolution no later than when the written resolution is sent to
them. See also section 224, which provides that the accidental failure to send to one or more members
a copy of such a memorandum would not invalidate such approval (subject to any provision in the
company's articles).

Subsection (6) provides that approval is never required on the part of a member of a wholly-owned   **10.188.16**
subsidiary or on the part of the members of an overseas company.

Subsection (7) provides that 'employment' in this section means any employment under a director's   **10.188.17**
service contract, which means the section as in the case of its predecessor applies to a contract for
services as well as a contract of service.[329]

---

director, this is not to say that the articles cannot subsequently be amended by special resolution under s 21
(leaving the service contract unaffected): cf *Southern Foundries (1926) Limited v Shirlaw* [1940] AC 701, followed
in *Shindler v Northern Raincoat Co. Limited* [1960] 1 WLR 1038. A term providing for payment in lieu of notice
(and drafted to exclude mitigation) may also be subject to challenge under the common law rules restricting the
effect of liquidated damages clauses that operate as penalties.
   [322]  S 225. Approval may be given for both purposes by a single resolution.
   [323]  See s 188(5)(a). The company's articles may however impose restrictions on the use of this procedure.
   [324]  [1999] 2 BCLC 301, distinguishing *Re R W Peak (Kings Lynn) Limited* [1998] 1 BCLC 193. See also more
generally *Re Torvale Group Ltd* [1999] 2 BCLC 605 and *BDG Roof-Bond Ltd v Douglas* [2001] 1 BCLC 401.
   [325]  Cf s 281(4), which leaves the common law principle of unanimous shareholder consent unaffected.
   [326]  Whether or not that guaranteed term is or may be longer than two years.
   [327]  Oddly, this restriction apparently does not apply where, under the fresh agreement, the director is to be
employed by a subsidiary. See also s 227, under which a 'service contract' is defined to include a contract under
which a director undertakes to perform services for a subsidiary. It therefore appears that while a further contract
with the company in respect of services to be performed for its subsidiary would be covered by this provision, on
a strict reading of the Act a new contract with the subsidiary would not. It is suggested that it would be unwise to
place much reliance on this loophole.
   [328]  If the original agreement may be continued at the instance of the director: see s 188(3)(a)(i).
   [329]  See s 227, which defines the expression 'service contract' for the purposes of Part 10 of CA 2006. Indeed,
that expression includes not only a contract of service and a contract for services but has been broadened to
include also a contract under which services that a director undertakes personally to perform are made available
by a third party to the company (or a subsidiary of the company) (s 227(1)(b)), thereby removing an area of doubt
that existed under CA 1985. The expression also extends to a letter of appointment, hence the terms upon which
non-executive directors are appointed are within the ambit of s 188.

### 189 Directors' long-term service contracts: civil consequences of contravention

**10.189.01**   If a company agrees to provision in contravention of section 188 (directors' long-term service contracts: requirement of members' approval)—

(a) the provision is void, to the extent of the contravention, and

(b) the contract is deemed to contain a term entitling the company to terminate it at any time by the giving of reasonable notice.

COMMENCEMENT DATE 1 October 2007[330]

**10.189.02**   The civil[331] consequences of a contravention of section 188 are penal in that the effect of this section, which substantially repeats section 319(6) of the Companies Act 1985, is that a director's service contract that was entered into without shareholder approval incorporating a term that made it necessary to obtain such approval is deemed to have been made for two years subject to its being determinable at the behest of the company at any time within that period by reasonable notice[332]. Although the offending provision is void (subject to these limitations), the remainder of the agreement of which it is a provision is not.

**10.189.03**   See also section 222 (dealing with the civil consequences of a breach of sections 217, 218, or 219).

## *Substantial property transactions*

**10.0.06**   Sections 190 to 196 concern substantial property transactions and replaced sections 320 to 322 of the 1985 Act, the main provisions of which had been introduced by the Companies Act 1980[333] following a number of DTI inspectors' reports of fraudulent asset stripping during the late 1970s.[334]

**10.0.07**   Under the 1985 Act, in addition to a director's obligation to disclose interests in contracts to the board under section 317, prior shareholder consent[335] was required where a public or private company intended to make an 'arrangement'[336] either to acquire non-cash assets[337] of the requisite value[338] from, or to transfer such assets to, a director of the company or its holding company, or a person 'connected'[339] with such a director.

---

[330] Companies Act 2006 (Commencement No 3, etc) Order 2007, SI 2007/2194, art 2. For transitional provisions, see SI 2007/2194, art 9, Sch 3, para 6. This section has been disapplied in respect of certain specified persons while Northern Rock, Bradford & Bingley and Deposits Management (Heritable) are wholly owned by the Treasury, pursuant to the Northern Rock plc Transfer Order 2008, SI 2008/432, art 17, Sch, para 2(g), the Bradford & Bingley plc Transfer of Securities and Property etc Order 2008, SI 2008/2546, art 13(1), Sch, para 2(g) and the Heritable Bank plc Transfer of Certain Rights and Liabilities Order 2008, SI 2008/2644, art 26, Sch 2, para 2(g), respectively.

[331] There are no criminal penalties for a failure to comply with the requirements of Part 10, Chapter 4; but contrast the position as regards the directors' remuneration report provisions in Part 15.

[332] Cf *Bain v The Rangers Football Club plc* [2011] CSOH 158 (Outer House, Court of Session), where it was held arguable that a twelve-month notice period would have been reasonable in the circumstances.

[333] Sections 48 and 63(1).

[334] See The Law Commission, Consultation Paper 153 and The Scottish Law Commission Discussion Paper No 105: 'Company Directors: Regulating Conflicts of Interests and Formulating a Statement of Duties. A Joint Consultation Paper' 4.172.

[335] Applying the principle in *Re Duomatic Ltd* [1969] 2 Ch 365, Park J held that the informal approval of a director as sole shareholder was sufficient: see *NBH Ltd & NBH Group Ltd v Kevin Hoare & Others* [2006] BCLC 649. As noted by Mummery LJ in *Euro Brokers Holdings Ltd v Monecor (London) Ltd* [2003] EWCA Civ 105; [2003] BCC 573; [2003] 1 BCLC 506, what matters 'is that all of the members have reached an agreement. If they have, they cannot be heard to say that they are not bound by it because the formal procedure was not followed'. The principle has been summarized and applied by Etherton LJ in the Court of Appeal in *Schofield v Schofield* [2011] EWCA Civ 154.

[336] The expression was not limited to and was clearly broader than 'transactions'. It included understandings which had no contractual effect. The defining feature of an 'arrangement' under ss 320–322 is that each party regards itself as being to some degree under a duty to act, or not to act, as the case may be, in a particular way: see *Re British Basic Slag Ltd's Agreements* [1963] 1 WLR 727, *Re Duckwari plc* [1999] Ch 253, and *Murray v Leisureplay plc* [2004] EWHC 1927 (QB), [106] (the latter decision went on appeal to the Court of Appeal but not in respect of this point, see *Murray v Leisureplay* [2005] EWCA Civ 963, [86]). Note the exceptions in ss 192–194 below.

[337] See s 739 of the 1985 Act.

[338] Which meant not less than £2,000 *and* either exceeding £100,000 or 10 per cent of the company's net asset value: see s 320(2) of the 1985 Act. The onus of establishing that a non-cash asset or a series of non-cash assets is of the requisite value lies with the person invoking the section.

[339] See s 346 of the 1985 Act.

The purpose of the provisions is to avoid the company entering into arrangements and transactions   **10.0.08**
which might benefit the director(s) to the detriment of the company. It protects a company against
distortions of judgment caused by directors' conflicts of interest: see *British Racing Drivers' Club v
Hextall Erskine*.[340]

The most significant reforms effected by sections 190 to 196 are (i) the introduction of an ability to   **10.0.09**
enter into an arrangement which is conditional on the approval of the company's members (thereby
enacting a recommendation of the Law Commission);[341] and (ii) while raising the minimum value of
a relevant asset from £2,000 to £5,000, providing for the aggregation of non-cash assets to determine
whether the thresholds have been exceeded.[342]

### 190  Substantial property transactions: requirement of members' approval

(1)  A company may not enter into an arrangement under which—   **10.190.01**
   (a)  a director of the company or of its holding company, or a person connected with such a
        director, acquires or is to acquire from the company (directly or indirectly) a substantial
        non-cash asset, or
   (b)  the company acquires or is to acquire a substantial non-cash asset (directly or indirectly) from
        such a director or a person so connected,
   unless the arrangement has been approved by a resolution of the members of the company or is
   conditional on such approval being obtained.
   For the meaning of 'substantial non-cash asset' see section 191.
(2)  If the director or connected person is a director of the company's holding company or a person
     connected with such a director, the arrangement must also have been approved by a resolution
     of the members of the holding company or be conditional on such approval being obtained.
(3)  A company shall not be subject to any liability by reason of a failure to obtain approval required
     by this section.
(4)  No approval is required under this section on the part of the members of a body corporate that—
   (a)  is not a UK-registered company, or
   (b)  is a wholly-owned subsidiary of another body corporate.
(5)  For the purposes of this section—
   (a)  an arrangement involving more than one non-cash asset, or
   (b)  an arrangement that is one of a series involving non-cash assets,
   shall be treated as if they involved a non-cash asset of a value equal to the aggregate value of all the
   non-cash assets involved in the arrangement or, as the case may be, the series.
(6)  This section does not apply to a transaction so far as it relates—
   (a)  to anything to which a director of a company is entitled under his service contract, or
   (b)  to payment for loss of office as defined in section 215 (payments requiring members'
        approval).
COMMENCEMENT DATE  1 October 2007[343]

Section 190 imposes the basic requirement of shareholder approval in connection with substantial   **10.190.02**
property transactions.

Subsection (1) prohibits a company from entering into an 'arrangement'[344] under which a director[345]   **10.190.03**
of that company or of its holding company (or a person 'connected'[346] with such a director) acquires or
is to acquire from the company (whether directly or indirectly) a substantial[347] non-cash asset or under

---

[340]  [1997] BCLC 182, 198 per Carnwath J.
[341]  See 'Company Directors: Regulating Conflicts of Interests and Formulating a Statement of Duties' (Sept 1999) The Law Commission and Scottish Law Commission (Law Com 261 and Scot Law Com No 171) 10.10.
[342]  Where a company's equity shares are listed on the premium segment of the Official List maintained by the UK Listing Authority and it enters into a transaction or arrangement with a director out of the ordinary course of business it will, in addition to the requirements of the 2006 Act, need to consider Chapter 11 of the Listing Rules on related party transactions. Similarly, a company listed on the Alternative Investment Market (AIM) will need to have regard to the related party transaction provisions in rule 13 of the AIM rules.
[343]  The Companies Act 2006 (Commencement No 3, etc) Order 2007, SI 2007/2194, art 2.
[344]  'Arrangement' is not defined, but there is no reason to suppose that it bears anything other than the meaning attributed to it in the context of s 320 of the 1985 Act. Accordingly, these provisions are not limited to 'transactions', and include 'understandings' of no contractual effect: see *Re British Basic Slag Ltd's Agreements* [1963] 1 WLR 727, *Re Duckwari plc* [1999] Ch 253, and *Murray v Leisureplay plc* [2004] EWHC 1927 (QB), [106] (the latter decision went on appeal to the Court of Appeal but not in respect of this point, see *Murray v Leisureplay* [2005] EWCA Civ 963, [86]).
[345]  'Director' includes 'shadow director': see s 223(1).
[346]  See s 252.
[347]  See s 191.

which the company acquires or is to acquire such an asset from such a person unless[348] either the arrangement has been approved by a resolution of the company's members or is conditional on such approval being obtained.

10.190.04    The principal change effected by this subsection is the introduction of the ability to enter into an arrangement which is conditional on the approval of the company's members. This implements the recommendation of the Law Commission.[349] The purpose of this reform is to deal with the commercial disadvantage otherwise encountered by a company where the other party to the arrangement will or may not continue to remain willing to make the arrangement in the period before the passing of the proposed resolution. If a conditional arrangement is made, but approval is *not* given by the members, the company will incur no liability by reason of that failure: subsection (3).[350]

10.190.05    The subsection applies whether the acquisition was or will be 'direct' or 'indirect' (see also section 195(3)). Again, this is a new provision, echoing section 322 of the 1985 Act, and is clearly intended to expand the scope of the prohibition or at least to prevent its avoidance by the simple expedient of transferring an asset through an intermediary.

10.190.06    The meaning of 'acquisition' is defined at section 1163(2) to include (the definition is not exhaustive) the creation or extinction of an estate or interest in, or a right over, any property, and the discharge of a liability of any person, other than a liability for a liquidated sum. This definition is in terms identical to that previously contained in section 739 of the 1985 Act.[351]

10.190.07    'Non-cash asset' is defined at section 1163(1) to mean any property or interest in property, other than cash (which expressly includes foreign currency). The definition is in terms identical to that previously stated in section 739(1) of the 1985 Act, and therefore includes interests created by the arrangement in question and interests which come into existence after the arrangement in question but by the time of the acquisition: see *Ultraframe (UK) Limited v Fielding*[352] (in which it was held that the grant of a lease fell within section 320 of the 1985 Act, and that an exclusive licence to exploit a design right was a creation of a right over property and therefore similarly amounted to a non-cash asset for the purposes of that section 320), and *Micro Leisure Ltd v County Properties & Developments Ltd*,[353] in which Lord Hamilton held that the transfer of a share of the profits in a proposed development was a creation of an interest to the requisite value for the purposes of section 320.[354]

10.190.08    The subsection provides for the arrangement to be approved by or to be conditional upon a resolution of the members. Section 320(1) of the 1985 Act similarly provided for (prior) approval by resolution of the company in general meeting. In connection with section 320, it was held, by Park J in *NBH Ltd & NBH Group Ltd v Kevin Hoare & Others*,[355] that the informal approval[356] of a director as sole shareholder was sufficient (applying the principle in *Re Duomatic Ltd*)[357] to comply with the requirements of the section. There is no reason to suppose that the provisions of section 190 will not be similarly construed.[358]

10.190.09    Moreover, for the purposes of section 320 of the 1985 Act, the general meeting had to approve the central aspects, but not necessarily every detail of the arrangement: see *Demite Ltd v Protec Health*

---

[348] And see also s 196 which provides for the effect of a subsequent ratification within a reasonable period where there has been an arrangement made in breach of s 190.

[349] See The Law Commission Paper 153 and The Scottish Law Commission Discussion Paper No 105; 'Company Directors: Regulating Conflicts of Interests and Formulating a Statement of Duties. A Joint Consultation Paper' 4.192.

[350] The Explanatory Notes to the 2006 Act state that the effect of subs (3) is that the company will not be liable under the contract if approval is not forthcoming. However, more correctly, the subsection restricts liability under an 'arrangement' where shareholder approval is not obtained. As noted above, 'arrangement' is to be interpreted widely and it need not be of contractual effect.

[351] Which was itself derived from CA 1980, s 87(1) and (4)(b). See *Duckwari plc v Offerventure Ltd* [1997] 2 BCLC 713, where it was held for the purposes of s 320 of the 1985 Act that, despite there being no formal assignment, a company had 'acquired' the benefit of a contract.

[352] [2005] EWHC 1638 (Ch) [1369], [1373]–[1387], and [1390]–[1394].

[353] 1999 SLT 1307.

[354] The definition of 'non-cash asset' includes an assignment of a right (chose in action) under a pre-existing contract but does not cover property or interests in property which have been brought into existence by the arrangement itself.

[355] [2006] BCLC 649

[356] See also *Re Conegrade Ltd* [2002] EWHC 2411, where approval was given at a directors' meeting, and each of the members was also a director.

[357] [1969] 2 Ch 365.

[358] See also Chapter 2 of Part 13 which provides for written resolutions to be passed by private companies without the need for a meeting, and see also s 281(4).

*Ltd*,[359] where Park J said that in the case of an acquisition by sale, one such feature would be the price, or possibly the minimum price, or at least a yardstick by which the price would be fixed. Park J stressed the importance of the congruence between the nature of the transaction which takes place and the description of the transaction approved by the shareholders. Once more, there is no reason to suppose that the requirements of section 190 will be differently understood.

Subsection (2) provides (in common with its predecessor, section 320(1) of the 1985 Act) that if the director or connected person is a director of the company's holding company, or is a person connected with such a director, the arrangement must also be approved by the holding company's members, or be conditional on their approval. **10.190.10**

Subsection (4) provides that approval under section 190(1) or (2) is not required by non-UK registered companies or by companies which are wholly-owned subsidiaries of another body corporate. This provision is of similar effect to section 321(1) of the 1985 Act which stated that approval under section 320 was not required *unless* the body corporate was a company within the meaning of the 1985 Act or was registered under section 680, and was not in any event required if the company was a wholly-owned subsidiary of any body corporate, wherever located (in which case, the parent was taken to have or to be able to exercise adequate control over its subsidiary). **10.190.11**

Subsection (5) is new to the 2006 Act. It provides for the aggregation of non-cash assets where either the arrangement itself involves or is one of a 'series' of arrangements that involves more than one non-cash asset. In such a case, the arrangement will be treated as if it involved a single non-cash asset of a value equal to the aggregate value of all the non-cash assets involved in the arrangement or series. The obvious points of difficulty in the application of this provision will concern the meaning of a 'series of arrangements' and the characterization of an event involving more than one asset as nonetheless comprising for these purposes a single 'arrangement'. The answer is likely to lie in a proper understanding of the purpose of section 190(1) and (2):[360] subsection (5) appears to be intended to prevent the avoidance of the section's basic purpose by restructuring an arrangement involving the acquisition of an asset as either (i) an arrangement involving the acquisition of a number of assets, or (ii) a number of connected arrangements intended ultimately to achieve the same or substantially the same effect as could have been achieved in a single step. **10.190.12**

Subsection (6) is new to the 2006 Act, and enacts a recommendation of the Law Commission.[361] It excludes from the regime 'transactions'[362] insofar as they relate to anything to which a director is entitled under his service contract[363] or to payment for loss of office[364] as defined at section 215 (which in any event requires member approval: see section 217). Under the 1985 Act, neither the discharge by a company of its own liability for damages for breach of a director's service contract (see *Gooding v Carter*[365]) nor covenanted payments made by the company under such a contract, for example by way of 'golden parachute' payment (see *Lander v Pict Petroleum Ltd*,[366] where payment was held to comprise the acquisition of a cash asset) fell within the scope of section 320. **10.190.13**

## 191  Meaning of 'substantial'

(1) This section explains what is meant in section 190 (requirement of approval for substantial property transactions) by a 'substantial' non-cash asset. **10.191.01**

(2) An asset is a substantial asset in relation to a company if its value—

   (a) exceeds 10% of the company's asset value and is more than £5,000, or

   (b) exceeds £100,000.

(3) For this purpose a company's 'asset value' at any time is—

---

[1998] BCC 638, 649E.

[360] As to which, see *British Racing Drivers' Club v Hextall Erskine* [1997] 1 BCLC 182, 198.

[361] 'Company Directors: Regulating Conflicts of Interests and Formulating a Statement of Duties' (September 1999) The Law Commission and Scottish Law Commission (Law Com 261 and Scot Law Com No 171) 10.13. See also The Law Commission Consultation Paper 153 and The Scottish Law Commission Discussion Paper No 105: 'Company Directors: Regulating Conflicts of Interests and Formulating a Statement of Duties. A Joint Consultation Paper' 4.193.

[362] It is not obvious why this exemption does not relate to 'arrangements'. If strictly construed, the subsection as enacted will not apply to an event properly described as an 'arrangement' but not as a 'transaction'. Presumably the Government did not intend to make a distinction between the two expressions and they can be applied *mutatis mutandis*. See also s 192.

[363] As defined at s 227 for the purposes of Part 10 of the 2006 Act.

[364] Note s 223(2): loss of office does not include loss of status as a shadow director.

[365] (Unreported) 13 March 1989.

[366] [1998] 2 BCC 248.

    (a)  the value of the company's net assets determined by reference to its most recent statutory accounts, or

    (b)  if no statutory accounts have been prepared, the amount of the company's called-up share capital.

  (4)  A company's 'statutory accounts' means its annual accounts prepared in accordance with Part 15, and its 'most recent' statutory accounts means those in relation to which the time for sending them out to members (see section 424) is most recent.

  (5)  Whether an asset is a substantial asset shall be determined as at the time the arrangement is entered into.

COMMENCEMENT DATE 1 October 2007[367]

**10.191.02**   This section explains what is meant in section 190 by 'substantial' in connection with the term 'substantial non-cash asset'. In effect, it replaces the provisions of section 320(2) of the 1985 Act.

**10.191.03**   By subsection (2), an asset is 'substantial' if its value either (i) exceeds 10 per cent of the company's asset value *and* is more than £5,000, or (ii) it exceeds £100,000. Under the 1985 Act, the asset was of the requisite value if its value was not less than £2,000 and it either exceeded £100,000 or 10 per cent of the company's asset value. In this regard, the effect of the 2006 Act is therefore to increase the *de minimis* threshold by £3,000.

**10.191.04**   Subsection (3) defines the company's 'asset value' at any given time as the value of its net assets by reference to its most recent statutory accounts, or, if no such accounts have been prepared, the amount of its called-up share capital. The company's 'statutory accounts' are defined at subsection (4) to mean annual accounts prepared in accordance with Part 15, and 'most recent' statutory accounts as those in relation to which the time for sending them out to members is most recent. This substantially re-enacts the provisions of section 320(2) of the 1985 Act. Difficult issues of valuation (and of the appropriate basis of valuation) will inevitably arise. For example, in *Ultraframe (UK) Ltd v Fielding*[368] Lewison J held that on the grant of a debenture, the company parts with nothing of value, and that the consideration it receives (since it cannot be valued in money or money's worth) cannot be a non-cash asset of the requisite value. However, he also held[369] that where a charged asset is sold, the equity of redemption is the relevant asset, and can be valued for the purposes of the statutory regime.

**10.191.05**   Subsection (5) requires that the value of the asset be determined 'as at the time' the arrangement is made. This was not a new provision (see section 320(2) of the 1985 Act and *Ultraframe (UK) Ltd v Fielding*).[370] Its rationale is that member approval is to be given once only, at the outset. The inevitable effect is that if it is impossible to tell, at the inception, when the arrangement is entered into, whether the arrangement will one day involve the acquisition of a substantial non-cash asset, then it will not fall within the section, and approval will not be required.[371] Note, however, as discussed below in connection with section 195, that in the assessment of losses for which liability might be imposed, depreciation in value as a result of market fluctuation *subsequent* to the arrangement can be relevant: see *Re Duckwari plc*.[372]

### 192 Exception for transactions with members or other group companies

**10.192.01**   Approval is not required under section 190 (requirement of members' approval for substantial property transactions)—

    (a)  for a transaction between a company and a person in his character as a member of that company, or

    (b)  for a transaction between—

       (i)  a holding company and its wholly-owned subsidiary, or

      (ii)  two wholly-owned subsidiaries of the same holding company.

COMMENCEMENT DATE 1 October 2007[373]

---

[367] Companies Act 2006 (Commencement No 3, etc) Order 2007, SI 2007/2194, art 2.

[368] [2005] EWHC 1638 (Ch), [1388]–[1389] (relying on *Re MC Bacon Ltd* [1990] BCLC 324, 339 which concerned the provisions of s 238 of the Insolvency Act 1986).

[369] [2005] EWHC 1638 (Ch), [1388]-[1389], [1408]–[1410].

[370] [2005] EWHC 1638 (Ch), [1392].

[371] See also *Lander v Premier Pict Petroleum Ltd* [1998] BCC 248 where it was held that if the 'non-cash asset' is not capable of valuation at the time the arrangement is entered into, it would not be possible to ascertain whether the arrangement is of the requisite value within what was CA 1985, s 320 and hence that section did not apply.

[372] [1999] Ch 253.

[373] Companies Act 2006 (Commencement No 3, etc) Order 2007, SI 2007/2194, art 2.

Under this section, approval is not required for 'transactions'[374] between a company and a person 'in   **10.192.02**
his character as' a member of the company (rather than as a director or person connected with a
director) or between a holding company and its wholly-owned subsidiary or two wholly-owned
subsidiaries of the same holding company (this appears to have been enacted because otherwise section
252 might cause one group company to be a person connected with the director of the other group
company and thus come within the scope of the regime, but in any event, see section 190(4)(b) which
on its face appears to be wide enough to deal with the point).

This section effectively re-enacts section 320(2)(a) and (3) of the 1985 Act. Thus, for example, the   **10.192.03**
payment of a dividend *in specie* will not fall within the scope of the regime. It will of course in most cases
be very difficult to demonstrate that an arrangement was entered into by the director in his character
as a member.

### 193  Exception in case of company in winding up or administration

(1)  This section applies to a company—                                                              **10.193.01**
    (a)  that is being wound up (unless the winding up is a members' voluntary winding up), or
    (b)  that is in administration within the meaning of Schedule B1 to the Insolvency Act 1986 (c. 45)
        or the Insolvency (Northern Ireland) Order 1989 (SI 1989/2405 (N.I. 19)).
(2)  Approval is not required under section 190 (requirement of members' approval for substantial
    property transactions)—
    (a)  on the part of the members of a company to which this section applies, or
    (b)  for an arrangement entered into by a company to which this section applies.

COMMENCEMENT DATE 1 October 2007[375]

This section re-enacts section 321(2)(b) in respect of companies in liquidation (other than members'   **10.193.02**
voluntary liquidation)[376] and adds a new provision, on the recommendation of the Law Commission,
which concluded that the conflict of interest ordinarily faced by directors does not arise when an
administrator contracts on behalf of the company.[377] The Law Commission also recommended
expanding a qualified exception to cover administrative receivers[378] enabling them to apply to the
court for approval or for some other substantial reason.[379]

### 194  Exception for transactions on recognised investment exchange

(1)  Approval is not required under section 190 (requirement of members' approval for substantial   **10.194.01**
    property transactions) for a transaction on a recognised investment exchange effected by a
    director, or a person connected with him, through the agency of a person who in relation to the
    transaction acts as an independent broker.
(2)  For this purpose—
    (a)  'independent broker' means a person who, independently of the director or any person
        connected with him, selects the person with whom the transaction is to be effected; and
    (b)  'recognised investment exchange' has the same meaning as in Part 18 of the Financial
        Services and Markets Act 2000 (c. 8).

COMMENCEMENT DATE 1 October 2007[380]

---

[374]  As with s 190(6) 'transaction' rather than the wider expression 'arrangement' has been used. Presumably,
it is not intended to make a distinction. See also s 321(2)(a) and (3) of the 1985 Act which in the context of the
same exception as previously enacted used the expression 'arrangement', consistently with s 320.

[375]  Companies Act 2006 (Commencement No 3, etc) Order 2007, SI 2007/2194, art 2.

[376]  See *Walker v W A Personnel Ltd* [2002] BPIR 621 in which the application of what was s 320 of the 1985 Act
was contested in the circumstances in which a company was insolvent. For further discussion see Goddard, 'The
Duomatic Principle and ss 320–322 of the Companies Act' [2004] JBL 121.

[377]  'Company Directors: Regulating Conflicts of Interests and Formulating a Statement of Duties' (September
1999) The Law Commission and Scottish Law Commission (Law Com 261 and Scot Law Com No 171)
10.17–10.19. See also *Hansard* HL Report Stage vol 681 (2 May 2006).

[378]  The proposal to include administrative receivers within the statutory exception was discussed in the House
of Lords (in its legislative capacity) and it was rejected on the basis of representations from Margaret Hodge MP
to the effect that it may be subject to abuse in circumstances where an administrative receiver, who in the case of
an LPA receiver need not necessarily be a licensed Insolvency Practitioner, is appointed by a director or a
connected person. See *Hansard*, HL, Pt II, col 632 (11 July 2006).

[379]  This was recommended to address a concern raised by *Demite Limited v Protec Health Limited* [1998] BCC
638, in which the court held that a company in liquidation could invoke s 320 of the 1985 Act to invalidate a sale
entered into with a company connected to one of its directors by an administrative receiver prior to liquidation.

[380]  Companies Act 2006 (Commencement No 3, etc) Order 2007, SI 2007/2194, art 2.

**10.194.02**    This section excepts from the requirements of section 190 'transactions'[381] on a 'recognised investment exchange' effected through the agency of a person acting as an 'independent broker'.

**10.194.03**    Subsection (2) defines 'recognised investment exchange' and 'independent broker'.

**10.194.04**    In effect this section re-enacts section 321(4) of the 1985 Act. Its purpose is to preserve transactions which came about through the decision of an independent broker and thus does not raise the conflict at which the requirements of section 190(1) and (2) are aimed.

### 195 Property transactions: civil consequences of contravention

**10.195.01**

(1) This section applies where a company enters into an arrangement in contravention of section 190 (requirement of members' approval for substantial property transactions).

(2) The arrangement, and any transaction entered into in pursuance of the arrangement (whether by the company or any other person), is voidable at the instance of the company, unless—

   (a) restitution of any money or other asset that was the subject matter of the arrangement or transaction is no longer possible,

   (b) the company has been indemnified in pursuance of this section by any other persons for the loss or damage suffered by it, or

   (c) rights acquired in good faith, for value and without actual notice of the contravention by a person who is not a party to the arrangement or transaction would be affected by the avoidance.

(3) Whether or not the arrangement or any such transaction has been avoided, each of the persons specified in subsection (4) is liable—

   (a) to account to the company for any gain that he has made directly or indirectly by the arrangement or transaction, and

   (b) (jointly and severally with any other person so liable under this section) to indemnify the company for any loss or damage resulting from the arrangement or transaction.

(4) The persons so liable are—

   (a) any director of the company or of its holding company with whom the company entered into the arrangement in contravention of section 190,

   (b) any person with whom the company entered into the arrangement in contravention of that section who is connected with a director of the company or of its holding company,

   (c) the director of the company or of its holding company with whom any such person is connected, and

   (d) any other director of the company who authorised the arrangement or any transaction entered into in pursuance of such an arrangement.

(5) Subsections (3) and (4) are subject to the following two subsections.

(6) In the case of an arrangement entered into by a company in contravention of section 190 with a person connected with a director of the company or of its holding company, that director is not liable by virtue of subsection (4)(c) if he shows that he took all reasonable steps to secure the company's compliance with that section.

(7) In any case—

   (a) a person so connected is not liable by virtue of subsection (4)(b), and

   (b) a director is not liable by virtue of subsection (4)(d),

   if he shows that, at the time the arrangement was entered into, he did not know the relevant circumstances constituting the contravention.

(8) Nothing in this section shall be read as excluding the operation of any other enactment or rule of law by virtue of which the arrangement or transaction may be called in question or any liability to the company may arise.

COMMENCEMENT DATE 1 October 2007[382]

**10.195.02**    Section 195 states the civil liabilities which arise from a breach of section 190. In substance, subject to one point,[383] it re-enacts section 322 of the 1985 Act, and the 2006 Act has not changed the pre-existing law.

**10.195.03**    First, and most significantly, by subsection (2), subject to exceptions,[384] the 'arrangement'[385] (and any 'transaction'[386] entered into in pursuance of the arrangement) is voidable at the instance of the

---

[381] As in respect of s 190(6) it is not clear why this rather than the wider expression 'arrangement' has been used. Presumably, it is not intended to make a distinction. However, see also s 321(4) of the 1985 Act which in the context of the same exception as previously enacted also used the expression 'transaction'.

[382] Companies Act 2006 (Commencement No 3, etc) Order 2007, SI 2007/2194, art 2.

[383] As to which, see the discussion in respect of subs (7) below.

[384] The court otherwise appears not to have discretion: *Demite Ltd v Protec Health Ltd* [1988] BCC 638, 650C.

[385] To be understood, presumably, in the expanded sense provided for at s 190(5)(b).

[386] To be understood, presumably, as an expression less wide than 'arrangement'.

company. If rescinded it would appear to be avoided as against all parties.[387] However, it is neither void *ab initio* (*Guinness v Saunders*)[388] nor illegal (*Niltan Carson Ltd v Hawthorne*),[389] although following rescission, the company may retain (or thereby acquire) an equitable title sufficient to found a tracing claim: see *El Ajou v Dollar Land Holdings plc*[390] and section 196(8).

Subsection (2) also contains an exhaustive[391] list of the bars to rescission. They are as follows.          **10.195.04**

First, that restitution is impossible: subsection (2)(a). However, what is possible need not be 'perfect'          **10.195.05**
restitution: *Ultraframe (UK) Ltd v Fielding & Others*.[392]

Secondly, that pursuant to section 190,[393] the company has been indemnified for any loss or damage:          **10.195.06**
subsection (2)(b). This provision would only make sense if the indemnity would place the company in
the position equivalent to that which it would have been in if rescission had been ordered.[394]

Thirdly, that rights acquired in good faith for value without actual (rather than constructive or          **10.195.07**
imputed) notice by a third party would be affected by rescission.

By subsections (3) and (4), subject to subsections (5), (6) and (7), but regardless of rescission, specified          **10.195.08**
persons are liable to account to the company for any gain made whether directly or indirectly by the
arrangement or transaction, and to indemnify the company for resultant loss or damage.

Those specified (by subsection(4)) are the director of the company or holding company with whom the          **10.195.09**
arrangement was made, or the connected person with whom the arrangement was made, or the
director with whom that connected person was connected, or any other director who authorized the
arrangement or transaction made pursuant to that arrangement.

The identification and quantification of (i) a relevant 'gain' whether made 'directly or indirectly' 'by'          **10.195.10**
the arrangement or transaction, or (ii) any relevant 'loss or damage' 'resulting from' the arrangement
or transaction have not always been straightforward, and the proper construction of these provisions
has become confused: see for example, *NBH Ltd v Hoare and Others*[395] and *Re Duckwari plc*,[396] which
among other things considered the impact of changes in value caused by fluctuations in the market. In
the former, Park J held that a 'gain' made in consequence of an increase in the value of the asset before
the sale of that asset to the company, was not a gain made by the director 'by' the arrangement for the
purposes of section 320 of the 1985 Act. On a sale, for the purposes of these provisions, he held that the
relevant gain is the amount by which the price exceeds the value of the asset. However, he also accepted
that the identification of a *loss* 'resulting from' (as opposed to 'by') an arrangement might be different:
he cited *Re Duckwari plc* in which the Court of Appeal (drawing an analogy with remedies for breach
of fiduciary duty and the misapplication of funds by a trustee) had assessed the extent of the indemnity
*as at the time of judgment*, and had thus taken account of a decrease in the value of the asset *subsequent*
to its transfer to the company in calculating the company's loss. He attributed the different approach to
the difference between the expressions 'by' and 'resulting from'.

However, in the identification of a relevant gain, although the expression 'by' was held by Park J to be          **10.195.11**
narrower than the expression 'resulting from', the court must also consider the meaning of the
qualification 'directly or indirectly', the effect of which is, presumably, to expand the scope of the
indemnity. Difficulty is most likely to arise in the identification of gains said to have been made
'indirectly' by the arrangement. In *Murray v Leisureplay plc*,[397] Stanley Burnton J said (in connection
with the 1985 Act) that the words indicated that Parliament had intended to 'cast its net wide', although,
equally, the provision required that the gain be made or received 'immediately on the making of' the
arrangement. In the same case, in the Court of Appeal,[398] it was held that there is a contrast between

---

[387]  Compare s 41(6) which provides for affirmation, setting aside or severance by the court on terms, which
might include avoidance against some but not all parties.
[388]  [1990] 2 AC 663, 698E.
[389]  [1988] BCLC 298, 322.
[390]  [1993] 3 All ER 717, 743d–e (and [1994] 2 All ER 685).
[391]  See *Demite Ltd v Protec Health Ltd* [1988] BCC 638, 650C–D, but see also s 196 which now contains that
which was previously at s 322(2)(c).
[392]  [2005] EWHC 1638 (Ch), [1424] *per* Lewison J.
[393]  On the wording it is clear that the company is barred from seeking the primary remedy of rescission where
it has already been indemnified under s 195(3) against any loss or damage suffered. This suggests that the
company is not barred from seeking rescission where it has been indemnified pursuant to a right other than
under this section.
[394]  Per Nourse J, *Re Duckwari plc (No 1)* [1997] BCLC 713.
[395]  [2006] EWHC 73, [44]–[49].
[396]  [1999] Ch 253.
[397]  [2004] EWHC 1927, [110].
[398]  At [2005] EWCA Civ 963, [98].

'directly or indirectly by' and 'resulting from' and that the court was bound by the decision in *Re Duckwari (No 2)*[399] that indirect losses were not losses 'resulting from' an arrangement.

**10.195.12**    By subsection (6), where an arrangement is made with a person connected with a director of the company or its holding company, the director is not liable to account or indemnify if he can show that he took 'all reasonable steps' to secure the company's compliance with the provisions of section 190. This replaces section 322(5) of the 1985 Act, and its application will depend on the facts and circumstances, including the particular role of the director within the management structure of the company, and his knowledge of the arrangement.[400] This provision has no effect on the ability of the company to rescind the arrangement.

**10.195.13**    Further, by subsection (7): (i) where an arrangement is made with a person connected with a director of the company or its holding company, that person will avoid liability if he can show that *at the time* when the arrangement was made he did not know the relevant circumstances constituting the contravention; and (ii) similarly, any director who authorized a contravening arrangement or transaction made pursuant to such an arrangement will avoid liability if he can show that *at the time* when the arrangement was made he did not know the relevant circumstances constituting the contravention. Again, this will be a question of fact. It is clearly not enough to be ignorant of the provisions of the Act. What is required is ignorance of some fact necessary to establish the breach. Neither does the subsection limit the exemption by reference to facts which, for example, ought to have been known or could have been discovered.[401] If the defendant establishes his ignorance as a fact, he will avoid liability. On the face of the statute, if a director is ignorant of the facts at the time of the arrangement, but comes to learn of them before a subsequent transaction made by the company on his authority but pursuant to that 'arrangement', he will nonetheless escape liability.

**10.195.14**    There appears to be no exemption based on ignorance of the relevant facts for either a director with whom the contravening arrangement is made or a director otherwise liable by virtue of his connection with the person with whom the arrangement was made, although in the latter case subsection (6) might provide a defence. This would seem to have narrowed the defence as previously expressed, at section 322(6), which conferred the defence on 'any such other director as is mentioned in subsection (3)'. The retention of the introductory words, 'in any case' (found in both section 322(6) of the 1985 Act and section 195(7) of the 2006 Act) suggests that this change might not have been intended.

**10.195.15**    Finally, by subsection (8), none of the statutory remedies or consequences otherwise arising is excluded by the provisions of section 195. This might be significant: it might, for example, permit a company to argue that it has proprietary rights to trace into the product of a transferred asset.

## 196  Property transactions: effect of subsequent affirmation

**10.196.01**    Where a transaction or arrangement is entered into by a company in contravention of section 190 (requirement of members' approval) but, within a reasonable period, it is affirmed—

    (a)  in the case of a contravention of subsection (1) of that section, by resolution of the members of the company, and

    (b)  in the case of a contravention of subsection (2) of that section, by resolution of the members of the holding company, the transaction or arrangement may no longer be avoided under section 195.

COMMENCEMENT DATE  1 October 2007[402]

**10.196.02**    By this section (which substantially re-enacts section 322(2)(c)) subsequent affirmation within a reasonable time by resolution of the company's or holding company's members as appropriate will avoid any right to rescind. It has no effect on other remedies. There does not appear to be any reason why the resolution need be passed at a meeting formally held, rather than by means of informal unanimous consent or by means of the procedure for written resolutions: see also *NBH Ltd & NBH*

---

[399] [1999] Ch 268.

[400] See *Lexi Holdings (In Administration) v Monuza Akthar Luqman, Zaurian Parveen Luqman* [2008] EWHC 1639 in which Briggs J held that directors will not be exempt from liability under s 320 if they simply do nothing when a fellow director is breaching his or her duties as director and they knew or should have known of the breach. This position was affirmed by the Court of Appeal in *Lexi Holdings (In Administration) v Monuza Akthar Luqman, Zaurian Parveen Luqman* [2009] EWCA CIV 117, [2009] BCC 716, in which it was held that had the directors been discharging their functions correctly, the company would not have suffered losses. The directors were therefore liable to compensate the company.

[401] Again see *Lexi Holdings (In Administration) v Monuza Akthar Luqman, Zaurian Parveen Luqman* [2009] EWCA Civ 117, [2009] BCC 716.

[402] Companies Act 2006 (Commencement No 3, etc) Order 2007, SI 2007/2194, art 2.

*Group Ltd v Kevin Hoare & Others*,[403] in which it was held, by Park J, that the informal (prior) approval[404] of a director as sole shareholder was sufficient to comply with the requirements of section 320(1) of the 1985 Act. Note also that section 196 makes no reference to approval at a 'general meeting', and is in that respect different from section 322(2)(c) of the 1985 Act. In any case, it is thought that to be an effective affirmation, the members will need to be fully informed of the relevant facts.[405]

## Loans, quasi-loans and credit transactions

Sections 197 to 214 replace the provisions regulating loans and quasi-loans to directors formerly contained in the 1985 Act, sections 330 to 342. The basic statutory prohibition preventing a company, subject to exceptions, making a loan to its directors (or to directors of its holding company) was first introduced in 1947, following the recommendations of the Cohen Committee.[406] The reason underlying the prohibition was identified by the Law Commission[407] as being 'to protect creditors and minority shareholders from the depletion in corporate assets through the making of loans, which if they were being made on arm's length terms, could usually be raised from third parties'. The Jenkins Committee, which reported in 1962, took a similar view to that of the Cohen Committee. It recommended that the provisions be extended to prohibit loans by a company to another company in which one or more directors of the lending company held, singly or collectively, and whether directly or indirectly, a controlling interest.[408] Following a number of corporate scandals at the end of the 1970s, the Companies Act (1980) created extensive further controls on loans and similar transactions between a company and its directors. The regime as consolidated into the Companies Act (1985) contained four main elements: (i) prohibitions; (ii) exemptions; (iii) civil remedies; and (iv) criminal penalties. The provisions applied differently to different types of company. The Law Commission described the result as 'complex and inaccessible'. The Company Law Review Steering Group concluded that (a) there was insufficient support for the general repeal or replacement of the prohibitions with disclosure obligations; (b) that certain restrictions applicable only to 'relevant companies' (that is public companies and their associates), should be extended to all companies; (c) that the monetary limits for certain exceptions should be raised; (d) that there should be a new exception for transactions approved by the company in general meeting; and (e) that attention should be given to simplifying the drafting of the relevant prohibitions and their exceptions.[409]                                                         **10.0.10**

The main changes in fact made by the Companies Act 2006 are (i) to limit the prohibition to cases   **10.0.11**
where members' consent has not been obtained; (ii) to abolish criminal penalties; and (iii) to widen the previous exemptions. There still remain separate regimes for private and public companies.[410]

## 197  Loans to directors: requirement of members' approval

(1)  A company may not—                                                                          **10.197.01**
   (a)  make a loan to a director of the company or of its holding company, or
   (b)  give a guarantee or provide security in connection with a loan made by any person to such a
        director,
   unless the transaction has been approved by a resolution of the members of the company.
(2)  If the director is a director of the company's holding company, the transaction must also have been
     approved by a resolution of the members of the holding company.

---

[403]  [2006] BCLC 649.

[404]  See also *Re Conegrade Ltd* [2002] EWHC 2411, where approval was given at a directors' meeting, and each of the members was also a director.

[405]  See *Euro Brokers Holdings Ltd v Monecor (London) Ltd* [2003] EWCA Civ 105; [2003] BCC 573 [2003]; 1 BCLC 506 in which it was held that if all members reach an agreement they cannot say they are not bound by it because formal procedures were not followed.

[406]  See the Report of the Committee on Company Law Amendment (June 1945) Cmnd 6659.

[407]  See The Law Commission, Consultation Paper 153 and The Scottish Law Commission Discussion Paper No 105: 'Company Directors: Regulating Conflicts of Interests and Formulating a Statement of Duties. A Joint Consultation Paper', Part 6.

[408]  Report of the Company Law Committee (June 1962) (Cmnd 1749).

[409]  The Company Law Review Steering Group 'Modern Company Law for a Competitive Economy' in: 'Developing the Framework' (March 2000), paras 28–30; 'Completing the Structure' (Nov 2000) (para 4.21); and 'Final Report' (June 2001) paras 6.15–6.16.

[410]  Where a company's equity shares are listed on the premium segment of the Official List maintained by the UK Listing Authority and it enters into a transaction or arrangement with a director out of the ordinary course of business it will, in addition to the requirements of the 2006 Act, need to consider Chapter 11 of the Listing Rules on related party transactions. Similarly, a company listed on the Alternative Investment Market (AIM) will need to have regard to the related party transaction provisions in rule 13 of the AIM rules.

(3) A resolution approving a transaction to which this section applies must not be passed unless a memorandum setting out the matters mentioned in subsection (4) is made available to members—

    (a) in the case of a written resolution, by being sent or submitted to every eligible member at or before the time at which the proposed resolution is sent or submitted to him;

    (b) in the case of a resolution at a meeting, by being made available for inspection by members of the company both—

        (i) at the company's registered office for not less than 15 days ending with the date of the meeting, and

        (ii) at the meeting itself.

(4) The matters to be disclosed are—

    (a) the nature of the transaction,

    (b) the amount of the loan and the purpose for which it is required, and

    (c) the extent of the company's liability under any transaction connected with the loan.

(5) No approval is required under this section on the part of the members of a body corporate that—

    (a) is not a UK-registered company, or

    (b) is a wholly-owned subsidiary of another body corporate.

COMMENCEMENT DATE 1 October 2007.[411]

**10.197.02**   The prohibition contained in this section is that a company, whether public or private, may not (i) provide a loan[412] to any of its directors[413] nor to any director of its holding company;[414] nor (ii) give a guarantee or provide any security in respect of any loan made to any of its directors or any director of its holding company, unless the transaction has first been approved by a resolution of members (subsection (1)). Where the director concerned is also a director of a holding company, there is an additional requirement that the transaction be approved by a resolution of members of the holding company (subsection (2)). The requirement to obtain approval of its members does not apply to any company which is not a UK-registered company, nor to any company which is a wholly-owned subsidiary of another body corporate (subsection (6)). The prohibition which applies to public companies (or companies associated with such companies) regarding loans made to persons connected with directors is now contained in section 200. Section 203 sets out a related prohibition. There are a number of specific exceptions to the general prohibition contained in section 197. These are contained in sections 204 to 209.

**10.197.03**   Approval of members is obtained by a resolution which may be passed either at a meeting or by way of written resolution, following disclosure of certain required matters by way of written memorandum (subsections (1), (3) and (4)). The matters which must be disclosed are: (a) the nature of the transaction; (b) the amount of the loan and the purpose for which it is required; and (c) the extent of the company's liability under any transaction connected with the loan (subsection (4)).[415] It appears that the disclosure to members of the holding company required by the section is solely disclosure of the subsidiary company's liability under any transaction connected with the loan rather than also, or alternatively, requiring disclosure of any liability of the holding company under any such connected transaction. It is suggested that in practice both will have to be disclosed to the members of the holding company.[416] In the case of a written resolution, the written memorandum containing the disclosed matters must be sent or submitted to every eligible member before or at the same time as the written resolution is sent or submitted to him.[417] In the case of a resolution at a meeting, the written memorandum containing the prescribed matters must be made available for inspection by members of the company both (i) at the company's registered office for a period of not less than 15 days ending with the date of the meeting, and (ii) at the meeting itself (subsection (3)).

---

[411] Companies Act 2006 (Commencement No 3, Consequential Amendments, Transitional Provisions and Savings) Order 2007 SI 2007/2194, art 2.

[412] The word 'loan' would appear to be limited to a situation where a company advances money on terms that it is to be repaid in money or money's worth. In *Champagne Perrier-Jouet SA v Finch* [1982] 1 WLR 1359 it was said that a company which had paid director's bills and supplied goods, on credit, to a company that he controlled had not made a 'loan' to him, within the meaning of the relevant articles of association of the company in question. The judge held that the same meaning would be applied to the word 'loan' in the statutory predecessor of what is now s 197.

[413] For the purposes of this section, a shadow director is treated as a director: see s 223.

[414] 'Holding company' is defined in s 1159.

[415] Note that in comparison to the requirements under s 337 of the 1985 Act the company is also required to disclose the nature of the transaction (s 197(4)(a)).

[416] As regards 'accidental failure to send memorandum': see s 224.

[417] Note a similar provision at s 203(3).

The direct statutory consequences of breach of the section are set out in section 213. The consequences   **10.197.04**
are civil only. In broad terms, the transaction may be voidable and certain persons are liable to account
for any gains or to indemnify the company against any losses. Where a valid resolution approving the
transaction has not been obtained in time, the transaction may be affirmed within a reasonable time by
a subsequent resolution or resolutions. If approval is retrospectively given in this manner the transaction may no longer be avoided, but any liability to account for gains or indemnify against losses
remains (see section 214).

## 198  Quasi-loans to directors: requirement of members' approval

    (1)  This section applies to a company if it is—          **10.198.01**
        (a)  a public company, or
        (b)  a company associated with a public company.
    (2)  A company to which this section applies may not—
        (a)  make a quasi-loan to a director of the company or of its holding company, or
        (b)  give a guarantee or provide security in connection with a quasi-loan made by any person to
            such a director,
       unless the transaction has been approved by a resolution of the members of the company.
    (3)  If the director is a director of the company's holding company, the transaction must also have been
       approved by a resolution of the members of the holding company.
    (4)  A resolution approving a transaction to which this section applies must not be passed unless a
       memorandum setting out the matters mentioned in subsection (5) is made available to
       members—
        (a)  in the case of a written resolution, by being sent or submitted to every eligible member at or
            before the time at which the proposed resolution is sent or submitted to him;
        (b)  in the case of a resolution at a meeting, by being made available for inspection by members
            of the company both—
            (i)  at the company's registered office for not less than 15 days ending with the date of the
               meeting, and
            (ii)  at the meeting itself.
    (5)  The matters to be disclosed are—
        (a)  the nature of the transaction,
        (b)  the amount of the quasi-loan and the purpose for which it is required, and
        (c)  the extent of the company's liability under any transaction connected with the quasi-loan.
    (6)  No approval is required under this section on the part of the members of a body corporate that—
        (a)  is not a UK-registered company, or
        (b)  is a wholly-owned subsidiary of another body corporate.

    COMMENCEMENT DATE 1 October 2007.[418]

The prohibition contained in this section is that a public company, or a company associated with such   **10.198.02**
a company,[419] may not (i) make a quasi-loan[420] to any of its directors[421] nor to any director of its
holding company;[422] nor (ii) give a guarantee or provide any security in connection with any quasi-
loan made by any person to such a director, unless the transaction has first been approved by a
resolution of members (subsection (2)). Where the director concerned is also a director of a holding
company, there is an additional requirement that the transaction is approved by a resolution of
members of the holding company (subsection (2)). The requirement to obtain approval of its members
does not apply to any company which is not a UK-registered company nor to any company which is a
wholly-owned subsidiary of another body corporate (subsection (6)). The prohibition regarding
quasi-loans made to persons connected with directors is now contained in section 200. Section 203 sets
out a related prohibition.

There are a number of specific exceptions to the general prohibition contained in section 198. These   **10.198.03**
are contained in sections 204 to 209.

Approval of members is obtained by a resolution which may be passed either at a meeting or by way of   **10.198.04**
written resolution, following disclosure of certain required matters by way of written memorandum
(subsections (1), (3) and (4)).

---

[418]  Companies Act 2006 (Commencement No 3, Consequential Amendments, Transitional Provisions and
Savings) Order 2007 SI 2007/2194, art 2.
[419]  As to the meaning of a company 'associated' with another: see s 256(b).
[420]  'Quasi-loan' is defined in s 199.
[421]  For the purposes of this section, a shadow director is treated as a director: see s 223.
[422]  'Holding company' is defined in s 1159.

**10.198.05** The matters which must be disclosed[423] to members are:

(i) the nature of the transaction;
(ii) the amount of the quasi-loan and the purpose for which it is required; and
(iii) the extent of the company's liability under any transaction connected with the quasi-loan (subsection (4)).

It appears that the disclosure to members of the holding company required by subsection (5) is solely disclosure of the subsidiary company's liability under any transaction connected with the quasi-loan rather than also, or alternatively, requiring disclosure of any liability of the holding company under any such connected transaction. It is suggested that in practice both will have to be disclosed to the members of the holding company.[424] In the case of a written resolution, the written memorandum containing the disclosed matters must be sent or submitted to every eligible member before or at the same time as the written resolution is sent or submitted to him.[425] In the case of a resolution at a meeting, the written memorandum containing the prescribed matters must be made available for inspection by members of the company both at the company's registered office for a period of not less than 15 days ending with the date of the meeting and at the meeting itself (subsection (3)).

**10.198.06** The direct statutory consequences of breach of the section are set out in section 213. The consequences are civil only. In broad terms, the transaction may be voidable and certain persons are liable to account for any gains or to indemnify the company against any losses. Where a valid resolution approving the transaction has not been obtained in time, the transaction may be affirmed within a reasonable time by a subsequent resolution or resolutions. If approval is retrospectively given in this manner the transaction may no longer be avoided, but any liability to account for gains or indemnify against losses remains (see section 214).

### 199 Meaning of 'quasi-loan' and related expressions

**10.199.01** (1) A 'quasi-loan' is a transaction under which one party ('the creditor') agrees to pay, or pays otherwise than in pursuance of an agreement, a sum for another ('the borrower') or agrees to reimburse, or reimburses otherwise than in pursuance of an agreement, expenditure incurred by another party for another ('the borrower')—
(a) on terms that the borrower (or a person on his behalf) will reimburse the creditor; or
(b) in circumstances giving rise to a liability on the borrower to reimburse the creditor.
(2) Any reference to the person to whom a quasi-loan is made is a reference to the borrower.
(3) The liabilities of the borrower under a quasi-loan include the liabilities of any person who has agreed to reimburse the creditor on behalf of the borrower.

COMMENCEMENT DATE 1 October 2007.[426]

**10.199.02** The wording of section 199 tracks that formerly contained within section 331(3) and (4) of the 1985 Act. A quasi-loan will exist where the creditor (C) pays or agrees to pay a sum for another (the borrower B) or reimburses or agrees to reimburse someone (A) who has incurred expenditure on another's behalf (the borrower B), either on terms that the borrower (or someone on his behalf) will reimburse the creditor or in circumstances where there arises a liability on the borrower so to reimburse the creditor. The concept of quasi-loan was adopted to bring within the scope of the basic prohibition on loans, in the case of public companies, transactions such as those considered in *Champagne Perrier-Jouet SA v Finch*.[427] In that case a company which had paid director's bills was held not to have made a 'loan' to him within the meaning of the relevant articles of association of the company in question.

### 200 Loans or quasi-loans to persons connected with directors: requirement of members' approval

**10.200.01** (1) This section applies to a company if it is—
(a) a public company, or
(b) a company associated with a public company.
(2) A company to which this section applies may not—
(a) make a loan or quasi-loan to a person connected with a director of the company or of its holding company, or

---

[423] Note that in comparison to the requirements under s 337 of the 1985 Act the company is also required to disclose the nature of the transaction (s 197(4)(a)).
[424] As regards 'accidental failure to send memorandum': see s 224.
[425] Note a similar provision at s 203(3).
[426] Companies Act 2006 (Commencement No 3, Consequential Amendments, Transitional Provisions and Savings) Order 2007 SI 2007/2194, art 2.
[427] [1982] 1 WLR 1359.

    (b)  give a guarantee or provide security in connection with a loan or quasi-loan made by any person to a person connected with such a director,

    unless the transaction has been approved by a resolution of the members of the company.

(3)  If the connected person is a person connected with a director of the company's holding company, the transaction must also have been approved by a resolution of the members of the holding company.

(4)  A resolution approving a transaction to which this section applies must not be passed unless a memorandum setting out the matters mentioned in subsection (5) is made available to members—

    (a)  in the case of a written resolution, by being sent or submitted to every eligible member at or before the time at which the proposed resolution is sent or submitted to him;

    (b)  in the case of a resolution at a meeting, by being made available for inspection by members of the company both—

      (i)  at the company's registered office for not less than 15 days ending with the date of the meeting, and

      (ii)  at the meeting itself.

(5)  The matters to be disclosed are—

    (a)  the nature of the transaction,

    (b)  the amount of the loan or quasi-loan and the purpose for which it is required, and

    (c)  the extent of the company's liability under any transaction connected with the loan or quasi-loan.

(6)  No approval is required under this section on the part of the members of a body corporate that—

    (a)  is not a UK-registered company, or

    (b)  is a wholly-owned subsidiary of another body corporate.

COMMENCEMENT DATE  1 October 2007.[428]

This section extends the prohibition on public companies (and companies associated with such companies)[429] making loans or quasi-loans to directors without members' approval, as contained in sections 197 and 198, so that it extends to persons connected with directors[430] of the company or the holding company.[431] The prohibition contained in this section is that a public company, or a company associated with such a company,[432] may not (i) make a loan [433] or quasi-loan[434] to any person connected[435] to any of its directors or to any director of its holding company; nor (ii) give a guarantee or provide any security in connection with any loan or quasi-loan made by any person to such a connected person, unless the transaction has first been approved by a resolution of members (subsection (1)). Where the connected person in question is connected to a director of a holding company, there is an additional requirement that the transaction is approved by a resolution of members of the holding company (subsection (3)). The requirement to obtain approval of its members does not apply to any company which is not a UK-registered company nor to any company which is a wholly-owned subsidiary of another body corporate (subsection (6)). Section 203 sets out a related prohibition. There are a number of specific exceptions to the general prohibition contained in section 200. These are contained in sections 204 to 209. **10.200.02**

Approval of members is obtained by a resolution which may be passed either at a meeting or by way of written resolution, following disclosure of certain required matters by way of written memorandum (subsections (1), (3) and (4)). The matters which must be disclosed[436] are: (i) the nature of the transaction; (ii) the amount of the quasi-loan and the purpose for which it is required; and (iii) the extent of the company's liability under any transaction connected with the quasi-loan (subsection (4)). It appears that the disclosure to members of the holding company required by subsection (5) is solely disclosure of the subsidiary company's liability under any transaction connected with the quasi-loan **10.200.03**

---

[428] Companies Act 2006 (Commencement No 3, Consequential Amendments, Transitional Provisions and Savings) Order 2007 SI 2007/2194, art 2.

[429] As to the meaning of a company 'associated' with another: see s 256 (b).

[430] For the purposes of this section, a shadow director is treated as a director: see s 223.

[431] 'Holding company' is defined in s 1159.

[432] As to the meaning of a company 'associated' with another: see s 256(b).

[433] The word 'loan' would appear to be limited to a situation where a company advances money on terms that it is to be repaid in money or money's worth. In *Champagne Perrier-Jouet SA v Finch* [1982] 1 WLR 1359 it was said that a company which had paid director's bills and supplied goods, on credit, to a company that he controlled had not made a 'loan' to him, within the meaning of the relevant articles of association of the company in question. The judge held that the same meaning would be applied to the word 'loan' in the statutory predecessor of what is now s 197.

[434] 'Quasi-loan' is defined in s 199.

[435] 'Connected' persons are defined in ss 252 *et seq.*

[436] Note that in comparison to the requirements under s 337 of the 1985 Act the company is also required to disclose the nature of the transaction (s 197(4)(a)).

rather than also, or alternatively, requiring disclosure of any liability of the holding company under any such connected transaction. It is suggested that in practice both will have to be disclosed to the members of the holding company.[437] In the case of a written resolution, the written memorandum containing the disclosed matters must be sent or submitted to every eligible member before or at the same time as the written resolution is sent or submitted to him.[438] In the case of a resolution at a meeting, the written memorandum containing the prescribed matters must be made available for inspection by members of the company both at the company's registered office for a period of not less than 15 days ending with the date of the meeting and at the meeting itself (subsection (3)).

**10.200.04** The direct statutory consequences of breach of the section are set out in section 213. The consequences are civil only. In broad terms, the transaction may be voidable and certain persons are liable to account for any gains or to indemnify the company against any losses. Where a valid resolution approving the transaction has not been obtained in time, the transaction may be affirmed within a reasonable time by a subsequent resolution or resolutions. If approval is retrospectively given in this manner the transaction may no longer be avoided, but any liability to account for gains or indemnify against losses remains (see section 214).

### 201 Credit transactions: requirement of members' approval

**10.201.01**
    (1) This section applies to a company if it is—
        (a) a public company, or
        (b) a company associated with a public company.
    (2) A company to which this section applies may not—
        (a) enter into a credit transaction as creditor for the benefit of a director of the company or of its holding company, or a person connected with such a director, or
        (b) give a guarantee or provide security in connection with a credit transaction entered into by any person for the benefit of such a director, or a person connected with such a director,
        unless the transaction (that is, the credit transaction, the giving of the guarantee or the provision of security, as the case may be) has been approved by a resolution of the members of the company.
    (3) If the director or connected person is a director of its holding company or a person connected with such a director, the transaction must also have been approved by a resolution of the members of the holding company.
    (4) A resolution approving a transaction to which this section applies must not be passed unless a memorandum setting out the matters mentioned in subsection (5) is made available to members—
        (a) in the case of a written resolution, by being sent or submitted to every eligible member at or before the time at which the proposed resolution is sent or submitted to him;
        (b) in the case of a resolution at a meeting, by being made available for inspection by members of the company both—
            (i) at the company's registered office for not less than 15 days ending with the date of the meeting, and
            (ii) at the meeting itself.
    (5) The matters to be disclosed are—
        (a) the nature of the transaction,
        (b) the value of the credit transaction and the purpose for which the land, goods or services sold or otherwise disposed of, leased, hired or supplied under the credit transaction are required, and
        (c) the extent of the company's liability under any transaction connected with the credit transaction.
    (6) No approval is required under this section on the part of the members of a body corporate that—
        (a) is not a UK-registered company, or
        (b) is a wholly-owned subsidiary of another body corporate.
    COMMENCEMENT DATE 1 October 2007.[439]

**10.201.02** The prohibition contained in this section is that a public company, or a company associated with such a company,[440] may not (i) enter into a credit transaction[441] as creditor[442] for the benefit of[443] any of its

---

[437] As regards 'accidental failure to send memorandum': see s 224.
[438] Note a similar provision at s 203(3).
[439] Companies Act 2006 (Commencement No 3, Consequential Amendments, Transitional Provisions and Savings) Order 2007 SI 2007/2194, art 2.
[440] As to the meaning of a company 'associated' with another: see s 256(b).
[441] 'Credit transaction' is defined in s 202.
[442] 'Creditor' is defined in s 202(1).
[443] See s 202(2).

directors,[444] any director of its holding company,[445] or any person connected[446] with such a director; nor (ii) give a guarantee or provide any security in connection with any credit transaction entered into by anyone in favour of such a director or person connected with such director, unless the relevant transaction has first been approved by a resolution of members (subsection (2)). Where the director or person connected with the director is also a director of a holding company or a person connected with such a holding company director, there is an additional requirement that the transaction is approved by a resolution of members of the holding company (subsection (3)). The requirement to obtain approval of its members does not apply to any company which is not a UK-registered company nor to any company which is a wholly-owned subsidiary of another body corporate (subsection (6)).

There are a number of specific exceptions to the general prohibition contained in section 201. These are contained in sections 204 to 209. **10.201.03**

Approval of members is obtained by a resolution which may be passed either at a meeting or by way of written resolution, following disclosure of certain required matters by way of written memorandum (subsections (1), (4) and (5)). **10.201.04**

The matters which must be disclosed[447] to members are: (i) the nature of the transaction entered into by the company; (ii) the value[448] of the credit transaction and the purpose for which the land, goods, or services sold or otherwise disposed of, leased, hired, or supplied under the credit transaction are required; and (iii) the extent of the company's liability under any transaction connected with the credit transaction (subsection (5)). It appears that the disclosure to members of the holding company required by subsection (5) is solely disclosure of the subsidiary company's liability under any transaction connected with the credit transaction rather than also, or alternatively, requiring disclosure of any liability of the holding company under any such connected transaction. It is suggested that in practice both will have to be disclosed to the members of the holding company.[449] In the case of a written resolution, the written memorandum containing the disclosed matters must be sent or submitted to every eligible member before or at the same time as the written resolution is sent or submitted to him.[450] In the case of a resolution at a meeting, the written memorandum containing the prescribed matters must be made available for inspection by members of the company both at the company's registered office for a period of not less than 15 days ending with the date of the meeting and at the meeting itself (subsection (3)). **10.201.05**

The direct statutory consequences of breach of the section are set out in section 213. The consequences are civil only. In broad terms, the transaction may be voidable and certain persons are liable to account for any gains or to indemnify the company against any losses. Where a valid resolution approving the transaction has not been obtained in time, the transaction may be affirmed within a reasonable time by a subsequent resolution or resolutions. If approval is retrospectively given in this manner the transaction may no longer be avoided, but any liability to account for gains or indemnify against losses remains (see section 214). **10.201.06**

## 202  Meaning of 'credit transaction'

(1) A 'credit transaction' is a transaction under which one party ('the creditor')— **10.202.01**

    (a) supplies any goods or sells any land under a hire-purchase agreement or a conditional sale agreement,

    (b) leases or hires any land or goods in return for periodical payments, or

    (c) otherwise disposes of land or supplies goods or services on the understanding that payment (whether in a lump sum or instalments or by way of periodical payments or otherwise) is to be deferred.

(2) Any reference to the person for whose benefit a credit transaction is entered into is to the person to whom goods, land or services are supplied, sold, leased, hired or otherwise disposed of under the transaction.

(3) In this section—

    'conditional sale agreement' has the same meaning as in the Consumer Credit Act 1974 (c. 39); and

    'services' means anything other than goods or land.

---

[444] For the purposes of this section, a shadow director is treated as a director: see s 223.

[445] 'Holding company' is defined in s.1159.

[446] 'Connected' persons are defined in ss 252 *et seq.*

[447] Note that in comparison to the requirements under s 337 of the 1985 Act the company is also required to disclose the nature of the transaction (s 197(4)(a)).

[448] See s 211.

[449] As regards 'accidental failure to send memorandum': see s 224.

[450] Note a similar provision at s 203(3).

COMMENCEMENT DATE 1 October 2007.[451]

**10.202.02**    This definition largely tracks that formerly contained in section 330(7) of the 1985 Act. The concept of 'credit transaction' was adopted to bring within the scope of the basic prohibition on loans, transactions such as those considered in *Champagne Perrier-Jouet SA v Finch*.[452] In that case a company supplied goods on credit to a company controlled by the supplying company's director. This transaction was held not to be a 'loan' to the director, within the meaning of the relevant articles of association of the company in question. The definition largely catches transactions where there is credit or deferred consideration.

### 203  Related arrangements: requirement of members' approval

**10.203.01**    (1)  A company may not—
   (a)  take part in an arrangement under which—
      (i)  another person enters into a transaction that, if it had been entered into by the company, would have required approval under section 197, 198, 200 or 201, and
      (ii)  that person, in pursuance of the arrangement, obtains a benefit from the company or a body corporate associated with it, or
   (b)  arrange for the assignment to it, or assumption by it, of any rights, obligations or liabilities under a transaction that, if it had been entered into by the company, would have required such approval,
   unless the arrangement in question has been approved by a resolution of the members of the company.
(2)  If the director or connected person for whom the transaction is entered into is a director of its holding company or a person connected with such a director, the arrangement must also have been approved by a resolution of the members of the holding company.
(3)  A resolution approving an arrangement to which this section applies must not be passed unless a memorandum setting out the matters mentioned in subsection (4) is made available to members—
   (a)  in the case of a written resolution, by being sent or submitted to every eligible member at or before the time at which the proposed resolution is sent or submitted to him;
   (b)  in the case of a resolution at a meeting, by being made available for inspection by members of the company both—
      (i)  at the company's registered office for not less than 15 days ending with the date of the meeting, and
      (ii)  at the meeting itself.
(4)  The matters to be disclosed are—
   (a)  the matters that would have to be disclosed if the company were seeking approval of the transaction to which the arrangement relates,
   (b)  the nature of the arrangement, and
   (c)  the extent of the company's liability under the arrangement or any transaction connected with it.
(5)  No approval is required under this section on the part of the members of a body corporate that—
   (a)  is not a UK-registered company, or
   (b)  is a wholly-owned subsidiary of another body corporate.
(6)  In determining for the purposes of this section whether a transaction is one that would have required approval under section 197, 198, 200 or 201 if it had been entered into by the company, the transaction shall be treated as having been entered into on the date of the arrangement.

COMMENCEMENT DATE 1 October 2007.[453]

**10.203.02**    This section largely replicates provisions which were formerly contained in section 330(6) and (7) of the 1985 Act. The main change is that, in parallel with the other new provisions, the prohibition is limited to cases where members' informed approval has not been obtained.

**10.203.03**    Section 203(1)(a) is an anti-avoidance provision. It is directed at the situation where a company does not itself enter into a transaction otherwise regulated under these provisions regarding loans etc but instead is party to an arrangement under which it (or an associated body corporate)[454] confers a benefit on another party, who enters such a transaction, effectively in its place. For these purposes it is unclear

[451] Companies Act 2006 (Commencement No 3, Consequential Amendments, Transitional Provisions and Savings) Order 2007, SI 2007/2194, art 2.
[452] [1982] 1 WLR 1359.
[453] Companies Act 2006 (Commencement No 3, Consequential Amendments, Transitional Provisions and Savings) Order 2007 SI 2007/2194, art 2.
[454] As to the meaning of a company 'associated' with another: see s 256(b).

whether the arrangement must be legally enforceable even if informally agreed and even if comprising a series of agreements rather than a single agreement.[455]

Section 203(1)(b) is directed at the situation where the company acquires the obligation of a third party under a transaction which it could not itself enter into by reason of the provisions regarding loans etc.  10.203.04

In the case of each of section 203(1)(a) and (b), the time for testing whether the transaction in question entered into by the third party was one that the company could not have entered into is judged by reference to the date on which the arrangement is entered into by the company. The date of the transaction is deemed to be the date of the arrangement in question (subsection (6)).  10.203.05

Where the director[456] or person connected with the director[457] is also a director of a holding company[458] or a person connected with such a holding company director, there is an additional requirement that the transaction is approved by a resolution of members of the holding company (subsection (2)). The requirement to obtain approval of its members does not apply to any company which is not a UK-registered company nor to any company which is a wholly-owned subsidiary of another body corporate (subsection (5)).  10.203.06

There are a number of specific exceptions to the general prohibition contained in section 203. These are contained in sections 204 to 209.  10.203.07

Approval of members is obtained by a resolution which may be passed either at a meeting or by way of written resolution, following disclosure of certain required matters by way of written memorandum (subsections (1), (3) and (4)).  10.203.08

The matters which must be disclosed[459] to members are: (i) the matters that would have to be disclosed if the company were seeking approval of the transaction to which the arrangement relates; (ii) the nature of the arrangement; and (iii) the extent of the company's liability under the arrangement or any transaction connected with it (subsection (4)). It appears that the disclosure to members of the holding company required by subsection (4) is solely disclosure of the extent of the subsidiary company's liability under any connected transaction or arrangement, rather than also, or alternatively, requiring disclosure of any liability of the holding company under any such connected transaction or arrangement. It is suggested that in practice both will have to be disclosed to the members of the holding company. In the case of a written resolution, the written memorandum containing the disclosed matters must be sent or submitted to every eligible member before or at the same time as the written resolution is sent or submitted to him.[460] In the case of a resolution at a meeting, the written memorandum containing the prescribed matters must be made available for inspection by members of the company both at the company's registered office for a period of not less than 15 days ending with the date of the meeting and at the meeting itself (subsection (3)).  10.203.09

The direct statutory consequences of breach of the section are set out in section 213. The consequences are civil only. In broad terms, the transaction may be voidable and certain persons are liable to account for any gains or to indemnify the company against any losses. Where a valid resolution approving the transaction has not been obtained in time, the transaction may be affirmed within a reasonable time by a subsequent resolution or resolutions. If approval is retrospectively given in this manner the transaction may no longer be avoided, but any liability to account for gains or indemnify against losses remains (see section 214).  10.203.10

## 204  Exception for expenditure on company business

(1) Approval is not required under section 197, 198, 200 or 201 (requirement of members' approval  10.204.01
for loans etc) for anything done by a company—
   (a) to provide a director of the company or of its holding company, or a person connected with
       any such director, with funds to meet expenditure incurred or to be incurred by him—
       (i) for the purposes of the company, or

---

[455]  See views of Law Commission, relying on *Re British Slag Ltd's Agreements* [1963] 1 WLR 727, contained in The Law Commission, Consultation Paper 153 and The Scottish Law Commission Discussion Paper No 105: 'Company Directors: Regulating Conflicts of Interests and Formulating a Statement of Duties. A Joint Consultation Paper' para 6.11. See also *Re Duckwari plc* [1999] Ch 253 and *Murray v Leisureplay plc* [2004] EWHC 1927 (QB).

[456]  For the purposes of this section, a shadow director is treated as a director: see s 223.

[457]  'Connected' persons are defined in s 252 *et seq*.

[458]  'Holding company' is defined in s 1159.

[459]  Note that in comparison to the requirements under s 337 of the 1985 Act the company is also required to disclose the nature of the transaction (s 197(4)(a)).

[460]  As regards 'accidental failure to send memorandum': see s 224.

(ii) for the purpose of enabling him properly to perform his duties as an officer of the company, or
(b) to enable any such person to avoid incurring such expenditure.
(2) This section does not authorise a company to enter into a transaction if the aggregate of—
    (a) the value of the transaction in question, and
    (b) the value of any other relevant transactions or arrangements, exceeds £50,000.

COMMENCEMENT DATE 1 October 2007[461]

**10.204.02**  This provision has its origins in section 50 of the Companies Act 1980 and, later, section 337 of the 1985 Act. The main changes are (i) to remove the requirement of approval by the company in general meeting;[462] (ii) to extend the exception to cover the provision of funds in relation to company expenditure, incurred or otherwise anticipated, not just to a director of the company but also to a director of its holding company or a person connected with either such director; and (iii) to increase the applicable financial limits to £50,000.[463]

**10.204.03**  The requirement to obtain informed shareholder approval does not apply to funds provided by a company to meet expenditure incurred or to be incurred or anything else done to avoid the incurring of certain types of expenditure by a set category of persons. The categories of person in question are (i) a director[464] of the company in question; (ii) a director of the holding company[465] of the company; and (iii) a person connected[466] with any such director. In each case the expenditure in question must be expenditure for the purposes of the company or for the purposes of enabling the person concerned to perform his duties as an officer of the company. The aggregate of the value of the transaction[467] and any other relevant transactions or arrangements[468] must not exceed £50,000.[469]

## 205 Exception for expenditure on defending proceedings etc

**10.205.01**
(1) Approval is not required under section 197, 198, 200 or 201 (requirement of members' approval for loans etc) for anything done by a company—
    (a) to provide a director of the company or of its holding company with funds to meet expenditure incurred or to be incurred by him—
        (i) in defending any criminal or civil proceedings in connection with any alleged negligence, default, breach of duty or breach of trust by him in relation to the company or an associated company, or
        (ii) in connection with an application for relief (see subsection (5)), or
    (b) to enable any such director to avoid incurring such expenditure,
    if it is done on the following terms.
(2) The terms are—
    (a) that the loan is to be repaid, or (as the case may be) any liability of the company incurred under any transaction connected with the thing done is to be discharged, in the event of—
        (i) the director being convicted in the proceedings,
        (ii) judgment being given against him in the proceedings, or
        (iii) the court refusing to grant him relief on the application; and
    (b) that it is to be so repaid or discharged not later than—
        (i) the date when the conviction becomes final,
        (ii) the date when the judgment becomes final, or
        (iii) the date when the refusal of relief becomes final.
(3) For this purpose a conviction, judgment or refusal of relief becomes final—
    (a) if not appealed against, at the end of the period for bringing an appeal;
    (b) if appealed against, when the appeal (or any further appeal) is disposed of.
(4) An appeal is disposed of—
    (a) if it is determined and the period for bringing any further appeal has ended, or
    (b) if it is abandoned or otherwise ceases to have effect.

---

[461] Companies Act 2006 (Commencement No 3, Consequential Amendments, Transitional Provisions and Savings) Order 2007 SI 2007/2194, art 2.

[462] And the related requirement of repayment if there was no prior approval and subsequent approval was not forthcoming. Removal of this requirement reflects the fact that this exception is now an exception to various prohibitions on transactions without informed shareholder consent.

[463] Under the 1985 Act, as amended by SI 1990/1393, the limit was £20,000.

[464] For the purposes of this section, a shadow director is treated as a director: see s 223.

[465] 'Holding company' is defined in s 1159.

[466] 'Connected' persons are defined in s 252 et seq.

[467] 'The value of the transaction' is further defined by s 211.

[468] 'Other relevant arrangements or transactions' are defined by s 210.

[469] Note the ability of the Secretary of State to increase this sum by order made under s 258.

(5)  The reference in subsection (1)(a)(ii) to an application for relief is to an application for relief under—

    section 661(3) or (4) (power of court to grant relief in case of acquisition of shares by innocent nominee), or

    section 1157 (general power of court to grant relief in case of honest and reasonable conduct).

COMMENCEMENT DATE  1 October 2007.[470]

This section largely replicates what was section 337A of the 1985 Act, as inserted by section 20 of the Companies (Audit, Investigations and Community Enterprise) Act 2004. The main changes are (i) to extend the exception to cover not only a director of the company but also a director of its holding company; and (ii) to extend the exception to cover relevant proceedings relating to associated companies as well as proceedings relating to the company in question.    **10.205.02**

The requirement to obtain informed shareholder approval does not apply to funds provided by a company to meet expenditure incurred or to be incurred or anything else done to avoid the incurring of certain types of expenditure by a set category of persons. The categories of person in question are a director[471] of the company in question or a director of the holding company[472] of the company. Connected persons are not covered. In each case the expenditure in question must be expenditure (i) in defending any criminal or civil proceedings in connection with any alleged negligence, default, breach of duty, or breach of trust by him in relation to the company or an associated company; or (ii) in connection with an application for relief under sections 661(3), (4) or 1157 (see subsections (1) and (5)). The precise scope of the application for relief is somewhat unclear but if read together with subsection (1)(a)(i) presumably covers an application for relief in relation to an associated company in addition to an application for relief in relation to the company in question. Anything done by the company under this section must be on terms that funds provided by the company, or any liability incurred by it, will be discharged in the event that, and as soon as, the proceedings are finally determined against the director. For these purposes, the section defines when proceedings are deemed to have finally determined against the director (see subsections (2) to (4)).    **10.205.03**

## 206  Exception for expenditure in connection with regulatory action or investigation

Approval is not required under section 197, 198, 200 or 201 (requirement of members' approval for loans etc) for anything done by a company—    **10.206.01**

(a)  to provide a director of the company or of its holding company with funds to meet expenditure incurred or to be incurred by him in defending himself—

    (i)   in an investigation by a regulatory authority, or

    (ii)  against action proposed to be taken by a regulatory authority, in connection with any alleged negligence, default, breach of duty or breach of trust by him in relation to the company or an associated company, or

(b)  to enable any such director to avoid incurring such expenditure.

COMMENCEMENT DATE  1 October 2007.[473]

This is a new provision which is a logical extension to the exception contained in section 205.    **10.206.02**

The requirement to obtain informed shareholder approval does not apply to funds provided by a company to meet expenditure incurred or to be incurred or anything else done to avoid the incurring of certain types of expenditure relating to regulatory investigations or proceedings by a set category of persons. The categories of person in question are a director[474] of the relevant company or a director of the holding company[475] of the company. Connected persons are not covered. In each case the expenditure in question must be expenditure in the relevant person defending himself (i) in an investigation by a regulatory authority, or (ii) against action proposed to be taken by a regulatory authority, in each case in connection with any alleged negligence, default, breach of duty, or breach of trust by him in relation to the company or an associated company.[476]    **10.206.03**

---

[470]  Companies Act 2006 (Commencement No 3, Consequential Amendments, Transitional Provisions and Savings) Order 2007 SI 2007/2194, art 2.

[471]  For the purposes of this section, a shadow director is treated as a director: see s 223.

[472]  'Holding company' is defined in s 1159.

[473]  Companies Act 2006 (Commencement No 3, Consequential Amendments, Transitional Provisions and Savings) Order 2007 SI 2007/2194, art 2.

[474]  For the purposes of this section, a shadow director is treated as a director: see s 223.

[475]  'Holding company' is defined in s 1159.

[476]  As to the meaning of a company 'associated' with another: see s 256(b).

**10.206.04**    The concept of 'defending' oneself and of 'allegations' of negligence and the like in an investigation which is not, in most cases,[477] an adversarial proceeding, is novel. It is to be presumed that the expenditure which is referred to is not limited to the stage (if it happens) where, say, provisional criticisms are advanced. However, it is possible that fine distinctions will be drawn as to when a director may properly be said to be 'defending' himself and as regards the question of whether 'allegations' have been made. Will it be sufficient if the factual background could give rise to an allegation of, say, breach of duty, even if such a breach is not alleged in terms? The description of 'action proposed to be taken' is also problematic. In some cases the proposed disciplinary action may be capable of being taken by the regulatory authority itself. However, in other cases the disciplinary action may be disciplinary proceedings which may lead to sanction being imposed by a tribunal. In such a case does the section cease to apply once disciplinary proceedings are instituted? If that is so, the exception under section 205 would apparently not be capable of applying because it appears to be restricted to court proceedings. It would be strange if assistance could be given where civil or criminal proceedings were running but not in relation to regulatory proceedings.

### 207 Exceptions for minor and business transactions

**10.207.01**    (1) Approval is not required under section 197, 198 or 200 for a company to make a loan or quasi-loan, or to give a guarantee or provide security in connection with a loan or quasi-loan, if the aggregate of—
   (a) the value of the transaction, and
   (b) the value of any other relevant transactions or arrangements,
   does not exceed £10,000.

   (2) Approval is not required under section 201 for a company to enter into a credit transaction, or to give a guarantee or provide security in connection with a credit transaction, if the aggregate of—
   (a) the value of the transaction (that is, of the credit transaction, guarantee or security), and
   (b) the value of any other relevant transactions or arrangements,
   does not exceed £15,000.

   (3) Approval is not required under section 201 for a company to enter into a credit transaction, or to give a guarantee or provide security in connection with a credit transaction, if—
   (a) the transaction is entered into by the company in the ordinary course of the company's business, and
   (b) the value of the transaction is not greater, and the terms on which it is entered into are not more favourable, than it is reasonable to expect the company would have offered to, or in respect of, a person of the same financial standing but unconnected with the company.

   COMMENCEMENT DATE 1 October 2007.[478]

**10.207.02**    This section brings together a number of exceptions previously contained in separate sections of the 1985 Act. It also extends those exceptions.

**10.207.03**    Subsection (1) extends former sections 332 and 334 of the 1985 Act. It permits the making of a loan, a quasi-loan, or the giving of a guarantee or the provision of security in connection with a loan or quasi-loan,[479] without informed members' consent,[480] provided that the defined value of the relevant transactions does not exceed the sum of £10,000.[481] For these purposes, the value in question is the aggregate of the value of the transaction and the value of any other relevant transactions or arrangements.[482] The new exception is wider than that under section 332 of the 1985 Act because it extends to quasi-loans made to connected persons and does not require the quasi-loan to be a short-term one.[483]

**10.207.04**    Subsection (2) essentially re-enacts the former section 335(1) of the 1985 Act, save that it has increased the value ceiling from £10,000[484] to £15,000. The subsection permits the entry into a credit transaction or the giving of a guarantee or the provision of security, without the obtaining of informed members' consent,[485] in connection with a credit transaction provided that the defined value of the relevant

---

[477]  See eg *Three Rivers DC v Bank of England (No 6)* [2004] UKHL 48, [2005] 1 AC 610, esp [10].

[478]  Companies Act 2006 (Commencement No 3, Consequential Amendments, Transitional Provisions and Savings) Order 2007 SI 2007/2194, art 2.

[479]  The exception under the 1985 Act, ss 332 and 334 only extended to loans and quasi-loans.

[480]  See ss 197–200.

[481]  Note the ability of the Secretary of State to increase this sum by order made under s 258.

[482]  'Other relevant arrangements or transactions' are defined by s 210.

[483]  That is there had to be a term requiring reimbursement within two months of the quasi-loan being incurred: see the 1985 Act, s 332(1)(a).

[484]  As inserted by SI 1990/1393.

[485]  See s 201.

transactions does not exceed the sum of £15,000.[486] For these purposes, the value in question is the aggregate of the value of the transaction (that is the credit transaction, guarantee, or security) and the value of any other relevant transactions or arrangements.[487]

Subsection (3) effectively re-enacts section 335(2) of the 1985 Act. The subsection permits the entry into a credit transaction or the giving of a guarantee or the provision of security in connection with a credit transaction, without obtaining informed members' consent,[488] provided that (i) the transaction is entered into by the company in the ordinary course of its[489] business; and (ii) the value of the transaction and its terms are no more favourable than the company might reasonably be expected to have offered in the case of an unconnected person of the same financial standing. A related exception is to be found in section 209.  **10.207.05**

## 208  Exceptions for intra-group transactions

(1) Approval is not required under section 197, 198 or 200 for—  **10.208.01**
  (a) the making of a loan or quasi-loan to an associated body corporate, or
  (b) the giving of a guarantee or provision of security in connection with a loan or quasi-loan made to an associated body corporate.
(2) Approval is not required under section 201—
  (a) to enter into a credit transaction as creditor for the benefit of an associated body corporate, or
  (b) to give a guarantee or provide security in connection with a credit transaction entered into by any person for the benefit of an associated body corporate.

COMMENCEMENT DATE  1 October 2007.[490]

This section essentially re-enacts and widens the exception formerly contained in sections 333 and 336 of the 1985 Act.  **10.208.02**

The section permits the making of loans and quasi-loans to an associated body corporate,[491] and the giving of guarantees or the provision of security in connection with loans or quasi-loans made to an associated body corporate, without obtaining informed members' consent.[492] The section also permits the entry into a credit transaction as creditor for the benefit of an associated body corporate or the giving of a guarantee or provision of security in connection with a credit transaction entered into by any person for the benefit of an associated body corporate, in each case without obtaining informed members' consent.[493]  **10.208.03**

## 209  Exceptions for money-lending companies

(1) Approval is not required under section 197, 198 or 200 for the making of a loan or quasi-loan, or the giving of a guarantee or provision of security in connection with a loan or quasi-loan, by a money-lending company if—  **10.209.01**
  (a) the transaction (that is, the loan, quasi-loan, guarantee or security) is entered into by the company in the ordinary course of the company's business, and
  (b) the value of the transaction is not greater, and its terms are not more favourable, than it is reasonable to expect the company would have offered to a person of the same financial standing but unconnected with the company.
(2) A 'money-lending company' means a company whose ordinary business includes the making of loans or quasi-loans, or the giving of guarantees or provision of security in connection with loans or quasi-loans.
(3) The condition specified in subsection (1)(b) does not of itself prevent a company from making a home loan—
  (a) to a director of the company or of its holding company, or
  (b) to an employee of the company,
if loans of that description are ordinarily made by the company to its employees and the terms of the loan in question are no more favourable than those on which such loans are ordinarily made.

[486]  Note the ability of the Secretary of State to increase this sum by order made under s 258.
[487]  'Other relevant arrangements or transactions' are defined by s 210.
[488]  See s 201.
[489]  See *Steen v Law* [1964] AC 287, esp [302]. The section refers to the ordinary course of the company's business not the ordinary course of business. As noted by Viscount Radcliffe, '[the relevant advances] should be of a scale and for a purpose similar to those regularly made by the company in carrying out its business'.
[490]  Companies Act 2006 (Commencement No 3, Consequential Amendments, Transitional Provisions and Savings) Order 2007 SI 2007/2194, art 2.
[491]  As to the meaning of a company 'associated' with another: see s 256(b).
[492]  See ss 197–200.
[493]  See s 201.

(4)  For the purposes of subsection (3) a 'home loan' means a loan—

(a)  for the purpose of facilitating the purchase, for use as the only or main residence of the person to whom the loan is made, of the whole or part of any dwelling-house together with any land to be occupied and enjoyed with it,

(b)  for the purpose of improving a dwelling-house or part of a dwelling-house so used or any land occupied and enjoyed with it, or

(c)  in substitution for any loan made by any person and falling within paragraph (a) or (b).

COMMENCEMENT DATE 1 October 2007.[494]

**10.209.02**  This section re-enacts and extends the exception formerly contained in section 338 of the 1985 Act. The main changes are to abolish the maximum amounts permitted and to widen the exception for 'home loans' to include connected persons who are employees.

**10.209.03**  The section applies to money-lending companies. That is companies whose ordinary business includes the making of loans or quasi-loans, or the giving of guarantees or provision of security in connection with loans or quasi-loans (see subsection (2)). Such companies are permitted to make loans and quasi-loans (and to give guarantees and provide security in connection with loans or quasi-loans) without obtaining the informed approval of members provided two conditions are met. The conditions are (i) that the transaction is entered into in the ordinary course of the company's business;[495] and (ii) the value of the transaction is no greater, and its terms are no more favourable, than the company might reasonably have been expected to offer to an unconnected person of the same financial standing. The section has parallels with section 207(3).

**10.209.04**  The requirement regarding the value and terms of the loan does not need to be met in the case of certain 'home loans'. 'Home loans' are loans made to facilitate the purchase or improvement of a main dwelling-house[496] or which is in substitution for such a loan made by any person (see subsection (4)). The home loans in question are those made to directors[497] of the company (or of its holding company) or employees of the company provided that loans of that description are ordinarily made by the company to its employees and the terms of the loan in question are no more favourable than those on which such loans are ordinarily made (see subsection (3)).

### 210  Other relevant transactions or arrangements

**10.210.01**
(1)  This section has effect for determining what are 'other relevant transactions or arrangements' for the purposes of any exception to section 197, 198, 200 or 201. In the following provisions 'the relevant exception' means the exception for the purposes of which that falls to be determined.

(2)  Other relevant transactions or arrangements are those previously entered into, or entered into at the same time as the transaction or arrangement in question in relation to which the following conditions are met.

(3)  Where the transaction or arrangement in question is entered into—

(a)  for a director of the company entering into it, or

(b)  for a person connected with such a director,

the conditions are that the transaction or arrangement was (or is) entered into for that director, or a person connected with him, by virtue of the relevant exception by that company or by any of its subsidiaries.

(4)  Where the transaction or arrangement in question is entered into—

(a)  for a director of the holding company of the company entering into it, or

(b)  for a person connected with such a director,

the conditions are that the transaction or arrangement was (or is) entered into for that director, or a person connected with him, by virtue of the relevant exception by the holding company or by any of its subsidiaries.

(5)  A transaction or arrangement entered into by a company that at the time it was entered into—

(a)  was a subsidiary of the company entering into the transaction or arrangement in question, or

(b)  was a subsidiary of that company's holding company,

is not a relevant transaction or arrangement if, at the time the question arises whether the transaction or arrangement in question falls within a relevant exception, it is no longer such a subsidiary.

---

[494]  Companies Act 2006 (Commencement No 3, Consequential Amendments, Transitional Provisions and Savings) Order 2007 SI 2007/2194, art 2.

[495]  See *Steen v Law* [1964] AC 287, esp 302. The section refers to the ordinary course of the company's business not the ordinary course of business. As noted by Viscount Radcliffe, '[the relevant advances] should be of a scale and for a purpose similar to those regularly made by the company in carrying out its business'.

[496]  Including improvement of part of a main dwelling-house or land occupied or enjoyed with such a dwelling-house.

[497]  For the purposes of this section, a shadow director is treated as a director: see s 223.

Commencement Date  1 October 2007.[498]

This section largely re-enacts the concepts formerly contained in section 339 of the 1985 Act. It is a **10.210.02** definitional section which is relevant to the exceptions contained in sections 204 and 207(1) and (2) to the requirement to obtain the informed approval of members to certain transactions. Those exceptions place monetary limits on the value of the benefits that can be conferred without obtaining the informed approval of members. The relevant exceptions are drafted so as to avoid their being abused by the splitting of transactions or arrangements into smaller transactions or arrangements. Accordingly, each of the exceptions in question requires the ascertainment of the aggregate of the value of the relevant transaction and the value of any 'other relevant transactions or arrangements'. That aggregate value must not exceed the relevant monetary ceiling laid down by the particular exception in question.

An 'other relevant transaction or arrangement' is any which meets two conditions. The first relates to **10.210.03** the time at which it was (or is) entered into. The second relates to the person(s) for whom[499] it is entered into.

As regards the time at which an 'other transaction or arrangement' must have been entered into in **10.210.04** order to fall within the definition, the transaction or arrangement must have been entered into before, or be entered into at the same time as, the proposed new transaction which falls to be considered under the relevant exception provided for by any of section 204 and 207(1) and (2) (referred to in the section as 'the transaction or arrangement in question').

As regards the person(s) for whom the other transaction or arrangement must have been entered into, **10.210.05** the identification of that person(s) depends upon identifying for whom the proposed new transaction which falls to be considered under the relevant exception under any of section 204 and 207(1) and (2) (referred to in the section as 'the transaction or arrangement in question') is to be entered into. For present purposes such proposed new transaction or arrangement is referred to as 'the New Transaction'.

If the New Transaction is to be entered into by a company for one of its own directors[500] or for a person **10.210.06** connected[501] with such director, then a transaction or arrangement entered into earlier or at the same time must be brought into account as an 'other relevant transaction or arrangement' if it was (or is) entered into (i) for that director or a person connected with that director, (ii) under the same statutory exception, (iii) by that company or any of its subsidiaries (see subsection (3)).

If the New Transaction is to be entered into by a company for a director of its holding company[502] or **10.210.07** for a person connected with such director, then a transaction or arrangement entered into earlier or at the same time must be brought into account as an 'other relevant transaction or arrangement' if it was (or is) entered into (i) for that holding company director or a person connected with that director, (ii) under the same statutory exception, (iii) by the holding company or any of its subsidiaries[503] (see subsection (4)).

However, a transaction or arrangement which was entered into by a company at a time when it was (i) **10.210.08** a subsidiary of the company which is now entering into the New Transaction, or (ii) a subsidiary of the holding company of the company which is now entering into the New Transaction is left out of account and not treated as an 'other relevant transaction or arrangement', if it is no longer such a subsidiary at the time when it is being considered whether the New Transaction falls within the exception (see subsection (5)).

### 211  The value of transactions and arrangements

(1)  For the purposes of section 197 to 214 (loans etc)—                    **10.211.01**
    (a)  the value of a transaction or arrangement is determined as follows, and
    (b)  the value of any other relevant transaction or arrangement is taken to be the value so determined reduced by any amount by which the liabilities of the person for whom the transaction or arrangement was made have been reduced.
(2)  The value of a loan is the amount of its principal.

---

[498]  Companies Act 2006 (Commencement No 3, Consequential Amendments, Transitional Provisions and Savings) Order 2007 SI 2007/2194, art 2.
[499]  The person 'for whom' a transaction or arrangement is entered into is further defined by s 212. It is a concept much used in this section.
[500]  For the purposes of this section, a shadow director is treated as a director: see s 223.
[501]  'Connected' persons are defined in s 252 *et seq.*
[502]  'Holding company' is defined in s 1159.
[503]  'Subsidiary' is defined by s 1159.

(3) The value of a quasi-loan is the amount, or maximum amount, that the person to whom the quasi-loan is made is liable to reimburse the creditor.

(4) The value of a credit transaction is the price that it is reasonable to expect could be obtained for the goods, services or land to which the transaction relates if they had been supplied (at the time the transaction is entered into) in the ordinary course of business and on the same terms (apart from price) as they have been supplied, or are to be supplied, under the transaction in question.

(5) The value of a guarantee or security is the amount guaranteed or secured.

(6) The value of an arrangement to which section 203 (related arrangements) applies is the value of the transaction to which the arrangement relates.

(7) If the value of a transaction or arrangement is not capable of being expressed as a specific sum of money—

(a) whether because the amount of any liability arising under the transaction or arrangement is unascertainable, or for any other reason, and

(b) whether or not any liability under the transaction or arrangement has been reduced, its value is deemed to exceed £50,000.

COMMENCEMENT DATE 1 October 2007.[504]

**10.211.02** This section largely re-enacts section 340 of the 1985 Act. The main change is a decrease in the deemed value of an unascertainable value from £100,000[505] to £50,000. The section is of relevance to the exceptions to the requirement of the informed approval of members which are contained in section 204 (exception for expenditure on company business) and 207[506] (exceptions for minor and business transactions).

### 212 The person for whom a transaction or arrangement is entered into

**10.212.01** For the purposes of sections 197 to 214 (loans etc) the person for whom a transaction or arrangement is entered into is—

(a) in the case of a loan or quasi-loan, the person to whom it is made;

(b) in the case of a credit transaction, the person to whom goods, land or services are supplied, sold, hired, leased or otherwise disposed of under the transaction;

(c) in the case of a guarantee or security, the person for whom the transaction is made in connection with which the guarantee or security is entered into;

(d) in the case of an arrangement within section 203 (related arrangements), the person for whom the transaction is made to which the arrangement relates.

COMMENCEMENT DATE 1 October 2007.[507]

**10.212.02** This definitional section largely re-enacts section 331(9) of the 1985 Act.

### 213 Loans etc: civil consequences of contravention

**10.213.01** (1) This section applies where a company enters into a transaction or arrangement in contravention of section 197, 198, 200, 201 or 203 (requirement of members' approval for loans etc).

(2) The transaction or arrangement is voidable at the instance of the company, unless—

(a) restitution of any money or other asset that was the subject matter of the transaction or arrangement is no longer possible,

(b) the company has been indemnified for any loss or damage resulting from the transaction or arrangement, or

(c) rights acquired in good faith, for value and without actual notice of the contravention by a person who is not a party to the transaction or arrangement would be affected by the avoidance.

(3) Whether or not the transaction or arrangement has been avoided, each of the persons specified in subsection (4) is liable—

(a) to account to the company for any gain that he has made directly or indirectly by the transaction or arrangement, and

(b) (jointly and severally with any other person so liable under this section) to indemnify the company for any loss or damage resulting from the transaction or arrangement.

(4) The persons so liable are—

(a) any director of the company or of its holding company with whom the company entered into the transaction or arrangement in contravention of section 197, 198, 201 or 203,

---

[504] Companies Act 2006 (Commencement No 3, Consequential Amendments, Transitional Provisions and Savings) Order 2007 SI 2007/2194, art 2.

[505] As inserted by SI 1990/1393.

[506] But note the exception contained in s 207(3).

[507] Companies Act 2006 (Commencement No 3, Consequential Amendments, Transitional Provisions and Savings) Order 2007, SI 2007/2194, art 2.

(b)  any person with whom the company entered into the transaction or arrangement in contravention of any of those sections who is connected with a director of the company or of its holding company,

(c)  the director of the company or of its holding company with whom any such person is connected, and

(d)  any other director of the company who authorised the transaction or arrangement.

(5)  Subsection (3) and (4) are subject to the following two subsections.

(6)  In the case of a transaction or arrangement entered into by a company in contravention of section 200, 201 or 203 with a person connected with a director of the company or of its holding company, that director is not liable by virtue of subsection (4)(c) if he shows that he took all reasonable steps to secure the company's compliance with the section concerned.

(7)  In any case—

(a)  a person so connected is not liable by virtue of subsection (4)(b), and

(b)  a director is not liable by virtue of subsection (4)(d),

if he shows that, at the time the transaction or arrangement was entered into, he did not know the relevant circumstances constituting the contravention.

(8)  Nothing in this section shall be read as excluding the operation of any other enactment or rule of law by virtue of which the transaction or arrangement may be called in question or any liability to the company may arise.

COMMENCEMENT DATE  1 October 2007.[508]

This section largely replicates section 341 of the 1985 Act. It should also be considered in conjunction with section 195 (dealing with the civil consequences of contravention of the provisions regarding substantial property transactions) and section 41 (dealing with the consequences of transactions with directors in the context of constitutional limitations on their powers). In broad terms the section provides for two remedies. First, but subject to exceptions, the transaction or arrangement may be avoided by the company. Secondly, certain classes of person are liable to account to the company for any gain made and to indemnify the company for any loss or damage resulting from the transaction or arrangement. These remedies are without prejudice to any other remedy that may exist (see subsection (8)).  **10.213.02**

Where there has been a contravention of any of section 197, 198, 200, 201, or 203 the transaction or arrangement will be voidable at the instance of the company, subject to a number of exceptions. However, if and for as long as it is not avoided, the company is still able to sue on it: see *Currencies Direct Limited v Ellis*.[509] If the transaction or arrangement is avoided it is doubtful that any trust arises by virtue of the avoidance over assets transferred by the company under the arrangement or transaction, the transaction being voidable rather than void.[510] It has been held[511] that funds applied in breach of what was section 330 of the 1985 Act will be held by the recipient on trust for the company but this is probably explicable on the basis that the directors acted in breach of fiduciary duties in transferring assets in breach of section 330 and that the recipient therefore held such funds as trustee. The section specifically preserves other remedies that the company may have (see subsection (8)).  **10.213.03**

The company has no right to avoid the transaction or arrangement in the circumstances set out in subsection (2) (and also section 214). These circumstances are probably exhaustive.[512] The circumstances under subsection (2) are as follows.  **10.213.04**

- First, that restitution is no longer possible: subsection (2)(a). However, what is possible need not be 'perfect' restitution.[513]
- Secondly, that the company has been indemnified for any loss or damage resulting from the transaction or arrangement: subsection (2)(b). Unlike the former section 341(2)(b) of the 1985 Act

---

[508]  Companies Act 2006 (Commencement No 3, Consequential Amendments, Transitional Provisions and Savings) Order 2007 SI 2007/2194, art 2.

[509]  [2002] 1 BCLC 193, esp [35].

[510]  In respect of voidable contracts the company can elect to avoid or confirm the contract. For the position in equity as opposed to statute see *Guinness plc v Saunders* [1990] 2 AC 663, esp [668] and as regards the comparable position under s 320 of the 1985 Act see *Demite Limited v Protec Health Limited (No 2)* (16 November 1998, unreported Park J). In this case Park J held that since it was not expressly stated in the statute, lapse of time would not render the contract voidable.

[511]  *Budge v A F Budge (Contractors) Ltd* [1997] BPIR 366. See also *Cox v Cox* [2006] EWHC 1077 (Ch).

[512]  As regards the comparable provision under what was CA 1985, s 322 see *Demite Limited v Protect Health Limited* [1998] BCC 638.

[513]  See, by analogy with what was s 322 of CA 1985, *Ultraframe (UK) Ltd v Fielding and Others* [2005] EWHC (Ch) 1638, [1424] *per* Lewison J.

it is no longer necessary that the indemnification be in pursuance of the statutory remedy for indemnification.[514]

- Thirdly, that relevant third party rights have intervened (subsection 2(c)). The rights in question must have been acquired in good faith, for value, and without actual notice of the contravention by a person who is not a party to the transaction or arrangement, and such rights must be ones that would be affected by the avoidance.
- Finally, under section 214 the right to avoid the transaction will be lost where the transaction or arrangement is affirmed within a reasonable period by the members of the company and/or the members of the company's holding company, depending upon what was the precise contravention.

**10.213.05**    Whether or not the transaction or arrangement entered into in breach of the relevant statutory provisions is avoided, monetary liabilities are imposed on the persons set out in subsection (4). Those persons are as follows.

- First, any director of the company or its holding company with whom the company entered into the transaction or arrangement in contravention of section 197, 198, 201 or 203 (subsection (4)(a)).
- Secondly, any person with whom the company entered into the transaction or arrangement in contravention of any of section 197, 198, 201 or 203 and who is connected with a director of the company or the holding company (subsection (4)(b)). However, such a connected person is not liable under this subsection if he shows that, at the time the relevant arrangement or transaction was entered into, he did not know the relevant circumstances constituting the contravention (subsections (5), (7)(a)).[515]
- Thirdly, the director of the company or of its holding company with whom any such person is connected (subsection (4)(c)). However, if the transaction or arrangement was entered into in contravention of section 200, 201 or 203 with a person connected with a director, that director is not liable under this subsection if he shows that he took all reasonable steps to secure the company's compliance with the section concerned (subsections (5),(6)).[516]
- Fourthly, any other director of the company who authorized the transaction or arrangement (subsection (4)(d)). However, such a director is not liable under this subsection if he shows that, at the time the relevant arrangement or transaction was entered into, he did not know the relevant circumstances constituting the contravention (subsections (5), (7)(a)).

**10.213.06**    The monetary obligation is one on the relevant person to account for any gain made by him directly or indirectly by the transaction or arrangement and (jointly and severally with any other person liable under the section)[517] to indemnify the company for any loss or damage resulting from the transaction or arrangement. The extent of the monetary liability can give rise to difficult questions of causation and some guidance can be gained from the cases in the context of what was section 322 of the Companies Act 1985.[518]

### 214 Loans etc: effect of subsequent affirmation

**10.214.01**    Where a transaction or arrangement is entered into by a company in contravention of section 197, 198, 200, 201 or 203 (requirement of members' approval for loans etc) but, within a reasonable period, it is affirmed—

>    (a)  in the case of a contravention of the requirement for a resolution of the members of the company, by a resolution of the members of the company, and

---

[514] Compare s 195(2)(b) under which a company is expressly barred from rescission only when indemnified pursuant to that section (see also n 369 to para 10.195.06). In this case it would appear that when the company has been indemnified under this section or otherwise the company will not be able to avoid the transaction or arrangement.

[515] See *Lexi Holdings (In Administration) v Monuza Akthar Luqman, Zaurian Parveen Luqman* [2009] EWCA Civ 117, [2009] BCC 716. The onus of proof is on the individual invoking the defence.

[516] See above.

[517] See *Neville (as administrator of Unigreg Ltd) and Anor v Krikorian and Others* [2006] EWCA Civ 943 in which the court held that a director who knew his company operated a loan account in favour of another director in breach of s 330 of CA 1985 was jointly and severally liable to repay all sums loaned after he became aware of the existence of the loan account even though he did not know details of the individual loans which were made. See also *Lexi Holdings (In Administration) v Monuza Akthar Luqman, Zaurian Parveen Luqman* [2009] EWCA Civ 117, [2009] BCC 716.

[518] See eg *Re Duckwari plc* [1999] Ch 253; *Murray v Leisureplay plc* [2004] EWHC 1927 (QB), and, on appeal, [2005] EWCA Civ 963.

(b)  in the case of a contravention of the requirement for a resolution of the members of the company's holding company, by a resolution of the members of the holding company,

the transaction or arrangement may no longer be avoided under section 213.

COMMENCEMENT DATE  1 October 2007.[519]

Now that the prohibitions under section 197 *et seq* are limited to cases where appropriate members' consent has not been obtained, section 214 introduces a further limit on the company's statutory right to avoid transactions entered into in breach of the prohibition. That mirrors what is now section 196 (which substantially re-enacts section 322(2)(c) of the 1985 Act). Subsequent affirmation within a reasonable time by resolution of the company's or holding company's members as appropriate will avoid any right to rescind. It has no effect on other remedies. There does not appear to be any reason why the resolution need be passed at a meeting formally held, rather than by means of informal unanimous consent or by means of the procedure for written resolutions: see also *NBH Ltd & NBH Group Ltd v Kevin Hoare & Others*,[520] in which it was held by Park J that the informal (prior) approval[521] of a director as sole shareholder was sufficient to comply with the requirements of section 320(1) of the 1985 Act. Note also that neither section 196 nor section 214 make reference to approval at a 'general meeting', and they are in that respect different from section 322(2)(c) of the 1985 Act. In any event, it is thought that to be an effective affirmation, the members will need to be fully informed of the relevant facts.     **10.214.02**

## Payments for loss of office

### 215  Payments for loss of office

(1)  In this Chapter a 'payment for loss of office' means a payment made to a director or past director of a company—     **10.215.01**
- (a)  by way of compensation for loss of office as director of the company,
- (b)  by way of compensation for loss, while director of the company or in connection with his ceasing to be a director of it, of—
  - (i)  any other office or employment in connection with the management of the affairs of the company, or
  - (ii)  any office (as director or otherwise) or employment in connection with the management of the affairs of any subsidiary undertaking of the company,
- (c)  as consideration for or in connection with his retirement from his office as director of the company, or
- (d)  as consideration for or in connection with his retirement, while director of the company or in connection with his ceasing to be a director of it, from—
  - (i)  any other office or employment in connection with the management of the affairs of the company, or
  - (ii)  any office (as director or otherwise) or employment in connection with the management of the affairs of any subsidiary undertaking of the company.

(2)  The references to compensation and consideration include benefits otherwise than in cash and references in this Chapter to payment have a corresponding meaning.

(3)  For the purposes of section 217 to 221 (payments requiring members' approval)—
- (a)  payment to a person connected with a director, or
- (b)  payment to any person at the direction of, or for the benefit of, a director or a person connected with him,

is treated as payment to the director.

(4)  References in those sections to payment by a person include payment by another person at the direction of, or on behalf of, the person referred to.

COMMENCEMENT DATE  1 October 2007[522]

---

[519]  Companies Act 2006 (Commencement No 3, Consequential Amendments, Transitional Provisions and Savings) Order 2007 SI 2007/2194, art 2.

[520]  [2006] BCLC 649.

[521]  See also *Re Conegrade Ltd* [2002] EWHC 2411 (Ch), where approval was given at a directors' meeting and each of the members was also a director.

[522]  Companies Act 2006 (Commencement No 3, etc) Order 2007, SI 2007/2194, art 2. For transitional provisions, see SI 2007/2194, art 9, Sch 3, para 12. This and the following seven sections (ss 216–222) have been disapplied in respect of certain specified persons while Northern Rock, Bradford & Bingley and Deposits Management (Heritable) are wholly owned by the Treasury, pursuant to the Northern Rock plc Transfer Order 2008, SI 2008/432, art 17, Sch, para 2(j), the Bradford & Bingley plc Transfer of Securities and Property etc Order 2008, SI 2008/2546, art 13(1), Sch, para 2(j) and the Heritable Bank plc Transfer of Certain Rights and Liabilities Order 2008, SI 2008/2644, art 26, Sch 2, para 2(j), respectively.

**10.215.02** A director[523] or former director may not be made an *ex gratia* payment for loss of office without a resolution of the members.[524]

**10.215.03** Sections 215 to 222 replace sections 312 to 316 of the Companies Act 1985. Sections 215 and 216 are definitions sections for the general restrictions regarding payments for loss of office contained in section 217 to 219. Exceptions to those restrictions are contained in sections 220 and 221. The civil consequences of a payment made in contravention of section 217, 218, or 219 are contained in section 222.

**10.215.04** Under section 316(4) of the Companies Act 1985 there was an express saving provision to the effect that nothing in section 313 to 315 prejudiced the operation of any rule of law requiring disclosure to be made with respect to any such payments as were there mentioned. This has not been repeated in the 2006 Act, presumably reflecting the fact that the scheme of the 2006 Act has been to shift focus from member disclosure to member approval. Clearly regard must still be had to the reporting and other disclosure obligations under the Act[525] and elsewhere[526] in respect of any duly approved payments for loss of office.

**10.215.05** Subsection (1): Payments for loss of office are payments made to a director or former director[527] to compensate them for losing their office as a director, or for losing any other office or employment with the company or with a subsidiary of the company. They also include payments made in connection with retirement. In the case of loss of employment or retirement from employment, the employment must relate to the management of the affairs of the company or a subsidiary.

**10.215.06** Subsection (2): It is immaterial whether payment is made in cash or the provision of other benefits.[528]

**10.215.07** Subsection (3): The restriction on payments for loss of office extends to payments to the nominee of, or otherwise for the benefit of, the director or a person connected with him.

**10.215.08** The restriction on payments to persons connected with a director is an anti-avoidance measure introduced for the first time in CA 2006. For the meaning of that expression see section 252.

**10.215.09** Subsection (4): See the note to section 217(2).

### 216 Amounts taken to be payments for loss of office

**10.216.01**
(1) This section applies where in connection with any such transfer as is mentioned in section 218 or 219 (payment in connection with transfer of undertaking, property or shares) a director of the company—
    (a) is to cease to hold office, or
    (b) is to cease to be the holder of—
        (i) any other office or employment in connection with the management of the affairs of the company, or
        (ii) any office (as director or otherwise) or employment in connection with the management of the affairs of any subsidiary undertaking of the company.
(2) If in connection with any such transfer—

---

[523] For the purposes of this and the following seven sections a shadow director is treated as a director: s 223(1)(d). However, any reference in those provisions to loss of office as a director does not apply in relation to loss of a person's status as a shadow director. The expressions director and shadow director are defined in ss 250 and 251, respectively.

[524] In Scotland, it has been held that compliance with the requirements of member approval in respect of an *ex gratia* payment does not exempt the directors from their duty to act bona fide in the best interests of the company and not for an improper purpose in deciding whether to make such a payment: *Gibson's Executor v Gibson* [1980] SLT 2. See also, by analogy, *Wilton Group plc v Abrams and others* [1991] BCLC 315 at 322–323 (an English decision in the context of s 188).

[525] Eg, in the company's accounts (under s 412(2)(c)) and, in the case of quoted companies, in the directors' remuneration report (under s 421).

[526] Eg, in a report to shareholders made under Listing Rules 9.8.6R(7) and 9.8.8R in the case of a UK-listed company incorporated in the UK.

[527] Any references in ss 216 to 222 to directors are thus references also to former directors. It does not matter if the recipient of the payment is no longer a director at the time the payment is made: what matters is the reason for the payment, and the provisions cannot be evaded by the device of resignation prior to the payment. In a decision of the Outer House under s 312 of CA 1985, it has been held that a payment made in connection with a new, honorary, appointment taking effect immediately after retirement was not within s 312: *Mercer v Heart of Midlothian plc* 2001 SLT 945. It is submitted that that decision, already criticized by some, should not be followed in claims brought under CA 2006, at any rate not in circumstances where the court makes a finding that the resignation and the payment are in substance elements of a single transaction.

[528] See also *Mercer v Heart of Midlothian plc* 2001 SLT 945.

(a)  the price to be paid to the director for any shares in the company held by him is in excess of the price which could at the time have been obtained by other holders of like shares, or

(b)  any valuable consideration is given to the director by a person other than the company,

the excess or, as the case may be, the money value of the consideration is taken for the purposes of those sections to have been a payment for loss of office.

COMMENCEMENT DATE  1 October 2007[529]

This section, which is derived from section 316(2) of the Companies Act 1985, treats certain payments as payments for loss of office for the purposes of section 218 and 219. It is intended to apply to the same set of circumstances as section 215, namely loss of office as a director, retirement from office as a director, and loss of, or retirement from, any other office or employment in connection with the management of the affairs of the company or a subsidiary.          **10.216.02**

Subsection (2): The payments brought within the restrictions contained in section 218 and 219 are those where, in connection with a transfer of the undertaking or property or shares of the company the director gets given more for the shares than other holders of like shares, or other valuable consideration. In such cases, the excess, or the money value of the consideration, is taken to have been a payment for loss of office.          **10.216.03**

## 217  Payment by company: requirement of members' approval

(1)  A company may not make a payment for loss of office to a director of the company unless the payment has been approved by a resolution of the members of the company.          **10.217.01**

(2)  A company may not make a payment for loss of office to a director of its holding company unless the payment has been approved by a resolution of the members of each of those companies.

(3)  A resolution approving a payment to which this section applies must not be passed unless a memorandum setting out particulars of the proposed payment (including its amount) is made available to the members of the company whose approval is sought—

(a)  in the case of a written resolution, by being sent or submitted to every eligible member at or before the time at which the proposed resolution is sent or submitted to him;

(b)  in the case of a resolution at a meeting, by being made available for inspection by the members both—

(i)  at the company's registered office for not less than 15 days ending with the date of the meeting, and

(ii)  at the meeting itself.

(4)  No approval is required under this section on the part of the members of a body corporate that—

(a)  is not a UK-registered company, or

(b)  is a wholly-owned subsidiary of another body corporate.

COMMENCEMENT DATE  1 October 2007[530]

Member approval is required if a company wishes to make a payment for loss of office to one of its directors or a director of its holding company. Section 217 is in most respects a continuation of section 312 of the Companies Act 1985.          **10.217.02**

Subsection (1): Although the approval required is an ordinary resolution[531] the company's articles may impose more stringent requirements.[532] Furthermore, where approval is also required under another provision of Chapter 4 of this Part, the requirements of each applicable provision must be met.[533] The approval must pre-date the payment.[534] A director who is also a voting member is ordinarily not debarred from voting on the proposed resolution, even if he is the intended beneficiary of the proposed payment.[535]          **10.217.03**

---

[529]  Companies Act 2006 (Commencement No 3, etc) Order 2007, SI 2007/2194, art 2. For transitional provisions, see SI 2007/2194, art 9, Sch 3, para 12. For the disapplication of this section in respect of certain specified persons while Northern Rock, Bradford & Bingley and Deposits Management (Heritable) are wholly owned by the Treasury, see note to s 215 above.

[530]  Companies Act 2006 (Commencement No 3, etc) Order 2007, SI 2007/2194, art 2. For transitional provisions, see SI 2007/2194, art 9, Sch 3, para 12. For the disapplication of this section in respect of certain specified persons while Northern Rock, Bradford & Bingley and Deposits Management (Heritable) are wholly owned by the Treasury, see note to s 215 above.

[531]  S 281(3).

[532]  Ibid. In addition to setting out requirements for member approval, the articles may themselves contain restrictions as to payments made to a director for loss of office.

[533]  S 225. Approval may be given for both purposes by a single resolution.

[534]  See however s 239 (ratification of acts of directors).

[535]  Re Duomatic Limited [1969] 2 Ch 365. However, regard should be had to the Listing Rules and the City Code on Takeovers and Mergers, where appropriate.

**10.217.04**    In the case of private companies, approval may be given by written resolution[536] or, it seems, informal unanimous consent.[537]

**10.217.05**    See further, in relation to charitable companies in England and Wales, section 201 of the Charities Act 2011 (as amended by the Companies Act 2006, section 226), which provides that any member approval under section 217[538] is ineffective without the prior written consent of the Charity Commission for England and Wales.

**10.217.06**    Subsection (2): Where the relevant payment is made by a subsidiary of the company of which the recipient is a director, resolutions are now required both in the case of the company and its subsidiary.[539]

**10.217.07**    Note that unlike section 218 and 219, section 217 does not apply to transactions entered into between a company that is neither the company of which the person is a director nor a subsidiary of the company of which the person is a director. However such a transaction may nevertheless be caught by the operation of section 215(4) if a transaction between a company and the director of a fellow subsidiary is entered into at the direction of, or on behalf of, the latter company.

**10.217.08**    Subsection (3): A memorandum setting out certain particulars about the transaction requiring approval of the members must be made available to the members whose approval is sought[540] if their approval is to be valid. If the approval is to be given by way of written resolution, the memorandum must be sent to the members able to vote on the written resolution no later than when the written resolution is sent to them. See also section 224, which provides that the accidental failure to send to one or more members a copy of such a memorandum would not invalidate such approval (subject to any provision in the company's articles).

**10.217.09**    Subsection (4): Approval is never required on the part of a member of a wholly-owned subsidiary or on the part of the members of an overseas company.

### 218 Payment in connection with transfer of undertaking etc: requirement of members' approval

**10.218.01**
(1) No payment for loss of office may be made by any person to a director of a company in connection with the transfer of the whole or any part of the undertaking or property of the company unless the payment has been approved by a resolution of the members of the company.

(2) No payment for loss of office may be made by any person to a director of a company in connection with the transfer of the whole or any part of the undertaking or property of a subsidiary of the company unless the payment has been approved by a resolution of the members of each of the companies.

(3) A resolution approving a payment to which this section applies must not be passed unless a memorandum setting out particulars of the proposed payment (including its amount) is made available to the members of the company whose approval is sought—
  (a) in the case of a written resolution, by being sent or submitted to every eligible member at or before the time at which the proposed resolution is sent or submitted to him;
  (b) in the case of a resolution at a meeting, by being made available for inspection by the members both—
    (i) at the company's registered office for not less than 15 days ending with the date of the meeting, and
    (ii) at the meeting itself.

(4) No approval is required under this section on the part of the members of a body corporate that—
  (a) is not a UK-registered company, or
  (b) is a wholly-owned subsidiary of another body corporate.

(5) A payment made in pursuance of an arrangement—

---

[536] See s 217(3)(a). The company's articles may, however, impose restrictions on the use of this procedure.

[537] *Re Duomatic Limited* [1969] 2 Ch 365; and see also *Wright v Atlas Wright (Europe) Ltd* [1999] 2 BCLC 301. Again, the use of this procedure is only available where permitted by the company's articles.

[538] A similar restriction applies to payments made under s 218.

[539] Unless the subsidiary is wholly-owned, in which case only a resolution of the holding company is required: s 217(4)(b). This exception extends to any body corporate that is a wholly-owned subsidiary of another body corporate. The requirement for a resolution of the holding company is a new anti-avoidance provision introduced in CA 2006, aimed at preventing a relevant payment to the director by the subsidiary with merely the approval of the holding company given as shareholder.

[540] This represents a departure from the position under CA 1985, which required disclosure of the proposed payment to all members regardless of whether they were entitled to receive notice of or attend at general meetings: see *Re Duomatic Limited* [1969] 2 Ch 365.

(a)  entered into as part of the agreement for the transfer in question, or within one year before or two years after that agreement, and

(b)  to which the company whose undertaking or property is transferred, or any person to whom the transfer is made, is privy,

is presumed, except in so far as the contrary is shown, to be a payment to which this section applies.

COMMENCEMENT DATE  1 October 2007[541]

Member approval is required if any person (including the company) wishes to make a payment for loss of office to a director of the company in connection with the transfer of the whole or any part of the undertaking or the property of the company or of a subsidiary of the company. Section 218 is in most respects a continuation of section 313 of the Companies Act 1985. **10.218.02**

Subsection (1): This prohibition extends to a payment for loss of office made by 'any person': unlike most of the other transactions covered in Chapter 4, its scope accordingly includes transactions between a company and the director of a fellow subsidiary. **10.218.03**

The requirements for member approval follow the same pattern as those contained in section 217(1). Where approval is also required under that provision, the requirements of both provisions must be met.[542] **10.218.04**

Subsection (2): The extension of the scope of the restriction contained in section 218 to include transfers of the undertaking or property of a subsidiary is an anti-avoidance measure introduced for the first time in the Companies Act 2006. **10.218.05**

Subsection (3): See also section 224 (accidental failure to send memorandum). **10.218.06**

Subsection (4): Approval is never required on the part of a member of a wholly-owned subsidiary or on the part of the members of an overseas company. **10.218.07**

Subsection (5) substantially repeats section 316(1) of the Companies Act 1985. **10.218.08**

### 219  Payment in connection with share transfer: requirement of members' approval

(1)  No payment for loss of office may be made by any person to a director of a company in connection with a transfer of shares in the company, or in a subsidiary of the company, resulting from a takeover bid unless the payment has been approved by a resolution of the relevant shareholders. **10.219.01**

(2)  The relevant shareholders are the holders of the shares to which the bid relates and any holders of shares of the same class as any of those shares.

(3)  A resolution approving a payment to which this section applies must not be passed unless a memorandum setting out particulars of the proposed payment (including its amount) is made available to the members of the company whose approval is sought—

(a)  in the case of a written resolution, by being sent or submitted to every eligible member at or before the time at which the proposed resolution is sent or submitted to him;

(b)  in the case of a resolution at a meeting, by being made available for inspection by the members both—

(i)  at the company's registered office for not less than 15 days ending with the date of the meeting, and

(ii)  at the meeting itself.

(4)  Neither the person making the offer, nor any associate of his (as defined in section 988), is entitled to vote on the resolution, but—

(a)  where the resolution is proposed as a written resolution, they are entitled (if they would otherwise be so entitled) to be sent a copy of it, and

(b)  at any meeting to consider the resolution they are entitled (if they would otherwise be so entitled) to be given notice of the meeting, to attend and speak and if present (in person or by proxy) to count towards the quorum.

(5)  If at a meeting to consider the resolution a quorum is not present, and after the meeting has been adjourned to a later date a quorum is again not present, the payment is (for the purposes of this section) deemed to have been approved.

(6)  No approval is required under this section on the part of shareholders in a body corporate that—

(a)  is not a UK-registered company, or

(b)  is a wholly-owned subsidiary of another body corporate.

(7)  A payment made in pursuance of an arrangement—

---

[541] Companies Act 2006 (Commencement No 3, etc) Order 2007, SI 2007/2194, art 2. For transitional provisions, see SI 2007/2194, art 9, Sch 3, para 12. For the disapplication of this section in respect of certain specified persons while Northern Rock, Bradford & Bingley and Deposits Management (Heritable) are wholly owned by the Treasury, see note to s 215 above.

[542] S 225. Approval may be given for both purposes by a single resolution.

(a) entered into as part of the agreement for the transfer in question, or within one year before or two years after that agreement, and

(b) to which the company whose shares are the subject of the bid, or any person to whom the transfer is made, is privy,

is presumed, except in so far as the contrary is shown, to be a payment to which this section applies.

COMMENCEMENT DATE 1 October 2007[543]

**10.219.02**    This section, like its predecessor sections 314 and 315 of the Companies Act 1985, is directed specifically to takeovers. It is aimed at avoiding the risk that directors may obtain advantageous payments from a person launching a takeover bid which should in fact go towards the shareholders in return for their shares. Shareholder approval is thus required if any person wishes to make a payment for loss of office to a director of the company in connection with the transfer of shares in the company or in a subsidiary of the company resulting from a takeover bid. Approval is required of the holders of the shares to which the bid relates and of any other holders of the same class.

**10.219.03**    Unlike its predecessor sections, section 219 no longer places a positive duty on the director to take all reasonable steps to secure that particulars of the proposed payment are brought to the attention of shareholders at the time that an offer is made for their shares.[544]

**10.219.04**    Oddly, the expression 'takeover bid' has not been defined for the purposes of Part 10, presumably by oversight. In section 971, the expression is defined for the purposes of Chapter 2 of Part 28 (impediments to takeovers) as having the same meaning as in the Takeovers Directive;[545] and see, similarly, sections 943 and 953 (in Part 28, Chapter 1). There is no reason to think it would bear a different or significantly different meaning in the present context, though the matter remains subject to clarification.[546]

**10.219.05**    Subsection (1): As in the case of section 218, this prohibition extends to a payment for loss of office made by 'any person': unlike most of the other transactions covered in Chapter 4, its scope accordingly includes transactions between a company and the director of a fellow subsidiary.

**10.219.06**    The extension of the scope of the restriction contained in section 219 to include all transfers of shares in the company or in a subsidiary resulting from a takeover bid is an anti-avoidance measure introduced for the first time in the Companies Act 2006.

**10.219.07**    Subsection (2): Aside from the specific requirements imposed by this subsection, the requirements for member approval follow the same pattern as those contained in section 217(1). Where approval is also required under that provision, the requirements of both provisions must be met.[547]

**10.219.08**    Subsection (3): See also section 224 (accidental failure to send memorandum).

**10.219.09**    Subsection (4): Neither the person making the offer, nor any associate of his, may vote on the resolution to approve the payment to the director. This is a new provision which implements a recommendation of the Law Commissions, aimed at providing essential protection for shareholders.

**10.219.10**    Subsection (6): Approval is never required on the part of a shareholder of a wholly-owned subsidiary or on the part of the shareholders of an overseas company.

**10.219.11**    Subsection (7) substantially repeats section 316(1) of the Companies Act 1985.

### 220 Exception for payments in discharge of legal obligations etc

**10.220.01**    (1) Approval is not required under section 217, 218 or 219 (payments requiring members' approval) for a payment made in good faith—

(a) in discharge of an existing legal obligation (as defined below),

(b) by way of damages for breach of such an obligation,

(c) by way of settlement or compromise of any claim arising in connection with the termination of a person's office or employment, or

(d) by way of pension in respect of past services.

---

[543] Companies Act 2006 (Commencement No 3, etc) Order 2007, SI 2007/2194, art 2. For transitional provisions, see SI 2007/2194, art 9, Sch 3, para 12. For the disapplication of this section in respect of certain specified persons while Northern Rock, Bradford & Bingley and Deposits Management (Heritable) are wholly owned by the Treasury, see note to s 215 above.

[544] See s 314(2) of CA 1985. This requirement was considered to be over-regulatory, given that shareholder approval must be obtained in any event, and its removal is in line with the shift in focus under CA 2006 from disclosure to approval.

[545] See Art 2 of Directive 2004/25/EC of the European Parliament and of the Council.

[546] Under s 314 of CA 1985, the relevant offer for shares was defined within the section.

[547] S 225. Approval may be given for both purposes by a single resolution.

(2) In relation to a payment within section 217 (payment by company) an existing legal obligation means an obligation of the company, or any body corporate associated with it, that was not entered into in connection with, or in consequence of, the event giving rise to the payment for loss of office.

(3) In relation to a payment within section 218 or 219 (payment in connection with transfer of undertaking, property or shares) an existing legal obligation means an obligation of the person making the payment that was not entered into for the purposes of, in connection with or in consequence of, the transfer in question.

(4) In the case of a payment within both section 217 and section 218, or within both section 217 and section 219, subsection (2) above applies and not subsection (3).

(5) A payment part of which falls within subsection (1) above and part of which does not is treated as if the parts were separate payments.

COMMENCEMENT DATE 1 October 2007[548]

Sections 217 to 219 are aimed at restricting *ex gratia* payments for loss of office. Payments made in discharge of certain (mainly existing legal) obligations are not intended to fall within the ambit of the restrictions, and this principle has now been set out more fully[549] in statutory form in the Companies Act 2006. Contractual obligations to pay compensation for loss of office, including so-called 'golden parachute' payments, may, however, be subject to other restrictions, for example those contained in section 188. **10.220.02**

Subsection (1)(d): 'pension' is not defined[550] and does not appear to be restricted to one to which there is a contractual entitlement. **10.220.03**

Subsection (2) and (3) specify the existing legal obligations of the company or its subsidiaries (or, in the case of payments otherwise falling within section 218 or 219, any other persons making such payments). For the meaning of associated bodies corporate see section 256. **10.220.04**

Subsection (4): The exception for payments otherwise falling within section 218 or 219 is somewhat narrower than the exception for payments otherwise falling within section 217, in that the payment must be in respect of a legal obligation of the person making the payment. As a result there is potentially room for uncertainty as to the position where a payment would, but for the exception, fall within both section 217 and 218 or 219. Subsection (4) is designed to resolve this by providing that, where a payment would, but for the exception, fall within section 217, the exception is available if section 220(2) is satisfied, regardless of whether the payment would also fall within section 218 or 219. **10.220.05**

Subsection (5): The effect of this provision, which is new, is to sever a single payment into lawful and unlawful elements. **10.220.06**

## 221 Exception for small payments

(1) Approval is not required under section 217, 218 or 219 (payments requiring members' approval) if— **10.221.01**

    (a) the payment in question is made by the company or any of its subsidiaries, and

    (b) the amount or value of the payment, together with the amount or value of any other relevant payments, does not exceed £200.

(2) For this purpose 'other relevant payments' are payments for loss of office in relation to which the following conditions are met.

(3) Where the payment in question is one to which section 217 (payment by company) applies, the conditions are that the other payment was or is paid—

    (a) by the company making the payment in question or any of its subsidiaries,

    (b) to the director to whom that payment is made, and

    (c) in connection with the same event.

---

[548] Companies Act 2006 (Commencement No 3, etc) Order 2007, SI 2007/2194, art 2. For transitional provisions, see SI 2007/2194, art 9, Sch 3, para 12. For the disapplication of this section in respect of certain specified persons while Northern Rock, Bradford & Bingley and Deposits Management (Heritable) are wholly owned by the Treasury, see note to s 215 above.

[549] Under CA 1985 bona fide payments by way of damages for breach of contract or by way of pension in respect of past services were exempted under s 316(3). Although payments made by the company pursuant to the terms of a director's service contract were not expressly exempted under the terms of the statute, it had been held by the Privy Council that the provisions of s 191 of the New Zealand Companies Act 1955, which was identically worded to s 312 of CA 1985, did not impose a restriction on such payments: *Taupo Totara Timber Co v Rowe* [1978] AC 537, subsequently followed in Scotland in *Lander v Premier Pict Petroleum Ltd* [1998] BCC 248.

[550] Contrast s 316(3) of CA 85.

(4) Where the payment in question is one to which section 218 or 219 applies (payment in connection with transfer of undertaking, property or shares), the conditions are that the other payment was (or is) paid in connection with the same transfer—
   (a) to the director to whom the payment in question was made, and
   (b) by the company making the payment or any of its subsidiaries.

COMMENCEMENT DATE 1 October 2007[551]

**10.221.02**  The exception for small payments was introduced for the first time in the Companies Act 2006.

**10.221.03**  The exception is limited to small payments of £200 (or the equivalent value in kind) or less. As a rule of thumb, the exception would cover a case of reasonably good wine or a single bottle of very good wine at 2006 values.

**10.221.04**  The small payments exception applies only to payments made by the company or subsidiaries and not, for example, to a payment made by a person making a takeover bid.

**10.221.05**  Subsection (1): The value of all relevant payments for loss of office, if there are more than one, needs to be aggregated in order to determine whether, in relation to any one such payment, the £200 exception may be used.

**10.221.06**  Subsection (2) to (4): In essence, relevant payments for loss of office are payments made to the same director, in connection with the same event (in the case of a payment falling within section 217) or transfer of undertaking, property, or shares (in the case of a payment falling within section 218 or 219), by the same company or any of its subsidiaries. The effect of section 221(1)(b) and subsections (2) to (4) is thus to prevent a series of connected payments, the individual values of which fall below £200, from coming within the exception.

### 222  Payments made without approval: civil consequences

**10.222.01**
(1) If a payment is made in contravention of section 217 (payment by company)—
   (a) it is held by the recipient on trust for the company making the payment, and
   (b) any director who authorised the payment is jointly and severally liable to indemnify the company that made the payment for any loss resulting from it.
(2) If a payment is made in contravention of section 218 (payment in connection with transfer of undertaking etc), it is held by the recipient on trust for the company whose undertaking or property is or is proposed to be transferred.
(3) If a payment is made in contravention of section 219 (payment in connection with share transfer)—
   (a) it is held by the recipient on trust for persons who have sold their shares as a result of the offer made, and
   (b) the expenses incurred by the recipient in distributing that sum amongst those persons shall be borne by him and not retained out of that sum.
(4) If a payment is in contravention of section 217 and section 218, subsection (2) of this section applies rather than subsection (1).
(5) If a payment is in contravention of section 217 and section 219, subsection (3) of this section applies rather than subsection (1), unless the court directs otherwise.

COMMENCEMENT DATE 1 October 2007[552]

**10.222.02**  The civil[553] consequences of a contravention of section 217, 218 or 219 are now grouped together in a single section, and clarified in certain respects.

**10.222.03**  Subsection (1) codifies the common law rule that an unapproved payment for loss of office by the company (now falling within the restriction contained in section 217), as a misapplication of company funds, renders the directors who authorized it (as well as the director who received it) liable to replace those funds: *Re Duomatic Limited*;[554] *Re Sharpe*.[555] While it was unclear, under the Companies Act

---

[551] Companies Act 2006 (Commencement No 3, etc) Order 2007, SI 2007/2194, art 2. For transitional provisions, see SI 2007/2194, art 9, Sch 3, para 12. For the disapplication of this section in respect of certain specified persons while Northern Rock, Bradford & Bingley and Deposits Management (Heritable) are wholly owned by the Treasury, see note to s 215 above.

[552] Companies Act 2006 (Commencement No 3, etc) Order 2007, SI 2007/2194, art 2. For transitional provisions, see SI 2007/2194, art 9, Sch 3, para 12. For the disapplication of this section in respect of certain specified persons while Northern Rock, Bradford & Bingley and Deposits Management (Heritable) are wholly owned by the Treasury, see note to s 215 above.

[553] There are no criminal penalties for a failure to comply with the requirements of Part 10, Chapter 4.

[554] [1969] 2 Ch 365.

[555] [1892] 1 Ch 154 at 165–166.

1985, whether it was necessary to demonstrate knowledge on the part of a director authorizing the payment (and if so the level of such knowledge), it now seems that there is no such requirement.

Subsection (2) now makes it clear that a payment received in contravention of section 218 (a payment **10.222.04** made by any person in connection with the transfer of the undertaking or property of a company or its subsidiary) is held on trust for the company whose undertaking or property is or is proposed to be transferred and not the company making the payment, removing an area of doubt that had existed under section 313(2) of the Companies Act 1985.

Subsection (3) substantially repeats section 315(1) of the Companies Act 1985 in respect of a payment **10.222.05** received in contravention of section 219 (a payment made by any person in connection with the transfer of shares in a company or its subsidiary).[556]

Subsection (4) and (5) resolve conflicts between remedies where the requirements of more than one of **10.222.06** these sections is breached. For example, if the payment contravenes both section 217 and section 219 because it was a payment by a company to one of its directors and it was a payment in connection with a takeover bid, and neither of the required member approvals was obtained, then the payment is held on trust for the persons who have sold their shares as a result of the offer (with the expense of so doing to be borne by the director or former director or other recipient of the payment) and not on trust for the company making the payment.[557] Note that in the case of payments contravening both section 217 and 219 (but not in the case of payments contravening both section 217 and 218) the court is given a jurisdiction to resolve the conflict between remedies in a different manner. There seems no reason in principle why a court in such circumstances should not direct a hybrid remedy.

## *Supplementary*

### 223  Transactions requiring members' approval: application of provisions to shadow directors

(1)  For the purposes of—                                                                **10.223.01**
    (a)  sections 188 and 189 (directors' service contracts),
    (b)  sections 190 to 196 (property transactions),
    (c)  sections 197 to 214 (loans etc), and
    (d)  sections 215 to 222 (payments for loss of office),
    a shadow director is treated as a director.
(2)  Any reference in those provisions to loss of office as a director does not apply in relation to loss of a person's status as a shadow director.

Commencement Date  1 October 2007[558]

By subsection (1), subject to subsection (2), the effect of this section is to apply the provisions of **10.223.02** sections 188 to 222 to shadow as well as to *de jure* directors. The meaning of 'shadow director' is found at section 251.

However, by subsection (2), references to 'loss of office as a director' do not apply in respect of the loss **10.223.03** by a person of his status as a shadow director. Such references are to be found at sections 190(6), 215 (which defines the meaning of 'payments for loss of office' for the purposes of Chapter 4 of Part 10), and sections 216 to 221.

### 224  Approval by written resolution: accidental failure to send memorandum

(1)  Where—                                                                              **10.224.01**
    (a)  approval under this Chapter is sought by written resolution, and
    (b)  a memorandum is required under this Chapter to be sent or submitted to every eligible member before the resolution is passed,
    any accidental failure to send or submit the memorandum to one or more members shall be disregarded for the purpose of determining whether the requirement has been met.

---

[556]  See also *General Exchange Bank v Horner* (1870) LR 9 Eq 480, in which it was held that a director was debarred, on general principles, from acquiring any secret profit coming to him in the course of or as a result of an offer for the company's shares. The statutory provision ensures that the payment is held on trust for the true victims of the transaction (ie the selling shareholders) and not the company (and hence the purchaser—as would otherwise be the position on the application of the principle in *Regal (Hastings) Ltd v Gulliver* [1942] 1 All ER 378).

[557]  This resolves an uncertainty that existed under ss 312 and 315 of CA 1985. Query whether the directors who authorized the payment (but did not benefit from it) would remain liable under sub-s 1(b).

[558]  Companies Act 2006 (Commencement No 3, Consequential Amendments, Transitional Provisions and Savings) Order 2007, SI 2007/2194, art 2.

(2) Subsection (1) has effect subject to any provision of the company's articles.

COMMENCEMENT DATE 1 October 2007[559]

**10.224.02**  This section applies to Chapter 4 of Part 10 (sections 188 to 226) which deals with transactions with directors requiring members' approval. It is a new provision, the need for which arises because, although under the 1985 Act a written resolution was only effective where signed by all members (see section 381A of the 1985 Act), this is not so under the 2006 Act (see section 296(4)). In the case of circulation of written resolutions, sections 291(7) and 293(7) provide that a failure to circulate relevant papers to all members may result in an offence being committed but that it will not affect the validity of any resolution provided it has been passed by the relevant majority signifying their agreement to it.

**10.224.03**  Similarly, section 224 provides that (subject to the articles of the company) in cases where approval of members is sought by written resolution and the Act requires that a 'memorandum' be sent or submitted to eligible members prior to passing the resolution, any 'accidental failure' to do so shall be disregarded for the purposes of determining whether the requirement has been satisfied.[560]

**10.224.04**  The provision will apply therefore in connection with section 188(5) (directors' long-term service contracts), section 197(3) (loans to directors), section 198(4) (quasi-loans to directors), section 200(4) (loans and quasi-loans to persons connected with directors), section 201(4) (credit transactions with directors and persons connected with directors), section 203(3) (related arrangements), section 217(3) (payments for loss of office), section 218(3) (payment in connected with transfer of undertaking) and section 219(3) (payment in connection with share transfer).

**10.224.05**  'Accidental failure' will presumably be interpreted in accordance with the words 'accidental omission' as found in the 1985 Act, Table A regulation 39 (and see now section 313 of the Act). Thus, the failure must arise as a result of an accident, not an error: see *Musselwhite v CH Musselwhite & Son Ltd*,[561] *Re West Canadian Collieries Ltd*[562], *Re Estate Acquisition & Development Ltd*,[563] and *Peninsular and Oriental Steam Navigation Co v Eller*.[564] If a company fails to send a memorandum to any, or even a majority, of its members, it is unclear whether section 224 would still apply. It may be that the procedural failure would be overlooked if the shareholder vote could be shown to be properly informed.[565]

### 225 Cases where approval is required under more than one provision

**10.225.01**  (1) Approval may be required under more than one provision of this Chapter.
(2) If so, the requirements of each applicable provision must be met.
(3) This does not require a separate resolution for the purposes of each provision.

COMMENCEMENT DATE 1 October 2007[566]

**10.225.02**  This section applies to cases under Chapter 4 of Part 10 where approval is required under more than one provision of the Chapter. The requirements are cumulative, and in such cases the requirements of each provision must be met, albeit not necessarily by means of separate resolutions.

**10.225.03**  Thus, for example, a substantial property transaction by means of the discharge of a person's liability (see sections 190 and 1163(2)) might also amount to a transaction (or be part of a transaction) by which a loan is made to that person. In such a case, approval would be required under both sections 190 and 197. Although part of the same resolution, it would have to be ensured that the members gave separate consideration to the requirements of each provision. However, if the transaction is both a payment for loss of office and a substantial property transaction, section 190(6)(b) provides that the rules on substantial property transactions do not apply and the rules on payment for loss of office apply in the usual manner.[567]

---

[559] Companies Act 2006 (Commencement No 3, Consequential Amendments, Transitional Provisions and Savings) Order 2007, SI 2007/2194, art 2.

[560] Introduced at the report stage of the House of Lords to ensure that accidental failure to send the memorandum would not necessarily invalidate the approval. *Hansard*, HL Report Stage, col 871 (9 May 2006).

[561] [1962] Ch 964.

[562] [1962] Ch 370.

[563] [1995] BCC 338.

[564] [2006] EWCA Civ 432.

[565] Compare *Euro Brokers Holdings Ltd v Monecor (London) Ltd* [2003] EWCA Civ 105; [2003] BCC 573; [2003] 1 BCLC 506 and *NBH Ltd & NBH Group Ltd v Kevin Hoare and Others* [2006] BCLC 649 in relation to ss 320–32 of the 1985 Act.

[566] Companies Act 2006 (Commencement No 3, Consequential Amendments, Transitional Provisions and Savings) Order 2007, SI 2007/2194, art 2.

[567] See *Hansard* HL, vol, 678, col 360 (9 February 2006), *per* Lord Sainsbury.

226  Requirement of consent of Charity Commission: companies that are charities[568]

## CHAPTER 5
## DIRECTORS' SERVICE CONTRACTS

Chapter 5 contains the provisions which replace section 318 of the Companies Act 1985,[569] under **10.227.01** which copies or memoranda of directors' 'contracts of service' (not defined)[570] had to be kept by the company and kept open for inspection by shareholders, without charge, unless either (i) the unexpired portion of the term for which the contract was to be in force was less than 12 months, or (ii) the contracts could, within the next 12 months following, have been terminated by the company without payment of compensation (section 318(11)). Where applicable it had been suggested that these exceptions were being used as a means of directors keeping secret the amount of their pay.[571] There was, in addition to those at section 318(11) of the 1985 Act, a more limited exception relating to contracts of service requiring work wholly or 'mainly'[572] outside the UK (section 318(5)). Both the exceptions in section 318(5) and (11) had been criticized,[573] although in practice they only applied to those companies who were not subject to the old requirements of the Listing Rules concerning public inspection of directors' service contracts. Note that these requirements under paragraphs 16.9 to 16.11 were repealed on the basis that the inspection of directors' service contracts is more appropriately regulated by company law and the Financial Reporting Council's Combined Code on Corporate Governance.[574]

The principal changes effected by the 2006 Act are: **10.227.02**

(i)   the introduction of a definition of a director's 'service contract' which expands the term as previously understood;
(ii)  the introduction of a shareholder's right to request a copy of the contract on payment of a fee; and
(iii) the repeal of the exceptions and limitations previously contained in section 318(5) and (11) of the 1985 Act.

Accordingly, the obligations on the company have been increased by the 2006 Act. **10.227.03**

### 227  Directors' service contracts

(1)  For the purposes of this Part a director's 'service contract', in relation to a company, means a **10.227.04** contract under which—
(a)  a director of the company undertakes personally to perform services (as director or otherwise) for the company, or for a subsidiary of the company, or
(b)  services (as director or otherwise) that a director of the company undertakes personally to perform are made available by a third party to the company, or to a subsidiary of the company.
(2)  The provisions of this Part relating to directors' service contracts apply to the terms of a person's appointment as a director of a company.
They are not restricted to contracts for the performance of services outside the scope of the ordinary duties of a director.

COMMENCEMENT DATE 1 October 2007[575]

This section contains a new provision: it defines for the purposes of Part 10 of the 2006 Act a director's **10.227.05** 'service contract' in relation to a company.[576] The definition at subsection (1)(a) is sufficiently broad to

[568] *Repealed by Schedule 10 of the Charities Act 2011.*
[569] S 26 of CA 1967 had introduced, for the first time, statutory provisions whereby a company's members could inspect its directors' service contracts.
[570] Although there was an obvious contrast with the use of the term 'agreement' in s 319 of CA 1985, and see also s 319(7) of the 1985 Act.
[571] See Brian R Cheffins, *Company Law, Theory, Structure and Operation* (1997), 664, n 83.
[572] As to which, see *Fawcett Properties Limited v Buckingham* [1961] AC 636, HL: 'mainly' bears its normal meaning of more than half, *per* Lord Morton of Henryton at 667.
[573] See The Law Commission, Consultation Paper 153 and The Scottish Law Commission Discussion Paper No 105: 'Company Directors: Regulating Conflicts of Interests and Formulating a Statement of Duties. A Joint Consultation Paper' at 4.140 and 4.145.
[574] See Financial Services Authority, Consultation Paper 04/16: 'The Listing Review and implementation of the Prospectus Rules' at 4.18. See now the UK Corporate Governance Code, June 2010.
[575] The Companies Act 2006 (Commencement No 3, etc) Order 2007, SI 2007/2194, art 2.
[576] The expression is found also at ss 177, 182, 188, and 190.

include contracts of employment or service (as, for example, an executive director) and contracts for services. It applies to contracts either with the company or with a subsidiary of the company.

**10.227.06**  Subsection (1)(b) covers services made available to the company or a subsidiary through a third party, for example, a personal services company.

**10.227.07**  However, in either case, it is important to understand that the contract must provide for the director to perform the service or services personally.

**10.227.08**  Sections 228 to 230 apply to service contracts within section 227(1) entered into, on or after 1 October 2007, appointments within section 227(2) made on or after that date, and to contracts to which section 318(1) of the 1985 Act applied immediately before that date.[577]

**10.227.09**  Subsection (2) expressly provides that Part 10 is also to be applied to the terms of a director's appointment, including, therefore, a letter of appointment (regardless, presumably, of whether the director is appointed to act as an executive or non-executive director), and furthermore, ensures that the definition of a 'service contract' is not restricted to services which fall outside the scope of a director's ordinary duties.

### 228  Copy of contract or memorandum of terms to be available for inspection

**10.228.01**
(1)  A company must keep available for inspection—
    (a)  a copy of every director's service contract with the company or with a subsidiary of the company, or
    (b)  if the contract is not in writing, a written memorandum setting out the terms of the contract.
(2)  All the copies and memoranda must be kept available for inspection at—
    (a)  the company's registered office, or
    (b)  a place specified in regulations under section 1136.
(3)  The copies and memoranda must be retained by the company for at least one year from the date of termination or expiry of the contract and must be kept available for inspection during that time.
(4)  The company must give notice to the registrar—
    (a)  of the place at which the copies and memoranda are kept available for inspection, and
    (b)  of any change in that place,
    unless they have at all times been kept at the company's registered office.
(5)  If default is made in complying with subsection (1), (2) or (3), or default is made for 14 days in complying with subsection (4), an offence is committed by every officer of the company who is in default.
(6)  A person guilty of an offence under this section is liable on summary conviction to a fine not exceeding level 3 on the standard scale and, for continued contravention, a daily default fine not exceeding one-tenth of level 3 on the standard scale.
(7)  The provisions of this section apply to a variation of a director's service contract as they apply to the original contract.

COMMENCEMENT DATE 1 October 2007[578]

**10.228.02**  Under this section, a company must keep available for inspection a copy of all directors' service contracts, or, if not in writing, a memorandum of their terms: subsection (1).

**10.228.03**  By subsection (2), the copy or memorandum must be kept at the company's registered office or at a place specified in regulations made under section 1136 (which came into force on 1 October 2009).[579] In essence, these provisions replace section 318(2) and (3) of the 1985 Act, and repeal the obligation to keep all copies or memoranda 'at the same place' (section 318(2) of the 1985 Act). Under the regulations issued by the Secretary of State pursuant to the power conferred under section 1136, an alternative location may be used instead of the registered office for inspection of company records, such as the copy or memorandum. The alternative location (which must be the same place for all company records listed in section 1136(2)), is a single location situated in the same part of the UK as the company's registered office.[580] A company is required to notify the registrar of such alternative inspection location and, additionally, is required to disclose the address of that location and the type of records kept to any person it deals with in the course of business who makes a written request for that information. A written response must be sent by the company to that person within five working days of receiving the request.[581]

[577]  The Companies Act 2006 (Commencement No 3, etc) Order 2007, SI 2007/2194, Sch 3, para 13.
[578]  The Companies Act 2006 (Commencement No 3, etc) Order 2007, SI 2007/2194, art 2.
[579]  The Companies Act 2006 (Commencement No 8, etc) Order 2008, SI 2008/2860, art 3(t).
[580]  The Companies (Company Records) Regulations 2008 (SI 2008/3006), reg 3.
[581]  The Companies (Trading Disclosures) Regulations 2008 (SI 2008/495), reg 9.

Subsection (3) contains a new provision: copies and memoranda must be retained and kept available **10.228.04** for inspection for at least one year *after* they have terminated or expired, but the subsection does not require the copies to be retained thereafter. This contrasts sharply with the repealed exception previously contained at section 318(11) of the 1985 Act which disapplied that section where the unexpired portion of the contract term was less than 12 months, or where the contract could, within the next 12 months following, have been terminated by the company without payment of compensation.

By subsection (4), notice must be given to the registrar of the place where the copies and memoranda **10.228.05** are kept and of any change to that place, unless they have at all times been kept at the registered office. This mirrors precisely the previous provision at section 318(4) of the 1985 Act.

Subsection (5) provides that a breach of subsection (1), (2), or (3) or a 14-day default in complying with **10.228.06** subsection (4) is an offence, committed by every officer[582] of the defaulting company. Subsection (6) provides for the penalty, being a fine,[583] and a daily default fine[584] for continuing contravention. Under section 318 of the 1985 Act the company was also criminally liable to pay a fine. This provision has been repealed. However, in common with the 1985 Act, the validity of contracts is not affected by breach of this section.

By subsection (7), the provisions of section 228 apply also to a variation of a director's service contract, **10.228.07** whether written or not. This is unsurprising, and simply re-enacts the provision previously contained at section 318(10) of the 1985 Act.

## 229  Right of member to inspect and request copy

(1) Every copy or memorandum required to be kept under section 228 must be open to inspection by **10.229.01** any member of the company without charge.

(2) Any member of the company is entitled, on request and on payment of such fee as may be prescribed, to be provided with a copy of any such copy or memorandum.
The copy must be provided within seven days after the request is received by the company.

(3) If an inspection required under subsection (1) is refused, or default is made in complying with subsection (2), an offence is committed by every officer of the company who is in default.

(4) A person guilty of an offence under this section is liable on summary conviction to a fine not exceeding level 3 on the standard scale and, for continued contravention, a daily default fine not exceeding one-tenth of level 3 on the standard scale.

(5) In the case of any such refusal or default the court may by order compel an immediate inspection or, as the case may be, direct that the copy required be sent to the person requiring it.

COMMENCEMENT DATE 1 October 2007[585]

This section confers on members the basic right to inspect copies or memoranda of directors' service **10.229.02** contracts kept pursuant to section 228, without payment of a fee: subsection (1). In this respect, it mirrors section 318(7) of the 1985 Act. Unlike the Combined Code,[586] this section does not enable inspection by a member of the public, whatever the nature of his interest in the company.

In addition, subsection (2) confers a new right on members, on payment of a prescribed fee, to be **10.229.03** provided with a copy of the contract or memorandum. As to the fee prescribed, see The Companies (Fees for Inspection and Copying of Company Records) Regulations 2007, SI 2007/2612, regulation 4. Although not previously contained in the 1985 Act, a member's right to copy was previously conferred by the Companies (Inspection and Copying of Registers, Indices and Documents) Regulations 1991, SI 1991/1998, regulation 3(2)(b).

Subsection (3) provides that a breach of subsection (1) or (2) is an offence committed by every officer[587] **10.229.04** of the company who is in default. Subsection (4) provides for the penalty, being a fine,[588] and a daily default fine[589] for continuing contravention. Under section 318 of the 1985 Act the company was also criminally liable to pay a fine; this provision has been repealed. The validity of contracts is not affected by breach of this section.

---

[582] See s 1121 for the meaning of 'officer' and 'in default' in this context.
[583] Not exceeding £1,000, according to the scale as currently drawn.
[584] Not exceeding £100, according to the scale as currently drawn.
[585] The Companies Act 2006 (Commencement No 3, etc) Order 2007, SI 2007/2194, art 2.
[586] See the Combined Code on Corporate Governance (June 2008) at A.4.4 and Sch C. See now the UK Corporate Governance Code, June 2010.
[587] See s 1121 for the meaning of 'in default' and 'officer' in this context.
[588] Not exceeding £1,000, according to the scale as currently drawn.
[589] Not exceeding £100, according to the scale as currently drawn.

**10.229.05** Subsection (5) grants to the court a power to compel immediate inspection or direct the provision of a copy of the copy or memorandum. To the extent that it deals with inspection, it mirrors section 318(9) of the 1985 Act. Although the company is not criminally liable under either section 228(5) or 229(3), if it fails to comply with an order made under section 229(5) it will be in contempt of court, as would any director who wilfully fails to take reasonable steps to ensure that the company complies with the order: see *Templeton Insurance Ltd v Motorcare Warranties Ltd and others*[590] and *Attorney-General for Tuvalu v. Philatelic Distribution Corp Limited*,[591] which held that a director is under a duty to take reasonable care to secure compliance with an order, and that a failure to do so will expose a director to liability to punishment for contempt even without personal participation in the breach.

### 230 Directors' service contracts: application of provisions to shadow directors

**10.230.01** A shadow director is treated as a director for the purposes of the provisions of this Chapter.

COMMENCEMENT DATE 1 October 2007[592]

**10.230.02** This section applies the provisions of Chapter 5 to shadow directors (defined at section 251) as previously did section 318(6) of the Companies Act 1985. As to the position in respect of *de facto* directors, see section 250, which provides that any reference to 'director' includes reference to a person occupying the position of director, by whatever name called.

## CHAPTER 6
## CONTRACTS WITH SOLE MEMBERS WHO ARE DIRECTORS

### 231 Contract with sole member who is also a director

**10.231.01** (1) This section applies where—
   (a) a limited company having only one member enters into a contract with the sole member,
   (b) the sole member is also a director of the company, and
   (c) the contract is not entered into in the ordinary course of the company's business.
(2) The company must, unless the contract is in writing, ensure that the terms of the contract are either—
   (a) set out in a written memorandum, or
   (b) recorded in the minutes of the first meeting of the directors of the company following the making of the contract.
(3) If a company fails to comply with this section an offence is committed by every officer of the company who is in default.
(4) A person guilty of an offence under this section is liable on summary conviction to a fine not exceeding level 5 on the standard scale.
(5) For the purposes of this section a shadow director is treated as a director.
(6) Failure to comply with this section in relation to a contract does not affect the validity of the contract.
(7) Nothing in this section shall be read as excluding the operation of any other enactment or rule of law applying to contracts between a company and a director of the company.

COMMENCEMENT DATE 1 October 2007[593]

**10.231.02** This section replaces section 322B[594] of the 1985 Act which implemented Article 5 of the 12th Company Law Directive (89/667/EEC). The 12th Company Law Directive constituted a more stringent regime, as Article 5 applied to contracts between the sole member and the company regardless of whether the sole member is a director (or sole director) of the company.

**10.231.03** Section 231 applies to companies which have a single member who is also a director,[595] whether or not he is the *sole* director. As the 2006 Act permits public companies to have a single shareholder, section 231 applies to both private and public companies.[596]

**10.231.04** Its purpose is to ensure that there is a proper record of contracts made in circumstances where there is some risk of confusion (and conflict) between the directorial and personal capacities of the person with whom the contract is made. It applies where:

---

[590] [2012] EWHC 795 (Comm).
[591] [1990] 1 WLR 926, CA.
[592] The Companies Act 2006 (Commencement No 3, etc) Order 2007, SI 2007/2194, art 2.
[593] The Companies Act 2006 (Commencement No 3, etc) Order 2007, SI 2007/2194, art 2.
[594] Inserted by the Companies (Single Member Private Limited Companies) Regulations 1992, SI 1992/1699, reg 2(1)(b), Sch 3(1), as from 15 July 1992.
[595] Including a shadow director: subs (5).
[596] See ss 7, 38, and 123.

(i) a contract is entered into otherwise than in writing;

(ii) between the company and its sole member, where that member is also a director of the company[597] or a shadow director (see subsection (5) and sections 250 and 251); and

(iii) the contract is not entered into 'in the ordinary course of the company's business'.

In those circumstances, by subsection (2), the company must either ensure that the terms of the contract are set out in a written memorandum, or are recorded in the minutes of the first meeting of the company's directors following the making of the contract. Compliance will be of obvious benefit where, for example, the company subsequently goes into liquidation or administration and the relevant insolvency practitioner requires evidence of extraordinary agreements made by the company. A breach would be relevant to an allegation of unfit conduct under the Company Directors Disqualification Act 1986.   **10.231.05**

The 'ordinary course of the company's business' will be determined by an examination of all the surrounding facts and circumstances: see *Steen v Law*,[598] and note that the section refers to the ordinary course of *the company's* business and not merely the ordinary course of business generally (see, for example, *Intercontinental Bank v Erastus Bankole Oladipo Akingbola and others*[599] and *Countrywide Banking Corporation Ltd v Dean*[600] ). Similar expressions are found in other areas of the law.[601] For example, in connection with (i) freezing orders, where respondents are usually permitted to meet their ordinary living or business expenses (see, for example, *TDK Tape Distributor (UK) Ltd v Videochoice Ltd*);[602] (ii) the standard form of the prospective validation order made under section 127 of the Insolvency Act 1986 which refers to payments made 'in the ordinary course of the business of the company' (see Practice Direction 49b: Order under section 127 Insolvency Act 1986); and (iii) floating charges, where the charge would be on a class of assets which, in the ordinary course of business of the company, would change from time to time (see *Re Yorkshire Woolcombers Association Ltd*).[603]   **10.231.06**

The consequences of breach of the section are criminal, not civil. The validity of the contract is not affected[604] (see subsection (6)) although by subsection (7) these provisions do not exclude the operation of any other rule of law or enactment, for example, section 182 and 190. Although it will be appreciated that if the contract is with a sole member, and subject to the decision in *Neptune (Vehicle Washing Equipment) Ltd v Fitzgerald (No 2)*,[605] then the principle in *Re Duomatic Ltd*[606] is likely to apply.   **10.231.07**

The criminal consequences affect the company's officers only, unlike section 322B of the 1985 Act which also imposed penalties on the company. By subsection (3), an offence is committed by 'every officer of the company who is in default'.[607]   **10.231.08**

Subsection (4) sets an upper limit on the amount of the fine, currently at £5,000.   **10.231.09**

# CHAPTER 7
## DIRECTORS' LIABILITIES

### Provision protecting directors from liability

There are two major issues which are addressed in this Chapter. First, a substantive reform of the law on ratification of acts giving rise to liability on the part of a director introduced in section 239 below. Secondly, the chapter restates section 309A to 309C and section 337A of the Companies Act 1985 (provisions relating to directors' liability) as inserted by the Companies (Audit, Investigations and Community Enterprise) Act 2004, amending section 310 of the Companies Act 1985. The 2004 Act made some important reforms in this area. The starting point for the reform package was a principle going back to section 152 of the Companies Act 1929,[608] namely that companies should be prohibited from exempting directors from, or indemnifying them against, liability for negligence, default, breach   **10.232.01**

---

[597] For the applicability to *de facto* directors, see s 250.

[598] [1964] AC 287, PC at 302.

[599] [2011] EWHC 605, paras 14–23.

[600] [1998] 2 WLR 441, PC.

[601] See s 207.

[602] [1986] 1 WLR 141, 146 per Skinner J.

[603] [1903] 2 Ch 284, 295.

[604] See *Re Horsley & Weight Ltd* [1982] Ch 442.

[605] [1995] BCC 1000.

[606] [1969] 2 Ch 365.

[607] See s 1121 for meaning of 'officer' and 'in default' in this context.

[608] Which became s 205 of CA 1948.

of duty or breach of trust in relation to the company.[609] However, the reform package also recognized that companies should be permitted to indemnify directors in respect of third-party claims in most circumstances, that is, claims not brought against them by their own company but claims by third parties that might have been, and some would say should have been, brought against the company.[610] The reforms permitted companies to pay directors' defence costs as they are incurred, even if the action is brought by the company itself.[611]

**10.232.02**    There were four main exceptions contained in the 2004 Act to indemnification which reflect the need to strike a careful balance in this area.[612] These are:[613]

(i)   criminal penalties;
(ii)  penalties imposed by regulatory bodies;
(iii) costs incurred by the director in defending criminal proceedings in which he is convicted; and
(iv)  costs incurred by the director in defending civil proceedings brought by the company in which final judgment is given against him.

**10.232.03**    The 2004 reforms also addressed some specific concerns relating to exposure to third party liabilities, particularly from the United States, and the cost of lengthy court proceedings.[614]

**10.232.04**    Although this chapter restates section 309A to 309C of the Companies Act 1985, there are three key changes to those sections introduced by this Chapter. First, the creation of a right for members to request a copy of a qualifying third party indemnity provision (section 238 below); secondly, the removal of criminal liability on the part of the company for failures to comply with the requirements of section 237 (copy of qualifying third party indemnity provision to be available for inspection); and, finally, a requirement for all qualifying third party indemnity provisions to be retained by a company for at least one year after they have expired (section 237(4) below).

**10.232.05**    It is noteworthy that the Companies Act 2006 (Commencement No. 3, Consequential Amendments, Transitional Provisions and Savings) Order 2007, SI 2007/2194, includes transitional provisions in art 9, Sch 3, in relation to ss 232–239 which came into effect on 1 October 2007.

### 232 Provisions protecting directors from liability

**10.232.06**
(1)  Any provision that purports to exempt a director of a company (to any extent) from any liability that would otherwise attach to him in connection with any negligence, default, breach of duty or breach of trust in relation to the company is void.
(2)  Any provision by which a company directly or indirectly provides an indemnity (to any extent) for a director of the company, or of an associated company, against any liability attaching to him in connection with any negligence, default, breach of duty or breach of trust in relation to the company of which he is a director is void, except as permitted by—
   (a) section 233 (provision of insurance),
   (b) section 234 (qualifying third party indemnity provision), or
   (c) section 235 (qualifying pension scheme indemnity provision).
(3)  This section applies to any provision, whether contained in a company's articles or in any contract with the company or otherwise.
(4)  Nothing in this section prevents a company's articles from making such provision as has previously been lawful for dealing with conflicts of interest.

COMMENCEMENT DATE 1 October 2007[615]

**10.232.07**    This section restates section 309A of the Companies Act 1985, as inserted by the Companies (Audit, Investigations and Community Enterprise) Act 2004. It prohibits a company from exempting a

---

[609] See, Official Report, 9/2/2006; coll GC364 (Lord Goldsmith).
[610] Ss 309B and 309C of CA 1985.
[611] S 337A of CA 1985 as inserted by the Companies (Audit, Investigations and Community Enterprise) Act 2004 permitted companies to pay the legal costs of directors upfront, provided that the directors repay such sums if convicted or judgment is given against them in any civil proceedings brought by the company or an associated company. See also, White Paper *Company Law Reform* Cm 6456 (DTI, London, March 2005) s 3.3.
[612] See, Official Report, 9/2/2006; coll GC364 (Lord Goldsmith).
[613] See ss 309A–309C and 337A of CA 1985.
[614] See, Official Report, 9/2/2006; coll GC364 (Lord Goldsmith).
[615] Companies Act 2006 (Commencement No 3, etc) Order 2007, SI 2007/2194, art 2. The section applies to any provision made on or after 1 October 2007. Ss 309A, 309B, and 309C(1), (3) and (6) of the 1985 Act or art 318 of the 1986 Order (so far as it relates to directors) continue to apply in relation to any provision to which they applied immediately before that date. See Sch 3 to the Companies Act 2006 (Commencement No. 3, Consequential Amendments, Transitional Provisions and Savings) Order 2007, SI 2007/2194.

director from, or indemnifying him against, any liability in connection with any negligence, default, breach of duty, or breach of trust by him in relation to the company. The prohibition on such exemptions dates back to the recommendations of the Greene Committee on Company Law,[616] which, in this respect, were implemented by section 152 of the Companies Act (1929), that later became section 310 of the Companies Act (1985).

Subsection (1) and (3) provide that any provision, whether in the company's articles of association, in **10.232.08** a contract, or otherwise, attempting to exempt or indemnify a director in breach of this section is void. These provisions address the issue that arose in *Movitex v Bulfield*,[617] where Vinelott J sought to reconcile section 310 of the Companies Act (1985), which similarly rendered void any provision in the articles which exempted a director from liability for breach of duty, with Article 85 of Table A which, subject to disclosure to being made to the board, permitted a director to be a party to a conflict transaction. As we saw above, the judge reconciled these two provisions by reasoning that the no-conflict rule was not a duty as such but a disability and, therefore, fell outside of section 310 of the 1985 Act. In this regard, it is noteworthy that the substantive duties codified in Part 10 of the 2006 Act are listed as 'duties'. The effect is that any article in the form of Article 85 of Table A will be caught by section 232(1) and (3). For companies who continue to adopt Article 85 of Table A, subsection (2) prohibits indemnification by an associated company[618] as well as by his own company.[619] However, this is subject to three exceptions. Section 233 (see below) permits the purchase of insurance, section 234 (see below) creates an exception for qualifying third party indemnity provisions, and thirdly, section 235 creates an exception for qualifying pension scheme indemnity provisions. Finally, subsection (4) makes it clear that nothing in this section prevents a company's articles from making such provision as has previously been lawful for dealing with conflicts of interest.

### 233  Provision of insurance

Section 232(2) (voidness of provisions for indemnifying directors) does not prevent a company from **10.233.01** purchasing and maintaining for a director of the company, or of an associated company, insurance against any such liability as is mentioned in that subsection.

    COMMENCEMENT DATE  1 October 2007[620]

This section restates section 309A(5) of the Companies Act 1985, as inserted by the Companies (Audit, **10.233.02** Investigations and Community Enterprise) Act 2004. It permits a company to purchase and maintain insurance for its directors (so-called D & O liability insurance), or the directors of an associated company,[621] against any liability attaching to them in connection with any negligence, default, breach of duty, or breach of trust by them in relation to the company of which they are a director. In practice, policies of insurance contain a range of exclusions which, therefore, leave directors exposed to a range of liabilities. In any case, liabilities resulting from fraudulent and illegal conduct cannot be covered. It is also noteworthy that the wording of the section suggests that it does *not* permit a company to meet the cost of any excess which the policy may provide for. This will need to be paid personally by the director.

### 234  Qualifying third party indemnity provision

  (1)  Section 232(2) (voidness of provisions for indemnifying directors) does not apply to qualifying **10.234.01** third party indemnity provision.
  (2)  Third party indemnity provision means provision for indemnity against liability incurred by the director to a person other than the company or an associated company.
      Such provision is qualifying third party indemnity provision if the following requirements are met.

---

[616]  Cmnd 2657, paras 46–47. See also, *Re Brazilian Rubber Plantations and Estates Ltd* [1911] 1 Ch 425; *Re City Equitable Fire Insurance Co Ltd* [1925] Ch 407.
[617]  [1988] BCLC 104, discussed above, at para 10.175.07
[618]  'Associated company' is defined in s 256 as, in effect, a company in the same group. The inclusion of this term is a change in the law which was not included in the amendments to the Companies Acts made by the Companies (Audit, Investigations and Community Enterprise) Act 2004. The reason for the change is unclear. See the Law Society's 'Proposed Amendments and Briefing for Parts 10 & 11' (issued 23 Jan 2006) 11.
[619]  It should be noted that the scope of subs (2) is again returned to in s 233 (see below), s 234(1) (see below), and s 235 (see below).
[620]  Companies Act 2006 (Commencement No 3, etc) Order 2007, SI 2007/2194, art 2. The section applies to any provision made on or after 1 October 2007. Ss 309A, 309B, and 309C(1)–(3) and (6) of the 1985 Act or art 318 of the 1986 Order (so far as it relates to directors) continue to apply in relation to any provision to which they applied immediately before that date. See Sch 3 to the Companies Act 2006 (Commencement No. 3, Consequential Amendments, Transitional Provisions and Savings) Order 2007, SI 2007/2194.
[621]  'Associated company' is defined in s 256 as, in effect, a company in the same group.

(3) The provision must not provide any indemnity against—
  (a) any liability of the director to pay—
    (i) a fine imposed in criminal proceedings, or
    (ii) a sum payable to a regulatory authority by way of a penalty in respect of non-compliance with any requirement of a regulatory nature (however arising); or
  (b) any liability incurred by the director—
    (i) in defending criminal proceedings in which he is convicted, or
    (ii) in defending civil proceedings brought by the company, or an associated company, in which judgment is given against him, or
    (iii) in connection with an application for relief (see subsection (6)) in which the court refuses to grant him relief.
(4) The references in subsection (3)(b) to a conviction, judgment or refusal of relief are to the final decision in the proceedings.
(5) For this purpose—
  (a) a conviction, judgment or refusal of relief becomes final—
    (i) if not appealed against, at the end of the period for bringing an appeal, or
    (ii) if appealed against, at the time when the appeal (or any further appeal) is disposed of; and
  (b) an appeal is disposed of—
    (i) if it is determined and the period for bringing any further appeal has ended, or
    (ii) if it is abandoned or otherwise ceases to have effect.
(6) The reference in subsection (3)(b)(iii) to an application for relief is to an application for relief under—
  section 661(3) or (4) (power of court to grant relief in case of acquisition of shares by innocent nominee) or section 1157 (general power of court to grant relief in case of honest and reasonable conduct).

COMMENCEMENT DATE 1 October 2007[622]

**10.234.02** This section restates section 309B and 337A of the Companies Act 1985, as inserted by the Companies (Audit, Investigations and Community Enterprise) Act 2004. It permits, but does not require, companies to indemnify directors in respect of proceedings brought by third parties (such as class actions in the US).[623] An indemnity that complies with the conditions set out in this section is described as a qualifying third party indemnity provision.

**10.234.03** Subsection (2) provides that the indemnity may cover liability incurred by the director to any person other than the company or an associated company.[624] This may include both legal costs and the financial costs of an adverse judgment. However, the indemnity must *not* cover liabilities to the company or to any associated company.[625]

**10.234.04** Subsection (3) provides that the indemnity must not cover criminal fines, penalties imposed by regulatory bodies (such as the Financial Services Authority), the defence costs of criminal proceedings where the director is found guilty, the defence costs of civil proceedings successfully brought against the director by the company or an associated company, and the costs of unsuccessful applications by the director for relief.[626] Subsection (3)(b)(iii) and (6) taken together, also permit, but do not require, companies to indemnify directors in respect of applications for relief from liability made under section 661(3) or (4) (power of court to grant relief in case of acquisition of shares by innocent nominee), or under section 1157 (general power of court to grant relief in case of honest and reasonable conduct).[627]

**10.234.05** Subsection (4) and (5) restate section 337A(5) and (6) of the Companies Act 1985 by stating when legal proceedings will be considered to have concluded for the purpose of the conditions imposed by subsection (3). As such, subsection (4) makes it clear that the references in subsection (3)(b) to a conviction, judgment, or refusal of relief are to the final decision in the proceedings. Subsection (5) provides further that for this purpose, a conviction, judgment, or refusal of relief becomes final if not appealed against, at the end of the period for bringing an appeal, or if appealed against, at the time when

---

[622] Companies Act 2006 (Commencement No 3, etc) Order 2007, SI 2007/2194, art 2. The section applies to any provision made on or after 1 October 2007. Sections 309A, 309B, and 309C(1)–(3) and (6) of the 1985 Act or art 318 of the 1986 Order (so far as it relates to directors) continue to apply in relation to any provision to which they applied immediately before that date. See Sch 3 to the Companies Act 2006 (Commencement No. 3, Consequential Amendments, Transitional Provisions and Savings) Order 2007, SI 2007/2194.
[623] See the Explanatory Notes to the Act, para 429.
[624] 'Associated company' is defined in s 256 as, in effect, a company in the same group.
[625] See the Explanatory Notes to the Act, para 430.
[626] See the Explanatory Notes to the Act, para 431.
[627] This was formerly contained in s 337A (1)(b) and (2) of CA 1985.

the appeal (or any further appeal) is disposed of. Likewise, an appeal is disposed of if it is determined and the period for bringing any further appeal has ended, or if it is abandoned or otherwise ceases to have effect.

## 235 Qualifying pension scheme indemnity provision

(1) Section 232(2) (voidness of provisions for indemnifying directors) does not apply to qualifying pension scheme indemnity provision.  **10.235.01**

(2) Pension scheme indemnity provision means provision indemnifying a director of a company that is a trustee of an occupational pension scheme against liability incurred in connection with the company's activities as trustee of the scheme.
Such provision is qualifying pension scheme indemnity provision if the following requirements are met.

(3) The provision must not provide any indemnity against—
   (a) any liability of the director to pay—
      (i) a fine imposed in criminal proceedings, or
      (ii) a sum payable to a regulatory authority by way of a penalty in respect of non-compliance with any requirement of a regulatory nature (however arising); or
   (b) any liability incurred by the director in defending criminal proceedings in which he is convicted.

(4) The reference in subsection (3)(b) to a conviction is to the final decision in the proceedings.

(5) For this purpose—
   (a) a conviction becomes final—
      (i) if not appealed against, at the end of the period for bringing an appeal, or
      (ii) if appealed against, at the time when the appeal (or any further appeal) is disposed of; and
   (b) an appeal is disposed of—
      (i) if it is determined and the period for bringing any further appeal has ended, or
      (ii) if it is abandoned or otherwise ceases to have effect.

(6) In this section 'occupational pension scheme' means an occupational pension scheme as defined in section 150(5) of the Finance Act 2004 (c. 12) that is established under a trust.

COMMENCEMENT DATE 1 October 2007[628]

This is a new section. It is concerned with the indemnification of a director of a company acting as a trustee of an occupational pension scheme. It was first introduced during the Standing Committee stage of the Companies Bill 2006.[629] It addresses worries that such directors perform a vital role, often for little direct financial reward, and that so-called D & O liability insurance currently available affords limited protection.[630] In view of that, the section permits companies to indemnify the directors of associated companies acting as trustees of occupational pension schemes. As such,[631] this section is one of the three exceptions to the rule prohibiting indemnification referred to in section 232(2) (see above).[632]  **10.235.02**

Subsection (2) defines 'pension scheme indemnity provision' as meaning provision indemnifying a director of a company that is a trustee of an occupational pension scheme against liability incurred in connection with the company's activities as trustee of the scheme. Subsection (6) further provides that 'occupational pension scheme' means an occupational pension scheme as defined in section 150(5) of the Finance Act 2004 (c. 12), that is established under a trust.  **10.235.03**

A provision is qualifying pension scheme indemnity provision if the requirements set out in subsection (3) are met. First, the provision must not provide any indemnity against any liability of the director to pay a fine imposed in criminal proceedings, or a sum payable to a regulatory authority by way of a penalty in respect of non-compliance with any requirement of a regulatory nature however arising  **10.235.04**

---

[628] Companies Act 2006 (Commencement No 3, etc) Order 2007, SI 2007/2194, art 2. The section applies to any provision made on or after 1 October 2007. Sections 309A, 309B, and 309C(1)–(3) and (6) of the 1985 Act or art 318 of the 1986 Order (so far as it relates to directors) continue to apply in relation to any provision to which they applied immediately before that date. See Sch 3 to the Companies Act 2006 (Commencement No. 3, Consequential Amendments, Transitional Provisions and Savings) Order 2007, SI 2007/2194.

[629] Amendment No 310 introduced on 11 July 2006. See Official Report, 11/7/2006; colls 635–636.

[630] See Official Report, 11/7/2006; coll 636 (the Solicitor-General): 'We made it clear … that the Government attach importance to the work of such directors and that we were aware that it can sometimes be difficult to recruit high-quality directors for companies acting as trustees of occupational pension schemes'.

[631] See subs (1).

[632] The other two exceptions are contained in s 233 which permits the purchase of insurance subject to certain qualifications (see above) and s 234 which creates an exception for qualifying third party indemnity provisions (see above).

(subsection (3)(a)). The provision must not provide any indemnity against any liability incurred by the director in defending criminal proceedings in which he is convicted (subsection (3)(b)).

**10.235.05**     Subsection (4) and (5) restate section 337A(5) and (6) of the Companies Act 1985 by stating when legal proceedings will be considered to have concluded for the purpose of the conditions imposed by subsection (3). As such, subsection (4) makes it clear that the reference in subsection (3)(b) to a conviction is to the final decision in the proceedings. Subsection (5) provides further that for this purpose, a conviction becomes final if not appealed against, at the end of the period for bringing an appeal, or if appealed against, at the time when the appeal (or any further appeal) is disposed of. Likewise, an appeal is disposed of if it is determined and the period for bringing any further appeal has ended, or if it is abandoned or otherwise ceases to have effect.

### 236 Qualifying indemnity provision to be disclosed in directors' report

**10.236.01**     (1)  This section requires disclosure in the directors' report of—
                      (a)  qualifying third party indemnity provision, and
                      (b)  qualifying pension scheme indemnity provision.
                      Such provision is referred to in this section as 'qualifying indemnity provision'.
               (2)  If when a directors' report is approved any qualifying indemnity provision (whether made by the company or otherwise) is in force for the benefit of one or more directors of the company, the report must state that such provision is in force.
               (3)  If at any time during the financial year to which a directors' report relates any such provision was in force for the benefit of one or more persons who were then directors of the company, the report must state that such provision was in force.
               (4)  If when a directors' report is approved qualifying indemnity provision made by the company is in force for the benefit of one or more directors of an associated company, the report must state that such provision is in force.
               (5)  If at any time during the financial year to which a directors' report relates any such provision was in force for the benefit of one or more persons who were then directors of an associated company, the report must state that such provision was in force.

               COMMENCEMENT DATE 1 October 2007[633]

**10.236.02**     This section restates section 309C of the Companies Act 1985, as inserted by the Companies (Audit, Investigations and Community Enterprise) Act 2004. Subsection (2) provides that if a qualifying third party indemnity provision is in force for the benefit of one or more directors or was in force during the previous year, this must be disclosed by the company in the directors' report.[634] Where the director is of one company but the qualifying third party indemnity provision is provided by an associated company,[635] then it must be disclosed in the directors' reports of both companies. The Explanatory Notes to the Act make it clear that companies which choose not to indemnify directors will not have to make any disclosure.[636]

### 237 Copy of qualifying indemnity provision to be available for inspection

**10.237.01**     (1)  This section has effect where qualifying indemnity provision is made for a director of a company, and applies—
                      (a)  to the company of which he is a director (whether the provision is made by that company or an associated company), and
                      (b)  where the provision is made by an associated company, to that company.
               (2)  That company or, as the case may be, each of them must keep available for inspection—
                      (a)  a copy of the qualifying indemnity provision, or
                      (b)  if the provision is not in writing, a written memorandum setting out its terms.
               (3)  The copy or memorandum must be kept available for inspection at—
                      (a)  the company's registered office;
                      (b)  a place specified in regulations under section 1136.
               (4)  The copy or memorandum must be retained by the company for at least one year from the date of termination or expiry of the provision and must be kept available for inspection during that time.

---

[633]  Companies Act 2006 (Commencement No 3, etc) Order 2007, SI 2007/2194, art 2. The section applies to any provision made on or after 1 October 2007. Sections 309A, 309B, and 309C(1)–(3) and (6) of the 1985 Act or art 318 of the 1986 Order (so far as it relates to directors) continue to apply in relation to any provision to which they applied immediately before that date. See Sch 3 to the Companies Act 2006 (Commencement No. 3, Consequential Amendments, Transitional Provisions and Savings) Order 2007, SI 2007/2194.

[634]  Directors' report is dealt with in Ch 5 of Pt 15.

[635]  'Associated company' is defined in s 256 as, in effect, a company in the same group.

[636]  Para 435.

(5)  The company must give notice to the registrar—
  (a)  of the place at which the copy or memorandum is kept available for inspection, and
  (b)  of any change in that place,
  unless it has at all times been kept at the company's registered office.
(6)  If default is made in complying with subsection (2), (3) or (4), or default is made for 14 days in complying with subsection (5), an offence is committed by every officer of the company who is in default.
(7)  A person guilty of an offence under this section is liable on summary conviction to a fine not exceeding level 3 on the standard scale and, for continued contravention, a daily default fine not exceeding one-tenth of level 3 on the standard scale.
(8)  The provisions of this section apply to a variation of a qualifying indemnity provision as they apply to the original provision.
(9)  In this section 'qualifying indemnity provision' means—
  (a)  qualifying third party indemnity provision, and
  (b)  qualifying pension scheme indemnity provision.

COMMENCEMENT DATE  1 October 2007[637]

This is a new section. Although this chapter restates section 309A to 309C and section 337A of the Companies Act 1985, as inserted by the Companies (Audit, Investigations and Community Enterprise) Act 2004, this section introduces a number of key changes to those sections. The section requires a company to keep copies of all the qualifying third party indemnity provisions (see section 234 above) and qualifying pension scheme indemnity provisions (see section 235 above) it has made for its own directors,[638] and also copies of all those it has made for directors of associated companies.[639] It should be read in conjunction with section 238 below, which creates a right for members to request a copy of a qualifying third party indemnity provision. **10.237.02**

Subsection (3) explains where the copy or memorandum must be kept available for inspection, namely, at the company's registered office or at a place specified in regulations under section 1136 (regulations about where certain company records to be kept available for inspection, see below). **10.237.03**

Subsection (4) is a new provision. It requires all qualifying third party indemnity provisions to be retained and made available for inspection for a further year after they have expired or terminated. But the company is not required by this section to retain copies of the indemnity provision thereafter.[640] Subsection (5) adds that the company must give notice to the registrar of the place at which the copy or memorandum is kept available for inspection, as well as of any change in that place, unless it has at all times been kept at the company's registered office. **10.237.04**

Subsection (6) makes a failure to comply with the requirements of this section a criminal offence. The consequences of this criminal offence are outlined in subsection (7), which provides that the maximum penalty that can be imposed on summary conviction is a fine not exceeding level 3 on the standard scale (currently £1,000) or, in cases of continued contravention, a daily default fine not exceeding one-tenth of that. It should be noted that in a change from the previous position under section 309C of the 1985 Act, the company will *no longer* be liable under the criminal offence. **10.237.05**

Finally, subsection (8) makes it clear that the provisions of this section apply to a variation of a qualifying third party indemnity provision as they apply to the original provision. **10.237.06**

---

[637] Companies Act 2006 (Commencement No 3, etc) Order 2007, SI 2007/2194, art 2. This section applies to: (a) qualifying indemnity provision within the meaning of s 237 made on or after 1 October 2007, and (b) qualifying third party indemnity provision within the meaning of s 309B(1) of the 1985 Act to which s 309C(4) and (5) of that Act applied immediately before that date. Before regulations under s 1136 of the Companies Act 2006 were in force specifying a place for the purposes of s 237(3)(b), the copies and memoranda referred to in s 237 could be kept by a company (a) at any place where its register of members is kept, or (b) at its principal place of business, provided that place is situated in the part of the United Kingdom in which the company is registered. See now the Companies (Company Records) Regulations 2008, SI 2008/3006, in force from 1 October 2009 and para 10.228.03. The provisions of s 318 of the 1985 Act, as applied by s 309C(4) and (5), continue to apply in relation to (a) any default before 1 October 2007 in complying with s 318(1) or (5), as so applied; (b) any request for inspection under s 318(7), as so applied, made before that date; (c) any duty to give notice under s 318(4), as so applied, arising before that date. See Sch 3 to the Companies Act 2006 (Commencement No. 3, Consequential Amendments, Transitional Provisions and Savings) Order 2007, SI 2007/2194.

[638] This is by reason of subs (9) which defines 'qualifying indemnity provision' as meaning (a) qualifying third party indemnity provision, and (b) qualifying pension scheme indemnity provision.

[639] 'Associated company' is defined in s 256 as, in effect, a company in the same group.

[640] Explanatory Notes to the Act, para 437.

### 238  Right of member to inspect and request copy

**10.238.01**   (1)  Every copy or memorandum required to be kept by a company under section 237 must be open to inspection by any member of the company without charge.

(2)  Any member of the company is entitled, on request and on payment of such fee as may be prescribed, to be provided with a copy of any such copy or memorandum.
The copy must be provided within seven days after the request is received by the company.

(3)  If an inspection required under subsection (1) is refused, or default is made in complying with subsection (2), an offence is committed by every officer of the company who is in default.

(4)  A person guilty of an offence under this section is liable on summary conviction to a fine not exceeding level 3 on the standard scale and, for continued contravention, a daily default fine not exceeding one-tenth of level 3 on the standard scale.

(5)  In the case of any such refusal or default the court may by order compel an immediate inspection or, as the case may be, direct that the copy required be sent to the person requiring it.

COMMENCEMENT DATE  1 October 2007[641]

**10.238.02**   This is a new section. It gives members a right to inspect *without* charge the copies of the qualifying third party indemnity provisions (or where they are not in writing, the written memorandum of their terms) held by the company in accordance with section 237 (see above).

**10.238.03**   Subsection (2) provides that such copies must be provided within seven days after the request is received by the company. Subsection (2) also creates a new right for members on payment of a fee (which is set by regulations made under section 1137)[642] to request a copy of the copy or memorandum held by the company.

**10.238.04**   Subsection (3) and (4) make a failure to comply with the requirements of this section a criminal offence. The maximum penalty that can be imposed on summary conviction is a fine not exceeding level 3 on the standard scale (currently £1,000) or, in cases of continued contravention, a daily default fine not exceeding one-tenth of that.

**10.238.05**   Finally, subsection (5) provides the court with discretion if an inspection required under subsection (1) is refused, or default is made in complying with subsection (2). The court may by order compel an immediate inspection or, as the case may be, direct that the copy required be sent to the person requiring it.

## *Ratification of acts giving rise to liability*

### 239  Ratification of acts of directors

**10.239.01**   (1)  This section applies to the ratification by a company of conduct by a director amounting to negligence, default, breach of duty or breach of trust in relation to the company.

(2)  The decision of the company to ratify such conduct must be made by resolution of the members of the company.

(3)  Where the resolution is proposed as a written resolution neither the director (if a member of the company) nor any member connected with him is an eligible member.

(4)  Where the resolution is proposed at a meeting, it is passed only if the necessary majority is obtained disregarding votes in favour of the resolution by the director (if a member of the company) and any member connected with him.
This does not prevent the director or any such member from attending, being counted towards the quorum and taking part in the proceedings at any meeting at which the decision is considered.

(5)  For the purposes of this section—
(a)  'conduct' includes acts and omissions;
(b)  'director' includes a former director;
(c)  a shadow director is treated as a director; and
(d)  in section 252 (meaning of 'connected person'), subsection (3) does not apply (exclusion of person who is himself a director).

(6)  Nothing in this section affects—
(a)  the validity of a decision taken by unanimous consent of the members of the company, or
(b)  any power of the directors to agree not to sue, or to settle or release a claim made by them on behalf of the company.

---

[641]  Companies Act 2006 (Commencement No 3, etc) Order 2007, SI 2007/2194, art 2. This section applies to: (a) qualifying indemnity provision within the meaning of s 237 made on or after 1 October 2007, and (b) qualifying third party indemnity provision within the meaning of s 309B(1) of the 1985 Act to which s 309C(4) and (5) of that Act applied immediately before that date.

[642]  Explanatory Notes to the Act, para 440.

(7)  This section does not affect any other enactment or rule of law imposing additional requirements for valid ratification or any rule of law as to acts that are incapable of being ratified by the company.

COMMENCEMENT DATE  1 October 2007[643]

In some situations, certain acts of directors can, as a matter of substantive law, be cured by ratification.[644] This process, like many of those found in company law, seems to have originated in trust law. In simple terms, ratification has been explained as the process by which 'those to whom duties are owed may release those who owe the duties from their legal obligations… prospectively or retrospectively.'[645] However, at common law it was not always clear when ratification will be effective,[646] as it is impossible to reconcile all the decided cases with any simple set of propositions. At the same time, English law has recognized a category of non-ratifiable wrongs. Many of these instances of non-ratifiability can be explained on the basis that the shareholders cannot ratify the wrong done to the company, either because the wrong is not done to the company but to the shareholders in their personal capacity (and the company is not, therefore, the proper plaintiff) or because the company itself is not 'legally competent' to deal with the question and therefore it is not possible for the company to ratify the act.[647]    **10.239.02**

The section preserves the previous law on ratification of acts of directors, but with one significant change.[648] Subsection (1) and (2) taken together make it clear that any decision by a company to ratify conduct by a director amounting to negligence, default, breach of duty, or breach of trust in relation to the company[649] must be taken by the members, and without reliance on the votes of the director or any connected person[650] with a personal interest in the ratification. A member may have a personal interest in the ratification if, for example, they stand to obtain personal advantage (whether directly or indirectly) from a vote in favour of the ratification.[651] This section has far-reaching implications on the law relating to derivative claims.[652] The former bar to derivative claims where the wrong is ratifiable is likely to be diluted because the possibilities for ratification have been significantly tightened by this    **10.239.03**

---

[643] Companies Act 2006 (Commencement No 3, etc) Order 2007, SI 2007/2194, art 2. The section applies to conduct by a director on or after 1 October 2007. Conduct by a director before that date is subject to the law relating to ratification that applied immediately before that date. See Sch 3 to the Companies Act 2006 (Commencement No. 3, Consequential Amendments, Transitional Provisions and Savings) Order 2007, SI 2007/2194.

[644] Law Commission, *Shareholder Remedies,* Consultation Paper No 142, 1996, para 5.2–5.17.

[645] PL Davies, *Gower's Principles of Modern Company Law*, (6th ed, London, 1997) 644.

[646] And thus, eg, what are the exact circumstances in which ratification may bar a derivative claim, on which see Part 11 below.

[647] Eg, acts of illegality, such as providing financial assistance by a public company for the purchase of its own shares in contravention of ss 677–683 below. It should be noted that some old cases implicitly accepted that deciding not to sue was the functional equivalent of ratification (so that the same rules should determine whether action by an individual was permitted or collective decision making was required). However, in *Smith v Croft (No 2)* [1988] Ch 114, Knox J draw a distinction between ratifying a breach of duty (in the sense that it ceases to be a wrongful act) and deciding not to sue in respect of the wrong.

[648] Explanatory Notes to the Act, para 441.

[649] These words are extremely wide and raised some questions during the Grand Committee Stage. Eg, there is the question of whether ratification should be able to apply to a breach of duty that amounts to market abuse. Lord Goldsmith clarified that whether or not the decision was ratified would not affect the question of whether the action was unlawful. The members could not make the action lawful by ratifying it if it was unlawful under the Financial Services and Markets Act 2000, or indeed any other legislation. Eg, they could not, by somehow ratifying insider dealing, prevent that from being a wrongful act. See Official Report, 9/2/2006; coll GC368 (Lord Goldsmith).

[650] The term 'connected person' is defined in s 252, see below.

[651] Explanatory Notes to the Bill, para 428. The intention is to capture those members who are motivated or influenced by personal advantage or gain arising from a vote in favour of ratification. It is intended to be a narrower test than just having an interest in the resolution because, arguably, all the shareholders will have an interest in the resolution. See Official Report, 9/2/2006; coll GC369 (Lord Goldsmith).

[652] One of the main ways in which the company can take legal action against a director (or, more usually, a former director) for breach of duty is through 'a derivative claim' brought by one or more shareholders to enforce a right which is vested not in himself or herself but in the company. For 'derivative claims' see Part 11 of the Act, ss 260–269 below.

provision.[653] This section now prohibits self-interested members from participating in the ratification vote, thereby reversing the old case law holding to the contrary.[654]

**10.239.04**    Subsection (2) provides that the decision of the company to ratify such conduct must be made by resolution of the members of the company. It is worth noting that the section does not specify whether this should be an ordinary resolution or whether a higher majority (or unanimity) is required.[655]

**10.239.05**    Subsection (3) provides that if the ratification decision is taken by way of a written resolution,[656] members with a personal interest in the ratification may not take part in the written resolution procedure. This means that the company does not need to send them a copy of the written resolution, and they are not counted when determining the number of votes required for the written resolution to be passed.[657]

**10.239.06**    Subsection (4) provides that if the ratification decision is taken at a meeting, members with a personal interest in the ratification may still attend the meeting, take part in the meeting, and count towards the quorum for the meeting (if their membership gives them the right to do so).

**10.239.07**    Subsection (5) provides a number of definitions for the purposes of this section. Thus, 'conduct' includes acts and omissions; 'director' includes a former director; a shadow director is treated as a director; and in section 252 (meaning of 'connected person', see below), subsection (3) does not apply (exclusion of person who is himself a director).

**10.239.08**    Subsection (6) makes it clear that nothing in this section changes the law on unanimous consent, so the restrictions imposed by this section as to who may vote on a ratification resolution will not apply when every member votes (informally or otherwise) in favour of the resolution. Subsection (6) also makes it clear that nothing in this section removes any powers of the directors that they may have to manage the affairs of the company.[658]

**10.239.09**    Finally, subsection (7) makes it clear that the requirements imposed by this section are in addition to any other limitations or restrictions imposed by the law as to what may or may not be ratified and when.[659] In *Franbar Holdings Ltd v Patel and others* [2008] EWHC 1534 (Ch), the High Court considered the operation of the statutory derivative action introduced by Part 11 of the Companies Act 2006 and made specific reference to this subsection. It was argued that section 239 had replaced the principle that directors' acts cannot be ratified where they constitute a fraud on the minority and the wrongdoers are in control of the company. However, the trial judge (Mr William Trower QC, sitting as a Deputy Judge of the High Court) rejected this argument, relying upon section 239(7):[660]

> ... the [following] words of Sir Richard Baggalay ... in *North-West Transportation v Beatty* (1887) 12 App Cas 589, 594, describing the circumstances in which a company cannot ratify breaches of duty by its directors, remain good law:
>
> '... provided such affirmance or adoption is not brought about by unfair or improper means, and is not illegal or fraudulent or oppressive towards those shareholders who oppose it.'
>
> It follows that, where the question of ratification arises in the context of an application to continue a derivative claim, the question which the court must still ask itself is whether the ratification has the effect that the claimant is being improperly prevented from bringing the claim on behalf of the company ... That may still be the case where the new connected person provisions are not satisfied, but there is still actual wrongdoer control pursuant to which there has been a diversion of assets to persons associated with the wrongdoer, albeit not connected in the sense for which provision is made by section 239(4).

---

[653]  It should be noted, however, that it is likely that cases where the wrong in question has been ratified will be surrounded with old arguments relating to whether the ratification is valid since s 263 (see below) clearly suggests that leave to bring a derivative claim should not be granted if the wrong has been ratified. This means that in many instances the effectiveness of a purported ratification will dominate the hearing for leave. This is a difficult and controversial issue. See further, Part 11 of the Act, ss 260–269.

[654]  See, eg, *North-West Transportation Co Ltd v Beatty* (1887) 12 App Cas 589.

[655]  Interestingly, the draft of this section as introduced in the Companies Bill (formerly the Company Law Reform Bill) in the House of Lords in November 2005 did specify that the decision of the company to ratify such conduct 'may be taken by ordinary resolution, subject to anything in the company's articles requiring a higher majority (or unanimity)'; however, this was omitted by the time the Companies Bill received royal assent on 8 November 2006.

[656]  See Chapter 2 of Part 14.

[657]  Explanatory Notes to the Act, para 442.

[658]  Explanatory Notes to the Act, para 444.

[659]  Explanatory Notes to the Act, para 445.

[660]  At para [45].

It is questionable whether the need to show 'actual wrongdoer control' survived the 2006 Act. The Government specifically insisted it did not want the claimant to have to show 'wrongdoer control', that is to show that the company is controlled by the directors whom the claimant believes to have acted in breach of their duties, as that might make it impossible for a derivative claim to be brought successfully by a member of a widely held company, including almost all major quoted companies.[661] It follows that the above remarks sit uneasily with this.

CHAPTER 8

DIRECTORS' RESIDENTIAL ADDRESSES: PROTECTION
FROM DISCLOSURE

## 240  Protected information

(1) This Chapter makes provision for protecting, in the case of a company director who is an        **10.240.01**
    individual—
    (a) information as to his usual residential address;
    (b) the information that his service address is his usual residential address.
(2) That information is referred to in this Chapter as 'protected information'.
(3) Information does not cease to be protected information on the individual ceasing to be a director
    of the company.
    References in this Chapter to a director include, to that extent, a former director.

COMMENCEMENT DATE  1 October 2009[662]

Chapter 8 (section 240 to 246) makes new provision for the protection from disclosure of the usual   **10.240.02**
residential address of a director who is an individual. Under the Companies Act 1985 the general rule
was that a director's usual residential address constituted part of the information placed in the public
domain.[663] The exception was where a confidentiality order[664] was made by the Secretary of State on
the application of the director or proposed director (an individual) concerned.[665] In order to obtain a
confidentiality order the director had to satisfy the Secretary of State that the public availability of his
usual residential address created or was likely to create a serious risk that the director or a person living
with him would be subject to violence or intimidation.[666] The regime created by the Companies Act
2006 provides generally for the non-disclosure of a director's usual residential address by both the
registrar of companies and the company concerned.[667] This general rule of non-disclosure is subject to
specific exceptions.[668]

The Companies Act 2006 accordingly seeks to reduce the scope for misuse of information in the public   **10.240.03**
domain relating to directors, while permitting disclosure where it is considered justified in particular

---

[661] *Prudential Assurance Co Ltd v Newman Industries Ltd (No 2)* [1982] Ch 204, 211.

[662] Companies Act 2006 (Commencement No 8, Transitional Provisions and Savings) Order 2008, SI 2008/2860, art 3(i).

[663] These addresses were to be notified to the registrar of companies (pursuant to CA 1985, ss 10(2), 288(2)) and were therefore available for inspection and copying from the public record maintained by the registrar (under CA 1985, s 709). The directors' usual residential addresses were required by CA 1985, s 288 to be stated in the register of directors (and secretaries); a register open to inspection by the public: CA 1985, ss 288, 289. These provisions are repealed with effect from 1 October 2009 by CA 2006, s 1295, Sch 16; Companies Act 2006 (Commencement No 8, Transitional Provisions and Savings) Order 2008, SI 2008/2860, art 4, Sch 1.

[664] CA 1985, s 723B, repealed with effect from 1 October 2009 by CA 2006, s 1295, Sch 16; Companies Act 2006 (Commencement No 8, Transitional Provisions and Savings) Order 2008, SI 2008/2860, art 4, Sch 1. Continued protection is given to directors in whose favour confidentiality orders were in force before 1 October 2009: Companies Act 2006 (Commencement No 8, Transitional Provisions and Savings) Order 2008, SI 2008/2860, art 5, Sch 2, paras 36–37. These directors will be treated as successful applicants for orders under CA 2006, s 1088 (application to make address unavailable for public inspection) and CA 2006, s 243(4) (application to prevent disclosure of protected information by registrar to a credit reference agency). Applications for confidentiality orders outstanding on 30 September 2009 will be determined and (if granted) attract the same protection as those in force before 1 October 2009: Companies Act 2006 (Commencement No 8, Transitional Provisions and Savings) Order 2008, SI 2008/2860, art 5, Sch 2, para 38.

[665] The effect of a confidentiality order is stated in CA 1985, s 723C, repealed with effect from 1 October 2009: CA 2006, s 1295, Sch 16; Companies Act 2006 (Commencement No 8, Transitional Provisions and Savings) Order 2008, SI 2008/2860, art 4, Sch 1. See n 652 above for the effect of pre-1 October 2009 confidentiality orders.

[666] CA 1985, s 723B(3) repealed from 1 October 2009.

[667] Sections 240–242.

[668] Sections 243–246.

circumstances. Significantly, the Companies Act 2006 does not require the registrar of companies to remove from the public record anything registered before the coming into force of Chapter 8.[669]

**10.240.04**   The information which is generally protected from use or disclosure by the company concerned and the registrar of companies is referred to as 'protected information,'[670] this information being the director's usual residential address and (where applicable) that his service address[671] is his usual residential address.[672] A director may designate the company's registered office as his service address.[673]

**10.240.05**   The restrictions on the use or disclosure of protected information do not end when the individual ceases to be a director.[674] Nor do these restrictions cease on the dissolution of the company concerned.[675]

### 241 Protected information: restriction on use or disclosure by company

**10.241.01**   (1)  A company must not use or disclose protected information about any of its directors, except—
  (a)  for communicating with the director concerned,
  (b)  in order to comply with any requirement of the Companies Acts as to particulars to be sent to the registrar, or
  (c)  in accordance with section 244 (disclosure under court order).
(2)  Subsection (1) does not prohibit any use or disclosure of protected information with the consent of the director concerned.

COMMENCEMENT DATE  1 October 2009[676]

**10.241.02**   This section limits the use and disclosure by a company of protected information relating to its directors. The requirements referred to in section 241(1)(b) will include those imposed under section 12(2)(a) and 167(1)(b).

**10.241.03**   The consent referred to in subsection (2) need not be written. This exception to the general prohibition may therefore lead to debate as to whether or not a director has impliedly consented to the use or disclosure of protected information in circumstances where he may be said to have acquiesced in its use or disclosure.

**10.241.04**   No sanction is prescribed by this Act for the breach of this prohibition.[677]

### 242 Protected information: restriction on use or disclosure by registrar

**10.242.01**   (1)  The registrar must omit protected information from the material on the register that is available for inspection where—
  (a)  it is contained in a document delivered to him in which such information is required to be stated, and
  (b)  in the case of a document having more than one part, it is contained in a part of the document in which such information is required to be stated.
(2)  The registrar is not obliged—
  (a)  to check other documents or (as the case may be) other parts of the document to ensure the absence of protected information, or
  (b)  to omit from the material that is available for public inspection anything registered before this Chapter comes into force.
(3)  The registrar must not use or disclose protected information except—
  (a)  as permitted by section 243 (permitted use or disclosure by registrar), or
  (b)  in accordance with section 244 (disclosure under court order).

COMMENCEMENT DATE  1 October 2009[678]

---

[669]  Section 242(2)(b).
[670]  Section 240(2).
[671]  CA 2006, s 1141.
[672]  Section 240.
[673]  CA 2006, s 163(5).
[674]  Section 240(3).
[675]  See s 244(2)(b).
[676]  Companies Act 2006 (Commencement No 8, Transitional Provisions and Savings) Order 2008, SI 2008/2860, art 3(i).
[677]  Presumably this has been left to data protection law.
[678]  Companies Act 2006 (Commencement No 8, Transitional Provisions and Savings) Order 2008, SI 2008/2860, art 3(i).

This section contains a specific prohibition relating to the public register[679] maintained by the registrar **10.242.02**
of companies;[680] and a general prohibition on the use or disclosure of protected information outside of
the exceptions created by section 243 and 244.[681]

The specific prohibition relates only to protected information contained in a document or (if it has **10.242.03**
more than one part) part of a document delivered to the registrar in which such information is required
to be stated. It is expressly stated that the registrar is not obliged to check other documents or parts of
documents to ensure the absence of protected information.[682] Similarly, as mentioned above, the
registrar is not required to remove from the register protected information registered before the
coming into force of Chapter 8.[683]

The Secretary of State may, however, make regulations[684] requiring the registrar, on application, to **10.242.04**
make an address on the register unavailable for public inspection.[685] The Companies (Disclosure of
Address) Regulations 2009 provide for such applications.[686] The application must relate to an address
placed on the register on or after 1 January 2003.[687] The grounds of this application are similar to those
set out in these regulations in relation to applications to prevent the registrar disclosing protected
information to a credit reference agency.[688]

This section (like the preceding section) prescribes no sanction for its breach. **10.242.05**

## 243  Permitted use or disclosure by the registrar

(1)  The registrar may use protected information for communicating with the director in question. **10.243.01**
(2)  The registrar may disclose protected information—
    (a)  to a public authority specified for the purposes of this section by regulations made by the
        Secretary of State, or
    (b)  to a credit reference agency.
(3)  The Secretary of State may make provision by regulations—
    (a)  specifying conditions for the disclosure of protected information in accordance with this
        section, and
    (b)  providing for the charging of fees.
(4)  The Secretary of State may make provision by regulations requiring the registrar, on application,
    to refrain from disclosing protected information relating to a director to a credit reference agency.
(5)  Regulations under subsection (4) may make provision as to—
    (a)  who may make an application,
    (b)  the grounds on which an application may be made,
    (c)  the information to be included in and documents to accompany an application, and
    (d)  how an application is to be determined.
(6)  Provision under subsection (5)(d) may in particular—
    (a)  confer a discretion on the registrar;
    (b)  provide for a question to be referred to a person other than the registrar for the purposes of
        determining the application.
(7)  In this section—
    'credit reference agency' means a person carrying on a business comprising the furnishing of
    information relevant to the financial standing of individuals, being information collected by
    the agency for that purpose; and
    'public authority' includes any person or body having functions of a public nature.
(8)  Regulations under this section are subject to negative resolution procedure.

COMMENCEMENT DATE  1 October 2009[689]

---

[679]  CA 2006, s 1080. The contents of the register are generally open to inspection and copying: ss 1085, 1086.
[680]  Section 242(1).
[681]  Section 242(3).
[682]  Section 242(2)(a).
[683]  See also the terms of s 1087(1)(b) which refer to protected information within s 242(1), rather than
protected information within s 240.
[684]  Subject to affirmative resolution procedure.
[685]  CA 2006, s 1088.
[686]  The Companies (Disclosure of Address) Regulations 2009, SI 2009/214 (in force from 1 October 2009), reg
9 in relation to an application by an individual whose usual residential address was placed on the register under
provisions including CA 1985, ss 10, 288 and 363 and CA 2006, ss 12, 167 and 855.
[687]  Editing the records maintained before this date was not considered practical, given their form.
[688]  CA 2006, s 243(4); Companies (Disclosure of Address) Regulations 2009, regs 5–8.
[689]  Companies Act 2006 (Commencement No 8, Transitional Provisions and Savings) Order 2008, SI
2008/2860, art 3(i).

**10.243.02**  This section permits the disclosure by the registrar of protected information to a public authority[690] specified in regulations and to a credit reference agency.[691] The Secretary of State may make regulations imposing conditions on the disclosure of information under this section, providing for fees[692] and requiring the registrar on application to refrain from disclosing protected information to a credit reference agency.

**10.243.03**  The Companies (Disclosure of Address) Regulations 2009 specify the public authorities to whom the registrar may disclose protected information if certain conditions are satisfied. A broad range of public authorities, including those with powers to regulate, tax and prosecute, are specified.[693] The conditions which must be satisfied are set out in paragraphs 2 and 3 of Schedule 2. The public authority must deliver to the registrar a statement that it intends to use the protected information only for the purpose of facilitating the carrying-out by itself of a public function.[694] The public authority[695] must also deliver to the registrar a statement that it will, where it supplies a copy of the protected information to a processor for the purpose of processing the information for use in respect of this purpose, take the data protection steps set out in Schedule 2, paragraph 3.[696] It appears that the registrar may, but is not required to, treat these statements as sufficient evidence of the matters stated in them.[697] The registrar may require further information or evidence (verified in such manner as he may direct) for the purpose of enabling his determination, in accordance with the regulations, whether to disclose protected information to a specified public authority.[698]

**10.243.04**  The regulations provide that the specified public authority must inform the registrar immediately of any change in respect of any statement, information or evidence provided for the purpose of enabling him to determine whether to disclose protected information.[699] This requirement is presumably a continuing one, rather than one which does not extend beyond the date of a particular disclosure determination. On this basis, the registrar will be assisted in his approach to subsequent disclosure determinations.

**10.243.05**  The conditions on which protected information may be disclosed by the registrar to a credit reference agency are set out in paragraphs 6–10 of Schedule 2 to the Companies (Disclosure of Address) Regulations 2009.[700] In relation to the conditions specified in paragraph 6: a statement[701] that these conditions are met may be treated as sufficient by the registrar. Alternatively, he may direct further evidence or information in relation to these conditions: regulation 3(3), (4). A credit reference agency must inform the registrar immediately of any change in respect of any statement, information or evidence provided for his determination.[702] In relation to the like requirement imposed on public authorities, see paragraph 10.243.04 above.

**10.243.06**  These regulations provide that a credit reference agency may disclose protected information to a public authority which has satisfied the requirements of paragraphs 2 and 3 of Schedule 2; or a credit reference agency which has satisfied the requirements of paragraphs 6–10 of Schedule 2.[703] This presumably means that the registrar must have been satisfied that these requirements have been satisfied and that disclosure should be allowed.[704]

**10.243.07**  The Companies (Disclosure of Address) Regulations 2009 make provision, pursuant to section 243(4)–(6) of the Act, for applications requiring the registrar to refrain from disclosing protected information relating to a director to a credit reference agency. (Unsurprisingly, there is no facility for such an application in relation to disclosure to specified public authorities.) The grounds[705] on which this application may be made by an individual who is (or proposes to become) a director are that he considers that there is a serious risk that he (or a person who lives with him) will be subjected to

---

[690]  Defined (inclusively) by s 243(7).

[691]  Defined in s 243(7), the definition being that found in the Consumer Credit Act 1974.

[692]  See The Registrar of Companies (Fees)(Companies, Overseas Companies & Limited Liability Partnerships) Regulations 2012, SI 2012/1907, reg 6, Sch 3.

[693]  SI 2009/214, Sch 1. The Companies (Disclosure of Address) Regulations 2010, SI 2010/2156 (in force from 1 October 2010) makes a minor amendment to Sch 1.

[694]  Schedule 2, para 2. 'Public function' is defined at Sch 2, para 11(1).

[695]  Subject to the exceptions specified at Sch 2, para 4.

[696]  Schedule 2, para 3.

[697]  Although reg 2 does not contain an express provision in the terms of reg 3(2).

[698]  Regulation 2(2),(3).

[699]  Regulation 2(4).

[700]  See reg 3(1).

[701]  See Sch 2, para 10.

[702]  Regulation 3(5).

[703]  See Sch 2, para 7(d).

[704]  Taking into account any requirements imposed under regs 2(2) and 3(3).

[705]  Regulation 5(2).

violence or intimidation as a result of the activities of at least one of the companies or limited liability partnerships identified;[706] alternatively that he is or has been employed by a relevant organization.[707] If the applicant is a company applying on behalf of any of its directors (who are individuals) or a subscriber to a memorandum of association, on behalf of any proposed directors (who are individuals), the grounds of the application are limited to the violence/intimidation ground in respect of the particular company (or proposed company) concerned.[708]

An application for an order preventing disclosure of protected information to a credit reference agency is made to the registrar. The application must be accompanied by evidence supporting the grounds relied upon.[709] The registrar may refer to a relevant body (which includes any police force[710] ) any question relating to assessment of the nature and extent of any risk of violence/intimidation relied upon; likewise (in a regulation 5 case) whether the applicant is an employee (or former employee) of a relevant organization.[711]    **10.243.08**

The following points may be made in relation to the serious risk of violence/intimidation ground. First, this ground is expressed in subjective terms.[712] (Subjective language was also found in CA 1985, section 723B(2)(b)[713] (confidentiality order applications), but the governing test was expressed in objective terms at section 723B(3).) It seems clear, however, that an objective basis for the perceived risk is required.[714] Secondly, the risk must result from the activities of at least one of the entities identified in regulation 5(2)(a) (where the director or proposed director applies under regulation 5), or of the company concerned (in the case of applications under regulations 6 and 7). (By comparison, CA 1985, section 723B (confidentiality order applications) did not require a link between the risk and the activities of a particular entity.) It would seem that there is good reason to construe a company's activities broadly, taking into account matters such as its trading relationships with other businesses, the effect of which may render its directors vulnerable to violent intimidation.    **10.243.09**

The Regulations provide for an appeal, subject to leave being granted, against an adverse decision of the registrar on an application for an order preventing the disclosure of protected information by the registrar to a credit reference agency.[715] The grounds of appeal stated in regulation 14 are similar to judicial review grounds. The registrar may, on the ground set out in regulation 16, revoke a decision to refrain from disclosing protected information relating to a director to a credit reference agency.    **10.243.10**

## 244  Disclosure under court order

(1)  The court may make an order for the disclosure of protected information by the company or by the registrar if—    **10.244.01**
   (a)  there is evidence that service of documents at a service address other than the director's usual residential address is not effective to bring them to the notice of the director, or
   (b)  it is necessary or expedient for the information to be provided in connection with the enforcement of an order or decree of the court, and the court is otherwise satisfied that it is appropriate to make the order.
(2)  An order for disclosure by the registrar is to be made only if the company—
   (a)  does not have the director's usual residential address, or
   (b)  has been dissolved.
(3)  The order may be made on the application of a liquidator, creditor or member of the company, or any other person appearing to the court to have a sufficient interest.
(4)  The order must specify the persons to whom, and purposes for which, disclosure is authorised.

COMMENCEMENT DATE  1 October 2009[716]

---

[706]  These being: the companies of which he is or proposes to become a director; the companies of which he was a director; the overseas companies of which he is or has been a director, secretary or permanent representative; or the limited liability partnerships of which he is or has been a member: reg 5(2)(a).

[707]  Government Communications Headquarters, the Secret Intelligence Service, the Security Service or a police force: reg 1(2).

[708]  See regs 6(2) and 7(2).

[709]  Regulation 5(3)(b). Similarly regs 6(3)(b) and 7(3)(b).

[710]  See reg 1(2).

[711]  Regulations 5(4)(a), 6(4) and 7(4): reg 5(4)(b).

[712]  See regs 5(2)(a), 6(2) and 7(2).

[713]  Repealed (subject to transitional provisions) with effect from 1 October 2009 by CA 2006, s 1295, Sch 16: Companies Act 2006 (Commencement No 8, Transitional Provisions and Savings) Order 2008, SI 2008/2860, art 4, Sch 1.

[714]  See eg reg 5(3)(b)(i), (4)(a).

[715]  Regulation 14.

[716]  Companies Act 2006 (Commencement No 8, Transitional Provisions and Savings) Order 2008, SI 2008/2860, art 3(i).

**10.244.02** The court has a discretion to order disclosure of protected information if there is evidence that the service of documents at a service address (other than the director's usual residential address) is ineffective or if it is necessary or expedient for the information to be provided in connection with the enforcement of a court order or decree. The court must also be satisfied that it is appropriate to make the order for disclosure sought.[717] The application for disclosure may be made by a liquidator, creditor, member, or any other person appearing to have a sufficient interest.[718] Disclosure by the registrar is a last resort, only to be ordered if the company does not have the director's usual residential address or if it has been dissolved.[719]

**10.244.03** Where disclosure is ordered, the court must specify the persons to whom and the purposes for which disclosure is authorized.[720] The precise terms of the disclosure ordered will govern the disclosure which is permissible so far as the registrar is concerned.[721]

**10.244.04** There is then the question of the impact of the terms of the court order on the person to whom disclosure is made. This person is not otherwise subject to any express statutory prohibition regarding his use or disclosure of the protected information. It may be that in these circumstances the court requires an undertaking from the recipient not to use or disclose the protected information except as permitted under the terms of the order; or alternatively makes an order directed at a recipient (who is before the court) to this effect.

### 245 Circumstances in which registrar may put address on the public record

**10.245.01** (1) The registrar may put a director's usual residential address on the public record if—
  (a) communications sent by the registrar to the director and requiring a response within a specified period remain unanswered, or
  (b) there is evidence that service of documents at a service address provided in place of the director's usual residential address is not effective to bring them to the notice of the director.
(2) The registrar must give notice of the proposal—
  (a) to the director, and
  (b) to every company of which the registrar has been notified that the individual is a director.
(3) The notice must—
  (a) state the grounds on which it is proposed to put the director's usual residential address on the public record, and
  (b) specify a period within which representations may be made before that is done.
(4) It must be sent to the director at his usual residential address, unless it appears to the registrar that service at that address may be ineffective to bring it to the individual's notice, in which case it may be sent to any service address provided in place of that address.
(5) The registrar must take account of any representations received within the specified period.
(6) What is meant by putting the address on the public record is explained in section 246.

COMMENCEMENT DATE 1 October 2009[722]

**10.245.02** The registrar may put a director's usual residential address on the public record[723] if either communications sent by the registrar to the director requiring a response within a specified period remain unanswered or there is evidence that service of documents at a service address provided in place of the director's usual residential address is not effective to bring them to the notice of the director.[724] The second alternative is not materially different from the ground on which the court may order disclosure in section 244(1)(a).[725]

**10.245.03** The exercise of this administrative power by the registrar may well have a greater impact than a disclosure order made by the court under section 244. A disclosure order will provide only for

---

[717] Section 244(1).
[718] Section 244(3).
[719] Section 244(2).
[720] Section 244(4).
[721] Section 242(3)(b).
[722] Companies Act 2006 (Commencement No 8, Transitional Provisions and Savings) Order 2008, SI 2008/2860, art 3(i).
[723] An expression defined by s 246(1).
[724] Section 245(1).
[725] The wording of s 245(1)(b) where it refers to 'a service address provided in place of the director's usual residential address' is not particularly apt to describe a service address. This wording appears to have escaped amendment when this Chapter was revised (pre-enactment).

disclosure to specific persons for particular purposes.[726] In contrast, putting the director's usual residential address on the public record will make it available to all for a period of five years.[727]

If the registrar proposes to exercise this power, notice must first be given to the director and to any **10.245.04** company of which the registrar has been notified he is a director, stating the grounds on which it is proposed to exercise this power and specifying a period within which representations may be made.[728] The registrar must take account of any representations received during the period specified.[729]

Whether the registrar will regard this administrative power as one which ought to be exercised in **10.245.05** certain circumstances where the ground on which it may be exercised has been dealt with (at least for the time being) in response to the notice given to the director and company remains to be seen. The registrar may in some cases take the view, having taken into account the track record of the director concerned and the representations received, that the power ought to be exercised in the interests of seeking to ensure that the director remains contactable in the future—or perhaps to deter directors in general from allowing the grounds for the exercise of this power to arise.

### 246  Putting the address on the public record

(1)  The registrar, on deciding in accordance with section 245 that a director's usual residential address   **10.246.01**
   is to be put on the public record, shall proceed as if notice of a change of registered particulars had been given—
   (a)  stating that address as the director's service address, and
   (b)  stating that the director's usual residential address is the same as his service address.
(2)  The registrar must give notice of having done so—
   (a)  to the director, and
   (b)  to the company.
(3)  On receipt of the notice the company must—
   (a)  enter the director's usual residential address in its register of directors as his service address, and
   (b)  state in its register of directors' residential addresses that his usual residential address is the same as his service address.
(4)  If the company has been notified by the director in question of a more recent address as his usual residential address, it must—
   (a)  enter that address in its register of directors as the director's service address, and
   (b)  give notice to the registrar as on a change of registered particulars.
(5)  If a company fails to comply with subsection (3) or (4), an offence is committed by—
   (a)  the company, and
   (b)  every officer of the company who is in default.
(6)  A person guilty of an offence under subsection (5) is liable on summary conviction to a fine not exceeding level 5 on the standard scale and, for continued contravention, a daily default fine not exceeding one-tenth of level 5 on the standard scale.
(7)  A director whose usual residential address has been put on the public record by the registrar under this section may not register a service address other than his usual residential address for a period of five years from the date of the registrar's decision.

COMMENCEMENT DATE  1 October 2009[730]

This section specifies the steps the registrar and the company concerned are to take when the registrar **10.246.02** exercises the power under section 245 to put a director's usual residential address on the public record. The registrar will proceed on the basis that notice of a change of registered particulars had been given,[731] stating the usual residential address as the director's service address and that the director's usual residential address is the same as his service address.[732] The registrar must give notice that this step has been taken to the director and company concerned.[733]

On receipt of this notice the company must enter the director's usual residential address in its register **10.246.03** of directors as his service address[734] and state in the register of directors' residential addresses[735] that

---

[726]  Section 244(4).
[727]  Section 246(7).
[728]  Section 245(2), (3).
[729]  Section 245(5).
[730]  Companies Act 2006 (Commencement No 8, Transitional Provisions and Savings) Order 2008, SI 2008/2860, art 3(i).
[731]  See s 167(1).
[732]  Section 246(1).
[733]  Section 246(2).
[734]  See s 163(1).
[735]  Section 165.

the director's usual residential address is the same as his service address. If the company has been notified by the director of a more recent usual residential address, it must enter that address as the director's service address in the register of directors; and must give notice to the registrar as on a change of registered particulars.[736] The company and any officer of the company who is in default commit an offence if the company fails to take these steps.[737]

**10.246.04**   The registrar's act of putting a director's usual residential address on the public record is effective for five years from the date of the registrar's decision.[738] During this period the director may not register a service address other than his usual residential address. There is no provision under which the director may invite the registrar to review the decision in the light of new circumstances. The power given to the Secretary of State to make regulations requiring the registrar to make an address on the register unavailable for public inspection[739] would not seem to cover regulations permitting the removal of a usual residential address before the expiry of the five-year period, given the clear terms of section 246(7).

CHAPTER 9

SUPPLEMENTARY PROVISIONS

*Provision for employees on cessation or transfer of business*

### 247 Power to make provision for employees on cessation or transfer of business

**10.247.01**
(1) The powers of the directors of a company include (if they would not otherwise do so) power to make provision for the benefit of persons employed or formerly employed by the company, or any of its subsidiaries, in connection with the cessation or the transfer to any person of the whole or part of the undertaking of the company or that subsidiary.
(2) This power is exercisable notwithstanding the general duty imposed by section 172 (duty to promote the success of the company).
(3) In the case of a company that is a charity it is exercisable notwithstanding any restrictions on the directors' powers (or the company's capacity) flowing from the objects of the company.
(4) The power may only be exercised if sanctioned—
   (a) by a resolution of the company, or
   (b) by a resolution of the directors, in accordance with the following provisions.
(5) A resolution of the directors—
   (a) must be authorised by the company's articles, and
   (b) is not sufficient sanction for payments to or for the benefit of directors, former directors or shadow directors.
(6) Any other requirements of the company's articles as to the exercise of the power conferred by this section must be complied with.
(7) Any payment under this section must be made—
   (a) before the commencement of any winding up of the company, and
   (b) out of profits of the company that are available for dividend.

COMMENCEMENT DATE 1 October 2009[740]

**10.247.02**   This section replaces Companies Act 1985, section 719.[741] The directors are given power to make provision for the benefit of employees and former employees of the company and any of its subsidiaries in connection with the cessation or the transfer to any person of the whole or part of the undertaking of the company or subsidiary. The power conferred on the directors by this section is conditional. Its exercise must be sanctioned either by a resolution of the company or by a resolution of the directors if

---

[736]  See s 167(1)(b).

[737]  Section 246(5).

[738]  Section 246(7).

[739]  Section 1088.

[740]  Companies Act 2006 (Commencement No 8, Transitional Provisions and Savings) Order 2008, SI 2008/2860, art 3(i). (The Companies Act 2006 (Commencement No 3, etc) Order 2007, SI 2007/2194, art 2(1)(d) had originally provided for the commencement of this provision on 1 October 2007. This commencement date was subsequently cancelled by The Companies Act 2006 (Commencement No. 4 and Commencement No. 3 (Amendment) Order 2007, SI 2007/2607, art 4(1).)

[741]  Repealed with effect 1 October 2009: CA 2006, s 1295, Sch 16; Companies Act 2006 (Commencement No 8, Transitional Provisions and Savings) Order 2008, art 4, Sch 1. This Order provides that CA 1985, s 719 continues to apply to provisions made before 1 October 2009 and to any provision sanctioned in accordance with CA 1985, s 719(3) before this date: art 5, Sch 2, para 40(2). A similar provision was first introduced by the CA 1980, s 74, reversing *Parke v Daily News* [1962] Ch 927.

this is authorized by the company's articles and there are no payments to or for the benefit of directors, former directors, or shadow directors.[742] The section does not provide that a board resolution is insufficient in the case of payments to or for the benefit of persons connected with directors, although it may be arguable on the facts that such a payment is also for the benefit of directors.

The company must comply with any requirements in its articles relating to the exercise of this statutory **10.247.03** power. Any payment under this section must be made before the commencement of the winding up of the company[743] and out of the company's profits available for distribution as dividend.[744]

The power conferred by this section is exercisable notwithstanding the directors' duty to promote the **10.247.04** success of the company.[745] There may, however, be potential for a shareholder to complain under section 994 (unfairly prejudicial conduct) if he alleges that a proposed payment under this provision is, in all the circumstances, excessive.

## Records of meetings of directors

### 248 Minutes of directors' meetings

(1) Every company must cause minutes of all proceedings at meetings of its directors to be recorded. **10.248.01**
(2) The records must be kept for at least ten years from the date of the meeting.
(3) If a company fails to comply with this section, an offence is committed by every officer of the company who is in default.
(4) A person guilty of an offence under this section is liable on summary conviction to a fine not exceeding level 3 on the standard scale and, for continued contravention, a daily default fine not exceeding one-tenth of level 3 on the standard scale.

COMMENCEMENT DATE 1 October 2007[746]

Minutes of all proceedings at directors' meetings must be recorded and that record must be kept for at **10.248.02** least ten years from the meeting date.[747] The requirement under section 382(1) of the Companies Act 1985[748] to record and maintain minutes of managers' meetings (where there are managers)[749] has been dropped. A breach of this section by the company gives rise to an offence by every officer of the company who is in default, but the company is not made liable for the breach.[750]

### 249 Minutes as evidence

(1) Minutes recorded in accordance with section 248, if purporting to be authenticated by the **10.249.01** chairman of the meeting or by the chairman of the next directors' meeting, are evidence (in Scotland, sufficient evidence) of the proceedings at the meeting.
(2) Where minutes have been made in accordance with that section of the proceedings of a meeting of directors, then, until the contrary is proved—
(a) the meeting is deemed duly held and convened,
(b) all proceedings at the meeting are deemed to have duly taken place, and
(c) all appointments at the meeting are deemed valid.

COMMENCEMENT DATE 1 October 2007[751]

The minutes of a directors' meeting recorded in accordance with section 248, which purport to be **10.249.02** authenticated by the chairman of that or the next directors' meeting, are evidence of the proceedings at the meeting.[752] Where minutes have been made pursuant to section 248, it is presumed (subject to proof to the contrary) that the meeting was duly held and convened, that all proceedings at the meeting

---

[742] Section 247(1), (4)–(6).
[743] The Insolvency Act 1986, s 187 makes provision for the circumstances in which similar payments may be made to employees (and former employees) where there is a surplus on a liquidation.
[744] Section 247(6), (7).
[745] Section 172.
[746] Companies Act 2006 (Commencement No 3, etc) Order 2007, SI 2007/2194, art 2. Board meetings held on or after 1 October 2007 are governed by this section: Companies Act 2006 (Commencement No 3, etc) Order, 2007, SI 2007/2194, art 9, Sch 3, para 19(1).
[747] Section 248(1), (2).
[748] Repealed with effect from 1 October 2007: CA 2006, s 1295, Sch 16; Companies Act 2006 (Commencement No 3, etc) Order 2007, SI 2007/2194, art 8, Sch 2. Subject to the transitional provision relating to board meetings held before this date: Companies Act 2006 (Commencement No 3, etc) Order 2007, art 9, Sch 3, para 19(2).
[749] CA 1985, s 382(1).
[750] CA 2006, s 248(3). Compare CA 1985, s 382(5), under which the company is also liable for the default.
[751] Companies Act 2006 (Commencement No 3, etc) Order 2007, SI 2007/2194, art 2.
[752] Section 249(1).

were duly held, and that all appointments at the meeting were validly made.[753] This presumption will apply irrespective of whether the minutes purport to have been authenticated by a chairman.

## Meaning of 'director' and 'shadow director'

### 250 'Director'

**10.250.01**  In the Companies Acts 'director' includes any person occupying the position of director, by whatever name called.

COMMENCEMENT DATE 1 October 2007[754]

**10.250.02**  This section reiterates wording found in section 741 of the Companies Act 1985,[755] section 251 of the Insolvency Act 1986, and section 22(4) of the Company Directors Disqualification Act 1986. Where those duly appointed to conduct the affairs of a company are referred to in the company's constitution by some name other than directors (eg governors) it is clear from this section that these persons are directors for the purposes of the Companies Acts: see *Re Lo-Line Electric Motors Ltd*.[756]

**10.250.03**  Is a 'de facto director' within this definition? A de facto director is an individual who acts as director, although not appointed as such. In determining whether an individual has acted as a director to the extent required for him to be characterized as a de facto director, no single matter is decisive. The question is very much one of fact and degree. The matters to be taken into account include: whether or not the individual was held out as a director by the company concerned; whether the individual used the title director;[757] whether he had proper information on which to base decisions; and whether he had to make major decisions. Taking all relevant factors (including those mentioned) into account, it may be asked whether or not the individual was part of the corporate governing structure.[758] Another relevant test is whether the individual was the sole person directing the affairs of the company (or acting with others equally lacking in a valid appointment); or, if there were others who were true directors, whether he was acting on an equal footing with those others in directing its affairs.[759] It is possible that the meaning of 'de facto director' may vary according to context, the purpose of the provision imposing liability (if the individual is held to be a de facto director) being taken into account.[760] Where an individual is a de jure director of a corporate director (company A) of company B, he will not be held to be a de facto director of company B on the basis of things done in his capacity as a director of company A.[761]

**10.250.04**  In *Lo-Line* the court rejected an argument that the words *'any person occupying the position of director'* in the statutory definition of director[762] covered a de facto director, so that a de facto director was to be treated as a director throughout the Companies Act 1985. It was held that the question of whether 'director' in a particular section of the Companies Act 1985 included a de facto director was to be determined as a matter of construction, having regard to language and purpose of the particular provision. Properly construed, the directors' disqualification provision then found at section 300 of the Companies Act 1985 did apply to de facto directors.[763]

---

[753]  Section 249(2).

[754]  Companies Act 2006 (Commencement No 3, etc) Order 2007, SI 2007/2194, art 2.

[755]  Repealed by CA 2006, s 1295, Sch 16 with effect from 1 October 2007: Companies Act 2006 (Commencement No 3, etc) Order 2007, SI 2007/2194, art 8, Sch 2.

[756]  [1988] 1 Ch 477, 488D–H, *per* Sir Nicholas Browne-Wilkinson VC (as he then was) in relation to CA 1985, s 741(1).

[757]  But the fact that this title is not used, or the absence of a holding out, is not decisive. See *Re Paycheck Services 3 Ltd, Revenue and Customs Commissioners v Holland* [2010] UKSC 51, [2010] 1 WLR 2793, [2011] 1 All ER 430 at [32], [90] and [108]. Conduct is of primary importance.

[758]  See *Re Hydrodan (Corby) Ltd* [1994] BCC 161, 163B–F; *Secretary of State for Trade and Industry v Tjolle* [1998] BCC 282, at 290C–E; *Re Kaytech International plc* [1999] BCC 390, at 401H–402D; *Secretary of State for Trade and Industry v Hollier* [2006] EWHC 1804, esp [66], [75] and [81]; *Re Mea Corp Limited* [2007] BCC 288; *Re Gemma Limited (In Liquidation)* [2008] EWHC 546, esp [40(2)]; *Re Paycheck Services 3 Ltd, Revenue and Customs Commissioners v Holland* [2010] UKSC 51, at [31], [39] and [91].

[759]  See *In re Richborough Furniture Ltd* [1996] 1 BCLC 507, at 524; *Re Paycheck Services 3 Ltd, Revenue and Customs Commissioners v Holland* [2010] UKSC 51, at [91].

[760]  *Re Paycheck Services 3 Ltd, Revenue and Customs Commissioners v Holland* [2010] UKSC 51, at [93]. See also the reference to the purpose of the relevant section, at [39].

[761]  *Re Paycheck Services 3 Ltd, Revenue and Customs Commissioners v Holland* [2010] UKSC 51.

[762]  S 741(1) Companies Act 1985, in materially the same terms as s 250 Companies Act 2006.

[763]  [1988] 1 Ch 477, 489A–C. *Re Paycheck Services 3 Ltd, Revenue and Customs Commissioners v Holland* [2010] UKSC 51, at [21].

In *Re Eurostem Maritime Ltd*[764] (which was cited in *Lo-Line*) the definition of director now found at section 250 of the Companies Act 2006 was held[765] to include de facto directors. In *Re Sykes (Butchers) Ltd*,[766] Ferris J referred without criticism to the legal basis upon which the (disqualification) proceedings before him had been determined below—that as a de facto director the appellant fell within the definition of director in section 22(4) of the Company Directors Disqualification Act 1986.[767] *Lo-Line* and *Eurostem* do not appear to have been cited in *Sykes*; and it does not appear that there was any debate as to the precise legal basis on which a de facto director fell within section 6 of the Company Directors Disqualification Act 1986. It may be argued that the point did not really arise because in the disqualification context it was clear that references to directors included de facto directors (as *Lo-Line* held).

10.250.05

The position as stated in *Lo-Line* probably continues to apply, so that it cannot be assumed that all references to directors in the Companies Act 2006 apply to de facto directors, the question being one of construction having regard to the language and purpose of the particular section. The general (now codified) fiduciary duties owed by directors are owed by de facto directors.[768] In *Re Paycheck Services 3 Ltd, Revenue and Customs Commissioners v Holland*[769] it was conceded that a de facto director was a director for the purposes of section 212 of the Insolvency Act 1986,[770] a procedural provision available on a winding up, which applies to a wide range of breaches of directors' duties.

10.250.06

## 251 'Shadow director'

(1) In the Companies Acts 'shadow director', in relation to a company, means a person in accordance with whose directions or instructions the directors of the company are accustomed to act.

(2) A person is not to be regarded as a shadow director by reason only that the directors act on advice given by him in a professional capacity.

(3) A body corporate is not to be regarded as a shadow director of any of its subsidiary companies for the purposes of—

Chapter 2 (general duties of directors),
Chapter 4 (transactions requiring members' approval), or
Chapter 6 (contract with sole member who is also a director),

by reason only that the directors of the subsidiary are accustomed to act in accordance with its directions or instructions.

10.251.01

COMMENCEMENT DATE 1 October 2007[771]

The definition in subsections (1) and (2) is the same[772] as that found in the section 741(1), (2) of the Companies Act 1985, section 251 of the Insolvency Act 1986, and section 22(5) of the Company Directors Disqualification Act 1986. The provisos relating to professional advice and subsidiaries[773] have been maintained.

10.251.02

The statutory definition of shadow director was considered by the Court of Appeal in *Secretary of State for Trade and Industry v Deverell*.[774] The following propositions emerged:

10.251.03

(i) The purpose of the provision is to identify those, other than professional advisers, with real influence in the corporate affairs of the company. It is not necessary however that this influence be exercised over the whole field of its corporate activities.

(ii) Whether any particular communication from the alleged shadow director is to be classified as a direction or instruction is to be ascertained objectively in the light of all the evidence. It is not necessary to prove the understanding or expectation of either the giver or the receiver. In many cases, if not most, it will be sufficient to prove the communication and its consequence. Evidence of the understanding or expectation may be relevant but it is not conclusive. The label attached to the communication by the parties is no more than a factor in considering whether the communication is within the statutory description of direction or instruction.

(iii) Non-professional advice may come within the statutory description of direction or instruction.

---

[764] [1987] PCC 190. Like *Lo-Line*, these were disqualification proceedings.
[765] *Per* Mervyn Davies J.
[766] [1998] BCC 484.
[767] [1998] BCC 484, 490H.
[768] See *Ultraframe (UK) Ltd v Fielding* [2005] EWHC 1638 (Ch) at [1257] and the cases there cited.
[769] [2010] UKSC 51.
[770] See [21].
[771] Companies Act 2006 (Commencement No 3, etc) Order 2007, SI 2007/2194, art 2.
[772] Subject to minor linguistic changes.
[773] The subsidiaries exception applies to sections with similar subject matter to those specified in CA 1985, s 741(3).
[774] [2000] 2 WLR 907.

(iv) It is not necessary to show that the properly appointed directors or some of them cast themselves in a subservient role or surrendered their discretions to the alleged shadow director. This will no doubt be sufficient, but to add such a requirement would be to put a gloss on the statutory wording.[775]

**10.251.04**    The role of a shadow director need not be covert. A person who openly instructs the board of a company may be a shadow director.[776] It is now clear that the categories of shadow director and de facto director are not mutually exclusive. In *In re Hydrodam (Corby) Ltd*[777] Millett J referred to these categories as alternatives, which were 'in most and perhaps all cases are mutually exclusive'. Millett J contrasted a de facto director—one who claims to act and purports to act as a director although not validly appointed as such—with a shadow director—one who does not claim or purport to act as a director, but (on the contrary) claims not to be a director, lurking in the shadows and sheltering behind others who he claims are the only directors of the company.[778]

**10.251.05**    In *Re Paycheck Services 3 Ltd, Revenue and Customs Commissioners v Holland*[779] the Supreme Court confirmed previous observations[780] to the effect that *Hydrodam* overstated the differences between de facto and shadow directors as these terms were now understood.[781] Although the stereotypical shadow director assumes a covert role, as noted above this is not necessarily the case.[782] And a de facto director may take major decisions by giving instructions to the de jure directors.[783] As Robert Walker LJ observed in *In re Kaytech International plc*:[784]

> However the two concepts do have at least this much in common, that an individual who was not a de jure director is alleged to have exercised real influence (otherwise than as a professional adviser) in the corporate governance of a company. Sometimes that influence may be concealed and sometimes it may be open. Sometimes it may be something of a mixture, as the facts of the present case show.

**10.251.06**    The directors of the company must be 'accustomed to act' in accordance with the directions or instructions of the alleged shadow director. In *Re Unisoft Group Ltd (No 3)*[785] Harman J held that this wording must refer to acts not on one individual occasion but over a period of time and as a regular course of conduct. In *Ultraframe (UK) Ltd v Fielding*[786] Lewison J concluded that where shadow directorship is established, it does not relate back to the first influenced act, but takes effect from the date when the directors first became 'accustomed to act'.[787]

**10.251.07**    As to whether it is sufficient that a governing majority of the board (rather than the whole board) are accustomed to act, Hart J accepted in *Lord v Sinai Securities Ltd*[788] that it must be shown that all the directors, or at least a consistent majority of them, had been accustomed to act on the directions of the alleged shadow director. In *Ultraframe (UK) Ltd v Fielding*[789] Lewison J concluded that a person at whose direction a governing majority of the board is accustomed to act is capable of being a shadow director. It appears, then, that a governing majority of the board is sufficient.[790]

---

[775]   [2000] 2 WLR 907, 919–920, [35] A further proposition was that the (same) statutory definition of shadow director in the Company Directors Disqualification Act (s 22(5)) is not to be strictly construed on the basis that this Act has quasi-penal consequences.
[776]   [2000] 2 WLR 907, 920, [36].
[777]   [1994] 2 BCLC 180, 182–183.
[778]   [1994] 2 BCLC 180, 183.
[779]   [2010] UKSC 51.
[780]   Eg *In re Kaytech International plc* [1999] 2 BCLC 351 at 423; *Ultraframe (UK) Ltd v Fielding* [2005] EWHC 1638 (Ch) at [1263].
[781]   [2010] UKSC 51, at [91], [110].
[782]   *Secretary of State for Trade and Industry v Deverell* [2000] 2 WLR 907, 920, at [36].
[783]   *Re Paycheck Services 3 Ltd, Revenue and Customs Commissioners v Holland* [2010] UKSC 51, at [91].
[784]   [1999] 2 BCLC 351, at 423.
[785]   [1994] 1 BCLC 609, 620.
[786]   [2005] EWHC 1638 (Ch).
[787]   Compare the suggestion of Pumfrey J in *Re London Citylink Ltd* [2005] EWHC 2875, [2005] All ER (D) 188, [15]: 'that it is possible for a shadow director to exist even where the board had done no acts at all, provided that the *de jure* directors have so fettered their discretion as to oblige themselves to act in accordance with the instructions of the shadow director: in other words, a company may have a shadow director from its inception'. See also para 16.
[788]   [2004] EWHC 1764 (Ch), [2005] 1 BCLC 295, 303.
[789]   [2005] EWHC 1638 (Ch), [1272].
[790]   In *Ultraframe* Lewison J accepted that this was a purposive, rather a literal construction of the words used—'the directors'. In *Re Unisoft Group Ltd (No 3)* [1994] 1 BCLC 609, 620 Harman J indicated his preference (without deciding the point) for the literal construction of these words, as referring to the whole board.

The general duties owed by a director of a company to the company (sections 170 to 177 of the  **10.251.08**
Companies Act 2006) only apply to shadow directors where, and to the extent that the corresponding
common law rules or equitable principles apply: section 170(5) of the Companies Act 2006. In
*Ultraframe (UK) Ltd v Fielding*[791] Lewison J concluded that the indirect influence exerted by a
paradigm shadow director who does not directly deal with or claim the right to deal with the company's
assets will not usually be enough to impose fiduciary duties on him.[792]

## *Other definitions*

### 252 Persons connected with a director

(1) This section defines what is meant by references in this Part to a person being 'connected' with a  **10.252.01**
director of a company (or a director being 'connected' with a person).

(2) The following persons (and only those persons) are connected with a director of a company—
   (a) members of the director's family (see section 253);
   (b) a body corporate with which the director is connected (as defined in section 254);
   (c) a person acting in his capacity as trustee of a trust—
      (i) the beneficiaries of which include the director or a person who by virtue of paragraph (a) or (b) is connected with him, or
      (ii) the terms of which confer a power on the trustees that may be exercised for the benefit of the director or any such person, other than a trust for the purposes of an employees' share scheme or a pension scheme;
   (d) a person acting in his capacity as partner—
      (i) of the director, or
      (ii) of a person who, by virtue of paragraph (a), (b) or (c), is connected with that director;
   (e) a firm that is a legal person under the law by which it is governed and in which—
      (i) the director is a partner,
      (ii) a partner is a person who, by virtue of paragraph (a), (b) or (c) is connected with the director, or
      (iii) a partner is a firm in which the director is a partner or in which there is a partner who, by virtue of paragraph (a), (b) or (c), is connected with the director.

(3) References in this Part to a person connected with a director of a company do not include a person who is himself a director of the company.

COMMENCEMENT DATE 1 October 2007[793]

This section provides the definition of a person 'connected' with a director (or a director 'connected'  **10.252.02**
with a person) for the purpose of Part 10.[794] This section, together with section 253 to 255, replace
section 346 of the Companies Act (1985).

### 253 Members of a director's family

(1) This section defines what is meant by references in this Part to members of a director's family.  **10.253.01**

(2) For the purposes of this Part the members of a director's family are—
   (a) the director's spouse or civil partner;
   (b) any other person (whether of a different sex or the same sex) with whom the director lives as partner in an enduring family relationship;
   (c) the director's children or step-children;
   (d) any children or step-children of a person within paragraph (b) (and who are not children or step-children of the director) who live with the director and have not attained the age of 18;
   (e) the director's parents.

(3) Subsection (2)(b) does not apply if the other person is the director's grandparent or grandchild, sister, brother, aunt or uncle, or nephew or niece.

COMMENCEMENT DATE 1 October 2007[795]

This definition of family members covers a broader range of individuals than those within section  **10.253.02**
346(2)(a) of the Companies Act 1985. Added to the list of those treated as connected by reason of a

---

[791] [2005] EWHC 1638 (Ch).

[792] See para 1289. Specific fiduciary duties may arise where control is exercised over corporate assets: paras 1290, 1291.

[793] Companies Act 2006 (Commencement No 3, etc) Order 2007, SI 2007/2194, art 2.

[794] See eg s 185 (general notice of interest), s 190 (requirement for members' approval of substantial property transactions), s 200 (requirement for members' approval of loans, quasi-loans), s 215 (payments for loss of office), s 239 (ratification of directors' acts).

[795] Companies Act 2006 (Commencement No 3, etc) Order 2007, SI 2007/2194, art 2.

family relationship are those identified at section 253(2)(b), (d), and (e). Children and step-children who have attained the age of 18 are no longer excluded.[796]

### 254 Director 'connected with' a body corporate

**10.254.01**

(1) This section defines what is meant by references in this Part to a director being 'connected with' a body corporate.

(2) A director is connected with a body corporate if, but only if, he and the persons connected with him together—

    (a) are interested in shares comprised in the equity share capital of that body corporate of a nominal value equal to at least 20% of that share capital, or

    (b) are entitled to exercise or control the exercise of more than 20% of the voting power at any general meeting of that body.

(3) The rules set out in Schedule 1 (references to interest in shares or debentures) apply for the purposes of this section.

(4) References in this section to voting power the exercise of which is controlled by a director include voting power whose exercise is controlled by a body corporate controlled by him.

(5) Shares in a company held as treasury shares, and any voting rights attached to such shares, are disregarded for the purposes of this section.

(6) For the avoidance of circularity in the application of section 252 (meaning of 'connected person')—

    (a) a body corporate with which a director is connected is not treated for the purposes of this section as connected with him unless it is also connected with him by virtue of subsection (2)(c) or (d) of that section (connection as trustee or partner); and

    (b) a trustee of a trust the beneficiaries of which include (or may include) a body corporate with which a director is connected is not treated for the purposes of this section as connected with a director by reason only of that fact.

COMMENCEMENT DATE 1 October 2007[797]

**10.254.02** This definition is in similar terms to section 346(4) of the Companies Act 1985. 'Body corporate' includes a body incorporated outside the UK but not a corporation sole or a partnership not regarded as a body corporate under the law by which it is governed, whether or not it is a legal person.[798]

### 255 Director 'controlling' a body corporate

**10.255.01**

(1) This section defines what is meant by references in this Part to a director 'controlling' a body corporate.

(2) A director of a company is taken to control a body corporate if, but only if—

    (a) he or any person connected with him—

        (i) is interested in any part of the equity share capital of that body, or

        (ii) is entitled to exercise or control the exercise of any part of the voting power at any general meeting of that body, and

    (b) he, the persons connected with him and the other directors of that company, together—

        (i) are interested in more than 50% of that share capital, or

        (ii) are entitled to exercise or control the exercise of more than 50% of that voting power.

(3) The rules set out in Schedule 1 (references to interest in shares or debentures) apply for the purposes of this section.

(4) References in this section to voting power the exercise of which is controlled by a director include voting power whose exercise is controlled by a body corporate controlled by him.

(5) Shares in a company held as treasury shares, and any voting rights attached to such shares, are disregarded for the purposes of this section.

(6) For the avoidance of circularity in the application of section 252 (meaning of 'connected person')—

    (a) a body corporate with which a director is connected is not treated for the purposes of this section as connected with him unless it is also connected with him by virtue of subsection (2)(c) or (d) of that section (connection as trustee or partner); and

    (b) a trustee of a trust the beneficiaries of which include (or may include) a body corporate with which a director is connected is not treated for the purposes of this section as connected with a director by reason only of that fact.

COMMENCEMENT DATE 1 October 2007[799]

---

[796] See CA 1985, s 346(3)(a).
[797] Companies Act 2006 (Commencement No 3, etc) Order 2007, SI 2007/2194, art 2.
[798] CA 2006, s 1173(1).
[799] Companies Act 2006 (Commencement No 3, etc) Order 2007, SI 2007/2194, art 2.

This section defines references to a director 'controlling' a body corporate[800] for the purpose section 254.[801]

**10.255.02**

### 256 Associated bodies corporate

For the purposes of this Part—

(a) bodies corporate are associated if one is a subsidiary of the other or both are subsidiaries of the same body corporate, and

(b) companies are associated if one is a subsidiary of the other or both are subsidiaries of the same body corporate.

COMMENCEMENT DATE 1 October 2007[802]

**10.256.01**

This definition of associated bodies corporate and associated companies is new. These terms are used in the provisions relating to the duty not to accept third party benefits,[803] directors' loans,[804] and directors' liabilities.[805]

**10.256.02**

### 257 References to company's constitution

(1) References in this Part to a company's constitution include—

(a) any resolution or other decision come to in accordance with the constitution, and

(b) any decision by the members of the company, or a class of members, that is treated by virtue of any enactment or rule of law as equivalent to a decision by the company.

(2) This is in addition to the matters mentioned in section 17 (general provision as to matters contained in company's constitution).

COMMENCEMENT DATE 1 October 2007[806]

**10.257.01**

The general definition of constitution in section 17 is extended for the purpose of Part 10 by this section.[807]

**10.257.02**

## General

### 258 Power to increase financial limits

(1) The Secretary of State may by order substitute for any sum of money specified in this Part a larger sum specified in the order.

(2) An order under this section is subject to negative resolution procedure.

(3) An order does not have effect in relation to anything done or not done before it comes into force. Accordingly, proceedings in respect of any liability incurred before that time may be continued or instituted as if the order had not been made.

COMMENCEMENT DATE 1 October 2007[808]

**10.258.01**

The Secretary of State may by order increase the financial limits in Part 10. These financial limits are all found in Chapter 4 (transactions requiring members' approval).

**10.258.02**

### 259 Transactions under foreign law

For the purposes of this Part it is immaterial whether the law that (apart from this Act) governs an arrangement or transaction is the law of the United Kingdom, or a part of it, or not.

COMMENCEMENT DATE 1 October 2007[809]

**10.259.01**

Part 10 applies irrespective of the law applicable to a transaction or arrangement: these provisions cannot be circumvented by a choice of law clause.[810]

**10.259.02**

---

[800] Section 1173(1) defines 'body corporate'.

[801] In similar terms to CA 1985, s 346(5).

[802] Companies Act 2006 (Commencement No 3, etc) Order 2007, SI 2007/2194, art 2.

[803] Section 176.

[804] Including quasi-loans and credit transactions, including ss 198, 200, 201, 203.

[805] Sections 232, 236.

[806] Companies Act 2006 (Commencement No 3, etc) Order 2007, SI 2007/2194, art 2.

[807] The sections in Part 10 referring to the constitution include ss 171, 173, 175, 177, 180, 181 (general duties of directors), and s 182 (declaration of interest).

[808] Companies Act 2006 (Commencement No 3, etc) Order 2007, SI 2007/2194, art 2.

[809] Companies Act 2006 (Commencement No 3, etc) Order 2007, SI 2007/2194, art 2.

[810] Similar provision was made in CA 1985, by s 347.

# 11

## DERIVATIVE CLAIMS AND PROCEEDINGS BY MEMBERS

**Companies Act 2006**

## PART 11
### DERIVATIVE CLAIMS AND PROCEEDINGS BY MEMBERS

## CHAPTER 1
### DERIVATIVE CLAIMS IN ENGLAND AND WALES OR NORTHERN IRELAND

### 260 Derivative claims

(1) This Chapter applies to proceedings in England and Wales or Northern Ireland by a member of a company—

    (a) in respect of a cause of action vested in the company, and

    (b) seeking relief on behalf of the company.

This is referred to in this Chapter as a 'derivative claim'.

(2) A derivative claim may only be brought—

    (a) under this Chapter, or

    (b) in pursuance of an order of the court in proceedings under section 994 (proceedings for protection of members against unfair prejudice).

(3) A derivative claim under this Chapter may be brought only in respect of a cause of action arising from an actual or proposed act or omission involving negligence, default, breach of duty or breach of trust by a director of the company.

The cause of action may be against the director or another person (or both).

(4) It is immaterial whether the cause of action arose before or after the person seeking to bring or continue the derivative claim became a member of the company.

(5) For the purposes of this Chapter—

    (a) 'director' includes a former director;

    (b) a shadow director is treated as a director; and

**11.260.01**

(c)  references to a member of a company include a person who is not a member but to whom shares in the company have been transferred or transmitted by operation of law.

COMMENCEMENT DATE  1 October 2007[1]

## Background

**11.260.02**  It has been the case since the earliest days of modern company law that a member could institute proceedings to protect his financial interest in the company against harm being done by those running the company, but this possibility was tightly controlled, most famously by the court in *Foss v Harbottle*.[2] Under English law such a claim could only be instituted under the following four grounds:

(i)  The company was acting *ultra vires*. This has become an increasing rarity these days with the progressive erosion of the *ultra vires* rule by Companies Acts 1985 and 1989, with the latest position reflected by section 39 of the 2006 Act which came into force on 1 October 2009.

(ii)  Breach of a special majority requirement (eg a 75 percent majority requirement— see *Baillie v Oriental Telephone and Electric Co Ltd*[3] and *Edwards v Halliwell*[4] for authorities on this exception).

(iii)  Fraud on the company/minority by controller. This is the paradigm scenario, discussed in authorities such as *Menier v Hoopers Telegraph Works*,[5] *Cook v Deeks*,[6] and more recently *Estmanco (Kilner House) Ltd v GLC*.[7]

(iv)  Infringement of a personal right. Personal rights are rights which are enforceable under the statutory contract—see Companies Act 2006, section 33 (which came into force on 1 October 2009). For example, a shareholder has a personal right to vote (see *Pender v Lushington*)[8] and to receive a properly declared dividend (*Wood v Odessa Waterworks*),[9] but there is not generally a personal right to have the value of one's shareholding protected against depreciation caused by damage to the company as this would fundamentally undermine the basic rule in *Foss v Harbottle*.[10] This latter principle, often characterized as the reflective loss rule, was confirmed by the House of Lords in *Johnson v Gore Wood & Co Ltd*.[11]

**11.260.03**  Unlike in many Commonwealth corporate law systems there was no fifth exception based upon the interests of justice—*Estmanco v GLC*.[12] This is because such an exception is deemed too vague and potentially damaging to the basic rule.

**11.260.04**  These substantive grounds were restrictive and did not reflect the needs of modern company law where there may be instances in which it would be appropriate for a shareholder to bring a claim—a derivative claim—to enforce a cause of action vested in the company in circumstances where the company itself was failing to bring such a claim. The difficulties of a shareholder using a derivative claim procedure successfully were exemplified by the views expressed by the Court of Appeal in *Prudential Assurance v Newman Industries (No 2)*.[13] This case illustrated the procedural complexity of the law and the hostility

---

[1]  Companies Act 2006 (Commencement No 3, etc) Order 2007, SI 2007/2194, art 2. Note that this, and the other sections in Part 11, do not apply in respect of certain persons while Northern Rock is wholly owned by the Treasury: see Northern Rock plc Transfer Order 2008, SI 2008/432. For a comprehensive review of the new regime on derivative claims, see A Reisberg, *Derivative Actions and Corporate Governance* (OUP, 2007). In-depth judicial consideration of this reform is provided by Lewison J in *Iesini v Westrip Holdings Ltd* [2009] EWHC 2526 (Ch), [2010] BCC 420. The Act does not extend to a double derivative claim—ie a claim by a member of a parent company in respect of a cause of action vested in a subsidiary company—but for the question whether such a claim may be available at common law, see the discussion in the judgment of the Court of Final Appeal in Hong Kong (including Lord Millett sitting as a non-permanent judge) in *Waddington Ltd v Chan Chun Hoo Thomas* [2009] 2 BCLC 82.

[2]  (1843) 2 Hare 461.

[3]  [1915] 1 Ch 503.

[4]  [1950] 2 All ER 1064.

[5]  (1874) LR 9 Ch 350.

[6]  [1916] AC 554.

[7]  [1982] 1 WLR 2.

[8]  (1877) 6 Ch D 70.

[9]  (1889) 42 Ch D 636.

[10]  (1843) 2 Hare 461.

[11]  [2002] 2 AC 1. For recent discussion, see *Webster v Sandersons Solicitors* [2009] EWCA Civ 830, [2009] 2 BCLC 542.

[12]  [1982] 1 WLR 2.

[13]  [1982] 2 WLR 31.

of the courts to derivative claims. Since that date few derivative claims were successfully initiated—for illustrations see *Knight v Frost*[14] and *Clark v Cutland*.[15]

The Law Commission, *Shareholder Remedies*[16] called for change. In particular it suggested a return to the drawing board with the introduction of a statutory derivative claims procedure modelled upon the Canadian system (see Canadian Business Corporations Act, sections 239 to 242) (which has since been adopted in New Zealand under the Companies Act 1993, sections 165 to 168 and in Australia under the Corporations Act 2001, sections 236 to 242). These recommendations were supported by the Company Law Review,[17] and by the subsequent White Paper,[18] and are now given effect to by sections 260 to 264. There is a useful body of literature on this subject.[19]   **11.260.05**

For parliamentary discussion see the debate in Grand Committee 27 February 2006. The Explanatory Notes to the Act (paragraphs 483 to 504) are also informative.   **11.260.06**

The section came into force on 1 October 2007. If a derivative claim is sought to be based on conduct which occurred before this date, the court can allow the claim to proceed only if such a claim could have been brought under the law which applied before 1 October 2007. A number of reported cases now throw light on how these transitional issues can be handled.[20]   **11.260.07**

## Relationship with other remedies: Unfair prejudice remedy; just and equitable winding-up

It should be appreciated that derivative claims form only part of the picture on shareholder protection. Of much greater importance is the statutory remedy for unfair prejudice conferred by Companies Act 2006, section 994[21] and, to a lesser extent, the possibility of winding up on the 'just and equitable' ground under section 122(1)(g) of the Insolvency Act 1986.[22]   **11.260.08**

## Jurisdiction

Subsection (1) defines the territorial scope of the derivative claim procedure in England and Wales and Northern Ireland. Separate provision is made by sections 265 to 269 for derivative proceedings in Scotland (where the procedural rules differ).   **11.260.09**

Subsection (2) makes it clear that apart from derivative claims initiated under this Chapter such claims may arise as a relief option on a successful unfair prejudice petition— see section 996 of the Companies Act 2006.   **11.260.10**

## Claimant

The claimant must be a member and sues on behalf of the company to enforce a cause of action vested in the company. Thus, the claimant must be one of the original subscribers to the memorandum of association or a person who has agreed to become a member and whose name is on the register of members: see the definition of 'member' in section 112. Note that by section 260(5)(c), a 'member' for the purposes of the section is also taken to include a person who is not a member but to whom shares in the company have been transferred or transmitted by operation of law. This mirrors the similar provision in section 994(2) in relation to the unfair prejudice remedy.[23]   **11.260.11**

Subsection (4) stresses that the status of the claimant when the cause of action arose is immaterial. Presumably an activist could join the company simply in order to litigate—but quaere whether the court would grant permission/leave in such a case.   **11.260.12**

---

[14] [1999] 1 BCLC 364.

[15] [2003] EWCA Civ 810.

[16] (1997) LC No. 246, Cm 3769, para 6.111 (see Poole and Roberts [1999] JBL 99).

[17] See *Final Report*, URN 01/942, paras 7.46–7.51.

[18] *Company Law Reform* (Cm 6456) in 2005 (para 3.4).

[19] See Arden [2002] JBL 579, 594 for expert insight into the thinking of the Company Law Review on this matter. For an overview of how the new statutory derivative claims procedure is working in Australia, see Legg and Jordan [2007] (19) *Sweet and Maxwell's Company Law Newsletter* 1.

[20] See for example *Iesini v Westrip Holdings Ltd* [2009] EWHC 2526 (Ch), [2010] BCC 420, *Parry v Bartlett* [2011] EWHC 3146 (Ch), *Hughes v Weiss* [2012] EWHC 2363 (Ch).

[21] See paras 30.994.01 *et seq.*

[22] See paras 30.994.27–29.

[23] See the discussion at para 30.994.09 for an explanation of what the provision means.

## Defendants

**11.260.13**   The claim may be against a director and/or a third party (subsection (3)).

**11.260.14**   Directors include current directors, former directors (subsection (5)(a)), de jure directors, de facto directors (section 250) and shadow directors (subsection (5)(b), as defined in section 251).

**11.260.15**   Third parties can be the subject of derivative claims provided that (section 260(3)) the claim against them is 'in respect of a cause of action arising from an actual or proposed act or omission involving negligence, default, breach of duty or breach of trust by a director of the company'—for example on the grounds that the third parties have wrongfully received company property or have facilitated a breach of duty. Where a third party has committed a wrong against the company but the only negligence, default, etc, of the directors lies in failing to rectify matters by bringing a claim against the third party, a derivative claim under section 260 will lie against the directors but not against the third party—though in such circumstances it may be possible to procure the company to bring a claim against the third party by the circuitous route of obtaining an order for the bringing of such a claim in proceedings under section 994.[24] For example on the grounds that they have wrongfully received company property or have facilitated a breach of duty. A derivative claim against a third party may also be possible where that party has committed a wrong against the company and the directors in breach of duty have failed to rectify matters. For discussion, see the Explanatory Notes to the Act at paragraph 494, which emphasize that derivative claims against third parties would be permitted only in very narrow circumstances; and the discussion in Grand Committee in the House of Lords (*Hansard*, column GC 10) (27 February 2006)).

## Grounds

**11.260.16**   By subsection (3), the claim must be in respect of a cause of action arising from negligence, default, breach of duty (common law or fiduciary), or breach of trust by a director. There is a change in the law here from the previous common law position. At common law pure negligence by a director could not found a derivative claim (*Pavlides v Jensen*[25] ) unless the director also profited from his own incompetence (*Daniels v Daniels*[26] ). Under the 2006 Act pure negligence will now suffice and so the potential exposure of directors to risk is broadened. The subsection also makes clear that a claim may be brought in respect of an act or an omission, and regardless whether it has already happened or is proposed for the future.[27]

## Costs

**11.260.17**   CPR rule 19.9E provides that the court may order the company to indemnify the claimant against liability for costs incurred in bringing the derivative claim (and also for costs incurred in the application for permission to bring the claim, which is discussed below). Under the old common law derivative claims procedure (eg *Wallersteiner v Moir (No 2)*[28] and *Smith v Croft*[29], the court would make such an order only in limited cases and it appears that under the new statutory jurisdiction the court is likely to exercise the power more frequently. In *Iesini v Westrip Holdings Ltd*, Lewison J confirmed that an indemnity as to costs in a derivative claim 'is not limited to impecunious defendants' and explained that 'Once the court has reached the conclusion that the claim ought to proceed for the benefit of the company, it ought normally to order the company to indemnify the claimant against his costs.'[30]

---

[24]   *Iesini v Westrip Holdings Ltd* [2009] EWHC 2526 (Ch), [2010] BCC 420 per Lewison J at [75] & [81]–[82].

[25]   [1956] Ch 565.

[26]   [1978] 2 All ER 89.

[27]   For further reading, see Keay and Loughrey (2008) 124 LQR 469. Note also Lowry and Dignam, *Company Law* (3rd edn, OUP, 2005), Chap 10.

[28]   [1975] QB 373.

[29]   [1986] 1 WLR 580.

[30]   [2009] EWHC 2526 (Ch), [2010] BCC 420 [125]. The burden that this imposes upon the company is a factor which the court will take into account in considering whether the claimant should be required to pursue some other remedy which would not impose such a burden on the company (such as an 'unfair prejudice' claim under CA 2006, s 994) and therefore whether permission for the derivative claim should be refused: [2009] EWHC 2526 (Ch), [126]. The decision in *Iesini* also explains, by reference to *Smith v Croft* [1986] 1 WLR 580, that while it may be the normal practice to order a costs indemnity in the sense that the claimant will recover his costs from the company at the end of the proceedings, it is less usual to make an order that the claimant may recover his costs from the company at intervals while the proceedings are ongoing. To obtain an order of the latter type, the claimant would need to show that he does not have sufficient resources to fund the ongoing proceedings and therefore needs to be reimbursed at regular intervals rather than waiting until the proceedings are concluded.

In *Kiani v Cooper*[31] the court ordered that the claimant's costs should be borne by the company save that the indemnity was not to extend to any adverse costs order which may be made in favour of the defendant against the claimant, though this latter aspect was to be reviewed further by the court after disclosure had taken place in the action.

If the claimant does seek an order that the company indemnify him against the costs of the claim (and    **11.260.18** the permission application), this should be stated in the claim form (and in the permission application): CPR Part 19, Practice Direction 19C, paragraph 2(2).

## Other bodies corporate; trade unions

Section 260 applies only in respect of companies within the meaning of the Companies Act 2006, as    **11.260.19** defined in section 1 of the Act. Derivative claims can, however, also be brought in respect of other bodies corporate and trade unions quite apart from the provisions of section 260; the procedure for such claims is governed by CPR rule 19.9C which adopts the same procedure as that for applications under sections 261, 262 and 264.

## Improper political donations/expenditure

There is a separate statutory procedure for the pursuit of claims against directors brought by autho-    **11.260.20** rized members on behalf of the company under sections 370 to 373 in respect of improper political donations or improper political expenditure. This latter procedure has a specific statutory provision (section 372) enabling advance indemnity orders to be obtained to require the company to indemnify the members in respect of the costs of the proceedings.[32]

## 261 Application for permission to continue derivative claim

    (1)  A member of a company who brings a derivative claim under this Chapter must apply to the court    **11.261.01**
         for permission (in Northern Ireland, leave) to continue it.
    (2)  If it appears to the court that the application and the evidence filed by the applicant in support of
         it do not disclose a prima facie case for giving permission (or leave), the court—
        (a)  must dismiss the application, and
        (b)  may make any consequential order it considers appropriate.
    (3)  If the application is not dismissed under subsection (2), the court—
        (a)  may give directions as to the evidence to be provided by the company, and
        (b)  may adjourn the proceedings to enable the evidence to be obtained.
    (4)  On hearing the application, the court may—
        (a)  give permission (or leave) to continue the claim on such terms as it thinks fit,
        (b)  refuse permission (or leave) and dismiss the claim, or
        (c)  adjourn the proceedings on the application and give such directions as it thinks fit.

COMMENCEMENT DATE 1 October 2007[33]

## Requirement for permission

There is an important safety valve involved in derivative claims—permission (or leave, if the claim is    **11.261.02** brought in Northern Ireland) must be obtained from the court *to continue* the claim. Section 263 (discussed below) identifies the criteria to be applied by the court. At common law such a control mechanism existed for some time in the former version of the Civil Procedure Rules—see cases such as *Mumbray v Lapper*,[34] *Portfolios of Distinction Ltdv Laird*,[35] *Jafari-Fini v Skillglass Ltd*,[36] and *Harley Street Capital Ltd v Tchigirinsky*.[37] The relevant rules are now set out in CPR rules 19.9 to 19.9F and Practice Direction 19C, discussed below.

In an amendment made at Report Stage in the House of Lords the need for a *prima facie* case to be made    **11.261.03** out was added in the form of what is now subsection (2), thus introducing in effect a *two-stage* procedure. If the application does not appear to disclose a prima facie case, the court must dismiss it at

---

   [31]  [2010] EWHC 577 (Ch), [2010] 2 BCLC 427 [47]–[49]. See also *Stainer v Lee* [2010] EWHC 1539 (Ch), [2011] BCC 134 where a capped advance indemnity was made available, limiting the indemnity to £40,000 with permission to apply to increase it at subsequent stages of the proceedings, per Roth J at [56].
   [32]  See the discussion at paras 14.370.01 *et seq.*
   [33]  Companies Act 2006 (Commencement No 3, etc) Order 2007, SI 2007/2194, art 2.
   [34]  [2005] BCC 90.
   [35]  [2005] BCC 16.
   [36]  [2005] EWCA Civ 365.
   [37]  [2006] BCC 209. See also *Reeves v Sprecher* [2007] EWHC 117 (Ch), [2008] BCC 49 where Lewison J considered whether a derivative claim should be allowed to continue where questions of whether England was the appropriate forum were raised.

the outset and can make any relevant consequential orders, which would presumably relate to costs. For parliamentary debate see *Hansard*, 9 May 2006, columns 883 to 885. If the claimant surmounts this first hurdle of a prima facie case, the court will give directions under subsection (3) leading to a further hearing at which the application for permission will be determined. It is important that this procedure is followed, a point emphasized by the court in *Langley Ward Ltd v Trevor*.[38]

**11.261.04** Permission was refused under section 261(1) by William Trower QC (sitting as a deputy High Court judge) in *Franbar Holdings Ltd v Patel*.[39] For discussion of various procedural aspects of derivative claims in general, see *Roberts v Gill & Co*.[40]

### Grant of permission, refusal of permission, or adjournment

**11.261.05** Subsection (4) makes it clear that on the hearing of the application for permission/leave the court has a full range of dispositive options available to it. The court may grant permission, refuse permission, or adjourn the application. An adjournment may be appropriate, for example, where the company wishes to have an opportunity to see whether the relevant conduct can be ratified or where the court considers that the board should consider further a particular matter affecting the question whether a derivative claim should be brought.[41]

### Procedure

**11.261.06** The procedural rules are contained in CPR rules 19.9 to 19.9F and Practice Direction 19C.

**11.261.07** A derivative claim is brought by way of a claim form (which must be headed 'Derivative claim'), with the company being made a defendant to the claim in addition to the director(s) and any relevant third parties.

**11.261.08** When the claim form is issued, the claimant must file an application notice under CPR Part 23 for permission to continue the claim in accordance with section 261, supported by written evidence. The company is not to be made a respondent to the permission application but the claimant must as soon as reasonably practicable send to the company the prescribed form of notice set out at the end of Practice Direction 19C together with copies of the claim form, the application notice and the evidence, and must then file with the court a witness statement confirming that he has done so. The claimant may, however, apply to the court for permission not to notify the company of the issue of the claim form and of the permission application where to do so would be likely to frustrate some part of the remedy sought, and in an appropriate case the claimant may also make an urgent application for interim relief (rules 19.9A(7) and 19.9(4)(b)).

**11.261.09** Following the issue of the application, the court will decide whether the application shows the requisite prima facie case under section 261(2). The court may do this just on a paper application, without a hearing; if the claimant's application is dismissed by the court without a hearing at this first stage, the claimant may within seven days ask the court for an oral hearing to reconsider the decision provided he notifies the company that he is doing so.

**11.261.10** At this first stage under subsection (2), the company is allowed to volunteer a submission (and attend an oral hearing if there is one) if it wishes so to do, but will not normally be allowed its costs: see Practice Direction 19C, paragraph 5.

**11.261.11** If the court decides at this first stage under subsection (2) that the permission application does show a prima facie case, it will order the company and any other appropriate parties to be made respondents to the application and will give directions for the filing of further evidence and for a further hearing at which the application will be determined.

**11.261.12** As to the costs of the permission application, CPR rule 19.9E provides that the claimant may seek from the court an order that the company indemnify the claimant in respect of such costs.[42]

### Discontinuance/settlement

**11.261.13** Where the court gives permission to continue a derivative claim, it may order that the claim may not be discontinued or settled without the court's permission: see CPR r 19.9F and Practice Direction 19C, paragraph 7. This would enable the court to ensure that any proposed discontinuance or settlement would first be brought to the attention of other members of the company who might have an interest

---

[38] [2011] EWHC 1893 (Ch).

[39] [2008] EWHC 1534 (Ch), [2009] 1 BCLC 1.

[40] [2008] EWCA Civ 803, [2009] 1 WLR 531, affirmed [2010] UKSC 22, [2011] 1 AC 240.

[41] *Iesini v Westrip Holdings Ltd* [2009] EWHC 2526 (Ch), [2010] BCC 420 [105]–[110] is an example of the latter situation.

[42] See paras 11.260.17–18 above.

in taking over the claim. The consultation paper published by the Courts Service on 23 May 2007 in advance of the implementation of CPR rr 19.9 to 19.9F noted that the intention behind the court being given this power is to discourage the development of so-called 'greenmail' claims where a person buys shares in a company and brings a claim which is settled on terms that include a purchase of the claimant's shares at a price above their market value.

### 262 Application for permission to continue claim as a derivative claim

(1) This section applies where—     **11.262.01**
    (a) a company has brought a claim, and
    (b) the cause of action on which the claim is based could be pursued as a derivative claim under this Chapter.
(2) A member of the company may apply to the court for permission (in Northern Ireland, leave) to continue the claim as a derivative claim on the ground that—
    (a) the manner in which the company commenced or continued the claim amounts to an abuse of the process of the court,
    (b) the company has failed to prosecute the claim diligently, and
    (c) it is appropriate for the member to continue the claim as a derivative claim.
(3) If it appears to the court that the application and the evidence filed by the applicant in support of it do not disclose a prima facie case for giving permission (or leave), the court—
    (a) must dismiss the application, and
    (b) may make any consequential order it considers appropriate.
(4) If the application is not dismissed under subsection (3), the court—
    (a) may give directions as to the evidence to be provided by the company, and
    (b) may adjourn the proceedings to enable the evidence to be obtained.
(5) On hearing the application, the court may—
    (a) give permission (or leave) to continue the claim as a derivative claim on such terms as it thinks fit,
    (b) refuse permission (or leave) and dismiss the application, or
    (c) adjourn the proceedings on the application and give such directions as it thinks fit.

COMMENCEMENT DATE 1 October 2007[43]

### Change of carriage of claim from company to a member

Subsections (1) and (2) must be read together. They enable a member in defined circumstances to take     **11.262.02**
over as a derivative claim the carriage of a claim initially initiated by the company. The claim as originally constituted must qualify as one which could be brought as a derivative claim—ie it must satisfy the requirements in section 260(3).

The ground on which such a change in the nature of proceedings will be permitted is identified by     **11.262.03**
section 262(2)(a)–(c), all of which must be satisfied. The Explanatory Notes to the Act suggest at paragraph 496 that an example of a claim being commenced by the company as an abuse of the process would be where the company brought the claim with a view to preventing a member bringing a derivative claim.[44]

### Procedure

In the same way as with a claim brought under section 260, there is a two-stage procedure for obtaining     **11.262.04**
permission. The claimant must satisfy the court that the application shows a prima facie case before being allowed to proceed to a full-blown permission hearing: section 262(3). This was a requirement added at Report Stage in the House of Lords to enable the court to make a speedy decision to dismiss—see *Hansard*, column 885 (9 May 2006).

For the procedural rules, see CPR rules 19.9 to 19.9F and Practice Direction 19C. By rule 19.9B, the     **11.262.05**
procedure for continuing a claim as a derivative claim under section 262 is similar to that for bringing a derivative claim under section 261.[45]

### Change of carriage of claim from one member to another

For the similar change of carriage scenario where a member wishes to take over a derivative claim     **11.262.06**
brought by another member, see section 264 below.

---

[43] Companies Act 2006 (Commencement No 3, etc) Order 2007, SI 2007/2194, art 2.
[44] See also the Law Commission's report at para 6.63, referred to in *Iesini v Westrip Holdings Ltd* [2009] EWHC 2526 (Ch), [2010] BCC 420 at [80].
[45] See therefore the discussion at paras 11.261.01–13 above.

## 263 Whether permission to be given

**11.263.01**

(1) The following provisions have effect where a member of a company applies for permission (in Northern Ireland, leave) under section 261 or 262.

(2) Permission (or leave) must be refused if the court is satisfied—

    (a) that a person acting in accordance with section 172 (duty to promote the success of the company) would not seek to continue the claim, or

    (b) where the cause of action arises from an act or omission that is yet to occur, that the act or omission has been authorised by the company, or

    (c) where the cause of action arises from an act or omission that has already occurred, that the act or omission—

        (i) was authorised by the company before it occurred, or

        (ii) has been ratified by the company since it occurred.

(3) In considering whether to give permission (or leave) the court must take into account, in particular—

    (a) whether the member is acting in good faith in seeking to continue the claim;

    (b) the importance that a person acting in accordance with section 172 (duty to promote the success of the company) would attach to continuing it;

    (c) where the cause of action results from an act or omission that is yet to occur, whether the act or omission could be, and in the circumstances would be likely to be—

        (i) authorised by the company before it occurs, or

        (ii) ratified by the company after it occurs;

    (d) where the cause of action arises from an act or omission that has already occurred, whether the act or omission could be, and in the circumstances would be likely to be, ratified by the company;

    (e) whether the company has decided not to pursue the claim;

    (f) whether the act or omission in respect of which the claim is brought gives rise to a cause of action that the member could pursue in his own right rather than on behalf of the company.

(4) In considering whether to give permission (or leave) the court shall have particular regard to any evidence before it as to the views of members of the company who have no personal interest, direct or indirect, in the matter.

(5) The Secretary of State may by regulations—

    (a) amend subsection (2) so as to alter or add to the circumstances in which permission (or leave) is to be refused;

    (b) amend subsection (3) so as to alter or add to the matters that the court is required to take into account in considering whether to give permission (or leave).

(6) Before making any such regulations the Secretary of State shall consult such persons as he considers appropriate.

(7) Regulations under this section are subject to affirmative resolution procedure.

COMMENCEMENT DATE 1 October 2007[46]

## *Introduction*

**11.263.02** Subsection (1) indicates that the following two subsections set out important requirements and guidance on when a derivative claim should be allowed to proceed under section 261, or a change of carriage permitted under section 262. Section 263 is not relevant where a change of carriage from one member to another is sought under section 264, because in such a situation section 263 will already have operated when the original member brought the claim.

## *Grounds on which permission must be refused*

**11.263.03** Subsection (2) is particularly important. If *any* of the three conditions identified in this subsection are present permission/leave *must* be refused.

**11.263.04** First (per subsection (2)(a), by reference to section 172), permission must be refused if a director would not have commenced the claim because to pursue it would not promote the success of the company.[47] Thus the test in most cases will be that permission must be refused if the claim is not in the interests of the members as a whole (having regard in particular to the matters identified in section 172(1)(a)–(f), and there may be occasional cases where it will be necessary also to have regard to some additional purpose of the company (section 172(2)) or the interests of the company's creditors (section 172(3)).[48]

---

[46] Companies Act 2006 (Commencement No 3, etc) Order 2007, SI 2007/2194, art 2.

[47] See the discussion of s 172 at paras 10.172.01 *et seq* above.

[48] In *Franbar Holdings Ltd v Patel* [2008] EWHC 1534 (Ch), [2009] 1 BCLC 1 the court concluded that not all directors would necessarily take the same view and that, on the facts of that case, the court could not be satisfied that a hypothetical director would conclude that the claim was insufficiently cogent to justify continuation.

To develop the point further, this absolute bar will only apply if no director would support the derivative claim.[49] This insight severely limits the scope of the absolute bar with the result that the matter will normally become the subject of discretion under section 263(3). It should also be noted that the absolute bar might be applied to some of the defendants in the proposed derivative claim, but not to others.[50]

Secondly (subsection (2)(b)), permission must be refused if the relevant act or omission has not yet **11.263.05** occurred and has been authorized by the company. For example, a company may in certain circumstances authorize a situation where a director has a conflict of interest.[51]

Thirdly (subsection (2)(c)), permission must be refused if the relevant act or omission has already **11.263.06** occurred and either was authorized by the company before it occurred or has been ratified by the company since it occurred. Again, for example, a company might have authorized a conflict of interest under section 175. As to ratification, see section 239 (at para 10.239.01 above), dealing with the ability of a company's members in certain circumstances to ratify a director's negligence, default, breach of duty, or breach of trust provided that the director himself and any members connected with him shall not be counted in the voting on such ratification. Section 239(7) preserves, however, the common law rules that certain acts are incapable of ratification; thus, acts ultra vires the company cannot be ratified, nor can a purported ratification be effective where it would result in a fraud on the minority in the sense that it would improperly prevent the claimant bringing a claim on behalf of the company such as a claim based on an improper diversion of business: see *Franbar Holdings Ltd v Patel*.[52]

### *Other relevant factors*

Subsection (3) offers general guidelines for the court.[53] These owe much to the Canadian model, **11.263.07** though they do not represent an exact replication—see the Canadian Business Corporations Act, section 239(2). Note the court's requirement of the need for good faith,[54] utilitarian considerations,[55] the possibility of authorization or ratification, and whether the member can pursue some other cause of action in his own right.[56] The court must have regard not only to whether authorization/ratification could be effected, but also to whether it is likely that it would be effected. If the claim could be pursued as a personal claim, rather than as a derivative claim, that fact might influence the court to refuse permission.[57] See the discussion at Report Stage *Hansard*, column 889 (9 May 2006). It is not a requirement to show that the alleged wrongdoers control the company.

Subsection (4) requires the court to have particular regard to any evidence of views of other members **11.263.08** of the company who have no personal interest in the matter.[58]

---

Nonetheless, the court refused permission having regard to other factors under s 263(3). See also *Stimpson v Southern Private Landlords Association* [2009] EWHC 2072 (Ch), [2010] BCC 387.

[49]  *Iesini v Westrip Holdings Ltd* [2009] EWHC 2526 (Ch), [2010] BCC 420, *Langley Ward Ltd v Trevor* [2011] EWHC 1893 (Ch), *Parry v Bartlett* [2011] EWHC 3146 (Ch), *Hughes v Weiss* [2012] EWHC 2363 (Ch).

[50]  For discussion of this point see *Kleanthous v Paphitis* [2011] EWHC 2287 (Ch).

[51]  See s 175 at para 10.175.01 above. Note also that s 180(4)(a) preserves the common law rules relating to authorization of conduct that otherwise would be a breach of duty.

[52]  [2008] EWHC 1534 (Ch), [2009] 1 BCLC 1, [43]–[47].

[53]  The court is required to have particular regard to these factors but is not precluded from also taking into account other factors: *Franbar Holdings Ltd v Patel* [2008] EWHC 1534 (Ch), [2009] 1 BCLC 1, [31].

[54]  If the claimant has some ulterior motive for bringing the claim, this may indicate a lack of good faith: [2009] 1 BCLC 1, [32]–[33]. See also *Stimpson v Southern Private Landlords Association* [2009] EWHC 2072 (Ch), [2010] BCC 387.

[55]  In considering the importance a director acting in accordance with s 172 would attach to continuing the claim, a hypothetical director would be likely to take into account a wide range of considerations, such as the prospects of success of the claim, the ability of the company to make a recovery on any award of damages, the disruption which would be caused to the development of the company's business by having to concentrate on the proceedings, the costs of the proceedings, any damage to the company's reputation and business if the proceedings were to fail, and so on: *Franbar Holdings Ltd v Patel* [2008] EWHC 1534 (Ch), [2009] 1 BCLC 1, [36].

[56]  It was on the basis of this latter ground that the court refused permission to continue a derivative claim in *Franbar Holdings Ltd v Patel* [2008] EWHC 1534 (Ch), [2009] 1 BCLC 1, [49]–[54], holding that the claimant should confine itself to the causes of action it was already pursuing by way of an unfair prejudice petition under s 994 of the Act and by way of an action alleging breaches of a shareholders' agreement.

[57]  Discussed in *Iesini v Westrip Holdings Ltd* [2009] EWHC 2526 (Ch), [2010] BCC 420 [123]–[126], highlighting in particular the relevance of the costs burden which may be imposed on a company by a derivative claim in contrast to an 'unfair prejudice' claim under CA 2006, s 994. See also *Kiani v Cooper* [2010] EWHC 577 (Ch), [2010] 2 BCLC 427 [38]–[41].

[58]  Discussed in *Iesini v Westrip Holdings Ltd* [2009] EWHC 2526 (Ch), [2010] BCC 420 [127]–[130], which notes that the interpretation of this provision is not straightforward but that it probably requires the court to have

**11.263.09** Cases are now being reported which illuminate how the courts are dealing with applications to continue derivative claims under these new provisions.[59] In *Mission Capital plc v Sinclair*[60] permission was refused. Although the application was in good faith and the question of whether a director acting in pursuance of duties imposed by section 172 would seek to continue the claim was not seen as a barrier to the claim, the critical issues were that a notional director would not have attached much importance to the claim and that the remedy which the claimant was seeking could have been better reviewed on an application under section 994 (the unfair prejudice jurisdiction).[61] Again, in *Fan-mailuk.com v Cooper*[62] permission was refused because there were linked proceedings which, if successful, would make the derivative claim superfluous. Permission to continue the derivative claim was also refused in *Iesini v Westrip Holdings Ltd*[63] where the possibility of a section 172 defence was decisive. This latter case contains a useful discussion generally of the derivative claims procedure. Specifically in relation to the interface between section 263(2)(a) and section 263(3)(b), the case confirms that section 263(2)(a) will debar a claim only where *no* director acting in accordance with section 172 would seek to continue the claim; if some directors would seek to continue the claim and others would not, the case is one for the application of section 263(3)(b).[64] The judgment in *Iesini* also includes a discussion of the 'good faith' requirement of section 263(3)(a), noting that if the claimant is pursuing the claim genuinely for the benefit of the company, he will not necessarily be debarred from pursuing the claim just because there may also be other benefits he will derive from it.[65] The claimant will, however, be likely to be debarred from pursuing the claim if he participated in the wrong of which he complains or if the claim is brought to escape the consequences of his own misdeeds.[66] In comparison with many of the above cases, permission to proceed was granted by the court in *Hughes v Weiss*,[67] a ruling of HHJ Keyser QC. This case is significant for explaining how pre-October 2007 conduct should be viewed by the court. Once again the point was made that the existence of an alternative remedy did not necessarily bar a derivative claim.[68] Much depends on the precise remedy that is being sought.

**11.263.10** In some cases the circumstances may be such that the court will give permission for a limited period only, for example, to the stage of disclosure of documents in the proceedings, with a further application then to be made to the court to extend the permission.[69]

## Amendments to the section

**11.263.11** Subsections (5) to (7) allow the Secretary of State to modify by regulation any of the conditions/criteria outlined in subsections (2) and (3)—perhaps if concerns arise that derivative actions are being abused. Proper consultation is required (subsection (6)) and regulations must use the affirmative resolution procedure (subsection (7)). This flexibility has raised concerns (voiced in Grand Committee in the House of Lords) about the inherent uncertainty as to the exposure of directors to litigation, but is probably a necessary responsive facility.

**11.263.12** For the affirmative resolution procedure see section 1290 below.

---

regard to any evidence of the views of members who (as it seems to the court, doing the best it can on an interim application) are not implicated in the alleged wrongdoing and who do not stand to benefit otherwise than in their capacity as members of the company.

[59] For example *Franbar Holdings Ltd v Patel* [2008] EWHC 1534 (Ch), [2009] 1 BCLC 1.

[60] [2008] BCC 866.

[61] See also *Stimpson v Southern Landlords Association* [2009] EWHC 2072 (Ch) in relation to the test of whether a hypothetical director would continue the claim.

[62] [2008] BCC 877. Applied in *Iesini v Westrip Holdings Ltd* [2009] EWHC 2526 (Ch), [2010] BCC 420, which notes (at para 79) that while the court will not embark on a 'mini-trial' when considering whether to grant permission at the second stage (assuming the first stage of the 'prima facie' hurdle under s 261(2) has been surmounted), the court nonetheless will have to form a provisional view on the strength of the claim in order properly to consider the requirements of s 263(2)(a) and (b).

[63] [2009] EWHC 2526 (Ch), [2010] BCC 420. See also *Stimpson v Southern Private Landlords Association* [2009] EWHC 2072 (Ch), [2010] BCC 387. In *Langley Ward Ltd v Trevor* [2011] EWHC 1893 (Ch) permission was refused.

[64] [2009] EWHC 2526 (Ch), [86]. Examples of the factors to be considered both in relation to s 263(2)(a) and s 263(3)(b) are given at para 85 of the judgment.

[65] [2009] EWHC 2526 (Ch), [113]–[121].

[66] *Iesini v Westrip Holdings Ltd* [2009] EWHC 2526 (Ch), [2010] BCC 420 [122].

[67] [2012] EWHC 2363 (Ch).

[68] Compare *Kleanthous v Paphitis* [2011] EWHC 2287 (Ch), where the existence of a possible alternative remedy was a significant consideration in blocking the derivative claim.

[69] *Stainer v Lee* [2010] EWHC 1539 (Ch), [2011] BCC 134 is a case where permission was given, in the first instance, just to the conclusion of disclosure, per Roth J at [55].

**264  Application for permission to continue derivative claim brought by another member**

(1)  This section applies where a member of a company ('the claimant')—                            **11.264.01**
    (a)  has brought a derivative claim,
    (b)  has continued as a derivative claim a claim brought by the company, or
    (c)  has continued a derivative claim under this section.
(2)  Another member of the company ("the applicant") may apply to the court for permission (in
    Northern Ireland, leave) to continue the claim on the ground that—
    (a)  the manner in which the proceedings have been commenced or continued by the claimant
       amounts to an abuse of the process of the court,
    (b)  the claimant has failed to prosecute the claim diligently, and
    (c)  it is appropriate for the applicant to continue the claim as a derivative claim.
(3)  If it appears to the court that the application and the evidence filed by the applicant in support of
    it do not disclose a prima facie case for giving permission (or leave), the court—
    (a)  must dismiss the application, and
    (b)  may make any consequential order it considers appropriate.
(4)  If the application is not dismissed under subsection (3), the court—
    (a)  may give directions as to the evidence to be provided by the company, and
    (b)  may adjourn the proceedings to enable the evidence to be obtained.
(5)  On hearing the application, the court may—
    (a)  give permission (or leave) to continue the claim on such terms as it thinks fit,
    (b)  refuse permission (or leave) and dismiss the application, or
    (c)  adjourn the proceedings on the application and give such directions as it thinks fit.

COMMENCEMENT DATE 1 October 2007[70]

## *Change of carriage of claim from one member to another*

Subsections (1) and (2) deal with change of carriage of a derivative claim in circumstances where the    **11.264.02**
claim had originally been initiated by another *member*. For the similar scenario where the claim had
originally been initiated by the company, see section 262 above. The grounds on which such a
procedural transition from one member to another can occur are identified in section 264(2) and
mirror those in section 262 above. The Explanatory Notes to the Act suggest at paragraph 503 that an
example of a claim being commenced by a member as an abuse of the process would be where the
member brought the claim with a view to preventing another member from bringing it.

## *Procedure*

As with sections 260 and 262, there is a two-stage procedure for obtaining permission. The claimant    **11.264.03**
must satisfy the court that the application shows a prima facie case before being allowed to proceed to
a full-blown permission hearing: section 264(3). This was a requirement added at Report Stage in the
House of Lords.

For the procedural rules, see CPR rule 19.9 to 19.9F and Practice Direction 19C. By rules 19.9B, the    **11.264.04**
procedure for taking over a derivative claim under section 264 is similar to that for bringing a derivative
claim under section 261.[71]

# CHAPTER 2
## DERIVATIVE PROCEEDINGS IN SCOTLAND

**265  Derivative proceedings**

(1)  In Scotland, a member of a company may raise proceedings in respect of an act or omission    **11.265.01**
    specified in subsection (3) in order to protect the interests of the company and obtain a remedy
    on its behalf.
(2)  A member of a company may raise such proceedings only under subsection (1).
(3)  The act or omission referred to in subsection (1) is any actual or proposed act or omission involving
    negligence, default, breach of duty or breach of trust by a director of the company.
(4)  Proceedings may be raised under subsection (1) against (either or both)—
    (a)  the director referred to in subsection (3), or
    (b)  another person.
(5)  It is immaterial whether the act or omission in respect of which the proceedings are to be raised
    or, in the case of continuing proceedings under section 267 or 269, are raised, arose before or
    after the person seeking to raise or continue them became a member of the company.

---

[70]  Companies Act 2006 (Commencement No 3, etc) Order 2007, SI 2007/2194, art 2.
[71]  See, therefore, the discussion at paras 11.261.01–11.261.12 above.

(6) This section does not affect—

    (a) any right of a member of a company to raise proceedings in respect of an act or omission specified in subsection (3) in order to protect his own interests and obtain a remedy on his own behalf, or

    (b) the court's power to make an order under section 996(2)(c) or anything done under such an order.

(7) In this Chapter—

    (a) proceedings raised under subsection (1) are referred to as 'derivative proceedings',

    (b) the act or omission in respect of which they are raised is referred to as the 'cause of action',

    (c) 'director' includes a former director,

    (d) references to a director include a shadow director, and

    (e) references to a member of a company include a person who is not a member but to whom shares in the company have been transferred or transmitted by operation of law.

COMMENCEMENT DATE 1 October 2007[72]

**11.265.02**  Subsection (1) enables members to raise proceedings[73] in order to protect the interests of the company and obtain a remedy on its behalf. The effect of subsection (2) is to remove the common law basis for such an action.[74] Any derivative action must now be founded on subsection (1).

**11.265.03**  The grounds on which derivative proceedings may be raised (subsection (3)) follow those specified in section 260(3) for other parts of the UK. The inclusion of pure negligence represents a change in the law which expands the potential exposure of directors to liability (see commentary on section 260).

**11.265.04**  Subsection (4) provides, following the approach of the provisions applicable in other parts of the UK, that derivative proceedings can be brought against a director or another person. It may well be necessary in some cases to take action against other persons who hold assets that are the subject of the derivative action (eg where it is alleged that directors have improperly removed assets that are held by another person) or who have facilitated a breach of duty in some other way. Subsection (5) makes clear that derivative proceedings may be based on conduct which occurs before or after the person seeking to raise or continue them becomes a member.

**11.265.05**  Subsection (6) clarifies the relationship between the new (statutory) derivative proceedings and the enforcement of personal rights by a member. It provides that derivative proceedings do not affect the enforcement of personal rights by a member. It does not, however, resolve the issue of what rights are considered to fall within the category of personal rights.[75] It also makes clear that the section does not affect the power of the court to make an order under section 996(2) of the Companies Act 2006 (pursuant to the 'unfairly prejudicial conduct' provisions of section 994 of the Companies Act 2006) authorizing civil proceedings to be brought in the name and on behalf of the company by such person or persons and on such terms as the court may direct.

**11.265.06**  Subsection (7) makes clear, *inter alia*, that derivative proceedings may be brought against a former director or a shadow director.

**11.265.07**  While there is no counterpart in Scotland to the procedural rules in England relating to costs in a derivative action (see para 11.261.12), the decision of the Inner House of the Court of Session in *Wishart v Castlecroft Securities and Others*[76] makes clear that costs in a derivative action fall within the general principle of Scots law that representative persons are entitled to the costs necessarily incurred in the interests of their constituents. The indemnity can cover both the first and second stage of the

---

[72] Companies Act 2006 (Commencement No 3, etc) Order 2007, SI 2007/2194, art 2.

[73] The Bill originally referred to derivative 'action' but this was amended at the committee stage in the House of Lords so as to allow for the possibility of proceedings by way of petition procedure, such as interdict, in some circumstances: see *Hansard*, HL, col GC35 (27 February 2006).

[74] The common law basis for such proceedings was recognized in *Anderson v Hogg* 2002 SC 190 (IH) and *Wilson v Inverness Retail & Business Park Ltd* 2003 SLT 301. While these cases focused on derivative actions based on 'fraud on the minority' (see commentary on s 260), there has been no suggestion of any substantive difference between English and Scots law as regards the other common law grounds for a derivative action.

[75] The issue of what constitutes personal rights has not been clarified by the Act. The Company Law Review Steering Group (CLRSG) recommended that all obligations imposed by the constitution should be enforceable by individual members unless the contrary is provided in the constitution: see Vol 8 of the CLRSG's Review, Completing the Structure (Nov 2000 URN 00/1355, available at ⟨http://www.dti.gov.uk/bbf/co-act-2006/clr-review/page 22794.html⟩), para 5.73.

[76] *Wishart v Castlecroft Securities and Others* [2009] CSOH 20, [2009] CSIH 65 at para 58, and for the award of costs in the same case see [2010] CSIH 2.

proceedings. Prospective orders can be made so as to limit the risks to minority shareholders, but that does not prejudice the court's control over the actual costs that will be awarded in any particular case.[77]

## 266 Requirement for leave and notice

(1) Derivative proceedings may be raised by a member of a company only with the leave of the court.     **11.266.01**

(2) An application for leave must—

    (a) specify the cause of action, and

    (b) summarise the facts on which the derivative proceedings are to be based.

(3) If it appears to the court that the application and the evidence produced by the applicant in support of it do not disclose a prima facie case for granting it, the court—

    (a) must refuse the application, and

    (b) may make any consequential order it considers appropriate.

(4) If the application is not refused under subsection (3)—

    (a) the applicant must serve the application on the company,

    (b) the court—

        (i) may make an order requiring evidence to be produced by the company, and

        (ii) may adjourn the proceedings on the application to enable the evidence to be obtained, and

    (c) the company is entitled to take part in the further proceedings on the application.

(5) On hearing the application, the court may—

    (a) grant the application on such terms as it thinks fit,

    (b) refuse the application, or

    (c) adjourn the proceedings on the application and make such order as to further procedure as it thinks fit.

COMMENCEMENT DATE 1 October 2007[78]

Subsection (1) provides that a member of a company may raise derivative proceedings only with the leave of the court. This represents a change in the law as the leave of the court was not previously required[79] and distinguishes the procedure in Scotland from that in England (see commentary on section 261). Subsection (2) provides that the application for leave must specify the cause of action and summarize the facts on which the derivative proceedings are to be based. The court then decides whether leave should be granted. In the first case under the new statutory procedure the court, stressed the limited nature of the burden placed on the petitioner at the first stage in the following terms: 'It is to be noted that no onus is placed on the applicant to satisfy the court that there is a prima facie case: rather the court is to refuse the application if it is satisfied that there is not a prima facie case.'[80] If leave is granted, the court may order the production of evidence and adjourn the proceedings. As provided for by subsection 4(c) the company is entitled to take part in the second-stage proceedings (having had the application served on it) but directors are not, even if they are implicated in the breach of duty that is the subject of the application.[81] On hearing the application the court may grant or refuse it or adjourn the proceedings as it thinks fit. It may also make an order for payment of the petitioners expenses by the company.[82] However, in *Wishart*, the court was not willing to underwrite all future costs but instead framed its order in terms that the applicants first stage costs would be covered and reserving the right of the applicant to apply for a similar order in respect of subsequent stages. If the application is granted, directors who are implicated in a breach of duty will have the opportunity to defend the subsequent proceedings.[83]     **11.266.02**

As is the case in England (see commentary on section 261), there is now in effect a two-stage process, the difference being that in Scotland the application for leave and the raising of derivative proceedings are procedurally distinct, whereas in England the latter is a continuation of the former. The differences between the first and second stages were explained as follows in *Wishart*:     **11.266.03**

'There are thus three significant differences between the first stage and the second stage: at the first stage, the material before the court is confined to the application and the supporting evidence     **11.266.04**

---

[77] See *Wishart v Castlecroft Securities and Others* [2009] CSOH 20, [2009] CSIH 65 at para 68. For example, a reasonable offer of settlement may result in no further award of costs to the petitioner.

[78] Companies Act 2006 (Commencement No 3, etc) Order 2007, SI 2007/2194, art 2.

[79] *Anderson v Hogg* 2002 SC 190 (IH); *Wilson v Inverness Retail & Business Park Ltd* 2003 SLT 301.

[80] *Wishart v Castlecroft Securities and Others* [2009] CSOH 20, [2009] CSIH 65 at para 31.

[81] *Wishart v Castlecroft Securities and Others* [2009] CSOH 20, [2009] CSIH 65 at para 21.

[82] *Wishart v Castlecroft Securities and Others* [2009] CSIH 65. While it was noted that there was no express statutory power to require the company to provide an indemnity for costs, the court held that a shareholder fell within the general principle that representative persons are entitled to the costs necessarily incurred in the interests of their constituents (at para 59).

[83] *Wishart v Castlecroft Securities and Others* [2009] CSOH 20, [2009] CSIH 65 at para 21.

produced by the applicant, whereas at the second stage the court may also have material placed before it by the company; at the first stage any hearing will normally be *ex parte*, whereas at the second stage the company is entitled to be heard; and at the first stage the court need only consider whether there is a *prima facie* case for granting the application, whereas at the second stage the court must decide whether the application should actually be granted. The matters which are in principle relevant to the court's decision are however the same at each stage: in particular, it is necessary at both stages to consider the requirements of sec 265 and the factors listed in sec 268, together with any other relevant circumstances.'

### 267  Application to continue proceedings as derivative proceedings

**11.267.01**
(1) This section applies where—
  (a) a company has raised proceedings, and
  (b) the proceedings are in respect of an act or omission which could be the basis for derivative proceedings.
(2) A member of the company may apply to the court to be substituted for the company in the proceedings, and for the proceedings to continue in consequence as derivative proceedings, on the ground that—
  (a) the manner in which the company commenced or continued the proceedings amounts to an abuse of the process of the court,
  (b) the company has failed to prosecute the proceedings diligently, and
  (c) it is appropriate for the member to be substituted for the company in the proceedings.
(3) If it appears to the court that the application and the evidence produced by the applicant in support of it do not disclose a prima facie case for granting it, the court—
  (a) must refuse the application, and
  (b) may make any consequential order it considers appropriate.
(4) If the application is not refused under subsection (3)—
  (a) the applicant must serve the application on the company,
  (b) the court—
    (i) may make an order requiring evidence to be produced by the company, and
    (ii) may adjourn the proceedings on the application to enable the evidence to be obtained, and
  (c) the company is entitled to take part in the further proceedings on the application.
(5) On hearing the application, the court may—
  (a) grant the application on such terms as it thinks fit,
  (b) refuse the application, or
  (c) adjourn the proceedings on the application and make such order as to further procedure as it thinks fit.

COMMENCEMENT DATE 1 October 2007[84]

**11.267.02**   This section (introduced at Committee stage in the House of Lords) is the equivalent in Scotland of section 262. The reference to a member being 'substituted' for the company differs to the formulation used in section 262 which refers to a member being permitted to 'continue the claim as a derivative claim', and reflects the absence in Scotland of a concept of a claim being continued in that manner.

**11.267.03**   The grounds on which a member may apply to be substituted for the company in the proceedings are the same as those in section 262. The Department of Trade and Industry (DTI) Explanatory Notes to the Bill cite as an example of the first ground for substitution mentioned in subsection (2) that the company brought the claim with a view to preventing a member bringing a derivative action.[85] The court has a wide discretion under subsection (5) in disposing of the application.

### 268  Granting of leave

**11.268.01**
(1) The court must refuse leave to raise derivative proceedings or an application under section 267 if satisfied—
  (a) that a person acting in accordance with section 172 (duty to promote the success of the company) would not seek to raise or continue the proceedings (as the case may be), or
  (b) where the cause of action is an act or omission that is yet to occur, that the act or omission has been authorised by the company, or

---

[84]  Companies Act 2006 (Commencement No 3, etc) Order 2007, SI 2007/2194, art 2.
[85]  See para 485.

   (c) where the cause of action is an act or omission that has already occurred, that the act or omission—
       (i)  was authorised by the company before it occurred, or
       (ii) has been ratified by the company since it occurred.
(2) In considering whether to grant leave to raise derivative proceedings or an application under section 267, the court must take into account, in particular—
   (a) whether the member is acting in good faith in seeking to raise or continue the proceedings (as the case may be),
   (b) the importance that a person acting in accordance with section 172 (duty to promote the success of the company) would attach to raising or continuing them (as the case may be),
   (c) where the cause of action is an act or omission that is yet to occur, whether the act or omission could be, and in the circumstances would be likely to be—
       (i)  authorised by the company before it occurs, or
       (ii) ratified by the company after it occurs,
   (d) where the cause of action is an act or omission that has already occurred, whether the act or omission could be, and in the circumstances would be likely to be, ratified by the company,
   (e) whether the company has decided not to raise proceedings in respect of the same cause of action or to persist in the proceedings (as the case may be),
   (f) whether the cause of action is one which the member could pursue in his own right rather than on behalf of the company.
(3) In considering whether to grant leave to raise derivative proceedings or an application under section 267, the court shall have particular regard to any evidence before it as to the views of members of the company who have no personal interest, direct or indirect, in the matter.
(4) The Secretary of State may by regulations—
   (a) amend subsection (1) so as to alter or add to the circumstances in which leave or an application is to be refused,
   (b) amend subsection (2) so as to alter or add to the matters that the court is required to take into account in considering whether to grant leave or an application.
(5) Before making any such regulations the Secretary of State shall consult such persons as he considers appropriate.
(6) Regulations under this section are subject to affirmative resolution procedure.

COMMENCEMENT DATE 1 October 2007[86]

This section replicates the grounds for the granting of leave set out in section 263 for England and    **11.268.02**
Wales and Northern Ireland (see para 11.263.06). Thus, the decision in *Franbar Holdings Ltd v Patel*[87]
would likely be followed in Scotland, albeit that an earlier Scottish case[88] provided a firm indication
that the availability of the unfair prejudice remedy (under section 994) did not preclude the bringing of
a derivative action.

Subsection (1) sets out several grounds on which the court must refuse leave to raise derivative    **11.268.03**
proceedings. The first is that a person acting in accordance with section 172 (a director's duty to
promote the success of the company) would not seek to continue the claim. This means that a member
or members bringing a derivative action must be acting in a way that benefits the members as a whole.
It was previously the case that a minority raising derivative proceedings did not act on behalf of the
shareholders as a whole.[89] In *Wishart*, the court noted that the scale of the potential recovery through
derivative proceedings justified the cost of the proceedings (which will be borne by the company if the
case against the wrongdoing directors does not ultimately succeed).[90]

Subsection (1)(a) is a different test to that established in *Smith v Croft (No 2)*,[91] where it was held that    **11.268.04**
an appropriate independent organ of the company (such as a majority within the minority who bring
the derivative action) must decide if it is in the interests of a company to bring an action. While the
court could determine whether that decision was made fairly, it was not for the court to decide if it was
right or wrong. The new statutory test would appear to suggest that it is for the court to decide (it must
be 'satisfied') whether the decision on taking action is taken in the interests of the members as a
whole.[92] However, subsection (3) requires, in line with *Smith v Croft (No 2)*, that the court must pay
'particular regard' to the views of the independent minority.

---

[86]  Companies Act 2006 (Commencement No 3, etc) Order 2007, SI 2007/2194, art 2.
[87]  [2008] EWHC 1534 (Ch).
[88]  *Wilson v Inverness Retail & Business Park Ltd* 2003 SLT 30, [26], per Lord Eassie.
[89]  *Smith v Glasgow etc Railway Co* (1897) 4 SLT 327.
[90]  *Wishart v Castlecroft Securities and Others* [2009] CSIH 65 at para 51.
[91]  [1988] Ch 114.
[92]  Whether the courts choose to intervene in any substantial manner in reviewing the merits of such decisions remains to be seen. The experience in other fields in which there is the potential for courts to review members'

**11.268.05**   Another ground on which the court must refuse leave to raise derivative proceedings is that, where the cause of action is an act or omission that is yet to occur, the act or omission has been authorized by the company, or where the cause of action is an act or omission that has already occurred, that the act or omission was authorized by the company before it occurred or has been ratified by the company since it occurred. The first case is linked with, but not limited to, the provisions of section 175(4)(b), which allow a company to authorize the existence of a conflict of interest on the part of a director. The second case is linked with section 239 which governs ratification of acts of directors. Under section 239(7), the existing law relating to the requirements for a valid ratification[93] and to acts that are capable of being ratified[94] remains relevant to any ratification of a cause of a derivative action. It will therefore remain the case that, for example, a breach of duty involving a lack of *bona fides* on the part of a director or one that involves a fraud on the minority cannot be ratified.

**11.268.06**   There are also several considerations that the court is required to take into account in deciding whether to grant leave to raise derivative proceedings. The court must consider whether the member is acting in good faith in bringing the action. Some, though not necessarily all, of the elements of this consideration may overlap with the court's assessment under subsection (1)(a) of whether a person acting in accordance with section 172 (a director's duty to promote the success of the company) would seek to continue the claim. The second is the importance that a person acting in accordance with section 172 would attach to raising a derivative action. By comparison with the section 172-related test in subsection (1)(a), this test appears rather opaque. However, it does allow the court to take into account issues such as the potential outcome of an action and the costs associated with it.

**11.268.07**   The third of these considerations relates to the possibility of authorization or ratification of an act or omission that has yet to occur. In this context, the link between the possibility of ratification and the availability of derivative proceedings differs from the previous law, which did not permit proceedings to be brought if the act or omission is capable of being ratified.[95] The new law does not in terms prevent access to derivative proceedings on the basis that the cause of action can be ratified. It focuses instead on the possibility of an actual ratification occurring, which is as much a factual as a legal issue in that not only must the act or omission be capable of ratification but there must also be some evidence that this will in fact occur. In that sense, issues coming before the courts relating to ratification of future acts are likely to be quite complex.

**11.268.08**   A similar comment can be made regarding the fourth consideration, which is that where the cause of action has already occurred, whether it could be and would be ratified by the company. This provision is even more problematic in that it potentially runs counter to the judicial policy of declining to adjudicate on issues that can be decided within a company through the normal operation of the principle of majority rule.[96] It does not seem clear what purpose would be served by the court doing anything other than declining to grant leave when the matter could be resolved by referring it back to a meeting of the members. However, when the cause of action cannot be ratified, this consideration does serve the clear purpose of permitting leave to raise a derivative action. In those circumstances, the old common law approach is followed.

**11.268.09**   The fifth consideration is whether the company has decided not to raise an action in respect of the same cause of action. If it has, there is clearly no need for derivative proceedings. A similar comment can be made in regard to the sixth consideration, which is that the cause of action is one which the member could pursue in his own right rather than on behalf of the company. Such an action would be based on a personal right and could not be said to be capable of being pursued in good faith so as to promote the interests of the company. While there is no express reference to the relevance of the unfair prejudice remedy in section 994, the court in *Wishart* did not regard the availability of that remedy as a 'compelling consideration'.[97]

**11.268.10**   A specific power is given to the Secretary of State by subsection (3) to amend subsections (1) and (2), subject to an obligation to consult such persons as he considers appropriate.

---

actions against a standard of acting in the best interests of the members as a whole (eg cases, such as *Allen v Gold Reefs of West Africa* [1900] 1 Ch 656 dealing with changes to the articles) suggest that the emphasis will remain on procedure rather than the substance of the decision.

[93]   In some cases ratification may require a special majority: see eg CA 1985, s 35(3), requiring a special resolution for ratification of a breach of duty on the part of directors in entering into an *ultra vires* contract.

[94]   See the commentary on s 239. Note the exclusion of self-interested votes of directors on a ratification resolution.

[95]   *MacDougall v Gardiner* (1875) 1 Ch D 13.

[96]   *MacDougall v Gardiner* (1875) 1 Ch D 13, 25, *per* Mellish LJ.

[97]   *Wishart v Castlecroft Securities and Others* [2009] CSOH 20, [2009] CSIH 65 at para 46. However, the court's reasoning does not rule out the possibility that the availability of the unfair prejudice remedy may be a 'compelling consideration'.

## 269 Application by member to be substituted for member pursuing derivative proceedings

(1) This section applies where a member of a company ('the claimant')—

  (a) has raised derivative proceedings,

  (b) has continued as derivative proceedings raised by the company, or

  (c) has continued derivative proceedings under this section.

(2) Another member of the company ('the applicant') may apply to the court to be substituted for the claimant in the action on the ground that—

  (a) the manner in which the proceedings have been commenced or continued by the claimant amounts to an abuse of the process of the court,

  (b) the claimant has failed to prosecute the proceedings diligently, and

  (c) it is appropriate for the applicant to be substituted for the claimant in the proceedings.

(3) If it appears to the court that the application and the evidence produced by the applicant in support of it do not disclose a prima facie case for granting it, the court—

  (a) must refuse the application, and

  (b) may make any consequential order it considers appropriate.

(4) If the application is not refused under subsection (3)—

  (a) the applicant must serve the application on the company,

  (b) the court—

    (i) may make an order requiring evidence to be produced by the company, and

    (ii) may adjourn the proceedings on the application to enable the evidence to be obtained, and

  (c) the company is entitled to take part in the further proceedings on the application.

(5) On hearing the application, the court may—

  (a) grant the application on such terms as it thinks fit,

  (b) refuse the application, or

  (c) adjourn the proceedings on the application and make such order as to further procedure as it thinks fit.

COMMENCEMENT DATE 1 October 2007[98]

**11.269.01**

This section is the equivalent of section 264 in the remainder of the UK. **11.269.02**

The grounds on which a member can apply to be substituted for another member in derivative proceedings are the same as those which apply to substitution of a member for the company (section 267 above). The court enjoys the same discretion as it does under section 267 (above) in disposing of the application. **11.269.03**

[98] Companies Act 2006 (Commencement No 3, etc) Order 2007, SI 2007/2194, art 2.

# 12

## COMPANY SECRETARIES

## Companies Act 2006

### PART 12
### COMPANY SECRETARIES

The inclusion in the Act of a part dedicated specifically to company secretaries was new in 2006. Whilst the Companies Act 1985 did contain various provisions relating to company secretaries they were contained within Part IX concerned with a company's management in general and directors in particular. Many of the changes in the law relating to company secretaries derive from recommendations made by the Company Law Review in their Final Report. Part 12 of the Act does not, however, contain any provisions relating to the function, duties, or authority of a company secretary. Thus, unlike the case of directors where their duties have been codified,[1] these aspects of the role of company secretary remain the sole preserve of the common law and other extra-statutory rules and regulations.[2] The secretary of a company remains an officer of that company for the purposes of the Act[3] and is liable for any offence committed by the company if he personally is in default.[4]   **12.0.01**

The company secretary is generally the officer of the company responsible for the administration of the company, including matters such as ensuring the correct maintenance of the registers required under the Act, filing documents with the registrar, and all matters relating to meetings including issuing notices, preparing agendas, and taking minutes. He will be subject to the same fiduciary duties as previously applied to directors (and which have now been codified).[5] Knowledge acquired by him in the course of carrying out the company's business may be attributed to the company and the secretary will have usual authority to bind his company in certain circumstances.[6] Given the administrative nature of his role this authority will extend to matters connected with the administration of the   **12.0.02**

---

[1]  Companies Act (CA) 2006, ss 171–177.

[2]  Paragraph A.1.4 of the Combined Code produced by the Committee on Corporate Governance provides that the board of a public company should have access to the advice and services of a company secretary who is responsible to the board for ensuring that board procedures are followed and rules and regulations are complied with. See now the UK Corporate Governance Code, June 2010. Companies House also issues some limited guidance about the role and responsibilities of a company secretary, the latest version of which was available from October 2008.

[3]  CA 2006, s 1173 and Sch 8. The definition of officer is the same as that previously found in CA 1985, s 744.

[4]  CA 2006, s 1121 which replaces CA 1985, s 733(2). In order to be liable the secretary must have authorized, permitted, participated in, or failed to take all reasonable steps to prevent the offence. This reflects a change from the wording of CA 1985, s 733(2) which included references to concepts such as 'connivance in'.

[5]  *McKay's Case* (1876) 2 Ch D 1 and *De Ruvigne's Case* (1877) 5 Ch D 306.

[6]  The secretary is an 'authorised signatory' of his company for the purposes of CA 2006, s 44.

company.[7] The court in *Panorama Development* left open whether the secretary's authority would, in the absence of a wider holding out, extend to matters such as the commercial management of the company. This will obviously depend on the particular circumstances of each secretary. However, given the increasing importance (particularly in large companies) of the role played by the secretary, the usual authority of a company secretary is likely to continue to expand, a point which the court in *Panorama Development* recognized. An attempt to rely on the authority of a company secretary was rejected on the facts in *Magical Marketing Limited v Holly* [2008] EWHC 2428.

## Private companies

### 270  Private company not required to have secretary

**12.270.01**
(1)  A private company is not required to have a secretary.

(2)  References in the Companies Acts to a private company 'without a secretary' are to a private company that for the time being is taking advantage of the exemption in subsection (1); and references to a private company 'with a secretary' shall be construed accordingly.

(3)  In the case of a private company without a secretary —

(a)  anything authorised or required to be given or sent to, or served on, the company by being sent to its secretary—

(i)   may be given or sent to, or served on, the company itself, and

(ii)  if addressed to the secretary shall be treated as addressed to the company; and

(b)  anything else required or authorised to be done by or to the secretary of the company may be done by or to—

(i)   a director, or

(ii)  a person authorised generally or specifically in that behalf by the directors.

COMMENCEMENT DATE 6 April 2008[8]

**12.270.02**  This section was new. It provides the most significant change introduced by Part 12, the abolition of the previous requirement[9] that all companies, including private companies, had to have a secretary. This implements the recommendation of the Company Law Review in paragraph 4.7 of their Final Report. Accordingly many of the remaining provisions of Part 12 are relevant only to public companies and to private companies which choose to have a secretary: the early drafts of the Companies Bill did restrict the subsequent sections to public companies but amendments made at a relatively late stage of the passing of the Act extended then to all companies with a secretary. Subsection (3)(b) is based on the provisions of the previous law[10] where the office of secretary was vacant or there was no secretary capable of acting. In particular any act which would otherwise be done by the secretary can be done by a director or some other person authorized by the directors to do the act. In addition service on the company itself will suffice where the addressee would otherwise have been the secretary.

## Public companies

### 271  Public company required to have secretary

**12.271.01**     A public company must have a secretary.

COMMENCEMENT DATE 6 April 2008[11]

**12.271.02**  This provision replaced but repeated the requirement for public companies to have a secretary.[12] As a public company must have at least two directors,[13] there is no longer any need for the provisions

---

[7] This extends to the hiring of cars for use by a company: *Panorama Development (Guildford) Ltd v Fidelis Furnishing Fabrics Ltd* [1971] 3 WLR 440. Lord Denning held that the statement of Lord Esher in *Barnett, Hoares & Co v South London Tramways Co* (1887) 18 QBD 815 that 'no person can assume that he [the company secretary] has any authority to represent anything at all' was no longer applicable. His Lordship went on to describe a company secretary as having 'extensive duties and responsibilities'. Salmon LJ echoed these comments in a concurring judgment.

[8] Companies Act 2006 (Commencement No 5, Transitional Provisions and Savings) Order 2007, SI 2007/3495, art 3(1)(c).

[9] CA 1985, s 283(1).

[10] CA 1985, s 283(3).

[11] Companies Act 2006 (Commencement No. 5, Transitional Provisions and Savings) Order 2007, SI 2007/3495, art 3(1)(c).

[12] CA 1985, s 283(1).

[13] CA 2006, s 154(2).

preventing a sole director from also acting as secretary or a corporation from being secretary where the sole director of the company is also the sole director of the corporation acting as secretary as under the previous law.[14]

## 272 Direction requiring public company to appoint secretary

(1) If it appears to the Secretary of State that a public company is in breach of section 271 (requirement to have secretary), the Secretary of State may give the company a direction under this section.                                                                                   **12.272.01**

(2) The direction must state that the company appears to be in breach of that section and specify—
  (a) what the company must do in order to comply with the direction, and
  (b) the period within which it must do so.
  That period must be not less than one month or more than three months after the date on which the direction is given.

(3) The direction must also inform the company of the consequences of failing to comply.

(4) Where the company is in breach of section 271 it must comply with the direction by—
  (a) making the necessary appointment, and
  (b) giving notice of it under section 276,
  before the end of the period specified in the direction.

(5) If the company has already made the necessary appointment, it must comply with the direction by giving notice of it under section 276 before the end of the period specified in the direction.

(6) If a company fails to comply with a direction under this section, an offence is committed by—
  (a) the company, and
  (b) every officer of the company who is in default.
  For this purpose a shadow director is treated as an officer of the company.

(7) A person guilty of an offence under this paragraph is liable on summary conviction to a fine not exceeding level 5 on the standard scale and, for continued contravention, a daily default fine not exceeding one-tenth of level 5 on the standard scale.

COMMENCEMENT DATE 6 April 2008[15]

This section was new. There was previously no penalty specified for a failure by a company to satisfy the requirement to have a secretary. The Act has remedied this but, rather than simply creating an offence committed by the failure to have a secretary, the Act creates a preliminary stage before any offence aimed at first remedying the situation. In the first instance, it is for the Secretary of State to give the public company which has no secretary a 'direction' as to what it must do to remedy the breach. Presumably this will be a relatively simple matter of telling the company that it must appoint a secretary who satisfies the eligibility requirements within a specified period which must be between one and three months. Where the direction requires the appointment of a secretary this requires both the appointment and the notification of the appointment by the company to the registrar to be completed within the time limit. It is only if there is a failure to follow the direction that an offence is committed.      **12.272.02**

## 273 Qualifications of secretaries of public companies

(1) It is the duty of the directors of a public company to take all reasonable steps to secure that the secretary (or each joint secretary) of the company—                                    **12.273.01**
  (a) is a person who appears to them to have the requisite knowledge and experience to discharge the functions of secretary of the company, and
  (b) has one or more of the following qualifications.

(2) The qualifications are—
  (a) that he has held the office of secretary of a public company for at least three of the five years immediately preceding his appointment as secretary;
  (b) that he is a member of any of the bodies specified in subsection (3);
  (c) that he is a barrister, advocate or solicitor called or admitted in any part of the United Kingdom;
  (d) that he is a person who, by virtue of his holding or having held any other position or his being a member of any other body, appears to the directors to be capable of discharging the functions of secretary of the company.

(3) The bodies referred to in subsection (2)(b) are—
  (a) the Institute of Chartered Accountants in England and Wales;
  (b) the Institute of Chartered Accountants of Scotland;
  (c) the Chartered Association of Certified Accountants;
  (d) the Institute of Chartered Accountants in Ireland;

---

[14] CA 1985, s 283(2) and (4)(a).

[15] Companies Act 2006 (Commencement No 5, Transitional Provisions and Savings) Order 2007, SI 2007/ 3495, art 3(1)(c).

    (e)  the Institute of Chartered Secretaries and Administrators;
    (f)  the Chartered Institute of Management Accountants;
    (g)  the Chartered Institute of Public Finance and Accountancy.

COMMENCEMENT DATE 6 April 2008[16]

**12.273.02**   This provision substantially repeated and replaced the provisions making it the duty of the directors of public companies to appoint a suitably knowledgeable, experienced, and qualified secretary and setting out the required qualifications.[17] The only changes are:

   (i)   It is no longer sufficient for a person to have been the secretary, assistant secretary, or deputy secretary of the company in question on 22 December 1980.[18]
   (ii)  The substitution of the Chartered Institute of Management Accountants (referred to in (3)(f)) for the Institute of Cost and Management Accountants[19] following a change of name by this institute.

        12.273.03Given the continuing important role of the company secretary in public companies (in particular in large public companies where the company secretary plays a central role in the satisfaction of the increasingly onerous corporate governance requirements), the satisfaction of the knowledge and experience requirements will require a wider range of skills. There is no penalty specified if the directors fail to appoint an appropriate person as secretary, although they may be the subject of civil action if the failure results in any loss to the company.

## *Provisions applying to private companies with a secretary and to public companies*

### 274  Discharge of functions where office vacant or secretary unable to act

**12.274.01**   Where in the case of a public company the office of secretary is vacant, or there is for any other reason no secretary capable of acting, anything required or authorised to be done by or to the secretary may be done—

   (a)  by or to an assistant or deputy secretary (if any), or
   (b)  if there is no assistant or deputy secretary or none capable of acting, by or to any person authorised generally or specially in that behalf by the directors.

COMMENCEMENT DATE 6 April 2008[20]

**12.274.02**   This replaced but substantially repeated, in respect of public companies, the rules for the discharge of the functions of the secretary where the office is vacant or there is no secretary able to act.[21] In such a case the assistant or deputy secretary is the next in line. If there is no such person, the identification of the person entitled to act is for the directors. The only material change from the old law is that, in the absence of a deputy or assistant secretary capable of acting, the directors may authorize any *person* to carry out the act to be done by or to the secretary. Previously the directors could only so authorize an *officer* of the company.[22]

### 275  Duty to keep register of secretaries

**12.275.01**   (1)  A company must keep a register of its secretaries.
   (2)  The register must contain the required particulars (see sections 277 to 279) of the person who is, or persons who are, the secretary or joint secretaries of the company
   (3)  The register must be kept available for inspection—
      (a)  at the company's registered office, or
      (b)  at a place specified in regulations under section 1136.
   (4)  The company must give notice to the registrar—
      (a)  of the place at which the registrar is kept available for inspection, and
      (b)  of any change in that place,
   unless it has at all times been kept at the company's registered office.
   (5)  The register must be open to the inspection—
      (a)  of any member of the company without charge, and
      (b)  of any other person on payment of such fee as may be prescribed.

---

   [16]  Companies Act 2006 (Commencement No 5, Transitional Provisions and Savings) Order 2007, SI 2007/3495, art 3(1)(c).
   [17]  CA 1985, s 286.
   [18]  Previously allowed under CA 1985, s 286(1)(a).
   [19]  CA 1985, s 286(2)(f).
   [20]  Companies Act 2006 (Commencement No 5, Transitional Provisions and Savings) Order 2007, SI 2007/3495, art 3(1)(c).
   [21]  CA 1985, s 283(3) which applied to all companies.
   [22]  CA 1985, s 283(3).

(6) If default is made in complying with subsection (1), (2) or (3), or if default is made for 14 days in complying with subsection (4), or if an inspection required under subsection (5) is refused, an offence is committed by—
   (a) the company, and
   (b) every officer of the company who is in default.
   For this purpose a shadow director is treated as an officer of the company.
(7) A person guilty of an offence under this section is liable on summary conviction to a fine not exceeding level 5 on the standard scale and, for continued contravention, a daily default fine not exceeding one-tenth of level 5 on the standard scale.
(8) In the case of a refusal of inspection of the register, the court may by order compel an immediate inspection of it.

COMMENCEMENT DATE 1 October 2009 save as necessary to enable regulations to be made by statutory instrument, for which purpose this section came into force on 20 January 2007.[23]

This section replaced but substantially repeated the requirement to keep a register of the company's   **12.275.02** secretary or secretaries and making it an offence to fail to do so.[24] This provision applies to all companies. Whilst a private company without a secretary has no secretaries to enter into such a register, the directors of such a company may choose to retain an empty register particularly if the company has made an express decision to have no secretary as permitted under section 270(1). This will apply particularly where an existing private company (which presently has a secretary) chooses to dispense with its secretary after Part 12 was brought into force.

The register must be kept available for inspection at the company's registered office or at some other   **12.275.03** place specified in regulations to be made under the Act. The prospect of this register being kept other than at the company's registered office is new. As a result, if this option is utilized by the company, notice of the place where the register is kept (and any changes to this location) must be notified to the Registrar of Companies within 14 days of the change, a provision which is also new. Members are entitled to inspect the register free of charge whilst others must, from 1 October 2009, pay £3.50 per hour or part thereof.[25] A failure by the company to satisfy any of the subsections in section 275 is an offence. As noted in paragraph 12.01 above, a secretary is an officer of the company and will, accordingly, also be liable if he personally is in default.

Section 275 also contains one other material difference from the provisions of the Companies Act 1985.   **12.275.04** Section 288(5A) of the Companies Act 1985 limited the right to inspect the register or to obtain a court order compelling inspection where particulars of the secretary's usual residential address were subject to such a confidentiality order under section 723B. As there is no longer any requirement for the register to include a secretary's usual residential address (see section 255(5) below), section 275 does not contain any provision corresponding to the Companies Act 1985, section 288(5A).

Part 38 of the Act (and in particular sections 1134 to 1135) set out the form of the register.[26] It may be   **12.275.05** kept in hard copy or electronic form[27] provided that the information is adequately recorded for future reference. However, if the register is kept in electronic form it must be capable of being reproduced in hard copy form[28] and where it is maintained other than in bound books, adequate precautions must be taken to guard against falsification and to facilitate the discovery of any falsification.[29]

## 276  Duty to notify registrar of changes

(1) A company must, within the period of 14 days from—                                           **12.276.01**
   (a) a person becoming or ceasing to be its secretary or one of its joint secretaries, or
   (b) the occurrence of any change in the particulars contained in its register of secretaries,
   give notice to the registrar of the change and of the date on which it occurred.
(2) Notice of a person having become secretary, or one of joint secretaries, of the company must be accompanied by that person to act in the relevant capacity.
(3) If default is made in complying with this section, an offence is committed by every officer of the company who is in default.
   For this purpose a shadow director is treated as an officer of the company.

---

[23] Companies Act 2008 (Commencement No 8, Transitional Provisions and Savings) Order 2008, SI 2008/2860, art 3(j).
[24] CA 1985, s 288(1) and (3)–(5) which applied to all companies.
[25] Companies (Fees for Inspection of Companies Records) Regulations 2008, SI 2008/3007.
[26] Replacing CA 1985, s 722.
[27] CA 2006, s 1135(1)(a).
[28] CA 2006, s 1135(2).
[29] CA 2006, s 1138.

(4)  A person guilty of an offence under this section is liable on summary conviction to a fine not exceeding level 5 on the standard scale and, for continued contravention, a daily default fine not exceeding one-tenth of level 5 on the standard scale.

COMMENCEMENT DATE  1 October 2009[30]

**12.276.02**  Section 276(1) and (3) to (4) replaced and repeated the provisions requiring notice to be given to the registrar of companies[31] of any change of company secretary (or the registered particulars of any such secretary) and making it an offence to fail to comply with these requirements.[32] These requirements apply to all public companies and any private companies which choose to have a secretary. Thus any existing private company which chooses to dispense with its secretary after Part 12 came into force will need to file a notification under this section. A period of 14 days is allowed for the notification to be given. As noted in paragraph 12.01 above, a secretary is an officer of the company and will, accordingly, be liable for the offence provided under this section if he personally is in default.

**12.276.03**  Section 276(2) was a new provision. Previously a written consent was only required from the person or persons who were to act as the first secretary or secretary of the company.[33] Now each new secretary or joint secretary must provide consent. Unlike the position for first secretaries,[34] there is no provision that where all the partners in a firm are (by way of a change or addition to the existing secretaries of a company) to act as joint secretaries, the consent may be given by one partner on behalf of all of the partners. It is likely however that such a consent will satisfy the requirements of section 276(2) as there is no obvious basis for distinguishing between the consent of a first secretary and that of any subsequent secretary. Form 288A[35] already contained provision for the incoming secretary to sign to indicate his or her consent to acting and therefore the requirements of section 276(2) will be satisfied by completion of a form in the current format.[36]

### 277  Particulars of secretaries to be registered: individuals

**12.277.01**  (1)  A company's register of secretaries must contain the following particulars in the case of an individual—
　　(a)  name and any former name;
　　(b)  address.
(2)  For the purposes of this section 'name' means a person's Christian name (or other forename) and surname, except that in the case of—
　　(a)  a peer or
　　(b)  an individual usually known by a title
　　the title may be stated instead of his Christian name (or other forename) and surname or in addition to either or both of them.
(3)  For the purposes of this section a 'former name' means a name by which the individual was formerly known for business purposes.
　　Where a person is or was formerly known by more than one such name, each of them must be stated.
(4)  It is not necessary for the register to contain particulars of a former name in the following cases—
　　(a)  in the case of a peer or an individual normally known by a British title, where the name is one by which the person was known previous to the adoption of or succession to the title;
　　(b)  in the case of any person, where the former name—
　　　(i)  was changed or disused before the person attained the age of 16 years, or
　　　(ii)  has been changed or disused for 20 years or more.
(5)  The address required to be stated in the register is a service address. This may be stated to be 'The company's registered office'.

COMMENCEMENT DATE  1 October 2009[37]

---

[30]  Companies Act 2008 (Commencement No 8, Transitional Provisions and Savings) Order 2008, SI 2008/2860, art 3(j).
[31]  'Registrar' is defined as the Registrar of Companies: CA 2006, s 1060(3).
[32]  CA 1985, s 288(2)–(4).
[33]  CA 1985, s 10(2)–(3). This requirement is retained by CA 2006, s 12(3) although the consent no longer has to be signed by the person becoming secretary. It simply has to be 'by' that person.
[34]  CA 2006, s 12(3).
[35]  The form prescribed under the corresponding provision of CA 1985, s 288(2).
[36]  Although, unlike CA 1985, s 288(2), CA 2006, s 276 does not provide for the Registrar of Companies to prescribe a form for the notification of changes.
[37]  Companies Act 2008 (Commencement No 8, Transitional Provisions and Savings) Order 2008, SI 2008/2860, art 3(j).

Subsection (1)(a) replaced and repeated the requirement to provide particulars of the secretary's name **12.277.02** and all former names.[38] Subsection (1)(b) contains a significant change. The new requirement is to provide an individual's *address*. Subsection (5), which is new, makes it clear that this requirement is intended to provide a service address for that individual rather than allowing access to personal information about his home address. Previously the register had to include the individual's *usual residential address*[39] and the only way in which this information could be withheld was by means of a confidentiality order imposed by the Secretary of State under section 723B of the Companies Act 1985 where there was a serious risk of violence or intimidation to the secretary or anyone living with him. Secretaries now have the ability to withhold their residential address if they so choose and elect to use their company's registered office as their address for service. This implements the recommendation of the Company Law Review in paragraph 11.46 of their Final Report.

Subsection (2) replaces and repeats the definition of 'name' for the purposes of the particulars to be **12.277.03** provided.[40]

Subsection (3) is new. A definition of 'former name' is provided for the first time: it appears to limit **12.277.04** former names to any name or names previously used for business subject to the long-stop date of 20 years in section (4)(b)(ii). It will also now include a married woman's maiden name if she previously used that name for business. This was previously expressly excluded from the particulars required by section 289(2)(b)(iii) of the Companies Act 1985 which has not been repeated. This change implements the recommendation of the Company Law Review in their Final Report.

Subsection (4) replaced and repeated the limitations on the requirement to register particulars of a **12.277.05** secretary's former name in the case of peers and minor or long disused names.[41] As noted in paragraph 12.277.03 above subsection (4) does not repeat the provision which excluded a married woman's unmarried name from the requirement to include particulars of former names.[42]

As explained in paragraph 12.277.02 above subsection (5) was new. **12.277.06**

### 278 Particulars of secretaries to be registered: corporate secretaries and firms

(1) A company's register of secretaries must contain the following particulars in the case of a body **12.278.01** corporate, or a firm that is legal person under the law by which it is governed—
  (a) corporate or firm name;
  (b) registered or principal office;
  (c) in the case of an EEA company to which the First Company Law Directive applies, particulars of—
    (i) the register in which the company file mentioned in Article 3 of that Directive is kept (including details of the relevant state), and
    (ii) the registration number in that register;
  (d) in any other case, particulars of—
    (i) the legal form of the company or firm and the law by which it is governed, and
    (ii) if applicable, the register in which it is entered (including details of the state) and its registration number in that register.
(2) If all the partners in a firm are joint secretaries it is sufficient to state the particulars that would be required if the firm were a legal person and the firm had been appointed secretary.

COMMENCEMENT DATE 1 October 2009[43]

Subsection (1) expanded on the previous provisions setting out the particulars to be registered where **12.278.02** the secretary is a body corporate or a firm with legal personality.[44] Under the previous law the register had to contain only the name and address of the registered or principal office of a corporation or Scottish firm acting as secretary. These requirements are repeated in (1)(a) and (b). The principal office is the place where the business of the relevant corporate body is managed and controlled.[45] Section (1)(b) and (c) add additional requirements for the particulars to include the identity of the register and registration number (if any) on which a company or firm is registered, and, for non-EEA companies,

---

[38] CA 1985, s 290(1)(a) and (3).
[39] CA 1985, s 290(1)(a).
[40] CA 1985, s 289(2)(a).
[41] CA 1985, s 289(2)(b)(i) and (ii).
[42] CA 1985, s 289(2)(b)(iii).
[43] Companies Act 2008 (Commencement No 8, Transitional Provisions and Savings) Order 2008, SI 2008/2860, art 3(j).
[44] CA 1985, s 290(1)(b).
[45] *Garton v Great Western Rly Co* (1858) EB &E 837 and *Palmer v Caledonian Rly Co* (1892) 1 QB 823.

the legal form and governing law of the company or firm. The additions in respect of EEA companies[46] implement the recommendation of the Company Law Review in paragraph 11.39 of their Final Report.

**12.278.03**   Subsection (2) replaced and repeated section 290(2) of the Companies Act 1985. There is no requirement to list the names and addresses of every member of a firm where all the partners are joint secretaries. In such cases the firm is to be treated as if it were a legal person and had been appointed as secretary.

### 279   Particulars of secretaries to be registered: power to make regulations

**12.279.01**
    (1)  The Secretary of State may make provision by regulations amending—
        section 277 (particulars of secretaries to be registered: individuals), or
        section 278 (particulars of secretaries to be registered: corporate secretaries and firms),
        so as to add to or remove items from the particulars required to be contained in a public company's register of secretaries.
    (2)  Regulations under this section are subject to affirmative resolution procedure.

COMMENCEMENT DATE 1 October 2009 save as necessary to enable regulations to be made by statutory instrument, for which purpose this section came into force on 20 January 2007.[47]

**12.279.02**   This was a new provision. It replicates section 166 of the Act which allows the Secretary of State to make regulations in relation to the particulars of directors to be registered.

### 280   Acts done by person in dual capacity

**12.280.01**   A provision requiring or authorizing a thing to be done by or to a director and the secretary of a company is not satisfied by its being done by or to the same person acting both as director and as, or in place of, the secretary.

COMMENCEMENT DATE 6 April 2008[48]

**12.280.02**   This repeated and replaced the provision preventing an individual who is both a director and the secretary of a company from effectively carrying out an act in both capacities where that act is required to be done to or by both a director *and* the secretary of that company.[49] Thus the act must be done to or carried out by two separate persons.

---

[46] EEA company is defined in CA 2006, s 1170.

[47] Companies Act 2008 (Commencement No 8, Transitional Provisions and Savings) Order 2008, SI 2008/2860, art 3(j).

[48] Companies Act 2006 (Commencement No 5, Transitional Provisions and Savings) Order 2007, SI 2007/3495, art 3(1)(c)

[49] CA 1985, s 284.

# 13

## RESOLUTIONS AND MEETINGS

## Companies Act 2006

# PART 13
## RESOLUTIONS AND MEETINGS

**13.0.01**    The provisions in this Part are based on parts of Part 11 Chapter 4 of the Companies Act 1985, but with considerable expansion to give effect to the need for changes in the law which were identified principally in the recommendations in Chapters 2, 6, and 7 of the Company Law Review Steering Group's Final Report. These provisions are intended to provide a comprehensive statement of the practice and procedure relating to company resolutions and meetings, when read together with the communication provisions in sections 1143 to 1148 and Schedules 4 and 5. In addition to implementing detailed policy changes that seek in particular to enhance shareholder involvement in public companies, this Part brings about two important changes for private companies. First, it makes the previous 'elective' regime the default regime for private companies, so that, for example, such companies no longer need to 'elect' to dispense with an annual general meeting (AGM) as they are not required to hold an AGM in the first place unless required by their Articles (or the company is a traded company). Secondly, this Part takes as its starting point in relation to private companies an assumption that they may prefer to take decisions by way of written resolutions rather than in general meetings, and accordingly the previous provisions regarding written resolutions have been redrafted and strengthened.

The structure of this Part is that it deals with (i) general matters relating to resolutions of all companies **13.0.02** (sections 281 to 287); (ii) written resolutions, for which the provisions apply only to private companies (sections 288 to 300); (iii) general meetings of all companies (sections 301 to 335); (iv) additional requirements for meetings of public companies (sections 336 to 340) and quoted companies (sections 341 to 354 and 361); and (v) record keeping (sections 355 to 359).

Provisions relating to resolutions and meetings may also be contained in a company's Articles. See the **13.0.03** 1985 Table A, which was amended on 1 October 2007 by The Companies (Tables A to F) (Amendment) Regulations 2007, SI 2007/2541 and The Companies (Tables A to F) (Amendment) (No 2) Regulations 2007, SI 2007/2826 to bring it into line with this Part of the Companies Act 2006. See also the Model Articles brought into effect on 1 October 2009 by the Companies (Model Articles) Regulations 2008, SI 2008/3229 and which replace the 1985 Table A as the default Articles for companies which do not register Articles of their own when they apply to be incorporated.

A number of amendments have been made to this Part by the Companies (Shareholders' Rights) **13.0.04** Regulations 2009, SI 2009/1632, to give effect to the European Shareholder Rights Directive, ie the Directive on 'the exercise of certain rights of shareholders in listed companies' (Directive 2007/36/EC). These amendments came into force on 3 August 2009 and apply in relation to meetings of which notice is given, or first given, on or after that date. They are intended to facilitate the exercise of basic shareholders' rights and to solve certain problems in the cross-border exercise of such rights, particularly voting rights. A UK public consultation was held between October 2008 and July 2009: see the consultation document and the Government's response to the consultation at ⟨http://www.berr.gov.uk/consultations/page48666.html⟩. The Government has published a number of FAQs relating to the amendments, at ⟨http://www.berr.gov.uk/whatwedo/businesslaw/co-act-2006/faq Act 2006/page52173.html⟩. Guidance has also been given by the ICSA, at ⟨http://www.icsasoftware.com/dl/Shareholder_Rights_Directive.pdf⟩. The amendments also tidy up some small areas where there was thought to be a lack of clarity in certain sections of the Companies Act 2006.

# CHAPTER 1
## GENERAL PROVISIONS ABOUT RESOLUTIONS

### 281 Resolutions

(1) A resolution of the members (or of a class of members) of a private company must be passed— **13.281.01**
    (a) as a written resolution in accordance with Chapter 2, or
    (b) at a meeting of the members (to which the provisions of Chapter 3 apply).
(2) A resolution of the members (or of a class of members) of a public company must be passed at a meeting of the members (to which the provisions of Chapter 3 and, where relevant, Chapter 4 apply).
(3) Where a provision of the Companies Acts—
    (a) requires a resolution of a company, or of the members (or a class of members) of a company, and
    (b) does not specify what kind of resolution is required,
    what is required is an ordinary resolution unless the company's articles require a higher majority (or unanimity).
(4) Nothing in this Part affects any enactment or rule of law as to—
    (a) things done otherwise than by passing a resolution,
    (b) circumstances in which a resolution is or is not treated as having been passed, or
    (c) cases in which a person is precluded from alleging that a resolution has not been duly passed.

COMMENCEMENT DATE 1 October 2007[1]

There was no equivalent to subsections (1) and (2) in the previous legislation. The subsections are **13.281.02** consistent with the aim of the Companies Act 2006 to set out core provisions regarding private companies before those relating to public companies. Subsection (1) provides that private companies can pass a resolution either by way of a written resolution or at a meeting, whereas by subsection (2) public companies can pass a resolution only by way of a meeting. These principles apply whether the resolution is to be passed by the members generally or by a class of members.

Despite the mandatory tone of both these subsections, they only apply to 'resolutions of the members' **13.281.03** (or of a class of members). Subsection (4) (which is based on section 381C of the Companies Act 1985) preserves the unanimous consent rule that is recognized at common law. This rule has two slightly different but related limbs. The first is that if all the members of a company are present at a meeting and

---

[1] Companies Act 2006 (Commencement No 3, etc) Order 2007, SI 2007/2194, art 2(1). For the transitional provisions, see Sch 3, paras 22–23 to this Order.

unanimously give their consent to a proposal, it is irrelevant that a formal resolution was not passed.[2] Secondly, it is not necessary that all the members should have met provided that they have in fact assented to a proposal. Perhaps the best-known example is from the decision in *Re Duomatic Ltd*,[3] where the assent to their own remuneration of the two directors who held all the voting shares met the requirements of the articles for general meeting approval of such remuneration. The rule was applied to a unanimous agreement to alter the articles in *Cane v Jones*[4] and to a reduction of capital in *Re Barry Artist plc*.[5] Although in the latter case the principle was applied reluctantly and the judge gave a warning that the procedure would not be accepted in future reductions, this view seems unlikely to be followed given the 'deregulatory' thrust of the modern legislation, not just in respect of the provisions that assume that private companies do not act by way of formal resolutions at meetings but also because the procedure for reduction of capital is also eased by the Act.[6]

**13.281.04**    Recently, the unanimous consent rule has been applied to a requirement for preference shareholders to give their assent before a charge over assets was created,[7] to the statutory requirement for directors' long-term service contracts to be approved by resolution of the company in general meeting,[8] to the formalities required for an allotment of shares and the disapplication of statutory pre-emption rights[9] and to provisions in a shareholders' agreement.[10]

**13.281.05**    However, unanimous consent cannot validate something that a general meeting itself cannot do, such as a purported ratification of a director's breach of duty that is not ratifiable even with the consent of all shareholders.[11] In addition the principle probably requires the agreement of all registered shareholders, because it is concerned with the position of all members entitled to attend and vote at a general meeting and it is therefore not sufficient to show the agreement of the shareholders with the beneficial interest in the shares.[12]

**13.281.06**    If a resolution is of a type listed in section 29 of the Companies Act 2006, the fact that it is passed either as a written resolution or by the informal procedure explained above does not remove the requirements for it to be forwarded to the registrar of companies in accordance with section 30 of the Companies Act 2006. This requirement is required to be satisfied however such a resolution is passed, whether as a written resolution, at a meeting, or informally.[13] The record-keeping requirements of sections 362 to 366 of the Companies Act 2006 should also be noted and must be complied with.

## 282 Ordinary resolutions

**13.282.01**
    (1) An ordinary resolution of the members (or of a class of members) of a company means a resolution that is passed by a simple majority.
    (2) A written resolution is passed by a simple majority if it is passed by members representing a simple majority of the total voting rights of eligible members (see Chapter 2).
    (3) A resolution passed at a meeting on a show of hands is passed by a simple majority if it is passed by [a simple majority of the votes cast by those entitled to vote].[a]
    (4) A resolution passed on a poll taken at a meeting is passed by a simple majority if it is passed by members representing a simple majority of the total voting rights of members who (being entitled to do so) vote [in person, by proxy or in advance (see section 322A)][b] on the resolution.
    (5) Anything that may be done by ordinary resolution may also be done by special resolution.

---

[2]  See in particular *Re Express Engineering Works Ltd* [1920] 1 Ch 466.
[3]  [1969] 2 Ch 365.
[4]  [1980] 1 WLR 1451.
[5]  [1985] BCLC 283.
[6]  For other authorities, see *Baroness Wenlock v River Dee Co* (1883) 36 Ch D 675n at 681 *per* Cotton LJ, *Re Oxted Motor Co Ltd* [1921] 3 KB 32 (waiving a notice requirement) and *Parker and Cooper Ltd v Reading* [1926] Ch 975. But see Re *Oceanrose Investments Ltd* [2008] EWHC 3475 (Ch), where the Court held that the *Duomatic* principle did not apply where a statutory provision specifically required a meeting to be held, in that case the Companies (Cross-Border Mergers) Regulations 2007, reg 13(1). For recent discussion of *Duomatic*, see eg *Schofield v Schofield* [2011] EWCA Civ 154 [2011] 2 BCLC 319, confirming that the relevant agreement may be express or by implication, verbal or by conduct, given at the relevant time or later, but must be an unqualified agreement that may objectively be established.
[7]  *Re Torvale Group Ltd* [1999] 2 BCLC 605.
[8]  *Wright v Atlas Wright (Europe) Ltd* [1999] 2 BCLC 301.
[9]  *Peña v Dale* [2004] 2 BCLC 508.
[10]  *Euro Brokers Holdings Ltd v Monecor (London) Ltd* [2003] 1 BCLC 506.
[11]  *Bowthorpe Holdings Ltd v Hills* [2003] 1 BCLC 226.
[12]  *Domoney v Godinho* [2004] 2 BCLC 15.
[13]  Depending on the particular resolution which has been passed, other requirements of CA 2006 may also need to be satisfied: eg, a change in a company's name is required formally to be notified to the registrar under CA 2006, s 78 in addition to the requirement to forward to him a copy of the resolution.

AMENDMENTS

[a] Substituted by the Companies (Shareholders' Rights) Regulations 2009, SI 2009/1632, reg 2(1), with effect from 3 August 2009 in relation to meetings of which notice is given, or first given, on or after that date.

[b] Substituted by the Companies (Shareholders' Rights) Regulations 2009, SI 2009/1632, reg 5(2), with effect from 3 August 2009 in relation to meetings of which notice is given, or first given, on or after that date.

COMMENCEMENT DATE 1 October 2007[14]

This section is a new statement by the Companies Act 2006, as the previous legislation did not contain a definition of an ordinary resolution, namely that it requires a simple majority of over 50 per cent. It applies both to resolutions of all members and to members of a class. The section is self-explanatory. It allows appropriate written resolutions of a private company[15] to be passed by a simple majority;[16] under the previous legislation, such resolutions had to be agreed by all those entitled to vote. **13.282.02**

The 1985 Table A formerly contained a provision in regulation 50 entitling the chairman of a general meeting to exercise a casting vote in the case of an equality of votes. This was revoked on 1 October 2007 by The Companies (Tables A to F) (Amendment) (No 2) Regulations 2007, SI 2007/2826, art 3: the Explanatory Note to this statutory instrument explains that the revocation is because regulation 50 conflicted with Companies Act 2006, sections 281 and 282. **13.282.03**

## 283 Special resolutions

(1) A special resolution of the members (or of a class of members) of a company means a resolution passed by a majority of not less than 75%. **13.283.01**

(2) A written resolution is passed by a majority of not less than 75% if it is passed by members representing not less than 75% of the total voting rights of eligible members (see Chapter 2).

(3) Where a resolution of a private company is passed as a written resolution—
   (a) the resolution is not a special resolution unless it stated that it was proposed as a special resolution, and
   (b) if the resolution so stated, it may only be passed as a special resolution.

(4) A resolution passed at a meeting on a show of hands is passed by a majority of not less than 75% if it is passed by [not less than 75% of the votes cast by those entitled to vote].[a]

(5) A resolution passed on a poll taken at a meeting is passed by a majority of not less than 75% if it is passed by members representing not less than 75% of the total voting rights of the members who (being entitled to do so) vote [in person, by proxy or in advance (see section 322A)][b] on the resolution.

(6) Where a resolution is passed at a meeting—
   (a) the resolution is not a special resolution unless the notice of the meeting included the text of the resolution and specified the intention to propose the resolution as a special resolution, and
   (b) if the notice of the meeting so specified, the resolution may only be passed as a special resolution.

AMENDMENTS

[a] Substituted by the Companies (Shareholders' Rights) Regulations 2009, SI 2009/1632, reg 2(2), with effect from 3 August 2009 in relation to meetings of which notice is given, or first given, on or after that date.

[b] Substituted by the Companies (Shareholders' Rights) Regulations 2009, SI 2009/1632, reg 5(2), with effect from 3 August 2009 in relation to meetings of which notice is given, or first given, on or after that date.

COMMENCEMENT DATE 1 October 2007[17]

This section is based on section 378 of the Companies Act 1985 insofar as it provided for a definition of a special resolution, whether of the members generally or of a class of members. A 75 per cent majority is required. In the case of private companies, the section provides that a special resolution can **13.283.02**

---

[14] Companies Act 2006 (Commencement No 3, etc) Order 2007, SI 2007/2194, art 2(1). For the transitional provisions, see Sch 3, paras 22–23 to this Commencement Order.

[15] See ss 288–300.

[16] i.e. a simple majority of the total voting rights of 'eligible members': see s 289 (para 13.289.02 below).

[17] Companies Act 2006 (Commencement No 3, etc) Order 2007, SI 2007/2194, art 2(1). For the transitional provisions, see Sch 3, paras 22–23 to this Commencement Order.

be passed by way of a written resolution agreed by such a percentage,[18] unlike the previous position for a written resolution where unanimity was required. Where a resolution is passed at a meeting, the requirement of 75 per cent means 75 per cent of those who are present and actually vote, rather than 75 per cent of those who are present whether they vote or not. A proposed special resolution to be passed as a written resolution must be identified as such in the text (subsection (3)(a)). The text of a special resolution to be proposed at a meeting must be included in the notice of the meeting, which must also specify the intention to propose the resolution as a special resolution (subsection (6)(a)). Where a resolution is proposed as a special resolution, it can only be passed as such (subsections (3)(b) and (6)(b)). Failure to set out the resolution or to specify that it is to be a special resolution will invalidate the resolution even if it is passed by a 75 per cent majority.[19]

**13.283.03**   Where a special resolution is passed by written resolution, there can be no issue as to any conflict between the proposal and the actual resolution. Where a special resolution is passed at a general meeting, the question might arise as to whether or not the resolution passed must be identical to that proposed, given that subsection (6)(a), unlike the previous section 378(2) of the Companies Act 1985, requires the notice to include 'the text of the resolution'. In a decision under the previous provision,[20] it was held that there had to be substantial concordance between the notice of a special resolution and the terms of the resolution passed and that there was no room for the application of the *de minimis* principle. However, a resolution as passed could properly be regarded as the resolution identified in the preceding notice, even though it departed in some respects from the text of the resolution set out in the notice (for example, by correcting grammatical or clerical errors which could be corrected as a matter of construction, or by reducing the words to more formal language), or it was reduced into the form of a new text which was not included in the notice, provided that in either case there is no departure whatever from the substance.

**13.283.04**   The main other difference from the previous legislation is that there is no longer a requirement for 21 days' notice of a special resolution to be passed at a meeting. The length of notice will be that required for the meeting itself.[21]

**13.283.05**   Special resolutions are required by the Companies Act 2006 in the following situations (they are also required by the Insolvency Act 1986 in certain winding up situations[22] and the articles may impose the requirements for such resolutions in other situations):

1.   Alteration of the articles.[23]
2.   Change of name.[24]
3.   Change of location of registered office to become or cease to be a Welsh company.[25]
4.   Re-registration of private company as public.[26]
5.   Re-registration of public company as private.[27]
6.   Re-registration of unlimited company as private limited company.[28]
7.   Disapplication of pre-emption rights.[29]
8.   Redenomination of capital by cancellation.[30]
9.   Variation of class rights.[31]
10.   Reduction of capital.[32]
11.   Authorization for off-market purchase of own shares.[33]

---

[18] i.e. not less than 75 per cent of the total voting rights of 'eligible members': see s 289 and para 13.289.02 below.

[19] *Macconnell v E Prill & Co Ltd* [1916] 2 Ch 57.

[20] *Re Moorgate Mercantile Holdings Ltd* [1980] 1 WLR 227. See also *Uniq plc* [2011] EWHC 749 (Ch) per David Richards J at [26]–[29], explaining that a resolution which contains an obvious error may be construed as if the error had not been made.

[21] See ss 307 and 312 as to the length of notice for meetings.

[22] See ss 84, 110, 111, and 122 of the 1986 Act.

[23] CA 2006, s 21.

[24] CA 2006, ss 77–78.

[25] CA 2006, s 88.

[26] CA 2006, s 90.

[27] CA 2006, s 97.

[28] CA 2006, s 105. (The converse situation—re-registration of a private limited company as an unlimited company—requires unanimity: CA 2006, s 102.)

[29] CA 2006, s 569.

[30] CA 2006, s 626.

[31] CA 2006, ss 630 and 631.

[32] CA 2006, s 641.

[33] CA 2006, s 694.

12.   Authorization of contingent contract for off-market purchase of own shares.[34]
13.   Variation of contract for off-market purchase of own shares.[35]
14.   Release of rights under contract for off-market purchase.[36]
15.   Approval of payment out of capital for redemption or purchase of own shares.[37]
16.   Opting in or opting out of Part 28 Chapter 2 Companies Act 2006 in relation to impediments to takeovers.[38]

It should be noted that the legislation no longer provides for an extraordinary resolution. Given the    **13.283.06**
removal of the requirement of 21 days' notice for a special resolution, an extraordinary resolution has
ceased to be of any separate relevance.[39]

## 284  Votes: general rules

(1)  On a vote on a written resolution—    **13.284.01**
    (a)  in the case of a company having a share capital, every member has one vote in respect of each
        share or each £10 of stock held by him, and
    (b)  in any other case, every member has one vote.
(2)  [On a vote on a resolution on a show of hands at a meeting, each member present in person has
    one vote.][a]
(3)  On a vote on a resolution on a poll taken at a meeting—
    (a)  in the case of a company having a share capital, every member has one vote in respect of each
        share or each £10 of stock held by him, and
    (b)  in any other case, every member has one vote.
(4)  The provisions of this section have effect subject to any provision of the company's articles.
[(5)  Nothing in this section is to be read as restricting the effect of—
    section 152 (exercise of rights by nominees),
    section 285 (voting by proxy),
    section 322 (exercise of voting rights on poll),
    section 322A (voting on a poll: votes cast in advance), or
    section 323 (representation of corporations at meetings).][b]

AMENDMENTS

[a]  Substituted by the Companies (Shareholders' Rights) Regulations 2009, SI 2009/1632, reg 2(3),
with effect from 3 August 2009 in relation to meetings of which notice is given, or first given, on or
after that date.

[b]  Inserted by the Companies (Shareholders' Rights) Regulations 2009, SI 2009/1632, reg 2(4), with
effect from 3 August 2009 in relation to meetings of which notice is given, or first given, on or after
that date.

COMMENCEMENT DATE  1 October 2007[40]

This section, which is self-explanatory, re-enacts the provisions in sections 370(1) and (6) of the    **13.284.02**
Companies Act 1985 and incorporates some provisions that inform the 1985 Table A, especially
regulation 54 in the 1985 Table A, and specifies the general rules on votes of members taken by written
resolution, on a show of hands at a meeting, or on a poll taken at a meeting. Subsection (4) allows these
general rules to be varied by the company's articles. Regulation 54 of the 1985 Table A was amended on
1 October 2007 by the Companies (Tables A to F) (Amendment) (No 2) Regulations 2007, SI
2007/2826 to make provision for proxies to vote on a show of hands.

The amendments to subsections (2) and (5) are to clarify the voting powers of proxies.    **13.284.03**

## [285  Voting by proxy

(1)  On a vote on a resolution on a show of hands at a meeting, every proxy present who has been duly    **13.285.01**
    appointed by one or more members entitled to vote on the resolution has one vote.
    This is subject to subsection (2).

---

[34]  CA 2006, s 694.
[35]  CA 2006, s 697.
[36]  CA 2006, s 700.
[37]  CA 2006, s 716.
[38]  CA 2006, s 966.
[39]  Subject to the savings provision in Sch, 3 para 23 to the Companies Act 2006 (Commencement No 3, etc)
Order 2007, SI 2007/2194, in relation to references to an extraordinary resolution in a company's memorandum
or articles or a contract.
[40]  Companies Act 2006 (Commencement No 3, etc) Order 2007, SI 2007/2194, art 2(1). For the transitional
provisions, see Sch 3, paras 22–23 to this Commencement Order.

(2) On a vote on a resolution on a show of hands at a meeting, a proxy has one vote for and one vote against the resolution if—

   (a) the proxy has been duly appointed by more than one member entitled to vote on the resolution, and

   (b) the proxy has been instructed by one or more of those members to vote for the resolution and by one or more other of those members to vote against it.

(3) On a poll taken at a meeting of a company all or any of the voting rights of a member may be exercised by one or more duly appointed proxies.

(4) Where a member appoints more than one proxy, subsection (3) does not authorise the exercise by the proxies taken together of more extensive voting rights than could be exercised by the member in person.

(5) Subsections (1) and (2) have effect subject to any provision of the company's articles.][a]

AMENDMENTS

[a] Substituted by the Companies (Shareholders' Rights) Regulations 2009, SI 2009/1632, reg 3, with effect from 3 August 2009 in relation to meetings of which notice is given, or first given, on or after that date.

**13.285.02**    This section replaces the original section 285 with effect from 3 August 2009 as a result of amendments made by the Companies (Shareholders' Rights) Regulations 2009, SI 2009/1632, to clarify the voting rights of proxies.

### [285A  Voting rights on poll or written resolution

**13.285A.01**    In relation to a resolution required or authorised by an enactment, if a private company's articles provide that a member has a different number of votes in relation to a resolution when it is passed as a written resolution and when it is passed on a poll taken at a meeting—

   (a) the provision about how many votes a member has in relation to the resolution passed on a poll is void, and

   (b) a member has the same number of votes in relation to the resolution when it is passed on a poll as the member has when it is passed as a written resolution.][a]

AMENDMENTS

[a] Substituted by the Companies (Shareholders' Rights) Regulations 2009, SI 2009/1632, reg 3, with effect from 3 August 2009 in relation to meetings of which notice is given, or first given, on or after that date. As noted below, the provisions were originally contained within s.285 and have been separated into this separate s.285A by the Companies (Shareholders' Rights) Regulations, SI 2009/1632.

**13.285A.02**    This repeats provisions that were formerly contained in section 285(3) when the Companies Act 2006 was enacted. The amendments made to section 285 by the Companies (Shareholders' Rights) Regulations 2009 led to the provisions being separated out into a free-standing section for clarity. The provisions cater for the fact that written resolutions in private companies no longer have to be passed unanimously. They ensure that the articles cannot provide that a member has a different number of votes on a written resolution from the number he would have when voting on a poll at a general meeting. A member, therefore, cannot be disadvantaged if one procedure is followed rather than the other.

### 286  Votes of joint holders of shares

**13.286.01**    (1) In the case of joint holders of shares of a company, only the vote of the senior holder who votes (and any proxies duly authorised by him) may be counted by the company.

   (2) For the purposes of this section, the senior holder of a share is determined by the order in which the names of the joint holders appear in the register of members.

   (3) Subsections (1) and (2) have effect subject to any provision of the company's articles.

COMMENCEMENT DATE  1 October 2007[41]

**13.286.02**    There was no statutory provision to this effect under earlier legislation, but standard articles of association were to the same effect.[42] Where shares are jointly held, only the votes of the senior holder (or any proxy appointed by him) count, the senior holder being the person whose name appears first in the register of members. The articles may provide to the contrary.

---

[41] Companies Act 2006 (Commencement No 3, etc) Order 2007, SI 2007/2194, art 2(1). For the transitional provisions, see Sch 3, paras 22–23 to this Commencement Order.

[42] See, eg, regulation 55 in the 1985 Table A.

## 287  Saving for provisions of articles as to determination of entitlement to vote

Nothing in this Chapter affects—                                                                                    **13.287.01**

    (a)  any provision of a company's articles—

        (i)  requiring an objection to a person's entitlement to vote on a resolution to be made in accordance with the articles, and

        (ii)  for the determination of any such objection to be final and conclusive, or

    (b)  the grounds on which such a determination may be questioned in legal proceedings.

COMMENCEMENT DATE 1 October 2007[43]

This section did not have a predecessor in the previous legislation. It is designed to preserve provisions    **13.287.02**
in companies' articles which impose a procedure for objecting to someone's entitlement to vote and
only applies in that event. Articles commonly contain such a procedure to provide certainty as to the
outcome of a meeting. For example regulation 58 in the 1985 Table A provides that any objection to a
vote at a meeting can only be raised at the meeting or adjourned meeting at which the vote is tendered
and gives the chairman of the meeting the right to adjudicate conclusively. The Model Articles which
came into effect on 1 October 2009 are to similar effect: see article 43 of the Model Articles for private
companies limited by shares, article 29 of the Model Articles for private companies limited by
guarantee, and article 35 of the Model Articles for public companies.

## CHAPTER 2
## WRITTEN RESOLUTIONS

Sections 288 to 300 amend, expand, and clarify the former Companies Act 1985 provisions relating to    **13.288.01**
written resolutions. They retain the rule that such resolutions can be passed only by private companies,
not public companies. It has been possible for private companies to act in this way since rules relating
to written resolutions extending beyond the provisions commonly found in a private company's
articles (see regulation 53 of the 1985 Table A, now revoked with effect from 1 October 2007 by The
Companies (Tables A to F) (Amendment) Regulations 2007, SI 2007/2541) were introduced in 1990 by
an amendment to the Companies Act 1985 made by the Companies Act 1989, introducing the
Companies Act 1985, sections 381A to 381C. These provisions in the Companies Act 2006 relax the old
rule by removing the former requirement that such resolutions had to be passed unanimously: it is
sufficient that they are approved by the appropriate percentage relating to the particular resolution in
question (ie more than 50 per cent for an ordinary resolution; not less than 75 per cent for a special
resolution). In addition to the general requirements of sections 288 to 300 for written resolutions, the
Companies Act 2006 prescribes additional formalities for certain particular written resolutions, which
are identified in the sections relating to such resolutions, such as sections 188 to 226 (transactions with
directors), section 571 (disapplication of pre-emption rights), sections 696 and 699 (purchase of own
shares), and section 718 (payment out of capital).[44]

### General provisions about written resolutions

## 288  Written resolutions of private companies

    (1)  In the Companies Acts a 'written resolution' means a resolution of a private company proposed    **13.288.02**
and passed in accordance with this Chapter.

    (2)  The following may not be passed as a written resolution—

        (a)  a resolution under section 168 removing a director before the expiration of his period of office;

        (b)  a resolution under section 510 removing an auditor before the expiration of his term of office.

    (3)  A resolution may be proposed as a written resolution—

        (a)  by the directors of a private company (see section 291), or

        (b)  by the members of a private company (see sections 292 to 295).

    (4)  References in enactments passed or made before this Chapter comes into force to—

        (a)  a resolution of a company in general meeting, or

---

[43]  Companies Act 2006 (Commencement No 3, etc) Order 2007, SI 2007/2194, art 2(1). For the transitional
provisions, see Sch 3, paras 22–23 to this Commencement Order.

[44]  Ss 300A–300D Companies Act 2006 contain transitional provisions for the period through to 1 October
2009 relating to disapplication of pre-emption rights, financial assistance, purchase of own shares, and payment
out of capital: see Companies Act 2006 (Commencement No 3, etc) Order 2007, SI 2007/2194, art 6 and Sch 1
para 13(4).

      (b)  a resolution of a meeting of a class of members of the company,
      have effect as if they included references to a written resolution of the members, or of a class of
      members, of a private company (as appropriate).
    (5)  A written resolution of a private company has effect as if passed (as the case may be)—
      (a)  by the company in general meeting, or
      (b)  by a meeting of a class of members of the company, and references in enactments passed or
          made before this section comes into force to a meeting at which a resolution is passed or to
          members voting in favour of a resolution shall be construed accordingly.

COMMENCEMENT DATE 1 October 2007[45]

**13.288.03**    The section contains some important background provisions relating to written resolutions.

**13.288.04**    First, by subsection (1) the written resolution procedure can be used only by private companies. It is not available to public companies; they must still take the procedural step of holding a meeting. While, as noted above, the ability for private companies to deal with matters by way of written resolution is not a new one, its retention and clarification in the Companies Act 2006 is consistent with the overall policy of deregulating the affairs and procedures of private companies.

**13.288.05**    Secondly, the written resolution procedure applies both to resolutions to be passed by the members as a whole and to resolutions to be passed by a class of members: see sections 281(1) and 288(4) and (5).

**13.288.06**    Thirdly, private companies have the right to use the written resolution procedure for all resolutions apart from the two exceptions stated in subsection (2) (and which are the same as those formerly in the Companies Act 1985, section 381A(7) and Part 1 of Schedule 15A). The written resolution procedure cannot be used for the removal of a director before the expiration of his period of office under section 168 of the Companies Act 2006 or for the removal of an auditor before the expiration of his term of office under section 510 of the Companies Act 2006. These two types of resolution are excluded from the procedure for written resolutions because the director or the auditor (as the case may be) has the right to protest against his proposed removal and thus a meeting must be held to consider any such protest. Where one or other of these two exceptions applies, even a private company must still hold a meeting, with all its associated procedural paraphernalia.

**13.288.07**    Fourthly, subsection (3) introduces the rule that a written resolution may be proposed either by the company's directors or by its members. The particular requirements of the rule are dealt with as a matter of substance by sections 291 and 292 to 295: see below.

**13.288.08**    Fifthly, subsections (4) and (5) ensure that the ability for private companies to pass resolutions as written resolutions extends to all resolutions referred to in any existing legislation.[46] There is thus no need for such legislation to be amended; existing references to resolutions are in the case of private companies to be read as if they included references to written resolutions.

**13.288.09**    It should also be noted that the auditor is entitled to receive communications sent to a member in relation to a written resolution: see section 502(1) Companies Act 2006.[47]

### 289 Eligible members

**13.289.01**    (1)  In relation to a resolution proposed as a written resolution of a private company, the eligible members are the members who would have been entitled to vote on the resolution on the circulation date of the resolution (see section 290).
    (2)  If the persons entitled to vote on a written resolution change during the course of the day that is the circulation date of the resolution, the eligible members are the persons entitled to vote on the resolution at the time that the first copy of the resolution is sent or submitted to a member for his agreement.

COMMENCEMENT DATE 1 October 2007[48]

---

[45] Companies Act 2006 (Commencement No 3, etc) Order 2007, S1 2007/2194, art 2(1). Note the transitional adaptations in Sch 1, para 13 to the Order which (i) substitutes CA 1985, s 391 for s 510 in subs (2)(b), (ii) adds a reference to CA 1985, s 80A in a new subs (2)(c) and (iii) adds a new subs (3) which applies the transitional requirements of ss 300A–300D inserted by Sch 1, para 13(4) to the Order. See also the transitional provisions in Sch 3, para 24 to this Commencement Order.

[46] As the terms of these provisions make clear, they apply only in relation to legislation that preceded the Companies Act 2006, not subsequent legislation, as noted in *Re Oceanrose Investments Ltd* [2008] EWHC 3475 (Ch) at [22].

[47] See also the explanatory notes to Companies Act 2006 at para 762, stating that s 502 requires a private company to send to its auditor all the information about any written resolution that it sends to its shareholders.

[48] Companies Act 2006 (Commencement No 3, etc) Order 2007, S1 2007/2194, art 2(1). For the transitional provisions, see Sch 3, para 24 to this Commencement Order.

This section is intended to create certainty as to the identities of the persons who are entitled to vote on     **13.289.02**
a written resolution. The key is to identify the 'circulation date': this is discussed in the commentary to
section 290 below and is, in short, the first day on which copies of the resolution are sent or submitted
to the members. Subsection (2) goes on to recognize that identifying the relevant *day* might not by itself
be sufficient: shares might be transferred during the course of that day, with the consequence that it will
be necessary to identify whether it is the transferor or the transferee who has the voting right. In such
circumstances it is necessary to identify the *time* that the resolution was first sent or submitted: the
member eligible to vote is the person who was entitled to vote at that particular time.

## *Circulation of written resolutions*

### 290  Circulation date

References in this Part to the circulation date of a written resolution are to the date on which copies     **13.290.01**
of it are sent or submitted to members in accordance with this Chapter (or if copies are sent or
submitted to members on different days, to the first of those days).

COMMENCEMENT DATE 1 October 2007[49]

It is important to be able to identify the 'circulation date' of the resolution for a number of reasons. In     **13.290.02**
particular, the date is relevant to the identification of the persons entitled to vote on a written resolution
(section 289), to the date when a proposed resolution lapses if it is not passed (section 297), and to the
period for which a proposed resolution must be displayed on the company's website if the company
chooses to circulate it by such means (section 299). The section explains that the circulation date is the
date on which copies of the resolution are sent or submitted to members, and if the copies are not all
sent or submitted on the same day it is the first of those days. A resolution can be 'sent' or 'submitted'
in a number of ways: see the commentary to section 291 below.[50]

### 291  Circulation of written resolutions proposed by directors

(1)  This section applies to a resolution proposed as a written resolution by the directors of the     **13.291.01**
     company.
(2)  The company must send or submit a copy of the resolution to every eligible member.
(3)  The company must do so—
     (a)  by sending copies at the same time (so far as reasonably practicable) to all eligible members
          in hard copy form, in electronic form or by means of a website, or
     (b)  if it is possible to do so without undue delay, by submitting the same copy to each eligible
          member in turn (or different copies to each of a number of eligible members in turn),
     or by sending copies to some members in accordance with paragraph (a) and submitting a copy or
     copies to other members in accordance with paragraph (b).
(4)  The copy of the resolution must be accompanied by a statement informing the member—
     (a)  how to signify agreement to the resolution (see section 296), and
     (b)  as to the date by which the resolution must be passed if it is not to lapse (see section 297).
(5)  In the event of default in complying with this section, an offence is committed by every officer of
     the company who is in default.
(6)  A person guilty of an offence under this section is liable—
     (a)  on conviction on indictment, to a fine;
     (b)  on summary conviction, to a fine not exceeding the statutory maximum.
(7)  The validity of the resolution, if passed, is not affected by a failure to comply with this section.

COMMENCEMENT DATE 1 October 2007[51]

There are two ways in which a written resolution can be proposed: by the directors, or by the members.     **13.291.02**
This section deals with the procedure for a proposal by the directors; sections 292 to 295 deal with the
procedure for a proposal by the members.

For a resolution to be proposed by the directors under this section, the company must 'send' or 'submit'     **13.291.03**
a copy to every eligible member, ie to all the persons entitled to vote on the resolution as determined in
accordance with the definition of 'eligible members' in section 289.

---

[49] The Companies Act 2006 (Commencement No 3, etc) Order 2007, SI 2007/2194, art 2(1). For the
transitional provisions, see Sch 3, para 24 to this Commencement Order.

[50] Sch 5, para 13(2) is also to be noted, for a particular timing point in the case where a resolution is circulated
by means of being made available on a website: it is not to be taken to have been sent to the members until the later
of the date on which notification is given to the members that it is so available or it first appears on the website.

[51] Companies Act 2006 (Commencement No 3, etc) Order 2007, SI 2007/2194, art 2(1). For the transitional
provisions, see Sch 3, para 24 to this Commencement Order.

**13.291.04** The requirement for a copy to be 'sent' is satisfied if it is sent in hard copy form, or in electronic form, or by means of a website: section 291(3)(a). This terminology needs to be read in conjunction with the definitions in section 1168 of the Companies Act 2006 and the communication provisions in sections 1143 to 1148 and Schedules 4 and 5 of the Companies Act 2006. In short, the definitions in section 1168 are as follows. First, a document or information is sent or supplied in hard copy form if it is sent or supplied in a paper copy or similar form capable of being read. Secondly, a document or information is sent or supplied in electronic form if it is sent or supplied by electronic means such as email or fax or by any other means while in an electronic form (such as by sending a disk by post). Thirdly, a document or information is sent or supplied by electronic means if it is sent initially and received at its destination by means of electronic equipment for the processing or storage of data and entirely transmitted, conveyed and received by wire, by radio, by optical means, or by other electromagnetic means. Fourthly, a document or information sent or supplied in electronic form must be sent or supplied in a form and by a means that the sender or supplier reasonably considers will enable the recipient to read it and to retain a copy of it. Fifthly, a document or information can be read only if it can be read with the naked eye or, to the extent that it consists of images, it can be seen with the naked eye.

**13.291.05** Where a document is sent by post, the provisions of section 1147(2) of the Companies Act 2006 will apply as to when it is deemed to have been received by the recipient. In short, and subject to any contrary provision in the company's articles, a document or information sent by post to an address in the UK is deemed to have been received 48 hours after it was posted provided the company can show it was properly addressed, prepaid, and posted. Where a document is sent by electronic means, the provisions of section 1147(3) of the Companies Act 2006 will apply. In short, and subject to any contrary provision in the company's articles, a document or information sent or supplied by electronic means is deemed to have been received 48 hours after it was sent provided the company can show it was properly addressed. As to the 'sending' of a document by means of a website, see section 299 below and section 1147(4) as to when the document is deemed to have been received by the recipient. In short, and subject to any contrary provision in the company's articles, a document or information sent or supplied by means of a website is deemed to have been received when it was first made available on the website or, if later, when the recipient received or is deemed to have received notice of the fact that the material was available on the website.

**13.291.06** Section 291(3)(a) imposes the requirement that so far as reasonably practicable all the copies of the resolution should be sent to the eligible members at the same time, but it is apparent, for example, from section 290 (which contemplates that copies might be sent on different days) that the legislation appreciates that there may be circumstances in which this requirement of reasonable practicability cannot be satisfied.

**13.291.07** The requirement for a copy to be 'submitted' contemplates that a copy is given to a member, and that if it is possible to do so without undue delay it is passed from member to member by way of a round-robin. Such a process of 'submission' can be by way of the company passing round a paper document or an email: see the explanatory notes to Companies Act 2006 at paragraph 534.

**13.291.08** A combination of 'sending' and 'submitting' can be used (section 291(3)), so that the company can tailor-make the procedure to suit the particular circumstances. For example, where the directors are themselves members, it would be pointless for the company to have to send them a copy of the resolution if they have themselves approved it at a board meeting and it is sitting in front of them; in such circumstances it could be 'submitted' to them at that time and then 'sent' to all the other members as soon as possible afterwards.

**13.291.09** To ensure that the members understand how to respond to the resolution and the date by which they should do so, the copy of the resolution which is provided to each member must be accompanied by a statement informing the member how to signify agreement to the resolution and as to the date by which the resolution must be passed if it is not to lapse. In other words, the accompanying statement must explain the matters set out in sections 296 and 297: see the commentary to these sections below.

**13.291.10** If there is default in complying with any of the requirements of this section, the criminal consequences in subsections (5) and (6) will follow in respect of every officer of the company who is in default. See sections 1121 to 1133 of the Companies Act 2006 for provisions relating to offences under the Companies Act 2006, and note in particular that for the purposes of section 291(5) the term 'officer' includes any director, manager, or secretary, and 'in default' means authorizing or permitting, participating in, or failing to take all reasonable steps to prevent the contravention of section 291.[52]

**13.291.11** However, a failure to comply with the section does not invalidate a resolution which has been passed: subsection (7). Nonetheless, depending on the particular circumstances giving rise to the failure to

---

[52] CA 2006, s 1121.

comply, other consequences may follow. For example, if the directors were deliberately to fail to circulate the resolution to certain members, those members might have grounds for seeking relief on the 'unfair prejudice' ground under section 994 of the Companies Act 2006, or there might be a basis for the company to bring a claim based on a breach by the directors of their fiduciary duties, or for a member to bring a derivative claim under section 260 of the Companies Act 2006.

## 292  Members' power to require circulation of written resolution

(1)  The members of a private company may require the company to circulate a resolution that may properly be moved and is proposed to be moved as a written resolution.          **13.292.01**

(2)  Any resolution may properly be moved as a written resolution unless—

    (a)  it would, if passed, be ineffective (whether by reason of inconsistency with any enactment or the company's constitution or otherwise),

    (b)  it is defamatory of any person, or

    (c)  it is frivolous or vexatious.

(3)  Where the members require a company to circulate a resolution they may require the company to circulate with it a statement of not more than 1,000 words on the subject matter of the resolution.

(4)  A company is required to circulate the resolution and any accompanying statement once it has received requests that it do so from members representing not less than the requisite percentage of the total voting rights of all members entitled to vote on the resolution.

(5)  The 'requisite percentage' is 5% or such lower percentage as is specified for this purpose in the company's articles.

(6)  A request—

    (a)  may be in hard copy form or in electronic form,

    (b)  must identify the resolution and any accompanying statement, and

    (c)  must be authenticated by the person or persons making it.

COMMENCEMENT DATE  1 October 2007[53]

This deals with the important power of the members of a company to propose a written resolution and to require it to be circulated.[54] The power is given to them by section 288(3)(b), and this section together with sections 293 to 295 deal with its procedural aspects.          **13.292.02**

The power is not an unfettered one. The legislation recognizes that if the power were unrestricted, it might be used for improper mischief-making. Thus three limitations are placed upon it: it cannot be used to propose a resolution which (i) would be ineffective, (ii) is defamatory, or (iii) is frivolous or vexatious: subsection (2).[55] These limitations may give rise to litigation as members will from time to time test their boundaries. The limitations should not, however, cause any particular difficulties of interpretation: it should generally be tolerably clear whether a proposed resolution would be ineffective,[56] or is defamatory, and although the concept of a 'frivolous or vexatious' resolution is potentially a more elastic one, it is a concept with which the courts are familiar having had to apply it for many years in the context of strike-out applications under Order 18 rule 19 of the old Rules of the Supreme Court.          **13.292.03**

A further fetter is imposed by the provision in subsections (4) and (5) that the company is required to circulate a resolution only where a request is made by members with the requisite voting power: they must have at least 5 per cent of the total voting rights of all members entitled to vote on the resolution, or such lower percentage as is specified in the company's articles. Even if they can surmount this hurdle, the requisitionists will then find that (subject to any contrary resolution by the company) they will have to pay the costs of circulating the resolution: section 294 below.          **13.292.04**

Provided the member or members proposing the resolution can satisfy these requirements, the company must circulate the resolution and the requisitionists can also require the resolution to be accompanied by a statement—of no more than 1,000 words—on the subject matter of the resolution.          **13.292.05**

---

[53]  Companies Act 2006 (Commencement No 3, etc) Order 2007, SI 2007/2194, art 2(1). For the transitional provisions, see Sch 3, para 24 to this Commencement Order.

[54]  The power is a similar one to that given to members of a public company to require a resolution to be circulated for consideration at the company's AGM: see CA 2006, s 338.

[55]  The same restrictions are placed on the power given to members of a public company to require a resolution to be circulated for consideration at the company's AGM: see CA 2006, s 338(2).

[56]  See by analogy *Rose v McGivern* [1998] 2 BCLC 593, which concerned similar wording in the old CA 1985, s 368 and where the directors were not required to call a meeting if the resolution proposed by the requisitioning members could not be of legal effect even if it were passed.

So the requisitionists have an opportunity to explain to the other members what the resolution is about and why they believe it to be a good thing.[57]

**13.292.06**  In keeping with the general trend toward electronic communication, a request to the company for a resolution to be circulated can be made either in hard copy form or in electronic form,[58] provided that in either case it identifies the resolution and any accompanying statement and that the request is authenticated.[59] It should be noted, however, that by Schedule 4 paragraph 6 of the Companies Act 2006 a member is permitted to send documents or information to a company in electronic form only if (i) the company has agreed (either generally or specifically) that the document or information may be sent electronically; or (ii) the company is deemed to have so agreed by a provision in the Companies Act 2006. Section 292 is not such a deeming provision (contrast for example section 298) and accordingly, despite the apparently clear wording of section 292(6)(a), a request under this section cannot be made in electronic form unless the company has agreed (either generally or specifically) to such a procedure. As to the requirement that the request be 'authenticated', see section 1146 of the Companies Act 2006 and its commentary below; in short, a document in hard copy form is authenticated if it is signed by the person sending or supplying it, and a document in electronic form is authenticated if the identity of the sender is confirmed in a manner specified by the company or (where no such manner has been specified by the company) if the document contains or is accompanied by a statement of the identity of the sender and the company has no reason to doubt the truth of the statement.

### 293  Circulation of written resolution proposed by members

**13.293.01**  (1)  A company that is required under section 292 to circulate a resolution must send or submit to every eligible member—
  (a)  a copy of the resolution, and
  (b)  a copy of any accompanying statement.
  This is subject to section 294(2) (deposit or tender of sum in respect of expenses of circulation) and section 295 (application not to circulate members' statement).
(2)  The company must do so—
  (a)  by sending copies at the same time (so far as reasonably practicable) to all eligible members in hard copy form, in electronic form or by means of a website, or
  (b)  if it is possible to do so without undue delay, by submitting the same copy to each eligible member in turn (or different copies to each of a number of eligible members in turn),
  or by sending copies to some members in accordance with paragraph (a) and submitting a copy or copies to other members in accordance with paragraph (b).
(3)  The company must send or submit the copies (or, if copies are sent or submitted to members on different days, the first of those copies) not more than 21 days after it becomes subject to the requirement under section 292 to circulate the resolution.
(4)  The copy of the resolution must be accompanied by guidance as to—
  (a)  how to signify agreement to the resolution (see section 296), and
  (b)  the date by which the resolution must be passed if it is not to lapse (see section 297).
(5)  In the event of default in complying with this section, an offence is committed by every officer of the company who is in default.
(6)  A person guilty of an offence under this section is liable—
  (a)  on conviction on indictment, to a fine;
  (b)  on summary conviction, to a fine not exceeding the statutory maximum.
(7)  The validity of the resolution, if passed, is not affected by a failure to comply with this section.

COMMENCEMENT DATE  1 October 2007[60]

**13.293.02**  This deals with the procedure by which a resolution proposed by members under section 292 and its accompanying statement are to be circulated to all the members eligible to vote on the resolution. As to who is an 'eligible member' for the purposes of subsection (1), see the commentary to section 289 above.

---

[57]  This is similar to the power given to members by CA 2006, s 314 to require a statement to be circulated in advance of a meeting, where a resolution is to be proposed at a meeting rather than as a written resolution.
[58]  As to 'hard copy form' and 'electronic form' see the definitions in CA 2006, s 1168 and the communication provisions in ss 1143–1148 and Schs 4 and 5, and the summary at para 13.291.04 above.
[59]  Where shares are in the names of joint holders, both or all of them must authenticate the request, unless under the company's articles one joint holder has authority to sign for all of them: *Patent Wood Keg Syndicate Ltd v Pearse* [1906] WN 164.
[60]  Companies Act 2006 (Commencement No 3, etc) Order 2007, S1 2007/2194, art 2(1). For the transitional provisions, see Sch 3, para 24 to this Commencement Order.

The requirements are much the same as for the circulation of a resolution proposed by directors under   **13.293.03**
section 291 above:

(i)   for the manner in which the resolution is to be sent or submitted to members, see paragraphs
      13.291.03 to 13.291.08 above;
(ii)  for the need for an accompanying statement to explain how agreement to the resolution is to be
      signified and by when this must be done, see paragraph 13.291.09 above;
(iii) for the criminal consequences of non-compliance with the section, see paragraph 13.291.10
      above; and
(iv)  for the result that a resolution is valid even if the section is not complied with, see paragraph
      13.291.11 above.

The additional requirements imposed in relation to a resolution proposed by members in contrast to   **13.293.04**
one proposed by directors are threefold. First, the company is not required to circulate the resolution
unless a sufficient amount is deposited or tendered to cover the expenses of circulation in accordance
with section 294: see section 294 below. Secondly, the company is not required to circulate the
accompanying statement if a successful application to prevent circulation has been made under section
295: see section 295 below. Thirdly, the company must circulate the resolution and any accompanying
statement within 21 days of being required to do so, or at least must circulate the first copy if for some
good reason copies are to be circulated on different days.[61] This time runs from the day when the
company has received requests to circulate the resolution from members holding the requisite voting
power, because it is at this point that the company is required to circulate the resolution and any
accompanying statements under section 292(4).

## 294 Expenses of circulation

(1)  The expenses of the company in complying with section 293 must be paid by the members who   **13.294.01**
     requested the circulation of the resolution unless the company resolves otherwise.
(2)  Unless the company has previously so resolved, it is not bound to comply with that section unless
     there is deposited with or tendered to it a sum reasonably sufficient to meet its expenses in
     doing so.

COMMENCEMENT DATE  1 October 2007[62]

This is self-explanatory: unless the company resolves otherwise, the expenses of circulating a resolu-   **13.294.02**
tion proposed by members must be paid by the proposers, and the company can require a sufficient
sum to be deposited with it or tendered to it in advance of circulation. This is intended to be a further
safeguard to prevent the company's time and money being spent on mischief-making: a member or
members wishing to propose a resolution will (in the absence of a resolution to the contrary by the
company) be required to put his money where his mouth is.[63]

## 295 Application not to circulate members' statement

(1)  A company is not required to circulate a members' statement under section 293 if, on an   **13.295.01**
     application by the company or another person who claims to be aggrieved, the court is satisfied
     that the rights conferred by section 292 and that section are being abused.
(2)  The court may order the members who requested the circulation of the statement to pay the
     whole or part of the company's costs (in Scotland, expenses) on such an application, even if they
     are not parties to the application.

COMMENCEMENT DATE  1 October 2007[64]

This enables the company or any aggrieved person to apply to court to prevent the circulation of a   **13.295.02**
statement proposed to accompany a written resolution under section 292(3), if the section is being

---

[61]  Sch 5, para 13(2) is to be noted for a particular timing point in the case where a resolution is circulated by
means of being made available on a website: it is not to be taken to have been sent to the members until the later
of the date on which notification is given to the members that it is so available or it first appears on the website.
[62]  The Companies Act 2006 (Commencement No 3, etc) Order 2007, S1 2007/2194, art 2(1). For the
transitional provisions, see Sch 3, para 24 to this Commencement Order.
[63]  Similar provision is made in relation to a member's request for a statement to be circulated prior to a
meeting (CA 2006, s 316) and in relation to a member's request for a resolution to be circulated for consideration
at a public company's AGM (CA 2006, s 340).
[64]  Companies Act 2006 (Commencement No 3, etc) Order 2007, S1 2007/2194, art 2(1). For the transitional
provisions, see Sch 3, para 24 to this Commencement Order.

abused.[65] The section does not enable an application to be made to prevent the circulation of the proposed resolution itself; it can only be to prevent the circulation of the accompanying statement. There may, however, be other grounds on which a person might seek to prevent the circulation of a proposed resolution; for example, he might seek injunctive relief if the resolution defamed him.

**13.295.03** The court can order the costs of such an application to be borne by the members who requested the circulation of the statement.

### Agreeing to written resolutions

### 296 Procedure for signifying agreement to written resolution

**13.296.01**
(1) A member signifies his agreement to a proposed written resolution when the company receives from him (or from someone acting on his behalf) an authenticated document—
    (a) identifying the resolution to which it relates, and
    (b) indicating his agreement to the resolution.
(2) The document must be sent to the company in hard copy form or in electronic form.
(3) A member's agreement to a written resolution, once signified, may not be revoked.
(4) A written resolution is passed when the required majority of eligible members have signified their agreement to it.

COMMENCEMENT DATE 1 October 2007[66]

**13.296.02** This deals with the manner in which a member signifies his agreement to a written resolution. There is no particular magic to it; he must identify the resolution he is dealing with, and indicate that he agrees to it. He does this by sending the relevant document to the company, in an 'authenticated' form, as to which see section 1146 and its commentary below.[67] As to the meanings of 'hard copy form' and 'electronic form', see the definitions in section 1168 of the Companies Act 2006 and the communication provisions in sections 1143 to 1148 and Schedules 4 and 5 of the Companies Act 2006, and see the summary at paragraph 13.291.04 above. Although subsection (2) suggests that the member will always have the option of sending the document in hard copy form or in electronic form, it needs to be read with section 298 and Schedule 4, paragraph 6: the member can send his document in electronic form only if (i) the company has given an electronic address in any document containing or accompanying a proposed written resolution (which may be subject to conditions or limitations specified in the document), or (ii) the company has agreed (either generally or specifically) that the document may be sent electronically.

**13.296.03** Clearly it is sufficient (as it was under section 381A(2) of the Companies Act 1985) for the members to indicate their agreement to the resolution by signing or otherwise authenticating more than one document; they do not all need to sign the same piece of paper.

**13.296.04** If the member does not agree to the resolution, he does not need to do anything. There is no need for him to return the document signifying that he is voting against the resolution; because a written resolution can be passed only if approved by the requisite percentage of members entitled to vote (sections 282(2) and 283(2)), a member who does not signify his agreement to the resolution will thereby automatically be counted within the percentage of members who are against it.

**13.296.05** It is important for a member to note that he cannot revoke his agreement once he has given it; he must make up his mind once and for all: subsection (3). He must also note that his agreement to the resolution is effective only when the relevant document is *received* by the company. Thus the member must make sure not only that he sends the document within the time limit specified in section 297, but also that it is received by the company within that time limit.

---

[65] The section is in the same terms as s 317, which deals with a statement to be circulated prior to a meeting at which a resolution is to be proposed.

[66] The Companies Act 2006 (Commencement No 3, etc) Order 2007, SI 2007/2194, art 2(1). For the transitional provisions, see Sch 3, para 24 to this Commencement Order.

[67] In short, a document in hard copy form is authenticated if it is signed by the person sending or supplying it, and a document in electronic form is authenticated if the identity of the sender is confirmed in a manner specified by the company or (where no such manner has been specified by the company) if the document contains or is accompanied by a statement of the identity of the sender and the company has no reason to doubt the truth of the statement. Where shares are in the names of joint holders, both or all of them must authenticate the request, unless under the company's articles one joint holder has authority to sign for all of them: *Patent Wood Keg Syndicate Ltd v Pearse* [1906] WN 164.

As to the 'required majority' for the passing of a written resolution, an ordinary resolution requires a   **13.296.06** simple majority of the total voting rights of eligible members, and a special resolution requires at least 75 per cent of the total voting rights of eligible members: see sections 282(2) and 283(2). The term 'eligible member' is defined in section 289.

### 297  Period for agreeing to written resolution

(1) A proposed written resolution lapses if it is not passed before the end of—      **13.297.01**
    (a)  the period specified for this purpose in the company's articles, or
    (b)  if none is specified, the period of 28 days beginning with the circulation date.
(2) The agreement of a member to a written resolution is ineffective if signified after the expiry of that period.

COMMENCEMENT DATE 1 October 2007[68]

Clearly it is sensible that there is a time limit imposed for members to respond to a proposed written   **13.297.02** resolution. The period will be whatever is specified in the company's articles. If the articles are silent on the point, it will be 28 days beginning with the 'circulation date'. The circulation date is the day when copies of the resolution are sent or submitted to members (or the first such day if copies are sent or submitted on different days): see section 290 above. In calculating 'the period of 28 days beginning with the circulation date', the circulation date is itself taken into account.[69] So, for example, if the circulation date is Wednesday 6 September, the proposed resolution will lapse at midnight on the night of Tuesday 3/Wednesday 4 October if it has not by then been passed. The section does not give the court power to extend the 28-day period.

## *Supplementary*

### 298  Sending documents relating to written resolutions by electronic means

(1) Where a company has given an electronic address in any document containing or accompanying   **13.298.01** a proposed written resolution, it is deemed to have agreed that any document or information relating to that resolution may be sent by electronic means to that address (subject to any conditions or limitations specified in the document).
(2) In this section 'electronic address' means any address or number used for the purposes of sending or receiving documents or information by electronic means.

COMMENCEMENT DATE 1 October 2007[70]

By Schedule 4, paragraph 6 a member is permitted to send documents or information to a company in   **13.298.02** electronic form only if (i) the company has agreed (either generally or specifically) that the document or information may be sent electronically, or (ii) the company is deemed to have so agreed by a provision in the Companies Act 2006. This section contains such a deeming provision: a member is entitled to send in electronic form a document or information relating to a proposed written resolution if the company has given an electronic address in any document containing or accompanying the proposed resolution (although the company may also specify that certain conditions or limitations are to be complied with).

An 'electronic address' is simply an address or number for sending or receiving documents or   **13.298.03** information by electronic means; so this will include an email address and a fax number. It might also include, for example, a mobile telephone number to which text messages can be sent; it would seem to be less likely that a company would use this as a means of communication, but it might do so, for example, in the case of a small company with one director and in circumstances where this is the easiest means of contacting him.

### 299  Publication of written resolution on website

(1) This section applies where a company sends—      **13.299.01**
    (a)  a written resolution, or
    (b)  a statement relating to a written resolution,
    to a person by means of a website.

---

[68]  Companies Act 2006 (Commencement No 3, etc) Order 2007, S1 2007/2194, art 2(1). For the transitional provisions, see Sch 3, para 24 to this Commencement Order.
[69]  *Zoan v Rouamba* [2000] 1 WLR 1509 at paras 23–24.
[70]  Companies Act 2006 (Commencement No 3, etc) Order 2007, S1 2007/2194, art 2(1). For the transitional provisions, see Sch 3, para 24 to this Commencement Order.

(2)  The resolution or statement is not validly sent for the purposes of this Chapter unless the resolution is available on the website throughout the period beginning with the circulation date and ending on the date on which the resolution lapses under section 297.

COMMENCEMENT DATE 1 October 2007[71]

**13.299.02**  The section applies where in accordance with section 291(3)(a) and (4) or section 293(2)(a) and (4), a company chooses to send a proposed resolution or accompanying statement by means of a website. Such a method is valid only if the resolution or statement are available on the website throughout the relevant period—ie from the circulation date to the day when the proposed resolution lapses if it has not already been passed.

**13.299.03**  The requirements which a company must meet in order for a communication validly to be sent by means of a website are spelt out in Schedule 5, Part 4. In particular, such a method of communication can be used only (i) if the member to whom the communication is being made has agreed (generally or specifically) to such a method; or (ii) if a resolution has been passed by the members permitting such a method (and that section 30 of the Companies Act 2006 has been complied with in relation to such resolution) or the company's articles permit such a method and the member has been asked by the company to agree to such a method and either has agreed or has failed to respond within 28 days of the request. The information must be made available on the website in such a way that the member can read it (in the sense that he can see it with the naked eye) and can retain a copy of it. And the company must notify the member that the information is on the website, by telling him that it is there, and what the relevant address is and how it may be accessed.[72]

**13.299.04**  As to subsection (2), cases may arise in which a company's website temporarily becomes unavailable as a result of a system 'crashing'. These are dealt with by Schedule 5, paragraph 14(2): notwithstanding what would otherwise appear to be the mandatory wording of section 299(2) that the information is to be 'available on the website throughout the period', there will not be a failure to comply with the section if the information is available for part of the period and the failure to make it available throughout the period is wholly attributable to circumstances that it would not be reasonable to have expected the company to prevent or avoid. Thus, for example, it would appear that a short unavailability caused by a system 'crash' wholly outside the company's control would not lead to invalidity, but unavailability caused by the fact that the company had set up a website which was clearly inadequate to cope with the number of hits it was likely to receive and therefore could not readily and regularly be accessed would be likely to lead to invalidity.

**13.299.05**  Finally, the section requires the resolution and statement to be available on the website throughout the period ending on 'the date on which the resolution lapses'. In many cases, however, the proposed resolution will not lapse; instead, it will be passed some time during that period. This latter situation is not expressly covered by the section and it is thus unclear whether a resolution which has been passed can be taken off the website even though the notional date at which it would have lapsed has not yet been reached.

### 300  Relationship between this Chapter and provisions of company's articles

**13.300.01**  A provision of the articles of a private company is void in so far as it would have the effect that a resolution that is required by or otherwise provided for in an enactment could not be proposed and passed as a written resolution.

COMMENCEMENT DATE 1 October 2007[73]

**13.300.02**  This is self-explanatory. It is a development of the point in sections 288(4) and (5) discussed in paragraph 13.288.08 above. References to resolutions in any enactment are to include references to written resolutions, and by this section any provision to the contrary in a private company's articles is void.

## CHAPTER 3
## RESOLUTIONS AT MEETINGS

**13.301.01**  Sections 301 to 335 contain provisions relating to general meetings of all companies, whether private or public. They apply to general meetings of all shareholders and also in most respects, by sections 334

---

[71] Companies Act 2006 (Commencement No 3, etc) Order 2007, S1 2007/2194, art 2(1). For the transitional provisions, see Sch 3, para 24 to this Commencement Order.

[72] Sch 5, para 13.

[73] Companies Act 2006 (Commencement No 3, etc) Order 2007, S1 2007/2194, art 2(1). For the transitional provisions, see Sch 3, para 24 to this Commencement Order.

to 335, to class meetings.[74] The sections are based on sections 368 to 377, 379, and 381 of the Companies Act 1985, with expansion and amendment, for example, to reflect the fact that private companies are no longer required to hold an AGM (whereas under the former regime such companies were required to hold an AGM unless they elected not to do so). The power which formerly existed for the Secretary of State to call an AGM where a company has failed to hold one (section 367 of the Companies Act 1985) has been repealed and not carried over into the Companies Act 2006.

## General provisions about resolutions at meetings

### 301  Resolutions at general meetings

A resolution of the members of a company is validly passed at a general meeting if—          **13.301.02**

(a)  notice of the meeting and of the resolution is given, and

(b)  the meeting is held and conducted,

in accordance with the provisions of this Chapter (and, where relevant, Chapter 4) and the company's articles.

COMMENCEMENT DATE  1 October 2007[75]

This section is an extension of section 378(6) of the Companies Act 1985 (which applied to special   **13.301.03** resolutions and the old-style extraordinary resolutions) and is self-explanatory. For a resolution to be validly passed at a general meeting, it is necessary to comply with the relevant procedures relating to the giving of notice of the meeting and the resolution, and to the manner in which the meeting is held and conducted, both in so far as such procedures are set out in the Companies Act 2006 and in so far as they are set out in the company's articles. The requirements are cumulative: both the Companies Act 2006 and the articles must be complied with, so the mandatory requirements of the Companies Act 2006 cannot be disapplied by the articles.

## Calling meetings

### 302  Directors' power to call general meetings

The directors of a company may call a general meeting of the company.          **13.302.01**

COMMENCEMENT DATE  1 October 2007[76]

This is self-explanatory. It gives statutory effect to part of regulation 37 of the 1985 Table A. For the   **13.302.02** directors to take a decision to call a meeting, they must act in accordance with the decision-making procedure laid down in the company's articles.[77] It will not be sufficient if the secretary of the company calls a meeting without the directors first having taken the decision that a meeting should be called.[78]

### 303  Members' power to require directors to call general meeting

(1)  The members of a company may require the directors to call a general meeting of the company.          **13.303.01**

(2)  The directors are required to call a general meeting once the company has received requests to do so from—

   (a)  members who hold at least [5%][a] of such of the paid up capital of the company as carries the right of voting at general meetings of the company (excluding any paid up capital held as treasury shares); or

   (b)  in the case of a company not having a share capital, members who represent at least [5%][b] of the total voting rights of all the members having a right to vote at general meetings.

(3)  […][c]

(4)  A request—

   (a)  must state the general nature of the business to be dealt with at the meeting, and

   (b)  may include the text of a resolution that may properly be moved and is intended to be moved at the meeting.

---

[74]  In relation to class meetings, ss 334(2) and 335(2) exclude the operation of ss 303–305 and 306 and ss 334(3) and 335(3) limit the operation of ss 318 and 321.

[75]  Companies Act 2006 (Commencement No 3, etc) Order 2007, S1 2007/2194, art 2(1).

[76]  Companies Act 2006 (Commencement No 3, etc) Order 2007, S1 2007/2194, art 2(1).

[77]  Although if the directors unanimously agree to call a meeting, albeit they have not formally considered the matter, this will apparently be sufficient: *Re Bonelli's Telegraph Company, Collie's Claim* (1871) LR 12 Eq 246 at 258–260; *H L Bolton (Engineering) Co Ltd v T J Graham & Sons Ltd* [1957] 1 QB 159; *Runciman v Walter Runciman plc* [1992] BCLC 1084; *Hunter v Senate Support Services Ltd* [2005] 1 BCLC 175. But cf *Re Haycraft Gold Reduction and Mining Co* [1900] 2 Ch 230 distinguished in *Boschoek Proprietary Co Ltd v Fuke* [1906] 1 Ch 148. It should also be checked whether there are provisions in the company's articles relaxing the requirements for the directors to meet formally.

[78]  *Re State of Wyoming Syndicate* [1901] 2 Ch 431.

(5) A resolution may properly be moved at a meeting unless—
    (a) it would, if passed, be ineffective (whether by reason of inconsistency with any enactment or the company's constitution or otherwise),
    (b) it is defamatory of any person, or
    (c) it is frivolous or vexatious.
(6) A request—
    (a) may be in hard copy form or in electronic form, and
    (b) must be authenticated by the person or persons making it.

AMENDMENTS

<sup>a</sup> Substituted by the Companies (Shareholders' Rights) Regulations 2009, SI 2009/1632, reg 4(2), with effect from 3 August 2009 in relation to meetings of which notice is given, or first given, on or after that date.

<sup>b</sup> Substituted by the Companies (Shareholders' Rights) Regulations 2009, SI 2009/1632, reg 4(2), with effect from 3 August 2009 in relation to meetings of which notice is given, or first given, on or after that date.

<sup>c</sup> Repealed by the Companies (Shareholders' Rights) Regulations 2009, SI 2009/1632, reg 4(3), with effect from 3 August 2009 in relation to meetings of which notice is given, or first given, on or after that date.

COMMENCEMENT DATE 1 October 2007[79]

**13.303.02**　This empowers the members to require the calling of a general meeting, and—in conjunction with sections 304 and 305 discussed below—is similar in effect to the former provision in section 368 of the Companies Act 1985. The section does not apply to class meetings: sections 334(2) and 335(2) of the Companies Act 2006.

**13.303.03**　The member or members seeking such a meeting must comply with various requirements in order for their request to be a valid one which the directors must act upon.

**13.303.04**　First, they must hold the required percentage of voting power, ie 5%; see subsection (2).

**13.303.05**　Secondly, by subsection (4) their request must state the general nature of the business to be dealt with at the meeting and may include the text of a proposed resolution. This is an extension of the previous legislation, which (cf section 368(3) of the Companies Act 1985) did not contain provision for the members to provide the text of a resolution.

**13.303.06**　Thirdly, by subsection (5) they may not put forward a resolution which (i) would be ineffective;[80] (ii) is defamatory; or (iii) is frivolous or vexatious.[81] These mirror the requirements of section 292(2) which deal with the members' power to require circulation of a written resolution: see the commentary at paragraph 13.292.03 above.

**13.303.07**　Fourthly, by subsection (6) their request may be made either in hard copy form or in electronic form,[82] and must be authenticated.[83] It would seem that the request does not need to be in a single document or communication; subsection (2) refers to 'requests' rather than 'a request', and under the former provision in section 368(3) of the Companies Act 1985 it was permissible for the relevant requisition to be contained in several documents in like form.[84]

---

[79] Companies Act 2006 (Commencement No 3, etc) Order 2007, SI 2007/2194, art 2(1). For the transitional provisions, see Sch 3, para 25 to this Commencement Order.

[80] This gives statutory effect to the interpretation placed by the court on CA 1985, s 368, under which the directors were not required to call a meeting if the resolution proposed by the requisitioning members could not be of legal effect even if it were passed: *Rose v McGivern* [1998] 2 BCLC 593.

[81] If a resolution is put forward which does fall foul of one of these three requirements, the requisitioning members cannot amend the resolution and thereby continue with the procedure: *Rose v McGivern* (above). They will have to start the procedure all over again, with a properly worded resolution.

[82] As to the meanings of 'hard copy form' and 'electronic form', see the definitions in CA 2006, s 1168 and the communication provisions in CA 2006, ss 1143–1148 and Schs 4 and 5, and see the summary at para 13.291.04 above.

[83] As to authentication, see s 1146 below and its commentary: in short, a document in hard copy form is authenticated if it is signed by the person sending or supplying it, and a document in electronic form is authenticated if the identity of the sender is confirmed in a manner specified by the company or (where no such manner has been specified by the company) if the document contains or is accompanied by a statement of the identity of the sender and the company has no reason to doubt the truth of the statement.

[84] Where shares are in the names of joint holders, both or all of them must sign or otherwise authenticate the request, unless under the company's articles one joint holder has authority to sign for all of them: *Patent Wood Keg Syndicate Ltd v Pearse* [1906] WN 164.

Provided the members satisfy these requirements, the court will not grant an injunction to restrain a   **13.303.08**
meeting being called in accordance with this section.[85]

## 304  Directors' duty to call meetings required by members

(1) Directors required under section 303 to call a general meeting of the company must call a   **13.304.01**
    meeting—
    (a) within 21 days from the date on which they become subject to the requirement, and
    (b) to be held on a date not more than 28 days after the date of the notice convening the
        meeting.
(2) If the requests received by the company identify a resolution intended to be moved at the
    meeting, the notice of the meeting must include notice of the resolution.
(3) The business that may be dealt with at the meeting includes a resolution of which notice is given
    in accordance with this section.
(4) If the resolution is to be proposed as a special resolution, the directors are treated as not having
    duly called the meeting if they do not give the required notice of the resolution in accordance with
    section 283.

COMMENCEMENT DATE 1 October 2007[86]

The section gives effect to the power given to the members by section 303, based on the former   **13.304.02**
provisions in section 368 of the Companies Act 1985. The section does not apply to class meetings:
sections 334(2) and 335(2) of the Companies Act 2006. The directors are required to act promptly on
the requisition by the members: they must call the meeting within 21 days from the date on which they
become subject to the requirement (ie within 21 days of the company receiving the appropriate request
from members holding the required percentage of votes in accordance with section 303(2)), and they
must call it to be held no later than 28 days after the date of the notice convening it.[87]

The directors are no longer required 'forthwith' to call the meeting, as they were under section 368(1)   **13.304.03**
of the Companies Act 1985.[88] The statutory requirement is only to call it within 21 days of being
required so to do. Nonetheless it is possible that in an appropriate case, if there were some real urgency
in requiring a meeting but the directors nonetheless waited until the end of the 21-day period to call it
and then called it for a date right at the end of the 28-day period, a member might have grounds for
complaining on the 'unfair prejudice' basis under section 994 of the Companies Act 2006: see, by
analogy, the position under the former provision as explained in *McGuinness v Bremner plc* [1988]
BCLC 673.

Where the request by the members has identified a proposed resolution in accordance with section   **13.304.04**
303(4), the notice of the meeting must include notice of the resolution, and the business which may
then be dealt with at the meeting includes such a resolution. If the resolution is to be proposed as a
special resolution, subsection (4) imposes the additional requirement that notice of the resolution
must be given in accordance with section 283(6).

In calling the meeting the directors are entitled, and indeed under a duty, to inform all the members   **13.304.05**
whether they believe the proposed resolution to be in the interests of the company, and are entitled to
use the company's monies for paying for such information to be circulated to the members.[89]

## 305  Power of members to call meeting at company's expense

(1) If the directors—   **13.305.01**
    (a) are required under section 303 to call a meeting, and
    (b) do not do so in accordance with section 304,
    the members who requested the meeting, or any of them representing more than one half of the
    total voting rights of all of them, may themselves call a general meeting.
(2) Where the requests received by the company included the text of a resolution intended to be
    moved at the meeting, the notice of the meeting must include notice of the resolution.

---

[85] *Cumbrian Newspapers Group Ltd v Cumberland & Westmorland Herald Newspaper & Printing Co Ltd*
[1987] Ch 1 at 24.
[86] Companies Act 2006 (Commencement No 3, etc) Order 2007, SI 2007/2194, art 2(1). For the transitional
provisions, see Sch 3, para 25 to this Commencement Order.
[87] Regulation 37 of the 1985 Table A was amended on 1 October 2007 to remove the provision allowing the
directors a period of 8 weeks to call a requisitioned meeting: see the Companies (Tables A to F) (Amendment)
Regulations 2007, SI 2007/2541, art 5. The provision was inconsistent with s 305 and would in any event have
been overridden by s 305.
[88] In the context of CA 1985, s 368 the term 'forthwith' meant 'as soon as practicable': *Re Windward Islands
(Enterprises) UK Ltd* [1983] BCLC 293.
[89] *Peel v London and North Western Railway Co* [1907] 1 Ch 5.

(3)  The meeting must be called for a date not more than three months after the date on which the directors become subject to the requirement to call a meeting.

(4)  The meeting must be called in the same manner, as nearly as possible, as that in which meetings are required to be called by directors of the company.

(5)  The business which may be dealt with at the meeting includes a resolution of which notice is given in accordance with this section.

(6)  Any reasonable expenses incurred by the members requesting the meeting by reason of the failure of the directors duly to call a meeting must be reimbursed by the company.

(7)  Any sum so reimbursed shall be retained by the company out of any sums due or to become due from the company by way of fees or other remuneration in respect of the services of such of the directors as were in default.

COMMENCEMENT DATE 1 October 2007[90]

**13.305.02**  This empowers the members to call a general meeting where the directors have failed to do so in response to a request under section 303. In the same way as sections 303 and 304, it is similar in effect to the former provisions in section 368 of the Companies Act 1985. The section does not apply to class meetings: sections 334(2) and 335(2) of the Companies Act 2006.

**13.305.03**  Such a meeting can be called by the members who made the request under section 303, or any of them representing more than half of the total voting rights of all of them. If the request under section 303 included the text of a proposed resolution (ie per section 303(4)(b)), the notice of the meeting called by the members must include notice of that resolution.

**13.305.04**  The time limit for such a meeting to be held is that the members must call it for a date not more than three months after the date on which the directors became subject to the requirement to call a meeting, ie not more than three months after the company received the appropriate request from members holding the required percentage of votes in accordance with section 303(2). Where it does not become apparent until the expiry of the 21-day period in section 304(1)(a) that the directors have failed to call a meeting, the members will then need to move promptly to ensure that a meeting can be called and held within the three-month period, of which 21 days will already have ticked by. It is not sufficient for the meeting to be called within the three-month period: it must be held within that period. Given that at least 14 days' notice is required of a general meeting (section 307 below), the members will have about eight weeks in which to send out the relevant notice.

**13.305.05**  By subsection (4), the procedure which the members are to follow in calling the meeting is, as nearly as possible, the same as that for meetings which are required to be called by the directors.[91] This brings into play in particular the provisions in sections 307 to 313: see below. Section 305 does not expressly state any particular requirements in relation to the calling of a meeting at which a resolution is to be proposed as a special resolution, but it would appear that by virtue of subsection (4) the members calling such a meeting must also comply with section 283(6).

**13.305.06**  Given that the need for the members to call a meeting under this section will arise only where the directors have failed in their obligation to do so, and that if the directors had complied with their obligation the expenses incurred in calling the meeting would have been borne by the company, subsection (6) provides that any reasonable expenses incurred by the members must be reimbursed by the company. And in order to ensure that it is the defaulting directors rather than the company which ultimately bears the cost, subsection (7) provides for the relevant amount to be recovered by the company by deducting it from monies which it otherwise would have to pay to such directors.

### 306  Power of court to order meeting

**13.306.01**  (1)  This section applies if for any reason it is impracticable—

(a)  to call a meeting of a company in any manner in which meetings of that company may be called, or

(b)  to conduct the meeting in the manner prescribed by the company's articles or this Act.

(2)  The court may, either of its own motion or on the application—

(a)  of a director of the company, or

(b)  of a member of the company who would be entitled to vote at the meeting,

order a meeting to be called, held and conducted in any manner the court thinks fit.

(3)  Where such an order is made, the court may give such ancillary or consequential directions as it thinks expedient.

---

[90] Companies Act 2006 (Commencement No 3, etc) Order 2007, SI 2007/2194, art 2(1). For the transitional provisions, see Sch 3, para 25 to this Commencement Order.

[91] *Re Windward Islands (Enterprises) UK Ltd* [1983] BCLC 293. So, eg, the relevant provisions as to the length of time for notice to be given of the meeting must be complied with.

(4)  Such directions may include a direction that one member of the company present at the meeting be deemed to constitute a quorum.

(5)  A meeting called, held and conducted in accordance with an order under this section is deemed for all purposes to be a meeting of the company duly called, held and conducted.

COMMENCEMENT DATE  1 October 2007[92]

This repeats the provision formerly in section 371 of the Companies Act 1985, with a few stylistic **13.306.02** changes. The section does not apply to class meetings: sections 334(2) and 335(2) of the Companies Act 2006. The section can apply only where it is 'impracticable' for a meeting to be called or conducted in the usual manner: subsection (1). For the test of impracticability to be satisfied, it is not necessary to show that it would be impossible to call or conduct a meeting: thus the section can be invoked even where it would be possible to call and conduct a meeting, but there is some factor which as a practical matter means it is appropriate to seek the assistance of the court.

An example of a situation where such impracticability can arise is where an attempt has been made to **13.306.03** hold a meeting in the usual manner but the meeting has had to be closed by the police because of a risk of a breach of the peace.[93] In contrast, the impracticability requirement will not be satisfied simply because there may be a concern whether the chairman has a conflict of interest, as there is ordinarily no requirement for the chairman to be free from conflict.[94] Nor can the section be used to override a shareholder's substantive rights or class rights.[95]

A difficult situation and one that may arise quite often in practice is where a company has become **13.306.04** deadlocked, for example where there are only two members, the quorum required for a meeting is two, and the member who has the minority shareholding refuses to attend a meeting so that the quorum requirement cannot be satisfied and the meeting cannot take place. In such circumstances the court will usually be prepared to direct a meeting, in particular by using the power given to it by subsection (4) to direct that the presence of one member is sufficient to constitute a quorum. The business of the company will thus be able to move forward; the general principle adopted by the court is that minority shareholders are not to be able to stultify the company's business by invoking the quorum provisions, at least where the majority are seeking to exercise a statutory right such as the right to remove a director. Thus in *Re El Sombrero Ltd*[96] the court directed a meeting to be held at which a quorum of one would be sufficient, against the background that there were three shareholders, the articles provided for a quorum of two, the holder of 90 per cent of the shares wanted to call and hold a meeting so that he could exercise his statutory right to remove the two directors who were also the other two shareholders, but those other two shareholders were unsurprisingly attempting to avoid their fate by refusing to agree to a meeting being held and thereby using the quorum provisions to block the meeting.

Other examples are *Re Opera Photographic Ltd*,[97] where the court directed a meeting so that the holder **13.306.05** of 51 per cent of the shares could proceed with a resolution to remove as a director the person who held the other 49 per cent, and *Union Music Ltd v Watson*,[98] where the court directed a meeting with a quorum of one even where there was a shareholders' agreement requiring a quorum of two, because the term in the shareholders' agreement was properly to be regarded as in the nature of a quorum provision rather than a class right or a substantive right. See also *Vectone Entertainment Holding Ltd v South Entertainment Ltd*,[99] which has a summary of the principles at paragraphs 32 to 33. In such circumstances the applicant is entitled to bring the matter before the court under section 306 rather than having to use what may be the more complicated route of a claim under section 994 of the Companies Act 2006.[100]

[92]  Companies Act 2006 (Commencement No 3, etc) Order 2007, S1 2007/2194, art 2(1). Note the transitional adaptation in Sch 1, para 14 to the Order making subs (1)(b) applicable also to requirements of CA 1985.

[93]  *Re British Union for the Abolition of Vivisection* [1995] 2 BCLC 1, where the court directed the holding of a meeting at which the votes of most members were to be cast by post rather than by attendance in person, so as to avoid the risk of further disorderly conduct.

[94]  *Might SA v Redbus Interhouse plc* [2004] 2 BCLC 449.

[95]  *Harman v BML Group Ltd* [1994] 1 WLR 893; *Union Music Ltd v Watson* [2003] 1 BCLC 453; *Vectone Entertainment Holding Ltd v South Entertainment Ltd* [2004] 2 BCLC 224; *Alvona Developments Ltd v Manhattan Loft Corporation (AC) Ltd* [2005] EWHC 1567.

[96]  [1958] Ch 900.

[97]  [1989] 1 WLR 634.

[98]  [2003] 1 BCLC 453.

[99]  [2004] 2 BCLC 224. For recent examples, see *Wheeler v Ross* [2011] EWHC 2527 (Ch), *Smith v Butler* [2011] EWHC 2301 (Ch) [2012] 1 BCLC 444, upheld at [2012] EWCA Civ 314.

[100]  *Union Music Ltd v Watson* [2003] 1 BCLC 453.

**13.306.06**    In granting such relief, however, the court ordinarily will have regard to the fact that one or other of the members might have grounds for a claim under the 'unfair prejudice' provisions of what is now section 994 of the Companies Act 2006 (formerly section 459 of the Companies Act 1985). Thus if a section 994 claim is up and running or is threatened, the court will in an appropriate case seek to ensure that the order which it makes will preserve the status quo pending the petition being heard: see *Re Sticky Fingers Restaurant Ltd*,[101] where directions were given for the calling of a meeting to appoint additional directors but subject to the proviso that they would undertake not to exclude from his directorship the petitioner who was claiming relief on the unfairly prejudicial ground, and cf *Re Whitchurch Insurance Consultants Ltd*.[102] If proceedings under section 994 are not yet under way or on the horizon, the court ordinarily will just direct a meeting to be held, leaving it to any member who claims to be aggrieved to present a petition under section 994 if he thinks he has grounds so to do.

**13.306.07**    Contrast, however, the situation where two members each hold 50 per cent of the company's shares, and one of them is seeking to invoke the section in order to push through a resolution which the other is opposed to. In such circumstances the court ordinarily will not allow the section to be invoked, because it is not the purpose of the section to enable one equal shareholder to be preferred over the other.[103]

**13.306.08**    An application can be made by a director of the company or by any member who would be entitled to vote at the meeting.[104] The relevant procedure is by way of claim form under CPR Part 8. Or the court can act of its own motion even in the absence of any such person making an application.[105]

## *Notice of meetings*

### 307    Notice required of general meeting

**13.307.01**         [(A1) This section applies to—
            (a)  a general meeting of a company that is not a traded company; and
            (b)  a general meeting of a traded company that is an opted-in company (as defined by section 971(1)), where—
                 (i)   the meeting is held to decide whether to take any action that might result in the frustration of a takeover bid for the company; or
                 (ii)  the meeting is held by virtue of section 969 (power of offeror to require general meeting to be held).
         (A2) For corresponding provision in relation to general meetings of traded companies (other than meetings within subsection (A1)(b)), see section 307A.] [a]

         (1)  A general meeting of a private company (other than an adjourned meeting) must be called by notice of at least 14 days.
         (2)  A general meeting of a public company (other than an adjourned meeting) must be called by notice of—
              (a)  in the case of an annual general meeting, at least 21 days, and
              (b)  in any other case, at least 14 days.
         (3)  The company's articles may require a longer period of notice than that specified in subsection (1) or (2).
         (4)  A general meeting may be called by shorter notice than that otherwise required if shorter notice is agreed by the members.
         (5)  The shorter notice must be agreed to by a majority in number of the members having a right to attend and vote at the meeting, being a majority who—
              (a)  together hold not less than the requisite percentage in nominal value of the shares giving a right to attend and vote at the meeting (excluding any shares in the company held as treasury shares), or
              (b)  in the case of a company not having a share capital, together represent not less than the requisite percentage of the total voting rights at that meeting of all the members.
         (6)  The requisite percentage is—
              (a)  in the case of a private company, 90% or such higher percentage (not exceeding 95%) as may be specified in the company's articles;
              (b)  in the case of a public company, 95%.
         (7)  Subsections (5) and (6) do not apply to an annual general meeting of a public company (see instead section 337(2)).

---

[101]  [1992] BCLC 84.
[102]  [1994] BCC 53. See also *Re Woven Rugs Ltd* [2002] 1 BCLC 324.
[103]  *Ross v Telford* [1998] 1 BCLC 82.
[104]  Subs (2).
[105]  Subs (2).

AMENDMENTS

<sup>a</sup> Inserted by the Companies (Shareholders' Rights) Regulations 2009, SI 2009/1632, reg 9(1), with
effect from 3 August 2009 in relation to meetings of which notice is given, or first given, on or after
that date.

COMMENCEMENT DATE  1 October 2007[106]

These provisions are self-explanatory, dealing with the notice required to be given for general meetings
of (i) companies which are not traded companies, and (ii) companies which are traded companies if
they are opted-in companies and the meeting is of one or other of the two types mentioned in
subsection (A1)(b). For an explanation of 'traded' companies and 'opted-in' companies see sections
360C and 971: a 'traded' company is a company any shares of which carry rights to vote at general
meetings and are admitted to trading on a regulated market in an EEA State by or with the consent of
the company, and an 'opted-in' company is a company in relation to which an opting-in resolution
under section 966(1) has effect and the conditions in section 966(2) and (4) are met. For the notice
required for other meetings of traded companies, see section 307A below.     **13.307.02**

The provisions are based on parts of the provisions formerly in section 369 of the Companies Act 1985,     **13.307.03**
but with some amendments.[107] In short—subject to any longer period stated in the articles[108] or shorter
period agreed by the members[109] —the period is always 14 days unless the meeting is the AGM of a
public company in which case it is 21 days.[110]

Particular points to note are as follows. First, it is only in relation to a public company that a notice     **13.307.04**
period is specified for an AGM, because private companies are no longer required to hold an AGM
unless required by their Articles (or the company is a traded company). Secondly, a company's articles
can require a longer period of notice than that stated in subsections (1) and (2) but cannot permit a
shorter period. Thirdly, a shorter period is however permitted under this section if it is agreed by the
required majority of the members as explained in subsections (5) and (6)[111] (save that in relation to a
public company's AGM, the period can be shortened only if all the members who are entitled to attend
and vote at the meeting so agree: section 337(2), see below).

Once notice has been given, the date of the meeting cannot be postponed simply by giving a further     **13.307.05**
notice: the meeting must be held on the due date and then adjourned to the proposed later date.[112]

## [307A  Notice required of general meeting: certain meetings of traded companies

(1)  A general meeting of a traded company must be called by notice of—     **13.307A.01**
    (a)  in a case where conditions A to C (set out below) are met, at least 14 days;
    (b)  in any other case, at least 21 days.
(2)  Condition A is that the general meeting is not an annual general meeting.
(3)  Condition B is that the company offers the facility for members to vote by electronic means
    accessible to all members who hold shares that carry rights to vote at general meetings.
    This condition is met if there is a facility, offered by the company and accessible to all such
    members, to appoint a proxy by means of a website.
(4)  Condition C is that a special resolution reducing the period of notice to not less than 14 days has
    been passed—
    (a)  at the immediately preceding annual general meeting, or

---

[106] Companies Act 2006 (Commencement No 3, etc) Order 2007, SI 2007/2194, art 2(1). For the transitional
provisions, see Sch 3, para 26 to this Commencement Order.
[107] The 14-day period is now of general application, whereas for unlimited companies it was previously only
seven days. The period is also 14 days for a meeting at which a special resolution is to be proposed: previously it
was 21 days.
[108] CA 2006, s 307(3).
[109] CA 2006, ss 307(4) and 337(2).
[110] The references to 'at least 14 days' and 'at least 21 days' mean that both the day on which the notice is given
and the day of the meeting are to be excluded, ie that there must be 14 or 21 clear days: see CA 2006, s 360 below,
reflecting the common law rule (*Re Hector Whaling Ltd* [1936] Ch 208) and regulation 38 of the 1985 Table A. So
if notice is given on Wednesday 6 September, a meeting requiring at least 14 days notice cannot be held until
Thursday 21 September, and a meeting requiring at least 21 days cannot be held until Thursday 28 September.
[111] The level of 90 per cent in relation to a private company is a change from the previous legislation which
required 95 per cent although the company could elect to lower the percentage to 90 per cent (cf CA 1985, s 369(3)
and (4)). The provision is now the other way around: the percentage is 90 per cent unless the articles state a higher
percentage up to 95 per cent. As to treasury shares, referred to in s 307(5)(a), see CA 2006, ss 724–732 below. Note
also the principles discussed in the commentary to s 281 above, by virtue of which business can be dealt with
without there being any meeting at all if the members unanimously agree to such matters.
[112] *Smith v Paringa Mines Ltd* [1906] 2 Ch 193.

(b)  at a general meeting held since that annual general meeting.

(5)  In the case of a company which has not yet held an annual general meeting, condition C is that a special resolution reducing the period of notice to not less than 14 days has been passed at a general meeting.

(6)  The company's articles may require a longer period of notice than that specified in subsection (1).

(7)  Where a general meeting is adjourned, the adjourned meeting may be called by shorter notice than required by subsection (1).

But in the case of an adjournment for lack of a quorum this subsection applies only if—

(a)  no business is to be dealt with at the adjourned meeting the general nature of which was not stated in the notice of the original meeting, and

(b)  the adjourned meeting is to be held at least 10 days after the original meeting.

(8)  Nothing in this section applies in relation to a general meeting of a kind mentioned in section 307(A1)(b) (certain meetings regarding takeover of opted-in company).]ª

AMENDMENTS

ª  Inserted by the Companies (Shareholders' Rights) Regulations 2009, SI 2009/1632, reg 9(2), with effect from 3 August 2009 in relation to meetings of which notice is given, or first given, on or after that date.

COMMENCEMENT DATE  3 August 2009

**13.307A.02**  This section was inserted by the Companies (Shareholders' Rights) Regulations 2009, SI 2009/1632, to set out the notice required of meetings of traded companies (save for the two particular types of meetings mentioned in section 307(A1)(b)).[113] For an explanation of 'traded' companies, see section 360C: a 'traded' company is a company any shares of which carry rights to vote at general meetings and are admitted to trading on a regulated market in an EEA State by or with the consent of the company.

**13.307A.03**  In the same way as in section 307, the references to 'at least 14 days' and 'at least 21 days' mean that both the day on which the notice is given and the day of the meeting are to be excluded, ie there must be 14 or 21 clear days: see Companies Act 2006, section 360 below.

## 308  Manner in which notice to be given

**13.308.01**  Notice of a general meeting of a company must be given—

(a)  in hard copy form,

(b)  in electronic form, or

(c)  by means of a website (see section 309),

or partly by one such means and partly by another.

COMMENCEMENT DATE  20 January 2007[114]

**13.308.02**  This is self-explanatory. The various means by which notice may be given of a general meeting are the same as the means by which various other corporate communications can be given. The section must be read in conjunction with the definitions in section 1168 of the Companies Act 2006 and the communication provisions in sections 1143 to 1148 and Schedules 4 and 5 of the Companies Act 2006: see the summary at paragraph 13.291.04 above.

## 309  Publication of notice of meeting on website

**13.309.01**  (1)  Notice of a meeting is not validly given by a company by means of a website unless it is given in accordance with this section.

(2)  When the company notifies a member of the presence of the notice on the website the notification must—

(a)  state that it concerns a notice of a company meeting,

(b)  specify the place, date and time of the meeting, and

(c)  in the case of a public company, state whether the meeting will be an annual general meeting.

(3)  The notice must be available on the website throughout the period beginning with the date of that notification and ending with the conclusion of the meeting.

COMMENCEMENT DATE  20 January 2007[115]

**13.309.02**  This is self-explanatory, dealing with particular requirements to be complied with when notice of a meeting is given by means of a website. There were similar provisions in the former section 369(4B) to

---

[113]  In s 307A(4) and (5) references to annual general meetings and general meetings include ones held before 3 August 2009: the Companies (Shareholders' Rights) Regulations 2009, SI 2009/1632, reg 23.

[114]  Companies Act 2006 (Commencement No 1, etc) Order 2006, S1 2006/3428, art 3(1)(a).

[115]  Companies Act 2006 (Commencement No 1, etc) Order 2006, S1 2006/3428, art 3(1)(a).

(4D) of the Companies Act 1985. The section must be read in conjunction with the communication provisions in sections 1143 to 1148 and Schedules 4 and 5 of the Companies Act 2006. As to the requirement in subsection (3) that the notice must be 'available on the website throughout the period', see the commentary at paragraphs above in relation to the similarly worded requirement in section 299(2).

## 310  Persons entitled to receive notice of meetings

(1) Notice of a general meeting of a company must be sent to—

  (a) every member of the company, and

  (b) every director.

(2) In subsection (1), the reference to members includes any person who is entitled to a share in consequence of the death or bankruptcy of a member, if the company has been notified of their entitlement.

(3) In subsection (2), the reference to the bankruptcy of a member includes—

  (a) the sequestration of the estate of a member;

  (b) a member's estate being the subject of a protected trust deed (within the meaning of the Bankruptcy (Scotland) Act 1985 (c. 66)).

(4) This section has effect subject to—

  (a) any enactment, and

  (b) any provision of the company's articles.

COMMENCEMENT DATE 1 October 2007[116]

**13.310.01**

This section is based in part on section 370 of the Companies Act 1985 and gives statutory effect to part of regulation 38 of the 1985 Table A. This section does not pick up the requirement in regulation 38 that notice be given to the company's auditor; this is addressed separately in section 502(2) of the Companies Act 2006 (below) which provides that the auditor is entitled to receive all notices of, and other communications relating to, any general meeting which a member of the company is entitled to receive.[117] Notice of general meetings must be sent to (i) every member, (ii) every director, and (iii) any person entitled to a share in consequence of the death or bankruptcy of a member. As to (iii), such persons must be notified even if they have not yet had their names entered into the register of members, provided that the company has been notified of their entitlement. But these notification requirements are subject to the provisions of any other enactments or of the company's articles to the contrary; for example, the articles may provide that notice does not need to be sent to any members for whom the company no longer has a valid address.

**13.310.02**

## 311  Contents of notices of meetings

(1) Notice of a general meeting of a company must state—

  (a) the time and date of the meeting, and

  (b) the place of the meeting.

(2) Notice of a general meeting of a company must state the general nature of the business to be dealt with at the meeting.

  [In relation to a company other than a traded company, this subsection has effect subject to any provision of the company's articles.]ᵃ

[(3) Notice of a general meeting of a traded company must also include—

  (a) a statement giving the address of the website on which the information required by section 311A (traded companies: publication of information in advance of general meeting) is published;

  (b) a statement—

    (i) that the right to vote at the meeting is determined by reference to the register of members, and

    (ii) of the time when that right will be determined in accordance with section 360B(2) (traded companies: share dealings before general meetings);

  (c) a statement of the procedures with which members must comply in order to be able to attend and vote at the meeting (including the date by which they must comply);

  (d) a statement giving details of any forms to be used for the appointment of a proxy;

  (e) where the company offers the facility for members to vote in advance (see section 322A) or by electronic means (see section 360A), a statement of the procedure for doing so (including the date by which it must be done, and details of any forms to be used); and

**13.311.01**

---

[116] Companies Act 2006 (Commencement No 3, etc) Order 2007, S1 2007/2194, art 2(1). For the transitional provisions, see Sch 3, para 26 to this Commencement Order.

[117] See also the explanatory notes to Companies Act 2006 at para 762, stating that the auditor must receive all communications relating to general meetings.

(f)   a statement of the right of members to ask questions in accordance with section 319A (traded companies: questions at meetings).][b]

AMENDMENTS

[a] Substituted by the Companies (Shareholders' Rights) Regulations 2009, SI 2009/1632, reg 10(2), with effect from 3 August 2009 in relation to meetings of which notice is given, or first given, on or after that date.

[b] Inserted by the Companies (Shareholders' Rights) Regulations 2009, SI 2009/1632, reg 10(3), with effect from 3 August 2009 in relation to meetings of which notice is given, or first given, on or after that date.

COMMENCEMENT DATE 1 October 2007[118]

**13.311.02**   This gives statutory effect to part of regulation 38 of the 1985 Table A. As is apparent from subsection (2), the requirement for the notice to state the general nature of the business to be dealt with at the meeting is subject to any provision of the company's articles.

**13.311.03**   The notice must be a fair and sufficiently informative statement of the business to be conducted. In addition to the matters specified in this section, the notice must contain a statement of the rights to appoint a proxy: section 325 of the Companies Act 2006. Further, if a special resolution is to be proposed at the meeting, the notice must also include the text of the resolution and specify the intention to propose it as a special resolution: section 283(6) of the Companies Act 2006. If the notice contains an electronic address for the company, then the company is thereby deemed to have agreed that any document or information relating to proceedings at the meeting may be sent by electronic means to that address (subject to any limitations or conditions specified in the notice): section 333 of the Companies Act 2006.

**13.311.04**   Additional information is required to be given in advance of general meetings of traded companies, and the requirements of section 311A below must also be complied with. For an explanation of 'traded' companies, see section 360C: a 'traded' company is a company any shares of which carry rights to vote at general meetings and are admitted to trading on a regulated market in an EEA State by or with the consent of the company.

### [311A  Traded companies: publication of information in advance of general meeting

**13.311A.01**

(1)   A traded company must ensure that the following information relating to a general meeting of the company is made available on a website—
   (a)   the matters set out in the notice of the meeting;
   (b)   the total numbers of—
      (i)   shares in the company, and
      (ii)   shares of each class,
      in respect of which members are entitled to exercise voting rights at the meeting;
   (c)   the totals of the voting rights that members are entitled to exercise at the meeting in respect of the shares of each class;
   (d)   members' statements, members' resolutions and members' matters of business received by the company after the first date on which notice of the meeting is given.
(2)   The information must be made available on a website that—
   (a)   is maintained by or on behalf of the company, and
   (b)   identifies the company.
(3)   Access to the information on the website, and the ability to obtain a hard copy of the information from the website, must not be conditional on payment of a fee or otherwise restricted.
(4)   The information—
   (a)   must be made available—
      (i)   in the case of information required by subsection (1)(a) to (c), on or before the first date on which notice of the meeting is given, and
      (ii)   in the case of information required by subsection (1)(d), as soon as reasonably practicable, and
   (b)   must be kept available throughout the period of two years beginning with the date on which it is first made available on a website in accordance with this section.
(5)   A failure to make information available throughout the period specified in subsection (4)(b) is disregarded if—
   (a)   the information is made available on the website for part of that period, and
   (b)   the failure is wholly attributable to circumstances that it would not be reasonable to have expected the company to prevent or avoid.

---

[118] Companies Act 2006 (Commencement No 3, etc) Order 2007, SI 2007/2194, art 2(1). For the transitional provisions, see Sch 3, para 26 to this Commencement Order.

(6)  The amounts mentioned in subsection (1)(b) and (c) must be ascertained at the latest practicable time before the first date on which notice of the meeting is given.

(7)  Failure to comply with this section does not affect the validity of the meeting or of anything done at the meeting.

(8)  If this section is not complied with as respects any meeting, an offence is committed by every officer of the company who is in default.

(9)  A person guilty of an offence under this section is liable on summary conviction to a fine not exceeding level 3 on the standard scale.][a]

AMENDMENTS

[a]  Inserted by the Companies (Shareholders' Rights) Regulations 2009, SI 2009/1632, reg 11, with effect from 3 August 2009 in relation to meetings of which notice is given, or first given, on or after that date.

COMMENCEMENT DATE  3 August 2009

This section sets out certain information which must be published by a traded company in advance of a general meeting. For an explanation of 'traded' companies, see section 360C: a 'traded' company is a company any shares of which carry rights to vote at general meetings and are admitted to trading on a regulated market in an EEA State by or with the consent of the company.                    **13.311A.02**

## 312  Resolution requiring special notice

(1)  Where by any provision of the Companies Acts special notice is required of a resolution, the resolution is not effective unless notice of the intention to move it has been given to the company at least 28 days before the meeting at which it is moved.          **13.312.01**

(2)  The company must, where practicable, give its members notice of any such resolution in the same manner and at the same time as it gives notice of the meeting.

(3)  Where that is not practicable, the company must give its members notice at least 14 days before the meeting—
  (a)  by advertisement in a newspaper having an appropriate circulation, or
  (b)  in any other manner allowed by the company's articles.

(4)  If, after notice of the intention to move such a resolution has been given to the company, a meeting is called for a date 28 days or less after the notice has been given, the notice is deemed to have been properly given, though not given within the time required.

COMMENCEMENT DATE  1 October 2007[119]

This repeats the provision formerly in section 379 of the Companies Act 1985, with one change in that the notice period under subsection (3) is 14 days whereas formerly it was 21 days. 'At least 14 days' and 'at least 28 days' means clear days, ie both the day on which the notice is given and the day of the meeting are to be excluded: see section 360 of the Companies Act 2006.          **13.312.02**

The resolutions of which special notice is required, and thus to which this section applies, are resolutions (i) to remove a director (section 168), (ii) to remove an auditor (section 511), and (iii) in relation to failure to re-appoint an auditor (section 515). The section deals only with special notice to be given in relation to such a resolution which is to be passed at a meeting, because such resolutions under sections 168, 511, and 515 can only be passed at a meeting. A resolution under section 514 is a written resolution, but has its own particular procedural requirements.          **13.312.03**

## 313  Accidental failure to give notice of resolution or meeting

(1)  Where a company gives notice of—          **13.313.01**
  (a)  a general meeting, or
  (b)  a resolution intended to be moved at a general meeting,
  any accidental failure to give notice to one or more persons shall be disregarded for the purpose of determining whether notice of the meeting or resolution (as the case may be) is duly given.

(2)  Except in relation to notice given under—
  (a)  section 304 (notice of meetings required by members),
  (b)  section 305 (notice of meetings called by members), or
  (c)  section 339 (notice of resolutions at AGMs proposed by members),
  subsection (1) has effect subject to any provision of the company's articles.

COMMENCEMENT DATE  1 October 2007[120]

---

[119]  Companies Act 2006 (Commencement No 3, etc) Order 2007, SI 2007/2194, art 2(1). For the transitional provisions, see Sch 3, para 27 to this Commencement Order.

[120]  Companies Act 2006 (Commencement No 3, etc) Order 2007, SI 2007/2194, art 2(1). For the transitional provisions, see Sch 3, para 28 to this Commencement Order.

**13.313.02**    This is based on regulation 39 of the 1985 Table A, with expansion. It is to be noted that although subsection (2) permits a company to make different provision in its articles, it cannot do so in the three cases identified in subsections (2)(a) to (c). The section can be relied upon only if the failure to give notice is 'accidental'; a deliberate failure to give notice to a member will not be saved by this section, even if the failure arose from a mistaken belief that the member was not entitled to notice.

**13.313.03**    Thus in *Re West Canadian Collieries Ltd*,[121] the court held that a meeting had been properly held and a resolution for a reduction of capital properly passed in circumstances where notices sent to share-holders were posted by means of the members' addresses being affixed by the use of plates on an 'Addressograph' machine. The plates for nine members had some time before been extracted and stored separately, as communications to those members had previously been returned and the company did not want to send future dividend warrants to addresses which might no longer be valid in case the warrants went astray, and in sending out the notices of the meeting to approve the reduction of capital, the plates for the nine members were inadvertently not put back and therefore notices were not sent to them. In contrast, in *Musselwhite v G H Musselwhite & Son Ltd*[122] a meeting could not be saved by a provision in similar terms to section 313, where the directors did not give notice to certain members because they erroneously thought the members were not entitled to notice as they had executed transfers of their shares under an agreement for sale, even though the transfers had not yet been registered and accordingly the register still showed the members as the holders of the shares.

## Members' statements

### 314  Members' power to require circulation of statements

**13.314.01**        (1)  The members of a company may require the company to circulate, to members of the company entitled to receive notice of a general meeting, a statement of not more than 1,000 words with respect to—
            (a)  a matter referred to in a proposed resolution to be dealt with at that meeting, or
            (b)  other business to be dealt with at that meeting.
        (2)  A company is required to circulate a statement once it has received requests to do so from—
            (a)  members representing at least 5% of the total voting rights of all the members who have a relevant right to vote (excluding any voting rights attached to any shares in the company held as treasury shares), or
            (b)  at least 100 members who have a relevant right to vote and hold shares in the company on which there has been paid up an average sum, per member, of at least £100.
            See also section 153 (exercise of rights where shares held on behalf of others).
        (3)  In subsection (2), a 'relevant right to vote' means—
            (a)  in relation to a statement with respect to a matter referred to in a proposed resolution, a right to vote on that resolution at the meeting to which the requests relate, and
            (b)  in relation to any other statement, a right to vote at the meeting to which the requests relate.
        (4)  A request—
            (a)  may be in hard copy form or in electronic form,
            (b)  must identify the statement to be circulated,
            (c)  must be authenticated by the person or persons making it, and
            (d)  must be received by the company at least one week before the meeting to which it relates.
        COMMENCEMENT DATE  1 October 2007[123]

**13.314.02**    Sections 314 to 317 replaced and expanded the provisions of the Companies Act 1985, sections 376 and 377 to the extent that they dealt with the circulation of members' statements. The circulation of resolutions requisitioned by members (which was also covered in sections 376 and 377 of the Companies Act 1985) is dealt with in sections 290 to 295 of the Act. These provisions apply to requests for the circulation of statements made on or after 1 October 2007. When the relevant requests were made on more than one day, the relevant date is that on which sufficient requests have been made so as to require the company to act.[124]

**13.314.03**    Section 314(1) and (2) is, with one exception, in materially the same terms as section 376(1)(b) and (2) respectively and allows the members of a company to require that company to circulate, in advance of

---

    [121] [1962] Ch 370. For a more recent example, see *Re Halcrow Holdings Ltd* [2011] EWHC 3662 (Ch).
    [122] [1962] Ch 964. On a different aspect of the decision, *Musselwhite v G H Musselwhite & Son Ltd* must be read subject to the explanation given of it in *Michaels v Harley House (Marylebone) Ltd* [2000] Ch 104, but this does not affect its applicability to s 313.
    [123] Companies Act 2006 (Commencement No 3, etc) Order 2007, SI 2007/2194, art 2(1). For the transitional provisions, see Sch 3, para 29 to this Order.
    [124] Ibid.

a meeting of the company, a statement of not more than 1,000 words relating either to a matter referred to in a proposed resolution or to the other business of the meeting. Subsections (2) and (3) provide that, in order to be included as a member for the purposes of requesting the circulation of a statement, the relevant member must, where the statement refers to matters in a proposed resolution, have a right to vote in respect of that proposed resolution or, in other cases, the right to vote at the meeting generally. Previously, where the requisitioning members numbered more than 100 with the requisite shareholdings there was no requirement that those members have any right to vote at the meeting.[125] Further where the requisitioning members amounted to 5 per cent or more they only had to have the right to vote at the meeting to which the statement related rather than, as now, in relation to any specific resolution.[126] If a company's shares are denominated in a currency other than sterling[127] the question of whether a member satisfies the criteria in subsection (2)(b) will be determined by reference to the most practical date and rate of exchange.[128]

Section 314(4) expands upon the procedural requirements for a members' request. As before, the **13.314.04** request must be received by the company at least one week before the meeting to which it relates.[129] This period remains a very short one and the provision of a request so close to a meeting is likely to cause significant practical difficulties if an application is made under section 324 below. However the request now does not have to be signed by the requesting members but authenticated and it may be in electronic form as well as hard copy.[130] Previously where members had a joint shareholding all of them must have signed the requisition but this authority will now be subject to the new requirement of authentication.[131]

As regards public companies and those which have their registered office in a Member State and which **13.314.05** are traded on a regulated market situated or operating within a Member State, reference should be made to sections 338 to 340 below and to the amendments to CA 2006 necessitated by the Shareholder Rights Directive (Directive 2007/36). The Directive was the subject of a consultation by BERR in 2008 and was implemented by the Companies (Shareholders' Rights) Regulations (SI 2009/1632) which came into force on 3 August 2009.

## 315  Company's duty to circulate members' statement

   (1)  A company that is required under section 314, to circulate a statement must send a copy of it to **13.315.01** each member of the company entitled to receive notice of the meeting—
      (a)  in the same manner as the notice of the meeting, and
      (b)  at the same time as, or as soon as reasonably practicable after, it gives notice of the meeting.
   (2)  Subsection (1) has effect subject to section 316(2) (deposit or tender of sum in respect of expenses of circulation) and section 317 (application not to circulate members' statement).
   (3)  In the event of default in complying with this section, an offence is committed by every officer of the company who is in default.
   (4)  A person guilty of an offence under this section is liable—
      (a)  on conviction on indictment, to a fine;
      (b)  on summary conviction, to a fine not exceeding the statutory maximum

COMMENCEMENT DATE 1 October 2007[132]

Section 315 is in materially the same terms as the Companies Act, 1985 section 376(3), (5), and (7). It **13.315.02** makes it clear that the members' statement must, if practicable, be circulated at the same time and in the same manner as the notice of the meeting. Failure to circulate a members' statement remains an offence for every officer of the company who is in default.[133] Under subsection (2) the duty of the company is subject to the exceptions set out in section 316(2) and 317.

---

[125]  CA 1985, s 376(2)(b).
[126]  CA 1985, s 376(2)(a).
[127]  As permitted by s 542(3).
[128]  *Obiter* in *Re Scandinavian Bank Group Plc* [1988] Ch 87 at 104 citing *In re Simo Securities Trust Limited* [1971] 1 WLR 1455.
[129]  CA 1985, s 377(1)(a).
[130]  Compare s 321(4)(a) and (c) with CA 1985, s 377(1)(a).
[131]  *Patent Wood Keg Syndicate Ltd v Pearse* [1906] WN 164.
[132]  Companies Act 2006 (Commencement No 3, etc) Order 2007, SI 2007/2194, art 2(1). For the transitional provisions, see Sch 3, para 29 to this Order.
[133]  CA, s 315(3) and (4). Officer in default is defined in ss 1121–1122.

### 316  Expenses of circulating members' statement

**13.316.01**

(1) The expenses of the company in complying with section 315 need not be paid by the members who requested the circulation of the statement if—

    (a) the meeting to which the requests relate is an annual general meeting of a public company, and

    (b) requests sufficient to require the company to circulate the statement are received before the end of the financial year preceding the meeting.

(2) Otherwise—

    (a) the expenses of the company in complying with that section must be paid by the members who requested the circulation of the statement unless the company resolves otherwise, and

    (b) unless the company has previously so resolved, it is not bound to comply with that section unless there is deposited with or tendered to it, not later than one week before the meeting, a sum reasonably sufficient to meet its expenses in doing so.

COMMENCEMENT DATE 1 October 2007[134]

**13.316.02**  Section 316 replaced section 377 of the Companies Act 1985 and expands upon the previous position that the circulation of a members' statement would, unless the company resolved otherwise, be at the expense of the requisitioning members.[135] In the most significant change made to the old law, the requisitioning members need not now pay the expenses if the relevant meeting is an AGM of a public company and the requisition is received by the company before the end of the financial year preceding the meeting (subsection (1)). If these conditions are not satisfied the old position continues to apply and the requesting members must pay unless the company resolves otherwise (subsection (2)(a)). Further, as before, a company is not obliged to circulate a members' statement unless a sum reasonably sufficient to meet its expenses of circulation is deposited with or tendered to it or the company has resolved otherwise.[136] However, the sum now only has to be tendered not later than one week before the meeting to which it relates rather than with the requisition.[137] The provision does not identify how the reasonable amount is to be ascertained.

### 317  Application not to circulate members' statement

**13.317.01**

(1) A company is not required to circulate a members' statement under section 315 if, on an application by the company or another person who claims to be aggrieved, the court is satisfied that the rights conferred by section 314 and that section are being abused.

(2) The court may order the members who requested the circulation of the statement to pay the whole or part of the company's costs (in Scotland, expenses) on such an application, even if they are not parties to the application.

COMMENCEMENT DATE 1 October 2007[138]

**13.317.02**  Section 317 replaced section 377(3) of the Companies Act 1985. It expands upon the second exception to the obligation of the company to circulate a members' statement created by that section, namely the power of the court to prevent the abuse by members of their rights to require the circulation of a members' statement. Under subsection (1) (and in contrast to the position under the Companies Act 1985)[139] the power of the court is not limited to circumstances where the rights are being abused to secure needless publicity for defamatory material, but is a general one to prevent the abuse of rights otherwise provided. It is likely that the courts will be slow to interfere with the exercise of members' rights, but the expanded exception may now cover matters such as statements the purpose of which is to ventilate or continue disputes between members or where the statement repeats matters which have been raised and dealt with at previous meetings. The purpose for which a member requests the circulation of a statement is therefore likely to be particularly relevant to the determination of whether or not it is an abuse of the right to require such circulation. The requesting member or members also remain potentially liable for the company's costs on such an application even if they are not parties to that application (subsection (2)).[140]

---

[134] Companies Act 2006 (Commencement No 3, etc) Order 2007, SI 2007/2194, art 2(1). For the transitional provisions, see Sch 3, para 29 to this Order.

[135] CA 1985, s 376(1).

[136] CA 1985, s 377(1)(b).

[137] Compare s 316(2)(b) with CA 1985, s 377(1)(b).

[138] Companies Act 2006 (Commencement No 3, etc) Order 2007, SI 2007/2194, art 2(1). For the transitional provisions, see Sch 3, para 29 to this Order.

[139] See CA 1985, s 324(1).

[140] CA 1985, s 324(2).

## *Procedure at meetings*

### 318  Quorum at meetings

(1)  In the case of a company limited by shares or guarantee and having only one member, one qualifying person present at a meeting is a quorum.

(2)  In any other case, subject to the provisions of the company's articles, two qualifying persons present at a meeting are a quorum, unless—

    (a)  each is a qualifying person only because he is authorised under section 323 to act as the representative of a corporation in relation to the meeting, and they are representatives of the same corporation; or

    (b)  each is a qualifying person only because he is appointed as proxy of a member in relation to the meeting, and they are proxies of the same member.

(3)  For the purposes of this section a 'qualifying person' means—

    (a)  an individual who is a member of the company,

    (b)  a person authorised under section 323 (representation of corporations at meetings) to act as the representative of a corporation in relation to the meeting, or

    (c)  a person appointed as proxy of a member in relation to the meeting.

**13.318.01**

COMMENCEMENT DATE 1 October 2007[141]

Section 318 replaced the provisions in relation to the quorum at company meetings previously found in sections 370(4) and 370A of the Companies Act 1985. It applies to meetings of which notice is given on or after 1 October 2007. When notice is given over more than one day, the relevant day is the first on which notice is given.[142]   **13.318.02**

Subsection (1) replaced and repeated in all material terms section 370A of the Companies Act 1985 in relation to single member private companies. A quorum is constituted by one qualifying person being present. Such a person is either the individual member, a proxy for such member, or a person authorized to act as the representative of a corporate member, as defined in subsection (3).   **13.318.03**

Subsection (2) replaced the provisions of section 370(4) of the Companies Act 1985. Whereas previously two members personally present constituted a quorum, now a quorum is constituted by two qualifying persons, which will include members personally present but is not so limited. Thus proxies and representatives of corporate members can count towards the quorum whereas previously they could not. The new provisions are (as with the old law)[143] expressly subject to any provision of the company's articles.[144] A quorum cannot be constituted by two persons acting as representative of the same corporate member or as proxy for the same member. In order for a meeting to transact business validly it has previously been held that there must be at least two members present throughout[145] but that, otherwise, if the meeting falls below the quorum (if set higher than two by the articles of association) the business transacted at the meeting is valid.[146] Paragraph 38 of the model private company articles and paragraph 30 of the model public company articles (as to which see Chapter 51) each appear to envisage that an inquorate meeting may appoint a chairman of the meeting but may transact no other business.   **13.318.04**

Subsection (3) defines the concept of a 'qualifying person'. Member is defined in section 112 of the Act.   **13.318.05**

### 319  Chairman of meeting

(1)  A member may be elected to be the chairman of a general meeting by a resolution of the company passed at the meeting.

**13.319.01**

---

[141]  Companies Act 2006 (Commencement No 3, etc) Order 2007, SI 2007/2194, art 2(1). For the transitional provisions, see Sch 3, para 30 of this Order.

[142]  Ibid.

[143]  CA 1985, s 370(1)

[144]  Regulation 40 of 1985 Table A (as amended by the Companies (Tables A to F) (Amendment) Regulations 2007) provides that, save in the case of a company with a single member, two persons entitled to vote constitute a quorum. The model private company articles and model public company articles contain no equivalent provisions as to quorum requirements for general meetings.

[145]  *Re London Flats Ltd* [1969] 1 WLR 711, a decision based on the premise that it is not possible to have a meeting of one person. Thus where one of the two members attending a meeting left, the resolution passed thereafter was not valid.

[146]  *Re Hartley Baird Ltd* [1955] Ch 143 in which the quorum requirement of 10 was satisfied but during the meeting the number of members present dropped to 9. Regulation 34 referred to in n 2 above provides that the quorum must be 'participating' for the meeting to be quorate and is entitled 'Quorum must participate'. The wording of this provision and in particular the use of the word 'participating' suggests that the meeting must remain quorate throughout and that there has been a change to the law.

(2)  Subsection (1) is subject to any provision of the company's articles that states who may or may not be chairman.

COMMENCEMENT DATE 1 October 2007[147]

**13.319.02**  Section 319 replaced section 370(5) of the Companies Act 1985. Subject to any provision in the company's articles[148] (subsection (2)), any member may be elected as chairman[149] of the meeting by an ordinary resolution of the company. This is intended to be a default provision.

**13.319.03**  The right to be chairman is not extended by this section to a 'qualifying person' (which includes a proxy or corporate representative). However, section 328 separately provides that, subject to any provision in the company's articles, a proxy can be elected as chairman by a resolution of the meeting. Further, section 323 provides that a corporate representative is entitled to exercise all the rights of the corporation as it if were an individual member. Thus it appears that, subject to the provisions of the company's articles, every qualifying person may be elected as chairman. It is regrettable that this is not made clear in the section of the Act dealing with the appointment of a chairman. Similar issues arise with the provisions relating to a demand for a poll.

**13.319.04**  The model private company articles (in Chapter 51) make express provision for the appointment of the chairman of general meetings. Paragraph 39 provides for a range of methods of appointment. In the first instance, under subparagraph (1), if the directors have appointed a chairman that person shall, if present and willing, chair general meetings. Under subparagraph (2), if the chairman appointed by the director is not present within 10 minutes of the start time for the meeting or is unwilling to chair the meeting, then the directors, or if no directors are present, the meeting itself, shall appoint a director or shareholder to chair the meeting. The model public company articles provide, in paragraph 31, for the same methods of appointment. These provisions do not appear to allow for either a proxy holder or a corporate representative to act as chairman as neither would be a shareholder.

**13.319.05**  Paragraph 38 of the model private company articles and paragraph 30 of the model public company articles (in Chapter 52) each provides that the only business which may be transacted at an inquorate meeting is the appointment of a chairman.

## [319A  Traded companies: questions at meetings

**13.319A.01**  (1)  At a general meeting of a traded company, the company must cause to be answered any question relating to the business being dealt with at the meeting put by a member attending the meeting.
(2)  No such answer need be given—
    (a)  if to do so would—
        (i)   interfere unduly with the preparation for the meeting, or
        (ii)  involve the disclosure of confidential information;
    (b)  if the answer has already been given on a website in the form of an answer to a question; or
    (c)  if it is undesirable in the interests of the company or the good order of the meeting that the question be answered.][a]

AMENDMENTS

[a]  Inserted by the Companies (Shareholders' Rights) Regulations 2009, reg 12.

COMMENCEMENT DATE 3 August 2009[150]

**13.319A.02**  This section, which was inserted by reg 12 of the Companies (Shareholders' Rights) Regulations 2009, implements article 9 of the Shareholder Rights Directive requiring a traded company to answer any question put by a member at a general meeting and relating to the business being dealt with at the meeting unless (a) to do so would (i) interfere unduly with the preparation for the meeting or (ii) involve the disclosure of confidential information; (b) the answer has already been given on a website

---

[147]  Companies Act 2006 (Commencement No 3, etc) Order 2007, S1 2007/2194, art 2(1).
[148]  Regulations 42 and 43 of 1985 Table A provide different provisions for the chairmanship of general meetings.
[149]  The position of chairman is an important one as it is for the chairman to conduct the proceedings at the meeting subject to the overriding consent of those present at the meeting. The duties of the chairman include keeping order, controlling the debate on the business at the meeting (including curtailing it if necessary) to ensure that the interested parties are given a fair opportunity to be heard, putting the resolutions to the meeting, and determining the process and result of votes (whether by show of hands or poll). For an example of the chairman's duty to allow the minority to be heard and his right to bring the discussion to an end to allow a vote to take place see *Wall v London and Northern Assets Corporation* [1898] 2 Ch 469.
[150]  The Companies (Shareholders' Rights) Regulations 2009, reg 1(2).

in the form of an answer to a question; (c) it is undesirable in the interests of the company of the good order of the meeting. It applies to meetings for which notice is given, or first given, on or after 3 August 2009.[151]

## 320  Declaration by chairman on a show of hands

(1)  On a vote on a resolution at a meeting on a show of hands, a declaration by the chairman that the resolution—                                                                                                  **13.320.01**
  (a)  has or has not been passed, or
  (b)  passed with a particular majority,
  is conclusive evidence of that fact without proof of the number or proportion of the votes recorded in favour of or against the resolution.
(2)  An entry in respect of such a declaration in minutes of the meeting recorded in accordance with section 355 is also conclusive evidence of that fact without such proof.
(3)  This section does not have effect if a poll is demanded in respect of the resolution (and the demand is not subsequently withdrawn).

COMMENCEMENT DATE 1 October 2007[152]

Section 320 replaced section 378(4)[153] of the Companies Act 1985 and enacted into primary legislation    **13.320.02**
provisions previously contained in Regulation 47[154] of Table A. It provides that a declaration by a chairman as to the result of a vote taken by a show of hands is conclusive evidence of that fact without further proof unless a poll is demanded and that demand is not subsequently withdrawn (subsection (3)). Previously the deeming provision in relation to special and extraordinary resolutions did not apply where a demand for a poll was made even if that demand was subsequently withdrawn. Subsection (2) is drawn from Regulation 47 (there was no equivalent provision in section 378(4)) and affords the company even greater certainty by providing that a record[155] of the chairman's declaration in the minutes of the meeting is also conclusive evidence. This provision is subject to demonstrating that the chairman's declaration is tainted by fraud.[156] It has also been held not to apply where there is a manifest error on the face of the chairman's declaration.[157] At the Standing Committee stage, the Government recognized the common law obligation of the chairman of the meeting to call a poll if he considered that a different result would be obtained than under the show of hands, but suggested that there was no consensus that this obligation needed to be codified. Paragraph 42 of the model private company articles and paragraph 34 of the model public company articles (in Chapter 52) each provide that a resolution put to a vote at a general meeting must be decided on a show of hands unless a poll is duly demanded in accordance with the articles.

This provision can be contrasted with amendments made to section 341 of CA 2006 by reg 20 of the    **13.320.03**
Companies (Shareholders' Rights) Regulations 2009 to implement article 14 of the Shareholder Rights Directive, which requires the result of a vote taken on a poll and details of the constituent parts of that result to be published by a traded company.

---

[151] The Companies (Shareholders' Rights) Regulations 2009, reg 1(2).
[152] Companies Act 2006 (Commencement No 3, etc) Order 2007, SI 2007/2194, art 2(1). For the transitional provisions, see Sch 3, para 29 to this Order.
[153] This provision dealt with extraordinary or special resolutions.
[154] This provision dealt with all resolutions. Neither the Plc articles nor the private company articles contain any provisions relating to this topic.
[155] S 355 of the Act sets out a company's record-keeping obligations.
[156] *Re Hadleigh Castle Gold Mines Ltd* [1900] 2 Ch 419, in which Cozens-Hardy J disagreed with an earlier decision of Kekewich J in *Young v South African and Australian Exploration and Development Syndicate* [1896] 2 Ch 268, is cited as authority for this principle and the head-note supports this. However, the judgment does not contain reasoning on this point which appears only to have been raised in argument. The case did not concern allegations of fraud. Similar points apply to *Arnot v United African Lands Ltd* [1901] 1 Ch 518 in which *Re Hadleigh* was approved. See instead *Kerr v John Mottram Ltd* [1940] Ch 657 for an authority dealing expressly with the exception for fraud.
[157] In *re Caratal (New) Mines Ltd* [1902] 2 Ch 498 the chairman said, following a poll, that the resolution had been passed by virtue of 200 votes given in favour of the resolution by proxy. Of the members voting in person, the totals were 23 against and only 6 for. The votes by proxy should not have been admitted and the court held that the resolution had not been passed as the declaration contained a mistake on its face. Where the minutes of a meeting contained a reference to the notice of the meeting having been read the court was entitled to look at the notice to see whether the decision of the meeting was legitimate notwithstanding a provision in the articles of the company deeming them conclusive: *Betts & Co Ltd v MacNaughton* [1910] 1 Ch 430.

### 321  Right to demand a poll

**13.321.01**

(1)  A provision of a company's articles is void in so far as it would have the effect of excluding the right to demand a poll at a general meeting on any question other than—

    (a)  the election of the chairman of the meeting, or

    (b)  the adjournment of the meeting.

(2)  A provision of a company's articles is void in so far as it would have the effect of making ineffective a demand for a poll on any such question which is made—

    (a)  by not less than 5 members having the right to vote on the resolution; or

    (b)  by a member or members representing not less than 10% of the total voting rights of all the members having the right to vote on the resolution (excluding any voting rights attached to any shares in the company held as treasury shares); or

    (c)  by a member or members holding shares in the company conferring a right to vote on the resolution, being shares on which an aggregate sum has been paid up equal to not less than 10% of the total sum paid up on all the shares conferring that right (excluding shares in the company conferring a right to vote on the resolution which are held as treasury shares).

COMMENCEMENT DATE 1 October 2007[158]

**13.321.02**  Section 321 replaced section 373 of the Companies Act 1985. A company's articles cannot remove or qualify the right to demand a poll on questions other than the election of chairman of the meeting or the adjournment of the meeting.[159] It might have been better for the provisions expressly to create a right to demand such a poll rather than leaving such a right as a common law right. However, at the Standing Committee stage it was made clear that Part 13 of the Act was not a comprehensive code for meetings which would remain subject also to common law rules and would allow flexibility for companies to deal with meeting in their articles. As to this, most companies' articles provide more generous rights in relation to the demand of a poll.[160] and, indeed, paragraph 44 of the model private company articles and paragraph 36 of the model public company articles (in Chapter 52) provide broad rights to demand a poll on any resolution.

**13.321.03**  Subsection (2) does not adopt the concept of the qualifying person in setting out the requirements for a demand for a poll. However, section 329 separately provides that a person holding a proxy is entitled to demand a poll whilst section 323(2) provides that a representative of a corporate member has all the powers as if the corporation were an individual member. Thus a proxy or corporate representative also counts towards the requirements of subsections (2)(a) to (c). It would have been clearer if these provisions had been included or at least cross-referred to in section 321(2).[161]

**13.321.04**  The Act does not provide any right to withdraw a demand for a poll. However, this is usually provided by the articles of association and such a provision is made in paragraphs 44(3) and 36(3) of the model private company articles and model public company articles respectively (for which see Chapter 52).[162] Further, subject to the company's articles, the procedure on a poll is generally to be determined by the chairman of the meeting.[163]

---

[158]  Companies Act 2006 (Commencement No 3, etc) Order 2007, SI 2007/2194, art 2(1). For the transitional provisions, see Sch 3, para 29 to this Order.

[159]  Regulations 46 and 51 of 1985 Table A provide for a poll on these issues as well as all others. The model private company articles and model public company articles each provide for a poll on any resolution. The failure to take a poll after one has been properly demanded renders the resolution subject to the demand invalid: *R v Cooper* (1870) LR 5 QB 457.

[160]  Regulation 46 of 1985 Table A provides for a poll on the demand of (i) the chairman, (ii) at least two members having a right to vote, (iii) by a member or members representing not less than one-tenth of the total voting rights of all members, or (iv) a member or members holding shares on which the aggregate sum paid up is not less than one-tenth of the total sum paid up on all shares. Paragraph 44(2) of the model private company articles and para 36(2) of the model public company articles each repeats points (i), (ii), and (iii). In addition, they provide for a poll to be demanded by the directors at the meeting. Each of the methods by which a poll can be demanded can be invoked either in advance of the general meeting or at the meeting either before a show of hands or immediately after the result of a show of hands is declared.

[161]  CA 1985 contained an express provision in s 373(2) for the inclusion of proxies in such calculations.

[162]  It is also provided by reg 48 of 1985 Table A.

[163]  Regulations 49–52 of 1985 Table A and now para 44(4) of the model private company articles. Section 37 of the model public company articles sets out a more detailed procedure for a poll. See Chapter 52 for the model articles.

### 322  Voting on a poll

> On a poll taken at a general meeting of a company, a member entitled to more than one vote need not, if he votes, use all his votes or cast all the votes he uses in the same way.

　　**13.322.01**

COMMENCEMENT DATE  1 October 2007[164]

Section 322 replaced section 374 of the Companies Act 1985 in relation to meetings of the company.[165]  This section recognizes (as did its predecessors) that a shareholder may act in more than one capacity. For example, a trust corporation may hold shares for more than one person and may receive different instructions as to how to vote the shares held on behalf of its various beneficiaries.

　　**13.322.02**

### [322A  Voting on a poll: votes cast in advance

> (1)  A company's articles may contain provision to the effect that on a vote on a resolution on a poll taken at a meeting, the votes may include votes cast in advance.
> (2)  In the case of a traded company any such provision in relation to voting at a general meeting may be made subject only to such requirements and restrictions as are—
>    (a)  necessary to ensure the identification of the person voting, and
>    (b)  proportionate to the achievement of that objective.
>    Nothing in this subsection affects any power of a company to require reasonable evidence of the entitlement of any person who is not a member to vote.
> (3)  Any provision of a company's articles is void in so far as it would have the effect of requiring any document casting a vote in advance to be received by the company or another person earlier than the following time—
>    (a)  in the case of a poll taken more than 48 hours after it was demanded, 24 hours before the time appointed for the taking of the poll;
>    (b)  in the case of any other poll, 48 hours before the time for holding the meeting or adjourned meeting.
> (4)  In calculating the periods mentioned in subsection (3), no account is to be taken of any part of a day that is not a working day.][a]

　　**13.322A.01**

AMENDMENTS

[a]  Inserted by the Companies (Shareholders' Rights) Regulations 2009, reg 5.

COMMENCEMENT DATE  3 August 2009[166]

This section, which was added by regulation 5 of the Companies (Shareholders' Rights) Regulations 2009, implements article 12 of the Shareholder Rights Directive (voting by correspondence). It allows a company's articles to include provision that, on a vote on a resolution on a poll taken at a meeting, the votes may include votes cast in advance. Further, in the case of traded companies any such provision may only be subject to such requirements and restrictions as are necessary to ensure the identification of the person voting and are proportionate to that objective. Companies will also be subject to restrictions on the time they can fix for receipt of any document casting a vote in advance.

　　**13.322A.02**

### 323  Representation of corporations at meetings

> (1)  If a corporation (whether or not a company within the meaning of this Act) is a member of a company, it may by resolution of its directors or other governing body authorise a person or persons to act as its representative or representatives at any meeting of the company.
> [(2)  A person authorised by a corporation is entitled to exercise (on behalf of the corporation) the same powers as the corporation could exercise if it were an individual member of the company. Where a corporation authorises more than one person, this subsection is subject to subsections (3) and (4).
> (3)  On a vote on a resolution on a show of hands at a meeting of the company, each authorised person has the same voting rights as the corporation would be entitled to.
> (4)  Where subsection (3) does not apply and more than one authorised person purport to exercise a power under subsection (2) in respect of the same shares—
>    (a)  if they purport to exercise the power in the same way as each other, the power is treated as exercised in that way;

　　**13.323.01**

---

[164]  Companies Act 2006 (Commencement No 3, etc) Order 2007, SI 2007/2194, art 2(1). For the transitional provisions, see Sch 3, para 29 to this Order.
[165]  For an explanation of the rationale behind s 108 of the CA 1948, the precursor of both this section and s 374 of CA 1985, see *Northern Counties Securities Ltd v Jackson and Steeple Ltd* [1974] 1 WLR 1133 at 1147. The provisions of s 374 of CA 1985 in relation to class meetings are covered in ss 334–335 of the Act.
[166]  The Companies (Shareholders' Rights) Regulations 2009, SI 2009/1632, reg 1(2).

(b) if they do not purport to exercise the power in the same way as each other, the power is treated as not exercised.]ᵃ

Amendments

ᵃ Inserted by the Companies (Shareholders' Rights) Regulations 2009, SI 2009/1632, reg 6.

Commencement Date Section 323(1): 1 October 2007[167] Section 323(2)–(4): 3 August 2009[168]

**13.323.02** Subsection (1) replaced section 375(1)(a) of the Companies Act 1985. A corporation is now entitled to appoint one or more persons to act as its representative at a meeting. The old provision referred only to the appointment of 'such person' in the singular and although this was interpreted as allowing the appointment of multiple representatives, section 375 made no provision for the effect of such appointments. The reference to 'other governing body' in relation to a company is retained but without any elucidation as to what is meant thereby given that the directors are expressly and separately referred to. It is suggested that it should be construed as a reference to a situation in which the directors are completely or partially divested of control such as liquidation[169] (where a liquidator will be in control) or administration (where an administrator will be in control).

**13.323.03** Subsections (2) to (4) were amended by regulation 6 of the Companies (Shareholders' Rights) Regulations 2009 which implements article 13.4 of the Shareholder Rights Directive (split votes by nominee shareholders).

**13.323.04** Subsection (2) in its original form repeated section 375(2) of the Companies Act 1985 save that the word 'member' was substituted for 'shareholder'. It made it clear that an authorized corporate representative could exercise all the powers the corporation could exercise if it were an individual member. The original subsection (3) was new and made the same provision for corporate representatives where a corporation appointed more than one. These provisions are now consolidated into one provision, subsection (2). Subject to subsections (3) and (4), all representatives of a corporate member have all powers as if that corporation were an individual member. These include such matters as the right to speak at a meeting, to vote on a show of hands, to demand a poll, and to act as chairman of the meeting. The provisions of the Act in relation to these matters need to be read accordingly. Previously appointment as a representative of a corporate member had advantages over appointment as a proxy, the latter being unable to speak at a meeting of a public company.[170] However, section 323 effectively (but somewhat obliquely) removes this distinction by providing that a member may appoint a proxy to exercise all of his rights as a member and attend, speak, and vote at a meeting of the company.

**13.323.05** The original subsection (4) was new and reflected the fact that, as referred to above, a corporate member could now expressly appoint more than one person as its representative. The amended subsections (3) and (4) make express provision for cases where a corporation authorizes more than one person.

**13.323.06** Pursuant to subsection (3) as amended, on a vote on a resolution on a show of hands at a meeting of the company, each authorized person has one vote if the corporation is entitled to vote on the resolution.

**13.323.07** Subsection (4) as amended provides the mechanism to deal with cases where there are multiple corporate representatives and they each purport to exercise a particular power. The amendments make it clear that these provisions only apply where the exercise of the power is *in respect of the same shares in the company*, the italicized words reflecting the material change. Where this requirement is satisfied, the subsection provides that the power is treated as exercised where the corporate representatives act in the same way, but as not exercised where the corporate representatives act in different ways.

*Proxies*

### 324 Rights to appoint proxies

**13.324.01**
    (1) A member of a company is entitled to appoint another person as his proxy to exercise all or any of his rights to attend and to speak and vote at a meeting of the company.

    (2) In the case of a company having a share capital, a member may appoint more than one proxy in relation to a meeting, provided that each proxy is appointed to exercise the rights attached to a

---

[167] The Companies Act 2006 (Commencement No 3, etc) Order 2007, SI 2007/2194, art 2(1). For the transitional provisions, see Sch 3, para 29 to this Order.

[168] The Companies (Shareholders' Rights) Regulations 2009, SI 2009/1632, reg 1(2).

[169] *Hillman v Crystal Bowl Amusements Ltd* [1973] 1 WLR 162 in which the court considered s 139 of CA 1948, the predecessor of s 375 of CA 1985. The liquidator may not fall within the definition of a 'governing body' if there is a creditors' committee in existence or the court has given directions to the liquidator inconsistent with the liquidator appointing himself as representative of a corporate member.

[170] CA 1985, s 372(1).

different share or shares held by him, or (as the case may be) to a different £10, or multiple of £10, of stock held by him.

COMMENCEMENT DATE  1 October 2007[171]

Sections 324 to 331 contain new provisions dealing with the appointment of proxies. These sections replace and considerably extend section 372 of the Companies Act 1985 and put on a statutory footing a number of matters that had been left to companies' articles. In doing so, they confer a minimum level of rights upon shareholders and proxies. It is always open to companies by their articles to confer more extensive rights.[172] As with the provisions at sections 318 to 323, the provisions at sections 324 to 331 apply to meetings of which notice is given on or after 1 October 2007. When notice is given over more than one day, the relevant day is the first on which notice is given.[173]    **13.324.02**

Under section 324(1), a member of any company is entitled to appoint another person[174] as a proxy to exercise all the member's rights to attend, speak, and vote at a meeting of the company. Under the Companies Act 1985, the statutory entitlement to appoint a proxy was limited to companies with share capital. Whether or not there was such a right for members of other companies depended upon the terms of the articles.    **13.324.03**

Section 324 also needs to be read together with sections 284(2) and 285(1) and (2), which provide new rules relating to voting by proxies on a show of hands. Proxies are entitled to vote on a resolution on a show of hands. Under the previous legislation they had no entitlement to do so unless the articles provided for it. The combined effect of sections 324, 284, and 285 is intended to be that the articles of a company can no longer disadvantage a member who votes by proxy.    **13.324.04**

Section 324(2) is a new provision entitling a member to appoint more than one proxy, provided that each proxy is appointed to exercise the rights attached to a different share (or shares of the member), or a different £10 (or multiple of £10) block of stock. This has to be read with sections 284(2) and 285(2), both of which have been amended by the Companies (Shareholders' Rights) Regulations 2009 with reference to meetings of which notice is given, or first given, on or after 3 August 2009.    **13.324.05**

## [324A  Obligation of proxy to vote in accordance with instructions

A proxy must act in accordance with any instructions given by the member by whom the proxy is appointed.][a]    **13.324A.01**

AMENDMENTS
[a]  Inserted by the Companies (Shareholders' Rights) Regulations 2009, SI 2009/1632, reg 7.

COMMENCEMENT DATE  3 August 2009[175]

This section requiring a proxy to act in accordance with the appointing member's instructions was inserted by the Companies (Shareholders' Rights) Regulations 2009 (implementing the EU Shareholder Rights Directive (2007/36/EC)), which came into force on 3 August 2009 and applies in relation to meetings of which notice is given, or first given, on or after that date.    **13.324A.02**

## 325  Notice of meeting to contain statement of rights

(1)  In every notice calling a meeting of a company there must appear, with reasonable prominence, a statement informing the member of—    **13.325.01**
    (a)  his rights under section 324, and
    (b)  any more extensive rights conferred by the company's articles to appoint more than one proxy.
(2)  Failure to comply with this section does not affect the validity of the meeting or of anything done at the meeting.
(3)  If this section is not complied with as respects any meeting, an offence is committed by every officer of the company who is in default.
(4)  A person guilty of an offence under this section is liable on summary conviction to a fine not exceeding level 3 on the standard scale.

COMMENCEMENT DATE  1 October 2007[176]

---

[171]  Companies Act 2006 (Commencement No 3, etc) Order 2007, SI 2007/2194, art 2(1).
[172]  See s 331.
[173]  Schedule 3, para 30 to the Companies Act 2006 (Commencement No 3, etc) Order 2007, SI 2007/2194.
[174]  Who need not be a member.
[175]  The Companies (Shareholders' Rights) Regulations 2009, SI 2009/1632, reg 1(2).
[176]  Companies Act 2006 (Commencement No 3, etc) Order 2007, SI 2007/2194, art 2(1). For the transitional provisions, see Sch 3, para 30 to this Order; and see para13.324.02 above.

**13.325.02**   This section replaces section 372(3) and (4) of the Companies Act 1985, with changes that are consequential upon the extended rights to appoint proxies that are conferred by section 324.

**13.325.03**   Section 325(1) requires the notice calling a meeting of the company to inform the member both of his rights under section 324 and of any more extended rights under the company's articles. There is no express repetition of the provision in section 372(3) of the Companies Act 1985 to the effect that the notice must state that the proxy need not be a member.

**13.325.04**   Section 325(2) provides that failure to comply with this section does not affect the validity of the meeting or anything done at it. This contrasts with the approach that has been taken, at least in Canada, to provisions equivalent to section 372(3) of the Companies Act 1985.[177]

**13.325.05**   Failure to comply will attract a fine for every officer of the company found in default.

### 326  Company-sponsored invitations to appoint proxies

**13.326.01**
   (1)  If for the purposes of a meeting there are issued at the company's expense invitations to members to appoint as proxy a specified person or a number of specified persons, the invitations must be issued to all members entitled to vote at the meeting.
   (2)  Subsection (1) is not contravened if—
       (a)  there is issued to a member at his request a form of appointment naming the proxy or a list of persons willing to act as proxy, and
       (b)  the form or list is available on request to all members entitled to vote at the meeting.
   (3)  If subsection (1) is contravened as respects a meeting, an offence is committed by every officer of the company who is in default.
   (4)  A person guilty of an offence under this section is liable on summary conviction to a fine not exceeding level 3 on the standard scale.

   COMMENCEMENT DATE 1 October 2007[178]

**13.326.02**   This section reproduces the effect of section 372(6) of the Companies Act 1985. It is common for the company's funds to be used in printing and sending out proxy forms so as to enable members to appoint directors or other nominees as proxies. However, if this is to happen both the Companies Act 1985 and the new provision at section 326 require the invitations to be issued to all members.[179]

**13.326.03**   There is an exception at section 326(2), which was also contained at section 372(6) of the Companies Act 1985, for the situation where a member requests a form of appointment naming the proxy, or a list of persons willing to act as proxy, provided that the form or list is available on request to all members.

**13.326.04**   Failure to comply will render all the officers of the company liable to a fine.

**13.326.05**   It should be noted that this section applies only to invitations sent out at the company's expense. It is possible for other interested persons, such as large shareholders, to send out proxy forms, provided they comply with the Companies Acts and the articles of the company. Section 326 does not apply to that situation.

### 327  Notice required of appointment of proxy etc

**13.327.01**
   [(A1)  In the case of a traded company—
       (a)  the appointment of a person as proxy must be notified to the company in writing; and
       (b)  the member is not required to provide the company with anything relating to the appoint-
             ment of a proxy other than reasonable evidence of—
           (i)   the identity of the member and of the proxy, and
           (ii)  the member's instructions (if any) as to how the proxy is to vote, and
           (iii) where the proxy is appointed by a person acting on behalf of the member, authority of
                 that person to make the appointment;
   but may not require to be provided with anything else relating to the appointment.][a]

   (1)  [The following provisions apply to traded companies and other companies as regards][b]
       (a)  the appointment of a proxy, and
       (b)  any document necessary to show the validity of, or otherwise relating to, the appointment of
             a proxy.

---

[177] See *Babic v Milinkovich* (1971) 22 DLR (3d) 732, SC (BC).
[178] Companies Act 2006 (Commencement No 3, etc) Order 2007, SI 2007/2194, art 2(1). For the transitional provisions, see Sch 3, para 30 to this Order; and see 13.324.02 above.
[179] In *Wilson v LMS Rly Co* [1940] Ch 393 it was held that stamped proxies could be sent at the company's expense to large shareholders only. This has been overruled by statute.

(2) Any provision of the company's articles is void in so far as it would have the effect of requiring any such appointment or document to be received by the company or another person earlier than the following time—

(a) in the case of a meeting or adjourned meeting, 48 hours before the time for holding the meeting or adjourned meeting;

(b) in the case of a poll taken more than 48 hours after it was demanded, 24 hours before the time appointed for the taking of the poll;

(c) in the case of a poll taken not more than 48 hours after it was demanded, the time at which it was demanded.

(3) In calculating the periods mentioned in subsection (2) no account shall be taken of any part of a day that is not a working day.

AMENDMENTS

[a]Inserted by the Companies (Shareholders' Rights) Regulations 2009, SI 2009/1632, reg 13.

[b]Amended by the Companies (Shareholders' Rights) Regulations 2009, SI 2009/1632, reg 13.

COMMENCEMENT DATE 1 October 2007[180]; 3 August 2009[181]

Section 327(1) to (3) replaces section 372(5) of the Companies Act 1985 and achieves the same effect of invalidating provisions in a company's articles that purport to require an appointment of a proxy (or any document showing the validity of the appointment or otherwise relating to it) to be received by the company more than 48 hours before the time for holding a meeting or any adjourned meeting[182] (see section 327(1) and (2)(a)). **13.327.02**

Section 327(1) to (3) differs from the section 372(5) of the Companies Act 1985 in two material respects. First, there are specific provisions with regard to polls. In the case of a poll taken more than 48 hours after it is demanded, a company cannot require notice of more than 24 hours before the time appointed for the taking of the poll: section 327(2)(b). In the case of a poll taken nor more than 48 hours after it is demanded, the company cannot require notice any earlier than the time at which the poll is demanded: section 327(2)(c). **13.327.03**

The second material difference lies in the calculation of the time periods at section 327(2). As distinct from the position under the Companies Act 1985, no account shall be taken of any part of a day that is not a working day. Weekends, bank holidays, Christmas Day, Good Friday (and the like) are accordingly excluded from the 48-hour and 24-hour periods stipulated by section 327(2). **13.327.04**

The provisions at section 327(A1) dealing with the appointment of a proxy in relation to traded companies were inserted by the Companies (Shareholders' Rights) Regulations 2009 (implementing the EU Shareholder Rights Directive (2007/36/EC)) which came into force on 3 August 2009 and apply in relation to meetings of which notice is given, or first given, on or after that date. A 'traded company' is defined at section 360C. **13.327.05**

## 328  Chairing meetings

(1) A proxy may be elected to be the chairman of a general meeting by a resolution of the company passed at the meeting. **13.328.01**

(2) Subsection (1) is subject to any provision of the company's articles that states who may or who may not be chairman.

COMMENCEMENT DATE 1 October 2007[183]

This is a new provision. It provides a default rule whereby a proxy may be elected as chairman of a meeting by resolution of the company passed at the meeting. However, this is subject to any provision of the articles which provides who may or may not be chairman. In the absence of such provision in the articles, a proxy can be appointed chairman under this section. **13.328.02**

## 329  Right of proxy to demand a poll

(1) The appointment of a proxy to vote on a matter at a meeting of a company authorises the proxy to demand, or join in demanding, a poll on that matter. **13.329.01**

---

[180]  Except subs (2)(c): Companies Act 2006 (Commencement No 3, etc) Order 2007, SI 2007/2194, art 2(1)(f).

[181]  As regards the amendments referred to in notes a and b above.

[182]  If a shareholder's proxy is in time for the adjourned meeting, then irrespective of the provisions of the company's articles it cannot now be held invalid simply on the grounds that it was not received in time at the original meeting: contrast *McLaren v Thomson* [1917] 2 Ch 261.

[183]  Companies Act 2006 (Commencement No 3, etc) Order 2007, SI 2007/2194, art 2(1). For the transitional provisions, see Sch 3, para 30 to this Order; and see para 13.324.02 above.

(2) In applying the provisions of section 321(2) (requirements for effective demand), a demand by a proxy counts—
    (a) for the purposes of paragraph (a), as a demand by the member;
    (b) for the purposes of paragraph (b), as a demand by a member representing the voting rights that the proxy is authorised to exercise;
    (c) for the purposes of paragraph (c), as a demand by a member holding the shares to which those rights are attached.

COMMENCEMENT DATE 1 October 2007[184]

**13.329.02** This provision substantially reproduces section 373(2) of the Companies Act 1985. The provision needs to be read together with section 321, which (like its predecessor section 373(1) of the Companies Act 1985) restricts the ability of a company to exclude members' rights to call a poll.

**13.329.03** As with the predecessor provision in the Companies Act 1985, section 329 provides that the appointment of a proxy to vote on a matter at a meeting authorizes the proxy to demand, or join in demanding, a poll on that matter. Whereas section 373(2) of the Companies Act 1985 went on simply to provide that a demand by a person as proxy for a member is the same as a demand by a member, the new section 329(2) spells out precisely how a demand by a proxy counts as a demand by the member, with reference to the three specific requirements in section 321(2)(a), (b), and (c).

### 330 Notice required of termination of proxy's authority

**13.330.01** [(A1) In the case of a traded company the termination of the authority of a person to act as proxy must be notified to the company in writing.][a]
    (1) [The following provisions apply in the case of traded companies and other companies as regards][b] notice that the authority of a person to act as proxy is terminated ('notice of termination').
    (2) The termination of the authority of a person to act as proxy does not affect—
        (a) whether he counts in deciding whether there is a quorum at a meeting,
        (b) the validity of anything he does as chairman of a meeting, or
        (c) the validity of a poll demanded by him at a meeting, unless the company receives notice of the termination before the commencement of the meeting.
    (3) The termination of the authority of a person to act as proxy does not affect the validity of a vote given by that person unless the company receives notice of the termination—
        (a) before the commencement of the meeting or adjourned meeting at which the vote is given, or
        (b) in the case of a poll taken more than 48 hours after it is demanded, before the time appointed for taking the poll.
    (4) If the company's articles require or permit members to give notice of termination to a person other than the company, the references above to the company receiving notice have effect as if they were or (as the case may be) included a reference to that person.
    (5) Subsections (2) and (3) have effect subject to any provision of the company's articles which has the effect of requiring notice of termination to be received by the company or another person at a time earlier than that specified in those subsections.
        This is subject to subsection (6).
    (6) Any provision of the company's articles is void in so far as it would have the effect of requiring notice of termination to be received by the company or another person earlier than the following time—
        (a) in the case of a meeting or adjourned meeting, 48 hours before the time for holding the meeting or adjourned meeting;
        (b) in the case of a poll taken more than 48 hours after it was demanded, 24 hours before the time appointed for the taking of the poll;
        (c) in the case of a poll taken not more than 48 hours after it was demanded, the time at which it was demanded.
    (7) In calculating the periods mentioned in subsections (3)(b) and (6) no account shall be taken of any part of a day that is not a working day.

AMENDMENTS

[a] Inserted by the Companies (Shareholders' Rights) Regulations 2009, SI 2009/1632, reg 13.

[b] Amended by the Companies (Shareholders' Rights) Regulations 2009, SI 2009/1632, reg 13.

COMMENCEMENT DATE 1 October 2007[185]; 3 August 2009[186]

---

[184] Companies Act 2006 (Commencement No 3, etc) Order 2007, S1 2007/2194, art 2(1). For the transitional provisions, see Sch 3, para 30 to this Order; and see para 13.324.02 above.

[185] Except subs (6)(c): Companies Act 2006 (Commencement No 3, etc) Order 2007, SI 2007/2194, art 2(1)(f). For the transitional provisions see Sch 3, para 30 to this Order; and see para 13.324.02 above.

[186] As regards the amendments referred to in notes a and b.

This section provides a default position, which replaces article 63 of Table A to the Companies Act    **13.330.02**
1985. In summary, the default position is that unless the company receives notice of the termination of
a proxy before the commencement of the meeting then that termination has no effect on whether the
proxy counts for quorum purposes, on the validity of any act of his as chairman, or on the validity of
any poll demanded by him (section 330(2)). Where a company is a traded company, section 330(A1)
requires that the termination be notified to the company in writing.[187] So far as voting is concerned, the
validity of a proxy's vote is not affected unless the company receives notice of the termination before
the commencement of the meeting, or adjourned meeting, or, in the case of a poll taken, more than 48
hours after it is demanded, before the time appointed for taking the poll (section 330(3)).

By virtue of section 330(4), if a company's articles require or permit notice of termination to be given    **13.330.03**
by some person other than the company, the default provisions of section 330(2) and (3) apply as if they
included a reference to that person.

As stated in the previous paragraph, this is a default position. A company's articles may require notice    **13.330.04**
of termination to be received by the company (or another person) at some time earlier than that
specified by section 330(2) and (3): section 330(5). However, any provision in a company's articles will
be void if it requires notice to be given any earlier than the timescales prescribed in section 330(6),
namely (a) in the case of a meeting or adjourned meeting, 48 hours before the time for holding the
meeting; (b) in the case of poll taken more than 48 hours after it is demanded, 24 hours before the time
appointed for taking of the poll; and (c) in the case of a poll taken not more than 48 hours after it was
demanded, the time at which it was demanded.[188] In each case, days (or parts of days) that are not
working days are not to be counted.[189]

The question arises, what if the shareholder wishes to attend and vote, but has not given notice of    **13.330.05**
termination in accordance with section 330. Where regulation 63 of Table A (or similar) applied, it was
always open to a shareholder to attend and vote at a meeting notwithstanding that he had not given
prior notice under the articles of his revocation of the proxy.[190] By attending and voting, the shareholder supersedes the proxy, irrespective of whether prior notice of termination or revocation has been
given. In that event the vote of the shareholder would be counted and any vote of the proxy would not
(although the position might be different if the articles made some express provision that disallowed
the shareholder from voting unless notice of termination had been given).[191] It is submitted that this
remains the position under the new Act.[192]

## 331  Saving for more extensive rights conferred by articles

> Nothing in sections 324 to 330 (proxies) prevents a company's articles from conferring more extensive    **13.331.01**
> rights on members or proxies than are conferred by those sections.
>
> COMMENCEMENT DATE  1 October 2007[193]

This section makes it clear that the provisions relating to proxies at sections 324 to 330 confer a    **13.331.02**
minimum level of rights upon shareholders and proxies. There is nothing to prevent a company's
articles from conferring more extensive rights on members or proxies.

---

[187]  For the definition of 'traded company' see s 360C. The provisions in relation to traded companies were
introduced by the Companies (Shareholders' Rights) Regulations 2009, which implement the EU Shareholder
Rights Directive (2007/36/EC) and came into force on 3 August 2009.

[188]  The effect of the provisions in relation to polls is that the reasoning in *Spiller v Mayo (Rhodesia) Co* [1926]
WN 78 could no longer apply.

[189]  Article 46(3) of the Model Articles for private companies provides that a notice revoking a proxy
appointment only takes effect if it is delivered before the start of the meeting or adjourned meeting to which it
relates. See the Companies (Model Articles) Regulations 2008, SI 2008/3229. These came into force as model
articles on 1 October 2009.

[190]  See *Cousins v International Brick Co Ltd* [1931] Ch 90.

[191]  See *Cousins v International Brick Co Ltd* [1931] 2 Ch 90, 101.

[192]  In this context, art 46(1) of the Model Articles for private companies provides that a person who is entitled
to attend, speak, or vote (either on a show of hands or on a poll) at a general meeting remains so entitled in respect
of that meeting or any adjournment of it, even though a valid proxy notice has been delivered to the company by
or on behalf of that person. See the Companies (Model Articles) Regulations 2008, SI 2008/3229. These came into
force as model articles on 1 October 2009.

[193]  Companies Act 2006 (Commencement No 3, etc) Order 2007, SI 2007/2194, art 2(1). For the transitional
provisions, see Sch 3, para 30 to this Order; and see para 13.324.02 above.

*Adjourned meetings*

### 332  Resolution passed at adjourned meeting

**13.332.01**    Where a resolution is passed at an adjourned meeting of a company, the resolution is for all purposes to be treated as having been passed on the date on which it was in fact passed, and is not to be deemed passed on any earlier date.

COMMENCEMENT DATE 1 October 2007[194]

**13.332.02**    This section reproduces the effect of section 381 of the Companies Act 1985 as it applies to members' meetings. The provisions of this section are applied also to class meetings, by virtue of section 334. There is no material difference between the provision of this section relating to members' meetings and the wording of section 381 of the Companies Act 1985. The provision was first included in the 1929 Act, and is designed to address the fact that an adjourned meeting is regarded in law as a single and continuous meeting, such that absent a provision to this effect, a resolution passed at an adjourned meeting would be deemed to have been passed on the day fixed for the original meeting.[195]

*Electronic communications*

### 333  Sending documents relating to meetings etc in electronic form

**13.333.01**    (1)  Where a company has given an electronic address in a notice calling a meeting, it is deemed to have agreed that any document or information relating to proceedings at the meeting may be sent by electronic means to that address (subject to any conditions or limitations specified in the notice).

(2)  Where a company has given an electronic address—
  (a)  in an instrument of proxy sent out by the company in relation to the meeting, or
  (b)  in an invitation to appoint a proxy issued by the company in relation to the meeting,
  it is deemed to have agreed that any document or information relating to proxies for that meeting may be sent by electronic means to that address (subject to any conditions or limitations specified in the notice).

(3)  In subsection (2), documents relating to proxies include—
  (a)  the appointment of a proxy in relation to a meeting,
  (b)  any document necessary to show the validity of, or otherwise relating to, the appointment of a proxy, and
  (c)  notice of the termination of the authority of a proxy.

(4)  In this section 'electronic address' means any address or number used for the purposes of sending or receiving documents or information by electronic means.

COMMENCEMENT DATE 20 January 2007

**13.333.02**    This section needs to be read together with the provisions regarding electronic communications to companies in Part 3 of Schedule 5. This section came into force on 20 January 2007.[196]

**13.333.03**    These provisions (taken together) permit a member to communicate with a company by electronic means to the following extent. Where the company has given an electronic address in a notice of meeting, it is deemed to have agreed that any document or information relating to proceedings at the meeting can be sent by electronic means to that address. Where the company has given an electronic address in an instrument of proxy or invitation to appoint a proxy, it is deemed to have agreed that any document or information relating to proxies (including those identified at subsections (a) to (c)) may be sent to that address. In each case, the deeming provision is subject to any conditions or limitations specified in the notice.

**13.333.04**    These provisions supersede the provisions for electronic communication inserted into section 372 of the Companies Act 1985 by the Companies Act 1985 (Electronic Communications) Order 2000. Those provisions were in less specific terms than the current provision, and they did not expressly contain a deeming provision in the manner that section 333 of the Act now does.

### [333A  Traded company: duty to provide electronic address for receipt of proxies etc

**13.333A.01**    (1)  A traded company must, when sending out an instrument of proxy for the purposes of a general meeting or issuing an invitation to appoint a proxy for those purposes, give an electronic address for the receipt of any document or information relating to proxies for the meeting.

---

[194]  Companies Act 2006 (Commencement No 3, etc) Order 2007, SI 2007/2194, art 2(1).
[195]  See *Neuschild v British Equatorial Oil Co* [1925] 1 Ch 346.
[196]  See Companies Act 2006 (Commencement No 1, Transitional Provisions and Savings) Order 2006, SI 2006/3428, art 3(b).

(2) The company is deemed to have agreed that any document or information relating to proxies for the meeting may be sent by electronic means to that address (subject to any limitation specified by the company when giving the address).

(3) Section 333(3) and (4) apply for the purposes of this section.]ᵃ

AMENDMENTS

ᵃ Inserted by the Companies (Shareholders' Rights) Regulations 2009, SI 2009/1632, reg 13.

COMMENCEMENT DATE 3 August 2009[197]

This section applies to traded companies (defined at section 360C) and requires them to provide an electronic address for receipt of proxies. It was introduced by the Companies (Shareholders' Rights) Regulations 2009 (implementing the EU Shareholder Rights Directive (2007/36/EC)), which came into force on 3 August 2009.    **13.333A.02**

## Application to class meetings

### 334  Application to class meetings

(1) The provisions of this Chapter apply (with necessary modifications) in relation to a meeting of holders of a class of shares as they apply in relation to a general meeting.    **13.334.01**
This is subject to subsections (2) [to]ᵃ(3).

(2) The following provisions of this Chapter do not apply in relation to a meeting of holders of a class of shares—
  (a) sections 303 to 305 (members' power to require directors to call general meeting),
  (b) section 306 (power of court to order meeting)[, and
  (c) sections 311(3), 311A, 319A, 327(A1), 330(A1) and 333(A) (additional requirements relating to traded companies).

(2A) Section 307(1) to (6) apply in relation to a meeting of holders of a class of shares in a traded company as they apply in relation to a meeting of holders of a class of shares in a company other than a traded company (and, accordingly, section 307A does not apply in relation to such a meeting)].ᵇ

(3) The following provisions (in addition to those mentioned in subsection (2)) do not apply in relation to a meeting in connection with the variation of rights attached to a class of shares (a 'variation of class rights meeting')—
  (a) section 318 (quorum), and
  (b) section 321 (right to demand a poll).

(4) The quorum for a variation of class rights meeting is—
  (a) for a meeting other than an adjourned meeting, two persons present holding at least one-third in nominal value of the issued shares of the class in question (excluding any shares of that class held as treasury shares);
  (b) for an adjourned meeting, one person present holding shares of the class in question.

(5) For the purposes of subsection (4), where a person is present by proxy or proxies, he is treated as holding only the shares in respect of which those proxies are authorised to exercise voting rights.

(6) At a variation of class rights meeting, any holder of shares of the class in question present may demand a poll.

(7) For the purposes of this section—
  (a) any amendment of a provision contained in a company's articles for the variation of the rights attached to a class of shares, or the insertion of any such provision into the articles, is itself to be treated as a variation of those rights, and
  (b) references to the variation of rights attached to a class of shares include references to their abrogation.

AMENDMENTS

ᵃ Amended by the Companies (Shareholders' Rights) Regulations 2009, SI 2009/1632, reg 14.

ᵇ Inserted by the Companies (Shareholders' Rights) Regulations 2009, SI 2009/1632, reg 14.

COMMENCEMENT DATE 1 October 2007[198]; 3 August 2009[199]

This section prescribes how the various provisions under this chapter of Part 13 (Resolutions at meetings) are applicable to meetings of holders of a class of shares. Class rights and variations of class    **13.334.02**

---

[197] See The Companies (Shareholders' Rights) Regulations 2009, SI 2009/1632, reg 1(2).
[198] Companies Act 2006 (Commencement No 3, etc) Order 2007, SI 2007/2194, art 2(1). The provisions at ss 334–335 apply to meetings of which notice is given on or after 1 October 2007. When notice is given over more than one day, the relevant day is the first on which notice is given (Sch 3, para 31 to Commencement No 3 Order, SI 2007/2194).
[199] As regards the amendments referred to in notes a and b.

rights are dealt with in Chapter 9 of Part 17 of the Act (Classes of shares and class rights). Whereas the Companies Act 1985 contained no definition of what constitutes a class of shares,[200] section 629 of the Act contains a definition of class rights for the purposes of Chapter 9 of Part 17; namely, that shares are to be regarded as one class if the rights attaching to them are in all respects uniform.[201] See, in more detail, paragraph 17.623.03 below.

**13.334.03** So far as concerns the provisions relating to resolutions to meetings of classes of shares, these were to be found in different places in the Companies Act 1985. Section 125(6) of the Companies Act 1985 provided that the provisions of section 369 (length of notice for calling company meetings), section 370 (general provisions as to meetings and votes), sections 376 and 377 (circulation of members resolutions) of that Act, and the provisions of articles relating to general meetings, applied 'so far as applicable' to meetings in connection with the variations of the rights attached to a class of shares.[202] However, this was considered to be a default provision which applied subject to the provision of the articles of the company. Separately, the proxy provisions under section 372 of the Companies Act 1985 were applied to all class meetings by virtue of section 372(7) of that Act.

**13.334.04** Under section 334 of the new Act, all the provisions of Chapter 3 of Part 13 apply (with the necessary modifications) to meetings of holders of a class of shares, subject to the following three exceptions.

**13.334.05** First, the powers of the members to requisition a meeting (under section 303 to 305 of the Act) and of the court to order a meeting (under section 306 of the Act) do not apply to class meetings. See section 334(2).

**13.334.06** Secondly, the quorum provisions at section 318 of the Act do not apply to any meeting in connection with the variation of rights attached to a class of shares: see section 334(3)(a). Instead, section 334(4) provides that the quorum for a variation of class rights meeting is two persons present, holding at least one-third in nominal value of the issued shares (excluding treasury shares). The position is different for an adjourned meeting, where one person present holding shares of the class in question will form a quorum. This quorum provision is materially the same as that provided under section 125(6)(a) of the Companies Act 1985. As for what constitutes a variation of rights, see the discussion in relation to section 630 of the Act at paragraph 17.630.03 below.

**13.334.07** Thirdly, the right to demand a poll at section 321 of the Act does not apply to any meeting in connection with the variation of rights attached to a class of shares: see section 334(3)(b). Instead, section 334(6) provides that any holder of shares of the class in question present may demand a poll. The effect of this provision is materially the same as that of section 125(6)(b) of the Companies Act 1985.

**13.334.08** Section 334(7)(a) and (b) reproduces (to materially the same effect) the provisions of section 125(7) and (8) respectively of the Companies Act 1985. By virtue of section 334(7)(a): any alteration of a provision for the variation of class rights, or the insertion of such a provision, is itself to be treated as a variation of those rights. By virtue of section 334(7)(b) references to the variation of rights attached to a class of shares include reference to their abrogation. These sections (as with predecessor sections under the Companies Act 1985) reflect the previous law.

**13.334.09** Section 334(2A) relates to traded companies (defined at section 360C). It was introduced by the Companies (Shareholders' Rights) Regulations 2009 (implementing the EU Shareholder Rights Directive (2007/36/EC)) and provides for the application of section 307(1) to (6) (and the non-application of the new section 307A) to the holders of a class of shares in a traded company. Section 334(2) has also been amended by the same regulations so as to disapply, in the case of class meetings, certain of the additional provisions relating to traded companies which were introduced by those regulations.

### 335 Application to class meetings: companies without share capital

**13.335.01**       (1) The provisions of this Chapter apply (with necessary modifications) in relation to a meeting of a class of members of a company without a share capital as they apply in relation to a general meeting.
      This is subject to subsections (2) and (3).
      (2) The following provisions of this Chapter do not apply in relation to a meeting of a class of members—
          (a) sections 303 to 305 (members' power to require directors to call general meeting), and

---

[200] As to which, see *per* Scott J in *Cumbrian Newspapers Group Ltd v Cumberland and Westmorland Herald Newspapers & Printing Co Ltd* [1987] Ch 1, 22.
[201] Save that shares are not to be treated as being of different classes simply because they do not carry the same rights to dividend in the 12 months following allotment; see s 643(2),
[202] Subject to the provisions of s 125(6)(a) and (b), as to which see para 13.334.06–07 below.

    (b)  section 306 (power of court to order meeting).

(3)  The following provisions (in addition to those mentioned in subsection (2)) do not apply in relation to a meeting in connection with the variation of the rights of a class of members (a 'variation of class rights meeting')—

    (a)  section 318 (quorum), and

    (b)  section 321 (right to demand a poll).

(4)  The quorum for a variation of class rights meeting is—

    (a)  for a meeting other than an adjourned meeting, two members of the class present (in person or by proxy) who together represent at least one-third of the voting rights of the class;

    (b)  for an adjourned meeting, one member of the class present (in person or by proxy).

(5)  At a variation of class rights meeting, any member present (in person or by proxy) may demand a poll.

(6)  For the purposes of this section—

    (a)  any amendment of a provision contained in a company's articles for the variation of the rights of a class of members, or the insertion of any such provision into the articles, is itself to be treated as a variation of those rights, and

    (b)  references to the variation of rights of a class of members include references to their abrogation.

COMMENCEMENT DATE 1 October 2007[203]

This section applies the provisions of this chapter to class meetings of companies without share capital. **13.335.02**
Section 335 duplicates the provisions of section 334, save that the quorum provision at section 335(4)(a) requires two persons to be present holding at least one-third of the voting rights (as opposed to one third of the nominal value of the issued share capital, as specified by section 334(4)(a). The comments above at the commentary to section 334 therefore apply *mutatis mutandis* to this section.

So far as concerns variation of class rights in companies without share capital, this is dealt with at **13.335.03**
section 631 of the Act, and commented on at paragraph 17.631.02 below.

## CHAPTER 4
## PUBLIC COMPANIES [AND TRADED COMPANIES][a]:
## ADDITIONAL REQUIREMENTS FOR AGMS

### 336  Public companies [and traded companies]:[b] annual general meeting

(1)  Every public company must hold a general meeting as its annual general meeting in each period **13.336.01**
of 6 months beginning with the day following its accounting reference date (in addition to any other meetings held during that period).

[(1A) Every private company that is a traded company must hold a general meeting as its annual general meeting in each period of 9 months beginning with the day following its accounting reference date (in addition to any other meetings held during that period).] [c]

(2)  A company that fails to comply with subsection (1) [or (1A)][d] as a result of giving notice under section 392 (alteration of accounting reference date)—

    (a)  specifying a new accounting reference date, and

    (b)  stating that the current accounting reference period or the previous accounting reference period is to be shortened,

    shall be treated as if it had complied with subsection (1) [or (1A)][e] if it holds a general meeting as its annual general meeting within 3 months of giving that notice.

(3)  If a company fails to comply with subsection (1) [or (1A)][f], an offence is committed by every officer of the company who is in default.

(4)  A person guilty of an offence under this section is liable—

    (a)  on conviction on indictment, to a fine;

    (b)  on summary conviction, to a fine not exceeding the statutory maximum

AMENDMENTS

[a]  Amended by the Companies (Shareholders' Rights) Regulations 2009, SI 2009/1632, reg 15.

[b]  Amended by the Companies (Shareholders' Rights) Regulations 2009, SI 2009/1632, reg 15.

[c]  Inserted by the Companies (Shareholders' Rights) Regulations 2009, SI 2009/1632, reg 15.

[d]  Amended by the Companies (Shareholders' Rights) Regulations 2009, SI 2009/1632, reg 15.

---

[203]  Companies Act 2006 (Commencement No 3, etc) Order 2007, SI 2007/2194, art 2(1). For the transitional provisions, see Sch 3, para 30 to this Order.

      [e] Amended by the Companies (Shareholders' Rights) Regulations 2009, SI 2009/1632, reg 15.

      [f] Amended by the Companies (Shareholders' Rights) Regulations 2009, SI 2009/1632, reg 15.

      COMMENCEMENT DATE 1 October 2007[204]; 3 August 2009[205]

**13.336.02** One of the recommendations of the Company Law Review Steering Group was that private companies should not be obliged to hold AGMs. Although the Companies Act 1985 provided for an elective regime whereby private companies could unanimously elect to dispense with holding general meetings and with the statutory activities usually conducted at AGMs (laying accounts and the appointment of auditors),[206] there was a concern that many private companies were deterred from dispensing with AGMs by the need for unanimity and the complex adaptations of the Companies Act 1985 that applied to the elective regime. As a result, the recommendation from the Steering Group, which has been adopted in the Act, was that the default position for private companies should be that they are not required to hold AGMs (albeit that they may elect to do so). This is reflected in the Act: the provisions relating to annual meetings at Chapter 4 of Part 13 apply only to public companies. There is nothing to prevent a private company from holding an annual general meeting, but there is no longer any statutory obligation to do so, unless the company is a traded company (as to which see section 336(1A) and 13.336.04 below). The repeal of section 366 of the 1985 Act does not affect any provision of a private company s memorandum or articles that expressly requires the company to hold an annual general meeting.[207] However, a company is not to be treated as one whose articles require it to hold an annual general meeting if immediately before 1 October 2007 an elective resolution to dispense with annual general meetings pursuant to section 366A of the Companies Act 1985 was in force.[208]

**13.336.03** The definition of a public company is at section 4 of the Act, and the provisions relating to the minimum share capital requirement for public companies are at Part 20.

**13.336.04** Subsection (1A) dealing with private traded companies was introduced by the Companies (Shareholders' Rights) Regulations 2009 (implementing the EU Shareholder Rights Directive (2007/36/EC)), which came into force on 3 August 2009. A 'traded company' is defined at section 360C.

**13.336.05** Under section 336(1), a public company is required to hold a general meeting as its AGM in each period of six months from its accounting reference date. The six-month period was recommended by the Company Law Review Steering Group. The period is considerably shorter than the period applying under the previous regime and is intended to ensure that shareholders have a more timely opportunity to hold the directors of a public company to account. The Companies Act 1985 provided (by section 366) that an AGM should be held each year and not more than 15 months after the previous AGM.[209]

**13.336.06** Any officer of a company which is in default of this requirement commits an offence: section 336(3) of the Act.

**13.336.07** Section 336(2) provides for an exception for companies who give notice under section 392 specifying a new accounting reference date and specifying that the current accounting reference period or the previous accounting reference period is to be shortened. In that event a company shall be treated as

---

  [204] Companies Act 2006 (Commencement No 3, etc) Order 2007, SI 2007/2194, art 2(1). Note the transitional adaptations in Sch 1, para 15 of the Order, which replace '6 months' in subs (1) with '7 months' and the reference in subs (2) to s 392 with a reference to Companies Act 1985, s 225. Paragraph 35 of Sch 3 to the Order provides that in the case of an existing public company (being a company formed and registered before 1 October 2007 which was a public company immediately before that date), s 366 of the Companies Act 1985 continues to apply to determine the date by which the company must hold its first annual general meeting after 30 September 2007. Section 336 of the Act applies in relation to subsequent annual general meetings.

  [205] As regards the amendments referred to in notes a to f.

  [206] See ss 366A and 379A of the Companies Act 1985, inserted by ss 115(2) and 116 of the Companies Act 1989 as from 1 April 1990 (subject to transitional provisions).

  [207] Schedule 3, para 32 to Commencement No 3 Order, SI 2007/2194. This paragraph also makes it clear that any provision specifying that one or more directors are to retire at an annual general meeting of the company is not a provision expressly requiring the company to hold an annual general meeting.

  [208] See Sch 5, para 2(6) to Commencement No 5 Order, SI 2007/3495.

  [209] The repeal of s 367 of the Companies Act 1985 (which contained a default power of the Secretary of State to call an annual general meeting) is subject to transitional provisions contained at Sch 3, para 33 to Commencement No 3 Order, SI 2007/2194, which provides that the repeal has effect in relation to a private company as from 1 October 2007 even if an application under that section has been made, or the Secretary of State has called or directed the calling of a meeting under that section before that date. So far as concerns public companies, the repeal of s 367 of the Companies Act 1985 does not affect the operation of that section in relation to a public company where an application was made before 1 October 2007 (see Sch 3, para 36).

having complied with section 336(1) if it holds an AGM within three months of giving that notice. As regards alterations of accounting reference dates under section 392 of the Act, see paragraph 15.392.02 below.

### 337  Public companies [and traded companies]:ᵃ notice of AGM

(1) A notice calling an annual general meeting of a public company [or a private company that is a traded company]ᵇ must state that the meeting is an annual general meeting.      **13.337.01**

(2) An annual general meeting [of a public company that is not a traded company]ᶜ may be called by shorter notice than that required by section 307(2) or by the company's articles (as the case may be), if all the members entitled to attend and vote at the meeting agree to the shorter notice.

[(3) Where a notice calling an annual general meeting of a traded company is given more than 6 weeks before the meeting, the notice must include—

   (a) if the company is a public company, a statement of the right under section 338 to require the company to give notice of a resolution to be moved at the meeting, and

   (b) whether or not the company is a public company, a statement of the right under section 338A to require the company to include a matter in the business to be dealt with at the meeting.]ᵈ

AMENDMENTS

ᵃ Amended by the Companies (Shareholders' Rights) Regulations 2009, SI 2009/1632, reg 16.

ᵇ Amended by the Companies (Shareholders' Rights) Regulations 2009, SI 2009/1632, reg 16.

ᶜ Amended by the Companies (Shareholders' Rights) Regulations 2009, SI 2009/1632, reg 16.

ᵈ Inserted by the Companies (Shareholders' Rights) Regulations 2009, SI 2009/1632, reg 16.

COMMENCEMENT DATE 1 October 2007[210]; 3 August 2009[211]

The provisions in relation to public companies in this section reproduce the effect of those parts of   **13.337.02**
sections 366(1) and section 369 of the Companies Act 1985 dealing with notice of an AGM. Section 337(3) and the additional provisions relating to traded companies in this section were introduced with effect from 3 August 2009 by The Companies (Shareholders' Rights) Regulations 2009 (which implement the EU Shareholder Rights Directive (2007/36/EC) and require traded companies (including private traded companies) to hold an AGM. A 'traded company' is defined at section 360C.

So far as concerns the notice itself, this must state that the meeting is an AGM (section 337(1),   **13.337.03**
reproducing the effect of section 366(1) of the Companies Act 1985).

So far as concerns length of notice, section 307(2) provides that an AGM must be called by notice of at   **13.337.04**
least 21 days, unless the articles provide for longer notice (a minimum of 14 days being required for notices of other general meetings). Section 307(4) and (5) provides that the 14-day time period for meetings other than an AGM may be shortened subject to the majority voting requirements of section 307(5). Section 337(2) of the Act deals with the circumstances in which the 21-day (or longer)[212] period of notice for holding an AGM may be shortened: this can only be achieved with the agreement of all the members entitled to attend and vote at the meeting. This reproduces the effect of section 369(3)(a) of the Companies Act 1985.

### 338  Public companies: members' power to require circulation of resolutions for AGMs

(1) The members of a public company may require the company to give, to members of the company   **13.338.01**
entitled to receive notice of the next annual general meeting, notice of a resolution which may properly be moved and is intended to be moved at that meeting.

(2) A resolution may properly be moved at an annual general meeting unless—

   (a) it would, if passed, be ineffective (whether by reason of inconsistency with any enactment or the company's constitution or otherwise),

   (b) it is defamatory of any person, or

   (c) it is frivolous or vexatious.

---

[210] Companies Act 2006 (Commencement No 3, etc) Order 2007, S1 2007/2194, art 2(1). For the transitional provisions, see Sch 3, para 37 to this Order. Section 337 of the Act applies to meetings of which notice is given on or after 1 October 2007, and s 369 applies to meetings of which notice is given before that date. Where notice is given over more than one day it is treated as having been given on the first of those days.

[211] As regards the amendments referred to in notes a to d.

[212] i.e. under the company's articles.

(3)  A company is required to give notice of a resolution once it has received requests that it do so from—

    (a)  members representing at least 5% of the total voting rights of all the members who have a right to vote on the resolution at the annual general meeting to which the requests relate (excluding any voting rights attached to any shares in the company held as treasury shares), or

    (b)  at least 100 members who have a right to vote on the resolution at the annual general meeting to which the requests relate and hold shares in the company on which there has been paid up an average sum, per member, of at least £100.

See also section 153 (exercise of rights where shares held on behalf of others).

(4)  A request—

    (a)  may be in hard copy form or in electronic form,

    (b)  must identify the resolution of which notice is to be given,

    (c)  must be authenticated by the person or persons making it, and

    (d)  must be received by the company not later than—

        (i)  6 weeks before the annual general meeting to which the requests relate, or

        (ii)  if later, the time at which notice is given of that meeting.

COMMENCEMENT DATE 1 October 2007[213]

**13.338.02**    This and the next two sections replace sections 376 and 377 of the Companies Act 1985, dealing with the members' power to require circulation of members' resolutions at AGMs, and the company's duty to comply.

**13.338.03**    There are some material differences between sections 338 to 340 and the previous regime. In particular, section 340 provides that the expenses of circulation are no longer to be met by the members, provided that sufficient requests to circulate the resolution are received before the end of the financial year preceding the meeting. Further, it is now made clear by sections 338 and 339 that only those members who are entitled to vote on the relevant resolution are to be counted in determining whether sufficient requests have been received so as to oblige the company to circulate the relevant resolution.

**13.338.04**    Under section 338, a company is required to give notice of a resolution which may be moved at the AGM, if it has received requests to do so from members representing at least 5 per cent of the total voting rights of members having a right to vote at the AGM on the resolution (excluding any shares in the company held as treasury shares), or from at least 100 members having a right to vote on the resolution and on whose shares there has been paid up an average sum, per member, of at least £100: see section 338(3). The inclusion of the requirement that the members (and qualifying shares) must have a right to vote on the resolution has been introduced by the Act. The requirements are otherwise the same as those that pertained under section 376(2) of the Companies Act 1985.

**13.338.05**    The request may be in hard copy or electronic form, must identify the resolution of which notice is given, and must be authenticated by the person or persons making the request. The request must also be received by the company no later than six weeks before the AGM to which the requests relate,[214] or, if later, the time at which notice is given of the meeting: see section 338(4).

**13.338.06**    Section 338(2) provides that a resolution may properly be moved at an AGM unless it falls within any of the descriptions at subsection (2)(a) to (c). Although the drafting of section 338(1) to (3) is somewhat loose in this regard, the section is to be read such that in the event that any of the conditions at subsections (2)(a) to (c) apply, the company is relieved from any obligation that it would otherwise have had by virtue of section 338(3).

**13.338.07**    Section 338(2)(a) relates to resolutions which would, if passed, be ineffective (whether by reason of inconsistency with the company's constitution or otherwise). Under section 367(1) of the Companies Act 1985, it was implicit in the words 'any resolution which may properly be moved' that the statutory entitlement (and obligation) applied only to those resolutions that were *intra vires* the company. This

---

[213]  Companies Act 2006 (Commencement No 3, etc) Order 2007, SI 2007/2194, art 2(1). For the transitional provisions, see Sch 3, para 34 to this Order. Sections 376 and 377 of the Companies Act 1985 continue to apply requisitions made under s 376(1)(a) to a private company before 1 October 2007 (unless the company is not required to comply with the requisition), and, for so long as such a requisition has not been complied with, s 366 of the 1985 Act also continues to apply. Where copies of the requisition are deposited on more than one day, the requisition is deemed to have been made on the first day on which the copies deposited were sufficient to require the company to act. So far as concerns public companies, ss 338–340 of the Act apply to requests made on or after 1 October 2007, and ss 376 and 377 continue to apply to requisitions made before that date. Again, where requests are made or copies of a requisition deposited on more than one day, the request or requisition will be deemed to have been made on the first day on which the requests made or copies deposited are sufficient to require the company to act (Sch 3, para 38 to the Order).

[214]  Excluding the day of the meeting and the day on which the request is received: see s 360(1).

has now been made clear by subsection 338(2)(a). The subsection also relates to resolutions which would be 'ineffective' not only because they are inconsistent with a statute of the company's constitution but also 'otherwise'. It is unclear how far this is intended to extend. It is submitted that 'ineffective' should be construed strictly and *sui generis* with the two examples given in the parentheses in section (2)(a), such that the subsection will only apply if the proposed resolution would, if passed, be ineffective in the sense of incapable of taking effect consistently with the law, the company's constitution and the like. Under the equivalent of the previous legislation, there is commonwealth authority to the effect that it is open to the directors to decline to give notice of a resolution where the matter is one exclusively within the competence of the board.[215] It is submitted that a resolution which was of this character would not be 'ineffective' within the sense of subsection (2)(a). Arguably, however, it may be possible for a resolution of this sort to be characterized as falling within subsection (2)(c), dealt with below.

Subsection (2)(b) relates to resolutions which are defamatory of any person. This seems to represent a change in the law which was not referred to in the explanatory notes to the Company Law Reform Bill, and which does not appear to have been foreshadowed in the various steering group reports or other publications leading up to publication of the bill. Under the Companies Act 1985, it was open to directors to apply to the court to be relieved from circulating a members' circular (ie a statement) which was defamatory: see section 377(3) of the Companies Act 1985. Members' circulars are now dealt with in sections 314 to 317, which appear to provide wider grounds on which the company may apply for relief from the court (ie on the grounds that the rights under the section are being abused, as opposed to it being defamatory). Section 338(2)(b) now provides that a resolution may not properly be moved if it is defamatory of any person. There was no such provision under the previous law. Moreover, it is not expressly necessary for the company to seek to come before the court to apply for dispensation. Under section 338 the members have no entitlement to require circulation of a resolution that is defamatory. This means that the company and its board could, if sufficiently confident, decide not to comply with members' requests under section 338 on the ground that the resolution was defamatory. The matter would then be left to the court, if anyone applied to the court, to determine whether that decision was correct. Given the penalty provisions of section 339(4) and (5), this approach may present a risk that the board may not wish to take, and it may accordingly be that in the event that a resolution is *prima facie* defamatory, a prudent board would wish to seek a direction from the court before deciding not to comply with the members' request. **13.338.08**

Under the previous law relating to circulation of members' circulars that were defamatory there is Commonwealth authority to the effect that 'defamatory' means *prima facie* defamatory. This means that the possibility that the requisition might have a valid defence in an action for defamation should be disregarded.[216] **13.338.09**

## [338A  Traded companies: members' power to include other matters in business dealt with at AGM

(1)  The members of a traded company may require the company to include in the business to be dealt with at an annual general meeting a matter (other than a proposed resolution) which may properly be included in the business. **13.338A.01**

(2)  A matter may properly be included in the business at an annual general meeting unless—
   (a)  it is defamatory of any person, or
   (b)  it is frivolous or vexatious.

(3)  A company is required to include such a matter once it has received requests that it do so from—
   (a)  members representing at least 5% of the total voting rights of all the members who have a right to vote at the meeting, or
   (b)  at least 100 members who have a right to vote at the meeting and hold shares in the company on which there has been paid up an average sum, per member, of at least £100.
   See also section 153 (exercise of rights where shares held on behalf of others).

(4)  A request—
   (a)  may be in hard copy form or in electronic form,
   (b)  must identify the matter to be included in the business,
   (c)  must be accompanied by a statement setting out the grounds for the request, and
   (d)  must be authenticated by the person or persons making it.

(5)  A request must be received by the company not later than—
   (i)  6 weeks before the meeting to which it relates, or
   (ii)  if later, the time at which notice is given of that meeting.][a]

---

[215]  See *Credit Development Pte Ltd v IMO Pte Ltd* [1993] 2 SLR 370 HC.
[216]  See *NRMA v Snodgrass* (2002) 170 FLR 175, SC (NSW).

ᵃ Inserted by the Companies (Shareholders' Rights) Regulations 2009, SI 2009/1632, reg 17.

COMMENCEMENT DATE 3 August 2009[217]

**13.338A.02** This section applies to traded companies (defined at section 360C) and entitles members to require that matters other than proposed resolutions be properly included in the business of an AGM. The section was introduced by the Companies (Shareholders' Rights) Regulations 2009, which came into force on 3 August 2009 and implement the EU Shareholder Rights Directive (2007/36/EC). The detailed provisions substantially mirror those of section 338 dealing with the rights of members of public companies to require circulation of proposed resolutions for AGMs.

### 339 Public companies: company's duty to circulate members' resolutions for AGMs

**13.339.01**
   (1) A company that is required under section 338 to give notice of a resolution must send a copy of it to each member of the company entitled to receive notice of the annual general meeting—
      (a) in the same manner as notice of the meeting, and
      (b) at the same time as, or as soon as reasonably practicable after, it gives notice of the meeting.
   (2) Subsection (1) has effect subject to section 340(2) (deposit or tender of sum in respect of expenses of circulation).
   (3) The business which may be dealt with at an annual general meeting includes a resolution of which notice is given in accordance with this section.
   (4) In the event of default in complying with this section, an offence is committed by every officer of the company who is in default.
   (5) A person guilty of an offence under this section is liable—
      (a) on conviction on indictment, to a fine;
      (b) on summary conviction, to a fine not exceeding the statutory maximum.

COMMENCEMENT DATE 1 October 2007[218]

**13.339.02** This section reproduces the effect of the provisions of section 376(3) to (5) of the Companies Act 1985, specifying the company's obligations to circulate a notice of a members' resolution in the same manner as the notice of the meeting and at the same time as (or as soon as reasonably practicable after) it gives notice.

**13.339.03** Failure to comply with this section gives rise to an offence on the part of every officer of the company in default.

**13.339.04** The company is, however, not obliged to circularize any notice in circumstances where a sum for expenses is required but has not been tendered or deposited. This is dealt with at section 340 of the Act.

### 340 Public companies: expenses of circulating members' resolutions for AGM

**13.340.01**
   (1) The expenses of the company in complying with section 339 need not be paid by the members who requested the circulation of the resolution if requests sufficient to require the company to circulate it are received before the end of the financial year preceding the meeting.
   (2) Otherwise—
      (a) the expenses of the company in complying with that section must be paid by the members who requested the circulation of the resolution unless the company resolves otherwise, and
      (b) unless the company has previously so resolved, it is not bound to comply with that section unless there is deposited with or tendered to it, not later than—
         (i) six weeks before the annual general meeting to which the requests relate, or
         (ii) if later, the time at which notice is given of that meeting, a sum reasonably sufficient to meet its expenses in complying with that section.

COMMENCEMENT DATE 1 October 2007[219]

**13.340.02** This section marks a change from the regime under the Companies Act 1985. Under the previous regime all requisitionists were required to deposit or tender a sum reasonably sufficient to meet the company's expenses in complying with the requisition (see section 377(1) of the Companies Act 1985). Under section 340 of the Act there is no need for the requisitionists to pay the company's expenses, provided that sufficient requests (ie sufficient to comply with the provisions of section 338(3) of the Act) have been received before the end of the financial year preceding the meeting.

---

[217] See the Companies (Shareholders' Rights) Regulations 2009, SI 2009/1632, reg 1(2).
[218] Companies Act 2006 (Commencement No 3, etc) Order 2007, S1 2007/2194, art 2(1). For the transitional provisions, see fn 212 to para 13.338.01 above.
[219] Companies Act 2006 (Commencement No 3, etc) Order 2007, S1 2007/2194, art 2(1). For the transitional provisions, see fn 212 to para 13.338.01 above.

It is always open to the company to resolve that the expenses of complying with the request should not    **13.340.03**
be met by the members: see section 340(2). Unless this happens, or the deadline under section 340(1)
is met, the position will be the same as that under the previous regime. In other words, the company is
not obliged to comply with the request unless there is deposited with it, or tendered to it, a sum
reasonably sufficient to meet its expenses in complying with section 339. The sum must be deposited
with or tendered to the company no later than six weeks before the AGM to which the requests
relate,[220] or the time at which notice is given of the meeting, if later.

## [340A  Traded companies: duty to circulate members' items for AGM

(1) A company that is required under section 338A to include any matter in the business to be dealt    **13.340A.01**
with at an annual general meeting must—
   (a) give notice of it to each member of the company entitled to receive notice of the annual
       general meeting—
       (i) in the same manner as notice of the meeting, and
       (ii) at the same time as, or as soon as reasonably practicable after, it gives notice of the
            meeting, and
   (b) publish it on the same website as that on which the company published the information
       required by section 311A.
(2) Subsection (1) has effect subject to section 340B(2) (deposit or tender of sum in respect of
    expenses of circulation).
(3) In the event of default in complying with this section, an offence is committed by every officer of
    the company who is in default.
(4) A person guilty of an offence under this section is liable—
   (a) on conviction on indictment, to a fine;
   (b) on summary conviction, to a fine not exceeding the statutory maximum.][a]

AMENDMENTS

[a] Inserted by the Companies (Shareholders' Rights) Regulations 2009, SI 2009/1632, reg 18.

COMMENCEMENT DATE  3 August 2009[221]

This section applies to traded companies (defined at section 360C) and provides for the obligation    **13.340A.02**
which corresponds to the entitlements of members of traded companies under section 338A to require
that matters other than proposed resolutions be properly included in the business of an AGM. The
section was introduced by the Companies (Shareholders' Rights) Regulations 2009, which came into
force on 3 August 2009 and implement the EU Shareholder Rights Directive (2007/36/EC).

## [340B  Traded companies: expenses of circulating other matters to be dealt with at AGM

(1) The expenses of the company in complying with section 340A need not be paid by the members    **13.340B.01**
who requested the inclusion of the matter in the business to be dealt with at the annual general
meeting if requests sufficient to require the company to include the matter are received before the
end of the financial year preceding the meeting.
(2) Otherwise—
   (a) the expenses of the company in complying with that section must be paid by the members
       who requested the inclusion of the matter unless the company resolves otherwise, and
   (b) unless the company has previously so resolved, it is not bound to comply with that section
       unless there is deposited with or tendered to it, not later than—
       (i) six weeks before the annual general meeting to which the requests relate, or
       (ii) if later, the time at which notice is given of that meeting,
       a sum reasonably sufficient to meet its expenses in complying with that section.][a]

AMENDMENTS

[a] Inserted by the Companies (Shareholders' Rights) Regulations 2009, SI 2009/1632, reg 18.

COMMENCEMENT DATE  3 August 2009[222]

This section applies to traded companies (defined at section 360C) and relates to the company's    **13.340B.02**
expenses of complying with a request under section 338A (in substance mirroring the provisions of
section 340 which relate to a public company's expenses of circulating members' resolutions). The
section was introduced by the Companies (Shareholders' Rights) Regulations 2009, which came into
force on 3 August 2009 and implements the EU Shareholder Rights Directive (2007/36/EC).

---

[220] Excluding the day of the meeting and the day on which notice is received: see s 360(1).
[221] See the Companies (Shareholders' Rights) Regulations 2009, SI 2009/1632, reg 1(2).
[222] See the Companies (Shareholders' Rights) Regulations 2009, SI 2009/1632, reg 1(2).

CHAPTER 5

ADDITIONAL REQUIREMENTS FOR QUOTED COMPANIES
[AND TRADED COMPANIES][a]

*Website publication of poll results*

### 341  Results of poll to be made available on website

**13.341.01**    (1)  Where a poll is taken at a general meeting of a quoted company [that is not a traded company],[b] the company must ensure that the following information is made available on a website—
    (a)  the date of the meeting,
    (b)  the text of the resolution or, as the case may be, a description of the subject matter of the poll,
    (c)  the number of votes cast in favour, and
    (d)  the number of votes cast against.
  [(1A) Where a poll is taken at a general meeting of a traded company, the company must ensure that the following information is available on a website—
    (a)  the date of the meeting,
    (b)  the text of the resolution or, as the case may be, a description of the subject matter of the poll,
    (c)  the number of votes validly cast,
    (d)  the proportion of the company's issued share capital at close of business on the day before the meeting represented by those votes;
    (e)  the number of votes cast in favour,
    (f)  the number of votes cast against,
    (g)  the number of abstentions (if counted).
  (1B)  A traded company must comply with subsection (1A) not later than—
    (a)  the end of the 16 days beginning with the day of the meeting, or
    (b)  if later, the end of the first working day following the day on which the results of the poll were declared.][c]
  (2)  The provisions of section 353 (requirements as to website availability) apply.
  (3)  In the event of default in complying with this section (or with the requirements of section 353 as it applies for the purposes of this section), an offence is committed by every officer of the company who is in default.
  (4)  A person guilty of an offence under subsection (3) is liable on summary conviction to a fine not exceeding level 3 on the standard scale.
  (5)  Failure to comply with this section (or the requirements of section 353) does not affect the validity of—
    (a)  the poll, or
    (b)  the resolution or other business (if passed or agreed to) to which the poll relates.
  (6)  This section only applies to polls taken after this section comes into force.

AMENDMENTS

[a]  Amended by the Companies (Shareholders' Rights) Regulations 2009, SI 2009/1632, reg 19.

[b]  Amended by the Companies (Shareholders' Rights) Regulations 2009, SI 2009/1632, reg 19.

[c]  Inserted by the Companies (Shareholders' Rights) Regulations 2009, SI 2009/1632, reg 19.

COMMENCEMENT DATE 1 October 2007[223]; 3 August 2009[224]

**13.341.02**    This Chapter of Part 13 introduces two new requirements for quoted companies. The first comprises an obligation to publish the results of polls at general meetings on an internet website. The second comprises an obligation on quoted companies to obtain an independent report on a poll if sufficient members demand one (and to publish that report on a website). Both these measures were recommended by the Company Law Review Steering Group in their Final Report (paragraph 6.39(ii) and (iv)).

**13.341.03**    The expression 'quoted company' in Part 13 has the same meaning as that given in Part 15 of the Act (see section 361). Part 15 explains the meaning of quoted company at section 385. Section 385(2) specifies the markets as the official list, the equivalents in EEA States, the New York Stock Exchange, and Nasdaq. The Secretary of State may extend or limit the ambit of section 385(1) and (2) so as to expand or restrict the categories of companies that are quoted companies.

---

[223]  Companies Act 2006 (Commencement No 3, etc) Order 2007, SI 2007/2194, art 2(1).
[224]  As regards the amendments referred to in notes a to c.

Where a poll has been taken at a general meeting of a quoted company, section 341 of the Act obliges **13.341.04** the company to publish on a website (as a minimum) the date of the meeting, the text of the resolution (or description of the subject matter of the poll), and the number of votes cast for and against the resolution. It is obviously open to a company to provide more information if it wishes to.

The provisions at section 341(A) and (B) contain separate requirements in relation to the matters to be **13.341.05** made available on a website in the case of traded companies. These were introduced with effect from 3 August 2009 by the Companies (Shareholders' Rights) Regulations 2009 (which implement the EU Shareholder Rights Directive (2007/36/EC)). A 'traded company' is defined at section 360(C) and means a company any shares of which carry rights to vote at general meetings and are admitted to trading on a regulated market in an EEA State by or with the consent of the company.

Under section 353, the website must be maintained by or on behalf of the quoted company and must **13.341.06** identify the company. Access to information of the website, and the ability to obtain a hard copy of the information on the site, must not be conditional on the payment of a fee or otherwise restricted (see section 353(2) and (3)). In addition, the information must be made available as soon as reasonably practicable and must be kept available throughout a two-year period beginning with the date the information is first made available (section 353(3)). However, a failure to make information available throughout that period may be disregarded if the information is available on the website for part of the period and the failure is wholly attributable to circumstances that it would not be reasonable to have expected the company to prevent or avoid (see section 353(5)). This would presumably include interruption of the service provided by the third party service providers, provided that the provider and system selected by the company is itself a reasonable one.

Failure to comply with the obligations in section 341 will render all the officers of the company in **13.341.07** default guilty of an offence (section 341(3) and (4)). However, it will not affect the validity of the poll or the resolution or other business to which the poll relates (section 341(5)).

### *Independent report on a poll*

### 342  Members' power to require independent report on poll

(1)  The members of a quoted company may require the directors to obtain an independent report on **13.342.01** any poll taken, or to be taken, at a general meeting of the company.

(2)  The directors are required to obtain an independent report if they receive requests to do so from—

    (a)  members representing not less than 5% of the total voting rights of all the members who have a right to vote on the matter to which the poll relates (excluding any voting rights attached to any shares in the company held as treasury shares), or

    (b)  not less than 100 members who have a right to vote on the matter to which the poll relates and hold shares in the company on which there has been paid up an average sum, per member, of not less than £100.

    See also section 153 (exercise of rights where shares held on behalf of others).

(3)  Where the requests relate to more than one poll, subsection (2) must be satisfied in relation to each of them.

(4)  A request—

    (a)  may be in hard copy form or in electronic form,

    (b)  must identify the poll or polls to which it relates,

    (c)  must be authenticated by the person or persons making it, and

    (d)  must be received by the company not later than one week after the date on which the poll is taken.

COMMENCEMENT DATE  1 October 2007[225]

Under this new provision of the Act, the directors of a quoted company must obtain an independent **13.342.02** report on any poll taken (or to be taken) at a general meeting of the company, if they receive requests to do so from members representing at least 5 per cent of the total voting rights of members having a right to vote on the matter to which the poll relates (excluding any shares in the company held as treasury shares), or from at least 100 members having a right to vote on the matter to which the poll relates and on whose shares there has been paid up an average sum, per member, of at least £100: see section 342(1) and (2).

---

[225]  Companies Act 2006 (Commencement No 3, etc) Order 2007, SI 2007/2194, art 2(1). Sections 342–354 of the Act apply to polls taken at meetings of which notice was given on or after 1 October 2007. Where notice of a meeting is given over more than one day, it is treated as given on the first of those days. See Sch 3, para 39 to this Order.

**13.342.03**    The content of the independent report is explained at section 347 of the Act (see paragraph 13.347.02 below). The maker of the report and the independence requirement are dealt with at sections 343 to 346 of the Act, considered below.

**13.342.04**    Although the request may be made in advance of the meeting, unless it is clear (say) from the quoted company's articles that a poll will be called, the members may need to take steps to ensure that a poll is called. As to this, see section 321 of the Act dealt with above.

**13.342.05**    Where the requests relate to more than one poll, the conditions in subsection (2) must be met in relation to each of them (section 342(3)).

**13.342.06**    As for the request itself, this may be in hard copy or electronic form, but must identify the poll or polls to which it relates, must be authenticated by the person making the request, and must be received by the quoted company no later than one week after the date on which the poll is taken.

### 343 Appointment of independent assessor

**13.343.01**
(1) Directors who are required under section 342 to obtain an independent report on a poll or polls must appoint a person they consider to be appropriate (an 'independent assessor') to prepare a report for the company on it or them.
(2) The appointment must be made within one week after the company being required to obtain the report.
(3) The directors must not appoint a person who—
  (a) does not meet the independence requirement in section 344, or
  (b) has another role in relation to any poll on which he is to report (including, in particular, a role in connection with collecting or counting votes or with the appointment of proxies).
(4) In the event of default in complying with this section, an offence is committed by every officer of the company who is in default.
(5) A person guilty of an offence under this section is liable on summary conviction to a fine not exceeding level 5 on the standard scale.
(6) If at the meeting no poll on which a report is required is taken—
  (a) the directors are not required to obtain a report from the independent assessor, and
  (b) his appointment ceases (but without prejudice to any right to be paid for work done before the appointment ceased).

COMMENCEMENT DATE 1 October 2007[226]

**13.343.02**    Following requests that trigger the obligation under section 342, the directors of the quoted company must, within one week, appoint an independent assessor they consider to be 'appropriate'. The Act does not give guidance as to the factors that would render a person appropriate, save that it lists exclusionary factors (namely that he must be independent and already involved in the voting process of the quoted company). The independence requirement is dealt with in more detail at section 344.

**13.343.03**    Under section 343(3), the directors must not appoint anyone who does not meet the independence requirement in section 344 (see paragraph 13.344.02–04 below). Nor may they appoint any person who has any other role in relation to the poll on which he is to report. This will include, in particular, any role in connection with collecting or counting votes or appointing proxies.

**13.343.04**    In those situations where the obligation under section 342 is triggered before the meeting takes place it is possible when the meeting happens that no poll will actually be required to be taken. In these circumstances there is no obligation on the directors to obtain a report (see section 343(6)(a)) and any existing appointment ceases (without prejudice to the assessor's right to be paid for work done)—see section 343(6)(b).

### 344 Independence requirement

**13.344.01**
(1) A person may not be appointed as an independent assessor—
  (a) if he is—
    (i) an officer or employee of the company, or
    (ii) a partner or employee of such a person, or a partnership of which such a person is a partner;
  (b) if he is—
    (i) an officer or employee of an associated undertaking of the company, or
    (ii) a partner or employee of such a person, or a partnership of which such a person is a partner;

---

[226] Companies Act 2006 (Commencement No 3, etc) Order 2007, SI 2007/2194, art 2(1). For the transitional provisions, see fn 224 to para 13.342.01 above.

(c) if there exists between—
   (i) the person or an associate of his, and
   (ii) the company or an associated undertaking of the company, a connection of any such description as may be specified by regulations made by the Secretary of State.
(2) An auditor of the company is not regarded as an officer or employee of the company for this purpose.
(3) In this section—
   'associated undertaking' means—
   (a) a parent undertaking or subsidiary undertaking of the company, or
   (b) a subsidiary undertaking of a parent undertaking of the company; and
   'associate' has the meaning given by section 345.
(4) Regulations under this section are subject to negative resolution procedure.

COMMENCEMENT DATE 1 October 2007[227]

This section explains the independence requirement in more detail. The persons excluded from appointment as independent assessors include the quoted company's officers and employees and their respective partners and employees (including, in the latter case, employees of any partnership of which any officer or employee of the company is partner): section 344(1)(a). Section 344(1)(b) extends the restriction in like terms to officers and employees of associated undertakings of the quoted company (and their respective partners and employees). Both these provisions are to substantially the same effect as (and are in similar terms to) the provisions in section 27 of the Companies Act 1989 relating to the ineligibility of a person for appointment as a company auditor on the grounds of lack of independence.                                                                                                 **13.344.02**

The extended restriction at 344(1)(c) will apply where there is between a person or an associate of his (which is defined by section 345 of the Act) and the quoted company or an associated undertaking of the company (as defined at section 344(3)) a 'connection of any such description' as may be specified by regulations made by the Secretary of State, those being subject to the negative resolution procedure (section 344(4)). This section also echoes the provisions of section 27(2) of the Companies Act 1989 in relation to auditors, now reproduced at section 1214(4) of the Act. In fact, no regulations were ever made under section 27(2) of the Companies Act 1989.                                                  **13.344.03**

An auditor of the company is not regarded as an officer or employee of the quoted company for the purposes of this section and an auditor may accordingly act as independent assessor. However, statutory auditors are subject to their own independence requirements under section 1214 of the Act.        **13.344.04**

## 345  Meaning of 'associate'

(1) This section defines 'associate' for the purposes of section 344 (independence requirement).          **13.345.01**
(2) In relation to an individual, 'associate' means—
   (a) that individual's spouse or civil partner or minor child or step-child,
   (b) any body corporate of which that individual is a director, and
   (c) any employee or partner of that individual.
(3) In relation to a body corporate, 'associate' means—
   (a) any body corporate of which that body is a director,
   (b) any body corporate in the same group as that body, and
   (c) any employee or partner of that body or of any body corporate in the same group.
(4) In relation to a partnership that is a legal person under the law by which it is governed, 'associate' means—
   (a) any body corporate of which that partnership is a director,
   (b) any employee of or partner in that partnership, and
   (c) any person who is an associate of a partner in that partnership.
(5) In relation to a partnership that is not a legal person under the law by which it is governed, 'associate' means any person who is an associate of any of the partners.
(6) In this section, in relation to a limited liability partnership, for 'director' read 'member'.

COMMENCEMENT DATE 1 October 2007[228]

This section defines 'associate' for the purposes of section 344 of the Act. It substantially reproduces the provisions of section 52 of the Companies Act 1989, relating to the definition of associate for the purposes of the Part of that Act dealing with eligibility for appointment as a company auditor. For that     **13.345.02**

---

[227] Companies Act 2006 (Commencement No 3, etc) Order 2007, SI 2007/2194, art 2(1). For the transitional provisions, see fn 224 to para 13.342.01 above.
[228] Companies Act 2006 (Commencement No 3, etc) Order 2007, SI 2007/2194, art 2(1). For the transitional provisions, see fn 224 to para 13.342.01 above.

purpose substantially the same definition is also reproduced at section 1260 of this Act in connection with the eligibility of persons for appointment as a company auditor.

### 346 Effect of appointment of a partnership

**13.346.01**
(1) This section applies where a partnership that is not a legal person under the law by which it is governed is appointed as an independent assessor.

(2) Unless a contrary intention appears, the appointment is of the partnership as such and not of the partners.

(3) Where the partnership ceases, the appointment is to be treated as extending to—

    (a) any partnership that succeeds to the practice of that partnership, or

    (b) any other person who succeeds to that practice having previously carried it on in partnership.

(4) For the purposes of subsection (3)—

    (a) a partnership is regarded as succeeding to the practice of another partnership only if the members of the successor partnership are substantially the same as those of the former partnership, and

    (b) a partnership or other person is regarded as succeeding to the practice of a partnership only if it or he succeeds to the whole or substantially the whole of the business of the former partnership.

(5) Where the partnership ceases and the appointment is not treated under subsection (3) as extending to any partnership or other person, the appointment may with the consent of the company be treated as extending to a partnership, or other person, who succeeds to—

    (a) the business of the former partnership, or

    (b) such part of it as is agreed by the company is to be treated as comprising the appointment.

COMMENCEMENT DATE 1 October 2007[229]

**13.346.02** This provision is (*mutatis mutandis*) to substantially the same effect as, and is in very similar terms to, the provisions of section 26 of the Companies Act 1989, dealing with the effect of the appointment of a partnership as company auditor.

**13.346.03** Unless the contrary intention appears, the appointment is of the partnership, rather than the partners. When the partnership ceases the appointment is to be taken as extending to any successor partnership (where the successor partnership has substantially the same members of the former partnership) or to any of the former partnership carrying on the practice on his own. In both cases, however, the partnership or person must succeed to the whole or substantially the whole of the business of the former partnership.

**13.346.04** Where the above conditions cannot be met, the appointment may with the consent of the quoted company be treated as extending to a partnership or other person who succeeds to the business of the former partnership, or to such part of it as is agreed by the company to be treated as comprising the appointment.

**13.346.05** In relation to the eligibility of auditors, section 1216 of the Act contains very similar provisions to those at section 346 relating to the appointment of an independent assessor.

### 347 The independent assessor's report

**13.347.01**
(1) The report of the independent assessor must state his opinion whether—

    (a) the procedures adopted in connection with the poll or polls were adequate;

    (b) the votes cast (including proxy votes) were fairly and accurately recorded and counted;

    (c) the validity of members' appointments of proxies was fairly assessed;

    (d) the notice of the meeting complied with section 325 (notice of meeting to contain statement of rights to appoint proxy);

    (e) section 326 (company-sponsored invitations to appoint proxies) was complied with in relation to the meeting.

(2) The report must give his reasons for the opinions stated.

(3) If he is unable to form an opinion on any of those matters, the report must record that fact and state the reasons for it.

(4) The report must state the name of the independent assessor.

COMMENCEMENT DATE 1 October 2007[230]

---

[229] Companies Act 2006 (Commencement No 3, etc) Order 2007, SI 2007/2194, art 2(1). For the transitional provisions, see fn 224 to para 13.342.01 above.

[230] Companies Act 2006 (Commencement No 3, etc) Order 2007, SI 2007/2194, art 2(1). For the transitional provisions, see fn 224 to para 13.342.01 above.

This section provides for the minimum amount of information that must be contained in the    **13.347.02**
independent assessor's report. The report must contain the independent assessor's opinion, with
reasons, as to each of the five matters set out in section 347(1). So far as concerns the taking of the poll,
the votes should be taken in writing, and it should be recorded how many votes each shareholder is
entitled to cast and does cast. In this context, a shareholder need not cast all his votes, and may cast
certain votes in different ways. This is particularly the case with trust corporations or similar institutional shareholders which may hold shares in different trusts or funds. If there is more than one
resolution, the poll must be taken on each resolution separately (although this can be done on one
piece of paper, provided that the votes can clearly mark their votes separately on the different
resolutions).[231]

In forming his opinion under section 347(1), the independent assessor will have to have regard to the    **13.347.03**
requirements of the Act, as well as the provisions of the relevant quoted company's articles of
association dealing with the taking of polls. As a general matter, the chairman should fix the hours
during which the poll is to be taken, and if he does not do so he cannot close the poll for so long as
shareholders continue to cast their votes. He may, however, close the poll if there are no more votes
coming in, and he has waited a reasonable time.[232]

## 348  Rights of independent assessor: right to attend meeting etc

(1) Where an independent assessor has been appointed to report on a poll, he is entitled to attend—    **13.348.01**
   (a) the meeting at which the poll may be taken, and
   (b) any subsequent proceedings in connection with the poll.
(2) He is also entitled to be provided by the company with a copy of—
   (a) the notice of the meeting, and
   (b) any other communication provided by the company in connection with the meeting to
     persons who have a right to vote on the matter to which the poll relates.
(3) The rights conferred by this section are only to be exercised to the extent that the independent
   assessor considers necessary for the preparation of his report.
(4) If the independent assessor is a firm, the right under subsection (1) to attend the meeting and any
   subsequent proceedings in connection with the poll is exercisable by an individual authorised by
   the firm in writing to act as its representative for that purpose.

COMMENCEMENT DATE 1 October 2007[233]

This section provides the independent assessor (and, in the case of a firm, its authorized representative)    **13.348.02**
with rights as against the quoted company to attend any meeting in connection with the poll and to be
provided with the notice of the meeting and any other communication in connection with the meeting
provided by the company to persons entitled to vote. The right is only to be exercised to the extent that
the independent assessor considers necessary for the preparation of his report.

This section is to be read in conjunction with section 349, which provides further rights of access to    **13.348.03**
information on the part of the independent assessor.

## 349  Rights of independent assessor: right to information

(1) The independent assessor is entitled to access to the company's records relating to—    **13.349.01**
   (a) any poll on which he is to report;
   (b) the meeting at which the poll or polls may be, or were, taken.
(2) The independent assessor may require anyone who at any material time was—
   (a) a director or secretary of the company,
   (b) an employee of the company,
   (c) a person holding or accountable for any of the company's records,
   (d) a member of the company, or
   (e) an agent of the company,
   to provide him with information or explanations for the purpose of preparing his report.
(3) For this purpose 'agent' includes the company's bankers, solicitors and auditor.
(4) A statement made by a person in response to a requirement under this section may not be used
   in evidence against him in criminal proceedings except proceedings for an offence under section
   350 (offences relating to provision of information).

---

[231]  See *Re RE Jones Ltd* (1933) 50 TLR 31.
[232]  See *R v St Pancras* (1839) 11 A&E 15; *R v Lambeth* (1838) 8 A&E 356.
[233]  Companies Act 2006 (Commencement No 3, etc) Order 2007, S1 2007/2194, art 2(1). For the transitional
provisions, see fn 224 to 13.342.01 above.

(5) A person is not required by this section to disclose information in respect of which a claim to legal professional privilege (in Scotland, to confidentiality of communications) could be maintained in legal proceedings.

COMMENCEMENT DATE 1 October 2007[234]

**13.349.02** This section provides two wide sets of powers to the independent assessor. The first, under section 349(1), entitles him to assess to the quoted company's records relating to any poll on which he is to report, and relating to the meeting at which any poll may be, or has been taken. The latter power in particular is wide on its face and is not expressly restricted by any qualification of the sort provided at section 348(3). However, although this is not expressly stated in the section, the right is only provided for the purpose of compiling the independent assessor's report, and the entitlement under section 349(1) should be seen accordingly.

**13.349.03** The right to information under section 349(2) is expressly limited to information or explanations required for the purpose of preparing the independent assessor's report, but the request may be made of a wide class of persons. In particular, these include employees of the quoted company, shareholders, and an 'agent' of the company (which, by virtue of section 349(3), includes the company's bankers, solicitors, and auditors).

**13.349.04** This section does not oblige any person to disclose information to which a claim to legal professional privilege can be maintained, which will be of particular relevance in connection with requests made of a company's solicitors (section 349(5)). Section 349(4) also provides that any statement made by a person in response to a requirement under section 349 may not be used in evidence against him in criminal proceedings, except (of course) in proceedings for an offence under section 350, which relates to failures to comply with a requirement under section 349.

### 350 Offences relating to provision of information

**13.350.01**
(1) A person who fails to comply with a requirement under section 349 without delay commits an offence unless it was not reasonably practicable for him to provide the required information or explanation.
(2) A person guilty of an offence under subsection (1) is liable on summary conviction to a fine not exceeding level 3 on the standard scale.
(3) A person commits an offence who knowingly or recklessly makes to an independent assessor a statement (oral or written) that—
  (a) conveys or purports to convey any information or explanations which the independent assessor requires, or is entitled to require, under section 349, and
  (b) is misleading, false or deceptive in a material particular.
(4) A person guilty of an offence under subsection (3) is liable—
  (a) on conviction on indictment, to imprisonment for a term not exceeding two years or a fine (or both);
  (b) on summary conviction—
    (i) in England and Wales, to imprisonment for a term not exceeding twelve months or to a fine not exceeding the statutory maximum (or both);
    (ii) in Scotland or Northern Ireland, to imprisonment for a term not exceeding six months, or to a fine not exceeding the statutory maximum (or both).
(5) Nothing in this section affects any right of an independent assessor to apply for an injunction (in Scotland, an interdict or an order for specific performance) to enforce any of his rights under section 348 or 349.

COMMENCEMENT DATE 1 October 2007[235]

**13.350.02** This section provides for two distinct offences relating to the provision of information to an independent assessor.

**13.350.03** Section 350(1) makes it an offence for any person to fail to comply with a requirement under section 349 without delay, unless it was not reasonably practicable for him to provide the required information or explanation. Section 349 provides no timetable for the provision of information requested, but it is clear from section 350 that the information must be provided 'without delay'. It is suggested that what

---

[234] Companies Act 2006 (Commencement No 3, etc) Order 2007, SI 2007/2194, art 2(1). For the transitional provisions, see fn 224 to para 13.342.01 above.
[235] Companies Act 2006 (Commencement No 3, etc) Order 2007, SI 2007/2194, art 2(1). For the transitional provisions, see fn 224 to para 13.342.01 above.

will constitute a delay will in practice vary according to the circumstances. In any event, if it is not reasonably practicable to provide information earlier than it is in fact provided, it is submitted that closing words of subsection 350(1) will operate to provide a defence under the subsection. A person committing an offence under this subsection is liable on summary conviction to a fine.

Section 350(3) makes it an indictable offence for a person knowingly or recklessly to make an oral or **13.350.04** written statement to an independent assessor which is misleading, false, or deceptive in any material particular, and which conveys (or purports to convey) information or explanations which the independent assessor requires or is entitled to require under section 349. It should be noted that this offence covers not only statements that are a response to any request under section 349. It also covers statements that are made to the independent assessor voluntarily or without request, provided that the statements convey information or explanations that the independent assessor could have required under section 349.

The criminal sanctions do not affect any right of an independent assessor to seek an injunction to **13.350.05** enforce his rights under section 348 and 349.

## 351  Information to be made available on website

    (1)  Where an independent assessor has been appointed to report on a poll, the company must ensure **13.351.01** that the following information is made available on a website—
        (a)  the fact of his appointment,
        (b)  his identity,
        (c)  the text of the resolution or, as the case may be, a description of the subject matter of the poll to which his appointment relates, and
        (d)  a copy of a report by him which complies with section 347.
    (2)  The provisions of section 353 (requirements as to website availability) apply.
    (3)  In the event of default in complying with this section (or with the requirements of section 353 as it applies for the purposes of this section), an offence is committed by every officer of the company who is in default.
    (4)  A person guilty of an offence under subsection (3) is liable on summary conviction to a fine not exceeding level 3 on the standard scale.
    (5)  Failure to comply with this section (or the requirements of section 353) does not affect the validity of—
        (a)  the poll, or
        (b)  the resolution or other business (if passed or agreed to) to which the poll relates.

COMMENCEMENT DATE 1 October 2007[236]

This section requires the quoted company to publish the report of the independent assessor on a **13.351.02** website, and sets out the minimum requirements as to the information that is to be provided. These include that the fact of his appointment, his identity, the text of the resolution (or, as the case may be, a description of the subject matter) of the poll to which his appointment relates, and a copy of his report duly complying with section 347.

The requirements as to website availability are contained in section 353 (which deals also with the **13.351.03** requirements of website availability for the purposes of section 341) and are expressly applied to this section by subsection 351(3). Under section 353, the website must be maintained by or on behalf of the quoted company and must identify the company. Access to information of the website, and the ability to obtain a hard copy of the information on the site, must not be conditional on the payment of a fee or otherwise restricted (see section 353(2) and (3)). In addition, the information must be made available as soon as reasonably practicable and must be kept available throughout a two-year period beginning with the date the information is first made available (section 353(3)). However, a failure to make information available throughout that period may be disregarded if the information is available on the website for part of the period and the failure is wholly attributable to circumstances that it would not be reasonable to have expected the company to prevent or avoid (see section 353(5)). This would presumably include interruption of the service provided by the third party service providers, provided that the provider and system selected by the company is itself a reasonable one.

Failure to comply with this section gives rise to an offence by every officer of the company which is in **13.351.04** default, but does not affect the validity of any poll or resolution or other business to which the poll relates.

---

[236]  Companies Act 2006 (Commencement No 3, etc) Order 2007, SI 2007/2194, art 2(1). For the transitional provisions, see fn 224 to para 13.342.01 above.

## *Supplementary*

### 352 Application of provisions to class meetings

**13.352.01**   [(1) The provisions of section 341 (results of poll to be made available on website) apply (with any necessary modifications) in relation to a meeting of holders of a class of shares of a quoted company or traded company in connection with the variation of the rights attached to such shares as they apply in relation to a general meeting of the company.

(1A) The provisions of sections 342 to 351 (independent report on poll) apply (with any necessary modifications) in relation to a meeting of holders of a class of shares of a quoted company in connection with the variation of the rights attached to such shares as they apply in relation to a general meeting of the company.][a]

(2) For the purposes of this section—

(a) any amendment of a provision contained in a company's articles for the variation of the rights attached to a class of shares, or the insertion of any such provision into the articles, is itself to be treated as a variation of those rights, and

(b) references to the variation of rights attached to a class of shares include references to their abrogation.

AMENDMENTS

[a]  Amended by the Companies (Shareholders' Rights) Regulations 2009, SI 2009/1632, reg 19.

COMMENCEMENT DATE  1 October 2007[237]; 3 August 2009[238]

**13.352.02**   So far as quoted companies are concerned, this section applies substantially all the provisions of Chapter 5 (additional requirements for quoted and traded companies) to any class meetings of a company in connection with the variation of the rights attaching to the class of shares. As for traded companies, the provisions of section 341 (results of poll to be made available on a website) apply in relation to class meetings of those companies. The provisions in relation to traded companies were introduced by the Companies (Shareholders' Rights) Regulations 2009, which implement the EU Shareholder Rights Directive (2007/36/EC). A 'traded company' is defined at section 360C.

**13.352.03**   Class rights, and variations of class rights, are dealt with in Chapter 9 of Part 17 of the Act (classes of shares and class rights). Whereas the Companies Act 1985 contained no definition of what constitutes a class of shares,[239] section 629 of the Act contains a definition of class rights for the purposes of Chapter 9 of Part 17; namely, that shares are to be regarded as one class if the rights attaching to them are in all respects uniform.[240]

**13.352.04**   As for what constitutes a variation of rights, see the discussion in relation to section 630 of the Act in Division 17 below. In this regard, section 352(2)(a) and (b) reproduce (to materially the same effect) the provisions of section 125(7) and (8) respectively of the Companies Act 1985. By virtue of section 352(2)(a) any alteration of a provision for the variation of class rights, or the insertion of such a provision, is itself to be treated as a variation of those rights. By virtue of section 352(2)(b) references to the variation of rights attached to a class of shares include reference to their abrogation. These sections (as with predecessor sections under the Companies Act 1985) reflect the previous law.

### 353 Requirements as to website availability

**13.353.01**   (1) The following provisions apply for the purposes of—

section 341 (results of poll to be made available on website), and

section 351 (report of independent observer to be made available on website).

(2) The information must be made available on a website that—

(a) is maintained by or on behalf of the company, and

(b) identifies the company in question.

(3) Access to the information on the website, and the ability to obtain a hard copy of the information from the website, must not be conditional on the payment of a fee or otherwise restricted.

(4) The information—

(a) must be made available as soon as reasonably practicable, and

(b) must be kept available throughout the period of two years beginning with the date on which it is first made available on a website in accordance with this section.

---

[237]  Companies Act 2006 (Commencement No 3, etc) Order 2007, SI 2007/2194, art 2(1). For the transitional provisions, see fn 224 to para 13.342.01 above.

[238]  As regards the amendments referred to in note a.

[239]  As to which see *per* Scott J in *Cumbrian Newspapers Group Ltd v Cumberland and Westmorland Herald Newspapers & Printing Co Ltd* [1987] Ch 1, 22.

[240]  Save that shares are not to be treated as being of different classes simply because they do not carry the same rights to dividend in the 12 months following allotment; see s 643(2).

(5)  A failure to make information available on a website throughout the period specified in subsection (4)(b) is disregarded if—

    (a)  the information is made available on the website for part of that period, and

    (b)  the failure is wholly attributable to circumstances that it would not be reasonable to have expected the company to prevent or avoid.

COMMENCEMENT DATE  1 October 2007[241]

This section sets out the minimum requirements that should apply to information to be published on a quoted company's website under section 341 and 351. The requirements of the section are discussed in more detail in the commentary in relation to each of those sections above.    **13.353.02**

### 354  Power to limit or extend the types of company to which provisions of this Chapter apply

(1)  The Secretary of State may by regulations—    **13.354.01**

    (a)  limit the types of company to which some or all of the provisions of this Chapter apply, or

    (b)  extend some or all of the provisions of this Chapter to additional types of company.

(2)  Regulations under this section extending the application of any provision of this Chapter are subject to affirmative resolution procedure.

(3)  Any other regulations under this section are subject to negative resolution procedure.

(4)  Regulations under this section may—

    (a)  amend the provisions of this Chapter (apart from this section);

    (b)  repeal and re-enact provisions of this Chapter with modifications of form or arrangement, whether or not they are modified in substance;

    (c)  contain such consequential, incidental and supplementary provisions (including provisions amending, repealing or revoking enactments) as the Secretary of State thinks fit.

COMMENCEMENT DATE  1 October 2007[242]

In its original form, the provisions of this Chapter of Part 13 applied to any 'quoted company'. The expression 'quoted company' in Part 13 has the same meaning as that given in Part 15 of the Act (see section 361). Part 15 explains the meaning of quoted company at section 385. The Secretary of State may extend or limit the ambit of section 385(1) and (2) so as to expand or restrict the categories of companies that are quoted companies.    **13.354.02**

Section 354 provides for a further power on the part of the Secretary of State to make regulations to limit or extend the types of company to which some or all of the provisions of this Chapter of Part 13 applies. This is additional to the Secretary of State's powers under section 385 to expand or restrict the categories of companies that are quoted companies. Following the coming into force of the Companies (Shareholders' Rights) Regulations 2009, SI 2009/1632, which implement the EU Shareholder Rights Directive (2007/36/EC), Chapter 5 now applies also to 'traded companies' as defined at section 360C.    **13.354.03**

## CHAPTER 6
## RECORDS OF RESOLUTIONS AND MEETINGS

### 355  Records of resolutions and meetings etc

(1)  Every company must keep records comprising—    **13.355.01**

    (a)  copies of all resolutions of members passed otherwise than at general meetings,

    (b)  minutes of all proceedings of general meetings, and

    (c)  details provided to the company in accordance with section 357 (decisions of sole member).

(2)  The records must be kept for at least ten years from the date of the resolution, meeting or decision (as appropriate).

(3)  If a company fails to comply with this section, an offence is committed by every officer of the company who is in default.

(4)  A person guilty of an offence under this section is liable on summary conviction to a fine not exceeding level 3 on the standard scale and, for continued contravention, a daily default fine not exceeding one-tenth of level 3 on the standard scale

COMMENCEMENT DATE  1 October 2007[243]

---

[241] Companies Act 2006 (Commencement No 3, etc) Order 2007, SI 2007/2194, art 2(1). For the transitional provisions, see fn 224 to para 13.342.01 above.

[242] Companies Act 2006 (Commencement No 3, etc) Order 2007, SI 2007/2194, art 2(1). For the transitional provisions, see fn 224 to para 13.342.01 above.

[243] Companies Act 2006 (Commencement No 3, etc) Order 2007, SI 2007/2194, art 2(1). For the transitional provisions, see Sch 3, para 40 to this Order.

**13.355.02**    Section 355 consolidates and simplifies record keeping provisions previously split amongst sections 382 and 382A of the Companies Act 1985 and expands the obligations of a company in respect of decisions of a sole member. As a general point, companies are now required to keep records of resolutions and meetings rather than minute books.[244] The manner in which records may be kept is set out in detail in Part 37, sections 1134 to 1135 of the Act. This section and sections 356 to 359 apply to resolutions passed, meetings held or decisions taken on or after 1 October 2007.[245]

**13.355.03**    Subsection (1) replaces sections 382A(1) (in respect of resolutions of the members passed other than by general meeting) and 382(1) (in respect of proceedings at general meetings). In addition it provides that a company must keep the details provided to it by a sole member in compliance with section 357. Previously the obligation lay only on the sole member to provide details of decisions to the company.[246] There was no express obligation to retain such details. Records of class meetings are also covered by this section.[247] Meetings of directors are covered by sections 248 and 249 of the Act.

**13.355.04**    Subsection (2) limits the period for which such records have to be kept to 10 years. Previously records of general meetings had to be retained indefinitely by virtue of the Companies Act 1985, section 383(1) which provided that a company had to keep available for inspection the books containing the minutes of a general meeting held on or after 1 November 1929.

**13.355.05**    Subsections (3) and (4) create an offence for any officer of a company who is in default of the obligations under subsections (1) and (2). They replace the Companies Act 1985, sections 382(5) (in relation to proceedings at general meetings) and 382A(3) (in respect of written resolutions). The failure to maintain a record of a particular resolution does not preclude proof that the resolution was passed.[248]

### 356  Records as evidence of resolutions etc

**13.356.01**    (1)  This section applies to the records kept in accordance with section 355.
(2)  The record of a resolution passed otherwise than at a general meeting, if purporting to be signed by a director of the company or by the company secretary, is evidence (in Scotland, sufficient evidence) of the passing of the resolution.
(3)  Where there is a record of a written resolution of a private company, the requirements of this Act with respect to the passing of the resolution are deemed to be complied with unless the contrary is proved.
(4)  The minutes of proceedings of a general meeting, if purporting to be signed by the chairman of that meeting or by the chairman of the next general meeting, are evidence (in Scotland, sufficient evidence) of the proceedings at the meeting.
(5)  Where there is a record of proceedings of a general meeting of a company, then, until the contrary is proved—
    (a)  the meeting is deemed duly held and convened,
    (b)  all proceedings at the meeting are deemed to have duly taken place, and
    (c)  all appointments at the meeting are deemed valid.

COMMENCEMENT DATE  1 October 2007[249]

**13.356.02**    Section 356 replaces provisions previously spread amongst sections 382 and 382A of the Companies Act 1985.

**13.356.03**    Subsections (2) and (3) replace section 382A(2) of the Companies Act 1985. Subsection (2) applies an evidentiary presumption in favour of records of a resolution passed otherwise than at a general meeting which purports to be signed by a director of the company or its secretary. Subsection (3) provides that where there is a record of a written resolution of a private company the requirements of the Act in relation to such resolutions[250] are deemed to be complied with. This is a rebuttable presumption.

**13.356.04**    Three notable points arise from these two subsections. First, subsection (2) applies to all companies whereas subsection (3) applies only to private companies as only such companies are provided with the

---

[244]  Company law has long imposed a duty on a company to maintain records of general meetings: *Re British Provident Life and Fire Insurance Society, Lane's case* (1863) 1 De GJ & S 504. The obligation to keep minutes in books kept for that purpose imposed by s 382 of CA 1985 was qualified by the provisions of CA 1985, s 723 which allowed records to be kept other than in a bound book.

[245]  As to which, see fn 242 to para 13.355.01 above.

[246]  CA 1985, s 382B(1).

[247]  S 359 of the Act.

[248]  Applying *Neptune v Fitzgerald* [1995] 3 WLR 108 (at 115–116) which concerned the records of a directors' meeting. These were previously covered along with general meetings by CA 1985, s 382.

[249]  Companies Act 2006 (Commencement No 3, etc) Order 2007, SI 2007/2194, art 2(1).

[250]  These requirements are set out in Part 13, Chapter 2 (ss 288–300) of the Act.

ability to pass written resolutions. Secondly, whereas under the Companies Act 1985 the signature of a director or company secretary was evidence of the proceedings in agreeing to the resolutions, such a signature is now evidence of the passing of the resolution (subsection (2)). It is suggested that the change in wording is not intended to alter the position which existed previously but to make it clear that the signature is direct evidence of the resolution itself. Third, the Companies Act 1985 only applied the presumption in favour of written resolutions where the other requirements of the section were satisfied, such as the entry of the resolutions and the members' signatures in a minute book. Subsection (3) applies the presumption to any record of a written resolution of a private company.

Subsection (4) replaces and repeats in material terms the provisions of section 382(2) of the Companies   **13.356.05**
Act 1985. Minutes of proceedings of a general meeting, if signed by the chairman of that meeting or the subsequent general meeting, are evidence of the proceedings. This provision can be contrasted with subsections (3) and (5) which create presumptions (albeit rebuttable) in favour of certain types of record and with section 320 of the Act which renders a chairman's declaration on a show of hands conclusive evidence.[251] Accordingly, minutes are not conclusive or presumptive evidence of the proceedings thereat. Thus a matter may be proved by the company or against it if there is no entry in the record of the proceedings.[252]

Subsection (5) replaces and repeats in material terms the provisions of section 382(4) of the Companies   **13.356.06**
Act 1985. Provided that a record of the proceedings of a general meeting is kept by the company, the meeting is presumed to have been properly held and convened,[253] the proceedings at the meeting are deemed to have duly taken place and all appointments are deemed valid. This provision is of particular importance given the practice, particularly in relation to public companies, of preparing draft minutes in advance of the meeting. This is perfectly proper but care should be taken to ensure that the meeting deals with all of the proposed business.[254] Further, the question of whether a meeting actually took place remains one of fact.[255]

## 357  Records of decisions by sole member

(1) This section applies to a company limited by shares or by guarantee that has only one member.   **13.357.01**
(2) Where the member takes any decision that—
    (a) may be taken by the company in general meeting, and
    (b) has effect as if agreed by the company in general meeting, he must (unless that decision is taken by way of a written resolution) provide the company with details of that decision.
(3) If a person fails to comply with this section he commits an offence.
(4) A person guilty of an offence under this section is liable on summary conviction to a fine not exceeding level 2 on the standard scale.
(5) Failure to comply with this section does not affect the validity of any decision referred to in subsection (2).

COMMENCEMENT DATE  1 October 2007[256]

Section 357 replaces and repeats in material terms the provisions of section 382B of the Companies Act   **13.357.02**
1985 in relation to single member companies. Where a sole member takes a decision (being one which may be taken in general meeting and which has effect as if agreed by the company at such a meeting) other than by way of written resolution or at a general meeting he must provide the company with details of that decision. In turn the company must retain a record of those details for 10 years.[257] The failure by a sole member to provide details is an offence (subsections (3) and (4)). However, under subsection (5), such a failure is not fatal to the validity of the decision.[258]

---

[251]  See also Article 47 of Table A. *Kerr v John Mottram Ltd* [1940] Ch 657 explains (in the context of a provision of the articles of a 1929 Act company) that the words 'conclusive evidence' are to be given their natural meaning and therefore, as between parties bound by the minutes, no further evidence can be led. This is subject to an exception where it can be demonstrated that the minutes were fraudulently written up.

[252]  *Re Pyle Works (No 2)* [1891] 1 Ch 173 and *Re Fireproof Doors Ltd* [1916] 2 Ch 142 relying on *Knight's Case* (1866) LR 2 Ch 321. See also *Neptune v Fitzgerald* [1995] 3 WLR 108.

[253]  Eg, it is presumed that the requisite notice of the meeting was given: *Re Portuguese Consolidated Copper Mines ex p Badman* (1890) 45 Ch D 16. The decision related to a meeting of directors rather than a general meeting but the provision relied upon (s 67 of the 1862 Act) applied the same presumptions to both types of meeting.

[254]  See *R (on the application of the IRC) v Kingston Crown Court* [2001] EWHC Admin 581 at para 22 for comments on this practice in the context of criminal proceedings.

[255]  *Glatzer and Warick Shipping Ltd v Bradstone Ltd* [1997] 1 Lloyd's Rep 449 at 471.

[256]  Companies Act 2006 (Commencement No 3, etc) Order 2007, S1 2007/2194, art 2(1).

[257]  S 362(1)(c).

[258]  See also *Neptune v Fitzgerald* [1995] 3 WLR 108 referred to under s 355 above.

**13.357.03**   This provision is linked to the line of authorities under which the courts have upheld decisions taken unanimously by the shareholders of a company but without a proper meeting or written resolution.[259] It remains to be seen whether these authorities will survive the enactment of this Act.

### 358 Inspection of records of resolutions and meetings

**13.358.01**
    (1) The records referred to in section 355 (records of resolutions etc) relating to the previous ten years must be kept available for inspection—
        (a) at the company's registered office, or
        (b) at a place specified in regulations under section 1136.
    (2) The company must give notice to the registrar—
        (a) of the place at which the records are kept available for inspection, and
        (b) of any change in that place,
      unless they have at all times been kept at the company's registered office.
    (3) The records must be open to the inspection of any member of the company without charge.
    (4) Any member may require a copy of any of the records on payment of such fee as may be prescribed.
    (5) If default is made for 14 days in complying with subsection (2) or an inspection required under subsection (3) is refused, or a copy requested under subsection (4) is not sent, an offence is committed by every officer of the company who is in default.
    (6) A person guilty of an offence under this section is liable on summary conviction to a fine not exceeding level 3 on the standard scale and, for continued contravention, a daily default fine not exceeding one-tenth of level 3 on the standard scale.
    (7) In a case in which an inspection required under subsection (3) is refused or a copy requested under subsection (4) is not sent, the court may by order compel an immediate inspection of the records or direct that the copies required be sent to the persons who requested them.

COMMENCEMENT DATE 1 October 2007[260]

**13.358.02**   Section 358 replaces and expands upon sections 383 and 382B(3) of the Companies Act 1985 and requires a company to keep available for inspection the records it must maintain under section 355.

**13.358.03**   Subsections (1) and (3) replace section 383(1) and 382B(3) of the Companies Act 1985. Records and minutes of meetings must still be kept available for inspection by members of the company free of charge (subsection (3)). However, the time period for which records must be kept available for inspection has been reduced. Under subsection (1) only records for the previous 10 years must be available. This mirrors the 10-year period for record retention set out in section 355 of the Act. Previously all minutes of proceedings of any general meeting held on or after 1 November 1929 had to be retained and made available for inspection. Subsection (1) also covers details of decisions by a sole member provided under section 357(2) which must be available for inspection. A member exercising his right under the Companies Act 1985, section 383(1) was entitled to be accompanied by an adviser.[261] The new provision in subsection (3) does not suggest any reason why this position should change.

**13.358.04**   These records must be available for inspection at the company's registered office or at some other place specified under regulations which can be made under section 1136 of the Act (subsection (1)). Subsection (2) imposes a new obligation on a company which arises from the right to keep records other than at its registered office. If this option is exercised, then the company must notify the registrar of companies of the location of the records and of any change of that place. This would include the movement of the records back to the registered office from some other permitted location as the obligation arises unless the records have, at all times, been kept at the company's registered office.

**13.358.05**   Subsection (4) replaces section 383(3) of the Companies Act 1985. A member is still entitled to be provided with a copy of the records upon payment of the prescribed fee. However, the Act removes the time-limit of seven days which previously applied to the provision of the copies of the requested records.[262]

**13.358.06**   Subsections (5) and (6) replace section 383(4) of the Companies Act 1985 making refusal to allow inspection or the failure to provide a requested copy an offence committed by every officer of the company in default. Previously the offence was also committed by the company.[263] Section 1137

---

[259] See Part 13, Chapter 2 for consideration of these authorities.
[260] Companies Act 2006 (Commencement No 3, etc) Order 2007, SI 2007/2194, art 2(1).
[261] *McCasker v Rae* (1966) SC 253.
[262] The relevant fee is prescribed by the Companies (Fees for Inspection and Copying of Company Records) Regulations 2007 at 10p per 500 words or part thereof.
[263] CA 1985, s 383(4).

provides the Secretary of State with the power to make regulations relating to this obligation (amongst others). Failure to comply with any such regulations is treated as a relevant failure for the purposes of the offence created under section 358: see section 1137(2).

Pursuant to subsection (7),[264] the court can compel immediate inspection of the records and the provision of copies if inspection is refused or a requested copy is not sent.     **13.358.07**

### 359 Records of resolutions and meetings of class of members

The provisions of this Chapter apply (with necessary modifications) in relation to resolutions and meetings of—     **13.359.01**

(a) holders of a class of shares, and

(b) in the case of a company without a share capital, a class of members, as they apply in relation to resolutions of members generally and to general meetings.

COMMENCEMENT DATE 1 October 2007[265]

Section 359 is new. It expressly applies the obligations to keep records and make them open to inspection to meetings of holders of a class of share or of a class of members. Where it is not possible to apply sections 355 to 358 as they stand, they apply with necessary modifications which will have to be determined by the court after the event.     **13.359.02**

### 360 Computation of periods of notice etc: clear day rule

(1) This section applies for the purposes of the following provisions of this Part—     **13.360.01**

section 307(1) and (2) (notice required of general meeting),

[section 307A(1), (4), (5) and (7)(b) (notice required of general meeting of traded company),][a]

section 312(1) and (3) (resolution requiring special notice),

section 314(4)(d) (request to circulate members' statement),

section 316(2)(b) (expenses of circulating statement to be deposited or tendered before meeting),

[section 337(3) (contents of notice of AGM of traded company),][b]

section 338(4)(d)(i) (request to circulate member's resolution at AGM of public company),

[section 338(A)(5) (request to include matter in the business to be dealt with at AGM of traded company),][c]

section 340(2)(b)(i) (expenses of circulating statement to be deposited or tendered before meeting), [and

[section 340B(2)(b) (traded companies: duty to circulate members' matters for AGM).][d]

(2) Any reference in those provisions to a period of notice, or to a period before a meeting by which a request must be received or sum deposited or tendered, is to a period of the specified length excluding—

(a) the day of the meeting, and

(b) the day on which the notice is given, the request received or the sum deposited or tendered.

AMENDMENTS

[a] Amended by the Companies (Shareholders' Rights) Regulations 2009, SI 2009/1632, reg 9.

[b] Amended by the Companies (Shareholders' Rights) Regulations 2009, SI 2009/1632, reg 16.

[c] Amended by the Companies (Shareholders' Rights) Regulations 2009, SI 2009/1632, reg 17.

[d] Amended by the Companies (Shareholders' Rights) Regulations 2009, SI 2009/1632, reg 18.

COMMENCEMENT DATE 1 October 2007[266]; 3 August 2009[267]

### [360A Electronic meetings and voting

(1) Nothing in this Part is to be taken to preclude the holding and conducting of a meeting in such a way that persons who are not present together at the same place may by electronic means attend and speak and vote at it.     **13.360A.01**

(2) In the case of a traded company the use of electronic means for the purpose of enabling members to participate in a general meeting may be made subject only to such requirements and restrictions as are—

(a) necessary to ensure the identification of those taking part and the security of the electronic communication, and

---

[264] Which replaces CA 1985, s 383(5).

[265] Companies Act 2006 (Commencement No 3, etc) Order 2007, S1 2007/2194, art 2(1).

[266] Companies Act 2006 (Commencement No 3, etc) Order 2007, S1 2007/2194, art 2(1).

[267] As regards the amendments referred to in notes a to d.

(b) proportionate to the achievement of those objectives.

(3) Nothing in subsection (2) affects any power of a company to require reasonable evidence of the entitlement of any person who is not a member to participate in the meeting.][a]

AMENDMENTS

[a] Inserted by the Companies (Shareholders' Rights) Regulations 2009, SI 2009/1632, reg 8.

COMMENCEMENT DATE 3 August 2009[268]

**13.360A.02**    This section was inserted by the Companies (Shareholders' Rights) Regulations 2009 (implementing the EU Shareholder Rights Directive (2007/36/EC)), which came into force on 3 August 2009. The intention of this provision is to implement Article 8 of that Directive (participation in general meetings by electronic means) by preventing anything in Part 13 of the Act from being an obstacle to meetings being held electronically. Section 360A(2) deals with the limited requirements and restrictions in respect of electronic participation that may be applied in the case of a 'traded company', that expression being defined at 360C of the Act.

### [360B Traded companies: requirements for participating in and voting at general meetings

**13.360B.01**    (1) Any provision of a traded company's articles is void in so far as it would have the effect of—

(a) imposing a restriction on a right of a member to participate in and vote at a general meeting of the company unless the member's shares have (after having been acquired by the member and before the meeting) been deposited with, or transferred to, or registered in the name of another person, or

(b) imposing a restriction on the right of a member to transfer shares in the company during the period of 48 hours before the time for the holding of a general meeting of the company if that right would not otherwise be subject to that restriction.

(2) A traded company must determine the right to vote at a general meeting of the company by reference to the register of members as at a time (determined by the company) that is not more than 48 hours before the time for the holding of the meeting.

(3) In calculating the period mentioned in subsection (1)(b) or (2), no account is to be taken of any part of a day that is not a working day.

(4) Nothing in this section affects—

(a) the operation of—

(i) Part 22 of this Act (information about interests in a company's shares),

(ii) Part 15 of the Companies Act 1985(a) (orders imposing restrictions on shares), or

(iii) any provision in a company's articles relating to the application of any provision of either of those Parts; or

(b) the validity of articles prescribed, or to the same effect as articles prescribed, under section 19 of this Act (power of Secretary of State to prescribe model articles).][a]

AMENDMENTS

[a] Inserted by the Companies (Shareholders' Rights) Regulations 2009, SI 2009/1632, reg 20.

COMMENCEMENT DATE 3 August 2009[269]

**13.360B.02**    This section was inserted by the Companies (Shareholders' Rights) Regulations 2009 (implementing the EU Shareholder Rights Directive (2007/36/EC)), which came into force on 3 August 2009. The intention of this provision is to implement Article 7 of that Directive (requirements for participation and voting at general meetings) in respect of 'traded companies'. The definition of a 'traded company' is at section 360C of the Act.

### [360C Meaning of 'traded company'

**13.360C.01**    In this Part, 'traded company' means a company any shares of which—

(a) carry rights to vote at general meetings, and

(b) are admitted to trading on a regulated market in an EEA State by or with the consent of the company.][a]

AMENDMENTS

[a] Inserted by the Companies (Shareholders' Rights) Regulations 2009, SI 2009/1632, reg 21.

COMMENCEMENT DATE 3 August 2009[270]

---

[268] The Companies (Shareholders' Rights) Regulations 2009, SI 2009/1632, reg 1(2).

[269] The Companies (Shareholders' Rights) Regulations 2009, SI 2009/1632, reg 1(2).

[270] The Companies (Shareholders' Rights) Regulations 2009, SI 2009/1632, reg 1(2).

This section provides the definition of the expression 'traded company' which appears in many of the **13.360C.02**
amendments made to the Act by the Companies (Shareholders' Rights) Regulations 2009 with effect
from 3 August 2009. Those regulations implement the EU Shareholder Rights Directive (2007/36/EC)
which relates to the exercise of shareholder rights attaching to voting shares in relation to general
meetings of companies which have their registered office in a Member State and whose shares are
admitted to trading on a regulated market situated or operating within a Member State. Under section
360C a company with traded voting shares is defined as a 'traded company' if the shares are admitted
to trading by or with consent of the company. A 'traded company' may (but need not) also be a 'quoted
company' within the meaning of sections 361 and 385 of the Act (as to which see the commentary to
those sections below) and vice versa.

## 361  Meaning of 'quoted company'

In this Part 'quoted company' has the same meaning as in Part 15 of this Act.                 **13.361.01**

COMMENCEMENT DATE  1 October 2007[271]

The expression 'quoted company' in Part 13 has the same meaning as that given in Part 15 of the Act. **13.361.02**
Part 15 explains the meaning of quoted company at section 385. In summary, the expression means a
company whose share capital has been included in the official list in accordance with Part 6 of the
Financial Services and Markets Act 2000, is officially listed in an EEA State, or is admitted to dealing on
either the New York Stock Exchange or the NASDAQ.

The Secretary of State may extend or limit the ambit of section 385(1) and (2) so as to expand or restrict **13.361.03**
the categories of companies that are quoted companies.

---

[271]  Companies Act 2006 (Commencement No 3, etc) Order 2007, SI 2007/2194, art 2(1).

# 14

# CONTROL OF POLITICAL DONATIONS AND EXPENDITURE

## Companies Act 2006

## PART 14
### CONTROL OF POLITICAL DONATIONS AND EXPENDITURE

Prior to the Political Parties, Elections and Referendums Act 2000, the *ultra vires* rule was employed to **14.0.01** control the making of political donations and expenditure by companies. The question of the capacity of the company to make such donations turned on the scope of the objects clause—and on the often complex distinctions between objects and powers. The Companies Act 1985, sections 35 and 35A offered effective protection to recipients of such donations as such activity constituted an 'act' of the company[1] and, although any such donations might have been subject to disclosure (depending on their amount), this was regarded as insufficient protection for shareholders where it was feared that directors might engage in subsidizing political parties and organizations for personal reasons rather than because such support was in the legitimate interests of the company.[2] In addition, although such donations might involve a breach of fiduciary duty by the directors, the ability to pursue action for breach of duty was circumscribed by the fact that this duty was owed to the company and acts in breach of duty might be ratified. It was therefore considered that specific regulation and accountability provisions were required. The Government chose to follow a recommendation made by the Committee on Standards in Public Life[3] that corporate donations[4] to political parties should require prior

---

[1] See the discussion of ss 39 and 40 of the Companies Act (CA) 2006. It appears that such donations would no longer be challengeable on the basis that the company has exceeded its capacity but s 40 would still be relevant in relation to the fact that such payments might involve a breach of authority by the directors.

[2] The Government maintains that this is the rationale underpinning these legislative provisions (Comm, SCD, Ninth Sitting, 29 June 2006, col 346).

[3] The Neill Committee, *The Funding of Political Parties in the United Kingdom*, Cm 4057, October 1998.

[4] These included donations in cash, or kind, any form of sponsorship or loans or any transactions at favourable rates.

authorization by the company's shareholders[5] and, by the Political Parties, Elections and Referendums Act 2000 (PPERA 2000), introduced Part XA (sections 347A to 347K) into the Companies Act 1985 to achieve this objective.[6]

**14.0.02** The provisions in Part 14 of the Companies Act 2006 largely reproduce the previous Part XA of the Companies Act 1985, while extending the scope of their application to include Northern Ireland. There is also some extension of the operation of these provisions to include donations to independent election candidates, and not just political parties and other political organizations. In addition, there are consequential amendments to reflect other substantive and presentational changes in the Companies Act 2006, eg on resolutions, and there is some clarification of the exemptions to add an exemption in favour of trade unions. The most significant amendment relates to the remedial consequences where unauthorized donations are made or unauthorized political expenditure occurs as the previous provision exempting the directors from their liability in specified circumstances has been removed from the 2006 legislation and there are important changes to the rules on ratification.

**14.0.03** In general terms, the order of the provisions in the Companies Act 2006 is more logical, neater and improves the clarity of the presentation of the applicable law. However, the prior shareholder authorization scheme has been criticized for its complexity and as imposing excessive burdens and costs on companies, especially the large corporate group, which may consider that the safest route is to pass precautionary resolutions in order to avoid later liability being imposed on its directors.

**14.0.04** Such precautionary resolutions have been passed by many public, listed companies since 2008. In large part this was because of the uncertainty surrounding the definitions of 'political donation' and 'political expenditure' (see commentary to sections 364 to 365 below). Shareholders were often informed that there were no plans to make direct donations to political parties. This is consistent with best practice guidance published by the Association of British Insurers, which also recommends that authorization is sought on an annual basis.[7]

**14.0.05** The disclosure of political donations and expenditure is required within the directors' report. The content of the directors' report is prescribed by the Companies Act 2006, Part 15, chapter 5, and the regulations made by the Secretary of State under section 416(4) of the Act,[8] discussed in Chapter 15 of this work.

**14.0.06** In 2010 the Committee on Standards in Public Life began an inquiry into the financing of political parties and in 2011 published a report containing twenty-four recommendations, including a cap on donations and a requirement that companies giving donations should have trading activities in the UK and sufficient income to fund the donation.[9] In its annual report, published in September 2012, the Committee noted that it had not received a formal response from the Government in respect of its recommendations.[10]

*Introductory*

### 362 Introductory[a]

**14.362.01** This Part has effect for controlling—

(a) political donations made by companies to political parties, to other political organisations and to independent election candidates, and

(b) political expenditure incurred by companies.

---

[5] *The Funding of Political Parties in the United Kingdom*, Cm 4057, October 1998, recommendation 34. See also *Political Donations by Companies*, Consultative Document of March 1999 (URN 99/757).

[6] Inserted by PPERA 2000, s 139 and Sch 19. The key provision was CA 1985 s 347C, requiring prior shareholder resolution to approve the donation or expenditure, although (i) this did not apply to aggregate donations of less than £5,000 in the period and (ii) any resolution would constitute general approval rather than approval limited to a specific transaction, would cover a four-year period and would stipulate a maximum figure for such donations in the period.

[7] ABI guidance: Companies Act and Articles of Association, October 2009 (available at ⟨http://www.ivis.co.uk/ArticlesOfAssociation.aspx⟩, last accessed 30 September 2012)..

[8] Small Companies and Groups (Accounts and Directors' Report) Regulations 2008, SI 2008/409, Part 3 and the Large and Medium-sized Companies and Groups (Accounts and Reports) Regulations 2008, SI 2008/410, Part 3.

[9] See ⟨http://www.public-standards.gov.uk/OurWork/Party_Political_Finance.html⟩, last accessed 30 September 2012.

[10] See ⟨http://www.public-standards.gov.uk/Library/Annual_Report_FINAL.pdf⟩, last accessed 30 September 2012.

AMENDMENTS AND NOTES

<sup>a</sup> This section applies without modification to unregistered companies by reg 3 of and Sch 1 to the Unregistered Companies Regulations 2009, SI 2009/2436 and, by Sch 2, applies to donations made or expenditure incurred on or after 1 October 2007.

COMMENCEMENT DATE 1 October 2007 (Great Britain), 1 November 2007 (Northern Ireland)[11]

This section explains the general purpose of the provisions in Part 14 and is based on Companies Act 1985, section 347A(1). In addition to controlling the company's expenditure on its own political activities, the provisions also control any donations made by companies to political parties and political organizations other than political parties.[12] The 2006 Act also extends the control to donations to independent election candidates at any election to public office,[13] who previously fell outside the scope of the legislative control and therefore represented an unintentional anomaly, particularly as independent candidates might stand on a single issue agenda of direct interest to the company in question. **14.362.02**

## *Donations and expenditure to which this Part applies*

### 363 Political parties, organisations etc to which this Part applies<sup>a</sup>

(1) This Part applies to a political party if— **14.363.01**
  (a) it is registered under Part 2 of the Political Parties, Elections and Referendums Act 2000 (c. 41), or
  (b) it carries on, or proposes to carry on, activities for the purposes of or in connection with the participation of the party in any election or elections to public office held in a member State other than the United Kingdom.
(2) This Part applies to an organisation (a 'political organisation') if it carries on, or proposes to carry on, activities that are capable of being reasonably regarded as intended—
  (a) to affect public support for a political party to which, or an independent election candidate to whom, this Part applies, or
  (b) to influence voters in relation to any national or regional referendum held under the law of the United Kingdom or another member State.
(3) This Part applies to an independent election candidate at any election to public office held in the United Kingdom or another member State.
(4) Any reference in the following provisions of this Part to a political party, political organisation or independent election candidate, or to political expenditure, is to a party, organisation, independent candidate or expenditure to which this Part applies.

AMENDMENTS AND NOTES

<sup>a</sup> This section applies without modification to unregistered companies by reg 3 of and Sch 1 to the Unregistered Companies Regulations 2009, SI 2009/2436 and, by Sch 2, applies to donations made or expenditure incurred on or after 1 October 2007.

COMMENCEMENT DATE 1 October 2007 (Great Britain), 1 November 2007 (Northern Ireland)[14]

As subsection (4) makes clear, this is a definitional section. Section 363(1) and (2) corresponds in terms of outcome to Companies Act 1985, section 347A(6), (7), and (9), although the relevant definitions are integrated into each subsection, with the exception of the definition of 'organisation' which appears in the minor definitions section, section 379(1). Section 363(3) is new. **14.363.02**

Subsection (1) of section 363 defines a political party as being a political party registered under PPERA 2000, Part II or, if it fulfils a more purpose-based definition,[15] ie if it 'carries on activities for the purpose of or in connection with the participation of the party' in any election for public office either in the UK or in any European Union Member State. Given the scope of this definition, all references to the previous terminology of 'registered party'[16] have been dropped so that if a political party satisfies either part of the subsection (1) definition, it is treated as a 'political party' for the purposes of this legislation. **14.363.03**

Subsection (2) defines a political organization, other than a political party, in the same terms as the Companies Act 1985, section 347A(7)(b) and (c). The wording is reorganized to avoid repetition. **14.363.04**

---

[11] Companies Act 2006 (Commencement No 3, etc) Order 2007, SI 2007/2194, arts 2(2) and 3(1), but the reference to 'independent election candidates' takes effect on 1 October 2008 (art 5 of the Order).
[12] As defined in CA 2006, s 363(1) and (2).
[13] CA 2006, s 363(3).
[14] Companies Act 2006 (Commencement No 3, etc) Order 2007, SI 2007/2194, arts 2(2) and 3(1), but the reference to 'independent election candidates' takes effect on 1 October 2008 (art 5 of the Order).
[15] CA 2006, s 363(1)(b).
[16] CA 1985, s 347A(9).

Section 379(1) (minor definitions section) defines 'organisation' as including a company, unincorporated association, or any combination of persons, and in order to be 'political' that organization must carry on, or aim to carry on, activities that 'are capable of being reasonably regarded' as having one of two purposes: either affecting public support for a political party (section 363(2)(a)) or for an independent election candidate;[17] or influencing voters in any referendum held in the UK or in any EU Member State (section 363(2)(b)). However, section 374(2) of the Companies Act 2006 provides that a trade union is not a political organization for the purposes of section 365 (meaning of 'political expenditure'), although corporate donations to a trade union's political fund require prior shareholder authorization.[18]

**14.363.05**    Subsection (3) is new and reflects the extended coverage in section 362 to include independent election candidates for any public office in the UK or other Member State.

### 364  Meaning of 'political donation'[a]

**14.364.01**    (1)  The following provisions have effect for the purposes of this Part as regards the meaning of 'political donation'.

(2)  In relation to a political party or other political organisation—

    (a)  'political donation' means anything that in accordance with sections 50 to 52 of the Political Parties, Elections and Referendums Act 2000—

        (i)  constitutes a donation for the purposes of Chapter 1 of Part 4 of that Act (control of donations to registered parties), or

        (ii)  would constitute such a donation reading references in those sections to a registered party as references to any political party or other political organisation,

    and

    (b)  section 53 of that Act applies, in the same way, for the purpose of determining the value of a donation.

(3)  In relation to an independent election candidate—

    (a)  'political donation' means anything that, in accordance with sections 50 to 52 of that Act, would constitute a donation for the purposes of Chapter 1 of Part 4 of that Act (control of donations to registered parties) reading references in those sections to a registered party as references to the independent election candidate,

    and

    (b)  section 53 of that Act applies, in the same way, for the purpose of determining the value of a donation.

(4)  For the purposes of this section, sections 50 and 53 of the Political Parties, Elections and Referendums Act 2000 (c. 41) (definition of 'donation' and value of donations) shall be treated as if the amendments to those sections made by the Electoral Administration Act 2006 (which remove from the definition of 'donation' loans made otherwise than on commercial terms) had not been made.

AMENDMENTS AND NOTES

[a]  This section applies without modification to unregistered companies by reg 3 of and Sch 1 to the Unregistered Companies Regulations 2009, SI 2009/2436 and, by Sch 2, applies to donations made or expenditure incurred on or after 1 October 2007.

COMMENCEMENT DATE 1 October 2007 (Great Britain),1 November 2007 (Northern Ireland)[19]

**14.364.02**    Political donations in relation to political parties or other political organizations are defined in accordance with the definitions in the PPERA 2000, sections 50 to 52, although disregarding the amendments to these definitions in sections 61 to 63 of the Electoral Administration Act 2006 in relation to loans (section 364(4)). These amendments remove loans which are made otherwise than on commercial terms from the definition of 'donations' within the PPERA 2000, sections 50 to 52. However, it follows that 'donations' for the purposes of the Companies Act 2006, which are subject to the prior approval by shareholders, will continue to include loans that are not made on commercial lending terms since, unlike the position with individual donations, the company's decision to lend money on non-commercial terms is made by the directors, and prior shareholder agreement therefore operates as protection for members.

---

[17]  Interestingly, the original version in CA 1985 s 347A(7)(b) also included reference to support for independent candidates although the provisions did not directly affect donations to such candidates.

[18]  CA 2006, s 374(1). It follows that all other corporate donations to a trade union are now exempt from the application of the legislation.

[19]  Companies Act 2006 (Commencement No 3, etc) Order 2007, SI 2007/2194, arts 2(2) and 3(1), but the reference to 'independent election candidates' takes effect on 1 October 2008 (art 5).

Thus, 'donations' as defined in the PPERA, disregarding amendments in the Electoral Administration **14.364.03**
Act 2006, include gifts of money or property (or transfers at less than market value, PPERA 2000,
section 50(3)), any sponsorship,[20] subscription or fees for affiliation or membership of the party
(although see the exemption in section 375), payments to cover expenses incurred directly or indirectly
by the political party or organization, any money lent other than on commercial terms, or the provision
of property services or facilities for the use or benefit of the party or organization which are made
otherwise than on commercial terms. The definition of 'donations' also includes such gifts or transfers
to any officers, members, trustees, or agents where made to such persons in that capacity, rather than
for that person's own use or benefit.

However, this definition is extremely wide and inherently uncertain so that it is unlikely to encourage **14.364.04**
the abandonment of precautionary resolutions. For example, the Law Society has questioned whether
it would include corporate entertainment where some of the guests are members of political parties,
amounts paid to politicians at commercial rates for speaking engagements at conferences and semi-
nars, and free attendance for politicians at conferences where other attendees are charged an attendance fee.[21] Although further guidance on the meaning of 'political donations' in the corporate context
might have been helpful, none was forthcoming.[22]

Section 364(3) is a new provision which is necessary to extend the coverage of this definition of **14.364.05**
'political donation' to donations made to an independent election candidate.

It follows that section 364 substantially reproduces Companies Act 1985, section 347A(4), with this **14.364.06**
additional extension to the scope of the definition.

## 365  Meaning of 'political expenditure'[a]

(1)  In this Part 'political expenditure', in relation to a company, means expenditure incurred by the **14.365.01**
company on—
  (a)  the preparation, publication or dissemination of advertising or other promotional or publicity
       material—
       (i)   of whatever nature, and
       (ii)  however published or otherwise disseminated,
       that, at the time of publication or dissemination, is capable of being reasonably regarded as
       intended to affect public support for a political party or other political organisation, or an
       independent election candidate, or
  (b)  activities on the part of the company that are capable of being reasonably regarded as
       intended—
       (i)   to affect public support for a political party or other political organisation, or an
             independent election candidate, or
       (ii)  to influence voters in relation to any national or regional referendum held under the law
             of a member State.
(2)  For the purposes of this Part a political donation does not count as political expenditure.

AMENDMENTS AND NOTES

[a]  This section applies without modification to unregistered companies by reg 3 of and Sch 1 to the
     Unregistered Companies Regulations 2009, SI 2009/2436 and, by Sch 2, applies to donations made
     or expenditure incurred on or after 1 October 2007.

COMMENCEMENT DATE 1 October 2007 (Great Britain), 1 November 2007 (Northern Ireland)[23]

This section substantially reproduces Companies Act 1985, section 347A(5), whilst extending the **14.365.02**
definition of 'political expenditure' to apply also to independent election candidates.

The definition of 'political expenditure' includes the costs of advertising or other promotional material **14.365.03**
where that publication is capable of being reasonably regarded as intended to affect public support for
the party, organization, or independent candidate, or expenditure incurred in relation to other
activities which are capable of being reasonably regarded as having the same aim, or to influence voters

---

[20]  As defined in PPERA 2000, s 51 to cover the expenses of meetings, publications, study, or research, other
than charges for admission, payment of the price for publications, or payment at commercial rates for
advertising.
[21]  Law Society Parliamentary Brief of 11 Jan 2006.
[22]  In debate at the Grand Committee Stage in the Lords (Official Report, House of Lords, Sixth Day, 1 March
2006: vol 679, GC144) Lord McKenzie had agreed to look at providing further guidance on the meaning of
'political donations'. However, this had not been provided by the time of the Committee Stage in the Commons
(Comm, SCD, Ninth Sitting, 29 June 2006, col 345–6) and no such guidance was added at the Report Stage.
[23]  Companies Act 2006 (Commencement No 3, etc) Order 2007, SI 2007/2194, arts 2(2) and 3(1), but the
reference to 'independent election candidates' takes effect on 1 October 2008 (art 5 of the Order).

in any referendum. However, the breadth of this definition has also proved controversial since the publication of promotional material need not be for the primary purpose of affecting public support for a political party or organization, or primarily to influence voters in any referendum; this might be only a subsidiary intention, the main intention being to promote the interests of the company.[24] Nevertheless, such publication will require a prior authorizing resolution and, since there is the possibility for delay in securing such a resolution before proceeding, this provision simply encourages the making of many precautionary resolutions.[25] The answer to this criticism may be the existence of the power in section 377 to exempt political expenditure by order, but this requires specific legislation for each difficulty subsequently identified by a company or sector and will not address the problems of delay when seeking to pursue the business interests of the company. The argument must, however, be that this definition has been in operation since 2000 so that the need for exemptions for general difficulties must surely have been identified already. The real difficulties in practice are therefore likely to relate to specific policy issues affecting the business and interests of the company, and it is at least arguable that precautionary resolutions ensuring shareholder approval are preferable to the adoption of a test to distinguish primary and subsidiary intentions behind particular expenditure.

**14.365.04**   Section 374(2) provides that trade unions are not 'political organisations' in relation to corporate 'political expenditure' within section 365. It follows that prior authorization is not required, and there is no protection mechanism to guard against, corporate expenditure on trade union promotion or other activities that might be perceived as political. However, this is unsurprising given the general exemption for corporate donations to trade unions.[26]

**14.365.05**   Subsection (2) avoids the duplication that might occur if a political donation within section 364 was also regarded as political expenditure within section 365.

### *Authorisation required for donations or expenditure*

**14.366.01**   The applicable provisions have been streamlined to avoid unnecessary duplication of procedures and requirements.

### 366 Authorisation required for donations or expenditure[a]

**14.366.02**
(1) A company must not—
   (a) make a political donation to a political party or other political organisation, or to an independent election candidate, or
   (b) incur any political expenditure,
   unless the donation or expenditure is authorised in accordance with the following provisions.
(2) The donation or expenditure must be authorised—
   (a) in the case of a company that is not a subsidiary of another company, by a resolution of the members of the company;
   (b) in the case of a company that is a subsidiary of another company by—
      (i) a resolution of the members of the company, and
      (ii) a resolution of the members of any relevant holding company.
(3) No resolution is required on the part of a company that is a wholly-owned subsidiary of a UK-registered company.
(4) For the purposes of subsection (2)(b)(ii) a 'relevant holding company' means a company that, at the time the donation was made or the expenditure was incurred—
   (a) was a holding company of the company by which the donation was made or the expenditure was incurred,
   (b) was a UK-registered company, and
   (c) was not a subsidiary of another UK-registered company.
(5) The resolution or resolutions required by this section—
   (a) must comply with section 367 (form of authorising resolution), and
   (b) must be passed before the donation is made or the expenditure incurred.
(6) Nothing in this section enables a company to be authorised to do anything that it could not lawfully do apart from this section.

---

[24] See comments by Lord Hodgson of Astley Abbotts in Grand Committee in the Lords (Official Report, House of Lords, Sixth Day, 1 March 2006, GC138-140) although it would be extremely difficult to devise an effective test to distinguish primary and subsidiary intentions.
[25] See the debate at Comm, SCD, Ninth Sitting, 29 June 2006, cols 347–9, criticizing the breadth of the definition of 'political expenditure'. On the other hand, the Government rejected an attempt at Committee stage (cols 357–61) to extend the definition of 'political expenditure' to include lobbying activities on the company's behalf. See also the unsuccessful attempt to include such a provision (as NC76) at Report Stage, 11 October 2006, 686.
[26] CA 2006, s 374(1).

AMENDMENTS AND NOTES

[a]  This section applies without modification to unregistered companies by reg 3 of and Sch 1 to the Unregistered Companies Regulations 2009, SI 2009/2436 and, by Sch 2, applies to donations made or expenditure incurred on or after 1 October 2007.

COMMENCEMENT DATE 1 October 2007 (Great Britain), 1 November 2007 (Northern Ireland)[27]

Section 366 is the key regulatory provision in this Part. It prohibits a company from making a political donation or incurring political expenditure without *prior* shareholder authorization by means of a resolution (defined by section 366(5) as needing to comply with the rules on form in section 367 and having to be passed before the donation is made or the expenditure is incurred). This section largely reproduces Companies Act 1985, section 347C(1). It is also clear that a resolution for these purposes can include a written resolution in the case of a private company.[28]    **14.366.03**

The other provision substantially reproduced here is Companies Act 1985, section 347C(6), since Companies Act 2006, section 366(6) also makes it clear that such a resolution cannot authorize the company to do anything that it could not otherwise do. However, section 366 does not contain a provision equivalent to Companies Act 1985, section 347C(5), stating that subsequent ratification of unauthorized donations or expenditure cannot nullify the contravention of the section. It therefore follows that subsequent ratification will excuse the directors under the new regime.    **14.366.04**

The Act contains special rules applicable to authorization in the group context. By subsection (2) of section 366, where the company is a subsidiary of another company,[29] there must be both a resolution of that subsidiary and a resolution of the members of 'any relevant holding company' (subsection (4)), defined as a UK holding company[30] of the company making the donation or incurring the expenditure and which must not itself be a subsidiary company or a subsidiary of a subsidiary company. It therefore follows that 'relevant holding company' refers to the ultimate UK holding company at the top of the group pyramid or, where that ultimate holding company is not a UK company, then the highest UK company in the pyramid. However, there is no separate requirement for a resolution by a wholly-owned subsidiary of a UK holding company since, to avoid unnecessary bureaucratic duplication, the holding company resolution alone will suffice (subsection (3)). This differs from Companies Act 1985, section 347D, which had permitted resolution by the holding company alone in the cases of *all* wholly-owned subsidiaries, ie even where the holding company was not registered under the Companies Act. The Companies Act 2006 limits the possibility of holding company resolution alone to donations or expenditure by wholly-owned subsidiaries of a UK holding company.    **14.366.05**

Equally, the previous Companies Act 1985, section 347E, applying to all subsidiary companies incorporated or established outside the jurisdiction, had required the holding company to pass the subsidiary approval resolution. This requirement has not been retained so that the general rules in section 366(2) and (3) will apply, ie a UK holding company at the top of the pyramid with an overseas subsidiary, not wholly-owned, would need to comply with section 366(2) and secure resolutions of the subsidiary company and the holding company. If there is no UK-registered holding company, section 366(2)(b) and (3) will not apply (subsection (4) definition), and only a resolution of the UK-registered subsidiary company would be required (section 366(2)(a)). If there is a UK-registered holding company in the pyramid, that company would need to authorize the donation or expenditure, in addition to the authorization by the subsidiary, despite the fact that the ultimate holding company is an overseas company (definition of 'relevant holding company' in subsection (4)).    **14.366.06**

## 367  Form of authorising resolution[a]

    (1)  A resolution conferring authorisation for the purposes of this Part may relate to—    **14.367.01**
        (a)  the company passing the resolution,
        (b)  one or more subsidiaries of that company, or
        (c)  the company passing the resolution and one or more subsidiaries of that company.
    (2)  A resolution may be expressed to relate to all companies that are subsidiaries of the company passing the resolution—
        (a)  at the time the resolution is passed, or
        (b)  at any time during the period for which the resolution has effect, without identifying them individually.

---

[27]  Companies Act 2006 (Commencement No 3, etc) Order 2007, SI 2007/2194, arts 2(2) and 3(1), but the reference to 'independent election candidates' takes effect on 1 October 2008 (art 5 of the Order).
[28]  See CA 2006, Pt 13, Ch 2, particularly s 288.
[29]  As defined in CA 2006, s 1159 and Sch 6.
[30]  'UK-registered company' is defined in CA 2006, s 1158 as a company registered under that Act and as excluding overseas companies.

    (3) The resolution may authorise donations or expenditure under one or more of the following heads—

        (a) donations to political parties or independent election candidates;

        (b) donations to political organisations other than political parties;

        (c) political expenditure.

    (4) The resolution must specify a head or heads—

        (a) in the case of a resolution under subsection (2), for all of the companies to which it relates taken together;

        (b) in the case of any other resolution, for each company to which it relates.

    (5) The resolution must be expressed in general terms conforming with [subsection (3)]$^b$ and must not purport to authorise particular donations or expenditure.

    (6) For each of the specified heads the resolution must authorise donations or, as the case may be, expenditure up to a specified amount in the period for which the resolution has effect (see section 368).

    (7) The resolution must specify such amounts—

        (a) in the case of a resolution under subsection (2), for all of the companies to which it relates taken together;

        (b) in the case of any other resolution, for each company to which it relates.

AMENDMENTS AND NOTES

[a] This section applies without modification to unregistered companies by reg 3 of and Sch 1 to the Unregistered Companies Regulations 2009, SI 2009/2436 and, by Sch 2, applies to donations made or expenditure incurred on or after 1 October 2007.

[b] Amended by the Companies Act 2006 (Consequential Amendments, Transitional Provisions and Savings) Order 2009, SI 2009/1941, art 2(1), Sch 1, para 260(1), (2).

COMMENCEMENT DATE 1 October 2007 (Great Britain), 1 November 2007 (Northern Ireland)[31]

**14.367.02** Subsection (1) is new and seeks to minimize the number of resolutions in the group context by providing that a single authorizing resolution may be limited to the company passing the resolution, or may be a resolution of a holding company which covers a number of subsidiaries, or a resolution which covers one or more subsidiaries and the holding company itself. It follows (subsection (2)) that it is possible to have a resolution which simply states that it covers all of a holding company's subsidiaries at the date of the resolution and the subsection expressly states that there is no need to identify those subsidiaries individually by naming them in the resolution. In the case of a subsection (2) all-inclusive resolution, the resolution must specify the subsection (3) head or heads (see below) for all of the companies covered as a single head and corresponding single authorized amount (subsection (7)(a)). This represents some attempt to reduce the bureaucracy and costs of the procedure in the context of the corporate group.

**14.367.03** Subsection (3) indicates the form of any approval resolution and states that the resolution *may* authorize donations or expenditure under broad heads of (i) donations to political parties or to independent candidates, (ii) donations to other political organizations,[32] or (iii) political expenditure.[33] It follows that a company could also pass a separate approval resolution for separate heads of expenditure, eg for donations to political parties and political expenditure.

**14.367.04** By subsection (4) the resolution must also specify a head or heads for each company to which it relates (although see the 'all-inclusive' resolutions of a holding company, covered by subsection (2); section 367(4)(a)).

**14.367.05** There is no equivalent within Companies Act 2006, section 367 of Companies Act 1985, section 347C(3), which had provided for the default position to require an ordinary resolution for authorization. Such a provision was contained in the original Bill but was removed at Report Stage since it is superfluous. Section 281(3) provides more generally that an ordinary resolution will be the default position 'unless the company's articles require a higher majority (or unanimity)'. Companies Act 1985, section 347C(3) had given the directors the power to increase the majority required for approval unless the articles provided otherwise or prevented this. The removal of this possibility is to be welcomed as it added unnecessary uncertainty and complexity to the position when in practice the directors were unlikely to want a higher majority requirement for such approval. Finally, it is clear that the resolution

---

[31] Companies Act 2006 (Commencement No 3, etc) Order 2007, SI 2007/2194, arts 2(2) and 3(1), but the reference to 'independent election candidates' takes effect on 1 October 2008 (art 5 of the Order).

[32] See CA 2006, s 364.

[33] See CA 2006, s 365.

can be a written resolution in the case of a private company since there is no specific requirement or reference to a general meeting.[34]

The key subsections here are subsections (5) and (6) which broadly correspond to Companies Act 1985, section 347C(2) and (4). Subsection (5) provides that the resolution must be expressed in general terms, ie in accordance with the general heads in subsection (3) without authorizing particular donations or expenditure. Subsection (5) originally stated that the general terms must conform to the requirements of subsection (2), a drafting error corrected by the Companies Act 2006 (Consequential Amendments, Transitional Provisions and Savings) Order 2009, which substitutes the reference to subsection (2) with one to subsection (3). Notwithstanding this change it might have been preferable to separate the provisions relating to form in a general sense from those relating to form in the context of resolutions applicable to companies in a group.[35]   **14.367.06**

Subsection (6) states that for each of the specified heads, the resolution must authorize the head of donations or expenditure (see subsection (3)) up to a specified amount in the period for which the resolution operates. The determination of this period is the subject of section 368. It follows that any resolution should specify a maximum figure for each general head in the period in question, and, with the exception of the subsection (2) all-inclusive resolution applicable to a holding company, for each company to which it relates (subsection (7)), and should not specify particular figures for specific donations or expenditures. If greater detail had been required, the prior authorization resolution procedure would have been a logistical and bureaucratic nightmare for companies and have greatly increased the costs of managing these accountability procedures.   **14.367.07**

### 368  Period for which resolution has effect[a]

(1) A resolution conferring authorisation for the purposes of this Part has effect for a period of four years beginning with the date on which it is passed unless the directors determine, or the articles require, that it is to have effect for a shorter period beginning with that date.   **14.368.01**

(2) The power of the directors to make a determination under this section is subject to any provision of the articles that operates to prevent them from doing so.

AMENDMENTS AND NOTES

[a] This section applies without modification to unregistered companies by reg 3 of and Sch 1 to the Unregistered Companies Regulations 2009, SI 2009/2436 and, by Sch 2, applies to donations made or expenditure incurred on or after 1 October 2007.

COMMENCEMENT DATE 1 October 2007 (Great Britain), 1 November 2007 (Northern Ireland)[36]

This section reproduces the effect of Companies Act 1985, section 347C(3)(b), although not its exact wording. Section 368 retains some discretion for the directors to control the effective period of operation of the approval resolution. The four-year authorization period is retained as the default position, running from the date on which the resolution is passed, unless the articles provide for a shorter period or the directors determine that the period shall be shorter. However, the directors possess this discretion only where there is nothing in the articles denying this discretion or preventing it from operating.   **14.368.02**

### *Remedies in case of unauthorised donations or expenditure*

### 369  Liability of directors in case of unauthorised donation or expenditure[a]

(1) This section applies where a company has made a political donation or incurred political expenditure without the authorisation required by this Part.   **14.369.01**

(2) The directors in default are jointly and severally liable—
  (a) to make good to the company the amount of the unauthorised donation or expenditure, with interest, and
  (b) to compensate the company for any loss or damage sustained by it as a result of the unauthorised donation or expenditure having been made.

(3) The directors in default are—
  (a) those who, at the time the unauthorised donation was made or the unauthorised expenditure was incurred, were directors of the company by which the donation was made or the expenditure was incurred, and
  (b) where—
    (i) that company was a subsidiary of a relevant holding company, and

---

[34] See CA 2006, s 288.
[35] As, eg, in relation to the CA 2006, s 370 enforcement action, s 370(1)(a) and (b).
[36] Companies Act 2006 (Commencement No 3, etc) Order 2007, SI 2007/2194, arts 2(2) and 3(1).

(ii) the directors of the relevant holding company failed to take all reasonable steps to prevent the donation being made or the expenditure being incurred,

the directors of the relevant holding company.

(4) For the purposes of subsection (3)(b) a 'relevant holding company' means a company that, at the time the donation was made or the expenditure was incurred—

(a) was a holding company of the company by which the donation was made or the expenditure was incurred,

(b) was a UK-registered company, and

(c) was not a subsidiary of another UK-registered company.

(5) The interest referred to in subsection (2)(a) is interest on the amount of the unauthorised donation or expenditure, so far as not made good to the company—

(a) in respect of the period beginning with the date when the donation was made or the expenditure was incurred, and

(b) at such rate as the Secretary of State may prescribe by regulations.

Section 379(2) (construction of references to date when donation made or expenditure incurred) does not apply for the purposes of this subsection.

(6) Where only part of a donation or expenditure was unauthorised, this section applies only to so much of it as was unauthorised.

AMENDMENTS AND NOTES

[a] This section applies with modification to unregistered companies by reg 3 of and Sch 1 to the Unregistered Companies Regulations 2009, SI 2009/2436 and, by Sch 2, applies to donations made or expenditure incurred on or after 1 October 2007.

COMMENCEMENT DATE 1 October 2007 (Great Britain), and 1 November 2007 (Northern Ireland)[37] with the exception of the enabling power in respect of section 369(5) for the Secretary of State to set the interest rate by regulations. The enabling power has been effective since 20 January 2007 (the Companies Act 2006 (Commencement No 1, Transitional Provisions and Savings) Order2006, SI 2006/3428, article 3(3)). The Companies (Interest Rate for Unauthorised Political Donation or Expenditure) Regulations 2007, SI 2007/2242, have a commencement date of 1 October 2007 (Great Britain) and 1 November 2007 (Northern Ireland).

**14.369.02**  In the event that unauthorized donations are made or expenditure is incurred, civil liability is imposed on directors, ie the directors are personally liable to reimburse the company for the amount of the unauthorized payment with interest (subsection (2)(a)), and also to compensate the company for any consequential loss suffered (subsection (2)(b)). By subsection (5), interest in respect of the unauthorized payment runs from that date when the donation was made or the expenditure incurred (and not the usual date under this Part of when the contract incurring the obligation to make payment was entered into, section 379(2)) until such time as the company is reimbursed (section 369(5)(a)), and the applicable interest rate is that stipulated by the Secretary of State via regulations, currently 8 per cent per annum.[38] Subsection (6) explains that severance is permitted so that if part of a donation or expenditure was unauthorized, eg a particular head (Companies Act 2006, section 367(3)) then the liability will apply only in respect of the unauthorized payment. It is unclear from the section whether it was intended also to permit severance of amount, eg if political donations to a political party are permitted to £20,000 but actual donations made amounted to £29,000. It would appear that the personal liability would extend only to the unauthorized £9,000 (so permitting severance of amount) since subsection (7) implies that liability ceases when the company is reimbursed and it ought therefore to follow that only unauthorized expenditure needs to be reimbursed and compensated. Thus, liability in this section is limited to compensation and is not designed to have any punitive element.

**14.369.03**  Subsections (3) to (5) define 'director' for the purposes of section 369 liability as any director of the company at the time the unauthorized donation was made or expenditure occurred and, where the company in question was a subsidiary of a holding company, the directors of 'the relevant holding company' (defined as in section 366(4) as the UK holding company at the top of the group pyramid or highest UK holding company) where those directors failed to take reasonable steps to prevent the unauthorized donation or expenditure. This extension of liability reflects the rules on the authorizing resolution in the group context in section 366 and the fact that the authority in this context must be given by a resolution of the ultimate UK holding company (section 366(4)). The lack of authorization could well relate to the absence of the required resolution by the members of the holding company. This is particularly controversial in principle as it involves lifting the veil to impose liability on directors of the holding company for the actions of all subsidiaries[39] and is seen as further evidence of

---

[37] Companies Act 2006 (Commencement No 3, etc) Order 2007, SI 2007/2194, arts 2(2) and 3(1).

[38] Companies (Interest Rate for Unauthorised Political Donation or Expenditure) Regulations 2007, SI 2007/2242, reg 2.

[39] Official Report, House of Lords, Sixth Sitting, 1 March 2006, GC 151–153.

the encroachment of the imposition of liability on directors which, it is feared, will discourage suitable candidates from taking up such positions.[40] However, only a director of a 'relevant holding company' which should have provided authorization can be liable, not directors of other holding companies in the group pyramid.

Significantly, there is no specific provision providing exemption from the joint and several liability of directors under subsection (2). In particular, the previous section 347F(7) in the 1985 Companies Act has not been retained. Section 347F(7) had provided that the provisions imposing personal liability on directors did not apply to directors of the holding company where the subsidiary was not wholly-owned. The removal of this exemption and application of liability to all directors of the 'relevant holding company', subject to the 'reasonable steps' excuse, has proved particularly controversial on the basis that such a holding company is not in complete control of the subsidiary.[41] However, the contrary argument is that if the subsidiary company satisfies the definition of a subsidiary, the holding company has voting control or is able to effectively control the board of the subsidiary company so that, in such circumstances, the holding company directors ought to be held accountable for its actions unless able to show that they took reasonable steps to prevent the unauthorized payment but were unable to do so. **14.369.04**

In addition, this relaxation in director protection is counter-balanced by the fact that section 366 does not contain a provision equivalent to Companies Act 1985, section 347C(5), stating that subsequent ratification of unauthorized donations or expenditure cannot nullify the contravention of the section. Therefore it appears that ratification will absolve the directors from liability despite the reference to the need for *prior* shareholder resolution. The absence of a prohibition on ratification is a major change in the new Act and goes some considerable way to addressing the concerns about apparent extensions of liability to UK holding company directors where the subsidiary is not wholly owned. **14.369.05**

The previous legislation had also included exemptions from liability in Companies Act 1985, section 347H, but in the new legislative regime the protections are limited to: (i) ratification of the unauthorized donation or expenditure; (ii) the protection in subsection (3)(b) for directors of the relevant holding company who are permitted to establish that they took all reasonable steps to prevent the subsidiary making the unauthorized donation or incurring the unauthorized expenditure and so are not held to be personally liable; and (iii) the general provision whereby the court can relieve the director from liability if satisfied that the director has established that he or she acted honestly and reasonably and, having regard to all the circumstances, ought fairly to be excused.[42] This latter form of protection recognizes the existence of personal liability but allows the court to excuse or relieve the director from that liability. It also applies in principle to all directors, not just directors of the relevant holding company. **14.369.06**

Remedial action for lack of authorization rests with the company and it is for the company to pursue this remedy as an exercise of their management powers. It follows that the general duties owed by the directors[43] are applicable. However, sections 370 and 371 provide a specific mechanism[44] whereby an authorized group of shareholders may enforce the liability under section 369 on behalf of the company. **14.369.07**

There is no criminal sanction applicable in instances of unauthorized political donations and expenditure. **14.369.08**

## 370 Enforcement of directors' liabilities by shareholder action[a]

(1) Any liability of a director under section 369 is enforceable— **14.370.01**
   (a) in the case of a liability of a director of a company to that company, by proceedings brought under this section in the name of the company by an authorised group of its members.
   (b) in the case of a liability of a director of a holding company to a subsidiary, by proceedings brought under this section in the name of the subsidiary by
      (i) an authorised group of members of the subsidiary, or
      (ii) an authorised group of members of the holding company.
(2) This is in addition to the right of the company to which the liability is owed to bring proceedings itself to enforce the liability.
(3) An 'authorised group' of members of a company means—
   (a) the holders of not less than 5% in nominal value of the company's issued share capital,
   (b) if the company is not limited by shares, not less than 5% of its members, or

---

[40] Official Report, House of Lords, Sixth Sitting, 1 March 2006, GC 155-6.
[41] See eg debate in Committee in the House of Commons (Comm, SCD, Ninth Sitting, 29 June 2006, cols 361–3).
[42] CA 2006, s 1157; previously CA 1985, s 727, which had been explicitly excluded from operating in this context by s 347F(8).
[43] See CA 2006, Pt 10, Ch 2, ss 170–81.
[44] Outside the derivative claim procedure, CA 2006, Part 11.

(c)  not less than 50 of the company's members.
(4)  The right to bring proceedings under this section is subject to the provisions of section 371.
(5)  Nothing in this section affects any right of a member of a company to bring or continue proceedings under Part 11 of this Act (derivative claims or proceedings).

AMENDMENTS AND NOTES

ª  This section applies without modification to unregistered companies by reg 3 of and Sch 1 to the Unregistered Companies Regulations 2009, SI 2009/2436 and, by Sch 2, applies to donations made or expenditure incurred on or after 1 October 2007.

COMMENCEMENT DATE 1 October 2007 (Great Britain), 1 November 2007 (Northern Ireland)[45]

**14.370.02**    This section, taken with section 371, substantially reproduces Companies Act 1985, section 347I and allows for a specific additional shareholder action by an authorized group of shareholders to enforce the liability imposed on directors under section 369 for default of the authorization rules under section 366 (subsection (1)). As originally drafted in the Bill, this appeared to refer only to the shareholders of 'the donor company' and not the relevant holding company.[46] However, this provision was amended at Report Stage in the Commons[47] to clarify that in the context of liability of a director of a holding company to a subsidiary, this could mean action by an authorized group of members of the subsidiary or members of that holding company (section 370(1)(b)). This represents an amendment to the previous coverage in the Companies Act 1985 provision, namely section 347I.

**14.370.03**    It is made clear that this enforcement is an additional mechanism to the usual enforcement action by the company (subsection (2)) and is subject to ultimate supervisory control by the court (section 371(3)). It is also a separate and specific enforcement procedure and does not detract from the general availability of the derivative claim[48] (subsection (5)) which an individual shareholder(s) may wish to pursue on the company's behalf. However, the grant of permission to continue in such a general derivative claim,[49] where it relates to an infringement of Part 14, will inevitably be affected by the procedures and requirements of sections 370, 371, and 372.

**14.370.04**    The section details the procedure for shareholder action and the meaning of an 'authorised group of members' for this purpose:

**14.370.05**    Subsection (3) identifies the 'authorised group' as constituting either at least 50 shareholders or the holders of at least 5 per cent in nominal value of the company's issued share capital or, in the case of a company not limited by shares, at least 5 per cent of the company's members. This is identical to the requirements in Companies Act 1985, section 347I(2), but sets out the identification in this context rather than by cross-reference to a section in a different part of the legislation which ostensibly dealt with shareholder action in a different context.[50]

**14.370.06**    The procedure for this enforcement action (subsection (4)) is set out in section 371.

### 371  Enforcement of directors' liabilities by shareholder action: supplementary[a]

**14.371.01**    (1)  A group of members may not bring proceedings under section 370 in the name of a company unless—
(a)  the group has given written notice to the company stating—
(i)   the cause of action and a summary of the facts on which the proceedings are to be based,
(ii)  the names and addresses of the members comprising the group, and
(iii) the grounds on which it is alleged that those members constitute an authorised group; and
(b)  not less than 28 days have elapsed between the date of the giving of the notice to the company and the bringing of the proceedings.
(2)  Where such a notice is given to a company, any director of the company may apply to the court within the period of 28 days beginning with the date of the giving of the notice for an order directing that the proposed proceedings shall not be brought, on one or more of the following grounds—
(a)  that the unauthorised amount has been made good to the company;
(b)  that proceedings to enforce the liability have been brought, and are being pursued with due diligence, by the company;

---

[45]  Companies Act 2006 (Commencement No 3, etc) Order 2007, SI 2007/2194, arts 2(2) and 3(1).
[46]  Comm, SCD, Ninth Sitting, 29 June 2006, cols 364–5.
[47]  Commons Amendment at Report Stage, 11 October 2006, 702, NC80.
[48]  CA 2006, Part 11.
[49]  CA 2006, s 261.
[50]  CA 1985, s 347I(2) made reference to the meaning in CA 1985, s 54(2), whereby shareholders were permitted to object to the re-registration of a public company as a private company.

(c) that the members proposing to bring proceedings under this section do not constitute an authorised group.

(3) Where an application is made on the ground mentioned in subsection (2)(b), the court may as an alternative to directing that the proposed proceedings under section 370 are not to be brought, direct—

    (a) that such proceedings may be brought on such terms and conditions as the court thinks fit, and

    (b) that the proceedings brought by the company—

        (i) shall be discontinued, or

        (ii) may be continued on such terms and conditions as the court thinks fit.

(4) The members by whom proceedings are brought under section 370 owe the same duties to the company in relation to the proceedings as would be owed by the directors of the company if the proceedings were being brought by the company itself.

But proceedings to enforce any such duty may be brought by the company only with the permission of the court.

(5) Proceedings brought under section 370 may not be discontinued or settled by the group except with the permission of the court, which may be given on such terms as the court thinks fit.

AMENDMENTS AND NOTES

[a] This section applies without modification to unregistered companies by reg 3 of and Sch 1 to the Unregistered Companies Regulations 2009, SI 2009/2436 and, by Sch 2, applies to donations made or expenditure incurred on or after 1 October 2007.

COMMENCEMENT DATE 1 October 2007 (Great Britain), 1 November 2007 (Northern Ireland)[51]

This section sets out the procedure (subsections (1)–(3)) for enforcement proceedings and in so doing reproduces the effect of Companies Act 1985, section 347I.  **14.371.02**

Subsection (1) provides that no such action can be commenced without written notice being given to the company which states the facts, cause of action, details of the group members, and the basis on which they satisfy the definition of 'authorised group' in section 370(3). There then follows a period of 28 days during which the proceedings may not be brought (section 371(1)(b)) but any director of the company can apply to the court for an order prohibiting the bringing of these proceedings on one of three specified grounds, namely that the company has been reimbursed the unauthorized amount (subsection (2)(a)), or that the members do not satisfy the definition of an 'authorised group' (subsection (2)(c)), or that the company is already pursuing proceedings with due diligence (subsection (2)(b)). The court may then order that the proposed proceedings should not be brought or, where the ground was that in section 371(2)(b) (company already pursuing proceedings with due diligence), as an alternative to the order prohibiting the authorized group proceedings, the court may direct that such proceedings may be brought on the terms and conditions specified by the court and that the proceedings by the company must either be discontinued or may be continued only on the terms and conditions laid down by the court (subsection (3)). The subsection (3) discretion enables the court to make a decision on whether it considers that the company is pursuing the proceedings with due diligence and make an order to reflect its findings.  **14.371.03**

If there is no application to the court by any director within the 28-day period or the court permits the shareholder proceedings to be commenced, the court has control of the action in the sense that the group of shareholders may not discontinue or settle the action without the court's permission, and the court can impose any terms it wishes on the grant of this permission (subsection (5)).  **14.371.04**

Since the members are acting on behalf of the company in order to secure a remedy for the company, they owe the same duties as would apply to the directors in these circumstances. However, since there is a danger that the directors may feel aggrieved at the action of these members, any proceedings by the company to enforce these duties owed by the group members can only be brought with the permission of the court (subsection (4)).  **14.371.05**

## 372  Costs of shareholder action[a]

(1) This section applies in relation to proceedings brought under section 370 in the name of a company ('the company') by an authorised group ('the group').  **14.372.01**

(2) The group may apply to the court for an order directing the company to indemnify the group in respect of costs incurred or to be incurred by the group in connection with the proceedings. The court may make such an order on such terms as it thinks fit.

(3) The group is not entitled to be paid any such costs out of the assets of the company except by virtue of such an order.

---

[51]  Companies Act 2006 (Commencement No 3, etc) Order 2007, SI 2007/2194, arts 2(2) and 3(1).

(4) If no such order has been made with respect to the proceedings, then—

    (a) if the company is awarded costs in connection with the proceedings, or it is agreed that costs incurred by the company in connection with the proceedings should be paid by any defendant, the costs shall be paid to the group; and

    (b) if any defendant is awarded costs in connection with the proceedings, or it is agreed that any defendant should be paid costs incurred by him in connection with the proceedings, the costs shall be paid by the group.

(5) In the application of this section to Scotland for 'costs' read 'expenses' and for 'defendant' read 'defender'.

AMENDMENTS AND NOTES

[a] This section applies without modification to unregistered companies by reg 3 of and Sch 1 to the Unregistered Companies Regulations 2009, SI 2009/2436 and, by Sch 2, applies to donations made or expenditure incurred on or after 1 October 2007.

COMMENCEMENT DATE 1 October 2007 (Great Britain), 1 November 2007 (Northern Ireland)[52]

**14.372.02**    Section 372 is identical in its effect to Companies Act 1985, section 347J.

**14.372.03**    Since the section 370 action is a group action on behalf of the company by some of its shareholders in order to secure reimbursement and compensation for the company's losses, section 372 allows the court to make an indemnity order in favour of the 'authorized group'. Therefore in order to guarantee that the group will be reimbursed its existing and prospective costs, the group will need to exercise its subsection (2) discretion, apply to the court for the order, and the court will need to grant that indemnity order, although it may choose to grant the order on any terms it thinks fit. Thus, there is no automatic right for the members to have the costs of the action reimbursed by the company.

**14.372.04**    If there is no such order in place then no costs are to be paid to the group by the company (subsection (3)). However, if the company is awarded costs in relation to the shareholder proceedings, or the defendant is held liable for the costs, then the costs recovered are to be paid to the group (subsection (4)(a)). It follows that if the defendant is awarded costs or it is agreed that the defendant's costs should be paid, the group will be responsible for payment of those costs (subsection (4)(b)).

### 373  Information for purposes of shareholder action[a]

**14.373.01**    (1) Where proceedings have been brought under section 370 in the name of a company by an authorised group, the group is entitled to require the company to provide it with all information relating to the subject matter of the proceedings that is in the company's possession or under its control or which is reasonably obtainable by it.

    (2) If the company, having been required by the group to do so, refuses to provide the group with all or any of that information, the court may, on an application made by the group, make an order directing—

    (a) the company, and

    (b) any of its officers or employees specified in the application,

    to provide the group with the information in question in such form and by such means as the court may direct.

AMENDMENTS AND NOTES

[a] This section applies without modification to unregistered companies by reg 3 of and Sch 1 to the Unregistered Companies Regulations 2009, SI 2009/2436 and, by Sch 2, applies to donations made or expenditure incurred on or after 1 October 2007.

COMMENCEMENT DATE 1 October 2007 (Great Britain), 1 November 2007 (Northern Ireland)[53]

**14.373.02**    Section 373 is identical to Companies Act 1985, section 347K.

**14.373.03**    Subsection (1) gives the 'authorised group' the right to require the company to provide it with all information in its possession or control, or which the company can reasonably obtain, relating to the subject matter of the proceedings, ie the political donation or expenditure and the circumstances surrounding the absence of an applicable authorizing resolution. However, this right to information arises only when 'proceedings have been brought' (subsection (1)) so that it will not apply before the written notice has been given to the company and the 28-day period has elapsed. Both are required (section 371) before proceedings can be commenced by the authorized group.

**14.373.04**    Subsection (2) provides for what is to happen if the company defaults in any way. The authorized group will need to apply to the court for an order directing the company and any named officers or employees

---

[52] Companies Act 2006 (Commencement No 3, etc) Order 2007, SI 2007/2194, arts 2(2) and 3(1).
[53] Companies Act 2006 (Commencement No 3, etc) Order 2007, SI 2007/2194, arts 2(2) and 3(1).

to provide the information in accordance with the requirements of the applicable court order. Failure to comply will constitute a contempt of court.

## Exemptions

### 374  Trade unions[a]

(1) A donation to a trade union, other than a contribution to the union's political fund, is not a political donation for the purposes of this Part.

14.374.01

(2) A trade union is not a political organisation for the purposes of section 365 (meaning of 'political expenditure').

(3) In this section—

'trade union' has the meaning given by section 1 of the Trade Union and Labour Relations (Consolidation) Act 1992 (c. 52) or Article 3 of the Industrial Relations (Northern Ireland) Order 1992 (S.I. 1992/807 (N.I. 5));

'political fund' means the fund from which payments by a trade union in the furtherance of political objects are required to be made by virtue of section 82(1)(a) of that Act or Article 57(2)(a) of that Order.

AMENDMENTS AND NOTES

[a] This section applies without modification to unregistered companies by reg 3 of and Sch 1 to the Unregistered Companies Regulations 2009, SI 2009/2436 and, by Sch 2, applies to donations made or expenditure incurred on or after 1 October 2007.

COMMENCEMENT DATE 1 October 2007 (Great Britain), 1 November 2007 (Northern Ireland)[54]

This is a new provision creating a new, and controversial, exemption for donations to trade unions in the UK and elsewhere, although it is clear that some trade union activities are political. Despite the nature of these activities the intention of the legislation is to exclude donations (other than contributions to the trade unions' political fund) (subsection (1)), and expenditure on trade union activities (subsection (2)) from the regulation in this Part. The explanatory note[55] indicates the practical rationale behind this exemption: it is designed to remove from regulation such expenditure as paid time off for trade union officials and use of company meeting rooms for meetings of the trade union which would previously have fallen within the scope of the authorization in Companies Act 1985, Part XA. The note also states that this includes the use of company vehicles by trade union officials, although such use is not specifically linked to union activities.

14.374.02

It proved to be a particularly controversial provision at Committee Stage in the Commons[56] on the basis that the total exemption went further than this limited objective concerning meeting rooms, etc.[57] Much of the concern was party political because of the perceived links between the Labour Party and funding by trade unions, eg that if a trade union received corporate donations in the form of use of rooms and vehicles, it could use the saved resources for political donations despite the legislative prohibition of transfers from trade union general funds to the 'political fund', and it was also suggested that non-members, such as companies, might make direct donations to the political fund. It was argued that since trade unions require the periodical consent of their members in respect of the political fund levy, then companies should obtain shareholder approval for any donations or expenditure in favour of trade unions. The Government's attempt to address these concerns has been limited to spelling out that contributions to a trade union's 'political fund' are not exempt.[58] However, this would not, it seems, prevent corporate donations having indirect effects on the sums spent in pursuit of political objectives by a trade union despite the absence of shareholder approval for such action, or even contrary to the shareholders' wishes. The answer, although requiring slightly more complex drafting, might have been to permit political expenditure in favour of trade unions without a resolution (along similar lines to subsection (2)), but to require donations to trade unions to fall within the regulation in this Part. However, it must be helpful that the final version of this provision has distinguished, in explicit terms, between donations to trade unions and political expenditure in their favour; nevertheless, the stated rationale for this exemption provision would seem to relate only to the latter.

14.374.03

---

[54] Companies Act 2006 (Commencement No 3, etc) Order 2007, SI 2007/2194, arts 2(2) and 3(1).
[55] Explanatory Notes to the Act, 630.
[56] Although not in the Lords.
[57] Comm, SCD, Ninth Sitting, 29 June 2006, cols 365–70 and Tenth Sitting, 4 July 2006, cols 373–82.
[58] Added at Report Stage, 11 October 2006, 711 (NC83).

## 375  Subscription for membership of trade association[a]

**14.375.01**
(1)  A subscription paid to a trade association for membership of the association is not a political donation for the purposes of this Part.
(2)  For this purpose—
'trade association' means an organisation formed for the purpose of furthering the trade interests of its members, or of persons represented by its members, and
'subscription' does not include a payment to the association to the extent that it is made for the purpose of financing any particular activity of the association.

AMENDMENTS AND NOTES

[a]  This section applies without modification to unregistered companies by reg 3 of and Sch 1 to the Unregistered Companies Regulations 2009, SI 2009/2436 and, by Sch 2, applies to donations made or expenditure incurred on or after 1 October 2007.

COMMENCEMENT DATE 1 October 2007 (Great Britain), 1 November 2007 (Northern Ireland)[59]

**14.375.02**  Although subscriptions are covered within the scope of 'political donations' in Companies Act 2006, section 364, since subscriptions to trade associations may have considerable benefits for the company and its business, the actual subscription for membership is exempted by section 375. However, subsection (2) makes it clear that the subscription must be limited to the amount necessary for membership and any payment made to a trade association in order to finance any particular activity of the association will be a 'donation' and subject to the authorization resolution.

**14.375.03**  This section corresponds to the exemption previously contained in the Companies Act 1985, section 347B(1) and (2), although it is no longer limited in jurisdictional terms to EU trade associations.

## 376  All-party parliamentary groups[a]

**14.376.01**
(1)  An all-party parliamentary group is not a political organisation for the purposes of this Part.
(2)  An 'all-party parliamentary group' means an all-party group composed of members of one or both of the Houses of Parliament (or of such members and other persons).

AMENDMENTS AND NOTES

[a]  This section applies without modification to unregistered companies by reg 3 of and Sch 1 to the Unregistered Companies Regulations 2009, SI 2009/2436 and, by Sch 2, applies to donations made or expenditure incurred on or after 1 October 2007.

COMMENCEMENT DATE 1 October 2007 (Great Britain), 1 November 2007 (Northern Ireland)[60]

**14.376.02**  This section restates the exemption in Companies Act 1985, section 347B(3) in respect of donations or expenditure to an 'all-party parliamentary group' (as defined in subsection (2)) by declaring that such groups are not 'political organisations' for the purposes of Part 14.[61]

## 377  Political expenditure exempted by order[a]

**14.377.01**
(1)  Authorisation under this Part is not needed for political expenditure that is exempt by virtue of an order of the Secretary of State under this section.
(2)  An order may confer an exemption in relation to—
(a)  companies of any description or category specified in the order, or
(b)  expenditure of any description or category so specified (whether framed by reference to goods, services or other matters in respect of which such expenditure is incurred or otherwise),
or both.
(3)  If or to the extent that expenditure is exempt from the requirement of authorisation under this Part by virtue of an order under this section, it shall be disregarded in determining what donations are authorised by any resolution of the company passed for the purposes of this Part.
(4)  An order under this section is subject to affirmative resolution procedure.

AMENDMENTS

[a]  This section applies with modification to unregistered companies by reg 3 of and Sch 1 to the Unregistered Companies Regulations 2009, SI 2009/2436 and, by Sch 2, applies to donations made or expenditure incurred on or after 1 October 2007.

---

[59]  Companies Act 2006 (Commencement No 3, etc) Order 2007, SI 2007/2194, arts 2(2) and 3(1).
[60]  Companies Act 2006 (Commencement No 3, etc) Order 2007, 51 2007/2194, arts 2(2) and 3(1).
[61]  Comm, SCD, Tenth Sitting, 4 July 2006, cols 384–8.

COMMENCEMENT DATE 1 October 2007 (Great Britain), 1 November 2007 (Northern Ireland)[62] with the exception of the enabling power in section 377 which has been effective since 20 January 2007

Section 377 provides for the Secretary of State to exempt other categories of political expenditure by statutory instrument. The order may limit exemption to particular companies or to particular expenditure. Such an order was made under the previous exemption by order provisions, Companies Act 1985, section 347B(8) to (11), in relation to the publication of newspapers which by their very nature involve the publication or dissemination of material which seeks to influence the views of the public.[63] The 2001 Exemption Order has been replaced by the Companies (Political Expenditure Exemption) Order 2007[64] which came into force in Great Britain on 1 October 2007 and in Northern Ireland on 1 November 2007. It exempts 'news material' (art 1(2)), which means 'material relating to news, public and political affairs, public and political events or views, opinion or comment on such news, affairs or events'. The exemption applies to expenditure 'incurred in the preparation, publication and dissemination of news material which is capable of being reasonably regarded as intended to affect public support for a political party or other political organization, or an independent election candidate, or to influence voters in relation to any national or regional referendum held under the law of a member State' (art 3) where the material is published by 'any company whose ordinary course of business includes, or is proposed to include' the publication or dissemination of such material for public consumption (art 4). However, since the impact of all Part 14 provisions in relation to independent election candidates did not come into force until 1 October 2008, the same applied to this Exemption Order (art 3(2)).

14.377.02

### 378 Donations not amounting to more than £5,000 in any twelve-month period[a]

(1) Authorisation under this Part is not needed for a donation except to the extent that the total amount of—
    (a) that donation, and
    (b) other relevant donations made in the period of 12 months ending with the date on which that donation is made,
exceeds £5,000.
(2) In this section—
    'donation' means a donation to a political party or other political organisation or to an independent election candidate; and
    'other relevant donations' means—
    (a) in relation to a donation made by a company that is not a subsidiary, any other donations made by that company or by any of its subsidiaries;
    (b) in relation to a donation made by a company that is a subsidiary, any other donations made by that company, by any holding company of that company or by any other subsidiary of any such holding company.
(3) If or to the extent that a donation is exempt by virtue of this section from the requirement of authorisation under this Part, it shall be disregarded in determining what donations are authorised by any resolution passed for the purposes of this Part.

14.378.01

AMENDMENTS AND NOTES

[a] This section applies without modification to unregistered companies by reg 3 of and Sch 1 to the Unregistered Companies Regulations 2009, SI 2009/2436 and, by Sch 2, applies to donations made or expenditure incurred on or after 1 October 2007.

COMMENCEMENT DATE 1 October 2007 (Great Britain), 1 November 2007 (Northern Ireland)[65]

This section restates the exemption in Companies Act 1985, section 347B(4). It is a *de minimis* exemption, ie in order to avoid excessive bureaucracy, no authorization is required if the aggregate amount of the donations by the company does not exceed £5,000 in a 12-month period. This relates to the aggregate amount of donations to a particular party or political organization or independent election candidate, as opposed to the total amount of expenditure under a particular head, eg all donations to political organizations other than political parties. However, in calculating this aggregate figure, the donations made by other companies in a corporate group must be taken into account, eg by the company's subsidiaries, by any holding company or by any other subsidiary of the holding company (subsection (2)).

14.378.02

---

[62] Companies Act 2006 (Commencement No 3, etc) Order 2007, SI 2007/2194, arts 2(2) and 3(1).
[63] Companies (EU Political Expenditure) Exemption Order 2001, SI 2001/445.
[64] SI 2007/2081.
[65] Companies Act 2006 (Commencement No 3, etc) Order 2007, SI 2007/2194, arts 2(2) and 3(1), but the reference to 'independent election candidates' took effect on 1 October 2008 (art 5 of the Order).

**14.378.03**　Since subsection (3) states that exempt donations are to be disregarded for the purposes of calculating whether donations are authorized by a resolution,[66] it appears to follow that if there is an authorizing resolution covering donations to political party X of £60,000 in a four-year period from 2008 to 2011 but only £3,000 is donated in 2008, £60,000, rather than £57,000, is the authorized total donation permitted for 2009 to 2011.

*Supplementary provisions*

### 379　Minor definitions[a]

**14.379.01**　(1)　In this Part—
　　　　　'director' includes shadow director; and
　　　　　'organisation' includes any *body* corporate or unincorporated association and any combination of persons.
　　(2)　Except as otherwise provided, any reference in this Part to the time at which a donation is made or expenditure is incurred is, in a case where the donation is made or expenditure incurred in pursuance of a contract, any earlier time at which that contract is entered into by the company.

AMENDMENTS

[a] This section applies with modification to unregistered companies by reg 3 of and Sch 1 to the Unregistered Companies Regulations 2009, SI 2009/2436 and, by Sch 2, applies to donations made or expenditure incurred on or after 1 October 2007.

COMMENCEMENT DATE 1 October 2007 (Great Britain), 1 November 2007 (Northern Ireland)[67]

**14.379.02**　This section organizes some of the definitions that were previously scattered around Companies Act 1985, section 347A. In subsection (1) the fact that 'director' includes a 'shadow director'[68] corresponds with the previous provision in Companies Act 1985, section 347A(3). The definition of 'organisation' is that previously contained in Companies Act 1985, section 347A(8), although it is difficult to see why this was not included in the general definitional section for 'political organisations' in section 363(2) of the 2006 Act.

**14.379.03**　There is a minor adjustment to the definition of 'relevant time' since this expression has disappeared in favour of references to the time when the donation was made or the expenditure was incurred. However, where this occurs in pursuance of the terms of a contract, the time when the donation was made or expenditure incurred is taken to be the date on which the contract was entered into (section 379(2)). Equally, it follows that for the purposes of calculating interest for reimbursement by the director(s) under section 369(2)(a), time runs from the date of the donation or expenditure rather than the date of any contract (section 369(5)).

[66] See also CA 2006, s 377(3) (expenditure exempted by order) to similar effect.
[67] Companies Act 2006 (Commencement No 3, etc) Order 2007, SI 2007/2194, arts 2(2) and 3(1).
[68] As defined in CA 2006, s 251.

# 15

## ACCOUNTS AND REPORTS

## Companies Act 2006

# PART 1
## ACCOUNTS AND REPORTS

# CHAPTER 1
## INTRODUCTION

### General

## 380  Scheme of this Part

(1)  The requirements of this Part as to accounts and reports apply in relation to each financial year of      **15.380.01**
     a company.

(2)  In certain respects different provisions apply to different kinds of company.

(3)  The main distinctions for this purpose are—

    (a)  between companies subject to the small companies regime (see section 381) and companies
     that are not subject to that regime; and

    (b)  between quoted companies (see section 385) and companies that are not quoted.

(4)  In this Part, where provisions do not apply to all kinds of company—

    (a)  provisions applying to companies subject to the small companies regime appear before the
     provisions applying to other companies,

    (b)  provisions applying to private companies appear before the provisions applying to public
     companies, and

    (c)  provisions applying to quoted companies appear after the provisions applying to other
     companies.

COMMENCEMENT DATE  6 April 2008[1]

Prior to this Act it was a frequent complaint that companies' legislation was not very helpfully laid out    **15.380.02**
so far as smaller companies were concerned. This was especially so of the 1985 Act's Part VII, the
predecessor to this Part 15. It was framed as a set of standard requirements for all companies, together
with a number of exceptions thereto available to smaller companies. In contrast, in this Act the small
companies regime is the standard or base case, and additional requirements for other companies are
added on top of it. This section advertises the structuring of Part 15 to achieve that end. However, the
comparatively neat arrangement of the requirements has been disturbed by the introduction of the
small companies exemption[2]—applying some aspects of the small companies regime to companies

---

[1]  Companies Act 2006 (Commencement No 5, Transitional Provisions and Savings) Order 2007, SI 2007/
3495, art 3(1) for financial years beginning on or after 6 April 2008.
[2]  Further to the Companies Act 2006 (Amendment) (Accounts and Reports) Regulations 2008, SI 2008/ 393,
regs 6 and 7.

that fail to qualify for that regime for certain reasons—which is mentioned briefly below and discussed in greater detail in the commentary to section 415A.

**15.380.03**   The following commentary gives on overview of the differing requirements of this Part for each type of company.[3]

**15.380.04**   A company subject to the small companies regime is required to prepare only a directors' report (without a business review) and individual accounts (ie, not group accounts as well).[4] Many, but not necessarily all, such companies will not require an audit report of those accounts and report.[5] They are required to circulate those accounts and reports to members but not to lay them in general meeting; and they need only to deliver to the registrar an abbreviated copy of those accounts and reports (or a copy omitting certain parts of the accounts and reports).[6]

**15.380.05**   A public company is subject to the same requirements save that its directors' report must include a business review (as must those of all companies outside the small companies regime), it must have an audit (unless dormant), it must prepare group accounts in certain circumstances, it must lay accounts before members in general meeting, and it must deliver to the registrar those accounts and reports, and do so within a tighter timetable than applicable to private companies (six months instead of nine).[7]

**15.380.06**   The requirements for a quoted company go further still and require it to prepare a directors' remuneration report, and to publish its annual accounts and reports on its website as soon as reasonably practicable.[8]

**15.380.07**   These, however, are not the only categories of companies for which Part 15 makes different provision. It provides for a company entitled to the small companies exemption,[9] ie, a company that would be in the small companies regime save for its being a member of an ineligible group.[10] Taking the exemption entitles the company to certain exemptions from disclosing particular information within the directors' report,[11] and from filing the directors' report with the Registrar.[12] It also makes different provision for medium-sized companies.[13] Different provision is made in relation to certain measures in their directors' reports, and they are permitted to deliver to the registrar an abbreviated copy of their annual accounts and reports,[14] but otherwise must comply with all requirements in relation to private companies. There is also a further class of company—a company that would be medium-sized save by reason only of its having been a member of an ineligible group within the financial year in question[15]—which is afforded certain exemptions from disclosure of non-financial key performance indicators in its directors' report.[16]

**15.380.08**   Companies that have any of their securities admitted to trading on a regulated market in an EEA State[17] are subject to occasional special provisions. For example, their group accounts must be prepared as IAS

---

[3]   Readers should note that many of the provisions in Parts 15 and 16 of the Act apply, with modifications, to limited liability partnerships by virtue of the Limited Liability Partnerships (Accounts and Audit) (Application of Companies Act 2006) Regulations 2008, SI 2008/1911. Readers should also note that many of the provisions of Parts 15 and 16 apply to insurance undertakings specified in reg 2(2)–(4) of the Insurance Accounts Directive (Miscellaneous Insurance Undertakings) Regulations 2008, SI 2008/565, and qualifying banks specified in reg 3 of the Bank Accounts Directive (Miscellaneous Banks) Regulations 2008, SI 2008/567.

[4]   See ss 381–384 (small companies regime); s 415 (requirement to prepare directors' report) and s 417(1) (requirement to prepare business review); s 394 (duty to prepare individual accounts); and s 398 (option to prepare group accounts).

[5]   See ss 477–479.

[6]   See s 423 (duty to circulate copies of annual accounts and reports) and s 444 (filing obligations).

[7]   See ss 480–481 (dormant companies' audit exemption); ss 399–402 (duty to prepare group accounts); s 437 (laying of accounts); and s 442 (period allowed for filing accounts).

[8]   See s 385 (quoted company); s 420 (duty to prepare directors' remuneration report); and s 430 (website publication).

[9]   See s 415A.

[10]   See s 384(2).

[11]   See ss 416(3) and 417.

[12]   See s 444A.

[13]   Defined in ss 465–467.

[14]   See s 417(7) (medium-sized company exemptions with regard to the business review) and s 445 (filing obligations of medium-sized companies).

[15]   See s 467(4).

[16]   See s 417(7).

[17]   See s 1173 (regulated market) and s 1170 (EEA State).

group accounts,[18] and they usually cannot be exempt from the requirement to prepare group accounts.[19]

It should also be noted that the various categories of company are not all necessarily mutually exclusive. **15.380.09** Thus all companies subject to the small companies regime are also medium-sized companies, although this does not have the effect of imposing additional requirements on such companies. Another example is quoted companies and those with securities admitted to trading on a regulated market in an EEA State. There is much in common between the two since many of the securities and markets referred to in their respective definitions are common. However, some quoted companies may be so by virtue of quotation on markets that are not regulated markets in an EEA State, such as the New York Stock Exchange;[20] or a company may have securities admitted to trading on an EEA regulated market that are not within the definition of quoted because the securities are not equity share capital or because the regulated market does not constitute the official list of the EEA State concerned.[21] There could even be the rare case of a company with securities admitted to trading on a regulated market in an EEA State that is not a public company. Section 755 permits a private company to issue shares to the public where it undertakes, as part of the offer, to re-register as a public company within six months of the offer date.[22] Furthermore, section 755's prohibition of public offers by a private company applies only in respect of private companies limited by shares or by guarantee—it does not apply to a private company that is an unlimited company. Finally, it is possible that the issuer was a public company at the time of the offer but later re-registered as a private company.

## Companies subject to the small companies regime

### 381   Companies subject to the small companies regime

The small companies regime [...]^a applies to a company for a financial year in relation to which the **15.381.01** company—

(a)  qualifies as small (see sections 382 and 383), and
(b)  is not excluded from the regime (see section 384).

AMENDMENTS
^a   Words omitted by the Companies Act 2006 (Amendment) (Accounts and Reports) Regulations 2008, SI 2008/393, reg 6.

COMMENCEMENT DATE  6 April 2008[23]

This section and the following three set out the basis for a company to be subject to the small companies **15.381.02** regime. The requirements in these sections are complicated and a careful reading is needed before concluding that a company is within the small companies regime.

It is important to distinguish between a company's qualifying as small and its being subject to the small **15.381.03** companies regime. Qualification as small is determined, more or less, by financial size in certain financial years; the thresholds (turnover, assets, and employees) for determining qualification are given by sections 382 and 383. However, qualification as small is not enough to be within the small companies regime: the company must not be excluded from the regime under section 384. Therefore, qualification for the small companies regime has two limbs and both must be met. This approach occasionally causes confusion because directors and accountants typically refer to a 'small company' when, properly speaking, a company within the small companies regime is intended.

A further distinction needs to be made between companies subject to the small companies regime and **15.381.04** companies entitled to the small companies exemption. As discussed in more detail in the commentary to section 415A, the small companies exemption entitles a company to certain exemptions from disclosing particular information within the directors' report,[24] and from filing the directors' report with the Registrar;[25] it applies, as explained at section 415A, to a company that would be in the small

---

[18]  Under Regulation (EC) No 1606/2002 at [2002] OJ/L243/1, as amended, acknowledged at s 403(1).
[19]  See ss 400(4) and 401(4), but subject to all subsidiary undertakings' falling to be excluded from consolidation under ss 402 and 405.
[20]  See s 385(2)(c).
[21]  See s 548 (equity share capital) and s 385 (qualification as a quoted company).
[22]  See s 755(3), (4).
[23]  Companies Act 2006 (Commencement No 5, Transitional Provisions and Savings) Order 2007, SI 2007/3495, art 3(1). This provision applies to accounts and reports for financial years beginning on or after 6 April 2008.
[24]  See ss 416(3) and 417.
[25]  See s 444A.

companies regime but for failure of the test in section 384(2) (excluded because it is a member of a group containing members that engage in certain types of activity or status).

### 382   Companies qualifying as small: general

**15.382.01**    (1)  A company qualifies as small in relation to its first financial year if the qualifying conditions are met in that year.

(2)  A company qualifies as small in relation to a subsequent financial year—

(a)  if the qualifying conditions are met in that year and the preceding financial year;

(b)  if the qualifying conditions are met in that year and the company qualified as small in relation to the preceding financial year;

(c)  if the qualifying conditions were met in the preceding financial year and the company qualified as small in relation to that year.

(3)  The qualifying conditions are met by a company in a year in which it satisfies two or more of the following requirements—

| | |
|---|---|
| 1.  Turnover | Not more than £[6.5][a] million |
| 2.  Balance sheet total | Not more than £[3.26][b] million |
| 3.  Number of employees | Not more than 50 |

(4)  For a period that is a company's financial year but not in fact a year the maximum figures for turnover must be proportionately adjusted.

(5)  The balance sheet total means the aggregate of the amounts shown as assets in the company's balance sheet.

(6)  The number of employees means the average number of persons employed by the company in the year, determined as follows—

(a)  find for each month in the financial year the number of persons employed under contracts of service by the company in that month (whether throughout the month or not),

(b)  add together the monthly totals, and

(c)  divide by the number of months in the financial year.

(7)  This section is subject to section 383 (companies qualifying as small: parent companies).

AMENDMENTS

[a]   Amendments made by the Companies Act 2006 (Amendment) (Accounts and Reports) Regulations 2008, SI 2008/393, reg 3(1).

[b]   Amendments made by the Companies Act 2006 (Amendment) (Accounts and Reports) Regulations 2008, SI 2008/393, reg 3(1).

COMMENCEMENT DATE  6 April 2008[26]

**15.382.02**    This section sets out the requirements that a company must meet to qualify as small. When a company is a parent company,[27] in addition to this section it must also meet the qualification requirements for parent companies under section 383.[28] As discussed under section 381, qualification as small is a prerequisite for being within the small companies regime but it is not the only consideration: the company must not be excluded from the regime under section 384.

**15.382.03**    Before addressing the provisions in detail, the terminology of this section bears examination, as it can be a source of difficulty. This section determines whether a company 'qualifies' as small.[29] It does so if the 'qualifying conditions' are met in certain periods. In turn the 'qualifying conditions' are 'met' if at least two of three 'requirements' of subsection (3) are 'satisfied'. For clarity in this commentary, subsection (3)'s three 'requirements' are referred to as thresholds.

**15.382.04**    This section can be separated into two distinct parts. Subsections (1) and (2) set out the periods in which the qualifying conditions must be met. Subsections (3) to (6) set out the qualifying thresholds themselves, as a set of thresholds,[30] together with supplementary provisions on their application.[31] The provisions of subsections (1) and (2) are a little complicated, although much less so than their predecessors under the 1985 Act.[32] The effect of these subsections can be stated in the following two propositions.

---

[26]  Companies Act 2006 (Commencement No 5, Transitional Provisions and Savings) Order 2007, SI 2007/3495, art 3(1) for financial years beginning on or after 6 April 2008.

[27]  See s 1173.

[28]  Subsection (7).

[29]  Subsections (1), (2).

[30]  Subsection (3).

[31]  Subsections (4)–(6).

[32]  Companies Act (CA) 1985, s 247.

- A company *first* qualifies as a small company in the second of two consecutive financial years[33] in which it meets any two of the thresholds in subsection (3), save that a company becomes small if it meets two such thresholds in its first financial year. Once a company has qualified as small, it *continues* to be so qualified until the following applies.
- A company *ceases* to qualify as small if it fails to satisfy any two of the thresholds in subsection (3) in two consecutive financial years. Once it has ceased to be a small company, it can qualify again only when the above applies again.

It should be noted that a company may meet different combinations of the subsection (3) thresholds in each relevant financial year—it need not meet the same two out of three every time. **15.382.05**

The effect described above is achieved by subsections (1) and (2) in the following manner. Subsection (1) is a straightforward statement that a company qualifies as small in its first financial year if it meets any two of the thresholds in that year. Subsection (2)(a) is a straightforward statement that a company qualifies as small in relation to any other financial year if that is the second consecutive year in which it meets any two of the thresholds. Subsection (2)(c) provides that if a company does not meet the thresholds in the financial year in question it can still qualify as small if it qualified as small in the previous financial year; that is to say, a failure in the current year alone does not cause a company to cease to qualify as small. Subsection (2)(b) provides that a company qualifies as small in relation to a financial year in which it meets any two of the thresholds if the company qualified as small in the previous year; it is not necessary that the prior year qualification arose from meeting any two thresholds in that year, but could have been qualification under subsection (2)(c); thus it can be seen that failure to meet any two thresholds in the previous financial year alone does not cause a company to cease to qualify as small. In addition, it can be seen that if the company failed to meet any two thresholds in the current and the preceding financial year, there is no provision of subsection (2) within which it falls and thus it does not qualify as small. **15.382.06**

The effect of these provisions can also be illustrated by example. In the following table it is assumed that year 1 is not the company's first financial year and that the company has never previously met the thresholds. **15.382.07**

| Year | Are any two of subsection (3)'s thresholds met this year? | Qualification as small for this year | Subsection under which qualified |
|------|-----------------------------------------------------------|--------------------------------------|----------------------------------|
| 1 | No | No | – |
| 2 | No | No | – |
| 3 | Yes | No | – |
| 4 | Yes | Yes | (2)(a) |
| 5 | No | Yes | (2)(c) |
| 6 | Yes | Yes | (2)(b) |
| 7 | No | Yes | (2)(c) |
| 8 | Yes | Yes | (2)(b) |
| 9 | No | Yes | (2)(c) |
| 10 | No | No | – |

Thus it can be seen that the company had to meet any two thresholds in two consecutive years—years 3 and 4—in order *first* to qualify as small (in year 4). Thereafter in years 5 to 9 it *continued* to be qualified as small notwithstanding that in those years it met any two thresholds in only one of any two consecutive years. Finally, the company *ceased* to qualify in year 10 when it had failed to meet any two thresholds for two consecutive years.

Subsection (3) gives the three thresholds (turnover, balance sheet total, employees) and to meet the qualifying conditions in a particular financial year the company must not exceed at least two of them. Turnover is defined in section 474(1) and is readily apparent in Companies Act individual accounts.[34] A caption labelled 'turnover' will not necessarily appear in IAS individual accounts[35] as different terminology may be used; however, the amount that corresponds with 'turnover' will usually be readily **15.382.08**

---

[33] See s 390.

[34] 'Turnover' is a line item in the profit and loss account under regulations made under s 396(3), as it was in the predecessor, CA 1985, Sch 4. See nn 170 and 171 to para 15.396.03 below.

[35] See s 395.

apparent. The balance sheet total means the aggregate of the carrying value of a company's assets (eg, *not* the company's net assets after deducting liabilities). The calculation of the numbers of employees is performed in the same manner as for the average staff number disclosures required by section 411.

**15.382.09**　When a financial year is not 12 months, the threshold for turnover is adjusted pro rata to reflect the actual financial year.[36] Thus when trading is seasonal the length of the financial year may play a part in deciding whether the turnover threshold is met in a short or a long financial year.

**15.382.10**　It is evident that it is not possible to determine conclusively whether a company qualifies as small until the accounts for the financial year are on the point of being approved. However, the directors should be able to make, for planning purposes, a reasonably accurate assessment before the accounts are prepared given the requirements to maintain adequate accounting records.[37]

### 383　Companies qualifying as small: parent companies

**15.383.01**
(1)　A parent company qualifies as a small company in relation to a financial year only if the group headed by it qualifies as a small group.

(2)　A group qualifies as small in relation to the parent company's first financial year if the qualifying conditions are met in that year.

(3)　A group qualifies as small in relation to a subsequent financial year of the parent company—
　　(a)　if the qualifying conditions are met in that year and the preceding financial year;
　　(b)　if the qualifying conditions are met in that year and the group qualified as small in relation to the preceding financial year;
　　(c)　if the qualifying conditions were met in the preceding financial year and the group qualified as small in relation to that year.

(4)　The qualifying conditions are met by a group in a year in which it satisfies two or more of the following requirements—

| | |
|---|---|
| 1. Aggregate turnover | Not more than £[6.5]a million net (or £[7.8]b million gross) |
| 2. Aggregare balance sheet total | Not more than £[3.26]c million net (or £[3.9]d million gross) million |
| 3. Aggregate number of employees | Not more than 50 |

(5)　The aggregate figures are ascertained by aggregating the relevant figures determined in accordance with section 382 for each member of the group.

(6)　In relation to the aggregate figures for turnover and balance sheet total—'net' means after any set-offs and other adjustments made to eliminate group transactions—
　　(a)　in the case of Companies Act accounts, in accordance with regulations under section 404,
　　(b)　in the case of IAS accounts, in accordance with international accounting standards; and 'gross' means without those set-offs and other adjustments.
A company may satisfy any relevant requirement on the basis of either the net or the gross figure.

(7)　The figures for each subsidiary undertaking shall be those included in its individual accounts for the relevant financial year, that is—
　　(a)　if its financial year ends with that of the parent company, that financial year, and
　　(b)　if not, its financial year ending last before the end of the financial year of the parent company.
If those figures cannot be obtained without disproportionate expense or undue delay, the latest available figures shall be taken.

AMENDMENTS

[a]　Amendments made by the Companies Act 2006 (Amendment) (Accounts and Reports) Regulations 2008, SI 2008/393, reg 3(2).

[b]　Amendments made by the Companies Act 2006 (Amendment) (Accounts and Reports) Regulations 2008, SI 2008/393, reg 3(2).

[c]　Amendments made by the Companies Act 2006 (Amendment) (Accounts and Reports) Regulations 2008, SI 2008/393, reg 3(2).

[d]　Amendments made by the Companies Act 2006 (Amendment) (Accounts and Reports) Regulations 2008, SI 2008/393, reg 3(2).

COMMENCEMENT DATE　6 April 2008[38]

---

[36]　A financial year does not have to be 12 months; see s 390.

[37]　See s 386.

[38]　Companies Act 2006 (Commencement No 5, Transitional Provisions and Savings) Order 2007, SI 2007/3495, art 3(1). This provision applies to accounts and reports for financial years beginning on or after 6 April 2008.

This section applies to any company that is a parent company.[39] Therefore, a parent company is   **15.383.02**
required to meet both section 382 and this section if it is to qualify as small.

In essence, this section takes the same threshold tests, and rules for applying them in particular   **15.383.03**
financial years,[40] that section 382 applies to an individual company,[41] and applies them to the group[42]
headed by the company. By extending these tests to the parent's group the section thus prevents what
would otherwise be a relatively straightforward exercise for a company (that would not qualify as
small) to divide its business between itself and various subsidiary undertakings, each of which could
qualify as small, with the aim of avoiding the more onerous reporting requirements applicable outwith
the small companies regime.

Subsections (2) and (3) are the equivalents of sections 382(1) and (2) and their application follows that   **15.383.04**
described earlier. Subsections (4) to (7) set out the qualifying conditions; their operation is broadly the
same as their equivalents in section 382. However, as the qualifying conditions—the satisfaction of
certain thresholds—apply on a group basis, some modification is needed to the requirements and these
are discussed below.

The thresholds for aggregate turnover and aggregate balance sheet total are given as net and gross   **15.383.05**
alternatives (the gross amount being 20 per cent greater than its equivalent net amount). The crucial
difference is that the basis of calculating the group's turnover and balance sheet amount under the gross
method is different from the basis of calculation under the net method. Considering the gross basis
first, the calculation is performed by adding together the respective amounts for each member of the
group without adjustment. If the company meets a threshold on this basis, there is no need to consider
the net basis. This is advantageous as the net basis requires more work to calculate the necessary figures,
as follows. Many groups in the normal course of events undertake intragroup transactions (eg, a
manufacturing company in the group selling to a retailing company in the group) such that the
turnover of group companies is increased by those intragroup transactions and, if balances are not
settled immediately, the assets of group members are increased by receivables from the other group
members. The net basis is after adjustments necessary to render the turnover and balance sheet total
onto the same basis as group accounts under either of the accounting options in section 403 (elimi-
nating intragroup effects). It is not entirely clear as to which of the Companies Act or IAS set
offs/adjustments is required by subsection (6). After all, if a company is within the small companies
regime then it need not prepare group accounts at all;[43] and even if it chooses to prepare IAS individual
accounts[44] that would not prejudice the choice for group accounts were they required.[45] However, this
uncertainty is unlikely to have much effect in practice as the eliminations required under either
accounting choice—essentially of intragroup trading and balances—will yield the same result.

Each threshold (qualifying condition) is considered separately such that a company may meet one   **15.383.06**
threshold on the gross basis and another on the net basis.

The threshold with respect to staff numbers is simply the sum of each company's employees. The   **15.383.07**
numbers for each company are calculated in accordance with section 382 (5). No adjustment is made
in the event that the same person is employed by more than one group company.

Subsection (7) sets out which of a subsidiary undertaking's financial years' figures should be used in the   **15.383.08**
calculation for the three thresholds. When its financial year ends on same day as the parent's, then that
financial year should be used. When the subsidiary undertaking's financial year does not end on the
same day as the parent's, the last financial year ending before the parent's financial year should be used.
It also follows from the requirement of subsection (7) that if its financial year is of a different length
from the parent's,[46] regardless of its end-date, no adjustment is made.

A dispensation from obtaining the subsidiary undertaking's financial information is given by subsec-   **15.383.09**
tion (7) when it 'cannot be obtained without disproportionate expense or undue delay'; in such
circumstances the Act requires that the 'latest available figures shall be taken'. It is not immediately clear

---

[39]  See s 1173.

[40]  See s 390.

[41]  More detail is given under s 382 above.

[42]  Defined in s 474(1) as a parent undertaking and its subsidiary undertakings, for which see s 1162. This
definition is based on the Act's definition of the parent and subsidiary undertakings even if the parent company
prepares IAS group accounts under s 403 in the event of its being required or choosing to prepare group accounts.

[43]  See s 398.

[44]  See s 395.

[45]  The choices under ss 395 and 403 are independent.

[46]  A financial year as defined by the Act does not have to be 12 months—see s 390—including the case where
the subsidiary undertaking is not a company under this Act, eg a foreign company.

what 'latest available figures' means and, in any case, it is expected that the dispensation will be used infrequently as the test of disproportionate expense and undue delay seems to set a high hurdle.

## 384  Companies excluded from the small companies regime

**15.384.01**

(1) The small companies regime does not apply to a company that is, or was at any time within the financial year to which the accounts relate—

  (a) a public company,

  (b) a company that—

    (i) is an authorised insurance company, a banking company, an e-money issuer, [a MiFID investment firm][a] or a UCITS management company, or

    (ii) carries on insurance market activity, or

  (c) a member of an ineligible group.

(2) A group is ineligible if any of its members is—

  (a) a public company,

  (b) a body corporate (other than a company) whose shares are admitted to trading on a regulated market in an EEA State,

  (c) a person (other than a small company) who has permission under Part 4 of the Financial Services and Markets Act 2000 (c.8) to carry on a regulated activity,

  (d) a small company that is an authorised insurance company, a banking company, an e-money issuer, [a MiFID investment firm][b] or a UCITS management company, or

  (e) a person who carries on insurance market activity.

(3) A company is a small company for the purposes of subsection (2) if it qualified as small in relation to its last financial year ending on or before the end of the financial year to which the accounts relate.

AMENDMENTS

[a] Words in square brackets substituted by the Markets in Financial Instruments Directive (Consequential Amendments) Regulations 2007, SI 2007/2932, reg 3(2).

[b] Words in square brackets substituted by the Markets in Financial Instruments Directive (Consequential Amendments) Regulations 2007, SI 2007/2932, reg 3(2).

COMMENCEMENT DATE  6 April 2008[47]

**15.384.02**  This section prohibits certain companies, notwithstanding that they qualify as small under sections 382 and 383, from being within the small companies regime. Subsections (1)(a) and (b) set out the exclusion tests applicable to the status of the company itself.

**15.384.03**  Subsections (1)(c) and (2) set out similar exclusion tests but applicable to the status of any member of any group[48] of which the company forms a part. Thus the tests apply not only by reference to the company's own subsidiary undertakings,[49] but also its parent undertakings[50] and its fellow subsidiary undertakings,[51] and whether they are UK companies or not. If the company fails to be within the small companies regime only by reason of exclusion under subsections (1)(c) and (2) then it will instead fall within section 415A's small companies exemption in relation to certain aspects of the directors' report.

**15.384.04**  It should be noted that the periods in respect of which exclusion applies are different from the periods in which the qualification as small is assessed. Qualification as small is assessed on what might be termed a two-year rolling basis.[52] On the other hand, a company is excluded in respect of a specific financial year if an exclusion test is met either at any time during that one financial year or, by virtue of the word 'is' in subsection (1), at the time of taking advantage of a provision in the small companies regime. For example, if the company wished that the copy of the accounts delivered to the registrar under section 444 be in the form of abbreviated accounts under that section and approved by the directors under section 450, then the company must not be ineligible at the times of approval and of delivery of those abbreviated accounts.

**15.384.05**  Of the conditions that result in exclusion, subsection (2)(a), which makes any group that contains a public company ineligible, has by far the widest effect. A public company means a UK public company.[53] Subsection (2)(b) may also have wide effect. It aims chiefly at foreign companies and does not apply to companies under the Act. A foreign company makes a group ineligible if its shares are

---

[47] Companies Act 2006 (Commencement No 5, Transitional Provisions and Savings) Order 2007, SI 2007/3495, art 3(1). This provision applies to accounts and reports for financial years beginning on or after 6 April 2008.

[48] For 'group' see ss 474(1) and 1162.

[49] See s 1162.

[50] See s 1162.

[51] Ie subsidiary undertakings of its parent undertaking that are not its own subsidiary undertakings; see s 1161.

[52] See ss 382 and 383.

[53] See s 4.

admitted to trading on a regulated market[54] in an EEA State.[55] The condition in subsection (2)(b), which requires shares to be admitted to trading on an EEA-regulated market, is narrower that those of subsections (1)(a) and (2)(a), since under those a public company need not actually have offered its shares to the public to cause exclusion from the small companies regime.

Subsections (1)(b) and (2)(c), (d) merit some explanation. First of all, the terms employed in them are **15.384.06** defined in section 474 (e-money issuer, a MiFID investment firm, regulated activity and UCITS management company), section 1164 (banking company), and section 1165 ('authorised insurance company'). It should be noted that the definition of 'regulated activity' is narrower than that of the Financial Services and Markets Act 2000, as section 474 excludes, for the purposes of this Part, certain activities that are regulated under that other Act.[56] The five activities specified in subsections (1)(b)(i) and (2)(d) is narrower still than regulated activities (ie, than those treated as regulated activities for the purposes of this Part). The effect of those two subsections, taken together with subsection (2)(c), is to render the company ineligible if it or, regardless of its size, its own subsidiary undertaking or a fellow group undertaking carries on one of that subset of five regulated activities. Subsection (2)(c) also has the effect that if the company's own subsidiary undertaking, or a fellow group undertaking that does not qualify as small,[57] carries on any other regulated activity (ie, one that is treated as a regulated activity for the purposes of this Part), the company is ineligible. This aspect of the provision is unlikely to have a practical effect in relation to the company's own subsidiary undertaking, as if that did not qualify as small, then following section 383's assessment of the company's own size on a group basis, neither would the company. For the avoidance of doubt, the carrying on of insurance market activity[58] by the company or its own subsidiary undertaking or a fellow group undertaking, will render the company ineligible.[59]

## Quoted and unquoted companies

### 385   Quoted and unquoted companies

(1)  For the purposes of this Part a company is a quoted company in relation to a financial year if it is   **15.385.01**
a quoted company immediately before the end of the accounting reference period by reference
to which that financial year was determined.

(2)  A 'quoted company' means a company whose equity share capital—
  (a)  has been included in the official list in accordance with the provisions of Part 6 of the Financial
       Services and Markets Act 2000 (c.8), or
  (b)  is officially listed in an EEA State, or
  (c)  is admitted to dealing on either the New York Stock Exchange or the exchange known as
       Nasdaq.

In paragraph (a) 'the official list' has the meaning given by section 103(1) of the Financial Services and
Markets Act 2000.

(3)  An 'unquoted company' means a company that is not a quoted company.

(4)  The Secretary of State may by regulations amend or replace the provisions of subsections (1) to (2)
     so as to limit or extend the application of some or all of the provisions of this Part that are
     expressed to apply to quoted companies.

(5)  Regulations under this section extending the application of any such provision of this Part are
     subject to affirmative resolution procedure.

(6)  Any other regulations under this section are subject to negative resolution procedure.

COMMENCEMENT DATE subsections (4)–(6) from 20 January 2007,[60] 1 October 2007 for certain
purposes[61] and 6 April 2008 for all other purposes[62]

Subsection (1) defines a quoted company, for the purposes of a particular financial year, as one that  **15.385.02**
meets the conditions in subsection (2) immediately before the end of the accounting reference period
upon which the financial year is based. By virtue of the so-called seven-day rule of section 390 a

---

[54]  See s 1173.

[55]  See s 1170.

[56]  Elsewhere in this Act the meaning of regulated activity is the same as in the Financial Services and Markets Act 2000; see s 1173.

[57]  Subsection (2)(d) refers to 'small company', defined by subs (3) as one qualifying as small—ie, one meeting ss 382 and 383.

[58]  See s 1165.

[59]  Subsections (1)(c), (2)(e).

[60]  Companies Act 2006 (Commencement No 1, etc) Order 2006, SI 2006/3428, art 3(3).

[61]  Companies Act 2006 (Commencement No 3, etc) Order 2007, SI 2007/2194, 2(3), for the purposes of the provisions in art 2(1) and (2).

[62]  Companies Act 2006 (Commencement No 5, Transitional Provisions and Savings) Order 2007, SI 2007/3495, art 3(1). This provision applies to accounts and reports for financial years beginning on or after 6 April 2008.

financial year may end up to seven days either side of the end of the accounting reference period, ie either side of the accounting reference date.[63]

**15.385.03**    Subsection (2) specifies the markets on which a company's equity share capital[64] must be traded for it to receive quoted company status. Thus, the admission to trading of debt or non-equity shares does not affect the status under this section.

**15.385.04**    Subsection (2) specifies the markets as the official list, equivalents in EEA States,[65] the New York Stock Exchange and Nasdaq. Thus, for example, having shares traded on the AIM does not make a company quoted.

CHAPTER 2

ACCOUNTING RECORDS

### 386  Duty to keep accounting records

**15.386.01**

(1)  Every company must keep adequate accounting records.

(2)  Adequate accounting records means records that are sufficient—

    (a)  to show and explain the company's transactions,

    (b)  to disclose with reasonable accuracy, at any time, the financial position of the company at that time, and

    (c)  to enable the directors to ensure that any accounts required to be prepared comply with the requirements of this Act (and, where applicable, of Article 4 of the IAS Regulation).

(3)  Accounting records must, in particular, contain—

    (a)  entries from day to day of all sums of money received and expended by the company and the matters in respect of which the receipt and expenditure takes place, and

    (b)  a record of the assets and liabilities of the company.

(4)  If the company's business involves dealing in goods, the accounting records must contain—

    (a)  statements of stock held by the company at the end of each financial year of the company,

    (b)  all statements of stocktakings from which any statement of stock as is mentioned in paragraph (a) has been or is to be prepared, and

    (c)  except in the case of goods sold by way of ordinary retail trade, statements of all goods sold and purchased, showing the goods and the buyers and sellers in sufficient detail to enable all these to be identified.

(5)  A parent company that has a subsidiary undertaking in relation to which the above requirements do not apply must take reasonable steps to secure that the undertaking keeps such accounting records as to enable the directors of the parent company to ensure that any accounts required to be prepared under this Part comply with the requirements of this Act (and, where applicable, of Article 4 of the IAS Regulation).

COMMENCEMENT DATE  6 April 2008[66]

**15.386.02**    This section requires all companies to keep adequate accounting records[67] and specifies what such records should achieve.[68] Whilst subsections (3) and (4) set out some particular requirements as to the contents, form, and organization of accounting records, this section is generally silent in that respect. The important matter of electronic accounting records is not dealt with in this section but, as provided by sections 1134 and 1135, accounting records may be in electronic form. Further guidance on the meaning of adequate accounting records and the other matters in this section can be found in guidance issued by the Institute of Chartered Accountant in England and Wales (ICAEW).[69]

**15.386.03**    Before dealing with the detail of the section, it might be queried as to why the legislation should require of companies that they keep records which it is in any event in their commercial interests to keep for the efficient running of their businesses. An answer becomes clear when one considers that others may at some stage need to use the records, such as a liquidator, an inspector, the Secretary of State, or, looking ahead to the offence in section 387, prosecutors. This section only sets minimum standards for accounting records and it is worth bearing in mind the comments of the ICAEW regarding this matter: 'the Act does not mandate that companies adopt the highest possible standards of record keeping

---

[63]  See ss 390–392 for financial years, accounting reference periods, and accounting reference dates.

[64]  See s 548.

[65]  See s 1170.

[66]  Companies Act 2006 (Commencement No 5, Transitional Provisions and Savings) Order 2007, SI 2007/ 3495, art 3(1). This provision applies to accounts and reports for financial years beginning on or after 6 April 2008.

[67]  Subsection (1).

[68]  Subsection (2).

[69]  *TECH 01/11—Guidance for directors on accounting records under the Companies Act 2006* (ICAEW, 2011).

systems, but sets only a minimum threshold as to the records that must be kept'.[70] Nevertheless, most companies keep accounting records that are more sophisticated than the Act's requirements. Furthermore, this section does not make provisions for the wider system of internal controls, which is far broader in scope than the accurate recording of transactions.[71] As noted in the Turnbull Guidance on Internal Controls, which has been incorporated in the UK corporate governance code, accounting records are a sub-category of financial controls, which are themselves part (although an important part) of internal controls.[72]

The duty in this section falls upon the company. In part this is to facilitate a wider range of persons    **15.386.04** within the company upon whom the sanction for non-compliance may fall.[73] However, it also raises a question in relation to outsourcing. Had the language of the 1948 Act been perpetuated—'every company shall cause to be kept'[74]—then it would have been clear that outsourcing of the keeping of accounting records was eminently possible. However the present formulation in subsection (1)—'every company must keep'—does not leave matters on such a certain footing.

Turning to subsection (2), there are three elements to what must be achieved by adequate accounting    **15.386.05** records. First, subsection (2)(a) requires that they should show and explain the company's transactions. It is clearly a prerequisite to subsections (2)(b) and (c). The ICAEW guidance is helpful in this area. It states that 'the accounting records should comprise an orderly, classified collection of information capable of timely retrieval, containing details of the company's transactions, assets and liabilities'.[75]

Second, subsection (2)(b) requires that the accounting records should disclose with reasonable    **15.386.06** accuracy at any time the financial position of the company at that time. This means that the accounting records must be written up within a reasonable time; in some cases, it will thus be necessary for the accounting records to be written up on a frequent basis.[76]

Third, subsection (2)(c) requires that the accounting records must be sufficient for the directors to    **15.386.07** prepare any accounts required by this Act and by the IAS Regulation when that regulation has direct effect to require a company to prepare IAS group accounts.[77] However, in contrast with subsection (2)(b), this subsection does not set any requirement for the timeliness of writing up of the accounting records in contemplation of the preparation of those accounts. Thus, it does not mean that the company is required to maintain financial information at any time that is as complete as is required to prepare annual accounts.[78] The ICAEW guidance states that 'the accounting records should therefore contain the primary material on which a set of accounts would be based. However they need not contain whatever additional items of information it would be necessary to know in order to make those accounts true and fair'.[79] The guidance also recognizes that some accounting entries are made only at the end of a financial year, for example depreciation, bad debts, or other losses; it explains that subsection (2)(b) 'will normally be satisfied if the basic data are recorded and a procedure exists to be applied to those data, so that when the financial position needs to be ascertained an adequate record is made and retained—for example by way of memorandum—of any expected loss, liability or contingency material to an assessment of the current position'.[80]

Finally, it follows from the ends at which adequate accounting records are aimed, that the sophistica-    **15.386.08** tion of a company's accounting records will need to be commensurate with the size and complexity of its activities.

Subsections (3) and (4) set out some specific content for accounting records in terms that will be    **15.386.09** familiar to accountants and bookkeepers. A company is required to maintain a cash book that

---

[70] *TECH 01/11—Guidance for directors on accounting records under the Companies Act 2006* (ICAEW, 2011), para 2.

[71] Ibid

[72] *UK corporate governance code* (Financial Reporting Council, 2010), ; *Internal Control: revised guidance for directors on internal controls* (Turnbull Guidance) (Financial Reporting Council, October 2005), para 4.

[73] 'Every officer of the company who is in default'—see ss 387(1) and 1121.

[74] CA 1948, s 147(1).

[75] *TECH 01/11—Guidance for directors on accounting records under the Companies Act 2006* (ICAEW, 2011), para 14.

[76] *TECH 01/11—Guidance for directors on accounting records under the Companies Act 2006* (ICAEW, 2011), para 18.

[77] See ss 403(1) and 474.

[78] *TECH 01/11Guidance for directors on accounting records under the Companies Act 2006* (ICAEW, 2011), para 19.

[79] *TECH 01/11Guidance for directors on accounting records under the Companies Act 2006* (ICAEW, 2011), para 20.

[80] *TECH 01/11Guidance for directors on accounting records under the Companies Act 2006* (ICAEW, 2011), para 23.

summarizes monies received and paid, with explanations given of each transaction; and a record of assets and liabilities, which is typically maintained as a nominal or general ledger and should be capable of producing a trial balance. A company dealing in goods—for example, a retailer—is required to maintain certain stock records. Although the language of these subsections is a little antiquated, there should be little difficulty in applying these requirements in practice. Moreover, many companies will in practice require, simply to run their businesses, more sophisticated records than are required by subsections (3) and (4).

**15.386.10**   Subsection (5) requires that where a company has a subsidiary undertaking[81] to which the requirements of this section do not apply—for example, a partnership[82] or a body corporate established overseas—the directors are required to take reasonable steps to secure that the accounting records of that undertaking are sufficient to enable the directors to prepare accounts in accordance with the requirements of the Act. This requirement applies in respect both of individual[83] and of group accounts.[84] However, in the case of a company's individual accounts, it is unlikely that the contents, form and organization of a subsidiary undertaking's accounting records would play a part in the preparation of the parent's individual accounts.

### 387  Duty to keep accounting records: offence

**15.387.01**
(1)  If a company fails to comply with any provision of section 386 (duty to keep accounting records), an offence is committed by every officer of the company who is in default.
(2)  It is a defence for a person charged with such an offence to show that he acted honestly and that in the circumstances in which the company's business was carried on the default was excusable.
(3)  A person guilty of an offence under this section is liable—
   (a)  on conviction on indictment, to imprisonment for a term not exceeding two years or a fine (or both);
   (b)  on summary conviction—
      (i)  in England and Wales, to imprisonment for a term not exceeding twelve months or to a fine not exceeding the statutory maximum (or both);
      (ii)  in Scotland or Northern Ireland, to imprisonment for a term not exceeding six months, or to a fine not exceeding the statutory maximum (or both).

COMMENCEMENT DATE  6 April 2008[85]

**15.387.02**   This section makes an offence of not keeping accounting records in accordance with the requirements of section 386, although it is a defence for an officer of the company to show that he acted honestly and that in the circumstances the default was excusable.

**15.387.03**   There are two matters arising from this section that are worth further consideration. The first is the persons on whom the penalty falls. It applies to any officer of the company who is in default[86] and thus the scope of the persons within penalty is wider than merely the directors. The second is that the penalty for failure to keep adequate accounting records can be a custodial one. This is understandable given that a fraudster will often falsify or destroy accounting records to conceal the facts. Thus, the penalty in this section offers one route by which the law can deal with this problem.

**15.387.04**   Any failure by the company under section 386 is a matter to which the courts are required to have regard when determining whether a director's conduct is unfit.[87]

### 388  Where and for how long records to be kept

**15.388.01**
(1)  A company's accounting records—
   (a)  must be kept at its registered office or such other place as the directors think fit, and
   (b)  must at all times be open to inspection by the company's officers.
(2)  If accounting records are kept at a place outside the United Kingdom, accounts and returns with respect to the business dealt with in the accounting records so kept must be sent to, and kept at, a place in the United Kingdom, and must at all times be open to such inspection.

---

[81]  See s 1162.
[82]  But not a GB limited liability partnership—which is in any case a body corporate—as the requirements of this section apply to those entities. See the Limited Liability Partnerships (Accounts and Audit) (Application of Companies Act 2006) Regulations 2008, SI 2008/1911 for financial years beginning on or after 1 October 2008.
[83]  See s 394.
[84]  See s 399.
[85]  Companies Act 2006 (Commencement No 5, Transitional Provisions and Savings) Order 2007, SI 2007/3495, art 3(1) for financial years beginning on or after 6 April 2008.
[86]  See s 1121.
[87]  Company Directors Disqualification Act 1986, s 9 and Sch 1, as amended by Companies Act 2006 (Consequential Amendments etc) Order 2008, SI 2008/948, art 106(8).

(3) The accounts and returns to be sent to the United Kingdom must be such as to—
    (a) disclose with reasonable accuracy the financial position of the business in question at intervals of not more than six months, and
    (b) enable the directors to ensure that the accounts required to be prepared under this Part comply with the requirements of this Act (and, where applicable, of Article 4 of the IAS Regulation).

(4) Accounting records that a company is required by section 386 to keep must be preserved by it—
    (a) in the case of a private company, for three years from the date on which they are made;
    (b) in the case of a public company, for six years from the date on which they are made.

(5) Subsection (4) is subject to any provision contained in rules made under section 411 of the Insolvency Act 1986 (c. 45) (company insolvency rules) or Article 359 of the Insolvency (Northern Ireland) Order 1989 (S.I. 1989/2405 (N.I. 19)).

COMMENCEMENT DATE   6 April 2008[88]

This section sets out the requirements as to where accounting records may be located and the length of time for which they should be preserved.   **15.388.02**

Subsection (1) permits accounting records to be maintained either at the registered office or such other places as the directors see fit. In many cases, a company's registered office will not be where its operations are based—for example, the registered office might be that of a law or accounting firm which provides company secretarial services. Furthermore, the volume of accounting records and common business-continuity planning considerations will often cause the records to be located in archives at sites separate from the business operations.   **15.388.03**

The accounting records are, under this section, open to inspection by the company's officers[89] only. Thus, members of the company or the general public have no statutory right to inspect the accounting records. Nevertheless, the members may, through the articles[90] or some other contractual arrangement,[91] acquire access to the accounting records.   **15.388.04**

In relation to a director's right of inspection, the Court of Appeal in *Oxford Legal Group Ltd v Sibbasbridge Services plc and another*[92] preferred the view that the right is conferred by the common law but is recognized by statute in what is now this section 388. In the same case it was stated very clearly that the right may only be exercised *qua* director; that is to say, to enable the person to discharge the duties of director and not for some other and improper purpose whether injurious to the company or not. Furthermore, *Kang v Kang and others*[93] confirms that the obligation upon the company is simply one to produce the documents. It does not extend to compelling the company, or any other officers, to answer requests for further information arising out of a review of the documents produced; the obligation is to produce documents, not to provide a narrative account of them.   **15.388.05**

A question arises, in relation to subsection (1)(b), as to the status of the auditor. The Act does not expressly put the auditor within the definition of an officer; on the other hand, neither is he excluded.[94] However, in *R v Shacter*[95] it was found that an auditor was an officer, in part because the legislation referred to his holding office.[96] Thus, it appears that the auditor, as an officer of the company, has access to the accounting records of the company. In any case, the auditor's right of access is put beyond doubt at other places in the Act.[97]   **15.388.06**

---

[88] Companies Act 2006 (Commencement No 5, Transitional Provisions and Savings) Order 2007, SI 2007/3495, art 3(1) for financial years beginning on or after 6 April 2008.

[89] See s 1173.

[90] Whilst Art 109, Table A (1985, as amended) denies the members access to the accounting records, there is no reason why this provision cannot be varied. This position is preserved in model articles of association eg art 50 for private companies limited by shares, see Chapter 51.

[91] For example, a joint venture agreement.

[92] [2008] EWCA Civ 387.

[93] See, for example, <http://www.11sb.com/member-cases-and-bulletins/kang-v-kang-and-others-(2012).-company..asp>.

[94] See s 1173.

[95] [1960] 2 QB 252 CCA.

[96] This was found in the context of CA 1948, s 159: 'Every company shall at each annual general meeting appoint an auditor to hold office from the conclusion of that, until the conclusion of the next, annual general meeting.' This provision's successors at sections 487 and 491 continue to refer to holding office.

[97] S 499 gives the auditor a right of access at all times to the company's books, accounts and vouchers and the right to require certain persons (including the directors) to provide information and explanations. Moreover, s 418 provides that the directors make a directors' report disclosure that, in effect, requires the directors to volunteer all necessary information to the company's auditor.

**15.388.07**    In addition to the company's officers' access, the Secretary of State has wide ranging powers to instigate investigations into companies through which an inspector appointed by him has the right to demand that the company present him with any of its documents,[98] and the Secretary of State has similar direct powers.[99]

**15.388.08**    Where accounting information is maintained outside the UK, for example in respect of an overseas branch, accounts and returns must be made to a place of business in the UK every six months.[100]

**15.388.09**    Under this section accounting records must be kept for three years by a private company and six years by a public company. However, it must not be overlooked that there are provisions in other legislation that may require some or all of those records to be preserved for longer periods.[101]

### 389  Where and for how long records to be kept: offences

**15.389.01**
    (1)  If a company fails to comply with any provision of subsections (1) to (3) of section 388 (requirements as to keeping of accounting records), an offence is committed by every officer of the company who is in default.

    (2)  It is a defence for a person charged with such an offence to show that he acted honestly and that in the circumstances in which the company's business was carried on the default was excusable.

    (3)  An officer of a company commits an offence if he—

        (a)  fails to take all reasonable steps for securing compliance by the company with subsection (4) of that section (period for which records to be preserved), or

        (b)  intentionally causes any default by the company under that subsection. (4) A person guilty of an offence under this section is liable—

        (a)  on conviction on indictment, to imprisonment for a term not exceeding two years or a fine (or both);

        (b)  on summary conviction—

            (i)  in England and Wales [or Scotland],[a] to imprisonment for a term not exceeding twelve months or to a fine not exceeding the statutory maximum (or both);

            (ii)  in […] Northern Ireland, to imprisonment for a term not exceeding six months, or to a fine not exceeding the statutory maximum (or both).

AMENDMENTS AND NOTES

[a]  Inserted by the Limited Liability Partnerships (Application of Companies Act 2006) Regulations 2009, SI 2009/1804, Sch 3.

COMMENCEMENT DATE  6 April 2008[102]

**15.389.02**    This section creates an offence for default with respect to location and inspection[103] and another for default with respect to the preservation[104] of accounting records. The precise formulations differ between the two offences. As with the offence under section 387 the sanctions fall more widely than upon directors[105] and can involve a custodial penalty.

**15.389.03**    Any failure by the company is a matter to which the courts are required to have regard when determining whether a director's conduct is unfit.[106]

CHAPTER 3A

COMPANY'S FINANCIAL YEAR

### 390  A company's financial year[a]

**15.390.01**
    (1)  A company's financial year is determined as follows.

    (2)  Its first financial year—

        (a)  begins with the first day of its first accounting reference period, and

---

[98]  CA 1985, s 434.

[99]  CA 1985, s 447.

[100]  Subsection (3).

[101]  For example the Limitation Act 1980; eg, the Taxes Management Act 1970.

[102]  Companies Act 2006 (Commencement No 5, Transitional Provisions and Savings) Order 2007, SI 2007/3495, art 3(1) for financial years beginning on or after 6 April 2008.

[103]  Subsections (1), (2).

[104]  Subsection (3).

[105]  Upon the officers in default—for which see s 1121—for the offence in relation to location and inspection; and upon officers whose acts and omissions fall within subs (3) for the offence in relation to preservation of records.

[106]  Company Directors Disqualification Act 1986, s 9 and Sch 1, as amended by Companies Act 2006 (Consequential Amendments etc) Order 2008, SI 2008/948, art 106(8).

(b) ends with the last day of that period or such other date, not more than seven days before or after the end of that period, as the directors may determine.

(3) Subsequent financial years—

    (a) begin with the day immediately following the end of the company's previous financial year, and

    (b) end with the last day of its next accounting reference period or such other date, not more than seven days before or after the end of that period, as the directors may determine.

(4) In relation to an undertaking that is not a company, references in this Act to its financial year are to any period in respect of which a profit and loss account of the undertaking is required to be made up (by its constitution or by the law under which it is established), whether that period is a year or not.

(5) The directors of a parent company must secure that, except where in their opinion there are good reasons against it, the financial year of each of its subsidiary undertakings coincides with the company's own financial year.

AMENDMENTS AND NOTES

<sup>a</sup> This section applies with modifications to overseas companies by reg 37 of the Overseas Companies Regulations 2009, 2009/1801.

COMMENCEMENT DATE  6 April 2008[107]

A matter of some importance in the preparation of accounts is the period to which they relate. This matter is dealt with in this section and the following two. It is worth noting at the outset that the effect of these provisions is, for the most part, to give a company successive, 12-month financial years, thereby putting the production of the accounts on an annual cycle. Nevertheless, the provisions may be used to generate a financial year from as short as one day to a maximum of 18 months.[108]   **15.390.02**

First, a company's financial year always commences on the day immediately following the end of its previous financial year or on the day of the company's incorporation in the case of its first financial year.[109] Second, the end of the financial year, subject to the so-called 'seven-day rule' discussed below, is the last day of the accounting reference period (ARP), which is usually[110] the next occurrence of the accounting reference date (ARD).[111] For example, consider the case of a company with an ARD of 31 December. If the ARD remains unchanged, the company's financial years will be successive 12-month periods ending every 31 December (but subject to the aforesaid seven-day rule). If, however, the ARD is changed under section 392 then, on that occasion, the financial year will be either a shorter or a longer period to the first or second next occurrence of the ARD, as the company may choose,[112] and subject to the seven-day rule.   **15.390.03**

The seven-day rule provides that a particular financial year need not end on the ARD itself (being the last day of the ARP) but on a date within not more than seven days of that date as the directors may determine.[113] The effect of the seven-day rule is to allow directors to adjust the financial year so that it does not, for example, end mid-week, which may not be desirable for some businesses that have weekly trading and bookkeeping cycles.[114]   **15.390.04**

When the financial year is not 12 months it is important to disclose in the accounts the period covered, including where this is owing to the seven-day rule.   **15.390.05**

Subsection (4) defines the financial year in the context of undertakings that are not companies under the Act.[115] This is relevant to subsection (5) and to some other provisions of the Act or of regulations expected to be made under this Act.[116]   **15.390.06**

---

[107] Companies Act 2006 (Commencement No 5, Transitional Provisions and Savings) Order 2007, SI 2007/3495, art 3(1).

[108] See s 392(5).

[109] Subsection (2)(a) refers to the first day of its first accounting reference date but s 391 provides that this is the date of its incorporation.

[110] The exception occurs when the financial year is lengthened or shortened by changing the ARD, as described at s 392.

[111] See s 391.

[112] See s 392(2).

[113] Subsections (2)(b), (3)(b).

[114] For example the retail trade.

[115] Eg, partnerships or overseas companies.

[116] For example s 392(3)(a) on alignment of financial years of subsidiary undertakings; eg, s 383 (companies qualifying as small: parent companies) requires data in respect of subsidiary undertakings with reference to financial years.

**15.390.07** The requirement of subsection (5) is that the financial year of a company's subsidiary undertakings[117] should be the same as that of the company unless there are good reasons against it. A parent and its subsidiary undertakings normally have coterminous financial years, which is certainly more practical for the purpose of preparing group accounts.[118] There are circumstances in which different financial years are unavoidable—for example, in some overseas jurisdictions the financial year may be determined by law and thus the parent may not be permitted to change it.[119] In the case of UK subsidiary undertakings, examples do exist of different financial years. In such circumstances, each case should be judged on its own merits in determining whether a different financial year is justified.

### 391 Accounting reference periods and accounting reference date[a]

**15.391.01**
(1) A company's accounting reference periods are determined according to its accounting reference date in each calendar year.

(2) The accounting reference date of a company incorporated in Great Britain before 1st April 1996 is—
  (a) the date specified by notice to the registrar in accordance with section 224(2) of the Companies Act 1985 (c. 6) (notice specifying accounting reference date given within nine months of incorporation), or
  (b) failing such notice—
    (i) in the case of a company incorporated before 1st April 1990, 31st March, and
    (ii) in the case of a company incorporated on or after 1st April 1990, the last day of the month in which the anniversary of its incorporation falls.

(3) The accounting reference date of a company incorporated in Northern Ireland before 22nd August 1997 is—
  (a) the date specified by notice to the registrar in accordance with article 232(2) of the Companies (Northern Ireland) Order 1986 (S.I. 1986/1032(N.I. 6)) (notice specifying accounting reference date given within nine months of incorporation), or
  (b) failing such notice—
    (i) in the case of a company incorporated before the coming into operation of Article 5 of the Companies (Northern Ireland) Order 1990 (S.I. 1990/593 (N.I. 5)), 31st March, and
    (ii) in the case of a company incorporated after the coming into operation of that Article, the last day of the month in which the anniversary of its incorporation falls.

(4) The accounting reference date of a company incorporated—
  (a) in Great Britain on or after 1st April 1996 and before the commencement of this Act,
  (b) in Northern Ireland on or after 22nd August 1997 and before the commencement of this Act, or
  (c) after the commencement of this Act,
  is the last day of the month in which the anniversary of its incorporation falls.

(5) A company's first accounting reference period is the period of more than six months, but not more than 18 months, beginning with the date of its incorporation and ending with its accounting reference date.

(6) Its subsequent accounting reference periods are successive periods of twelve months beginning immediately after the end of the previous accounting reference period and ending with its accounting reference date.

(7) This section has effect subject to the provisions of section 392 (alteration of accounting reference date).

AMENDMENTS AND NOTES

[a] This section applies with modifications to overseas companies by reg 37 of the Overseas Companies Regulations 2009, 2009/1801.

COMMENCEMENT DATE 6 April 2008[120]

**15.391.02** This section determines a company's accounting reference date (ARD) and thus its accounting reference period (ARP) which, in turn, forms the basis of the financial year under the provisions of section 390. Put simply, subsections (1) and (6) have the effect that the ARD is an anniversary date in each calendar year at which each ARP ends; a new ARP begins on the next day.

---

[117] See s 1162.

[118] Even where the financial years of undertakings included in the consolidation differ, accounting standards—both UK standards applicable to Companies Act group accounts and EU-adopted IFRS applicable to IAS group accounts, for which see ss 404 and 403(1), (2)(b) respectively—require adjustments to make the consolidated information coterminous.

[119] Of course, the parent could change all the other group companies' financial years but this is a rather extreme solution and not usually thought necessary owing to the 'good reasons' dispensation.

[120] Companies Act 2006 (Commencement No 5, Transitional Provisions and Savings) Order 2007, SI 2007/3495, art 3(1).

The ARD is nowadays automatically assigned on incorporation,[121] but may be subsequently changed   **15.391.03**
by the company under section 392. Subsections (2) and (3) are complicated requirements that preserve
the rules for determining, by reference to incorporation dates and procedures, the ARDs of companies
incorporated in Great Britain before 1 April 1996 or in Northern Ireland before 22 August 1997.
Subsection (4) sets out the requirement applicable to companies incorporated after those dates and to
companies incorporated under this Act, that the ARD will be the last day of the month in which the
anniversary of its incorporation falls. In both cases—companies incorporated under previous Acts and
under this Act—the company may change the ARD in accordance with section 392. Where a company
has previously changed its ARD under the predecessor to section 392,[122] the effect of such changes
appears to be preserved (notwithstanding that subsections (2) and (3) might otherwise appear to reset
the ARD to an incorporation basis) by virtue of section 1297(3).

The requirement of subsection (5) that a company's first ARP is a period of more than six months is   **15.391.04**
often misunderstood. It is not a prohibition on a company's having a first ARP of less than six months
on the occasion of a change in the ARD; section 392, which qualifies this section,[123] permits any ARP
(including the first) to be of any length of less than 12 months. Rather, subsection (5)'s effect is to ensure
that a company does not automatically have a very short first ARP. For example, if a company were
incorporated on 9 August 2009, its ARD would be 31 August and, absent subsection (5), its first ARP
might be the 23-day period to 31 August 2009; it would be onerous for the legislation to force a
company into that position, and so subsection (5)'s minimum and maximum lengths of the first ARP
instead have the result that its first ARP is the 12 months and 23 days to 31 August 2010. The subsection
(5) minimum period is, however, as noted earlier, subject to the provisions of section 392. Thus there
is nothing to prevent this company from immediately availing itself of the facility in section 392 to
change its ARD to, say, 31 December and to choose that its first ARP to be the four months and 23 days
to 31 December 2009.[124]

## 392   Alteration of accounting reference date[a]

    (1)  A company may by notice given to the registrar specify a new accounting reference date having   **15.392.01**
        effect in relation to—
        (a)  the company's current accounting reference period and subsequent periods, or
        (b)  the company's previous accounting reference period and subsequent periods. A company's
               'previous accounting reference period' means the one immediately preceding its current
               accounting reference period.
    (2)  The notice must state whether the current or previous accounting reference period—
        (a)  is to be shortened, so as to come to an end on the first occasion on which the new accounting
               reference date falls or fell after the beginning of the period, or
        (b)  is to be extended, so as to come to an end on the second occasion on which that date falls
               or fell after the beginning of the period.
    (3)  A notice extending a company's current or previous accounting reference period is not effective
        if given less than five years after the end of an earlier accounting reference period of the company
        that was extended under this section.
        This does not apply—
        (a)  to a notice given by a company that is a subsidiary undertaking or parent undertaking of
               another EEA undertaking if the new accounting reference date coincides with that of the
               other EEA undertaking or, where that undertaking is not a company, with the last day of its
               financial year, or
        (b)  where the company is in administration under Part 2 of the Insolvency Act 1986 (c. 45) or Part
               3 of the Insolvency (Northern Ireland) Order 1989 (S.I. 1989/2405 (N.I. 19)), or
        (c)  where the Secretary of State directs that it should not apply, which he may do with respect to
               a notice that has been given or that may be given.
    (4)  A notice under this section may not be given in respect of a previous accounting reference period
        if the period for filing accounts and reports for the financial year determined by reference to that
        accounting reference period has already expired.
    (5)  An accounting reference period may not be extended so as to exceed 18 months and a notice
        under this section is ineffective if the current or previous accounting reference period as extended
        in accordance with the notice would exceed that limit.
        This does not apply where the company is in administration under Part 2 of the Insolvency Act
        1986 (c.45) or Part 3 of the Insolvency (Northern Ireland) Order 1989 (S.I.1989/2405 (N.I. 19)).

---

[121]  Subsection (4).
[122]  CA 1985, s 225.
[123]  Subsection (7).
[124]  See s 392(2)(a).

(6)  In this section 'EEA undertaking' means an undertaking established under the law of any part of the United Kingdom or the law of any other EEA State.

AMENDMENTS AND NOTES

a  This section applies with modifications to overseas companies by reg 37 of the Overseas Companies Regulations 2009, 2009/1801.

COMMENCEMENT DATE  6 April 2008[125]

**15.392.02**  This section permits a company to change its accounting reference date (ARD) and so change its accounting reference periods (ARPs) and its financial year under sections 391 and 390 respectively.

**15.392.03**  Subsections (1) and (2) set out the main provision that a company may, by notifying the registrar, change its ARD.[126] The change is effected by the act of giving valid notice. That is to say, it is not a mere request to the registrar.

**15.392.04**  The change in ARD does not in general change historical ARPs. Instead the change takes effect going forward with either the current ARP, or (subject to time limits) the one immediately preceding it, being shortened or lengthened (subject to limits) as the company may choose, in order to effect the change.

**15.392.05**  The current ARP means that prevailing at the time notification is made but before taking account of the notice itself. For example, for a company with an ARD of 31 December and giving notice on 11 May 2009, the current ARP is the year ending 31 December 2009; the previous ARP is the year ended 31 December 2008. However, the ability to change the previous ARP is restricted as discussed below.

**15.392.06**  There are no restrictions as to the occasion on which the ARD may be changed so as to lengthen or shorten the current ARP. However, the *previous* ARP may be changed only during the period for filing the annual accounts and reports for that period.[127] Those filing periods, as given by section 442, are nine months for a private company and six months for a public company from the end of the ARP in question. This restriction operates by reference to the ARP before the change intended by the notice. The effect of this restriction is to prevent the company and its directors from lengthening the previous ARP to obtain more time, based on the new ARP, to file accounts and reports and thus to avoid the respective civil penalties and fines for late filing.[128]

**15.392.07**  In terms of the length of the ARP chosen to effect the change, there is no prohibition as to how short it may be, nor as respects the number of times ARPs are shortened. Indeed, daily ARPs are feasible under this chapter. However, subsection (5) limits a lengthened period to no more than 18 months[129] and subsection (3) restricts the number of times a company may extend its ARP to once in every five years subject to three exceptions. The restriction of the period by which, and the number of times that, the ARP may be lengthened is presumably to give effect to a policy that a company should routinely prepare and publish its accounts and reports at least annually. Of the three exceptions, the most important is that of subsection (3)(a) which covers the case where the company aligns its ARD with that of an EEA undertaking[130] that is its subsidiary undertaking or its parent undertaking.[131] This exception does not, however, make any stipulation as to whether the other undertaking needs to be active. It would thus appear that the existence of a dormant parent or subsidiary undertaking, perhaps newly acquired from a company formation agent, would suffice to qualify for this exception.

CHAPTER 4
ANNUAL ACCOUNTS
*General*

### 393  Accounts to give true and fair view

**15.393.01**  (1)  The directors of a company must not approve accounts for the purposes of this Chapter unless they are satisfied that they give a true and fair view of the assets, liabilities, financial position and profit or loss—

---

125  Companies Act 2006 (Commencement No 5, Transitional Provisions and Savings) Order 2007, SI 2007/3495, art 3(1).
126  See s 1060 for the registrar. The registrar has under the power granted to it at s 1068, specified Form AA01 for notices on or after 1 October 2009. For notices before 1 October 2009, a savings provision (Sch 4, para 8 of SI 2007/3495, as referred to at n 1 to para 15.392.01 above) requires the old 1985 Act form (Form 225) to continue to be used.
127  Subsection (4).
128  See ss 451 and 453.
129  Unless the company is in administration—see subs (5).
130  See s 1170.
131  See s 1162.

      (a)  in the case of the company's individual accounts, of the company;

      (b)  in the case of the company's group accounts, of the undertakings included in the consolida-
          tion as a whole, so far as concerns members of the company.

   (2)  The auditor of a company in carrying out his functions under this Act in relation to the company's
      annual accounts must have regard to the directors' duty under subsection (1). Commencement
      Date 6 April 2008[132]

This section was introduced in this Act in response to concerns about the state of the previous **15.393.02**
legislation[133] after the introduction of accounting under EU-adopted IFRS[134] as now embodied in
sections 395(1)(b) and 403(1) and (2)(b) of this Act.

The concept of a true and fair view has long been a key part of accounting in the UK and has been the **15.393.03**
standard to which accounts are required to be prepared since the 1948 Act.[135] As more fully explained
in the context of Companies Act individual accounts at section 396, whilst the true and fair standard in
effect brings with it the need to comply with accounting standards—in that case UK accounting
standards—such compliance is necessary but may not be sufficient; this is because the true and fair
view is not qualified in any way, and since no set of accounting standards can cater for the kaleidoscope
of commercial transactions that exist in practice, professional judgment is required to identify
additional disclosures or accounting. The requirement thus encompasses more than bare compliance
with accounting standards.

In the 1985 Act after amendment to introduce accounting under EU-adopted IFRS,[136] the legislation **15.393.04**
contained no true and fair requirement in respect of IAS individual accounts or of IAS group accounts;
the only requirements under that legislation were that such accounts be in accordance with EU-
adopted IFRS.[137] Although EU-adopted IFRS contains a requirement which accountants in the UK,
and more recently a legal opinion obtained and published by the Financial Reporting Council (the
Moore opinion),[138] accept as equivalent to the true-and-fair requirement,[139] concern has been expressed, for example by institutional investors, first that the continuation of the true and fair standard
was not enshrined in law for IAS individual or group accounts. Second, a concern was expressed that
there may have been some uncertainty in relation to auditors' reports because the 1985 Act (in a
provision in similar terms to section 495 of this Act)[140] specifically required auditors to report by
reference to the true and fair standard, whereas the requirement placed upon the directors in relation
to the preparation of the accounts was not in the same terms.

In response to these concerns this section of the 2006 Act was introduced. It applies to all **15.393.05**
accounts—that is, Companies Act individual accounts, Companies Act group accounts, IAS individual
accounts, and IAS group accounts—and it requires that they give a true and fair view in respect of the
company or the undertakings included in the consolidation as the case may be.[141] Thus bare compliance with the standards, whether those are UK accounting standards or EU-adopted IFRS, continues
not necessarily to be sufficient. This matter was also addressed by Martin Moore in his Opinion, in
which he concludes that this new section is a clarification of the primary of the true and fair concept,

---

[132] Companies Act 2006 (Commencement No 5, Transitional Provisions and Savings) Order 2007, SI
2007/3495, art 3(1) for financial years beginning on or after 6 April 2008.

[133] CA 1985, ss 226(2)(b), 227(2), (3)(b).

[134] This is the term used by the accountancy profession for the international accounting standards defined in
s 474(1) and with which IAS individual accounts and IAS group accounts must comply.

[135] CA 1948, ss 149 and 150.

[136] The amendments under the Companies Act 1985 (International Accounting Standards and Other Accounting Amendments) Regulations 2004, SI 2004/2947 had effect for financial years commencing on or after 1
Jan 2005.

[137] See para 15.393.02 above, n 129.

[138] Martin Moore QC, 'The true and fair requirement revisited' (FRC, 2008), para 4C. The opinion is available
at <www.frc.org.uk>.

[139] For accounting periods beginning before 1 January 2009, see *IAS 1 Presentation of financial statements*
(International Accounting Standards Board, 2003, as amended; see Commission Regulation (EC) No 1126/2008
at [2008] OJ/L320/1), as amended, requires a fair presentation (para 13). For accounting periods beginning on or
after 1 January 2009, a revised version of IAS 1 applies although the requirement (para 15) is the same, see
Commission Regulation 2009 (EC) No 1274/2008 at [2008] OJ/L339/3 as amended.

[140] CA 1985, s 235.

[141] The section uses the term 'undertakings included in the consolidation' rather than 'group' as the latter is
defined in s 474(1) as the company and its subsidiary undertakings (see s 1162), whereas if the accounts are IAS
group accounts the population of consolidated undertakings may very occasionally be slightly different. The
more general terminology used here thus accommodates both Companies Act group accounts and IAS group
accounts.

rather than a substantive change in the requirements of law in this area;[142] and that the provisions of the 2006 Act 'underline and reinforce the centrality of the true and fair requirement to the preparation of financial statements'.[143]

**15.393.06**   It should be added, however, that the true and fair requirement of this section is not overriding. That is to say, there is no requirement *within the Act* to depart from (override) a provision of EU-adopted IFRS in IAS individual or IAS group accounts even when compliance with that provision would not result in a true and fair view in the particular circumstances; in such a case the override in EU-adopted IFRS must instead be looked to.[144] The case is different for Companies Act individual accounts and Companies Act group accounts as sections 396 and 404 contain an override provision.

## *Individual accounts*

### 394   Duty to prepare individual accounts[a]

**15.394.01**   The directors of every company must prepare accounts for the company for each of its financial years unless the company is exempt from that requirement under section 394A [b].

Those accounts are referred to as the company's 'individual accounts'. AMENDMENTS AND NOTES

[a]  This section applies with modifications to overseas companies by reg 38 of the Overseas Companies Regulations 2009, 2009/1801.

[b]  Inserted by the Companies and Limited Liability Partnerships (Accounts and Audit Exemptions and Change in Accounting Framework) Regulations 2012, SI 2012/2301

COMMENCEMENT DATE in relation to the exemption referred to in section 394A, from 1 October 2012[145]; otherwise, 6 April 2008[146]

**15.394.02**   This section requires all companies – save for certain dormant companies guaranteed by a parent undertaking as set out in section 394A – to prepare 'accounts for the company', called 'individual accounts'; the form and content of those accounts, which may be prepared as Companies Act individual accounts or IAS individual accounts, is determined by later sections.[147] The responsibility for preparing the accounts falls upon the directors.

**15.394.03**   In the context of Companies Act individual accounts,[148] 'accounts for the company' is well understood to mean accounts that deal with only the company's income, expenses, assets, and liabilities, in particular dealing with the company's interest in other entities as investments. This stands in contrast with consolidated (group) accounts for which separate provision is made under sections 398 and 399.

**15.394.04**   The commentary at section 395 addresses the meaning of 'accounts for the company' in the context of IAS individual accounts.

### 394A   Individual accounts: exemption for dormant subsidiaries

**15.394A.01**
(1)  A company is exempt from the requirement to prepare individual accounts for a financial year if—
  (a)  it is itself a subsidiary undertaking,
  (b)  it has been dormant throughout the whole of that year, and
  (c)  its parent undertaking is established under the law of an EEA State.
(2)  Exemption is conditional upon compliance with all of the following conditions—
  (a)  all members of the company must agree to the exemption in respect of the financial year in question,
  (b)  the parent undertaking must give a guarantee under section 394C in respect of that year,
  (c)  the company must be included in the consolidated accounts drawn up for that year or to an earlier date in that year by the parent undertaking in accordance with—
    (i)  the provisions of the Seventh Directive (83/349/EEC), or
    (ii)  international accounting standards,

---

[142]  'The true and fair requirement revisited' (FRC, 2008), para 56.

[143]  Ibid, para 4K.

[144]  *IAS 1*; see para 15.393.04 above, n 133, para 17 for financial years beginning before 1 January 2009; para 19 for financial years beginning on or after 1 January 2009.

[145]  Companies and Limited Liability Partnerships (Accounts and Audit Exemptions and Change of Accounting Framework) Regulations 2012, SI 2012/2301 for financial years ending on or after 1 October 2012.

[146]  Companies Act 2006 (Commencement No 5, Transitional Provisions and Savings) Order 2007, SI 2007/3495, art 3(1) for financial years beginning on or after 6 April 2008.

[147]  See ss 395–397.

[148]  See s 396.

(d) the parent undertaking must disclose in the notes to the consolidated accounts that the company is exempt from the requirement to prepare individual accounts by virtue of this section, and

(e) the directors of the company must deliver to the registrar within the period for filing the company's accounts and reports for that year—
  (i) a written notice of the agreement referred to in subsection (2)(a),
  (ii) the statement referred to in section 394C(1),
  (iii) a copy of the consolidated accounts referred to in subsection (2)(c),
  (iv) a copy of the auditor's report on those accounts, and
  (v) a copy of the consolidated annual report drawn up by the parent undertaking.

COMMENCEMENT DATE  1 October 2012[149]

This exemption, which was introduced in 2012, may be summarized as being conditional upon three   **15.394A.02**
principal matters: that the company is dormant throughout the entire financial year that it is a subsidiary undertaking; that it is guaranteed by an EEA parent undertaking; and that it is not one of certain categories of company set out in section 394B. As to the first condition, the definition of a dormant company is dealt with in section 1169. As to the latter two conditions, these are in the same terms as the sections 448A-448C dormant, guaranteed subsidiaries' filing exemption and the sections 479A-479C guaranteed subsidiaries' audit exemption. These exemption conditions are dealt with in the commentary at sections 479A-479C.

The combined effect of sections 394A-394C, 448A-448C and 479A-479C is that a dormant, guaranteed   **15.394A.03**
subsidiary undertaking may, at one extreme, choose to prepare no annual accounts at all, or, at the other, to prepare, have audited and deliver annual accounts to the registrar; or various combinations in between. Note, however, that there is no equivalent exemption in relation to the preparation of a directors' report under section 415. Nor is there any exception in relation to delivering the directors' report under section 441 (unless the company *also* falls within one of the other exemptions following that section, i.e. sections 444 and 444A in relation to the small companies regime/small companies).

Whether or not this exemption will be widely taken up may be doubtful. Companies might weigh up   **15.394A.04**
the time and effort required to fulfill all the requirements of sections 394A to 394C against the time needed to prepare and file accounts (which will almost by definition, be virtually identical to the accounts for the previous financial year) and decide that continue to prepare them requires less effort. This may be so especially when it is considered that this new exemption does not give any exemption in relation to the directors' report.

## 394B   Companies excluded from the dormant subsidiaries exemption

A company is not entitled to the exemption conferred by section 394A (dormant subsidiaries) if it was   **15.394B.01**
at any time within the financial year in question—

(a) a quoted company as defined in section 385(2) of this Act,
(b) a company that—
  (i) is an authorised insurance company, a banking company, an e-money issuer, a MiFID investment firm or a UCITS management company, or
  (ii) carries on insurance market activity, or
(c) a special register body as defined in section 117(1) of the Trade Union and Labour Relations (Consolidation) Act 1992 (c 52) or an employers' association as defined in section 122 of that Act or Article 4 of the Industrial Relations (Northern Ireland) Order 1992 (S.I. 1992/807) (NI 5).

COMMENCEMENT DATE  1 October 2012[150]

This section excludes certain categories of companies for the section 394A exemption, in identical   **15.394B.02**
terms to sections 448B and 479B.

## 394C   Dormant subsidiaries exemption: parent undertaking declaration of guarantee

(1) A guarantee is given by a parent undertaking under this section when the directors of the   **15.394C.01**
subsidiary company deliver to the registrar a statement by the parent undertaking that it guarantees the subsidiary company under this section.
(2) The statement under subsection (1) must be authenticated by the parent undertaking and must specify—
  (a) the name of the parent undertaking,

---

[149] Companies and Limited Liability Partnerships (Accounts and Audit Exemptions and Change of Accounting Framework) Regulations 2012, SI 2012/2301, for financial years ending on or after 1 October 2012.
[150] Companies and Limited Liability Partnerships (Accounts and Audit Exemptions and Change of Accounting Framework) Regulations 2012, SI 2012/2301, for financial years ending on or after 1 October 2012.

    (b) if the parent undertaking is incorporated in the United Kingdom, its registered number (if any),

    (c) if the parent undertaking is incorporated outside the United Kingdom and registered in the country in which it is incorporated, the identity of the register on which it is registered and the number with which it is so registered,

    (d) the name and registered number of the subsidiary company in respect of which the guarantee is being given,

    (e) the date of the statement, and

    (f) the financial year to which the guarantee relates.

(3) A guarantee given under this section has the effect that—

    (a) the parent undertaking guarantees all outstanding liabilities to which the subsidiary company is subject at the end of the financial year to which the guarantee relates, until they are satisfied in full, and

    (b) the guarantee is enforceable against the parent undertaking by any person to whom the subsidiary company is liable in respect of those liabilities.

COMMENCEMENT DATE 1 October 2012[151]

**15.394C.02**    The guarantee arrangements required by this section, as a condition for the section 394A exemption, is in identical terms to that of sections 448C and 479C. The commentary on the latter deals with the guarantee.

### 395  Individual accounts: applicable accounting framework[a]

**15.395.01**

(1) A company's individual accounts may be prepared—

    (a) in accordance with section 396 ('Companies Act individual accounts'), or

    (b) in accordance with international accounting standards ('IAS individual accounts'). This is subject to the following provisions of this section and to section 407 (consistency of financial reporting within group).

(2) The individual accounts of a company that is a charity must be Companies Act individual accounts.

(3) After the first financial year in which the directors of a company prepare IAS individual accounts ('the first IAS year'), all subsequent individual accounts of the company must be prepared in accordance with international accounting standards unless there is a relevant change of circumstance. [This is subject to subsection (4A)][c].

(4) There is a relevant change of circumstance if, at any time during or after the first IAS year—

    (a) the company becomes a subsidiary undertaking of another undertaking that does not prepare IAS individual accounts,

    [(aa) the company ceases to be a subsidiary undertaking,][b]

    (b) the company ceases to be a company with securities admitted to trading on a regulated market in an EEA State, or

    (c) a parent undertaking of the company ceases to be an undertaking with securities admitted to trading on a regulated market in an EEA State.

[(4A) After a financial year in which the directors of a company prepare IAS individual accounts for the company, the directors may change to preparing Companies Act individual accounts for a reason other than a relevant change of circumstance provided they have not changed to Companies Act individual accounts in the period of five years preceding the first day of that financial year].[c]

[(4B) In calculating the five year period for the purpose of subsection (4A), no account should be taken of a change due to a relevant change of circumstance][c].

(5) If, having changed to preparing Companies Act individual accounts [][c], the directors again prepare IAS individual accounts for the company, subsections (3) and (4) apply again as if the first financial year for which such accounts are again prepared were the first IAS year.

AMENDMENTS AND NOTES

  [a] This section applies with modifications to overseas companies by reg 37 of the Overseas Companies Regulations 2009, 2009/1801.

  [b] Inserted by the Companies Act 2006 (Amendment) (Accounts and Reports) Regulations 2008, SI 2008/393, reg 9.

  [c] Inserted or deleted by the Companies and Limited Liability Partnerships (Accounts and Audit Exemptions and Change in Accounting Framework) Regulations 2012, SI 2012/2301, for financial years ending on or after 1 October 2012.

---

[151] Companies and Limited Liability Partnerships (Accounts and Audit Exemptions and Change of Accounting Framework) Regulations 2012, SI 2012/2301, for financial years ending on or after 1 October 2012, as corrected.

COMMENCEMENT DATE in relation to subsections 4A and 4 B, from 1 October 2012[152]; otherwise, 6 April 2008[153]

Subsection (1) gives a company (other than a charity) the choice of preparing its individual accounts under either of two accounting frameworks: Companies Act individual accounts, or in accordance with international accounting standards[154] ('IAS individual accounts'). For reasons explained below these standards are known by the accountancy profession as 'EU-adopted IFRS'. The choice by the company's directors is, however, subject to section 407 that imposes upon the directors of certain parent companies a duty to secure a consistent choice among that parent company,[155] and its subsidiary undertakings.[156] In permitting this choice the section implements a Member State option in EC legislation.[157] A similar choice is granted by section 403 with respect to group accounts, but the two choices are independent of each other. **15.395.02**

Subsection (2) provides that a company that is a charity must prepare Companies Act individual accounts. **15.395.03**

Whichever choice is made, the accounts disclosure requirements of sections 409 to 413[158] apply; and the approval, and the signature requirements of section 414 apply. **15.395.04**

Section 396 makes provision for the main form and content of Companies Act individual accounts and the standard to which they must be prepared—true and fair. As discussed at that section this brings with it the need normally to comply with UK accounting standards,[159] and the true and fair requirement is an overriding one. In contrast, the main form and content of IAS individual accounts is driven by the direct requirement of subsection (1)(b) that such accounts be in accordance with EU-adopted IFRS, and by the true and fair requirement of section 393, which, as discussed there, is not an overriding one. Thus the choice offered by this section is largely characterized as one between UK accounting standards (sometimes known as 'UK GAAP')[160] and those of EU-adopted IFRS. **15.395.05**

As more fully explained under section 474, IFRS are accounting standards issued by the International Accounting Standards Board (IASB).[161] EU-adopted IFRS are those IFRS that have been adopted by the European Commission under what is known as the IAS Regulation.[162] IFRS and EU-adopted IFRS are not necessarily precisely the same, mainly because there will be a time lag (albeit a matter of months) between the IASB's issuing a standard and the European Commission's adopting it. However, there has also been an instance of the Commission's explicitly modifying a standard on adoption[163] and, as described below, it appears that IFRS requirements for the preparation of consolidated accounts are implicitly modified on adoption. The adoption process is described under section 474. **15.395.06**

Whilst the general application of EU-adopted IFRS is not the subject of this commentary, the interaction of those standards with this section can give rise, occasionally, to two questions as to the appropriate provisions of standards to be applied. The questions are more fully described below – Briefly put, however, they are this: is it possible that IAS individual accounts may, through the application of EU-adopted IFRS, have to be in consolidated form (or be accompanied by consolidated accounts); or in some cases be in unconsolidated form but nevertheless include (or be accompanied by accounts including) certain interests in other entities by equity accounting[164] or proportionate **15.395.07**

---

[152] Companies and Limited Liability Partnerships (Accounts and Audit Exemptions and Change of Accounting Framework) Regulations 2012, SI 2012/2301, for financial years ending on or after 1 October 2012.

[153] Companies Act 2006 (Commencement No 5, Transitional Provisions and Savings) Order 2007, SI 2007/3495, art 3(1) for financial years beginning on or after 6 April 2008.

[154] See s 474(1).

[155] See s 1173.

[156] See s 1162.

[157] Art 5 of Regulation (EC) No 1606/2002 at [2002] OJ/L243/1, as amended (called in this Act, 'the IAS Regulation').

[158] Related undertakings, off balance sheet arrangements, employee numbers and costs (but not applicable for the small companies regime), directors' benefits.

[159] Those issued by the Accounting Standards Board. See s 396.

[160] As in, generally accepted accounting practice.

[161] International Accounting Standards (IAS), International Financial Reporting Standards (IFRS), and related interpretations (SIC, IFRIC). The whole body of these is also known as 'IFRS'.

[162] Regulation (EC) No 1606/2002 at [2002] OJ/L243/1, as amended.

[163] *IAS 39 Financial instruments: recognition and measurement* (International Accounting Standards Board, 2005), adopted by the European Commission in 2005. See Commission Regulation (EC) No 1864/2005 at [2005] OJ/L299/45.

[164] Meaning reporting the investee entity's profits and net assets as single lines in the profit and loss account and balance sheet respectively.

consolidation,[165] which are forms of accounting hitherto employed under UK companies legislation only in group (consolidated) accounts? The European Commission's Accounting Regulatory Committee (ARC)[166] has considered these two questions. On the first, its view is that it does not require or permit consolidation in relation to individual accounts, but it has yet to form a view on the second.[167]

**15.395.08**   The questions arise because IFRS (ie, as issued by the IASB) do not always require accounts that deal with interests in other entities as investments, which is otherwise the familiar basis of individual accounts. In particular, first of all, IFRS require that the accounts of a company with a subsidiary must, subject to exceptions, be consolidated accounts; such a company *may* also prepare 'separate financial statements' that deal with subsidiaries as simple investments, but it is not required by IFRS to do so; and IFRS prohibit preparation by such a company only of 'separate financial statements'.[168]

**15.395.09**   The question arises then as to whether a such a company, if it is exempt under this Act from preparing group (consolidated) accounts,[169] must nevertheless prepare its IAS individual accounts as consolidated accounts (or additionally prepare consolidated accounts) in order for those IAS individual accounts to comply with standards. The summary record of the ARC meeting records the Commission's view as follows: 'where, under the 7th Company Law Directive [ie, national law implementing the same, in this case sections 398 to 402] a parent company is exempted from preparing consolidated accounts, but chooses to prepare its annual accounts [being the directive's terminology for individual accounts] in accordance with IFRS as adopted by the EU, those provisions of IAS 27 setting out the requirement to prepare consolidated accounts do not apply. Such annual accounts [individual accounts] are described as having been prepared in accordance with 'IFRS as adopted by the EU'. In other words, in EU-adopted IAS 27, the consolidation requirement of that standard is implicitly struck out; accordingly IAS individual accounts, prepared on the familiar basis of dealing with a subsidiary as an investment (under the 'separate financial statements' provisions of EU-adopted IFRS), comply with EU-adopted IFRS.

**15.395.10**   The summary record of the ARC meeting also records that a further issue was put to the Commission in relation to the appropriate provisions of EU-adopted IFRS to be applied in individual accounts. It is inferred that the question relates to the rare instance of a company with certain investee interests, other than in subsidiaries (as defined in IAS 27), and whether the relevant IFRS, when adopted for use in the EU, have the effect of requiring the transactions, assets, and liabilities of those investee entities to be reflected, to some extent, directly in IAS individual accounts.[170] The summary record does not set out a view on the matter.

**15.395.11**   Returning more directly to this section, once a company has prepared IAS individual accounts for a financial year, subsection (3) requires that IAS individual accounts in all subsequent financial years[171]

---

[165]   Meaning reporting the company's share of the investee entity's transactions, assets, and liabilities as if they were transactions, assets, and liabilities of the company. The IASB has recently issued a new standard IFRS 11, *Joint arrangements*, which will remove the option in IFRS for proportionate consolidation. At the time of writing, this standard had not been endorsed by the EU; see the commentary at s 474 for a discussion of the endorsement process. If endorsed, the new standard would be expected to apply for financial years beginning on or after 1 January 2014.

[166]   This committee is responsible for adoption of IFRS, as more fully described in the commentary at s 474. Its members also carry out the functions of the Contact Committee established under the EC Fourth and Seventh Company Law Directives to facilitate harmonized application of those directives (see art 52 of EC Fourth Company Law Directive 78/660/EEC at [1978] OJ/L222/11, as amended and art 47 of EC Seventh Company Law Directive 83/349/EEC at [1983] OJ/L193/1, as amended).

[167]   See Agenda Paper (Document ARC/19/2006) and the Summary Record of the Meetings of the Accounting Regulatory Committee and Contact Committee of 24 November 2006, 2 February 2007 and 6 June 2007, available from <http://ec.europa.eu/internal_market/accounting/committees_En. htm>.

[168]   IAS 27 *Consolidated and separate financial statements* (International Accounting Standards Board, 2004, revised 2008), see Commission Regulation (EC) No 1126/2008 at [2008] OJ/L320/1, as amended, defines 'subsidiary' for this purpose. The relevant accounting requirements are set out at paras 5–11. If endorsed by the EU IFRS 10 *Consolidated Financial Statements* makes similar provisions.

[169]   See ss 398–402.

[170]   The investee entities in question are termed by IAS 28 (IASB, 2004) and IAS 31 (IASB, 2004) as 'associates' and 'jointly-controlled entities' and the case occurs where the company has such an investee but does not have what IAS 27 (see para 15.395.08 above, n 158) terms a 'subsidiary' and fails certain conditions. In a similar manner to the IAS 27 requirement for consolidated accounts, those standards, as issued by the IASB, would require what they term 'equity accounting' or (jointly-controlled entities) proportionate consolidation, whereas 'separate financial statements' that adopt simpler investment accounting would be optional. The issue is whether those requirements are to be read as effective in EU-adopted IAS 28 and EU-adopted IAS 31 (adopted by Commission Regulation (EC) No 1126/2008 at [2008] OJ/L320/1, as amended).

[171]   See s 390.

unless one of the exceptions in subsection (4) applies or, for financial years ending on or after 1 October 2012, subsection (5) applies. This promotes consistency over time in the basis of financial information presented, which is generally held to be an important concept in financial reporting.

Subsection (4) provides four exceptions. The first applies where the company becomes a subsidiary undertaking[172] of another undertaking that does not prepare IAS individual accounts. This provision removes an administrative burden on the acquiring group by enabling it to avoid having some companies using EU-adopted IFRS whilst the rest do not. The second exception applies where the company ceases to be a subsidiary undertaking. As the choice of EU-adopted IFRS would have been determined previously on a group-wide basis,[173] it is reasonable to offer the directors of the former subsidiary undertaking the choice of reverting to Companies Act individual accounts when it is no longer a subsidiary undertaking. If the company that ceases to be a subsidiary undertaking is itself a parent company, its subsidiary undertakings would be permitted to revert to Companies Act individual accounts by virtue of subsection (4)(a).   **15.395.12**

The third and fourth exceptions are related: they apply where either the company or its parent undertaking ceases to have securities admitted to trading on a regulated market in an EEA state.[174] This recognizes that an undertaking that is required by the IAS Regulation to prepare IAS group accounts,[175] owing to having securities so traded, may also have chosen EU-adopted IFRS for its own individual accounts and for those of all other of its subsidiary undertakings to avoid the preparation of financial information under two different accounting frameworks. When the requirement to prepare IAS group accounts ceases to apply to such a parent undertaking, it is reasonable to permit a revisiting of the choice of IAS individual accounts or Companies Act individual accounts by that company for its own individual accounts and its subsidiary undertaking in relation to its individual accounts.[176]   **15.395.13**

For financial years ending on or after 1 October 2012, subsection (5) introduces an additional facility to switch back to Companies Act individual accounts, (ie. accounts under 'UK GAAP'). This new facility allows a company's individual accounts prepared in accordance with EU-adopted IFRS to switch back to 'UK GAAP' provided that the company had 'not changed' to UK GAAP accounts in the period of five years preceding the first day of the financial year in which it is now intended to switch to 'UK GAAP'. In the calculation of whether a previous change to 'UK GAAP' has occurred in the previous five years, any change due to a 'relevant change in circumstances' under section 395(4) is ignored. In other words, there is now a free choice for an entity to revert to 'UK GAAP' from EU-adopted IFRS as long as the company had not in the last five years made such a free choice to revert to UK GAAP.   **15.395.14**

The new switching facility was introduced for two reasons. First, the Financial Reporting Council has proposed an overhaul of UK GAAP. To permit those companies that already use EU-adopted IFRS to prepare their accounts to have the ability to use the revised 'UK GAAP', this change in the law was needed. In addition there is a current anomaly in that if a company withdraws from AIM, then, under the current law, it would not be able to revert to UK GAAP, since AIM is not a regulated market in an EEA state. The new 'five year' rule should allow former AIM companies to revert to 'UK GAAP' (ie. it is not a relevant change in circumstances under subsection (4)).   **15.395.15**

## 396   Companies Act individual accounts[a]

(1) Companies Act individual accounts must comprise—   **15.396.01**
    (a) a balance sheet as at the last day of the financial year, and
    (b) a profit and loss account.

(2) The accounts must—
    (a) in the case of the balance sheet, give a true and fair view of the state of affairs of the company as at the end of the financial year, and
    (b) in the case of the profit and loss account, give a true and fair view of the profit or loss of the company for the financial year.

(3) The accounts must comply with provision made by the Secretary of State by regulations as to—
    (a) the form and content of the balance sheet and profit and loss account, and
    (b) additional information to be provided by way of notes to the accounts.

(4) If compliance with the regulations, and any other provision made by or under this Act as to the matters to be included in a company's individual accounts or in notes to those accounts, would

---

[172] See s 1162.
[173] See s 407, which requires consistency of financial reporting within a group.
[174] See s 1173 (regulated market) and s 1170 (EEA State).
[175] See s 403(1).
[176] Subs (4)(b); subs (4)(c).

not be sufficient to give a true and fair view, the necessary additional information must be given in the accounts or in a note to them.

(5)  If in special circumstances compliance with any of those provisions is inconsistent with the requirement to give a true and fair view, the directors must depart from that provision to the extent necessary to give a true and fair view.

Particulars of any such departure, the reasons for it, and its effect must be given in a note to the accounts.

AMENDMENTS AND NOTES

ᵃ  This section applies with modifications to overseas companies by reg 38 of the Overseas Companies Regulations 2009, 2009/1801.

COMMENCEMENT DATE  subsection (3) in relation to the regulation-making power, from 20 January 2007;[177] otherwise, 6 April 2008[178]

**15.396.02**   This important section, which is derived from the 1985 Act and its predecessors,[179] governs the form and content of Companies Act individual accounts and sets out the standard to which they are to be prepared, namely that they must give a true and fair view of the state of affairs at the end of the financial year and of the profit or loss for that year.

**15.396.03**   The basic form and content is for a balance sheet, profit or loss account, and notes, with the format and some accounting rules and disclosures prescribed by regulations under subsection (3). These regulations deal separately with the requirements for companies subject to the small companies regime[180] and for other companies,[181] and are in substantially the same form as the requirements of 1985 Act.[182] All companies must still meet the true and fair requirement discussed below.

**15.396.04**   The most important aspect of this section, not least in that it effectively provides considerably more by way of requirements as to form and content, is the true and fair requirement of subsections (2), (4), and (5). This requirement has three different elements: in the context of Companies Act individual accounts, in effect it requires compliance with accounting standards issued by the Financial Reporting Council;[183] but that whilst that is normally necessary, it may not be sufficient; and the requirement is overriding. Each of these elements is described in more detail in the following paragraphs.

**15.396.05**   In 1993 the ASB[184] obtained and published a legal opinion from Mary Arden QC[185] on the relationship between accounting standards and the true and fair requirement[186] following on from the earlier joint opinions she had written with Leonard Hoffmann QC.[187] In 2008, the Financial Reporting Council (FRC) obtained and published an opinion from Martin Moore QC addressing the question of whether this Act (and other developments in EC law) requires any revision in the approach set out in the Arden opinion.[188] The commentary below sets out the key features of the Arden opinion, supplemented where necessary by reference to the Moore opinion.

**15.396.06**   The Arden opinion explains that the question of whether accounts satisfy the true and fair requirement is of course a question of law for the courts and that, without qualifying that requirement in any way, the courts will look to the practices and views of accountants to interpret that requirement, and the more authoritative those views and practices then the more ready the court will be to follow them; in the case of *Lloyd Cheyham v Littlejohn*[189] it was held that standards, at that time those of the ASB's predecessor, were very strong evidence as to what is the proper standard that should be adopted. It

---

[177]  Companies Act 2006 (Commencement Order No 1, etc) Order 2006, SI 2006/3428, art 3(3).

[178]  Companies Act 2006 (Commencement No 5,Transitional Provisions and Savings) Order 2007, SI 2007/3495, art 3(1) for financial years beginning on or after 6 April 2008.

[179]  Ultimately from the CA 1948, s 149.

[180]  Small Companies and Groups (Accounts and Directors' Report) Regulations 2008, SI 2008/409.

[181]  Large and Medium-sized Companies and Groups (Accounts and Reports) Regulations 2008, SI 2008/410.

[182]  CA 1985, schs 4, 8, 9 and 9A.

[183]  See the commentary at section 464 for the authority of the FRC to issue such standards. The standards issued by the FRC and its predecessors are Statement of Standard Accounting Practice (SSAPs), Financial Reporting Standards (FRSs), Abstracts of the Urgent Issues Task Force (UITFs) and, for companies subject to the small companies regime, the Financial Reporting Standard for Smaller Entities (FRSSE).

[184]  Accounting Standards Board – the body prescribed under section 464 for setting accounting standards until July 2012, from when the Financial Reporting Council was prescribed in its place.

[185]  Now the Rt Hon Dame Mary Arden DBE, LJ.

[186]  Mary Arden QC, 'Accounting Standards Board—the true and fair requirement', 1993; as appended to the *Foreword to accounting standards* (ASB, 1993).

[187]  Now Lord Hoffmann.

[188]  Martin Moore QC, 'The true and fair requirement revisited', (FRC, 2008). The opinion is available at www.frc.org.uk.

[189]  [1987] BCLC 303 at 313.

offers the opinion that changes brought about by the Companies Act 1989[190] and in the arrangements for setting accounting standards—which continue to this day—have increased the likelihood that the courts will hold that, in general, compliance with accounting standards is necessary to meet the true and fair requirement; and it observed that it is the norm for accounts to comply. The Moore opinion finds no change to this, noting that 'the approach to the true and fair requirement in the Opinions [the Arden opinion and earlier Hoffmann and Arden joint opinions] … has been affirmed by the English courts.'[191]

The Arden opinion was written at a time when there was only one system of accounting standards in use in the UK, namely those of the ASB (which at the time was the body setting accounting standards[192]). There are now EU-adopted IFRS also.[193] The question arises as to whether those alternative standards might have any authority in relation to Companies Act individual accounts under the true and fair requirement. It seems rather unlikely to be so: the Financial Reporting Council (FRC) – the successor to the ASB and its standards have statutory recognition for Companies Act individual accounts; and the Act provides an alternative facility (IAS individual accounts) specifically to enable the use of EU-adopted IFRS and explicitly requires compliance therewith.   **15.396.07**

The second element of the true and fair requirement is that whilst, in effect, it is necessary for Companies Act individual accounts to comply with (FRC) standards, the true and fair requirement is not limited or qualified in any respect by this. That is to say, compliance with standards is necessary but not necessarily sufficient. Accounting standards cannot be expected to cater for all eventualities in the kaleidoscope of commercial transactions that exist in practice, and professional judgment must be applied where they do not provide a complete answer. This is partly codified by subsection (4)'s provision that where the information given in accounts would not be sufficient to give a true and fair view, then such additional information as would give a true and fair view must be given in the accounts.   **15.396.08**

The final element of the true and fair requirement of this section is that it is overriding. That is to say, if in special circumstances compliance with some aspect of the regulations under subsection (3) or other requirements of this Act, supplemented by additional disclosure, is not consistent with giving a true and fair view, then that aspect must be departed from in order to adopt an alternative course of action that does give a true and fair view. It should be emphasized that there is no choice in subsection (5). Rather departure in such circumstances is mandatory. Moreover, this mandatory requirement to depart from the requirements of regulations or other requirements of this Act applies only when compliance therewith would positively fail to give a true and fair view. Accordingly subsection (5) does not permit departure to adopt an alternative course of action on the grounds that it gives a truer and fairer view. Accounting standards themselves include an equivalent override provision to cover cases where a requirement of standards would not in exceptional circumstances give a true and fair view.[194]   **15.396.09**

### 397   IAS individual accounts[a]

Where the directors of a company prepare IAS individual accounts, they must state in the notes to the accounts that the accounts have been prepared in accordance with international accounting standards.   **15.397.01**

AMENDMENTS AND NOTES

[a]   This section applies with modifications to overseas companies by reg 38 of the Overseas Companies Regulations 2009, 2009/1801.

COMMENCEMENT DATE   6 April 2008[195]

This section requires that a company preparing IAS individual accounts[196] includes within them a statement that they are prepared in accordance with international accounting standards. This reference to international accounting standards is normally formulated as 'International Financial Reporting Standards (IFRSs) as adopted by the EU'[197] and thus the standards are also known by the abbreviated term 'EU-adopted IFRS'.   **15.397.02**

---

[190]   Eg, the introduction of CA 1985, Sch 4, para 36A, requiring disclosure of compliance with applicable accounting standards or an explanation of any departure, has been re-enacted at para 45 of the Large and Medium-sized Companies and Groups (Accounts and Reports) Regulations 2008, SI 2008/410; and the recognition of the ASB under CA 1985, s 256, re-enacted at s 464 of this Act.

[191]   *The true and fair requirement revisited*, para 17.

[192]   See commentary to s 464.

[193]   See s 395(1)(b).

[194]   *Foreword to accounting standards* (ASB, 1993), para 19.

[195]   Companies Act 2006 (Commencement No 5, Transitional Provisions and Savings) Order 2007, SI 2007/3495, art 3(1) for financial years beginning on or after 6 April 2008.

[196]   See s 395.

[197]   This is the phrase used in the Auditing Practices Board (APB) literature for use in audit reports—see *APB Bulletin 2009/02 Auditor's Reports on Financial Statements in the United Kingdom* (APB, 2009)—eg and so, for

**15.397.03**    As more fully explained under section 474, IFRS are accounting standards issued by the International Accounting Standards Board (IASB). EU-adopted IFRS are those IFRS that have been adopted by the European Commission. IFRS and EU-adopted IFRS are not necessarily precisely the same, mainly because there will be a time lag between the IASB's issuing a standard and the European Commission's adopting it but also because, less frequently, the Commission might adopt an IFRS in modified form (or fail to adopt it). Where a company's accounts comply with both EU-adopted IFRS and IFRS issued by the IASB the company may want to make clear that they comply with those IFRS issued by the IASB. In particular, for certain companies subject to the US Securities Exchange Commission's rules,[198] an exemption from providing a reconciliation of the company's IFRS annual accounts to US accounting rules (US GAAP) is available where, among other things, a statement is made as to compliance with IFRS issued by the IASB.[199] This is of course acceptable but such a statement must be in addition to the required statement of compliance with EU-adopted IFRS. When contemplating making such an additional compliance statement it should be borne in mind that it will not be automatically the case that such an additional statement can be made in every subsequent year; for example, the time lag for Commission adoption may prevent dual compliance on some occasions.

**15.397.04**    Where a company, having also prepared group accounts,[200] takes advantage of the facility in section 408 not to include within the annual accounts the profit and loss account of the IAS individual accounts, the framing of the disclosure under this section 397 will require care, as more fully explained at section 408.

### Group accounts: small companies

### 398    Option to prepare group accounts

**15.398.01**    If at the end of a financial year a company subject to the small companies regime is a parent company the directors, as well as preparing individual accounts for the year, may prepare group accounts for the year. COMMENCEMENT DATE  6 April 2008[201]

**15.398.02**    There is no requirement for companies within the small companies regime[202] to prepare group accounts, but under this section such a company's directors may choose do so, in addition to preparing the individual accounts. This option applies only where, at the end of its financial year,[203] the company is a parent company–ie, a company with one or more subsidiary undertakings.[204]

**15.398.03**    In so providing, this section preserves part, but not all, of the 1985 Act regime. There are two significant changes, however. First, medium-sized companies[205] are now required to prepare group accounts (they are outwith this section but within the duty in section 399); there was no such requirement in the 1985 Act. The explanation given by the Government for this change was that the 1985 Act's size limits for small and medium had been substantially increased in 2004.[206]

**15.398.04**    Second, as explained at section 384, a company is excluded from the small companies regime if it or any member of a group of which it forms a part—whether that is its own subsidiary undertaking, its own parent undertaking, or its fellow subsidiary undertaking—is ineligible (for example, because it is a public company). Under the previous legislation,[207] a company could not use the equivalent size-based exemption from preparing group accounts on grounds of ineligibility only if itself or one of its subsidiary undertakings was ineligible.

**15.398.05**    The form and content of the group accounts that may be prepared under this section are specified at section 404 for Companies Act group accounts and at section 403 for IAS group accounts. It is, however, worth observing at this stage that the effect of those sections is that the group accounts are consolidated accounts; consolidation is a well understood concept, whereby the company's interests in certain other undertakings are accounted for by treating the company and those other undertakings as

---

consistency, is used in accounts themselves also. For commentary on the authority of APB pronouncements see s1217.

[198]  Known as foreign private issuers.

[199]  This exemption is available for financial years ending after 15 November 2007.

[200]  See ss 398 and 399.

[201]  Companies Act 2006 (Commencement No 5,Transitional Provisions and Savings) Order 2007, SI 2007/3495, art 3(1) for financial years beginning on or after 6 April 2008.

[202]  See ss 381–384.

[203]  See s 390. Reference should also be made to *FRS 2 Accounting for subsidiary undertakings* (ASB, 1992).

[204]  See ss 1173 and 1162.

[205]  See ss 465–467.

[206]  Explanatory Notes to the CA 2006 (DTI/HMSO, 2006), para 649.

[207]  CA 1985, s 248.

if they were a single entity. Although it is the existence of a subsidiary undertaking that triggers the facility to prepare group accounts, if the company chooses under section 403 to prepare such accounts as IAS group accounts it is the requirements of EU-adopted IFRS[208] that determine the population of undertakings included in the consolidation.

## Group accounts: other companies

### 399   Duty to prepare group accounts[a]

(1) This section applies to companies that are not subject to the small companies regime.            **15.399.01**

> (2) If at the end of a financial year the company is a parent company the directors, as well as preparing individual accounts for the year, must prepare group accounts for the year unless the company is exempt from that requirement.
> (3) There are exemptions under—
> section 400 (company included in EEA accounts of larger group),
> section 401 (company included in non-EEA accounts of larger group), and
> section 402 (company none of whose subsidiary undertakings need be included in the consolidation).
> (4) A company to which this section applies but which is exempt from the requirement to prepare group accounts, may do so.

AMENDMENTS AND NOTES

> a   This section applies with modifications to overseas companies by reg 38 of the Overseas Companies Regulations 2009, 2009/1801.

COMMENCEMENT DATE  6 April 2008[209]

This section applies to all companies other than those which fall within the small companies regime. It    **15.399.02**
requires the directors of a company which, at the end of its financial year, is a parent company—a company with one or more subsidiary undertakings[210]—to prepare group accounts. Thus, for example, if a parent company, which had previously been required to prepare group accounts, disposed of its subsidiary undertakings part way through its financial year such that it had no subsidiary undertakings at the end of its financial year, there would be no requirement or facility for that company to prepare consolidated accounts, notwithstanding the fact that during the financial year it had subsidiary undertakings.

The duty to prepare group accounts is subject to the three exemptions set out in sections 400 to 402,    **15.399.03**
whereby the company need not prepare group accounts but may choose to do so.

The form and content of the group accounts that may be prepared under this section are specified at    **15.399.04**
section 404 for Companies Act group accounts and at section 403 for IAS group accounts. It is, however, worth observing at this stage that the effect of those sections is that the group accounts are consolidated accounts; consolidation is a well understood concept, whereby the company's interests in certain other undertakings are accounted for by treating the company and those other undertakings as if they were a single entity. Although it is the existence of a subsidiary undertaking that triggers the facility to prepare group accounts, if the company chooses under section 403 to prepare such accounts as IAS group accounts it is the requirements of EU-adopted IFRS[211] that determine the population of undertakings included in the consolidation.

### 400   Exemption for company included in EEA group accounts of larger group

(1) A company is exempt from the requirement to prepare group accounts if it is itself a subsidiary    **15.400.01**
undertaking and its immediate parent undertaking is established under the law of an EEA State, in the following cases—

> (a)  where the company is a wholly-owned subsidiary of that parent undertaking;
> (b)  where that parent undertaking holds more than 50% of the allotted shares in the company and notice requesting the preparation of group accounts has not been served on the company by shareholders holding in aggregate—
> (i)   more than half of the remaining allotted shares in the company, or

---

[208] A customary name for the international accounting standards defined in s 474(1) with which IAS group accounts must, under the IAS Regulation (see s 474) or under s 403(2)(b), comply.
[209] Companies Act 2006 (Commencement No 5, Transitional Provisions and Savings) Order 2007, SI 2007/3495, art 3(1) for financial years beginning on or after 6 April 2008.
[210] See ss 390 (financial year), 1173 (parent company), and 1162 (subsidiary undertaking). Reference should also be made to *FRS 2 Accounting for subsidiary undertakings* (ASB, 1992).
[211] A customary name for the international accounting standards defined in s 474(1) with which IAS group accounts must, under the IAS Regulation (see s 474) or under s 403(2)(b), comply.

(ii) 5% of the total allotted shares in the company.

Such notice must be served not later than six months after the end of the financial year before that to which it relates.

(2) Exemption is conditional upon compliance with all of the following conditions—

    (a) the company must be included in consolidated accounts for a larger group drawn up to the same date, or to an earlier date in the same financial year, by a parent undertaking established under the law of an EEA State;

    (b) those accounts must be drawn up and audited, and that parent undertaking's annual report must be drawn up, according to that law—

        (i) in accordance with the provisions of the Seventh Directive (83/349/EEC) (as modified, where relevant, by the provisions of the Bank Accounts Directive (86/635/EEC) or the Insurance Accounts Directive (91/674/EEC)), or

        (ii) in accordance with international accounting standards;

    (c) the company must disclose in its individual accounts that it is exempt from the obligation to prepare and deliver group accounts;

    (d) the company must state in its individual accounts the name of the parent undertaking that draws up the group accounts referred to above and—

        (i) if it is incorporated outside the United Kingdom, the country in which it is incorporated, or

        (ii) if it is unincorporated, the address of its principal place of business;

    (e) the company must deliver to the registrar, within the period for filing its accounts and reports for the financial year in question, copies of—

        (i) those group accounts, and

        (ii) the parent undertaking's annual report,

together with the auditor's report on them;

    (f) any requirement of Part 35 of this Act as to the delivery to the registrar of a certified translation into English must be met in relation to any document comprised in the accounts and reports delivered in accordance with paragraph (e).

(3) For the purposes of subsection (1)(b) shares held by a wholly-owned subsidiary of the parent undertaking, or held on behalf of the parent undertaking or a wholly-owned subsidiary, shall be attributed to the parent undertaking.

(4) The exemption does not apply to a company any of whose securities are admitted to trading on a regulated market in an EEA State.

(5) Shares held by directors of a company for the purpose of complying with any share qualification requirement shall be disregarded in determining for the purposes of this section whether the company is a wholly-owned subsidiary.

(6) In subsection (4) 'securities' includes—

    (a) shares and stock,

    (b) debentures, including debenture stock, loan stock, bonds, certificates of deposit and other instruments creating or acknowledging indebtedness,

    (c) warrants or other instruments entitling the holder to subscribe for securities falling within paragraph (a) or (b), and

    (d) certificates or other instruments that confer—

        (i) property rights in respect of a security falling within paragraph (a), (b) or (c),

        (ii) any right to acquire, dispose of, underwrite or convert a security, being a right to which the holder would be entitled if he held any such security to which the certificate or other instrument relates, or

        (iii) a contractual right (other than an option) to acquire any such security otherwise than by subscription.

COMMENCEMENT DATE  6 April 2008[212]

**15.400.02**    This section, derived from the 1985 Act,[213] provides a widely used exemption from preparing group accounts. Put at its briefest, it applies for parent companies that are themselves subsidiary undertakings and have an immediate parent undertaking[214] which is established in an EEA State[215] *and* are consolidated into the group accounts of an undertaking established in an EEA State (not necessarily the immediate parent). The circumstances and conditions[216] for exemption are detailed and care is needed when taking advantage of the exemption to ensure that all of its requirements are met. It is worth

---

[212] Companies Act 2006 (Commencement No 5, Transitional Provisions and Savings) Order 2007, SI 2007/3495, art 3(1) for financial years beginning on or after 6 April 2008.

[213] CA 1985, s 228.

[214] See s 1162 for subsidiary undertaking and parent undertaking.

[215] See s 1170. The EEA comprises the Member States of the EU, Norway, Iceland, and Liechtenstein.

[216] See subs (1) for circumstances; see subss (2) and (4) for conditions.

emphasizing the effect of one of those conditions immediately: a company that has any of its securities (subsection (6) provides an extensive definition of securities) admitted to trading on a regulated market[217] in an EEA State cannot use this exemption.[218]

Subsection (1)(a) addresses the basic circumstance of the exemption. It requires that the *immediate* parent undertaking of the company in question be established under the law of an EEA state. The company must be a wholly owned subsidiary[219] of this undertaking. This requires that the company has no members except its immediate parent company or that immediate parent undertaking's other wholly owned subsidiaries or persons acting on its/their behalf, but disregarding shares held by directors for a share qualification requirement.[220] Thus, for example, if the company has in issue preference shares held otherwise than by the immediate parent (or its wholly owned subsidiaries), then subsection (1)(a) is failed.  **15.400.03**

Subsection (1)(b) extends the circumstances of the exemption to cover cases where the immediate parent, established under the law of an EEA State, holds over 50 per cent of the company, subject to minority protection measures as set out in the subsection. Subsection (3) provides that shares held by the immediate parent's wholly owned subsidiaries or on behalf of them or of the company, count towards the 50 per cent. This percentage is in respect of 'the allotted shares', and thus it follows that it refers to 50 per cent by number of shares. So, for example, a single preference share counts equally in this calculation with a single ordinary share notwithstanding the different economic or voting entitlements that each might represent.  **15.400.04**

Subsections (2)(a) and (b) set out a number of conditions that the company claiming exemption must meet: that it must be included within the consolidated accounts of a higher parent undertaking (higher consolidated accounts) established in an EEA State; that those higher consolidated accounts must be drawn up to the same or an earlier date in the same financial year;[221] that they must be prepared pursuant to a law that is in accordance with the EC Seventh Company Law Directive[222] or be prepared in accordance with international accounting standards (also known as EU-adopted IFRS);[223] that they are audited pursuant to a law that is in accordance with the EC Seventh Company Law Directive; and that this higher EEA parent undertaking draws up an annual report pursuant to a law that is in accordance with that directive.  **15.400.05**

The first of subsection (2)'s condition bears examination in connection with the requirement of subsection (1) for an *immediate* parent undertaking established under the law of an EEA State. It is neither necessary for that immediate parent to prepare the consolidated accounts referred to subsection (2), nor for the company to be a wholly owned subsidiary of the higher parent that does prepare such accounts. For example, a company might be immediately wholly owned by a Danish company which is in turn ultimately majority owned by a French company that prepares consolidated accounts including the company. This would be sufficient for subsections (1)(a) and (2)(a). However, if the company is immediately wholly owned by an undertaking incorporated in the United States which is in turn ultimately majority owned by a French company that prepares consolidated accounts including the company, subsection (1) would be failed—the immediate parent undertaking is not established in the EEA—and the exemption is not available.[224]  **15.400.06**

Subsection (2)(a) requires the company to be 'included' in these higher consolidated accounts. The term 'included in consolidated accounts' means that the assets, liabilities, and trading of the subsidiary must be included in full in the group accounts.[225] Thus, proportionate consolidation or equity accounting is not sufficient.  **15.400.07**

---

[217]  See s 1173.

[218]  Subs (4).

[219]  See s 1159 for 'subsidiary', 'holding company', and 'wholly owned subsidiary'; and note that the meanings of these terms are different from, and on occasion narrower than, those of 'parent undertaking', 'parent company', and 'subsidiary company', which are defined in ss 1162 and 1173 of this Act.

[220]  Subs (5).

[221]  See s 390.

[222]  Directive 83/349/EEC at [1983] OJ/L193/1, as amended, modified where relevant by the EC Bank Accounts Directive (86/635/EEC) at [1986] OJ/L372/1 or the EC Insurance Accounts Directive (91/ 674/EEC) at [1991] OJ/L374/7 if relevant. Compliance with the EC Seventh Company Law Directive includes (see Arts 17 and 29) compliance with much of the EC Fourth Company Law Directive 78/ 660/EEC at [1978] OJ/L222/11, as amended, as if the group were a single company.

[223]  See s 474.

[224]  However, such a company may be able to benefit from the exemption in s 401.

[225]  See s 474(1).

**15.400.08**   It is also necessary for the higher consolidated accounts to be drawn up to the same date (as the accounts of the company seeking to use the exemption) or to an earlier date in the same financial year. However, as it is not always practical to align financial years immediately after acquisition, the exemption might not be available initially. For example, if a parent company with a financial year ended 31 March 2010 were acquired in February 2010 by a company with a 31 December year end, the acquired company would *not* be included in the acquirer's 31 December 2009 consolidation and would be prohibited under section 392 from extending its financial year to 31 December 2010 (as this would result in a financial year of 21 months). Thus, it would have to prepare consolidated accounts for the year ended 31 March 2010 notwithstanding the fact that it was acquired during that period.

**15.400.09**   However, it appears that it is only necessary for one day of the financial year of the company claiming exemption to be included in the higher consolidated accounts. For example, if a company with a financial year ending on 31 December 2009 is acquired on 30 December 2009 by a company that also has a financial year to 31 December 2009, it would be consolidated into that higher parent's consolidated accounts for one day and would meet the condition.

**15.400.10**   Further to subsection (2)(b), the higher consolidated accounts must be drawn up according to the law of an EEA Member State either in accordance with the EC Seventh Company Law Directive, which provides the European company law framework for consolidated accounts, or in accordance with EU-adopted IFRS. If the higher parent undertaking is a company it is a simple prerequisite that the EEA State has implemented that directive into its national law[226] or has permitted the use of EU-adopted IFRS under the IAS Regulation[227] as the case may be. In both cases—the directive and EU-adopted IFRS—it is of course necessary that the accounts do in fact comply with the relevant framework.

**15.400.11**   The 'annual report' requirement of subsection (2)(b) uses the terminology of the EC Seventh Company Law Directive,[228] which has been implemented in the UK, together with additional UK requirements, as the directors' report. It should be noted that the directive requirements include elements of the so-called enhanced business review, including the need for non-financial key performance indicators where appropriate.[229] This requirement should not be overlooked.

**15.400.12**   Subsection (2)(c) and (d) requires disclosures in the accounts of the company claiming exemption. Subsection (2)(e) and (f) requires the higher consolidated accounts to be delivered to the registrar. This requirement should not be overlooked. Thus, for example, when dealing with a group of companies the requirement appears to need each group company that is taking advantage of the exemption to deliver a copy of the higher consolidated accounts; in a large group with many intermediate parent companies, this might prove to be a large exercise (albeit made easier by the broader availability of electronic delivery under this Act).[230] When those higher consolidated accounts are prepared in a language other than English, then by virtue of subsection (2)(f) and sections 1102 to 1107 (of Part 35) a certified translation[231] must be delivered also (subject to section 1104 where the company concerned is Welsh).

### 401   Exemption for company included in non-EEA group accounts of larger group

**15.401.01**
   (1)  A company is exempt from the requirement to prepare group accounts if it is itself a subsidiary undertaking and its parent undertaking is not established under the law of an EEA State, in the following cases—

     (a)  where the company is a wholly-owned subsidiary of that parent undertaking;

     (b)  where that parent undertaking holds more than 50% of the allotted shares in the company and notice requesting the preparation of group accounts has not been served on the company by shareholders holding in aggregate—

       (i)  more than half of the remaining allotted shares in the company, or

       (ii)  5% of the total allotted shares in the company.

---

[226]  Under the Agreement on the European Economic Area (Oporto, 2 May 1992) the EEA States that are not within the EU agree to implement certain EC law within their national law. The company law directives, including the EC Seventh Company Law Directive, are such laws.

[227]  For companies not directly within the IAS Regulation (Regulation (EC) No 1606/2002), as amended, Art 5 thereof gives Member States the option of allowing the use of EU-adopted IFRS in lieu of directives-based national provision. Companies that are directly within the IAS Regulation are only so if they are first required by directive-based provisions of national law to prepare consolidated accounts which the IAS Regulation then requires to be in accordance with EU-adopted IFRS.

[228]  Art 36.

[229]  See s 417. However, it should be noted that the requirements of s 417(5) are not derived from that directive. See s 417(6) for non-financial key performance indicators.

[230]  See ss 441 and 1068.

[231]  See s 1107.

Such notice must be served not later than six months after the end of the financial year before that to which it relates.

(2) Exemption is conditional upon compliance with all of the following conditions—

    (a) the company and all of its subsidiary undertakings must be included in consolidated accounts for a larger group drawn up to the same date, or to an earlier date in the same financial year, by a parent undertaking;

    (b) those accounts and, where appropriate, the group's annual report, must be drawn up—

       (i) in accordance with the provisions of the Seventh Directive (83/349/EEC) (as modified, where relevant, by the provisions of the Bank Accounts Directive (86/635/EEC) or the Insurance Accounts Directive (91/674/EEC)), or

       (ii) in a manner equivalent to consolidated accounts and consolidated annual reports so drawn up;

    (c) the group accounts must be audited by one or more persons authorised to audit accounts under the law under which the parent undertaking which draws them up is established;

    (d) the company must disclose in its individual accounts that it is exempt from the obligation to prepare and deliver group accounts;

    (e) the company must state in its individual accounts the name of the parent undertaking which draws up the group accounts referred to above and—

       (i) if it is incorporated outside the United Kingdom, the country in which it is incorporated, or

       (ii) if it is unincorporated, the address of its principal place of business;

    (f) the company must deliver to the registrar, within the period for filing its accounts and reports for the financial year in question, copies of—

       (i) the group accounts, and

       (ii) where appropriate, the consolidated annual report, together with the auditor's report on them;

    (g) any requirement of Part 35 of this Act as to the delivery to the registrar of a certified translation into English must be met in relation to any document comprised in the accounts and reports delivered in accordance with paragraph (f).

(3) For the purposes of subsection (1)(b), shares held by a wholly-owned subsidiary of the parent undertaking, or held on behalf of the parent undertaking or a wholly-owned subsidiary, are attributed to the parent undertaking.

(4) The exemption does not apply to a company any of whose securities are admitted to trading on a regulated market in an EEA State.

(5) Shares held by directors of a company for the purpose of complying with any share qualification requirement shall be disregarded in determining for the purposes of this section whether the company is a wholly-owned subsidiary.

(6) In subsection (4) 'securities' includes—

    (a) shares and stock,

    (b) debentures, including debenture stock, loan stock, bonds, certificates of deposit and other instruments creating or acknowledging indebtedness,

    (c) warrants or other instruments entitling the holder to subscribe for securities falling within paragraph (a) or (b), and

    (d) certificates or other instruments that confer—

       (i) property rights in respect of a security falling within paragraph (a), (b) or (c),

       (ii) any right to acquire, dispose of, underwrite or convert a security, being a right to which the holder would be entitled if he held any such security to which the certificate or other instrument relates, or

       (iii) a contractual right (other than an option) to acquire any such security otherwise than by subscription.

COMMENCEMENT DATE   6 April 2008[232]

This section provides, in a similar manner to the preceding section, an exemption from preparing group accounts for parent companies that are themselves subsidiary undertakings of a parent undertaking,[233] in this case established under the law of a non-EEA State,[234] and are included in the consolidated accounts of a higher parent undertaking (higher consolidated accounts). This section is, to a large extent, based upon section 400, which provided the template.     **15.401.02**

There are three key differences between sections 400 and 401. First, whilst it is necessary under subsection (1) for a parent undertaking to be established in a non-EEA State, it requires only one parent     **15.401.03**

---

[232] Companies Act 2006 (Commencement No 5, Transitional Provisions and Savings) Order 2007, SI 2007/3495, art 3(1) for financial years beginning on or after 6 April 2008.

[233] See s 1162 for subsidiary undertaking and parent undertaking.

[234] Ie, not in an EEA State. See s 1170 for EEA State.

undertaking to be so established. This rule contrasts with section 400(1), where the place of establishment of the immediate parent undertaking is specified (in that case, in an EEA State); and with section 400(2) which specifies the place of establishment (in that case, in an EEA State) of the parent undertaking preparing the higher consolidated accounts. Under this section, however, and provided the company is a wholly-owned subsidiary[235] and other conditions set out in subsections (2) to (4) are met, all that is necessary is that the company has *a* parent undertaking that is established in a non-EEA State and that *a* parent undertaking, which may be the same one or another one, prepares the higher consolidated accounts. Thus within this exemption (provided all other conditions are met) are cases such as a company with an immediate, wholly owning parent undertaking established in, say, the United States or Switzerland, but which is included in higher consolidated accounts of an ultimate parent undertaking established elsewhere, whether that is outwith the EEA or not, provided those higher consolidated accounts meet the conditions of subsection (2).

15.401.04    Where the company seeking exemption is a non-wholly-owned subsidiary of an undertaking established in a non-EEA State, it might be thought to be the case that it is necessary that a non-EEA-undertaking should in fact be the immediate parent undertaking (although as described above the higher consolidated accounts could be prepared by a higher parent undertaking established within or without the EEA). This would be because in such a case subsection (1)(b) refers to the holding by 'that parent undertaking'—ie, by the non-EEA undertaking mentioned in subsection (1)—of more than 50 per cent of the allotted shares in the company. However, in interpreting 'subsidiary undertaking' and 'parent undertaking', paragraph 9 of Schedule 7 provides that rights held by a parent undertaking are treated as including those held by its subsidiary undertakings, and thus any rights held by the company's immediate parent undertaking (eg, established in the EEA) will be attributed to its parent undertaking (eg, established outside the EEA). If the holding of shares is viewed as a right—and the UK accounting standard that interprets these provisions takes that view[236]—then an immediate EEA-established parent undertaking's partial holding in the company would be attributed to a higher non-EEA parent undertaking and the test of the latter's holding more than 50 per cent could be met.

15.401.05    Whilst such an interpretation could be easily applied where the minority interest is directly at the level of the holdings in the company seeking exemption, its applicability is less clear where the minority arises at a higher level in the group (but below the non-EEA established parent undertaking in question). This is because subsection (1)(b) contemplates a right for the holders of the other shares in the company itself, whereas these shares would be wholly held by the immediate parent undertaking in a case where the minority arises higher in the group.

15.401.06    Turning to the second difference from section 400, subsection (2)(b) requires the higher consolidated accounts, in which the company is included, to be in accordance with the EC Seventh Company Law Directive[237] or 'drawn up in a manner equivalent to'. If the relevant parent undertaking is a company established in an EEA State (eg, it is the ultimate parent undertaking albeit there is an intermediate parent established outside the EEA), then this requirement should not present any real obstacle. This includes the case where that higher parent undertaking has used EU-adopted IFRS[238] since, as set out below, this would be considered 'equivalent'.

15.401.07    Where the higher consolidated accounts are drawn up by a parent undertaking outside of the EEA the issue of equivalence falls to be addressed. The issue is a difficult one and has been dealt with, albeit not comprehensively, by Urgent Issues Task Force (UITF) Abstract 43[239] in relation to the same provision

---

[235]  See s 1159.

[236]  *FRS 2 Accounting for subsidiary undertakings* (ASB, 1992, revised June 2009). At para 14, in reference to para 9 of Sch 7, it states that 'any shares held, or powers exercisable, by a subsidiary undertaking should be treated as held or exercisable by its parent undertaking'.

[237]  At [1983] OJ/L193/1, as amended, and EC Bank Accounts Directive (86/635/EEC) at [1986] OJ/L372/1, as amended, and EC Insurance Accounts Directive (91/674/EEC) at [1991] OJ/L374/7, as amended, if relevant. Compliance with the EC Seventh Company Law Directive includes (see Arts 17 and 29) compliance with much of the EC Fourth Company Law Directive (78/660/EEC) at [1978] OJ/L222/11, as amended, as if the group were a single company.

[238]  The customary name for international accounting standards defined in s 474(1).

[239]  *UITF Abstract No 43 The interpretation of equivalence for the purposes of section 228A of the Companies Act 1985* (ASB, 2006). Until July 2012 The Urgent Issues Task Force (UITF) was a committee of the then Accounting Standards Board (ASB) that assisted the ASB in areas where an accounting standard or Companies Act provision existed but where unsatisfactory or conflicting interpretations had developed or seemed likely to develop. If the UITF reached a consensus on such an issue, the ASB published an abstract of the consensus, and this had the same authority as an accounting standard issued by the ASB. Following the reorganization of the Financial Reporting Council, the role and responsibilities of the UITF was transferred to the Accounting Council which under the new structure of the FRC amongst other things is tasked with developing accounting standards. The Accounting Council has stated its intention to form a new Committee which will address the issues that have previously been

in the predecessor legislation. In short, it states a consensus view that the use of EU-adopted IFRS will always result in equivalence.[240] The use of IFRS[241] themselves will also result in equivalence subject to one point, as follows: if the European Commission has not adopted a standard (issued by the IASB) because it considers that it is not in conformity with the Fourth or Seventh Directive, this may preclude equivalence depending on the relevance of that standard to the consolidated accounts in question.[242] It also provides that national accounting standards will result in equivalence where these are based directly on IFRS, but are more restrictive. Where they are based on IFRS but differ in other ways, the abstract requires consideration of the effect of the particular differences from the EU-adopted IFRS;[243] reference should be made to UITF 43 itself. Note also that the European Commission's occasional decision on equivalence of other national accounting standards for the purposes of the Transparency[244] and Prospectus[245] Directives have no direct bearing on the determination of equivalence under this section—eg, the Commission's assessments are not based on a technical analysis of the standards as they currently stand.

The third difference from section 400 is that subsection (2) requires not only the company but all of its    **15.401.08**
subsidiary undertakings to be included in the higher consolidated accounts. This provision, for all of the company's subsidiary undertakings, has no equivalent in section 400.

### 402  Exemption if no subsidiary undertakings need be included in the consolidation[a]

A parent company is exempt from the requirement to prepare group accounts if under section 405 all of    **15.402.01**
its subsidiary undertakings could be excluded from consolidation in Companies Act group accounts.

AMENDMENTS AND NOTES

[a]  This section applies with modifications to overseas companies by reg 38 of the Overseas Companies Regulations 2009, 2009/1801.

COMMENCEMENT DATE  6 April 2008[246]

The section provides an exemption to a company from preparing group accounts when all of the    **15.402.02**
company's subsidiary undertakings[247] could be excluded from the consolidation in Companies Act group accounts—notwithstanding that the group accounts that the company might otherwise prepare would be IAS group accounts.[248] The circumstances in which a subsidiary undertaking may be so excluded are given by section 405.

### *Group accounts: general*

### 403  Group accounts: applicable accounting framework[a]

(1)  The group accounts of certain parent companies are required by Article 4 of the IAS Regulation to    **15.403.01**
be prepared in accordance with international accounting standards ('IAS group accounts').
(2)  The group accounts of other companies may be prepared—
   (a)  in accordance with section 404 ('Companies Act group accounts'), or
   (b)  in accordance with international accounting standards ('IAS group accounts'). This is subject to the following provisions of this section.
(3)  The group accounts of a parent company that is a charity must be Companies Act group accounts.
(4)  After the first financial year in which the directors of a parent company prepare IAS group accounts ('the first IAS year'), all subsequent group accounts of the company must be prepared in accordance with international accounting standards unless there is a relevant change of circumstance. [This is subject to subsection (5A)][b].
(5)  There is a relevant change of circumstance if, at any time during or after the first IAS year—
   (a)  the company becomes a subsidiary undertaking of another undertaking that does not prepare IAS group accounts,

---

dealt with by the UITF. Based on the transitional and savings provisions in regulation 24 of the Statutory Auditors (Amendment of Companies Act 2006 and Delegation of Functions etc) Order 2012, SI 2012/1741 UITFs currently in existence will remain in force until withdrawn.
[240]  *UITF 43*, paras 10, 26(b)(ii).
[241]  Ie, standards issued by the IASB. These are to a very high degree coextensive with EU-adopted IFRS; however, time lags in adoption of IFRS by the European Commission into EU-adopted IFRS, or modifications on adoption, mean that that are not always identical in every respect. See the commentary at s 474.
[242]  *UITF 43*, paras 11, 26(b)(iii).
[243]  *UITF 43*, paras 12, 26(b)(iv).
[244]  2004/109/EC at [2004] OJ/L390/38.
[245]  Commission Regulation (EC) No 809/2004 implementing Directive 2003/71/EC at [2004] OJ/L149/1.
[246]  Companies Act 2006 (Commencement No 5, Transitional Provisions and Savings) Order 2007, SI 2007/3495, art 3(1) for financial years beginning on or after 6 April 2008.
[247]  See s 1162.
[248]  See s 403(1), (2)(b).

(b)  the company ceases to be a company with securities admitted to trading on a regulated market in an EEA State, or

(c)  a parent undertaking of the company ceases to be an undertaking with securities admitted to trading on a regulated market in an EEA State.

[(5A) After a financial year in which the directors of a parent company prepare IAS group accounts for the company, the directors may change to preparing Companies Act group accounts for a reason other than a relevant change of circumstance provided they have not changed to Companies Act group accounts in the period of five years preceding the first day of that financial year.

(5B)  In calculating the five year period for the purpose of subsection (5A), no account should be taken of a change due to a relevant change of circumstance][b].

(6)  If, having changed to preparing Companies Act group accounts [ ], the directors again prepare IAS group accounts for the company, subsections (4) and (5) apply again as if the first financial year for which such accounts are again prepared were the first IAS year.

AMENDMENTS AND NOTES

[a]  This section applies with modifications to overseas companies by reg 38 of the Overseas Companies Regulations 2009, 2009/1801.

[b]  Inserted or deleted by the Companies and Limited Liability Partnerships (Accounts and Audit Exemptions and Change in Accounting Framework) Regulations 2012, SI 2012/2301, for financial years ending on or after 1 October 2012.[249]

COMMENCEMENT DATE  in relation to subsections 4A and 4B, from 1 October 2012[250]; otherwise, 6 April 2008[251]

**15.403.02**   This section and the following two provide the form and content of group accounts for those companies preparing them. Subject to one proviso (dealt with later in this commentary), this section offers a similar choice to that afforded by section 395 for individual accounts, namely to prepare those group accounts either in accordance with regulations under section 404 and, in effect, UK accounting standards (Companies Act Group Accounts), or in accordance with EU-adopted IFRS[252] (IAS Group Accounts). The effect of this section is that group accounts must take one of these two forms, thereby ruling out all other possibilities. In both cases a true and fair requirement applies either through section 404 or 393.

**15.403.03**   The choices made by a parent company for its individual accounts and its group accounts are not linked; Companies Act may be chosen for one and IAS for the other. In addition, unlike the individual accounts choice, there is no requirement in relation to consistency of choice among companies within a group (if more than one company in a group prepared group accounts, say because an intermediate holding company chose to do so); that is, there is no equivalent of section 407 for group accounts.

**15.403.04**   As with the case of individual accounts, there are some restrictions placed upon the choice: a charity cannot choose IAS group accounts; and, once IAS group accounts are chosen, there can be no reverting to Companies Act group accounts save on the occasion of defined changes in circumstances or, for financial years ending on or after 1 October 2012, subsection (6) applies. These restrictions are in the same form as for individual accounts under section 395 save that there is no equivalent of the provision in section 395(4)(aa). As discussed in the commentary to section 395(4)(aa), this provides that a company's ceasing to be a subsidiary undertaking is a change of circumstance in connection with its individual accounts. It is not immediately clear why this section omits an equivalent to section 395(4)(aa) as such a company might also be a parent company. A further point of note in relation, in particular, to group accounts, for financial years ending before 1 October 2012 in connection with section 403(5)(b) and former AIM companies. In order for a company to take advantage of that section, it must cease to have securities admitted to trading on a regulated market of an EEA state.[253] Therefore, withdrawing from AIM will not lead to a relevant change of circumstance because AIM is not such a regulated market. This is unfortunate given that on such an occasion the company will cease to fall under the AIM requirement to prepare IAS group accounts (ie, the AIM rules forced the company into making that choice under this section). Notwithstanding the freedom from this AIM rule, the company

---

[249]  Companies and Limited Liability Partnerships (Accounts and Audit Exemptions and Change of Accounting Framework) Regulations 2012, SI 2012/2301, for financial years ending on or after 1 October 2012.

[250]  Companies and Limited Liability Partnerships (Accounts and Audit Exemptions and Change of Accounting Framework) Regulations 2012, SI 2012/2301, for financial years ending on or after 1 October 2012.

[251]  Companies Act 2006 (Commencement No 5, Transitional Provisions and Savings) Order 2007, SI 2007/3495, art 3(1) for financial years beginning on or after 6 April 2008.

[252]  A customary name for the international accounting standards defined in s 474(1) with which IAS group accounts must, under the IAS Regulation (see s 474) or under s 403(2)(b), comply.

[253]  See s 1173 (regulated market) and s 1170 (EEA State).

is not free to revert to preparing Companies Act group accounts as its circumstances do not fall within subsection (5)(b).[254] However, for subsequent financial years this problem is resolved, as explained in the following paragraphs.

For financial years ending on or after 1 October 2012, subsection (6) introduces an additional facility to switch back to Companies Act group accounts, (ie. accounts under 'UK GAAP'). This new facility allows a company's group accounts prepared in accordance with EU-adopted IFRS to switch back to 'UK GAAP' provided that the group had 'not changed' to UK GAAP accounts in the period of five years preceding the first day of the financial year in which it is now intended to switch to 'UK GAAP'. In the calculation of whether a previous change to 'UK GAAP' has occurred in the previous five years, any change due to a 'relevant change in circumstances' under section 395(4) is ignored. In other words, there is now a free choice for a company to revert to 'UK GAAP' from EU-adopted IFRS as long as the group had not in the last five years made such a free choice to revert to UK GAAP.   **15.403.05**

The new switching facility was introduced for two reasons. First, the Financial Reporting Council has proposed an overhaul of UK GAAP. To permit those companies that already use EU-adopted IFRS to prepare their accounts to have the ability to use the revised 'UK GAAP', this change in the law was needed. Moreover, with particular relevance to group accounts, if a company withdraws from AIM, then, hitherto, it would not have been able to revert to UK GAAP, since AIM is not a regulated market in an EEA state. The new 'five year' rule should allow former AIM companies to revert to 'UK GAAP'.   **15.403.06**

Reverting to a more general comparison with section 395, there is one major difference between the case of group accounts and that of individual accounts; and this is the proviso mentioned at the start of this commentary. It is that the IAS Regulation,[255] which has direct effect in the UK, forces certain parent companies' group accounts to be prepared in accordance with EU-adopted IFRS, ie they must prepare IAS group accounts. Accordingly subsection (1) acknowledges that certain companies fall within the IAS Regulation—which has direct effect in Member States—and thus do not fall within the option provided by subsection (2) for other companies.   **15.403.07**

The 'certain parent companies' to which subsection (1) refers are identified by article 4 of that regulation: 'companies governed by the law of a Member State shall prepare their consolidated accounts in conformity with the international accounting standards adopted in accordance with the procedure laid down in Article 6(2) if, at their balance sheet date, their securities are admitted to trading on a regulated market of any Member State within the meaning of [Article 4(14) of Directive 2004/39/EC of 21 April 2004 on markets in financial instruments[256]].'[257] It is worth noting that this article governs only the manner of preparation of group accounts. Whether group accounts are to be prepared at all remains a matter for this Act.[258]   **15.403.08**

It is sometimes queried whether the traded securities referred to in that article are those of any undertaking falling to be included within the group accounts, on the grounds that they are group securities and the article is concerned with group accounts. It is clear, however, that the securities in question are those only of the parent company itself.   **15.403.09**

## 404   Companies Act group accounts[a]

    (1)  Companies Act group accounts must comprise—   **15.404.01**
        (a)  a consolidated balance sheet dealing with the state of affairs of the parent company and its subsidiary undertakings, and
        (b)  a consolidated profit and loss account dealing with the profit or loss of the parent company and its subsidiary undertakings.

---

[254]  AIM Rule 19.

[255]  Regulation (EC) No 1606/2002 at [2002] OJ/L243/1, as amended, and see s 474(1).

[256]  At [2004] OJ/L145/1, known as 'MiFID'. This directive replaces Council Directive 93/22/EEC of 10 May 1993 ('ISD'), to which the original text of the IAS Regulation referred. Art 69 of MiFID states that references to terms in, or articles of, the ISD directive shall be construed as references to the equivalents in MiFID. The text in square brackets has been inserted accordingly.

[257]  'International accounting standards adopted in accordance with the procedure laid down in Article 6(2)' are the same as international accounting standards as defined in s 474(1), known as EU-adopted IFRS. The European Commission publishes an annual list of regulated markets referred to in this article. These are the same regulated markets as defined in this Act at s 1173.

[258]  See ss 398 to 402 for the requirement (or option) to prepare group accounts. See the commentary at s 395 where it is noted that the view of the European Commission's Accounting Regulatory Committee is that provisions of EU-adopted IFRS do *not* have the effect of displacing or negating the authority of national law implementing the EC Seventh Company Law Directive 83/349/EEC at [1983] OJ/L193/1, as amended, in this case the sections first mentioned, to determine whether group accounts are prepared.

(2)  The accounts must give a true and fair view of the state of affairs as at the end of the financial year, and the profit or loss for the financial year, of the undertakings included in the consolidation as a whole, so far as concerns members of the company.

(3)  The accounts must comply with provision made by the Secretary of State by regulations as to—

    (a)  the form and content of the consolidated balance sheet and consolidated profit and loss account, and

    (b)  additional information to be provided by way of notes to the accounts.

(4)  If compliance with the regulations, and any other provision made by or under this Act as to the matters to be included in a company's group accounts or in notes to those accounts, would not be sufficient to give a true and fair view, the necessary additional information must be given in the accounts or in a note to them.

(5)  If in special circumstances compliance with any of those provisions is inconsistent with the requirement to give a true and fair view, the directors must depart from that provision to the extent necessary to give a true and fair view.

Particulars of any such departure, the reasons for it and its effect must be given in a note to the accounts.

AMENDMENTS AND NOTES

ᵃ  This section applies with modifications to overseas companies by reg 38 of the Overseas Companies Regulations 2009, 2009/1801.

COMMENCEMENT DATE subsection (3) in relation to the regulation-making power, from 20 January 2007;[259] otherwise 6 April 2008[260]

**15.404.02**  This section is in substantially the same form as section 396 but in relation to Companies Act group accounts rather than individual accounts. Subsection (1) specifies that the Companies Act group accounts must be consolidated accounts dealing with the parent company and its subsidiary undertakings (but see section 405 for those subsidiary undertakings that must or may be excluded). Consolidation is a well understood accounting concept, whereby the company's interests in certain other undertakings are accounted for by treating the company and those other undertakings as if they were a single entity.

**15.404.03**  The form and content of the consolidated accounts are determined in accordance with regulations made under subsection (3), which have been made on the commencement of this section in substantially the same form as schedules 4A, 9, and 9A to the 1985 Act.[261] As with section 396, much the most important element of this section is that the standard to which the accounts are required to be prepared is true-and-fair. As explained in the context of that earlier section, this means in effect that the consolidated accounts must comply with UK accounting standards; but that while such compliance may be necessary it is not necessarily sufficient; and that the need for a true and fair view is overriding.

**15.404.04**  In connection with the overriding nature of the true and fair requirement, the relationship between subsection (5) and section 405 merits attention: can the override require exclusion from the consolidation where section 405 would not? Subsection (5) is the authority— indeed the requirement—for departure from certain provisions if compliance therewith would be inconsistent with a true and fair view. The subsection refers to departure from 'those provisions', which is a reference to those cited in the previous subsection, ie 'the regulations [under sub section (3)] and any other provision made by or under this Act *as to the matters* to be included in the company's group accounts or in notes to those accounts'. Section 405 deals with the question as to which subsidiary undertakings are to be included in the consolidation. The question arises as to whether section 405 is a provision which should, in appropriate circumstances, be departed from pursuant to the overriding requirement for a true and fair view in subsection (5). This turns on whether a subsidiary undertaking can be viewed as a 'matter'. Whilst at first sight this might be unclear, reference to the EC Seventh Company Law Directive,[262] which sections 404 and 405 (among others) implement, provides clarity on the question: Article 16(5) of that Directive sets out the true and fair override in the case of consolidated accounts and specifies departure only from certain articles[263] which do not include the articles[264] which are implemented by section 405.

**15.404.05**  Thus section 405's limits on the exclusion of subsidiary undertakings from consolidation may not be overridden. However, it is thought that the manner in which they are included is a 'matter' within

---

[259]  Companies Act 2006 (Commencement No 1, etc) Order 2006, SI 2006/3428, art 3(3).

[260]  Companies Act 2006 (Commencement No 5, Transitional Provisions and Savings) Order 2007, SI 2007/3495, art 3(1) for financial years beginning on or after 6 April 2008.

[261]  See para 15.396.03, nn 170 and 171.

[262]  Directive (EEC) 83/349 [1983] OJ L193/1, as amended.

[263]  Articles 17–35, 39.

[264]  Articles 3 and 13.

subsection (5) and can therefore be overridden. Thus in appropriate circumstances it could be necessary to include a subsidiary undertaking by the method of proportional consolidation rather than the full consolidation otherwise required by section 405.[265]

## 405  Companies Act group accounts: subsidiary undertakings included in the consolidation[a]

(1)  Where a parent company prepares Companies Act group accounts, all the subsidiary undertakings of the company must be included in the consolidation, subject to the following exceptions.

(2)  A subsidiary undertaking may be excluded from consolidation if its inclusion is not material for the purpose of giving a true and fair view (but two or more undertakings may be excluded only if they are not material taken together).

(3)  A subsidiary undertaking may be excluded from consolidation where—

(a)  severe long-term restrictions substantially hinder the exercise of the rights of the parent company over the assets or management of that undertaking, or

(b)  the information necessary for the preparation of group accounts cannot be obtained without disproportionate expense or undue delay, or

(c)  the interest of the parent company is held exclusively with a view to subsequent resale.

(4)  The reference in subsection (3)(a) to the rights of the parent company and the reference in subsection (3)(c) to the interest of the parent company are, respectively, to rights and interests held by or attributed to the company for the purposes of the definition of 'parent undertaking' (see section 1162) in the absence of which it would not be the parent company.

**15.405.01**

AMENDMENTS AND NOTES

[a]  This section applies with modifications to overseas companies by reg 38 of the Overseas Companies Regulations 2009, 2009/1801.

COMMENCEMENT DATE  6 April 2008[266]

This section serves two functions. First it determines the scope of undertakings included in the consolidation in Companies Act group accounts.[267] Second, by virtue of section 402 it can in effect determine whether group accounts, be they Companies Act group accounts or IAS group accounts, are required at all. If no undertaking would fall to be included in a Companies Act group accounts consolidation under this section then no group accounts —Companies Act or IAS—are required by section 402.

**15.405.02**

Where IAS group accounts are in fact prepared, this section does not apply to the preparation of those IAS group accounts; instead the scope of undertakings included in any IAS group accounts that are prepared is determined by EU-adopted IFRS.[268]

**15.405.03**

The section is a case where UK accounting standards, with which compliance is in effect required by the true and fair requirement,[269] provide more detailed requirements that are consistent with the Act but also narrow down some of the choices otherwise available in the Act. In this case the relevant standard is FRS 2;[270] its effect is noted throughout the following paragraphs.

**15.405.04**

Subsection (1) sets out the basic proposition that all subsidiary undertakings[271] must be 'included in the consolidation', which is defined in section 474(1) as full rather than proportional consolidation. As noted at sections 398 and 399, FRS 2 provides further detail as to how the definition of a 'subsidiary undertaking' is to be applied. FRS 2 also sets out more detail as to the method of full consolidation, eg how intragroup transactions are to be eliminated, or the questions of uniform accounting policies and periods.

**15.405.05**

Subsections (2) and (3) set out exceptions whereby a subsidiary undertaking need not be consolidated into its parent's group accounts. In practice these exceptions in subsection (3) result only occasionally in the exclusion of a subsidiary undertaking. Moreover, when they are under consideration the effect of

**15.405.06**

[265]  Articles 18 and 22 of that Directive specify the method of full consolidation but are within the scope of the override—see n 246, above.

[266]  Companies Act 2006 (Commencement No 5, Transitional Provisions and Savings) Order 2007, SI 2007/3495, art 3(1) for financial years beginning on or after 6 April 2008.

[267]  See s 404.

[268]  A customary name for the international accounting standards defined in s 474(1) with which IAS group accounts must, under the IAS Regulation (see s 474) or under s 403(2)(b), comply.

[269]  See commentary at s 404.

[270]  FRS 2 Accounting for subsidiary undertakings (ASB, 1992).

[271]  See s 1162.

FRS 2 is important since it identifies the cases where directors must use the facility to exclude and where they must not.

**15.405.07**  Before dealing with the exceptions it is worth noting that the effect of this section and section 1162 is that non-consolidation of an undertaking is not synonymous with failure to meet the test of being a subsidiary undertaking—although it is an occasional misconception that it is so; an undertaking can be a subsidiary undertaking but nevertheless be excluded from consolidation.

**15.405.08**  The first exception is on the grounds of materiality and exclusion is optional. The test of immateriality has to be met in relation to all of such subsidiary undertakings taken together. The effect of this is to require consolidation of subsidiary undertakings when taken together they are material, which might not be the case if each subsidiary undertaking were evaluated singly.

**15.405.09**  Subsections (3)(a) and (4) provide an option to exclude a subsidiary undertaking that is subject to severe long-term restrictions that substantially hinder the exercise of those rights of the parent company by virtue of which it is the parent company. FRS 2 determines cases of severe long-term restrictions and it *requires* exclusion in these cases.

**15.405.10**  Severe long-term restrictions mean that the parent has, in effect, lost control of the subsidiary undertaking; however, they are identified by their effect in practice, not by the way they are imposed.[272] For example, it applies in joint venture arrangements if one party holds a majority of the share capital but, as explained in accounting standards, 'contractual arrangements with the other shareholder mean that in practice the shareholders share control over their investee. In such a case the interests of the minority shareholder amount to 'severe long-term restrictions' that 'substantially hinder the exercise of the rights of the parent undertaking over the assets or management of the subsidiary undertaking'.[273] However, whilst it is optional to exclude a subsidiary on these grounds under this section, accounting standards[274] prohibit the consolidation of any subsidiary undertaking to which severe long-term restrictions apply.

**15.405.11**  The optional exclusion in subsection (3)(b)—on the grounds of disproportionate expense or undue delay—is not, in fact, available because FRS 2 prohibits its use. FRS 2 takes the view that the benefit of consolidation of material subsidiaries is always greater than the costs and delays of obtaining the necessary information.[275]

**15.405.12**  The final exception is that of subsection (3)(c) and (4) where the interest of the parent company is held exclusively with a view to subsequent sale. One of the situations that this exemption deals with is that where a group of companies is acquired but the purchaser does not intend to retain every member of the acquired group, eg it intends to sell incidental undertakings. Another situation is where a bank acquires a subsidiary undertaking as a result of the enforcement of security and the bank does not intend it to become a continuing part of its group's activities. However, although the exception is potentially wide, restrictive parameters for its use are given by accounting standards.[276] Thus, whilst this section makes the use of this exception optional, FRS 2 prohibits its use when the subsidiary undertaking has been previously consolidated, and requires its use when the subsidiary undertaking has not been consolidated previously. It also applies a time limit for the view to resale (one year approximately).[277]

### 406   IAS group accounts[a]

**15.406.01**  Where the directors of a company prepare IAS group accounts, they must state in the notes to those accounts that the accounts have been prepared in accordance with international accounting standards.

AMENDMENTS AND NOTES

[a]  This section applies with modifications to overseas companies by reg 38 of the Overseas Companies Regulations 2009, 2009/1801.

COMMENCEMENT DATE  6 April 2008[278]

**15.406.02**  This section requires that a company preparing IAS group accounts includes within them a statement that they are prepared in accordance with international accounting standards. This reference to international accounting standards is normally formulated as 'International Financial Reporting

---

[272]  Para 78(c), FRS 2.
[273]  *FRS 9 Associates and joint ventures* (ASB, 1997), para 11.
[274]  Para 25, FRS 2; and para 11, FRS 9.
[275]  Para 24, FRS 2.
[276]  Paras 11 and 25, FRS 2.
[277]  Para 11, FRS 2.
[278]  Companies Act 2006 (Commencement No 5, Transitional Provisions and Savings) Order 2007, SI 2007/3495, art 3(1) for financial years beginning on or after 6 April 2008.

Standards (IFRSs) as adopted by the EU'[279] and thus the standards are also known by the abbreviated term 'EU-adopted IFRS'.

As more fully explained under section 474, IFRS are accounting standards issued by the International Accounting Standards Board (IASB). EU-adopted IFRS are those IFRS that have been adopted by the European Commission. IFRS and EU-adopted IFRS are not necessarily precisely the same, mainly because there will be a time lag between the IASB's issuing a standard and the European Commission's adopting it, but also because, less frequently, the Commission might adopt an IFRS in modified form (or fail to adopt it). Where a company's accounts comply with both EU-adopted IFRS and IFRS issued by the IASB the company may want to make clear that they comply with those IFRS issued by the IASB. This is of course acceptable but such a statement must be in addition to the required statement of compliance with EU-adopted IFRS. When contemplating making such an additional compliance statement it should be borne in mind that it will not be automatically the case that such an additional statement can be made in every subsequent year; for example, the time lag for Commission adoption may prevent dual compliance on some occasions.

**15.406.03**

## 407   Consistency of financial reporting within group

(1)  The directors of a parent company must secure that the individual accounts of—

    (a)  the parent company, and

    (b)  each of its subsidiary undertakings,

    are all prepared using the same financial reporting framework, except to the extent that in their opinion there are good reasons for not doing so.

(2)  Subsection (1) does not apply if the directors do not prepare group accounts for the parent company.

(3)  Subsection (1) only applies to accounts of subsidiary undertakings that are required to be prepared under this Part.

(4)  Subsection (1) does not require accounts of undertakings that are charities to be prepared using the same financial reporting framework as accounts of undertakings which are not charities.

(5)  Subsection (1)(a) does not apply where the directors of a parent company prepare IAS group accounts and IAS individual accounts.

**15.407.01**

COMMENCEMENT DATE  6 April 2008[280]

This section aims at ensuring that a consistent choice is made within certain groups, and subject to exceptions, in the matter of the 'financial reporting framework' used in the preparation of the individual accounts of those undertakings. Although 'financial reporting framework' is not defined, it refers to the applicable accounting framework[281] chosen under section 395—namely Companies Act or IAS individual accounts. It is not entirely clear why the legislation should aim at this consistency, but it is widely supposed that it would be helpful to the taxation authorities in respect of intragroup trading.

**15.407.02**

First of all, subsections (1) and (2) place the duty to secure consistency of choice, by the company itself and by its subsidiary undertakings, upon the directors of a parent company that prepares group accounts. Thus if a parent company does not prepare group accounts, for example, because it is itself included in the consolidated accounts of a higher parent undertaking in another EEA State,[282] then there is no requirement for consistency of choice for individual accounts; but if a parent company is required to prepare consolidated accounts, for example if its higher parent undertaking is incorporated outside of the EEA but its consolidated accounts are not drawn up in a manner equivalent to that under the EC Seventh Company Law Directive,[283] or it has no higher parent, then the duty to secure consistency applies.

**15.407.03**

When this duty does apply, it applies to the directors of the parent company that is preparing the group accounts. Thus it does not apparently fall directly upon the directors of any subsidiary undertaking of that parent company, notwithstanding that those directors are the ones who are charged by section 394 with preparing the individual accounts of that company and thus for making the choice under section 395 as to the applicable accounting framework. However, section 395(1) does make the choice

**15.407.04**

---

[279]  This is the phrase used in the Auditing Practices Board (APB) literature in audit reports—eg see APB Bulletin 2010/02 (Revised) *Compendium of illustrative auditor's reports on United Kingdom private sector financial statements for periods ended on or after 15 December 2010* (APB, 2011)—and so, for consistency, is also used in accounts themselves. See commentary on the authority of APB pronouncements at s 1217.

[280]  Companies Act 2006 (Commencement No 5, Transitional Provisions and Savings) Order 2007, SI 2007/3495, art 3(1) for financial years beginning on or after 6 April 2008.

[281]  The terms 'financial reporting' and 'accounting' are sometimes used interchangeably in the accountancy profession.

[282]  See s 400.

[283]  See s 401.

exercised by those directors 'subject to the … provisions of… section 407', thus bringing the consistency principle somewhat awkwardly into the subsidiary undertaking directors' consideration.

**15.407.05**  Subsections (3) to (5) contain a number of specific exceptions from the consistency rule. The first makes clear that the consistency rule applies only to undertakings whose accounts preparation is governed by Part 15 of this Act. Thus, for example, subsidiary undertakings that are foreign companies are excluded. The common case of a UK company that is a subsidiary undertaking is of course included. There are, however, likely to be a small number of other UK undertakings that prepare their accounts under this Part. For example, limited liability partnerships and certain partnerships are required to prepare their accounts in accordance with Part 15 of this Act.[284]

**15.407.06**  Subsection (4) disapplies the consistency rule with respect to subsidiary undertakings that are charities since by section 395(2) these are always required to prepare Companies Act individual accounts.

**15.407.07**  The effect of subsection (5) is to modify the consistency rule so that it applies only to a parent company's subsidiary undertakings but not to the parent company itself, in the case where the parent company prepares IAS group accounts and IAS individual accounts. This exception is made to enable parent companies that prepare IAS group accounts—say, because they are listed companies—to choose to prepare the individual accounts of the parent company on the same basis without triggering the need for all subsidiary undertakings to move to IAS individual accounts.

**15.407.08**  Subsection (1), however, contains a much more general exception: the consistency rule may be departed from to the extent that the directors of the parent company are of the opinion that there are good reasons for so departing. Following the introduction of the consistency requirement in the predecessor Act, the Department of Trade and Industry (DTI) published some views on the operation of the good-reasons exception, as follows:

> This provision is intended to provide a degree of flexibility where there are genuine (including cost/benefit) grounds for using different accounting frameworks within a group of companies. Examples of 'good reasons' could include: A group using IAS acquired a subsidiary undertaking that had not been using IAS; in the first year of acquisition, it might not be practical for the newly acquired company to switch to IAS straight away.

> The group contains subsidiary undertakings that are themselves publicly traded, in which case market pressures or regulatory requirements to use IAS might come into play, without necessarily justifying a switch to IAS by the non-publicly traded subsidiaries.

> A subsidiary undertaking or the parent was planning to apply for a listing and so might wish to convert to IAS in advance, but the rest of group was not planning to apply for a listing. The group contains minor or dormant subsidiaries where the costs of switching accounting framework would outweigh the benefits.

> The key point is that the directors of the parent company must be able to justify any inconsistency, to shareholders, regulators or other interested parties.[285]

**15.407.09**  Beyond these remarks provided by the DTI (as it then was) it is difficult to generalize upon the operation of the 'good reasons' exception.

### 408  Individual profit and loss account where group accounts prepared

**15.408.01**  (1)  This section applies where—
  (a) a company prepares group accounts in accordance with this Act, and
  (b) the notes to the company's individual balance sheet show the company's profit or loss for the financial year determined in accordance with this Act.
(2)  The [company's individual][a] profit and loss account need not contain the information specified in section 411 (information about employee numbers and costs).
(3)  The company's individual profit and loss account must be approved in accordance with section 414(1) (approval by directors) but may be omitted from the company's annual accounts for the purposes of the other provisions of the Companies Acts.
(4)  The exemption conferred by this section is conditional upon its being disclosed in the company's annual accounts that the exemption applies.

---

[284] See the Partnership (Accounts) Regulations 2008, SI 2008/569, reg 4 for partnerships for financial years beginning on or after 6 April 2008; see the Limited Liability Partnerships (Accounts and Audit) (Application of Companies Act 2006) Regulations 2008, SI 2008/1911 for limited liability partnerships for financial years beginning on or after 1 October 2008.

[285] Guidance for UK companies on accounting and reporting: Requirements under the Companies Act 2006 and the application of the IAS regulation (DBERR, 2008), para 9.17.

AMENDMENTS AND NOTES

ª Inserted by the Companies Act 2006 (Amendment) (Accounts and Reports) Regulations 2008, SI
2008/393, reg 10.

COMMENCEMENT DATE   6 April 2008[286]

This section provides a widely-used exemption from including in the 'annual accounts' the company's      **15.408.02**
individual profit and loss account (sometimes known as the parent company profit and loss account)
when the company prepares group accounts. By virtue of section 472(2) the exemption extends to the
notes to the individual profit and loss account also, since that section provides that the term 'profit and
loss account' refers also to the notes thereto. The section also contains an exemption from providing
information required by section 411 (employee numbers and costs).

The exemptions themselves are set out in subsections (2) and (3) whilst conditions for their use are set      **15.408.03**
out in subsections (1) and (4). The disclosure conditions of those subsections should not be overlooked: the use of the exemption must be stated in the annual accounts, as must be the figure for parent
company's individual accounts' profit or loss for the financial year—the figure required here being
profit or loss before deduction of any distributions but subject to accounting standards.[287]

Taking first the simpler, subsection (3) exemption, a company's annual accounts are defined in section      **15.408.04**
471 as, subject to this section, its individual accounts together with, if any, its group accounts. The
exemption in subsection (3) thus permits omission from these 'annual accounts' of the company's
individual profit and loss account. This is an important exemption since it is in relation only to the
annual accounts that the Act's requirements for audit, publication, laying (for public companies), and
delivery to the registrar apply.[288] Thus under this exemption there is no requirement for the company's
individual profit and loss account to be audited, published, laid (for public companies), or delivered to
the registrar.

It should be noted that the exemption is in respect only of *inclusion* of the parent company's own profit      **15.408.05**
and loss account in the annual accounts. Thus, the preparation and approval of that profit and loss
account is still required by subsection (3) and this matter should not be overlooked.

The subsection (3) exemption is available in respect both of Companies Act individual accounts and      **15.408.06**
IAS individual accounts.[289] Where the company prepares IAS accounts, the profit and loss account is
typically called something else-eg income statement or statement of comprehensive income. This is
acknowledged at section 474(1), which states that in relation to a company that prepares IAS accounts,
'profit and loss account' means an income statement or other equivalent financial statement required
to be prepared by EU-adopted IFRS. However, where the company prepares IAS individual accounts,
this section, taken together with section 397, presents a problem. Section 397 requires IAS individual
accounts to include a statement that those individual accounts are prepared in accordance with
EU-adopted IFRS.[290] EU-adopted IFRS do not permit the inclusion of a statement of compliance with
EU-adopted IFRS unless all of the requirements of EU-adopted IFRS are met;[291] and EU-adopted IFRS
would not be complied with in a set of accounts that did not include a profit and loss account. It
therefore appears that the section 397 statement cannot be made in relation to the incomplete
individual accounts included in the annual accounts. Rather, the statement should make clear that it is
in relation to individual accounts prepared by the directors—ie the complete individual
accounts[292]—albeit that a part thereof has been omitted from the version included within the annual
accounts.

---

[286] Companies Act 2006 (Commencement No 5, Transitional Provisions and Savings) Order 2007, SI
2007/3495, art 3(1) for financial years beginning on or after 6 April 2008.
[287] This is so because a distribution does not form part of the accounting profit or loss for the year. However,
under accounting standards—both UK standards and EU-adopted IFRS (the standards used for IAS individual
and group accounts)—certain shares are classified as liabilities of the company and distributions thereon are
classified as interest charges; such distributions are accounted for accounting purposes as deductions in arriving
at profit or loss for the financial year.
[288] See ss 475, 423 and 430, 437, and 441–447 respectively.
[289] See s 395.
[290] The customary name for the international accounting standards, defined in s 474, in accordance with
which IAS individual accounts are required to be prepared.
[291] For accounting periods beginning before 1 January 2009, see *IAS 1 Presentation of financial statements*
(International Accounting Standards Board, 2003, 2003, as amended; Commission Regulation (EC) No 1126/
2008 at [2008] OJ/L320/1, as amended, so stipulates at para 14. For accounting periods beginning on or after 1
January 2009, a revised version of IAS 1 applies although the requirement (para 16) is the same, see Commission
Regulation 2009 (EC) No 1274/2008 at [2008] OJ/L339/3, as amended.
[292] Since, as per subs (3), the individual profit and loss account must nevertheless be prepared and approved.

**15.408.07**    Accounting standards also require additional information to be presented as part of the profit and loss account or its IFRS equivalent.[293] This additional information is viewed as part of the profit and loss account, or a note thereto, and the exemption is available in respect of that additional information.

**15.408.08**    The exemption available in subsection (2) addresses the disclosures that would otherwise be required by section 411 in relation to employee numbers and costs. That section requires these figures in relation to the individual accounts and group accounts—ie unconsolidated and consolidated bases. However, this section 408 allows that the individual accounts disclosures are not required—ie not just that they need not be included in annual accounts, but that they need not even be included in the unpublished individual profit and loss account.

### *Information to be given in notes to the accounts*

### 409   Information about related undertakings

**15.409.01**    (1)  The Secretary of State may make provision by regulations requiring information about related undertakings to be given in notes to a company's annual accounts.

(2)  The regulations—
   (a)  may make different provision according to whether or not the company prepares group accounts, and
   (b)  may specify the descriptions of undertaking in relation to which they apply, and make different provision in relation to different descriptions of related undertaking.

(3)  The regulations may provide that information need not be disclosed with respect to an undertaking that—
   (a)  is established under the law of a country outside the United Kingdom, or
   (b)  carries on business outside the United Kingdom, if the following conditions are met.

(4)  The conditions are—
   (a)  that in the opinion of the directors of the company the disclosure would be seriously prejudicial to the business of—
      (i)   that undertaking,
      (ii)  the company,
      (iii) any of the company's subsidiary undertakings, or
      (iv)  any other undertaking which is included in the consolidation;
   (b)  that the Secretary of State agrees that the information need not be disclosed.

(5)  Where advantage is taken of any such exemption, that fact must be stated in a note to the company's annual accounts.

COMMENCEMENT DATE subsections (1) to (4), from 20 January 2007;[294] otherwise 6 April 2008[295]

**15.409.02**    This section and the following section deal with the disclosure of related undertakings in every set of annual accounts. It applies regardless of whether the individual accounts and any group accounts comprising the annual accounts are prepared as Companies Act or IAS individual or group accounts.

**15.409.03**    'Related undertakings' are not defined in the section. They are instead specified in regulations made under subsection (2)(b), which also provide the details to be disclosed.[296] The regulations[297] are in a form very similar to the Companies Act 1985's Schedule 5, the predecessor to this section. Broadly speaking, the regulations require disclosure in relation to a company's interests in certain other companies (simplifying somewhat, those where the interest is over 20 per cent) and in relation to the company's ultimate parent company and to certain group accounts in which the company is included. Where a company has subsidiary undertakings but does not prepare group accounts, as might be the

---

[293]  Under UK GAAP, companies are required to present a statement of total recognized gains and losses in addition to the profit and loss account: see FRS 3 *Reporting financial performance* (ASB, 1993; revised 1993 and 1999), para 27. Under EU-adopted IFRSs, companies may choose to adopt a 'two-statement' approach. When this approach is taken, the company will present, in addition to an income statement, a statement of comprehensive income: see IAS 1 *Presentation of financial statements* (IASB, 2003; revised 2007). See Commission Regulation (EC) 1274/2008 of 17 December 2008 amending Regulation (EC) 1126/2008 adopting certain international accounting standards in accordance with Regulation (EC) 1606/2002 as regards International Accounting Standard (IAS) 1 [2008] OJ L339/3 (as amended), para 81.

[294]  Companies Act 2006 (Commencement No 1, etc) Order 2006, SI 2006/3428, art 3(3).

[295]  Companies Act 2006 (Commencement No 5, Transitional Provisions and Savings) Order 2007, SI 2007/3495, art 3(1) for financial years beginning on or after 6 April 2008.

[296]  Subsection (1).

[297]  See the regulations referred to in para 15.396.03, nn 170 and 171.

case when a parent company falls within the small companies regime[298] under this Act, more extensive disclosures are required of the company's interests in its subsidiary undertaking.

Subsections (3) to (5) permit, in certain circumstances, non-disclosure of information relating to undertakings established outside the UK or carrying on a business overseas where the information—which is essentially of the ownership link between one undertaking and another—would in the opinion of the directors be seriously prejudicial to the business of any of the undertakings specified in subsection (4) and, most importantly, if the Secretary of State so agrees. Under section 729 of the 1985 Act, the DTI (now DBIS) published statistics regarding the applications made to it under miscellaneous provisions of the Companies Act 1985. According to those statistics, no exemptions were agreed by the Secretary of State as at 31 March 2006 with respect to applications made under section 231(3) of the 1985 Act, which was the predecessor to subsection (4).[299]   **15.409.04**

This section's disclosure is subject, in certain cases, to the derogation/alternative compliance offered by section 410.   **15.409.05**

## 410   Information about related undertakings: alternative compliance

(1) This section applies where the directors of a company are of the opinion that the number of undertakings in respect of which the company is required to disclose information under any provision of regulations under section 409 (related undertakings) is such that compliance with that provision would result in information of excessive length being given in notes to the company's annual accounts.   **15.410.01**

>   (2)   The information need only be given in respect of—
>     (a)   the undertakings whose results or financial position, in the opinion of the directors, principally affected the figures shown in the company's annual accounts, and
>     (b)   where the company prepares group accounts, undertakings excluded from consolidation under section 405(3) (undertakings excluded on grounds other than materiality).
>   (3)   If advantage is taken of subsection (2)—
>     (a)   there must be included in the notes to the company's annual accounts a statement that the information is given only with respect to such undertakings as are mentioned in that subsection, and
>     (b)   the full information (both that which is disclosed in the notes to the accounts and that which is not) must be annexed to the company's next annual return.
>   For this purpose the 'next annual return' means that next delivered to the registrar after the accounts in question have been approved under section 414.
>   (4)   If a company fails to comply with subsection (3)(b), an offence is committed by—
>     (a)   the company, and
>     (b)   every officer of the company who is in default.
>   (5)   A person guilty of an offence under subsection (4) is liable on summary conviction to a fine not exceeding level 3 on the standard scale and, for continued contravention, a daily default fine not exceeding one-tenth of level 3 on the standard scale.
>   COMMENCEMENT DATE   6 April 2008[300]

This section permits a company to reduce the number of related undertakings in relation to which disclosure in the annual accounts is required under section 409. This is a necessary relaxation: there are some parent companies that have many hundreds of related undertakings such that a disclosure running for many pages would otherwise be required.   **15.410.02**

Subsections (1) and (2) set out the basic requirement that, if in the opinion of the directors, the disclosure required by section 409 would be of excessive length, then the directors may choose to disclose information in relation only to those that they consider to be the principal related undertakings of the company and to those material undertakings that, if the company prepares group accounts, have been excluded from the consolidation.[301] The latter requirement is presumably on the grounds that such exclusion may be noteworthy.   **15.410.03**

If this exemption is taken, a full list of related undertakings, and the required information, must be annexed to the next annual return delivered to the registrar[302] and the fact of exemption must be   **15.410.04**

---

[298]   See ss 381–384.
[299]   *Companies in 2005–2006* (DTI, 2006), p 27.
[300]   Companies Act 2006 (Commencement No 5, Transitional Provisions and Savings) Order 2007, SI 2007/3495, art 3(1) for financial years beginning on or after 6 April 2008.
[301]   See s 405 for exclusion of subsidiary undertakings from consolidation.
[302]   See s 854.

disclosed in the annual accounts.[303] Neither of these requirements should be overlooked and an offence is committed if the requirements of subsection (3) is not complied with.[304]

## [410A   Information about off-balance sheet arrangements

**15.410A.01**

(1)  In the case of a company that is not subject to the small companies regime, if in any financial year—
   (a)  the company is or has been party to arrangements that are not reflected in its balance sheet, and
   (b)  at the balance sheet date the risks or benefits arising from those arrangements are material, the information required by this section must be given in notes to the company's annual accounts.

(2)  The information required is—
   (a)  the nature and business purpose of the arrangements, and
   (b)  the financial impact of the arrangements on the company.

(3)  The information need only be given to the extent necessary for enabling the financial position of the company to be assessed.

(4)  If the company qualifies as medium-sized in relation to the financial year (see sections 465 to 467) it need not comply with subsection (2)(b).

(5)  This section applies in relation to group accounts as if the undertakings included in the consolidation were a single company.][a]

AMENDMENTS

[a]  Inserted by the Companies Act 2006 (Amendment) (Accounts and Reports) Regulations 2008, SI 2008/393, reg 8.

COMMENCEMENT DATE  6 April 2008[305]

**15.410A.02**   This new section is derived from changes made to the Fourth and Seventh Directives [306] by Directive (EC) 2006/46,[307] and makes provision for disclosure requirements relating to off-balance sheet arrangements. It applies to all companies, irrespective of whether they prepare Companies Act or IAS accounts,[308] other than those in the small companies regime; the disclosures are relaxed slightly for companies able to take advantage of exemptions for medium-sized companies.

**15.410A.03**   No clear definition is given in the Directive or in this Act of an off-balance sheet arrangement. This section provides only a general indication, ie that it refers to arrangements not reflected on the company's balance sheet and for which the risks and benefits are material.[309] However, in providing guidance on this matter,[310] DBERR (now DBIS) has stated that one of the Directive's goals is to increase transparency in off-balance sheet arrangements, and referred to recital (9) of Directive 2006/46 for examples of the types of transaction that might be caught by this requirement.[311] Recital (9) says:

> Such off-balance-sheet arrangements could be any transactions or agreements which companies may have with entities, even unincorporated ones, that are not included in the balance sheet. Such off-balance-sheet arrangements may be associated with the creation or use of one or more Special Purpose Entities (SPEs) and offshore activities designed to address, inter alia, economic, legal, tax or accounting objectives. Examples of such off-balance-sheet arrangements include risk and benefit-sharing arrangements or obligations arising from a contract such as debt factoring, combined sale and repurchase agreements, consignment stock arrangements, take or pay arrangements, securitization

---

[303]  Subsection (3).

[304]  Subsection (4).

[305]  Companies Act 2006 (Amendment) (Accounts and Reports) Regulations 2008, SI 2008/393 reg 2(2) for financial years beginning on or after 6 April 2008.

[306]  Directive (EEC) 78/660 [1978] OJ L222/11, as amended; and Directive (EEC) 83/349 [1983] OJ L193/1, as amended.

[307]  At [2006] OJ/L224/1

[308]  See ss 396 and 397.

[309]  Subsection (1)(a), (b)

[310]  *Guidance for UK companies on accounting and reporting: Requirements under the Companies Act 2006 and the application of the IAS Regulation* (DBERR, 2008), para 5.10.

[311]  The Urgent Issues Task Force (UIFT) made a similar observation in its press notice dated 30 June 2008. Until July 2012 The Urgent Issues Task Force (UITF) was a committee of the then Accounting Standards Board (ASB) that assisted the ASB in areas where an accounting standard or Companies Act provision existed but where unsatisfactory or conflicting interpretations had developed or seemed likely to develop. If the UITF reached a consensus on such an issue, the ASB published an abstract of the consensus, and this had the same authority as an accounting standard issued by the ASB. Press notices, such as referred to here, had no official standing.

arranged through separate companies and unincorporated entities, pledged assets, operating leasing arrangements, outsourcing and the like. Appropriate disclosure of the material risks and benefits of such arrangements that are not included in the balance sheet should be set out in the notes to the accounts or the consolidated accounts.

Turning to the requirements, section 410A applies where two conditions are met. The first is that **15.410A.04** that arrangement is 'not reflected in its balance sheet', indicating that an arrangement that results in any asset or a liability in the balance sheet would be outside the scope of this section. Thus, lease arrangements and special purpose vehicles are outside these disclosure requirements when they are brought on to the balance sheet (typically, by application of accounting standards). The second condition is that the risks and benefits are material, which will require the directors to apply judgment in assessing this matter.

In meeting the disclosure requirements, it is likely that accounting standards—and for Companies Act **15.410A.05** accounts, the regulations made under section 396(3)—will capture many off-balance sheet arrangements, requiring either recognition in the balance sheet or some measure of disclosure. Nevertheless, there will be arrangements which are not caught by either the recognition or disclosure requirements of accounting standards. Some of these arrangements will, no doubt, be complicated, and could involve special purchase vehicles. However, as indicated above in the extract from the Directive, the scope of these requirements may include some commonplace arrangements that hitherto have not been considered off-balance sheet arrangements at all, such as some outsourcings, and hence not disclosed. Whilst it is not possible here to set out the wide variety of arrangements that are found in practice that might qualify as off-balance sheet arrangements under section 410A, directors should consider these requirements when preparing accounts.

The disclosure requirements themselves are high-level requirements calling for information as to the **15.410A.06** arrangement, its business purpose, and the financial effect; the information is required only to the extent necessary to enable the financial position of the company to be assessed. As noted above, many off-balance sheet arrangements will also fall within the disclosure requirements of accounting standards. However, it should not be overlooked that section 410A may address more arrangements and may require more disclosure for an arrangement, than do accounting standards.

Where group (consolidated) accounts are prepared, subsection (5) requires that the undertakings **15.410A.07** included in the consolidation are treated as a single company. That is to say, where annual accounts include group accounts as well as individual accounts, then disclosure is given on both the group and individual bases.

## 411   Information about employee numbers and costs

(1) In the case of a company not subject to the small companies regime, the following information **15.411.01** with respect to the employees of the company must be given in notes to the company's annual accounts—

   (a)   the average number of persons employed by the company in the financial year, and
   (b)   the average number of persons so employed within each category of persons employed by the company.

(2)   The categories by reference to which the number required to be disclosed by subsection (1)(b) is to be determined must be such as the directors may select having regard to the manner in which the company's activities are organised.

(3)   The average number required by subsection (1)(a) or (b) is determined by dividing the relevant annual number by the number of months in the financial year.

(4)   The relevant annual number is determined by ascertaining for each month in the financial year—
   (a)   for the purposes of subsection (1)(a), the number of persons employed under contracts of service by the company in that month (whether throughout the month or not);
   (b)   for the purposes of subsection (1)(b), the number of persons in the category in question of persons so employed; and adding together all the monthly numbers.

(5)   In respect of all persons employed by the company during the financial year who are taken into account in determining the relevant annual number for the purposes of subsection (1)(a) there must also be stated the aggregate amounts respectively of—
   (a)   wages and salaries paid or payable in respect of that year to those persons;
   (b)   social security costs incurred by the company on their behalf; and
   (c)   other pension costs so incurred.
   This does not apply in so far as those amounts, or any of them, are stated elsewhere in the company's accounts.

(6) In subsection (5)—

'pension costs' includes any costs incurred by the company in respect of—

(a) any pension scheme established for the purpose of providing pensions for persons currently or formerly employed by the company,

(b) any sums set aside for the future payment of pensions directly by the company to current or former employees, and

(c) any pensions paid directly to such persons without having first been set aside;

'social security costs' means any contributions by the company to any state social security or pension scheme, fund or arrangement.

(7) [This section applies in relation to group accounts][a] as if the undertakings included in the consolidation were a single company.

AMENDMENTS

[a] Inserted by the Companies Act 2006 (Amendment) (Accounts and Reports) Regulations 2008, SI 2008/393, reg 11.

COMMENCEMENT DATE 6 April 2008[312]

**15.411.02** This section does not apply to companies subject to the small companies regime. For other companies it applies regardless of whether the individual accounts and any group accounts comprising the annual accounts are prepared as Companies Act or IAS individual or group accounts.[313]

**15.411.03** The employee numbers disclosures are required by subsection (1) to be made in the annual accounts, which comprise the individual accounts and any group accounts.[314] The requirements of subsections (1) to (6) are in terms of the company's employees and thus require individual accounts figures. Subsection (7) specifies the basis of disclosure in relation to any group accounts included in the annual accounts; it specifies that the section applies as if the undertakings included in the consolidation were a single company—ie a group basis of disclosure. In practice, in a case where there are group accounts, the group basis is the only basis that need be calculated and disclosed. This arises because where group accounts are prepared, advantage is almost always taken of the section 408(2) exemption from providing these disclosures in the parent's individual profit and loss account.

**15.411.04** Few problems generally arise in practice with respect to these disclosure requirements. However, some matters merit remark. The first relates to part-time employees. By virtue of the calculation method set out in subsection (4), a part-time employee counts fully towards the average staff number as the calculation is in fact one of the average number of contracts of service. As a practical matter, many companies with large numbers of part-time staff voluntarily disclose *additional* figures for the average full-time equivalent staff numbers, so as to provide data that is consistent with staff costs disclosed under subsection (5).

**15.411.05** Second, in calculating employee numbers where group accounts are prepared, the calculation is performed 'as if the undertakings included in the consolidation were a single company'. Thus, where an employee is employed by a number of companies in the group, he would be counted only once for the purpose of disclosures under this section, rather than the section aggregating the figures for each group member (in which he would count as a part-time employee more than once).[315]

**15.411.06** The status of non-executive directors will have to be considered carefully. In most cases, these directors are contracted under a contract *for* services[316] and are not, therefore, within the disclosures.

**15.411.07** The requirement of subsection (1)(b) to analyse the staff numbers by category invites consideration. Subsection (2) provides that these categories should be determined by the directors after 'having regard to the manner in which the company's activities are organised'. In practice, this requirement has been interpreted broadly and a number of different approaches have been adopted, including disclosure by business unit (ie according to segments identified under accounting standards on segmental analysis of results and position), disclosure by function (administrative, sales, and marketing), and, for some international firms, by country of employment.

**15.411.08** The costs disclosures of subsections (5) and (6) address the aggregate amounts in respect of wages and salaries, social security costs, and pension costs. These disclosures should be given on an accruals basis, as indicated by the reference in subsection (5)(a) for wages and salaries 'paid and payable'. The determination of pension costs for accounting purposes, which then fall to be disclosed, is a complex

---

[312] Companies Act 2006 (Commencement No 5, Transitional Provisions and Savings) Order 2007, SI 2007/3495, art 3(1) for financial years beginning on or after 6 April 2008.

[313] See ss 395 and 403.

[314] See s 471.

[315] Cf ss 383 and 466 in relation to employee numbers for qualification for small or medium-sized companies.

[316] Not a contract *of* service, as required by subs (4)(a).

matter for final-salary type schemes and is handled in detail by the relevant accounting standard.[317] The relevant accounting standard will be determined by reference to whichever accounting framework[318] has been chosen for the individual accounts, in addition to amounts for the company alone, or for the group accounts in relation to consolidated figures.

Finally, subsection (5) provides that the cost disclosures are not required 'in so far as those amounts, or    **15.411.09** any of them, are stated elsewhere in the company's accounts'. This provision is meant to apply when a particular format of the profit and loss account[319] is used, which gives the information required by subsection (5), as there is little to be gained from duplicating the disclosure.

## 412  Information about directors' benefits: remuneration

(1)  The Secretary of State may make provision by regulations requiring information to be given in      **15.412.01** notes to a company's annual accounts about directors' remuneration.

(2)  The matters about which information may be required include—
  (a)  gains made by directors on the exercise of share options;
  (b)  benefits received or receivable by directors under long-term incentive schemes;
  (c)  payments for loss of office (as defined in section 215);
  (d)  benefits receivable, and contributions for the purpose of providing benefits, in respect of past services of a person as director or in any other capacity while director;
  (e)  consideration paid to or receivable by third parties for making available the services of a person as director or in any other capacity while director.

(3)  Without prejudice to the generality of subsection (1), regulations under this section may make any such provision as was made immediately before the commencement of this Part by Part 1 of Schedule 6 to the Companies Act 1985 (c. 6).

(4)  For the purposes of this section, and regulations made under it, amounts paid to or receivable by—
  (a)  a person connected with a director, or
  (b)  a body corporate controlled by a director, are treated as paid to or receivable by the director. The expressions 'connected with' and 'controlled by' in this subsection have the same meaning as in Part 10 (company directors).

(5)  It is the duty of—
  (a)  any director of a company, and
  (b)  any person who is or has at any time in the preceding five years been a director of the company, to give notice to the company of such matters relating to himself as may be necessary for the purposes of regulations under this section.

(6)  A person who makes default in complying with subsection (5) commits an offence and is liable on summary conviction to a fine not exceeding level 3 on the standard scale. Commencement Date subsections (1) to (3) from 20 January 2007;[320] otherwise 6 April 2008[321]

This section makes provision for the disclosure of directors' remuneration in the annual accounts. It      **15.412.02** applies to all companies. It applies regardless of whether the individual accounts and any group accounts comprising the annual accounts are prepared as Companies Act or IAS individual or group accounts.[322]

The section does not itself effect any annual accounts disclosure requirement. It simply gives the       **15.412.03** Secretary of State power to make regulations that do so. Regulations have been made in the form of the predecessor requirements of Part I of Schedule 6 to the 1985 Act, and this is specifically adverted to in subsection (3)[323] One anti-avoidance provision of the former Schedule 6 has, however, been reenacted in this section itself: subsection (4) provides that amounts paid to or receivable by a person connected with a director or a body corporate controlled by a director[324] are attributed to the director concerned for these disclosures.

---

[317]  *FRS 17 Retirement benefits* (ASB, 2000); or *IAS 19 Employee benefits* (International Accounting Standards Board, 2003, revised 2011); see Commission Regulation (EC) No 1126/2008 at [2008] OJ/L320/1, as amended.

[318]  See ss 395 and 403.

[319]  Regulations under ss 396(3) and 404(3) (see nns 1 and 2 to para 15.396.03) provide a format for the profit and loss account (called format 2) that includes these costs on the face of the profit and loss account.

[320]  Companies Act 2006 (Commencement No 1, etc) Order 2006, SI 2006/3428, art 3(3).

[321]  Companies Act 2006 (Commencement No 5, Transitional Provisions and Savings) Order 2007, SI 2007/3495, art 3(1) for financial years beginning on or after 6 April 2008.

[322]  See ss 395 and 403.

[323]  See the regulations referred to in nn 170 and 171 to para 15.396.03.

[324]  See ss 252 to 255.

**15.412.04**    The regulations made under this section, however, are much less detailed than the requirement upon a quoted company[325] for a directors' remuneration report under sections 420 to 422. However, quoted companies must comply with this section and with sections 420 to 422. In order to avoid duplication of disclosure, a common practice is for quoted companies to make modest format changes to the directors' remuneration report so as to incorporate Schedule 6's lesser disclosures and then to cross refer from the annual accounts to that report, thereby fulfilling their obligations under this section.

**15.412.05**    Subsection (5) requires a director and certain past directors to notify the company of any matter relating to himself as may be necessary for the purposes of complying with the regulations. This provision is needed because information concerning directors' remuneration may not be known by the company, in particular, the Accounts and Reports Regulations[326] required disclosure of remuneration paid to a director, in respect of services to the company, by third parties. Subsection (5) provides that this disclosure obligation continues for five years after the director leaves office because, for example, the Accounts and Reports Regulations required disclosure of certain retirement benefits and compensation of past directors. Failure by a director to comply with these provisions is an offence as provided by subsection (6).

### 413  Information about directors' benefits: advances, credit and guarantees

**15.413.01**
(1) In the case of a company that does not prepare group accounts, details of—
   (a) advances and credits granted by the company to its directors, and
   (b) guarantees of any kind entered into by the company on behalf of its directors, must be shown in the notes to its individual accounts.
(2) In the case of a parent company that prepares group accounts, details of—
   (a) advances and credits granted to the directors of the parent company, by that company or by any of its subsidiary undertakings, and
   (b) guarantees of any kind entered into on behalf of the directors of the parent company, by that company or by any of its subsidiary undertakings, must be shown in the notes to the group accounts.
(3) The details required of an advance or credit are—
   (a) its amount,
   (b) an indication of the interest rate,
   (c) its main conditions, and
   (d) any amounts repaid.
(4) The details required of a guarantee are—
   (a) its main terms,
   (b) the amount of the maximum liability that may be incurred by the company (or its subsidiary), and
   (c) any amount paid and any liability incurred by the company (or its subsidiary) for the purpose of fulfilling the guarantee (including any loss incurred by reason of enforcement of the guarantee).
(5) There must also be stated in the notes to the accounts the totals—
   (a) of amounts stated under subsection (3)(a),
   (b) of amounts stated under subsection (3)(d),
   (c) of amounts stated under subsection (4)(b), and
   (d) of amounts stated under subsection (4)(c).
(6) References in this section to the directors of a company are to the persons who were a director at any time in the financial year to which the accounts relate.
(7) The requirements of this section apply in relation to every advance, credit or guarantee subsisting at any time in the financial year to which the accounts relate—
   (a) whenever it was entered into,
   (b) whether or not the person concerned was a director of the company in question at the time it was entered into, and
   (c) in the case of an advance, credit or guarantee involving a subsidiary undertaking of that company, whether or not that undertaking was such a subsidiary undertaking at the time it was entered into.
(8) Banking companies and the holding companies of credit institutions need only state the details required by [subsection (5)(a) and (5)(c)].[327]

---

[325]  See s 385.
[326]  See the regulations referred to in nn 170 and 171 to para 15.396.03.
[327]  Inserted by the Companies Act 2006 (Amendment of Section 413) Regulations 2009, SI 2009/3022, reg 2, for financial years ending on or after 23 December 2009.

COMMENCEMENT DATE  6 April 2008[328]

Part 10 of this Act determines whether a company may enter into certain transactions with a director    **15.413.02**
of the company or with certain other persons (its holding company's directors or connected persons).
This section provides for disclosure in the annual accounts of certain transactions, albeit using
different terminology, with directors (regardless of whether those transactions are lawfully made
under Part 10).

Within Part 10, sections 197 to 214 of this Act determine whether a company may make a loan or    **15.413.03**
quasi-loan to, or enter into a credit transaction for the benefit of, a director[329] of the company; and
whether the company may give a guarantee or provide security in connection with such a transaction;
or whether the company may enter into such transactions, guarantees, or provision of security for a
director of the company's holding company,[330] for a person connected[331] with a director of the
company or for a person connected with a director of the company's holding company. The applicability of the rules varies depending on whether the company is, or is associated with, a public company.
Section 211 defines the value of such transactions for the purposes of the financial limits applying
under those sections in certain cases. This section 413 is not, however, consistent in its construction or
language with those earlier sections.[332]

The commentary that follows later deals in turn with each of this section's transaction types, persons    **15.413.04**
involved, and disclosure details. However, before embarking upon that, three further background
points should be noted. First, this section replaces the disclosure requirements of Parts II and III of
Schedule 6 to the 1985 Act and results in a narrowing down of disclosure, in particular in respect of the
persons with whom transactions fall to be disclosed, but also due to the lack of disclosure requirements
in this section for other transactions or arrangements in which a director has a material interest; Parts
II and III of Schedule 6 were written in what was often criticized as, for the layman, overly technical and
perhaps abstruse language; the text of this section is, in comparison, considerably simpler but at times
not as precise as the former requirements. In that regard, it is worth noting that terminology used in,
and requirements of, this section appears to be a reimplementation of the relevant provisions in the EC
Fourth and Seventh Company Law Directives[333] in a form much more akin to a straight 'copy out' of
the Directives than hitherto. It can be inferred that the requirements of this section are intended to
conform to the minimum required by EC legislation.[334]

Secondly, the effect of accounting standards[335] is to supplement this section's disclosures. This in effect    **15.413.05**
broadens out again the disclosure beyond the narrow range of persons within this section and to other
transactions and arrangements.

Thirdly, the Act makes separate provision for the disclosure of certain forms of indemnity given for the    **15.413.06**
benefit of a director against third party claims—qualifying third party indemnity provisions under
section 234 and qualifying pension scheme indemnity provisions under section 235. Disclosure of such
arrangements is required by section 236 to be made in the directors' report.

Turning to the transaction types covered by this section, they are advances, credits, and guarantees of    **15.413.07**
any kind. These terms are not defined in the Act. Nevertheless, it appears that the terms 'advances' and
'credits' capture many transactions. An 'advance' would appear to cover any arrangement under which
funds are made available. A 'credit' is, arguably given normal commercial usage, a transaction in which
a director receives credit. It seems therefore that the full range of loans, quasi-loans, and credit
transactions will be caught by these disclosure requirements. Specific examples might include mortgage loans, advances to cover business expenses, or advance payment of remuneration.

---

[328]  Companies Act 2006 (Commencement No 5, Transitional Provisions and Savings) Order 2007, SI
2007/3495, art 3(1) for financial years beginning on or after 6 April 2008.
[329]  See s 199 (meaning of 'quasi loan' and related expressions), s 202 (meaning of 'credit transactions'), and s
250 (meaning of 'director').
[330]  See s 1159.
[331]  See s 1159 (holding company) and s 254 (directors 'connected with' a body corporate).
[332]  At the time of writing the Government is consulting on whether to revise the section to become more
consistent in that regard. See *Disclosure of loans to directors in company accounts* (DBIS, 2009).
[333]  Fourth Company Law Directive (EEC) 78/660 [1978] OJ L222/11 (as amended), Art 43(13); EC Seventh
Company Law Directive (EEC) 83/349 [1985] OJ L193/1 (as amended), Art 34(13).
[334]  The consultation noted at n 314 to para 15.413.03 also covers the question of whether to extend the
requirements beyond the EC minimum.
[335]  *FRS 8 Related party disclosures* (ASB, 1995, as amended); *IAS 24 Related party disclosures* (International
Accounting Standards Board, 2003, as revised 2011); see Commission Regulation (EC) No 1126/2008 at [2008]
OJ/L320/1, as amended).

**15.413.08**  'Guarantee' is not defined. However, given the words 'guarantee or provide security' in, for example, section 197(1), it appears not to encompass the provision of security, not withstanding that the commercial effect of providing security is close to that of giving a guarantee. In addition, a guarantee does not include an indemnity.[336]

**15.413.09**  To be within the disclosure requirement an advance, credit, or guarantee, *inter alia*, need only have subsisted at any time during the financial year[337] between persons within the scope of the section during the financial year. This is regardless of whether the transaction was originally entered at an earlier time and regardless of whether the parties to the transaction would at that earlier time have been within the scope of the section.

**15.413.10**  Turning to the parties to the transaction, the first point to address is the party that grants the advance or credit, or that enters into the guarantee (called hereafter, for convenience, the 'lender/guarantor'). This differs depending upon the form of accounts. If only individual accounts are prepared, the lender/guarantor must be the company. If group accounts are prepared, the lender/guarantor must be the company or any of its subsidiary undertakings.[338]

**15.413.11**  The other party to the transaction must be a director of the company at any time during the financial year. So, for example, if a person resigned as a director during the financial year and a relevant transaction occurred with him during the financial year but after his resignation, nevertheless it is within the disclosure requirement. The term 'director' does not include a shadow director.[339]

**15.413.12**  When the transaction in question is an advance or credit the disclosure applies if the advance or credit is from the lender to a director. When the transaction in question is a guarantee it must be made by the guarantor 'on behalf of a director'. This language is somewhat curious. One might normally speak of a guarantor's giving a guarantee to a principal debtor in relation to his debt receivable. For example, section 197(1) addresses 'a guarantee ... in connection with a loan ... to ... a director'. This section's language differs and closely follows that of the above-mentioned Directives. However, these were hitherto implemented by the 1985 Act as, for example, 'guarantee in connection with a loan made by any person to such a director'.[340] If it can be assumed that the previous legislation was a proper implementation of the Directives, then it may be surmised that the effect of the Directive's language, as now employed in this section, is the same as hitherto. That is to say, a guarantee on behalf of a director must refer to a guarantee of the performance of a director in a transaction between the director and a third party, for example the company's guaranteeing a loan payable by a director to a third party.

**15.413.13**  To conclude, in relation to the transacting parties, it will be readily apparent that the disclosures never apply where the transacting party is not a director, for example where he is a person connected with a director; nor do they ever apply where the lender/guarantor is not the company but is a parent undertaking or fellow subsidiary undertaking of the company.

**15.413.14**  Moving on to the required details in subsections (3) and (4), first of all it is clear that separate disclosure should be made for each advance, credit, and guarantee, and that there is no requirement to name the director to whom the disclosure relates.

**15.413.15**  For the most part the required details under subsections (3) and (4) do not raise any issues. However, the requirements of subsection (3)(a) and (d) merit attention. When an advance or credit subsists over a number of years with progressive repayments the necessary disclosure is not immediately clear. An example might be a mortgage loan where a substantial sum would have been lent perhaps a decade or more ago and the balance will now be much reduced. Is the appropriate disclosure the original advance and the cumulative repayment to date? In most practical cases of mortgage loans the company concerned is likely to be a banking company, or the holding company of a credit institution.[341] In such a case subsection (8) requires less detailed disclosure; all that need be given are aggregate amounts—that is, director by director disclosure is not required of advance or credit amounts and the

---

[336] For example s 677(1)(b) (financial assistance in relation to the acquisition of shares) makes mention of indemnities separately from guarantees. The distinction depends essentially on whether the liability of the party under a guarantee or indemnity is primary or secondary. It is a guarantee if liability is secondary, that is, it is dependent on failure of the debtor to pay; see eg *Yeoman Credit Ltd v Latimer* [1961] 2 All ER 294 at 296. That said, the distinction may be easier to state than to apply. For discussion, see Goode, *Legal Problems of Credit and Security* (3rd edn, 2003), Chap 8.

[337] See s 390.

[338] See s 1162.

[339] See ss 250 and 251.

[340] CA 1985, Sch 6, paras 15(a) and 16(a) required disclosure in relation to any arrangement of a kind set out in that Act's s 330 which, for example, referred to guarantees of loans in the form quoted above.

[341] See s 1164 (banking company), s 1159 (holding company), and s 1173 (credit institution).

maximum liability under guarantees.[342] (It is commonplace for such companies to enter into lending arrangements with their employees, either on an arm's length basis or subsidized. As a result, disclosure might otherwise be unnecessarily lengthy and of no great import.) Nevertheless, a question remains as to what subsection (3)(a) means. If it were the case that subsection (3)(a) required disclosures of the original loan amount this would result in a disclosure of little relevance or utility as it would be disconnected from the directors' indebtedness during and at the end of the financial year. Once again implementation of the Directives in the predecessor legislation may be of assistance. The Directives are similarly unclear as to the point in time at which the advance amount, for example, is to be computed; the 1985 Act implemented them by requiring disclosure of the balances at the beginning and end of the financial year and of the maximum balance.[343]

## Approval and signing of accounts

### 414  Approval and signing of accounts[a]

(1)  A company's annual accounts must be approved by the board of directors and signed on behalf of the board by a director of the company.                                              **15.414.01**

(2)  The signature must be on the company's balance sheet.

(3)  If the accounts are prepared in accordance with the provisions applicable to companies subject to the small companies regime, the balance sheet must contain a statement to that effect in a prominent position above the signature.

(4)  If annual accounts are approved that do not comply with the requirements of this Act (and, where applicable, of Article 4 of the IAS Regulation), every director of the company who—

    (a)  knew that they did not comply, or was reckless as to whether they complied, and

    (b)  failed to take reasonable steps to secure compliance with those requirements or, as the case may be, to prevent the accounts from being approved, commits an offence.

(5)  A person guilty of an offence under this section is liable—

    (a)  on conviction on indictment, to a fine;

    (b)  on summary conviction, to a fine not exceeding the statutory maximum.

AMENDMENTS AND NOTES

[a]  This section applies with modifications to overseas companies by reg 39 of the Overseas Companies Regulations 2009, 2009/1801.

COMMENCEMENT DATE  6 April 2008[344]

This section makes provision for the approval and signature of the annual accounts. It applies to all companies. It applies regardless of whether the individual accounts and any group accounts comprising the annual accounts are prepared as Companies Act or IAS individual or group accounts.[345]                **15.414.02**

The approval is by the board collectively but the signature, on the company's balance sheet, is by a director on behalf of the board.[346] The section does not require the signature to be accompanied by the date of approval. However, the date of approval is a significant matter in terms of accounting, and thus the date of approval (and the identification of the body approving the accounts) is required by accounting standards to be disclosed.[347] The practice is therefore for the signature at the foot of the balance sheet to be preceded by a statement to the effect that the annual accounts were approved by the board, with the date disclosed, and that they were signed on its behalf by the director concerned. This also provides clarity, for a reader of the balance sheet, that it is the board collectively that is approving the annual accounts rather than solely the signing director.                **15.414.03**

Subsection (3) requires a specific statement to be made on the balance sheet if the annual accounts have been prepared under the small companies regime. Section 475 contains a similar, related requirement. Where, under that section, a company takes advantage of the exemption from audit (some, but not necessarily all, companies within the small companies regime may be in this position), it is required to include on the balance sheet a statement to that effect, and a statement by the directors acknowledging                **15.414.04**

---

[342]  For financing years ending before 23 December 2009, owing to a drafting error in the legislation, banking companies and holding companies of credit institutions are required to disclose individual advance or credit amounts and the maximum liability under each individual guarantee. This error has been corrected by the Companies Act 2006 (Amendment of Section 413) Regulations 2009, SI 2009/3022.

[343]  CA 1985, Sch 6, para 22(2)(d).

[344]  Companies Act 2006 (Commencement No 5,Transitional Provisions and Savings) Order 2007, SI 2007/3495, art 3(1) for financial years beginning on or after 6 April 2008.

[345]  See ss 395 and 403.

[346]  Subsection (1).

[347]  FRS 21 *Events after the balance sheet date* (ASB, 2004) para 17; IAS 10 *Events after the balance sheet date* (IASB, 2003, as amended), adopted by the European Commission [2004], see Commission Regulation (EC) No 1126/2008 at [2008] OJ/L320/1, as amended, para 17.

their responsibility to ensure that the annual accounts and accounting records comply with the Act. These statements are required to appear above the signature.

**15.414.05** It should be noted that only one director is required to sign although it is common practice, particularly among quoted companies, for two directors to sign. This is, of course, entirely acceptable; indeed, the whole board could sign the balance sheet if they so desired.

**15.414.06** The balance sheet on which the signature is required to appear is 'the company's balance sheet'. This is the individual accounts balance sheet.[348] However, it is common practice for both the individual and group accounts balance sheets to be signed. Where the individual and group accounts are prepared under different accounting frameworks—typically as Companies Act individual accounts and IAS group accounts—arguably both ought as a matter of accounting practice to include approval/dating statements and signatures. This is because they are prepared under separate accounting frameworks and so each ought *separately* to comply with the requirements of the respective accounting standards to state the date of approval and the body by which the accounts were approved. In addition, where auditors issue separate reports on Companies Act individual accounts and IAS group accounts contained within annual accounts,[349] they are likely to insist that their clients include a separate approval/dating statement in each of the individual and group accounts.

**15.414.07** For some companies the FSA's Disclosure and Transparency Rules (DTR) make provisions related to the approval of the annual accounts. Put simply, these rules apply to companies with transferable securities admitted to trading on a regulated market;[350] and require a 'responsibility statement' by those responsible within the company, which would normally be the company's board. The responsibility statement must contain the following assertions: that the financial statements give a true and fair view of the assets, liabilities, financial position, and profit and loss of the company and the undertakings included in the consolidation taken as a whole.[351]

**15.414.08** It would be open to a company to combine such a statement with the approval statement, but as yet there seems little sign of such a practice after the recent introduction of this rule in the DTR.[352]

**15.414.09** Where accounts are approved that do not comply with the requirements of the Act or of Article 4 of the IAS Regulation,[353] each director who knew they did not comply or was reckless as to whether they complied and did not take reasonable steps to secure compliance commits an offence. An example might be where the directors are told by the auditor he will qualify his report if the directors prepare the annual accounts using a particular accounting treatment, but the directors nevertheless go ahead and a court subsequently finds the annual accounts to be defective. More generally, as with the case of the offences in connection with audit reports,[354] there is a practical concern for directors as to the meaning of 'reckless' in this context and what conduct will amount to recklessness.

**15.414.10** In terms of the civil consequences of defective annual accounts, whilst there is no express authority on the point, it is sometimes suggested[355] that under common law the directors owe a duty of care, and can be liable for negligence, in the same way as auditors under the so-called *Caparo* rule. Briefly put, there is no general duty of care to individual members or to members of the public at large, in particular in respect of a decision to invest in the company; there is only a general duty to the actual members, as a body, in respect of their governance rights. In addition, however, if the company has securities admitted to trading on a securities market, section 90A of the Financial Services and Markets Act 2000[356] makes provision for the company to compensate third parties in relation to losses sustained in reliance on untrue or misleading statements or omissions in the annual accounts published pursuant

---

[348] S 394 requires 'accounts for the company', which are the individual accounts.
[349] See the commentary on s 485.
[350] Having the same meaning as at s 1173 of this Act.
[351] For the scope of these rules see DTR 4.1.1R and 4.4.2R; for the responsibility statement see DTR 4.1.12R.
[352] The requirements of the DTR apply to financial years beginning on or after 20 January 2007.
[353] See s 403(1).This addresses cases where the IAS Regulation applies directly and so requires IAS group accounts. Where the company prepares IAS individual accounts or IAS group accounts as a matter of choice under ss 395(1) or 403(2) respectively, then it is compliance with the Act that in turn requires compliance with the IAS Regulation.
[354] See s 507.
[355] For example see para 2.11 of *Issue 76—Transparency obligations directive* (Financial Markets Law Committee, 2004).
[356] From 1 October 2010, the scope of section 90A (further to the Financial Services and Markets Act 2000 (Liability of Issuers) Regulations 2010, SI 2010/1192) has been extended to apply to any issuer with securities that, with the consent of the issuer, are admitted to trading on a market i) situated or operating in the United Kingdom, or ii) that has the UK as its home state. 'Securities market' means a regulated market, a multilateral trading facility (MTF) or a market or facility of a corresponding description outside the EEA (FSMA, Sch 10, para 8(1)(b). This contrasts with the previous version of section 90A (before 1 October 2010) that applied only to companies that

to the DTR. If the company sustained a loss under that provision then it would appear that the company may have a right of action, under *Caparo* principles, against its directors particularly given the test in section 90A(4) of that Act requiring knowledge on the part of a director as to the untrue or misleading statement or omission.

## CHAPTER 5
## DIRECTORS' REPORT

*Directors' report*

### 415   Duty to prepare directors' report

(1) The directors of a company must prepare a directors' report for each financial year of the company.   **15.415.01**

(2) For a financial year in which—
    (a) the company is a parent company, and
    (b) the directors of the company prepare group accounts,
    the directors' report must be a consolidated report (a 'group directors' report') relating to the undertakings included in the consolidation.

(3) A group directors' report may, where appropriate, give greater emphasis to the matters that are significant to the undertakings included in the consolidation, taken as a whole.

(4) In the case of failure to comply with the requirement to prepare a directors' report, an offence is committed by every person who—
    (a) was a director of the company immediately before the end of the period for filing accounts and reports for the financial year in question, and
    (b) failed to take all reasonable steps for securing compliance with that requirement.

(5) A person guilty of an offence under this section is liable—
    (a) on conviction on indictment, to a fine;
    (b) on summary conviction, to a fine not exceeding the statutory maximum.

COMMENCEMENT DATE   6 April 2008[357]

Under this section all companies are required to prepare a directors' report. Where a company prepares group accounts the directors' report must deal with the company and the undertakings included in the consolidation.[358] This is in contrast to the requirements for accounts. A company preparing group accounts will also at the same time prepare individual accounts. The directors' report, however, is a single report in all cases. Moreover, by virtue of subsection (3) the report need not deal with matters of significance to the company alone to the same depth with which it deals with matters that are significant to the company and the undertakings included in the consolidation as a whole.   **15.415.02**

The requirements for the contents of the directors' report are spread among sections 416 to 418, in regulations made under section 416(4) and in section 236. Section 416, broadly speaking, requires information about the directors and a collection of other matters as may be stipulated by regulations (eg creditor payment policy is required by regulations made under section 416). Section 417 requires a review of the company's or the group's business, and is in many ways the core of the directors' report. Section 418 requires a disclosure about the completeness of provision of information from the directors to the auditor of the company. Section 236 requires disclosure of qualifying third party indemnity provisions[359] and qualifying pension scheme indemnity provisions[360] for the benefit of the company's directors or otherwise provided by the company (eg for a director of the company's subsidiary).[361]   **15.415.03**

Under subsections (4) and (5) it is an offence to fail to prepare a directors' report. This is in addition to the offence in section 419 of preparing a defective directors' report.   **15.415.04**

In practice many directors' reports go beyond the content required by the Act. For example, certain listed companies are required by the Listing Rules to disclose in their annual financial report that the   **15.415.05**

---

had securities admitted to trading on a regulated market. Thus, for example, companies listed on AIM are now caught within section 90A because AIM is an MTF.

[357] Companies Act 2006 (Commencement No 5, Transitional Provisions and Savings) Order 2007, SI 2007/3495, art 3(1) for financial years beginning on or after 6 April 2008.

[358] See s 474(1) for the meaning of 'included in the consolidation', as distinct from group.

[359] See s 234.

[360] See s 235.

[361] See ss 232 and 256 of this Act and for 'subsidiary' see s 1159.

company is a going concern with assumptions or qualifications as necessary[362] and how they have applied the principles of the UK Corporate Governance Code;[363] whether they complied with the provisions of that code with any departures explained For financial years beginning on or after 1 October 2012, compliance with the Code would require the company's directors also to make a statement about, broadly, speaking, the fairness of the whole annual financial report (see the commentary at section 417) and give a description of how the audit committee (a non-statutory sub-committee of the board, with responsibilities as described in the Code) has discharged its responsibilities, including the significant issues considered by the audit committee in relation to the annual accounts, and how these issues were addressed.[364] Many listed companies include (or are expected to include) these disclosures in their directors' reports. Furthermore, as discussed in the commentary on section 472A, Chapter 7 of the FSA's Disclosure and Transparency Rules requires companies with securities admitted to trading on a regulated market to make certain corporate governance disclosures in either the directors' report or in a separate corporate governance statement. Many companies choose to incorporate these disclosures into the director's report.

### [415A Directors' report: small companies exemption

**15.415A.01**     (1)  A company is entitled to small companies exemption in relation to the directors' report for a financial year if—
        (a)  it is entitled to prepare accounts for the year in accordance with the small companies regime, or
        (b)  it would be so entitled but for being or having been a member of an ineligible group.
     (2)  The exemption is relevant to—
        • section 416(3) (contents of report: statement of amount recommended by way of dividend),
        • section 417 (contents of report: business review), and
        • sections 444 to 446 (filing obligations of different descriptions of company).][a]

AMENDMENTS

[a]   Inserted by the Companies Act 2006 (Amendment) (Accounts and Reports) Regulations 2008, SI 2008/393, reg 6.

COMMENCEMENT DATE  6 April 2008[365]

**15.415A.02**   Part 15 as originally enacted addressed first the case of companies subject to the small companies regime before providing additional requirements for other companies. In other words, there was one definition (albeit a multipart one) of a category of company that had a significantly different set of requirements—the small companies regime.

**15.415A.03**   The insertion of this section has fractured the hitherto clean distinctions in Part 15 between the small company regime and others. It has introduced a new class of company, a company entitled to the small companies exemption, the effect of which is to extend certain exemptions from disclosing particular information within the directors' report, and from filing the directors' report with the registrar, to certain companies that are outside the small companies regime. (This extension maintains, as far as possible, the position that existed in the 1985 Act.[366]) It should be noted from the outset that these exemptions were, as originally enacted, available to companies within the small companies regime, and such companies thus remain in exactly the same position as they were before.

**15.415A.04**   Subsection (1) sets out the qualification criteria for the small companies exemption. These are that the company is either within the small companies regime (see sections 381 to 384) or would otherwise qualify for the small companies regime save for its being a member of an ineligible group (ie under section 384(2)). Thus, the company must meet the size thresholds set out in section 382 and, if a parent company, section 383; and the company itself must not qualify as an ineligible company further to section 384(1)(a) and (b). However, unlike the small companies regime, the company is not disqualified if it is a member of a group that contains certain categories of company (eg a public company).

**15.415A.05**   Once qualified, a company within the small companies exemption may, in fact, take advantage of three exemptions: the first two relate to omission of information from the directors' report, and the third

---

[362]  Listing Rules LR 9.8.6 (3), (5) and (6) contain these disclosure requirements; LR 9.1.1 to 9.1.4 set out the scope of their application. These are examples of disclosures required under the Listing Rules; there are others.
[363]  See *UK Corporate Governance Code* (Financial Reporting Council, June 2010).
[364]  Listing Rule LR 9.8.6R
[365]  Companies Act 2006 (Amendment) (Accounts and Reports) Regulations 2008, SI2008/393, reg 2(2) for financial years beginning on or after 6 April 2008.
[366]  See Companies Act 1985, s 247A(1A)(a), which extended certain exemptions from giving information in, and filing, the directors' report to companies that otherwise would not qualify for the special provisions available to small companies under the 1985 Act.

provides an exemption from the filing of the directors' report. Each of these exemptions may be used independently of the others—for example, a company may take advantage of the exemptions allowing certain information to be omitted from the directors' report but nevertheless decide on filing the report with the Registrar.

Turning to the exemptions relating to the contents of the directors' report, a company entitled to the small companies exemption is permitted to take advantage of the exemption in section 416(3), which provides an exemption from providing information regarding the amount recommended by way of dividend, and section 417(1), which provides an exemption from the requirement for a business review. The latter is particularly useful because, for example, it provides relief to those subsidiary undertakings that are excluded from the small companies regime only by virtue of their being subsidiary undertakings of a public company. Many public companies, especially those that are listed, have numerous subsidiary undertakings which have little or no activity in them. For such companies, it is questionable what benefit the preparation of a business review would have. **15.415A.06**

The third exemption relates to the filing of the directors' report. Section 444A relieves companies entitled to the small companies exemption from delivering a directors' report to the registrar. This exemption relates only to the filing of the directors' report; a directors' report, albeit modified by virtue of the other provisions of this section, must still be prepared and circulated to members. **15.415A.07**

### 416   Contents of directors' report: general

(1)  The directors' report for a financial year must state— **15.416.01**
  (a)  the names of the persons who, at any time during the financial year, were directors of the company, and
  (b)  the principal activities of the company in the course of the year.
(2)  In relation to a group directors' report subsection (1)(b) has effect as if the reference to the company was to the undertakings included in the consolidation.
(3)  Except in the case of a company [entitled to the small companies exemption]ª the report must state the amount (if any) that the directors recommend should be paid by way of dividend.
(4)  The Secretary of State may make provision by regulations as to other matters that must be disclosed in a directors' report.
  Without prejudice to the generality of this power, the regulations may make any such provision as was formerly made by Schedule 7 to the Companies Act 1985.

AMENDMENTS

ª  Amendment made by the Companies Act 2006 (Amendment) (Accounts and Reports) Regulations 2008, SI 2008/393, reg 6.

COMMENCEMENT DATE  subsection (4) from 20 January 2007;[367] otherwise 6 April 2008[368]

Whilst subsections (1) to (3) require three specific pieces of content in the directors' report, it is regulations under subsection (4) that contain the most detailed specification under this section. **15.416.02**

In terms of the content specified directly by this section, that of subsection (1)(a) invites consideration. It requires a statement of the names of those who served as directors of the company at any time during the financial year. Even where group accounts are prepared, this requirement applies only to the directors of the parent company and not to any undertakings included in the consolidation. When a director has been in office for only part of the financial year, it is not necessary to state the date of his appointment or/and resignation, although this information is customarily given. Likewise, it is not necessary to disclose details of directors who were appointed after the end of the financial year, although this is often customarily provided. **15.416.03**

On the commencement of Part 15 regulations have been made under subsection (4) in similar form to the provisions of Schedule 7 to the 1985 Act—indeed, the subsection specifically refers to this.[369] That schedule required disclosure in a number of areas including political donations and expenditure, charitable donations, employment-related matters, and policy and practice on payment of creditors. **15.416.04**

For some categories of company additional contents of the directors' report may be prescribed by other instruments. In particular, chapter 7 of the FSA's Disclosure and Transparency Rules (DTR) require, subject to an alternative, the inclusion of certain corporate governance disclosures; the alternative is for these to be given in a separate corporate governance statement (the authority for which thereby resides in the DTR but for which an approval process is provided by this Act at section 419A). (The chosen **15.416.05**

---

[367]  Companies Act 2006 (Commencement No 1, etc) Order 2006, SI 2006/3428, art 3(3).
[368]  Companies Act 2006 (Commencement No 5, Transitional Provisions and Savings) Order 2007, SI 2007/3495, art 3(1) for financial years beginning on or after 6 April 2008.
[369]  See the regulations referred to in para 15.396.03, nn 170 and 171.

alternative may affect questions of the directors' liability in relation to the disclosures; see the commentaries at sections 419 and 419A.) The companies upon which this DTR requirement falls are those with securities admitted to trading on a regulated market.[370, 371] Whilst this DTR requirement implements EC directives,[372] it is substantially a repetition of Listing Rule disclosure requirements[373] in relation to the UK Corporate Governance Code,[374] as more fully explained in the commentary at section 472A.

## 417  Contents of directors' report: business review

**15.417.01**

(1) Unless the company is [entitled to the small companies exemption][a], the directors' report must contain a business review.[b]

(2) The purpose of the business review is to inform members of the company and help them assess how the directors have performed their duty under section 172 (duty to promote the success of the company).

(3) The business review must contain—
    (a) a fair review of the company's business, and
    (b) a description of the principal risks and uncertainties facing the company.

(4) The review required is a balanced and comprehensive analysis of—
    (a) the development and performance of the company's business during the financial year, and
    (b) the position of the company's business at the end of that year, consistent with the size and complexity of the business.

(5) In the case of a quoted company the business review must, to the extent necessary for an understanding of the development, performance or position of the company's business, include—
    (a) the main trends and factors likely to affect the future development, performance and position of the company's business; and
    (b) information about—
        (i) environmental matters (including the impact of the company's business on the environment),
        (ii) the company's employees, and
        (iii) social and community issues,
    including information about any policies of the company in relation to those matters and the effectiveness of those policies; and
    (c) subject to subsection (11), information about persons with whom the company has contractual or other arrangements which are essential to the business of the company.
    If the review does not contain information of each kind mentioned in paragraph (b) (i), (ii) and (iii), it must state which of those kinds of information it does not contain.

(6) The review must, to the extent necessary for an understanding of the development, performance or position of the company's business, include—
    (a) analysis using financial key performance indicators, and
    (b) where appropriate, analysis using other key performance indicators, including information relating to environmental matters and employee matters.
    'Key performance indicators' means factors by reference to which the development, performance or position of the company's business can be measured effectively.

(7) Where a company qualifies as medium-sized in relation to a financial year (see sections 465 to 467), the directors' report for the year need not comply with the requirements of subsection (6) so far as they relate to non-financial information.[c]

(8) The review must, where appropriate, include references to, and additional explanations of, amounts included in the company's annual accounts.

(9) In relation to a group directors' report this section has effect as if the references to the company were references to the undertakings included in the consolidation.

(10) Nothing in this section requires the disclosure of information about impending developments or matters in the course of negotiation if the disclosure would, in the opinion of the directors, be seriously prejudicial to the interests of the company.

(11) Nothing in subsection (5)(c) requires the disclosure of information about a person if the disclosure would, in the opinion of the directors, be seriously prejudicial to that person and contrary to the public interest.

---

370  As defined in the FSA's Handbook Glossary, being essentially the same as that in s 1173 of this Act.
371  For financial years beginning on or after 29 June 2008.
372  Directive (EEC) 78/660 [1978] OJ L222/11 as amended and Directive (EEC) 83/349 [1983] OJ L193/1, as amended.
373  LR9.8.6R (6).
374  See the *UK Corporate Governance Code* (Financial Reporting Council, June 2010).

AMENDMENTS AND NOTES

ᵃ Amendment made by the Companies Act 2006 (Amendment) (Accounts and Reports) Regulations 2008, SI 2008/393, reg 6.

ᵇ Transitional provision: Companies Act 2006 (Commencement No 3, Transitional Provisions and Savings) Order 2007, SI 2007/2194, Sch 1, para 16 makes the following adaptation.

'For subsection (1) substitute—

"(1) Unless the company is entitled to small companies exemption in relation to the directors' report, the report must contain a business review.

(1A) A company is entitled to the small companies exemption in relation to the directors' report for a financial year if it—

    (a) qualifies as small in relation to that year under Part 7 of the Companies Act 1985 or Part 8 of the Companies (Northern Ireland) Order 1986, and

    (b) is not, and was not at any time within that year, an ineligible company as defined in section 247A(1B) of that Act or Article 255A(1B) of that Order."'.

    The above transitional provision has been repealed by the Companies Act 2006 (Commencement No 5, Transitional Provisions and Savings) Order 2007, SI 2007/3495, art 10(1)(b) from 6 April 2008; it is presumed that the intention here is to repeal for financial years beginning on or after 6 April 2008 since that is the basis of commencement of the small companies exemption (s 415A) as referred to in this subs (1) after the transitional adaptation falls away.

    ᶜ Transitional Provision: Paragraph 16 of Schedule 1 of The Companies Act 2006 (Commencement No 3, Transitional Provisions and Savings) Order 2007, SI 2007/2194 makes the following adaptation. 'For subsection (7) substitute—

"(7) Where a company—

    (a) qualifies as medium-sized in relation to a financial year under Part 7 of the Companies Act 1985 or Part 8 of the Companies (Northern Ireland) Order 1986, and

    (b) is not, and was not at any time within that year, an ineligible company as defined in section 247A(1B) of that Act or Article 255A(1B) of that Order,

    the directors' report for the year need not comply with the requirements of subsection (6) so far as they relate to non-financial information…

    The above transitional provision has been repealed by the Companies Act 2006 (Commencement No 5, Transitional Provisions and Savings) Order 2007, SI 2007/3495, art 10(1)(b) from 6 April 2008; it is presumed that the intention here is to repeal for financial years beginning on or after 6 April 2008.

COMMENCEMENT DATE 1 October 2007[375]

This section sets the requirement for one of the main components of the content of the directors' report—the business review. Put simply, it is a narrative report of the company's business to accompany the figures as shown in the annual accounts. The section is the product of much development in the way in which the requirement for such a report is articulated, such that the business review now required is known in practice as the 'enhanced business review'. It arises both from the debate about narrative reporting conducted by the Company Law Review and subsequently by the Department of Trade and Industry (now BIS)—including on the occasion of the repeal of the short-lived statutory operating and financial review (OFR)[376]—and from requirements of the so-called EC Modernization Directive.[377] Note that for certain listed companies these requirements are, in effect, to be supplemented by developments in the UK Corporate Governance Code, as described at the end of this section's commentary.    **15.417.02**

The scope of application of this section differs depending upon the type of company concerned. For companies entitled to the small companies exemption[378] the section does not apply at all. For    **15.417.03**

---

[375] Companies Act 2006 (Commencement No 3, etc) Order 2007, SI 2007/2194, art 2(1) for directors' reports for financial years beginning on or after 1 October 2007.

[376] The enhanced business review has much in common with the repealed statutory OFR and thus the Accounting Standards Board's (ASB's) best practice *Reporting statement—Operating and financial review* (ASB, 2006) will be a useful reference in relation to the enhanced business review. In January 2008, the ASB issued a table showing how the guidance in the Reporting statement can be applied to the requirements of this section.

[377] Directive (EC) 2003/51 [2003] OJ L178/16. This Directive amended various accounting directives that, *inter alia*, set the requirement, in European legislation, for the directors' report (eg the Fourth Company Law Directive (EEC) 78/660 [1978] OJ L222/11, as amended).

[378] See s 415A

companies that are medium-sized,[379] or would be medium-sized save by reason only of its having been a member of an ineligible group within the financial year in question,[380] subsections (5)[381] and (6)(b) do not apply. For larger but unquoted companies[382] subsection (5) does not apply. For quoted companies the entire section applies.

**15.417.04**    Subsection (2) is a statement of the purpose of the business review. On the face of the matter, this is a declaration rather than a requirement falling upon the directors. However, this declaration may colour the way in which the requirements of the remainder of the section need to be met, perhaps in particular those of subsections (5) and (6); those subsections refer to certain matters being included to the extent necessary for an understanding of the development, performance, or position of the company's business, which may be thought to have something in common with informing the members of the company about the directors' performance of their duty under section 172 as referred to in subsection (2). Section 172 requires the directors to promote the success of the company for the benefit of its members as a whole. In doing so, however, that section requires, among other things, that the directors have regard to likely long-term consequences of their decisions, the interests of company's employees, fostering business relationships, the company's impact on the community and the environment, and standards of business conduct.

**15.417.05**    Subsections (3) to (11) then articulate the requirement for the business review but do not do so in any highly detailed fashion. That is to say, they are not a checklist of specific matters that should or should not be included. Given that the requirements apply to a wide range of companies, from owner-managed business to quoted multinationals, and carrying on business across a wide range of commercial activities, it is entirely understandable that the legislation does not aim at detailed prescription—such an object would have been unattainable.

**15.417.06**    The first substantive requirement of the section is that of subsection (3) as amplified by subsection (4). The relationship between the two is not, however, entirely clear. Subsection (3) requires that the 'business review' must contain a 'fair review' of the business and a description of the risks and uncertainties faced. The Financial Review Reporting Panel (FRRP) has commented on what it considers shortcomings in the application of this particular requirement, noting that disclosure is often generic or inconsistent with the annual accounts. The FRRP also stated that, in its opinion, companies should disclose how they manage risks.[383] Subsection (4) then makes further provision about 'the review' (that it be balanced, comprehensive, and cover the business's development, performance, and position). It is not clear whether this refers to the 'business review' of subsections (3)(a) and (b) or only the 'fair review' of subsection (3)(a). Indeed, the risks and uncertainties facing the company can be an inherent part of both the performance during the year and the position at the end of the year. Thus taking subsections (3) and (4) together the intent may appear to be to require disclosure of the business's development, performance, and position at the end of the year including risks and uncertainties faced.

**15.417.07**    Three other points from subsection (4) warrant some emphasis. First, the review must be balanced and comprehensive. So, for example, it might be necessary to give information that puts the company's performance in an unwelcome light. Second, the analysis needs to be consistent with the size and complexity of the business. Thus, that for a multinational conglomerate may be in greater detail and of greater length than that of a company with a single and unsophisticated line of business in the UK. Third, the risk and uncertainties inherent in the position of the business at the end of the year will require an element of forward-looking disclosure, a point also noted in a DTI publication on the business review.[384]

**15.417.08**    In compiling the review required by subsections (3) and (4), subsection (6) requires the use of key performance indicators (KPIs), both financial KPIs and—for companies other than those that are medium-sized—KPIs relating to environmental and employee matters. Financial KPIs might include measures drawn from, or based upon, the annual accounts—for example, interest cover or gearing—and hitherto unpublished internal measures that the directors use to monitor performance,

---

[379]  See ss 465–467.

[380]  See s 467(4).

[381]  Subsection (5) does not apply to unquoted companies and since a medium-sized company must not be a public company—see s 467(1)(a)—it is highly unlikely that it could be a quoted company as defined in s 385.

[382]  For quoted and unquoted companies, see s 385.

[383]  FRRP Press Notice 130, February 2011. The FRRP was the body authorized under section 457 to make an application to court in relation to a defective directors' report. Since July 2012 it has been succeeded as authorized body by the Conduct Committee of the Financial Reporting Council.

[384]  *Guidance on the changes to the Directors' report requirements in the Companies Act 1985* (DTI, 2005), which provided guidance on the application of CA 1985, s 234ZZB(2) and (3).The requirements of s 234ZZB included the equivalent of the current subs (4).

for example sales per square foot of retail space. Non-financial KPIs might deal with, for example, carbon emissions or staff turnover.[385] The particular KPIs used are left to the discretion of the directors. They must be factors that are effective in measuring the development, performance, or position of the business. Moreover, KPI analysis is required only to the extent necessary for an understanding of the development, performance, or position of the business. Thus if the use of KPIs does not, in the directors' judgment, add anything to the understanding of the development, performance, or position of the business otherwise successfully conveyed by the business review, then KPIs need not be used; however, in most practical circumstances it is difficult to envisage a meaningful discussion of performance without the use of key measures.

For a quoted company subsection (5) gives yet further specification in three areas. First of all, **15.417.09** subsection (5)(a) gives a strong forward-looking aspect to the review (trends and factors affecting the future). Second, subsection (5)(b) specifies environmental, employment, and social and community issues for potential coverage; that coverage would include, but not necessarily be limited to, the company's policies on such matters and their effectiveness. Third, subsection (5)(c) requires (subject to a narrow exemption discussed below) information about persons with whom there are contractual or other arrangements essential to the business. This subsection received a certain amount of publicity prior to Royal Assent owing to the subsection's effect, in some cases, of requiring disclosure of a company's relationship with its suppliers. However, it is by no means restricted to that class. Indeed, its language could encompass, among others, customers and employees, although the latter are already referred to in the earlier provision in subsection (5)(b). However, all of the matters identified by subsection (5) are required only to the extent that they are necessary for an understanding of the development, performance, or position of the business. Whether such information is necessary for an understanding of the business can only be judged in relation to the specific business in question. Thus the onus falls upon the directors of the company in the first instance to determine the extent to which the information noted in subsection (5) is necessary. With respect to environmental, employment, and social and community issues, and contractual and other arrangements, even if it is judged that information upon these issues is not necessary, the business review cannot be silent upon them. Rather, the subsection requires the review to state that it does not cover those matters—in effect an overt assertion by the directors that such matters are not necessary for an understanding of the business.

It is also interesting to consider the positions of quoted companies and unquoted companies including **15.417.10** medium-sized companies. A quoted company must include the subsection (5) and (6) information to the extent necessary for an understanding of the business; and an unquoted company is not subject to subsection (5) or, if medium-sized, to the subsection (6)(b) requirement for non-financial KPIs. The implication for an unquoted company is that, apparently, it need not include subsection (5) type information even where it would be necessary for an understanding of the business; and for a medium-sized company that it need not include non-financial KPI's even where they would be necessary for such an understanding. Thus whilst the legislation appears to expect less of an unquoted company and even less of one that is medium-sized, nevertheless owing to the subjective terms in which the section is framed and the potential for overlap among the provisions of subsections (2) to (6), the legislation is unclear; thus unquoted and medium-sized companies may need, to some extent, to provide disclosure that goes further than the apparent minimums in subsections (6) and (6)(a) respectively. Indeed the DTI (now DBIS) itself has in effect drawn attention to the absence of clear dividing lines between the different provisions. At a time when the OFR had been repealed, and when what are now the subsection (5) trends-and-factors etc requirements had not yet been introduced, the DTI stated that: the OFR specified in detail additional areas in respect of which disclosures might be required. These areas included trends and factors likely to affect the future development, performance and position of the business, and information about environmental, employee, social and community issues and policies. Companies producing a business review are not specifically required to make disclosures in as many additional areas, but will need to considering [sic] doing so where information is material to understanding the development, performance and position of the company, the principal risks and uncertainties facing it, or to provide an indication of likely future developments in the business of the company. Moreover, key performance indicators must be used where appropriate (including specifically those relating to environmental and employee issues).[386]

---

[385] In connection with non-financial KPIs, the DTI draws attention (in *Guidance on the changes to the Directors' report requirements in the Companies Act 1985* (DTI, 2005)) to *Environmental key performance indicators: reporting guidelines for UK business* (DEFRA, 2006), *Guidance on how to report your greenhouse gas emissions* (DEFRA, 2009), and *Accounting for people: report of the task force on human capital management* (presented to the Secretary of State for Trade and Industry, 2003).

[386] Guidance on the changes to the Directors' report requirements in the Companies Act 1985 (DTI, 2005).

**15.417.11**    Subsections (8) to (11) contain supplementary provisions of which the most important are the last two. In recognition of the forward-looking nature of the business review, subsection (10) allows the directors to omit certain matters, the inclusion of which would, in the opinion of the directors, be seriously prejudicial to the company's interests. Those matters are impending developments and matters in the course of negotiation.

**15.417.12**    The disclosures required by subsection (5)(c) may occasionally prejudice the person of whom it is made. In order to avoid this, subsection (11) permits a company to avoid disclosure where two conditions are met: first, the disclosure must be seriously prejudicial to that person (not the company); and, second, the disclosure would be contrary to the public interest. Thus, the circumstances in which this exemption is available are very limited.[387]

**15.417.13**    Over and above these requirements in section 417, certain listed companies are required by the Listing Rules to disclose in their annual financial report whether they have complied with the provisions of the UK Corporate Governance Code (the Code) with any departures explained.[388] For financial years beginning on or after 1 October 2012 a new Code provision requires (for compliance with the Code – note that the company may instead choose to explain its non-compliance) that the directors make a statement that they consider the annual report and annual accounts, taken as a whole, to be fair, balanced and understandable and that it provides the information necessary for shareholders to assess the company's performance, business model and strategy.[389] In effect this is, for companies within its scope, a requirement for narrative reporting – and the directors' report seems the natural place to fulfill this requirement – with an objective similar to, but potentially different from, the principles of the business review set out in subsections (3) and (4); and it is a requirement for the directors explicitly to confirm that the narrative reporting that they have provided does indeed meet that objective.

### 418   Contents of directors' report: statement as to disclosure to auditors

**15.418.01**    (1) This section applies to a company unless—

    (a)   it is exempt for the financial year in question from the requirements of Part 16 as to audit of accounts, and

    (b)   the directors take advantage of that exemption.

(2) The directors' report must contain a statement to the effect that, in the case of each of the persons who are directors at the time the report is approved—

    (a)   so far as the director is aware, there is no relevant audit information of which the company's auditor is unaware, and

    (b)   he has taken all the steps that he ought to have taken as a director in order to make himself aware of any relevant audit information and to establish that the company's auditor is aware of that information.

(3) 'Relevant audit information' means information needed by the company's auditor in connection with preparing his report.

(4) A director is regarded as having taken all the steps that he ought to have taken as a director in order to do the things mentioned in subsection (2)(b) if he has—

    (a)   made such enquiries of his fellow directors and of the company's auditors for that purpose, and

    (b)   taken such other steps (if any) for that purpose,

    as are required by his duty as a director of the company to exercise reasonable care, skill and diligence.

(5) Where a directors' report containing the statement required by this section is approved but the statement is false, every director of the company who—

    (a)   knew that the statement was false, or was reckless as to whether it was false, and

    (b)   failed to take reasonable steps to prevent the report from being approved, commits an offence.

(6) A person guilty of an offence under subsection (5) is liable—

    (a)   on conviction on indictment, to imprisonment for a term not exceeding two years or a fine (or both);

---

[387]   The example given by the Government, on the introduction of this exemption, was in relation to persons at risk from 'animal rights activists', *Hansard*, HL, vol 686, col 456 (2 Nov 2006).

[388]   Listing Rule LR 9.8.6R

[389]   *UK Corporate Governance Code* (FRC, 2012). It is intended by the FRC that this version of the Code will be applicable for financial years beginning on or after 1 October 2012. However, for this to be so it will require the UK Listing Authority to make a change to Listing Rule LR 9.8.6R so that relevant listed companies will be required to state that they have complied with this 2012 version of the Code (or to explain why they have not). At present the Listing Rules refer to an earlier version of the Code.

(b)  on summary conviction—
    (i)   in England and Wales, to imprisonment for a term not exceeding twelve months or to a fine not exceeding the statutory maximum (or both);
    (ii)  in Scotland or Northern Ireland, to imprisonment for a term not exceeding six months, or to a fine not exceeding the statutory maximum (or both).

COMMENCEMENT DATE  6 April 2008[390]

This section is derived from a recommendation of the Company Law Review that the duty of directors to provide information and explanations to the auditor on request[391] be extended to require the directors to volunteer information to the auditor. The Company Law Review also considered that failure in such a duty should involve civil liability, with vicarious liability for the company, so as to provide clarity on the auditor's right to a contribution or to assert contributory negligence, for example in a case where the auditor is sued by the company in relation to defective accounts prepared by the directors.[392]    **15.418.02**

The section requires that the directors' report of a company subject to audit must contain a statement that *each* of the directors, at the time of approving the report, has taken steps to make themselves aware of relevant audit information and to establish that the company's auditor is aware of the information. Thus the section in effect places a duty upon the directors to volunteer all necessary information to the company's auditor. However, it would not appear to provide the clarity sought by the Company Law Review in terms of contribution.    **15.418.03**

A key part of the provision is that each director is obliged to take steps to apprise himself of relevant audit information and to establish the auditor is aware of it.[393] These steps may include, but are not limited to, the director's making such enquiries, commensurate with the duty to exercise reasonable care, skill, and diligence[394] of his fellow directors and of the auditor for that purpose. The effect of this, for the board as a whole, is not to change significantly its collective responsibilities; after all, they are collectively responsible for preparing the annual accounts etc and in order to do so properly the board must satisfy itself that the annual accounts etc meet the relevant requirements, and thus satisfying the auditor on the same is not a great extension of duty. However, the main change effected is to emphasize a measure of individual responsibility for each director. This may promote more dialogue amongst the directors; for example one might imagine the finance director being asked by his fellow directors to provide a picture, in more depth perhaps than hitherto, of matters that are material to the annual accounts etc and of the information communicated by him, and his finance function staff, to the auditor and the processes for doing so. Indeed, subsection (4)(a) recognizes that the making of enquiries with fellow directors will be relevant.    **15.418.04**

It might be thought that a director could, under subsection (4)(a), simply ask the auditor whether he has received all the information that he needs from the directors. Setting aside the question of whether such an approach would be commensurate with the director's duty, no auditor is likely to answer an open question such as this (nor is the auditor under any duty to answer at all) given that the policy purpose behind the provision is to promote the volunteering of information from directors to auditors. Rather, a director's questions for the auditor are more likely to be directed at establishing whether the auditor is aware of specific matters.    **15.418.05**

Relevant audit information is defined in subsection (3) as information needed by the company's auditor in connection with his report. It is evident from this that relevant audit information means any information which the auditor would consider, if he was aware of it, relevant to any of the opinions to be given in his report under sections 495 to 497.    **15.418.06**

As with the original duty to provide information and explanations on request, default under this section is a criminal offence.[395]    **15.418.07**

### 419  Approval and signing of directors' report

(1)  The directors' report must be approved by the board of directors and signed on behalf of the board by a director or the secretary of the company.    **15.419.01**

---

[390]  Companies Act 2006 (Commencement No 5, Transitional Provisions and Savings) Order 2007, SI 2007/3495, art 3(1) for financial years beginning on or after 6 April 2008.
[391]  See ss 499–501.
[392]  The issue of contributory negligence, including the rule in *Re Hampshire Land Co* [1896] 2 Ch 743, is discussed in *Modern company law for a competitive economy—Final report* (The Company Law Review Steering Group, July 2001), para 8.139 *et seq*.
[393]  Subsections (2)(b), (4).
[394]  This is the duty set out in s 174 although, oddly, this section does not explicitly cross-refer to it.
[395]  Subsections (5), (6).

(2) If [in preparing the report advantage is taken of the small companies exemption]ᵃ, it must contain a statement to that effect in a prominent position above the signature.

(3) If a directors' report is approved that does not comply with the requirements of this Act, every director of the company who—

    (a) knew that it did not comply, or was reckless as to whether it complied, and

    (b) failed to take reasonable steps to secure compliance with those requirements or, as the case may be, to prevent the report from being approved, commits an offence.

(4) A person guilty of an offence under this section is liable—

    (a) on conviction on indictment, to a fine;

    (b) on summary conviction, to a fine not exceeding the statutory maximum.

AMENDMENTS

ᵃ Amendment by the Companies Act 2006 (Amendment) (Accounts and Reports) Regulations 2008, SI 2008/393, reg 6.

COMMENCEMENT DATE 6 April 2008[396]

**15.419.02** This section requires that the directors' report be approved by the board and signed on the board's behalf by a director or the company secretary. The director signing the report need not be the same one who signs the balance sheet under section 414; indeed, the directors' report may be signed by the company secretary whereas the balance sheet may not. There is no requirement to date the directors' report although this is always done.

**15.419.03** The offence and related penalty for approving a defective directors' report are the same as provided under section 414 with respect to annual accounts. However, no offence is committed by the company secretary if he signs a defective directors' report on behalf of the board—the offence relates to approval by the directors, not to the act of signing. In addition, there may be civil consequences of approving a defective directors' report. First, under section 463 the directors may be liable to the company in relation to false or misleading statements or to omissions; but the section confines the directors' liability to that case alone (cf, the annual accounts where the general law of negligence continues to apply). Second, if the company has securities admitted to trading on a securities market,[397] section 90A of the Financial Services and Markets Act 2000[398] makes provision for the company, in certain cases, to compensate third parties in relation to losses sustained in reliance on untrue or misleading statement or on omissions in the directors' report.[399] If such a company sustained a loss under that provision then it may be able to seek recovery from its directors under section 463, particularly given the test in section 90A(4) of that Act requiring knowledge on the part of a director as to the untrue or misleading statement or omission, and thus the scope of directors' liability may, albeit indirectly, be wider than otherwise appears on the face of section 463.

### [419A Approval and signing of separate corporate governance statement

**15.419A.01** Any separate corporate governance statement must be approved by the board of directors and signed on behalf of the board by a director or the secretary of the company.]ᵃ

AMENDMENTS

ᵃ Inserted by the Companies Act 2006 (Accounts, Reports and Audit) Regulations 2009, SI 2009/1581, reg 2, as from 27 June 2009, in relation to financial years beginning on or after 29 June 2008 which have not ended before 27 June 2009.

COMMENCEMENT DATE 27 June 2009

---

[396] Companies Act 2006 (Commencement No 5, Transitional Provisions and Savings) Order 2007, SI 2007/3495, art 3(1) for financial years beginning on or after 6 April 2008.

[397] From 1 October 2010, the scope of section 90A (further to the Financial Services and Markets Act 2000 (Liability of Issuers) Regulations 2010, SI 2010/1192) has been extended to apply to any issuer with securities that, with the consent of the issuer, are admitted to trading on a market i) situated or operating in the United Kingdom, or ii) that has the UK as its home state. 'Securities market' means a regulated market, a multilateral trading facility (MTF) or a market or facility of a corresponding description outside the EEA (FSMA, Sch 10, para 8(1)(b). This contrasts with the previous version of section 90A (before 1 October 2010) that applied only to companies that had securities admitted to trading on a regulated market. Thus, for example, companies listed on AIM are now caught within section 90A because AIM is an MTF.

[398] Inserted into that Act by s 1270 of this Act.

[399] Before 1 October 2010, for certain companies the directors' report is a document required to be published in response to a requirement mentioned in s 90A(1)(a) of that Act and is thus within that section's liability regime. From 1 October 2010, s 90A has been extended to include any document published by 'recognised means', including information published on a recognized information service (see Financial Services and Markets Act Sch 10A, para 4).

This new section is derived from changes made to the Fourth and Seventh Directives,[400] and requires **15.419A.02**
that where a company prepares a separate corporate governance statement (that is, outside of the
directors' report)[401] that statement must be approved and signed on the board's behalf by a director or
the company secretary.

This section is unusual in as much as it requires the approval of this statement, whereas the require- **15.419A.03**
ment to prepare the statement is not contained within this Act. Rather, chapter 7 of the FSA's Disclosure
and Transparency Rules (DTR) require the inclusion of certain corporate governance disclosures
either within the directors' report[402] or in a separate corporate governance statement.[403] Thus the
authority and requirement for this statement resides in the DTR but this section provides for its
approval.

The director signing the report need not be the same one who signs the balance sheet under section 414. **15.419A.04**
There is no requirement to date the corporate governance statement, although this is expected always
to be done.

The section provides no offence in relation to default in compliance with this section. It should also be **15.419A.05**
noted that the statement is not covered by the provisions of section 463 of this Act or of section 90A of
the Financial Services and Market Act 2000 (unless published by recognized means);[404], [405] the general
law, eg as to negligence, will apply. It is worth noting that if a company's directors choose to include the
required DTR disclosure within the directors' report rather than in a separate corporate governance
statement, then the liability position described in the commentary at section 419 would apply.

# CHAPTER 6
## QUOTED COMPANIES: DIRECTORS' REMUNERATION REPORT

### 420 Duty to prepare directors' remuneration report

(1) The directors of a quoted company must prepare a directors' remuneration report for each **15.420.01**
financial year of the company.
(2) In the case of failure to comply with the requirement to prepare a directors' remuneration report,
every person who—
   (a) was a director of the company immediately before the end of the period for filing accounts
   and reports for the financial year in question, and
   (b) failed to take all reasonable steps for securing compliance with that requirement, commits an
   offence.
(3) A person guilty of an offence under this section is liable—
   (a) on conviction on indictment, to a fine;
   (b) on summary conviction, to a fine not exceeding the statutory maximum.

COMMENCEMENT DATE 6 April 2008[406]

This section is derived from provisions of the 1985 Act introduced in 2002[407] to increase certain **15.420.02**
companies' transparency in relation to policies and amounts of directors' remuneration. This section
requires every quoted company[408] to prepare a directors' remuneration report. The contents of this
report are given by section 421. In contrast with all other accounts and reports required by this Part,
section 422 creates a statutory requirement for the directors' remuneration report to be voted upon by
members.

Subsections (2) and (3) make an offence of failure to prepare a directors' remuneration report. This **15.420.03**
offence is separate from, and in addition to, the offence for approval of a defective directors' remu-

---

[400] Directive (EEC) 78/660 [1978] OJ L222/11, as amended; and Directive (EEC) 83/349 [1983] OJ L193/1, as
amended.
[401] See s 472(A)(3).
[402] See s 416.
[403] See s 472A.
[404] Inserted into that Act by s 1270 of this Act.
[405] For recognized means, see n 386.
[406] Companies Act 2006 (Commencement No 5, Transitional Provisions and Savings) Order 2007, SI
2007/3495, art 3(1) for financial years beginning on or after 6 April 2008.
[407] CA 1985, s 234B; introduced by the Directors' Remuneration Report Regulations 2002, SI 2002/1986.
[408] See s 385.

neration report.[409] The offence falls on those who were directors of the company immediately before the end of the period for filing accounts and reports.[410]

### 421 Contents of directors' remuneration report

**15.421.01**
(1) The Secretary of State may make provision by regulations as to—
 (a) the information that must be contained in a directors' remuneration report,
 (b) how information is to be set out in the report, and
 (c) what is to be the auditable part of the report.
(2) Without prejudice to the generality of this power, the regulations may make any such provision as was made, immediately before the commencement of this Part, by Schedule 7A to the Companies Act 1985 (c. 6).
(3) It is the duty of—
 (a) any director of a company, and
 (b) any person who is or has at any time in the preceding five years been a director of the company,
 to give notice to the company of such matters relating to himself as may be necessary for the purposes of regulations under this section.
(4) A person who makes default in complying with subsection (3) commits an offence and is liable on summary conviction to a fine not exceeding level 3 on the standard scale.

COMMENCEMENT DATE subsections (1) and (2) from 20 January 2007;[411] otherwise 6 April 2008[412]

**15.421.02**  The content of the directors' remuneration report is determined by regulations made under the power in subsection (1).[413]

**15.421.03**  Under those regulations, which are broadly the same as the 1985 Act's Schedule 7A, the directors' remuneration report is split into two parts: an unaudited part and a part subject to audit. The unaudited part contains, among other matters, detailed narrative disclosures of remuneration policy and a graph of the total shareholder return in respect of the company's quoted equity shares compared with that of a broad equity market index. The part of the report subject to audit contains detailed information concerning all aspects of the directors' remuneration: salaries and bonus, compensation for loss of office, share option schemes, and other long term incentive schemes and pension arrangements.[414] This detailed information has to be given in tabular form. Thus, the provisions in subsection (1)(b) and (c) are intelligible in light of the requirements of the regulations. Subsection (1)(b) permits regulations to determine the form of disclosure—for example, by specifying a line graph or by requiring a tabular form.

**15.421.04**  Subsection (1)(c) allows the regulations to split the content into unaudited and auditable parts. In presenting a report it is of practical importance clearly to distinguish these parts. This is because both the members reading the report and the auditors reporting upon it will want to be clear as to what is and is not subject to audit. Furthermore, the designation of the appropriate portion of the report as 'audited' would be incorrect as the report must exist, ie be approved by the directors, before it can then be audited, such that it never falls to be described as 'audited' at the time of its preparation/approval. A more appropriate designation might be either 'auditable'[415] or another designation that conveys the same meaning—eg 'subject to audit'.

**15.421.05**  Subsection (3) requires a director and certain past directors to notify the company of any matter relating to himself as may be necessary for the purposes of complying with the regulations. This provision is needed because information concerning directors' remuneration may not be known by the company. In particular, the regulations require disclosure of remuneration paid to a director, in respect

---

[409] See s 422.

[410] For a public company, six months after the end of the relevant accounting reference period. See s 442.

[411] Companies Act 2006 (Commencement No 1, etc) Order 2006, SI 2006/3428, art 3(3).

[412] Companies Act 2006 (Commencement No 5, Transitional Provisions and Savings) Order 2007, SI 2007/3495, art 3(1) for financial years beginning on or after 6 April 2008.

[413] See the Large and Medium-sized Companies and Groups (Accounts and Reports) Regulations 2008, SI 2008/410, Sch 8.

[414] The Listing Rules also make provision for disclosures with regard to directors' remuneration (see LR 9.8.6R (7), 9.8.8R which complement, but differ very slightly from, those in the regulation. The Financial Services Authority (FSA) had previously indicated that it intended to delete those provisions in the Listing Rules that overlap the Companies Act provisions when this Act's provisions were brought into force (*Policy Statement 06/11 Implementation of the Transparency Directive*, FSA 2006; paras 2.31 and 2.32). However, the Listing Rules remain as yet unchanged in this regard.

[415] See s 497.

of services to the company, by third parties.[416] Subsection (3) provides that this disclosure obligation continues for five years after the director leaves office because, for example, the regulations require disclosure of certain retirement benefits and compensation of past directors.[417] Failure to comply with these provisions is an offence as provided by subsection (4).

### 422 Approval and signing of directors' remuneration report

(1) The directors' remuneration report must be approved by the board of directors and signed on behalf of the board by a director or the secretary of the company.

(2) If a directors' remuneration report is approved that does not comply with the requirements of this Act, every director of the company who—
    (a) knew that it did not comply, or was reckless as to whether it complied, and
    (b) failed to take reasonable steps to secure compliance with those requirements or, as the case may be, to prevent the report from being approved, commits an offence.

(3) A person guilty of an offence under this section is liable—
    (a) on conviction on indictment, to a fine;
    (b) on summary conviction, to a fine not exceeding the statutory maximum.

15.422.01

COMMENCEMENT DATE 6 April 2008[418]

This section requires that the directors' remuneration report be approved by the board and signed on the board's behalf by a director or the company secretary. The director signing the report need not be the same one who signs the balance sheet under section 414; indeed, the directors' remuneration report may be signed by the company secretary whereas the balance sheet may not. There is no requirement to date the directors' remuneration report although this is always done.

15.422.02

The offence and related penalty for approving a defective directors' remuneration report are the same as provided under section 414 with respect to annual accounts. However, no offence is committed by the company secretary if he signs a defective directors' remuneration report on behalf of the board—the offence relates to approval by the directors, not to the act of signing. As with the directors' report, there may also be civil consequences of approving a defective directors' remuneration report under section 463 (liability of the directors to the company in relation to false or misleading statement or omissions); but the section confines the directors' liability to that case alone (cf, the annual accounts where the general law of negligence continues to apply).

15.422.03

## CHAPTER 7
## PUBLICATION OF ACCOUNTS AND REPORTS
### *Duty to circulate copies of accounts and reports*

### 423 Duty to circulate copies of annual accounts and reports

(1) Every company must send a copy of its annual accounts and reports for each financial year to—
    (a) every member of the company,
    (b) every holder of the company's debentures, and
    (c) every person who is entitled to receive notice of general meetings.

(2) Copies need not be sent to a person for whom the company does not have a current address.

(3) A company has a 'current address' for a person if—
    (a) an address has been notified to the company by the person as one at which documents may be sent to him, and
    (b) the company has no reason to believe that documents sent to him at that address will not reach him.

(4) In the case of a company not having a share capital, copies need not be sent to anyone who is not entitled to receive notices of general meetings of the company.

(5) Where copies are sent out over a period of days, references in the Companies Acts to the day on which copies are sent out shall be read as references to the last day of that period.

(6) This section has effect subject to section 426 (option to provide summary financial statement).

15.423.01

---

[416] See the Large and Medium-sized Companies and Groups (Accounts and Reports) Regulations 2008, SI 2008/410, Sch 8, para 16.

[417] Large and Medium-sized Companies and Groups (Accounts and Reports) Regulations 2008, SI 2008/410, Sch 8, para 15.

[418] Companies Act 2006 (Commencement No 5, Transitional Provisions and Savings) Order 2007, SI 2007/3495, art 3(1) for financial years beginning on or after 6 April 2008.

COMMENCEMENT DATE  6 April 2008[419]

**15.423.02**   This section is the first of four provisions requiring circulation or publication of the annual accounts and reports.[420] This section requires circulation chiefly to members; section 430 requires quoted companies to make the annual accounts and reports available on a website; section 437 requires public companies to lay them in general meeting; and section 441 requires them to be placed on the public record, *viz* the register.[421]

**15.423.03**   This section applies in relation to the annual accounts as defined in section 471. With one exception, this amounts to all of the documents prepared under this Part and any auditor's report under Part 16. The exception is that sections 419A and 472A refer to a separate corporate governance statement that is potentially required (albeit required by the FSA's Disclosure and Transparency Rules (DTR)), but such a statement is not covered by the circulation duty in this section. This omission is of little practical relevance as companies of the type that may have to prepare such a statement customarily circulate corporate governance information (eg when its inclusion sprang purely from the Listing Rules) and much other material (eg chairman's letter etc) with the annual accounts and reports for circulation.

**15.423.04**   Subsection (1), taken together with subsection (4), provides that a company having a share capital must circulate its annual accounts and reports to every member, every debenture holder,[422] and each person entitled to receive notice of general meetings. Those persons entitled to notice include the members and the directors, subject to the company's articles, and such persons as are entitled under the articles,[423] and the auditor.[424] Hitherto, articles typically provided, under Table A (1985, as amended), article 112, that in the case of joint holders, the company need give notice only to the first named joint holder in the register of members; and that, in the case of overseas members who have not provided an address within the UK (or an electronic address), no notice need be given. However, the model articles[425] made under section 19 are silent on the matter.

**15.423.05**   For a company not having a share capital—ie most guarantee companies—subsections (1) and (4) provide that copies need only be sent to those entitled to receive notice of general meetings. The practical effect is that debenture holders in such companies do not under this section receive a copy. Of course, the debenture trust deed might require a copy to be provided to holders and, failing that, the debenture holder may exercise his right under section 431 or 432 to demand a copy of the annual accounts and reports.

**15.423.06**   The persons to whom the annual accounts and report must be sent can be extended by virtue of section 145 or section 146, each of which has a different effect. Section 145(1) permits a company's articles to provide that a member may nominate another person to enjoy or exercise all or specified rights of the member. The right to receive a copy of the annual accounts under this section is one that is specifically referred to in section 145(3). Section 146 (applying to a company whose shares are admitted to trading on a regulated market)[426] permits a member to nominate another person to enjoy 'information rights', which includes the right to receive a copy of the company's annual accounts and reports.

**15.423.07**   The section does not detail the timing or manner of sending. Timing is dealt with in section 424. The manner of sending is addressed at sections 1143 to 1148 and Schedule 5, which permits sending by hard copy,[427] in electronic form,[428] or by use of a website, all subject to detailed provisions in those sections. However, in the case of a section 146 nominee, the default method is by means of a website.[429]

**15.423.08**   Subsection (2) does not require a company to send the annual accounts and reports to any person for whom it does not have a current address,[430] as determined under subsection (3). Having had an address notified to it, the burden of proof is put on the company to determine that it has no reason to believe that the documents will not reach the person at that address. The section provides no further information as to how directors might judge this. However, the Explanatory Notes to the Act give the example of where copies are returned marked 'not known at this address' or an electronic equivalent.

---

[419] Companies Act 2006 (Commencement No 5, Transitional Provisions and Savings) Order 2007, SI 2007/3495, art 3(1) for financial years beginning on or after 6 April 2008.

[420] See s 471 for meaning of 'annual accounts and reports'.

[421] See s 1080.

[422] See s 738 for 'debenture'.

[423] See s 310.

[424] See s 502.

[425] See Chapter 51.

[426] See s 1173.

[427] See s 1168.

[428] See s 1168.

[429] See s 147.

[430] See s 1148 for 'address'.

Some practical factors also suggest themselves for consideration—for example, whether dividend cheques sent to that address are not presented. The policy motive behind this provision, described in the Explanatory Notes, is to relieve companies from sending out in circumstances of that nature.

Subsection (6) provides that, rather than sending the annual accounts and reports, a company might send out a summary financial statement[431] to a person mentioned in subsection (1) or to a nominated person[432] if the company and the person opt for these statements. This facility is particularly useful to quoted companies, thereby avoiding the expense of printing and distributing what might amount to a very large document in cases where the entitled person is content with a shorter one; where the sending out is in electronic form or by means of a website, the recipient will benefit from reduced printing costs (because the document he receives and prints himself will be shorter).  **15.423.09**

### 424  Time allowed for sending out copies of accounts and reports

(1)  The time allowed for sending out copies of the company's annual accounts and reports is as follows.   **15.424.01**

(2)  A private company must comply with section 423 not later than—
  (a)  the end of the period for filing accounts and reports, or
  (b)  if earlier, the date on which it actually delivers its accounts and reports to the registrar.

(3)  A public company must comply with section 423 at least 21 days before the date of the relevant accounts meeting.

(4)  If in the case of a public company copies are sent out later than is required by subsection (3), they shall, despite that, be deemed to have been duly sent if it is so agreed by all the members entitled to attend and vote at the relevant accounts meeting.

(5)  Whether the time allowed is that for a private company or a public company is determined by reference to the company's status immediately before the end of the accounting reference period by reference to which the financial year for the accounts in question was determined.

(6)  In this section the 'relevant accounts meeting' means the accounts meeting of the company at which the accounts and reports in question are to be laid. Commencement Date  6 April 2008[433]

This section sets the time limits for sending out annual accounts and reports[434] under section 423. It makes different provisions for public and for private companies. The applicable provision is based on the status of a company as public or private at the end of the accounting reference period (ARP)[435] in relation to which the annual accounts and reports are drawn up.[436]  **15.424.02**

For a public company subsection (3) requires the sending-out to be completed[437] at least 21 days before the relevant accounts meeting, ie the meeting at which the annual accounts and reports are to be laid before members.[438] If the annual accounts and reports are sent out too late to meet the 21-day rule, the section may, nevertheless, be deemed to be met if the members so agree at the accounts meeting. The 21-day rule is aligned with that for giving notice of the annual general meeting (AGM)[439] since it is standard practice for a company to lay its annual accounts and reports at the AGM and also simultaneously to send out the notice and these documents. It should be noted that if the accounts meeting is not the AGM—and it need not be—then the notice period is at least 14 days,[440] unless the public company in question is also a traded company[441] and the conditions in section 307A(2) to (5) have not been met.[442] Perhaps more importantly, for a listed public company, the Corporate Governance Code asks that notice of the AGM, and related papers, be sent at least 20 working days, ie usually  **15.424.03**

---

[431]  See s 426.

[432]  S 426(5) confirms that the Summary Financial Statement option applies in relation to persons nominated under s 146 but is silent in relation to s 145.

[433]  Companies Act 2006 (Commencement No 5, Transitional Provisions and Savings) Order 2007, SI 2007/3495, art 3(1) for financial years beginning on or after 6 April 2008.

[434]  See s 471.

[435]  See s 391.

[436]  See s 390. By virtue of the seven-day rule in that section, the financial year for which the annual accounts and reports are drawn up may end on a date not more than seven days before or after the end of the ARP.

[437]  See s 423(5). If the exercise takes more than one day, the requirement to send out is met on the last such day.

[438]  See s 437.

[439]  See ss 307, 307A and 337.

[440]  See s 307.

[441]  See s 360C.

[442]  In which case, the notice period will be at least 21 days. See s 307A(1)(b).

28 calendar days before the meeting.[443] Thus in practice a listed public company will usually send out its annual accounts and reports no later than 28 days before the accounts meeting.

**15.424.04**  Since a private company is not required to lay annual accounts and reports before members in general meeting, the Act makes different provision for the timing of sending-out by such companies, by linking it with the delivery to the registrar (filing).[444] Thus such a company is required to send out its annual accounts and reports on the earlier of the end of the period for filing, which is usually nine months after the end of the ARP,[445] and the date that it actually files the annual accounts and reports.

### 425  Default in sending out copies of accounts and reports: offences

**15.425.01**  (1)  If default is made in complying with section 423 or 424, an offence is committed by—
   (a)  the company, and
   (b)  every officer of the company who is in default.
(2)  A person guilty of an offence under this section is liable—
   (a)  on conviction on indictment, to a fine;
   (b)  on summary conviction, to a fine not exceeding the statutory maximum.

COMMENCEMENT DATE  6 April 2008[446]

**15.425.02**  This section provides that failure to comply with the duty to circulate annual accounts and reports within the specified time (sections 423 and 424) is an offence by the company and every officer in default.[447]

### *Option to provide summary financial statement*

### 426  Option to provide summary financial statement

**15.426.01**  (1)  A company may—
   (a)  in such cases as may be specified by regulations made by the Secretary of State, and
   (b)  provided any conditions so specified are complied with,

provide a summary financial statement instead of copies of the accounts and reports required to be sent out in accordance with section 423.
(2)  Copies of those reports and accounts must, however, be sent to any person entitled to be sent them in accordance with that section and who wishes to receive them.
(3)  The Secretary of State may make provision by regulations as to the manner in which it is to be ascertained, whether before or after a person becomes entitled to be sent a copy of those accounts and reports, whether he wishes to receive them.
(4)  A summary financial statement must comply with the requirements of— section 427 (form and contents of summary financial statement: unquoted companies), or section 428 (form and contents of summary financial statement: quoted companies).
(5)  This section applies to copies of accounts and reports required to be sent out by virtue of section 146 to a person nominated to enjoy information rights as it applies to copies of accounts and reports required to be sent out in accordance with section 423 to a member of the company.
(6)  Regulations under this section are subject to negative resolution procedure. Commencement Date subsections (3) and (6) from 20 January 2007;[448] otherwise 6 April 2008[449]

**15.426.02**  The requirement of section 423 that a company send out its annual accounts and reports[450] to the persons entitled thereunder is made subject to this section.[451] The persons entitled under that section include persons nominated under section 145 or 146,[452] although, oddly, subsection (5) of this section

---

[443]  Under Listing Rule LR 9.8.6R (6) certain listed companies are required to state whether they comply with the provisions of the *UK Corporate Governance Code* (Financial Reporting Council, June 2010). See provision E.2.4 of that Code for AGM notice.
[444]  See ss 442 and 443.
[445]  See s 442 for the periods allowed and s 443 for the calculation of the end of that period.
[446]  Companies Act 2006 (Commencement No 5, Transitional Provisions and Savings) Order 2007, SI 2007/3495, art 3(1) for financial years beginning on or after 6 April 2008.
[447]  See s 1121.
[448]  Companies Act 2006 (Commencement No 1, etc) Order 2006, SI 2006/3428, art 3(3).
[449]  Companies Act 2006 (Commencement No 5, Transitional Provisions and Savings) Order 2007, SI 2007/3495, art 3(1) for financial years beginning on or after 6 April 2008.
[450]  See s 471.
[451]  See s 423(6).
[452]  S 145 allows a company's articles to provide for a member to nominate another person to enjoy or exercise all or specified rights of the member, including the right to receive a copy of the annual accounts. S 146 permits

adverts only to the latter nominees. This does not appear of any consequence because section 145 states that a person so nominated should be treated 'as if he were a member'.[453] Thus, the position of a person nominated by virtue of section 145 appears to be no different from that of a member such that this section is applicable to section 145 nominees.

Under this section a company can, in some cases, send out under section 423, in lieu of the annual accounts and reports, a summary financial statement (SFS) if that is the wish of the entitled person or nominated person in question. These SFS provisions apply regardless of whether the individual accounts and any group accounts comprising the annual accounts are prepared as Companies Act or IAS individual or group accounts. The form and content of an SFS is determined by the following two sections; in general terms it is a summary version of, but derived from, the full documents. In practice an SFS is considerably shorter than the full documents, particularly for quoted companies. The manner of sending out is, as under section 423, dealt with by sections 1143 to 1148 and Schedule 5 (eg including in electronic form or by means of a website). However, in the case of a section 146 nominee, the default method is by means of a website.[454]    **15.426.03**

It should be emphasized that the sending out of an SFS is a substitute only for the sending out of the full documents under section 423 and where the entitled person so wishes. Thus, first, a company still has to prepare the 'full' annual accounts and reports. Second, the matter of whether to send an SFS or the full documents has to be determined for each entitled person individually—there is no facility for the blanket sending out of SFS's (but see the following paragraph). Third, it is the full annual accounts and reports, not the SFS, that are required to be delivered to the registrar.[455] Fourth, the rights in sections 431 and 432 of members and debenture holders to demand a (single) copy of the annual accounts and reports are unaffected. In addition, subsection (2) provides that those persons entitled to receive a copy of the annual accounts and reports under section 423 do not lose the right to have the full document sent to them under section 423 if they wish it.    **15.426.04**

The key matters of the cases and conditions under which an SFS may be provided, and the manner of ascertainment of each entitled person's wishes, are dealt with by regulations under subsections (1) and (3),[456] which are in similar form to the regulations under the predecessor provision in the 1985 Act. Broadly speaking these limit the facility to send an SFS to those companies which had their annual accounts audited; and they provide that a company may notify an entitled person of the intention to send him an SFS, and, if the person fails to respond requesting the full documents, that person's wishes are treated as being to have an SFS.    **15.426.05**

### 427  Form and contents of summary financial statement: unquoted companies

(1)  A summary financial statement by a company that is not a quoted company must—    **15.427.01**
   (a)  be derived from the company's annual accounts, and
   (b)  be prepared in accordance with this section and regulations made under it.
(2)  The summary financial statement must be in such form, and contain such information, as the Secretary of State may specify by regulations.
   The regulations may require the statement to include information derived from the directors' report.
(3)  Nothing in this section or regulations made under it prevents a company from including in a summary financial statement additional information derived from the company's annual accounts or the directors' report.
(4)  The summary financial statement must—
   (a)  state that it is only a summary of information derived from the company's annual accounts;
   (b)  state whether it contains additional information derived from the directors' report and, if so, that it does not contain the full text of that report;
   (c)  state how a person entitled to them can obtain a full copy of the company's annual accounts and the directors' report;
   (d)  contain a statement by the company's auditor of his opinion as to whether the summary financial statement—
      (i)  is consistent with the company's annual accounts and, where information derived from the directors' report is included in the statement, with that report, and
      (ii)  complies with the requirements of this section and regulations made under it;

---

a member of a certain type of company to nominate another person to enjoy 'information rights', which include the right to receive a copy of the company's annual accounts and report.

[453]  See s 145(2).
[454]  See s 147.
[455]  See s 441.
[456]  See the Companies (Summary Financial Statement) Regulations 2008 SI 2008/374.

(e)  state whether the auditor's report on the annual accounts was unqualified or qualified and, if it was qualified, set out the report in full together with any further material needed to understand the qualification;

(f)  state whether, in that report, the auditor's statement under section 496 (whether directors' report consistent with accounts) was qualified or unqualified and, if it was qualified, set out the qualified statement in full together with any further material needed to understand the qualification;

(g)  state whether that auditor's report contained a statement under—

(i)  section 498(2)(a) or (b) (accounting records or returns inadequate or accounts not agreeing with records and returns), or

(ii)  section 498(3) (failure to obtain necessary information and explanations), and if so, set out the statement in full.

(5)  Regulations under this section may provide that any specified material may, instead of being included in the summary financial statement, be sent separately at the same time as the statement.

(6)  Regulations under this section are subject to negative resolution procedure. Commencement Date subsections (2), (5), and (6) from 20 January 2007;[457] otherwise 6 April 2008[458]

**15.427.02**  This section governs the form and content of the summary financial statement (SFS) for unquoted companies.[459] These SFS are required to contains certain minimum content prescribed by regulation;[460] to be derived from the annual accounts[461] and, possibly, from the directors' report;[462] to contain disclosures in relation to its being only a summary and advertising the right to a copy of the full annual accounts and reports;[463] to contain a statement by the auditor;[464] and to contain information in relation to the auditor's report on the full annual accounts and reports if it was qualified or contained certain statements.[465]

**15.427.03**  The minimum contents are specified by regulations under subsection (2) detailing the derivation from the annual accounts.[466] The regulations are in substantially the same form as those under the predecessor legislation. The regulations require a condensed version of the profit and loss account and balance sheet, whereas virtually all of the accompanying notes to the accounts are not required;[467] no provision is made for any summary of, or minimum contents derived from, the directors' report; and a cautionary disclosure is also required (referred to further below).

**15.427.04**  The regulations thus provide only a minimum content for SFS. Under subsection (3) additional information may be included, but such information must be derived from the annual accounts or directors' report. This means that 'new' information—that is to say, information that was not contained within the annual accounts or directors' report— cannot be introduced into the SFS, although there appears to be no restriction on circulating the SFS, subject to an appropriate demarcation, as part of a more comprehensive document that contains information that is not derived from the annual accounts or directors' report.

**15.427.05**  Under subsections (4)(a) to (c) a company is required to advertise the status of the SFS as being only a summary derived from the annual accounts and, if relevant, the directors' report; and to state how an entitled person can obtain the full documents. In addition, the regulations under subsection (2) require that the SFS include a statement in a prominent position that they are not sufficient for an understanding of the results and state of affairs of the company or the undertakings included in the consolidation as the case may be.

**15.427.06**  Under subsection (4)(d) the SFS must include a statement from the auditor giving his opinion as to whether the information contained in the SFS is consistent with the annual accounts (and directors' report, if relevant) and complies with this section and its regulations. Auditing Practices Board

---

[457] Companies Act 2006 (Commencement No 1, etc) Order 2006, SI 2006/3428, art 3(3).

[458] Companies Act 2006 (Commencement No 5, Transitional Provisions and Savings) Order 2007, SI 2007/3495, art 3(1) for financial years beginning on or after 6 April 2008.

[459] See s 385.

[460] Subsections (1), (2).

[461] For the annual accounts, see s 471.

[462] Subsections (1), (3). For the directors' report itself, see ss 415–419.

[463] Subsection (4)(a)–(c).

[464] Subsection (4)(d).

[465] Subsection (4)(e)–(g).

[466] See the Companies (Summary Financial Statement) Regulations 2008 SI 2008/374.

[467] Some limited information is required in relation to directors' emoluments.

literature[468] provides more detail in relation to the auditor's statement.[469] In terms of this subsection, two points are worth noting. First, if the auditor qualifies his statement on the SFS, then the company may nevertheless circulate the SFS. This is because the requirement is not for a positive opinion as to consistency and compliance but for an opinion as to whether the SFS are consistent and comply.[470] Second, it is peculiar that the SFS must *contain* a statement from the auditor rather than being *accompanied by* a statement from the auditor. Thus it seems that no SFS could be consistent with the annual accounts (and directors' report) owing to the inclusion of the auditor's statement within the SFS (such a statement not being part of the annual accounts) and thus all auditors' statements would automatically be qualified ones; auditors do not, however, customarily qualify their statements in this regard.

Subsections (4)(e) and (f) require that *the company* state in the SFS whether or not the auditor's report on the annual accounts and directors' report was qualified or unqualified.[471] If it was qualified *the company* is required to reproduce in the SFS the qualification and any further material needed to understand it. Usually the text of the qualification itself will be sufficient for an understanding thereof. However, where the qualification includes a reference to a note to the annual accounts, but does not reproduce the relevant information from that note, then that information would need to be reproduced in the SFS.[472] Subsection(4)(g) makes similar provision for the company to state in SFS whether certain statements were included in the auditor's report on the annual accounts and if so to reproduce them.    **15.427.07**

The offence and related penalty for approving a defective SFS are provided under section 429. However, there may also be civil consequences of approving a defective SFS owing to the provisions of section 463, under which the directors may be liable to the company in relation to false or misleading statements or to omissions in relation to content derived from the directors' report.    **15.427.08**

## 428  Form and contents of summary financial statement: quoted companies

(1) A summary financial statement by a quoted company must—    **15.428.01**
    (a) be derived from the company's annual accounts and the directors' remuneration report, and
    (b) be prepared in accordance with this section and regulations made under it.
(2) The summary financial statement must be in such form, and contain such information, as the Secretary of State may specify by regulations.
The regulations may require the statement to include information derived from the directors' report.
(3) Nothing in this section or regulations made under it prevents a company from including in a summary financial statement additional information derived from the company's annual accounts, the directors' remuneration report or the directors' report.
(4) The summary financial statement must—
    (a) state that it is only a summary of information derived from the company's annual accounts and the directors' remuneration report;
    (b) state whether it contains additional information derived from the directors' report and, if so, that it does not contain the full text of that report;
    (c) state how a person entitled to them can obtain a full copy of the company's annual accounts, the directors' remuneration report or the directors' report;
    (d) contain a statement by the company's auditor of his opinion as to whether the summary financial statement—
        (i) is consistent with the company's annual accounts and the directors' remuneration report and, where information derived from the directors' report is included in the statement, with that report, and
        (ii) complies with the requirements of this section and regulations made under it;
    (e) state whether the auditor's report on the annual accounts and the auditable part of the directors' remuneration report was unqualified or qualified and, if it was qualified, set out the report in full together with any further material needed to understand the qualification;
    (f) state whether that auditor's report contained a statement under—
        (i) section 498(2) (accounting records or returns inadequate or accounts or directors' remuneration report not agreeing with records and returns), or

---

[468] The Auditing Practices Board (APB) has been replaced, following the reorganization of the Financial Reporting Council (FRC) from July 2012, by the FRC Board. Its literature remains in place, however.

[469] *APB Bulletin 2008/03 The auditor's statement on the summary financial statement in the United Kingdom* (APB, 2008).

[470] Cf the case for the auditor's special report on abbreviated accounts for filing at s 449.

[471] See s 495 for a discussion of the meaning of 'qualified'.

[472] For example this is the approach that an auditor would take in assessing the consistency of the SFS with the annual accounts. See *APB Bulletin 2008/03 The auditor's statement on the summary financial statement in the United Kingdom* (APB, 2008), para 28.

(ii)  section 498(3) (failure to obtain necessary information and explanations), and if so, set out the statement in full;

(g)  state whether, in that report, the auditor's statement under section 496 (whether directors' report consistent with accounts) was qualified or unqualified and, if it was qualified, set out the qualified statement in full together with any further material needed to understand the qualification.

(5)  Regulations under this section may provide that any specified material may, instead of being included in the summary financial statement, be sent separately at the same time as the statement.

(6)  Regulations under this section are subject to negative resolution procedure.

COMMENCEMENT DATE  subsections (2), (5), and (6) from 20 January 2007;[473] otherwise 6 April 2008[474]

**15.428.02**  This section governs the form and content of the summary financial statement (SFS) for quoted companies.[475] It is in substantially the same form as that of section 427 in relation to unquoted companies' SFS. The difference is that the full annual accounts and reports[476] required of a quoted company include a directors' remuneration report[477] and so the SFS for such a company is required to contain certain minimum information derived from that additional report.

**15.428.03**  These SFS are required to contains certain minimum contents prescribed by regulation;[478] to be derived from the annual accounts, directors' remuneration report, and, possibly, from the directors' report;[479] to contain disclosures in relation to its being only a summary and advertising the right to a copy of the full annual accounts and reports;[480] to contain a statement by the auditor;[481] and to contain information in relation to the auditor's report on the full annual accounts and reports if it was qualified or contained certain statements.[482]

**15.428.04**  The regulations under this section are in substantially the same form as those under the predecessor legislation.[483] Under the regulations, the minimum contents derived from the directors' remuneration report are in relation to the company's remuneration policies and the performance graph.[484]

**15.428.05**  In other respects the commentary set out in relation to section 427 provides more detail on the equivalent provisions of this section.

### 429  Summary financial statements: offences

**15.429.01**  (1)  If default is made in complying with any provision of section 426, 427 or 428, or of regulations under any of those sections, an offence is committed by—
(a)  the company, and
(b)  every officer of the company who is in default.
(2)  A person guilty of an offence under this section is liable on summary conviction to a fine not exceeding level 3 on the standard scale.

COMMENCEMENT DATE  6 April 2008[485]

**15.429.02**  This section provides that default in compliance with the provisions of section 426 (circulation of summary financial statement), or of section 427 or section 428 (form and content of summary financial statement), is an offence by the company and every officer in default.[486]

---

[473] Companies Act 2006 (Commencement No 1, etc) Order 2006, SI 2006/3428, art 3(3).
[474] Companies Act 2006 (Commencement No 5, Transitional Provisions and Savings) Order 2007, SI 2007/3495, art 3(1) for financial years beginning on or after 6 April 2008.
[475] See s 385.
[476] See s 471.
[477] See s 420.
[478] Subsections (1), (2).
[479] Subsections (1), (3).
[480] Subsection (4)(a)–(c).
[481] Subsection (4)(d).
[482] Subsection (4)(e)–(g).
[483] See the Companies (Summary Financial Statement) Regulations 2008, SI 2008/374.
[484] See commentary at s 421.
[485] Companies Act 2006 (Commencement No 5, Transitional Provisions and Savings) Order 2007, SI 2007/3495, art 3(1) for financial years beginning on or after 6 April 2008.
[486] See s 1121.

*Quoted companies: requirements as to website publication*

## 430   Quoted companies: annual accounts and reports to be made available on website[a]

(1)  A quoted company must ensure that its annual accounts and reports—                    **15.430.01**
    (a)  are made available on a website, and
    (b)  remain so available until the annual accounts and reports for the company's next financial year are made available in accordance with this section.

(2)  The annual accounts and reports must be made available on a website that—
    (a)  is maintained by or on behalf of the company, and
    (b)  identifies the company in question.

(3)  Access to the annual accounts and reports on the website, and the ability to obtain a hard copy of the annual accounts and reports from the website, must not be—
    (a)  conditional on the payment of a fee, or
    (b)  otherwise restricted, except so far as necessary to comply with any enactment or regulatory requirement (in the United Kingdom or elsewhere).

(4)  The annual accounts and reports—
    (a)  must be made available as soon as reasonably practicable, and
    (b)  must be kept available throughout the period specified in subsection (1)(b).

(5)  A failure to make the annual accounts and reports available on a website throughout that period is disregarded if—
    (a)  the annual accounts and reports are made available on the website for part of that period, and
    (b)  the failure is wholly attributable to circumstances that it would not be reasonable to have expected the company to prevent or avoid.

(6)  In the event of default in complying with this section, an offence is committed by every officer of the company who is in default.

(7)  A person guilty of an offence under subsection (6) is liable on summary conviction to a fine not exceeding level 3 on the standard scale.

AMENDMENTS AND NOTES

[a]  This section applies without modification to unregistered companies by reg 10 of the Unregistered Companies Regulations 2009, SI 2009/2436.

COMMENCEMENT DATE   6 April 2008[487]

Sections 430 of the Companies Act 2006 is a new provision providing for the publication of quoted   **15.430.02**
companies' annual accounts and reports. These provisions implement a recommendation made by the Company Law Review Steering Committee for a mandatory requirement to make this information electronically available.[488]

These provisions do not extend to prior year accounts. Prior year accounts are available from   **15.430.03**
Companies House. The accounts must remain available on the website until replaced by the subsequent year's accounts. There is, however, nothing in the Act that would prevent a company from maintaining such archives on its website.

Section 430(3) provides that the information and the ability to print a hard copy must be available on   **15.430.04**
the website free of charge and without any restriction, unless such restrictions are necessary to comply with any UK statutory or regulatory requirements but also any foreign statutory or regulatory requirements.

The information must be available on the website 'as soon as reasonably practicable' and available   **15.430.05**
'throughout' the required time period (section 430(4)). Given that the information will most likely have been prepared in electronic form and the ease with which such electronic documents can be uploaded to a website, one would imagine that the Act envisions a short time frame within which the information must be available on the company website. Section 430(5) addresses disruption to the availability of the website. Any period in which the information is not available will be ignored, provided that the information has been available for part of the required time period, and any period when it is not available is 'wholly attributable' to 'circumstances that it would not be reasonable to have expected the company to prevent or avoid'. The language 'prevent or avoid' suggests that website downtime attributable to unforeseen technical problems or to resolve such problems will benefit from this provision. The word avoid would suggest that regular unavailability due to the failure to remedy

---

[487] Companies Act 2006 (Commencement No 5, Transitional Provisions and Savings) Order 2007, SI 2007/3495, art 6.
[488] CLRSG, *Final Report*, paras 8.91–8.99.

the technical problems or make the required investment in order to remedy such problems may not benefit from this exception.

**15.430.06**   Failure to comply with section 430 is a criminal offence punishable by a fine.

*Right of member or debenture holder to demand copies of accounts and reports*

### 431   Right of member or debenture holder to copies of accounts and reports: unquoted companies

**15.431.01**

(1)   A member of, or holder of debentures of, an unquoted company is entitled to be provided, on demand and without charge, with a copy of—
 (a)   the company's last annual accounts,
 (b)   the last directors' report, and
 (c)   the auditor's report on those accounts (including the statement on that report).
(2)   The entitlement under this section is to a single copy of those documents, but that is in addition to any copy to which a person may be entitled under section 423.
(3)   If a demand made under this section is not complied with within seven days of receipt by the company, an offence is committed by—
 (a)   the company, and
 (b)   every officer of the company who is in default.
(4)   A person guilty of an offence under this section is liable on summary conviction to a fine not exceeding level 3 on the standard scale and, for continued contravention, a daily default fine not exceeding one-tenth of level 3 on the standard scale.

COMMENCEMENT DATE   6 April 2008[489]

**15.431.02**   This section gives a member or debenture holder in an unquoted company,[490] or a person so nominated under section 145, or a person nominated under section 146, a right to demand that a (single) copy of the annual accounts,[491] directors' report, and auditor's report (see below) be provided to him free of charge. This right may be exercised even if he has already received a copy of the annual accounts and reports under section 423.[492] The persons who have this right are slightly fewer than those covered by section 423; that section also includes persons other than the members and debenture holders if they are entitled to notice of general meetings.[493]

**15.431.03**   The requirement in subsection (1)(c) is to provide 'the auditor's report on those accounts (including the statement on that report)'. It is not immediately obvious which report is being referred to in parentheses. However, it would be odd for it to refer to the auditor's report itself, and thus it appears that it is a reference to the directors' report as specified in subsection (1)(b). Thus the statement referred to in parentheses is the auditor's statement as to the consistency of the directors' report with the annual accounts.[494]

**15.431.04**   The means of provision of a copy of the annual accounts and reports fall within the scope of sections 1143 to 1148 and Schedule 5. It may therefore be provided, for example, in electronic form or by means of a website. However, in the case of a section 146 nominee, the default method is by means of a website.[495]

### 432   Right of member or debenture holder to copies of accounts and reports: quoted companies

**15.432.01**

(1)   A member of, or holder of debentures of, a quoted company is entitled to be provided, on demand and without charge, with a copy of—
 (a)   the company's last annual accounts,
 (b)   the last directors' remuneration report,
 (c)   the last directors' report, and
 (d)   the auditor's report on those accounts (including the report on the directors' remuneration report and on the directors' report).

---

[489] Companies Act 2006 (Commencement No 5, Transitional Provisions and Savings) Order 2007, SI 2007/3495, art 3(1) for financial years beginning on or after 6 April 2008.

[490] See s 385.

[491] See s 471.

[492] Subsection (2).

[493] See s 423(1). Such other persons are the directors, the auditors, and anyone stipulated by the articles.

[494] The equivalent requirement in s 432(1)(d) makes it clear that the report which is being referred to there is the directors' report. See s 496 for the auditor's statement on the directors' report.

[495] See s 147.

(2)  The entitlement under this section is to a single copy of those documents, but that is in addition to any copy to which a person may be entitled under section 423.

(3)  If a demand made under this section is not complied with within seven days of receipt by the company, an offence is committed by—
   (a)  the company, and
   (b)  every officer of the company who is in default.

(4)  A person guilty of an offence under this section is liable on summary conviction to a fine not exceeding level 3 on the standard scale and, for continued contravention, a daily default fine not exceeding one-tenth of level 3 on the standard scale.

COMMENCEMENT DATE  6 April 2008[496]

This section gives a member or debenture holder in a quoted company,[497] or a person so nominated **15.432.02** under sections 145 or a person nominated under section 146, a right to demand a (single) copy of the annual accounts,[498] directors' report, directors' remuneration report, and auditor's report to be provided to him free of charge. This right may be exercised even if he has already received a copy of the annual accounts and reports under section 423.[499] The persons who have this right are slightly fewer than those covered by section 423; that section also includes persons other than the members and debenture holders if they are entitled to notice of general meetings.[500]

The means of provision of a copy of the annual accounts and reports fall within the scope of sections **15.432.03** 1143 to 1148 and Schedule 5. It may therefore be provided, for example, in electronic form or by means of a website. However, in the case of a section 146 nominee, the default method is by means of a website.[501]

## Requirements in connection with publication of accounts and reports

### 433  Name of signatory to be stated in published copies of accounts and reports

(1)  Every copy of a document to which this section applies that is published by or on behalf of the **15.433.01** company must state the name of the person who signed it on behalf of the board.

(2)  In the case of an unquoted company, this section applies to copies of—
   (a)  the company's balance sheet, and
   (b)  the directors' report.

(3)  In the case of a quoted company, this section applies to copies of—
   (a)  the company's balance sheet,
   (b)  the directors' remuneration report, and
   (c)  the directors' report.

(4)  If a copy is published without the required statement of the signatory's name, an offence is committed by—
   (a)  the company, and
   (b)  every officer of the company who is in default.

(5)  A person guilty of an offence under this section is liable on summary conviction to a fine not exceeding level 3 on the standard scale.

COMMENCEMENT DATE  6 April 2008[502]

This section consolidates the various requirements of the 1985 Act with respect to stating the **15.433.02** signatories' names on copies of a company's balance sheet, directors' report, and, in the case of a quoted company, the directors' remuneration report, that are published by or on behalf of the company. Similar provision is made in relation to the auditor's report at section 505, albeit subject to certain exceptions set out therein.

The definition of 'published' is given in section 436. It means, 'publishes, issues or circulates it [the **15.433.03** document in question] or otherwise makes it available for public inspection in a manner calculated to invite members of the public generally, or any class of members of the public, to read it'. This has the effect of bringing within this section, for example, the copies of the annual accounts and reports sent

---

[496]  Companies Act 2006 (Commencement No 5, Transitional Provisions and Savings) Order 2007, SI 2007/3495, art 3(1) for financial years beginning on or after 6 April 2008.

[497]  See s 385.

[498]  See s 471.

[499]  Subsection (2).

[500]  See s 423(1). Such other persons are the directors, the auditors, and anyone stipulated by the articles.

[501]  See s 147.

[502]  Companies Act 2006 (Commencement No 5, Transitional Provisions and Savings) Order 2007, SI 2007/3495, art 3(1) for financial years beginning on or after 6 April 2008.

out under section 423, those laid under section 437 (public companies only), any that may be delivered to the registrar under section 441,[503] and those made available on a website.[504]

### 434　Requirements in connection with publication of statutory accounts

**15.434.01**　　(1)　If a company publishes any of its statutory accounts, they must be accompanied by the auditor's report on those accounts (unless the company is exempt from audit and the directors have taken advantage of that exemption).

(2)　A company that prepares statutory group accounts for a financial year must not publish its statutory individual accounts for that year without also publishing with them its statutory group accounts.

(3)　A company's 'statutory accounts' are its accounts for a financial year as required to be delivered to the registrar under section 441.

(4)　If a company contravenes any provision of this section, an offence is committed by—
　　(a)　the company, and
　　(b)　every officer of the company who is in default.

(5)　A person guilty of an offence under this section is liable on summary conviction to a fine not exceeding level 3 on the standard scale.

(6)　This section does not apply in relation to the provision by a company of a summary financial statement (see section 426).

Commencement Date　6 April 2008[505]

**15.434.02**　Before addressing this section, it is necessary to summarize the effect of three other sections. Sections 423, 437, and 441 address the circulation of the annual accounts and reports[506] (including any auditor's report) to entitled persons, their laying before members in general meeting (public companies only), and their delivery to the registrar for placing on the public record. The whole of the annual accounts, comprising the individual accounts and any group accounts that are required, form a single document which, together with any auditor's report, are the subject of those requirements. Thus for the purposes of those sections the annual accounts cannot be separated into their individual and group accounts components nor separated from any auditor's report. They must be kept together.

**15.434.03**　This section 434 is concerned with the keeping together on the occasion of publication, as defined in section 436, of the statutory accounts, as defined in section (3) of this section, with any auditor's report. Its practical effect, however, is limited to cases outside of the circulation, laying, or filing required by the more specific and restrictive provisions of sections 423, 437, and 441.

**15.434.04**　The statutory accounts defined by subsection (3) are those required to be filed under section 441. For companies within the small companies regime[507] and those able to take advantage of the provisions for medium-sized companies,[508] these need not be the 'full' annual accounts but may be abbreviated accounts and a special auditor's report.[509] Thus the abbreviated accounts are statutory accounts and this section applies to them. The full annual accounts and reports of such companies are also within the filing requirement of section 441 as the company may choose to file them and would thus also appear to be statutory accounts; were it not so then the unusual situation would arise that the full annual accounts would not be subject to this section. Companies that are neither in the small companies regime nor are medium-sized are required by section 441 to file their full annual accounts and so similar issues do not arise.

**15.434.05**　Furthermore, the filing requirement relates to the annual accounts, or abbreviated accounts, that comprise both individual accounts and any group accounts in a single package; and some of the accounts disclosure requirements of Chapter 4 of this Part relate to the annual accounts rather than specifically the individual or group accounts.[510] Notwithstanding this, the implication of subsection (2) is that there can be separate statutory individual accounts and statutory group accounts. Thus other than on the occasions covered by sections 423, 437, and 441, the effect of subsections (1) and (2) would appear to be that whilst the individual accounts may be published only with the group accounts and with the auditor's report, the group accounts and the auditor's report may nevertheless be published without the individual accounts. In the latter case the auditor's report will deal with both the individual

---

[503]　This is also specifically required under each of ss 444–447.

[504]　Required for quoted companies by s 430.

[505]　Companies Act 2006 (Commencement No 5, Transitional Provisions and Savings) Order 2007, SI 2007/3495, art 3(1) for financial years beginning on or after 6 April 2008.

[506]　See s 471.

[507]　See ss 381–384.

[508]　See ss 465–467.

[509]　See ss 449 and 450.

[510]　See ss 409–413.

and group accounts and thus it is unlikely that an auditor would be content with having his report published without the full document upon which it reports.

The introduction of IAS group accounts[511] has focused attention on this requirement in subsection (2). It might be thought that it is untidy to put together Companies Act individual accounts[512] with IAS group accounts and instead seek to keep the two entirely separate. However, as mentioned, sections 423, 437, and 441 apply in respect of the annual accounts as a whole, thus preventing separate presentation for those purposes; and for publication covered by this section 434 separate publication of individual accounts is prohibited by subsection (2).    **15.434.06**

Subsection (6) states that the requirements of this section do not apply to a summary financial statement.[513] It is not immediately clear why this appears here because it is clear that the summary financial statement is not the company's statutory accounts.    **15.434.07**

### 435  Requirements in connection with publication of non-statutory accounts

(1) If a company publishes non-statutory accounts, it must publish with them a statement indicating—    **15.435.01**
   (a) that they are not the company's statutory accounts,
   (b) whether statutory accounts dealing with any financial year with which the non-statutory accounts purport to deal have been delivered to the registrar,
   (c) whether an auditor's report has been made on the company's statutory accounts for any such financial year, and if so whether the report—
      (i) was qualified or unqualified, or included a reference to any matters to which the auditor drew attention by way of emphasis without qualifying the report, or
      (ii) contained a statement under section 498(2) (accounting records or returns inadequate or accounts or directors' remuneration report not agreeing with records and returns), or section 498(3) (failure to obtain necessary information and explanations).
(2) The company must not publish with non-statutory accounts the auditor's report on the company's statutory accounts.
(3) References in this section to the publication by a company of 'non-statutory accounts' are to the publication of—
   (a) any balance sheet or profit and loss account relating to, or purporting to deal with, a financial year of the company, or
   (b) an account in any form purporting to be a balance sheet or profit and loss account for a group headed by the company relating to, or purporting to deal with, a financial year of the company,
   otherwise than as part of the company's statutory accounts.
(4) In subsection (3)(b) 'a group headed by the company' means a group consisting of the company and any other undertaking (regardless of whether it is a subsidiary undertaking of the company) other than a parent undertaking of the company.
(5) If a company contravenes any provision of this section, an offence is committed by—
   (a) the company, and
   (b) every officer of the company who is in default.
(6) A person guilty of an offence under this section is liable on summary conviction to a fine not exceeding level 3 on the standard scale.
(7) This section does not apply in relation to the provision by a company of a summary financial statement (see section 426).

COMMENCEMENT DATE  6 April 2008[514]

This section has the effect that the auditor's report on statutory accounts, as defined in section 434(3), is not published with non-statutory accounts,[515] which are defined in subsection (3) of this section; and that any non-statutory accounts contain disclosures making clear their status and relation to the statutory accounts, thereby avoiding any confusion that might arise if different kinds of financial information is in the public domain.[516] The disclosures themselves present few issues in practice.    **15.435.02**

---

[511] See s 403.
[512] See s 395.
[513] See ss 426–429.
[514] Companies Act 2006 (Commencement No 5, Transitional Provisions and Savings) Order 2007, SI 2007/3495, art 3(1) for financial years beginning on or after 6 April 2008.
[515] Subsection (2).
[516] Subsection (1).

However, where the company is not subject to audit[517] the disclosure pursuant to subsection (1)(c) might be made in such a way as to clarify that no auditor's report has been made as there is no audit required.

**15.435.03**    Non-statutory accounts are defined by subsection (3). The definition is wide and, as a consequence, many forms of financial information, if they relate to or purport to deal with a financial year[518] of the company, will be captured. It follows from this definition that to be non-statutory accounts, financial information must relate to the same financial year as statutory accounts. There are four common examples of this. The first is a condensed annual financial statement information under the Financial Services Authority's Disclosure and Transparency Rules[519] (also known as an annual financial reporting announcement) and, where given voluntarily, a preliminary announcement under the Financial Services Authority's Listing Rules.[520] It consists, *inter alia*, of a balance sheet and profit and loss account for the financial year and comparatives. It therefore amounts to non-statutory accounts with respect to the current and comparative figures. The disclosures of subsection (1) are given in respect of both years.[521]

**15.435.04**    The second example is any full year comparative balance sheet or profit and loss account figures contained in a half-yearly financial report required under the Disclosure and Transparency Rules.[522] The figures for the half year (current and comparative) are not non statutory accounts because they do not cover the whole financial year. The disclosures of subsection (1) are given in respect only of the full year comparatives.

**15.435.05**    The third example is a prospectus. Where the three financial years' figures in this document are restated—eg, the three years' annual accounts are not merely reproduced because a change in accounting policy is necessary—the disclosures are given for the relevant years.

**15.435.06**    The final common example is the case of a company that is registered with the Securities and Exchange Commission (SEC) in the United States. Such a company is required annually to file with the SEC, in accordance with US law, an annual report on Form 20-F. The contents of Form 20-F are the broadly the same basic information as in the statutory accounts, for the financial year dealt with in the statutory accounts, but reformatted and with additional US disclosures including a second year of comparatives for the profit and loss account. It therefore amounts to non-statutory accounts with respect to the current and both years' comparative figures. The disclosures of subsection (1) are given in respect of all three years.[523]

**15.435.07**    Although a summary financial statement[524] meets the definition of non-statutory accounts, it is excluded from the requirements of this section by subsection (7). This is, however, of little practical significance because the requirements of sections 427 and 428 are similar to those of this section.

**15.435.08**    Although this section usually does not give rise to difficulties of interpretation, subsection (4) invites consideration. It addresses the meaning of the 'group headed by the company' in subsection (3)(b) (which refers to any accounts in relation to such a group and whether they are non-statutory accounts). Were it not for subsection (4), then 'group' in subsection (3) would have had the meaning given in section 474 as being the company and its subsidiary undertakings.[525] That meaning, as explained in the commentary on that section, relates to the undertakings included in the consolidation in Companies Act group accounts whereas those included in IAS group accounts may very occasionally differ slightly. In order not to be restricted to a meaning associated with Companies Act group accounts, subsection (4) has adopted much more general language. In fact the language is such that accounts of a group headed by the company might even extend to accounts that include a sister company of the company.

---

[517] See s 475.

[518] See s 390.

[519] DTR 6.3.5(2).

[520] A preliminary announcement is voluntary under LR 9.7A.1R. Condensed annual financial statement information under DTR 6.3.5R(2) may be disseminated via a Regulatory Information Service in lieu of the full accounts.

[521] The requirements of DTR 6.3.5 may also be met by disseminating the entire annual accounts in unedited form. If that approach is taken, the audit report must be attached, see s 434.

[522] DTR 4.2.

[523] Some companies include sufficient information in their statutory accounts to enable them to file that with the SEC in satisfaction of the Form 20-F requirement. This section does not apply in such cases.

[524] See ss 426–429.

[525] See s 1162.

### 436  Meaning of 'publication' in relation to accounts and reports

(1)  This section has effect for the purposes of—                                                    **15.436.01**
 section 433 (name of signatory to be stated in published copies of accounts and reports),
 section 434 (requirements in connection with publication of statutory accounts), and
 section 435 (requirements in connection with publication of non-statutory accounts).
(2)  For the purposes of those sections a company is regarded as publishing a document if it publishes,
 issues or circulates it or otherwise makes it available for public inspection in a manner calculated
 to invite members of the public generally, or any class of members of the public, to read it.

COMMENCEMENT DATE  6 April 2008[526]

This section provides a definition of 'publication' for sections 433 to 435.                          **15.436.02**

The definition is a wide one and embraces, for example, the copies of the annual accounts and reports   **15.436.03**
delivered to the registrar under section 441, as the registrar will put those documents on the public
record. It is also clear that making the annual accounts and reports available on a website[527] will invite
members of the public to read them and so thus is covered.

However, in the case of copies of the annual accounts and reports circulated to entitled persons under   **15.436.04**
section 423, and laid before members in general meeting under section 437 (public companies only),
the construction of section 436(2) invites consideration. Whilst such publication would clearly fall
within the phrase 'publishes, issues or circulates it', the question arises as to whether this is the subject
to the qualifying words, 'for public inspection [etc]' and whether, if so, the members are a class of the
public. However, the natural grammatical reading appears to be that those qualifying words relate only
to 'or otherwise makes it available' and not to 'publishes, issues or circulates it'. Thus copies circulated
under section 423 and laid under section 437 (public companies only) are within the definition of
'publication'.

CHAPTER 8

PUBLIC COMPANIES: LAYING OF ACCOUNTS AND REPORTS
BEFORE GENERAL MEETING

### 437 Public companies: laying of accounts and reports before general meeting

(1)  The directors of a public company must lay before the company in general meeting copies of its      **15.437.01**
 annual accounts and reports.
(2)  This section must be complied with not later than the end of the period for filing the accounts and
 reports in question.
(3)  In the Companies Acts 'accounts meeting', in relation to a public company, means a general
 meeting of the company at which the company's annual accounts and reports are (or are to be)
 laid in accordance with this section.

COMMENCEMENT DATE  6 April 2008[528]

This section requires the directors of a public company to lay copies of the company's annual accounts   **15.437.02**
and reports[529] before the company in general meeting. There is no such requirement for private
companies and, in contrast to the 1985 Act, there is no statutory provision to cover a case where a
private company wishes to do so.[530]

This section applies in relation to the annual accounts and reports as defined in section 471. With one   **15.437.03**
exception, this amounts to all of the documents prepared under this Part and any auditor's report
under Part 16. The exception is that sections 419A and 472A refer to a separate corporate governance
statement that is potentially required (albeit required by the FSA's Disclosure and Transparency Rules
(DTR)), but such a statement is not covered by this section's duty to lay. This omission is of little
practical relevance as companies of the type that may have to prepare such a statement customarily

---

[526] Companies Act 2006 (Commencement No 5, Transitional Provisions and Savings) Order 2007, SI
2007/3495, art 3(1) for financial years beginning on or after 6 April 2008.
[527] Required for quoted companies by s 430.
[528] Companies Act 2006 (Commencement No 5, Transitional Provisions and Savings) Order 2007, SI
2007/3495, art 3(1) for financial years beginning on or after 6 April 2008.
[529] See s 471.
[530] As part of a simplifying measure, statute no longer includes any requirement for a private company to hold
an annual general meeting (s 336 applies only to public companies), to lay annual accounts and reports or to take
steps to appoint auditors annually (under s 487 the auditor of a private company is usually deemed to be
re-appointed each year). A private company could, of course, provide in its articles that its annual accounts and
reports are to be laid in general meeting etc.

include corporate governance information (eg, when its inclusion sprang purely from the Listing Rules), and much other material (eg, chairman's letter etc) with the annual accounts and reports that are laid.

**15.437.04**    The requirement in subsection (1) to 'lay before the company' is expressed in terms that may appear antiquated; how exactly are the annual accounts and reports to be laid before members? In practice companies take a straightforward, clear approach to laying: at the general meeting they make available copies of the annual accounts and reports (although of course copies have already been sent to members under sections 423 and 424); and they include on the agenda a resolution to consider and accept them.

**15.437.05**    Subsection (2) provides that the time limit for compliance be the same as that for filing—ie, usually six months after the end of the accounting reference period to which the annual accounts and reports relate.[531]

**15.437.06**    Although it is invariably the case in practice that the accounts of a public company are laid before the company at the annual general meeting (AGM),[532] subsection (1) permits the annual accounts and reports to be laid at any general meeting of the company. Thus, it is possible for the accounts meeting and the AGM to be different meetings of the company although this is highly unlikely to arise in practice—indeed the time limits for holding the AGM reproduce those for the accounts meeting.

### 438  Public companies: offence of failure to lay accounts and reports

**15.438.01**
    (1)  If the requirements of section 437 (public companies: laying of accounts and reports before general meeting) are not complied with before the end of the period allowed, every person who immediately before the end of that period was a director of the company commits an offence.
    (2)  It is a defence for a person charged with such an offence to prove that he took all reasonable steps for securing that those requirements would be complied with before the end of that period.
    (3)  It is not a defence to prove that the documents in question were not in fact prepared as required by this Part.
    (4)  A person guilty of an offence under this section is liable on summary conviction to a fine not exceeding level 5 on the standard scale and, for continued contravention, a daily default fine not exceeding one-tenth of level 5 on the standard scale.

COMMENCEMENT DATE  6 April 2008[533]

**15.438.02**    This section provides for an offence for failure to lay the annual accounts and reports before the company in general meeting. It raises no particular difficulties but it is notable that this section, together with the offences for failure to circulate or to file,[534] are in effect also a sanction for failure to prepare annual accounts.[535]

## CHAPTER 9
## QUOTED COMPANIES: MEMBERS' APPROVAL OF DIRECTORS' REMUNERATION REPORT

### 439  Quoted companies: members' approval of directors' remuneration report

**15.439.01**
    (1)  A quoted company must, prior to the accounts meeting, give to the members of the company entitled to be sent notice of the meeting notice of the intention to move at the meeting, as an ordinary resolution, a resolution approving the directors' remuneration report for the financial year.
    (2)  The notice may be given in any manner permitted for the service on the member of notice of the meeting.
    (3)  The business that may be dealt with at the accounts meeting includes the resolution. This is so notwithstanding any default in complying with subsection (1) or (2).
    (4)  The existing directors must ensure that the resolution is put to the vote of the meeting.

---

[531]  Under s 442 the time allowed to a public company for filing is six months, but subject to the rules relating to changes in accounting reference date. For accounting reference period and accounting reference date, see ss 391 and 392.

[532]  See s 336.

[533]  Companies Act 2006 (Commencement No 5, Transitional Provisions and Savings) Order 2007, SI 2007/3495, art 3(1) for financial years beginning on or after 6 April 2008.

[534]  See ss 425 and 451–453.

[535]  Chapter 4 of this Part contains no explicit sanction for failure to prepare annual accounts (cf, s 415(4), (5) in relation to the directors' report and s 420(2), (3) in relation to the directors' remuneration report).

(5)  No entitlement of a person to remuneration is made conditional on the resolution being passed by reason only of the provision made by this section.

(6)  In this section—

'the accounts meeting' means the general meeting of the company before which the company's annual accounts for the financial year are to be laid; and

'existing director' means a person who is a director of the company immediately before that meeting.

COMMENCEMENT DATE  6 April 2008[536]

This section requires that the directors of a quoted company[537] give notice of, and put to the vote at, the accounts meeting, a resolution to approve the directors' remuneration report. This requirement was introduced[538] at the same time as the directors' remuneration report. Its policy motive is to promote dialogue between the directors and investor groups by offering the shareholders an opportunity to express an opinion on the company's directors' remuneration policies and actual practice.          **15.439.02**

The failure of the members to approve the directors' remuneration report is largely confined to negative publicity. The directors' remuneration report stands as approved as by the board;[539] and there is no effect on the remuneration of any person as a result of failure of the members to approve the report[540] (although it would be open to a company to contract with a director to make his remuneration conditional to some degree on this resolution).          **15.439.03**

The 'accounts meeting' to which this section relates is defined in subsection (6) in the same form as the definition for a public company in section 437(3). It is presumed that the definition is repeated here to cover the unlikely possibility of an unlimited private company's being a quoted company.[541]          **15.439.04**

## 440  Quoted companies: offences in connection with procedure for approval

(1)  In the event of default in complying with section 439(1) (notice to be given of resolution for approval of directors' remuneration report), an offence is committed by every officer of the company who is in default.          **15.440.01**

(2)  If the resolution is not put to the vote of the accounts meeting, an offence is committed by each existing director.

(3)  It is a defence for a person charged with an offence under subsection (2) to prove that he took all reasonable steps for securing that the resolution was put to the vote of the meeting.

(4)  A person guilty of an offence under this section is liable on summary conviction to a fine not exceeding level 3 on the standard scale.

(5)  In this section—

'the accounts meeting' means the general meeting of the company before which the company's annual accounts for the financial year are to be laid; and

'existing director' means a person who is a director of the company immediately before that meeting.

COMMENCEMENT DATE  6 April 2008[542]

This section provides for two offences with regard to the members' approval of the directors' remuneration report: failure to give notice of a resolution for approving the directors' remuneration report at the accounts meeting; and failure to put that resolution to a vote at the accounts meeting.          **15.440.02**

---

[536] Companies Act 2006 (Commencement No 5, Transitional Provisions and Savings) Order 2007, SI 2007/3495, art 3(1) for financial years beginning on or after 6 April 2008.

[537] See s 385.

[538] CA 1985, s 241A, introduced by the Directors' Remuneration Report Regulations 2002, SI 2002/1986.

[539] Under s 422.

[540] Subsection (5).

[541] Section 755's prohibition on a private company's offering its securities to the public applies only to private limited companies and thus not to unlimited private companies.

[542] Companies Act 2006 (Commencement No 5, Transitional Provisions and Savings) Order 2007, SI 2007/3495, art 3(1) for financial years beginning on or after 6 April 2008.

CHAPTER **10**

FILING OF ACCOUNTS AND REPORTS

*Duty to file accounts and reports*

**441   Duty to file accounts and reports with the registrar**[a]

15.441.01

(1) The directors of a company must deliver to the registrar for each financial year the accounts and reports required by—

section 444 (filing obligations of companies subject to small companies regime),

[section 444A (filing obligations of companies entitled to small companies exemption in relation to directors' report)],[b]

section 445 (filing obligations of medium-sized companies),

section 446 (filing obligations of unquoted companies), or

section 447 (filing obligations of quoted companies).

(2) This is subject to—

section 448 (unlimited companies exempt from filing obligations) [and

section 448A (dormant subsidiaries exempt from filing obligations).][c]

AMENDMENTS AND NOTES

[a] This section applies with modifications to overseas companies by reg 40 of the Overseas Companies Regulations 2009, 2009/1801.

[b] Inserted by the Companies Act 2006 (Accounts and Reports) Regulations 2008, SI 2008/393, reg 6.

[c] Inserted by the Companies and Limited Liability Partnerships (Accounts and Audit Exemptions and Change in Accounting Framework) Regulations 2012, SI 2012/2301, for financial years ending on or after 1 October 2012.

COMMENCEMENT DATE in relation to subsections (2), from 1 October 2012[543]; otherwise, 6 April 2008[544]

15.441.02   This section requires the directors of a company to deliver to the registrar[545] such accounts and reports as specified by sections 444 to 448. This delivery of accounts and reports is also known as filing of accounts and reports, as in the heading to this section. Certain unlimited companies are exempt from this requirement.[546]

15.441.03   The five sections referred to specify the accounts and reports by reference to companies falling into different categories—those in the small companies regime,[547] those entitled to the small companies exemption,[548] medium-sized companies,[549] unquoted companies, and quoted companies;[550] and, perhaps oddly, each of those five sections repeats the requirement to file. The construction of each of sections 444 to 448 is such as to place each company in the most advantageous category; for example, a medium-sized company will also be unquoted, but it nevertheless falls only within the section for medium-sized companies.

15.441.04   To put it briefly, in respect of unquoted companies not falling within the small companies regime, the small companies exemption, or within the provisions for medium sized companies, and for quoted companies, the documents that must be filed are simply those annual accounts and reports[551] that have been prepared for the members and sent to them under section 423. However, for companies in the small companies regime and for medium-sized companies, together with any separate governance statement prepared pursuant to the FSA's DTR,[552] sections 444 and 445 permit the omission of certain reports and certain parts of the annual accounts, and for those within the small companies exemption,

---

[543] Companies and Limited Liability Partnerships (Accounts and Audit Exemptions and Change of Accounting Framework) Regulations 2012, SI 2012/2301, for financial years ending on or after 1 October 2012.

[544] Companies Act 2006 (Commencement No 5, Transitional Provisions and Savings) Order 2007, SI 2007/3495, art 3(1) for financial years beginning on or after 6 April 2008.

[545] See s 1060.

[546] Subsection (2), and see s 448.

[547] See ss 381–384.

[548] See ss 415A and 441A.

[549] See ss 465–467. As more fully explained at the commentary on those sections, in order to take advantage of the provisions of this Part for medium-sized companies, such as s 445, a company that qualifies as medium-sized under ss 465–466 must not be excluded from so doing by s 467. That is to say, notwithstanding the language of the legislation in this section, qualification as medium-sized alone, under ss 465–466, is not enough.

[550] See s 385.

[551] See s 471.

[552] See ss 419A, 472A.

section 444A permits the omission of the directors' report; naturally, the filing of the full annual accounts and reports would be always sufficient to meet such companies' filing obligations.

As is apparent from each of sections 444 to 447, it is only a copy of the relevant accounts and reports  **15.441.05**
that is required to be delivered and, save as required by the registrar for authentication (see below), it need not be signed.[553] All of those sections provide, however, that the copies of the balance sheet, directors' report, directors' remuneration report (if relevant), and auditor's report (if relevant) must state the name of the person that signed the originals.[554]

The manner of delivery to the registrar is specified in sections 1068 to 1071. Hitherto, where accounts  **15.441.06**
were subject to audit, only signed, hard copies were accepted by the registrar:[555] faxed or electronic copies were not permitted. It is now the case that companies may deliver certain documents electronically, including any accounts and reports under this section.[556] The registrar has power to specify the precise manner of electronic delivery and to require and specify the means of authentication. The requirements are contained in what are known as the Registrar's Rules made under section 1068.[557] Electronic delivery is by means of a submission of a completed 'pdf' accounts template provided by Companies House[558] (known as webfiling) or in an extensible markup language (XML or XBRL) schema specified by Companies House (known as software filing), in which case the company is responsible for ensuring the compatibility of its data. The first method is likely to be useful only for simpler accounts. The registrar does not have power to compel electronic delivery, but the Secretary of State has regulation-making power to do so.[559] Companies House had previously announced that it intends, subject to the outcome of a consultation and to subsequent regulations being approved by Parliament,[560] to accept only electronic filings for the vast majority of companies (over 98 per cent according to Companies House) by March 2013.[561] Following the outcome of the consultation confirming the Government's intention not to add new regulations that affect small companies it will not introduce mandatory electronic filing until 2014.[562]

As noted above, the primary legislation no longer requires that the filed copies of accounts and reports  **15.441.07**
be signed copies of each of the individual documents in the suite.[563] This is to facilitate electronic filing. Where electronic means are used, the Registrar's Rules[564] specify the manner of authentication. In the case of hard copy filing, a director's signature (in black ink) is required at the end of the balance sheet; no person's signature is required elsewhere (eg, not on any director's report or auditor's report). This signature is intended to attest to the authenticity of the copy of the whole suite of documents comprising the filed accounts and reports. It appears that it is not necessary to state the name of this signatory.

Delivery means that the documents, whether they be in hard copy or electronic form, must be received  **15.441.08**
by the registrar.[565] Thus, for example, the posting of the documents is not sufficient for the directors to fulfill their obligation with respect to delivery; it is their receipt by the registrar that satisfies the requirement.

---

[553] However, copies delivered to the registrar before 1 October 2009 are required to be signed owing to transitional adaptations (see ss 444–447 and 449) made by the Companies Act 2006 (Commencement No 5, Transitional Provisions and Savings) Order 2007, SI 2007/3495. The transitional adaptations require a signed copy of the balance sheet, the directors' report and any auditor's report to be delivered to the registrar. This transitional adaptation was revoked on 1 October 2009, see the Companies Act 2006 (Commencement No 8, Transitional Provisions and Savings) Order 2008, SI 2008/2860, reg(6)(1).

[554] Subject, in the case of the auditors' report, to the provisions of s 506.

[555] As discussed in n 527 to para 15.441.05 above, copies delivered to the registrar before 1 October 2009 are required to be signed owing to transitional adaptations of the Companies Act 2006 (Commencement No 5, Transitional Provisions and Savings) Order 2007. CA 1985, s 707B permitted electronic communication to be used for the delivery of any document under that Act provided that such delivery was in such form and manner as was directed by the registrar. However, the registrar did not accept the electronic filing of accounts that were subject to audit.

[556] See ss 1068(5) and 1078. The electronic delivery facility in those sections commenced with effect from 1 January 2007.

[557] The full, final rules were in force from 1 October 2009. See <http://www.companieshouse.gov.uk/about/policyDocuments/registrarsRules.shtml>.

[558] The Government agency that assists the Registrar in the discharge of his duties.

[559] Ss 1068(7) and 1069 respectively.

[560] The regulations will be subject to the affirmative resolution procedure – see s 1069(3).

[561] *Register 72 online* (Companies House, Spring 2011).

[562] <http://www.companieshouse.gov.uk/about/electronicServices.shtml>.

[563] See n 525 to para 15.441.04 above in relation to filing prior to 1 October 2009.

[564] The full, final rules were in force from 1 October 2009.

[565] See s 1071.

**15.441.09** Furthermore, the registrar has made rules under the power specifying the form of documents delivered.[566] In relation to filing of accounts and reports, this requires white paper and black typescript or manuscript in black ink; this, presumably, is to facilitate the electronic scanning of the documents. It is also specified that the company's registered number must appear on one of the suite of documents comprising the accounts and reports, and, if the accounts themselves are chosen, it must appear on the face of the balance sheet or profit and loss account; it is no longer permitted for the number to appear on the front cover of the suite as a whole.

### 442 Period allowed for filing accounts[a]

**15.442.01**
(1) This section specifies the period allowed for the directors of a company to comply with their obligation under section 441 to deliver accounts and reports for a financial year to the registrar. This is referred to in the Companies Acts as the 'period for filing' those accounts and reports.

(2) The period is—
   (a) for a private company, nine months after the end of the relevant accounting reference period, and
   (b) for a public company, six months after the end of that period. This is subject to the following provisions of this section.

(3) If the relevant accounting reference period is the company's first and is a period of more than twelve months, the period is—
   (a) nine months or six months, as the case may be, from the first anniversary of the incorporation of the company, or
   (b) three months after the end of the accounting reference period, whichever last expires.

(4) If the relevant accounting reference period is treated as shortened by virtue of a notice given by the company under section 392 (alteration of accounting reference date), the period is—
   (a) that applicable in accordance with the above provisions, or
   (b) three months from the date of the notice under that section, whichever last expires.

(5) If for any special reason the Secretary of State thinks fit he may, on an application made before the expiry of the period otherwise allowed, by notice in writing to a company extend that period by such further period as may be specified in the notice.

(6) Whether the period allowed is that for a private company or a public company is determined by reference to the company's status immediately before the end of the relevant accounting reference period.

(7) In this section 'the relevant accounting reference period' means the accounting reference period by reference to which the financial year for the accounts in question was determined.

AMENDMENTS AND NOTES

[a] This section applies with modifications to overseas companies by reg 40 of the Overseas Companies Regulations 2009, 2009/1801.

COMMENCEMENT DATE 6 April 2008[567]

**15.442.02** This section determines the period allowed to the directors to deliver the accounts and reports to the registrar under section 441. This is known as the 'period for filing'.[568] The documents required to be delivered by section 441 may be delivered at any time during the period for filing. As noted under section 441, delivery means receipt by the registrar.

**15.442.03** The period for filing begins the day after the relevant accounting reference period[569] (ARP) ends. In normal circumstances it ends, for private limited companies, nine months after the end of the relevant ARP; and for public companies, six months after the end of the relevant ARP. Thus the period for filing is not based on the end of the financial year; if it were, the registrar would have to track each company's financial year—an onerous administrative task—owing to the seven-day rule in section 390.[570] Section 443 specifies the manner of calculating the day of the month on which falls the end of the period for filing.

**15.442.04** Subsections (3) and (4) deal with two special cases. The first is that of the first ARP that is longer than twelve months.[571] If the normal rule of subsection (2) applied, a period of up to 27 months could elapse

---

[566] Registrar's Rules made under s 1068. The full, final rules were in force from 1 October 2009.

[567] Companies Act 2006 (Commencement No 5, Transitional Provisions and Savings) Order 2007, SI 2007/3495, art 3(1) for financial years beginning on or after 6 April 2008.

[568] Subsection (1).

[569] See s 391.

[570] Accounts and reports are prepared in relation to a financial year which ends on any date of the directors' choosing not more than seven days before or after the end of the ARP.

[571] See s 391(5).

between incorporation and the filing of the first accounts and reports.[572] The effect of subsection (3) is to limit this: the period for filing ends six or nine months, as the case may be, after the first anniversary of incorporation, or three months after the end of the ARP if later.

The other special case relates to that of a company that shortens an ARP under section 392. Without any special rule this might result in the directors being in immediate default; ie, the period for filing by reference to the new, short ARP could already have expired since the company is allowed to change a previous ARP at any time up to the end of the period for filing in relation to the original ARP. Thus subsection (4) provides that the period for filing is determined as that under the normal rule of subsection (2) or, if later, is three months after the date of the notice given under section 392. For example, a public company could, by notice given on 11 May 2010, shorten its ARP from being the 12 months to 31 December 2009 to become the three months to 31 March 2009; without subsection (4), the period for filing for the new ARP would already have expired on 30 September 2009; under subsection (4)(b), the period for filing will end on 11 August 2010, being three months after the notice to change.          **15.442.05**

There may be occasions on which a company's directors cannot meet the filing deadlines under this section. Under subsection (5), the directors may, within the period for filing, apply to the Secretary of State for an extension of the period for filing and, if he believes there is a special reason for doing so, he may extend that period. In practice the application is made to Government officials employed by the registrar. It appears that extensions are not granted lightly: 9,123 companies applied for an extension under this section's predecessor in the 1985 Act during the year ended 31 March 2006, of which only 3,061 were granted.[573]          **15.442.06**

### 443   Calculation of period allowed

(1) This section applies for the purposes of calculating the period for filing a company's accounts and reports which is expressed as a specified number of months from a specified date or after the end of a specified previous period.          **15.443.01**

> (2)   Subject to the following provisions, the period ends with the date in the appropriate month corresponding to the specified date or the last day of the specified previous period.
> (3)   If the specified date, or the last day of the specified previous period, is the last day of a month, the period ends with the last day of the appropriate month (whether or not that is the corresponding date).
> (4)   If—
>> (a)   the specified date, or the last day of the specified previous period, is not the last day of a month but is the 29th or 30th, and
>> (b)   the appropriate month is February, the period ends with the last day of February.
> (5)   'The appropriate month' means the month that is the specified number of months after the month in which the specified date, or the end of the specified previous period, falls.

COMMENCEMENT DATE   6 April 2008[574]

This section sets out the method by which the last day of the period for filing (as defined in section 442) is determined. Put simply, if the accounting reference period (ARP) ends on a month-end date (30 September, say), the six- or nine-month period for filing for that ARP, as the case may be,[575] ends on the month-end date six or nine month later (the following 31 March or 30 June); if the ARP does not end on a month-end date (12 November, say), then the filing period ends on the corresponding day in the month six or nine months later (the following 12 May or 12 August). In so providing, the section overturns, in respect of the period for filing, the case law that hitherto applied.[576]          **15.443.02**

The section is drafted in terms of determining a date a specified number of months from a 'specified date' or 'after the end of a specified period'. The 'specified date' refers to the cases covered by section 442(3)(a) and (4)(b): ie, a period measured from the anniversary of incorporation, and one measured from the date of notice to shorten the ARP, respectively. The phrase 'after the end of a specified period' refers to cases covered by section 442(2), (3)(b), and (4)(a): ie, the specified period is the ARP in relation to which filing is required.          **15.443.03**

---

[572]   If a private company arranged its affairs so as to have a first ARP of the maximum 18 months and then took the maximum nine months to file.

[573]   *Companies in 2005–2006* (DTI, 2006), p 27.

[574]   Companies Act 2006 (Commencement No 5, Transitional Provisions and Savings) Order 2007, SI 2007/3495, art 3(1) for financial years beginning on or after 6 April 2008.

[575]   Taking, by way of example, the usual periods under s 442(2).

[576]   Under *Dodds v Walker* [1981] 2 All ER 609 the corresponding day rule always applied even when the ARP was on a month-end. Thus with an ARP ending on 30 September, a public company would have had to have filed by the following 30 March, not 31 March.

**15.443.04**    Subsection (3) deals with the most common case of a company with an ARP ending on a month-end date. It provides the simple month-end-to-month-end calculation rule.

**15.443.05**    Subsections (3) and (4) deal with the unusual case of a company with an ARP ending during a month. They provide the corresponding date rule, subject to special provision where the period for filing would, according to that rule, otherwise end on a non-existent date in February. For example, if a private company's ARP ends on 30 May, then there is no corresponding date nine months later in February, and subsection (4) provides that the period for filing instead ends on the last day of February.

## Filing obligations of different descriptions of company

### 444   Filing obligations of companies subject to small companies regime

**15.444.01**
(1)  The directors of a company subject to the small companies regime—
  (a)  must deliver to the registrar for each financial year a copy of a balance sheet drawn up as at the last day of that year, and
  (b)  may also deliver to the registrar—
    (i)  a copy of the company's profit and loss account for that year, and
    (ii)  a copy of the directors' report for that year.
(2)  The directors must also deliver to the registrar a copy of the auditor's report on [the accounts (and any directors' report that it delivers)].[a] This does not apply if the company is exempt from audit and the directors have taken advantage of that exemption.
(3)  The copies of accounts and reports delivered to the registrar must be copies of the company's annual accounts and reports, except that where the company prepares Companies Act accounts—
  (a)  the directors may deliver to the registrar a copy of a balance sheet drawn up in accordance with regulations made by the Secretary of State, and
  (b)  there may be omitted from the copy profit and loss account delivered to the registrar such items as may be specified by the regulations.
  These are referred to in this Part as 'abbreviated accounts'.
(4)  If abbreviated accounts are delivered to the registrar the obligation to deliver a copy of the auditor's report on the accounts is to deliver a copy of the special auditor's report required by section 449.
(5)  Where the directors of a company subject to the small companies regime deliver to the registrar IAS accounts, or Companies Act accounts that are not abbreviated accounts, and in accordance with this section—
  (a)  do not deliver to the registrar a copy of the company's profit and loss account, or
  (b)  do not deliver to the registrar a copy of the directors' report,
  the copy of the balance sheet delivered to the registrar must contain in a prominent position a statement that the company's annual accounts and reports have been delivered in accordance with the provisions applicable to companies subject to the small companies regime.
(6)  The copies of the balance sheet and any directors' report delivered to the registrar under this section must state the name of the person who signed it on behalf of the board.[b]
(7)  The copy of the auditor's report delivered to the registrar under this section must—
  (a)  state the name of the auditor and (where the auditor is a firm) the name of the person who signed it as senior statutory auditor, or
  (b)  if the conditions in section 506 (circumstances in which names may be omitted) are met, state that a resolution has been passed and notified to the Secretary of State in accordance with that section.[c]

AMENDMENTS AND NOTES

[a]  Words inserted by the Companies Act 2006 (Amendment) (Accounts and Reports) Regulations 2008, SI 2008/393, reg 12.

[b]  Transitional provision: The Companies Act 2006 (Commencement No 5, Transitional Provisions and Savings) Order 2007, SI 2007/3495, Sch 1, para 6 contained a transitional provision that was revoked with effect from 1 October 2009. No detail is given here.

[c]  Transitional provision: The Companies Act 2006 (Commencement No 5, Transitional Provisions and Savings) Order 2007, SI 2007/3495, Sch 1, para 6 made certain adaptations that were revoked with effect from 1 October 2009. No detail is given here.

COMMENCEMENT DATE  subsection (3) from 20 January 2007;[577] otherwise 6 April 2008[578]

---

[577]  Companies Act 2006 (Commencement No 1, etc) Order 2006, SI 2006/3428, art 3(3).
[578]  Companies Act 2006 (Commencement No 5, Transitional Provisions and Savings) Order 2007, SI 2007/3495, art 3(1) for financial years beginning on or after 6 April 2008.

This section applies only to companies within the small companies regime.[579] Where such companies    **15.444.02**
are also entitled to the small companies exemption or are medium-sized and unquoted, they are not
within sections 444A, 445 and 446 on small companies exemption, medium-sized, and unquoted
companies' filings respectively.[580]

It should be noted first of all that the documents to be filed are copies rather than signed originals. As    **15.444.03**
discussed at section 441, this is to facilitate electronic filing; however, as also noted in that commentary,
if the filing is in hard copy then the Registrar's Rules (under section 1068) require the filing to be
authenticated by a director's signature on one of the documents comprising the filed accounts and
reports. The names of the original signatories of the relevant original documents must nevertheless be
stated with respect to the balance sheet and any directors' report[581] but section 506 provides an
exception for certain cases in relation to the auditor's report.[582]

Turning to the documents that are to be delivered, the filing obligations of companies subject to the    **15.444.04**
small companies regime are much lighter than those of other companies. Under this section such a
company has three options. First, it need file only certain selected parts of the annual accounts and
reports (as sent to members under section 423); it need file only the balance sheet and the auditor's
report (if there is one), or it may file those with one or other of the profit and loss account or the
directors' report.[583] In such a case a statement must be made on the balance sheet in a prominent
position that they 'have been delivered' in accordance with the provisions applicable to companies
subject to the small companies regime. The requirement to state that they 'have been delivered' is
rather awkward, as it is plainly the case that they have not been delivered when the statement is made.

If the directors take this route, a difficult issue arises for the auditor. His report deals not only with the    **15.444.05**
balance sheet but with the profit and loss account and the directors' report. Indeed, the profit and loss
account is a fundamental part of the annual accounts[584] on which the auditor reported.[585] No auditor
is likely to be content to have published his report upon documents without its being accompanied by
all of those documents in full. However, that is precisely the report that the auditor has given and it is
required to be attached to the selected portions of the annual accounts delivered to the registrar.
Notwithstanding his discomfort, it appears that the auditor is powerless to prevent his report's being so
filed. In response to this issue, the Auditing Practices Board (APB) [586]suggests that the auditor insert an
explanatory preface (in the filing copy) to alert readers to the fact that the company has taken advantage
of the facility in section 444, and has proposed some illustrative wording.[587]

The second option for a company subject to the small companies regime is that it could file 'abbreviated    **15.444.06**
accounts'.[588] The abbreviated accounts option is available only where the full annual accounts are
Companies Act accounts[589]—that is, it is not possible to file an abbreviated accounts version of annual
accounts that include either IAS individual or IAS group accounts (but presumably such a company
would instead avail itself of its choices under subsection (1)). The form and content of abbreviated
accounts are determined by separate regulations under subsection (3),[590] the form and content of
which are much the same as that under the 1985 Act;[591] no profit and loss account is required to be
presented and limited information is required to be presented in the notes to the accounts. Under the
regulations there is no facility for abbreviated group accounts, if the company chooses to prepare group
accounts at all.

Section 450 sets out the approval and signing requirements for the (original copy of) abbreviated    **15.444.07**
accounts, including the requirement for a statement on the balance sheet to the effect that they are
prepared in accordance with special provisions. In addition, where abbreviated accounts are to be filed,

---

[579]  See ss 381–384.

[580]  See ss 444A(5), 445(7) and 446(5).

[581]  Subsection (6) and see s 433.

[582]  Subsection (7).

[583]  Subsections (1)(a), (2). See s 475 for the requirement for audit.

[584]  See s 471.

[585]  See s 495.

[586]  The Auditing Practices Board (APB) has been replaced, following the reorganization of the Financial
Reporting Council (FRC) from July 2012 by the FRC Board. Its literature remains in place, however.

[587]  See Bulletin 2008/04 *The special auditor's report on abbreviated accounts in the United Kingdom* (APB,
2008), paras 10–12. For the authority of APB material, see the commentary on s 1217.

[588]  Subsection (3).

[589]  See ss 395 and 403.

[590]  The Small Companies and Groups (Accounts and Directors' Report) Regulations 2008.

[591]  Previously contained within the CA 1985, s 246(5), (6), and Sch 8A.

the auditor's report (if any) on the full annual accounts is not filed with them; it would be inappropriate to require the filing of a report in association with a different set of accounts from those on which the auditor reported. Hence a special auditor's report is required instead[592] as further specified by section 449.

**15.444.08**   It should be noted that the option to file abbreviated accounts does not alter the obligation of directors under section 394 to prepare the company's full individual accounts for the year and send those individual accounts to members and others further to section 423.

**15.444.09**   The final choice available to a company subject to the small companies regime is to file the same, full annual accounts, directors' report, and auditor's report (if there is one) as was sent to members and others under section 423. To do so the company would choose under subsection (1)(b) to file the directors' report and the profit and loss account.

## [444A   Filing obligations of companies entitled to small companies exemption in relation to directors' report[a]

**15.444A.01**
    (1)   The directors of a company that is entitled to small companies exemption in relation to the directors' report for a financial year—
        (a)  must deliver to the registrar a copy of the company's annual accounts for that year, and
        (b)  may also deliver to the registrar a copy of the directors' report.
    (2)   The directors must also deliver to the registrar a copy of the auditor's report on the accounts (and any directors' report) that it delivers.
       This does not apply if the company is exempt from audit and the directors have taken advantage of that exception.
    (3)   The copies of the balance sheet and directors' report delivered to the registrar under this section must state the name of the person who signed it on behalf of the board.
    [(4) The copy of the auditor's report delivered to the registrar under this section must—
        (a)  state the name of the auditor and (where the auditor is a firm) the name of the person who signed it as senior statutory auditor, or
        (b)  if the conditions in section 506 (circumstances in which names may be omitted) are met, state that a resolution has been passed and notified to the Secretary of State in accordance with that section.][b]
    (5)   This section does not apply to companies within section 444 (filing obligations of companies subject to the small companies regime).]

AMENDMENTS AND NOTES

[a]   Inserted by the Companies Act 2006 (Amendment) (Accounts and Reports) Regulations 2008, SI 2008/393, reg 6 for financial years beginning on or after 6 April 2008 (reg 2(2)).

[b]   Subsection (4): substituted by the Companies Act 2006 (Accounts, Reports and Audit) Regulations 2009, SI 2009/1581, reg 10, as from 1 October 2009. No detail of the former provision is given here.

COMMENCEMENT DATE   6 April 2008

**15.444A.02**   This section applies only to companies that qualify for the small companies exemption of section 415A but are not within the small companies' regime.[593]

**15.444A.03**   Where companies within this section are also medium-sized and/or unquoted, they are not within sections 445 and 446 on medium-sized and unquoted companies' filings.[594]

**15.444A.04**   It should be noted first of all that the documents to be filed are copies rather than signed originals. As discussed at section 441, this is to facilitate electronic filing; however, as also noted in that commentary, if the filing is in hard copy then the Registrar's Rules (under section 1068) require the filing to be authenticated by a director's signature on one of the documents comprising the filed accounts and reports. The names of the original signatories of the relevant original documents must nevertheless be stated with respect to the balance sheet and any directors' report;[595] but section 506 provides an exception for certain cases in relation to the auditor's report.[596]

**15.444A.05**   This section has been inserted to relieve companies entitled to the small companies exemption from delivering a directors' report to the registrar. The exemption given by subsection (1) relates only to the filing of the directors' report; a directors' report, albeit modified by virtue of the other provisions of this

---

[592]   Subsection (4).
[593]   Subsection (4).
[594]   See ss 445(7) and 446(5).
[595]   Subsection (3) and see s 433.
[596]   Subsection (4).

section, must still be prepared and circulated to members. The annual accounts and any auditor's report thereon are required to be filed.

### 445   Filing obligations of medium-sized companies

(1) The directors of a company that qualifies as a medium-sized company in relation to a financial year (see sections 465 to 467) must deliver to the registrar a copy of—    **15.445.01**
   (a) the company's annual accounts, and
   (b) the directors' report.

(2) They must also deliver to the registrar a copy of the auditor's report on those accounts (and on the directors' report).
   This does not apply if the company is exempt from audit and the directors have taken advantage of that exemption.

(3) Where the company prepares Companies Act accounts, the directors may deliver to the registrar a copy of the company's annual accounts for the financial year—
   (a) that includes a profit and loss account in which items are combined in accordance with regulations made by the Secretary of State, and
   (b) that does not contain items whose omission is authorised by the regulations. These are referred to in this Part as 'abbreviated accounts'.

(4) If abbreviated accounts are delivered to the registrar the obligation to deliver a copy of the auditor's report on the accounts is to deliver a copy of the special auditor's report required by section 449.

(5) The copies of the balance sheet and directors' report delivered to the registrar under this section must state the name of the person who signed it on behalf of the board.[a]

(6) The copy of the auditor's report delivered to the registrar under this section must—
   (a) state the name of the auditor and (where the auditor is a firm) the name of the person who signed it as senior statutory auditor, or
   (b) if the conditions in section 506 (circumstances in which names may be omitted) are met, state that a resolution has been passed and notified to the Secretary of State in accordance with that section.[b]

(7) This section does not apply to companies within [(a)] section 444 (filing obligations of companies subject to the small companies regime) [, or (b) section 444A (filing obligations of companies entitled to small companies exemption in relation to directors report)[c]].

AMENDMENTS AND NOTES

[a] Transitional provision: Companies Act 2006 (Commencement No 5, Transitional Provisions and Savings) Order 2007, SI 2007/3495, Sch 1, para 7 made certain adaptations that were revoked with effect from 1 October 2009. No detail is given here.

[b] Transitional provision: Companies Act 2006 (Commencement No 5, Transitional Provisions and Savings) Order 2007, SI 2007/3495, Sch 1, para 7 made certain adaptations that were revoked with effect from 1 October 2009. No detail is given here..

[c] Amendment made by the Commencement Act 2006, (Amendment) (Accounts and Reports) Regulations 2008, SI 2008/393

COMMENCEMENT DATE   subsection (3) from 20 January 2007;[597] otherwise 6 April 2008[598]

This section applies only to companies that qualify as medium-sized but are not within the small **15.445.02** companies' regime or entitled to the small companies exemption. It should be noted that although the section uses the term 'qualifies as a medium-sized company', the effect of section 467 is that not only must a company so qualify under sections 465 and 466, but it must not be excluded under section 467 from taking advantage of provisions relating to companies qualifying as medium-sized.

Where companies within this section are also unquoted, they are not within section 446 on unquoted **15.445.03** companies' filing.[599]

It should be noted first of all that the documents to be filed are copies rather than signed originals. As **15.445.04** discussed at section 441, this is to facilitate electronic filing; however, as also noted in that commentary, if the filing is in hard copy then the Registrar's Rules (under section 1068) require the filing to be authenticated by a director's signature on one of the documents comprising the filed accounts and reports. The names of the original signatories of the relevant original documents must nevertheless be

---

[597] Companies Act 2006 (Commencement No 1, etc) Order 2006, SI 2006/3428, art 3(3).
[598] Companies Act 2006 (Commencement No 5, Transitional Provisions and Savings) Order 2007, SI 2007/3495, art 3(1) for financial years beginning on or after 6 April 2008.
[599] See s 446(5).

stated with respect to the balance sheet and any directors' report;[600] but section 506 provides an exception for certain cases in relation to the auditor's report.[601]

**15.445.05**   A medium-sized company has two choices with respect to the documents to be filed. First, it may file the same, full annual accounts and directors' report with the auditor's report thereon (unless exempt from audit)[602] that were sent to members and others under section 423. Alternatively, it may choose to file 'abbreviated accounts'.

**15.445.06**   The abbreviated accounts option is available only where the full annual accounts are Companies Act accounts[603]—that is, it is not possible to file an abbreviated accounts version of IAS individual or group accounts. The form and content of abbreviated accounts is determined by separate regulations under subsection (3)[604] and only very limited omissions are permitted. In particular, the major dispensation provided by the 1985 Act[605] —the omission of the company's turnover—is not provided by these regulations.[606] Section 450 sets out the approval and signing requirements for the (original copy of) abbreviated accounts, including the requirement for a statement on the balance sheet to the effect that they are prepared in accordance with special provisions. In addition, where abbreviated accounts are to be filed, the auditor's report (if any) on the full annual accounts is not filed with them; it would be inappropriate to require the filing of a report in association with a different set of accounts from those on which the auditor reported. Hence a special auditor's report is required instead[607] as further specified by section 449.

**15.445.07**   It should be noted that the option to file abbreviated accounts does not alter the obligations of directors under sections 394 and 399 to prepare the company's full annual accounts for the year and to send those to members and others further to section 423.

### 446   Filing obligations of unquoted companies

**15.446.01**
(1)   The directors of an unquoted company must deliver to the registrar for each financial year of the company a copy of—
  (a)   the company's annual accounts,
  (b)   the directors' report [, and
  (c)   any separate corporate governance statement].[a]
(2)   The directors must also deliver to the registrar a copy of the auditor's report on those accounts (and the directors' report [and any separate corporate governance statement][b]
     This does not apply if the company is exempt from audit and the directors have taken advantage of that exemption.
(3)   The copies of the balance sheet[, directors' report and any separate corporate governance statement][c] delivered to the registrar under this section must state the name of the person who signed it on behalf of the board.[d]
(4)   The copy of the auditor's report delivered to the registrar under this section must—
  (a)   state the name of the auditor and (where the auditor is a firm) the name of the person who signed it as senior statutory auditor, or
  (b)   if the conditions in section 506 (circumstances in which names may be omitted) are met, state that a resolution has been passed and notified to the Secretary of State in accordance with that section.[e]
(5)   This section does not apply to companies within—
  (a)   section 444 (filing obligations of companies subject to the small companies regime),
  [(aa) section 444A (filing obligations of companies entitled to the small companies exemption in relation to directors' report), or][f]
  (b)   section 445 (filing obligations of medium-sized companies).

AMENDMENTS AND NOTES

[a]   Inserted by the Companies Act 2006 (Accounts, Reports and Audit) Regulations 2009, SI 2009/ 1581, reg 3(1), (2), as from 27 June 2009, in relation to financial years beginning on or after 29 June 2008 which have not ended before 27 June 2009.

[b]   Inserted by regulations noted at note a above.

---

[600]   Subsection (5) and see s 433.
[601]   Subsection (6).
[602]   See s 475.
[603]   See ss 395 and 403.
[604]   Large and Medium-sized Companies and Groups (Accounts and Reports) Regulations 2008, SI 2008/ 410.
[605]   Previously contained within the CA 1985, ss 246A(3).
[606]   Although particulars of turnover may still be omitted.
[607]   Subsection (4).

<sup>c</sup> Amended by regulations noted at note a above.

<sup>d</sup> Transitional provision: Companies Act 2006 (Commencement No 5, Transitional Provisions and Savings) Order 2007, SI 2007/3495, Sch 1, para 8 made certain adaptations that were revoked with effect from 1 October 2009. No detail is given here.

<sup>e</sup> Transitional provision: Companies Act 2006 (Commencement No 5, Transitional Provisions and Savings) Order 2007, SI 2007/3495, Sch 1, para 8 made certain adaptations that were revoked with effect from 1 October 2009. No detail is given here.

<sup>f</sup> Inserted by the Companies Act 2006 (Amendment) (Accounts and Reports) Regulations 2008, SI 2008/393, reg 6.

COMMENCEMENT DATE  6 April 2008[608]

The effect of this section is that an unquoted company,[609] which is not a company subject to the small companies regime, not entitled to the small companies exemption, or not one able to take advantage of provisions for medium-sized companies,[610] must deliver to the registrar the same, full set of annual accounts and reports that were required to be sent to members and others under section 423, together with any separate corporate governance statement.[611]     **15.446.02**

It should be noted that the documents to be filed are copies rather than signed originals. As discussed at section 441, this is to facilitate electronic filing; however, as also noted in that commentary, if the filing is in hard copy then the Registrar's Rules (under section 1068) require the filing to be authenticated by a director's signature on one of the documents comprising the filed accounts and reports. The names of the original signatories of the relevant original documents must nevertheless be stated with respect to the balance sheet and any directors' report;[612] but section 506 provides an exception for certain cases in relation to the auditor's report.[613]     **15.446.03**

## 447  Filing obligations of quoted companies

(1)  The directors of a quoted company must deliver to the registrar for each financial year of the company a copy of—     **15.447.01**
   (a)  the company's annual accounts,
   (b)  the directors' remuneration report,
   (c)  the directors' report [, and
   (d)  any separate corporate governance statement].<sup>a</sup>
(2)  They must also deliver a copy of the auditor's report on those accounts (and on the directors' remuneration report, [the directors' report and any separate corporate governance statements]<sup>b</sup>.
(3)  The copies of the balance sheet, the directors' remuneration report, [the directors report and any separate corporate governance statement]<sup>c</sup> delivered to the registrar under this section must state the name of the person who signed it on behalf of the board.<sup>d</sup>
(4)  The copy of the auditor's report delivered to the registrar under this section must—
   (a)  state the name of the auditor and (where the auditor is a firm) the name of the person who signed it as senior statutory auditor, or
   (b)  if the conditions in section 506 (circumstances in which names may be omitted) are met, state that a resolution has been passed and notified to the Secretary of State in accordance with that section.<sup>e</sup>

AMENDMENTS AND NOTES

<sup>a</sup> Inserted by the Companies Act 2006 (Accounts, Reports and Audit) Regulations 2009, SI 2009/1581, reg 4(1), (2), as from 27 June 2009, in relation to financial years beginning on or after 29 June 2008 which have not ended before 27 June 2009.

<sup>b</sup> Inserted by regulations as noted at note a above.

<sup>c</sup> Inserted by regulations as noted at note a above.

<sup>d</sup> Transitional provision: Companies Act 2006 (Commencement No 5, Transitional Provisions and Savings) Order 2007, SI 2007/3495, Sch 1, para 9 made certain adaptations that were revoked with effect from 1 October 2009. No detail is given here.

---

[608] Companies Act 2006 (Commencement No 5, Transitional Provisions and Savings) Order 2007, SI 2007/3495, art 3(1) for financial years beginning on or after 6 April 2008.

[609] See s 385.

[610] Subsection (5).

[611] See ss 419A, 472A.

[612] Subsection (3) and see s 433.

[613] Subsection (4).

e  Transitional provision: Companies Act 2006 (Commencement No 5, Transitional Provisions and Savings) Order 2007, SI 2007/3495, Sch 1, para 9 made certain adaptations that were revoked with effect from 1 October 2009. No detail is given here.

COMMENCEMENT DATE  6 April 2008[614]

**15.447.02**  The effect of this section is that a quoted company[615] must deliver to the registrar the same, full set of annual accounts and reports that were required to be sent to members and others under section 423 together with any separate corporate governance statement.[616]

**15.447.03**  It should be noted that the documents to be filed are copies rather than signed originals. As discussed at section 441, this is to facilitate electronic filing; however, as also noted in that commentary, if the filing is in hard copy then the Registrar's Rules (under section 1068) require the filing to be authenticated by a director's signature on one of the documents comprising the filed accounts and reports. The names of the original signatories of the relevant original documents must nevertheless be stated with respect to the balance sheet and any directors' report;[617] but section 506 provides an exception for certain cases in relation to the auditor's report.[618]

### 448  Unlimited companies exempt from obligation to file accounts

**15.448.01**
(1)  The directors of an unlimited company are not required to deliver accounts and reports to the registrar in respect of a financial year if the following conditions are met.

(2)  The conditions are that at no time during the relevant accounting reference period—
  (a)  has the company been, to its knowledge, a subsidiary undertaking of an undertaking which was then limited, or
  (b)  have there been, to its knowledge, exercisable by or on behalf of two or more undertakings which were then limited, rights which if exercisable by one of them would have made the company a subsidiary undertaking of it, or
  (c)  has the company been a parent company of an undertaking which was then limited.
  The references above to an undertaking being limited at a particular time are to an undertaking (under whatever law established) the liability of whose members is at that time limited.

(3)  The exemption conferred by this section does not apply if—
  (a)  the company is a banking or insurance company or the parent company of a banking or insurance group, or
  (b)  [each of the members of the company is —
    (i)  a limited company
    (ii)  another unlimited company each of whose members is a limited company,
    (iii)  a Scottish partnership each of whose member is a limited company.
  The references in paragraph (b) to a limited company, another unlimited company or a Scottish partnership include a comparable undertaking incorporated in or formed under the law of a country or territory outside the United Kingdom.][a]

(4)  Where a company is exempt by virtue of this section from the obligation to deliver accounts—
  (a)  section 434(3) (requirements in connection with publication of statutory accounts: meaning of 'statutory accounts') has effect with the substitution for the words 'as required to be delivered to the registrar under section 441' of the words 'as prepared in accordance with this Part and approved by the board of directors'; and
  (b)  section 435(1)(b) (requirements in connection with publication of non-statutory accounts: statement whether statutory accounts delivered) has effect with the substitution for the words from 'whether statutory accounts' to 'have been delivered to the registrar' of the words 'that the company is exempt from the requirement to deliver statutory accounts'.

(5)  In this section the 'relevant accounting reference period', in relation to a financial year, means the accounting reference period by reference to which that financial year was determined.

AMENDMENTS

a  Words substituted by the Companies Act 2006 (Amendment) (Accounts and Reports) Regulations 2008, SI 2008/393, reg 13.

COMMENCEMENT DATE  6 April 2008[619]

---

[614]  Companies Act 2006 (Commencement No 5, Transitional Provisions and Savings)Order 2007, SI 2007/3495, art 3(1) for financial years beginning on or after 6 April 2008.

[615]  See s 385.

[616]  See ss 419A, 472A.

[617]  Subsection (3) and see s 433.

[618]  Subsection (4).

[619]  Companies Act 2006 (Commencement No 5, Transitional Provisions and Savings) Order 2007, SI 2007/3495, art 3(1) for financial years beginning on or after 6 April 2008.

Except as provided by this section, the obligations of this Part, and of Part 16, relating to an unlimited company are the same as in relation to a limited company. Thus the directors of an unlimited company must, for example, prepare accounts, have them audited if necessary, and send them to the company's members and others as required by section 423.   **15.448.02**

An exception is, nevertheless, made with regard to the filing of an unlimited company's annual accounts with the registrar.[620] Thus if conditions of this section are met, an unlimited company is not required to file its annual accounts, although the directors may still choose to do so.[621] It would appear that the policy motive behind this exemption is that as the members have unlimited liability, then the creditors are not solely reliant on the solvency of the company itself, and so the company is granted privacy of its financial affairs.   **15.448.03**

However, an exception from filing might otherwise easily lead to unintended uses and so subsection (2) provides conditions. The effect is, for example, to prevent a group from operating through unlimited companies with limited companies as their immediate holding companies (the accounts of which would be of little interest, being simply those of a holding company); this would otherwise mean that whilst each individual operation in effect had limited liability, yet no accounts for those individual operations would be on public record. Thus subsection (2)(a) applies when the unlimited company is a subsidiary undertaking[622] of an undertaking[623] that has limited liability, even if the unlimited company has other members who have unlimited liability. This test is applied to all parent undertakings and, therefore, the wider group of which the unlimited company is a member, must be considered. Subsection (2)(b) requires that all members which have limited liability are considered together, thus dealing with circumstances in which subsection (2)(a) would be circumvented by the rights that would be exercisable by a parent being exercisable by two or more undertakings with limited liability.   **15.448.04**

Subsection (2)(c) requires an unlimited company to file accounts when it is a parent undertaking.[624] This provision ensures that group accounts are filed if otherwise required by the Act—ie, it prevents a group of limited companies from being headed by an unlimited company, being a pure holding company, and therefore not providing consolidated information on public record.   **15.448.05**

The condition in subsection (3)(a) prevents advantage from being taken of the exception for certain type of activities—ie, banking or insurance companies or groups.[625]   **15.448.06**

The provision in subsection (3)(b) that the unlimited company does not meet those conditions is of little practical significance as subsections (2)(a) and (b) appear to cover all potential circumstances in which subsection (3)(b) is met.   **15.448.07**

## 448A   Dormant subsidiaries exempt from obligation to file accounts

(1)  The directors of a company are not required to deliver a copy of the company's individual accounts to the registrar in respect of a financial year if—   **15.448A.01**
   (a)  the company is a subsidiary undertaking,
   (b)  it has been dormant throughout the whole of that year, and
   (c)  its parent undertaking is established under the law of an EEA State.
(2)  Exemption is conditional upon compliance with all of the following conditions—
   (a)  all members of the company must agree to the exemption in respect of the financial year in question,
   (b)  the parent undertaking must give a guarantee under section 448C in respect of that year,
   (c)  the company must be included in the consolidated accounts drawn up for that year or to an earlier date in that year by the parent undertaking in accordance with—
     (i)  the provisions of the Seventh Directive (83/349/EEC), or
     (ii)  international accounting standards,
   (d)  the parent undertaking must disclose in the notes to the consolidated accounts that the directors of the company are exempt from the requirement to deliver a copy of the company's individual accounts to the registrar by virtue of this section, and
   (e)  the directors of the company must deliver to the registrar within the period for filing the company's accounts and reports for that year—
     (i)  a written notice of the agreement referred to in subsection (2)(a),
     (ii)  the statement referred to in section 448C(1),

---

[620]  See s 1060.
[621]  It is highly unlikely they would choose to do so since the exception is one of the few advantages of an unlimited company.
[622]  See s 1162.
[623]  See s 1161.
[624]  See s 1162.
[625]  See ss 1164 and 1165.

    (iii) a copy of the consolidated accounts referred to in subsection (2)(c),

    (iv) a copy of the auditor's report on those accounts, and

    (v) a copy of the consolidated annual report drawn up by the parent undertaking.

COMMENCEMENT DATE 1 October 2012[626]

**15.448A.02** This exemption, which was introduced in 2012, may be summarized as being conditional upon three principal matters: that the company is dormant throughout the entire financial year that it is a subsidiary undertaking; that it is guaranteed by an EEA parent undertaking; and that it is not one of certain categories of company set out in section 448B. As to the first condition, the definition of a dormant company is dealt with in section 1169. As to the latter two conditions, these are in the same terms as the sections 394A-4394C dormant, guaranteed subsidiaries' annual accounts preparation exemption and the sections 479A-479C guaranteed subsidiaries' audit exemption. These exemption conditions are dealt with in the commentary at sections 479A-479C.

**15.448A.03** The combined effect of sections 394A-394C, 448A-448C and 479A-479C is that a dormant, guaranteed subsidiary undertaking may, at one extreme, choose to prepare no annual accounts at all, or, at the other, to prepare, have audited and deliver annual accounts to the registrar; or various combinations in between, such as preparing annual accounts but, under this section, not delivering them. Note, however, that there is no equivalent exemption in relation to the preparation of a directors' report under section 415. Nor is there any exception in relation to delivering the directors' report under section 441 (unless the company *also* falls within one of the other exemptions following that section, i.e. sections 444 and 444A in relation to the small companies regime/ small companies).

### 448B Companies excluded from the dormant subsidiaries exemption

**15.448B.01** The directors of a company are not entitled to the exemption conferred by section 448A (dormant subsidiaries) if the company was at any time within the financial year in question—

(a) a quoted company as defined in section 385(2) of this Act,

(b) a company that—

    (i) is an authorised insurance company, a banking company, an e-Money issuer, a MiFID investment firm or a UCITS management company, or

    (ii) carries on insurance market activity, or

(c) a special register body as defined in section 117(1) of the Trade Union and Labour Relations (Consolidation) Act 1992 (c 52) or an employers' association as defined in section 122 of that Act or Article 4 of the Industrial Relations (Northern Ireland) Order 1992 (S.I. 1992/807) (NI 5).

COMMENCEMENT DATE 1 October 2012[627]

**15.448B.02** This section excludes certain categories of companies for the section 394A exemption, in identical terms to sections 448B and 479B.

### 448C Dormant subsidiaries filing exemption: parent undertaking declaration of guarantee

**15.448C.01** (1) A guarantee is given by a parent undertaking under this section when the directors of the subsidiary company deliver to the registrar a statement by the parent undertaking that it guarantees the subsidiary company under this section.

(2) The statement under subsection (1) must be authenticated by the parent undertaking and must specify—

    (a) the name of the parent undertaking,

    (b) if the parent undertaking is incorporated in the United Kingdom, its registered number (if any),

    (c) if the parent undertaking is incorporated outside the United Kingdom and registered in the country in which it is incorporated, the identity of the register on which it is registered and the number with which it is so registered,

    (d) the name and registered number of the subsidiary company in respect of which the guarantee is being given,

    (e) the date of the statement, and

    (f) the financial year to which the guarantee relates.

---

[626] Companies and Limited Liability Partnerships (Accounts and Audit Exemptions and Change of Accounting Framework) Regulations 2012, SI 2012/2301, for financial years ending on or after 1 October 2012.

[627] Companies and Limited Liability Partnerships (Accounts and Audit Exemptions and Change of Accounting Framework) Regulations 2012, SI 2012/2301, for financial years ending on or after 1 October 2012.

(3)  A guarantee given under this section has the effect that—
    (a)  the parent undertaking guarantees all outstanding liabilities to which the subsidiary company is subject at the end of the financial year to which the guarantee relates, until they are satisfied in full, and
    (b)  the guarantee is enforceable against the parent undertaking by any person to whom the subsidiary company is liable in respect of those liabilities.

COMMENCEMENT DATE  1 October 2012[628]

The guarantee arrangements required by this section, as a condition for the section 394A exemption, are in identical terms to those of sections 448C and 479C. The commentary on the latter deals with the guarantee.     **15.448C.02**

## *Requirements where abbreviated accounts delivered*

## 449   Special auditor's report where abbreviated accounts delivered

(1)  This section applies where—     **15.449.01**
    (a)  the directors of a company deliver abbreviated accounts to the registrar, and
    (b)  the company is not exempt from audit (or the directors have not taken advantage of any such exemption).
(2)  The directors must also deliver to the registrar a copy of a special report of the company's auditor stating that in his opinion—
    (a)  the company is entitled to deliver abbreviated accounts in accordance with the section in question, and
    (b)  the abbreviated accounts to be delivered are properly prepared in accordance with regulations under that section.
(3)  The auditor's report on the company's annual accounts need not be delivered, but—
    (a)  if that report was qualified, the special report must set out that report in full together with any further material necessary to understand the qualification, and
    (b)  if that report contained a statement under—
        (i)   section 498(2)(a) or (b) (accounts, records or returns inadequate or accounts not agreeing with records and returns), or
        (ii)  section 498(3) (failure to obtain necessary information and explanations), the special report must set out that statement in full.
(4)  The provisions of—
    sections 503 to 506 (signature of auditor's report), and
    sections 507 to 509 (offences in connection with auditor's report),
    apply to a special report under this section as they apply to an auditor's report on the company's annual accounts prepared under Part 16.[a]
(5)  If abbreviated accounts are delivered to the registrar, the references in section 434 or 435 (requirements in connection with publication of accounts) to the auditor's report on the company's annual accounts shall be read as references to the special auditor's report required by this section.

AMENDMENTS AND NOTES

[a]  Transitional provision: Companies Act 2006 (Commencement No 5, Transitional Provisions and Savings) Order 2007, SI 2007/3495, Sch 1, para 10 made certain adaptations that were revoked with effect from 1 October 2009. No detail is given here.

COMMENCEMENT DATE  6 April 2008[629]

Sections 444 and 445 permit companies subject to the small companies regime, or those able to take     **15.449.02** advantage of provisions for medium-sized companies, to file abbreviated accounts. These are a version of the full annual accounts but with certain specified omissions. Those sections provide that the auditor's report (if any) on the full annual accounts is not filed with them;[630] it would be inappropriate to require the filing of a report in association with a different set of accounts from those on which the

---

[628]  Companies and Limited Liability Partnerships (Accounts and Audit Exemptions and Change of Accounting Framework) Regulations 2012, SI 2012/2301, for financial years ending on or after 1 October 2012, as corrected.

[629]  Companies Act 2006 (Commencement No 5, Transitional Provisions and Savings) Order 2007, SI 2007/3495, art 3(1) for financial years beginning on or after 6 April 2008.

[630]  See ss 444(4) and 445(4), which impose an obligation only to deliver the special report under this section. This section provides (subs (3)) that the auditor's report on the full accounts 'need not' be delivered, perhaps implying that it may nevertheless be delivered. In practice an auditor is not likely to consent to his report being so delivered.

auditor reported. Instead a special auditor's report under this section is required in cases where the full annual accounts were subject to audit.

**15.449.03**   Section 449 sets out the general form and content of the special auditor's report. Further form and content is specified by the Auditing Practices Board.[631]

**15.449.04**   Subsection (2) determines the basic form of the opinion. It requires that the auditor must report that it is his opinion that the company is entitled to deliver abbreviated accounts under the appropriate section (entitlement being based on measures taken from, or apparent in, annual accounts)[632] and that the abbreviated accounts comply with the relevant regulations. Thus if the auditor is unable so to report, the company is not entitled to file abbreviated accounts.[633]

**15.449.05**   Where the auditor's report on the full annual accounts was qualified, there is no prohibition on the filing of abbreviated accounts. However, the subject matter of the qualification could well be relevant to the abbreviated accounts. Accordingly, subsection (3) requires the reproduction of any qualified report, or similar statement made under section 498(2)(a), (b), or (3), in the auditor's report on the abbreviated accounts. However, the qualification may call into question measures in the annual accounts by reference to which the entitlement to deliver abbreviated accounts is determined; if in such a case the auditor is unable to conclude upon the company's entitlement, then as mentioned above, the company is not entitled.[634]

**15.449.06**   Subsection (4) applies the provisions that apply to all auditors' reports, with respect to signature and to offences, to the special auditor's report on abbreviated accounts. Thus, the special auditor's report is on an equal footing with other auditor's reports in this regard.

**15.449.07**   When abbreviated accounts are prepared, they become statutory accounts[635] of the company, and thus the requirements in sections 434 and 435, with respect to the presentation of the auditor's report, are read as referring to the special auditor's report prepared under this section.

### 450   Approval and signing of abbreviated accounts

**15.450.01**   (1)   Abbreviated accounts must be approved by the board of directors and signed on behalf of the board by a director of the company.
(2)   The signature must be on the balance sheet.
(3)   The balance sheet must contain in a prominent position above the signature a statement to the effect that it is prepared in accordance with the special provisions of this Act relating (as the case may be) to companies subject to the small companies regime or to medium-sized companies.
(4)   If abbreviated accounts are approved that do not comply with the requirements of regulations under the relevant section, every director of the company who—
    (a)   knew that they did not comply, or was reckless as to whether they complied, and
    (b)   failed to take reasonable steps to prevent them from being approved, commits an offence.
(5)   A person guilty of an offence under subsection (4) is liable—
    (a)   on conviction on indictment, to a fine;
    (b)   on summary conviction, to a fine not exceeding the statutory maximum.

COMMENCEMENT DATE  6 April 2008[636]

**15.450.02**   This section makes provision for the approval of the abbreviated accounts. The approval is by the board collectively, but the signature, on the company's balance sheet, is by a director on behalf of the board.[637] It should be noted that only one director is required to sign although two (or more) may do so.

**15.450.03**   The section does not require the signature to be accompanied by the date of approval, but it is done for the following reasons. First of all, as described at section 414, the full annual accounts state the date of their approval; this is because the date of approval is a significant matter in terms of accounting and is

---

[631] The Auditing Practices Board (APB) has been replaced, following the reorganization of the Financial Reporting Council (FRC) from July 2012 by the FRC Board. Its literature remains in place, however. APB *Bulletin 2008/04 The special auditor's report on abbreviated accounts in the United Kingdom* (APB, 2008). For the authority of APB material, see the commentary on s 1217.

[632] See ss 381–384 and 465–467.

[633] For example see APB *Bulletin 2008/04*, para 40.

[634] For example see APB *Bulletin 2008/04*, para 40.

[635] See s 434(3).

[636] Companies Act 2006 (Commencement No 5, Transitional Provisions and Savings) Order 2007, SI 2007/3495, art 3(1) for financial years beginning on or after 6 April 2008.

[637] Subsection (1).

required by accounting standards to be disclosed.[638] It is of such significance that it ought also to be stated in the abbreviated accounts derived from the full annual accounts. Thus it would be considered good practice for the signature at the foot of the balance sheet to be preceded by a statement to the effect that the abbreviated accounts were approved by the board, with the date disclosed, and that they were signed on its behalf by the director concerned. This also provides clarity, for a reader of the balance sheet, that it is the board collectively that is approving the abbreviated accounts rather than solely the signing director. If the abbreviated accounts are not approved on the same date as the full annual accounts—which is not in fact the usual arrangement—then it would be considered good practice also to state the date of approval of the abbreviated accounts and to note that the abbreviated accounts do not consider the effects of any events between the two dates.[639]

Subsection (3) requires a specific statement to be made on the balance sheet that the abbreviated accounts are prepared in accordance with the special provisions of the Act relating to companies subject to the small companies regime or to medium-sized companies. The registrar enforces this regularly and rejects the delivery of accounts if the required statement is not made.    **15.450.04**

## Failure to file accounts and reports

### 451   Default in filing accounts and reports: offences[a]

(1) If the requirements of section 441 (duty to file accounts and reports) are not complied with in    **15.451.01**
    relation to a company's accounts and reports for a financial year before the end of the period for
    filing those accounts and reports, every person who immediately before the end of that period
    was a director of the company commits an offence.

(2) It is a defence for a person charged with such an offence to prove that he took all reasonable steps
    for securing that those requirements would be complied with before the end of that period.

(3) It is not a defence to prove that the documents in question were not in fact prepared as required
    by this Part.

(4) A person guilty of an offence under this section is liable on summary conviction to a fine not
    exceeding level 5 on the standard scale and, for continued contravention, a daily default fine not
    exceeding one-tenth of level 5 on the standard scale.

AMENDMENTS

[a] This section applies with modifications to overseas companies by reg 41 of the Overseas Companies
Regulations 2009, 2009/1801.

COMMENCEMENT DATE  6 April 2008[640]

An offence is committed by each person who is a director of the company at end of the period for    **15.451.02**
filing[641] if the relevant accounts and reports are not delivered during the period for filing. The filing of
the accounts and reports after expiry of the period for filing has no bearing on the matter. The purpose
of subsection (3) is to deny the directors a defence by their not preparing the accounts and reports at
all.[642]

The registrar takes late filing seriously and does undertake prosecution of directors, albeit less    **15.451.03**
frequently than the levying of civil penalties on companies.[643] For example, although information is
not available for prosecutions under this section, during the year ended 31 March 2010, the registrar
sought in England and Wales 2,879 prosecutions under the Companies Act 1985, section 242(2) (the
predecessor to this section), of which 1,397 were successful.[644]

### 452   Default in filing accounts and reports: court order

(1) If—    **15.452.01**
    (a) the requirements of section 441 (duty to file accounts and reports) are not complied with in
        relation to a company's accounts and reports for a financial year before the end of the period
        for filing those accounts and reports, and

---

[638] FRS 21 *Events after the balance sheet date* (ASB, 2004, as amended) para 17; IAS 10 *Events after the balance sheet date* (International Accounting Standards Board, 2003, as amended), see Commission Regulation (EC) 1126/2008 at [2008] OJ L320/1, as amended,

[639] For example this is required of the auditors in relation to the s 449 special report by *APB Bulletin 2008/04*.

[640] Companies Act 2006 (Commencement No 5, Transitional Provisions and Savings) Order 2007, SI 2007/3495, art 3(1) for financial years beginning on or after 6 April 2008.

[641] See ss 442 and 443.

[642] A similar argument was successfully made in the case of *Stockdale v Coulson* [1974] 3 All ER 154, as a response to which the predecessor to subs (3) was introduced.

[643] See s 453.

[644] *Statistical tables on companies registration activities* (BIS, 2010), p 19.

(b) the directors of the company fail to make good the default within 14 days after the service of a notice on them requiring compliance, the court may, on the application of any member or creditor of the company or of the registrar, make an order directing the directors (or any of them) to make good the default within such time as may be specified in the order.

(2) The court's order may provide that all costs (in Scotland, expenses) of and incidental to the application are to be borne by the directors.

COMMENCEMENT DATE 6 April 2008[645]

**15.452.02**   This section provides a legal mechanism for any member of the company, a creditor, or the registrar[646] to apply to court for the purpose of requiring the directors to file accounts and reports. Whilst the provisions of this section are available to members and creditors, they are rarely used by them, and its relevance is largely confined to the registrar.

### 453   Civil penalty for failure to file accounts and reports

**15.453.01**   (1) Where the requirements of section 441 are not complied with in relation to a company's accounts and reports for a financial year before the end of the period for filing those accounts and reports, the company is liable to a civil penalty.

This is in addition to any liability of the directors under section 451.

(2) The amount of the penalty shall be determined in accordance with regulations made by the Secretary of State by reference to—

(a) the length of the period between the end of the period for filing the accounts and reports in question and the day on which the requirements are complied with, and

(b) whether the company is a private or public company.

(3) The penalty may be recovered by the registrar and is to be paid into the Consolidated Fund.

(4) It is not a defence in proceedings under this section to prove that the documents in question were not in fact prepared as required by this Part.

(5) Regulations under this section having the effect of increasing the penalty payable in any case are subject to affirmative resolution procedure.

Otherwise, the regulations are subject to negative resolution procedure.

COMMENCEMENT DATE subsections (2) and (5) from 20 January 2007;[647] otherwise 6 April 2008[648]

**15.453.02**   This section makes a company liable for a civil penalty if it has failed to file its accounts and reports within the period for filing.[649] Subsection (4) prevents a company's avoiding liability by its not preparing the annual accounts and reports.[650] This civil penalty should be distinguished from the criminal offence that falls on the directors, as provided by section 451.

**15.453.03**   The penalty applies whether the filing has been made late or whether it remains outstanding. The scale of penalties is determined by regulations under subsection (2).[651] Under the regulations, a company is liable immediately after the period for filing expires without filing being made; if the company continues in default, further liabilities arise in certain time intervals; public companies are liable at a higher rate than private companies. However, in contrast to the predecessor to this section,[652] a new category has been introduced (more than one month late but not more than three months late), penalties have been increased, and the penalties are doubled for failure to file on time where there was also a failure in relation to the previous financial year.

---

[645] Companies Act 2006 (Commencement No 5, Transitional Provisions and Savings) Order 2007, SI 2007/3495, art 3(1) for financial years beginning on or after 6 April 2008.

[646] See s 1060.

[647] Companies Act 2006 (Commencement No 1, etc) Order 2006, SI 2006/3428, art 3(3).

[648] Companies Act 2006 (Commencement No 5, Transitional Provisions and Savings) Order 2007, SI 2007/3495, art 3(1) for financial years beginning on or after 6 April 2008.

[649] See ss 442 and 443.

[650] As note 613 at para 15.451.02 above.

[651] See the Companies (Late Filing Penalties) and Limited Liability Partnerships (Filing Periods and Late Filing Penalties) Regulations 2008, SI 2008/497. The increased penalties apply to filings on or after 1 February 2009; the doubling of penalties applies where the first of two consecutive late filings was in respect of a financial year commencing on or after 6 April 2008.

[652] CA 1985, s 242A.

During the year ended 31 March 2010, the registrar issued 231,291 penalty notices against companies   **15.453.04**
registered in the United Kingdom; the aggregate value of these civil penalties was £111.78 million.[653]
Monies collected are paid into the consolidated fund rather than being available as a source of income
solely for the BIS.

## CHAPTER 11 REVISION OF DEFECTIVE ACCOUNTS AND REPORTS

### *Voluntary revision*

### 454   Voluntary revision of accounts etc

   (1)  If it appears to the directors of a company that—                                        **15.454.01**
      (a)  the company's annual accounts,
      (b)  the directors' remuneration report or the directors' report, or
      (c)  a summary financial statement of the company,
      did not comply with the requirements of this Act (or, where applicable, of Article 4 of the IAS
      Regulation), they may prepare revised accounts or a revised report or statement.
   (2)  Where copies of the previous accounts or report have been sent out to members, delivered to the
      registrar or (in the case of a public company) laid before the company in general meeting, the
      revisions must be confined to—
      (a)  the correction of those respects in which the previous accounts or report did not comply with
         the requirements of this Act (or, where applicable, of Article 4 of the IAS Regulation), and
      (b)  the making of any necessary consequential alterations.
   (3)  The Secretary of State may make provision by regulations as to the application of the provisions
      of this Act in relation to—
      (a)  revised annual accounts,
      (b)  a revised directors' remuneration report or directors' report, or
      (c)  a revised summary financial statement.
   (4)  The regulations may, in particular—
      (a)  make different provision according to whether the previous accounts, report or statement are
         replaced or are supplemented by a document indicating the corrections to be made;
      (b)  make provision with respect to the functions of the company's auditor in relation to the
         revised accounts, report or statement;
      (c)  require the directors to take such steps as may be specified in the regulations where the
         previous accounts or report have been—
         (i)   sent out to members and others under section 423,
         (ii)  laid before the company in general meeting, or
         (iii) delivered to the registrar,
      or where a summary financial statement containing information derived from the previous
      accounts or report has been sent to members under section 426;
      (d)  apply the provisions of this Act (including those creating criminal offences) subject to such
         additions, exceptions and modifications as are specified in the regulations.
   (5)  Regulations under this section are subject to negative resolution procedure.

COMMENCEMENT DATE  6 April 2008[654]

This section and the three following are derived from measures introduced by the 1989 Act following   **15.454.02**
the recommendations of what was known as the Dearing Report[655]. This section gives the directors of
a company the facility to correct errors in the annual accounts[656], directors' report[657], directors'
remuneration report[658] or summary financial statement[659] by issuing revised versions of these documents; the three following sections give the Secretary of State, or a body authorized by him, a power to
seek a court order to compel the directors to do so, but only in relation to annual accounts and
directors' reports. This enables a regime to be set up whereby apparent errors in annual accounts and

---

[653] *Statistical tables on companies registration activities* (BIS, 2010), p 33.
[654] Companies Act 2006 (Commencement No 5, Transitional Provisions and Savings) Order 2007, SI
2007/3495, art 3. This provision applies to accounts and reports for financial years beginning on or after 6 April
2008.
[655] *The Making of Accounting Standards – Report of the Review Committee under the Chairmanship of Sir Ron
Dearing CB* (Institute of Chartered Accountants in England and Wales, September 1988).
[656] See s 471.
[657] See s 415.
[658] See s 420.
[659] See s 426.

directors' reports could be looked into and corrected. The objective of the regime is 'not to punish or penalize, but to provide arrangements that will lead to the provision of good accounting information when it is lacking – the only objective is good financial reporting'[660]

**15.454.03**   Sub-section (1) gives the directors the facility to prepare a revised version of the company's annual accounts, or other specified documents, if it appears to them that the document in question did not comply with the requirements of the Act or with the IAS Regulation[661] as the case may be; this would include non-compliance with accounting standards since IAS accounts are required to comply with EU-adopted IFRS[662] and since one of the effects of the true-and-fair requirement in relation to Companies Act accounts is tantamount to making it necessary to comply with UK accounting standards[663].

**15.454.04**   Thus revision can only be undertaken where there is non-compliance. There are three points to bear in mind here. First, it follows that the directors are unable to prepare, for example, revised annual accounts where the original accounts comply with the Act but the directors wish they had used a different form of words to describe a particular matter or had omitted unnecessary material; if the annual accounts comply with the Act, then they cannot be subject to revision no matter how desirable that might appear for other reasons, and this rule has been upheld by the courts[664]. Second if, for example, there is an error in the annual accounts then whilst they may be subject to revision, the directors' report that accompanied those annual accounts cannot be revised unless the directors' report is also in error (which might occur if, for example, it quotes a figure from the annual accounts that is now found to be in error). Third, by preparing revised annual accounts, or one of the other specified documents, the directors are opening themselves to the risk of sanctions in respect of their apparent approval of defective originals, which would be a criminal offence[665]. Having said that, it must be remembered that the policy behind the regime when originally enacted was 'not to punish or penalize, but to provide arrangements that will lead to provision of good accounting information when it is lacking – the only objective is good financial reporting[666]; no instances are known of those sanctions being applied on the occasion of revision, although there have been cases of disciplinary enquiry by professional bodies in respect of their members who have been directors (or auditors) of companies revising annual accounts.

**15.454.05**   Since sub-section (1) provides that the directors 'may' prepare revised accounts and reports then it would appear that revision is a voluntary matter, although the Secretary of State or a body authorized by him has power under sections 456 to 457 to seek to compel directors to do so. Aside from such compulsion, the directors' choice is likely to be influenced by factors such as whether the annual distribution procedures for the annual accounts and reports are yet complete, how soon the following year's annual accounts and reports are to be produced, how serious is the error and what requirements there are upon the company in relation to the accounts in other fields of law and regulation (eg, dissemination of information under the Disclosure and Transparency Rules). For example, if the error is discovered before the annual accounts have been delivered to the Registrar then it would seem difficult for the directors to go ahead and deliver annual accounts which they now know to be in error; revision would seem appropriate. On the other hand, it might be that all of the circulation, laying and delivery of the annual accounts has been completed, at the time that the error is discovered the next year's set of annual accounts is soon to be prepared and circulated and the company has no securities traded on any market. Since entirely new and updated accounting information is about to be published it may be appropriate not to prepare a revised version of the previous year's annual accounts but to deal with the matter by restating the comparative figures in the following year's annual accounts; accounting standards, both UK standards applying to Companies Act accounts and EU-adopted IFRS applying to IAS accounts[667] require disclosures on the occasion of correcting errors by restatement of comparatives.

**15.454.06**   Sub-section (2) sets out the limits of the revision. In the circumstances specified the revision must be limited to correcting the error and any consequential changes. This applies where the annual accounts or other specified document have been sent out to members, delivered to the registrar or (for a public

---

[660] Para 15.1, *Dearing Report.*
[661] This covers the case where the group accounts are directly required by the IAS Regulation to comply with that regulation. See s 403(1).
[662] See ss 395(1)(b) and 403(1), (2)(b).
[663] See ss 396 and 404.
[664] See *Re A Company (No 1389920)* [2004] All ER (D) 115 (Jan).
[665] For annual accounts, see s 414; for the directors' report, s 419; for the directors' remuneration report, s 442; and for the summary financial statement, s 429.
[666] Para 15.1, *Dearing Report.*
[667] See ss 395 and 403.

company) laid in general meeting. This begs the question as to whether additional changes can be made in revised accounts where the original accounts had not been sent out to members, to the registrar or (for a public company) laid in general meeting. Seemingly they can. However, as explained in the next paragraph, they cannot in any case be changed with the benefit of hindsight.

The Secretary of State has made regulations[668] under subsection (3) for the application of this section.   **15.454.07**
These regulations permit that revision may be either by way of replacement of the entire document or by supplementary note; that prominent disclosure is required of their replacing the original document and as to the original failure and its correction; and (unless exempt from audit under section 477, 479A or 480) that an auditor's report is required. In addition a key provision of the regulations is that the revised accounts are to be prepared as at the date of approval of the original accounts. This makes clear that the revised accounts are not required to (and are prohibited from) taking account of hindsight since the date of approval of the original accounts.

## Secretary of State's notice

### 455   Secretary of State's notice in respect of accounts or reports

(1)   This section applies where—                                                                                **15.455.01**
    (a)   copies of a company's annual accounts or directors' report have been sent out under section 423, or
    (b)   a copy of a company's annual accounts or directors' report has been delivered to the registrar or (in the case of a public company) laid before the company in general meeting, and it appears to the Secretary of State that there is, or may be, a question whether the accounts or report comply with the requirements of this Act (or, where applicable, of Article 4 of the IAS Regulation).

(2)   The Secretary of State may give notice to the directors of the company indicating the respects in which it appears that such a question arises or may arise.

(3)   The notice must specify a period of not less than one month for the directors to give an explanation of the accounts or report or prepare revised accounts or a revised report.

(4)   If at the end of the specified period, or such longer period as the Secretary of State may allow, it appears to the Secretary of State that the directors have not—
    (a)   given a satisfactory explanation of the accounts or report, or
    (b)   revised the accounts or report so as to comply with the requirements of this Act (or, where applicable, of Article 4 of the IAS Regulation), the Secretary of State may apply to the court.

(5)   The provisions of this section apply equally to revised annual accounts and revised directors' reports, in which case they have effect as if the references to revised accounts or reports were references to further revised accounts or reports.

COMMENCEMENT DATE   6 April 2008[669]

This section specifies procedures that the Secretary of State must go through prior to making an   **15.455.02**
application to court under section 456 seeking a court order to compel the directors of a company to use section 454 to prepare revised accounts or a revised directors' report. The scope of this section (and the following two, which deal with an application and with other persons authorized to apply) is thus narrower than that of section 454 which facilitates the directors' revising also a directors' remuneration report or a summary financial statement.

The Secretary of State must notify the company's directors of the respects in which the annual accounts   **15.455.03**
or directors' reports may not comply with the Act or the IAS Regulation[670], and seek an explanation or a revision within a period of not less than one month. The section does not compel the directors either to provide an explanation or to make a revision. However, if the directors fail to make a revision or give a satisfactory explanation, the Secretary of State has discretion to apply to court for an order.

In practice the Secretary of State's powers under the section are exercised by officials at Companies   **15.455.04**
House[671]. Further, the powers are exercised only in respect of companies subject to the small companies regime and those qualifying for exemption for medium-sized companies[672]; scrutiny in relation to

---

[668]   Companies (Revision of Defective Accounts and Reports) Regulations 2008, SI 2008/373.

[669]   Companies Act 2006 (Commencement No 5, Transitional Provisions and Savings) Order 2007, SI 2007/3495, art 3. This provision applies to accounts and reports for financial years beginning on or after 6 April 2008.

[670]   This covers the case where the group accounts are directly required by the IAS regulation to comply with that regulation. See section 403(2)(b).

[671]   Companies House is the BIS agency that assists the registrar to carry out the Secretary of State's duties.

[672]   See ss 381 to 384 and s 465 to 467.

other companies is left to the person authorized under section 457[673]. This division of responsibility arises not from the legislation or section 457 authorization order but from custom and practice on the part of the BIS[674] and the authorized person[675]. Note, however, that an authorized person is not required to go through procedures equivalent to those of this section before making an application to court; in practice the authorized person does go through similar procedures as explained in the commentary at section 457.

## Application to court

### 456 Application to court in respect of defective accounts or reports

**15.456.01**

(1) An application may be made to the court—
  (a) by the Secretary of State, after having complied with section 455, or
  (b) by a person authorised by the Secretary of State for the purposes of this section, for a declaration (in Scotland, a declarator) that the annual accounts of a company do not comply, or a directors' report does not comply, with the requirements of this Act (or, where applicable, of Article 4 of the IAS Regulation) and for an order requiring the directors of the company to prepare revised accounts or a revised report.

(2) Notice of the application, together with a general statement of the matters at issue in the proceedings, shall be given by the applicant to the registrar for registration.

(3) If the court orders the preparation of revised accounts, it may give directions as to—
  (a) the auditing of the accounts,
  (b) the revision of any directors' remuneration report, directors' report or summary financial statement, and
  (c) the taking of steps by the directors to bring the making of the order to the notice of persons likely to rely on the previous accounts, and such other matters as the court thinks fit.

(4) If the court orders the preparation of a revised directors' report it may give directions as to—
  (a) the review of the report by the auditors,
  (b) the revision of any summary financial statement,
  (c) the taking of steps by the directors to bring the making of the order to the notice of persons likely to rely on the previous report, and
  (d) such other matters as the court thinks fit.

(5) If the court finds that the accounts or report did not comply with the requirements of this Act (or, where applicable, of Article 4 of the IAS Regulation) it may order that all or part of—
  (a) the costs (in Scotland, expenses) of and incidental to the application, and
  (b) any reasonable expenses incurred by the company in connection with or in consequence of the preparation of revised accounts or a revised report,
  are to be borne by such of the directors as were party to the approval of the defective accounts or report.
  For this purpose every director of the company at the time of the approval of the accounts or report shall be taken to have been a party to the approval unless he shows that he took all reasonable steps to prevent that approval.

(6) Where the court makes an order under subsection (5) it shall have regard to whether the directors party to the approval of the defective accounts or report knew or ought to have known that the accounts or report did not comply with the requirements of this Act (or, where applicable, of Article 4 of the IAS Regulation), and it may exclude one or more directors from the order or order the payment of different amounts by different directors.

(7) On the conclusion of proceedings on an application under this section, the applicant must send to the registrar for registration a copy of the court order or, as the case may be, give notice to the registrar that the application has failed or been withdrawn.

(8) The provisions of this section apply equally to revised annual accounts and revised directors' reports, in which case they have effect as if the references to revised accounts or reports were references to further revised accounts or reports.

COMMENCEMENT DATE 6 April 2008[676]

---

[673] For further commentary on authorized person see s 457.

[674] Department for Business, Innovation and Skills

[675] See *The Conduct Committee Operating Procedures for Reviewing Corporate Reporting* (Financial Reporting Council, July 2012), para 15. The division is, in fact, slightly more complicated than described in the main body of the text because the FRRP may also review any private company within a group which does not qualify as a small or medium-sized group, and that group might include small and medium private sized companies.

[676] Companies Act 2006 (Commencement No 5, Transitional Provisions and Savings) Order 2007, SI 2007/3495, art 3. This provision applies to accounts and reports for financial years beginning on or after 6 April 2008.

This section provides the facility for the Secretary of State, or a person authorized by him under section   **15.456.02**
457, to apply to court for an order that the directors of a company prepare revised accounts or a revised
directors' report. In practice the existence of this facility serves to promote cooperation of directors
with the Secretary of State or the authorized person in the course of their enquiries into matters relating
to the compliance of annual accounts or director's reports. Since this facility was introduced through
the 1989 Act no application to court has been known to have been made although it is thought that the
authorized person has come close to doing so on more than one occasion.

The ability of the Secretary of State to apply to court for a declaration and order is contingent on   **15.456.03**
compliance with section 455 (section 456(1)(a)). The authorized person's authority to make an
application is not contingent on the provision of a prior notice by either the Secretary of State pursuant
to section 455 or otherwise.

Before the Secretary of State may make an application to court he must have been through the   **15.456.04**
procedures specified by section 456; however, where the application is made by the authorized person,
there is no requirement for any specified prior procedures to have been followed. However, as
explained in the commentary at section 457, the Financial Reporting Council's Conduct Committee
(being the authorized person) does in practice go through a set of procedures.

As well as having the power to make the order, the court also has powers over specific consequential   **15.456.05**
matters that may need to be attended to, such as the auditing of any revised accounts, but also with
respect to such other matters as the court thinks fit. Furthermore, if the annual accounts or directors'
report are found not to have complied then the courts may order that the directors party to the original
approval should bear some or all of the costs of the applicant in making the application and of the
company in relation to the preparation of the revised accounts or report. The purpose of the directors'
bearing the company's costs would appear to be to prevent the members of the company from
effectively bearing the costs of rectifying a failure on the part of the directors in their duty to the
members of the company to provide them with accounts and reports. If a director is able to show that
he took all reasonable steps to prevent the approval of the defective accounts or report then he cannot
be ordered to bear the costs. This 'reverse burden of proof' is in the same form as that in connection
with the criminal offence for approval of defective accounts or directors' reports at sections 414
and 419.

Since an application to court for revision of annual accounts or a directors' report is a significant   **15.456.06**
matter, the section provides that the applicant (the Secretary of State or the authorized person as the
case may be) must notify the registrar of the application, any subsequent order, any failure of the
application or its withdrawal.

### 457   Other persons authorised to apply to the court

(1) The Secretary of State may by order (an 'authorisation order') authorise for the purposes of section   **15.457.01**
456 any person appearing to him—

    (a) to have an interest in, and to have satisfactory procedures directed to securing, compliance
        by companies with the requirements of this Act (or, where applicable, of Article 4 of the IAS
        Regulation) relating to accounts and directors' reports,

    (b) to have satisfactory procedures for receiving and investigating complaints about companies'
        annual accounts and directors' reports, and

    (c) otherwise to be a fit and proper person to be authorised.

(2) A person may be authorised generally or in respect of particular classes of case, and different
persons may be authorised in respect of different classes of case.

(3) The Secretary of State may refuse to authorise a person if he considers that his authorisation is
unnecessary having regard to the fact that there are one or more other persons who have been
or are likely to be authorised.

(4) If the authorised person is an unincorporated association, proceedings brought in, or in connection with, the exercise of any function by the association as an authorised person may be brought
by or against the association in the name of a body corporate whose constitution provides for the
establishment of the association.

(5) An authorisation order may contain such requirements or other provisions relating to the exercise
of functions by the authorised person as appear to the Secretary of State to be appropriate.
No such order is to be made unless it appears to the Secretary of State that the person would, if
authorised, exercise his functions as an authorised person in accordance with the provisions
proposed.

(6)  Where authorisation is revoked, the revoking order may make such provision as the Secretary of State thinks fit with respect to pending proceedings.

(7)  An order under this section is subject to negative resolution procedure.

COMMENCEMENT DATE 6 APRIL 2008[677]

**15.457.02**  This section, and its predecessor introduced by the 1989 Act, has allowed the creation and operation, through to July 2012, of the Financial Reporting Review Panel (FRRP); since then this same role has been carried out by the Conduct Committee of the Financial Reporting Council. Indeed, the main purpose of what is now chapter 11 of Part 15 of this Act was to set up this body and give it power, under what is now section 456, to apply to court for an order for revision of the accounts.

**15.457.03**  There is no precise or exhaustive criteria set out in this section for authorization of a person. Sub-section (1) gives wide discretion to the Secretary of State to determine what he thinks are satisfactory procedures that a body should have, and that it should otherwise appear to him to be a fit and proper person. Moreover, sub-section (5) allows the Secretary of State to insert conditions, to be complied with by the authorized person, in the Authorisation Order. The Secretary of State may, it appears, authorize more than one person.

**15.457.04**  Like its predecessor the FRRP, the Conduct Committee is authorized under subsection (1)[678]. The Conduct Committee[679] is in fact a committee established under the Articles of Association of a guarantee company named the Financial Reporting Council Limited. However, under sub-section (4) an application for a Court Order under section 456 would, be made in the name of the Financial Reporting Council Limited.

**15.457.05**  The Conduct Committee is, and the FRRP was under previous authorization orders, authorized in respect of all companies, although by custom and practice on its part and that of the Secretary of State it does not look at companies subject to the small companies regime or qualifying for exemptions for as medium-sized companies.[680, 681] The category of companies with which it may deal is therefore not confined to listed companies, although this remains its main area of effort, but it also, for example, extends to large private groups or to private company subsidiaries of listed companies.

**15.457.06**  The Conduct Committee publishes its operating procedures, which are based on those of its predecessor the FRRP, on its website.[682] First of all, the Conduct Committee (through its corporate reporting review team) looks into a company's annual accounts either because a complaint, made directly to the Conduct Committee or in press comment, appears to raise a valid question about the compliance of the annual accounts; because the company is selected by the Conduct Committee through a risk-based assessment procedure; or because it has been notified that a qualified audit report on the company's accounts has been filed with the Registrar.[683] With respect to the risk-based assessment, the Conduct Committee selects companies falling into a business sector that is either under strain or likely to give rise to difficult accounting issues. Generic list of business sectors that the Conduct Committee focuses upon are published annually.

**15.457.07**  If a company has been selected on the risk-based selection, or as a result of complaint/press comment, the Conduct Committee's staff will review the annual accounts and determine whether there appears to be a question of non-compliance in one or more areas. (When the Conduct Committee is notified of a qualified audit report, the question of non-compliance will normally be answered if the accounts are qualified for disagreement or an adverse opinion is given[684].) If so then the staff of the Conduct Committee will write to the company to seek information and explanations so as to assist the Conduct

[677] Companies Act 2006 (Commencement No 5, Transitional Provisions and Savings) Order 2007, SI 2007/3495, art 3. This provision applies to accounts and reports for financial years beginning on or after 6 April 2008.

[678] In relation to the FRRP, the Companies (Defective Accounts and Directors' Reports) (Authorised Person) and Supervision of Accounts and Reports (Prescribed Body) Order 2008, SI 2008/623 was revoked, and authorizing instead the Conduct Committee, by the Supervision of Accounts and Reports (Prescribed Body) and Companies (Defective Accounts and Directors' Reports) (Authorised Person) Order 2012, coming into force 2 July 2012.

[679] *The Conduct Committee Operating Procedures for Reviewing Corporate Reporting* (Financial Reporting Council, July 2012), para 15.

[680] See ss 381 to 384 and ss 465 to 467.

[681] See *The Conduct Committee Operating Procedures for Reviewing Corporate Reporting*, para 15.

[682] <http://www.frc.org.uk>.

[683] The Conduct Committee (previously FRRP) is provided with information on qualified audit reports by an independent data provider. See FRRP Press Notice No. 111.

[684] The FRRP stated that a qualified audit report is 'a strong indicator that the financial statements may not be properly prepared in accordance with the law and do not give a true and fair view.' See FRRP Press Notice No. 111.

Committee chairman and deputy chairman to decide whether an enquiry should be opened into an alleged breach. This exploratory stage is sometimes known as a preliminary enquiry. Even if deficiencies in the annual accounts are acknowledged by the company, an actual or formal enquiry would not be opened if the company agreed to appropriate corrective action (see below). This process is usually carried on entirely by correspondence between the company and the Conduct Committee.

If the Conduct Committee Chairman or Deputy Chairman is not satisfied by the preliminary enquiries **15.457.08**
then a formal Review Group Enquiry is instituted. In such a case a Review Group of five or more people is called together to conduct the enquiry. The five people are drawn from a panel, known (confusingly) as the Financial Reporting Review Panel) which consists of approximately 30 persons who usually either are or have recently been accountants in professional practice, accountants in business, solicitors or barristers. This Review Group of five persons will enquire into the matter both by correspondence with the company's directors and by meetings with the directors who will usually be accompanied by accountancy advisors. Companies in this situation sometimes take legal advice at this stage. If the Review Group is not satisfied that the annual accounts comply then it will advise the Conduct Committee accordingly. It will then be for the Conduct Committee to decide what corrective action to seek or, ultimately, to determine that an application to court be made.

In practice the Conduct Committee accepts a variety of corrective action by the directors depending **15.457.09**
upon the particular circumstances. For example, with relatively minor matters the Conduct Committee may be satisfied with an undertaking by the company to improve disclosure in future years' annual accounts; in other cases it may be satisfied by the directors' restating the accounts by way of prior year adjustment in the following year's annual accounts; in other cases it may want the annual accounts in question to be revised—in one case a company prepared and issued five years' worth of revised accounts in order to satisfy the FRRP.[685]

The proceedings of the Conduct Committee (and any Review Group) are kept confidential (in **15.457.10**
connection with which, see also sections 460 and 461). However, where the company agrees to undertake corrective action or were the Conduct Committee to make an application to court, then the Conduct Committee puts out a press release naming the company, describing the matter under enquiry and, in the former case, the corrective action agreed to be taken.

## 458  Disclosure of information by tax authorities

(1) The Commissioners for Her Majesty's Revenue and Customs may disclose information to a person **15.458.01**
     authorised under section 457 for the purpose of facilitating—
    (a) the taking of steps by that person to discover whether there are grounds for an application
        to the court under section 456 (application in respect of defective accounts etc), or
    (b) a decision by the authorised person whether to make such an application.
(2) This section applies despite any statutory or other restriction on the disclosure of information.
    Provided that, in the case of personal data within the meaning of the Data Protection Act 1998 (c.
    29), information is not to be disclosed in contravention of that Act.
(3) Information disclosed to an authorised person under this section—
    (a) may not be used except in or in connection with—
        (i) taking steps to discover whether there are grounds for an application to the court under
            section 456, or
        (ii) deciding whether or not to make such an application, or in, or in connection with,
            proceedings on such an application; and
    (b) must not be further disclosed except—
        (i) to the person to whom the information relates, or
        (ii) in, or in connection with, proceedings on any such application to the court.
(4) A person who contravenes subsection (3) commits an offence unless—
    (a) he did not know, and had no reason to suspect, that the information had been disclosed
        under this section, or
    (b) he took all reasonable steps and exercised all due diligence to avoid the commission of the
        offence.
(5) A person guilty of an offence under subsection (4) is liable—
    (a) on conviction on indictment, to imprisonment for a term not exceeding two years or a fine (or
        both);
    (b) on summary conviction—
        (i) in England and Wales, to imprisonment for a term not exceeding twelve months or to a
            fine not exceeding the statutory maximum (or both);

---

[685] The 1996 to 2000 annual accounts of Wiggins Group Plc. See FRRP Press Notice No. 65. The directors also voluntarily revised the 1995 annual accounts, although these were not subject to the FRRP's enquiry.

  (ii) in Scotland or Northern Ireland, to imprisonment for a term not exceeding six months, or to a fine not exceeding the statutory maximum (or both).

[(6) Where an offence under this section is committed by a body corporate, every officer of the body who is in default also commits the offence. For this purpose—

  (a) any person who purports to act as director, manager or secretary of the body is treated as an officer of the body, and

  (b) if the body is a company, any shadow director is treated as an officer of the company.][a]

AMENDMENTS AND NOTES

[a] Inserted by the the Companies Act 2006 (Consequential Amendments etc) Order 2008, SI 2008/948, Sch 1, para 244.

COMMENCEMENT DATE 6 April 2008[686]

**15.458.02** This section re-enacts a provision introduced by the 2004 Act following a recommendation of the Co-ordinating Group on Audit and Accounting Issues[687]. This group was set up by the government in response to accounting scandals in the United States. One of its key recommendations was the strengthening of the role of the person authorized under (what is now) section 457, i.e. what is now the Conduct Committee of the Financial Reporting Council. In particular it reported that the examination of annual accounts by accountants at Her Majesty's Revenue and Customs (HMRC) identified instances of non-compliance with the UK accounting standards and proposed that the government should examine the possibility of opening an information gateway between HMRC and the authorized person (the Conduct Committee). This section effects such a gateway.

**15.458.03** The section permits the disclosure of information only to a person authorized under section 457, ie, the Conduct Committee. It does not cover disclosure of information to the Secretary of State.

**15.458.04** Sub-sections (1) to (3) set out the purposes for which information may be disclosed by the Commissioners, restrictions upon that disclosure and restrictions upon the use and further disclosure of the information by the authorized person receiving it. Further details relating to provision of information under this framework were agreed between HMRC and the FRRP (the predecessor body of the Conduct Committee) in a memorandum of understanding dated June 2005 and published on the FRC's website[688]. The memorandum did not change on the occasion of the Conduct Committee succeeding to the role of authorized person. Presumably the memorandum is to be taken as indicating the Conduct Committee's intentions.

## *Power of authorised person to require documents etc*

### 459 Power of authorised person to require documents, information and explanations

**15.459.01** (1) This section applies where it appears to a person who is authorised under section 457 that there is, or may be, a question whether a company's annual accounts or directors' report comply with the requirements of this Act (or, where applicable, of Article 4 of the IAS Regulation).

  (2) The authorised person may require any of the persons mentioned in subsection (3) to produce any document, or to provide him with any information or explanations, that he may reasonably require for the purpose of—

   (a) discovering whether there are grounds for an application to the court under section 456, or

   (b) deciding whether to make such an application.

  (3) Those persons are—

   (a) the company;

   (b) any officer, employee, or auditor of the company;

   (c) any persons who fell within paragraph (b) at a time to which the document or information required by the authorised person relates.

  (4) If a person fails to comply with such a requirement, the authorised person may apply to the court.

  (5) If it appears to the court that the person has failed to comply with a requirement under subsection (2), it may order the person to take such steps as it directs for securing that the documents are produced or the information or explanations are provided.

  (6) A statement made by a person in response to a requirement under subsection (2) or an order under subsection (5) may not be used in evidence against him in any criminal proceedings.

---

[686] Companies Act 2006 (Commencement No 5,Transitional Provisions and Savings) Order 2007, SI 2007/3495, art 3. This provision applies to accounts and reports for financial years beginning on or after 6 April 2008.

[687] *Final report to the Secretary of State for Trade and Industry and the Chancellor of the Exchequer* (Co-ordinating Group on Audit and Accounting Issues, January 2003)

[688] *Memorandum of understanding between HM Revenue & Customs and the Financial Reporting Review Panel* (Financial Review Reporting Panel, 2005). See FRRP Press Notice No. 86.

(7)  Nothing in this section compels any person to disclose documents or information in respect of which a claim to legal professional privilege (in Scotland, to confidentiality of communications) could be maintained in legal proceedings.

(8)  In this section 'document' includes information recorded in any form.

COMMENCEMENT DATE   6 April 2008[689]

Prior to the commencement of the 2004 Act the authorized person, being now the Conduct Committee   **15.459.02** of the Financial Reporting Council, had no powers other than to seek a court order under the predecessor to section 456[690]. There was, however, understood to be some concern that the need to rely on this single, very serious power had unnecessarily slowed down the pace of its enquiries in some cases. In addition, a report at European level recommended that bodies such as the Conduct Committee should have adequate powers.[691] Accordingly, the 2004 Act introduced the powers that are now set out in this section 459.

The powers are available only where the Conduct Committee considers that there is or may be a   **15.459.03** question of whether the annual accounts or directors' report comply with the Act (or IAS Regulation, if applicable). Thus the Conduct Committee must have some grounds – eg, information contained in a complaint or possible non-compliance that is apparent simply from reading the accounts – for using these powers; it cannot simply indulge in a 'fishing expedition' by demanding explanations or documents about a set of accounts over which no question of compliance has otherwise been raised or become apparent.

The powers enable the Conduct Committee to require of a wide category of persons any information   **15.459.04** or explanations or document that the Conduct Committee may reasonably require for the widely defined purpose of discovering whether there are grounds for application to the court under section 456. Since the grounds for application to court, in relation to annual accounts, would be that the Conduct Committee had formed the opinion that the annual accounts did not comply with the Act (or the IAS Regulation), then it is in effect a power to seek whatever is reasonably required in order to discover whether the accounts do or do not comply. Subsection (2)(b) also gives as a further purpose the making of a decision as to whether to make an application. However, this seems unlikely to extend the power much beyond its already wide-ranging extent.

As well as the powers ensuring that the Conduct Committee can obtain answers to its questions, it also   **15.459.05** enables it to demand documents. Thus if it is enquiring into a particular transaction it could demand the legal documentation by which the transaction was effected (say, a lease). It might also demand correspondence with third parties in relation to the accounting for a transaction, eg, an accountant's opinion. The power would also extend to obtaining internal company correspondence in relation to the accounting for the matter under consideration.

The persons from whom information, explanations and documents may be demanded are not   **15.459.06** restricted to the directors of the company. It includes other officers of the company, its employees, its auditor and the company itself. Former officers, employees or auditors are also within the scope of this power. Thus the Conduct Committee is provided with many alternative avenues of enquiry if the directors of the company were not to cooperate with it, although this might be thought to be an over-provision and that tackling the recalcitrant directors would have been the better policy response.

The section does not lay down any particular procedures for the exercise of the powers contained   **15.459.07** within it. For example, it would not appear to be necessary for the Conduct Committee specifically to notify the person to whom the request is made that it made under this section.

The powers to require information, explanations and documents are backed up by the facility in   **15.459.08** sub-sections (4) and (5) for the Conduct Committee to apply for a court order where a person fails to comply with a request.

Set against these wide powers, sub-section (7) ensures that disclosure cannot be made of material   **15.459.09** covered by legal professional privilege[692]; and sub-section (6) deals with the human rights aspects, *viz*

---

[689]  Companies Act 2006 (Commencement No 5, Transitional Provisions and Savings) Order 2007, SI 2007/3495, art 3. This provision applies to accounts and reports for financial years beginning on or after 6 April 2008.

[690]  Companies Act 1985, s 245B.

[691]  *Standard No 1 on financial information – enforcement of standards on financial information in Europe* (Committee of European Securities Regulations, March 2003).

[692]  Art 8.1 of the Convention for the Protection of Human Rights and Fundamental Freedoms (Council of Europe, 1950) addresses, *inter alia*, the rights of companies to respect for their correspondence and is a convention right within the scope of the Human Rights Act 1998.

that a statement by a person (but not documents supplied by him) cannot be used in evidence against that person in criminal proceedings[693].

## 460   Restrictions on disclosure of information obtained under compulsory powers

**15.460.01**

(1)   This section applies to information (in whatever form) obtained in pursuance of a requirement or order under section 459 (power of authorised person to require documents etc) that relates to the private affairs of an individual or to any particular business.

(2)   No such information may, during the lifetime of that individual or so long as that business continues to be carried on, be disclosed without the consent of that individual or the person for the time being carrying on that business.

(3)   This does not apply—

   (a)   to disclosure permitted by section 461 (permitted disclosure of information obtained under compulsory powers), or

   (b)   to the disclosure of information that is or has been available to the public from another source.

(4)   A person who discloses information in contravention of this section commits an offence, unless—

   (a)   he did not know, and had no reason to suspect, that the information had been disclosed under section 459, or

   (b)   he took all reasonable steps and exercised all due diligence to avoid the commission of the offence.

(5)   A person guilty of an offence under this section is liable—

   (a)   on conviction on indictment, to imprisonment for a term not exceeding two years or a fine (or both);

   (b)   on summary conviction—

      (i)   in England and Wales, to imprisonment for a term not exceeding twelve months or to a fine not exceeding the statutory maximum (or both);

      (ii)   in Scotland or Northern Ireland, to imprisonment for a term not exceeding six months, or to a fine not exceeding the statutory maximum (or both).

[(6)   Where an offence under this section is committed [by a body corporate, every officer of the body who is in default also commits the offence. For this purpose—

   (a)   any person who purports to act as director, manager or secretary of the body is treated as an officer of the body, and

   (b)   if the body is a company, any shadow director is treated as an officer of the company.][a]

AMENDMENTS AND NOTES

[a]   Inserted by the the Companies Act 2006 (Consequential Amendments etc) Order 2008, SI 2008/948, Sch 1, para 245.

COMMENCEMENT DATE   6 April 2008[694]

**15.460.02**   This section provides a safeguard in relation to the wide powers of section 459 to obtain information, explanations and documents, by restricting the use and disclosure of information so obtained. The practical effect of the section is that, first of all, commercially confidential information divulged to the person authorized under section 457 ie, the Conduct Committee of the Financial Reporting Council may not be used or disclosed by them otherwise than for purposes specified in section 461 for so long as the information remains commercially confidential. Since it is likely that information provided to the Conduct Committee will from time to time contain such commercially confidential matters then the section is rightly valuable to companies.

**15.460.03**   The other effect of the section is to provide similar protection where information relates to the private affairs of an individual during that individual's lifetime. Although it is less likely that information of this nature could be provided to the Conduct Committee, it is not out of the question. For example, the matter being enquired into may relate to a transaction between a company and a director that is not otherwise to be disclosed under the Act.

**15.460.04**   It should be noted that the restrictions provided for in this section apply only in respect of information given in response to a request from the Conduct Committee under section 459. Thus information given voluntarily is not covered, although the common law on confidentiality may have some effect.

---

[693]   Art 6.1 of the Convention for the Protection of Human Rights and Fundamental Freedoms (Council of Europe, 1950) addresses, *inter alia*, the right to be free of coerced self-incrimination, and is a convention right with the scope of the Human Rights Act 1998.

[694]   Companies Act 2006 (Commencement No 5, Transitional Provisions and Savings) Order 2007, SI 2007/3495, art 3. This provision applies to accounts and reports for financial years beginning on or after 6 April 2008.

However under its operating procedures[695] the Conduct Committee states that it treats all information received as if it were acquired under its statutory powers; but this Conduct Committee undertaking is subject to the Conduct Committee's limited public reporting of its activities – eg, a public announcement that a company under review has agreed to change its accounting in relation to a particular matter – which are described in the commentary at section 457.

### 461  Permitted disclosure of information obtained under compulsory powers

(1) The prohibition in section 460 of the disclosure of information obtained in pursuance of a requirement or order under section 459 (power of authorised person to require documents etc) that relates to the private affairs of an individual or to any particular business has effect subject to the following exceptions.

(2) It does not apply to the disclosure of information for the purpose of facilitating the carrying out by the authorised person of his functions under section 456.

(3) It does not apply to disclosure to—
   (a)  the Secretary of State,
   (b)  the Department of Enterprise, Trade and Investment for Northern Ireland,
   (c)  the Treasury,
   (d)  the Bank of England,
   (e)  the Financial Services Authority, or
   (f)  the Commissioners for Her Majesty's Revenue and Customs.

(4) It does not apply to disclosure—
   (a)  for the purpose of assisting a body designated by an order under section 1252 (delegation of functions of the Secretary of State) to exercise its functions under Part 42;[a]
   (b)  with a view to the institution of, or otherwise for the purposes of, disciplinary proceedings relating to the performance by an accountant or auditor of his professional duties;
   (c)  for the purpose of enabling or assisting the Secretary of State or the Treasury to exercise any of their functions under any of the following—
        (i)   the Companies Acts,
        (ii)  Part 5 of the Criminal Justice Act 1993 (c. 36) (insider dealing),
        (iii) the Insolvency Act 1986 (c. 45) or the Insolvency (Northern Ireland) Order 1989 (S.I. 1989/2405 (N.I. 19)),
        (iv)  the Company Directors Disqualification Act 1986 (c. 46) or the Company Directors Disqualification (Northern Ireland) Order 2002 (S.I. 2002/3150 (N.I. 4)),
        (v)   the Financial Services and Markets Act 2000 (c. 8);
   (d)  for the purpose of enabling or assisting the Department of Enterprise, Trade and Investment for Northern Ireland to exercise any powers conferred on it by the enactments relating to companies, directors' disqualification or insolvency;
   (e)  for the purpose of enabling or assisting the Bank of England to exercise its functions;
   (f)  for the purpose of enabling or assisting the Commissioners for Her Majesty's Revenue and Customs to exercise their functions;
   (g)  for the purpose of enabling or assisting the Financial Services Authority to exercise its functions under any of the following—
        (i)   the legislation relating to friendly societies or to industrial and provident societies,
        (ii)  the Building Societies Act 1986 (c. 53),
        (iii) Part 7 of the Companies Act 1989 (c. 40),
        (iv)  the Financial Services and Markets Act 2000; or
   (h)  in pursuance of any Community obligation.

(5) It does not apply to disclosure to a body exercising functions of a public nature under legislation in any country or territory outside the United Kingdom that appear to the authorised person to be similar to his functions under section 456 for the purpose of enabling or assisting that body to exercise those functions.

(6) In determining whether to disclose information to a body in accordance with subsection (5), the authorised person must have regard to the following considerations—
   (a)  whether the use which the body is likely to make of the information is sufficiently important to justify making the disclosure;
   (b)  whether the body has adequate arrangements to prevent the information from being used or further disclosed other than—
        (i)   for the purposes of carrying out the functions mentioned in that subsection, or
        (ii)  for other purposes substantially similar to those for which information disclosed to the authorised person could be used or further disclosed.

(7) Nothing in this section authorises the making of a disclosure in contravention of the Data Protection Act 1998 (c. 29).

**15.461.01**

---

[695]  *The Conduct Committee Operating Procedures for Reviewing Corporate Reporting* (Financial Reporting Council, July 2012), para 59.

AMENDMENTS AND NOTES

ᵃ Amended by the Companies Act 2006 (Consequential Amendments etc) Order 2008, SI 2008/ 948, Sch 1, para 246.

COMMENCEMENT DATE  6 April 2008[696]

**15.461.02**  This section details the exceptions to the restriction in section 460 on the use by the person authorized under section 457, which is the Conduct Committee of the Financial Reporting Review Council, of information obtained under its compulsory powers set out in section 459. The principal exception is, of course, the disclosure for the purpose of obtaining a court order under section 456 to revise the annual accounts or directors' report.

**15.461.03**  The other exceptions are, broadly speaking, public authorities (sub-section (3)), or for the exercise of functions of a public nature (sub-section (4)) or to a body that exercises a function similar to that of the Conduct Committee abroad (sub-sections (5) and (6)). It should be noted that the permitted disclosures in sub-sections (3), (4) and (5) are independent of each other. Thus, for example, information can be passed to the Secretary of State under sub-section (3)(a) without consideration of the purpose of disclosure under sub-section (4).

**15.461.04**  Thus information could, for example, be passed to BIS to enable them to undertake an action to disqualify a person as a director; or to The Commissioners for Her Majesty's Revenue and Customs (HMRC), say where the information suggests that the tax computations may be based on annual accounts that do not give a true and fair view; or to the United States Securities and Exchange Commission (SEC) say to facilitate a co-ordinated approach to a company which, through a registration with the SEC, is also subject to SEC oversight of its accounting compliance. The Conduct Committee is also subject to non-statutory arrangements with each of HMRC and the SEC[697]. However the former relates only to provision of information from the HMRC to the Conduct Committee, rather than *vice versa*. The Conduct Committee is also party to arrangements with the Financial Services Authority (FSA)[698]; these envisage, however, the transmission from the Conduct Committee to the FSA only of information relating to the fact that a company's annual accounts are under review and similar matters, rather than of information obtained from the company.

### 462  Power to amend categories of permitted disclosure

**15.462.01**  (1)  The Secretary of State may by order amend section 461(3), (4) and (5).
(2)  An order under this section must not—
   (a)  amend subsection (3) of that section (UK public authorities) by specifying a person unless the person exercises functions of a public nature (whether or not he exercises any other function);
   (b)  amend subsection (4) of that section (purposes for which disclosure permitted) by adding or modifying a description of disclosure unless the purpose for which the disclosure is permitted is likely to facilitate the exercise of a function of a public nature;
   (c)  amend subsection (5) of that section (overseas regulatory authorities) so as to have the effect of permitting disclosures to be made to a body other than one that exercises functions of a public nature in a country or territory outside the United Kingdom.
(3)  An order under this section is subject to negative resolution procedure. Commencement Date 6 April 2008[699]

[696] Companies Act 2006 (Commencement No 5, Transitional Provisions and Savings) Order 2007, SI 2007/3495, art 3. This provision applies to accounts and reports for financial years beginning on or after 6 April 2008.
[697] *Memorandum of Understanding between HM Revenue & Customs (HMRC) and the Financial Reporting Review Panel (the Panel)* dated June 2005; *Protocol between the Financial Services Authority, UK, the Financial Reporting Council, UK, and the SEC, US to facilitate implementation of the CESR/SEC work plan,* dated April 2007. Both are available on the FRC's website at <http://www.frc.org.uk>. Whilst the first mentioned document was entered into by the Conduct Committee's predecessor, the Financial Reporting Review Panel, and has not been amended on the occasion of the Conduct Committee's succession, it is assumed that it reflects the Conduct Committee's intentions.
[698] *Memorandum of understanding between the Financial Reporting Review Panel and the Financial Services Authority,* dated April 2005 available from the FRC's website at <http://www.frc.org.uk>. Whilst the document was entered into by the Conduct Committee's predecessor, the Financial Reporting Review Panel, and has not been amended on the occasion of the Conduct Committee's succession, it is assumed that it reflects the Conduct Committee's intentions.
[699] Companies Act 2006 (Commencement No 5, Transitional Provisions and Savings) Order 2007, SI 2007/3495, art 3. This provision applies to accounts and reports for financial years beginning on or after 6 April 2008

This section gives the Secretary of State a limited power to amend the permitted disclosure, under **15.462.02** section 461, of information obtained under section 460 by the person authorized under section 457 (ie, the Conduct Committee of the Financial Reporting Council). However, sub-section (2) ensures that any amendments to section 461 follow the principle that disclosure is permitted only to persons exercising functions of a public nature (including in relation to countries or territories outside the UK) or for the purpose of the exercise of a function of a public nature.

## CHAPTER 12
### SUPPLEMENTARY PROVISIONS
#### *Liability for false or misleading statements in reports*

### 463  Liability for false or misleading statements in reports

(1) The reports to which this section applies are—    **15.463.01**
   (a) the directors' report,
   (b) the directors' remuneration report, and
   (c) a summary financial statement so far as it is derived from either of those reports.
(2) A director of a company is liable to compensate the company for any loss suffered by it as a result of—
   (a) any untrue or misleading statement in a report to which this section applies, or
   (b) the omission from a report to which this section applies of anything required to be included in it.
(3) He is so liable only if—
   (a) he knew the statement to be untrue or misleading or was reckless as to whether it was untrue or misleading, or
   (b) he knew the omission to be dishonest concealment of a material fact.
(4) No person shall be subject to any liability to a person other than the company resulting from reliance, by that person or another, on information in a report to which this section applies.
(5) The reference in subsection (4) to a person being subject to a liability includes a reference to another person being entitled as against him to be granted any civil remedy or to rescind or repudiate an agreement.
(6) This section does not affect—
   (a) liability for a civil penalty, or
   (b) liability for a criminal offence.

COMMENCEMENT DATE  20 January 2007[700]

This section was introduced in this Act in connection with the expansion of the directors' report    **15.463.02** business review requirement to its present extent in section 417 and at the same time as the introduction of section 90A of the Financial Services and Markets Act 2000 (FSMA) as inserted by section 1270 of this Act.

The business review has, as noted at section 417, a strong forward looking element. Its development    **15.463.03** was accompanied by calls for some form of protection for directors from liability in relation to the report in order not to inhibit transparent and meaningful narrative reporting under that section.[701] Indeed, introducing this section the Government cited the encouragement of meaningful reporting as an objective.[702] In terms of protecting directors, the section might, as the Government observed when it introduced this section,[703] be more correctly characterized as one which provides a degree of certainty for directors as to the extent of their liability. Nevertheless, the section has become commonly known as the 'safe harbour'.

Related to the introduction of this section was the simultaneous introduction of section 90A of FSMA.    **15.463.04** That section provides, *inter alia*, that the company, where it has securities admitted to trading on a securities market,[704] is liable to compensate a person who suffered loss as a result of acquiring, continuing to hold, or disposing of such securities in reasonable reliance on a statement in the

---

[700] Companies Act 2006 (Commencement No 1, etc) Order 2006, SI 2006/3428, art 3(1).

[701] Eg, this was recommended by the Company Law Review in relation to their earlier proposal for extended narrative reporting, *Modern Company Law for a Competitive Economy—Final Report* (Company Law Review Steering Group, 2001, para 8.38).

[702] *Hansard*, HL, vol 682, col 740 (23 May 2006).

[703] Ibid.

[704] From 1 October 2010, the scope of section 90A (further to the Financial Services and Markets Act 2000 (Liability of Issuers) Regulations 2010, SI 2010/1192) has been extended to apply to any issuer with securities that, with the consent of the issuer, are admitted to trading on a market i) situated or operating in the United Kingdom, or ii) that has the UK as its home state. 'Securities market' means a regulated market, a multilateral trading facility

directors' report which has proved to be untrue or misleading or on a directors' report containing an omission. The company is not liable unless, in addition, a director of the company knew or was reckless as to whether the statement was untrue or misleading, or knew that the omission was a dishonest concealment. This provision of the FSMA added to the need to have a degree of certainty as to the persons to whom, and occasions on which, directors are liable in relation to the directors' report.

**15.463.05**    Turning then to this section itself, although it was conceived with the directors' report in mind, as set out in subsection (1) it applies in relation to a wider range of documents: it applies in relation to a directors' remuneration report (if any)[705] and a summary financial statement (if any)[706] to the extent derived from the directors' report or directors' remuneration report. It does not cover the annual accounts themselves, which are therefore still covered by common law. As noted briefly at section 414, whilst there is no express authority on the point it is sometimes suggested that under common law the directors owe a duty of care, in relation to the annual accounts, to the actual members of the company as a body in respect of their governance rights, and accordingly can be liable for negligence to those members as a body.[707] Commenting on the different positions of the directors' report and the annual accounts, the Government noted in debate before the introduction of this section that reporting in the latter was objectively determinable to a greater extent than in the former, given the inherent uncertainties in the forward-looking element to the directors' report.[708] It should also be noted that this section does not cover any separate corporate governance statement; since the directors have a choice as to whether to include the relevant corporate governance disclosures in the directors' report or in a separate corporate governance statement,[709] then in effect the directors have a choice as to whether to bring them within this section. However, if the corporate governance statement is published by recognized means,[710] it will be brought within the scope of section 90A of FSMA.

**15.463.06**    The person to whom the directors may be civilly liable is, by subsection (2), the company. By virtue of subsection (4) the case is limited to their being liable to the company; accordingly, the directors cannot have civil liability to any other person as a result of reliance on the relevant report. In relation to the business review contained within the directors' report this is reinforced by section 417(2)'s provision that the purpose of such a review is to assist the members to assess the discharge by the directors of their duty under section 172 (duty to promote success of the company), that duty being owed to the company.[711]

**15.463.07**    Civil liability to the company arises under subsections (2) if the company has suffered loss as a result of an untrue or misleading statement or omission, subject to the mental test set out in subsection (3). The terms of these subsections are virtually identical to those of the FSMA provision mentioned earlier.[712] One effect of this is that if the company is liable under the FSMA to compensate an investor for his investment losses (arising from a defective directors' report), that compensation may be a loss of the company for which a director could under this section be civilly liable to compensate the company.

**15.463.08**    Although the section is mainly concerned with the position of directors, it also affects the position of other persons by virtue of subsection (4). That subsection's limitation covers any person who might otherwise be thought to be liable to a person, other than the company, who relied upon the relevant report; it provides that such a person could not be liable other than to the company. The chief practical effect of this is likely to confirm that an auditor remains open to civil liability to the company, but only the company, in relation to his report in relation to the directors' report, directors' remuneration report, or summary financial statement derived therefrom.[713]

---

(MTF) or a market or facility of a corresponding description outside the EEA (FSMA, Sch 10, para 8(1)(b). This contrasts with the previous version of section 90A (before 1 October 2010) that applied only to companies that had securities admitted to trading on a regulated market. Thus, for example, companies listed on AIM are now caught within section 90A because AIM is an MTF.

[705]    Quoted companies only. See ss 385 and 420.

[706]    See s 426.

[707]    Eg, see para 2.11 of *Issue 76—Transparency obligations directive* (Financial Markets Law Committee, 2004).

[708]    *Hansard*, HL, vol 681, col 939 (10 May 2006).

[709]    See ss 419, 419A, 472A.

[710]    Before 1 October 2010, for certain companies the directors' report is a document required to be published in response to a requirement mentioned in s 90A(1)(a) of that Act and is thus within that section's liability regime. From 1 October 2010, s 90A has been extended to include any document published by 'recognised means', including information published on a recognized information service (see FSMA, Sch 10A, para 4).

[711]    See s 170(1).

[712]    FSMA, s 90A(3)(b), (4), (9)(a).

[713]    See the commentary at Part 16, Chap 6 for the question of an auditor's liability more generally.

## *Accounting and reporting standards*

### 464  Accounting standards

(1)  In this Part 'accounting standards' means statements of standard accounting practice issued by such body or bodies as may be prescribed by regulations.                              **15.464.01**

(2)  References in this Part to accounting standards applicable to a company's annual accounts are to such standards as are, in accordance with their terms, relevant to the company's circumstances and to the accounts.

(3)  Regulations under this section may contain such transitional and other supplementary and incidental provisions as appear to the Secretary of State to be appropriate.

COMMENCEMENT DATE subsections (1) and (3) from 20 January 2007;[714] otherwise 6 April 2008[715]

Under the regulations made under section 396(3),[716] companies other than those that are subject to the small companies regime or those that are medium-sized, are required to state in Companies Act individual accounts and Companies Act group accounts that those accounts were prepared in accordance with applicable accounting standards subject to any departures that were disclosed and explained.[717] Until July 2012 the Accounting Standards Board (ASB) was prescribed as the body issuing such standards.[718] Following reorganization, the Financial Reporting Council (FRC) has become the prescribed body issuing such standards.[719] In issuing such standards the FRC will take advice from its newly established Accounting Council, the membership and daily activities of what are otherwise essentially the same as the former ASB, but the ultimate authority rests with the FRC. Transitional and savings provisions ensure that accounting standards issued or adopted by the ASB (and its predecessor bodies) are treated as being issued by the Financial Reporting Council and remain in force until withdrawn.[720] These provisions are part of the way in which the legislation gives statutory recognition to the issue of accounting standards and compliance with them, adding to the need to comply with such accounting standards in order for Companies Act individual and group accounts to comply with the true and fair requirements.[721]          **15.464.02**

Under a provision of the 2004 Act the Secretary of State is empowered to make grants to bodies concerned with issuing accounting standards,[722] although the Government announced on 14 October 2010 that the Financial Reporting Council will in the future be entirely funded by market participants.[723]          **15.464.03**

## *Companies qualifying as medium-sized*

### 465  Companies qualifying as medium-sized: general

(1)  A company qualifies as medium-sized in relation to its first financial year if the qualifying conditions are met in that year.                              **15.465.01**

(2)  A company qualifies as medium-sized in relation to a subsequent financial year— (a) if the qualifying conditions are met in that year and the preceding financial year;

    (b)  if the qualifying conditions are met in that year and the company qualified as medium-sized in relation to the preceding financial year;

    (c)  if the qualifying conditions were met in the preceding financial year and the company qualified as medium-sized in relation to that year.

(3)  The qualifying conditions are met by a company in a year in which it satisfies two or more of the following requirements—

| | |
|---|---|
| 1. Turnover | Not more than £[25.9] million |
| 2. Balance sheet total | Not more than £[12.9]a million |
| 3. Number of employees | Not more than 250 |

---

[714]  Companies Act 2006 (Commencement No 1, etc) Order 2006, SI 2006/3428, art 3(3).

[715]  Companies Act 2006 (Commencement No 5, Transitional Provisions and Savings) Order 2007, SI 2007/3495, art 3(1) for financial years beginning on or after 6 April 2008.

[716]  Large and Medium-sized Companies and Groups (Accounts and Reports) Regulations 2008, SI 2008/410.

[717]  Large and Medium-sized Companies and Groups (Accounts and Reports) Regulations 2008, SI 2008/410, Sch 1, para 45; Sch 2, para 54; Sch 3, para 62.

[718]  See the Accounting Standards (Prescribed Body) Regulations 2008, SI 2008/651.

[719]  See the Statutory Auditors (Amendment of Companies Act 2006 and Delegation of Functions etc) Order 2012, SI 2012/1741.

[720]  See regulation 24, ibid.

[721]  See the commentary on ss 396 and 404.

[722]  Companies (Audit Investigations and Community Enterprise) Act 2004, s 16.

[723]  FRC Press Notice 310.

(4) For a period that is a company's financial year but not in fact a year the maximum figures for turnover must be proportionately adjusted.

(5) The balance sheet total means the aggregate of the amounts shown as assets in the company's balance sheet.

(6) The number of employees means the average number of persons employed by the company in the year, determined as follows—

(a) find for each month in the financial year the number of persons employed under contracts of service by the company in that month (whether throughout the month or not),

(b) add together the monthly totals, and

(c) divide by the number of months in the financial year.

(7) This section is subject to section 466 (companies qualifying as medium-sized: parent companies).

AMENDMENTS AND NOTES

[a] Amendments in square brackets made by the Companies Act 2006 (Amendment) (Accounts and Reports) Regulations 2008, SI 2008/393, reg 4.

COMMENCEMENT DATE  6 April 2008[724]

15.465.02  This section and the next two are in virtually identical form to sections 382 to 384 which define a company subject to the small companies' regime; as with the small companies regime, the application of this section and the next two is a little complicated and reference should be made to the commentary on the small companies regime under sections 382 to 384. The differences are that the size limits of subsection (3) are naturally much larger than the corresponding limits in section 382(3); and the range of financial services activities which render a company ineligible are a little wider at section 467 than in the corresponding section 384. In addition, the terminology is not wholly consistent. A company 'qualifies as medium sized' if it meets the size tests of this section and, where relevant, section 466. This does indeed correspond with 'qualifying as small' under sections 382 and 383. A company that qualifies as small, and is not excluded by section 384, is said to be one subject to the small companies regime.[725]. There is no useful equivalent terminology of a medium-sized companies regime—the equivalent is a company that is medium-sized and not excluded by section 467 (corresponding to section 384) from taking advantage of the exemptions of this Part for such companies.

15.465.03  The exemptions are, first, that the copy of its annual accounts and directors' report to be delivered to the registrar may be an abbreviated version of those prepared for and circulated to the members.[726] Second, such a company does not fall directly within that element of the business review contained within the directors' report that relates to non-financial measures (environmental, employment, social, and community issues).[727]

15.465.04  The application of this section follows that described in respect of section 382 earlier on. In short, a company *first* qualifies as medium-sized in the second of two consecutive financial years[728] in which it meets any two of the conditions in subsection (3), save that a company becomes medium-sized if it meets two such conditions in its first financial year. Once a company has qualified as medium-sized, it *continues* to be so qualified until it *ceases* to satisfy any two of the conditions in subsection (3) in two consecutive financial years. If the company is a parent company,[729] it must also meet section 466.

### 466  Companies qualifying as medium-sized: parent companies

15.466.01  (1) A parent company qualifies as a medium-sized company in relation to a financial year only if the group headed by it qualifies as a medium-sized group.

(2) A group qualifies as medium-sized in relation to the parent company's first financial year if the qualifying conditions are met in that year.

(3) A group qualifies as medium-sized in relation to a subsequent financial year of the parent company—

(a) if the qualifying conditions are met in that year and the preceding financial year;

(b) if the qualifying conditions are met in that year and the group qualified as medium-sized in relation to the preceding financial year;

---

[724] Companies Act 2006 (Commencement No 5, Transitional Provisions and Savings) Order 2007, SI 2007/3495, art 3(1) for financial years beginning on or after 6 April 2008.

[725] See s 381.

[726] See s 445.

[727] See s 417(7). As discussed in the commentary on that section, the boundary between what a medium-sized company must present in its business review and what other companies must present is not as clear as it might seem

[728] See s 390.

[729] See s 1173.

(c)   if the qualifying conditions were met in the preceding financial year and the group qualified as medium-sized in relation to that year.

(4)   The qualifying conditions are met by a group in a year in which it satisfies two or more of the following requirements—

| | |
|---|---|
| 1. Aggregate turnover | Not more than £[25.9] million net (or £[31.1] million gross) |
| 2. Aggregate balance sheet total | Not more than £[12.9] million net (or £[15.1]a million gross) |
| 3. Aggregate number of employees | Not more than 250 |

(5)   The aggregate figures are ascertained by aggregating the relevant figures determined in accordance with section 465 for each member of the group.

(6)   In relation to the aggregate figures for turnover and balance sheet total— 'net' means after any set-offs and other adjustments made to eliminate group transactions—

(a)   in the case of Companies Act accounts, in accordance with regulations under section 386,

(b)   in the case of IAS accounts, in accordance with international accounting standards; and 'gross' means without those set-offs and other adjustments.

A company may satisfy any relevant requirement on the basis of either the net or the gross figure.

(7)   The figures for each subsidiary undertaking shall be those included in its individual accounts for the relevant financial year, that is—

(a)   if its financial year ends with that of the parent company, that financial year, and

(b)   if not, its financial year ending last before the end of the financial year of the parent company.

If those figures cannot be obtained without disproportionate expense or undue delay, the latest available figures shall be taken.

AMENDMENTS AND NOTES

a   Amendments in square brackets made by the Companies Act 2006 (Amendment) (Accounts and Reports) Regulations 2008, SI 2008/393, reg 4.

COMMENCEMENT DATE   6 April 2008[730]

This section is in identical form to section 383 with respect to small companies, save that the size requirements of subsection (4) are naturally much larger. The application of this section follows that described for section 383 earlier on.          **15.466.02**

## 467   Companies excluded from being treated as medium-sized

(1)   A company is not entitled to take advantage of any of the provisions of this Part relating to companies qualifying as medium-sized if it was at any time within the financial year in question—          **15.467.01**

(a)   a public company,

(b)   a company that—

(i)   has permission under Part 4 of the Financial Services and Markets Act 2000 (c. 8) to carry on a regulated activity, or

(ii)   carries on insurance market activity, or

(c)   a member of an ineligible group.

(2)   A group is ineligible if any of its members is—

(a)   a public company,

(b)   a body corporate (other than a company) whose shares are admitted to trading on a regulated market,

(c)   a person (other than a small company) who has permission under Part 4 of the Financial Services and Markets Act 2000 to carry on a regulated activity,

(d)   a small company that is an authorised insurance company, a banking company, an e-money issuer, [a MiFID investment firm]a or a UCITS management company, or

(e)   a person who carries on insurance market activity.

(3)   A company is a small company for the purposes of subsection (2) if it qualified as small in relation to its last financial year ending on or before the end of the financial year in question.

[(4)   This section does not prevent a company from taking advantage of section 417(7) (business review: non-financial information) by reason only of its having been a member of an ineligible group within the financial year in question.]b

AMENDMENTS AND NOTES

a   Words in square brackets substituted by the Markets in Financial Instruments Directive (Consequential Amendments) Regulations 2007, SI 2007/2932, reg 3(3).

---

[730]   Companies Act 2006 (Commencement No 5, Transitional Provisions and Savings) Order 2007, SI 2007/3495, art 3(1) for financial years beginning on or after 6 April 2008.

<sup>b</sup>  Subsection (4) added by the Companies Act 2006 (Amendment) (Accounts and Reports) Regula-
tions 2008, SI 2008/393, reg 7.

COMMENCEMENT DATE  6 April 2008[731]

**15.467.02**  This section is in virtually identical form to section 384 in respect of companies excluded from the
small companies' regime. Save for the four differences discussed below, its application follows that
described in respect of section 384.

**15.467.03**  The first difference is that the exclusion in this section operates only by reference to the status of the
company, and members of a group[732] of which it forms a part, at any time during the financial year[733]
in relation to which the company seeks to use a provision for medium-sized companies. By way of
contrast, a company is additionally excluded from the small companies regime if it is, at the time of
seeking to use a small companies regime provision, ineligible.[734]

**15.467.04**  The second difference is that subsection (2)(b) refers to a body corporate's[735] shares being traded on a
regulated market. Section 384(2)(b) refers to their being traded on a regulated market *in an EEA State*.
This, however, is a difference of drafting rather than of effect. A regulated market is defined in section
1173 as having the same meaning as in the EC Markets in Financial Instruments Directive and thus
covers a market that is regulated pursuant to that directive wherever in the EEA it is situated. Thus
unless regulated markets is explicitly stated as applying only to markets in certain EEA States—and
here it is not—then it refers to all EEA States.[736]

**15.467.05**  The third difference is more substantive. The type of activities rendering the company ineligible under
subsection (1)(b)(i) is wider than that of the corresponding section 384 (1)(b)(i). For medium-sized
companies, all regulated activity (for the purposes of this Part)[737] by the company itself leads to
ineligibility whereas for companies qualifying as small[738] it is only five particular regulated activities
that do so. Those five are in fact the same as the five specified by subsection (2)(d) in relation to
activities carried on by another group member that itself qualifies as small.[739] Thus in summary in
relation to regulated activity, the company is rendered ineligible: under subsection (1)(b)(i) if it carries
on any regulated activity (regulated for the purposes of this Part); under subsection (2)(c) if any group
member, that does not itself qualify as small, carries on any regulated activity (regulated for the
purposes of this Part); or if any group member, that does qualify as small, carries on one of the five
activities specified in subsection (2)(d).[740]

**15.467.06**  Subsection (4) reinstates the position that existed in the 1985 Act[741] permitting companies that are
otherwise excluded from using special provisions for medium-sized companies from taking advantage
of the exemption in section 417(7) from providing non-financial key performance indicators in their
business reviews.[742]

## *General power to make further provision about accounts and reports*

### 468  General power to make further provision about accounts and reports

**15.468.01**      (1)  The Secretary of State may make provision by regulations about—
        (a)  the accounts and reports that companies are required to prepare;
        (b)  the categories of companies required to prepare accounts and reports of any description;
        (c)  the form and content of the accounts and reports that companies are required to prepare;
        (d)  the obligations of companies and others as regards—
            (i)   the approval of accounts and reports,
            (ii)  the sending of accounts and reports to members and others,
            (iii) the laying of accounts and reports before the company in general meeting,

---

    [731]  Companies Act 2006 (Commencement No 5, Transitional Provisions and Savings) Order 2007, SI
2007/3495, art 3(1) for financial years beginning on or after 6 April 2008.
    [732]  See s 474.
    [733]  See s 390.
    [734]  Contrast subs (1)'s 'if it was at any time within the financial year in question,' to s 384(1)'s 'that it *is*, or was
at any time within the financial year in question'.
    [735]  See s 1173.
    [736]  Eg, there are several provisions elsewhere in this Act that qualify the term as relation to regulated markets
in the UK.
    [737]  See s 474.
    [738]  See ss 382 and 383.
    [739]  i.e. one that meets ss 382 and 383.
    [740]  For definitions of those five activities, see ss 474, 1164, and 1165.
    [741]  Companies Act 1985, s 247A(1A) in relation to s 246(2A).
    [742]  See s 417 for further information on the requirement to provide non-financial key performance indicators.

> (iv) the delivery of copies of accounts and reports to the registrar, and
> (v) the publication of accounts and reports.
>
> (2) The regulations may amend this Part by adding, altering or repealing provisions.
> (3) But they must not amend (other than consequentially)—
>   (a) section 393 (accounts to give true and fair view), or
>   (b) the provisions of Chapter 11 (revision of defective accounts and reports).
> (4) The regulations may create criminal offences in cases corresponding to those in which an offence is created by an existing provision of this Part.
>   The maximum penalty for any such offence may not be greater than is provided in relation to an offence under the existing provision.
> (5) The regulations may provide for civil penalties in circumstances corresponding to those within section 453(1) (civil penalty for failure to file accounts and reports).
> The provisions of section 453(2) to (5) apply in relation to any such penalty.

COMMENCEMENT DATE  20 January 2007[743]

This section replaces the widely drafted secondary legislative power in the 1985 Act's Part VII, to which Part 15 of this Act is the successor. The previous power was used on a number of occasions over the years, for example to update the accounting requirements as accounting practice developed or as EC directives demanded change in this area. In respect of the latter, the power was used in conjunction with that of the European Communities Act 1972, section 2(2), where the latter alone might have been insufficient to make desirable consequential changes in relation to new directive requirements. The power was also used to effect developments in corporate governance and the reporting of corporate governance, such as the introduction of the directors' remuneration report.[744]    **15.468.02**

The power in this section appears more targeted than its predecessor and is explicit in its coverage of most of the subject matter of Part 15, but leaving out the true and fair requirement of section 393 and the regime for the enquiry into, and revision of, defective accounts and reports. The continuation of the former is considered so important as a matter of accounting practice that its being outwith the scope of this power is entirely understandable.    **15.468.03**

### Other supplementary provisions

### 469  Preparation and filing of accounts in euros

(1) The amounts set out in the annual accounts of a company may also be shown in the same accounts translated into euros.    **15.469.01**

> (2) When complying with section 441 (duty to file accounts and reports), the directors of a company may deliver to the registrar an additional copy of the company's annual accounts in which the amounts have been translated into euros.
> (3) In both cases—
>   (a) the amounts must have been translated at the exchange rate prevailing on the date to which the balance sheet is made up, and
>   (b) that rate must be disclosed in the notes to the accounts.
> (4) For the purposes of sections 434 and 435 (requirements in connection with published accounts) any additional copy of the company's annual accounts delivered to the registrar under subsection (2) above shall be treated as statutory accounts of the company.
>   In the case of such a copy, references in those sections to the auditor's report on the company's annual accounts shall be read as references to the auditor's report on the annual accounts of which it is a copy.

COMMENCEMENT DATE  6 April 2008[745]

This section (like its predecessor)[746] is little used. It implements an EC Fourth Company Law Directive[747] measure that originally facilitated the use of ECU figures in accounts, whereas strictly the ECU was not in fact a currency. Within the European and UK legislation the ECU has now been replaced with the euro,[748] and arguably the directive provision and this section are redundant.    **15.469.02**

---

[743] Companies Act 2006 (Commencement No 1, etc) Order 2006, SI 2006/3428, art 3(3).
[744] Introduced by the Directors' Remuneration Report Regulations 2002, SI 2002/1986.
[745] Companies Act 2006 (Commencement No 5, Transitional Provisions and Savings) Order 2007, SI 2007/3495, art 3(1) for financial years beginning on or after 6 April 2008.
[746] CA 1985, s 242B.
[747] Directive 78/660/EEC at [1978] OJ/L222/11, as amended.
[748] Per EC Regulation 1103/97/EC at [1997] OJ/L162/1, Art 2.

**15.469.03**   There is no explicit requirement of law that prohibits the preparation of accounts in a currency other than Sterling. If IAS individual or group accounts are prepared then in fact EU-adopted IFRS[749] explicitly permit a choice of currency.[750] Under those standards the figures are translated from the currency of the primary economic environment in which the company operates into the chosen presentation currency in the following way: the balance sheet amounts are translated at the exchange rate prevailing at balance sheet date; and the profit and loss account is translated at (put simply) an average rate for the period concerned.

**15.469.04**   The occasion and method of translation provided by this section are different. First of all, subsection (1) provides that in the annual accounts—ie, those prepared under sections 394, 398, and 399—there may be an additional presentation of the figures in euros; and subsection (2) permits the original figures in the annual accounts prepared under those sections to be removed from the copy delivered to the registrar and to have euro figures substituted. In both cases the method of translation is to convert all figures—both those relating to the balance sheet and those relating to the profit and loss account—at a single rate, being the rate prevailing at the balance sheet date.

### 470   Power to apply provisions to banking partnerships

**15.470.01**   (1)  The Secretary of State may by regulations apply to banking partnerships, subject to such exceptions, adaptations and modifications as he considers appropriate, the provisions of this Part (and of regulations made under this Part) applying to banking companies.
(2)  A 'banking partnership' means a partnership which has permission under Part 4 of the Financial Services and Markets Act 2000 (c. 8).
But a partnership is not a banking partnership if it has permission to accept deposits only for the purpose of carrying on another regulated activity in accordance with that permission.
(3)  Expressions used in this section that are also used in the provisions regulating activities under the Financial Services and Markets Act 2000 have the same meaning here as they do in those provisions.
See section 22 of that Act, orders made under that section and Schedule 2 to that Act.
(4)  Regulations under this section are subject to affirmative resolution procedure.

COMMENCEMENT DATE  20 January 2007[751]

**15.470.02**   This section flows from the Bank Accounts Directive[752] that requires accounts for credit institutions,[753] and governs the form and content thereof. This Act implements its requirements for companies by virtue of requiring accounts[754] and regulations under sections 396(3) and 404(3) (form and content of Companies Act individual accounts and Companies Act group accounts) make special provision for banking companies. However, the scope of credit institutions within the Bank Accounts Directive is potentially wider than companies. Thus this section gives the Secretary of State power to apply this Act's requirements for banking companies to another form of undertaking, *viz* banking partnerships, should the need to do so ever arise.

### 471   Meaning of 'annual accounts' and related expressions[a]

**15.471.01**   (1)  In this Part a company's 'annual accounts', in relation to a financial year, means—
(a)  [any individual accounts prepared by the company] for that year (see section 394)[b], and
(b)  any group accounts prepared by the company for that year (see sections 398 and 399).
This is subject to section 390 (option to omit individual profit and loss account from annual accounts where information given in group accounts).
(2)  In the case of an unquoted company, its 'annual accounts and reports' for a financial year are—
(a)  its annual accounts,
(b)  the directors' report, and
(c)  the auditor's report on those accounts and the directors' report (unless the company is exempt from audit).
(3)  In the case of a quoted company, its 'annual accounts and reports' for a financial year are—
(a)  its annual accounts,
(b)  the directors' remuneration report,
(c)  the directors' report, and

---

[749]  The customary name for 'international accounting standards' defined in s 474 in compliance with which IAS individual and IAS group accounts are required to be prepared.
[750]  *IAS 21 The effects of changes in foreign exchange rates* (International Accounting Standards Board, 2003, as amended). See Commission Regulation (EC) No 1126/2008 at [2008] OJ/L320/1 as amended.
[751]  Companies Act 2006 (Commencement No 1, etc) Order 2006, SI 2006/3428, art 3(3).
[752]  Directive 86/635/EEC at [1986] OJ/L372/1, as amended.
[753]  Defined in Directive 2006/48/EC at [2006] OJ/L177/1, as amended.
[754]  See ss 394, 398, and 399.

(d)   the auditor's report on those accounts, on the auditable part of the directors' remuneration report and on the directors' report.

AMENDMENTS AND NOTES

a   This section applies with modifications to overseas companies by reg 42 of the Overseas Companies Regulations 2009, 2009/1801.

b   Substituted by the Companies and Limited Liability Partnerships ( Accounts and Audit Exemptions and Change in Accounting Framework) Regulations 2012, SI 2012/ 2301, for financial years ending on or after 1 October 2012.

COMMENCEMENT DATE in relation to subsections (1)(a) from 1 October 2012[755]; otherwise, 6 April 2008[756].

The concept of the 'annual accounts' is an important one since the requirement to have accounts audited, published, laid (for public companies), and delivered to the registrar all apply in respect of annual accounts.[757]   **15.471.02**

Where a company prepares only individual accounts, then the annual accounts consist only of those accounts. Where the company prepares individual accounts and group accounts, then the annual accounts consist of those group accounts together with the individual accounts save for the individual profit and loss account and related notes where the company takes advantage of section 408 (to prepare the profit and loss account etc but not to include it). In such a case there is therefore no requirement to have the individual profit and loss account audited, published, laid (for public companies), or delivered to the registrar.   **15.471.03**

The 'annual accounts and reports' consist of the annual accounts and such of the following reports as are required to be prepared: directors' report, directors' remuneration report, and auditors' report. The term 'annual accounts and reports' does not, however, embrace any separate corporate governance statement. Whilst separate provision is made for such a statement to be reviewed by the auditor and delivered to the registrar,[758] no provision is made for circulation to members etc or for laying before members (in relation to public companies).[759] As noted at the relevant sections, this omission is unlikely to have any practical effect: companies will almost certainly circulate and lay such a statement anyway.   **15.471.04**

## 472   Notes to the accounts[a]

(1)   Information required by this Part to be given in notes to a company's annual accounts may be contained in the accounts or in a separate document annexed to the accounts.   **15.472.01**

(2)   References in this Part to a company's annual accounts, or to a balance sheet or profit and loss account, include notes to the accounts giving information which is required by any provision of this Act or international accounting standards, and required or allowed by any such provision to be given in a note to company accounts.

AMENDMENTS AND NOTES

a   This section applies with modifications to overseas companies by reg 42 of the Overseas Companies Regulations 2009, 2009/1801.

COMMENCEMENT DATE   6 April 2008[760]

The facility in subsection (1)—to present notes to the accounts in a separate document albeit annexed to the accounts—is not known ever to be used. One reason for this is that, for example, it is almost always the case that the balance sheet gives a true and fair view of the company's state of affairs only when taken together with the notes that amplify certain matters dealt with in the balance sheet. There would thus be considerable reluctance upon the part of accountants to present the notes in a separate document notwithstanding that it might be annexed to the accounts.   **15.472.02**

Subsection (2) makes clear that, for example, references to a balance sheet include notes related to the balance sheet. Without this provision it would often be impossible, for example, to meet the require-   **15.472.03**

---

[755]   Companies and Limited Liability Partnerships (Accounts and Audit Exemptions and Change of Accounting Framework) Regulations 2012, SI 2012/2301, for financial years ending on or after 1 October 2012.

[756]   Companies Act 2006 (Commencement No 5, Transitional Provisions and Savings) Order 2007, SI 2007/3495, art 3(1) for financial years beginning on or after 6 April 2008.

[757]   See ss 475, 423 and 430, 437, and 441–447 respectively.

[758]   See ss 497A, 498A and ss 447, 448.

[759]   See ss 423, 437.

[760]   Companies Act 2006 (Commencement No 5, Transitional Provisions and Savings) Order 2007, SI 2007/3495, art 3(1) for financial years beginning on or after 6 April 2008.

ment for the balance sheet to give a true and fair view of the company's state of affairs since notes amplifying certain aspects of the balance sheet are an integral part of that true and fair view.

### 472A Meaning of 'corporate governance statement' etc

**15.472A.01**   [(1) In this Part 'corporate governance statement' means the statement required by rules 7.2.1 to 7.2.11 in the Disclosure Rules and Transparency Rules sourcebook issued by the Financial Services Authority.

(2) Those rules were inserted by Annex C of the Disclosure Rules and Transparency Rules Sourcebook (Corporate Governance Rules) Instrument 2008 made by the Authority on 26 June 2008 (FSA 2008/32).

(3) A 'separate' corporate governance statement means one that is not included in the directors' report.]ᵃ

AMENDMENTS AND NOTES

ᵃ Inserted by the Companies Act 2006 (Accounts, Reports and Audit) Regulations 2009, SI 2009/1581, reg 5, as from 27 June 2009, in relation to financial years beginning on or after 29 June 2008 which have not ended before 27 June 2009.

COMMENCEMENT DATE  27 June 2009

**15.472A.02**   This section is part of the implementation of changes made to the Fourth and Seventh Directives.[761] Taken together, this section, section 419A, and chapter 7 of the FSA's Disclosure and Transparency Rules (DTR) require certain companies to publish annually a statement explaining certain elements of their corporate governance structure and practices.

**15.472A.03**   Chapter 7 of the DTR applies to companies with securities admitted to trading on a regulated market. It requires that certain corporate governance disclosures (exemptions from many of the disclosures are available to certain debt issuers[762]) be made either in the directors' report or in a separate corporate governance statement. Where the latter option is taken then that statement is subject to approval under provisions of this Act's section 419A; ie, the separate corporate governance statement arises under the DTR but requires Companies Act approval. This section 472A serves as a definition to connect that section 419A with the statement made under the DTR.

**15.472A.04**   The disclosures required by the DTR are substantially a repetition of those in Listing Rule LR 9.8.6R (5), (6). Those require that a listed company disclose how it has applied the principles of the UK Corporate Governance Code[763] and whether it has complied with the Code's provisions, with any departures explained. In addition the DTR repeats disclosure requirements applicable to the directors' report in regulations made under section 416 (in relation to share capital).

### 473  Parliamentary procedure for certain regulations under this Part

**15.473.01**   (1) This section applies to regulations under the following provisions of this Part—
    section 396 (Companies Act individual accounts),
    section 404 (Companies Act group accounts),
    section 409 (information about related undertakings),
    section 412 (information about directors' benefits: remuneration, pensions and compensation for loss of office),
    section 416 (contents of directors' report: general),
    section 421 (contents of directors' remuneration report),
    section 444 (filing obligations of companies subject to small companies regime),
    section 445 (filing obligations of medium-sized companies),
    section 468 (general power to make further provision about accounts and reports).
(2) Any such regulations may make consequential amendments or repeals in other provisions of this Act, or in other enactments.
(3) Regulations that—
    (a) restrict the classes of company which have the benefit of any exemption, exception or special provision,
    (b) require additional matter to be included in a document of any class, or
    (c) otherwise render the requirements of this Part more onerous, are subject to affirmative resolution procedure.
(4) Otherwise, the regulations are subject to negative resolution procedure.

---

[761] Directive 78/660/EEC at [1978] OJ/L222/11, as amended; and Directive 83/349/EEC at [1983] OJ/L193/1, as amended.
[762] DTR 1B.1.6.
[763] *UK Corporate Governance Code* (Financial Reporting Council, 2010).

COMMENCEMENT DATE   20 January 2007[764]

This section reflects the usual policy of requiring the affirmative resolution procedure[765] for secondary   **15.473.02**
legislation that increases the regulatory burden, and the negative resolution procedure[766] in other
cases.

## 474   Minor definitions[a]

(1)   In this Part—                                                                   **15.474.01**

'e-money issuer' means a person who has permission under Part 4 of the Financial Services and
Markets Act 2000 (c.8) to carry on the activity of issuing electronic money within the meaning
of article 9B of the Financial Services and Markets Act 2000 (Regulated Activities) Order 2001
(S.I. 2001/544);

'group' means a parent undertaking and its subsidiary undertakings;

'IAS Regulation' means EC Regulation No. 1606/2002 of the European Parliament and of the
Council of 19 July 2002 on the application of international accounting standards;

'included in the consolidation', in relation to group accounts, or 'included in consolidated group
accounts', means that the undertaking is included in the accounts by the method of full (and
not proportional) consolidation, and references to an undertaking excluded from consolidation
shall be construed accordingly;

'international accounting standards' means the international accounting standards, within the
meaning of the IAS Regulation, adopted from time to time by the European Commission in
accordance with that Regulation;

['MiFID investment firm' means an investment firm within the meaning of Article 4.1.1 of
Directive 2004/39/EC of the European Parliament and of the Council of 21 April 2004 on
markets in financial instruments, other than—

(a)   a company to which that Directive does not apply by virtue of Article 2 of that Directive,

(b)   a company which is an exempt investment firm within the meaning of regulation
224A(3) of the Financial Services and Markets Act 2000 (Markets in Financial Instruments) Regulations 2007, and

(c)   any other company which fulfils all the requirements set out in regulation 4C(3) of those
Regulations;][b]

'profit and loss account', in relation to a company that prepares IAS accounts, includes an income
statement or other equivalent financial statement required to be prepared by international
accounting standards;

'regulated activity' has the meaning given in section 22 of the Financial Services and Markets Act
2000, except that it does not include activities of the kind specified in any of the following
provisions of the Financial Services and Markets Act 2000 (Regulated Activities) Order 2001 (S.I.
2001/544)—

(a)   article 25A (arranging regulated mortgage contracts),

(b)   article 25B (arranging regulated home reversion plans),

(c)   article 25C (arranging regulated home purchase plans),

[(ca) article 25E (arranging regulated sale and rent back agreements),][c]

(d)   article 39A (assisting administration and performance of a contract of insurance),

(e)   article 53A (advising on regulated mortgage contracts),

(f)   article 53B (advising on regulated home reversion plans),

(g)   article 53C (advising on regulated home purchase plans), [(ga)article 53D (advising on
regulated sale and rent back agreements),][d]

(h)   article 21 (dealing as agent), article 25 (arranging deals in investments) or article 53
(advising on investments) where the activity concerns relevant investments that are not
contractually based investments (within the meaning of article 3 of that Order), or

(i)   article 64 (agreeing to carry on a regulated activity of the kind mentioned in paragraphs
(a) to (h));

'turnover', in relation to a company, means the amounts derived from the provision of goods and
services falling within the company's ordinary activities, after deduction of—

(a)   trade discounts,

(b)   value added tax, and

(c)   any other taxes based on the amounts so derived;

'UCITS management company' has the meaning given by the Glossary forming part of the
Handbook made by the Financial Services Authority under the Financial Services and Markets
Act 2000 (c.8).

---

[764]  Companies Act 2006 (Commencement No 1, etc) Order 2006, SI 2006/3428, art 3(3).
[765]  See s 1290.
[766]  See s 1289.

(2) In the case of an undertaking not trading for profit, any reference in this Part to a profit and loss account is to an income and expenditure account. References to profit and loss and, in relation to group accounts, to a consolidated profit and loss account shall be construed accordingly.

AMENDMENTS AND NOTES

ᵃ This section applies with modifications to overseas companies by reg 42 of the Overseas Companies Regulations 2009, 2009/1801.

ᵇ Words in square brackets substituted by the Markets in Financial Instruments Directive (Consequential Amendments) Regulations 2007, SI 2007/2932, reg 3(4).

ᶜ Amended by the Financial Services and Markets 2000 (Regulated Activities) (Amendment) Order 2009, SI 2009/1342, art 26.

ᵈ Amended by the Financial Services and Markets 2000 (Regulated Activities) (Amendment) Order 2009, SI 2009/1342, art 26.

COMMENCEMENT DATE 6 April 2008[767]

**15.474.02** This section defines a number of terms that recur at a number of places throughout Part 15. Three particularly important terms are 'international accounting standards', 'group', and 'included in the consolidation'.

**15.474.03** 'International accounting standards' are customarily known in the accounting profession as 'EU-adopted IFRS' and are best explained by taking each of 'IFRS' as 'EU-adopted' in turn. IFRS are accounting standards issued by the International Accounting Standards Board (IASB).[768] EU-adopted IFRS are those IFRS that have been adopted by the European Commission under the IAS regulation[769] as also defined in this section. IFRS and EU-adopted IFRS are not necessarily precisely the same, for three reasons. The main reason is that there will be a time lag (albeit a matter of months) between the IASB's issuing a standard and the Commission's adopting it. Second, EU-adopted IFRS do not include certain ancillary material that is included in IFRS as issued by the IASB, such as appended material detailing the basis for the IASB's conclusions (ie, explaining the IASB's decision to incorporate particular requirements within the standard).[770] However, it would be difficult to conclude that an EU-adopted IFRS should be interpreted any differently from an IFRS simply due to this omission. Finally, there has also been an instance of the Commission's explicitly modifying a standard on adoption[771] because of a disagreement between some Member States and the IASB as to the appropriateness of certain detailed provisions of the standard and, as described at section 395, it appears that IFRS requirements for the preparation of consolidated accounts are implicitly modified on adoption.

**15.474.04** The IAS Regulation gives the Commission power to adopt the IASB's standards (individually) and specifies the procedure for so doing.[772] The process is known as 'comitology', and the specific procedure called 'Regulatory procedure with scrutiny', which was introduced in 2008[773] and is in effect a secondary legislative procedure at EC level. Under this there is a committee, known as the Accounting Regulatory Committee (ARC) chaired by the Commission and consisting of representatives of each the Member States' governments.

**15.474.05** The Commission controls the agenda of the ARC but only the Member States may vote, with the usual weightings. However, the Commission need not propose such a Regulation in relation to any particular standard. The first stage of the procedure is to put a proposal to the ARC. Once ARC has voted on the proposal, whether in favour (by qualified majority) or not, the matter is referred to the European Parliament and the Council. Unless the European Parliament or Council votes against it by their usual majorities (eg, by a qualified majority in the case of the Council), within a certain time of its being put to them, then the Commission Regulation is carried. There is thus considerable bias in favour of any

---

[767] Companies Act 2006 (Commencement No 5, Transitional Provisions and Savings) Order 2007, SI 2007/3495, art 3(1) for financial years beginning on or after 6 April 2008.

[768] International Accounting Standards (IAS), International Financial Reporting Standards (IFRS) and related interpretations (SIC, IFRIC). The whole body of these is also known as 'IFRS'.

[769] Regulation (EC) No 1606/2002 at [2002] OJ/L243/1, as amended.

[770] This exclusion is presumably for expediency's sake in view of the need for the Commission to make translations into all official languages.

[771] IAS 39 Financial instruments: recognition and measurement, adopted by the European Commission in 2005. See Commission Regulation (EC) No 1864/2005 at [2005] OJ/L299/45.

[772] Art 3(1) contains the power and Art 6 specifies Arts 5a and 7 of Decision 1999/468/EC at [1999] OJ/L184/23 as the procedure, as amended by Decision 2006/512/EC at [2006] OJ/L200/11.

[773] Decision 2006/512/EC at [2006] OJ/L200/11, which amended Decision 1999/468/EC at [1999] OJ/L184/23 by introducing 'Regulatory procedure with scrutiny' (Art 5a).

proposal put forward by the Commission. However, as a practical matter the Commission seeks to build a substantial consensus among Member States before making a formal proposal to the ARC.

Once a Commission Regulation adopting a standard is made, it does not enter into force until it is published in the Official Journal in all official languages; and such a standard, once it is in force, will have its own effective date set out within it. Notwithstanding that the IASB issues IFRS in English, all of the official language versions of EU-adopted IFRS have equal standing. The Commission maintains on its website a listing of all EU-adopted IFRS with links to the relevant Commission Regulations.[774] **15.474.06**

The IAS regulation sets out the criteria by which the question of adoption is to be determined. A standard can only be adopted if it is consistent with the true and fair requirements of the EC Fourth and Seventh Company Law Directives;[775] if it is conducive to the European public good; and if the resulting financial information would meet certain qualitative criteria in relation to an assessment of steward-ship and to economic decision-making.[776] The test of public good has not yet been cited as a reason for rejecting a standard (or part thereof) but the implication of this test is that at some stage a company's members might be denied accounts that give a true and fair view because such accounts would not serve the public good—notwithstanding that one might suppose that having true and fair accounts is overwhelmingly good public policy itself. **15.474.07**

In making the assessment of the technical accounting aspects of a standard, the ARC receives reports from a body known as the European Financial Reporting Advisory Group (EFRAG). This body, and its reports, have no formal standing under EC law; it was set up at the behest of the Commission to provide these reports of technical assessment. Its members are drawn from bodies that set accounting stan-dards at national level within Member States. For example, the UK's Accounting Standards Board is represented upon it. However, it must be emphasized that the Commission and the ARC are under no legal obligation to follow EFRAG recommendations and it must be recognized that the ARC's deliberations can have a political aspect. **15.474.08**

Turning to the definition of 'group', it is worth emphasizing that it refers to the parent undertaking and its subsidiary undertakings as identified according to other definitions in this Act.[777] UK accounting standards also address further aspects of the application of these definitions.[778] However, EU-adopted IFRS have a definition of a group which, whilst in a great many cases will result in the group consisting of the same undertakings as under the Act, may in some cases result in minor differences. It is therefore important to appreciate that any provision of this Act that refers to the 'group' is referring to the group defined by the Act, notwithstanding that the requirement might relate to IAS group accounts. **15.474.09**

On the other hand, the term 'included in the consolidation' refers to those undertakings that are in fact included, whether the basis of inclusion was determined under the Act or under EU-adopted IFRS. For example, the requirement that directors do not approve group accounts unless they give a true and fair view is stated in these terms.[779] **15.474.10**

---

[774] See <http://ec.europa.eu/internal_market/accounting/legal_framework/regulations_adopting_ias_text_En.htm> for the listing.
[775] Directive 78/660/EEC at [1978] OJ/L222/11, as amended and Directive 83/349/EEC at [1983] OJ/ L193/1, as amended.
[776] Art 3(2).
[777] See s 1162.
[778] *FRS 2 Accounting for subsidiary undertakings* (ASB, 1992).
[779] See s 393(1)(b).

# 16

## AUDIT

## Companies Act 2006

# PART 16
## AUDIT

# CHAPTER 1
## REQUIREMENT FOR AUDITED ACCOUNTS

*Requirement for audited accounts*

### 475  Requirement for audited accounts

**16.475.01**

(1) A company's annual accounts for a financial year must be audited in accordance with this Part unless the company—

    (a)  is exempt from audit under—

        section 477 (small companies), [section 479A (subsidiary companies)]ᵃ or

        section 480 (dormant companies); or

    (b)  is exempt from the requirements of this Part under section 482 (non profit-making companies subject to public sector audit).

  (2)  A company is not entitled to any such exemption unless its balance sheet contains a statement by the directors to that effect.

  (3)  A company is not entitled to exemption under any of the provisions mentioned in subsection (1)(a) unless its balance sheet contains a statement by the directors to the effect that—

    (a)  the members have not required the company to obtain an audit of its accounts for the year in question in accordance with section 476, and

    (b)  the directors acknowledge their responsibilities for complying with the requirements of this Act with respect to accounting records and the preparation of accounts.

  (4)  The statement required by subsection (2) or (3) must appear on the balance sheet above the signature required by section 414.

AMENDMENTS

ᵃ Inserted by the Companies and Limited Liability Partnerships (Accounts and Audit Exemptions and Change in Accounting Framework) Regulations 2012, SI 2012/2301, for financial years ending on or after 1 October 2012.

COMMENCEMENT DATE   in relation to subsections (1)(a), from 1 October 2012;[1] otherwise 6 April 2008

This section provides for the requirement that each company's annual accounts[2] should be audited, but subject to exemptions for those companies named under subsection (1)(a) and (b).[3]  **16.475.02**

The requirement and the exemptions are articulated as being in relation to 'audit' of the 'annual accounts' in accordance with this Part 16. 'Audit' is not defined in this Part or in the Act. However, section 495 provides that the function of an auditor is to make a report on the annual accounts, and sections 496 to 498 require a number of other matters to be included within that report, in particular in relation to the directors' report[4] and, if one is required, the directors' remuneration report.[5] Thus it follows that a company that is exempt from audit of its annual accounts is in fact exempt from obtaining any auditor's report on any of its annual accounts or reports.  **16.475.03**

Of those exempted companies named by subsection (1)(a) and (b), small companies[6] — which are not necessarily synonymous with companies subject to Part 15's small companies regime—and dormant companies[7] are by far the most numerous. These companies represent the majority of all companies registered, such that these exemptions are important and widely used. For example, during the year ended 31 March 2010, 71.3 per cent of all accounts filed at Companies House were audit exempt and 19.0 per cent were dormant.[8]  **16.475.04**

The detailed conditions for each category of exemption are discussed in more detail under later sections;[9] and exemption is also conditional upon the members not exercising their section 476 right to require an audit and upon the making of the disclosure under subsections (2) and, if relevant, subsection (3). However, it is important to note that there may be a non-statutory requirement for an audit—for example, within the company's articles or a shareholders' agreement, or there may be a professional obligation to file audited accounts with a professional body—such that the company may not be able to take advantage of the audit exemption under the Act. In addition, other legislation may  **16.475.05**

---

[1] Companies and Limited Liability Partnerships (Accounts and Audit Exemptions and Change of Accounting Framework) Regulations 2012, SI 2012/2301, for financial years ending on or after 1 October 2012.

[2] Companies Act 2006 (Commencement No 5, Transitional Provisions and Savings) Order 2007, SI 2007/3495, art 3(1) for financial years beginning on or after 6 April 2008.

[3] See s 471.

[4] Readers should note that many of the provisions in Parts 15 and 16 of the Act apply, with modifications, to limited liability partnerships by virtue of the Limited Liability Partnerships (Accounts and Audit) (Application of Companies Act 2006) Regulations 2008, SI 2008/1911. Readers should note that many of the provisions of Parts 15 and 16 apply to insurance undertakings specified in reg 2(2)–(4) of the Insurance Accounts Directive (Miscellaneous Insurance Undertakings) Regulations 2008, SI 2008/565, and qualifying banks specified in reg 3 of the Bank Accounts Directive (Miscellaneous Banks) Regulations 2008, SI 2008/567.

[5] See s 415.

[6] See s 420.

[7] See s 477.

[8] See s 480.

[9] Statistical tables on companies registration activities (BIS, 2011/2012), p 34.

require an audit. For example, those exempt under subsection (1)(b) are instead subject to public sector audit under various enactments.[10]

**16.475.06** A company may only take advantage of the audit exemption to which it is otherwise entitled, if the company's balance sheet contains a statement that the company is taking advantage of the exemptions given by subsection (1). The form of that statement, for companies exempt under subsection (1)(a), is given by subsection (3).[11] It is likely, although not necessarily automatic, that a company in this situation will also be required to include on its balance sheet the statement as to accounts preparation under the small companies regime and to include a further statement on the copy delivered to the registrar if the company takes advantage of the facility to deliver incomplete annual accounts and reports.[12] The presence of these statements is routinely checked by Companies House; their absence will lead to rejection of the annual accounts.

**16.475.07** A company that under subsection (1)(b) is exempt from audit under this Part 16, and thus instead is subject to public section audit, must nevertheless include upon the balance sheet a directors' statement of Part 16 exemption. In the interests of clarity such a statement might be drafted to make clear that the company is instead subject to public sector audit.

**16.475.08** A company may claim exemption from audit but retain an auditor—that is to say, it is not a necessary requirement of taking the exemption for an incumbent auditor to resign from office, although it is the usual practice to do so.

**16.475.09** On some occasions a company may need to have an auditor even though its annual accounts are exempt from audit. A private company wishing to purchase its own shares out of capital (ie, make a permissible capital payment) under section 709 *et seq* must obtain an auditor's report upon the directors' section 714 statement. In practice an auditor is appointed where such a need arises and resigns when the report is completed.

### 476 Right of members to require audit

**16.476.01**
(1) The members of a company that would otherwise be entitled to exemption from audit under any of the provisions mentioned in section 475(1)(a) may by notice under this section require it to obtain an audit of its accounts for a financial year.
(2) The notice must be given by—
    (a) members representing not less in total than 10% in nominal value of the company's issued share capital, or any class of it, or
    (b) if the company does not have a share capital, not less than 10% in number of the members of the company.
(3) The notice may not be given before the financial year to which it relates and must be given not later than one month before the end of that year.

COMMENCEMENT DATE 6 April 2008[13]

**16.476.02** This section gives the members of a company the right to require an audit of the annual accounts subject to conditions set out in subsections (2) and (3), and it thereby affords members—in particular, members who form a minority—a degree of protection. Nevertheless, the use of this right is uncommon because many of the companies to which the audit exemption is available are either owner-managed or dormant, wholly-owned subsidiary companies.

**16.476.03** Subsection (2) provides which or how many members may require the company to obtain an audit. For companies with share capital, a member or members who hold 10 per cent or more in nominal value of any class of the company's shares—for example, a class of preference shares—may require an audit. For companies without a share capital—that is to say, guarantee companies—members who form 10 per cent or more of the members of the company may require an audit.

---

[10] See ss 477–483.
[11] See ss 482 and 483.
[12] This statement appears less forceful than the previous requirement under the Companies Act (CA) 1985, s 249B(4) where the directors had to acknowledge their responsibilities for 'preparing accounts which give a true and fair view of the state of affairs of the company as at the end of the financial year and of its profit or loss for the financial year'. Nevertheless, the change in wording has no practical effect and the directors' duty to prepare true and fair accounts is unchanged by the use of the exemption conferred by this section.
[13] A company that is exempt under s 477 is likely to have employed special provisions for the preparation of accounts under the small companies regime; see s 414. It may also intend to use the special filing provisions of s 444(1)(a).

The effect of subsection (3)'s timing rule is to prevent multiple year notices and to avoid imposing the    **16.476.04**
audit requirement too close to, or after, the end of the financial year,[14] which otherwise might cause
problems for the auditor with respect to obtaining certain audit evidence—for example, attendance at
the year end stock take in some cases.

## *Exemption from audit: small companies*

### 477  Small companies: conditions for exemption from audit[a]

(1)  A company that [qualifies as a small company in relation to][b] a financial year is exempt from the    **16.477.01**
requirements of this Act relating to the audit of accounts for that year.

(2)  []c

(3)  []c

(4)  For the purposes of this section—

  (a)  whether a company qualifies as a small company shall be determined in accordance with
section 382(1) to (6),

  (b)  []c

(5)  This section has effect subject to—

  section 475(2) and (3) (requirements as to statements to be contained in balance sheet),

  section 476 (right of members to require audit),

  section 478 (companies excluded from small companies exemption), and

  section 479 (availability of small companies exemption in case of group company).

AMENDMENTS and Notes

ª   Amended by the Companies and Limited Liability Partnerships (Accounts and Audit Exemptions
and Change in Accounting Framework) Regulations 2012, SI 2012/2301 for financial years ending
on or after 1 October 2012, and previously read:

(1)  A company that meets the following conditions in respect of a financial year is exempt from the
requirements of this Act relating to the audit of accounts for that year.

(2)  The conditions are:

  (a)  that the company qualifies as small company in relation to that year,

  (b)  that its turnover in that year is not more than £[6.5] million, and

  (c)  that its balance sheet total for that year is not more than £[3.26] million

(3)  For a period which is a company's financial yaer but not in fact a year the maximum figure for
turnover shall be proportionately adjusted.

(4)  For the purposes of this section-

  (a)  whether a company qualifies as a small company shall be determined in accordance with
section 382(1) to (6),

  (b)  ['balance sheet total]' has the same meaning as in that section.

(5)  This section has effect subject to-

  section 475(2) and (3) (requirements as to statements to be contained in balance sheet),

  section 476 (right of members to require audit),

  section 478 (companies excluded from small companies exemption), and

  section 479 (availability of small companies exemption in case of group company).

ᵇ   Inserted by the Companies and Limited Liability Partnerships (Accounts and Audit Exemptions
and Change in Accounting Framework) Regulations 2012, SI 2012/2301, for financial years ending
on or after 1 October 2012.

ᶜ   Repealed by the Companies and Limited Liability Partnerships (Accounts and Audit Exemptions
and Change of Accounting Framework) Regulations 2012, SI 2012/2301, for financial years ending
on or after1 October 2012.

COMMENCEMENT DATE    in relation to the amendments in section (1) to (4) from 1 October 2012;[15]
otherwise, 6 April 2008[16]

This section deals with the availability of the exemption from audit for what the section heading refers    **16.477.02**
to as a small company. However, this section does not, on its own, determine whether a company is
exempt from audit: it should be considered together with section 478, which excludes certain companies from availing themselves of this audit exemption. Further, if the company is a member of a group

---

[14]  Companies Act 2006 (Commencement No 5, Transitional Provisions and Savings) Order 2007, SI 2007/
3495, art 3(1) for financial years beginning on or after 6 April 2008.
[15]  See s 390.
[16]  Companies and Limited Liability Partnerships (Accounts and Audit Exemptions and Change of Accounting Framework) Regulations 2012, SI 2012/2301 for financial years ending on or after 1 October 2012.

as defined in section 479, the qualifying conditions in that section must also be met. Prior to the amendment effective for financial year ending on or after 1 October 2012, the effect of these sections (as they stood, as set out above, before amendment) was to create an exemption that applies in similar but by no means identical circumstances to the small companies regime for accounting (and other related matters) under Part 15.[17]

**16.477.03**    These sections, and their relationship with Part 15, were, however, complex. Before commenting in detail upon them it is worth noting the terminology and the broad effect compared with Part 15. The terminology of Part 15 is that a 'small companies regime' for accounting is available to some but not all small companies; in this Part 16 what might be termed a 'small companies audit exemption' was available to some but not all small companies; and this latter population will be a subset of those within the small companies regime. Comparing the two, one could say that, broadly, to be within the small companies regime for accounting the company must meet a two limb test: the company, *and any group headed by it*, must meet size tests; and any group of which the company forms a part (eg a higher group) must not contain certain categories of company (including that the company itself must not fall into those categories). The small companies audit exemption, broadly speaking, was a two-limb test as follows: the company, *and any group of which it forms a part* (eg a higher group), must meet similar but not identical size tests; and such a group must not contain the same certain categories of company, and the company itself must not fall within an *extended* list of categories.

**16.477.04**    Turning to the detail of the provisions, subsection (2) previously set out the size conditions in relation to the company. The first condition was that the company must qualify as a small company as determined by section 382(1) to (6), which was part of the first limb of the small companies regime for accounts. Section 382(7) addresses qualification as small for parent companies but is not brought within this section 477 because section 479 makes separate and different provision for companies within groups.

**16.477.05**    The second and third conditions were that, in the financial year[18] in question, being those ending before 1 October 2012, the turnover was not more than £6.5 million and the balance sheet total[19] was not more than £3.26 million. These conditions were the same as two of the 'thresholds' that are given by section 382(3).

**16.477.06**    At first sight, it may appear odd that these thresholds were repeated in this section when they are identical to thresholds given by section 382(3). However, on closer inspection it can be seen that the manner of inclusion of these thresholds in subsection (2)(b) and (c) made the test more stringent. First, for the purposes of section 382(3), it was possible to qualify as a small company by meeting only one of the turnover or balance sheet total thresholds (if the employee numbers threshold is also met). However, it was not possible to qualify for audit exemption without meeting both. Second, as explained at section 382, that test of qualification as a small company was based on what could be described as a 'two-year rolling basis', whereas qualification for the exemption from audit required the thresholds in subsection (2)(b) and (c) to be met in each financial year for which exemption from audit is sought. Thus, taking these two points together, unlike section 382(3), to qualify for audit exemption (for financial years ending before 1 October 2012) a company must, inter alia, have met both the turnover and balance sheet total thresholds and have done so in the financial year in which exemption was sought.

**16.477.07**    For financial years ending on or after 1 October 2012, these complex rules have been simplified. The additional need to meet turnover and the balance sheet total tests in the year in question, as discussed above, is removed. Instead, it is now the case that to fall within this small companies audit exemption it is merely a requirement to be within the small companies regime for accounting, subject to the additional conditions in section 477(5).

## 478 Companies excluded from small companies exemption

**16.478.01**    A company is not entitled to the exemption conferred by section 477 (small companies) if it was at any time within the financial year in question—

> (a)  a public company,
> (b)  a company that—
>> (i)   is an authorised insurance company, a banking company, an e-money issuer, [a MiFID investment firm][a] or a UCITS management company, or
>> (ii)  carries on insurance market activity, or

---

[17]  Companies Act 2006 (Commencement No 5, Transitional Provisions and Savings) Order 2007, SI 2007/3495, art 3(1) for financial years beginning on or after 6 April 2008.
[18]  See s 381.
[19]  See s 390.

(c) a special register body as defined in section 117(1) of the Trade Union and Labour Relations (Consolidation) Act 1992 (c. 52) or an employers' association as defined in section 122 of that Act or Article 4 of the Industrial Relations (Northern Ireland) Order 1992 (S.I. 1992/807 (N.I. 5)).

AMENDMENTS and Notes

a Substituted by the Markets in Financial Instruments Directive (Consequential Amendments) Regulations 2007, SI 2007/2932, reg 3(5).

COMMENCEMENT DATE  6 April 2008[20]

This section excludes certain categories of company from taking advantage of the small companies audit exemption given by section 477. The excluded categories are the same as those that are excluded from the Part 15 small companies regime under section 384 (in relation to the company itself), save for those additional categories named in subsection (c) to which exclusion is extended.    **16.478.02**

It should be noted that section 479(2)(a)(ii) and (5)(b) contains a similar exclusion test based upon the Part 15 excluded categories, but in relation to the members of any group of which the company forms a part, but without any equivalent of the extension made by subsection (c).    **16.478.03**

## 479  Availability of small companies exemption in case of group company[a]

(1) A company is not entitled to the exemption conferred by section 477 (small companies) in respect of a financial year during any part of which it was a group company unless—    **16.479.01**
    (a) [the group—
        (i) qualifies as a small group in relation to that financial year, and
        (ii) was not at any time in that year an ineligible group, or][b]
    (b) subsection (3) applies.
(2) []][b]
(3) A company is not excluded by subsection (1) if, throughout the whole of the period or periods during the financial year when it was a group company, it was both a subsidiary undertaking and dormant.
(4) In this section—
    (a) 'group company' means a company that is a parent company or a subsidiary undertaking, and
    (b) 'the group', in relation to a group company, means that company together with all its associated undertakings.
For this purpose undertakings are associated if one is a subsidiary undertaking of the other or both are subsidiary undertakings of a third undertaking.
(5) For the purposes of this section—
    (a) whether a group qualifies as small shall be determined in accordance with section 383 (companies qualifying as small: parent companies);
    (b) 'ineligible group' has the meaning given by section 384(2) and (3);
    (c) []][c]
(6) The provisions mentioned in subsection (5) apply for the purposes of this section as if all the bodies corporate in the group were companies.

AMENDMENTS and Notes

a Amended by the Companies and Limited Liability Partnerships (Accounts and Audit Exemptions and Change in Accounting Framework) Regulations 2012, SI 2012/2301 for financial years ending on or after 1 October 2012, and previously read:

(1) A company is not entitled to the exemption conferred by section 477 (small companies) in respect of a financial year during any part of which it was a group company unless-
    (a) the conditions specified in subsection (2) below are met, or
    (b) subsection (3) applies.
(2) The conditions are-
    (a) that the group-
        (i) qualifies as a small group in relation to that financial year, and
        (ii) was not at any time in that year an ineligible group;
    (b) that the group's aggregate turnover in that year is not more than £[6.5] million net (or £[7.8] million gross);
    (c) that the group's aggregate balance sheet total for that year is not more than £[3.26] million net (or £[3.9]a million gross).

---

[20] These have the same meanings as in s 382. The definition of balance sheet total is specifically read across from that section by subs (4)(b), whereas turnover is defined for the purposes of Part 16 at s 539 in identical terms to Part 15's definition at s 474.

 (3) A company is not excluded by subsection (1) if, throughout the whole of the period or periods during the financial year when it was a group company, it was both a subsidiary undertaking and dormant.

 (4) In this section-

  (a) 'group company' means a company that is a parent company or a subsidiary undertaking, and

  (b) 'the group', in relation to a group company, means that company together with all its associated undertakings.

   For this purpose undertakings are associated if one is a subsidiary undertaking of the other or both are subsidiary undertakings of a third undertaking.

 (5) For the purposes of this section-

  (a) whether a group qualifies as small shall be determined in accordance with section 383 (companies qualifying as small: parent companies);

  (b) 'ineligible group' has the meaning given by section 384(2) and (3);

  (c) a group's aggregate turnover and aggregate balance sheet total shall be determined as for the purposes of section 383;

  (d) 'net' and 'gross' have the same meaning as in that section;

  (e) a company may meet any relevant requirement on the basis of either the gross or the net figure.

 (6) The provisions mentioned in subsection (5) apply for the purposes of this section as if all the bodies corporate in the group were companies.

 <sup>b</sup> Inserted by the Companies and Limited Liability Partnerships (Accounts and Audit Exemptions and Change of Accounting Framework) Regulations 2012, SI 2012/2301, reg 5, for financial years ending on or after 1 October 2012.

 <sup>c</sup> Repealed by the Companies and Limited Liability Partnerships (Accounts and Audit Exemptions and Change of Accounting Framework) Regulations 2012, SI 2012/2301, reg 5, for financial years ending on or after from 1 October 2012.

 COMMENCEMENT DATE in relation to subsections (1)(a),(2) and (5)(c), from 1 October 2012;[21] otherwise, 6 April 2008[22]

**16.479.02** This section sets out conditions, additional to those of sections 477 and 478, that must be met in relation to a group company in order for that company to qualify for the 'small company' exemption from audit. The test is similar to that in relation to groups for Part 15's small companies regime save that its thresholds were, for financial years ending before 1 October 2012, applied in a different way and that they applied to any group of which the company forms a part (eg a higher group), whereas in Part 15 the size test is applied to the group headed by the company.

**16.479.03** First of all, the section applies where the company was a group company *at any time during the financial year* for which exemption is sought, and subsection (3) (see below) deals with a particular consequence of this timing rule.

**16.479.04** A group company is defined in subsection (4) as one that is either a parent company[23] or a subsidiary undertaking.[24] The definition of the group is given by subsection (4)(b) and may be described as comprising the company and all undertakings which are the company's parent undertakings, subsidiary undertakings and fellow subsidiary undertakings.[25] Prior to financial years ending on or after 1 October 2012, the size conditions of subsection (2) applied to this group. For subsequent financial years, the effect of subsection (1)(a)(i) is to apply the section 383 size tests. Thus in contrast with Part 15's small companies regime, the size tests applied to any higher group of which the company forms a part. The effect of this is that a group could not, by dividing its business between various subsidiary undertakings, arrange that they individually meet the exemption conditions.

---

 [21] Companies Act 2006 (Commencement No 5, Transitional Provisions and Savings) Order 2007, SI 2007/3495, art 3(1). This provision applies to accounts and reports for financial years beginning on or after 6 April 2008.
 [22] Companies and Limited Liability Partnerships (Accounts and Audit Exemptions and Change of Accounting Framework) Regulations 2012, SI 2012/2301, for financial years ending on or after 1 October 2012.
 [23] Companies Act 2006 (Commencement No 5, Transitional Provisions and Savings) Order 2007, SI 2007/3495, art 3(1). This provision applies to accounts and reports for financial years beginning on or after 6 April 2008.
 [24] See s 1173.
 [25] See s 1162.

For financial years ending before 1 October 2012, subsection (2) then applied conditions to this group.    **16.479.05**
The first[26] was that the group qualified as small, as determined by section 383, and was not at any time
in the financial year an ineligible group, as determined by section 384(2) and (3).

The second and third conditions[27] were that the group's aggregate turnover was not more than £6.5    **16.479.06**
million net or £7.8 million gross and its balance sheet total was not more than £3.26 million net or £3.9
million gross. These conditions were the same as two of the thresholds in section 383, albeit, as
discussed above, applied to a different group. The meaning of 'aggregate turnover', 'balance sheet total',
'net' and 'gross' is given by section 383, and reference should be made to that section for a discussion
of the difference between these two methods of calculation.

As discussed under section 477, it may appear odd that these Part 15 thresholds were repeated in this    **16.479.07**
section when they are identical to thresholds given by section 383(4). However, on closer inspection it
can be seen that the manner of inclusion of these thresholds in subsection (2)(b) and (c) made the test
more stringent. First, for the purposes of section 383(4), it is possible to qualify as a small company by
meeting only one of the turnover or balance sheet total thresholds (if the employee numbers threshold
is also met). However, it was not possible to qualify for audit exemption without meeting both. Second,
as explained at section 383, that test of qualification as a small company is based on what could be
described as a 'two-year rolling basis', whereas qualification for the exemption from audit requires the
thresholds in subsection (2)(b) and (c) were to be met in each financial year for which exemption from
audit was sought. Thus, taking these two points together, unlike section 382(3), to qualify for audit
exemption (for financial years ending before 1 October 2012), a company must, inter alia, have met
both the turnover and balance sheet total thresholds and done so in the financial year in which
exemption was sought.[28]

For financial years ending on or after 1 October 2012, these complex rules have been simplified. The    **16.479.08**
additional need to meet turnover and the balance sheet total tests in the year in question, as discussed
above, is removed. Instead, it is now the case that to fall within this small companies audit exemption
it is merely a requirement to be within the small companies regime for accounting, subject to the
additional conditions in section 479(5).

Subsection (3) gave an important exception from the previous group size limits of subsection (2) and    **16.479.09**
now from group size limits applied under subsection (1). The main effect of this subsection is to put
'off-the-shelf' companies purchased from formation agents on an equal footing with other newly
formed, freestanding companies. The problem that would be faced by 'off-the-shelf' companies absent
subsection (3) arises from the fact that the requirements of this section apply if a company is a group
company at any time during its financial year. 'Off-the-shelf' companies are formed as subsidiary
undertakings of their formation agents and those formation agents' groups almost always breach the
conditions in what was subsection (2) or now in subsection (1). This leads to an issue when an
'off-the-shelf' company is sold, during its financial year, by the formation agent to an individual who
then carries on a small business in the company. Without subsection (3), an 'off-the-shelf' company,
that would otherwise meet the conditions set out in sections 477 to 478, would fail to meet the
qualifying conditions for exemption from audit in its first financial year owing to its membership of the
formation agent's large group during part of that year. That would be an unwelcome outcome from the
standpoint of the new owner of an 'off-the-shelf' company and, it seems, of little logic if the company
would be in a position to claim exemption from audit in subsequent financial years. This problem is
solved by subsection (3), which provides that the group conditions of subsection (2), or now the group
conditions of subsection (1), were not required to be met if throughout the periods of its being a group
company it was a dormant[29] subsidiary undertaking.[30] The benefit for an 'off-the-shelf' company is
that the period of its being within the formation agents' large group, provided it was dormant during
that period (which is almost always the case in practice), is ignored in determining whether it may
claim exemption from audit. This is of considerable assistance to individuals who purchase 'off-the-
shelf' companies. However, where a small group purchases such a company, it appears that the
subsection (3) exemption might not apply, since the company is also a member of the acquirer's small
group but is not—presumably—dormant during that period; accordingly, former subsection (2) tests
appeared, and now the subsection (1) tests appear to apply both in relation to the acquirer's small group
and to the vendor formation agent's group. This would stand in contrast to the position under the

---

[26]  See s 1161.

[27]  Subsection (2)(a).

[28]  Subsection (2)(b), (c).

[29]  See s 1169.

[30]  But not if the company is a parent company as this might result in its not preparing audited group accounts
when audited group accounts would otherwise be required.

predecessor legislation[31] where the period of dormant membership of a non-small group (ie one that fails subsection (2)) was ignored for the purpose of applying the predecessor to subsection (2); an 'off-the-shelf' company purchased by a small group would clearly have been audit exempt. To overcome this apparent problem, one course of action might be to change the accounting reference date[32] such that the end of one financial year coincides with the date of purchase, thus putting the company under subsection (3) in the first financial year and subsection (2) in the second financial year without that second financial year being affected by membership of the large formation agent's group.

### *Exemption from audit: qualifying subsidiaries*

### 479A  Subsidiary companies: conditions for exemption from audit

**16.479A.01**

(1) A company is exempt from the requirements of this Act relating to the audit of individual accounts for a financial year if-
  (a)  it is itself a subsidiary undertaking, and
  (b)  its parent undertaking is established under the law of an EEA State.
(2) Exemption is conditional upon compliance with all of the following conditions-
  (a)  all members of the company must agree to the exemption in respect of the financial year in question,
  (b)  the parent undertaking must give a guarantee under section 479C in respect of that year,
  (c)  the company must be included in the consolidated accounts drawn up for that year or to an earlier date in that year by the parent undertaking in accordance with-
    (i)  the provisions of the Seventh Directive (83/349/EEC)(d), or
    (ii)  international accounting standards,
  (d)  the parent undertaking must disclose in the notes to the consolidated accounts that the company is exempt from the requirements of this Act relating to the audit of individual accounts by virtue of this section, and
  (e)  the directors of the company must deliver to the registrar on or before the date that they file the accounts for that year-
    (i)  a written notice of the agreement referred to in subsection (2)(a),
    (ii)  the statement referred to in section 479C(1),
    (iii) a copy of the consolidated accounts referred to in subsection (2)(c),
    (iv) a copy of the auditor's report on those accounts, and
    (v)  a copy of the consolidated annual report drawn up by the parent undertaking.
(3) This section has effect subject to-
  section 475(2) and (3) (requirements as to statements contained in balance sheet), and
  section 476 (right of members to require audit).

Commencement Date   1 October 2012[33]

**16.479A.02**    This section, which applies in relation to financial years ending on or after 1 October 2012, enables some subsidiary undertakings to be exempt from audit, and in doing so it implements a member state option in Article 57 of the EC Fourth Company Law Directive[34]. The principal conditions for exemption are that all of the members agree and that an EEA parent provides a guarantee of the company's liabilities as at the financial year end in question. The guarantee is described more fully at section 479C. However, the cardinal points are that it is apparently very broad and potentially very long-lasting.

**16.479A.03**    The policy behind this exemption is, presumably, that the members' interest is protected by the requirement that they agree unanimously; that the interests of the creditors, who might deal with the company after, inter alia, having looked at its annual accounts, are protected by a guarantee from the company's parent; and that, based on such protections, there may be no reason to impose the cost of audit provided that audited accounts of the guarantor are also publically available in the same way as are the company's annual accounts.

**16.479A.04**    There are, however, three inherent tensions or questions in relation to such a policy. First, those who extend credit to the company after, inter alia, having consulted audit-exempt annual accounts will not, in fact, benefit from the guarantee. The guarantee covers only the liabilities as at the financial year-end of those accounts. Self-evidently, a person consulting these accounts must necessarily be doing so after the financial year end in question. Second, if one can dispense with assurance over the quality of the

[31]  CA 1985, ss 249AA and 249B.
[32]  See s 391.
[33]  Companies and Limited Liability Partnerships (Accounts and Audit Exemptions and Change of Accounting Framework) Regulations 2012, SI 2012/2301, for financial years ending on or after 1 October 2012.
[34]  Directive 78/660/EEC at [1978] OJ/L222/11, as amended.

information in the annual accounts, then this begs the questions as to why the legislation should require the information in the first place. Finally, the activities of the company will not be entirely free of audit. The group accounts of a higher part must be audited, and thus some audit procedures, and costs, will arise in relation to the company's activities included in those group accounts.[35] Notwithstanding these points, the exemption has been introduced to the statute book.

For a group contemplating this exemption it is worth noting, first, the effect of spreading liability around the group. After all, a presumed purpose of currently conducting parts of the group's business through limited liability subsidiary undertakings is to restrict the assets against which creditors can claim (ie, ring-fence liabilities and assets into separate 'pots'). This guarantee regime would negate such a purpose. This is so even if the guarantor is a holding company. In such a case, holding company's assets, available to meet claims under the guarantee, would include the holding company's shareholdings in other subsidiary undertakings. A second point to note is that, although this guarantee would remove that advantage of conducting business through limited liability subsidiaries, it would not remove any other rules of company law relating to limited liability subsidiaries. For example, the normal rules restricting and controlling distributions by the subsidiary undertaking to the parent would still apply, notwithstanding the parent's guarantee.     **16.479A.05**

Turning to the detail of the section, first of all the company must be a subsidiary undertaking, for which see section 1162. Second, the guarantor must be a parent undertaking established in an EEA state. It need not necessarily be the immediate or the ultimate parent undertaking. Moreover, a parent undertaking need not, as is evident from its definition in sections 1161, be a company. Third, the exemption extends only to the company's individual accounts and not to any group accounts. However, it is likely that the company would not be required to prepare group accounts, as a company that is exempt under this section 479A is likely to be exempt from preparing group accounts under section 400 (exemption for company included in EEA group, which is in similar terms but without the need for a guarantee).     **16.479A.06**

Taking, next, the other conditions of subsection (2) (ie, other than the guarantee itself, for which see section 479C), the first (subsection (2)(a)) is that all of the members agree the exemption. (For resolutions of members, see section 281.) This is, obviously, a requirement for unanimous agreement of all members, whether, eg, ordinary shareholders or preference shareholders. If all of the shares are owned by the parent undertaking (or others controlled by it), then this presents little problem. Any external shareholders may present more of a problem. Note also that, as advertised in subsection (3), even after giving this agreement a member could, in effect, change its view and seek to use section 476 to require an audit (provided that it met the voting and timing rules of that section).     **16.479A.07**

Subsection (2)(c) requires that the company is included in the consolidated accounts of the guarantor. The term 'included in consolidated accounts' means that the assets, liabilities, and trading of the subsidiary must be included in full in the group accounts.[36] Thus, proportionate consolidation or equity accounting is not sufficient.     **16.479A.08**

It is also necessary for the guarantor parent's consolidated accounts to be drawn up to the same date (as the accounts of the company) or to an earlier date in the same financial year. However, as it is not always practical to align financial years immediately after acquisition, the exemption might not be available initially. For example, if a company with a financial year ended 31 March 2013 were acquired in February 2013 by a new parent with a 31 December year end, the acquired company would *not* be included in the acquirer's 31 December 2012 consolidation and would be prohibited under section 392 from extending its financial year to 31 December 2013 (as this would result in a financial year of 21 months). Thus, it would have to be subject to audit for the financial year ended 31 March 2013.     **16.479A.09**

However, it appears that it is only necessary for one day of the financial year of the company claiming exemption to be included in the guarantor parent's consolidated accounts. For example, if a company with a financial year ending on 31 December 2012 were acquired on 30 December 2012 by a company that also has a financial year to 31 December 2012, it would be consolidated into that guarantor parent's consolidated accounts for one day and would meet the condition.     **16.479A.10**

Further, these consolidated accounts of the guarantor parent must be drawn up either in accordance with the EC Seventh Company Law Directive[37] or in accordance with EU-adopted IFRS. If the     **16.479A.11**

---

[35] See, for example, the UK auditing standard *ISA (UK & Ir) 600 Special considerations-audits of group financial statements (including the work of component auditors)* (Auditing Practices Board, 2010).

[36] See s 474(1).

[37] Directive 83/849/EEC at [1983] OJ/L193/1, as amended. Compliance with the EC Seventh Company Law Directive includes (see arts 17 and 29) compliance with much of the EC Fourth Company Law Directive 78/660/EEC at [1978] OJ/L222/11, as amended, as if the group were a single company.

guarantor parent is a company, it is a simple prerequisite that the EEA state has implemented that directive into its national law[38] or has permitted the use of EU-adopted IFRS under the IAS Regulation,[39] as the case may be. In both cases-the directive and EU-adopted IFRS-it is of course necessary that the accounts do in fact comply with the relevant framework. It should not be overlooked, however, that these consolidated accounts must also disclose that the company-so, presumably, naming the company-is to be exempt from audit under this section 479A. These consolidated accounts of the guarantor parent must be delivered to the registrar and, inter alia, they must, under subsections (2)(e)(iii), (iv), (v) be accompanied by an audit report on those consolidated accounts and by a consolidated annual report. Accordingly, it is required that those consolidated accounts are audited. There must also be drawn up an 'annual report'. 'Annual report' in this context (implementation of an EC Fourth Company Law Directive member state option) is the terminology of the EC company law directives and has been implemented in the UK as the directors' report. However, since this section does not specifically refer to the annual report's being in accordance with the provisions of that directive, it is left unclear as to what might be the minimum contents necessary to establish that the document can be regarded as an annual report for section 479A. Provided that the parent undertaking is a company, and that the relevant EEA state has implemented those directives and the company has complied with them, then it should be straightforward to deal with this point, as those directives would require an annual report of such a company.

**16.479A.12**  Subsection (3) provides that, together, with those consolidated accounts, audit report, and annual report, the directors of the company must deliver to the registrar a notice of the members' agreement and the guarantee statement under section 479C. Importantly, these must be delivered on or before the date that the annual accounts of the company are delivered. Unusually, the operation of this section 479A is unaffected by any late delivery of the company's own annual accounts. That is, it appears that the company's annual accounts might be delivered late (after the timing required by sections 442, 443) and yet this audit exemption will still be available so long as the subsection (3) filings are not made later still. On the other hand, any failure to deliver the relevant section 479A documents on or before the delivery of the annual accounts of the company will preclude the company from using this exemption. Note, finally, that there is no exemption from preparing and delivering the annual accounts of the company itself (unless the company is also dormant, for which see sections 394A to 394C and 448A to 448C).

### 479B  Companies excluded from the subsidiary companies audit exemption

**16.479B.01**  A company is not entitled to the exemption conferred by section 479A (subsidiary companies) if it was at any time within the financial year in question-

    (a)  a quoted company as defined in section 385(2) of this Act,
    (b)  a company that-
        (i)  is an authorised insurance company, a banking company, an e-money issuer, a MiFID investment firm or a UCITS management company, or
        (ii)  carries on insurance market activity, or
    (c)  a special register body as defined in section 117(1) of the Trade Union and Labour Relations (Consolidation) Act 1992 (c 52)(a) or an employers' association as defined in section 122 of that Act or Article 4 of the Industrial Relations (Northern Ireland) Order 1992 (SI 1992/807) (NI 5).

    COMMENCEMENT DATE  1 October 2012[40]

**16.479B.02**  This section excludes from the audit exemption certain specified categories of company. The categories are similar to some elements of other exclusions elsewhere in Parts 15 and 16 (in sections 384, 478, and 481). Note, first, that these exclusions, unlike some others, are based only upon the status of the company itself (the company seeking audit exemption) and not on that of any group of which it forms a part.

---

[38]  Under the Agreement on the European Economic Area (Oporto, 2 May 1992) the EEA States that are not within the EU agree to implement certain EC law within their national law. The company law directives, including the EC Seventh Company Law Directive, are such laws.

[39]  For companies not directly within the IAS Regulation (Regulation (EC) No 1606/2002), as amended, Art 5 thereof gives Member States the option of allowing the use of EU-adopted IFRS in lieu of directives-based national provision. Companies that are directly within the IAS Regulation are only so if they are first required by directive-based provisions of national law to prepare consolidated accounts which the IAS Regulation then requires to be in accordance with EU-adopted IFRS.

[40]  Companies and Limited Liability Partnerships (Accounts and Audit Exemptions and Change of Accounting Framework) Regulations 2012, SI 2012/2301, for financial years ending on or after 1 October 2012.

Subsections (a) and (b) are the most important exclusions. The term 'quoted' used in subsection (a) is    **16.479B.03**
defined in section 385. Note that the quotation is, inter alia, only of equity share capital. So, for example,
a company with listed debt would not, by reason only of that listed debt, be precluded from using the
exemption.

Subsection (b) excludes companies carrying on specified types of financial services business. The    **16.479B.04**
relevant definitions are set out in section 539, 1164, and 1165.

## 479C  Subsidiary companies audit exemption: parent undertaking declaration of guarantee

(1)  A guarantee is given by a parent undertaking under this section when the directors of the    **16.479C.01**
subsidiary company deliver to the registrar a statement by the parent undertaking that it
guarantees the subsidiary company under this section.

(2)  The statement under subsection (1) must be authenticated by the parent undertaking and must
specify-
  (a)  the name of the parent undertaking,
  (b)  if the parent undertaking is incorporated in the United Kingdom, its registered number (if
    any),
  (c)  if the parent undertaking is incorporated outside the United Kingdom and registered in the
    country in which it is incorporated, the identity of the register on which it is registered and the
    number with which it is so registered,
  (d)  the name and registered number of the subsidiary company in respect of which the
    guarantee is being given,
  (e)  the date of the statement, and
  (f)  the financial year to which the guarantee relates.

(3)  A guarantee given under this section has the effect that-
  (a)  the parent undertaking guarantees all outstanding liabilities to which the subsidiary company
    is subject at the end of the financial year to which the guarantee relates, until they are
    satisfied in full, and
  (b)  the guarantee is enforceable against the parent undertaking by any person to whom the
    subsidiary company is liable in respect of those liabilities.

COMMENCEMENT DATE  1 October 2012[41]

This section provides for a parent undertaking of a company to put itself in the position of guarantor    **16.479C.02**
of that company's liabilities in order that the company might take advantage of the section 479A audit
exemption, for which such a guarantee is one of the principal conditions.

Whilst subsection (2) sets out some procedural matters, the key matters of interest are subsections (1)    **16.479C.03**
and (3). First of all, subsection (1) makes clear that the parent undertaking puts itself into the position
of guarantor by the simple act of delivering a statement to that effect (plus other specified details) to the
registrar, and subsection (3) provides that the consequence of doing so is that the parent undertaking
thereby becomes liable as guarantor, enforceable against that parent by any person to whom the
company is liable. That is to say, the parent undertaking's liability as guarantor is a liability by operation
of statute law (this section). So the guarantee is not effected as a matter of contract law between
guarantor and beneficiary. This makes the giving of the guarantee much easier than would have been
the case if the parent undertaking has been required to contract to that effect with each and every party
with a claim upon the company.

Second, it will be apparent from subsection (3) that the scope of the parent undertaking's liability is very    **16.479C.04**
broad and potentially long-lasting. This guarantee covers 'all outstanding liabilities'. It is interesting to
contrast this with other formulations in this Act, such as those of sections 643(2) (solvency statement
for a private company's capital reduction) and 714(4) (permissible capital payment by a private
company), which use the formulation, 'all of the company's liabilities (including any contingent and
prospective liabilities)'. The question might arise as to whether, because this section 479C omits those
sections' explanations of the inclusion of contingent and prospective liabilities within 'liabilities',
contingent and prospective liabilities are covered by this guarantee or not. In other words, does a lack
of emphatic description, as to what is included, amount to an exclusion? Whilst this has not yet been
tested in practice, it appears that, since contingent liabilities and prospective liabilities are themselves
a variety of liability, then they are included within the guarantee. If so, then, for example, litigation
liabilities would be included, as would all future rentals under a lease.

---

[41]  The Companies and Limited Liability Partnerships (Accounts and Audit Exemptions and Change of
Accounting Framework) Regulations 2012. This provision applies to accounts and reports for financial years
ending on or after 1 October 2012, as corrected.

**16.479C.05**    Note also that some of these liabilities could be very 'long tail', for example leases or the company's obligation in relation to defined benefit pensions schemes. Note in this connection that, whilst the liabilities are those only as at the end of the financial year in question, there is no provision for the guarantee in respect of the related financial year to be withdrawn. So once the guarantee has been given, it would stand in perpetuity (including in the event that the company is sold by the guarantor's group) until the guaranteed liabilities, however 'long-tail', have been satisfied. So, in the case of defined benefit pension scheme obligations, it would stand until the benefits accrued as at the financial year-end by pensioners, deferred members, and current employee scheme members have been paid in full, which would occur when the last such person has died and (any death benefits have been paid).

**16.479C.06**    Whilst the guarantee is potentially very long-lasting, it is not a rolling guarantee, ie it does not cover new liabilities that arise after the financial year end in question. However, should the company wish to be exempt from audit for future financial years, then the parent undertaking will have to go through the section 479A, 479C process, and give a fresh guarantee, for every such financial year end.

## *Exemption from audit: dormant companies*

### 480  Dormant companies: conditions for exemption from audit

**16.480.01**    (1)  A company is exempt from the requirements of this Act relating to the audit of accounts in respect of a financial year if—

    (a)  it has been dormant since its formation, or
    (b)  it has been dormant since the end of the previous financial year and the following conditions are met.

(2)  The conditions are that the company—

    (a)  as regards its individual accounts for the financial year in question—
        (i)  is entitled to prepare accounts in accordance with the small companies regime (see sections 381 to 384), or
        (ii)  would be so entitled but for having been a public company or a member of an ineligible group, and
    (b)  is not required to prepare group accounts for that year.

(3)  This section has effect subject to—

        section 475(2) and (3) (requirements as to statements to be contained in balance sheet),
        section 476 (right of members to require audit), and
        section 481 (companies excluded from dormant companies exemption).

COMMENCEMENT DATE  6 April 2008[42]

**16.480.02**    This and the following section deal with the audit exemption for dormant companies. The legislation is presumably based upon a policy that there is little to be gained from auditing dormant companies: the auditor's principal task would be to examine the directors' assertion that the company is dormant. Thus, the Act permits most but not all dormant companies an exemption.

**16.480.03**    Put simply, the overall effect of the two sections is that if a company is dormant and is not of a type specified in section 481, then subject to one proviso it is exempt from audit. The proviso is that if the company has not always been dormant (since formation) then it must both meet section 382 and 383's small company size tests and not be required to prepare group accounts.

**16.480.04**    Turning to the detail of the section, the definition of a dormant company is given by section 1169 and is not dealt with here. Once it has been determined that a company is dormant, it is necessary to turn to subsection (1), which provides for two classes of dormant companies. The first are those which have been dormant since formation. A company in this class will qualify for the audit exemption, unless it is of a type that is excluded by virtue of section 481, without consideration of section 480(2).

**16.480.05**    The second class are those which have become dormant—ie at some point in their histories they were not dormant. A company in this class must have been dormant from the end of the financial year preceding the one in question—ie for the entire financial year[43] for which the audit exemption is claimed; and once this has been established, it is necessary for such a company to turn to the conditions set out in subsection (2).

**16.480.06**    The first condition of subsection (2) is that the company is, subject to one modification, entitled to prepare accounts in accordance with Part 15's small companies regime.[44] Qualification for the small companies regime has two parts. The first part is that the company qualifies as small in accordance with

---

[42]  Companies Act 2006 (Commencement No 5, Transitional Provisions and Savings) Order 2007, SI 2007/3495, art 3(1) for financial years beginning on or after 6 April 2008.
[43]  See s 390.
[44]  See s 381.

size tests in section 382 and, if it is a parent company, in section 383. A dormant company will almost always meet the section 382 test because its turnover must be nil and it is highly unlikely to have any employees whatsoever. However, it is worthwhile noting that being dormant is not synonymous with qualification as a small company. As discussed at section 382, qualification for the small companies regime is based on what may be described as a 'two year rolling basis'. Thus, it is possible that in its first year of dormancy it will not qualify as a small company owing to the size of its business in either or both of the two preceding financial years. The second part of qualification for the small companies regime is that the company is not excluded from that regime by virtue of its being, or its being a member of a group that contains, a company in one of the categories specified in section 384. For the purposes of this section 480, subsection (2)(a)(ii) varies the application of section 384. The result is that the only categories that cannot take advantage of the subsection (1)(b) dormant exemption are those named in section 384(1)(b), ie if the company *itself* carries on one of five specified financial services activities or carries on insurance market activity; and these are in fact the same categories of exclusion that apply by virtue of section 481; thus, the advantage conferred by this subsection flows mainly to dormant companies, provided they are not one of those named here, even though they are subsidiary under-takings of a 'large' group. The terms in section 384 (1)(b) (and section 481) are defined in sections 474 (and section 539), 1164, and 1165.

The second condition of subsection (2) is that the company is not required to prepare group accounts     **16.480.07**
for that financial year. It is presumably a matter of public policy that where group accounts are required by law, they should be audited; after all, the group may not be dormant. However, this condition in subsection (2)(b) does not appear to be breached where a dormant company subject to Part 15's small companies regime opts to prepare group accounts, since this is a result of a choice by the company rather than a requirement of the Act.[45] This is presumably because the company could anyway validly avoid having audited group accounts by choosing not to prepare group accounts at all.

### 481  Companies excluded from dormant companies exemption

A company is not entitled to the exemption conferred by section 480 (dormant companies) if it was at     **16.481.01**
any time within the financial year in question a company that—

  (a) is an authorised insurance company, a banking company, an e-money issuer, [a MiFID investment firm][a] or a UCITS management company, or
  (b) carries on insurance market activity.

A MENDMENTS

  [a] Words in square brackets substituted by the Markets in Financial Instruments Directive (Consequential Amendments) Regulations 2007, SI 2007/2932, reg 3(6).

C OMMENCEMENT D ATE  6 April 2008[46]

This section prohibits all dormant[47] companies, where they are permitted to provide specified financial     **16.481.02**
services,[48] from taking advantage of the dormant company audit exemption of section 480.

For companies that have become dormant after formation, this section is a duplication of section     **16.481.03**
480(2)(a)(ii).

## Companies subject to public sector audit

### 482  Non-profit-making companies subject to public sector audit

  (1) The requirements of this Part as to audit of accounts do not apply to a company for a financial year     **16.482.01**
       if it is non-profit-making and its accounts—
  (a) are subject to audit [by the Comptroller and Auditor General by virtue of an order under section 25(6) of the Government Resources and Accounts Act 2000 (c. 20), or; by
  (ab) are subject to audit by the Auditor General for Wales by virtue of—
       (i)  an order under section 144 of the Government of Wales Act 1998, or
       (ii) paragraph 18 of Schedule 8 to the Government of Wales Act 2006;][a]
  (b) are accounts—
       (i)  in relation to which section 21 of the Public Finance and Accountability (Scotland) Act 2000 (asp 1) (audit of accounts: Auditor General for Scotland) applies, or
       (ii) that are subject to audit by the Auditor General for Scotland by virtue of an order under section 483 (Scottish public sector companies: audit by Auditor General for Scotland); or

---

  [45] See s 398.
  [46] Companies Act 2006 (Commencement No 5, Transitional Provisions and Savings) Order 2007, SI 2007/3495, art 3(1) for financial years beginning on or after 6 April 2008.
  [47] See s 1169.
  [48] Defined in ss 539, 1164, and 1165.

    (c)   are subject to audit by the Comptroller and Auditor General for Northern Ireland by virtue of an order under Article 5(3) of the Audit and Accountability (Northern Ireland) Order 2003 (S.I. 2003/418 (N.I. 5)).

  (2)  In the case of a company that is a parent company or a subsidiary undertaking, subsection (1) applies only if every group undertaking is non-profit-making.

  (3)  In this section 'non-profit-making' has the same meaning as in Article 54 of the Treaty on the Functioning of the European Union.[b]

  (4)  This section has effect subject to section 475(2) (balance sheet to contain statement that company entitled to exemption under this section).

AMENDMENTS and Notes

[a]  Subsection (1) amended by the Government of Wales Act 2006 (Consequential Modifications, Transitional Provisions and Savings) Order 2009, SI 2009/, art 10(2).

[b]  Subsection (3) amended by The Treaty of Lisbon (Changes in Terminology or Numbering) Order 2012, SI 2012/1809, from 1 August 2012.

COMMENCEMENT DATE 1 April 2008[49]

**16.482.02** This section introduces a new exemption from audit under Part 16 for certain non-profit-making companies—broadly, those that are non-departmental public bodies—that are instead subject to public sector audit. Before this Act, the UK did not to take advantage of what is, in effect, the EC Treaty's exemption[50] for non-profit-making companies; all non-profit-making companies were hitherto subject to the audit requirements of predecessor legislation, even those public sector companies that were subject to the scrutiny of the Comptroller and Auditor General.[51]

**16.482.03** The facility to leave out such companies arises from Article 48 of the EC Treaty which defines 'companies or firms' in such a way so as to exclude those that are non-profit-making. Thus non-profit-making companies are outside the EC Fourth[52] and Seventh[53] Company Law Directives, being based on Article 44(2)(g) of that treaty; and so the Act is able to exclude a non-profit-making company from its audit requirements.

**16.482.04** No definition is given in the EC Treaty of 'non-profit making'. However, this is unlikely to lead to significant practical issues as the orders referred to in subsection (1) will provide the detail. It may be noted that in relation to England and Wales and Northern Ireland the orders are made under other legislation,[54] whereas in relation to Scotland the orders are made under section 483 of this Act[55] (or are covered directly under Scottish legislation).

**16.482.05** Where a company that would otherwise qualify for audit exemption under subsection (1) is a parent company[56] or subsidiary undertaking,[57] every group undertaking[58] must be non-profit-making. However, it is simply enough to be non-profit-making—that is to say, it is not necessary that each such undertaking be subject to public sector audit under subsection (1).

---

[49]  Companies Act 2006 (Commencement No 5, Transitional Provisions and Savings) Order 2007, SI 2007/3495, art 3(1) for financial years beginning on or after 1 April 2008. In relation to accounts for financial years beginning on or after 1 April 2008 and before 6 April 2008, the reference to the requirements of Part 16 of the Companies Act 2006 shall be read as a reference to the requirements of Part 7 of the Companies 1985 Act or Part 8 of the Companies (Northern Ireland) 1986 Order.

[50]  EC Treaty (Treaty of Rome, as amended), Art 48 (previously Art 58).

[51]  The duplication for public sector companies was dealt with in *Holding to account: the review of audit and accountability for central government* (Report by Lord Sharman of Redlynch, February 2001). Its proposal was that the Comptroller and Auditor General (and equivalents) be allowed to perform audits for the purpose of companies legislation, thereby removing the duplication. This has been taken up in this Act, which, in addition to this s 482 exemption, also permits an Auditor General to act as a company's auditor (see Chapter 3, Part 42) under Part 16 in the normal way.

[52]  Fourth Council Directive (EEC) 78/660 based on Article 54(3)(g) of the Treaty on the annual accounts of certain types of companies [1978] OJ L222/11, as amended, Art 1.

[53]  Seventh Council Directive (EEC) 83/349 based on Article 54(3)(g) of the Treaty on consolidated accounts [1983] OJ L193/1, as amended, Art 4.

[54]  Subsection (1)(a), (ab)(i), (c).

[55]  Subsection (1)(b)(ii).

[56]  See s 1173.

[57]  See s 1162.

[58]  See s 1161.

Where a company takes advantage of the exemption conferred by this section, a statement is required **16.482.06** to be made on the balance sheet to that effect.[59] However, the precise form of that statement is not dictated by the Act.[60]

### 483  Scottish public sector companies: audit by Auditor General for Scotland

(1)  The Scottish Ministers may by order provide for the accounts of a company having its registered **16.483.01** office in Scotland to be audited by the Auditor General for Scotland.

(2)  An order under subsection (1) may be made in relation to a company only if it appears to the Scottish Ministers that the company—

    (a)  exercises in or as regards Scotland functions of a public nature none of which relate to reserved matters (within the meaning of the Scotland Act 1998 (c. 46)), or

    (b)  is entirely or substantially funded from a body having accounts falling within paragraph (a) or (b) of subsection (3).

(3)  Those accounts are—

    (a)  accounts in relation to which section 21 of the Public Finance and Accountability (Scotland) Act 2000 (asp 1) (audit of accounts: Auditor General for Scotland) applies,

    (b)  accounts which are subject to audit by the Auditor General for Scotland by virtue of an order under this section.

(4)  An order under subsection (1) may make such supplementary or consequential provision (including provision amending an enactment) as the Scottish Ministers think expedient.

(5)  An order under subsection (1) shall not be made unless a draft of the statutory instrument containing it has been laid before, and approved by resolution of, the Scottish Parliament.

COMMENCEMENT DATE  20 January 2007[61]

This section confers new powers on Scottish Ministers[62] to provide by order for the accounts of a **16.483.02** company which has a registered office in Scotland to be audited by the Auditor General for Scotland. The effect is to put that company outside Part 16 by virtue of section 482(1)(b)(ii).

Those companies to which these provisions apply are given by subsection (2) and fall into two **16.483.03** categories. The first covers companies that have public functions in relation to Scotland and do not operate in any areas that are reserved.[63] The second covers companies that are entirely or substantially funded from a body having accounts falling within subsection (3) (no definition is given as to 'substantially funded'). Those accounts are ones audited by the Auditor General for Scotland either directly under the Public Finance and Accountability (Scotland) Act 2000 or because they are themselves the subject of an order under this section.[64]

Put simply, this section contains a power to enable a company that is a Scottish non-departmental **16.483.04** public body, not operating in a reserved area (which would instead be covered by section 482 directly), to be made subject to public sector audit instead of audit under Part 16.

*General power of amendment by regulations*

### 484  General power of amendment by regulations

(1)  The Secretary of State may by regulations amend this Chapter or section 539 (minor definitions) **16.484.01** so far as applying to this Chapter by adding, altering or repealing provisions.

(2)  The regulations may make consequential amendments or repeals in other provisions of this Act, or in other enactments.

(3)  Regulations under this section imposing new requirements, or rendering existing requirements more onerous, are subject to affirmative resolution procedure.

(4)  Other regulations under this section are subject to negative resolution procedure.

COMMENCEMENT DATE  20 January 2007[65]

---

[59]  Subsection (4).

[60]  In contrast to other companies that are exempt from audit and for which s 475(3) makes further specific provision.

[61]  Companies Act 2006 (Commencement No 1, etc) Order 2006, SI 2006/3428, art 3(3).

[62]  Scotland Act 1998, s 44(2).

[63]  Further to the Scotland Act 1998.

[64]  See Companies Act 2006 (Scottish Public Sector Companies to be Audited by the Auditor General for Scotland) Order 2008, SSI 2008/144, Schedule.

[65]  Companies Act 2006 (Commencement No 1, etc) Order 2006, SI 2006/3428, art 3(3).

**16.484.02** This section reflects the usual policy of requiring the affirmative resolution procedure[66] for secondary legislation that increases the regulatory burden, and the negative resolution procedure[67] in other cases. It should be noted that this is the only general amendment power in Part 16 and thus only this Chapter—essentially the requirement for audit and exemptions therefrom—is subject to amendment without recourse to primary legislation.

## CHAPTER 2
## APPOINTMENT OF AUDITORS

### Private companies

### 485 Appointment of auditors of private company: general

**16.485.01**

(1) An auditor or auditors of a private company must be appointed for each financial year of the company, unless the directors reasonably resolve otherwise on the ground that audited accounts are unlikely to be required.

(2) For each financial year for which an auditor or auditors is or are to be appointed (other than the company's first financial year), the appointment must be made before the end of the period of 28 days beginning with—

    (a) the end of the time allowed for sending out copies of the company's annual accounts and reports for the previous financial year (see section 424), or[a]

    (b) if earlier, the day on which copies of the company's annual accounts and reports for the previous financial year are sent out under section 423.

    This is the 'period for appointing auditors'.[b]

(3) The directors may appoint an auditor or auditors of the company—

    (a) at any time before the company's first period for appointing auditors,

    (b) following a period during which the company (being exempt from audit) did not have any auditor, at any time before the company's next period for appointing auditors, or

    (c) to fill a casual vacancy in the office of auditor.

(4) The members may appoint an auditor or auditors by ordinary resolution—

    (a) during a period for appointing auditors,

    (b) if the company should have appointed an auditor or auditors during a period for appointing auditors but failed to do so, or

    (c) where the directors had power to appoint under subsection (3) but have failed to make an appointment.

(5) An auditor or auditors of a private company may only be appointed—

    (a) in accordance with this section, or

    (b) in accordance with section 486 (default power of Secretary of State).

    This is without prejudice to any deemed re-appointment under section 487.

AMENDMENTS

[a] Transitional provision: Companies Act 2006 (Commencement No 3, Transitional Provisions and Savings) Order 2007, SI 2007/2194, Sch 1, para 17 makes the following adaptations.

'For paragraph (a) of subsection (2) substitute:

    "(a) the end of the period allowed for delivering accounts and reports under section 244 of the Companies Act 1985 or Article 252 of the Companies (Northern Ireland) Order 1986, or".'

[b] Transitional provision: Companies Act 2006 (Commencement No 3, Transitional Provisions and Savings) Order 2007, SI 2007/2194, Sch 1, para 17 makes the following adaptations.

'In paragraph (b) of subsection (2), for "section 423" substitute:

    "section 238 of the Companies Act 1985 or Article 246 of the Companies (Northern Ireland) Order 1986".'

The above transitional provision has been repealed by the Companies Act 2006 (Commencement No. 5, Transitional Provisions and Savings) Order 2007, SI 2007/3495, art 10(1)(b) from 6 April 2008; it is presumed that the intention here is repeal for financial years beginning on or after 6 April 2008 since that is the basis of commencement of ss 424 and 423 as referred to in this subs (2) after the transitional adaptation falls away.

---

[66] See s 1290.
[67] See s 1289.

COMMENCEMENT DATE  1 October 2007[68]

This and the following three sections set out the requirements relating to the appointment of an auditor  **16.485.02**
of a private company; the rules relating to a public company are given by sections 489 to 491.

Private companies, unlike public companies, are not required to lay the annual accounts and reports  **16.485.03**
before members in general meeting (although their articles may require it). Instead this section
identifies an annual 'period for appointing auditors' in order to afford an annual opportunity for
auditor appointment or re-appointment. However, the rules in this section and in section 487 have the
effect of permitting continuous tenure for the auditor as the default position. Whilst these rules appear
intricate they are best understood by considering the typical case: the company will send to members
(and others) its annual accounts and reports[69] for the previous financial year,[70] including the auditor's
report in relation to that year; 28 days thereafter the auditor is deemed to be re-appointed under section
487(2) in relation to the next financial year. There are a number of exceptions to this typical case. The
principal ones are where the annual accounts and reports are sent out after the time limit allowed by
section 424, in which case re-appointment occurs 28 days after the expiry of that time limit; and where
the auditor was appointed by the directors, in which case he must be actually re-appointed by the
members. Aside from these, and other exceptions set out in section 487(2)(b) to (e), the directors will
generally not exercise their rights given by subsection (3), nor will the members exercise their rights
given by subsection (4), and thus the administrative task of re-appointing an auditor will in most cases
be fulfilled by the members and directors doing nothing.

It is interesting to note that there is no sanction on either the company or its directors for failure to  **16.485.04**
appoint an auditor. However, failure to obtain an audit report (unless exempt) would lead to various
failures, and sanctions, in relation to obligations in Part 15.[71]

Turning to subsection (1), its requirement refers to appointing 'an auditor or auditors'. Thus, a single  **16.485.05**
audit firm may be appointed or two or more may be appointed jointly. Joint auditors are, however, only
rarely encountered in practice. The remainder of this commentary refers, for convenience, to a single
auditor.

Subsection (1) provides for one circumstance where the appointment of an auditor is not required:  **16.485.06**
when 'the directors reasonably resolve otherwise on the grounds that audited accounts are unlikely to
be required'. First of all, the language of this provision indicates the passing of a directors' resolution.
Second, the provision is necessarily forward looking: it covers those occasions on which exemption
from audit on the grounds either of being a dormant company[72] or a small company[73] is anticipated
(both of which could not be conclusively determined until after the end of the financial year in
question).

As noted above, in order to effect an annual appointment opportunity, the section specifies an annual  **16.485.07**
'period for appointing auditors'. Subsection (2)(a) and (b) gives two possible dates, related to the
sending out of the annual accounts and reports for the previous financial year, on which the period for
appointing auditors might begin: the earlier is taken automatically. An effect of this rule is that where
a company has failed to send out its previous year's annual accounts and reports by the time limit
specified in section 424, the 28-day period for appointing auditors will commence on the expiry of that
time limit. This is so notwithstanding that the auditor, in all practical likelihood, will not yet have
fulfilled his duties—eg most probably those annual accounts and reports have not been sent out
because the annual accounts' preparation, and consequently their audit, are not yet completed.

The subsection (2) rule does not apply in respect of appointment for the company's first financial year.  **16.485.08**
This is because in such a case there is no previous financial year by reference to which a period for
appointing auditors could be derived. Instead subsection (3)(a) deals with this case. Under it the
directors may appoint the auditor at any time before the first period for appointing auditors—ie before
the company's first annual accounts and reports are sent out, or before the time limit for so doing if
earlier. Clearly, if the directors leave the matter to such a late stage it is highly unlikely that the auditor
will have sufficient time to undertake his work and report to the members before the filing deadline.
The normal state of affairs is for the appointment to be made at a considerably earlier date. Indeed,

---

[68]  Companies Act 2006 (Commencement No 3, etc) Order 2007, SI 2007/2194, art 2(1) for financial years
beginning on or after 1 October 2007.

[69]  See s 471.

[70]  See s 390.

[71]  Eg, offences in relation to default in sending out copies of accounts and reports, s 425; and failure to file
accounts and reports, s 451.

[72]  See s 480.

[73]  See s 477.

depending upon the nature of the company's business it may be necessary to appoint an auditor during the year, if the scope of his audit work is not to be limited (eg inability to attend the year-end stock take, where appropriate) and lead to a qualification of his report.[74]

**16.485.09**    The timing of an appointment by the directors under subsection (3)(b) and (c) would be subject to similar practical issues. It is worth noting that subsection (3)(c) will apply when the auditor is removed[75] or resigns.[76] The directors' rights to appoint auditors in subsection (3) share one key characteristic: by virtue of section 487(2)(a) and subsection (4)(a) of this section, the subsequent re-appointment of the directors' choice will fall to the members during the next period for appointing auditors before the system of deemed annual re-appointment could come into effect.

**16.485.10**    The members may appoint an auditor in any of the circumstances given by subsection (4). As described above, the members will generally exercise their rights only on the occasion of a change in auditor because, in the typical case, the auditor will be deemed to be re-appointed thereafter by virtue of section 487(2). With respect to the first appointment by members, the appointment is made by the passing of an ordinary resolution[77] of the members, either in general meeting or by passing a written resolution.[78]

**16.485.11**    The rights of the members in subsection (4)(b) and (c) are likely to be used to rectify an earlier administrative oversight although, on occasions, it may be the result of a dispute between directors and members. Subsection (4)(b) confers the right on the members to appoint an auditor if one is not appointed during the period for appointing auditors. This could happen, for example, if the directors do not propose a replacement for an auditor who has resigned; or if the members fail to pass an ordinary resolution to appoint or reappoint an auditor under subsection (4)(a). In this case, the right of members to appoint an auditor appears to co-exist with that of the Secretary of State under section 486 and the interaction between these rights is uncertain.[79] A similar issue arises with respect to the members' right to appoint an auditor under section (4)(c) where the directors fail to do so under subsection (3). It is not immediately clear under subsection (4)(c) where the boundary lies between the right of the directors to appoint the auditor and the right of the members—that is to say, whether the right given to members in subsection (4)(c) can only be exercised when the directors have failed to make an appointment after an unreasonably long period; the legislation is not clear in that regard.

### 486  Appointment of auditors of private company: default power of Secretary of State

**16.486.01**    (1)  If a private company fails to appoint an auditor or auditors in accordance with section 485, the Secretary of State may appoint one or more persons to fill the vacancy.

(2)  Where subsection (2) of that section applies and the company fails to make the necessary appointment before the end of the period for appointing auditors, the company must within one week of the end of that period give notice to the Secretary of State of his power having become exercisable.

(3)  If a company fails to give the notice required by this section, an offence is committed by—
    (a)  the company, and
    (b)  every officer of the company who is in default.

(4)  A person guilty of an offence under this section is liable on summary conviction to a fine not exceeding level 3 on the standard scale and, for continued contravention, a daily default fine not exceeding one-tenth of level 3 on the standard scale.

COMMENCEMENT DATE  1 October 2007[80]

**16.486.02**    Subsection (1) gives the Secretary of State the right to appoint an auditor when a private company fails to appoint one in accordance with section 485. However, it is not immediately clear what 'fails to appoint ... in accordance with section 485' means given that the right to appoint an auditor falls to the directors and members at different times. Nevertheless, subsection (2) requires that the Secretary of State be given notice of his power's having become exercisable after failure to appoint an auditor before the end of the period for appointing auditors.[81] The practical effect of these provisions, then, is that the

---

[74]  See s 495.

[75]  See s 510.

[76]  See s 516.

[77]  See s 282.

[78]  See s 288.

[79]  Under the old legislation (CA 1985, s 387), the Secretary of State's powers did not appear to co-exist with that of the members or directors; and it was under that legislation that there occurred the case referred to at para 16.489.10, n 96 below.

[80]  Companies Act 2006 (Commencement No 3, etc) Order 2007, SI 2007/2194, art 2(1). This provision applies to accounts and reports for financial years beginning on or after 1 October 2007.

[81]  See s 485.

Secretary of State's powers are likely to be employed if the members fail to appoint an auditor before the end of the period for appointing auditors.

This section's obligation upon the company to notify the Secretary of State, when the company fails to **16.486.03** appoint an auditor before the end of the period for appointing auditors as required by subsection 485(2), is the only statutory obligation that falls upon the company as a result of its not appointing auditors. The company's failure to notify the Secretary of State results in the company and every officer in default[82] committing an offence.

The powers of the Secretary of State, under this section, would probably be exercised by officials at **16.486.04** Companies House.[83]

### 487  Term of office of auditors of private company

(1) An auditor or auditors of a private company hold office in accordance with the terms of their     **16.487.01**
    appointment, subject to the requirements that—
    (a) they do not take office until any previous auditor or auditors cease to hold office, and
    (b) they cease to hold office at the end of the next period for appointing auditors unless
        re-appointed.
(2) Where no auditor has been appointed by the end of the next period for appointing auditors, any
    auditor in office immediately before that time is deemed to be re-appointed at that time, unless—
    (a) he was appointed by the directors, or
    (b) the company's articles require actual re-appointment, or
    (c) the deemed re-appointment is prevented by the members under section 488, or
    (d) the members have resolved that he should not be re-appointed, or
    (e) the directors have resolved that no auditor or auditors should be appointed for the financial
        year in question.
(3) This is without prejudice to the provisions of this Part as to removal and resignation of auditors.[a]
(4) No account shall be taken of any loss of the opportunity of deemed re-appointment under this
    section in ascertaining the amount of any compensation or damages payable to an auditor on his
    ceasing to hold office for any reason.

AMENDMENTS and Notes

[a] Transitional provision: Companies Act 2006 (Commencement No. 3, Transitional Provisions and Savings) Order 2007, SI 2007/2194, Sch 1, para 18 makes the following adaptation. 'In subsection (3) for "the provisions of this Part" substitute "the provisions of Chapter 5 of Part 11 of the Companies Act 1985 or Chapter 5 of Part 12 of the Companies (Northern Ireland) Order 1986".' This transitional provision has been repealed by the Companies Act 2006 (Commencement No 5, Transitional Provisions and Savings) Order 2007, SI 2007/3495, art 10(1)(b) from 6 April 2008; it is presumed that the intention here is to repeal with immediate effect on that date (eg, not on a financial years beginning basis) since that is the basis of commencement of the removal and resignation provisions of this Part as referred to in subs (3) after the transitional adaptation falls away.

COMMENCEMENT DATE 1 October 2007[84]

This section specifies the term of office for an auditor of a private company. It is an important section **16.487.02** for such companies as, together with section 485, it creates the default regime whereby, subject to certain exceptions, an auditor of a private company continues in office by virtue of deemed re-appointment for each succeeding year.

This section's requirements have no effect on the members' right to remove the auditor[85] or on the **16.487.03** auditor's right to resign from office.[86]

Subsection (1)(a) provides for the point in time at which an auditor takes office and subsection (1)(b) **16.487.04** provides that the auditor will continue to hold office until the end of the next period for appointing auditors. The effect is that the offices of outgoing and incoming auditors do not overlap. This applies

---

[82] See s 1121.
[83] 'Companies House' is the name given to the BIS agency that assists the registrar to fulfil his obligations under Part 35.
[84] Companies Act 2006 (Commencement No 3, etc) Order 2007, SI 2007/2194, art 2(1) for financial years beginning on or after 1 October 2007.
[85] See s 510.
[86] See s 516.

however he is appointed, whether by the passing of an ordinary resolution during the period for appointing auditors,[87] by the directors,[88] or by the members outside the period for appointing auditors.[89]

**16.487.05**   When taken together with section 485(2)(a), subsection (1) invites some consideration. Suppose that firm A was appointed as auditor in relation to the financial year[90] ending on 31 December 2009, but it is intended that it be replaced by firm B in relation to the financial year ending on 31 December 2010. Suppose, further, that the company is late in preparing its 2009 annual accounts such that they have not been sent out to members (and others) by 30 September 2010 as required by sections 423 and 424. Consequently, firm A is not in a position to complete its audit at that date. However, by virtue of section 485(2)(a) the 28-day period for appointing auditors in relation to 2010 begins at that time. If the annual accounts and audit are expected still to be incomplete 28 days later, complications may arise if it is proposed that the members appoint firm B under section 485(4)(a) during that period: it would appear to be the case that under subsection (1)(b), A's term would end on 28 October 2010, and B would be appointed in relation to 2010, notwithstanding that A had not yet fulfilled its duties under, eg section 495 to report upon the 2009 annual accounts; how then, and by whom, would the 2009 annual accounts be audited? Accordingly it may be advisable not to pass a resolution during the period for appointing auditors and instead allow A to be deemed re-appointed under subsection (2). Firm A could then resign, or be removed, after it had completed its report in relation to 2009. The appointment of B could then be made by the directors' exercising their right to fill a casual vacancy under section 485(3)(c).

**16.487.06**   Returning to the main practical effect of this section, the chapeau to subsection (2) sets out the rule, subject to exceptions given by subsections (2)(a) to (e), that the auditor is deemed to be re-appointed each year if no further action is taken. However, the exceptions are important and provide a degree of protection to the members who may not desire the incumbent auditor to continue in office. Of these exceptions, subsection (2)(a) is of some practical importance: its effect is to require that an auditor's appointment made by the directors can only be re-appointed by the passing of an ordinary resolution of the members. The exception in subsection (2)(e) may also be of practical relevance: section 485(1) requires the appointment of an auditor unless the directors reasonably resolve that audit accounts are unlikely to be required; thus if the directors so resolve, eg because they reasonably expect the company to qualify for the small company audit exemption[91] for the first time, then there will be no automatic re-appointment of the auditor in relation to that financial year.

**16.487.07**   Subsection (4) is worth further consideration. If an auditor ceases to hold office and puts in a claim for damages, compensation, or similar, subsection (4) puts beyond doubt that he is not permitted to take account of lost income from future years for which he might otherwise have been deemed to be re-appointed.

### 488  Prevention by members of deemed re-appointment of auditor

**16.488.01**   (1)  An auditor of a private company is not deemed to be re-appointed under section 487(2) if the company has received notices under this section from members representing at least the requisite percentage of the total voting rights of all members who would be entitled to vote on a resolution that the auditor should not be re-appointed.

(2)  The 'requisite percentage' is 5%, or such lower percentage as is specified for this purpose in the company's articles.

(3)  A notice under this section—

(a)  may be in hard copy or electronic form,

(b)  must be authenticated by the person or persons giving it, and

(c)  must be received by the company before the end of the accounting reference period immediately preceding the time when the deemed re-appointment would have effect.

COMMENCEMENT DATE  1 October 2007[92]

**16.488.02**   This section provides a mechanism by which a minority of the members may challenge the continuance in office of an auditor by requiring the re-appointment to be made by ordinary resolution[93] of the members as under section 485(4)(a).

---

[87]  Further to s 485(4)(a).
[88]  Further to s 485(3).
[89]  Further to s 485(4)(b) and (c).
[90]  See s 390.
[91]  See s 477.
[92]  Companies Act 2006 (Commencement No 3, etc) Order 2007, SI 2007/2194, art 2(1) for financial years beginning on or after 1 October 2007.
[93]  See s 282.

Subsection (2) sets the 'requisite percentage'—that is to say, the percentage of such voting rights   **16.488.03**
represented by those giving notice—at 5 per cent. Whilst the requisite percentage is permitted to be
reduced in the articles, it may not be increased. Those who are entitled to vote will be determined by the
company's articles; in most cases, it will be the ordinary shareholders who hold such a right but there
may be circumstances in which other shareholders also hold this right—for example, preference
shareholders are typically afforded voting rights if their dividends are in arrears.

Subsection (3)(c) limits the period in which such a notice may be given to that before the end of the   **16.488.04**
accounting reference period (ARP)[94] immediately preceding the time when deemed re-appointment
would otherwise have taken place. For example, take a company with a 31 December year end. If a
minority wishes to avoid deemed appointment in 2010, which would be in relation to the 2010 ARP
(see section 485(1) and (2)), they must give notice to the company before 31 December 2009. Reference
is made to the ARP as this ends on the accounting reference date,[95] whereas the financial year[96] may
end up to seven days either side[97] thereof at the directors' discretion. Thus the time limit for the
minority to exercise their rights could not be frustrated by the seven days' discretion for directors.

*Public companies*

### 489  Appointment of auditors of public company: general

(1)  An auditor or auditors of a public company must be appointed for each financial year of the   **16.489.01**
company, unless the directors reasonably resolve otherwise on the ground that audited accounts
are unlikely to be required.

(2)  For each financial year for which an auditor or auditors is or are to be appointed (other than the
company's first financial year), the appointment must be made before the end of the accounts
meeting of the company at which the company's annual accounts and reports for the previous
financial year are laid.

(3)  The directors may appoint an auditor or auditors of the company—

(a)  at any time before the company's first accounts meeting;

(b)  following a period during which the company (being exempt from audit) did not have any
auditor, at any time before the company's next accounts meeting;

(c)  to fill a casual vacancy in the office of auditor.

(4)  The members may appoint an auditor or auditors by ordinary resolution—

(a)  at an accounts meeting;

(b)  if the company should have appointed an auditor or auditors at an accounts meeting but
failed to do so;

(c)  where the directors had power to appoint under subsection (3) but have failed to make an
appointment.

(5)  An auditor or auditors of a public company may only be appointed—

(a)  in accordance with this section, or

(b)  in accordance with section 490 (default power of Secretary of State).

COMMENCEMENT DATE  6 April 2008[98]

The requirements with respect to the appointment of an auditor of a public company are set out in this   **16.489.02**
and the following section. Unlike a private company, a public company is required to hold a general
meeting, the accounts meeting,[99] at which the annual accounts and reports for the previous financial
year[100] are laid before the company. Thus, whilst the rules for appointing an auditor appear intricate,
they are, perhaps, best understood by considering the typical case of the accounts meeting: the auditor's
report on the previous financial year's annual accounts and reports is laid before members at the
accounts meeting and he is re-appointed by the passing of an ordinary resolution[101] at that meeting,
holding office from the end of that meeting until the end of the next accounts meeting.

---

[94]  See s 391.

[95]  See s 391.

[96]  See s 390.

[97]  See s 390(2)(b) and (3)(b).

[98]  Companies Act 2006 (Commencement No 5, Transitional Provisions and Savings) Order 2007, SI 2007/
3495, art 3(1) with respect to appointments for financial years beginning on or after 6 April 2008.

[99]  See s 437.

[100]  See s 390.

[101]  Subsection (4)(a).

**16.489.03**    It is interesting to note that there is no sanction on either the company or its directors for failure to appoint an auditor. However, failure to obtain an audit report (unless exempt) would lead to various failures, and sanctions, in relation to obligations in Part 15.[102]

**16.489.04**    Turning to subsection (1), its requirement refers to appointing 'an auditor or auditors'. Thus, a single audit firm may be appointed, or two or more may be appointed jointly. Joint auditors are, however, only rarely encountered in practice. The remainder of this commentary refers, for convenience, to a single auditor.

**16.489.05**    Subsection (1) provides for one circumstance where the appointment of an auditor is not required: when the 'directors reasonably resolve otherwise on the ground that audited accounts are unlikely to be required'. First of all, the language of this provision indicates the passing of a directors' resolution. Second, the provision is necessarily forward looking: it covers those occasions on which the qualification as a dormant company[103] is anticipated and the company is otherwise expected to meet the audit exemption requirements of section 480.

**16.489.06**    Subsection (2) sets out the general rule as to the timing of appointment, ie that it is done by the end of the accounts meeting for the previous financial year; as discussed above it is almost always done at this meeting. The subsection (2) rule does not, however, apply in respect of a company's first financial year. This is because in such a case there is no previous financial year.

**16.489.07**    Subsection (3)(a) deals with the first financial year. The directors appoint the auditor at any time before the first accounts meeting. Since that is the accounts meeting at which the auditor would report upon the company's first annual accounts and reports, it is clearly a practical imperative that he be appointed considerably in advance of that accounts meeting. Indeed, depending upon the nature of the company's business it may be necessary to appoint an auditor during the year, if the scope of his audit work is not to be limited (eg inability to attend the year-end stock take, where appropriate) and lead to a qualification of his report.[104]

**16.489.08**    The timing of an appointment by the directors under subsection (3)(b) and (c) would be subject to similar practical issues—ie the directors would be unwise to wait until the next accounts meeting. It is worth noting that subsection (3)(c) will apply when the auditor is removed[105] or resigns[106] —that is to say, ceases to hold office other than by failing to be re-appointed at the accounts meeting.

**16.489.09**    The members may appoint an auditor in any of the circumstances given by subsection (4). As described above, the circumstance of subsection (4)(a) is the normal state of affairs for most companies. Thus, either the directors will put forward the existing auditor for re-appointment or the members will be asked to appoint a new auditor proposed by the directors. The appointment, nevertheless, is made by the passing of an ordinary resolution[107] of the members. This procedure, therefore, gives the members the right to reject the appointment of an auditor, say, if they are dissatisfied with the service provided or have other concerns over his suitability.

**16.489.10**    The rights of the members in subsection (4)(b) and (c) are likely to be used when there has been a breakdown in the relationship between members and directors of the company and, therefore, would rarely be seen in practice. Subsection (4)(b), as mentioned above, confers the right on the members to appoint an auditor if one is not appointed at the accounts meeting. This could happen, for example, if the directors do not propose a replacement for an outgoing one; or if the resolution to appoint or re-appoint an auditor is put to the meeting but is rejected by the members.[108] In this case, the right of members to appoint an auditor co-exists with that of the Secretary of State under section 490, and the interaction between these rights is uncertain.[109] A similar issue arises with respect to the members' right to appoint an auditor under section (4)(c) where the directors fail to do so under subsection (3). It is not immediately clear under subsection (4)(c) where the boundary lies between the right of the directors to appoint the auditor and the right of the members—that is to say, whether the right given to

---

[102]   Eg, offences in relation to default in sending out copies of accounts and reports, s 425; failure to lay accounts and reports, s 438; and failure to file accounts and reports, s 451.

[103]   See s 1169.

[104]   See s 495.

[105]   See s 510.

[106]   See s 516.

[107]   See s 282. Unlike a private company, a public company cannot avail itself of a written resolution under s 288.

[108]   A rare example of such shareholder action at a listed company is the annual general meeting of Eurotunnel plc on 7 April 2004.

[109]   Under the old legislation (CA 1985, s 387), the Secretary of State's powers did not appear to co-exist with those of the members or directors; and it was under that legislation that the case referred to in n 96 above occurred.

members in subsection (4)(c) can only be exercised when the directors have failed to make an appointment after an unreasonably long period; the legislation is not clear in that regard.

When an auditor is appointed under subsection (4)(b) or (c), the resolution to appoint him will be at **16.489.11** a general meeting of the company other than the accounts meeting. In certain circumstances, special notice[110] of the resolution must be given to the company when the auditor proposed to be appointed is replacing an outgoing auditor by virtue of section 515.

## 490  Appointment of auditors of public company: default power of Secretary of State

(1) If a public company fails to appoint an auditor or auditors in accordance with section 489, the **16.490.01** Secretary of State may appoint one or more persons to fill the vacancy.

(2) Where subsection (2) of that section applies and the company fails to make the necessary appointment before the end of the accounts meeting, the company must within one week of the end of that meeting give notice to the Secretary of State of his power having become exercisable.

(3) If a company fails to give the notice required by this section, an offence is committed by—
   (a) the company, and
   (b) every officer of the company who is in default.

(4) A person guilty of an offence under this section is liable on summary conviction to a fine not exceeding level 3 on the standard scale and, for continued contravention, a daily default fine not exceeding one-tenth of level 3 on the standard scale.

COMMENCEMENT DATE  6 April 2008[111]

Subsection (1) gives the Secretary of State the right to appoint an auditor when a public company fails **16.490.02** to appoint one in accordance with section 489. However, it is not immediately clear what 'fails to appoint … in accordance with section 489' means given that the right to appoint an auditor falls to the directors and members in different circumstances —for example, before the first accounts meeting, to fill a causal vacancy, at the accounts meeting, or at another meeting convened by the members for the purpose of appointing an auditor. Nevertheless, subsection (2) requires that the Secretary of State be given notice of his power having become exercisable after failure to appoint an auditor before the end of the accounts meeting,[112] which indicates that the practical effect of these provisions is that the Secretary of State's powers are likely to be employed if the members fail to appoint an auditor at the accounts meeting.

This might happen when either a serious dispute exists between the directors and members such that **16.490.03** the members reject all nominees put forward by the directors, or through administrative oversight by the directors and members. However, the equivalent right under the previous legislation[113] was rarely exercised and this is likely to remain the case.

This section's obligation upon the company, to notify the Secretary of State when the company fails to **16.490.04** appoint an auditor before the end of the accounts meeting as required by section 489(2), is the only statutory obligation that falls upon the company from its not appointing auditors. The company's failure to notify the Secretary of State results in the company and every officer in default[114] committing an offence.

The powers of the Secretary of State, under this section, would probably be exercised by officials at **16.490.05** Companies House.[115]

## 491  Term of office of auditors of public company

(1) The auditor or auditors of a public company hold office in accordance with the terms of their **16.491.01** appointment, subject to the requirements that—
   (a) they do not take office until the previous auditor or auditors have ceased to hold office, and
   (b) they cease to hold office at the conclusion of the accounts meeting next following their appointment, unless re-appointed.

(2) This is without prejudice to the provisions of this Part as to removal and resignation of auditors.

---

[110] See s 312.
[111] Companies Act 2006 (Commencement No 5, Transitional Provisions and Savings) Order 2007, SI 2007/3495, art 3(1) with respect to appointments for financial years beginning on or after 6 April 2008.
[112] See s 437.
[113] CA 1985, s 387.
[114] See s 1121.
[115] 'Companies House' is the name given to the BIS agency that assists the registrar to fulfil his obligations under Part 35.

COMMENCEMENT DATE  6 April 2008[116]

**16.491.02**    This section specifies the term of office for an auditor of a public company.

**16.491.03**    Subsection (1)(a) provides for the point in time at which an auditor takes office and subsection (1)(b) provides that the auditor will continue to hold office until the end of the next accounts meeting[117] after his appointment. The effect is that the offices of outgoing and incoming auditors do not overlap. This applies however he is appointed, whether at an accounts meeting, by the directors,[118] or at another general meeting of the company.[119] It is this provision that, in contrast with that for private companies,[120] ensures that auditor appointment for public companies is an annual matter and that it occurs at the accounts meeting.

**16.491.04**    The requirements of subsection (1) have no effect on the members' right to remove the auditor[121] or on the auditor's right to resign from office.[122]

## *General provisions*

### 492  Fixing of auditors' remuneration

**16.492.01**    (1)  The remuneration of an auditor appointed by the members of a company must be fixed by the members by ordinary resolution or in such manner as the members may by ordinary resolution determine.

(2)  The remuneration of an auditor appointed by the directors of a company must be fixed by the directors.

(3)  The remuneration of an auditor appointed by the Secretary of State must be fixed by the Secretary of State.

(4)  For the purposes of this section 'remuneration' includes sums paid in respect of expenses.

(5)  This section applies in relation to benefits in kind as to payments of money.

COMMENCEMENT DATE  6 April 2008[123]

**16.492.02**    The requirements of this section govern the fixing of an auditor's remuneration for both private and public companies.

**16.492.03**    Subsection (1) applies to the remuneration of an auditor who is appointed by the members of the company.[124] The members have two choices: by ordinary resolution[125] either to fix the remuneration themselves, or to agree on some other manner of fixing it—for example, by delegating the task to the directors. In practice, the authority to fix the auditor's remuneration is almost always given to the directors by the passing of a resolution, typically in terms 'that the directors be hereby authorized to determine the auditor's remuneration' or some other suitable form of authority. In the case of listed companies, a particular group of directors, eg the audit committee,[126] is sometimes named in the resolution.

**16.492.04**    The direct right of the directors to fix the auditor's remuneration is limited to those circumstances in which they appoint the auditor,[127] although as noted above, in practice the authority to do so is almost

---

[116] Companies Act 2006 (Commencement No 5, Transitional Provisions and Savings) Order 2007, SI 2007/3495, art 3(1) with respect to auditors appointed for financial years beginning on or after 6 April 2008.

[117] See s 437.

[118] Further to s 489(3).

[119] Further to s 489(4)(b) and (c).

[120] See s 487

[121] See s 510.

[122] See s 516.

[123] Companies Act 2006 (Commencement No 5, Transitional Provisions and Savings) Order 2007, SI 2007/3495, art 3(1) with respect to auditors appointed for financial years beginning on or after 6 April 2008.

[124] Further to ss 485(4) or 489(4).

[125] See s 282.

[126] The audit committee is a sub-committee of the board with a particular focus on audit and accounting—see the *UK Corporate Governance Code* (Financial Reporting Council, September 2012, provision C.3.1. Although the audit committee is not recognized in the Act, issuers with securities admitted to trading on a regulated market that are required to appoint an auditor are required by the FSA's Disclosure and Transparency Rule (DTR) 1B.1.2 to appoint an audit committee (whose members and functions are governed by DTR 7.1), although exemptions for certain issuers are given by DTR 1B.1.3. These DTR requirements implement the Audit Directive 2006/43/EC of the European Parliament and of the Council [2006], OJ L157/87, as amended, art 41.

[127] See ss 485(3) and 489(3).

always delegated to them in other cases. When the auditor is appointed by the Secretary of State (although it is rare for this to occur), the Secretary of State fixes the remuneration.[128]

When the auditor is deemed to be re-appointed,[129] the section is not explicit as to the fixing of his remuneration. This is of some practical importance given that deemed re-appointment is likely to be the commonplace for private companies. Where, for example, the members originally appointed the auditor and chose to delegate the fixing to the directors, it appears that the resolution to authorize the directors to fix the auditor's remuneration need not be put to the members again unless actual re-appointment is required under section 487(2) (including that a previous 1985 Act resolution continues to have effect on commencement of this Act[130] ). This proposition is based on the observation that the members appoint the auditor only once and, thereafter, the auditor is deemed to be re-appointed. Moreover, it is thought that this section acts as a restriction, in certain cases, upon the persons who may fix the remuneration rather than as a comprehensive statement of the authority for fixing auditor remuneration. Thus, the alternative view is that since the section does not address fixing in the deemed re-appointment case, there is, in that case, no restriction as to who may fix the remuneration and, thus, the directors may, in the normal course of events as agents of the company, fix the auditor's remuneration. Indeed, in practice it is the directors who do so.    **16.492.05**

### 493  Disclosure of terms of audit appointment

(1)  The Secretary of State may make provision by regulations for securing the disclosure of the terms    **16.493.01**
on which a company's auditor is appointed, remunerated or performs his duties. Nothing in the following provisions of this section affects the generality of this power.

(2)  The regulations may—
  (a)  require disclosure of—
    (i)  a copy of any terms that are in writing and
    (ii)  a written memorandum setting out any terms that are not in writing;
  (b)  require disclosure to be at such times, in such places and by such means as are specified in the regulations;
  (c)  require the place and means of disclosure to be stated—
    (i)  in a note to the company's annual accounts (in the case of its individual accounts) or in such manner as is specified in the regulations (in the case of group accounts),
    (ii)  in the directors' report, or
    (iii)  in the auditor's report on the company's annual accounts.

(3)  The provisions of this section apply to a variation of the terms mentioned in subsection (1) as they apply to the original terms.

(4)  Regulations under this section are subject to affirmative resolution procedure.

COMMENCEMENT DATE  20 January 2007[131]

This section gives the Secretary of State power to require the disclosure of the terms of an auditor's    **16.493.02**
appointment. This power is new and no precedent exists for the regulations that may be made under this section. Whilst there can be no certainty as to the categories of companies that will be covered by any eventual regulations, the Government has indicated that regulations would require website publication of the terms of auditor appointment by quoted companies.[132]

Auditing standards require the contractual terms to be put in writing in what is commonly known as    **16.493.03**
an 'engagement letter'.[133] Thus, in most cases, it is the engagement letter that may be subject to the disclosure requirements of regulations made under this section. When the contractual terms are not expressed in writing, or when the engagement letter does not contain all substantive terms, the regulation-making power may be used to require the company to prepare a memorandum of those unwritten terms. Such memoranda are expected to be rare.

---

[128]  However, on the rare occasions that the Secretary of State exercises his powers of appointment, the fixing of the remuneration is likely to be delegated to the directors, as happened in the case of Eurotunnel plc (see para 16.489.10, n 96 above).

[129]  Private companies only—by virtue of s 487(2).

[130]  See savings provision of the Companies Act 2006 (Commencement No 5, Transitional Provisions and Savings) Order 2007, SI 2007/3495, Sch 4, para 11. This provision applies to accounts and reports for financial years beginning on or after 6 April 2008.

[131]  Companies Act 2006 (Commencement No 1, etc) Order 2006, SI 2006/3428, art 3(3).

[132]  *Hansard*, HL, vol 681, col 1019 (10 May 2006).

[133]  *International Standard on Auditing (UK & Ireland) 210 Terms of audit engagements* (Auditing Practices Board, 2004). See in particular para 2-1.

**494 Disclosure of services provided by auditor or associates and related remuneration**

**16.494.01**     (1)  The Secretary of State may make provision by regulations for securing the disclosure of—

   (a)  the nature of any services provided for a company by the company's auditor (whether in his capacity as auditor or otherwise) or by his associates;

   (b)  the amount of any remuneration received or receivable by a company's auditor, or his associates, in respect of any such services.

   Nothing in the following provisions of this section affects the generality of this power.

   (2)  The regulations may provide—

   (a)  for disclosure of the nature of any services provided to be made by reference to any class or description of services specified in the regulations (or any combination of services, however described);

   (b)  for the disclosure of amounts of remuneration received or receivable in respect of services of any class or description specified in the regulations (or any combination of services, however described);

   (c)  for the disclosure of separate amounts so received or receivable by the company's auditor or any of his associates, or of aggregate amounts so received or receivable by all or any of those persons.

   (3)  The regulations may—

   (a)  provide that 'remuneration' includes sums paid in respect of expenses;

   (b)  apply to benefits in kind as well as to payments of money, and require the disclosure of the nature of any such benefits and their estimated money value;

   (c)  apply to services provided for associates of a company as well as to those provided for a company;

   (d)  define 'associate' in relation to an auditor and a company respectively.

   (4)  The regulations may provide that any disclosure required by the regulations is to be made—

   (a)  in a note to the company's annual accounts (in the case of its individual accounts) or in such manner as is specified in the regulations (in the case of group accounts),

   (b)  in the directors' report, or

   (c)  in the auditor's report on the company's annual accounts.

   (5)  If the regulations provide that any such disclosure is to be made as mentioned in subsection (4)(a) or (b), the regulations may require the auditor to supply the directors of the company with any information necessary to enable the disclosure to be made.

   (6)  Regulations under this section are subject to negative resolution procedure.

   COMMENCEMENT DATE  20 January 2007[134]

**16.494.02**     This section permits the Secretary of State to make regulations concerning the disclosure of an auditor's and his associates' total remuneration. Regulations have been made under this section which require the disclosure by the company in the annual accounts of the auditor's remuneration broken down into fees for the audit of the annual accounts and, for companies other than those that are subject to the small companies regime or are able to take advantage of exemptions for medium-sized companies, eight categories of non-audit fees (including fees for the audits of subsidiary undertakings).[135] Guidance on the application of the regulations has been issued by the Institute of Chartered Accountants in England and Wales (ICAEW)[136].

**16.494.03**     Regulations made under this section aim at providing transparency in relation to auditor's remuneration and are generally considered to make a contribution to demonstrating auditor independence.

# CHAPTER 3
## FUNCTIONS OF AUDITOR

### *Auditor's report*

**495 Auditor's report on company's annual accounts**

**16.495.01**     (1)  A company's auditor must make a report to the company's members on all annual accounts of the company of which copies are, during his tenure of office—

   (a)  in the case of a private company, to be sent out to members under section 423;

---

[134]  Companies Act 2006 (Commencement No 1, etc) Order 2006, SI 2006/3428, art 3(3).

[135]  See the Companies (Disclosure of Auditor Remuneration and Liability Limitation Agreements) Regulations 2008, SI 2008/489, as amended by the Companies (Disclosure of Auditor Remuneration and Liability Limitation Agreements (Amendment) Regulations 2011, SI 2011/2198, for financial years beginning on or after 1 October 2011.

[136]  *TECH 04/11 Disclosure of auditor remuneration (Revised)* (ICAEW, 2011).

    (b)  in the case of a public company, to be laid before the company in general meeting under section 437.

(2)  The auditor's report must include—

    (a)  an introduction identifying the annual accounts that are the subject of the audit and the financial reporting framework that has been applied in their preparation, and

    (b)  a description of the scope of the audit identifying the auditing standards in accordance with which the audit was conducted.

(3)  The report must state clearly whether, in the auditor's opinion, the annual accounts—

    (a)  give a true and fair view—

        (i)  in the case of an individual balance sheet, of the state of affairs of the company as at the end of the financial year,

        (ii)  in the case of an individual profit and loss account, of the profit or loss of the company for the financial year,

        (iii)  in the case of group accounts, of the state of affairs as at the end of the financial year and of the profit or loss for the financial year of the undertakings included in the consolidation as a whole, so far as concerns members of the company;

    (b)  have been properly prepared in accordance with the relevant financial reporting framework; and

    (c)  have been prepared in accordance with the requirements of this Act (and, where applicable, Article 4 of the IAS Regulation).

Expressions used in this subsection that are defined for the purposes of Part 15 (see section 474) have the same meaning as in that Part.

(4)  The auditor's report—

    (a)  must be either unqualified or qualified, and

    (b)  must include a reference to any matters to which the auditor wishes to draw attention by way of emphasis without qualifying the report.

COMMENCEMENT DATE  6 April 2008[137]

If a company's annual accounts[138] are subject to audit,[139] this Part requires the appointment of an auditor[140] and Part 15 requires the directors to publish the auditor's report, lay it before members (public companies), and (usually) to deliver it to the registrar, in all cases together with the annual accounts.[141]     **16.495.02**

This section places a duty upon the appointed auditor to report. It does not specify the work that an auditor must undertake to support his report, which is instead the subject of auditing standards,[142] but specifies the matters as to which his opinion is to attest (subsection (3)). It also specifies certain technical drafting matters in relation to the report (subsections (2) and (4)(b)) that are also dealt with by auditing standards. Such standards do, however, continue to make much more detailed provision in relation to such reports, including extending the opinions to be given.[143] This commentary deals first with the requirements of the section before turning briefly to auditing standards and other matters that affect the drafting of an auditor's report.     **16.495.03**

Subsection (1) identifies the annual accounts in relation to which the auditor has a duty to report, and the persons to whom he reports. It is worth noting that the duty to report is not triggered by the preparation of annual accounts but by their being put to the company's members as a whole, either by sending out (private companies) or laying in general meeting (public companies).[144] This is because the section requires the auditor to make his report to the members. Indeed, the fact of the auditor's statutory duty being to report to the members, as a body, is of great importance in the matter of the     **16.495.04**

---

[137] Companies Act 2006 (Commencement No 5, Transitional Provisions and Savings) Order 2007, SI 2007/3495, art 3(1) with respect to auditors' reports on accounts or reports for financial years beginning on or after 6 April 2008.

[138] See s 471.

[139] See s 475.

[140] See ss 485–491.

[141] See ss 423 and 430, 437 and 441 *et seq*. Under s 441 *et seq* an alternative report may sometimes be delivered in relation to abbreviated accounts of certain companies.

[142] The applicable auditing standards are those issued by the Auditing Practices Board (APB) and from July 2012, those issued by its successor, the Financial Reporting Council (FRC). These are known as International Standards on Auditing (UK & Ireland) (ISA's (UK & Ir)). They are so called because they reproduce International Standards on Auditing (issued by the International Auditing and Assurance Standards Board) with additional material suitable to the legal environment of the UK (and that of Ireland). The APB also published Practice Notes and Bulletins. For commentary on the authority of the FRC and APB pronouncements, see s 1217.

[143] See *ISA (UK & Ir) 700 (Revised) The auditor's report on financial statements* (APB, 2011: FRC, 2012).

[144] There is no requirement for private companies to lay annual accounts before members in general meeting. Thus the duty to make an auditor's report is triggered by a different event in relation to members, ie sending-out.

persons to whom the auditor owes a duty of care and thus to whom he may be liable for negligence. Although a leading case in this area is that of *Caparo* in 1990[145] (and a line of cases before that), following the more recent *Bannerman* case[146] it has become the practice of auditors to include a paragraph in their reports, known as a Bannerman paragraph, emphasizing that the statutory duty is to report solely to the members, as a body, and disclaiming any duty or liability to any other persons.[147] In the *Bannerman* case a bank contended that it had continued to provide overdraft facilities to a company, which had subsequently gone into receivership, in reliance on audited accounts; that in the course of its ordinary audit work, in relation to whether the company was a going concern, the company's auditor had, or ought to have, read the facility letters between the bank and the company which required the company to provide a copy of the audited accounts to the bank; and that, accordingly, the auditor knew, or ought to have known, that the bank intended to rely upon the audit report; and that the auditor consequently owed a duty of care to the bank. The judge refused the auditor's application to have the claim struck out; the auditor's failure to disclaim liability to the bank was an important circumstance supporting the finding of a duty of care; the case was allowed to proceed to trial, although it is understood that there was subsequently a settlement.

16.495.05    Subsection (2)'s requirements are technical drafting matters. The annual accounts are usually identified by page numbers or by the titles of the component parts that make up the annual accounts (eg profit and loss account etc). The description of the audit is achieved in one of two ways: either by a cross-reference to a generic description of an audit maintained on the website of the Financial Reporting Council (FRC); or the inclusion directly in the auditor's report of a short, generic description. The most important matter, here, however, is the identification of the 'relevant financial reporting framework'. This refers to what the headings to sections 395 and 403 call the 'applicable accounting framework'. That is to say, it identifies whether the individual or group accounts, as the case may be, are prepared as Companies Act or IAS individual or group accounts. As discussed at those earlier sections, this is essentially a question of whether the accounts employ UK accounting standards[148] (and the provisions of regulations under sections 396(3) or 404(3)) or EU-adopted International Financial Reporting Standards (IFRS).[149] Since there is a choice as between the two, it is most important to make clear what choice the company has made.

16.495.06    Subsection (3) is the heart of this section. It specifies the matters upon which the auditor should give his opinion. First of all, his opinion is to be given in relation to the annual accounts. These are defined[150] as the individual accounts; or, where group accounts are prepared, the individual accounts and the group accounts together, but subject to the option in section 408 for the directors to omit the individual accounts profit and loss account (which must nevertheless be prepared and approved by the directors).

16.495.07    The standards of preparation of the accounts, to which the auditor's opinion must attest, are set out in subsection (3)(a) to (c) and are the same standards to which the directors are required to prepare the accounts. The true-and-fair requirements of section 393 (IAS individual or group accounts) or sections 396(2) and 404(2), (Companies Act individual and group accounts) correspond with those of subsection (3)(a).[151] The commentary on those earlier sections discusses the concept of a true and fair view. It should be noted that in a case where the company has taken advantage of section 408 not to include its individual profit and loss account in the annual accounts, subsection (3)(a)(ii) is accordingly of no effect.

16.495.08    Subsection (3)(a)(iii) includes the words, 'so far as concerns the members of the company', in relation to the profit or loss of the undertakings included in the consolidation. This arises because the undertakings whose profits and losses are so included need not be wholly owned (eg a subsidiary

---

[145] *Caparo Industries plc v Dickman* [1990] 1 All ER 568, HL.

[146] *Royal Bank of Scotland plc v Bannerstone Johnstone Maclay and others* [2003] SC 125.

[147] *AUDIT 01/03 The audit report and auditors' duty of care to third parties* (Institute of Chartered Accountants in England and Wales (ICAEW), 2003) provides further detail in relation to this, including an illustrative disclaimer paragraph in the context of the 1985 Act that then applied.

[148] Those issued by the Accounting Standards Board before July 2012 and any issued by the Financial Reporting Council after that date. See s 396.

[149] This is the term used by the accountancy profession for the international accounting standards defined in s 474(1) and with which IAS individual accounts and IAS group accounts must comply (see ss 395(1)(b) and 403(1), (2)(b)).

[150] See s 471.

[151] This is in contrast to the position under CA 1985 as it had been amended by the Companies Act 1985 (International Accounting Standards and Other Accounting Amendments) Regulations 2004, SI 2004/ 2947 with effect for financial years commencing on or after 1 Jan 2005. As discussed at s 393, this omitted in relation to IAS individual and group accounts any direct, statutory true-and-fair requirement upon the directors with respect to the preparation of such accounts.

undertaking need not be wholly owned).[152] The practical significance of this is that in determining whether his report should refer to a consolidated profit or a consolidated loss, the figure an auditor refers to is that stated after excluding amounts attributable to minority (or non-controlling) interests.

The opinion under subsection (3)(b) in relation to the 'relevant financial reporting framework' refers to whether Companies Act individual or group accounts, as the case may be, are properly prepared in accordance with UK accounting standards; or whether IAS individual or group accounts, as the case may be, are properly prepared in accordance with EU-adopted IFRS.  **16.495.09**

Where, as is almost universally the case, the company has taken advantage of section 408 to omit the individual accounts profit and loss account, this requirement presents a problem in relation to IAS individual accounts. EU-adopted IFRS do not permit a claim of compliance with EU-adopted IFRS unless all of the requirements of EU-adopted IFRS are met.[153] EU-adopted IFRS would not be complied with in a set of accounts that did not include a profit and loss account. It therefore appears that a positive opinion as to proper preparation in accordance with EU-adopted IFRS might not be given in relation to the incomplete individual accounts included in the annual accounts under section 408. The Department for Business Enterprise and Regulatory Reform (DBERR)—now Department for Business Innovation and Skills (BIS) has addressed this matter in guidance.[154] It did not contemplate a qualified opinion but noted that 'auditors will also need to describe the accounting framework that has been used within their audit reports. In respect of the individual accounts, the reference to the framework will need to make clear that its basis is IAS as adopted for use in the EU and as applied in accordance with the provisions of the 2006 Act'. The phrase 'as applied in accordance with the provisions of the 2006 Act' has been adopted in practice by auditors and reflected in authoritative auditing literature.[155] In effect the phase signifies that the incomplete individual accounts, as presented, comply with EU-adopted IFRS only insofar as required by UK statute.  **16.495.10**

It is worth noting that subsection (3)(a) and (b) is differently constructed compared with the previous legislation.[156] Under the predecessor provision the opinion was as to a true and fair view in accordance with the relevant financial reporting framework (ie conflating what are now the separate opinions under (3)(a) and (b)). This may have given the appearance of the true and fair view's being qualified as meaning no more than bare compliance with UK accounting standards or EU-adopted IFRS as the case may be, whereas a true and fair view means more than bare compliance.[157] The provision has been modified in this Act to remove that appearance by separating true-and-fair and framework compliance into separate opinions.  **16.495.11**

Subsection (3)(c) corresponds, first, with all other requirements of Part 15 in relation to the annual accounts form and content. It therefore relates to the requirement that annual accounts consist of individual accounts and group accounts (unless in relation to group accounts the company is within the small companies regime[158] or can take advantage of one of the exemptions in sections 400 to 402); compliance of Companies Act individual or group accounts with relevant regulations or of IAS individual accounts with the IAS Regulation,[159] and to the requirements of section 407 (consistency of choice of Companies Act or IAS individual accounts within a group), section 408 (disclosures that are conditions precedent for the individual profit and loss account omission under that section), sections 409 to 413 (disclosures in annual accounts concerning related undertakings, off-balance sheet arrangements, employee numbers/costs and directors' remuneration/advances etc), and section 414 (signing of the balance sheet).  **16.495.12**

In relation to subsection (3)(c)'s requirement for an opinion on compliance with Article 4 of the IAS Regulation,[160] the question arises at to when this is applicable. As explained at section 403, the group accounts of certain companies are directly within the IAS Regulation and it is in relation only to those that the IAS Regulation compliance opinion is required. It does not apply in relation to group accounts voluntarily prepared as IAS group accounts under the choice at section 403(2).  **16.495.13**

---

[152]  See s 1162.

[153]  *IAS 1 Presentation of financial statements* (International Accounting Standards Board, 2003, revised 2007); see Commission Regulation (EC) 1126/2008—at [2008] OJ/L320/1, as amended.

[154]  See *Guidance for UK companies on accounting and reporting: Requirements under the* Companies Act 2006 *and the application of the IAS regulation* (DBERR, 2008), para 9.24.

[155]  *APB Bulletin 2010/02 Compendium of illustrative auditor's reports on United Kingdom private sector financial statements for periods ended on or after 15 December 2010* (APB, 2010), para 27.

[156]  CA 1985, s 235(2).

[157]  See ss 396 and 404.

[158]  See s 398.

[159]  See ss 395(1)(b), 396(3), 403(1), 403(2)(b), and 404(3).

[160]  See s 474.

**16.495.14**  It might be supposed that subsection (3) calls either for an opinion that, for example, the accounts do give a true and fair view or that they do not. Although it was always understood to be so, subsection (4)(a) now makes clear that a qualified opinion may be given. Section 539 defines a qualified report as one that does not state an unqualified opinion that the accounts are prepared in accordance with this Act or with other legislation; the latter would include the IAS Regulation. The definition thus covers all of the opinions required by subsection (3). Auditing standards have much to say on qualified reports. They explain that the auditor should express a qualified opinion where, first, the auditor concludes that the accounts contain misstatements but that whilst the effect is material it is not so pervasive as to render the accounts misleading or incomplete; or, second, the auditor is unable to obtain sufficient appropriate audit evidence on which to base his audit opinion and the auditor concludes that the possible effects could be material but not pervasive.[161]

**16.495.15**  An example of the first type of qualified opinion would be where the auditor concludes that a debtor balance should have been provided against but was not. Another example would be a case where the auditor concludes that the directors should not have taken advantage of an exemption from preparing group accounts (the qualification would be of the opinion under subsection (3)(c)—ie non-compliance with the Act). In such a case the opinion is expressed on an 'except for basis' (eg except for the matter referred to, the accounts give a true and fair view).

**16.495.16**  An example of the second type of qualified opinion (commonly known as a limitation in scope because this term was used in earlier versions of auditing standards, although it has now been discarded) might be the case where the auditor is unable to observe the counting of physical stocks, say because he was appointed only after the count had taken place. In such cases the auditor expresses his opinion on an 'except for the possible effects of' basis.[162] In the case of a limitation in scope the auditor would also need to include in his report a statement under section 498(3) to the effect that he has not received all the information and explanations necessary for the purposes of his audit.

**16.495.17**  If the effect of a misstatement is both material and pervasive, auditing standards require the auditor to give an adverse opinion,[163] eg that the accounts do not give a true and fair view.[164] In contrast to the qualified opinions named above, auditing standards do not include an adverse opinion within the category of qualified opinions, but rather included it within a wider category called modified opinions.[165] However, notwithstanding the terminology used by auditing standards, an adverse opinion is for the purposes of the Act a qualified opinion as defined by section 539.

**16.495.18**  Auditing standards also provide for an auditor to give a disclaimer of opinion. This arises where the auditor is unable to obtain sufficient appropriate audit evidence on which to base an opinion, and the auditor concludes that the possible effects on the accounts could be both material and persuasive. Accordingly, the auditor is unable to express an opinion.[166] In such a case he would make a report to that effect; the report would also include the section 498(3) statement. It might be thought that the legislation requires an auditor to give an opinion on the matters specified in subsection (3) and that to give a disclaimer report is to fail to do so. However, subsection (4), taken together with the definition of 'qualified' in section 539, appears to admit of a report in terms other than an unqualified opinion. Thus it is long-standing practice, and fully in accordance with auditing standards, to give a disclaimer report in appropriate circumstances, albeit such circumstances may be rare. In common with adverse opinions, auditing standards do not include disclaimers within the category of qualified opinions but include them within the wider category of modified opinions,[167] notwithstanding that a disclaimer is a qualified opinion as defined by section 539.

**16.495.19**  Whatever type of modified opinion the auditor gives, auditing standards require a clear description of the substantive reasons and, where possible, the quantification of the matter for which the report is qualified.[168]

**16.495.20**  Subsection (4)(b) has the appearance of a redundant provision. If the auditor wishes to draw attention to a matter by way of emphasis without qualifying his report, he would undoubtedly do so anyway. What this subsection does is merely recognize what auditing standards refer to as an 'emphasis of matter' paragraph. (or, rather rarely, an 'other matter' paragraph). These deal with matters that, in the auditor's judgment, are of such importance that it is fundamental to the reader's understanding of the

---

[161]  *ISA (UK & Ir) 700 (Revised)*, paras 57(a), 61, and 66.
[162]  *ISA (UK & Ir) 705*, para 23.
[163]  *ISA (UK & Ir) 705*, para 8.
[164]  *ISA (UK & Ir) 705*, para 24.
[165]  *ISA (UK & Ir) 705*, para 5(b).
[166]  *ISA (UK & Ir) 705*, para 25.
[167]  *ISA (UK & Ir) 705*, para 5(b).
[168]  *ISA (UK & Ir) 705*, paras 16 to 21.

accounts or the auditor's responsibilities and report.[169] These matters typically relate to significant uncertainties that could affect the annual accounts and the resolutions of which are dependent on future events, particularly going concern issues.[170] They do not qualify the opinion. That is not to say that significant uncertainties and going concern issues always result in an emphasis of matter. The detailed determination of whether such an issue should give rise to a modified opinion is an auditing matter outside the scope of this work. It is sufficient to say that such a matter, if accounted for (or disclosed) inappropriately, would lead to a qualified opinion; that the difference between a significant uncertainty and a 'limitation in scope' form of qualified opinion is that the former is outside the control of the company and thus goes beyond the point where the auditor could require the production of evidence; and that multiple significant uncertainties result in a disclaimer.

This section 495 is not a complete statement of what falls to be included in an auditor's report. As already noted, auditing standards give more detailed specification. In addition to the matters already referred to at various places above, they require the report to include a statement of the respective responsibilities of the directors and of the auditors,[171] and, for financial years on or after 1 October 2012, the opinions referred to in the next paragraph. Illustrative report wordings are also provided.[172] Furthermore, Auditing Practices Board literature provides for an auditor to discharge his responsibilities under section 495 in two reports in cases where the individual accounts are under one financial reporting framework (eg Companies Act individual accounts) and the group accounts are under another (eg IAS group accounts);[173] this is so notwithstanding the requirement of subsection (1) for 'a report' on the annual accounts that comprise both the individual and group accounts.    **16.495.21**

In relation to financial years beginning on or after 1 October 2012, certain revised auditing standards will be applicable in relation to certain listed companies.[174] These come into effect at the same time as it is intended that revisions to the UK Corporate Governance Code (the Code) become effective for those companies.[175] Compliance with that version of the Code would require the company's directors to report certain matters in documents containing the annual accounts-ie, within the rest of what is known colloquially as the annual report. The revised auditing standards will require the auditor to give an opinion in relation to that Code-based reporting by directors. This appears to go further than the legislation, ie than this section 495, requires. However, as explained at section 1217, the requirements of auditing standards may be said to have some statutory backing through Part 42's statutory-based regime for the regulation of auditors and audits.    **16.495.22**

As noted at sections 415 and 417, the matters reported by the directors would be, first, a statement that they consider the annual report and annual accounts, taken as a whole, to be fair, balanced, and understandable, and that it provides the information necessary for shareholders to assess the company's performance, business model, and strategy. Second, the directors would give a description of how the audit committee (a non-statutory sub-committee of the board, with responsibilities as described in the Code) has discharged its responsibilities, including the significant issues considered by the audit committee in relation to the annual accounts, and how these issues were addressed.    **16.495.23**

The revised auditing standards require that the auditor communicates to the audit committee what is the auditor's rationale and supporting evidence for its professional judgment as to various matters, including, but not limited to, the company's significant accounting policies and the directors' valuations of material assets and liabilities and related disclosures.[176] Turning to the audit report itself, the revised auditing standards require the auditor to report by exception, or explicitly to confirm that there is no exception to report, in relation to whether: the directors' 'fair etc' statement is inconsistent with the knowledge acquired by the auditor in the course of performing the audit; the directors' description    **16.495.24**

---

[169] *ISA (UK & Ir) 706 Emphasis of matter paragraphs and other matter paragraphs in the independent auditor's report* (APB, 2009), para 5.

[170] *ISA (UK & Ir) 706*, para A1. *ISA (UK & Ir) 570 Going concern* (APB, 2009), para 19.

[171] *ISA (UK & Ir) 700 (Revised)*, para 15.

[172] *APB Bulletin 2010/02*. Note that this has not been updated for the additional reporting for financial years beginning on or after 1 October 2012.

[173] *APB Bulletin 2010/02* para 22.

[174] ISA (UK & Ir) 260 (Revised, 2012) Communication with those charged with governance (FRC, 2012); ISA (UK & Ir) 700 (Revised, 2012) The auditor's report on financial statements (FRC, 2012); and ISA (UK & Ir) 720 (Revised, 2012) Section A-other information in documents containing audited financial statements (FRC, 2012).

[175] UK Corporate Governance Code (FRC, September 2012). It is intended by the FRC that this version of the Code will be applicable for financial years beginning on or after 1 October 2012. However, for this to be so, it will require the UK Listing Authority to make a change to Listing Rule LR 9.8.6R so that relevant listed companies will be required to state that they have complied with this 2012 version of the Code (or to explain why they have not). At present the Listing Rules refer to an earlier version of the Code.

[176] *ISA (UK & Ir) 260 (Revised, 2012)*, paras 16-1, A20-1, A20-2, A20-4.

of the work of the audit committee appropriately addresses matters communicated by the auditor to the audit committee;[177] and whether any other financial or non-financial information, in the auditor's judgment, is materially inconsistent with the information in the audited annual accounts or is apparently materially incorrect based on, or materially inconsistent with, the knowledge acquired by the auditor in the course of performing the audit or that is otherwise misleading.[178]

**16.495.25**    The key effect of these major changes is, broadly speaking, to require a new assurance to shareholders from the auditor, based on the audit of the annual accounts, about the propriety of the entire annual report and accounts (the 'fair etc' statement), and in particular to report to shareholders as to whether the annual report gives the shareholders transparency about details of issues discussed between the auditor and the audit committee.

**16.495.26**    At the same time, the Listing Rules of the Financial Services Authority have, for many years, made provision for other, lesser matters to be included in an auditor's report. They require certain listed companies to disclose in documents accompanying their annual accounts (or in those annual accounts) whether they have complied with the provisions of the UK corporate governance code.[179] They then require the company's auditor to review the company's compliance statement in respect of nine particular provisions of that Code and to report if in their opinion the company's statement does not reflect its compliance.[180]

**16.495.27**    Finally, elsewhere this Act makes further provision for matters to be included in the auditor's report. Sections 496, 497, and 497A require opinions in relation to the directors' report, any directors' remuneration report, and any separate corporate governance statement. Section 498 requires certain matters to be reported by exception. As explained at that section, auditing standards go beyond that too, including for financial years beginning on or after 1 October 2012. Sections 503 to 505 deal with the signature of the report. Dating of the report is dealt with only by auditing standards; this is commented on at section 503.

## 496 Auditor's report on directors' report

**16.496.01**    The auditor must state in his report on the company's annual accounts whether in his opinion the information given in the directors' report for the financial year for which the accounts are prepared is consistent with those accounts.

COMMENCEMENT DATE    6 April 2008[181]

**16.496.02**    The opinion required of an auditor by this section is required to be included in his report upon the annual accounts under section 495, ie there is no requirement for a separate report. Auditing standards make further provision for the work to be done by an auditor to support this opinion and the wording of the opinion.[182]

## 497 Auditor's report on auditable part of directors' remuneration report

**16.497.01**    (1) If the company is a quoted company, the auditor, in his report on the company's annual accounts for the financial year, must—
(a) report to the company's members on the auditable part of the directors' remuneration report, and
(b) state whether in his opinion that part of the directors' remuneration report has been properly prepared in accordance with this Act.
(2) For the purposes of this Part, 'the auditable part' of a directors' remuneration report is the part identified as such by regulations under section 421.

---

[177] If the directors choose not to comply with the Code's requirement to make the statement and give the description, then the Listing Rules would, when amended to refer to this 2012 version of the Code, require the directors to explain why they have not complied. The auditing standards would then require the auditor to report as to whether the directors' explanation is materially inconsistent with the knowledge acquired by the auditor in the course of performing the audit.

[178] ISA (UK& Ir) 700 (Revised, 2012), paras 22A, 22B; ISA (UK & Ir) 720 (Revised, 2012) Section A, paras 5, 6, 6-1.

[179] UK Corporate Governance Code (Financial Reporting Council, June 2010). Listing Rules LR 9.8.6R (6) contain these disclosure requirements; LR 9.1.1R to 9.1.4R set out the scope of their application.

[180] Listing Rule LR 9.8.10R (2).

[181] Companies Act 2006 (Commencement No 5, Transitional Provisions and Savings) Order 2007, SI 2007/3495, art 3(1) with respect to auditors' reports on accounts or reports for financial years beginning on or after 6 April 2008.

[182] ISA 720 (UK&Ir) (Revised) Section A—Other information in documents containing audited financial statements, Section B—The auditor's statutory reporting responsibility in relation to director's reports (Auditing Practices Board, 2009); APB Bulletin 2010/02 Compendium of illustrative auditor's reports on United Kingdom private sector financial statements for periods ended on or after 15 December 2010 (APB, 2010).

COMMENCEMENT DATE  6 April 2008[183]

The directors of a quoted company[184] are required by section 420 to prepare a directors' remuneration report. The content of that report is determined by regulations made under the power in section 421 (and which reproduce the requirements under the predecessor legislation),[185] and those regulations may identify parts of the content as subject to audit. It is thus that part of the directors' remuneration report that is auditable and hence subject to this section 497.     **16.497.02**

The opinion required of an auditor by this section is required to be included in his report upon the annual accounts under section 495, ie there is no requirement for a separate report. Auditing literature makes further provision for the wording of the opinion.[186]     **16.497.03**

## [497A  Auditor's report on separate corporate governance statement

(1)  Where the company prepares a separate corporate governance statement in respect of a financial year the auditor must state in his report on the company's annual accounts for that year whether in his opinion the information given in the statement in compliance with rules 7.2.5 and 7.2.6 in the Disclosure Rules and Transparency Rules sourcebook issued by the Financial Services Authority (information about internal control and risk management systems in relation to financial reporting processes and about share capital structures) is consistent with those accounts.     **16.497A.01**

(2)  The rules referred to above were inserted by Annex C of the Disclosure Rules and Transparency Rules Sourcebook (Corporate Governance Rules) Instrument 2008 made by the Authority on 26 June 2008 (FSA 2008/32).][a]

AMENDMENTS and Notes

[a]  Inserted by the Companies Act 2006 (Accounts, Reports and Audit) Regulations 2009, SI 2009/1581, reg 6, as from 27 June 2009, in relation to financial years beginning on or after 29 June 2008 which have not ended before 27 June 2009.

COMMENCEMENT DATE  27 June 2008

This new section is derived from changes made to the Fourth and Seventh Directives,[187] and requires that where a company prepares a separate corporate governance statement (that is, outside of the directors' report) the auditor must, in the auditor's report, state whether in his opinion certain of the information required to be disclosed by the FSA's Disclosure Rules and Transparency Rules (DTR) is consistent with the company's accounts. As explained in the commentaries on sections 416, 472A, and 538A, the DTR in effect give companies that are within the scope of those particular rules (see section 498A) the choice of making certain corporate governance disclosures within the directors' report or within a separate corporate governance statement. If the former route is taken then the disclosures fall within section 496 requiring the auditor to review and report upon the entire directors' report for consistency with the accounts. This section ensures that the same level of auditor review applies in cases where a separate corporate governance statement is chosen.     **16.497A.02**

The particular disclosures that are the subject of this section's auditor's review—DTR 7.2.5R and 7.2.6R—are the main part but not the totality of the content of a corporate governance statement. They relate to a description of the main features of the company's internal control and risk management systems in relation to the financial reporting process and certain disclosures about share capital. However, auditing standards go further and have the effect of requiring the auditor to review the rest of a separate corporate governance statement, by virtue of its being published together with the audited accounts, but do not require reporting in cases of consistency.[188]     **16.497A.03**

The opinion required of an auditor by this section is to be included in his report upon the annual accounts under section 495, ie there is no requirement for a separate report. Auditing standards make further provision for the work to be done by an auditor to support this opinion.[189]     **16.497A.04**

---

[183]  Companies Act 2006 (Commencement No 5, Transitional Provisions and Savings) Order 2007, SI 2007/3495, art 3(1) with respect to auditors' reports on accounts or reports for financial years beginning on or after 6 April 2008.

[184]  See s 385.

[185]  CA 1985, Sch 7A.

[186]  *APB Bulletin 2010/02 Compendium of illustrative auditor's reports on United Kingdom private sector financial statements for periods ended on or after 15 December 2010* (APB, 2010).

[187]  Directive (EEC) 78/660 [1978] OJ L222/11, as amended; and Directive (EEC) 83/349 [1983] OJ L193/1, as amended.

[188]  *ISA 720(UK & IR) (Revised) Section A—Other information in documents containing audited financial statements* (APB, 2009).

[189]  *ISA 720 (UK & IR) (Revised) Section A—Other information in documents containing audited financial statements* (APB, 2009).

*Duties and rights of auditors*

### 498 Duties of auditor

**16.498.01**

(1) A company's auditor, in preparing his report, must carry out such investigations as will enable him to form an opinion as to—

   (a) whether adequate accounting records have been kept by the company and returns adequate for their audit have been received from branches not visited by him, and

   (b) whether the company's individual accounts are in agreement with the accounting records and returns, and

   (c) in the case of a quoted company, whether the auditable part of the company's directors' remuneration report is in agreement with the accounting records and returns.

(2) If the auditor is of the opinion—

   (a) that adequate accounting records have not been kept, or that returns adequate for their audit have not been received from branches not visited by him, or

   (b) that the company's individual accounts are not in agreement with the accounting records and returns, or

   (c) in the case of a quoted company, that the auditable part of its directors' remuneration report is not in agreement with the accounting records and returns,

the auditor shall state that fact in his report.

(3) If the auditor fails to obtain all the information and explanations which, to the best of his knowledge and belief, are necessary for the purposes of his audit, he shall state that fact in his report.

(4) If—

   (a) the requirements of regulations under section 412 (disclosure of directors' benefits: remuneration, pensions and compensation for loss of office) are not complied with in the annual accounts, or

   (b) in the case of a quoted company, the requirements of regulations under section 421 as to information forming the auditable part of the directors' remuneration report are not complied with in that report,

the auditor must include in his report, so far as he is reasonably able to do so, a statement giving the required particulars.

[(5) If the directors of the company—

   (a) have prepared accounts in accordance with the small companies regime, or

   (b) have taken advantage of small companies exemption in preparing the directors' report,

and in the auditor's opinion they were not entitled to do so, the auditor shall state that fact in his report.][a]

AMENDMENTS and Notes

[a] New subs (5) inserted by the Companies Act 2006 (Amendment) (Accounts and Reports) Regulations 2008, SI 2008/393, reg 6.

COMMENCEMENT DATE   6 April 2008[190]

**16.498.02**    Although the heading to this section refers to the duties of an auditor it does not address the work that is to be done by an auditor to support his opinion, which is the subject of auditing standards;[191] nor does it address the question as to whom he owes a duty in making his report, for which see the commentary at section 495. Instead this section specifies further opinions or statements that an auditor may be required to include in his report. The report referred to throughout this section is the report required of the auditor under section 495, ie his report upon the annual accounts. This section 498 does not require a separate report.

**16.498.03**    Subsections (1), (2), and (5) require the auditor to give an opinion by exception on five specified matters (accounting records; branch returns; agreement of records and accounts; agreement of records and directors' remuneration report; and use of the small companies regime). Subsection (3) requires, by exception, a statement in relation, in effect, to the adequacy of audit evidence received. Subsection (4) requires the auditor to make a statement, by exception, making good certain of the company's disclosures in some cases.

---

[190] Companies Act 2006 (Commencement No 5, Transitional Provisions and Savings) Order 2007, SI 2007/3495, art 3(1) with respect to auditors' reports on accounts or reports for financial years beginning on or after 6 April 2008.

[191] The applicable auditing standards are those of the Auditing Practices Board (APB), known as International Standards on Auditing (UK & Ireland) (ISA's (UK & Ir)). They are so called because they reproduce International Standards on Auditing (issued by the International Auditing and Assurance Standards Board) with additional material suitable to the legal environment of the UK (and that of Ireland). The APB also publishes Practice Notes and Bulletins. For commentary on the authority of the FRC and APB pronouncements, see s 1217.

As mentioned, the reporting under this section is by exception. However, auditing standards require an   **16.498.04**
auditor to go further. They require the auditor to state whether there are any matters to report in
respect of these matters.[192] In effect, there is positive rather than exception reporting.

Dealing first with the opinions on the five specified matters, subsections (1) and (2) are structured to   **16.498.05**
require the auditor to carry out such investigations as will enable him to form an opinion on four of
those (the use of the small companies regime is left out at this point), with subsection (2) then requiring
the resulting opinion or opinions to be stated if negative. Subsection (1) thus adds very
little—subsection (2) seems entirely workable without subsection (1)—and it is perhaps odd that the
legislation refers here to the need to carry out work to support the opinion whereas no equivalent
provision is necessary in relation to the far more important opinions required by section 495 (the main
opinion upon the true and fair view and compliance with the Act).

The most significant of subsection (2)'s specified matters is the keeping of adequate accounting   **16.498.06**
records. Section 386 places a duty upon the directors to keep adequate accounting records and the
meaning of that term is dealt with in the commentary on that earlier section. The previous legislation
required an auditor's opinion in relation to 'proper' accounting records.[193] The change from 'proper' to
'adequate' does not, however, appear to be a great change. The previous legislation placed substantially
the same duty upon the directors as to the standard of maintenance of accounting records as that in
section 386. Section 386's change is to refer to that substantially similar duty as one to keep 'adequate'
accounting records. Thus notwithstanding the change in terminology the standard to which accounting records are required to be maintained and to which an auditor may need to attest, is substantially
unchanged.

It should be noted that it is unlikely that an opinion as to inadequate accounting records would be made   **16.498.07**
without there also being a qualification, for a limitation of scope, or in extreme cases there being a
disclaimer of the auditor's opinion upon the accounts themselves.[194] That is to say, if there is an
inadequacy of record keeping it is unlikely therefore to have been practical for the auditor to have
obtained sufficient evidence concerning material matters in the individual accounts.[195] The reverse is
not, however, necessarily true—a limitation in the scope of audit evidence may arise otherwise than
from inadequate accounting records.

It should be noted that the accounting records referred to in this section 498 are those of the company   **16.498.08**
itself. Thus if there were a failure in the accounting records at an undertaking included in the
consolidation this would not require a statement of inadequacy of accounting records in the auditor's
report in relation either to the company's individual accounts (they are unaffected) or its group
accounts (they are not addressed by this section), although of course it is likely that the failure could
lead to a qualification of the opinion upon the group accounts.

Subsection (2) also refers to the adequacy, for audit purposes, of returns from branches not visited by   **16.498.09**
the auditor. This is arguably an unnecessary provision given modern auditing practice. Auditing
standards require the auditor to obtain sufficient appropriate audit evidence so as to be able to draw
reasonable conclusions upon which to base his audit opinion.[196] This applies regardless of the location
of any branch forming part of the company. Auditing standards also address the use by the auditor of
the work of another auditor, eg an auditor of an overseas branch.[197]

The other two matters in subsection (2) are perhaps otiose. The auditor is required to state if the   **16.498.10**
individual accounts or auditable part of the directors' remuneration report do not agree with the
accounting records, if that is his opinion. If such a situation obtained then either his opinion on the
individual accounts or the auditable part of the directors remuneration, on the one hand, or the
adequacy of the accounting records on the other, would in any event be qualified—ie if the two disagree
then both cannot be correct; the additional statements required by subsection (2)(b) and (c) thus
appear to add little.

Subsection (5) adds little in relation to the accounts but has some effect in relation to the directors'   **16.498.11**
report. If the auditor is of the opinion that the company, having prepared accounts under the small

---

[192]  *ISA 700 (UK&Ir) (Revised) The auditor's report on financial statements* (APB, 2011), paras 21, 22, and A15
to A17.
[193]  CA 1985, s 237(2).
[194]  See s 495.
[195]  *ISA (UK & Ir) 700 (Revised)*, para A18.
[196]  *ISA (UK & Ir) 500 Audit evidence* (APB, 2009), para 6.
[197]  *ISA (UK & Ir) 600 Special considerations—audits of group financial statements* (including the work of
component auditors) (APB, 2009); para A2 refers to branches.

companies regime,[198] was not entitled to do so, then he would in any event have to qualify his opinion, pursuant to section 495(3)(c) (preparation of accounts in compliance with the Act). To that extent subsection (5) is a duplication. Where this subsection creates an additional reporting obligation is in connection with the directors' report, since the propriety of its preparation is not otherwise subject to audit:[199] if the directors' report has been prepared in accordance with the small companies exemption,[200] whereas it is the auditor's opinion that it should not have been so, the auditor must give his opinion that it is not so.

16.498.12    A statement under subsection (3) will be required whenever the auditor is unable to obtain what auditing standards term sufficient appropriate audit evidence—information and explanation necessary for the purposes of his audit, in the language of the Act—and, accordingly, makes a report which is qualified for what is commonly known as a limitation in scope or is a disclaimer of opinion on any of the matters on which he is or may be required to report (ie principally the annual accounts under section 495). The section may also have a bearing on the question of the discharge of the duties of directors and others under section 499(1)(b) to provide the auditor with information and explanations on request; and on the propriety of the directors' statements in the directors' report under section 418 to the effect that so far as the directors are each aware the auditor has all the information needed in connection with his report.

16.498.13    Subsection (4) requires the auditor to make good, in his report, any deficiencies in the company's disclosure of directors' remuneration under section 412 (all companies) or section 421 (quoted companies directors' remuneration report) that have led the auditor to qualify his report in that regard. The obligation to make good applies only insofar as the auditor is reasonably able to do so. For example, if the auditor disagrees with a disclosure then he is likely to have an opinion as to what should have been disclosed. However, this will not always be so. The auditor may be of the opinion that a disclosure is omitted but may be unable to obtain the information that should have been disclosed.

### [498A Auditor's duties in relation to separate corporate governance statement

16.498A.01    Where the company is required to prepare a corporate governance statement in respect of a financial year and no such statement is included in the directors' report—

> (a)  the company's auditor, in preparing his report on the company's annual accounts for that year, must ascertain whether a corporate governance statement has been prepared, and
>
> (b)  if it appears to the auditor that no such statement has been prepared, he must state that fact in his report.][a]

AMENDMENTS

[a] Inserted by the Companies Act 2006 (Accounts, Reports and Audit) Regulations 2009, SI 2009/1581, reg 7, as from 27 June 2009, in relation to financial years beginning on or after 29 June 2008 which have not ended before 27 June 2009.

COMMENCEMENT DATE    27 June 2008

16.498A.02    This new section is derived from changes made to the Fourth and Seventh Directives[201] and requires that where a company has not prepared a separate corporate governance statement and is required to do so, this fact shall be stated by the auditor in his report. As noted at section 538A, a corporate governance statement is required not by this Act but by chapter 7 of the FSA's Disclosure and Transparency Rules (DTR), although approval of a separate such statement (see section 419A) and auditor review thereof (see section 497A) are required by this Act. The DTR requirement falls upon companies with securities admitted to trading on a regulated market.[202] The disclosures comprising the statement may be made within the directors' report or in a separate statement. This section requires the auditor to report where the company fails to give a separate statement in lieu of one incorporated within the directors' report, ie to report by exception. However, auditing standards go further: they require the auditor to state whether he has anything to report in respect of this matter (being the

---

[198] See s 381 for the qualification for the small companies regime; and see s 380 for a commentary on the different requirements of Part 15 for different types of company.

[199] Under s 496 the auditor is required to report on the consistency of the directors' report with the annual accounts.

[200] See ss 415A, 416 and 417 for the differences in directors' report requirements for companies within the small companies exemption.

[201] Directive (EEC) 78/660 [1978] OJ L222/11, as amended; and Directive (EEC) 83/349 [1983] OJ L193/1, as amended.

[202] As defined in the FSA's Handbook Glossary, being essentially the same as that of s 1173 of this Act.

approach taken to all exception reporting).[203] That additional reporting under auditing standards will thus apply to all cases where the statement is not incorporated within the directors' report.

## 499  Auditor's general right to information

(1)  An auditor of a company—                                                                          **16.499.01**

    (a)  has a right of access at all times to the company's books, accounts and vouchers (in whatever form they are held), and

    (b)  may require any of the following persons to provide him with such information or explanations as he thinks necessary for the performance of his duties as auditor.

(2)  Those persons are—

    (a)  any officer or employee of the company;

    (b)  any person holding or accountable for any of the company's books, accounts or vouchers;

    (c)  any subsidiary undertaking of the company which is a body corporate incorporated in the United Kingdom;

    (d)  any officer, employee or auditor of any such subsidiary undertaking or any person holding or accountable for any books, accounts or vouchers of any such subsidiary undertaking;

    (e)  any person who fell within any of paragraphs (a) to (d) at a time to which the information or explanations required by the auditor relates or relate.

(3)  A statement made by a person in response to a requirement under this section may not be used in evidence against him in criminal proceedings except proceedings for an offence under section 501.

(4)  Nothing in this section compels a person to disclose information in respect of which a claim to legal professional privilege (in Scotland, to confidentiality of communications) could be maintained in legal proceedings.

COMMENCEMENT DATE  6 April 2008[204]

This section grants an auditor two important rights, one of access to the books etc and the other to require information etc. Both of these underpin the performance of his work. However, whilst these rights are fundamental, it is rare for the auditor formally to exercise them; if the auditor's relationship with the company and its directors had deteriorated such that it was necessary to do so, it is unlikely that he would choose to continue in office. Rather, these rules could be seen as setting the overall statutory framework for the provision of information to auditors.  **16.499.02**

Subsections (1)(a) and (b) provide these rights. The terminology in subsection (1)(a) bears examination. The word 'voucher' is undefined and may appear somewhat dated, but its meaning is commonly thought to be the documents which vouch for or provide evidence of a transaction such as invoices and receipts.[205]  **16.499.03**

The auditor has here a right of access to the company's 'books, accounts and vouchers' rather than a right of access to the 'accounting records'; however, as an officer of the company he has a right of access to the accounting records under section 388. The form in which the books, accounts, and vouchers are maintained, paper or electronic, has no effect on the application of subsection (1)(a).  **16.499.04**

Subsection (1)(b) gives the auditor the right to require the persons named in subsection (2) to provide information and explanations for the purpose of his work. It is noteworthy that the obligation falls on a class of persons wider than merely the directors. This is a relatively new development that was first introduced by the 2004 Act, following a Company Law Review recommendation.[206] The policy intention is to strengthen the hand of the auditor by giving him more extensive rights to require information and explanations.[207]  **16.499.05**

What is required as information or explanations is a matter to be determined by the auditor, not the directors or other persons named in subsection (2). The effect of this is to prevent such persons from turning down the auditor's requests for information or explanation as being in their view unnecessary  **16.499.06**

---

[203]  *ISA 700 (UK&Ir) (Revised). The auditor's report on financial statements* (APB, 2011), paras 21, 22 and A15 to A17.

[204]  Companies Act 2006 (Commencement No 5, Transitional Provisions and Savings) Order 2007, SI 2007/3495, art 3(1) with respect to auditors appointed for financial years beginning on or after 6 April 2008.

[205]  Eg, see the remarks of Lords Sainsbury and Sharman at *Hansard*, HL, vol 659, col 72 (16 March 2004), during the passage of the Companies (Audit, Investigations and Community Enterprise) Act 2004. Lord Sharman added, 'take [the vouchers] away from the auditor and there is no audit.'

[206]  *Modern Company Law for a Competitive Economy—Final Report* (Company Law Review Steering Group, 2001), para 8.119.

[207]  Explanatory Notes to the Companies (Audit, Investigations and Community Enterprise Act 2004 (DTI/HMSO, 2004), para 45.

for the performance of the auditor's duties and instead to allow the auditor to pursue any line of enquiry that he thinks necessary.

**16.499.07**    The form of a request for information is not specified and thus it may be verbal or written.

**16.499.08**    Notwithstanding the prescriptive language of subsection (1)(b), no person is compelled by this section to provide the requested information or explanation to the auditor, although failure to do so is an offence under section 501(3) unless compliance is not reasonably practicable. However, directors are subject to further requirements under section 418, which require them to make a statement in the directors' report with respect to their having volunteered relevant audit information to the auditor.

**16.499.09**    As noted above, the right conferred on the auditor by subsection (1)(b) is broad and the information and explanations may be provided in many different ways. For example, an auditor may ask to view, or for the directors to obtain, a valuation report that evidences the amount at which an asset is recorded in the company's books.

**16.499.10**    Those persons who are required to provide information and explanations to the auditor are determined by subsection (2) which casts a wide net. At subsection (2)(a) officers and employees are caught. Subsection (2)(b) catches those who are responsible for the books or accounts but are otherwise not employees—for example, where the accounting function is outsourced. Subsection (2)(c) applies only to subsidiary undertakings[208] that are bodies corporate incorporated in the United Kingdom, as the Act does not claim to extend to overseas jurisdictions. Provisions for other subsidiary undertakings, which would include overseas subsidiary undertakings and, eg UK partnerships,[209] are dealt with under section 500. The requirement in subsection (2)(c) would be of little practical use to the auditor if it applied only to artificial persons: thus, subsection 2(d) extends the obligation to provide information and explanations to the officers, employees, and auditors of bodies corporate caught by subsection (2)(c).

**16.499.11**    Subsection (2)(e) has the effect that the right of the auditor to require information or explanations from the persons named in subsection (2)(a) to (d) exists regardless of whether they no longer fall within the categories of such persons at the date of the auditor's enquiries. Thus, for example, a company's employee could not be removed from the duty even by the company's terminating his employment.

**16.499.12**    Subsection (3) provides that information obtained under subsection (2) cannot be used against the person who provided it in criminal proceedings (other than for section 501's offence in relation to this section itself), thereby respecting the provisions of the Human Rights Act 1998.[210]

**16.499.13**    The auditor's right to information is not an absolute right. Subsection (4) provides that the auditor has no right to information that is subject to legal professional privilege. This provision provides clarity that the common law on such privilege is unaffected by this section; and that the section respects the Human Rights Act 1998,[211] both of which recognize legal professional privilege. The inability of the auditor to obtain privileged information might cause difficulties for the auditor's obtaining audit evidence regarding provisions and disclosures relating to pending legal matters. This has been addressed by the Institute of Chartered Accountants in England and Wales (ICAEW), which provides guidance on appropriate audit procedures in its Handbook Statement 3.903 supplemented by its guidance in AUDIT 2/95.[212] Where the auditor is nevertheless unable to obtain sufficient appropriate audit evidence, his report will be qualified for a limitation in scope or, in an extreme case, to give a disclaimer of opinion;[213] the auditor would also make the statement under section 498(3) that he has not obtained all the information and explanations necessary for the purposes of his audit; and the directors' report statement under section 418, intended to be to the effect that the directors have provided to the auditor all information necessary in connection with his report, would need to be suitably qualified.

---

[208]  See s 1162.

[209]  But not limited liability partnerships, which are bodies corporate and thus within subs (2)(c).

[210]  Art 6.1 of the Convention for the Protection of Human Rights and Fundamental Freedoms (Council of Europe, 1950) addresses, *inter alia*, the right to be free of coerced self-incrimination, and is a convention right within the scope of the Human Rights Act 1998.

[211]  Art 8.1 of the Convention for the Protection of Human Rights and Fundamental Freedoms (Council of Europe, 1950) addresses, *inter alia*, the rights of companies to respect for their correspondence and is a convention right within the scope of the Human Rights Act 1998.

[212]  *The ascertainment and confirmation of contingent liabilities arising from pending legal matters* (ICAEW, 1970 and 1995).

[213]  See s 495.

## 500  Auditor's right to information from overseas subsidiaries

(1) Where a parent company has a subsidiary undertaking that is not a body corporate incorporated in the United Kingdom, the auditor of the parent company may require it to obtain from any of the following persons such information or explanations as he may reasonably require for the purposes of his duties as auditor.    **16.500.01**

(2) Those persons are—
   (a) the undertaking;
   (b) any officer, employee or auditor of the undertaking;
   (c) any person holding or accountable for any of the undertaking's books, accounts or vouchers;
   (d) any person who fell within paragraph (b) or (c) at a time to which the information or explanations relates or relate.

(3) If so required, the parent company must take all such steps as are reasonably open to it to obtain the information or explanations from the person concerned.

(4) A statement made by a person in response to a requirement under this section may not be used in evidence against him in criminal proceedings except proceedings for an offence under section 501.

(5) Nothing in this section compels a person to disclose information in respect of which a claim to legal professional privilege (in Scotland, to confidentiality of communications) could be maintained in legal proceedings.

COMMENCEMENT DATE  6 April 2008[214]

This section gives the auditor a right to information with respect to any subsidiary undertaking that is not a body corporate incorporated in the United Kingdom. It is, therefore, evident that despite the title of the section this right to information applies to subsidiary undertakings that are UK partnerships[215] as well as to subsidiary undertakings, incorporated or otherwise, established under foreign jurisdictions.    **16.500.02**

The auditor's right in this section is of a different nature to his right in section 499. First, the auditor has no direct right of access to the subsidiary undertaking's books, accounts, and vouchers; the auditor could, however, use his right to seek information contained in the relevant subsidiary undertaking's books, accounts, and vouchers. Second, the obligation to provide information and explanations falls upon the parent company and not on those persons named in subsection (2). These differences are necessary to avoid extraterritoriality of the Act's provisions.    **16.500.03**

The parent company's obligation to obtain information from the subsidiary undertakings in question is not an absolute obligation, and subsection (3) requires that the parent company take 'all such steps as are reasonably open to it to obtain the information or explanations'. The effect of subsections (4) and (5) is the same as described above under section 499.    **16.500.04**

## 501  Auditor's rights to information: offences[a]

(1) A person commits an offence who knowingly or recklessly makes to an auditor of a company a statement (oral or written) that—    **16.501.01**
   (a) conveys or purports to convey any information or explanations which the auditor requires, or is entitled to require, under section 499, and
   (b) is misleading, false or deceptive in a material particular.

(2) A person guilty of an offence under subsection (1) is liable—
   (a) on conviction on indictment, to imprisonment for a term not exceeding two years or a fine (or both);
   (b) on summary conviction—
     (i) in England and Wales [or Scotland],[b] to imprisonment for a term not exceeding twelve months or to a fine not exceeding the statutory maximum (or both);
     (ii) in Northern Ireland, to imprisonment for a term not exceeding six months or to a fine not exceeding the statutory maximum (or both).

(3) A person who fails to comply with a requirement under section 499 without delay commits an offence unless it was not reasonably practicable for him to provide the required information or explanations.

(4) If a parent company fails to comply with section 500, an offence is committed by—
   (a) the company, and
   (b) every officer of the company who is in default.

---

[214] Companies Act 2006 (Commencement No 5, Transitional Provisions and Savings) Order 2007, SI 2007/3495, art 3(1) with respect to auditors appointed for financial years beginning on or after 6 April 2008.

[215] Ie partnerships formed under the Partnership Act 1890 and the Limited Partnerships Act 1907 but not one under the Limited Liability Partnerships Act 2000 as such a body is a corporate one.

(5)  A person guilty of an offence under subsection (3) or (4) is liable on summary conviction to a fine not exceeding level 3 on the standard scale.

(6)  Nothing in this section affects any right of an auditor to apply for an injunction (in Scotland, an interdict or an order for specific performance) to enforce any of his rights under section 499 or 500.

AMENDMENTS and Notes

a  This section applies with modifications to LLPs by reg 85 of the Limited Liability Partnerships (Application of Companies Act 2006) Regulations 2009, SI 2009/1804.

b  Amended by the Limited Liability Partnerships (Application of Companies Act 2006) Regulations 2009, SI 2009/1804, Sch 3.

COMMENCEMENT DATE  6 April 2008[216]

**16.501.02**  This section sets out the offences that relate to section 499(1)(b) and section 500. It is notable that no offence is committed by denying the auditor a right of access to the company's books, accounts, and vouchers (the right set out in section 499(1)(a)), although the auditor may apply for an injunction to obtain access to them by virtue of subsection (6).[217]

**16.501.03**  Subsections (1) to (3) deal with offences that relate to section 499(1)(b). It is apparent that there are two offences contained within these subsections. The first is of a person's providing information that is, or explanations that are, 'misleading, false or deceptive in a material particular'. The penalty for this offence, which may be custodial, is given by subsection (2).

**16.501.04**  The second offence, given by subsection (3), is of a person's not providing information or explanations without delay, although a defence exists where it was not reasonably practicable for that person to provide the required information or explanations. This defence appears to provide, for example, an appropriate degree of protection to junior employees of the company, who may not be privy to all the details of a transaction in question and, as a consequence, may be unable to respond to the auditor's enquiry.

**16.501.05**  Subsection (4) provides for an offence relating to failing to comply with section 500 (company to obtain information from certain subsidiary undertakings). The offence is committed by both the company and every officer of the company in default.[218]

### 502 Auditor's rights in relation to resolutions and meetings

**16.502.01**  (1)  In relation to a written resolution proposed to be agreed to by a private company, the company's auditor is entitled to receive all such communications relating to the resolution as, by virtue of any provision of Chapter 2 of Part 13 of this Act, are required to be supplied to a member of the company.

(2)  A company's auditor is entitled—

(a)  to receive all notices of, and other communications relating to, any general meeting which a member of the company is entitled to receive,

(b)  to attend any general meeting of the company, and

(c)  to be heard at any general meeting which he attends on any part of the business of the meeting which concerns him as auditor.

(3)  Where the auditor is a firm, the right to attend or be heard at a meeting is exercisable by an individual authorised by the firm in writing to act as its representative at the meeting.

COMMENCEMENT DATE  6 April 2008[219]

**16.502.02**  This section gives the auditor the right to receive all communications with respect to written resolutions and general meetings, to attend general meetings, and to speak at them on any matters which concern him as auditor. The latter right is exercisable by a duly authorized individual where the auditor is a firm.[220]

**16.502.03**  There are no penalties for failing to comply with this section. Furthermore, whilst auditors do from time to time attend such meetings, it is rare for the auditor to exercise his right under section 502(2)(c) by addressing the meeting.

---

[216]  Companies Act 2006 (Commencement No 5, Transitional Provisions and Savings) Order 2007, SI 2007/3495, art 3(1) with respect to auditors appointed for financial years beginning on or after 6 April 2008.

[217]  It is, of course, unlikely that an auditor would choose to make such an application. If the relationship has deteriorated to that degree, it is unlikely that the auditor would choose to continue in office.

[218]  See s 1121.

[219]  Companies Act 2006 (Commencement No 5, Transitional Provisions and Savings) Order 2007, SI 2007/3495, art 3(1) with respect to auditors appointed on or after 6 April 2008.

[220]  See s 1173.

## Signature of auditor's report

### 503  Signature of auditor's report

(1)  The auditor's report must state the name of the auditor and be signed and dated.  **16.503.01**
(2)  Where the auditor is an individual, the report must be signed by him.
(3)  Where the auditor is a firm, the report must be signed by the senior statutory auditor in his own name, for and on behalf of the auditor.

COMMENCEMENT DATE  6 April 2008[221]

This section implements a requirement of the EC Statutory Audit Directive,[222] and a recommendation  **16.503.02** of the Audit Quality Forum,[223] that the audit report be signed in the name of the individual in the audit firm that was responsible for the audit. The policy intention is for this transparency measure to enhance confidence in the audit.

Subsection (1) requires, first of all, that the name of the auditor be stated in the report. Where the  **16.503.03** auditor is a firm,[224] it is thus the firm's name that falls to be stated. Subsection (1) then requires the report to be signed, but it is subsections (2) and (3) that govern the manner of signature. Where the auditor is a firm it is here that the name of an individual within the firm—the senior statutory auditor, for which see section 504—first becomes relevant. That person must sign in his own name, for and on behalf of his firm; it should be emphasized, however, that the report remains that of the firm and section 504 provides that no additional liability may be attached to the individual by virtue of his personal signature. The section does not, however, require this person's name to be stated (although his signature may of course be legible). However, auditing literature employs, in the report, a statement under the signature giving both names (eg '[individual name], for and on behalf of [audit firm name]').[225] In addition, section 505 requires (subject to section 506) that the individual's name be stated in published *copies* of the report, whereas this section addresses the original report.

Subsection (1) then requires the report to be dated.[226] The date as at which accounting information is  **16.503.04** prepared (by directors) or considered (by an auditor) is a significant matter. In making his report the auditor should consider the effect of events and transactions up to the date of his report.[227] It is therefore very widespread practice for the auditor to sign his report on the same day on which the directors approve the annual accounts[228] so as to avoid the possibility of an occurrence between the two dates requiring adjustment to reported amounts or to disclosures; if that were to occur then the auditor would have to take it into account, whereas the directors did not have the opportunity to do so. In terms of determining the date entered upon the audit report, auditing standards make very clear that the date is to be that on which the report was actually signed;[229] it is *not* permitted to give an earlier date, eg as at which the remainder of the audit work, other than the signing of the report, was completed.

These requirements as to the signing of the report relate only to the original report. There is no longer  **16.503.05** a statutory requirement for the copy delivered to the registrar to be a signed copy; this is to facilitate electronic filing. Sections 444 to 447 deal with the need to state, in the filed copy, the name of the auditor and the signatory. Section 505 deals with the need to state the name of the auditor and signatory in copies generally. Both are subject to the exception in section 506.

---

[221] Companies Act 2006 (Commencement No 5, Transitional Provisions and Savings) Order 2007, SI 2007/3495, art 3(1) with respect to auditors' reports on accounts or reports for financial years beginning on or after 6 April 2008.

[222] Directive (EC) 2006/43 on statutory audits of annual accounts and consolidated accounts, amending Council Directives (EEC) 78/660 and (EEC) 83/349 and repealing Council (EEC) Directive 84/253 [2006] OJ L157/87, Art 28.

[223] *Audit quality: Shareholder involvement—identifying the audit partner* (ICAEW, 2005). The Audit Quality Forum was convened by the ICAEW at the request of the Secretary of State for Trade and Industry; it brings together the audit profession, investors, business, and regulators to work together to generate policy proposals that will further enhance confidence in the independent audit by promoting transparency and accountability.

[224] See s 1173.

[225] *APB Bulletin 2010/02 Compendium of illustrative auditor's reports on United Kingdom private sector financial statements for periods ended on or after 15 December 2010* (APB, 2010).

[226] Cf, the lack of statutory provision for, eg, the directors to state the date of their approval of the annual accounts under s 414.

[227] *International Standards on Auditing (UK & Ireland)* (ISA (UK & Ir)) *560 Subsequent events* (APB, 2009).

[228] See s 414.

[229] *ISA (UK & Ir) 700 (Revised) The auditor's report on financial statements* (APB, 2011) para 26.

### 504 Senior statutory auditor

**16.504.01**    (1)  The senior statutory auditor means the individual identified by the firm as senior statutory auditor in relation to the audit in accordance with—
   (a)  standards issued by the European Commission, or
   (b)  if there is no applicable standard so issued, any relevant guidance issued by—
      (i)   the Secretary of State, or
      (ii)  a body appointed by order of the Secretary of State.
(2)  The person identified as senior statutory auditor must be eligible for appointment as auditor of the company in question (see Chapter 2 of Part 42 of this Act).
(3)  The senior statutory auditor is not, by reason of being named or identified as senior statutory auditor or by reason of his having signed the auditor's report, subject to any civil liability to which he would not otherwise be subject.
(4)  An order appointing a body for the purpose of subsection (1)(b)(ii) is subject to negative resolution procedure.

COMMENCEMENT DATE  Subsections (2)(b)(i), (4) in relation to the order-making power, from 20 January 2007;[230] otherwise 6 April 2008[231]

**16.504.02**    The 'senior statutory auditor' is the term given to the individual within a firm[232] who, under section 503, signs the audit report in his own name for and on behalf of his firm. The term is not one drawn from auditing practice but is new coinage under this Act, reflecting the terminology of EC law.[233] As facilitated in subsection (1), the precise arrangements for defining this person were originally set out in UK guidance issued by the Auditing Practices Board (APB).[234] which states that 'senior statutory auditor' has the same meaning as 'engagement partner' as provided by auditing standards,[235] ie 'the partner or other person in the firm who is responsible for the audit engagement and its performance, and for the auditor's report that is issued on behalf of the firm, and who, where required, has the appropriate authority from a professional, legal or regulatory body'.[236] The APB was, until July 2012, the body appointed under subsection (1)(b)(ii). From July 2012, the Financial Reporting Council (FRC) is the appointed body.[237] The FRC has not issued guidance on the meaning of senior statutory auditor. However, under the transitional and savings provisions of the order appointing the FRC, the APB guidance is treated as if issued by the FRC and therefore remains in force.[238]

**16.504.03**    Subsection (3) makes important provision that the senior statutory auditor does not have his civil liability extended by virtue of his signing under section 503 or of his being named or identified as the senior statutory auditor.

### 505 Names to be stated in published copies of auditor's report

**16.505.01**    (1)  Every copy of the auditor's report that is published by or on behalf of the company must—
   (a)  state the name of the auditor and (where the auditor is a firm) the name of the person who signed it as senior statutory auditor, or
   (b)  if the conditions in section 506 (circumstances in which names may be omitted) are met, state that a resolution has been passed and notified to the Secretary of State in accordance with that section.

---

[230]  Companies Act 2006 (Commencement No 1, etc) Order 2006, SI 2006/3428, art 3(3).
[231]  Companies Act 2006 (Commencement No 5, Transitional Provisions and Savings) Order 2007, SI 2007/3495, art 3(1) with respect to auditors' reports on accounts or reports for financial years beginning on or after 6 April 2008.
[232]  See s 1173.
[233]  Statutory Audit Directive (EC) 2006/43 [2006] OJ L157/87)), Art 2(2) defines the 'statutory auditor' as the natural person who is approved in accordance with that directive by the competent authorities of a Member State to carry out the audit of individual and group accounts required by community law.
[234]  *APB Bulletin 2008/6 The 'Senior Statutory Auditor' under the United Kingdom Companies Act 2006* (APB, 2008).
[235]  The applicable auditing standards are those of the Auditing Practices Board (APB), known as International Standards on Auditing (UK & Ireland) (ISA's (UK & Ir)). They are so called because they reproduce International Standards on Auditing (issued by the International Auditing and Assurance Standards Board) with additional material suitable to the legal environment of the UK (and that of Ireland). The APB also publishes practice notes and bulletins.
[236]  *APB Bulletin 2008/6*, para 6, referring to ISA (UK & Ir) 220 *Quality control for audits of historical financial information* (APB, 2004).
[237]  The Statutory Auditors (Amendment of Companies Act 2006 and Delegation of Functions etc) Order 2012, SI 2012/1741, reg 15.
[238]  Ibid, reg 16(2).

(2) For the purposes of this section a company is regarded as publishing the report if it publishes, issues or circulates it or otherwise makes it available for public inspection in a manner calculated to invite members of the public generally, or any class of members of the public, to read it.

(3) If a copy of the auditor's report is published without the statement required by this section, an offence is committed by—

(a) the company, and

(b) every officer of the company who is in default.

(4) A person guilty of an offence under this section is liable on summary conviction to a fine not exceeding level 3 on the standard scale.

COMMENCEMENT DATE  6 April 2008[239]

This section requires, subject to the exception in section 506, that the name of the auditor and, in the case of a firm,[240] the name of the individual in the firm who signed on behalf of his firm (termed the senior statutory auditor in the preceding sections) be stated in copies of the auditor's report published by or on behalf of the company. **16.505.02**

Subsection (2) defines 'published' for this purpose. It has the effect that a copy of the audit report forming part of annual accounts and reports delivered to the registrar under section 441 must state the relevant name or names, as the registrar will put those documents on the public record; to that extent it is a duplication of the provisions of sections 444 to 447 that address filing specifically. It is also clear that making a copy of the audit report, as part of a set of annual accounts and reports, available on a website (eg for quoted companies pursuant to section 430) will invite members of the public to read it and so the name or names must be stated. **16.505.03**

However, in the case of copies of the audit report forming part of the annual accounts and reports circulated to entitled persons under section 423, and laid before members in general meeting under section 437 (public companies only), the construction of subsection (2) invites consideration. Whilst such publication would clearly fall within the phrase 'publishes, issues or circulates it', the question arises as to whether this is the subject to the qualifying words, 'for public inspection [etc]' and whether, if so, the members are a class of the public. However, the natural grammatical reading appears to be that those qualifying words relate only to 'or otherwise makes it available' and not to 'publishes, issues or circulates it'. Thus copies circulated under section 423 (quoted companies only) or section 430 (quoted companies only) and laid under section 437 (public companies only) are within this section's requirement to state the auditor's and signatory's names. In any event, as explained at section 503, it may become a practice for the original of the audit report to state the names of the firm and the individual, and thus any copy would automatically include that also. **16.505.04**

## 506  Circumstances in which names may be omitted

(1) The auditor's name and, where the auditor is a firm, the name of the person who signed the report as senior statutory auditor, may be omitted from— **16.506.01**

(a) published copies of the report, and

(b) the copy of the report delivered to the registrar under Chapter 10 of Part 15 (filing of accounts and reports),

if the following conditions are met.

(2) The conditions are that the company—

(a) considering on reasonable grounds that statement of the name would create or be likely to create a serious risk that the auditor or senior statutory auditor, or any other person, would be subject to violence or intimidation, has resolved that the name should not be stated, and

(b) has given notice of the resolution to the Secretary of State, stating—

(i) the name and registered number of the company,

(ii) the financial year of the company to which the report relates, and

(iii) the name of the auditor and (where the auditor is a firm) the name of the person who signed the report as senior statutory auditor.

COMMENCEMENT DATE  6 April 2008[241]

---

[239] Companies Act 2006 (Commencement No 5, Transitional Provisions and Savings) Order 2007, SI 2007/3495, art 3(1) with respect to auditors' reports on accounts or reports for financial years beginning on or after 6 April 2008.

[240] See s 1173.

[241] Companies Act 2006 (Commencement No 5, Transitional Provisions and Savings) Order 2007, SI 2007/3495, art 3(1) with respect to auditors' reports on accounts or reports for financial years beginning on or after 6 April 2008.

**16.506.02**    This section has the effect of providing protection for an audit firm[242] and its personnel where that firm is auditor of a company that is subject to a campaign of violence and intimidation. In this it is motivated by similar considerations to those behind the provisions at sections 163, 167 and 240 to 246 permitting directors' residential addresses to be kept out of the public domain.

**16.506.03**    The permission to omit the name or names applies only in relation to copies of the report that are otherwise required to state the name or names under section 505 or under filing requirements in Part 15.[243] It does not apply to the original audit report. The original report, furnished to the company, must still state the name of the firm under section 503(1). As, however, it is not the original report that is circulated, but copies, this does not pose a problem.

**16.506.04**    The conditions for this exemption are set out in subsection (2). It should be emphasized that subsection (2)(a) requires the company to resolve that the name should not be stated, but it does not require the resolution to include that name (which might otherwise defeat the purpose). Subsection (2)(b) requires the name to be included on a notice of the resolution given to the Secretary of State. This notice should not be confused with the notice of the resolution in the sense of the company's governance procedures; rather it is a notice in the sense of a notification to the Secretary of State of a matter resolved upon by the company.

## *Offences in connection with auditor's report*

### 507  Offences in connection with auditor's report

**16.507.01**    (1) A person to whom this section applies commits an offence if he knowingly or recklessly causes a report under section 495 (auditor's report on company's annual accounts) to include any matter that is misleading, false or deceptive in a material particular.

(2) A person to whom this section applies commits an offence if he knowingly or recklessly causes such a report to omit a statement required by—

(a) section 498(2)(b) (statement that company's accounts do not agree with accounting records and returns),

(b) section 498(3) (statement that necessary information and explanations not obtained), or

(c) section 498(5) (statement that directors wrongly took advantage of exemption from obligation to prepare group accounts).

(3) This section applies to—

(a) where the auditor is an individual, that individual and any employee or agent of his who is eligible for appointment as auditor of the company;

(b) where the auditor is a firm, any director, member, employee or agent of the firm who is eligible for appointment as auditor of the company.

(4) A person guilty of an offence under this section is liable—

(a) on conviction on indictment, to a fine;

(b) on summary conviction, to a fine not exceeding the statutory maximum.

COMMENCEMENT DATE  6 April 2008[244]

**16.507.02**    This section creates a criminal offence in relation to auditing, where hitherto there was none. It was introduced as part of the UK response to high profile failures in the United States[245] and as part of a package of measures that included the facility for auditors to negotiate to limit their liability.[246]

**16.507.03**    The offence addresses failures in relation to all of the requirements of section 495 and certain requirements of section 498. Section 495 requires the auditor to give his opinion on a number of matters in relation to the company's annual accounts, which can be broadly summarized as whether those accounts give a true and fair view; whether they comply with the relevant financial reporting framework (accounting standards); and whether they comply with the Act or, in the case of companies whose group accounts fall directly within the IAS Regulation,[247] whether they comply with Article 4 thereof. That section also stipulates some matters that can be characterized as technical drafting matters in relation to the form of the report, although it seems unlikely that failure in this regard would result in a report that met subsection (1)'s test of being misleading, false, or deceptive in a material particular. By virtue of sections 496 and 497, the section 495 report also includes opinions on the

---

[242] See s 1173.

[243] See ss 444(7), 445(6), 446(4), and 447(4).

[244] Companies Act 2006 (Commencement No 5, Transitional Provisions and Savings) Order 2007, SI 2007/3495, art 3(1) with respect to auditors' reports on accounts or reports for financial years beginning on or after 6 April 2008.

[245] The US company Enron failed in 2001, and its auditor, Arthur Andersen LLP, subsequently collapsed.

[246] See ss 532–538.

[247] See ss 495 and 403(1).

directors' report and any directors' remunerations report (quoted companies[248] only). These opinions, being matters included in a report under section 495, are also within the scope of the offence. It may be noted that the offence arises in relation to matters included in the report but not to omissions. Since section 495 (and sections 496 and 497) simply requires opinions on a fixed set of matters, any question of omissions is irrelevant. Omissions are, however, relevant to reporting under section 498, since that section requires that an opinion or statement be given only where it is negative (see below for details).

The offence is expressed in a 'knowingly or recklessly' formulation. There is a practical concern for      **16.507.04**
auditors as to the meaning of 'reckless' in this context and what conduct will amount to recklessness and how this will interrelate with possible disciplinary actions by regulators. Sections 508 and 509 are intended as a response to those latter concerns.

Of the several matters upon which reporting might be required under section 498, the offence is      **16.507.05**
attracted in relation to omission of an opinion or statement only in respect of the three matters stated in subsection (2) of this section. The offence is again expressed in a 'knowingly or recklessly' formulation. In addition, it is a matter of some concern that an omission will trigger the offence without any regard to the significance of that omission to the audit report as a whole. That is to say, there is no equivalent of subsection (1)'s test of its rendering the audit report misleading, false, or deceptive in a material particular.

The persons who may be found to have committed these offences, on the 'knowingly or recklessly'      **16.507.06**
basis, are set out in subsection (3). This category of persons is not restricted to those leading the firm or the audit in question but is defined broadly so as to cover any person who is eligible for appointment as auditor of the company, ie under Part 42 of this Act.[249] The firm[250] itself is not within the scope of the offence. The penalty is an unlimited fine.

## 508  Guidance for regulatory and prosecuting authorities: England, Wales and Northern Ireland

(1) The Secretary of State may issue guidance for the purpose of helping relevant regulatory and      **16.508.01**
    prosecuting authorities to determine how they should carry out their functions in cases where behaviour occurs that—
   (a) appears to involve the commission of an offence under section 507 (offences in connection with auditor's report), and
   (b) has been, is being or may be investigated pursuant to arrangements—
      (i) under paragraph 15 of Schedule 10 (investigation of complaints against auditors and supervisory bodies), or
      (ii) of a kind mentioned in paragraph 24 of that Schedule (independent investigation for disciplinary purposes of public interest cases).
(2) The Secretary of State must obtain the consent of the Attorney General before issuing any such guidance.
(3) In this section 'relevant regulatory and prosecuting authorities' means—
   (a) supervisory bodies within the meaning of Part 42 of this Act,
   (b) bodies to which the Secretary of State may make grants under section 16(1) of the Companies (Audit, Investigations and Community Enterprise) Act 2004 (c. 27) (bodies concerned with accounting standards etc),
   (c) the Director of the Serious Fraud Office,
   (d) the Director of Public Prosecutions or the Director of Public Prosecutions for Northern Ireland, and
   (e) the Secretary of State.
(4) This section does not apply to Scotland.

COMMENCEMENT DATE 6 April 2008[251]

One of the issues raised by the existence, in section 507, of a criminal offence in relation to audit      **16.508.02**
reporting is that the facts could give rise to disciplinary proceedings by a body with regulatory functions in relation to auditors and also to a prosecution. This section permits the Secretary of State, with the consent of the Attorney General, to issue guidance to the regulatory bodies (those specified in subsection (3)(a) and (b)) and to prosecuting authorities (those specified in subsection (3)(c) to (e)) for the purpose of helping relevant regulatory and prosecuting authorities to determine how they should

---

[248]  See s 385.
[249]  In particular, see s 1211.
[250]  See s 1173.
[251]  Companies Act 2006 (Commencement No 5, Transitional Provisions and Savings) Order 2007, SI 2007/3495, art 3(1) with respect to auditors' reports on accounts or reports for financial years beginning on or after 6 April 2008.

carry out their functions, and such guidance was issued in February 2010 by BIS.[252] This guidance helps prosecutors to decide not to prosecute in a case where disciplinary proceedings would be a better response. In particular, the guidance states that where the offence concerns recklessness and the evidential test is met by relying on inference only, it is highly unlikely that prosecution would be appropriate where the public interest may be met by referring the matter to disciplinary action by the appropriate regulatory body.[253]

**16.508.03**      This section applies only in England, Wales, and Northern Ireland. Scotland is covered in similar terms by section 509.

### 509   Guidance for regulatory authorities: Scotland

**16.509.01**

(1) The Lord Advocate may issue guidance for the purpose of helping relevant regulatory authorities to determine how they should carry out their functions in cases where behaviour occurs that—

    (a) appears to involve the commission of an offence under section 507 (offences in connection with auditor's report), and

    (b) has been, is being or may be investigated pursuant to arrangements—

        (i) under paragraph 15 of Schedule 10 (investigation of complaints against auditors and supervisory bodies), or

        (ii) of a kind mentioned in paragraph 24 of that Schedule (independent investigation for disciplinary purposes of public interest cases).

(2) The Lord Advocate must consult the Secretary of State before issuing any such guidance.

(3) In this section 'relevant regulatory authorities' means—

    (a) supervisory bodies within the meaning of Part 42 of this Act,

    (b) bodies to which the Secretary of State may make grants under section 16(1) of the Companies (Audit, Investigations and Community Enterprise) Act 2004 (c. 27) (bodies concerned with accounting standards etc), and

    (c) the Secretary of State.

(4) This section applies only to Scotland.

COMMENCEMENT DATE 6 April 2008[254]

**16.509.02**      This section, applying in Scotland, is similar to section 508 (England, Wales, and Northern Ireland), to which commentary reference should be made. However, under this section the guidance would be issued by the Lord Advocate after consultation with the Secretary of State; and among those to whom the guidance would be addressed, the prosecuting authorities are limited to the Secretary of State. To date no guidance has been issued by the Lord Advocate.[255]

# CHAPTER 4
# REMOVAL, RESIGNATION, ETC OF AUDITORS

## *Removal of auditor*

**16.510.01**      Chapter 4 of Part 16 of the Companies Act 2006 restates, reorders and amends sections 391 to 394A of the Companies Act 1985. The 2006 Act now addresses removal, failure to re-appoint, and resignation separately.

### 510   Resolution removing auditor from office

**16.510.02**

(1) The members of a company may remove an auditor from office at any time.

(2) This power is exercisable only—

    (a) by ordinary resolution at a meeting, and

    (b) in accordance with section 511 (special notice of resolution to remove auditor).

(3) Nothing in this section is to be taken as depriving the person removed of compensation or damages payable to him in respect of the termination—

    (a) of his appointment as auditor, or

    (b) of any appointment terminating with that as auditor.

---

[252] *Companies Act 2006, Section 508—Guidance for Regulatory and Prosecuting Authorities in England, Wales and Northern Ireland—Offences in Connection with Auditors' Reports (Section 507)* (BIS, 2010).

[253] *Companies Act 2006, Section 508—Guidance for Regulatory and Prosecuting Authorities in England, Wales and Northern Ireland—Offences in Connection with Auditors' Reports (Section 507)* (BIS, 2010), para 8.

[254] Companies Act 2006 (Commencement No 5, Transitional Provisions and Savings) Order 2007, SI 2007/3495, art 3(1) with respect to auditors' reports on accounts or reports for financial years beginning on or after 6 April 2008.

[255] Although guidance has been issued by BIS for England, Wales and Northern Ireland. See s 508.

(4)  An auditor may not be removed from office before the expiration of his term of office except by resolution under this section.

COMMENCEMENT DATE  6 April 2008[256]

Section 510 restates and amends section 391(1) and (3) of the Companies Act 1985. It provides that an auditor may only be removed during the period of his term in office by an ordinary resolution passed at a meeting provided that special notice was given of the intention to move such a resolution at the meeting and the other procedural requirements of section 511 are complied with.[257] Section 510(3) clarifies that removal does not affect any compensation or damages entitlement arising from the termination of office or any appointment which terminates upon loss of office as the company's auditor.    **16.510.03**

Section 510(4) adds a new provision that makes clear that any other arrangement for mid-term removal of the auditor from office is ineffective and unenforceable.    **16.510.04**

## 511  Special notice required for resolution removing auditor from office

(1)  Special notice is required for a resolution at a general meeting of a company removing an auditor from office.    **16.511.01**

(2)  On receipt of notice of such an intended resolution the company must immediately send a copy of it to the auditor proposed to be removed.

(3)  The auditor proposed to be removed may make with respect to the intended resolution representations in writing to the company (not exceeding a reasonable length) and request their notification to members of the company.

(4)  The company must (unless the representations are received by it too late for it to do so)—
   (a)  in any notice of the resolution given to members of the company, state the fact of the representations having been made, and
   (b)  send a copy of the representations to every member of the company to whom notice of the meeting is or has been sent.

(5)  If a copy of any such representations is not sent out as required because received too late or because of the company's default, the auditor may (without prejudice to his right to be heard orally) require that the representations be read out at the meeting.

(6)  Copies of the representations need not be sent out and the representations need not be read at the meeting if, on the application either of the company or of any other person claiming to be aggrieved, the court is satisfied that the auditor is using the provisions of this section to secure needless publicity for defamatory matter.
   The court may order the company's costs (in Scotland, expenses) on the application to be paid in whole or in part by the auditor, notwithstanding that he is not a party to the application.

COMMENCEMENT DATE  6 April 2008[258]

Section 511 restates and amends section 391A of the Companies Act 1985. In addition to the requirement of special notice, section 511 requires that the auditor receives notice of the intended resolution. The company must send such notice to the auditor immediately upon receipt of notice of the intended resolution. The auditors may prepare written representations in relation to the proposed removal resolution which the company must distribute to the members unless the company receives such representation too late for them to do so (section 511(4)(b)). If the representations are received prior to any notice of the resolution given by the company to its members, the company must inform its members in the notice that the auditor has made representations (section 511(4)(a)). Where such representations are not distributed to the shareholders, the auditor may insist that the representations be read out at the shareholders' meeting (section 511(5)).    **16.511.02**

Section 511(6) provides that the representations do not have to be read out nor distributed to members if on application the court orders that the representations are being used by the auditor to 'secure needless publicity for defamatory matter' (section 511 (6)). The application may be made by the company or another person who claims to be 'aggrieved'. The predecessor to section 511(6), section 391(A)(6) of the Companies Act 1985, provided that the court could make such an order where 'rights conferred by this section are being abused' *to* 'secure needless publicity for defamatory matter'. There are no decided cases under section 391(A)(6). However, there is limited authority on the meaning of 'using the provisions of this section to secure needless publicity for defamatory matter'    **16.511.03**

---

[256] Companies Act 2006 (Commencement No 5, Transitional Provisions and Savings) Order 2007, SI 2007/3495, art 3. This provision applies where notice of the intended resolution is given after 6 April 2008.

[257] See s 312 of CA (resolution requiring special notice).

[258] Companies Act 2006 (Commencement No 5, Transitional Provisions and Savings) Order 2007, SI 2007/3495, art 3.

from cases dealing with section 394 of the Companies Act 1985. Section 394 relates to the statement of circumstances provided by an auditor when he ceases to hold office. Under section 394(6) the court may order that the statement is not distributed to members where 'the auditor is using the statement to secure needless publicity for defamatory matter'. In *Jarvis plc v PricewaterhouseCoopers*,[259] *dicta* from Lightman J suggests that for proceedings instituted under this section 'the company must allege that the auditor acted in bad faith in using the statement'. He noted further that 'this is a most serious allegation, tantamount to an allegation of dishonesty, against professional accountants'. In *Easier v Deloitte Touche LLP*,[260] the defendant successfully struck out an application under section 394 which did not contain any supporting evidence of *mal fides*. Evans-Lombe J held that allegations 'that were tantamount to allegations of fraud ... should be supported by evidence of mala fides'.

**16.511.04**    In *Jarvis plc v PricewaterhouseCoopers* the court noted that there was scope to abuse section 394 because by instituting proceedings the distribution of the statement is delayed. There is similar scope for abuse by the company in connection with section 511(6), especially when combined with the exemption from distribution of the representations to members where it is too late to do so. Lightman J noted that applicants under section 394 should cooperate in obtaining an expedited trial. It is anticipated that the courts would have a similar expectation in relation to section 511(6).

**16.511.05**    Section 511(6) provides a discretion to the court to order the auditor to pay the costs of the application. Such an order may be made even if the auditor is not a party to the application. No such order has been made in a reported case. Note that in *Jarvis v PricewaterhouseCoopers* the late discontinuance of the application by the company, together with Lightman J's concern about the applicant's behaviour, resulted in an award of costs against the company on an indemnity basis.

## 512 Notice to registrar of resolution removing auditor from office

**16.512.01**    (1) Where a resolution is passed under section 510 (resolution removing auditor from office), the company must give notice of that fact to the registrar within 14 days.
(2) If a company fails to give the notice required by this section, an offence is committed by—
(a) the company, and
(b) every officer of it who is in default.
(3) A person guilty of an offence under this section is liable on summary conviction to a fine not exceeding level 3 on the standard scale and, for continued contravention, a daily default fine not exceeding one-tenth of level 3 on the standard scale.

COMMENCEMENT DATE  6 April 2008[261]

**16.512.02**    This section restates section 391(2) of the Companies Act 1985. It provides that the company must give notice to the registrar of the resolution removing the auditor from office. Such notice must be given within 14 days of it being passed. Failure to comply with the notice obligation is an offence committed by both the company and any officer in default.

## 513 Rights of auditor who has been removed from office

**16.513.01**    (1) An auditor who has been removed by resolution under section 510 has, notwithstanding his removal, the rights conferred by section 502(2) in relation to any general meeting of the company—
(a) at which his term of office would otherwise have expired, or
(b) at which it is proposed to fill the vacancy caused by his removal.
(2) In such a case the references in that section to matters concerning the auditor as auditor shall be construed as references to matters concerning him as a former auditor.

COMMENCEMENT DATE  6 April 2008[262]

**16.513.02**    This section restates section 391(2) of the Companies Act 1985. It ensures that an auditor who has been removed pursuant to section 510 retains the rights conferred on him by section 502(2). Please see further section 502(2) of the Companies Act 2006 and accompanying commentary.

---

[259] [2000] 2 BCLC 368.
[260] [2004] All ER (D) 378.
[261] Companies Act 2006 (Commencement No 5, Transitional Provisions and Savings) Order 2007, SI 2007/3495, art 3.
[262] Companies Act 2006 (Commencement No 5, Transitional Provisions and Savings) Order 2007, SI 2007/3495, art 3. The Order provides that in relation to auditors appointed before 6 April 2008 'the reference to rights under section 502(2) shall be read as a reference to rights under section 390(1) of the 1985 Act or Article 398(1) of the 1986 Order' (Sch 4, para 13).

*Failure to re-appoint auditor*

## 514  Failure to re-appoint auditor: special procedure required for written resolution

(1)  This section applies where a resolution is proposed as a written resolution of a private company whose effect would be to appoint a person as auditor in place of a person (the 'outgoing auditor') whose term of office has expired, or is to expire, at the end of the period for appointing auditors.

(2)  The following provisions apply if—

    (a)  no period for appointing auditors has ended since the outgoing auditor ceased to hold office, or

    (b)  such a period has ended and an auditor or auditors should have been appointed but were not.

(3)  The company must send a copy of the proposed resolution to the person proposed to be appointed and to the outgoing auditor.

(4)  The outgoing auditor may, within 14 days after receiving the notice, make with respect to the proposed resolution representations in writing to the company (not exceeding a reasonable length) and request their circulation to members of the company.

(5)  The company must circulate the representations together with the copy or copies of the resolution circulated in accordance with section 291 (resolution proposed by directors) or section 293 (resolution proposed by members).

(6)  Where subsection (5) applies—

    (a)  the period allowed under section 293(3) for service of copies of the proposed resolution is 28 days instead of 21 days, and

    (b)  the provisions of section 293(5) and (6) (offences) apply in relation to a failure to comply with that subsection as in relation to a default in complying with that section.

(7)  Copies of the representations need not be circulated if, on the application either of the company or of any other person claiming to be aggrieved, the court is satisfied that the auditor is using the provisions of this section to secure needless publicity for defamatory matter.

The court may order the company's costs (in Scotland, expenses) on the application to be paid in whole or in part by the auditor, notwithstanding that he is not a party to the application.

(8)  If any requirement of this section is not complied with, the resolution is ineffective.

COMMENCEMENT DATE  6 April 2008[263]

**16.514.01**

Section 514 sets out the procedural steps that must be complied with where a written resolution is proposed appointing another auditor other than the company's auditor for the previous financial year (the outgoing auditor). If these procedural steps are not complied with the resolution is *ineffective* (section 514(8)).  **16.514.02**

The section provides that both the outgoing auditor and the new auditor must be sent a copy of the written resolution proposing to appoint the new auditor. Within a 14-day period of *receipt* of this notice the outgoing auditor may make representations regarding the proposed appointment of another auditor and request their circulation (section 514(4)). The company is required to circulate these representations with the proposed written resolutions unless the court orders otherwise in accordance with section 514(7).  **16.514.03**

Section 514(7) provides that the representations need not be circulated if the auditor 'is using the provisions of these sections to secure needless publicity or defamatory matter'. On the meaning of this term as well as the costs implications of making a strategic rather than well founded application see commentary in paragraphs 16.511.03 to 16.511.05 above.  **16.514.04**

Section 514(6) extends the time for service of written resolution proposed by the company's members to 28 days. The offences set forth in section 293(5) and (6) apply to the failure to comply with section 514(5). See further commentary to section 293(5) and (6).  **16.514.05**

## 515  Failure to re-appoint auditor: special notice required for resolution at general meeting

(1)  This section applies to a resolution at a general meeting of a company whose effect would be to appoint a person as auditor in place of a person (the 'outgoing auditor') whose term of office has ended, or is to end—  **16.515.01**

    (a)  in the case of a private company, at the end of the period for appointing auditors;

    (b)  in the case of a public company, at the end of the next accounts meeting.

---

[263] Companies Act 2006 (Commencement No 5, Transitional Provisions and Savings) Order 2007, SI 2007/3495, art 3. This provision applies to the appointments for financial years beginning after 6 April 2008.

(2) Special notice is required of such a resolution if—
  (a) in the case of a private company—
      (i) no period for appointing auditors has ended since the outgoing auditor ceased to hold office, or
      (ii) such a period has ended and an auditor or auditors should have been appointed but were not;
  (b) in the case of a public company—
      (i) there has been no accounts meeting of the company since the outgoing auditor ceased to hold office, or
      (ii) there has been an accounts meeting at which an auditor or auditors should have been appointed but were not.
(3) On receipt of notice of such an intended resolution the company shall forthwith send a copy of it to the person proposed to be appointed and to the outgoing auditor.
(4) The outgoing auditor may make with respect to the intended resolution representations in writing to the company (not exceeding a reasonable length) and request their notification to members of the company.
(5) The company must (unless the representations are received by it too late for it to do so)—
  (a) in any notice of the resolution given to members of the company, state the fact of the representations having been made, and
  (b) send a copy of the representations to every member of the company to whom notice of the meeting is or has been sent.
(6) If a copy of any such representations is not sent out as required because received too late or because of the company's default, the outgoing auditor may (without prejudice to his right to be heard orally) require that the representations be read out at the meeting.
(7) Copies of the representations need not be sent out and the representations need not be read at the meeting if, on the application either of the company or of any other person claiming to be aggrieved, the court is satisfied that the auditor is using the provisions of this section to secure needless publicity for defamatory matter.
  The court may order the company's costs (in Scotland, expenses) on the application to be paid in whole or in part by the outgoing auditor, notwithstanding that he is not a party to the application.

COMMENCEMENT DATE  6 April 2008[264]

**16.515.02**  Section 515 sets out the procedural steps that must be complied with where a resolution is intended to be moved at a general meeting to appoint another auditor other than the company's auditor for the previous financial year (the outgoing auditor).

**16.515.03**  Special notice will in the vast majority of cases be required (see section 515(2) on the conditions for the special notice requirement).[265]

**16.515.04**  The company must immediately send a copy of the intended resolution to both the outgoing auditor and the new auditor. The auditors may prepare written representations in relation to the intended resolution which the company must distribute to the members unless the company receives such representation too late for them to do so (section 515(5)(b)). If the representations are received prior to any notice of the resolution given by the company to its members, the company must inform its members in the notice that the auditor has made representations (section 515(5)(a)). Where such representations are not distributed to the shareholders, the auditor may insist that the representations be read out at the shareholders' meeting (section 515(6)).

**16.515.05**  Section 515(7) provides that the representations do not have to be read out or distributed to members if on application the court orders that the representations are being used by the auditor to 'secure needless publicity for defamatory matter'. The application may be made by the company or a person who claims she is 'aggrieved'. This provision is identical to section 511(6). Accordingly, please see paragraphs 16.511.03 to 16.511.05 regarding its interpretation and the applicable case law.

## Resignation of auditor

### 516  Resignation of auditor

**16.516.01**
(1) An auditor of a company may resign his office by depositing a notice in writing to that effect at the company's registered office.
(2) The notice is not effective unless it is accompanied by the statement required by section 519.

---

[264] Companies Act 2006 (Commencement No 5, Transitional Provisions and Savings) Order 2007, SI 2007/3495, art 3. This provision applies to the appointments for financial years beginning after 6 April 2008.
[265] See s 312 of the Companies Act 2006 (resolution requiring special notice).

(3)  An effective notice of resignation operates to bring the auditor's term of office to an end as of the date on which the notice is deposited or on such later date as may be specified in it.

COMMENCEMENT DATE  6 April 2008[266]

Sections 516 and 517 restate section 392 of the Companies Act 1985. Section 516 provides that an auditor may resign by depositing a notice of resignation with the company. That notice of resignation will not come into effect, however, unless accompanied by the auditor's statement of circumstances connected to the resignation or, in the alternative for a private company *only*, a statement that there are no such circumstances (section 519).                                                                                      **16.516.02**

## 517  Notice to registrar of resignation of auditor

(1)  Where an auditor resigns the company must within 14 days of the deposit of a notice of resignation send a copy of the notice to the registrar of companies.                                              **16.517.01**
(2)  If default is made in complying with this section, an offence is committed by—
    (a)  the company, and
    (b)  every officer of the company who is in default.
(3)  A person guilty of an offence under this section is liable—
    (a)  on conviction on indictment, to a fine;
    (b)  on summary conviction, to a fine not exceeding the statutory maximum and, for continued contravention, a daily default fine not exceeding one-tenth of the statutory maximum.

COMMENCEMENT DATE  6 April 2008[267]

Section 517 provides that the notice of resignation must be sent by the company to the registrar of companies within 14 days of deposit with the company. Failure to comply with this obligation is an offence committed by both the company and any officer in default.                                         **16.517.02**

## 518  Rights of resigning auditor

(1)  This section applies where an auditor's notice of resignation is accompanied by a statement of the circumstances connected with his resignation (see section 519).                                         **16.518.01**
(2)  He may deposit with the notice a signed requisition calling on the directors of the company forthwith duly to convene a general meeting of the company for the purpose of receiving and considering such explanation of the circumstances connected with his resignation as he may wish to place before the meeting.
(3)  He may request the company to circulate to its members—
    (a)  before the meeting convened on his requisition, or
    (b)  before any general meeting at which his term of office would otherwise have expired or at which it is proposed to fill the vacancy caused by his resignation,
a statement in writing (not exceeding a reasonable length) of the circumstances connected with his resignation.
(4)  The company must (unless the statement is received too late for it to comply)—
    (a)  in any notice of the meeting given to members of the company, state the fact of the statement having been made, and
    (b)  send a copy of the statement to every member of the company to whom notice of the meeting is or has been sent.
(5)  The directors must within 21 days from the date of the deposit of a requisition under this section proceed duly to convene a meeting for a day not more than 28 days after the date on which the notice convening the meeting is given.
(6)  If default is made in complying with subsection (5), every director who failed to take all reasonable steps to secure that a meeting was convened commits an offence.
(7)  A person guilty of an offence under this section is liable—
    (a)  on conviction on indictment, to a fine;
    (b)  on summary conviction to a fine not exceeding the statutory maximum.
(8)  If a copy of the statement mentioned above is not sent out as required because received too late or because of the company's default, the auditor may (without prejudice to his right to be heard orally) require that the statement be read out at the meeting.
(9)  Copies of a statement need not be sent out and the statement need not be read out at the meeting if, on the application either of the company or of any other person who claims to be aggrieved, the court is satisfied that the auditor is using the provisions of this section to secure needless publicity for defamatory matter.

---

[266] Companies Act 2006 (Commencement No 5, Transitional Provisions and Savings) Order 2007, SI 2007/3495, art 3. This provision applies to resignations occurring on or after 6 April 2008.
[267] Companies Act 2006 (Commencement No 5, Transitional Provisions and Savings) Order 2007, SI 2007/3495, art 3.

The court may order the company's costs (in Scotland, expenses) on such an application to be paid in whole or in part by the auditor, notwithstanding that he is not a party to the application.

(10) An auditor who has resigned has, notwithstanding his resignation, the rights conferred by section 502(2) in relation to any such general meeting of the company as is mentioned in subsection (3)(a) or (b) above.

In such a case the references in that section to matters concerning the auditor as auditor shall be construed as references to matters concerning him as a former auditor.

COMMENCEMENT DATE 6 April 2008[268]

**16.518.02** This section restates section 392A of the Companies Act 1985. The auditor's rights set forth in section 518 apply where the auditor has deposited a statement of the circumstances connected with his ceasing to be the company's auditor.

**16.518.03** The section provides the auditors with the right to call upon the directors to call a meeting to consider the auditor's explanation of the circumstances connected with the loss of office (section 518(2)). The directors must call such a meeting within 21 days of *the date the auditor's requisition was deposited* with the company for a date not later than 28 days from the date of the *notice convening the meeting*. Any director who does not take 'reasonable steps' to ensure that such a meeting is called is guilty of an offence (section 518(6)) and liable to a fine (section 518(7)). There are no reported cases on section 392A and, therefore, no judicial guidance on the meaning of 'reasonable steps' that would insulate directors from liability where no meeting is called.

**16.518.04** In addition, this section also provides auditors with a right to have the statement of circumstances distributed prior to the shareholder meeting, whether it is a requisitioned meeting or another meeting at which the auditors term would have expired or another auditor would be appointed (section 518(3)). Furthermore, any notice of the meeting must refer to the fact that a statement of circumstances has been deposited by the auditor (section 518(4)(b)). If the statement is not distributed as a result of late deposit or default on the part of the company the auditor has the right to require that the statement be read out at the meeting (section 518(8)).

**16.518.05** Section 518(9) provides that the statement of circumstances does not have to be read out or distributed to members if on application the court orders that the representations are being used by the auditor to 'secure needless publicity for defamatory matter'. The application may be made by the company or a person who claims she is 'aggrieved'. This provision is identical to section 511(6). Accordingly, please see paragraphs 16.511.03 to 16.511.05 regarding its interpretation and the applicable case law.

**16.518.06** Section 518(10) ensures that the rights conferred on the auditor by section 502(2) to receive notices and communications regarding, to attend and to be heard at shareholder meetings apply to the requisitioned meeting or other meeting at which the auditor's term would have expired or at which another auditor would be appointed. This is the case even though the auditor is no longer the company's auditor following his effective resignation.

### *Statement by auditor on ceasing to hold office*

### 519 Statement by auditor to be deposited with company

**16.519.01**
(1) Where an auditor of an unquoted company ceases for any reason to hold office, he must deposit at the company's registered office a statement of the circumstances connected with his ceasing to hold office, unless he considers that there are no circumstances in connection with his ceasing to hold office that need to be brought to the attention of members or creditors of the company.

(2) If he considers that there are no circumstances in connection with his ceasing to hold office that need to be brought to the attention of members or creditors of the company, he must deposit at the company's registered office a statement to that effect.

(3) Where an auditor of a quoted company ceases for any reason to hold office, he must deposit at the company's registered office a statement of the circumstances connected with his ceasing to hold office.

(4) The statement required by this section must be deposited—
(a) in the case of resignation, along with the notice of resignation;
(b) in the case of failure to seek re-appointment, not less than 14 days before the end of the time allowed for next appointing an auditor;
(c) in any other case, not later than the end of the period of 14 days beginning with the date on which he ceases to hold office.

---

[268] Companies Act 2006 (Commencement No 5, Transitional Provisions and Savings) Order 2007, SI 2007/3495, art 3. This provision applies to resignations occurring on or after 6 April 2008.

(5)  A person ceasing to hold office as auditor who fails to comply with this section commits an offence.

(6)  In proceedings for such an offence it is a defence for the person charged to show that he took all reasonable steps and exercised all due diligence to avoid the commission of the offence.

(7)  A person guilty of an offence under this section is liable—

(a)  on conviction on indictment, to a fine;

(b)  on summary conviction, to a fine not exceeding the statutory maximum.

[(8)  Where an offence under this section is committed by a body corporate, every officer of the body who is in default also commits the offence.

For this purpose—

(a)  any person who purports to act as director, manager or secretary of the body is treated as an officer of the body, and

(b)  if the body is a company, any shadow director is treated as an officer of the company.]ᵃ

AMENDMENTS

ᵃ  Inserted by the Companies Act 2006 (Consequential AMENDMENTS etc) Order 2008, SI 2008/948.

COMMENCEMENT DATE  6 April 2008[269]

This section, together with sections 520 and 521 of the Companies Act 2006 restate and amend section 394 of the Companies Act 1985. In contrast to section 394 of the 1985 Act, section 519 imposes different obligations on unquoted (section 519(1)) and quoted (section 519(3)) companies in relation to the statement of circumstances. No separate definition of quoted company is provided for Chapter 4 of Part 16. One presumes that the definition set forth in section 531 for Chapter 5 of Part 16 would be applicable.   **16.519.02**

Previously, under section 394 of the 1985 Act, in relation to quoted and unquoted companies, auditors were required to deposit a 'statement of *any* circumstances connected with his ceasing to hold office which *he considers* should be brought to the attention of the members or creditors of the company' or, in the alternative, '*if he considers* that there are no such circumstances, a statement that there are none' (emphasis added). Both of these options were grounded in the auditor's subjective opinion. In contrast, in relation to unquoted companies, the new section 519(1) removes the element of subjectivity from the first but not the second option. Accordingly, section 519(1) imposes an obligation on the auditors of an unquoted company to deposit a statement of *the* circumstances connected with his loss of office. These circumstances are not qualified by what he considers ought to be brought to the members' or creditors' attention. However, this mandatory obligation is subject to a subjective exception where the auditor 'considers that there are no circumstances ... that *need* to be brought to the attention of members or creditors' (emphasis added). The Government submitted that these changes alter the balance in favour of disclosure of circumstances because it provides for mandatory disclosure with a subjective exception, whereas the prior regulation under section 394 rendered the disclosure obligation contingent on the auditor's consideration. This is correct. Unless the exception applies—where there are *no* circumstances—the auditor has no discretion about what should be disclosed, he must disclose 'the circumstances', which is to be objectively assessed (see further paragraph 16.519.05 below). However, the use of the word 'need' instead of 'should' (as in section 394 of the Companies Act 1985) seems to undermine the Government's stated intention of encouraging disclosure. Arguably, what one needs to know is less than what one should know.   **16.519.03**

Where the auditor considers that there are no circumstances that the auditor needs to bring to the members' or creditors' attention, then he is required by section 519(2) to make a statement that there are no such circumstances.   **16.519.04**

Auditors of quoted companies are not provided with the exception which benefits auditors of private companies. The auditor of a quoted company must deposit a statement of the circumstances connected with his ceasing to hold office. In contrast to section 394 of the 1985 Act, the circumstances require an objective assessment. Section 519 does not provide auditors with a discretion to qualify these circumstances according to what they would consider to be material, or relevant, or that *should* be brought to the members and creditors attention. This provision was intentionally crafted to remove a role for auditor subjectivity. However, this creates some difficulty. Any assessment or report of circumstances involves the exercise of discretion in the determination of detail and, to some extent, relevance. Judicial guidance will be required to determine the scope and extent of the required disclosure.   **16.519.05**

Although section 519(5), which provides that an auditor fails to comply with this section is guilty of an offence, merely restates section 394A(1) of the Companies Act 1985, it takes on much more important significance with an objectively determined statement of circumstances. In this regard, the defence   **16.519.06**

---

[269]  Companies Act 2006 (Commencement No 5, Transitional Provisions and Savings) Order 2007, SI 2007/3495, art 3. This provision applies where the auditor ceases to hold office on or after 6 April 2008.

provided by section 519(6) is of particular importance, which provides a defence for auditors who can show that they took 'all reasonable steps' and exercised 'all due diligence' in the preparation and deposit of the statement or, in the case of a private company, a statement that there are no such circumstances.

### 520 Company's duties in relation to statement

**16.520.01**
(1) This section applies where the statement deposited under section 519 states the circumstances connected with the auditor's ceasing to hold office.

(2) The company must within 14 days of the deposit of the statement either—
  (a) send a copy of it to every person who under section 423 is entitled to be sent copies of the accounts, or
  (b) apply to the court.

(3) If it applies to the court, the company must notify the auditor of the application.

(4) If the court is satisfied that the auditor is using the [provisions of section 519] to secure needless publicity for defamatory matter—
  (a) it shall direct that copies of the statement need not be sent out, and
  (b) it may further order the company's costs (in Scotland, expenses) on the application to be paid in whole or in part by the auditor, even if he is not a party to the application.

The company must within 14 days of the court's decision send to the persons mentioned in subsection (2)(a) a statement setting out the effect of the order.

(5) If no such direction is made the company must send copies of the statement to the persons mentioned in subsection (2)(a) within 14 days of the court's decision or, as the case may be, of the discontinuance of the proceedings.

(6) In the event of default in complying with this section an offence is committed by every officer of the company who is in default.

(7) In proceedings for such an offence it is a defence for the person charged to show that he took all reasonable steps and exercised all due diligence to avoid the commission of the offence.

(8) A person guilty of an offence under this section is liable—
  (a) on conviction on indictment, to a fine;
  (b) on summary conviction, to a fine not exceeding the statutory maximum.

COMMENCEMENT DATE 6 April 2008[270]

**16.520.02**    Section 520 restates and amends section 394(4), (6), and (7) of the Companies Act 1985. It sets forth the obligations of the company where the auditor has deposited a statement of circumstances connected with his ceasing to hold office.

**16.520.03**    The primary duty placed on the company is to send a copy of the statement to every person who would, under section 423 of the Companies Act 2006, be entitled to receive a copy of the company's accounts (section 520(2)(a)). However, this obligation is suspended if the company applies to the court to obtain an order that the statement must not be sent out on the basis that the auditor is using the statement to 'secure needless publicity for defamatory matter' (section 520(2)(b) and (4)).

**16.520.04**    Under section 520(2) the company has 14 days from receipt of the statement of circumstances to either send out copies or make an application to court. In *P&P Design plc v PricewaterhouseCoopers*,[271] following its resignation as auditor, PricewaterhouseCoopers deposited a statement of circumstances. The company made an application to court on day 15, one day later than the 14-day time period under section 394 of the Companies Act 1985. The court held that the time period is a mandatory time period that cannot be extended by the court. Accordingly, an application made outside of the 14-day time period is an invalid application for the purposes of section 520(2), and if a company has not at such point sent out a copy of the statement pursuant to section 520(2) then its officers in default have committed an offence (section 520(6)).

**16.520.05**    If the company makes an application to court it must notify the auditor that it has done so (section 520(3)). To obtain an order relieving the company of its obligation to send out a copy of the statement and preventing the auditor from sending a copy to the registrar of companies (see section 521), the company must demonstrate that the auditor is using the 'provisions of section 519 to secure needless publicity for defamatory matter'. Apart from replacing the word 'statement' with 'provisions of section 519' (see square brackets), section 520(4) is identical to section 394(6) of the Companies Act 1985. Authority on the meaning of 'secure publicity for defamatory matter' under section 394(6) is, therefore, directly applicable. In *Jarvis plc v PricewaterhouseCoopers*,[272] *dicta* from Lightman J suggests that for proceedings instituted under section 394(6) 'the company must allege that the auditor acted in bad

---

[270] Companies Act 2006 (Commencement No 5, Transitional Provisions and Savings) Order 2007, SI 2007/3495, art 3. This provision applies where the auditor ceases to hold office on or after 6 April 2008.
[271] [2002] 2 BCLC 648.
[272] [2000] 2 BCLC 368.

faith in using the statement'. He noted further that 'this is a most serious allegation, tantamount to an allegation of dishonesty, against professional accountants'. In *Easier v Deloitte Touche LLP*,[273] the defendant successfully struck out an application under section 394 which did not contain any supporting evidence of *mal fides*. Evans-Lombe J held that allegations 'that were tantamount to allegations of fraud … should be supported by evidence of mala fides'.

In *Jarvis plc v PricewaterhouseCoopers*, the court noted that there was scope to abuse section 394 as by instituting proceeding the distribution of the statement is delayed. Lightman J noted that applicants under section 394 should cooperate in obtaining an expedited trial.    **16.520.06**

Where the company is successful in its application it must, within 14 days of the court's decision, send out statement detailing the effect of the court order to all persons who would be entitled to receive the accounts under section 423 of the Companies Act 2006 (section 520(4)). If the company is unsuccessful then a copy of the statement of circumstances must be sent 14 days of the decision (section 520(5)). Section 520(5) also clarifies that if there is a discontinuance of the application the 14 days clock commences from the date of discontinuance.    **16.520.07**

Section 520(4) provides a discretion to the court to order the auditor to pay the costs of the application. Such an order may be made even if the auditor is not a party to the application. No such order has been made in a reported case. Note that in *Jarvis v PricewaterhouseCoopers* the late discontinuance of the application by the company, together with Lightman J's concern about the applicant's behaviour, resulted in an award of costs against the company on an indemnity basis.    **16.520.08**

Section 520(6) provides that if the company fails to comply with the obligations set forth in section 520, every officer in default is guilty of an offence and liable to a fine. Previously under section 394A(4) it was the company *and* every officer in default who were guilty of an offence. Section 520(7) makes an important additional amendment by providing for a reasonable steps and due diligence defence that was not available under the Companies Act 1985.    **16.520.09**

### 521  Copy of statement to be sent to registrar

(1) Unless within 21 days beginning with the day on which he deposited the statement under section 519 the auditor receives notice of an application to the court under section 520, he must within a further seven days send a copy of the statement to the registrar.    **16.521.01**
(2) If an application to the court is made under section 520 and the auditor subsequently receives notice under subsection (5) of that section, he must within seven days of receiving the notice send a copy of the statement to the registrar.
(3) An auditor who fails to comply with subsection (1) or (2) commits an offence.
(4) In proceedings for such an offence it is a defence for the person charged to show that he took all reasonable steps and exercised all due diligence to avoid the commission of the offence.
(5) A person guilty of an offence under this section is liable—
  (a) on conviction on indictment, to a fine;
  (b) on summary conviction, to a fine not exceeding the statutory maximum.
[(6) Where an offence under this section is committed by a body corporate, every officer of the body who is in default also commits the offence.
  For this purpose—
  (a) any person who purports to act as director, manager or secretary of the body is treated as an officer of the body, and
  (b) if the body is a company, any shadow director is treated as an officer of the company.][a]

AMENDMENTS
[a] Inserted by the Companies Act 2006 (Consequential AMENDMENTS etc) Order 2008, SI 2008/948.

COMMENCEMENT DATE  6 April 2008[274]

Section 521(1) reformulates but does not substantively amend section 394(5) of the Companies Act 1985. It provides that if after 21 days from the date the auditor deposited the statement of circumstances with the company the auditor has received no notification of any court application, the auditor must send a copy of the statement to the registrar of companies within seven days of the expiry of the 21-day period. In *P&P design plc v PricewaterhouseCoopers*[275] the court addressed the situation where an application was made outside the 14-day period under section 520(2) but where the auditor received    **16.521.02**

---

[273] [2004] All ER (D) 378. 258 Companies Act 2006 (Commencement No 5, Transitional Provisions and Savings) Order 2007, SI 2007/3495, art 3. This provision applies where the auditor ceases to hold office on or after 6 April 2008.
[274] Companies Act 2006 (Commencement No 5, Transitional Provisions and Savings) Order 2007, SI 2007/3495, art 3. This provision applies where the auditor ceases to hold office on or after 6 April 2008.
[275] [2002] 2BCLC 648.

notice of the application prior to the expiry of the 21-day period under section 394(5) of the Companies Act. The court held that the auditor was still under an obligation to forward the statement to the registrar as although notice was received prior to the 21-day period it was an invalid application and the notice under section 394(5), and, therefore, under new section 520(1), must be a notice of a valid application.

**16.521.03**    If the company's application under section 520 fails or is discontinued the auditor must send a copy of the statement to the registrar of companies within seven days of notice of the court's decision or the discontinuance (section 521(2)).

**16.521.04**    The auditor commits an offence punishable by a fine if he fails to comply with section 521(1) or (2). The Act makes a reasonable steps and all due diligence defence available to the auditor (section 521(5)).

### 522  Duty of auditor to notify appropriate audit authority[276]

**16.522.01**
(1) Where—
   (a) in the case of a major audit, an auditor ceases for any reason to hold office, or
   (b) in the case of an audit that is not a major audit, an auditor ceases to hold office before the end of his term of office,
the auditor ceasing to hold office must notify the appropriate audit authority.
(2) The notice must—
   (a) inform the appropriate audit authority that he has ceased to hold office, and
   (b) be accompanied by a copy of the statement deposited by him at the company's registered office in accordance with section 519.
(3) If the statement so deposited is to the effect that he considers that there are no circumstances in connection with his ceasing to hold office that need to be brought to the attention of members or creditors of the company, the notice must also be accompanied by a statement of the reasons for his ceasing to hold office.
(4) The auditor must comply with this section—
   (a) in the case of a major audit, at the same time as he deposits a statement at the company's registered office in accordance with section 519;
   (b) in the case of an audit that is not a major audit, at such time (not being earlier than the time mentioned in paragraph (a)) as the appropriate audit authority may require.
(5) A person ceasing to hold office as auditor who fails to comply with this section commits an offence.
(6) If that person is a firm an offence is committed by—
   (a) the firm, and
   (b) every officer of the firm who is in default.
(7) In proceedings for an offence under this section it is a defence for the person charged to show that he took all reasonable steps and exercised all due diligence to avoid the commission of the offence.
(8) A person guilty of an offence under this section is liable—
   (a) on conviction on indictment, to a fine;
   (b) on summary conviction, to a fine not exceeding the statutory maximum.

COMMENCEMENT DATE  6 April 2008[277]

**16.522.02**    This new section imposes on the auditors new notification requirements to regulatory authorities following the auditor's loss of office. This section, together with section 523 of the Companies Act 2006, ensures the compliance of UK company law with Article 38(2) of the EU Directive 2006/43 on statutory audits of annual accounts and consolidated accounts.[278]

**16.522.03**    The obligations imposed by section 522 on auditors distinguish between major audits and non-major audits. The obligations apply both to auditors who provide major audits and cease to hold office for *any reason* and auditors who provide non-major audits and *either* resign or are dismissed.

**16.522.04**    Major audits are defined in section 525 of the Companies Act 2006 as being audits of *either* companies which are admitted to the official list *or* 'any other person in whose financial condition there is a major public interest' (section 525(2)). 'Major public interest' is not defined. The Act provides for further guidance in regard to the meaning of major audit to be provided by the 'appropriate audit authority' (section 525(3)), which in this case is expected to be the Professional Oversight Board for Accounting, a subsidiary of the Financial Reporting Council (section 525(3)). Accordingly, these obligations apply

---

[276] For a very useful flowchart explaining CA 2006, ss 522–525 see the FRC's website at ⟨http://www.frc.org.uk/pob/regulation/auditfirms.cfm⟩.
[277] Companies Act 2006 (Commencement No 5, Transitional Provisions and Savings) Order 2007, SI 2007/3495, art 3. This provision applies where the auditor ceases to hold office on or after 6 April 2008.
[278] [2006] OJ L157/87.

to, amongst others, auditors of listed companies who resign, are dismissed, or are not re-appointed, or auditors of non-listed companies who either resign or are dismissed. They do not apply to auditors of non-listed companies that are not re-appointed following the expiry of the term in office.

Where the provisions of section 522 apply, the auditor must inform the 'appropriate audit authority that he has ceased to hold office'. The appropriate audit authority is defined in section 525. In relation to a major audit, the appropriate audit authority is either the Secretary of State or a person to whom the Secretary of State delegates his authority (section 525(1)(a)(ii)). It is expected that this person will be the Professional Oversight Board for Accounting. In relation to a non-major audit, it is expected that the appropriate audit authority will be the professional association, such as the Institute of Chartered Accountants in England and Wales, of which the auditor is a member. Section 522(4) sets forth the time periods for complying with this notification requirement.          **16.522.05**

Where the auditor has deposited a statement of circumstances in accordance with section 519 of the Companies Act 2006 he must also include a copy of that statement with the notice to the appropriate audit authority (section 522(2)). However, where the auditor has deposited a statement that there are no such circumstances, then he must provide the appropriate audit authority with a 'statement of reasons for his ceasing to hold office'.          **16.522.06**

It should be noted that the fact that the company has made an application to court to obtain an order that the statement of representations does not have to be sent to the persons entitled to receive copies of accounts under section 423 or even where it has obtained such a court order, has no effect on the auditor's obligation to notify the appropriate audit authority or to attach a copy of such statement.          **16.522.07**

Failure to comply with this section is an offence punishable by a fine. The section makes clear that the audit firm as well as every officer of the firm who is in default may commit an offence. Officer is defined in section 1261(1) to include a manager or the members of a body corporate where the members manage the body corporate. Certainly this would include the engagement partner, and arguably any other partner involved in the audit or the supervision of the audit. Both audit firm and officer may benefit from a reasonable steps and due diligence defence (section 522(7)).          **16.522.08**

## 523  Duty of company to notify appropriate audit authority

(1)  Where an auditor ceases to hold office before the end of his term of office, the company must notify the appropriate audit authority.          **16.523.01**

(2)  The notice must—
    (a)  inform the appropriate audit authority that the auditor has ceased to hold office, and
    (b)  be accompanied by—
        (i)  a statement by the company of the reasons for his ceasing to hold office, or
        (ii)  if the copy of the statement deposited by the auditor at the company's registered office in accordance with section 519 contains a statement of circumstances in connection with his ceasing to hold office that need to be brought to the attention of members or creditors of the company, a copy of that statement.

(3)  The company must give notice under this section not later than 14 days after the date on which the auditor's statement is deposited at the company's registered office in accordance with section 519.

(4)  If a company fails to comply with this section, an offence is committed by—
    (a)  the company, and
    (b)  every officer of the company who is in default.

(5)  In proceedings for such an offence it is a defence for the person charged to show that he took all reasonable steps and exercised all due diligence to avoid the commission of the offence.

(6)  A person guilty of an offence under this section is liable—
    (a)  on conviction on indictment, to a fine;
    (b)  on summary conviction, to a fine not exceeding the statutory maximum.

COMMENCEMENT DATE  6 April 2008[279]

This new section imposes on the company new notification requirements to regulatory authorities following the auditor's loss of office before the end of his term in office. This section, together with section 522 of the Companies Act 2006, ensures the compliance of UK company law with Article 38(2) of the Directive (EC) 2006/43 on statutory audits of annual accounts and consolidated accounts.[280]          **16.523.02**

The obligations imposed by section 523 on companies do not, in contrast to section 522, explicitly distinguish between major audits and non-major audits. However, they only apply to companies when          **16.523.03**

---

[279] Companies Act 2006 (Commencement No 5, Transitional Provisions and Savings) Order 2007, SI 2007/3495, art 3. This provision applies where the auditor ceases to hold office on or after 6 April 2008.
[280] [2006] OJ L157/87.

the auditors *either* resign or are dismissed. They do not apply to auditors that are not re-appointed following the expiry of his term in office.

**16.523.04**   Section 523(2) provides that when the auditor has ceased to hold office the company must notify the appropriate audit authority and such notification must include *either* a statement by the company of the reasons why the auditor ceases to hold office or a copy of statement of circumstances deposited by the auditor, if he deposited such a statement. In contrast to section 522, which makes the statement of reasons conditional on there being no statement of circumstances, section 523(2) appears to provide the company with a choice even where there is such a statement of circumstances. One would have thought that the company may take this option where the auditor's statement of circumstances cast negative light over the company's accounting practices and the company wishes to present additional information or an alternative viewpoint.

**16.523.05**   Although section 523(2) does not rely explicitly on the distinction between major and non-major audit, it implicitly relies upon it to determine the appropriate authority to whom notification may be made. As per section 525 in relation to a major audit, this will be either the Secretary of State or, it is expected, the Public Accounting Oversight Board; and in the case of a non-major audit the appropriate audit authority will be the professional association, such as the Institute of Chartered Accountants in England and Wales, of which the auditor is a member.

**16.523.06**   The company must comply with its notification obligations to the appropriate audit authority within 14 days of the auditor depositing the statement of circumstances or the statement that there are no such circumstances (section 523(3)).

**16.523.07**   The company as well as every officer in default commits an offence punishable by fine if they fail to comply with these notification provisions (section 523(4)). A reasonable steps and all due diligence defence is made available (section 523(5)).

### 524 Information to be given to accounting authorities

**16.524.01**   (1) The appropriate audit authority on receiving notice under section 522 or 523 of an auditor's ceasing to hold office—
     (a) must inform the accounting authorities, and
     (b) may if it thinks fit forward to those authorities a copy of the statement or statements accompanying the notice.
   (2) The accounting authorities are—
     (a) the Secretary of State, and
     (b) any person authorised by the Secretary of State for the purposes of section 456 (revision of defective accounts: persons authorised to apply to court).
   (3) If either of the accounting authorities is also the appropriate audit authority it is only necessary to comply with this section as regards any other accounting authority.
   (4) If the court has made an order under section 520(4) directing that copies of the statement need not be sent out by the company, sections 460 and 461 (restriction on further disclosure) apply in relation to the copies sent to the accounting authorities as they apply to information obtained under section 459 (power to require documents etc).

COMMENCEMENT DATE 6 April 2008[281]

**16.524.02**   This new section provides that the appropriate audit authority must inform the accounting authorities about the auditor's loss of office. This is a mandatory requirement (section 524(1)(a)). The accounting authorities are both the Secretary of State and, currently, the Financial Reporting Review Panel (FRRP). In addition, the section provides the appropriate audit authority with a discretion as to whether, along with the information regarding loss of office, it also forwards any statement of circumstances and/or any statement of reasons which accompanied the notice provided by the auditor and/or the company (section 524(1)(b)). The appropriate audit authority may do so 'if it thinks fit'. No further guidance is provided on how this discretion should be exercised. Given the Financial Reporting Council's focus on 'joined-up regulation',[282] one would expect in relation to the Professional Oversight Board, the FRRP's sister organization, a readiness to forward this information to the FRRP.

**16.524.03**   Where the company obtains an order under section 520(4) providing that copies of the statement of circumstances need not be sent out, the restrictions on information disclosure imposed by sections 460 and 461 apply to the copy of the statements sent to the Secretary of State and the FRRP.

---

[281] Companies Act 2006 (Commencement No 5, Transitional Provisions and Savings) Order 2007, SI 2007/3495, art 3. This provision applies where the auditor ceases to hold office on or after 6 April 2008.

[282] See comments from Sir Bryan Nicholson, the Chairman of the Financial Reporting Council reported in 'MG Rover may have to restate accounts regulatory inquiry', *Financial Times* (18 April 2005).

## 525  Meaning of 'appropriate audit authority' and 'major audit'

<sup>a</sup>(1) In sections 522, 523 and 524 'appropriate audit authority' means—

    (a) in the case of a major audit [(other than one conducted by an Auditor General)]—

        (i) the Secretary of State, or

        (ii) if the Secretary of State has delegated functions under section 1252 to a body whose functions include receiving the notice in question, that body;

    (b) in the case of an audit [(other than one conducted by an Auditor General)] that is not a major audit, the relevant supervisory body.

    (c) in the case of an audit conducted by an Auditor General, the Independent Supervisor.

'Supervisory body' and 'Independent Supervisor' have the same meaning as in Part 42 (statutory auditors) (see section 1217 and 1228).]

(2) In sections 522 and this section 'major audit' means a statutory audit conducted in respect of—

    (a) a company any of whose securities have been admitted to the official list (within the meaning of Part 6 of the Financial Services and Markets Act 2000 (c. 8)), or

    (b) any other person in whose financial condition there is a major public interest.

(3) In determining whether an audit is a major audit within subsection (2)(b), regard shall be had to any guidance issued by any of the authorities mentioned in subsection (1).

AMENDMENTS

<sup>a</sup> As amended by the Statutory Auditors and Third Country Auditors Regulations 2007, SI 2007/3494.

COMMENCEMENT DATE  6 April 2008[283]

This is a new section. For commentary on the appropriate audit authority please see paragraph 16.522.05 above.  **16.525.02**

For commentary on the meaning of major audit please see paragraph 16.522.04 above.  **16.525.03**

*Supplementary*

## 526  Effect of casual vacancies

If an auditor ceases to hold office for any reason, any surviving or continuing auditor or auditors may continue to act.  **16.526.01**

COMMENCEMENT DATE  6 April 2008[284]

This section restates section 388(2) of the Companies Act 1985. Where there are two or more joint auditors and one of them ceases to hold office this section provides that the surviving auditors may continue to act.  **16.526.02**

# CHAPTER 5
# QUOTED COMPANIES: RIGHT OF MEMBERS TO RAISE AUDIT CONCERNS AT ACCOUNTS MEETING

## 527  Members' power to require website publication of audit concerns

(1) The members of a quoted company may require the company to publish on a website a statement setting out any matter relating to—  **16.527.01**

    (a) the audit of the company's accounts (including the auditor's report and the conduct of the audit) that are to be laid before the next accounts meeting, or

    (b) any circumstances connected with an auditor of the company ceasing to hold office since the previous accounts meeting,

that the members propose to raise at the next accounts meeting of the company.

(2) A company is required to do so once it has received requests to that effect from—

    (a) members representing at least 5% of the total voting rights of all the members who have a relevant right to vote (excluding any voting rights attached to any shares in the company held as treasury shares), or

    (b) at least 100 members who have a relevant right to vote and hold shares in the company on which there has been paid up an average sum, per member, of at least £100.

---

[283] Companies Act 2006 (Commencement No 5, Transitional Provisions and Savings) Order 2007, SI 2007/3495, art 3. This provision applies where the auditor ceases to hold office on or after 6 April 2008.
[284] Companies Act 2006 (Commencement No 5, Transitional Provisions and Savings) Order 2007, SI 2007/3495, art 3. This provision applies where the vacancy occurs on or after 6 April 2008.

See also section 153 (exercise of rights where shares held on behalf of others).

(3)  In subsection (2) a 'relevant right to vote' means a right to vote at the accounts meeting.

(4)  A request—

(a)  may be sent to the company in hard copy or electronic form,

(b)  must identify the statement to which it relates,

(c)  must be authenticated by the person or persons making it, and

(d)  must be received by the company at least one week before the meeting to which it relates.

(5)  A quoted company is not required to place on a website a statement under this section if, on an application by the company or another person who claims to be aggrieved, the court is satisfied that the rights conferred by this section are being abused.

(6)  The court may order the members requesting website publication to pay the whole or part of the company's costs (in Scotland, expenses) on such an application, even if they are not parties to the application.

COMMENCEMENT DATE  6 April 2008[285]

**16.527.02**    Section 527 is a new section and provides shareholders in quoted companies[286] with a new right to require the company to publish on a website maintained by or on behalf of the company (section 528(2)) a statement that relates either to the audit of the company's accounts to be addressed at the next accounts meeting or to the circumstances connected to the auditor ceasing to hold office and which the shareholders intend to raise at the next accounts meeting.

**16.527.03**    This section requires that the company is only required to place such a statement on the website where requested by the requisite number of shareholders. The function of this provision is similar to the obligation placed upon the company to circulate members' statements under section 292(3) of the Companies Act 2006, namely, to facilitate shareholder communication and activism. Section 527(2) requires that the company must publish the statement on the website where it receives requests *either* from members representing at least 5 per cent of the members' voting rights (excluding any shares held in treasury) or at least 100 members who have the right to vote at an accounts meeting and whose shares in aggregate have a minimum average paid up share capital of £100.

**16.527.04**    A request from shareholders sent to the company may be sent in hard copy or electronic form (section 527(4)(a)) and only amounts to a 'request' for the purposes of section 527 that would require the company to act where it identifies the statement that is to be published on the website, it is authenticated by the person making the statement, and it is received at least one week prior to the meeting. Accordingly, where the person making the posted statement is not a member of shareholder group making the request, a form of authentication will be required from the maker of the statement before it is posted.

**16.527.05**    Whilst encouraging shareholder communication and activism, arguably this provision also generates scope for abusive or vexatious activity by minority shareholders who may wish to publish information that damages the company and whose web publication would not be viewed as in the best interests of the company. To address these concerns, section 527(5) provides for the company to make an application to court to obtain an order that the company is not required to publish the statement. The court will grant such an order where it is satisfied that that the rights conferred by this section are being abused. No further guidance on 'being abused' is provided by the section. The notion of rights being abused was deployed in the Companies Act 1985 in several contexts, for example, in relation to the similar context in which the court may order that shareholders' statements do not have to be circulated.[287] However, there were no reported cases on the meaning of abuse of rights in those differing contexts. If the company makes such an application to prevent website publication, the court has a discretion to make an award of costs against the requesting shareholders, even though they may not be party to the application. The threat of a costs award represents a degree of deterrence against an abuse of these rights.

### 528  Requirements as to website availability

**16.528.01**    (1)  The following provisions apply for the purposes of section 527 (website publication of members' statement of audit concerns).

(2)  The information must be made available on a website that—

(a)  is maintained by or on behalf of the company, and

---

[285] Companies Act 2006 (Commencement No 5, Transitional Provisions and Savings) Order 2007, SI 2007/3495, art 3. Subsection (1)(a) and (b) applies to accounts and auditors appointed for financial years beginning after 6 April 2008, respectively.

[286] Defined in s 531 of CA 2006.

[287] S 377(3) of CA 1985 (see s 295 of CA 2006). See also s 304(4) (directors right to protest removal), s 391A(6) (rights of auditors who are removed or not re-appointed); s 392A(7) (rights of resigning auditors) of CA 1985.

     (b)  identifies the company in question.
(3)  Access to the information on the website, and the ability to obtain a hard copy of the information from the website, must not be conditional on the payment of a fee or otherwise restricted.
(4)  The statement—
     (a)  must be made available within three working days of the company being required to publish it on a website, and
     (b)  must be kept available until after the meeting to which it relates.
(5)  A failure to make information available on a website throughout the period specified in subsection (4)(b) is disregarded if—
     (a)  the information is made available on the website for part of that period, and
     (b)  the failure is wholly attributable to circumstances that it would not be reasonable to have expected the company to prevent or avoid.

COMMENCEMENT DATE  6 April 2008[288]

This section regulates the availability of the website on which the shareholder statement must be posted.   **16.528.02**

Section 528(3) provides that the information posted pursuant to section 527 must be available on the website free of charge, and access to it must not be restricted in any way, including any restriction on printing a hard copy of the information from the website.   **16.528.03**

The information must be available on the website within three working days of the company being required to publish it, ie three days from the date it receives a request that complies with requirements set forth in section 527(2) and (4). It must remain available on the website until after the relevant shareholder meeting. Failure to comply with section 528's availability provisions is an offence committed by any officer in default punishable by fine (section 530). Any period in which the information is not available will be disregarded and will not, therefore, amount to a breach of section 528, provided that the information has been available for part of the required time period, and any period when it is not available is 'wholly attributable' to 'circumstances that it would not be reasonable to have expected the company to prevent or avoid'. The language 'prevent or avoid' suggests that website downtime attributable to unforeseen technical problems or to resolve such problems will benefit from this provision. The word avoid would suggest that regular unavailability due to the failure to remedy the recurrent technical problems or to make the required investment in order to remedy such problems may not benefit from this exception.   **16.528.04**

### 529  Website publication: company's supplementary duties

(1)  A quoted company must in the notice it gives of the accounts meeting draw attention to—   **16.529.01**
     (a)  the possibility of a statement being placed on a website in pursuance of members' requests under section 527, and
     (b)  the effect of the following provisions of this section.
(2)  A company may not require the members requesting website publication to pay its expenses in complying with that section or section 528 (requirements in connection with website publication).
(3)  Where a company is required to place a statement on a website under section 527 it must forward the statement to the company's auditor not later than the time when it makes the statement available on the website.
(4)  The business which may be dealt with at the accounts meeting includes any statement that the company has been required under section 527 to publish on website.

COMMENCEMENT DATE  6 April 2008[289]

This is a new section. Section 529(1) imposes an obligation on a quoted company, when it gives notice of the accounts meeting, to inform shareholders that a statement may be placed on the website. It also requires, at the time of giving notice of the meeting, that the company inform the shareholders that any expenses of website publication of a shareholder statement will not be borne by the members; the auditors will be informed about the statement; and the statement may be addressed at the shareholder meeting (section 529(1)(b)). Section 529(2) prevents the company from deterring shareholder requests pursuant to section 527 by preventing the imposition of the costs of posting the statement on the requesting shareholders. Section 529(3) provides that the company must forward the shareholder statement to be posted on the website to the company's auditor and must do so not later that the time   **16.529.02**

---

[288] Companies Act 2006 (Commencement No 5, Transitional Provisions and Savings) Order 2007, SI 2007/3495, art 3.
[289] Companies Act 2006 (Commencement No 5, Transitional Provisions and Savings) Order 2007, SI 2007/3495, art 3.

it posts the statement on the website. Section 529(4) clarifies that the accounts meeting may deal with the posted statement.

### 530  Website publication: offences

**16.530.01**
    (1)  In the event of default in complying with
        (a)  section 528 (requirements as to website publication), or
        (b)  section 529 (companies' supplementary duties in relation to request for website publication),
        an offence is committed by every officer of the company who is in default.
    (2)  A person guilty of an offence under this section is liable—
        (a)  on conviction on indictment, to a fine;
        (b)  on summary conviction, to a fine not exceeding the statutory maximum.

COMMENCEMENT DATE  6 April 2008[290]

**16.530.02**    This is a new section. Any failure to comply with section 528 or section 529 is an offence committed by every officer in default and is a default punishable by fine.

### 531  Meaning of 'quoted company'

**16.531.01**
    (1)  For the purposes of this Chapter a company is a quoted company if it is a quoted company in accordance with section 385 (quoted and unquoted companies for the purposes of Part 15) in relation to the financial year to which the accounts to be laid at the next accounts meeting relate.
    (2)  The provisions of subsections (4) to (6) of that section (power to amend definition by regulations) apply in relation to the provisions of this Chapter as in relation to the provisions of that Part.

COMMENCEMENT DATE  6 April 2008[291]

**16.531.02**    This is a new section. See commentary to section 385.

## CHAPTER 6
## AUDITORS' LIABILITY

### *Voidness of provisions protecting auditors from liability*

### 532  Voidness of provisions protecting auditors from liability

**16.532.01**
    (1)  This section applies to any provision—
        (a)  for exempting an auditor of a company (to any extent) from any liability that would otherwise attach to him in connection with any negligence, default, breach of duty or breach of trust in relation to the company occurring in the course of the audit of accounts, or
        (b)  by which a company directly or indirectly provides an indemnity (to any extent) for an auditor of the company, or of an associated company, against any liability attaching to him in connection with any negligence, default, breach of duty or breach of trust in relation to the company of which he is auditor occurring in the course of the audit of accounts.
    (2)  Any such provision is void, except as permitted by—
        (a)  section 533 (indemnity for costs of successfully defending proceedings), or
        (b)  sections 534 to 536 (liability limitation agreements).
    (3)  This section applies to any provision, whether contained in a company's articles or in any contract with the company or otherwise.
    (4)  For the purposes of this section companies are associated if one is a subsidiary of the other or both are subsidiaries of the same body corporate.

COMMENCEMENT DATE  6 April 2008[292]

**16.532.02**    Section 532 restates and amends section 310 of the Companies Act 1985 as amended by section 19(2) of the Companies (Audit, Investigations and Community Enterprise) Act 2004. It provides that any provision, whether set forth in the articles or in a contract or otherwise, (section 532(3)) which purports to exempt or to directly or indirectly indemnify[293] the auditor from liability for negligence,

---

[290] Companies Act 2006 (Commencement No 5, Transitional Provisions and Savings) Order 2007, SI 2007/3495, art 3.
[291] Companies Act 2006 (Commencement No 5, Transitional Provisions and Savings) Order 2007, SI 2007/3495, art 3.
[292] Companies Act 2006 (Commencement No 5, Transitional Provisions and Savings) Order 2007, SI 2007/3495, art 3.
[293] In *The Fanti and Padre Island (No 2)* [1991] 2 AC 1, Lord Goff held that 'a promise of indemnity is simply a promise to hold the indemnified person harmless against a specified loss or expense'.

default, breach of duty, or breach of trust arising from the audit of the company's accounts is void unless such exemption or indemnification is the product of a permitted limited liability agreement pursuant to sections 534 to 536 or is permitted indemnification for costs where the auditor successfully defends proceedings (section 533). The prohibition on indemnification extends to indemnifying the auditor of an associated company. Associated companies are those companies that have a parent-subsidiary[294] relationship or share the same parent company.

The prohibition applies to provisions contained in the 'company's articles or in any contract with the company or otherwise' (section 532(3)). This restates the scope of the prohibition set forth in section 310 of the Companies Act 1985. In *Burgoine v Waltham Forest London Council*[295] the court, *obiter dicta*, considered the meaning of the words of 'or otherwise' in relation to section 310 prior to its amendment by the 2004 Act.[296] The question was whether the reference to 'or otherwise' extends the prohibition on indemnification to parties other than the company. Neuberger J held that the words 'or otherwise' are to be interpreted 'eiusdem generic with the preceding words' and, therefore, that 'it can be said with some force that there is a genus, namely an arrangement between the company and its officers, which restricts what might otherwise be said to be a very wide meaning of the words "or otherwise"'. **16.532.03**

## *Indemnity for costs of defending proceedings*

### 533  Indemnity for costs of successfully defending proceedings

Section 532 (general voidness of provisions protecting auditors from liability) does not prevent a company from indemnifying an auditor against any liability incurred by him— **16.533.01**

   (a)  in defending proceedings (whether civil or criminal) in which judgment is given in his favour or he is acquitted, or
   (b)  in connection with an application under section 1157 (power of court to grant relief in case of honest and reasonable conduct) in which relief is granted to him by the court.

COMMENCEMENT DATE  6 April 2008[297]

Section 533 restates section 310(3)(b) of the Companies Act 1985. This section provides a specific exemption to the general prohibition under section 532 and allows the company to indemnify the auditor for costs incurred in civil or criminal proceedings where the auditor prevails or for the costs incurred in relation to an application for relief from liability pursuant to section 1157 of the Companies Act 2006, where the auditors acted honestly and reasonably. It does not, however, permit the company to advance any costs to the auditor prior to judgment being given in his favour.[298] **16.533.02**

Under section 310(3)(a) of the Companies Act 1985 the company was authorized to purchase insurance for the auditor against any liability covered by section 310. This exemption is not repeated in section 533 or elsewhere in the Companies Act 2006. Given that the prohibition in section 532 extends to any indirect indemnification, this option of purchasing insurance is no longer available. **16.533.03**

## *Liability limitation agreements*

### 534  Liability limitation agreements

   (1)  A 'liability limitation agreement' is an agreement that purports to limit the amount of a liability owed to a company by its auditor in respect of any negligence, default, breach of duty or breach of trust, occurring in the course of the audit of accounts, of which the auditor may be guilty in relation to the company. **16.534.01**
   (2)  Section 532 (general voidness of provisions protecting auditors from liability) does not affect the validity of a liability limitation agreement that—
      (a)  complies with section 535 (terms of liability limitation agreement) and of any regulations under that section, and
      (b)  is authorised by the members of the company (see section 536).
   (3)  Such an agreement—
      (a)  is effective to the extent provided by section 537, and
      (b)  is not subject—

---

[294]  Defined in s 1159 of CA 2006. This definition includes subsidiaries of subsidiaries.
[295]  [1997] 2 BCLC 612.
[296]  Prior to the amendment of CA 1985 by the Companies (Audit, Investigation and Community Enterprise) Act 2004, the prohibition set forth in s 310 was applicable to both officers of the company and auditors.
[297]  Companies Act 2006 (Commencement No 5, Transitional Provisions and Savings) Order 2007, SI 2007/3495, art 3.
[298]  See further *Branch v Bagley* [2004] EWHC 426.

(i)  in England and Wales or Northern Ireland, to section 2(2) or 3(2)(a) of the Unfair Contract Terms Act 1977 (c. 50);

(ii) in Scotland, to section 16(1)(b) or 17(1)(a) of that Act.

COMMENCEMENT DATE  6 April 2008[299]

### 535  Terms of liability limitation agreement

**16.535.01**

(1)  A liability limitation agreement—

(a)  must not apply in respect of acts or omissions occurring in the course of the audit of accounts for more than one financial year, and

(b)  must specify the financial year in relation to which it applies.

(2)  The Secretary of State may by regulations—

(a)  require liability limitation agreements to contain specified provisions or provisions of a specified description;

(b)  prohibit liability limitation agreements from containing specified provisions or provisions of a specified description.

'Specified' here means specified in the regulations.

(3)  Without prejudice to the generality of the power conferred by subsection (2), that power may be exercised with a view to preventing adverse effects on competition.

(4)  Subject to the preceding provisions of this section, it is immaterial how a liability limitation agreement is framed.

In particular, the limit on the amount of the auditor's liability need not be a sum of money, or a formula, specified in the agreement.

(5)  Regulations under this section are subject to negative resolution procedure.

COMMENCEMENT DATE  6 April 2008[300]

**16.535.02**  Section 534 defines a 'liability limitation agreement' and provides that irrespective of the general prohibition of exemption from and indemnification of liability set forth in section 532, such agreements are valid to the extent that they comply with the regulation of its terms set forth in section 535 and are duly authorized pursuant to section 536.

**16.535.03**  Pursuant to the definition set forth in section 534(1), a liability limitation agreement relates to liability owed by the auditor to the company in relation to *any* negligence, default, breach of duty, or breach of trust arising in relation to the audit of the company's accounts. It does not exclude any type of egregious breach such as a willful breach of duty. However, the nature of the negligence or the breach could affect the effectiveness of the limitation (see commentary on section 537 of the Companies Act 2006).

**16.535.04**  The definition provides that it is an agreement that 'purports' to limit liability rather than actually limits liability. Therefore, a valid liability limitation agreement is not necessarily effective in accordance with its terms. Its effectiveness is subject to section 537 which overrides the provisions of the agreement to the extent that they limit liability to less than what 'is fair and reasonable in all the circumstances of the case' (see further paragraphs 16.537.02 to 16.537.05 below).

**16.535.05**  Section 534(3) clarifies that regulation of exclusion clauses in sections 2(2) and 3(2)(a) of the Unfair Contract Terms Act 1977 are inapplicable to liability limitation agreements.

**16.535.06**  Section 535(1) requires a liability limitation agreement may only apply to acts or omissions that could result in liability in any one financial year. It also provides that the agreement must set forth the financial year to which it is applicable. There is nothing currently in section 535 that would prevent the company entering into several agreements relating to acts or omissions in previous financial years (one agreement for each year). However, apart from the time restriction set forth in section 535(1), section 535 contains no other restrictions on the terms of a liability limitation agreement. To the contrary, section 535(4) clarifies that there are currently no such restrictions: 'subject to the preceding provisions of this section, it is immaterial how a limited liability agreement is framed'. During the consideration of the Companies Bill in the Grand Committee of the House of Lords concern was raised that the use of the word 'amount' in several sections of the Act (for example, section 534(1)) placed an implicit prohibition on proportionate liability agreements that aimed to limit the auditors liability to his proportionate share of the responsibility for any loss incurred by the company. The reasoning behind this observation was that amount indicates a specific sum or cap and would not enable the flexibility inherent in a proportionate liability agreement. Several members of the House of Lords suggested that the word 'amount' should be replaced with 'extent'. The Government did not accept this proposal;

---

[299] Companies Act 2006 (Commencement No 5, Transitional Provisions and Savings) Order 2007, SI 2007/3495, art 3.

[300] Companies Act 2006 (Commencement No 5, Transitional Provisions and Savings) Order 2007, SI 2007/3495, art 3.

however, to clarify that a liability limitation agreement could adopt a proportionate liability approach section 535(4) now provides that a liability limitation need not refer to 'a sum of money' (a cap) or 'a formula' (for example, a fee multiple). In this regard, see also the evolution of the definition of 'principal terms' (section 536(4) below). It should be noted that given the flexibility which the Act provides in relation to the terms of an agreement, the agreement could provide for both a proportionality and a cap or fee multiple restriction, for example, proportional liability not to exceed of a specified fee multiple.[301]

Although, as noted above, the only restrictions on the terms of the liability limitation agreement are the time period restrictions in section 535(1), section 535(2) provides the power to make regulations which specify additional required or prohibited terms in a liability limitation agreement. One of the motivating factors for introducing this power was concern that the evolution of these agreements could negatively impact on the ability of audit firms outside of the Big Four to compete. This concern receives legislative expression in section 535(3) which explicitly provides that this power may be exercised to address such competitive problems.

**16.535.07**

### 536  Authorisation of agreement by members of the company

(1) A liability limitation agreement is authorised by the members of the company if it has been authorised under this section and that authorisation has not been withdrawn.

**16.536.01**

(2) A liability limitation agreement between a private company and its auditor may be authorised—
    (a) by the company passing a resolution, before it enters into the agreement, waiving the need for approval,
    (b) by the company passing a resolution, before it enters into the agreement, approving the agreement's principal terms, or
    (c) by the company passing a resolution, after it enters into the agreement, approving the agreement.

(3) A liability limitation agreement between a public company and its auditor may be authorised—
    (a) by the company passing a resolution in general meeting, before it enters into the agreement, approving the agreement's principal terms, or
    (b) by the company passing a resolution in general meeting, after it enters into the agreement, approving the agreement.

(4) The 'principal terms' of an agreement are terms specifying, or relevant to the determination of—
    (a) the kind (or kinds) of acts or omissions covered,
    (b) the financial year to which the agreement relates, or
    (c) the limit to which the auditor's liability is subject.

(5) Authorisation under this section may be withdrawn by the company passing an ordinary resolution to that effect—
    (a) at any time before the company enters into the agreement, or
    (b) if the company has already entered into the agreement, before the beginning of the financial year to which the agreement relates. Paragraph (b) has effect notwithstanding anything in the agreement.

COMMENCEMENT DATE  6 April 2008[302]

This is a new section. Pursuant to section 534(2)(b) the validity of a liability limitation agreement is dependent on authorization by the company's shareholders. Section 536 sets out the specific requirements of such approval. For both private companies (section 536(2)(b) and (c)) and public companies (section 536(3)) the agreement may be authorized by *either* a resolution which approves the 'principal terms' of the agreement prior to the company entering into the agreement or approving the agreement once it has been entered into. In addition, for private companies only (section 536(2)(a)) the agreement may be authorized by a resolution passed prior to entering into the agreement which waives the approval requirement.

**16.536.02**

Section 536(4) provides a definition of the 'principal terms' which could be approved by the general meeting of a public or private company. They include the acts and omissions covered, the applicable financial year, and the liability limit. The original Company Law Reform Bill referred to 'the amount to which the auditor's liability is limited'. The final text of this section reflects the concern noted above that such a reference to amount excluded a proportionate liability agreement. It is clear that from the

**16.536.03**

---

[301] For specimen terms of Liability Limitation Agreements, see FRC Guidance on Auditor Liability Limitation Agreements (FRC, 2008), appendices B–D ⟨http://www.frc.org.uk/documents/pagemanager/frc/Auditor_Liability_Limitation_Agreements/FRC%20ALLA%20Guidance%20June%202008%20final.pdf⟩.

[302] Companies Act 2006 (Commencement No 5, Transitional Provisions and Savings) Order 2007, SI 2007/3495, art 3. The Order provides that 'a resolution passed before 6 April 2008 authorizing a liability limitation agreement is effective for the purpose of section 536 if it complies with the requirements of that section'.

current wording of section 536(4)(c) and section 535(4) that such proportionate liability agreements are valid provided they comply with the requirements of section 534(2).

**16.536.04**    The authorization granted by the shareholders in accordance with section 536 may be revoked by ordinary resolution to that effect at any time prior to the company entering into the agreement or, where the agreement has been entered into, prior to the commencement of the financial year, that is prior to the auditor being able to commence work for the financial year to which the agreement relates.

### 537  Effect of liability limitation agreement

**16.537.01**    (1)  A liability limitation agreement is not effective to limit the auditor's liability to less than such amount as is fair and reasonable in all the circumstances of the case having regard (in particular) to—
  (a)  the auditor's responsibilities under this Part,
  (b)  the nature and purpose of the auditor's contractual obligations to the company, and
  (c)  the professional standards expected of him.
(2)  A liability limitation agreement that purports to limit the auditor's liability to less than the amount mentioned in subsection (1) shall have effect as if it limited his liability to that amount.
(3)  In determining what is fair and reasonable in all the circumstances of the case no account is to be taken of—
  (a)  matters arising after the loss or damage in question has been incurred, or
  (b)  matters (whenever arising) affecting the possibility of recovering compensation from other persons liable in respect of the same loss or damage.

COMMENCEMENT DATE  6 April 2008[303]

**16.537.02**    A liability limitation agreement will only be effective in limiting the auditor's liability to the company to the extent that the limitation does not result in auditor liability which is less than what is 'fair and reasonable in all the circumstances of the case'. If such liability is less than what is 'fair and reasonable in all the circumstances of the case' the limitation agreement is not voided, thereby removing any limitation; rather the limitation in the agreement will be replaced by such a 'fair and reasonable' amount (section 537(2)). However, if the terms of any liability limitation agreement result in the auditor being liable for more than what would be 'fair and reasonable in all the circumstances of the case' then section 537 will not alter such liability.

**16.537.03**    The central issues in section 537 are first, how to determine what is 'fair and reasonable', and second, how to identify what types of circumstance will affect what is fair and reasonable. Other statutory provisions that deploy the 'fair and reasonable' standard in relation to contractual limitations on liability are of no direct assistance in the application of the standard under section 537. However, the approach that the courts should take to the assessment of 'fair and reasonable' under the Unfair Contract Terms Act 1977 is instructive as to how the courts may approach the 'fair and reasonable' assessment under section 537 of the Companies Act 2006. In *George Mitchell (Chesterhall) Ltd v Finney Lock Seeds Ltd*,[304] Lord Goff summarized the approach as follows:

> It would not be accurate to describe such a decision as an exercise of discretion. But a decision under any of the provisions referred to will have this in common with the exercise of a discretion, that, in having regard to the various matters to which ... section 11 of the Act of 1977 direct attention, the court must entertain a whole range of considerations, put them in the scales on one side or the other, and decide at the end of the day on which side the balance comes down.

**16.537.04**    As compared to the Unfair Contract Terms Act 1977, which uses 'fair and reasonable' to determine whether a contractual liability limitation is valid (rather than effective),[305] the Companies Act 2006 provides a more limited non-exclusive list of factors that are relevant to the determination of whether the liability limitation is fair and reasonable. Specifically the Act mentions the auditor's responsibilities under Part 16 of the Companies Act 2006, 'the nature and purpose of the auditor's contractual obligations to the company', and the professional standards expected of the auditor. The wording of the provision suggests that these three factors must always be considered; however, they represent a non-exclusive list of factors and other considerations may be relevant to the court's determination. The Act provides no other guidelines in this regard and leaves it to the courts to make a case by case assessment. It is submitted, however, that this 'fair and reasonable' test provides the courts with an opportunity to consider, as one of several factors, the auditor's proportionate fault. In making a

---

[303]  Companies Act 2006 (Commencement No 5, Transitional Provisions and Savings) Order 2007, SI 2007/3495, art 3.
[304]  [1983] 2 AC 803.
[305]  See s 11 of and Sch 2 to the Unfair Contract Terms Act 1977.

determination about fairness, the extent of the auditor's blame or responsibility for the loss would seem a natural consideration. Such an approach would, however, imply an element of proportionality into those agreements that rely on caps or fee multiples.

Interestingly, these specified factors mirror certain of the rules/considerations that determine the       **16.537.05**
extent of the auditor's liability in negligence or the breach of the contractual duty of skill and care in the first place. For example, failure to comply with professional standards may be relevant to whether or not the auditor's contractual duty of skill and care has been breached. Furthermore, as the House of Lords in *South Australia Asset Management Corp v York Montague Ltd* (SAAMCO)[306] clarified, breach of this duty of care does not result in the auditor being liable for all the consequences of this breach.[307] A company may not have continued to trade and incur losses *but for* the auditor's negligence, but this does not mean that the auditor is responsible for all or part of these losses. To determine which consequences the auditor would be responsible for, the court must determine what is the scope of the auditor's duty of care. In relation to the contractual duty of care a central consideration in this determination is the auditor's contractual obligations to the company. Lord Hoffmann put it as follows: 'the scope of the duty, in the sense of the consequences for which the [service provider] is responsible is that which the law regards as best giving effect to the express obligations assumed by the [service provider].'[308] Accordingly, to the extent that the terms of the auditor's engagement delimit the types of risk for which the auditors can be held responsible, for example, continued trading losses, the concept of the scope of the duty of care performs a type of proportionate liability limitation function. Accordingly, having been taken account of in the determination of liability these contractual under-takings will be reconsidered by the court in determining whether any liability limitation is 'fair and reasonable'. Given the current state of English duty of care jurisprudence, to the extent that the courts place particular weight on this contractual factor one wonders whether the impact of liability limitation agreements will be significant. If the contractual delimitation of risk is a central factor in the determi-nation of minimum auditor liability exposure (that is, what is fair and reasonable) then in many instances this will be very similar to the actual liability pursuant to a contractually delimited scope of the duty of care.

Any decision made by a court as to what is fair and reasonable is, it is submitted, likely to treated       **16.537.06**
deferentially by an appeal court. The approach taken to appellate review under the 'fair and reasonable' standard set forth in the Unfair Contracts Terms Act 1977 is apposite to section 537. In this regard, in *George Mitchell (Chesterhall) Ltd v Finney Lock Seeds Ltd*,[309] Lord Goff held:

> There will sometimes be room for a legitimate difference of judicial opinion as to what the answer should be, where it will be impossible to say that one view is demonstrably wrong and the other demonstrably right. It must follow, in my view, that, when asked to review such a decision on appeal, the appellate court should treat the original decision with the utmost respect and refrain from interference with it unless satisfied that it proceeded upon some erroneous principle or was plainly and obviously wrong.

Section 537(3) provides that in assessing what is 'fair and reasonable in all the circumstances of the       **16.537.07**
case', neither matters which arise after the loss has been incurred nor the scope to recover damages from other potentially responsible persons, may be taken into account.

## 538  Disclosure of agreement by company

(1)  A company which has entered into a liability limitation agreement must make such disclosure in       **16.538.01**
    connection with the agreement as the Secretary of State may require by regulations.
(2)  The regulations may provide, in particular, that any disclosure required by the regulations shall be made—
    (a)  in a note to the company's annual accounts (in the case of its individual accounts) or in such manner as is specified in the regulations (in the case of group accounts), or
    (b)  in the directors' report.
(3)  Regulations under this section are subject to negative resolution procedure.

COMMENCEMENT DATE  6 April 2008[310]

---

[306]  [1997] AC 191.

[307]  [1997] AC 191, 214.

[308]  [1997] AC 191, 212. See also, *Aneco Reinsurance Undertaking v Johnson & Higgins* [2002] 1 Lloyd's Rep 157, 163.

[309]  [1983] 2 AC 803.

[310]  Companies Act 2006 (Commencement No 5, Transitional Provisions and Savings) Order 2007, SI 2007/3495, art 3.

**16.538.02**   Section 538 is a new section and provides that companies who enter into a liability limitation agreement must disclose such agreement in accordance with regulations issued by the Secretary of State. Section 538(2) provides, non-exclusively, that such regulations may require disclosure in a note to the company's annual accounts or in the director's report. The Companies (Disclosure of Auditor Remuneration and Liability Limitation Agreements) Regulations 2008, SI 2008/489 provide for such disclosure through a note to the company's accounts.[311] The accounts in which the disclosure of the agreement is made must be the accounts for the financial year to which the agreement relates, unless agreement is reached too late for it to be 'reasonably practicable to do so', in which case it should be be made in the following year's accounts.[312]

### [538A  Meaning of 'corporate governance statement' etc

**16.538A.01**
    (1)  In this Part 'corporate governance statement' means the statement required by rules 7.2.1 to 7.2.11 in the Disclosure Rules and Transparency Rules sourcebook issued by the Financial Services Authority.

    (2)  Those rules were inserted by Annex C of the Disclosure Rules and Transparency Rules Sourcebook (Corporate Governance Rules) Instrument 2008 made by the Authority on 26 June 2008 (FSA 2008/32).

    (3)  A 'separate' corporate governance statement means one that is not included in the directors' report.][a]

AMENDMENTS

[a]  Inserted by the Companies Act 2006 (Accounts, Reports and Audit) Regulations 2009 SI 2009/1581, reg 8, as from 27 June 2009, in relation to financial years beginning on or after 29 June 2008 which have not ended before 27 June 2009.

COMMENCEMENT DATE  27 June 2009

**16.538A.02**   Where a company prepares a separate corporate governance statement, the auditor has a duty under section 497A to report on that corporate governance statement and state whether it is consistent with the annual accounts.[313] This section defines 'corporate governance statement' and 'separate' corporate governance statement for the purposes of this Part. A more detailed discussion of this definition can be found in the commentary on section 472A.

### 539  Minor definitions[a]

**16.539.01**   In this Part—

'e-money issuer' means a person who has permission under Part 4 of the Financial Services and Markets Act 2000 (c. 8) to carry on the activity of issuing electronic money within the meaning of article 9B of the Financial Services and Markets Act 2000 (Regulated Activities) Order 2001 (S.I. 2001/544);

    […][b]

['MiFID investment firm' means an investment firm within the meaning of Article 4.1.1 of Directive 2004/39/EC of the European Parliament and of the Council of 21 April 2004 on markets in financial instruments, other than—

    (a)  a company to which that Directive does not apply by virtue of Article 2 of that Directive,

    (b)  a company which is an exempt investment firm within the meaning of regulation 4A(3) of the Financial Services and Markets Act 2000 (Markets in Financial Instruments) Regulations 2007, and

    (c)  any other company which fulfils all the requirements set out in regulation 4C(3) of those Regulations;][c]

'qualified', in relation to an auditor's report (or a statement contained in an auditor's report), means that the report or statement does not state the auditor's unqualified opinion that the accounts have been properly prepared in accordance with this Act or, in the case of an undertaking not required to prepare accounts in accordance with this Act, under any corresponding legislation under which it is required to prepare accounts; 'turnover', in relation to a company, means the amounts derived from the provision of goods and services falling within the company's ordinary activities, after deduction of—

    (a)  trade discounts,

    (b)  value added tax, and

    (c)  any other taxes based on the amounts so derived;

---

[311]  Companies (Disclosure of Auditor Remuneration and Liability Limitation Agreements) Regulations 2008, SI 2008/489 reg 8(1).

[312]  Companies (Disclosure of Auditor Remuneration and Liability Limitation Agreements) Regulations 2008, SI 2008/489, reg 8(2) and (3).

[313]  See s 471.

'UCITS management company' has the meaning given by the Glossary forming part of the Handbook made by the Financial Services Authority under the Financial Services and Markets Act 2000.

AMENDMENTS and Notes

[a] This section applies with modification to LLPs by reg 47 of the Limited Liability Partnerships (Accounts and Audit) (Application of Companies Act 2006) Regulations 2008, SI 2008/1911.

[b] Repealed by the Markets in Financial Instruments Directive (Consequential Amendments) Regulations 2007, SI 2007/2932.

[c] Inserted by the Markets in Financial Instruments Directive (Consequential Amendments) Regulations 2007, SI 2007/2932.

COMMENCEMENT DATE   6 April 2008[314]

Section 539 defines several terms used in Part 16 of the ActIt should be noted that in 2013 legislation   **16.539.02**
will come into force creating two new regulatory authorities, the Prudential Regulation Authority and Financial Conduct Authority, and the Financial Services Authority will cease to exist. The FSA Handbook will be subsumed, with amendments, into the Handbooks of the new authorities. It should also be noted that in October 2011 the European Commission published legislative proposals, known as MiFID II, which will result in the repeal of Directive 2004/39/EC.

---

[314] Companies Act 2006 (Commencement No 5, Transitional Provisions and Savings) Order 2007, SI 2007/3495, art 3(1) for financial years beginning on or after 6 April 2008.

# 17

# A COMPANY'S SHARE CAPITAL

## Companies Act 2006

## PART 17
## A COMPANY'S SHARE CAPITAL

This Part of the Act, together with Part 18, sets out the detailed statutory law relating to the shares and **17.0.01** share capital of a company. It is clearly only applicable to companies with a share capital. One of the key aims of the Company Law Review was to modernize and simplify the law relating to shares and share capital, although to some extent this was constrained by the provisions of the Second Company Law Directive.[1] This has been the subject of an amending Directive in 2006.[2] Most of the changes under this amending Directive were optional, but UK law has been amended to reflect them, as described later in this chapter and Chapter 18.[3] This was mostly done on final implementation of Parts 17 and 18 of the Act on 1 October 2009.[4]

The Second Directive requires, among other things, public companies to file statements of their issued **17.0.02** share capital if there is no authorized capital and to have par value shares, and it restricts their ability to provide financial assistance for an acquisition of their shares. Although the Companies Act 2006 abolished the prohibition on private companies providing financial assistance, and made other changes for their benefit, including introducing the ability for them to reduce capital without going to court, and although it also abolished the concept of authorized capital for both public and private limited companies, it does not distinguish between the different types of company in most other ways. So, in particular, the shares in private companies limited by shares, as well as in public companies, must still have a par value and all companies limited by shares must file statements of capital on incorporation and following any alteration.

---

[1] Directive (EEC) 77/91 on coordination of safeguards which, for the protection of the interests of members and others, are required by Member States of companies within the meaning of the second paragraph of Article 58 of the Treaty, in respect of the formation of public limited liability companies and the maintenance and alteration of their capital, with a view to making such safeguards equivalent [1977] OJ L26/1.

[2] Directive (EC) 2006/68 amending Council Directive 77/91/EEC as regards the formation of public limited liability companies and the maintenance and alteration of their capital [2006] OJ L264/32.

[3] The one change that was compulsory was originally implemented by amending the Companies Act 1985, s 136(3) with effect from 6 April 2008, requiring creditors objecting to a reduction of capital to show that there was a real likelihood that the reduction would result in the company being unable to discharge its debt or claim when it fell due: the Companies (Reduction of Capital) (Creditor Protection) Regulations 2008, SI 2008/719. See now s 646(1), as amended.

[4] See the Companies (Share Capital and Acquisition by Company of its Own Shares) Regulations 2009, SI 2009/2022, which amended ss 562(5), 646(1), 694(5), 697(4), 700(4), and 701(5) and repealed s 725.

CHAPTER 1
SHARES AND SHARE CAPITAL OF A COMPANY

*Shares*

### 540 Shares

**17.540.01**
  (1) In the Companies Acts 'share', in relation to a company, means share in the company's share capital.
  (2) A company's shares may no longer be converted into stock.
  (3) Stock created before the commencement of this Part may be reconverted into shares in accordance with section 620.
  (4) In the Companies Acts—
      (a) references to shares include stock except where a distinction between share and stock is express or implied, and
      (b) references to a number of shares include an amount of stock where the context admits of the reference to shares being read as including stock.

COMMENCEMENT DATE 1 October 2009[5]

**17.540.02**   This section had no equivalent in previous companies legislation, although much of it was derived from the definition section (section 744) in the Companies Act 1985, in particular the meaning of 'share' for the purpose of the legislation in subsection (1) and the references in subsection (4). Subsection (1) is more of a description than a definition of a share in a company, a matter that is further discussed in the notes to section 541.

**17.540.03**   As recommended by the Steering Group of the Company Law Review (CLRG),[6] the long-standing ability to convert shares into stock was abolished by subsection (2) with effect from 1 October 2009,[7] and section 620 no longer permits an alteration of share capital to that effect. Stock existing on that date may be reconverted into shares under that section.

### 541 Nature of shares

**17.541.01**
  The shares or other interest of a member in a company are personal property (or, in Scotland, moveable property) and are not in the nature of real estate (or heritage).

COMMENCEMENT DATE 1 October 2009[8]

**17.541.02**   This section was derived from section 182(1)(a) of the Companies Act 1985 and its predecessors. It describes the fundamental attribute of a share or other interest of a member in a company, namely that it is personal (or, in Scotland, moveable) property and not real property.[9] As such it is a chose in action.[10] Neither this section nor section 540 provides a real definition of a 'share' for which it is necessary to look at the case law. Perhaps the best-known definition is that of Farwell J in *Borland's Trustee v Steel Brothers & Co Ltd*:[11] 'A share is the interest of a shareholder in the company, measured by a sum of money for the purpose of liability in the first place and of interest in the second, but also consisting of a series of mutual covenants entered into by all the shareholders inter se in accordance with section 16 of the Companies Act 1862.'[12]

**17.541.03**   The fact that a share is an item of property means that *prima facie* the rights attached to it, particularly any voting rights, can be exercised without regard to the interests of other shareholders, although there are limits on this principle in the context of certain resolutions of shareholders, especially resolutions

---

[5] Companies Act 2006 (Commencement No 8, Transitional Provisions and Savings) Order 2008, SI 2008/2860, art 3(k).
   [6] See *Modern Company Law for a Competitive Economy: Company Formation and Capital Maintenance*, October 1999, para 3.13.
   [7] See also the Companies Act 2006 (Commencement No 8, Transitional Provisions and Savings) Order 2008, SI 2008/2860, Sch 2, para 41.
   [8] Companies Act 2006 (Commencement No 8, Transitional Provisions and Savings) Order 2008, SI 2008/2860, art 3(k).
   [9] Note that the phrase 'personal property' is used rather than 'personal estate' in the previous legislation, although the word 'estate' is kept in relation to 'real estate'.
   [10] *R v Williams* [1942] AC 541 at 549; *Colonial Bank v Whinney* (1886) 11 App Cas 426.
   [11] [1901] 1 Ch 279 at 288.
   [12] This is now s 33 of the 2006 Act; see para 3.33.02.

to amend the articles of association[13] and resolutions ratifying directors' breaches of duty where the votes of the relevant directors cannot be counted.[14] The principle is also subject to the exercise by the court of its powers under various provisions, particularly Part 30 of the Act concerning unfair prejudice claims.[15]

The other basic characteristic of a share, namely its transferability, is covered separately in section 554.  **17.541.04**

## 542  Nominal value of shares

(1)  Shares in a limited company having a share capital must each have a fixed nominal value.  **17.542.01**

(2)  An allotment of a share that does not have a fixed nominal value is void.

(3)  Shares in a limited company having a share capital may be denominated in any currency, and different classes of shares may be denominated in different currencies.
      But see section 765 (initial authorised minimum share capital requirement for public company to be met by reference to share capital denominated in sterling or euros).

(4)  If a company purports to allot shares in contravention of this section, an offence is committed by every officer of the company who is in default.

(5)  A person guilty of an offence under this section is liable—
      (a)  on conviction on indictment, to a fine;
      (b)  on summary conviction, to a fine not exceeding the statutory maximum.

COMMENCEMENT DATE 1 October 2009[16]

This section had no equivalent in earlier Companies Acts. The requirement in subsection (1) that  **17.542.02** shares have a fixed nominal value is a consequence of the abolition of the requirement for companies limited by shares to have an authorized or nominal share capital in their memorandum of association[17] and because of the EC requirement for public companies to have shares that have nominal or par values.[18] It was decided to apply this requirement to all companies limited by shares. It should be noted that although the concept of authorized share capital has been abolished, an application for registration of a company limited by shares must still include a statement of initial shareholdings detailing the number and nominal value of the shares to be taken by the subscribers to the memorandum.[19] Subsequent sections impose an obligation to file a statement of capital in the event of an alteration. Any allotment of a no par value share is void and officers responsible are guilty of a criminal offence. The nominal value (and any premium payable) is the limit of the liability of a member of a company limited by shares.[20] There is no requirement that the nominal value corresponds with the lowest or any particular denomination of a currency.[21]

At the same time the opportunity has been taken to put into statutory form the principle that shares  **17.542.03** may be denominated in any currency[22] and that different classes of shares may be denominated in different currencies. However, the minimum capital required of public companies[23] must be satisfied in pounds sterling or euros, as the proviso to subsection (3) indicates.

## 543  Numbering of shares

(1)  Each share in a company having a share capital must be distinguished by its appropriate number,  **17.543.01** except in the following circumstances.

(2)  If at any time—
      (a)  all the issued shares in a company are fully paid up and rank *pari passu* for all purposes, or
      (b)  all the issued shares of a particular class in a company are fully paid up and rank *pari passu* for all purposes,

---

[13]  See para 3.21.02

[14]  See s 239; see para 10.239.02.

[15]  See para 30.994.02.

[16]  Companies Act 2006 (Commencement No 8, Transitional Provisions and Savings) Order 2008, SI 2008/2860, art 3(k).

[17]  See para 2.8.02.

[18]  See Second Company Law Directive 77/91, Art 8.

[19]  See s 10 at para 2.10.02.

[20]  Insolvency Act 1986, s 74.

[21]  *Re Rotaprint plc*, unreported, 21 July 1986, cited in *Re Scandinavian Bank Group plc* [1987] BCLC 220 at 224, where a reduction of capital divided a share capital into shares of ½p each after that sum had ceased to be legal tender. See also the Australian decision in *Re Australian Pacific Technology Ltd* (1994) 13 ACSR 478, where shares had a nominal value of 0.01 cents each.

[22]  *Re Scandinavian Bank Group plc* [1987] BCLC 220.

[23]  See ss 761–767; see paras 20.761.01–20.767.04.

none of those shares need thereafter have a distinguishing number so long as it remains fully paid up and ranks *pari passu* for all purposes with all shares of the same class for the time being issued and fully paid up.

COMMENCEMENT DATE 1 October 2009[24]

**17.543.02**   This section is derived from section 182(2) of the Companies Act 1985, but has been restated in a rather more expansive way. The requirement for the numbering of shares is self-explanatory, but it is in practice unlikely to apply in many cases, as the vast majority of shares today are issued as fully paid up, and thus the exception in subsection (2) will apply.

### 544  Transferability of shares

**17.544.01**
(1)  The shares or other interest of any member in a company are transferable in accordance with the company's articles.
(2)  This is subject to—
    (a)  the Stock Transfer Act 1963 (c. 18) or the Stock Transfer Act (Northern Ireland) 1963 (c.24 (N.I.)) (which enables securities of certain descriptions to be transferred by a simplified process), and
    (b)  regulations under Chapter 2 of Part 21 of this Act (which enable title to securities to be evidenced and transferred without a written instrument).
(3)  See Part 21 of this Act generally as regards share transfers.

COMMENCEMENT DATE 6 April 2008[25]

**17.544.02**   This section is derived from section 182(1)(b) of the 1985 Act and has been redrafted in a more modern manner, also incorporating the reference to the Northern Irish Stock Transfer Act. In cross-referring to Part 21, subsection (3) incorporates the other formalities required for a transfer of shares.

**17.544.03**   As an item of property, a share or other interest in a company is *prima facie* freely transferable.[26] Provided the transferee is legally competent to take the shares,[27] a transferor can, for example, transfer shares in order to increase his voting power.[28] As subsection (1) makes clear, the manner of transfer is to be determined by the articles, subject to the Stock Transfer Act 1963 and the Uncertificated Securities Regulations 2001.[29] In practice the shares in a private company are often subject to restrictions on transfer.[30] These will commonly take one or both of two forms, namely articles giving directors the power to refuse registration of a transfer and articles conferring rights of pre-emption on other shareholders. There is considerable case law concerning the nature and effect of such restrictions,[31] but attention is drawn now to section 771 which requires a company refusing to register a transfer to provide reasons for that.

### 545  Companies having a share capital

**17.545.01**   References in the Companies Acts to a company having a share capital are to a company that has power under its constitution to issue shares.

COMMENCEMENT DATE 1 October 2009[32]

**17.545.02**   There was no equivalent to this section in the previous legislation. It is self-explanatory and is obviously relevant to the many provisions, especially in Part 17, that apply only to companies with a share capital.

---

[24]  Companies Act 2006 (Commencement No 8, Transitional Provisions and Savings) Order 2008, SI 2008/2860, art 3(k).

[25]  Companies Act 2006 (Commencement No 5, Transitional Provisions and Savings) Order 2007, SI 2007/3495, art 2.

[26]  *Re Smith, Knight & Co, Weston's Case* (1868) 4 Ch App 20; *Re National Provincial Marine Insurance, Gilbert's Case* (1870) 5 Ch App 559, 565; *Re Cawley & Co* (1889) 42 Ch D 209; *Pinkett v Wright* (1842) 2 Hare 120, 130; *Re Copal Varnish Co Ltd* [1917] 2 Ch 349; *Re Bede Steam Shipping Co Ltd* [1917] 1 Ch 123; *Re Smith & Fawcett Ltd* [1942] Ch 304; *Greenhalgh v Mallard* [1943] 2 All ER 234.

[27]  *Re Blakely Ordnance Co, Lumsden's Case* (1868) 4 Ch App 31, 34.

[28]  *Re Stranton Iron and Steel Co* (1873) LR 16 Eq 559; *Moffatt v Farquhar* (1878) 7 Ch D 591; *Cannon v Trask* (1875) LR 20 Eq 669; *Pender v Lushington* (1877) 6 Ch D 70; *Re Bede Steam Shipping Co Ltd* [1917] 1 Ch 123.

[29]  SI 2001/3755. See Chapter 49. These were made under s 209 of the Companies Act (CA) 1989. They still apply for the purposes of Chapter 2 of Part 21.

[30]  Before amendments made by the CA 1980, a restriction on transfer was compulsory for private companies.

[31]  See eg *Gore-Browne on Companies*, Ch 23.

[32]  Companies Act 2006 (Commencement No 8, Transitional Provisions and Savings) Order 2008, SI 2008/2860, art 3(k).

## 546  Issued and allotted share capital

17.546.01

(1)  References in the Companies Acts—
    (a)  to 'issued share capital' are to shares of a company that have been issued;
    (b)  to 'allotted share capital' are to shares of a company that have been allotted.
(2)  References in the Companies Acts to issued or allotted shares, or to issued or allotted share capital, include shares taken on the formation of the company by the subscribers to the company's memorandum.

COMMENCEMENT DATE  1 October 2009[33]

This section did not have an equivalent in the previous legislation, but it provides a useful introduction to the later provisions on share capital, particularly in the light of the abolition of the concept of authorized share capital,[34] which means that a company with the power to issue shares will henceforth have only allotted share capital and issued share capital.[35] Obviously this Part of the Act dealing with share capital is applicable only to companies limited by shares. The descriptions in subsection (1) of issued share capital and allotted share capital must be read in the light of section 558, which provides that shares are allotted when a person acquires the unconditional right to be included in the company's register of members in respect of them. Thus, the time when shares are allotted is governed by the formation of a binding contract between the company and the prospective shareholder, but they are not issued until the allottee's name is entered in the register of members.[36]  **17.546.02**

Note that by subsection (2) any references to issued or allotted shares or share capital includes shares taken by the subscribers to the memorandum on the formation of the company.  **17.546.03**

### *Share capital*

## 547  Called-up share capital

In the Companies Acts—  **17.547.01**

'called-up share capital', in relation to a company, means so much of its share capital as equals the aggregate amount of the calls made on its shares (whether or not those calls have been paid), together with—
    (a)  any share capital paid up without being called, and
    (b)  any share capital to be paid on a specified future date under the articles, the terms of allotment of the relevant shares or any other arrangements for payment of those shares; and
'uncalled share capital' is to be construed accordingly.

COMMENCEMENT DATE  1 October 2009[37]

These definitions of called-up share capital and uncalled-up share capital were previously in the interpretation part of the Companies Acts, most recently section 737 of the Companies Act 1985. Called-up share capital is of particular importance in the context of the share capital that must be stated in a company's balance sheet, and is also of particular relevance for public companies that become subject to a serious loss of capital within section 656. It is thought that this does not just refer to the amount of the nominal value of shares that have been allotted or issued. Frequently a shareholder is liable under the terms on which shares were allotted to pay more than the nominal value of those shares, in other words including a premium, so that the amount called-up or uncalled will refer to his total liability, and the price of shares may well be paid without there being a 'call';[38] as paragraph (a) makes clear, shares paid for other than in response to a call are nonetheless included in the definition of called-up share capital. Further it does not matter that calls have actually been paid.  **17.547.02**

---

[33]  Companies Act 2006 (Commencement No 8, Transitional Provisions and Savings) Order 2008, SI 2008/2860, art 3(k).

[34]  See para 2.8.02.

[35]  Note also that reserve capital, previously permitted by s 120 of CA 1985, can no longer be created, that section having been repealed and not replaced. However, the validity of a special resolution passed to create reserve capital before 1 October 2009 is preserved: the Companies Act 2006 (Commencement No 8, Transitional Provisions and Savings) Order 2008, SI 2008/2860, Sch 2, para 67.

[36]  See *National Westminster Bank v IRC* [1995] 1 AC 119. There is Canadian authority to the effect that shares can be issued before share certificates are prepared: *Associated Stevedoring Co v Callanan* (1968) 70 DLR (2d) 687.

[37]  Companies Act 2006 (Commencement No 8, Transitional Provisions and Savings) Order 2008, SI 2008/2860, art 3(k).

[38]  Calls are not specifically referred to in the Act, but standard articles (see eg Art 16 of the Table A produced under the 1985 Act) and art 54 of the model articles for public companies prescribed under the 2006 Act) will give the directors the power to make calls.

**17.547.03** In addition called-up share capital does not either refer just to the actual amount already paid or called in respect of such shares, since by paragraph (b) it includes any amounts that a shareholder is already contractually obliged to pay at a defined date, whether that is under the articles, the terms on which the shares were allotted, or any other arrangements.

### 548 Equity share capital

**17.548.01** In the Companies Acts 'equity share capital', in relation to a company, means its issued share capital excluding any part of that capital that, neither as respects dividends nor as respects capital, carries any right to participate beyond a specified amount in a distribution.

COMMENCEMENT DATE 1 October 2009[39]

**17.548.02** This definition of equity share capital was previously contained in the general definition section (section 744) of the Companies Act 1985. It is what is also often referred to as ordinary share capital, thus excluding shares that have specified and limited participation rights *either* as regards profits *or* as regards return of capital or both. So shares that are preferred as to dividend, but not as to capital, are not equity shares, and vice versa. The same is true as regards shares that have any other limited rights as to dividend, return of capital, or both, eg rights that are deferred to the rights of other shares. Preference shares that have preferred rights in both respects are clearly not equity shares.

# CHAPTER 2
## ALLOTMENT OF SHARES: GENERAL PROVISIONS

### *Power of directors to allot shares*

### 549 Exercise by directors of power to allot shares etc

**17.549.01**
(1) The directors of a company must not exercise any power of the company—
   (a) to allot shares in the company, or
   (b) to grant rights to subscribe for, or to convert any security into, shares in the company,
   except in accordance with section 550 (private company with single class of shares) or section 551 (authorisation by company).
(2) Subsection (1) does not apply—
   (a) to the allotment of shares in pursuance of an employees' share scheme, or
   (b) to the grant of a right to subscribe for, or to convert any security into, shares so allotted.
(3) [Subsection (1) does not apply to the allotment of shares pursuant to a right to subscribe for, or to convert any security into, shares in the company.][a]
(4) A director who knowingly contravenes, or permits or authorises a contravention of, this section commits an offence.
(5) A person guilty of an offence under this section is liable—
   (a) on conviction on indictment, to a fine;
   (b) on summary conviction, to a fine not exceeding the statutory maximum.
(6) Nothing in this section affects the validity of an allotment or other transaction.

AMENDMENTS AND NOTES

[a] Amended by the Companies Act 2006 (Allotment of Shares and Right of Pre-emption) (Amendment) Regulations 2009, SI 2009/2561, reg 2(1).

COMMENCEMENT DATE 1 October 2009[40]

**17.549.02** This section replaces section 80(1), (2), (9), and (10) of the 1985 Act. It restates the prohibition, derived from the Second Company Law Directive[41] against directors exercising any power of the company to allot shares or to grant rights to subscribe for, or to convert any security into, shares in the company, except in accordance with section 550 (private company with a single class of shares) or section 551 (authorization by the company). The section therefore applies, as did its predecessor, to the allotment of securities such as warrants and convertible bonds that contain such rights. As was the case with its predecessor, the section does not apply to the allotment of shares pursuant to an employees' share scheme or to the grant of a right to subscribe for or convert any security into shares so allotted. Nor does it apply in any circumstances[42] when a right, to which the section applies, is exercised to subscribe for

---

[39] Companies Act 2006 (Commencement No 8, Transitional Provisions and Savings) Order 2008, SI 2008/2860, art 3(k).
[40] Companies Act 2006 (Commencement No 8, Transitional Provisions and Savings) Order 2008, SI 2008/2860, art 3(k).
[41] Directive (EEC) 77/91 [1977] OJ L26/1.
[42] The amendment of subs (3) by art 2(1) of SI 2009/2561 makes this point clear.

or to convert any security into shares. In those circumstances the grant of the right will already have fallen under the control of the section and therefore there is no need to control the exercise of the right.

The requirement for companies to have 'authorised' share capital was abolished by the Companies Act 2006 but for companies incorporated under the Companies Act 1985 (or an earlier Act), the authorized share capital in the memorandum (now taken to be part of the articles) will continue (subject to section 551) to operate as a limit unless removed by special resolution.     **17.549.03**

The consequences of non-compliance with the section remain the same as under its predecessor: a director may be guilty of an offence and may be liable to a fine but the validity of an allotment or other transaction is not affected.     **17.549.04**

## 550  Power of directors to allot shares etc: private company with only one class of shares

Where a private company has only one class of shares, the directors may exercise any power of the company—     **17.550.01**

> (a)  to allot shares of that class, or
> (b)  to grant rights to subscribe for or to convert any security into such shares,
> except to the extent that they are prohibited from doing so by the company's articles.

COMMENCEMENT DATE 1 October 2009[43]

As noted by the Company Law Review (CLR),[44] the basic prohibition now contained in section 549 was imposed on private companies when the UK implemented the Second EC Directive, which applies only to public companies. In line with the CLRG's view that the provision does not meet the needs of most private companies, this section removes private companies from the prohibition where the private company will have only one class of share following the allotment. The section is formulated as a default rule as it is possible for the articles to prohibit or limit the power of the directors in this context. The definition of classes of share is given in section 629. The section removes the need for the elective regime applicable to private companies that was previously contained in section 80A of the Companies Act 1985.     **17.550.02**

The section applies to companies formed before 1 October 2009 only if the members have resolved that the directors should have the power under it, although such resolution can be an ordinary resolution even if it alters the company's articles.[45] Such a resolution must be filed under Chapter 3 of Part 3[46] and one passed before 1 October 2009 is treated as if passed on that date. Any subsequent restriction on the directors' power must be effected by an alteration of the articles in the normal way. For the purposes of the section, provisions of the articles of a company registered before 1 October 2009 authorizing the directors to allot shares under section 80A of the 1985 Act or added following an appropriate elective resolution under that section are not to be treated as provisions prohibiting the directors from exercising the powers under the section in cases to which the authority does not extend.[47]     **17.550.03**

## 551  Power of directors to allot shares etc: authorisation by company

> (1)  The directors of a company may exercise a power of the company—     **17.551.01**
>     (a)  to allot shares in the company, or
>     (b)  to grant rights to subscribe for or to convert any security into shares in the company,
>     if they are authorised to do so by the company's articles or by resolution of the company.
> (2)  Authorisation may be given for a particular exercise of the power or for its exercise generally, and may be unconditional or subject to conditions.
> (3)  Authorisation must—
>     (a)  state the maximum amount of shares that may be allotted under it, and
>     (b)  specify the date on which it will expire, which must be not more than five years from—
>         (i)  in the case of authorisation contained in the company's articles at the time of its original incorporation, the date of that incorporation;
>         (ii)  in any other case, the date on which the resolution is passed by virtue of which the authorisation is given.

---

[43]  Companies Act 2006 (Commencement No 8, Transitional Provisions and Savings) Order 2008, SI 2008/2860, art 3(k).

[44]  *Final Report*, para 4.5.

[45]  Companies Act 2006 (Commencement No 8, Transitional Provisions and Savings) Order 2008, SI 2008/2860, Sch 2, para 43.

[46]  See para 3.29.01.

[47]  Companies Act 2006 (Commencement No 8, Transitional Provisions and Savings) Order 2008, SI 2008/2860, Sch 2, para 44.

(4) Authorisation may—

    (a) be renewed or further renewed by resolution of the company for a further period not exceeding five years, and

    (b) be revoked or varied at any time by resolution of the company.

(5) A resolution renewing authorisation must—

    (a) state (or restate) the maximum amount of shares that may be allotted under the authorisation or, as the case may be, the amount remaining to be allotted under it, and

    (b) specify the date on which the renewed authorisation will expire.

(6) In relation to rights to subscribe for or to convert any security into shares in the company, references in this section to the maximum amount of shares that may be allotted under the authorisation are to the maximum amount of shares that may be allotted pursuant to the rights.

(7) The directors may allot shares, or grant rights to subscribe for or to convert any security into shares, after authorisation has expired if—

    (a) the shares are allotted, or the rights are granted, in pursuance of an offer or agreement made by the company before the authorisation expired, and

    (b) the authorisation allowed the company to make an offer or agreement which would or might require shares to be allotted, or rights to be granted, after the authorisation had expired.

(8) A resolution of a company to give, vary, revoke or renew authorisation under this section may be an ordinary resolution, even though it amends the company's articles.

(9) Chapter 3 of Part 3 (resolutions affecting a company's constitution) applies to a resolution under this section.

COMMENCEMENT DATE 1 October 2009[48]

**17.551.02**    This section replaces section 80(1) and (3) to (8) of the 1985 Act and applies both to public companies and to private companies which will have more than one class of shares after a proposed allotment.[49] It authorizes directors to issue shares (or grant rights to subscribe for shares or to convert any security into shares) if they have been given prior authorization for the proposed allotment by ordinary resolution or by the articles of association. An ordinary resolution suffices to give authority to the directors even when it has the effect of altering the company's articles (which normally requires a special resolution). That remains so even if the articles contain an authorized capital clause (see para 17.549.03 above). The authorization can be general or limited to a specific issue of shares, and the choice between the two carries implications for the power of the directors to make share issues other than on a pre-emptive basis (see commentary on sections 570 and 571). Neither the Model Articles[50] for public companies nor the Model Articles for private companies limited by shares give directors such authority.[51]

**17.551.03**    The authority must state the maximum number of shares (or shares that may be allotted under rights granted by the company) that may be allotted under it, and specify the date on which it will expire, which must be no more than five years from the relevant dates referred to in subsection (3)(b). In the case of listed companies, institutional investors are expected to follow the Statement of Principles adopted by the Pre-Emption Group, which represents the interests of institutional investors. The Statement of Principles indicates that the number of shares which the directors should be authorized to issue should be the lesser of (a) the unissued ordinary share capital, and (b) a sum equal to one-third[52] of the issued ordinary share capital. The circular issued in connection with a resolution under this section must, in the case of a listed company, include, *inter alia*, a statement by the directors as to whether they have any present intention of exercising the authority and, if so, for what purpose.[53]

**17.551.04**    Any authority may be renewed by the company by ordinary resolution for further successive periods not exceeding five years. A company may vary or revoke an authority by ordinary resolution.

**17.551.05**    Even though any authority required by the section has expired, the directors may allot shares (or grant rights) if they are allotted in pursuance of an offer or agreement made by the company before the authority expired. However, the authority must have allowed the company to make an offer or agreement which would or might require shares to be allotted after the authority expired.

---

[48] Companies Act 2006 (Commencement No 8, Transitional Provisions and Savings) Order 2008, SI 2008/2860, art 3(k).

[49] An authorization under s 80 of the 1985 Act has effect on and after 1 October 2009 as if made under this section: Companies Act 2006 (Commencement No 8, Transitional Provisions and Savings) Order 2008, SI 2008/2860, Sch 2, para 45.

[50] See SI 2008/3229 and Chapter 52.

[51] See Art 43 of the former and Art 22 of the latter.

[52] Two-thirds in the case of fully pre-emptive rights issues. This guidance relates to the number of shares that directors are authorized to issue. Whether shareholders will approve a non pre-emptive issue is a separate matter (see sections 567–571).

[53] See FSA Listing Rule LR 13.8.1R.

## Prohibition of commissions, discounts and allowances

### 552  General prohibition of commissions, discounts and allowances

(1) Except as permitted by section 553 (permitted commission), a company must not apply any of its shares or capital money, either directly or indirectly, in payment of any commission, discount or allowance to any person in consideration of his—    **17.552.01**
  (a) subscribing or agreeing to subscribe (whether absolutely or conditionally) for shares in the company, or
  (b) procuring or agreeing to procure subscriptions (whether absolute or conditional) for shares in the company.
(2) It is immaterial how the shares or money are so applied, whether by being added to the purchase money of property acquired by the company or to the contract price of work to be executed for the company, or being paid out of the nominal purchase money or contract price, or otherwise.
(3) Nothing in this section affects the payment of such brokerage as has previously been lawful.

COMMENCEMENT DATE  1 October 2009[54]

This section replaces section 98 of the Companies Act 1985. The general principle that a company    **17.552.02**
cannot apply any of its shares or capital money in paying commissions, discounts, or allowances in
connection with a share issue is made subject to the exceptions contained in section 553 (below).

### 553  Permitted commission

(1) A company may, if the following conditions are satisfied, pay a commission to a person in    **17.553.01**
consideration of his subscribing or agreeing to subscribe (whether absolutely or conditionally) for shares in the company, or procuring or agreeing to procure subscriptions (whether absolute or conditional) for shares in the company.
(2) The conditions are—
  (a) the payment of the commission is authorised by the company's articles;
  (b) the commission paid or agreed to be paid does not exceed—
    (i)  10% of the price at which the shares are issued, or
    (ii) the amount or rate authorised by the articles,
    whichever is the less.
(3) A vendor to, or promoter of, or other person who receives payment in money or shares from, a company may apply any part of the money or shares so received in payment of any commission the payment of which directly by the company would be permitted by this section.

COMMENCEMENT DATE  1 October 2009[55]

This section replaces section 97 of the Companies Act 1985. It permits a company to pay commission    **17.553.02**
in connection with a share issue if such payment is permitted by the articles and does not exceed 10 per
cent of the price of the shares issued.

## Registration of allotment

### 554  Registration of allotment

(1) A company must register an allotment of shares as soon as practicable and in any event within    **17.554.01**
two months after the date of the allotment.
(2) This does not apply if the company has issued a share warrant in respect of the shares (see section 779).
(3) If a company fails to comply with this section, an offence is committed by—
  (a) the company, and
  (b) every officer of the company who is in default.
(4) A person guilty of an offence under this section is liable on summary conviction to a fine not exceeding level 3 on the standard scale and, for continued contravention, a daily default fine not exceeding one-tenth of level 3 on the standard scale.
(5) For the company's duties as to the issue of share certificates etc, see Part 21 (certification and transfer of securities).

COMMENCEMENT DATE  1 October 2009[56]

---

[54] Companies Act 2006 (Commencement No 8, Transitional Provisions and Savings) Order 2008, SI 2008/2860, art 3(k).
[55] Companies Act 2006 (Commencement No 8, Transitional Provisions and Savings) Order 2008, SI 2008/2860, art 3(k).
[56] Companies Act 2006 (Commencement No 8, Transitional Provisions and Savings) Order 2008, SI 2008/2860, art 3(k).

**17.554.02**  This section introduces a new requirement for an allotment of shares to be registered as soon as practicable and in any event within two months after the date of an issue.[57] For companies falling within the scope of section 555, it represents an additional requirement that does not appear to have an obvious purpose (as a return of the allotment must be registered in any case). However, for other companies (such as unlimited companies with a share capital) it does mean that there will now be a record of all allotments (see also section 556 regarding the additional requirements for allotments by unlimited companies of a new class of shares).

## *Return of allotment*

### 555  Return of allotment by limited company

**17.555.01**
    (1) This section applies to a company limited by shares and to a company limited by guarantee and having a share capital.
    (2) The company must, within one month of making an allotment of shares, deliver to the registrar for registration a return of the allotment.
    (3) The return must—
        (a) contain the prescribed information, and
        (b) be accompanied by a statement of capital.
    (4) The statement of capital must state with respect to the company's share capital at the date to which the return is made up—
        (a) the total number of shares of the company,
        (b) the aggregate nominal value of those shares,
        (c) for each class of shares—
            (i) prescribed particulars of the rights attached to the shares,
            (ii) the total number of shares of that class, and
            (iii) the aggregate nominal value of shares of that class, and
        (d) the amount paid up and the amount (if any) unpaid on each share (whether on account of the nominal value of the share or by way of premium).

COMMENCEMENT DATE 1 October 2009[58]

**17.555.02**  This section replaces section 88 of the 1985 Act.[59] The requirement to make a return of allotments to the registrar follows its predecessor. The prescribed information to be included in the return is—

    (a) the number of shares allotted;
    (b) the amount paid up and the amount (if any) unpaid on each allotted share (whether on account of the nominal value of the share or by way of premium); and
    (c) where the shares are allotted as fully or partly paid up (as to their nominal value or any premium on them) otherwise than in cash, the consideration for the allotment.[60]

**17.555.03**  There is a new requirement for a statement of capital. The latter requirement is a consequence of the abolition of the requirement for companies to have an authorized share capital[61] taken together with the requirement of Article 2 of the Second EC Directive that the constitution should show, when the company has no authorized capital, the amount of the subscribed capital. The statement of capital will therefore show a company's total subscribed capital at the date to which the return of allotments is made up. It is a more extensive statement than that previously required by section 88 of the 1985 Act, which related only to shares that had been allotted. For example, the new statement of capital will take account of the cumulative effect of allotments, as well as any redemption or purchase by the company of its own shares. While the Second Directive applies only to public companies, this section applies to a private company limited by shares and to a private company limited by guarantee and having a share capital.

**17.555.04**  The information to be included in the statement of capital includes prescribed particulars of the rights attached to each class of share, which was previously required by section 123 of the 1985 Act in respect of an increase in authorized share capital. The prescribed particulars are—

---

    [57] It only applies to an allotment on or after 1 October 2009: Companies Act 2006 (Commencement No 8, Transitional Provisions and Savings) Order 2008, SI 2008/2860, Sch 2, para 46.
    [58] Companies Act 2006 (Commencement No 8, Transitional Provisions and Savings) Order 2008, SI 2008/2860, art 3(k).
    [59] It only applies to an allotment on or after 1 October 2009: Companies Act 2006 (Commencement No 8, Transitional Provisions and Savings) Order 2008, SI 2008/2860, Sch 2, para 47.
    [60] Companies (Shares and Share Capital) Order 2009, SI 2009/388, art 3.
    [61] See s 8 of the Act, removing the requirement for the memorandum to state the authorized share capital, and para 7.30 of the CLR *Final Report*.

    (a)  particulars of any voting rights attached to the shares, including rights that arise only in certain circumstances;

    (b)  particulars of any rights attached to the shares, as respects dividends, to participate in a distribution;

    (c)  particulars of any rights attached to the shares, as respects capital, to participate in a distribution (including on winding up); and

    (d)  whether the shares are to be redeemed or are liable to be redeemed at the option of the company or the shareholder.[62]

Section 88(2)(b) of the 1985 Act required, in the case of shares allotted as fully or partly paid otherwise than in cash, that the contract with the allottee be returned to the registrar. That contract might well contain commercially sensitive information that a company would not wish to disclose. There is no similar requirement in this section but the Secretary of State does have the power to prescribe the information which must be included in the return of allotments and could therefore require that such information be included.   **17.555.05**

## 556  Return of allotment by unlimited company allotting new class of shares

(1)  This section applies to an unlimited company that allots shares of a class with rights that are not in all respects uniform with shares previously allotted.   **17.556.01**

(2)  The company must, within one month of making such an allotment, deliver to the registrar for registration a return of the allotment.

(3)  The return must contain the prescribed particulars[a] of the rights attached to the shares.

(4)  For the purposes of this section shares are not to be treated as different from shares previously allotted by reason only that the former do not carry the same rights to dividends as the latter during the twelve months immediately following the former's allotment.

AMENDMENTS AND NOTES

a  The prescribed particulars are the same as in the case of s 555(4)(c)(i): the Companies (Shares and Share Capital) Order 2009, SI 2009/388, art 2(2)(e).

COMMENCEMENT DATE 1 October 2009[63]

This section restates, in terms applicable specifically to unlimited companies, the provisions of section 128(1) and (2) of the 1985 Act, which require a company to make a return of an allotment of a new class of shares to the registrar within one month.[64]   **17.556.02**

## 557  Offence of failure to make return

(1)  If a company makes default in complying with—   **17.557.01**
      section 555 (return of allotment of shares by limited company), or
      section 556 (return of allotment of new class of shares by unlimited company),
    an offence is committed by every officer of the company who is in default.

(2)  A person guilty of an offence under this section is liable—
    (a)  on conviction on indictment, to a fine;
    (b)  on summary conviction, to a fine not exceeding the statutory maximum and, for continued contravention, a daily default fine not exceeding one-tenth of the statutory maximum.

(3)  In the case of default in delivering to the registrar within one month after the allotment the return required by section 555 or 556—
    (a)  any person liable for the default may apply to the court for relief, and
    (b)  the court, if satisfied—
        (i)  that the omission to deliver the document was accidental or due to inadvertence, or
        (ii)  that it is just and equitable to grant relief,
      may make an order extending the time for delivery of the document for such period as the court thinks proper.

COMMENCEMENT DATE 1 October 2009[65]

This section replaces sections 88(5) and 128(5) of the 1985 Act. It imposes criminal liability on directors and officers who are in default when a company fails to make a return under section 555 or   **17.557.02**

---

62  Companies (Shares and Share Capital) Order 2009, SI 2009/388, art 2(2)(d).

63  Companies Act 2006 (Commencement No 8, Transitional Provisions and Savings) Order 2008, SI 2008/2860, art 3(k).

64  It only applies to an allotment on or after 1 October 2009: Companies Act 2006 (Commencement No 8, Transitional Provisions and Savings) Order 2008, SI 2008/2860, Sch 2, para 48.

65  Companies Act 2006 (Commencement No 8, Transitional Provisions and Savings) Order 2008, SI 2008/2860, art 3(k).

section 556. Such persons can apply to the court for relief and the court can make an order extending the time for delivery of the documents for such period as the court thinks proper.

## *Supplementary provisions*

### 558 When shares are allotted

**17.558.01**     For the purposes of the Companies Acts shares in a company are taken to be allotted when a person acquires the unconditional right to be included in the company's register of members in respect of the shares.

COMMENCEMENT DATE 1 October 2009[66]

**17.558.02**     This section replaces the (interpretation) provision previously contained in section 738(1) of the Companies Act 1985.

### 559   Provisions about allotment not applicable to shares taken on formation

**17.559.01**     The provisions of this Chapter have no application in relation to the taking of shares by the subscribers to the memorandum on the formation of the company.

COMMENCEMENT DATE 1 October 2009[67]

**17.559.02**     This section is a new provision which was not contained in the 1985 Act. Shares taken by the subscribers to the memorandum are recorded in the memorandum which constitutes a public record of the allotment to the subscribers.

## CHAPTER 3
## ALLOTMENT OF EQUITY SECURITIES: EXISTING SHAREHOLDERS' RIGHT OF PRE-EMPTION

### *Introductory*

### 560   Meaning of 'equity securities' and related expressions

**17.560.01**     (1) In this Chapter—
'equity securities' means—
   (a) ordinary shares in the company, or
   (b) rights to subscribe for, or to convert securities into, ordinary shares in the company;
'ordinary shares' means shares other than shares that as respects dividends and capital carry a right to participate only up to a specified amount in a distribution.
   (2) [References in this Chapter to the allotment of equity securities—
     (a) include the grant of a right to subscribe for, or to convert any securities into, ordinary shares in the company, and
     (b) do not include the allotment of shares pursuant to such a right.
   (3) References in this Chapter to the allotment of equity securities include the sale of ordinary shares in the company that immediately before the sale were held by the company as treasury shares.][a]

AMENDMENTS AND NOTES

[a] Amended by the Companies Act 2006 (Allotment of Shares and Right of Pre-emption) (Amendment) Regulations 2009, SI 2009/2561, reg 2(2).

COMMENCEMENT DATE 1 October 2009[68]

**17.560.02**     This section adapts, for the purposes of this Chapter, some of the definitions previously contained in section 94 of the Companies Act 1985. The definition of allotment includes the grant of rights referred to in subsection (2)(a) but not the allotment of shares pursuant to such rights (which are thereby excluded from existing shareholders' right of pre-emption). The exceptions relating to bonus shares and shares taken by a subscriber to the memorandum are contained in sections 564 and 577 respectively.

---

[66] Companies Act 2006 (Commencement No 8, Transitional Provisions and Savings) Order 2008, SI 2008/2860, art 3(k).

[67] Companies Act 2006 (Commencement No 8, Transitional Provisions and Savings) Order 2008, SI 2008/2860, art 3(k).

[68] Companies Act 2006 (Commencement No 8, Transitional Provisions and Savings) Order 2008, SI 2008/2860, art 3(k).

## Existing shareholders' right of pre-emption

### 561  Existing shareholders' right of pre-emption

(1) A company must not allot equity securities to a person on any terms unless—       **17.561.01**

    (a) it has made an offer to each person who holds ordinary shares in the company to allot to him on the same or more favourable terms a proportion of those securities that is as nearly as practicable equal to the proportion in nominal value held by him of the ordinary share capital of the company, and

    (b) the period during which any such offer may be accepted has expired or the company has received notice of the acceptance or refusal of every offer so made.

(2) Securities that a company has offered to allot to a holder of ordinary shares may be allotted to him, or anyone in whose favour he has renounced his right to their allotment, without contravening subsection (1)(b).

(3) [...]ᵃ

(4) Shares held by the company as treasury shares are disregarded for the purposes of this section, so that—

    (a) the company is not treated as a person who holds ordinary shares, and

    (b) the shares are not treated as forming part of the ordinary share capital of the company.

(5) This section is subject to—

    (a) sections 564 to 566 (exceptions to pre-emption right),

    (b) sections 567 and 568 (exclusion of rights of pre-emption),

    (c) sections 569 to 573 (disapplication of pre-emption rights), and

    (d) section 576 (saving for certain older pre-emption procedures).

AMENDMENTS AND NOTES

ᵃ Deleted by the Companies Act 2006 (Allotment of Shares and Right of Pre-emption) (Amendment) Regulations 2009, SI 2009/2561, reg 2(3). Amendment of s 560 by art 2(2) of that instrument made the original provision in this subsection redundant.

COMMENCEMENT DATE 1 October 2009[69]

This section consolidates most of the provisions previously contained in section 89 of the Companies    **17.561.02** Act 1985.[70] It requires offers of equity securities (defined in section 560) to be made first to shareholders on a pre-emptive basis. Historically, there was no such common law rule or statutory requirement in the UK, although it had been common for such provisions to be included in the articles of companies and the Stock Exchange Listing Rules had applied such a rule to listed companies. The Second EC Directive required offers to be made on a pre-emptive basis (at least in the case of public companies) and UK Company law has, since 1980, given effect to this requirement. Although not required by the directive, the rule in this section is stated so as to apply to a private company, although there are special provisions in section 567 relating to the disapplication of the rule in the case of private companies.

The meaning of a pre-emptive offer is set out in subsection (1). The effect of the rule requiring that any    **17.561.03** offer of equity securities be on a pre-emptive basis is that a company is not able to offer such securities to any other person unless an offer on the same or more favourable terms has been made to holders of ordinary shares.[71] In that sense, the pre-emption rule allows a shareholder to maintain his proportionate shareholding in the company when an allotment of new shares is made. If that were not the case, a shareholder would face the prospect of dilution of the relative voting power of his shareholding following an allotment of new shares. He might also face the possibility of dilution in the value of his shares if the allotment were made at less than market value. In setting the price for a pre-emptive issue of shares (a 'rights issue') directors must consider the potential dilution in the value of the shareholding of shareholders unable to take up the offer (at least where that is known or foreseeable). An issue at par

---

[69] Companies Act 2006 (Commencement No 8, Transitional Provisions and Savings) Order 2008, SI 2008/2860, art 3(k).

[70] Section 561 only applies to an allotment on or after 1 October 2009: Companies Act 2006 (Commencement No 8, Transitional Provisions and Savings) Order 2008, SI 2008/2860, Sch 2, para 49(1). When it applies, s 562 applies to offers made on or after 1 October 2009 and s 90 of the 1985 Act applies to offers made before that date and the requirements of the section may be met by offers within either s 562 or s 90: Companies Act 2006 (Commencement No 8, Transitional Provisions and Savings) Order 2008, SI 2008/2860, Sch 2, para 49(2).

[71] For example, in the case of a company with a share capital of 100 ordinary shares that proposes to allot 20 new shares, it will be obliged to offer five of those new shares to a holder of 25 shares. The rule also has the effect that an offer of 'equity securities' to the holders of a particular class of share must be made to all ordinary shareholders unless the exception in s 568 applies.

in circumstances where a higher price could have been obtained is a breach of fiduciary duty and may be 'unfairly prejudicial' for the purposes of section 994.[72]

**17.561.04**   A company is prohibited from allotting securities in respect of which a pre-emptive offer to shareholders is required unless the period during which the offer may be accepted has expired or the company has received notice of the acceptance or refusal of every offer so made. Irrespective of this element of the prohibition, it is in any case only when the outcome of all pre-emptive offers are known that the company would be in a position to determine the scale of an offer that might be made to other persons.

**17.561.05**   The effect of subsection (4) is that Treasury shares are disregarded for the purposes of this section. This reflects the rationale of shares being held in treasury by the company, which is primarily to manage the capital requirements of the company rather than to exercise ownership rights.

**17.561.06**   In addition to the requirements of this section, listed companies need to take account of the Listing Rules. In one respect the Listing Rules appear to relax the requirement to offer equity securities to holders of relevant shares on a *pro rata* basis. This results from the provision that the requirement to make a pre-emptive offer does not apply if the company considers it necessary or expedient to exclude shares from the offer on account of the laws or regulatory requirements of another territory.[73] That provision is intended to allow companies to exclude from a pre-emptive offer shares held by persons resident in territories (such as the United States) that impose onerous requirements in relation to an offer. However, that provision of the Listing Rules cannot itself modify the requirement of subsection (1), since even for a listed company Listing Rules cannot override requirements of the Companies Act. To comply with subsection (1) while taking advantage of the exclusion permitted by the Listing Rules a company would have to rely on either the 'as nearly as practicable' provision in subsection (1) or the decision in *Mutual Life Insurance Company of New York v Rank Organisation*,[74] holding that it was possible to exclude shareholders resident in the United States from an offer.

**17.561.07**   The Listing Rules also require that securities not taken up by existing holders in a rights issue must be offered for subscription or purchase on terms that any premium obtained over the subscription or purchase price (net of expenses) is to be for the account of the holders.[75] This is normally achieved through the sale by the company of 'nil paid' rights, which entitle the purchaser to subscribe for shares in the same manner as the existing holders who have declined to take up their rights. A premium normally attaches to 'nil paid' rights on the basis that a rights issue is normally priced at a discount to the prevailing market price of a company's shares.

### 562 Communication of pre-emption offers to shareholders

**17.562.01**   (1) This section has effect as to the manner in which offers required by section 561 are to be made to holders of a company's shares.
(2) The offer may be made in hard copy or electronic form.
(3) If the holder—
  (a) has no registered address in an EEA State and has not given to the company an address in an EEA State for the service of notices on him, or
  (b) is the holder of a share warrant,
the offer may be made by causing it, or a notice specifying where a copy of it can be obtained or inspected, to be published in the Gazette.
(4) The offer must state a period during which it may be accepted and the offer shall not be withdrawn before the end of that period.
(5) The period must be a period of at least [14]ᵃ days beginning—
  (a) in the case of an offer made in hard copy form, with the date on which the offer is sent or supplied;
  (b) in the case of an offer made in electronic form, with the date on which the offer is sent;
  (c) in the case of an offer made by publication in the Gazette, with the date of publication.

---

[72]  *Re Sunrise Radio Ltd (Kohli v Lit)* [2009] EWHC 2893 (Ch). In that case the court held that where it was foreseen that a minority shareholder would not or might not have the money or inclination to subscribe to a rights issue, the directors should consider the price that could and should be paid by shareholders willing to subscribe. Failure to do so, such as by issuing new shares at par, would represent a breach of fiduciary duty and would be unfairly prejudicial to the minority (since their shareholding would be diluted by an under-priced issue of shares).

[73]  FSA Listing Rule LR 9.3.12R.

[74]  [1985] BCLC 11. The court held, in respect of a challenge to the exclusion of shareholders resident in the United States from an offer for sale that included a preferential element for existing shareholders, that no overriding term could be implied into the contract of membership that shareholders of the same class were to be treated equally.

[75]  FSA Listing Rule LR 9.5.4R.

(6)  The Secretary of State may by regulations made by statutory instrument—
   (a)  reduce the period specified in subsection (5) (but not to less than 14 days), or
   (b)  increase that period.
(7)  A statutory instrument containing regulations made under subsection (6) is subject to affirmative resolution procedure.

AMENDMENTS AND NOTES

<sup>a</sup> Substituted by the Companies (Share Capital and Acquisition by a Company of its Own Shares) Regulations 2009, SI 2009/2022, reg 2.

COMMENCEMENT DATE 1 October 2009[76]

This section replaces section 90 of the Companies Act 1985. A pre-emptive offer required by section 561 must be in writing and must remain open for acceptance for at least 14 days.[77] It can be delivered in hard copy or electronic form. A company is required to give individual notice to all shareholders who have given a service address in the EEA (rather than just the UK, as was the case under the 1985 Act). There are transitional provisions to cover the situations where offers and allotments straddle the commencement of this section.[78]    **17.562.02**

## 563  Liability of company and officers in case of contravention

(1)  This section applies where there is a contravention of—          **17.563.01**
      section 561 (existing shareholders' right of pre-emption), or
      section 562 (communication of pre-emption offers to shareholders).
(2)  The company and every officer of it who knowingly authorised or permitted the contravention are jointly and severally liable to compensate any person to whom an offer should have been made in accordance with those provisions for any loss, damage, costs or expenses which the person has sustained or incurred by reason of the contravention.
(3)  No proceedings to recover any such loss, damage, costs or expenses shall be commenced after the expiration of two years—
      (a)  from the delivery to the registrar of companies of the return of allotment, or
      (b)  where equity securities other than shares are granted, from the date of the grant.

COMMENCEMENT DATE 1 October 2009[79]

This section replaces section 92 of the Companies Act 1985. It provides a civil, but not a criminal, sanction for a contravention of sections 561 and 562.[80] The company, and every officer of the company who knowingly authorized or permitted the contravention, are jointly and severally liable to compensate any person to whom an offer should have been made for any loss, damage, costs, or expenses which that person has sustained or incurred by reason of that contravention. The section does not appear to invalidate any allotment not complying with shareholders' pre-emptive rights, although the decision in *Re Thundercrest*[81] raises the possibility that the court may in some circumstances order rectification of the register under section 125 of the Act. In that case, the court set aside an allotment made by the directors of the company to themselves of shares which were subject to the pre-emptive rights of the only other shareholder in the company who had not been given proper notice (under section 90 of the Companies Act 1985) of the issue. Doubt has been expressed, however, over whether a similar decision would be reached in the context of an issue to a larger number of shareholders.[82]    **17.563.02**

---

[76] Companies Act 2006 (Commencement No 8, Transitional Provisions and Savings) Order 2008, SI 2008/2860, art 3(k).

[77] Note that the period of 14 days was substituted for the previous period of 21 days by the Companies (Share Capital and Acquisition by a Company of its Own Shares) Regulations 2009, SI 2009/2022. The shortening of the offer timetable was recommended by the Rights Issue Review Group in its Report to the Chancellor of the Exchequer (November 2008) to reduce uncertainty arising from share price volatility during an extended offer period.

[78] Companies Act 2006 (Commencement No 8, Transitional Provisions and Savings) Order 2008, SI 2008/2860, Sch 2, para 49.

[79] Companies Act 2006 (Commencement No 8, Transitional Provisions and Savings) Order 2008, SI 2008/2860, art 3(k).

[80] The reference to s 562 is to be read as including a reference to s 90 of the 1985 Act in cases where offers and allotments straddle 1 October 2009: Companies Act 2006 (Commencement No 8, Transitional Provisions and Savings) Order 2008, SI 2008/2860, Sch 2, para 49(3).

[81] [1995] 1 BCLC 117.

[82] In *Re Thundercrest* it was doubted (Baker P at 125) whether rectification (as opposed to damages under s 92 of the 1985 Act) would be available in other circumstances, such as where the allotment was made to outside investors.

**17.563.03**    Subsection (2) provides that no such proceedings to recover any such loss, damage, costs, or expenses shall be commenced after the expiry of two years from the delivery to the registrar of companies of the return of allotments in question. Where equity securities other than shares are granted, the two-year period runs from the date of the grant.

## *Exceptions to right of pre-emption*

### 564  Exception to pre-emption right: bonus shares

**17.564.01**    Section 561(1) (existing shareholders' right of pre-emption) does not apply in relation to the allotment of bonus shares.

COMMENCEMENT DATE 1 October 2009[83]

**17.564.02**    This section consolidates the exception from pre-emption rights that was previously contained in section 94(2) of the Companies Act 1985. It means that there is no right of pre-emption in relation to bonus shares, but as bonus shares[84] can by definition only be allotted to members, the exception does not have any significant effect.

### 565  Exception to pre-emption right: issue for non-cash consideration

**17.565.01**    Section 561(1) (existing shareholders' right of pre-emption) does not apply to a particular allotment of equity securities if these are, or are to be, wholly or partly paid up otherwise than in cash.

COMMENCEMENT DATE 1 October 2009[85]

**17.565.02**    This section consolidates the exception from pre-emption rights previously contained in section 89(4) of the Companies Act 1985. It means that in the case of other forms of consideration for an allotment, such as, for example, land, buildings, or securities, an offer can be made directly to other persons without a pre-emptive offer having to be made to shareholders. Why non-cash offers should be excluded is not entirely clear[86] as the same risk of dilution of a shareholder's proportionate shareholding is present in the case of an allotment for a non-cash consideration. It seems likely that the main consideration is that allotments for a non-cash consideration allow a company to respond more quickly to opportunities to acquire assets or businesses without facing the uncertainty of first making an offer to shareholders, which may or may not be taken up.

**17.565.03**    The exception contained in this section led to the development of the technique known as 'vendor placing'. The technique is applied to transactions in which a buyer wishes to issue shares as payment for assets, an entire undertaking, or shares in another company. Since the vendor in such a transaction provides payment for the new shares in a form other than cash, the issue of shares is not subject to the principle of pre-emption in section 561. Moreover, since the vendor will often not want to hold shares in the buyer, an arrangement is normally made with an investment bank to place the newly issued shares with investors. In those circumstances, the risk that shareholders will be diluted by an issue of shares for a consideration that is less than the prevailing market price is addressed by several controls. First, the provisions of section 593 relating to the valuation of non-cash consideration will apply unless the exceptions in sections 594 and 595 are applicable. Secondly, in the case of listed companies (where the technique is of most relevance) the Listing Rules limit the discount on any issue of shares to 10 per cent.[87] Thirdly, a 'clawback' provision may be included in the vendor placing enabling shareholders to subscribe for shares, thereby providing them with an opportunity to take up shares that would otherwise be allotted to and remain with placees.

### 566  Exception to pre-emption right: securities held under employees' share scheme

**17.566.01**    Section 561 (existing shareholders' right of pre-emption) does not apply to the allotment of [equity] securities that would, apart from any renunciation or assignment of the right to their allotment, be held under [or allotted or transferred pursuant to] an employees' share scheme.[a]

AMENDMENTS AND NOTES

[a] Amended by the Companies Act 2006 (Allotment of Shares and Right of Pre-emption) (Amendment) Regulations 2009, SI 2009/2561, reg 2(4).

---

[83] Companies Act 2006 (Commencement No 8, Transitional Provisions and Savings) Order 2008, SI 2008/2860, art 3(k).

[84] See the commentary on s 582 for a definition of bonus shares.

[85] Companies Act 2006 (Commencement No 8, Transitional Provisions and Savings) Order 2008, SI 2008/2860, art 3(k).

[86] They are also excluded from the relevant provision (Art 29) of the Second EC Directive.

[87] FSA Listing Rule LR 9.5.10.

COMMENCEMENT DATE  1 October 2009[88]

This section consolidates the provision previously contained in section 89(5) of the Companies Act **17.566.02**
1985. Its meaning is clear. The amendment removes doubt over the scope of the exception so far as
allotments and transfers are concerned.

## Exclusion of right of pre-emption

### 567  Exclusion of requirements by private companies

(1)  All or any of the requirements of—    **17.567.01**
    (a)  section 561 (existing shareholders' right of pre-emption), or
    (b)  section 562 (communication of pre-emption offers to shareholders)
may be excluded by provision contained in the articles of a private company.
(2)  They may be excluded—
    (a)  generally in relation to the allotment by the company of equity securities, or
    (b)  in relation to allotments of a particular description.
(3)  Any requirement or authorisation contained in the articles of a private company that is inconsistent with either of those sections is treated for the purposes of this section as a provision excluding
that section.
(4)  A provision to which section 568 applies (exclusion of pre-emption right: corresponding right
conferred by articles) is not to be treated as inconsistent with section 561.

COMMENCEMENT DATE  1 October 2009[89]

This section replaces section 91 of the Companies Act 1985. It provides that the articles of a private **17.567.02**
company may exclude pre-emption rights and/or the provisions of section 562 (communication of a
pre-emptive offer). A requirement or authority contained in the articles of a private company, if it is
inconsistent with the requirements of sections 561 or 562, shall have effect as a provision excluding that
section. This exclusion does not extend to provisions in the articles conferring pre-emptive rights of
the type referred to by section 568. Any exclusion in force immediately before 1 October 2009 under
section 91 of the 1985 Act has effect as if effective under this section.[90]

### 568  Exclusion of pre-emption right: articles conferring corresponding right

(1)  The provisions of this section apply where, in a case in which section 561 (existing shareholders' **17.568.01**
right of pre-emption) would otherwise apply—
    (a)  a company's articles contain provision ('pre-emption provision') prohibiting the company
from allotting ordinary shares of a particular class unless it has complied with the condition
that it makes such an offer as is described in section 561(1) to each person who holds ordinary
shares of that class, and
    (b)  in accordance with that provision—
        (i)  the company makes an offer to allot shares to such a holder, and
        (ii)  he or anyone in whose favour he has renounced his right to their allotment accepts the
offer.
(2)  In that case, section 561 does not apply to the allotment of those shares and the company may
allot them accordingly.
(3)  The provisions of section 562 (communication of pre-emption offers to shareholders) apply in
relation to offers made in pursuance of the pre-emption provision of the company's articles.
This is subject to section 567 (exclusion of requirements by private companies).
(4)  If there is a contravention of the pre-emption provision of the company's articles, the company,
and every officer of it who knowingly authorised or permitted the contravention, are jointly and
severally liable to compensate any person to whom an offer should have been made under the
provision for any loss, damage, costs or expenses which the person has sustained or incurred by
reason of the contravention.
(5)  No proceedings to recover any such loss, damage, costs or expenses may be commenced after the
expiration of two years—
    (a)  from the delivery to the registrar of companies of the return of allotment, or
    (b)  where equity securities other than shares are granted, from the date of the grant.

---

[88] Companies Act 2006 (Commencement No 8, Transitional Provisions and Savings) Order 2008, SI 2008/
2860, art 3(k).
[89] Companies Act 2006 (Commencement No 8, Transitional Provisions and Savings) Order 2008, SI 2008/
2860, art 3(k).
[90] Companies Act 2006 (Commencement No 8, Transitional Provisions and Savings) Order 2008, SI 2008/
2860, Sch 2, para 50.

COMMENCEMENT DATE 1 October 2009[91]

**17.568.02**  This section consolidates the provisions previously contained in section 89(3) and (4) of the Companies Act 1985.[92] Special provision is made to meet the situation where a company's articles confer pre-emptive rights which require a company proposing to allot equity securities of a particular class to offer those shares on a pre-emptive basis. Where that is the case, subsection (2) provides that an offer to allot in compliance with such a provision will prevent the application of section 561 in the event that the recipient, or anyone in whose favour the recipient has renounced his right to allotment, accepts the offer. In that sense, the section narrows the pre-emption rule in section 561, which would otherwise require an offer of any 'equity securities' to be made to all ordinary shareholders. The communication of such a limited offer (as is referred to by subsection (1)(b)(i)) is governed by section 562. The company and its officers are jointly and severally liable for loss caused by contravention of the pre-emption provisions of a company's articles.

**17.568.03**  This section does not, however, make clear whether it excludes the contractual remedy of specific performance in respect of pre-emption rights derived from the articles. Contractual obligations to issue or take up shares in a company have been enforced in a number of cases[93] and there would seem no reason in principle to treat a contractual obligation derived from the articles as being different. If that view is taken, it would follow that the failure of the subsection to exclude specific performance means that the remedy is available.

## Disapplication of pre-emption rights

### 569 Disapplication of pre-emption rights: private company with only one class of shares

**17.569.01**  (1)  The directors of a private company that has only one class of shares may be given power by the articles, or by a special resolution of the company, to allot equity securities of that class as if section 561 (existing shareholders' right of pre-emption)—
 (a)  did not apply to the allotment, or
 (b)  applied to the allotment with such modifications as the directors may determine.
 (2)  Where the directors make an allotment under this section, the provisions of this Chapter have effect accordingly.

COMMENCEMENT DATE 1 October 2009[94]

**17.569.02**  Reflecting the wider powers given to directors to allot shares under section 550, this section provides that the directors of a private company that has only one class of shares may be given power by the articles or by special resolution to allot shares otherwise than on a pre-emptive basis. The power to allot shares in this manner may be exercised by the directors even if there is no exclusion of pre-emption rights under section 567. However, even when there is exclusion of pre-emption rights under section 567, it may be that a particular issue of shares has to be authorized by the company because the directors have not been given the power available under this section or the default power contained in section 556 (allowing directors of a private company with only one class of shares to issue shares without the authority of the company) has been deleted or altered by the company's articles.

**17.569.03**  The reference in subsection (2) to this Chapter having effect 'accordingly' means that its provisions are excluded only when the offer has no pre-emptive element, but that in other cases they do apply so long as some part of the offer is on a pre-emptive basis.

### 570 Disapplication of pre-emption rights: directors acting under general authorisation

**17.570.01**  (1)  Where the directors of a company are generally authorised for the purposes of section 551 (power of directors to allot shares etc: authorisation by company), they may be given power by the articles, or by a special resolution of the company, to allot equity securities pursuant to that authorisation as if section 561 (existing shareholders' right of pre-emption)—
 (a)  did not apply to the allotment, or
 (b)  applied to the allotment with such modifications as the directors may determine.

---

[91] Companies Act 2006 (Commencement No 8, Transitional Provisions and Savings) Order 2008, SI 2008/2860, art 3(k).

[92] As to the transitional provisions, see Companies Act 2006 (Commencement No 8, Transitional Provisions and Savings) Order 2008, SI 2008/2860, Sch 2, para 51.

[93] See eg *New Brunswick etc v Muggeridge* (1860) 62 ER 418; *Oriental Inland Steam Co v Briggs* (1861) 70 ER 1209; and *Odessa Tramways Co v Mendel* (1878) 8 Ch D 235.

[94] Companies Act 2006 (Commencement No 8, Transitional Provisions and Savings) Order 2008, SI 2008/2860, art 3(k).

(2)  Where the directors make an allotment under this section, the provisions of this Chapter have effect accordingly.

(3)  The power conferred by this section ceases to have effect when the authorisation to which it relates—

(a)  is revoked, or

(b)  would (if not renewed) expire.

But if the authorisation is renewed the power may also be renewed, for a period not longer than that for which the authorisation is renewed, by a special resolution of the company.

(4)  Notwithstanding that the power conferred by this section has expired, the directors may allot equity securities in pursuance of an offer or agreement previously made by the company if the power enabled the company to make an offer or agreement that would or might require equity securities to be allotted after it expired.

COMMENCEMENT DATE  1 October 2009[95]

This section, together with sections 571 to 573, replaces the provisions of section 95 of the 1985 Act that dealt with circumstances in which the directors are generally authorized to allot shares. In that sense it covers circumstances that form a subset of those covered by section 571, which also applies to circumstances in which directors are authorized to make a specified allotment. Provision made under section 95 of the 1985 Act has effect on and after 1 October 2009 as if it had been made under this section and the power conferred thereby may be renewed under subsection (3).[96] A general authorization is authority given to the directors under section 551 (previously section 80 of the 1985 Act) to allot shares which is not limited to a particular issue. In these circumstances, directors may be given power by the articles or by a special resolution to allot shares otherwise than on a pre-emptive basis. As was the case with its predecessor, the duration of this power is linked (by subsection (3)) to the duration of the general authority to allot shares, and provision is made for the power to be renewed (by special resolution) if the authority is renewed. An allotment can be made after the power conferred by the section has expired in pursuance of an agreement made while it was effective.   **17.570.02**

While the FSA's Listing Rules do not restrict disapplication of statutory pre-emption rights, self-regulation on the part of institutional investors does. Guidelines drawn up by the Stock Exchange Pre-Emption Group[97] in 1987[98] limit the size of share issues not involving pre-emption rights that will be approved by ABI/NAPF members when voting on a disapplication resolution and control the price at which such an issue can be made. Such resolutions for an annual disapplication of pre-emptive rights will be approved by ABI/NAPF members provided they do not exceed 5 per cent of the issued ordinary share capital shown in the latest published annual accounts. A cumulative limit is also applied to restrict issues made over a three-year period by a company using its disapplication entitlement to 7.5 per cent of issued ordinary share capital shown by the latest published annual accounts. As regards the price of an issue to non-shareholders, the Pre-Emption Guidelines provide that any discount should not exceed 5 per cent and the Stock Exchange monitors this guideline both before and after an issue is made.[99]   **17.570.03**

### 571  Disapplication of pre-emption rights by special resolution

(1)  Where the directors of a company are authorised for the purposes of section 551 (power of directors to allot shares etc: authorisation by company), whether generally or otherwise, the company may by special resolution resolve that section 561 (existing shareholders' right of pre-emption)—   **17.571.01**

(a)  does not apply to a specified allotment of equity securities to be made pursuant to that authorisation, or

(b)  applies to such an allotment with such modifications as may be specified in the resolution.

(2)  Where such a resolution is passed the provisions of this Chapter have effect accordingly.

---

[95]  Companies Act 2006 (Commencement No 8, Transitional Provisions and Savings) Order 2008, SI 2008/2860, art 3(k).

[96]  Companies Act 2006 (Commencement No 8, Transitional Provisions and Savings) Order 2008, SI 2008/2860, Sch 2, paras 52 and 53.

[97]  The group comprises representatives of institutional investors, investment banks, and listed companies.

[98]  For the current version see 'Disapplying pre-emption rights, a statement of principles' (July 2008) at <http://www.pre-emptiongroup.org.uk/pre-emptiongroup/media/Documents/Statement-of-Principles-July-2008.pdf>.

[99]  The Pre-Emption Guidelines require companies to complete a form showing the projected discount at which the new shares will be issued and the actual discount at which the shares are issued. The actual discount will reflect market conditions at the time that the pricing decision is made.

(3) A special resolution under this section ceases to have effect when the authorisation to which it relates—
  (a) is revoked or
  (b) would (if not renewed) expire.
But if the authorisation is renewed the resolution may also be renewed, for a period not longer than that for which the authorisation is renewed, by a special resolution of the company.
(4) Notwithstanding that any such resolution has expired, the directors may allot equity securities in pursuance of an offer or agreement previously made by the company if the resolution enabled the company to make an offer or agreement that would or might require equity securities to be allotted after it expired.
(5) A special resolution under this section, or a special resolution to renew such a resolution, must not be proposed unless—
  (a) it is recommended by the directors, and
  (b) the directors have complied with the following provisions.
(6) Before such a resolution is proposed, the directors must make a written statement setting out—
  (a) their reasons for making the recommendation,
  (b) the amount to be paid to the company in respect of the equity securities to be allotted, and
  (c) the directors' justification of that amount.
(7) The directors' statement must—
  (a) if the resolution is proposed as a written resolution, be sent or submitted to every eligible member at or before the time at which the proposed resolution is sent or submitted to him;
  (b) if the resolution is proposed at a general meeting, be circulated to the members entitled to notice of the meeting with that notice.

COMMENCEMENT DATE 1 October 2009[100]

**17.571.02**    This section replaces the provisions of section 95(2) of the 1985 Act and deals with circumstances in which the directors have any form of authority to allot shares under section 551. This means that, as well as covering the general authority dealt with by section 570, it covers authority given for a specific allotment only. In such circumstances, directors may be given power by a special resolution to make an offer otherwise than on a pre-emptive basis. The resolution must be recommended by the directors, who must make a written statement setting out, *inter alia*, their reasons for their recommendation.[101] The written statement must be circulated to members in accordance with subsection (7), which seeks to ensure that members have adequate time to consider the statement before voting on the associated resolution (to disapply pre-emption rights). As was the case with its predecessor, the duration of this power is linked (by subsection (3)) to the duration of the authority to allot shares, and provision is made for the power to be renewed (by special resolution) if the authority is renewed. An allotment can be made after the power conferred by the section has expired in pursuance of an agreement made while it was effective.

**17.571.03**    Similar considerations apply under this section with regard to the role of self-regulation by institutional investors as with section 570. Disapplication of pre-emption rights may be considered so as to facilitate the making of an 'open offer', which is similar to a rights issue, except that it is not made by a renounceable letter of allotment. The main attractions of an open offer are the possibility of a shorter timetable for the offering and the possibility of excluding overseas shareholders from the offer.

**572 Liability for false statement in directors' statement**

**17.572.01**    (1) This section applies in relation to a directors' statement under section 571 (special resolution disapplying pre-emption rights) that is sent, submitted or circulated under subsection (7) of that section.
(2) A person who knowingly or recklessly authorises or permits the inclusion of any matter that is misleading, false or deceptive in a material particular in such a statement commits an offence.
(3) A person guilty of an offence under this section is liable—
  (a) on conviction on indictment, to imprisonment for a term not exceeding two years or a fine (or both);
  (b) on summary conviction—
    (i) in England and Wales, to imprisonment for a term not exceeding twelve months or to a fine not exceeding the statutory maximum (or both);

[100] Companies Act 2006 (Commencement No 8, Transitional Provisions and Savings) Order 2008, SI 2008/2860, art 3(k).
[101] It is irrelevant whether this statement is made or sent, submitted or circulated before, on, or after 1 October 2009: Companies Act 2006 (Commencement No 8, Transitional Provisions and Savings) Order 2008, SI 2008/2860, Sch 2, para 54(1).

(ii)  in Scotland or Northern Ireland, to imprisonment for a term not exceeding six months, or to a fine not exceeding the statutory maximum (or both).

COMMENCEMENT DATE  1 October 2009[102]

This section replaces section 95(6) of the Companies Act 1985 and has the same effect. Criminal liability under the section may attach to any person, not just directors, although the statement to which the section relates is one made by the directors (under section 571(7)). There is no liability for statements that are simply negligent without being reckless, nor is there express provision providing for liability in respect of omissions, although it might be argued that some omissions fall within 'misleading' material.      **17.572.02**

### 573  Disapplication of pre-emption rights: sale of treasury shares

(1)  This section applies in relation to a sale of shares that is an allotment of equity securities by virtue of section [560(3)][a] (sale of shares held by company as treasury shares).      **17.573.01**

(2)  The directors of a company may be given power by the articles, or by a special resolution of the company, to allot equity securities as if section 561 (existing shareholders' right of pre-emption)—
    (a)  did not apply to the allotment, or
    (b)  applied to the allotment with such modifications as the directors may determine.

(3)  The provisions of section 570(2) and (4) apply in that case as they apply to a case within subsection (1) of that section.

(4)  The company may by special resolution resolve that section 561—
    (a)  shall not apply to a specified allotment of securities, or
    (b)  shall apply to the allotment with such modifications as may be specified in the resolution.

(5)  The provisions of section 571(2) and (4) to (7) apply in that case as they apply to a case within subsection (1) of that section.

AMENDMENTS AND NOTES

[a]  Amended by the Companies Act 2006 (Allotment of Shares and Right of Pre-emption) (Amendment) Regulations 2009, SI 2009/2561, reg 2(5).

COMMENCEMENT DATE  1 October 2009[103]

Holding shares in treasury is a technique for managing the share capital of a company that was introduced in 2003.[104] It enables certain companies (principally those which are listed or whose shares are admitted to trading on the Alternative Investment Market and equivalent companies in the EEA) to buy back qualifying shares and hold them 'in treasury', without being subject to the normal requirement for such shares to be cancelled. Shares held in treasury can subsequently be sold, and it is the ability of the company to adjust shares so held that provides a technique for adjusting the share capital according to the needs of the company. In principle, the pre-emptive rights contained in section 561 apply to sales of treasury shares and this section therefore deals with disapplication of pre-emption rights in these circumstances.[105]      **17.573.02**

Subsection (2) permits a general power to be given by the articles or by special resolution to the directors to allot shares held in treasury otherwise than on a pre-emptive basis. Subsection (4) permits a power to be given by special resolution to make a specific allotment of shares held in treasury.      **17.573.03**

Subsections (3) and (5) have the effect that, following a disapplication of pre-emption rights in respect of treasury shares, the provisions of sections 570 and 571 which relate to the making of an allotment following disapplication of pre-emption rights apply.      **17.573.04**

### *Supplementary*

### 574  References to holder of shares in relation to offer

(1)  In this Chapter, in relation to an offer to allot securities required by—      **17.574.01**
    (a)  section 561 (existing shareholders' right of pre-emption), or
    (b)  any provision to which section 568 applies (articles conferring corresponding right),

---

[102]  Companies Act 2006 (Commencement No 8, Transitional Provisions and Savings) Order 2008, SI 2008/2860, art 3(k).

[103]  Companies Act 2006 (Commencement No 8, Transitional Provisions and Savings) Order 2008, SI 2008/2860, art 3(k).

[104]  Companies (Acquisition of Own Shares) (Treasury Shares) Regulations 2003, SI 2003/1116 amended the 1985 Act to allow for the introduction of the technique.

[105]  As to the transitional provisions, see Companies Act 2006 (Commencement No 8, Transitional Provisions and Savings) Order 2008, SI 2008/2860, Sch 2, para 55.

a reference (however expressed) to the holder of shares of any description is to whoever was the holder of shares of that description at the close of business on a date to be specified in the offer.

(2)   The specified date must fall within the period of 28 days immediately before the date of the offer.

COMMENCEMENT DATE 1 October 2009[106]

**17.574.02**   This section defines a holder of shares for the purposes of this Chapter.

### 575 Saving for other restrictions on offer or allotment

**17.575.01**
(1)   The provisions of this Chapter are without prejudice to any other enactment by virtue of which a company is prohibited (whether generally or in specified circumstances) from offering or allotting equity securities to any person.
(2)   Where a company cannot by virtue of such an enactment offer or allot equity securities to a holder of ordinary shares of the company, those shares are disregarded for the purposes of section 561 (existing shareholders' right of pre-emption), so that—
(a)   the person is not treated as a person who holds ordinary shares, and
(b)   the shares are not treated as forming part of the ordinary share capital of the company.

COMMENCEMENT DATE 1 October 2009[107]

**17.575.02**   Subsection (1) provides that the provisions of this Chapter are without prejudice to any enactment by virtue of which a company is prohibited (whether generally or in specified circumstances) from offering or allotting equity securities to any person. This refers to the possibility that a restriction may be imposed on shares under section 794, which provides for an order to be made by the court when notice is served by the company under section 802 on a person who is or was interested in shares of the company, and that person fails to give the company any information required by the notice within the time specified within it. Section 445 of the 1985 Act provides a similar power to the Secretary of State when, in connection with an investigation under sections 442 or 444, there is difficulty in finding out the relevant facts about shares. One of the restrictions imposed under section 797 as a consequence of an order under section 794 is that no further shares shall be issued in right of them or in pursuance of any offer made to their holder.

**17.575.03**   Subsection (2) provides that where a company cannot by virtue of such an enactment offer or allot equity securities to a holder of relevant shares or relevant employee shares, those sections have effect as if the shares held by that holder are disregarded for the purposes of section 561.

### 576 Saving for certain older pre-emption requirements

**17.576.01**
(1)   In the case of a public company the provisions of this Chapter do not apply to an allotment of equity securities that are subject to a pre-emption requirement in relation to which section 96(1) of the Companies Act 1985 (c. 6) or Article 106(1) of the Companies (Northern Ireland) Order 1986 applied immediately before the commencement of this Chapter.
(2)   In the case of a private company a pre-emption requirement to which section 96(3) of the Companies Act 1985 or Article 106(3) of the Companies (Northern Ireland) Order 1986, Order applied immediately before the commencement of this Chapter shall have effect, so long as the company remains a private company, as if it were contained in the company's articles.
(3)   A pre-emption requirement to which section 96(4) of the Companies Act 1985 or Article 106(4) of the Companies (Northern Ireland) Order 1986 applied immediately before the commencement of this section shall be treated for the purposes of this Chapter as if it were contained in the company's articles.

COMMENCEMENT DATE 1 October 2009[108]

**17.576.02**   Subsection (1) preserves the effect of section 96(1) of the Companies Act 1985, which provided that sections 89 to 95 of the Companies Act 1985 (the old pre-emptive rights regime) did not apply to a 'pre-1982 pre-emption requirement' of a public company. Such a requirement is in essence a pre-emptive provision imposed by the memorandum, articles, or otherwise before the relevant date by virtue of which the company must make an allotment of equity securities which is inconsistent with sections 89 to 94 of the Companies Act 1985. The effect is that the company remains able to make such an issue.

---

[106] Companies Act 2006 (Commencement No 8, Transitional Provisions and Savings) Order 2008, SI 2008/2860, art 3(k).
[107] Companies Act 2006 (Commencement No 8, Transitional Provisions and Savings) Order 2008, SI 2008/2860, art 3(k).
[108] Companies Act 2006 (Commencement No 8, Transitional Provisions and Savings) Order 2008, SI 2008/2860, art 3(k).

Subsection (2) preserves the effect of section 96(3) of the Companies Act 1985, which provides that in          **17.576.03**
the case of a private company a 'pre-1982 pre-emption requirement' is to be treated as if it were in its
memorandum or articles so long as it remains a private company. This is subject to the proviso that the
requirement is capable, under section 91 of the 1985 Act, of excluding any relevant provisions of
sections 89 to 94 of the 1985 Act. Subsection (3) has the same effect in relation to Northern Ireland.

### 577  Provisions about pre-emption not applicable to shares taken on formation

The provisions of this Chapter have no application in relation to the taking of shares by the subscribers          **17.577.01**
to the memorandum on the formation of the company.

COMMENCEMENT DATE  1 October 2009[109]

This section makes clear that this Chapter has no application to the taking of shares by the subscribers          **17.577.02**
to the memorandum on the formation of a company.

# CHAPTER 4
## PUBLIC COMPANIES: ALLOTMENT WHERE ISSUE NOT FULLY SUBSCRIBED

### 578  Public companies: allotment where issue not fully subscribed

(1)  No allotment shall be made of shares of a public company offered for subscription unless—          **17.578.01**
  (a)  the issue is subscribed for in full, or
  (b)  the offer is made on terms that the shares subscribed for may be allotted—
    (i)  in any event, or
    (ii)  if specified conditions are met (and those conditions are met).
(2)  If shares are prohibited from being allotted by subsection (1) and 40 days have elapsed after the
first making of the offer, all money received from applicants for shares must be repaid to them
forthwith, without interest.
(3)  If any of the money is not repaid within 48 days after the first making of the offer, the directors
of the company are jointly and severally liable to repay it, with interest at the rate for the time
being specified under section 17 of the Judgments Act 1838 (c. 110) from the expiration of the
48th day.
A director is not so liable if he proves that the default in the repayment of the money was not
due to any misconduct or negligence on his part.
(4)  This section applies in the case of shares offered as wholly or partly payable otherwise than in cash
as it applies in the case of shares offered for subscription.
(5)  In that case—
  (a)  the references in subsection (1) to subscription shall be construed accordingly;
  (b)  references in subsections (2) and (3) to the repayment of money received from applicants for
shares include—
    (i)  the return of any other consideration so received (including, if the case so requires, the
release of the applicant from any undertaking), or
    (ii)  if it is not reasonably practicable to return the consideration, the payment of money
equal to its value at the time it was so received;
  (c)  references to interest apply accordingly.
(6)  Any condition requiring or binding an applicant for shares to waive compliance with any
requirement of this section is void.

COMMENCEMENT DATE  1 October 2009[110]

This section replaces section 84 of the Companies Act 1985.[111] The purpose of the rule, which is in          **17.578.02**
mandatory form and implements Article 28 of the Second EC Company Law Directive, is to protect
persons who apply for shares by ensuring that if the increase in capital is not fully subscribed, the
capital will be increased by the amount of the subscriptions only if the offer is made on terms that so
provide. An under-subscribed offer made without reference to such terms poses the risk to subscribers
that the purpose for which the offer was made will not be capable of being pursued by the company. A
40-day period following the making of the offer is permitted to determine if an allotment can be made
under subsection (1). If it cannot, all money received from applicants for shares must be repaid,

---

[109]  Companies Act 2006 (Commencement No 8, Transitional Provisions and Savings) Order 2008, SI
2008/2860, art 3(k).
[110]  Companies Act 2006 (Commencement No 8, Transitional Provisions and Savings) Order 2008, SI
2008/2860, art 3(k).
[111]  As to the transitional provisions, see Companies Act 2006 (Commencement No 8, Transitional Provisions
and Savings) Order 2008, SI 2008/2860, Sch 2, para 56.

without interest. If repayment has not taken place by the 48th day after making the offer[112] the directors are jointly and severally liable to repay the money, with interest. The rate of interest will be as specified under section 17 of the Judgments Act 1838 (currently 8 per cent): this represents a change from the rate of 5 per cent specified by section 84(3) of the 1985 Act. However, a director is not so liable if he proves that the default in the repayment of the money was not due to any misconduct or negligence on his part. The section applies equally to shares offered as wholly or partly payable otherwise than in cash (eg shares offered as consideration for assets purchased by the company).

### 579  Public companies: effect of irregular allotment where issue not fully subscribed

**17.579.01**
(1) An allotment made by a public company to an applicant in contravention of section 578 (public companies: allotment where issue not fully subscribed) is voidable at the instance of the applicant within one month after the date of the allotment, and not later.

(2) It is so voidable even if the company is in the course of being wound up.

(3) A director of a public company who knowingly contravenes, or permits or authorises the contravention of, any provision of section 578 with respect to allotment is liable to compensate the company and the allottee respectively for any loss, damages, costs or expenses that the company or allottee may have sustained or incurred by the contravention.

(4) Proceedings to recover any such loss, damages, costs or expenses may not be brought more than two years after the date of the allotment.

COMMENCEMENT DATE 1 October 2009[113]

**17.579.02**    This section replaces section 85 of the 1985 Act.[114] It allows an applicant to whom an allotment is made in contravention of section 578 to avoid the allotment within one month of the date of the allotment. A director who knowingly permits or authorizes a breach of section 578 is liable to compensate the company and the allottee. A limitation period of two years applies to proceedings to recover such compensation.

## CHAPTER 5
## PAYMENT FOR SHARES

### *General rules*

### 580  Shares not to be allotted at a discount

**17.580.01**
(1) A company's shares must not be allotted at a discount.

(2) If shares are allotted in contravention of this section, the allottee is liable to pay the company an amount equal to the amount of the discount, with interest at the appropriate rate.

COMMENCEMENT DATE 1 October 2009[115]

**17.580.02**    Subsection (1) prohibits the allotment of shares at a discount. A discount refers to the possibility of shares being allotted at less than their nominal or 'par' value. The basis of the rule, which was recognized by the common law,[116] is that a company should not overstate the size of its share capital. The rule applies whether the shares are issued fully paid or partly paid in the first instance. Shares can be issued partly paid but that does not represent a mechanism for allotting at less than the nominal value.

**17.580.03**    Any liability to pay the amount of a discount may be enforced in a winding-up for the benefit of creditors or other shareholders,[117] as the case may be, but the mere fact that some members received their shares at a discount does not entitle other members holding shares properly issued to bring a winding-up petition.[118] As an alternative to these remedies, the company may make the directors who

---

[112] Under s 84 of the 1985 Act, the 40- and 48-day periods ran from the date of issue of the prospectus.

[113] Companies Act 2006 (Commencement No 8, Transitional Provisions and Savings) Order 2008, SI 2008/2860, art 3(k).

[114] As to the transitional provisions, see Companies Act 2006 (Commencement No 8, Transitional Provisions and Savings) Order 2008, SI 2008/2860, Sch 2, para 56.

[115] Companies Act 2006 (Commencement No 8, Transitional Provisions and Savings) Order 2008, SI 2008/2860, art 3(k).

[116] See *Ooregum Gold Mining Co of India v Roper* [1892] AC 125, HL.

[117] *Welton v Saffery* [1897] AC 299, HL.

[118] *Re Pioneers of Mashonaland Syndicate* [1893] 1 Ch 731.

were responsible for the share issue liable to pay the amount of the discount as damages for breach of duty.[119]

The rule that a proper consideration must be obtained for issued shares is applicable in a wide range of   **17.580.04**
situations which clearly survive the statutory confirmation of the principle. For example, the issue of £1
debentures at a discount with a provision that they may be exchanged for fully paid £1 shares
immediately or at any time before a fixed date, is unlawful, as the shares would be issued at a discount.
A company cannot issue 200 £1 shares in satisfaction of a debt of £100,[120] nor can it allot 200 £1 shares
for 50p each in consideration of the allottee making a loan of £100 to the company.[121]

Subsection (2) provides that if shares are allotted in contravention of subsection (1) the allottee is liable   **17.580.05**
to pay the company an amount equal to the amount of the discount, with interest at the appropriate
rate. See the commentary on section 588 for the position of a subsequent holder of the shares.

### 581  Provision for different amounts to be paid on shares

A company, if so authorised by its articles, may—   **17.581.01**

  (a)  make arrangements on the issue of shares for a difference between the shareholders in the
       amounts and times of payment of calls on their shares;
  (b)  accept from any member the whole or part of the amount remaining unpaid on any shares
       held by him, although no part of that amount has been called up;
  (c)  pay dividend in proportion to the amount paid up on each share where a larger amount is
       paid up on some shares than on others.

COMMENCEMENT DATE 1 October 2009[122]

This section consolidates the provisions previously contained in section 119 of the Companies Act   **17.581.02**
1985. It permits a company, if so authorized by its articles, to make provision for different amounts to
be paid on shares and to pay dividends in proportion to the amount paid up on each share.

The first paragraph of the section does not refer to the creation of different classes of share. The   **17.581.03**
nominal value and rights attaching to a class of shares remains unaltered even if an issue of shares of
that class establishes different arrangements in respect of the amount and times of payments of calls.
Article 17 of Table A[123] authorizes a company to make an issue of shares on such terms.

The second paragraph refers to the company accepting from any member the whole or part of the   **17.581.04**
amount remaining unpaid on any shares held by him although no part of that amount has been called
up. Table A contains no provision permitting a company to do this.

The third paragraph provides that a company can pay dividends in proportion to the amount paid up   **17.581.05**
on each share where a larger amount is paid up on some shares than on others. Article 104 of Table A
requires a company to do this, except as otherwise provided by the rights attached to shares.

### 582  General rule as to means of payment

  (1)  Shares allotted by a company, and any premium on them, may be paid up in money's   **17.582.01**
       worth (including goodwill and know-how).
  (2)  This section does not prevent a company—
       (a)  from allotting bonus shares to its members, or
       (b)  from paying up, with sums available for the purpose, any amounts for the time being unpaid
            on any of its shares (whether on account of the nominal value of the shares or by way of
            premium).
  (3)  This section has effect subject to the following provisions of this Chapter (additional rules for
       public companies).

COMMENCEMENT DATE 1 October 2009[124]

This section consolidates the provisions previously contained in section 99(1) and (4) of the Compa-   **17.582.02**
nies Act 1985. Subsection (1) establishes that payment for shares allotted by a company may be in
money or money's worth. This applies both to the nominal value of the shares and any premium that

---

[119]  *Hirsche v Sims* [1894] AC 654.
[120]  *Moseley v Koffyfontein Mines Ltd (No 1)* [1904] 2 Ch 108, CA.
[121]  *Re Wragg Ltd* [1897] 1 Ch 796, 831, CA.
[122]  *Re James Pitkin & Co Ltd* [1916] WN 112.
[123]  Companies Act 2006 (Commencement No 8, Transitional Provisions and Savings) Order 2008, SI
2008/2860, art 3(k).
[124]  See the Companies (Tables A to F) Regulations 1985 (SI 1985/805).

is paid on allotment. Subsection (2) provides that this section does not prevent a company from allotting bonus shares to its members or from paying up, with sums available for the purpose, any amount for the time being unpaid on any of its shares. The concept of a bonus share is that it is a share that is paid up from funds made available by the company and not the members. The designation 'bonus' reflects the appearance that members are receiving something for nothing, but in reality the issue of bonus shares is no more than a re-designation of a company's net assets, which are already attributable to (although not directly owned by) members. A crucial phrase in the subsection is 'sums available for the purpose'. The operation of the principle of maintenance of capital means that in order to allot bonus shares a company must have reserves that can be capitalized (see commentary on section 610). A bonus issue involves such reserves being used to pay up an allotment of new bonus shares to members *pro rata* to their existing holding. As the net assets of the company are unaltered (other then as regards their classification in the balance sheet) following a bonus issue, it can be expected that the value of each share will fall *pro rata* to the scale of the issue (eg a bonus issue of one new share for every four held will, *ceteris paribus*, lead to a 25 per cent decline in value as the number of shares in issue has increased by 25 per cent with no change in net assets).

### 583  Meaning of payment in cash

**17.583.01**
(1) The following provisions have effect for the purposes of the Companies Acts.
(2) A share in a company is deemed paid up (as to its nominal value or any premium on it) in cash, or allotted for cash, if the consideration received for the allotment or payment up is a cash consideration.
(3) A 'cash consideration' means—
    (a) cash received by the company,
    (b) a cheque received by the company in good faith that the directors have no reason for suspecting will not be paid,
    (c) a release of a liability of the company for a liquidated sum,
    (d) an undertaking to pay cash to the company at a future date, or
    (e) payment by any other means giving rise to a present or future entitlement (of the company or a person acting on the company's behalf) to a payment, or credit equivalent to payment, in cash.
(4) The Secretary of State may by order provide that particular means of payment specified in the order are to be regarded as falling within subsection (3)(e).
(5) In relation to the allotment or payment up of shares in a company—
    (a) the payment of cash to a person other than the company, or
    (b) an undertaking to pay cash to a person other than the company, counts as consideration other than cash.
    This does not apply for the purposes of Chapter 3 (allotment of equity securities: existing shareholders' right of pre-emption).
(6) For the purpose of determining whether a share is or is to be allotted for cash, or paid up in cash, 'cash' includes foreign currency.
(7) An order under this section is subject to negative resolution procedure.

COMMENCEMENT DATE 1 October 2009[125]

**17.583.02**  This section consolidates and extends the definition of 'cash' previously contained in section 738 of the Companies Act 1985. Subsection (3)(e) applies only in relation to consideration received in respect of an obligation entered into on or after 1 October 2009.[126] Subsection (4) permits the Secretary of State to designate other forms of payment in cash. One such form of payment that has been designated is a settlement bank's obligation to make a payment in respect of the allotment or payment-up of shares under the CREST settlement system.[127]

---

[125] Companies Act 2006 (Commencement No 8, Transitional Provisions and Savings) Order 2008, SI 2008/2860, art 3(k).

[126] Companies Act 2006 (Commencement No 8, Transitional Provisions and Savings) Order 2008, SI 2008/2860, art 3(k).

[127] Companies Act 2006 (Commencement No 8, Transitional Provisions and Savings) Order 2008, SI 2008/2860, Sch 2, para 57(1).

*Additional rules for public companies*

### 584  Public companies: shares taken by subscribers of memorandum

Shares taken by a subscriber to the memorandum of a public company in pursuance of an undertaking    **17.584.01**
of his in the memorandum, and any premium on the shares, must be paid up in cash.

    COMMENCEMENT DATE  1 October 2009[128]

This section replaces section 106 of the Companies Act 1985.    **17.584.02**

### 585  Public companies: must not accept undertaking to do work or perform services

(1) A public company must not accept at any time, in payment up of its shares or any premium on    **17.585.01**
them, an undertaking given by any person that he or another should do work or perform services
for the company or any other person.

(2) If a public company accepts such an undertaking in payment up of its shares or any premium on
them, the holder of the shares when they or the premium are treated as paid up (in whole or in
part) by the undertaking is liable—

  (a) to pay the company in respect of those shares an amount equal to their nominal value,
together with the whole of any premium or, if the case so requires, such proportion of that
amount as is treated as paid up by the undertaking; and

  (b) to pay interest at the appropriate rate on the amount payable under paragraph (a).

(3) The reference in subsection (2) to the holder of shares includes a person who has an unconditional
right—

  (a) to be included in the company's register of members in respect of those shares, or

  (b) to have an instrument of transfer of them executed in his favour.

    COMMENCEMENT DATE  1 October 2009[129]

This section consolidates the provisions previously contained in section 99(2), (3), and (4) of the    **17.585.02**
Companies Act 1985. Subsection (2) prohibits a public company from accepting as payment for shares
an undertaking given by any person that he or she should do work or perform services for the company
or any other person. It remains open to a private company to accept such an undertaking in payment
for shares as any valuable consideration *prima facie* suffices.[130] The court will not normally enquire
into the adequacy of the payment relative to the shares unless there is evidence that the payment was
illusory or that there is an obvious imbalance between the payment and the value of the shares.[131] In
England, the doctrine of consideration prevents a company accepting as payment past service for
which the company was not obliged to pay[132] but in Scotland such payment is acceptable.[133]

Subsection (2) provides that if a public company does accept an undertaking referred to in subsection    **17.585.03**
(1) as payment for shares, the holder is liable to pay up the shares and any premium on them when they
or the premium are treated as paid up by the company. The holder is also required to pay interest at the
appropriate rate on the amount payable. Subsection (3) makes clear that a 'holder' for this purpose
includes any person who has an unconditional right to be included in the company's register of
members in respect of those shares or to have an instrument of transfer of them executed in his favour.
This encompasses a buyer in a contract for the sale of shares when the transfer of title (ie the change of
registered holder) has not yet occurred as well as a buyer (eg in a sale outside a market in which
standard settlement procedures apply) who has a contractual right to demand that the seller execute an
instrument of transfer in his favour. The reference to an unconditional right to be included in the
register may be problematic in those instances where a company's articles reserve a power to the
directors to approve a transfer of shares to a new member. A prohibited undertaking remains *prima
facie* enforceable under section 591, but as enforcement would result in the company receiving
payment twice for an allotment of shares (following payment by the holder), relief under section 589
would seem appropriate in those circumstances.[134]

---

[128] Companies (Shares and Share Capital) Order 2009, SI 2009/388, art 4.

[129] Companies Act 2006 (Commencement No 8, Transitional Provisions and Savings) Order 2008, SI
2008/2860, art 3(k).

[130] Companies Act 2006 (Commencement No 8, Transitional Provisions and Savings) Order 2008, SI
2008/2860, art 3(k).

[131] See eg *Re Theatrical Trust Ltd, Chapman's Case* [1895] 1 Ch 771, where payment was in the form of an
agreement to become manager for five years.

[132] *Re Wragg Ltd* [1897] 1 Ch 796.

[133] See *Re Eddystone Marine Insurance Co* [1893] 3 Ch 9, CA.

[134] *Park Business Interiors Ltd v Park* [1990] BCC 914.

### 586  Public companies: shares must be at least one-quarter paid up

**17.586.01**
(1)  A public company must not allot a share except as paid up at least as to one-quarter of its nominal value and the whole of any premium on it.

(2)  This does not apply to shares allotted in pursuance of an employees' share scheme.

(3)  If a company allots a share in contravention of this section—

(a)  the share is to be treated as if one-quarter of its nominal value, together with the whole of any premium on it, had been received, and

(b)  the allottee is liable to pay the company the minimum amount which should have been received in respect of the share under subsection (1) (less the value of any consideration actually applied in payment up, to any extent, of the share and any premium on it), with interest at the appropriate rate.

(4)  Subsection (3) does not apply to the allotment of bonus shares, unless the allottee knew or ought to have known the shares were allotted in contravention of this section.

COMMENCEMENT DATE  1 October 2009[135]

**17.586.02**  This section replaces section 101 of the Companies Act 1985. Subsection (1) provides that a public company must not allot a share except as paid up at least as to one-quarter of its nominal value and the whole of any premium on it. For example, if shares of £1 nominal value are allotted at a price of £2, the allotment price must be at least £1.25. A consequence of the rule is to limit the extent to which a rights issue can be discounted when the market value of shares has risen to a level that represents a multiple of the nominal value. In those circumstances, a bonus issue, which has the effect of bringing the market value closer into line with the nominal value, may be required prior to a rights issue to avoid the limiting effect of the rule.

**17.586.03**  Subsection (2) provides that subsection (1) does not apply to shares allotted in pursuance of an employees' share scheme.

**17.586.04**  Subsection (3) provides that if a company allots a share in contravention of subsection (1) the share is to be treated as if one-quarter of its nominal value, together with the whole of any premium on it, had been received. It provides further that the allottee is then liable to pay the company the minimum amount specified in subsection (1) less any payment actually made with interest at the appropriate rate.

**17.586.05**  Subsection (4) provides that subsection (3) does not apply to the allotment of bonus shares, unless the allottee knew or ought to have known the shares were allotted in contravention of subsection (1). The rationale for this approach is presumably that in an allotment of bonus shares the allottee is not called on to make any payment, meaning that he normally relies on the company's internal procedures to satisfy the rule in subsection (1) as to payment. However, it may be that the allottee is implicated (eg by being a director) in the company's failure to observe subsection (1), in which case it is appropriate to hold him responsible for payment.

### 587  Public companies: payment by long-term undertaking

**17.587.01**
(1)  A public company must not allot shares as fully or partly paid up (as to their nominal value or any premium on them) otherwise than in cash if the consideration for the allotment is or includes an undertaking which is to be, or may be, performed more than five years after the date of the allotment.

(2)  If a company allots shares in contravention of subsection (1), the allottee is liable to pay the company an amount equal to the aggregate of their nominal value and the whole of any premium (or, if the case so requires, so much of that aggregate as is treated as paid up by the undertaking), with interest at the appropriate rate.

(3)  Where a contract for the allotment of shares does not contravene subsection (1), any variation of the contract that has the effect that the contract would have contravened the subsection, if the terms of the contract as varied had been its original terms, is void.

This applies also to the variation by a public company of the terms of a contract entered into before the company was re-registered as a public company.

(4)  Where—

(a)  a public company allots shares for a consideration which consists of or includes (in accordance with subsection (1)) an undertaking that is to be performed within five years of the allotment, and

(b)  the undertaking is not performed within the period allowed by the contract for the allotment of the shares,

---

[135]  Another possibility might be to argue that the statutory payment provided for by the section discharges the obligation to provide services. That analysis is not inconsistent with s 591 since that section refers to the undertaking being enforceable by the company apart from this chapter, thereby leaving open the possibility that there may be other impediments to the enforcement of the obligation.

the allottee is liable to pay the company, at the end of the period so allowed, an amount equal to the aggregate of the nominal value of the shares and the whole of any premium (or, if the case so requires, so much of that aggregate as is treated as paid up by the undertaking), with interest at the appropriate rate.

(5) References in this section to a contract for the allotment of shares include an ancillary contract relating to payment in respect of them.

COMMENCEMENT DATE 1 October 2009[136]

This section replaces section 102 of the Companies Act 1985. Subsection (1) prohibits a public company from allotting shares as fully or partly paid up (as to their nominal value or any premium on them) otherwise than in cash if the consideration for the allotment is or includes an undertaking which is to be, or may be, performed more than five years after the date of the allotment. The rationale for the prohibition is presumably to prevent a company accepting as payment for shares an undertaking in respect of which there is some uncertainty as to its performance should the position of the allottee change prior to performance of the undertaking.    **17.587.02**

Subsection (2) provides that if a company allots shares in contravention of subsection (1) the allottee is liable to pay the company an amount equal to the aggregate of their nominal value and the whole of the premium (or, if the case so requires, so much of that aggregate as is treated as paid up by the undertaking), with interest at the appropriate rate. The sanction for contravention is therefore effectively imposed on the allottee, who is required to pay up the shares. The undertaking remains *prima facie* valid under section 591 (see commentary on that section).    **17.587.03**

Subsection (3) is an anti-evasion provision. It provides that any (subsequent) variation of a contract complying with subsection (1) which has the effect of making it non-compliant, is void. This rules out the possibility of using changes to contracts of allotment as a technique to avoid the effect of subsection (1). Subsection (3) applies also to the variation by a public company of the terms of a contract entered into before the company was re-registered as a public company. This covers the situation where a private company is re-registered as a public company and the terms of a contract of allotment are altered so that they would not, if they had been original terms, comply with subsection (1).    **17.587.04**

Subsection (4) refers to the consequences of non-performance by an allottee of an undertaking to be performed within five years that is legitimately accepted by the company as payment for shares. It makes clear that the allottee in these circumstances is liable to pay to the company an amount equal to the value of the shares and the whole of any premium with interest at the appropriate rate. In these circumstances, the payment made to the company can be regarded as a statutory form of liquidated damages, with the result that the obligation to perform the undertaking is discharged.    **17.587.05**

## Supplementary provisions

### 588 Liability of subsequent holders of shares

(1) If a person becomes a holder of shares in respect of which—    **17.588.01**
    (a) there has been a contravention of any provision of this Chapter, and
    (b) by virtue of that contravention another is liable to pay any amount under the provision contravened,
that person is also liable to pay that amount (jointly and severally with any other person so liable), subject as follows.

(2) A person otherwise liable under subsection (1) is exempted from that liability if either—
    (a) he is a purchaser for value and, at the time of the purchase, he did not have actual notice[a] of the contravention concerned, or
    (b) he derived title to the shares (directly or indirectly) from a person who became a holder of them after the contravention and was not liable under subsection (1).

(3) References in this section to a holder, in relation to shares in a company, include any person who has an unconditional right—
    (a) to be included in the company's register of members in respect of those shares, or
    (b) to have an instrument of transfer of the shares executed in his favour.

(4) This section applies in relation to a failure to carry out a term of a contract as mentioned in section 587(4) (public companies: payment by long-term undertaking) as they apply in relation to a contravention of a provision of this Chapter.

AMENDMENTS AND NOTES

---

[136] Companies Act 2006 (Commencement No 8, Transitional Provisions and Savings) Order 2008, SI 2008/2860, art 3(k).

<sup>a</sup> The reference to 'actual notice' strengthens the position of the holder of the shares since it excludes constructive notice: see eg *Eagle Trust plc v SBC Securities Ltd* [1991] BCLC 438.

COMMENCEMENT DATE 1 October 2009[137]

17.588.02      This section replaces section 112 of the Companies Act 1985. Subsection (1) provides that if a person becomes a holder of shares in respect of which there has been a breach of this chapter and by virtue of that contravention another is liable to pay any amount under the section contravened, that person is also liable to pay that amount (jointly and severally with any other person so liable) unless he is exempted from liability by subsection (2). This means that, subject to the exceptions created by subsection (2), a holder is subject to the same liability as an allottee.

17.588.03      Subsection (2) exempts a person otherwise liable under subsection (1) if either:

(i) he is a purchaser for value and, at the time of the purchase, he did not have actual notice of the contravention concerned; or

(ii) he derived title to the shares (directly or indirectly) from a person who became a holder of them after the contravention and was not liable under subsection (1).

17.588.04      A purchaser is not required to enquire as to whether there has been a breach of the relevant provisions and will not be taken to have constructive notice. Therefore, it seems that other than in circumstances in which a purchaser is informed by the seller (unlikely) or the company that there has been a contravention, it will be difficult to show actual notice. A person deriving title to the shares from a holder who is exempt from liability as a purchaser for value is also exempt from liability.

17.588.05      Subsection (3) provides that references in this section to a holder of shares includes a person who has an unconditional right to be included in the company's register of members in respect of those shares or to have an instrument of transfer executed in his favour. This appears to extend the liability (and exemptions) in this section to (i) a buyer of shares in a 'settled' transaction[138] who has not yet been registered as the holder, and (ii) a buyer of shares in an 'unsettled' transaction who has not yet had an instrument of transfer executed in his favour. In the former case, the buyer is the beneficial but not the legal owner. In the latter case, there is only a contract for sale of the shares and therefore only a contractual right to require a transfer.

### 589 Power of court to grant relief

17.589.01

(1) This section applies in relation to liability under—

     section 585(2) (liability of allottee in case of breach by public company: of prohibition on accepting undertaking to do work or perform services),

     section 587(2) or (4) (liability of allottee in case of breach by public company of prohibition on payment by long-term undertaking), or

     section 588 (liability of subsequent holders of shares) as it applies in relation to a contravention of those sections.

(2) A person who—

     (a) is subject to any such liability to a company in relation to payment in respect of shares in the company, or

     (b) is subject to any such liability to a company by virtue of an undertaking given to it in, or in connection with, payment for shares in the company,

may apply to the court to be exempted in whole or in part from the liability.

(3) In the case of a liability within subsection (2)(a), the court may exempt the applicant from the liability only if and to the extent that it appears to the court just and equitable to do so [having regard to—

     (a) whether the applicant has paid, or is liable to pay, any amount in respect of—

         (i) any other liability arising in relation to those shares under any provision of this Chapter or Chapter 6, or

         (ii) any liability arising by virtue of any undertaking given in or in connection with payment for those shares;

     (b) whether any person other than the applicant has paid or is likely to pay, whether in pursuance of any order of the court or otherwise, any such amount;

---

<sup>137</sup> Companies Act 2006 (Commencement No 8, Transitional Provisions and Savings) Order 2008, SI 2008/2860, art 3(k).

<sup>138</sup> Companies Act 2006 (Commencement No 8, Transitional Provisions and Savings) Order 2008, SI 2008/2860, art 3(k).

     (c) whether the applicant or any other person—
         (i) has performed in whole or in part, or is likely so to perform any such undertaking, or
         (ii) has done or is likely to do any other thing in payment or part payment for the shares.]ᵃ

(4) In the case of a liability within subsection (2)(b), the court may exempt the applicant from the liability only if and to the extent that it appears to the court just and equitable to do so [having regard to—
     (a) whether the applicant has paid or is liable to pay any amount in respect of liability arising in relation to the shares under any provision of this Chapter or Chapter 6;
     (b) whether any person other than the applicant has paid or is likely to pay, whether in pursuance of any order of the court or otherwise, any such amount.]ᵇ

(5) In determining whether it should exempt the applicant in whole or in part from any liability, the court must have regard to the following overriding principles—
     (a) a company that has allotted shares should receive money or money's worth at least equal in value to the aggregate of the nominal value of those shares and the whole of any premium or, if the case so requires, so much of that aggregate as is treated as paid up;
     (b) subject to that, where a company would, if the court did not grant the exemption, have more than one remedy against a particular person, it should be for the company to decide which remedy it should remain entitled to pursue.

(6) If a person brings proceedings against another ('the contributor') for a contribution in respect of liability to a company arising under any provision of this Chapter or Chapter 6 and it appears to the court that the contributor is liable to make such a contribution, the court may, if and to the extent that it appears to it, just and equitable to do so having regard to the respective culpability (in respect of the liability to the company) of the contributor and the person bringing the proceedings—
     (a) exempt the contributor in whole or in part from his liability to make such a contribution, or
     (b) order the contributor to make a larger contribution than, but for this subsection, he would be liable to make.

AMENDMENTS AND NOTES

ᵃ Words in square brackets are omitted in relation to a decision whether to grant relief in respect of a liability arising before 1 October 2009: Companies Act 2006 (Commencement, Transitional Provisions and Savings) Order 2008, SI 2008/2860, Sch 2, para 58.

ᵇ Words in square brackets are omitted in relation to a decision whether to grant relief in respect of a liability arising before 1 October 2009: Companies Act 2006 (Commencement, Transitional Provisions and Savings) Order 2008, SI 2008/2860, Sch 2, para 58.

COMMENCEMENT DATE 1 October 2009

This section replaces section 113(1) to (8) of the Companies Act 1985 and extends its provisions. **17.589.02**
Subsection (2) provides that where a person is liable to a company as a result of a contravention relating to the provisions set out in subsection (1) he may make an application to the court to be exempted in whole or in part from the liability. Subsection (3) sets out the requirements that must be met before the court exempts a person from liability under subsection (2)(a). Subsection (4) sets out the matters to be taken into account by the court in granting relief from a liability falling within subsection (2)(b).[139] Subsection (5) is new and sets out two overriding principles which apply when the court determines whether it should exempt the applicant in whole or part from any liability. The second principle emphasis that it is for the company and not the court to decide what remedy it should pursue against an allottee or holder of shares: the effect presumably is to prevent the court granting relief on the sole basis that the company has another remedy available to it.

## 590 Penalty for contravention of this Chapter

(1) If a company contravenes any of the provisions of this Chapter, an offence is committed by— **17.590.01**
     (a) the company, and
     (b) every officer of the company who is in default.

(2) A person guilty of an offence under this section is liable—
     (a) on conviction on indictment, to a fine;
     (b) on summary conviction, to a fine not exceeding the statutory maximum.

COMMENCEMENT DATE 1 October 2009[140]

---

[139] i.e one in which payment has been made and an instrument of transfer executed in the buyer's favour (or in CREST, an authorized instruction requiring a change to the Operator register of members issued on his behalf).

[140] Companies Act 2006 (Commencement No 8, Transitional Provisions and Savings) Order 2008, SI 2008/2860, art 3(k). See *Re Bradford Investments plc (No 2)* [1991] BCC 224, stressing that it is for the applicants

**17.590.02**    This section provides for the imposition of a penalty, in the form of a fine, on a company and its officers if the company contravenes any of the provisions of Chapter 5.

### 591  Enforceability of undertakings to do work etc

**17.591.01**    (1)  An undertaking given by any person, in or in connection with payment for shares in a company, to do work or perform services or to do any other thing, if it is enforceable by the company apart from this Chapter, is so enforceable notwithstanding that there has been a contravention in relation to it of a provision of this Chapter or Chapter 6.

(2)  This is without prejudice to section 589 (power of court to grant relief etc in respect of liabilities).

COMMENCEMENT DATE  1 October 2009[141]

**17.591.02**    This section provides that, subject to section 589, a contravention of this Chapter does not in itself render unenforceable an undertaking given by any person to do work or perform services or do any other thing in connection with payment for shares. This would in principle allow for the company to receive payment twice for the same allotment of shares as it could enforce the undertaking and also require payment under section 587(4). In these circumstances exemption from liability under section 589 would seem the sensible solution to the extent necessary to avoid the company receiving more than full payment for an allotment of shares.

### 592  The appropriate rate of interest

**17.592.01**    (1)  For the purposes of this Chapter the 'appropriate rate' of interest is 5% per annum or such other rate as may be specified by order made by the Secretary of State.

(2)  An order under this section is subject to negative resolution procedure.

COMMENCEMENT DATE  1 October 2009[142]

**17.592.02**    This section fixes the appropriate rate of interest for this Chapter.

# CHAPTER 6
## PUBLIC COMPANIES: INDEPENDENT VALUATION OF NON-CASH CONSIDERATION

### *Non-cash consideration for shares*

### 593  Public company: valuation of non-cash consideration for shares

**17.593.01**    (1)  A public company must not allot shares as fully or partly paid up (as to their nominal value or any premium on them) otherwise than in cash unless—

(a)  the consideration for the allotment has been independently valued in accordance with the provisions of this Chapter,

(b)  the valuer's report has been made to the company during the six months immediately preceding the allotment of the shares, and

(c)  a copy of the report has been sent to the proposed allottee.

(2)  For this purpose the application of an amount standing to the credit of—

(a)  any of a company's reserve accounts, or

(b)  its profit and loss account,

in paying up (to any extent) shares allotted to members of the company, or premiums on shares so allotted, does not count as consideration for the allotment.

(3)  If a company allots shares in contravention of subsection (1) and either—

(a)  the allottee has not received the valuer's report required to be sent to him, or

(b)  there has been some other contravention of the requirements of this section or section 596 that the allottee knew or ought to have known amounted to a contravention,

the allottee is liable to pay the company an amount equal to the aggregate of the nominal value of the shares and the whole of any premium (or, if the case so requires, so much of that aggregate as is treated as paid up by the consideration), with interest at the appropriate rate.

---

to make out a good case for relief and that it will be very difficult to meet the 'just and equitable' requirement of subsection (4) when the company has not received full value (in the form of non-cash consideration) for shares.

[141] Companies Act 2006 (Commencement No 8, Transitional Provisions and Savings) Order 2008, SI 2008/2860, art 3(k).

[142] Companies Act 2006 (Commencement No 8, Transitional Provisions and Savings) Order 2008, SI 2008/2860, art 3(k).

(4) This section has effect subject to—

> section 594 (exception to valuation requirement: arrangement with another company), and
>
> section 595 (exception to valuation requirement: merger [or division][143]).

COMMENCEMENT DATE 1 October 2009[144]

This section consolidates some of the provisions previously contained in section 103 of the Companies Act 1985. Subsection (1) sets out three requirements that must be met before a public company can allot shares for a non-cash consideration. Cash is defined by section 583 (above). Non-cash consideration is therefore a form of payment for shares that falls outside this definition or is a payment, or an undertaking to pay cash, to a person other than the company. The requirements apply whether the shares are fully or partly paid up and also when an allotment of shares is mixed with other consideration given by the company in exchange for non-cash consideration. In those circumstances the valuer must also value the other consideration to determine what proportion of the consideration provided by the allottee is attributable to the shares (see commentary on section 596). The three requirements of subsection (1) are first that the consideration for the allotment must be independently valued in accordance with this Chapter; second, that a report with respect to its value is made to the company within the prescribed timescale; and third, that a copy of the report has been sent to the proposed allottee.  **17.593.02**

Subsection (3) provides that if the company allots shares in contravention of subsection (1) and either the allottee has not received the valuer's report required by that subsection or there has been some other contravention of this Chapter, which the allottee knew or ought to have known amounted to a contravention, the allottee is liable to pay up the shares with interest at the appropriate rate. Paying up refers to paying up the nominal value and any premium or, if the case so requires, so much of the aggregate as is treated as paid up by the consideration. Failure to pay on the part of the allottee may result in the disenfranchisement of the relevant shares where the articles contain a relevant provision.[145]  **17.593.03**

While section 565 provides that allotments of equity securities for non-cash consideration need not be on a pre-emptive basis, it remains open to a company to make such an allotment on a pre-emptive basis. If it does, then the requirements of this section apply in the normal way, subject to the exceptions provided by sections 594 and 595. However, the constraints imposed by a pre-emptive offer, both in respect of the sources of new capital (limited to existing shareholders) and the offer timetable, are likely to make this option unattractive in most cases.  **17.593.04**

### 594 Exception to valuation requirement: arrangement with another company

(1) Section 593 (valuation of non-cash consideration) does not apply to the allotment of shares by a company ('company A') in connection with an arrangement to which this section applies.  **17.594.01**

(2) This section applies to an arrangement for the allotment of shares in company A on terms that the whole or part of the consideration for the shares allotted is to be provided by—
   (a) the transfer to that company, or
   (b) the cancellation,
   of all or some of the shares, or of all or some of the shares of a particular class, in another company ('company B').

(3) It is immaterial whether the arrangement provides for the issue to company A of shares, or shares of any particular class, in company B.

(4) This section applies to an arrangement only if under the arrangement it is open to all the holders of the shares in company B (or, where the arrangement applies only to shares of a particular class, to all the holders of shares of that class) to take part in the arrangement.

(5) In determining whether that is the case, the following shall be disregarded—
   (a) shares held by or by a nominee of company A;
   (b) shares held by or by a nominee of a company which is—
      (i) the holding company, or a subsidiary, of company A, or
      (ii) a subsidiary of such a holding company;
   (c) shares held as treasury shares by company B.

[143] Inserted by the Companies (Reporting Requirements in Mergers and Divisions) Regulations 2011 SI 2011/1606 Part 2, reg 2(4)(b).
[144] Companies Act 2006 (Commencement No 8, Transitional Provisions and Savings) Order 2008, SI 2008/2860, art 3(k).
[145] Companies Act 2006 (Commencement No 8, Transitional Provisions and Savings) Order 2008, SI 2008/2860, art 3(k).

(6) In this section—

    (a) 'arrangement' means any agreement, scheme or arrangement (including an arrangement sanctioned in accordance with—

        (i) Part 26 (arrangements and reconstructions), or

        (ii) section 110 of the Insolvency Act 1986 (c. 45) or Article 96 of the Insolvency (Northern Ireland) Order 1989 (S.I. 1989/2405 (N.I. 19)) (liquidator in winding up accepting shares as consideration for sale of company property), and

    (b) 'company', except in reference to company A, includes any body corporate.

COMMENCEMENT DATE 1 October 2009[146]

**17.594.02**    This section consolidates the provisions previously contained in sections 103(3) and (4) of the Companies Act 1985. It excludes from the scope of section 593 allotments that are made in connection with takeovers or other arrangements (eg under Part 26 or section 110 of the Insolvency Act 1986) when some or all of the consideration for the allotment of the bidder's shares is the transfer of shares in the target to the bidder or cancellation of shares in the target. The rationale for this exclusion is presumably that there is an adequate mechanism for the valuation of the non-cash consideration provided by the freedom of the target's shareholders to accept or decline the bidder's offer according to its perceived adequacy. Subsection (4) limits the exclusion established by subsection (3) to circumstances in which the arrangement is open to all the shareholders in the target company or, where the offer is in respect of a particular class, all the members of that class. Subsection (5) refers to certain shares that are to be excluded in determining whether the arrangement is open to all the holders.

### 595 Exception to valuation requirement: merger [or division][147]

**17.595.01**    (1) Section 593 (valuation of non-cash consideration) does not apply to the allotment of shares by a company [as part of a scheme to which Part 27 (mergers and divisions of public companies) applies if-

    (a) in the case of a scheme involving a merger, an expert's report is drawn up as required by section 909, or

    (b) in the case of a scheme involving a division, an expert's report is drawn up as required by section 924.][148]

    (2) [...](3) [...][149]

COMMENCEMENT DATE 1 October 2009[150]

**17.595.02**    This section consolidates the provisions previously contained in section 103(5) of the Companies Act 1985. It excludes from the scope of section 593 an allotment by a company in connection with its proposed merger with another company. Merger in this context is taken to be an arrangement whereby one company proposes to acquire all the assets and liabilities of the other in exchange for an issue of shares or other securities to the shareholders of the other, with or without any cash payment to shareholders. This differs from an arrangement referred to in section 594(2) in that the consideration is in the form of business assets, leaving the 'target' as a 'shell' whose shares are still held by its shareholders. In this case, the rationale for exclusion from the scope of section 593 is presumably the same as that referred to above in the commentary on section 594.

### 596 Non-cash consideration for shares: requirements as to valuation and report

**17.596.01**    (1) The provisions of sections 1150 to 1153 (general provisions as to independent valuation and report) apply to the valuation and report required by section 593 (public company: valuation of non-cash consideration for shares).

---

[146] See *Re Bradford investments plc* [1990] RCC 224, for a case in which disenfranchisement operated as a result of such a provision in the articles. Article 41 of the Model Articles for public companies (SI 2008/3229) could have the same effect.

[147] Inserted by the Companies (Reporting Requirements in Mergers and Divisions) Regulations 2011, SI 2011/1606 Part 2, reg 2(4)(a).

[148] Inserted by the Companies (Reporting Requirements in Mergers and Divisions) Regulations 2011, SI 2011/1606 Part 2, reg 2(2).

[149] Subsections (2) and (3) repealed by the Companies (Reporting Requirements in Mergers and Divisions) Regulations 2011, SI 2011/1606, reg 2(3).

[150] Companies Act 2006 (Commencement No 8, Transitional Provisions and Savings) Order 2008, SI 2008/2860, art 3(k).

(2) The valuer's report must state—
  (a) the nominal value of the shares to be wholly or partly paid for by the consideration in question;
  (b) the amount of any premium payable on the shares;
  (c) the description of the consideration and, as respects so much of the consideration as he himself has valued, a description of that part of the consideration, the method used to value it and the date of the valuation;
  (d) the extent to which the nominal value of the shares and any premium are to be treated as paid up—
     (i) by the consideration;
     (ii) in cash.
(3) The valuer's report must contain or be accompanied by a note by him—
  (a) in the case of a valuation made by a person other than himself, that it appeared to himself reasonable to arrange for it to be so made or to accept a valuation so made,
  (b) whoever made the valuation that the method of valuation was reasonable in all the circumstances,
  (c) that it appears to the valuer that there has been no material change in the value of the consideration in question since the valuation, and
  (d) that, on the basis of the valuation, the value of the consideration, together with any cash by which the nominal value of the shares or any premium payable on them is to be paid up, is not less than so much of the aggregate of the nominal value and the whole of any such premium as is treated as paid up by the consideration and any such cash.
(4) Where the consideration to be valued is accepted partly in payment up of the nominal value of the shares and any premium and partly for some other consideration given by the company, section 593 and the preceding provisions of this section apply as if references to the consideration accepted by the company included the proportion of that consideration that is properly attributable to the payment up of that value and any premium.
(5) In such a case—
  (a) the valuer must carry out, or arrange for, such other valuations as will enable him to determine that proportion, and
  (b) his report must state what valuations have been made under this subsection and also the reason for, and method and date of, any such valuation and any other matters which may be relevant to that determination.

COMMENCEMENT DATE 1 October 2009[151]

This section replaces section 108 of the Companies Act 1985. Subsection (2) sets out the requirements **17.596.02** for the valuation report. It is required to state the following:

(a) The nominal value of the shares to be wholly or partly paid for by the consideration in question.
(b) The amount of any premium payable on the shares.

These two elements are necessary in order that an assessment can be made of the adequacy of the non-cash consideration to be paid to the company in return for the allotment. They also allow an assessment to be made as to whether the company is issuing the shares at an appropriate price. That issue is important because even if the non-cash consideration does represent the value that is claimed for it by the company making the allotment, shareholders will suffer dilution in their shareholding if shares are allotted at less than the full market price. In the case of companies whose shares are not listed, the determination of the allotment price may pose a greater problem in that there may be no recent transactions that will act as a guide to market value.

(c) A description of the (non-cash) consideration and, as respects so much of the consideration as the valuer has valued, a description of that part of the consideration, the method used to value it and the date of the valuation.
(d) The extent to which the nominal value of the shares and any premium are to be treated as paid up by the (non-cash) consideration and in cash. This also carries implications for the adequacy of the non-cash consideration since the general objective of the valuation report is to ensure that the value of the non-cash consideration matches the aggregate of the nominal value and premium that are to be treated as paid up by that form of consideration. While the process of matching is transparent in the case of cash consideration, it can only be assessed in the case of non-cash consideration with the benefit of a valuation.

Subsection (3) requires that the valuer's report shall contain or be accompanied by a note which **17.596.03** justifies and explains any part of a valuation made by a delegate. Paragraph (d) focuses on the adequacy

---

[151] Companies Act 2006 (Commencement No 8, Transitional Provisions and Savings) Order 2008, SI 2008/2860, art 3(k).

of the consideration and is intended to ensure that non-cash consideration does indeed represent full payment for that part of an allotment in respect of which it is given as consideration.

**17.596.04**   Subsections (4) and (5) deal with the situation in which non-cash consideration is accepted by a company partly in payment for an allotment of shares and partly for some other consideration. It provides that the provisions of section 593 and the preceding provisions of this section apply equally to the part of the non-cash consideration that is attributable to the allotment of shares. The valuer is required to carry out, or arrange for, such other valuations as will enable him to determine that proportion. His report is required to state what valuations have been made under this subsection and also the reason for, and method of, any such valuation and any other matters which may be relevant to the determination.

### 597 Copy of report to be delivered to registrar

**17.597.01**   (1)  A company to which a report is made under section 593 as to the value of any consideration for which, or partly for which, it proposes to allot shares must deliver a copy of the report to the registrar for registration.

(2)  The copy must be delivered at the same time that the company files the return of the allotment of those shares under section 555 (return of allotment by limited company).

(3)  If default is made in complying with subsection (1) or (2), an offence is committed by every officer of the company who is in default.

(4)  A person guilty of an offence under this section is liable—

    (a)  on conviction on indictment, to a fine;

    (b)  on summary conviction, to a fine not exceeding the statutory maximum and, for continued contravention, a daily default fine not exceeding one-tenth of the statutory maximum.

(5)  In the case of default in delivering to the registrar any document as required by this section, any person liable for the default may apply to the court for relief.

(6)  The court, if satisfied—

    (a)  that the omission to deliver the document was accidental or due to inadvertence, or

    (b)  that it is just and equitable to grant relief,

    may make an order extending the time for delivery of the document for such period as the court thinks proper.

COMMENCEMENT DATE 1 October 2009[152]

**17.597.02**   This section replaces section 111 of the Companies Act 1985. Subsection (1) requires that a report made under section 593 shall be delivered to the registrar of companies for registration at the same time as a company files the return of allotments of the relevant shares. Under section 555 the time-limit for the making of a return following an allotment is one month.

### *Transfer of non-cash asset in initial period*

### 598 Public company: agreement for transfer of non-cash asset in initial period

**17.598.01**   (1)  A public company formed as such must not enter into an agreement —

    (a)  with a person who is a subscriber to the company's memorandum,

    (b)  for the transfer by him to the company, or another, before the end of the company's initial period of one or more non-cash assets, and

    (c)  under which the consideration for the transfer to be given by the company is at the time of the agreement equal in value to one-tenth or more of the company's issued share capital.

    unless the conditions referred to below have been complied with.

(2)  The company's 'initial period' means the period of two years beginning with the date of the company being issued with a certificate under section 761 (trading certificate).

(3)  The conditions are those specified in—

    section 599 (requirement of independent valuation), and

    section 601 (requirement of approval by members).

(4)  This section does not apply where—

    (a)  it is part of the company's ordinary business to acquire, or arrange for other persons to acquire, assets of a particular description, and

    (b)  the agreement is entered into by the company in the ordinary course of that business.

(5)  This section does not apply to an agreement entered into by the company under the supervision of the court or of an officer authorised by the court for the purpose.

---

[152] Companies Act 2006 (Commencement No 8, Transitional Provisions and Savings) Order 2008, SI 2008/2860, art 3(k).

COMMENCEMENT DATE 1 October 2009[153]

This section consolidates some of the provisions previously contained in section 104 of the Companies **17.598.02**
Act 1985: the remaining provisions have been taken to sections 599, 600, and 601. It regulates
agreements whereby a public company enters into agreements with a subscriber to the memorandum
for the transfer by him to the company or another person of one or more non-cash assets equal to
one-tenth or more of the company's issued share capital within what is described as the 'initial period'.
The objective of the section appears to be to the prevention of fraud on the part of promoters of public
companies, although the extent to which it is capable of achieving that objective has been questioned
on the basis that public companies are rarely formed as such and that potential fraudsters can place
themselves outside the reach of the section by avoiding being a member of the company at the
appropriate time.[154] The section is more broadly formulated than section 593 because it applies
irrespective of whether or not the consideration given by the company for the transfer of non-cash
assets is an allotment of shares or not. Subsection (1) prohibits a public company from entering into an
agreement of the type referred to above within the initial period unless the conditions specified in
sections 599 and 601 are complied with if the consideration for the transfer to be given to the company
is equal in value at the time of the agreement to one-tenth or more of the company's nominal share
capital issued at the time.

## 599  Agreement for transfer of non-cash asset: requirement of independent valuation

(1)  The following conditions must have been complied with—                                **17.599.01**
  (a)  the consideration to be received by the company, and any consideration other than cash to
       be given by the company, must have been independently valued in accordance with the
       provisions of this Chapter,
  (b)  the valuer's report must have been made to the company during the six months immediately
       preceding the date of the agreement, and
  (c)  a copy of the report must have been sent to the other party to the proposed agreement not
       later than the date on which copies have to be circulated to members under section 601(3).
(2)  The reference in subsection (1)(a) to the consideration to be received by the company is to the
     asset to be transferred to it or, as the case may be, to the advantage to the company of the asset's
     transfer to another person.
(3)  The reference in subsection (1)(c) to the other party to the proposed agreement is to the person
     referred to in section 598(1)(a).
     If he has received a copy of the report under section 601 in his capacity as a member of the
     company, it is not necessary to send another copy under this section.
(4)  This section does not affect any requirement to value any consideration for purposes of section
     593 (valuation of non-cash consideration for shares).

COMMENCEMENT DATE 1 October 2009[155]

This section requires an independent valuation as a condition for the making of a transfer which would **17.599.02**
otherwise be prohibited by section 598. Subsection (2) clarifies the requirement to have valued the
non-cash asset being transferred to the company by providing that it includes a requirement to value
the benefit to the company when the agreement provides for the transfer of the non-cash asset to a
person other than the company. This would apply, for example, where a company entered into an
agreement for the transfer of a non-cash asset to its subsidiary. In those circumstances, the valuation
would require to take into account the percentage shareholding in the subsidiary. Subsection (4) makes
clear that the requirement to value a non-cash asset under this section is without prejudice to any
requirement to value any consideration for the purposes of section 593.

## 600  Agreement for transfer of non-cash asset: requirements as to valuation and report

(1)  The provisions of sections 1150 to 1153 (general provisions as to independent valuation and **17.600.01**
     report) apply to the valuation and report required by section 599 (public company: transfer of
     non-cash asset).
(2)  The valuer's report must state—

---

[153] Companies Act 2006 (Commencement No 8, Transitional Provisions and Savings) Order 2008, SI
2008/2860, art 3(k).
[154] See J Birds, AJ Boyle, B Clark, I MacNeil, G McCormack, C Twigg-Flesner, C Villiers (eds), *Boyle & Birds'
Company Law* (8th edn, 2011, Bristol, Jordans), para 7.14.4
[155] Companies Act 2006 (Commencement No 8, Transitional Provisions and Savings) Order 2008, SI
2008/2860, art 3(k).

(a)  the consideration to be received by the company, describing the asset in question (specifying the amount to be received in cash) and the consideration to be given by the company (specifying the amount to be given in cash), and

(b)  the method and date of valuation.

(3)  The valuer's report must contain or be accompanied by a note by him—

(a)  in the case of a valuation made by a person other than himself, that it appeared to himself reasonable to arrange for it to be so made or to accept a valuation so made,

(b)  whoever made the valuation, that the method of valuation was reasonable in all the circumstances,

(c)  that it appears to the valuer that there has been no material change in the value of the consideration in question since the valuation, and

(d)  that, on the basis of the valuation, the value of the consideration to be received by the company is not less than the value of the consideration to be given by it.

(4)  Any reference in section 599 or this section to consideration given for the transfer of an asset includes consideration given partly for its transfer.

(5)  In such a case—

(a)  the value of any consideration partly so given is to be taken as the proportion of the consideration properly attributable to its transfer,

(b)  the valuer must carry out or arrange for such valuations of anything else as will enable him to determine that proportion, and

(c)  his report must state what valuations have been made for that purpose and also the reason for and method and date of any such valuation and any other matters which may be relevant to that determination.

COMMENCEMENT DATE 1 October 2009[156]

**17.600.02**   This section consolidates the provisions previously contained in section 104(4)(a) of the Companies Act 1985. It sets out the requirements for the valuation that is required by section 599. It follows the pattern of section 596 in respect of elements of a valuation made by a delegate and circumstances in which the non-cash asset represents only part of the consideration to be received by the company.

### 601  Agreement for transfer of non-cash asset: requirement of approval by members

**17.601.01**   (1)  The following conditions must have been complied with—

(a)  the terms of the agreement must have been approved by an ordinary resolution of the company,

[(b) copies of the valuer's report must have been circulated to the members entitled to notice of the meeting at which the resolution is proposed, not later than the date on which notice of the meeting is given, and][a]

(c)  a copy of the proposed resolution must have been sent to the other party to the proposed agreement.

(2)  The reference in subsection (1)(c) to the other party to the proposed agreement is to the person referred to in section 598(1)(a).

(3)  [...][b]

AMENDMENTS AND NOTES

[a]  Amended by the Companies Act 2006 (Consequential Amendments, Transitional Provisions and Savings) Order 2009, SI 2009/1941, art 2(1), Sch 1, para 260(3)(a).

[b]  Repealed by the Companies Act 2006 (Consequential Amendments, Transitional Provisions and Savings) Order 2009, SI 2009/1941, art 2(1), Sch 1, para 260(3)(b).

COMMENCEMENT DATE 1 October 2009[157]

**17.601.02**   This section consolidates the provisions previously contained in section 104(4)(c) and (d) of the Companies Act 1985. The reference in subsection (3)(b) to the giving of notice to members and the other person (if not a member) is to 21 days notice if the resolution required by subsection (1)(a) is to be proposed at the annual general meeting or 14 days if it is to be proposed at a general meeting (see section 307).

---

[156] Companies Act 2006 (Commencement No 8, Transitional Provisions and Savings) Order 2008, SI 2008/2860, art 3(k).

[157] Companies Act 2006 (Commencement No 8, Transitional Provisions and Savings) Order 2008, SI 2008/2860, art 3(k).

## 602  Copy of resolution to be delivered to registrar

(1) A company that has passed a resolution under section 601 with respect to the transfer of an asset must, within 15 days of doing so, deliver to the registrar a copy of the resolution together with the valuer's report required by that section.    **17.602.01**

(2) If a company fails to comply with subsection (1), an offence is committed by—
  (a) the company, and
  (b) every officer of the company who is in default.

(3) A person guilty of an offence under this section is liable on summary conviction to a fine not exceeding level 3 on the standard scale and, for continued contravention, to a daily default fine not exceeding one-tenth of level 3 on the standard scale.

COMMENCEMENT DATE 1 October 2009[158]

This section consolidates the provisions previously contained in section 111(2) and (4) of the Companies Act 1985.    **17.602.02**

## 603  Adaptation of provisions in relation to company re-registering as public

The provisions of sections 598 to 602 (public companies: transfer of non-cash assets) apply with the following adaptations in relation to a company re-registered as a public company—    **17.603.01**

  (a) the reference in section 598(1)(a) to a person who is a subscriber to the company's memorandum shall be read as a reference to a person who is a member of the company on the date of re-registration;
  (b) the reference in section 598(2) to the date of the company being issued with a certificate under section 761 (trading certificate) shall be read as a reference to the date of re-registration.

COMMENCEMENT DATE 1 October 2009[159]

This section consolidates the provisions previously contained in section 116 of the Companies Act 1985. The effect of paragraph (a) is that, in the case of a company which re-registers as a public company, a member at the date of re-registration is treated for the purposes of section 598(1)(a) as equivalent to a subscriber. Given that most companies are formed initially as private companies and later re-register, the effect is to extend the rules on transfers of non-cash assets in the initial period to members at the time of re-registration.    **17.603.02**

## 604  Agreement for transfer of non-cash asset: effect of contravention

(1) This section applies where a public company enters into an agreement in contravention of section 598 and either—    **17.604.01**
  (a) the other party to the agreement has not received the valuer's report required to be sent to him, or
  (b) there has been some other contravention of the requirements of this Chapter that the other party to the agreement knew or ought to have known amounted to a contravention.

(2) In those circumstances—
  (a) the company is entitled to recover from that person any consideration given by it under the agreement, or an amount equal to the value of the consideration at the time of the agreement, and
  (b) the agreement, so far as not carried out, is void.

(3) If the agreement is or includes an agreement for the allotment of shares in the company, then—
  (a) whether or not the agreement also contravenes section 593 (valuation of non-cash consideration for shares), this section does not apply to it in so far as it is for the allotment of shares, and
  (b) the allottee is liable to pay the company an amount equal to the aggregate of the nominal value of the shares and the whole of any premium (or, if the case so requires, so much of that aggregate as is treated as paid up by the consideration), with interest at the appropriate rate.

COMMENCEMENT DATE 1 October 2009[160]

This section replaces section 105 of the Companies Act 1985. Subsection (1) sets out the circumstances in which a contravention of section 598 leads to the consequences provided for in subsections (2) and    **17.604.02**

---

[158] Companies Act 2006 (Commencement No 8, Transitional Provisions and Savings) Order 2008, SI 2008/2860, art 3(k).
[159] Companies Act 2006 (Commencement No 8, Transitional Provisions and Savings) Order 2008, SI 2008/2860, art 3(k).
[160] Companies Act 2006 (Commencement No 8, Transitional Provisions and Savings) Order 2008, SI 2008/2860, art 3(k).

(3). The circumstances are that there has been a contravention of section 598 and the appropriate person (with whom the agreement is made) has not received the valuer's report or there has been some other contravention of the requirements of this Chapter which he knew or ought to have known amounted to a contravention. The reference to 'ought to have known' clearly implies an objective test, meaning that ignorance of the relevant provisions will not prevent the consequences provided for by subsections (2) and (3) taking effect.

**17.604.03**   Subsection (2) provides that the company is then entitled to recover from that person any consideration given by it under the agreement, or an amount equal to the value of the consideration at the time of the agreement; and the agreement, so far as not carried out, is void. There is no express provision in respect of the property ('non-cash asset') received by the company, but the consequence of the transaction being void must be that the company is required to return the property to the person with whom the agreement was made.

**17.604.04**   Subsection (3) modifies the application of subsection (2) in circumstances where the agreement is or includes an agreement for the allotment of shares in the company. It provides that whether or not the agreement also contravenes section 593, this section does not apply to it so far as it is for the allotment of shares. The result is that when an agreement contravening section 598 is not entirely an agreement for the allotment of shares, this section is applicable only to that part of the agreement that does not relate to an allotment of shares. The part of the agreement that represents an allotment of shares remains valid (subject to the liability provisions of section 593). However, the subsection goes on to provide that, in those circumstances, the allottee is liable to pay to the company an amount equal to the aggregate of the nominal value of the shares and the whole of any premium (or, if the case so requires, so much of that aggregate as is treated as paid up by the consideration) with interest at the appropriate rate. No specific provision is made in respect of the property transferred to the company in breach of section 598 following the paying up of the shares by the allottee, but it would seem correct to follow the analysis suggested above in respect of subsection (2), with the result that the company would be required to return the property to the allottee.

## *Supplementary provisions*

### 605  Liability of subsequent holders of shares

**17.605.01**         (1)  If a person becomes a holder of shares in respect of which—
             (a)  there has been a contravention of section 593 (public company: valuation of non-cash consideration for shares), and
             (b)  by virtue of that contravention another is liable to pay any amount under the provision contravened,
          that person is also liable to pay that amount (jointly and severally with any other person so liable), unless he is exempted from liability under subsection (3) below.
          (2)  If a company enters into an agreement in contravention of section 598 and—
             (a)  the agreement is or includes an agreement for the allotment of shares in the company,
             (b)  a person becomes a holder of shares allotted under the agreement, and
             (c)  by virtue of the agreement and allotment under it another person is liable to pay an amount under section 604,
          the person who becomes the holder of the shares is also liable to pay that amount (jointly and severally with any other person so liable), unless he is exempted from liability under subsection (3) below.
          This applies whether or not the agreement also contravenes section 593.
          (3)  A person otherwise liable under subsection (1) or (2) is exempted from that liability if either—
             (a)  he is a purchaser for value and, at the time of the purchase, he did not have actual notice[a] of the contravention concerned, or
             (b)  he derived title to the shares (directly or indirectly) from a person who became a holder of them after the contravention and was not liable under subsection (1) or (2).
          (4)  References in this section to a holder, in relation to shares in a company, include any person who has an unconditional right—
             (a)  to be included in the company's register of members in respect of those shares, or
             (b)  to have an instrument of transfer of the shares executed in his favour.

AMENDMENTS AND NOTES

   [a]  The reference to 'actual notice' strengthens the position of the holder of the shares since it excludes constructive notice: see eg *Eagle Trust plc v SBC Securities Ltd* [1991] BCLC 438.

COMMENCEMENT DATE  1 October 2009[161]

---

[161] Companies Act 2006 (Commencement No 8, Transitional Provisions and Savings) Order 2008, SI 2008/2860, art 3(k).

This section replaces section 112 of the Companies Act 1985. Subsection (1) provides that if a person **17.605.02** becomes a holder of shares in respect of which there has been a breach of section 593 and by virtue of that contravention another is liable to pay any amount under the section contravened, that person is also liable to pay that amount (jointly and severally with any other person so liable) unless he is exempted from liability by subsection (3). This means that, subject to the exceptions created by subsection (3), a holder is subject to the same liability as a person who is allotted shares in contravention of the relevant provision.

Subsection (2) contains a special provision applicable to contravention of section 598. It deals with **17.605.03** circumstances in which one person becomes a holder of shares allotted in contravention of section 598 while another person has an obligation to make a payment under section 604. Those circumstances might arise if a contravention of section 598 required the allottee to make a payment under section 604(2) but the relevant shares were transferred before the payment was made. The subsection provides that in such circumstances the holder is liable jointly and severally to pay that amount unless exempted by subsection (3); and this applies whether or not the agreement also contravenes section 593.

Subsection (3) exempts a person otherwise liable under subsection (1) or (2) if either: **17.605.04**

(i)   he is a purchaser for value and, at the time of the purchase, he did not have actual notice of the contravention concerned; or

(ii)  he derived title to the shares (directly or indirectly) from a person who became a holder of them after the contravention and was not liable under subsection (1) or (2).

A purchaser is not required to enquire as to whether there has been a breach of the relevant provisions **17.605.05** and will not be taken to have constructive notice. Therefore, it seems that other than in circumstances that a purchaser is informed by the seller (unlikely) or the company that there has been a contravention, it will be difficult to show actual notice. A person deriving title to the shares from a holder who is exempt from liability as a purchaser for value is also exempt from liability.

Subsection (4) provides that references in this section to a holder of shares includes a person who has **17.605.06** an unconditional right to be included in the company's register of members in respect of those shares or to have an instrument of transfer executed in his favour. This extends the liability (and exemptions) in this section to (i) a buyer of shares who has not yet been registered[162] as the holder, and (ii) a buyer of shares who has not yet had an instrument of transfer executed in his favour.[163]

## 606  Power of court to grant relief

(1)  A person who—                                                                    **17.606.01**
  (a)  is liable to a company under any provision of this Chapter in relation to payment in respect of any shares in the company, or
  (b)  is liable to a company by virtue of an undertaking given to it in, or in connection with, payment for any shares in the company,
may apply to the court to be exempted in whole or in part from the liability.

(2)  In the case of a liability within subsection (1)(a), the court may exempt the applicant from the liability only if and to the extent that it appears to the court just and equitable to do so [having regard to—
  (a)  whether the applicant has paid, or is liable to pay, any amount in respect of—
    (i)   any other liability arising in relation to those shares under any provision of this Chapter or Chapter 5, or
    (ii)  any liability arising by virtue of any undertaking given in or in connection with payment for those shares;
  (b)  whether any person other than the applicant has paid or is likely to pay, whether in pursuance of any order of the court or otherwise, any such amount;
  (c)  whether the applicant or any other person—
    (i)   has performed in whole or in part, or is likely so to perform any such undertaking, or
    (ii)  has done or is likely to do any other thing in payment or part payment for the shares.]ᵃ

(3)  In the case of a liability within subsection (1)(b), the court may exempt the applicant from the liability only if and to the extent that it appears to the court just and equitable to do so [having regard to—
  (a)  whether the applicant has paid or is liable to pay any amount in respect of liability arising in relation to the shares under any provision of this Chapter or Chapter 5;

---

[162] Companies Act 2006 (Commencement No 8, Transitional Provisions and Savings) Order 2008, SI 2008/2860, art 3(k).

[163] This presumably refers to a 'settled' transaction, in which the buyer is the beneficial but not yet the legal owner of the shares.

(b) whether any person other than the applicant has paid or is likely to pay, whether in pursuance of any order of the court or otherwise, any such amount.]ᵇ

(4) In determining whether it should exempt the applicant in whole or in part from any liability, the court must have regard to the following overriding principles—

(a) that a company that has allotted shares should receive money or money's worth at least equal in value to the aggregate of the nominal value of those shares and the whole of any premium or, if the case so requires, so much of that aggregate as is treated as paid up;

(b) subject to this, that where such a company would, if the court did not grant the exemption, have more than one remedy against a particular person, it should be for the company to decide which remedy it should remain entitled to pursue.

(5) If a person brings proceedings against another ('the contributor') for a contribution in respect of liability to a company arising under any provision of this Chapter or Chapter 5 and it appears to the court that the contributor is liable to make such a contribution, the court may, if and to the extent that it appears to it, just and equitable to do so having regard to the respective culpability (in respect of the liability to the company) of the contributor and the person bringing the proceedings—

(a) exempt the contributor in whole or in part from his liability to make such a contribution, or

(b) order the contributor to make a larger contribution than, but for this subsection, he would be liable to make.

(6) Where a person is liable to a company under section 604(2) (agreement for transfer of non-cash asset: effect of contravention), the court may, on application, exempt him in whole or in part from that liability if and to the extent that it appears to the court to be just and equitable to do so having regard to any benefit accruing to the company by virtue of anything done by him towards the carrying out of the agreement mentioned in that subsection.

AMENDMENTS AND NOTES

ᵃ Words in square brackets are omitted in relation to a decision whether to grant relief in respect of a liability arising before 1 October 2009: Companies Act 2006 (Commencement, Transitional Provisions and Savings) Order 2008, SI 2008/2860, Sch 2, para 58.

ᵇ Words in square brackets are omitted in relation to a decision whether to grant relief in respect of a liability arising before 1 October 2009: Companies Act 2006 (Commencement, Transitional Provisions and Savings) Order 2008, SI 2008/2860, Sch 2, para 58.

COMMENCEMENT DATE 1 October 2009[164]

**17.606.02** This section replaces section 113 of the Companies Act 1985. Subsection (1) provides for the possibility of a person liable under certain of the provisions of this Chapter to apply to the court for exemption. Subsection (2) sets out two requirements that must be met before the court exempts a person from liability under subsection (1)(a). The primary consideration is that it is just and equitable to do so having regard to the matters subsequently listed. The first requirement takes account of the possibility that the applicant may already have a liability to pay for the shares under the relevant sections or under an undertaking given in connection with payment for the shares. The second takes account of the possibility that another person has paid or is likely to pay any such amount. The third takes account of the possibility that the applicant has performed or is likely to perform any undertaking or do any other thing in payment for the shares.

**17.606.03** Liability under subsection (1)(b) arises other than under the provisions of this Chapter—this is the implication of 'or' at the end of subsection (1)(a) and the reference to 'any shares' in subsection (1)(b). It follows that the liability (and relief) referred to in subsection (1)(b) is not limited to share issues made by a public company for a non-cash consideration or transfers of non-cash assets to a public company in the initial period. The conditions for granting relief follow those that apply in respect of liability under subsection (1)(a) with the omission of the third (the likelihood of an undertaking being performed).

### 607 Penalty for contravention of this Chapter

**17.607.01**
(1) This section applies where a company contravenes—
    section 593 (public company allotting shares for non-cash consideration), or
    section 598 (public company entering into agreement for transfer of non-cash asset).
(2) An offence is committed by—
    (a) the company, and
    (b) every officer of the company who is in default.

---

[164] This presumably refers to an 'unsettled' transaction in which the buyer has the contractual right to demand that an instrument of transfer (or its electronic equivalent in CREST, an authorized instruction) be executed on his behalf.

(3) A person guilty of an offence under this section is liable—
    (a) on conviction on indictment, to a fine;
    (b) on summary conviction, to a fine not exceeding the statutory maximum.

COMMENCEMENT DATE 1 October 2009[165]

This section replaces section 114 of the Companies Act 1985. It provides for the imposition of a penalty, **17.607.02**
in the form of a fine, on a company and its officers if the company contravenes any of the provisions of
sections 593 or 598.

## 608 Enforceability of undertakings to do work etc

(1) An undertaking given by any person, in or in connection with payment for shares in a company, **17.608.01**
to do work or perform services or to do any other thing, if it is enforceable by the company apart
from this Chapter, is so enforceable notwithstanding that there has been a contravention in
relation to it of a provision of this Chapter or Chapter 5.
(2) This is without prejudice to section 606 (power of court to grant relief etc in respect of liabilities).

COMMENCEMENT DATE 1 October 2009[166]

This section replaces section 115 of the Companies Act 1985. It provides that, subject to section 606, a **17.608.02**
contravention of the provisions of this Chapter does not in itself render unenforceable an undertaking
given by any person to do work or perform services or do any other thing in connection with payment
for shares. This would in principle allow for the company to receive payment twice for the same
allotment of shares as it could enforce the undertaking and also require payment under section 593(3).
In these circumstances exemption from liability under section 606 would seem the sensible solution to
the extent necessary to avoid the company receiving more than full payment for an allotment of shares.

## 609 The appropriate rate of interest

(1) For the purposes of this Chapter the 'appropriate rate' of interest is 5% per annum or such other **17.609.01**
rate as may be specified by order made by the Secretary of State.
(2) An order under this section is subject to negative resolution procedure.

COMMENCEMENT DATE 1 October 2009[167]

This section sets 'the appropriate rate' of interest in respect of relevant provisions of this Chapter at 5 **17.609.02**
per cent per annum or such other rate as may be specified by order.

## CHAPTER 7
## SHARE PREMIUMS

### *The share premium account*

## 610 Application of share premiums

(1) If a company issues shares at a premium, whether for cash or otherwise, a sum equal to the **17.610.01**
aggregate amount or value of the premiums on those shares must be transferred to an account
called 'the share premium account'.
(2) Where, on issuing shares, a company has transferred a sum to the share premium account, it may
use that sum to write off—
    (a) the expenses of the issue of those shares;
    (b) any commission paid on the issue of those shares.
(3) The company may use the share premium account to pay up new shares to be allotted to
members as fully paid bonus shares.
(4) Subject to subsections (2) and (3), the provisions of the Companies Acts relating to the reduction
of a company's share capital apply as if the share premium account were part of its paid up share
capital.

---

[165] Companies Act 2006 (Commencement No 8, Transitional Provisions and Savings) Order 2008, SI 2008/2860, art 3(k).
[166] Companies Act 2006 (Commencement No 8, Transitional Provisions and Savings) Order 2008, SI 2008/2860, art 3(k).
[167] Companies Act 2006 (Commencement No 8, Transitional Provisions and Savings) Order 2008, SI 2008/2860, art 3(k).

(5)  This section has effect subject to—

section 611 (group reconstruction relief);

section 612 (merger relief);

section 614 (power to make further provisions by regulations).

(6)  In this Chapter 'the issuing company' means the company issuing shares as mentioned in subsection (1) above.

COMMENCEMENT DATE 1 October 2009[168]

**17.610.02**  Subsection (1) requires a company that issues shares at a premium, whether for cash or otherwise, to transfer the premium to the share premium account. A premium refers to any payment for shares made to a company that is greater than the nominal value of the shares. Whether a company is able to obtain a premium is a matter that can only be determined in the marketplace and there is no legal obligation to obtain a premium,[169] although directors who fail to do so when it is available may be acting in breach of duty. The share premium account must appear on the liabilities side of the balance sheet, just like share capital. Indeed, as noted below, it is treated in many respects similarly to share capital.

**17.610.03**  Following the recommendation of the CLR,[170] subsection (2) is now more restrictive as regards the use of the share premium account. It can be used to write off the expenses of the issue[171] of the shares that gave rise to the premium or any commission paid on the issue of those shares or to pay up an allotment of shares to members as fully paid bonus shares. In its old form, subsection (2) (of section 130 of the 1985 Act) had also permitted the share premium to be applied to writing off:

- preliminary expenses on the formation of a company;
- the expenses of or commission paid or discount allowed on, any issue of debentures of the company;
- the provision of a premium on the redemption of debentures.

**17.610.04**  The more restrictive application of the share premium account permitted under the new version means that it is more effectively ring-fenced and becomes even more similar to share capital than it had been in the past.

### *Relief from requirements as to share premiums*

### 611  Group reconstruction relief

**17.611.01**  (1)  This section applies where the issuing company—

(a)  is a wholly-owned subsidiary of another company ('the holding company'), and

(b)  allots shares—

(i)  to the holding company or

(ii)  to another wholly-owned subsidiary of the holding company,

in consideration for the transfer to the issuing company of non-cash assets of a company ('the transferor company') that is a member of the group of companies that comprises the holding company and all its wholly-owned subsidiaries.

(2)  Where the shares in the issuing company allotted in consideration for the transfer are issued at a premium, the issuing company is not required by section 610 to transfer any amount in excess of the minimum premium value to the share premium account.

(3)  The minimum premium value means the amount (if any) by which the base value of the consideration for the shares allotted exceeds the aggregate nominal value of the shares.

(4)  The base value of the consideration for the shares allotted is the amount by which the base value of the assets transferred exceeds the base value of any liabilities of the transferor company assumed by the issuing company as part of the consideration for the assets transferred.

(5)  For the purposes of this section—

(a)  the base value of assets transferred is taken as—

(i)  the cost of those assets to the transferor company, or

(ii)  if less, the amount at which those assets are stated in the transferor company's accounting records immediately before the transfer;

---

[168] Companies Act 2006 (Commencement No 8, Transitional Provisions and Savings) Order 2008, SI 2008/2860, art 3(k).

[169] Companies Act 2006 (Commencement No 8, Transitional Provisions and Savings) Order 2008, SI 2008/2860, art 3(k).

[170] *Hilder v Dexter* [1902] AC 474, HL.

[171] CLR, *Completing the Structure*, para 7.8.

(b)  the base value of the liabilities assumed is taken as the amount at which they are stated in the transferor company's accounting records immediately before the transfer.

COMMENCEMENT DATE  1 October 2009[172]

This section replaces section 132 of the Companies Act 1985. Its purpose is to limit the effect of section **17.611.02** 610 in the case of allotments of shares at a premium which form part of a group reconstruction. The section applies where a wholly-owned subsidiary of another company (the holding company) allots shares to the holding company or another wholly-owned subsidiary of the holding company in consideration for the transfer to the issuing company of assets other than cash, being assets of any company (the transferor company) which is a member of the group of companies which comprises the holding company and all its wholly-owned subsidiaries.

Subsection (2) makes clear that in these circumstances the issuing company is not required by section **17.611.03** 610 to transfer any amount in excess of the 'minimum premium value' to the share premium account.

Subsections (3), (4), and (5) clarify the meaning of the minimum premium value. The minimum **17.611.04** premium value (MPV) can be stated in algebraic form as follows:

$$\text{MPV} = [(\text{the lower of TAC or TAA}) - \text{TLA}] - \text{INVS}$$

Where:

Tac is the (historic) cost of the assets being transferred from the transferor company

Taa is the amount at which those assets are stated in the transferor company's accounting records immediately before the transfer

Tla is the accounting value of liabilities of the transferor company to be assumed by the issuing company as part of the consideration for the assets transferred

Invs is the aggregate nominal value of the shares allotted by the issuing company.

It can be seen that the formula establishes a value for the consideration paid by the transferor company **17.611.05** to the issuing company and that the MPV represents the excess of that consideration over the nominal value of shares issued. The combined effect of subsections (2) to (5) is that the issuing company can ignore any rise in the value of the assets being transferred over their original cost for the purposes of the calculation of share premium. The MPV can be minimized by the use of the original cost of the relevant assets, thereby limiting the share premium that must be entered in the issuer's accounts (since there is no obligation to transfer any amount in excess of the MPV to the share premium account).

## 612  Merger relief

(1)  This section applies where the issuing company has secured at least a 90% equity holding in **17.612.01** another company in pursuance of an arrangement providing for the allotment of equity shares in the issuing company on terms that the consideration for the shares allotted is to be provided—
(a)  by the issue or transfer to the issuing company of equity shares in the other company, or
(b)  by the cancellation of any such shares not held by the issuing company.
(2)  If the equity shares in the issuing company allotted in pursuance of the arrangement in consideration for the acquisition or cancellation of equity shares in the other company are issued at a premium, section 610 does not apply to the premiums on those shares.
(3)  Where the arrangement also provides for the allotment of any shares in the issuing company on terms that the consideration for those shares is to be provided—
(a)  by the issue or transfer to the issuing company of non-equity shares in the other company, or
(b)  by the cancellation of any such shares in that company not held by the issuing company,
relief under subsection (2) extends to any shares in the issuing company allotted on those terms in pursuance of the arrangement.
(4)  This section does not apply in a case falling within section 611 (group reconstruction relief).

COMMENCEMENT DATE  1 October 2009[173]

This section replaces section 131 of the Companies Act 1985. It provides relief, in respect of mergers **17.612.02** falling within its scope, from the section 610 obligation to create a share premium account. The need for such relief arises as a result of the possibility that a bidder which has made a successful share-for-share offer to the shareholders of another company might be required to create a large share premium account and suffer the consequences that follow from the restricted application of that account permitted by section 610. That risk is particularly acute when the nominal value of a bidder's shares is substantially lower than their market value. There would also be a risk in those circumstances that the

---

[172]  As opposed to any issue under the 1985 Act.
[173]  Companies Act 2006 (Commencement No 8, Transitional Provisions and Savings) Order 2008, SI 2008/2860, art 3(k).

creation of a share premium account, which would of necessity have to come from existing reserves, would limit the capacity of a bidder to pay dividends.

**17.612.03**  Subsection (1) determines that the section applies where the issuing company has secured at least a 90 per cent equity holding in another company in pursuance of a share-for-share offer made to the shareholders of the other company or an agreement for the cancellation of shares not held by the issuing company. For example, if A offers 1 share in A for every 2 shares in B held by the shareholders of B and secures a 90 per cent acceptance, the section applies. Equally, if A holds 10 per cent of B and offers to issue one new share in A to the shareholders in B as payment for the cancellation of each remaining share in B, the section applies if A secures a 90 per cent shareholding (ie when, following cancellation, A holds 90 per cent of all the shares in B).

**17.612.04**  Subsection (2) provides that in the circumstances set out in subsection (1), section 610 does not apply to the premiums on shares issued by A as consideration to the holders of shares in B. This alleviates the potential problems referred to in the first paragraph above. Subsection (3) provides that subsection (2) applies also to arrangements under which 'non-equity shares' are to be transferred to the issuing company or cancelled as consideration for the issue of equity shares.

### 613  Merger relief: meaning of 90% equity holding

**17.613.01**  (1)  The following provisions have effect to determine for the purposes of section 612 (merger relief) whether a company ('company A') has secured a 90% equity holding in another company ('company B') in pursuance of such an arrangement as is mentioned in subsection (1) of that section.

(2)  Company A has a 90% equity holding in company B if in consequence of an acquisition or cancellation of equity shares in company B (in pursuance of that arrangement) it holds equity shares in company B of an aggregate amount equal to 90% or more of the nominal value of that company's equity share capital.

(3)  For this purpose—
    (a)  it is immaterial whether any of those shares were acquired in pursuance of the arrangement; and
    (b)  shares in company B held by the company as treasury shares are excluded in determining the nominal value of company B's share capital.

(4)  Where the equity share capital of company B is divided into different classes of shares, company A is not regarded as having a 90% equity holding in company B unless the requirements of subsection (2) are met in relation to each of those classes of shares taken separately.

(5)  For the purposes of this section shares held by—
    (a)  a company that is company A's holding company or subsidiary, or
    (b)  a subsidiary of company A's holding company, or
    (c)  its or their nominees,
are treated as held by company A.

COMMENCEMENT DATE  1 October 2009[174]

**17.613.02**  This section consolidates the provisions previously contained in section 130(4), (5), (6), and (7) of the Companies Act 1985. Subsection (1) clarifies when the issuing company reaches the 90 per cent equity-holding threshold in another company specified in section 612. It makes clear (i) that all shares held by the issuer count, not just those acquired under the offer; (ii) that the effect of a cancellation on the part of the other company must be taken into account in calculating the holding of the issuing company (see the example above in the commentary on section 612); and (iii) that shares held by company B in treasury are excluded from the calculation.

**17.613.03**  Subsection (2) provides that where the equity share capital of the other company is divided into different classes of shares, this section does not apply unless the requirements of subsection (1) are satisfied in relation to each of those classes of shares taken separately.

**17.613.04**  Subsection (5) clarifies the circumstances in which the issuing company will be taken to hold shares for the purposes of the 90 per cent threshold. In all these circumstances (including nominees) the registered holder (and therefore legal owner) will be a person other than the issuing company.

### 614  Power to make further provision by regulations

**17.614.01**  (1)  The Secretary of State may by regulations make such provision as he thinks appropriate—
    (a)  for relieving companies from the requirements of section 610 (application of share premiums) in relation to premiums other than cash premiums;

---

[174] Companies Act 2006 (Commencement No 8, Transitional Provisions and Savings) Order 2008, SI 2008/2860, art 3(k).

    (b)  for restricting or otherwise modifying any relief from those requirements provided by this Chapter.

(2)  Regulations under this section are subject to affirmative resolution procedure.

COMMENCEMENT DATE 1 October 2009[175]

This section replaces section 134 of the Companies Act 1985. It authorizes the Secretary of State to make regulations relieving companies from the requirements of section 610 in relation to premiums other than cash premiums, or for restricting or otherwise modifying any relief from those requirements provided by this Chapter.     **17.614.02**

### 615 Relief may be reflected in company's balance sheet

An amount corresponding to the amount representing the premiums, or part of the premiums, on shares issued by a company that by virtue of any relief under this Chapter is not included in the company's share premium account may also be disregarded in determining the amount at which any shares or other consideration provided for the shares issued is to be included in the company's balance sheet.     **17.615.01**

COMMENCEMENT DATE 1 October 2009[176]

This section consolidates the provision previously contained in section 133(1) of the Companies Act 1985. Its effect is that the amount of any premium which benefits from relief under this Chapter does not have to be shown as part of share capital in a company's balance sheet. This has the effect, *inter alia*, that the investment (represented by the share issue) in the (newly acquired) subsidiary can be shown at a lower figure in the parent's accounts, with the result that pre-acquisition profits within the subsidiary may be available for distribution.     **17.615.02**

*Supplementary provisions*

### 616 Interpretation of this Chapter

(1)  In this Chapter—     **17.616.01**
    'arrangement' means any agreement, scheme or arrangement (including an arrangement sanctioned in accordance with—
    (a)  Part 26 (arrangements and reconstructions), or
    (b)  section 110 of the Insolvency Act 1986 (c. 45) or Article 96 of the Insolvency (Northern Ireland) Order 1989 (S.I. 1989/2405 (N.I. 19)) (liquidator in winding up accepting shares as consideration for sale of company property));
    'company', except in reference to the issuing company, includes any body corporate;
    'equity shares' means shares comprised in a company's equity share capital, and 'non-equity shares' means shares (of any class) that are not so comprised;
    'the issuing company' has the meaning given by section 610(6).
(2)  References in this Chapter (however expressed) to—
    (a)  the acquisition by a company of shares in another company, and
    (b)  the issue or allotment of shares to, or the transfer of shares to or by, a company,
    include (respectively) the acquisition of shares by, and the issue or allotment or transfer of shares to or by, a nominee of that company.
    The reference in section 611 to the transferor company shall be read accordingly.
(3)  References in this Chapter to the transfer of shares in a company include the transfer of a right to be included in the company's register of members in respect of those shares.

COMMENCEMENT DATE 1 October 2009[177]

This section sets out a number of definitions that apply for the purposes of this Chapter.     **17.616.02**

---

[175] Companies Act 2006 (Commencement No 8, Transitional Provisions and Savings) Order 2008, SI 2008/2860, art 3(k).

[176] Companies Act 2006 (Commencement No 8, Transitional Provisions and Savings) Order 2008, SI 2008/2860, art 3(k).

[177] Companies Act 2006 (Commencement No 8, Transitional Provisions and Savings) Order 2008, SI 2008/2860, art 3(k).

# CHAPTER 8
## ALTERATION OF SHARE CAPITAL

### *How share capital may be altered*

### 617 Alteration of share capital of limited company

**17.617.01**

   (1)  A limited company having a share capital may not alter its share capital except in the following ways.

   (2)  The company may—

      (a)  increase its share capital by allotting new shares in accordance with this Part, or

      (b)  reduce its share capital in accordance with Chapter 10.

   (3)  The company may—

      (a)  sub-divide or consolidate all or any of its share capital in accordance with section 618, or

      (b)  reconvert stock into shares in accordance with section 620.

   (4)  The company may redenominate all or any of its shares in accordance with section 622, and may reduce its share capital in accordance with section 626 in connection with such a redenomination.

   (5)  Nothing in this section affects—

      (a)  the power of a company to purchase its own shares, or to redeem shares, in accordance with Part 18;

      (b)  the power of a company to purchase its own shares in pursuance of an order of the court under—

         (i)  section 98 (application to court to cancel resolution for re-registration as a private company),

         (ii)  section 721(6) (powers of court on objection to redemption or purchase of shares out of capital),

         (iii)  section 759 (remedial order in case of breach of prohibition of public offers by private company), or

         (iv)  Part 30 (protection of members against unfair prejudice);

      (c)  the forfeiture of shares, or the acceptance of shares surrendered in lieu, in pursuance of the company's articles, for failure to pay any sum payable in respect of the shares;

      (d)  the cancellation of shares under section 662 (duty to cancel shares held by or for a public company);

      (e)  the power of a company—

         (i)  to enter into a compromise or arrangement in accordance with Part 26 (arrangements and reconstructions), or

         (ii)  to do anything required to comply with an order of the court on an application under that Part.

COMMENCEMENT DATE 1 October 2009[178]

**17.617.02**    Unlike the previous provision on alteration of capital,[179] which was worded in a permissive way, subsection (1) prohibits alterations of share capital except those specified in subsections (2), (3), and (4). The difference from the previous legislation is that conversions of shares into stock and cancellations of shares that have not been taken up are no longer permitted.[180] Further, as companies no longer have an authorized capital,[181] there is no longer any need for a power to increase that and any increase in share capital can be done, as subsection (2)(a) makes clear, simply by allotting new shares in accordance with Chapter 2 of this Part.

**17.617.03**    The other alterations that a company may now effect are (i) a reduction of share capital; (ii) a sub-division or consolidation of share capital; (iii) a reconversion of stock into shares; (iv) a redenomination of shares and any associated reduction; (v) a purchase or redemption of its own shares under Part 18; (vi) a forfeiture of shares or acceptance of surrender in lieu for non-payment, provided this is permitted by the articles;[182] and (vii) a cancellation of shares under section 662.

---

[178] Companies Act 2006 (Commencement No 8, Transitional Provisions and Savings) Order 2008, SI 2008/2860, art 3(k).

[179] Companies Act 2006 (Commencement No 8, Transitional Provisions and Savings) Order 2008, SI 2008/2860, art 3(k).

[180] Companies Act 1985, s 121.

[181] As to the abolition of the power to convert shares into stock, see also s 554(2).

[182] See para 2.8.02.

Subsection (5) makes it clear that the prohibition does not affect the various other statutory provisions    **17.617.04**
that can have an effect on share capital following a court order under the provisions mentioned in
subsection (5)(b) or court approval under Part 26 dealing with arrangements and reconstructions.

### *Subdivision or consolidation of shares*

### 618  Sub-division or consolidation of shares

(1) A limited company having a share capital may—    **17.618.01**
  (a) sub-divide its shares, or any of them, into shares of a smaller nominal amount than its existing
    shares, or
  (b) consolidate and divide all or any of its share capital into shares of a larger nominal amount
    than its existing shares.
(2) In any sub-division, consolidation or division of shares under this section, the proportion between
  the amount paid and the amount (if any) unpaid on each resulting share must be the same as it
  was in the case of the share from which that share is derived.
(3) A company may exercise a power conferred by this section only if its members have passed a
  resolution authorising it to do so.
(4) A resolution under subsection (3) may authorise a company—
  (a) to exercise more than one of the powers conferred by this section;
  (b) to exercise a power on more than one occasion;
  (c) to exercise a power at a specified time or in specified circumstances.
(5) The company's articles may exclude or restrict the exercise of any power conferred by this section.

COMMENCEMENT DATE 1 October 2009[183]

This section spells out the power to sub-divide or consolidate shares much more expansively than the    **17.618.02**
previous provision.[184] It also abolishes the requirement for a company to have authority in its articles
for such an alteration of capital, although as subsection (5) provides, the power can be excluded or
restricted in the articles.

By subsection (2), where shares are sub-divided or consolidated, the proportion between the amount    **17.618.03**
paid and the amount unpaid (if any) on the original share(s) must remain the same in relation to the
share(s) resulting from the sub-division or consolidation. If, for example, £2 is unpaid on a £10 share
that is subsequently sub-divided into ten £1 shares, there will be 20p unpaid on each of those ten shares.
Note, however, that this may be affected by a scheme sanctioned as a reduction of capital. In *Re
Doloswella Rubber and Tea Estates Ltd*,[185] a company was permitted to divide £500 shares, on which
£185 was paid up, into three £100 shares with £38 6s 8d unpaid and two unpaid £100 shares and to
accept a surrender of the latter shares for future issue.

Subsection (3) does not spell out the type of resolution necessary, but it is clear from the general    **17.618.04**
provision on resolutions, section 281(3), that an ordinary resolution will suffice unless the articles
require a higher majority or unanimity. A difference from the previous position is that the resolution
does not itself have to authorize a sub-division or consolidation; it can now confer a power to do so, in
the terms permitted by subsection (4), which can be actually exercised by the directors.

Subsection (4)(a) confirms that a single resolution may authorize both a consolidation and sub-    **17.618.05**
division of shares,[186] which may be necessary if, for example, a reduction of capital has resulted in
shares having what is regarded as an inconvenient nominal value. If, say, a reduction has resulted in
shares with a nominal value of[187]/3 pence each, six of such shares can be consolidated into shares of £4
each and the resulting shares subdivided into four £1 shares.

Subsections (4)(b) and (c) go further than the previous law. Under paragraph (b) it will be possible for    **17.618.06**
the company to give the directors power to sub-divide or consolidate in the future without having to
seek the sanction of a further resolution. Paragraph (c) permits resolutions that are conditional, for
example, on the passing of a subsequent resolution reorganizing capital, say by way of reduction or
redenomination.

---

[183]  This is not something covered by the legislation, but valid provided that the articles so provide.
[184]  Companies Act 2006 (Commencement No 8, Transitional Provisions and Savings) Order 2008, SI
2008/2860, art 3(k).
[185]  CA 1985, s 121(2)(b) and (d).
[186]  [1917] 1 Ch 213.
[187]  As was permitted in *Re North Cheshire Brewery* [1920] WN 149.

### 619 Notice to registrar of sub-division or consolidation

**17.619.01**

(1) If a company exercises the power conferred by section 618 (sub-division or consolidation of shares) it must within one month after doing so give notice to the registrar, specifying the shares affected.

(2) The notice must be accompanied by a statement of capital.

(3) The statement of capital must state with respect to the company's share capital immediately following the exercise of the power—

  (a) the total number of shares of the company,

  (b) the aggregate nominal value of those shares,

  (c) for each class of shares—

    (i) prescribed particulars of the rights attached to the shares,

    (ii) the total number of shares of that class, and

    (iii) the aggregate nominal value of shares of that class, and

  (d) the amount paid up and the amount (if any) unpaid on each share (whether on account of the nominal value of the share or by way of premium).

(4) If default is made in complying with this section, an offence is committed by—

  (a) the company, and

  (b) every officer of the company who is in default.

(5) A person guilty of an offence under this section is liable on summary conviction to a fine not exceeding level 3 on the standard scale and, for continued contravention, a daily default fine not exceeding one-tenth of level 3 on the standard scale.

COMMENCEMENT DATE 1 October 2009[188]

**17.619.02** This section repeats and replaces the previous requirement[189] to notify the registrar within one month of the exercise of the power to sub-divide or consolidate shares under section 618, with the criminal penalty specified in subsections (4) and (5) on the company and every officer in default. However, the requirement at the same time to file a statement of capital is new and is imposed consequent upon the abolition of the requirement for a company limited by shares to have an authorized capital,[190] because of the requirements of Article 2 of the Second Company Law Directive[191] —'the statutes or instruments of incorporation of the company shall always give at least the following information … (c) when the company has no authorized capital, the amount of the subscribed capital …'. Although the Directive only applies to public companies, the requirement here is being imposed on all companies limited by shares.

**17.619.03** The contents of the statement of capital are the same as those required for the original statement to be filed on application for registration under section 10,[192] and on other capital alterations. A detailed description can be found in the annotations to section 10.

### *Reconversion of stock into shares*

### 620 Reconversion of stock into shares

**17.620.01**

(1) A limited company that has converted paid-up shares into stock (before the repeal by this Act of the power to do so) may reconvert that stock into paid-up shares of any nominal value.

(2) A company may exercise the power conferred by this section only if its members have passed an ordinary resolution authorising it to do so.

(3) A resolution under subsection (2) may authorise a company to exercise the power conferred by this section—

  (a) on more than one occasion;

  (b) at a specified time or in specified circumstances.

COMMENCEMENT DATE 1 October 2009[193]

---

[188] Companies Act 2006 (Commencement No 8, Transitional Provisions and Savings) Order 2008, SI 2008/2860, art 3(k).

[189] CA 1985, s 122. Note that the repeal of s 122(1)(a) and (d) and (2) does not affect the operation of those provisions in relation to a consolidation and division or sub-division of shares effected before 1 October 2009: Companies Act 2006 (Commencement, Transitional Provisions and Savings) Order 2008, SI 2008/2860, Sch 2, para 59.

[190] See para 2.8.02.

[191] Directive (EEC) 77/91 [1977] OJ L26/1.

[192] See para 2.10.02.

[193] Companies Act 2006 (Commencement No 8, Transitional Provisions and Savings) Order 2008, SI 2008/2860, art 3(k).

The previous power to convert shares into stock was abolished by the repeal and non-replacement of the previous provision,[194] but as companies existing at the time that this section was commenced (1 October 2009) may have had stock which they wish to convert back into shares, this section gives them power to do so. It can only be used to convert stock into fully paid shares, but that can be of any nominal value. There is no longer any requirement that the articles contain power for a company to reconvert stock into shares and only an ordinary resolution is required.

**17.620.02**

Subsections (2) and (3) go further than the previous law in terms of the nature of an ordinary resolution, which under them confers authority, no doubt normally on the directors, rather than actually itself authorizing the conversion. Under subsection (3)(a) it will be possible for the company to give the directors power to convert in the future without having to seek the sanction of an additional ordinary resolution. Paragraph (c) permits resolutions that confer conditional authority, for example, on the passing of a subsequent resolution reorganizing capital, say by way of reduction or redenomination.

**17.620.03**

### 621  Notice to registrar of reconversion of stock into shares

(1) If a company exercises a power conferred by section 620 (reconversion of stock into shares) it must within one month after doing so give notice to the registrar, specifying the stock affected.

**17.621.01**

(2) The notice must be accompanied by a statement of capital.

(3) The statement of capital must state with respect to the company's share capital immediately following the exercise of the power—
  (a) the total number of shares of the company,
  (b) the aggregate nominal value of those shares,
  (c) for each class of shares—
    (i) prescribed particulars of the rights attached to the shares,
    (ii) the total number of shares of that class, and
    (iii) the aggregate nominal value of shares of that class, and
  (d) the amount paid up and the amount (if any) unpaid on each share (whether on account of the nominal value of the share or by way of premium).

(4) If default is made in complying with this section, an offence is committed by—
  (a) the company, and
  (b) every officer of the company who is in default.

(5) A person guilty of an offence under this section is liable on summary conviction to a fine not exceeding level 3 on the standard scale and, for continued contravention, a daily default fine not exceeding one-tenth of level 3 on the standard scale.

COMMENCEMENT DATE 1 October 2009[195]

Where a company re-converts stock into shares under section 620, it must within one month give notice of the alteration to the registrar, together with a statement of capital, with the criminal penalty specified in subsections (4) and (5) on the company and every officer in default. This section replaced section 122 of the 1985 Act.[196]

**17.621.02**

The requirement at the same time to file a statement of capital was new and was imposed consequent upon the abolition of the requirement for a company limited by shares to have an authorized capital,[197] because of the requirements of Article 2 of the Second Company Law Directive[198] —'the statutes or instruments of incorporation of the company shall always give at least the following information…(c) when the company has no authorized capital, the amount of the subscribed capital…'. Although the Directive only applies to public companies, the requirement here is imposed on all companies limited by shares. The contents of the statement of capital are the same as that required for the original statement to be filed on application for registration under section 10,[199] and on other capital alterations. A detailed description can be found in the annotations to section 10.

**17.621.03**

---

[194] CA 1985, s 121(1)(c). There is a saving for conversions into stock effected before 1 October 2009: the Companies Act 2006 (Commencement No 8, Transitional Provisions and Savings) Order 2008, SI 2008/2860, Sch 2, para 41.

[195] Companies Act 2006 (Commencement No 8, Transitional Provisions and Savings) Order 2008, SI 2008/2860, art 3(k).

[196] Note that the repeal of s 122(1)(c) and (2) did not affect the operation of those provisions in relation to a reconversion effected before 1 October 2009: Companies Act 2006 (Commencement No 8, Transitional Provisions and Savings) Order 2008, SI 2008/2860, Sch 2, para 60.

[197] See para 2.10.02.

[198] Directive (EEC) 77/91 [1977] OJ L26/1.

[199] See para 2.10.02.

*Redenomination of share capital*

**622  Redenomination of share capital**

**17.622.01**
    (1)  A limited company[200] having a share capital may by resolution redenominate its share capital or any class of its share capital.
        'Redenominate' means convert shares from having a fixed nominal value in one currency to having a fixed nominal value in another currency.
    (2)  The conversion must be made at an appropriate spot rate of exchange specified in the resolution.
    (3)  The rate must be either—
        (a)  a rate prevailing on a day specified in the resolution, or
        (b)  a rate determined by taking the average of rates prevailing on each consecutive day of a period specified in the resolution.
    The day or period specified for the purposes of paragraph (a) or (b) must be within the period of 28 days ending on the day before the resolution is passed.
    (4)  A resolution under this section may specify conditions which must be met before the redenomination takes effect.
    (5)  Redenomination in accordance with a resolution under this section takes effect—
        (a)  on the day on which the resolution is passed, or
        (b)  on such later day as may be determined in accordance with the resolution.
    (6)  A resolution under this section lapses if the redenomination for which it provides has not taken effect at the end of the period of 28 days beginning on the date on which it is passed.
    (7)  A company's articles may prohibit or restrict the exercise of the power conferred by this section.
    (8)  Chapter 3 of Part 3 (resolutions affecting a company's constitution) applies to a resolution under this section.

COMMENCEMENT DATE 1 October 2009[201]

**17.622.02**  Sections 623 to 625 introduce a new simple procedure whereby a company having a share capital may redenominate its share capital from one currency to another without court involvement. Until the introduction of this procedure,[202] the only course available to a public company wishing to redenominate its issued share capital was to follow the reduction of capital process set out in Companies Act 1985 sections 135ff, cancelling those shares which it wished to redenominate and issuing new shares in the required currency in their place. A private company could choose to follow this course or to follow the share buy-back procedure prescribed by sections 171ff, again issuing new shares in the relevant currency.

**17.622.03**  Section 622 permits a limited company to redenominate its share capital by simply passing a resolution to that effect. 'Resolution', for the purpose, means an ordinary resolution[203] although a company may specify in its articles that the resolution requires a higher majority or unanimity.[204]

**17.622.04**  The company's articles need not confer a specific authority for the company to be entitled to avail itself of this procedure:[205] a company whose articles are silent will be deemed to have the requisite power. However, a company may if it so wishes prohibit or restrict the exercise of the power to redenominate under this section.[206]

**17.622.05**  The resolution must specify the spot rate of exchange at which the conversion is to take place[207] and that rate must be either (i) a rate prevailing on a day specified in the resolution, or (ii) a rate determined by taking the average of rates prevailing on each consecutive day of a period specified in the resolution. In either case, the day or period specified must be within the period of 28 days ending on the day before the resolution is passed.[208] It appears that a company wishing to follow this procedure has three choices: (a) to specify in the resolution that the conversion is to take place at the spot rate of exchange prevailing on [specified date A]; (b) to specify in the resolution that the conversion is to take place at a rate determined by taking the average of rates prevailing on each consecutive day of the period between [specified date A] and [specified date B] inclusive; or (c) to stipulate the rate of exchange at which the

---

[200]  The section does not apply to an unlimited company having a share capital which is and will remain able freely to redenominate its share capital as it sees fit.
[201]  Companies Act 2006 (Commencement No 8, Transitional Provisions and Savings) Order 2008, SI 2860/2008, art 3(k).
[202]  From October 2009.
[203]  S 281.
[204]  S 281(3).
[205]  Cf CA 1985, s 135(1).
[206]  S 622(7).
[207]  S 623(2).
[208]  S 623(3).

conversion is to take place, provided that rate is the actual spot rate prevailing on a particular day or the average of rates prevailing on consecutive days of a period before the notice containing the resolution is sent or circulated to shareholders, and provided that that day or period in either case fell within the period of 28 days ending on the day before the resolution is passed. If a company follows this route, it must specify in the resolution the day or period on which the chosen rate was the prevailing rate or by reference to which the rate was determined.[209]

Where a company passes a redenomination resolution pursuant to section 623, the redenomination   **17.622.06**
takes place either (i) on the day on which the resolution is passed, or (ii) on such later date as may be determined in accordance with the resolution.[210] However, if a company proposes to provide for the redenomination to take place on a date later than that on which the resolution is passed, then it must take care that the effective date is before the end of the period of 28 days beginning with the date on which the resolution is passed: this is because a resolution passed under section 622(1) will lapse if the redenomination for which it provides has not taken effect at the end of that period.[211]

The use of the phrase 'determined in accordance with the resolution' allows the company to fix the date   **17.622.07**
by reference to conditions which must be met before the redenomination takes effect[212] rather than simply specifying a precise date in the resolution. However, if it chooses to do so, and the redenomination does not take effect before the end of the period of 28 days beginning with the day on which the resolution is passed, then the resolution will lapse and the redenomination cannot take effect.[213]

Chapter 3 of Part 3 (resolutions affecting a company's constitution) applies to a redenomination   **17.622.08**
resolution.[214] *Inter alia*, this will require that a copy of the resolution be forwarded to the registrar within 15 days after it is passed or made.[215]

### 623  Calculation of new nominal values

For each class of share the new nominal value of each share is calculated as follows:   **17.623.01**

**Step One**

Take the aggregate of the old nominal values of all the shares of that class.

**Step Two**

Translate that amount into the new currency at the rate of exchange specified in the resolution.

**Step Three**

Divide that amount by the number of shares in the class.

COMMENCEMENT DATE 1 October 2009[216]

This section sets out how the new nominal value of the shares within each class the subject of the   **17.623.02**
redenomination resolution is to be calculated. There are three steps: first, aggregate the nominal values of all the shares of the class; second, convert that into the new currency at the rate specified in the resolution; and third, divide the product by the number of shares in the class. The three steps are more easily explained by reference to worked examples:

First example: this supposes that there are 150,000 ordinary shares of £1 each within the class of shares   **17.623.03**
to be redenominated.

*Step One* (aggregate nominal values of all the shares of that class):150,000×1=£150,000
*Step Two* (translate that amount into new currency at rate of exchange specified in resolution): 150,000 ×1.98 ($/£rate on10 Feb 2007)= $297,000
*Step Three* (divide that amount by the number of shares in the class): 297,000÷150,000=$1.98
Accordingly, the new nominal value of each of the 150,000 ordinary shares is $1.98

Second example: this supposes that there are 150,000 ordinary shares of 5 pence each within the class   **17.623.04**
of shares to be redenominated.

---

[209] S 622(3).
[210] S 622(5).
[211] S 622(6).
[212] S 622(4).
[213] S 622(6).
[214] S 622(8).
[215] S 30(1).
[216] Companies Act 2006 (Commencement No 8, Transitional Provisions and Savings) Order 2008, SI 2860/2008, art 3(k).

*Step One* (aggregate nominal values of all the shares of that class): 150,000 × 5p (0.05) = £7,500

*Step Two* (translate that amount into new currency at rate of exchange specified in resolution): 7,500×1.49(£/€rate on/10Feb2007)=€11,175

*Step Three* (divide that amount by the number of shares in the class)11,175÷150,000=€ 0.0745 Accordingly, the new nominal value of each of the 150,000 ordinary shares is € 0.0745.[217]

### 624   Effect of redenomination

**17.624.01**
(1) The redenomination of shares does not affect any rights or obligations of members under the company's constitution, or any restrictions affecting members under the company's constitution. In particular, it does not affect entitlement to dividends (including entitlement to dividends in a particular currency), voting rights or any liability in respect of amounts unpaid on shares.
(2) For this purpose the company's constitution includes the terms on which any shares of the company are allotted or held.
(3) Subject to subsection (1), references to the old nominal value of the shares in any agreement or statement, or in any deed, instrument or document, shall (unless the context otherwise requires) be read after the resolution takes effect as references to the new nominal value of the shares.

COMMENCEMENT DATE 1 October 2009[218]

**17.624.02**  This section makes it clear that redenomination does not affect the rights and obligations of members or any restrictions which may affect them under the company's constitution. 'Constitution' for this purposes includes the terms on which any shares of the company are allotted or held whether or not those terms are in fact set out in the company's articles of association or any resolution or agreement.[219] In particular, redenomination does not affect entitlement to dividends (including entitlement to dividends in a particular currency) or voting rights. Any liability in respect of amounts unpaid on shares will also remain unaffected by redenomination. The Explanatory Notes accompanying this section suggest that the liability to pay uncalled capital remains a liability payable in the original currency.

**17.624.03**  After a redenomination, references in any agreement or statement, or in any deed, instrument, or document to the old nominal value of the shares, are to be read as references to the new nominal value of the shares unless the particular context otherwise requires.[220] This will avoid the need for the company to recast such documents following a redenomination.

### 625   Notice to registrar of redenomination

**17.625.01**
(1) If a limited company having a share capital redenominates any of its share capital, it must within one month after doing so give notice to the registrar, specifying the shares redenominated.
(2) The notice must—
    (a) state the date on which the resolution was passed, and
    (b) be accompanied by a statement of capital.
(3) The statement of capital must state with respect to the company's share capital as redenominated by the resolution—
    (a) the total number of shares of the company,
    (b) the aggregate nominal value of those shares,
    (c) for each class of shares—
        (i) prescribed particulars of the rights attached to the shares,
        (ii) the total number of shares of that class, and
        (iii) the aggregate nominal value of shares of that class, and
    (d) the amount paid up and the amount (if any) unpaid on each share (whether on account of the nominal value of the share or by way of premium).
(4) If default is made in complying with this section, an offence is committed by—
    (a) the company, and
    (b) every officer of the company who is in default.

---

[217] This is an example of a case where the company might wish to avail itself of the new reduction of capital procedure set out in s 626 in order to adjust the nominal values of the redenominated shares to obtain a more suitable value.

[218] Companies Act 2006 (Commencement No 8, Transitional Provisions and Savings) Order 2008, SI 2860/2008, art 3(k).

[219] Cf the definition in s 17 which, however, is not exhaustive of the meaning of a company's constitution.

[220] S 624(3).

(5) A person guilty of an offence under this section is liable on summary conviction to a fine not exceeding level 3 on the standard scale and, for continued contravention, a daily default fine not exceeding one-tenth of level 3 on the standard scale.

COMMENCEMENT DATE 1 October 2009[221]

Section 625 requires a company to give notice to the registrar of companies specifying the shares redenominated. Notice must be given within one month of the redenomination.[222] Although ambiguous, it appears that time is to be measured from the date on which the redenomination resolution is passed.[223] The 'registrar' for this purpose is the registrar of companies for England and Wales, Scotland, or Northern Ireland 'as the case may require',[224] presumably by reference to the company's place of incorporation. **17.625.02**

The requirement for notice to be given of a redenomination is in addition to the requirement that a copy of the redenomination resolution be forwarded to the registrar within 15 days after it is passed.[225] **17.625.03**

The notice to the registrar must be accompanied by a statement of capital[226] which must contain the specified details with respect to the company's capital as redenominated.[227] **17.625.04**

A failure to comply with the requirements of section 625(1) to (3) will not invalidate the redenomination since filing is not a condition of the redenomination taking effect.[228] However, failure to comply is an offence[229] and the company and every officer of it in default is liable to the penalties prescribed by section 625(5). The offence is a summary offence and carries a fine not exceeding level 3 on the standard scale and, for continued contravention, a daily default fine not exceeding one-tenth of level 3 on the standard scale.[230] For the purpose of this section, an 'officer' includes any director, manager, or secretary and any person who is to be treated as an officer for the purposes of the provision in question.[231] An officer will be 'in default' if he authorizes or permits, participates, or fails to take all reasonable steps to prevent, the contravention.[232] A company which is an officer of another company, within the meaning supplied by section 1121(2), will not commit an offence as an officer in default unless one of its officers is in default.[233] **17.625.05**

## 626 Reduction of capital in connection with redenomination

(1) A limited company that passes a resolution redenominating some or all of its shares may, for the purpose of adjusting the nominal values of the redenominated shares to obtain values that are, in the opinion of the company, more suitable, reduce its share capital under this section. **17.626.01**

(2) A reduction of capital under this section requires a special resolution of the company.

(3) Any such resolution must be passed within three months of the resolution effecting the redenomination.

(4) The amount by which a company's share capital is reduced under this section must not exceed 10% of the nominal value of the company's allotted share capital immediately after the reduction.

---

[221] Companies Act 2006 (Commencement No 8, Transitional Provisions and Savings) Order 2008, SI 2860/2008, art 3(k).

[222] S 625(1).

[223] Cf the words in s 622(1) 'may by resolution redenominate its share capital' and s 622(4), (5), and (6) where the reference is to the redenomination taking effect but further cf the words of s 627(1).

[224] S 1060(3).

[225] S 30(1) which applies to the resolution by virtue of s 622(8) above.

[226] S 625(2)(b). Following a consultation on the subject of statements of capital which closed on 11 January 2010, in May 2011 the government indicated that it would be introducing legislation to simplify the financial information requirements for all companies in statements of capital, except those required on formation and in the Annual Return, to require the following information: the total number of shares of the company, the aggregate nominal value of those shares, the aggregate amount unpaid on those shares (whether on account of nominal value of the shares or by way of premium), the total number of shares in each class, the aggregate nominal value of shares in each class and the aggregate amount unpaid on shares in each class (whether on account of nominal value of the shares or by way of premium).

[227] S 625(3). The prescribed particulars of the rights attached to shares to be included in the notice are those prescribed in the Companies (Shares and Share Capital) Order 2009, SI 2009/388: by art 2 these particulars are the voting, dividend and distribution, and return on winding-up rights, and rights to redemption. In practice, form SH14 available from Companies House for use in connection with a redenomination of share capital combines both the notice required by s 625(1) and the Statement of Capital required under s 625(2).

[228] Cf s 649(3).

[229] S 624(4).

[230] S 625(5).

[231] The definition, which is not exhaustive of who may be an officer, is found in s 1121(2).

[232] S 1121(3).

[233] S 1122(1).

(5) A reduction of capital under this section does not extinguish or reduce any liability in respect of share capital not paid up.

(6) Nothing in Chapter 10 applies to a reduction of capital under this section.

COMMENCEMENT DATE 1 October 2009[234]

**17.626.02**  This section provides a special process which enables a company to reduce its share capital in order to adjust the nominal values of redenominated shares in order to obtain more suitable values. The process, to which none of the provisions of Chapter 10 of this Part (reduction of share capital) applies,[235] is only available where a company has passed a redenomination resolution and is limited to achieving the purpose specified.[236] It is also limited to the case where the amount proposed to be written off the capital by the reduction does not exceed 10 per cent of the nominal value of the company's allotted share capital immediately after the reduction.[237]

**17.626.03**  The relevant resolution reducing the company's capital ('the reduction resolution'), which must be a special resolution,[238] must be passed within three months of the resolution effecting the redenomination.[239] There is no need for it to be accompanied by a solvency statement[240] or for the company to seek the confirmation of the Court.[241] However, the reduction will not take effect unless and until the notice and the statement of capital required by section 627 to be given to the registrar of companies is registered by him.[242]

**17.626.04**  The reserve arising on the reduction must be carried to a special undistributable reserve called a 'redenomination reserve' in accordance with section 628 below.[243]

### 627 Notice to registrar of reduction of capital in connection with redenomination

**17.627.01**  (1) A company that passes a resolution under section 626 (reduction of capital in connection with redenomination) must within 15 days after the resolution is passed give notice to the registrar stating—
  (a) the date of the resolution, and
  (b) the date of the resolution under section 622 in connection with which it was passed.
  This is in addition to the copies of the resolutions themselves that are required to be delivered to the registrar under Chapter 3 of Part 3.
  (2) The notice must be accompanied by a statement of capital.
  (3) The statement of capital must state with respect to the company's share capital as reduced by the resolution—
  (a) the total number of shares of the company,
  (b) the aggregate nominal value of those shares,
  (c) for each class of shares—
    (i) prescribed particulars of the rights attached to the shares,
    (ii) the total number of shares of that class, and
    (iii) the aggregate nominal value of shares of that class, and
  (d) the amount paid up and the amount (if any) unpaid on each share (whether on account of the nominal value of the share or by way of premium).
  (4) The registrar must register the notice and the statement on receipt.
  (5) The reduction of capital is not effective until those documents are registered.
  (6) The company must also deliver to the registrar, within 15 days after the resolution is passed, a statement by the directors confirming that the reduction in share capital is in accordance with section 626(4) (reduction of capital not to exceed 10% of nominal value of allotted shares immediately after reduction).
  (7) If default is made in complying with this section, an offence is committed by—
  (a) the company, and
  (b) every officer of the company who is in default.
  (8) A person guilty of an offence under this section is liable—

---

[234] Companies Act 2006 (Commencement No 8, Transitional Provisions and Savings) Order 2008, SI 2860/2008, art 3(k).
[235] S 626(6).
[236] S 626(1).
[237] S 626(4). This 10 per cent cap is required in the case of public companies by the Second Company Law Directive (77/91/EEC).
[238] S 626(2).
[239] S 626(3).
[240] Cf s 642.
[241] Cf s 645ff.
[242] S 627(5).
[243] S 628(1).

(a) on conviction on indictment to a fine, and

(b) on summary conviction to a fine not exceeding the statutory maximum.

COMMENCEMENT DATE 1 October 2009[244]

Section 627 requires a company to give notice to the registrar of companies of a reduction of capital carried out under section 626. Notice must be given within 15 days of the passing of the resolution.[245] The 'registrar' for this purpose is the registrar of companies for England and Wales, Scotland, or Northern Ireland 'as the case may require'.[246] **17.627.02**

The requirement for notice to be given of a reduction carried out in this context is in addition to the requirement that a copy of the reduction resolution be forwarded to the registrar within 15 days after it is passed.[247] **17.627.03**

The notice to the registrar must be accompanied by a statement of capital[248] which must contain the specified details with respect to the company's capital as reduced. These include certain prescribed particulars as to share rights.[249] **17.627.04**

The reduction of capital is not effective until the notice and the statement required by this section to be given are registered by the registrar.[250] The registrar must register the notice and statement on receipt.[251] The registrar may make rules[252] providing when a document is to be regarded as received.[253] **17.627.05**

The company must also deliver to the registrar a statement by its directors confirming that the reduction does not exceed 10 per cent of the nominal value of the company's allotted share capital immediately after the reduction.[254] The delivery of this statement is not a condition of the reduction taking effect, but failure to file such a statement is an offence[255] punishable as prescribed in section 627(8). **17.627.06**

Failure to comply with the requirements of section 627 is an offence[256] and the company and every officer of it in default is liable to the penalties prescribed by section 627(8). The offence is triable either way,[257] a summary offence and carries a fine.[258] For the purpose of this section, an 'officer' includes any director, manager, or secretary and any person who is to be treated as an officer for the purposes of the provision in question.[259] An officer will be 'in default' if he authorizes or permits, participates, or fails to take all reasonable steps to prevent, the contravention.[260] A company which is an officer of another company, within the meaning supplied by section 1121(2), will not commit an offence as an officer in default unless one of its officers is in default.[261] **17.627.07**

## 628 Redenomination reserve

(1) The amount by which a company's share capital is reduced under section 626 (reduction of capital in connection with redenomination) must be transferred to a reserve, called 'the redenomination reserve'. **17.628.01**

(2) The redenomination reserve may be applied by the company in paying up shares to be allotted to members as fully paid bonus shares.

---

[244] Companies Act 2006 (Commencement No 8, Transitional Provisions and Savings) Order 2008, SI 2860/2008, art 3(k).

[245] S 627(1).

[246] S 1060(3).

[247] S 30(1) which applies to the resolution by virtue of s 622(8) above.

[248] S 627(2).

[249] S 627(3). The prescribed particulars of the rights attached to shares to be included in the notice are those prescribed in the Companies (Shares and Share Capital) Order 2009, SI 2009/388: by art 2 these particulars are the voting, dividend and distribution, and return on winding-up rights, and rights to redemption. In practice, form SH15 available from Companies House for use in connection with a redenomination of share capital combines both the notice required by s 627(1) and the Statement of Capital required under s 627(2). Please see footnote 27 above as to anticipated future legislation concerning Statements of Capital.

[250] S 627(5).

[251] S 627(4).

[252] Pursuant to the power conferred by s 1117.

[253] S 1071(2).

[254] S 627(6).

[255] S 627(7).

[256] S 627(7).

[257] S 627(8).

[258] S 627(8).

[259] The definition, which is not exhaustive, of who may be an officer, is found in s 1121(2).

[260] S 1121(3).

[261] S 1122(1).

(3)  Subject to that, the provisions of the Companies Acts relating to the reduction of a company's share capital apply as if the redenomination reserve were paid up share capital of the company.

COMMENCEMENT DATE 1 October 2009[262]

**17.628.02**    Where a company reduces its share capital using the procedure prescribed by section 626, the amount whereby the capital is reduced must be transferred to a 'redenomination reserve'.[263]

**17.628.03**    The redenomination reserve is an undistributable reserve and, save that it may be used by the company to pay up shares to be allotted to the company's members as bonus shares,[264] it is to be treated as if it were paid up share capital.[265] In this sense, the redenomination reserve is similar to the capital redemption reserve[266] arising on a diminution of capital on the redemption or purchase of shares. A company which wishes to reduce or cancel the redenomination reserve must do so in accordance with the procedures prescribed by the Act with respect to reduction of share capital:[267] section 626 does not apply to that reserve.[268]

CHAPTER 9

CLASSES OF SHARE AND CLASS RIGHTS

*Introductory*

### 629  Classes of shares

**17.629.01**    (1)  For the purpose of this Chapter shares are of one class if the rights attached to them are in all respects uniform.

                (2)  For this purpose the rights attached to shares are not regarded as different from those attached to other shares by reason only that they do not carry the same rights to dividends in the twelve months immediately following their allotment.

COMMENCEMENT DATE 1 October 2009[269]

**17.629.02**    This section defines a class of shares and class rights for the purposes of this Chapter.

**17.629.03**    The only reported case properly to consider the meaning of the term 'class right' for the purposes of the superseded provision of the Companies Act 1985 (section 125) was *Cumbrian Newspapers Group Ltd v Cumberland & Westmoreland Herald Newspaper and Printing Co Ltd*.[270] The focus in that case was on rights contained in the articles, but it is clear that such rights can also be contained in the memorandum, the terms of issue, or the resolution authorizing the issue (as originally framed or subsequently varied). Three different types of rights contained in the articles were identified in the *Cumbrian Newspapers* case. The first was where rights or benefits are attached to particular shares. Examples of such rights are dividend rights and rights to participate in surplus assets on a winding-up. Such rights create conventional classes of shares and the court had little difficulty in holding that they fell within the scope of section 125 of the 1985 Act. The second category was where rights are conferred on individuals not in the capacity of members but for ulterior reasons connected with the administration of the company or the conduct of its business. Such rights were not considered to be class rights for the purposes of section 125.[271] The third category was rights or benefits that were not attached to any particular shares but were nonetheless conferred on the beneficiary in the capacity of member of the company. Such rights were held to be class rights within the meaning of section 125. In the *Cumbrian Newspapers* case, the rights in question were contingent on the member holding 10 per cent of the issued ordinary shares of the defendant and included a pre-emptive right regarding the transfer of any shares in the defendant and the right to nominate a director to the board. The special voting rights of

---

[262] Companies Act 2006 (Commencement No 8, Transitional Provisions and Savings) Order 2008, SI 2860/2008, art 3(k).

[263] S 628(1).

[264] S 628(2).

[265] S 628(3).

[266] See s 733.

[267] Part 17 Chapter 10 with effect from a date to be fixed or, pending that, CA 1985, ss 135–138.

[268] S 628(3).

[269] Companies Act 2006 (Commencement No 8, Transitional Provisions and Savings) Order 2008, SI 2008/2860, art 3(k).

[270] [1986] 2 All ER 816.

[271] Scott J gave as an example of such rights those given to the company solicitor in *Eley v Positive Government Security Life Assurance Co Ltd* (1875) 1 Ex D 20.

a director on a resolution for his dismissal which were the subject of dispute in the case of *Bushell v Faith*[272] were cited as examples of rights that fell within this third category and therefore within section 125.

The effect of the decision in *Cumbrian Newspapers* was to extend, for the purposes of section 125 of the Companies Act 1985, the meaning of a class of shares beyond what may be regarded as conventionally different classes (category one in the analysis above). This carried implications particularly for private companies, in which the third category of class rights (above) is most commonly found. The effect was to bring within the procedure for variation of class rights a wider range of rights than would be the case if only conventional classes were to be included. **17.629.04**

While the DTI Explanatory Notes to the Companies Act 2006 do not indicate any intention to change the law in respect of class rights, it is arguable that the reference in subsection (1) to rights attached to shares (as opposed to members) has the effect of excluding the third category of rights in *Cumbrian Newspapers*.[273] The second category can certainly be excluded from the definition because the rights are not attached to shares but to persons holding them. The section leaves open the issue of whether class rights are only the rights that are unique to a particular class or whether they extend beyond that to include some or all of the rights attached to the relevant shares. While there is very little judicial comment on this point, despite its fundamental importance, the middle position, whereby class rights extend beyond the unique rights of a class to include rights relating to voting, dividends, and return of capital on a winding-up, has attracted academic support.[274] **17.629.05**

## Variation of class rights

### 630 Variation of class rights: companies having a share capital

(1) This section is concerned with the variation of the rights attached to a class of shares in a company having a share capital. **17.630.01**
(2) Rights of a class of members may only be varied—
(a) in accordance with provision in the company's articles for the variation of those rights, or
(b) where the company's articles contain no such provision, if the members of that class consent to the variation in accordance with this section.
(3) This is without prejudice to any other restrictions on the variation of the rights.
(4) The consent required for the purposes of this section on the part of the holders of a class of a company's shares is—
(a) consent in writing from the holders of at least three-quarters in nominal value of the issued shares of that class (excluding any shares held as treasury shares), or
(b) a special resolution passed at a separate general meeting of the holders of that class sanctioning the variation.
(5) Any amendment of a provision contained in a company's articles for the variation of the rights attached to a class of shares, or the insertion of any such provision into the articles, is itself to be treated as a variation of those rights.
(6) In this section, and (except where the context otherwise requires) in any provision in a company's articles for the variation of the rights attached to a class of shares, references to the variation of those rights include references to their abrogation.

COMMENCEMENT DATE 1 October 2009[275]

The CLR recommended that the existing provisions of section 125 of the Companies Act 1985 (which were introduced in 1980, implementing part of the Second Company Law Directive[276]) be simplified.[277] That recommendation reflected an underlying policy that company law should facilitate the creation of different classes of shares to meet diverse financing requirements. This section certainly does contain a simpler set of procedural requirements for a variation in class rights. However, it leaves **17.630.02**

---

[272] [1969] 1 All ER 1002.
[273] That distinction was of relevance for taxation purposes in *Grays Timber Products Ltd v Revenue and Customs Commissioners* [2010] UKSC 4. In that case the managing director of a company held shares with enhanced rights set out in the subscription agreement but those rights were not assignable. The rights were termed 'personal' and were worthless to a purchaser (meaning that they were to be ignored in determining the market value of the shares for taxation purposes).
[274] See PL Davies, *Gower and Davies Principles of Modern Company Law* (8th edn, 2008, Sweet & Maxwell), 671.
[275] Companies Act 2006 (Commencement No 8, Transitional Provisions and Savings) Order 2008, SI 2008/2860, art 3(k).
[276] Directive (EEC) 77/91 [1977] OJ L26/1.
[277] See CLR *Final Report*, para 7.28 and *Developing the Framework*, paras 4.1.47–4.1.51.

largely unanswered the contentious issue of the meaning of a 'variation', which remains subject to interpretation by the courts.

**17.630.03**    In contrast with the broad interpretation given to class rights under the Companies Act 1985, a restrictive approach was adopted to the meaning of a variation or abrogation.[278] While some cases identified instances in which class rights were varied[279], the instances in which a variation was not recognized provide a clearer impression of the restrictive meaning applied to the term. A variation or abrogation has been held not to occur in the following circumstances:[280]

(1)  an issue of new shares ranking *pari passu* with class X;[281]

(2)  an issue ranking in priority to class X,[282] there being no extrinsic contractual promise to the holders of class X that this would not be done;[283]

(3)  an issue of bonus shares (whether ordinary or preference) to the holders in class Y (ordinary shares), when it had the effect of greatly increasing their voting power as against that of the holders in class X (preference shares),[284] or of reducing the amount which would come in a liquidation, on a distribution of surplus assets, to the holders in class X (preference shares);[285]

(4)  a subdivision of shares in class Y so that the holders in that class acquired a greatly increased voting power in comparison to class X;[286]

(5)  the cancellation of paid-up capital to an equal extent on both class X (preference shares) and class Y (ordinary shares), with the result that the fixed preferential dividend payable to class X, though unaltered in percentage, was substantially reduced in amount, whereas the dividend for class Y remained at large;[287] and

(6)  the alteration of the place of payment (and thus the currency) of dividends from England to Australia, causing the fixed preferential dividend payable to class X to be of lesser value because the Australian pound was worth less than the English pound sterling.[288]

**17.630.04**    In several of the instances cited in the previous paragraph (both instances in 3; 4) the reasoning employed in reaching the conclusion that there was no variation was based on a distinction between varying a right and affecting the enjoyment of a right. Even if it is accepted that the concept of a variation should be defined narrowly so as to limit the capacity for obstruction by minorities, this approach is problematic since it permits functional equivalents of a variation to be implemented without triggering the requirements applicable to a variation. For example, it was observed in *Greenhalgh v Arderne Cinemas Ltd*[289] that had the proposal been to increase the votes attached to shares rather than to sub-divide the shares, it would have amounted to a variation. Since the voting position of shareholders would ultimately be the same in either case it is difficult to rationalize a distinction between a variation of rights and enjoyment of rights. Nevertheless, the risk to a class posed by the possibility of a proposal falling within the latter rather than the former can be mitigated by an appropriately drafted variation provision in the articles which, if formulated so as to cover the enjoyment of rights (or at least specific instances), will govern the proposal according to subsection (2).

**17.630.05**    Subsection (2) sets out the requirement that a variation may occur only in accordance with a provision in the articles or (where no provision is made) if the holders of shares of that class consent to the variation in accordance with this section. The new form of abbreviated memorandum (see section 8) will mean that neither class rights nor provision for their variation will in future be contained in the memorandum. Where such rights or provisions for their variation are currently specified in the memorandum they will be treated under section 28 as part of the articles.

**17.630.06**    The consent required is specified by subsection (4) as being that of three quarters in nominal value of the issued shares of that class or a special resolution passed at a general meeting of the holders of that

---

[278]  As noted below, an abrogation has been and will continue to be treated as functionally equivalent to a variation for the purposes of this section.

[279]  See eg *Re Old Silkstone Collieries Ltd.* [1954] Ch 169, CA and *Scottish Insurance Corp Ltd v Wilsons & Clyde Coal Co Ltd* [1949] AC 462, HL (Sc).

[280]  This follows the list shown in *Boyle & Birds' Company Law* (6th edn) 270.

[281]  *Re Schweppes Ltd* [1914] 1 Ch 322, CA (a decision under the Companies (Consolidation) Act 1908).

[282]  *Pulbrook v New Civil Service Co-operation* (1878) 26 WR 11; *Underwood v London Music Hall Ltd* [1901] 2 Ch 309; *Hodge v James Howell & Co Ltd* [1958] CLY 446, CA.

[283]  See *Allen v Gold Reefs of West Africa Ltd* [1900] 1 Ch 656, pp 673–674 and 679, CA.

[284]  *White v Bristol Aeroplane Co Ltd* [1953] Ch 65; *Re John Smith's Tadcaster Brewery Co Ltd* [1953] Ch 308.

[285]  *Dimbula Valley (Ceylon) Tea Co Ltd v Laurie* [1961] Ch 353.

[286]  *Greenhalgh v Arderne Cinemas Ltd* [1946] 1 All ER 512, CA.

[287]  *Re Mackenzie & Co Ltd* [1916] 2 Ch 450.

[288]  *Adelaide Electric Supply Co Ltd v Prudential Assurance Co* [1934] AC 122, HL.

[289]  [1946] 1 All ER 512, 515, per Lord Greene MR.

class sanctioning the variation. However, this is stated by subsection (3) to be without prejudice to any other (more demanding) restrictions on the variation. For example, it would be possible for the articles to specify a higher percentage of votes than that required to pass a special resolution. If class rights are entrenched under section 22, it may not be possible to vary them at all, or only under certain circumstances.

Subsections (5) and (6) replace subsections (7) and (8) of section 125 of the 1985 Act. Subsection (5) **17.630.07** treats as functionally equivalent to a variation of rights an alteration of a provision contained in a company's articles for the variation of the rights attached to a class of shares or the insertion of any such provision into the articles. Subsection (6) does the same as regards an abrogation of class rights. The significance of these provisions is that the procedure for variation of class rights is itself a class a right and cannot be varied without following the procedure set out above. Were it otherwise, the requirement to follow the procedure could be circumvented.

## 631 Variation of class rights: companies without a share capital

(1) This section is concerned with the variation of the rights of a class of members of a company **17.631.01** where the company does not have a share capital.
(2) Rights of a class of members may only be varied—
  (a) in accordance with provision in the company's articles for the variation of those rights, or
  (b) where the company's articles contain no such provision, if the members of that class consent to the variation in accordance with this section.
(3) This is without prejudice to any other restrictions on the variation of the rights.
(4) The consent required for the purposes of this section on the part of the members of a class is—
  (a) consent in writing from at least three-quarters of the members of the class, or
  (b) a special resolution passed at a separate general meeting of the members of that class sanctioning the variation.
(5) Any amendment of a provision contained in a company's articles for the variation of the rights of a class of members, or the insertion of any such provision into the articles, is itself to be treated as a variation of those rights.
(6) In this section, and (except where the context otherwise requires) in any provision in a company's articles for the variation of the rights of a class of members, references to the variation of those rights include references to their abrogation.

COMMENCEMENT DATE 1 October 2009[290]

Section 125 of the Companies Act 1985 did not make provision for the alteration of class rights of **17.631.02** members who were not shareholders. The result was that the procedure to be followed to give effect to a variation of class rights in those circumstances was complex and surrounded by some uncertainty.[291] The effect of this section is to apply to companies without share capital provisions similar to those found in section 630, which apply to a company with a share capital.

## 632 Variation of class rights: saving for court's powers under other provisions

Nothing in section 630 or 631 (variation of class rights) affects the power of the court under— **17.632.01**

section 98 (application to cancel resolution for public company to be re-registered as private),
Part 26 (arrangements and reconstructions), or
Part 30 (protection of members against unfair prejudice).

COMMENCEMENT DATE 1 October 2009[292]

This section is consequential on sections 630 and 631 and preserves the court's rights under other **17.632.02** provisions. Those other provisions provide alternative and, assuming the restrictive interpretation of the meaning of a variation of class rights continues, possibly more effective remedies for the protection of class rights.

## 633 Right to object to variation: companies having a share capital

(1) This section applies where the rights attached to any class of shares in a company are varied under **17.633.01** section 630 (variation of class rights: companies having a share capital).

---

[290] Companies Act 2006 (Commencement No 8, Transitional Provisions and Savings) Order 2008, SI 2008/2860, art 3(k).
[291] See generally P Davies, *Gower and Davies' Principles of Modern Company Law* (7th edn, 2003, Sweet & Maxwell) 501–502.
[292] Companies Act 2006 (Commencement No 8, Transitional Provisions and Savings) Order 2008, SI 2008/2860, art 3(k).

(2)  The holders of not less in the aggregate than 15% of the issued shares of the class in question (being persons who did not consent to or vote in favour of the resolution for the variation) may apply to the court to have the variation cancelled.
     For this purpose any of the company's share capital held as treasury shares is disregarded.

(3)  If such an application is made, the variation has no effect unless and until it is confirmed by the court.

(4)  Application to the court—
     (a)  must be made within 21 days after the date on which the consent was given or the resolution was passed (as the case may be), and
     (b)  may be made on behalf of the shareholders entitled to make the application by such one or more of their number as they may appoint in writing for the purpose.

(5)  The court, after hearing the applicant and any other persons who apply to the court to be heard and appear to the court to be interested in the application, may, if satisfied having regard to all the circumstances of the case that the variation would unfairly prejudice the shareholders of the class represented by the applicant, disallow the variation, and shall if not satisfied confirm it.
     The decision of the court on any such application is final.

(6)  References in this section to the variation of the rights of holders of a class of shares include references to their abrogation.

COMMENCEMENT DATE  1 October 2009[293]

**17.633.02**  This section replaces section 127 of the Companies Act 1985 and provides for the right of a minority within a class to object to a variation of their class rights under section 630. It applies only to a variation (or abrogation) within the meaning of section 630 and therefore the restrictive meaning given to that term for the purposes of that section limits the extent to which a minority can challenge the decision of the majority.

**17.633.03**  The minority must comprise holders of at least 15 per cent of the issued shares of the class in question and that once an application is made to the court the variation has no effect unless and until it is confirmed by the court. Subsection (4) requires an application to be made within 21 days of consent being given to the variation or the resolution passed (as the case may be).

**17.633.04**  Subsection (5) provides that the basis on which the court is to review the variation is whether it would be unfairly prejudicial to the minority in the class in respect of which a variation has been approved. The court is required, on the basis of that criterion, to approve or disallow the variation, and the decision of the court on any such application is final.

**17.633.05**  As there is no reported use of the superseded provisions of the 1985 Act (section 127), the meaning of unfairly prejudicial to the minority in a class remains unclear. Another option open to the minority, which is not excluded by this section and does not require a 15 per cent shareholding, is to challenge a variation on the basis of a lack of good faith on the part of the majority in adopting a class resolution.[294]

### 634  Right to object to variation: companies without a share capital

**17.634.01**  (1)  This section applies where the rights of any class of members of a company are varied under section 631 (variation of class rights: companies without a share capital).

(2)  Members amounting to not less than 15% of the members of the class in question (being persons who did not consent to or vote in favour of the resolution for the variation) may apply to the court to have the variation cancelled.

(3)  If such an application is made, the variation has no effect unless and until it is confirmed by the court.

(4)  Application to the court must be made within 21 days after the date on which the consent was given or the resolution was passed (as the case may be) and may be made on behalf of the members entitled to make the application by such one or more of their number as they may appoint in writing for the purpose.

(5)  The court, after hearing the applicant and any other persons who apply to the court to be heard and appear to the court to be interested in the application, may, if satisfied having regard to all the circumstances of the case that the variation would unfairly prejudice the members of the class represented by the applicant, disallow the variation, and shall if not satisfied confirm it.
     The decision of the court on any such application is final.

---

[293]  Companies Act 2006 (Commencement No 8, Transitional Provisions and Savings) Order 2008, SI 2008/2860, art 3(k).

[294]  See, as regards the general principle, *Carruth v Imperial Chemical Industries Ltd* [1937] AC 707, 756 and 765; and, for a decision setting aside a class resolution (in the context of a reduction of capital) on the basis that the majority had not voted with a view to the interests of the class, *Re Holders Investment Trust Ltd* [1971] 1 WLR 583.

**17.637.02**    This section replaces section 128(3) of the 1985 Act and removes the exceptions contained in that section, which had the effect that a variation in class rights did not always have to be notified to the registrar. It requires a company to register a variation of rights attached to shares within a month.

### 638  Notice of new class of members

**17.638.01**    (1)  If a company not having a share capital creates a new class of members, the company must within one month from the date on which the new class is created deliver to the registrar a notice containing particulars of the rights attached to that class.

(2)  If default is made in complying with this section, an offence is committed by—

(a)  the company, and

(b)  every officer of the company who is in default.

(3)  A person guilty of an offence under this section is liable on summary conviction to a fine not exceeding level 3 on the standard scale and, for continued contravention, a daily default fine not exceeding one-tenth of level 3 on the standard scale.

COMMENCEMENT DATE  1 October 2009[299]

**17.638.02**    This section replaces section 129(1) of the 1985 Act. It requires a company without a share capital to register details of a new class of members within one month of its creation.

### 639  Notice of name or other designation of class of members

**17.639.01**    (1)  Where a company not having a share capital assigns a name or other designation, or a new name or other designation, to any class of its members, it must within one month from doing so deliver to the registrar a notice giving particulars of the name or designation so assigned.

(2)  If default is made in complying with this section, an offence is committed by—

(a)  the company, and

(b)  every officer of the company who is in default.

(3)  A person guilty of an offence under this section is liable on summary conviction to a fine not exceeding level 3 on the standard scale and, for continued contravention, a daily default fine not exceeding one-tenth of level 3 on the standard scale.

COMMENCEMENT DATE  1 October 2009[300]

**17.639.02**    This section replaces section 129(3) of the 1985 Act. It requires a company without a share capital to register a name or other designation, or a new name or other designation given to a class of shares within one month.

### 640  Notice of particulars of variation of class rights

**17.640.01**    (1)  If the rights of any class of members of a company not having a share capital are varied, the company must within one month from the date on which the variation is made deliver to the registrar a notice containing particulars of the variation.

(2)  If default is made in complying with this section, an offence is committed by—

(a)  the company, and

(b)  every officer of the company who is in default.

(3)  A person guilty of an offence under this section is liable on summary conviction to a fine not exceeding level 3 on the standard scale and, for continued contravention, a daily default fine not exceeding one-tenth of level 3 on the standard scale.

COMMENCEMENT DATE  1 October 2009[301]

**17.640.02**    This section replaces section 129(2) of the 1985 Act and removes the exceptions contained in that section, which had the effect that a variation in class rights did not always have to be notified to the registrar. It requires a company without a share capital to register a variation of rights attached to shares within a month.

---

[299] Companies Act 2006 (Commencement No 8, Transitional Provisions and Savings) Order 2008, SI 2008/2860, art 3(k).

[300] Companies Act 2006 (Commencement No 8, Transitional Provisions and Savings) Order 2008, SI 2008/2860, art 3(k).

[301] Companies Act 2006 (Commencement No 8, Transitional Provisions and Savings) Order 2008, SI 2008/2860, art 3(k).

(6)  References in this section to the variation of the rights of a class of members include references to their abrogation.

COMMENCEMENT DATE  1 October 2009[295]

This section provides for members of a company without a share capital to object to a variation in class   **17.634.02**
rights. The procedure for making the objection and the basis on which the court is to reach its decision
is the same as for section 633.

## 635  Copy of court order to be forwarded to the registrar

(1)  The company must within 15 days after the making of an order by the court on an application   **17.635.01**
under section 633 or 634 (objection to variation of class rights) forward a copy of the order to the
registrar.
(2)  If default is made in complying with this section an offence is committed by—
    (a)  the company, and
    (b)  every officer of the company who is in default.
(3)  A person guilty of an offence under this section is liable on summary conviction to a fine not
exceeding level 3 on the standard scale and, for continued contravention, a daily default fine not
exceeding one-tenth of level 3 on the standard scale.

COMMENCEMENT DATE  1 October 2009[296]

This section replaces section 127(5) of the 1985 Act. It requires the company to register a copy of an   **17.635.02**
order made by the court under section 633 or 634 within 15 days.

### *Matters to be notified to the registrar*

## 636  Notice of name or other designation of class of shares

(1)  Where a company assigns a name or other designation, or a new name or other designation, to   **17.636.01**
any class of its shares, it must within one month from doing so deliver to the registrar a notice
giving particulars of the name or designation so assigned.
(2)  If default is made in complying with this section, an offence is committed by—
    (a)  the company, and
    (b)  every officer of the company who is in default.
(3)  A person guilty of an offence under this section is liable on summary conviction to a fine not
exceeding level 3 on the standard scale and, for continued contravention, a daily default fine not
exceeding one-tenth of level 3 on the standard scale.

COMMENCEMENT DATE  1 October 2009[297]

This section replaces section 128(4) of the Companies Act 1985. It requires a company to register a   **17.636.02**
name or other designation, or a new name or other designation given to a class of shares within one
month.

## 637  Notice of particulars of variation of rights attached to shares

(1)  Where the rights attached to any shares of a company are varied, the company must within one   **17.637.01**
month from the date on which the variation is made deliver to the registrar a notice giving
particulars of the variation.
(2)  If default is made in complying with this section, an offence is committed by—
    (a)  the company, and
    (b)  every officer of the company who is in default.
(3)  A person guilty of an offence under this section is liable on summary conviction to a fine not
exceeding level 3 on the standard scale and, for continued contravention, a daily default fine not
exceeding one-tenth of level 3 on the standard scale.

COMMENCEMENT DATE  1 October 2009[298]

---

[295] Companies Act 2006 (Commencement No 8, Transitional Provisions and Savings) Order 2008, SI
2008/2860, art 3(k).
[296] Companies Act 2006 (Commencement No 8, Transitional Provisions and Savings) Order 2008, SI
2008/2860, art 3(k).
[297] Companies Act 2006 (Commencement No 8, Transitional Provisions and Savings) Order 2008, SI
2008/2860, art 3(k).
[298] Companies Act 2006 (Commencement No 8, Transitional Provisions and Savings) Order 2008, SI
2008/2860, art 3(k).

# CHAPTER 10
## REDUCTION OF SHARE CAPITAL

### *Introductory*

### 641  Circumstances in which a company may reduce its share capital[a]

(1) A limited company having a share capital may reduce its share capital—     **17.641.01**

    (a) in the case of a private company limited by shares, by special resolution supported by a solvency statement (see sections 642 to 644);

    (b) in any case, by special resolution confirmed by the court (see sections 645 to 651).

(2) A company may not reduce its capital under subsection (1)(a) if as a result of the reduction there would no longer be any member of the company holding shares other than redeemable shares.

(3) Subject to that, a company may reduce its share capital under this section in any way.

(4) In particular, a company may—

    (a) extinguish or reduce the liability on any of its shares in respect of share capital not paid up, or

    (b) either with or without extinguishing or reducing liability on any of its shares—

        (i) cancel any paid-up share capital that is lost or unrepresented by available assets, or

        (ii) repay any paid-up share capital in excess of the company's wants.

(5) A special resolution under this section may not provide for a reduction of share capital to take effect later than the date on which the resolution has effect in accordance with this Chapter.

(6) This Chapter (apart from subsection (5) above) has effect subject to any provision of the company's articles restricting or prohibiting the reduction of the company's share capital.

AMENDMENTS AND NOTES

[a] Replaced CA 1985, s 135(1) and (2) while introducing the new 'non-court route' share capital reduction procedure for private companies. The introduction of this procedure was 1 October 2008.

COMMENCEMENT DATE 1 October 2008 (section 641(1)(a) and (2)–(6)—private companies: reduction of share capital supported by solvency statement);[302] 1 October 2009 (remaining provisions)[303]

This section implements, for private companies, the proposal of the Company Law Review (CLR) that     **17.641.02**
companies be permitted to reduce their capital with the sanction of a special resolution supported by a declaration of solvency by the directors. This proposal was first canvassed in its consultation document, *Modern Company Law, The Strategic Framework*.[304] The CLR proposed that a similar route be made available to public companies, subject to a statutory right, necessary to comply with the requirements with respect to public companies imposed by Article 32 of the Second Company Law Directive,[305] permitting an objecting creditor to apply to the court in opposition to the reduction. It was proposed that creditors would have such a right in any case save for a capital reduction proposed simply for the purpose of writing off existing losses or one which would create an undistributable reserve of not more than 10 per cent of the reduced capital. In the event, the CLR's proposal with respect to public companies has not been followed through and a public company wishing to reduce its capital will still have to apply to the court for sanction in order to effect a lawful reduction of capital under this chapter.[306]

The new procedure whereby a private company may reduce its capital by special resolution supported     **17.641.03**
by a solvency statement is set out in detail in sections 642 to 644. Section 641 also preserves, for both private and public companies having a share capital, the existing procedure[307] whereby a company may reduce its capital by special resolution followed by Court approval. This procedure appears in this Act in sections 645 to 649.

Section 641(2) provides a limitation on the use of the special resolution and solvency statement (the     **17.641.04**
so-called 'non-court route') procedure. A private company may not reduce its capital using this process if, as a result of the reduction, there would no longer be any member of the company holding

---

[302] Companies Act 2006 (Commencement No 7, Transitional Provisions and Savings) Order 2008, SI 2008/1886, art 2.

[303] Companies Act 2006 (Commencement No 8, Transitional Provisions and Savings) Order 2008, SI 2008/2860, art 3(k).

[304] URN 99/654, February 1999, paras 5.4.4–5.4.13.

[305] Directive (EEC) 77/91 [1977] OJ L26/1.

[306] Section 641(1)(b) and ss 645–649.

[307] Currently set out in CA 1985, ss 135–139.

shares other than redeemable shares. When this sub-clause was introduced,[308] it qualified both court-approved and non-court route reductions. The qualification, so far as the court-approved reductions is concerned, was removed from the Bill, following the debate in the Grand Committee of the House of Lords.[309] The Explanatory Notes[310] state that 'a private company limited by shares should not be capable of reducing its share capital to zero unless the reduction of capital is sanctioned by the Court'. It is clear, therefore, that the presence of this section will preclude a private company from carrying out a reduction of capital which requires the capital to be reduced to zero, even momentarily.[311] In such a case, the court procedure must be adopted.

**17.641.05**    The words of section 641(3) preserve, subject to the qualification the subject of subsection 641(2), the permissive terms of section 135(1) of the Companies Act 1985 which permit a company to reduce its share capital 'in any way'. Those words have appeared in successive Companies Acts since the Companies (Consolidation) Act 1908.[312]

**17.641.06**    The words of section 641(4) follow the CLR's recommendation[313] that the non-exhaustive list of examples of how a reduction of capital might be achieved should remain in the legislation, subject to amendment to remove the reference to the memorandum. In fact, the words mirror closely the words of section 135(2) of the Companies Act 1985 (which, in turn, replicated, with one minor amendment, those of the 1948 Act).

**17.641.07**    A special resolution which provides for the reduction of a company's capital may not provide for the reduction to take effect later than the date on which it has effect as provided by sections 644 and 649. This provision is directed to preventing the members of a company circumventing the provisions of the Act which prescribe when the reduction of capital takes effect by providing in the terms of their resolution that it should take effect at a later date.

**17.641.08**    Formerly, in the absence of an express authority in its articles of association, a company had no power to reduce its capital.[314] Article 34 in 1985 Table A[315] supplied such authority by default in the case of companies incorporated after the introduction of the Companies Act 1985. However, this section now supplies the authority by statute unless the company by its articles expressly prohibits a reduction of capital or restricts it to particular circumstances. Under transitional provisions, existing companies whose articles are silent will, however, be entitled to continue to rely on that silence prohibiting a reduction of capital unless and until the members resolve to amend the constitution to include permission.

**17.641.09**    As regards the use a company may make of any reserve arising on a reduction of capital, reference should be made to section 654(1) of the Companies Act 2006, and the Companies (Reduction of Share Capital) Order 2008.[316] The prohibition in that section came into effect on 1 October 2008.[317] However, in relation to certain reductions, notably reductions of capital of private companies using the 'non-court route' procedure, the restriction is disapplied and the reserve 'is to be treated for the purposes of Part 23' of the Companies Act 2006 as a realized profit. In the case of court-sanctioned reductions the prohibition is disapplied unless the court orders otherwise. The disapplication is subject to any contrary provision of any order or undertaking given to the court, the resolution or any other resolution relevant to the reduction, or the company's articles of association.

---

[308] Company Law Reform Bill Clause 561(3) as printed on 1 Nov 2005, amending CA 1985, inserting s 135(1B).

[309] See the debate on Lords Amendment No A67A: *Hansard*, HL, col GC4 (20 March 2006).

[310] Paragraph 953.

[311] An example of a case where a company might wish to reduce its capital to zero momentarily would be where it has a number of different classes of shares of par values and wishes to tidy up its capital prior to a flotation: it might choose to cancel its entire issued capital and issue new shares of a single class to its existing shareholders in numbers reflecting the proportionate rights and values of their former holdings in the capital of the company.

[312] Chapter 69.

[313] *Company Formation and Capital Maintenance*, para 3.28.

[314] CA 1985, s 135(1).

[315] SI 1985/805.

[316] SI 2008/1915.

[317] Companies Act 2008 (Commencement No 7, Transitional Provisions and Savings) Order 2008, SI 2008/1886, art 2.

*Private companies: reduction of capital supported by solvency statement*

### 642  Reduction of capital supported by solvency statement[a]

(1)  A resolution[b] for reducing share capital of a private company limited by shares is supported by a solvency statement if—    **17.642.01**

    (a)  the directors of the company make a statement of the solvency of the company in accordance with section 643 (a 'solvency statement') not more than 15 days before the date on which the resolution is passed, and

    (b)  the resolution and solvency statement are registered in accordance with section 644.

(2)  Where the resolution is proposed as a written resolution, a copy of the solvency statement must be sent or submitted to every eligible member at or before the time at which the proposed resolution is sent or submitted to him.

(3)  Where the resolution is proposed at a general meeting, a copy of the solvency statement must be made available for inspection by members of the company throughout that meeting.

(4)  The validity of a resolution is not affected by a failure to comply with subsection (2) or (3).

AMENDMENTS AND NOTES

[a]  CA 2006, s 641(1)(a) and ss 642–644 introduce the new 'non-court route' share capital reduction procedure for private companies.

[b]  The relevant resolution must be a special resolution: s 641(1)(a).

COMMENCEMENT DATE  1 October 2008[318]

The requirements of section 642(1) incorporate by reference the requirements of sections 643 and the    **17.642.02**
registration provisions of section 644. A resolution will be supported by a solvency statement if the
solvency statement is made in accordance with section 643 not more than 15 days before the date on
which the resolution is passed, and both the resolution and the solvency statement are registered in
accordance with section 644.

No specific penalty is prescribed by the Act for breach of the requirement that the solvency statement    **17.642.03**
be made not more than 15 days before the date on which the resolution is passed. However, since the
15-day requirement is one of the conditions by reference to which the Act defines when a resolution is
supported by a solvency statement, it would be unwise for directors to do otherwise than strictly
comply with the 15 day deadline.

Section 642(2) and (3) provides for the solvency statement to be made available to members, either by    **17.642.04**
sending or submitting it to them at or before the time at which the proposed resolution is sent or
submitted to them if the resolution is to be proposed as a written resolution, or simply by making
it available for inspection by members of the company throughout the meeting if the resolution is to be
proposed at a general meeting. Section 644(5) requires the directors of the company to deliver a
statement to the registrar of companies confirming (*inter alia*) that the statement was provided to
members in accordance with these sections[319] and if the company delivers to the registrar a solvency
statement which was not provided to members in accordance with section 642(2) or (3) an offence is
committed by every officer of the company who is in default.[320]

Accordingly, although the making available to members of the solvency statement might be thought to    **17.642.05**
be central to the solvency statement process, section 642(4) makes it clear that the validity of the special
resolution does not depend on members having had an opportunity to scrutinize the statement. The
scheme of the Act is to penalize, by rendering it a criminal offence,[321] failure to comply with the
requirements of section 642(2) and (3) but not to impugn the resolution.[322]

### 643  Solvency statement

(1)  A solvency statement is a statement that each of the directors—    **17.643.01**

    (a)  has formed the opinion, as regards the company's situation at the date of the statement, that there is no ground on which the company could then be found to be unable to pay (or otherwise discharge) its debts; and

---

[318]  Companies Act 2006 (Commencement No 7, Transitional Provisions and Savings) Order 2008, SI 2008/1886, art 2.

[319]  Section 644(5).

[320]  Section 644(7).

[321]  See s 644(7)

[322]  See the debate on this point in Grand Committee in the House of Lords, *Hansard*, HL, col GC12 (20 March 2006). It appears that the Government's view was that the threat of criminal sanction would be sufficient encouragement for company officers to comply with the procedural requirements of this section.

(b)  has also formed the opinion—
    (i)   if it is intended to commence the winding up of the company within twelve months of
          that date, that the company will be able to pay (or otherwise discharge) its debts in full
          within twelve months of the commencement of the winding up; or
    (ii)  in any other case, that the company will be able to pay (or otherwise discharge) its debts
          as they fall due during the year immediately following that date.
(2)  In forming those opinions, the directors must take into account all of the company's liabilities
     (including any contingent or prospective liabilities).
(3)  The solvency statement must be in the prescribed form and must state—
    (a)  the date on which it is made, and
    (b)  the name of each director of the company.
(4)  If the directors make a solvency statement without having reasonable grounds for the opinions
     expressed in it, and the statement is delivered to the registrar, an offence is committed by every
     director who is in default.
(5)  A person guilty of an offence under subsection (4) is liable—
    (a)  on conviction on indictment, to imprisonment for a term not exceeding two years or a fine (or
         both);
    (b)  on summary conviction—
        (i)   in England and Wales, to imprisonment for a term not exceeding twelve months or to a
              fine not exceeding the statutory maximum (or both);
        (ii)  in Scotland or Northern Ireland, to imprisonment for a term not exceeding six months, or
              to a fine not exceeding the statutory maximum (or both).

COMMENCEMENT DATE  1 October 2008[323]

**17.643.02**  This section 643 prescribes the content of the solvency statement; the form of the statement is
prescribed by article 2 of the Companies (Reduction of Share Capital) Order 2008 which, so far as
material, provides only that the statement must '(a) be in writing, (b) indicate that it is a solvency
statement for the purposes of section 642 of the Act, and (c) be signed by each of the directors'. The
statement is simply that, a statement, and not a statutory declaration.[324] Whilst the section itself refers
to the statement in the singular (as does the Reduction of Share Capital Order), the Explanatory
Notes[325] state that there is no requirement that the directors must all be in the same place when they
make the statement. This tends to suggest that, a 'solvency statement' could take the form of more than
one statement, on general principles of construction, the singular including the plural, unless the
context requires otherwise, provided that each was in exactly the same terms and was made on the same
date and were submitted together to the registrar[326] as one single 'solvency statement' complying with
the relevant requirements.

**17.643.03**  As indicated in the Explanatory Note,[327] all the directors of the company for the time being must make
the statement jointly. This requirement is confirmed by article 2(c) of the Companies (Reduction of
Share Capital) Order 2008.[328] In the absence of unanimity among the directors the 'non-court route'
procedure will not be available.

**17.643.04**  It is unclear precisely what test or tests Parliament intended to include by selecting, in section 643(1)(a),
the phrase 'no ground on the company could then be found to be unable to pay (or otherwise
discharge) its debts'.[329] The words are not dissimilar to those used in the Companies Act 1985 section
156(2), although the opinions to be formed under that section were directed to the position immediately following the relevant event (in that case, the giving of the financial assistance). The reference to
'then' in this section is clearly to the date of the solvency statement.[330]

**17.643.05**  The test imposed in section 643(1)(b) is *in addition* to that in section 643(1)(a).

---

[323] Companies Act 2006 (Commencement No 7, Transitional Provisions and Savings) Order 2008, SI
2008/1886, art 2.
[324] This follows the CLR's recommendation in Company Formation and Capital Maintenance, para 3.30 and
Completing the Structure, Chap 7.
[325] Para 960.
[326] Under s 644.
[327] Para 958.
[328] SI 2008/1915.
[329] Indeed, during Grand Committee in the House of Lords, when invited to indicate whether a 'balance sheet'
test was intended, Lord Sainsbury expressed the Government's position to be that it did 'not consider it
appropriate to include a specific test or rule in the clause, as that may be more restrictive on the company in some
circumstances and could be open to potential abuses in others—for example, where the assets in the balance sheet
are revalued at the higher end of a range of possible valuations for the sole purpose of supporting the capital
reduction exercise'.
[330] See *Hansard*, HL, col GC13 (20 March 2006).

The requirement that the directors, in making the solvency statement, take into account the company's **17.643.06** contingent and prospective liabilities, means that the directors must take into account in forming their opinion under sections 1(a) and (b), those liabilities of the company which, although not presently due and payable, will or may become payable on the occurrence of some future event. A contingent creditor is 'a person towards whom under an existing obligation, the company may or will become subject to a present liability on the happening of some future event or at some future date'[331] and a prospective creditor, 'a creditor in respect of a debt which will certainly become due in the future, either on some date which has been already determined or on some date determinable by reference to future events'.[332]

## 644 Registration of resolution and supporting documents

(1) Within 15 days after the resolution for reducing share capital is passed the company must deliver **17.644.01** to the registrar—
  (a) a copy of the solvency statement, and
  (b) a statement of capital.
  This is in addition to the copy of the resolution itself that is required to be delivered to the registrar under Chapter 3 of Part 3.
(2) The statement of capital must state with respect to the company's share capital as reduced by the resolution—
  (a) the total number of shares of the company,
  (b) the aggregate nominal value of those shares,
  (c) for each class of shares—
    (i) prescribed particulars of the rights attached to the shares,
    (ii) the total number of shares of that class, and
    (iii) the aggregate nominal value of shares of that class, and
  (d) the amount paid up and the amount (if any) unpaid on each share (whether on account of the nominal value of the share or by way of premium).
(3) The registrar must register the documents delivered to him under subsection (1) on receipt.
(4) The resolution does not take effect until those documents are registered.
(5) The company must also deliver to the registrar, within 15 days after the resolution is passed, a statement by the directors confirming that the solvency statement was—
  (a) made not more than 15 days before the date on which the resolution was passed, and
  (b) provided to members in accordance with section 642(2) or (3).
(6) The validity of a resolution is not affected by—
  (a) a failure to deliver the documents required to be delivered to the registrar under subsection (1) within the time specified in that subsection, or
  (b) a failure to comply with subsection (5).
(7) If the company delivers to the registrar a solvency statement that was not provided to members in accordance with section 642(2) or (3), an offence is committed by every officer of the company who is in default.
(8) If default is made in complying with this section, an offence is committed by—
  (a) the company, and
  (b) every officer of the company who is in default.
(9) A person guilty of an offence under subsection (7) or (8) is liable—
  (a) on conviction on indictment, to a fine;
  (b) on summary conviction, to a fine not exceeding the statutory maximum.

COMMENCEMENT DATE 1 October 2008[333]

Section 644 sets out the publicity requirements which apply where a company has adopted the solvency **17.644.02** statement route. Within 15 days after the resolution has been passed, the company must deliver to the registrar a copy of the solvency statement, a statement of capital containing the information specified in section 644(2),[334] and a statement by the directors confirming that the solvency statement was made

---

[331] See *Re William Hockley Ltd* [1962] 1 WLR 555, 558, *per* Pennycuick J.
[332] See *Stonegate Securities v Gregory* [1980] 1 Ch 576, 579, *per* Buckley LJ.
[333] Companies Act 2006 (Commencement No 7, Transitional Provisions and Savings) Order 2008, SI 2008/1886, art 2.
[334] Companies (Shares and Share Capital) Order 2009, SI 2009/388, art 2(2)(j) and (3) prescribe particulars as to share rights, namely voting, dividend and distribution, and winding-up capital return rights, as well as redemption rights. Following a consultation on the subject of statements of capital which closed on 11 January 2010, in May 2011 the government indicated that it would be introducing legislation to simplify the financial information requirements for all companies in statements of capital, except those required on formation and in the Annual Return, to require the following information: the total number of shares of the company, the aggregate nominal value of those shares, the aggregate amount unpaid on those shares (whether on account of nominal value of the shares or by way of premium), the total number of shares in each class, the aggregate

not more than 15 days before the date on which the resolution was passed, and was provided to members in accordance with section 642(2) or (3). Failure to comply with the filing requirement is made a criminal offence by section 644(8), and the penalties are as prescribed in section 644(9). The validity of the resolution is not affected by a failure to comply with the filing requirements of this section. However, the combined effect of section 644(3) and (4) is that, unless and until the solvency statement and statement of capital are delivered to the registrar and registered by him, the reduction of capital does not take effect. Accordingly, whilst the resolution is valid, it is without effect so far as it purports to reduce the company's issued capital until the solvency statement and statement of capital are registered.

**17.644.03** Although section 644(3) imposes an obligation on the registrar to register the solvency statement and statement of capital delivered to him, and on whose registration the taking effect of the reduction depends, there is no provision in this section equivalent to those in section 649(5) which require him to certify such registration.

## *Reduction of capital confirmed by the court*

### 645 Application to court for order of confirmation

**17.645.01**
(1) Where a company has passed a resolution for reducing share capital, it may apply to the court for an order confirming the reduction.
(2) If the proposed reduction of capital involves either—
   (a) diminution of liability in respect of unpaid share capital, or
   (b) the payment to a shareholder of any paid-up share capital,
   section 646 (creditors entitled to object to reduction) applies unless the court directs otherwise.[a]
(3) The court may, if having regard to any special circumstances of the case it thinks proper to do so, direct that section 646 is not to apply as regards any class or classes of creditors.[335]
(4) The court may direct that section 646 is to apply in any other case.

AMENDMENTS AND NOTES

[a] Section 645(2) and (4) reproduce, without material amendment, the provisions of CA 1985, ss 136(2).

COMMENCEMENT DATE 1 October 2009[336]

**17.645.02** Sections 645 to 649 replaced Companies Act 1985, sections 135 to 139 with effect from 1 October 2009. These sections prescribe the procedure to be followed by a company seeking the court's confirmation of a reduction of capital. Public companies will still be bound to follow the route following the implementation of the 2006 Act, as will private companies where the reduction involves a reduction of capital to zero, even where that reduction is only momentary,[337] and where a private company wishes to reduce its capital for the purpose of making a return of capital to members or a distribution to members[338] in circumstances where it is not able to comply with Part 23 of the Act, even having regard to the disapplication of the restrictions in section 654(1) made by the Companies (Reduction of Share Capital) Order 2008. The provisions preserve, with small amendments, the procedure prescribed by the Companies Act 1985.

**17.645.03** Section 645(2) states, as did its immediate predecessor, Companies Act 1985, section 136(2), that where the proposed reduction of capital involves either a diminution of liability in respect of unpaid share capital or the repayment to a shareholder of any paid-up share capital, the provisions of the Act which require settlement of a list of creditors entitled to object to the reduction of capital[339] will apply unless the court directs otherwise. In any other case, as section 645(4) states, the burden, so to speak, is reversed, and the court may direct that section 646 is to apply. Accordingly, in all cases, the court will consider whether the provisions of section 646 are to apply.

---

nominal value of shares in each class and the aggregate amount unpaid on shares in each class (whether on account of nominal value of the shares or by way of premium).

[335] Section 645(3) mirrors the provisions of CA 1985, s 136(6).

[336] Companies Act 2006 (Commencement No 8, Transitional Provisions and Savings) Order 2008, SI 2008/2860, art 3(k).

[337] Section 641(2)—see para 17.641.04 above.

[338] This would appear to be the intention for the regulations made under s 654 of the Act: see *Implementation of Companies Act 2006: A Consultative Document*, paras 2.199–2.207, and see para 17.653.03 below.

[339] For this purpose, being the creditors entitled to object to the reduction of capital and therefore including every creditor of the company who at the date fixed by the court is entitled to any debt or claim that, if that date were the commencement of the winding up of the company would be admissible in proof against the company, is entitled to object to the reduction of capital: s 646(1).

The philosophy underlying the difference is that, whilst creditors are taken to assume the risk that the **17.645.04** company's capital may be lost in carrying on its business and in operations incidental thereto, they are also entitled to assume that its capital will otherwise remain available for the discharge of its liabilities and, in particular, that capital will not be returned to shareholders. This is known as the 'capital maintenance rule', sometimes also known as the rule in *Trevor v Whitworth*.[340] Accordingly, where by a reduction of capital confirmed by the court, capital is to be returned to shareholders, or their liability to pay calls is to be forgiven, stringent conditions are prescribed by the Act to ensure that creditors' interests are not compromised thereby. Where, on the other hand, the reduction of capital is proposed because capital has been lost in the course of the company's business, creditors' rights are not prejudiced by the reduction of capital, which simply brings the company's balance sheet in line with reality. In this regard, however, a distinction must be drawn between a genuine loss of capital, where the loss is permanent, and mere trading losses which may be recoverable. In this latter case, a reduction of capital against such a loss could result in the company subsequently being able to distribute capital if, in fact, the loss is recovered and, accordingly, the court is astute in such cases to ensure creditors' interests are safeguarded by requiring suitable protection to be put in place in a similar manner as it does in cases where capital is being returned.

Notwithstanding the provisions of section 645(2), the practice of the court has long been[341] to 'direct **17.645.05** otherwise' in the exercise of its discretion under the equivalent of section 645(3). In order to be satisfied that it is a 'proper case' in which to make such a direction, the court must be satisfied (i) that the creditors of the company who would be entitled to object have been properly identified in the evidence before it; (ii) that the nature and amount of their debts are adequately stated; and (iii) that the provision proposed by the company as regards those debts is sufficient to allow the court to dispense with the formal procedure which would allow the creditors to require those debts which are admitted by the company to be discharged in full, secured, or adjudicated.[342] In practice, the court has developed a series of standard undertakings and accepted forms of guarantees and other forms of security which it will accept as sufficient and upon the strength of which it will direct that the process prescribed by section 646 and its predecessors is not to apply as regards any class or classes of creditors. However, those forms are not set in stone and, the court will consider other forms of security provided they meet the objective of adequately protecting creditors.

The position is similar as respects the court's discretion under section 645(3). As noted above,[343] where **17.645.06** the reduction of capital is proposed in connection with a permanent loss of capital, creditors' interests are not prejudiced thereby. However, cases where the loss sought to be written off is represented solely by losses of this type are exceptional. In the usual case the losses against which the capital is to be reduced may be capable of being recovered, either by trading recoveries or because the balance sheet relied on contains hidden values, for example in the form of assets included at less than the value at which they may be subsequently realized or liabilities included at values greater than that at which they may subsequently be called. In such cases, the court will also expect the company to make provision for its creditors before it will make a direction that the provisions of section 646 shall not apply.

## 646  Creditors entitled to object to reduction

    (1)  Where this section applies (see section 645(2) and (4)), every creditor of the company who— **17.646.01**

    [(a)] at the date fixed by the court is entitled to any debt or claim that, if that date were the commencement of the winding up of the company would be admissible in proof against the company, and

      (b)  can show that there is a real likelihood that the reduction would result in the company being unable to discharge his debt or claim when it fell due][a] is entitled to object to the reduction of capital.

    (2)  The court shall settle a list of creditors entitled to object.

    (3)  For that purpose the court—

      (a)  shall ascertain, as far as possible without requiring an application from any creditor, the names of those creditors and the nature and amount of their debts or claims, and

      (b)  may publish notices fixing a day or days within which creditors not entered on the list are to claim to be so entered or are to be excluded from the right of objecting to the reduction of capital.

    (4)  If a creditor entered on the list whose debt or claim is not discharged or has not determined does not consent to the reduction, the court may, if it thinks fit, dispense with the consent of that creditor on the company securing payment of his debt or claim.

---

[340]  See *Trevor v Whitworth* (1887) 12 App Cas 409, 57 LJ Ch 28, HL.
[341]  Anecdotal evidence suggests that the last such direction was made around 60 years ago.
[342]  See s 646.
[343]  See para 17.645.02 above.

(5) For this purpose the debt or claim must be secured by appropriating (as the court may direct) the following amount—

    (a) if the company admits the full amount of the debt or claim or, though not admitting it, is willing to provide for it, the full amount of the debt or claim;

    (b) if the company does not admit, and is not willing to provide for, the full amount of the debt or claim, or if the amount is contingent or not ascertained, an amount fixed by the court after the like enquiry and adjudication as if the company were being wound up by the court.

AMENDMENTS AND NOTES

a Inserted by the Companies (Share Capital and Acquisition by a Company of its Own Shares) Regulations 2009, SI 2009/2022, reg 3.

COMMENCEMENT DATE 1 October 2009[344]

**17.646.02**  The creditors entitled to object include all those creditors of the company who would be entitled to claim in a winding up of the company at the date fixed by the court. They are not therefore confined to the creditors whose debts may appear on a balance sheet drawn up at that date but extend to contingent and prospective creditors of the company whose claims would be admissible to proof in a liquidation of the company taking effect at that date. The expression 'contingent creditor' means a creditor in respect of a debt which will only become due in an event which may or may not occur; and a 'prospective creditor' is a creditor in respect of a debt which will certainly become due in the future, either on some date which has been already determined or on some date determinable by reference to future events.[345] Accordingly, in considering its creditor position, liabilities which would fall to be included by a company would extend, for example, to contingent liabilities under contractual warranties given in sale of goods contracts even where no notified breach has occurred and to covenants to repair in long term leases which take effect only on termination or surrender. The amendment to subsection (1) requires a creditor, in order to be entitled to object to a reduction of capital, to show that there is a real likelihood that the reduction would result in the company being unable to discharge his debt or claim when it fell due.[346] This requires a creditor to demonstrate a particular present assessment about a future state of affairs. Such an assessment must be grounded in the facts as they are known at the time the objection is raised and must avoid the purely speculative. Although the period in relation to which the assessment is to be made will be affected by the nature and duration of the liability in question, in general, the more remote in time the contemplated event that will make payment fall due the more difficult it will be to establish the reality of the likelihood that the return of capital will result in inability to discharge the debt. Further, whilst the section obviously does not require a creditor to prove that a future event will happen, it is concerned that the chance of the company's being unable to discharge the debt because it has returned capital be evaluated as a 'real likelihood', and therefore requires the objecting creditor to show the chance to be beyond the merely possible, but short of the probable.[347]

**17.646.03**  As noted above,[348] in practice the procedure prescribed by section 646(2) for settling a list of creditors has fallen into disuse. However, it is by reference to the rights of the creditors for which this procedure allows that the court considers the alternatives offered for the protection of creditors in cases under section 645(2) or (4). Accordingly, where the court is satisfied that there are, in fact, no creditors who would be able to persuade the court that there was a 'real likelihood' that, if the reduction of capital was confirmed and a distribution made as proposed, that return of capital would result in the company being unable to discharge its debts, the court may, in its discretion, dispense with the requirement that a list of creditors be settled and with any alternative form of protection. However, where protection is to be put in place, the date at which the court will require the relevant protection to be in place is customarily the date upon which the reduction of capital takes effect under section 649(3) (its predecessor, being Companies Act 1985, section 138(2)), that being the date upon which the creditors are affected by the reduction.

**17.646.04**  It is the practice of the court to require that the company advertise the date and time of the hearing of the petition seeking the court's confirmation of the proposed reduction of capital together with brief details of the substance of the relief claimed in advance of the court hearing in order to allow any

---

[344] Companies Act 2006 (Commencement No 8, Transitional Provisions and Savings) Order 2008, SI 2008/2860, art 3(k).

[345] See *Stonegate Securities Ltd v Gregory* [1980] Ch 576, 579, *per* Buckley LJ.

[346] This seeks to implement Art 1(9) of the Simplification of Capital Maintenance Directive (EC) 2006/68 [2006] OJ L264/32, the purpose of which is to standardize creditor protection in the EU.

[347] *Re Liberty International Plc* [2010] EWHC 1060 (Ch) [2011] Bus. L.R. D17 per Norris J at paragraphs 17–20, cited with approval by the Court of Session in *Royal Scottish Assurance Plc* (Petitioner) [2011] CSOH 2.

[348] See para 17.645.03 above.

creditor or member of the company wishing to object to the proposed reduction to appear at the hearing and to put before the court any objection which he may have.

### 647  Offences in connection with list of creditors

(1)  If an officer of the company—                                                              **17.647.01**
    (a)  intentionally or recklessly—
        (i)   conceals the name of a creditor entitled to object to the reduction of capital, or
        (ii)  misrepresents the nature or amount of the debt or claim of a creditor, or
    (b)  is knowingly concerned in any such concealment or misrepresentation, he commits an offence.
(2)  A person guilty of an offence under this section is liable—
    (a)  on conviction on indictment, to a fine;
    (b)  on summary conviction, to a fine not exceeding the statutory maximum.

COMMENCEMENT DATE  1 October 2009[349]

Although, as stated above,[350] the procedure for settling a list of creditors is not, in practice, used, the    **17.647.02**
criminal penalty prescribed by this section emphasizes the seriousness with which the legislature treats the concealment or misrepresentation of creditor claims on a reduction of capital. Where the court made an order confirming a reduction of capital on the basis of an intentional or reckless misrepresentation of fact, which might include misrepresenting the nature or amount of the debt or claim of a creditor, then the court's order sanctioning the reduction of capital might be set aside on the grounds of fraud.[351]

### 648  Court order confirming reduction

(1)  The court may make an order confirming the reduction of capital on such terms and conditions as    **17.648.01**
it thinks fit.
(2)  The court must not confirm the reduction unless it is satisfied, with respect to every creditor of the company who is entitled to object to the reduction of capital that either—
    (a)  his consent to the reduction has been obtained, or
    (b)  his debt or claim has been discharged, or has determined or has been secured.
(3)  Where the court confirms the reduction, it may order the company to publish (as the court directs) the reasons for reduction of capital, or such other information in regard to it as the court thinks expedient with a view to giving proper information to the public, and (if the court thinks fit) the causes that led to the reduction.
(4)  The court may, if for any special reason it thinks proper to do so, make an order directing that the company must, during such period (commencing on or at any time after the date of the order) as is specified in the order, add to its name as its last words the words 'and reduced'.
    If such an order is made, those words are, until the end of the period specified in the order, deemed to be part of the company's name.

COMMENCEMENT DATE  1 October 2009[352]

The words of section 648(1) (which mirror the opening and closing words of the Companies Act 1985,    **17.648.02**
section 137(1))[353] make it clear that the exercise of the court's power is discretionary. The court will usually confirm a reduction of capital provided four tests are satisfied: namely, that shareholders are treated equitably; that the reduction proposals have been properly explained to shareholders; that the company's creditors are safeguarded; and that the reduction is for a discernible purpose.[354]

So far as the first requirement is concerned—that the shareholders are to be treated equitably—the    **17.648.03**
usual rule is that where capital is being reduced in order to be returned to shareholders, the shares to be reduced and to receive the returned capital will be those entitled to priority on a winding up or other return of capital (typically preference shares[355] ); and where the capital has been lost, the shares to be reduced will be those on which the loss would fall on a winding up (typically ordinary shares).

---

[349] Companies Act 2006 (Commencement No 8, Transitional Provisions and Savings) Order 2008, SI 2008/2860, art 3(k).
[350] See para 17.645.03 above.
[351] See *Fletcher v RAC* [2000] 1 BCLC 331.
[352] Companies Act 2006 (Commencement No 8, Transitional Provisions and Savings) Order 2008, SI 2008/2860, art 3(k).
[353] Which it has replaced.
[354] See *Re Thorn EMI plc* [1989] BCLC 612.
[355] See *Re Saltdean Estate Co Ltd* [1968] 1 WLR 1844, a case where preference shareholders whose capital was to be repaid were objecting on the ground that they were also entitled to participate in distributions of profit along with the ordinary shareholders, and repayment would deprive them of that income.

**17.648.04**    As to the second requirement, it will be a ground for refusing to confirm the reduction if there has been a material misstatement to shareholders in any explanatory circular or notice seeking their approval for the necessary special resolution.[356]

**17.648.05**    The third requirement—that the company's creditors are to be safeguarded—is reinforced by subsection (2). Subsection (2)[357] emphasizes that, before the court's discretion under section 648(1) arises, it must satisfy itself with respect to every creditor of the company who is entitled to object to the reduction of capital[358] has either consented to the reduction or that his debt or claim has been discharged, or has determined or has been secured. In practice, the question of creditor consent is invariably dealt with at an interlocutory stage, convened on an application issued at the same time as the company's petition seeking the court's confirmation of the reduction. As a result, by the time the court comes to consider the exercise of its discretion under section 648(1), the issue of creditor protection has already been fully ventilated at a hearing in chambers, and relevant undertakings extracted from the company as a condition of the petition being permitted to proceed to a hearing. The court hearing the petition nevertheless looks at the matter afresh in order to satisfy itself that the exercise of its discretion is appropriate in all of the circumstances.[359]

**17.648.06**    The fourth requirement—that the reduction must be for a discernible purpose[360] —is usually of importance only where the reduction serves merely to achieve a tax saving on what would otherwise be a simple transaction needing no assistance from the court.[361] In practice, however, the court takes a generous view of what will constitute a discernible purpose. The mere fact that the reduction provides a fiscally efficient way of implementing a transaction will not matter, so long as the reduction makes some difference to the company.

**17.648.07**    Until the introduction of the predecessor of a section to similar effect to section 648(4) in Companies Act 1929, in all cases of reduction of capital, the words 'and reduced' had to be added to a company's subject to a power for the court to dispense with the addition in cases where creditors were not affected. In practice, the court has not for many years exercised its power to require a company to add the words 'and reduced' to its name and now simply exercises its power under section 649(4).

### 649  Registration of order and statement of capital

**17.649.01**    (1)  The registrar, on production of an order of the court confirming the reduction of a company's share capital and the delivery of a copy of the order and of a statement of capital (approved by the court), shall register the order and statement.

           This is subject to section 650 (public company reducing capital below authorised minimum).

      (2)  The statement of capital must state with respect to the company's share capital as altered by the order—

           (a)  the total number of shares of the company,

           (b)  the aggregate nominal value of those shares,

           (c)  for each class of shares—

               (i)  prescribed particulars of the rights attached to the shares,

               (ii)  the total number of shares of that class, and

               (iii)  the aggregate nominal value of shares of that class, and

           (d)  the amount paid up and the amount (if any) unpaid on each share (whether on account of the nominal value of the share or by way of premium).

      (3)  The resolution for reducing share capital, as confirmed by the court's order, takes effect—

           (a)  in the case of a reduction of share capital that forms part of a compromise or arrangement sanctioned by the court under Part 26 (arrangements and reconstructions)—

               (i)  on delivery of the order and statement of capital to the registrar, or

               (ii)  if the court so orders, on the registration of the order and statement of capital;

---

[356]  See *Re European Home Products Ltd* [1988] BCLC 690.

[357]  Which replaced the condition contained in CA 1985, s 137(1).

[358]  ie those identified in s 646(1) or, otherwise, those who would be entitled to prove in a liquidation taking effect on the date the reduction takes effect.

[359]  See also para 17.648.02 above for the matters which the court will consider.

[360]  See also This requirement was explained by Harman J as being that the court will not confirm a reduction which is pointless or hollow: see *Re Ratners Group plc* [1988] BCLC 685, a case concerned with a reduction of share premium account purely to enable reserves to be included in consolidated accounts against which goodwill arising on consolidation could be written off.

[361]  As was the case in *Re Rylands Whitecross Ltd* (unreported, 21 December 1973) in which Brightman J refused to confirm a reduction where a company with three members could have achieved the substance of the transaction by their unanimous agreement.

(b)  in any other case, on the registration of the order and statement of capital.

(4)  Notice of the registration of the order and statement of capital must be published in such manner as the court may direct.

(5)  The registrar must certify the registration of the order and statement of capital.

(6)  The certificate—

    (a)  must be signed by the registrar or authenticated by the registrar's official seal, and

    (b)  is conclusive evidence—

        (i)  that the requirements of this Act with respect to the reduction of share capital have been complied with, and

        (ii)  that the company's share capital is as stated in the statement of capital.

COMMENCEMENT DATE  1 October 2009[362]

The 'registrar' referred to in these sections is the registrar of companies for England and Wales, Scotland, or Northern Ireland 'as the case may require'[363] presumably by reference to the company's place of incorporation.  **17.649.02**

The requirement that the company submit a statement of capital has replaced the requirement, in the Companies Act 1985 section 138(1), for delivery of a minute, approved by the court, showing with respect to the company's share capital as reduced by the order (i) the amount of the share capital; (ii) the number of shares into which it is to be divided, and the amount of each share; and (iii) the amount (if any) at the date of the registration deemed to be paid up on each share. The requirement in section 649(2)(c)(i) that the statement contain prescribed particulars of the rights attached to the shares for each class of shares (prescribed here referring to the fact that the Secretary of State is empowered to make orders or regulations prescribing what is to be supplied in the statement of capital in this regard)[364] was new and in addition to the remaining information (which had to be provided in the minute). The new requirement mirrors the provisions elsewhere in the Act where statements of capital are required to be filed (as, for example, in section 644(2)).[365]  **17.649.03**

Under Companies Act 1985, section 138(2), the reduction of capital took effect 'on the registration of the order and minute, and not before', and that was so whether or not the reduction formed part of a scheme of arrangement or compromise with members or creditors under Part XIII of Companies Act 1985 which, by virtue of Companies Act 1985, section 425(3) would have effect on delivery to the registrar. Under Companies Act 2006, section 649(3), if the reduction of capital forms part of a compromise or arrangement sanctioned by the court under Part 26 of the Act, the reduction will take effect either (i) on delivery of the order and statement of capital to the registrar; or (ii) if the court so orders, on the registration of the order and statement of capital. This accords with the recommendation of the CLR.[366] 'Delivery' is dealt with in Companies Act 2006, section 1071 which provides that  **17.649.04**

(1)  A document is not delivered to the registrar until it is received by the registrar.

(2)  Provision may be made by registrar's rules as to when a document is to be regarded as received.

As to section 649(4), the court's practice has been to require the company to publish an advertisement in the same periodical as it published the date and time of the hearing of the petition following registration of the court's order notifying the fact of registration of the order and of any minute required under the Companies Act 1985, section 138(1) to be registered. The usual form of advertisement records the fact that the order was made on the petition, the date of the order, together with summary details of the order made, and states the company's capital as reduced.[367] It is anticipated that, under this provision, the court's practice will remain the same save that the advertisement will refer to the statement of capital rather than to the minute as previously.  **17.649.05**

Under the predecessors of section 649(6)(b),[368] the authorities demonstrate that the effect of the section is that the registrar's certificate will be conclusive even if, for example, there was as a matter of fact no valid resolution of the company to reduce capital.[369] Under the Companies Act 2006, section  **17.649.06**

---

[362]  Companies Act 2006 (Commencement No 8, Transitional Provisions and Savings) Order 2008, SI 2008/2860, art 3(k).

[363]  Section 1060(3).

[364]  Section 1167.

[365]  The relevant particulars are prescribed by the Companies (Shares and Share Capital) Order 2009, SI 2009/388, art 2(2)(k) and (3): what is to be stated are voting, dividend and distribution, and winding-up capital return rights, as well as redemption rights. See, however, footnote 33 above.

[366]  *Modern Company Law For a Competitive Economy*: Vol 1, para 13.11(iv).

[367]  See *Re Oceana Development Co* [1912] WN 121, 138.

[368]  Latterly CA 1985, s 138(4)(b) but going back to CA 1867, s 15.

[369]  See *Ladies' Dress Association v Pulbrook* [1900] 2 QB 376.

1095 and 1096, it is possible that in similar circumstances the company or its officers might be able to procure the removal of the certificate from the register.

*Public company reducing capital below authorised minimum*

### 650 Public company reducing capital below authorised minimum[370]

**17.650.01**
    (1) This section applies where the court makes an order confirming a reduction of a public company's capital that has the effect of bringing the nominal value of its allotted share capital below the authorised minimum.
    (2) The registrar must not register the order unless either—
       (a) the court so directs, or
       (b) the company is first re-registered as a private company.
    (3) Section 651 provides an expedited procedure for re-registration in these circumstances.

COMMENCEMENT DATE 1 October 2009[371]

**17.650.02** The authorized minimum in relation to the nominal value of the allotted capital of a public company is £50,000 or the prescribed euro equivalent.[372] There are two cases in which a public company's capital may be reduced below the authorized minimum on a reduction of capital. The first is when the company's capital is reduced *scintilla temporis*, that is, for a moment in time only, before immediately being increased to its former level in excess of the authorized minimum.[373] An example of such a case would be where, in a takeover situation, as part of a scheme of arrangement, a company reduces its issued capital to zero before immediately increasing it, usually to its former level, allotting the new shares to the bidder, the former shareholders being satisfied in cash, shares in the bidder, or other consideration according to the terms of the scheme. In such a case, the court's current practice is to direct that the registrar register the order notwithstanding that the company's capital is reduced below the authorized minimum, but the minute will usually record the resolution of the company providing for the subsequent increase of capital and issue of shares. The second such case is where the company's intention is to permanently reduce its capital to below the authorized minimum. In that event, given that it must pass the special resolution under section 645(1), it will usually be the case that the company will pass the necessary resolution to re-register as a private company under section 97(1)(a) at the same time as it passes the reduction resolution under section 645. However, for a number of reasons,[374] the company may not have in fact achieved re-registered status by the time it wishes to register the order of the court confirming the reduction of its capital. Section 645 permits the court to direct that the registrar register an order which reduces the company's capital below the authorized minimum, notwithstanding that the company will remain a public company after the reduction takes effect. It must be emphasized that the court's powers under this section are not limited to the situation where the company has passed a resolution to re-register as a private company. However, save in the first identified case above, where there is no intention on the part of the company to make such an application, the court is likely to be reluctant to exercise its powers under this section in view of the requirements of the Second Company Law Directive.[375]

### 651 Expedited procedure for re-registration as a private company

**17.651.01**
    (1) The court may authorise the company to be re-registered as a private company without its having passed the special resolution required by section 97.
    (2) If it does so, the court must specify in the order the changes to the company's name and articles to be made in connection with the re-registration.
    (3) The company may then be re-registered as a private company if an application to that effect is delivered to the registrar together with—
       (a) a copy of the court's order, and

---

[370] This section replaces the provisions of CA 1985, s 139(1) and (2) with effect from October 2009.
[371] Companies Act 2006 (Commencement No 8, Transitional Provisions and Savings) Order 2008, SI 2008/2860, art 3(k).
[372] Section 763(1). Detailed provisions as to when a company with, or a company that will have, allotted share capital denominated in more than one currency has the value of such share capital reduced below the authorized minimum are set out in the Companies (Authorised Minimum) Regulations 2009, SI 2009/2425, regs 3 and 4. Those Regulations (reg 5) also set out circumstances in which the registrar may assume that a company with allotted share capital denominated in more than one currency has had the value of that share capital reduced below the authorized minimum, if the court has not directed that the order confirming the reduction of the company's share capital be registered.
[373] For an example of such a case see *Re MB Group plc* [1989] BCLC 672.
[374] See commentary on ss 97–101.
[375] Directive (EEC) 77/91 [1977] OJ L26/2, Art 34.

    (b)  notice of the company's name, and a copy of the company's articles, as altered by the court's order.

(4)  On receipt of such an application the registrar must issue a certificate of incorporation altered to meet the circumstances of the case.

(5)  The certificate must state that it is issued on re-registration and the date on which it is issued.

(6)  On the issue of the certificate—

    (a)  the company by virtue of the issue of the certificate becomes a private company, and

    (b)  the changes in the company's name and articles take effect.

(7)  The certificate is conclusive evidence that the requirements of this Act as to re-registration have been complied with.

COMMENCEMENT DATE 1 October 2009[376]

Section 651(1) only applies where the court makes an order confirming a reduction of a public **17.651.02** company's capital that has the effect of bringing the nominal value of its allotted share capital below the authorized minimum. In any other case, the company must follow the procedure prescribed by sections 97 to 101 which allows, *inter alia*, a dissentient minority of the prescribed number or value[377] to apply to the court to quash the necessary special resolution. On such an application, the court may cancel or confirm the resolution for re-registration[378] or may make an order subject to terms and conditions or adjourn the proceedings in order that an arrangement can be made to the court's satisfaction for the purchase of the dissentient members' shares.[379] The expedited procedure conferred on the court by sections 650 and 651 necessarily excludes the right afforded to dissentients under section 98.

A public company's name[380] must end with 'public limited company' or 'p.l.c.',[381] or, in the case of a **17.651.03** Welsh public company which so chooses, with 'cwmni cyfyngedig cyhoeddus' or 'c.c.c.'.[382] A private company,[383] save for charities and others exempted as provided by section 60 of this Act, must have a name that ends with 'limited' or 'ltd.', or, in the case of a Welsh company, if it so chooses, with 'cyfyngedig' or 'cyf.'. So far as its articles of association are concerned, there is nothing in the 2006 Act which requires a company to include within its articles any indication of its status.[384] However, where the Articles do require amendment to reflect the company's new status, section 651(2) confers power on the court to specify the necessary changes in its order.

In order to effect the re-registration under this section, the company must deliver an application to that **17.651.04** effect under this section together with a copy of the court's order, notice of the company's name, and a copy of the company's articles as altered by the court's order. There is no indication on the face of the section that the form of the application is to be the subject of prescription in rules to be made by the Secretary of State,[385] and the Explanatory Notes confirm[386] that the application need not be signed by a director or secretary as was required by Companies Act 1985.

## *Effect of reduction of capital*

### 652  Liability of members following reduction of capital

(1)  Where a company's share capital is reduced, a member of the company (past or present) is not **17.652.01** liable in respect of any share to any call or contribution exceeding in amount the difference (if any) between—

    (a)  the nominal amount of the share as notified to the registrar in the statement of capital delivered under section 644 or 649, and

    (b)  the amount paid on the share or the reduced amount (if any) which is deemed to have been paid on it, as the case may be.[a]

---

[376]  Companies Act 2006 (Commencement No 8, Transitional Provisions and Savings) Order 2008, SI 2008/2860, art 3(k).

[377]  See s 98(1).

[378]  Section 98(3).

[379]  Section 98(4).

[380]  Save in the case of Community interest companies, but see s 33(3) and (4) of the Companies (Audit, Investigations and Community Enterprise) Act 2004: s 58(3).

[381]  Section 58(1).

[382]  Section 58(2).

[383]  Again, excepting Community interest companies, but see s 33(1) and (2) of the Companies (Audit, Investigations and Community Enterprise) Act 2004: s 59(3).

[384]  Neither do the default model articles for public companies.

[385]  Cf CA 1985, s 139(4).

[386]  Paragraph 972.

(2) This is subject to section 653 (liability to creditor in case of omission from list).

(3) Nothing in this section affects the rights of the contributories among themselves.[b]

AMENDMENTS AND NOTES

[a] The words of this subsection mirror those of CA 1985, s 140(1) with the substitution of the reference to the statement of capital for the reference in the former to the minute

[b] This preserves the qualification present in CA 1985, s 140(5).

COMMENCEMENT DATE 1 October 2008 (s 652(1) and (3)); 1 October 2009 (remaining provisions)[387]

**17.652.02** The provisions of section 652 apply both to reductions of capital supported by a solvency statement and to those sanctioned by the court. The purpose of this provision is to limit the sum which a member or past member of the company is liable to pay on a call on a partly paid share following a reduction of capital. Its effect is to limit members' liability to pay to the difference (if any) between the reduced nominal value of the share as set out in the statement of capital delivered under sections 644 or 649, and the amount paid up thereon or the reduced amount deemed to have been paid up thereon. This section is subject to the overriding provision of section 653 where the reduction of capital is one confirmed by the court and the circumstances are those identified in that section.

### 653 Liability to creditor in case of omission from list of creditors[388]

**17.653.01**
(1) This section applies where, in the case of a reduction of capital confirmed by the court—
   (a) a creditor entitled to object to the reduction of share capital is by reason of his ignorance—
      (i) of the proceedings for reduction of share capital, or
      (ii) of their nature and effect with respect to his debt or claim,
      not entered on the list of creditors, and
   (b) after the reduction of capital the company is unable to pay the amount of his debt or claim.
(2) Every person who was a member of the company at the date on which the resolution for reducing capital took effect under section 649(3) is liable to contribute for the payment of the debt or claim an amount not exceeding that which he would have been liable to contribute if the company had commenced to be wound up on the day before that date.
(3) If the company is wound up, the court on the application of the creditor in question, and proof of ignorance as mentioned in subsection (1)(a), may if it thinks fit—
   (a) settle accordingly a list of persons liable to contribute under this section, and
   (b) make and enforce calls and orders on them as if they were ordinary contributories in a winding up.
(4) The reference in subsection (1)(b) to a company being unable to pay the amount of a debt or claim has the same meaning as in section 123 of the Insolvency Act 1986 (c. 45) or Article 103 of the Insolvency (Northern Ireland) Order 1989 (S.I. 1989/2405 (N.I. 19)).

COMMENCEMENT DATE 1 October 2009[389]

**17.653.02** Section 653 applies where (i) the reduction of capital is one confirmed by the court; (ii) a creditor falling within the class identified in section 646(1) has not been entered on the list of creditors because of his lack of knowledge of the proceedings for reduction of share capital or of their nature and effect with respect to his debt or claim; and (iii) following the reduction, the company is unable to pay the amount of his debt or claim.[390] A company is 'unable to pay' the creditor's debt only if it satisfies the definition in section 123 of the Insolvency Act 1986 or Article 103 of the Insolvency (Northern Ireland) Order 1989.[391] The phrase therefore has a somewhat narrow, legal, meaning.

**17.653.03** If the conditions specified are satisfied, then those persons who were members of the company on the date on which the reduction of capital took effect are liable to contribute to the assets of the company for the payment of the debt or claim to the same extent as if the company had gone into liquidation on that day:[392] that is to say, *pari passu* between themselves up to the full uncalled amount due on their respective shares at their pre-reduction values or, if less, until the debt is discharged in full.[393]

---

[387] Companies Act 2006 (Commencement No 7, Transitional Provisions and Savings) Order 2008, SI 2008/1886, art 2; Companies Act 2006 (Commencement No 8, etc) Order 2008, SI 2008/2860, art 3(k).

[388] Subsections (1)–(3) of this section mirror, without material amendment, the words of CA 1985, s 140(2)–(4).

[389] Companies Act 2006 (Commencement No 8, Transitional Provisions and Savings) Order 2008, SI 2008/2860, art 3(k).

[390] Section 654(1).

[391] Section 643(4).

[392] Section 653(2).

[393] Insolvency Act 1986, s 74.

If the company is wound up, the court is given supplementary powers under section 653(3) to settle a **17.653.04** list of persons liable to contribute, that is, a list of every person who was a member of the company on the date on which the reduction of capital took effect,[394] and to make and enforce calls and orders on them as if they were ordinary contributories in a winding up.[395] A member may be liable under section 653 where he would escape liability as a contributory under the Insolvency Act: under the latter, a past member of the company will not be liable to contribute if he has ceased to be a member one year or more before the commencement of the winding up. Here, he will remain liable if he was a member at the date the reduction took effect, notwithstanding that the winding up may occur long after that one year is accomplished.

## CHAPTER 11
## MISCELLANEOUS AND SUPPLEMENTARY PROVISIONS

### 654  Treatment of reserve arising from reduction of capital

(1)  A reserve arising from the reduction of a company's share capital is not distributable, subject to     **17.654.01** any provision made by order under this section.

(2)  The Secretary of State may by order specify cases in which—
(a)  the prohibition in subsection (1) does not apply, and
(b)  the reserve is to be treated for the purposes of Part 23 (distributions) as a realised profit.

(3)  An order under this section is subject to affirmative resolution procedure.

COMMENCEMENT DATE  1 October 2008[396]

This section had no precursor in the previous legislation and was introduced at a very late stage in the **17.654.02** passage of the Bill through Parliament. It was introduced to provide a further safeguard and reinforce the principle of maintenance of capital. It applies, subject to the exceptions described below, in relation to any reduction of capital taking effect on or after 1 October 2008, whether under the Companies Act 1985 (irrespective of when the special resolution for the reduction was passed) or the Companies Act 2006.[397] Thus, in the event that a reduction of capital produces a reserve, this is not distributable except to the extent that orders made under subsection (2) so provide, as described in paragraph 17.654.03. Although this section appears in Part 18 of the Act, it must be read in conjunction with the general provisions on distributions in Part 23.

The Companies (Reduction of Share Capital) Order 2008[398] provides for complete exemption from the **17.654.03** effect of the section as regards an unlimited company and a private company reducing capital supported by a solvency statement when there has been no application to the court for an order confirming the reduction. The section also does not apply to a public company when the court confirms the reduction and so orders. In these circumstances the reserve is to be treated as a realized profit for the purposes of Part 23 of the Act. However, these exemptions are subject to an order of, or undertaking given to, the court, anything to the contrary in the resolution reducing capital or any other relevant resolution and anything to the contrary in the company's articles.

### 655  Shares no bar to damages against company

A person is not debarred from obtaining damages or other compensation from a company by reason **17.655.01** only of his holding or having held shares in the company or any right to apply or subscribe for shares or to be included in the company's register of members in respect of shares.

COMMENCEMENT DATE  1 October 2009[399]

This section restates what was section 111A of the 1985 Act.[400] It reverses the common law rule,[401] **17.655.02** introduced in order to reinforce the principle of maintenance of capital, that a shareholder could not recover damages in a claim against the company. There are likely to be few situations when a

---

[394]  Section 653(2).

[395]  For the relevant powers of the court in a compulsory winding-up, see Insolvency Act 1986, ss 148–154 (England and Wales), s 161 (Scotland). The same powers are exercisable by the liquidator in a voluntary winding-up: see Insolvency Act 1986, s 165(4).

[396]  Companies Act 2006 (Commencement No 7, Transitional Provisions and Savings) Order 2008, SI 2008/1886, art 2.

[397]  See ibid, art 7(2).

[398]  SI 2008/1915, art 3.

[399]  Companies Act 2006 (Commencement No 8, Transitional Provisions and Savings) Order 2008, SI 2008/2860, art 3(k).

[400]  It was introduced by CA 1989, s 131.

[401]  *Houldsworth v City of Glasgow Bank* (1880) 5 App Cas 317.

shareholder would seek damages as a remedy. The most likely would be in an action on a misstatement in a prospectus.[402] In other cases, such as to enforce rights under the articles, it is far more likely that the remedy sought is an injunction or a declaration, or, as when claiming unpaid dividends, for a debt.

### 656  Public companies: duty of directors to call meeting on serious loss of capital

**17.656.01**

(1)  Where the net assets of a public company are half or less of its called-up share capital, the directors must call a general meeting of the company to consider whether any, and if so what, steps should be taken to deal with the situation.

(2)  They must do so not later than 28 days from the earliest day on which that fact is known to a director of the company.

(3)  The meeting must be convened for a date not later than 56 days from that day.

(4)  If there is a failure to convene a meeting as required by this section, each of the directors of the company who—

    (a)  knowingly authorises or permits the failure, or

    (b)  after the period during which the meeting should have been convened, knowingly authorises or permits the failure to continue,

commits an offence.

(5)  A person guilty of an offence under this section is liable—

    (a)  on conviction on indictment, to a fine;

    (b)  on summary conviction, to a fine not exceeding the statutory maximum.

(6)  Nothing in this section authorises the consideration at a meeting convened in pursuance of subsection (1) of any matter that could not have been considered at that meeting apart from this section.

COMMENCEMENT DATE 1 October 2009[403]

**17.656.02** This section was introduced initially in the Companies Act 1980 in order to implement the Second EC Company Law Directive[404] and was consolidated as section 142 in the Companies Act 1985. The restatement in this Act removes the previous reference to convening an extraordinary general meeting, as that type of meeting has been abolished. The only other substantive change made by the 2006 Act is an increase in the penalty for breach.

**17.656.03** It should be noted that the section applies only to public companies, but that the obligation to call a meeting arises as soon as one director is aware of the loss of capital. The fact that the value of net assets must fall to half or less of the company's called-up share capital for the obligation to arise must presumably depend on the valuation of the assets according to the latest accounts that have been prepared. Called-up share capital is defined in section 547,[405] and amounts to so much of a company's capital as equals the aggregate amount of calls made, whether or not they have been paid, together with any share capital paid up without being called and any capital to be paid on a specified date.[406] It is not wholly clear whether this includes any premium paid or to be paid on the shares or is confined to their nominal value. A literal interpretation might suggest the latter, but it is thought that a more sensible interpretation would include premiums, given that for most purposes they are treated as capital.[407]

**17.656.04** It is clear from subsection (4) that only a deliberate failure to call an extraordinary general meeting will render a director guilty of an offence. Equally clearly the meeting can consider any proposal to deal with the situation or even not to do anything, given the wording of subsection (1). However, if there is to be formal consideration of, for example, a resolution to reduce capital, proper notice must be given according to the terms of subsection (6).

### 657  General power to make further provision by regulations

**17.657.01**

(1)  The Secretary of State may by regulations modify the following provisions of this Part—

    sections 552 and 553 (prohibited commissions, discounts and allowances),

    Chapter 5 (payment for shares),

    Chapter 6 (public companies: independent valuation of non-cash consideration),

    Chapter 7 (share premiums),

    sections 622 to 628 (redenomination of share capital),

    Chapter 10 (reduction of capital), and

---

[402]  This was the subject of the *Houdsworth* case, above.

[403]  Companies Act 2006 (Commencement No 8, Transitional Provisions and Savings) Order 2008, SI 2008/2860, art 3(k).

[404]  77/91/EEC, Art 17.

[405]  See para 17.547.02.

[406]  Whether under the articles, the terms of allotment or any other arrangement for payment of the shares.

[407]  See para 17.610.02.

section 656 (public companies: duty of directors to call meeting on serious loss of capital).

(2) The regulations may—

   (a) amend or repeal any of those provisions, or

   (b) make such other provision as appears to the Secretary of State appropriate in place of any of those provisions.

(3) Regulations under this section may make consequential amendments or repeals in other provisions of this Act, or in other enactments.

(4) Regulations under this section are subject to affirmative resolution procedure.

COMMENCEMENT DATE 1 October 2009[408]

In giving the Secretary of State the power to amend by regulations many provisions in Part 17 relating to share capital, this section was a new insertion into the 2006 Act. The power is a wide one, but approval of the regulations must be by affirmative resolution in both Houses of Parliament. The power has been used to effect changes consequential upon the agreed modifications to the Second EC Directive.[409]     **17.657.02**

---

[408] Companies Act 2006 (Commencement No 8, Transitional Provisions and Savings) Order 2008, SI 2008/2860, art 3(k).

[409] Directive 77/91. The changes are effected by Directive 2006/68/EC. They cover the valuation of non-cash consideration, purchase of own shares, and the prohibition on financial assistance (the provisions concerning the last two matters are in Part 18, which also contains, in s 737, an amending power). The changes should have been implemented by 15 April 2009, but, except as regards an amendment concerning reductions of capital (made originally to s 136(2) of the 1985 Act by the Companies (Reduction of Capital) Creditor Protection) Regulations 2008, SI 2008/719) were not implemented until 1 October 2009: see the Companies (Share Capital and Acquisition by Company of its Own Shares) Regulations 2009, SI 2009/2022.

# 18

# ACQUISITION BY LIMITED COMPANY OF ITS OWN SHARES

# Companies Act 2006

## PART 18
## ACQUISITION BY LIMITED COMPANY OF ITS OWN SHARES

**18.0.01**  This Part of the Act separates the provisions dealing with a company's acquisition of its own shares and providing financial assistance to another for an acquisition of its shares from the other rules that are concerned with the principle of maintenance of capital in Part 17. Until relatively recently, the general prohibition was a common law rule,[1] supplemented by a statutory rule on financial assistance. However, the implementation, originally in 1980, of the Second Company Law Directive[2] required statutory rules, not least to cover the provisions applicable only to public companies, and those were followed, in 1981, by statutory exceptions permitting the issue of redeemable shares and, subject to strict conditions, the purchase by a company of its own shares. The restating and amendment of these provisions in this Act has led to some simplification, especially for private companies, in line with the general objective of deregulation.

## CHAPTER 1
## GENERAL PROVISIONS
### *Introductory*

### 658  General rule against limited company acquiring its own shares

**18.658.01**
(1)  A limited company must not acquire its own shares, whether by purchase, subscription or otherwise, except in accordance with the provisions of this Part.
(2)  If a company purports to act in contravention of this section—
     (a)  an offence is committed by—

---

[1]  *Trevor v Whitworth* (1887) 12 App Cas 409.
[2]  Directive (EEC) 77/91 [1977] OJ L26/1.

      (i) the company, and

      (ii) every officer of the company who is in default, and

   (b) the purported acquisition is void.

(3) A person guilty of an offence under this section is liable—

   (a) on conviction on indictment, to imprisonment for a term not exceeding two years or a fine (or both);

   (b) on summary conviction—

      (i) in England and Wales, to imprisonment for a term not exceeding twelve months or a fine not exceeding the statutory maximum (or both);

      (ii) in Scotland or Northern Ireland, to imprisonment for a term not exceeding six months or a fine not exceeding the statutory maximum (or both).

COMMENCEMENT DATE 1 October 2009[3]

This section *prima facie* renders void acquisitions of its own shares by any limited company. It also imposes potentially severe criminal penalties on the company and every officer in default. It applies to a company limited by shares or limited by guarantee and having a share capital,[4] but a number of situations are exempt by virtue of the exceptions in section 659 and the other provisions of Part 18. With just minor drafting changes, the section restates the prohibition formerly in section 143 of the 1985 Act. The differences in criminal penalties as between England and Wales, on the one hand, and Scotland and Northern Ireland, on the other, are due to the different maxima that courts of summary jurisdiction can impose. **18.658.02**

In implementing Article 18 of the Second Company Law Directive, section 658 confirms the common law rule established by the House of Lords in *Trevor v Whitworth*,[5] that, because of the principle of maintenance of capital, it was unlawful for a limited company[6] to purchase its own shares except by a proper reduction of capital. The effect of the section can be seen from the decision in *Vision Express (UK) Ltd v Wilson*,[7] where it was held that part of a *Tomlin* order under which a company was to purchase all the rights in shares in itself held by the other party was void. On the other hand, it does not apply when company A acquires the whole of the issued share capital of company B and the sole asset of the company B is a shareholding in company A.[8] At common law it has been held that a guarantee of an agreement by a company to acquire its own shares is enforceable if, properly construed, it was intended to relate to all promises made by the company irrespective of their legality or only to such promises as are unlawful.[9] There seems no reason why the same result should not follow from a breach of the section. **18.658.03**

However, today the principle confirmed by this section is subject to a number of very important exceptions, as seen in the following section and subsequent Chapters of this Part, not least the provisions allowing a limited company to redeem or purchase its own shares under the provisions of Chapters 3 to 6. A failure, though, to comply with the requirements of those provisions will render an acquisition void under this section.[10] **18.658.04**

## 659 Exceptions to general rule

(1) A limited company may acquire any of its own fully paid shares otherwise than for valuable consideration. **18.659.01**

(2) Section 658 does not prohibit—

   (a) the acquisition of shares in a reduction of capital duly made;

   (b) the purchase of shares in pursuance of an order of the court under—

      (i) section 98 (application to court to cancel resolution for re-registration as a private company),

      (ii) section 721(6) (powers of court on objection to redemption or purchase of shares out of capital),

---

[3] Companies Act 2006 (Commencement No 8, Transitional Provisions and Savings) Order 2008, SI 2008/2860, art 3(1).

[4] Since 1980 it has not been possible to form a guarantee company with a share capital, but there may be ones surviving from before the implementation of the Companies Act (CA) 1980.

[5] (1887) 12 App Cas 409.

[6] The rule never applied to unlimited companies (*Re Borough Commercial Building Society* [1893] 2 Ch 242), nor does the section.

[7] [1995] 2 BCLC 419.

[8] *Acatos & Hutchinson plc v Watson* [1995] BCC 446; as to the consequence of B becoming a subsidiary of A, see Chapter 4 of Part 8, ss 136–144.

[9] *Garrard v James* [1925] Ch 616, *Heald v O'Connor* [1971] 1 WLR 497.

[10] *Re R W Peak (King's Lynn) Ltd* [1998] 1 BCLC 193.

(iii) section 759 (remedial order in case of breach of prohibition of public offers by private company), or

(iv) Part 30 (protection of members against unfair prejudice);

(c) the forfeiture of shares, or the acceptance of shares surrendered in lieu, in pursuance of the company's articles, for failure to pay any sum payable in respect of the shares.

COMMENCEMENT DATE 1 October 2009[11]

**18.659.02**     This section repeats and expands the exceptions to the general prohibition on a company acquiring its own shares that were previously in section 143(3) of the 1985 Act. As is made clear by subsection (1), a company can acquire its own shares as a gift—other than for valuable consideration. This exception was first introduced particularly to assist companies that act as executors or trustees, although if the company is a public company, it will be subject to the provisions of sections 662ff below. Previously its own fully paid shares could be held on trust for, or by a nominee for, a company,[12] but this is not necessary by virtue of subsection (1).

**18.659.03**     The exceptions in subsection (2)(a) and (b) permit acquisitions effected in accordance with statutory provisions under court supervision (in the case of reductions of capital) or by court order, although perhaps it is somewhat odd to refer to an 'acquisition' of shares in a reduction of capital, since they are cancelled in such a situation. With regard to reductions of capital, it should be noted that private companies may now reduce capital without court confirmation under sections 642 to 644, but this must still be within the meaning of a reduction 'duly made'.

**18.659.04**     Subsection (2)(c) recognizes that shares may be forfeited or surrendered in lieu of forfeiture following failure to pay any sum due on them. There has never been, or at least, never been any other, clear statutory recognition of the power to forfeit shares or accept surrenders in lieu of forfeiture except that Table A has long contained provisions permitting these. However, it has for many years been established[13] that shares may be forfeited or surrendered for non-payment of calls, provided that there is authority in the articles.[14] Forfeiture for any other reason is invalid,[15] as is a forfeiture that does not comply with the articles.[16] The details of shares forfeited or surrendered must be disclosed in the directors' report.[17]

## *Shares held by company's nominee*

### 660 Treatment of shares held by nominee

**18.660.01**     (1) This section applies where shares in a limited company—

(a) are taken by a subscriber to the memorandum as nominee of the company,

(b) are issued to a nominee of the company, or

(c) are acquired by a nominee of the company, partly paid up, from a third person.

(2) For all purposes—

(a) the shares are to be treated as held by the nominee on his own account, and

(b) the company is to be regarded as having no beneficial interest in them.

(3) This section does not apply—

(a) to shares acquired otherwise than by subscription by a nominee of a public company, where—

(i) a person acquires shares in the company with financial assistance given to him, directly or indirectly, by the company for the purpose of or in connection with the acquisition, and

(ii) the company has a beneficial interest in the shares;

(b) to shares acquired by a nominee of the company when the company has no beneficial interest in the shares.

COMMENCEMENT DATE 1 October 2009[18]

---

[11] Companies Act 2006 (Commencement No 8, Transitional Provisions and Savings) Order 2008, SI 2008/2860, art 3(l).

[12] *Kirby v Wilkins* [1929] 2 Ch 444, *Re Castiglione's Will Trusts* [1958] Ch 549.

[13] *Lane's Case* (1862) 1 De G J & S 504, *Kipling v Todd* (1878) 3 CPD 350.

[14] *Trevor v Whitworth* (1887) 12 App Cas 409, 417, 429, 438.

[15] *Hopkinson v Mortimer, Harley & Co Ltd* [1917] 1 Ch 646 (non-payment of debt), *Hope v International Financial Society* (1876) 4 Ch D 327 (article invalid that provided for forfeiture of shares of member who instituted or supported proceedings against the company or any of its directors).

[16] *Houldsworth v Evans* (1868) LR 3 HL 263.

[17] This is not expressly provided for in the Act (compare Sch 7 to the 1985 Act), but regulations include the matters formerly contained in that Schedule; see para 15.416.04.

[18] Companies Act 2006 (Commencement No 8, Transitional Provisions and Savings) Order 2008, SI 2008/2860, art 3(l).

This section and section 661, which implement Article 18 of the Second Company Law Directive, are    **18.660.02**
the restated provisions formerly in sections 144 and 145 of the 1985 Act. The drafting is a considerable
improvement on the former sections.[19] They deal with what are likely to be very limited situations,
principally[20] where shares are issued to a nominee of a limited company with a share capital or where
a nominee acquires partly paid shares in such a company from a third person. In these cases, subject to
the exceptions provided for in subsection (3), the shares are treated as held by the nominee in his own
account and the company has no beneficial interest in them.[21]

Having said that, the section is not free from difficulties of interpretation. One concern is its relation-    **18.660.03**
ship with section 658, since it could be argued that any purported dealing with shares in the circumstances described in this section would be void under the earlier section as an acquisition by the
company of its own shares. On the other hand, a better interpretation would be to regard it as an
exception to that provision so that any transaction covered is not void but instead imposes liability on
the nominee and the others under section 661. Although the wording of the former provision led to
some argument about whether the second circumstance in subsection (1), namely the issue of shares to
a nominee, would cover fully paid shares as well as partly paid shares, its inclusion in a separate
sub-paragraph now clearly indicates that it does; this matters in a case where the nominal value of the
shares was fully paid, but a premium was not, since section 661 imposes liability for any premium.

Subsection (3) excludes some cases from the effect of subsection (2) and hence from imposing liability    **18.660.04**
under section 661. The most straightforward case is that in subsection (3)(b), namely where a nominee
of the company has acquired shares in the company but the company has no beneficial interest in them.
In this respect the definition of beneficial interest in sections 671 to 676 is important, since it permits
companies to hold interests such as residual interests under a pension scheme or an employees' share
scheme where shares in it are vested in trustees without falling foul of the section.[22]

The other exclusion, in subsection (3)(b) is in effect from this section only and not from liability under    **18.660.05**
section 661.[23] Here the company must be a public company, the shares must have been acquired by its
nominee other than by being issued to him, the company must have provided financial assistance for
the purposes of or in connection with the acquisition,[24] and the company must have a beneficial
interest in the shares.[25] Note that section 661, below, will apply to this situation, which in practice is
likely, it is thought, to be very rare.

## 661  Liability of others where nominee fails to make payment in respect of shares

(1)  This section applies where shares in a limited company—    **18.661.01**
    (a)  are taken by a subscriber to the memorandum as nominee of the company,
    (b)  are issued to a nominee of the company, or
    (c)  are acquired by a nominee of the company, partly paid up, from a third person.
(2)  If the nominee, having been called on to pay any amount for the purposes of paying up, or paying
    any premium on, the shares, fails to pay that amount within 21 days from being called on to do
    so, then—
    (a)  in the case of shares that he agreed to take as subscriber to the memorandum, the other
        subscribers to the memorandum, and
    (b)  in any other case, the directors of the company when the shares were issued to or acquired
        by him,
    are jointly and severally liable with him to pay that amount.
(3)  If in proceedings for the recovery of an amount under subsection (2) it appears to the court that
    the subscriber or director—
    (a)  has acted honestly and reasonably, and
    (b)  having regard to all the circumstances of the case, ought fairly to be relieved from liability,
    the court may relieve him, either wholly or in part, from his liability on such terms as the court
    thinks fit.

---

[19]  The former exception in respect of shares issued in consequence of an application made before 22
December 1980, or transferred in pursuance of an agreement to acquire them made before that date (previously
s 145(2)(b) of the 1985 Act) no longer appears, presumably on the grounds that it is now of no relevance.
  [20]  It is difficult to envisage the situation in subs (1)(a) occurring in the UK.
  [21]  The common law was to the same effect: *Cree v Somervail* (1879) 4 App Cas 648.
  [22]  See further para 18.671.01–18.676.02 below.
  [23]  See s 661(5), which exempts from that section only the exception in subs (3)(b).
  [24]  As to financial assistance generally, see ss 677–683, but note that this provision is wider than those
provisions, since it may be given in connection with the acquisition and not just for the purpose of the acquisition.
Further, there is no definition of financial assistance for the purposes of this section.
  [25]  Beneficial interest again being construed in accordance with ss 671–676.

(4) If a subscriber to a company's memorandum or a director of a company has reason to apprehend that a claim will or might be made for the recovery of any such amount from him—
(a) he may apply to the court for relief, and
(b) the court has the same power to relieve him as it would have had in proceedings for recovery of that amount.

(5) This section does not apply to shares acquired by a nominee of the company when the company has no beneficial interest in the shares.

COMMENCEMENT DATE 1 October 2009[26]

**18.661.02** As is the case with section 671, this section restates part of the previous sections 144 and 145 of the 1985 Act, but in a much clearer fashion. Liability for future calls on shares acquired by subscribers to the memorandum and nominees, including for any premium, is imposed jointly and severally by subsection (2) on the persons there mentioned, namely (a) the other subscribers to the memorandum if the shares were issued to the nominee pursuant to an obligation therein, or (b) the directors of the company at the time of the issue or acquisition in any other cases. Although likely to be rare in application, the section does preserve the principle of maintenance of capital by ensuring that a company does not indirectly pay for its own shares. Note the exception in subsection (5) and see the comment on this situation in the notes to section 671.

**18.661.03** Relief against liability under subsection (3), which can be applied for prospectively under subsection (4), can be granted by the court on the same basis as it can relieve a director or officer from liability generally under section 1157.[27]

## *Shares held by or for public company*

### 662 Duty to cancel shares in public company held by or for the company

**18.662.01** (1) This section applies in the case of a public company—
(a) where shares in the company are forfeited, or surrendered to the company in lieu of forfeiture, in pursuance of the articles, for failure to pay any sum payable in respect of the shares;
(b) where shares in the company are surrendered to the company in pursuance of section 102C(1)(b) of the Building Societies Act 1986 (c. 53);
(c) where shares in the company are acquired by it (otherwise than in accordance with this Part or Part 30 (protection of members against unfair prejudice)) and the company has a beneficial interest in the shares;
(d) where a nominee of the company acquires shares in the company from a third party without financial assistance being given directly or indirectly by the company and the company has a beneficial interest in the shares; or
(e) where a person acquires shares in the company, with financial assistance given to him, directly or indirectly, by the company for the purpose of or in connection with the acquisition, and the company has a beneficial interest in the shares.

(2) Unless the shares or any interest of the company in them are previously disposed of, the company must—
(a) cancel the shares and diminish the amount of the company's share capital by the nominal value of the shares cancelled, and
(b) where the effect is that the nominal value of the company's allotted share capital is brought below the authorised minimum, apply for re-registration as a private company, stating the effect of the cancellation.

(3) It must do so no later than—
(a) in a case within subsection (1)(a) or (b), three years from the date of the forfeiture or surrender;
(b) in a case within subsection (1)(c) or (d), three years from the date of the acquisition;
(c) in a case within subsection (1)(e), one year from the date of the acquisition.

(4) The directors of the company may take any steps necessary to enable the company to comply with this section, and may do so without complying with the provisions of Chapter 10 of Part 17 (reduction of capital).
See also section 664 (re-registration as private company in consequence of cancellation).

(5) Neither the company nor, in a case within subsection (1)(d) or (e), the nominee or other shareholder may exercise any voting rights in respect of the shares.

---

[26] Companies Act 2006 (Commencement No 8, Transitional Provisions and Savings) Order 2008, SI 2008/2860, art 3(l).

[27] See the comments on that section at para 37.1157.02.

(6)  Any purported exercise of those rights is void.

COMMENCEMENT DATE  1 October 2009[28]

This and the following sections 663 to 669 implement Articles 20 to 22 of the Second Company Law    **18.662.02**
Directive and impose a special regime only for public companies that have acquired their own shares
or a beneficial interest in their own shares.[29] This section is the restatement of section 146 of the 1985
Act and there is no doubt that it is much more clearly drafted. 'Beneficial interest' is construed in
accordance with sections 671 to 676[30] and the effect is that a company will not be subject to the regime
of these sections if it holds its own shares as trustee. Section 662 applies both where an event mentioned
in subsection (1) or section 668(1)(a) to (d) occurs on or after 1 October 2009 and where an event
mentioned in section 146(1) of the 1985 Act or section 148(1)(a) to (d) of the 1985 Act, which is
replaced by section 668(1)(a) to (d), occurred before that date unless, before then, the company has
complied with section 146(2) (replaced by section 662(2)) or the period for compliance specified in
section 146(3) (replaced by section 662(3)) has expired.[31]

In essence, in the situations prescribed by the section, companies must either dispose of or cancel the    **18.662.03**
relevant shares within three years, or one year in the case covered by subsection (1)(e), and during that
period any voting rights attached to the shares cannot be exercised. Any cancellation of shares under
the section will be a reduction of capital, but it is governed by this section, rather than by the usual
procedures for reducing capital, so that the directors may so resolve and there is no need to obtain the
consent of members and the confirmation of the court as in the usual case of a reduction by a public
company.[32]

The situations when shares must be disposed of or cancelled within three years are (a) following    **18.662.04**
forfeiture or surrender for failure to pay a call on shares; (b) where the company itself acquires its own
shares other than in the situations permitted, which includes redemptions or purchases under
Chapters 3 and 4, and it has a beneficial interest in them; and (c) where a nominee of the company
acquires shares from a third person without being financially assisted by the company and the
company has a beneficial interest in them. Forfeiture and surrender were described in the notes to
section 659, above. Situation (b) would appear to include an acquisition by the company without it
providing consideration, even though that is not prohibited by section 658. It seems arguable that
situation (c) would be in breach of the basic prohibition in section 658(1).

The situation where shares must be disposed of or cancelled within one year is where a person acquires    **18.662.05**
shares with financial assistance and the company has a beneficial interest in them. It should be noted
here, again,[33] that there is no definition of 'financial assistance' for this purpose and that the wording
is broader than that of the general prohibition on financial assistance in sections 678 and 679.[34] There
appears to be scope for a conflict between these sections. If section 678 or 679 is breached, the
consequences are that the acquisition of shares is void and illegal, but section 662 appears to sanction
an acquisition within subsection (1)(e) for the one-year period before the shares must be disposed of or
cancelled, so that, if it disposes of the shares, the company would be entitled to the value of its beneficial
interest, unless the shares were partly paid and the case falls within section 660(1).

### 663  Notice of cancellation of shares

(1)  Where a company cancels shares in order to comply with section 662, it must within one month    **18.663.01**
     after the shares are cancelled give notice to the registrar, specifying the shares cancelled.
(2)  The notice must be accompanied by a statement of capital.
(3)  The statement of capital must state with respect to the company's share capital immediately
     following the cancellation—
     (a)  the total number of shares of the company,
     (b)  the aggregate nominal value of those shares,

---

[28]  Companies Act 2006 (Commencement No 8, Transitional Provisions and Savings) Order 2008, SI 2008/
2860, art 3(l).
[29]  The section does not apply to an old public company: the Companies Act 2006 (Consequential Amendments, Transitional Provisions and Savings) Order 2009, SI 2009/1941, Sch 3, para 7(1). As to the meaning of 'old
public company', see ibid, para 1.
[30]  See paras 18.671.01–02 below.
[31]  Companies Act 2006 (Commencement No 8, Transitional Provisions and Savings) Order 2008, SI 2008/
2860, Sch 2, para 70.
[32]  See para 17.641.02.
[33]  See the commentary to s 660, above.
[34]  See paras 18.678.02 and 18.679.02 below.

        (c)   for each class of shares—
           (i)   prescribed particulars of the rights attached to the shares,
           (ii)  the total number of shares of that class, and
           (iii) the aggregate nominal value of shares of that class, and
        (d)  the amount paid up and the amount (if any) unpaid on each share (whether on account of the nominal value of the share or by way of premium).

    (4)  If default is made in complying with this section, an offence is committed by—
        (a)  the company, and
        (b)  every officer of the company who is in default.

    (5)  A person guilty of an offence under this section is liable on summary conviction to a fine not exceeding level 3 on the standard scale and, for continued contravention, a daily default fine not exceeding one-tenth of level 3 on the standard scale.

COMMENCEMENT DATE  1 October 2009[35]

**18.663.02**    The obligation to file notice of a cancellation of shares effected under section 663 is here specifically imposed in this Part of the Act rather than, as before, being subsumed under the general obligation to file notice of any cancellation under the former section 122 of the 1985 Act.[36] The requirement is straightforward. The associated obligation to file a statement of capital mirrors the similar obligation imposed when a company is registered or alters its capital in any way. See the notes to section 10.

### 664  Re-registration as private company in consequence of cancellation

**18.664.01**    (1)  Where a company is obliged to re-register as a private company to comply with section 662, the directors may resolve that the company should be so re-registered.
        Chapter 3 of Part 3 (resolutions affecting a company's constitution) applies to any such resolution.

    (2)  The resolution may make such changes—
        (a)  in the company's name, and
        (b)  in the company's articles,
        as are necessary in connection with its becoming a private company.

    (3)  The application for re-registration must contain a statement of the company's proposed name on re-registration.

    (4)  The application must be accompanied by—
        (a)  a copy of the resolution (unless a copy has already been forwarded under Chapter 3 of Part 3),
        (b)  a copy of the company's articles as amended by the resolution, and
        (c)  a statement of compliance.

    (5)  The statement of compliance required is a statement that the requirements of this section as to re-registration as a private company have been complied with.

    (6)  The registrar may accept the statement of compliance as sufficient evidence that the company is entitled to be re-registered as a private company.

COMMENCEMENT DATE  1 October 2009[37]

**18.664.02**    This and the following section provides for the consequences of a public company being subject to section 662 and being compelled to reduce capital under that section because it has not disposed of shares acquired by it or its nominee in the circumstances described therein.[38] If the effect of the reduction is that the company no longer has the minimum capital required to be a public company, the directors can take the necessary steps to apply for re-registration as a private company and make the necessary alterations to the company's name and in the articles. Obviously the first will replace 'public

---

[35] Companies Act 2006 (Commencement No 8, Transitional Provisions and Savings) Order 2008, SI 2008/2860, art 3(l).

[36] Section 663 applies where shares are cancelled on or after 1 October 2009; filing in respect of shares cancelled before then was governed by s 122 of the 1985 Act: Companies Act 2006 (Commencement No 8, Transitional Provisions and Savings) Order 2008, SI 2008/2860, Sch 2, para 71. The section does not apply to an old public company: the Companies Act 2006 (Consequential Amendments, Transitional Provisions and Savings) Order 2009, SI 2009/1941, Sch 3, para 7(1). As to the meaning of 'old public company', see Sch 3, para 1.

[37] Companies Act 2006 (Commencement No 8, Transitional Provisions and Savings) Order 2008, SI 2008/2860, art 3(l).

[38] The section does not apply to an old public company: the Companies Act 2006 (Consequential Amendments, Transitional Provisions and Savings) Order 2009, SI 2009/1941, Sch 3, para 7(1). As to the meaning of 'old public company', see Sch 3, para 1.

limited company' or 'plc' with 'limited' or 'ltd'.[39] What changes to the articles are necessary will depend on the circumstance of the particular company.[40]

There has been no reported case arising out of the predecessor to this section and it does not seem likely **18.664.03** to be of common application, if only because the minimum share capital requirement for public companies is a relatively low amount. It may be assumed, though, that the directors' resolution amending the articles would be potentially open to challenge under the general law that allows an amendment by special resolution to be challenged.[41]

The procedure differs slightly from that described in the former section 147 of the 1985 Act, which this **18.664.04** section in part replaces. The previous reference to changes in the memorandum has been omitted, given the fact that the memorandum no longer has any continuing purpose.[42] The requirement for a statement of compliance replaces the previous requirement for completion of the prescribed form.

## 665  Issue of certificate of incorporation on re-registration

(1) If on an application under section 664 the registrar is satisfied that the company is entitled to be **18.665.01** re-registered as a private company, the company shall be re-registered accordingly.
(2) The registrar must issue a certificate of incorporation altered to meet the circumstances of the case.
(3) The certificate must state that it is issued on re-registration and the date on which it is issued.
(4) On the issue of the certificate—
    (a) the company by virtue of the issue of the certificate becomes a private company, and
    (b) the changes in the company's name and articles take effect.
(5) The certificate is conclusive evidence that the requirements of this Act as to re-registration have been complied with.

COMMENCEMENT DATE 1 October 2009[43]

This section restates the obligations imposed on the registrar and the consequences of re-registration **18.665.02** as a private company formerly contained in section 147(4) of the 1985 Act. In addition to removing any references to changes in the memorandum, which are no longer necessary, the section is worded more clearly.

Any unjustified refusal by the registrar to re-register the company would be challengeable by way of **18.665.03** judicial review. The effect of the new certificate of incorporation, namely as to its being conclusive evidence, is the same as an original certificate of incorporation as described in the notes to section 15.

## 666  Effect of failure to re-register

(1) If a public company that is required by section 662 to apply to be re-registered as a private **18.666.01** company fails to do so before the end of the period specified in subsection (3) of that section, Chapter 1 of Part 20 (prohibition of public offers by private company) applies to it as if it were a private company.
(2) Subject to that, the company continues to be treated as a public company until it is so re-registered.

COMMENCEMENT DATE 1 October 2009[44]

This section restates what was formerly in section 149(1) of the 1985 Act. That is, a company that fails **18.666.02** to apply for re-registration continues to be a public company for the purposes of the Act, except that it cannot offer any shares to the public.[45] This means that, among other things, it cannot take effect of the

---

[39] Or the Welsh equivalents.
[40] Under transitional arrangements, this section and ss 665–667 apply in any case where s 662 applies: Companies Act 2006 (Commencement No 8, Transitional Provisions and Savings) Order 2008, SI 2008/2860, Sch 2, para 72; see para 18.662.02 above. For the purposes of an application under s 664 in respect of a resolution agreed under s 147 of the 1985 Act before 1 October 2009, amendments of a company's memorandum may be treated as amendments of its articles: Ibid.
[41] See para 3.21.02. The actions of the directors would also potentially be open to challenge under the unfair prejudice provisions (Part 30).
[42] See para 2.8.02.
[43] Companies Act 2006 (Commencement No 8, Transitional Provisions and Savings) Order 2008, SI 2008/2860, art 3(l).
[44] Companies Act 2006 (Commencement No 8, Transitional Provisions and Savings) Order 2008, SI 2008/2860, art 3(l).
[45] See para 20.755.02. The section does not apply to an old public company: the Companies Act 2006 (Consequential Amendments, Transitional Provisions and Savings) Order 2009, SI 2009/1941, Sch 3, para 7(1). As to the meaning of 'old public company', see Sch 3, para 1.

deregulatory provisions introduced by the 2006 Act relating to written resolutions, the abolition of the annual general meeting for private companies, the abolition of the prohibition on private companies providing financial assistance for an acquisition of their own shares, and the easier procedure for a reduction of capital.

### 667 Offence in case of failure to cancel shares or re-register

**18.667.01**      (1) This section applies where a company, when required to do by section 662—
      (a) fails to cancel any shares, or
      (b) fails to make an application for re-registration as a private company,
     within the time specified in subsection (3) of that section.
    (2) An offence is committed by—
      (a) the company, and
      (b) every officer of the company who is in default.
    (3) A person guilty of an offence under this section is liable on summary conviction to a fine not exceeding level 3 on the standard scale and, for continued contravention, a daily default fine not exceeding one-tenth of level 3 on the standard scale.

COMMENCEMENT DATE 1 October 2009[46]

**18.667.02**   This section restates what was previously section 149(2) of the 1985 Act. It provides the specified criminal sanction on the company and every officer in default for non-compliance with the requirements of section 662 regarding the cancellation of shares and, where appropriate, the requirement to apply for re-registration as private company.[47]

### 668 Application of provisions to company re-registering as public company

**18.668.01**      (1) This section applies where, after shares in a private company—
      (a) are forfeited in pursuance of the company's articles or are surrendered to the company in lieu of forfeiture,
      (b) are acquired by the company (otherwise than by any of the methods permitted by this Part or Part 30 (protection of members against unfair prejudice)), the company having a beneficial interest in the shares,
      (c) are acquired by a nominee of the company from a third party without financial assistance being given directly or indirectly by the company, the company having a beneficial interest in the shares, or
      (d) are acquired by a person with financial assistance given to him, directly or indirectly, by the company for the purpose of or in connection with the acquisition, the company having a beneficial interest in the shares,
     the company is re-registered as a public company.
    (2) In that case the provisions of sections 662 to 667 apply to the company as if it had been a public company at the time of the forfeiture, surrender or acquisition, subject to the following modification.
    (3) The modification is that the period specified in section 662(3)(a), (b) or (c) (period for complying with obligations under that section) runs from the date of the re-registration of the company as a public company.

COMMENCEMENT DATE 1 October 2009[48]

**18.668.02**   In restating section 149(1) to (3) of the 1985 Act, this section subjects a private company that has been re-registered as a public company to the regime of sections 662 to 667 if its shares have been forfeited or surrendered or acquired in the circumstances specified in subsection (1)(b) to (d), which mirror the circumstances in section 662(1)(c) to (e).[49] The only difference, by subsection (3), is that the periods allowed for disposal or cancellation of the shares commence from the date of re-registration and not the date of forfeiture, surrender, or acquisition.[50]

---

[46] Companies Act 2006 (Commencement No 8, Transitional Provisions and Savings) Order 2008, SI 2008/2860, art 3(l).

[47] The section does not apply to an old public company: the Companies Act 2006 (Consequential Amendments, Transitional Provisions and Savings) Order 2009, SI 2009/1941, Sch 3, para 7(1). As to the meaning of 'old public company', see Sch 3, para 1.

[48] Companies Act 2006 (Commencement No 8, Transitional Provisions and Savings) Order 2008, SI 2008/2860, art 3(l).

[49] See the notes to the earlier sections for discussion of the meaning of these circumstances. The section applies to an old public company as to a private company: the Companies Act 2006 (Consequential Amendments, Transitional Provisions and Savings) Order 2009, SI 2009/1941, Sch 3, para 7(2). As to the meaning of 'old public company', see Sch 3, para 1.

[50] As to the transitional provisions affecting this section, see para 18.662.02 above.

### 669  Transfer to reserve on acquisition of shares by public company or nominee

(1) Where—                                                                                                    **18.669.01**
    (a)  a public company, or a nominee of a public company, acquires shares in the company, and
    (b)  those shares are shown in a balance sheet of the company as an asset,
    an amount equal to the value of the shares must be transferred out of profits available for
    dividend to a reserve fund and is not then available for distribution.
(2) Subsection (1) applies to an interest in shares as it applies to shares.
    As it so applies the reference to the value of the shares shall be read as a reference to the value
    to the company of its interest in the shares.

COMMENCEMENT DATE  1 October 2009[51]

This section, which restates section 149(4) of the 1985 Act, applies to public companies only[52] and   **18.669.02**
requires the capitalization of an amount equal to the value of its own shares acquired by the company
or its nominee or the value of the company's interest where the shares or interest are shown as an asset
on the balance sheet. The funds must be provided out of distributable profits and are not available for
distribution.[53]

## *Charges of public company on own shares*

### 670  Public companies: general rule against lien or charge on own shares

(1) A lien or other charge of a public company on its own shares (whether taken expressly or         **18.670.01**
    otherwise) is void, except as permitted by this section.
(2) In the case of any description of company, a charge is permitted if the shares are not fully paid up
    and the charge is for an amount payable in respect of the shares.
(3) In the case of a company whose ordinary business—
    (a)  includes the lending of money, or
    (b)  consists of the provision of credit or the bailment (in Scotland, hiring) of goods under a
         hire-purchase agreement, or both,
    a charge is permitted (whether the shares are fully paid or not) if it arises in connection with a
    transaction entered into by the company in the ordinary course of that business.
(4) In the case of a company that has been re-registered as a public company, a charge is permitted
    if it was in existence immediately before the application for re-registration.

COMMENCEMENT DATE  1 October 2009[54]

This section, which restates section 150 of the 1985 Act,[55] controls what liens or other charges a public   **18.670.02**
company can have over its own shares. This will apply whatever its articles may provide because the
effect of the section is to render impermissible charges void. There may well be, or at least have been,
public companies whose articles were adopted before this section first came into force,[56] and which
provided, for example, for a lien on shares for any debt owing by a shareholder.

The three permissible liens or charges are set out in subsections (2), (3), and (4). A lien or charge on   **18.670.03**
partly paid shares in respect of any amount payable on them, which will include any premium as well
as in respect of their nominal value, is generally allowed. The phrase 'every description of company' in
subsection (2) is clearly in contrast to money lending and the other companies covered by subsection
(3). Such companies are permitted to have charges on their own shares, whether fully or partly paid, in
connection with a transaction entered into in the ordinary course of business. The exception in
subsection (4) concerns companies re-registered as public,[57] in respect of charges on their own shares
existing immediately before their re-registration.[58]

---

[51]  Companies Act 2006 (Commencement No 8, Transitional Provisions and Savings) Order 2008, SI 2008/
2860, art 3(l).
[52]  The section does not apply to an old public company: the Companies Act 2006 (Consequential Amendments, Transitional Provisions and Savings) Order 2009, SI 2009/1941, Sch 3, para 7(1). As to the meaning of 'old
public company', see Sch 3, para 1.
[53]  See generally Part 23 and the annotations thereto.
[54]  Companies Act 2006 (Commencement No 8, Transitional Provisions and Savings) Order 2008, SI 2008/
2860, art 3(l).
[55]  Except for the omission of any reference to pre-1980 'old public companies', but see n 58 to para 18.670.03
below.
[56]  As s 38 of CA 1980.
[57]  As to these, see para 7.90.02.
[58]  In addition, in respect of a company that, after 22 March 1982 in the case of a GB registered company or after
30 September 1984 in the case of a Northern Irish company, remained an old public company and did not before
that date apply to be registered as a public company, any charge on its own shares that was in existence on or

*Supplementary provisions*

### 671 Interests to be disregarded in determining whether company has beneficial interest

**18.671.01**     In determining for the purposes of this Chapter whether a company has a beneficial interest in shares, there shall be disregarded any such interest as is mentioned in—

> section 672 (residual interest under pension scheme or employees' share scheme),
> section 673 (employer's charges and other rights of recovery), or
> section 674 (rights as personal representative or trustee).

COMMENCEMENT DATE 1 October 2009[59]

**18.671.02**    Sections 671 to 676 provide for the situations where a company is not regarded as having a beneficial interest in shares for the purposes of the previous provisions of this Chapter, particularly where shares are held by a nominee for the company. They were previously contained in Schedule 2 to the Companies Act 1985. Broadly, they permit a company to have an interest that amounts to a residual interest under a pension scheme or employees' share scheme, and where a company acts as personal representative or trustee without falling foul of sections 660 and 661 concerning the treatment of shares in any company held by a nominee and sections 662 to 668 requiring public companies or private companies re-registering as public companies to cancel or dispose of shares in which they have an interest.

### 672 Residual interest under pension scheme or employees' share scheme

**18.672.01**     (1)  Where the shares are held on trust for the purposes of a pension scheme or employees' share scheme, there shall be disregarded any residual interest of the company that has not vested in possession.

(2)  A 'residual interest' means a right of the company to receive any of the trust property in the event of—

   (a)  all the liabilities arising under the scheme having been satisfied or provided for, or
   (b)  the company ceasing to participate in the scheme, or
   (c)  the trust property at any time exceeding what is necessary for satisfying the liabilities arising or expected to arise under the scheme.

(3)  In subsection (2)—

   (a)  the reference to a right includes a right dependent on the exercise of a discretion vested by the scheme in the trustee or another person, and
   (b)  the reference to liabilities arising under a scheme includes liabilities that have resulted, or may result, from the exercise of any such discretion.

(4)  For the purposes of this section a residual interest vests in possession—

   (a)  in a case within subsection (2)(a), on the occurrence of the event mentioned there (whether or not the amount of the property receivable pursuant to the right is ascertained);
   (b)  in a case within subsection (2)(b) or (c), when the company becomes entitled to require the trustee to transfer to it any of the property receivable pursuant to that right.

(5)  Where by virtue of this section shares are exempt from section 660 or 661 (shares held by company's nominee) at the time they are taken, issued or acquired but the residual interest in question vests in possession before they are disposed of or fully paid up, those sections apply to the shares as if they had been taken, issued or acquired on the date on which that interest vests in possession.

(6)  Where by virtue of this section shares are exempt from sections 662 to 668 (shares held by or for public company) at the time they are acquired but the residual interest in question vests in possession before they are disposed of, those sections apply to the shares as if they had been acquired on the date on which the interest vests in possession.

COMMENCEMENT DATE 1 October 2009[60]

**18.672.02**    This section defines what is meant by a residual interest under a pension scheme, defined in section 675, or employees' share scheme, defined in section 1166, so that such an interest of a company does not amount to a beneficial interest for the purposes of the Chapter, provided that it has not vested in possession.

---

immediately before that date is a permitted charge and not void under this section: the Companies Act 2006 (Consequential Amendments, Transitional Provisions and Savings) Order 2009, SI 2009/1941, Sch 3, para 7(3) and (4). As to the meaning of 'old public company', see Sch 3, para 1.

[59] Companies Act 2006 (Commencement No 8, Transitional Provisions and Savings) Order 2008, SI 2008/2860, art 3(l).

[60] Companies Act 2006 (Commencement No 8, Transitional Provisions and Savings) Order 2008, SI 2008/2860, art 3(l).

A residual interest is defined as a right of the company to receive any of the trust property    **18.672.03**

(i)  if all the liabilities, including liabilities that have resulted or may result from the exercise of any discretion vested by the scheme in the trustee or another person, arising under the scheme have been satisfied or provided for;

(ii)  if the company ceases to participate in the scheme; or

(iii)  if the trust property at any time exceeds what is necessary to satisfy the liabilities arising or expected to arise under the scheme.

It does not matter whether or not the right is dependent on the exercise of a discretion vested by the scheme in the trustee or in any other person. Vesting in possession occurs in case (i) if all the liabilities arising under the scheme have been satisfied or provided for, whether or not the amount of property receivable by the company is then ascertained, or, in cases within (ii) and (iii) above, when the company becomes entitled to require the trustee to transfer to it any of the property receivable by it.

## 673  Employer's charges and other rights of recovery

(1)  Where the shares are held on trust for the purposes of a pension scheme there shall be disregarded—    **18.673.01**

    (a)  any charge or lien on, or set-off against, any benefit or other right or interest under the scheme for the purpose of enabling the employer or former employer of a member of the scheme to obtain the discharge of a monetary obligation due to him from the member;

    (b)  any right to receive from the trustee of the scheme, or as trustee of the scheme to retain, an amount that can be recovered or retained—

        (i)  under section 61 of the Pension Schemes Act 1993 (c. 48), or otherwise, as reimbursement or partial reimbursement for any contributions equivalent premium paid in connection with the scheme under Part 3 of that Act, or

        (ii)  under section 57 of the Pension Schemes (Northern Ireland) Act 1993 (c. 49), or otherwise, as reimbursement or partial reimbursement for any contributions equivalent premium paid in connection with the scheme under Part 3 of that Act.

(2)  Where the shares are held on trust for the purposes of an employees' share scheme, there shall be disregarded any charge or lien on, or set-off against, any benefit or other right or interest under the scheme for the purpose of enabling the employer or former employer of a member of the scheme to obtain the discharge of a monetary obligation due to him from the member.

COMMENCEMENT DATE  1 October 2009[61]

This section provides for other interests of a company arising under a pension scheme or employees'    **18.673.02**
share scheme, where the shares are held on trust, to be disregarded for the purposes of determining whether or not it has a beneficial interest in its own shares.

If the trust is for the purposes of a pension scheme, the relevant rights are (i) any charge or lien on, or    **18.673.03**
set-off against, any benefit or other right or interest under the scheme for the purpose of enabling the employer or former employer of a member of the scheme to obtain the discharge of a monetary obligation due to him from the member; and (ii) any right to receive from the trustee of the scheme, or as trustee of the scheme to retain, any amount that can be recovered or retained under the Acts mentioned in subsection (1)(b). If the trust is for the purpose of an employees' share scheme the relevant rights are those in (i).

## 674  Rights as personal representative or trustee

Where the company is a personal representative or trustee, there shall be disregarded any rights that    **18.674.01**
the company has in that capacity including, in particular—

    (a)  any right to recover its expenses or be remunerated out of the estate or trust property, and

    (b)  any right to be indemnified out of that property for any liability incurred by reason of any act or omission of the company in the performance of its duties as personal representative or trustee.

COMMENCEMENT DATE  1 October 2009[62]

This section provides for a general exemption from the meaning of a beneficial interest in shares for the    **18.674.02**
purposes of the Chapter where a company is a personal representative or trustee in respect of the rights it has in that capacity. Such a situation could arise where, for example, a bank becomes the personal

---

[61]  Companies Act 2006 (Commencement No 8, Transitional Provisions and Savings) Order 2008, SI 2008/2860, art 3(l).

[62]  Companies Act 2006 (Commencement No 8, Transitional Provisions and Savings) Order 2008, SI 2008/2860, art 3(l).

representative of a deceased person who was a shareholder in it. Clearly any such rights as personal representative or trustee are covered, but the section specifies in particular rights to expenses or remuneration out of the estate or trust property and rights to be indemnified against liabilities arising out of its performance as personal representative or trustee.

### 675 Meaning of 'pension scheme'

**18.675.01**
(1) In this Chapter 'pension scheme' means a scheme for the provision of benefits consisting of or including relevant benefits for or in respect of employees or former employees.

(2) In subsection (1) 'relevant benefits' means any pension, lump sum, gratuity or other like benefit given or to be given on retirement or on death or in anticipation of retirement or, in connection with past service, after retirement or death.

COMMENCEMENT DATE 1 October 2009[63]

**18.675.02** This section defines 'pension scheme' for the purposes of the Chapter and in particular for the purposes of sections 672 and 673 concerning when a company's interest in its own shares held under such a scheme can be disregarded. The broad definition seems apt to cover every possible type of scheme, whether provided by the company or another person.

### 676 Application of provisions to directors

**18.676.01** For the purposes of this Chapter references to 'employer' and 'employee', in the context of a pension scheme or employees' share scheme, shall be read as if a director of a company were employed by it.

COMMENCEMENT DATE 1 October 2009[64]

**18.676.02** This section makes it clear that a director is to be treated as an employee of the company for the purpose of the preceding provisions regarding a company's interests in its own shares arising under a pension scheme or employees' share scheme. In practice many directors will also be employees by virtue of having a contract of service in addition to their holding the office of director; however, it is clear that for the purposes of this Chapter, they do not have to have such a contract.

## CHAPTER 2
## FINANCIAL ASSISTANCE FOR PURCHASE OF OWN SHARES

### *Introductory*

### 677 Meaning of 'financial assistance'[a]

**18.677.01**
(1) In this Chapter 'financial assistance' means—
   (a) financial assistance given by way of gift,
   (b) financial assistance given—
      (i) by way of guarantee, security or indemnity (other than an indemnity in respect of the indemnifier's own neglect or default), or
      (ii) by way of release or waiver,
   (c) financial assistance given—
      (i) by way of a loan or any other agreement under which any of the obligations of the person giving the assistance are to be fulfilled at a time when in accordance with the agreement any obligation of another party to the agreement remains unfulfilled, or
      (ii) by way of the novation of, or the assignment (in Scotland, assignation) of rights arising under, a loan or such other agreement, or
   (d) any other financial assistance given by a company where—
      (i) the net assets of the company are reduced to a material extent by the giving of the assistance, or
      (ii) the company has no net assets.

(2) [b]'Net assets' here means the aggregate amount of the company's assets less the aggregate amount of its liabilities.

(3) For this purpose a company's liabilities include—
   (a) where the company draws up Companies Act individual accounts, any provision of a kind specified for the purposes of this subsection by regulations under section 396, and
   (b) where the company draws up IAS individual accounts, any provision made in those accounts.

AMENDMENTS AND NOTES

---

[63] Companies Act 2006 (Commencement No 8, Transitional Provisions and Savings) Order 2008, SI 2008/2860, art 3(l).

[64] Companies Act 2006 (Commencement No 8, Transitional Provisions and Savings) Order 2008, SI 2008/2860, art 3(l).

ª  Section 677(1) replaces CA 1985, s 152(1)(a) without material amendment.
ᵇ  Section 677(2) and (3) replaces CA 1985, s 152(2) without material amendment.
COMMENCEMENT DATE  1 October 2009[65]

Part 18 Chapter 2 (sections 677 to 683) replaced the Companies Act 1985, sections 151 to 154 in their  **18.677.02**
entirety from 1 October 2009; but those sections and sections 155 to 158 (containing the so-called
'whitewash' provisions available for private companies) were repealed in relation to private companies
from 1 October 2008. Section 151 contained a general prohibition[66] on the giving of financial assistance
by a company or any of its subsidiaries for the purpose of the acquisition of shares in the company
either at or before the acquisition[67] or after the acquisition.[68] One of the principal features of the 2006
Act, highlighted by the Department of Business, Innovation and Skills (BIS) as a 'key benefit to private
companies'[69] is the removal of the prohibition against private companies providing financial assistance
for the purchase of their own shares. The saving of transaction costs to private companies resulting
from the change in the legislation has been estimated as being as much as £20 million per annum.[70]
This was introduced from 1 October 2008, but with the financial assistance prohibition being retained
for public companies.[71] This is in order to comply with the Second Company Law Directive.[72]

The general prohibition found in the 1985 Act had its origins in section 16 of the Companies Act 1928[73]  **18.677.03**
in which a statutory prohibition against the provision by a company of financial assistance for the
purpose of or in connection with a purchase made or to be made by any person of shares in the
company was first introduced into English statute law. The same prohibition, extended so as to apply
to a subscription for shares as well as to a purchase[74] and to financial assistance provided by a
subsidiary, was repeated in the Companies Act 1948, section 54, amended by the Companies Act
1980,[75] and in the Companies Act 1981, section 43. It was the 1981 Act which introduced the
conditional exemption for private companies which permitted them to give financial assistance in
connection with the acquisition of its own shares or of shares in its holding company provided that the
company had net assets which were not reduced thereby or, to the extent that its net assets were
reduced, where the assistance was provided out of distributable profits.[76] The 1981 Act supplied a
detailed procedure with which a private company had to comply before it could lawfully provide the
financial assistance[77] which was the precursor of the 'whitewash' procedure supplied in the Companies
Act 1985, sections 155 to 158.

The central aim of the prohibition is to prevent resources of a target company or its subsidiaries being  **18.677.04**
used to finance an acquisition of shares in the target to the detriment of creditors or shareholders.
Although it is a criminal offence for a company to give prohibited financial assistance, the courts have
generally taken a broad view of the prohibition, this being most apparent in the judgment of Arden LJ
in *Chaston v SWP Group plc*,[78] declining to use a purposive construction to limit the scope of the
provisions (as explained in the judgment of Ward LJ in *Chaston* at [62]). But the courts have also, by
applying the 'commercial realities' test (referred to below at paragraph 18.677.06 and n 80), introduced
a mechanism which, in practice, gives a discretion to exclude from the scope of the prohibition genuine
commercial transactions which might otherwise have been technically illegal.

When considering whether or not the prohibition is applicable in any given case, it may be useful to ask  **18.677.05**
the following questions: First is there proposed, or has there been, an acquisition of shares in a target

---

[65]  Companies Act 2006 (Commencement No 8, Transitional Provisions and Savings) Order 2008, SI 2008/
2860, art 3(l).
[66]  Subject to exceptions set out in s 153 and to the relaxation for solvent private companies under the so-called
whitewash procedure in ss 155–158.
[67]  Section 151(1).
[68]  Section 151(2).
[69]  CA 2006: Major Business Benefits.
[70]  According to the Regulatory Impact Assessment URN 06/2234 Jan 2007, based on estimates provided by the
Law Society to the CLR.
[71]  Companies Act 2006 (Commencement No 5, Transitional Provisions and Savings) Order 2007, SI 2007/
3495, art 5(2), and see Sch 4, paras 51 and 52.
[72]  Directive (EEC) 77/91 [1977] OJ L26/1, Art 23.
[73]  Replaced, in turn, by CA 1929, s 45.
[74]  A statutory reversal of the decision in *Re VGM Holdings Limited* [1942] 1 Ch 235 in which the Court of
Appeal had held that the acquisition of shares in a company by application and allotment was not a 'purchase' and
so fell outside the prohibition, which was held not to cover a transaction by which a company provides money to
assist a subscription for its own shares.
[75]  Section 88 and Sch 3.
[76]  CA 1981, s 43(1)–(2).
[77]  CA 1981, ss 43(4)–(9) and 44.
[78]  [2003] 1 BCLC 675.

which is a public company, or a private company with a public company subsidiary (sections 678(1), (3); 679(1), (3))? Secondly, if so, is there something to be done by (i) the target or a subsidiary company, where the target is a public company, or (ii) by a public company subsidiary where the target is a private company, which can qualify as 'financial assistance' (section 677)? Thirdly, if so, is what is to be done being done either (i) for the purpose of the proposed acquisition (sections 678(1), 679(1)), or (ii) for the purpose of reducing or discharging a liability incurred for the purpose of the previous acquisition (sections 678(3), 679(3), 683(2)? Fourthly, if so, is the transaction nevertheless lawful by reason of some exemption (sections 678(2), (4), 679(2), (4), 681, 682)?

**18.677.06**    Although the opening words of section 677(1) (the section material for the second of the questions) suggest that it supplies the definition of 'financial assistance', the fact that each identified class itself uses the words 'financial assistance' as part of its definition means that in practice the section does little to define it.[79] Accordingly, the question whether or not a particular transaction constitutes 'financial assistance' within the scope of the prohibition will remain one to be resolved by reference to the 'commercial realities' of the situation on a case by case basis.[80] The transaction must be 'financial' and it must be 'assistance'. As to the latter, "assistance" involves something in the nature of aid or help. It cannot exist in a vacuum; it must be given to someone'.[81] Further, the 'commercial realities' test is to be applied in deciding whether the transaction was 'for the purpose' of a prohibited disposition (which it may be if it was to 'smooth the path'[82] to the disposition), or whether it was merely 'in connection with' the disposition.[83]

**18.677.07**    The term 'gift' used in relation to the first category of what may be financial assistance will include transactions which are gifts in substance: ie payments for which the company does not receive any consideration.[84] Depending on the circumstances, an undervalue transfer by the company may be a gift;[85] and overpayment may also amount to a gift.[86]

**18.677.08**    Both 'guarantee' and 'indemnity', used in relation to the second category, are recognized legal terms[87] and are to be given their ordinary legal meaning in section 677. An indemnity involves a contract by one party to protect the other against loss.[88] A guarantee is 'a contract to answer for the debt, default or miscarriage of another who is to be primarily liable to the promisee'.[89] It is to be noted that an indemnity in respect of the indemnifier's own neglect or default is outside this second category of financial assistance. This exclusion may be significant in any case where a company is raising share capital and is required to give an indemnity to an underwriter. The exclusion will not necessarily remove the relevant indemnity from the residual category of financial assistance—the fourth category referred to below.

---

[79]  *Cf AMG Global Nominees (private) Ltd v Africa Resources Ltd* [2009] 1 BCLC 281, [22], *per* Sir Andrew Morritt C: 'Though s 151(1)(a) purports to define "financial assistance" it does not do so because in the purported definitions it repeats the word "financial"'.

[80]  This was the approach of Hoffmann J in *Charterhouse v Tempest Diesels* [1986] BCLC 1, 5, when he held that the words 'financial assistance' in CA 1948, s 54 'have no technical meaning and their frame of reference is in my judgment the language of ordinary commerce. One must examine the commercial realities of the transaction and decide whether it can properly be described as the giving of financial assistance by the company, bearing in mind that the section is a penal one and should not be strained to cover transactions which are not fairly within it'. This approach, of treating the expression 'financial assistance' as being non-technical and commercial, and allowing the court to examine the 'the commercial substance' of the transaction or look at 'commercial realities' has been endorsed by the Court of Appeal in *Chaston v SWP Group plc* [2003] 1 BCLC 675, [17]; *MT Realisations v Digital Equipment* [2003] 2 BCLC 117, [28]; and *Anglo Petroleum Ltd v TFB (Mortgages) Ltd* [2008] 1 BCLC 185, [26]ff upholding Peter Smith J [2006] EWHC 258, [131].

[81]  The quoted words are from *Sterileair Pty Ltd v Papallo* (unreported 16 November 1998), Federal Court of Australia, cited by Mummery LJ in *MT Realisations v Digital Equipment* [2003] 2 BCLC 117, [28] See also *Corporate Development Partners LLC v E-Relationship Marketing Ltd* [2007] EWHC 436 (Ch), [29], *per* Rimer J and the *obiter* remarks of Christopher Nugee QC in *Makram Barsoum Estafnous v London & Leeds Business Centres Limited* [2009] EWHC 1308 (Ch), [80].

[82]  Per Arden LJ in *Chaston v SWP Group plc* [2003] 1 BCLC 675, [38].

[83]  See per Rimer J in *Corporate Development Partners LLC v E-Relationship Marketing Ltd* [2007] EWHC 436 (Ch), [29].

[84]  *Plaut v Steiner* (1989) 5 BCC 352.

[85]  *Plaut v Steiner* (1989) 5 BCC 352, 364.

[86]  *Barclays Bank plc v British & Commonwealth Holdings plc* [1996] 1 BCLC 1, 41.

[87]  See *Barclays Bank plc v British & Commonwealth Holdings plc* [1996] 1 BCLC 1, 39.

[88]  *Yeoman Credit Ltd v Latter* [1961] 1 WLR 828, 831, *per* Holroyd Pearce LJ.

[89]  *Yeoman Credit Ltd v Latter* [1961] 1 WLR 828, 831, *per* Holroyd Pearce LJ.

The third category of transaction which can qualify as financial assistance is that of making a loan or any other agreement under which in effect credit is provided.[90] Essentially what is required is that the company acquires a debt, although the assignment of the benefit of a debt may also come within this category.

Where a company has no net assets, any form of financial assistance is prohibited.[91] This is because the final residual category of 'any other financial assistance' is not confined to transactions of the same type as the three other specified categories. This means that a case where a company's net assets are unaffected by the relevant transaction, or even if they are improved, potentially falls within the scope of the definition if the company has no net assets.[92]

Where a company has net assets, whether or not a reduction of net assets is 'material' is one of degree to be answered on the facts of the particular case.[93] However, while showing a reduction in a company's net assets to a material extent is necessary to qualify the company as a possible provider of financial assistance, this alone is insufficient; it remains necessary to identify the disposition of assets or assumption of liabilities by the company which are to count as the giving of financial assistance by the company.[94]

Section 677(2) and (3) make it clear that it is the actual value of the assets and liabilities and not merely their book value which is to be taken into account in determining the company's net asset position.[95]

## Circumstances in which financial assistance prohibited

### 678 Assistance for acquisition of shares in public company

(1) Where a person is acquiring or proposing to acquire shares in a public company, it is not lawful for that company, or a company that is a subsidiary of that company, to give financial assistance directly or indirectly for the purpose of the acquisition before or at the same time as the acquisition takes place.

(2) Subsection (1) does not prohibit a company from giving financial assistance for the acquisition of shares in it or its holding company if—
(a) the company's principal purpose in giving the assistance is not to give it for the purpose of any such acquisition, or
(b) the giving of the assistance for that purpose is only an incidental part of some larger purpose of the company,
and the assistance is given in good faith in the interests of the company.

(3) Where—
(a) a person has acquired shares in a company, and
(b) a liability has been incurred (by that or another person) for the purpose of the acquisition,
it is not lawful for that company, or a company that is a subsidiary of that company, to give financial assistance directly or indirectly for the purpose of reducing or discharging the liability if, at the time the assistance is given, the company in which the shares were acquired is a public company.

(4) Subsection (3) does not prohibit a company from giving financial assistance if—
(a) the company's principal purpose in giving the assistance is not to reduce or discharge any

---

[90] In *The Law Debenture Trust Corporation plc v The Ural Caspian Oil Corporation Ltd* (unreported, 21 July 1994) consideration was given to the meaning of 'any other agreement under with any of the obligations of the person giving the assistance are to be fulfilled at a time when in accordance with the agreement any obligation of another party to the agreement remains unfulfilled'. Vinelott J held that a future obligation to make a payment in unlikely circumstances contained in a commercial agreement under which a present asset was sold did not cause the agreement to amount to financial assistance within the category.

[91] Section 677(1)(d)(ii).

[92] Cf the decision of Laddie J in *MT Realisations Ltd (in liquidation) v Digital Equipment Co Ltd* [2003] BCC 415 on the wording of CA 1985, s 152(iv) (which read 'any other financial assistance given by a company the net assets of which are thereby reduced to a material extent or which has no net assets') where he held that the words 'which are thereby reduced' as they were placed in that section applied to both companies with net assets and those without. This was doubted by Arden LJ in *Chaston v SWP Group plc* [2003] 1 BCLC 675, [41], and not followed by Richard Sheldon QC in *Re Hill & Tyler Ltd* [2004] BCC 732. But in any event the rewording, rephrasing, and new punctuation which appear in s 677(1)(d) suggest that that argument is no longer available.

[93] *Parlett v Guppy's (Bridport) Ltd* [1996] 2 BCLC 34, 36, *per* Nourse LJ. Christopher Nugee QC in *Makram Barsoum Estafnous v London & Leeds Business Centres Limited* [2009] EWHC 1308 (Ch), [82](i) emphasized that the issue is not whether the acquisition as a whole causes the material reduction, but whether the financial assistance itself does so.

[94] *AMG Global Nominees (Private) Ltd v Africa Resources Ltd* [2009] 1 BCLC 281, [22].

[95] *Parlett v Guppy's (Bridport) Ltd* [1996] 2 BCLC 34, 42. Although in some cases the accounts of a company will sufficiently indicate the scale of the company's net assets: *Makram Barsoum Estafnous v London & Leeds Business Centres Limited* [2009] EWHC 1308 (Ch), [82](i).

liability incurred by a person for the purpose of the acquisition of shares in the company or its holding company, or

(b) the reduction or discharge of any such liability is only an incidental part of some larger purpose of the company,

and the assistance is given in good faith in the interests of the company.

(5) This section has effect subject to sections 681 and 682 (unconditional and conditional exceptions to prohibition).

COMMENCEMENT DATE 1 October 2009[96]

**18.678.02**    Subsections (1) and (3) of this section replicate the prohibition contained in the Companies Act 1985, sections 151(1) and (2) but confine it to the case where the shares the subject of the actual or proposed acquisition are shares in a company which is (or is at the time the financial assistance was given) a public company. Subsection (3) therefore catches the case where financial assistance is given for the acquisition of shares in a company which was a private company at the time the shares were acquired but which, at the time the post-acquisition assistance is given, has re-registered as a public company.

**18.678.03**    A 'public company' for this purpose is defined in the Companies Act 2006, section 4 and means a company limited by shares or limited by guarantee and having a share capital whose certificate of incorporation states that it is a public company, and in relation to which the requirements of the Companies Act 2006, or the former Companies Acts, as to registration or re-registration as a public company have been complied with on or after the relevant date. The 'former Companies Acts' is defined by section 1171 and means the Joint Stock Companies Acts, the Companies Act 1862 the Companies Consolidation Act 1908, the Companies Act 1929, the Companies Acts 1948 to 1983 and the provisions of the Companies Act 1985 and the Companies Consolidation (Consequential Provisions) Act 1985 that are no longer in force, and certain Northern Irish equivalents. 'Company' is defined by the Companies Act 2006, section 1 as meaning:

a company formed and registered under this Act, that is—

(a) a company so formed and registered after the commencement of this Part, or

(b) a company that immediately before the commencement of this Part—

(i) was formed and registered under the Companies Act 1985 (c. 6) or the Companies (Northern Ireland) Order 1986 (S.I. 1986/1032 (N.I. 6)), or

(ii) was an existing company for the purposes of that Act or that Order,

(which is to be treated on commencement as if formed and registered under this Act).[97]

**18.678.04**    An 'existing company' for the purposes of the Companies Act 1985 was defined[98] as meaning a company formed and registered under the former Companies Acts, but excluded a company registered under the Joint Stock Companies Acts, the Companies Act 1862, or the Companies (Consolidation) Act 1908 in what was then Ireland. The 'former Companies Acts' as that phrase is used in the Companies Act 1985 means the Joint Stock Companies Acts, the Companies Act 1862, the Companies (Consolidation) Act 1908, the Companies Act 1929, and the Companies Acts 1948 to 1983. The relevant date in relation to registration or re-registration in Great Britain is 22 December 1980, and in relation to registration or re-registration in Northern Ireland, 1 July 1983.[99] The section will therefore apply to targets which are (or were at the time the assistance is given) public companies registered under the UK Acts. However, where the relevant acquisition is or was of shares in a non-UK registered company, then the prohibition does not bite even if the assistance is given by a UK registered subsidiary.[100]

**18.678.05**    It appears, according to Arden LJ in *Chaston v SWP Group plc*,[101] that a 'person', for the purposes of section 678 may include the company itself.[102] Although a redemption of shares under Chapter 3 of Part 18 or purchase by a company of its own shares under Chapter 4 of Part 18 are expressly excluded from the prohibition by section 681(2)(d),[103] that section by itself does not exclude from the prohibition financial assistance given for the purpose of such an acquisition which would otherwise fall within the scope of section 678(1) or (3). Suppose, for example, a company is proposing to make a lawful own share purchase, having sufficient distributable profits. If, nevertheless, the company has to provide

---

[96] Companies Act 2006 (Commencement No 8, Transitional Provisions and Savings) Order 2008, SI 2008/2860, art 3(l).

[97] CA 2006, s 1(1).

[98] By s 735(1).

[99] CA 2006, s 4(3).

[100] See also Explanatory Notes, para 992.

[101] [2003] 1 BCLC 675, [47].

[102] See *Chaston v SWP Group plc* [2003] BCC 140, 154.

[103] Section 681(1).

security to its bank (but not if the bank already has security) in order to borrow the money to make the redemption, arguably the company will be giving financial assistance by way of security (section 677(1)(b)(i)) for the purpose of its own purchase of its own shares. This would be a surprising result: it is suggested that it cannot have been intended by Arden LJ.

The inclusion of the phrase 'proposing to acquire shares' in section 678(1)[104] means that a transaction may fall foul of the prohibition even if the proposed acquisition does not come to fruition.[105] It also means that transactions carried out by a company to groom itself for a sale may be caught, provided only that there is a proposing purchaser. It follows that a commitment by a target to pay a break fee, or to pay for an acquirer's due diligence, is likely to be found to be given for the purpose of the acquirer's proposed acquisition, not merely as an irrelevant inducement. However, what is likely to matter in this case is whether the target has no net assets or its commitment results in a material reduction in net assets so as to amount to 'financial assistance' within the residual category in section 677(1)(d).[106]

**18.678.06**

'Acquire' and 'acquiring' are not confined to a purchase of shares but extend the prohibition to cover a subscription or exchange of shares.[107]

**18.678.07**

The inclusion of the words 'a company that is' in the phrase 'a company that is a subsidiary of that company' are directed to clearing up an ambiguity which had existed under section 151.[108] As explained above,[109] 'company', as defined by the Companies Act 2006, section 1, means a company formed and registered under the Companies Act 2006 or under the other UK legislation referred to in that section. A non-UK registered company, although it may be a 'subsidiary' of the target,[110] will not therefore be '*a company* that is a subsidiary'. It follows that the prohibition does not extend to financial assistance given by subsidiary incorporated in an overseas jurisdiction.[111]

**18.678.08**

Central to the prohibition is the 'purpose' for which the financial assistance is given. The court will have regard to the commercial realities in deciding on the 'purpose' of the transaction alleged as involving prohibited financial assistance.[112] The practical consequence of an agreement infringing the prohibition will usually be that the court will not enforce it as an agreement to do something in breach of a statute. [113]

**18.678.09**

Section 678(2) and (4) contains the 'principal purpose' and 'incidental part of a larger purpose' exemptions formerly contained in the Companies Act 1985, section 153(1) and (2). It is a question of fact, in any case, whether the assistance given is for a 'larger purpose'. However, it is important to distinguish between the 'reasons' for the assistance and the 'purpose' for which it is given.[114] To qualify as a 'larger purpose' for the purposes of section 678(2), the purpose must be an independent purpose to which the provision of the assistance is an incident. It follows that the financial or commercial advantages flowing from the acquisition will not qualify as a 'larger purpose' as they are part only of the reason for forming the purpose of providing the assistance as opposed to constituting a purpose

**18.678.10**

---

[104] Replicating the use of that phrase in CA 1985, s 151(1)

[105] See *Chaston v SWP Group plc* [2003] 1 BCLC 675, [42], and also *Parlett v Guppy's (Bridport) Ltd* [1996] 2 BCLC 34, 47, per Nourse LJ (*obiter*) where he indicated that he would have rejected an argument that if no transfer of shares is made, no financial assistance is given. In *Makram Barsoum Estafnous v London & Leeds Business Centres Limited* [2009] EWHC 1308 (Ch), [77] Christopher Nugee QC (*obiter*) referred to the decision in *Chaston* and stated that 'a person can I think be described as proposing to acquire a company even if they have not carried out due diligence and reserve the right not to proceed if the due diligence might turn up something that would cause them to abandon the proposal'.

[106] The 1 per cent of the value of an offer contemplated under Rule 21.2 of the City Code on Takeovers and Mergers as the maximum permitted 'de minimis' inducement fee is not necessarily appropriate as a guide to the maximum reduction in the target's net assets which would not be regarded as 'material'. As to break fees, see the judgment of Jonathan Hirst QC sitting as a Deputy Judge of the High Court in *ParOS Plc v Worldlink Group Plc* [2012] EWHC 394 (Comm), [2012] All ER (D) 133 (Mar) at [69]-[72] (decided under the CA 1985 provisions).

[107] Cf *Re VGM Holdings Ltd* [1942] Ch 235 construing the words of CA 1929, s 45 which used the word 'purchase'. The words 'purchase' was replaced by 'purchase or subscription' in CA 1948, s 54(1) and that was replaced by 'acquire' and 'acquiring' in CA 1981, s 42.

[108] The words of which were 'it is not lawful for the company or any of its subsidiaries'.

[109] Paragraph 18.678.02 above.

[110] Subsidiary being defined in CA 2006, s 1159 and Sch 6.

[111] This reflects the decision of Millet J in *Arab Bank plc v Mercantile Holdings Ltd* [1994] 1 BCLC 330, applied by the Court of Appeal in *AMG Global Nominees (Private) Ltd v Africa Resources Ltd* [2009] 1 BCLC 281.

[112] See eg *Corporate Development Partners LLC v E-Relationship Marketing Ltd* [2007] EWHC 436 (Ch), [29] and [35], per Rimer J; see also *Anglo Petroleum Ltd v TFB (Mortgages) Ltd* [2008] 1 BCLC 185, and *Dyment v Boyden* [2005] BCC 79.

[113] *Makram Barsoum Estafnous v London & Leeds Business Centres Limited* [2009] EWHC 1308 (Ch), [82](iii), per Christopher Nugee QC (*obiter*).

[114] See per Lord Oliver in *Brady v Brady* [1989] AC 755, 779; and see also *Chaston v SWP* [2003] 1 BCLC 675.

distinct from and larger than it.[115] 'In good faith in the interests of the company' postulates a requirement that those responsible for procuring the company to provide the assistance act in the genuine belief that it is being done in the company's interests.[116]

**18.678.11**  Section 678(5) makes it clear that a transaction which would otherwise infringe the prohibition will fall outside it if any of the unconditional or conditional exceptions contained in sections 681 or 682 apply to it.

### 679 Assistance by public company for acquisition of shares in its private holding company

**18.679.01**
   (1)  Where a person is acquiring or proposing to acquire shares in a private company, it is not lawful for a public company that is a subsidiary of that company to give financial assistance directly or indirectly for the purpose of the acquisition before or at the same time as the acquisition takes place.

   (2)  Subsection (1) does not prohibit a company from giving financial assistance for the acquisition of shares in its holding company if—

     (a)  the company's principal purpose in giving the assistance is not to give it for the purpose of any such acquisition, or

     (b)  the giving assistance for that purpose is only an incidental part of some larger purpose of the company.

   and the assistance is given in good faith in the interests of the company.

   (3)  Where—

     (a)  a person has acquired shares in a private company, and

     (b)  a liability has been incurred (by that or another person) for the purpose of the acquisition,

   it is not lawful for a public company that is a subsidiary of that company to give financial assistance directly or indirectly for the purpose of reducing or discharging the liability.

   (4)  Subsection (3) does not prohibit a company from giving financial assistance if—

     (a)  the company's principal purpose in giving the assistance is not to reduce or discharge any liability incurred by a person for the purpose of the acquisition of shares in its holding company, or

     (b)  the reduction or discharge of any such liability is only an incidental part of some larger purpose of the company,

   and the assistance is given in good faith in the interests of the company.

   (5)  This section has effect subject to sections 681 and 682 (unconditional and conditional exceptions to prohibition).

COMMENCEMENT DATE  1 October 2009[117]

**18.679.02**  Section 679(1) extends the prohibition to financial assistance given by a public company which is a subsidiary of a private company for the purpose of an acquisition of shares in that private company before or at the same time as the acquisition takes place. Section 679(3) extends the prohibition to after the event financial assistance given by a public company to its private holding company.

**18.679.03**  As in section 678, the language of the section ('private company', 'public company that is a subsidiary of that company') makes it clear that the section will not apply to assistance given where the target parent company is not a UK company or by a company which is not UK registered. Further, this section will not apply where the company giving the assistance is not a public company, even if the assisting company is a UK-registered subsidiary of a public company. This is because the section only prohibits public companies from giving assistance.

**18.679.04**  As with section 678, in both cases, the prohibition is subject to 'principal purpose' and 'larger purpose' exemptions[118] and, section 679(5) makes it clear, this section has effect subject to sections 681 and 682 (unconditional and conditional exceptions to prohibition).

### 680 Prohibited financial assistance an offence

**18.680.01**
   (1)  If a company contravenes section 678(1) or (3) or section 679(1) or (3) prohibited financial assistance) an offence is committed by—

     (a)  the company, and

     (b)  every officer of the company who is in default.

   (2)  A person guilty of an offence under this section is liable—

---

[115]  *Brady v Brady* [1989] AC 755, 780.
[116]  *Brady v Brady* [1989] AC 755, 777.
[117]  Companies Act 2006 (Commencement No 8, Transitional Provisions and Savings) Order 2008, SI 2008/2860, art 3(1).
[118]  Section 679(2) and (4). See para 18.678.09 above.

(a)  on conviction on indictment, to imprisonment for a term not exceeding two years or a fine (or both);

(b)  on summary conviction—

(i)  in England and Wales, to imprisonment for a term not exceeding twelve months or to a fine not exceeding the statutory maximum (or both);

(ii)  in Scotland or Northern Ireland, to imprisonment for a term not exceeding six months, or to a fine not exceeding the statutory maximum (or both).

COMMENCEMENT DATE  1 October 2009[119]

This section creates the criminal offence and prescribes the criminal sanctions which flow from a breach of section 678(1) or (3) or section 679(1) or (3). For the purposes of this section, an 'officer' includes any director manager or secretary and any person who is to be treated as an officer for the purposes of the provision in question.[120] An officer will be 'in default' if he authorizes or permits, participates or fails to take all reasonable steps to prevent, the contravention.[121] A company which is an officer of another company, within the meaning supplied by section 1121(2), will not commit an offence as an officer in default unless one of its officers is in default.[122]    **18.680.02**

In addition to the criminal sanction for breach of the prohibition, a transaction which infringes the prohibition will be unenforceable between the parties and possibly void as unlawful.[123] In addition, any director of the company who is party to a breach of the prohibition is guilty of breaching the fiduciary duty which he owes to the company and is liable to the company in respect of any loss it suffers.[124]    **18.680.03**

*Exceptions from prohibition*

## 681  Unconditional exceptions

(1)  Neither section 678 nor section 679 prohibits a transaction to which this section applies.    **18.681.01**

(2)  Those transactions are—

(a)  a distribution of the company's assets by way of—

(i)  dividend lawfully made, or

(ii)  distribution in the course of a company's winding up;

(b)  an allotment of bonus shares;

(c)  a reduction of capital under Chapter 10 of Part 17;

(d)  a redemption of shares under Chapter 3 or a purchase of shares under Chapter 4 of this Part;

(e)  anything done in pursuance of an order of the court under Part 26 (order sanctioning compromise or arrangement with members or creditors);

(f)  anything done under an arrangement made in pursuance of section 110 of the Insolvency Act 1986 (c. 45) or Article 96 of the Insolvency (Northern Ireland) Order 1989 (S.I. 1989/2405 (N.I. 19)) (liquidator in winding up accepting shares as consideration for sale of company's property);

(g)  anything done under an arrangement made between a company and its creditors that is binding on the creditors by virtue of Part 1 of the Insolvency Act 1986 or Part 2 of the Insolvency (Northern Ireland) Order 1989 (S.I. 1989/2405 (N.I. 19)).

COMMENCEMENT DATE  1 October 2009[125]

Section 681[126] supplies a number of exceptions to the prohibition contained in sections 678 and 679. The conditions prescribed in this section are 'unconditional',[127] that is to say, they apply to both private and public companies and irrespective of the assisting company's net asset position. Whilst the section removes the listed transactions from the scope of the sections, it does not mention financial assistance    **18.681.02**

---

[119]  Companies Act 2006 (Commencement No 8, Transitional Provisions and Savings) Order 2008, SI 2008/2860, art 3(l).

[120]  The definition, which is not exhaustive of who may be an officer, is found in s 1121(2).

[121]  Section 1121(3).

[122]  Section 1122(1).

[123]  See *Heald v O'Connor* [1971] 1 WLR 497 (not following *Victor Battery Co Ltd v Curry's Ltd* [1946] Ch 242), *Brady v Brady* [1989] AC 755, and *Neilson v Stewart* [1991] BCC 713, 1991 SC, (HL) 22 For a discussion of the distinction between 'unenforceable' and 'void' in this context, and relevant authorities, see also the judgment of Jonathan Hirst QC, sitting as a Deputy Judge of the High Court in *ParOS Plc v Worldlink Group Plc* [2012] EWHC 394 (Comm), [2012] All ER (D) 133 (Mar) at [74]-[81].

[124]  *Re VGM Holdings Ltd* [1942] Ch 235, *Steen v Law* [1964] AC 287, *Selangor Rubber Estates Ltd v Craddock (No 3)* [1968] 1 WLR 1555, 1655.

[125]  Companies Act 2006 (Commencement No 8, Transitional Provisions and Savings) Order 2008, SI 2008/2860, art 3(l).

[126]  Which replaces CA 1985, s 153(3) without material amendment.

[127]  Cf those contained in s 682.

given for the purpose of those of the listed transactions which entail an acquisition of shares.[128] The exception provided for by section 681(2)(e) has been described as an unqualified power of the court in *Re Uniq Plc*.[129] In that case David Richards J declined to lay down a test for the exercise of the power since it was said that a general approach will develop as a result of its exercise in the circumstances of individual cases. In that particular case the financial assistance was sanctioned since it was commercially necessary for restructuring which was itself in the interests of creditors and members.

### 682 Conditional exceptions

**18.682.01**

(1) Neither section 678 nor section 679 prohibits a transaction to which this section applies—

    (a) if the company giving the assistance is a private company, or

    (b) if the company giving the assistance is a public company and—

        (i) the company has net assets that are not reduced by the giving of the assistance, or

        (ii) to the extent that those assets are so reduced, the assistance is provided out of distributable profits.

(2) The transactions to which this section applies are—

    (a) where the lending of money is part of the ordinary business of the company, the lending of money in the ordinary course of the company's business;

    (b) the provision by the company, in good faith in the interests of the company or its holding company, of financial assistance for the purposes of an employees' share scheme;

    (c) the provision of financial assistance by the company for the purposes of or in connection with anything done by the company (or another company in the same group) for the purpose of enabling or facilitating transactions in shares in the first-mentioned company or its holding company between, and involving the acquisition of beneficial ownership of those shares by—

        (i) bona fide employees or former employees of that company (or another company in the same group), or

        (ii) spouses or civil partners, widows, widowers or surviving civil partners, or minor children or step-children of any such employees or former employees;

    (d) the making by the company of loans to persons (other than directors) employed in good faith by the company with a view to enabling those persons to acquire fully paid shares in the company or its holding company to be held by them by way of beneficial ownership.

(3) The references in this section to 'net assets' are to the amount by which the aggregate of the company's assets exceeds the aggregate of its liabilities.

(4) For this purpose—

    (a) the amount of both assets and liabilities shall be taken to be as stated in the company's accounting records immediately before the financial assistance is given, and

    (b) 'liabilities' includes any amount retained as reasonably necessary for the purpose of providing for a liability the nature of which is clearly defined and that is either likely to be incurred or certain to be incurred but uncertain as to amount or as to the date on which it will arise.

(5) For the purposes of subsection (2)(c) a company is in the same group as another company if it is a holding company or subsidiary of that company or a subsidiary of a holding company of that company.

C OMMENCEMENT  D ATE  1 October 2009[130]

**18.682.02**    This section supplies exceptions to the prohibition contained in sections 678 and 679 where the conditions identified in subsection (2) are satisfied. The exceptions apply without restriction where the company giving the assistance is a private company. However, they apply where the company giving the assistance is a public company only if that company has net assets and either (i) those assets are not

---

[128] See *Chaston v SWP Group plc* [2003] 1 BCLC 675, 692, in which Arden LJ suggested that financial assistance given for the purpose of an acquisition by a company of its own shares might infringe the prohibition in s 151 giving as her example the case of an *unlimited* company and hence one to which the s 153(3) exemption (now, so far as material, the CA 2006, s 681(2) exemption) has no, at any rate no express, application. In *Re Hill & Tyler Ltd* [2004] BCC 732 Richard Sheldon QC held that where a company borrowed on security to raise money which would then be advanced by the company for the purpose of giving financial assistance, the giving of the security was indirectly for that purpose and prohibited. It is therefore possible that a transaction of the type in *Re Hill & Tyler Ltd* (for example, giving security by a company to enable the company to raise funds to be used in a transaction expressly permitted under s 681(2)) would be prohibited. However, in the light of *Anglo Petroleum Ltd v TFB (Mortgages) Ltd* [2008] 1 BCLC 185, [42] and [47]–[51] such a conclusion is unlikely. In this last case the Court of Appeal left open the question whether *Re Hill & Tyler Ltd* had been wrongly decided.

[129] [2011] EWHC 749 (Ch).

[130] Companies Act 2006 (Commencement No 8, Transitional Provisions and Savings) Order 2008, SI 2008/2860, art 3(l).

reduced by the giving of the assistance, or (ii) if and to the extent that its net assets are reduced, that the assistance is provided out of distributable profits.[131]

'Net assets' for the purpose of section 682, means the amount by which the aggregate of the company's **18.682.03** assets exceeds the amount of its liabilities[132] and the values to be placed on both is to be taken to be that as stated in the company books immediately before the financial assistance is given.[133] 'Liabilities' will include amounts retained against liabilities provided that the nature of the liability is clearly defined and one either likely to be incurred or certain to be incurred but uncertain as to amount or as to the date on which it will arise.[134]

'Distributable profits' is defined in section 683(1) and means those profits out of which the company **18.682.04** could lawfully make a distribution equal in value to that assistance. In addition, where the financial assistance consists of or includes, or is treated as arising in consequence of, the sale, transfer, or other disposition of a non-cash asset, any profit which the company would be entitled to treat as available for the purpose of such a transaction is included.[135] In each case, 'distribution', bears the same meaning as in Part 23.

In order to rely on the exemption contained in section 682(2)(a), the words of the subsection make it **18.682.05** clear that the company giving the assistance must be satisfy the following conditions:

(i)   where ordinary business of the company must include the lending of money;
(ii)  the financial assistance must be given by way of loan; and
(iii) the loan must be given in the ordinary course of the company's business.

> Only lending consistent with the normal course of the company's business and of a kind which the company ordinarily practised will qualify.[136] To be part of the ordinary business of a company, the lending of money must be a general lending of money, so that money so lent is at the borrower's free disposition and not, save in special circumstances, confined to special uses or restricted to particular and defined purposes.[137]

The exemption in clause 682(2)(b) will only apply where the financial assistance is given for the **18.682.06** purposes of an employees share scheme *and* that assistance is given in good faith in the interests of the company or its holding company.[138] An employees share scheme[139] is a scheme for encouraging or facilitating the holding of shares in or debentures of a company, any of its subsidiaries, the company's holding company or any of its subsidiaries, a subsidiary of the company's holding company, by or for the benefit of bona fide employees or former employees of the company, their spouses, civil partners, surviving spouses, surviving civil partners, minor children, or step-children.

The exemption in section 682(2)(c) is directed to removing from the ambit of the prohibition financial **18.682.07** assistance given for the purpose of or in connection with anything done by it for the purpose of enabling or facilitating transactions in shares between the company (or its holding company) between employees or former employees of the company or of another company in the same group as the company, or their spouses, civil partners, minor children, or step-children. This exemption is not confined to the case where there is a scheme in place provided the purpose is as set out in the subsection. There is no comparable requirement in this subsection that the assistance be given in good faith in the interests of the company or its holding company. However, the employees or former employees must be 'bona fide' and the transaction assisted must involve the acquisition by them of beneficial ownership in the shares. For the purposes of this subsection, a company is in the same group as another if it is a holding company or a subsidiary of that company or a subsidiary of a holding company of that company: section 682(5).

The last conditional exemption supplied by section 682 applies to loans given by the company to **18.682.08** persons (other than directors) employed in good faith by the company with a view to enabling them to acquire fully paid shares in the company or its holding company. Again, the transaction assisted must involve the acquisition by the employees of beneficial ownership in the shares. This exemption is

---

[131]  This replaces CA 1985, s 154(1).
[132]  Section 682(3), cf s 677(2).
[133]  Section 683(4)(a), cf s 677(3).
[134]  Section 682(4)(b).
[135]  Section 683(1)(b). For which profits, otherwise unrealized, may be so included, see s 846.
[136]  *Steen v Law* [1964] AC 287, 301–302.
[137]  *Steen v Law* [1964] AC 287, 302. The Privy Council in that case concluded that it was 'virtually impossible to see how loans, big or small, deliberately made by a company for the direct purpose of financing a purchase of its shares could ever be described as made in the ordinary course of its business'.
[138]  The words of CA 1985, s 153(4)(b) confined the interests to be considered to those of the company itself.
[139]  As defined in s 1166.

confined to financial assistance given by way of loan[140] and to employees of the company, employed by it in good faith. It does not extend to former employees or spouses etc of the employees.[141]

## *Supplementary*

### 683 Definitions for this Chapter

**18.683.01**
    (1) In this Chapter—
        'distributable profits', in relation to the giving of any financial assistance—
        (a) means those profits out of which the company could lawfully make a distribution equal in value to that assistance, and
        (b) includes, in a case where the financial assistance consists of or includes, or is treated as arising in consequence of, the sale, transfer or other disposition of a non-cash asset, any profit that, if the company were to make a distribution of that character would be available for that purpose (see section 846); and
        'distribution' has the same meaning as in Part 23 (distributions) (see section 829).
    (2) In this Chapter—
        (a) a reference to a person incurring a liability includes his changing his financial position by making an agreement or arrangement (whether enforceable or unenforceable, and whether made on his own account or with any other person) or by any other means, and
        (b) a reference to a company giving financial assistance for the purposes of reducing or discharging a liability incurred by a person for the purpose of the acquisition of shares includes its giving such assistance for the purpose of wholly or partly restoring his financial position to what it was before the acquisition took place.

COMMENCEMENT DATE 1 October 2009[142]

**18.683.02**    Section 683(1) supplies the definitions of 'distributable profits' and of 'distribution' for the purposes of section 677 to 682. The term 'distributable profits' appears in section 682(1)(b) and defines the profits out of which a public company may lawfully provide financial assistance where its net assets are reduced for the purposes of the conditional exemptions contained in that section.[143]

**18.683.03**    The term 'distribution' appears in section 681(1)(a) and in section 683 and carries the same meaning as in Part 23 of the Act.

**18.683.04**    Section 683(2) has replaced the Companies Act 1985, section 152(3) in the same terms. The effect of the section is to extend the meaning of the phrase 'incurring a liability' and 'reducing or discharging a liability'. 'Incurring a liability' will include a person changing his financial position by making an agreement or arrangement, whether or not the agreement or arrangement is enforceable and whether he makes it on his own account or with another person. 'Discharging a liability' includes the whole or partial restoration of the position of the accountable person to what it was before the acquisition of shares took place.

## CHAPTER 3
## REDEEMABLE SHARES

### 684 Power of limited company to issue redeemable shares

**18.684.01**
    (1) A limited company having a share capital may issue shares that are to be redeemed or are liable to be redeemed at the option of the company or the shareholder ('redeemable shares'), subject to the following provisions.
    (2) The articles of a private limited company may exclude or restrict the issue of redeemable shares.
    (3) A public limited company may only issue redeemable shares if it is authorised to do so by its articles.
    (4) No redeemable shares may be issued at a time when there are no issued shares of the company that are not redeemable.

COMMENCEMENT DATE 1 October 2009[144]

---

[140] Cf s 682(2)(b) and (c) which covers any type of financial assistance.

[141] Cf s 682(2)(b) and (c) both of which extend to such a class.

[142] Companies Act 2006 (Commencement No 8, Transitional Provisions and Savings) Order 2008, SI 2008/2860, art 3(l).

[143] See para 18.682.04 above.

[144] Companies Act 2006 (Commencement No 8, Transitional Provisions and Savings) Order 2008, SI 2008/2860, art 3(l).

This and the following five sections replaced the previous sections 159 and 160 of the 1985 Act. As well 　**18.684.02**
as involving some redrafting, they liberalized and redrafted the power of a limited company to issue
redeemable shares. Companies have long been allowed to issue redeemable preference shares and the
general power in this section to issue redeemable shares of any class was first introduced in the
Companies Act 1981.[145] It was recognized that allowing this did not infringe the principle of maintenance of capital, provided that appropriate safeguards were introduced.[146] It should be noted that all
the provisions apply only to limited companies; unlimited companies have never been subject to the
strict capital maintenance principles and would be free as a matter of common law to issue redeemable
shares.

As one of the measures intended to deregulate the law applying to private companies, there is no longer 　**18.684.03**
any need for them to have authority for such an issue in their articles, although, under subsection (3),
this remains a requirement for public companies and, under subsection (2), a private company's
articles can exclude or restrict the power.

It is possible to issue shares on terms that they will be redeemed or on terms that either the company or 　**18.684.04**
the shareholder has the option to redeem them. However, by virtue of subsection (4), a company must
have issued shares that are not redeemable, but clearly it would suffice if there was only one such issued
share. It is not possible to change the terms of an issue of shares to convert them into redeemable
shares,[147] but this is effectively academic now given the general power for a company to purchase any
of its own shares under Chapter 4 of this Part.

## 685  Terms and manner of redemption

(1) The directors of a limited company may determine the terms, conditions and manner of 　**18.685.01**
redemption of shares if they are authorised to do so—
  (a) by the company's articles, or
  (b) by a resolution of the company.
(2) A resolution under subsection (1)(b) may be an ordinary resolution, even though it amends the
company's articles.
(3) Where the directors are authorised under subsection (1) to determine the terms, conditions and
manner of redemption of shares—
  (a) they must do so before the shares are allotted, and
  (b) any obligation of the company to state in a statement of capital the rights attached to the
    shares extends to the terms, conditions and manner of redemption.
(4) Where the directors are not so authorised, the terms, conditions and manner of redemption of
any redeemable shares must be stated in the company's articles.

COMMENCEMENT DATE  1 October 2009[148]

This section liberalizes the previous requirements for the terms and manner in which shares are to be 　**18.685.02**
redeemed (referred to here as the 'redemption conditions'). Experience since the ability to issue
redeemable shares of any class was first introduced in 1980 showed that increased liberality was
desirable. Previously, these terms, conditions, and manner of redemption had in all cases to be
provided in the articles, but now the directors may determine them if authorized by resolution of the
company or by the articles, provided they do so before the shares are allotted. Clearly a company can
still choose to prescribe the redemption conditions in its articles and not give the directors authority to
do so, although it seems unlikely that many companies would do so. For the avoidance of doubt,
subsection (4) makes it clear that, if the directors are not so authorized, the terms, conditions, and
manner of redemption must be stated in the articles.

Whether the directors have authority or the matter is covered by the company's articles, the full details 　**18.685.03**
of redemption must clearly be set out. It is easy to appreciate the distinction between 'terms and
conditions' and 'manner' of redemption, but it is perhaps not so easy to understand the distinction
between 'terms' and 'conditions', when 'terms' is usually understood to include 'conditions'. On the
other hand, given the reference to 'terms' in section 686, below, concerning the date of payment for
redemption, perhaps this word should be understood as referring to this aspect, with 'conditions'
being, for example, provisions that determine how the price for redemption is to be determined.

The reference in subsection (2) to the possibility of an authorizing resolution altering the articles is 　**18.685.04**
clearly aimed primarily at companies registered before this Part of the Act came into force on 1 October

---

[145] The Act does not repeat the savings in s 180 of the 1985 Act.
[146] See the following sections.
[147] *Re St James' Court Estate Ltd* [1944] Ch 6.
[148] Companies Act 2006 (Commencement No 8, Transitional Provisions and Savings) Order 2008, SI
2008/2860, art 3(l).

2009, whose articles contain the redemption conditions and have not been otherwise amended. Publicity for the redemption conditions is ensured by the fact that they must be included in the statement of capital that will have to be included with the return of allotment of redeemable shares.[149]

### 686  Payment for redeemable shares

**18.686.01**      (1)  Redeemable shares in a limited company may not be redeemed unless they are fully paid.
         (2)  The terms of redemption of shares in a limited company may provide that the amount payable on redemption may, by agreement between the company and the holder of the shares, be paid on a date later than the redemption date.
         (3)  Unless redeemed in accordance with a provision authorised by subsection (2), the shares must be paid for on redemption.

COMMENCEMENT DATE  1 October 2009[150]

**18.686.02**    As under the previous law, redeemable shares can only be redeemed if they are fully paid up, but this section relaxes some former requirements. Whereas previously redeemable shares always had to be paid for on redemption, it is now possible under subsection (2) for the terms of redemption, that is the terms on which the shares were issued, to provide that the amount payable is, if both the company and the shareholder agree, to be paid for at a later date. Otherwise, under subsection (3), they must be paid for on redemption, and an agreement to pay by instalments will be illegal and void.[151] This additional flexibility was recommended by the Steering Group of the Company Law Review. It applies not just to shares issued on and after 1 October 2009 but also to shares issued before that date where the terms of redemption have been amended on or after that date to allow for payment on a date later than the redemption date.[152] If there is no such amendment, so much of the former provision (section 159(3) of the 1985 Act) as requires payment on redemption continues to apply in any other case.[153]

**18.686.03**    Payment for redeemable shares includes payment in kind as well as payment in money.[154]

### 687  Financing of redemption

**18.687.01**      (1)  A private limited company may redeem redeemable shares out of capital in accordance with Chapter 5.
         (2)  Subject to that, redeemable shares in a limited company may only be redeemed out of—
             (a)  distributable profits of the company, or
             (b)  the proceeds of a fresh issue of shares made for the purposes of the redemption.
         (3)  Any premium payable on redemption of shares in a limited company must be paid out of distributable profits of the company, subject to the following provision.
         (4)  If the redeemable shares were issued at a premium, any premium payable on their redemption may be paid out of the proceeds of a fresh issue of shares made for the purposes of the redemption, up to an amount equal to—
             (a)  the aggregate of the premiums received by the company on the issue of the shares redeemed, or
             (b)  the current amount of the company's share premium account (including any sum transferred to that account in respect of premiums on the new shares),
             whichever is the less.
         (5)  The amount of the company's share premium account is reduced by a sum corresponding (or by sums in the aggregate corresponding) to the amount of any payment made under subsection (4).
         (6)  This section is subject to section 735(4) (terms of redemption enforceable in a winding up).

COMMENCEMENT DATE  1 October 2009[155]

**18.687.02**    This section deals with the financing of a redemption of redeemable shares. It re-enacts without any changes in substance the requirements in the former section 160 of the 1985 Act, although the drafting is a little different, in particular subsection (1) drawing attention to the ability of a private company to finance a redemption out of capital.

---

[149]  As to this, see para 17.555.02 above.
[150]  Companies Act 2006 (Commencement No 8, Transitional Provisions and Savings) Order 2008, SI 2008/2860, art 3(l).
[151]  *Pena v Dale* [2004] 2 BCLC 508, [107]–[114].
[152]  Companies Act 2006 (Commencement No 8, Transitional Provisions and Savings) Order 2008, SI 2008/2860 Sch 2, para 73.
[153]  Companies Act 2006 (Commencement No 8, Transitional Provisions and Savings) Order 2008, SI 2008/2860 Sch 2, para 73.
[154]  *BDG Roof-Bond Ltd v Douglas* [2000] 1 BCLC 401.
[155]  Companies Act 2006 (Commencement No 8, Transitional Provisions and Savings) Order 2008, SI 2008/2860, art 3(l).

So, unless a private company uses capital under Chapter 5, a company must fund a basic redemption **18.687.03** out of distributable profits or the proceeds of a fresh issue made for the purpose. If distributable profits are used,[156] they have to be assessed in accordance with the general requirements relating to distributions,[157] including being supported by an unqualified auditor's report.[158]

If a premium is payable on redemption, then it must, by subsection (3) be paid out of distributable **18.687.04** profits, except that it can be funded out of any premium received from a fresh issue up to the amount of the premium originally received when the shares were issued or out of the share premium account, which is then reduced in accordance with subsection (4). The amount of the share premium account available for this purpose is the current amount including any amount represented by the premium on the new shares issued.[159] In this way capital is maintained despite the redemption.

It has been held in New Zealand, that it is not permissible for a company to give security over its assets **18.687.05** for a redemption of redeemable shares, as this would violate the principle of maintenance of capital;[160] this seems correct in principle.

### 688  Redeemed shares treated as cancelled

Where shares in a limited company are redeemed—                                        **18.688.01**

    (a)   the shares are treated as cancelled, and
    (b)   the amount of the company's issued share capital is diminished accordingly by the nominal value of the shares redeemed.

COMMENCEMENT DATE  1 October 2009[161]

This section repeats the substance of what was previously in section 160(4) of the 1985 Act, although it **18.688.02** does not repeat the fact that authorized capital is not affected by a redemption, since the concept of authorized capital has been abolished.[162] Although the amount of the company's issued capital is diminished by the nominal value of the shares redeemed, because the shares redeemed are treated as cancelled, in many cases the company will be obliged to create a capital redemption reserve under section 733.[163]

### 689  Notice to registrar of redemption

    (1)  If a limited company redeems any redeemable shares it must within one month after doing so give **18.689.01** notice to the registrar, specifying the shares redeemed.
    (2)  The notice must be accompanied by a statement of capital.
    (3)  The statement of capital must state with respect to the company's share capital immediately following the redemption—
        (a)   the total number of shares of the company,
        (b)   the aggregate nominal value of those shares,
        (c)   for each class of shares—
            (i)   prescribed particulars of the rights attached to the shares,
            (ii)  the total number of shares of that class, and
            (iii) the aggregate nominal value of shares of that class, and
        (d)   the amount paid up and the amount (if any) unpaid on each share (whether on account of the nominal value of the share or by way of premium).
    (4)  If default is made in complying with this section, an offence is committed by—
        (a)   the company, and
        (b)   every officer of the company who is in default.
    (5)  A person guilty of an offence under this section is liable on summary conviction to a fine not exceeding level 3 on the standard scale and, for continued contravention, a daily default fine not exceeding one-tenth of level 3 on the standard scale.

COMMENCEMENT DATE  1 October 2009[164]

---

[156]  Distributable profits are defined in s 736 by reference to the general definition in s 830; see para 28.830.02.
[157]  See Part 23.
[158]  *BDG Roof-Bond Ltd v Douglas* [2000] 1 BCLC 401.
[159]  As to the share premium account, see para 17.610.02 above.
[160]  *Supercool Refrigeration & Air Conditioning v Hoverd Industries Ltd* [1994] 3 NZLR 300.
[161]  Companies Act 2006 (Commencement No 8, Transitional Provisions and Savings) Order 2008, SI 2008/2860, art 3(l).
[162]  See para 2.8.02.
[163]  See para 18.733.02 below.
[164]  Companies Act 2006 (Commencement No 8, Transitional Provisions and Savings) Order 2008, SI 2008/2860, art 3(l). As to transitional arrangements, see Ibid, Sch 2, para 74.

**18.689.02**    This section imposes the filing obligations on a company that has redeemed any redeemable shares. It is spelt out separately from other filing obligations, consistent with the general scheme of the Act. The notice must be filed within one month of the redemption, specifying the shares redeemed, and be accompanied by the usual up-to-date statement of capital, the requirements for which are the same as for the original statement under section 10 and other subsequent capital changes.[165]

**18.689.03**    The penalties for default fall on both the company and every officer in default.[166]

# CHAPTER 4
## PURCHASE OF OWN SHARES

### *General provisions*

### 690  Power of limited company to purchase own shares

**18.690.01**    (1)  A limited company having a share capital may purchase its own shares (including any redeemable shares), subject to—
     (a)  the following provisions of this Chapter, and
     (b)  any restriction or prohibition in the company's articles.
    (2)  A limited company may not purchase its own shares if as a result of the purchase there would no longer be any issued shares of the company other than redeemable shares or shares held as treasury shares.

COMMENCEMENT DATE  1 October 2009[167]

**18.690.02**    The ability of limited companies to purchase their own shares[168] was first introduced in the Companies Act 1981. Although *prima facie* a departure from traditional principles regarding the maintenance of capital, so that the common law forbad such a purchase,[169] there is in fact no breach of the principle if the payment is not made out of capital, which will always be the case for a public limited company, as made clear by the following sections. A private limited company may pay for its own shares out of capital as explained further in the annotations to sections 709 to 723.

**18.690.03**    The original provisions were subsequently amended to liberalize the law further, in particular by allowing publicly traded shares purchased by a company to be held in treasury. They were further amended, as well as restated, in this Act, in removing the previous requirement for authority to be given by a company's articles. However, as subsection 1(b) indicates, the power can be restricted or prohibited in the articles. By virtue of subsection (2), following such a purchase there must always be at least one issued share in the company that is not a redeemable share or a treasury share.

### 691  Payment for purchase of own shares

**18.691.01**    (1)  A limited company may not purchase its own shares unless they are fully paid.
    (2)  Where a limited company purchases its own shares, the shares must be paid for on purchase.

COMMENCEMENT DATE  1 October 2009[170]

**18.691.02**    The meaning of this section is clear, so that partly paid shares cannot be purchased by the company and payment must be made on purchase. There is no provision for payment by instalments, in contrast with the position regarding redeemable shares[171] and an agreement to pay by instalments will be illegal and void.[172] However, the company will not be able to recover the money paid to a shareholder

---

[165] For detailed consideration, see the commentary to s 10.

[166] As to the meaning of 'officer in default', see s 1121.

[167] Companies Act 2006 (Commencement No 8, Transitional Provisions and Savings) Order 2008, SI 2008/2860, art 3(l).

[168] Unlimited companies have always been able to do so: *Re Borough Commercial Building Society* [1893] 2 Ch 242.

[169] *Trevor v Whitworth* (1887) 12 App Cas 409. The principle is confirmed generally in s 658; see para 18.658.02.

[170] Companies Act 2006 (Commencement No 8, Transitional Provisions and Savings) Order 2008, SI 2008/2860, art 3(l).

[171] See s 686. Obviously there is a clear difference because the terms of redemption, that is part of the original bargain, can so provide, whereas this would be impossible in the case of a purchase.

[172] *Pena v Dale* [2004] 2 BCLC 508, [107]–[114]; *Kinlan v Crimmin* [2006] EWHC 779 (Ch), [2007] BCC 106, [46]–[50].

in breach of this requirement because of a mistake of law or fact, if the latter has changed his position.[173]

## 692  Financing of purchase of own shares

(1) A private limited company may purchase its own shares out of capital in accordance with Chapter 5.

(2) Subject to that—

    (a) a limited company may only purchase its own shares out of—

        (i) distributable profits of the company, or

        (ii) the proceeds of a fresh issue of shares made for the purpose of financing the purchase, and

    (b) any premium payable on the purchase by a limited company of its own shares must be paid out of distributable profits of the company, subject to subsection (3).

(3) If the shares to be purchased were issued at a premium, any premium payable on their purchase by the company may be paid out of the proceeds of a fresh issue of shares made for the purpose of financing the purchase, up to an amount equal to—

    (a) the aggregate of the premiums received by the company on the issue of the shares purchased, or

    (b) the current amount of the company's share premium account (including any sum transferred to that account in respect of premiums on the new shares),

    whichever is the less.

(4) The amount of the company's share premium account is reduced by a sum corresponding (or by sums in the aggregate corresponding) to the amount of any payment made under subsection (3).

(5) This section has effect subject to section 735(4) (terms of purchase enforceable in a winding up).

COMMENCEMENT DATE 1 October 2009[174]

18.692.01

This section repeats the basic requirements for financing a purchase of shares out of capital in the same terms as are provided for by section 687 regarding redeemable shares. The restatement of the provision highlights in subsection (1) the ability of private companies to finance a purchase out of capital.

18.692.02

So, unless a private company uses capital under Chapter 5, a company must fund a purchase of its own shares out of distributable profits or the proceeds of a fresh issue made for the purpose. If distributable profits are used,[175] they have to be assessed in accordance with the general requirements relating to distributions,[176] including being supported by an unqualified auditor's report.[177]

18.692.03

If a premium is payable on a purchase, then it must, by subsection (2)(b) be paid out of distributable profits, except that it can be funded out of any premium received from a fresh issue up to the amount of the premium originally received when the shares were issued or out of the share premium account, which is then reduced in accordance with subsection (4). The amount of the share premium account available for this purpose is the current amount including any amount represented by the premium on the new shares issued.[178]

18.692.04

## *Authority for purchase of own shares*

## 693  Authority for purchase of own shares

(1) A limited company may only purchase its own shares—

    (a) by an off-market purchase, in pursuance of a contract approved in advance in accordance with section 694;

    (b) by a market purchase, authorised in accordance with section 701.

(2) A purchase is 'off-market' if the shares either—

    (a) are purchased otherwise than on a recognised investment exchange, or

    (b) are purchased on a recognised investment exchange but are not subject to a marketing arrangement on the exchange.

18.693.01

---

[173] *Kinlan v Crimmin* [2006] EWHC 779 (Ch), [56]–[60], [2007] BCC 106, applying the principle established in *Lipkin Gorman v Karpale Ltd* [1991] 2 AC 548 and *Kleinwort Benson Ltd v Lincoln City Council* [1999] 2 AC 349.

[174] Companies Act 2006 (Commencement No 8, Transitional Provisions and Savings) Order 2008, SI 2008/2860, art 3(l).

[175] Distributable profits are defined in s 736 by reference to the general definition in s 930; see para 23.830.02.

[176] See Part 23.

[177] *BDG Roof-Bond Ltd v Douglas* [2000] 1 BCLC 401.

[178] As to the share premium account, see para 17.610.02 above.

(3) For this purpose a company's shares are subject to a marketing arrangement on a recognised investment exchange if—
   (a) they are listed under Part 6 of the Financial Services and Markets Act 2000 (c. 8), or
   (b) the company has been afforded facilities for dealings in the shares to take place on the exchange—
      (i) without prior permission for individual transactions from the authority governing that investment exchange, and
      (ii) without limit as to the time during which those facilities are to be available.
(4) A purchase is a 'market purchase' if it is made on a recognised investment exchange and is not an off-market purchase by virtue of subsection (2)(b).
(5) In this section 'recognised investment exchange' means a recognised investment exchange (within the meaning of Part 18 of the Financial Services and Markets Act 2000) other than an overseas exchange (within the meaning of that Part).

COMMENCEMENT DATE 1 October 2009[179]

**18.693.02** This section restates the two types of purchase by a company of its own shares that are permitted as previously provided in section 163 of the 1985 Act, namely an off-market purchase under a contract approved in advance or a market purchase authorized in advance. Subsection (1), in imposing this requirement, was added for additional clarity in the 2006 Act. The detailed requirements for the two different types of purchase are spelt out in the following sections. Section 693(1)(a) applies to contracts entered into on or after 1 October 2009 and to contracts entered into before then which provide that no shares may be purchased in pursuance of the contract until its terms have been authorized by special resolution and are in fact so authorized on or after that date.[180]

**18.693.03** A purchase will be a market purchase only if it is actually made on a recognized investment exchange, so that a purchase by a company with traded shares by means of a privately negotiated contract—an over-the-counter purchase—will be an off-market purchase. A recognized investment exchange is one that is recognized by the Financial Services Authority under the Financial Services and Markets Act 2000,[181] other than an overseas exchange, but any market purchase of shares that are listed under Part 6 of that Act will be a market purchase.

## *Authority for off-market purchase*

### 694 Authority for off-market purchase

**18.694.01**
(1) A company may only make an off-market purchase of its own shares in pursuance of a contract approved prior to the purchase in accordance with this section.
(2) Either—
   (a) the terms of the contract must be authorised by a special resolution of the company before the contract is entered into, or
   (b) the contract must provide that no shares may be purchased in pursuance of the contract until its terms have been authorised by a special resolution of the company.
(3) The contract may be a contract, entered into by the company and relating to shares in the company, that does not amount to a contract to purchase the shares but under which the company may (subject to any conditions) become entitled or obliged to purchase the shares.
(4) The authority conferred by a resolution under this section may be varied, revoked or from time to time renewed by a special resolution of the company.
(5) In the case of a public company a resolution conferring, varying or renewing authority must specify a date on which the authority is to expire, which must not be later than [five years][a] after the date on which the resolution is passed.
(6) A resolution conferring, varying, revoking or renewing authority under this section is subject to—
   section 695 (exercise of voting rights), and
   section 696 (disclosure of details of contract).

AMENDMENTS AND NOTES

[a] Substituted by the Companies (Share Capital and Acquisition by Company of its Own Shares) Regulations 2009, SI 2009/2022, reg 4.

COMMENCEMENT DATE 1 October 2009[182]

---

[179] Companies Act 2006 (Commencement No 8, Transitional Provisions and Savings) Order 2008, SI 2008/2860, art 3(l).
[180] Companies Act 2006 (Commencement No 8, Transitional Provisions and Savings) Order 2008, SI 2008/2860, Sch 2, para 76.
[181] As to these, see the registers part of the FSA's website, ⟨http://www.fsa.gov.uk⟩.
[182] Companies Act 2006 (Commencement No 8, Transitional Provisions and Savings) Order 2008, SI 2008/2860, art 3(l).

This and the following two sections lay down the detailed requirements for authorizing an off-market purchase of a company's own shares. In doing so, they recast the former sections 164 and 165 of the 1985 Act and set out the requirements in a clearer way. Where a resolution under those sections of the 1985 Act is in force immediately before 1 October 2009, it has effect on and after that date as if passed under these sections of the 2006 Act, and may be varied, revoked, or renewed accordingly.[183] Section 694 applies to contracts entered into on or after 1 October 2009 and to contracts entered into before then which provide that no shares may be purchased in pursuance of the contract until its terms have been authorized by special resolution and are in fact so authorized on or after that date.[184]                        **18.694.02**

As section 694(1) makes clear, and subsections (2) and (3) spell out in more detail, an off-market purchase can only be effected pursuant to either a contract authorized in advance or a contract that is conditional on general meeting authorization. As is made clear by subsection (3),[185] a conditional contract covers the situation where a company, which is likely to mean the directors of the company, wishes to enter into an option to purchase its own shares, whether it will have the right to purchase or be subject to an obligation to purchase. The previous legislation used the description 'contingent purchase contract' to cover this sort of conditional contract, but the 2006 Act dispensed with this description.                        **18.694.03**

The terms of a proposed contract or a purchase under a conditional contract require prior approval by special resolution.[186] Voting on the resolution is restricted by what is now section 695 and the details must be available for inspection in accordance with section 696. There is no time limit specified for private companies in respect of how long the authority lasts, but, by subsection (5), public companies must complete an authorized purchase within five years of the passing of the resolution. This period was introduced pursuant to liberalization measures in Directive (EC) 2006/68.[187] By subsection (4), any variation, revocation, or renewal of an authority similarly requires special resolution sanction.                        **18.694.04**

There are no specific criminal or civil penalties prescribed for breach of the requirements in this and the following sections, but it is clear that a contract purportedly entered into in pursuance of a resolution that does not comply with the section is void as a contract to perform an unlawful act, namely an unauthorized purchase by a company of its own shares,[188] and the criminal penalties specified in section 658[189] will apply. An agreement between the company and a shareholder for the purchase of his shares is not enforceable until it has been sanctioned under the section,[190] but specific performance of such a contract, for example under a *Tomlin* order, may be granted that is contingent on such sanction.[191]                        **18.694.05**

There is an important point of general application to this and the ensuing sections, which it is convenient to discuss here. As is clear from section 695, and indeed might be expected in many cases, an off-market purchase by a private company may be approved by written resolution rather than by the passing of a special resolution at a general meeting.[192] However, the extent to which the informal asset of all members to an off-market purchase, a principle that is expressly preserved by the Act,[193] will satisfy the requirements is not entirely clear. In *Re R W Peak (Kings Lynn) Ltd*,[194] the view was expressed that the various requirements of what was section 164 of the 1985 Act could not be waived, but more recent authority[195] suggests that the disclosure requirements now contained in section 696 can be dispensed with. In *Kinlan v Crimmin*,[196] the judge distinguished between requirements existing for the benefit of the members of the company, in particular the requirement of what is now section 696(2)(b) regarding disclosure at the registered office, and requirements imposed for the protection of creditors                        **18.694.06**

---

[183] Companies Act 2006 (Commencement No 8, Transitional Provisions and Savings) Order 2008, SI 2008/2860, Sch 2, para 75.

[184] Companies Act 2006 (Commencement No 8, Transitional Provisions and Savings) Order 2008, SI 2008/2860, Sch 2, para 76.

[185] This was previously separately defined in the former s 165.

[186] As to special resolutions and written resolutions that can be used by private companies, see s 283 and ss 288–300.

[187] [2006] OJ 264/32. See the Companies (Share Capital and Acquisition by Company of its Own Shares) Regulations 2009, SI 2009/2022, reg 4. Previously the period was 18 months.

[188] *Re R W Peak (Kings Lynn) Ltd* [1998] 1 BCLC 193.

[189] See para 18.658.02.

[190] *Western v Rigblast Holdings Ltd* 1989 GWD 23–950 (SC).

[191] *Vision Express (UK) Ltd v Wilson* [1998] BCC 173.

[192] As to written resolutions, see ss 288–300.

[193] Section 281(4); see para 13.281.03.

[194] [1998] 1 BCLC 193, esp 204–205.

[195] *BDG Roof-Bond Ltd v Douglas* [2000] 1 BCLC 401, 416–417 and *Kinlan v Crimmin* [2006] EWHC 779 (Ch), [2007] BCC 106, [40]–[45].

[196] See above.

of the company. The former could be waived by unanimous consent of the members, the latter could not be. This seems a sensible result provided that there is genuine agreement to a proper resolution approving the terms of the proposed contract, which is filed with the registrar.[197] Whether this is now permitted by the terms of section 696(5) is further discussed in the notes to that section.

### 695 Resolution authorising off-market purchase: exercise of voting rights

**18.695.01**
(1) This section applies to a resolution to confer, vary, revoke or renew authority for the purposes of section 694 (authority for off-market purchase of own shares).
(2) Where the resolution is proposed as a written resolution, a member who holds shares to which the resolution relates is not an eligible member.
(3) Where the resolution is proposed at a meeting of the company, it is not effective if—
   (a) any member of the company holding shares to which the resolution relates exercises the voting rights carried by any of those shares in voting on the resolution, and
   (b) the resolution would not have been passed if he had not done so.
(4) For this purpose—
   (a) a member who holds shares to which the resolution relates is regarded as exercising the voting rights carried by those shares not only if he votes in respect of them on a poll on the question whether the resolution shall be passed, but also if he votes on the resolution otherwise than on a poll;
   (b) any member of the company may demand a poll on that question;
   (c) a vote and a demand for a poll by a person as proxy for a member are the same respectively as a vote and a demand by the member.

COMMENCEMENT DATE  1 October 2009[198]

**18.695.02**  The effect of this section, the requirements of which were previously in section 164(5) of the 1985 Act, is that the member whose shares are the subject of the proposed contract or contingent purchase contract for an off-market purchase is disenfranchised from voting, whether on a show of hands or a poll and in person or by proxy, on the special resolution. If he does vote, his votes must not be counted. It applies to any variation, revocation, or renewal of authority as well as the original sanctioning of such a contract.

**18.695.03**  If the resolution is proposed as a written resolution, the same effect applies under subsection (2) by providing that a member in question is not an eligible member.[199]

**18.695.04**  Any member and their proxy have a statutory right to demand a poll, whatever the company's articles provide.

### 696 Resolution authorising off-market purchase: disclosure of details of contract

**18.696.01**
(1) This section applies in relation to a resolution to confer, vary, revoke or renew authority for the purposes of section 694 (authority for off-market purchase of own shares).
(2) A copy of the contract (if it is in writing) or a memorandum setting out its terms (if it is not) must be made available to members—
   (a) in the case of a written resolution, by being sent or submitted to every eligible member at or before the time at which the proposed resolution is sent or submitted to him;
   (b) in the case of a resolution at a meeting, by being made available for inspection by members of the company both—
     (i) at the company's registered office for not less than 15 days ending with the date of the meeting, and
     (ii) at the meeting itself.
(3) A memorandum of contract terms so made available must include the names of the members holding shares to which the contract relates.
(4) A copy of the contract so made available must have annexed to it a written memorandum specifying such of those names as do not appear in the contract itself.
(5) The resolution is not validly passed if the requirements of this section are not complied with.

COMMENCEMENT DATE  1 October 2009[200]

---

[197] Under s 707; see para 18.707.02 below.
[198] Companies Act 2006 (Commencement No 8, Transitional Provisions and Savings) Order 2008, SI 2008/2860, art 3(l).
[199] See s 289 for the general definition of eligible member in relation to a written resolution.
[200] Companies Act 2006 (Commencement No 8, Transitional Provisions and Savings) Order 2008, SI 2008/2860, art 3(l).

This section specifies the disclosure requirements that must be complied with in connection with a proposed contract to purchase a company's own shares or a proposed purchase under a conditional contract, whether it concerns an original proposal or the variation, revocation, or renewal of such a proposal.    **18.696.02**

In cases under the provision that this section replaces, it has been held that the unanimous consent of the members can in effect dispense with these requirements, because they are for the benefit of members only.[201] Presumably any such assent must be properly informed assent though. What is not clear is whether these authorities are effectively reversed by subsection (5), providing that a resolution is not validly passed if the requirements of the section are not complied with. There was no exact equivalent to this subsection in the previous provisions, although they did contain clearly mandatory requirements that were satisfied by unanimous consent. Given that some of the principal purposes of the 2006 Act were said to be simplification and deregulation, it would be strange if fully informed unanimous consent were not permitted to override the detailed requirements.    **18.696.03**

Because a written resolution can be used by a private company to sanction an off-market purchase, subsection (2)(a) modifies the requirements of the section appropriately, in particular by providing that the disclosure requirements must be satisfied by the supply of the relevant documents to each relevant member at or before the time the resolution is given to him for signature. Although this is expressed as a mandatory requirement, presumably the unanimous consent principle could dispense with it.    **18.696.04**

In the case of a resolution at a meeting, a copy of the contract if it is in writing, or a written memorandum of its terms if it is not, must be available for inspection by members at the company's registered office for at least 15 days before the meeting and at the meeting itself. Any memorandum must include the names of all the members whose shares are the subject of the proposal (subsection (3)) and any contract that does not contain all the names must have a written memorandum attached that does include the names not in the contract (subsection (4)).    **18.696.05**

### 697 Variation of contract for off-market purchase

(1) A company may only agree to a variation of a contract authorised under section 694 (authority for off-market purchase) if the variation is approved in advance in accordance with this section.    **18.697.01**

(2) The terms of the variation must be authorised by a special resolution of the company before it is agreed to.

(3) That authority may be varied, revoked or from time to time renewed by a special resolution of the company.

(4) In the case of a public company a resolution conferring, varying or renewing authority must specify a date on which the authority is to expire, which must not be later than [five years][a] after the date on which the resolution is passed.

(5) A resolution conferring, varying, revoking or renewing authority under this section is subject to—
    section 698 (exercise of voting rights), and
    section 699 (disclosure of details of variation).

AMENDMENTS AND NOTES

[a] Substituted by the Companies (Share Capital and Acquisition by Company of its Own Shares) Regulations 2009, SI 2009/2022, reg 4.

COMMENCEMENT DATE 1 October 2009[202]

This and the following two sections make special provision for the situation where it is proposed to vary a contract to purchase a company's own shares by an off-market purchase or under a conditional contract. However, the requirements for a special resolution to approve the variation in advance are in effect identical to those imposed by section 694 concerning an original proposal, and the notes to that section should be consulted for commentary. Note that the previous period of 18 months in subsection (4) was extended to five years.[203]    **18.697.02**

### 698 Resolution authorising variation: exercise of voting rights

(1) This section applies to a resolution to confer, vary, revoke or renew authority for the purposes of section 697 (variation of contract for off-market purchase of own shares).    **18.698.01**

---

[201] *BDG Roof-Bond Ltd v Douglas* [2000] 1 BCLC 401, 416–417 and *Kinlan v Crimmin* [2006] EWHC 779 (Ch), [2007] BCC 106, [40]–[45], discussed in the notes to s 694.
[202] Companies Act 2006 (Commencement No 8, Transitional Provisions and Savings) Order 2008, SI 2008/2860, art 3(l).
[203] See the Companies (Share Capital and Acquisition by Company of its Own Shares) Regulations 2009, SI 2009/2022, reg 4.

(2) Where the resolution is proposed as a written resolution, a member who holds shares to which the resolution relates is not an eligible member.

(3) Where the resolution is proposed at a meeting of the company, it is not effective if—

(a) any member of the company holding shares to which the resolution relates exercises the voting rights carried by any of those shares in voting on the resolution, and

(b) the resolution would not have been passed if he had not done so.

(4) For this purpose—

(a) a member who holds shares to which the resolution relates is regarded as exercising the voting rights carried by those shares not only if he votes in respect of them on a poll on the question whether the resolution shall be passed, but also if he votes on the resolution otherwise than on a poll;

(b) any member of the company may demand a poll on that question;

(c) a vote and a demand for a poll by a person as proxy for a member are the same respectively as a vote and a demand by the member.

COMMENCEMENT DATE 1 October 2009[204]

**18.698.02** This section has the same effect concerning a proposed variation of an off-market contract to purchase its own shares as section 695 and is in virtually identical terms. It disenfranchises the members whose shares are the subject of the proposal and confers the same rights as does section 695. See the commentary to that section.

### 699 Resolution authorising variation: disclosure of details of variation

**18.699.01** (1) This section applies in relation to a resolution under section 697 (variation of contract for off-market purchase of own shares).

(2) A copy of the proposed variation (if it is in writing) or a written memorandum giving details of the proposed variation (if it is not) must be made available to members—

(a) in the case of a written resolution, by being sent or submitted to every eligible member at or before the time at which the proposed resolution is sent or submitted to him;

(b) in the case of a resolution at a meeting, by being made available for inspection by members of the company both—

(i) at the company's registered office for not less than 15 days ending with the date of the meeting, and

(ii) at the meeting itself.

(3) There must also be made available as mentioned in subsection (2) a copy of the original contract or, as the case may be, a memorandum of its terms, together with any variations previously made.

(4) A memorandum of the proposed variation so made available must include the names of the members holding shares to which the variation relates.

(5) A copy of the proposed variation so made available must have annexed to it a written memorandum specifying such of those names as do not appear in the variation itself.

(6) The resolution is not validly passed if the requirements of this section are not complied with.

COMMENCEMENT DATE 1 October 2009[205]

**18.699.02** This section imposes the disclosure requirements regarding a proposed variation of an approved contract for an off-market purchase of a company's own shares. It mirrors the requirements of section 696 save that, of necessity, it refers to disclosure of the proposed variation and, by subsection (3), requires disclosure at the same time of the original contract or memorandum of its terms.

### 700 Release of company's rights under contract for off-market purchase

**18.700.01** (1) An agreement by a company to release its rights under a contract approved under section 694 (authorisation of off-market purchase) is void unless the terms of the release agreement are approved in advance in accordance with this section.

(2) The terms of the proposed agreement must be authorised by a special resolution of the company before the agreement is entered into.

(3) That authority may be varied, revoked or from time to time renewed by a special resolution of the company.

(4) In the case of a public company a resolution conferring, varying or renewing authority must specify a date on which the authority is to expire, which must not be later than [five years][a] after the date on which the resolution is passed.

---

[204] Companies Act 2006 (Commencement No 8, Transitional Provisions and Savings) Order 2008, SI 2008/2860, art 3(1).

[205] Companies Act 2006 (Commencement No 8, Transitional Provisions and Savings) Order 2008, SI 2008/2860, art 3(1).

(5)  The provisions of—

>   section 698 (exercise of voting rights), and
>
>   section 699 (disclosure of details of variation),apply to a resolution authorising a proposed release agreement as they apply to a resolution authorising a proposed variation.

AMENDMENTS AND NOTES

^a  Substituted by the Companies (Share Capital and Acquisition by Company of its Own Shares) Regulations 2009, SI 2009/2022, reg 4.

COMMENCEMENT DATE  1 October 2009[206]

This section replaced section 167(2) of the 1985 Act. Where a resolution under section 167(2) was in force immediately before 1 October 2009, it has effect on and after that date as if passed under section 700 of the 2006 Act, and may be varied, revoked or renewed accordingly.[207] The section prohibits and renders void any release of the rights of the company in respect of an off-market purchase of a company's own shares unless the agreement to release rights is approved by special resolution. It contains the same basic requirements as section 694 and subsection (5) applies the provisions of sections 698 and 699 regarding voting rights and disclosure to a proposed release.     **18.700.02**

## *Authority for market purchase*

## 701  **Authority for market purchase**

(1)  A company may only make a market purchase of its own shares if the purchase has first been authorised by a resolution of the company.     **18.701.01**

(2)  That authority—
   (a)  may be general or limited to the purchase of shares of a particular class or description, and
   (b)  may be unconditional or subject to conditions.

(3)  The authority must—
   (a)  specify the maximum number of shares authorised to be acquired, and
   (b)  determine both the maximum and minimum prices that may be paid for the shares.

(4)  The authority may be varied, revoked or from time to time renewed by a resolution of the company.

(5)  A resolution conferring, varying or renewing authority must specify a date on which it is to expire, which must not be later than [five years]^a after the date on which the resolution is passed.

(6)  A company may make a purchase of its own shares after the expiry of the time limit specified if—
   (a)  the contract of purchase was concluded before the authority expired, and
   (b)  the terms of the authority permitted the company to make a contract of purchase that would or might be executed wholly or partly after its expiration.

(7)  A resolution to confer or vary authority under this section may determine either or both the maximum and minimum price for purchase by—
   (a)  specifying a particular sum, or
   (b)  providing a basis or formula for calculating the amount of the price (but without reference to any person's discretion or opinion).

(8)  Chapter 3 of Part 3 (resolutions affecting a company's constitution) applies to a resolution under this section.

AMENDMENTS AND NOTES

^a  Substituted by the Companies (Share Capital and Acquisition by Company of its Own Shares) Regulations 2009, SI 2009/2022, reg 4.

COMMENCEMENT DATE  1 October 2009[208]

This section replaced section 166 of the 1985 Act with some drafting changes, but no changes in effect other than the increase in the period in subsection (5). The requirements for authorizing a market purchase that it imposes are much more liberal than those required for an off-market purchase. There is no question of authorization of specific contracts, rather a general authority is conferred by ordinary resolution. Where a resolution under section 166 of the 1985 Act was in force immediately before 1     **18.701.02**

---

[206] Companies Act 2006 (Commencement No 8, Transitional Provisions and Savings) Order 2008, SI 2008/2860, art 3(l).

[207] Companies Act 2006 (Commencement No 8, Transitional Provisions and Savings) Order 2008, SI 2008/2860, Sch 2, para 75.

[208] Companies Act 2006 (Commencement No 8, Transitional Provisions and Savings) Order 2008, SI 2008/2860, art 3(l).

October 2009, it has effect on and after that date as if passed under this section of the 2006 Act, and may be varied, revoked, or renewed accordingly.[209]

**18.701.03**  The authority may be general or specific in the sense of being limited to the purchase of shares of a particular class or description. It may be unconditional or subject to conditions. The resolution must specify the maximum number of shares covered by the authority and the maximum and minimum prices to be paid. By subsection (7), price specification can be by the identification of particular sums of money or by the use of a basis or formula, provided that this is not linked to any person's opinion or discretion.

**18.701.04**  By subsection (5), the resolution must also give a date for expiry of the authority, which is five years from the date of the resolution. This period was introduced as a result of liberalization measures introduced by Directive (EC) 2006/68.[210] Even though the resolution required is only an ordinary one, it has to be filed under Chapter 3 of Part 3.[211]

**18.701.05**  Clearly a market purchase effected without authority or in breach of an authority would be void under section 658 as an illegal purchase by a company of its own shares.[212]

## *Supplementary provisions*

### 702  Copy of contract or memorandum to be available for inspection

**18.702.01**
(1)  This section applies where a company has entered into—
   (a)  a contract approved under section 694 (authorisation of contract for off-market purchase), or
   (b)  a contract for a purchase authorised under section 701 (authorisation of market purchase).
(2)  The company must keep available for inspection—
   (a)  a copy of the contract, or
   (b)  if the contract is not in writing, a written memorandum setting out its terms.
(3)  The copy or memorandum must be kept available for inspection from the conclusion of the contract until the end of the period of ten years beginning with—
   (a)  the date on which the purchase of all the shares in pursuance of the contract is completed, or
   (b)  the date on which the contract otherwise determines.
(4)  The copy or memorandum must be kept available for inspection—
   (a)  at the company's registered office, or
   (b)  at a place specified in regulations under section 1136.
(5)  The company must give notice to the registrar—
   (a)  of the place at which the copy or memorandum is kept available for inspection, and
   (b)  of any change in that place,
unless it has at all times been kept at the company's registered office.
(6)  Every copy or memorandum required to be kept under this section must be kept open to inspection without charge—
   (a)  by any member of the company, and
   (b)  in the case of a public company, by any other person.
(7)  The provisions of this section apply to a variation of a contract as they apply to the original contract.

COMMENCEMENT DATE  1 October 2009[213]

**18.702.02**  This section, which replaced parts of the former section 169 of the 1985 Act, imposes the obligation on the company to keep a record of purchases of its own shares (that is a copy of any contract or a written memorandum of its terms, together with any variations) at its registered office, or a place specified under section 1136,[214] for a period of ten years. If any such contract or memorandum is not kept at the registered office, the company must give notice of its location and any change therein to the registrar under subsection (5). The obligation was previously required under the same section as that imposing the filing obligations.[215] The ten-year period runs from the date of completion of the contract or the

---

[209] Companies Act 2006 (Commencement No 8, Transitional Provisions and Savings) Order 2008, SI 2008/2860, Sch 2, para 75.
[210] [2006] OJ L264/32. See the Companies (Share Capital and Acquisition by Company of its Own Shares) Regulations 2009, SI 2009/2022, reg 4. Previously the period was 18 months.
[211] See subs (8). As to these filing requirements, see para 3.30.02.
[212] See the commentary to s 694 above.
[213] Companies Act 2006 (Commencement No 8, Transitional Provisions and Savings) Order 2008, SI 2008/2860, art 3(1).
[214] This is the general provision regarding the location of company records; see para 37.1136.01.
[215] The filing obligation is now imposed by s 707.

date on which the contract otherwise determines; the latter must refer to a date later than that of completion, otherwise the obligation to keep records of purchases could be easily avoided.

A member of any company has the right to inspect the copy of the contract or written memorandum **18.702.03** of its terms without charge, and any person can inspect the records of a public company without charge. The consequences of breach are specified in section 703, below.

### 703  Enforcement of right to inspect copy or memorandum

(1)  If default is made in complying with section 702(2), (3) or (4) or default is made for 14 days in    **18.703.01** complying with section 702(5), or an inspection required under section 702(6) is refused, an offence is committed by—
   (a)  the company, and
   (b)  every officer of the company who is in default.
(2)  A person guilty of an offence under this section is liable on summary conviction to a fine not exceeding level 3 on the standard scale and, for continued contravention, a daily default fine not exceeding one-tenth of level 3 on the standard scale.
(3)  In the case of refusal of an inspection required under section 702(6) the court may by order compel an immediate inspection.

COMMENCEMENT DATE  1 October 2009[216]

The right to inspect the copies or memoranda relating to a company's purchase of its own shares,    **18.703.02** conferred by section 702, is backed up by the criminal penalty on every officer in default[217] specified in subsection (2) of this section. There is also under subsection (3) the right to ask the court for an order to compel an immediate inspection.

In respect of the latter right, the court clearly has a discretion that it would no doubt exercise on a    **18.703.03** similar basis to the right of inspection of the register of members under section 118(3),[218] which, *mutatis mutandis*, is worded identically.

### 704  No assignment of company's right to purchase own shares

The rights of a company under a contract authorised under—    **18.704.01**

   (a)  section 694 (authority for off-market purchase), or
   (b)  section 701 (authority for market purchase)

are not capable of being assigned.

COMMENCEMENT DATE  1 October 2009[219]

This section prohibits the assignment of the company's rights to purchase its own shares conferred    **18.704.02** under the sections authorizing either off-market or market purchases of its own shares. There are no difficulties of interpretation here. Obviously any purported assignment would be void and unenforceable, although no other penalty is specified.

### 705  Payments apart from purchase price to be made out of distributable profits

(1)  A payment made by a company in consideration of—    **18.705.01**
   (a)  acquiring any right with respect to the purchase of its own shares in pursuance of a contingent purchase contract approved under section 694 (authorisation of off-market purchase),
   (b)  the variation of any contract approved under that section, or
   (c)  the release of any of the company's obligations with respect to the purchase of any of its own shares under a contract—
     (i)  approved under section 694, or
     (ii)  authorised under section 701 (authorisation of market purchase),
   must be made out of the company's distributable profits.
(2)  If this requirement is not met in relation to a contract, then—
   (a)  in a case within subsection (1)(a), no purchase by the company of its own shares in pursuance of that contract may be made under this Chapter;
   (b)  in a case within subsection (1)(b), no such purchase following the variation may be made under this Chapter;

---

[216] Companies Act 2006 (Commencement No 8, Transitional Provisions and Savings) Order 2008, SI 2008/2860, art 3(l).
[217] As to the meaning of 'officer in default', see s 1121.
[218] See para 8.118.02.
[219] Companies Act 2006 (Commencement No 8, Transitional Provisions and Savings) Order 2008, SI 2008/2860, art 3(l).

(c)  in a case within subsection (1)(c), the purported release is void.

COMMENCEMENT DATE  1 October 2009[220]

**18.705.02**  This section repeats, with some drafting changes, the effect of the former section 168 of the 1985 Act. Whereas the price for a purchase of a company's own shares may be funded out of a fresh issue of shares and, in the case of a private company, out of capital, in addition to distributable profits, any other payment made by a company of the sort identified in subsection (1) must be made out of distributable profits.[221]

**18.705.03**  In the case of the first two types of payment, namely payments to acquire rights under a contract for an off-market purchase or payments to vary an off-market purchase, then if these are not funded by distributable profits, the company cannot purchase its own shares under this Chapter. The wording here differs from the former section 168, which provided for the contract to be illegal, but the effect is the same as a purchase not made under this Chapter would be illegal under section 658.

**18.705.04**  A payment to release any of the company's obligations with respect to any type of purchase of its own shares that is not funded out of distributable profits is void.

### 706  Treatment of shares purchased

**18.706.01**  Where a limited company makes a purchase of its own shares in accordance with this Chapter, then—

(a)  if section 724 (treasury shares) applies, the shares may be held and dealt with in accordance with Chapter 6;
(b)  if that section does not apply—
(i)   the shares are treated as cancelled, and
(ii)  the amount of the company's issued share capital is diminished accordingly by the nominal value of the shares cancelled.

COMMENCEMENT DATE  1 October 2009[222]

**18.706.02**  This section provides for the consequences, so far as the shares themselves are concerned, when a company purchases its own shares under this Chapter. Shares that can be held as treasury shares, which basically means publicly traded shares,[223] and which have been purchased out of distributable profits, can be 'kept alive' on that basis. However, as far as a company's purchases of all other shares are concerned, the shares are treated as cancelled and the issued capital is diminished by the nominal value of the shares. Thus there is in effect a statutory reduction of capital. The filing requirement consequential on this result is provided for in section 708.

### 707  Return to registrar of purchase of own shares

**18.707.01**  (1)  Where a company purchases shares under this Chapter, it must deliver a return to the registrar within the period of 28 days beginning with the date on which the shares are delivered to it.
(2)  The return must distinguish—
(a)  shares in relation to which section 724 (treasury shares) applies and shares in relation to which that section does not apply, and
(b)  shares in relation to which that section applies—
(i)   that are cancelled forthwith (under section 729 (cancellation of treasury shares)), and
(ii)  that are not so cancelled.
(3)  The return must state, with respect to shares of each class purchased—
(a)  the number and nominal value of the shares, and
(b)  the date on which they were delivered to the company.
(4)  In the case of a public company the return must also state—
(a)  the aggregate amount paid by the company for the shares, and
(b)  the maximum and minimum prices paid in respect of shares of each class purchased.
(5)  Particulars of shares delivered to the company on different dates and under different contracts may be included in a single return.
In such a case the amount required to be stated under subsection (4)(a) is the aggregate amount paid by the company for all the shares to which the return relates.
(6)  If default is made in complying with this section an offence is committed by every officer of the company who is in default.

---

[220]  Companies Act 2006 (Commencement No 8, Transitional Provisions and Savings) Order 2008, SI 2008/2860, art 3(l).
[221]  Distributable profits are defined in s 736 by reference to the general definition in s 830; see para 23.830.02.
[222]  Companies Act 2006 (Commencement No 8, Transitional Provisions and Savings) Order 2008, SI 2008/2860, art 3(l).
[223]  See further para 18.724.02 below.

(7) A person guilty of an offence under this section is liable—

    (a) on conviction on indictment, to a fine;

    (b) on summary conviction to a fine not exceeding the statutory maximum and, for continued contravention, a daily default fine not exceeding one-tenth of the statutory maximum.

COMMENCEMENT DATE 1 October 2009[224]

This section prescribes the filing requirements following a company's purchase of its own shares; these were formerly in part of section 169 of the 1985 Act.[225] A filing must be made of any purchase by any type of company within 28 days of the shares being delivered to the company, although it is permissible to include in a single return shares delivered on different dates and under different contracts. The return must distinguish shares that fall within the definition of treasury shares under section 724, which means basically publicly traded shares, from any other shares. As far as treasury shares are concerned, the return must distinguish between those that have been cancelled under section 729 and those that are not so cancelled. Where shares have been cancelled, notice must also be given under section 708.    **18.707.02**

A public company only is required to disclose the details of the price(s) paid under subsection (4). This is both the aggregate amount paid for the shares covered by the return and the maximum and minimum prices paid in respect of shares of each class purchased.    **18.707.03**

The penalty for a failure to give notice in accordance with the section falls on every officer of the company in default.[226]    **18.707.04**

### 708 Notice to registrar of cancellation of shares

(1) If on the purchase by a company of any of its own shares in accordance with this Part—    **18.708.01**

    (a) section 724 (treasury shares) does not apply (so that the shares are treated as cancelled), or

    (b) that section applies but the shares are cancelled forthwith (under section 729 (cancellation of treasury shares)),

    the company must give notice of cancellation to the registrar, within the period of 28 days beginning with the date on which the shares are delivered to it, specifying the shares cancelled.

(2) The notice must be accompanied by a statement of capital.

(3) The statement of capital must state with respect to the company's share capital immediately following the cancellation—

    (a) the total number of shares of the company,

    (b) the aggregate nominal value of those shares,

    (c) for each class of shares—

        (i) prescribed particulars of the rights attached to the shares,

        (ii) the total number of shares of that class, and

        (iii) the aggregate nominal value of shares of that class, and

    (d) the amount paid up and the amount (if any) unpaid on each share (whether on account of the nominal value of the share or by way of premium).

(4) If default is made in complying with this section, an offence is committed by—

    (a) the company, and

    (b) every officer of the company who is in default.

(5) A person guilty of an offence under this section is liable on summary conviction to a fine not exceeding level 3 on the standard scale and, for continued contravention, a daily default fine not exceeding one-tenth of level 3 on the standard scale.

COMMENCEMENT DATE 1 October 2009[227]

This section specifies the additional filing requirements when shares are cancelled following a company's purchase of its own shares.[228] This will apply in every case (see section 706) except a purchase of shares that fall within the definition of treasury shares in section 724, that is basically publicly traded shares, and which are not cancelled. The major change from the position under the former require-    **18.708.02**

---

[224] Companies Act 2006 (Commencement No 8, Transitional Provisions and Savings) Order 2008, SI 2008/2860, art 3(l).

[225] It applies in relation to shares delivered to the company on or after 1 October 2009; s 169 of the 1985 Act applies to shares delivered before that date: Companies Act 2006 (Commencement No 8, Transitional Provisions and Savings) Order 2008, SI 2008/2860, Sch 2, para 77.

[226] As to the meaning of 'officer in default', see s 1121.

[227] Companies Act 2006 (Commencement No 8, Transitional Provisions and Savings) Order 2008, SI 2008/2860, art 3(l).

[228] It applies in relation to shares delivered to the company on or after 1 October 2009; s 169 of the 1985 Act applies to shares delivered before that date: Companies Act 2006 (Commencement No 8, Transitional Provisions and Savings) Order 2008, SI 2008/2860, Sch 2, para 77.

ments is the additional requirement to file an up-to-date statement of capital under subsections (2) and (3). Commentary on this requirement, which applies to all capital alterations, can be found elsewhere.[229]

**18.708.03**   Note that the penalty for failure to comply with this filing obligation falls on the company as well as every officer in default,[230] but is a lower penalty than that specified under section 707.

CHAPTER 5

REDEMPTION OR PURCHASE BY PRIVATE COMPANY
OUT OF CAPITAL

*Introductory*

### 709 Power of private limited company to redeem or purchase own shares out of capital

**18.709.01**   (1) A private limited company may in accordance with this Chapter, but subject to any restriction or prohibition in the company's articles, make a payment in respect of the redemption or purchase of its own shares otherwise than out of distributable profits or the proceeds of a fresh issue of shares.
     (2) References below in this Chapter to payment out of capital are to any payment so made, whether or not it would be regarded apart from this section as a payment out of capital.

COMMENCEMENT DATE  1 October 2009[231]

**18.709.02**   The predecessors to this and the following sections 710 to 723 were first introduced to allow private companies to use capital to fund a redemption or purchase of their own shares, in effect providing an alternative mechanism for reducing capital to the traditional one,[232] and allowing them, for example, more easily to satisfy the wishes of a retiring or deceased shareholder if there were no existing shareholder willing or able to purchase their shares. Previously this was not permitted without authority in the articles, although now under subsection (1) the position has been reversed and such purchases are permitted in any case, provided that the articles do not restrict or prohibit the use of capital. Sections 709 to 723 apply where the directors' statement referred to in section 714 is made on or after 1 October 2009.[233]

**18.709.03**   The restatement in this Act has resulted in a much clearer layout of the provisions.

*The permissible capital payment*

### 710 The permissible capital payment

**18.710.01**   (1) The payment that may, in accordance with this Chapter, be made by a company out of capital in respect of the redemption or purchase of its own shares is such amount as, after applying for that purpose—
       (a) any available profits of the company, and
       (b) the proceeds of any fresh issue of shares made for the purposes of the redemption or purchase,
       is required to meet the price of redemption or purchase.
     (2) That is referred to below in this Chapter as 'the permissible capital payment' for the shares.

COMMENCEMENT DATE  1 October 2009[234]

**18.710.02**   This section, which was derived from part of section 171 of the 1985 Act, defines what can be paid out of capital in order to finance a redemption or purchase of its own shares by a private company. However, there appears to a subtle change in the wording of subsection (1) as compared to its predecessor, section 171(3) of the 1985 Act. The latter subsection referred to the permissible capital payment as being the payment out of capital 'taken together' with any available profits and the proceeds of any fresh issue of shares as was required to meet the price of redemption or purchase. The restated

---

[229] See the commentary to s 10.

[230] As to the meaning of 'officer in default', see s 1121.

[231] Companies Act 2006 (Commencement No 8, Transitional Provisions and Savings) Order 2008, SI 2008/2860, art 3(l).

[232] As to this, see para 17.641.01 above.

[233] Companies Act 2006 (Commencement No 8, Transitional Provisions and Savings) Order 2008, SI 2008/2860, Sch 2, para 78. Until that date, the former requirements of ss 171–178 of the 1985 Act, requiring, *inter alia*, a statutory declaration by directors, applied.

[234] Companies Act 2006 (Commencement No 8, Transitional Provisions and Savings) Order 2008, SI 2008/2860, art 3(l).

definition refers to the amount of capital as 'after applying' available profits and the proceeds of a fresh issue is required to meet the price of redemption or purchase.

However, it remains clear, and indeed arguably it is clearer because of the change in wording, that a company wishing to use capital must first use any available profits, so that a redemption made out of 'distributable profits' is not within the section.[235] What are available profits is determined under sections 711 and 712. The accounting consequences of a payment out of capital are now contained in section 734.

**18.710.03**

The total of any available profits, any funds obtained from a fresh issue, and the payment out of capital is 'the permissible capital payment for the shares'.

**18.710.04**

## 711 Available profits

(1) For the purposes of this Chapter the available profits of the company, in relation to the redemption or purchase of any shares, are the profits of the company that are available for distribution (within the meaning of Part 23).

(2) But the question whether a company has any profits so available, and the amount of any such profits, shall be determined in accordance with section 712 instead of in accordance with sections 836 to 842 in that Part.

**18.711.01**

COMMENCEMENT DATE 1 October 2009[236]

This section, taken together with section 712, both of which restate the former section 172 of the 1985 Act, determine the crucial question of whether or not a private company has available profits that have to be used to finance a redemption or purchase of its own shares before capital can be used. The term incorporates the general definition of distributable profits in Part 23,[237] but they are to be determined in accordance with section 712 rather than in accordance with the general provisions defining distributable profits.

**18.711.02**

## 712 Determination of available profits

(1) The available profits of the company are determined as follows.

(2) First, determine the profits of the company by reference to the following items as stated in the relevant accounts—
(a) profits, losses, assets and liabilities,
(b) provisions of the following kinds—
(i) where the relevant accounts are Companies Act accounts, provisions of a kind specified for the purposes of this subsection by regulations under section 396;
(ii) where the relevant accounts are IAS accounts, provisions of any kind;
(c) share capital and reserves (including undistributable reserves).

(3) Second, reduce the amount so determined by the amount of—
(a) any distribution lawfully made by the company, and
(b) any other relevant payment lawfully made by the company out of distributable profits,
after the date of the relevant accounts and before the end of the relevant period.

(4) For this purpose 'other relevant payment lawfully made' includes—
(a) financial assistance lawfully given out of distributable profits in accordance with Chapter 2,
(b) payments lawfully made out of distributable profits in respect of the purchase by the company of any shares in the company, and
(c) payments of any description specified in section 705 (payments other than purchase price to be made out of distributable profits) lawfully made by the company.

(5) The resulting figure is the amount of available profits.

(6) For the purposes of this section 'the relevant accounts' are any accounts that—
(a) are prepared as at a date within the relevant period, and
(b) are such as to enable a reasonable judgment to be made as to the amounts of the items mentioned in subsection (2).

(7) In this section 'the relevant period' means the period of three months ending with the date on which the directors' statement is made in accordance with section 714.

**18.712.01**

COMMENCEMENT DATE 1 October 2009[238]

---

[235] *Quayle Munro Ltd, Petitioners* 1993 SLT 723.
[236] Companies Act 2006 (Commencement No 8, Transitional Provisions and Savings) Order 2008, SI 2008/2860, art 3(l).
[237] See para 23.830.01.
[238] Companies Act 2006 (Commencement No 8, Transitional Provisions and Savings) Order 2008, SI 2008/2860, art 3(l).

**18.712.02** This section restates in a rather different way what was previously section 172(2) to (6) of the 1985 Act. The effect is that the accounts that are to be relied on to determine the available profits that must be used before a payment out of capital are accounts prepared within three months before the directors' statement under section 714. Available profits are first determined by reference to the items listed in subsection (2) in those accounts. The available profits are then reduced by the amount of any lawful distribution with the extended meaning in subsection (4) made after the accounts are prepared and before the date of the statement. As well as a normal distribution, subsection (4) includes a payment out of distributable profits to assist a purchase of the company's own shares and a payment made under section 705. The retention of the former type of payment seems curious given that a private company is no longer prohibited in any circumstances from providing financial assistance for an acquisition of its own shares.

**18.712.03** The resulting figure is the amount of available profits and, because of this, a company has the opportunity to exhaust its distributable profits by the time of the payment out of capital.

**18.712.04** As to the different types of accounts referred to in subsection (2)(b)(i), see sections 395 to 397 and the commentary thereto.[239]

## *Requirements for payment out of capital*

### 713 Requirements for payment out of capital

**18.713.01**
(1) A payment out of capital by a private company for the redemption or purchase of its own shares is not lawful unless the requirements of the following sections are met—
  section 714 (directors' statement and auditor's report);
  section 716 (approval by special resolution);
  section 719 (public notice of proposed payment);
  section 720 (directors' statement and auditor's report to be available for inspection).
(2) This is subject to any order of the court under section 721 (power of court to extend period for compliance on application by persons objecting to payment).

COMMENCEMENT DATE 1 October 2009[240]

**18.713.02** This section introduces the procedural requirements that have to be complied with in order for a private company to finance a redemption or purchase of its own shares out of capital. It is the equivalent of section 173(1) of the 1985 Act and usefully highlights the fact that any such payment is not lawful unless all the conditions are met. In addition to the specific penalties provided for breach of the various requirements, a payment of capital in breach of these requirements would clearly be treated as recoverable in accordance with general principles governing illegality.

### 714 Directors' statement and auditor's report

**18.714.01**
(1) The company's directors must make a statement in accordance with this section.
(2) The statement must specify the amount of the permissible capital payment for the shares in question.
(3) It must state that, having made full inquiry into the affairs and prospects of the company, the directors have formed the opinion—
  (a) as regards its initial situation immediately following the date on which the payment out of capital is proposed to be made, that there will be no grounds on which the company could then be found unable to pay its debts, and
  (b) as regards its prospects for the year immediately following that date, that having regard to—
    (i) their intentions with respect to the management of the company's business during that year, and
    (ii) the amount and character of the financial resources that will in their view be available to the company during that year,
  the company will be able to continue to carry on business as a going concern (and will accordingly be able to pay its debts as they fall due) throughout that year.
(4) In forming their opinion for the purposes of subsection (3)(a), the directors must take into account all of the company's liabilities (including any contingent or prospective liabilities).
(5) The directors' statement must be in the prescribed form and must contain such information with respect to the nature of the company's business as may be prescribed.
(6) It must in addition have annexed to it a report addressed to the directors by the company's auditor stating that—
  (a) he has inquired into the company's state of affairs,

---

[239] See para 15.395.01.
[240] Companies Act 2006 (Commencement No 8, Transitional Provisions and Savings) Order 2008, SI 2008/2860, art 3(l).

(b) the amount specified in the statement as the permissible capital payment for the shares in question is in his view properly determined in accordance with sections 710 to 712, and

(c) he is not aware of anything to indicate that the opinion expressed by the directors in their statement as to any of the matters mentioned in subsection (3) above is unreasonable in all the circumstances.

COMMENCEMENT DATE 1 October 2009[241]

This section, which replaces the majority of section 173 of the 1985 Act with minor redrafting and changes mentioned below, is concerned with the directors' statement of solvency as confirmed by the auditors. In this respect the 2006 Act deregulated the requirements to some extent by requiring the directors to make this statement rather than, as before, a statutory declaration. So the need for a swearing before a commissioner for oaths was abolished.[242]     **18.714.02**

The section (subsections (2) to (4)) closely prescribes the contents of that statement, with a relatively heavy criminal penalty in section 715 for directors who make it without having reasonable grounds for their belief. It is essentially a statement that in their opinion the company is solvent at the time—that is, it will be able to pay its debts immediately after the payment out of capital—and that, having regard to their intentions regarding the management of the business and taking account of all liabilities including contingent and prospective liabilities,[243] it will remain so for a year.     **18.714.03**

By subsection (5), the prescribed form has to be followed and may prescribe further information regarding the nature of the company's business. However, at the time of writing no form has been prescribed under this section, so it must simply follow the wording required by subsections (2) and (3).     **18.714.04**

Directors of a company that is wound up insolvent within one year of a payment out of capital will be liable to contribute to the assets of the company under section 76 of the Insolvency Act 1986, unless they can show that they had reasonable grounds for forming the opinion set out in the statement. The former shareholder from whom shares were purchased with a payment out of capital will also be liable to repay the amount of that payment and the directors will be jointly and severally liable with him.     **18.714.05**

As well as confirming that the directors' statement is reasonable, by subsection (6), the auditors must confirm that in their view the permissible capital payment for the shares[244] has been properly determined.     **18.714.06**

### 715 Directors' statement: offence if no reasonable grounds for opinion

(1) If the directors make a statement under section 714 without having reasonable grounds for the opinion expressed in it, an offence is committed by every director who is in default.     **18.715.01**

(2) A person guilty of an offence under this section is liable—

(a) on conviction on indictment, to imprisonment for a term not exceeding two years or a fine (or both);

(b) on summary conviction—

(i) in England and Wales, to imprisonment for a term not exceeding twelve months or a fine not exceeding the statutory maximum (or both);

(ii) in Scotland or Northern Ireland, to imprisonment for a term not exceeding six months or a fine not exceeding the statutory maximum (or both).

COMMENCEMENT DATE 1 October 2009[245]

This section prescribes a potentially heavy criminal penalty on directors who make a statement under section 714 without having reasonable grounds for their opinion.[246] The reason for the difference in the maximum penalties in subsection (2)(b) that can be imposed summarily is because the relevant courts in England and Wales have greater sentencing powers than those in Scotland or Northern Ireland.     **18.715.02**

---

[241] Companies Act 2006 (Commencement No 8, Transitional Provisions and Savings) Order 2008, SI 2008/2860, art 3(l).

[242] This applies only to statements made on or after 1 October 2009: Companies Act 2006 (Commencement No 8, Transitional Provisions and Savings) Order 2008, SI 2008/2860, Sch 2, para 78.

[243] As to the meaning of these, see para 17.643.06 above.

[244] See s 710.

[245] Companies Act 2006 (Commencement No 8, Transitional Provisions and Savings) Order 2008, SI 2008/2860, art 3(l).

[246] As to the meaning of director in default, see s 1121.

### 716 Payment to be approved by special resolution

**18.716.01**
(1) The payment out of capital must be approved by a special resolution of the company.
(2) The resolution must be passed on, or within the week immediately following, the date on which the directors make the statement required by section 714.
(3) A resolution under this section is subject to—
section 717 (exercise of voting rights), and
section 718 (disclosure of directors' statement and auditors' report).

COMMENCEMENT DATE 1 October 2009[247]

**18.716.02** This section prescribes the special resolution necessary to approve a payment out of capital for a redemption or purchase of the company's own shares, which must be an additional resolution to that required under section 694 approving the actual contract in the case of a purchase. The resolution must be passed on or within a week of the date of the directors' statement under section 714.[248] Subsection (3) indicates the additional requirements under sections 717 and 718.

### 717 Resolution authorising payment: exercise of voting rights

**18.717.01**
(1) This section applies to a resolution under section 716 (authority for payment out of capital for redemption or purchase of own shares).
(2) Where the resolution is proposed as a written resolution, a member who holds shares to which the resolution relates is not an eligible member.
(3) Where the resolution is proposed at a meeting of the company, it is not effective if—
(a) any member of the company holding shares to which the resolution relates exercises the voting rights carried by any of those shares in voting on the resolution, and
(b) the resolution would not have been passed if he had not done so.
(4) For this purpose—
(a) a member who holds shares to which the resolution relates is regarded as exercising the voting rights carried by those shares not only if he votes in respect of them on a poll on the question whether the resolution shall be passed, but also if he votes on the resolution otherwise than on a poll;
(b) any member of the company may demand a poll on that question;
(c) a vote and a demand for a poll by a person as proxy for a member are the same respectively as a vote and a demand by the member.

COMMENCEMENT DATE 1 October 2009[249]

**18.717.02** This section disenfranchises, whether voting on a show of hands or on a poll, in person or by proxy, the member or members who hold shares that are the subject of a proposed redemption or purchase out of capital. In the case of a resolution proposed as a written resolution, subsection (2) achieves this by excluding the member in question from being an eligible member.[250] Any member and any proxy for a member has a statutory right under subsection (4)(b) to demand a poll on the resolution.

### 718 Resolution authorising payment: disclosure of directors' statement and auditor's report

**18.718.01**
(1) This section applies to a resolution under section 716 (resolution authorising payment out of capital for redemption or purchase of own shares).
(2) A copy of the directors' statement and auditor's report under section 714 must be made available to members—
(a) in the case of a written resolution, by being sent or submitted to every eligible member at or before the time at which the proposed resolution is sent or submitted to him;
(b) in the case of a resolution at a meeting, by being made available for inspection by members of the company at the meeting.
(3) The resolution is ineffective if this requirement is not complied with.

COMMENCEMENT DATE 1 October 2009[251]

---

[247] Companies Act 2006 (Commencement No 8, Transitional Provisions and Savings) Order 2008, SI 2008/2860, art 3(l).
[248] The time limits regarding the actual payment following the special resolution are now separately specified in s 723.
[249] Companies Act 2006 (Commencement No 8, Transitional Provisions and Savings) Order 2008, SI 2008/2860, art 3(l).
[250] See generally s 289.
[251] Companies Act 2006 (Commencement No 8, Transitional Provisions and Savings) Order 2008, SI 2008/2860, art 3(l).

The directors' statement and auditor's report required by section 714 must be made available to members of the company voting on the special resolution to approve a payment out of capital. If not, the resolution is ineffective. If the resolution is proposed as a written resolution, this requirement is satisfied if the documents are supplied to each eligible member[252] at the time or before he receives the resolution for signature. Otherwise, the documents must be available for inspection at the meeting where the resolution is proposed.    **18.718.02**

It might be arguable that the unanimous consent of all the members could dispense with these formalities, by analogy with the decisions under what are now sections 694 *et seq.*[253] However, given that this part of the Act is concerned with a payment out of capital and given the rights of creditors conferred under the following sections, it is thought that there would not be the same force in such an argument in the context of the requirements under this section.    **18.718.03**

## 719  Public notice of proposed payment

(1)  Within the week immediately following the date of the resolution under section 716 the company must cause to be published in the Gazette a notice—    **18.719.01**
    (a)  stating that the company has approved a payment out of capital for the purpose of acquiring its own shares by redemption or purchase or both (as the case may be),
    (b)  specifying—
        (i)   the amount of the permissible capital payment for the shares in question, and
        (ii)  the date of the resolution,
    (c)  stating where the directors' statement and auditor's report required by section 714 are available for inspection, and
    (d)  stating that any creditor of the company may at any time within the five weeks immediately following the date of the resolution apply to the court under section 721 for an order preventing the payment.
(2)  Within the week immediately following the date of the resolution the company must also either—
    (a)  cause a notice to the same effect as that required by subsection (1) to be published in an appropriate national newspaper, or
    (b)  give notice in writing to that effect to each of its creditors.
(3)  'An appropriate national newspaper' means a newspaper circulating throughout the part of the United Kingdom in which the company is registered.
(4)  Not later than the day on which the company—
    (a)  first publishes the notice required by subsection (1), or
    (b)  if earlier, first publishes or gives the notice required by subsection (2),
    the company must deliver to the registrar a copy of the directors' statement and auditor's report required by section 714.

COMMENCEMENT DATE  1 October 2009[254]

As well as restating the law, this section of necessity amends its predecessor (section 175 of the 1985 Act) by replacing the previous references to the directors' statutory declaration to the directors' statement that is now required by section 713.[255]    **18.719.02**

It imposes specific publicity requirements when a company is proposing to pay for its own shares out of capital, obviously for the protection of the creditors of the company. These are quite extensive, requiring, within one week of the special resolution approving the payment, notice in the Gazette in the terms of subsection (1), as well as, under subsection (2) a similar notice in an appropriate national newspaper or to every creditor. Subsection (4) also requires delivery of the directors' statement and auditor's report under section 714 to the registrar.    **18.719.03**

The notice must state the approval of the payment out of capital and specify the amount of the permissible capital payment and the date of the resolution. Of particular importance is the fact that the notice must state the right of any member and creditor to inspect the statement and report at the registered office, enforceable by court order under section 720(7), and the right of any creditor to apply for an order under section 721 preventing the payment.    **18.719.04**

---

[252]  See s 289.
[253]  See the commentary to s 694.
[254]  Companies Act 2006 (Commencement No 8, Transitional Provisions and Savings) Order 2008, SI 2008/2860, art 3(l).
[255]  Note also the reference in subsection (3) to a newspaper circulating throughout the part of the UK in which the company is registered, rather than the previous references to England and Wales or Scotland, because of the fact that the Act applies to the whole of the UK (see para 44.1299.01).

### 720 Directors' statement and auditor's report to be available for inspection

**18.720.01**
    (1) The directors' statement and auditor's report must be kept available for inspection throughout the period—
        (a) beginning with the day on which the company—
            (i)  first publishes the notice required by section 719(1), or
            (ii) if earlier, first publishes or gives the notice required by section 719(2), and
        (b) ending five weeks after the date of the resolution for payment out of capital.
    (2) They must be kept available for inspection—
        (a) at the company's registered office, or
        (b) at a place specified in regulations under section 1136.
    (3) The company must give notice to the registrar—
        (a) of the place at which the statement and report are kept available for inspection, and
        (b) of any change in that place,
    unless they have at all times been kept at the company's registered office.
    (4) They must be open to the inspection of any member or creditor of the company without charge.
    (5) If default is made for 14 days in complying with subsection (3), or an inspection under subsection (4) is refused, an offence is committed by—
        (a) the company, and
        (b) every officer of the company who is in default.
    (6) A person guilty of an offence under this section is liable on summary conviction to a fine not exceeding level 3 on the standard scale and, for continued contravention, a daily default fine not exceeding one-tenth of level 3 on the standard scale.
    (7) In the case of a refusal of an inspection required by subsection (4), the court may by order compel an immediate inspection.

COMMENCEMENT DATE 1 October 2009[256]

**18.720.02**  This section, which restates part of the former section 175 of the 1985 Act, imposes the obligation to keep the directors' statement and auditor's report under section 714 available for inspection by any member or creditor of the company without charge. They must be kept either at the company's registered office or at a place (the alternative inspection location) specified in regulations made under section 1136.[257] The right to inspect is enforceable by court order under subsection (7).

**18.720.03**  The five-week period for inspection, which will run from the earlier of the publication of the notice in the Gazette on the one hand, or newspaper publication or written notice to all creditors on the other, relates to both the period that a member or creditor has for applying to the court to cancel the resolution under section 721 and to the period within which a payment of capital may be made, as laid down in section 723, namely only between five and seven weeks after the passing of the special resolution.

**18.720.04**  The criminal penalty for breach, which is imposed on both the company and any officer in default,[258] was reduced by the 2006 Act, the previous penalty being stated as simply a fine.

### *Objection to payment by members or creditors*

### 721 Application to court to cancel resolution

**18.721.01**
    (1) Where a private company passes a special resolution approving a payment out of capital for the redemption or purchase of any of its shares—
        (a) any member of the company (other than one who consented to or voted in favour of the resolution), and
        (b) any creditor of the company,
    may apply to the court for the cancellation of the resolution.
    (2) The application—
        (a) must be made within five weeks after the passing of the resolution, and
        (b) may be made on behalf of the persons entitled to make it by such one or more of their number as they may appoint in writing for the purpose.

---

[256] Companies Act 2006 (Commencement No 8, Transitional Provisions and Savings) Order 2008, SI 2008/2860, art 3(1).
[257] This is the general provision regarding the location of company records; see para 37.1136.01. See the Companies (Company Records) Regulations 2008, SI 2008/3006.
[258] As to the meaning of 'officer in default', see s 1121.

(3)  On an application under this section the court may if it thinks fit—

    (a)  adjourn the proceedings in order that an arrangement may be made to the satisfaction of the court—

        (i)  for the purchase of the interests of dissentient members, or

        (ii)  for the protection of dissentient creditors, and

    (b)  give such directions and make such orders as it thinks expedient for facilitating or carrying into effect any such arrangement.

(4)  Subject to that, the court must make an order either cancelling or confirming the resolution, and may do so on such terms and conditions as it thinks fit.

(5)  If the court confirms the resolution, it may by order alter or extend any date or period of time specified—

    (a)  in the resolution, or

    (b)  in any provision of this Chapter applying to the redemption or purchase to which the resolution relates.

(6)  The court's order may, if the court thinks fit—

    (a)  provide for the purchase by the company of the shares of any of its members and for the reduction accordingly of the company's capital, and

    (b)  make any alteration in the company's articles that may be required in consequence of that provision.

(7)  The court's order may, if the court thinks fit, require the company not to make any, or any specified, amendments of its articles without the leave of the court.

COMMENCEMENT DATE  1 October 2009[259]

This section confers the potentially very important right of any dissenting member and any creditor to apply to the court within five weeks of the passing of a special resolution approving a purchase out of capital.  **18.721.02**

It confers very wide powers on the court. Because of subsection (3), the emphasis is very clearly on an arrangement that purchases the interests of the members if the application is from one or more of them or protects the interests of the dissentient creditors, backed up by an order to that effect. If the interests of dissentient members are to be purchased, that can be by the company, with the consequential reduction in capital referred to in subsection (6); obviously alternatively the purchase could be by continuing members.  **18.721.03**

As far as creditors are concerned, whether they are protected by an arrangement under subsection (3) or by order under subsection (4), there has been no reported decision hitherto regarding how their interests should be regarded. Presumably, though, unless the dissentient creditors can persuade the court that there is something wrong with the directors' statement or auditor's report, there is very little, if any, chance of their succeeding. Although a payment out of capital may be regarded in some respects as the equivalent of a formal reduction of capital, in respect of which there are well-established procedures for the protection of creditors,[260] the procedure is nonetheless not the same and it should be noted that there is no provision for the protection of creditors under the new procedure for private companies formally to reduce capital following a directors' statement of solvency,[261] which suggests that the court should interfere only if there can be shown to be some defect in the statement or report.  **18.721.04**

## 722  Notice to registrar of court application or order

(1)  On making an application under section 721 (application to court to cancel resolution) the applicants, or the person making the application on their behalf, must immediately give notice to the registrar.  **18.722.01**

This is without prejudice to any provision of rules of court as to service of notice of the application.

(2)  On being served with notice of any such application, the company must immediately give notice to the registrar.

(3)  Within 15 days of the making of the court's order on the application, or such longer period as the court may at any time direct, the company must deliver to the registrar a copy of the order.

(4)  If a company fails to comply with subsection (2) or (3) an offence is committed by—

    (a)  the company, and

    (b)  every officer of the company who is in default.

---

[259]  Companies Act 2006 (Commencement No 8, Transitional Provisions and Savings) Order 2008, SI 2008/2860, art 3(l).

[260]  See para 17.645.03 above.

[261]  See para 17.642.01 above.

(5) A person guilty of an offence under this section is liable on summary conviction to a fine not exceeding level 3 on the standard scale and, for continued contravention, a daily default fine not exceeding one-tenth of level 3 on the standard scale.

COMMENCEMENT DATE 1 October 2009[262]

**18.722.02**   This section imposes the filing obligations in the event of a dissentient member or a creditor applying to the court for cancellation of a resolution approving a payment out of capital. It replaced, with drafting amendments, the former section 176(3) and (4) of the 1985 Act but also made an important change.

**18.722.03**   The change is the new obligation on the applicant to give notice to the registrar under subsection (1). As before, the company must itself immediately file notice with the registrar on being served with notice of the application,[263] and there is a separate filing requirement within 15 days following the court's order. The penalties for the company failing to comply with either filing obligation fall both on it and on any officer in default.[264]

## Supplementary provisions

### 723  When payment out of capital to be made

**18.723.01**
(1) The payment out of capital must be made—
   (a) no earlier than five weeks after the date on which the resolution under section 716 is passed, and
   (b) no more than seven weeks after that date.
(2) This is subject to any exercise of the court's powers under section 721(5) (power to alter or extend time where resolution confirmed after objection).

COMMENCEMENT DATE 1 October 2009[265]

**18.723.02**   This section closely prescribes the times within which a payment of capital can be made, unless the time is altered pursuant to court order under section 721. It replaced part of section 174(1) of the 1985 Act.

**18.723.03**   The minimum five weeks after the passing of the special resolution is to allow for the appropriate publicity and rights of dissenting members and creditors to apply to the court, as governed by sections 719 to 721. The further two weeks allowed for the payment actually to be made is to ensure that not too long a period elapses from the date of the directors' statement and auditor's report; in total no more than eight weeks can elapse from that date to the date of payment, because of the requirement in section 716 that the special resolution approving the payment must be made within a week of the directors' statement.

## CHAPTER 6
## TREASURY SHARES

### 724  Treasury shares

**18.724.01**
(1) This section applies where—
   (a) a limited company makes a purchase of its own shares in accordance with Chapter 4,
   (b) the purchase is made out of distributable profits, and
   (c) the shares are qualifying shares.
(2) For this purpose 'qualifying shares' means shares that—
   (a) are included in the official list in accordance with the provisions of Part 6 of the Financial Services and Markets Act 2000 (c. 8),
   (b) are traded on the market known as the Alternative Investment Market established under the rules of London Stock Exchange plc,
   (c) are officially listed in an EEA State, or
   (d) are traded on a regulated market.
   In paragraph (a) 'the official list' has the meaning given in section 103(1) of the Financial Services and Markets Act 2000.

---

[262] Companies Act 2006 (Commencement No 8, Transitional Provisions and Savings) Order 2008, SI 2008/2860, art 3(l).

[263] The wording here has been clarified from the provision this section replaces to make it clear that the company's obligation can arise only once it has been served.

[264] As to the meaning of 'officer in default', see s 1121.

[265] Companies Act 2006 (Commencement No 8, Transitional Provisions and Savings) Order 2008, SI 2008/2860, art 3(l).

(3) Where this section applies the company may—
    (a) hold the shares (or any of them), or
    (b) deal with any of them, at any time, in accordance with section 727 or 729.
(4) Where shares are held by the company, the company must be entered in its register of members as the member holding the shares.
(5) In the Companies Acts references to a company holding shares as treasury shares are to the company holding shares that—
    (a) were (or are treated as having been) purchased by it in circumstances in which this section applies, and
    (b) have been held by the company continuously since they were so purchased (or treated as purchased).

COMMENCEMENT DATE 1 October 2009[266]

This and the following sections are substantially the provisions first introduced in 2003[267] by way of amendment to the former provisions of the 1985 Act to allow publicly traded shares purchased by a company to be held in treasury, so that they can if appropriate be re-issued or otherwise dealt with according to sections 727 or 729, provided that payment for the purchase is made out of distributable profits and not out of the proceeds of a fresh issue of shares. The shares that qualify for this treatment are widely defined in subsection (2).[268]   **18.724.02**

The section allows a company that has purchased qualifying shares in accordance with Chapter 4 of this Part to hold all or any of the shares as treasury shares, in which case the company must be entered as the member in its register of members,[269] or to deal with them. But shares are only regarded as treasury shares if they have been purchased in accordance with Chapter 4 and held continuously by the company since then (subsection (5)). There was a limit on the number of shares that could be held in treasury as prescribed by section 725, but that section was repealed from 1 October 2009, and the rights attaching to treasury shares held by the company are severely restricted under section 726.   **18.724.03**

## [725 Treasury shares: maximum holdings

(1) Where a company has shares of only one class, the aggregate nominal value of shares held as treasury shares must not at any time exceed 10% of the nominal value of the issued share capital of the company at that time.   **18.725.01**
(2) Where the share capital of a company is divided into shares of different classes, the aggregate nominal value of the shares of any class held as treasury shares must not at any time exceed 10% of the nominal value of the issued share capital of the shares of that class at that time.
(3) If subsection (1) or (2) is contravened by a company, the company must dispose of or cancel the excess shares, in accordance with section 727 or 729, before the end of the period of twelve months beginning with the date on which that contravention occurs.
    The 'excess shares' means such number of the shares held by the company as treasury shares at the time in question as resulted in the limit being exceeded.
(4) Where a company purchases qualifying shares out of distributable profits in accordance with section 724, a contravention by the company of subsection (1) or (2) above does not render the acquisition void under section 658 (general rule against limited company acquiring its own shares).][a]

AMENDMENTS AND NOTES
  [a] Repealed by the Companies (Share Capital and Acquisition by Company of its Own Shares) Regulations 2009, SI 2009/2022, reg 5.

COMMENCEMENT DATE 1 October 2009[270]

Previously, companies could retain their own shares as treasury shares only up to the maximum levels specified in this section, so that they could not exceed 10 per cent of the nominal value of the issued share capital or 10 per cent of any class of shares see subsections (1) and (2).   **18.725.02**

---

[266] Companies Act 2006 (Commencement No 8, Transitional Provisions and Savings) Order 2008, SI 2008/2860, art 3(l).
[267] Companies (Acquisition of Own Shares) (Treasury Shares) Regulations 2003, SI 2003/1116.
[268] For the meaning of 'regulated market', see s 1173, which adopts the definition in Art 4.1(14) of Directive 2004/39/EC.
[269] See Chapter 2 of Part 8 for the register of members.
[270] Companies Act 2006 (Commencement No 8, Transitional Provisions and Savings) Order 2008, SI 2008/2860, art 3(l).

**18.725.03** However, as a result of liberalization measures introduced by Directive (EC) 2006/68,[271] the section was repealed with effect from 1 October 2009,[272] curiously the same date as it was commenced. The section is retained here because of a transitional provision preserving criminal liability under section 732 where the 12-month period ended before 1 October 2009.[273]

### 726 Treasury shares: exercise of rights

**18.726.01**
    (1) This section applies where shares are held by a company as treasury shares.
    (2) The company must not exercise any right in respect of the treasury shares, and any purported exercise of such a right is void.
        This applies, in particular, to any right to attend or vote at meetings.
    (3) No dividend may be paid, and no other distribution (whether in cash or otherwise) of the company's assets (including any distribution of assets to members on a winding up) may be made to the company, in respect of the treasury shares.
    (4) Nothing in this section prevents—
        (a) an allotment of shares as fully paid bonus shares in respect of the treasury shares, or
        (b) the payment of any amount payable on the redemption of the treasury shares (if they are redeemable shares).
    (5) Shares allotted as fully paid bonus shares in respect of the treasury shares are treated as if purchased by the company, at the time they were allotted, in circumstances in which section 724(1) (treasury shares) applied.

    COMMENCEMENT DATE 1 October 2009[274]

**18.726.02** This section imposes important restrictions on shares held as treasury shares, so that for the period they are so held, the company has no rights in respect of them, including the right to attend or vote at meetings (subsection (2)) and rights to dividends or other distributions (subsection (3)), except in respect of bonus shares or any amount payable on the redemption of treasury shares that are redeemable shares (subsection (4)). The reference in subsection (2) to rights to attend or vote at meetings is clearly not exhaustive and must comprehend any other right given, for example, by the company's articles, to the shares in question.

**18.726.03** The effect of subsection (5) is that any bonus shares allotted in respect of treasury shares will themselves be regarded as treasury shares, so that they can be retained or dealt with under the Act. The penalties for breach are contained in section 732.

### 727 Treasury shares: disposal

**18.727.01**
    (1) Where shares are held as treasury shares, the company may at any time—
        (a) sell the shares (or any of them) for a cash consideration, or
        (b) transfer the shares (or any of them) for the purposes of or pursuant to an employees' share scheme.
    (2) In subsection (1)(a) 'cash consideration' means—
        (a) cash received by the company, or
        (b) a cheque received by the company in good faith that the directors have no reason for suspecting will not be paid, or
        (c) a release of a liability of the company for a liquidated sum, or
        (d) an undertaking to pay cash to the company on or before a date not more than 90 days after the date on which the company agrees to sell the shares, or
        (e) payment by any other means giving rise to a present or future entitlement (of the company or a person acting on the company's behalf) to a payment, or credit equivalent to payment, in cash.
        For this purpose 'cash' includes foreign currency.
    (3) The Secretary of State may by order provide that particular means of payment specified in the order are to be regarded as falling within subsection (2)(e).
    (4) If the company receives a notice under section 979 (takeover offers: right of offeror to buy out minority shareholders) that a person desires to acquire shares held by the company as treasury shares, the company must not sell or transfer the shares to which the notice relates except to that person.

---

[271] [2006] OJ L254/32.

[272] See the Companies (Share Capital and Acquisition by Company of its Own Shares) Regulations 2009, SI 2009/2022.

[273] Companies (Share Capital and Acquisition by Company of its Own Shares) Regulations 2009, SI 2009/2022, reg 5(3).

[274] Companies Act 2006 (Commencement No 8, Transitional Provisions and Savings) Order 2008, SI 2008/2860, art 3(l).

(5)  An order under this section is subject to negative resolution procedure.

COMMENCEMENT DATE  1 October 2009[275]

This section spells out what a company can do with treasury shares if it decides that it no longer wishes to hold them as such. An alternative is cancellation under section 729.                                **18.727.02**

First the company can sell them for a cash consideration, with the consequences specified in section 731. Although cash consideration is broadly defined in subsection (2), obviously the company cannot sell them for any other form of consideration, for example property of any sort including shares in another company. Otherwise cash consideration, in any currency, includes a cheque received in good faith, the discharge of a liability of the company, an undertaking to pay cash within 90 days and payment by any other means giving rise to an entitlement to a payment or credit equivalent to payment in cash. The last of these types of cash consideration was newly introduced in the 2006 Act[276] and in this respect there is power to specify in regulations (see subsections (3) and (5)) particular means of payment that are to be regarded as falling within it.                **18.727.03**

Secondly the company can transfer them for the purposes of or pursuant to an employees' share scheme.[277]                                                                                         **18.727.04**

Subsection (4) is designed to prevent the company frustrating a takeover when the offeror has achieved a 90 per cent holding and seeks to exercise its right of compulsory acquisition under section 979.  **18.727.05**

## 728  Treasury shares: notice of disposal

(1)  Where shares held by a company as treasury shares—                                             **18.728.01**
    (a)  are sold, or
    (b)  are transferred for the purposes of an employees' share scheme,
    the company must deliver a return to the registrar not later than 28 days after the shares are disposed of.
(2)  The return must state with respect to shares of each class disposed of—
    (a)  the number and nominal value of the shares, and
    (b)  the date on which they were disposed of.
(3)  Particulars of shares disposed of on different dates may be included in a single return.
(4)  If default is made in complying with this section an offence is committed by every officer of the company who is in default.
(5)  A person guilty of an offence under this section is liable—
    (a)  on conviction on indictment, to a fine;
    (b)  on summary conviction, to a fine not exceeding the statutory maximum and, for continued contravention, a daily default fine not exceeding one-tenth of the statutory maximum.

COMMENCEMENT DATE  1 October 2009[278]

This section imposes a special filing requirement in respect of treasury shares which were not immediately cancelled following their purchase by the company. It applies if shares are subsequently sold or transferred under an employees' share scheme, pursuant to section 727. The return must be completed within 28 days of disposal of the shares, but can include particulars disposed of on different dates (subsection (3)).                                                                              **18.728.02**

The penalty for breach falls on every officer of the company in default.[279]                       **18.728.03**

## 729  Treasury shares: cancellation

(1)  Where shares are held as treasury shares, the company may at any time cancel the shares (or any of them).                                                                                       **18.729.01**
(2)  If shares held as treasury shares cease to be qualifying shares, the company must forthwith cancel the shares.

---

[275]  Companies Act 2006 (Commencement No 8, Transitional Provisions and Savings) Order 2008, SI 2008/2860, art 3(l).
[276]  It applies only where the contract for the sale of the shares is entered into on or after 1 October 2009: Companies Act 2006 (Commencement No 8, Transitional Provisions and Savings) Order 2008, SI 2008/2860, Sch 2, para 79.
[277]  As defined in s 1166.
[278]  Companies Act 2006 (Commencement No 8, Transitional Provisions and Savings) Order 2008, SI 2008/2860, art 3(l).
[279]  For the meaning of this, see s 1121.

    (3) For this purpose shares are not to be regarded as ceasing to be qualifying shares by virtue only of—

        (a) the suspension of their listing in accordance with the applicable rules in the EEA State in which the shares are officially listed, or

        (b) the suspension of their trading in accordance with—

            (i) in the case of shares traded on the market known as the Alternative Investment Market, the rules of London Stock Exchange plc, and

            (ii) in any other case, the rules of the regulated market on which they are traded.

    (4) If company cancels shares held as treasury shares, the amount of the company's share capital is reduced accordingly by the nominal amount of the shares cancelled.

    (5) The directors may take any steps required to enable the company to cancel its shares under this section without complying with the provisions of Chapter 10 of Part 17 (reduction of share capital).

COMMENCEMENT DATE 1 October 2009[280]

**18.729.02** This section covers two circumstances in which treasury shares are cancelled. First the company has a right at any time to cancel all or any of the shares it currently holds in treasury (subsection (1)). Secondly, subsection (2) prescribes the circumstances in which shares held in treasury must be cancelled, namely if they cease to be qualifying shares. However, they must be permanently withdrawn from being listed or traded on a relevant market; merely being suspended does not require their cancellation (subsection (3)).

**18.729.03** Either form of cancellation will result in a reduction of share capital, by the nominal value of the shares in question, but the directors have authority under subsection (5) to take the necessary steps without going through the normal reduction of capital procedure.[281] The filing requirements are imposed by section 730, below.

### 730 Treasury shares: notice of cancellation

**18.730.01** (1) Where shares held by a company as treasury shares are cancelled, the company must deliver a return to the registrar not later than 28 days after the shares are cancelled.

        This does not apply to shares that are cancelled forthwith on their acquisition by the company (see section 708).

    (2) The return must state with respect to shares of each class cancelled—

        (a) the number and nominal value of the shares, and

        (b) the date on which they were cancelled.

    (3) Particulars of shares cancelled on different dates may be included in a single return.

    (4) The notice must be accompanied by a statement of capital.

    (5) The statement of capital must state with respect to the company's share capital immediately following the cancellation—

        (a) the total number of shares of the company,

        (b) the aggregate nominal value of those shares,

        (c) for each class of shares—

            (i) prescribed particulars of the rights attached to the shares,

            (ii) the total number of shares of that class, and

            (iii) the aggregate nominal value of shares of that class, and

        (d) the amount paid up and the amount (if any) unpaid on each share (whether on account of the nominal value of the share or by way of premium).

    (6) If default is made in complying with this section, an offence is committed by—

        (a) the company, and

        (b) every officer of the company who is in default.

    (7) A person guilty of an offence under this section is liable on summary conviction to a fine not exceeding level 3 on the standard scale and, for continued contravention, a daily default fine not exceeding one-tenth of level 3 on the standard scale.

COMMENCEMENT DATE 1 October 2009[282]

**18.730.02** This section imposes a special filing requirement in respect of treasury shares which were not immediately cancelled following their purchase by the company. It applies if shares are subsequently

---

[280] Companies Act 2006 (Commencement No 8, Transitional Provisions and Savings) Order 2008, SI 2008/2860, art 3(l).

[281] As to this, see para 17.641.01 above.

[282] Companies Act 2006 (Commencement No 8, Transitional Provisions and Savings) Order 2008, SI 2008/2860, art 3(l).

cancelled.[283] The return must be completed within 28 days of disposal of the shares, but can include particulars disposed of on different dates (subsection (3)). It must be accompanied by a statement of capital in the standard form, further explanation of which can be found in the commentary to section 10.[284]

The penalty for breach falls on the company and every officer of the company in default.[285]            **18.730.03**

## 731  Treasury shares: treatment of proceeds of sale

(1) Where shares held as treasury shares are sold, the proceeds of sale must be dealt with in accordance with this section.                                                                                **18.731.01**
(2) If the proceeds of sale are equal to or less than the purchase price paid by the company for the shares, the proceeds are treated for the purposes of Part 23 (distributions) as a realised profit of the company.
(3) If the proceeds of sale exceed the purchase price paid by the company—
   (a) an amount equal to the purchase price paid is treated as a realised profit of the company for the purposes of that Part, and
   (b) the excess must be transferred to the company's share premium account.
(4) For the purposes of this section—
   (a) the purchase price paid by the company must be determined by the application of a weighted average price method, and
   (b) if the shares were allotted to the company as fully paid bonus shares, the purchase price paid for them is treated as nil.

COMMENCEMENT DATE  1 October 2009[286]

This section prescribes what happens to the proceeds of sale of any treasury shares and facilitates their   **18.731.02**
disposal in order to boost a company's distributable profits. Up to the amount that the company paid for the shares, determined in accordance with subsection (4)(a),[287] is treated as realized profit for the purposes of the requirements of the Act governing distributions.[288] Any excess above that amount has to be transferred to the share premium account.[289] Obviously if the company receives less than it paid for the shares, there will be nothing to transfer to the share premium account.

Any treasury shares that were allotted as bonus shares have a nil value for this purpose (subsection   **18.731.03**
(4)(b)).

## 732  Treasury shares: offences

(1) If a company contravenes any of the provisions of this Chapter (except section 730 (notice of   **18.732.01**
cancellation)), an offence is committed by—
   (a) the company, and
   (b) every officer of the company who is in default.
(2) A person guilty of an offence under this section is liable—
   (a) on conviction on indictment, to a fine;
   (b) on summary conviction to a fine not exceeding the statutory maximum.

COMMENCEMENT DATE  1 October 2009[290]

This section prescribes the relatively steep penalties (which can include an unlimited fine) for the   **18.732.02**
company or any officer of a company in default[291] under the sections dealing with treasury shares, except that for failure to deliver notice of cancellation under section 730, which has its own specific penalty. The 2006 Act introduced the penalty on the company in order to emphasize the importance of due compliance with the provisions; there was no such provision in the original sections dealing with treasury shares.

---

[283] It applies to shares cancelled on or after 1 October 2009: Companies Act 2006 (Commencement No 8, Transitional Provisions and Savings) Order 2008, SI 2008/2860, Sch 2, para 80. The requirements of s 169A of the 1985 Act applied to shares cancelled before that date.

[284] See para 2.10.02.

[285] For the meaning of officer in default, see s 1121.

[286] Companies Act 2006 (Commencement No 8, Transitional Provisions and Savings) Order 2008, SI 2008/2860, art 3(l).

[287] The Act does not define 'weighted average price method'.

[288] See para 23.830.02.

[289] As to this, see para 17.610.01 above.

[290] Companies Act 2006 (Commencement No 8, Transitional Provisions and Savings) Order 2008, SI 2008/2860, art 3(l).

[291] As to the meaning of 'officer in default', see s 1121.

# CHAPTER 7
## SUPPLEMENTARY PROVISIONS

### 733 The capital redemption reserve

**18.733.01**

(1) In the following circumstances a company must transfer amounts to a reserve, called the 'capital redemption reserve'.

(2) Where under this Part shares of a limited company are redeemed or purchased wholly out of the company's profits, the amount by which the company's issued share capital is diminished in accordance with—

    (a) section 688(b) (on the cancellation of shares redeemed), or

    (b) section 706(b)(ii) (on the cancellation of shares purchased),

    must be transferred to the capital redemption reserve.

(3) If—

    (a) the shares are redeemed or purchased wholly or partly out of the proceeds of a fresh issue, and

    (b) the aggregate amount of the proceeds is less than the aggregate nominal value of the shares redeemed or purchased,

    the amount of the difference must be transferred to the capital redemption reserve.

    This does not apply in the case of a private company if, in addition to the proceeds of the fresh issue, the company applies a payment out of capital under Chapter 5 in making the redemption or purchase.

(4) The amount by which a company's share capital is diminished in accordance with section 729(4) (on the cancellation of shares held as treasury shares) must be transferred to the capital redemption reserve.

(5) The company may use the capital redemption reserve to pay up new shares to be allotted to members as fully paid bonus shares.

(6) Subject to that, the provisions of the Companies Acts relating to the reduction of a company's share capital apply as if the capital redemption reserve were part of its paid up share capital.

COMMENCEMENT DATE 1 October 2009[292]

**18.733.02**  This section restates section 170 of the 1985 Act with drafting amendments and imposes capital maintenance requirements following a company's redemption or purchase of its own shares. It is designed to ensure that where a company redeems or purchases its own shares (a) by using distributable profits, or (b) to the extent that it uses distributable profits where a new issue is also used, or (c) where the proceeds of a new issue are less than the nominal value of the shares, capital is maintained by the creation of or increase in its capital redemption reserve. Case (c) does not apply where a private company uses a payment out of capital to fund a purchase in addition to the proceeds of a new issue (subsection (3)). Similarly, by subsection (4), the same capital maintenance requirement applies where treasury shares are cancelled under section 729.

**18.733.03**  The capital redemption reserve is treated as capital. It can be used to fund an issue of fully paid bonus shares (subsection (5)), but otherwise can be dealt with only in accordance with the provisions on reduction of capital (subsection (6)).[293]

### 734 Accounting consequences of payment out of capital

**18.734.01**

(1) This section applies where a payment out of capital is made in accordance with Chapter 5 (redemption or purchase of own shares by private company out of capital).

(2) If the permissible capital payment is less than the nominal amount of the shares redeemed or purchased, the amount of the difference must be transferred to the company's capital redemption reserve.

(3) If the permissible capital payment is greater than the nominal amount of the shares redeemed or purchased—

    (a) the amount of any capital redemption reserve, share premium account or fully paid share capital of the company, and

    (b) any amount representing unrealised profits of the company for the time being standing to the credit of any revaluation reserve maintained by the company,

    may be reduced by a sum not exceeding (or by sums not in total exceeding) the amount by which the permissible capital payment exceeds the nominal amount of the shares.

---

[292] Companies Act 2006 (Commencement No 8, Transitional Provisions and Savings) Order 2008, SI 2008/2860, art 3(l).

[293] As to reduction of capital, see para 17.641.01 above.

(4) Where the proceeds of a fresh issue are applied by the company in making a redemption or purchase of its own shares in addition to a payment out of capital under this Chapter, the references in subsections (2) and (3) to the permissible capital payment are to be read as referring to the aggregate of that payment and those proceeds.

COMMENCEMENT DATE 1 October 2009[294]

This section restates what was formerly in section 171 of the 1985 Act regarding the effect of a private company redeeming or purchasing its shares out of capital on the company's share capital in its accounts. **18.734.02**

If the permissible capital payment, as described in section 710, is less than the nominal value of the shares, the difference must be transferred to the capital redemption reserve,[295] so maintaining capital. Where it is greater than the nominal value of the shares, the company's capital accounts (that is its fully paid share capital, capital redemption reserve, and share premium account) and any reserve representing unrealized profits may be reduced by the difference. **18.734.03**

Where a fresh issue is used to fund a redemption or purchase, in addition to a payment out of capital, then the permissible capital payment is the aggregate of the payment and the proceeds of the fresh issue. **18.734.04**

## 735 Effect of company's failure to redeem or purchase

(1) This section applies where a company— **18.735.01**
    (a) issues shares on terms that they are or are liable to be redeemed, or
    (b) agrees to purchase any of its shares.
(2) The company is not liable in damages in respect of any failure on its part to redeem or purchase any of the shares.
    This is without prejudice to any right of the holder of the shares other than his right to sue the company for damages in respect of its failure.
(3) The court shall not grant an order for specific performance of the terms of redemption or purchase if the company shows that it is unable to meet the costs of redeeming or purchasing the shares in question out of distributable profits.
(4) If the company is wound up and at the commencement of the winding up any of the shares have not been redeemed or purchased, the terms of redemption or purchase may be enforced against the company.
    When shares are redeemed or purchased under this subsection, they are treated as cancelled.
(5) Subsection (4) does not apply if—
    (a) the terms provided for the redemption or purchase to take place at a date later than that of the commencement of the winding up, or
    (b) during the period—
        (i) beginning with the date on which the redemption or purchase was to have taken place, and
        (ii) ending with the commencement of the winding up,
    the company could not at any time have lawfully made a distribution equal in value to the price at which the shares were to have been redeemed or purchased.
(6) There shall be paid in priority to any amount that the company is liable under subsection (4) to pay in respect of any shares—
    (a) all other debts and liabilities of the company (other than any due to members in their character as such), and
    (b) if other shares carry rights (whether as to capital or as to income) that are preferred to the rights as to capital attaching to the first-mentioned shares, any amount due in satisfaction of those preferred rights.
    Subject to that, any such amount shall be paid in priority to any amounts due to members in satisfaction of their rights (whether as to capital or income) as members.

COMMENCEMENT DATE 1 October 2009[296]

This section, which restates section 178 of the 1985 Act with minor drafting changes, restricts the rights that a shareholder has against a company that fails to redeem or purchase his shares in breach of either **18.735.02**

---

[294] Companies Act 2006 (Commencement No 8, Transitional Provisions and Savings) Order 2008, SI 2008/2860, art 3(1).

[295] See s 733.

[296] Companies Act 2006 (Commencement No 8, Transitional Provisions and Savings) Order 2008, SI 2008/2860, art 3(1).

the terms of redemption, in the case of redeemable shares, or of a contract to buy shares.[297] The main effect is that a shareholder cannot claim damages for breach of the company's duty to redeem or purchase shares, although it is only for that breach that damages are prohibited by subsection (2) and he can maintain other claims for damages if appropriate, for example for breach of a covenant to redeem shares.[298] Other remedies for a failure to redeem or purchase, for example, an order for specific performance, are available, although specific performance cannot be ordered, under subsection (3), if the company shows that it is unable to meet the cost out of distributable profits.

**18.735.03**    Subsections (4) to (6) deal with the situation where the company has been wound up having failed before the commencement of the winding up to redeem or purchase in breach of the terms of redemption or an agreement to purchase. The shareholder can enforce payment provided that between the due date and the date of winding up the company could have made a distribution equal to the price at which the shares were to have been redeemed or purchased, but ranks for payment after all other creditors and after shareholders having preferential rights to the return of capital before the class of shares held by the shareholder. Shares that are redeemed or purchased in this way are treated as cancelled.

### 736  Meaning of 'distributable profits'

**18.736.01**    In this Part (except in Chapter 2 (financial assistance): see section 683) 'distributable profits', in relation to the making of any payment by a company, means profits out of which the company could lawfully make a distribution (within the meaning given by section 830) equal in value to the payment.

COMMENCEMENT DATE  1 October 2009[299]

**18.736.02**    This section repeats the definition of 'distributable profits' previously in section 181(a) of the 1985 Act. The definition applies for the whole of Part 18, except for Chapter 2 dealing with financial assistance. It has a wide application throughout the Part, but is by itself unproblematic as it simply refers to the general provision on distributions, namely section 830.[300]

### 737  General power to make further provision by regulations

**18.737.01**
(1)  The Secretary of State may by regulations modify the provisions of this Part.
(2)  The regulations may—
    (a)  amend or repeal any of the provisions of this Part, or
    (b)  make such other provision as appears to the Secretary of State appropriate in place of any of the provisions of this Part.
(3)  Regulations under this section may make consequential amendments or repeals in other provisions of this Act, or in other enactments.
(4)  Regulations under this section are subject to affirmative resolution procedure.

COMMENCEMENT DATE  1 October 2009[301]

**18.737.02**    This section confers wide powers to alter, by statutory instrument subject to affirmative resolution procedure, any of the provisions in this Part dealing with a company's acquisition of its own shares. It replaces more limited powers that were contained in section 179 of the 1985 Act, which were exercised in order first to introduce the provisions dealing with treasury shares. The powers are obviously very extensive.

---

[297]  The former s 178 referred to redemptions or purchases after 15 June 1982, which was the date that the original provisions in the CA 1981 allowing the redemption and purchase of a company's own shares came into force. Previously only redeemable preference shares were permitted under the CA 1948. The removal of the reference to the date is no doubt to the fact that the limitation period for any claims before then has long expired.

[298]  *Barclays Bank plc v British & Commonwealth Holdings plc* [1996] 1 BCLC 1.

[299]  Companies Act 2006 (Commencement No 8, Transitional Provisions and Savings) Order 2008, SI 2008/2860, art 3(l).

[300]  See para 23.830.01.

[301]  Companies Act 2006 (Commencement No 8, Transitional Provisions and Savings) Order 2008, SI 2008/2860, art 3(l).

# 19

## DEBENTURES

## Companies Act 2006

### PART 19

### DEBENTURES

### *General provisions*

### 738 Meaning of 'debenture'[a]

In the Companies Acts 'debenture' includes debenture stock, bonds and any other securities of a company, whether or not constituting a charge on the assets of the company.     **19.738.01**

AMENDMENTS AND NOTES

[a] Section 738 also applies (with appropriate modifications) to LLPs by virtue of the Limited Liability Partnerships (Application of Companies Act 2006) Regulations 2009, SI 2009/1804, Pt 6.

COMMENCEMENT DATE 6 April 2008[1]

Formerly contained in section 744 (general definition section) of the Companies Act 1985. This provision from the former section 744 has been re-allocated for the convenience of the reader and puts the definition of 'debenture' alongside the main sections of the Act which regulate the issue of debentures.     **19.738.02**

The definition makes it clear that it is designed to be non-exhaustive[2] and it does not matter whether or not the debenture (be it in the form of debenture stock, bonds, or other securities of the company) constitutes a charge on the assets of the company. It will remain a question of construction in every case where it is alleged that a 'debenture' has been created by a company but, although the courts have     **19.738.03**

---

[1] Companies Act 2006 (Commencement No 5, Transitional Provisions and Savings) Order 2007, SI 2007/3495, art 3.

[2] The section uses the word 'includes'.

refused to give an exhaustive definition to the term[3] (a policy reflected in the Act), any transaction which creates or acknowledges a debt will, in general, suffice to come within the wide parameters of the definition.[4]

### 739  Perpetual debentures[a]

**19.739.01**
(1)  A condition contained in debentures, or in a deed for securing debentures, is not invalid by reason only that the debentures are made—
  (a)  irredeemable, or
  (b)  redeemable only—
    (i)  on the happening of a contingency (however remote), or
    (ii)  on the expiration of a period (however long),
  any rule of equity to the contrary notwithstanding.
(2)  Subsection (1) applies to debentures whenever issued and to deeds whenever executed.

AMENDMENTS AND NOTES

[a]  Section 739 also applies (with appropriate modifications) to LLPs by virtue of the Limited Liability Partnerships (Application of Companies Act 2006) Regulations 2009, SI 2009/1804, Pt 6.

COMMENCEMENT DATE  6 April 2008[5]

**19.739.02**  Formerly section 193 of the Companies Act 1985. This section makes it clear that an issue of debentures or a deed securing an issue of debentures is not invalidated if either type of issue is made irredeemable or, redeemable only if a remote contingency occurs or a long period of time elapses.

**19.739.03**  The section was originally introduced to make it clear that the general equitable rules designed to protect impecunious mortgagors did not apply to companies which could be presumed to contract on an equal footing.[6] Therefore, a company can clog the equity of redemption[7] and exclude the rule against perpetuities when issuing debentures.

### 740  Enforcement of contract to subscribe for debentures[a]

**19.740.01**
A contract with a company to take up and pay for debentures of the company may be enforced by an order for specific performance.

AMENDMENTS AND NOTES
[a]  Section 740 also applies (with appropriate modifications) to LLPs by virtue of the Limited Liability Partnerships (Application of Companies Act 2006) Regulations 2009, SI 2009/1804, Pt 6.
COMMENCEMENT DATE  6 April 2008[8]

**19.740.02**  Formerly section 195 of the Companies Act 1985. This section makes it clear that the remedy of specific performance will be available against a party who refuses to perform a contract to either issue or pay for debentures of a company.[9] However, the remedy will not be available if the company forfeits the debenture for non-payment of calls.[10]

### 741  Registration of allotment of debentures[a]

**19.741.01**
(1)  A company must register an allotment of debentures as soon as practicable and in any event within two months after the date of the allotment.
(2)  If a company fails to comply with this section, an offence is committed by—
  (a)  the company, and
  (b)  every officer of the company who is in default.
(3)  A person guilty of an offence under this section is liable on summary conviction to a fine not exceeding level 3 on the standard scale and, for continued contravention, a daily default fine not exceeding one-tenth of level 2 on the standard scale.

---

[3]  See *Knightsbridge Estates Trust v Byrne* [1940] AC 613, 621–622, *per* Viscount Maugham.
[4]  See *Levy v Abercorris Slate & Slab Co* (1887) 37 Ch D 260, 264, *per* Chitty J.
[5]  Companies Act 2006 (Commencement No 5, Transitional Provisions and Savings) Order 2007, SI 2007/3495, art 3.
[6]  See *Knightsbridge Estates Trust Ltd v Byrne* [1940] AC 613, 622–623, *per* Viscount Maugham.
[7]  Prior to the introduction of the Companies Act (CA) 1907, s 14 perpetual debentures were invalid as clogs on the equity of redemption.
[8]  Companies Act 2006 (Commencement No 5, Transitional Provisions and Savings) Order 2007, SI 2007/3495, art 3.
[9]  At common law the remedy of specific performance was not available in this situation; see *South African Territories v Wallington* [1898] AC 309. The common law position was originally changed by virtue of the CA 1907, s 16 (effective as of 1 July 1908).
[10]  See *Kuala Pahi Rubber Estates Ltd v Mowbray* (1914) 111 LT 1072, CA.

(4)  For the duties of the company as to the issue of the debentures, or certificates of debenture stock, see Part 21 (certification and transfer of securities).

AMENDMENTS AND NOTES

a  Section 741 also applies (with appropriate modifications) to LLPs by virtue of the Limited Liability Partnerships (Application of Companies Act 2006) Regulations 2009, SI 2009/1804, Pt 6.

COMMENCEMENT DATE  6 April 2008[11]

This is a new section and imposes a duty upon the company to register an allotment of debentures 'as **19.741.02** soon as practical' after they have been allotted but, in any event, within two months of the allotment.[12] It is an offence not to comply with this requirement and failure will render the company and any responsible officer of the company liable to a fine.[13] It should be noted that where an issue of debentures is secured by a charge then that will require a separate act of registration under the company charge registration provisions of the Act.[14]

## 742  Debentures to bearer (Scotland)[a]

Notwithstanding anything in the statute of the Scots Parliament of 1696, chapter 25, debentures to **19.742.01** bearer issued in Scotland are valid and binding according to their terms.

AMENDMENTS AND NOTES

a  Section 742 also applies (with appropriate modifications) to LLPs by virtue of the Limited Liability Partnerships (Application of Companies Act 2006) Regulations 2009, SI 2009/1804, Pt 6.

COMMENCEMENT DATE  6 April 2008[15]

Formerly section 197 of the Companies Act 1985. Debentures to bearer have been widely accepted **19.742.02** under English law since the 19th century. However, in Scotland there was doubt whether they were valid or not due to difficulties in construing the Scottish Bankruptcy Act 1696 (c 25). This provision was introduced into the Act to make it clear that bearer debentures are valid under Scottish law.

## *Register of debenture holders*

## 743  Register of debenture holders[a]

(1)  Any register of debenture holders of a company that is kept by the company must be kept **19.743.01** available for inspection—
    (a)  at the company's registered office, or
    (b)  at a place specified in regulations under section 1136.
(2)  A company must give notice to the registrar of the place where any such register is kept available for inspection and of any change in that place.
(3)  No such notice is required if the register has, at all times since it came into existence, been kept available for inspection at the company's registered office.
(4)  If a company makes default for 14 days in complying with subsection (2), an offence is committed by—
    (a)  the company, and
    (b)  every officer of the company who is in default.
(5)  A person guilty of an offence under this section is liable on summary conviction to a fine not exceeding level 3 on the standard scale and, for continued contravention, a daily default fine not exceeding one-tenth of level 3 on the standard scale.
(6)  References in this section to a register of debenture holders include a duplicate—
    (a)  of a register of debenture holders that is kept outside the United Kingdom, or
    (b)  of any part of such a register.

---

[11]  Companies Act 2006 (Commencement No 5, Transitional Provisions and Savings) Order 2007, SI 2007/3495, art 3.
[12]  See s 741(1). Note also s 769(1) which obliges the company to complete and have ready for delivery the debentures allotted or any certificates of debenture stock within two months after the allotment. The section applies to allotments of debentures made on or after 6 April 2008; see SI 2007/3496, art 20.
[13]  See s 741(2), (3).
[14]  On which see Part 25 of the Act, discussed below.
[15]  Companies Act 2006 (Commencement No 5, Transitional Provisions and Savings) Order 2007, SI 2007/3495, art 3.

AMENDMENTS AND NOTES

ᵃ Section 743 also applies (with appropriate modifications) to LLPs by virtue of the Limited Liability
Partnerships (Application of Companies Act 2006) Regulations 2009, SI 2009/1804, Pt 6.

COMMENCEMENT DATE 6 April 2008[16]

**19.743.02**   Formerly (in part) section 190 of the Companies Act 1985. In circumstances where a company keeps a
register of its debenture holders[17] then, by virtue of this section, a duty is imposed upon the company
to keep that register available for inspection[18] at either its registered office, or at another place specified
by the Secretary of State.[19] The company is also required to inform the registrar of companies of the
location of the register of debenture holders or any change in that location.[20] If a company or any
relevant officer fails to give notice to the registrar of the location of the register or any change thereof
within 14 days of the register being established or its location changed then both parties commit an
offence punishable by way of fine.[21]

### 744  Register of debenture holders: right to inspect and require copyᵃ

**19.744.01**   (1)  Every register of debenture holders of a company must, except when duly closed, be open to the
inspection—
(a) of the registered holder of any such debentures, or any holder of shares in the company,
without charge, and
(b) of any other person on payment of such fee as may be prescribed.
(2)  Any person may require a copy of the register, or any part of it, on payment of such fee as may be
prescribed.
(3)  A person seeking to exercise either of the rights conferred by this section must make a request to
the company to that effect.
(4)  The request must contain the following information—
(a) in the case of an individual, his name and address;
(b) in the case of an organisation, the name and address of an individual responsible for making
the request on behalf of the organisation;
(c) the purpose for which the information is to be used; and
(d) whether the information will be disclosed to any other person, and if so—
(i)   where that person is an individual, his name and address,
(ii)  where that person is an organisation, the name and address of an individual responsible
for receiving the information on its behalf, and
(iii) the purpose for which the information is to be used by that person.
(5)  For the purposes of this section a register is 'duly closed' if it is closed in accordance with provision
contained—
(a) in the articles or in the debentures,
(b) in the case of debenture stock in the stock certificates, or
(c) in the trust deed or other document securing the debentures or debenture stock.
The total period for which a register is closed in any year must not exceed 30 days.
(6)  References in this section to a register of debenture holders include a duplicate—
(a) of a register of debenture holders that is kept outside the United Kingdom, or
(b) of any part of such a register.

AMENDMENTS AND NOTES

ᵃ Section 744 also applies (with appropriate modifications) to LLPs by virtue of the Limited Liability
Partnerships (Application of Companies Act 2006) Regulations 2009, SI 2009/1804, Pt 6.

COMMENCEMENT DATE 6 April 2008[22]

[16] Companies Act 2006 (Commencement No 5, Transitional Provisions and Savings) Order 2007, SI 2007/
3495, art 3.
[17] This phrase includes a duplicate register of debenture holders (or any part of such a register) that is kept
outside the UK; see s 743(6).
[18] As to inspection rights generally see s 744 below.
[19] See s 743(1)(b). For the Secretary of State's powers to specify places where the register of debenture holders
may be kept see s 1136. See the Companies (Company Record) Regulations 2008, SI 2008/3006 which require one
'alternative inspection location' for all registers not kept at the registered office.
[20] See s 743(2). However, notification to the registrar is not required if the register has, at all times since it came
into existence, been kept available for inspection at the company's registered office; see s 743(3). The notice
referred to in this section is prescribed by the registrar under powers conferred by s 1068(1) of the Act.
[21] See s 743(4)(5).
[22] Companies Act 2006 (Commencement No 5, Transitional Provisions and Savings) Order 2007, SI 2007/
3495, art 3.

Formerly section 191 of the Companies Act 1985.[23] This section imposes a duty upon a company **19.744.02** keeping a register of debenture holders to allow certain parties[24] access to that register in order to inspect it.[25] However, such parties do not have a right of access on days (not to exceed 30 in any year) when the register is 'duly closed' as set out in accordance with provisions contained in the company's articles or in the relevant document creating the debentures.[26] Any person may also require the company to provide them, upon payment of a fee,[27] with a copy of the register or any part of it.[28] However, a party inspecting the register does not have a right to make their own copies of the register but must, instead, request that the company make any copies required on their behalf.[29]

A new provision in the section is that a party wishing to either inspect the register of debenture holders **19.744.03** or make a copy of it (in whole or in part) must now first make a request of the company to that effect.[30] The party making the request is required to furnish the company with detailed information about themselves and the reason for the request, including the purpose for which the inspection of, or copies from, the register is being made.[31] The latter is a new requirement added to the Act in order that the company is not required to supply delicate information 'blind' to any third party. Instead, the company is allowed to vet applications in advance in order to determine whether they consider the request is made for a 'proper purpose'.[32] Should the company believe that a request is being made for an improper purpose[33] then the company may apply to the court to request that it be relieved from the duty to comply.[34] In all other cases the company is obliged to grant the request.

### 745  Register of debenture holders: response to request for inspection or copy[a]

(1)  Where a company receives a request under section 744 (register of debenture holders: right to **19.745.01** inspect and require copy), it must within five working days either—
    (a)  comply with the request, or
    (b)  apply to the court.
(2)  If it applies to the court it must notify the person making the request.
(3)  If on an application under this section the court is satisfied that the inspection or copy is not sought for a proper purpose—
    (a)  it shall direct the company not to comply with the request, and
    (b)  it may further order that the company's costs (in Scotland, expenses) on the application be paid in whole or in part by the person who made the request, even if he is not a party to the application.
(4)  If the court makes such a direction and it appears to the court that the company is or may be subject to other requests made for a similar purpose (whether made by the same person or different persons), it may direct that the company is not to comply with any such request.
    The order must contain such provision as appears to the court appropriate to identify the requests to which it applies.
(5)  If on an application under this section the court does not direct the company not to comply with the request, the company must comply with the request immediately upon the court giving its decision or, as the case may be, the proceedings being discontinued.

---

[23]  The new ss 744–747 and s 749 (discussed below) will apply to any requests for information made on or after 6 April 2008. However, in relation to requests made before that date the previous provisions of the Companies Act 1985, s 191(1)–(6) or, in relation to Northern Ireland, the Companies Order 1986, art 200(1)–(6) will continue to apply: see SI 2007/3495, art 22.

[24]  See s 744(1)(a), (b) for these parties. Note also *Lemon v Austin Friars Investment Trust Ltd* [1926] Ch 1.

[25]  See s 744(1).

[26]  See generally s 744(5).

[27]  The fees for inspecting and taking a copy of the register of debenture holders are set out in the Companies (Fees for Inspection and Copying of Company Records) (No 2) Regulations 2007, SI 2007/3535.

[28]  See s 744(2).

[29]  See *Re Balaghat Gold Mining Co* [1901] 2 KB 665, CA.

[30]  See s 745(3).

[31]  This information is also required of any other person the applicant will pass the information on to; see s 757(4)(d).

[32]  On which see s 745(3) below.

[33]  Eg the company may believe that the application is being made by, or on behalf of, a terrorist organization in order to access the names and addresses of those providing finance for the company who will then become the targets of criminal actions.

[34]  See generally s 745 below.

AMENDMENTS AND NOTES

<sup>a</sup> Section 745 also applies (with appropriate modifications) to LLPs by virtue of the Limited Liability Partnerships (Application of Companies Act 2006) Regulations 2009, SI 2009/1804, Pt 6.

COMMENCEMENT DATE 6 April 2008[35]

**19.745.02** This is a new section governing the company's responses to requests for inspection of the register of debenture holders or copies therefrom. Where a section 744 request is made to inspect the register or to have a copy of it made the company is given five working days to consider it and then either comply with the request, or apply to the court for an order directing the company not to comply with it.[36] Should the company decide to seek a non-compliance order then it must notify the person making the section 744 request.[37]

**19.745.03** It is for the company to demonstrate to the satisfaction of the court that 'the inspection or a copy is not sought for a proper purpose'.[38] The court has a wide discretion when considering such applications and there is no prescribed criteria as to what might constitute a 'proper purpose' or, indeed, an 'improper purpose'. We will have to wait for case law before the boundaries of this become clear. However, any person seeking to gain information from the register to be used for criminal purposes will necessarily not be seeking them for a 'proper purpose' and will have their request denied.[39]

**19.745.04** In order to prevent companies' time being wasted processing what might be termed 'floodgate' section 744 requests, the court is given power, when making a section 745 order in a given case, to order the company to also refuse any other requests made 'for a similar purpose'.[40] In addition, in cases where the court directs the company to comply with the request, the court is given a discretion to order that the company's costs in making the section 745 application be met by the party making the original section 744 request.[41]

**19.745.05** Should the court refuse to make a section 745 order, the company having failed to establish that the section 744 request was not for a 'proper purpose', then the company must comply with the request 'immediately upon the court giving its decision'[42] unless the proceedings are continued by the company appealing.

### 746 Register of debenture holders: refusal of inspection or default in providing copy[a]

**19.746.01**   (1) If an inspection required under section 744 (register of debenture holders: right to inspect and require copy) is refused or default is made in providing a copy required under that section, otherwise than in accordance with an order of the court, an offence is committed by—
    (a) the company, and
    (b) every officer of the company who is in default.
  (2) A person guilty of an offence under this section is liable on summary conviction to a fine not exceeding level 3 on the standard scale and, for continued contravention, a daily default fine not exceeding one-tenth of level 3 on the standard scale.
  (3) In the case of any such refusal or default the court may by order compel an immediate inspection or, as the case may be, direct that the copy required be sent to the person requesting it.

AMENDMENTS AND NOTES

<sup>a</sup> Section 746 also applies (with appropriate modifications) to LLPs by virtue of the Limited Liability Partnerships (Application of Companies Act 2006) Regulations 2009, SI 2009/1804, Pt 6.

COMMENCEMENT DATE 6 April 2008[43]

**19.746.02** Formerly (in part) section 191 of the Companies Act 1985. This section makes it an offence, punishable by way of a fine, for the company and any relevant officer to refuse to meet a section 745 request (unless authorized by the court).[44]

---

[35] Companies Act 2006 (Commencement No 5, Transitional Provisions and Savings) Order 2007, SI 2007/3495, art 3.

[36] See s 745(1).

[37] See s 745(2).

[38] See s 745(3).

[39] Cf *Daiichi UK Ltd v SHAC* [2005] 1 BCLC 27.

[40] See s 745(4). When making such an additional order the court must ensure that the order contains such provision as appears to the court appropriate to identify the requests to which it relates.

[41] See s 745(3)(b).

[42] See s 745(5).

[43] Companies Act 2006 (Commencement No 5, Transitional Provisions and Savings) Order 2007, SI 2007/3495, art 3.

[44] i.e. a s 745 order is made in favour of the company.

If the company continues to refuse to meet a section 745 request then the court is given a discretion to make an order compelling the company to allow an inspection of the register of debenture holders or, as the case may be, that the company makes copies from the register as requested.[45]                    **19.746.03**

## 747   Register of debenture holders: offences in connection with request for or disclosure of information[a]

(1)   It is an offence for a person knowingly or recklessly to make in a request under section 744 (register of debenture holders: right to inspect and require copy) a statement that is misleading, false or deceptive in a material particular.                    **19.747.01**

(2)   It is an offence for a person in possession of information obtained by exercise of either of the rights conferred by that section—

   (a)   to do anything that results in the information being disclosed to another person, or

   (b)   to fail to do anything with the result that the information is disclosed to another person, knowing or having reason to suspect that person may use the information for a purpose that is not a proper purpose.

(3)   A person guilty of an offence under this section is liable—

   (a)   on conviction on indictment, to imprisonment for a term not exceeding two years or a fine (or both);

   (b)   on summary conviction—

      (i)   in England and Wales, to imprisonment for a term not exceeding twelve months or to a fine not exceeding the statutory maximum (or both);

      (ii)   in Scotland or Northern Ireland, to imprisonment for a term not exceeding six months, or to a fine not exceeding the statutory maximum (or both).

AMENDMENTS AND NOTES

[a]   Section 747 also applies (with appropriate modifications) to LLPs by virtue of the Limited Liability Partnerships (Application of Companies Act 2006) Regulations 2009, SI 2009/1804, Pt 6.

COMMENCEMENT DATE  6 April 2008[46]

This is a new provision. This section is designed to ensure that any information gained from a section 745 request is only used for a 'proper purpose' and generally remains with the person who made the request. It is an offence, punishable by way of imprisonment, or a fine, or both, for a person to make a section 745 request and in the process make a statement 'that is misleading, false or deceptive in a material particular'.[47]                    **19.747.02**

An offence is also committed if a person obtains information from a section 745 request and either does something, or fails to do something, which results in that information being disclosed to another person who the person obtaining the information knows or has reason to suspect that the other person may use the information for an improper purpose.[48] The punishment for this offence is a fine (not to exceed the statutory maximum) and/or imprisonment (not to exceed 12 months).[49]                    **19.747.03**

## 748   Time limit for claims arising from entry in register[a]

(1)   Liability incurred by a company—                    **19.748.01**

   (a)   from the making or deletion of an entry in the register of debenture holders, or

   (b)   from a failure to make or delete any such entry,

   is not enforceable more than ten years after the date on which the entry was made or deleted or, as the case may be, the failure first occurred.

(2)   This is without prejudice to any lesser period of limitation (and, in Scotland, to any rule that the obligation giving rise to the liability prescribes before the expiry of that period).

AMENDMENTS AND NOTES

[a]   Section 748 also applies (with appropriate modifications) to LLPs by virtue of the Limited Liability Partnerships (Application of Companies Act 2006) Regulations 2009, SI 2009/1804, Pt 6.

COMMENCEMENT DATE  6 April 2008[50]

---

[45]   See s 746(3).

[46]   Companies Act 2006 (Commencement No 5, Transitional Provisions and Savings) Order 2007, SI 2007/3495, art 3.

[47]   See s 747(1).

[48]   See s 747(2).

[49]   See s 747(3).

[50]   Companies Act 2006 (Commencement No 5, Transitional Provisions and Savings) Order 2007, SI 2007/3495, art 3.

**19.748.02** Formerly section 191(7) of the Companies Act 1985. This section imposes a ten-year period of limitation[51] for bringing claims against the company for either:

(i) the company's failure in making or deleting an entry to, or from, its register of debentures; or

(ii) the company's failure to make or delete an entry to, or from, its register of debentures.

Formerly the period of limitation was 20 years under the 1985 Act.[52] However, this new ten-year limitation period does not apply where any shorter period is rendered applicable.[53]

**19.748.03** It remains a matter of debate as to the precise ambit of section 748(1), as to whether it is confined to preventing claims against the company for damages after ten years have expired from the company's failure in maintaining the register of debenture holders, or whether it also applies so as to prevent claims, for example, as to the rightful title to debentures.

## *Supplementary provisions*

### 749 Right of debenture holder to copy of deed[a]

**19.749.01**
(1) Any holder of debentures of a company is entitled, on request and on payment of such fee as may be prescribed, to be provided with a copy of any trust deed for securing the debentures.

(2) If default is made in complying with this section, an offence is committed by every officer of the company who is in default.

(3) A person guilty of an offence under this section is liable on summary conviction to a fine not exceeding level 3 on the standard scale and, for continued contravention, a daily default fine not exceeding one-tenth of level 3 on the standard scale.

(4) In the case of any such default the court may direct that the copy required be sent to the person requiring it.

AMENDMENTS AND NOTES

[a] Section 749 also applies (with appropriate modifications) to LLPs by virtue of the Limited Liability Partnerships (Application of Companies Act 2006) Regulations 2009, SI 2009/1804, Pt 6.

COMMENCEMENT DATE 6 April 2008[54]

**19.749.02** Formerly section 191(3), (4), and (5) of the Companies Act 1985. This, slightly revised, section establishes the right of any holder of debentures to be provided by the company with a copy of any trust deed (if it exists) for securing those debentures upon request and the payment of a prescribed fee.[55]

**19.749.03** Failure to comply with a request is an offence committed by the relevant officers of the company[56] and renders those in default liable to a fine.[57]

**19.749.04** Continued failure to meet a request by a debenture holder allows the courts discretion to direct that a copy of the trust deed be sent to the person requiring it.[58]

### 750 Liability of trustees of debentures[a]

**19.750.01**
(1) Any provision contained in—

(a) a trust deed for securing an issue of debentures, or

(b) any contract with the holders of debentures secured by a trust deed,

is void in so far as it would have the effect of exempting a trustee of the deed from, or indemnifying him against, liability for breach of trust where he fails to show the degree of care and diligence required of him as trustee, having regard to the provisions of the trust deed conferring on him any powers, authorities or discretions.

---

[51] The new 10-year period of limitation applies in respect of causes of action arising on or after 6 April 2008. In respect of causes of action arising before that date the time limit for causes of action is: (a) 10 years from 6 April 2008; or (b) 20 years (as provided by s 191(7) of the Companies Act 1985 or, in respect of Northern Ireland companies, the Companies Order 1986, art 200(7)) from when the cause of action arose, which ever expires first: see generally SI 2007/3495, art 23.

[52] See CA 1985, s 191(7).

[53] See s 748(2).

[54] Companies Act 2006 (Commencement No 5, Transitional Provisions and Savings) Order 2007, SI 2007/3495, art 3.

[55] See s 749(1). The prescribed fee is set out in the Companies (Fees for Inspection of Company Records) (No 2) Regulations 2007, SI 2007 3535, reg 4.

[56] See s 749(2).

[57] See s 749(3).

[58] See s 749(4).

(2) Subsection (1) does not invalidate—
  (a) a release otherwise validly given in respect of anything done or omitted to be done by a trustee before the giving of the release;
  (b) any provision enabling such a release to be given—
    (i) on being agreed to by a majority of not less than 75% in value of the debenture holders present and voting in person or, where proxies are permitted, by proxy at a meeting summoned for the purpose, and
    (ii) either with respect to specific acts or omissions or on the trustee dying or ceasing to act.
(3) This section is subject to section 751 (saving for certain older provisions).

AMENDMENTS AND NOTES

ᵃ Section 750 also applies (with appropriate modifications) to LLPs by virtue of the Limited Liability Partnerships (Application of Companies Act 2006) Regulations 2009, SI 2009/1804, Pt 6.

COMMENCEMENT DATE 6 April 2008[59]

Formerly section 192(1) and (2) of the Companies Act 1985. This section renders void any provision contained in either a trust deed for securing an issue of debentures, or any contract with debenture holders (secured by a trust deed) which purports to exempt the trustee from liability for breach of trust where he fails to show the desired degree of skill and care when performing his duties under the relevant trust deed. The section also applies so as to render void any attempt to indemnify such a trustee against liability in similar circumstances.[60]     **19.750.02**

However, the section is subject to two exceptions:     **19.750.03**

(i) a release (otherwise valid) given to the trustee in respect of anything done, or omitted to be done, by him before the release was given is valid;[61] or
(ii) any provision which enables a release to be given to a trustee in respect of past defaults (as in (i)) above) if 75 per cent or more in value of the debenture holders present and voting in person agree to the release at a meeting called for that purpose and, that release is in respect of specific acts or, omissions of the trustee or, because the trustee has died or ceased to act as trustee is also valid.[62]

A third exception is found under the Trustee Act 1925[63] which gives the court a discretion to excuse a trustee 'wholly or partly' from personal liability for breach of trust if the trustee can demonstrate to the court that he acted 'honestly and reasonably' and 'ought fairly to be excused'.[64]

Section 750 is subject to section 751; see below.     **19.750.04**

## 751 Liability of trustees of debentures: saving for certain older provisionsᵃ

(1) Section 750 (liability of trustees of debentures) does not operate—     **19.751.01**
  (a) to invalidate any provision in force on the relevant date so long as any person—
    (i) then entitled to the benefit of the provision, or
    (ii) afterwards given the benefit of the provision under subsection (3) below, remains a trustee of the deed in question, or
  (b) to deprive any person of any exemption or right to be indemnified in respect of anything done or omitted to be done by him while any such provision was in force.
(2) The relevant date for this purpose is—
  (a) 1st July 1948 in a case where section 192 of the Companies Act 1985 (c. 6) applied immediately before the commencement of this section;
  (b) 1st July 1961 in a case where Article 201 of the Companies (Northern Ireland) Order 1986 (S.I. 1986/1032 (N.I. 6)) then applied.
(3) While any trustee of a trust deed remains entitled to the benefit of a provision saved by subsection (1) above the benefit of that provision may be given either—
  (a) to all trustees of the deed, present and future, or
  (b) to any named trustees or proposed trustees of it,

---

[59] Companies Act 2006 (Commencement No 5, Transitional Provisions and Savings) Order 2007, SI 2007/3495, art 3.

[60] See generally s 750(1).

[61] See generally s 750(2)(a).

[62] See generally s 750(2)(b).

[63] See s 61.

[64] See generally *National Trustees Co of Australia Ltd v General Finance Co. of Australia Ltd* [1905] AC 373, 381–382, PC (a higher standard is expected of a trustee for reward than of a private person acting as a gratuitous trustee before relief will be granted under s 61 of the Trustee Act 1925). Note also CA 2006, s 1157 (power of court to grant relief to corporate officers or breach of duty, trust, negligence or other default).

by a resolution passed by a majority of not less than 75% in value of the debenture holders present in person or, where proxies are permitted, by proxy at a meeting summoned for the purpose.

(4)  A meeting for that purpose must be summoned in accordance with the provisions of the deed or, if the deed makes no provision for summoning meetings, in a manner approved by the court.

AMENDMENTS AND NOTES

[a]  Section 751 also applies (with appropriate modifications) to LLPs by virtue of the Limited Liability Partnerships (Application of Companies Act 2006) Regulations 2009, SI 2009/1804, Pt 6.

COMMENCEMENT DATE  6 April 2008[65]

**19.751.02**  Formerly section 192(3) and (4) of the Companies Act 1985. This section is a general saving section to protect provisions contained in older debenture trusts (ie prior to 1 July 1948/1961 depending on the Companies legislation governing the trust).[66] The section operates to save from avoidance under section 750 any provision[67] which was in force on 1 July 1948[68] and exempted, or indemnified, a trustee from, or against, liability for breach of trust so long as that trustee still remains a trustee. The protection also extends in favour of trustees who have had the benefit conferred upon them by virtue of section 751(3) and (4).[69] Under the latter provisions the protection given to trustees can be extended from trustees appointed prior to 1 July 1948[70] to either:

(i)   all trustees of the deed, present or future; or,
(ii)  to any named trustees or proposed trustees;

if 75 per cent in value of the debenture holders present vote in favour at a meeting[71] called for that purpose.[72]

**19.751.03**  The protection also operates in favour of a trustee who breached the trust and had a right to be exempted or indemnified from or against that breach of trust prior to such clauses being rendered void from 1 July 1948.[73]

### 752  Power to re-issue redeemed debentures[a]

**19.752.01**  (1)  Where a company has redeemed debentures previously issued, then unless—
   (a)  provision to the contrary (express or implied) is contained in the company's articles or in any contract made by the company, or
   (b)  the company has, by passing a resolution to that effect or by some other act, manifested its intention that the debentures shall be cancelled,
   the company may re-issue the debentures, either by re-issuing the same debentures or by issuing new debentures in their place. This subsection is deemed always to have had effect.

(2)  On a re-issue of redeemed debentures the person entitled to the debentures has (and is deemed always to have had) the same priorities as if the debentures had never been redeemed.

(3)  The re-issue of a debenture or the issue of another debenture in its place under this section is treated as the issue of a new debenture for the purposes of stamp duty.
   It is not so treated for the purposes of any provision limiting the amount or number of debentures to be issued.

(4)  A person lending money on the security of a debenture re-issued under this section which appears to be duly stamped may give the debenture in evidence in any proceedings for enforcing his security without payment of the stamp duty or any penalty in respect of it, unless he had notice (or, but for his negligence, might have discovered) that the debenture was not duly stamped. In that case the company is liable to pay the proper stamp duty and penalty.

---

[65]  Companies Act 2006 (Commencement No 5, Transitional Provisions and Savings) Order 2007, SI 2007/3495, art 3.

[66]  On which see s 751(2).

[67]  On which see s 750(1).

[68]  Or, in the case of debentures formerly governed by the Companies (Northern Ireland) Order 1986, s 201, 1 July 1961. See generally s 751(2) for the meaning of 'relevant date'. Both dates are when provisions first became operative under past Companies legislation outlawing exemptions or indemnities from, or against, liability for breach of trust in favour of trustees of debentures. The latter used to be very popular in debenture trusts.

[69]  See s 751(1).

[70]  Or 1 July 1961 in the case of Northern Ireland trustees, see paras 19.751.02–19.751.03 below.

[71]  A meeting called for this purpose must be summoned in accordance with the provisions of the deed or, if there are no provisions, then in a manner approved by the court; see s 751(4).

[72]  See s 751(3).

[73]  Or 1 July 1961 in respect of debenture trusts governed by the Companies (Northern Ireland) Order 1986, s 201.

AMENDMENTS AND NOTES

a Section 752 also applies (with appropriate modifications) to LLPs by virtue of the Limited Liability
Partnerships (Application of Companies Act 2006) Regulations 2009, SI 2009/1804, Pt 6.

COMMENCEMENT DATE 6 April 2008[74]

Formerly section 194 of the Companies Act 1985. This section makes clear that a company, which has **19.752.02**
redeemed debentures previously issued, has power to either:

(i) re-issue those debentures, or
(ii) issue new debentures in their place.[75]

> At common law this was not the case and where a company redeemed its debentures then they were deemed
> to be extinguished at the point of redemption such that they could not be re-issued.[76] The Companies Act
> was amended to permit debentures to be re-issued in this situation.[77] However, the power to re-issue
> debentures, which have been redeemed by the company, is subject to two limitations.

(i) No re-issue will be permitted where the company's articles forbid it or, the company has made a
contract preventing the re-issue of debentures.[78]
(ii) The company has either passed a resolution, or done some other act, cancelling the redeemed
debentures.[79]

A company may now re-issue redeemed debentures and when this is done those debentures have the **19.752.03**
same rights and priority attached to them as if they had never been redeemed.[80] A subscriber to
re-issued debentures is entitled to the same rights and priority as the holders of the other debentures in
the series, and it follows that the company, on re-issuing them, may not seek to vary these rights.[81]
Should a company purport to re-issue debentures upon different terms to the original issue then the
debentures will be treated as not belonging to the original series. Therefore, the holder of the newly
're-issued' debenture will not be entitled to the benefit of any security charge securing the original issue.
In reality the 're-issue' will be treated as a fresh issue of debentures subject to its own terms as noted at
the time of issue but, independent of any terms relating to the former issue of debentures, such that any
reference to a purported benefit in the form of a security charge contained in the former issue will be
subordinated to the claims of the holders of the original (ie former) issue. Should either:

(i) a redeemed debenture be re-issued; or
(ii) a new debenture be issued in place of a redeemed debenture;

> then, in both cases, for the purposes of stamp duty the issue is treated as a new issue of a debenture.[82]
> However, for all other purposes the re-issue of debentures will not be treated as a new issue.[83]

Where a person has lent a company money and taken a re-issued debenture (which appeared to be duly **19.752.04**
stamped) as security for that loan, then that person may use the debenture in evidence in any
proceedings to enforce the security against the company despite the fact that stamp duty had not in fact
been paid. The holder of the debenture is relieved of having to pay stamp duty and, instead, the
company re-issuing the debenture is placed under a duty to pay the duty and any penalty.[84] This
remains the case unless it can be shown that the person taking the debenture as security had notice, or
would have discovered the fact (but for his negligence) that no stamp duty had been paid. Quite often,
on a re-issue of debentures which were originally stamped on their first issue, it is overlooked that duty
is repayable on the re-issue and the debentures are not stamped a second time.

## 753 Deposit of debentures to secure advances[a]

Where a company has deposited any of its debentures to secure advances from time to time on current **19.753.01**
account or otherwise, the debentures are not treated as redeemed by reason only of the company's
account having ceased to be in debit while the debentures remained so deposited.

---

[74] Companies Act 2006 (Commencement No 5, Transitional Provisions and Savings) Order 2007, SI 2007/
3495, art 3.
[75] See s 752(1).
[76] See *Re George Routledge & Sons Ltd* [1904] 2 Ch 474.
[77] By virtue of CA 1907, s 15; a feature found in successive Companies Acts and now found in s 752.
[78] See s 752(1)(a).
[79] See s 752(1)(b).
[80] See s 752(2).
[81] See *Re Antofagasta (Chili) and Bolivia Rly Co Ltd's Trust Deed* [1939] Ch 732.
[82] See s 752(3).
[83] See s 752(3).
[84] See s 752(4).

AMENDMENTS AND NOTES

ᵃ Section 753 also applies (with appropriate modifications) to LLPs by virtue of the Limited Liability
Partnerships (Application of Companies Act 2006) Regulations 2009, SI 2009/1804, Pt 6.

COMMENCEMENT DATE  6 April 2008[85]

**19.753.02**  Formerly section 194(3) of the Companies Act 1985. This section is intended to remove any doubt that
debentures deposited to secure a current account might become redeemed by virtue of the account
moving from deficit to credit. The very nature of a current account is that it will fluctuate from time to
time moving in and out of credit/deficit depending on the company's trading success/failure. The
section is intended to promote debenture deposits as a security device particularly in the banking
world. Because of this section it will require an express statement by the company in order that
debentures, deposited by way of security, can be deemed to have been redeemed.

### 754  Priorities where debentures secured by floating chargeᵃ

**19.754.01**
(1) This section applies where debentures of a company registered in England and Wales or Northern
Ireland are secured by a charge that, as created, was a floating charge.

(2) If possession is taken, by or on behalf of the holders of the debentures, of any property comprised
in or subject to the charge, and the company is not at that time in the course of being wound up,
the company's preferential debts shall be paid out of assets coming to the hands of the persons
taking possession in priority to any claims for principal or interest in respect of the debentures.

(3) 'Preferential debts' means the categories of debts listed in Schedule 6 to the Insolvency Act 1986
(c. 45) or Schedule 4 to the Insolvency (Northern Ireland) Order 1989 (S.I. 1989/2405 (N.I. 19)).
For the purposes of that Schedule 'the relevant date' is the date of possession being taken as
mentioned in subsection (2).

(4) Payments under this section shall be recouped, as far as may be, out of the assets of the company
available for payment of general creditors.

AMENDMENTS AND NOTES

ᵃ Section 754 also applies (with appropriate modifications) to LLPs by virtue of the Limited Liability
Partnerships (Application of Companies Act 2006) Regulations 2009, SI 2009/1804, Pt 6.

COMMENCEMENT DATE  6 April 2008[86]

**19.754.02**  Formerly section 196 of the Companies Act 1985. This section applies in a situation where an issue of
debentures is secured by a floating charge[87] and the holders of the floating charge seek to enforce it
against a company in default, but the company is not in the course of being wound up. In this situation,
if the holders of the floating charge take possession[88] of any property of the company subject to the
charge then they are obliged to pay the holders of the company's preferential debts in priority to the
claims of the debenture holders.[89] Any payments made under this section to the holders of preferential
debts are to be recouped by the floating charge holder from the assets of the company which are
available to meet the claims of general creditors.[90]

**19.754.03**  However, the holders of a floating charge can only ever seek to recoup their debt if there are assets
available to meet their claim. The determination of this question will be dependant upon the normal

---

[85] Companies Act 2006 (Commencement No 5, Transitional Provisions and Savings) Order 2007, SI 2007/
3495, art 3.

[86] Companies Act 2006 (Commencement No 5, Transitional Provisions and Savings) Order 2007, SI 2007/
3495, art 3.

[87] That is to say a charge which was created as a floating charge such that it matters not if the nature of the
charge is expressed to change at a later date on the happening of some event/contingency into a fixed charge. It
is the moment of creation, rather than enforcement, that determines the nature of the charge as being a floating
charge for the purposes of the section; see s 754(1). Cf *Re Woodroffes (Musical Instruments) Ltd* [1986] Ch 366; *Re
Brightlife Ltd* [1987] Ch 200. As to the meaning and identification of a floating charge see generally *Re Spectrum
Plus Ltd* [2005] UKHL 41.

[88] The holders of any preferential debts will also gain priority if the holders of a floating charge appoint a
receiver; see Insolvency Act 1986 (as amended), s 40. But note also the effects of s 72A (abolition of right of
floating charge holder to appoint an administrative receiver).

[89] See s 754(2). For these purposes 'preferential debts' means certain payments due to: occupational pension
schemes; employees; levies on coal and steel production; see: s 754(3) and Insolvency Act 1986 (as amended), s
386, and Sch 6. Prior to the amendment of the Insolvency Act, Sch 6, by the Enterprise Act 2002, s 251 the
categories of 'preferential debt' were quite large and could, in many cases, serve to undermine the quality of
security held by the debenture holders. For companies registered in Northern Ireland see Insolvency (Northern
Ireland) Order 1989 for the categories of 'preferential debt'.

[90] See s 754(4).

rules of priority applicable to competing claims against corporate property[91] under general insolvency[92] and property law.[93] Basically, however, a fixed charge will take priority over a floating charge[94] and over the claims of preferential debt holders.[95] Therefore, a floating charge holder may find that there is little left when he seeks to realize his interest.[96]

---

[91] On the question of general priorities see WJ Gough, *Company Charges* (2nd edn, 1995, London, Butterworths).

[92] See also: Insolvency Act 1986, s 40 (preferential debts priority where a receiver appointed), s 175 (preferential debts priority in a winding up).

[93] The reader should consult the standard works on this topic; see generally, WJ Gough, *Company Charges* (2nd edn, 1995, London, Butterworths).

[94] See *English and Scottish Mercantile Investment Co Ltd v Brunton* [1892] 2 QB 700, CA.

[95] Cf *Griffiths v Yorkshire Bank Plc* [1994] 1 WLR 1427.

[96] Note also the effects on a floating charge in corporate insolvency of the Insolvency Act 1986 (as amended), s 176A.

# 20

# PRIVATE AND PUBLIC COMPANIES

## Companies Act 2006

### PART 20
### PRIVATE AND PUBLIC COMPANIES

### CHAPTER 1
### PROHIBITION OF PUBLIC OFFERS BY PRIVATE COMPANIES

#### *Introduction*

Chapter 1 of Part 20 prohibits private companies from raising capital through the sale of their securities to the public. It replaces similar restrictions which were imposed by section 81(1) of the Companies Act 1985. It may be said that this prohibition reinforces one of the basic distinctions between private companies and public companies. In the case of the former there is no minimum capital requirement for formation; their membership is usually small and often restricted, with limitations frequently being placed on the transfer of shares; and they face less onerous accounting requirements. To allow private companies to make public offers of their securities would be to undermine their 'private' character. It may also be argued, given the lighter regulatory burden placed on private companies and the attendant risks, that it should not be permissible for such companies to offer their securities to the public. Instead, investment in private companies should be restricted to those who may be thought to have some understanding of its affairs, such as its existing shareholders and debenture holders, and employees. **20.0.01**

A contravention of the prohibition created by this chapter is not a criminal offence (as was a contravention of section 81(1) of the Companies Act 1985); though there are potentially serious civil consequences (eg compulsory winding up). Nonetheless, a breach of the prohibition does not itself invalidate any allotment or sale of securities. **20.0.02**

#### 755 Prohibition of public offers by private company

(1) A private company limited by shares or limited by guarantee and having a share capital must not— **20.755.01**
    (a) offer to the public any securities of the company, or
    (b) allot or agree to allot any securities of the company with a view to their being offered to the public.

(2) Unless the contrary is proved, an allotment or agreement to allot securities is presumed to be made with a view to their being offered to the public if an offer of the securities (or any of them) to the public is made—

(a) within six months after the allotment or agreement to allot, or

(b) before the receipt by the company of the whole of the consideration to be received by it in respect of the securities.

(3) A company does not contravene this section if—

(a) it acts in good faith in pursuance of arrangements under which it is to re-register as a public company before the securities are allotted, or

(b) as part of the terms of the offer it undertakes to re-register as a public company within a specified period, and that undertaking is complied with.

(4) The specified period for the purposes of subsection (3)(b) must be a period ending not later than six months after the day on which the offer is made (or, in the case of an offer made on different days, first made).

(5) In this Chapter 'securities' means shares or debentures.

COMMENCEMENT DATE 6 April 2008[1]

**20.755.02** This section introduces the basic prohibition on private companies[2] offering their securities to the public or allotting,[3] or agreeing to allot, their securities with a view their being offered to the public.

**20.755.03** Subsection (1) imposes a restriction on private companies offering their securities to the public.[4] However, the restriction only applies to private companies limited by shares or limited by guarantee and having a share capital. The restriction does not apply, therefore, to other kinds of private company, for example private companies limited by guarantee not having a share capital, or unlimited private companies. The scope of this subsection is subtly different from that of section 81(1) of the Companies Act which applied to all private companies other than those limited by guarantee and not having a share capital.

**20.755.04** Subsection (1)(a) prohibits a private company from offering any of its securities to the public itself. 'Securities' are defined in section 755(5) (see below) as meaning 'shares' or 'debentures'. The predecessor provision in section 81(1)(a) of the Companies Act 1985 expressly stated that the prohibition in section 81(1) applied whether the private company offered its shares or debentures for cash or otherwise. It is considered that the prohibition in subsection (1)(a) also applies whether a private company seeks to offer its shares or debentures for cash or otherwise.

**20.755.05** Subsection (1)(b) addresses the situation where a private company allots, or agrees to allot, its securities with a view to their then being offered to the public by someone else. For example, a company might allot its securities with a view to the allotee then offering them to the public, or to a third party for the third party then to offer them to the public. The prohibition in subsection (1)(a) cannot therefore be circumvented by allotting securities with a view to a subsequent offer by the allotee to the public, directly or indirectly. The scope of this provision is further explained by subsection (2).

**20.755.06** Subsection (2) creates a rebuttable presumption that a private company has allotted its securities, or agreed to offer its securities, with a view to their being offered to the public (contrary to subsection (1)(b)) in two situations.

**20.755.07** First, by virtue of subsection (2)(a), a private company will be presumed (unless the contrary is proved) to have allotted its securities with a view to their being offered to the public where it has allotted its securities and the securities (or any of them) have then been offered to the public within six months of the allotment or agreement to allot.

**20.755.08** Second, by virtue of subsection (2)(b), a private company will be presumed (unless the contrary is proved) to have allotted its securities, or agreed to allot its securities, with a view to their being offered to the public where there is an offer to the public of the securities (or any of them) made before receipt by the private company of the whole of the consideration due in respect of the allotment or agreement to allot. For example, where an allotee does not have to pay for securities allotted to him before there is onward offer to the public (whenever made), there is a presumption that the allotment to the allotee was made with a view to an offer to the public.

**20.755.09** The predecessor provision was section 58(3) of the Companies Act 1985. However, section 58(3) provided that the arrangements described in subsection (2) above were evidence (unless the contrary was proved) of an offer in breach of the prohibition; as opposed to a rebuttable presumption. It is suggested that there is no practical difference between these two formulations.

---

[1] Companies Act 2006 (Commencement No 5, Transitional Provisions and Savings) Order 2007, SI 2007/3495, art 3.

[2] As to the definition of 'private company', see s 4.

[3] As to the definition of allotment and related expressions, see Sch 8.

[4] As to the definition of 'offer to the public', see s 756 below.

Subsection (3) creates two exceptions from the prohibition contained in subsection (1) for companies　**20.755.10**
that are planning to re-register as public companies. First, a private company does not contravene
subsection (1) by offering its securities to the public provided that it is acting in good faith in pursuance
of arrangements under which it will re-register as a public company before they are allotted (subsection
(3)(a). This exception applies even if, ultimately, the re-registration does not take place, provided that
it was genuinely and reasonably intended that the company would be re-registered. Second, a private
company does not contravene subsection (1) in offering its securities to the public provided that it is a
term of the offer that the company undertakes to re-register as a public company within a specified
period within the meaning of subsection (4) (see below) and the undertaking is complied with
(subsection (3)(b)). Although subsection (3) does not say so expressly, it seems implicit that this second
exception should apply where the securities are allotted before the company re-registers as a public
company, provided that the undertaking to register is complied with within the specified period.

There was no equivalent provision in the Companies Act 1985.　**20.755.11**

Subsection (4) defines the specified period within which a private company must re-register as a public　**20.755.12**
company for the purposes of the exception created by subsection (3)(b). The specified period by which
the company must undertake to re-register as a public company must be a period no longer than six
months, starting on the day after the day on which the offer to the public is made. Where the offer to the
public is made on different days, the period of six months starts from the day after the day that the offer
was first made.

Subsection (5) defines 'securities' for the purposes of this Chapter. 'Securities' means shares or　**20.755.13**
debentures.[5] In the context of a company with share capital, a 'share' means a share in the share capital
of the company, and includes stock.[6] A 'debenture' is defined as including debenture stock, bonds, and
any other securities of a company, whether or not constituting a charge on assets of the company.[7]

## 756  Meaning of 'offer to the public'

(1) This section explains what is meant in this Chapter by an offer of securities to the public.　**20.756.01**
(2) An offer to the public includes an offer to any section of the public, however selected.
(3) An offer is not regarded as an offer to the public if it can properly be regarded, in all the
circumstances, as—
   (a) not being calculated to result, directly or indirectly, in securities of the company becoming
   available to persons other than those receiving the offer, or
   (b) otherwise being a private concern of the person receiving it and the person making it.
(4) An offer is to be regarded (unless the contrary is proved) as being a private concern of the person
receiving it and the person making it if—
   (a) it is made to a person already connected with the company and, where it is made on terms
   allowing that person to renounce his rights, the rights may only be renounced in favour of
   another person already connected with the company; or
   (b) it is an offer to subscribe for securities to be held under an employees' share scheme and,
   where it is made on terms allowing that person to renounce his rights, the rights may only be
   renounced in favour of—
      (i) another person entitled to hold securities under the scheme, or
      (ii) a person already connected with the company.
(5) For the purposes of this section 'person already connected with the company' means—
   (a) an existing member or employee of the company,
   (b) a member of the family of a person who is or was a member or employee of the company,
   (c) the widow or widower, or surviving civil partner, of a person who was a member or employee
   of the company,
   (d) an existing debenture holder of the company, or
   (e) a trustee (acting in his capacity as such) of a trust of which the principal beneficiary is a person
   within any of paragraphs (a) to (d).

---

　[5]  See s 755(5).
　[6]  See Sch 8 and s 540(4). See also s 1161(2) for the meaning of 'share' in the context of a company with capital,
but no share capital, and in the context of an undertaking without capital. Although the definitions in s 1161(2)
are not expressly disapplied from ss 755 et seq, given that the prohibition in s 755 refers only to companies having
a share capital, they can be of no practical application.
　[7]  See Sch 8 and s 738. See further *Lemon v Austin Friars Investment Trust Limited* [1926] 1 Ch 1 and *NV
Slavenburg's Bank v Intercontinental Natural Resources Ltd* [1985] 1 All ER 955 for a discussion of the meaning of
'debenture'.

(6)  For the purposes of subsection (5)(b) the members of a person's family are the person's spouse or civil partner and children (including step-children) and their descendants.

COMMENCEMENT DATE  6 April 2008[8]

**20.756.02**  Subsection (1) defines what is meant by an offer to the public for the purposes of this Chapter (the prohibition on public offers by private companies). The equivalent provision in the Companies Act 1985 was section 742A.

**20.756.03**  Subsection (2) provides that an offer to the public includes an offer to any section of the public however selected. For example, an offer to persons within a particular region, or to a persons within a particular economic group (eg those drawing old-age pensions), would most likely beregarded as offers to the public. It is suggested that this is because the offer would be open to be accepted by *any* person within the selected group.[9] Such an offer is to be contrasted with the kind of offers described in subsection (3)(a).

**20.756.04**  Subsection (3) is the first of three subsections which set out particular circumstances in which an offer of securities is not to be regarded as an offer to the public. Subsection (3) thus sets out two sets of circumstances where an offer of securities is not to be regarded as an offer to the public.

**20.756.05**  By virtue of subsection (3)(a) an offer will not be regarded as an offer to the public where it is not calculated to result, directly or indirectly, in the securities becoming available to persons other than those receiving the offer.[10] Subsection (3)(a) would therefore cover an offer to particular persons, where it was intended that only those persons could accept the offer, for example, an offer to a small number of named institutions. Section 742A(2)(a) of the Companies Act 1985 provided a similar exception from the prohibition on private companies offering their shares etc to the public. Further, case law under similar earlier companies legislation suggested that the essential characteristic of an offer to the public was that it was open to anyone who should wish to subscribe.[11] Therefore, an offer made only to associates of the members of the board of directors on the other hand, for example, was not.[12]

**20.756.06**  Additionally, by virtue of subsection (3)(b), an offer is not regarded as an offer to the public where it may be properly regarded as being a 'private concern' of the person making the offer and the person receiving it. There is no definition of the term 'private concern' as such, (and Companies Act 1985, section 742A referred to a 'domestic concern'). However, subsection (4) (see below) sets out a series of situations where an offer is to be regarded as being a 'private concern' unless the contrary is proved.

**20.756.07**  Neither subsection (3)(a) nor subsection (3)(b) imposes any limit on the maximum number of persons to whom an offer may be made and still benefit from either provision. However, in practice one would expect that there must be a point at which an offer to a large number of persons, albeit specifically directed at each person, becomes an offer to a section of the public within subsection (2).[13]

**20.756.08**  Subsection (4) has the effect that an offer is to be regarded (unless the contrary is proved) as being a 'private concern' of the person receiving it and the person making it (and therefore not an offer to the public) in certain defined situations. (Subsection (5) sets out the meaning of the term 'persons already connected to the company'.) Subsection (4) is similar to section 742A(2)(b) Companies Act 1985, which had the effect of allowing private companies to make offers to persons if such offer was a 'domestic concern' of the private company making the offer and the persons receiving it.

---

[8]  Companies Act 2006 (Commencement No 5, Transitional Provisions and Savings) Order 2007, SI 2007/3495, art 3.

[9]  See *Lee v Evans* (1964) 112 CLR 276, where the High Court of Australia considered the South Australian statutory prohibition on offers to the public, and, after reviewing the English cases, held that, 'the basic concept (of a public invitation) is that the invitation, though maybe not universal, is general; that it is an invitation to all and sundry of some segment of the community at large.'

[10]  In *Governments Stocks and Other Investment Securities Ltd v Christopher* [1956] 1 All ER 490, a case concerning Companies Act 1948, ss 55(2) and 455 and the meaning of 'prospectus', it was held that whether there had been an offer to the public was to be determined by reference to the number of persons who could accept the offer, not to the number of persons who received the offer document.

[11]  See *In re South of England Natural Gas and Petroleum Company, Limited* [1911] 1 Ch 573.

[12]  See *Sleigh v The Glasgow and Transvaal Options, Limited* (1904) 6 F 420; *Sherwell v Combined Incandescent Mantels Syndicate Ltd* [1907] WN 110; *Nash v Lynde* [1928] AC 158.

[13]  See *Securities and Exchange Commission v Sunbeam Gold Mines Co* 9 Cir, 1938, 95F 2d 699, where the American court considered the exemption in Securities Act 1933, s 4(1), which permits transactions by an issuer 'not involving any public offering' for a discussion. The court held that: 'To determine the distinction between "public" and "private" in any particular context, it is essential to examine the circumstances under which the distinction is sought to be established, and to consider the purposes sought to be achieved by such distinction.'

First, by virtue of subsection (4)(a), an offer will be regarded (unless the contrary is proved) as a 'private concern' of the persons receiving and making it where it is made to 'persons already connected to the company' (as defined in subsection (5)) and, if the offer is renounceable by the person to whom it was made, it is renounceable only in favour of other persons who are also 'persons already connected to the company'. Second, by virtue of subsection (4)(b), an offer will also be regarded (unless the contrary is proved) as a 'private concern' of the persons receiving and making it where the offer concerns securities to be held under an 'employees' share scheme'[14] and, if the offer is renounceable by the person to whom it is made, it is renounceable only in favour another person entitled to hold securities under the 'employees' share scheme' or a person already connected to the company. An 'employees' share scheme' is defined in Schedule 8 and section 1166 and is, broadly, a scheme for encouraging or facilitating the holding of shares or debentures in a company by or for the benefit of its employees and members of their families.    **20.756.09**

Further, the language of section 756(3)(b) suggests that the list of offers in subsection (4) which are to be regarded as a private concern of the persons receiving and making it is not exhaustive. It may be argued, for example, that an offer to a small and closed group of persons with some pre-existing connection with the company could also be a private concern of the company and the recipients of the offer.    **20.756.10**

Subsection (5) defines the term 'persons already connected to the company' for the purposes of subsection (4). A person is already connected to the company if he is an existing member (ie shareholder) or an employee of the company; or a member of the 'family' (as defined by subsection (6)) of a person who is, or was, a member of the company or is, or was, an employee of the company; or the widow, widower, or surviving civil partner, of a person who was a member or employee of the company; or an existing debenture holder of the company; or a trustee of a trust whose principal beneficiary is any of the foregoing persons. In broad terms, therefore, a 'person already connected to the company' is a shareholder or an employee of the company, or member of the family of a shareholder or an employee or former shareholder or former employee, or a person holding debentures of the company, or a trustee holding for any such persons.    **20.756.11**

Subsection (6) defines, for the purposes of subsection (5), who the members of a person's family are. They are the person's spouse, civil partner, children (including step-children), and their descendants.    **20.756.12**

### 757  Enforcement of prohibition: order restraining proposed contravention

(1)  If it appears to the court—    **20.757.01**
   (a)  on an application under this section, or
   (b)  in proceedings under Part 30 (protection of members against unfair prejudice),
   that a company is proposing to act in contravention of section 755 (prohibition of public offers by private companies), the court shall make an order under this section.
(2)  An order under this section is an order restraining the company from contravening that section.
(3)  An application for an order under this section may be made by—
   (a)  a member or creditor of the company, or
   (b)  the Secretary of State.

COMMENCEMENT DATE  6 April 2008[15]

Section 757 grants to the court certain powers in respect of a private company which proposes to offer its securities to the public in contravention of section 755. These procedures are new. Section 81 of the Companies Act 1985 had no equivalent provision.    **20.757.02**

Subsection (1) requires the court to make an order under subsection (2) if it appears to the court on an application that a private company proposes to contravene section 755 (prohibition of public offers by private companies). The application may be made either under this section or under Part 30 in the context of proceedings to protect members against unfair prejudice.    **20.757.03**

Subsection (2) specifies the order that the court shall make in the circumstances described in subsection (1) is an order restraining the company from contravening section 755.    **20.757.04**

Subsection (3) sets out the persons who may apply for an order under section 757. An application may be made by a member or creditor of the private company concerned or by the Secretary of State. No criteria are specified as to the exercise by the Secretary of State of his powers under this section.    **20.757.05**

---

[14]  As to the definition of 'employees' share scheme', see Sch 8 and s 1166.
[15]  Companies Act 2006 (Commencement No 5, Transitional Provisions and Savings) Order 2007, SI 2007/ 3495, art 3.

**758 Enforcement of prohibition: orders available to the court after contravention**

**20.758.01**    (1)  This section applies if it appears to the court—
        (a)  on an application under this section, or
        (b)  in proceedings under Part 30 (protection of members against unfair prejudice),
        that a company has acted in contravention of section 755 (prohibition of public offers by private companies).
    (2)  The court must make an order requiring the company to re-register as a public company unless it appears to the court—
        (a)  that the company does not meet the requirements for re-registration as a public company, and
        (b)  that it is impractical or undesirable to require it to take steps to do so.
    (3)  If it does not make an order for re-registration, the court may make either or both of the following—
        (a)  a remedial order (see section 759), or
        (b)  an order for the compulsory winding up of the company.
    (4)  An application under this section may be made by—
        (a)  a member of the company who—
           (i)  was a member at the time the offer was made (or, if the offer was made over a period, at any time during that period), or
           (ii)  became a member as a result of the offer,
        (b)  a creditor of the company who was a creditor at the time the offer was made (or, if the offer was made over a period, at any time during that period), or
        (c)  the Secretary of State.

COMMENCEMENT DATE 6 April 2008[16]

**20.758.02**    Section 758 grants to the court certain powers in respect of a private company that has offered its securities to the public in contravention of section 755. These procedures are new. section 81 of the Companies Act 1985 had no equivalent provision.

**20.758.03**    Subsection (1) provides that the court has certain powers under subsection (2) if it appears to the court that a private company has contravened section 755 (prohibition of public offers by private companies). The application may be made either under this section or under Part 30 in the context of proceedings to protect members against unfair prejudice.

**20.758.04**    Subsection (2) specifies the orders that the court shall make on an application of the kind described in subsection (1). By subsection (2), the court must order the private company to re-register as a public company unless the company does not meet the requirements to re-register as a public company (under Part 7) (subsection (2)(a)) and it would be impractical or undesirable to require the company to take the necessary steps to re-register (subsection (2)(b)). In those circumstances, by virtue of subsection (3) the court has a discretion to make one or both of two orders. The court may make a remedial order under section 759 (see below) (subsection (3)(a)). Alternatively or additionally, the court may make an order winding up the company (subsection (3)(b)). The explanatory notes suggest that a court may wish to decline to make such orders where, although the company has breached section 755, it has not allotted shares and where it has withdrawn the offer and undertaken not to do it again.

**20.758.05**    Taking subsections (2) and (3) together, the preferred remedy where a private company has contravened section 755 is an order that the company re-register as a public company, rather than a remedial order under section 759 (see below) or an order winding up the company.

**20.758.06**    Subsection (4) sets out the persons who may apply for an order under section 758. There are three categories of person. An application may be made by a person who was a member of the company at the time that the public offer was made (or at any time during the period that the offer was open) or who became a member as a result of the public offer (subsection (4)(a)). An application may also be made by a creditor of the company at the time that the public offer was made (or at any time during the period which the offer was open) (subsection (4)(b)). Finally, an application may be made by the Secretary of State (subsection (4)(c)). No criteria are specified as to the exercise by the Secretary of State of his powers under this section.

**759 Enforcement of prohibition: remedial order**

**20.759.01**    (1)  A 'remedial order' is an order for the purpose of putting a person affected by anything done in contravention of section 755 (prohibition of public offers by private company) in the position he would have been in if it had not been done.

---

[16]  Companies Act 2006 (Commencement No 5, Transitional Provisions and Savings) Order 2007, SI 2007/3495, art 3.

(2)  The following provisions are without prejudice to the generality of the power to make such an order.

(3)  Where a private company has—

(a)  allotted securities pursuant to an offer to the public, or

(b)  allotted or agreed to allot securities with a view to their being offered to the public,

a remedial order may require any person knowingly concerned in the contravention of section 755 to offer to purchase any of those securities at such price and on such other terms as the court thinks fit.

(4)  A remedial order may be made—

(a)  against any person knowingly concerned in the contravention, whether or not an officer of the company;

(b)  notwithstanding anything in the company's constitution (which includes, for this purpose, the terms on which any securities of the company are allotted or held);

(c)  whether or not the holder of the securities subject to the order is the person to whom the company allotted or agreed to allot them.

(5)  Where a remedial order is made against the company itself, the court may provide for the reduction of the company's capital accordingly.

COMMENCEMENT DATE  6 April 2008[17]

Section 759 introduces the new concept of a 'remedial order' to remedy breaches of section 755.  **20.759.02**

Subsection (1) defines a 'remedial order'. It is essentially an order to put any person affected by a breach  **20.759.03**
of section 755 into the position he would have been in had the breach not occurred.

Subsection (2) makes clear that the following subsections which describe the scope of a remedial order  **20.759.04**
are without prejudice to the generality of the court's power to make such an order.

Subsection (3) provides that where a private company has allotted securities pursuant to an offer made  **20.759.05**
in contravention of section 755 (see section 755(1)(a)), or where a private company has allotted or
agreed to allot securities with a view to their being offered to the public in contravention of section 755
(see section 755(1)(b)), the court may order any person knowingly concerned in such contraventions
to purchase the securities in question at such price and terms as the court shall think fit.

Subsection (4) and subsection (5) make clear the potential breadth of a remedial order. By virtue of  **20.759.06**
subsection (4) a remedial order may be made against any person knowingly concerned in the
contravention, whether or not he is an officer of the company[18] (subsection (4)(a)). A remedial order
may be made notwithstanding anything in the company's constitution; that is to say, it may override
provisions in a company's memorandum or articles concerning the terms on which securities are
allotted or held (subsection (4)(b)). A remedial order may be made whether or nor the holder of the
securities subject to the order is the person to whom the company allotted or agreed to allot the
securities. This would seem to allow the court to make an order concerning subsequent purchasers of
securities offered in breach of section 755. Subsection (5) empowers the court, where it makes an order
against the company itself, to make provision for a reduction of the company's capital accordingly.[19]

## 760  Validity of allotment etc not affected

Nothing in this Chapter affects the validity of any allotment or sale of securities or of any agreement  **20.760.01**
to allot or sell securities.

COMMENCEMENT DATE  6 April 2008[20]

Section 760 provides that a public offer made in contravention of section 760 does not affect the validity  **20.760.02**
of any allotment or sale of securities or of any agreement to allot or sell securities.

section 81(3) of the Companies Act 1985 made a similar provision in respect of offers which contra-  **20.760.03**
vened section 81(1) of that Act.

---

[17]  Companies Act 2006 (Commencement No 5, etc) Order 2007, SI 2007/3495, art 4.

[18]  See *Securities and Investments Board v Pantell (No 2)* [1991] Ch 256 for a discussion of how a solicitor could
be 'knowingly concerned' in a contravention of the Financial Services Act 1986.

[19]  See ss 641 *et seq* for reduction of capital generally.

[20]  Companies Act 2006 (Commencement No 5, etc) Order 2007, SI 2007/3495, art 3.

# CHAPTER 2
## MINIMUM SHARE CAPITAL REQUIREMENT
## FOR PUBLIC COMPANIES

### 761 Public company: requirement as to minimum share capital

**20.761.01**

(1) A company that is a public company (otherwise than by virtue of re-registration as a public company) must not do business or exercise any borrowing powers unless the registrar has issued it with a certificate under this section (a 'trading certificate').

(2) The registrar shall issue a trading certificate if, on an application made in accordance with section 762, he is satisfied that the nominal value of the company's allotted share capital is not less than the 'authorised minimum'.

(3) For this purpose a share allotted in pursuance of an employees' share scheme shall not be taken into account unless paid up as to—

    (a) at least one-quarter of the nominal value of the share, and

    (b) the whole of any premium on the share.

(4) A trading certificate has effect from the date on which it is issued and is conclusive evidence that the company is entitled to do business and exercise any borrowing powers.

COMMENCEMENT DATE 6 April 2008[21]

**20.761.02** This section replaces sections 117(1), (2), (4), (6) and (8) of the Companies Act 1985. It does not make any substantive changes to those provisions and, like these, only applies to public companies that are formed as such on their original incorporation under the Companies Act 2006 (as opposed to companies that re-register from private limited to public)[22] and to existing public companies, which were formed as such, and which have not obtained a trading certificate at the date that the Companies Act 2006 comes into force. The section retains the requirement for such companies to obtain a trading certificate from the Registrar of Companies before commencing business.

**20.761.03** Subsections (1) and (2) confirm that, as under the Companies Act 1985, the registrar will only issue a trading certificate if he is satisfied that certain conditions are met and in particular that there is a minimum share capital requirement known as 'the authorised minimum' (see section 763 below).

**20.761.04** Subsection (3) makes it clear that a share allotted in pursuance of an employees' share scheme shall not be taken into account for the purposes of establishing the nominal value of the company's allotted share capital under subsection (2). There is an exception under which a share allotted in pursuance of an employees' share scheme shall be taken into account for the above purposes when (a) it is paid up as to at least one-quarter of the nominal value of the share, and (b) it is paid up as to the whole of any premium on the share.

**20.761.05** Subsection (4) provides that a trading certificate has effect from the date that it is *issued* and is *conclusive evidence* that the company is entitled to do business as a public company. Where a public company that is formed under this section, or under section 117 of the Companies Act 1985, has not obtained a trading certificate within a year of its incorporation, it may be wound up by the court.[23]

### 762 Procedure for obtaining certificate

**20.762.01**

(1) An application for a certificate under section 761 must—

    (a) state that the nominal value of the company's allotted share capital is not less than the authorised minimum,

    (b) specify the amount, or estimated amount, of the company's preliminary expenses,

    (c) specify any amount or benefit paid or given, or intended to be paid or given, to any promoter of the company, and the consideration for the payment or benefit, and

    (d) be accompanied by a statement of compliance.

(2) The statement of compliance is a statement that the company meets the requirements for the issue of a certificate under section 761.

(3) The registrar may accept the statement of compliance as sufficient evidence of the matters stated in it.

COMMENCEMENT DATE 6 April 2008[24]

---

[21] Companies Act 2006 (Commencement No 5, etc) Order 2007, SI 2007/3495, art 3.

[22] Under the provisions of Part 7 of the CA 2006.

[23] See s 122(1)(b) of the Insolvency Act 1986.

[24] Companies Act 2006 (Commencement No 5, etc) Order 2007, SI 2007/3495, art 3.

This section details the procedure for obtaining a trading certificate.[25] It replaces section 117(3) of the    **20.762.02**
Companies Act 1985. Subsection (1) prescribes the contents of the application for a trading certificate,
which, *inter alia*, must include a statement that the nominal value of the company's share capital is not
less than the authorised minimum which is defined under section 763 (see below).

Subsections (2) and (3) make a new provision for a statement of compliance.[26] This replaces the    **20.762.03**
requirement for a statutory declaration under section 117(3) of the Companies Act 1985 (or 'electronic
statement' under section 117(3A) Companies Act 1985) when an application is made for a trading
certificate. According to the Explanatory Notes to the Companies Act 2006,[27] this statement does not
need to be witnessed and may be made in paper or electronic form. According to Form SH50 (issued
by Companies House) the statement of compliance may be signed by a director, secretary, a person
authorized[28] or CIC (Community Interest Companies) manager.[29]

### 763  The authorised minimum

(1)  'The authorised minimum', in relation to the nominal value of a public company's allotted share    **20.763.01**
     capital is—
     (a)  £50,000, or
     (b)  the prescribed euro equivalent.
(2)  The Secretary of State may by order prescribe the amount in euros that is for the time being to be
     treated as equivalent to the sterling amount of the authorised minimum.
(3)  This power may be exercised from time to time as appears to the Secretary of State to be
     appropriate.
(4)  The amount prescribed shall be determined by applying an appropriate spot rate of exchange to
     the sterling amount and rounding to the nearest 100 euros.
(5)  An order under this section is subject to negative resolution procedure.
(6)  This section has effect subject to any exercise of the power conferred by section 764 (power to
     alter authorised minimum).

COMMENCEMENT DATE  6 April 2008[30]

This section, which is self-explanatory, retains the requirement contained in sections 117 and 118 of    **20.763.02**
the Companies Act 1985 that before a public company may do business, a minimum share capital,
known as the 'authorized minimum', must be subscribed. The main difference from the previous
legislation is that, unlike the Companies Act 1985 which permitted denomination only in sterling, it
was concluded during Commons passage of the Companies Bill (formerly the Company Law Reform
Bill) that there was a case for permitting the authorized minimum to be denominated in sterling or an
equivalent amount expressed in euros (see subsection (1)(a) and (b). Indeed, Article 6 of the Second
Company Law Directive[31] from which that requirement derives, permits the authorized minimum to
be denominated in euros or sterling (see below).

The section retains the authorized minimum at £50,000 as recommended by the Company Law Review    **20.763.03**
(CLR)[32] or the prescribed euro equivalent. There is the same minimum share capital requirement
where a private company re-registers as a public company under Part 7 of the Companies Act 2006 (or
formerly under section 43 of the Companies Act 1985). This implements Article 6 of the Second
Company Law Directive[33] which requires that in order that a public company may be incorporated or
obtain authorization to commence business, a minimum capital shall be subscribed, the amount of
which shall be not less than 25,000 ECU expressed in the domestic currency of the Member State.[34] The
ECU was replaced by the euro with effect from 1 January 1999. While the Second Company Law
Directive does not prescribe that the minimum share capital requirements for a public company must

---

[25]  The form (SH50) required to be submitted under this section when applying for a trading certificate as a
public    company    is    available    at:    ⟨http://www.companieshouse.gov.uk/forms/generalForms/
SH50_application_for_trading_certificate_for_a_public_company.pdf⟩.

[26]  See section 5 of form SH50 available at: ⟨http://www.companieshouse.gov.uk/forms/generalForms/
SH50_application_for_trading_certificate_for_a_public_company.pdf⟩.

[27]  Para 830.

[28]  Under either section 270 or 274 of the Companies Act 2006.

[29]  See section 5 of form SH50.

[30]  Companies Act 2006 (Commencement No 5, etc) Order 2007, SI 2007/3495, art 3.

[31]  77/91/EEC.

[32]  *Completing the Structure*, para 7.6.

[33]  77/91/EEC.

[34]  The directive goes on to lay down how the equivalent of 25,000 ECU in the Member State's national
currency is to be calculated.

be met in the Member States' domestic currency,[35] in a decision under the previous provision,[36] Harman J took the view that Article 6 seemed to require EU Member States to impose on public companies incorporated within the EU a minimum share capital in their own national currency.[37] There does not, however, appear to be anything in Article 6 of the Second Company Law Directive that requires the authorized minimum to continue to be denominated in sterling once a public company has been registered or re-registered.[38]

**20.763.04**  Turning to the substance of this section, the following should be noted. For the purposes of the definition of 'the authorised minimum' in subsection (1), the amount in euros to be treated as equivalent to the sterling amount(e) is currently €57,100.[39] Subsection (2) provides the Secretary of State with a new power to prescribe by order the authorized minimum figure in euros which for the time being is to be treated as equivalent to the relevant sterling amount. This power is necessary due to exchange rate fluctuations and in order to achieve parity between the prescribed sterling and euro amounts. Subsection (3) states that this power may be exercised from time to time in order to maintain approximate parity between the euro figure and the specified sterling amount if, due to exchange rate fluctuations, the specified euro figure exceeds or falls below £50,000. It is not, however, anticipated that this power would be exercised unless the difference between the two values became significant.[40] Subsection (4) explains how the amount prescribed shall be determined under the new power, namely, the euro amount to be prescribed is to be determined by applying an appropriate spot rate of exchange to the sterling amount and rounding to the nearest 100 euros. As this power could only be used for the express purpose of prescribing the amount expressed in euros which, after applying an appropriate exchange rate, equates to £50,000,[41] subsection (5) provides that this power should be subject to the negative resolution procedure.[42]

**20.763.05**  Finally, it should be noted that the power to alter the authorized minimum is contained in section 764 (see below).

### 764  Power to alter authorised minimum

**20.764.01**  (1) The Secretary of State may by order—
  (a) alter the sterling amount of the authorised minimum, and
  (b) make a corresponding alteration of the prescribed euro equivalent.
(2) The amount of the prescribed euro equivalent shall be determined by applying an appropriate spot rate of exchange to the sterling amount and rounding to the nearest 100 euros.
(3) An order under this section that increases the authorised minimum may—
  (a) require a public company having an allotted share capital of which the nominal value is less than the amount specified in the order to—
    (i) increase that value to not less than that amount, or
    (ii) re-register as a private company;

---

[35] It would certainly be convenient for some companies if their authorized share capital could be denominated in a currency other than pounds sterling. The most obvious example would be the euro.
[36] CA 1985, s 118. See *Re Scandinavian Bank Group plc* [1988] Ch 87.
[37] It should be noted that the opportunity has been taken to put into statutory form (see s 542(2) above) the principle that shares may be denominated in any currency (*Re Scandinavian Bank Group plc*, Ibid) and that different classes of shares may be denominated in different currencies, subject to s 765 (initial authorized minimum share capital requirement for public company to be met by reference to share capital denominated in sterling or euros, see below).
[38] Official Report, 15/3/06; Col GC481–482 (Lord McKenzie). Ss 622 to 628 (see above) contain new provisions that enable both public and private companies alike to easily redenominate their share capital from one currency to another. Those provisions enable a public company to redenominate all of its share capital, including the authorized minimum, into another currency of the company's choosing as soon as the company has been registered or re-registered. The practical effect is that shares in a limited company having a share capital could end up denominated in whatever currency the company chooses.
[39] Companies (Authorised Minimum) Regulations 2009, SI 2009/2424. This is reduced from the €65,600 prescribed by the Companies (Authorised Minimum) Regulations 2008, SI 2008/729, reg 2 which were revoked on 1 October 2009. However, the figure of €57,100 in reg 2 is to be read as €65,600 where that regulation applies to determine whether the nominal value of a public company's allotted share capital is less than the authorized minimum for the purposes of an application for a trading certificate under s 761 where the application was received by the registrar before 1 October 2009. See reg 9(1) and (2)(a) of the Companies (Authorised Minimum) Regulations 2009.
[40] See HL Paper 264, published by the Delegated Powers and Regulatory Reform Committee, House of Lords on 1 Nov 2006, para. 42.
[41] Ibid, para 43.
[42] For negative resolution procedure see s 1289 below.

  (b) make provision in connection with any such requirement for any of the matters for which provision is made by this Act relating to—
    (i) a company's registration, re-registration or change of name,
    (ii) payment for shares comprised in a company's share capital, and
    (iii) offers to the public of shares in or debentures of a company,
    including provision as to the consequences (in criminal law or otherwise) of a failure to comply with any requirement of the order;
  (c) provide for any provision of the order to come into force on different days for different purposes.
  (4) An order under this section is subject to affirmative resolution procedure.

COMMENCEMENT DATE 6 April 2008[43]

This section replaces section 118 of the Companies Act 1985 which contained a power for the Secretary **20.764.02** of State to alter the authorized minimum[44] (which was set at £50,000). This power was not carried forward in the Companies Bill (formerly the Company Law Reform Bill) when it was first introduced in the House of Lords in November 2005, as it was originally envisaged that any alteration to the authorized minimum could be achieved by other existing or then-proposed powers. However, in light of the decision to permit the authorized minimum to be satisfied in euros and the power to prescribe the euro amount (see section 763 above) it was thought to be sensible to reinstate the express power to alter the authorized minimum and to make corresponding changes to the euro equivalent rather than relying on the section 2(2) of the European Communities Act 1972 power.[45] The section was therefore introduced as part of amendments made during the Bill's passage through the House of Commons on 1 November 2006.[46]

Subsection (1) provides, as under section 118 of the Companies Act 1985, that the Secretary of State **20.764.03** may by order alter the sterling amount of the authorized minimum and also make a corresponding alteration of the prescribed euro equivalent. This may be necessary, for example, because of changes to the prescribed minimum capital requirement for public companies at EU level, or desirable, for example, if it was considered appropriate for business reasons to raise or lower the minimum share capital requirement for public companies within the limits permitted by the Second Company Law Directive.[47] Subsection (2) states that the amount of the prescribed euro equivalent shall be determined by applying an appropriate spot rate of exchange to the sterling amount and rounding to the nearest 100 euros. Subsection (3) provides, as was the case under section 118 of the Companies Act 1985, that an order made pursuant to this power which increases the authorized minimum may require a public company to increase the value of its allotted share capital (such that it satisfies the authorized minimum as revised) or to re-register as a private company, and may make provision in connection with any such requirement for any of the matters for which provision is made in the Companies Act 2006 relating to a company's registration, re-registration, or change of name, to payment for any share comprised in a company's share capital, and offers to the public of shares or debentures in a company. As was the case under section 118(3) of the Companies Act 1985, subsection (4) states that the power is subject to affirmative resolution procedure.[48]

## 765 Authorised minimum: application of initial requirement

  (1) The initial requirement for a public company to have allotted share capital of a nominal value not **20.765.01** less than the authorised minimum, that is—
    (a) the requirement in section 761(2) for the issue of a trading certificate, or
    (b) the requirement in section 91(1)(a) for re-registration as a public company,
    must be met either by reference to allotted share capital denominated in sterling or by reference to allotted share capital denominated in euros (but not partly in one and partly in the other).
  (2) Whether the requirement is met is determined in the first case by reference to the sterling amount and in the second case by reference to the prescribed euro equivalent.
  (3) No account is to be taken of any allotted share capital of the company denominated in a currency other than sterling or, as the case may be, euros.

---

[43] Companies Act 2006 (Commencement No 5, etc) Order 2007, SI 2007/3495, art 3.
[44] The 'authorised minimum' is defined in s 763 above.
[45] See HL paper 264, published by the Delegated Powers and Regulatory Reform Committee, House of Lords on 1 Nov 2006, para 46.
[46] See HL paper 264, published by the Delegated Powers and Regulatory Reform Committee, House of Lords on 1 Nov 2006.
[47] Explanatory Notes to the CA 2006, para 1081.
[48] For affirmative resolution procedure see s 1290 below.

(4)  If the company could meet the requirement either by reference to share capital denominated in sterling or by reference to share capital denominated in euros, it must elect in its application for a trading certificate or, as the case may be, for re-registration as a public company which is to be the currency by reference to which the matter is determined.

COMMENCEMENT DATE  6 April 2008[49]

**20.765.02**  This section prescribes how the authorized minimum is to be met. It was first introduced as part of amendments made during the Companies Bill's passage through the House of Commons on 1 November 2006[50] in light of the decision to permit the 'authorised minimum' to be denominated in sterling or an equivalent amount expressed in euros (see section 763 above).

**20.765.03**  The Companies Act permits shares in a limited company having a share capital to be denominated in any currency, and different classes of shares may be denominated in different currencies (see section 542(3) above). Likewise, the Companies Act permits the 'authorised minimum' of a public company to be denominated in sterling or an equivalent amount expressed in euros (see section 763(1)(a) and (b) above). However, this section states that the initial requirement for a public company to have allotted share capital of a nominal value not less than the authorized minimum,[51] must be met *either* by reference to allotted share capital denominated in sterling or by reference to allotted share capital denominated in euros, but, importantly, *not* partly in one and partly in the other (see subsection (1)). Subsection (2) determines how this requirement is met, namely, in the first case by reference to the sterling amount and in the second case by reference to the prescribed euro equivalent. For example, if a company has allotted sterling shares to the total value of £25,000 and euro shares to the equivalent of £60,000, the authorized minimum will have been satisfied in euros. If the same company had allotted sterling shares to the total value of £10,000 and euro shares to the equivalent of £40,000 it would not have satisfied the minimum share capital requirement for a public company as the authorized minimum may be satisfied in sterling or euro but not partly in sterling and partly in euro.[52] Subsection (3) adds that no account is to be taken of any allotted share capital of the company denominated in a currency other than sterling or, as the case may be, euros. Finally, subsection (4) makes it clear that if the company could meet the requirement either by reference to share capital denominated in sterling or by reference to share capital denominated in euros, it must elect in its application for a trading certificate or, as the case may be, for re-registration as a public company which is to be the currency by reference to which the matter is determined.[53]

### 766  Authorised minimum: application where shares denominated in different currencies etc

**20.766.01**
(1)  The Secretary of State may make provision by regulations as to the application of the authorised minimum in relation to a public company that—
    (a)  has shares denominated—[54]
        (i)   in more than one currency, or
        (ii)  in a currency other than sterling or euros.
    (b)  redenominates the whole or part of its allotted share capital, or
    (c)  allots new shares.
(2)  The regulations may make provision as to the currencies, exchange rates and dates by reference to which it is to be determined whether the nominal value of the company's allotted share capital is less than the authorised minimum.
(3)  The regulations may provide that where—
    (a)  a company has redenominated the whole or part of its allotted share capital, and

---

[49]  Companies Act 2006 (Commencement No 5, etc) Order 2007, SI 2007/3495, art 3. Note that on the same commencement date of 6 April 2008, the section applied by 1985 c 9, s 3(2A) (as inserted by the Companies Act 2006 (Consequential Amendments etc) Order 2008 (SI 2008/948), art 3(1), Sch 1 para 95(3) (with arts 6, 11, 12)). The section was also applied by SI 1986/1032 (NI 6), art 22(b) (as substituted by the Companies Act 2006 (Consequential Amendments etc) Order 2008 (SI 2008/948), art 3(1), Sch 1 para 114 (with arts 6, 11, 12)).

[50]  See HL Paper 264, published by the Delegated Powers and Regulatory Reform Committee, House of Lords on 1 Nov 2006.

[51]  Ie the requirement in s 761(2) for the issue of a trading certificate, or the requirement in s 91(1)(a) for re-registration as a public company.

[52]  Explanatory Notes to the CA 2006, para 1083.

[53]  See form RR01 available at: ⟨http://www.companieshouse.gov.uk/forms/generalForms/RR01_application_by_a_private_company_for_reregisration_as_public_company.pdf⟩.

[54]  Inserted by the Companies Act 2006 (Consequential Amendments and Transitional Provisions) Order 2011, SI 2011/1265 art 28 made on 12 May 2011.

(b)  the effect of the redenomination is that the nominal value of the company's allotted share capital is less than the authorised minimum,

the company must re-register as a private company.

(4)  Regulations under subsection (3) may make provision corresponding to any provision made by sections 664 to 667 (re-registration as private company in consequence of cancellation of shares).

(5)  Any regulations under this section have effect subject to section 765 (authorised minimum: application of initial requirement).

(6)  Regulations under this section are subject to negative resolution procedure.

COMMENCEMENT DATE 6 April 2008[55]

This is a new section which provides the Secretary of State with the power to make provision by regulations to prescribe how references to the authorized minimum[56] are to be applied. The Companies Act permits companies to redenominate (ie convert) their share capital from one currency to another, eg from sterling to dollars (or vice versa).[57] Companies may wish to redenominate their share capital for a number of reasons, for example, in order to match the company's allotted share capital with the currency in which its assets are held, or because (notwithstanding the fact that the company was formed and registered in the UK) the vast majority of the company's shareholders are resident overseas.[58] There are also provisions in the Companies Act which require a company to re-register as a private company if, as a result of the company either reducing its share capital pursuant to a court order, or cancelling its shares in circumstances where it is required to do so, the value of the company's allotted share capital is brought below the authorized minimum.[59]     **20.766.02**

The power granted under subsection (1a) gives the Secretary of State power to make regulations which specify how the authorized minimum test would apply where all the shares of a public company are denominated in a currency other than sterling or euros. Subsection (1a) previously granted the Secretary of State the power in relation only to companies who had shares denominated in more than one currency. [60] The power granted under subsection (2) to the Secretary of State to make provision by regulations to prescribe how references to the authorized minimum are to be applied is necessary to prescribe how this is to be ascertained where a company has redenominated its share capital into a different currency, for example, in prescribing what currency should apply (whether it be sterling or euros), the relevant exchange rate, and the date by reference to which it is to be determined. The type of scenario that the power in this section is intended for, to take an extreme example,[61] is the situation where a public company incorporates with a share capital of £50,000 (expressed in sterling), allots additional dollar shares, subsequently redenominates part of its share capital into euros, and then applies to the court to reduce its share capital. It will be necessary in such circumstances to determine what test should be applied to ascertain whether the company's allotted share capital has fallen below the authorized minimum. In other words what exchange rates must be applied, as at what date they should be applied, and as between what currencies. Regulations made pursuant to subsection (2) will deal with this type of issue.     **20.766.03**

Whilst a company is free under the Companies Act 2006 to redenominate all of its share capital, including the authorized minimum, subsequent to its registration or re-registration as a public company, there is an issue as to what is to happen where a company has redenominated its share capital and, owing to subsequent exchange rate fluctuations, the value of the currency in which the company's shares are now held has fallen such that if the company were to redenominate its share capital back into sterling or euros it would fail to satisfy the authorized minimum. In these circumstances, subsection (3) provides the power to the Secretary of State to make provision by regulations to require the company to re-register as a private company, whereas subsection (4) provides that these regulations may correspond to any provision made by sections 664 to 667 (re-registration as a private company in consequence of cancellation of shares).[62] An application by a public company for re-registration as a private company following a reduction of capital due to redenomination needs to be done using Form     **20.766.04**

[55] Companies Act 2006 (Commencement No 5, etc) Order 2007, SI 2007/3495, art 3.

[56] See s 763 above.

[57] See ss 622–628 above.

[58] See HL Paper 264, published by the Delegated Powers and Regulatory Reform Committee, House of Lords on 1 Nov 2006, para 47.

[59] See ss 664–667 (re-registration as private company in consequence of cancellation of shares) above.

[60] Companies (Authorised Minimum) Regulations 2009, SI 2009/2424 which was initially used on 12 March 2008 and came into force on 6 April 2008. The Companies (Authorised Minimum) Regulations 2008, SI 2008/729 were revoked on 1 October 2009. See s 763 above.

[61] Explanatory Notes to the CA 2006, para 1086.

[62] See regulation 5 of the Companies (Shares, Share Capital and Authorised Minimum) Regulations 2008, SI 2008/0000.

RR10 (issued by Companies House).[63] This form may be signed by a director, secretary, a person authorized,[64] administrator, administrative receiver, receiver, receiver manager or CIC (Community Interest Companies) manager.[65]

**20.766.05**   Subsection (5) states that any regulations under this section have effect subject to section 765 (authorized minimum: application of initial requirement, see above). Finally, subsection (6) states that the power to make provision by regulations under this section should be subject to the negative resolution procedure. This is deemed to be appropriate owing to the technical nature of these regulations, and the fact that this power may only be exercised for the express purpose of dealing with exchange rate fluctuations subsequent to a redenomination of share capital.[66]

### 767 Consequences of doing business etc without a trading certificate

**20.767.01**
(1) If a company does business or exercises any borrowing powers in contravention of section 761, an offence is committed by—
   (a) the company, and
   (b) every officer of the company who is in default.
(2) A person guilty of an offence under subsection (1) is liable—
   (a) on conviction on indictment, to a fine;
   (b) on summary conviction, to a fine not exceeding the statutory maximum.
(3) A contravention of section 761 does not affect the validity of a transaction entered into by the company, but if a company—
   (a) enters into a transaction in contravention of that section, and
   (b) fails to comply with its obligations in connection with the transaction within 21 days from being called on to do so,
   the directors of the company are jointly and severally liable to indemnify any other party to the transaction in respect of any loss or damage suffered by him by reason of the company's failure to comply with its obligations.
(4) The directors who are so liable are those who were directors at the time the company entered into the transaction.

COMMENCEMENT DATE 6 April 2008[67]

**20.767.02**   This section reinstates the penalty that was prescribed in section 117(7) and Schedule 24 of the Companies Act 1985. It also reunites the criminal sanction with the civil penalty that was prescribed in section 117(8) of the Companies Act 1985 and ensures that the consequences of a company acting in contravention of section 761 (see above) can be found in one place.

**20.767.03**   By reason of subsections (1) and (2), as was the case under the Companies Act 1985, where a public company that is required to obtain a trading certificate enters into a transaction without first obtaining such a certificate, the directors are jointly and severally liable for any loss or damage caused to the other party to the transaction as a result of the company failing to meet its obligations. In addition, the company and every officer of the company who is in default commit an offence. However, subsection (4) qualifies the above liability when it specifies that a director will only be jointly and severally liable with the company if he was a director at the time that the transaction was entered into, and if the company has failed to meet its obligations under the transaction in question within 21 days of being called on to do so (subsection (3)(b)). Subsection (3) also confirms that, notwithstanding the fact that the company should not have entered into the transaction, the transaction itself is valid.

**20.767.04**   Finally, it should be noted that, in addition to the consequences prescribed by this section, according to section 122(1)(b) of the Insolvency Act 1986, where a public company has not obtained a trading certificate[68] within a year of its incorporation, it may be wound up by the court.

---

[63] The form is available at: ⟨http://www.companieshouse.gov.uk/forms/generalForms/RR10_application_by_a_public_company_for_reregistration_as_a_private_company_following.pdf⟩. See also regulation 6 of the Companies (Shares, Share Capital and Authorised Minimum) Regulations 2008, SI 2008/0000.

[64] Under either section 270 or 274 of the Companies Act 2006.

[65] See section 3 of form RR10.

[66] See HL Paper 264, published by the Delegated Powers and Regulatory Reform Committee, House of Lords on 1 Nov 2006, para 51.

[67] Companies Act 2006 (Commencement No 5, etc) Order 2007, SI 2007/3495, art 3.

[68] See s 761 above.

# 21

## CERTIFICATION AND TRANSFER OF SECURITIES

*See also Chapter 49: Uncertified Securities Regulations.*

## Companies Act 2006

### PART 21
### CERTIFICATION AND TRANSFER OF SECURITIES

### CHAPTER 1
### CERTIFICATION AND TRANSFER OF SECURITIES: GENERAL

*Share certificates*

### 768 Share certificate to be evidence of title

**21.768.01**
(1) In the case of a company registered in England and Wales or Northern Ireland, a certificate under the common seal of the company specifying any shares held by a member is prima facie evidence of his title to the shares.

(2) In the case of a company registered in Scotland—

    (a) a certificate under the common seal of the company specifying any shares held by a member, or

    (b) a certificate specifying any shares held by a member and subscribed by the company in accordance with the Requirements of Writing (Scotland) Act 1995 (c. 7),

is sufficient evidence, unless the contrary is shown, of his title to the shares.

COMMENCEMENT DATE 6 April 2008[1]

**21.768.02**   This section, which restates section 186 of the 1985 Act with minor drafting changes, states the effect of a share certificate and obviously applies only when shares are issued in certificated form.[2] The reference to the common seal in subsection (1) includes an official seal under section 50,[3] but the section cannot apply if a company is not required by its articles to fix a seal to its share certificates.[4] The certificate is *prima facie*, or in Scotland sufficient, evidence of the legal title of the holder of the shares, but it is not evidence of an indefeasible title,[5] so proof that the holder obtained the shares from someone who could not give him title to them will mean the holder losing the shares and the name of the true owner being retained on or restored to the register.[6] Someone with possession of or an immediate right to possession of a share certificate can bring a claim in conversion.[7]

**21.768.03**   However, case law has long established that a share certificate creates an estoppel in favour of a person who relies on it in good faith either in buying the shares comprised in it or as regards a statement on it that the shares are fully paid up.[8] This is an unusual form of estoppel since it confers a right to damages against the company. The measure of damages in a case of a wrongful refusal to register the person who has relied on the certificate is the value of the shares at the date of the refusal to register.[9] Where the person who has relied on the certificate resells them and is liable to his purchaser in damages or has to buy other shares in order to perform the contract to resell, he can recover his loss from the company.[10] It has been held, however, that this does not apply if a certificate is a forgery, even if the forgery was

---

[1] Companies Act 2006 (Commencement No 5, Transitional Provisions and Savings) Order 2007, SI 2007/3495, art 3.

[2] That is, not under the CREST system; see para 21.785.01.

[3] See para 4.50.02.

[4] It is not necessary for a company to have a seal; see s 45.

[5] *Johnston v Renton* (1870) LR 9 Eq 181; *Simm v Anglo-American Telegraph Co* (1879) 5 QBD 188.

[6] *Barton v London & North-Western Railway Co* (1890) 24 QBD 77; *Welch v Bank of England* [1955] Ch 508; *Hart v Frontino and Bolivia South American Gold Mining Co Ltd* (1870) LR 5 Ex 111.

[7] *MCC Proceeds Inc v Lehman Brothers International (Europe)* [1998] 2 BCLC 659. This does not apply to someone with merely an equitable title to shares.

[8] See *Re Bahia and San Francisco Railway Co* (1868) LR 3 QB 584 and *Re Ottos Kopje Diamond Mines Ltd* [1893] 1 Ch 618 for illustrations of the first proposition and *Burkinshaw v Nicolls* (1878) 3 App Cas 1004 and *Re British Farmers' Pure Linseed Cake Co* (1878) 7 Ch D 533 for illustrations of the second proposition.

[9] *Re Ottos Kopje Diamond Mines*, above.

[10] *Balkis Consolidated Co Ltd v Tomkinson* [1893] AC 396.

committed by the company secretary,[11] and a similar result was reached where the certificate was signed by two directors and the secretary without authority.[12]

If a certificate is correct in stating that a certain person is the registered holder of the shares, the company will not be liable to a purchaser from that person by virtue of having certified a previous transfer of the shares to another person, even though the company gave the certificate back to the registered holder after certifying the transfer, thus enabling the registered holder to deal with the shares again. The real cause of the loss by the purchaser is the fraud of the registered holder and not the negligence, if any, of the company. Furthermore, any duty of the company to ensure that the certificate is sent to the registered holder is owed to the registered holder only, not to third parties such as purchasers.[13]    **21.768.04**

As regards someone protected by a statement that the shares are fully paid up, the estoppel prevents the company from claiming any further amount from him. Clearly the original holder of a certificate will normally be unable to prove either reliance or ignorance of the true position,[14] but the position may be different if he is not the person who actually applied for the shares and was ignorant of the true position.[15] It has been held that if a transferee who is entitled to rely on the estoppel sells the shares, even a purchaser who was aware that the shares were not fully paid can also rely on the estoppel,[16] although this decision has been doubted.[17] A director who relied on the certificate in good faith was protected even when he had signed the certificate.[18] In *Re MacDonald, Sons & Co,*[19] the estoppel extended to a letter accompanying the share certificate stating that the shares were fully paid, even though the certificate was silent on this. Knowledge sufficient to disentitle the transferee from relying on the estoppel may arise from an indication of irregularity on the certificate, for example where the word 'bonus' was printed on it,[20] or from knowledge of facts that the shares have not been paid for in cash.[21] However, only actual knowledge will suffice in this context; it is not enough that the transferee ought to have known that the shares were not fully paid.[22]    **21.768.05**

## *Issue of certificates etc on allotment*

### 769  Duty of company as to issue of certificates etc on allotment

(1)  A company must, within two months after the allotment of any of its shares, debentures or debenture stock, complete and have ready for delivery—    **21.769.01**
    (a)  the certificates of the shares allotted,
    (b)  the debentures allotted, or
    (c)  the certificates of the debenture stock allotted.
(2)  Subsection (1) does not apply—
    (a)  if the conditions of issue of the shares, debentures or debenture stock provide otherwise,
    (b)  in the case of allotment to a financial institution (see section 778), or
    (c)  in the case of an allotment of shares if, following the allotment, the company has issued a share warrant in respect of the shares (see section 779).
(3)  If default is made in complying with subsection (1) an offence is committed by every officer of the company who is in default.

---

[11]  *Ruben v Great Fingall Consolidated* [1906] AC 439. However, it is by no means certain that this decision would be followed today, given the fact that a company secretary may well be regarded as having apparent authority to represent the certificate as genuine: *Panorama Developments (Guildford) Ltd v Fidelis Furnishing Fabrics Ltd* [1971] 2 QB 711 and see the Australian High Court decision in *Northside Developments Pty Ltd v Registrar-General* (1990) 64 ALJR 427.

[12]  *South London Greyhound Racecourses Ltd v Wake* [1931] 1 Ch 496. This decision is even less likely to be followed given the much wider concept of apparent authority that applies today. In addition the claimant ought to be able to rely upon s 44; see para 4.44.02.

[13]  *Longman v Bath Electric Tramways Ltd* [1905] 1 Ch 646.

[14]  *Re Vulcan Ironworks Co* [1885] WN 120.

[15]  *Re Building Estates Brickfield Co, Parbury's Case* [1896] 1 Ch 100.

[16]  *Re Stapleford Colliery Co, Barrow's Case* (1880) 14 ChD 432.

[17]  *Re London Celluloid Co* (1888) 39 ChD 190 at 197; *Re Railway Time Tables Publishing Co* (1889) 42 Ch D 98 at 110.

[18]  *Re Coasters Ltd* [1911] 1 Ch 86.

[19]  [1894] 1 Ch 89.

[20]  *Re Eddystone Marine Insurance Co (No 2)* [1894] WN 30; *ex p Bloomenthal* [1896] 2 Ch 525, reversed on the facts, sub nom *Bloomenthal v Ford* [1897] AC 156.

[21]  *Re Caribbean Co* (1875) 10 Ch App 614; *Re London Celluloid Co* (1888) 39 Ch D 190; *Bloomenthal v Ford,* above; *Re African Gold Concessions and Market Development Co, Markham and Darter's Case* [1899] 1 Ch 414.

[22]  *Bloomenthal v Ford,* above.

(4) A person guilty of an offence under subsection (3) is liable on summary conviction to a fine not exceeding level 3 on the standard scale and, for continued contravention, a daily default fine not exceeding one-tenth of level 3 on the standard scale.

COMMENCEMENT DATE 6 April 2008[23]

**21.769.02**  This section restates the obligation on a company to issue a certificate following an allotment of shares, debentures or debenture stock that was previously in section 185 of the 1985 Act. The latter section also applied on a transfer of such securities, but that matter is now dealt with separately in section 776. At the same time, the requirements were amended by the 2006 Act in two respects. First subsection (2)(c) was inserted to clarify that the obligation to issue a certificate does not apply to bearer shares. Secondly, breach of the requirements remains an offence by any officer in default,[24] but there is no longer an offence committed by the company. The other sanction is the power of the court to order compliance under section 782.

**21.769.03**  Unless the conditions of issue provide otherwise and subject to the cases in subsection (2) covered by sections 778 and 779, the section requires a company to have an appropriate certificate ready within two months of the allotment of shares or debentures. Shares are allotted when someone acquires the unconditional right to be included in the company's register of members in respect of them,[25] which basically means when the contract to allot them is fully executed. The same would clearly apply in respect of debentures.

**21.769.04**  Whether or not a shareholder or debenture holder can require a number of certificates where they hold more than one share or debenture depends on the articles.[26] The normal practice is to include all the shares or debentures held by one person in one certificate. The form of the certificate will also be determined by the articles.[27] Even if the certificate is issued under seal, it is not a deed.[28] A share certificate is likely to state the amount paid up on the shares represented, but should not state that the shares are subject to a lien in the company's favour.[29]

## Transfer of securities

### 770  Registration of transfer

**21.770.01**  (1) A company may not register a transfer of shares in or debentures of the company unless—
    (a) a proper instrument of transfer has been delivered to it, or
    (b) the transfer—
        (i) is an exempt transfer within the Stock Transfer Act 1982 (c. 41), or
        (ii) is in accordance with regulations under Chapter 2 of this Part.
(2) Subsection (1) does not affect any power of the company to register as shareholder or debenture holder a person to whom the right to any shares in or debentures of the company has been transmitted by operation of law.

COMMENCEMENT DATE 6 April 2008[30]

**21.770.02**  This section restates, with drafting amendments, what was section 183(1) and (2) of the 1985 Act. The drafting amendments include the omission of the previous statement that a transfer of shares or debentures in breach of the section was not lawful, but this would seem implied by the wording of subsection (1). There is also no longer any reference to the section applying notwithstanding anything in the company's articles, but it is thought again that this is implicit from the mandatory nature of subsection (1).

---

[23] Companies Act 2006 (Commencement No 5, Transitional Provisions and Savings) Order 2007, SI 2007/3495, art 3.

[24] For the meaning of this, see s 1121.

[25] S 558.

[26] *Sharpe v Tophams Ltd* [1939] Ch 373. See Art 6 in Table A to the Companies Act (CA) 1985 and Art 24 of the model articles for a private company (see Chapter 52 at 51.MA.49).

[27] Table A to CA 1985 requires it to be under seal and signed by the director and the secretary or by two directors, but the model articles for a private company (Art 24) allow the alternative of execution in accordance with the Act which (in s 44(2)(c)) allows execution by one director with an attestation clause.

[28] *South London Greyhound Racecourses v Wake* [1931] 1 Ch 496; *R v Williams* [1942] AC 541. The Listing Rules do not require a certificate to be sealed.

[29] *Re W Key & Son Ltd* [1902] Ch 467.

[30] Companies Act 2006 (Commencement No 5, Transitional Provisions and Savings) Order 2007, SI 2007/3495, art 3.

The section ensures that there are appropriate formalities for the transfer of a share[31] or debenture by **21.770.03** means of a 'proper instrument of transfer', and that an oral transfer is ineffective, as is a provision for automatic transfer, for example from a deceased member to his widow.[32] However, this applies only to the transfer of legal title, not to the disposition of a beneficial interest, which will be governed by the requirements of the law of trusts, nor to an equitable mortgage or charge on shares or debentures, which can be created simply by deposit of the certificate or an appropriate agreement.[33]

A 'proper instrument of transfer' is a written document that will attract stamp duty, but there are no **21.770.04** other implications regarding its form.[34] Standard articles used to provide that a transfer had to be signed by, or on behalf of, both the transferor and transferee,[35] but the version of Table A prescribed under the 1985 Act requires[36] only that it be executed by or on behalf of the transferor, except where a share is only partly paid. The model articles issued for a private company limited by shares under the 2006 Act state[37] only that shares may be transferred by means of an instrument of transfer in a form permitted by law. Any signatures should be witnessed, the document must give the amount of the consideration and the numbers, if any, of the shares, and the names, addresses, and occupations of the parties.

In practice transfers of shares and debentures issued by private companies limited by shares and **21.770.05** unquoted public companies use the forms provided by the Stock Transfer Act 1963 or forms corresponding to these.[38] These must be executed by the transferor but need not be executed by the transferee. They must contain particulars of the transferor, the description and number or amount of the shares or stock, the nature and amount of the consideration, and the full name and address of the transferee, but attestation is unnecessary.

The exemptions in subsection (1)(b) relate to shares and debentures in quoted companies will either be **21.770.06** transferred via the CREST system, that is under the Uncertificated Securities Regulations made under Chapter 2, or, in increasingly rare cases, under the Stock Exchange's Talisman system. Transfers exempted under the Stock Transfer Act 1982 are transfers of government and related securities.

Subsection (2) refers to cases where a member dies or becomes bankrupt and thus exempts from the **21.770.07** formal requirements the transmission of shares or debentures to the personal representatives or trustee in bankruptcy, as appropriate.

## 771  Procedure on transfer being lodged

(1)  When a transfer of shares in or debentures of a company has been lodged with the company, the **21.771.01** company must either—
  (a)  register the transfer, or
  (b)  give the transferee notice of refusal to register the transfer, together with its reasons for the refusal,
  as soon as practicable and in any event within two months after the date on which the transfer is lodged with it.

(2)  If the company refuses to register the transfer, it must provide the transferee with such further information about the reasons for the refusal as the transferee may reasonably request.
  This does not include copies of minutes of meetings of directors.

(3)  If a company fails to comply with this section, an offence is committed by—
  (a)  the company, and
  (b)  every officer of the company who is in default.

(4)  A person guilty of an offence under this section is liable on summary conviction to a fine not exceeding level 3 on the standard scale and, for continued contravention, a daily default fine not exceeding one-tenth of level 3 on the standard scale.

---

[31]  Except bearer shares, which are governed by s 779.
[32]  *Re Greene* [1949] Ch 333. Exceptionally, if the company is in liquidation and the liquidator is satisfied that the transferee would be able to compel the transfer, although he is not obliged to recognize the title of the transferee, the liquidator may dispense with the formalities: *Re Baku Consolidated Oilfields Ltd* [1994] 1 BCLC 173.
[33]  *Harrold v Plenty* [1907] 2 Ch 314; *Stubbs v Slater* [1910] 1 Ch 632.
[34]  *Re Paradise Motor Co Ltd* [1968] 1 WLR 1125 at 1141; *Nisbet v Shepherd* [1994] 1 BCLC 300. There is no need for a deed unless the articles require one, which is most unlikely these days: *Re Tahiti Cotton Co* (1873) LR 6 HL 37.
[35]  See Table A in the Companies Act 1948, Art 22.
[36]  Art 23.
[37]  Art 22.
[38]  These forms cannot be used in respect of unlimited companies and companies limited by guarantee.

    (5) This section does not apply—

      (a) in relation to a transfer of shares if the company has issued a share warrant in respect of the shares (see section 779);

      (b) in relation to the transmission of shares or debentures by operation of law.

COMMENCEMENT DATE 6 April 2008[39]

**21.771.02** In dealing with the requirements when a transfer of shares or debentures is lodged with a company, this section replaces in part section 183(4), (5), and (6) of the 1985 Act, but it also modifies the former provision in important ways.

**21.771.03** The obligation to register a transfer is within the same time period, namely with an absolute deadline of two months of the date of the lodging of the transfer. However, the duty to act as soon as practicable is a new requirement, although the two-month deadline was the maximum period allowed for registration of a transfer under the former section 183(5). As it was held that a company is obliged to take a decision to refuse to register a transfer within a reasonable time,[40] with the statutory two months being the maximum such time,[41] the slight change in wording seems to produce no real difference in effect.

**21.771.04** The articles of a private company will commonly give the directors the right to refuse to register a transfer of shares.[42] The previous requirement merely to send notice of such a refusal has been replaced by the requirement to give notice with reasons and such further information as the transferee reasonably requests other than minutes of directors' meetings. This requirement was recommended by the Company Law Review Steering Group,[43] and may have the effect of qualifying the right of refusal. Previously, if the articles gave the directors an absolute discretion to refuse to register, it was challengeable only if they could be shown to have acted in bad faith[44] or if they acted outside a reasonable time, and they were not required to give their reasons.[45] Clearly the fact that reasons must be disclosed will make it more possible to challenge a refusal. Under the former section 183(5) it has been held[46] that a failure to communicate a proper refusal to register a transfer within the two-month period did not render the decision void, but given the new requirement to give reasons within that time period, it seems arguable that this decision does not survive the rewording.

### 772 Transfer of shares on application of transferor

**21.772.01** On the application of the transferor of any share or interest in a company, the company shall enter in its register of members the name of the transferee in the same manner and subject to the same conditions as if the application for the entry were made by the transferee.

COMMENCEMENT DATE 6 April 2008[47]

**21.772.02** This section repeats what was formerly in section 183(4) of the 1985 Act, with the effect that either the transferor or the transferee can lodge a transfer for registration, the section giving the transferor this right as if the application were made by the transferee.

### 773 Execution of share transfer by personal representative

**21.773.01** An instrument of transfer of the share or other interest of a deceased member of a company—

    (a) may be made by his personal representative although the personal representative is not himself a member of the company, and

    (b) is as effective as if the personal representative had been such a member at the time of the execution of the instrument.

COMMENCEMENT DATE 6 April 2008[48]

---

[39] Companies Act 2006 (Commencement No 5, Transitional Provisions and Savings) Order 2007, SI 2007/3495, art 3. This section applies to transfers lodged with the company on or after 6 April 2008: Ibid, Sch 4, para 30.

[40] *Re Joint Discount Co, Shepherd's Case* (1866) 2 Ch App 16.

[41] *Re Swaledale Cleaners Ltd* [1968] 1 WLR 1710; *Tett v Phoenix Property and Investment Co Ltd* [1984] BCLC 599; *Re Inverdeck Ltd* [1998] BCC 256.

[42] See Art 26(2) of the model articles for a private company limited by shares (see Chapter 52 at MA.101). For discussion see, for example, *Gore-Browne on Companies*, chap 23.

[43] See *Completing the Structure*, para 5.80.

[44] *Re Smith & Fawcett Ltd* [1942] Ch 304; *Charles Forte Investments Ltd v Amanda* [1964] Ch 240; *Village Cay Marina Ltd v Acland* [1998] 2 BCLC 327.

[45] *Ex p Penney* (1873) 8 Ch App 446; *Berry v Tottenham Hotspur Football and Athletic Co Ltd* [1935] Ch 718.

[46] *Popely v Planarrive Ltd* [1997] 1 BCLC 8.

[47] Companies Act 2006 (Commencement No 5, Transitional Provisions and Savings) Order 2007, SI 2007/3495, art 3.

[48] Companies Act 2006 (Commencement No 5, Transitional Provisions and Savings) Order 2007, SI 2007/3495, art 3.

This section was formerly section 183(3) of the 1985 Act. It allows the personal representatives of a **21.773.02** deceased member to transfer shares or debentures as if they were registered members, that is, for the purpose of executing an instrument of transfer. It does not give them any right to transfer if the articles restrict their rights.

## 774  Evidence of grant of probate etc

The production to a company of any document that is by law sufficient evidence of the grant of— **21.774.01**

(a)  probate of the will of a deceased person,

(b)  letters of administration of the estate of a deceased person, or

(c)  confirmation as executor of a deceased person,

shall be accepted by the company as sufficient evidence of the grant.

COMMENCEMENT DATE  6 April 2008[49]

This section, which restates section 187 of the 1985 Act, deals with the specific situation of a company **21.774.02** recognizing the title of an executor or administrator of a deceased person as regards their rights as shareholder or debenture holder. The reference to documents that 'by law' are sufficient evidence is a reference to the law of the appropriate part of the UK. A company may not recognize a personal representative until they have obtained probate or letters of administration in this country and, if a company recognizes the title of a foreign executor, it will be regarded as an 'executor de son tort'.[50]

Despite this, it has been held that a liquidator does not need to insist on an English grant if he is satisfied **21.774.03** that the personal representatives would be entitled, but he would be better advised to obtain an indemnity or insist on an English grant being obtained.[51]

## 775  Certification of instrument of transfer

(1)  The certification by a company of an instrument of transfer of any shares in, or debentures of, the **21.775.01** company is to be taken as a representation by the company to any person acting on the faith of the certification that there have been produced to the company such documents as on their face show a prima facie title to the shares or debentures in the transferor named in the instrument.

(2)  The certification is not to be taken as a representation that the transferor has any title to the shares or debentures.

(3)  Where a person acts on the faith of a false certification by a company made negligently, the company is under the same liability to him as if the certification had been made fraudulently.

(4)  For the purposes of this section—

(a)  an instrument of transfer is certificated if it bears the words 'certificate lodged' (or words to the like effect);

(b)  the certification of an instrument of transfer is made by a company if—

(i)  the person issuing the instrument is a person authorised to issue certificated instruments of transfer on the company's behalf, and

(ii)  the certification is signed by a person authorised to certificate transfers on the company's behalf or by an officer or employee either of the company or of a body corporate so authorised;

(c)  a certification is treated as signed by a person if—

(i)  it purports to be authenticated by his signature or initials (whether handwritten or not), and

(ii)  it is not shown that the signature or initials was or were placed there neither by himself nor by a person authorised to use the signature or initials for the purpose of certificating transfers on the company's behalf.

COMMENCEMENT DATE  6 April 2008[52]

This section restates section 184 of the 1985 Act. Certification of transfers of shares or debentures is a **21.775.02** procedure used when not all the shares or debentures represented by one certificate are being transferred. In such a situation, the certificate is lodged with the company and the fact that this has been done is noted on the transfer form by the words 'certificate lodged' or words to the same effect.[53] This certified transfer is returned to the transferor who will then deliver it to the transferee. After the transfer is lodged with the company and the registration of the transferee, two new certificates will be

---

[49]  Companies Act 2006 (Commencement No 5, Transitional Provisions and Savings) Order 2007, SI 2007/ 3495, art 3.

[50]  *New York Breweries Co Ltd v Attorney-General* [1899] AC 62.

[51]  *Re Baku Consolidated Oilfields Ltd* [1994] 1 BCLC 173.

[52]  Companies Act 2006 (Commencement No 5, Transitional Provisions and Savings) Order 2007, SI 2007/ 3495, art 3.

[53]  See subs (3)(a).

prepared and issued appropriately to the transferor and transferee. The legitimacy of the procedure was established in *Bishop v Balkis Consolidated Co.*[54] This section is concerned with the position of persons such as the transferee who act in reliance on a certification on the form of transfer.

**21.775.03**    However, what the section does is to establish a representation that documents have been produced showing a *prima facie* title to the shares or debentures in question. It is not a representation that the transferor has any title to those shares or debentures, so that, for example, it will not cure a forged transfer.[55] However, it has been held that a certified transfer that purports to relate to fully paid shares will bind the company even if the shares are only partly paid.[56] The effect of subsection (2) is to impose the same liability on the company in the case of a negligent certification as if the certification had been made fraudulently.[57]

**21.775.04**    The main purpose of the section is the provision in subsection (3)(b). Decisions made before this was first introduced in the Companies Act 1948 held that a certification by an agent of the company with authority to certify transfers but who did so fraudulently was not the act of the company.[58] Now, provided the person issuing the instrument is authorized to issue certificated transfers and the certification is signed, in the manner indicated by subsection (3)(c), by a person or another company authorized to certificate transfers or by any officer or servant of the company, the certification is deemed to be made by the company. Therefore, the company will be bound if such a person acts fraudulently. However, it is still the case under subsection (3)(b)(i) that the person must have authority to issue certificated transfers, which must be either by express or implied authority conferred by the directors or where the directors have conferred apparent authority on that person.[59] In the absence of that, subsection (3)(b) cannot apply.

## *Issue of certificates etc on transfer*

### 776  Duty of company as to issue of certificates etc on transfer

**21.776.01**        (1)  A company must, within two months after the date on which a transfer of any of its shares, debentures or debenture stock is lodged with the company, complete and have ready for delivery—
          (a)  the certificates of the shares transferred,
          (b)  the debentures transferred, or
          (c)  the certificates of the debenture stock transferred.
        (2)  For this purpose a 'transfer' means—
          (a)  a transfer duly stamped and otherwise valid, or
          (b)  an exempt transfer within the Stock Transfer Act 1982 (c. 41),
        but does not include a transfer that the company is for any reason entitled to refuse to register and does not register.
        (3)  Subsection (1) does not apply—
          (a)  if the conditions of issue of the shares, debentures or debenture stock provide otherwise,
          (b)  in the case of a transfer to a financial institution (see section 778), or
          (c)  in the case of a transfer of shares if, following the transfer, the company has issued a share warrant in respect of the shares (see section 779).
        (4)  Subsection (1) has effect subject to section 777 (cases where the Stock Transfer Act 1982 applies).
        (5)  If default is made in complying with subsection (1) an offence is committed by every officer of the company who is in default.
        (6)  A person guilty of an offence under this section is liable on summary conviction to a fine not exceeding level 3 on the standard scale and, for continued contravention, a daily default fine not exceeding one-tenth of level 3 on the standard scale.

COMMENCEMENT DATE  6 April 2008[60]

---

[54]  (1890) 25 QBD 512.

[55]  As to these, see the commentary to s 768, above.

[56]  *Re Concessions Trust, McKay's Case* [1896] 2 Ch 757.

[57]  It should be remembered that this was introduced at a time when tortious liability for negligent misstatements was very limited. On the other hand, because negligence liability is equated with fraudulent liability, that is liability for the tort of deceit, presumably the measure of damages would be greater.

[58]  See the House of Lords' decisions in *George Whitechurch Ltd v Cavanagh* [1902] AC 117 and *Kleinwort v Associated Automatic Machine Corp* (1934) 50 TLR 244, which were in accordance with the general law regarding the liability of a principal for the fraud of his agent.

[59]  Apparent authority would almost certainly be regarded as conferred on a company secretary, in the absence of actual authority: *Panorama Developments (Guildford) Ltd v Fidelis Furniture Fabrics Ltd* [1971] 2 QB 711.

[60]  Companies Act 2006 (Commencement No 5, Transitional Provisions and Savings) Order 2007, SI 2007/ 3495, art 3.

This section restates section 182 of the 1985 Act in so far as it applies to the issue of certificates on the transfer of shares. That former provision also covered the issue of certificates on allotment, but this is now covered separately by section 769.   **21.776.02**

The obligation is to have certificates complete and ready for delivery within two months of a transfer being lodged. The transfer must be properly stamped and otherwise valid or be exempt under the Stock Transfer Act 1982 (subsection (2)), but there is obviously no obligation when a company properly refuses to register a transfer. Similarly there is no obligation if the conditions of the issue provide that the securities in question are not evidenced by a certificate nor in the cases in subsection (2) covered by sections 778 and 779, that is cases of transfer to a financial institution and cases where the company has issued a share warrant in respect of transferred shares. Cases covered by section 777 are also exempt (subsection (4)).   **21.776.03**

Breach of the requirements is an offence by any officer in default,[61] but there is no longer an offence committed by the company, as was previously the case. The other sanction is the power of the court to order compliance under section 782.   **21.776.04**

## 777  Issue of certificates etc: cases within the Stock Transfer Act 1982

(1)  Section 776(1) (duty of company as to issue of certificates etc on transfer) does not apply in the case of a transfer to a person where, by virtue of regulations under section 3 of the Stock Transfer Act 1982, he is not entitled to a certificate or other document of or evidencing title in respect of the securities transferred.   **21.777.01**

(2)  But if in such a case the transferee—

    (a)  subsequently becomes entitled to such a certificate or other document by virtue of any provision of those regulations, and

    (b)  gives notice in writing of that fact to the company,

section 776 (duty to company as to issue of certificates etc) has effect as if the reference in subsection (1) of that section to the date of the lodging of the transfer were a reference to the date of the notice.

COMMENCEMENT DATE  6 April 2008[62]

This section restates section 185(3) of the 1985 Act. The Stock Transfer Act 1982 provides that transfers of certain gilt-edged securities, mostly those issued by governments and other public authorities, but including some that are issued by registered companies,[63] set out in Schedule 1 to that Act are effective without the need for an instrument in writing and without certificates.   **21.777.02**

## *Issue of certificates etc on allotment or transfer to financial institution*

## 778  Issue of certificates etc: allotment or transfer to financial institution

(1)  A company—   **21.778.01**

    (a)  of which shares or debentures are allotted to a financial institution,

    (b)  of which debenture stock is allotted to a financial institution, or

    (c)  with which a transfer for transferring shares, debentures or debenture stock to a financial institution is lodged,

is not required in consequence of that allotment or transfer to comply with section 769(1) or 776(1) (duty of company as to issue of certificates etc).

(2)  A 'financial institution' means—

    (a)  a recognised clearing house acting in relation to a recognised investment exchange, or

    (b)  a nominee of—

        (i)  a recognised clearing house acting in that way, or

        (ii)  a recognised investment exchange,

designated for the purposes of this section in the rules of the recognised investment exchange in question.

(3)  Expressions used in subsection (2) have the same meaning as in Part 18 of the Financial Services and Markets Act 2000 (c. 8).

COMMENCEMENT DATE  6 April 2008[64]

---

[61]  For the meaning of this, see s 1121.

[62]  Companies Act 2006 (Commencement No 5, Transitional Provisions and Savings) Order 2007, SI 2007/3495, art 3.

[63]  These include debentures issued by the Agricultural Mortgage Corporation PLC, the Commonwealth Development Finance Company Limited, Finance for Industry Public Limited Company, or the Scottish Agricultural Securities Corporation Limited.

[64]  Companies Act 2006 (Commencement No 5, Transitional Provisions and Savings) Order 2007, SI 2007/3495, art 3.

**21.778.02** This section provides further exemptions from the requirements to issue certificates, either on allotment or on transfer of shares, debentures or debenture stock to a financial institution as defined in subsection (2).The situations covered are those where securities are held in uncertificated form under the CREST system.[65]

## Share warrants

### 779 Issue and effect of share warrant to bearer

**21.779.01**
    (1) A company limited by shares may, if so authorised by its articles, issue with respect to any fully paid shares a warrant (a 'share warrant') stating that the bearer of the warrant is entitled to the shares specified in it.

    (2) A share warrant issued under the company's common seal or (in the case of a company registered in Scotland) subscribed in accordance with the Requirements of Writing (Scotland) Act 1995 (c. 7) entitles the bearer to the shares specified in it and the shares may be transferred by delivery of the warrant.

    (3) A company that issues a share warrant may, if so authorised by its articles, provide (by coupons or otherwise) for the payment of the future dividends on the shares included in the warrant.

COMMENCEMENT DATE 6 April 2008[66]

**21.779.02** This section allows for the issue of share warrants or bearer shares, that is shares issued without a certificate and transferable simply by delivery.[67] Share warrants are negotiable instruments, with the result that the title of a holder whose warrant is stolen is likely to be defeated by a subsequent purchaser in good faith.[68] The section must be read in conjunction with section 122, which, in providing how bearer shares are to be treated in the company's register of members, makes it clear that shares can be originally issued in bearer form.[69] Table A made no provision authorizing the issue of bearer shares, but the model articles for public companies prescribed under the 2006 Act do so provide, giving the directors the power to decide the form of the warrant, how dividends are to be paid, and the extent to which the holders of bearer shares have the rights of membership of the company.[70] The clear implication of this, taken together with the fact that fiscal restrictions on the issue of bearer shares no longer exist, is that their greater use is to be encouraged.

### 780 Duty of company as to issue of certificates on surrender of share warrant

**21.780.01**
    (1) A company must, within two months of the surrender of a share warrant for cancellation, complete and have ready for delivery the certificates of the shares specified in the warrant.

    (2) Subsection (1) does not apply if the company's articles provide otherwise.

    (3) If default is made in complying with subsection (1) an offence is committed by every officer of the company who is in default.

    (4) A person guilty of an offence under subsection (3) is liable on summary conviction to a fine not exceeding level 3 on the standard scale and, for continued contravention, a daily default fine not exceeding one-tenth of level 3 on the standard scale.

COMMENCEMENT DATE 6 April 2008[71]

**21.780.02** Under section 122(4), unless the company's articles provide otherwise, the holder of a share warrant is entitled to surrender it and have his name entered in the register of members. This section imposes the parallel right to have a share certificate in respect of the shares, although again this is subject to the articles (subsection (2)). The penalty for breach falls on any officer in default.[72]

---

[65] See further Chapter 2 to this Part and the commentary thereto. The requirements will apply if securities are converted into certificated form: Uncertificated Securities Regulations 2001 SI 2001/3755, reg 32(8).

[66] Companies Act 2006 (Commencement No 5, Transitional Provisions and Savings) Order 2007, SI 2007/3495, art 3.

[67] It also allows the issue of stock warrants: *Pilkington v United Railways of Havana and Regla Warehouses Ltd* [1930] 2 Ch 108—although a company can no longer convert shares into stock; see para 17.620.02.

[68] *Rumball v Metropolitan Bank* (1876) 2 QBD 194; *Webb, Hale & Co v Alexandra Water Co* (1905) 93 LT 339.

[69] Previously it was thought that shares had to be issued with a certificate and could only subsequently be converted to bearer form.

[70] See Art 51 of the model articles. See Chapter 52 at MA.318.

[71] Companies Act 2006 (Commencement No 5, Transitional Provisions and Savings) Order 2007, SI 2007/3495, art 3. This section applies to share warrants surrendered on or after 6 April 2008: Ibid, Sch 4, para 31.

[72] As to the meaning of this, see s 1121.

## 781  Offences in connection with share warrants (Scotland)

(1)  If in Scotland a person—          **21.781.01**

  (a)  with intent to defraud, forges or alters, or offers, utters, disposes of, or puts off, knowing the same to be forged or altered, any share warrant or coupon, or any document purporting to be a share warrant or coupon issued in pursuance of this Act, or

  (b)  by means of any such forged or altered share warrant, coupon or document—

    (i)  demands or endeavours to obtain or receive any share or interest in a company under this Act, or

    (ii)  demands or endeavours to receive any dividend or money payment in respect of any such share or interest,

  knowing the warrant, coupon or document to be forged or altered,

  he commits an offence.

(2)  If in Scotland a person without lawful authority or excuse (of which proof lies on him) —

  (a)  engraves or makes on any plate, wood, stone, or other material, any share warrant or coupon purporting to be—

    (i)  a share warrant or coupon issued or made by any particular company in pursuance of this Act, or

    (ii)  a blank share warrant or coupon so issued or made, or

    (iii)  a part of such a share warrant or coupon, or

  (b)  uses any such plate, wood, stone, or other material, for the making or printing of any such share warrant or coupon, or of any such blank share warrant or coupon or of any part of such a share warrant or coupon, or

  (c)  knowingly has in his custody or possession any such plate, wood, stone, or other material, he commits an offence.

(3)  A person guilty of an offence under subsection (1) is liable on summary conviction to imprisonment for a term not exceeding six months or to a fine not exceeding level 5 on the standard scale (or both).

(4)  A person guilty of an offence under subsection (2) is liable—

  (a)  on conviction on indictment, to imprisonment for a term not exceeding seven years or a fine (or both);

  (b)  on summary conviction, to imprisonment for a term not exceeding six months or a fine not exceeding the statutory maximum (or both).

COMMENCEMENT DATE  6 April 2008[73]

The penalties for the offences under this section, which only applies in Scotland, were amended by the          **21.781.02**
2006 Act. There appears to be no reported case involving a prosecution for the particular offences in it, which are directed at forgeries of share warrants in particular, and it would seem that the acts described would be covered by more general offences in any event.

## *Supplementary provisions*

## 782  Issue of certificates etc: court order to make good default

(1)  If a company on which a notice has been served requiring it to make good any default in          **21.782.01**
complying with—

  (a)  section 769(1) (duty of company as to issue of certificates etc on allotment),

  (b)  section 776(1) (duty of company as to issue of certificates etc on transfer), or

  (c)  section 780(1) (duty of company as to issue of certificates etc on surrender of share warrant), fails to make good the default within ten days after service of the notice, the person entitled to have the certificates or the debentures delivered to him may apply to the court.

(2)  The court may on such an application make an order directing the company and any officer of it to make good the default within such time as may be specified in the order.

(3)  The order may provide that all costs (in Scotland, expenses) of and incidental to the application are to be borne by the company or by an officer of it responsible for the default.

COMMENCEMENT DATE  6 April 2008[74]

This section separates out the powers of the court that were previously in section 185(6) and (7) of the          **21.782.02**
1985 Act, making them also applicable to the situation in subsection (1)(c), that is the failure to issue a certificate on the surrender of a share warrant.

---

[73]  Companies Act 2006 (Commencement No 5, Transitional Provisions and Savings) Order 2007, SI 2007/3495, art 3.

[74]  Companies Act 2006 (Commencement No 5, Transitional Provisions and Savings) Order 2007, SI 2007/3495, art 3.

**21.782.03**   Before someone applies to the court to enforce his right to a certificate (or, where appropriate, to a debenture) under the provisions mentioned in subsection (1), he must serve a notice on the company requiring it to provide him with it. If that request is not complied with after 10 days of service of the notice, he may apply to the court, which may order the company and any officer of it to comply (subsection (2)) and provide that the company or an officer responsible for the default bears the applicant's costs (or expenses) (subsection (3)). There appears to be no reported use of this provision.

## CHAPTER 2
## EVIDENCING AND TRANSFER OF TITLE TO SECURITIES WITHOUT WRITTEN INSTRUMENT

### *Introductory*

### 783  Scope of this Chapter

**21.783.01**   In this Chapter—
(a) 'securities' means shares, debentures, debenture stock, loan stock, bonds, units of a collective investment scheme within the meaning of the Financial Services and Markets Act 2000 (c. 8) and other securities of any description;
(b) references to title to securities include any legal or equitable interest in securities;
(c) references to a transfer of title include a transfer by way of security;
(d) references to transfer without a written instrument include, in relation to bearer securities, transfer without delivery.

COMMENCEMENT DATE  6 April 2008[75]

**21.783.02**   This section contains definitions that were previously contained in section 207(1) of the Companies Act 1985.

### 784  Power to make regulations

**21.784.01**   (1) The power to make regulations under this Chapter is exercisable by the Treasury and the Secretary of State, either jointly or concurrently.
(2) References in this Chapter to the authority having power to make regulations shall accordingly be read as references to both or either of them, as the case may require.
(3) Regulations under this Chapter are subject to affirmative resolution procedure.

COMMENCEMENT DATE  6 April 2008[76]

**21.784.02**   This section defines who may exercise the power to make regulations which is contained in section 785. The power to make regulations was previously limited to the Secretary of State but has now been extended to the Treasury.

### *Powers exercisable*

### 785  Provision enabling procedures for evidencing and transferring title

**21.785.01**   (1) Provision may be made by regulations for enabling title to securities to be evidenced and transferred without a written instrument.
(2) The regulations may make provision—
(a) for procedures for recording and transferring title to securities, and
(b) for the regulation of those procedures and the persons responsible for or involved in their operation.
(3) The regulations must contain such safeguards as appear to the authority making the regulations appropriate for the protection of investors and for ensuring that competition is not restricted, distorted or prevented.
(4) The regulations may, for the purpose of enabling or facilitating the operation of the procedures provided for by the regulations, make provision with respect to the rights and obligations of persons in relation to securities dealt with under the procedures.
(5) The regulations may include provision for the purpose of giving effect to—
(a) the transmission of title to securities by operation of law;

---

[75] Companies Act 2006 (Commencement No 5, Transitional Provisions and Savings) Order 2007, SI 2007/3495.
[76] Companies Act 2006 (Commencement No 5, Transitional Provisions and Savings) Order 2007, SI 2007/3495.

(b)  any restriction on the transfer of title to securities arising by virtue of the provisions of any enactment or instrument, court order or agreement;

(c)  any power conferred by any such provision on a person to deal with securities on behalf of the person entitled.

(6)  The regulations may make provision with respect to the persons responsible for the operation of the procedures provided for by the regulations—

(a)  as to the consequences of their insolvency or incapacity, or

(b)  as to the transfer from them to other persons of their functions in relation to those procedures.

COMMENCEMENT DATE  6 April 2008[77]

This section contains the provisions previously contained in subsections (2), (3), (5), and (6) of section 207 of the Companies Act 1989. It provides for a power to make regulations for enabling title to securities to be evidenced and transferred without a written instrument and defines their scope. This process is generally referred to as 'dematerialisation'. Subsection (2) permits the regulations to govern the operation and procedures of the (dematerialized) transfer system and the persons responsible for it. Additional controls are imposed under the Financial Services and Markets Act 2000[78] as sending dematerialized instructions on behalf of another person is a regulated activity for the purposes of the Act and therefore requires authorization and compliance with the regulatory rules of the Financial Services Authority.[79] Subsection (3) requires the regulations to contain safeguards for the protection of investors and for ensuring that competition is not restricted. Subsection (6) provides that the regulations may make provision with respect to the persons responsible for the operation of the new procedures as to the consequences of their insolvency or incapacity, or as to the transfer from them to other persons of their functions.

**21.785.02**

## 786  Provision requiring arrangements to be adopted

(1)  Regulations under this Chapter may make provision—

**21.786.01**

(a)  enabling the members of a company or of any designated class of companies to adopt, by ordinary resolution, arrangements under which title to securities is required to be evidenced and transferred without a written instrument; or

(b)  requiring companies, or any designated class of companies, to adopt such arrangements.

(2)  The regulations may make such provision—

(a)  in respect of all securities issued by a company, or

(b)  in respect of all securities of a specified description.

(3)  The arrangements provided for by regulations making such provision as is mentioned in subsection (1)—

(a)  must not be such that a person who but for the arrangements would be entitled to have his name entered in the company's register of members ceases to be so entitled, and

(b)  must be such that a person who but for the arrangements would be entitled to exercise any rights in respect of the securities continues to be able effectively to control the exercise of those rights.

(4)  The regulations may—

(a)  prohibit the issue of any certificate by the company in respect of the issue or transfer of securities,

(b)  require the provision by the company to holders of securities of statements (at specified intervals or on specified occasions) of the securities held in their name, and

(c)  make provision as to the matters of which any such certificate or statement is, or is not, evidence.

(5)  In this section—

(a)  references to a designated class of companies are to a class designated in the regulations or by order under section 787; and

(b)  'specified' means specified in the regulations.

COMMENCEMENT DATE  6 April 2008[80]

---

[77]  Companies Act 2006 (Commencement No 5, Transitional Provisions and Savings) Order 2007, SI 2007/3495.

[78]  See the Financial Services and Markets Act 2000 (Regulated Activities) Order 2001 (SI 2001/544), Regs 45–48.

[79]  Nominees and custodians with a direct link to CREST (see below) are likely to undertake this activity for clients who do not have such a link.

[80]  Companies Act 2006 (Commencement No 5, Transitional Provisions and Savings) Order 2007, SI 2007/3495.

**21.786.02**   Subsection (1) provides that regulations made under section 785 (i) may enable the members of a company or any designated class of company to adopt an ordinary resolution requiring securities to be held and transferred in dematerialized form; or (ii) may require companies to adopt such arrangements. The first option envisages a company itself adopting a mandatory system of dematerialized holding and transfer of securities (which would have no effect on other companies opting to retain a combination of certificated and uncertificated holdings), while the second option envisages that the regulations will impose such a mandatory system on companies or a particular class of company.[81] Subsection (2) makes clear that the relevant regulations may apply to all securities issued by a company or all securities of a specified description.

**21.786.03**   Subsection (3) is designed to protect certain rights of investors following dematerialization. Paragraph (a) is intended to preserve the possibility of a true owner of shares asserting his right to be entered as a member against a person recorded as a member who is not the true owner. This might occur within a dematerialized system as a result of error or fraud and the Regulations make provision for rectification in both cases.[82] Paragraph (b) ensures that the beneficial owner of a security held in dematerialized form remains able to instruct the nominee (legal owner) in respect of issues such as voting. Such a right is derived from the general law of trust or contract,[83] not the regulations.

**21.786.04**   Subsection (4) provides that the regulations will be able to prohibit the issue of share certificates by relevant companies. This would result in shareholders in such companies losing the option of continuing to hold certificates and transfer their shares by paper-based methods. It also provides that the regulations may require companies to provide to shareholders statements of the securities held in their name. Finally it allows the regulations to make provision as to the matters of which any such certificate or statement is, or is not, evidence: this includes the power to deprive existing share certificates of any evidential status.

### 787 Provision requiring arrangements to be adopted: order-making powers

**21.787.01**   (1)  The authority having power to make regulations under this Chapter may by order—
    (a)  designate classes of companies for the purposes of section 786 (provision enabling or requiring arrangements to be adopted);
    (b)  provide that, in relation to securities of a specified description—
       (i)   in a designated class of companies, or
       (ii)  in a specified company or class of companies,
       specified provisions of regulations made under this Chapter by virtue of that section either do not apply or apply subject to specified modifications.
    (2)  In subsection (1) 'specified' means specified in the order.
    (3)  An order under this section is subject to negative resolution procedure.

COMMENCEMENT DATE 6 April 2008[84]

**21.787.02**   This section provides additional flexibility by enabling ministers to designate the classes of company to which the regulations are to apply by order as well as in the regulations themselves. This power can also be used to exempt classes of company from the regulations or to modify their application.

### *Supplementary*

### 788 Provision that may be included in regulations

**21.788.01**   Regulations under this Chapter may—
    (a)  modify or exclude any provision of any enactment or instrument, or any rule of law;
    (b)  apply, with such modifications as may be appropriate, the provisions of any enactment or instrument (including provisions creating criminal offences);
    (c)  require the payment of fees, or enable persons to require the payment of fees, of such amounts as may be specified in the regulations or determined in accordance with them;

---

[81]  For a proposal that would require all listed companies to dematerialize the holding and transfer of their shares see ICSA Consultation *The Dematerialisation of Shares and Share Transfers* at ⟨http://www.icsa.org.uk/index.php?option=com_content&task=view&id=480&Itemid=2512⟩ (11 April 2006).

[82]  See the commentary on Parts 3 and 4 of the Regulations below.

[83]  While the right to instruct a nominee (who is a trustee) is established in trust law, it may also be provided for contractually, typically in an agreement between a nominee (such as a stockbroker or custodian) and the ultimate investor.

[84]  Companies Act 2006 (Commencement No 5, Transitional Provisions and Savings) Order 2007, SI 2007/3495.

(d) empower the authority making the regulations to delegate to any person willing and able to discharge them any functions of the authority under the regulations.

COMMENCEMENT DATE 6 April 2008[85]

This section contains the provisions previously contained in section 207(7) of the Companies Act 1989. **21.788.02** In particular, paragraph (a) provides authority to modify or exclude any provision, enactment, or rule of law. This power has been used in making the Uncertificated Securities Regulations[86] so as to disapply and modify the provisions of the Companies Act 1985 which relate to holding and transfer of shares in certificated form and which are not applicable to holding and transfer in uncertificated form.

## 789 Duty to consult

Before making— **21.789.01**

(a) regulations under this Chapter, or

(b) any order under section 787,

the authority having power to make regulations under this Chapter must carry out such consultation as appears to it to be appropriate.

COMMENCEMENT DATE 6 April 2008[87]

This section requires that, before making regulations or designating a class of companies, Ministers are **21.789.02** obliged to consult such persons as they consider appropriate. The rationale is presumably to ensure that the broad powers that are now available are exercised in an appropriate manner and take due account of established market practices.

The regulations deal with the status of these registers and the relationship between the registers and the **21.789.03** obligation imposed by section 113 of the Companies Act 2006 to maintain a register of members. They also deal with the issue of the evidential value of entries in the registers as regards title to securities and the process by which title is transferred. As will become clear from the discussion below, it is the policy of the regulations to give priority to the operator register of members in respect of these issues in the event of a conflict between the two registers. The underlying rationale is a policy of minimizing the risks that arise in settlement when transfer of legal title takes place after settlement of a transaction (delivery of evidence of title in exchange for payment). In these circumstances the buyer faces the risk (at least temporarily) of paying and not being the registered owner.[88] This risk is minimized if priority in determining legal title is given to the operator register as the transfer will be recorded first in that register.

As regards the status of the registers, the regulations provide that in respect of a participating issuer any **21.789.04** reference in an enactment or instrument to a company's register of members shall, unless the context requires otherwise, be taken to refer to the two registers.[89] However, in the event of a conflict between the two registers, it is the entry in the operator register of members that prevails.[90] The obligation to maintain a (conventional) register of members under section 113 of the 2006 Act is disapplied in the case of participating issuers, but the sanctions for failing to maintain the section 113 register apply equally to failure to maintain the issuer register of members.[91] The rationale for disapplying the obligation to maintain a conventional register under section 113 is presumably that the relevant information is now shown in the new registers.

An entry on either the operator or issuer register of members has the same legal effect in respect of title **21.789.05** to dematerialized shares as does a certificate in respect of certificated shares.[92] The entry or certificate is *prima facie* evidence (in Scotland sufficient evidence unless the contrary is shown) of legal title to shares. However, in the event of a conflict between the two registers, the operator register prevails, but even that entry is not conclusive as ownership of shares ultimately rests with the person who is entitled

---

[85] Companies Act 2006 (Commencement No 5, Transitional Provisions and Savings) Order 2007, SI 2007/3495.

[86] Uncertificated Securities Regulations 2001, SI 2001/3755.

[87] Companies Act 2006 (Commencement No 5, Transitional Provisions and Savings) Order 2007, SI 2007/3495.

[88] In a 'real time' delivery-versus-payment settlement system that risk is eliminated as transfer of title occurs at the same time as payment but in any other system (including those that are described as implementing the principle of delivery-versus-payment but have not implemented a 'real time' version) the risk will be present.

[89] See eg s 116 of the 2006 Act, providing for the right to inspect the register of members.

[90] This is the effect of regulation 20(5).

[91] Regulation 20 and Sch 4 (para 5) to the regulations.

[92] Regulation 24 and s 768 of the 2006 Act.

to be registered.[93] In the case of securities other than shares, an entry in the operator register alone (there is no equivalent to the issuer register in the case of such securities which are 'eligible debt securities') has the same effect.

**21.789.06**   Provision is made in the regulations for rectification of the registers. As an entry provides only *prima facie* and not conclusive evidence in respect of the matters to which it refers (primarily membership and securities held), it may be that the entries in the register will be disputed. While membership is completed by registration, it also requires agreement[94] and there will be no agreement if the requirements for membership in the articles are not met.[95] The regulations envisage rectification of the registers by agreement between the issuer and operator or alternatively as a result of a court order made under section 125 of the Companies Act 2006.[96]

**21.789.07**   Transfer of title to uncertificated shares is effected by the operator who, having verified the relevant electronic settlement instructions that are input by intermediaries following the making of a bargain, effects the transfer by making the appropriate changes in the operator register. The operator then gives an operator-instruction to the issuer to register the transfer (or transmission) in the issuer register of members and the record of uncertificated shares.[97] However, it is clear that transfer of legal title occurs as a result of the entry in the operator register and therefore any delay between the making of that entry and the entry in the issuer register is of no consequence. A participating issuer is required, unless it is impracticable to do so by virtue of circumstances beyond its control, to ensure that the record of uncertificated shares is regularly reconciled with the operator register of members.[98] In the case of 'eligible debt securities', transfer or transmission occurs simply by the making and deletion of entries on the relevant operator register. The regulations specify circumstances in which the operator must[99] or may[100] refuse to register a transfer, in which case notice of the refusal must be sent to the transferee.

### Part 4   Dematerialized instructions etc.

**21.789.08**   This part deals with the liability of senders and recipients of properly authenticated dematerialized instructions. Subject to limited exceptions, the recipient is entitled to act on the instruction and the person by whom or on behalf of whom it was sent may not deny that it was sent with proper authority and contained accurate information.[101] This appears to have the result that a transfer resulting from an unauthorized or erroneous instruction will stand so long as it appears to emanate from within the system (in which case it will appear to be a 'properly authenticated dematerialised instruction'). That outcome, however, is without prejudice to any liability of any person for causing or permitting a dematerialized instruction to have been sent without authority or to contain information which is incorrect or to be expressed to have been sent by a person who did not send it. Thus, a remedy (eg in damages for negligence) may be available but not rectification of the register as a matter of right.

**21.789.09**   This part also deals with liability in respect of forged instructions. The regulations adopt a limited definition of forged instructions in the sense that a forged transfer does not include one that is fabricated by a person operating within the system. Such an instruction would be treated as unauthorized and dealt with as described above. 'Forged instructions' for the purposes of the regulations are those that emanate from outside the system or from computers other than those from which it purported to be sent. The operator may be liable for loss (capped at £50,000 per instruction) resulting from forged instructions that lead to changes on the register but not if the operator identifies a person as being responsible for the relevant instruction. The transferor has no right to rectification of the register in these circumstances. In effect, the rights of the transferee are prioritized and the operator is made liable for security defects in the system (which lead to 'forged instructions') but not for unauthorized use within the system.

---

[93]   While the regulations do not in terms modify that principle, the provisions of Part 4 (below) limit the extent to which a true owner who has been removed from the register can be restored.

[94]   CA 2006, s 112(2).

[95]   Admittedly, this is less likely for listed companies than for other companies as restrictions on transfer are the most obvious source of difficulty and such restrictions are not permitted in the case of listed companies.

[96]   Regulation 25.

[97]   Regulation 27.

[98]   The standard practice is that at the end of each business day issuers' registrars combine a copy of the record of dematerialized holdings maintained by CREST with their records of certificated holdings to form the full registers.

[99]   Regulation 27(2).

[100]   Regulation 27(4).

[101]   Regulation 35.

## Part 5  Miscellaneous and supplemental

This part deals with a number of issues in respect of which the regulations carry implications.    **21.789.10**

The provisions of regulations 40 and 46 to 48 are of particular significance. Regulation 40 exonerates    **21.789.11**
trustees and personal representatives from any liability for breach of trust or default in dealing with
uncertificated securities unless they are expressly prohibited. It also follows the general principle of
company law (section 126 of the Companies Act 2006)[102] in providing that the operator is not bound
or compelled to recognize any express, implied, or constructive trust or other interest in respect of
uncertificated units of a security, even if he has actual or constructive notice of the said trust or interest.
Regulation 40 also makes provision for a trustee of a trust deed for securing an issue of debentures to
assent to an amendment of the trust deed without liability for breach of trust so as to permit holding
and transfer of debentures in uncertificated form.

Regulation 46 sets out a number of contraventions of the regulations which are actionable as breaches    **21.789.12**
of statutory duty. Such an action is without prejudice to any other liability which any person may incur.
Regulation 47 provides for liability on the part of officers of participating issuers and officers of an
operator for knowingly and wilfully authorizing or permitting certain defaults or contraventions.
Regulation 48 provides for exemption from liability in respect of certain regulations for the Crown and
various bodies associated with the Crown.

## 790  Resolutions to be forwarded to registrar

> Chapter 3 of Part 3 (resolutions affecting a company's constitution) applies to a resolution passed by    **21.790.01**
> virtue of regulations under this Chapter.
>
> COMMENCEMENT DATE  6 April 2008[103]

This section has the effect that a resolution passed by virtue of regulations under this Chapter must be    **21.790.02**
forwarded to the registrar within 15 days after it is passed or made. If a company fails to do so, an
offence is committed by the company and every officer who is in default.

---

[102] Note that s 126 does not apply to Scotland and that reg 40 does not prevent an operator giving notice of a
trust to a company.
[103] Companies Act 2006 (Commencement No 5, Transitional Provisions and Savings) Order 2007, SI
2007/3495.

# 22

## INFORMATION ABOUT INTERESTS IN A COMPANY'S SHARES

---

## Companies Act 2006

### PART 22

### INFORMATION ABOUT INTERESTS IN A COMPANY'S SHARES

This part of the Act contains provisions regarding a public company's right to investigate those who **22.0.01** have an interest in its shares. It re-enacts the disclosure obligations resulting from a notice issued by the company under sections 212 to 219 of the Companies Act 1985. Crucially there is no change to the definition of 'interest in shares' for this purpose.

**22.0.02** The key changes to the disclosure obligations in this Part of the Act are:

- disclosure notices need not be in hard copy but can be in electronic form (section 793 and Part 37 on the service of notices);
- provision in section 808 for unknown shareholders and ownerless shares to be entered on the register;
- the removal in section 817 of the onerous condition that a company verify third party information that was obtained in response to a section 893 disclosure notice before placing that information on the register;
- the removal in section 816 of the need to keep the disclosure notice information on the register after six years.

## *Introductory*

### 791 Companies to which this Part applies

**22.791.01** This Part applies only to public companies.

COMMENCEMENT DATE 20 January 2007[1]

**22.791.02** Section 791 specifies that this Part applies only to public companies. It replicates section 198 of the Companies Act 1985 which applied the disclosure regime to public companies.

### 792 Shares to which this Part applies

**22.792.01** (1) References in this Part to a company's shares are to the company's issued shares of a class carrying rights to vote in all circumstances at general meetings of the company (including any shares held as treasury shares).

(2) The temporary suspension of voting rights in respect of any shares does not affect the application of this Part in relation to interests in those or any other shares.

COMMENCEMENT DATE 20 January 2007[2]

**22.792.02** Section 792 sets out the type of shares (those carrying the rights to vote in all circumstances at general meetings) that can engage a section 793 notice (below). In using this definition it is simply restating the position in section 198(2) of the Companies Act 1985. Section 792 (2) will mean that shares held by a company 'in treasury' following a purchase of its own shares are covered by the disclosure notice provisions in section 793. If a company does wish to purchase its own shares and avoid the disclosure notice provisions in section 793 then it will need to cancel those shares.

## *Notice requiring information about interests in shares*

### 793 Notice by company requiring information about interests in its shares

**22.793.01** (1) A public company may give notice under this section to any person whom the company knows or has reasonable cause to believe—

(a) to be interested in the company's shares, or

(b) to have been so interested at any time during the three years immediately preceding the date on which the notice is issued.

(2) The notice may require the person—

(a) to confirm that fact or (as the case may be) to state whether or not it is the case, and

(b) if he holds, or has during that time held, any such interest, to give such further information as may be required in accordance with the following provisions of this section.

(3) The notice may require the person to whom it is addressed to give particulars of his own present or past interest in the company's shares (held by him at any time during the three year period mentioned in subsection (1)(b)).

(4) The notice may require the person to whom it is addressed, where—

(a) his interest is a present interest and another interest in the shares subsists, or

(b) another interest in the shares subsisted during that three year period at a time when his interest subsisted,

to give, so far as lies within his knowledge, such particulars with respect to that other interest as may be required by the notice.

---

[1] Companies Act 2006 (Commencement No 1, etc) Order 2006, SI 2006/3428, art 3.
[2] Companies Act 2006 (Commencement No 1, etc) Order 2006, SI 2006/3428, art 3.

(5)  The particulars referred to in subsections (3) and (4) include—
   (a)  the identity of persons interested in the shares in question, and
   (b)  whether persons interested in the same shares are or were parties to—
       (i)  an agreement to which section 824 applies (certain share acquisition agreements), or
       (ii)  an agreement or arrangement relating to the exercise of any rights conferred by the holding of the shares.
(6)  The notice may require the person to whom it is addressed, where his interest is a past interest, to give (so far as lies within his knowledge) particulars of the identity of the person who held that interest immediately upon his ceasing to hold it.
(7)  The information required by the notice must be given within such reasonable time as may be specified in the notice.

COMMENCEMENT DATE  20 January 2007[3]

Section 793 confers on a public company the ability to issue a notice requiring a person who it knows, or has reasonable cause to believe, has an interest in its shares (or to have had an interest in the previous three years) to confirm or deny the fact, and, if they confirm the interest to disclose information about the interest, including information about any other person with an interest in the shares.   **22.793.02**

It serves a useful purpose for companies in that it allows them to find out the identity of those with voting rights (direct or indirect) that are below the thresholds for automatic disclosure, and it also enables companies (and members of the company) to ascertain the underlying beneficial owners of shares.   **22.793.03**

Additionally the section allows a company to follow a chain of disclosure information by requiring information from nominees about the person they are acting for. The company can additionally construct a chain of ownership by requiring in subsection (6) information from past owners as to the person they sold the shares to. The company can also require information on any share acquisition agreements, or any agreement or arrangement as to how the rights attaching to those shares should be exercised (section 825). Section 793 restates section 212(1) to (4) of the Companies Act 1985.   **22.793.04**

According to the guidance notes attached to the section, unlike section 212 of the 1985 Act notice does not have to be in hard copy but can be in electronic form.[4] The subject of a disclosure notice must be given a reasonable time to respond. In *Re Lonrho Plc*[5] the court found that one day was not a reasonable time but that two days in the particular circumstances was reasonable. In that same case Vinelott J expressed the opinion that the drafting of section 212 was defective in compelling the company issuing the notice to specify a reasonable time. Oddly, given this view, section 793 replicates the reasonable time provisions of section 212. The guidance notes on the section offers the following explanation: 'what is reasonable has not been defined so as to allow flexibility according to the circumstances, but if the time given is not reasonable, the company will not have served a valid notice'.   **22.793.05**

## 794  Notice requiring information: order imposing restrictions on shares

(1)  Where—   **22.794.01**
   (a)  a notice under section 793 (notice requiring information about interests in company's shares) is served by a company on a person who is or was interested in shares in the company, and
   (b)  that person fails to give the company the information required by the notice within the time specified in it,
   the company may apply to the court for an order directing that the shares in question be subject to restrictions.
   For the effect of such an order see section 797.
(2)  If the court is satisfied that such an order may unfairly affect the rights of third parties in respect of the shares, the court may, for the purpose of protecting those rights and subject to such terms as it thinks fit, direct that such acts by such persons or descriptions of persons and for such purposes as may be set out in the order shall not constitute a breach of the restrictions.
(3)  On an application under this section the court may make an interim order.
   Any such order may be made unconditionally or on such terms as the court thinks fit.
(4)  Sections 798 to 802 make further provision about orders under this section.

COMMENCEMENT DATE  20 January 2007[6]

This section provides that an application may be made to the court, if a person fails to comply with a disclosure notice, for a direction that the shares in question are to be subject to the restrictions set out in section 797. It re-enacts section 216(1) of the Companies Act 1985. A failure to give a full and truthful   **22.794.02**

---

[3]  Companies Act 2006 (Commencement No 1, etc) Order 2006, SI 2006/3428, art 3.
[4]  See the provisions on sending or supplying documents or information in Part 37 of the Act.
[5]  [1989] BCLC 315.
[6]  Companies Act 2006 (Commencement No 1, etc) Order 2006, SI 2006/3428, art 3.

answer to an inquiry under the former section 212 was deemed a failure to comply with a notice: see *Re TR Technology Investment Trust Plc.*[7]

**22.794.03**    While it is clear that the court may protect the rights of third parties who would be unfairly affected by the order it is also required to protect the interests of the company. For example in *Re Ricardo Group Ltd (No 3)*[8] the court found that it must have regard to the interests of the company as a whole when being asked to place a restriction on shares for failure to comply with a disclosure notice and not just the interests of those wishing to use the disclosure provisions to remain in control. It is worth noting that when considering the initial restriction order, where the interests of third parties will be prejudiced, the courts have in the past required undertakings from the respondents, instead of making a restriction order.[9]

### 795 Notice requiring information: offences

**22.795.01**    (1)  A person who—
    (a)  fails to comply with a notice under section 793 (notice requiring information about interests in company's shares), or
    (b)  in purported compliance with such a notice—
      (i)   makes a statement that he knows to be false in a material particular, or
      (ii)  recklessly makes a statement that is false in a material particular,
    commits an offence.
    (2)  A person does not commit an offence under subsection (1)(a) if he proves that the requirement to give information was frivolous or vexatious.
    (3)  A person guilty of an offence under this section is liable—
    (a)  on conviction on indictment, to imprisonment for a term not exceeding two years or a fine (or both);
    (b)  on summary conviction—
      (i)   in England and Wales, to imprisonment for a term not exceeding twelve months or to a fine not exceeding the statutory maximum (or both);
      (ii)  in Scotland or Northern Ireland, to imprisonment for a term not exceeding six months, or to a fine not exceeding the statutory maximum (or both).

COMMENCEMENT DATE  20 January 2007[10]

**22.795.02**    Section 795 specifies the penalties ranging from a fine to imprisonment for failure to provide information when served with a notice under section 793. It re-enacts section 216(3) and (4) of the Companies Act 1985. As with section 216(3) and (4) a failure to give a full and truthful answer to an inquiry will be deemed a failure to comply with a notice.[11] Under the previous penalty regime in section 216(3) if a corporate entity was guilty of an offence then shareholders, directors, and managers might also be liable: section 733(2) and (3) of the Companies Act 1985.

### 796 Notice requiring information: persons exempted from obligation to comply

**22.796.01**    (1)  A person is not obliged to comply with a notice under section 793 (notice requiring information about interests in company's shares) if he is for the time being exempted by the Secretary of State from the operation of that section.
    (2)  The Secretary of State must not grant any such exemption unless—
    (a)  he has consulted the Governor of the Bank of England, and
    (b)  he (the Secretary of State) is satisfied that, having regard to any undertaking given by the person in question with respect to any interest held or to be held by him in any shares, there are special reasons why that person should not be subject to the obligations imposed by that section.

COMMENCEMENT DATE  20 January 2007[12]

**22.796.02**    Section 796 gives the Secretary of State a power to exempt someone from complying with a section 793 notice. In order to exercise this power the Secretary of State must consult the Governor of the Bank of England. If having done this he is satisfied that there are special reasons for an exemption he may, having regard to any undertaking given, exempt the person from the obligation to comply. It re-states section 216(5) of the Companies Act 1985.

---

[7]  [1988] BCLC 256.
[8]  [1989] BCLC 771.
[9]  See *Re Malaga Investments Ltd* (1987) 3 BCC 569.
[10]  Companies Act 2006 (Commencement No 1, etc) Order 2006, SI 2006/3428, art 3.
[11]  *Re TR Technology Investment Trust Plc* [1988] BCLC 256.
[12]  Companies Act (Commencement No 1, etc) Order 2006, SI 2006/3428, art 3.

*Orders imposing restrictions on shares*

## 797  Consequences of order imposing restrictions

(1)  The effect of an order under section 794 that shares are subject to restrictions is as follows—          **22.797.01**
    (a)  any transfer of the shares is void;
    (b)  no voting rights are exercisable in respect of the shares;
    (c)  no further shares may be issued in right of the shares or in pursuance of an offer made to their holder;
    (d)  except in a liquidation, no payment may be made of sums due from the company on the shares, whether in respect of capital or otherwise.
(2)  Where shares are subject to the restriction in subsection (1)(a), an agreement to transfer the shares is void.
    This does not apply to an agreement to transfer the shares on the making of an order under section 800 made by virtue of subsection (3)(b) (removal of restrictions in case of court-approved transfer).
(3)  Where shares are subject to the restriction in subsection (1)(c) or (d), an agreement to transfer any right to be issued with other shares in right of those shares, or to receive any payment on them (otherwise than in a liquidation), is void.
    This does not apply to an agreement to transfer any such right on the making of an order under section 800 made by virtue of subsection (3)(b) (removal of restrictions in case of court-approved transfer).
(4)  The provisions of this section are subject—
    (a)  to any directions under section 794(2) or section 799(3) (directions for protection of third parties), and
    (b)  in the case of an interim order under section 794(3), to the terms of the order.

COMMENCEMENT DATE  20 January 2007[13]

Section 797 sets out the range of impacts an order under section 794 has on the shares concerned. Thus    **22.797.02**
voting rights are suspended, a share transfer or agreement to transfer is void, and no further issues of shares or payments due (save in a liquidation) may be made to the holder. This section was formerly contained in section 454 of the Companies Act 1985. Under the previous provision, for example in *Re Geers Gross Plc*,[14] such a restriction under section 216(1) prevented the registered owner, who was holding the shares on behalf of a Swiss bank who had refused to answer a disclosure notice, from selling his shares. In *Re Ashbourne Investments*[15] shares subject to a restriction were subsequently the target of a compulsory transfer as the result of a successful takeover of the company. The court held that it could order the compulsory transfer but restrict the payment of the proceeds to the owner of the shares. See also *F H Lloyd Holdings*[16] on the application of restrictions to a foreign shareholder.

## 798  Penalty for attempted evasion of restrictions

(1)  This section applies where shares are subject to restrictions by virtue of an order under section    **22.798.01**
794.
(2)  A person commits an offence if he—
    (a)  exercises or purports to exercise any right—
        (i)  to dispose of shares that to his knowledge, are for the time being subject to restrictions, or
        (ii)  to dispose of any right to be issued with any such shares, or
    (b)  votes in respect of any such shares (whether as holder or proxy), or appoints a proxy to vote in respect of them, or
    (c)  being the holder of any such shares, fails to notify of their being subject to those restrictions a person whom he does not know to be aware of that fact but does know to be entitled (apart from the restrictions) to vote in respect of those shares whether as holder or as proxy, or
    (d)  being the holder of any such shares, or being entitled to a right to be issued with other shares in right of them, or to receive any payment on them (otherwise than in a liquidation), enters into an agreement which is void under section 797(2) or (3).
(3)  If shares in a company are issued in contravention of the restrictions, an offence is committed by—
    (a)  the company, and
    (b)  every officer of the company who is in default.

---

[13]  Companies Act 2006 (Commencement No 1, etc) Order 2006, SI 2006/3428, art 3.
[14]  [1987] 1 WLR 1649, CA.
[15]  [1978] 1 WLR 1346.
[16]  (1985) PCC 268.

(4)  A person guilty of an offence under this section is liable—
    (a)   on conviction on indictment, to a fine;
    (b)   on summary conviction, to a fine not exceeding the statutory maximum.
(5)  The provisions of this section are subject—
    (a)   to any directions under—
        section 794(2) (directions for protection of third parties), or
        section 799 or 800 (relaxation or removal of restrictions), and
    (b)   in the case of an interim order under section 794(3), to the terms of the order.

COMMENCEMENT DATE 20 January 2007[17]

**22.798.02**  This section sets out the range of penalties for evasion of a restriction imposed under section 794. The section covers both a person exercising or purporting to exercise rights over the restricted shares and the company should the company issue shares in contravention of the restriction. These provisions are a restatement of the penalties formerly contained in section 455 of the Companies Act 1985.

### 799  Relaxation of restrictions

**22.799.01**
(1)  An application may be made to the court on the ground that an order directing that shares shall be subject to restrictions unfairly affects the rights of third parties in respect of the shares.
(2)  An application for an order under this section may be made by the company or by any person aggrieved.
(3)  If the court is satisfied that the application is well-founded, it may, for the purpose of protecting the rights of third parties in respect of the shares, and subject to such terms as it thinks fit, direct that such acts by such persons or descriptions of persons and for such purposes as may be set out in the order do not constitute a breach of the restrictions.

COMMENCEMENT DATE 20 January 2007[18]

**22.799.02**  Section 799 provides the court with a power to relax a restriction over shares should third party rights be unfairly affected. The application can be made by the company or the third party concerned. The provisions for relaxation and removal of restrictions were formerly contained in section 456 of the Companies Act 1985 as one single provision. In the consolidation process undertaken for the Companies Act 2006 the relaxation and removal provisions are enacted as separate provisions in sections 799 and 800 (below). It is worth noting that when considering the initial restriction order under section 794 the court can, under section 794(2), protect such third party rights as it is aware of. Additionally where the interests of third parties will be prejudiced instead of making a restriction order the courts have in the past required undertakings from the respondents designed to protect third parties: see *Re Malaga Investments Ltd.*[19]

### 800  Removal of restrictions

**22.800.01**
(1)  An application may be made to the court for an order directing that the shares shall cease to be subject to restrictions.
(2)  An application for an order under this section may be made by the company or by any person aggrieved.
(3)  The court must not make an order under this section unless—
    (a)   it is satisfied that the relevant facts about the shares have been disclosed to the company and no unfair advantage has accrued to any person as a result of the earlier failure to make that disclosure, or
    (b)   the shares are to be transferred for valuable consideration and the court approves the transfer.
(4)  An order under this section made by virtue of subsection (3)(b) may continue, in whole or in part, the restrictions mentioned in section 797(1)(c) and (d) (restrictions on issue of further shares or making of payments) so far as they relate to a right acquired or offer made before the transfer.
(5)  Where any restrictions continue in force under subsection (4)—
    (a)   an application may be made under this section for an order directing that the shares shall cease to be subject to those restrictions, and
    (b)   subsection (3) does not apply in relation to the making of such an order.

COMMENCEMENT DATE 20 January 2007[20]

**22.800.02**  Section 800 provides the court with a general power to remove a restriction over shares should disclosure have subsequently occurred or where an approved transfer for value is at issue. The

---

[17]  Companies Act 2006 (Commencement No 1, etc) Order 2006, SI 2006/3428, art 3.
[18]  Companies Act 2006 (Commencement No 1, etc) Order 2006, SI 2006/3428, art 3.
[19]  (1987) 3 BCC 569.
[20]  Companies Act 2006 (Commencement No 1, etc) Order 2006, SI 2006/3428, art 3.

application can be made by the company or any aggrieved person. It is worth noting that under subsection (4) the court can approve a transfer but retain some or all of the restriction on the shares. The provisions for relaxation and removal of restrictions were formerly contained in section 456 of the Companies Act 1985 as one single provision. In the consolidation process undertaken for the Companies Act 2006 the relaxation and removal provisions are enacted as separate provisions in sections 799 (above) and 800. The original wording of this section in the 1985 Act used the word 'sale' which was held to mean 'sale' for cash and not exchange for other shares: see *Re Westminster Property Group PLC*.[21] The section was then reworded to change 'sale' for 'transfer' to cover such transactions. This wording is continued in the Companies Act 2006.

## 801  Order for sale of shares

(1)  The court may order that the shares subject to restrictions be sold, subject to the court's approval as to the sale.    **22.801.01**
(2)  An application for an order under subsection (1) may only be made by the company.
(3)  Where the court has made an order under this section, it may make such further order relating to the sale or transfer of the shares as it thinks fit.
(4)  An application for an order under subsection (3) may be made—
   (a)  by the company,
   (b)  by the person appointed by or in pursuance of the order to effect the sale, or
   (c)  by any person interested in the shares.
(5)  On making an order under subsection (1) or (3) the court may order that the applicant's costs (in Scotland, expenses) be paid out of the proceeds of sale.

COMMENCEMENT DATE  20 January 2007[22]

Section 801 provides the court with a power to order the sale of the shares subject to a restriction order    **22.801.02** on application by the company. The court may also make a further order regarding the sale or transfer as it thinks fit—for example, in *Re Ashbourne Investments*[23] shares subject to a restriction were subsequently the target of a compulsory transfer as the result of a successful takeover of the company. The court held that it could order the compulsory transfer but restrict the payment of the proceeds to the owner of the shares. Section 801 was formerly part of section 456 of the Companies Act 1985.

## 802  Application of proceeds of sale under court order

(1)  Where shares are sold in pursuance of an order of the court under section 801, the proceeds of    **22.802.01** the sale, less the costs of the sale, must be paid into court for the benefit of the persons who are beneficially interested in the shares.
(2)  A person who is beneficially interested in the shares may apply to the court for the whole or part of those proceeds to be paid to him.
(3)  On such an application the court shall order the payment to the applicant of—
   (a)  the whole of the proceeds of sale together with any interest on them, or
   (b)  if another person had a beneficial interest in the shares at the time of their sale, such proportion of the proceeds and interest as the value of the applicant's interest in the shares bears to the total value of the shares.
   This is subject to the following qualification.
(4)  If the court has ordered under section 801(5) that the costs (in Scotland, expenses) of an applicant under that section are to be paid out of the proceeds of sale, the applicant is entitled to payment of his costs (or expenses) out of those proceeds before any person interested in the shares receives any part of those proceeds.

COMMENCEMENT DATE  20 January 2007[24]

Section 802 provides for the proceeds of a sale order under section 801 to be paid into court to be held    **22.802.02** for those beneficially interested in the shares. On application from those beneficially interested in the shares the court will disperse the proceeds less costs. These provisions were formerly contained in section 457 of the Companies Act 1985.

---

[21]  [1985] BCLC 188.
[22]  Companies Act 2006 (Commencement No 1, etc) Order 2006, SI 2006/3428, art 3.
[23]  [1978] 1 WLR 1346.
[24]  Companies Act 2006 (Commencement No 1, etc) Order 2006, SI 2006/3428, art 3.

*Power of members to require company to act*

### 803  Power of members to require company to act

**22.803.01**
(1) The members of a company may require it to exercise its powers under section 793 (notice requiring information about interests in shares).

(2) A company is required to do so once it has received requests (to the same effect) from members of the company holding at least 10 per cent of such of the paid-up capital of the company as carries a right to vote at general meetings of the company (excluding any voting rights attached to any shares in the company held as treasury shares).

(3) A request—
   (a) may be in hard copy form or in electronic form,
   (b) must—
      (i) state that the company is requested to exercise its powers under section 793,
      (ii) specify the manner in which the company is requested to act, and
      (iii) give reasonable grounds for requiring the company to exercise those powers in the manner specified, and
   (c) must be authenticated by the person or persons making it.

COMMENCEMENT DATE  20 January 2007[25]

**22.803.02**   Section 803 provides a procedure for a member or group of members to instigate a section 793 notice. It restates section 214(1) and (2) of the Companies Act 1985 but differs from its predecessor in two ways. First, the 10 per cent threshold can be achieved through multiple requests from small shareholders which equals 10 per cent or more of the paid up capital rather than needing a single member request or single collective request as was the case under section 214. Secondly, the notice can be served electronically as well as in hard copy.

**22.803.03**   The purpose of section 214 was to allow shareholders to demand information in situations where the directors or management may not have an interest in seeking that information. Section 803 is intended to carry on in the same way as section 214; indeed the guidance notes provide an example of a section 803 situation where 'the members might want to act where they suspect that the directors are involved in building a holding from behind the shelter of nominees'. However, under the 1985 Act procedure, section 214 requests were highly unusual even in these situations. One of the difficulties was that those making a request under the old section must not only specify the manner in which they require the powers to be exercised, but must also give reasonable grounds for requiring the company to exercise the powers in the manner specified. The determination of whether the shareholders had 'reasonable grounds' was in the absence of any specification in the Act left to the company to determine. The new section 803 simply repeats the section 214 procedure, so in the situation described in the guidance notes, where the shareholders request the company to require information that they suspect relates to the directors, it is likely that the directors will be the ones to determine whether there are reasonable grounds for the request. There is, however, a difference in the penalty for default by an officer of the company[26] which may make hostile directors think carefully or more carefully than under the 1985 regime about the reasonableness of a shareholder request.

### 804  Duty of company to comply with requirement

**22.804.01**
(1) A company that is required under section 803 to exercise its powers under section 793 (notice requiring information about interests in company's shares) must exercise those powers in the manner specified in the requests.

(2) If default is made in complying with subsection (1) an offence is committed by every officer of the company who is in default.

(3) A person guilty of an offence under this section is liable—
   (a) on conviction on indictment, to a fine;
   (b) on summary conviction, to a fine not exceeding the statutory maximum.

COMMENCEMENT DATE  20 January 2007[27]

**22.804.02**   Section 804 compels a company to act as requested in a section 803 request and sets out the range of penalties for default in compliance with a request under section 803. Section 804 is based on section 214(4) and (5) of the Companies Act 1985. It should be noted that requests from shareholders under the previous section 214 procedure (see section 803 above) were unusual. This it is to be suspected was because management was often hostile to such requests and determined that they were unreasonable.

---

[25] Companies Act 2006 (Commencement No 1, etc) Order 2006, SI 2006/3428, art 3.
[26] See s 804 below.
[27] Companies Act 2006 (Commencement No 1, etc) Order 2006, SI 2006/3428, art 3.

In the previous penalty regime under the 1985 Act the company and an officer were liable to a fine[28] but under section 804 the offence of non-compliance is a criminal one confined to the company's officers which results in a fine.

## 805 Report to members on outcome of investigation

(1) On the conclusion of an investigation carried out by a company in pursuance of a requirement under section 803 the company must cause a report of the information received in pursuance of the investigation to be prepared.
The report must be made available for inspection within a reasonable period (not more than 15 days) after the conclusion of the investigation.

(2) Where—
   (a) a company undertakes an investigation in pursuance of a requirement under section 803, and
   (b) the investigation is not concluded within three months after the date on which the company became subject to the requirement,
   the company must cause to be prepared in respect of that period, and in respect of each succeeding period of three months ending before the conclusion of the investigation, an interim report of the information received during that period in pursuance of the investigation.

(3) Each such report must be made available for inspection within a reasonable period (not more than 15 days) after the end of the period to which it relates.

(4) The reports must be retained by the company for at least six years from the date on which they are first made available for inspection and must be kept available for inspection during that time—
   (a) at the company's registered office, or
   (b) at a place specified in regulations under section 1136.

(5) The company must give notice to the registrar—
   (a) of the place at which the reports are kept available for inspection, and
   (b) of any change in that place,
   unless they have at all times been kept at the company's registered office.

(6) The company must within three days of making any report prepared under this section available for inspection, notify the members who made the requests under section 803 where the report is so available.

(7) For the purposes of this section an investigation carried out by a company in pursuance of a requirement under section 803 is concluded when—
   (a) the company has made all such inquiries as are necessary or expedient for the purposes of the requirement, and
   (b) in the case of each such inquiry—
      (i) a response has been received by the company, or
      (ii) the time allowed for a response has elapsed.

COMMENCEMENT DATE 20 January 2007[29]

**22.805.01**

Section 805 requires a company that has carried out an investigation as a result of a section 803 request to prepare and retain a report, and sets out the procedures for members to access that report. It restates section 215 of the Companies Act 1985. The only substantial difference between section 215 and section 805 is that the requirement in section 215(4) that '[s]uch a report shall not include any information with respect to a company entitled to avail itself of the benefit conferred by [section] 231(3) (disclosure of shareholdings not required if it would be harmful to company's business); but where any such information is omitted, that fact shall be stated in the report'. This provision has been enacted separately in section 826 with the same effect.

**22.805.02**

## 806 Report to members: offences

(1) If default is made for 14 days in complying with section 805(5) (notice to registrar of place at which reports made available for inspection) an offence is committed by—
   (a) the company, and
   (b) every officer of the company who is in default.

(2) A person guilty of an offence under subsection (1) is liable on summary conviction to a fine not exceeding level 3 on the standard scale and, for continued contravention, a daily default fine not exceeding one-tenth of level 3 on the standard scale.

(3) If default is made in complying with any other provision of section 805 (report to members on outcome of investigation), an offence is committed by every officer of the company who is in default.

(4) A person guilty of an offence under subsection (3) is liable—

**22.806.01**

---

[28] S 214 (5).
[29] Companies Act 2006 (Commencement No 1, etc) Order 2006, SI 2006/3428, art 3.

(a)  on conviction on indictment, to a fine;

(b)  on summary conviction, to a fine not exceeding the statutory maximum.

COMMENCEMENT DATE  20 January 2007[30]

**22.806.02**  Section 806 sets out the range of penalties for default in compliance with section 805. It restates section 215(8) of the Companies Act 1985. In the previous penalty regime under the 1985 Act the company and an officer were liable to a fine, but, under section 806 where default is with regard to reporting to the members, the offence of non-compliance is a criminal one confined to the company's officers which results in a fine.

### 807  Right to inspect and request copy of reports

**22.807.01**
(1) Any report prepared under section 805 must be open to inspection by any person without charge.

(2) Any person is entitled, on request and on payment of such fee as may be prescribed, to be provided with a copy of any such report or any part of it. The copy must be provided within ten days after the request is received by the company.

(3) If an inspection required under subsection (1) is refused, or default is made in complying with subsection (2), an offence is committed by—
   (a) the company, and
   (b) every officer of the company who is in default.

(4) A person guilty of an offence under this section is liable on summary conviction to a fine not exceeding level 3 on the standard scale and, for continued contravention, a daily default fine not exceeding one-tenth of level 3 on the standard scale.

(5) In the case of any such refusal or default the court may by order compel an immediate inspection or, as the case may be, direct that the copy required be sent to the person requiring it.

COMMENCEMENT DATE  20 January 2007[31]

**22.807.02**  Section 807 restates section 219 of the Companies Act 1985. It compels the company to make freely available to any person a report prepared under section 805. A copy can also be requested if a fee is paid. It also sets out the criminal penalties for non-compliance and makes provision for the courts to compel disclosure.

## *Register of interests disclosed*

### 808  Register of interests disclosed

**22.808.01**
(1) The company must keep a register of information received by it in pursuance of a requirement imposed under section 793 (notice requiring information about interests in company's shares).

(2) A company which receives any such information must, within three days of the receipt, enter in the register—
   (a) the fact that the requirement was imposed and the date on which it was imposed, and
   (b) the information received in pursuance of the requirement.

(3) The information must be entered against the name of the present holder of the shares in question or, if there is no present holder or the present holder is not known, against the name of the person holding the interest.

(4) The register must be made up so that the entries against the names entered in it appear in chronological order.

(5) If default is made in complying with this section an offence is committed by—
   (a) the company, and
   (b) every officer of the company who is in default.

(6) A person guilty of an offence under this section is liable on summary conviction to a fine not exceeding level 3 on the standard scale and, for continued contravention, a daily default fine not exceeding one-tenth of level 3 on the standard scale.

(7) The company is not by virtue of anything done for the purposes of this section affected with notice of, or put upon inquiry as to, the rights of any person in relation to any shares.

COMMENCEMENT DATE  20 January 2007[32]

**22.808.02**  Previously under the 1985 Act regime the register kept by virtue of section 211 of the Companies Act 1985 contained all interests notified; that is those under the automatic disclosure rules and those arising as a result of a notice served under section 212 (see section 793 above). Under the 1985 regime section 212 interests were held in a separate part of the register of interests in shares. The Government

---

[30] Companies Act 2006 (Commencement No 1, etc) Order 2006, SI 2006/3428, art 3.
[31] Companies Act 2006 (Commencement No 1, etc) Order 2006, SI 2006/3428, art 3.
[32] Companies Act 2006 (Commencement No 1, etc) Order 2006, SI 2006/3428, art 3.

intends, both through section 811 and in future regulations under the Financial Services and Markets Act 2000, to specify how interests that arise under the automatic disclosure rules will be distinguished from each other.

Section 808 compels the company to keep a register of section 793 information, timescales for entry onto the register, how the information is to be registered, and penalties for non-compliance. The important distinction between the previous regime and the section 808 register is that the details of the section 793 compulsion are registered as well as the information received. Additionally there is provision in section 808 for how unknown shareholders and ownerless shares are to be entered on the register. The penalties for default are also criminal in nature and apply both to the company and its officers. **22.808.03**

## 809  Register to be kept available for inspection

(1)  The register kept under section 808 (register of interests disclosed) must be kept available for inspection—    **22.809.01**
    (a)  at the company's registered office, or
    (b)  at a place specified in regulations under section 1136.
(2)  A company must give notice to the registrar of companies of the place where the register is kept available for inspection and of any change in that place.
(3)  No such notice is required if the register has at all times been kept available for inspection at the company's registered office.
(4)  If default is made in complying with subsection (1), or a company makes default for 14 days in complying with subsection (2), an offence is committed by—
    (a)  the company, and
    (b)  every officer of the company who is in default.
(5)  A person guilty of an offence under this section is liable on summary conviction to a fine not exceeding level 3 on the standard scale and, for continued contravention, a daily default fine not exceeding one-tenth of level 3 on the standard scale.

COMMENCEMENT DATE  20 January 2007[33]

Section 809 compels the company to make the section 808 register of interests disclosed available for inspection, specifies the location of the register, and the criminal penalties the company and its officers are liable to for default. It restates part of section 211 of the Companies Act 1985. **22.809.02**

## 810  Associated index

(1)  Unless the register kept under section 808 (register of interests disclosed) is kept in such a form as itself to constitute an index, the company must keep an index of the names entered in it.    **22.810.01**
(2)  The company must make any necessary entry or alteration in the index within ten days after the date on which any entry or alteration is made in the register.
(3)  The index must contain, in respect of each name, a sufficient indication to enable the information entered against it to be readily found.
(4)  The index must be at all times kept available for inspection at the same place as the register.
(5)  If default is made in complying with this section, an offence is committed by—
    (a)  the company, and
    (b)  every officer of the company who is in default.
(6)  A person guilty of an offence under this section is liable on summary conviction to a fine not exceeding level 3 on the standard scale and, for continued contravention, a daily default fine not exceeding one-tenth of level 3 on the standard scale.

COMMENCEMENT DATE  20 January 2007[34]

Section 810 compels the company to have an index to the section 808 register unless the register is itself a searchable database. It restates part of section 211 of the Companies Act 1985. **22.810.02**

## 811  Rights to inspect and require copy of entries

(1)  The register required to be kept under section 808 (register of interests disclosed), and any associated index, must be open to inspection by any person without charge.    **22.811.01**
(2)  Any person is entitled, on request and on payment of such fee as may be prescribed, to be provided with a copy of any entry in the register.
(3)  A person seeking to exercise either of the rights conferred by this section must make a request to the company to that effect.

---

[33]  Companies Act 2006 (Commencement No 1, etc) Order 2006, SI 2006/3428, art 3.
[34]  Companies Act 2006 (Commencement No 1, etc) Order 2006, SI 2006/3428, art 3.

(4) The request must contain the following information—
 (a) in the case of an individual, his name and address;
 (b) in the case of an organisation, the name and address of an individual responsible for making the request on behalf of the organisation;
 (c) the purpose for which the information is to be used; and
 (d) whether the information will be disclosed to any other person, and if so—
  (i) where that person is an individual, his name and address,
  (ii) where that person is an organisation, the name and address of an individual responsible for receiving the information on its behalf, and
  (iii) the purpose for which the information is to be used by that person.

COMMENCEMENT DATE 20 January 2007 (subs (1)–(3));[35] 6 April 2008 (subs (4))[36]

**22.811.02** Section 811 compels the company to make available without charge to any person the register and its index. A fee can be charged for a copy of a register entry. Anyone requesting access to the register must provide their name and address and the purpose for which the information is to be used. It restates section 219 and part of section 211 of the Companies Act 1985. One difference between the section 211 of the 1985 Act inspection regime and section 811 is that the requirement in section 211(9) that '[n]either the register nor any associated index shall be available for inspection in accordance with that section in so far as it contains information with respect to a company for the time being entitled to avail itself of the benefit conferred by section 231(3)'[37] has been enacted separately in section 826 with the same effect. It is worth noting that there is no requirement to inform the person requesting access under section 811 that refusal is due to the provisions of section 826 (see section 826 below).

### 812 Court supervision of purpose for which rights may be exercised

**22.812.01** (1) Where a company receives a request under section 811 (register of interests disclosed: right to inspect and require copy), it must—
 (a) comply with the request if it is satisfied that it is made for a proper purpose, and
 (b) refuse the request if it is not so satisfied.
(2) If the company refuses the request, it must inform the person making the request, stating the reason why it is not satisfied.
(3) A person whose request is refused may apply to the court.
(4) If an application is made to the court—
 (a) the person who made the request must notify the company, and
 (b) the company must use its best endeavours to notify any persons whose details would be disclosed if the company were required to comply with the request.
(5) If the court is not satisfied that the inspection or copy is sought for a proper purpose, it shall direct the company not to comply with the request.
(6) If the court makes such a direction and it appears to the court that the company is or may be subject to other requests made for a similar purpose (whether made by the same person or different persons), it may direct that the company is not to comply with any such request.
 The order must contain such provision as appears to the court appropriate to identify the requests to which it applies.
(7) If the court does not direct the company not to comply with the request, the company must comply with the request immediately upon the court giving its decision or, as the case may be, the proceedings being discontinued.

COMMENCEMENT DATE 6 April 2008[38]

**22.812.02** Section 812 compels the company to allow access if satisfied that it is for a proper purpose. If it refuses on the basis that the request was not for a proper purpose then an application can be made to court by the person refused access. If such proceedings are instigated the company must use its best endeavours to notify any persons whose details might be disclosed. Section 812 restates part of section 219 of the Companies Act 1985. Under the previous regime the company could refuse access but the section never specified the ground for refusal.

---

[35] Companies Act 2006 (Commencement No 1, etc) Order 2006, SI 2006/3428, art 3.
[36] Companies Act 2006 (Commencement No 5, Transitional Provisions and Savings) Order 2007, SI 2007/3495, art 3.
[37] Now s 409(3) (disclosure of shareholdings not required if it would be harmful to company's business).
[38] Companies Act 2006 (Commencement No 5, Transitional Provisions and Savings) Order 2007, SI 2007/3495, art 3.

### 813 Register of interests disclosed: refusal of inspection or default in providing copy

(1) If an inspection required under section 811 (register of interests disclosed: right to inspect and require copy) is refused or default is made in providing a copy required under that section, otherwise than in accordance with an order of the court, an offence is committed by—
    (a) the company, and
    (b) every officer of the company who is in default.
(2) A person guilty of an offence under this section is liable on summary conviction to a fine not exceeding level 3 on the standard scale and, for continued contravention, a daily default fine not exceeding one-tenth of level 3 on the standard scale.
(3) In the case of any such refusal or default the court may by order compel an immediate inspection or, as the case may be, direct that the copy required be sent to the person requesting it.

COMMENCEMENT DATE 20 January 2007[39]

22.813.01

Section 813 sets out the criminal penalties and gives the court a power to remedy the default. It restates section 219(3) and (4) of the Companies Act 1985.

22.813.02

### 814 Register of interests disclosed: offences in connection with request for or disclosure of information

(1) It is an offence for a person knowingly or recklessly to make in a request under section 811 (register of interests disclosed: right to inspect or require copy) a statement that is misleading, false or deceptive in a material particular.
(2) It is an offence for a person in possession of information obtained by exercise of either of the rights conferred by that section—
    (a) to do anything that results in the information being disclosed to another person, or
    (b) to fail to do anything with the result that the information is disclosed to another person,
    knowing, or having reason to suspect, that person may use the information for a purpose that is not a proper purpose.
(3) A person guilty of an offence under this section is liable—
    (a) on conviction on indictment, to imprisonment for a term not exceeding two years or a fine (or both);
    (b) on summary conviction—
        (i) in England and Wales, to imprisonment for a term not exceeding twelve months or to a fine not exceeding the statutory maximum (or both);
        (ii) in Scotland or Northern Ireland, to imprisonment for a term not exceeding six months, or to a fine not exceeding the statutory maximum (or both).

COMMENCEMENT DATE 6 April 2008[40]

22.814.01

Section 814 provides for severe criminal penalties for misleading, false, or deceptive statements given when making a request under section 811 and for misuse of that information obtained. The section marks a continuance of a trend begun by the Criminal Justice and Police Act 2001 of protecting individuals or companies who have information on the public registers which could be misused. The Criminal Justice and Police Act 2001 allows directors at risk of potential or actual violence or intimidation to have their names and addresses removed from the public register (see now Chapter 8 of part 10 of this Act). The concern here in section 814 is a similar one in that it is aimed at preventing organizations such as the Animal Liberation Front obtaining information which could be used to intimidate or harm participants in the company.

22.814.02

### 815 Entries not to be removed from register

(1) Entries in the register kept under section 808 (register of interests disclosed) must not be deleted except in accordance with—
    section 816 (old entries), or
    section 817 (incorrect entry relating to third party).
(2) If an entry is deleted in contravention of subsection (1), the company must restore it as soon as reasonably practicable.
(3) If default is made in complying with subsection (1) or (2), an offence is committed by—
    (a) the company, and
    (b) every officer of the company who is in default.

22.815.01

---

[39] Companies Act 2006 (Commencement No 1, etc) Order 2006, SI 2006/3428, art 3.
[40] Companies Act 2006 (Commencement No 5, Transitional Provisions and Savings) Order 2007, SI 2007/3495, art 3.

(4) A person guilty of an offence under this section is liable on summary conviction to a fine not exceeding level 3 on the standard scale and, for continued contravention of subsection (2), a daily default fine not exceeding one-tenth of level 3 on the standard scale.

COMMENCEMENT DATE 20 January 2007[41]

**22.815.02** Section 815 compels companies not to delete entries on the section 808 register unless they are old or incorrect. A wrongly deleted entry must be restored as soon as practicable and failure to comply will result in a criminal offence. It restates section 218 of the Companies Act 1985.

### 816 Removal of entries from register: old entries

**22.816.01** A company may remove an entry from the register kept under section 808 (register of interests disclosed) if more than six years have elapsed since the entry was made.

COMMENCEMENT DATE 20 January 2007[42]

**22.816.02** Section 816 re-enacts section 217(1) of the Companies Act 1985 in a much simpler and easy to use form. Previously under section 217(1) a company could remove an entry after six years if either:

(a) that entry recorded the fact that the person in question had ceased to have an interest notifiable under this Part in relevant share capital of the company, or

(b) it has been superseded by a later entry made under section 211 against the same person's name; and in a case within paragraph (a) the company may also remove that person's name from the register.

Section 816 simply allows removal after six years.

### 817 Removal of entries from register: incorrect entry relating to third party

**22.817.01** (1) This section applies where in pursuance of an obligation imposed by a notice under section 793 (notice requiring information about interests in company's shares) a person gives to a company the name and address of another person as being interested in shares in the company.

(2) That other person may apply to the company for the removal of the entry from the register.

(3) If the company is satisfied that the information in pursuance of which the entry was made is incorrect, it shall remove the entry.

(4) If an application under subsection (3) is refused, the applicant may apply to the court for an order directing the company to remove the entry in question from the register.
The court may make such an order if it thinks fit.

COMMENCEMENT DATE 20 January 2007[43]

**22.817.02** Section 817 provides for the removal of an incorrect entry regarding a third party from the register. Section 817 restates section 217 of the Companies Act 1985 with one significant difference. Section 817 removed the onerous condition that a company verify third party information that was obtained in response to a section 211[44] disclosure notice before placing that information on the register. If that information does turn out to be incorrect the third party can apply to court to have the entry removed.

### 818 Adjustment of entry relating to share acquisition agreement

**22.818.01** (1) If a person who is identified in the register kept by a company under section 808 (register of interests disclosed) as being a party to an agreement to which section 824 applies (certain share acquisition agreements) ceases to be a party to the agreement, he may apply to the company for the inclusion of that information in the register.

(2) If the company is satisfied that he has ceased to be a party to the agreement, it shall record that information (if not already recorded) in every place where his name appears in the register as a party to the agreement.

(3) If an application under this section is refused (otherwise than on the ground that the information has already been recorded), the applicant may apply to the court for an order directing the company to include the information in question in the register.
The court may make such an order if it thinks fit.

COMMENCEMENT DATE 20 January 2007[45]

---

[41] Companies Act 2006 (Commencement No 1, etc) Order 2006, SI 2006/3428, art 3.
[42] Companies Act 2006 (Commencement No 1, etc) Order 2006, SI 2006/3428, art 3.
[43] Companies Act 2006 (Commencement No 1, etc) Order 2006, SI 2006/3428, art 3.
[44] Now s 793.
[45] Companies Act 2006 (Commencement No 1, etc) Order 2006, SI 2006/3428, art 3.

Section 818 provides that if a person previously identified on the register as a party to a section 824 **22.818.02**
share acquisition agreement[46] later ceases to be such a party then he may ask for the register to be
amended. In the event that the company refuses, the individual may seek a court order to compel the
company to rectify the register. It restates section 217(4) and (5) of the Companies Act 1985.

### 819 Duty of company ceasing to be public company

(1) If a company ceases to be a public company, it must continue to keep any register kept under **22.819.01**
section 808 (register of interests disclosed), and any associated index, until the end of the period
of six years after it ceased to be such a company.
(2) If default is made in complying with this section, an offence is committed by—
  (a) the company, and
  (b) every officer of the company who is in default.
(3) A person guilty of an offence under this section is liable on summary conviction to a fine not
exceeding level 3 on the standard scale and, for continued contravention, a daily default fine not
exceeding one-tenth of level 3 on the standard scale.

COMMENCEMENT DATE 20 January 2007[47]

Section 819 requires the company to keep its section 808 register for six years after ceasing to be a public **22.819.02**
company. As such it restates part of section 211(7) and (10) of the Companies Act 1985 and provides
for criminal penalties for non-compliance.

### *Meaning of interest in shares*

### 820 Interest in shares: general

(1) This section applies to determine for the purposes of this Part whether a person has an interest in **22.820.01**
shares.
(2) In this Part—
  (a) a reference to an interest in shares includes an interest of any kind whatsoever in the shares,
and
  (b) any restraints or restrictions to which the exercise of any right attached to the interest is or
may be subject shall be disregarded.
(3) Where an interest in shares is comprised in property held on trust, every beneficiary of the trust is
treated as having an interest in the shares.
(4) A person is treated as having an interest in shares if—
  (a) he enters into a contract to acquire them, or
  (b) not being the registered holder, he is entitled—
    (i) to exercise any right conferred by the holding of the shares, or
    (ii) to control the exercise of any such right.
(5) For the purposes of subsection (4)(b) a person is entitled to exercise or control the exercise of a
right conferred by the holding of shares if he—
  (a) has a right (whether subject to conditions or not) the exercise of which would make him so
entitled, or
  (b) is under an obligation (whether subject to conditions or not) the fulfilment of which would
make him so entitled.
(6) A person is treated as having an interest in shares if—
  (a) he has a right to call for delivery of the shares to himself or to his order, or
  (b) he has a right to acquire an interest in shares or is under an obligation to take an interest in
shares.
This applies whether the right or obligation is conditional or absolute.
(7) Persons having a joint interest are treated as each having that interest.
(8) It is immaterial that shares in which a person has an interest are unidentifiable.

COMMENCEMENT DATE 20 January 2007[48]

Section 820 restates the definition of 'interest in shares' from section 208 of the Companies Act 1985 as **22.820.02**
including 'an interest of any kind whatsoever'. This definition it is worth noting is deliberately very
wide and has been noted by the courts to have been so defined 'to counter the limitless ingenuity of
persons who prefer to conceal their interests behind trusts and corporate entities'.[49] While there is no
EU element to these provisions, definitional aspects of the Transparency Directive had the potential to
cause confusion here. As a result, in order to implement the Transparency Directive, the automatic

---

[46] This may also include a concert party agreement.
[47] Companies Act 2006 (Commencement No 1, etc) Order 2006, SI 2006/3428, art 3.
[48] Companies Act 2006 (Commencement No 1, etc) Order 2006, SI 2006/3428, art 3.
[49] *Re TR Technology Investment Trust plc* [1988] BCLC 256 at 261.

disclosure obligations in sections 198 to 211 of Part VI of the Companies Act 1985 were repealed and replaced by regulations under the Financial Services and Markets Act 2000. In doing this a different concept of an 'interest in voting rights' has been adopted for the purposes of the Transparency Directive.[50]

### 821 Interest in shares: right to subscribe for shares

**22.821.01**
(1) Section 793 (notice by company requiring information about interests in its shares) applies in relation to a person who has, or previously had, or is or was entitled to acquire, a right to subscribe for shares in the company as it applies in relation to a person who is or was interested in shares in that company.
(2) References in that section to an interest in shares shall be read accordingly.

COMMENCEMENT DATE 20 January 2007[51]

**22.821.02** Section 821 provides that a notice under section 793 applies in relation to rights to subscribe for shares. It restates section 212(6) of the Companies Act 1985.

### 822 Interest in shares: family interests

**22.822.01**
(1) For the purposes of this Part a person is taken to be interested in shares in which—
  (a) his spouse or civil partner, or
  (b) any infant child or step-child of his,
  is interested.
(2) In relation to Scotland 'infant' means a person under the age of 18 years.

COMMENCEMENT DATE 20 January 2007[52]

**22.822.02** Section 822 relates to certain family interests which will be attributed to connected persons for the purpose of disclosure in this Part of the Act. Thus an interest by a spouse/civil partner or infant child or step-child will confer an interest in shares for the purposes of this Part of the Act. It restates section 203 (1) of the Companies Act 1985.

### 823 Interest in shares: corporate interests

**22.823.01**
(1) For the purposes of this Part a person is taken to be interested in shares if a body corporate is interested in them and—
  (a) the body or its directors are accustomed to act in accordance with his directions or instructions, or
  (b) he is entitled to exercise or control the exercise of one-third or more of the voting power at general meetings of the body.
(2) For the purposes of this section a person is treated as entitled to exercise or control the exercise of voting power if—
  (a) another body corporate is entitled to exercise or control the exercise of that voting power, and
  (b) he is entitled to exercise or control the exercise of one-third or more of the voting power at general meetings of that body corporate.
(3) For the purposes of this section a person is treated as entitled to exercise or control the exercise of voting power if—
  (a) he has a right (whether or not subject to conditions) the exercise of which would make him so entitled, or
  (b) he is under an obligation (whether or not subject to conditions) the fulfilment of which would make him so entitled.

COMMENCEMENT DATE 20 January 2007[53]

**22.823.02** This section outlines certain corporate interests which will be attributed to connected persons for the purpose of disclosure in this Part of the Act. Thus a person will be interested in shares if a body corporate which is controlled by that person has an interest in the shares. Section 823 restates section 203(2) to (4) of the Companies Act 1985.

---

[50] See the Disclosure and Transparency Rules of the Financial Services Authority.
[51] Companies Act 2006 (Commencement No 1, etc) Order 2006, SI 2006/3428, art 3.
[52] Companies Act 2006 (Commencement No 1, etc) Order 2006, SI 2006/3428, art 3.
[53] Companies Act 2006 (Commencement No 1, etc) Order 2006, SI 2006/3428, art 3.

## 824  Interest in shares: agreement to acquire interests in a particular company

(1)  For the purposes of this Part an interest in shares may arise from an agreement between two or          **22.824.01**
more persons that includes provision for the acquisition by any one or more of them of interests
in shares of a particular public company (the 'target company' for that agreement).

(2)  This section applies to such an agreement if—

  (a)  the agreement includes provision imposing obligations or restrictions on any one or more of
the parties to it with respect to their use, retention or disposal of their interests in the shares
of the target company acquired in pursuance of the agreement (whether or not together
with any other interests of theirs in the company's shares to which the agreement relates),
and

  (b)  an interest in the target company's shares is in fact acquired by any of the parties in pursuance
of the agreement.

(3)  The reference in subsection (2) to the use of interests in shares in the target company is to the
exercise of any rights or of any control or influence arising from those interests (including the right
to enter into an agreement for the exercise, or for control of the exercise, of any of those rights
by another person).

(4)  Once an interest in shares in the target company has been acquired in pursuance of the
agreement, this section continues to apply to the agreement so long as the agreement continues
to include provisions of any description mentioned in subsection (2).
This applies irrespective of—

  (a)  whether or not any further acquisitions of interests in the company's shares take place in
pursuance of the agreement;

  (b)  any change in the persons who are for the time being parties to it;

  (c)  any variation of the agreement.

References in this subsection to the agreement include any agreement having effect (whether
directly or indirectly) in substitution for the original agreement.

(5)  In this section—

  (a)  'agreement' includes any agreement or arrangement, and

  (b)  references to provisions of an agreement include—

    (i)   undertakings, expectations or understandings operative under an arrangement, and

    (ii)  any provision whether express or implied and whether absolute or not.

References elsewhere in this Part to an agreement to which this section applies have a corresponding meaning.

(6)  This section does not apply—

  (a)  to an agreement that is not legally binding unless it involves mutuality in the undertakings,
expectations or understandings of the parties to it; or

  (b)  to an agreement to underwrite or sub-underwrite an offer of shares in a company, provided
the agreement is confined to that purpose and any matters incidental to it.

COMMENCEMENT DATE  20 January 2007[54]

Section 824 provides that an interest in shares will arise where any agreement or arrangement, legally    **22.824.02**
binding or not, exists which involves undertakings, expectations, or understandings that interests in
shares will be acquired and that they will be subject to certain restrictions while the agreement exists.
Such agreements or arrangements may include groups of persons acting in concert to prepare the way
for a takeover offer for the company or to support a pending takeover offer. Section 824 runs parallel
to the City Code rules on 'Concert Parties'. Section 824 restates section 204 of the Companies Act 1985.

## 825  Extent of obligation in case of share acquisition agreement

(1)  For the purposes of this Part each party to an agreement to which section 824 applies is treated    **22.825.01**
as interested in all shares in the target company in which any other party to the agreement is
interested apart from the agreement (whether or not the interest of the other party was acquired,
or includes any interest that was acquired, in pursuance of the agreement).

(2)  For those purposes an interest of a party to such an agreement in shares in the target company is
an interest apart from the agreement if he is interested in those shares otherwise than by virtue
of the application of section 824 (and this section) in relation to the agreement.

(3)  Accordingly, any such interest of the person (apart from the agreement) includes for those
purposes any interest treated as his under section 822 or 823 (family or corporate interests) or by
the application of section 824 (and this section) in relation to any other agreement with respect
to shares in the target company to which he is a party.

(4)  A notification with respect to his interest in shares in the target company made to the company
under this Part by a person who is for the time being a party to an agreement to which section 824
applies must—

---

[54]  Companies Act 2006 (Commencement No 1, etc) Order 2006, SI 2006/3428, art 3.

(a)  state that the person making the notification is a party to such an agreement,
(b)  include the names and (so far as known to him) the addresses of the other parties to the agreement, identifying them as such, and
(c)  state whether or not any of the shares to which the notification relates are shares in which he is interested by virtue of section 824 (and this section) and, if so, the number of those shares.

COMMENCEMENT DATE  20 January 2007[55]

**22.825.02**   The section provides a set of rules for determining the extent of the interests in a target company of persons who are party to an agreement to which section 824 applies. Section 825 restates section 205 of the Companies Act 1985.

## *Other supplementary provisions*

### 826  Information protected from wider disclosure

**22.826.01**       (1)  Information in respect of which a company is for the time being entitled to any exemption conferred by regulations under section 409(3) (information about related undertakings to be given in notes to accounts: exemption where disclosure harmful to company's business)—
            (a)  must not be included in a report under section 805 (report to members on outcome of investigation), and
            (b)  must not be made available under section 811 (right to inspect and request copy of entries).
        (2)  Where any such information is omitted from a report under section 805, that fact must be stated in the report.

COMMENCEMENT DATE  20 January 2007[56]

**22.826.02**   Section 409(3) and (4) confers on the Secretary of State the power to make regulations exempting a company from the need to disclose information relating to its holdings in related undertakings in notes to its accounts, where that information would be seriously prejudicial to the business of the undertaking. The Secretary of State must then agree to such an exemption. Section 826 adds to that exemption by precluding such information from a section 805 report and by excluding such information on the register from inspection under section 811. In only the case of an exclusion from a section 805 report must the fact that the information is missing be disclosed in the report. Section 409(5) requires the fact of the exemption in all cases to be disclosed in a note to the annual accounts. Section 826 restates section 211(9) and 215(4) of the Companies Act 1985.

### 827  Reckoning of periods for fulfilling obligations

**22.827.01**       Where the period allowed by any provision of this Part for fulfilling an obligation is expressed as a number of days, any day that is not a working day shall be disregarded in reckoning that period.

COMMENCEMENT DATE  20 January 2007[57]

**22.827.02**   Section 827 outlines how to calculate the period of days with regard to an obligation in this Part of the Act. It restates section 220(2) of the Companies Act 1985.

### 828  Power to make further provision by regulations

**22.828.01**       (1)  The Secretary of State may by regulations amend—
            (a)  the definition of shares to which this Part applies (section 792),
            (b)  the provisions as to notice by a company requiring information about interests in its shares (section 793), and
            (c)  the provisions as to what is taken to be an interest in shares (sections 820 and 821).
        (2)  The regulations may amend, repeal or replace those provisions and make such other consequential amendments or repeals of provisions of this Part as appear to the Secretary of State to be appropriate.
        (3)  Regulations under this section are subject to affirmative resolution procedure.

COMMENCEMENT DATE  20 January 2007[58]

**22.828.02**   Section 828 confers powers on the Secretary of State to make regulations amending provisions of this Part of the Act. It restates section 210A of the Companies Act 1985.

---

[55]  Companies Act 2006 (Commencement No 1, etc) Order 2006, SI 2006/3428, art 3.
[56]  Companies Act 2006 (Commencement No 1, etc) Order 2006, SI 2006/3428, art 3.
[57]  Companies Act 2006 (Commencement No 1, etc) Order 2006, SI 2006/3428, art 3.
[58]  Companies Act 2006 (Commencement No 1, etc) Order 2006, SI 2006/3428, art 3.

# 23

## DISTRIBUTIONS

## Companies Act 2006

### PART 23
### DISTRIBUTIONS

### CHAPTER 1
### RESTRICTIONS ON WHEN DISTRIBUTIONS MAY BE MADE

#### Introductory

### 829 Meaning of 'distribution'

(1) In this Part 'distribution' means every description of distribution of a company's assets to its members, whether in cash or otherwise, subject to the following exceptions.    **23.829.01**

(2) The following are not distributions for the purposes of this Part—

(a) an issue of shares as fully or partly paid bonus shares;

     (b)  the reduction of share capital—
        (i)  by extinguishing or reducing the liability of any of the members on any of the company's shares in respect of share capital not paid up, or
        (ii)  by repaying paid-up share capital;
     (c)  the redemption or purchase of any of the company's own shares out of capital (including the proceeds of any fresh issue of shares) or out of unrealised profits in accordance with Chapter 3, 4 or 5 of Part 18;
     (d)  a distribution of assets to members of the company on its winding up.

COMMENCEMENT DATE 6 April 2008[1]

**23.829.02**    This section consolidates the definition of a distribution previously contained in section 263(2) of the Companies Act 1985. It provides that a distribution includes every transfer of a company's assets to its members except those falling within the excluded categories referred to in paragraphs (a) to (d) of subsection (2).

## General rules

### 830 Distributions to be made only out of profits available for the purpose

**23.830.01**    (1)  A company may only make a distribution out of profits available for the purpose.
        (2)  A company's profits available for distribution are its accumulated, realised profits, so far as not previously utilised by distribution or capitalisation, less its accumulated, realised losses, so far as not previously written off in a reduction or reorganisation of capital duly made.
        (3)  Subsection (2) has effect subject to sections 832 and 835 (investment companies etc: distributions out of accumulated revenue profits).

COMMENCEMENT DATE 6 April 2008[2]

**23.830.02**    This section consolidates the prohibition previously contained in section 263 of the Companies Act 1985. It codifies the common law rule that a distribution of a company's assets to a shareholder, except in accordance with specific statutory procedures, is a return of capital, which is unlawful and ultra vires the company.[3] The Supreme Court of Appeal has interpreted this provision to mean that an issue of shares at an undervalue is not a distribution if it is made in circumstances where the company and the shareholder genuinely did not know that the issue was at an undervalue.[4] This approach recognizes that in some cases it may be difficult to establish the fair value of assets that form the consideration for a share issue and that transactions should not in those circumstances face the risk of re-characterization as a distribution simply as a result of an arithmetical difference between the consideration and a subsequent valuation of assets.[5] Subsection (2) sets out the definition of profits available for distribution. Following the approach of the Second Company Law Directive,[6] it follows the 'balance sheet surplus' method of determining profits available for distribution. This allows a company to distribute net profits on both capital and revenue at the particular time, that is according to the relevant accounts. It provides that a company's profits available for distribution are its accumulated, realized profits (on both capital and revenue) not previously distributed or capitalized,[7] less its accumulated realized losses (on both revenue and capital) not written off in a proper reduction or reorganization of capital.[8] The reference to 'accumulated' makes clear that the ability to make a distribution is not

---

[1]  Companies Act 2006 (Commencement No 5, Transitional Provisions and Savings) Order 2007, SI 2007/3495, art 3.
[2]  Companies Act 2006 (Commencement No 5, Transitional Provisions and Savings) Order 2007, SI 2007/3495, art 3.
[3]  *Progress Property Co Ltd v Moore and another* [2009] EWCA Civ 629 (CA), citing *Aveling Barford v Perion Ltd* (1989) 5 BCC 677 and *Re Halt Garage* (1964) Ltd [1982] 3 All ER 1016.
[4]  *Progress Property Co Ltd v Moore and another* [2009] EWCA Civ 629 (CA); affirmed on appeal at [2010] UKSC 55. In this context, constructive knowledge as to the adequacy of property forming the consideration for the issue of shares is not to be imputed to the issuing company (Mummery LJ at para 27 (CA)).
[5]  See in this context the approval by Lord Walker in *Progress Property Co Ltd v Moore and another* [2010] UKSC 55 (at para 31) of the comments made by Lord Hamilton in *Clydebank Football Club v Steedman* 2002 SLT 109.
[6]  Directive (EC) 77/91 (1977) OJ L26/1.
[7]  Capitalization of profits refers to the process by which profits are used to pay up an allotment of shares to the members of a company (see s 582).
[8]  A company is able to 'write off' losses by reducing capital under Chapter 10 of Part 17 of the 2006 Act. The resulting fall in share capital shown in the balance sheet is intended to bring the residual claims of shareholders (as represented by share capital) more closely into line with the assets of the company. What is being 'written off' is essentially shareholders' residual claims: the company cannot unilaterally adjust the claims of its creditors, which remain unchanged throughout this process.

dependent only on the current year's financial position: if reserves created from previous years' profits are sufficiently large, a company may be able to sustain dividend payments for some time despite recording trading losses. Unrealized profits, such as those arising on a revaluation of assets, are not available for distribution until they are realized. There is no definition of 'realised' and hence difficulties may arise in some cases, such as where conditions (eg a retention of title clause) are attached to a transfer of property. Some guidance is available from FRS18, which sets out how companies should select, apply, and disclose accounting policies. According to that standard, realized profits include both profits realized in the form of cash or of other assets, the ultimate cash realization of which can be assessed with reasonable certainty.[9]

## 831 Net asset restriction on distributions by public companies

(1) A public company may only make a distribution—                                   **23.831.01**
   (a) if the amount of its net assets is not less than the aggregate of its called up share capital and undistributable reserves, and
   (b) if, and to the extent that, the distribution does not reduce the amount of those assets to less than that aggregate.
(2) For this purpose a company's 'net assets' means the aggregate of the company's assets less the aggregate of its liabilities.
(3) 'Liabilities' here includes—
   (a) where the relevant accounts are Companies Act accounts, provisions of a kind specified for the purposes of this subsection by regulations under section 396;
   (b) where the relevant accounts are IAS accounts, provisions of any kind.
(4) A company's undistributable reserves are—
   (a) its share premium account;
   (b) its capital redemption reserve;
   (c) the amount by which its accumulated, unrealised profits (so far as not previously utilised by capitalisation) exceed its accumulated, unrealised losses (so far as not previously written off in a reduction or reorganisation of capital duly made);
   (d) any other reserve that the company is prohibited from distributing—
      (i) by any enactment (other than one contained in this Part), or
      (ii) by its articles.
   The reference in paragraph (c) to capitalisation does not include a transfer of profits of the company to its capital redemption reserve.
(5) A public company must not include any uncalled share capital as an asset in any accounts relevant for purposes of this section.
(6) Subsection (1) has effect subject to sections 832 and 835 (investment companies etc: distributions out of accumulated revenue profits).

COMMENCEMENT DATE 6 April 2008[10]

This section consolidates the provisions previously contained in section 264 of the Companies Act   **23.831.02**
1985. It imposes an additional capital maintenance requirement on a public company making a distribution. The purpose of requiring that net assets following a distribution be not less than the aggregate of a company's share capital and undistributable reserves is to give effect to the principle of maintenance of capital. This principle aims to ensure that share capital and certain reserves are 'locked-in' to the company so as to provide a fund to meet creditors' claims. If distributions were permitted in contravention of that principle, it would no longer be accurate to regard share capital, in principle, as a fixed fund that acts as a cushion for creditors' claims.

Subsection (2) clarifies the meaning of 'net assets', making clear that liabilities include provisions as   **23.831.03**
defined by regulations made under section 402 and any provision that is made in IAS accounts.[11]

Subsection (4) defines a company's undistributable reserves.                          **23.831.04**

---

[9] See FRS18, para 28. See also 'Guidance on the determination of realised profits and losses in the context of distributions under the Companies Act 2006' (TECH 01/09, Institute of Chartered Accountants in England and Wales and Institute of Chartered Accountants of Scotland, July 2009).
[10] Companies Act 2006 (Commencement No 5, Transitional Provisions and Savings) Order 2007, SI 2007/3495, art 3.
[11] The latter are accounts drawn up according to International Financial Reporting Standards. All listed companies are required to prepare accounts according to these standards after 1 Jan 2005.

*Distributions by investment companies*

### 832  Distributions by investment companies out of accumulated revenue profits

**23.832.01**
(1)  An investment company may make a distribution out of its accumulated, realised revenue profits if the following conditions are met.

(2)  It may make such a distribution only if, and to the extent that, its accumulated, realised revenue profits, so far as not previously utilised by a distribution or capitalisation, exceed its accumulated revenue losses (whether realised or unrealised), so far as not previously written off in a reduction or reorganisation of capital duly made.

(3)  It may make such a distribution only—
(a)  if the amount of its assets is at least equal to one and a half times the aggregate of its liabilities to creditors, and
(b)  if, and to the extent that, the distribution does not reduce that amount to less than one and a half times that aggregate.

(4)  For this purpose a company's liabilities to creditors include—
(a)  in the case of Companies Act accounts, provisions of a kind specified for the purposes of this subsection by regulations under section 396;
(b)  in the case of IAS accounts, provisions for liabilities to creditors.

(5)  The following conditions must also be met—
(a)  [the company's shares must be shares admitted to trading on a regulated market;][12]
(b)  during the relevant period it must not have—
(i)  [...][13]
(ii)  applied any unrealised profits or any capital profits (realised or unrealised) in paying up debentures or amounts unpaid on its issued shares;[14]
(c)  it must have given notice to the registrar under section 833(1) (notice of intention to carry on business as an investment company)—
(i)  before the beginning of the relevant period, or
(ii)  as soon as reasonably practicable after the date of its incorporation.

(6)  For the purposes of this section—
(a)  [...][15]
(b)  the 'relevant period' is the period beginning with—
(i)  the first day of the accounting reference period immediately preceding that in which the proposed distribution is to be made, or
(ii)  where the distribution is to be made in the company's first accounting reference period, the first day of that period,
and ending with the date of the distribution.

(7)  The company must not include any uncalled share capital as an asset in any accounts relevant for purposes of this section.

COMMENCEMENT DATE  6 April 2008[16]

**23.832.02**  This section consolidates the provisions previously contained in section 265 of the Companies Act 1985. It has the effect of exempting investment companies (defined in section 833), subject to conditions, from the provisions of section 830, which limit distributions that can be made by a company. Subsection (2) provides that an investment company may make a distribution by reference to the accumulated position in respect of its revenue profits. Subsection (2) then extends the distributions that can be made by an investment company (from its revenue profits) beyond those permitted by section 830. It permits such additional distributions to be made by reference to a formula that relates its assets to its liabilities to creditors. The purpose of this requirement is presumably to act as a form of capital maintenance so as to protect creditors from the relaxation of section 830 by ensuring that creditors' claims are always covered by an appropriate margin. A distribution is permitted if assets are at least equal to one and a half times liabilities to creditors and to the extent that the distribution does not reduce that multiple.

---

[12] Amended by the Companies Act 2006 (Amendment of Part 23) (Investment Companies) Regulations 2012, SI 2012/952, reg 2(2)(a).

[13] Deleted by the Companies Act 2006 (Amendment of Part 23) (Investment Companies) Regulations 2012, SI 2012/952, reg 2(2)(b).

[14] Amended by the Companies Act 2006 (Amendment of Part 23) (Investment Companies) Regulations 2012, SI 2012/952, reg 2(2)(c).

[15] Deleted by the Companies Act 2006 (Amendment of Part 23) (Investment Companies) Regulations 2012, SI 2012/952, reg 2(2)(3).

[16] Companies Act 2006 (Commencement No 5, Transitional Provisions and Savings) Order 2007, SI 2007/3495, art 3.

In what sense does this relax the rule in section 830? An example of an investment company with a **23.832.03** simple structure can be used to illustrate the point. Assume that company A, which has just been established, has assets (in the form of a portfolio) of 200 that are represented by share capital of 180 and loans of 20. During the first year of operation, the investment portfolio falls in value by 30 per cent, generating a capital loss of 60. The company receives income (dividends, etc) of 10 and has operating costs of 5, leaving a revenue profit of 5. At the end of its first year of operation, it has no distributable profit for the purposes of section 830 (taking account of both capital and revenue profits) but it can distribute the revenue profit of 5 under this section because assets cover creditors' claims by more than one and a half times. If the portfolio were to rise in value by 15 per cent during the following year and the same revenue profit were recorded, the company would still have no distributable profit for the purposes of section 830 (as the rise of 21 in the value of the portfolio plus the accumulated revenue profits of 10 would be offset by the loss of 60 carried forward) but would once again be able to distribute the revenue profit of 5. Moreover, if no revenue profit were distributed in the first year, the accumulated revenue profit of 10 could be distributed in the second year.

Subsection (5) sets out further conditions that must be met by an investment company that makes a **23.832.04** distribution under subsection (1). First, its shares must be listed on a regulated market (as defined in section 1173). Second, the company must not have applied any unrealized profits or any capital profits (realized or unrealized) in paying up debentures or amounts unpaid on its issued shares.

## 833  Meaning of 'investment company'

(1)  In this Part an 'investment company' means a public company that—                        **23.833.01**
    (a)  has given notice (which has not been revoked) to the registrar of its intention to carry on business as an investment company, and
    (b)  since the date of that notice has complied with the following requirements.[17]
(2)  This requirements is—
    (a)  that the business of the company consists of investing its funds in shares, land or other assets, with the aim of spreading investment risk and giving members of the company the benefit of the results of the management of its funds;
    (b)  [...]
    (c)  [...]
    (d)  [...][18]
(3)[19]
(4)  Notice to the registrar under this section may be revoked at any time by the company on giving notice to the registrar that it no longer wishes to be an investment company within the meaning of this section.
(5)  On giving such a notice, the company ceases to be such a company.

COMMENCEMENT DATE  6 April 2008[20]

This section consolidates some of the provisions previously found in section 266 of the Companies Act **23.833.02** 1985. It sets out the requirements that must be met for a company to be considered an investment company. The model that is envisaged by these requirements is that of a company that acts as an indirect investment vehicle for its members and distributes the bulk of its income (eg in the form of dividends, interest, and rents) to its members. So-called 'investment trusts' are the main example of investment companies, although such a company also has to satisfy the requirements of section 842 of the Income and Corporation Taxes Act 1988 in order to be classified as an investment trust. While an investment company as defined in this section bears a strong resemblance to other forms of pooled investments funds such as unit trusts and investment companies with variable capital (ICVC), there are two important differences. First, a section 833 investment company is a closed-end fund, meaning that the capital of such a company can only be adjusted by following the standard procedures set by company law. This is not the case for unit trusts or open-ended investment companies,[21] which are open-ended funds and can adjust their capital (through the process of creation and redemption of units) according to the demand for investment in the fund. Second, a section 833 investment company

---

[17] Amended by the Companies Act 2006 (Amendment of Part 23) (Investment Companies) Regulations 2012, SI 2012/952, reg 2(4).

[18] Subsections (b), (c), and (d) deleted by the Companies Act 2006 (Amendment of Part 23) (Investment Companies) Regulations 2012, SI 2012/952, reg 2(5)(c).

[19] Subsections (b), (c), and (d) deleted by the Companies Act 2006 (Amendment of Part 23) (Investment Companies) Regulations 2012, SI 2012/952, reg 2(6).

[20] Companies Act 2006 (Commencement No 5, Transitional Provisions and Savings) Order 2007, SI 2007/3495, art 3.

[21] These companies ('OEICs' in the EC regulatory scheme) are referred to as 'ICVCs' (investment companies with variable capital) in the UK.

does not fall within the definition of a 'collective investment scheme' for the purposes of the Financial Services and Markets Act 2000,[22] with the result that the Financial Services authority is not involved in authorizing or supervising such a company.[23]

**23.833.03**   The restriction on distribution of capital profits previously contained in this section was removed as part of the package of measures in SI 2012/952 that liberalized the operation of investment companies. Thus capital profits are now in principle available for distribution so long as they are realized (see section 830).

**23.833.04**   Subsection (3) provides that an investment company need not be prohibited by its memorandum or articles from redeeming or purchasing its own shares in accordance with Part 18 out of its capital profits. This relaxation of the rule in subsection (2)(c) was introduced in 1999[24] in response to concern that investment companies were unable to take effective action to reduce the 'discount' at which the shares of such companies typically traded by comparison with their net asset value. The relaxation allows investment companies to redeem and purchase shares from distributable profits as defined for the purposes of section 830, meaning that realized capital profits can be used for that purpose.

### 834 Investment company: condition as to holdings in other companies

**23.834.01**   [...][25]

### 835 Power to extend provisions relating to investment companies

**23.835.01**   [...][26]

## Chapter 2
## Justification of Distribution by Reference to Accounts

### *Justification of distribution by reference to accounts*

### 836 Justification of distribution by reference to relevant accounts

**23.836.01**

(1) Whether a distribution may be made by a company without contravening this Part, and the amount of a distribution that may be so made, is determined by reference to the following items as stated in the relevant accounts—
   (a) profits, losses, assets and liabilities;
   (b) provisions of the following kinds—
       (i) where the relevant accounts are Companies Act accounts, provisions of a kind specified for the purposes of this subsection by regulations under section 396;
       (ii) where the relevant accounts are IAS accounts, provisions of any kind;
   (c) share capital and reserves (including undistributable reserves).

(2) The relevant accounts are the company's last annual accounts, except that—
   (a) where the distribution would be found to contravene this Part by reference to the company's last annual accounts, it may be justified by reference to interim accounts, and
   (b) where the distribution is proposed to be declared during the company's first accounting reference period, or before any accounts have been circulated in respect of that period, it may be justified by reference to initial accounts.

(3) The requirements of—
   section 837 (as regards the company's last annual accounts),
   section 838 (as regards interim accounts), and
   section 839 (as regards initial accounts),
   must be complied with, as and where applicable.

---

[22] See the definition of a collective investment scheme in s 235 and the 'carve out' for funds organized as companies other than OEICs in Art 21 of the FSMA 2000 (Collective Investment Schemes) Order 2001, SI 2001/1062.

[23] If a s 833 investment company becomes a listed company, as many do (in the form of 'investment trusts'), the listing regime under FSMA 2000 will become applicable in the normal way.

[24] By the Companies Act 1985 (Investment Companies) (Distribution of Profits) Regulations 1999, SI 1999/2770.

[25] Section 834 was repealed by the Companies Act 2006 (Amendment of Part 23) (Investment Companies) Regulations 2012, SI 2012/952, reg 2(7).

[26] Section 835 was repealed by the Companies Act 2006 (Amendment of Part 23) (Investment Companies) Regulations 2012, SI 2012/952, reg 2(7).

(4)  If any applicable requirement of those sections is not complied with, the accounts may not be relied on for the purposes of this Part and the distribution is accordingly treated as contravening this Part.

COMMENCEMENT DATE  6 April 2008[27]

This section consolidates the provisions previously contained in section 270 of the Companies Act 1985. It deals with the issue of whether a distribution may be made by a company without contravening this Part. Subsection (1) sets out the items in a company's accounts by reference to which the permissible amount of a distribution is determined.    **23.836.02**

Subsection (2) sets out the principle that the relevant accounts for this purpose are the last annual accounts except when (a) reference only to those accounts would result in a contravention of this Part, in which case reference may be made to interim accounts (eg when the last annual accounts show less distributable profit than a proposed distribution but subsequent interim accounts show an adequate distributable profit); or (b) a distribution is proposed to be declared during the company's first accounting reference period or before any accounts are laid in respect of that period, in which case reference may be made to initial accounts.    **23.836.03**

Subsection (4) provides that the relevant section (837, 838, or 839) is treated as contravened in the case of a distribution unless the statutory requirements about the relevant accounts (in this and the following sections) are complied with in relation to that distribution. This means that even if the substance of the relevant sections is complied with, contravention of the requirements relating to relevant accounts will result in the distribution being unlawful. Moreover, it is not open to the members to waive the requirements relating to relevant accounts: see *Precision Dippings v Precision Dippings Marketing Ltd.*[28]    **23.836.04**

*Requirements applicable in relation to relevant accounts*

### 837  Requirements where last annual accounts used

(1)  The company's last annual accounts means the company's individual accounts—    **23.837.01**
    (a)  that were last circulated to members in accordance with section 423 (duty to circulate copies of annual accounts and reports), or
    (b)  if in accordance with section 426 the company provided a summary financial statement instead, that formed the basis of that statement.
(2)  The accounts must have been properly prepared in accordance with this Act, or have been so prepared subject only to matters that are not material for determining (by reference to the items mentioned in section 836(1)) whether the distribution would contravene this Part.
(3)  Unless the company is exempt from audit and the directors take advantage of that exemption, the auditor must have made his report on the accounts.
(4)  If that report was qualified—
    (a)  the auditor must have stated in writing (either at the time of his report or subsequently) whether in his opinion the matters in respect of which his report is qualified are material for determining whether a distribution would contravene this Part, and
    (b)  a copy of that statement must—
        (i)  in the case of a private company, have been circulated to members in accordance with section 423, or
        (ii)  in the case of a public company have been laid before the company in general meeting.
(5)  An auditor's statement is sufficient for the purposes of a distribution if it relates to distributions of a description that includes the distribution in question, even if at the time of the statement it had not been proposed.

COMMENCEMENT DATE  6 April 2008[29]

This section consolidates the provisions previously contained in section 271 of the Companies Act 1985. It sets out the statutory requirements which apply when a company's last annual accounts constitute the only accounts relevant under section 836.    **23.837.02**

Subsection (2) permits some deviation from the principle that the accounts should have been properly prepared under the Act. Items that are not material for determining if there has been a breach of section 836(1) are ignored in determining if accounts are properly prepared for the purposes of this section.    **23.837.03**

---

[27]  Companies Act 2006 (Commencement No 5, Transitional Provisions and Savings) Order 2007, SI 2007/ 3495, art 3.
[28]  [1986] Ch 447.
[29]  Companies Act 2006 (Commencement No 5, Transitional Provisions and Savings) Order 2007, SI 2007/ 3495, art 3.

Subsection (3) requires the auditor to have made his report on the accounts unless the company is exempt from audit and the directors take advantage of that exemption. Subsection (4) provides that in the case of a 'qualified report', the auditors must also have stated in writing (either at the time of their report or subsequently) whether, in their opinion, the matter in respect of which their report is qualified is material for determining whether a distribution would contravene this Part. A copy of the relevant part of the report must have been laid before the company in general meeting in the case of a public company or, in the case of a private company, circulated to members in accordance with section 423.

**23.837.04**    Subsection (5) provides that a statement under subsection (4) may provide that a qualification to an audit report is not material for a future distribution of any description which includes that particular distribution, even if at the time of the statement such a distribution has not been proposed.

### 838  Requirements where interim accounts used

**23.838.01**
(1)  Interim accounts must be accounts that enable a reasonable judgment to be made as to the amounts of the items mentioned in section 836(1).

(2)  Where interim accounts are prepared for a proposed distribution by a public company, the following requirements apply.

(3)  The accounts must have been properly prepared, or have been so prepared subject to matters that are not material for determining (by reference to the items mentioned in section 836(1)) whether the distribution would contravene this Part.

(4)  'Properly prepared' means prepared in accordance with sections 395 to 397 (requirements for company individual accounts), applying those requirements with such modifications as are necessary because the accounts are prepared otherwise than in respect of an accounting reference period.

(5)  The balance sheet comprised in the accounts must have been signed in accordance with section 414.

(6)  A copy of the accounts must have been delivered to the registrar.

Any requirement of Part 35 of this Act as to the delivery of a certified translation into English of any document forming part of the accounts must also have been met.

COMMENCEMENT DATE  6 April 2008[30]

**23.838.02**    This section set out the statutory requirements in respect of interim accounts prepared for a proposed distribution by a public company. Company law does not require a company to prepare interim accounts, but there are two reasons why such accounts might be prepared: first, if the company is a listed company it will be required to prepare such accounts even if no distribution is proposed;[31] and second, a company may wish to prepare such accounts so as to be able to make a distribution if the distribution cannot be made on the basis of the previous annual accounts.

**23.838.03**    Subsection (3) follows the same approach as section 837(2) while subsection (4) permits such modifications to the accounts as are necessary to reflect the fact that interim accounts are not prepared in respect of an accounting reference period. There is, however, no equivalent in this section to section 837(3), as there is no requirement for interim accounts to be audited.[32] However, subsection (6) requires a copy of the interim accounts to have been delivered to the registrar of companies.

### 839  Requirements where initial accounts used

**23.839.01**
(1)  Initial accounts must be accounts that enable a reasonable judgment to be made as to the amounts of the items mentioned in section 836(1).

(2)  Where initial accounts are prepared for a proposed distribution by a public company, the following requirements apply.

(3)  The accounts must have been properly prepared, or have been so prepared subject to matters that are not material for determining (by reference to the items mentioned in section 836(1)) whether the distribution would contravene this Part.

(4)  'Properly prepared' means prepared in accordance with sections 395 to 397 (requirements for company individual accounts), applying those requirements with such modifications as are necessary because the accounts are prepared otherwise than in respect of an accounting reference period.

(5)  The company's auditor must have made a report stating whether, in his opinion, the accounts have been properly prepared.

---

[30] Companies Act 2006 (Commencement No 5, Transitional Provisions and Savings) Order 2007, SI 2007/3495, art 3.

[31] See UKLA Listing Rule LR 9.9.1R.

[32] See UKLA Listing Rules, LR 9.9.1R. Note that if the interim accounts are audited, the auditors' report must be reproduced in full in the interim report: LR 9.9.9R.

(6) If that report was qualified—

    (a) the auditor must have stated in writing (either at the time of his report or subsequently) whether in his opinion the matters in respect of which his report is qualified are material for determining whether a distribution would contravene this Part, and

    (b) a copy of that statement must [have been laid before the company in general meeting[a]].

(7) A copy of the accounts, of the auditor's report and of any auditor's statement must have been delivered to the registrar.

Any requirement of Part 35 of this Act as to the delivery of a certified translation into English of any of those documents must also have been met.

AMENDMENTS

    [a] Amended by the Companies Act 2006 (Consequential Amendments, Transitional Provisions and Savings) Order 2009, SI 2009/1941, art 2(1), Sch 1, para 260(4).

COMMENCEMENT DATE 6 April 2008[33]

This section consolidates the provisions previously contained in section 273 of the Companies Act **23.839.02** 1985. It deals with the statutory requirements in respect of initial accounts prepared for a proposed distribution by a public company. Subsection (3) follows sections 837(2) and 838(3) in requiring that the accounts are 'properly prepared'. Subsection (5) requires that the company's auditors must have made a report stating whether, in their opinion, the accounts have been properly prepared. Subsection (6) requires that if the auditor's report is qualified, the auditor must also state in writing whether, in his opinion, the matter in respect of which his report is qualified is material for determining whether the distribution would contravene this Part. A copy of that statement must have been laid before the company in general meeting.

Subsection (7) requires that a copy of the accounts, of the auditor's report under subsection (5), and of **23.839.03** the auditor's statement (if any) under subsection (6) must have been delivered to the registrar of companies.

## *Application of provisions to successive distributions etc*

## 840 Successive distributions etc by reference to the same accounts

(1) In determining whether a proposed distribution may be made by a company in a case where— **23.840.01**

    (a) one or more previous distributions have been made in pursuance of a determination made by reference to the same relevant accounts, or

    (b) relevant financial assistance has been given, or other relevant payments have been made, since those accounts were prepared,

    the provisions of this Part apply as if the amount of the proposed distribution was increased by the amount of the previous distributions, financial assistance and other payments.

(2) The financial assistance and other payments that are relevant for this purpose are—

    (a) financial assistance lawfully given by the company out of its distributable profits;

    (b) financial assistance given by the company in contravention of section 678 or 679 (prohibited financial assistance) in a case where the giving of that assistance reduces the company's net assets or increases its net liabilities;

    (c) payments made by the company in respect of the purchase by it of shares in the company, except a payment lawfully made otherwise than out of distributable profits;

    (d) payments of any description specified in section 705 (payments apart from purchase price of shares to be made out of distributable profits).

(3) In this section 'financial assistance' has the same meaning as in Chapter 2 of Part 18 (see section 677).

(4) For the purpose of applying subsection (2)(b) in relation to any financial assistance—

    (a) 'net assets' means the amount by which the aggregate amount of the company's assets exceeds the aggregate amount of its liabilities, and

    (b) 'net liabilities' means the amount by which the aggregate amount of the company's liabilities exceeds the aggregate amount of its assets,

    taking the amount of the assets and liabilities to be as stated in the company's accounting records immediately before the financial assistance is given.

---

[33] Companies Act 2006 (Commencement No 5, Transitional Provisions and Savings) Order 2007, SI 2007/ 3495, art 3.

(5) For this purpose a company's liabilities include any amount retained as reasonably necessary for the purposes of providing for any liability—
  (a) the nature of which is clearly defined, and
  (b) which is either likely to be incurred or certain to be incurred but uncertain as to amount or as to the date on which it will arise.

COMMENCEMENT DATE 6 April 2008[34]

**23.840.02**  This section consolidates the provisions previously contained in section 274 of the Companies Act 1985. It deals with two or more distributions (including those listed in subsection (2)) that are made by reference to a single set of relevant accounts. It provides that in this case, a proposed distribution is increased by the amount of previous distributions for the purposes of applying the provisions of this Part.

**23.840.03**  Subsection (2) makes clear that the reference to distributions in subsection (1) includes several forms of financial assistance and some payments made by a company in respect of the purchase of its own shares. The rationale for inclusion of these distributions is that they are either made from distributable profits, which is the same 'fund' from which distributions can be drawn, or that they are analogous to a distribution in that they reduce the net assets of the company and therefore pose a threat to the interests of creditors.

# CHAPTER 3
## SUPPLEMENTARY PROVISIONS

### *Accounting matters*

### 841 Realised losses and profits and revaluation of fixed assets

**23.841.01**
(1) The following provisions have effect for the purposes of this Part.
(2) The following are treated as realised losses—
  (a) in the case of Companies Act accounts, provisions of a kind specified for the purposes of this paragraph by regulations under section 396 (except revaluation provisions);
  (b) in the case of IAS accounts, provisions of any kind (except revaluation provisions).
(3) A 'revaluation provision' means a provision in respect of a diminution in value of a fixed asset appearing on a revaluation of all the fixed assets of the company, or of all of its fixed assets other than goodwill.
(4) For the purpose of subsections (2) and (3) any consideration by the directors of the value at a particular time of a fixed asset is treated as a revaluation provided—
  (a) the directors are satisfied that the aggregate value at that time of the fixed assets of the company that have not actually been revalued is not less than the aggregate amount at which they are then stated in the company's accounts, and
  (b) it is stated in a note to the accounts—
    (i) that the directors have considered the value of some or all of the fixed assets of the company without actually revaluing them,
    (ii) that they are satisfied that the aggregate value of those assets at the time of their consideration was not less than the aggregate amount at which they were then stated in the company's accounts, and
    (iii) that accordingly, by virtue of this subsection, amounts are stated in the accounts on the basis that a revaluation of fixed assets of the company is treated as having taken place at that time.
(5) Where—
  (a) on the revaluation of a fixed asset, an unrealised profit is shown to have been made, and
  (b) on or after the revaluation, a sum is written off or retained for depreciation of that asset over a period,
  an amount equal to the amount by which that sum exceeds the sum which would have been so written off or retained for the depreciation of that asset over that period, if that profit had not been made, is treated as a realised profit made over that period.

COMMENCEMENT DATE 6 April 2008[35]

**23.841.02**  This section consolidates the provisions previously found in section 275 of the Companies Act 1985. It provides for the identification of realized losses and profits by reference to assets in the 'relevant

---

[34] Companies Act 2006 (Commencement No 5, Transitional Provisions and Savings) Order 2007, SI 2007/3495, art 3.
[35] Companies Act 2006 (Commencement No 5, Transitional Provisions and Savings) Order 2007, SI 2007/3495, art 3.

accounts' (see section 836). This carries implications for the identification of distributable profits under section 830 since both realized profits and losses must be included in the computation of distributable profits.

Subsection (1) requires, in the case of Companies Acts accounts, certain provisions to be treated as realized losses. Such provisions include those for depreciation and contingent liabilities that are likely to be incurred or certain to be incurred but uncertain as to amount or as to the date on which it will arise (eg the cost of recalling faulty products or paying compensation to buyers). In the case of accounts prepared under International Financial Reporting Standards (IAS accounts), provisions of any kind (other than revaluation provisions) must be treated as realized losses. Subsection (3) makes clear that the revaluation provisions being referred to in this section are provisions in respect of a diminution in value of a fixed asset appearing on a revaluation of all the fixed assets of the company, or all of its fixed assets other than goodwill. **23.841.03**

Subsection (4) provides for what can be termed a 'deemed revaluation' of the company's assets. This is not an actual valuation but operates when the directors have considered the value of fixed assets of the company and are satisfied that their aggregate value at the time in question is not less than the aggregate amount at which they are for the time being stated in the company's accounts. Such a 'deemed revaluation' can be considered to be a revaluation for the purposes of subsections (2) and (3) and can therefore have the effect of creating a profit available for distribution. **23.841.04**

Subsection (5) deals with the situation in which an unrealized profit arises following a revaluation of a fixed asset, and at the same time or subsequently a provision is made for depreciation of that asset. Such a situation might arise if, for example, a company's policy was to depreciate its plant and machinery on a 'straight line' basis over 10 years. If the original cost of the plant were 100, a depreciation provision of 10 would be made each year. If, in year 5 (with the plant now valued at 60 in the balance sheet), the plant were revalued at 80, then this section allows a realized profit of 10 to be recognized. The realized profit is the amount by which the revaluation (20) exceeds the sum retained or written off for depreciation (10). **23.841.05**

## 842 Determination of profit or loss in respect of asset where records incomplete

In determining for the purposes of this Part whether a company has made a profit or loss in respect of an asset where— **23.842.01**

(a)  there is no record of the original cost of the asset, or

(b)  a record cannot be obtained without unreasonable expense or delay,

its cost is taken to be the value ascribed to it in the earliest available record of its value made on or after its acquisition by the company.

COMMENCEMENT DATE 6 April 2008[36]

This section consolidates the provision previously contained in section 275(3) of the Companies Act 1985. **23.842.02**

## 843 Realised profits and losses of long-term insurance business

(1)  The provisions of this section have effect for the purposes of this Part as it applies in relation to an authorised insurance company [other than an insurance special purpose vehicle][a] carrying on long-term business. **23.843.01**

(2)  An amount included in the relevant part of the company's balance sheet that—

(a)  represents a surplus in the fund or funds maintained by it in respect of its long term business, and

(b)  has not been allocated to policy holders or, as the case may be, carried forward unappropriated in accordance with asset identification rules made under section 142(2) of the Financial Services and Markets Act 2000 (c. 8),

is treated as a realised profit.

(3)  For the purposes of subsection (2)—

(a)  the relevant part of the balance sheet is that part of the balance sheet that represents accumulated profit or loss;

(b)  a surplus in the fund or funds maintained by the company in respect of its long term business means an excess of the assets representing that fund or those funds over the liabilities of the company attributable to its long term business, as shown by an actuarial investigation.

(4)  A deficit in the fund or funds maintained by the company in respect of its long-term business is treated as a realised loss.

---

[36]  Companies Act 2006 (Commencement No 5, Transitional Provisions and Savings) Order 2007, SI 2007/3495, art 3.

For this purpose a deficit in any such fund or funds means an excess of the liabilities of the company attributable to its long term business over the assets representing that fund or those funds, as shown by an actuarial investigation.

(5) Subject to subsections (2) and (4), any profit or loss arising in the company's long term business is to be left out of account.

(6) For the purposes of this section an 'actuarial investigation' means an investigation made into the financial condition of an authorised insurance company in respect of its long term business—

(a) carried out once in every period of twelve months in accordance with rules made under Part 10 of the Financial Services and Markets Act 2000, or

(b) carried out in accordance with a requirement imposed under section 166 of that Act,

by an actuary appointed as actuary to the company.

(7) In this section 'long-term business' means business that consists of effecting or carrying out contracts of long-term insurance.

This definition must be read with section 22 of the Financial Services and Markets Act 2000, any relevant order under that section and Schedule 2 to that Act.

[(8) In this section insurance special purpose vehicle means a special purpose vehicle within the meaning of Article 2.1(p) of Directive 2005/68/EC of the European Parliament and of the Council of 16 November 2005 on reinsurance and amending Council Directives 73/239/EEC, 92/49/EEC as well as Directives 98/78/EC and 2002/83/EC.][b]

AMENDMENTS AND NOTES

[a] Amended by the Reinsurance Directive Regulations 2007 (SI 2007/3253).

[b] Inserted by the Reinsurance Directive Regulations 2007, SI 2007/3253.

COMMENCEMENT DATE 6 April 2008[37]

**23.843.02**   This section consolidates the provisions previously contained in section 268 of the Companies Act 1985. It makes special provision for insurance companies with long-term business as regards their distributable profits. The need for such provision arises from the method by which profits within a life fund are attributed to policyholders on the one hand and members of the company on the other.[38] Normally the articles of such a company stipulate the proportion of profits that are attributable to policyholders (whose premiums constitute the fund) and shareholders respectively. Profits are identified through the calculation of actuarial surplus (or deficit), which represents essentially the difference between the value of the fund and the present value of all liabilities (future claims on the fund by policyholders). The effect of this section is that an actuarial surplus or deficit within a long-term fund is to be treated as either a realized profit (and therefore in principle available for distribution or as a loss). The limiting effect of the section is that an actuarial investigation (as defined in subsection (6)) is required to identify a surplus before any distribution is made. This carries implications in particular for listed companies who wish to distribute interim dividends but undertake actuarial valuations on an annual basis: in these circumstances, it will only be possible to make an interim distribution when there is sufficient distributable surplus carried forward from the last valuation.

## 844  Treatment of development costs

**23.844.01**   (1) Where development costs are shown or included as an asset in a company's accounts, any amount shown in respect of those costs is treated—

(a) for the purposes of section 830 (distributions to be made out of profits available for the purpose) as a realised loss, and

(b) for the purposes of section 832 (distributions by investment companies out of accumulated revenue profits) as a realised revenue loss.

This is subject to the following exceptions.

(2) Subsection (1) does not apply to any part of that amount representing an unrealised profit made on revaluation of those costs.

(3) Subsection (1) does not apply if—

(a) there are special circumstances in the company's case justifying the directors in deciding that the amount there mentioned is not to be treated as required by subsection (1),

(b) it is stated—

(i) in the case of Companies Act accounts, in the note required by regulations under section 396 as to the reasons for showing development costs as an asset, or

(ii) in the case of IAS accounts, in any note to the accounts,

that the amount is not to be so treated, and

---

[37] Companies Act 2006 (Commencement No 5, Transitional Provisions and Savings) Order 2007, SI 2007/3495, art 3.

[38] In the case of a mutual life company, the members are the policyholders, but in other cases policyholders are not automatically members.

    (c)  the note explains the circumstances relied upon to justify the decision of the directors to that effect.

COMMENCEMENT DATE  6 April 2008[39]

This section consolidates the provisions previously contained in section 269 of the Companies Act **23.844.02** 1985. It deals with the issue of how development costs should be treated for the purpose of distributions. The rationale for inclusion of such costs as an asset in the company's balance sheet is that the cost is an investment made by the company that will yield at least an equivalent revenue return over time. However, from the perspective of distributions, the concern is that if that expectation is not fulfilled, the company may be left without sufficient assets to cover creditors' claims as a result of distributions having been made to members based on the recognition of development costs as assets rather than (in conventional accounting terms) as costs in the profit and loss account.

Subsection (1) provides that where development costs are shown as an asset in a company's accounts, **23.844.03** any amount shown in respect of those costs is to be treated under section 830 as a realized loss and under section 832 as a realized revenue loss. The result is that, for the purpose of dividend distributions, development costs must be counted as a loss for the purpose of calculating distributable profits. This avoids the risk associated with classifying those costs as assets, referred to above.

Subsection (2) establishes an exception to the rule established in subsection (1), which does not apply **23.844.04** to any part of development costs that represent an unrealized profit made on revaluation of those costs.

Another exception is provided by subsection (3), which provides that subsection (1) does not apply if **23.844.05** the directors decide that there are special circumstances that justify departure from the rule. In this case, the notes to the accounts must record that the amount is not treated according to subsection (1) and explain the circumstances relied upon to justify the decision of the directors to that effect.

## Distributions in kind

### 845  Distributions in kind: determination of amount

(1)  This section applies for determining the amount of a distribution consisting of or including, or **23.845.01** treated as arising in consequence of, the sale, transfer or other disposition by a company of a non-cash asset where—
    (a)  at the time of the distribution the company has profits available for distribution, and
    (b)  if the amount of the distribution were to be determined in accordance with this section, the company could make the distribution without contravening this Part.
(2)  The amount of the distribution (or the relevant part of it) is taken to be—
    (a)  in a case where the amount or value of the consideration for the disposition is not less than the book value of the asset, zero;
    (b)  in any other case, the amount by which the book value of the asset exceeds the amount or value of any consideration for the disposition.
(3)  For the purposes of subsection 1(a) the company's profits available for distribution are treated as increased by the amount (if any) by which the amount or value of any consideration for the disposition exceeds the book value of the asset.
(4)  In this section 'book value', in relation to an asset, means—
    (a)  the amount at which the asset is stated in the relevant accounts, or
    (b)  where the asset is not stated in those accounts at any amount, zero.
(5)  The provisions of Chapter 2 (justification of distribution by reference to accounts) have effect subject to this section.

COMMENCEMENT DATE  6 April 2008[40]

This section applies for the purpose of determining the amount of a distribution where it takes the form **23.845.02** of the disposition of a non-cash asset. It was introduced to remove doubts arising from the case of *Aveling Barford Ltd v Perion Ltd*[41] over whether a transfer of an asset to members amounts to a distribution. For the section to apply, the company must have profits available for distribution and if the amount of the distribution were determined in accordance with this section, the company could make a distribution without contravening this Part. If those requirements are not met the distribution will be illegal. This preserves the position as determined in *Aveling Barford*,[42] holding that

---

[39]  Companies Act 2006 (Commencement No 5, Transitional Provisions and Savings) Order 2007, SI 2007/ 3495, art 3.
[40]  Companies Act 2006 (Commencement No 5, Transitional Provisions and Savings) Order 2007, SI 2007/ 3495, art 3.
[41]  [1989] BCLC 626.
[42]  Ibid.

a distribution at an undervalue when the company has no distributable profits is illegal. The consequences of an illegal distribution are governed by section 847.

**23.845.03** Subsection (2)(b) provides that when the book value of the asset (in the 'relevant accounts') exceeds the amount or the value of the consideration for the disposition, the amount of the distribution is the excess. For example a distribution to members of an asset shown in the relevant accounts at 100 would be treated as a distribution of 100 if there is no consideration paid for the disposition. Where the book value is equal to or less than any consideration received by the company the value of the distribution is zero (subsection (2)(a)).

**23.845.04** Subsection (3) provides that, in calculating distributable profits, the amount, if any, by which the amount or value of the consideration for the disposition exceeds the book value of the asset, is treated as profit. So, in the above example, if the distribution to members were in the form of a sale of property for which the company received consideration of 120, its distributable profits would be increased by 20.

### 846 Distributions in kind: treatment of unrealised profits

**23.846.01**
(1) This section applies where—
   (a) a company makes a distribution consisting of or including, or treated as arising in consequence of, the sale, transfer or other disposition by the company of a non-cash asset, and
   (b) any part of the amount at which that asset is stated in the relevant accounts represents an unrealised profit.
(2) That profit is treated as a realised profit—
   (a) for the purpose of determining the lawfulness of the distribution in accordance with this Part (whether before or after the distribution takes place), and
   (b) for the purpose of the application, in relation to anything done with a view to or in connection with the making of the distribution, of any provision of regulations under section 396 under which only realised profits are to be included in or transferred to the profit and loss account.

COMMENCEMENT DATE 6 April 2008[43]

**23.846.02** This section consolidates the provisions previously contained in section 276 of the Companies Act 1985. It makes special provision for distributions other than in the form of cash. It provides in essence that where such a distribution (or any part of it) represents an unrealized profit in the relevant accounts, that profit is to be treated as a realized profit for determining the lawfulness of the distribution. It is also to be so treated for the purposes of determining whether a transfer of the profit can be made to the profit and loss account in connection with the distribution. It is normally only realized profits that can be transferred to the profit and loss account and distributed.

## Consequences of unlawful distribution

### 847 Consequences of unlawful distribution

**23.847.01**
(1) This section applies where a distribution, or part of one, made by a company to one of its members is made in contravention of this Part.
(2) If at the time of the distribution the member knows or has reasonable grounds for believing that it is so made, he is liable—
   (a) to repay it (or that part of it, as the case may be) to the company, or
   (b) in the case of a distribution made otherwise than in cash, to pay the company a sum equal to the value of the distribution (or part) at that time.
(3) This is without prejudice to any obligation imposed apart from this section on a member of a company to repay a distribution unlawfully made to him.
(4) This section does not apply in relation to—
   (a) financial assistance given by a company in contravention of section 678 or 679, or
   (b) any payment made by a company in respect of the redemption or purchase by the company of shares in itself.

COMMENCEMENT DATE 6 April 2008[44]

**23.847.02** This section consolidates the provisions previously contained in section 277 of the Companies Act 1985. Subsection (2) provides that a member who knows or has reasonable grounds to believe that a distribution or part of it is unlawful is liable to repay it or that part of it, but it does not specify any

---

[43] Companies Act 2006 (Commencement No 5, Transitional Provisions and Savings) Order 2007, SI 2007/3495, art 3.
[44] Companies Act 2006 (Commencement No 5, Transitional Provisions and Savings) Order 2007, SI 2007/3495, art 3.

further consequences of an improper dividend. Whether or not a distribution is unlawful is determined in the first instance by reference to the definition of distributable profits in section 830. Furthermore, a distribution must be justified by reference to the relevant accounts (see section 836) and it is not possible to look behind those accounts to determine if distributable profits exist.[45] This remedy does not apply to any unlawful financial assistance given to members in contravention of section 678 or section 679 or to payments in respect of the redemption or purchase of a company's own shares.

Subsection (3) makes clear that the additional remedies provided by the common law in respect of a dividend paid out of capital will apply to a payment illegal under the Act. Thus directors are liable to compensate the company if they know or should know that a distribution is illegal.[46] However, the courts have recognized that in circumstances where directors act honestly and reasonably and in reliance on the advice of auditors, they may benefit from exemption from liability under section 1157 (previously section 727 of the Companies Act 1985). That exemption will be available only where the directors are not implicated in the falsification of the accounts[47] and where exemption will not result in the enrichment of directors (as a result of the distribution) at the expense of creditors.[48]

**23.847.03**

Any member can restrain a proposed illegal distribution by injunction,[49] but a member who has knowingly received such a distribution cannot bring a derivative action against the directors,[50] and will be liable to account to the company as a constructive trustee.[51] It is not possible for the members to ratify an illegal distribution or absolve directors from their liability in making such a distribution.[52] Rather curiously, perhaps, a creditor has no *locus standi* to restrain an illegal distribution, unless he has an enforceable security which is thereby put in jeopardy.[53] His only remedy is to seek a winding-up.

**23.847.04**

## *Other matters*

### 848 Saving for certain older provisions in articles

(1) Where immediately before the relevant date a company was authorised by a provision of its articles to apply its unrealised profits in paying up in full or in part unissued shares to be allotted to members of the company as fully or partly paid bonus shares, that provision continues (subject to any alteration of the articles) as authority for those profits to be so applied after that date.

(2) For this purpose the relevant date is—
    (a) for companies registered in Great Britain, 22nd December 1980;
    (b) for companies registered in Northern Ireland, 1st July 1983.

**23.848.01**

COMMENCEMENT DATE 6 April 2008[54]

This section consolidates the provision previously contained in section 278 of the Companies Act 1985. The background to this provision is that the capitalization of undistributed profits (whether realized or unrealized), although not a distribution for the purposes of section 829, requires express sanction in the memorandum or articles. As regards companies that have adopted the standard articles in Table A,[55] Article 110 provides such authorization. For companies that are governed by the Model Articles[56] made under the 2006 Act, similar provision is made by Article 36 in the case of private companies and

**23.848.02**

---

[45] *Bairstow and Others v Queens Moat Houses plc* [2001] 2 BCLC 531, CA. However, in the case of a share issue at an undervalue, the effect of *Progress Property Co Ltd v Moore and another* [2009] EWCA Civ 629 (CA), affirmed on appeal at [2010] UKSC 55, appears to be that it is not necessary to demonstrate that there are distributable profits. In those circumstances there is no distribution if the parties genuinely believe that the share issue is not at an undervalue. (See also the annotation to s 830 above).

[46] See eg *Flitcroft's Case* (1882) 21 Ch D 519 and *Bairstow and Others v Queens Moat Houses plc* [2001] 2 BCLC 531, CA.

[47] *Bairstow and Others v Queens Moat Houses plc* [2001] 2 BCLC 531, [65]–[66], per Walker LJ.

[48] In *Re Marini Ltd* [2004] BCC 172, the court declined to exercise its discretion to exempt directors from liability for an unlawful distribution, despite concluding that they acted honestly following advice from the company's auditor, on the basis that it would result in a depletion of the assets of the company available to creditors of the company, which was in the hands of a liquidator.

[49] See eg *Hoole v Great Western Railway Co* (1867) 3 Ch App 262.

[50] *Towers v African Tug Co* [1904] 1 Ch 558.

[51] *Precision Dippings Ltd v Precision Dippings Marketing Ltd* [1985] 3 WLR 812, CA.

[52] *Aveling Barford Ltd v Perion* [1989] BCLC 626.

[53] *Mills v Northern Railway of Buenos Aires* (1870) 5 Ch App 621.

[54] Companies Act 2006 (Commencement No 5, Transitional Provisions and Savings) Order 2007, SI 2007/3495, art 3.

[55] Table A contained in The Companies (Tables A to F) Regulations 1985 (SI 1985/805).

[56] These articles were made under the authority conferred by section 19(1) of the Companies Act 2006 and are contained in The Companies (Model Articles) Regulations 2008, SI 2008/3229.

Article 78 in the case of public companies. Those provisions permit the company to capitalize any undivided profits not required for paying any preferential dividend (whether or not they are available for distribution) or any sum standing to the credit of the company's share premium account or capital redemption reserve. They may then appropriate the capitalized sum to the members who would have been entitled to it by way of dividend, by issuing fully paid-up bonus shares to them. If the capitalization is of distributable profits, it can also be used to fund the issue of fully paid-up debentures and to pay up, wholly or partly, any amount owing on hitherto partly paid-up shares.[57]

**23.848.03**   The effect of this section is that pre-Companies Act 1980 provisions in a company's articles empowering a company to apply unrealized profits in paying up bonus shares remain effective, whenever the relevant shares are issued.

### 849  Restriction on application of unrealised profits

**23.849.01**   A company must not apply an unrealised profit in paying up debentures or any amounts unpaid on its issued shares.

COMMENCEMENT DATE 6 April 2008[58]

**23.849.02**   This section consolidates the provision previously contained in section 263(4) of the Companies Act 1985. The differing treatment of debentures by comparison with bonus shares (see section 848 above) can be justified on the basis that debentures represent a new and different type of claim against the company, whereas bonus shares represent an accounting restatement of a shareholder's claim that does not change the economic value of the claim (because shareholders' net assets remain the same after a bonus issue).

### 850  Treatment of certain older profits or losses

**23.850.01**   (1)  Where the directors of a company are, after making all reasonable enquiries, unable to determine whether a particular profit made before the relevant date is realised or unrealised, they may treat the profit as realised.
(2)  Where the directors of a company, after making all reasonable enquiries, are unable to determine whether a particular loss made before the relevant date is realised or unrealised, they may treat the loss as unrealised.
(3)  For the purposes of this section the relevant date is—
(a)  for companies registered in Great Britain, 22nd December 1980;
(b)  for companies registered in Northern Ireland, 1st July 1983.

COMMENCEMENT DATE 6 April 2008[59]

**23.850.02**   This section consolidates the provision previously found in section 263(5) of the Companies Act 1985.

### 851  Application of rules of law restricting distributions

**23.851.01**   (1)  Except as provided in this section, the provisions of this Part are without prejudice to any rule of law restricting the sums out of which, or the cases in which, a distribution may be made.
(2)  For the purposes of any rule of law requiring distributions to be paid out of profits or restricting the return of capital to members—
(a)  section 845 (distributions in kind: determination of amount) applies to determine the amount of any distribution or return of capital consisting of or including, or treated as arising in consequence of the sale, transfer or other disposition by a company of a non-cash asset; and
(b)  section 846 (distributions in kind: treatment of unrealised profits) applies as it applies for the purposes of this Part.
(3)  In this section references to distributions are to amounts regarded as distributions for the purposes of any such rule of law as is referred to in subsection (1).

COMMENCEMENT DATE 6 April 2008[60]

**23.851.02**   This section consolidates and extends part of the provisions previously contained in section 281 of the Companies Act 1985. It makes clear that the provisions of this Part are without prejudice to any rule of law restricting the sums out of which, or the cases in which, a distribution may be made. Sections 845

---

[57]  The option to pay up unpaid shares is not applicable to a private company (and is not included in art 36) as the concept of unpaid capital is not recognized in the Model Articles for Private Companies Limited by Shares.
[58]  Companies Act 2006 (Commencement No 5, Transitional Provisions and Savings) Order 2007, SI 2007/3495, art 3.
[59]  Companies Act 2006 (Commencement No 5, Transitional Provisions and Savings) Order 2007, SI 2007/3495, art 3.
[60]  Companies Act 2006 (Commencement No 5, Transitional Provisions and Savings) Order 2007, SI 2007/3495, art 3.

and 846 are relevant, within their field of application, to determining the amount under any rule of law requiring distributions to be paid out of profits or restricting the return of capital to members.

## 852  Saving for other restrictions on distributions

The provisions of this Part are without prejudice to any enactment, or any provision of a company's articles, restricting the sums out of which, or the cases in which, a distribution may be made.     **23.852.01**

COMMENCEMENT DATE  6 April 2008[61]

This section consolidates the remainder of the provisions previously contained in section 281 of the   **23.852.02** Companies Act 1985 (see section 851 above).

## 853  Minor definitions

(1)  The following provisions apply for the purposes of this Part.     **23.853.01**

(2)  References to profit or losses of any description—
    (a)  are to profits or losses of that description made at any time, and
    (b)  except where the context otherwise requires, are to profits or losses of a revenue or capital character.

(3)  'Capitalisation', in relation to a company's profits, means any of the following operations (whenever carried out)—
    (a)  applying the profits in wholly or partly paying up unissued shares in the company to be allotted to members of the company as fully or partly paid bonus shares, or
    (b)  transferring the profits to capital redemption reserve.

(4)  References to 'realised profits' and 'realised losses', in relation to a company's accounts, are to such profits or losses of the company as fall to be treated as realised in accordance with principles generally accepted at the time when the accounts are prepared, with respect to the determination for accounting purposes of realised profits or losses.

(5)  Subsection (4) is without prejudice to—
    (a)  the construction of any other expression (where appropriate) by reference to accepted accounting principles or practice, or
    (b)  any specific provision for the treatment of profits or losses of any description as realised.

(6)  'Fixed assets' means assets of a company which are intended for use on a continuing basis in the company's activities.

COMMENCEMENT DATE  6 April 2008[62]

This section provides definitions for this Part.     **23.853.02**

---

[61] Companies Act 2006 (Commencement No 5, Transitional Provisions and Savings) Order 2007, SI 2007/3495, art 3.
[62] Companies Act 2006 (Commencement No 5, Transitional Provisions and Savings) Order 2007, SI 2007/3495, art 3.

# 24

## A COMPANY'S ANNUAL RETURN

---

## Companies Act 2006

### PART 24
### A COMPANY'S ANNUAL RETURN

### 854 Duty to deliver annual returns[a]

(1) Every company must deliver to the registrar successive annual returns each of which is made up to a date not later than the date that is from time to time the company's return date.

(2) The company's return date is—

    (a) the anniversary of the company's incorporation, or

    (b) if the company's last return delivered in accordance with this Part was made up to a different date, the anniversary of that date.

(3) Each return must—

    (a) contain the information required by or under the following provisions of this Part, and

    (b) be delivered to the registrar within 28 days after the date to which it is made up.

**24.854.01**

AMENDMENTS

[a] This section applies with modification to LLPs by reg 30 of the Limited Liability Partnerships (Application of Companies Act 2006) Regulations 2009, SI 2009/1804. It applies without modification to unregistered companies by reg 3 of and Sch 1 to the Unregistered Companies Regulations 2009, SI 2009/2436.

COMMENCEMENT DATE 1 October 2009[1]

Sections 854 to 858 provide for the submission by registered companies of an annual return. The annual return is a disclosure document which is delivered to the Registrar of Companies and is thereafter publicly available. The annual return contains very general information about the company, its activities, and its officers and directors, and more detailed information about a company's share capital, the members of the company, and their shareholdings. Some of this information may be available from other public documents filed with the Registrar of Companies, for example, if the company has recently filed a statement of capital details of the company's share capital will be available therein. The advantage of the annual return is that it brings together this information in one document which is up-to-date as of the date of the return. Companies House publishes regularly updated information about the annual return requirements in guidance booklet GP2 Life of a Company-Part 1 Annual

**24.854.02**

---

[1] Companies Act 2006 (Commencement No 8, Transitional Provisions and Savings) Order 2008, SI 2008/2860, art 3(m).

Requirements.[2] A fee is payable for filing the annual return.[3] Sections 854 to 858 apply to annual returns made up to a date on or after 1 October 2009.[4, 5]

**24.854.03**    Section 854 restates and amends subsection 363(1) of the Companies Act 1985. The provision provides that a company must deliver an annual return which contains the prescribed information up to a date which is no later than the 'return date'. The return date is either the anniversary of the date when the company was incorporated or the anniversary of the date up to which the previous year's annual report was made, provided that such annual return was delivered in accordance with the Act. The annual return must be delivered within 28 days of the date it is made up to. Notable amendments from the 1985 Act are the absence of a prescribed form for the annual return (section 363(2)(a) of the 1985 Act) and that section 854 does not require a director or officer to sign the return as was required by section 363(1) of the Companies Act 1985. The information required to be included in the annual return is set forth in sections 855 and 856 of the 2006 Act.

**24.854.04**    The failure to file a return can result in the commission of an offence (see section 858 below). In addition, the failure to file a return may be a ground to strike the company off the Company Register (see Part 31, Chapter 1 of the 2006 Act). Persistent failure to deliver a return could be a ground to disqualify a person from acting as a director pursuant to section 3 of the Company Directors Disqualification Act 1986 and is relevant to a determination of unfitness to act as a director pursuant to that Act (Schedule 1, Part 1, paragraph 4).

### 855 Contents of annual return: general[a]

**24.855.01**    (1) Every annual return must state the date to which it is made up and contain the following information—
    (a) the address of the company's registered office;
    (b) the type of company it is and its principal business activities;
    (c) [the required particulars (see section 855A)][a] of—
      (i) the directors of the company, and
      (ii) in the case of a private company with a secretary or a public company, the secretary or joint secretaries;
    [(d) if any company records are (in accordance with regulations under section 1136) kept at a place other than the company's registered office, the address of that place and the records that are kept there;][b, c]
    (2) The information as to the company's type must be given by reference to the classification scheme prescribed for the purposes of this section.
    (3) The information as to the company's principal business activities may be given by reference to one or more categories of any prescribed system of classifying business activities.
    [(4) In this Part—
      'DTR5 issuer' means an issuer to which Chapter 5 of the Disclosure Rules and Transparency Rules sourcebook issued by the Financial Services Authority applies;][d]
      ['relevant market' means any of the markets mentioned in article 4(1) of the Financial Services and Markets Act 2000 (Prescribed Markets and Qualifying Investments) Order 2001;][e] and
      'return period', in relation to an annual return, means the period beginning immediately after the date to which the last return was made up (or, in the case of the first return, with the incorporation of the company) and ending with the date to which the return is made up.

AMENDMENTS AND NOTES

[a] This section applies with modification to LLPs by reg 30 of the Limited Liability Partnerships (Application of Companies Act 2006) Regulations 2009, SI 2009/1804. It applies with modification to unregistered companies by reg 3 of and Sch 1 to the Unregistered Companies Regulations 2009, SI 2009/2436.

---

  [2] See ⟨http://www.companieshouse.gov.uk/about/gbhtml/gp2.shtml⟩ (last accessed 5 October 2012). In respect of LLPs see ⟨http://www.companieshouse.gov.uk/about/gbhtml/gpllp2.shtml⟩ (last accessed 5 October 2012).

  [3] Registrar of Companies ( Fees) ( Companies, Overseas Companies and Limited Liability Partnerships) Regulations 2012, SI 2012/ 1907.

  [4] Companies Act 2006 (Commencement No 8, Transitional Provisions and Savings) Order 2008, SI 2008/ 2860, Sch 2, para 81.

  [5] Annual returns made up to a prior date are governed by the Companies Act 1985 and applicable secondary legislation, including the Companies Act 1985 (Annual Return) and Companies (Principal Business Activities) (Amendment) Regulations 2008, SI 2008/1659.

b   Amended by the Companies Act 2006 (Annual Return and Service Addresses) Regulations 2008, SI
    2008/3000, reg 2.

c   Inserted by the Companies Act 2006 (Annual Return and Service Addresses) Regulations 2008, SI
    2008/3000, reg 3.

d   Inserted by the Companies Act 2006 (Annual Return and Service Addresses) Regulations 2008, SI
    2008/3000, reg 4. Legislation is due to come into force in 2013 under which the Financial Services
    Authority's role and responsibilities will be assumed by two new authorities: the Financial Conduct
    Authority and Prudential Regulation Authority. Each authority will have its own Handbook, into
    which the current FSA Handbook, with amendments, will be subsumed.

e   Inserted by the Companies Act 2006 (Annual Returns) Regulations 2011 reg 2.

f   Inserted by the Companies Act 2006 (Annual Returns) Regulations 2011 reg 2.

COMMENCEMENT DATE  1 October 2009[6]

## [855A  Required particulars of directors and secretaries[a]

(1)  For the purposes of section 855(1)(c) the required particulars of a director are—                **24.855A.01**
    (a)  where the director is an individual, the particulars required by section 163 to be entered in the
        register of directors (subject to subsection (2) below); and
    (b)  where the director is a body corporate or a firm that is a legal person under the law by which
        it is governed, the particulars required by section 164 to be entered in the register of
        directors.
(2)  The former name of a director who is an individual is a required particular in relation to an annual
    return only if the director was known by the name for business purposes during the return period.
(3)  For the purposes of section 855(1)(c)(ii) the required particulars of a secretary are—
    (a)  where a secretary is an individual, the particulars required by section 277 to be entered in the
        register of secretaries (subject to subsection (4) below); and
    (b)  where a secretary is a body corporate or a firm that is a legal person under the law by which
        it is governed, the particulars required by section 278(1) to be entered in the register of
        secretaries.
(4)  The former name of a secretary who is an individual is a required particular in relation to an annual
    return only if the secretary was known by the name for business purposes during the return
    period.
(5)  Where all the partners in a firm are joint secretaries, the required particulars are the particulars
    that would be required to be entered in the register of secretaries if the firm were a legal person
    and the firm had been appointed secretary.][b]

AMENDMENTS AND NOTES

a   This section applies with modification to LLPs by reg 30 of the Limited Liability Partnerships
    (Application of Companies Act 2006) Regulations 2009, SI 2009/1804. It applies to unregistered
    companies by reg 3 of and Sch 1 to the Unregistered Companies Regulations 2009, SI 2009/2436.

b   Inserted by the Companies Act 2006 (Annual Return and Service Addresses) Regulations 2008, SI
    2008/3000, reg 2.

COMMENCEMENT DATE  1 October 2009[7]

Section 855 of the Act restates and amends section 364 of the Companies Act 1985. This provision sets     **24.855A.02**
forth the general information which must be provided in the annual return. This includes the address
of the company's registered office, what type of company it is, for example, whether it is a private
company limited by shares or a public company limited by shares, and the company's principal
business activities. The Companies Act 2006 (Annual Return and Service Addresses) Regulations 2008
provide for company type and business activity classifications. Pursuant to regulation 6, as amended by
the Companies Act 2006 (Annual Returns) Regulations 2011, the business activity classification should
be made according to the UK Standard Industrial Classification of Economic Activities 207 prepared
by the Office for National Statistics and published by Palgrave Macmillan. The listing of principal
business activities in the annual return does not restrict the company to undertaking only those
activities.[8]

---

    [6] Companies Act 2006 (Commencement No 8, Transitional Provisions and Savings) Order 2008, SI 2008/
2860, art 3(m).
    [7] Companies Act 2006 (Commencement No 8, Transitional Provisions and Savings) Order 2008, SI 2008/
2860, art 3(m).
    [8] MB *Inspection Ltd v Hi-Rope Ltd* [2010] RPC 18; *Zurich Insurance Co v Zurich Investments Ltd* [2011] RPC 6.

**24.855A.03**   With regard to the information about directors and officers, section 855 makes reference to the required particulars. With regard to these particulars, the Companies Act 2006 (Annual Return and Service Addresses) Regulations 2008 amended the Act by inserting section 855A. This provides that the annual return information is the same information as set forth in the register of directors and the register of secretaries. Please refer to the commentary on sections 163, 164, 277 and 278 of the Act in this regard.

**24.855A.04**   Section 855 also provides that where the register of members and/or of debenture holders are not available for inspection at the company's registered office, then the annual return must provide the address of where they are available for inspection.

## 856 Contents of annual return: information about [shares and] share capital [ . . . ]ª

**24.856.01**
(1) The annual return of a company having a share capital must also contain the following information.
(1A) The return must contain a statement of capital[b]
(2) The statement of capital must state with respect to the company's share capital at the date to which the return is made up—
    (a) the total number of shares of the company,
    (b) the aggregate nominal value of those shares,
    (c) for each class of shares—
        (i) [the voting rights][c] attached to the shares,
        (ii) the total number of shares of that class, and
        (iii) the aggregate nominal value of shares of that class, and
    (d) the amount paid up and the amount (if any) unpaid on each share (whether on account of the nominal value of the share or by way of premium).
(2A) The annual return must also state whether any of the company's shares were, at any time during the return period, shares admitted to trading on a relevant market or on any other market which is outside the United Kingdom.
(2B) If any of the company's shares were shares admitted to trading as mentioned in subsection (2A), the annual return must also state whether both of the following conditions were satisfied throughout the return period—
    (a) there were shares of the company which were shares admitted to trading on a relevant market;
    (b) the company was a DTR5 issuer.[d]
    [ . . . ][e]

AMENDMENTS AND NOTES

ª   This section applies to unregistered companies by reg 3 of and Sch 1 to the Unregistered Companies Regulations 2009, SI 2009/2436. The words inserted were done so by the Companies Act 2006 (Annual Returns) Regulations 2011, reg 3. The deleted words were repealed by the Companies Act 2006 (Annual Return and Service Addresses) Regulations 2008, SI 2008/3000, reg 7.

b   Amended by the Companies Act 2006 (Annual Returns) Regulations 2011 reg 3.

c   Amended by the Companies Act 2006 (Annual Return and Service Addresses) Regulations 2008, SI 2008/3000, reg 7.

d   Inserted by the Companies Act 2006 (Annual Returns) Regulations 2011 reg 3.

e   Repealed by the Companies Act 2006 (Annual Return and Service Addresses) Regulations 2008, SI 2008/3000, reg 7.

COMMENCEMENT DATE 1 October 2009[9]

## [856A Contents of annual return: information about shareholders: non-traded companies

**24.856A.01**
(1) This section applies to the annual return of a company none of whose shares were, at any time during the return period, shares admitted to trading on a relevant market or on any other market which is outside the United Kingdom.[a]
(2) The return must [also][b] contain the name (as it appears in the company's register of members) of every person who was a member of the company at any time during the return period.
    The return must conform to the following requirements for the purpose of enabling the entries relating to any given person to be easily found—
    (a) the entries must be listed in alphabetical order by name; or

---

9   Companies Act 2006 (Commencement No 8, Transitional Provisions and Savings) Order 2008, SI 2008/2860, art 3(m).

    (b)  the return must have annexed to it an index that is sufficient to enable the name of the person in question to be easily found.

(3)  The return must also state—

    (a)  the number of shares of each class held at the end of the date to which the return is made up by each person who was a member of the company at that time,

    (b)  the number of shares of each class transferred during the return period by or to each person who was a member of the company at any time during that period, and

    (c)  the dates of registration of those transfers.

(4)  If either of the two immediately preceding returns has given the full particulars required by subsections (2) and (3), the return need only give such particulars as relate—

    (a)  to persons who became, or ceased to be, members during the return period, and

    (b)  to shares transferred during that period.][c]

AMENDMENTS AND NOTES

[a]  Inserted by the Companies Act 2006 (Annual Returns) Regulations 2011 reg 4.

[b]  Inserted by the Companies Act 2006 (Annual Returns) Regulations 2011 reg 4.

[c]  Inserted by the Companies Act 2006 (Annual Return and Service Addresses) Regulations 2008, SI 2008/3000, reg 7.

COMMENCEMENT DATE  1 October 2009[10]

## [856B  *Contents of annual return: information about shareholders: certain traded companies*[a]

(1)  This section applies to the annual return of a company any of whose shares were, at any time during the return period, shares admitted to trading on a relevant market or on any other market which is outside the United Kingdom.                                                          **24.856B.01**

(2)  But this section does not apply to the annual return of a company if throughout the return period—

    (a)  there were shares of the company which were shares admitted to trading on a relevant market, and

    (b)  the company was a DTR5 issuer.

(3)  The annual return of a company to which this section applies must also state, in respect of each person who held at least 5% of the issued shares of any class of the company at the end of the date to which the return is made up—

    (a)  the person's name and address (as they appear in the company's register of members); and

    (b)  the number of shares of each class held by the person at that time.

(4)  The return must conform to the following requirements for the purpose of enabling entries relating to any given person to be easily found—

    (a)  the entries must be listed in alphabetical order by name; or

    (b)  the return must have annexed to it an index that is sufficient to enable the name of the person in question to be easily found.][b]

AMENDMENTS AND NOTES

[a]  This section applies to unregistered companies by reg 3 of and Sch 1 to the Unregistered Companies Regulations 2009, SI 2009/2436.

[b]  Inserted by the Companies Act 2006 (Annual Return and Service Addresses) Regulations 2008, SI 2008/3000, reg 7.

COMMENCEMENT DATE  1 October 2009[11]

Sections 856, 856A and 856B restate and amend section 364A of the Companies Act 1985. The sections    **24.856B.02**
specify the information that the company must provide about its share capital and its shareholders.

The company's annual return must contain a statement of capital which is up-to-date as of the date the    **24.856B.03**
return is made up. The statement of capital must provide detailed information on the number of the
company's shares, the classes of shares, the aggregate nominal value of the shares as a whole as well as
for each class of share, and the amount paid and unpaid on each share. Following the abolition of the

---

[10]  Companies Act 2006 (Commencement No 8, Transitional Provisions and Savings) Order 2008, SI 2008/2860, art 3(m) and Companies Act 2006 (Annual Return and Service Addresses) Regulations 2008, SI 2008/3000, reg 1.

[11]  Companies Act 2006 (Commencement No 8, Transitional Provisions and Savings) Order 2008, SI 2008/2860, art 3(m) and Companies Act 2006 (Annual Return and Service Addresses) Regulations 2008, SI 2008/3000, reg 1.

concept of authorized share capital and, therefore, the distinction between authorized and issued share capital, the statement of capital refers only to the shares of the company. In relation to each class, the statement must provide information on the voting rights that attach to each class.

**24.856B.04**   Sections 856A and 856B require that the return contain prescribed information on the members of the company. The extent of the prescribed information varies depending on whether or not the company is traded on a relevant market (as defined in section 855) or is an issuer that must comply with the FSA's Disclosure Rules and Transparency Rules Sourcebook ('DTR 5 Issuer'). If the company is not traded on a relevant market then the annual return must provide details of all names of persons who were members during the return period (defined in section 855(4), as amended) and details of number of shares held by each person who was a member at the end of the return period. On the other hand, if the company is traded on a relevant market and is *not* a DTR 5 Issuer then these disclosure obligations only apply to all members who hold more than five per cent of issued shares of any class of the company's shares. In relation to such companies the disclosure requirement relates to the name and address of the relevant members, whereas for a company not traded on a relevant market the disclosure of only the name is required. Note, in relation to companies which are not traded on a relevant market, that if either of the two preceding annual returns provided this information then, in the alternative, the company can simply provide information on those persons who ceased to be or became members or five per cent members, respectively.

### 857 Contents of annual return: power to make further provision by regulations

**24.857.01**   (1)  The Secretary of State may by regulations make further provision as to the information to be given in a company's annual return.
(2)  The regulations may—
   (a)  amend or repeal the provisions of sections 855 and 856, and
   (b)  provide for exceptions from the requirements of those sections as they have effect from time to time.
(3)  Regulations under this section are subject to negative resolution procedure.

COMMENCEMENT DATE 1 October 2009[12]

**24.857.02**   Section 857 restates and amends section 365(1) and (2) of the Companies Act 1985. This section provides authority for the Secretary of State to make regulations amending or repealing sections 855 and 856 of the Companies Act 2006. As detailed above, this power was exercised through the Companies Act 2006 (Annual Return and Service Addresses) Regulations 2008 and Companies Act 2006 (Annual Returns) Regulations 2011. Section 857 enables regulations to amend the content of the annual return but does not enable the regulations to alter the duty to deliver a return (section 854) or the implications of the failure to deliver a return (section 858). In addition, the regulations may provide for exceptions from the obligations set forth in sections 855 and 856. This power to except was not provided in section 365 of the 1985 Act.

### 858 Failure to deliver annual return[a]

**24.858.01**   (1)  If a company fails to deliver an annual return before the end of the period of 28 days after a return date, an offence is committed by—
   (a)  the company,
   (b)  subject to subsection (4)—
     (i)  every director of the company, and
     (ii)  in the case of a private company with a secretary or a public company, every secretary of the company, and
   (c)  every other officer of the company who is in default.
[For this purpose a shadow director is treated as a director.][b]
(2)  A person guilty of an offence under subsection (1) is liable on summary conviction to a fine not exceeding level 5 on the standard scale and, for continued contravention, a daily default fine not exceeding one-tenth of level 5 on the standard scale.
(3)  The contravention continues until such time as an annual return made up to that return date is delivered by the company to the registrar.
(4)  It is a defence for a director or secretary charged with an offence under subsection (1)(b) to prove that he took all reasonable steps to avoid the commission or continuation of the offence.
(5)  In the case of continued contravention, an offence is also committed by every officer of the company who did not commit an offence under subsection (1) in relation to the initial contravention but is in default in relation to the continued contravention. A person guilty of an offence

---

[12] Companies Act 2006 (Commencement No 8, Transitional Provisions and Savings) Order 2008, SI 2008/2860, art 3(m). However, the power to make Regulations came into force at an earlier date (20 January 2007): Companies Act 2006 (Commencement No 1, Transitional Provisions and Savings) Order 2006/3428, art 3(3).

under this subsection is liable on summary conviction to a fine not exceeding one-tenth of level 5 on the standard scale for each day on which the contravention continues and he is in default.

AMENDMENTS AND NOTES

<sup>a</sup> This section applies with modification to LLPs by reg 30 of the Limited Liability Partnerships (Application of Companies Act 2006) Regulations 2009, SI 2009/1804. It applies to unregistered companies by reg 3 of and Sch 1 to the Unregistered Companies Regulations 2009, SI 2009/2436.

<sup>b</sup> Inserted by the Companies Act 2006 (Annual Return and Service Addresses) Regulations 2008, SI 2008/3000, reg 8.

COMMENCEMENT DATE  1 October 2009[13]

Section 858 restates and amends section 363(3) and (4) of the Companies Act 1985. It provides that the  **24.858.02** company, directors (including shadow directors), other officers in default, and company secretaries are guilty of an offence and liable to a fine if the return is not delivered within 28 days of the return date. Subsection (3) provides a reasonable steps defence for a director or company secretary in relation to the original failure to deliver with 28 days. Where no offence was committed by an officer in relation to the original failure to deliver, if he is in default in relation to the continued contravention he is guilty of an offence.

## 859  Application of provisions to shadow directors [ . . . ]<sup>a</sup>

AMENDMENTS  **24.859.01**

<sup>a</sup> Repealed by the Companies Act 2006 (Annual Return and Service Addresses) Regulations 2008, SI 2008/3000, reg 8.

---

[13]  Companies Act 2006 (Commencement No 8, Transitional Provisions and Savings) Order 2008, SI 2008/2860, art 3(m).

# 25

## COMPANY CHARGES

## Companies Act 2006

### PART 25
### COMPANY CHARGES

The provisions relating to company charges amount to a substantive re-enactment of the old provisions found in Part XII, Chapter 1, sections 395 to 409 of the Companies Act 1985. However, there are minor changes in the new Act and the contents of the old sections have been re-arranged, perhaps in an attempt to be user friendly. The most notable addition to the new provisions is that they have been **25.0.01**

5<br>

extended to embrace charges created by companies registered in Northern Ireland which was previously governed by a separate regime.[1] A notable omission in the new Act is that the company charge provisions no longer expressly extend so as to cover charges on property created, or acquired by, companies incorporated outside Great Britain but which have an established place of business in England and Wales.[2] It should be noted that the previous attempt to reform this area by virtue of the Companies Act 1989, Part IV, sections 93 to 107 was never brought into force and has now been repealed.[3] The 'new' sections relating to charge registration are based on the 1985 Act alone.

**25.0.02**   A public register of company charges has been in existence since 1900. The purpose of establishing the register was to provide a means by which the public could ascertain, independent of the company, which, if any, of its assets were encumbered by certain types of security charge.[4] Therefore, the 'mischief'[5] of companies being able to create successive charges over the same property in favour of different creditors could be prevented. In other cases, especially in relation to unsecured creditors, the public register would allow them to assess the creditworthiness of the company by ascertaining its net worth minus any property encumbered by security charge.[6]

**25.0.03**   There have been several attempts to reform company charges in recent years. The most important of these recommendations came in 1989 by virtue of the Diamond Report[7] and, more recently: in 2002 by virtue of Law Commission Consultation Paper No 164;[8] and in 2004 Law Commission Consultation Paper No 176;[9] and, finally, in 2005 with Law Commission Report No 296.[10] However, none of these measures found favour with the Government and are not reflected (to any substantive degree) in the new Act.[11] The need for reform has not escaped judicial notice, and problems with the current regime have led one senior judge to remark that 'this is an unsatisfactory area of law' such that a new 'structured personal property security legislation' may be desirable.[12] However, the Government is presently considering the need to amend this area and the registration provisions may be revised in the near future.[13] The following sections of the Act in relation to company charges all come into force on 1 October 2009.[14]

---

[1]   See Companies Act (CA) 2006, ss 861(3) definition of 'company' and 1284. It should be noted that a separate regime (albeit under the CA) still exists with regard to Scottish companies; on which see Part 25, Ch 2, ss 878–892 discussed below. However, it should be noted that the government are currently considering proposals which would integrate the system such that it applied equally to both jurisdictions; see commentary to s 894 below.

[2]   See: CA 1985, s 409; *Slavenburg's Bank v Intercontinental Natural Resources Ltd* [1980] 1 WLR 1076. However, by virtue of s 1052 the Secretary of State has power to make regulations concerning company charges insofar as they affect overseas registered companies. A charge registration scheme similar to that imposed by ss 860–892 now also applies to overseas companies by virtue of the Overseas Companies (Execution of Documents and Registration of Charges) Regulations 2009, SI 2009/1917 as amended by the 2011 Amendment Regulations, see SI 2011/2194.

[3]   See CA 2006, s 1295 and Sch 16.

[4]   See *Esberger & Son Ltd v Capital and Counties Bank* [1913] 2 Ch 366, 374, per Sargant J.

[5]   See *Re Yolland, Husson and Birkett Ltd* [1908] 1 Ch 152, 156, *per* Cozens-Hardy MR. Note also *Smith v Bridgend County Borough Council* [2001] UKHL 58 at [19], *per* Lord Hoffmann.

[6]   See *Smith v Bridgend County Council* [2001] UKHL 58 at [19], *per* Lord Hoffmann who questions whether this aim was 'a realistic form of protection and whether the choice of registrable charges was entirely logical'.

[7]   See the Report *A Review of Security Interests in Property* (London, DTI, 1989) Chairman Professor AL Diamond. Regard should also be had to the Crowther Report at Part 5; see Report of the Committeee on Consumer Credit *Consumer Credit* (1971) Cmnd 4396 (London, HMSO, 1971) Chairman Lord Crowther.

[8]   See *Registration of Security Interests: Company Charges and Property other than Land* (London, TSO, 2002).

[9]   See *Company Security Interests: A Consultative Report* (London, TSO, 2004); see further McCormack (2005) 68 MLR 286.

[10]   See *Company Security Interests* Cm 6654 (London, TSO, 2005).

[11]   For background discussion of the 1985 provisions see de Lacy, Chapter 15, in John de Lacy (ed) *The Reform of United Kingdom Company Law* (London, Cavendish Publishing, 2002).

[12]   See *National Westminster Bank plc v Spectrum plus Ltd* [2004] EWCA Civ 670, [99], *per* Lord Phillips MR. For a comprehensive treatment of the need to revise UK security interest law in relation to personal property security assignments, see John de Lacy (ed), *The Reform of UK Personal Property Security Law: Comparative Perspectives* (London, Routledge-Cavendish, 2010).

[13]   See further the commentary to s 894 below.

[14]   See the Companies Act 2006 (Commencement No 8, Transitional Provisions and Savings) Order 2008, SI 2008/2860, art 3(n). The Act only applies to charges created after 1 October 2009; all charges created previous to this date will remain governed by CA 1985.

# Chapter 1
## Companies Registered in England and Wales or in Northern Ireland
### Requirement to register company charges

## 860  Charges created by a company[a]

(1)  A company that creates a charge to which this section applies must deliver the prescribed particulars of the charge, together with the instrument (if any) by which the charge is created or evidenced, to the registrar for registration before the end of the period allowed for registration.

(2)  Registration of a charge to which this section applies may instead be effected on the application of a person interested in it.

(3)  Where registration is effected on the application of some person other than the company, that person is entitled to recover from the company the amount of any fees properly paid by him to the registrar on registration.

(4)  If a company fails to comply with subsection (1), an offence is committed by—
   (a)  the company, and
   (b)  every officer of it who is in default.

(5)  A person guilty of an offence under this section is liable—
   (a)  on conviction on indictment, to a fine;
   (b)  on summary conviction, to a fine not exceeding the statutory maximum.

(6)  Subsection (4) does not apply if registration of the charge has been effected on the application of some other person.

(7)  This section applies to the following charges—
   (a)  a charge on land or any interest in land, other than a charge for any rent or other periodical sum issuing out of land,
   (b)  a charge created or evidenced by an instrument which, if executed by an individual, would require registration as a bill of sale,
   (c)  a charge for the purposes of securing any issue of debentures,
   (d)  a charge on uncalled share capital of the company,
   (e)  a charge on calls made but not paid,
   (f)  a charge on book debts of the company,
   (g)  a floating charge on the company's property or undertaking,
   (h)  a charge on a ship or aircraft, or any share in a ship,
   (i)  a charge on goodwill or on any intellectual property.

**25.860.01**

Amendments and Notes

[a]  Section 860 also applies (with appropriate modifications) to LLPs by virtue of the Limited Liability Partnerships (Application of Companies Act 2006) Regulations 2009, SI 2009/1804, Pt 9.

Commencement Date  1 October 2009[15]

This section replaces sections 395(1), 396(1), and 399 of the Companies Act 1985 in providing for the registration of certain types of company charge. A duty is imposed upon the chargor company and its relevant officer/s to deliver the 'prescribed particulars'[16] of the charge together with the instrument creating the charge (if there is one) to the registrar within the prescribed time limit[17] (ie registration) otherwise the charge will become void against certain parties. Avoidance can only ever come into play if the 'prescribed particulars' are not sent to the registrar of companies for registration by the company; it does not matter if, in fact, the registrar fails to register those particulars so long as they are supplied in the first place.[18] Failure to deliver the prescribed particulars within the required time limit will also render the chargor company (and its relevant officer/s) liable to a fine.[19] For these purposes the 'prescribed particulars' are:[20]

**25.860.02**

---

[15]  Companies Act 2006 (Commencement No 8, Transitional Provisions and Savings) Order 2008, SI 2008/2860, art 3(n).

[16]  On which see s 869 below.

[17]  See further s 870 below on the time periods for registration.

[18]  See: *National Provincial and Union Bank of England v Charnley* [1924] 1 KB 431, at 447, *per* Scrutton LJ; *Slavenburg's Bank v Intercontinental Natural Resources Ltd* [1980] 1 WLR 1076, at 1086C, *per* Lloyd J. This in fact happened in *First City Corp Ltd v Downsview Nominees Ltd* [1990] 3 NZLR 265 (New Zealand CA); affirmed, sub nom, *Downsview Nominees Ltd v First City Corp. Ltd* [1993] AC 295, PC.

[19]  On which see s 860(4) and (5).

[20]  See Companies (Particulars of Company Charges) Regulations 2008, SI 2008/2996. The 'prescribed particulars' remain the same under the new Act as under the former Companies Act 1985.

(a) the date of the creation of the charge;

(b) a description of the instrument (if any) creating or evidencing the charge;

(c) the amount secured by the charge;

(d) the name and address of the person entitled to the charge; and

(e) short particulars of the property charged.

**25.860.03**   In practice the importance of the section falls upon the chargee as beneficiary of the charge because if registration is not made on time the chargee will face the possibility of having their security charge avoided. The latter point is recognized by the section because although it places a duty upon the chargor company it also allows a person interested in the charge (in practice the chargee) to effect registration in place of the chargor[21] and that person will be able to recover from the chargor any fees payable in respect of the registration.[22] If registration is made by some other person then the chargor and its officer/s will also be relieved of the financial penalty for default.[23]

**25.860.04**   The section requires all transactions creating a type of charge listed[24] to be registered. Therefore, oral charges of a type listed require registration and it is not confined to those charges created by an instrument.[25] The section only applies to consensual charges of the type expressly listed in the Act by virtue of subsection (7)(a) to (i); any type of charge which is not listed will not require registration under the section and will not be liable to avoidance. Therefore, many types of company property which are routinely subject to charge security interests are immune from the registration requirement such as charges over shares[26] or insurance policies.[27] Because the Act only requires consensual charges of a type listed to be registered it follows that charges arising by operation of law are automatically excluded from the registration requirement.[28] A further significant limitation on the ambit of the registration provisions concerns the fact that they do not apply to quasi-security interests. In this situation because the debtor ('chargor') has no proprietary right to convey to his creditor ('chargee') by way of security then no charge interest is recognized by the law. This has meant that common finance-raising devices, such as retention of title clauses,[29] hire purchase agreements,[30] chattel leases, and Quistclose trusts[31] have all escaped the registration scheme despite the fact that their existence imperils a proper credit rating of the company and means that the register of charges is, by its very nature, a somewhat limited tool in assessing the financial wellbeing of a company. The Act only applies to security interests operating by way of 'charge' and, although this has been extended so as to cover security arising by way of mortgage,[32] it does not cover possessory security interests such as the pledge[33] or lien.[34] However, the Act will apply to purchase money security (pms)

---

[21] See s 860(2).

[22] See s 860(3).

[23] See s 860(6).

[24] On which see s 860(7).

[25] See: *Re CL Nye Ltd* [1971] Ch 442,466C, *per* Harman LJ.; *Sun Tai Cheung Credits Ltd v Attorney-General* [1987] 1 WLR 948, PC.

[26] See *Re Sugar Properties (Derisly Wood) Ltd* [1988] BCLC 146.

[27] See *Paul & Frank Ltd v Discount Bank (Overseas) Ltd* [1967] Ch 348.

[28] See *London & Cheshire Insurance Co Ltd v Laplagrene Property Co Ltd* [1971] 1 Ch 499.

[29] See *Clough Mill Ltd v Martin* [1985] 1 WLR 110; *Armour v Thyssen Edelstahlwerke AG* [1991] AC 339. However, although at one time it appeared as if these clauses would provide an excellent and far-ranging finance device (ie in the immediate aftermath of the Court of Appeal decision in the case of *Aluminium Industrie Vaassen BV v Romalpa Aluminium Ltd* [1976] 1 WLR 676) the courts have since proved hostile to *Romalpa* clauses as they became known, and it now appears as if such clauses will only escape the need to register them as security charges under the Act if the seller of goods seeks only to use the clause to recover his original goods as supplied to the buyer. Any attempt by a seller of goods to use a *Romalpa* clause to claim proceeds of sub-sale (*Tatung (UK) Ltd v Galex Telesure Ltd* (1989) 5 BCC 325), manufactured goods (*Borden (UK) Ltd v Scottish Timber Products Ltd* [1981] Ch 25), or, goods where some form of process has been used on them by the buyer) *Re Peachdart Ltd* [1984] Ch 131), will be classified by the courts as a registrable company charge and the clause will, therefore, be void if it is not registered (as will invariably be the case) under the Act. Only if the goods can be returned to their original condition, without material damage, will a *Romalpa* seller be allowed by the courts to assert his interest so as to recover the goods without his claim being rejected as an unregistered security charge interest under the Act; see *Hendy Lennox Ltd v Graham Puttick Ltd* [1984] 1 WLR 485. For a detailed and critical review of this area see de Lacy (1995) 24 Anglo-American Law Review 327.

[30] See *Stoneleigh Finance Ltd v Phillips* [1965] 2 QB 537.

[31] See *Carreras Rothmans Ltd v Freeman Mathews Treasure Ltd* [1985] Ch 207.

[32] See s 861(5).

[33] See *Barrett & Co Ltd v Livesey* (1981) 131 NLJ 1213.

[34] See *Re Cosslett (Contractors) Ltd* [1998] Ch 495; *Re Hamlet International Ltd* [1999] 2 BCLC 506; *Trident International Ltd v Barlow* [2000] BCC 602.

charges[35] despite the absence of any *scintilla temporis* between the company's acquisition of property and the charging of it in favour of the chargee.[36] The pms charge is purely a priority device given sanction by the courts in order to promote the provision of secured finance by guaranteeing fairness of outcome.[37]

It is a question of law in any given case whether or not a registrable charge has been created. There is 'no    **25.860.05** one clear touchstone by which it can necessarily and inevitably be said that a document' expressed to be an absolute disposition of property is, in reality, a security charge.[38] Nor is the fact that parties have deliberately sought to avoid the registration requirement by adopting a form of financing transaction that does not create a charge, but in effect mimics its nature, affect the issue.[39] Parties are generally free to adopt whatever finance-raising techniques they like so long as they are legal. The effects of the technique they adopt in practice will differ, but these differences do not affect the determination of the type of transaction adopted by them in the first place. Therefore, the identification of a charge interest is to be determined by ordinary methods of interpretation starting by looking at the words used by the parties and then by looking at the general circumstances of the parties at the time of the transaction. In most cases the wording used by parties in their contracts will be sufficient to decide the issue. The identification of a debtor's conveyance of a proprietary interest by way of security to a creditor with the retention of an equity of redemption will be enough to dispose of the issue as disclosing it operates as a charge.[40] However, in a small number of cases it might not be easy to distinguish between an absolute assignment of property and one intended to operate by way of security (ie company charge). In the latter situation it is ultimately for the courts to determine the issue and, in extreme cases, they will not shirk from their task. For example, in one case a retention of title clause was construed by the court (contrary to its express wording) so that property was deemed to have passed to a buyer and then been re-conveyed by way of (registrable) security charge to the seller to cover payment of outstanding obligations between the parties. In reaching this decision the court noted that it did 'violence' to the express wording of the contract under consideration.[41] Such cases have caused much difficulty, and the dividing line between sale and security is not always easy to determine.[42] As a result the certainty that we all strive for in the law can be lost[43] and so-called established practice turned on its head.[44] Even in cases where the issue of establishing the existence of a security interest was clear such problems have also presented themselves regularly. The best example of this is the continuing difficulty in distinguishing between a fixed and floating charge.[45] A recent decision of the House of Lords has had the effect of turning 25 years of established banking practice on its head by classifying (what was believed to be) a 'fixed' charge over a debtor company's book debts in favour of its bank as, in reality, a floating charge.[46] In another case decided in 1985[47] it was decided that the so-called shipowner's lien on sub-freight was a registrable charge on book debts and void for non-registration. This was despite the fact that the general shipping community did not regard it as a charge and certainly had never contemplated the need to register this type of interest. The fact that this type of interest had been around since the 19th century and until 1985 had never been challenged as a registrable interest was to no avail, nor the fact that the judgment would 'come as a shock to those who deal with matters of this kind'.[48] In 1986 the judgment was followed and the equitable lien on sub-freights found to be a floating charge on book debts (if the sub-freights were not in existence at the time of the time charter's execution) which would be void if not registered within 21 days of the charterparty being executed.[49] In 2001 it was found *obiter*

---

[35]  On which see *Abbey National Building Society v Cann* [1991] AC 56; *Whale v Viasystems Technograph Ltd* [2002] EWCA Civ 480.

[36]  See *Stroud Architectural Systems Ltd v John Laing Construction Ltd* [1994] BCC 18; discussed by de Lacy [1994] Conv 242.

[37]  For a comprehensive treatment of this issue see de Lacy [1991] LMCLQ 531.

[38]  See *Welsh Development Agency v Export Finance Co Ltd* [1992] BCC 270, 280B, *per* Dillon LJ.

[39]  See *Welsh Development Agency v Export Finance Co Ltd* [1992] 270, 302H, *per* Staughton LJ.

[40]  See *Swiss Bank Corporation v Lloyds Bank* [1982] AC 584, 594–595, *per* Buckley LJ. Once a security charge has been identified it will then have to be of a type listed by s 860(7) in order to be registrable under the Act.

[41]  See *In re Peachdart Ltd* [1984] Ch 131, 143A, *per* Vinelott J.

[42]  See, eg, *Curtain Dream plc v Churchill Merchanting Ltd* [1990] BCC 341; *Welsh Development Agency v Export Finance Co Ltd* [1992] BCC 270.

[43]  Contrast *Clough Mill Ltd v Martin* [1984] 1 WLR 1067 first instance decision of Judge O'Donoghue holding that a simple retention of title clause is a registrable company charge with the Court of Appeal decision overturning him at [1985] 1 WLR 111.

[44]  See, by way of analogy, *Re Spectrum Plus Ltd* [2005] UKHL 41; *Re Welsh Irish Ferries Ltd* [1986] Ch 471.

[45]  See generally *Re Spectrum Plus Ltd* [2005] UKHL and the authorities there cited.

[46]  *Re Spectrum Plus Ltd* [2005] UKHL.

[47]  See *Re Welsh Irish Ferries Ltd* [1986] Ch 471.

[48]  See *Re Welsh Irish Ferries Ltd* [1986] Ch 471, 480C, *per* Nourse J.

[49]  See *Annangel Glory Compania Naviera SA v Golodetz Ltd* [1988] PCC 37.

by the Privy Council that both these decisions were wrong and the equitable lien on sub-freights is not a registrable company charge.[50] A further area of difficulty is found with the so-called charge-back security interest. In 1986 it was found that an agreement to charge an indebtedness by A to B in favour of B by A is a conceptual impossibility.[51] This decision caused much controversy and again threatened established practice, particularly in banking circles where the practice was common and the priority of a charge-back was potentially imperilled. The debate raged for nearly a decade before the House of Lords established the legality of the practice,[52] although the question of whether such charges are registrable or not remains an open one.[53]

**25.860.06**    It should be noted that many of the types of charge listed as requiring registration under the Companies Act also require registration under other legislation if the relevant charge is to be fully enforceable.[54] This is particularly important as the Companies Act does not seek to regulate priorities of competing charge security interests. Therefore, if a chargee is to have priority they must not only comply with the Companies Act registration provisions but also those laid down in the other legislation. For these purposes the other legislation is in the case of:

(a)    land—registered land, Land Registration Act 1925 (as amended) and, now more rarely, unregistered land, Land Charges Act 1972.[55]

(b)    a charge on a ship or aircraft, or any share in a ship—in respect of a charge over a ship or a share in a ship registration will also have to be made under the Merchant Shipping (Registration etc) Act 1993;—in relation to a charge over an aircraft registration will also have to be made under the Mortgaging of Aircraft Order 1972.[56]

(c)    a charge on intellectual property (or a licence covering it)[57] —in respect of a charge over 'intellectual property' meaning[58] a charge over: a patent;[59] a trade mark;[60] a registered design;[61] copyright or design right; registration will also have to be made under the relevant legislation listed at the accompanying footnote.

**25.860.07**    Certain types of charge are also expressly exempted from other registration provisions or the company charges register:

(a)    A charge created or evidenced by an instrument which, if executed by an individual, would require registration as a bill of sale; this type of charge is exempted from the Bills of Sale Acts 1878–1891.[62]

(b)    A floating charge covering unregistered land is excluded from the land charge register.[63]

---

[50]    See *Agnew v Commissioner of Inland Revenue* [2001] UKPC 28, [39], judgment delivered by Lord Millett.

[51]    See *Re Charge Card Services Ltd* [1987] Ch 150.

[52]    See *Re BCCI (No 8)* [1998] AC 214.

[53]    It is best practice to register such arrangements in order to assure priority and the registrar of companies will accept such charges for registration. Outside banking circles such charges should be registered since the debt will be classified as a charge on book debts. In banking circles it is arguable that such charges do not constitute a charge on book debts; see *Northern Bank Ltd v Ross* [1990] BCC 883; *Re Brightlife Ltd* [1987] Ch 200. In *Re BCCI (No 8)* [1998] AC 214, 227 Lord Hoffmann was cautious on this issue stating that it was for the banks to 'make up their own mind' whether to register charge-backs or not.

[54]    Reference should also be made to s 893 which allows the Secretary of State to make information-sharing arrangements in respect of special registers which is discussed below. For an example of the need for dual registration and the consequences of failure to do so see *Burston Finance Ltd v Speirway Ltd* [1974] 1 WLR 1648 (charge over land registered under Land Registration Act 1925 but chargee failed to register under CA; charge avoided in chargor's liquidation and chargee could not fall back on unpaid vendor's lien).

[55]    A floating charge which covers registered land will also have to be registered at the land registry if it is to be fully effective. Under the Land Registration Act 1925, the floating charge should be registered as a notice or caution against dealing; see ss 49, 54. A floating charge covering unregistered land is excluded from the land charges register by virtue of Land Charges Act 1972, s 3(7). All non-floating charges require dual registration under both the CA and relevant land registration Act. Note also *Re Wallis & Simmonds (Builders) Ltd* [1974] 1 WLR 391 (Equitable deposit of title deeds to land requires registration under CA as a charge over land otherwise it will be liable to be avoided under that Act).

[56]    See SI 1972/1268.

[57]    See s 861(4) below for the meaning of 'intellectual property'.

[58]    By virtue of s 865(4).

[59]    See Patents Act 1977, ss 32–33.

[60]    See Trade Marks Act 1994, s 25.

[61]    See Registered Designs Act 1949, s 19.

[62]    See Bills of Sale Act (1878) Amendment Act 1882, s 17; *Re Standard Manufacturing Co* [1891] 1 Ch 627; *Slavenburg's Bank v Intercontinental Natural Resources Ltd* [1980] 1 WLR 1076, 1098H, *per* Lloyd J.

[63]    See Land Charges Act 1972, s 3(7). Prior to 1970 all charges were excluded from the land charge register by virtue of Land Charges Act 1925, s 10(5); see *Property Discount Corporation Ltd v Lyon Group Ltd* [1981] 1 WLR

(c) The Secretary of State is given power under section 893 to make 'information-sharing arrangements' between the registrar of companies and persons responsible for keeping any 'special
register'.[64] Under this section the Secretary of State is given far-reaching powers to make orders
regulating the registration of company charges which are also covered by a separate register such
that the Secretary of State may order that the charge does not have to be registered on the company
charges register[65] if he is satisfied that certain conditions are met. As yet no such orders have been
made.[66]

### 861  Charges which have to be registered: supplementary[a]

(1) The holding of debentures entitling the holder to a charge on land is not, for the purposes of        **25.861.01**
   section 860(7)(a), an interest in the land.
(2) It is immaterial for the purposes of this Chapter where land subject to a charge is situated.
(3) The deposit by way of security of a negotiable instrument given to secure the payment of book
   debts is not, for the purposes of section 860(7)(f), a charge on those book debts.
(4) For the purposes of section 860(7)(i), 'intellectual property' means—
   (a)  any patent, trade mark, registered design, copyright or design right;
   (b)  any licence under or in respect of any such right.
(5) In this Chapter—
   'charge' includes mortgage, and
   'company' means a company registered in England and Wales or in Northern Ireland.

AMENDMENTS AND NOTES

[a]   Section 861 also applies (with appropriate modifications) to LLPs by virtue of the Limited Liability
   Partnerships (Application of Companies Act 2006) Regulations 2009, SI 2009/1804, Pt 9.

COMMENCEMENT DATE  1 October 2009[67]

This section replaces the former section 396 of the Companies Act 1985. The section provides for   **25.861.02**
additional situations in which certain types of charge will not require registration and also for
definitions of the type of property and company which are covered by the registration scheme.

Subsections (1) and (2) make it clear that the holder of debentures entitling the holder to a charge on   **25.861.03**
land will not have to register that interest as a charge on land;[68] and also makes it clear that for the
purposes of Chapter 1, in the case of a charge over land, it is immaterial where the land subject to a
charge is located. Therefore, the fact that a company may own land located overseas, which it
subsequently charges, is irrelevant with regard to the issue of the need to register that charge in order
that it does not become liable to avoidance.

Subsection (3) preserves the negotiability of a negotiable instrument to secure the payment of book   **25.861.04**
debts by removing the need to register such an instrument as a charge on those book debts, as would
otherwise have been required.[69]

Subsection (4) provides a useful definition of 'intellectual property' and makes clear the types of   **25.861.05**
property that are caught by the registration duty.[70]

Subsection (5) extends the registration duty to cover mortgages as well as charges which are to be   **25.861.06**
treated the same for the purposes of the Chapter. It also limits the application of the Chapter to those
charges created by companies registered in England and Wales or in Northern Ireland.[71] Therefore, a
separate scheme exists for charges created by Scottish companies.[72]

---

300. However, the exclusion was narrowed to only floating charges and charges created before 1970 by virtue of
Law of Property Act 1969, s 26.
   [64]  On which see s 893(1) below.
   [65]  See s 893(3)(a).
   [66]  See generally the commentary of s 893 below.
   [67]  Companies Act 2006 (Commencement No 8, Transitional Provisions and Savings) Order 2008, SI 2008/
2860, art 3(n).
   [68]  The charge will, however, require registration if it secures an issue of debentures; see s 860(7)(c).
   [69]  By virtue of s 860(7)(f). The chargee must ensure that they take actual possession of the negotiable
instrument in order to avoid the need for registration, an agreement for the deposit of such an instrument
without possession is not enough; see *Chase Manhattan Asia Ltd v Official Receiver* [1990] 1 WLR 1181, 1184G,
*per* Lord Templeman.
   [70]  That is the registration duty imposed by s 860(7)(i).
   [71]  This is a new provision including Northern Ireland; previously Northern Ireland was covered by separate
legislation.
   [72]  On which see ss 878–892 below.

### 862 Charges existing on property acquired[a]

**25.862.01**
(1) This section applies where a company acquires property which is subject to a charge of a kind which would, if it had been created by the company after the acquisition of the property, have been required to be registered under this Chapter.
(2) The company must deliver the prescribed particulars of the charge, together with a certified copy of the instrument (if any) by which the charge is created or evidenced, to the registrar for registration.
(3) Subsection (2) must be complied with before the end of the period allowed for registration.
(4) If default is made in complying with this section, an offence is committed by—
    (a) the company, and
    (b) every officer of it who is in default.
(5) A person guilty of an offence under this section is liable—
    (a) on conviction on indictment, to a fine, and
    (b) on summary conviction, to a fine not exceeding the statutory maximum.

AMENDMENTS AND NOTES

[a] Section 862 also applies (with appropriate modifications) to LLPs by virtue of the Limited Liability Partnerships (Application of Companies Act 2006) Regulations 2009, SI 2009/1804, Pt 9.

COMMENCEMENT DATE 1 October 2009[73]

**25.862.02**
Formerly section 400 of the Companies Act 1985. The section applies retroactively to impose a registration duty in situations where a company acquires property that is already subject to a charge at the time of acquisition.[74] However the duty will only apply if the property is subject to the type of charge already listed in section 860(7) and it would have required registration had that company created it in the first place after its acquisition.

**25.862.03**
Failure to comply with the section will render the company acquiring the property and any of its officers responsible for the omission to register liable to a fine. However, in contrast to the situation where the company creates the charge and fails to register it[75] (or someone on their behalf) the charge will not be liable for avoidance by reason only of non-compliance with the section. For the purposes of section 862(2) the 'prescribed particulars' are the same as under section 860(1) with the additional requirement that the date the property subject to the charge is acquired also has to be supplied.[76]

## *Special rules about debentures*

### 863 Charge in series of debentures[a]

**25.863.01**
(1) Where a series of debentures containing, or giving by reference to another instrument, any charge to the benefit of which debenture holders of that series are entitled pari passu is created by a company, it is for the purposes of section 860(1) sufficient if the required particulars, together with the deed containing the charge (or, if there is no such deed, one of the debentures of the series), are delivered to the registrar before the end of the period allowed for registration.
(2) The following are the required particulars—
    (a) the total amount secured by the whole series, and
    (b) the dates of the resolutions authorising the issue of the series and the date of the covering deed (if any) by which the series is created or defined, and
    (c) a general description of the property charged, and
    (d) the names of the trustees (if any) for the debenture holders.
(3) Particulars of the date and amount of each issue of debentures of a series of the kind mentioned in subsection (1) must be sent to the registrar for entry in the register of charges.
(4) Failure to comply with subsection (3) does not affect the validity of the debentures issued.
(5) Subsections (2) to (6) of section 860 apply for the purposes of this section as they apply for the purposes of that section, but as if references to the registration of the charge were a reference to the registration of the series of debentures.

---

[73] Companies Act 2006 (Commencement No 8, Transitional Provisions and Savings) Order 2008, SI 2008/2860, art 3(n).
[74] Ie the company acquiring the property was not responsible for the initial creation of the charge.
[75] On which see ss 860 and 874.
[76] See SI 2008/2996, reg 4.

AMENDMENTS AND NOTES

ª  Section 863 also applies (with appropriate modifications) to LLPs by virtue of the Limited Liability
   Partnerships (Application of Companies Act 2006) Regulations 2009, SI 2009/1804, Pt 9.

COMMENCEMENT DATE  1 October 2009[77]

Formerly section 397(1) of the Companies Act 1985. This section lists the 'required particulars' that   **25.863.02**
have to be delivered to the registrar for registration in respect of an issue of debentures secured by a
charge which the holders of the debentures are entitled *pari passu*. These 'required particulars'[78] are
slightly different to the 'prescribed particulars'[79] that have to be delivered in respect of a charge which
does not secure an issue of debentures. Apart from matters listed in section 863(2), the company
issuing the debentures also has to supply the registrar with particulars of the date and amount of each
issue of debentures of a series.[80] However, with respect to the latter information, failure to supply the
registrar with such information does not affect the validity of the debentures issued.[81]

Failure to comply with the requirement to supply the registrar with information relating to the issue of   **25.863.03**
debentures is an offence and both the company issuing the debentures and its relevant officials
responsible for compliance will be liable for a fine.[82]

The 'time period allowed for registration'[83] is, in the case where there is a deed containing the charge,   **25.863.04**
21 days beginning with the day after the day on which that deed was executed; or, if there is no such
deed, then 21 days beginning with the day after the day on which the first debenture of the series was
executed.[84]

The purpose of the section is to make life easier in respect of registration in relation to charges securing   **25.863.05**
an issue of debentures where, but for these provisions, it might be difficult to have to register details of
the same charge every time a debenture in the series was issued by the company. By virtue of these
provisions only one act of registration is required: either at the date the day after the date the deed
creating the charge is executed, or the date the day after the date the first debenture is issued.[85]

## 864  Additional registration requirement for commission etc in relation to debentures[a]

(1)  Where any commission, allowance or discount has been paid or made either directly or indirectly   **25.864.01**
     by a company to a person in consideration of his—
     (a)  subscribing or agreeing to subscribe, whether absolutely or conditionally, for debentures in a
          company, or
     (b)  procuring or agreeing to procure subscriptions, whether absolute or conditional, for such
          debentures,
     the particulars required to be sent for registration under section 860 shall include particulars as to
     the amount or rate per cent. of the commission, discount or allowance so paid or made.
(2)  The deposit of debentures as security for a debt of the company is not, for the purposes of this
     section, treated as the issue of debentures at a discount.
(3)  Failure to comply with this section does not affect the validity of the debentures issued.

AMENDMENTS AND NOTES

ª  Section 864 also applies (with appropriate modifications) to LLPs by virtue of the Limited Liability
   Partnerships (Application of Companies Act 2006) Regulations 2009, SI 2009/1804, Pt 9.

COMMENCEMENT DATE  1 October 2009[86]

Formerly section 397(2)(3) of the Companies Act 1985. Subsection (1) makes it clear that in a situation   **25.864.02**
where the company issuing debentures has paid or made (either directly or indirectly) any commission, allowance, or discount to a person in consideration of his subscribing (etc) for those debentures
or procuring subscriptions from others for those debentures then, in relation to the 'required particu-

---

77  Companies Act 2006 (Commencement No 8, Transitional Provisions and Savings) Order 2008, SI 2008/
2860, art 3(a).
78  See s 863(2) for the 'required particulars'.
79  See ss 860(1) and 869(4) for the 'prescribed particulars'. For the meaning of 'prescribed particulars' see n 20
above.
80  See s 863(3).
81  See s 863(4).
82  See s 863(5) applying s 860(2)–(6). However, if a person other than the company issuing the debentures
effects registration with the registrar then no offence will be committed by the company.
83  See s 870(1).
84  See s 870(3).
85  See s 870(3).
86  Companies Act 2006 (Commencement No 8, Transitional Provisions and Savings) Order 2008, SI 2008/
2860, art 3(n).

lars' that have to be sent to the registrar for registration, details of the amount, or rate per cent, of the commission, discount, or allowance paid, shall also be sent to the registrar. However, failure to comply with this requirement by the company does not affect the validity of any debentures issued.[87]

**25.864.03**  For purposes of clarity of application it is also made clear that where debentures are deposited as security for the debt of the company that is not to be treated as an issue of debentures at a discount for the purposes of section 864 and will not, therefore, be a particular that has to be supplied to the registrar.[88]

### 865 Endorsement of certificate on debentures[a]

**25.865.01**
(1) The company shall cause a copy of every certificate of registration given under section 869 to be endorsed on every debenture or certificate of debenture stock which is issued by the company, and the payment of which is secured by the charge so registered.

(2) But this does not require a company to cause a certificate of registration of any charge so given to be endorsed on any debenture or certificate of debenture stock issued by the company before the charge was created.

(3) If a person knowingly and wilfully authorises or permits the delivery of a debenture or certificate of debenture stock which under this section is required to have endorsed on it a copy of a certificate of registration, without the copy being so endorsed upon it, he commits an offence.

(4) A person guilty of an offence under this section is liable on summary conviction to a fine not exceeding level 3 on the standard scale.

AMENDMENTS AND NOTES

[a] Section 865 also applies (with appropriate modifications) to LLPs by virtue of the Limited Liability Partnerships (Application of Companies Act 2006) Regulations 2009, SI 2009/1804, Pt 9.

COMMENCEMENT DATE 1 October 2009[89]

**25.865.02**  Formerly section 402 of the Companies Act 1985. This section imposes a requirement that a company issuing a debenture or a certificate of debenture stock endorses on it a copy of the certificate of registration issued by the registrar of companies in respect of the charge securing it.[90] The purpose of the section is to provide the company with a means of proving to parties subscribing to the debenture that a valid charge exists[91] complying with the registration requirements laid down by the Act.[92] However, the company is not required to endorse a copy of the certificate of registration on any debenture issued before the charge has been created.[93]

**25.865.03**  Any person who 'knowingly and wilfully authorises or permits' the delivery of a debenture or certificate of debenture stock without the certificate of registration being endorsed on it commits an offence liable on summary conviction to a fine.[94]

### *Charges in other jurisdictions*

### 866 Charges created in, or over property in, jurisdictions outside the United Kingdom[a]

**25.866.01**
(1) Where a charge is created outside the United Kingdom comprising property situated outside the United Kingdom, the delivery to the registrar of a verified copy of the instrument by which the charge is created or evidenced has the same effect for the purposes of this Chapter as the delivery of the instrument itself.

(2) Where a charge is created in the United Kingdom but comprises property outside the United Kingdom, the instrument creating or purporting to create the charge may be sent for registration under section 860 even if further proceedings may be necessary to make the charge valid or effectual according to the law of the country in which the property is situated.

---

[87] See s 864(3).

[88] See s 864(2).

[89] Companies Act 2006 (Commencement No 8, Transitional Provisions and Savings) Order 2008, SI 2008/2860, art 3(n).

[90] See s 869(5).

[91] Ie a valid charge securing the debenture or certificate of debenture stock issued by the company.

[92] See *Re Yolland, Husson and Birkett Ltd* [1908] 1 Ch 152, 158, *per* Cozens-Hardy MR (explaining the purpose of the certificate of registration in respect of company charges issued in relation to a series of debentures).

[93] See s 865(2).

[94] See s 865(3) and (4).

AMENDMENTS AND NOTES

<sup>a</sup> Section 866 also applies (with appropriate modifications) to LLPs by virtue of the Limited Liability Partnerships (Application of Companies Act 2006) Regulations 2009, SI 2009/1804, Pt 9.

COMMENCEMENT DATE 1 October 2009[95]

Formerly section 398(1) and (3) of the Companies Act 1985. Subsection (1) makes it clear that in a case where an English[96] company creates a charge outside the UK comprising of property also outside the UK, the company does not have to deliver to the registrar[97] the actual instrument creating that charge but, instead, may deliver a verified copy of that instrument.[98] In this context 'United Kingdom' means Great Britain and Northern Ireland.[99] The purpose of this section is to make life easier for the company[100] because the original instrument might be needed in the country where the charge was created for the purpose of ensuring its validity under the law of that jurisdiction. If this concession were not available then the charge might become liable to avoidance due to non-compliance with the strict time period imposed for registering charges by virtue of section 870. The registration provisions apply to all charges created by English companies even if the law governing the instrument which creates the charge is governed by another jurisdiction.[101]     **25.866.02**

Subsection (2) allows the company[102] to send the instrument creating the charge covering (in part) property located outside the UK to the registrar where that charge is created in the UK, despite the fact that further proceedings might be required to make the charge valid in the country (outside the UK) where the property is located. Once again this provision is necessary due to the strict time period in which charges have to be registered in order to remain fully enforceable.[103]     **25.866.03**

### 867  Charges created in, or over property in, another United Kingdom jurisdiction<sup>a</sup>

(1) Subsection (2) applies where—     **25.867.01**
   (a) a charge comprises property situated in a part of the United Kingdom other than the part in which the company is registered, and
   (b) registration in that other part is necessary to make the charge valid or effectual under the law of that part of the United Kingdom.
(2) The delivery to the registrar of a verified copy of the instrument by which the charge is created or evidenced, together with a certificate stating that the charge was presented for registration in that other part of the United Kingdom on the date on which it was so presented has, for the purposes of this Chapter, the same effect as the delivery of the instrument itself.

AMENDMENTS AND NOTES

<sup>a</sup> Section 867 also applies (with appropriate modifications) to LLPs by virtue of the Limited Liability Partnerships (Application of Companies Act 2006) Regulations 2009, SI 2009/1804, Pt 9.

COMMENCEMENT DATE 1 October 2009[104]

Formerly section 398(4) of the Companies Act 1985. This section is designed to make it easier for a company[105] to comply with the registration requirement[106] in a situation where the property subject to the charge is located in another part of the UK[107] to the company and a further registration is also necessary in that other part of the UK in order to make the charge valid or effectual under the law of that other part. If these conditions are satisfied then the company need only send a verified copy of the     **25.867.02**

---

[95] Companies Act 2006 (Commencement No 8, Transitional Provisions and Savings) Order 2008, SI 2008/2860, art 3(n).

[96] This also applies where a Northern Ireland or Welsh company creates a charge; see s 861(5). All further references to an English company should be construed accordingly.

[97] Ie in order to comply with the duty imposed by s 860(1).

[98] The company has 21 days beginning the day after the day on which the instrument could have been received in the UK if it had been posted and dispatched with due diligence from the country where the charge was in fact created; see s 870(1)(b).

[99] See Interpretation Act 1978, s 5.

[100] Or, indeed, the chargee.

[101] See *Re Weldtech Equipment Ltd* [1991] BCC 16,17F, *per* Hoffmann J.

[102] Or, indeed, the chargee.

[103] On which see s 870.

[104] Companies Act 2006 (Commencement No 8, Transitional Provisions and Savings) Order 2008, SI 2008/2860, art 3(n).

[105] Or, indeed, the chargee.

[106] See s 860.

[107] 'UK' means Great Britain and Northern Ireland; see Interpretation Act 1978, s 5. In other words we are dealing with charges created in England, Wales, Northern Ireland, and Scotland.

instrument creating[108] the charge together with a certificate stating that the charge was presented for registration in that other part of the UK on the date on which it was so presented. If the company does this, then this will have the same effect as if the company had presented the original instrument creating the charge to the registrar as required by section 860(1).

## Orders charging land: Northern Ireland

### 868 Northern Ireland: registration of certain charges etc affecting land[a]

**25.868.01**

(1) Where a charge imposed by an order under Article 46 of the 1981 Order or notice of such a charge is registered in the Land Registry against registered land or any estate in registered land of a company, the Registrar of Titles shall as soon as may be cause two copies of the order made under Article 46 of that Order or of any notice under Article 48 of that Order to be delivered to the registrar.

(2) Where a charge imposed by an order under Article 46 of the 1981 Order is registered in the Registry of Deeds against any unregistered land or estate in land of a company, the Registrar of Deeds shall as soon as may be cause two copies of the order to be delivered to the registrar.

(3) On delivery of copies under this section, the registrar shall—

(a) register one of them in accordance with section 869, and

(b) not later than 7 days from that date of delivery, cause the other copy together with a certificate of registration under section 869(5) to be sent to the company against which judgment was given.

(4) Where a charge to which subsection (1) or (2) applies is vacated, the Registrar of Titles or, as the case may be, the Registrar of Deeds shall cause a certified copy of the certificate of satisfaction lodged under Article 132(1) of the 1981 Order to be delivered to the registrar for entry of a memorandum of satisfaction in accordance with section 872.

(5) In this section—

'the 1981 Order' means the Judgments Enforcement (Northern Ireland) Order 1981 (S.I.1981/226 (N.I. 6));

'the Registrar of Deeds' means the registrar appointed under the Registration of Deeds Act (Northern Ireland) 1970 (c.25),

'Registry of Deeds' has the same meaning as in the Registration of Deeds Acts,

'Registration of Deeds Acts' means the Registration of Deeds Act (Northern Ireland) 1970 and every statutory provision for the time being in force amending that Act or otherwise relating to the registry of deeds, or the registration of deeds, orders or other instruments or documents in such registry,

'the Land Registry' and 'the Registrar of Titles' are to be construed in accordance with section 1 of the Land Registration Act (Northern Ireland) 1970 (c. 18),

'registered land' and 'unregistered land' have the same meaning as in Part 3 of the Land Registration Act (Northern Ireland) 1970.

AMENDMENTS AND NOTES

[a] Section 868 also applies (with appropriate modifications) to LLPs by virtue of the Limited Liability Partnerships (Application of Companies Act 2006) Regulations 2009, SI 2009/1804, Pt 9.

COMMENCEMENT DATE  1 October 2009[109]

**25.868.02**   This is a completely new provision which only applies in respect of judgments under Article 46 of the Northern Ireland Judgments Enforcement Order 1981 which have been granted against the land[110] of a company in Northern Ireland. Where this happens then either the Registrar of Titles (in the case of registered land) or the Registrar of Deeds (in the case of unregistered land) shall cause two copies of the charge imposed against the land by virtue of the judgment order to be delivered to the registrar of companies. The registrar of companies is then obliged to register one of the copies on the company charges register[111] and send the other copy to the company against whom the judgment was given.[112] Should the judgment charge later be vacated then either the Registrar of Titles or Registrar of Deeds is then obliged to inform the registrar of companies of this event, and a memorandum of satisfaction will then be entered on the company charges register.[113]

---

[108]  Or instrument evidencing the charge; see s 867(2).

[109]  Companies Act 2006 (Commencement No 8, Transitional Provisions and Savings) Order 2008, SI 2008/2860, art 3(n).

[110]  This covers both registered and unregistered land; see s 868(1) and (2).

[111]  See ss 868(3)(a) and 869.

[112]  See s 868(3)(b).

[113]  See ss 868(4) and 872.

The purpose of this new section is to allow searchers of the company charges register to discover the    **25.868.03**
existence of judgment charges against land held by companies in Northern Ireland.

## The register of charges

### 869  Register of charges to be kept by registrar[a]

(1) The registrar shall keep, with respect to each company, a register of all the charges requiring     **25.869.01**
registration under this Chapter.

(2) In the case of a charge to the benefit of which holders of a series of debentures are entitled, the
registrar shall enter in the register the required particulars specified in section 863(2).

(3) In the case of a charge imposed by the Enforcement of Judgments Office under Article 46 of the
Judgments Enforcement (Northern Ireland) Order 1981, the registrar shall enter in the register the
date on which the charge became effective.

(4) In the case of any other charge, the registrar shall enter in the register the following particulars—

    (a) if it is a charge created by a company, the date of its creation and, if it is a charge which was
existing on property acquired by the company, the date of the acquisition,

    (b) the amount secured by the charge,

    (c) short particulars of the property charged, and

    (d) the persons entitled to the charge.

(5) The registrar shall give a certificate of the registration of any charge registered in pursuance of this
Chapter, stating the amount secured by the charge.

(6) The certificate—

    (a) shall be signed by the registrar or authenticated by the registrar's official seal, and

    (b) is conclusive evidence that the requirements of this Chapter as to registration have been
satisfied.

(7) The register kept in pursuance of this section shall be open to inspection by any person.

AMENDMENTS AND NOTES

[a] Section 869 also applies (with appropriate modifications) to LLPs by virtue of the Limited Liability
Partnerships (Application of Companies Act 2006) Regulations 2009, SI 2009/1804, Pt 9.

COMMENCEMENT DATE  1 October 2009[114]

Formerly section 401 of the Companies Act 1985. This section establishes the public register of charges   **25.869.02**
maintained by the registrar of companies who is under a duty to keep a register of those charges
mandated for registration.[115] The register is open for inspection by any member of the public.[116]

The section details the information, the 'prescribed particulars',[117] which is to be entered on the register   **25.869.03**
and is supplied to the registrar for this purpose by the company creating the charge.[118] In most cases[119]
the information entered on the public register is:[120]

(a) the date the charge is created; in general this will be the date the contract creating the charge was
entered into no matter if the moneys that it was intended to secure were advanced by the creditor
at a later date.[121] However, care must be taken in distinguishing between an agreement to create a
charge with immediate effect and an agreement to create a charge should a contingency occur. In
the latter situation no charge will be created until the contingency occurs which will also be the
date for registration purposes.[122] In simple terms the moment the parties to the contract intended
the creditor to benefit from the security charge is the date it was created for registration purposes;[123]

(b) the amount secured by the charge; although the purpose of this is to disclose to searchers of the
register the amount owing to the secured creditor, it is not a requirement that a specific figure of

---

[114] Companies Act 2006 (Commencement No 8, Transitional Provisions and Savings) Order 2008, SI
2008/2860, art 3(n).

[115] On which see ss 860(1) and (7), 862(1).

[116] See s 869(7).

[117] See s 860(1).

[118] See s 860(1) and (2).

[119] See s 869(2) (charge securing a series of debentures) and s 869(3) (judgment charge over land in Northern
Ireland) being the exceptions.

[120] See s 869(4).

[121] See *Esberger & Son Ltd v Capital and Counties Bank* [1913] 2 Ch 366, 374, *per* Sargant J.

[122] See *Williams v Burlington Investments Ltd* (1977) 121 Sol J 424, HL.

[123] In *Esberger & Son Ltd v Capital and Counties Bank* [1913] 2 Ch 366, 374 Sargant J explained that there must
be 'one definite period of time from which the twenty-one days must be or can be readily calculated by the
registrar.'

the outstanding debt is entered on the register.[124] Therefore, although in some cases a specific figure might be disclosed, in many cases the reference will be to 'all moneys due for the time being whether in the present or future'.[125] In other cases a specific figure of debt might be mentioned, but it is also stated the charge will cover future advances such that the searcher will not know from looking at the register the exact figure of the outstanding debt at any particular time;[126]

(c)    short particulars of the property charged; the company must supply the registrar with short particulars describing the property which is subject to the charge so that it is possible to identify which types of property are encumbered. However, the description might be quite general and need not be specific in the sense of particularising every item covered. So, for example, it would suffice to describe the charge as covering 'all book debts' of the chargor company without having to describe each and every debt owed to the company at the time of registration. The charge might also be expressed to cover future property of the chargor company;

(d)    the persons entitled to the charge; it is a requirement that the name of the chargee is entered on the register.[127]

**25.869.04**    Following receipt of the prescribed particulars and instrument (if any) creating the charge the registrar is required to enter the details listed above on the public register and issue a signed certificate, stating the amount secured by the charge, to the person who supplied the particulars.[128] Any certificate issued by the registrar is 'conclusive evidence that the requirements of this Chapter as to registration have been satisfied'.[129] The reason for making the certificate conclusive has been explained as:

> It seems to me that section [869(6)(b)] should be taken as meaning what it says. There is good reason for this. Section [874] puts into a charge by a company a weakness; this weakness limits a chargee of the company in dealing with his charge; it is to be expected that the group of sections should not sterilize a chargee of a company in dealing with his charge; it is therefore to be expected that the group of sections should provide in absolute terms for a marketable security, which cannot be achieved unless the certificate of the registrar is in every respect conclusive and unassailable.[130]

**25.869.05**    If it were otherwise and the certificate were not conclusive then 'no lender on the faith of the charge could be secure and sure that it would not thereafter be attacked by somebody…'.[131] The conclusive nature of the registrar's certificate can have far-reaching consequences. Therefore, it matters not if either the chargor or the registrar makes a mistake when entering details of the charge on either the prescribed particulars form or the register of charges (including the certificate of registration); in both cases the chargee will be protected from having his charge avoided once the certificate of registration has been issued no matter how misleading the details of the registered charge may be. So, for example, in a case where the registrar mistakenly recorded the details of an issue of debentures as being entitled to the same priority when, in fact, the series contained two different classes of priority, the issue of the certificate was held to be conclusive that the requirements of the Act had been complied with and a liquidator of the chargor company was unable to benefit from the avoidance power.[132] Likewise, in cases where the chargee has supplied erroneous particulars to the registrar which have then been entered on the register conveying false or misleading information, the chargee has still retained a fully enforceable charge immune from avoidance once the registrar issued a certificate of registration.[133] The courts will not go behind the certificate issued by the registrar—the Act states that it is 'conclusive'

---

[124]  See *National Provincial and Union Bank of England v Charnley* [1924] 1 KB 431, 444, *per* Bankes; 448, *per* Scrutton LJJ.

[125]  This will be particularly the case where there is a floating charge given to secure the repayment of a current account.

[126]  This will also be the case where the secured debt includes interest. 'In order to discover the terms and effect of the charge … one must look at the document creating the charge and not at the register. It is from that document that one will discover what moneys are secured and what is the total amount secured by the charge.'; *Re Mechanisations (Eaglescliffe) Ltd* [1966] Ch 20, 35–36, *per* Buckley J.

[127]  However, this only extends to the name of the chargee at the time of registration following the creation of the charge. Therefore, should the first chargee assign his interest there is no requirement that the name of the assignee be substituted such that the register would become out of date following an assignment of the charge. Cf s 872 below.

[128]  See s 869(5).

[129]  See s 869(6)(b).

[130]  See *Re CL Nye Ltd* [1971] Ch 442, 474D, *per* Russell LJ.

[131]  See *Re CL Nye Ltd* [1971] Ch 442, 469H–470A, *per* Harman LJ.

[132]  See *Re Yolland, Husson & Birkett Ltd* [1908] 1 Ch 152, CA.

[133]  See *Cunard Steamship Co Ltd v Hopwood* [1908] 2 Ch 564 (no date of creation given in particulars); *National Provincial & Union Bank of England v Charnley* [1924] 1 KB 431, CA (fact that charge covered chattels as well as land not mentioned in particulars); *Re Eric Holmes (Property) Ltd* [1965] Ch 1052 (false date of creation of charge supplied); *Re Mechanisations (Eaglescliffe) Ltd* [1966] Ch 20 (charge details only mention principal sum

and that is exactly what it means.[134] However, the certificate is only conclusive as regards the prescribed particulars and it is not conclusive as regards non-particulars. Thus, in a case where the chargee supplied the registrar with details of a charge but gave the wrong company registration number[135] such that the charge was registered against the wrong company it was held that the certificate could only be taken as being conclusive that the wrong company had registered a charge and was accordingly 'meaningless and worthless' as against the right company wishing to use the certificate as a defence.[136]

The certificate of registration will also be a defence to the chargor company and its officers in **25.869.06** proceedings brought under section 860(4).[137]

The conclusive nature of the certificate of registration also means that the courts will not allow judicial **25.869.07** review of the registrar's decision to issue the certificate even if the petitioner could demonstrate an error of fact or law on the part of the registrar in issuing the certificate.[138]

The strength of the conclusivity provision has meant that in cases where an application is granted for **25.869.08** late registration of a charge[139] and a *Re Charles* Order[140] is made then it is now implicit to the court's order granting an extension of time that the registrar will not issue a certificate of registration (despite registering the charge) until the time period given to challenge the order (normally 14 days) has expired.[141] However, in a case where the registrar issued a certificate in breach of that implied direction, then it was held that neither an administrator of the company nor any of its unsecured creditors could later seek to challenge the order granting an extension of time for registration since the certificate was conclusive that the requirements of the Act in respect of registration had been met by the chargee.[142]

The potentially harsh effects produced by the courts refusing to look behind the certificate of **25.869.09** registration has not escaped the courts.[143] Although at one time it appeared as if the courts would only offer sympathy to a party aggrieved at a fraudulent registration such that it could only be left to Parliament to intervene (if it thought fit),[144] in more recent times the courts appear to be prepared to intervene. There is now substantive *dicta* that a third party creditor, who can demonstrate a loss caused as a direct result of a prior chargee supplying false information to the registrar which was then entered on the register, 'may well be'[145] able to take proceedings 'in personam'[146] against the chargee such that the chargee cannot use the certificate of registration as a defence[147] and will be liable for damages to that creditor.[148] However, this authority does not quite go so far as to avoid *in toto* the certificate of registration; it serves only to prevent an unmeritorious chargee from using the certificate as a defence to a challenge to his security or, in a claim for damages brought by a creditor who can demonstrate a loss caused by the conduct of the chargee, in getting the charge registered so that he was misled by inaccurate or misleading particulars entered on the register.[149] Nevertheless, there is now Privy

---

of debt and omit to mention fact that interest and other sums also covered); *Re CL Nye Ltd* [1971] Ch 442, CA (false date of creation of charge supplied to registrar).

[134] See also *Exeter Trust Ltd v Screenways Ltd* [1991] 477, 481A *per* Nourse LJ.

[135] All companies are allocated a registration number at incorporation and they are required to use this number to identify them when sending documents to the registrar, but the number is not a particular of a charge for the purposes of the registration scheme; see *Re Advantage Healthcare (T10) Ltd* [2000] BCC 985, 988C, *per* Lightman J.

[136] See *Re Advantage Healthcare (T10) Ltd* [2000] BCC 985, 988B, *per* Lightman J.

[137] See *Re CL Nye Ltd* [1971] 1 Ch 442, 474B, *per* Russell LJ.

[138] See *R v Registrar of Companies ex p Central Bank of India* [1986] 1 QB 1114. However, this will not be the case where judicial review is sought by the Attorney-General since the CA is not expressed so as to bind the Crown; Ibid at 1169G, 1177E, *per* Lawton and Slade LJJ.

[139] See s 873 below.

[140] [1933] WN 15.

[141] See *Ali v Top Marques Car Rental Ltd* (2006) *Times Law Reports*, 10 Feb.

[142] See *Ali v Top Marques Car Rental Ltd* (2006) *Times Law Reports*, 10 Feb.

[143] In *Re Eric Holmes (Property) Ltd* [1965] Ch 1052, 1072A, *per* Pennycuick J remarked: 'It is, I think, possible that there is some lacuna in the Act here, inasmuch as the Act gives apparently, protection where the certificate is made upon the basis of particulars which are incorrect and might even be fraudulent.'

[144] See *Re Eric Holmes (Property) Ltd* [1965] Ch 1032, 1071, *per* Pennycuick J.

[145] See *Re CL Nye Ltd* [1971] 1 Ch 442, 474F, *per* Russell LJ; *Re Advantage Healthcare (T10) Ltd* [2000] 985, 988F–G, *per* Lightman J.

[146] See *Re CL Nye Ltd* [1971] 1 Ch 442, 474F, *per* Russell LJ; *Re Advantage Healthcare (T10) Ltd* [2000] 985, 988F-G, *per* Lightman J.

[147] See *National Provincial and Union Bank of England v Charnley* [1924] 1 KB 431, 454, *per* Atkin LJ.

[148] See *R v Registrar of Companies, ex p Central Bank of India* [1986] 1 QB 1114, 1117G, *per* Slade LJ.

[149] A possible problem with this argument is the situation where a creditor of the chargor company searches the register and makes an advance on the basis of the information revealed which he later learns to be inaccurate (due to the fault of the chargee) but a search of the original instrument of charge would have revealed the true

Council authority stating that: 'A mortgagee who knowingly applied for and obtained a certificate under section [869(6)] falsely affirming or implying … that his charge was created within the time limit would be liable to have his certificate set aside by the court on the grounds of fraud.'[150]

**25.869.10**   Likewise, where a person suffers a loss as a result of an entry (or non-entry) on the public register caused by the registrar then they 'may well have a remedy against the Registrar for issuing the certificate but he or she cannot dispute the conclusiveness of the certificate as issued.'[151]

**25.869.11**   Although a certificate of registration will protect the charge against challenge under the Companies Act avoidance provisions[152] it confers no other benefits. Thus, a charge will be vulnerable and open to challenge on grounds other than non-compliance with the registration provisions. Therefore, a charge obtained through fraud or duress[153] would be open to challenge. A charge protected by the certificate of registration has also been avoided at a later date as a preference.[154]

**25.869.12**   It has been stated that the doctrine of constructive notice applies to the public register of charges established by section 869. At least two separate views have emerged as to the scope of the constructive notice doctrine in this area.[155] The first, what might be termed, the wide view of constructive notice holds that registered information constitutes notice to the world of the contents of the public register of charges.[156] There is weak *obiter* case support for this viewpoint.[157] A second, what might be termed, the narrow view of constructive notice also exists.[158] This states that registered information constitutes notice only to those parties who might reasonably be expected to search the public register prior to dealing with the company. There is no case authority to support this viewpoint. The point still awaits definitive judgment but it is submitted that the doctrine of constructive notice does not apply to the company charges register. There is no substantive evidence to support the application of the doctrine and the establishment of the public register of charges in 1900[159] was purely intended as a means of supplying public information on charges. The question of priority was deliberately not addressed by the legislature and it is pushing matters too far to suggest that they intended the constructive notice doctrine to apply in the absence of an express priority point for competing charges (and other priority conflicts) contained in the legislation.[160]

### 870  The period allowed for registration[a]

**25.870.01**   (1) The period allowed for registration of a charge created by a company is—
(a) 21 days beginning with the day after the day on which the charge is created, or
(b) if the charge is created outside the United Kingdom, 21 days beginning with the day after the day on which the instrument by which the charge is created or evidenced (or a copy of it) could, in due course of post (and if despatched with due diligence) have been received in the United Kingdom.

---

picture. S 875 requires each company to keep a copy of instruments creating a registrable charge at its registered office which is open to inspection by creditors by virtue of s 877(4). However, the courts have made clear that creditors should not rely on the public register of charges as to the extent of the charge but should instead inspect the instrument; see: *National Provincial and Union Bank of England v Charnley* [1924] 1 KB 431, 444–445 *per* Bankes LJ; *Re Mechanisations (Eaglescliffe) Ltd* [1966] Ch 20, 35–36, *per* Buckley J.

[150] See *Sun Tai Cheung Credits Ltd v Attorney-General* [1987] 1 WLR 948, 953, a judgment of the Privy Council delivered by Lord Templeman. Note also *Esberger & Son Ltd v Capital and Counties Bank* [1913] 2 Ch 366 (charge registered with false date of creation held to be unenforceable, but authority of certificate of registration never argued). Cf *National Provincial and Union Bank of England v Charnley* [1924] 1 KB 431, 448, *per* Scrutton LJ.

[151] See *First City Corporation Ltd v Downsview Nominees Ltd* [1990] 3 NZLR 265, 272, line 25, *per* Richardson J. (New Zealand Court of Appeal) affirmed *sub nom Downsview Nominees Ltd v First City Corporation Ltd* [1993] AC 295; *Re Advantage Healthcare (T10) Ltd* [2000] BCC 985, 988F–G, *per* Lightman J.

[152] See ss 860, 874.

[153] See *R v Registrar of Companies ex p Central Bank of India* [1986] 1 QB 1114, 1183B, *per* Dillon J.

[154] See *Re Eric Holmes (Property) Ltd* [1965] Ch 1032; and note Insolvency Act 1986, ss 238, 239, 245 (provisions which might be utilized to avoid a registered charge).

[155] Consider also the following views on the scope of constructive notice: charge registration gives 'constructive notice to all those affected', *Gore-Browne On Companies* (Bristol, Jordans, 25th edn, 1992) Vol 1, para 18.13, n 6 and the main text threat; charge registration will bind a subsequent purchaser who will be taken to have constructive notice of it, *Palmer's Company Law* (London, Sweet & Maxwell, 25th edn, 1992) para 13.326, point 2. Interestingly, no one has sought to suggest that the doctrine of constructive notice might also apply to the register of charges maintained by the company itself which is also available for public inspection; see s 876 below.

[156] See generally WJ Gough, *Company Charges* (London, Butterworths, 2nd edn, 1995) 833–847.

[157] See *Earle v Hemsworth RDC* (1928) 44 TLR 605, 608, *per* Wright J.

[158] See R Goode, *Commercial Law* (London, Penguin, 3rd edn, 2004) 666(d).

[159] By virtue of CA 1900, s 14.

[160] For a complete review of the issues see de Lacy [2001] *The Conveyancer* 122.

(2) The period allowed for registration of a charge to which property acquired by a company is subject is—

    (a) 21 days beginning with the day after the day on which the acquisition is completed, or

    (b) if the property is situated and the charge was created outside the United Kingdom, 21 days beginning with the day after the day on which the instrument by which the charge is created or evidenced (or a copy of it) could, in due course of post (and if despatched with due diligence) have been received in the United Kingdom.

(3) The period allowed for registration of particulars of a series of debentures as a result of section 863 is—

    (a) if there is a deed containing the charge mentioned in section 863(1), 21 days beginning with the day after the day on which that deed is executed, or

    (b) if there is no such deed, 21 days beginning with the day after the day on which the first debenture of the series is executed.

AMENDMENTS AND NOTES

<sup>a</sup> Section 870 also applies (with appropriate modifications) to LLPs by virtue of the Limited Liability Partnerships (Application of Companies Act 2006) Regulations 2009, SI 2009/1804, Pt 9.

COMMENCEMENT DATE 1 October 2009[161]

This section is a new one and represents a change of approach in that it unifies all the former provisions[162] relating to the time period for registration of various types of charge into one section. This has been done as part of the attempt to be user friendly which is the theme behind the revised drafting of the charge registration provisions. **25.870.02**

The section tells us the time period for registering a charge in six different situations:[163] **25.870.03**

(i) Where a charge is created by a company registered in England, Wales, or Northern Ireland and covers property in those countries[164] then the time period is 21 days to register beginning the day after the charge was created.[165]

(ii) Where the charge is created outside the UK[166] then the time period is 21 days beginning with the day after the day[167] on which the instrument which created the charge[168] could have been received in the UK if posted with due diligence.[169]

(iii) Where a company acquires property subject to a charge the time period for registration is 21 days beginning with the day after the day[170] on which the property was acquired.[171]

(iv) Where a company acquires property subject to a charge and that property is situated, and the charge created, outside the UK, then the time period for registration is 21 days beginning with the day after the day[172] on which the instrument creating the charge[173] could have been received in the UK if posted with due diligence.[174]

(v) Where the company creates a charge in a deed to secure an issue of a series of debentures then the time period for registration is 21 days beginning with the day after the day on which the deed was executed.[175]

---

[161] Companies Act 2006 (Commencement No 8, Transitional Provisions and Savings) Order 2008, SI 2008/2860, art 3(n).

[162] On which see CA 1985, ss 395(1), 398(2), 400(2), 397(1).

[163] See generally ss 860, 862, and 863 for the substantive sections detailing the types of charge that require registration under the Act.

[164] This will also apply to property located in Scotland.

[165] This represents a change in the law. Under the old s 395(1) the time period for registration was 21 days beginning on the day the charge was created.

[166] Ie Great Britain and Northern Ireland; see Interpretation Act 1978, s 5.

[167] This represents a change in the old law of s 398(2) which provided for a time period of registration beginning with 21 days after the day the instrument of charge would have been received in the UK.

[168] *Quaere* the time period in a case where there is no instrument creating or evidencing the charge? Section 860(1) clearly requires such charges to be registered but this provision appears to have overlooked the eventuality.

[169] This represents a change in the old law which by virtue of s 398(2) required registration to be made within 21 days beginning with the day on which the instrument could have been received in the UK.

[170] This represents a change in the old law which by virtue of s 400(2) required registration to be made within 21 days after the day on which the property was acquired by the company.

[171] See s 870(2)(a).

[172] This changes the old law which by virtue of s 397(1) required registration to be made within 21 days beginning with the day on which the instrument could have been received in the UK.

[173] *Quaere* the status of a charge which was not created or evidenced by an instrument? See also at n 168 above.

[174] See s 870(2)(b).

[175] See s 870(3)(a).

(vi) Where the company creates a charge and there is no deed to secure a series of debentures then the time period for registration is 21 days beginning with the day after the day on which the first debenture of the series was executed.[176]

### 871 Registration of enforcement of security[a]

**25.871.01**
(1) If a person obtains an order for the appointment of a receiver or manager of a company's property, or appoints such a receiver or manager under powers contained in an instrument, he shall within 7 days of the order or of the appointment under those powers, give notice of the fact to the registrar.

(2) Where a person appointed receiver or manager of a company's property under powers contained in an instrument ceases to act as such receiver or manager, he shall, on so ceasing, give the registrar notice to that effect.

(3) The registrar must enter a fact of which he is given notice under this section in the register of charges.

(4) A person who makes default in complying with the requirements of this section commits an offence.

(5) A person guilty of an offence under this section is liable on summary conviction to a fine not exceeding level 3 on the standard scale and, for continued contravention, to a daily default fine not exceeding one-tenth of level 3 on the standard scale.

AMENDMENTS AND NOTES

[a] Section 871 also applies (with appropriate modifications) to LLPs by virtue of the Limited Liability Partnerships (Application of Companies Act 2006) Regulations 2009, SI 2009/1804, Pt 9.

COMMENCEMENT DATE 1 October 2009[177]

**25.871.02** Formerly section 405 of the Companies Act 1985. This section imposes a duty upon a person who obtains an order for the appointment of a receiver or manager of a company's property to give notice of that appointment to the registrar of companies within seven days of that fact.[178] Failure to give such notice is an offence[179] punishable by a fine.[180]

**25.871.03** Once appointed to act as a receiver or manager of a company's property, should the person appointed cease to act in the role then he is under a duty to inform the registrar of companies of that fact.[181]

**25.871.04** The registrar of companies is under a duty to enter details of the appointment of a receiver or manager, or of the fact that a person has ceased to act in either role, on the register of company charges.[182]

**25.871.05** The purpose of this section is to provide a source of information for those searching the register of charges in relation to a company whether or not any receiver or manager has been appointed over the company's property.[183]

### 872 Entries of satisfaction and release[a]

**25.872.01**
(1) Subsection (2) applies if a statement is delivered to the registrar verifying with respect to a registered charge—
(a) that the debt for which the charge was given has been paid or satisfied in whole or in part, or
(b) that part of the property or undertaking charged has been released from the charge or has ceased to form part of the company's property or undertaking.

(2) The registrar may enter on the register a memorandum of satisfaction in whole or in part, or of the fact part of the property or undertaking has been released from the charge or has ceased to form part of the company's property or undertaking (as the case may be).

(3) Where the registrar enters a memorandum of satisfaction in whole, the registrar shall if required send the company a copy of it.

[176] See s 870(3)(b).
[177] Companies Act 2006 (Commencement No 8, Transitional Provisions and Savings) Order 2008, SI 2008/2860, art 3(n).
[178] See s 871(1).
[179] See s 871(4).
[180] See s 871(5).
[181] See s 871(2).
[182] See s 871(3).
[183] See s 877 for rights to inspect the public register of charges.

Formerly section 403 of the Companies Act 1985. This section allows a party[185] to send to the registrar a statement declaring that either (i) the debt secured by the registered charge has been paid in full or in part; or (ii) the property subject to the charge has been released from the charge or disposed of by the chargor company.    **25.872.02**

Upon receipt of the statement the registrar has a discretion[186] to enter on the register of charges a memorandum of satisfaction disclosing the nature of the statement received such that a searcher of the register will then be able to form a better view as to the creditworthiness of the company. The registrar should satisfy himself as to the authenticity of the statement before making any entry on the register.[187] However, following making an entry on the register the registrar is only obliged to notify the company of an entry if it relates to the satisfaction of the debt in whole and the company requests it.[188]    **25.872.03**

## 873 Rectification of register of charges[a]

(1) Subsection (2) applies if the court is satisfied—    **25.873.01**
   (a) that the failure to register a charge before the end of the period allowed for registration, or the omission or misstatement of any particular with respect to any such charge or in a memorandum of satisfaction—
      (i)  was accidental or due to inadvertence or to some other sufficient cause, or
      (ii) is not of a nature to prejudice the position of creditors or shareholders of the company, or
   (b) that on other grounds it is just and equitable to grant relief.
(2) The court may, on the application of the company or a person interested, and on such terms and conditions as seem to the court just and expedient, order that the period allowed for registration shall be extended or, as the case may be, that the omission or misstatement shall be rectified.

Formerly section 404 of the Companies Act 1985. This section allows the chargor company or any person interested in a charge to seek an order of the court: (a) extending the time period for registration in a case where a charge has not been registered in the prescribed time period;[190] or (b) that any omission or misstatement in the registered particulars of a charge be rectified.    **25.873.02**

However, the court, before acceding to any such application must be satisfied that the failure to register or mistake in the particulars was: (a) accidental; or, due to inadvertence; or, some other sufficient cause;[191] or (b) is not of a nature to prejudice the position of creditors or shareholders of the company;[192] or (c) that on other grounds it is just and equitable to grant relief.[193]    **25.873.03**

An applicant who discovers that his charge has not been registered on time or that it has been registered containing some error or omission 'should apply without delay' to the court to have the matter dealt with. Failure to do so will cause the court to 'look askance at a chargee who deliberately defers his application in order to see which way the wind is going to blow' before then seeking to persuade the    **25.873.04**

---

[184] Companies Act 2006 (Commencement No 8, Transitional Provisions and Savings) Order 2008, SI 2008/2860, art 3(n).

[185] The section does not limit the categories of person who may deliver a statement to the registrar.

[186] Section 872(2) states that the registrar 'may' make an entry on the register following receipt of the statement.

[187] Cf s 887(2) below affecting Scotland alone (registrar must satisfy himself, in the case of floating charges, that the secured creditor agrees to the change).

[188] See s 874(3).

[189] Companies Act 2006 (Commencement No 8, Transitional Provisions and Savings) Order 2008, SI 2008/2860, art 3(n).

[190] On which see s 870.

[191] See s 873(1)(a)(i).

[192] See s 873(1)(a)(ii).

[193] See s 873(1)(b).

court to exercise its discretion in his favour.[194] If an applicant can satisfy the above listed criteria then the court is given a complete discretion[195] as to the remedy it might grant, and may impose 'such terms and conditions as seem to the court just and expedient'.[196] Although the section lists alternative and distinct grounds to justify the court exercising its discretion 'the underlying guide to the exercise of the discretion is whether for any reason, whether specified in the section or not, it would be just and equitable to grant relief.'[197]

**25.873.05**    Once an applicant can demonstrate to the court that he qualifies for an extension under one of the listed grounds then the court will generally accede to the application and grant an extension of time or rectify the register, as the case may be. However, as applications are made on an *ex parte* basis the normal practice where an extension of time is sought is to include in the order[198] extending the time period a provision protecting the rights of secured creditors who acquired their interest in the charged property in between the time of the creation of the original unregistered charge and the date at which it was eventually registered (pursuant to the court order). Such an order will not be granted, however, in favour of secured creditors where to do so would be inequitable or unconscionable. So, for example, should a director of the chargor company take and register a charge over the encumbered property of his company upon learning of the charge not being registered,[199] or a chargee who took his interest at the same time as the unregistered charge but upon express terms that it was to be at all times subject to that charge,[200] then, in both cases, the extension in time for registration will not be subject to those interests gaining priority. Nevertheless, the taking of a security charge with knowledge of the unregistered charge will not, by itself, amount to inequitable conduct such that the chargee should be denied his priority if and when the prior chargee applies for an extension in time.[201] Nor, where two charges are taken at the same time over the same property in favour of different persons one (which is not registered) expressed to take priority over the other (which is registered on time), does this agreement alter the nature of the avoidance power which will render a belated priority in favour of the latter since the parties are entitled to have presumed that both charges were valid and enforceable at law and would remain so in the absence of language to the contrary in their priority/subordination agreement.[202] An order will not be made to protect the interests of unsecured creditors since they have no proprietary rights against the assets of the chargor company (pending liquidation).[203]

**25.873.06**    Once a winding up of the company has commenced then only in exceptional circumstances[204] will a court grant an order extending time for registration, since upon the appointment of a liquidator the avoidance power will come into operation rendering the unregistered charge void against the liquidator.[205] Likewise, should an administration order be granted then an application should normally be denied.[206] However, the fact that a winding up of the company might appear likely does not, by itself, mean that an application for an extension of the time period should be denied. Rather, in normal circumstances an order for extending the time period for registration should be granted subject to a *Re*

---

[194]    See *Re Ashpurton Estates Ltd* [1983] Ch 110, 132A–B, *per* Lord Brightman. Note also *Re Telomatic Ltd* [1994] 1 BCLC 90 where a late application for an extension of the time period for registration would have been rejected for this reason had the grounds for exercising the discretion to grant an extension been made out.

[195]    Section 873(2) states that the court 'may' grant a remedy.

[196]    See s 873(2).

[197]    See *Re Braemar Investments Ltd* [1989] Ch 54, 61B, *per* Hoffmann J; and note: *Confiance Ltd v Timespan Images Ltd* [2005] 2 BCLC 693, 700i–701a, *per* Pumfrey J; *Re MIG Trust Ltd* [1933] Ch 542, 560, *per* Lord Hanworth MR.

[198]    See *Re Ashpurton Estates Ltd* [1983] Ch 110, 122H–123B *per* Lord Brightman for the rationale of this order.

[199]    See *Re Fablehill Ltd* [1991] BCC 590; *Confiance Ltd v Timespan Images Ltd* [2005] 2 BCLC 693.

[200]    See *Barclays Bank plc v Stuart Landon Ltd* [2002] BCC 917. This case should, however, be treated with caution since the case of *Bank of Scotland v TA Neilson & Co.* 1991 SLT 8 was not cited before the court nor does any substantive argument on the issue of priorities appear to have taken place.

[201]    See *Re Monolithic Building Co. Ltd* [1915] 1 Ch 643.

[202]    See *Bank of Scotland v TA Neilson & Co* 1991 SLT 8, 11D–F, *per* Lord Maclean. The case of *Barclays Bank plc v Stuart Landon Ltd* [2002] BCC 917 must be taken as an example of where the terms of the priority agreement could be taken to have covered the eventuality of non-registration or that the point was not taken in the case. The latter view should also be applied to the Irish case of *Re Clarets* [1978] IRLM 215.

[203]    See *Re Ashpurton Estates Ltd* [1983] Ch 110, 123C–F, *per* Lord Brightman.

[204]    See eg *Re RM Arnold & Co Ltd* [1984] BCLC 535, 540b–e, *per* Harman J.

[205]    See s 874(1)(a). Note also *Re Ashpurton Estates Ltd* [1983] Ch 110, 123F–G, *per* Lord Brightman 'It follows … that the courts must invariably refuse to extend the time for registration once the company has gone into liquidation.'

[206]    See *Re Barrow Borough Transport Ltd* [1990] Ch 227. An extension might be granted however, if the purpose of the administration order is to rescue or rehabilitate the company; Ibid and see Insolvency Act 1986 (as amended), s 248 and Sch B1, para 3(1)(a).

*Charles* Order[207] including the proviso that should the company later be wound up then the liquidator is at liberty to challenge the order granting the extension and have it set aside. The mere possibility that, at the time the application is made for an extension of time, there might be grounds for challenging the unregistered charge, for example as a preference, is not enough to deny the application.[208] The only time an application for late registration can be denied is if it can be shown that a later application to set aside the extension order 'would be bound to succeed'.[209] Were it otherwise then the unregistered charge holder would never be given the chance to show that his charge was valid and fully enforceable other than on the ground of non-registration.[210] Unsecured creditors have no general grounds for complaining about the grant of a charge by a company unless insolvency intervenes for they have no proprietary interest over the assets of the company and cannot, therefore, object to an unregistered charge being granted or registered late *per se*.[211]

Should the court grant an extension of time for registration and make it subject to a *Re Charles* Order **25.873.07** then the normal practice is for the registrar to register the charge but not to issue a certificate of registration until the time period for challenging the extension of time in favour of the liquidator or administrator has expired.[212] This is to ensure that the charge holder does not benefit from the conclusivity of the certificate of registration.[213] This practice is now so engrained that it has become an implied direction in every case where an extension is granted by the court.[214]

## Avoidance of certain charges

### 874 Consequence of failure to register charges created by a company[a]

(1) If a company creates a charge to which section 860 applies, the charge is void (so far as any **25.874.01**
security on the company's property or undertaking is conferred by it) against—
   (a) a liquidator of the company,
   (b) an administrator of the company, and
   (c) a creditor of the company,
   unless that section is complied with.
(2) Subsection (1) is subject to the provisions of this Chapter.
(3) Subsection (1) is without prejudice to any contract or obligation for repayment of the money secured by the charge; and when a charge becomes void under this section, the money secured by it immediately becomes payable.

AMENDMENTS AND NOTES

[a] Section 874 also applies (with appropriate modifications) to LLPs by virtue of the Limited Liability Partnerships (Application of Companies Act 2006) Regulations 2009, SI 2009/1804, Pt 9.

COMMENCEMENT DATE 1 October 2009[215]

Formerly section 395 of the Companies Act 1985. This section renders a charge which is not registered **25.874.02** within the prescribed time period[216] void against the three listed categories of interest. If the particulars of a charge are not delivered to the registrar within the prescribed time period[217] then the charge becomes subject to the avoidance power and the registrar can no longer accept the particulars.[218] In these circumstances the only remedy for the holder of the charge will be to make an application for registration out of time.[219]

A charge which is not registered in time is only rendered void against the parties listed, namely a **25.874.03** liquidator, an administrator, or a creditor. Therefore, outside of liquidation the unregistered charge

---

[207] [1933] WN 15.
[208] See *Barclays Bank plc v Stuart Landon Ltd* [2002] BCC 917, 921A–B, *per* Chadwick LJ.
[209] See *Barclays Bank plc v Stuart Landon Ltd* [2002] BCC 917, 921G, *per* Chadwick LJ.
[210] See *Barclays Bank plc v Stuart Landon Ltd* [2002] BCC 917, 921F, *per* Chadwick LJ.
[211] See *Re Ashpurton Estates Ltd* [1983] Ch 110, 123B–E, *per* Lord Brightman.
[212] See *Ali v Top Marques Car Rental Ltd* (2006) *Times Law Reports*, 10 February.
[213] See s 869(6)(b).
[214] See *Ali v Top Marques Car Rental Ltd* (2006) *Times Law Reports*, 10 February.
[215] Companies Act 2006 (Commencement No 8, Transitional Provisions and Savings) Order 2008, SI 2008/2860, art 3(n).
[216] See s 870 above.
[217] On which see s 870.
[218] See *R v Registrar of Companies ex p Central Bank of India* [1986] 1 QB 1114, 1170G–1171B and 1178D, *per* Lawton and Slade LJJ.
[219] On which see s 873.

remains fully enforceable against the company[220] and any other party.[221] The unregistered charge remains valid throughout the time period allowed for registration and if (following default) the chargee realizes his security within that time then he will be immune to challenge despite non-registration. A chargee who realizes his unregistered security charge after the expiration of the time period for registration will also be immune from challenge if, at the time of realization, none of the beneficiaries of the avoidance power had either been appointed[222] or gained a proprietary right[223] over the encumbered assets.[224] Likewise, an agreement creating a charge and providing that the chargor will create, every 21 days thereafter, another charge upon the same terms as the original but in substitution thereof until the debt is repaid, is a valid method of evading the registration requirement and thereby giving public notice of the charge.[225]

25.874.04    Although a company cannot utilize the avoidance power prior to liquidation[226] 'once the company is in liquidation and can only act by its liquidator, there seems to me little value in a distinction between whether the charge is void against the liquidator or void against the company. It is void against the company in liquidation'.[227] Likewise, when the section states that the unregistered charge is void against 'an administrator'[228] this 'means void against the company in administration or (another way of saying the same thing) against the company when acting by its administrator'.[229] Therefore, once the company has gone into liquidation or administration the company can invoke the avoidance power for non-registration.[230]

25.874.05    Regarding avoidance against 'a creditor', the mere fact of non-registration does not mean that the charge will be void if the company has creditors. Rather, it is only creditors with a proprietary right in, or against, the assets subject to the unregistered charge that can utilize the avoidance power.[231] Therefore, a second chargee with or without notice of the prior unregistered charge will take free of it[232] as will an unsecured creditor who has levied execution against the encumbered assets of the company.[233] Should the second chargee not register their interest, however, then they will not take priority over the prior charge. Instead (outside of the chargor company's insolvency and any question of fraud) the first chargee to register, having utilized the section 873 procedure, will prevail.

25.874.06    Should a charge become void due to non-registration it should be noted that the avoidance power only strikes so as to invalidate the enforceability of the security interest, it does not affect the underlying obligation to repay the money secured by that charge. Thus, the holder of the avoided charge can still bring an action to enforce his debt against the chargor company and, should insolvency intervene, the debt will be provable but will only rank *pari passu* with the other claims against the company. Given the fact that the Act places a duty upon the chargor company to register the charge[234] that company's failure to do so means that the money secured by the unregistered charge 'immediately becomes

---

[220] See *Bank of Scotland v TA Neilson & Co* 1991 SLT 8, 11A, *per* Lord Maclean, and, by way of analogy, *Independent Automatic Sales Ltd v Knowles and Foster* [1962] 1 WLR 974. Note also *Re Monolithic Building Co* [1915] 1 Ch 643, 667, *per* Cozens-Hardy MR and 667–668, *per* Phillimore LJ.

[221] Eg a purchaser for value without notice; *Stroud Architectural Systems Ltd v John Laing Construction Ltd* [1994] BCC 18, 24, *per* Judge John Newey QC.

[222] Ie a liquidator or administrator.

[223] Ie a secured creditor or an unsecured creditor who levied execution.

[224] See *Merchantile Bank of India Ltd v Chartered Bank of India, Australia and China, and Strauss & Co Ltd* [1937] 1 All ER 231; *Slavenburg's Bank v Intercontinental Natural Resources Ltd* [1980] 1 WLR 1076, 1090C–1091F, *per* Lloyd J.

[225] See *Re Renshaw & Co Ltd* [1908] WN 210. The device is not advisable since there is nothing to prevent a third party intervening and taking and registering a charge in priority. The device would also be vulnerable to challenge under Insolvency Act 1986, ss 239, 245 (in respect of a floating charge).

[226] See *Bank of Scotland v TA Neilson & Co* 1991 SLT 8, 11A, *per* Lord Maclean, and, by way of analogy, *Independent Automatic Sales Ltd v Knowles and Foster* [1962] 1 WLR 974. Note also *Re Monolithic Building Co* [1915] 1 Ch 643, 667, *per* Cozens-Hardy MR and 667–668, *per* Phillimore LJ.

[227] See *Smith v Bridgend County Borough Council* [2001] UKHL 58 at para h, *per* Lord Hoffmann.

[228] See s 874(1)(b).

[229] See *Smith v Bridgend County Borough Council* [2001] UKHL 58 at para h, *per* Lord Hoffmann. An administrator has an advantage that irrespective of the avoidance power he can deal with property encumbered by a charge (whether registered or not) by virtue of Insolvency Act 1986 (as amended), s 248 and Sch B1, paras 43(2), 70, 71, but, in the case of an unregistered charge, the avoidance power will operate to free the administrator of the obligation to apply the proceeds realized to the discharge of the secured debt.

[230] See *Smith v Bridgend County Borough Council* [2001] UKHL 58, at para f, *per* Lord Scott.

[231] See *Re Telomatic Ltd* [1994] 1 BCLC 90, 95a, *per* Judge Micklem; *Re Ehrmann Bros Ltd* [1906] 2 Ch 697.

[232] See *Re Monolithic Building Co* [1915] 1 Ch 643.

[233] See *Re Ashpurton Estates Ltd* [1983] Ch 110, 123E, *per* Lord Brightman.

[234] See s 860(1).

payable'.[235] A moot point regarding the point at which the money becomes repayable is whether that point is the expiration of the time period for registration[236] or the latter period plus the point at which a beneficiary of the avoidance power intervenes. There will be cases where the prescribed time period for registration expires but at that time there is no beneficiary of the avoidance power in place such that to all intents and purposes the holder of the unregistered charge will still have a fully effective security. In most cases this point will, perhaps, be more theoretical than real for such a party would, in all probability, seek a court order pursuant to section 873 rather than an order for the immediate repayment of any money secured by the charge. However, the latter point aside, a literal reading of section 874(3) would suggest that the avoidance time is the point of time at which a beneficiary of the avoidance power comes onto the scene rather than the mere expiration of the prescribed time period for registration. The section actually says 'and when a charge *becomes void* under this section, the money secured by it immediately becomes payable'.[237] A charge can only become void under the section as against a liquidator, an administrator, or a creditor, but if none of these parties exists then simple logic dictates that the charge is not void, and, if the charge is not void then the money secured by the charge cannot become repayable since the charge has to be void in order for that to happen.

Finally, it is submitted that the avoidance provision[238] is compliant with the European Convention on **25.874.07** Human Rights[239] (the Convention) and, in particular, Article 1 of the First Protocol[240] which aims to protect persons from being unlawfully deprived of their proprietary rights. The avoidance power serves to protect the integrity of the public register of company charges and thereby the interests of all parties who seek to rely on the information contained therein. Because of this it is a measure that is in, to use the language of the Convention,[241] the 'public interest' or 'the general interest' and, therefore, amounts to a proportionate deprivation of a proprietary right (ie the inability to assert an unregistered charge against prescribed parties) in the interests of the general community as is allowed under the Convention.[242]

## Companies' records and registers

### 875 Companies to keep copies of instruments creating charges[a]

(1) A company must keep available for inspection a copy of every instrument creating a charge **25.875.01** requiring registration under this Chapter, including any document delivered to the company under section 868(3)(b) (Northern Ireland: orders imposing charges affecting land).
(2) In the case of a series of uniform debentures, a copy of one of the debentures of the series is sufficient.

AMENDMENTS AND NOTES

[a] Section 875 also applies (with appropriate modifications) to LLPs by virtue of the Limited Liability Partnerships (Application of Companies Act 2006) Regulations 2009, SI 2009/1804, Pt 9.

COMMENCEMENT DATE 1 October 2009[243]

Formerly section 406 of the Companies Act 1985. This section imposes a duty on the company to keep **25.875.02** a copy of every instrument creating a charge that requires registration under the Act,[244] or a copy of a judgment charge against land in Northern Ireland,[245] at its registered office.[246] Therefore, the company will not be required to act in the case of an oral charge or any other charge arising out of a transaction

[235] See s 874(3).
[236] See s 870.
[237] See s 874(3) (emphasis added).
[238] See s 874(1).
[239] This became effective under UK law by virtue of the Human Rights Act 1998 which introduced parts of the Convention (including Art 1 of the First Protocol) directly into the UK as of 2 October 2000; see SI 2000/1815.
[240] This provides that: 'Every natural or legal person is entitled to the peaceful enjoyment of his possessions. No one shall be deprived of his possessions except in the public interest and subject to the conditions provided for by the law and by the general principles of international law.
The proceeding provisions shall not, however, in any way impair the right of a State to enforce such laws as it deems necessary to control the use of property in accordance with the general interest or to secure the payment of taxes or other contributions or penalties.'
[241] i.e. Art 1 of the First Protocol.
[242] For a detailed examination of the question of Convention compatibility and the avoidance power see de Lacy [2004] JBL 448.
[243] Companies Act 2006 (Commencement No 8, Transitional Provisions and Savings) Order 2008, SI 2008/2860, art 3(n).
[244] On which see ss 860(7), 876(1).
[245] See generally s 868 (covering both registered and unregistered land).
[246] By virtue of s 877(4) any creditor or member of the company has a right to inspect these instruments.

not involving a charge being created by an instrument.[247] Where a company has created a charge to secure an issue of uniform debentures then it only need keep a copy of one of those debentures at its registered office.[248]

## 876 Company's register of charges[a]

**25.876.01**
(1) Every limited company shall keep available for inspection a register of charges and enter in it—
(a) all charges specifically affecting property of the company, and
(b) all floating charges on the whole or part of the company's property or undertaking.
(2) The entry shall in each case give a short description of the property charged, the amount of the charge and, except in the cases of securities to bearer, the names of the persons entitled to it.
(3) If an officer of the company knowingly and wilfully authorises or permits the omission of an entry required to be made in pursuance of this section, he commits an offence.
(4) A person guilty of an offence under this section is liable—
(a) on conviction on indictment, to a fine;
(b) on summary conviction, to a fine not exceeding the statutory maximum.

AMENDMENTS AND NOTES

[a] Section 876 also applies (with appropriate modifications) to LLPs by virtue of the Limited Liability Partnerships (Application of Companies Act 2006) Regulations 2009, SI 2009/1804, Pt 9.

COMMENCEMENT DATE 1 October 2009[249]

**25.876.02** Formerly section 407 of the Companies Act 1985. This section imposes a duty on the company to keep at its registered office a register of charges. This is a separate and distinct register to that maintained by the registrar of companies.[250] The register is potentially much wider than that kept by the registrar of companies because it is a register of 'all charges',[251] including floating charges, specifically affecting the property of the company. Therefore, unlike the register maintained by the registrar, this register is not confined to consensual charges[252] but will also cover charges arising by operation of law. It also covers 'all charges' specifically affecting the property of the company[253] with no exceptions (unlike that kept by the registrar).[254] The register is, therefore, potentially the most comprehensive source of information on charges[255] affecting the property of the company.[256]

**25.876.03** The register of charges maintained by the company details[257] (a) all charges specifically affecting its property, and (b) all floating charges on the whole or part of its property.

**25.876.04** The register must also detail the following information[258] in relation to each charge[259]:

(i) a short description of the property covered by the charge;
(ii) the amount secured by the charge; and
(iii) the names of the persons entitled to the charge.[260]

**25.876.05** The section makes it an offence for an officer of the company to 'knowingly and wilfully' authorize or permit the company not to keep a register of charges as required by the section.[261] Therefore, in order for an offence to be committed by an officer, that officer must be shown to have knowledge of the omission to keep the register and an intention that the register is not kept by the company. It has been found that in a case where the officers of the company instructed the company secretary to register a

---

[247] Eg a charge created by the deposit of title deeds to land.
[248] See s 875(2).
[249] Companies Act 2006 (Commencement No 8, Transitional Provisions and Savings) Order 2008, SI 2008/2860, art 3(n).
[250] On which see s 869.
[251] See s 876(1)(a).
[252] See s 860(1) which makes it clear that the register kept by the registrar, by virtue of s 869, only applies to charges 'created' by the company.
[253] Unlike the s 869 register which is confined to the categories of charge listed in ss 860(7), 862, 868.
[254] On which see s 861.
[255] 'Charge' also includes 'mortgage' for these purposes; see s 860(5).
[256] In practice this register is rarely kept by companies nor is the requirement to keep it enforced; see de Lacy, *The Reform of United Kingdom Company Law* (London, Cavendish, 2002) 366 n 253, 367 n 255.
[257] See s 876(1).
[258] Contrast this with the information required to be kept on the public register of charges kept by the registrar of companies which is similar except that the date of the charges creation is also required; see s 869(4). Note also s 863(2) in relation to the information required in respect of a charge to secure an issue of debentures.
[259] By virtue of s 876(2).
[260] Except in the case of securities to bearer, where no names are required; see s 876(2).
[261] See s 876(3) and (4) (detailing the punishment for breach of the section).

charge, but he failed to do so, that no offence was committed by them.[262] Unlike the public register of charges,[263] should the company fail to keep a register of charges then the validity of the unregistered charges is in no way affected by non-registration and the charge will remain fully enforceable.[264] The only penalty for non-compliance is on the relevant company officers and is limited to a fine.[265] Although this register is available for public inspection[266] it is submitted that the doctrine of constructive notice does not apply to the contents of the register.[267]

## 877 Instruments creating charges and register of charges to be available for inspection[a]

(1) This section applies to—    **25.877.01**
  (a) documents required to be kept available for inspection under section 875 (copies of instruments creating charges), and
  (b) a company's register of charges kept in pursuance of section 876.
(2) The documents and register must be kept available for inspection—
  (a) at the company's registered office, or
  (b) at a place specified in regulations under section 1136.
(3) The company must give notice to the registrar—
  (a) of the place at which the documents and register are kept available for inspection, and
  (b) of any change in the place.
unless they have at all times been kept at the company's registered office.
(4) The documents and register shall be open to the inspection—
  (a) of any creditor or member of the company without charge, and
  (b) of any other person on payment of such fee as may be prescribed.
(5) If default is made for 14 days in complying with subsection (3) or an inspection required under subsection (4) is refused, an offence is committed by—
  (a) the company, and
  (b) every officer of the company who is in default.
(6) A person guilty of an offence under this section is liable on summary conviction to a fine not exceeding level 3 on the standard scale and, for continued contravention, a daily default fine not exceeding one-tenth of level 3 on the standard scale.
(7) If an inspection required under subsection (4) is refused the court may by order compel an immediate inspection.

AMENDMENTS AND NOTES

[a] Section 877 also applies (with appropriate modifications) to LLPs by virtue of the Limited Liability Partnerships (Application of Companies Act 2006) Regulations 2009, SI 2009/1804, Pt 9.

COMMENCEMENT DATE 1 October 2009[268]

Formerly section 408 of the Companies Act 1985. This section imposes a duty upon the company to    **25.877.02** keep available for inspection at its registered office[269] copies of instruments creating registrable charges and also a register of all charges affecting its property.[270] The section also creates a right to inspect these documents in respect of two separate categories of interest. Firstly, existing creditors[271] and members of the chargor company have a right to inspect both the register of charges[272] and any copies of instruments[273] that the company is required to keep without charge. Secondly, 'any other person'[274] also has the same inspection rights as existing creditors and members of the company but subject to

---

[262] See *Re Hackney Borough Newspaper Co* (1876) 3 Ch D 669.

[263] On which see s 874.

[264] See *Wright v Horton* (1887) 12 App Cas 371.

[265] See s 876(3)(4).

[266] By virtue of s 877(4).

[267] A similar argument is also advanced in connection with the public register of charges maintained by the registrar of companies pursuant to s 869, discussed above.

[268] Companies Act 2006 (Commencement No 8, Transitional Provisions and Savings) Order 2008, SI 2008/2860, art 3(n).

[269] See generally s 877(2). The company may also keep these documents at a place other than its registered office if authorized by the Secretary of State under s 1136.

[270] See generally s 877(1)(2). Unless the company keeps its documents at its registered office at all times then the company is required to inform the registrar of the place where the documents are kept or any change thereof; s 877(3).

[271] This does not cover potential creditors; see *Wright v Horton* (1887) 12 App Cas 371, 376, *per* Lord Halsbury LC who will have to exercise the inspection right conferred by s 877(4)(b) and, therefore, pay a fee.

[272] On which see s 876(1).

[273] On which see s 875.

[274] See s 877(4)(b). The prescribed fee is set out in the Companies (Fees for Inspection of Company Records) Regulations 2008, SI 2008/3007, reg 2(c).

payment of a prescribed fee.[275] This is a change in the law. Previously, under the old 1985 Act, the right to inspect copies of instruments creating charges was confined to creditors and members of the company.[276] Third parties only used to have a right to inspect the company's internal register of charges.[277] It is now clear that all parties have the same rights to access the company's charge information.[278] The right to inspect the register of charges has also been held to cover the right to make copies of the entries on that register.[279]

25.877.03    Should the company refuse a request to inspect the register of charges or copies of instruments by either of the two categories of party entitled to inspect them then both the company and any relevant officer making that refusal commit an offence[280] punishable by way of a fine.[281] Should the company repeatedly refuse access to its register and copies of instruments then an aggrieved party may seek an order of the court to compel the company to grant immediate access.[282]

# CHAPTER 2
## COMPANIES REGISTERED IN SCOTLAND

### *Introductory note*

25.878.01    The law relating to floating charges and receivers in Scotland falls within the legislative competence of the Scottish Parliament.[283] The Bankruptcy and Diligence etc (Scotland) Act 2007[284] will introduce fundamental changes, implementing the recommendations of the Scottish Law Commission.[285] That Act (referred to in the commentary below as the Scottish Act) provides that the Companies Act provisions be repealed in their entirety and replaced by the new provisions. Commencement of the Scottish Act has been delayed as a result of concerns expressed by certain stakeholders about the impact of commencement.[286] The changes will, in the main, apply only to charges[287] created after the coming into force of the relevant provisions.[288] Thus, subsisting charges will remain subject to the law as it stands before the changes take effect regarding this Chapter, which consolidates the registration provisions previously contained in Chapter II of Part XII of the Companies Act 1985, and Chapter 1 of Part XVIII of the 1985 Act. The most important changes introduced by the Scottish Act are referred to in the commentary below.

---

[275] See s 877(4)(b).

[276] See CA 1985, s 408(1).

[277] See CA 1985, s 408(2).

[278] See generally, s 877(4). The only point of distinction is that third parties will have to pay a prescribed fee to access the information.

[279] See *Nelson v Anglo-American Land Mortgage Agency Co* [1897] 1 Ch 130, 133 *per* Nelson J.

[280] See s 877(5).

[281] See s 877(6).

[282] See s 877(7). The court will also grant an injunction to prevent the company stopping a person inspecting the register of charges from taking copies of the entries; see *Nelson v Anglo-American Mortgage Agency Co* [1897] 1 Ch 130, 134, *per* Nelson J.

[283] The Scotland Act 1998 (s 30 and Sch 5 Pt II Head C) devolves to the Scottish Parliament power to legislate with respect to floating charges and receivers, excepting the law relating to preferential debts, the regulation of insolvency practitioners, and co-operation among insolvency courts

[284] The statute was passed by the Scottish Parliament on 30 Nov 2006 and Royal Assent was given on 15 Jan 2007.

[285] Scottish Law Commission, *Discussion Paper on Registration of Rights in Security by Companies* (No 121, Oct 2002) and Scottish Law Commission, *Report on Registration of Rights in Security by Companies* (No 197, Sept 2004).

[286] See Register of Floating Charges Technical Working Group Report to Scottish Government (August 2011). Concern focuses in particular on the (additional) requirement for registration in the proposed Scottish Register of Floating Charges and the potential for legal uncertainty to arise from the provisions of the Scottish Act, especially for English and overseas companies.

[287] The term 'charge' is derived from English law, whereas Scots law uses the generic term 'right in security' to describe the (real) right that is held by a secured creditor over and above a personal claim against a debtor. However, since the introduction of the floating charge to Scotland, the term 'charge' has become standard usage in respect of that particular form of security interest.

[288] It remains unclear whether the Scottish Act will be implemented as it stands or with the amendment proposed (as Option 2) in the Register of Floating Charges Technical Working Group Report to Scottish Government (August 2011). It is also unclear whether the registration provisions of the Scottish Act will be superseded by the proposals made by BIS for a UK-wide scheme of registration: see BIS, Revised Scheme for Registration of Charges Created by Companies and Limited Liability Partnerships, Proposed Revision of Part 25, Companies Act 2006 (August 2011).

*Charges requiring registration*

## 878  Charges created by a company

(1)  A company[a] that creates a charge to which this section applies must deliver the prescribed      **25.878.02**
particulars of the charge, together with a copy certified as a correct copy of the instrument (if any)
by which the charge is created or evidenced, to the registrar for registration before the end of the
period allowed for registration.

(2)  Registration of a charge to which this section applies may instead be effected on the application
of a person interested in it.

(3)  Where registration is effected on the application of some person other than the company, that
person is entitled to recover from the company the amount of any fees properly paid by him to the
registrar on the registration.

(4)  If a company fails to comply with subsection (1), an offence is committed by—
(a)  the company, and
(b)  every officer of the company who is in default.

(5)  A person guilty of an offence under this section is liable—
(a)  on conviction on indictment, to a fine, and
(b)  on summary conviction, to a fine not exceeding the statutory maximum.

(6)  Subsection (4) does not apply if registration of the charge has been effected on the application of
some other person.

(7)  This section applies to the following charges—
(a)  a charge on land or any interest in such land, other than a charge for any rent or other
periodical sum payable in respect of the land,
(b)  a security over incorporeal moveable property of any of the following categories—
(i)  goodwill,
(ii)  a patent or a licence under a patent,
(iii)  a trademark,
(iv)  a copyright or a licence under a copyright,
(v)  a registered design or a licence in respect of such a design,
(vi)  a design right or a licence under a design right,
(vii)  the book debts (whether book debts of the company or assigned to it), and
(viii) uncalled share capital of the company or calls made but not paid,
(c)  a security over a ship or aircraft or any share in a ship,
(d)  a floating charge.

AMENDMENTS AND NOTES

[a]  Including a limited liability partnership, by virtue of the Limited Liability Partnerships (Scotland)
Regulations 2001, SI 2001/128, art 3.

COMMENCEMENT DATE  1 October 2009[289]

This section consolidates provisions that were previously spread across several sections of Chapter II of    **25.878.03**
Part XII of the Companies Act 1985. Subsection (1) imposes on a company that creates a charge the
requirement to register prescribed particulars together with a copy (certified in the prescribed manner[290] to be a correct copy) of the instrument (if any) by which the charge is created or evidenced before
the end of the period allowed for registration. The purpose of registration is to give publicity to the fact
that a real right has been created over the property subject to the charge since the existence of the charge
is a matter of considerable importance not just for the granter and the holder of the security interest but
also for their respective creditors.

Subsections (2) and (3) (replacing section 415(1) and (2) of the Companies Act 1985) permit another    **25.878.04**
interested person to register the charge and to recover from the company the amount of any fee. This
would permit, *inter alia*, a lender to register the charge.

Subsections (4) and (5) set out the offences associated with non-registration, replacing section 415(3)    **25.878.05**
of the Companies Act 1985.

---

[289]  Companies Act 2006 (Commencement No 8, Transitional Provisions and Savings) Order 2008, SI
2008/2860, art 3(n).

[290]  Regulation 7 of the Companies (Forms) Regulations 1985 SI 1985/854 (as amended) requires that the copy
instrument must be certified by the company who created the charge. The person signing the certificate must be
an officer of the company (director or secretary). The copy instrument itself is not registered and is not available
to those searching the register, although shareholders and existing creditors have a right to inspect it: s 896. The
practice appears to be that the registrar neither keeps nor copies the (copy) instrument, merely using it at the time
of registration to check the accuracy of the particulars: see G Gretton 'Registration of Company Charges' 6 *Edin
LR* (2002) 146–175, p 156.

**25.878.06**    Subsection (7) sets out the charges to which the registration requirement applies. It is only in respect of the floating charge that reference is made to a specific type of security interest. The remaining references are to assets and it therefore follows that the registration requirement applies to any form of security interest created over those assets. The charge may secure not only the payment of a debt but any other obligation (subject to express exclusion, such as in paragraph (a)).

**25.878.07**    Charges on property within the United Kingdom but outside Scotland fall within the registration requirement in this section if the company is registered in Scotland, with the result that there is no need (nor any possibility) for further registration with the Registrar for England and Wales or Northern Ireland. Similarly, charges registered by companies in England and Wales or Northern Ireland with the Registrar of Companies under section 860 do not require to undergo any further registration procedure in Scotland. The position will change following implementation of the Scottish Act which requires registration of a floating charge in the new Register of Floating Charges irrespective of the location of incorporation of the granter. Section 893 contains a power which may be exercised so as to avoid the need for double registration.[291]

### 879    Charges which have to be registered: supplementary

**25.879.01**    (1)    A charge on land, for the purposes of section 878(7)(a), includes a charge created by a heritable security within the meaning of section 9(8) of the Conveyancing and Feudal Reform (Scotland) Act 1970.

(2)    The holding of debentures entitling the holder to a charge on land is not, for the purposes of section 878(7)(a), deemed to be an interest in land.

(3)    It is immaterial for the purposes of this Chapter where land subject to a charge is situated.

(4)    The deposit by way of security of a negotiable instrument given to secure the payment of book debts is not, for purposes of section 898(7)(c)(vii), to be treated as a charge on those book debts.

(5)    References in this Chapter to the date of the creation of a charge are—

(a)    in the case of a floating charge, the date on which the instrument creating the floating charge was executed by the company creating the charge, and

(b)    in any other case, the date on which the right of the person entitled to the benefit of the charge was constituted as a real right.

(6)    In this Chapter 'company' means an incorporated company registered in Scotland.

COMMENCEMENT DATE 1 October 2009[292]

**25.879.02**    This section consolidates a number of provisions that were previously spread across several sections of Chapter II of Part XII of the Companies Act 1985. Subsections (1) and (3) replace section 410(4)(a) of the 1985 Act; subsection (4) replaces section 412; and subsections (5) and (6) replace section 410(5).

**25.879.03**    Subsection (2) clarifies, in the context of debentures, the meaning of an 'interest in land'. It applies typically to circumstances in which company A grants a security interest to B over debentures it holds in company C, when those debentures are charged on land. The effect of subsection (2) is that the charge granted by company A to B is not an interest in land for the purposes of section 878(7). Moreover, as it is not one of the remaining security interests referred to in section 878(7), such a charge is not subject to the registration requirement in section 882(1).

**25.879.04**    The date of the creation of a floating charge is the date on which the instrument creating the floating charge was executed by the company creating the charge.[293] The date of the creation of any other security interest is the date on which the right of the person entitled to the benefit of the charge was constituted as a real right. In the case of a hertitable security over land (standard security) the real right is constituted by registration in the appropriate register (Land Register or Register of Sasines).[294] In the case of an assignation in security of incorporeal moveable property, the real right arises on intimation

---

[291]    The DTI Consultation Document 'Registration of Scottish Floating Charges' (May 2007) proposes to use the s 893 power to treat floating charges registered in the Scottish register of floating charges (to be created under the Bankruptcy and Diligence (Scotland) Act 2007) as if they had been registered with the Registrar of Companies.

[292]    Companies Act 2006 (Commencement No 8, Transitional Provisions and Savings) Order 2008, SI 2008/2860, art 3(n).

[293]    Under the Scottish Act, the date of creation of a floating charge will be the date of registration, subject to the operation of the principle of advance notice. When advance notice is given in the prescribed form, it will have the effect that the floating charge will be treated as having been created when the notice is registered. By way of contrast, the date of creation of a floating charge (or any security other than a standard security) under the BIS proposals for a new UK-wide registration scheme is generally the date of delivery to the lender (see the Draft Companies Act 2006 (Amendment of Part 25) Regulations 2012, Sch 1).

[294]    In the case of the Register of Sasines the date of recording can be confirmed by confirmation issued by the Keeper, whereas in the case of the Land Register the date is confirmed by a Charge Certificate.

to the account debtor.[295] Registration is not constitutive of the real right in the case of a floating charge as the registration requirement assumes that the security interest has already been created.[296]

## 880  Duty to register charges existing on property acquired

(1) Subsection (2) applies where a company acquires any property which is subject to a charge of any kind as would, if it had been created by the company after the acquisition of the property, have been required to be registered under this Chapter.       **25.880.01**

(2) The company must deliver the prescribed particulars of the charge, together with a copy (certified to be a correct copy) of the instrument (if any) by which the charge was created or is evidenced, to the registrar for registration before the end of the period allowed for registration.

(3) If default is made in complying with this section, an offence is committed by—
   (a) the company, and
   (b) every officer of it who is in default.

(4) A person guilty of an offence under this section is liable—
   (a) on conviction on indictment, to a fine;
   (b) on summary conviction, to a fine not exceeding the statutory maximum.

COMMENCEMENT DATE  1 October 2009[297]

Subsection (1) requires a company to register a charge over property which it acquires if such a charge would require registration if created after acquisition of the property by the company. The logic of this requirement is presumably twofold. First, it provides a means whereby the charge holder can identify the new owner of the property subject to the charge. Second, it brings the existence of the charge to the attention of the creditors of the new owner: if this did not occur, the creditors of the new owner might extend further credit on the basis that there were unencumbered assets available to satisfy their claims. The section applies most obviously to a fixed charge as a floating charge allows the debtor to transfer property subject to the charge in an unencumbered form to a third party prior to the attachment of the charge.       **25.880.02**

Subsection (3) provides for a fine to be imposed on a company and every officer in default for non-compliance with this section, and a daily default fine for continued contravention.       **25.880.03**

## 881  Charge by way of ex facie absolute disposition, etc

(1) For the avoidance of doubt, it is hereby declared that, in the case of a charge created by way of an ex facie absolute disposition or assignation qualified by a back letter or other agreement, or by a standard security qualified by an agreement, compliance with section 878(1) does not of itself render the charge unavailable as security for indebtedness incurred after the date of compliance.       **25.881.01**

(2) Where the amount secured by a charge so created is purported to be increased by a further back letter or agreement, a further charge is held to have been created by the ex facie absolute disposition or assignation or (as the case may be) by the standard security, as qualified by the further back letter or agreement.

(3) In that case, the provisions of this Chapter apply to the further charge as if—
   (a) references in this Chapter (other than in this section) to the charge were references to the further charge, and
   (b) references to the date of the creation of the charge were references to the date on which the further back letter or agreement was executed.

COMMENCEMENT DATE  1 October 2009[298]

Subsection (1) makes clear that registration in accordance with section 878(1) of an *ex facie* absolute disposition[299] qualified by a back letter or other form of agreement or a standard security qualified by an agreement does not render the charge unavailable as security for indebtedness incurred after the       **25.881.02**

---

[295]  This poses some difficulty in establishing the date on which the real right is constituted. The Registrar of Companies does require proof of intimation before such a charge can be registered: while there is in principle no restriction on the manner of proof, acceptable forms are the debtor's acknowledgement or a certificate of intimation with evidence of posting (eg recorded delivery). Under the Scottish Act, assignation of a floating charge will become effective on registration.

[296]  See para 1.7 of Scottish Law Commission Report No 121 (above n 285 to para 25.878.01).

[297]  Companies Act 2006 (Commencement No 8, Transitional Provisions and Savings) Order 2008, SI 2008/2860, art 3(n).

[298]  Companies Act 2006 (Commencement No 8, Transitional Provisions and Savings) Order 2008, SI 2008/2860, art 3(n).

[299]  The *ex facie* absolute disposition is not competent for new heritable securities since the entry into effect of s 9 of the Conveyancing and Feudal Reform (Scotland) Act 1970: it does, however, remain competent for assignations in security of incorporeal moveable property.

date of compliance. This provision overrides the common law rule that publication of the terms of the advance (by recording of the back letter or agreement along with the security interest) prevents the security being used to secure advances after the date of publication.[300] Thus, even if it were assumed that an 'all sums' security fell within the common law rule,[301] this subsection ensures that it remains capable of securing future advances following registration.

**25.881.03**    Subsection (2) deals with the situation in which the amount secured by a charge so created is increased by a further back letter or agreement. In these circumstances, a new charge is taken to have been created and the provisions of this Chapter apply to the further charge *mutatis mutandis* as they do to the original charge. This subsection does not, in terms, apply to a floating charge (being limited to the types of security referred to in subsection (1)). However, alteration of the amount secured by a floating charge is dealt with by section 466 of the Companies Act 1985, which makes similar provision. The remaining issue is whether non-registration results in the charge securing only the original amount. The logic of the principle that publicity is constitutive of the real right would suggest that the charge is so limited,[302] but some doubt must remain in the absence of specific statutory provision.[303]

## *Special rules about debentures*

### 882  Charge in series of debentures

**25.882.01**

(1)  Where a series of debentures containing, or giving by reference to any other instrument, any charge to the benefit of which the debenture-holders of that series are entitled pari passu, is created by a company, it is sufficient for purposes of section 878 if the required particulars, together with a copy of the deed containing the charge (or, if there is no such deed, of one of the debentures of the series) are delivered to the registrar before the end of the period allowed for registration.

(2)  The following are the required particulars—

    (a)  the total amount secured by the whole series,

    (b)  the dates of the resolutions authorising the issue of the series and the date of the covering deed (if any) by which the security is created or defined,

    (c)  a general description of the property charged,

    (d)  the names of the trustees (if any) for the debenture-holders, and

    (e)  in the case of a floating charge, a statement of any provisions of the charge and of any instrument relating to it which prohibit or restrict or regulate the power of the company to grant further securities ranking in priority to, or *pari passu* with, the floating charge, or which vary or otherwise regulate the order of ranking of the floating charge in relation to subsisting securities.

(3)  Where more than one issue is made of debentures in the series, particulars of the date and amount of each issue of debentures of the series must be sent to the registrar for entry in the register of charges.

(4)  Failure to comply with subsection (3) does not affect the validity of any of those debentures.

(5)  Subsections (2) to (6) of section 878 apply for the purposes of this section as they apply for the purposes of that section but as if for the reference to the registration of the charge there was substituted a reference to the registration of the series of debentures.

COMMENCEMENT DATE  1 October 2009[304]

**25.882.02**    This section replaces section 413(2) of the Companies Act 1985. It deals with the issue of a series of debentures secured *pari passu* by a single charge. The objective is to permit a company to raise finance by making an issue or issues of debentures on the basis that each debenture is secured *pari passu* by a single charge. This carries significant benefits for a company in accessing secured finance because it can do so on the basis of registering a single charge over the company's assets. In these circumstances a company is required to deliver to the registrar within 21 days of the execution of the deed containing the charge the prescribed particulars set out in subsection(2)(a) to (e).[305] A copy of the deed (there is no requirement for certification as in the case of section 878) must also be provided. Compliance with these requirements is taken to be compliance with the registration requirement in section 878. When

---

[300]  See WM Gloag and JW Irvine, *Law of Rights in Security* (W Green, Edinburgh, 1897), 156–7, citing the case of *Keith v Maxwell* 1795 Bell, *Folio Cases* 234. The rule does not apply to standard securities or assignations in security of incorporeal moveable property.

[301]  See Gloag and Irvine, ibid, 157 for the opposing views on the matter.

[302]  See, supporting this view, G Gretton, 'Registration of Company Charges' 6 *Edin LR* (2002) 146–175, 153.

[303]  For the contrary view, see *Palmer's Company Law* (Sweet & Maxwell) para 13.411 (release 82: Sept 2001).

[304]  Companies Act 2006 (Commencement No 8, Transitional Provisions and Savings) Order 2008, SI 2008/2860, art 3(n).

[305]  The information should be provided in Form 413(Scot). Forms can be found online at ⟨http://www.companieshouse.gov.uk/forms/formsOnline.shtml⟩.

more than one issue is made of debentures in the series, the prescribed particulars must be sent to the registrar in respect of each issue, but any omission to do this does not affect the validity of any of those debentures.

### 883  Additional registration requirement for commission etc in relation to debentures

(1) Where any commission, allowance or discount has been paid or made either directly or indirectly    **25.883.01**
by a company to a person in consideration of his—
  (a)  subscribing or agreeing to subscribe, whether absolutely or conditionally, for debentures in a company, or
  (b)  procuring or agreeing to procure subscriptions, whether absolute or conditional, for such debentures,
the particulars required to be sent for registration under section 878 shall include particulars as to the amount or rate per cent. of the commission, discount or allowance so paid or made.
(2) The deposit of debentures as security for a debt of the company is not, for the purposes of this section, treated as the issue of debentures at a discount.
(3) Failure to comply with this section does not affect the validity of the debentures issued.

COMMENCEMENT DATE  1 October 2009[306]

This section replaces section 413(3) of the Companies Act 1985. It deals with commission paid or    **25.883.02**
allowance or discount made in connection with an issue of debentures. In contrast to the position in respect of share issues,[307] there are no restrictions on the payment of commission in respect of debentures nor is there a prohibition on issue at a discount. However, any such commission, allowance, or discount must be included in the particulars sent to the registrar under section 878.

## Charges on property outside the United Kingdom

### 884  Charges on property outside United Kingdom

Where a charge is created in the United Kingdom but comprises property outside the United Kingdom,    **25.884.01**
the copy of the instrument creating or purporting to create the charge may be sent for registration under section 878 even if further proceedings may be necessary to make the charge valid or effectual according to the law of the country in which the property is situated.

COMMENCEMENT DATE  1 October 2009[308]

This section replaces section 411(2) of the Companies Act 1985. It deals with charges created in the UK    **25.884.02**
(by companies registered in Scotland) comprising property outside the UK. It permits but does not require registration to proceed under section 878, notwithstanding that further proceedings may be necessary to make the charge valid or effectual according to the law of the country in which the property is situated. The intention of the section is presumably to allow registration within the 21-day period prescribed by section 886, but it would be more consistent with section 878 to permit registration within 21 days of the security being constituted as a real right according to the *lex situs*.

## The register of charges

### 885  Register of charges to be kept by registrar

(1) The registrar shall keep, with respect to each company, a register of all the charges requiring    **25.885.01**
registration under this Chapter.
(2) In the case of a charge to the benefit of which holders of a series of debentures are entitled, the registrar shall enter in the register the required particulars specified in section 882(2).
(3) In the case of any other charge, the registrar shall enter in the register the following particulars—
  (a)  if it is a charge created by a company, the date of its creation and, if it is a charge which was existing on property acquired by the company, the date of the acquisition,
  (b)  the amount secured by the charge,
  (c)  short particulars of the property charged,
  (d)  the persons entitled to the charge, and

---

[306]  Companies Act 2006 (Commencement No 8, Transitional Provisions and Savings) Order 2008, SI 2008/2860, art 3(n).
[307]  See ss 552 and 553, replacing ss 97 and 98 of the Companies Act (CA) 1985.
[308]  Companies Act 2006 (Commencement No 8, Transitional Provisions and Savings) Order 2008, SI 2008/2860, art 3(n).

    (e)  in the case of a floating charge, a statement of any of the provisions of the charge and of any instrument relating to it which prohibit or restrict or regulate the company's power to grant further securities ranking in priority to, or *pari passu* with, the floating charge, or which vary or otherwise regulate the order of ranking of the floating charge in relation to subsisting securities.

  (4)  The registrar shall give a certificate of the registration of any charge registered in pursuance of this Chapter, stating—

    (a)  the name of the company and the person first-named in the charge among those entitled to the benefit of the charge (or, in the case of a series of debentures, the name of the holder of the first such debenture issued), and

    (b)  the amount secured by the charge.

  (5)  The certificate—

    (a)  shall be signed by the registrar or authenticated by the registrar's official seal, and

    (b)  is conclusive evidence that the requirements of this Chapter as to registration have been satisfied.

  (6)  The register kept in pursuance of this section shall be open to inspection by any person.

COMMENCEMENT DATE 1 October 2009[309]

**25.885.02**    This section replaces sections 417 and 418 of the Companies Act 1985.

**25.885.03**    Subsection (1) requires the registrar of companies to keep a register of all the charges requiring registration in this Chapter and to enter in it the particulars specified below. Under the Scottish Act, this requirement will end and floating charges will be registered in the (new) Register of Floating Charges which will be established and maintained by the Keeper of the Registers of Scotland.

**25.885.04**    Subsection (2) requires, in the case of a charge securing a series of debentures, entry in the register of the particulars specified in section 886(2).

**25.885.05**    In the case of any other charge the particulars to be registered are set out in subsection (3). The particulars must show the 'person entitled to the charge' but as no provision is made for the registration of an assignation it will be only the original holder that is shown and not an assignee.[310] In the case of a floating charge a 'negative pledge clause' or a 'ranking agreement' must be registered.[311] Failure to register any of the prescribed particulars results in the charge being 'void' (section 889 and section 878).[312] This information is submitted on form 410(Scot).[313] A certified copy of the instrument of charge must be also be submitted[314] but is not registered and is not available to those searching the register, although shareholders and existing creditors have a right to inspect it.[315] The practice appears to be that the registrar neither keeps nor copies the (copy) instrument, merely using it at the time of registration to check the accuracy of the particulars. Under the Scottish Act, the entire document will be recorded in the (new) Register of Floating Charges.

**25.885.06**    Subsection (4) requires the registrar of companies to give a certificate of the registration of any charge registered in pursuance of this Chapter. A crucial provision is that contained in subsection (5)(b) to the effect that the certificate is conclusive evidence that the requirements of this Chapter as to registration have been complied with. In England, it was held in respect of the parallel provision (section 410(2) of the Companies Act 1985) that the conclusive nature of the certificate is maintained even if the filed particulars omitted a class of asset covered by the security[316] or misstated the date of creation of the charge[317] or the amount secured.[318] In cases such as these, the conclusive nature of the certificate substantially erodes the principle that the Register of Charges should act as an accurate public record of charges granted by a company. The conclusive nature of the certificate does not, however, extend to

---

[309] Companies Act 2006 (Commencement No 8, Transitional Provisions and Savings) Order 2008, SI 2008/2860, art 3(n).

[310] It was suggested in *Libertas-Kommerz GmbH v Johnson* 1997 SC 191 that a company is bound to record an assignation in its internal (s 891) register but that has been disputed: see G Gretton, 'Registration of Company Charges' 6 *Edin LR* (2002) 146–175, 155. There is certainly no express statutory obligation to register an assignation. Under the Scottish Act, an assignation will require registration.

[311] For definition of these terms, see the commentary on s 464 of the CA 1985.

[312] The prescribed particulars should be distinguished from other terms of the charge. So long as the prescribed particulars are registered the conclusive nature of a certificate of registration will result in effect being given to the charge even when important terms are not disclosed in the particulars: see the commentary on subs (5).

[313] Companies (Forms) Regulations 1985, SI 1985/854.

[314] CA 2006, s 880(2).

[315] CA 2006, s 892(4).

[316] *National Provincial and Union Bank of England v Charnley* [1924] 1 KB 431.

[317] *Re Eric Holmes (Property) Ltd* [1965] Ch 1052.

[318] *Re Mechanisations (Eaglescliffe) Ltd* [1966] Ch 20.

matters beyond the registration requirements of the Act, such as the validity of the charge registered.[319] It is not necessary to secure valid registration that the registrar should register the charge and issue a certificate.[320] It is sufficient that the creditor has satisfactory evidence of having submitted the prescribed particulars and a certified copy of the instrument of charge within the statutory timescale.

Subsection (6) provides that the register maintained under this section is open to inspection by any person. **25.885.07**

## 886  The period allowed for registration

(1)  The period allowed for registration of a charge created by a company is— **25.886.01**
   (a)  21 days beginning with the day after the day on which the charge is created, or
   (b)  if the charge is created outside the United Kingdom, 21 days beginning with the day after the day on which a copy of the instrument by which the charge is created or evidenced could, in due course of post (and if despatched with due diligence) have been received in the United Kingdom.
(2)  The period allowed for registration of a charge to which property acquired by a company is subject is—
   (a)  21 days beginning with the day after the day on which the transaction is settled, or
   (b)  if the property is situated and the charge was created outside the United Kingdom, 21 days beginning with the day after the day on which a copy of the instrument by which the charge is created or evidenced could, in due course of post (and if despatched with due diligence) have been received in the United Kingdom.
(3)  The period allowed for registration of particulars of a series of debentures as a result of section 882 is—
   (a)  if there is a deed containing the charge mentioned in section 882(1), 21 days beginning with the day after the day on which that deed is executed, or
   (b)  if there is no such deed, 21 days beginning with the day after the day on which the first debenture of the series is executed.

COMMENCEMENT DATE 1 October 2009[321]

This section deals with the period permitted for registration. The standard rule is that registration must occur within 21 days of creation of the charge.[322] Sections 1(b) and 2(b) extend the 21-day period of registration in the case of a charge created out of the UK. In that case, the 21-day period begins to run from the date on which the copy of the instrument creating it could have been received in the UK. This provision inevitably leaves open-ended the period within which registration of the charge must occur. A duty to post the copy would seem to arise in the case of a floating charge when it is executed (abroad) by the company (applying section 879(5)), but in the case of a fixed charge the date on which the real right is constituted will depend on the *lex situs* of the property in question[323] and therefore the date on which the duty to post arises cannot be fixed by the law in the UK. **25.886.02**

## 887  Entries of satisfaction and relief

(1)  Subsection (2) applies if a statement is delivered to the registrar verifying with respect to any registered charge— **25.887.01**
   (a)  that the debt for which the charge was given has been paid or satisfied in whole or in part, or
   (b)  that part of the property charged has been released from the charge or has ceased to form part of the company's property.
(2)  If the charge is a floating charge, the statement must be accompanied by either—
   (a)  a statement by the creditor entitled to the benefit of the charge, or a person authorised by him for the purpose, verifying that the statement mentioned in subsection (1) is correct, or
   (b)  a direction obtained from the court, on the ground that the statement by the creditor mentioned in paragraph (a) could not be readily obtained, dispensing with the need for that statement.
(3)  The registrar may enter on the register a memorandum of satisfaction (in whole or in part) regarding the fact contained in the statement mentioned in subsection (1).
(4)  Where the registrar enters a memorandum of satisfaction in whole, he shall, if required, furnish the company with a copy of the memorandum.

---

[319] *Scottish & Newcastle Breweries Ltd v Liquidator of Rathburne Hotel Co Ltd* [1970] SLT 313.
[320] *NV Slavenburg's Bank v Intercontinental Natural Resources Limited* [1980] 1 All ER 955.
[321] Companies Act 2006 (Commencement No 8, Transitional Provisions and Savings) Order 2008, SI 2008/2860, art 3(n).
[322] See, as regards date of creation, s 879.
[323] Several foreign legal systems may be relevant in this context if the security interest covers property in different countries

---

(5) Nothing in this section requires the company to submit particulars with respect to the entry in the register of a memorandum of satisfaction where the company, having created a floating charge over all or any part of its property, disposes of part of the property subject to the floating charge.

COMMENCEMENT DATE 1 October 2009[324]

**25.887.02** This section replaces section 419 of the Companies Act 1985. It deals with the recording in the Register of Charges of memoranda of satisfaction and release. The former records payment in whole or in part of the debt which is secured by the charge. The latter records that part of the property has been released from the charge or has ceased to form part of the company's property.

**25.887.03** While the general purpose of these memoranda is no doubt to inform creditors, their utility and the formulation of the provisions have attracted considerable criticism.[325] In the first place, there is no obligation imposed on either debtor or creditor to ensure registration of these memoranda.[326] In that sense, they do not provide a reliable record for creditors as to payment of the underlying debt or the property that is subject to the charge. That characteristic is compounded by the fact that release of specified properties from the scope of a floating charge is effective without registration of a memorandum of release.[327] Second, the memoranda referred to in subsection (3) record the 'fact' of payment or release. In the case of payment, it has been noted that the memorandum of satisfaction does not state that the security has been discharged but assumes that it has been.[328] However, while that approach deals adequately with most circumstances in which a security is given for a fixed sum, it does not deal with circumstances in which security is given for 'all sums due or to become due' as in that case payment does not discharge the security.[329] In the case of a memorandum of release, no provision is made for the release of the entire property subject to the charge,[330] with the result that such a release could not be recorded under subsection (1)(b).

**25.887.04** Subsection (2) requires, in the case of a floating charge[331] that the registrar secure the certification by the creditor of the accuracy of the contents of the memorandum or, if that is not possible, that he secures the direction of the court in respect of registration. The purpose is clearly to ensure that the debtor company is not able unilaterally to have recorded a memorandum of satisfaction or release, to the potential prejudice of the creditor or third parties.[332]

**25.887.05** Subsection (3) requires the registrar to furnish the company with a copy of a memorandum entered in the Register of Charges pursuant to this section. The prescribed forms for the provision of information to the registrar under subsection (1) are Form 419a(Scot) and 419b(Scot).[333]

**25.887.06** Subsection (5) makes clear that a disposal of property subject to a floating charge does not require a company to submit particulars with respect to the entry in the register of a memorandum of satisfaction. This reflects the nature of the floating charge as a security interest that leaves a company with freedom to deal in property subject to the charge so long as the charge has not attached (crystallized).

---

[324] Companies Act 2006 (Commencement No 8, Transitional Provisions and Savings) Order 2008, SI 2008/2860, art 3(n).

[325] See generally Scottish Law Commission Report No 197 paras 2.24–2.26 and G Gretton, 'Registration of Company Charges' 6 *Edin LR* (2002) 146–175, 160–3.

[326] That conclusion is made clear both by the wording of subs (3) and the decision in *Scottish & Newcastle plc v Ascot Inns Ltd* 1994 SLT 1140. Under the Scottish Act it will be necessary for alterations to a floating charge to be registered but discharge will remain possible by other means.

[327] *Scottish & Newcastle plc v Ascot Inns Ltd* 1994 SLT 1140. This is so despite the presence of two different registration regimes for such a release: this section and s 466(4) of the CA 1985. The position will change under the Scottish Act, which provides that property may be released from a floating charge only on registration of an instrument of alteration to that effect (s 36).

[328] Following *Cameron v Williamson* (1895) 22 R 293, holding that repayment of a fixed-sum security discharges the security.

[329] The solution favoured by the Scottish Act is that a deed of discharge should replace the memorandum of satisfaction. Such a deed would discharge the security in whole or part but would be without prejudice to any other rule whereby a security may be discharged (eg repayment in the case of a loan for a fixed amount).

[330] As might occur for example if the creditor had taken standard securities over several properties and wishes to release one.

[331] The provision, in terms, applies only to floating charges but it has been suggested that it should be taken to apply to a creditor entitled to the benefit of any charge: see *Palmer's Company Law* para 13.412.1 and G Gretton, 'Registration of Company Charges' 6 *Edin LR* (2002) 146–175, 162.

[332] As to the issue of third parties' reliance on the content of memoranda of satisfaction or release, see the commentary on s 888 below.

[333] Forms can be found online at ⟨http://www.companieshouse.gov.uk/forms/formsOnline.shtml⟩.

## 888  Rectification of register of charges

(1)  Subsection (2) applies if the court is satisfied—                                    **25.888.01**
  (a)  that the failure to register a charge before the end of the period allowed for registration, or the omission or misstatement of any particular with respect to any such charge or in a memorandum of satisfaction—
    (i)   was accidental or due to inadvertence or to some other sufficient cause, or
    (ii)  is not of a nature to prejudice the position of creditors or shareholders of the company, or
  (b)  that on other grounds it is just and equitable to grant relief.
(2)  The court may, on the application of the company or a person interested, and on such terms and conditions as seem to the court just and expedient, order that the period allowed for registration shall be extended or, as the case may be, that the omission or misstatement shall be rectified.

COMMENCEMENT DATE 1 October 2009[334]

This section deals with two separate issues. The first is the power of the court to permit late registration    **25.888.02**
of a charge in the Register of Charges. The second is the power of the court to permit rectification of errors in a duly registered charge or memorandum of satisfaction.

The court's power to extend the period for registration of a charge may be exercised if the omission    **25.888.03**
meets one or more of the following criteria: (a) it was accidental, inadvertent, or due to some other sufficient cause; or (b) it is not of a nature to prejudice the position of creditors or shareholders of the company; or (c) that it is on other grounds just and equitable to grant relief.

It has been noted that there are some inherent problems in applying these criteria.[335] In particular, the    **25.888.04**
reference to 'sufficient cause' raises the question whether any cause that leads to omission to register is sufficient or whether (as seems likely) sufficiency must be assessed against some other standard: and if that other standard is not specified, there may be little difference between extension based on sufficient cause and extension based on just and equitable relief. Moreover, the reference to omission to register as prejudicing the interests of creditors and shareholders is difficult to rationalize. Shareholders will suffer the effect of a fine for non-registration under section 878(5), but will not in principle suffer because a creditor fails to constitute a security interest through registration. Similarly, creditors other than the holder of a charge do not in principle suffer as a result of failure to register the charge: in reality such creditors benefit as the charge holder will not have gained the priority that was sought through the medium of the charge.[336] While these issues remain unresolved, what is clear is that the creditor should make an application as soon as the omission is discovered, as substantial delay is likely to lead to refusal of permission.[337]

In principle, late registration permitted by the court validates the charge *ab initio*.[338] However, that    **25.888.05**
conclusion must be tempered by the proviso[339] that any extension may be given subject to such terms and conditions as seem to the court just and expedient. The effect of the proviso is normally that the order made by the court is stated to be without prejudice to the rights of parties acquired during the period between the date of the creation of the charge and the date of its actual registration.[340] Thus, the effect of the proviso is that a late-registered charge really takes effect only from the date of registration and not the date of creation (which would be the case if it were registered within the 21-day period).

---

[334] Companies Act 2006 (Commencement No 8, Transitional Provisions and Savings) Order 2008, SI 2008/2860, art 3(n).

[335] See G Gretton, 'Registration of Company Charges' 6 *Edin LR* (2002) 146–175, 169.

[336] It was held in respect of the parallel provision in England (s 404 of CA 1985) that an ordinary creditor has no sufficient interest to oppose an application to extend the time for registration and no interest which ought to be protected if an extension is granted: see *R v Registrar of Companies ex p Central Bank of India* [1986] QB 1114, CA.

[337] *Prior, Petitioner* 1989 SLT 840; *Salvesen, Petitioner* [2009] CSOH 161 (holding that late registration would not be allowed after a delay of more than three years and at a time when the company was in administration).

[338] This seems the logical conclusion of 'extending' the time permitted for registration and follows the approach taken in respect of late registration in England: see eg *Watson v Duff Morgan & Vermont (Holdings) Ltd* [1974] 1 All ER 794.

[339] This has become known as the 'Joplin' proviso, the reference being to *In re Joplin Bakery Co* [1902] Ch 79.

[340] G Gretton, 'Registration of Company Charges' 6 *Edin LR* (2002) 146–175, 171 provides the following example to illustrate the effect of the proviso:
'Thus, suppose that a company grants two floating charges, to banks A and B, on 1 and 2 March respectively. Bank B's charge is registered in the Charges Register on 10 March. Bank A's charge is registered in the Charges Register on 10 July, after a successful application for permission to register late. Although on 2 March, Bank A's charge was effective, the effect of the Joplin proviso is that it ranks from 10 July, not from 1 March. Probably any negative pledge clause that it contains also takes effect only from 10 July.'

25.888.06  Rectification of errors in the registered particulars of a charge or memorandum of satisfaction is possible on the same grounds as those mentioned above in connection with late registration. This possibility does not seem to be activated very often, largely as a result of the conclusive nature of a certificate of registration (see commentary on section 885 above), which has the effect thatneither the debtor nor the creditor has any real interest in correcting mistakes in the registered particulars, as they are generally of no consequence. Under the Scottish Act, rectification will be possible in accordance with the general law relating to rectification of registered documents.[341] The result of rectification will be that the document is treated as always so recorded as rectified. As there will be no certificate of registration under the Scottish Act (conclusive or otherwise) it seems that there may be greater use made of rectification as the parties are likely to be more concerned about inaccuracies in a registered charge.

## *Avoidance of certain charges*

### 889  Charges void unless registered

25.889.01  (1)  If a company creates a charge to which section 878 applies, the charge is void (so far as any security on the company's property or any part of it is conferred by the charge) against—
(a)  the liquidator of the company,
(b)  an administrator of the company, and
(c)  any creditor of the company
unless that section is complied with.
(2)  Subsection (1) is without prejudice to any contract or obligation for repayment of the money secured by the charge; and when a charge becomes void under this section the money secured by it immediately becomes payable.

COMMENCEMENT DATE  1 October 2009[342]

25.889.02  There are two sanctions prescribed by this section for failure to comply with the registration require-ment. Subsection (1) provides that the charge is 'void against the liquidator or administrator and any creditor of the company' and subsection (2) provides that the money secured by a charge becomes payable immediately. Under the Scottish Act, by way of contrast, the position will become simpler: only a registered charge can constitute a security interest and so a failure to register results in there being no security interest.

25.889.03  The effect of subsection (2) is that there is an automatic acceleration of any sum due and not simply an option to accelerate. This statutory provision does not therefore make allowance for the position of a creditor who may want to preserve the underlying loan agreement and perhaps reconstitute the security interest. No mention is made of the automatic acceleration provision being applicable to any obligation other than the payment of money which is secured by a floating charge. It should therefore be assumed that such an obligation will continue according to its terms.

25.889.04  The effect of subsection (1) appears to be that so long as the company is a going concern the charge remains valid against the company and only creditors who hold a security which competes with it have any locus to challenge it.[343] This would mean that if a creditor holding an unregistered fixed charge entered into possession of the subject of the security as creditor in possession following a company's failure to fulfil its obligations in respect of a loan, the company could not object to sale of the property on the grounds that the charge had not been registered.[344] A similar line of reasoning would lead to the conclusion that a receiver acting for a floating charge holder could also carry out such a sale and pass a valid title to a purchaser. The effect of a floating charge being void against the liquidator or administrator is that (irrespective of whether the company is insolvent or not) the charge holder cannot require the liquidator or administrator to recognize the charge as valid and it cannot therefore serve the purpose of giving the charge holder priority over the unsecured creditors. In those circum-stances, the general creditors are entitled to require the liquidator or administrator to ignore the

---

[341]  The relevant provision is contained in s 8 of the Law Reform (Miscellaneous Provisions) (Sc) Act 1985.
[342]  Companies Act 2006 (Commencement No 8, Transitional Provisions and Savings) Order 2008, SI 2008/2860, art 3(n).
[343]  *Bank of Scotland v TA Neilson & Co* 1991 SLT 8. While this interpretation corresponds with the accepted view of the parallel English provision in s 395 of CA 1985 (now s 874 of CA 2006) (see R Goode, *Commercial Law* (3rd edn, London, Penguin 2004), 667), it is not easy to reconcile with the formulation of subs (1): see generally G Gretton, 'Registration of Company Charges' 6 *Edin LR* (2002) 146–175.
[344]  *Bank of Scotland v TA Neilson & Co* 1991 SLT 8, *per* Lord MacLean at p 11. This interpretation is not, however, free from doubt: see G Gretton, 'Registration of Company Charges' 6 *Edin LR* (2002) 146–175, 167 for the alternative view that a sale by the charge holder cannot give good title to a buyer.

priority that would have arisen had the charge been properly registered: that is the sense in which the charge is 'void against any creditor'.

Even if a floating charge becomes void as a result of subsection (1), the underlying obligation (typically    **25.889.05**
a loan agreement) remains enforceable, with repayment being accelerated under subsection (2). In those circumstances, the creditor simply loses his priority as a secured creditor and will have to rank for payment in liquidation alongside other unsecured creditors.

## *Companies' records and registers*

### 890  Copies of instruments creating charges to be kept by company

(1)  Every company shall cause a copy of every instrument creating a charge requiring registration    **25.890.01**
under this Chapter to be kept available for inspection.
(2)  In the case of a series of uniform debentures, a copy of one debenture of the series is sufficient.

COMMENCEMENT DATE  1 October 2009[345]

This section replaces section 421 of the Companies Act 1985. It requires a company to keep available    **25.890.02**
for inspection a copy of every instrument creating a charge requiring registration under this Chapter. There is no such requirement under the Scottish Act.

Subsection (2) makes clear that, in the case of a series of uniform debentures, a copy of one debenture    **25.890.03**
of the series is sufficient.

### 891  Company's register of charges

(1)  Every company shall keep available for inspection a register of charges and enter in it all charges    **25.891.01**
specifically affecting property of the company, and all floating charges on any property of the company.
(2)  There shall be given in each case a short description of the property charged, the amount of the charge and, except in the case of securities to bearer, the names of the persons entitled to it.
(3)  If an officer of the company knowingly and wilfully authorises or permits the omission of an entry required to be made in pursuance of this section, he commits an offence.
(4)  A person guilty of an offence under this section is liable—
    (a)  on conviction on indictment, to a fine;
    (b)  on summary conviction, to a fine not exceeding the statutory maximum.

COMMENCEMENT DATE  1 October 2009[346]

This section replaces section 422 of the Companies Act 1985. It requires every company to keep    **25.891.02**
available for inspection a register of charges (sometimes referred to as the 'internal register'). This register is distinct from the Register of Charges maintained by the Registrar of Companies and differs from it in that the latter shows only charges requiring registration under this Chapter, whereas the internal register is required to show all charges granted by the company over its property. Subsection (2) sets out the information that must be shown in the internal register in respect of a charge. As with the Register of Charges at Companies House, there will be no record of an assignation.[347] An officer of the company (but not the company itself) who knowingly and wilfully authorizes or permits the omission of an entry required to be made by this section is liable to a fine.

### 892  Instruments creating charges and register of charges to be available for inspection

(1)  This section applies to-    **25.892.01**
    (a)  documents required to be kept available for inspection under section 890 (copies of instruments creating charges), and
    (b)  a company's register of charges kept in pursuance of section 891.
(2)  The documents and register must be kept available for inspection-
    (a)  at the company's registered office, or
    (b)  at a place specified in regulations under section 1136.
(3)  The company must give notice to the registrar-
    (a)  of the place at which the documents and register are kept available for inspection, and
    (b)  of any change in that place,
        unless they have at all times been kept at the company's registered office.

---

[345] Companies Act 2006 (Commencement No 8, Transitional Provisions and Savings) Order 2008, SI 2008/2860, art 3(n).
[346] Companies Act 2006 (Commencement No 8, Transitional Provisions and Savings) Order 2008, SI 2008/2860, art 3(n).
[347] See commentary on s 885.

(4) The documents and register shall be open to the inspection-
    (a) of any creditor or member of the company without charge, and
    (b) of any other person on payment of such fee as may be prescribed.
(5) If default is made for 14 days in complying with subsection (3) or an inspection required under subsection (4) is refused, an offence is committed by-
    (a) the company, and
    (b) every officer of the company who is in default.
(6) A person guilty of an offence under this section is liable on summary conviction to a fine not exceeding level 3 on the standard scale and, for continued contravention, a daily default fine not exceeding one-tenth of level 3 on the standard scale.
(7) If an inspection required under subsection (4) is refused the court may by order compel an immediate inspection.

COMMENCEMENT DATE 1 October 2009[348]

**25.892.02**    This section replaces section 423 of the Companies Act 1985. Subsection (4) provides for members and creditors to have free access to copies of instruments creating charges and the internal register kept by the company. It also provides for inspection by any other person on payment of a fee. If inspection is refused, the company and officers of the company who are in default may be fined under subsection (6). In the case of a refusal by a company to allow inspection, the court may by order compel an immediate inspection of the copies or register.

# CHAPTER 3
## POWERS OF THE SECRETARY OF STATE

### 893 Power to make provision for effect of registration in special register

**25.893.01**    (1) In this section a 'special register' means a register, other than the register of charges kept under this Part, in which a charge to which Chapter 1 or Chapter 2 applies is required or authorised to be registered.
(2) The Secretary of State may by order make provision for facilitating the making of information-sharing arrangements between the person responsible for maintaining a special register ('the responsible person') and the registrar that meet the requirement in subsection (4).
    'Information-sharing arrangements' are arrangements to share and make use of information held by the registrar or by the responsible person.
(3) If the Secretary of State is satisfied that appropriate information-sharing arrangements have been made, he may by order provide that—
    (a) the registrar is authorised not to register a charge of a specified description under Chapter 1 or Chapter 2,
    (b) a charge of a specified description that is registered in the special register within a specified period is to be treated as if it had been registered (and certified by the registrar as registered) in accordance with the requirements of Chapter 1 or, as the case may be, Chapter 2, and
    (c) the other provisions of Chapter 1 or, as the case may be, Chapter 2 apply to a charge so treated with specified modifications.
(4) The information-sharing arrangements must ensure that persons inspecting the register of charges—
    (a) are made aware, in a manner appropriate to the inspection, of the existence of charges in the special register which are treated in accordance with provision so made, and
    (b) are able to obtain information from the special register about any such charge.
(5) An order under this section may—
    (a) modify any enactment or rule of law which would otherwise restrict or prevent the responsible person from entering into or giving effect to information-sharing arrangements,
    (b) authorise the responsible person to require information to be provided to him for the purposes of the arrangements,
    (c) make provision about—
        (i) the charging by the responsible person of fees in connection with the arrangements and the destination of such fees (including provision modifying any enactment which would otherwise apply in relation to fees payable to the responsible person), and
        (ii) the making of payments under the arrangements by the registrar to the responsible person,
    (d) require the registrar to make copies of the arrangements available to the public (in hard copy or electronic form).
(6) In this section 'specified' means specified in an order under this section.

---

[348] Companies Act 2006 (Commencement No 8, Transitional Provisions and Savings) Order 2008, SI 2008/2860, art 3(n).

(7) A description of charge may be specified, in particular, by reference to one or more of the following—

   (a) the type of company by which it is created,

   (b) the form of charge which it is,

   (c) the description of assets over which it is granted,

   (d) the length of the period between the date of its registration in the special register and the date of its creation.

(8) Provision may be made under this section relating to registers maintained under the law of a country or territory outside the United Kingdom.

(9) An order under this section is subject to negative resolution procedure.

COMMENCEMENT DATE 1 October 2009[349]

This is a new provision which is designed to facilitate information sharing between the registrar of companies and persons responsible for maintaining other registers (ie 'special registers')[350] upon which registrable company charges also have to be registered in addition to the register of company charges.[351] The section gives the Secretary of State power to make new 'information-sharing arrangements' between the two persons provided that certain conditions are met.[352] These conditions are that any person inspecting the register of company charges must be made aware of the existence of any additional charges affecting the property of the company that are registered on the 'special register' and also that person must be able to obtain information from the 'special register' about such charges.[353]     **25.893.02**

Where the Secretary of State makes an information-sharing arrangement order then he is given wide powers as to the terms of any such order.[354] So, for example, the Secretary of State may order that: [355]     **25.893.03**

(i) the registrar of companies shall no longer register a charge of a type that would normally require registration under the Companies Act;

(ii) if a charge is registered on a 'special register' it shall be treated as if it had also been registered on the company charges register;

(iii) the registration of charge provisions under the Companies Act shall apply to charges registered on a 'special register' with special modifications as may be determined by the order.

To ensure that any new information-sharing arrangement is fully effective the Secretary of State is also given wide powers to 'modify any enactment or rule of law' or to 'authorise the responsible person to require information to be provided to him for the purposes of the arrangements'.[356] The Secretary of State is also given power to allow for the charging of fees and the provision of copies of charge information in connection with an order for a new information-sharing arrangement.[357]     **25.893.04**

Information-sharing arrangement orders may be made in respect of the company charge register and other registers of charges maintained in the UK or in relation to a territory outside the UK.[358] In relation to other UK registers such orders are most likely to be made in respect of the register of title to land transfers under the Land Registration Act 1925 or, in relation to mortgages of ships under the Merchant Shipping Act 1994. In Scotland it will be important in relation to floating charges registered under the Bankruptcy and Diligence (Scotland) Act 2007. This new section is designed to make the delivery of information in relation to company charges more efficient and to avoid the duplication of information where possible. Where an information-sharing arrangement is in place then, in theory, a searcher should only need to make one search of the company charges register in order to learn about the existence of relevant charges.     **25.893.05**

## 894  General power to make amendments to this Part

(1) The Secretary of State may by regulations under this section—     **25.894.01**

   (a) amend this Part by altering, adding or repealing provisions,

---

[349] Companies Act 2006 (Commencement No 8, Transitional Provisions and Savings) Order 2008, SI 2008/2860, art 3(n).

[350] See s 893(1).

[351] See s 893(2).

[352] See s 893(2).

[353] See s 893(4) for these conditions.

[354] See generally, s 893(3).

[355] See s 893(3). Note that the Secretary of State is given discretion as to the terms of any order he chooses to make.

[356] See generally s 893(5).

[357] See s 893(5).

[358] See s 893(8).

(b) make consequential amendments or repeals in this Act or any other enactment (whether passed or made before or after this Act).

(2) Regulations under this section are subject to affirmative resolution procedure.

COMMENCEMENT DATE 1 October 2009[359]

**25.894.02**  This is a new section and gives the Secretary of State a wide power to amend or repeal the sections in the Companies Act or any other enactment governing the registration of company charges. Given the complex nature of company charge law and its enormous commercial importance this is a welcome measure which will bring some flexibility in future to the issue of law reform. No longer will we have to wait for a new Companies Act in order to correct a mistake in the legislation or some decision of a court which was not expected.[360]

**25.894.03**  The Government explained the purpose of this new section as being:

The purpose of the power [in s 894] is to make changes within the confines of the existing system … We intend to use that power to address the many imperfections of the present system[361]

Therefore, the Government is of the view that the section cannot be used to bring about fundamental reforms to the present company charge registration system via the introduction of a notice file type scheme such as was canvassed by the Law Commission in 2002.[362] With respect to the latter, the Department for Business, Innovation and Skills has established a Secured Transactions Law Reform Project under the directorship of Professor Sir Roy Goode QC, which will report at a later date on the future shape of fundamental reforms to this area.[363] Instead, the Government has consulted on more modest reforms utilizing the s 894 power.

**25.894.04**  In March 2010 the Department published *Registration of Charges Created by Companies and LLPs*[364] which invited comments on the need and possible shape of reforms to the current registration scheme based on tidying up the present provisions. The consultation period for responses closed in June 2010. Following on from this paper, a further four discussion papers have been published, namely: URN 1230 (October 2010); URN 1336 (November 2010); URN 11/862 (April 2011); and finally URN 11/1108 (August 2011)—*Revised Scheme For Registration of Charges Created by Companies and Limited Liability Partnerships: Proposed Revision of Part 25, Companies Act 2006*. This latter document contains the main details of the latest thinking of the government on the reform of this area.

**25.894.05**  Finally the Department of Business published a separate stand-alone draft statutory instrument detailing their reform proposals to date (ie which would replace the current Part 25 of the Act) in 2012 and offered stakeholders a 'final opportunity' to make representations on the effects of the proposed reforms (by 7 September 2012) prior to their implementation. At the time of writing, the government have stated that it is their intention to place the final (revised) draft statutory instrument before both Houses of Parliament in the autumn of 2012, with a view to a new and revised law of company charges (ie replacing the current provisions of Part 25 discussed in the main text above) coming into force in April 2013, this new law to apply in equal measure to both companies incorporated in England/Wales and Scotland in a new unified regime. Nevertheless, readers are advised to proceed with caution on these reforms and potential implementation dates since this area has been fraught with difficulties and delays. Readers are advised to consult the Department of Business website[365] for updates on the progress of reform, and it would come as no surprise to learn that further delays in implementing reform may well occur before/if we eventually see a new scheme brought into effect. Even if reforms are made, then they will be of a highly technical nature and based on the current scheme, rather than any of the more modern Personal Property Security type schemes based upon Article 9 of the USA Uniform Commercial Code.[366]

---

[359] Companies Act 2006 (Commencement No 8, Transitional Provisions and Savings) Order 2008, SI 2008/2860, art 3(n).

[360] Cf *Re Welsh Irish Ferries Ltd* [1986] Ch 471.

[361] See (*Hansard* HL, col 480, *per* Lord Sainsbury (2 November 2006).

[362] See para 25.0.03, n 8 above.

[363] On which see ⟨http://www.bis.gov.uk/consultations/registration-of-charges⟩.

[364] Consultation Paper URN 10/697 (issued 12 March 2010, closing date for consultation responses 18 June 2010).

[365] See generally <http://www.bis.gov.uk> (company charge reform/consultation).

[366] Indeed the Department of Business website consultation framework document, 'Registration of charges created by companies and limited liability partnerships' under the heading 'Background to consultation', makes it clear that: 'Fundamental changes for the longer term are being considered by the Secured Transactions Law Reform Project; the project director is Professor Sir Roy Goode CBE, QC.' It seems that company charge reform is likely to remain on the agenda for some considerable time to come!

# 26

## ARRANGEMENTS AND RECONSTRUCTIONS

---

## Companies Act 2006

### PART 26
### ARRANGEMENTS AND RECONSTRUCTIONS

### *Introduction*

This Part is derived from the provisions of Part XIII of the Companies Act 1985, which in turn were **26.0.01** derived from previous Companies Acts.[1] It restates, with only minor additions, the provisions of sections 425 to 427 of the 1985 Act.

The Part applies to 'compromises or arrangements', which are commonly referred to as 'schemes of **26.0.02** arrangement' or, simply, 'schemes'. The uses for schemes of arrangement are varied. The procedure can be used, for example, to transfer incorporation to another jurisdiction, place a new holding company on top of an existing company, effect a merger or demerger, effect a takeover,[2] buy out minority interests, or effect a restructuring between a company in financial difficulties and its creditors. The main advantage of a scheme is that, once approved by the requisite majority and the court, it binds all who fall within its terms including those who objected and those who did not vote. This coercive effect, however, brings with it the scrutiny of the court to ensure that there is no unfairness or oppression of dissentients.

There are three stages to a scheme under this Part: first, the application to the court under section 896 **26.0.03** for an order that a meeting of the relevant members or creditors be called; second the convening and holding of the meeting of the relevant members or creditors; and third, if the meeting is approved by the requisite majority at the meeting, the application to the court for sanction of the scheme under section 899. Once the scheme is effective in accordance with this Part it binds the company and those affected by it. Applications are made in the Companies Court. The detail of the practice and procedure in relation to the applications to court for sanction in relation to schemes under this Part are outside the scope of this work.[3]

---

[1]  Schemes of arrangement were originally provided for, in respect of insolvent companies only, under the Joint Stock Companies Arrangement Act 1870. The power to promote a scheme in respect of all companies, not just those in liquidation, was introduced by the Companies (Consolidation) Act 1908.

[2]  See the Takeover Panel Statement 2008/1 and Takeover Code. See also *Re Expro International plc* [2008] EWHC 1543 (Ch) for a case involving the interaction of the Takeover Code and the scheme process.

[3]  For further information see the Civil Procedure Rules, particularly Practice Direction 49A (Applications under the Companies Acts and Related Legislation), the *Practice Statement (Companies Schemes of Arrangement)* [2002] 1 WLR 1345 and the Companies Court section of the Chancery Guide (Chapter 20 of the 2009 edition, especially paras 20.15–20.17).

*Application of this Part*

### 895  Application of this Part

**26.895.01**

(1) The provisions of this Part apply where a compromise or arrangement is proposed between a company and—

    (a) its creditors, or any class of them, or

    (b) its members, or any class of them.

(2) In this Part—

    'arrangement' includes a reorganisation of the company's share capital by the consolidation of shares of different classes or by the division of shares into shares of different classes, or by both of those methods; and

    'company'—

    (a) in section 900 (powers of court to facilitate reconstruction or amalgamation) means a company within the meaning of this Act, and

    (b) elsewhere in this Part means any company liable to be wound up under the Insolvency Act 1986 (c. 45) or the Insolvency (Northern Ireland) Order 1989 (S.I. 1989/2405 (N.I. 19)).

(3) The provisions of this Part have effect subject to Part 27 (mergers and divisions of public companies) where that Part applies (See sections 902 and 903).

COMMENCEMENT DATE 6 April 2008[4]

*Scope of this Part: 'compromises or arrangements'*

**26.895.02**  This section is derived from sections 425(1), (6) and 427(6) of the Companies Act 1985. Section 895(1) stipulates that the Part applies in respect of the proposal of any 'compromise or arrangement'. Neither of these terms has a definition under the Act (nor its predecessors) and there is no single definition arising from the case law. As such these terms do not have a fixed meaning. A power to 'compromise' rights presupposes some dispute about them or difficulty in enforcing them.[5] An 'arrangement', by contrast, does not presuppose some dispute. A number of decisions have recognized that 'arrangement' should not be limited to something analogous to a compromise. For a scheme to constitute a compromise or arrangement it is essential, however, that there is an element of accommodation, or 'give and take', between the parties.[6] It has been said that, beyond this, it is undesirable to attempt a definition.[7] Schemes therefore involve the giving up of one right and the replacement with another. For example, in a restructuring of a company in financial difficulties, the rights of bondholders may be converted into equity under a debt-for-equity swap effected by a scheme. In a takeover scheme, the rights of shareholders in the target may be cancelled in return for consideration (whether in the form of securities or cash) from the offeror.

**26.895.03**  A scheme under this Part requires the company to be party to the arrangement: it cannot be between creditors and members only.[8] There is nothing in the legislation that prescribes the subject matter of a scheme: a scheme could be a compromise or arrangement about anything which the company and its creditors or members may properly agree amongst themselves.

**26.895.04**  Section 895(2) expressly includes in the meaning of 'arrangement' a reorganization of share capital by the consolidation of shares of different classes or by the division of shares into shares of different classes or by both those methods.

**26.895.05**  In addition to schemes of compromise or arrangement under this Part, other compromises and arrangements are provided for in other legislation. In respect of transfers of insurance business or banking business, Part VII of the Financial Services and Markets Act 2000 (insurance business transfer schemes and banking business transfer schemes) provides a statutory mechanism for transfer of books

---

    [4] Companies Act 2006 (Commencement No 5, Transitional Provisions and Savings) Order 2007, SI 2007/3495.

    [5] *Sneath v Valley Gold Limited* [1893] 1 Ch 477 is taken as the leading authority on the point, although the facts of that case concerned power in a debenture trust deed not in respect of a scheme under the Companies Act. And see *Mercantile Investment and General Trust Co v International Co of Mexico* [1893] 1 Ch 484.

    [6] *Re NFU Development Trust Ltd* [1972] 1 WLR 1548, where the removal of membership rights as part of a scheme aimed at reducing administrative costs, but without offering members any compensating advantage, was not an 'arrangement'. In *Re Bluebrook Ltd* [2010] 1 BCLC 338 it was held that, where a scheme forms part of a wider restructuring, a court can look beyond the terms of the scheme in order to assess whether a compensating advantage is offered in the wider context. See also *In the Matter of Uniq plc* [2011] EWHC 749 (Ch), where it was held that it would be 'artificial' to confine the analysis of 'give and take' purely to the terms of a scheme itself if that scheme forms an integral part of a wider restructuring.

    [7] Nourse J in *Re Savoy Hotel Ltd* [1981] Ch 351 (in respect of the meaning of 'arrangement').

    [8] *Ex p Kaplan* 1987 (3) SA 413 PD (South Africa).

of business without the need to novate every contract in relation to the business separately. Further, corporate reconstructions are possible under provisions of the Insolvency Act 1986.[9]

## 'Creditors' and 'members'

'Creditor' includes every person who has a pecuniary claim against the company, whether the claim is  **26.895.06** actual or contingent[10] or whether it is preferential, secured,[11] or unsecured. 'Creditors' are not limited to those persons who would have a provable claim in the winding up of the company, although it clearly includes all those who would have such a claim Future asbestosis claimants who did not have accrued causes of action in tort at the date of a scheme would nonetheless be bound by the scheme as 'creditors'. As one of the reasons for schemes is to encourage arrangements so as to avoid insolvent liquidation and facilitate the financial rehabilitation of the company, as wide a meaning as possible should be given to the word 'creditors' in this section.[12] In *Re Lehman Brothers International (Europe) (In Administration) (No 2)* [2009] EWCA Civ 1161 the Court of Appeal held that it is not possible to use a scheme of arrangement to compromise proprietary rights, even where those rights might also overlap with rights as a creditor. A scheme can include some element of release of contractual rights or rights of action against related third parties necessary to give effect to the scheme.[13] However, the Court of Appeal held that it cannot extend to rights of creditors over their own property and the existence of a pecuniary claim in respect of the possible breach of trust or contract in respect of that property did not provide a gateway to provide jurisdiction to permit the variation of the proprietary rights.

Where it is impossible to identify all the creditors, an adjudication process can be established whereby  **26.895.07** claims are submitted by a set date and any disputed claims assessed by an independent adjudicator, 'in so far as the law allows'.[14] An adjudication process will not be an infringement of Article 6 of the European Convention on Human Rights (right of access to courts) as incorporated into English Law by the Human Rights Act 1998.[15]

The direct effect of a scheme under this Part in respect of obligations which are governed by foreign  **26.895.08** laws is limited. Although it seems certain that, as against assets within this jurisdiction, the scheme will bind them, as against assets abroad the foreign contract continues notwithstanding the approval of a scheme.[16] The question whether an obligation has been discharged is governed by its proper law.[17] In order to give a scheme concluded under this Part effect as against assets abroad, steps should be taken to make it binding according to the law of the place where the assets lie.[18] Often' if there are significant foreign assets or obligations, parallel schemes or analogous arrangements are proposed. In considering whether to sanction a scheme, the court might take into account any risk that foreign creditors could negate the effect of the scheme by action based on the foreign contract in the local courts and enforcing against foreign assets of the company.

---

[9] See further the commentary regarding schemes in liquidation and administrations under s 896 below.

[10] See the judgment of David Richards J in *Re T & N Ltd and ors* [2006] 1 WLR 1728 where the authorities are considered at length. See also *Re Atlantic Computers plc (In Administration)* [1995] BCC 696 for a case where letters of comfort were identified as not giving rise to a contractual right such that the holders of them could participate in a scheme.

[11] See *Re Empire Mining Co* (1890) 44 Ch D 402.

[12] *Re T & N Ltd and ors* [2005] EWHC 2870 (Ch).

[13] See, eg *Re T&N Limited and ors (No 3)* [2006] EWHC 1477 (Ch).

[14] See, eg, the schemes proposed in *Re Osiris Insurance Ltd* [1999] 1 BCLC 182, *Re Hawk Insurance Co Ltd* [2002] BCC 300 and *British Aviation Insurance Co Limited* [2006] BCC 14. The reference to 'in so far as the law allows' brings in the law in relation to the limitations on such a clause in relation to an expert determination in a private contract: see, eg, *Jones v Sherwood Computer Services plc* [1992] 1 WLR 277, CA.

[15] *Re Pan Atlantic Insurance Co Ltd* [2003] BCC 847.

[16] *Ellis v McHenry* (1871) LR 6 CP 228.

[17] *Wight and ors v Eckhardt Marine GmbH* [2004] 1 AC 147.

[18] US courts have recognized orders giving effect to UK schemes under Chapter 15 of the US Bankruptcy Code (see n 37 for more detail). Schemes will not benefit from automatic recognition under the Insolvency Regulation (Council Regulation (EC) No 1346/2000 of 29 May 2000) because they are not included in the list of applicable insolvency proceedings in Annex A to that regulation. The position in Europe under the Judgments Regulation (Council Regulation (EC) No 44/2001 of 22 December 2000) is uncertain. On 15 February 2012, the Federal Court of Justice of Germany (Bundesgerichtshof) (Ref: BGH, IV, and ZR 194/09) upheld a decision made by the Higher Regional Court in Celle (Ref: 8U 46/09), Germany in 2009, to decline recognition of an English scheme between an insurance company (Equitable Life) and its creditors because it did not constitute a 'judgment' under Article 32 of the Judgments Regulation.

**26.895.09**   Identifying who constitutes a *'member'* of a company for the purposes of this part should prove straightforward in cases of companies formed under the Companies Acts.[19] Issues might arise with regard to holders of share options and warrants. In Australian cases the trend has been to treat option-holders as creditors.[20]

### *'or any class of them'*

**26.895.10**   The proposed scheme need not be between the company and all of its members or creditors. Schemes are permitted as between the company and a class only of its members or creditors (section 895(1)(a) and (b)). The identification of the appropriate class at the outset of the scheme process is vital. Some transactions involve one or more schemes between the company and various different classes of creditors or members. Equally in some cases companies wish to treat all members or creditors alike and have only one class. Failure to properly identify different classes can be fatal to a scheme, as the court will lack jurisdiction to consider whether to exercise its discretion under section 899.[21] The identification of separate classes of creditors or members does not necessarily follow distinctions in the company's capital structure (whether as between different types of shareholders (as members) or types of bondholders (as creditors)), although that is a starting point for consideration. It is the obligation of the company to properly identify the relevant classes.

**26.895.11**   A class 'must be confined to those persons whose rights are not so dissimilar as to make it impossible for them to consult together with a view to their common interest' (Bowen LJ in *Sovereign Life Assurance Co v Dodd* [1892] 2 QB 573). Modern cases (following the judgment of Chadwick LJ in the Court of Appeal in *Re Hawk Insurance Co Ltd* [2002] BCC 300) make it clear that unless significant dissimilarities in legal rights are identified, all creditors and members are capable of consulting together. It is dissimilarity in legal *rights* not interests that matters. Differences in motives or interests do not give rise to separate classes. A broad approach is now taken and the differences might be material without leading to separate classes:[22] 'if one gets too picky about potential different classes, one could end up with virtually as many classes as there are members of a particular group' (*per* Neuberger J in *Re Anglo American Insurance Ltd* [2001] 1 BCLC 755). In *Re Hawk* Chadwick LJ warned about the risk of minority creditors being able to frustrate the wishes of the majority by an overzealous dissection of creditors into different classes. So-called 'class issues' should now be identified at the first stage of the scheme process.[23] In the context of creditor schemes, the modern approach in considering whether groups of creditors form different classes is to identify the appropriate 'comparator'. This is often an analysis of the rights of the relevant groups in an insolvent winding up in the case of companies in financial difficulties where the alternative to the scheme is likely to be such a process. In solvent schemes of arrangement for insurance companies, the appropriate comparator may be a continuing solvent run-off.[24]

### *Application to different types of companies*

**26.895.12**   The court's jurisdiction to sanction a scheme under section 895 hinges on its jurisdiction to wind up the scheme company in question. A 'company' for these purposes means a company incorporated under the Companies Acts or 'any company liable to be wound up' under what is now the Insolvency Act 1986. Foreign companies may also be wound up under the Insolvency Act on the basis that they are unregistered companies. Three preconditions, established by case law, must be fulfilled in order for the English court to exercise its discretion to grant a winding up order in respect of a foreign company. These are: (a) that the company has a sufficiently close connection with England (usually, but not invariably, in the form of assets within the jurisdiction); (b) that there is a reasonable possibility of benefit accruing to creditors from the making of the winding up order; and (c) that one or more

---

[19] As far as schemes between a foreign company and its members are concerned, see *Re Drax Holdings Ltd; Re Inpower Ltd* [2004] 1 WLR 1049 where Lawrence Collins J said that it would almost certainly be for the courts of the place of incorporation to consider any compromise of members' rights and that therefore it was very unlikely that the English court would take jurisdiction in such a case.

[20] See *MIA Group Ltd* [2004] NSWSC 712 in the New South Wales Supreme Court and *Re Sino Gold Mining Ltd* (ACN 093 518 579) 2009 FCA 1277 in the Federal Court of Australia, although see also *Re Niagara Mining Ltd* (2002) 47 ACSR (Australia) in the Federal Court.

[21] See instances of incorrect identification of classes having been fatal to the proposed scheme in *Re United Provident Assurance Co Ltd* [1910] 2 Ch 477 at 481, *Re Hellenic & General Trust Ltd* [1976] 1 WLR 123 and *Re British Aviation Insurance Co Ltd* [2006] BCC 14.

[22] See, eg, *Re Equitable Life Assurance Society (No 1)* [2002] BCC 319, *Re Perusahaan Perseroan (Persero) PT Perusahaan Penerbangan Garuda Indonesia* [2001] All ER (D) 53 (Oct) and *Re Telewest Communications plc (No 1)* [2004] BCC 342.

[23] See the *Practice Statement (Companies Schemes of Arrangement)*, discussed below under s 896.

[24] See *Re British Aviation Insurance Co Ltd* [2006] BCC 14.

persons interested in the distribution of assets are persons over whom the English court has jurisdiction.[25] The courts have decided that these preconditions are relevant to the exercise of the court's discretion (rather than its jurisdiction) in determining whether it should make a winding-up order and so do not have to be fulfilled in the case of a scheme, where the company is not necessarily insolvent. The 'sufficient connection' test should, however, be met as its practical effect is to ensure that a court declines to exercise 'exorbitant jurisdiction', save where it is appropriate to do so.[26] It is most relevant in the context of a court establishing whether it has jurisdiction to approve a scheme of arrangement under section 895(2).[27] Where the scheme of arrangement is between the foreign company and its creditors the connection might be shown in cases where, for example, the obligations to be varied under the scheme derive from an agreement which is governed by English law and subject to the exclusive jurisdiction of the English courts.[28]

## Impact of EU Regulations

The English court's jurisdiction to wind up insolvent foreign companies had been limited by article 3(2) of the Insolvency Regulation[29] in that it can only wind up companies whose centres of main interests ('COMIs') are situated in another EU Member State if they have an 'establishment' (as defined by article 2(h) of that Regulation) in the UK. The effects of such proceedings are restricted to the assets situated in the UK. Jurisdiction to wind up companies under the Insolvency Act 1986 is consequently confined to companies that fall outside the scope of the Insolvency Regulation. However, the English courts have found that article 3(2) did not prevent the English court from assuming jurisdiction to sanction a scheme of a company whose COMI was situated in another Member State.[30] This approach has since been adopted in cases such as *Re Tele Columbus GmbH & others* (No 7359 of 2010, 14 December 2010), concerning a scheme of a German company's obligations, and *Re Metrovacesa SA* [2011] EWHC 1014 (Ch), concerning a scheme of a Spanish company's obligations. The COMIs of both companies were situated in the Member State in which they had been incorporated, note England.   **26.895.13**

Briggs J examined the basis for the English Court's jurisdiction at length in *Re Rodenstock GmbH* [2011] EWHC 1104 (Ch), and that approach has been confirmed in *Primacom Holding GMBH v A Group of the Senior Lenders & Credit Agricole* at both the permission to convene ([2011] EWHC 3746 (Ch)) and sanction hearings ([2012] EWHC 164 (Ch)), concerning the scheme of a German company's obligations, which were governed by English law and with an English jurisdiction clause. The approach in *Rodenstock* was also adopted at the permission to convene hearing in *Re NEF Telecom Company BV and Bulgarian Telecommunications Company AD*, a scheme proposed by a Bulgarian telecoms operator and its indirect Dutch parent company.[31]   **26.895.14**

There is some uncertainty as to whether scheme proceedings will be granted automatic recognition under the Judgments Regulation[32] by the courts of other EU Member States. In the *Equitable Life* case, the German courts refused to recognize a solvent scheme of arrangement[33] in respect of obligations governed by German law. Article 1(2)(b) of that Regulation appears to exclude proceedings relating to 'juridical arrangements, compositions and analogous proceedings'. However, in *Rodenstock*[34] the court   **26.895.15**

---

[25] *Real Estate Development Co* [1991] BCLC 210; *Re Latreefers Inc.* [2001] BCC 174.

[26] *Re Drax Holdings Ltd* [2004] 1 WLR 1049 at paras 24 and 25; *Re Rodenstock* [2011] EWHC 1104 (Ch).

[27] Note that, for the purposes of s. 895(2)(b), a non-UK 'EEA insurer' (or a branch of a non-UK EEA insurer) is to be treated as a company liable to be wound up under the Insolvency Act 1986 if it would be liable to be so wound up but for the prohibition in regulation 4(1)(a) of the Insurers (Reorganisation and Winding Up) Regulations 2004 (SI 2004/353). Accordingly, the English courts have jurisdiction to sanction a scheme promoted by an insolvent non-UK EEA insurer (this was confirmed in the *Sovereign Marine* case). A similar carve out exists in relation to insolvent non-UK 'EEA credit institutions' under the Credit Institutions (Reorganisations and Winding Up) Regulations 2004 (SI 2004/1045).

[28] *Re Drax Holdings Ltd* [2004] 1 WLR 1049 at paras 29 and 30; *Re La Seda de Barcelona SA* [2010] EWHC 1364 (Ch); *Re Tele Columbus GmbH & others* (No 7359 of 2010, 14 December 2010, unreported); *Re Metrovacesa SA* [2011] EWHC 1014 (Ch); *Re Rodenstock* [2011] EWHC 1104 (Ch).

[29] Council Regulation (EC) No 1346/2000 of 29 May 2000 on insolvency proceedings, articles 1, 3(1) and 3(2).

[30] *Re DAP Holding NV* [2005] EWHC 2092 (Ch). In that case, Lewison J reasoned that, because circumstances such as an insolvency or an establishment within a Member State are transient and may change, there is nothing to prevent the courts of a Member State concluding that the company is liable to be wound up in the UK so long as there is sufficient connection with the UK.

[31] [2012 ] EWHC 2483 (Ch). The scheme was subsequently sanctioned by Vos J on 9 September 2012, although at the time of writing the judgment was not available.

[32] Council Regulation (EC) No. 44/2001 of 22 December 2000.

[33] See n 18 above.

[34] The case concerned a German company which had its COMI in Germany. It had no establishment or assets in the UK that were likely to be affected by the scheme. The company had incurred a significant debt under a

found that a proper construction of that provision was that proceedings before an English court to sanction a scheme of arrangement relating to a solvent company 'were plainly civil and commercial matters within article 1' and therefore benefited from the recognition and enforcement provisions in Chapter 3 of that Regulation. A more difficult question is whether a scheme of arrangement will fall within article 22(2) of the Judgments Regulation. Article 22(2) confers exclusive jurisdiction on the courts of the 'seat' of a company in proceedings that have as their object the 'dissolution' of the company, where that seat is located in an EU Member State. The conclusion in *Rodenstock* was that article 22(2) precluded the English court from assuming jurisdiction to wind up a solvent company whose seat was located in another EU Member State and which had no establishment in the UK.

**26.895.16** Although Briggs J in *Rodenstock* found that neither the Insolvency Regulation nor the Judgments Regulation conferred jurisdiction on the English court to wind up a solvent company whose COMI or seat was located in another EU Member State, this did not lead him to conclude that the English court had no jurisdiction to sanction schemes in relation to such companies. Instead, he found that the authority to do so lay in the phrase 'liable to be wound up' used in section 895(2)(b), which he described as a 'touchstone' for the court's jurisdiction, finding it improbable that on a purposive interpretation of those Regulations as part of English law any such narrowing of jurisdiction was intended in relation to schemes.[35] He agreed with Warren J's *obiter* remarks (in relation to companies incorporated in non-Member States) in *Re Sovereign Marine & General Insurance Co Ltd* [2006] BCC 774 to the effect that the phrase 'liable to be wound up' was designed simply to identify the types of company and association to which the jurisdiction applies and, at least so far as concerns solvent companies, nothing in either the Insolvency Regulation or the Judgments Regulation has narrowed the scope of the meaning of that phrase, or, therefore, the definition of 'company' which it provides. In essence, the expression was to be construed as defining the type of entity that was capable of being wound up.

**26.895.17** Briggs J went on to sanction the *Rodenstock* scheme, finding that the company had a sufficient connection to England because the facilities agreement was governed by English law and subject to the jurisdiction of the English courts. He distinguished the case from the 'Equitable Life case' (in which the first instance German court refused to recognize a solvent scheme of arrangement) on the basis that the underlying facility agreement in that case was governed by German law.[36] Briggs J relied on expert evidence to the effect that a decision by the English court to sanction the scheme would be legally effective in Germany because the German courts would, pursuant to the Rome Convention on the law applicable to contractual obligations, apply English law to the question of whether the senior lenders' rights against the company had been varied by the scheme. The use of expert evidence to confirm the effectiveness of the scheme in the jurisdiction of incorporation of the debtor company has previously been seen in relation to the *Tele Columbus* and *Metrovacesa* applications.[37] The court in both cases relied on the fact that the companies' finance documentation was subject to English governing law and jurisdiction clauses when establishing jurisdiction. Expert evidence as to enforceability has also been deployed in the other, more recent, jurisdiction cases referred to above.

**26.895.18** Note that, where the underlying contract is governed by the law of another jurisdiction, the risk of challenge by local creditors may be reduced by effecting a parallel scheme in that jurisdiction. However, this will only be possible if the debtor company has assets in that jurisdiction and the local law provides for an equivalent procedure.[38] This approach was adopted in the *Drax Holdings* case where simultaneous orders were made in the Jersey and Cayman Islands courts to ensure all creditors were bound.[39]

**26.895.19** As identified by Briggs J in *Rodenstock*, some areas of uncertainty remain to be clarified by the courts: (a) the ratio of the *Rodenstock* case only technically considered schemes of solvent companies so the position of insolvent companies under the Judgments Regulation remains unclear; (b) Briggs J

---

facilities agreement expressed to be governed by English law and subject to the exclusive jurisdiction of the English courts. The purpose of the scheme was to vary the terms of the agreement in order to enable the company to implement a restructuring plan. The company, which was described as solvent, was at risk of being placed into an insolvency process in Germany once the existing waiver of its breach of financial covenants under the agreement had expired.

[35] *Re Rodenstock* [2011] EWHC 1104 (Ch) at para 54.

[36] The judgment in this case was upheld by the Federal Court of Justice of Germany (Bundesgerichtshof) on appeal. See n 18 above.

[37] See n 29 above.

[38] See para 26.895.08 above.

[39] Alternatively, the debtor company could seek recognition of the scheme as a 'foreign proceeding' in the US courts under Chapter 15 of the US Bankruptcy Code if it has a connection with the US. Chapter 15 has none of the recognition problems associated with the EU legislation as it expressly provides, in its definition of 'foreign proceeding' for recognition of proceedings involving 'adjustment of debt', with the apparent intention of capturing solvent schemes.

acknowledged that a scheme sanctioned by an English court may not be automatically recognized by the courts of another Member State as a 'judgment' under the Judgments Regulation; and (c) he expressed a 'final reservation' that the Judgments Regulation could affect solvent schemes where a majority of creditors are domiciled outside England.[40]

This 'final reservation' has since been addressed in the sanction hearing of the *Primacom* scheme (*Primacom Holding GMBH v A Group of the Senior Lenders & Credit Agricole* [2012] EWHC 164 (Ch)), where none of the creditors was domiciled in England. In *Primacom*, Hildyard J held that the English court had jurisdiction because of the exclusive English jurisdiction clauses in the agreements with the creditors and on the ground that the parties had consented or submitted to the jurisdiction of the English court by participating in previous proceedings.[41] **26.895.20**

## Associated dealings

If the scheme involves a transaction for which other sections of the Companies Act or other legislation prescribe special formalities, then such formalities must also be complied with. For example, reductions of capital often form part of transactions involving schemes. **26.895.21**

## Meeting of creditors or members

### 896  Court order for holding of meeting

(1) The court may, on an application under this section, order a meeting of the creditors or class of creditors, or of the members of the company or class of members (as the case may be), to be summoned in such manner as the court directs. **26.896.01**

(2) An application under this section may be made by—

    (a) the company,

    (b) any creditor or member of the company, or

    [(c) if the company is being wound up, the liquidator, or

    (d) if the company is in administration, the administrator].[a]

[(3) Section 323 (representation of corporations at meetings) applies to a meeting of creditors under this section as to a meeting of the company (references to a member of the company being read as references to a creditor).][b]

AMENDMENTS AND NOTES

[a] Amended by the Companies Act 2006 (Consequential Amendments etc) Order 2008, SI 2008/948, arts 3(1)(b), 6, Sch 1, para 249(2).

[b] Inserted by the Companies Act 2006 (Consequential Amendments etc) Order 2008, SI 2008/948, arts 3(1)(b), 6, Sch 1, para 249(3).

COMMENCEMENT DATE  6 April 2008[42]

This section is derived from section 425(1) of the Companies Act 1985. It sets out the ability of the company, a member, creditor, liquidator, or administrator to apply to court to order the summonsing of the meeting at which the scheme will be proposed to members or creditors or any class of them.[43] Applying to court for an order that a meeting be summonsed is the first stage in the three-stage scheme process. **26.896.02**

---

[40] *Re Rodenstock* [2011] EWHC 1104 (Ch) at paras 57–62. This was on the basis that Chapter II of the Judgments Regulation generally allocates jurisdiction by reference to the domicile of the intended defendants and none of the exceptions were relevant to solvent schemes of arrangement.

[41] Counsel for the scheme company put forward four ways of resolving the jurisdictional issue: (i) art 2 of the Judgments Regulation has no application in the context of a scheme because no one is being sued; (ii) if art 2 does not apply, it is nevertheless subject expressly to the Judgments Regulation as a whole, including arts 23 and 24. Under art 23, the English court would have exclusive jurisdiction by virtue of the exclusive English jurisdiction clauses in the documentation; (iii) under art 24, a court of a Member State before which a defendant enters an appearance has jurisdiction. It was submitted that all the scheme creditors concerned had in one way or another submitted to the jurisdiction of the English court, in particular by their participation in proceedings before the High Court at the first scheme hearing; (iv) as canvassed by Briggs J in *Re Rodenstock*, the English court should accept jurisdiction by analogy with art 4. (Article 4 directs a Member State to apply domestic law when a defendant is not domiciled in a Member State.) Hildyard J held that he favoured the first solution offered by counsel but that, in any event, he accepted the second and third.

[42] Companies Act 2006 (Commencement No 5, Transitional Provisions and Savings) Order 2007, SI 2007/3495.

[43] The meaning of the words 'creditors', 'members', and 'class' and the scope of this Part generally have been considered above, under s 895.

*Schemes in a liquidation or administration*

26.896.03    There is no prohibition on schemes for companies being wound up or in administration[44] and section 896(2)(c) makes it clear that the liquidator or administrator can propose a scheme.[45] Schemes of arrangement can prove useful in compromising classes of creditor claims in insolvent situations. The Insolvency Act 1986 provides its own mechanisms for compromises or reconstructions (company voluntary arrangements under Part I, reconstructions under section 110, the power of compromise, or arrangements under Schedule 1, paragraph 18 (in administration) and Schedule 4, paragraph 2 (in winding-up)). It was held in *Re Trix Ltd* [1970] 1 WLR 1421, however, that where creditors were to be dealt with otherwise than strictly in accordance with their rights, the procedure to be used was that under what is now this Part of the Companies Act because that afforded the greatest protection to non-assenting creditors and allowed them to object formally to the proposals.[46]

26.896.04    A scheme can impose terms which are different from the statutory scheme of distributions on liquidations and such a scheme would bind the liquidator, although the court should be careful before making such an order.[47] A scheme between creditors and a company being wound up must have the approval of the liquidator.[48]

*The court's discretion to summons a meeting*

26.896.05    When determining whether to summon a meeting, the court is not concerned with the merits of the scheme.[49] The merits of the scheme are considered at the hearing for sanction following the meeting (under section 899(1)—see below). The court may, however, not summon a meeting or meetings of different classes where there is no prospect that the scheme will be approved by any of the meetings or where there is no prospect that the company will consent to the scheme.[50] Usually where the class is small and all its members consent to the scheme there is no need to hold a meeting as the compromise or arrangement can be achieved contractually. However, the court can convene a meeting of a class even though there is only one person in it, although such a one-person class could just as well contractually bind himself to the compromise or arrangement.[51] A meeting will not have been validly held, however, where the relevant class consists of more than one person but only one person attends.[52] It is also possible for the court to direct that the meeting should be held abroad.[53]

*Class issues*

26.896.06    In relation to the proper identification of classes, see the discussion under section 895 above. In response to *Re Hawk*,[54] in which class issues were raised at the hearing for sanction under the then equivalent of section 899 rather than at the application for permission to summons the meeting, the Chancery Division issued *Practice Statement (Companies Schemes of Arrangement)*.[55] The purpose of the Practice Statement is to enable issues concerning the composition of classes of creditor and the summoning of meetings to be identified and, if appropriate, resolved early in the proceedings. A failure to correctly identify the class will mean that the court lacks jurisdiction to give its sanction at the final hearing. It is the applicant's responsibility to determine whether more than one meeting of creditors is required by a scheme and if so to ensure that those meetings are properly constituted by class of creditor. Further the applicant is also responsible for drawing the court's attention as soon as possible to any issues concerning the constitution of the meetings of creditors or which affect the conduct of those meetings. If any such class issues are identified, the court should consider whether directions should be given for the resolution of that issue in advance of the proposed meetings. Where practicable

---

[44]  Although s 895 applies Part 26 to companies capable of being wound up under the Insolvency Act 1986, that simply identifies the types of company in respect of which a scheme can be proposed.

[45]  In fact schemes were originally only available in the case of companies being wound up: Joint Stock Companies Arrangement Act 1870.

[46]  See, however, *Re Bank of Credit and Commerce International SA (No 2)* [1992] BCC 715 where *Re Trix* was distinguished in what was said to be an 'exceptional case'.

[47]  *Re Anglo American Insurance Ltd* [2001] 1 BCLC 755.

[48]  *Re International Contract Co (Hankey's Case)* (1872) 26 LT 358.

[49]  *Re Telewest Communications plc* [2004] BCC 342, followed in *Re MyTravel Group plc* [2005] 1 WLR 2365.

[50]  *Re Savoy Hotel Ltd* [1981] Ch 351, where a hostile takeover was proposed by one shareholder and the Board (which also controlled a considerable proportion of the voting rights) opposed said takeover.

[51]  *Re RMCA Reinsurance Ltd* [1994] BCC 378.

[52]  *Re Altitude Scaffolding Ltd Re T&N Ltd and ors* [2006] EWHC 1401 (Ch).

[53]  *Re RMCA Reinsurance Ltd* [1994] BCC 378, where directions were sought for a meeting in Singapore.

[54]  Discussed above under s 899.

[55]  [2002] 1 WLR 1345

the applicant should give notice of the application to those affected by it so that their views can be taken into account at the hearing.

It is clear that, in practice, relevant jurisdictional issues may now be considered at the initial hearing.    **26.896.07**
These include all questions as to whether the court would have the power to sanction the scheme under the relevant sections.[56] Although the Practice Statement is couched mainly in terms of class issues arising in the context of creditor schemes, questions about the composition of classes of members could also arise, although that must be a much rarer occurrence. It would be good practice for such member class issues to also be ventilated at an early stage on the application for orders convening the meeting(s).

## The meeting

The section provides that the meeting shall be 'summoned in such manner as the court directs', but it    **26.896.08**
contains nothing express to give the court control over the proceedings at the meeting. The court has, however, an inherent jurisdiction to give directions as to how the meeting should be held and conducted. Directions are typically given as to where and when the meeting is to be held, who is to chair the meeting, and for advertisement in national or international newspapers. It is possible for the court to direct that the meeting should be held abroad.[57]

Voting is not on a show of hands but must be by poll, since the statutory majority under section 899(1)    **26.896.09**
is concerned, in part, with the value of the votes.[58] Proxies are permitted.[59] Although the court can seemingly order a meeting of a one-person class, a meeting will not have been validly held where the relevant class consists of more than one person but only one person attends.[60] The court can waive non-compliance with the direction given by it as to convening the meetings.[61]

Where either members or creditors or a class of them are not affected by the scheme, then no meeting    **26.896.10**
is required of that class and they are not entitled to notice of it or to vote at it.[62] For example, if the effect of the scheme will be that the rights of one class of shareholders will be altered, but the rights of another class of shareholders will be unaffected, a meeting of only those shareholders whose rights are being altered is required. Similarly, if a class of creditors have no interest because the whole value of the assets would be exhausted by those who have priority over them in a liquidation, the assent of that class at a meeting is not necessary,[63] and the court can sanction the arrangement notwithstanding their opposition.[64] When determining whether there are sufficient assets to meet the claims of particular creditors, the court is concerned with identifying real economic interests in the company: mere theoretical or fanciful possibilities of a sufficiency of assets can be discounted.[65]

If a creditor has two claims against the company but votes in respect of only one, he can nonetheless    **26.896.11**
participate in the scheme in respect of both claims.[66]

### 897  Statement to be circulated or made available

(1)  Where a meeting is summoned under section 896—    **26.897.01**
   (a)  every notice summoning the meeting that is sent to a creditor or member must be accompanied by a statement complying with this section, and
   (b)  every notice summoning the meeting that is given by advertisement must either—

---

[56]  As happened in *Re MyTravel Group plc* [2005] 1 WLR 2365.
[57]  *Re RMCA Reinsurance Ltd* [1994] BCC 378, where directions were sought for a meeting in Singapore.
[58]  As to how class meetings should be conducted see *Carruth v Imperial Chemical Industries Ltd* [1937] AC 707.
[59]  Proxies are expressly contemplated by s 899(1). In practice most attendance at meetings to consider scheme proposals is by proxy.
[60]  *Re Altitude Scaffolding Ltd Re T&N Ltd and ors* [2006] EWHC 1401 (Ch).
[61]  *Re Equitable Life Assurance Society (No 2)* [2002] BCC 319 at 328 at para 35 of the judgment and *Re Peninsular & Oriental Steam Navigation Company* [2006] EWHC 389 (Ch)
[62]  *Re British & Commonwealth Holdings plc (No 3)* [1992] 1 WLR 672.
[63]  Likewise, it is not necessary to serve notice on shareholders in an insolvent company whose rights are valueless: *Mercantile Investment and General Trust Co v International Co of Mexico* [1893] 1 Ch 484.
[64]  *Re Tea Corporation Ltd* [1904] 1 Ch 12; *Re MyTravel Group plc* [2005] 1 WLR 2365. Those creditors who are excluded from a scheme may nonetheless have the right to be heard on the sanction: see, eg *BAT Industries plc* unreported, September 3 1998), Ch D (Companies Court), Neuberger J and *Re Bluebrook Ltd* [2009] EWHC 2114 (Ch).
[65]  *Re MyTravel Group plc* [2005] 1 WLR 2365. And see *Re Bluebrook Ltd* [2009] EWHC 2114 (Ch) for an example of the court dealing with an alternative valuation put forward by a creditor excluded by the company from the scheme (and the restructuring) on the basis that it had no real economic interest.
[66]  *Curtis v BURT Co Ltd* [1912] 28 TLR 585.

       (i)   include such a statement, or

       (ii)  state where and how creditors or members entitled to attend the meeting may obtain copies of such a statement.

(2)  The statement must—

    (a)  explain the effect of the compromise or arrangement, and

    (b)  in particular, state—

       (i)   any material interests of the directors of the company (whether as directors or as members or as creditors of the company or otherwise), and

       (ii)  the effect on those interests of the compromise or arrangement, in so far as it is different from the effect on the like interests of other persons.

(3)  Where the compromise or arrangement affects the rights of debenture holders of the company, the statement must give the like explanation as respects the trustees of any deed for securing the issue of the debentures as it is required to give as respects the company's directors.

(4)  Where a notice given by advertisement states that copies of an explanatory statement can be obtained by creditors or members entitled to attend the meeting, every such creditor or member is entitled, on making application in the manner indicated by the notice, to be provided by the company with a copy of the statement free of charge.

(5)  If a company makes default in complying with any requirement of this section, an offence is committed by—

    (a)  the company, and

    (b)  every officer of the company who is in default.

This is subject to subsection (7) below.

(6)  For this purpose the following are treated as officers of the company—

    (a)  a liquidator or administrator of the company, and

    (b)  a trustee of a deed for securing the issue of debentures of the company.

(7)  A person is not guilty of an offence under this section if he shows that the default was due to the refusal of a director or trustee for debenture holders to supply the necessary particulars of his interests.

(8)  A person guilty of an offence under this section is liable—

    (a)  on conviction on indictment, to a fine;

    (b)  on summary conviction, to a fine not exceeding the statutory maximum.

COMMENCEMENT DATE 6 April 2008[67]

**26.897.02**    This section is derived from section 426 of the Companies Act 1985. There are three documents contemplated by this section: a notice convening the meeting which the court has ordered be convened (section 897(1)(a)); the explanatory statement accompanying such notice (section 897(1)); and an advertisement (section 897(1)(b)). It should be noted, however, that the section does not require both notice and advertisement in every case.

### Explanatory statement and notice

**26.897.03**    Section 897(1)(a) requires that with every notice summoning a scheme meeting, there shall be sent a statement explaining the effect of the compromise or arrangement, and if there is notice by advertisement, the explanatory statement must be included in the advertisement or details of where the explanatory statement might be obtained must be given (see section 897(4) for further explanation). In practice, the notice summonsing the meeting is often contained within the relevant explanatory statement.

**26.897.04**    The section gives little guidance as to what must be included other than an explanation of the effect of the proposed scheme.[68] The explanatory statement should, however, be clear, fair, and, so far as possible, give all information reasonably necessary to enable the recipient to determine how to vote.[69] What that requires in respect of an individual scheme will depend very much on the facts surrounding that particular scheme.

**26.897.05**    Section 897(2)(b)(i) and (ii) requires express disclosure of any material interests of the directors (whether in their capacity as directors or as members or creditors or otherwise), and if the effect of the scheme is different in respect of the directors' interests from its effect on the same interests of other persons, this must be stated. A statement that 'the directors have no interests in the scheme other than as members along with other members of the company', does not comply with this requirement.[70] The

---

[67] Companies Act 2006 (Commencement No 5, Transitional Provisions and Savings) Order 2007, SI 2007/3495.

[68] See s 897(2)(a).

[69] See *RAC Motoring Services Limited* [2000] 1 BCLC 307 at 328. Sending the petition by which the company sought leave to convene the meeting will be insufficient: *Rankin & Blackmore, Petitioners* 1950 SC 218.

[70] The precise extent of the interests must be disclosed: *Coltness Iron Co Limited, Petitioners* 1951 SC 476.

section requires that any differences in effect of the scheme be stated. If there are no differences, this need not be stated.[71] The requirement applies not only to the directors' beneficial interests, but also to interests as trustees.[72]

Where there has been a material change of fact or of directors' interests between the issue of the explanatory statement and the meeting, the company should consider whether the information would be such that a reasonable shareholder would be likely to be affected in his voting by the new fact. If it is, then a further explanatory statement would be necessary.[73] A failure to disclose information is not necessarily fatal to the sanction of the scheme if, had the information been provided, no consenting creditor would have changed his view.[74] **26.897.06**

No notice needs to be given to any class which is not affected by the scheme.[75] The court must be satisfied that sufficient steps have been taken to notify all those who are eligible to attend the meeting.[76] The fact that relevant documents were not sent to creditors because of either an accidental failure or impossibility will not necessarily invalidate the process.[77] The requirement of notification is not absolute. It has been accepted that time and expense are relevant factors when determining the extent of the notification.[78] Regard will be had to notification by letter but also by advertisement in the national, international, and specialist press. Deficiencies in notification can be taken into account when the court considers whether to sanction the scheme under section 899.[79] **26.897.07**

## Advertisement

Even if every member is sent a copy of the explanatory statement, the omission to state in the advertisement where a copy is obtainable will invalidate the scheme.[80] **26.897.08**

## Default

If the company fails to comply with its obligations under section 897, then every officer of the company who is in default is liable on conviction on indictment to a fine or on summary conviction to a fine not exceeding the statutory maximum (currently £5,000). **26.897.09**

## 898 Duty of directors and trustees to provide information

(1) It is the duty of— **26.898.01**
    (a) any director of the company, and
    (b) any trustee for its debenture holders,
    to give notice to the company of such matters relating to himself as may be necessary for purposes
    of section 897 (explanatory statement to be circulated or made available).
(2) Any person who makes default in complying with this section commits an offence.
(3) A person guilty of an offence under this section is liable on summary conviction to a fine not
    exceeding level 3 on the standard scale.

COMMENCEMENT DATE 6 April 2008[81]

This section is derived from section 426(7) of the Companies Act 1985. It places a positive duty on directors and trustees for a debenture holder to provide the company with information about himself as is required for the explanatory statement under section 897 (namely his material interests in the company (whether as director/trustee or as member or as creditor of the company or otherwise) and the effect on those interests of the proposed scheme in so far as it is different from the effect on the like interests of other persons). It is an offence for the director or trustee to fail to do so, triable summarily only, and punishable by a fine not exceeding level 3 on the standard scale (currently £1,000). **26.898.02**

---

[71] *City Property Investment Trust Corp Ltd, Petitioners* 1951 SC 570.
[72] *Second Scottish Investment Trust Co Ltd, Petitioners* 1962 SLT 392.
[73] See *Re MB Group plc* [1989] BCLC 672.
[74] *Re Heron International NV* [1994] 1 BCLC 667.
[75] See the discussion above under s 896.
[76] *Re Osiris Insurance Ltd* [1999] 1 BCLC 182.
[77] *Re Equitable Life Assurance Society (No 2)* [2002] BCC 319 at 328 at para 35 of the judgment; *Re Peninsula & Oriental Steam Navigation Company* [2006] EWHC 389 (Ch) and [2006] EWCA Civ 432; and Re Halcrow Holdings Limited [2011] EWHC 3662 (Ch).
[78] *Re British Aviation Insurance Co Ltd* [2006] BCC 14.
[79] *Re British Aviation Insurance Co Ltd* [2006] BCC 14.
[80] *City Property Investment Trust Corp Ltd, Petitioners* 1951 SC 570.
[81] Companies Act 2006 (Commencement No 5, Transitional Provisions and Savings) Order 2007, SI 2007/3495.

*Court sanction for compromise or arrangement*

**899   Court sanction for compromise or arrangement**

**26.899.01**
(1)  If a majority in number representing 75% in value of the creditors or class of creditors or members of class of members (as the case may be), present and voting either in person or by proxy at the meeting summoned under section 896, agree a compromise or arrangement, the court may, on an application under this section, sanction the compromise or arrangement.

(2)  An application under this section may be made by—
(a)  the company,
(b)  any creditor or member of the company, or
[(c)  if the company is being wound up, the liquidator, or
(d)  if the company is in administration, the administrator].ᵃ

(3)  A compromise or [arrangement]ᵇ sanctioned by the court is binding on—
(a)  all creditors or the class of creditors or on the members or class of members (as the case may be), and
(b)  the company or, in the case of a company in the course of being wound up, the liquidator and contributories of the company.

(4)  The court's order has no effect until a copy of it has been delivered to the registrar.

[(5)  Section 323 (representation of corporations at meetings) applies to a meeting of creditors under this section as to a meeting of the company (references to a member of the company being read as references to a creditor).]ᶜ

AMENDMENTS AND NOTES

ᵃ  Amended by the Companies Act 2006 (Consequential Amendments etc) Order 2008, SI 2008/948, arts 3(1)(b), 6, Sch 1, para 250(2).

ᵇ  Substituted by the Companies Act 2006 (Consequential Amendments and Transitional Provisions) Order 2011, SI 2011/1265, art 28(1), (3).

ᶜ  Inserted by the Companies Act 2006 (Consequential Amendments etc) Order 2008, SI 2008/948, arts 3(1)(b), 6, Sch 1, para 250(3).

COMMENCEMENT DATE  6 April 2008[82]

*The statutory majority*

**26.899.02**  The statutory majority for approval of a scheme at the meeting was formerly found in section 425(2) of the Companies Act 1985. It is now found here. The majority requirements remain the same. There must be a majority in number representing a 75 per cent majority in value of the relevant class present and voting at the meeting in favour of the arrangement. Thus, at least half those voting must vote in favour and their votes must represent 75 per cent by value of those voting. Those who do not vote may be ignored.[83] This majority provision seeks to strike a balance between those with large economic interests and those, possibly far greater in number, who have much smaller interests. If there is more than one class, all classes entitled to vote on the scheme must vote in favour of the scheme if it is to be binding upon each class.

**26.899.03**  In relation to classes of members, each member shall be counted individually and each separate share of the same class will have the same value. For creditor schemes, each creditor shall be counted individually but the value of votes will depend upon the amount of the debts held by each creditor which comes within the relevant class. Each claim must be properly valued[84] and as such a creditor will only be able to claim in respect of a debt which can have an estimate placed on it.[85] The court will have to be satisfied that the voting rights of the members or creditors were accurately calculated.[86] A person voting shares as a nominee or trustee for more than one member or creditor can split his vote, so as to vote parts of his overall interest differently in respect of different instructions received from his beneficiaries.[87]

[82]  Companies Act 2006 (Commencement No 5, Transitional Provisions and Savings) Order 2007, SI 2007/3495.
[83]  *Re Bessemer Steel and Ordnance Co* (1875) 1 Ch D 251.
[84]  *Re British Aviation Insurance Co Ltd* [2006] BCC 14.
[85]  *Re Albert Life Assurance Co* (1871) 6 Ch App 381.
[86]  *Re British Aviation Insurance Co Ltd* [2006] BCC 14.
[87]  *Re Equitable Life Assurance Society (No 1)* [2002] BCC 319.

## The application for sanction: the approach of the court to exercise of its discretion

The application to the court for sanction of the scheme following a meeting at which the necessary     **26.899.04**
majority is obtained is the third stage of the scheme process.

The court is not bound by the decision of the meeting and has an unfettered discretion whether to     **26.899.05**
approve it. Sanction is not a formality.[88] In considering whether to sanction the scheme, the court is
conscious that the effect of a scheme, when sanctioned, will be, by virtue of section 899(3), to bind those
who voted against it and those who did not vote at all. However, the court will be slow to depart from
the decision of the meeting and is unlikely to do so, as long as it is satisfied:[89] (a) that all relevant
formalities have been complied with; (b) the majority acted bona fide in supporting the scheme;[90] and
(c) the scheme is such that an intelligent and honest person, who is a member of the class concerned
and acting alone in respect of his interest as such member, might approve it. The court will, in practice,
hear objections to the scheme not only from members of the class affected by it, but other members or
creditors (including contingent creditors), although it has been said that the scheme essentially
remains a domestic matter between the company and those affected by it and the court does not have
a roving commission to interfere.[91]

Examples of situations where the court might refuse to sanction a proposed scheme include[92] situa-     **26.899.06**
tions where: the class or classes have been incorrectly identified and drawn such that a class affected has
not consented at a proper meeting;[93] those voting in favour were promoting a special interest which
differs from the interests of an independent and objective shareholder;[94] the court finds that the
scheme is unreasonable or has inherent unfairness in it;[95] the information given about the scheme may
not have been adequate; inducements were offered to significant members or creditors which were not
offered generally and which were not disclosed to the rest of the class;[96] the substance of the scheme
involves some expropriation of members' rights without some compensating advantage;[97] the scheme
was beyond the capacity of the company;[98] the scheme involves a transaction which conflicts with
companies legislation;[99] the scheme is part of a wider transaction the effect of which may be unlawful;[100] there has been inadequate notification of the scheme meeting; the scheme meeting was not fairly
and properly conducted;[101] a scheme made provision for costs and remuneration which were not

---

[88]  *Kempe v Ambassador Insurance Co* [1998] 1 WLR 271; *Re BTR plc* [2000] 1 BCLC 740 at 747.
[89]  *Re National Bank Limited* [1966] 1 WLR 819, at 829. Quoted with approval many times subsequently: see,
eg *Re Telewest* [2004] EWHC 1466 (Ch).
[90]  A court will not sanction a scheme if it appears that the majority have not voted bona fide in the interest of
the class (*Re Wedgwood Coal and Iron Co* (1877) 6 Ch D 627), or if in all the circumstances it does not approve of
it (*Re Hickman, ex p Strawbridge* (1883) 25 Ch D 266). For example if a holder of a substantial block of a class
concerned is offered some inducement to support the scheme, this may be sufficient to invalidate the purported
approval, unless the inducement is disclosed to the members of the class (*British American Nickel Corp Ltd v MJ
O'Brien Ltd* [1927] AC 369). If the disclosure is made, the court will, in appropriate circumstances, approve the
scheme and will even allow the votes of the person treated preferentially (*Goodfellow v Nelson Line (Liverpool)
Ltd* [1912] 2 Ch 324).
[91]  *Re BAT Industries plc* (unreported, September 3 1998), Ch D (Companies Court), Neuberger J; and see also
*Re MB Group plc* [1989] BCLC 672.
[92]  The examples given are intended to be illustrative of the types of arguments that might succeed, depending
on the facts of the particular case.
[93]  *Re Hellenic and General Trust Ltd* [1976] 1 WLR 123, although note that as stated above the court may
ignore classes of creditors where, if there was an immediate distribution of the corporate assets, none would be
available for that class: *Re Tea Corporation* [1904] 1 Ch 12 and *Re MyTravel plc* [2005] 1 WLR 2365. The failure
of a creditor to raise a class issue at the first stage (application for order to convene meeting) does not prevent the
class issue being raised at the sanction hearing: *British Aviation Insurance Co Ltd* [2006] BCC 14. The failure
to properly convene meetings of different classes is a matter of jurisdiction rather than discretion.
[94]  *Re BTR plc* [2000] BCLC 740. In the *British Aviation* case the court said that in that scheme reinsured
creditors who were also reinsurers of the company proposing the scheme had a different economic interest to
ordinary insureds: the effect of the scheme would be to cap these parties' liabilities (if the company's liabilities
were capped by the scheme so would the reinsurers' liabilities as reinsurers) whereas that would not be the case
with direct insureds.
[95]  *Re Telewest Communications plc (No 2)* [2005] BCC 36 and *Re British Aviation Insurance Co Ltd* [2006] BCC
14.
[96]  *British American Nickel Corp Ltd v M J O'Brien Ltd* [1927] AC 369.
[97]  *NFU Development Trust Limited* [1972] 1 WLR 1548.
[98]  *Re Oceanic Steam Navigation Company Limited* [1939] Ch 41.
[99]  *Re St James' Court Estate Ltd* [1944] Ch 6.
[100]  *Re BAT Industries plc* (unreported, September 3 1998), Ch D (Companies Court), Neuberger J.
[101]  *British Aviation Insurance Co Ltd* [2006] BCC 14.

subject to scrutiny by the court;[102] and a scheme gave a power to a majority of debenture holders to bind a minority by anything which the court could render binding under the Act, the objection being that this was a delegation to the majority of the powers of the court.[103]

**26.899.07** Although a scheme may be disadvantageous to some creditors, the fact that the overall advantages outweigh the disadvantages, that a significant number of creditors had voted unanimously in favour of the scheme, and that all creditors were fully informed of it justified the court in sanctioning the scheme.[104] The fact of a low turnout appears not to be a reason, in itself, to refuse to sanction a scheme. However it can be taken into account in considering other issues, in particular whether those who voted were pursuing a special interest.[105] A further factor which can be taken into account on sanction is whether there were any irrevocable undertakings to vote in favour. Although this appears to no longer be a class issue,[106] it could be a factor taken into account at the sanction stage.

**26.899.08** The court has an inherent discretion to correct any obvious mistakes in the document which set out the scheme, but it cannot alter the substance of the scheme and impose the parties to an arrangement to which they had not agreed,[107] although it can impose conditions before sanctioning the scheme.[108] The court has sanctioned a scheme which provided for future amendment of either the scheme itself or any other documents to be entered into pursuant to it.[109]

### Effect of sanction

**26.899.09** Once the scheme is sanctioned by the court (and registered) it becomes binding. Whether the scheme be a valid one or not, it cannot later be questioned by the company on the grounds of capacity or breach of some statutory provision.[110] It has been held that an order sanctioning a scheme can be set aside for fraud even though this may mean that the scheme must be unravelled, although a scheme will not, however, be set aside for fraud if it would still have been sanctioned had the fraud not been perpetrated.[111]

**26.899.10** A scheme binds only the company, its members, and its creditors to the arrangements made between them. Third parties to the scheme are unaffected, although they can voluntarily bind themselves to it as a matter of contract.[112] In some cases a formal scheme is proposed only in respect of a class or classes of creditors or members who have not signalled their assent to the proposed compromise or arrangements, with those classes of creditors or members who have already agreed to the transaction participating contractually.

**26.899.11** An appeal is possible, but only with the permission of the court sanctioning the scheme or the Court of Appeal.[113] Quite how a scheme which had become effective in accordance with section 899(4), so that the company and its members/creditors have relied on the effectiveness of the order, would be unravelled if an appeal was successful is unclear. It is more likely that some procedural mechanism would have to be adopted to stay the effectiveness of the scheme pending an urgent ruling from the Court of Appeal, so that there was no question of having to unravel the scheme after it had become effective.[114]

---

[102] *Re Mortgage Insurance Corporation* [1896] WN 4.

[103] *Re Land Mortgage Bank of Florida* [1898] 1 Ch 444.

[104] *Re Osiris Insurance Ltd* [1999] 1 BCLC 182.

[105] *British Aviation Insurance Co Ltd* [2006] BCC 14.

[106] *Re Telewest Communications plc* [2004] BCC 342.

[107] *Kempe v Amabassador Insurance Co* [1998] 1 WLR 271.

[108] *Re Canning Jarrah Timber Co (Western Australia Ltd)* [1900] 1 Ch 708.

[109] *Re Cape plc and others* [2006] EWHC 1316 (Ch) and [2006] EWHC 1446 (Ch). This case is probably exceptional as it involved long-tail asbestosis liabilities with an expected period of 40–50 years, which period would be covered by the scheme. The provisions for amendment reflected the fact that it was predictable that there would be legal, medical, and financial developments with a significant impact on the arrangement. It would not be practicable to propose a new scheme each time an amendment was reasonably required.

[110] A company which has become bound by a scheme cannot subsequently vary the scheme by agreement with other parties affected (*British & Commonwealth Holdings plc v Barclays Bank plc* [1996] 1 WLR 1).

[111] *Fletcher v Royal Automobile Club Ltd* [2000] 1 BCLC 331.

[112] *Re Glendale Land Development Ltd (In Liquidation)* [1982] 7 ACLR 171 (Australia) and *City of Swan & Ors v Lehman Bros Australia Limited* (2009) 260 ALR 199.

[113] Access to Justice Act, s 54 1999 and CPR 52.

[114] This was the solution in the appeal to the Court of Appeal in the *P&O* case: *Re Peninsula & Oriental Steam Navigation Company* [2006] EWHC 389 (Ch).

## Registration

The order of the court sanctioning the scheme must be delivered to the registrar of companies for **26.899.12** registration in accordance with section 899(4), otherwise the scheme will not be effective. Companies House will not register an order without being supplied with a copy of a letter from the Stamp Office confirming that no stamp duty is payable on the order (or, if it is, evidence that the duty has been paid).

## Reconstructions and amalgamations

### 900 Powers of court to facilitate reconstruction or amalgamation

(1) This section applies where application is made to the court under section 899 to sanction a **26.900.01** compromise or arrangement and it is shown that—

    (a) the compromise or arrangement is proposed for the purposes of, or in connection with, a scheme for the reconstruction of any company or companies, or the amalgamation of any two or more companies, and

    (b) under the scheme the whole or any part of the undertaking or the property of any company concerned in the scheme ('a transferor company') is to be transferred to another company ('the transferee company').

(2) The court may, either by the order sanctioning the compromise or arrangement or by a subsequent order, make provision for all or any of the following matters—

    (a) the transfer to the transferee company of the whole or any part of the undertaking and of the property or liabilities of any transferor company;

    (b) the allotting or appropriation by the transferee company of any shares, debentures, policies or other like interests in that company which under the compromise or arrangement are to be allotted or appropriated by that company to or for any person;

    (c) the continuation by or against the transferee company of any legal proceedings pending by or against any transferor company;

    (d) the dissolution, without winding up, of any transferor company;

    (e) the provision to be made for any persons who, within such time and in such manner as the court directs, dissent from the compromise or arrangement;

    (f) such incidental, consequential and supplemental matters as are necessary to secure that the reconstruction or amalgamation is fully and effectively carried out.

(3) If an order under this section provides for the transfer of property or liabilities—

    (a) the property is by virtue of the order transferred to, and vests in, the transferee company, and

    (b) the liabilities are, by virtue of the order, transferred to and become liabilities of that company.

(4) The property (if the order so directs) vests free from any charge that is by virtue of the compromise or arrangement to cease to have effect.

(5) In this section—

    'property' includes property, rights and powers of every description; and

    'liabilities' includes duties.

(6) Every company in relation to which an order is made under this section must cause a copy of the order to be delivered to the registrar within seven days after its making.

(7) If default is made in complying with subsection (6) an offence is committed by—

    (a) the company, and

    (b) every officer of the company who is in default.

(8) A person guilty of an offence under subsection (7) is liable on summary conviction to a fine not exceeding level 3 on the standard scale and, for continued contravention, a daily default fine not exceeding one-tenth of level 3 on the standard scale.

COMMENCEMENT DATE 6 April 2008[115]

This section applies only to companies incorporated under the Companies Act—see section 895(2)(a). **26.900.02** It does not therefore apply to proposed transfers to foreign companies. Its predecessor was section 427 of the Companies Act 1985.

This section gives power to the court to approve a scheme which involves the transfer of assets and **26.900.03** liabilities between one or more company and one or more other companies. A transfer under this section vests the transferred undertaking in the transferee by order of the court.

The powers to assist in the transfer and vesting are found in subsections (2) to (4). This type of so-called **26.900.04** 'transfer' scheme might be used, for example, when it is wished to merge the assets and undertakings of two companies into one company, or to split the businesses of an existing company by dissolving that company and transferring its businesses to two or more new companies in each of which the former shareholders will hold shares.

---

[115] Companies Act 2006 (Commencement No 5, Transitional Provisions and Savings) Order 2007, SI 2007/3495.

### Reconstruction

**26.900.05**   In *Re MyTravel Group plc* [2005] 1 WLR 2365 it was held that for, a scheme to be a 'reconstruction' for the purposes of what is now section 900, substantially the same persons must hold the shares of both the old and the new companies. The section could not therefore be used to effect a transfer of the undertaking and assets of a company in financial difficulties to a new company in which the shareholders of the old company would be allotted 4 per cent of the shares.

### 'Property'

**26.900.06**   The word 'property' has been held by the House of Lords to mean only those assets with which the company has the right to deal without obtaining the consent of a third party.[116] The scheme of arrangement could not be used to override the rights of third parties. Thus 'property' in this section does not include an employment contract, nor the benefit of a contract which requires a counterparty's consent before its assignment.

### Registration

**26.900.07**   Unlike the registration requirement under section 899(4), section 900(6) imposes a positive duty on the company and its officers to register the order and make it an offence not to register an order under section 900, punishable by a fine not exceeding level 3 on the standard scale (currently £1,000) and provides for a daily default fine of up to 10 per cent of the level 3 amount (thus, currently £100).

### Obligations of company with respect to articles etc

#### 901  Obligations of company with respect to articles etc

**26.901.01**
(1)  This section applies—
    (a)  to any order under section 899 (order sanctioning compromise or arrangement), and
    (b)  to any order under section 900 (order facilitating reconstruction or amalgamation) that alters the company's constitution.
(2)  If the order amends—
    (a)  the company's articles, or
    (b)  any resolution or agreement to which Chapter 3 of Part 3 applies (resolution or agreement affecting a company's constitution),
the copy of the order delivered to the registrar by the company under section 899(4) or section 900(6) must be accompanied by a copy of the company's articles, or the resolution or agreement in question, as amended.
(3)  Every copy of the company's articles issued by the company after the order is made must be accompanied by a copy of the order, unless the effect of the order has been incorporated into the articles by amendment.
(4)  In this section—
    (a)  references to the effect of the order include the effect of the compromise or arrangement to which the order relates; and
    (b)  in the case of a company not having articles, references to its articles shall be read as references to the instrument constituting the company or defining its constitution.
(5)  If a company makes default in complying with this section an offence is committed by—
    (a)  the company, and
    (b)  every officer of the company who is in default.
(6)  A person guilty of an offence under this section is liable on summary conviction to a fine not exceeding level 3 on the standard scale.

COMMENCEMENT DATE  6 April 2008[117]

**26.901.02**   The provisions of section 901(1) and (2) are new and were included for consistency with other provisions in the Act concerning such orders. Section 901(2) imposes an additional obligation on a company where the effect of the scheme is to alter a company's constitution. A copy of the relevant constitutional document must be lodged with the registrar, along with the order of the court in respect of the scheme. The remainder is derived from sections 425(3) and (4) of the Companies Act 1985. Default is an offence, triable summarily only and punishable by a fine not exceeding level 3 on the standard scale (currently £1,000).

---

[116]  *Nokes v Doncaster Amalgamated Collieries Ltd* [1940] AC 1014.
[117]  Companies Act 2006 (Commencement No 5, Transitional Provisions and Savings) Order 2007, SI 2007/3495.

# 27

## MERGERS AND DIVISIONS
## OF PUBLIC COMPANIES

# Companies Act 2006

## PART 27
### MERGERS AND DIVISIONS OF PUBLIC COMPANIES

### *Introduction*

**27.0.01**    Part 27 of the 2006 Act is essentially a restatement of section 427A and the provisions contained in Schedule 15B to the Companies Act 1985. This Part deals with the conditions under which public companies can apply to court for an order by using the procedures set out under Part 26 of the 2006 Act to sanction a scheme of arrangement or a reconstruction involving the merger or division of a public company or companies.

**27.0.02**    As discussed above, Part 26 enables a company to enter into a 'compromise or arrangement' with its creditors and/or its members subject to sanction by the Companies Court and the approval by creditors and members at class meetings.[1] Once sanctioned by the court, the scheme becomes effective and binding on the company itself and all relevant creditors and/or members and cannot afterwards be altered.[2]

**27.0.03**    Part 27 sets out additional (and more onerous) conditions to the requirements imposed by Part 26 for all mergers and divisions and applies in specific cases, as formerly set out in section 427A(2) of the 1985 Act. Part 27 mergers and divisions involve the transfer of the undertaking, property, and liabilities of public companies to other public companies or, as may be the case, other companies (whether or not public) which are formed for the purposes of the merger or division, in exchange for shares in the transferee company receivable by members of the transferor companies, with or without an additional cash payment. The court may only sanction a scheme of arrangement implementing a merger or division falling within Part 27 if all procedural requirements have been met and it complies with (or is able to exclude) the conditions of Part 26 and Part 27.

**27.0.04**    Section 427A and Schedule 15B of the 1985 Act[3] were inserted into the 1985 Act to modify sections 425 to 427 of the 1985 Act in accordance with the Companies (Mergers and Divisions) Regulations 1987,[4] which implemented the minimum requirements imposed by the Third Council Directive (EEC) 78/855[5] concerning mergers of public limited liability companies (the 'Third Directive') and the Sixth Council Directive (EEC) 82/891[6] (the 'Sixth Directive') concerning the division of public limited liability companies.

**27.0.05**    The provisions of the 1985 Act have been reorganized in the Act, departing from the original specific case-by-case approach to a separation of Chapters for both mergers and divisions. The separation leads to a clearer and simpler layout of provisions and a closer conformity to the form of the provisions set out in the Third Directive and the Sixth Directive. The Act also introduces new independence requirements for experts and valuers, as set out in sections 936 and 937.

---

[1]  See Part 26 for the effect of sanction by the court of a scheme.

[2]  Even if the members and creditors of the company agree to the alteration, as seen in *Devi v People's Bank of Northern India* [1938] 4 All ER 337.

[3]  Section 427A took effect from 1 January 1988. Schedule 15B was originally inserted as Sch 15A by the Companies (Mergers and Divisions) Regulations 1987, SI 1987/1991, reg 2(C), Schedule, Pt II, as from 1 January 1988 and renumbered by the Companies Act 1989, s 114(2), as from 1 April 1990.

[4]  SI 1987/1991.

[5]  [1978] OJ L295/36, as amended by Council Directive (EC) 2007/63 [2007] OJ L300/47 and Council Directive (EC) 2009/109 [2009] OJ L259/14.

[6]  [1982] OJ L378/47.

### The Third Directive and the Sixth Directive

**27.0.06** The Third Directive was implemented to aid cross-border mergers of public limited liability companies which were previously only permissible in certain EU Member States, involved complex legal processes, or were restrictively costly to undertake. It provides for monitoring of the merger process to be carried out by the national authority having jurisdiction over the merging companies, which will provide for the legal outcome. Where cross-border mergers are carried out, the national authority considered to have jurisdiction is the national authority of the company which results from the cross-border merger. Where the resulting company falls under UK jurisdiction, Part 26 and Part 27 of the Act must be applied to the merger.

**27.0.07** The Sixth Directive acknowledges the similarities that exist between operations involving mergers and divisions and makes equivalent provision for divisions to those set out for mergers in the Third Directive. Protection for members and creditors of companies involved in the division are extended so that such obligations to provide protection cannot be avoided—these methods of protection have been set out in Part 26 and Part 27.

**27.0.08** Implementation of the Third Directive and the Sixth Directive into UK law has resulted in the courts monitoring the processes involved in mergers and divisions, as detailed in Part 26.

### Directive (EC) 2005/56 on cross-border mergers of limited liability companies[7] (the 'Cross-Border Directive') and the Companies (Cross-Border Mergers) Regulations 2007[8] (the 'Cross-Border Regulations')

**27.0.09** The Cross-Border Regulations came into force in the UK on 15 December 2007 to implement the provisions of the Cross-Border Directive, which sets out specific rules for both private and public companies involved in cross-border mergers within the EEA. The implementation of the Cross-Border Directive should aid cross-border mergers by way of the introduction of a consistent and transparent framework for mergers throughout the EEA, reducing the cost of cross-border mergers as well as legal and administrative uncertainties and difficulties.[9]

**27.0.10** The provisions of the Cross-Border Regulations are based on the approach taken in the Third Directive in relation to domestic mergers of public limited companies, which is already reflected in Part 27 of the Act and the merger provisions in the European Company Statute (Regulation (EC) 2157/2001[10]). Part 27 of the Act, however, does not provide for cross-border mergers between UK companies and countries elsewhere in the EEA. Therefore the effect of the implementation of the Cross-Border Directive is substantially limited to the replication of the Part 27 provisions to encompass cross-border mergers, only making adjustments where regulatory requirements are required in relation to cross-border mergers differing to those already in place. As a result, the Cross-Border Regulations contain a number of additional, and more onerous, requirements than those set out in the Cross-Border Directive. The Cross-Border Regulations also implement the employee participation provisions outlined in the Cross-Border Directive,[11] which follow, as closely as possible, the European Public Limited-Liability Company Regulations 2004, SI 2004/2326 and the European Public Limited-Liability Company Regulations (Northern Ireland) 2004.

### Mergers under the Cross-Border Regulations

**27.0.11** The Cross-Border Regulations recognize three specific types of cross-border mergers,[12] in each case where a UK company is involved in a merger with one or more EEA companies. 'Company' includes public and private companies and unlimited companies, as well as unregistered companies and

---

[7] As amended by Council Directive (EC) 2009/109 [2009] OJ L259/14.
[8] SI 2007/2974, as amended by the Companies (Cross-Border Mergers) (Amendment) Regulations 2008, SI 2008/583.
[9] See DTI Consultative Document entitled 'Implementation of Directive 2005/56/EC on Cross-Border Mergers of Limited Liability Companies' (March 2007), which can be viewed at ⟨http://webarchive.nationalarchives.gov.uk/20070305115119/http://www.dti.gov.uk/files/file38049.pdf⟩, p 48.
[10] [2001] OJ L294/1
[11] This is a system which gives employees a statutory or contractual right to involvement at board level. Statutory rights exist in some EEA states, such as Germany, Austria, Sweden, and the Netherlands. Employees in the United Kingdom do not have a statutory right to involvement at board level but employers and employees can create such arrangements contractually. Where the arrangements meet the definition of employee participation, these will need to be retained following the merger.
[12] (i) A merger by absorption; (ii) a merger by formation of a new company; and (iii) a merger by absorption of a wholly owned subsidiary as set out in the Cross-Border Regulations, SI 2007/2974, reg 2(1). The merger must

companies in administration. An 'EEA company' is a body corporate governed by the law of an EEA state other than the United Kingdom.[13] Note that a UK company in administration may take part in a cross-border merger (and in such case the administrator's consent is required) but a UK company in liquidation may not.

**27.0.12**    The Cross-Border Regulations set out a two-stage procedure. In the first 'pre-merger' stage, mirroring the domestic regime set out in Part 27, each company involved in the merger must prepare and circulate adopted draft terms of merger, a directors' report and an independent expert's report to its shareholders. Copies of each of the documents need to be available for inspection for one month before the first shareholder (or class) meeting for inspection by shareholders and employee representatives and the directors' report must be delivered to the company's employee representatives (or, if none exist, the employees) two months before the first shareholder (or class) meeting. Once the documents are prepared, the UK company will apply to the court for it to convene a meeting of shareholders (or class of shareholders) to approve the merger.

**27.0.13**    In each of the jurisdictions where the merging companies are registered, the company registries have certain registration functions. In the United Kingdom, not less than two months before the date of the first shareholder (or class) meeting to approve the merger, the directors must deliver to the registrar of companies a copy of any court order convening the meeting(s), a copy of the draft terms of merger and certain particulars of each merging company set out in the 'Cross-Border Mergers Form'.[14] The registrar must publish details of the merger and the meeting(s) in the *Gazette* at least one month before the date of the first meeting.

**27.0.14**    The draft terms of merger must be approved by a majority of each class of shareholders, representing 75 per cent in value of each class. Where any of the creditors of the company have applied to court to require the convening of a creditor (or class of creditor) meeting, equivalent creditor approval must also be obtained. In certain circumstances shareholder approval is not required, for example in the case of a transferor company in a merger by absorption of a wholly owned subsidiary.

**27.0.15**    After gaining the necessary shareholder and creditor approvals, each merging company may apply to its relevant national competent authority for an order certifying the completion of the pre-merger requirements. In the United Kingdom, the courts are the competent authority, being the High Court in England, Wales and Northern Ireland and the Court of Session in Scotland.

**27.0.16**    In the second 'merger completion' stage, the competent authority of the country where the merged entity will be registered must approve the merger. The competent authority will fix a date when the merger takes place which is not less than 21 days after the order approving the merger, upon which date the registrar strikes the name of any transferor company from the register and makes a note on the register that the company's assets and liabilities have been transferred to a new company. The transferee company must take such steps as are required to effect the transfer of assets and liabilities of the transferor companies.

**27.0.17**    Following approval, a UK transferee company and every UK transferor company must deliver to the registrar of companies, within seven days of the date of the court order, a copy of such order and, where there is a transferor company that is an EEA company, details of the register in which it is entered and its registration number. If the approval is given by a competent authority of another EEA state, every UK transferor company must deliver a copy of the order to the registrar of companies within 14 days of its date. Certain information must also be provided to the registrar of companies if the UK company has amended its articles or if an order is made which affects its constitution in some way.

**27.0.18**    If the merger involves employee participation arrangements in one or more of the merging companies, final approval by the competent authority can only be given once the arrangements for the employee participation in the merged entity have been agreed in accordance with Part 4 of the Cross-Border Regulations. Negotiations to agree employee participation arrangements may take up to 12 months (the usual end date is six months but this can be extended up to 12 months) so cross-border mergers may take a considerable time to implement. Note that final approval by the court must be within six months of the order granting the pre-merger certificates (which certifies completion of all of the pre-merger requirements) so companies must ensure that the pre-merger certificate is only sought once it is clear that employee participation arrangements will be finalized within six months. The principle is that the merged entity will be subject to the rules in force concerning employee

---

involve at least one company formed and registered in the United Kingdom and at least one company formed and registered in an EEA state other than the United Kingdom.

[13]  SI 2007/2974, reg 3(1).

[14]  The Cross-Border Mergers Form is available on the website of the registrar of companies at ⟨http://www.companieshouse.gov.uk/forms/formsContinuation.shtml#CB01⟩.

participation, if any, in the EEA state where it will have its registered office. For example, subject to certain exceptions, where a UK company merges with a German company and the merged entity registers in Germany, then German national law on employee participation rights will apply throughout the newly merged company, including any establishments in the United Kingdom.[15]

While the Cross-Border Regulations have increased the choices available where a UK company wants to merge with a company from another EEA state, the lengthy process for approval could prove unwieldy, and existing structures, such as takeovers by offer or schemes of arrangement, are likely to be used instead.

**27.0.19**

The Government extended the legislation on cross-border mergers to limited liability partnerships (LLPs) with effect from 1 October 2009.[16] Part 26 of the Act (with appropriate amendments changing 'company' into 'LLP') applies to LLPs, as do the provisions of the Cross-Border Regulations, with the exception of the provisions relating to employee participation.

**27.0.20**

## Directive (EC) 2009/109 amending the Second Council Directive,[17] the Third Directive, the Sixth Directive, and the Cross-Border Directive as regards reporting and documentation requirements in mergers and divisions

In July 2007, the European Commission launched a consultation on its proposals to simplify existing EU law in the areas of company law, accounting and audit. The measures proposed were set out in a Communication[18] and aim to reduce or remove a range of administrative requirements imposed under European company law directives that are considered outdated or excessive in order to 'reduce the burdens weighing on companies within the Community to the minimum that is necessary to ensure the interests of the other stakeholders'.[19] It was decided that company law directives which mainly address issues that can be regulated at national level (such as the Second Directive, the Third Directive, and the Sixth Directive) would be simplified.

**27.0.21**

As part of this simplification process, Directive (EC) 2009/109[20] amending the Second Council Directive, the Third Directive, the Sixth Directive, and the Cross-Border Directive was adopted on 16 September 2009. The Directive was adopted to amend the costly reporting and administrative (publication and documentation) requirements in the case of mergers and divisions and to update methods to inform members about the merger or division to take into account technological developments. The implementation date of this Directive was 30 June 2011.

**27.0.22**

The main changes brought about by Directive 2009/109 are:

**27.0.23**

- allowing Member States to designate websites for publication of the draft terms of merger or division along with other documents which need to be made available as part of the process, which companies can use, free of charge, as an alternative to their own websites, subject only to necessary safeguards and security considerations;
- removing the requirements under the Third Directive and the Sixth Directive to draw up an accounting statement where the company is already producing a half-yearly financial statement under the Transparency Directive,[21] or where all the shareholders agree;
- removing the requirements under the Third Directive and the Sixth Directive for a management report where all the shareholders agree;
- allowing Member States to relieve companies from the requirement to produce an expert's report under the Second Directive where the company is already drawing one up in the context of a merger or division (under the Third Directive or the Sixth Directive), thereby removing the 'double reporting' requirements;

---

[15] See Guidance on the Companies (Cross-Border Mergers) Regulations 2007, which can be viewed at ⟨http://www.bis.gov.uk/files/file41862.doc⟩, 10, cl 10.6 which also provides more detailed guidance on employee participation in the context of the Cross-Border Regulations.

[16] See the SI 2009/1804, Part 10.

[17] Directive (EEC) 7/91 [1977] OJ L26/31.

[18] Communication from the Commission on a Simplified Business Environment for Companies in the Areas of Company Law, Accounting and Auditing, a copy of which can be found at ⟨http://ec.europa.eu/internal_market/company/docs/simplification/com2007_394_en.pdf⟩.

[19] European Parliament Legislative Resolution of 22 April 2009 on the Proposal for a Directive as regards Reporting and Documentation Requirements in the case of Mergers and Divisions, 4, para 2, which can be found at ⟨http://register.consilium.europa.eu/pdf/en/09/st08/st08883.en09.pdf⟩.

[20] [2009] OJ L259/14.

[21] Directive (EC) 2004/109 [2004] OJ L390/38 on the harmonisation of transparency requirements in relation to information about issuers whose securities are admitted to trading on a regulated market.

- reducing reporting and information requirements where the merger or division is taking place between parent companies and their subsidiaries; and
- amending the Third Directive and the Sixth Directive to reflect amendments to the creditor protection rules contained in the Second Directive, to allow creditors to apply to the courts for protection, as long as they can show that due to the merger or division their claim is at stake and they have not been adequately protected by company safeguards.

**27.0.24**    On 13 January 2011, BIS published draft regulations[22] to implement Directive 2009/109. BIS invited questions and comments on the draft regulations, which will expand the range of circumstances in which a company may dispense with certain of the requirements of a merger or division. Parliament approved the Companies (Reporting Requirements in Mergers and Divisions) Regulations 2011[23] on 1 July 2011. These regulations apply to mergers or divisions adopted on or after 1 August 2011. The regulations implement the changes brought about by Directive 2009/109, which fall into two broad categories: enabling companies to take advantage of new technology; and the removal of over regulation. In the explanatory memorandum to the regulations, BIS stated that the regulations will simplify the process of a division or merger, but will not impose additional costs or burdens on business.

### Directive 2011/35/EU codifying the Third Directive

**27.0.25**    On 5 April 2011, the European Parliament and Council adopted Directive 2011/35/EU.[24] This Directive repeals and replaces the Third Directive, save for the time limits for member states to transpose the provisions of the Third Directive into national law, which remain in place. The main objective of this Directive is for shareholders of merging companies to be kept adequately informed and for the rights of these shareholders to be suitably protected. The implementation date of this Directive was 1 July 2011.

**27.0.26**    The main differences between this Directive and the Third Directive, which it replaces, are:

- the publication of the draft terms of merger, which must take place one month prior to a general meeting to decide the merger, may now be effected by making them available on the website of a company free of charge for the public. Member states may require publication of the draft terms of merger to be effected through a central electronic platform referred to in the Sixth Directive;
- the administrative/management bodies which prepare a detailed written report explaining the draft terms of the merger are required to inform the general meeting of their company of any material change in the assets and liabilities between the date of preparation of the draft terms of merger and the date of the general meeting;
- the requirement for a detailed written report to be prepared by the administrative/management bodies of each merging company may be waived if all persons holding voting rights in the merging company so agree;
- the requirement for experts (acting on behalf of the merging companies, but independent of them) to examine the draft terms of the merger and prepare a written report to the shareholders may be waived if all persons holding voting rights in the merging company so agree;
- the requirement for a merging company to produce an accounting statement (in the event that the latest annual accounts for the merging company are not sufficiently recent) may be waived if all persons holding voting rights in the merging company so agree; and
- a merging company may satisfy its requirement to publish certain documents relating to the merger by: (i) emailing them to those shareholders who have consented to such form of correspondence; or (ii) making them available on the website of a company where they may be downloaded and printed.

**27.0.27**    Notwithstanding the above differences, this Directive is a codifying directive, and does not bring forward any new measures, and so is not required to be implemented by Member States which have already implemented all aspects required by the Third Directive. Therefore, the United Kingdom has not implemented this Directive.

---

[22] Draft Companies (Reporting Requirements in Mergers and Divisions) Regulations 2011. This is available, with explanatory text, at ⟨http://www.bis.gov.uk/policies/business-law/company-and-partnership-law/europe/eu-legislation/company-mergers-and-divisions-simplification-of-the-3rd-and-6th-company-law-directives⟩.

[23] SI 2011/1606.

[24] Directive 2011/35/EU [2011] OJ L110/1.

CHAPTER 1

INTRODUCTORY

## 902 Application of this Part

(1) This Part applies where—                                                                          27.902.01
   (a) a compromise or arrangement is proposed between a public company and—
      (i) its creditors or any class of them, or
      (ii) its members or any class of them,
      for the purposes of, or in connection with, a scheme for the reconstruction of any company
      or companies or the amalgamation of any two or more companies,
   (b) the scheme involves—
      (i) a merger (as defined in section 904), or
      (ii) a division (as defined in section 919), and
   (c) the consideration for the transfer (or each of the transfers) envisaged is to be shares in the
      transferee company (or one or more of the transferee companies) receivable by members of
      the transferor company (or transferor companies), with or without any cash payment to
      members.
(2) In this Part—
   (a) a 'new company' means a company formed for the purposes of, or in connection with, the
      scheme, and
   (b) an 'existing company' means a company other than one formed for the purposes of, or in
      connection with, the scheme.
(3) This Part does not apply where the company in respect of which the compromise or arrangement
   is proposed is being wound up.

COMMENCEMENT DATE 6 April 2008[25]

### *'Compromise or arrangement'*

Section 902 applies to compromises or arrangements,[26] which are commonly known as 'schemes of    27.902.02
arrangement', made between a public company and its creditors or members, or any class of them. No
scheme of arrangement will exist unless the company is also a party to the proposed arrangement. If the
scheme affects the contractual relationship subsisting between the company and its members, and the
rights and obligations between the company and its members are sufficiently affected by the proposed
scheme, the courts are likely to find that a scheme of arrangement exists between them.[27]

As more fully described in the commentary on Part 26 of the Act, a scheme of arrangement can relate    27.902.03
to any subject matter provided it is properly agreed between the company and its members or creditors
and an element of 'accommodation' is given on each side rather than a mere surrendering of rights by
the members or creditors.[28] Practically, a scheme's subject matter must be such that the court will
approve its sanction, although in general the courts have construed the term 'arrangement' broadly.[29]
However, the courts have no jurisdiction to sanction a scheme where the arrangements are *ultra vires*
the company[30] or where the scheme provisions fall outside of the general law. The courts are also
unlikely to sanction a scheme which is contrary to another statutory provision, such as section 110 of
the Insolvency Act 1986.[31] If a scheme involves a reduction of capital, then the arrangements should
comply with the relevant statutory provisions in Part 17, Chapter 10 of the Act.

---

[25] Companies Act 2006 (Commencement No 5, Transitional Provisions and Savings) Order 2007, SI 2007/
3495, art 3(1).
[26] See paras 26.895.02–05 for the meaning of 'compromise' and 'arrangement'.
[27] *Re Savoy Hotel Limited* [1981] 3 All ER 646 where it was argued that the scheme was not 'between' the
company and the members.
[28] Where the rights of members are being expropriated, there must be some kind of compensating advantage
for the members or it will not be held that they are entering into a scheme of arrangement with the company; *Re
NFU Development Trust Limited* [1973] 1 All ER 135.
[29] *Re Guardian Assurance Co* [1917] 1 Ch 431.
[30] *Re Oceanic Steam Navigation Company Limited* [1939] 1 Ch 41.
[31] Enabling a voluntary solvent winding up to be used to bring about the transfer or sale of the whole part of
the company's business or property to another company in exchange for shares, policies, or other like interests to
be distributed among the members of the liquidating company. The court is unlikely to sanction a scheme which
is brought under Part 26 rather than s 110 of the Insolvency Act 1986 in order to avoid the rights of dissentients
given under s 110. If the safeguards for dissentients contained in s 110 are retained, sanction is more likely to be
given.

**27.902.04**   In practice, with the exception of the insurance industry, schemes of arrangement are rarely, if ever, used to effect a merger. The requirements formerly set out under Schedule 15B of the 1985 Act and restated in Part 27 are detailed, onerous, and costly to comply with, and the merging of assets and liabilities may involve such issues as third party rights and consents and bank guarantees.

**27.902.05**   Part 27 is relatively easy to avoid in transactions where undertakings are transferred, for example if the consideration includes something other than shares combined with cash, the technical definition of a scheme set out in Part 27 is avoided, so Part 27 no longer applies. Generally, the acquisition of shares in the company by way of share-for-share takeover or hive down, rather than a scheme of arrangement, will more easily achieve what is required.

### 'Public company'

**27.902.06**   Part 27 applies where a compromise or arrangement is proposed between a public company and its creditors or members, or any class of them. To be a public company, a company must be limited by shares or by guarantee, have a share capital and a certificate of incorporation which states that it is a public company, and it must have complied with the Act and the 1985 Act (or former Companies Acts) as to its registration or re-registration as a public company on or after 22 December 1980 in Great Britain or 1 July 1983 in Northern Ireland.[32] In relation to a public company from Northern Ireland, 'public company' means a public company within the meaning of the Companies (Northern Ireland) Order 1986.

### 'Creditors' and 'members'

**27.902.07**   The meaning and identification of 'creditors' and 'members' is discussed in detail in the commentary on Part 26 of the Act. Generally, any person with a pecuniary claim against the company involved in the scheme capable of estimate will be considered to be a creditor.[33]

### 'Class'

**27.902.08**   The commentary on Part 26 of the Act considers what constitutes a 'class' for the purposes of schemes of arrangement which are proposed between the company and a class only of its members or creditors. Each class of members or creditors should be identified accurately by the company for the various meetings that the court has power to call under section 896(1) of the Act, and should fairly represent the divergent rights of members and creditors.

**27.902.09**   Determining the correct classes of creditors and/or members can give rise to the greatest difficulty when implementing a scheme. It is the company which determines the correct classes, and historically the court has not given guidance on identifying classes at the application stage.[34] However, a failure by the applicant to identify a class or classes of members or creditors where persons have dissimilar rights can mean that the court will refuse to sanction the scheme,[35] which can be costly in both expense and time. Occasionally, disputes have also been laid before the court to decide whether the identification of classes by the company has been too specific and whether too many classes have been formed.[36]

**27.902.10**   See paragraphs 26.895.10 and 26.896.06 for further commentary on the constitution of classes.

### 'Consideration'

**27.902.11**   The reference to consideration set out in section 902(1)(c) restates section 427A(1)(c) of the 1985 Act, under which the consideration payable for the transfer is to be shares transferred from the transferee company (or one or more of the transferee companies) to the members of the transferor company(ies). The members of the transferee company become members of the transferor company, with the effect of merging the businesses and pooling the ownership of the merging companies. Consideration in the

---

[32]   As set out in s 4(2) of CA 2006.

[33]   *Re Albert Life Assurance Co* (1871) 6 LR Ch App 381, 386.

[34]   Although a practice statement was issued in 2002 ([2002] 1 WLR 1345, effective from 15 April 2002), which intended to ensure that the correct classes of creditors could be identified early on in the proceedings.

[35]   As seen in *Sovereign Life Assurance Co v Dodd* [1892] 2 QB 573 where the court considered whether creditors of the company whose life insurance policies had matured and whose policies had not yet matured formed a single class or two distinct classes of creditors. The court held that separate meetings should have been summoned, and as only one meeting had been convened, the arrangement could not therefore be sanctioned. See also *Re British Aviation Insurance Co Ltd* [2005] EWHC 1621 (Ch), where the company convened a meeting of a single class of creditors when in reality two classes of creditors should have been formed and separate meetings held, the court held that it had no jurisdiction to sanction the scheme.

[36]   *PT Garuda Indonesia, Re* [2001] EWCA Civ 1696.

form of shares, if necessary or desired, can be combined with a cash payment to the members of the transferor companies by the transferee company.

## Companies being wound up

If a company is being wound up or has an administration order in force in relation to it, the liquidator or administrator of that company can apply to the court to order a meeting of the creditors or members or classes of them in respect of a scheme of arrangement under section 896 of the Act. Part 27 expressly states that if such a scheme of arrangement is proposed, the additional requirements imposed by Part 27 are not applicable.

**27.902.12**

### 903  Relationship of this Part to Part 26

(1)  The court must not sanction the compromise or arrangement under Part 26 (arrangements and reconstructions) unless the relevant requirements of this Part have been complied with.

(2)  The requirements applicable to a merger are specified in sections 905 to 914.
   Certain of those requirements, and certain general requirements of Part 26, are modified or excluded by the provisions of sections 915 to [918A]ª.

(3)  The requirements applicable to a division are specified in sections 920 to 930.
   Certain of those requirements, and certain general requirements of Part 26, are modified or excluded by the provisions of sections 931 to 934.

**27.903.01**

AMENDMENTS AND NOTES

ª  Amended by the Companies (Reporting Requirements in Mergers and Divisions) Regulations 2011, SI 2011/1606, reg 4.

COMMENCEMENT DATE 6 April 2008[37]

The Third Directive and the Sixth Directive, which dictate the procedures governing schemes involving mergers and divisions, do not require the involvement of the court in the process. However, the directives do require that unless the legality of a merger or division is supervised by a court or an administrative body, certain of the required documents would have to be certified in due legal form by a 'notary or other legal authority', who has to check the draft terms and that the formalities for the merger or division are being complied with. Note, however, that neither examination of the draft terms of a merger or division by an independent expert nor a written expert's report need be required, if all shareholders so agree. See further commentary on section 915.

**27.903.02**

The Third Directive and the Sixth Directive have therefore been interpreted such that the sanction of the court is needed for a scheme of arrangement involving a merger or division under Part 27. Such sanction will not be given unless Part 26 has been complied with (or excluded by the provisions of Part 27) and all of the additional requirements of Part 27 have also been fulfilled. Court sanction ensures that checks are imposed to ensure that the formalities are being dealt with and in such a manner that the court would approve.

**27.903.03**

# CHAPTER 2
## MERGER
### *Introductory*

### 904  Mergers and merging companies

(1)  The scheme involves a merger where under the scheme—

(a)  the undertaking, property and liabilities of one or more public companies, including the company in respect of which the compromise or arrangement is proposed, are to be transferred to another existing public company (a 'merger by absorption'), or

(b)  the undertaking, property and liabilities of two or more public companies, including the company in respect of which the compromise or arrangement is proposed, are to be transferred to a new company, whether or not a public company, (a 'merger by formation of a new company').

(2)  References in this Part to 'the merging companies' are—

(a)  in relation to a merger by absorption, to the transferor and transferee companies;

(b)  in relation to a merger by formation of a new company, to the transferor companies.

**27.904.01**

COMMENCEMENT DATE 6 April 2008[38]

---

**27.904.02**     Section 904 of the Act removes the 'case-by-case' approach taken under the 1985 Act setting out example factual structures of schemes of arrangement involving mergers. The section is basically a restatement and reorganization of section 427A of the 1985 Act, Cases 1 and 2, but introduces the definitions of 'merger by absorption' and 'merger by formation'.

**27.904.03**     The effect of a 'merger by absorption' under Part 27 would be for the business, assets, and liabilities of one or more of the public companies involved in the merger to be transferred to another existing public company, the former then being dissolved.

**27.904.04**     Alternatively, a 'merger by formation' takes place when the business, assets, and liabilities of one or more public companies are transferred into a new company (public or private) formed for the purpose of the merger so that the business of the original companies becomes the business of the single newly formed company and the original companies are dissolved. The shareholders of the 'transferor' company or companies become the shareholders of the 'transferee' company.

### Requirements applicable to merger

### 905 Draft terms of scheme (merger)

**27.905.01**       (1) A draft of the proposed terms of the scheme must be drawn up and adopted by the directors of the merging companies.

             (2) The draft terms must give particulars of at least the following matters—

                 (a) in respect of each transferor company and the transferee company—

                     (i) its name,

                     (ii) the address of its registered office, and

                     (iii) whether it is a company limited by shares or a company limited by guarantee and having a share capital;

                 (b) the number of shares in the transferee company to be allotted to members of a transferor company for a given number of their shares (the 'share exchange ratio') and the amount of any cash payment;

                 (c) the terms relating to the allotment of shares in the transferee company;

                 (d) the date from which the holding of shares in the transferee company will entitle the holders to participate in profits, and any special conditions affecting that entitlement;

                 (e) the date from which the transactions of a transferor company are to be treated for accounting purposes as being those of the transferee company;

                 (f) any rights or restrictions attaching to shares or other securities in the transferee company to be allotted under the scheme to the holders of shares or other securities in a transferor company to which any special rights or restrictions attach, or the measures proposed concerning them;

                 (g) any amount of benefit paid or given or intended to be paid or given—

                     (i) to any of the experts referred to in section 909 (expert's report), or

                     (ii) to any director of a merging company,

                 and the consideration for the payment of benefit.

             (3) The requirements in subsection (2)(b), (c) and (d) are subject to section 915 (circumstances in which certain particulars not required).

             COMMENCEMENT DATE 6 April 2008[39]

**27.905.02**     Under section 905, all the directors of the transferor and pre-existing transferee companies involved in the proposed scheme of arrangement need to prepare a draft of the proposed terms of the merger including all of the details specified under section 905(2), in accordance with the implementation into the UK of Article 5 of the Third Directive. The section sets out the minimum content requirements for the draft terms.

**27.905.03**     Note that for schemes involving a merger by absorption where all of the relevant securities of the transferor company(ies) are held by or on behalf of the transferee company, the draft terms do not need to include the details of the allotment of shares in the transferee company as specified in section 905(2)(b) to (d) inclusive.

**27.905.04**     The company should consider providing for a degree of flexibility in the proposed scheme so as to be able to agree to any modifications the court may approve as a condition of sanctioning the scheme without having to revert to shareholders for further approval. This may happen, for example, where justifiable objections have been raised at the hearing of the petition by minority shareholders. A good example of the use of conditions is seen in *Re Canning Jarrah Timber Company (Western Australia)*

---

[39] Companies Act 2006 (Commencement No 5, Transitional Provisions and Savings) Order 2007, SI 2007/3495, art 3(1).

*Limited*,[40] where a scheme was granted on the condition that the liquidator of the company paid out creditors in full before passing assets to the company, that shareholders who opposed the scheme could be entitled to all the statutory rights of dissident shareholders, and that the liquidator abandon a number of underwriting agreements.

## 906  Publication of draft terms [by registrar][a] (merger)

(1) The directors of each of the merging companies must deliver a copy of the draft terms to the registrar.

(2) The registrar must publish in the Gazette notice of receipt by him from that company of a copy of the draft terms.

(3) That notice must be published at least one month before the date of any meeting of that company summoned for the purpose of approving the scheme.

[(4) The requirements in this section are subject to section 906A (publication of draft terms on company website).][b]

**27.906.01**

AMENDMENTS AND NOTES

[a] Amended by the Companies (Reporting Requirements in Mergers and Divisions) Regulations 2011, SI 2011/1606, reg 5(2).

[b] Inserted by the Companies (Reporting Requirements in Mergers and Divisions) Regulations 2011, SI 2011/1606, reg 5(1).

COMMENCEMENT DATE 6 April 2008[41]

Once drafted, the directors of the transferor and pre-existing transferee companies involved must deliver the draft terms to the Registrar of Companies, who will publish a notice in the *London Gazette* (or in the case of a Northern Ireland company, the *Belfast Gazette*) of his receipt of that copy. There must be at least one month between the publication of the notice of receipt and the first of any meeting considering the scheme of either the transferor company or pre-existing transferee company(ies). These requirements do not apply to a company which complies with section 906A.

**27.906.02**

## [906A  Publication of draft terms on company website (merger)

(1) Section 906 does not apply in respect of a company if the conditions in subsections (2) to (6) are met.

(2) The first condition is that the draft terms are made available on a website which—
   (a) is maintained by or on behalf of the company, and
   (b) identifies the company.

(3) The second condition is that neither access to the draft terms on the website nor the supply of a hard copy of them from the website is conditional on payment of a fee or otherwise restricted.

(4) The third condition is that the directors of the company deliver to the registrar a notice giving details of the website.

(5) The fourth condition is that the registrar publishes the notice in the Gazette at least one month before the date of any meeting of the company summoned for the purpose of approving the scheme.

(6) The fifth condition is that the draft terms remain available on the website throughout the period beginning one month before, and ending on, the date of any such meeting.][a]

**27.906A.01**

AMENDMENTS AND NOTES

[a] Inserted by the Companies (Reporting Requirements in Mergers and Divisions) Regulations 2011, SI 2011/1606, reg 6.

COMMENCEMENT DATE 1 April 2011[42]

The directors of the transferor and pre-existing transferee companies involved are not required to deliver the draft terms to the Registrar of Companies if the draft terms are instead published on a website maintained by or on behalf of the relevant company which is available for free. Notice containing details of the website containing such draft terms must be delivered to the Registrar of Companies, who will publish a notice in the London Gazette (or in the case of a Northern Ireland company, the Belfast Gazette) of his receipt of that copy. The draft terms must remain available on the website for the period starting one month before and ending on the date of any meeting considering the scheme of either the transferor company or pre-existing transferee company(ies).

**27.906A.02**

---

[40] [1900] 1 Ch 708.

[41] Companies Act 2006 (Commencement No. 5, Transitional Provisions and Savings) Order 2007, SI 2007/3495, art 3(1).

[42] Companies (Reporting Requirements in Mergers and Divisions) Regulations 2011, SI 2011/1606, reg 1(2).

### 907  Approval of members of merging companies

**27.907.01**
    (1)  The scheme must be approved by a majority in number, representing 75 per cent. in value, of each class of members of each of the merging companies, present and voting either in person or by proxy at a meeting.

    (2)  This requirement is subject to sections 916, 917 and 918 (circumstances in which meetings of members not required).

    COMMENCEMENT DATE 6 April 2008[43]

**27.907.02**  Section 896 of Part 26 sets out the requirement for the company, its members or creditors or, if relevant, the liquidator or administrator to apply to court for directions for the convening and holding of meetings of each class of members or creditors of the transferor company(ies) to approve the proposed scheme.

**27.907.03**  Section 907 requires additional meetings of each class of members of each of the merging existing *transferee* companies to approve the scheme as well. It is assumed that the criteria for assessing different classes of members for transferee companies will be the same as is used for transferor companies (see commentary on section 902 above and on Part 26).

**27.907.04**  The need to hold members' meetings is subject to sections 916, 917, and 918 which set out the circumstances in which members' meetings are not required.

### Approval by members

**27.907.05**  There are two requirements for a successful vote from each class meeting.

**27.907.06**  The first is that the majority of that class who vote in favour of the scheme must be a majority in number of the members of that class, ie over half of the class of members or creditors who are present and vote at the meeting either in person or by virtue of a proxy.

**27.907.07**  The second requirement is that three quarters of the members of that class in value of holding must vote in favour of the scheme. The reasoning for this is explained in *NFU Development Trust Ltd*,[44] which considered the 75 per cent vote in value required under Part 26. Brightman J explained that 'in referring to three-fourths in value of the…members or class of members' [the section] is directing attention to the size of the stake which each member has in the company. The purpose is to prevent a numerical majority with a small stake outvoting a minority with a large stake, eg to prevent 51 members with one share each outvoting 49 members with ten shares each'.[45] The requirement dates back to the early 1900s when the procedure to approve schemes of arrangement applied only to compromises or arrangements with creditors, and prevented creditors with large claims from being able to push through a scheme to the detriment of creditors holding a minority in value of claims. In the current market, where members of listed companies often use nominee entities to hold shares and vote, it is questionable in these cases whether the decision of the members themselves bears any relation to the attainment of a majority in number.

**27.907.08**  As the statutory majority is concerned with the value of the votes, voting under section 907 must be on a poll. 'Value', in respect of creditors, means the amount of each creditor's debts within the relevant class and, in respect of shareholders, each share shall carry the same value.

**27.907.09**  Section 907 provides for the majorities to be satisfied by those who actually vote at the relevant meeting, rather than those who do not attend the meeting, or who are not entitled to vote, or those who attend the meeting in person or by proxy but do not vote, despite having the right to do so.

**27.907.10**  In the event that a class dissents but in circumstances where there are no assets available for such dissenting class, the court may use its discretion to decide whether or not the dissent should be ignored and if the scheme should be considered as a scheme between the company and its creditors and other contributories who do have an interest.[46]

**27.907.11**  After the meeting the chairman should report to the court on the outcome of the meeting, including particulars such as the number of members in person or in proxy and the results of the vote. Any particulars of proxies which have been rejected should also be included. In approving the scheme, amongst other things, the court will want to ensure that in each class meeting enough of the members

---

   [43]  Companies Act 2006 (Commencement No 5, Transitional Provisions and Savings) Order 2007, SI 2007/3495, art 3(1).

   [44]  [1973] 1 All ER 135.

   [45]  [1973] 1 All ER 135, 139.

   [46]  *Re Tea Corporation Limited* [1904] 1 Ch 12.

or creditors who are representative of that class vote (in person or in proxy), so that it is satisfied that the decision taken in each meeting is fairly representative of that class.

## 908 Directors' explanatory report (merger)

(1) The directors of each of the merging companies must draw up and adopt a report.     **27.908.01**

(2) The report must consist of—

    (a) the statement required by section 897 (statement explaining effect of compromise or arrangement), and

    (b) insofar as that statement does not deal with the following matters, a further statement—

      (i) setting out the legal and economic grounds for the draft terms, and in particular for the share exchange ratio, and

      (ii) specifying any special valuation difficulties.

(3) The requirement in this section is subject to section 915 (circumstances in which reports not required)[, section 915A (other circumstances in which reports and inspection not required) and section 918A (agreement to dispense with reports etc)]ᵃ.

AMENDMENTS AND NOTES

ᵃ Amended by the Companies (Reporting Requirements in Mergers and Divisions) Regulations 2011, SI 2011/1606, reg 7.

COMMENCEMENT DATE 6 April 2008[47]

Section 908 requires the directors of each of the merging companies to prepare a detailed explanatory    **27.908.02** report, the contents of which are set out in section 897 (as further explained in the commentary to Part 26), together with details of the legal and economic grounds for the draft terms (in particular for the share exchange ratio), specifying any special valuation difficulties if not already included within the section 897 explanatory statement. The explanatory report must be sent out with every notice summoning a meeting (section 897(1)).

The purpose of the explanatory statement is to set out as much information for shareholders or    **27.908.03** creditors as is needed to enable them to sufficiently understand the effect of the scheme of arrangement to be able to take a vote on it.[48] The significance of all of the statements must be explained and the statements must be fair. To assess its adequacy, the courts will examine the explanatory statement together with the notice summoning the meeting(s), and assess whether it provides a reasonably clear explanation of the scheme with sufficient information. It is important for cross-border mergers to disclose the new jurisdiction of the company to members and creditors.

Note that where there has been any material change to the directors' interests or to the facts in the    **27.908.04** explanatory statement between the issue of the explanatory report and the date of the meeting, and the company fails to inform the members, the court is unlikely to sanction the scheme if a reasonable member would have altered his decision on the scheme of arrangement had the issue been disclosed, even in the absence of bad faith.[49] However, in relation to the non-disclosure of a change to the directors' interests of which the court is satisfied that no reasonable member or creditor would change his decision, the scheme can still be sanctioned.[50]

Therefore, if a material change in circumstances occurs after the class meetings have been held, the    **27.908.05** company should consider sending out written details of such change to all of the creditors and members and applying to the court to order a second meeting, to avoid the court refusing to sanction the scheme on the basis that the creditors and/or members did not have all of the information on which to base their decision.

Although section 908 deals with the practicalities of the explanatory statement, the overriding objec-    **27.908.06** tive of the section is to provide an explanation of the effect of the scheme of arrangement to the members and creditors. The court cannot dispense with the requirements for the explanatory statement and a failure to comply will make it necessary to call new meetings with proper notice.

Failure to comply with all of the requirements of section 897 may also result in a fine for both the    **27.908.07** company itself and any of its officers, including any liquidator or administrator of the company.

---

[47] Companies Act 2006 (Commencement No. 5, Transitional Provisions and Savings) Order 2007, SI 2007/ 3495, art 3(1).

[48] See the Australian case of *Residues Treatment and Trading Co Ltd v Southern Resources Ltd* (1998) 14 ACLR 375, 394, later adopted in *Re RAC Motoring Services Ltd* [2000] 1 BCLC 307, 328 which stated 'it is sufficient if directors make a full and fair disclosure of all matters within the knowledge of the directors which would enable shareholders to make a properly informed judgment on the matters intended to be submitted to them'.

[49] *Re Jessel Trust Ltd* [1985] BCLC 119.

[50] *Re Heron International NV* [1994] 1 BCLC 200.

However, note there is a carve out under section 897(7) where the company and/or its officers will not be guilty of an offence under this section if they can show that the failure was a result of the refusal of a director or trustee for debenture holders to provide details of his interests.

### 909 Expert's report (merger)

**27.909.01**    (1)  An expert's report must be drawn up on behalf of each of the merging companies.

(2)  The report required is a written report on the draft terms to the members of the company.

(3)  The court may on the joint application of all the merging companies approve the appointment of a joint expert to draw up a single report on behalf of all those companies.

If no such appointment is made, there must be a separate expert's report to the members of each merging company drawn up by a separate expert appointed on behalf of that company.

(4)  The expert must be a person who—

(a)  is eligible for appointment as a statutory auditor (see section 1212), and

(b)  meets the independence requirement in section 936.

(5)  The expert's report must—

(a)  indicate the method or methods used to arrive at the share exchange ratio;

(b)  give an opinion as to whether the method or methods used are reasonable in all the circumstances of the case, indicate the values arrived at using each such method and (if there is more than one method) give an opinion on the relative importance attributed to such methods in arriving at the value decided on;

(c)  describe any special valuation difficulties that have arisen;

(d)  state whether in the expert's opinion the share exchange ratio is reasonable; and

(e)  in the case of a valuation made by a person other than himself (see section 935), state that it appeared to him reasonable to arrange for it to be so made or to accept a valuation so made.

(6)  The expert (or each of them) has—

(a)  the right of access to all such documents of all the merging companies, and

(b)  the right to require from the companies' officers all such information,

as he thinks necessary for the purposes of making his report.

(7)  The requirement in this section is subject to section 915 (circumstances in which reports not required)[, section 915A (other circumstances in which reports and inspection not required)][a] [and section 918A (agreement to dispense with expert's report).][b]

AMENDMENTS AND NOTES

[a]  Amended by the Companies (Reporting Requirements in Mergers and Divisions) Regulations 2011, SI 2011/1606, reg 8.

[b]  Amended by the Companies (Mergers and Divisions of Public Companies) (Amendment) Regulations 2008, SI 2008/690, reg 2(1).

COMMENCEMENT DATE 6 April 2008[51]

**27.909.02**    Section 909 implements the requirements of the Third Directive, which requires a report on the draft terms to be drawn up at a national level. The Third Directive also introduces the possibility of drawing up a joint expert's report intended for all of the members of companies taking part in the merger, rather than requiring an expert's report for all participating companies, in order to limit experts' costs in mergers.

**27.909.03**    The expert report provided to members is intended to justify the fairness of the merger terms and provide reassurance to the members that the share capital is fully made up of value. The independence requirement is new to the Act and is considered further in the discussion of section 936.

**27.909.04**    The expert must be given rights of access to all documents and has a right to require any necessary further information from the companies' officers.

**27.909.05**    As a result of section 915, in the case of a merger by absorption where all relevant securities of the transferor company(ies) are held by or on behalf of the transferee company, there is no need for an expert's report to be prepared at all.

**27.909.06**    A further exception to the requirement to prepare an independent expert's report is contained within section 918A, which was inserted by the Companies (Mergers and Divisions of Public Companies) (Amendment) Regulations 2008, SI 2008/690, regulation 2(1). As a result of section 918A, public companies may dispense with the requirement in circumstances where all of the shareholders agree. See paragraph 27.918A.02 below for a fuller discussion of this exception.

---

[51]  Companies Act 2006 (Commencement No. 5, Transitional Provisions and Savings) Order 2007, SI 2007/3495, art 3(1).

The exceptions to the expert's reports contained in section 915 and section 918A, together with the    **27.909.07**
opportunity for the preparation of a single expert's report in circumstances where the exceptions do
not apply, goes some way to relieve the burden of preparing expert reports, which can be considered as
onerous and not of particular use.

## 910  Supplementary accounting statement (merger)

[(1)  This section applies if the last annual accounts of any of the merging companies relate to a    **27.910.01**
financial year ending before—
(a)  the date seven months before the first meeting of the company summoned for the purposes
of approving the scheme, or
(b)  if no meeting of the company is required (by virtue of any of sections 916 to 918), the date
six months before the directors of the company adopt the draft terms of the scheme.
(1A)If the company has not made public a half-yearly financial report relating to a period ending on or
after the date mentioned in subsection (1), the directors of the company must prepare a
supplementary accounting statement.]ᵃ
(2)  That statement must consist of—
(a)  a balance sheet dealing with the state of affairs of the company as at a date not more than
three months before the draft terms were adopted by the directors, and
(b)  where the company would be required under section 399 to prepare group accounts if that
date were the last day of a financial year, a consolidated balance sheet dealing with the state
of affairs of the company and the undertakings that would be included in such a consolidation.
(3)  The requirements of this Act (and where relevant Article 4 of the IAS Regulation) as to the balance
sheet forming part of a company's annual accounts, and the matters to be included in notes to it,
apply to the balance sheet required for an accounting statement under this section, with such
modifications as are necessary by reason of its being prepared otherwise than as at the last day of
a financial year.
(4)  The provisions of section 414 as to the approval and signing of accounts apply to the balance
sheet required for an accounting statement under this section.
[(5)  In this section 'half-yearly financial report' means a report of that description required to be made
public by rules under section 89A of the Financial Services and Markets Act 2000⁵² (transparency
rules).
(6)  The requirement in this section is subject to section 915A (other circumstances in which reports
and inspection not required) and section 918A (agreement to dispense with reports etc).]ᵇ

AMENDMENTS AND NOTES

ᵃ  Substituted by the Companies (Reporting Requirements in Mergers and Divisions) Regulations
2011, SI 2011/1606, reg 9(2).

ᵇ  Inserted by the Companies (Reporting Requirements in Mergers and Divisions) Regulations 2011,
SI 2011/1606, reg 9(3).

COMMENCEMENT DATE 6 April 2008⁵³

Section 910 restates and amends the requirement formerly set out in paragraph 6 of Schedule 15B to the    **27.910.02**
1985 Act for the preparation of a supplementary accounting statement where the last annual accounts
of the merging companies relate to a financial year more than seven months (previously six months in
the 1985 Act) before the first meeting of the company to approve the scheme of arrangement or, where
no meeting is required, the date six months before the directors of the company adopt the draft terms
of the scheme. Provision is made in section 910(1A) for the company to use a half-yearly financial
report which it has published and made available to shareholders instead of preparing a supplementary
accounting statement.

In line with section 414 of the Act, the balance sheet required for the accounting statement must be    **27.910.03**
approved by the board of directors and signed on behalf of the board by a director of the company.

---

⁵²  2000 c. 8. Section 89A was inserted by section 1266 of the Companies Act 2006.
⁵³  Companies Act 2006 (Commencement No. 5, Transitional Provisions and Savings) Order 2007, SI 2007/
3495, art 3(1).

## 911 Inspection of documents (merger)

**27.911.01**
(1) The members of each of the merging companies must be able, during the period specified below—
    (a) to inspect at the registered office of that company copies of the documents listed below relating to that company and every other merging company, and
    (b) to obtain copies of those documents or any part of them on request free of charge.
(2) The period referred to above is the period—
    (a) beginning one month before, and
    (b) ending on the date of,
    the first meeting of the members, or any class of members, of the company for the purposes of approving the scheme.
(3) The documents referred to above are—
    (a) the draft terms;
    (b) the directors' explanatory report;
    (c) the expert's report;
    (d) the company's annual accounts and reports for the last three financial years ending on or before the first meeting of the members, or any class of members, of the company summoned for the purposes of approving the scheme;
    (e) any supplementary accounting statement required by section 910[; and
    (f) if no statement is required by section 910 because the company has made public a recent half-yearly financial report (see subsection (1A) of that section), that report.][a]
(3A) The requirement in subsection (1)(a) is subject to section 911A(1) (publication of documents on company website).][b]
(4) The requirements of subsection (3)(b) and (c) are subject to section 915 (circumstances in which reports not required) [and section 918A (agreement to dispense with reports etc).][c]
[(5) Section 1145 (right to hard copy) does not apply to a document sent or supplied in accordance with subsection (1)(b) to a member who has consented to information being sent or supplied by the company by electronic means and has not revoked that consent.
(6) Part 4 of Schedule 5 (communications by means of a website) does not apply for the purposes of subsection (1)(b) (but see section 911A(5)).
(7) The requirements in this section are subject to section 915A (other circumstances in which reports and inspection not required).].[d]

AMENDMENTS AND NOTES

[a] Amended by the Companies (Reporting Requirements in Mergers and Divisions) Regulations 2011, SI 2011/1606, reg 10(2).
[b] Inserted by the Companies (Reporting Requirements in Mergers and Divisions) Regulations 2011, SI 2011/1606, reg 10(3).
[c] Substituted by the Companies (Reporting Requirements in Mergers and Divisions) Regulations 2011, SI 2011/1606, reg 10(4).
[d] Inserted by the Companies (Reporting Requirements in Mergers and Divisions) Regulations 2011, SI 2011/1606, reg 10(5).

COMMENCEMENT DATE 6 April 2008[54]

**27.911.02** The purpose of giving the members the opportunity to inspect all of the scheme documents listed in section 911(3) is to protect the interests of those members. The company may satisfy this requirement through the publication of scheme documents on a website in accordance with section 911A, or copies of documents may be provided by electronic mail with shareholder consent. By explaining and justifying the legal and economic aspects of the merger and allowing the members adequate time before the meeting to inspect the documents, the members will be in a better position to take an informed decision at the class meetings.

**27.911.03** The court has a discretion over whether to sanction the scheme under section 899 of the Act following the holding of the statutory meeting(s). In approving the scheme, the court must satisfy itself, amongst other things, that approval at the class meetings was reasonable, the members were fully informed as to the implications of the scheme, and all statutory provisions have been complied with. Generally, the court will adopt an objective test in the exercise of its discretion, although in practice, if the members or creditors have been given full information, together with adequate time to digest such information and the scheme has been approved by the class meetings, the court is likely to provide sanction and will

---

[54] Companies Act 2006 (Commencement No. 5, Transitional Provisions and Savings) Order 2007, SI 2007/3495, art 3(1).

not substitute its own view for that of the meeting. In *Re Dorman Long and Company Limited*,[55] Maugham J stated: 'In my opinion ... what I have to see is whether the proposal is such that an intelligent and honest man, a member of the class concerned and acting in respect of his interest, might reasonably approve.'

Please see paragraph 26.896.05 for a fuller discussion of the court exercise of its discretion.    **27.911.04**

### [911A  Publication of documents on company website (merger)

(1) Section 911(1)(a) does not apply to a document if the conditions in subsections (2) to (4) are met    **27.911A.01**
in relation to that document. This is subject to subsection (6).

(2) The first condition is that the document is made available on a website which—
  (a) is maintained by or on behalf of the company, and
  (b) identifies the company.

(3) The second condition is that access to the document on the website is not conditional on payment of a fee or otherwise restricted.

(4) The third condition is that the document remains available on the website throughout the period beginning one month before, and ending on, the date of any meeting of the company summoned for the purpose of approving the scheme.

(5) A person is able to obtain a copy of a document as required by section 911(1)(b) if—
  (a) the conditions in subsections (2) and (3) are met in relation to that document, and
  (b) the person is able, throughout the period specified in subsection (4)—
    (i) to retain a copy of the document as made available on the website, and
    (ii) to produce a hard copy of it.

(6) Where members of a company are able to obtain copies of a document only as mentioned in subsection (5), section 911(1)(a) applies to that document even if the conditions in subsections (2) to (4) are met.][a]

AMENDMENTS AND NOTES

[a] Inserted by the Companies (Reporting Requirements in Mergers and Divisions) Regulations 2011, SI 2011/1606, reg 11.

COMMENCEMENT DATE 1 August 2011[56]

Companies are not required to make documents available at their registered office if the documents are    **27.911A.02**
available on a website maintained by or on behalf of them, and the documents remain available on the website for the period starting one month before and ending on the date of the meeting considering the scheme.

### [911B  Report on material changes of assets of merging companies

(1) The directors of each of the merging companies must report—    **27.911B.01**
  (a) to every meeting of the members, or any class of members, of that company summoned for the purpose of agreeing to the scheme, and
  (b) to the directors of every other merging company, any material changes in the property and liabilities of that company between the date when the draft terms were adopted and the date of the meeting in question.

(2) The directors of each of the other merging companies must in turn—
  (a) report those matters to every meeting of the members, or any class of members, of that company summoned for the purpose of agreeing to the scheme, or
  (b) send a report of those matters to every member entitled to receive notice of such a meeting.

(3) The requirement in this section is subject to section 915A (other circumstances in which reports and inspection not required) and section 918A (agreement to dispense with reports etc).][a]

AMENDMENTS AND NOTES

[a] Inserted by the Companies (Reporting Requirements in Mergers and Divisions) Regulations 2011, SI 2011/1606, reg 12.

COMMENCEMENT DATE 1 August 2011[57]

Directors must notify to the meeting considering the scheme material changes in the property and    **27.911B.02**
liabilities of the company which have occurred since the adoption of the draft terms.

---

[55] [1934] 1 Ch 635, 657.
[56] Companies (Reporting Requirements in Mergers and Divisions) Regulations 2011, SI 2011/1606, reg 1(2).
[57] Companies (Reporting Requirements in Mergers and Divisions) Regulations 2011, SI 2011/1606, reg 1(2).

### 912 Approval of articles of new transferee company (merger)

**27.912.01** In the case of a merger by formation of a new company, the articles of the transferee company, or a draft of them, must be approved by ordinary resolution of ... each of the transferor companies.[a]

AMENDMENTS AND NOTES

[a] Words omitted repealed by the Companies (Reporting Requirements in Mergers and Divisions) Regulations 2011, SI 2011/1606, reg 13.

COMMENCEMENT DATE 6 April 2008 [58]

**27.912.02** This section restates the requirement under Schedule 15B(3)(f) of the 1985 Act for the articles of association of any transferee company which is not a pre-existing transferee to be approved by the company by ordinary resolution. There are no exceptions to this requirement.

### 913 Protection of holders of securities to which special rights attached (merger)

**27.913.01** (1) The scheme must provide that where any securities of a transferor company (other than shares) to which special rights are attached are held by a person otherwise than as a member or creditor of the company, that person is to receive rights in the transferee company of equivalent value.
(2) Subsection (1) does not apply if—
   (a) the holder has agreed otherwise, or
   (b) the holder is, or under the scheme is to be, entitled to have the securities purchased by the transferee company on terms that the court considers reasonable.

COMMENCEMENT DATE 6 April 2008[59]

**27.913.02** This was formerly set out in paragraphs 8(1) and (2) of Schedule 15B of the 1985 Act. The section provides for holders of transferor securities with special rights, other than as members or creditors of the company, to receive equal rights in the transferee company, unless the holder agrees otherwise or is entitled to have his securities purchased on terms deemed reasonable by the court.

### 914 No allotment of shares to transferor company or [transferee company] (merger)

**27.914.01** The scheme must not provide for shares in the transferee company to be allotted to—

   (a) a transferor company (or its nominee) in respect of shares in the transferor company held by [the transferor company itself] (or its nominee)[; or
   (b) the transferee company (or its nominee) in respect of shares in a transferor company held by the transferee company (or its nominee).][a]

AMENDMENTS AND NOTES

[a] Amended by the Companies (Mergers and Divisions of Public Companies) (Amendment) Regulations 2008, SI 2008/690, reg 3.

COMMENCEMENT DATE 6 April 2008[60]

**27.914.02** Section 914(a) was formerly set out in paragraph 7 of Schedule 15B to the 1985 Act. This section 914 prevents a scheme subject to Part 27 being sanctioned by the court if it involves an allotment of shares in the transferee company to either the transferor company or the transferee company (or their nominees) in return for shares in a transferor company which are held by that transferor company or the transferee company (or their nominees).

### *Exceptions where shares of transferor company held by transferee company*

### 915 Circumstances in which certain particulars and reports not required (merger)

**27.915.01** (1) This section applies in the case of a merger by absorption where all of the relevant securities of the transferor company (or, if there is more than one transferor company, of each of them) are held by or on behalf of the transferee company.
(2) The draft terms of the scheme need not give the particulars mentioned in section 905(2)(b), (c), or (d) (particulars relating to allotment of shares to members of transferor company).
(3) Section 897 (explanatory statement to be circulated or made available) does not apply.
(4) The requirements of the following sections do not apply—

---

[58] Companies Act 2006 (Commencement No. 5, Transitional Provisions and Savings) Order 3495, SI 3495/3495, art 3(1).
[59] Companies Act 2006 (Commencement No. 5, Transitional Provisions and Savings) Order 2007, SI 2007/3495, art 3(1).
[60] Companies Act 2006 (Commencement No. 5, Transitional Provisions and Savings) Order 2007, SI 2007/3495, art 3(1).

      section 908 (directors' explanatory report),
      section 909 (expert's report).
(5)  The requirements of section 911 (inspection of documents) so far as relating to any document required to be drawn up under the provisions mentioned in subsection (4) above do not apply.
(6)  In this section 'relevant securities', in relation to a company, means shares or other securities carrying the right to vote at general meetings of the company.

COMMENCEMENT DATE 6 April 2008[61]

The exceptions laid out under sections 915 to 918 and 931 to 934 allow the court to sanction the proposed scheme even though certain requirements of Part 27 have not been met.  **27.915.02**

In 2006 and 2007, the EU Commission undertook an action programme[62] setting out how it proposed to reduce administrative burdens placed upon companies in certain situations by identifying over-burdensome and costly information obligations, judging whether such burdens were necessary, and removing or amending them where appropriate. The objective of reducing such administrative burdens was for 'improving the competitiveness of such enterprises and for achieving the objectives of the Lisbon agenda'.[63] Reduction measures were put into action,[64] one of which included simplifying the Third Directive and the Sixth Directive by easing the requirements to members of companies who were applying for a scheme of arrangement involving a merger or division. The aim was to make certain reporting requirements voluntary and to give the members of the companies involved in the merger or division the opportunity to decide whether certain written reports should be drawn up.[65]  **27.915.03**

This reduction measure is reflected in section 915 of the Act, whereby in schemes involving a merger by absorption where all of the voting shares in the transferor company(ies) are held by or on behalf of the transferee company, the explanatory report and expert's report are not needed, the requirements to be inserted into the draft terms are reduced, and the corresponding inspection and circulation requirements removed.  **27.915.04**

## [915A  Other circumstances in which reports and inspection not required (merger)

(1)  This section applies in the case of a merger by absorption where 90 per cent or more (but not all) of the relevant securities of the transferor company (or, if there is more than one transferor company, of each of them) are held by or on behalf of the transferee company.  **27.915A.01**
(2)  If the conditions in subsections (3) and (4) are met, the requirements of the following sections do not apply—
  (a)  section 908 (directors' explanatory report),
  (b)  section 909 (expert's report),
  (c)  section 910 (supplementary accounting statement),
  (d)  section 911 (inspection of documents), and
  (e)  section 911B (report on material changes of assets of merging company).
(3)  The first condition is that the scheme provides that every other holder of relevant securities has the right to require the transferee company to acquire those securities.
(4)  The second condition is that, if a holder of securities exercises that right, the consideration to be given for those securities is fair and reasonable.
(5)  The powers of the court under section 900(2) (power to facilitate reconstruction or amalgamation) include the power to determine, or make provision for the determination of, the consideration to be given for securities acquired under this section.
(6)  In this section—'other holder' means a person who holds securities of the transferor company otherwise than on behalf of the transferee company (and does not include the transferee company itself);'relevant securities', in relation to a company, means shares or other securities carrying the right to vote at general meetings of the company.]ᵃ

---

[61] Companies Act 2006 (Commencement No 5, Transitional Provisions and Savings) Order 2007, SI 2007/3495, art 3(1).
[62] Commission working document COM(3495)23: 'Communication from the Commission to the Council, the European Parliament, the European Economic and Social Committee and the Committee of the Regions': 'Action Programme for Reducing Administrative Burdens in the European Union', 24 January 2007.
[63] Directive (EC) 2007/63 [2007] OJ L300/47, Preamble.
[64] Eg reducing paperwork regarding export refunds for small farms by simplifying Commission Regulation (EC) 800/1999 of 15 April 1999 laying down common detailed rules for the application of the system of export refunds on agricultural products [1999] OJ L102/11.
[65] See 'Proposal for a Directive of the European Parliament and of the Council amending Council Directive 78/855/EEC concerning mergers of public limited liability companies and Council Directive 82/891/EEC concerning the division of public limited companies as regards the requirement for an independent expert's report on the occasion of a merger or a division', which can be viewed at ⟨http://eur-lex.europa.eu/LexUriServ/LexUriServ.do?uri=COM:2007:0091:FIN:EN:PDF⟩, published on 6 March 2007.

AMENDMENTS AND NOTES

ᵃ Inserted by the Companies (Reporting Requirements in Mergers and Divisions) Regulations 2011, SI 2011/1606, reg 14.

COMMENCEMENT DATE 1 August 2011⁶⁶

**27.915A.02**  In the case of a merger where one company owns 90 per cent or more of the company being acquired and minority shareholders have the right to have their shares acquired by the acquiring company for fair and reasonable consideration, those requirements referred to in section 915A(2) do not apply.

## 916 Circumstances in which meeting of members of transferee company not required (merger)

**27.916.01**
(1) This section applies in the case of a merger by absorption where 90% or more (but not all) of the relevant securities of the transferor company (or, if there is more than one transferor company, of each of them) are held by or on behalf of the transferee company.

(2) It is not necessary for the scheme to be approved at a meeting of the members, or any class of members, of the transferee company if the court is satisfied that the following conditions have been complied with.

[(3) The first condition is that either subsection (3A) or subsection 3(B) is satisfied.

(3A) This subsection is satisfied if publication of notice of receipt of the draft terms by the registrar took place in respect of the transferee company at least one month before the date of the first meeting of members, or any class of members, of the transferor company summoned for the purpose of agreeing to the scheme.

(3B) This subsection is satisfied if—
  (a) the conditions in section 906A(2) to (4) are met in respect of the transferee company,
  (b) the registrar published the notice mentioned in subsection (4) of that section in the Gazette at least one month before the date of the first meeting of members, or any class of members, of the transferor company summoned for the purpose of agreeing to the scheme, and
  (c) the draft terms remained available on the website throughout the period beginning one month before, and ending on, that date.]ᵃ

[(4) The second condition is that subsection (4A) or (4B) is satisfied for each of the documents listed in the applicable paragraphs of section 911(3)(a) to (f) relating to the transferee company and the transferor company (or, if there is more than one transferor company, each of them).

(4A) This subsection is satisfied for a document if the members of the transferee company were able during the period beginning one month before, and ending on, the date mentioned in subsection (3A) to inspect that document at the registered office of that company.

(4B) This subsection is satisfied for a document if—
  (a) the document is made available on a website which is maintained by or on behalf of the transferee company and identifies the company,
  (b) access to the document on the website is not conditional on the payment of a fee or otherwise restricted, and
  (c) the document remains available on the website throughout the period beginning one month before, and ending on, the date mentioned in subsection (3A).

(4C) The third condition is that the members of the transferee company were able to obtain copies of the documents mentioned in subsection (4), or any part of those documents, on request and free of charge, throughout the period beginning one month before, and ending on, the date mentioned in subsection (3A).

(4D) For the purposes of subsection (4C)—
  (a) section 911A(5) applies as it applies for the purposes of section 911(1)(b), and
  (b) Part 4 of Schedule 5 (communications by means of a website) does not apply.]ᵇ

(5) The [fourth]ᶜ condition is that—
  (a) one or more members of the transferee company, who together held not less than 5 per cent of the paid-up capital of the company which carried the right to vote at general meetings of the company (excluding any shares in the company held as treasury shares) would have been able, during that period, to require a meeting of each class of members to be called for the purpose of deciding whether or not to agree to the scheme, and
  (b) no such requirement was made.

(6) In this section 'relevant securities', in relation to a company, means shares or other securities carrying the right to vote at general meetings of the company.

AMENDMENTS AND NOTES

ᵃ Substituted by the Companies (Reporting Requirements in Mergers and Divisions) Regulations 2011, SI 2011/1606, reg 15(2).

ᵇ Substituted by the Companies (Reporting Requirements in Mergers and Divisions) Regulations 2011, SI 2011/1606, reg 15(3).

ᶜ Amended by the Companies (Reporting Requirements in Mergers and Divisions) Regulations 2011, SI 2011/1606, reg 15(4).

COMMENCEMENT DATE 6 April 2008[67]

Section 916 reduces the burden of holding members' meetings for *transferee* companies in cases where the scheme involves a merger by absorption, provided that certain conditions are met.     **27.916.02**

Where *90 per cent or more* of the voting shares in the transferor company are held by or on behalf of the transferee company, provided that:     **27.916.03**

(a)  a receipt of a copy of or details of the website making available the draft terms of the transferee company is published in the *Gazette* a month prior to the first meeting of the members of the transferor company;

(b)  the members of the transferee company(ies) have access to (i) the draft terms, (ii) the company's last three financial years accounts, and (iii) any supplementary accounting statement relating to both the transferee and transferor companies within that period, or, if no statement is required because the company has published a recent half-yearly financial report, that report;

(c)  those members have the right to receive free copies of the scheme documents (whether hard copies or by electronic means); and, finally

(d)  5 per cent or more of the members of the transferee company, or class of them, could have required a meeting to discuss the scheme but decided not to do so,

then there is no requirement to hold members (or class) meetings of the transferee company to approve the scheme.

The reasoning behind the reduction of reporting requirements is explored in the commentary to section 915.     **27.916.04**

## 917  Circumstances in which no meetings required (merger)

(1)  This section applies in the case of a merger by absorption where all of the relevant securities of the transferor company (or, if there is more than one transferor company, of each of them) are held by or on behalf of the transferee company.     **27.917.01**

(2)  It is not necessary for the scheme to be approved at a meeting of the members, or any class of members, of any of the merging companies if the court is satisfied that the following conditions have been complied with.

[(3)  The first condition is that either subsection (3A) or subsection (3B) is satisfied.

(3A) This subsection is satisfied if publication of notice of receipt of the draft terms by the registrar took place in respect of all the merging companies at least one month before the date of the court's order.

(3B) This subsection is satisfied if—

(a)  the conditions in section 906A(2) to (4) are met in respect of each of the merging companies,

(b)  in each case, the registrar published the notice mentioned in subsection (4) of that section in the Gazette at least one month before the date of the court's order, and

(c)  the draft terms remained available on the website throughout the period beginning one month before, and ending on, that date.]ᵃ

[(4)  The second condition is that subsection (4A) or (4B) is satisfied for each of the documents listed in the applicable paragraphs of section 911(3)(a) to (f) relating to the transferee company and the transferor company (or, if there is more than one transferor company, each of them).

(4A) This subsection is satisfied for a document if the members of the transferee company were able during the period beginning one month before, and ending on, the date mentioned in subsection (3A) to inspect that document at the registered office of that company.

(4B) This subsection is satisfied for a document if—

(a)  the document is made available on a website which is maintained by or on behalf of the transferee company and identifies the company,

(b)  access to the document on the website is not conditional on the payment of a fee or otherwise restricted, and

(c)  the document remains available on the website throughout the period beginning one month before, and ending on, the date mentioned in subsection (3A).

---

[67]  Companies Act 2006 (Commencement No. 5, Transitional Provisions and Savings) Order 2007, SI 2007/3495, art 3(1).

(4C) The third condition is that the members of the transferee company were able to obtain copies of the documents mentioned in subsection (4), or any part of those documents, on request and free of charge, throughout the period beginning one month before, and ending on, the date mentioned in subsection (3A).

(4D) For the purposes of subsection (4C)—

    (a)   section 911A(5) applies as it applies for the purposes of section 911(1)(b), and

    (b)   Part 4 of Schedule 5 (communications by means of a website) does not apply.][b]

(5)   The [fourth][c] condition is that—

    (a)   one or more members of the transferee company, who together held not less than 5 per cent of the paid-up capital of the company which carried the right to vote at general meetings of the company (excluding any shares in the company held as treasury shares) would have been able, during that period, to require a meeting of each class of members to be called for the purpose of deciding whether or not to agree to the scheme, and

    (b)   no such requirement was made.

(6)   In this section 'relevant securities', in relation to a company, means shares or other securities carrying the right to vote at general meetings of the company.

Amendments and Notes

[a]   Substituted by the Companies (Reporting Requirements in Mergers and Divisions) Regulations 2011, SI 2011/1606, reg 16(2).

[b]   Substituted by the Companies (Reporting Requirements in Mergers and Divisions) Regulations 2011, SI 2011/1606, reg 16(3).

[c]   Amended by the Companies (Reporting Requirements in Mergers and Divisions) Regulations 2011, SI 2011/1606, reg 16(4).

Commencement Date 6 April 2008[68]

**27.917.02**    Section 917 removes the requirement to hold *any* members' meetings in cases where the scheme involves a merger by absorption, under certain circumstances.

**27.917.03**    Where *all* of the voting shares in the transferor company are held by or on behalf of the transferee company, provided that:

    (a)   a receipt of a copy of or details of the website making available the draft terms on behalf of all of the merging companies is published in the *Gazette* a month prior to the date of the court's order;

    (b)   the members of the transferee company have access to *all of the scheme documents* set out in section 911(3) relating to both the transferee and transferor companies within that period;

    (c)   those members have the right to receive free copies of the scheme documents (whether hard copies or by electronic means); and, finally

    (d)   5 per cent or more of the members of the transferee company, or class of them, could have required a meeting to discuss the scheme but decided not to do so,

then there is no requirement to hold members (or class) meetings of any of the merging companies to approve the scheme.

**27.917.04**    The reasoning behind the reduction of reporting requirements is explored in the commentary to section 915.

### Other exceptions

### 918   Other circumstances in which meeting of members of transferee company not required (merger)

**27.918.01**    (1)   In the case of any merger by absorption, it is not necessary for the scheme to be approved by the members of the transferee company if the court is satisfied that the following conditions have been complied with.

[(2)   The first condition is that either subsection (2A) or subsection (2B) is satisfied.

(2A) This subsection is satisfied if publication of notice of receipt of the draft terms by the registrar took place in respect of the transferee company at least one month before the date of the first meeting of members, or any class of members, of the transferor company (or, if there is more than one transferor company, any of them) summoned for the purposes of agreeing to the scheme.

---

[68]   Companies Act 2006 (Commencement No. 5, Transitional Provisions and Savings) Order 2007, SI 2007/3495, art 3(1).

(2B) This subsection is satisfied if—
  (a) the conditions in section 906A(2) to (4) are met in respect of the transferee company,
  (b) the registrar published the notice mentioned in subsection (4) of that section in the Gazette at least one month before the date of the first meeting of members, or any class of members, of the transferor company (or, if there is more than one transferor company, any of them) summoned for the purposes of agreeing to the scheme, and
  (c) the draft terms remained available on the website throughout the period beginning one month before, and ending on, that date.]ᵃ
[(3) The second condition is that subsection (3A) or (3B) is satisfied for each of the documents listed in the applicable paragraphs of section 911(3) relating to the transferee company and the transferor company (or, if there is more than one transferor company, each of them).
(3A) This subsection is satisfied for a document if the members of the transferee company were able during the period beginning one month before, and ending on, the date of any such meeting as is mentioned in subsection (2A) to inspect that document at the registered office of that company.
(3B) This subsection is satisfied for a document if—
  (a) the document is made available on a website which is maintained by or on behalf of the transferee company and identifies the company,
  (b) access to the document on the website is not conditional on the payment of a fee or otherwise restricted, and
  (c) the document remains available on the website throughout the period beginning one month before, and ending on, the date of any such meeting as is mentioned in subsection (2A).
(3C) The third condition is that the members of the transferee company were able to obtain copies of the documents mentioned in subsection (3), or any part of those documents, on request and free of charge, throughout the period beginning one month before, and ending on, the date of any such meeting as is mentioned in subsection (2A).
(3D) For the purposes of subsection (3C)—
  (a) section 911A(5) applies as it applies for the purposes of section 911(1)(b), and
  (b) Part 4 of Schedule 5 (communications by means of a website) does not apply.]ᵇ
(4) The [fourth]ᶜ condition is that—
  (a) one or more members of that company, who together held not less than 5% of the paid-up capital of the company which carried the right to vote at general meetings of the company (excluding any shares in the company held as treasury shares) would have been able, during that period, to require a meeting of each class of members to be called for the purpose of deciding whether or not to agree to the scheme, and
  (b) no such requirement was made.

AMENDMENTS AND NOTES

ᵃ Substituted by the Companies (Reporting Requirements in Mergers and Divisions) Regulations 2011, SI 2011/1606, reg 17(2).
ᵇ Substituted by the Companies (Reporting Requirements in Mergers and Divisions) Regulations 2011, SI 2011/1606, reg 17(3).
ᶜ Amended by the Companies (Reporting Requirements in Mergers and Divisions) Regulations 2011, SI 2011/1606, reg 17(4).

COMMENCEMENT DATE 6 April 2008[69]

Section 918 allows an additional opportunity to reduce the burden of holding members' meetings for **27.918.02** *transferee* companies in cases where the scheme involves a merger by absorption, provided that certain conditions are met.

Provided that: **27.918.03**

(a) receipt of a copy of or details of the website making available the draft terms in respect of the transferee company is published in the *Gazette* a month prior to the first meeting of the members of the transferor company;
(b) the members of the transferee company have access to *all of the scheme documents* set out in section 911(3) relating to both the transferee and transferor companies within that period;
(c) those members have the right to receive free copies of the scheme documents (whether hard copies or by electronic means); and, finally

---

[69] Companies Act 2006 (Commencement No. 5, Transitional Provisions and Savings) Order 2007, SI 2007/3495, art 3(1).

(d)  5 per cent or more of the members of the transferee company, or class of them, could have required a meeting to discuss the scheme but decided not to do so,

then there is no requirement to hold members (or class) meetings of the transferee company to approve the scheme.

**27.918.04**  The reasoning behind the reduction of reporting requirements is explored in the commentary to section 915.

### [918A  Agreement to dispense with [reports etc]ᵃ (merger)

**27.918A.01**  (1)  If all members holding shares in, and all persons holding other securities of, [the merging companies],ᵇ being shares or securities that carry a right to vote in general meetings of the company in question, so agree, [the following requirements do not apply]ᶜ
(1A) The requirements that may be dispensed with under this section are—
　(a)  the requirements of—
　　(i)  section 908 (directors' explanatory report),
　　(ii)  section 909 (expert's report).
　　(iii)  section 910 (supplementary accounting statement), and
　　(iv)  section 911B (report on material changes of assets of merging company); and
　(b)  the requirements of section 911 (inspection of documents) so far as relating to any document required to be drawn up under sections 908, 909 or 910.]ᵈ
(2)  For the purposes of this section—
　(a)  the members, or holders of other securities, of a company, and
　(b)  whether shares or other securities carry a right to vote in general meetings of the company,
are determined as at the date of the application to the court under section 896.]ᵉ

AMENDMENTS AND NOTES

ᵃ  Amended by the Companies (Reporting Requirements in Mergers and Divisions) Regulations 2011, SI 2011/1606, reg 18(4).
ᵇ  Amended by the Companies (Reporting Requirements in Mergers and Divisions) Regulations 2011, SI 2011/1606, reg 18(2)(a).
ᶜ  Amended by the Companies (Reporting Requirements in Mergers and Divisions) Regulations 2011, SI 2011/1606, reg 18(2)(b).
ᵈ  Inserted by the Companies (Reporting Requirements in Mergers and Divisions) Regulations 2011, SI 2011/1606, reg 18(3).
ᵉ  Inserted by the Companies (Mergers and Divisions of Public Companies) (Amendment) Regulations 2008, SI 2008/690, reg 2(2).

COMMENCEMENT DATE 6 April 2008[70]

**27.918A.02**  Section 918A of the Act was inserted following an amendment to the Third Directive[71] (which sets out the rules and procedures for the mergers of public companies) as an administrative reduction measure following an EU Commission action programme undertaken in 2006 and 2007[72] which set out proposals to reduce administrative burdens placed upon companies applying for a scheme of arrangement involving a merger or division.

**27.918A.03**  As a result of section 918A, if all of the members with voting rights in general meetings of all the companies involved in the merger agree, the preparation of reports and supplemental accounting statement can be dispensed with. This exception relieves companies of the material cost imposed by the obligation to prepare reports and supplemental accounting statement but continues to protect all of the shareholders (including the minority shareholders) as all of the shareholders are required to agree for the disapplication to be applied.

**27.918A.04**  See paragraph 27.915.03 above for a fuller discussion of the EU Commission action programme and its aims and objectives.

---

[70]  Companies (Mergers and Divisions of Public Companies) (Amendment) Regulations 2008, SI 2008/690, reg 1.
[71]  By Directive (EC) 2007/63 [2007] OJ L300/47, Art 1.
[72]  Commission Working Document COM(3495)23: 'Communication from the Commission to the Council, the European Parliament, the European Economic and Social Committee and the Committee of the Regions': 'Action Programme for Reducing Administrative Burdens in the European Union', 24 January 2007.

# CHAPTER 3
## DIVISION

### *Introductory*

### 919  Divisions and companies involved in a division

(1) The scheme involves a division where under the scheme the undertaking, property and liabilities    **27.919.01**
of the company in respect of which the compromise or arrangement is proposed are to be divided
among and transferred to two or more companies each of which is either—

   (a) an existing public company, or

   (b) a new company (whether or not a public company).

(2) References in this Part to the companies involved in the division are to the transferor company and
any existing transferee companies.

COMMENCEMENT DATE 6 April 2008[73]

Section 919 essentially re-states Case 3 from section 427A(2) of the 1985 Act and introduces a    **27.919.02**
definition for a scheme of arrangement involving a 'division'. A division scheme (as referred to in Part
27) is a scheme whereby the transferee company transfers to more than one company (each being a
public company already in existence or a newly formed company being public or private which may be
specifically formed for that purpose) all of its undertakings, assets, and liabilities in accordance with the
allocation laid out in the draft terms of division required under section 920. The transferee company is
then dissolved. The transfer is in exchange for the allocation to the members of the company being
divided of shares in the companies receiving contributions of assets and liabilities as a result of the
division, with or without a cash payment.

### *Requirements to be complied with in case of division*

### 920  Draft terms of scheme (division)

(1) A draft of the proposed terms of the scheme must be drawn up and adopted by the directors of    **27.920.01**
each of the companies involved in the division.

(2) The draft terms must give particulars of at least the following matters—

   (a) in respect of the transferor company and each transferee company—

      (i) its name,

      (ii) the address of its registered office, and

      (iii) whether it is a company limited by shares or a company limited by guarantee and having
a share capital;

   (b) the number of shares in a transferee company to be allotted to members of the transferor
company for a given number of their shares (the 'share exchange ratio') and the amount of
any cash payment;

   (c) the terms relating to the allotment of shares in a transferee company;

   (d) the date from which the holding of shares in a transferee company will entitle the holders to
participate in profits, and any special conditions affecting that entitlement;

   (e) the date from which the transactions of the transferor company are to be treated for
accounting purposes as being those of a transferee company;

   (f) any rights or restrictions attaching to shares or other securities in a transferee company to be
allotted under the scheme to the holders of shares or other securities in the transferor
company to which any special rights or restrictions attach, or the measures proposed
concerning them;

   (g) any amount of benefit paid or given or intended to be paid or given—

      (i) to any of the experts referred to in section 924 (expert's report), or

      (ii) to any director of a company involved in the division,

   and the consideration for the payment of benefit.

(3) The draft terms must also—

   (a) give particulars of the property and liabilities to be transferred (to the extent that these are
known to the transferor company) and their allocation among the transferee companies;

   (b) make provision for the allocation among and transfer to the transferee companies of any
other property and liabilities that the transferor company has acquired or may subsequently
acquire; and

---

[73] Companies Act 2006 (Commencement No. 5, Transitional Provisions and Savings) Order 2007, SI 2007/
3495, art 3(1).

(c) specify the allocation to members of the transferor company of shares in the transferee companies and the criteria upon which that allocation is based.

COMMENCEMENT DATE 6 April 2008[74]

**27.920.02**  Section 920 deals with the preparation by the directors of each of the companies involved in the division of a draft of the proposed terms of the division. The draft terms must include all of the details specified under section 920(2) and (3), which deal in part with the transfer of the transferor company(ies) assets and liabilities and the criteria by which the allocation of transferee shares is to be made among the transferee companies. Note that this includes any assets and liabilities which will be subsequently acquired by the transferor between the point in time at which the draft terms are drafted to the point in time where the company being divided ceases to exist post-transfer.

**27.920.03**  The contents of draft terms are further discussed under the commentary for section 905 above.

### 921 Publication of draft terms [by registrar][a] (division)

**27.921.01**
(1) The directors of each company involved in the division must deliver a copy of the draft terms to the registrar.
(2) The registrar must publish in the Gazette notice of receipt by him from that company of a copy of the draft terms.
(3) That notice must be published at least one month before the date of any meeting of that company summoned for the purposes of approving the scheme.
(4) The requirements in this section are subject to [section 921A (publication of draft terms on company website) and][b] section 934 (power of court to exclude certain requirements).

AMENDMENTS AND NOTES

[a] Amended by the Companies (Reporting Requirements in Mergers and Divisions) Regulations 2011, SI 2011/1606, reg 19(2).

[b] Amended by the Companies (Reporting Requirements in Mergers and Divisions) Regulations 2011, SI 2011/1606, reg 19(1).

COMMENCEMENT DATE 6 April 2008[75]

**27.921.02**  Unless the court dispenses with the requirement (under section 934(1)(a)(i)), a copy of the draft terms of division must be delivered to the Registrar of Companies, who will publish a notice in the *Gazette* of his receipt of that copy at least a month prior to the first of any meetings considering the scheme of any of the companies involved in the division. These requirements do not apply to a company which complies with section 921A.

### [921A Publication of draft terms on company website (division)

**27.921A.01**
(1) Section 921 does not apply in respect of a company if the conditions in subsections (2) to (6) are met.
(2) The first condition is that the draft terms are made available on a website which—
    (a) is maintained by or on behalf of the company, and
    (b) identifies the company.
(3) The second condition is that neither access to the draft terms on the website nor the supply of a hard copy of them from the website is conditional on payment of a fee or otherwise restricted.
(4) The third condition is that the directors of the company deliver to the registrar a notice giving details of the website.
(5) The fourth condition is that the registrar publishes the notice in the Gazette at least one month before the date of any meeting of the company summoned for the purposes of approving the scheme.
(6) The fifth condition is that the draft terms remain available on the website throughout the period beginning one month before, and ending on, the date of any such meeting.][a]

AMENDMENTS AND NOTES

[a] Inserted by the Companies (Reporting Requirements in Mergers and Divisions) Regulations 2011, SI 2011/1606, reg 20.

COMMENCEMENT DATE 1 August 2011[76]

---

[74] Companies Act 2006 (Commencement No. 5, Transitional Provisions and Savings) Order 2007, SI 2007/3495, art 3(1).
[75] Companies Act 2006 (Commencement No. 5, Transitional Provisions and Savings) Order 2007, SI 2007/3495, art 3(1).
[76] Companies (Reporting Requirements in Mergers and Divisions) Regulations 2011, SI 2011/1606, reg 1(2).

The directors of a company involved in the division are not required to deliver the draft terms to the **27.921A.02**
Registrar of Companies if the draft terms are instead published on a website maintained by or on behalf
of the relevant company which is available for free. Notice containing details of the website containing
such draft terms must be delivered to the Registrar of Companies, who will publish a notice in the
*London Gazette* (or in the case of a Northern Ireland company, the *Belfast Gazette*) of his receipt of that
copy. The draft terms must remain available on the website for the period starting one month before
and ending on the date of any meeting considering the scheme.

## 922  Approval of members of companies involved in the division

(1)  The compromise or arrangement must be approved by a majority in number, representing 75%     **27.922.01**
     in value, of each class of members of each of the companies involved in the division, present and
     voting either in person or by proxy at a meeting.
(2)  This requirement is subject to sections 931 and 932 (circumstances in which meeting of members
     not required).

COMMENCEMENT DATE 6 April 2008[77]

The holding of meetings of each class of members or creditors of the transferor company (ies) to   **27.922.02**
approve the proposed scheme is set out in section 896 of Part 26. Section 922 extends this requirement
to meetings of each class of members of each of the transferee companies to approve the scheme. There
is no requirement to hold meeting(s) of members if the circumstances set out in sections 931 and 932
are met—please see commentary on these sections for details.

As previously set out in Schedule 15B of the 1985 Act, the statutory majority for member approval of a   **27.922.03**
scheme involving a division is a majority in number, representing three quarters of the members of
each class in value of holding, voting in favour of the scheme.

For further discussion of the court's discretion over the calling of member meetings and approval by   **27.922.04**
members, please see the commentary for section 907 of the Act and section 896, Part 26.

## 923  Directors' explanatory report (division)

(1)  The directors of the transferor and each existing transferee company must draw up and adopt a   **27.923.01**
     report.
(2)  The report must consist of—
     (a)  the statement required by section 897 (statement explaining effect of compromise or
          arrangement), and
     (b)  insofar as that statement does not deal with the following matters, a further statement—
          (i)   setting out the legal and economic grounds for the draft terms, and in particular for the
                share exchange ratio and for the criteria on which the allocation to the members of the
                transferor company of shares in the transferee companies was based, and
          (ii)  specifying any special valuation difficulties.
(3)  The report must also state—
     (a)  whether a report has been made to any transferee company under section 593 (valuation of
          non-cash consideration for shares), and
     (b)  if so, whether that report has been delivered to the registrar of companies.
(4)  The requirement in this section is subject to section 933 (agreement to dispense with reports etc)
     [and section 933A (certain requirements excluded where shareholders given proportional rights)][a]

AMENDMENTS AND NOTES

[a]  Amended by the Companies (Reporting Requirements in Mergers and Divisions) Regulations
     2011, SI 2011/1606, reg 21.

COMMENCEMENT DATE 6 April 2008[78]

The reasoning behind the explanatory report is discussed in the commentaries for section 908 and   **27.923.02**
section 897 of Part 26. The section 897 report required for schemes involving a division of companies
must be supplemented with additional details on the legal and economic grounds of the scheme, and
must state whether a section 593 report has been made and delivered to the registrar (see Part 17 for
commentary on section 593 reports).

---

[77] Companies Act 2006 (Commencement No. 5, Transitional Provisions and Savings) Order 2007, SI 2007/
3495, art 3(1).
[78] Companies Act 2006 (Commencement No. 5, Transitional Provisions and Savings) Order 2007, SI 2007/
3495, art 3(1) and Sch 1, 'Transitional Adaptations of Provisions Brought into Force'.

### 924 Expert's report (division)

**27.924.01**
(1) An expert's report must be drawn up on behalf of each company involved in the division.

(2) The report required is a written report on the draft terms to the members of the company.

(3) The court may on the joint application of the companies involved in the division approve the appointment of a joint expert to draw up a single report on behalf of all those companies.
If no such appointment is made, there must be a separate expert's report to the members of each company involved in the division drawn up by a separate expert appointed on behalf of that company.

(4) The expert must be a person who—
   (a) is eligible for appointment as a statutory auditor (see section 1212), and
   (b) meets the independence requirement in section 936.

(5) The expert's report must—
   (a) indicate the method or methods used to arrive at the share exchange ratio;
   (b) give an opinion as to whether the method or methods used are reasonable in all the circumstances of the case, indicate the values arrived at using each such method and (if there is more than one method) give an opinion on the relative importance attributed to such methods in arriving at the value decided on;
   (c) describe any special valuation difficulties that have arisen;
   (d) state whether in the expert's opinion the share exchange ratio is reasonable; and
   (e) in the case of a valuation made by a person other than himself (see section 935), state that it appeared to him reasonable to arrange for it to be so made or to accept a valuation so made.

(6) The expert (or each of them) has—
   (a) the right of access to all such documents of the companies involved in the division, and
   (b) the right to require from the companies' officers all such information,
   as he thinks necessary for the purposes of making his report.

(7) The requirement in this section is subject to section 933 (agreement to dispense with reports etc) [and section 923A (certain requirements excluded where shareholders given proportional rights)]ᵃ.

AMENDMENTS AND NOTES

ᵃ Amended by the Companies (Reporting Requirements in Mergers and Divisions) Regulations 2011, SI 2011/1606, reg 22.

COMMENCEMENT DATE 6 April 2008[79]

**27.924.02**  Section 924 provides for the drawing up by an independent expert of a report based on the draft terms. The independence requirement is new to the Act and is discussed under the commentary for section 936. As is the case for the expert's report drawn up in the case of a scheme involving a merger, on a joint application of the companies involved in the division, a single expert's report intended for all of the members of companies taking part in the division can be prepared, rather than an expert's report for each participating company. The expert must be given rights of access to all documents and has a right to require any further information required for the report from the companies' officers.

**27.924.03**  If all of the members with voting rights in general meetings of all the companies involved in the division agree, no expert's report needs to be prepared.

**27.924.04**  Please see the commentary on sections 909 and 915 for further details.

### 925 Supplementary accounting statement (division)

**27.925.01**
[(1) This section applies if the last annual accounts of a company involved in the division relate to a financial year ending before—
   (a) the date seven months before the first meeting of the company summoned for the purposes of approving the scheme, or
   (b) if no meeting of the company is required (by virtue of section 931 or 931), the date six months before the directors of the company adopt the draft terms of the scheme.

(1A) If the company has not made public a half-yearly financial report relating to a period ending on or after the date mentioned in subsection (1), the directors of the company must prepare a supplementary accounting statement.]ᵃ

(2) That statement must consist of—
   (a) a balance sheet dealing with the state of affairs of the company as at a date not more than three months before the draft terms were adopted by the directors, and

---

[79] Companies Act 2006 (Commencement No. 5, Transitional Provisions and Savings) Order 2007, SI 2007/ 3495, art 3(1).

    (b)  where the company would be required under section 399 to prepare group accounts if that date were the last day of a financial year, a consolidated balance sheet dealing with the state of affairs of the company and the undertakings that would be included in such a consolidation.

(3)  The requirements of this Act (and where relevant Article 4 of the IAS Regulation) as to the balance sheet forming part of a company's annual accounts, and the matters to be included in notes to it, apply to the balance sheet required for an accounting statement under this section, with such modifications as are necessary by reason of its being prepared otherwise than as at the last day of a financial year.

(4)  The provisions of section 414 as to the approval and signing of accounts apply to the balance sheet required for an accounting statement under this section.

(4A)In this section 'half-yearly financial report' means a report of that description required to be made public by rules under section 89A of the Financial Services and Markets Act 2000 (transparency rules).]<sup>b</sup>

(5)  The requirement in this section is subject to section 933 (agreement to dispense with reports etc) [and section 933A (certain requirements excluded where shareholders given proportional rights)]<sup>c</sup>.

AMENDMENTS AND NOTES

<sup>a</sup> Substituted by the Companies (Reporting Requirements in Mergers and Divisions) Regulations 2011, SI 2011/1606, reg 23(2).

<sup>b</sup> Inserted by the Companies (Reporting Requirements in Mergers and Divisions) Regulations 2011, SI 2011/1606, reg 23(3).

<sup>c</sup> Amended by the Companies (Reporting Requirements in Mergers and Divisions) Regulations 2011, SI 2011/1606, reg 23(4).

COMMENCEMENT DATE 6 April 2008[80]

Section 925 restates and amends the requirement formerly set out in paragraph 6 of Schedule 15B to the 1985 Act for the preparation of a supplementary accounting statement in the situation where the last annual accounts of the companies involved in the division relate to a financial year more than seven months (previously six months in the 1985 Act) before the first meeting of the company to approve the scheme of arrangement, or, if no meeting is required, the date six months before the directors of the company adopt the draft terms of the scheme. Provision is made in section 925(1A) for the company to use a half-yearly financial report which it has published and made available to shareholders instead of preparing a supplementary accounting statement.   **27.925.02**

In line with section 414 of the Act, the balance sheet required for the accounting statement must be approved by the board of directors and signed on behalf of the board by a director of the company.   **27.925.03**

If all the members with voting rights in general meetings of all of the companies involved in the division agree, no supplementary accounting statements need be prepared.   **27.925.04**

## 926 Inspection of documents (division)

(1)  The members of each company involved in the division must be able, during the period specified below—   **27.926.01**

    (a)  to inspect at the registered office of that company copies of the documents listed below relating to that company and every other company involved in the division, and

    (b)  to obtain copies of those documents or any part of them on request free of charge.

(2)  The period referred to above is the period—

    (a)  beginning one month before, and

    (b)  ending on the date of,

  the first meeting of the members, or any class of members, of the company for the purposes of approving the scheme.

(3)  The documents referred to above are—

    (a)  the draft terms;

    (b)  the directors' explanatory report;

    (c)  the expert's report;

    (d)  the company's annual accounts and reports for the last three financial years ending on or before the first meeting of the members, or any class of members, of the company summoned for the purposes of approving the scheme;

    (e)  any supplementary accounting statement required by section 925[; and

---

[80]  Companies Act 2006 (Commencement No. 5, Transitional Provisions and Savings) Order 2007, SI 2007/3495, art 3(1).

(f)  if no statement is required by section 925 because the company has made public a recent half-yearly financial report (see subsection (1A) of that section), that report.][a]

[(3A)The requirement in subsection (1)(a) is subject to section 926A(1) (publication of documents on company website).][b]

(4)  The requirements in subsection (3)(b), (c), and (e) are subject to section 933 (agreement to dispense with reports etc) )[, section 933A (certain requirements excluded where shareholders given proportional rights)][c] and section 934 (power of court to exclude certain requirements).

[(5)  Section 1145 (right to hard copy) does not apply to a document sent or supplied in accordance with subsection (1)(b) to a member who has consented to information being sent or supplied by the company by electronic means and has not revoked that consent.

(6)  Part 4 of Schedule 5 (communication by means of a website) does not apply for the purposes of subsection 1(b) (but see section 926A(5)).][d]

AMENDMENTS AND NOTES

[a]  Amended by the Companies (Reporting Requirements in Mergers and Divisions) Regulations 2011, SI 2011/1606, reg 24(2).

[b]  Inserted by the Companies (Reporting Requirements in Mergers and Divisions) Regulations 2011, SI 2011/1606, reg 24(3).

[c]  Amended by the Companies (Reporting Requirements in Mergers and Divisions) Regulations 2011, SI 2011/1606, reg 24(4).

[d]  Inserted by the Companies (Reporting Requirements in Mergers and Divisions) Regulations 2011, SI 2011/1606, reg 24(5).

COMMENCEMENT DATE 6 April 2008[81]

**27.926.02**   The Sixth Directive stresses the importance of keeping members of companies involved in a division '... adequately informed in as objective a manner as possible and that their rights be suitably protected'.[82] Therefore when exercising its discretion to sanction the scheme, the court must be satisfied that approval given in the class meetings was reasonable and based on full information regarding the legal and economic aspects of the division, together with adequate time to digest such information.

**27.926.03**   Please see commentary on section 909 and Part 26 for a fuller discussion of the exercise by the court of its discretion.

## [926A  Publication of documents on company website (division)

**27.926A.01**
(1)  Section 926(1)(a) does not apply to a document if the conditions in subsections (2) to (4) are met in relation to that document. This is subject to subsection (6).

(2)  The first condition is that the document is made available on a website which—
   (a)  is maintained by or on behalf of the company, and
   (b)  identifies the company.

(3)  The second condition is that access to the document on the website is not conditional on payment of a fee or otherwise restricted.

(4)  The third condition is that the document remains available on the website throughout the period beginning one month before, and ending on, the date of any meeting of the company summoned for the purpose of approving the scheme.

(5)  A person is able to obtain a copy of a document as required by section 926(1)(b) if—
   (a)  the conditions in subsections (2) and (3) are met in relation to that document, and
   (b)  the person is able, throughout the period specified in subsection (4)—
      (i)   to retain a copy of the document as made available on the website, and
      (ii)  to produce a hard copy of it.

(6)  Where members of a company are able to obtain copies of a document only as mentioned in subsection (5), section 926(1)(a) applies to that document even if the conditions in subsections (2) and (4) are met.][a]

AMENDMENTS AND NOTES

[a]  Inserted by the Companies (Reporting Requirements in Mergers and Divisions) Regulations 2011, SI 2011/1606, reg 25.

COMMENCEMENT DATE 1 August 2011[83]

---

[81]  Companies Act 2006 (Commencement No. 5, Transitional Provisions and Savings) Order 2007, SI 2007/3495, art 3(1).

[82]  [1982] OJ L 378/47.

[83]  Companies (Reporting Requirements in Mergers and Divisions) Regulations 2011, SI 2011/1606, reg 1(2).

Companies are not required to make documents available at their registered office if the documents are **27.926A.02** available on a website maintained by or on behalf of them, and the documents remain available on the website for the period starting one month before and ending on the date of the meeting considering the scheme.

### 927 Report on material changes of assets of transferor company (division)

(1) The directors of the transferor company must report—                                                   **27.927.01**
  (a) to every meeting of the members, or any class of members, of that company summoned for the purpose of agreeing to the scheme, and
  (b) to the directors of each existing transferee company,
  any material changes in the property and liabilities of the transferor company between the date when the draft terms were adopted and the date of the meeting in question.
(2) The directors of each existing transferee company must in turn—
  (a) report those matters to every meeting of the members, or any class of members, of that company summoned for the purpose of agreeing to the scheme, or
  (b) send a report of those matters to every member entitled to receive notice of such a meeting.
(3) The requirement in this section is subject to section 933 (agreement to dispense with reports etc) [and section 933A (certain requirements excluded where shareholders given proportional rights)]ᵃ.

AMENDMENTS AND NOTES

ᵃ Amended by the Companies (Reporting Requirements in Mergers and Divisions) Regulations 2011, SI 2011/1606, reg 26.

COMMENCEMENT DATE 6 April 2008[84]

The requirement to produce a report on material changes in the property and liabilities of the **27.927.02** transferor company under section 927 previously only applied to schemes involving divisions of companies, but now applies equally to a merger of companies, pursuant to section 911B. If the members of all of the companies involved in the division who have a right to vote in general meetings agree, the requirement to produce the report on material changes may be dispensed with.

### 928 Approval of articles of new transferee company (division)

The articles of every new transferee company, or a draft of them, must be approved by ordinary **27.928.01** resolution of the transferor company.

COMMENCEMENT DATE 6 April 2008[85]

This section re-states the requirement under Schedule 15B(3)(f) of the 1985 Act for the memorandum **27.928.02** and articles of association of any transferee company which is not a pre-existing transferee to be approved by the company and be available for inspection (with Companies House) by the members. There are no exceptions to this requirement.

### 929 Protection of holders of securities to which special rights attached (division)

(1) The scheme must provide that where any securities of the transferor company (other than shares) **27.929.01** to which special rights are attached are held by a person otherwise than as a member or creditor of the company, that person is to receive rights in a transferee company of equivalent value.
(2) Subsection (1) does not apply if—
  (a) the holder has agreed otherwise, or
  (b) the holder is, or under the scheme is to be, entitled to have the securities purchased by a transferee company on terms that the court considers reasonable.

COMMENCEMENT DATE 6 April 2008[86]

This was formerly set out in paragraph 8 of Schedule 15B of the 1985 Act. The section provides for **27.929.02** holders of transferor securities with special rights, other than as members or creditors of the company, to receive equal rights in the transferee company, unless the holder agrees otherwise or is entitled to have his securities purchased on terms deemed reasonable by the court.

---

[84] Companies Act 2006 (Commencement No. 5, Transitional Provisions and Savings) Order 2007, SI 2007/3495, art 3(1).
[85] Companies Act 2006 (Commencement No. 5, Transitional Provisions and Savings) Order 2007, SI 2007/3495, art 3(1).
[86] Companies Act 2006 (Commencement No. 5, Transitional Provisions and Savings) Order 2007, SI 2007/3495, art 3(1).

### 930 No allotment of shares to transferor company or [to transferee company] (division)

**27.930.01**    The scheme must not provide for shares in a transferee company to be allotted to—

> [(a)]   the transferor company (or its nominee) in respect of shares in the transferor company held by [the transferor company itself] (or its nominee)[; or
>
>     (b)   a transferee company (or its nominee) in respect of shares in the transferor company held by the transferee company (or its nominee).]ᵃ

AMENDMENTS AND NOTES

> ᵃ   Amended by the Companies (Mergers and Divisions of Public Companies) (Amendment) Regulations 2008, SI 2008/690, reg 4.

COMMENCEMENT DATE 6 April 2008[87]

**27.930.02**    Section 930(a) was formerly set out in paragraph 7 of Schedule 15B to the 1985 Act. This section 930 prevents a scheme subject to Part 27 being sanctioned by the court if it involves an allotment of shares in the transferee company to either the transferor company or the transferee company (or their nominees) in return for shares in a transferor company which are held by that transferor company or the transferee company (or their nominees).

## *Exceptions where shares of transferor company held by transferee company*

### 931 Circumstances in which meeting of members of transferor company not required (division)

**27.931.01**      (1)   This section applies in the case of a division where all of the shares or other securities of the transferor company carrying the right to vote at general meetings of the company are held by or on behalf of one or more existing transferee companies.

             (2)   It is not necessary for the scheme to be approved by a meeting of the members, or any class of members, of the transferor company if the court is satisfied that the following conditions have been complied with.

             [(3)   The first condition is that either subsection (3A) or subsection (3B) is satisfied.

             (3A)This subsection is satisfied if publication of notice of receipt of the draft terms by the registrar took place in respect of all the companies involved in the division at least one month before the date of the court's order.

             (3B) This subsection is satisfied if—

>     (a)   the conditions in section 921A(2) to (4) are met in respect of each of the companies involved in the division,
>
>     (b)   in each case, the registrar published the notice mentioned in subsection (4) of that section in the Gazette at least one month before the date of the court's order, and
>
>     (c)   the draft terms remained available on the website throughout the period beginning one month before, and ending on, that date.]ᵃ

             [(4)   The second condition is that subsection (4A) or (4B) is satisfied for each of the documents listed in the applicable paragraphs of section 926(3) relating to every company involved in the division.

             (4A)This subsection is satisfied for a document if the members of every company involved in the division were able during the period beginning one month before, and ending on, the date of the court's order to inspect that document at the registered office of their company.

             (4B) This subsection is satisfied for a document if—

>     (a)   the document is made available on a website which is maintained by or on behalf of the company to which it relates and identifies the company,
>
>     (b)   access to the document on the website is not conditional on payment of a fee or otherwise restricted, and
>
>     (c)   the document remains available on the website throughout the period beginning one month before, and ending on, the date of the court's order.

             (4C)The third condition is that the members of every company involved in the division were able to obtain copies of the documents mentioned in subsection (4), or any part of those documents, on request and free of charge, throughout the period beginning one month before, and ending on, the date of the court's order.

             (4D)For the purposes of subsection (4C)—

>     (a)   section 926A(5) applies as it applies for the purposes of section 926(1)(b), and
>
>     (b)   Part 4 of Schedule 5 (communications by means of a website) does not apply.]ᵇ

             (5)   ...ᶜ

---

(6)  The fourth condition is that the directors of the transferor company have sent—
  (a)  to every member who would have been entitled to receive notice of a meeting to agree to the scheme (had any such meeting been called), and
  (b)  to the directors of every existing transferee company,
  a report of any material change in the property and liabilities of the transferor company between the date when the terms were adopted by the directors and the date one month before the date of the court's order.

AMENDMENTS AND NOTES

ᵃ  Substituted by the Companies (Reporting Requirements in Mergers and Divisions) Regulations 2011, SI 2011/1606, reg 27(2).
ᵇ  Substituted by the Companies (Reporting Requirements in Mergers and Divisions) Regulations 2011, SI 2011/1606, reg 27(3).
ᶜ  Repealed by the Companies (Reporting Requirements in Mergers and Divisions) Regulations 2011, SI 2011/1606, reg 27(4).

COMMENCEMENT DATE 6 April 2008[88]

Section 931 relates to the dispensing of members' meetings of the *transferor* company.     **27.931.02**

In the case of a division, if *all* of the voting shares in the transferor company are held by or on behalf of     **27.931.03**
the transferee company(ies), as long as:

(a)  notice of receipt of a copy of or details of the website making available the draft terms in respect of all of the companies involved in the division is published in the *Gazette* a month prior to the date of the court's order;
(b)  the members of every company involved in the division have access to all of the scheme documents set out in section 926(3) relating to every company involved in the division within that period;
(c)  those members have the right to receive free copies of the scheme documents (whether hard copies or by electronic means); and, finally
(d)  the directors of the transferor sent out a material change report to all members who would be entitled to receive it and to the directors of all existing transferee companies,

then there is no requirement to hold members (or class) meetings of the transferor company to approve the scheme.

The reasoning behind the reduction of reporting requirements is explored in the commentary to     **27.931.04**
section 915.

## *Other exceptions*

## 932  Circumstances in which meeting of members of transferee company not required (division)

(1)  In the case of a division, it is not necessary for the scheme to be approved by the members of a     **27.932.01**
transferee company if the court is satisfied that the following conditions have been complied with in relation to that company.
[(2)  The first condition is that either subsection (2A) or subsection (2B) is satisfied.
(2A) This subsection is satisfied if publication of notice of receipt of the draft terms by the registrar took place in respect of the transferee company at least one month before the date of the first meeting of members of the transferor company summoned for the purposes of agreeing to the scheme.
(2B) This subsection is satisfied if—
  (a)  the conditions in section 921A(2) to (4) are met in respect of the transferee company,
  (b)  the registrar published the notice mentioned in subsection (4) of that section in the Gazette at least one month before the date of the first meeting of members of the transferor company summoned for the purposes of agreeing to the scheme, and
  (c)  the draft terms remained available on the website throughout the period beginning one month before, and ending on, that date.]ᵃ
[(3)  The second condition is that subsection (3A) or (3B) is satisfied for each of the documents listed in the applicable paragraphs of section 926(3) relating to the transferee company and every other company involved in the division.

[88]  Companies Act 2006 (Commencement No 5, Transitional Provisions and Savings) Order 2007, SI 2007/ 3495, art 3(1).

(3A) This subsection is satisfied for a document if the members of the transferee company were able during the period beginning one month before, and ending on, the date mentioned in subsection (2A) to inspect that document at the registered office of that company.

(3B) This subsection is satisfied for a document if—

    (a)   the document is made available on a website which is maintained by or on behalf of the transferee company and identifies the company,

    (b)   access to the document on the website is not conditional on payment of a fee or otherwise restricted, and

    (c)   the document remains available on the website throughout the period beginning one month before, and ending on, the date mentioned in subsection (2A).

(3C) The third condition is that the members of the transferee company were able to obtain copies of the documents mentioned in subsection (3), or any part of those documents, on request and free of charge, throughout the period beginning one month before, and ending on, the date mentioned in subsection (2A).

(3D) For the purposes of subsection (3C)—

    (a)   section 926A(5) applies as it applies for the purposes of section 926(1)(b), and

    (b)   Part 4 of Schedule 5 (communications by means of a website) does not apply.][b]

(4)   The [fourth][c] condition is that—

    (a)   one or more members of that company, who together held not less than 5% of the paid-up capital of the company which carried the right to vote at general meetings of the company (excluding any shares in the company held as treasury shares) would have been able, during that period, to require a meeting of each class of members to be called for the purpose of deciding whether or not to agree to the scheme, and

    (b)   no such requirement was made.

(5)   The [first, second and third][d] conditions above are subject to section 934 (power of court to exclude certain requirements).

Amendments and Notes

[a]   Substituted by the Companies (Reporting Requirements in Mergers and Divisions) Regulations 2011, SI 2011/1606, reg 28(2).

[b]   Substituted by the Companies (Reporting Requirements in Mergers and Divisions) Regulations 2011, SI 2011/1606, reg 28(3).

[c]   Amended by the Companies (Reporting Requirements in Mergers and Divisions) Regulations 2011, SI 2011/1606, reg 28(4).

[d]   Amended by the Companies (Reporting Requirements in Mergers and Divisions) Regulations 2011, SI 2011/1606, reg 28(5).

Commencement Date 6 April 2008[89]

**27.932.02**     Section 932 relates to the dispensing of members' meetings of the *transferee* company.

**27.932.03**     It provides that in the case of a division, provided that:

    (a)   a notice of receipt of a copy of or details of the website making available the draft terms in respect of the transferee company is published in the *Gazette* a month prior to the first class meeting of the members of the transferor company;

    (b)   the members of the transferee company have access to all of the scheme documents set out in section 926(3) relating to every company involved in the division within that period;

    (c)   those members have the right to receive free copies of the scheme documents (whether hard copies or by electronic means); and, finally

    (d)   5 per cent or more of the members of the transferee company, or class of them, could have required a meeting to discuss the scheme but decided not to do so,

then there is no requirement to hold members' (or class) meetings of the transferee company to approve the scheme.

**27.932.04**     The reasoning behind the reduction of reporting requirements is explored in the commentary to section 915.

---

[89]   Companies Act 2006 (Commencement No 5, Transitional Provisions and Savings) Order 2007, SI 2007/3495, art 3(1).

## 933 Agreement to dispense with reports etc (division)

(1) If all members holding shares in, and all persons holding other securities of, the companies involved in the division, being shares or securities that carry a right to vote in general meetings of the company in question, so agree, the following requirements do not apply.

27.933.01

(2) The requirements that may be dispensed with under this section are—
  (a) the requirements of—
    (i) section 923 (directors' explanatory report),
    (ii) section 924 (expert's report),
    (iii) section 925 (supplementary accounting statement), and
    (iv) section 927 (report on material changes in assets of transferor company); and
  (b) the requirements of section 926 (inspection of documents) so far as relating to any document required to be drawn up under the provisions mentioned in paragraph (a)(i), (ii) or (iii) above.

(3) For the purposes of this section—
  (a) the members, or holders of other securities, of a company, and
  (b) whether shares or other securities carry a right to vote in general meetings of the company, are determined as at the date of the application to the court under section 896.

COMMENCEMENT DATE 6 April 2008[90]

In line with the Commission's administration reduction measures for schemes involving mergers and divisions as discussed under the commentary for section 915 above, section 933 allows, with the agreement of all members of the companies involved in the division, the explanatory report, expert's report, supplementary accounting statements, and material change report to be dispensed with unless the members explicitly ask for their production. The corresponding duty of the company to make these reports available to the members of the companies is also removed.

27.933.02

## [933A Certain requirements excluded where shareholders given proportional rights (division)

(1) This section applies in the case of a division where each of the transferee companies is a new company.

27.933A.01

(2) If all the shares in each of the transferee companies are to be allotted to the members of the transferor company in proportion to their rights in the allotted share capital of the transferor company, the following requirements do not apply.

(3) The requirements which do not apply are—
  (a) the requirements of—
    (i) section 923 (directors' explanatory report),
    (ii) section 924 (expert's report),
    (iii) section 925 (supplementary accounting statement), and
    (iv) section 927 (report on material changes in assets of transferor company); and
  (b) the requirements of section 926 (inspection of documents) so far as relating to any document required to be drawn up under the provisions mentioned in paragraph (a)(i), (ii) or (iii) above.][a]

AMENDMENTS AND NOTES

[a] Inserted by the Companies (Reporting Requirements in Mergers and Divisions) Regulations 2011, SI 2011/1606, reg 29.

COMMENCEMENT DATE 1 August 2011[91]

In the case of a division where each of the transferee companies is a new company and all the shares in each of the transferee companies are to be allotted to the members of the transferor company in proportion to their rights in the allotted share capital of the transferor company, those requirements referred to in section 933A(3) do not apply.

27.933A.02

## 934 Power of court to exclude certain requirements (division)

(1) In the case of a division, the court may by order direct that—

27.934.01

  (a) in relation to any company involved in the division, the requirements of—
    (i) section 921 (publication of draft terms), and
    (ii) section 926 (inspection of documents),
    do not apply, and
  (b) in relation to an existing transferee company, section 932 (circumstances in which meeting of members of transferee company not required) has effect with the omission of the [first,

---

second and third]ᵃ conditions specified in that section,

if the court is satisfied that the following conditions will be fulfilled in relation to that company.

(2)  The first condition is that the members of that company will have received, or will have been able to obtain free of charge, copies of the documents listed in section 926—

  (a)  in time to examine them before the date of the first meeting of the members, or any class of members, of that company summoned for the purposes of agreeing to the scheme, or

  (b)  in the case of an existing transferee company where in the circumstances described in section 932 no meeting is held, in time to require a meeting as mentioned in subsection (4) of that section.

(3)  The second condition is that the creditors of that company will have received or will have been able to obtain free of charge copies of the draft terms in time to examine them—

  (a)  before the date of the first meeting of the members, or any class of members, of the company summoned for the purposes of agreeing to the scheme, or

  (b)  in the circumstances mentioned in subsection (2)(b) above, at the same time as the members of the company.

(4)  The third condition is that no prejudice would be caused to the members or creditors of the transferor company or any transferee company by making the order in question.

AMENDMENTS AND NOTES

ᵃ Amended by the Companies (Reporting Requirements in Mergers and Divisions) Regulations 2011, SI 2011/1606, reg 30.

COMMENCEMENT DATE 6 April 2008[92]

**27.934.02**   Section 934 restates Schedule 15B paragraphs 11(1), (3), and (4)(a) to (d) and sets out where the court may use its discretion to remove some of the reporting, inspection, and publication requirements, as well as the conditions to remove the need to hold members' meetings of the transferee company.

# CHAPTER 4
# SUPPLEMENTARY PROVISIONS
## *Expert's report and related matters*

### 935  Expert's report: valuation by another person

**27.935.01**   (1)  Where it appears to an expert—

  (a)  that a valuation is reasonably necessary to enable him to draw up his report, and

  (b)  that it is reasonable for that valuation, or part of it, to be made by (or for him to accept a valuation made by) another person who—

    (i)   appears to him to have the requisite knowledge and experience to make the valuation or that part of it, and

    (ii)  meets the independence requirement in section 936,

  he may arrange for or accept such a valuation, together with a report which will enable him to make his own report under section 909 or 924.

(2)  Where any valuation is made by a person other than the expert himself, the latter's report must state that fact and must also—

  (a)  state the former's name and what knowledge and experience he has to carry out the valuation, and

  (b)  describe so much of the undertaking, property and liabilities as was valued by the other person, and the method used to value them, and specify the date of the valuation.

COMMENCEMENT DATE 6 April 2008[93]

**27.935.02**   Should the expert believe that a valuation is necessary and reasonable for the purposes of the expert's report, the expert can delegate that task to an appropriately skilled person who is neither an officer nor a servant of any of the companies involved in the scheme or of any member of those companies' groups, other than the auditor. Details of any such delegate, along with the method of valuation, the date such valuation took place, and what was valued must be included in the experts' report.

---

[92] Companies Act 2006 (Commencement No. 5, Transitional Provisions and Savings) Order 2007, SI 2007/3495, art 3(1).

[93] Companies Act 2006 (Commencement No. 5, Transitional Provisions and Savings) Order 2007, SI 2007/3495, art 3(1).

### 936 Experts and valuers: independence requirement

(1) A person meets the independence requirement for the purposes of section 909 or 924 (expert's    **27.936.01**
report) or section 935 (valuation by another person) only if—
   (a) he is not—
     (i) an officer or employee of any of the companies concerned in the scheme, or
     (ii) a partner or employee of such a person, or a partnership of which such a person is a
       partner;
   (b) he is not—
     (i) an officer or employee of an associated undertaking of any of the companies concerned
       in the scheme, or
     (ii) a partner or employee of such a person, or a partnership of which such a person is a
       partner; and
   (c) there does not exist between—
     (i) the person or an associate of his, and
     (ii) any of the companies concerned in the scheme or an associated undertaking of such a
       company,
     a connection of any such description as may be specified by regulations made by the Secretary
     of State.
(2) An auditor of a company is not regarded as an officer or employee of the company for this
purpose.
(3) For the purposes of this section—
   (a) the 'companies concerned in the scheme' means every transferor and existing transferee
     company;
   (b) 'associated undertaking', in relation to a company, means—
     (i) a parent undertaking or subsidiary undertaking of the company, or
     (ii) a subsidiary undertaking of a parent undertaking of the company; and
   (c) 'associate' has the meaning given by section 937.
(4) Regulations under this section are subject to negative resolution procedure.

COMMENCEMENT DATE 6 April 2008[94]

The independence requirements for experts and valuers are new to the Act and correspond to the    **27.936.02**
independence requirements set out for statutory auditors under section 1214 of the Act. The person
preparing the expert's report or carrying out the valuation needs to be independent of the companies
involved in the scheme. The provisions of section 936 widen the category of persons who would not
qualify as independent for these purposes.

The Secretary of State is given a new power under section 936 to make regulations specifying a    **27.936.03**
connection that a person may not have in order to determine whether that person is sufficiently
independent to be an expert or valuer under Part 27.

### 937 Experts and valuers: meaning of 'associate'

(1) This section defines 'associate' for the purposes of section 936 (experts and valuers: indepen-    **27.937.01**
dence requirement).
(2) In relation to an individual, 'associate' means—
   (a) that individual's spouse or civil partner or minor child or step-child,
   (b) any body corporate of which that individual is a director, and
   (c) any employee or partner of that individual.
(3) In relation to a body corporate, 'associate' means—
   (a) any body corporate of which that body is a director,
   (b) any body corporate in the same group as that body, and
   (c) any employee or partner of that body or of any body corporate in the same group.
(4) In relation to a partnership that is a legal person under the law by which it is governed, 'associate'
means—
   (a) any body corporate of which that partnership is a director,
   (b) any employee of or partner in that partnership, and
   (c) any person who is an associate of a partner in that partnership.
(5) In relation to a partnership that is not a legal person under the law by which it is governed,
'associate' means any person who is an associate of any of the partners.
(6) In this section, in relation to a limited liability partnership, for 'director' read 'member'.

COMMENCEMENT DATE 6 April 2008[95]

---

[94] Companies Act 2006 (Commencement No. 5, Transitional Provisions and Savings) Order 2007, SI 2007/
3495, art 3(1).
[95] Companies Act 2006 (Commencement No. 5, Transitional Provisions and Savings) Order 2007, SI 2007/
3495, art 3(1).

**27.937.02**    Section 937 is a new addition to the Act. It tracks section 52 of the Companies Act 1989 (with the exception of the references to Scottish firms set out in section 52(4) Companies Act 1989).

### *Powers of the court*

### 938   Power of court to summon meeting of members or creditors of existing transferee company

**27.938.01**
(1) The court may order a meeting of—
     (a) the members of an existing transferee company, or any class of them, or
     (b) the creditors of an existing transferee company, or any class of them,
to be summoned in such manner as the court directs.
(2) An application for such an order may be made by—
     (a) the company concerned,
     (b) a member or creditor of the company, or
[(c) if the company is being wound up, the liquidator, or
     (d) if the company is in administration, the administrator].[a]
[(3) Section 323 (representation of corporations at meetings) applies to a meeting of creditors under this section as to a meeting of the company (references to a member being read as references to a creditor).][b]

AMENDMENTS AND NOTES

[a] Amended by the Companies Act 2006 (Consequential Amendments, Transitional Provisions and Savings) Order 2009, SI 2009/1941, art 2(1), Sch 1, para 260(5).
[b] Inserted by the Companies Act 2006 (Consequential Amendments etc) Order 2008, SI 2008/948, art 3(1).

COMMENCEMENT DATE 6 April 2008[96]

**27.938.02**    The application to the court requesting that the court summons the necessary meetings of members or creditors can be made by the company, any member or creditor of the company, or, if applicable, the administrator. In theory, the application can be made without the consent of the company itself, although in practice, the court will not convene the meetings if the company is not in administration and the company has not approved it. In addition, the court does not have jurisdiction to sanction a scheme which the company has not approved either by the board or, as the case may be, by a simple majority of members in a general meeting.

**27.938.03**    Note that under section 938 and Part 26 the court has a discretion as to the calling of meetings and the manner in which the meetings are summoned. Such discretion goes some way to protecting the members and creditors of the company, particularly to ensure that the minority in each class meeting is not coerced by the majority into a favourable vote, and that a fair representation and number of class members attend and vote at the meeting, whether in person or by proxy. In relation to creditor class meetings called under section 938 and Part 26, where there are a number of creditors who are entitled to attend and vote at a meeting and only one creditor of that class attends in person or by proxy, no 'meeting' will be considered to have occurred. The position is different where there is just a single member of the class, or it can be established that it would be impossible for any other member of that class to attend, either in person or by proxy.[97] No meeting is required in the case of a class of members of creditors which has no real interests in the assets of the company[98] and the court may sanction the scheme without their consent.

**27.938.04**    The court also has the opportunity to prevent meetings being called which, from the outset, would obviously serve no purpose, as the holders of the majority of the votes oppose the proposed scheme and the necessary majority could never be obtained.[99]

---

[96] Companies Act 2006 (Commencement No. 5, Transitional Provisions and Savings) Order 2007, SI 2007/3495, art 3(1).
[97] *Re Altitude Scaffolding Ltd, Re T&N Ltd and other companies* [2006] All ER (D) 181 (Jun).
[98] In the case of ordinary shareholders see *Re Tea Corporation* [1904] 1 Ch 12.
[99] As held in *Re Savoy Hotel Ltd* [1981] Ch 351.

### 939  Court to fix date for transfer of undertaking etc of transferor company

(1) Where the court sanctions the compromise or arrangement, it must—          **27.939.01**
  (a) in the order sanctioning the compromise or arrangement, or
  (b) in a subsequent order under section 900 (powers of court to facilitate reconstruction or amalgamation),
fix a date on which the transfer (or transfers) to the transferee company (or transferee companies) of the undertaking, property and liabilities of the transferor company is (or are) to take place.
(2) Any such order that provides for the dissolution of the transferor company must fix the same date for the dissolution.
(3) If it is necessary for the transferor company to take steps to ensure that the undertaking, property and liabilities are fully transferred, the court must fix a date, not later than six months after the date fixed under subsection (1), by which such steps must be taken.
(4) In that case, the court may postpone the dissolution of the transferor company until that date.
(5) The court may postpone or further postpone the date fixed under subsection (3) if it is satisfied that the steps mentioned cannot be completed by the date (or latest date) fixed under that subsection.

COMMENCEMENT DATE 6 April 2008[100]

Petitions to sanction schemes of arrangement under Part 26 and Part 27 of the Act, whether the applicant is a creditor or member of the company, are heard by the Companies Court Judge. The requirement to obtain court sanction is essentially a way for the court to confirm that the formalities set out under Part 26 and Part 27 are being followed and the scheme is being dealt with in a manner in which the court approves.          **27.939.02**

Under section 939, the court must fix a single date on which the transfer of the undertaking, and also, if the company is to be dissolved, the dissolution of the company, will take place.          **27.939.03**

Straightforward schemes not involving a reduction of capital which proceed to plan could be completed in around two months from the date of the first application to court under Part 26, so the company should approach the Court Manager of the Companies Court by informal application early on in the process to settle a suitable timetable and decide on when to book court dates for the hearing.          **27.939.04**

A practice direction has been given[101] stating that, if possible, applications should be heard prior to the Long Vacation as for a hearing to be fixed during the Long Vacation, the application must be one in which for financial, commercial or economic reasons it would be desirable to fix the hearing before the end of the Long Vacation. The practice direction specifically includes mergers which arise during the summer which are likely to be affected by market fluctuations. Alternatively, it must be shown that the application could not with reasonable diligence have been made and prosecuted in time before the Long Vacation began.          **27.939.05**

## *Liability of transferee companies*

### 940  Liability of transferee companies for each other's defaults

(1) In the case of a division, each transferee company is jointly and severally liable for any liability transferred to any other transferee company under the scheme to the extent that the other company has made default in satisfying that liability.          **27.940.01**
  This is subject to the following provisions.
(2) If a majority in number representing 75% in value of the creditors or any class of creditors of the transferor company, present and voting either in person or by proxy at a meeting summoned for the purposes of agreeing to the scheme, so agree, subsection (1) does not apply in relation to the liabilities owed to the creditors or that class of creditors.
(3) A transferee company is not liable under this section for an amount greater than the net value transferred to it under the scheme.
  The 'net value transferred' is the value at the time of the transfer of the property transferred to it under the scheme less the amount at that date of the liabilities so transferred.

COMMENCEMENT DATE 6 April 2008[102]

Section 940 restates paragraph 19 of Schedule 15B of the 1985 Act and applies only to divisions.          **27.940.02**

---

[100] Companies Act 2006 (Commencement No. 5, Transitional Provisions and Savings) Order 2007, SI 2007/3495, art 3(1).
[101] Civil Procedure Rules, Practice Direction 49b, Part 8—Applications under CA 1985 and other legislation relating to companies (supplement to Part 49).
[102] Companies Act 2006 (Commencement No. 5, Transitional Provisions and Savings) Order 2007, SI 2007/3495, art 3(1).

**[940A  Disregard of website failures beyond control of company**

**27.940A.01**
(1) A failure to make information or a document available on the website throughout a period specified in any of the provisions mentioned in subsection (2) is to be disregarded if—
- (a) it is made available on the website for part of that period, and
- (b) the failure to make it available throughout that period is wholly attributable to circumstances that it would not be reasonable to have expected the company to prevent or avoid.

(2) The provisions referred to above are—
- (a) section 906A(6),
- (b) section 911A(4),
- (c) section 916(3B) and (4B),
- (d) section 917(3B) and (4B),
- (e) section 918(2B) and (3B),
- (f) section 921A(6),
- (g) section 926A(4),
- (h) section 931(3B) and (4B), and
- (i) section 932(2B) and (3B).]^a

AMENDMENTS AND NOTES

^a Inserted by the Companies (Reporting Requirements in Mergers and Divisions) Regulations 2011, SI 2011/1606, reg 31.

COMMENCEMENT DATE 1 August 2011[103]

**27.940A.02**
A company has not failed to make documents available on a website maintained by or on behalf of them if the documents do not remain available on the website throughout the period specified where the documents are available for part of the relevant period, and the failure to have the documents available throughout the period is due to circumstances that it would be unreasonable to have expected the company to prevent or avoid.

*Interpretation*

**941  Meaning of 'liabilities' and 'property'**

**27.941.01**
In this Part—

'liabilities' includes duties;
'property' includes property, rights and powers of every description.

COMMENCEMENT DATE 6 April 2008[104]

*Property*

**27.941.02**
See earlier discussion as to the meaning of 'property' in paragraph 26.900.06.

---

[103] Companies (Reporting Requirements in Mergers and Divisions) Regulations 2011, SI 2011/1606, reg 1(2).
[104] Companies Act 2006 (Commencement No. 5, Transitional Provisions and Savings) Order 2007, SI 2007/3495, art 3(1).

# 28

## TAKEOVERS ETC

## Companies Act 2006

### PART 28
### TAKEOVERS ETC

### CHAPTER 1
### THE TAKEOVER PANEL

**28.0.01**    Part 28 of the Act implements the EU Takeovers Directive[1] (the 'Takeovers Directive'). As the directive was required to be implemented by 20 May 2006 these provisions replace, with changes, the Takeovers Directive (Interim Implementation) Regulations 2006[2] (the 'Interim Regulations'). Part 28 places the Takeover Panel on a statutory footing, sets out rules applying to the conduct of takeover bids, makes provision to override barriers to takeovers in certain cases, imposes new disclosure requirements on companies, and regulates the position of minority shareholders following a successful takeover bid. The background to the provisions can be found in the Department of Trade and Industry (DTI) consultation document on Implementation of the European Directive on Takeover Bids.[3] The European Commission published a report on the Takeovers Directive in June 2012[4] which concluded that the regime created by the Takeovers Directive is working satisfactorily. However, there are areas where the rules could merit clarification to improve legal certainty. These include the concept of 'acting in concert', the mandatory bid rule, and the protection of rights of employees in a bid situation. It seems likely that the Commission will adopt a proposal to amend the Takeovers Directive in due course.

### *The Panel and its rules*

#### 942  The Panel

**28.942.01**
(1) The body known as the Panel on Takeovers and Mergers ('the Panel') is to have the functions conferred on it by or under this Chapter.
(2) The Panel may do anything that it considers necessary or expedient for the purposes of, or in connection with, its functions.
(3) The Panel may make arrangements for any of its functions to be discharged by—
    (a) a committee or subcommittee of the Panel, or
    (b) an officer or member of staff of the Panel, or a person acting as such.
This is subject to section 943(4) and (5).

COMMENCEMENT DATE 6 April 2007[5]

**28.942.02**    The Takeover Panel was established in 1968 to provide a framework for regulating takeovers in the UK. It is widely regarded as having been successful in applying a regime that is flexible, effective, and fair. The Panel was supported, since its creation, by the Bank of England and the Governor of the Bank of England nominated the chairman, deputy chairman, and four independent members of the Panel. Other members were provided by financial institutions and professionals involved in takeovers and mergers on secondment to the Panel. Following implementation of the Takeovers Directive, the senior members of the Panel and its independent members have been appointed on the recommendation of the Nominations Committee thereby assuring their independence from the Bank of England.

**28.942.03**    Section 942 places the Takeover Panel on a statutory basis. This was necessary to implement the Takeovers Directive. Subsection (1) confers on the Panel the functions set out in Part 28 of the Act. The Panel has the power to do anything 'necessary or expedient' for the purposes of or in connection with its functions.[6]

---

[1]  Directive (EC) 2004/25 [2004] OJ L142/12, 30.4.2004.
[2]  SI 2006/1183.
[3]  DTI, January 2005.
[4]  Report from the Commission to the European Parliament, the Council, the European Economic and Social Committee and the Committee of the Regions on the Application of Directive 2004/25/EC on Takeover Bids COM (2012) 347 final 28.6.2012.
[5]  Companies Act 2006 (Commencement No 2, etc) Order 2007, SI 2007/1093, art 2(1)(b).
[6]  In a series of decisions concerned with the construction of statutory powers to make defence regulations in wartime, the court held that it had no jurisdiction to investigate the reasons for the making of the regulations, or whether they were in fact necessary or expedient as this was a matter for the relevant minister. See *Minister of Agriculture and Fisheries v Price* [1941] 2 KB 116; *R v Comptroller-General of Patents ex p Bayer Products Ltd* [1941] 2 KB 306; *Progressive Supply Co v Dalton* [1943] Ch 54; *Horton v Owen* [1943] KB 111. In *Taylor v Brighton Borough Council* [1947] KB 736 the Court of Appeal regarded the question of whether a restriction in a planning scheme was necessary or expedient to be a matter for the council. However, it is considered that in the light of the development of judicial review since these cases were decided that the question of whether action by the panel is

The Act does not deal in substance with the Panel's constitution or internal arrangements, which continue in most respects to be a matter for the Panel.[7]

Subsection (3) permits delegation by the Panel. The day-to-day work of supervising takeovers is carried out by the Panel's executive (the Executive). In carrying out these functions, the Executive operates independently of the Panel. The Executive has responsibility for the conduct of investigations, the monitoring of dealings in connection with the Code, and the giving of rulings on the interpretation, application, or effect of the Code.[8] The Executive is staffed by employees, secondees from law firms, accountancy firms, corporate brokers, investment banks, and other organizations. It is led by its Director General who is assisted by permanent Deputy Directors General and Secretaries and other members of the Executive's permanent and seconded staff.[9] The Panel has up to 35 members including a chairman, up to three deputy chairmen, up to 20 other members, as well as individuals appointed by professional bodies.[10] The Panel as a whole assumes responsibility for the policy, financing, and administration of its functions, and for the functioning and operation of the Takeover Code (the Code)[11]. Otherwise, the Panel operates through a number of Committees[12] of which the most important are the Code Committee and the Hearings Committee. Membership of either committee is mutually exclusive and no member of the Code Committee may subsequently be a member of the Hearings Committee.[13]   **28.942.04**

The Code Committee exercises the rule-making functions of the Panel, and is responsible for keeping the Code under review and for proposing, consulting on, and making amendments to the Code.[14] The Hearings Committee reviews rulings by the Panel's Executive. It also hears disciplinary hearings brought by the Executive if the Executive considers that there has been a breach of the Code. The Hearings Committee is assisted by a secretary who is usually a partner in a law firm acting as an officer of the Panel.[15] The Nominations Committee monitors the size, composition, and balance of the Panel, and has taken over the Bank of England's former role in making senior appointments to the Panel.   **28.942.05**

Under the Directive, the UK is required to ensure at all times that there is a body to regulate takeovers. There is no procedure under the Act to replace the Panel should it cease to be an appropriate body to carry out this function, or if its rules cease to comply with the Directive. The Attorney-General stated in Parliament that '[t]he Government would retain the power through secondary legislation, particularly the European Communities Act 1972, either to remove and replace the panel as regulator or substitute rules made by the panel which were contrary to Community law ... In the event that the panel ceased to be an appropriate regulatory body or there were concerns about the compliance of the panel rules with the Directive, those powers could be exercised'.[16] The Solicitor General gave a commitment that the Government would consult before exercising such powers.[17]   **28.942.06**

## 943  Rules

(1)  The Panel must make rules giving effect to Articles 3.1, 4.2, 5, 6.1 to 6.3, 7 to 9 and 13 of the Takeovers Directive.   **28.943.01**

(2)  Rules made by the Panel may also make other provision—

---

'necessary or expedient' is justiciable, and therefore liable to challenge in the case of irrationality, bad faith or procedural impropriety. That said, the court is likely to defer to the judgment of the Panel, as a specialist regulatory body, on the question of whether any particular action is necessary or expedient for carrying out the Panel's functions.

[7] Section 943(5) presupposes the existence of a committee responsible for making rules and s 951 requires the existence of the Hearings Committee.

[8] Introduction to the Code, section 5

[9] R Gillespie, The Takeover Panel, p. 18 in *A Practitioner's Guide to the City Code on Takeovers and Mergers 2011/2012* (London, 2011).

[10] These include the Association for Financial Markets in Europe, the Association of British Insurers, the Association of Private Client Investment Managers and Stockbrokers, the British Bankers' Association, the Confederation of British Industry, the Institute of Chartered Accountants in England and Wales, the Investment Management Association, and the National Association of Pension Funds. See Introduction to the Code, section 4(a).

[11] Introduction to the Code, section 4(a).

[12] See ⟨http://www.thetakeoverpanel.org.uk⟩ for information on committees of the Panel.

[13] Introduction to the Code, section 4(d).

[14] See Introduction to the Code, section 4(b). The Code Committee was formed in 2001. Originally its members were not members of the Executive or the Panel. Following implementation of the Takeovers Directive they became members of the Panel. In certain exceptional cases, the Code Committee might consider it necessary to amend the Code on an expedited basis.

[15] Introduction to the Code, section 4(c).

[16] *Hansard*, HL, Grand Committee, col 286, Lord Goldsmith (28 March 2006).

[17] *Hansard*, HC, Standing Committee D, col 774 (18 July 2006).

(a) for or in connection with the regulation of—
(i) takeover bids,
(ii) merger transactions, and
(iii) transactions (not falling within sub-paragraph (i) or (ii)) that have or may have, directly or indirectly, an effect on the ownership or control of companies;
(b) for or in connection with the regulation of things done in consequence of, or otherwise in relation to, any such bid or transaction;
(c) about cases where—
(i) any such bid or transaction is, or has been, contemplated or apprehended, or
(ii) an announcement is made denying that any such bid or transaction is intended.
(3) The provision that may be made under subsection (2) includes, in particular, provision for a matter that is, or is similar to, a matter provided for by the Panel in the City Code on Takeovers and Mergers as it had effect immediately before the passing of this Act.
(4) In relation to rules made by virtue of section 957 (fees and charges), functions under this section may be discharged either by the Panel itself or by a committee of the Panel (but not otherwise).
(5) In relation to rules of any other description, the Panel must discharge its functions under this section by a committee of the Panel.
(6) Section 1 (meaning of 'company') does not apply for the purposes of this section.
(7) In this section 'takeover bid' includes a takeover bid within the meaning of the Takeovers Directive.
(8) In this Chapter 'the Takeovers Directive' means Directive 2004/25/EC of the European Parliament and of the Council.
(9) A reference to rules in the following provisions of this Chapter is to rules under this section.

COMMENCEMENT DATE 6 April 2007[18]

**28.943.02**   Under section 943, the Panel is required to make rules implementing requirements in the Takeovers Directive. These include: (i) general principles on the conduct of takeover bids; (ii) the authority competent to supervise bids; (iii) protection of minority shareholders; (iv) the provision of information about bids; (v) public disclosure; (vi) the obligations of the board of an offeree company; and (vii) other rules concerning bids. The imposition of a statutory duty on a private body to make rules is unusual and raises the question of how it is to be enforced. The Act does not include any mechanism for enforcement, although on normal principles of administrative law any person with a sufficient interest would be able to bring proceedings for judicial review in the event of a failure by the Panel to make the required rules.[19] as could the Attorney-General[20] Section 961 confers an exemption from liability in damages that would seem to apply to a failure to make appropriate rules implementing the Directive.[21]

**28.943.03**   In addition to the areas covered by the Directive, the Panel has wide powers to make rules for the regulation of takeover bids, mergers, and other transactions that may have an effect on the ownership of companies. This represents an expansion of the powers of the Panel compared with the Interim Regulations, although not from its traditional role before the implementation of the Takeovers Directive.[22] The Panel has the statutory authority to regulate mergers, takeovers of public companies whose shares are not quoted on a regulated market as well as certain types of corporate restructuring (eg mergers by scheme of arrangement). The Solicitor General explained in Parliament the objectives of the section:

> The second objective is that we wish to ensure that the panel's rule-making authority over other areas of corporate activity that it has traditionally regulated continues. That includes matters outside the scope of the Takeover Directive such as takeovers of public companies whose shares are not traded on regulated markets and mergers. We wish to preserve a unitary principle to the panel's regulatory functions. It would not have been right to create one set of rules applying to takeovers under

---

[18] Companies Act 2006 (Commencement No 2, etc) Order 2007, SI 2007/1093, art 2(1)(b).

[19] Senior Courts Act 1981, s 31(3) and CPR r 54.

[20] The Attorney-General has standing to prevent the law from being breached and need not show any injury: *Attorney-General v Cockermouth* Local Board (1874) LR 18 Eq 172.

[21] As a matter of Community law, the UK is responsible for implementation of the directive. A failure could therefore give rise to a claim for damages under the principle of state liability recognized in Joined Cases C-6/90 and C-9/90 *Francovich v Italy* [1991] ECR I-5357. If the breach of Community law is committed by the Takeover Panel, and it has immunity under the Act, then proceedings against the UK should be brought against the Government: *Kirklees MBC v Wickes Building Supplies Ltd* [1993] AC 227, 282.

[22] As the Interim Regulations were delegated legislation made under section 2(2) of the European Communities Act 1972 it was not possible to legislate for matters going beyond the scope of the Takeovers Directive: see *Oakley v Animal* [2006] Ch 337. The Panel did not cease to regulate other takeover bids in the interim; it continued to do so but on a non-statutory basis.

theDirective and another applying to other types of corporate controls transaction, so [the section] extends a right for the panel to make rules in areas of activity that are broadly regulated by the takeover code at present.[23]

The companies, transactions, and persons subject to the Code are currently set out in section 3 of the Introduction to the Code.

A further problem with the Interim Regulations has been corrected. As the Regulations were made **28.943.04** under section 2(2) of the European Communities Act 1972 it was not possible to confer a power on the Panel to amend its rules as this would have infringed the prohibition on the delegation of statutory powers (*delegatus non potest delegare*). Primary legislation was therefore needed once the rules had been given statutory force to enable amendments to be made by the Panel to the Code.

Subsection (4) specifies that rules about fees and charges may be made either by a committee of the **28.943.05** Panel, or by the Panel as a whole. This provision was inserted to enable the Panel to continue its practice of acting as a whole when making such rules. In all other cases, rules must be made by a committee of the Panel (currently, the Code Committee).[24]

## The Takeover Code

The Takeover Code consists of general principles supplemented by detailed rules. There are six general **28.943.06** principles taken from Article 3 of the Directive. The principles provide general guidelines for all takeovers.

1. All holders of the securities of an offeree company of the same class must be afforded equivalent treatment; moreover, if a person acquires control of a company, the other holders of securities must be protected.[25]
2. The holders of the securities of an offeree company must have sufficient time and information to enable them to reach a properly informed decision on the bid; where it advises the holders of securities, the board of the offeree company must give its views on the effects of implementation of the bid on employment, conditions of employment and the locations of the company's places of business.
3. The board of an offeree company must act in the interests of the company as a whole and must not deny the holders of securities the opportunity to decide on the merits of the bid.
4. False markets must not be created in the securities of the offeree company, of the offeror company or of any other company concerned by the bid in such a way that the rise or fall of the prices of the securities becomes artificial and the normal functioning of the markets is distorted.
5. An offeror must announce a bid only after ensuring that he/she can fulfil in full any cash consideration, if such is offered, and after taking all reasonable measures to secure the implementation of any other type of consideration.
6. An offeree company must not be hindered in the conduct of its affairs for longer than is reasonable by a bid for its securities.

   This is supplemented by 38 detailed rules, together with notes on the rules. The analysis of the Panel's rules is outside the scope of this commentary and the reader is referred to specialist works on takeovers.[26]

---

[23] *Hansard*, HC, Standing Committee D, col 781 (18 July 2006).

[24] *Hansard*, HL, Grand Committee, col. 287, Lord Goldsmith (28 March 2006).

[25] In Case C-101/08 *Audiolux* the European Court of Justice was asked whether art 3(1)(a) was a manifestation of a general principle of Community Law that existed prior to the entry into force of Directive 2004/25/EC and whether, if so, such principle applied to the relations between majority shareholders and the minority. The response of the Court was negative, ruling that 'Community law does not include any general principle of law under which minority shareholders are protected by an obligation on the dominant shareholder, when acquiring or exercising control of a company, to offer to buy their shares under the same conditions as those agreed when a shareholding conferring or strengthening the control of the dominant shareholder was acquired' [2009] ECR I9823. In para [51] the Court explained: '[I]t cannot be inferred from the use of the term "general principles" in Article 3 of that directive that the Community legislature thereby intends the principles mentioned in that article to be treated in the same way as general principles of Community law. As is clear from the words "for the purposes of implementing this Directive", they are only guiding principles for the implementation of that directive by the Member States.'

[26] Eg G Eaborn (ed), *Butterworths Takeovers: Law and Practice*, 1st edn (London, 2005) (2nd edn due 2012) and Weinberg and Blank on Takeovers and Mergers, 5th edn (London, 2012).

### 944 Further provisions about rules

**28.944.01**
(1) Rules may—
   (a) make different provision for different purposes;
   (b) make provision subject to exceptions or exemptions;
   (c) contain incidental, supplemental, consequential or transitional provision;
   (d) authorise the Panel to dispense with or modify the application of rules in particular cases and by reference to any circumstances.

   Rules made by virtue of paragraph (d) must require the Panel to give reasons for acting as mentioned in that paragraph.

(2) Rules must be made by an instrument in writing.

(3) Immediately after an instrument containing rules is made, the text must be made available to the public, with or without payment, in whatever way the Panel thinks appropriate.

(4) A person is not to be taken to have contravened a rule if he shows that at the time of the alleged contravention the text of the rule had not been made available as required by subsection (3).

(5) The production of a printed copy of an instrument purporting to be made by the Panel on which is endorsed a certificate signed by an officer of the Panel authorised by it for that purpose and stating—
   (a) that the instrument was made by the Panel,
   (b) that the copy is a true copy of the instrument, and
   (c) that on a specified date the text of the instrument was made available to the public as required by subsection (3),

   is evidence (or in Scotland sufficient evidence) of the facts stated in the certificate.

(6) A certificate purporting to be signed as mentioned in subsection (5) is to be treated as having been properly signed unless the contrary is shown.

(7) A person who wishes in any legal proceedings to rely on an instrument by which rules are made may require the Panel to endorse a copy of the instrument with a certificate of the kind mentioned in subsection (5).

COMMENCEMENT DATE 6 April 2007[27]

**28.944.02** Subsection (1) makes clear that the Panel's rule-making powers are very wide. The rules may make different provision for different purposes, and include exceptions or exemptions. The Panel may dispense with or modify the application of its rules in particular cases, although the Panel has a duty to give its reasons for doing so. Rules must be made in writing and must be made available to the public. The current rules are published on the Panel's website[28] as well as being published by the Panel as the Takeover Code (known as the Blue Book). As a body exercising public powers, the Panel is required, when making rules, to act rationally and in good faith, and to follow proper procedures.[29] A failure to do so could result in the rules being challenged by judicial review.[30]

**28.944.03** Subsection (4) provides a statutory defence to a person accused of a breach of a rule where the rule has not been published. It seems that this defence applies even if the person was aware of the relevant unpublished rule.

**28.944.04** Subsection (5) provides that the production of a printed copy of an instrument purporting to be made by the Panel on which is endorsed a certificate signed by an officer of the Panel is evidence of the facts stated in the certificate. A person involved in legal proceedings may require the Panel to provide such a certificate for the purposes of legal proceedings.[31]

### 945 Rulings

**28.945.01**
(1) The Panel may give rulings on the interpretation, application or effect of rules.

---

[27] Companies Act 2007 (Commencement No 2, etc) Order 2007, SI 2007/1093, art 2(1)(b).

[28] See ⟨http://www.thetakeoverpanel.org.uk⟩.

[29] Decisions by bodies exercising public law functions may be challenged on grounds of illegality, irrationality, or procedural unfairness: *Council of Civil Service Unions v Minister for the Civil Service* [1985] AC 374, 410–411. For detailed discussion of the grounds of judicial review see eg M Fordham, *Judicial Review Handbook* Handbook 5th edn (Oxford, 2008) and Woolf et al, *De Smith's Judicial Review*, 6th edn (London, 2007).

[30] Even before being placed on a statutory basis the Panel was subject to judicial review: *R v Panel on Takeovers and Mergers ex p Datafin plc* [1987] QB 815, although the court made clear that it was unlikely to intervene during the course of a bid, deferring its review until after the conclusion of procedures by the Panel. This approach is clearly inapplicable if judicial review is sought of a Panel rule although the person challenging the rule will still need to have a sufficient interest to bring proceedings for judicial review. The Attorney General confirmed in Parliament that judicial review continues to be available: *Hansard*, HL, Grand Committee, col 306 (28 March 2006). This is also stated in the explanatory notes on the Companies Act (CA) 2006, para 1178.

[31] Companies Act 2006, s 944(7).

(2)  To the extent and in the circumstances specified in rules, and subject to any review or appeal, a ruling has binding effect.

COMMENCEMENT DATE  6 April 2007[32]

Subsection (2) provides that any ruling by the Panel 'has binding effect'. This section gives statutory effect to rulings by the Panel (including the Executive) on the interpretation, application, and effect of its rules. This contrasts with the position before the implementation of the Takeovers Directive where contravention of the Code did not entail any direct legal consequences. Historically, the Panel sought to ensure compliance through a consensual approach with the parties engaged in takeovers.[33] In the event of a failure to comply with the Code, the Panel could (a) issue a private reprimand; (b) publicly censure the offender; (c) report the breach to a regulatory body (eg the Financial Services Authority (FSA), the London Stock Exchange, or the DTI); or (d) name the persons as someone not likely to comply with the Code. There were also indirect means of ensuring compliance. The FSA endorsed the Code under section 143 of the Financial Services and Markets Act 2000 (now repealed). The consequence was that the FSA could, at the request of the Panel, take disciplinary action, under its rules, against an authorized person who contravened the Code or a Panel ruling. An authorized person was (and remains today) prohibited from acting, or continuing to act, for any person in connection with a transaction to which the Code applies if he has reasonable grounds to believe that the person in question, or his principal, is not complying or is not likely to comply with the Code.[34] FSA Guidance states that a firm should keep itself informed of Panel notices and take them into account.[35] in 2010, the UK Government announced its plans to abolish the FSA and replace it with two new regulatory bodies: the Prudential Regulation Authority (PRA) and the Financial Conduct Authority (FCA) with effect from 2013. The Financial Policy Committee will be established to seek to remove or reduce systemic risks and thereby enhance the resilience of the financial system. The FSA's current responsibilities in connection with the Code will be taken over by the FCA, although whether this will lead to a change in approach remains to be seen.     **28.945.02**

An appeal has no automatic suspensory effect on a Panel ruling and the Panel may give directions to ensure compliance with its interpretation pending determination of the appeal.[36]     **28.945.03**

## 946  Directions

Rules may contain provision conferring power on the Panel to give any direction that appears to the Panel to be necessary in order—     **28.946.01**

(a)  to restrain a person from acting (or continuing to act) in breach of rules;
(b)  to restrain a person from doing (or continuing to do) a particular thing, pending determination of whether that or any other conduct of his is or would be a breach of rules;
(c)  otherwise to secure compliance with rules.

COMMENCEMENT DATE  6 April 2007[37]

This section enables the Panel to give legally enforceable directions pending a determination of whether or not conduct contravenes the Code. The Panel may also give directions to secure compliance with its rules. The Solicitor General explained the position in Parliament as follows:     **28.946.02**

> The [section] allows the panel to make provision in its rules giving directions preventing a person from breaching the rules in the interim while a matter awaits determination by the panel, or otherwise, to ensure compliance with the rules. This is an important facilitative provision, and once the panel has decided on the effect of a rule in a particular case, it can guarantee its interpretation by requiring relevant parties to do or not do certain things in accordance with the ruling…Persons affected by a decision of the panel on which a direction is issued will still be able to seek a review of that decision by the panel's own appeal processes. If circumstances arise in which the facts are only temporary, the panel may wish to deal with those temporary circumstances and ensure that its views are clear to those who might have to address them.[38]

---

[32]  Companies Act 2006 (Commencement No 2, etc) Order 2007, SI 2007/1093, art 2(1)(b).
[33]  G Eaborn (ed), *Butterworths Takeovers: Law and Practice* (London, 2005) 21.
[34]  FSA Handbook of Rules and Guidance MAR 4.3.1R.
[35]  FSA Handbook of Rules and Guidance MAR 4.3.2G(2).
[36]  See s 946 and commentary.
[37]  Companies Act 2006 (Commencement No 2, etc) Order 2007, SI 2007/1093, art 2(1)(b).
[38]  *Hansard*, HC, Standing Committee D, col 782 (18 July 2006).

*Information*

### 947 Power to require documents and information

**28.947.01**

(1) The Panel may by notice in writing require a person—
  (a) to produce any documents that are specified or described in the notice;
  (b) to provide, in the form and manner specified in the notice, such information as may be specified or described in the notice.

(2) A requirement under subsection (1) must be complied with—
  (a) at a place specified in the notice, and
  (b) before the end of such reasonable period as may be so specified.

(3) This section applies only to documents and information reasonably required in connection with the exercise by the Panel of its functions.

(4) The Panel may require—
  (a) any document produced to be authenticated, or
  (b) any information provided (whether in a document or otherwise) to be verified,
  in such manner as it may reasonably require.

(5) The Panel may authorise a person to exercise any of its powers under this section.

(6) A person exercising a power by virtue of subsection (5) must, if required to do so, produce evidence of his authority to exercise the power.

(7) The production of a document in pursuance of this section does not affect any lien that a person has on the document.

(8) The Panel may take copies of or extracts from a document produced in pursuance of this section.

(9) A reference in this section to the production of a document includes a reference to the production of—
  (a) a hard copy of information recorded otherwise than in hard copy form, or
  (b) information in a form from which a hard copy can be readily obtained.

(10) A person is not required by this section to disclose documents or information in respect of which a claim to legal professional privilege (in Scotland, to confidentiality of communications) could be maintained in legal proceedings.

COMMENCEMENT DATE 6 April 2007[39]

**28.947.02**   To exercise its statutory functions the Panel is given very wide powers to obtain information and require the production of documents. The only limitation is that the documents or information are reasonably required in connection with the exercise by the Panel of its functions. The reference to 'any person' implies that foreign companies or individuals may be subject to requests by the Panel for information or documents, although the effectiveness of any request outside the UK will depend on local law. The Panel has the right to make copies or extracts of documents which are incidental to the obtaining of information. Disclosure by the Panel is dealt with in section 948. The Panel may also authorize a person to exercise any of its powers under this section. This would permit the Panel to appoint a law or accountancy firm to help it collect and analyse documents.[40]

**28.947.03**   A person is not required to disclose any documents or information in respect of which a claim to legal professional privilege could be maintained in legal proceedings.[41] At common law privilege is not restricted to legal advice in connection with actual or contemplated legal proceedings.[42] This raises the question of whether the statutory reference to legal proceedings is intended to abrogate legal professional privilege in a non-litigation context. In *Three Rivers District Council v Governor and Company of the Bank of England*[43] Lord Scott referred to the policy underlying the law in this area:

> it is necessary in our society, a society in which the restraining and controlling framework is built upon a belief in the rule of law, that communications between clients and lawyers, whereby the clients are hoping for the assistance of the lawyers' legal skills in the management of their (the clients') affairs, should be secure against the possibility of any scrutiny from others, whether the police, the executive, business competitors, inquisitive busy-bodies or anyone else.

**28.947.04**   In *R (Morgan Grenfell & Co Ltd) v Special Commissioner of Income Tax*[44] the House of Lords held that legal professional privilege was a fundamental human right that could only be abrogated by express words or necessary implication. The European Court of Human Rights has held that legal professional

---

[39] Companies Act 2006 (Commencement No 2, etc) Order 2007, SI 2007/1093, art 2(1)(b).
[40] See explanatory notes on the Companies Act 2006, para 1190.
[41] The circumstances in which privilege arises is treated in specialist works. See eg C Passmore, *Privilege* 2nd edn (XPL Law, 2006) (3rd edn due 2012), and B Thanki et al, *Law of Privilege*, 2nd edn (Oxford, 2011).
[42] *Three Rivers District Council v Governor and Company of the Bank of England (No 6)* [2005] 1 AC 610.
[43] [2005] 1 AC 610, 649–650.
[44] [2003] 1 AC 563.

privilege can be invaded only in exceptional circumstances.[45] It is therefore considered that the reference to legal proceedings should not be interpreted as excluding by implication privilege in a non-litigation context.[46]

## 948  Restrictions on disclosure

   (1)   This section applies to information (in whatever form)—                                   **28.948.01**
       (a)  relating to the private affairs of an individual, or
       (b)  relating to any particular business,
      that is provided to the Panel in connection with the exercise of its functions.
   (2)   No such information may, during the lifetime of the individual or so long as the business continues to be carried on, be disclosed without the consent of that individual or (as the case may be) the person for the time being carrying on that business.
   (3)   Subsection (2) does not apply to any disclosure of information that—
       (a)  is made for the purpose of facilitating the carrying out by the Panel of any of its functions,
       (b)  is made to a person specified in Part 1 of Schedule 2,
       (c)  is of a description specified in Part 2 of that Schedule, or
       (d)  is made in accordance with Part 3 of that Schedule.
   (4)   The Secretary of State may amend Schedule 2 by order subject to negative resolution procedure.
   (5)   An order under subsection (4) must not—
       (a)  amend Part 1 of Schedule 2 by specifying a person unless the person exercises functions of a public nature (whether or not he exercises any other function);
       (b)  amend Part 2 of Schedule 2 by adding or modifying a description of disclosure unless the purpose for which the disclosure is permitted is likely to facilitate the exercise of a function of a public nature;
       (c)  amend Part 3 of Schedule 2 so as to have the effect of permitting disclosures to be made to a body other than one that exercises functions of a public nature in a country or territory outside the United Kingdom.
   (6)   Subsection (2) does not apply to—
       (a)  the disclosure by an authority within subsection (7) of information disclosed to it by the Panel in reliance on subsection (3);
       (b)  the disclosure of such information by anyone who has obtained it directly or indirectly from an authority within subsection (7).
   (7)   The authorities within this subsection are—
       (a)  the Financial Services Authority;[47]
       (b)  an authority designated as a supervisory authority for the purposes of Article 4.1 of the Takeovers Directive;
       (c)  any other person or body that exercises functions of a public nature, under legislation in an EEA State other than the United Kingdom, that are similar to the Panel's functions or those of the Financial Services Authority.
   (8)   This section does not prohibit the disclosure of information if the information is or has been available to the public from any other source.
   (9)   Nothing in this section authorises the making of a disclosure in contravention of the Data Protection Act 1998 (c. 29).

   COMMENCEMENT DATE  For the purposes of exercising the power to make orders: 20 January 2007. Otherwise 6 April 2007.[48]

This section sets out the circumstances in which the Panel is permitted to disclose information   **28.948.02** obtained pursuant to section 947 and proved one of the more controversial provisions during the Bill's passage through Parliament. Subsection (2) imposes a general duty of confidentiality on the disclosure of information relating to the private affairs of an individual or relating to any particular business. 'Private affairs' are undefined, although some guidance may be gained from the case law of the European Court of Human Rights under Article 8 of the European Convention on Human Rights.

---

   [45]  *Foxley v United Kingdom* (2000) 31 EHRR 637, 647.
   [46]  See however *Price Waterhouse v BCCI Holdings (Luxembourg) SA* [1992] BCLC 583, 593 where Millett J held that a provision of the Banking Act 1987 preventing the Bank of England from requiring production of a document by counsel or solicitors, was to be interpreted 'not only as making an exception to documents which may be required to be produced but also as marking the limits of that exception'. In *R (Morgan Grenfell & Co Ltd) v Special Commissioner of Income Tax* [2003] 1 AC 563 Lord Hoffmann considered the case to be wrong.
   [47]  When in force, Schedule 18, para 118 of the Financial Services Act 2012 will substitute references to the Financial Services Authority with references to '(a) the Financial Conduct Authority; (aa) the Prudential Regulation Authority; (ab) the Bank of England'.
   [48]  Companies Act 2006 (Commencement No 2, etc) Order 2007, SI 2007/1093, art 2(1)(b).

When questioned in Parliament, Lord McKenzie, for the Government, stated that 'private affairs' means non-business matters, and gave as examples information relating to an individual's remuneration, share options, or related party transactions.[49] However, subsection (8) confirms that confidentiality does not apply to any information that is or has been available to the public from any other source. This includes information that would otherwise be private but which is required to be disclosed under a regulatory rule or enactment.

**28.948.03**    It is notable that the restriction on disclosure of information relating to a business is not restricted to information that would, at common law, attract protection under the law of confidence, although, as mentioned, no protection attaches to information once it has entered into the public domain.[50] It is considered that the reference to 'any source' includes information made available abroad, or on the Internet.

**28.948.04**    In *Melton Medes Ltd v Securities and Investment Board*[51] the court held that an equivalent prohibition on disclosure in the Financial Services Act 1986 did not confer a private cause of action for damages in the event of an unauthorized disclosure. Lightman J held that the Financial Services Act 1986 created an elaborate scheme of duties backed by a mix of enforcement mechanisms with, in each case, the mechanism earmarked to the duty in question. The only sanction for breach was criminal prosecution.[52] The judge was also influenced by two further considerations that were inconsistent with the availability of a civil claim for damages:

> The first is that the role of the SIB[53] is of a senior regulator in the public interest and specifically in the interest and for the protection of investors. Section 179 (and in particular its protection of the subject, as well as the source, of information) is apt to control in the public interest the use and dissemination of information acquired rather than to subject the SIB in this respect to private law actions. The special interest of informants and the persons to whom information relates is safeguarded by affording them the necessary locus standi in judicial review proceedings to enforce this public duty. The second is that to recognize the creation of a statutory private right would be to recognize a new category of non-confidential information in respect of which a private right to non-disclosure exists, for information protected by section 179 need not be confidential.[54]

> The same considerations apply to the position of the Panel under the Act and it is therefore considered that no private right of action exists in the case of improper disclosure. The matter seems placed beyond doubt by section 956 which excludes any liability for the tort of breach of statutory duty.[55]

**28.948.05**    Subsection (3) permits a wide range of disclosures. The Panel may disclose information (a) for the purpose of facilitating the carrying out by the Panel of any of its functions, (b) made to a person specified in Part 1 of Schedule 2, (c) of a description specified in Part 2 of that Schedule, or (d) made in accordance with Part 3 of that Schedule. Part 1 of Schedule 2 lists a number of 'specified persons' to whom disclosure may be made. These include the Secretary of State, the Treasury, the Bank of England, the FSA,[56] Customs and Excise, the Director of Public Prosecutions, and the police. It has been amended to include equivalent governmental, regulatory, and law enforcement bodies (including the police). Similar lists apply in relation to Jersey, Guernsey, and the Isle of Man.

**28.948.06**    Part 2 of that schedule lists 53 types of disclosure that are permitted in relation to the United Kingdom, 13 in relation to Jersey, 8 in respect of Guernsey, and 17 in relation to the Isle of Man. There are also a number of general disclosures. In respect of the United Kingdom, most relate to either the performance of functions under the Financial Services and Markets Act 2000, investigations, law enforcement, or the functioning of government departments and public bodies. There is a general right of disclosure with a view to the institution of, or otherwise for the purposes of, criminal proceedings in the British Islands or elsewhere, which covers criminal proceedings worldwide.[57]

---

[49]  *Hansard*, HL, col 970 (10 May 2006).
[50]  Subsection (8).
[51]  [1995] Ch 137.
[52]  [1995] Ch 137, 146.
[53]  Securities and Investments Board.
[54]  [1995] Ch 137, 146.
[55]  Theoretically an action could be brought for negligence on the basis that the Panel owes a duty of care not to make an unauthorized disclosure, in which case the considerations set out in *Melton Medes* will be relevant. However, absent a specific assumption of responsibility it is considered that no duty will be owed: see, by analogy, *Stovin v Wise* [1996] AC 923; *Gorringe v Calderdale Metropolitan Borough Council* [2004] 1 WLR 1057 and *Customs and Excise Commissioners v Barclays Bank plc* [2007] 1 AC 181.
[56]  When in force, Schedule 18, para 118 of the Financial Services Act 2012 will substitute references to the Financial Services Authority with references to the Financial Conduct Authority and the Prudential Regulation Authority.
[57]  Sch 2, Part 2 (E), para 3.

Part 3 applies to disclosures made to overseas regulatory bodies. The body must exercise functions of **28.948.07** a public nature that appear to the Panel to be similar to its own functions, or those of the FSA.[58] The disclosure must be made for the purpose of enabling or assisting that person or body to exercise those functions.[59] The Panel is required to consider if the use the body is likely to make of the information is sufficiently important to justify making disclosure and whether the body has adequate arrangements to prevent the information being further used or disclosed otherwise than for the purposes of carrying out the functions mentioned or any other purposes that are substantially similar.[60] Subsections (4) and (5) make provision for the list in Schedule 2 to be amended. This has been done twice.[61]

The section permits disclosure by the Panel, but does not require it.[62] In Parliament, the Solicitor **28.948.08** General stated that the Panel may refuse a request where the information is confidential.[63] It is expected that the Panel will normally make disclosure in response to a request for information, although it has the power to make disclosures of its own motion.[64]

The restriction on disclosure does not apply to information provided by the Panel to the FSA, bodies **28.948.09** exercising functions equivalent to the Panel in other EEA States, or any other person or body that exercises functions of a public nature under legislation in other EEA States.

Subsection (9) imposes an overriding restriction on the disclosure of information. Regardless of the **28.948.10** availability of a power to disclose information under subsections (3) and (6) to (7), no disclosure may be made if it would involve a contravention of the Data Protection Act 1998. Such a limitation was thought necessary to avoid possible infringements of the EU Data Protection Directive,[65] although it may in practice be difficult for a person to prove such a breach.

### 949 Offence of disclosure in contravention of section 948

(1) A person who discloses information in contravention of section 948 is guilty of an offence, **28.949.01** unless—
    (a) he did not know, and had no reason to suspect, that the information had been provided as mentioned in section 948(1), or
    (b) he took all reasonable steps and exercised all due diligence to avoid the commission of the offence.

(2) A person guilty of an offence under this section is liable—
    (a) on conviction on indictment, to imprisonment for a term not exceeding two years or a fine (or both);
    (b) on summary conviction—
        (i) in England and Wales, to imprisonment for a term not exceeding twelve months or to a fine not exceeding the statutory maximum (or both);
        (ii) in Scotland or Northern Ireland, to imprisonment for a term not exceeding six months, or to a fine not exceeding the statutory maximum (or both).

(3) Where a company or other body corporate commits an offence under this section, an offence is also committed by every officer of the company or other body corporate who is in default.

COMMENCEMENT DATE 6 April 2007[66]

Section 949 imposes criminal sanctions for an infringement of section 948. Contravention is punished **28.949.02** by up to two years' imprisonment and/or an unlimited fine following conviction on indictment, and up to 12 months' imprisonment (six months in Scotland and Northern Ireland) and a fine up to the statutory maximum following summary trial. The statutory maximum is currently £5,000. However,

---

[58] Sch 2, Part 3, paras 1(1)(a) and 1(2). When in force, Schedule 18, para 118 of the Financial Services Act 2012 will substitute references to the Financial Services Authority with references to the functions of the 'Financial Conduct Authority or the Prudential Regulation Authority or similar to the regulatory functions of the Bank of England'.

[59] Sch 2, Part 3, para 1(1)(b).

[60] Sch 2, Part 3, para 2.

[61] Companies Act 2006 (Amendment of Schedule 2) Order 2009, SI 2009/202 (repealed) and the Companies Act 2006 (Amendment of Schedule 2) (No 2) Order 2009, SI 2009/1208.

[62] *Hansard*, HC, col 795, the Solicitor General (18 July 2006).

[63] *Hansard*, HC, col 796, the Solicitor General (18 July 2006). Confidentiality is not a bar to disclosure 'in cases in which the panel takes the view that it is important that that should happen'.

[64] *Hansard*, HC, col 796 (18 July 2006), where the Solicitor General gave as an example the Panel discovering that an offence has been committed.

[65] Directive (EC) 95/46 [1995] OJ L281/31 23.11.1995.

[66] Companies Act 2006 (Commencement No 2, etc) Order 2007, SI 2007/1093, art 2(1)(b).

by virtue of section 1131 in relation to an offence committed after commencement of that section and before commencement of section 154(1) of the Criminal Justice Act 2003, the reference to 'twelve months' is substituted by 'six months'. Section 154(1) of the Criminal Justice Act 2003 is not yet in force and will only enter into force at a date to be appointed.[67] The effect is that the maximum sentence is currently six months. See Chapter 36 for commentary on section 1131.

**28.949.03**     There are two separate defences. First, that the person did not know, and had no reason to expect, that the information had been provided to the Panel in connection with the exercise of its functions. Secondly, that the person making disclosure took all reasonable steps and exercised all due diligence to avoid committing the offence. Belief that the information was not confidential, or was in the public domain, is not, in itself, a defence. Nor is the belief that disclosure was in the public interest.

**28.949.04**     Where an offence is committed by a company or body corporate every officer of the company who is in default is also guilty. Section 1121(3) determines whether an officer is in default. This states that an officer is 'in default' if he authorizes or permits, participates in, or fails to take all reasonable steps to prevent, the contravention.

## Co-operation

### 950 Panel's duty of co-operation

**28.950.01**     (1) The Panel must take such steps as it considers appropriate to co-operate with—
    (a) the Financial Services Authority;[68]
    (b) an authority designated as a supervisory authority for the purposes of Article 4.1 of the Takeovers Directive;
    (c) any other person or body that exercises functions of a public nature, under legislation in any country or territory outside the United Kingdom, that appear to the Panel to be similar to its own functions or those of the Financial Services Authority.[69]
    (2) Co-operation may include the sharing of information that the Panel is not prevented from disclosing.

COMMENCEMENT DATE 6 April 2007[70]

**28.950.02**     This section implements Article 4(4) of the Takeovers Directive. It imposes a duty of co-operation on the Panel with (i) the FSA;[71] (ii) supervisors of takeover bids in other EEA States; and (iii) any other person or body exercising functions of a public nature similar to those of the FSA.[72] Failure could, in theory, be subject to judicial review, although the broad discretion granted to the Panel makes a successful challenge unlikely.

**28.950.03**     The form and manner of co-operation is as the Panel considers appropriate in the light of the circumstances, and may include sharing information which the Panel is not prevented from disclosing.[73] In the Government's view, the section gives the Panel great discretion and enables it to make whatever decision it feels is appropriate in particular circumstances.[74] The Panel's interpretation of this requirement is set out in section 12 of the Introduction to the Code (Co-operation and Information Sharing).

## Hearings and appeals

### 951 Hearings and appeals

**28.951.01**     (1) Rules must provide for a decision of the Panel to be subject to review by a committee of the Panel (the 'Hearings Committee') at the instance of such persons affected by the decision as are specified in the rules.
    (2) Rules may also confer other functions on the Hearings Committee.

---

[67] Criminal Justice Act 2003, s 336(3).

[68] When in force, Schedule 18, para 118 of the Financial Services Act 2012 will substitute references to the Financial Services Authority with references to '(a) the Financial Conduct Authority; (aa) the Prudential Regulation Authority; (ab) the Bank of England'.

[69] When in force, Schedule 18, para 118 of the Financial Services Act 2012 will substitute references to the Financial Services Authority with references to the 'Financial Conduct Authority or the Prudential Regulation Authority or similar to the regulatory functions of the Bank of England'.

[70] Companies Act 2006 (Commencement No 2, etc) Order 2007, SI 2007/1093, art 2(1)(b).

[71] See n 66 above for the replacement of the FSA by the FCA and PRA.

[72] See n 67 above.

[73] *Hansard*, HC, col 797, the Solicitor General (18 July 2006).

[74] *Hansard*, HC, col 799, the Solicitor General (18 July 2006).

    (3)  Rules must provide for there to be a right of appeal against a decision of the Hearings Committee to an independent tribunal (the 'Takeover Appeal Board') in such circumstances and subject to such conditions as are specified in the rules.

    (4)  Rules may contain—

        (a)  provision as to matters of procedure in relation to proceedings before the Hearings Committee (including provision imposing time limits);

        (b)  provision about evidence in such proceedings;

        (c)  provision as to the powers of the Hearings Committee dealing with a matter referred to it;

        (d)  provision about enforcement of decisions of the Hearings Committee and the Takeover Appeal Board.

    (5)  Rules must contain provision—

        (a)  requiring the Panel, when acting in relation to any proceedings before the Hearings Committee or the Takeover Appeal Board, to do so by an officer or member of staff of the Panel (or a person acting as such);

        (b)  preventing a person who is or has been a member of the committee mentioned in section 943(5) from being a member of the Hearings Committee or the Takeover Appeal Board;

        (c)  preventing a person who is a member of the committee mentioned in section 943(5), of the Hearings Committee or of the Takeover Appeal Board from acting as mentioned in paragraph (a).

Commencement Date 6 April 2007[75]

This section imposes a statutory duty on the Panel to make rules dealing with challenges to the Panel's decisions. Those rules must provide for a right of rehearing before the Hearings Committee and an appeal to the Takeover Appeal Board (the Appeal Board). Although the Hearings Committee is functionally a part of the Panel, members of the Panel who took the decision under challenge are precluded from being members of the Hearings Committee or of the Appeal Board.   **28.951.02**

As mentioned above in the commentary on section 943, the Panel is a body exercising public functions and as such is subject to judicial review.[76] It is therefore required to comply with the rules of natural justice and to reach a decision in a manner that is fair. It is not, however, subject to the rules of evidence that govern court proceedings. The same applies to the Appeal Board.   **28.951.03**

A further question is whether either or both of the Panel and the Appeal Board constitute a 'public authority' for the purposes of section 6 of the Human Rights Act 1998. Section 6 (1) of that Act states that it is unlawful for a public authority to act in a way which is incompatible with a Convention right. A 'public authority' includes (a) a court or tribunal and (b) any person certain of whose functions are functions of a public nature, but does not include either House of Parliament or a person exercising functions in connection with proceedings in Parliament.[77] In relation to a particular act, a person is not a public authority by virtue only of subsection (3)(b) if the nature of the act is private.[78]   **28.951.04**

It is considered that because of their public functions both the Panel and the Appeal Board are public authorities and are therefore subject to those Convention rights incorporated into English law by the Human Rights Act 1998. Article 6(1) of the European Convention on Human Rights states that 'In the determination of his civil rights and obligations …, everyone is entitled to a fair and public hearing within a reasonable time by an independent and impartial tribunal established by law'. There is an extensive jurisprudence on the requirements of Article 6 although it is outside the scope of this commentary to consider this further. In *Principle Capital Investment Trust PLC*,[79] the Appeal Board held that it was unnecessary to consider whether the Hearings Committee was an Article 6 compliant tribunal as the Appeal Board was constitutionally an independent public body. Moreover, as the Hearings Committee had adopted lawful and fair procedures, the Appeal Board was entitled to take into account the findings of the Hearings Committee.[80]   **28.951.05**

---

[75]  Companies Act 2006 (Commencement No 2, etc) Order 2007, SI 2007/1093, art 2(1)(b).

[76]  *R v Panel on Takeovers and Mergers ex p Datafin plc* [1987] QB 815. The court will usually wait until the conclusion of the Panel's processes.

[77]  Human Rights Act 1998, s 6(3).

[78]  Human Rights Act 1998, s 6(5).

[79]  Decision 2010/1, 30 April 2010.

[80]  Ibid, para 12.

*Hearings Committee*

**28.951.06**   The Hearings Committee may be convened in the following cases:

(i)   by a party to a takeover, or any other person affected by a ruling of the Executive with a sufficient interest in the matter who wishes to contest that ruling;

(ii)   by the Executive if it decides to refer a matter for review without itself giving a ruling where it considers that there is a particularly unusual, important, or difficult point at issue;

(iii)   if the Executive brings disciplinary proceedings for a breach of the Code or of a ruling of the Executive or of the Panel; or

(iv)   in other circumstances if the Executive, or the Hearings Committee, considers it appropriate to do so.[81]

The Panel must be informed as soon as possible, and in any event within one month from the event giving rise to the application for review. Where it considers it necessary, the Executive may stipulate a reasonable time within which the Panel must be notified, which, depending on the facts, may range from a few hours to the one-month period. The Executive may also extend the usual one-month period within which the Panel must be notified.[82]

**28.951.07**   The Hearings Committee of the Panel comprises[83] the Chairman, up to three Deputy Chairmen, up to eight other members designated by the Panel, and the individuals appointed by specified bodies.[84] The principal function of the Hearings Committee is to review rulings of the Executive. The Hearings Committee also hears disciplinary proceedings instituted by the Executive if the Executive considers there has been a breach of the Code.[85] The quorum for Hearings Committee proceedings is five. A case is usually presented in person by the parties or their advisers, although parties may be legally represented before the Hearings Committee if they wish. Proceedings are in private, although the chairman may, at his discretion, direct otherwise. Parties may also request that the hearing be held in public. It is the usual policy of the Hearings Committee to publish its rulings by means of a Panel Statement.[86]

*Takeover Appeal Board*

**28.951.08**   Any party may appeal to the Takeover Appeal Board.[87] The Takeover Appeal Board is an independent body that hears appeals against rulings of the Hearings Committee and replaced the former Appeal Committee. The Chairman and Deputy Chairman are appointed by the Master of the Rolls and usually have held high judicial office. The other members of the Takeover Appeal Board are appointed by the Chairman or Deputy Chairman and usually have relevant knowledge and experience of takeovers and the Code. The Takeover Appeal Board has its own rules which are published on its website.[88] The Government took the view, in implementing the Directive, that there was no need to place the Takeover Appeal Board itself on a statutory footing, or to provide for the Takeover Appeal Board to make rules governing appeals.[89] The compatibility of this with the Takeovers Directive may be doubted.[90]

**28.951.09**   Appeals are conducted on an informal basis by way of rehearing and no formal rules of evidence apply.[91] Proceedings before the Appeal Board are held in private, unless the chairman of the hearing, at his discretion, directs otherwise. Any party may, however, request that the hearing be held in public, and such a request shall be considered and ruled upon by the chairman of the hearing (or, at the discretion of the chairman of the hearing, by the Appeal Board itself).[92] Decisions are made by majority

---

[81]   Introduction to the Code, section 7(a).

[82]   Introduction to the Code, section 7(b).

[83]   Introduction to the Code, section 4(c).

[84]   As to which see Introduction to the Code, section 4(a)(iv).

[85]   Introduction to the Code, sections 4(c) and 11(a).

[86]   Introduction to the Code, section 7(c).

[87]   Appeal Board Rule 1.1.

[88]   The Appeal Board's website is at ⟨http://www.thetakeoverappealboard.org.uk⟩.

[89]   *Hansard*, HL, Grand Committee, col 303, Lord Goldsmith (28 March 2006).

[90]   See the cases cited in nn 193 and 194 to para 28.966.25 below. Where a directive creates rights in favour of individuals those rights must be capable of enforcement through binding legal rules. Mere administrative practices or ad hoc arrangements are insufficient.

[91]   Appeal Board Rules 2.8 and 2.9.

[92]   Appeal Board Rule 2.12.

vote with the chairman having a casting vote.[93] However, the Chairman may deal with appeals that he considers to have no reasonable prospect of success without convening the Appeal Board.[94] The Appeal Board may confirm, vary, set aside, annul, or replace the ruling of the Hearings Committee, and shall remit the matter to the Hearings Committee with such directions as the Appeal Board considers appropriate for giving effect to its decision. In an appeal in respect of a disciplinary matter, the Appeal Board may impose any sanction that is available to the Hearings Committee.[95] The Board will provide a written copy of its decision as soon as practicable.[96]

In *Principle Capital Investment Trust PLC*,[97] the Appeal Board held that an appeal is not a *de novo* hearing. The Appeal Board followed the guidance provided by Lindley MR in *Coghlan v Cumberland*:[98]    **28.951.10**

> Even where, as in this case, the appeal turns on a question of fact, the Court of Appeal has to bear in mind that its duty is to rehear the case, and the Court must reconsider the materials before the judge with such other materials as it may have decided to admit. The Court must then make up its own mind, not disregarding the judgment appealed from, but carefully weighing and considering it; and not shrinking from overruling it if on full consideration the Court comes to the conclusion that the judgment is wrong.

The Appeal Board stated that its members were entitled to weigh and consider the decision of the    **28.951.11**
Hearings Committee in order to make up their own minds.[99]

## *Contravention of rules etc*

### 952 Sanctions

(1) Rules may contain provision conferring power on the Panel to impose sanctions on a person who    **28.952.01**
has—
  (a) acted in breach of rules, or
  (b) failed to comply with a direction given by virtue of section 946.
(2) Subsection (3) applies where rules made by virtue of subsection (1) confer power on the Panel to impose a sanction of a kind not provided for by the City Code on Takeovers and Mergers as it had effect immediately before the passing of this Act.
(3) The Panel must prepare a statement (a 'policy statement') of its policy with respect to—
  (a) the imposition of the sanction in question, and
  (b) where the sanction is in the nature of a financial penalty, the amount of the penalty that may be imposed.
An element of the policy must be that, in making a decision about any such matter, the Panel has regard to the factors mentioned in subsection (4).
(4) The factors are—
  (a) the seriousness of the breach or failure in question in relation to the nature of the rule or direction contravened;
  (b) the extent to which the breach or failure was deliberate or reckless;
  (c) whether the person on whom the sanction is to be imposed is an individual.
(5) The Panel may at any time revise a policy statement.
(6) The Panel must prepare a draft of any proposed policy statement (or revised policy statement) and consult such persons about the draft as the Panel considers appropriate.
(7) The Panel must publish, in whatever way it considers appropriate, any policy statement (or revised policy statement) that it prepares.
(8) In exercising, or deciding whether to exercise, its power to impose a sanction within subsection (2) in the case of any particular breach or failure, the Panel must have regard to any relevant policy statement published and in force at the time when the breach or failure occurred.

COMMENCEMENT DATE 6 April 2007[100]

Subsection (1) gives the Panel the power to impose sanctions on persons who act in breach of its rules,    **28.952.02**
or fail to comply with a direction given by the Panel under section 946. Subsection (3) imposes a duty on the Panel to publish a policy statement where it proposes to impose a sanction of a type not provided for by the Code as it had effect immediately before the passing of the Act. Those sanctions were:

---

[93] Appeal Board Rule 2.18.
[94] Appeal Board Rule 1.6(b).
[95] Appeal Board Rule 2.19.
[96] Appeal Board Rule 2.20.
[97] Decision 2010/1 30 April 2010.
[98] [1898] 1 Ch 704, 704–705, CA.
[99] Decision 2010/1 30 April 2010, para 13.
[100] Companies Act 2006 (Commencement No 2, etc) Order 2007, SI 2007/1093, art 2(1)(b).

   (i)  issuing a private statement of censure;

   (ii)  issuing a public statement of censure;

   (iii)  suspending or withdrawing any exemption, approval or other special status which the Panel had granted to a person, or imposing conditions on the continuing enjoyment of such exemption, approval or special status, in respect of all or part of the activities to which such exemption, approval or special status relates;

   (iv)  reporting the offender's conduct to a United Kingdom or overseas regulatory authority or professional body (such as the Financial Services Authority) so that that authority or body can consider whether to take disciplinary or enforcement action; and

   (v)  publishing a statement indicating that the offender is someone who is not likely to comply with the Code. The rules of the FSA,[101] and certain professional bodies oblige their members, in certain circumstances, not to act for such a person in a transaction subject to the Code.[102]

**28.952.03**   It follows that the requirement to publish a policy statement only applies should the Panel decide to impose sanctions of a different kind from those listed above (for example, a fine).[103] In practice, the Panel is likely to consult on any changes to its sanctioning policy, as it has done in the past. The policy statement must include a statement of the Panel's policy with respect to the sanction and, if a financial penalty, the amount of the penalty that can be imposed. The Act also sets out factors that the Panel must have regard to when imposing sanctions. These include the seriousness of the breach or failure in question, the extent to which the breach was deliberate or reckless and whether the person subject to the penalty is an individual. Clearly, the first two factors are aggravating elements. The relevance of the third is less clear as there does not seem to be any reason *a priori* to consider a breach by an individual as less serious than a breach by a company, although the financial means of an individual may be less than those of a company.

**28.952.04**   The Panel has the power to revise a policy statement 'at any time'. However, the revision of a policy statement (as any other act by the Panel) is subject to judicial review, and it is considered that the Panel is not able to revise a policy statement so as to increase the penalty beyond that specified at the time that the relevant conduct was engaged in, at least save in exceptional cases.[104] Where the Panel proposes to adopt a new policy statement, or revise an existing policy statement, it is required to prepare a draft and to consult such persons as the Panel considers appropriate. The intention is that the Panel will seek, and have regard to, the view of interested parties, although it is not bound by any views that are expressed in the course of the consultation.

### 953  Failure to comply with rules about bid documentation

**28.953.01**   (1)  This section applies where a takeover bid is made for a company that has securities carrying voting rights admitted to trading on a regulated market in the United Kingdom.

   (2)  Where an offer document published in respect of the bid does not comply with offer document rules, an offence is committed by—

     (a)  the person making the bid, and

     (b)  where the person making the bid is a body of persons, any director, officer or member of that body who caused the document to be published.

   (3)  A person commits an offence under subsection (2) only if—

     (a)  he knew that the offer document did not comply, or was reckless as to whether it complied, and

     (b)  he failed to take all reasonable steps to secure that it did comply.

   (4)  Where a response document published in respect of the bid does not comply with response document rules, an offence is committed by any director or other officer of the company referred to in subsection (1) who—

---

  [101]  MAR 4.3.1R.

  [101]  Introduction to the Code, para 11(b).

  [103]  *Hansard*, HC, col 802, the Solicitor General (18 July 2006). Any change to the Panel's existing sanctions is a matter for the Panel.

  [104]  This is because such persons would have a legitimate expectation that the policy in force would be followed, at least where it is sufficiently clear. See *R v Liverpool Corporation ex p Liverpool Taxi Fleet Operators' Association* [1972] 2 QB 299; *Attorney-General of Hong Kong v Ng Yuen Shiu* [1983] 2 AC 629; *R v Secretary of State for the Home Department ex p Khan* [1984] 1 WLR 1337; *R v Secretary of State for the Home Department ex p Ruddock* [1987] 1 WLR 1482 and *R v North and East Devon Health Authority ex p Coughlan* [2001] QB 213. See, however, *R v Panel on Takeovers and Mergers ex p Fayed* [1992] BCLC 938 where the 'policy' was found to be insufficiently clearly stated and there were good reasons for departing from it in any event. The matter would seem to be put beyond doubt by subs (8) which requires the Panel to 'have regard to any relevant policy statement published and in force at the time when the breach or failure occurred'.

      (a)  knew that the response document did not comply, or was reckless as to whether it complied, and

      (b)  failed to take all reasonable steps to secure that it did comply.

  (5)  Where an offence is committed under subsection (2)(b) or (4) by a company or other body corporate ('the relevant body')—

      (a)  subsection (2)(b) has effect as if the reference to a director, officer or member of the person making the bid included a reference to a director, officer or member of the relevant body;

      (b)  subsection (4) has effect as if the reference to a director or other officer of the company referred to in subsection (1) included a reference to a director, officer or member of the relevant body.

  (6)  A person guilty of an offence under this section is liable—

      (a)  on conviction on indictment, to a fine;

      (b)  on summary conviction, to a fine not exceeding the statutory maximum.

  (7)  Nothing in this section affects any power of the Panel in relation to the enforcement of its rules.

  (8)  Section 1 (meaning of 'company') does not apply for the purposes of this section.

  (9)  In this section—

      'designated' means designated in rules;

      'offer document' means a document required to be published by rules giving effect to Article 6.2 of the Takeovers Directive;

      'offer document rules' means rules designated as rules that give effect to Article 6.3 of that Directive;

      'response document' means a document required to be published by rules giving effect to Article 9.5 of that Directive;

      'response document rules' means rules designated as rules that give effect to the first sentence of Article 9.5 of that Directive;

      'securities' means shares or debentures;

      'takeover bid' has the same meaning as in that Directive;

      'voting rights' means rights to vote at general meetings of the company in question, including rights that arise only in certain circumstances.

COMMENCEMENT DATE  6 April 2007[105]

This section creates two criminal offences where a person publishes an offer document or a response that does not comply with the documentation requirements in the Takeovers Directive. In the Government's view such an offence was necessary in order to properly implement Article 17 of the Directive, which requires sanctions to be 'effective, proportionate and dissuasive'.[106] For the section to apply there must be (a) a takeover bid (b) for a company (c) that has securities (d) carrying voting rights (e) admitted to trading (f) on a regulated market (g) in the UK. It is therefore restricted to those takeover bids regulated by the Directive. Other situations subject to the Code will be dealt with by either the Panel under its rules or through other legal or regulatory sanctions (eg offences of market manipulation or fraud, or through the imposition of penalties for market abuse under the Financial Services and Markets Act 2000). **28.953.02**

Under the Takeovers Directive, an 'offer document' is a document containing the information necessary to enable the holders of the offeree company's securities to reach a properly informed decision on the bid. Article 6(3) of the Directive requires it to contain at least the following information: **28.953.03**

(a)  the terms of the bid;

(b)  the identity of the offeror and, where the offeror is a company, the type, name and registered office of that company;

(c)  the securities or, where appropriate, the class or classes of securities for which the bid is made;

(d)  the consideration offered for each security or class of securities and, in the case of a mandatory bid, the method employed in determining it, with particulars of the way in which that consideration is to be paid;

(e)  the compensation offered for the rights which might be removed as a result of the breakthrough rule laid down in Article 11(4), with particulars of the way in which that compensation is to be paid and the method employed in determining it;

(f)  the maximum and minimum percentages or quantities of securities which the offeror undertakes to acquire;

(g)  details of any existing holdings of the offeror, and of persons acting in concert with him/her, in the offeree company;

(h)  all the conditions to which the bid is subject;

---

[105]  Companies Act 2006 (Commencement No 2, etc) Order 2007, SI 2007/1093, art 2(1)(b).

[106]  *Hansard*, HL, cols 205–208, Lord Goldsmith (16 May 2006).

(i) the offeror's intentions with regard to the future business of the offeree company and, insofar as it is affected by the bid, the offeror company and with regard to the safeguarding of the jobs of their employees and management, including any material change in the conditions of employment, and in particular the offeror's strategic plans for the two companies and the likely repercussions on employment and the locations of the companies' places of business;

(j) the time allowed for acceptance of the bid;

(k) where the consideration offered by the offeror includes securities of any kind, information concerning those securities;

(l) information concerning the financing for the bid;

(m) the identity of persons acting in concert with the offeror or with the offeree company and, in the case of companies, their types, names, registered offices and relationships with the offeror and, where possible, with the offeree company; and

(n) the national law which will govern contracts concluded between the offeror and the holders of the offeree company's securities as a result of the bid and the competent courts.

These requirements have been implemented through Rule 24 of the Code.

**28.953.04**  The 'response document' is a document prepared by the board of the offeree company setting out its opinion of the bid and the reasons on which it is based, including its views on the effects of implementation of the bid on all the company's interests, and specifically employment, and on the offeror's strategic plans for the offeree company and their likely repercussions on employment and the locations of the company's places of business. The relevant requirements are found in Rule 25 of the Takeover Code.

**28.953.05**  The *actus reus* of the offence is simply non-compliance with the relevant documentation requirements. There is no materiality threshold. Who is liable is governed by subsection (2). This states that an offence is committed by the person making the bid and, where the person making the bid is a body of persons, any director, officer or member of that body who caused the document to be published. In respect of individual defendants, the requirement that the director, officer or member must have caused the document to be published requires a causal nexus between the individual concerned and the publication of the offer document.

**28.953.06**  Concerns were expressed in Parliament as to the category of persons who could commit this offence, and, in particular, whether it extended to corporate advisers where they announce a bid on behalf of an offeror.[107] As a result, the clause was amended during its passage through the House of Lords. Lord Goldsmith, for the Government, stated that the intention was 'to restrict liability for the offence in respect of offer documents to the bidder or any director, officer or member of the bidder who caused the bid document to be published. This has the important consequence of relieving employees and agents of the bidder from potential liability for the offence and the additional costs that might have arisen from this; for example, to professional advisers'.[108] In the House of Commons the Solicitor General added:

> I have made clear our position on agents: we do not intend to criminalise them. We are aware that it has long been City practice that merchant banks deliver the relevant takeover documents. In implementing the Directive, a key objective has been to disturb as little as possible the existing system of takeover regulation in UK and City practice. It is not Government policy to make agents making bids on behalf of bidders potentially liable for the offence... We are aware that concerns remain that agents continue to be caught inadvertently by the offence provision. That stems from the use of the phrase 'person making the bid'. Might that include agents? We do not believe so. It must be taken to mean the person who intends to take over the target company; I say that knowing that the relevant people will refer to my comments.[109]

The Government's intention seems clear that these statements will be admissible under *Pepper v Hart*[110] as an aid to the construction of the section.

**28.953.07**  The *mens rea* is dealt with by subsection (3). There are two alternatives. First, a person will be guilty if he knew that the document did not comply. Secondly, he will be guilty if he was 'reckless'. Case law makes clear that where the word reckless is used as an ingredient in criminal liability this requires advertent recklessness (ie the defendant appreciated that there was a risk of non-compliance and

---

[107] *Hansard*, HL, Grand Committee, cols 307–310 (28 March 2006).
[108] *Hansard*, HL, col 211 (16 May 2006).
[109] *Hansard*, HC, cols 805–807 (18 July 2006).
[110] [1993] AC 593. The House of Lords permitted reference to Hansard where three conditions are met: (a) legislation was ambiguous or obscure or led to absurdity; (b) the material relied upon consisted of one or more statements by a Minister or other promoter of the Bill together if necessary with such other Parliamentary material as was necessary to understand such statements and their effect; and (c) the statements relied upon were clear. It is considered that all three requirements are met in this case.

decided to run the risk nonetheless).[111] Failure to give any thought to the matter is not recklessness, however negligent such conduct may be considered to be. The defendant must also have failed to take all reasonable steps to secure that the document did comply. This is an additional requirement. What is reasonable will depend on the circumstances and it is considered that the defendant's role in the preparation of the document, as well as his level of responsibility for the document, will be material. Clearly proper standards are expected to be maintained in the preparation of bid documentation and it is considered that the court will be slow to accept a defence based on alleged practical difficulties in complying with the requirements.

In terms of the response, as the Directive squarely places responsibility on the board of the offeree **28.953.08** company, it is likely to be a rare case for a director or officer to escape liability under subsection (4)(b) given the board's collective responsibility for the response. The prosecution will still need to satisfy subsection (4)(a) and show that the defendant knew or was reckless as to the infringement.

As with other criminal offences, the prosecution bears the burden of establishing guilt beyond **28.953.09** reasonable doubt. This, coupled with the delay and cost of criminal proceedings, compared with enforcement action by the Panel under the Code, suggests that prosecution is likely to be confined to clear cases of a failure to meet the necessary requirements, or to those situations where there is significant public detriment. Nonetheless, the existence of criminal sanctions may be expected to have a prophylactic effect in encouraging persons involved with bid documentation to maintain the required standards. One situation where the Government considered prosecution would be appropriate was in respect of serious or deliberate misstatements that come to light only some time after a bid has been completed. Another is where the misstatements related to third parties who may be affected by the bid but who have no contractual rights in respect of it (eg employees).[112]

Subsection (7) makes clear that the power to prosecute is without prejudice to the right of the Panel to **28.953.10** investigate and discipline persons for breaches of its rules.

## 954  Compensation

(1)  Rules may confer power on the Panel to order a person to pay such compensation as it thinks just       **28.954.01**
     and reasonable if he is in breach of a rule the effect of which is to require the payment of money.
(2)  Rules made by virtue of this section may include provision for the payment of interest (including
     compound interest).

COMMENCEMENT DATE  6 April 2007[113]

This section confers a statutory power on the Panel to make rules requiring the payment of compen- **28.954.02** sation for certain breaches of its rules. The Introduction to the Code states in this respect:

> Where a person has breached the requirements of any of Rules 6, 9, 11, 14, 15, 16.1 or 35.3 of the Code, the Panel may make a ruling requiring the person concerned to pay, within such period as is specified, to the holders, or former holders, of securities of the offeree company such amount as it thinks just and reasonable so as to ensure that such holders receive what they would have been entitled to receive if the relevant Rule had been complied with.[114]

The consideration of these rules is outside the scope of this commentary.

The Panel has no free-standing power to order the payment of compensation and the Attorney- **28.954.03** General stated in Parliament that the Government 'did not want the panel to become a body to whom any party with a grievance about a takeover bid process could turn in search of financial recompense'.[115]

## 955  Enforcement by the court

(1)  If, on the application of the Panel, the court is satisfied—                                              **28.955.01**
     (a)  that there is a reasonable likelihood that a person will contravene a rule-based requirement,
          or
     (b)  that a person has contravened a rule-based requirement or a disclosure requirement,
     the court may make any order it thinks fit to secure compliance with the requirement.
(2)  In subsection (1) 'the court' means the High Court or, in Scotland, the Court of Session.
(3)  Except as provided by subsection (1), no person—

---

[111]  *R v G* [2004] 1 AC 1034 departing from *R v Caldwell* [1982] AC 341. See, by way of confirmation, *Attorney General's Reference (No 3 of 2003)* [2005] 1 QB 73.
[112]  *Hansard*, HC, col 805, the Solicitor General (18 July 2006).
[113]  Companies Act 2006 (Commencement No 2, etc) Order 2007, SI 2007/1093, art 2(1)(b).
[114]  Section 10(c).
[115]  *Hansard*, HL, Grand Committee, col 311 (28 March 2006).

    (a)  has a right to seek an injunction, or

    (b)  in Scotland, has title or interest to seek an interdict or an order for specific performance,

to prevent a person from contravening (or continuing to contravene) a rule-based requirement or a disclosure requirement.

  (4)  In this section—

    'contravene' includes fail to comply;

    'disclosure requirement' means a requirement imposed under section 947;

    'rule-based requirement' means a requirement imposed by or under rules.

COMMENCEMENT DATE 6 April 2007[116]

**28.955.02**    This section bolsters the enforcement powers of the Panel by enabling the Panel to apply to the court to prevent or terminate infringements of its rules. This is intended as a long stop where the Panel's other powers prove inadequate to secure compliance with the Code and is only likely to be used as a matter of last resort or in urgent cases.[117] The Panel must satisfy the court (on the balance of probabilities) either (a) that there is a reasonable likelihood that a person will contravene a requirement imposed by or under the Panel's rules; (b) that a person has contravened such a requirement; or (c) that he has failed to make disclosure as required by section 947.

**28.955.03**    According to the explanatory notes on the Act, 'It is expected that in accordance with usual practice, the court will not, in exercising its jurisdiction under this section, rehear substantively the matter or examine the issues giving rise to the ruling or, as the case may be, the request for documents or information except on "judicial review principles", where there has been an error of law or procedure'.[118]

**28.955.04**    Subsection (3) makes clear that only the Panel has power to apply to the court for an injunction or (in Scotland) interdict. The intention is that the Panel should be the sole arbiter of infringements of its rules, and seems motivated by concerns that third parties might otherwise attempt to use the Panel's enforcement powers as a tactical device in a bid situation.

### 956  No action for breach of statutory duty etc

**28.956.01**    (1)  Contravention of a rule-based requirement or a disclosure requirement does not give rise to any right of action for breach of statutory duty.

  (2)  Contravention of a rule-based requirement does not make any transaction void or unenforceable or (subject to any provision made by rules) affect the validity of any other thing.

  (3)  In this section—

    (a)  'contravention' includes failure to comply;

    (b)  'disclosure requirement' and 'rule-based requirement' have the same meaning as in section 955.

COMMENCEMENT DATE 6 April 2007[119]

**28.956.02**    Section 956 is supplementary to section 955 and reinforces the position of the Panel as the sole body responsible for the enforcement of its rules. Subsection (1) provides that contravention of a 'rule-based requirement' (ie one of the Panel's rules) or a 'disclosure requirement' (a disclosure obligation under section 947) does not give rise to any action for breach of statutory duty. It follows that a third party will be unable to recover damages for any loss caused as a result of such breaches.

**28.956.03**    Subsection (2) provides that such contravention does not make any transaction void or unenforceable or (subject to any provision made by rules) affect the validity of any other thing. It follows that (subject to any provision to the contrary in the Code) no party will be able to argue that a breach of the Code, or an illegal disclosure, makes a contract illegal or unenforceable. This is without prejudice to any rights arising under the general law (eg rescission for misrepresentation).

*Funding*

### 957  Fees and charges

**28.957.01**    (1)  Rules may provide for fees or charges to be payable to the Panel for the purpose of meeting any part of its expenses.

---

[116]  Companies Act 2006 (Commencement No 2, etc) Order 2007, SI 2007/1093, art 2(1)(b).

[117]  G Morse, Proposed Amendments to the Takeovers Code to Implement the 13th EC Directive [2006] JBL 242, 244.

[118]  Para 1212.

[119]  Companies Act 2006 (Commencement No 2, etc) Order 2007, SI 2007/1093, art 2(1)(b).

(2) A reference in this section or section 958 to expenses of the Panel is to any expenses that have been or are to be incurred by the Panel in, or in connection with, the discharge of its functions, including in particular—

(a) payments in respect of the expenses of the Takeover Appeal Board;

(b) the cost of repaying the principal of, and of paying any interest on, any money borrowed by the Panel;

(c) the cost of maintaining adequate reserves.

COMMENCEMENT DATE  6 April 2007[120]

This section gives the Panel statutory authority to levy fees. This is necessary as at common law a   **28.957.02**
private or public body has no power to impose fees in the absence of a contractual agreement to do
so.[121] Currently the Panel is funded through charges on offer documents and the PTM Levy on certain
transactions and exempt/recognized intermediary charges.

## 958 Levy

(1) For the purpose of meeting any part of the expenses of the Panel, the Secretary of State may by   **28.958.01**
regulations provide for a levy to be payable to the Panel—

(a) by specified persons or bodies, or persons or bodies of a specified description, or

(b) on transactions, of a specified description, in securities on specified markets.

In this subsection 'specified' means specified in the regulations.

(2) The power to specify (or to specify descriptions of) persons or bodies must be exercised in such a way that the levy is payable only by persons or bodies that appear to the Secretary of State—

(a) to be capable of being directly affected by the exercise of any of the functions of the Panel, or

(b) otherwise to have a substantial interest in the exercise of any of those functions.

(3) Regulations under this section may in particular—

(a) specify the rate of the levy and the period in respect of which it is payable at that rate;

(b) make provision as to the times when, and the manner in which, payments are to be made in respect of the levy.

(4) In determining the rate of the levy payable in respect of a particular period, the Secretary of State—

(a) must take into account any other income received or expected by the Panel in respect of that period;

(b) may take into account estimated as well as actual expenses of the Panel in respect of that period.

(5) The Panel must—

(a) keep proper accounts in respect of any amounts of levy received by virtue of this section;

(b) prepare, in relation to each period in respect of which any such amounts are received, a statement of account relating to those amounts in such form and manner as is specified in the regulations.

Those accounts must be audited, and the statement certified, by persons appointed by the Secretary of State.

(6) Regulations under this section—

(a) are subject to affirmative resolution procedure if subsection (7) applies to them;

(b) otherwise, are subject to negative resolution procedure.

(7) This subsection applies to—

(a) the first regulations under this section;

(b) any other regulations under this section that would result in a change in the persons or bodies by whom, or the transactions on which, the levy is payable.

(8) If a draft of an instrument containing regulations under this section would, apart from this subsection, be treated for the purposes of the Standing Orders of either House of Parliament as a hybrid instrument, it is to proceed in that House as if it were not such an instrument.

COMMENCEMENT DATE  For the purpose of exercising the power to make regulations: 20 January 2007.
Otherwise 6 April 2007.[122]

Section 958 enables the Secretary of State to make regulations providing for a levy to be payable to the   **28.958.02**
Panel (a) by specified persons or bodies, or persons or bodies of a specified description, or (b) on
transactions, of a specified description, in securities on specified markets. The purpose is to enable the
costs of the Panel to be met by persons engaged in takeover-related activity. To ensure that only such

---

[120]  Companies Act 2006 (Commencement No 2, etc) Order 2007, SI 2007/1093, art 2(1)(b).

[121]  See *McCarthy & Stone (Developments) Ltd v Richmond-upon-Thames London Borough Council* [1992] 2
AC 48 and *Attorney General v Wilts United Dairies Ltd* (1922) 91 LJ KB 897 affg (1921) 37 TLR 884.

[122]  Companies Act 2006 (Commencement No 2, etc) Order 2007, SI 2007/1093, art 2(1)(b).

persons are required to pay the levy subsection (2) provides that power to specify persons or bodies must be exercised in such a way that the levy is payable only by persons or bodies that appear to the Secretary of State (a) to be capable of being directly affected by the exercise of any of the functions of the Panel, or (b) otherwise to have a substantial interest in the exercise of those functions. This is a subjective test as the levy is payable by persons or bodies *that appear to the Secretary of State* to be involved in such action, whether or not they in fact are. The purpose, apparently, is to insulate the Secretary of State's decision from judicial challenge, although the regulations are subject to Parliamentary scrutiny. No regulations have yet been made under this provision.

**28.958.03**   Subsection (3) deals with the amount of the levy. Regulations may specify the rate of the levy and the period in respect of which it is payable at that rate and make provision as to the times when, and the manner in which, payments are to be made. Subsection (4) requires the Secretary of State, when determining the rate of the levy, to take into account any other income received or expected by the Panel in respect of that period. Additionally, he may (but need not) take into account estimated as well as actual expenses of the Panel.

**28.958.04**   Subsection (5) imposes a statutory duty on the Panel to keep proper accounts and to prepare an audited statement of account in respect of amounts received through the levy.

**28.958.05**   The first regulations made under this section are subject to affirmative resolution. This requires an affirmative resolution by both Houses of Parliament.[123] The same applies to any amendments that would result in a change in the persons or bodies by whom, or the transactions on which, the levy is payable. In all other cases the negative resolution procedure applies in which case the regulations will come into effect unless annulled by either House of Parliament.[124]

**28.958.06**   Subsection (8) refers to Standing Orders of either House of Parliament dealing with hybrid instruments. Currently, only the House of Lords has in place such a standing order (Lords Private Business Standing Order 216). This states that where, in the opinion of the Chairman of Committees, an affirmative instrument is such that, apart from the provisions of the Act authorizing it to be made, it would require to be enacted by a private or hybrid bill, he shall report his opinion to the House and the Minister or other person responsible for it. The instrument is then subject to a petitioning procedure. Any petitions made not to affirm a hybrid instrument, together with the instrument, are then referred to the Hybrid Instruments Committee. This Committee may consider representations and hold hearings before reporting back to the House of Lords. If the Hybrid Instruments Committee considers that there ought to be a further inquiry, the House may refer any or all matters to a select committee of five lords with orders of reference specified by the House.[125] The reason for subsection (8) is to prevent this procedure from applying as it would otherwise be necessary given the Panel's status as a private law body exercising statutory powers.

### 959  Recovery of fees, charges or levy

**28.959.01**   An amount payable by any person or body by virtue of section 957 or 958 is a debt due from that person or body to the Panel, and is recoverable accordingly.

   COMMENCEMENT DATE 6 April 2007[126]

**28.959.02**   Section 959 enables fees and levies payable to the Panel under section 957 and 958 to be enforced as a debt in civil proceedings. The procedure is the same as that for liquidated claims under the Civil Procedure Rules 1998.

### *Miscellaneous and supplementary*

### 960  Panel as party to proceedings

**28.960.01**      The Panel is capable (despite being an unincorporated body) of—

      (a)  bringing proceedings under this Chapter in its own name;
      (b)  bringing or defending any other proceedings in its own name.

   COMMENCEMENT DATE 6 April 2007[127]

---

[123] Section 1290.
[124] Section 1289.
[125] This description is based on W McKay (ed), *Erskine May's Parliamentary Practice* (24th edn, London, 2011) 684–685.
[126] Companies Act 2006 (Commencement No 2, etc) Order 2007, SI 2007/1093, art 2(1)(b).
[127] Companies Act 2006 (Commencement No 2, etc) Order 2007, SI 2007/1093, art 2(1)(b).

At common law, an unincorporated association cannot sue or be sued in its own name.[128] However, **28.960.02**
where numerous persons have the same interest, proceedings can be begun and, unless the court orders
otherwise, continued by or against one or more of the members as representatives of the other
members or some of them.[129] This would clearly be inconvenient, so Parliament has provided that the
Panel can both sue and be sued in its own name. However, the Act does not incorporate the Panel or
otherwise affect its status or composition.

## 961   Exemption from liability in damages

(1)   Neither the Panel, nor any person within subsection (2), is to be liable in damages for anything      **28.961.01**
       done (or omitted to be done) in, or in connection with, the discharge or purported discharge of
       the Panel's functions.
(2)   A person is within this subsection if—
       (a)   he is (or is acting as) a member, officer or member of staff of the Panel, or
       (b)   he is a person authorised under section 947(5).
(3)   Subsection (1) does not apply—
       (a)   if the act or omission is shown to have been in bad faith, or
       (b)   so as to prevent an award of damages in respect of the act or omission on the ground that it
             was unlawful as a result of section 6(1) of the Human Rights Act 1998 (c. 42) (acts of public
             authorities incompatible with Convention rights).

COMMENCEMENT DATE  6 April 2007[130]

This is an example of a type of provision that has become increasingly common in recent years which    **28.961.02**
seeks to insulate public bodies from civil liability as a result of their negligence or breach of duty. Other
examples include the immunities conferred on the Financial Services Authority,[131] recognized investment exchanges, and recognized clearing houses.[132]

Subsection (1) gives immunity to the Panel for anything done (or omitted to be done) in or in    **28.961.03**
connection with the discharge, or purported discharge, of the Panel's functions. This is very broad and
it is difficult to imagine the Panel taking action related to the conduct of a bid that is not in or in
connection with the discharge, or purported discharge, of its functions. Arguably, running a separate
business connected to takeovers would also be covered (eg publishing statistics about takeover activity
in different countries). However, it is considered that running a commercial business unrelated to
takeover activity (eg a pizza parlour), or publishing a newspaper, would fall outside the scope of the
immunity.

Subsection (2) extends the immunity to members, officers, and staff of the Panel, as well as any person    **28.961.04**
authorized by the Panel to obtain information under section 947(5).

There are two exceptions to the statutory immunity. First, there is no immunity if the act or omission    **28.961.05**
is shown to have been in bad faith. It should be noted that while bad faith is a ground for judicial review
under English law, and is therefore a basis for challenging administrative action, it is not itself a ground
of civil liability. It follows that to bring a claim for damages against the Panel it is not sufficient to allege
bad faith. A specific tort will still need to be identified and pleaded in the claim form. In many cases the
appropriate cause of action is likely to be misfeasance in public office. The requirements of this tort
were authoritatively stated by the House of Lords in *Three Rivers District Council v Bank of England (No
3)*.[133] It requires the deliberate abuse of power by a public officer, either intending to injure the victim,
or in the knowledge that his actions are unlawful and that they will probably injure the victim. In
certain cases other intentional torts could also be relevant (eg conspiracy, libel, etc). Though 'bad faith'
will often involve dishonesty[134] the terms are not synonymous, as a member of the Panel could

---

[128]   *London Association for Protection of Trade v Greenlands Ltd* [1916] 2 AC 15; *Grossman v Granville Club*
(1884) 28 Sol Jo 513.
[129]   *Halsbury's Laws of England*, 5th edn (London, 2009), Clubs, para 279 citing CPR 19.6.
[130]   Companies Act 2006 (Commencement No 2, etc) Order 2007, SI 2007/1093, art 2(1)(b).
[131]   Financial Services and Markets Act 2000, Sch 1, para 19. The Financial Services Act 2013 will repeal Sch 1.
However, a similar immunity will apply to the FCA (Sch 1ZA, para 25) and the PRA (Sch 1ZB, para 33).
[132]   Financial Services and Markets Act 2000, s 291. For the Coalition Government's intention to continue this
approach see *A New Approach to Financial Regulation: the Blueprint for Reform*, Cm 8083, June 2011, para 2.37
(securities settlement systems) and para 2.39 (payment systems).
[133]   [2003] 2 AC 1.
[134]   For the conflict between *Twinsectra v Yardley* [2002] 2 AC 164 and *Barlow Clowes International Ltd v
Eurotrust* [2006] 1 WLR 1476, see *Abou-Rahmah v Abacha* [2007] 1 Lloyd's Rep 115, *Starglade Properties Ltd v
Roland Nash* [2011] Lloyd's Rep FC 102 and *Secretary of State for Justice v Topland Group PLC* [2011] EWHC 983
(QB) judgment dated 18 April 2011.

consider that unlawful conduct that injures a particular individual or company serves the public interest more generally. Such a belief will not negate a finding of bad faith.

**28.961.06**    The second exception to the immunity is where it would prevent an award of damages in respect of an act or omission that is unlawful under section 6(1) of the Human Rights Act 1998. This is intended to avoid the risk of any breach of the European Convention on Human Rights. The reader should consult specialist works on the Convention to determine when such a claim may be brought.[135]

### 962 Privilege against self-incrimination

**28.962.01**    (1) A statement made by a person in response to—
    (a) a requirement under section 947(1), or
    (b) an order made by the court under section 955 to secure compliance with such a requirement,
    may not be used against him in criminal proceedings in which he is charged with an offence to which this subsection applies.
    (2) Subsection (1) applies to any offence other than an offence under one of the following provisions (which concern false statements made otherwise than on oath)—
    (a) section 5 of the Perjury Act 1911 (c. 6);
    (b) section 44(2) of the Criminal Law (Consolidation) (Scotland) Act 1995 (c. 39);
    (c) Article 10 of the Perjury (Northern Ireland) Order 1979 (S.I. 1979/1714 (N.I. 19)).

COMMENCEMENT DATE 6 April 2007[136]

**28.962.02**    Section 962 preserves the common law privilege against self-incrimination. It provides that a statement made by a person pursuant to a request under section 947, or pursuant to a court order to comply with such a request, is inadmissible in criminal proceedings against him. The only exception is prosecution for perjury in making the statement. This gives effect to the judgment of the European Court of Human Rights in *Saunders v United Kingdom*.[137]

### 963 Annual reports

**28.963.01**    (1) After the end of each financial year the Panel must publish a report.
    (2) The report must—
    (a) set out how the Panel's functions were discharged in the year in question;
    (b) include the Panel's accounts for that year;
    (c) mention any matters the Panel considers to be of relevance to the discharge of its functions.

COMMENCEMENT DATE 6 April 2007[138]

**28.963.02**    This section requires the Panel to publish an annual report. The report must include the Panel's accounts as well as any matters the Panel considers to be of relevance to the discharge of its functions. The latter will enable the Panel to publish details of its activities. The Panel has in fact published an annual report since its inception and copies of the Panel's annual reports since 1969 are available on its website.

### 964 Amendments to Financial Services and Markets Act 2000

**28.964.01**    (1) The Financial Services and Markets Act 2000 (c. 8) is amended as follows.
    (2) Section 143 (power to make rules endorsing the City Code on Takeovers and Mergers etc) is repealed.
    (3) In section 144 (power to make price stabilising rules), for subsection (7) substitute—
    '(7) "Consultation procedures" means procedures designed to provide an opportunity for persons likely to be affected by alterations to those provisions to make representations about proposed alterations to any of those provisions.'
    (4) In section 349 (exceptions from restrictions on disclosure of confidential information), after subsection (3) insert—
      '(3A) Section 348 does not apply to—
      (a) the disclosure by a recipient to which subsection (3B) applies of confidential information disclosed to it by the Authority[139] in reliance on subsection (1);
      (b) the disclosure of such information by a person obtaining it directly or indirectly from a recipient to which subsection (3B) applies.

---

[135] See eg J Beatson et al, *Human Rights: Judicial Protection in the United Kingdom* (London, 2008) and A Lester et al *Human Rights Law and Practice* 3rd edn (London, 2009).
[136] Companies Act 2006 (Commencement No 2, etc) Order 2007, SI 2007/1093, art 2(1)(b).
[137] (1996) 23 EHRR 313.
[138] Companies Act 2006 (Commencement No 2, etc) Order 2007, SI 2007/1093, art 2(1)(b).
[139] The Financial Services Act 2012 will substitute for the reference to the Authority a reference to 'FCA or PRA' from such day as the Treasury may by order appoint: Sched 18, para 118.

        (3B) This subsection applies to—

           (a) the Panel on Takeovers and Mergers;

           (b) an authority designated as a supervisory authority for the purposes of Article 4.1 of the Takeovers Directive;

           (c) any other person or body that exercises public functions, under legislation in an EEA State other than the United Kingdom, that are similar to the Authority's[140] functions or those of the Panel on Takeovers and Mergers.'

     (5) In section 354 (Financial Services Authority's duty to co-operate with others), after subsection (1) insert—

   '(1A) The Authority must take such steps as it considers appropriate to cooperate with—

           (a) the Panel on Takeovers and Mergers;

           (b) an authority designated as a supervisory authority for the purposes of Article 4.1 of the Takeovers Directive;

           (c) any other person or body that exercises functions of a public nature, under legislation in any country or territory outside the United Kingdom, that appear to the Authority to be similar to those of the Panel on Takeovers and Mergers.'[141]

     (6) In section 417(1) (definitions), insert at the appropriate place—

       'Takeovers Directive' means Directive 2004/25/EC of the European Parliament and of the Council;'.

COMMENCEMENT DATE 6 April 2007[142]

Section 964 makes a number of amendments to the Financial Services and Markets Act 2000 as a result of placing the Panel on a statutory footing.    **28.964.02**

Subsection (2) repeals section 143. This section enabled the FSA to exercise disciplinary powers over authorized persons for breach of certain provisions of the Code and the rules on the Substantial Acquisition of Shares (SARs) (now repealed). The procedure involved the FSA designating provisions of the Code and SARs (which was done through MAR 4 in the Market Conduct volume of the FSA's Handbook of Rules and Guidance). Under section 143, the FSA could only take action where requested to do so by the Panel. This formed part of the indirect method for enforcement of the Panel's rules. Since the Panel may now take action directly for breaches of the Code the procedure set out in section 143 has become redundant. It should be noted that a breach by an authorized person of the Code may still be actionable by the FSA. This is because such a breach is likely to involve a contravention of the FSA's Principles for Business[143] (volume PRIN of the FSA's Handbook of Rules and Guidance). The Panel continues to be able to report breaches of the Code to the FSA. Once the FSA is abolished in 2013 this responsibility will pass to the FCA.    **28.964.03**

Subsection (3) follows on from the repeal of the definition of 'consultation procedures' in section 143. There is no change to the existing law.    **28.964.04**

Subsection (4) enables the FSA to share information with the Panel. Section 348 of the Financial Services and Markets Act 2000 sets out restrictions on the disclosure of confidential information by the FSA. The exceptions, which permit the sharing of information, are found in section 349. Subsections (3A) and (3B) (as inserted) enable disclosure by the FSA to the Panel, an authority designated as a supervisory authority for the purposes of Article 4.1 of the Takeovers Directive and any other person or body that exercises public functions, under legislation in an EEA State other than the UK, that are similar to the FSA's functions or those of the Panel. The Financial Services Act 2012 will substitute references to the FSA with references to the FCA and PRA following abolition of the FSA.[144]    **28.964.05**

Subsection (5) has a similar purpose. Section 354 of the Financial Services and Markets Act 2000 imposes a duty on the FSA to co-operate with other bodies exercising functions similar to the FSA, or involved in the prevention or detection of financial crime. Following the abolition of the FSA, this duty will pass to the FCA.    **28.964.06**

---

[140]  The Financial Services Act 2012 will substitute for the reference to the Authority's functions a reference to 'functions of the FCA or PRA' from such day as the Treasury may by order appoint: Sched 18, para 118 .

[141]  The Financial Services Act 2012 will repeal section 354 FSMA 2000 and add a new section 354A imposing an equivalent duty of co-operation on the FCA from such day as the Treasury may by order appoint: Sched 12, para 25.

[142]  Companies Act 2006 (Commencement No 2, etc) Order 2007, SI 2007/1093, art 2(1)(b).

[143]  Especially, Principle 5 (market conduct).

[144]  See nn 140 and 141 above.

**28.964.07** Subsection (5) adds to this list the Panel as well as other bodies in EEA States exercising similar powers. Subsection (6) adds a new definition in respect of the Takeovers Directive.

### 965　Power to extend to Isle of Man and Channel Islands

**28.965.01** Her Majesty may by Order in Council direct that any of the provisions of this Chapter extend, with such modifications as may be specified in the Order, to the Isle of Man or any of the Channel Islands.

> COMMENCEMENT DATE 20 January 2007 for the purpose of enabling the exercise of power to make regulations, and 6 April 2007 for all other purposes.[145]

**28.965.02** This section enables the provisions of Chapter 1 of Part 28 to be extended to the Isle of Man and the Channel Islands.

### Isle of Man

**28.965.03** The jurisdiction of the Panel was extended to the Isle of Man by the Companies Act 2006 (Extension of Takeover Provisions) (Isle of Man) Order 2008[146] ('the Order') with effect from 1 March 2009.[147] The Order makes a number of modifications to the application of Chapter 1 of Part 28 to reflect differences in the legal system and governmental and regulatory structures of the Isle of Man. The Order provides for the exchange of information about takeovers with the Panel and relevant authorities in the Isle of Man and elsewhere. The more important modifications are noted briefly below. The order was amended by the Companies Act 2006 (Extension of Takeover Panel Provisions) (Isle of Man) Order 2009, SI 2009/1378 with effect from 1 July 2009. This deleted the specific provisions in the Order dealing with disclosure of information arising from the exercise by the Panel of its functions and extended Schedule 2 to the Isle of Man. This was consequent to the replacement of Schedule 2 by the Companies Act 2006 (Amendment of Schedule 2) (No 2) Order 2009, SI 2009/1208.

### Restrictions on disclosure

**28.965.04** Subsections (4) and (5) of section 948, which permit the Secretary of State to modify the list of permitted disclosures set out in Schedule 2 by order, do not apply to the Isle of Man.[148] A disclosure may be made by the Financial Services Commission of the Isle of Man, as well as any other person or body who has obtained the information directly or indirectly from the Commission.[149] The reference to the Data Protection Act 1998 is substituted by a reference to the relevant Manx legislation.[150]

### Punishment for improper disclosure

**28.965.05** Section 949 is modified to reflect the Manx legal system.[151] The maximum penalty on summary conviction is custody for a term not exceeding six months and/or a fine not exceeding £5,000.[152]

### Panel's duty of co-operation

**28.965.06** The Panel has a duty of co-operation with the Financial Services Commission of the Isle of Man.[153]

### Failure to comply with rules about bid documentation

**28.965.07** Section 953(6) is modified to reflect the Manx legal system.[154] The maximum penalty on summary conviction is fixed at £5,000.[155]

---

[145]　Companies Act 2006 (Commencement No 2, etc) Order 2007, SI 2007/1093, art 2(1)(b).

[146]　SI 2008/3122.

[147]　Companies Act 2006 (Extension of Takeover Panel Provisions) (Isle of Man) Order 2008, SI 2008/3122, art 1.

[148]　Companies Act 2006 (Extension of Takeover Panel Provisions) (Isle of Man) Order 1008, SI 2008/3122, Sch, para 1(a).

[149]　Companies Act 2006 (Extension of Takeover Panel Provisions) (Isle of Man) Order 1008, SI 2008/3122, Sch, para 1(b). See para 28.948.09 below for commentary.

[150]　Companies Act 2006 (Extension of Takeover Panel Provisions) (Isle of Man) Order 1008, SI 2008/3122, Sch, para 1(c) referring to the Data Protection Act 2002 (an Act of Tynwald: c 2).

[151]　Companies Act 2006 (Extension of Takeover Panel Provisions) (Isle of Man) Order 1008, SI 2008/3122, Sch, para 2(a).

[152]　Companies Act 2006 (Extension of Takeover Panel Provisions) (Isle of Man) Order 1008, SI 2008/3122, Sch, para 2(b).

[153]　Companies Act 2006 (Extension of Takeover Panel Provisions) (Isle of Man) Order 1008, SI 2008/3122, Sch, para 3.

[154]　Companies Act 2006 (Extension of Takeover Panel Provisions) (Isle of Man) Order 1008, SI 2008/3122, Sch, para 4(a).

[155]　Ibid, Sch, para 4(b).

*Enforcement by the court*

The power in section 955 to enforce the Panel's rules in the Isle of Man is vested in the High Court of     **28.965.08**
the Isle of Man.[156] Judgments of the High Court, including the Staff of Government Division, are
enforceable by registration in the United Kingdom under Part I of the Foreign Judgments (Reciprocal
Enforcement) Act 1933,[157] but not otherwise.[158]

*Exemption from liability in damages*

The Panel's exemption from liability in damages under section 961 does not apply in respect of an act     **28.965.09**
or omission on the grounds that it was unlawful as a result of section 6(1) of the Human Rights Act 2001
(an Act of Tynwald: c 1).[159]

*Exceptions to the privilege against self-incrimination*

This exception applies to an offence under section 5 of the Perjury Act 1952 (an Act of Tynwald:     **28.965.10**
Volume XVIII of the Isle of Man Statutes, p 86).[160]

*Amendments to Financial Services Act 2008 (an Act of Tynwald)*

Section 964 amends the Financial Services and Markets Act 2000.[161] This Act does not apply to the Isle     **28.965.11**
of Man.[162] Paragraph 8(3) of the Schedule to the Order, however, makes a number of changes to the
equivalent legislation in the Isle of Man.

The functions of the Financial Supervision Commission are amended to include a duty to take such     **28.965.12**
steps as it considers appropriate to co-operate with (a) the Panel, (b) an authority designated as a
supervisory authority for the purposes of Article 4(1) of the Takeovers Directive, and (c) any other
person or body which exercises functions of a public nature, under legislation, in any country or
territory outside of the British Isles, that appear to the Commission to be similar to those of the
Panel.[163] This corresponds to section 964(5) of the Act. For commentary see paragraph 28.964.06
above.

Paragraph 8(4) amends the restrictions on disclosure in Schedule 5, paragraph 2 to the Financial     **28.965.13**
Services Act 2008 (an Act of Tynwald: c 8) to permit disclosure of confidential information to (a) the
Panel, (b) an authority designated as a supervisory authority for the purposes of Article 4(1) of the
Takeovers Directive, and (c) any other person or body which exercises functions of a public nature,
under legislation, in any country or territory outside of the British Isles, that appear to the Commission
to be similar to those of the Panel.[164] This corresponds to section 964(4) of the Act. For commentary see
paragraph 28.964.05 above.

*Application of Schedule 2 of the Act*

Paragraphs 9 and 10 of the Order made provision for the disclosure by the Panel of information. These     **28.965.14**
provisions have now been repealed and the ability of the Panel to make disclosures in relation to the Isle
of Man is found in Schedule 2, which has been extended to the Isle of Man.[165] See Chapter 48 and the
commentary on Schedule 2.

---

[156] Companies Act 2006 (Extension of Takeover Panel Provisions) (Isle of Man) Order 1008, SI 2008/3122,
Sch, para 5.

[157] Reciprocal Enforcement of Foreign Judgments (Isle of Man) Order 1973, SI 1973/611.

[158] Foreign Judgments (Reciprocal Enforcement) Act 1933, s 6 precludes a court in the United Kingdom from
entertaining proceedings for the recovery of a sum payable under a foreign judgment to which Part 1 of the 1933
Act applies other than through proceedings by way of registration of the judgment. Section 34 of the Civil
Jurisdiction and Judgments Act 1982 precludes a claim on the original cause of action.

[159] Companies Act 2006 (Extension of Takeover Panel Provisions) (Isle of Man) Order 2008, SI 2008/3122,
Sch, para 6.

[160] Companies Act 2006 (Extension of Takeover Panel Provisions) (Isle of Man) Order 1008, SI 2008/3122,
Sch, para 7.

[161] For text see para 28.964.01 above and commentary to paras 28.964.02–28.964.07 above.

[162] Financial Services and Markets Act 2000, s 430.

[163] Financial Services Act 2008 (an Act of Tynwald), Sch 1, para 2(1)(ea) and (1A); as substituted by
Companies Act 2006 (Extension of Takeover Panel Provisions) (Isle of Man) Order 2008, SI 2008/3122, Sch, para
8(3).

[164] Financial Services Act 2008 (an Act of Tynwald), Sch 5, para 2(A) and 4(B); as substituted by Companies
Act 2006 (Extension of Takeover Panel Provisions) (Isle of Man) Order 2008, SI 2008/3122, Sch, para 8(4).

[165] SI 2009/1378, art 2 with effect from 1 July 2009.

*Jersey*

**28.965.15**    The Panel has been appointed by the Companies (Appointment of Takeovers and Mergers Panel) (Jersey) Order 2009 under Article 2 of the Companies (Takeovers and Mergers Panel) (Jersey) Law 2009 to carry out certain functions in relation to takeovers and mergers under Jersey law. The rules set out in the Code have statutory effect in Jersey.[166]

*Guernsey*

**28.965.16**    The Panel has been appointed by the Companies (Guernsey) Law 2008 to carry out certain functions in relation to takeovers and mergers under Guernsey law. The rules set out in the Code have statutory effect in Guernsey.[167]

CHAPTER 2

IMPEDIMENTS TO TAKEOVERS

*Opting in and opting out*

### 966 Opting in and opting out

**28.966.01**    (1)  A company may by special resolution (an 'opting-in resolution') opt in for the purposes of this Chapter if the following three conditions are met in relation to the company.

(2)  The first condition is that the company has voting shares admitted to trading on a regulated market.

(3)  The second condition is that—

    (a)  the company's articles of association—

        (i)  do not contain any such restrictions as are mentioned in Article 11 of the Takeovers Directive, or

        (ii)  if they do contain any such restrictions, provide for the restrictions not to apply at a time when, or in circumstances in which, they would be disapplied by that Article,

        and

    (b)  those Articles do not contain any other provision which would be incompatible with that Article.

(4)  The third condition is that—

    (a)  no shares conferring special rights in the company are held by—

        (i)  a minister,

        (ii)  a nominee of, or any other person acting on behalf of, a minister, or

        (iii)  a company directly or indirectly controlled by a minister,

        and

    (b)  no such rights are exercisable by or on behalf of a minister under any enactment.

(5)  A company may revoke an opting-in resolution by a further special resolution (an 'opting-out resolution').

(6)  For the purposes of subsection (3), a reference in Article 11 of the Takeovers Directive to Article 7.1 or 9 of that Directive is to be read as referring to rules under section 943(1) giving effect to the relevant Article.

(7)  In subsection (4) 'minister' means—

    (a)  the holder of an office in Her Majesty's Government in the United Kingdom;

    (b)  the Scottish Ministers;

    (c)  a Minister within the meaning given by section 7(3) of the Northern Ireland Act 1998 (c. 47);

  [(d) the Welsh Ministers;][a]

    and for the purposes of that subsection 'minister' also includes the Treasury, the Board of Trade [and][b] the Defence Council […].[c]

(8)  The Secretary of State may by order subject to negative resolution procedure provide that subsection (4) applies in relation to a specified person or body that exercises functions of a public nature as it applies in relation to a minister.

    'Specified' means specified in the order.

AMENDMENTS AND NOTES

[a]  Amended by Sch 1, para 142 to the Government of Wales Act 2006 (Consequential Modifications and Transitional Provisions) Order 2007, SI 2007/1388, with effect from 25 May 2007.

[b]  Amended by Sch 1, para 142 to the Government of Wales Act 2006 (Consequential Modifications and Transitional Provisions) Order 2007, SI 2007/1388, with effect from 25 May 2007.

---

[166]  Introduction to the Code, section 15.
[167]  Introduction to the Code, section 16.

<sup>c</sup> Repealed by Sch 1, para 142 to the Government of Wales Act 2006 (Consequential Modifications and Transitional Provisions) Order 2007, SI 2007/1388, with effect from 25 May 2007.

COMMENCEMENT DATE For the purpose of exercising the power to make orders: 20 January 2007. Otherwise 6 April 2007.[168]

Historically, there have been no restrictions on the ability of English companies to structure their share    **28.966.02**
capital to place impediments on takeovers, although market pressures have ensured that there are few UK-listed companies with differential voting structures or restrictions on the transfer of shares or voting rights.[169] The purpose of section 966 is to enable a company, by special resolution, to override certain of these restrictions through adopting the provisions on 'breakthrough' in Article 11 of the Takeovers Directive.

Under the Takeovers Directive Member States have a right to apply the breakthrough provisions to all    **28.966.03**
listed companies. The Government considered that the mandatory application of Article 11 was inappropriate and could have a number of drawbacks. In particular, market forces had reduced the number of companies with differential share structures without the need for legislative intervention. Applying Article 11 might not have had the desired effect of promoting more open takeover markets and liberal one share/one vote structures, as companies could list outside of the EU or in an EU State that did not apply Article 11. Finally, applying Article 11 would restrict the current flexibility that enables companies and shareholders to construct share structures as they see fit.[170] Where a Member State does not apply Article 11 it must allow companies to opt in on an individual basis.[171] This is the approach taken in the UK.

Article 12 of the Takeovers Directive permits Member States to specify that Article 11 can only be relied    **28.966.04**
on by a bidder against a target company where the bidder company, and any controlling company, are similarly subject to Article 11 (ie there is reciprocity between the target and the bidder).[172] The Government decided against applying this provision for three main reasons. Firstly, consultees stated that they saw considerable benefits in an open takeover regime and that a policy of protectionism should not be pursued. Secondly, seeking to ring-fence UK companies from takeovers by third country companies could lead to retaliation and have adverse consequences for international trade and thirdly, adoption of the reciprocity provisions would add considerably to the complexity of the implementing provisions.[173]

### Article 11 of the Takeovers Directive

Article 11(2) provides that any restrictions on the transfer of securities in the articles of the offeree    **28.966.05**
company shall not apply to the offeror during the time allowed for acceptance of the bid. Equally, restrictions on the transfer of securities in contractual agreements between the offeree company and holders of its securities, or in contractual agreements between holders of the offeree company's securities entered into after the adoption of the Takeovers Directive, do not apply to the offeror.

Article 11(3) provides that restrictions on voting rights in the articles of the offeree company shall not    **28.966.06**
have effect at a general meeting of shareholders that decides on any defensive measures. Restrictions on voting rights provided for in contractual agreements between the offeree company and holders of its securities, or in contractual agreements between holders of the offeree company's securities entered into after the adoption of the Takeovers Directive, also do not have effect at a general meeting of shareholders which decides on any defensive measures. Multiple-vote securities carry only one vote at such meetings.

Under Article 11(4) where, following a bid, the offeror holds 75 per cent or more of the capital-carrying    **28.966.07**
voting rights, no restrictions on the transfer of securities, or on voting rights, nor any extraordinary rights of shareholders concerning the appointment or removal of board members apply. Multiple-vote

---

[168]  Companies Act 2006 (Commencement No 2, etc) Order 2007, SI 2007/1093, art 2(1)(b).
[169]  DTI, Implementation of the European Directive on Takeover Bids, A Consultation Document, January 2005, p 27.
[170]  DTI, Implementation of the European Directive on Takeover Bids, A Consultation Document, January 2005, pp 26–28. According to the consultation document, 'There are special cases where differential share structures may be argued to provide entrepreneurial or other advantages. For example, differential share structures may prove an incentive for entrepreneurs to bring new companies to the market whilst protecting special (eg founders') interests. Equally, differential share structures have themselves been used in facilitating restructuring opportunities such as dual holding companies.'
[171]  Takeovers Directive, Art 12(2).
[172]  Takeovers Directive, Art 12(3).
[173]  DTI, Implementation of the European Directive on Takeover Bids, A Consultation Document, Jan 2005, p 28.

securities each carry only one vote at the first general meeting of shareholders following closure of the bid in order to amend the articles or to remove or appoint board members.

**28.966.08**    Article 11(5) requires that where rights are removed as a result of Article 11(3) or 11(4) equitable compensation must be provided for any loss suffered by the holders of those rights. The terms for determining such compensation, and the arrangements for its payment, are to be set by Member States.

**28.966.09**    Article 11(6) states that the provisions of Articles 11(3) and 11(4) do not apply to securities where the restrictions on voting rights are compensated for by specific pecuniary advantages. This will normally be the case with preference shares, which usually have no voting rights so long as the specified dividend is paid. Article 11 also does not apply where Member States hold securities in the offeree company which confer special rights which are compatible with the Treaty on the Functioning of the European Union, or to special rights provided for in national law which are compatible with the Treaty, or to co-operatives.

### Procedure

**28.966.10**    The decision to opt in to Article 11 is taken by special resolution at a general meeting of the company. While the effect of applying Article 11 is, *inter alia*, to disable the holders of securities carrying multiple votes from exercising those rights, nothing in the section provides that such rights are not valid on a resolution whether or not to opt in. It follows that where the articles contain a *Bushell v Faith*[174] clause, a person with multiple voting rights may rely on those rights in order to defeat (or pass) a resolution to opt in. Equally, a shareholders' agreement containing a provision requiring the parties to vote against opting in would be enforceable by the parties to the agreement under *Russell v Northern Bank*.[175] That these rights are unaffected in a vote on a resolution was confirmed by the Government during the passage of the Companies Bill through Parliament.[176]

### The first condition

**28.966.11**    There are three conditions for a company to opt in. The first condition is that the company has voting shares admitted to trading on a regulated market. If the company only has debt securities, or securities not carrying voting rights, admitted to trading then the provisions on breakthrough do not apply. This is unsurprising as such shares could never confer control over the company, and the limitation is designed to prevent Article 11 being used in situations other than a takeover.

**28.966.12**    'Voting rights' are defined as 'rights to vote at general meetings of the company in question, including rights that arise only in certain circumstances'.[177] This may be contrasted with the definition of voting rights in Schedule 7, paragraph 2 of the Act as 'the rights conferred on shareholders in respect of their shares or, in the case of an undertaking not having a share capital, on members, to vote at general meetings of the undertaking on all, or substantially all, matters'.[178] It follows that for the purposes of section 966 contingent rights, such as those commonly included in preference shares, are taken into account in determining whether the company is eligible to opt in to Article 11. Obviously, the holders of such securities cannot vote on a resolution to opt in unless such contingent rights have become exercisable. Article 11(6) disapplies the provisions on breakthrough in respect of securities where the restrictions on voting rights are compensated for by specific pecuniary advantages. To comply with Article 11 there is therefore no need to modify the rights of holders of such securities.

**28.966.13**    The company must have securities that are admitted to trading on a regulated market. Regulated markets are defined in the Markets in Financial Instruments (MiFID) Directive.[179] It is not necessary

---

[174] [1970] AC 1099.

[175] [1992] 1 WLR 588.

[176] *Hansard*, HL, Grand Committee, col 316, Lord Goldsmith (28 March 2006).

[177] Section 971(1).

[178] See to similar effect Sch 6 para 2. These definitions apply for the purpose of determining membership of a corporate group.

[179] Art 1(1) of the Takeovers Directive refers to securities 'admitted to trading on a regulated market within the meaning of Directive 93/22/EEC in one or more Member States (hereinafter referred to as a "regulated market").' Directive 93/22/EEC was repealed with effect from 1 November 2007 by Art 69 of Directive 2004/39/EC on markets in financial instruments amending Council Directives 85/611/EEC and 93/6/EEC and Directive 2000/12/EC of the European Parliament and of the Council and repealing Council Directive 93/22/EEC (MiFID) (as substituted by Art 1(4) of Directive 2006/31/EC amending Directive 2004/39/EC on markets in financial instruments, as regards certain deadlines). Art 69 of MiFID continues: 'References to Directive 93/22/EEC shall be construed as references to this Directive. References to terms defined in, or Articles of, Directive 93/22/EEC shall be construed as references to the equivalent term defined in, or Articles of, this Directive.' A 'regulated market' is defined in Art 4(1)(14) of MiFID as 'a multilateral system operated and/or

that the regulated market be located in the UK, so provided that the company's securities are admitted to trading on a regulated market in the EEA it will be able to opt in to Article 11. However, a company whose securities are admitted to trading on a market that is not designated as a 'regulated market' is unable to opt in to Article 11. This includes companies whose securities are traded on the Alternative Investment Market (AIM). The same applies to public companies and, in certain circumstances, private companies, whose shares are not publicly traded, but are subject to the jurisdiction of the Panel.[180]

## The second condition

The second condition is that either the articles do not contain any of the restrictions that are mentioned in Article 11, or if they do contain such restrictions, the articles provide for the restrictions not to apply at a time when, or in circumstances in which, they would be disapplied by the Takeovers Directive. The restrictions referred to in Article 11 have been briefly summarized above. There seem to have been two main considerations in implementing the Directive this way. Firstly, the Government considered that companies should have the maximum flexibility in opting in. Secondly, if a company decides to opt in, its articles should be amended, where necessary, to reflect the opting in resolution.[181] Amending the articles is also intended to protect those shareholders whose rights would otherwise be overridden.[182]    **28.966.14**

Companies opting in have the choice *either* to remove any provisions from their articles that are incompatible with Article 11 *or* to provide that such provisions are inapplicable in the case of a bid covered by the Takeovers Directive. In the latter case the restrictions will remain valid and enforceable in all other situations. Subsection (3)(b) contains a catch-all provision requiring that the articles do not do not contain any other provision which would be incompatible with Article 11.    **28.966.15**

Subsection (6) states that the references in Article 11 of the Takeovers Directive to Article 7(1) or 9 is to be read as referring to rules made under section 943(1) to give effect to the relevant article. It follows that when considering references to the time for acceptance of a bid and to the obligations of the board of the offeree company one looks to the relevant Panel rules. This is necessary as the Takeovers Directive leaves the detailed determination of such matters to Member States.    **28.966.16**

## The third condition

The third condition, is that no shares conferring special rights in the company are held by (i) a government minister, (ii) a nominee of, or any other person acting on behalf of, a minister, (iii) a company directly or indirectly controlled by a minister, and no such rights are exercisable by or on behalf of a minister under any enactment. This implements Article 11(7) and takes outside the scope of the provisions companies where the Government retains a 'golden share' enabling it to object to changes in ownership or control. This used to be common in the case of privatized utility companies. Subsection (7) was amended with effect from 25 May 2007 to replace the reference to the National    **28.966.17**

---

managed by a market operator, which brings together or facilitates the bringing together of multiple third-party buying and selling interests – in financial instruments in the system and in accordance with its non-discretionary rules – in a way that results in a contract, in respect of the financial instruments admitted to trading under its rules and/or systems, and which is authorized and functions regularly and in accordance with the provisions of Title III'. Under Art 47 of MiFID (as substituted by Art 6(16) of Directive 2010/78/EU amending Directives 98/26/EC, 2002/87/EC, 2003/6/EC, 2003/41/EC, 2003/71/EC, 2004/39/EC, 2004/109/EC, 2005/60/ EC, 2006/48/EC, 2006/49/EC and 2009/65/EC in respect of the powers of the European Supervisory Authority (European Banking Authority), the European Supervisory Authority (European Insurance and Occupational Pensions Authority) and the European Supervisory Authority (European Securities and Markets Authority)) each Member State shall draw up a list of regulated markets for which it is the home Member State and forward that list to the other Member States and the European Securities and Markets Authority (ESMA). ESMA is required to publish and keep up to date a list of all regulated markets on its website (see ⟨http://mifiddatabase.esma.europa.eu/⟩). MiFID has been extended to the EEA (with modifications not relevant to this context): see Decision of the EEA Joint Committee No 65/2005 of 29 April 2005 amending Annex IX (Financial services) to the EEA Agreement OJ L239/50 15.9.2005. At the time of writing Directive 2010/78/EU had not yet been extended to the EEA, although it had been considered EEA relevant by EFTA experts. In practice, ESMA's database includes details on regulated markets in all EEA states.

[180]  Introduction to the Code, para 3.

[181]  *Hansard*, HL, Grand Committee, cols 315–316, Lord Goldsmith (28 March 2006). He gave the following example: 'Art 11.3 of the directive provides that multiple vote securities shall carry only one vote each at a meeting to decide upon defensive measures. Companies might make such an express provision in their Articles or they might decide to go further and ban multiple vote securities altogether. Either approach would be fully compliant with Article 11 of the directive and we do not see any reason to force a company down either of those routes' (col 315).

[182]  *Hansard*, HL, Grand Committee, col 316.

Assembly for Wales with a reference to Welsh Ministers.[183] The effect is to exclude from section 966 shares in a company held by the Welsh Ministers which confer special rights on those Ministers. The change follows the formal separation between the executive and legislative arms of the National Assembly for Wales made by the Government of Wales Act 2006.

**28.966.18**    Unlike the Directive, subsection (4) does not require that the relevant rights are compatible with the Treaty on the Functioning of the European Union.[184] However, given that the section has been enacted to implement the Takeovers Directive, it must be interpreted in a manner that conforms with the Directive.[185] It follows that where the relevant special rights are void, because they are incompatible with the Treaty,[186] the company concerned will be able to opt in.

**28.966.19**    Subsection (8) gives the Secretary of State the power, by order, to provide that subsection (4) applies in relation to a specified person or body that exercises functions of a public nature as it applies in relation to a minister. The effect is to bring outside the scope of the opt-in provisions companies where golden shares, or similar rights, are held by a public body other than a minister. Such a resolution is subject to annulment by either House of Parliament. Clearly, this power can only be exercised where it would be compatible with the Takeovers Directive and the Treaty on the Functioning of the European Union.

### Failure to satisfy the conditions

**28.966.20**    What is the effect of a resolution that is passed if the three conditions are not satisfied? Subsection (1) states that a company may opt in *if the following three conditions are met in relation to the company*. It is considered that this is a mandatory requirement, and that satisfaction of the three conditions at the relevant time (see section 967(3)) is a requirement for an opting-in resolution to be valid. It follows that if any of the three conditions is not met then the resolution is void and of no effect. This could cause hardship in some cases, for example if there is genuine doubt as to whether a particular provision in the articles contravenes Article 11, or whether a golden share is compatible with the Treaty. However, a company contemplating opting in will usually have access to legal advice, and it is possible to err on the side of caution when amending the articles. As an opting-in resolution may adversely affect third party rights, it seems correct that this should only be possible if the statutory conditions for such a resolution are strictly met.

### Opting out

**28.966.21**    A company that has opted in is able to opt out again through passing a special resolution revoking the earlier resolution to opt in.[187] Section 966(6) states that the effective date of an opting-out resolution may not be earlier than the first anniversary of the date on which a copy of the opting-in resolution was forwarded to the registrar. It follows that while a company may pass an opting out resolution at any time after it has opted in, the resolution may not take effect until the first anniversary of the date it was forwarded to the registrar.[188] This time limit is super-equivalent to the Takeovers Directive and was introduced to promote certainty. In the Government's view 'If a company, having carefully weighed the consequences, decides to opt in, it seems right to provide at least a limited time period—and this is all this is—of one year during which the company cannot reverse that decision to opt in. That will focus minds on whether it is the right decision to have made'.[189]

**28.966.22**    A more difficult question is whether a company that is subject to a bid could (after the one-year period) opt out as a tactical means to frustrate the bid. In most cases this is unlikely to be possible due to the time involved in calling a general meeting to pass a resolution revoking the earlier decision. However, in principle, there does not appear to be any prohibition on a company passing such a resolution during the course of a bid. However, the better view may be that such a resolution would be held to constitute a defensive measure for the purposes of Article 9 of the Takeovers Directive. In this case, Article 11 would itself apply to the resolution to opt out, with the result that holders of multiple voting rights, for example, would be unable to rely on such rights to pass a resolution.

---

[183]  Government of Wales Act 2006 (Consequential Modifications and Transitional Provisions) Order 2007, SI 2007/1388, Sch 1, para 142.

[184]  Takeovers Directive, Art 11(7).

[185]  *Litster v Forth Dry Dock and Engineering Co Ltd.* [1990] 1 AC 546; and *Webb v EMO Air Cargo (UK) Ltd (No 2)* [1995] 1 WLR 1454.

[186]  See eg Case C-4 83/99 *Commission v France* [2002] ECR I-4781; Case C-503/99 *Commission v Belgium* [2002] ECR I-4809; Case C-98/01 *Commission v United Kingdom* [2003] ECR I-4641; and Joined Cases C-282 and 283/04 *Commission v Netherlands* [2006] ECR I-9141. In only the second case were the special rights held to be compatible with the Treaty.

[187]  Subsection (5).

[188]  *Semble*, if the resolution purports to take effect at an earlier date it is null and void.

[189]  *Hansard*, HL, Grand Committee, col 317, Lord Goldsmith (28 March 2006).

An opting-out resolution cannot have retrospective effect so as to invalidate steps that have been taken **28.966.23**
in a bid prior to the effective date of the resolution.[190]

## Compensation

Article 11(5) requires the payment of compensation where rights are removed as a result of the opt-in **28.966.24**
resolution under Articles 11(3) and 11(4). The Government has not made any express provision for the
payment of compensation. The DTI consultation document stated 'there is no need to provide for
compensation in these circumstances. The decision to opt in will have been taken in accordance with
the usual rules involved for changing the articles (including protection of class rights). It will be open
to the parties to agree on terms, including any compensatory payment. There is, therefore, no loss
suffered by shareholders as a consequence of subsequent override of rights'.[191] In Parliament the
Government justified this approach:

> The starting point is that any decision to opt in will have to be taken in accordance with the usual rules
> for changing the Articles of Association of a company. That will include the safeguards that will apply
> to classes of shareholders, where those exist, and to minority shareholders. These provisions would be
> available for those who oppose an opting-in decision that would adversely affect their rights. But with
> regard to the specific issue of compensation, Article 11.5 provides that equitable compensation must
> be provided to those whose rights are overridden by virtue of the operation of the article. Again, we
> have tried to preserve the room for manoeuvre for companies and shareholders. It may be that in
> gaining the agreement of a shareholder with special rights to an opting-in resolution there has to be
> some form of financial settlement between the company and that shareholder or shareholders; or the
> Articles of Association might have to be amended to provide for compensation to be paid when any
> bid is made and the provisions of Article 11 take effect. The choice will be left to companies and their
> shareholders.[192]

It may be questioned whether this approach is compatible with the Takeovers Directive. The European **28.966.25**
Court of Justice has stressed the need for measures implementing a directive to be legally binding. For
this reason administrative practices and circulars are not regarded as adequate implementation.[193]
Where (as here) the provision is intended to create rights for individuals, it is necessary for implementation to take the form of binding legal rules.[194] Admirable as the Government's desire for flexibility
may be, Article 11(5) has not been implemented in this manner.

## Application to unregistered companies

The Provisions of Chapter 2 ('Impediments to Takeovers') and Chapter 3 ('Squeeze-Out and Sell-Out') **28.966.26**
have applied to unregistered companies since 6 April 2007.[195] An unregistered company means[196] a
body corporate incorporated in, and having a principal place of business in, the United Kingdom, other
than (1) a body incorporated by, or registered under, a public general enactment, (2) a body not formed
for the purpose of carrying on a business that has for its object the acquisition of gain by the body or its
individual members, (3) a body for the time being exempted from section 1043 of the Companies Act
2006 by a direction of the Secretary of State, or (4) an open-ended investment company.

Sections 966 to 973 of the Act (impediments to takeovers) apply to unregistered companies (as defined **28.966.27**
above).[197]

---

[190]  Section 967(1) and (2).
[191]  DTI, Implementation of the European Directive on Takeover Bids, A Consultation Document, January
2005, p 31.
[192]  *Hansard*, HL, Grand Committee, col 316, Lord Goldsmith (28 March 2006).
[193]  See eg Case 116/86 *Commission v Italy* [1988] ECR 1323; Case 236/85 *Commission v Netherlands* [1987]
ECR 3989; Case 239/85 *Commission v Belgium* [1986] ECR 3645; Case C-13/90 *Commission v France* [1991] ECR
I-4327; Case C-381/92 *Commission v Ireland* [1994] ECR I-215; Case C-96/95 *Commission v Germany* [1997]
ECR I-1653; Case C-145/99 *Commission v Italy* [2002] ECR I-2235; Case C-259/01 *Commission v France* [2002]
ECR I-11093.
[194]  Eg Case 102/79 *Commission v Belgium* [1980] ECR 1473; Case 96/81 *Commission v Netherlands* [1982]
ECR 1791; Case 97/81 *Commission v Netherlands* [1982] ECR 1819; Case C-361/88 *Commission v Germany*
[1991] ECR I-2567.
[195]  Companies Act (Unregistered Companies) Regulations 2007, SI 2007/318 (revoked with effect from 1
October 2009 by SI 2009/2436).
[196]  Unregistered Companies Regulations 2009, SI 2009/2436, reg 2(a), with effect from 1 October 2009. Prior
to that date, see the Companies Act (Unregistered Companies) Regulations 2007, SI 2007/318.
[197]  Unregistered Companies Regulations 2009, SI 2009/2436, reg 3, Sch 1, para 14(1).

**28.966.28**    Sections 974 to 991 ('Squeeze-Out' and 'Sell-Out') apply to unregistered companies, but so far as relating to the offeree company, only if the unregistered company has voting shares admitted to trading on a regulated market.[198]

### 967   Further provision about opting-in and opting-out resolutions

**28.967.01**      (1)   An opting-in resolution or an opting-out resolution must specify the date from which it is to have effect (the 'effective date').

         (2)   The effective date of an opting-in resolution may not be earlier than the date on which the resolution is passed.

         (3)   The second and third conditions in section 966 must be met at the time when an opting-in resolution is passed, but the first one does not need to be met until the effective date.

         (4)   An opting-in resolution passed before the time when voting shares of the company are admitted to trading on a regulated market complies with the requirement in subsection (1) if, instead of specifying a particular date, it provides for the resolution to have effect from that time.

         (5)   An opting-in resolution passed before the commencement of this section complies with the requirement in subsection (1) if, instead of specifying a particular date, it provides for the resolution to have effect from that commencement.

         (6)   The effective date of an opting-out resolution may not be earlier than the first anniversary of the date on which a copy of the opting-in resolution was forwarded to the registrar.

         (7)   Where a company has passed an opting-in resolution, any alteration of its articles of association that would prevent the second condition in section 966 from being met is of no effect until the effective date of an opting-out resolution passed by the company.

         COMMENCEMENT DATE 6 April 2007[199]

**28.967.02**    Section 967 makes further provision as to the procedure for opting in (or opting out). Subsection (1) provides that the resolution must specify the date from which it will take effect and subsection (2) precludes retrospective resolutions.

**28.967.03**    Subsection (3) sets out the temporal requirements for satisfaction of the three conditions in section 966 (see above). The requirement that the company's articles do not contain any provisions inconsistent with Article 11, and that there is no golden share or other special rights, must be satisfied at the time when the resolution is passed. However, there does not seem to be any reason why amendments to the company's articles cannot be dealt with at the same general meeting as the meeting which passes the opting-in resolution. Section 26 requires a company that amends its articles to send a copy of the amended articles to the Registrar within 15 days but does not prevent the resolution from taking effect at the time it is passed (or such later time as may be specified in the resolution).

**28.967.04**    The requirement that the company has voting shares admitted to trading on a regulated market must be satisfied at the date that the resolution takes effect. It follows that companies whose shares are to be admitted to trading on a registered market may pass a resolution opting in from the date of admission to trading. As this date may not be known in advance, subsection (4) provides that instead of specifying a particular date, the resolution will be valid if it provides for the resolution to take effect from the date of admission to trading.

**28.967.05**    Subsection (5) was a transitional provision designed to assist companies that wished to pass opting-in resolutions prior to the commencement date. It permitted companies to specify that the resolution would take effect from the date of the entry into force of section 967 (ie 6 April 2007). Its force is now spent.

**28.967.06**    Subsection (6) prevents a company opting out within 12 months. It has been considered in the commentary on section 966.

**28.967.07**    Subsection (7) prevents a company from amending its articles under section 21 so as to include provisions that are inconsistent with Article 11 of the Takeovers Directive. The section does not invalidate the change, but suspends its effects until the effective date of an opting out resolution. Once again, there does not seem to be any impediment to both resolutions being passed at the same meeting.

### *Consequences of opting in*

### 968   Effect on contractual restrictions[a]

**28.968.01**      (1)   The following provisions have effect where a takeover bid is made for an opted-in company.

         (2)   An agreement to which this section applies is invalid in so far as it places any restriction—

             (a)   on the transfer to the offeror, or at his direction to another person, of shares in the company

---

[198]   Unregistered Companies Regulations 2009, SI 2009/2436, reg 3, Sch 1, para 14(2).
[199]   Companies Act 2006 (Commencement No 2, etc) Order 2007, SI 2007/1093, art 2(1)(b).

during the offer period;

(b) on the transfer to any person of shares in the company at a time during the offer period when the offeror holds shares amounting to not less than 75% in value of all the voting shares in the company;

(c) on rights to vote at a general meeting of the company that decides whether to take any action which might result in the frustration of the bid;

(d) on rights to vote at a general meeting of the company that—

(i) is the first such meeting to be held after the end of the offer period, and

(ii) is held at a time when the offeror holds shares amounting to not less than 75% in value of all the voting shares in the company.

(3) This section applies to an agreement—

(a) entered into between a person holding shares in the company and another such person on or after 21st April 2004, or

(b) entered into at any time between such a person and the company,

and it applies to such an agreement even if the law applicable to the agreement (apart from this section) is not the law of a part of the United Kingdom.

(4) The reference in subsection (2)(c) to rights to vote at a general meeting of the company that decides whether to take any action which might result in the frustration of the bid includes a reference to rights to vote on a written resolution concerned with that question.

(5) For the purposes of subsection (2)(c), action which might result in the frustration of a bid is any action of that kind specified in rules under section 943(1) giving effect to Article 9 of the Takeovers Directive.

(6) If a person suffers loss as a result of any act or omission that would (but for this section) be a breach of an agreement to which this section applies, he is entitled to compensation, of such amount as the court considers just and equitable, from any person who would (but for this section) be liable to him for committing or inducing the breach.

(7) In subsection (6) 'the court' means the High Court or, in Scotland, the Court of Session.

(8) A reference in this section to voting shares in the company does not include—

(a) debentures, or

(b) shares that, under the company's articles of association, do not normally carry rights to vote at its general meetings (for example, shares carrying rights to vote that, under those articles, arise only where specified pecuniary advantages are not provided).

AMENDMENTS AND NOTES

ª Transitional provision: Companies Act 2006 (Commencement No 2, Consequential Amendments, Transitional Provisions and Savings) Order 2007, SI 2007/1093, Sch 1, para 4, made transitional provision for written resolutions. This provision was revoked by the Companies Act 2006 (Commencement No 3, Consequential Amendments, Transitional Provisions and Savings) Order 2007, SI 2007/2194, art 1(b), with effect from 1 October 2007 when the corresponding provisions of the Companies Act 2006 were brought into force.

COMMENCEMENT DATE 6 April 2007[200]

Sections 966 and 967 are concerned with restrictions in a company's constitution that could frustrate a bid. Section 968 concerns contractual restrictions not part of the company's articles. Legislation was necessary to override such provisions in relation to an opted-in company as there is no other means to override private contractual rights as a result of a constitutional decision by a company.[201] This follows from the rule that a company's constitution only binds the company and its members and does not affect the rights of third parties.

**28.968.02**

### *Invalidity of contractual provisions*

Subsection (2) sets out the consequences where such a resolution is in place:

**28.968.03**

(a) Any restriction on the transfer to the offeror, or at his direction to another person, of shares in the company during the offer period is invalid.

This covers contractual restrictions on transfer not included in the company's articles. An example is a provision in a shareholders' agreement where a shareholder grants other shareholders a right of pre-emption should he wish to sell his shares. Such restrictions could also, possibly, be included in a contractual arrangement with the company. The purpose is to enable the holder of such shares to accept the offer. However, where an equitable interest in shares has passed to a purchaser for value (for example, under a specifically enforceable contract for the sale of shares)

---

[200] Companies Act 2006 (Commencement No 2, etc) Order 2007, SI 2007/1093, art 2(1)(b).

[201] *Hansard*, HL, Grand Committee, col 315, Lord Goldsmith (28 March 2006).

then, as the legal owner holds a bare legal title, the inability of the registered shareholder to deal with the shares without the consent of the beneficial owner without committing a breach of trust should not be viewed as a 'restriction'. In this case the decision whether or not to accept the offer should lie with the equitable owner who has the economic interest in the shares. Likewise, where shares are held on trust it should be the equitable owner that determines whether to accept the offer.

**28.968.04**    (b)   Any restriction on the transfer to any person of shares in the company at a time during the offer period when the offeror holds shares amounting to not less than 75% in value of all the voting shares in the company is invalid.

There was some debate in Parliament as to the meaning of 'in value'. In the Grand Committee, Lord Goldsmith, for the Government, stated that 'we think it is clear what they mean: they refer to the nominal value of shares, so to achieve the breakthrough threshold the bidder must reach 75 per cent of the nominal value of the company's voting shares'.[202] The suggestion that the nominal value of shares was intended attracted criticism from the opposition. When the Bill was considered further on Report Lord Goldsmith stated:

> Article 11.4 of the takeover directive uses a concept unfamiliar to English company law in terms of its language; that is, it talks of the offeror holding 75 per cent or more of the capital carrying voting rights … If one is looking to see what is 75 per cent of the capital carrying voting rights, I stand by saying that in the majority of cases normally one would find that by looking at the nominal value of the shares and seeing whether they hold 75 per cent or more. Plainly in the case where we have only one class of share, no difficulty at all arises. In the situation where one has more than one class of share, no real difficulty may arise; there may be some difference in the market value of the shares at a particular stage but the voting rights may still appear to be broadly comparable to the nominal value. What will the court make of it? The words in the Bill do not say 'nominal value'; they say, 'value'. It has been left in that sense so that it will be for the court to interpret what is meant. I answered the question because I was asked and it is right that we should indicate what we think. How will the court interpret it? The court will need to interpret this provision in the same way as it would interpret other provisions in a statute where it is plain that the intention has been to implement a directive. So I have little doubt that they will look at the directive and say that in understanding it they need to understand that it is intended to implement the requirements of Article 11.4 … There may be some cases—this is where the concern may have arisen over what I said—where the structure of the company is such that the court would say that if we are really looking at 75 per cent of capital carrying voting rights, it is not appropriate on this occasion just to look at the nominal value because the structure of the company is extraordinary: someone has 90 per cent of the nominal value for virtually nothing and the rest of the shareholders, who have only 10 per cent of the nominal value, have the real bulk of the company. I can see that one could have such a company and in those circumstances the court may say that 75 per cent of value in that context is to be interpreted in a different way … So it is not straightforward: we do not know what the European Court of Justice would make of capital carrying voting rights, or 75 per cent of those in any event.[203]

**28.968.05**    The Government therefore decided on a formulation that leaves it to the national and European courts to determine the meaning of the section.[204] When the matter falls for decision it is considered that the court should adopt a purposive construction and reject the nominal value of the shares as this may be fortuitous and in the example Lord Goldsmith gave bears no relationship to the real value of the shares.

**28.968.06**    (c)   Any restriction on rights to vote at a general meeting of the company that decides whether to take any action which might result in the frustration of the bid is invalid.

          ?    This provision is aimed at contractual arrangements that restrict the ability of a shareholder to vote on a resolution at a general meeting that decides on defensive action.

**28.968.07**    Subsection (5) provides that action which might result in the frustration of a bid is any action of that kind specified in rules made under section 943(1) giving effect to Article 9 of the Takeovers Directive. It follows that the relevant Panel rules will apply. Subsection (4) makes clear that the reference to voting rights also includes rights to vote on a written resolution.

**28.968.08**    (d)   Any restriction on rights to vote at a general meeting of the company that (i) is the first such meeting to be held after the end of the offer period, and (ii) is held at a time when the offeror holds shares amounting to not less than 75% in value of all the voting shares in the company is invalid.

---

[202]  *Hansard*, HL, Grand Committee, col 318, Lord Goldsmith (28 March 2006).
[203]  *Hansard*, HL, col 213, Lord Goldsmith (16 May 2006).
[204]  See also *Hansard*, HC, col 811, the Solicitor General (18 July 2006).

This provision implements Article 11(4) of the Directive. The purpose is to enable the bidder, where he has acquired 75 per cent in value of the voting shares, to pass resolutions (i) amending the company's articles, and (ii) changing the composition of the company's board of directors. The intention is that the successful bidder should not be frustrated in his ability to run the company as a result of any restrictions on the exercise of the voting rights once he has acquired 75 per cent 'in value' of the company's shares. What constitutes 'value' is considered above.

The provision only applies to the first general meeting after the end of the offer period with the result **28.968.09** that if the bidder fails to exercise his rights at that meeting he will be bound by the relevant restrictions at any subsequent meeting. The objective is not to interfere with third party rights more than strictly necessary to enable the bidder to obtain control of the company. If he fails to exercise those rights at the first meeting the bidder has only himself to blame.

## Scope of application

The scope of section 968 is defined by subsection (3). This states that the section applies to an **28.968.10** agreement (a) entered into between a person holding shares in the company and another such person on or after 21 April 2004, or (b) entered into at any time between such a person and the company. Agreements entered into prior to 21 April 2004, which was the date of adoption of the Takeovers Directive, are exempted from the breakthrough provisions, and are therefore unaffected by the passing of an opting-in resolution. Where an agreement entered into before that date is amended after 21 April 2004 the question arises whether the exemption still applies. It is submitted that in this case the answer will depend on whether the effect of the amendment is to convert the former agreement into in substance a new agreement. Agreements made with the company are subject to section 968 regardless of the time that they were entered into.

Section 968 applies 'even if the law applicable to the agreement (apart from this section) is not the law **28.968.11** of a part of the United Kingdom'. It follows that it is not possible to contract out of the breakthrough provisions by subjecting the contract to a system of law that does not apply the Takeovers Directive. For the purposes of English private international law, it is a mandatory rule that applies regardless of the governing law of the contract.[205] It is possible that a jurisdiction clause in an agreement that selects the forum of a non-EEA State, coupled with the choice of a legal system that would not give effect to the rules in subsection (2), would be void on the grounds that it is contrary to public policy.[206]

## Compensation

The Takeovers Directive requires that persons whose rights are rendered void under the breakthrough **28.968.12** provisions are entitled to compensation. Article 11(5) goes on to state that the terms for determining such compensation, and the arrangements for its payment, are to be set by the Member States.

In the Government's view, the payment of compensation is likely to be determined in the first instance **28.968.13** by the bidder.[207] This is because the bidder is required to state in the bid documentation, 'the compensation offered for the rights which might be removed as a result of the breakthrough rule laid down in Article 11(4), with particulars of the way in which that compensation is to be paid and the method employed in determining it'.[208] This may facilitate negotiation of the appropriate level of compensation between the bidder and the party holding the rights that will be overridden.[209]

However, Article 11(5) requires the payment of compensation where the parties are unable to agree, **28.968.14** and requires a remedy for the person whose rights are taken away. Subsection (6) states that if a person suffers loss as a result of any act or omission that would (but for this section) be a breach of an agreement to which this section applies, he is entitled to compensation, of such amount as the court considers just and equitable, from any person who would (but for this section) be liable to him for committing or inducing the breach.

---

[205] The governing law of a contract concluded on or after 17 December 2009 is determined by applying the rules in Regulation 593/2008 on the law applicable to contractual obligations (Rome I). Art 9(2) states that, 'Nothing in this Regulation shall restrict the application of the overriding mandatory provisions of the law of the forum'. Section 968(3) imposes a duty on the English court to do this. Contracts concluded before 17 December 2009 are subject to the Rome Convention on the Law Applicable to Contractual Obligations (1980) which had the force of law under the Contracts (Applicable Law) Act 1990 in respect of contracts made after 1 April 1991. Contracts concluded prior to that date are subject to the common law.

[206] *The Hollandia* [1983] 1 AC 565.

[207] See also Explanatory Notes on the Companies Act 2006 para 1240.

[208] Takeovers Directive, art 6(3)(e).

[209] DTI, 'Implementation of the European Directive on Takeover Bids, A Consultation Document', January 2005, 31.

**28.968.15**    This creates two classes of persons who are liable to pay compensation: (i) the person who would have been guilty of a breach of contract (ie the other contracting party/parties), and (ii) any person who would be liable for inducing the breach of contract. Where the relevant agreement is entered into with the company, the effect is that the person will be entitled to compensation from the company. Where the contract is made with a third party, then the section gives a cause of action against any person who is relieved of the obligation to perform as a result of the resolution being passed. For example, a person who agrees in a shareholders' agreement to give another person a right of pre-emption will be relieved of this obligation once an opt-in resolution is passed. However, it is not obvious that he should be obliged to pay compensation as he may not have sought to be relieved of the obligation, and may even have voted against the relevant resolution. The same applies to a contractual agreement not to vote shares, or to exercise voting rights at the direction of a third party.

**28.968.16**    The second class of persons who are liable to pay compensation are persons who would be liable for 'inducing' the breach. Procuring or inducing a breach of contract is a recognized tort under England law.[210] The reference in subsection (6) to liability for inducing the breach appears intended to incorporate into the statutory cause of action the requirements of this common law tort. A claimant will therefore need to prove the existence (but for the section) of a 'breach' of contract and each of the other elements of the tort of inducing a breach of contract. Detailed discussion of this tort is outside the scope of the commentary and readers are referred to specialist works on the law of tort.[211] Basically, a claim requires (a) knowledge of the relevant contract, (b) an intention, (c) as to the relevant breach, and (d) resulting loss.[212] The law in this area is extremely complex and it may be regretted that the Government did not adopt a simpler statutory scheme when implementing the Directive.

**28.968.17**    The Government's intention seems to be that the bidder will be liable to pay compensation as an inducer. However, the drafting is curious in this case as the making of a takeover offer does not involve an actual, or even a notional, breach of the contractual provisions invalidated by section 968. Subsection (2) invalidates the relevant contractual rights for the duration of the offer period, and at the first meeting of the company held after the bidder has acquired 75 per cent of the shares by value. The real or proximate cause of the invalidity of the relevant rights following a bid is therefore the resolution. It is true that but for the bid there would have been no loss. However, the reason that the bid has this effect is because of the resolution. In *OBG Ltd v Allen*[213] the House of Lords rejected the possibility of liability for procuring a breach of contract where the actions of the defendant interfere with the performance of a contract short of actually causing a breach.[214] Such interference is actionable, if at all, as the tort of unlawful interference. Making a takeover bid is not unlawful interference[215] and this tort is not referred to in subsection (6). Moreover, whether there can be liability for the indirect procurement of a breach of contract[216] remains uncertain.[217]

**28.968.18**    A further difficulty is that the tort of procuring a breach of contract requires intention.[218] Lord Hoffmann stated in *OBG*:[219] 'It is necessary for this purpose to distinguish between ends, means and consequences. If someone knowingly causes a breach of contract, it does not normally matter that it is the means by which he intends to achieve some further end or even that he would rather have been able to achieve that end without causing a breach. ... On the other hand, if the breach of contract is neither an end in itself nor a means to an end, but merely a foreseeable consequence, then in my opinion it cannot for this purpose be said to have been intended.' It is difficult to see how the making of a bid constitutes an *intention* that the claimant's contractual rights will be breached.[220] Procuring a breach of contract is an illegal act, and where a bidder makes an offer for a company that has not opted in he does

---

[210]  *Lumley v Gye* (1853) 2 E & B 216.

[211]  See eg M Jones et al (general eds), *Clerk & Lindsell on Torts* (20th edn, London, 2010), Ch 24; H Carty, An *Analysis of the Economic Torts* (Oxford, 2001).

[212]  *OBG Ltd v Allan* [2008] 1 AC 1.

[213]  *Ibid.*

[214]  [2008] 1 AC 1, 31 (Lord Hoffmann), 62 (Lord Nicholls).

[215]  [2008] 1 AC 1, 32 'Unlawful means ... consists of acts intended to cause loss to the claimant by interfering with the freedom of a third party in a way which is unlawful as against that third party and which is intended to cause loss to the claimant' per Lord Hoffmann.

[216]  As suggested in *Thomson v Deakin* [1952] Ch 646, 697.

[217]  See the discussion in M Jones et al (general eds), *Clerk & Lindsell on Torts* (20th edn, London, 2010), paras 24–45 to 24–50

[218]  [2008] 1 AC 1, 30.

[219]  *Ibid.*

[220]  *Rookes v Barnard* [1964] AC 1129, 1212, *per* Lord Devlin and *Thomson v Deakin* [1952] Ch 646, 697, *per* Jenkins LJ.

not normally intend that the shareholders will breach their contractual obligations.[221] Why should he so intend where a company has opted in? Knowledge that an event may occur is not the same as an intention that it does occur,[222] unless it is the means by which his further end is achieved. In some cases the bidder will in any event lack knowledge of the relevant contracts.[223]

Another difficulty is that for loss to crystallize the person affected must decide not to comply with his **28.968.19** contractual obligations. Subsection (2) provides that the relevant restrictions are invalid. It follows that they cannot be enforced, and the person bound by them is free to disregard them. However, it does not require him to do so, and such a person is free to act in a way that is consistent with those restrictions. (The point of Article 11 is to permit shareholders to act as they see fit, not to compel them to accept a bid).

It follows that if the normal rules applicable to the tort of inducing a breach of contract apply it may be **28.968.20** difficult in practice to claim compensation from the bidder under the section. It is possible that a broader approach to the construction of the provision is called for. Yet even if correct, it remains difficult to see how the making of a bid will 'induce' non-performance of the relevant contractual obligations in the absence of an intention on the bidder's part that this should occur. There also remains the argument that it is the resolution, and not the bid, that is the real and proximate cause of loss. The courts may be able to square this circle, and hold that the bidder is liable, because he is the most appropriate person to pay compensation, and will be the ultimate beneficiary of the relevant rights being disapplied. Yet it seems that this conclusion is not required by the Takeovers Directive which leaves the terms and arrangements for the payment of compensation to the Member States. After all, a bidder could state in the offer that he proposes to pay no compensation to those whose rights are overridden under Article 11, in which case the matter is left to the court.

Persons, other than the bidder, may also be required to pay compensation under subsection (6). On the **28.968.21** view suggested above, the passing of the resolution to opt in to Article 11 is causative of the loss of the relevant rights. This raises the question of whether those involved in proposing and voting on the resolution will be liable as an 'inducer'. In principle, there seems no reason why such persons could not be caught. This could bring within subsection (6) persons who proposed and argued in favour of the resolution. It seems that shareholders are also potentially within the scope of subsection (6) as to pass a special resolution 75 per cent must have voted in favour. Should subsection (6) apply to those shareholders who voted in favour of the resolution, or should all shareholders be liable to pay compensation regardless of how they voted? It can be argued that only those who voted in favour of the resolution have the necessary intention that the contractual restrictions are rendered void. Against that, the vote will be taken in the context of a procedure under the Companies Act where those who vote against a special resolution agree (through becoming a shareholder) to be bound by the decision of a 75 per cent majority. Objecting shareholders benefit, as much as those who vote in favour, from the assumed increase in the value of their shares through facilitating successful bids being made.

If the directors of an opted-out company solicit a takeover bid are they at risk of personal liability under **28.968.22** this provision? In theory there seems no reason why directors could not be liable for inducement. If the making of a bid is regarded as an inducement (see above) then in principle directors that solicit a bid could be liable, even if they are acting in the best interests of the company. Liability under subsection (6) is not predicated on fault, or on a breach of duty, and the effect of the opt-in resolution is that there will not, in fact, be any breach of contract. However, it is considered that the fact that the directors acted properly in soliciting a bid will be relevant in deciding whether it is appropriate to order them to pay compensation.

Compensation is 'of such amount as the court considers just and equitable'. It follows that the court is **28.968.23** not bound, in assessing compensation, by the rules applicable to the quantification of damages for breach of contract or for the tort of inducing a breach of contract.[224] Neither will the rules on causation and remoteness of damages apply. Instead, the task of the court is to assess what is fair in all the circumstances. Given the large number of persons against whom an order to pay compensation may in

---

[221] *Pennzoil v Texaco* 729 SW 2d 768 (Tex App 1987) is an example where the defendant was found to have done so and mulcted of $3 billion in punitive damages as a result.

[222] *R v Moloney* [1985] AC 905; *R v Hancock and Shankland* [1986] AC 455; *R v Nedrick* [1986] 3 All ER 1; *R v Woollin* [1999] 1 AC 82. In *OBG Ltd v Allan* [2008] 1 AC 1 the House of Lords rejected the view that foreseeability was sufficient for liability.

[223] The defendant must know of the existence of the contract to intend its breach, but need not know the details. Wilful blindness also suffices: 'Even if they did not know the actual terms of the contract, but had the means of knowledge—which they deliberately disregarded—that would be enough.' *Emerald Construction Co Ltd v Lowthian* [1966] 1 WLR 691, 700 per Lord Denning MR. However, 'It is not the same as negligence or even gross negligence' *OBG Ltd v Allan* [2008] 1 AC 1, 30 per Lord Hoffmann.

[224] Compare *R v Investors Compensation Scheme Ltd ex p Bowden* [1996] 1 AC 261.

principle be made it is considered that in determining what is fair the court should have regard, amongst others, to the following factors: (i) the identity of the person against whom compensation is claimed; (ii) whether the person has benefited from the invalidity of the contractual provisions; and (iii) whether the person from whom compensation is sought was acting in the proper performance of his duty. The first and third factors would enable the court to decline to make an award against directors of the company where they were acting properly in the performance of their duties to the company. Given that compensation is awarded for the loss of legal rights it also seems fair that those who benefit from the resolution should, in most cases, pay the compensation. Apart from the bidder, this is likely to be the shareholders in the company and, in an appropriate case, persons relieved from liability to comply with the relevant restrictions.

**28.968.24**    In terms of quantum, the starting point would seem to be the amount that the claimant has lost as a result of the restrictions being invalid.[225] This may be difficult in some cases to quantify. It is possible that the court will develop guidelines as to the payment of compensation in such cases.

### 969  Power of offeror to require general meeting to be called

**28.969.01**    (1)  Where a takeover bid is made for an opted-in company, the offeror may by making a request to the directors of the company require them to call a general meeting of the company if, at the date at which the request is made, he holds shares amounting to not less than 75% in value of all the voting shares in the company.

(2)  The reference in subsection (1) to voting shares in the company does not include—

(a)  debentures, or

(b)  shares that, under the company's articles of association, do not normally carry rights to vote at its general meetings (for example, shares carrying rights to vote that, under those articles, arise only where specified pecuniary advantages are not provided).

(3)  Sections 303 to 305 (members' power to require general meetings to be called) apply as they would do if subsection (1) above were substituted for subsections (1) to (3) of section 303, and with any other necessary modifications.

COMMENCEMENT DATE 6 April 2007[226]

**28.969.02**    Section 969 provides a bidder with the right to require the directors of an opted-in company to call a general meeting of the company if he holds 75 per cent in value of all the voting shares in the company. The rights conferred by Article 11 would be of little practical value if the bidder was unable to exercise them by requiring the directors to call a general meeting.

**28.969.03**    Subsection (2) specifies that in determining whether the requirement that the bidder has 75 per cent in value of the voting shares, debentures, and shares that, under the company's articles, do not normally carry rights to vote at its general meetings (eg preference shares) are ignored. This overrides section 971(2) in accordance with which such securities may be treated as shares. The question of what 'value' means in this context is considered in the commentary on section 968 above.

**28.969.04**    Subsection (3) applies, with the necessary modifications, the procedure for holding general meetings called by members of the company. Section 304 requires the directors to call such a meeting within 21 days from the date on which the relevant request was received.[227] The meeting must be held on a date not more than 28 days after the date of the notice convening the meeting.[228] If the directors fail to call the meeting then the bidder is himself able to call the meeting.[229] The procedure for doing so is set out in section 305.

---

[225]  A gain-based measure focusing on the benefit derived by the person relieved of performance would not be appropriate as (1) quantification of the gain is unlikely to be possible and (2) the purpose of Art 11 is to facilitate takeover bids, thereby improving economic efficiency through facilitating operation of the market in corporate control. Gain-based damages are appropriate in cases of wrongdoing to strip the defendant of the benefit obtained (see eg *Penarth Dock Engineering Co Ltd v Pounds* [1963] 1 Lloyd's Rep 359; *Wrotham Park Estate Co v Parkside Homes* [1974] 1 WLR 798; *Attorney-General v Blake* [2001] 1 AC 268). This is not relevant in the case of a takeover bid as there is no wrongdoing.

[226]  Companies Act 2006 (Commencement No 2, etc) Order 2007, SI 2007/1093, art 2(1)(b).

[227]  Section 304(1)(a).

[228]  Section 304(1)(b).

[229]  Section 305(1).

## *Supplementary*

## 970 Communication of decisions

(1) A company that has passed an opting-in resolution or an opting-out resolution must notify— 28.970.01

    (a) the Panel, and

    (b) where the company—

        (i) has voting shares admitted to trading on a regulated market in an EEA State other than the United Kingdom, or

        (ii) has requested such admission,

    the authority designated by that state as the supervisory authority for the purposes of Article 4.1 of the Takeovers Directive.

(2) Notification must be given within 15 days after the resolution is passed and, if any admission or request such as is mentioned in subsection (1)(b) occurs at a later time, within 15 days after that time.

(3) If a company fails to comply with this section, an offence is committed by—

    (a) the company, and

    (b) every officer of it who is in default.

(4) A person guilty of an offence under this section is liable on summary conviction to a fine not exceeding level 3 on the standard scale and, for continued contravention, a daily default fine not exceeding one-tenth of level 3 on the standard scale.

COMMENCEMENT DATE 6 April 2007[230]

Section 937 imposes statutory a duty on an opted-in company that passes an opting-in or opting-out resolution to notify the Panel.[231] If the company has voting shares admitted to trading on a regulated market in an EEA State other than the UK, or has requested such admission, then it must notify the competent authority under the Takeovers Directive in that jurisdiction.[232] Notification must be made within 15 days of the passing of the resolution.[233] A notification must also be made if the company's securities are admitted to trading on a regulated market outside of the UK, or if the company requests admission, within 15 days of such admission or request.[234]  28.970.02

Failure to notify is an offence punishable by a fine currently not exceeding £1000. Continued contravention is punishable by a daily default fine which may not exceed £100.[235]  28.970.03

Where an offence is committed by a company or body corporate every officer of the company who is in default is also guilty.[236] Section 1121(3) determines whether an officer is in default. This states that an officer is 'in default' if he authorizes or permits, participates in, or fails to take all reasonable steps to prevent, the contravention.  28.970.04

## 971 Interpretation of this Chapter

(1) In this Chapter— 28.971.01

    'offeror' and 'takeover bid' have the same meaning as in the Takeovers Directive;

    'offer period', in relation to a takeover bid, means the time allowed for acceptance of the bid by—

    (a) rules under section 943(1) giving effect to Article 7.1 of the Takeovers Directive, or

    (b) where the rules giving effect to that Article which apply to the bid are those of an EEA State other than the United Kingdom, those rules;

    'opted-in company' means a company in relation to which—

    (a) an opting-in resolution has effect, and

    (b) the conditions in section 966(2) and (4) continue to be met;

    'opting-in resolution' has the meaning given by section 966(1);

    'opting-out resolution' has the meaning given by section 933(5);

---

[230] Companies Act 2006 (Commencement No 2, etc) Order 2007, SI 2007/1093, art 2(1)(b).

[231] Section 970(1)(a).

[232] Section 970(1)(b).

[233] Section 970(2).

[234] Section 970(2).

[235] Section 970(4). Section 87 of the Legal Aid, Sentencing and Punishment of Offenders Act 2012, when it enters into force, will enable the Secretary of State to to alter the sums specified as levels 1 to 4 on the standard scale of fines for summary offences. Subsection (1) provides that the Secretary of State may by order substitute for the sums specified as levels 1 to 4 on the standard scale, such sums as the Secretary of State considers appropriate. Subsection (2) prevents the Secretary of State from altering the sums in a way which alters the ratio of the levels to each other. Subsections (5) and (6) provide that orders made under this section are to be made by statutory instrument, using the affirmative resolution procedure.

[236] Section 970(3).

'the Takeovers Directive' means Directive 2004/25/EC of the European Parliament and of the Council;

'voting rights' means rights to vote at general meetings of the company in question, including rights that arise only in certain circumstances;

'voting shares' means shares carrying voting rights.

(2) For the purposes of this Chapter—

(a) securities of a company are treated as shares in the company if they are convertible into or entitle the holder to subscribe for such shares;

(b) debentures issued by a company are treated as shares in the company if they carry voting rights.

COMMENCEMENT DATE  6 April 2007[237]

**28.971.02**    Section 971 contains definitions used in Chapter 2 of Part 28 of the Act. These definitions have been considered, where appropriate, in the commentary on sections 966 to 970.

### 972  Transitory provision

**28.972.01**

(1) Where a takeover bid is made for an opted-in company, section 368 of the Companies Act 1985 (c.6) (extraordinary general meeting on members' requisition) and section 378 of that Act (extraordinary and special resolutions) have effect as follows until their repeal by this Act.

(2) Section 368 has effect as if a members' requisition included a requisition of a person who—

(a) is the offeror in relation to the takeover bid, and

(b) holds at the date of the deposit of the requisition shares amounting to not less than 75% in value of all the voting shares in the company.

(3) In relation to a general meeting of the company that—

(a) is the first such meeting to be held after the end of the offer period, and

(b) is held at a time when the offeror holds shares amounting to not less than 75% in value of all the voting shares in the company,

section 378(2) (meaning of 'special resolution') has effect as if '14 days' notice' were substituted for '21 days' notice'.

(4) A reference in this section to voting shares in the company does not include—

(a) debentures, or

(b) shares that, under the company's articles of association, do not normally carry rights to vote at its general meetings (for example, shares carrying rights to vote that, under those articles, arise only where specified pecuniary advantages are not provided).

COMMENCEMENT DATE  6 April 2007[238]

**28.972.02**    Section 972 introduced a transitional provision for opted-in companies pending the repeal of sections 368 and 378 of the Companies Act 1985, and the bringing into force of section 969. Section 368 made provision for the calling of an extraordinary general meeting on a members' requisition. The effect was to enable an offeror holding not less than 75 per cent in value of the shares in the company to require the directors to call a general meeting. If the directors failed to call the meeting within 21 days, or to convene a meeting more than 28 days after the notice, the offeror could convene the meeting himself.[239] The amendment to section 378(2) enabled the meeting to be called on 14 days notice instead of 21 days. The corresponding provisions of the Act (sections 303 to 305) entered into force on 1 October 2007, so the force of this section is now spent.

### 973  Power to extend to Isle of Man and Channel Islands

**28.973.01**    Her Majesty may by Order in Council direct that any of the provisions of this Chapter extend, with such modifications as may be specified in the Order, to the Isle of Man or any of the Channel Islands.

COMMENCEMENT DATE  For the purposes of exercising the power to make orders: 20 January 2007. Otherwise 6 April 2007.[240]

**28.973.02**    The section enables the provisions on 'breakthrough' to be extended to the Isle of Man and the Channel Islands. No order has yet been made.

---

[237]  Companies Act 2006 (Commencement No 2, etc) Order 2007, SI 2007/1093, art 2(1)(b).

[238]  Companies Act 2006 (Commencement No 2, etc) Order 2007, SI 2007/1093, art 2(1)(b).

[239]  CA 1985, s 368(4) and (8).

[240]  Companies Act 2006 (Commencement No 2, etc) Order 2007, SI 2007/1093, art 2(1)(b).

# CHAPTER 3
## 'SQUEEZE-OUT' AND 'SELL-OUT'

### *Introduction*

Where a 'takeover offer' has been made, sections 974 to 982 (inclusive) provide a mechanism for the **28.0.02** offeror to acquire compulsorily certain shares which are not assented to the offer ('squeeze-out rights'). In addition, and again where a 'takeover offer' has been made, sections 983 to 985 (inclusive) allow certain minority shareholders to require the offeror to acquire their shares ('sell-out rights'). If an offer is not a 'takeover offer' for the purposes of Chapter 3, then the squeeze-out and sell-out rights under that Chapter will not apply. Absent such an offer, there is therefore no statutory mechanism under English law for a majority shareholder to acquire compulsorily shares held by the minority or for minority shareholders to require a majority shareholder to acquire their shares, other than by way of a scheme of arrangement under Parts 26 and 27 of the Act (sections 895 to 941 (inclusive) (see commentaries above under those sections)) which effectively re-enacts sections 425 to 427A (inclusive) and Schedule 15B of the Companies Act 1985.

For the purposes of both the squeeze-out and the sell-out mechanisms, a 'takeover offer' is defined by **28.0.03** reference to sections 974 to 978 (inclusive). However, it must also be an 'offer' which is capable of acceptance by shareholders and which, when so accepted, gives rise to a binding conditional or unconditional contract: In *Re Chez Nico (Restaurants) Limited*[241] the court held that an invitation to shareholders to tender their shares for sale was not an 'offer' for these purposes.

Squeeze-out and sell-out rights have been in UK company legislation for many years. In the case of **28.0.04** squeeze-out rights legislation was first introduced in 1929.[242] Sell-out rights first appeared in 1987.[243] Both sets of rights appeared in Part XIIIA (sections 428 to 430F (inclusive)) of the Companies Act 1985, although the provisions of Chapter 3 of Part 28 of the Act differ from those of the Companies Act 1985 in a number of significant respects. The changes in the law reflect the requirement of the UK to implement Articles 15 and 16 of the Takeovers Directive (Directive (EC) 2004/25[244] ) and some additional changes recommended in the Company Law Review.[245] Like its predecessor provisions in the Companies Act 1985, the provisions of Chapter 3 of Part 28 of the Act apply with respect to 'takeover offers' for shares in public or private companies (and regardless of whether the Takeovers Directive or the Takeover Code applies), although in practice these provisions have been and will continue to be most heavily applied in the case of takeovers of public companies.

The provisions of Chapter 3 of Part 28 of the Act came into force on 6 April 2007. The Act repealed **28.0.05** sections 428 to 430F (inclusive) of the Companies Act 1985 and articles 421 to 423F of the Companies (Northern Ireland) Order 1986 save in relation to a takeover offer where the date of the offer was before 6 April 2007.[246]

It is worth noting that the provisions of Chapter 3 of Part 28 are not the only mechanism by which a **28.0.06** minority shareholding in a company may potentially be compulsorily acquired. In particular, and as already noted, it is possible to achieve such an acquisition with the sanction of the court by means of a

---

[241] [1992] BCLC 192.

[242] Companies Act (CA) 1929, s 155, subsequently reenacted in the CA 1948, s 209 and then substituted by ss 428–430 of the CA 1985, which were themselves amended and supplemented by the Financial Services Act 1986, s 172.

[243] CA 1985, ss 430A and 430B, inserted by s 172(1) of, and Sch 12 to, the Financial Services Act 1986 as from 30 April 1987, save in any case in which the offer was made before that date.

[244] [2004] OJ L142/12.

[245] See in particular Final Report (Chapter 13, 282–300). Relevant provisions of the Takeovers Directive (Directive (EC) 2004/25 [2004] OJ L142/12) were implemented in relation to companies with securities carrying voting rights admitted to trading on a regulated market by the Takeovers Directive (Interim Implementation) Regulations 2006 (SI 2006/1183, regs 23 and 30 and Sch 2), which disapplied ss 428–430F (inclusive) of the CA 1985 for takeover offers made on or after 20 May 2006 for such companies. Those regulations were revoked by Art 7 of and Sch 5 to the Companies Act 2006 (Commencement No 2, Consequential Amendments, Transitional Provisions and Savings) Order 2007, SI 2007/1093.

[246] The repeal is set out in Sch 16 to the Act and the saving provision is set out in Sch 6 to the Companies Act 2006 (Commencement No 2, Consequential Amendments, Transitional Provisions and Savings) Order 2007, SI 2007/1093. References to the 'date of the offer' are to be construed under s 428(1) of the CA 1985 or Art 421(1) of the Companies (Northern Ireland) Order 1986 (as applicable) for this purpose. The revocation of the Takeovers Directive (Interim Implementation) Regulations 2006 (SI 2006/1183) also took effect such that the operation of Part 5 of those regulations (squeeze-out and sell-out) would not be affected in relation to a takeover offer where the date of the offer was before 6 April 2007.

scheme of arrangement under Parts 26 and 27 of the Act (see above). In addition it may be possible to effect such an acquisition by virtue of provisions introduced into the relevant company's articles of association, although the courts have, both before and since 1929, adopted a guarded approach when determining the validity of such provisions.[247] Nevertheless, it remains necessary to consider such provisions in certain situations.[248]

### Application to unregistered companies

**28.0.07**  The Companies Acts (Unregistered Companies) Regulations 2007[249] have been repealed and replaced by the Unregistered Companies Regulations 2009,[250] which came into force on 1 October 2009. An 'unregistered company' means a body corporate incorporated in, and having a principal place of business in, the United Kingdom, other than: (i) a body incorporated by, or registered under, a public general enactment, (ii) a body not formed for the purpose of carrying on a business that has for its object the acquisition of gain by the body or its individual members, (iii) a body for the time being exempted from section 1043 of the Companies Act 2006 by a direction of the Secretary of State under subsection 1(c) of that section, and (iv) an open-ended investment company.

**28.0.08**  Paragraph 14(2) of Schedule 1 to the Unregistered Companies Regulations 2009 applies sections 974 to 991 of the Companies Act 2006 to unregistered companies, but 'so far as relating to the offeree company only if the unregistered company has voting shares admitted to trading on a regulated market'.

### Takeover offers

### 974 Meaning of 'takeover offer'

**28.974.01**
(1) For the purposes of this Chapter an offer to acquire shares in a company is a 'take-over offer' if the following two conditions are satisfied in relation to the offer.

(2) The first condition is that it is an offer to acquire—
   (a) all the shares in a company, or
   (b) where there is more than one class of shares in a company, all the shares of one or more classes,
other than shares that at the date of the offer are already held by the offeror.
   Section 975 contains provision supplementing this subsection.

(3) The second condition is that the terms of the offer are the same—
   (a) in relation to all the shares to which the offer relates, or
   (b) where the shares to which the offer relates include shares of different classes, in relation to all the shares of each class.
   Section 976 contains provision treating this condition as satisfied in certain circumstances.

(4) In subsections (1) to (3) 'shares' means shares, other than relevant treasury shares, that have been allotted on the date of the offer (but see subsection (5)).

---

[247] The leading pre-1929 case is often cited as *Allen v Gold Reefs of West Africa Ltd* [1900] 1 Ch 656 even though it was not strictly a case on 'squeeze-out' provisions but rather a case on the ability of a majority shareholder to alter the articles of association. In that case Lindley MR held that such a power must be exercised 'bona fide for the benefit of the company', and in *Brown v British Abrasive Wheel Co* [1919] 1 Ch 290 Astbury J distinguished the benefit of the company concerned from the benefit of the majority shareholder which had attempted to alter the articles of association. An important more recent case is the Australian case of *Gambotto v WCP Ltd* [1995] 13 ACLC 324 in which the majority proposed that an amendment to the articles introducing squeeze-out rights would be valid if it was introduced for a proper purpose and did not operate oppressively in relation to the minority shareholders. *Gambotto* has not yet been comprehensively considered in the English courts, although for an indication of the possible view of the English courts of the 'proper purpose' aspect of the test expounded in *Gambotto*, see *Rock Nominees Ltd v RCO Holdings plc* [2004] EWCA Civ 118. See also *Constable v Executive Connections Limited* [2005] 2 BCLC 638.

[248] One of the most common situations in which such provisions need to be considered is in the context of provisions which are often introduced into the articles of association of a target company prior to the close of a takeover offer allowing or requiring the company to acquire compulsorily any further shares which are issued in the future pursuant to the exercise of options (eg options issued under the terms of an employees' share scheme). Although this has not been tested fully in the court, the view generally taken is that, provided such a provision is inserted into the articles of association before the options are exercised, and its insertion and subsequent application is not inconsistent with the terms on which the options are in issue, the provision should be enforceable.

[249] SI 2007/318.

[250] SI 2009/2436.

(5) A takeover offer may include among the shares to which it relates—

    (a) all or any shares that are allotted after the date of the offer but before a specified date;

    (b) all or any relevant treasury shares that cease to be held as treasury shares before a specified date;

    (c) all or any other relevant treasury shares.

(6) In this section—

    'relevant treasury shares' means shares that—

        (a) are held by the company as treasury shares on the date of the offer, or

        (b) become shares held by the company as treasury shares after that date but before a specified date;

    'specified date' means a date specified in or determined in accordance with the terms of the offer.

(7) Where the terms of an offer make provision for their revision and for acceptances on the previous terms to be treated as acceptances on the revised terms, then, if the terms of the offer are revised in accordance with that provision—

    (a) the revision is not to be regarded for the purposes of this Chapter as the making of a fresh offer, and

    (b) references in this Chapter to the date of the offer are accordingly to be read as references to the date of the original offer.

COMMENCEMENT DATE 6 April 2007 (subject to saving provisions: see General Introductory Commentary to Chapter 3 above).[251]

Under section 974 an offer for shares in a company is a 'takeover offer' if two conditions are satisfied. **28.974.02**

The first condition, set out in subsection (2), is that the offer is for all the shares in a company, or, where **28.974.03** there is more than one class of shares in a company, all the shares of one or more classes, in either case other than shares that at the date of the offer are already held by the offeror. Section 975 contains provisions in this regard relating to shares which the offeror already holds or has, on certain terms, already contracted to acquire when the offer is made.

The reference in subsection (2) to 'all the shares' is to all shares (or, as the case may be, all issued shares **28.974.04** of the particular class in question) in issue at the date of the offer. It is common in public company takeovers for the relevant offer to be made both for shares in issue on the date of the offer and also for shares subsequently allotted (for example, pursuant to the exercise of options) before a specified date (with provision for the offeror to elect to alter that date after the offer is made). Such an extension will not prevent an offer from being a 'takeover offer' for the purposes of section 974. Indeed, subsection (5)[252] provides that a takeover offer may include among the shares to which it relates 'all or any shares that are allotted after the date of the offer but before a specified date', 'all or any relevant treasury shares that cease to be held as treasury shares before a specified date' and/or 'all or any other relevant treasury shares'. Under subsection (6), 'relevant treasury shares' are, for this purpose, shares that are held by the company as treasury shares on the date of the offer or that become shares held by the company as treasury shares after that date but before a date specified in the terms of the offer (for example, because the company purchases shares and holds them as treasury shares after the date of the offer).

One effect of this first condition is that a 'takeover offer' must be made to all shareholders, including **28.974.05** those overseas. However, within the constraints of section 976, it is possible to offer different forms of consideration to overseas shareholders. Where the law of an overseas jurisdiction would prohibit the sending of documents containing the terms of an offer to such an overseas shareholder then, provided the offer is, on its terms, addressed to all shareholders, the fact that those documents are not sent into that jurisdiction may not affect the offer's status as a takeover offer for the purposes of section 974. However, judicial opinion expressed in the context of Part XIIIA of the Companies Act 1985 did not completely settle this point.[253] Section 978 of the Act now clarifies the position a little by stating that where there are holders of shares in a company to whom an offer to acquire shares in the company is not communicated, that does not prevent the offer from being a takeover offer for the purposes of Chapter 3 of Part 28 if certain conditions are satisfied. Please refer to the commentary on section 978 below.

---

[251] Companies Act 2006 (Commencement No 2, etc) Order 2007, SI 2007/1093, art 2.

[252] These provisions replicate the provisions of s 428(2) and (2A) of the CA 1985, which were introduced pursuant to reg 5 of the Companies (Acquisition of Own Shares) (Treasury Shares) (No 2) Regulations 2003, SI 2003/3031 as from 18 December 2003.

[253] See *Winpar Holdings Ltd v Joseph Holt Group plc* [2001] 2 BCLC 604, in which this point was considered but no general right was conferred on an offeror to avoid sending documents containing the terms of an offer into such jurisdictions.

**28.974.06** For the purposes of Chapter 3 of Part 28:

- Securities of a company are treated as shares in the company if they are convertible into, or entitle the holder to subscribe for, such shares.[254] This means that a 'takeover offer' within the meaning of 974 could be made for such convertible securities and a minority of non-assenting holders of those securities squeezed-out in accordance with the provisions of Chapter 3 of Part 28. This does not require any securities to be treated as shares of the same class as those into which they are convertible or for which the holder is entitled to subscribe, or as shares of the same class as other securities by reason only that the shares into which they are convertible or for which the holder is entitled to subscribe are of the same class.[255] Therefore convertible securities of this type would be treated as a separate class and a separate 'takeover offer' would be made for them prior to invoking the squeeze-out or sell-out provisions of Chapter 3 of Part 28.
- Debentures issued by a company that has voting shares, or debentures carrying voting rights, which are admitted to trading on a regulated market are treated as shares in the company if they carry voting rights.[256] This means that a 'takeover offer' within the meaning of section 974 could be made for such debentures and a minority of non-assenting debenture holders could be squeezed-out in accordance with the provisions of Chapter 3 of Part 28.

**28.974.07** The second condition for an offer to be a 'takeover offer', which is set out in subsection (3), is that the terms of the offer are the same in relation to all the shares to which the offer relates, or, where the shares to which the offer relates include shares of different classes, the same in relation to all the shares of each class. Section 976 (see commentary below) details cases where this condition is to be treated as satisfied. This condition is discussed further below in the commentary on section 976.

**28.974.08** Subsection (7), which has the same effect as section 428(7) of the Companies Act 1985, makes clear that where the terms of an offer provide for revisions to the offer any such revision will not be regarded as a new offer for the purposes of Chapter 3 of Part 28.[257] This is relevant to the time limits in section 980(2) which are discussed below in the commentary on that section.[258]

### 975  Shares already held by the offeror etc

**28.975.01**
(1) The reference in section 974(2) to shares already held by the offeror includes a reference to shares that he has contracted to acquire, whether unconditionally or subject to conditions being met. This is subject to subsection (2).
(2) The reference in section 974(2) to shares already held by the offeror does not include a reference to shares that are the subject of a contract—
  (a) intended to secure that the holder of the shares will accept the offer when it is made, and
  (b) entered into—
    (i) by deed and for no consideration,
    (ii) for consideration of negligible value, or
    (iii) for consideration consisting of a promise by the offeror to make the offer.
(3) In relation to Scotland, this section applies as if the words 'by deed and' in subsection (2)(b)(i) were omitted.
(4) The condition in section 974(2) is treated as satisfied where—
  (a) the offer does not extend to shares that associates of the offeror hold or have contracted to acquire (whether unconditionally or subject to conditions being met), and
  (b) the condition would be satisfied if the offer did extend to those shares.
    (For further provision about such shares, see section 977(2)).

COMMENCEMENT DATE 6 April 2007 (subject to saving provisions: see General Introductory Commentary to Chapter 3 above).[259]

**28.975.02** Section 975 expands on the requirement in section 974(2), which provides that a 'takeover offer' within the meaning of section 974 need not be made in respect of 'shares that at the date of the offer are already

---

[254] Section 989(1).
[255] Section 989(2).
[256] Section 990(1) and (2). Voting rights are defined for these purposes in s 991(1) as 'rights to vote at general meetings of the company, including rights that arise only in certain circumstances'.
[257] This means that where such an offer is revised in accordance with its terms allowing such revision, references to the 'date of the offer' in Chapter 3 of Part 28 of the Act will continue to be to the date of the original offer. See also s 991(1) and its commentary below.
[258] The implication of this is that if the terms of an offer do not provide for revisions, and the offeror wishes to revise the offer, the offeror will have to make a new takeover offer and address the effect of acceptances received under the old offer: see Re Chez Nico (Restaurants) Limited [1992] BCLC 192.
[259] Companies Act 2006 (Commencement No 2, etc) Order 2007, SI 2007/1093, art 2.

held by the offeror'. In particular, shares already held by the offeror include shares that he has contracted to acquire, whether unconditionally or subject to conditions being met (subsection (1)) but they exclude shares that are subject to a contract of the type described in subsection (2). Subsection (2) encompasses the agreements referred to as 'irrevocable undertakings', 'irrevocable commitments', or 'lock-up agreements' which are commonly entered into shortly before a takeover offer is announced or made.[260]

Subsection (2)(a) refers to such a contract as a contract 'intended to secure that the holder of the shares **28.975.03** will accept the offer when it is made', which raises the question of whether the insertion of other provisions into such a contract would prevent it from remaining within the subsection.[261] Subsections (2)(b)(i) and (iii) echo the provisions formerly set out in section 428(5) of the Companies Act 1985 that such a contract may either be entered into by deed and for no consideration[262] or for consideration consisting of a promise by the offeror to make the offer.[263] To these possibilities subsection (2)(b)(ii) adds that such a contract may also be entered into 'for consideration of negligible value'.[264]

The effect of subsection (1) is that shares to which a contract within the meaning of subsection (2) **28.975.04** relates count towards the threshold for the exercise of squeeze-out rights (see section 979) once these shares are assented to the offer. One helpful feature of section 975 is that, unlike its predecessor section 428(5) of the Companies Act 1985, it has the effect that an irrevocable undertaking need not be signed by the registered holder of the shares concerned in order that the shares to which the undertaking relates be counted, once they are assented to the offer, towards the thresholds needed to exercise squeeze-out or sell-out rights.[265] This is of particular relevance where shares are held by a trustee or custodian on behalf of a beneficial owner and it is easier to obtain the agreement of the beneficial owner of the shares (or another person, such as an investment manager, with the requisite authority in relation to disposals of the relevant shares) to the undertaking than the registered holder. Under the previous Companies Act 1985 regime, it was always necessary for an irrevocable undertaking to be executed by the registered holder[266] but it was often not possible to obtain the registered owner's agreement to the undertaking without express written authority and instruction from or on behalf of the beneficial owner of the shares.

The effect of subsection (4) is that a 'takeover offer' does not cease to be such for the purposes of section **28.975.05** 974 merely because it is not extended to shares held by 'associates' of the offeror (defined in section 988, which substantially replicates the provisions of section 430E of the Companies Act 1985).

Section 977(2) (see commentary below under that section) states that for the purposes of Chapter 3 of **28.975.06** Part 28, shares that an associate of the offeror holds or has contracted to acquire, whether at the date of the offer or subsequently, are not treated as 'shares to which the offer relates', even if the offer extends to such shares.

---

[260]  Certain provisions of the Takeover Code have the result that, in the case of takeovers to which the Takeover Code applies, such agreements are normally entered into shortly before a firm intention to make the offer is announced, rather than simply at any time before the offer is made.

[261]  The corresponding provision in the CA 1985, s 428(5), referred to such a contract as 'a contract binding the holder to accept the offer when it is made'.

[262]  The reference to deeds is omitted in relation to Scotland: subs (3).

[263]  The arrangement most commonly chosen in relation to public company takeovers has been a contract entered into by deed and for no consideration, even though this carries the disadvantage that it may not be possible to obtain specific performance of the relevant shareholder's undertaking to accept the offer. Offerors often avoid seeking undertakings in the form of a contract entered into for consideration consisting of a promise by the offeror to make the offer because they may wish to preserve a residual right not to make the offer, however unlikely it might be that the Takeover Panel would allow such a right to be exercised: the Takeover Code contains stringent restrictions on failure to make an offer once a firm intention to make the offer has been announced so this is a more important consideration in relation to takeover offers to which the Takeover Code does not apply.

[264]  This allows the possibility that an offeror could obtain an irrevocable undertaking, executed other than by way of a deed, which may, subject to the availability of equitable remedies, be enforceable by way of specific performance, although the question of whether the consideration provided is of 'negligible value' would have to be addressed.

[265]  This is the case because subs (2)(a) refers to a contract 'intended to secure that the holder of the shares will accept the offer when it is made', which could refer to a contract to procure acceptance of the offer executed by the absolute beneficial owner of the relevant shares or by some other person who is entitled to bind the registered holder. It remains necessary to check that such a beneficial owner of shares, or other person, has the power to procure that the offer is accepted.

[266]  This was the case because s 428(5) of the CA 1985 referred to a contract 'binding the holder'; by contrast, s 975(2)(a) of the Act refers to a contract 'intended to secure that the holder of the shares will accept the offer when it is made'.

## 976 Cases where offer treated as being on same terms

**28.976.01**
    (1) The condition in section 974(3) (terms of offer to be the same for all shares or all shares of particular classes) is treated as satisfied where subsection (2) or (3) below applies.

    (2) This subsection applies where—

        (a) shares carry an entitlement to a particular dividend which other shares of the same class, by reason of being allotted later, do not carry,

        (b) there is a difference in the value of consideration offered for the shares allotted earlier as against that offered for those allotted later,

        (c) that difference merely reflects the difference in entitlement to the dividend, and

        (d) the condition in section 974(3) would be satisfied but for that difference.

    (3) This subsection applies where—

        (a) the law of a country or territory outside the United Kingdom—

            (i) precludes an offer of consideration in the form, or any of the forms, specified in the terms of the offer ('the specified form'), or

            (ii) precludes it except after compliance by the offeror with conditions with which he is unable to comply or which he regards as unduly onerous,

        (b) the persons to whom an offer of consideration in the specified form is precluded are able to receive consideration in another form that is of substantially equivalent value, and

        (c) the condition in section 974(3) would be satisfied but for the fact that an offer of consideration in the specified form to those persons is precluded.

COMMENCEMENT DATE 6 April 2007 (subject to saving provisions: see General Introductory Commentary to Chapter 3 above).[267]

**28.976.02** The second condition in section 974 to an offer being a 'takeover offer' for the purposes of Chapter 3 of Part 28 of the Act is that the terms of offer must be the same for all shares or all shares of particular classes. Section 976 lists a number of instances where that is treated to be the case.[268]

**28.976.03** Subsection (2) allows an offeror to offer consideration of a different value to different shareholders where the difference in value reflects a difference in entitlement to a particular dividend of the company which arises by virtue of the shares in question having been allotted later than other shares. Notwithstanding that the consideration differs between shareholders in this way, the offer will still be a 'takeover offer' for the purposes of section 974.[269] For example, where the terms on which a dividend is to be paid are such that only shareholders who are registered as such on a particular date are entitled to receive the dividend, and subsequent to that date (but before the dividend is actually paid) the company allots further shares, an offeror would be entitled to offer consideration of a different value to the holders of those subsequently allotted shares than to the holders of shares in respect of which the dividend was paid, the difference in value per share reflecting the dividend per share that is payable.

**28.976.04** Subsection (3) substantially replicates the effect of section 428(4) of the Companies Act 1985 and allows an offeror to offer consideration in another form 'of substantially equivalent value' to that offered to other shareholders where the law of a country or territory outside the UK precludes an offer of consideration in the form, or any of the forms, specified in the terms of the offer or precludes it except after compliance by the offeror with conditions with which he is unable to comply or which he regards as unduly onerous. For example, where the consideration under the offer is shares with a cash alternative, the terms of the offer may provide that residents of a non-UK jurisdiction may only accept the cash alternative where making the share alternative available in that jurisdiction would require the satisfaction of local legal requirements with which the offeror is unable to comply. If the offer does so provide then it should not, on this ground, cease to be a 'takeover offer' for the purposes of section 974. Where the consideration is shares only, with no cash alternative, it is thought that the offer could provide for relevant non-UK accepting shareholders to be deemed to have authorized the sale of their consideration shares for cash which would then be remitted to them, although there is no judicial authority on this point.

**28.976.05** Section 976 does not define 'substantially equivalent value' and there is no direct judicial authority on this point. There is a risk that, if the consideration is shares with a fixed value cash alternative, and only the cash alternative is made available to certain non-UK shareholders, a change in the value of the shares during the course of the offer may result in a violation of this requirement. There may also be commercial reasons why the value of share consideration may not be the same as the value of a cash alternative from the outset, reflecting such factors as the immediate value and convertibility of cash in

---

[267] Companies Act 2006 (Commencement No 2, etc) Order 2007, SI 2007/1093, art 2.

[268] It should be noted, in the context of takeover offers to which the Takeover Code applies, that Rule 16 of the Takeover Code imposes restrictions on differential offers being made to different shareholders.

[269] No such guidance appeared in the squeeze-out provisions of the CA 1985.

the hands of its recipients, and the marketability of, and market risks associated with the value of, the consideration shares. If these factors are relevant in determining the respective values of share consideration and a cash alternative then they will need to be assessed against the 'substantially equivalent value' criterion if section 976(3) is relevant.

The DTI Consultative Document on the Act[270] proposed that where some shareholders agree to accept    **28.976.06**
more onerous obligations than others, that ought not in itself to prevent the offer from being a 'takeover offer' allowing the application of the squeeze-out or sell-out mechanisms. However, this proposal has not been implemented in the Act. It therefore remains unclear, for example, whether an offer which involves some, but not all, shareholders giving warranties or indemnities to the offeror, would fall within the definition of a 'takeover offer' for the purposes of Chapter 3 of Part 28 of the Act. Accordingly, the issue to be considered remains that of whether such additional obligations amount to terms of the offer or not. This point can be of particular relevance where an offeror seeks warranties from shareholders who are involved in the management of the target company but does not seek warranties from other shareholders.

## 977  Shares to which an offer relates

(1)  Where a takeover offer is made and, during the period beginning with the date of the offer and    **28.977.01**
ending when the offer can no longer be accepted, the offeror—

    (a)  acquires or unconditionally contracts to acquire any of the shares to which the offer relates, but

    (b)  does not do so by virtue of acceptances of the offer,

those shares are treated for the purposes of this Chapter as excluded from those to which the offer relates.

(2)  For the purposes of this Chapter shares that an associate of the offeror holds or has contracted to acquire, whether at the date of the offer or subsequently, are not treated as shares to which the offer relates, even if the offer extends to such shares.

In this subsection 'contracted' means contracted unconditionally or subject to conditions being met.

(3)  This section is subject to section 979(8) and (9).

COMMENCEMENT DATE  6 April 2007 (subject to saving provisions: see General Introductory Commentary to Chapter 3 above).[271]

The expression 'shares to which the offer relates' is used in a number of contexts in Chapter 3 of Part    **28.977.02**
28 of the Act. The concept is particularly important in the context of the thresholds in sections 979(2) and (4) which an offeror must reach in order to exercise squeeze-out rights under that section. Subject to exceptions set out in section 979 (8) and (9), the effect of section 977 is to exclude from the 'shares to which the offer relates':

- shares which the offeror acquires or unconditionally contracts to acquire, other than by virtue of acceptances of the offer, during the period beginning with the date of the offer up to the time when the offer can no longer be accepted; and
- shares which an 'associate'[272] of the offeror holds or has contracted to acquire (whether before or after the offer is made), even if the offer extends to those shares.

    The principal implications of this, and of the provisions of sections 979(8) and (9), are as follows.

(i)  Shares held by an offeror or its associates at the date of the offer are excluded from the calculation of the percentage thresholds set out in sections 979(2) and (4). This means that, when calculating those thresholds, such shares are excluded from both the denominator and the numerator.

(ii)  Shares purchased by the offeror after that time (but before the time when the offer can no longer be accepted) may be counted towards those percentage thresholds (ie they should be included in both the denominator and the numerator in the calculation) where the requirements of section 979(8) are met. Where these requirements are not met, such shares are excluded from the calculation of the percentage threshold as stated in paragraph (i) above.

(iii)  Shares purchased by an associate of the offeror after the time referred to in paragraph (i) above (but again before the time when the offer can no longer be accepted) may also be counted towards the percentage thresholds (ie they should be included in both the denominator and the numerator in the calculation) where the requirements of section 979(9) are met and those shares are assented

---

[270]  See *Modern Company Law for a Competitive Economy: Completing the Structure* (DTI, November 2000) (Annex B) 378.

[271]  Companies Act 2006 (Commencement No 2, etc) Order 2007, SI 2007/1093, art 2.

[272]  'Associate' is defined in s 988. See the commentary below on that section.

to the offer. Where these requirements are not met, such shares are excluded from the calculation of the percentage threshold as stated in paragraph (i) above.

(iv) Only a holder of 'shares to which the offer relates' may invoke the sell-out provisions of sections 983 to 985 (inclusive). In other words, an associate of the offeror may not invoke those provisions.

### 978  Effect of impossibility etc of communicating or accepting offer

**28.978.01**

(1) Where there are holders of shares in a company to whom an offer to acquire shares in the company is not communicated, that does not prevent the offer from being a takeover offer for the purposes of this Chapter if—
  (a) those shareholders have no registered address in the United Kingdom,
  (b) the offer was not communicated to those shareholders in order not to contravene the law of a country or territory outside the United Kingdom, and
  (c) either—
    (i) the offer is published in the Gazette, or
    (ii) the offer can be inspected, or a copy of it obtained, at a place in an EEA State or on a website, and a notice is published in the Gazette specifying the address of that place or website.

(2) Where an offer is made to acquire shares in a company and there are persons for whom, by reason of the law of a country or territory outside the United Kingdom, it is impossible to accept the offer, or more difficult to do so, that does not prevent the offer from being a takeover offer for the purposes of this Chapter.

(3) It is not to be inferred—
  (a) that an offer which is not communicated to every holder of shares in the company cannot be a takeover offer for the purposes of this Chapter unless the requirements of paragraphs (a) to (c) of subsection (1) are met, or
  (b) that an offer which is impossible, or more difficult, for certain persons to accept cannot be a takeover offer for those purposes unless the reason for the impossibility or difficulty is the one mentioned in subsection (2).

COMMENCEMENT DATE  6 April 2007 (subject to saving provisions: see General Introductory Commentary to Chapter 3 above).[273]

**28.978.02**  Section 978 allows an offeror not to communicate an offer to certain shareholders whilst still maintaining the offer as a 'takeover offer' for the purposes of Chapter 3 of Part 28 of the Act. Specifically, it allows the offeror to avoid communicating the offeror to shareholders without registered addresses in the UK in order not to contravene the law of a country or territory outside the UK, provided the offer is published in the Gazette[274] or the offer can be inspected, or a copy of it obtained, at a place in an EEA state or on a website, and a notice is published in the Gazette specifying the address of that place or website, where, in either case, references to the 'offer' are to the offer and its terms. Many offerors are likely to decide that making a copy of the offer available for inspection, rather than publishing it on a website, is a more practicable arrangement because if an offeror proposed to publish the offer on a website it would have to check its compliance with securities and other law and regulation of jurisdictions from which the website is accessible and may, subject to local law and regulation, find onerous conditions attached to such compliance.

**28.978.03**  It is important to note that subsection (1) concerns the communication of an offer and does not affect the general requirement in section 974 that a 'takeover offer' be made for all shares (or all shares of the class in question). In other words the 'takeover offer' to which subsection (1) refers must still be made to the overseas shareholders concerned but it need not be communicated to them if the requirements of that section are fulfilled.

**28.978.04**  It may be the case that, where the offer is made to a shareholder, it may not be possible, or it may be more difficult, for that shareholder to accept the offer by reason of the law of a country or territory outside the UK. In that case subsection (2) provides that the offer will not, by virtue of that impossibility or greater difficulty, fail to be a 'takeover offer' for the purposes of Chapter 3 of Part 28. Difficulties with accepting the offer are to be considered separately from non-communication of the offer itself. The latter point is addressed in subsection (3)(a) (see below).

**28.978.05**  Subsection (3)(a) maintains the possibility that, where an offer is not communicated to one or more shareholders and the reason for that is not that stated in subsection (1) and/or the procedural

---

[273] Companies Act 2006 (Commencement No 2, etc) Order 2007, SI 2007/1093, art 2.
[274] This is a reference to the *London Gazette* for companies registered in England and Wales, the *Edinburgh Gazette* for companies registered in Scotland, and the *Belfast Gazette* for companies registered in Northern Ireland: s 1173(1).

requirements of subsection (1) have not been met, the offer will not necessarily fail to be a 'takeover offer', although the ability of an offeror simply to make the terms available for inspection at an address in the EEA notified in the Gazette should make it straightforward to avoid reliance on subsection (3)(a).

Similarly, subsection (3)(b) maintains the possibility that, where an offer is impossible, or more difficult, for certain persons to accept, and the reason for that impossibility or greater difficulty is not that stated in subsection (2), that also does not necessarily mean that the offer will fail to be a 'takeover offer'.  **28.978.06**

The effect of subsection (3) is effectively to confer an ability on the court to hold that an offer is a **28.978.07** 'takeover offer' notwithstanding that subsection (1) or (2) is not satisfied. For example, the court may, if presented with similar facts, choose to follow *Winpar Holdings Ltd v Joseph Holt Group plc*[275] in which it was held that an offeror could invoke the squeeze-out provisions of section 429 of the Companies Act 1985 notwithstanding that the offer document had not been communicated to a small number of overseas shareholders and had not otherwise been made available to them.

### *'Squeeze-out'*

### 979  Right of offeror to buy out minority shareholder

(1) Subsection (2) applies in a case where a takeover offer does not relate to shares of different  **28.979.01**
   classes.
(2) If the offeror has, by virtue of acceptances of the offer, acquired or unconditionally contracted to acquire—
   (a) not less than 90% in value of the shares to which the offer relates, and
   (b) in a case where the shares to which the offer relates are voting shares, not less than 90% of the voting rights carried by those shares,
   he may give notice to the holder of any shares to which the offer relates which the offeror has not acquired or unconditionally contracted to acquire that he desires to acquire those shares.
(3) Subsection (4) applies in a case where a takeover offer relates to shares of different classes.
(4) If the offeror has, by virtue of acceptances of the offer, acquired or unconditionally contracted to acquire—
   (a) not less than 90% in value of the shares of any class to which the offer relates, and
   (b) in a case where the shares of that class are voting shares, not less than 90% of the voting rights carried by those shares,
   he may give notice to the holder of any shares of that class to which the offer relates which the offeror has not acquired or unconditionally contracted to acquire that he desires to acquire those shares.
(5) In the case of a takeover offer which includes among the shares to which it relates—
   (a) shares that are allotted after the date of the offer, or
   (b) relevant treasury shares (within the meaning of section 974) that cease to be held as treasury shares after the date of the offer,
   the offeror's entitlement to give a notice under subsection (2) or (4) on any particular date shall be determined as if the shares to which the offer relates did not include any allotted, or ceasing to be held as treasury shares, on or after that date.
(6) Subsection (7) applies where—
   (a) the requirements for the giving of a notice under subsection (2) or (4) are satisfied, and
   (b) there are shares in the company which the offeror, or an associate of his, has contracted to acquire subject to conditions being met, and in relation to which the contract has not become unconditional.
(7) The offeror's entitlement to give a notice under subsection (2) or (4) shall be determined as if—
   (a) the shares to which the offer relates included shares falling within paragraph (b) of subsection (6), and
   (b) in relation to shares falling within that paragraph, the words 'by virtue of acceptances of the offer' in subsection (2) or (4) were omitted.
(8) Where—
   (a) a takeover offer is made,
   (b) during the period beginning with the date of the offer and ending when the offer can no longer be accepted, the offeror—
      (i) acquires or unconditionally contracts to acquire any of the shares to which the offer relates, but
      (ii) does not do so by virtue of acceptances of the offer, and
   (c) subsection (10) applies,

---

275 [2001] 2 BCLC 604.

then, for the purposes of this section, those shares are not excluded by section 977(1) from those to which the offer relates, and the offeror is treated as having acquired or contracted to acquire, them by virtue of acceptances of the offer.

(9) Where—

    (a)  a takeover offer is made,

    (b)  during the period beginning with the date of the offer and ending when the offer can no longer be accepted, an associate of the offeror acquires or unconditionally contracts to acquire any of the shares to which the offer relates, and

    (c)  subsection (10) applies,

then for the purposes of this section those shares are not excluded by section 977(2) from those to which the offer relates.

(10) This subsection applies if—

    (a)  at the time the shares are acquired or contracted to be acquired as mentioned in subsection (8) or (9) (as the case may be), the value of the consideration for which they are acquired or contracted to be acquired ('the acquisition consideration') does not exceed the value of the consideration specified in the terms of the offer, or

    (b)  those terms are subsequently revised so that when the revision is announced the value of the acquisition consideration, at the time mentioned in paragraph (a), no longer exceeds the value of the consideration specified in those terms.

COMMENCEMENT DATE 6 April 2007 (subject to saving provisions: see General Introductory Commentary to Chapter 3 above).[276]

**28.979.02**    Section 979 is the principal provision of Chapter 3 of Part 28 of the Act regarding 'squeeze-out' rights. The section, which is subject to the procedural requirements of sections 980 and 981, provides (at subsection (2)) that an offeror who has made a 'takeover offer' (within the meaning of section 974) may compulsorily acquire shares in respect of which that offer has not been accepted if the offeror has acquired or unconditionally contracted to acquire (a) at least 90 per cent in value of the shares to which the offer relates,[277] and (b) where those shares are voting shares, at least 90 per cent of the voting rights carried by those shares. The first limb of this test is the same as that which appeared in section 429 of the Companies Act 1985, save that this limb is now clarified to refer to shares acquired or *unconditionally*[278] contracted to be acquired; the second limb is new, although in most cases it is unlikely to alter the manner in which the test applies. The reason for the addition of the new second limb of the test is that it is required by Article 15(2) of the Takeovers Directive.

**28.979.03**    Circumstances in which the second limb of the test would alter the position are likely to be rare but could include a situation where some shares in a class subject to a takeover offer have been completely disenfranchised pursuant to provisions of the articles of association of the relevant company.

**28.979.04**    Where there is more than one class of share, the two-limb test described above applies on a class-by-class basis (subsection (4)).

**28.979.05**    Where the takeover offer extends to shares allotted after the date of the offer or to relevant treasury shares which cease to be held as such after that date,[279] the offeror's entitlement to give a notice under subsection (2) or (4) at any time is assessed without reference to shares allotted after that time or 'relevant treasury shares' (within the meaning of section 974) which cease to be held as such after that time. The effect of subsection (5) is that if shares are subsequently allotted, or 'relevant treasury shares' subsequently cease to be held as such, this would not affect the offeror's entitlement to serve the notice (even if the effect of the allotment or the treasury shares ceasing to be held as such means that the offeror falls below the acceptance threshold in subsection (2) or (4)):[280] the notice, once served, takes its course under the procedural provisions of sections 980 and 981. If the offeror wishes to serve further

---

[276]  Companies Act 2006 (Commencement No 2, etc) Order 2007, SI 2007/1093, art 2.

[277]  The term 'value' also appeared in this test as formulated in s 429 of CA 1985.

[278]  The word 'unconditionally' did not appear in s 429 of CA 1985, although so far as the application of the test in s 429(1) of CA 1985 was concerned (that the offeror must have 'acquired or contracted to acquire not less than nine-tenths in value of the shares to which the offer relates'), 'contracted to acquire' was generally accepted to mean 'unconditionally contracted to acquire', although the use of the phrase 'contracted to acquire' in other provisions of Part XIIIA of CA 1985 was less clear on this point. For the purposes of s 979 a person contracts unconditionally to acquire shares if his entitlement under the contract to acquire them is not (or is no longer) subject to conditions or if all conditions to which it was subject have been met: s 991(2). References in Chapter 3 of Part 28 of the Act to a contract becoming unconditional are to be read accordingly.

[279]  See s 974(5) and (6) and accompanying commentary above.

[280]  This is a welcome clarification of the position which pertained under s 429 of CA 1985, where subsequent allotments pursuant to the exercise of convertible securities or options required particularly careful consideration.

squeeze-out notices then it must satisfy the applicable 90 per cent thresholds by reference to shares (or shares in a class) then in issue and to which the offer relates at the time when those notices are given.

Where the acceptance threshold in subsection (2) or (4) has been reached and the offeror or his   **28.979.06**
associate has contracted to acquire shares to which the offer relates and the relevant contract is subject to one or more conditions which have not been fulfilled, those shares are, by virtue of subsection (7), included in the shares to which the offer relates for the purposes of determining the offeror's continuing entitlement to give a notice under this section.[281]

Subsections (8) and (9) address the treatment of shares to which the offer relates which are acquired or   **28.979.07**
unconditionally contracted to be acquired by the offeror other than by way of acceptances of the offer, or acquired or unconditionally contracted to be acquired by the offeror's associates, in either case while the offer remains open for acceptance. Where the shares subject to the offer are publicly traded, this would include, for example, shares which the offeror or its associates acquire in the market during this period. The offeror is treated as having acquired or contracted to acquire shares which it acquires in this manner by virtue of acceptances of the offer (and may therefore take them into account in assessing whether it has reached the applicable acceptance threshold for the purposes of subsection (2) or (4)) provided subsection (10) applies (see below). Similarly, shares which associates of the offeror acquire or unconditionally contract to acquire during that period are treated for the purposes of section 979 as shares to which the offer relates, again only if subsection (10) applies.

Subsection (10) specifies that the value of the consideration for which the offeror or its associate (as the   **28.979.08**
case may be) acquires or contracts to acquire such shares must not exceed the value of the consideration under the terms of the offer or, where it does exceed the offer consideration, the offer is revised so that this requirement is met.[282]

## 980  Further provision about notices given under section 979

(1) A notice under section 979 must be given in the prescribed manner.   **28.980.01**
(2) No notice may be given under section 979(2) or (4) after the end of—
    (a) the period of three months beginning with the day after the last day on which the offer can be accepted, or
    (b) the period of six months beginning with the date of the offer, where that period ends earlier and the offer is one to which subsection (3) below applies.
(3) This subsection applies to an offer if the time allowed for acceptance of the offer is not governed by rules under section 943(1) that give effect to Article 7 of the Takeovers Directive.
    In this subsection 'the Takeovers Directive' has the same meaning as in section 943.
(4) At the time when the offeror first gives a notice under section 979 in relation to an offer, he must send to the company—
    (a) a copy of the notice, and
    (b) a statutory declaration by him in the prescribed form, stating that the conditions for the giving of the notice are satisfied.
(5) Where the offeror is a company (whether or not a company within the meaning of this Act) the statutory declaration must be signed by a director.
(6) A person commits an offence if—
    (a) he fails to send a copy of a notice or a statutory declaration as required by subsection (4), or
    (b) he makes such a declaration for the purposes of that subsection knowing it to be false or without having reasonable grounds for believing it to be true.
(7) It is a defence for a person charged with an offence for failing to send a copy of a notice as required by subsection (4) to prove that he took reasonable steps for securing compliance with that subsection.
(8) A person guilty of an offence under this section is liable—
    (a) on conviction on indictment, to imprisonment for a term not exceeding two years or a fine (or both);
    (b) on summary conviction—
        (i) in England and Wales, to imprisonment for a term not exceeding twelve months or to a fine not exceeding the statutory maximum (or both) and, for continued contravention, a daily default fine not exceeding one-fiftieth of the statutory maximum;

---

[281] This means, in effect, that the squeeze-out right may not be exercised until the applicable 90 per cent thresholds have been reached on the basis of acceptances of the offer and unconditional acquisitions of shares.

[282] Where the Takeover Code applies, acquisitions of shares or interests in shares made while an offer remains open for acceptance will, in any event, trigger a requirement to increase the consideration under the terms of the offer where the highest price paid for such acquisitions exceeds that previously stated under the terms of the offer: Takeover Code, Rule 6.2.

(ii) in Scotland or Northern Ireland, to imprisonment for a term not exceeding six months, or to a fine not exceeding the statutory maximum (or both) and, for continued contravention, a daily default fine not exceeding one-fiftieth of the statutory maximum.

COMMENCEMENT DATE 6 April 2007 (subject to saving provisions: see General Introductory Commentary to Chapter 3 above).[283]

**28.980.02**  Section 980 sets out the manner and form in which a notice under section 979 is to be given.

**28.980.03**  The notice must be given to each non-assenting shareholder in a prescribed form.[284] Under subsection (2) no such notice may be served more than three months after the last day on which the offer may be accepted. This period is alternatively six months beginning with the date of the offer if this period ends earlier and subsection (3) applies to the offer. Subsection (3) will broadly apply where the takeover offer is not subject to the Takeovers Directive, for example takeovers of most private companies.

**28.980.04**  The time limits in section 980 which derive from Article 15(4) of the Takeovers Directive contrast with those that applied under section 429(3) of the Companies Act 1985, which provided that no notice could be given unless the applicable acceptance threshold had been reached within four months of the date of the offer and that no such notice could be given more than two months after the offeror had acquired or contracted to acquire shares which satisfied that threshold.[285]

**28.980.05**  Under subsection (4), when a notice is first given under section 979, the offeror must send a copy of the notice to the company together with a statutory declaration in the prescribed form[286] stating that the conditions for the giving of the notice are satisfied. Where, as is common in public takeovers, the offeror wishes to serve a number of such notices, practice is likely to continue to follow that adopted under the former section 429(4) of the Companies Act 1985 (which is substantially replicated in subsection (4)): a copy of the first such notice sent out is sent to the company.[287]

**28.980.06**  There are offences for failing to send the notice or statutory declaration to the company in accordance with subsection (4) and for making the statutory declaration knowing it to be false or without having reasonable grounds for believing it to be true (subsection (6)). It is a defence for a person charged with the offence of failing to send the notice as required by subsection (4) to prove that he took reasonable steps to do so (subsection (7)). These offences, and the available defence, are also the same as those that applied under sections 429(6) and (7) of the Companies Act 1985. The penalties, which are set out in subsection (8) of this section, are (a) on conviction on indictment, imprisonment for up to two years and/or an unlimited fine; and (b) on summary conviction, imprisonment for up to 12 months (six months in Scotland or Northern Ireland) or a fine not exceeding the statutory maximum (currently £5,000)[288] and, for continued contravention, a daily default fine of up to one-fiftieth of the statutory maximum (currently £100). However, by virtue of section 1131 in relation to an offence committed after commencement of that section and before commencement of section 154(1) of the Criminal Justice Act 2003, the reference to 'twelve months' is substituted by 'six months'. Section 154(1) of the Criminal Justice Act 2003 will enter into force at a date to be appointed.[289] See Chapter 36 for commentary on section 1131.

### 981 Effect of notice under section 979

**28.981.01**
(1) Subject to section 986 (applications to the court), this section applies where the offeror gives a shareholder a notice under section 979.
(2) The offeror is entitled and bound to acquire the shares to which the notice relates on the terms of the offer.

---

[283]  Companies Act 2006 (Commencement No 2, etc) Order 2007, SI 2007/1093, art 2.

[284]  The prescribed form is set out in the Companies (Forms) (Amendment) Regulations 1987, SI 1987/752, as amended by the Companies Act 2006 (Commencement No 2, Consequential Amendments, Transitional Provisions and Savings) Order 2007, SI 2007/1093.

[285]  In *Re Western Manufacturing Ltd* [1956] Ch 436, [1955] 3 All ER 733 it was held that the offeror was permitted to fix a shorter period than that which applied at the relevant time. This principle seems likely also to apply to the new time limits specified in subs (2).

[286]  Where the offeror is a company, the statutory declaration must be signed by a director: subs (5). The prescribed form is set out in the Companies (Forms) (Amendment) Regulations 1987 (SI 1987/752), as amended by the Companies Act 2006 (Commencement No 2, Consequential Amendments, Transitional Provisions and Savings) Order 2007, SI 2007/1093.

[287]  Therefore, where numerous such notices are sent out, copies of the other such notices are not sent to the company. The 'first notice' is often regarded as that sent to the non-assenting shareholder whose name appears first on the register of members of the company (but see also s 981(6)). Whether this practice complies with this section (or the former provision, s 429(4) of CA 1985) has not been tested in the court.

[288]  Magistrates' Courts Act 1980, s 32(9), as amended by the Criminal Justice Act 1991, s 17(2)(c).

[289]  Criminal Justice Act 2003, s 336(3).

(3) Where the terms of an offer are such as to give the shareholder a choice of consideration, the notice must give particulars of the choice and state –

    (a) that the shareholder may, within six weeks from the date of the notice, indicate his choice by a written communication sent to the offeror at an address specified in the notice, and

    (b) which consideration specified in the offer will apply if he does not indicate a choice.

The reference in subsection (2) to the terms of the offer is to be read accordingly.

(4) Subsection (3) applies whether or not any time-limit or other conditions applicable to the choice under the terms of the offer can still be complied with.

(5) If the consideration offered to or (as the case may be) chosen by the shareholder—

    (a) is not cash and the offeror is no longer able to provide it, or

    (b) was to have been provided by a third party who is no longer bound or able to provide it,

the consideration is to be taken to consist of an amount of cash, payable by the offeror, which at the date of the notice is equivalent to the consideration offered or (as the case may be) chosen.

(6) At the end of six weeks from the date of the notice the offeror must immediately—

    (a) send a copy of the notice to the company, and

    (b) pay or transfer to the company the consideration for the shares to which the notice relates.

Where the consideration consists of shares or securities to be allotted by the offeror, the reference in paragraph (b) to the transfer of the consideration is to be read as a reference to the allotment of the shares or securities to the company.

(7) If the shares to which the notice relates are registered, the copy of the notice sent to the company under subsection (6)(a) must be accompanied by an instrument of transfer executed on behalf of the holder of the shares by a person appointed by the offeror.

On receipt of that instrument the company must register the offeror as the holder of those shares.

(8) If the shares to which the notice relates are transferable by the delivery of warrants or other instruments, the copy of the notice sent to the company under subsection (6)(a) must be accompanied by a statement to that effect.

On receipt of that statement the company must issue the offeror with warrants or other instruments in respect of the shares, and those already in issue in respect of the shares become void.

(9) The company must hold any money or other consideration received by it under subsection (6)(b) on trust for the person who, before the offeror acquired them, was entitled to the shares in respect of which the money or other consideration was received.

Section 982 contains further provision about how the company should deal with such money or other consideration.

COMMENCEMENT DATE  6 April 2007 (subject to saving provisions: see General Introductory Commentary to Chapter 3 above).[290]

Section 981 sets out the effect of a squeeze-out notice given under section 979 and substantially replicates the provisions of section 430 of the Companies Act 1985. Once such a notice is given, the offeror is 'entitled and bound' to acquire the shares to which the notice relates 'on the terms of the offer': subsection (2).[291]   **28.981.02**

Under subsection (3), if there is a choice of consideration, the notice must give particulars of the choice and state that the shareholder may make his choice in writing to the offeror within six weeks from the date of the notice, and the notice must also state which consideration will apply if the shareholder does not indicate a choice. This can cause difficulties where one or more consideration choices are, by their nature, only available as a practical matter for a limited period and may not, therefore, continue to be available to non-assenting shareholders after the giving of notices under section 979. Subsection (4) provides in effect that the consideration choices made available to the assenting shareholders must be extended to the non-assenting shareholders, even if a time period within which one or more such choices had to be exercised has expired,[292] save that subsection (5) requires the offeror to substitute cash 'equivalent' for non-cash consideration offered to or chosen by the non-assenting shareholder in circumstances where the offeror is no longer able to provide that consideration or a third party who was to have provided that consideration is no longer bound or able to do so. Overall, then, where a takeover offer provides for cash and non-cash consideration choices, cash consideration must be preserved as a choice for non-assenting shareholders but non-cash consideration must be substituted with an 'equivalent' amount of cash if subsection (5) applies. The assessment of 'equivalence' for these purposes may give rise to difficult issues.   **28.981.03**

---

[290]  Companies Act 2006 (Commencement No 2, etc) Order 2007, SI 2007/1093, art 2.

[291]  There is nothing in Chapter 3 of Part 28 which allows a s 979 notice, once served, to be withdrawn. This was also the case in relation to Part XIIIA of the CA 1985 and notices under s 429 of that legislation, as noted in *Re Greythorn Ltd* [2002] 1 BCLC 437.

[292]  This provision also appeared in s 430(4) of CA 1985.

**28.981.04** For example, where the consideration is shares or other securities and the terms of the offer allow shareholders to elect to sell that consideration for cash on a basis underwritten by a financial institution, the offeror may not wish to incur underwriting fees in relation to those arrangements for the duration of the six week period in which non-assenting shareholders may make their choice pursuant to subsection (3). In that case, if the underwritten alternative ceases to exist, the offeror will still be required to provide cash from its own (or other acquired) resources to satisfy elections for that alternative which are made by shareholders who receive the section 979 notices. Under subsection (5) if the consideration offered or chosen by the relevant shareholder is not cash and the offeror is not able to provide it, or it was to have been provided by a third party who is no longer bound or able to provide it, the offeror must provide cash of 'equivalent value' to the value of that consideration as at the date of the section 979 notice.

**28.981.05** The position is more complicated where the offeror has made a so-called 'mix and match' offer, under which shareholders may elect to receive a mixture of securities and cash, with the degree to which each shareholder's choice is satisfied depending upon the choices of other shareholders, the total ratio of cash to securities available being fixed. Much thought was devoted to the proper interpretation of the provisions of section 430 of the Companies Act 1985 in determining how the terms of a mix and match offer should be extended to the recipients of notices under section 429 of that legislation. Section 981 does not clarify this point. In the past many offerors have offered the recipients of squeeze-out notices a free choice of securities and/or cash where 'mix and match' consideration was offered under the original takeover offer.[293]

**28.981.06** Under subsection (6), six weeks after the service of squeeze-out notices, the offeror must send a copy of all such notices to the company and pay or transfer to the company the consideration for the shares to which the notices relate (where applicable, complying with any elections made by non-assenting shareholders). Where consideration comprises shares or other securities to be allotted by the offeror, subsection (6) requires such allotment to be made to the company. In the case of shares in the offeror, this will result in the company holding shares in its holding company.[294] It should be noted that the operation of subsection (6) is suspended if an application under section 986(1) has been made and is pending at the end of the six-week period: please refer to the commentary below on section 986.

**28.981.07** Where the shares to which the squeeze-out notice relates are registered, the copy notices sent to the company under subsection (6) must be accompanied by an instrument of transfer executed on behalf of the relevant non-assenting shareholder by a person appointed by the offeror (subsection (7)). The offeror must also arrange for the stamping of such instruments of transfer with *ad valorem* stamp duty. If the shares concerned are held in the CREST system the procedure for their transfer to the offeror is governed by regulation 42 of the Uncertificated Securities Regulations 2001.[295]

---

[293] The principle, expounded in *Re Carlton Holdings Ltd* [1971] 1 WLR 918, that a dissentient shareholder should not be penalized as a result of his dissent, should be borne in mind here. Other approaches which have been proposed include (i) looking at the extent to which the elections of shareholders who accepted the offer were met under the terms of the 'mix and match' and satisfying the elections of recipients of squeeze-out notices to the same extent (which would mean that if all accepting shareholders received exactly the consideration for which they elected, the recipients of the squeeze-out notices would be given a free choice between the two forms of consideration or a mixture): under this proposal elections which non-assenting shareholders make would be treated as if they had been made pursuant to acceptances of the original takeover offer; (ii) organizing a new mix and match election arrangement within the pool of non-assenting shareholders to whom squeeze-out notices have been sent, under which those shareholders are free to make elections for one or other, or a mixture, of the two forms of consideration, but the total cash and total securities made available to such shareholders will be in the same ratio as that made available to the shareholders who accepted the original takeover offer: in the Company Law Review the opinion was expressed that the suggestion in (ii) would not satisfy the requirement that non-assented shares be acquired 'on the terms of the offer' and that the suggestion in (i) was preferable (*Modern Company Law for a Competitive Economy: Completing the Structure* (DTI, Nov 2000) Annex B, pp 387–388). It is also generally thought that, where one form of consideration under a mix and match offer has been 'used up' on account of elections made by accepting shareholders, it would not be acceptable to deny non-assenting shareholders that choice. Offerors should bear in mind that the effect of these arrangements may mean that more cash, or more securities, may need to be made available than would be anticipated based on elections made by assenting shareholders alone.

[294] Although this is generally prohibited by s 136 of the Act, s 138(1) provides that the prohibition does not apply where the subsidiary holds the relevant shares as trustee and neither the holding company nor a subsidiary of it is beneficially interested in the trust. S 981(9) provides that the consideration paid or transferred to the target company at the end of the six-week period stipulated in subs (6) is to be held on trust for the relevant non-assenting shareholder.

[295] SI 2001/3755 (as amended).

Subsection (8) makes provision for the treatment of shares which are transferable by warrants or other instruments.   **28.981.08**

The company must hold the consideration which the offeror pays or transfers to it under subsection (6) on trust for the relevant non-assenting shareholder (subsection (9)). Further provision concerning this trust is made in section 982.   **28.981.09**

## 982  Further provision about consideration held on trust under section 981(9)

(1) This section applies where an offeror pays or transfers consideration to the company under section 981(6).   **28.982.01**

(2) The company must pay into a separate bank account that complies with subsection (3)—
  (a) any money it receives under paragraph (b) of section 981(6), and
  (b) any dividend or other sum accruing from any other consideration it receives under that paragraph.

(3) A bank account complies with this subsection if the balance on the account—
  (a) bears interest at an appropriate rate, and
  (b) can be withdrawn by such notice (if any) as is appropriate.

(4) If—
  (a) the person entitled to the consideration held on trust by virtue of section 981(9) cannot be found, and
  (b) subsection (5) applies,
the consideration (together with any interest, dividend or other benefit that has accrued from it) must be paid into court.

(5) This subsection applies where—
  (a) reasonable enquiries have been made at reasonable intervals to find the person, and
  (b) twelve years have elapsed since the consideration was received, or the company is wound up.

(6) In relation to a company registered in Scotland, subsections (7) and (8) apply instead of subsection (4).

(7) If the person entitled to the consideration held on trust by virtue of section 981(9) cannot be found and subsection (5) applies—
  (a) the trust terminates,
  (b) the company or (if the company is wound up) the liquidator must sell any consideration other than cash and any benefit other than cash that has accrued from the consideration, and
  (c) a sum representing—
    (i) the consideration so far as it is cash,
    (ii) the proceeds of any sale under paragraph (b), and
    (iii) any interest, dividend or other benefit that has accrued from the consideration,
    must be deposited in the name of the Accountant of Court in a separate bank account complying with subsection (3) and the receipt for the deposit must be transmitted to the Accountant of Court.

(8) Section 58 of the Bankruptcy (Scotland) Act 1985 (c. 66) (so far as consistent with this Act) applies (with any necessary modifications) to sums deposited under subsection (7) as it applies to sums deposited under section 57(1)(a) of that Act.

(9) The expenses of any such enquiries as are mentioned in subsection (5) may be paid out of the money or other property held on trust for the person to whom the enquiry relates.

COMMENCEMENT DATE 6 April 2007 (subject to saving provisions: see General Introductory Commentary to Chapter 3 above).[296]

Section 982 contains provisions concerning the trust on which consideration paid or transferred to the target company under section 981 is to be held for non-assenting shareholders.   **28.982.02**

Moneys forming part of the consideration, and any income on such moneys and any dividend or other sum accruing on the consideration, are to be paid into a separate bank account under the terms of which interest is to accrue on the balance at 'an appropriate rate' and withdrawals are permitted 'by such notice (if any) as is appropriate' (subsections (2) and (3)). The company must maintain this trust for a period of 12 years, making reasonable enquiries to find the beneficiaries at 'reasonable intervals' during that period.[297] Cash and other consideration which remain unclaimed at the end of that period must be paid into court (subsections (4) and (5)).[298]   **28.982.03**

In practice in relation to cash consideration, and particularly where there are large numbers of corporate and individual beneficiaries of the trust alike, two separate bank accounts may be established   **28.982.04**

---

[296] Companies Act 2006 (Commencement No 2, etc) Order 2007, SI 2007/1093, art 2.
[297] The expense of such enquiries may be paid out of the trust property: subs (9).
[298] In Scotland the provisions of subss (7) and (8) are substituted for those of subss (4) and (5).

for administrative efficiency to take account of the differing UK withholding tax regimes for benefi-ciaries in respect of whom banks are required to deduct lower rate income tax at source and beneficiaries in respect of whom it is the trustee's obligation to withhold tax instead. Subject to the requirements of subsections (2) and (3), the Act contains no restrictions on the terms and conditions on which moneys are held in the account. In particular, there is no statutory requirement to inform the bank of the nature of the account, although there would appear to be no reason not to do so.

## 'Sell-out'

### 983  Right of minority shareholder to be bought out by offeror

**28.983.01**

(1) Subsections (2) and (3) apply in a case where a takeover offer relates to all the shares in a company. For this purpose a takeover offer relates to all the shares in a company if it is an offer to acquire all the shares in the company within the meaning of section 974.

(2) The holder of any voting shares to which the offer relates who has not accepted the offer may require the offeror to acquire those shares if, at any time before the end of the period within which the offer can be accepted—

(a) the offeror has by virtue of acceptances of the offer acquired or unconditionally contracted to acquire some (but not all) of the shares to which the offer relates, and

(b) those shares, with or without any other shares in the company which he has acquired or contracted to acquire (whether unconditionally or subject to conditions being met)—

  (i) amount to not less than 90% in value of all the voting shares in the company (or would do so but for section 990(1)), and

  (ii) carry not less than 90% of the voting rights in the company (or would do so but for section 990(1)).

(3) The holder of any non-voting shares to which the offer relates who has not accepted the offer may require the offeror to acquire those shares if, at any time before the end of the period within which the offer can be accepted—

(a) the offeror has by virtue of acceptances of the offer acquired or unconditionally contracted to acquire some (but not all) of the shares to which the offer relates, and

(b) those shares, with or without any other shares in the company which he has acquired or contracted to acquire (whether unconditionally or subject to conditions being met), amount to not less than 90% in value of all the shares in the company (or would do so but for section 990(1)).

(4) If a takeover offer relates to shares of one or more classes and at any time before the end of the period within which the offer can be accepted—

(a) the offeror has by virtue of acceptances of the offer acquired or unconditionally contracted to acquire some (but not all) of the shares of any class to which the offer relates, and

(b) those shares, with or without any other shares of that class which he has acquired or contracted to acquire (whether unconditionally or subject to conditions being met)—

  (i) amount to not less than 90% in value of all the shares of that class, and

  (ii) in a case where the shares of that class are voting shares, carry not less than 90% of the voting rights carried by the shares of that class,

the holder of any shares of that class to which the offer relates who has not accepted the offer may require the offeror to acquire those shares.

(5) For the purposes of subsections (2) to (4), in calculating 90% of the value of any shares, shares held by the company as treasury shares are to be treated as having been acquired by the offeror.

(6) Subsection (7) applies where—

(a) a shareholder exercises rights conferred on him by subsection (2), (3) or (4),

(b) at the time when he does so, there are shares in the company which the offeror has contracted to acquire subject to conditions being met, and in relation to which the contract has not become unconditional, and

(c) the requirement imposed by subsection (2)(b), (3)(b) or (4)(b) (as the case may be) would not be satisfied if those shares were not taken into account.

(7) The shareholder is treated for the purposes of section 985 as not having exercised his rights under this section unless the requirement imposed by paragraph (b) of subsection (2), (3) or (4) (as the case may be) would be satisfied if—

(a) the reference in that paragraph to other shares in the company which the offeror has contracted to acquire unconditionally or subject to conditions being met were a reference to such shares which he has unconditionally contracted to acquire, and

(b) the reference in that subsection to the period within which the offer can be accepted were a reference to the period referred to in section 984(2).

(8) A reference in subsection (2)(b), (3)(b), (4)(b), (6) or (7) to shares which the offeror has acquired or contracted to acquire includes a reference to shares which an associate of his has acquired or contracted to acquire.

COMMENCEMENT DATE  6 April 2007 (subject to saving provisions: see General Introductory Commentary to Chapter 3 above).[299]

Section 983 provides for minority shareholders to have a right to sell their shares to an offeror, the **28.983.02** so-called 'sell-out right'. Like the 'squeeze-out rights' of an offeror, sell-out rights are only exercisable if there has been a 'takeover offer' relating to 'all the shares' in the company (subsection (1)). As with squeeze-out rights, the terms 'takeover offer' and 'all the shares' are to be interpreted according to section 974. Thus there is no general statutory right under this section for minority shareholders to be bought out by a majority shareholder: there must first be a 'takeover offer' and the requisite thresholds described below must be reached. In addition, a shareholder who has accepted the offer may not exercise this right (subsections (2) and (3)) (although he may of course have rights in contract against the offeror if and when the offer becomes or is declared unconditional in all respects).

In relation to voting shares, under subsection (2) the threshold condition for the exercise of the sell-out **28.983.03** right is that, by virtue of acceptances of the offer, the offeror has, during the time when the offer is open for acceptances, acquired some (but not all) of the shares to which the offer relates and those shares, with or without any other shares in the company which the offeror and/or its associates[300] has acquired or contracted[301] to acquire, amount to at least 90 per cent in value[302] of all voting shares in the company and carry at least 90 per cent of the voting rights in the company (in each case disregarding debentures in the company which are treated as shares by virtue of section 990(1)).

In relation to non-voting shares, under subsection (3) the threshold condition for the exercise of the **28.983.04** sell-out right is the same as that for voting shares save for the obvious omission of a provision relating to the offeror acquiring or contracting to acquire at least 90 per cent of voting rights.

Where there is more than one class of shares to which the takeover offer relates, subsection (4) operates **28.983.05** to apply the 90 per cent thresholds referred to above on a class by class basis in determining whether the holder of a share of a particular class subject to the offer may exercise the sell-out right.

It is important to note that the threshold for the exercise of sell-out rights is different from the threshold **28.983.06** for the exercise of squeeze-out rights under section 979. In particular, the inclusion of shares already acquired, or contracted to be acquired, in the calculation of the threshold for the exercise of sell-out rights means that an offeror who, alone or together with associates, holds or acquires shares otherwise than by virtue of acceptances of the offer is likely to reach the sell-out threshold before the squeeze-out threshold is reached. The principal implication of this is that it may, in those circumstances, be necessary for the offeror to serve notices on non-assenting shareholders under section 984(3) (see below) if squeeze-out notices have not yet been served under section 979.

## 984  Further provision about rights conferred by section 983

(1)  Rights conferred on a shareholder by subsection (2), (3) or (4) of section 983 are exercisable by a **28.984.01** written communication addressed to the offeror.

(2)  Rights conferred on a shareholder by subsection (2), (3) or (4) of that section are not exercisable after the end of the period of three months from—

(a)  the end of the period within which the offer can be accepted, or

(b)  if later, the date of the notice that must be given under subsection (3) below.

---

[299]  Companies Act 2006 (Commencement No 2, etc) Order 2007, SI 2007/1093, art 2.

[300]  Subsection (8) addresses the inclusion of shares held or contracted to be acquired by associates of the offeror in the calculation of the 90 per cent sell-out thresholds.

[301]  The shares which the offeror already holds or has contracted to acquire, which count towards the 90 per cent thresholds for the exercise of the sell-out right, (i) include shares which an associate of the offeror has acquired or contracted to acquire (subs (8)); and (ii) may be shares which the offeror (or an associate of the offeror) has contracted to acquire conditionally as well as shares which the offeror has contracted to acquire unconditionally. The reference to conditional acquisitions counting towards the threshold was not an explicit feature of the former regime under s 430A of CA 1985. However, subss (6) and (7) have the effect that a shareholder is treated as not having exercised the sell-out right unless the 90 per cent threshold condition is satisfied on the basis of acceptances of the offer and other, *unconditional*, acquisitions of shares. In other words, the offeror does not have to purchase the shares of the person purporting to exercise the 'sell-out' right unless the offeror has acquired or unconditionally contracted to acquire such number of shares as meets the applicable 90% threshold(s) by the time the period referred to in s 984(2) ends. However, the requirement on the offeror to serve a notice on non-assenting shareholders under s 984(3) advising them of their rights under s 983 arises at the time referred to in s 983(2), (3), or (4) (as applicable), whether or not the condition(s) to acquisition have been satisfied.

[302]  In calculating 90 per cent of the value of any shares, shares held by the company as treasury shares are to be treated as acquired by the offeror: subs (5).

    (3)  Within one month of the time specified in subsection (2), (3) or (4) (as the case may be) of that section, the offeror must give any shareholder who has not accepted the offer notice in the prescribed manner of—
       (a)  the rights that are exercisable by the shareholder under that subsection, and
       (b)  the period within which the rights are exercisable.
       If the notice is given before the end of the period within which the offer can be accepted, it must state that the offer is still open for acceptance.
    (4)  Subsection (3) does not apply if the offeror has given the shareholder a notice in respect of the shares in question under section 979.
    (5)  An offeror who fails to comply with subsection (3) commits an offence.
       If the offeror is a company, every officer of that company who is in default or to whose neglect the failure is attributable also commits an offence.
    (6)  If an offeror other than a company is charged with an offence for failing to comply with subsection (3), it is a defence for him to prove that he took all reasonable steps for securing compliance with that subsection.
    (7)  A person guilty of an offence under this section is liable—
       (a)  on conviction on indictment, to a fine;
       (b)  on summary conviction, to a fine not exceeding the statutory maximum and, for continued contravention, a daily default fine not exceeding one-fiftieth of the statutory maximum.

COMMENCEMENT DATE 6 April 2007 (subject to saving provisions: see General Introductory Commentary to Chapter 3 above).[303]

**28.984.02**    There is no prescribed form in which non-assenting shareholders may exercise sell-out rights, other than that, under subsection (1) of this section, it be done by written communication to the offeror. In any event, under subsection (2), the right may not be exercised more than three months from: (i) the end of the period within which the offer can be accepted; or (ii) if later, the date of the notice required under subsection (3).

**28.984.03**    Subsection (3) requires that the offeror give a notice in prescribed form to non-assenting shareholders within one month of the time when the applicable threshold under section 983(2), (3) or (4) has been reached. The prescribed form[304] describes the rights that are exercisable by non-assenting shareholders under section 983 and states the period within which they are exercisable (which is, as noted above, three months from the date of the notice). If the notice is given at a time when the offer is still open for acceptance, the notice must state that this is the case: subsection (3). Where the 'takeover offer' included a choice of consideration, the notice under subsection (3) must notify the relevant non-assenting shareholder that the same choice will be available to him[305] and may indicate the 'default' consideration which will apply if the shareholder does not indicate a choice.[306]

**28.984.04**    There is no requirement to serve a notice under subsection (3) on a non-assenting shareholder if the offeror has given that shareholder a squeeze-out notice under section 979 (subsection (4). The requirement to give a notice under subsection (3) within one month of the relevant sell-out threshold being reached means that the offeror may have to give such notices before giving squeeze-out notices under section 979 if, on the latest date for giving the notice under subsection (3), the threshold for the exercise of the squeeze-out right under section 979 has not been reached. The giving of notices under subsection (3) does not preclude the subsequent giving of squeeze-out notices under section 979.

**28.984.05**    An offeror which fails to comply with subsection (3) commits an offence, and if the offeror is a company, every officer of that company who is in default or to whose neglect the failure is attributable also commits an offence (subsection (5)). There is a defence, which is available only to offerors that are not companies, that the offeror took all reasonable steps for securing compliance with subsection (3) (subsection (6)). The penalty on conviction on indictment is an unlimited fine, while that on summary conviction is a fine not exceeding the statutory maximum (currently £5,000)[307] and, for continued contravention, a daily default fine not exceeding one-fiftieth of the statutory maximum (currently £100). However, the commission of this offence does not appear to invalidate the subsequent giving of squeeze-out notices under section 979.

---

[303] Companies Act 2006 (Commencement No 2, etc) Order 2007, SI 2007/1093, art 2.
[304] See the Companies (Forms) (Amendment) Regulations 1987 (SI 1987/752), as amended by arts 4 and 5 of Sch 3 to the Companies Act 2006 (Commencement No 2, Consequential Amendments, Transitional Provisions and Savings) Order 2007, SI 2007/1093.
[305] Section 985(3)(b)(i).
[306] Section 985(3)(b)(ii).
[307] Magistrates' Courts Act 1980, s 32(9), as amended by the Criminal Justice Act 1991, s 17(2)(c).

### 985  Effect of requirement under section 983

(1)  Subject to section 986, this section applies where a shareholder exercises his rights under section 983 in respect of any shares held by him.

(2)  The offeror is entitled and bound to acquire those shares on the terms of the offer or on such other terms as may be agreed.

(3)  Where the terms of an offer are such as to give the shareholder a choice of consideration—

    (a)  the shareholder may indicate his choice when requiring the offeror to acquire the shares, and

    (b)  the notice given to the shareholder under section 984(3)—

        (i)   must give particulars of the choice and of the rights conferred by this subsection, and

        (ii)  may state which consideration specified in the offer will apply if he does not indicate a choice.

    The reference in subsection (2) to the terms of the offer is to be read accordingly.

(4)  Subsection (3) applies whether or not any time-limit or other conditions applicable to the choice under the terms of the offer can still be complied with.

(5)  If the consideration offered to or (as the case may be) chosen by the shareholder—

    (a)  is not cash and the offeror is no longer able to provide it, or

    (b)  was to have been provided by a third party who is no longer bound or able to provide it,

the consideration is to be taken to consist of an amount of cash, payable by the offeror, which at the date when the shareholder requires the offeror to acquire the shares is equivalent to the consideration offered or (as the case may be) chosen.

COMMENCEMENT DATE  6 April 2007 (subject to saving provisions: see General Introductory Commentary to Chapter 3 above).[308]

**28.985.01**

Section 985 provides for the terms on which shares are to be acquired pursuant to the exercise of the sell-out right provided by sections 983 and 984. As in the case where a squeeze-out notice has been served under section 979, the offeror becomes 'entitled and bound' to acquire the shares in respect of which the right is exercised 'on the terms of the offer', although, like its predecessor, section 430B of the Companies Act 1985, this section also allows the acquisition to take place 'on such other terms as may be agreed'.

**28.985.02**

In much the same manner as in relation to squeeze-out under section 981, if a choice of consideration was offered under the terms of the 'takeover offer' under subsections (3) and (4) then, unless subsection (5) applies in relation to non-cash consideration, the same choice must be made available to the shareholders exercising their sell-out rights under sections 983 and 984, even if a time period within which one or more such choices had to be exercised has expired. The commentary under section 981 contains some further remarks on the potential implications of these requirements.

**28.985.03**

## *Supplementary*

### 986  Applications to the court

(1)  Where a notice is given under section 979 to a shareholder the court may, on an application made by him, order—

    (a)  that the offeror is not entitled and bound to acquire the shares to which the notice relates, or

    (b)  that the terms on which the offeror is entitled and bound to acquire the shares shall be such as the court thinks fit.

(2)  An application under subsection (1) must be made within six weeks from the date on which the notice referred to in that subsection was given.

    If an application to the court under subsection (1) is pending at the end of that period, section 981(6) does not have effect until the application has been disposed of.

(3)  Where a shareholder exercises his rights under section 983 in respect of any shares held by him, the court may, on an application made by him or the offeror, order that the terms on which the offeror is entitled and bound to acquire the shares shall be such as the court thinks fit.

(4)  On an application under subsection (1) or (3)—

    (a)  the court may not require consideration of a higher value than that specified in the terms of the offer ('the offer value') to be given for the shares to which the application relates unless the holder of the shares shows that the offer value would be unfair;

    (b)  the court may not require consideration of a lower value than the offer value to be given for the shares.

(5)  No order for costs or expenses may be made against a shareholder making an application under subsection (1) or (3) unless the court considers that—

    (a)  the application was unnecessary, improper or vexatious,

    (b)  there has been unreasonable delay in making the application, or

**28.986.01**

---

[308]  Companies Act 2006 (Commencement No 2, etc) Order 2007, SI 2007/1093, art 2.

(c)  there has been unreasonable conduct on the shareholder's part in conducting the proceedings on the application.

(6)  A shareholder who has made an application under subsection (1) or (3) must give notice of the application to the offeror.

(7)  An offeror who is given notice of an application under subsection (1) or (3) must give a copy of the notice to—

(a)  any person (other than the applicant) to whom a notice has been given under section 979;

(b)  any person who has exercised his rights under section 983.

(8)  An offeror who makes an application under subsection (3) must give notice of the application to—

(a)  any person to whom a notice has been given under section 979;

(b)  any person who has exercised his rights under section 983.

(9)  Where a takeover offer has not been accepted to the extent necessary for entitling the offeror to give notices under subsection (2) or (4) of section 979 the court may, on an application made by him, make an order authorising him to give notices under that subsection if it is satisfied that—

(a)  the offeror has after reasonable enquiry been unable to trace one or more of the persons holding shares to which the offer relates,

(b)  the requirements of that subsection would have been met if the person, or all the persons, mentioned in paragraph (a) above had accepted the offer, and

(c)  the consideration offered is fair and reasonable.

This is subject to subsection (10).

(10) The court may not make an order under subsection (9) unless it considers that it is just and equitable to do so having regard, in particular, to the number of shareholders who have been traced but who have not accepted the offer.

Commencement Date 6 April 2007 (subject to saving provisions: see General Introductory Commentary to Chapter 3 above).[309]

**28.986.02**    Section 986 provides procedures for:

- non-assenting shareholders to challenge the application of the squeeze-out procedure (subsection (1)); and
- non-assenting shareholders or the offeror to challenge aspects of the application of the sell-out procedure (subsection (3)).

Such rights were also provided under the former legislation, section 430C of the Companies Act 1985, although section 986 differs in some respects from that earlier section.

### Challenges to the squeeze-out procedure under subsection (1)

**28.986.03**    An application to the court to challenge the squeeze-out procedure may only be made by a shareholder on whom the offeror has served a notice under section 979 and may only be made within six weeks from the date on which that notice was given (subsection (2)). If such an application is made then the operation of section 981(6) (requiring, *inter alia*, that the offeror pay or transfer to the company the consideration in respect of the shareholders to whom notices have been given under section 979, and that the non-assented shares be transferred to the offeror six weeks from the date of the notices) is suspended until the application has been disposed of (subsection (2)). Specifically, the application to challenge squeeze-out must request either that the offeror is not entitled and bound to acquire the shares to which the section 979 notice relates or that the terms on which the offeror is entitled and bound to acquire the shares are to be such as the court thinks fit (subsection (1)), although, as noted below, subsection (4) constrains the court somewhat as to its ability to vary the consideration due to the applicant non-assenting shareholder(s).

**28.986.04**    Subsection (4) provides that the court may not require consideration of a higher value than that specified in the terms of the offer ('the offer value') to be given for the shares to which the application relates unless the holder of the shares shows that the offer value would be unfair, and that the court may not require consideration of a lower value than the offer value to be given for the shares. The meaning of 'unfair' has not yet been tested in this context, although it might be expected that the court would decide to assess unfairness in relation to the non-assenting shareholders as a whole rather than the applicant in isolation.[310] Subsection (4) is a new provision which did not appear in section 430C of the Companies Act 1985.

**28.986.05**    Subsection (5) has the same effect as section 430C(4) of the Companies Act 1985 and constrains the court from making costs orders against applicant shareholders unless the application was unnecessary,

---

[309]  Companies Act 2006 (Commencement No 2, etc) Order 2007, SI 2007/1093, art 2.

[310]  The mere fact that the consideration under the offer could have been greater, but was not, might not in itself render the consideration 'unfair' for these purposes: see *Re Grierson, Oldham & Adams* [1968] Ch 17.

improper, or vexatious,[311] or there has been unreasonable delay in making the application,[312] or there has been unreasonable conduct on the shareholder's part in conducting the proceedings on the application. As under section 430C of the Companies Act 1985, this is likely to render an application under this section less risky for dissentient shareholders than other applications which may be available. An unsuccessful applicant may apply for interest on the consideration due to him under the terms of the compulsory purchase of his shares.[313]

A shareholder who has made an application under subsection (1) challenging the squeeze-out proce-   **28.986.06** dure must give notice that he has done so to the offeror (subsection (6)) and an offeror who is given such a notice must give a copy of that notice to any person (other than the applicant) to whom a squeeze-out notice has been given under section 979 and any person who has exercised his sell-out rights under section 983 (subsection (7)).

On the basis of case law on section 430C of the Companies Act 1985, a severe burden will be placed on   **28.986.07** a shareholder who applies for an order under subsection (1). Absent fraud or a pre-existing connection between the offeror and the shareholders who have accepted the takeover offer such that they effectively amount to one and the same person,[314] the court has generally adopted the starting position that special circumstances must be pleaded to persuade the court to prevent the application of statutory squeeze-out provisions such as section 979 or to interfere with the terms of the offer so far as it is addressed to the applicant. The burden is on the applicant to demonstrate that the order ought to be made. So great is this burden in most cases that many disgruntled non-assenting shareholders may prefer initially to investigate whether the application of the squeeze-out procedure may be challenged on some technical ground, such as an error in the calculation of the applicable threshold under section 979(2) or (4).

In order to discharge this burden it has been held that an applicant must demonstrate that the offer is   **28.986.08** 'obviously unfair, patently unfair, unfair to the meanest intelligence'.[315] However, it is not clear that this is the correct test, not least because as so formulated it would appear to nullify the protection afforded by subsection (1).[316]

In *Re Bugle Press*[317] the court came close to establishing a presumption of unfairness in cases where 90   **28.986.09** per cent of the company's shareholders are, in effect, the same person as the offeror, requiring in such cases that it be for the offeror to demonstrate that the application of the squeeze-out procedure is in the best interests of the target company. However, under the Act, in many cases where there is a close connection between the offeror and shareholders holding at least 90 per cent of the issued share capital and voting rights in a company (or, where there is more than one class of shares, in respect of the relevant class) the offeror and those shareholders will be 'associates' within the meaning of section 988, meaning that the 90 per cent shareholding would not, if acquired prior to the date of the offer, count towards the offeror's interest in the company for the purposes of assessing whether the offeror has reached the applicable threshold in section 979(2) or (4).

Other connections between the offeror and the target company and its shareholders may also establish   **28.986.10** unfairness. For example, where a director of the offeror is also a director of, and a shareholder in, the target company, and insufficient information has been provided to the target shareholders by the standards set in the Takeover Code, it has been held that the heavy burden on the applicant ought to be

---

[311]  See *Re Trafalgar House plc* (unreported, Chancery Division, 22 July 1996).
[312]  See *Re Lifecare International plc* [1990] BCLC 222.
[313]  *Re Hoare & Co Ltd* [1933] 150 LT 374.
[314]  See *Re Bugle Press* [1960] 3 All ER 791. When determining fairness in relation to offers to which the Takeover Code applies, the court also increasingly appears to be willing to have regard to the offeror's and the offeror's directors' compliance with the Takeover Code, such as the requirements in the Takeover Code to provide information to the shareholders to whom the offer is addressed: see the dicta of Browne-Wilkinson VC in *Re Chez Nico (Restaurants) Ltd* [1992] BCLC 192 and the *obiter dicta* of Peter Leaver QC (sitting as a Deputy Judge of the High Court) in *Fiske Nominees Ltd v Dwyka Diamond Ltd* [2002] EWHC 770 (Ch). The court may also take into account the offeror's breach of applicable legislation in assessing fairness: see *Re Chez Nico (Restaurants) Ltd* [1992] BCLC 192. It is likely that the court would also take into account breaches of the Takeover Code by the target company or its directors (such as a failure by those directors to advise the target company's shareholders on the merits of the offer, in breach of Rule 3 of the Takeover Code).
[315]  *Per* Vaisey J in *Re Sussex Brick Co* [1961] Ch 289.
[316]  A point made by Megarry J in *Marston Valley Brick Company* (unreported, Chancery Division, 1 July 1969), who suggested an alternative formulation of the test, that the court should intervene where the 'inadequacy' of the offer was demonstrated beyond all reasonable argument, the court being slow to interpret 'inadequacy' in this context simply in terms of the level of consideration accepted by the requisite majority of shareholders.
[317]  [1960] 3 All ER 791.

lifted.[318] This potentially has implications for the conduct of management buy-outs, where directors of a target company form a vehicle which makes an offer to acquire that company.

### Challenges to the sell-out procedure under subsection (3)

**28.986.11**   The provisions of subsections (4) to (7) (inclusive) described above also apply where the offeror makes an application to the court under subsection (3) challenging the application of the sell-out procedure. In that case the offeror must give notice of the application to any person to whom a squeeze-out notice has been given under section 979 and any person who has exercised his sell-out rights under section 983 (subsection (8)).

### Untraceable shareholders

**28.986.12**   Subsections (9) and (10), which have substantially the same effect as section 430C(5) of the Companies Act 1985, provide a mechanism for an offeror to apply for an order of the court authorizing the giving of squeeze-out notices under section 979 notwithstanding that the applicable thresholds (in section 979(2) or (4)) for the giving of such notices have not been met but would have been met had untraced shareholders accepted the offer. Section 430C(5) of the Companies Act 1985 was applied in *Re Joseph Holt plc*.[319] 'Untraced' in this context means the offeror must have been unable to trace the relevant shareholders 'after reasonable enquiry' (subsection (9)(a)). The consideration offered must be fair and reasonable (subsection (9)(c)) and the court may not make an order under subsection (9) unless it considers that it is just and equitable to do so having regard, in particular, to the number of shareholders who have been traced but who have not accepted the offer (subsection (10)).

### 987  Joint offers

**28.987.01**
(1)  In the case of a takeover offer made by two or more persons jointly, this Chapter has effect as follows.

(2)  The conditions for the exercise of the rights conferred by section 979 are satisfied—
   (a)  in the case of acquisitions by virtue of acceptances of the offer, by the joint offerors acquiring or unconditionally contracting to acquire the necessary shares jointly;
   (b)  in other cases, by the joint offerors acquiring or unconditionally contracting to acquire the necessary shares either jointly or separately.

(3)  The conditions for the exercise of the rights conferred by section 983 are satisfied—
   (a)  in the case of acquisitions by virtue of acceptances of the offer, by the joint offerors acquiring or unconditionally contracting to acquire the necessary shares jointly;
   (b)  in other cases, by the joint offerors acquiring or contracting (whether unconditionally or subject to conditions being met) to acquire the necessary shares either jointly or separately.

(4)  Subject to the following provisions, the rights and obligations of the offeror under sections 979 to 985 are respectively joint rights and joint and several obligations of the joint offerors.

(5)  A provision of sections 979 to 986 that requires or authorises a notice or other document to be given or sent by or to the joint offerors is complied with if the notice or document is given or sent by or to any of them (but see subsection (6)).

(6)  The statutory declaration required by section 980(4) must be made by all of the joint offerors and, where one or more of them is a company, signed by a director of that company.

(7)  In sections 974 to 977, 979(9), 981(6), 983(8) and 988 references to the offeror are to be read as references to the joint offerors or any of them.

(8)  In section 981(7) and (8) references to the offeror are to be read as references to the joint offerors or such of them as they may determine.

(9)  In sections 981(5)(a) and 985(5)(a) references to the offeror being no longer able to provide the relevant consideration are to be read as references to none of the joint offerors being able to do so.

(10) In section 986 references to the offeror are to be read as references to the joint offerors, except that—
   (a)  an application under subsection (3) or (9) may be made by any of them, and
   (b)  the reference in subsection (9)(a) to the offeror having been unable to trace one or more of the persons holding shares is to be read as a reference to none of the offerors having been able to do so.

COMMENCEMENT DATE  6 April 2007 (subject to saving provisions: see General Introductory Commentary to Chapter 3 above).[320]

---

[318] *Re Chez Nico (Restaurants) Ltd* [1992] BCLC 192 (see above).
[319] [2001] 2 BCLC 604.
[320] Companies Act 2006 (Commencement No 2, etc) Order 2007, SI 2007/1093, art 2.

Section 987 provides for takeover offers made by two or more persons jointly and introduces **28.987.02**
modifications to sections in Chapter 3 of Part 28 which apply in those circumstances. In practice the
application of section 987 is likely to be rare because where two or more persons wish to participate in
a takeover offer it is more common for them to procure that such an offer is made by a single company
in which they each hold shares (in which case this section would not apply to the offer).

*Interpretation*

## 988  Associates

(1)  In this Chapter 'associate', in relation to an offeror, means—                          **28.988.01**
    (a)  a nominee of the offeror,
    (b)  a holding company, subsidiary or fellow subsidiary of the offeror or a nominee of such a
       holding company, subsidiary or fellow subsidiary,
    (c)  a body corporate in which the offeror is substantially interested,
    (d)  a person who is, or is a nominee of, a party to a share acquisition agreement with the offeror,
       or
    (e)  (where the offeror is an individual) his spouse or civil partner and any minor child or step-child
       of his.
(2)  For the purposes of subsection (1)(b) a company is a fellow subsidiary of another body corporate
    if both are subsidiaries of the same body corporate but neither is a subsidiary of the other.
(3)  For the purposes of subsection (1)(c) an offeror has a substantial interest in a body corporate if—
    (a)  the body or its directors are accustomed to act in accordance with his directions or
       instructions, or
    (b)  he is entitled to exercise or control the exercise of one-third or more of the voting power at
       general meetings of the body.
    Subsections (2) and (3) of section 823 (which contain provision about when a person is treated as
    entitled to exercise or control the exercise of voting power) apply for the purposes of this
    subsection as they apply for the purposes of that section.
(4)  For the purposes of subsection (1)(d) an agreement is a share acquisition agreement if—
    (a)  it is an agreement for the acquisition of, or of an interest in, shares to which the offer relates,
    (b)  it includes provisions imposing obligations or restrictions on any one or more of the parties to
       it with respect to their use, retention or disposal of such shares, or their interests in such
       shares, acquired in pursuance of the agreement (whether or not together with any other
       shares to which the offer relates or any other interests of theirs in such shares), and
    (c)  it is not an excluded agreement (see subsection (5)).
(5)  An agreement is an 'excluded agreement'—
    (a)  if it is not legally binding, unless it involves mutuality in the undertakings, expectations or
       understandings of the parties to it, or
    (b)  if it is an agreement to underwrite or sub-underwrite an offer of shares in a company,
       provided the agreement is confined to that purpose and any matters incidental to it.
(6)  The reference in subsection (4)(b) to the use of interests in shares is to the exercise of any rights
    or of any control or influence arising from those interests (including the right to enter into an
    agreement for the exercise, or for control of the exercise, of any of those rights by another
    person).
(7)  In this section—
    (a)  'agreement' includes any agreement or arrangement;
    (b)  references to provisions of an agreement include—
       (i)  undertakings, expectations or understandings operative under an arrangement, and
       (ii)  any provision whether express or implied and whether absolute or not.

COMMENCEMENT DATE  6 April 2007 (subject to saving provisions: see General Introductory Commentary to Chapter 3 above).[321]

The complex definition of 'associate' in section 988 retains many of the features of that which was set **28.988.02**
out in section 430E of the Companies Act 1985. It is of principal relevance to the following matters
arising under the squeeze-out and sell-out provisions of sections 974 to 987 (inclusive):

• The condition in section 974(2) that a 'takeover offer' extend to all the shares in a company, or, where
there is more than one class of shares in a company, all the shares of one or more classes, is treated
as satisfied notwithstanding that the offer does not extend to shares that 'associates' of the offeror
hold or have contracted to acquire (whether unconditionally or subject to conditions being met) (see
section 975(4)(a)).
• Under section 977(2), and subject to section 979(9), for the purposes of Chapter 3 of Part 28 the Act,
shares that an 'associate' of the offeror holds or has contracted to acquire, whether at the date of the

---

[321]  Companies Act 2006 (Commencement No 2, etc) Order 2007, SI 2007/1093, art 2.

offer or subsequently, are not treated as shares to which the offer relates, even if the offer extends to such shares.

- Under section 979(6) and (7) the offeror's entitlement to give a squeeze-out notice under section 979 is determined as if the shares to which the takeover relates include shares which an associate of the offeror (as well as the offeror itself) has contracted to acquire subject to unfulfilled conditions.
- Under section 979(9), shares which 'associates' of the offeror acquire or unconditionally contract to acquire during that period are treated for the purposes of section 979 as shares to which the offer relates if section 979(10) applies. Section 979(10) specifies that the value of the consideration for which the offeror or its associate (as the case may be) acquires or contracts to acquire such shares must not exceed the value of the consideration under the terms of the offer or, where it does exceed the offer consideration, the offer is revised so that this requirement is met.[322]
- Under section 983(8) shares acquired or contracted to be acquired by 'associates' of the offeror are included in the calculation of the 90 per cent sell-out right thresholds specified in section 983.

## 989 Convertible securities

**28.989.01**
(1) For the purposes of this Chapter securities of a company are treated as shares in the company if they are convertible into or entitle the holder to subscribe for such shares.
References to the holder of shares or a shareholder are to be read accordingly.
(2) Subsection (1) is not to be read as requiring any securities to be treated—
(a) as shares of the same class as those into which they are convertible or for which the holder is entitled to subscribe, or
(b) as shares of the same class as other securities by reason only that the shares into which they are convertible or for which the holder is entitled to subscribe are of the same class.

COMMENCEMENT DATE 6 April 2007 (subject to saving provisions: see General Introductory Commentary to Chapter 3 above).

**28.989.02**
Section 989 is substantially the same as section 430F of the Companies Act 1985. It allows an offeror to avoid the potential difficulty which may be caused if securities convertible into shares undergo conversion while a takeover offer for shares of the same class is open for acceptances, by the offeror making a separate offer for the convertible securities themselves, treating them as a separate class. The treatment of such securities as a separate class (which is assisted by the provisions of subsection (2)) allows an offeror to apply the squeeze-out provisions of section 979 in relation to convertible securities which are not assented to that offer if the squeeze-out thresholds set out in that section are satisfied in relation to the convertible securities alone as a class.[323]

**28.989.03**
This section does not apply in relation to options to acquire shares in the company, which therefore need to be treated separately.

## 990 Debentures carrying voting rights

**28.990.01**
(1) For the purposes of this Chapter debentures issued by a company to which subsection (2) applies are treated as shares in the company if they carry voting rights.
(2) This subsection applies to a company that has voting shares, or debentures carrying voting rights, which are admitted to trading on a regulated market.
(3) In this Chapter, in relation to debentures treated as shares by virtue of subsection (1)—
(a) references to the holder of shares or a shareholder are to be read accordingly;
(b) references to shares being allotted are to be read as references to debentures being issued.

COMMENCEMENT DATE 6 April 2007 (subject to saving provisions: see General Introductory Commentary to Chapter 3 above).[324]

**28.990.02**
Section 990 is a new provision in the Act. Debentures issued by a company that has voting shares or debentures carrying voting rights, which are admitted to trading on a regulated market, are treated as shares for the purposes of Chapter 3 of Part 28 if those debentures carry voting rights. It is worth noting that under section 991(1), 'voting rights' are carried even if they only arise in certain circumstances.

---

[322] Where the Takeover Code applies, acquisitions of shares or interests in shares made while an offer remains open for acceptance will, in any event, trigger a requirement to increase the consideration under the terms of the offer where the highest price paid for such acquisitions exceeds that previously stated under the terms of the offer: Takeover Code, Rule 6.2.

[323] The ability of an offeror to acquire compulsorily such convertible securities is also subject to the procedural requirements of ss 980 and 981. Where the Takeover Code applies to a takeover offer, an appropriate offer or proposal for convertible securities is required under Rule 15 of the Takeover Code.

[324] Companies Act 2006 (Commencement No 2, etc) Order 2007, SI 2007/1093, art 2.

## 991 Interpretation

(1) In this Chapter—

'the company' means the company whose shares are the subject of a takeover offer;

'date of the offer' means—

(a) where the offer is published, the date of publication;

(b) where the offer is not published, or where any notices of the offer are given before the date of publication, the date when notices of the offer (or the first such notices) are given;

and references to the date of the offer are to be read in accordance with section 974(7) (revision of offer terms) where that applies;

'non-voting shares' means shares that are not voting shares;

'offeror' means (subject to section 987) the person making a takeover offer;

'voting rights' means rights to vote at general meetings of the company, including rights that arise only in certain circumstances;

'voting shares' means shares carrying voting rights.

(2) For the purposes of this Chapter a person contracts unconditionally to acquire shares if his entitlement under the contract to acquire them is not (or is no longer) subject to conditions or if all conditions to which it was subject have been met. A reference to a contract becoming unconditional is to be read accordingly.

COMMENCEMENT DATE 6 April 2007 (subject to saving provisions: see General Introductory Commentary to Chapter 3 above).[325]

Section 991 contains the definitions of certain terms used in Chapter 3 of Part 28 of the Act. Of particular note are the following:

- 'Date of the offer': This term was not explicitly defined in the Companies Act 1985.
- 'Voting rights': For the purposes of Chapter 3 of Part 28, shares or debentures carry 'voting rights' even if those rights only arise in certain circumstances. For example, on this basis, a class of preference shares the terms of which only confer voting rights on their holders where a dividend is in arrears would be 'voting shares' for the purposes of this Chapter.

28.991.01

28.991.02

## CHAPTER 4
### AMENDMENTS TO PART 7 OF THE COMPANIES ACT 1985

## 992 Matters to be dealt with in directors' report

(1) Part 7 of the Companies Act 1985 (c. 6) (accounts and audit) is amended as follows.

(2) In Schedule 7 (matters to be dealt with in directors' report), after Part 6 insert—

28.992.01

'PART 7
DISCLOSURE REQUIRED BY CERTAIN PUBLICLY-TRADED COMPANIES

13 (1) This Part of this Schedule applies to the directors' report for a financial year if the company had securities carrying voting rights admitted to trading on a regulated market at the end of that year.

(2) The report shall contain detailed information, by reference to the end of that year, on the following matters—

(a) the structure of the company's capital, including in particular—

(i) the rights and obligations attaching to the shares or, as the case may be, to each class of shares in the company, and

(ii) where there are two or more such classes, the percentage of the total share capital represented by each class;

(b) any restrictions on the transfer of securities in the company, including in particular—

(i) limitations on the holding of securities, and

(ii) requirements to obtain the approval of the company, or of other holders of securities in the company, for a transfer of securities;

(c) in the case of each person with a significant direct or indirect holding of securities in the company, such details as are known to the company of—

(i) the identity of the person,

(ii) the size of the holding, and

(iii) the nature of the holding;

(d) in the case of each person who holds securities carrying special rights with regard to control of the company—

(i) the identity of the person, and

---

[325] Companies Act 2006 (Commencement No 2, etc) Order 2007, SI 2007/1093, art 2.

       (ii)  the nature of the rights;
   (e)  where—
       (i)   the company has an employees' share scheme, and
       (ii)  shares to which the scheme relates have rights with regard to control of the company that are not exercisable directly by the employees,
       how those rights are exercisable;
   (f)  any restrictions on voting rights, including in particular—
       (i)   limitations on voting rights of holders of a given percentage or number of votes,
       (ii)  deadlines for exercising voting rights, and
       (iii)  arrangements by which, with the company's co-operation, financial rights carried by securities are held by a person other than the holder of the securities;
   (g)  any agreements between holders of securities that are known to the company and may result in restrictions on the transfer of securities or on voting rights;
   (h)  any rules that the company has about—
       (i)   appointment and replacement of directors, or
       (ii)  amendment of the company's articles of association;
   (i)  the powers of the company's directors, including in particular any powers in relation to the issuing or buying back by the company of its shares;
   (j)  any significant agreements to which the company is a party that take effect, alter or terminate upon a change of control of the company following a takeover bid, and the effects of any such agreements;
   (k)  any agreements between the company and its directors or employees providing for compensation for loss of office or employment (whether through resignation, purported redundancy or otherwise) that occurs because of a takeover bid.
  (3)  For the purposes of sub-paragraph (2)(a) a company's capital includes any securities in the company that are not admitted to trading on a regulated market.
  (4)  For the purposes of sub-paragraph (2)(c) a person has an indirect holding of securities if—
   (a)  they are held on his behalf, or
   (b)  he is able to secure that rights carried by the securities are exercised in accordance with his wishes.
  (5)  Sub-paragraph (2)(j) does not apply to an agreement if—
   (a)  disclosure of the agreement would be seriously prejudicial to the company, and
   (b)  the company is not under any other obligation to disclose it.
  (6)  In this paragraph—
'securities' means shares or debentures;
'takeover bid' has the same meaning as in the Takeovers Directive;
'the Takeovers Directive' means Directive 2004/25/EC of the European Parliament and of the Council;
'voting rights' means rights to vote at general meetings of the company in question, including rights that arise only in certain circumstances.'
  (4)  In section 234ZZA (requirements of directors' reports), at the end of subsection (4) (contents of Schedule 7) insert—
'Part 7 specifies information to be disclosed by certain publicly-traded companies.'
  (5)  After that subsection insert—
'(5)  A directors' report shall also contain any necessary explanatory material with regard to information that is required to be included in the report by Part 7 of Schedule 7.'
  (5)  In section 251 (summary financial statements), after subsection (2ZA) insert—
'(2ZB)  A company that sends to an entitled person a summary financial statement instead of a copy of its directors' report shall—
   (a)  include in the statement the explanatory material required to be included in the directors' report by section 234ZZA(5), or
   (b)  send that material to the entitled person at the same time as it sends the statement.
     For the purposes of paragraph (b), subsections (2A) to (2E) apply in relation to the material referred to in that paragraph as they apply in relation to a summary financial statement.'
  (6)  The amendments made by this section apply in relation to directors' reports for financial years beginning on or after 20th May 2006.

COMMENCEMENT DATE 6 April 2007[326]

**28.992.02**   Section 992 amended Part 7 of the Companies Act 1985 by requiring additional disclosures in the directors' reports of companies which had securities carrying voting rights admitted to trading on a regulated market (whether or not that included a listing on the London Stock Exchange) at the end of the financial year to which the directors' reports related. These amendments, which implemented Article 10 of the Takeovers Directive, applied in relation to directors' reports for financial years beginning on or after 20 May 2006.

---

[326] Companies Act 2006 (Commencement No 2, etc) Order 2007, SI 2007/1093, art 2.

The Small Companies and Groups (Accounts and Directors' Report) Regulations 2008 (SI 2008/409) **28.992.03** and the Large and Medium-Sized Companies and Groups (Accounts and Reports) Regulations 2008 (SI 2008/410) replaced the provisions previously contained in the Schedules to Part 7 of the Companies Act 1985 and Part 7 of the Companies (Northern Ireland) Order 1986 (SI 1986/1032). The Regulations came into force on 6 April 2008 and apply to financial years beginning on or after that date.

The Regulations were made by the Secretary of State under his power in section 416(4) of the Act to **28.992.04** make regulations as to the contents of the directors' report. Regulations under sections 427 and 428 may make provision for additional explanatory material when summary financial statements are distributed rather than full reports and accounts.

Breach of the requirement to prepare a directors' report attracts the criminal penalties under section **28.992.05** 415(5) of the Act.

# 29

## FRAUDULENT TRADING

---

### Companies Act 2006

### PART 29
### FRAUDULENT TRADING

#### 993  Offence of fraudulent trading[a]

(1) If any business of a company is carried on with intent to defraud creditors of the company or creditors of any other person, or for any fraudulent purpose, every person who is knowingly a party to the carrying on of the business in that manner commits an offence.

(2) This applies whether or not the company has been, or is in the course of being, wound up.

(3) A person guilty of an offence under this section is liable—

    (a) on conviction on indictment, to imprisonment for a term not exceeding ten years or a fine (or both);

    (b) on summary conviction—

        (i) in England and Wales, to imprisonment for a term not exceeding twelve months or a fine not exceeding the statutory maximum (or both);

        (ii) in Scotland or Northern Ireland, to imprisonment for a term not exceeding six months or a fine not exceeding the statutory maximum (or both).

**29.993.01**

AMENDMENTS AND NOTES

[a] This section applies with modifications to LLPs by reg 47 of the Limited Liability Partnerships (Application of Companies Act 2006) Regulations 2009, SI 2009/1804.

COMMENCEMENT DATE 1 October 2007[1]

This restated section 458 of Companies Act 1985, though the maximum period of imprisonment was increased from seven years to ten years (see Explanatory Notes to Act, paragraph 1264). Once again, this provision did not feature in the Bill as initially drafted, having only appeared at a late stage in the passage through the Commons.

**29.993.02**

The offence of fraudulent trading was introduced as a sanction to curb abuse of limited liability in Companies Act 1929. Its impact in that respect is limited, with only a modest number of successful prosecutions each year. Having said that, allegations of fraudulent trading are often the spur for a Department of Trade and Industry (DTI) (now Department of Business, Innovation and Skills (BIS)) investigation, and may result in companies being wound up in the public interest under section 124A of the Insolvency Act 1986.

**29.993.03**

The wording of the restated provision mirrors its statutory predecessor in terms of the substantive nature of the offence, though it has benefited from a cosmetic makeover. Significantly the maximum penalty for fraudulent trading has been increased from seven years imprisonment to ten years. The 'statutory maximum' fine is presently £5,000. The Proceeds of Crime Act 2002 might be brought into play against a convicted person. In 2005–06 official statistics show 25 prosecutions for fraudulent trading resulting in only seven convictions, a clear indication of the burdens facing the prosecution.

**29.993.04**

This offence of fraudulent trading mirrors the civil wrong of the same name as outlined in Insolvency Act 1986, section 213, though liability for the latter can only arise where the company is being wound up. Such a requirement is not necessary under section 993: see section 993(2).

**29.993.05**

Turning to the substantive elements of the offence there are *three* forms of modus operandi under section 993(1). The company's business must be carried on with intent either to:

**29.993.06**

---

[1] Companies Act 2006 (Commencement No 3, etc) Order 2007, SI 2007/2194, art 2.

(i)   Defraud the creditors of the company. The term creditors includes persons to whom a debt is not presently payable.[2]

(ii)  Defraud the creditors of other persons.

(iii) Or for any other fraudulent purpose. This could encompass frauds committed against *potential* creditors: see *R v Kemp*.[3] For other possibilities here see *Re Todd (Swanscombe) Ltd*.[4]

**29.993.07**   Generally, for any of these forms of conduct it is necessary to establish dishonesty—as the court stressed in *Re Patrick and Lyon Ltd*[5] the test is subjective and not objective. This requirement is the rock upon which many allegations of fraudulent trading founder. Defendants often cite incompetence as opposed to dishonesty as the plausible explanation for their behaviour. But, if the hurdle of proving dishonesty can be overcome, any person who is knowingly a party to such activities is potentially liable. However, active participation in the fraud is essential; mere passivity will not suffice. This point has been made in a number of cases including *Re Maidstone Buildings Provisions Ltd*.[6]

**29.993.08**   Having mentioned these qualifications there is no need to establish repetitive conduct; a single fraudulent act will suffice.[7] Furthermore the offence can be committed by any person—there is no need to show that the defendant was a director or even a shadow director.[8] Third parties dealing with the management of a company can thus be enmeshed—there are real problems of interpretation for the courts in dealing with such instances.[9]

**29.993.09**   There is no doubt that the courts are more inclined to find reasons for denying the existence of fraudulent trading, whether it be the criminal offence or civil liability, as a deconstruction of the judicial opinions expressed in the recent Court of Appeal ruling in *Morphitis v Bernasconi*[10] indicates.

---

[2]  *R v Smith* [1996] 2 Cr App R 1.

[3]  [1988] QB 646.

[4]  [1990] BCC 125.

[5]  [1933] Ch 786. But see *Re William C Leitch Ltd* [1932] 2 Ch 71 and *R v Grantham* [1984] QB 675 for a more flexible approach. On directions to the jury see *R v Lockwood* (1985) 2 BCC 99, 333.

[6]  [1971] 1 WLR 1085.

[7]  *Re Gerald Cooper Chemicals Ltd* [1978] Ch 262.

[8]  In *Re Augustus Barnett and Son Ltd* [1986] BCLC 170 an allegation that a parent company had participated in the fraudulent trading of the business of one of its subsidiaries failed to convince the court. See also *R v Miles* [1992] Crim LR 657.

[9]  See *Bank of India v Morris* [2005] EWCA Civ 693 for consideration of the difficult issues arising here in the civil context.

[10]  [2002] EWCA Civ 289. But for a rare civil case where fraudulent trading by some of the defendants was found to be present see *Re Overnight Ltd* [2010] EWHC 613 (Ch), [2010] 2 BCLC 186 (Roth J).

# 30

# PROTECTION OF MEMBERS AGAINST UNFAIR PREJUDICE

## Companies Act 2006

### PART 30

### PROTECTION OF MEMBERS AGAINST UNFAIR PREJUDICE

### *Main provisions*

### 994 Petition by company member

(1) A member of a company may apply to the court by petition for an order under this Part on the ground—

    (a) that the company's affairs are being or have been conducted in a manner that is unfairly prejudicial to the interests of members generally or of some part of its members (including at least himself), or

    (b) that an actual or proposed act or omission of the company (including an act or omission on its behalf) is or would be so prejudicial.

(1A) [For the purposes of subsection (1)(a), a removal of the company's auditor from office—

    (a) on grounds of divergence of opinions on accounting treatments or audit procedures, or

    (b) on any other improper grounds,

shall be treated as being unfairly prejudicial to the interests of some part of the company's members.][a]

(2) The provisions of this Part apply to a person who is not a member of a company but to whom shares in the company have been transferred or transmitted by operation of law as they apply to a member of a company.

(3) In this section, and so far as applicable for the purposes of this section in the other provisions of this Part, 'company' means—

    (a) a company within the meaning of this Act, or

    (b) a company that is not such a company but is a statutory water company within the meaning of the Statutory Water Companies Act 1991 (c. 58).

**30.994.01**

AMENDMENTS AND NOTES

[a] Subsection (1A) inserted by the Statutory Auditors and Third Country Auditors Regulations 2007, SI 2007/3494, reg 42(1), with effect from 6 April 2008. The amendment does not apply in relation to auditors appointed for financial years beginning before 6 April 2008: SI 2007/3494, reg 42(2). For judicial discussion of subs (1A), see the judgment of HHJ Purle QC in *Re Sunrise Radio Ltd* [2009] EWHC 2893 (Ch), [9]–[10].

COMMENCEMENT DATE 1 October 2007[1]

---

[1] Companies Act 2006 (Commencement No 3, etc) Order 2007, SI 2007/2194, art 2.

*Introduction and provenance*

**30.994.02**    This is the critical provision in the Companies Act 2006 dealing with shareholder rights and remedies. Most domestic disputes within companies will be dealt with under this particular statutory jurisdiction. The section gives shareholders a powerful weapon to obtain redress where their legitimate rights are being ignored or trampled upon. It is most often used to enable a shareholder to exit from a company by requiring his shares to be bought at a fair value in circumstances where he would otherwise find it difficult to sell them. A buy-out is not, however, the only relief the court can give; it has complete discretion under section 996 to grant whatever relief it thinks fit (discussed at paragraphs 30.996.01 *et seq* below) and so can tailor-make the remedy to suit the justice of the case. It should also be borne in mind that this section is not the only statutory protection given to shareholders; in an appropriate case shareholders may also be able to seek redress by way of a derivative claim under Part 11 of the Companies Act 2006 (discussed at paragraphs 11.260.01 *et seq*) or by a winding up of the company on the just and equitable ground under section 122(1)(g) of the Insolvency Act 1986. The interface between these remedies is discussed at paragraphs 30.994.27 *et seq* below.

**30.994.03**    The power given to the court by section 994 to intervene in corporate affairs at the behest of an aggrieved shareholder can be traced back to the Companies Act 1948, under which the governing provision for many years was Companies Act 1948, section 210 which offered a remedy in cases of 'oppression'. For many reasons, this provision did not operate successfully in practice, and, in the period up to 1980, there were only half a dozen instances of successful reported usage. The provision was therefore significantly remodelled in 1980 (in the form of Companies Act 1980, section 75), with the key change being the substitution of the concept of 'unfair prejudice' in lieu of oppression. That provision was then consolidated as section 459 of the 1985 Act, which was later extended by the Companies Act 1989 (and by the Water Act 1989). The version in Companies Act 2006, section 994 is the same in substance as the old section 459 but with minor stylistic modifications. The case law developed under section 459 is therefore directly applicable to the present section.

**30.994.04**    After a cautious start, the volume of case law under the section 459 provision grew exponentially. The courts, casting off their traditional antipathy towards intervention in the internal affairs of companies, suddenly felt able to adopt an interventionist role. In so doing, they were further encouraged by Parliament with the amendment made by Companies Act 1989, which extended the scope of the jurisdiction further by encompassing complaints of unfair prejudice to shareholders in general. By the middle of the 1990s, it had become apparent both to policy makers and the courts that this jurisdiction needed to be more tightly controlled. The Law Commission, in its report 'Shareholder Remedies',[2] suggested a number of potential methods of limiting the quantity of cases coming before the courts including the possibility of statutory presumptions of unfair prejudice in defined circumstances. As it happened, it was not necessary to introduce such measures by legislation, as the House of Lords in *O'Neill v Phillips*[3] placed significant curbs on the exploitation of the provision by highlighting that it did not provide an automatic exit option for every aggrieved and disappointed shareholder. As discussed at paragraphs 30.994.15 *et seq* below, what is required is some breach of the shareholder's legitimate rights. The conduct complained of does not, however, have to be unlawful quite apart from the section, as the concept embraced by the section is a wider one, with its focus on fairness. *O'Neill v Phillips* did damp down the fires of litigation, and was met with some criticism on the grounds that it reduced the protection on offer to minority shareholders. There were calls put to the Company Law Review for a statutory reversal of this authority, but they fell on deaf ears.[4] In recent years, there has been some evidence of another upsurge in interest in this remedial jurisdiction and many cases are still coming before the courts.

**30.994.05**    The remainder of the discussion in relation to this section addresses the following issues:

- To which companies and other entities does the section apply?
- Who can apply for relief?
- The nature of the interest protected; unfairly prejudicial conduct.
- Examples of unfairly prejudicial conduct.
- Relationship with other remedies: just and equitable winding up and derivative claims.
- The role of the company in proceedings under the section.
- Procedural matters.

The relief which the court may grant is considered in the discussion below relating to section 996.

---

2  (1997) (LC No 246, Cm 376).
3  [1999] 1 WLR 1092.
4  See para 7.41 of the Final Report (URN 01/942).

## To which companies and other entities does the section apply?

The section applies to any company within the meaning of Companies Act 2006 (see section 994(3)(a)): ie a company as defined by section 1 of the Companies Act 2006.[5] Nonetheless, virtually all instances of successful section 994 petitions relate to private, as opposed to public, companies. **30.994.06**

The section does not extend to foreign companies, but the respondents to proceedings in respect of a company to which the section does apply can include persons outside the jurisdiction provided that appropriate grounds for service out of the jurisdiction can be shown. The definition of 'company' in section 994(3)(a) is adapted for transitional purposes to cater for Northern Irish companies.[6] **30.994.07**

The section is also made applicable to limited liability partnerships unless the members of the partnership unanimously agree (by an agreement which must be recorded in writing) to exclude its operation.[7] **30.994.08**

## Who can apply for relief?

By subsections (1) and (2), the petitioner must be (i) a member of the company; or (ii) someone to whom shares in the company have been transferred or transmitted by operation of law. The former requirement is met by someone who is one of the original subscribers to the memorandum of association or who has agreed to become a member and whose name is on the register of members: section 112 of the Companies Act 2006. The latter requirement allows a petition to be brought, for example, by someone to whom shares in the company have been transferred by a proper instrument of transfer but who has been unable to obtain registration because the people who control the company are refusing to register the transfer, or by someone to whom shares have been transmitted on the death or bankruptcy of a shareholder but who similarly is being refused registration.[8] In such circumstances proceedings under section 994 could be coupled with a claim for rectification of the company's register of members under section 125 of the Companies Act 2006.[9] **30.994.09**

There may also be cases in which a person who holds shares only as a nominee may be entitled to seek relief under section 994, if he can show that his interests as shareholder are capable of including the economic and contractual interests of the beneficial owner of the shares, as was the case in *Re Brightview Ltd; Atlasview Ltd v Barton*.[10] **30.994.10**

Former members and prospective members are denied access to the jurisdiction. **30.994.11**

As a practical matter, where there is a dispute as to the standing of the petitioner, it may often be convenient and cost-effective for it to be resolved as a preliminary issue, so that if it is found that the petitioner does not have standing, the time and cost of proceedings on the substantive issues can be avoided.[11] **30.994.12**

There is no formal clean hands bar to seeking relief under section 994[12] but a petitioner with dirty hands may well find the court deciding that he has not been unfairly prejudiced[13] or refusing to grant relief even if unfair prejudice is established.[14] **30.994.13**

The court may have to consider whether recourse to a section 994 petition is permissible in circumstances where the parties have agreed that disputes should be referred to arbitration. Formerly, the state of the authorities here was unclear.[15] However, it is now apparent from the Court of Appeal ruling in *Fulham FC v Richards*[16] that an arbitration clause can oust the section 994 jurisdiction. **30.994.14**

---

[5] As is apparent from s 994(3)(b), the section also applies to statutory water companies.

[6] Companies Act 2006 (Commencement No 3, etc) Order 2007, SI 2007/2194, Sch 1, para 19.

[7] See the Limited Liability Partnerships (Application of Companies Act 2006) Regulations 2009, SI 2009/1804, Pt 12, regs 48–49. See Chapter 6 in Morse et al, *Palmer's Limited Liability Partnership Law* (2nd edn, 2011, Sweet & Maxwell) for general discussion. On the potential application of s 994 to LLPs see the discussion in *Eaton v Caulfield* [2011] EWHC 173 (Ch), [2011] BCC 385.

[8] *Re a Company* [1986] BCLC 391; *Re McCarthy Surfacing Ltd; Hecquet v McCarthy* [2006] EWHC 832 (Ch).

[9] The court may in an appropriate case order a stay of a s 994 petition to enable a claim for rectification to be brought under s 125 where retrospective rectification is sought to a date ante-dating the issue of the petition: *Re Starlight Developers Ltd* [2007] EWHC 1660 (Ch).

[10] [2004] EWHC 1056 (Ch), [2004] BCC 542.

[11] See eg the procedure followed in *Khan v Nallamothu* [2005] EWHC 2124 (Ch), where there were preliminary issues as to whether one or other of the parties had 'hijacked' the company by sending false returns to Companies House.

[12] *Re London School of Electronics Ltd* [1986] Ch 211.

[13] Eg *Kelly v Hussain* [2008] EWHC 1117 (Ch).

[14] *Re London School of Electronics Ltd* [1986] Ch 211; *Richardson v Blackmore* [2006] BCC 276.

[15] Compare *Exeter City AFC v The Football Conference* [2004] BCC 498 with *Re Vocam (Europe) Ltd* [1998] BCC 396.

[16] [2011] EWCA Civ 855.

*The nature of the interest protected; unfairly prejudicial conduct*

**30.994.15**   One of the problems with the original jurisdiction under section 210 Companies Act 1948 was that the remedy was only available to a member complaining of a wrong done to him or her *qua* member, and that this was interpreted in a strict and narrow sense. In the early cases under section 75 of the Companies Act 1980, there were suggestions that this artificial and limiting restriction would continue to be applied.[17] However, the courts eventually opted for a wider interpretation.[18] In so doing, they recognized that in the context of a member joining a private company, the expectations might go beyond those enjoyed strictly *qua* member in the narrow sense of the term. Thus, for example, there may be a legitimate expectation to participate in management. This wider view undoubtedly was one of the factors leading to the expansion of the jurisdiction in the late 1980s and early 1990s. However, it was placed in context by *O'Neill v Phillips*,[19] which made clear that 'legitimate expectations' was a concept to be interpreted strictly and in accordance with traditional equitable principles.

**30.994.16**   In particular Lord Hoffmann in *O'Neill v Phillips* explained the position as follows:

> Parliament has chosen fairness as the criterion by which the court must decide whether it has jurisdiction to grant relief. It is clear from the legislative history … that it chose this concept to free the court from technical considerations of legal right and to confer a wide power to do what appeared just and equitable. But this does not mean that the court can do whatever the individual judge happens to think fair. The concept of fairness must be applied judicially and the content which it is given by the courts must be based upon rational principles.…
>
> In the case of section 459 [now section 994], the background has the following two features. First, a company is an association of persons for an economic purpose, usually entered into with legal advice and some degree of formality. The terms of the association are contained in the articles of association and sometimes in collateral agreements between the shareholders. Thus the manner in which the affairs of the company may be conducted is closely regulated by rules to which the shareholders have agreed. Secondly, company law has developed seamlessly from the law of partnership, which was treated by equity, like the Roman *societas*, as a contract of good faith. One of the traditional roles of equity, as a separate jurisdiction, was to restrain the exercise of strict legal rights in certain relationships in which it considered that this would be contrary to good faith. These principles have, with appropriate modification, been carried over into company law.
>
> The first of these two features leads to the conclusion that a member of a company will not ordinarily be entitled to complain of unfairness unless there has been some breach of the terms on which he agreed that the affairs of the company should be conducted. But the second leads to the conclusion that there will be cases in which equitable considerations make it unfair for those conducting the affairs of the company to rely upon their strict legal powers. Thus unfairness may consist in a breach of the rules or in using the rules in a manner which equity would regard as contrary to good faith.
>
> This approach to the concept of unfairness in section 459 [now section 994] runs parallel to that which your Lordships' House, in ***Ebrahimi v Westbourne Galleries Ltd*** [1973] AC 360, adopted in giving content to the concept of 'just and equitable' as a ground for winding up. After referring to cases on the equitable jurisdiction to require partners to exercise their powers in good faith, Lord Wilberforce said at 379:
>
> > 'The words ['just and equitable'] are a recognition of the fact that a limited company is more than a mere legal entity, with a personality in law of its own: that there is room in company law for recognition of the fact that behind it, or amongst it, there are individuals, with rights, expectations and obligations inter se which are not necessarily submerged in the company structure. That structure is defined by the Companies Act 1948 and by the articles of association by which shareholders agree to be bound. In most companies and in most contexts, this definition is sufficient and exhaustive, equally so whether the company is large or small. The 'just and equitable' provision does not, as the respondents [the company] suggest, entitle one party to disregard the obligation he assumes by entering a company, nor the court to dispense him from it. It does, as equity always does, enable the court to subject the exercise of legal rights to equitable considerations; considerations, that is, of a personal character arising between one individual and another, which may make it unjust, or inequitable, to insist on legal rights, or to exercise them in a particular way.'

---

[17]   See eg *Re A Company (004475 of 1982)* [1983] Ch 178.
[18]   *Re A Company (00477 of 1986)* [1986] BCLC 376; *Re Haden Bill Electrical Ltd* [1995] 2 BCLC 280.
[19]   [1999] 1 WLR 1092.

I would apply the same reasoning to the concept of unfairness in section 459 [now section 994]. The Law Commission, in its report on *Shareholder Remedies* (Law Com No 246) (1997) para 4.11, p 43 expresses some concern that defining the content of the unfairness concept in the way I have suggested might unduly limit its scope and that 'conduct which would appear to be deserving of a remedy may be left unremedied'. In my view, a balance has to be struck between the breadth of the discretion given to the court and the principle of legal certainty. Petitions under section 459 [now section 994] are often lengthy and expensive. It is highly desirable that lawyers should be able to advise their clients whether or not a petition is likely to succeed. Lord Wilberforce, after the passage which I have quoted, said that it would be impossible 'and wholly undesirable' to define the circumstances in which the application of equitable principles might make it unjust, or inequitable (or unfair) for a party to insist on legal rights or to exercise them in a particular way. This of course is right. But that does not mean that there are no principles by which those circumstances may be identified. The way in which such equitable principles operate is tolerably well settled and in my view it would be wrong to abandon them in favour of some wholly indefinite notion of fairness.

See also *Re Guidezone Ltd*, per Jonathan Parker J:[20]　　　　　　　　　　　**30.994.17**

'unfairness' may arise from agreements or promises made, or understandings reached, during the life of the company which it would be unfair to allow the majority to ignore. Applying traditional equitable principles, equity will not hold the majority to an agreement, promise or understanding which is not enforceable at law unless and until the minority has acted in reliance on it. In the case of an agreement, promise or understanding made or reached when the company was formed, that requirement will almost always be fulfilled, in that the minority will have acted on the agreement, promise or understanding in entering into association with the majority and taking the minority stake. But the same cannot be said of agreements, promises or understandings made or reached subsequently, which are not themselves enforceable at law. In such a case, the majority will not as a general rule be regarded in equity as having acted contrary to good faith unless and until it has allowed the minority to act in reliance on such an agreement, promise or understanding. Absent some special circumstances, it will only be at that point, and not before, that equity will intervene by providing a remedy to the minority which is not available at law.

Therefore an assessment whether conduct is unfair must be made against the legal background of the relevant corporate structure. The conduct is not to be considered in a vacuum. This 'legal background' is usually the company's articles of association together with any collateral agreements between the shareholders. It will not be unfair for the affairs of a company to be conducted in accordance with the articles and any shareholders' agreement unless it would be inequitable for the articles and any such agreement to be enforced in the particular circumstances under consideration. The extracts from the case law set out above show that such 'inequitability' can arise from the fact that the legal background—both in the Articles and in any shareholders' agreement—can be subject to equitable principles which may moderate the exercise of strict legal rights when insistence on the enforcement of such rights would be unconscionable. There is less scope for unfairness and breach of legitimate expectation where sophisticated investors are involved.[21]　　　**30.994.18**

In order to satisfy this test of inequitability, or unconscionability, the conduct does not have to be unlawful. Nor does it have to be such as would justify the making of a winding-up order on the just and equitable ground under section 122(1)(g) of the Insolvency Act 1986 (in contrast to the position under the old section 210 of the Companies Act 1948). Thus conduct can be unfairly prejudicial even if it does not technically infringe the Companies Acts.[22]　　　**30.994.19**

In a broad sense, the test is as to whether the conduct renders it unjust for a party to insist on his strict legal rights. There can never be an exhaustive definition of what is capable of constituting such conduct and the concept of fairness in any particular case will depend upon the context in which it is being used, because what may constitute unfair prejudice is open-ended depending upon the precise circumstances of each case. Nonetheless, the courts will not apply some indefinite notion of fairness, but will instead apply the relevant principles according to the settled and established equitable rules. As a rule of thumb a useful test is to ask whether the exercise of the power or rights in question would involve a breach of an agreement or understanding between the parties which it would be unfair to allow a　　　**30.994.20**

---

[20] [2000] 2 BCLC 321, [175]. Although part of the reasoning in this case was overruled in *Hawkes v Cuddy (No 2)* [2009] EWCA Civ 291, [2009] 2 BCLC 427 on the point of the interface between the unfair prejudice and winding-up remedies, this observation in relation to 'unfairness' still holds true.

[21] See the comments of David Richards J in *Re Coroin* Ltd [2012] EWHC 2343 (Ch) at [635].

[22] Eg *McGuinness v Bremner plc* [1988] BCLC 673.

shareholder to ignore. Such agreements or understandings may arise by words or by conduct and do not have to be contractually binding in order to found the equity.[23]

**30.994.21**   Such agreements or understandings may often arise in the context of a private company, where there is scope for understandings and expectations to arise among the shareholders and management above and beyond the company's constitution.[24] This is particularly so where the company is a joint venture between two, or a few, individuals who at the outset expect that they will each be equally involved in the running of the business and that they will all share in the rewards which the business produces. There is unlikely to be any scope for such legitimate expectations in the context of a public listed company where all a shareholder can rely on is the public constitution of the company.[25]

**30.994.22**   To satisfy the test of 'unfair prejudice', it is self-evident that the petitioner must show conduct which is both unfair and prejudicial. Both criteria have to be met for a petition to succeed.[26] These are flexible concepts that need to be applied in the context of each individual case.[27] Although the concept of unfairness is flexible, it is not an unbounded concept.[28] Furthermore, the conduct must relate to the company's affairs.[29] The conduct does not, however, have to be a continuing one: in appropriate circumstances a single act or omission will be sufficient. In determining whether it is unfairly prejudicial, the conduct is to be interpreted from an objective perspective.[30] The fact that the alleged wrongdoer may not have intended it to be unfair and prejudicial is not decisive of the matter.

**30.994.23**   It is not enough merely to show that the relationship between the parties has irretrievably broken down and that trust and confidence between the shareholders no longer exists, as company law does not contain a concept of 'no-fault divorce'.[31] The breakdown in the relationship must have arisen from some underlying inequitability of the type described above, or there must have been some such inequitability subsequent to the breakdown.

### Examples of unfairly prejudicial conduct

**30.994.24**   By way of example, exclusion from participation in management may be regarded as unfairly prejudicial in circumstances where there is a legitimate expectation of being involved in management.[32] An unjustified refusal to pay a dividend may suffice, particularly where other shareholders are also directors and are extracting monies for themselves by inflated fees while starving the non-director shareholder of any return on his investment.[33] A breach of a director's fiduciary duties may in some circumstances form the basis of a successful petition, most obviously in cases where the company's business has been improperly diverted to another company controlled by the majority shareholders or the directors and the majority have in some other way been lining their pockets at the expense of the company and the petitioner.[34] Mismanagement would generally not suffice unless prolonged and

---

[23]  *O'Neill v Phillips* [1999] 1 WLR 1092; *Re Guidezone Ltd* [2000] 2 BCLC 321.

[24]  For the relevance of cultural considerations in assessing alleged unfair prejudice in the context of a family company, see *Rahman v Malik* [2008] 2 BCLC 403.

[25]  *Re Blue Arrow plc* [1987] BCLC 585; *Re Astec (BSR) plc* [1998] 2 BCLC 556.

[26]  *Nicholas v Soundcraft Electronics Ltd* [1993] BCLC 360 See also *Sikorski v Sikorski* [2012] EWHC 1613 (Ch) at para [55] per Briggs J..

[27]  See eg the comments of the court in *Re Sunrise Radio Ltd* [2009] EWHC 2893 (Ch), where HHJ Purle QC stressed the need for the court to retain a sense of proportion and to consider whether the matters complained of (even if established) could have affected the value of the petitioner's shareholding.

[28]  See the comments of Arden LJ in *Maidment v Attwood* [2012] EWCA Civ 998 at para [21].

[29]  *Re Legal Costs Negotiators Ltd* [1999] 2 BCLC 171; *Gross v Rackind* [2004] EWCA Civ 815, [2005] 1 WLR 3505. For further consideration of this point, see *Hawkes v Cuddy (No 2)* [2009] EWCA Civ 291, [2009] 2 BCLC 427. In *Re Coroin Ltd* [2012] EWHC 2343 (Ch), David Richards J made the point at [626] that, in general, disputes between shareholders personally cannot be characterized as relating to the company's affairs. See also *Sikorski v Sikorski* [2012] EWHC 1613 (Ch) at para [56] per Briggs J

[30]  *Re R A Noble & Sons Ltd* [1983] BCLC 273. See also *Fisher v Cadman* [2006] 1 BCLC 499 and *Wilson v Jaymarke Estates Ltd* [2007] UKHL 29, which show that acquiescence in unfairly prejudicial conduct can be brought to an end thereby justifying a petition. Conversely, passive behaviour on the part of the respondent may be relevant in establishing unfair prejudice—see the discussion in *Whillock v Henderson* [2009] BCC 291.

[31]  *O'Neill v Phillips* [1999] 1WLR 1092, 1104–1105, *per* Lord Hoffmann. Where the company has become deadlocked and is unable to carry on its business, the remedy of a winding-up on the just and equitable ground may be available under s 122(1)(g) of the Insolvency Act 1986. For consideration by the Court of Appeal of the relationship between this remedy and the remedy under s 994 Companies Act 2006, see *Hawkes v Cuddy (No 2)* [2009] EWCA Civ 291, [2009] 2 BCLC 427.

[32]  Eg *Oak Investment Partners XII, Limited Partnership v Boughtwood* [2009] 1 BCLC 453, upheld by the Court of Appeal, [2010] EWCA Civ 23, where there was a boardroom *coup d'état*.

[33]  *Grace v Biagioli* [2006] 2 BCLC 70. See also *Re McCarthy Surfacing Ltd* [2009] BCC 464.

[34]  See eg *O'Donnell v Shanahan* [2009] EWCA Civ 751, [2009] BCC 822 in relation to the so-called 'no profit' and 'no conflict' elements of fiduciary duties.

coupled with exceptional circumstances.[35] A shareholder could also petition where there is an attempt to squeeze him out by an improper issue of new shares to other shareholders, for example in circumstances where the company does not require further funds and the only purpose of the share issue is to dilute the petitioner's stake. Other examples may involve matters such as withholding information from the petitioner in circumstances where he has a legitimate right to be informed about, and perhaps even consulted on, various aspects of the company's business. The flexibility of the unfair prejudice remedy means that there can never been an exhaustive list of the types of conduct which may lead to relief.

In a group situation, conduct of the affairs of one company can in appropriate circumstances be conduct of the affairs of another company for the purpose of the section, and in particular conduct of the affairs of a subsidiary may be conduct of the affairs of the parent and vice versa.[36]     **30.994.25**

Subsection (1A) has introduced a specific statutory ground of unfair prejudice arising from the improper removal of a company's auditor.[37]     **30.994.26**

## Relationship with other remedies: just and equitable winding up and derivative claims

As mentioned at paragraph 30.994.02 above, a further statutory protection given to shareholders is the court's jurisdiction to wind up a company for 'just and equitable' reasons under section 122(1)(g) of the Insolvency Act 1986. Under the old law of shareholder remedies under section 210 of the Companies Act 1948, in order to qualify for relief against oppression, it was necessary to show that it would have been just and equitable to wind up the company. This illogical point of connection between the two shareholder remedial jurisdictions was removed by section 75 of the Companies Act 1980; therefore, for relief to be obtained under section 994 of the Companies Act 2006 it is irrelevant whether or not a winding-up order could also be obtained. Equally, the circumstances in which a 'just and equitable' winding-up order may be obtained do not depend upon showing that there is conduct which satisfies the 'unfair prejudice' test. The winding-up remedy may be granted where there is a deadlock in the company's affairs or where the so-called substratum of its business has ceased to exist, even in the absence of any unfairly prejudicial conduct. Thus for a remedy to be granted under section 994 of the Companies Act 2006, some form of wrongdoing must be established, but this is not a prerequisite for the winding-up remedy under section 122(1)(g) of the Insolvency Act 1986.     **30.994.27**

Where there is wrongdoing, there will be many cases in which the relevant conduct will give rise both to the jurisdiction under section 994 and to the jurisdiction under section 122(1)(g), in which case the petitioner must consider carefully the relief he really wants, bearing in mind that the winding-up remedy will mean the end of the company, whereas granting relief under the unfair prejudice jurisdiction offers a more humane and flexible option if it is possible to achieve it.[38] A court hearing a winding-up petition under section 122(1)(g) may refuse to wind up the company if it is of the opinion that some other remedy is available (particularly under section 994) and that the petitioner is acting unreasonably in seeking to have the company wound up instead of seeking to pursue the other remedy: section 125(2) of the Insolvency Act 1986. In this context a practical point to note is that a petitioner who wishes to bring claims for both the unfair prejudice remedy and the winding-up remedy must have regard to the requirements of the Practice Direction referred to at paragraph 30.994.34 below.     **30.994.28**

For a review of the interface between the unfair prejudice jurisdiction and the winding-up jurisdiction, see the Court of Appeal's decision in *Hawkes v Cuddy (No 2)*.[39]     **30.994.29**

A proposed petitioner under section 994 must also consider carefully whether the relief which he seeks (such as a buy-out of his shareholding) is one which is personal to him or whether (such as a claim that compensation should be paid) it is one which is more properly claimable by the company. In the former situation the claim is one which he can properly bring under section 994. In the latter situation he must consider whether the claim should instead be brought by way of a derivative claim under Part     **30.994.30**

---

[35] *Re Macro (Ipswich) Ltd* [1994] 2 BCLC 354. Compare *Re Saul D Harrison and Sons plc* [1995] 1 BCLC 14 where the court was supportive of the managerial prerogative and in particular the duty to have regard to employee interests even at the expense of certain shareholders.

[36] *Nicholas v Soundcraft Electronics Ltd* [1993] BCLC 360; *Gross v Rackind* [2004] EWCA Civ 815, [2005] 1 WLR 3505; *Re Grandactual Ltd* [2006] BCC 73; *Hawkes v Cuddy (No 2)* [2009] EWCA Civ 291, [2009] 2 BCLC 427. A wide view of what constitutes the company's affairs was taken in *Oak Investment Partners XII, Limited Partnership v Boughtwood* [2009] 1 BCLC 453, upheld by the Court of Appeal (see [2010] EWCA Civ 23).

[37] See the discussion of subs (1A) in the judgment of HHJ Purle QC in *Re Sunrise Radio Ltd* [2009] EWHC 2893 (Ch), [9]–[10].

[38] *Shah v Shah* [2010] EWHC 313 (Ch)

[39] [2009] EWCA Civ 291, [2009] 2 BCLC 427, [104]–[108].

11 of the Companies Act 2006 (discussed at paragraphs 11.260.11 *et seq*). A claimant who seeks to claim that damages or compensation should be paid to him rather than to the company (as an alternative to or in addition to a buy-out of his shares), should also be careful to ensure that he is not infringing the principle of reflective loss.[40] See *Clark v Cutland*,[41] *Re Chime Corporation Ltd*,[42] and *Gamlestaden Fastigheter AB v Baltic Partners Ltd*.[43]

### The role of the company in proceedings under the section

**30.994.31**   It is usually unnecessary and inappropriate for the company to play a part in the proceedings. The fight is between the shareholders and thus the company is usually the subject-matter of the dispute rather than an interested party. The practical consequence is that the company's monies must not be used to fund the dispute. Any attempt by the alleged wrongdoers to use the company as a litigation piggy-bank would simply be a further ground of unfairly prejudicial conduct of which the petitioner could properly complain and in relation to which the petitioner could obtain interim injunctive relief.[44]

**30.994.32**   Nonetheless there may sometimes be a case where it is necessary or expedient for the company to play some part in the proceedings, such as where disclosure is sought from it or where an order is sought that it should buy the petitioner's shares. In such a case the company may properly be involved and may use its monies to fund such involvement, although its role in the proceedings is likely to be a small one.[45]

**30.994.33**   In general, an unfair prejudice petition should not be presented once a company has become insolvent, because in that situation the shareholders will have lost any tangible interest in the company and also the issue of obtaining leave might arise. However, if an unfair prejudice petition has been presented some time before the descent into insolvency, proceedings might be permitted to continue with a remedy being ordered against a respondent which reflects the value of the shares at the time when the alleged unfair prejudice occurred.[46] It also has to be said that the courts are reluctant to see a deserving petitioner deprived of a remedy against an individual respondent simply because the company may be insolvent.[47]

### Procedural matters

**30.994.34**   For procedural aspects of an unfair prejudice petition, see the Companies (Unfair Prejudice Applications) Proceedings Rules 2009[48] which govern proceedings under section 994 and deal with matters such as the form of the petition, service of the petition, the issues the court will deal with on the first hearing of the petition, and so forth.

**30.994.35**   See also Practice Direction 49B to CPR Part 49 (entitled 'Order Under Section 127 Insolvency Act 1986') which notes in particular the undesirability of including within an unfair prejudice petition, a petition under section 122(1)(g) of the Insolvency Act 1986 to have the company wound up on the just and equitable ground. The Practice Direction explains that a claim for winding up should be included only if it is the relief which the petitioner prefers or it is thought that it may be the only relief to which the petitioner is entitled.[49] See the discussion of the interface between the unfair prejudice jurisdiction and the winding-up jurisdiction at paragraphs 30.994.27–29 above.

**30.994.36**   Once the proceedings have been issued, in the High Court all interim steps (except for injunction applications, which must be made to a judge) will be dealt with by the Companies Court registrars in proceedings in London or by the district registrars in proceedings in a district registry, at the

---

[40] *Johnson v Gore Wood & Co* [2002] 2 AC 1.

[41] [2004] 1 WLR 783.

[42] [2004] 3 HKLRD 922 (*sub nom Nina Kung v Tan Man Kou*), a decision of the Hong Kong Court of Final Appeal with Lord Scott of Foscote sitting as a non-permanent judge.

[43] [2007] UKPC 26, a decision of the Privy Council in relation to the equivalent provision of Jersey law, confirming that in certain circumstances the court does have power on an unfair prejudice application to make an order for the payment of damages or compensation to the company, and confirming also that on the particular facts of that case the petitioner was entitled to seek relief even where the company was insolvent.

[44] *Re Crossmore Electrical and Civil Engineering Ltd* [1989] BCLC 137.

[45] *Re a Company (No 1126 of 1992)* [1994] 2 BCLC 146.

[46] On this scenario see the discussion in Re Phoenix Contracts (Leicester) Ltd [2010 ] EWHC 2375 (Ch).

[47] See the observations of the court on this general issue in *Maidment v Attwood* [2012] EWCA Civ 998.

[48] SI 2009/2469.

[49] The Practice Direction is set out in the *White Book* (2010 edn Vol 2, 716). The petitioner was allowed by the court to retain a claim to a winding up as an alternative remedy in *Central Coating Ltd; Lad v Patel* [2004] EWHC 3472 (Ch).

conclusion of which the proceedings will be transferred to a judge for trial.[50] The general principles within the CPR are applicable to petitions under section 994, and thus the court will always give consideration to the most efficient and cost-effective way of disposing of the matter, including for example whether certain issues should be dealt with as preliminary issues.[51]

## 995  Petition by Secretary of State

(1)  This section applies to a company in respect of which—                                **30.995.01**
    (a)  the Secretary of State has received a report under section 437 of the Companies Act 1985 (c. 6) (inspector's report);
    (b)  the Secretary of State has exercised his powers under section 447 or 448 of that Act (powers to require documents and information or to enter and search premises);
    (c)  the Secretary of State or the Financial Services Authority has exercised his or its powers under Part 11 of the Financial Services and Markets Act 2000 (c. 8) (information gathering and investigations); or
    (d)  the Secretary of State has received a report from an investigator appointed by him or the Financial Services Authority under that Part.

(2)  If it appears to the Secretary of State that in the case of such a company—
    (a)  the company's affairs are being or have been conducted in a manner that is unfairly prejudicial to the interests of members generally or of some part of its members, or
    (b)  an actual or proposed act or omission of the company (including an act or omission on its behalf) is or would be so prejudicial, he may apply to the court by petition for an order under this Part.

(3)  The Secretary of State may do this in addition to, or instead of, presenting a petition for the winding up of the company.

(4)  In this section, and so far as applicable for the purposes of this section in the other provisions of this Part, 'company' means any body corporate that is liable to be wound up under the Insolvency Act 1986 (c. 45) or the Insolvency (Northern Ireland) Order 1989 (S.I. 1989/2405 (N.I. 19)).

COMMENCEMENT DATE  1 October 2007[52]

The statutory predecessor to this section (section 460 of the Companies Act 1985) was never used.    **30.995.02**
There are no changes in substance as compared to that statutory predecessor (which had been amended by the Financial Services and Markets Act 2000 (Consequential Amendments and Repeals) Order 2001 (SI 2001/3649)), though the format of the provision has been stylistically remodelled.[53] It remains to be seen whether the Secretary of State will ever make use of this power or whether the section will languish in the same way as its predecessor. The test in subsection (2) is the same as that in section 994(1) discussed above, though in one respect this section gives to the Secretary of State a wider jurisdiction than that given by section 994 to members because the definition of 'company' in section 995(4) includes a foreign company in contrast to the position under section 994, as noted in paragraph 30.994.07 above.[54]

## 996  Powers of the court under this Part

(1)  If the court is satisfied that a petition under this Part is well founded, it may make such order as    **30.996.01**
it thinks fit for giving relief in respect of the matters complained of.

(2)  Without prejudice to the generality of subsection (1), the court's order may—
    (a)  regulate the conduct of the company's affairs in the future;
    (b)  require the company—
      (i)   to refrain from doing or continuing an act complained of, or
      (ii)  to do an act that the petitioner has complained it has omitted to do;
    (c)  authorise civil proceedings to be brought in the name and on behalf of the company by such person or persons and on such terms as the court may direct;
    (d)  require the company not to make any, or any specified, alterations in its articles without the leave of the court;

---

[50]  The proceedings must be brought by petition. If incorrectly brought by claim form they will be stuck out as the Court does not have jurisdiction to treat them as if they had instead been by petition: *Re Osea Road Campsite Ltd; Bamber v Eaton* [2004] EWHC 2437 (Ch), [2005] 1 WLR 760.

[51]  Thus the statement by Morritt J in *Re United Cable Television (London South) plc* 1 July 1993 (unreported) that in any unfair prejudice petition of any complexity it would be appropriate to have a split trial so that the court would only have to go on to consider questions of share valuation if the petitioner were first to be able to show that he is entitled to relief under the section is still likely to be authoritative even though it was a pre-CPR decision.

[52]  Companies Act 2006 (Commencement No 3, etc) Order 2007, SI 2007/2194, art 2.

[53]  See also the Water Consolidation (Consequential Provisions) Act 1991, s 2(1), Sch 1, para 40(1).

[54]  The section is also made applicable to limited liability partnerships: see the Limited Liability Partnerships (Application of Companies Act 2006) Regulations 2009, SI 2009/1804, Pt 12, regs 48–49.

(e) provide for the purchase of the shares of any members of the company by other members or by the company itself and, in the case of a purchase by the company itself, the reduction of the company's capital accordingly.

COMMENCEMENT DATE 1 October 2007[55]

### Introduction and provenance

**30.996.02**    Section 996 deals with remedies available to a petitioner who has been successful in petitioning the court alleging unfair prejudice. The section is based upon the old section 461 of the Companies Act 1985. The substance is the same, though with some stylistic modifications and with some of the elements in that former provision now being reallocated to sections 997 and 998. The case law developed under section 461 is therefore directly applicable to the present section.

### Interim relief

**30.996.03**    Section 996 does not deal with interim relief, though in principle it is available under the court's usual powers to grant interim relief. A petitioner must always consider whether he requires interim relief to hold the ring during the period before his claim will come to trial, such as interim injunctive relief to restore the *status quo ante* in respect of conduct of which he complains or to preserve any rights he may to access to information. That said, the court may be reluctant to grant interim relief requiring the company to allow an excluded director to remain in post.[56] In an extreme case, the appointment of a receiver to run the company pending trial may be considered.

### Final relief

**30.996.04**    At the final disposal of the petition, the court has a free rein to grant whatever relief it thinks appropriate. Subsection (2) details a range of potential options open to the court but they are not exhaustive.[57] Most of these options are never utilized—for a rare instance of a derivative action under subsection (2)(c) resulting from an unfair prejudice petition see *Re Cyplon Development Ltd* (1982) (unreported).[58]

**30.996.05**    The over-arching aim of the court in granting relief is 'to put right and cure for the future the unfair prejudice which the petitioner has suffered': *Re Bird Precision Bellows Ltd*.[59] It is a prospective jurisdiction: 'the court must assess the appropriateness of any particular remedy as at the date of the hearing and not at the date of presentation of the petition; and may even take into account conduct which has occurred between those two dates. The court is entitled to look at the reality and practicalities of the overall situation, past, present and future': *Grace v Biagioli*.[60]

**30.996.06**    The main option in practice is that now specified in subsection (2)(e), namely a share purchase order. Typically, the court will order that the respondents (or, less usually, the company) buy out the petitioner at fair value.[61] There may also be cases where it would be wrong for the petitioner to be forced out of the company and in these cases, though unusual, the court may require the respondent to sell his shares to the petitioner.[62]

### Share valuation

**30.996.07**    When determining what is fair value, the court will have regard to whether or not the company was in effect a 'quasi-partnership'. If it was, then the general approach under section 996 will usually be to apply a pro rata formula (value of assets divided by percentage of shares held): *Re Bird Precision Bellows*

---

[55] Companies Act 2006 (Commencement No 3, etc) Order 2007, SI 2007/2194, art 2.

[56] The giving of undertakings may be a better way forward. On this, note the discussion in *Pringle v Callard* [2007] EWCA Civ 1075, [2008] 2 BCLC 505. Generally the courts favour a clean break via share buyout rather than allowing a contentious relationship to continue—see generally *Fowler v Gruber* [2009] CSOH 36, [2010] 1 BCLC 563.

[57] On the possibility of bespoke remedies see Briggs J in *Sikorski v Sikorski* [2012] EWHC 1613 (Ch) at para [75].

[58] Noted in Lowry and Dignam, *Company Law* (3rd edn, 2006, OUP) para 11.50. As to whether the court can make a declaration of illegality as part of s 994 proceedings, see *Cuddy v Hawkes* [2007] EWCA Civ 1072. For the outcome of the litigation, see *Hawkes v Cuddy (No 2)* [2009] EWCA Civ 291, [2009] 2 BCLC 427.

[59] [1986] Ch 658, 669, *per* Oliver LJ.

[60] [2005] EWCA Civ 1222, [73].

[61] *Grace v Biagioli* [2005] EWCA Civ 1222, [75].

[62] See eg *Re Nuneaton Borough FC Ltd* [1991] BCC 44; *Oak Investment Partners XII, Limited Partnership v Boughtwood* [2009] 1 BCLC 453, upheld by the Court of Appeal at [2010] EWCA Civ 23.

*Ltd.*[63] Thus, in such circumstances there is no discount applied for the fact that it is a minority shareholding that is being purchased, even though the market would normally operate such a discount. But if the company is not to be regarded as a 'quasi-partnership' and the petitioner's role was just that of an investor, a discount is applied. There may occasionally be a case of a company which is not a quasi-partnership but in respect of which there are exceptional circumstances which require a valuation on a pro rata basis rather than a discounted basis, but the courts have expressly said that it is difficult to envisage what such exceptional circumstances might be.[64] The difference between shares being valued on a pro rata basis or at a discount can be very substantial.

This raises the question of what is meant by the term 'quasi-partnership', but it is not a term capable of      **30.996.08**
precise definition. In general terms, it means a company where there is a relationship of mutual trust and confidence between the shareholders similar to that between the members of a partnership, such that equitable obligations arise which make it unjust or inequitable for the shareholders as between themselves to insist on their strict legal rights. As noted by the Privy Council in *CVC/Opportunity Equity Partners Ltd v Demarco Almeida*,[65] the characteristics of such companies will typically include (i) that there is a business association formed or continued on the basis of a personal relationship of mutual trust and confidence; (ii) that there is an understanding or agreement that all or some of the shareholders should participate in the management of the business; and (iii) that there are restrictions on the transfer of shares so that a member cannot realize his stake if he is excluded from the business.

The appellate court will be most reluctant to upset a valuation determined at first instance, as is      **30.996.09**
apparent from *Re Cumana Ltd.*[66]

For guidance generally as to the share valuation process, see *Profinance Trust v Gladstone*,[67] where full      **30.996.10**
consideration was given to the question of the timing of the valuation. Here the Court of Appeal indicated that shares should normally be valued as at the date of sale, but the court has power to select a different date if appropriate. Thus, for example, the court might select some earlier date where a company has been deprived of its business or has been reconstructed or had its business changed so significantly that it has a new economic identity, or where the petition has been on foot for some time and there has been a general fall in the market. Much of the latest case law on share buyouts is centred upon this critical issue of the date when the valuation should be taken.[68] Each case hinges very much upon its individual facts.

Where the valuation process has been delegated to an independent expert the court should be careful      **30.996.11**
about placing too many curbs on the exercise of expert discretion by that valuer.[69]

## Other matters

A successful section 994 petition is not a panacea, and there may be instances where a remedy is      **30.996.12**
deserved but cannot be awarded—on this scenario see *Re Full Cup International Ltd.*[70] Note that the court has no power under section 996 to grant a winding up order; this is a separate jurisdiction governed by section 122(1)(g) of the Insolvency Act 1986 as discussed at paragraphs 30.994.27*et seq* above.[71]

Finally, given that an order that the respondent should buy the petitioner's shares at a fair value is the      **30.996.13**
relief which is most commonly given, the court will in many cases be prepared to strike out a petition

---

[63]  [1986] Ch 658. *CVC/Opportunity Equity Partners Ltd v Demarco Almeida* [2002] 2 BCLC 108. Compare *Fowler v Gruber* [2009] CSOH 36, [2010] 1 BCLC 563—company had ceased to be a quasi partnership at relevant time.

[64]  *Strahan v Wilcock* [2006] 2 BCLC 555. So even a 49.96 per cent shareholding is to be valued at a discount where the company is not a quasi-partnership and there are no exceptional circumstances to require a pro rata valuation: *Re Campbell Irvine (Holdings) Ltd (No 2)*; *Irvine v Irvine* [2006] EWHC 583 (Ch). A discount was applied in *Re McCarthy Surfacing Ltd* [2009] BCC 464 as the quasi-partnership had come to an end prior to the application. For a rare example of a case where no discount was applied even though there was not a quasi-partnership, see *Re Sunrise Radio Ltd* [2009] EWHC 2893 Ch, [289]–[389].

[65]  [2002] 2 BCLC 108, [32]. See also *Strahan v Wilcock* [2006] 2 BCLC 555, [17]–[26].

[66]  [1986] BCLC 430.

[67]  [2002] 1 BCLC 141. See also *Re Sunrise Radio Ltd* [2009] EWHC 2893 (Ch).

[68]  See eg *DiGrado v D'Angelo (Re Abbington Hotel Ltd)* [2011] EWHC 635 (Ch); *Croly v Good* [2010] EWHC 1 (Ch), [2011] BCC 105; *Re Sctoitec Group Ltd* [2010] EWHC 1830 (Ch), [2011] 1 BCLC 277 and *Re Phoenix Contracts (Leicester) Ltd* [2010] EWHC 2375 (Ch).

[69]  *Boughtwood v Oak Investment Partners XII, Limited Partnership* [2010] EWCA Civ 23.

[70]  [1998] BCC 58.

[71]  *Re Full Cup International Ltd* [1998] BCC 58. See para 30.994.33 above as to the limited grounds on which it may be appropriate to combine a winding-up petition with an unfair prejudice petition.

if the respondent has offered such relief and the petitioner has unjustifiably refused to accept it. For a respondent's offer to be effective:

(i)   it should be at a fair value (and thus in a quasi-partnership situation it should be on a pro rata basis without any discount by virtue of the fact that the shareholding is a minority: see paragraph 30.996.08 above);

(ii)  if the value cannot be agreed between the parties, the respondent should offer to submit to a valuation by an independent expert, acting as an expert rather than as an arbitrator;

(iii) the offer should provide for both parties to have equal rights to information about the company and to make submissions to the expert; and

(iv)  if the offer has not been made promptly in response to the petitioner's complaints, it should include an offer to pay the costs incurred by the petitioner in pursuing the complaints.[72]

**30.996.14**   A respondent will be in a particularly strong position where, as is often the case, the company's articles contain a mechanism for the minority shareholder to offer up his shares for purchase at a price to be determined by an independent valuer, and the respondent agrees to operate such a mechanism. As Lord Hoffmann explained in *O'Neill v Phillips*, in a case where the minority shareholder has been excluded from involvement in management then 'If the respondent to a petition has plainly made a reasonable offer, then the exclusion as such will not be unfairly prejudicial and he will be entitled to have the petition struck out'.[73]

## *Supplementary provisions*

### 997  Application of general rule-making powers

**30.997.01**   The power to make rules under section 411 of the Insolvency Act 1986 (c. 45) or Article 359 of the Insolvency (Northern Ireland) Order 1989 (S.I. 1989/2405 (N.I. 19)), so far as relating to a winding-up petition, applies for the purposes of a petition under this Part.

COMMENCEMENT DATE  1 October 2007[74]

**30.997.02**   This is a remnant of a provision formerly contained in section 461 of the Companies Act 1985. It represents a curiosity in company law which links rule-making powers connected to this unfair prejudice remedy to winding up matters. This anomaly has persisted since the provision was introduced way back in the 1940s, where the substantive wording did indeed link this remedy to winding up and it is unfortunate that the opportunity was not taken to reconsider it.

### 998  Copy of order affecting company's constitution to be delivered to registrar

**30.998.01**   (1)  Where an order of the court under this Part—
        (a)  alters the company's constitution, or
        (b)  gives leave for the company to make any, or any specified, alterations to its constitution,
        the company must deliver a copy of the order to the registrar.
    (2)  It must do so within 14 days from the making of the order or such longer period as the court may allow.
    (3)  If a company makes default in complying with this section, an offence is committed by—
        (a)  the company, and
        (b)  every officer of the company who is in default.
    (4)  A person guilty of an offence under this section is liable on summary conviction to a fine not exceeding level 3 on the standard scale and, for continued contravention, a daily default fine not exceeding one-tenth of level 3 on the standard scale.

COMMENCEMENT DATE  1 October 2007[75]

**30.998.02**   This is not a new provision. Rather it is an amalgam of various residual and consequential matters hived off from section 461 of the Companies Act 1985. The type of order referred to in this section will rarely be granted on a successful section 994 petition.

---

[72] *O'Neill v Phillips* [1999] 1 WLR 1092. But an offer will not always be an effective answer to a petition, for example if the expert does not have the necessary independence or has not been supplied with the correct information: *Re Belfield Furnishings Ltd; Isaacs v Belfield Furnishings Ltd* [2006] EWHC 183 (Ch). Nor will it be an answer if the relief which the petitioner justifiably seeks and is likely to obtain is that he should be permitted to buy the respondent's shares rather than being forced out of the company by having to sell his own shares: *Oak Investment Partners XII, Limited Partnership v Boughtwood* [2009] 1 BCLC 453, upheld by the Court of Appeal at [2010] EWCA Civ 23.

[73] *O'Neill v Phillips* [1999] 1 WLR 1092 at 110.

[74] Companies Act 2006 (Commencement No 3, etc) Order 2007, SI 2007/2194, art 2.

[75] Companies Act 2006 (Commencement No 3, etc) Order 2007, SI 2007/2194, art 2.

The former provision, section 461(5) of the Companies Act 1985, contemplated the possibility of the     **30.998.03**
court making orders requiring alterations in the company's articles or in its memorandum. The
reference to the memorandum has not been included in section 998 because the new provisions in the
Companies Act 2006 relating to a company's memorandum, which make it a very much more limited
document than that formerly required under the Companies Act 1985, mean that there will be nothing
in the memorandum which it would be appropriate for the court to require to be altered: cf sections 8
and 28 of the Companies Act 2006.

## 999  Supplementary provisions where company's constitution altered

(1)  This section applies where an order under this Part alters a company's constitution.     **30.999.01**
(2)  If the order amends—
    (a)  a company's articles, or
    (b)  any resolution or agreement to which Chapter 3 of Part 3 applies (resolution or agreement
        affecting a company's constitution),
    the copy of the order delivered to the registrar by the company under section 998 must be
    accompanied by a copy of the company's articles, or the resolution or agreement in question, as
    amended.
(3)  Every copy of a company's articles issued by the company after the order is made must be
    accompanied by a copy of the order, unless the effect of the order has been incorporated into the
    articles by amendment.
(4)  If a company makes default in complying with this section an offence is committed by—
    (a)  the company, and
    (b)  every officer of the company who is in default.
(5)  A person guilty of an offence under this section is liable on summary conviction to a fine not
    exceeding level 3 on the standard scale.

COMMENCEMENT DATE  1 October 2007[76]

This further supplements section 998. It was introduced into the Bill at the eleventh hour and does not     **30.999.02**
appear to have a statutory predecessor (see Explanatory Notes to Act, paragraph 1266). However, its
future usage is likely to be minimal if only because, if previous experience with the unfair prejudice
jurisdiction is repeated, orders made under section 996(2)(d) will be rare birds. For 'constitution' see
section 17.

---

[76]  Companies Act 2006 (Commencement No 3, etc) Order 2007, SI 2007/2194, art 2. But note Sch 3, para 47,
which stresses that s 999 does not apply to court orders made before 1 October 2007.

# 31

## DISSOLUTION AND RESTORATION TO THE REGISTER

## Companies Act 2006

### PART 31
### DISSOLUTION AND RESTORATION TO THE REGISTER

### CHAPTER 1
### STRIKING OFF

*Registrar's power to strike off defunct company*

#### 1000 Power to strike off company not carrying on business or in operation[a]

**31.1000.01**

(1) If the registrar has reasonable cause to believe that a company is not carrying on business or in operation, the registrar may send to the company by post a letter inquiring whether the company is carrying on business or in operation.

(2) If the registrar does not within one month of sending the letter receive any answer to it, the registrar must within 14 days after the expiration of that month send to the company by post a registered letter referring to the first letter, and stating—

    (a) that no answer to it has been received, and

    (b) that if an answer is not received to the second letter within one month from its date, a notice will be published in the Gazette with a view to striking the company's name off the register.

(3) If the registrar—

    (a) receives an answer to the effect that the company is not carrying on business or in operation, or

    (b) does not within one month after sending the second letter receive any answer,

    the registrar may publish in the Gazette, and send to the company by post, a notice that at the expiration of three months from the date of the notice the name of the company mentioned in it will, unless cause is shown to the contrary, be struck off the register and the company will be dissolved.

(4) At the expiration of the time mentioned in the notice the registrar may, unless cause to the contrary is previously shown by the company, strike its name off the register.

(5) The registrar must publish notice in the Gazette of the company's name having been struck off the register.

(6) On the publication of the notice in the Gazette the company is dissolved.

(7) However—

    (a) the liability (if any) of every director, managing officer and member of the company continues and may be enforced as if the company had not been dissolved, and

    (b) nothing in this section affects the power of the court to wind up a company the name of which has been struck off the register.

AMENDMENTS AND NOTES

[a] This section applies with modifications to LLPs by reg 50 of the Limited Liability Partnerships (Application of Companies Act 2006) Regulations 2009, SI 2009/1804.

COMMENCEMENT DATE 1 October 2009[1]

**31.1000.02** For the rationale of Part 31 generally see the Explanatory Notes to the Act, paragraphs 1267 to 1285. Important transitional provisions are located in the Companies Act 2006 (Commencement No 8, Transitional Provisions and Savings) Order 2008,[2] Schedule 2, paragraphs 88 to 92.

**31.1000.03** This provision was partly based upon the Companies Act 1985, section 652. It confers discretion upon the registrar (see section 1060 for definition) to strike off companies that are not carrying on business, a scenario affirmed by their refusal to respond to correspondence from the registrar. It is estimated that many thousands of companies suffer this fate every year, though in some several hundred cases the striking off is later reversed. Section 1000 outlines the procedure to be adopted by the registrar before undertaking this draconian course of action. The sequence of events involving an initial letter followed by a more official communication and then a notice in the Gazette mirrors that employed under the former section 652. For 'Gazette' see section 1173.

**31.1000.04** This mode of striking off is used for dormant companies. It is essentially a bureaucratic procedure designed to slim down the number of companies appearing on the register. If the company indicates

---

[1] Companies Act 2006 (Commencement No 8, Transitional Provisions and Savings) Order 2008, SI 2008/2860, art 3(o). Part 13 of the Limited Liability Partnerships (Application of Companies Act 2006) Regulations 2009, SI 2009/1804 generally applies, with modifications, Pt 31 to LLPs.

[2] SI 2008/2860.

that it is not carrying on business, or does not reply to communications from the registrar, a notice can be dispatched to the effect that the company will be automatically struck off after the expiry of three months.

In *Steans Fashions Ltd v Legal and General Assurance Society Ltd*[3] the Court of Appeal indicated that where a defunct company had been struck off by the registrar under section 652 and proceedings had then been instituted against it the proper course of action was to stay such proceedings pending an application to the court for restoration under what used to be section 653. **31.1000.05**

## 1001 Duty to act in case of company being wound up[a]

(1) If, in a case where a company is being wound up— **31.1001.01**
   (a) the registrar has reasonable cause to believe—
      (i) that no liquidator is acting, or
      (ii) that the affairs of the company are fully wound up, and
   (b) the returns required to be made by the liquidator have not been made for a period of six consecutive months,
   the registrar must publish in the Gazette and send to the company or the liquidator (if any) a notice that at the expiration of three months from the date of the notice the name of the company mentioned in it will, unless cause is shown to the contrary, be struck off the register and the company will be dissolved.
(2) At the expiration of the time mentioned in the notice the registrar may, unless cause to the contrary is previously shown by the company, strike its name off the register.
(3) The registrar must publish notice in the Gazette of the company's name having been struck off the register.
(4) On the publication of the notice in the Gazette the company is dissolved.
(5) However—
   (a) the liability (if any) of every director, managing officer and member of the company continues and may be enforced as if the company had not been dissolved, and
   (b) nothing in this section affects the power of the court to wind up a company the name of which has been struck off the register.

AMENDMENTS AND NOTES

[a] This section applies with modifications to LLPs by reg 50 of the Limited Liability Partnerships (Application of Companies Act 2006) Regulations 2009, SI 2009/1804.

COMMENCEMENT DATE 1 October 2009[4]

Unlike the scenario described in section 1000, in this instance the registrar is *obliged* to act. This provision was hived off from the former section 652(4) of the Companies Act 1985. Naturally there are similarities to the procedure adopted for striking off under section 1000 but this procedure is less convoluted. For 'registrar' see section 1060 and for 'Gazette' see section 1173. **31.1001.02**

## 1002 Supplementary provisions as to service of letter or notice[a]

(1) A letter or notice to be sent under section 1000 or 1001 to a company may be addressed to the company at its registered office or, if no office has been registered, to the care of some officer of the company. **31.1002.01**
(2) If there is no officer of the company whose name and address are known to the registrar, the letter or notice may be sent to each of the persons who subscribed the memorandum (if their addresses are known to the registrar).
(3) A notice to be sent to a liquidator under section 1001 may be addressed to him at his last known place of business.

AMENDMENTS

[a] This section applies with modifications to LLPs by reg 50 of the Limited Liability Partnerships (Application of Companies Act 2006) Regulations 2009, SI 2009/1804.

COMMENCEMENT DATE 1 October 2009[5]

This provision deals with communication of notices under sections 1000 and 1001. 'Registrar' is defined by section 1060 and 'officer' by section 1173. For 'registered office' see the Companies Act 2006, section 86. **31.1002.02**

---

[3] [1995] 1 BCLC 332.
[4] Companies Act 2006 (Commencement No 8, Transitional Provisions and Savings) Order 2008, SI 2008/2860, art 3(o).
[5] Companies Act 2006 (Commencement No 8, Transitional Provisions and Savings) Order 2008, SI 2008/2860, art 3(o).

## 1003 Striking off on application by company[a]

**31.1003.01**
(1) On application by a company, the registrar of companies may strike the company's name off the register.
(2) The application—
    (a) must be made on the company's behalf by its directors or by a majority of them, and
    (b) must contain the prescribed information.
(3) The registrar may not strike a company off under this section until after the expiration of three months from the publication by the registrar in the Gazette of a notice—
    (a) stating that the registrar may exercise the power under this section in relation to the company, and
    (b) inviting any person to show cause why that should not be done.
(4) The registrar must publish notice in the Gazette of the company's name having been struck off.
(5) On the publication of the notice in the Gazette the company is dissolved.
(6) However—
    (a) the liability (if any) of every director, managing officer and member of the company continues and may be enforced as if the company had not been dissolved, and
    (b) nothing in this section affects the power of the court to wind up a company the name of which has been struck off the register.

AMENDMENTS AND NOTES

[a] This section applies with modifications to LLPs by reg 51 of the Limited Liability Partnerships (Application of Companies Act 2006) Regulations 2009, SI 2009/1804.

COMMENCEMENT DATE 1 October 2009[6]

**31.1003.02**
This is based upon section 652A of the Companies Act 1985. It allows companies to be stuck off by their own volition. This provision was originally introduced by the Deregulation and Contracting Out Act 1994, which indicates its policy pedigree. It, originally, permitted directors of a *private* company to apply to the registrar to have the company's name struck off the register. This power has been used extensively since its introduction—in 2003/04 it is estimated that some 66,000 companies were dissolved via this route. The registrar (section 1060) must gazette (section 1173) the fact that he has received such application to permit objections to be raised. Once three months have elapsed, the striking off can proceed. The power of the court to wind up a company struck off in such circumstances is explicitly preserved by subsection (6)(b).

**31.1003.03**
The White Paper, *Company Law Reform*[7] called for this facility to be extended to *public* companies (see paragraph 4.9). The Companies Act 2006 implemented this reform by the simple expedient of deleting the word 'private' from section 652A and then reconstituting the thus amended provision.

**31.1003.04**
For the declaration required on an application under section 1003 see The Registrar of Companies and Applications for Striking Off Regulations 2009.[8]

## 1004 Circumstances in which application not to be made: activities of company[a]

**31.1004.01**
(1) An application under section 1003 (application for voluntary striking off) on behalf of a company must not be made if, at any time in the previous three months, the company has—
    (a) changed its name,
    (b) traded or otherwise carried on business,
    (c) made a disposal for value of property or rights that, immediately before ceasing to trade or otherwise carry on business, it held for the purpose of disposal for gain in the normal course of trading or otherwise carrying on business, or
    (d) engaged in any other activity, except one which is—
        (i) necessary or expedient for the purpose of making an application under that section, or deciding whether to do so,
        (ii) necessary or expedient for the purpose of concluding the affairs of the company,
        (iii) necessary or expedient for the purpose of complying with any statutory requirement, or
        (iv) specified by the Secretary of State by order for the purposes of this subparagraph.
(2) For the purposes of this section, a company is not to be treated as trading or otherwise carrying on business by virtue only of the fact that it makes a payment in respect of a liability incurred in the course of trading or otherwise carrying on business.

---

[6] Companies Act 2006 (Commencement No 8, Transitional Provisions and Savings) Order 2008, SI 2008/2860, art 3(o).
[7] (2005) (Cm 6456).
[8] SI 2009/2009, reg 2.

(3)  The Secretary of State may by order amend subsection (1) for the purpose of altering the period in relation to which the doing of the things mentioned in paragraphs (a) to (d) of that subsection is relevant.

(4)  An order under this section is subject to negative resolution procedure.

(5)  It is an offence for a person to make an application in contravention of this section.

(6)  In proceedings for such an offence it is a defence for the accused to prove that he did not know, and could not reasonably have known, of the existence of the facts that led to the contravention.

(7)  A person guilty of an offence under this section is liable—

    (a)  on conviction on indictment, to a fine;

    (b)  on summary conviction, to a fine not exceeding the statutory maximum.

AMENDMENTS AND NOTES

a  This section applies with modifications to LLPs by reg 51 of the Limited Liability Partnerships (Application of Companies Act 2006) Regulations 2009, SI 2009/1804.

COMMENCEMENT DATE  1 October 2009[9]

This provision, which replicates parts of section 652B of the Companies Act 1985, imposes constraints upon applications made under section 1003. For example, the procedure is not to be used if the company has traded or has changed its name within the previous three months. What is regarded as trading is explained in subsections (1) and (2). These constraints are supported by criminal sanctions (subsections (5) to (7)). The statutory maximum referred to in subsection (7) is presently £5,000.   **31.1004.02**

The Secretary of State can modify the limitations outlined in subsection (1). For the negative resolution procedure specified in subsection (4) see section 1289.   **31.1004.03**

## 1005  Circumstances in which application not to be made: other proceedings not concluded[a]

(1)  An application under section 1003 (application for voluntary striking off) on behalf of a company must not be made at a time when—   **31.1005.01**

    (a)  an application to the court under Part 26 has been made on behalf of the company for the sanctioning of a compromise or arrangement and the matter has not been finally concluded;

    (b)  a voluntary arrangement in relation to the company has been proposed under Part 1 of the Insolvency Act 1986 (c. 45) or Part 2 of the Insolvency (Northern Ireland) Order 1989 (S.I. 1989/2405 (N.I. 19)) and the matter has not been finally concluded;

    (c)  the company is in administration under Part 2 of that Act or Part 3 of that Order;

    (d)  paragraph 44 of Schedule B1 to that Act or paragraph 45 of Schedule B1 to that Order applies (interim moratorium on proceedings where application to the court for an administration order has been made or notice of intention to appoint administrator has been filed);

    (e)  the company is being wound up under Part 4 of that Act or Part 5 of that Order, whether voluntarily or by the court, or a petition under that Part for winding up of the company by the court has been presented and not finally dealt with or withdrawn;

    (f)  there is a receiver or manager of the company's property;

    (g)  the company's estate is being administered by a judicial factor.

(2)  For the purposes of subsection (1)(a), the matter is finally concluded if—

    (a)  the application has been withdrawn,

    (b)  the application has been finally dealt with without a compromise or arrangement being sanctioned by the court, or

    (c)  a compromise or arrangement has been sanctioned by the court and has, together with anything required to be done under any provision made in relation to the matter by order of the court, been fully carried out.

(3)  For the purposes of subsection (1)(b), the matter is finally concluded if—

    (a)  no meetings are to be summoned under section 3 of the Insolvency Act 1986 (c. 45) or Article 16 of the Insolvency (Northern Ireland) Order 1989,

    (b)  meetings summoned under that section or Article fail to approve the arrangement with no, or the same, modifications,

    (c)  an arrangement approved by meetings summoned under that section, or in consequence of a direction under section 6(4)(b) of that Act or Article 19(4)(b) of that Order, has been fully implemented, or

    (d)  the court makes an order under section 6(5) of that Act or Article 19(5) of that Order revoking approval given at previous meetings and, if the court gives any directions under section 6(6) of that Act or Article 19(6) of that Order, the company has done whatever it is required to do under those directions.

(4)  It is an offence for a person to make an application in contravention of this section.

---

9  Companies Act 2006 (Commencement No 8, Transitional Provisions and Savings) Order 2008, SI 2008/2860, art 3(o).

(5) In proceedings for such an offence it is a defence for the accused to prove that he did not know, and could not reasonably have known, of the existence of the facts that led to the contravention.

(6) A person guilty of an offence under this section is liable—

   (a) on conviction on indictment, to a fine;

   (b) on summary conviction, to a fine not exceeding the statutory maximum.

AMENDMENTS AND NOTES

[a] This section applies with modifications to LLPs by reg 51 of the Limited Liability Partnerships (Application of Companies Act 2006) Regulations 2009, SI 2009/1804.

COMMENCEMENT DATE 1 October 2009[10]

**31.1005.02**   This again represents a fragment of the former section 652B of the Companies Act 1985 (in particular subsections (3) to (5) of section 652B). The voluntary striking off procedure cannot be used where an arrangement has been proposed or insolvency proceedings with respect to the company are afoot. This disability ends when the proceedings in question have been finally concluded.

**31.1005.03**   Again note the use of criminal sanctions dealt with by subsections (4) to (6). The statutory maximum mentioned in subsection (6) is £5,000 at present.

### 1006  Copy of application to be given to members, employees, etc.[a]

**31.1006.01**   (1) A person who makes an application under section 1003 (application for voluntary striking off) on behalf of a company must secure that, within seven days from the day on which the application is made, a copy of it is given to every person who at any time on that day is—

   (a) a member of the company,

   (b) an employee of the company,

   (c) a creditor of the company,

   (d) a director of the company,

   (e) a manager or trustee of any pension fund established for the benefit of employees of the company, or

   (f) a person of a description specified for the purposes of this paragraph by regulations made by the Secretary of State.

   Regulations under paragraph (f) are subject to negative resolution procedure.

(2) Subsection (1) does not require a copy of the application to be given to a director who is a party to the application.

(3) The duty imposed by this section ceases to apply if the application is withdrawn before the end of the period for giving the copy application.

(4) A person who fails to perform the duty imposed on him by this section commits an offence. If he does so with the intention of concealing the making of the application from the person concerned, he commits an aggravated offence.

(5) In proceedings for an offence under this section it is a defence for the accused to prove that he took all reasonable steps to perform the duty.

(6) A person guilty of an offence under this section (other than an aggravated offence) is liable—

   (a) on conviction on indictment, to a fine;

   (b) on summary conviction, to a fine not exceeding the statutory maximum.

(7) A person guilty of an aggravated offence under this section is liable—

   (a) on conviction on indictment, to imprisonment for a term not exceeding seven years or a fine (or both);

   (b) on summary conviction—

      (i) in England and Wales, to imprisonment for a term not exceeding twelve months or to a fine not exceeding the statutory maximum (or both);

      (ii) in Scotland or Northern Ireland, to imprisonment for a term not exceeding six months, or to a fine not exceeding the statutory maximum (or both).

AMENDMENTS AND NOTES

[a] This section applies with modifications to LLPs by reg 51 of the Limited Liability Partnerships (Application of Companies Act 2006) Regulations 2009, SI 2009/1804.

COMMENCEMENT DATE 1 October 2009[11]

**31.1006.02**   This is a procedural requirement largely founded upon elements of the Companies Act 1985, section 652B. The seven-day notification requirement replicates the former law. Note the concession granted by subsection (3) where the application for voluntary striking off is quickly withdrawn. The

---

[10] Companies Act 2006 (Commencement No 8, Transitional Provisions and Savings) Order 2008, SI 2008/2860, art 3(o).

[11] Companies Act 2006 (Commencement No 8, Transitional Provisions and Savings) Order 2008, SI 2008/2860, art 3(o).

notification obligations imposed herein are substantially underpinned by criminal sanctions including an aggravated offence in subsection (4). The statutory maximum cited in subsection (7) is £5,000. For 'creditor' see section 1011, for 'member' see section 112, and for 'director' see section 250.

## 1007  Copy of application to be given to new members, employees, etc[a]

(1) This section applies in relation to any time after the day on which a company makes an application under section 1003 (application for voluntary striking off) and before the day on which the application is finally dealt with or withdrawn.    **31.1007.01**

(2) A person who is a director of the company at the end of a day on which a person (other than himself) becomes—
   (a) a member of the company,
   (b) an employee of the company,
   (c) a creditor of the company,
   (d) a director of the company,
   (e) a manager or trustee of any pension fund established for the benefit of employees of the company, or
   (f) a person of a description specified for the purposes of this paragraph by regulations made by the Secretary of State,
   must secure that a copy of the application is given to that person within seven days from that day. Regulations under paragraph (f) are subject to negative resolution procedure.

(3) The duty imposed by this section ceases to apply if the application is finally dealt with or withdrawn before the end of the period for giving the copy application.

(4) A person who fails to perform the duty imposed on him by this section commits an offence.
   If he does so with the intention of concealing the making of the application from the person concerned, he commits an aggravated offence.

(5) In proceedings for an offence under this section it is a defence for the accused to prove—
   (a) that at the time of the failure he was not aware of the fact that the company had made an application under section 1003, or
   (b) that he took all reasonable steps to perform the duty.

(6) A person guilty of an offence under this section (other than an aggravated offence) is liable—
   (a) on conviction on indictment, to a fine;
   (b) on summary conviction, to a fine not exceeding the statutory maximum.

(7) A person guilty of an aggravated offence under this section is liable—
   (a) on conviction on indictment, to imprisonment for a term not exceeding seven years or a fine (or both);
   (b) on summary conviction—
      (i) in England and Wales, to imprisonment for a term not exceeding twelve months or to a fine not exceeding the statutory maximum (or both);
      (ii) in Scotland or Northern Ireland, to imprisonment for a term not exceeding six months, or to a fine not exceeding the statutory maximum (or both).

AMENDMENTS AND NOTES

[a] This section applies with modifications to LLPs by reg 51 of the Limited Liability Partnerships (Application of Companies Act 2006) Regulations 2009, SI 2009/1804.

COMMENCEMENT DATE  1 October 2009[12]

This appears to be based upon section 652C of the Companies Act 1985. It represents a continuing notification obligation imposed upon an applicant for voluntary striking off. Obligations here are once again supported by criminal sanctions including the aggravated offence under subsection (4). The statutory maximum noted in subsections (6) and (7) is £5,000 at present. Definitions of use are provided for 'creditor' (section 1011), 'director' (section 250), and 'member' (section 112).    **31.1007.02**

On the negative resolution procedure mentioned in subsection (2)(f) see section 1289 below.    **31.1007.03**

## 1008  Copy of application: provisions as to service of documents[a]

(1) The following provisions have effect for the purposes of—    **31.1008.01**
   section 1006 (copy of application to be given to members, employees, etc), and
   section 1007 (copy of application to be given to new members, employees, etc).

(2) A document is treated as given to a person if it is—
   (a) delivered to him, or
   (b) left at his proper address, or
   (c) sent by post to him at that address.

---

[12] Companies Act 2006 (Commencement No 8, Transitional Provisions and Savings) Order 2008, SI 2008/2860, art 3(o).

(3) For the purposes of subsection (2) and section 7 of the Interpretation Act 1978 (c. 30) (service of documents by post) as it applies in relation to that subsection, the proper address of a person is—

    (a) in the case of a firm incorporated or formed in the United Kingdom, its registered or principal office;

    (b) in the case of a firm incorporated or formed outside the United Kingdom—

        (i) if it has a place of business in the United Kingdom, its principal office in the United Kingdom, or

        (ii) if it does not have a place of business in the United Kingdom, its registered or principal office;

    (c) in the case of an individual, his last known address.

(4) In the case of a creditor of the company a document is treated as given to him if it is left or sent by post to him—

    (a) at the place of business of his with which the company has had dealings by virtue of which he is a creditor of the company, or

    (b) if there is more than one such place of business, at each of them.

Amendments and Notes

[a] This section applies with modifications to LLPs by reg 51 of the Limited Liability Partnerships (Application of Companies Act 2006) Regulations 2009, SI 2009/1804.

Commencement Date 1 October 2009[13]

**31.1008.02** This procedural provision, which has the Companies Act 1985, section 652D as its statutory predecessor, supports the obligations imposed by sections 1006 and 1007. For 'registered office' see section 86.

## 1009 Circumstances in which application to be withdrawn[a]

**31.1009.01** (1) This section applies where, at any time on or after the day on which a company makes an application under section 1003 (application for voluntary striking off) and before the day on which the application is finally dealt with or withdrawn—

    (a) the company—

        (i) changes its name,

        (ii) trades or otherwise carries on business,

        (iii) makes a disposal for value of any property or rights other than those which it was necessary or expedient for it to hold for the purpose of making, or proceeding with, an application under that section, or

        (iv) engages in any activity, except one to which subsection (4) applies;

    (b) an application is made to the court under Part 26 on behalf of the company for the sanctioning of a compromise or arrangement;

    (c) a voluntary arrangement in relation to the company is proposed under Part 1 of the Insolvency Act 1986 (c. 45) or Part 2 of the Insolvency (Northern Ireland) Order 1989 (S.I. 1989/2405 (N.I. 19));

    (d) an application to the court for an administration order in respect of the company is made under paragraph 12 of Schedule B1 to that Act or paragraph 13 of Schedule B1 to that Order;

    (e) an administrator is appointed in respect of the company under paragraph 14 or 22 of Schedule B1 to that Act or paragraph 15 or 23 of Schedule B1 to that Order, or a copy of notice of intention to appoint an administrator of the company under any of those provisions is filed with the court;

    (f) there arise any of the circumstances in which, under section 84(1) of that Act or Article 70 of that Order, the company may be voluntarily wound up;

    (g) a petition is presented for the winding up of the company by the court under Part 4 of that Act or Part 5 of that Order;

    (h) a receiver or manager of the company's property is appointed; or

    (i) a judicial factor is appointed to administer the company's estate.

(2) A person who, at the end of a day on which any of the events mentioned in subsection (1) occurs, is a director of the company must secure that the company's application is withdrawn forthwith.

(3) For the purposes of subsection (1)(a), a company is not treated as trading or otherwise carrying on business by virtue only of the fact that it makes a payment in respect of a liability incurred in the course of trading or otherwise carrying on business.

(4) The excepted activities referred to in subsection (1)(a)(iv) are—

    (a) any activity necessary or expedient for the purposes of—

        (i) making, or proceeding with, an application under section 1003 (application for voluntary striking off),

---

[13] Companies Act 2006 (Commencement No 8, Transitional Provisions and Savings) Order 2008, SI 2008/2860, art 3(o).

      (ii) concluding affairs of the company that are outstanding because of what has been necessary or expedient for the purpose of making, or proceeding with, such an application, or

      (iii) complying with any statutory requirement;

    (b) any activity specified by the Secretary of State by order for the purposes of this subsection. An order under paragraph (b) is subject to negative resolution procedure.

(5) A person who fails to perform the duty imposed on him by this section commits an offence.

(6) In proceedings for an offence under this section it is a defence for the accused to prove—

    (a) that at the time of the failure he was not aware of the fact that the company had made an application under section 1003, or

    (b) that he took all reasonable steps to perform the duty.

(7) A person guilty of an offence under this section is liable—

    (a) on conviction on indictment, to a fine;

    (b) on summary conviction, to a fine not exceeding the statutory maximum.

AMENDMENTS AND NOTES

ᵃ This section applies with modifications to LLPs by reg 51 of the Limited Liability Partnerships (Application of Companies Act 2006) Regulations 2009, SI 2009/1804.

COMMENCEMENT DATE 1 October 2009[14]

This provision, which contains elements of the former section 652C of the Companies Act 1985, imposes an obligation to withdraw an application for voluntary striking off where the circumstances change before the application is heard. The change of circumstances referred to involves the creation of conditions such as those specified in sections 1004 and 1005 which would have debarred the application in the first place. **31.1009.02**

The statutory maximum mentioned in subsection (7) is £5,000. **31.1009.03**

For the negative resolution procedure specified in subsection (4)(b) see section 1289. **31.1009.04**

## 1010 Withdrawal of applicationᵃ

An application under section 1003 is withdrawn by notice to the registrar. **31.1010.01**

AMENDMENTS AND NOTES

ᵃ This section applies with modifications to LLPs by reg 51 of the Limited Liability Partnerships (Application of Companies Act 2006) Regulations 2009, SI 2009/1804.

COMMENCEMENT DATE 1 October 2009[15]

This is self explanatory. For 'registrar' see section 1060. For statutory predecessor see the Companies Act 1985, section 652D(6). **31.1010.02**

## 1011 Meaning of 'creditor'ᵃ

In this Chapter 'creditor' includes a contingent or prospective creditor. **31.1011.01**

AMENDMENTS AND NOTES

ᵃ This section applies with modifications to LLPs by reg 51 of the Limited Liability Partnerships (Application of Companies Act 2006) Regulations 2009, SI 2009/1804.

COMMENCEMENT DATE 1 October 2009[16]

This interpretation of the concept of creditor is standard and is based upon the former section 652D(8) of the Companies Act 1985. It is relevant for sections 1006 and 1007. **31.1011.02**

---

[14] Companies Act 2006 (Commencement No 8, Transitional Provisions and Savings) Order 2008, SI 2008/2860, art 3(o).

[15] Companies Act 2006 (Commencement No 8, Transitional Provisions and Savings) Order 2008, SI 2008/2860, art 3(o).

[16] Companies Act 2006 (Commencement No 8, Transitional Provisions and Savings) Order 2008, SI 2008/2860, art 3(o).

CHAPTER 2
PROPERTY OF DISSOLVED COMPANY

*Property vesting as bona vacantia*

### 1012 Property of dissolved company to be bona vacantia[a]

31.1012.01
(1) When a company is dissolved, all property and rights whatsoever vested in or held on trust for the company immediately before its dissolution (including leasehold property, but not including property held by the company on trust for another person) are deemed to be bona vacantia and—
   (a) accordingly belong to the Crown, or to the Duchy of Lancaster or to the Duke of Cornwall for the time being (as the case may be), and
   (b) vest and may be dealt with in the same manner as other bona vacantia accruing to the Crown, to the Duchy of Lancaster or to the Duke of Cornwall.
(2) Subsection (1) has effect subject to the possible restoration of the company to the register under Chapter 3 (see section 1034).

AMENDMENTS AND NOTES

[a] This section applies with modifications to LLPs by reg 52 of the Limited Liability Partnerships (Application of Companies Act 2006) Regulations 2009, SI 2009/1804.

COMMENCEMENT DATE 1 October 2009[17]

31.1012.02
This is based upon the Companies Act 1985, section 654. '*Bona vacantia*' means literally 'vacant goods'. It is a common law concept dating back to Norman times, though in this area the law is naturally founded in statute. The Treasury Solicitors Department (TSD) has a Division dealing with *bona vacantia*—its website ⟨http://www.bonavacantia.gov.uk⟩ is a mine of helpful information on how the statutory rules operate in practice—various guidance booklets are available. Within the TSD's Division there is a special section dealing with dissolved companies. In the case of *bona vacantia* devolving to the Duchies of Lancaster and Cornwall the TSD does not act—instead the work is carried out by a nominated firm of solicitors. Looking at the TSD website it seems that domain names as *bona vacantia* has been a common phenomenon in recent years. Note the exception specified in subsection (1) where the company is acting as trustee (as opposed to being a beneficiary under a trust). Note transitional provisions relevant to sections 1012 to 1023 in the Companies Act 2006 (Commencement No 8, Transitional Provisions and Savings) Order 2008,[18] Schedule 2, paragraph 88.

31.1012.03
For the fate of property if the company is restored to the register see section 1034.

31.1012.04
Where a company is dissolved, the registrar of companies is obliged to keep its records for two years (formerly 10 years), after which they may be transferred to the Public Records Office—see section 1050.

### 1013 Crown disclaimer of property vesting as bona vacantia[a]

31.1013.01
(1) Where property vests in the Crown under section 1012, the Crown's title to it under that section may be disclaimed by a notice signed by the Crown representative, that is to say the Treasury Solicitor, or, in relation to property in Scotland, the Queen's and Lord Treasurer's Remembrancer.
(2) The right to execute a notice of disclaimer under this section may be waived by or on behalf of the Crown either expressly or by taking possession.
(3) A notice of disclaimer must be executed within three years after—
   (a) the date on which the fact that the property may have vested in the Crown under section 1012 first comes to the notice of the Crown representative, or
   (b) if ownership of the property is not established at that date, the end of the period reasonably necessary for the Crown representative to establish the ownership of the property.
(4) If an application in writing is made to the Crown representative by a person interested in the property requiring him to decide whether he will or will not disclaim, any notice of disclaimer must be executed within twelve months after the making of the application or such further period as may be allowed by the court.
(5) A notice of disclaimer under this section is of no effect if it is shown to have been executed after the end of the period specified by subsection (3) or (4).
(6) A notice of disclaimer under this section must be delivered to the registrar and retained and registered by him.
(7) Copies of it must be published in the Gazette and sent to any persons who have given the Crown representative notice that they claim to be interested in the property.

---

[17] Companies Act 2006 (Commencement No 8, Transitional Provisions and Savings) Order 2008, SI 2008/2860, art 3(o).
[18] SI 2008/2860.

(8) This section applies to property vested in the Duchy of Lancaster or the Duke of Cornwall under section 1012 as if for references to the Crown and the Crown representative there were respectively substituted references to the Duchy of Lancaster and to the Solicitor to that Duchy, or to the Duke of Cornwall and to the Solicitor to the Duchy of Cornwall, as the case may be.

AMENDMENTS AND NOTES

a  This section applies with modifications to LLPs by reg 52 of the Limited Liability Partnerships (Application of Companies Act 2006) Regulations 2009, SI 2009/1804.

COMMENCEMENT DATE  1 October 2009[19]

Based upon the Companies Act 1985, section 656 this provision recognizes that the Crown may, under section 1012, be left property that is worthless or worse. Accordingly the legal mechanism of disclaimer is made available to it. The Treasury Solicitor's Department website on *bona vacantia* contains useful illustrations of typical onerous property likely to be disclaimed. This provision outlines the procedure to be adopted by the Crown if it wishes to disclaim *bona vacantia*. Reference to case law involving liquidator's disclaimer under section 178 of the Insolvency Act 1986 might prove useful here to establish working principles.        **31.1013.02**

The changes made by section 1013 to the Companies Act 1985, section 656 give the Crown more time to disclaim—3 years rather than 12 months in standard cases, and 12 months rather than three months on receipt of notice from an interested party.        **31.1013.03**

## 1014  Effect of Crown disclaimer[a]

(1) Where notice of disclaimer is executed under section 1013 as respects any property, that property is deemed not to have vested in the Crown under section 1012.        **31.1014.01**
(2) The following sections contain provisions as to the effect of the Crown disclaimer—
 sections 1015 to 1019 apply in relation to property in England and Wales or Northern Ireland;
 sections 1020 to 1022 apply in relation to property in Scotland.

AMENDMENTS AND NOTES

a  This section applies with modifications to LLPs by reg 52 of the Limited Liability Partnerships (Application of Companies Act 2006) Regulations 2009, SI 2009/1804.

COMMENCEMENT DATE  1 October 2009[20]

This is based upon the Companies Act 1985, section 657. It introduces the detailed rules contained in sections 1015 to 1019 (for England and Wales) and 1020 to 1022 (for Scotland). Unlike section 657 there is no explicit cross reference to the provisions in the Insolvency Act 1986 on liquidator's disclaimer. The rules in the Companies Act 2006 are thus customized, though presumably case law on liquidator's disclaimer will continue to have value—see generally *Re Yarmarine (IW) Ltd.*[21]        **31.1014.02**

*Effect of Crown disclaimer: England and Wales and Northern Ireland*

## 1015  General effect of disclaimer[a]

(1) The Crown's disclaimer operates so as to terminate, as from the date of the disclaimer, the rights, interests and liabilities of the company in or in respect of the property disclaimed.        **31.1015.01**
(2) It does not, except so far as is necessary for the purpose of releasing the company from any liability, affect the rights or liabilities of any other person.

AMENDMENTS AND NOTES

a  This section applies with modifications to LLPs by reg 53 of the Limited Liability Partnerships (Application of Companies Act 2006) Regulations 2009, SI 2009/1804.

COMMENCEMENT DATE  1 October 2009[22]

Although disclaimer releases both the company and the Crown, third party obligations (for example those of guarantors and sureties) are not discharged. This is consistent with the view taken in the House of Lords in *Hindcastle Ltd v Barbara Attenborough Associates Ltd*[23] (the leading authority on liquidator's disclaimer).        **31.1015.02**

---

¹⁹ Companies Act 2006 (Commencement No 8, Transitional Provisions and Savings) Order 2008, SI 2008/2860, art 3(o).
²⁰ Companies Act 2006 (Commencement No 8, Transitional Provisions and Savings) Order 2008, SI 2008/2860, art 3(o).
²¹ [1992] BCLC 276.
²² Companies Act 2006 (Commencement No 8, Transitional Provisions and Savings) Order 2008, SI 2008/2860, art 3(o).
²³ [1997] AC 70.

## 1016 Disclaimer of leaseholds[a]

**31.1016.01**
(1) The disclaimer of any property of a leasehold character does not take effect unless a copy of the disclaimer has been served (so far as the Crown representative is aware of their addresses) on every person claiming under the company as underlessee or mortgagee, and either—
    (a) no application under section 1017 (power of court to make vesting order) is made with respect to that property before the end of the period of 14 days beginning with the day on which the last notice under this paragraph was served, or
    (b) where such an application has been made, the court directs that the disclaimer shall take effect.
(2) Where the court gives a direction under subsection (1)(b) it may also, instead of or in addition to any order it makes under section 1017, make such order as it thinks fit with respect to fixtures, tenant's improvements and other matters arising out of the lease.
(3) In this section the 'Crown representative' means—
    (a) in relation to property vested in the Duchy of Lancaster, the Solicitor to that Duchy;
    (b) in relation to property vested in the Duke of Cornwall, the Solicitor to the Duchy of Cornwall;
    (c) in relation to property in Scotland, the Queen's and Lord Treasurer's Remembrancer;
    (d) in relation to other property, the Treasury Solicitor.

AMENDMENTS AND NOTES

[a] This section applies with modifications to LLPs by reg 53 of the Limited Liability Partnerships (Application of Companies Act 2006) Regulations 2009, SI 2009/1804.

COMMENCEMENT DATE 1 October 2009[24]

**31.1016.02**  This mirrors the provision on liquidator's disclaimer in section 179 of the Insolvency Act 1986. The need to serve notices under subsection (1) on underlessees and mortgagees is particularly important as it enables such parties to intervene to protect their position.

## 1017 Power of court to make vesting order[a]

**31.1017.01**
(1) The court may on application by a person who—
    (a) claims an interest in the disclaimed property, or
    (b) is under a liability in respect of the disclaimed property that is not discharged by the disclaimer,
    make an order under this section in respect of the property.
(2) An order under this section is an order for the vesting of the disclaimed property in, or its delivery to—
    (a) a person entitled to it (or a trustee for such a person), or
    (b) a person subject to such a liability as is mentioned in subsection (1)(b) (or a trustee for such a person).
(3) An order under subsection (2)(b) may only be made where it appears to the court that it would be just to do so for the purpose of compensating the person subject to the liability in respect of the disclaimer.
(4) An order under this section may be made on such terms as the court thinks fit.
(5) On a vesting order being made under this section, the property comprised in it vests in the person named in that behalf in the order without conveyance, assignment or transfer.

AMENDMENTS AND NOTES

[a] This section applies with modifications to LLPs by reg 53 of the Limited Liability Partnerships (Application of Companies Act 2006) Regulations 2009, SI 2009/1804.

COMMENCEMENT DATE 1 October 2009[25]

**31.1017.02**  Again this appears to be based upon the vesting order model as found in section 181 of the Insolvency Act 1986. Cases decided under section 181 such as *Re Vedmay Ltd*,[26] *Lloyds Bank Nominees v Aladdin Ltd*,[27] and *Re Spirit Motorsport Ltd*,[28] may be relevant in defining the term 'interest' as found in subsection (1)(a). The court enjoys generous discretion with regard to vesting orders but note the constraint imposed by subsection (3). A vesting order automatically transfers the property without the need for a separate conveyance (subsection (5)).

---

[24] Companies Act 2006 (Commencement No 8, Transitional Provisions and Savings) Order 2008, SI 2008/2860, art 3(o).
[25] Companies Act 2006 (Commencement No 8, Transitional Provisions and Savings) Order 2008, SI 2008/2860, art 3(o).
[26] [1994] 1 BCLC 676.
[27] [1996] 1 BCLC 720.
[28] [1996] 1 BCLC 684.

## 1018  Protection of persons holding under a lease[a]

(1) The court must not make an order under section 1017 vesting property of a leasehold nature in a person claiming under the company as underlessee or mortgagee except on terms making that person—
  (a) subject to the same liabilities and obligations as those to which the company was subject under the lease, or
  (b) if the court thinks fit, subject to the same liabilities and obligations as if the lease had been assigned to him.
(2) Where the order relates to only part of the property comprised in the lease, subsection (1) applies as if the lease had comprised only the property comprised in the vesting order.
(3) A person claiming under the company as underlessee or mortgagee who declines to accept a vesting order on such terms is excluded from all interest in the property.
(4) If there is no person claiming under the company who is willing to accept an order on such terms, the court has power to vest the company's estate and interest in the property in any person who is liable (whether personally or in a representative character, and whether alone or jointly with the company) to perform the lessee's covenants in the lease.
(5) The court may vest that estate and interest in such a person freed and discharged from all estates, incumbrances and interests created by the company.

AMENDMENTS AND NOTES

[a] This section applies with modifications to LLPs by reg 53 of the Limited Liability Partnerships (Application of Companies Act 2006) Regulations 2009, SI 2009/1804.

COMMENCEMENT DATE  1 October 2009[29]

This deals with certain matters consequential upon a vesting order where the property is leasehold in nature. The underlessee or mortgagee cannot benefit from a vesting order without assuming the obligations of the tenant company with regard to the lease.

Cases on disclaimer by liquidators decided under section 182 of the Insolvency Act 1986, such as *Re ITM Corp Ltd*[30] might act as an aid to interpretation here.

## 1019  Land subject to rentcharge[a]

Where in consequence of the disclaimer land that is subject to a rentcharge vests in any person, neither he nor his successors in title are subject to any personal liability in respect of sums becoming due under the rentcharge, except sums becoming due after he, or some person claiming under or through him, has taken possession or control of the land or has entered into occupation of it.

AMENDMENTS AND NOTES

[a] This section applies with modifications to LLPs by reg 53 of the Limited Liability Partnerships (Application of Companies Act 2006) Regulations 2009, SI 2009/1804.

COMMENCEMENT DATE  1 October 2009[31]

This is a necessary transitional matter to prevent persons benefiting from a vesting order being saddled with accrued obligations of the company in respect of rentcharge payments. See the Insolvency Act 1986, section 180 for a comparator. For liability with respect to rentcharges where there is no disclaimer see section 1023 below.

## *Effect of Crown disclaimer: Scotland*

## 1020  General effect of disclaimer[a]

(1) The Crown's disclaimer operates to determine, as from the date of the disclaimer, the rights, interests and liabilities of the company, and the property of the company, in or in respect of the property disclaimed.
(2) It does not (except so far as is necessary for the purpose of releasing the company and its property from liability) affect the rights or liabilities of any other person.

AMENDMENTS AND NOTES

[a] This section applies with modifications to LLPs by reg 54 of the Limited Liability Partnerships (Application of Companies Act 2006) Regulations 2009, SI 2009/1804.

---

[29] Companies Act 2006 (Commencement No 8, Transitional Provisions and Savings) Order 2008, SI 2008/2860, art 3(o).

[30] [1997] BCC 554.

[31] Companies Act 2006 (Commencement No 8, Transitional Provisions and Savings) Order 2008, SI 2008/2860, art 3(o).

COMMENCEMENT DATE 1 October 2009[32]

**31.1020.02**    This is the Scottish counterpart of section 1015. For the statutory predecessor see the Companies Act 1985, section 657(4). In Scotland *bona vacantia* and disclaimer is handled by the Queen's and Lord Treasurer's Remembrancer.

### 1021  Power of court to make vesting order[a]

**31.1021.01**    (1)  The court may—
    (a)  on application by a person who either claims an interest in disclaimed property or is under a liability not discharged by this Act in respect of disclaimed property, and
    (b)  on hearing such persons as it thinks fit,
make an order for the vesting of the property in or its delivery to any persons entitled to it, or to whom it may seem just that the property should be delivered by way of compensation for such liability, or a trustee for him.
    (2)  The order may be made on such terms as the court thinks fit.
    (3)  On a vesting order being made under this section, the property comprised in it vests accordingly in the person named in that behalf in the order, without conveyance or assignation for that purpose.

AMENDMENTS AND NOTES

[a] This section applies with modifications to LLPs by reg 54 of the Limited Liability Partnerships (Application of Companies Act 2006) Regulations 2009, SI 2009/1804.

COMMENCEMENT DATE 1 October 2009[33]

**31.1021.02**    See comments on the Companies Act 2006, section 1017 for the English counterpart. See the former Companies Act 1985, section 657(5).

### 1022  Protection of persons holding under a lease[a]

**31.1022.01**    (1)  Where the property disclaimed is held under a lease the court must not make a vesting order in favour of a person claiming under the company, whether—
    (a)  as sub-lessee, or
    (b)  as creditor in a duly registered or (as the case may be) recorded heritable security over a lease, except on the following terms.
    (2)  The person must by the order be made subject—
    (a)  to the same liabilities and obligations as those to which the company was subject under the lease in respect of the property, or
    (b)  if the court thinks fit, only to the same liabilities and obligations as if the lease had been assigned to him.
In either event (if the case so requires) the liabilities and obligations must be as if the lease had comprised only the property comprised in the vesting order.
    (3)  A sub-lessee or creditor declining to accept a vesting order on such terms is excluded from all interest in and security over the property.
    (4)  If there is no person claiming under the company who is willing to accept an order on such terms, the court has power to vest the company's estate and interest in the property in any person liable (either personally or in a representative character, and either alone or jointly with the company) to perform the lessee's obligations under the lease.
    (5)  The court may vest that estate and interest in such a person the lease or in relation to the lease.
    (6)  For the purposes of this section a heritable security—
    (a)  is duly recorded if it is recorded in the Register of Sasines, and
    (b)  is duly registered if registered in accordance with the Land Registration (Scotland) Act 1979 (c. 33).

AMENDMENTS AND NOTES

[a] This section applies with modifications to LLPs by reg 54 of the Limited Liability Partnerships (Application of Companies Act 2006) Regulations 2009, SI 2009/1804.

COMMENCEMENT DATE 1 October 2009[34]

**31.1022.02**    This is a Scottish adaptation of the Companies Act 2006, section 1018. For the former provision see the Companies Act 1985, section 657(7).

---

[32] Companies Act 2006 (Commencement No 8, Transitional Provisions and Savings) Order 2008, SI 2008/2860, art 3(o).
[33] Companies Act 2006 (Commencement No 8, Transitional Provisions and Savings) Order 2008, SI 2008/2860, art 3(o).
[34] Companies Act 2006 (Commencement No 8, Transitional Provisions and Savings) Order 2008, SI 2008/2860, art 3(o).

## *Supplementary provisions*

### 1023  Liability for rentcharge on company's land after dissolution[a]

(1) This section applies where on the dissolution of a company land in England and Wales or Northern Ireland that is subject to a rentcharge vests by operation of law in the Crown or any other person ('the proprietor').

(2) Neither the proprietor nor his successors in title are subject to any personal liability in respect of sums becoming due under the rentcharge, except sums becoming due after the proprietor, or some person claiming under or through him, has taken possession or control of the land or has entered into occupation of it.

(3) In this section 'company' includes any body corporate.

**31.1023.01**

AMENDMENTS AND NOTES

[a] This section applies with modifications to LLPs by reg 55 of the Limited Liability Partnerships (Application of Companies Act 2006) Regulations 2009, SI 2009/1804.

COMMENCEMENT DATE  1 October 2009[35]

This provision, which is based upon the Companies Act 1985, section 658, deals with rentcharges. However, unlike its statutory predecessor it provides no formal linkage to section 180 of the Insolvency Act 1986, though principles developed under section 180 clearly may be relevant. For 'body corporate' in subsection (3) see section 1173.

**31.1023.02**

# CHAPTER 3
## RESTORATION TO THE REGISTER

### *Administrative restoration to the register*

### 1024  Application for administrative restoration to the register[a]

(1) An application may be made to the registrar to restore to the register a company that has been struck off the register under section 1000 or 1001 (power of registrar to strike off defunct company).

(2) An application under this section may be made whether or not the company has in consequence been dissolved.

(3) An application under this section may only be made by a former director or former member of the company.

(4) An application under this section may not be made after the end of the period of six years from the date of the dissolution of the company.
For this purpose an application is made when it is received by the registrar.

**31.1024.01**

AMENDMENTS AND NOTES

[a] This section applies with modifications to LLPs by reg 56 of the Limited Liability Partnerships (Application of Companies Act 2006) Regulations 2009, SI 2009/1804.

COMMENCEMENT DATE  1 October 2009[36]

This section was introduced when the Companies Bill entered the Commons in May 2006. The Company Law Review[37] gave enthusiastic backing to such a change which represents the converse of administrative striking off under section 1000. Lord McKenzie of Luton further explained the rationale.[38] This deregulated procedure was only to be used in limited circumstances as an alternative to an application to the court. There is a limited range of applicants—former directors and former members (subsection (3)). Applications under section 1024 can only be made within six years of dissolution (see subsection (4)). For 'registrar' see section 1060.

**31.1024.02**

### 1025  Requirements for administrative restoration[a]

(1) On an application under section 1024 the registrar shall restore the company to the register if, and only if, the following conditions are met.

(2) The first condition is that the company was carrying on business or in operation at the time of its striking off.

**31.1025.01**

---

[35] Companies Act 2006 (Commencement No 8, Transitional Provisions and Savings) Order 2008, SI 2008/2860, art 3(o).

[36] Companies Act 2006 (Commencement No 8, Transitional Provisions and Savings) Order 2008, SI 2008/2860, art 3(o).

[37] URN 01/942 para 11.19.

[38] See *Hansard*, cols 759–760 (23 May 2006).

(3) The second condition is that, if any property or right previously vested in or held on trust for the company has vested as ***bona vacantia***, the Crown representative has signified to the registrar in writing consent to the company's restoration to the register.

(4) It is the applicant's responsibility to obtain that consent and to pay any costs (in Scotland, expenses) of the Crown representative—

    (a) in dealing with the property during the period of dissolution, or

    (b) in connection with the proceedings on the application,

    that may be demanded as a condition of giving consent.

(5) The third condition is that the applicant has—

    (a) delivered to the registrar such documents relating to the company as are necessary to bring up to date the records kept by the registrar, and

    (b) paid any penalties under section 453 or corresponding earlier provisions (civil penalty for failure to deliver accounts) that were outstanding at the date of dissolution or striking off.

(6) In this section the 'Crown representative' means—

    (a) in relation to property vested in the Duchy of Lancaster, the Solicitor to that Duchy;

    (b) in relation to property vested in the Duke of Cornwall, the Solicitor to the Duchy of Cornwall;

    (c) in relation to property in Scotland, the Queen's and Lord Treasurer's Remembrancer;

    (d) in relation to other property, the Treasury Solicitor.

AMENDMENTS AND NOTES

[a] This section applies with modifications to LLPs by reg 56 of the Limited Liability Partnerships (Application of Companies Act 2006) Regulations 2009, SI 2009/1804.

COMMENCEMENT DATE 1 October 2009[39]

**31.1025.02** This was one of the later introduced reform clauses. It deals with the prerequisites that must be satisfied before a company can be restored to the register by administrative act. As noted in the annotation to section 1024, this deregulated option was meant to be tightly circumscribed. Note therefore the *three* preconditions outlined in subsections (1) (need for trading prior to striking off), (2) (Crown representative consent to be obtained in writing), and (5) (compliance with procedures and settlement of civil penalties). For 'registrar' see section 1060.

## 1026 Application to be accompanied by statement of compliance[a]

**31.1026.01** (1) An application under section 1024 (application for administrative restoration to the register) must be accompanied by a statement of compliance.

(2) The statement of compliance required is a statement—

    (a) that the person making the application has standing to apply (see subsection (3) of that section), and

    (b) that the requirements for administrative restoration (see section 1025) are met.

(3) The registrar may accept the statement of compliance as sufficient evidence of those matters.

AMENDMENTS AND NOTES

[a] This section applies with modifications to LLPs by reg 56 of the Limited Liability Partnerships (Application of Companies Act 2006) Regulations 2009, SI 2009/1804.

COMMENCEMENT DATE 1 October 2009[40]

**31.1026.02** This clause was introduced after the Bill had passed through the Lords for its initial scrutiny. It prescribes safeguards in the form of a statement of compliance before an administrative restoration under the Companies Act 2006, section 1024 can take place. Compliance relates to the *locus standi* of applicant and satisfaction of the three conditions outlined in section 1025. For 'registrar' see section 1060.

## 1027 Registrar's decision on application for administrative restoration[a]

**31.1027.01** (1) The registrar must give notice to the applicant of the decision on an application under section 1024 (application for administrative restoration to the register).

(2) If the decision is that the company should be restored to the register, the restoration takes effect as from the date that notice is sent.

(3) In the case of such a decision, the registrar must—

    (a) enter on the register a note of the date as from which the company's restoration to the register takes effect, and

    (b) cause notice of the restoration to be published in the Gazette.

---

[39] Companies Act 2006 (Commencement No 8, Transitional Provisions and Savings) Order 2008, SI 2008/2860, art 3(o).

[40] Companies Act 2006 (Commencement No 8, Transitional Provisions and Savings) Order 2008, SI 2008/2860, art 3(o).

(4) The notice under subsection (3)(b) must state—
- (a) the name of the company or, if the company is restored to the register under a different name (see section 1033), that name and its former name,
- (b) the company's registered number, and
- (c) the date as from which the restoration of the company to the register takes effect.

AMENDMENTS AND NOTES

ᵃ This section applies with modifications to LLPs by reg 56 of the Limited Liability Partnerships (Application of Companies Act 2006) Regulations 2009, SI 2009/1804.

COMMENCEMENT DATE 1 October 2009[41]

Again this represents a belated reform attempt having only surfaced in the final stages of the passage   **31.1027.02**
through the Lords. This provision deals with the effect of and consequences flowing from an administrative restoration to the register. The registrar, quite naturally, is obliged to notify the applicant of the decision, and if the application succeeds the restoration takes effect from the date when the notice is sent (subsection (2)). For 'Gazette' see section 1173. Contents of the official notification are specified by subsection (4). For the 'registered number' see section 1066 below.

## 1028 Effect of administrative restorationᵃ

- (1) The general effect of administrative restoration to the register is that the company is deemed to   **31.1028.01**
  have continued in existence as if it had not been dissolved or struck off the register.
- (2) The company is not liable to a penalty under section 453 or any corresponding earlier provision (civil penalty for failure to deliver accounts) for a financial year in relation to which the period for filing accounts and reports ended—
  - (a) after the date of dissolution or striking off, and
  - (b) before the restoration of the company to the register.
- (3) The court may give such directions and make such provision as seems just for placing the company and all other persons in the same position (as nearly as may be) as if the company had not been dissolved or struck off the register.
- (4) An application to the court for such directions or provision may be made any time within three years after the date of restoration of the company to the register.

AMENDMENTS AND NOTES

ᵃ This section applies with modifications to LLPs by reg 56 of the Limited Liability Partnerships (Application of Companies Act 2006) Regulations 2009, SI 2009/1804.

COMMENCEMENT DATE 1 October 2009[42]

This deals with the consequences attendant upon the administrative restoration of a company to the   **31.1028.02**
register under the Companies Act 2006, section 1024. This provision maintains the statutory fiction that the company was deemed never to have been struck off—for judicial comment on that fiction see *Tymans Ltd v Craven*,[43] *Re Priceland Ltd*,[44] and *Top Creative Ltd v St Alban's District Council*.[45] Note the broad powers of direction enjoyed by the court under subsection (3) but there is a three-year time limit prescribed by subsection (4) on applications to the court for the exercise of such powers.

## *Restoration to the register by the court*

## 1029 Application to court for restoration to the registerᵃ

- (1) An application may be made to the court to restore to the register a company—   **31.1029.01**
  - (a) that has been dissolved under Chapter 9 of Part 4 of the Insolvency Act 1986 (c. 45) or Chapter 9 of Part 5 of the Insolvency (Northern Ireland) Order 1989 (S.I. 1989/2405 (N.I. 19)) (dissolution of company after winding up),
  - (b) that is deemed to have been dissolved under paragraph 84(6) of Schedule B1 to that Act or paragraph 85(6) of Schedule B1 to that Order (dissolution of company following administration), or
  - (c) that has been struck off the register—
    - (i) under section 1000 or 1001 (power of registrar to strike off defunct company), or
    - (ii) under section 1003 (voluntary striking off),
    whether or not the company has in consequence been dissolved.

---

[41] Companies Act 2006 (Commencement No 8, Transitional Provisions and Savings) Order 2008, SI 2008/2860, art 3(o).
[42] Companies Act 2006 (Commencement No 8, Transitional Provisions and Savings) Order 2008, SI 2008/2860, art 3(o).
[43] [1952] 2 QB 100.
[44] [1997] 1 BCLC 467.
[45] [2000] 2 BCLC 379.

(2) An application under this section may be made by—
   (a) the Secretary of State,
   (b) any former director of the company,
   (c) any person having an interest in land in which the company had a superior or derivative interest,
   (d) any person having an interest in land or other property—
      (i) that was subject to rights vested in the company, or
      (ii) that was benefited by obligations owed by the company,
   (e) any person who but for the company's dissolution would have been in a contractual relationship with it,
   (f) any person with a potential legal claim against the company,
   (g) any manager or trustee of a pension fund established for the benefit of employees of the company,
   (h) any former member of the company (or the personal representatives of such a person),
   (i) any person who was a creditor of the company at the time of its striking off or dissolution,
   (j) any former liquidator of the company,
   (k) where the company was struck off the register under section 1003 (voluntary striking off), any person of a description specified by regulations under section 1006(1)(f) or 1007(2)(f) (persons entitled to notice of application for voluntary striking off),
or by any other person appearing to the court to have an interest in the matter.

AMENDMENTS AND NOTES

[a] This section applies with modifications to LLPs by reg 57 of the Limited Liability Partnerships (Application of Companies Act 2006) Regulations 2009, SI 2009/1804.

COMMENCEMENT DATE 1 October 2009[46]

**31.1029.02**  This consolidation measure was introduced as the Bill reached the conclusion of its passage through the Lords. It is based upon an attempt to *unify* the procedures formerly operating under the Companies Act 1985, section 651 and section 653 respectively. This welcome simplification of the law was recommended by the Company Law Review.[47] The Court of Appeal described the background to this change in *Peaktone Ltd v Joddrell*.[48] For explanation as to the underlying rationale see Lord McKenzie of Luton.[49] It deals with applications to the court for the restoration of a dissolved or struck off company to the register. The circumstances under which such an application may be made and the *locus standi* of potential applicants is explained by subsections (1) and (2). For the use of the former procedure to deal with overlooked assets on liquidation see *Re Oakleague Ltd*.[50] The list of applicants in subsection (2) is most extensive and certainly wider than that which operated under the former section 653 of the Companies Act 1985 which employed the 'aggrieved person' test to limit applicants. For transitional measures, see the Companies Act 2006 (Commencement No 8, Transitional Provisions and Savings) Order 2008,[51] Schedule 2, paragraphs 90 and 91.

**31.1029.03**  One problem with this unified provision will be the extent to which case law decided under sections 651 and 653 of the Companies Act 1985 is still relevant. For example, is the characterization of Harman J in *Re Portafram Ltd*[52] of restoration proceedings under section 653 as quasi-administrative rather than lis inter parties still apposite? On who might be regarded as a 'creditor' for the purposes of subsection (2)(i) see *Re Aga Estate Agencies Ltd*.[53] Note that the definition of 'creditor' laid down in section 1011 only applies explicitly to Chapter 1 of Part 31, but, presumably, a comparable meaning will be given to the term in this context.

### 1030  When application to the court may be made[a]

**31.1030.01**  (1) An application to the court for restoration of a company to the register may be made at any time for the purpose of bringing proceedings against the company for damages for personal injury.
(2) No order shall be made on such an application if it appears to the court that the proceedings would fail by virtue of any enactment as to the time within which proceedings must be brought.

---

[46] Companies Act 2006 (Commencement No 8, Transitional Provisions and Savings) Order 2008, SI 2008/2860, art 3(o).
[47] URN 01/942 para 11.17.
[48] [2012] EWCA Civ 1035.
[49] *Hansard*, cols 759–760 (23 May 2006).
[50] [1995] 2 BCLC 624.
[51] SI 2008/2860.
[52] [1986] BCLC 533.
[53] [1986] BCLC 346.

(3)  In making that decision the court must have regard to its power under section 1032(3) (power to give consequential directions etc) to direct that the period between the dissolution (or striking off) of the company and the making of the order is not to count for the purposes of any such enactment.

(4)  In any other case an application to the court for restoration of a company to the register may not be made after the end of the period of six years from the date of the dissolution of the company, subject as follows.

(5)  In a case where—

   (a)  the company has been struck off the register under section 1000 or 1001 (power of registrar to strike off defunct company),

   (b)  an application to the registrar has been made under section 1024 (application for administrative restoration to the register) within the time allowed for making such an application, and

   (c)  the registrar has refused the application,

   an application to the court under this section may be made within 28 days of notice of the registrar's decision being issued by the registrar, even if the period of six years mentioned in subsection (4) above has expired.

(6)  For the purposes of this section—

   (a)  'personal injury' includes any disease and any impairment of a person's physical or mental condition; and

   (b)  references to damages for personal injury include—

      (i)  any sum claimed by virtue of section 1(2)(c) of the Law Reform (Miscellaneous Provisions) Act 1934 (c. 41) or section 14(2)(c) of the Law Reform (Miscellaneous Provisions) Act (Northern Ireland) 1937 (1937 c. 9 (N.I.)) (funeral expenses)), and

      (ii)  damages under the Fatal Accidents Act 1976 (c. 30), the Damages (Scotland) Act 1976 (c. 13) or the Fatal Accidents (Northern Ireland) Order 1977 (S.I. 1977/1251 (N.I. 18)).

AMENDMENTS AND NOTES

[a]  This section applies with modifications to LLPs by reg 57 of the Limited Liability Partnerships (Application of Companies Act 2006) Regulations 2009, SI 2009/1804.

COMMENCEMENT DATE  1 October 2009[54]

This represents an amalgam of provisions formerly found in the Companies Act 1985, sections 651 and 653. Under the former provision the period in which application was required to be made was two years, whereas under section 653 it was 20 years; under the new unified procedure the application to the court to restore must be made within six years (see subsection (4)) with extra flexibility being offered in personal injury cases where the injury might not surface for many years after dissolution—these changes are in law with recommendations made by the Company Law Review in its *Final Report*.[55] Full information is given by subsections (4) and (5) on when an application may be made to the court for a dissolved company to be restored to the register. It particularly focuses on applications made in the personal injury context, a scenario explained in subsection (6). On personal injury cases authorities decided under the former law, such as *Re Workvale Ltd (No 2)*[56] might still be useful. For 'registrar' in subsection (5) see section 1060.   **31.1030.02**

## 1031  Decision on application for restoration by the court[a]

(1)  On an application under section 1029 the court may order the restoration of the company to the register—   **31.1031.01**

   (a)  if the company was struck off the register under section 1000 or 1001 (power of registrar to strike off defunct companies) and the company was, at the time of the striking off, carrying on business or in operation;

   (b)  if the company was struck off the register under section 1003 (voluntary striking off) and any of the requirements of sections 1004 to 1009 was not complied with;

   (c)  if in any other case the court considers it just to do so.

(2)  If the court orders restoration of the company to the register, the restoration takes effect on a copy of the court's order being delivered to the registrar.

(3)  The registrar must cause to be published in the Gazette notice of the restoration of the company to the register.

(4)  The notice must state—

   (a)  the name of the company or, if the company is restored to the register under a different name (see section 1033), that name and its former name,

---

[54]  Companies Act 2006 (Commencement No 8, Transitional Provisions and Savings) Order 2008, SI 2008/2860, art 3(o).

[55]  URN 01/942 para 11.18.

[56]  [1992] BCLC 544.

(b)  the company's registered number, and

(c)  the date on which the restoration took effect.

AMENDMENTS AND NOTES

<sup>a</sup> This section applies with modifications to LLPs by reg 57 of the Limited Liability Partnerships (Application of Companies Act 2006) Regulations 2009, SI 2009/1804.

COMMENCEMENT DATE 1 October 2009[57]

**31.1031.02**   This details the options open to the court where an application is made to the court for restoration under the Companies Act 2006, section 1029. The notification responsibilities of the registrar in the event of restoration are explained by subsections (2) to (4) with particular emphasis being given to the question of corporate name and registered number (see section 1066). For 'registrar' see section 1060 and 'Gazette' see section 1173.

### 1032  Effect of court order for restoration to the register[a]

**31.1032.01**
(1)  The general effect of an order by the court for restoration to the register is that the company is deemed to have continued in existence as if it had not been dissolved or struck off the register.

(2)  The company is not liable to a penalty under section 453 or any corresponding earlier provision (civil penalty for failure to deliver accounts) for a financial year in relation to which the period for filing accounts and reports ended—

(a)  after the date of dissolution or striking off, and

(b)  before the restoration of the company to the register.

(3)  The court may give such directions and make such provision as seems just for placing the company and all other persons in the same position (as nearly as may be) as if the company had not been dissolved or struck off the register.

(4)  The court may also give directions as to—

(a)  the delivery to the registrar of such documents relating to the company as are necessary to bring up to date the records kept by the registrar,

(b)  the payment of the costs (in Scotland, expenses) of the registrar in connection with the proceedings for the restoration of the company to the register,

(c)  where any property or right previously vested in or held on trust for the company has vested as *bona vacantia*, the payment of the costs (in Scotland, expenses) of the Crown representative—

(i)  in dealing with the property during the period of dissolution, or

(ii)  in connection with the proceedings on the application.

(5)  In this section the 'Crown representative' means—

(a)  in relation to property vested in the Duchy of Lancaster, the Solicitor to that Duchy;

(b)  in relation to property vested in the Duke of Cornwall, the Solicitor to the Duchy of Cornwall;

(c)  in relation to property in Scotland, the Queen's and Lord Treasurer's Remembrancer;

(d)  in relation to other property, the Treasury Solicitor.

AMENDMENTS AND NOTES

<sup>a</sup> This section applies with modifications to LLPs by reg 57 of the Limited Liability Partnerships (Application of Companies Act 2006) Regulations 2009, SI 2009/1804.

COMMENCEMENT DATE 1 October 2009[58]

**31.1032.02**   This details the effect of a restoration to the register. It mirrors the effect where an administrative restoration has taken place under section 1028 of the 2006 Act. Note the fiction maintained by subsection (1) that the company was deemed never to have been dissolved—for case law under the former regime on this point see *Tyman's Ltd v Craven*,[59] *Re Priceland Ltd*,[60] and *Top Creative Ltd v St Albans District Council*.[61] In *Peaktone Ltd v Joddrell*,[62] the Court of Appeal reviewed such authorities and came down in favour of the view taken in the old section 653 cases. Thus, the restoration to the register was capable under section 1032 of retrospectively validating proceedings commenced against the company when it was dissolved. The wide language of, and flexible jurisdiction under, section 1032 was stressed. The court is given extensive consequential powers of direction by subsections (3) and (4). For example, where property has been held by the Crown during the period post dissolution as *bona*

---

[57] Companies Act 2006 (Commencement No 8, Transitional Provisions and Savings) Order 2008, SI 2008/2860, art 3(o).

[58] Companies Act 2006 (Commencement No 8, Transitional Provisions and Savings) Order 2008, SI 2008/2860, art 3(o).

[59] [1952] 2 QB 100.

[60] [1997] 1 BCLC 467.

[61] [2000] 2 BCLC 379.

[62] [2012] EWCA Civ 1035.

*vacantia* the costs of handling it and of dealing with the restoration application are to be deducted from any restoration of property/funds to the company.

## *Supplementary provisions*

### 1033 Company's name on restoration[a]

(1) A company is restored to the register with the name it had before it was dissolved or struck off the register, subject to the following provisions.    **31.1033.01**

(2) If at the date of restoration the company could not be registered under its former name without contravening section 66 (name not to be the same as another in the registrar's index of company names), it must be restored to the register—

   (a) under another name specified—

     (i) in the case of administrative restoration, in the application to the registrar, or

     (ii) in the case of restoration under a court order, in the court's order, or

   (b) as if its registered number was also its name.

References to a company's being registered in a name, and to registration in that context, shall be read as including the company's being restored to the register.

(3) If a company is restored to the register under a name specified in the application to the registrar, the provisions of—

   section 80 (change of name: registration and issue of new certificate of incorporation), and

   section 81 (change of name: effect), apply as if the application to the registrar were notice of a change of name.

(4) If a company is restored to the register under a name specified in the court's order, the provisions of—

   section 80 (change of name: registration and issue of new certificate of incorporation), and

   section 81 (change of name: effect), apply as if the copy of the court order delivered to the registrar were notice of a change a name.

(5) If the company is restored to the register as if its registered number was also its name—

   (a) the company must change its name within 14 days after the date of the restoration,

   (b) the change may be made by resolution of the directors (without prejudice to any other method of changing the company's name),

   (c) the company must give notice to the registrar of the change, and

   (d) sections 80 and 81 apply as regards the registration and effect of the change.

(6) If the company fails to comply with subsection (5)(a) or (c) an offence is committed by—

   (a) the company, and

   (b) every officer of the company who is in default.

(7) A person guilty of an offence under subsection (6) is liable on summary conviction to a fine not exceeding level 5 on the standard scale and, for continued contravention, a daily default fine not exceeding one-tenth of level 5 on the standard scale.

Amendments and Notes

[a] This section applies with modifications to LLPs by reg 58 of the Limited Liability Partnerships (Application of Companies Act 2006) Regulations 2009, SI 2009/1804.

Commencement Date 1 October 2009[63]

This deals with a whole series of permutations relating to questions of corporate nomenclature in the event of restoration to the register. In particular it addresses the situation where the company cannot be restored under its former name because that name would be too similar to another corporate name registered in the interim—another name needs to be selected as part of the restoration process.    **31.1033.02**

For officer in default see sections 1121 to 1122. For the daily default fine specified in subsection (7) see the Companies Act 2006, section 1125. Details of level 5 of the standard scale are to be found in paragraph 1370 of the Explanatory Notes to the Bill when it entered the Commons in May 2006.    **31.1033.03**

For definitions of 'registered number' see section 1066, and for 'registrar' see section 1060.    **31.1033.04**

### 1034 Effect of restoration to the register where property has vested as bona vacantia[a]

(1) The person in whom any property or right is vested by section 1012 (property of dissolved company to be *bona vacantia*) may dispose of, or of an interest in, that property or right despite the fact that the company may be restored to the register under this Chapter.    **31.1034.01**

(2) If the company is restored to the register—

   (a) the restoration does not affect the disposition (but without prejudice to its effect in relation to any other property or right previously vested in or held on trust for the company), and

---

[63] Companies Act 2006 (Commencement No 8, Transitional Provisions and Savings) Order 2008, SI 2008/2860, art 3(o).

(b) the Crown or, as the case may be, the Duke of Cornwall shall pay to the company an amount equal to—

(i) the amount of any consideration received for the property or right or, as the case may be, the interest in it, or

(ii) the value of any such consideration at the time of the disposition,

or, if no consideration was received an amount equal to the value of the property, right or interest disposed of, as at the date of the disposition.

(3) There may be deducted from the amount payable under subsection (2)(b) the reasonable costs of the Crown representative in connection with the disposition (to the extent that they have not been paid as a condition of administrative restoration or pursuant to a court order for restoration).

(4) Where a liability accrues under subsection (2) in respect of any property or right which before the restoration of the company to the register had accrued as *bona vacantia* to the Duchy of Lancaster, the Attorney General of that Duchy shall represent Her Majesty in any proceedings arising in connection with that liability.

(5) Where a liability accrues under subsection (2) in respect of any property or right which before the restoration of the company to the register had accrued as *bona vacantia* to the Duchy of Cornwall, such persons as the Duke of Cornwall (or other possessor for the time being of the Duchy) may appoint shall represent the Duke (or other possessor) in any proceedings arising out of that liability.

(6) In this section the 'Crown representative' means—

(a) in relation to property vested in the Duchy of Lancaster, the Solicitor to that Duchy;

(b) in relation to property vested in the Duke of Cornwall, the Solicitor to the Duchy of Cornwall;

(c) in relation to property in Scotland, the Queen's and Lord Treasurer's Remembrancer;

(d) in relation to other property, the Treasury Solicitor.

AMENDMENTS AND NOTES

ᵃ This section applies with modifications to LLPs by reg 58 of the Limited Liability Partnerships (Application of Companies Act 2006) Regulations 2009, SI 2009/1804.

COMMENCEMENT DATE 1 October 2009[64]

**31.1034.02** This deals with the position of property treated as *bona vacantia* where a company is later restored to the register. Restoration does not affect intervening property dispositions, though the proceeds of sale might revert to the company. Crown costs of disposition also need to be taken into account (see subsection (3)). For transitional provisions, see the Companies Act 2006 (Commencement No 8, Transitional Provisions and Savings) Order 2008,[65] Schedule 2, paragraph 92.

---

[64] Companies Act 2006 (Commencement No 8, Transitional Provisions and Savings) Order 2008, SI 2008/2860, art 3(o).

[65] SI 2008/2860.

# 32

---

## COMPANY INVESTIGATIONS

---

## Companies Act 2006

# PART 32
## COMPANY INVESTIGATIONS

### Company investigations: amendments

**32.0.01**   Part 32 is not reproduced in full here because sections 1035 to 1038 merely amend/add to the relevant provisions on investigations in CA 1985 which are reproduced in their amended/supplemented form later in this chapter. Section 1039 is however reproduced in full as it makes a consequential amendment to section 8 of the Company Directors Disqualification Act 1986 (which is not included in this collection). Relevant legislation amending the CA 1985 is listed in reverse chronological order.

### 1035  Powers of Secretary of State to give directions to inspectors

**32.1035.01**   [This inserts sections 446A and 446B into the Companies Act 1985. Amendments are also made to sections 431, 432, and 437 of the Companies Act 1985]

COMMENCEMENT DATE 1 October 2007[1]

### 1036  Resignation, removal and replacement of inspectors

**32.1036.01**   [This inserts sections 446C and 446D into the Companies Act 1985]

COMMENCEMENT DATE 1 October 2007[2]

### 1037  Power to obtain information from former inspectors etc

**32.1037.01**   [This inserts section 446E into the Companies Act 1985 and makes minor amendments to sections 451A and 452 of the Companies Act 1985]

COMMENCEMENT DATE 1 October 2007[3]

### 1038  Power to require production of documents

**32.1038.01**   [This amends section 434(6) to (8) of the Companies Act 1985 and section 447(9) of the Companies Act 1985]

COMMENCEMENT DATE 1 October 2007[4]

### 1039  Disqualification orders: consequential amendments

**32.1039.01**   In section 8(1A)(b)(i) of the Company Directors Disqualification Act 1986 (c. 46) (disqualification after investigation of company: meaning of 'investigative material')—

(a)  after 'section' insert '437, 446E,', and
(b)  after '448' insert ', 451A'.

COMMENCEMENT DATE 1 October 2007[5]

**32.1039.02**   This amends section 8 of the Company Directors Disqualification Act 1986 by introducing references to sections 437, 446E, and 451A. This represents a consequential change resulting from amendments made by other provisions in the Companies Act 2006. Such disqualifications resulting from investigations are, however, rare, with only 19 cases officially recorded in 2003–2004, a figure placed in perspective by the hundreds of director disqualifications taking place every year. This figure increased

---

[1]  Companies Act (Commencement No 3, etc) Order 2007, SI 2007/2194, art 2.
[2]  Companies Act (Commencement No 3, etc) Order 2007, SI 2007/2194, art 2.
[3]  Companies Act (Commencement No 3, etc) Order 2007, SI 2007/2194, art 2.
[4]  Companies Act (Commencement No 3, etc) Order 2007, SI 2007/2194, art 2.
[5]  Companies Act (Commencement No 3, etc) Order 2007, SI 2007/2194, art 2.

to only 26 in 2005–2006 and it is therefore easy to see that the mechanism has untapped potential. The 2005 White Paper, *Company Law Reform*[6] (paragraph 6.3) was keen to expand usage of this control mechanism and to make it more effective by permitting usage of material not included in a final investigation report. See also the Explanatory Notes to the Bill when it entered the Commons in May 2006, paragraph 1231 for an explanation of the rationale behind section 1039.

## Companies (Audit, Investigations and Community Enterprise) Act 2004

### CHAPTER 4
### INVESTIGATIONS

## Companies Act 1989

### PART III
### INVESTIGATIONS AND POWERS TO OBTAIN INFORMATION

*Amendments of the Companies Act 1985*

**'124A Petition for winding up on grounds of public interest**
    (1)  Where it appears to the Secretary of State from—
        (a)  any report made or information obtained under Part XIV (except section 448A) of the Companies Act 1985 (company investigations, &c.),
        (b)  any report made by inspectors under—
            (i)  section 167, 168, 169 or 284 of the Financial Services and Markets Act 2000 or
            (ii)  where the company is an open-ended investment company (within the meaning of that Act), regulations made as a result of section 262(2)(k) of that Act,
        (bb) any information or documents obtained under section 165, 171, 172, 173 or 175 of that Act,

---

[6] Cm 6456.

(c) any information obtained under section 2 of the Criminal Justice Act 1987 or section 28 of the Criminal Law (Consolidation) (Scotland) Act 1995 (fraud investigations), or

(d) any information obtained under section 83 of the Companies Act 1989 (powers exercisable for purpose of assisting overseas regulatory authorities),

that it is expedient in the public interest that a company should be wound up, he may present a petition for it to be wound up if the court thinks it just and equitable for it to be so.

(2) This section does not apply if the company is already being wound up by the court.'

**32.CA89.05**  Section 124A(1)(b) was substituted and section 124(A)(1)(bb) was inserted by the Financial Services and Markets Act 2000 (Consequential Amendments and Repeals) Order 2001, SI 2001/3649.

**32.CA89.06**  This relocates the power of the Secretary of State to present a winding-up petition from section 440 of the Companies Act 1985 to the Insolvency Act 1986. This draconian step can only be taken in the light of information obtained through various investigation processes. The actual decision to present the winding-up petition does not have to be taken by the Secretary of State personally; it can be delegated to a responsible official according to *Re Golden Chemicals Ltd*.[7]

**32.CA89.07**  A winding-up petition under section 124A cannot be used if the company is already being wound up by the court (section 124A(2)). No such disability operates where the extant winding-up procedure is voluntary in nature—*Re Lubin, Rosen and Associates Ltd*.[8] The power now vested by section 124A of the Insolvency Act 1986 has been utilized extensively in recent years. For example it appears from the DTI Annual Companies Report for 2003–2004 that some 371 companies were wound up in exercise of this jurisdiction. It can be used against overseas companies. Leading cases on this particular jurisdiction would include *Re North West Holdings plc*[9] (liability of directors for costs), *Secretary of State for Trade and Industry v Bell Davies Trading Ltd*[10] (use of undertakings instead of winding up), and *Re Marann Brooks CSV Ltd*[11] (non-application of EC Regulation on Insolvency Proceedings 1346/2000). There is an extensive literature on this subject.[12]

### 61  Inspectors' reports as evidence

**32.CA89.08**  [This makes a minor referential amendment to the Companies Act 1985, section 441]

### 62  Investigation of company ownership

**32.CA89.09**  [This amends section 442 of the Companies Act 1985]

### 64  Entry and search of premises

**32.CA89.10**  [This substitutes section 448 of the Companies Act 1985. Consequential amendments to Schedule 24 of the Companies Act 1985 were also made by subsection (2) but that subsection was in turn repealed by Companies Act 2006]

### 66  Punishment for destroying, mutilating, &c. company documents

**32.CA89.11**  [This amends section 450 of the Companies Act 1985]

### 68  Disclosure of information by Secretary of State or inspector

**32.CA89.12**  [This substitutes a new section 451A of the Companies Act 1985]

### 69  Protection of banking information

**32.CA89.13**  [This amends section 452 of the Companies Act 1985]

### 70  Investigation of oversea companies

**32.CA89.14**  [This amends section 453 of the Companies Act 1985]

---

[7] [1976] Ch 300.

[8] [1975] 1 WLR 122.

[9] [2001] EWCA Civ 67.

[10] [2004] EWCA Civ 1066. See also *Secretary of State for BERR v Amway (UK) Ltd* [2009] BCC 781.

[11] [2003] BCC 239.

[12] For discussion see Keay (1999) 20 *Company Lawyer* 296; Campbell (2001) 17 IL & P 129; and Finch [2002] *Insolvency Lawyer* 157.

## Companies Act 1985

### PART XIV

### INVESTIGATION OF COMPANIES AND THEIR AFFAIRS; REQUISITION OF DOCUMENTS

#### *Appointment and functions of inspectors*

### 431  Investigation of a company on its own application or that of its members

(1)  The Secretary of State may appoint one or more competent inspectors to investigate the affairs of **32.CA85.01**
a company and to report the result of their investigations to him.

(2)  The appointment may be made—

    (a)  in the case of a company having a share capital, on the application either of not less than 200 members or of members holding not less than one-tenth of the shares issued [(excluding any shares held as treasury shares)],[a]

    (b)  in the case of a company not having a share capital, on the application of not less than one-fifth in number of the persons on the company's register of members, and

    (c)  in any case, on application of the company.

(3)  The application shall be supported by such evidence as the Secretary of State may require for the purpose of showing that the applicant or applicants have good reason for requiring the investigation.

(4)  The Secretary of State may, before appointing inspectors, require the applicant or applicants to give security, to an amount not exceeding £5,000, or such other sum as he may by order specify, for payment of the costs of the investigation.

    An order under this subsection shall be made by statutory instrument subject to annulment in pursuance of a resolution of either House of Parliament.

AMENDMENTS AND NOTES

[a]  Inserted by the Companies (Acquisition of Own Shares) (Treasury Shares) Regulations 2003, SI 2003/1116. Subsection (1) further amended by CA 2006, s 1035(2).

The right of the state to investigate companies is best seen as part of the quid pro quo for limited **32.CA85.02**
liability. This power of official investigation dates back to the Joint Stock Companies Act 1856 and has been upgraded on numerous occasions since then.[13] Investigation law reform did not feature in The Company Law Review, though the government itself did float ideas for reform in *Company Investigations: Powers for the 21st Century* (2001). The position today is that the investigation provisions, although superficially located in the rump of the 1985 Act have been heavily amended by the 1989, 2004, and 2006 Acts primarily with a view to enhancing the powers of investigators. It is rumoured that in the future they will be reconstituted into a single discrete piece of legislation. Recent statistical information on aspects of the investigation process are contained in *Companies in 2004– 05*, DTI (October 2005) (HC 544) pages 7–10.

Subsection (1) of section 431 authorizes the Secretary of State to appoint inspectors to investigate the **32.CA85.03**
affairs of a company. The 'affairs' of a company are to be interpreted widely.[14]

Subsection (2) identifies the circumstances under which an appointment of inspectors may be made **32.CA85.04**
under this subsection.

Subsections (3) and (4) deal with the necessary evidence required before the Secretary of State will **32.CA85.05**
appoint on application and with the possibility of security being required from the applicant.

### 432  Other company investigations

(1)  The Secretary of State shall appoint one or more competent inspectors to investigate the affairs of **32.CA85.06**
a company and report the result of their investigations to him, if the court by order declares that its affairs ought to be so investigated.[a]

(2)  The Secretary of State may make such an appointment if it appears to him that there are circumstances suggesting—

---

[13]  On investigations generally, see A Lidbetter, *Company Investigations and Public Law* (Hart Publishing, 1999). See also Lidbetter in de Lacy (ed), *The Reform of UK Company Law* (Cavendish, 2002) Ch 4 for a more up-to-date perspective. Useful historical insights may be gleaned from Fraser (1971) 34 MLR 260 and Sealy [1974] CLJ 225.

[14]  *R v Board of Trade ex p St Martin's Preservation Co Ltd* [1965] 1 QB 603.

(a)  that the company's affairs are being or have been conducted with intent to defraud its creditors or the creditors of any other person, or otherwise for a fraudulent or unlawful purpose, or in a manner which is unfairly prejudicial to some part of its members, or

(b)  that any actual or proposed act or omission of the company (including an act or omission on its behalf) is or would be so prejudicial, or that the company was formed for any fraudulent or unlawful purpose, or

(c)  that persons concerned with the company's formation or the management of its affairs have in connection therewith been guilty of fraud, misfeasance or other misconduct towards it or towards its members, or

(d)  that the company's members have not been given all the information with respect to its affairs which they might reasonably expect.

[(2A) Inspectors may be appointed under subsection (2) on terms that any report they may make is not for publication; and in such a case, the provisions of section 437(3) (availability and publication of inspectors' reports) do not apply.]$^b$

(3)  Subsections (1) and (2) are without prejudice to the powers of the Secretary of State under section 431; and the power conferred by subsection (2) is exercisable with respect to a body corporate notwithstanding that it is in course of being voluntarily wound up.

(4)  The reference in subsection (2)(a) to a company's members includes any person who is not a member but to whom shares in the company have been transferred or transmitted by operation of law.

AMENDMENTS AND NOTES

$^a$  Subsection (1) amended by CA 2006, s 1035(3).

$^b$  Subsection (2A) inserted by CA 1989, s 55.

**32.CA85.07**    Subsection (1) regulates appointments of inspectors under circumstances where the court asks for an investigation—such appointments are rare with barely one investigation being undertaken each year.

**32.CA85.08**    Subsection (2) deals with the more common scenario where the Secretary of State acting on his own initiative appoints inspectors. The criteria for such an appointment are outlined in subsection (2) but it should be noted by reference to subsection (3) that the fact that the company is in the process of being wound up is no barrier to such appointment. Section 432 investigations can be protracted affairs typically costing millions of pounds to complete. The most recent section 432 investigation to be completed and published looked into the collapse of MG Rover.[15] Other recent completed investigations initiated under section 432(2) include Mirror Group Newspapers plc (2001), TransTec plc (2003), and Queens Moat Houses plc (2004). It is made clear by subsection (2A) that an inspector may be appointed on the understanding that the final report will not be published. The power of appointment under section 432 is subordinate to any power/obligation to investigate arising under section 431 (see subsection (3)). However, a government investigation cannot be avoided by putting a company into voluntary liquidation. Subsection (4) is a definition provision. On discretion generally and government investigations see *Norwest Holst Ltd v Secretary of State for Trade and Industry*.[16]

### 433  Inspectors' powers during investigation

**32.CA85.09**    (1)  If inspectors appointed under section 431 or 432 to investigate the affairs of a company think it necessary for the purposes of their investigation to investigate also the affairs of another body corporate which is or at any relevant time has been the company's subsidiary or holding company, or a subsidiary of its holding company or a holding company of its subsidiary, they have power to do so; and they shall report on the affairs of the other body corporate so far as they think that the results of their investigation of its affairs are relevant to the investigation of the affairs of the company first mentioned above.

(2)  [...]$^a$

AMENDMENTS AND NOTES

$^a$  Subsection (2) repealed by the Financial Services Act 1986.

**32.CA85.10**    Subsection (1) represents an erosion of the fundamental principle that each company within a group is to be regarded as a separate legal entity. This reflects the practical facts of life within the modern business corporation operating a group structure.

**32.CA85.11**    Subsection (2) was repealed by the Financial Services Act 1986.

---

[15]  For initiation, see DTI Press Notice, 31 May 2005 and for publication of report see MacGregor and Newey, *Report on the Affairs of Phoenix Venture Holdings Ltd, MG Rover Group Ltd and 33 other companies*, Department of BIS, 11 September 2009. For follow up see BIS Press Notice 9 May 2011 (disqualification undertakings accepted).

[16]  [1978] Ch 201.

## 434 Production of documents and evidence to inspectors

(1) When inspectors are appointed under section 431 or 432, it is the duty of all officers and agents of the company, and of all officers and agents of any other body corporate whose affairs are investigated under section 433(1)—

  (a) to produce to the inspectors all [documents][a] of or relating to the company or, as the case may be, the other body corporate which are in their custody or power,

  (b) to attend before the inspectors when required to do so, and

  (c) otherwise to give the inspectors all assistance in connection with the investigation which they are reasonably able to give.

(2) If the inspectors consider that an officer or agent of the company or other body corporate, or any other person, is or maybe in possession of information relating to a matter which they believe to be relevant to the investigation, they may require him—

  (a) to produce to them any documents in his custody or power relating to that matter,

  (b) to attend before them, and

  (c) otherwise to give them all assistance in connection with the investigation which he is reasonably able to give;

and it is that person's duty to comply with the requirement.[b]

(3) An inspector may for the purposes of the investigation examine any person on oath, and may administer an oath accordingly.[c]

(4) In this section a reference to officers or to agents includes past, as well as present, officers or agents (as the case may be); and 'agents', in relation to a company or other body corporate, includes its bankers and solicitors and persons employed by it as auditors, whether these persons are or are not officers of the company or other body corporate.

(5) An answer given by a person to a question put to him in exercise of powers conferred by this section (whether as it has effect in relation to an investigation under any of sections 431 to 433, or as applied by any other section in this Part) may be used in evidence against him.

[(5A) However, in criminal proceedings in which that person is charged with an offence to which this subsection applies—

  (a) no evidence relating to the answer may be adduced, and

  (b) no question relating to it may be asked,

by or on behalf of the prosecution, unless evidence relating to it is adduced, or a question relating to it is asked, in the proceedings by or on behalf of that person.

(5B) Subsection (5A) applies to any offence other than—

  (a) an offence under section 2 or 5 of the Perjury Act 1911 (false statements made on oath otherwise than in judicial proceedings or made otherwise than on oath); or

  (b) an offence under section 44(1) or (2) of the Criminal Law (Consolidation) (Scotland) Act 1995 (false statements made on oath or otherwise than on oath).][d][; or

  (c) an offence under Article 7 or 10 of the Perjury (Northern Ireland) Order 1979 (false statements made on oath otherwise than in judicial proceedings or made otherwise than on oath).][e]

(6) In this section 'document' includes information recorded in any form.[f]

[(7) The power under this section to require its production of a document includes power, in the case of a document not in hard copy form, to require the production of a copy of the document.][g]

[(8) An inspector may take copies of or extracts from a document produced in pursuance of this section.][h]

AMENDMENTS AND NOTES

[a] Subsection (1)(a) amended by CA 1989, s 56.

[b] Subsection (2) substituted by CA 1989, s 56.

[c] Subsection (3) substituted by CA 1989, s 56.

[d] Subsections (5A) and (5B) inserted by the Youth Justice and Criminal Evidence Act 1999.

[e] Inserted by the Companies Act 2006 (Consequential Amendments, Transitional Provisions and Savings) Order 2009, SI 2009/1941, Sch 1 para 57.

[f] Subsection (6) inserted by subs (6) (since replaced). Subsection (6) then replaced by CA 2006, s 1038.

[g] Subsection (7) inserted by CA 2006, s 1038.

[h] Subsection (8) inserted by CA 2006, s 1038.

**32.CA85.13**    Subsections (1), (4), and (6) outline the duty of company officers (as defined by subsection (4)) to cooperate with the investigation.[17] Cooperation includes delivery up of documents (see subsection (6)).

**32.CA85.14**    Subsection (2) states that inspectors can compel an officer to cooperate. This obligation to assist the investigation is reinforced by section 436, which deals with liability for contempt. Subsection (3) relates to examinations on oath which can be conducted by an inspector.

**32.CA85.15**    Subsections (5), (5A), and (5B) relate to evidential matters and subsections (5A) and (5B) are designed to cater for the criticisms raised in the European Court of Human Rights in *Saunders v UK*.[18] In *R v Lyons et al*,[19] however, it was confirmed by the House of Lords that subsections (5A) and (5B) were not intended to have retrospective effect and therefore convictions based upon evidence deemed admissible by subsection (5) could not be overturned. On admissibility and subsection (5) see *Karak Rubber Co Ltd v Burden*.[20]

**32.CA85.16**    On the power to require the production of documents under subsections (7) and (8) see Explanatory Note to the Bill when it entered the Commons in May 2006, paragraph 1230.

### 436   Obstruction of inspectors treated as contempt of court

**32.CA85.17**    [(1) If any person—
       (a)   fails to comply with section 434(1)(a) or (c),
       (b)   refuses to comply with a requirement under section 434(1)(b) or (2), or
       (c)   refuses to answer any question put to him by the inspectors for the purposes of the investigation,
     the inspectors may certify that fact in writing to the court.][a]
   (2)   [...][b]
   (3)   The court may thereupon enquire into the case; and, after hearing any witnesses who may be produced against or on behalf of the alleged offender and after hearing any statement which may be offered in defence, the court may punish the offender in like manner as if he had been guilty of contempt of the court.

A MENDMENTS AND N OTES

   [a]   Subsection (1) amended by CA 1989, s 56(6).
   [b]   Subsection (2) repealed by CA 1989, s 56(6).

**32.CA85.18**    Subsections (1) and (3) relate to the use of the sanction of contempt of court to strengthen the hand of the inspectors. Subsection (3) in particular explains the procedural aspects of the matter. Subsection (2) was repealed by the Companies Act 1989, section 56(6).

### 437   Inspectors' reports

**32.CA85.19**    (1)   The inspectors may, and if so directed by the Secretary of State shall, make interim reports to the Secretary of State, and on the conclusion of their investigation shall make a final report to him. [...][a]
   [(1A) Any persons who have been appointed under section 431 or 432 may at any time and, if the Secretary of State directs them to do so, shall inform him of any matters coming to their knowledge as a result of their investigations.][b]
   (1B)   [...][c]
   (1C)   [...][d]
   (2)   If the inspectors were appointed under section 432 in pursuance of an order of the court, the Secretary of State shall furnish a copy of any report of theirs to the court.
   [(2A) If the company is registered under the Companies Act 2006 in Northern Ireland the Secretary of State must send a copy of any interim or final report by the inspectors to the Department of Enterprise, Trade and Investment in Northern Ireland.][e]
   (3)   In any case the Secretary of State may, if he thinks fit—
       (a)   forward a copy of any report made by the inspectors to the company's registered office,
       (b)   furnish a copy on request and on payment of the prescribed fee to—
          (i)   any member of the company or other body corporate which is the subject of the report,
          (ii)   any person whose conduct is referred to in the report,
          (iii)   the auditors of that company or body corporate,

---

[17]   For background comment, see McCormack [1993] JBL 425, 428 *et seq.*
[18]   [1997] BCC 872.
[19]   [2002] 3 WLR 1562.
[20]   [1971] 1 WLR 1748.

  (iv) the applicants for the investigation,
  (v)  any other person whose financial interests appear to the Secretary of State to be affected
       by the matters dealt with in the report, whether as a creditor of the company or body
       corporate, or otherwise, and
  (c)  cause any such report to be printed and published.

AMENDMENTS AND NOTES

[a]  Part of subs (1) repealed by CA 2006, Sch 16.

[b]  Subsection (1A) inserted by the Financial Services Act 1986.

[c]  Subsection (1B) repealed by CA 2006, Sch 16.

[d]  Subsection (1C) repealed by CA 2006, Sch 16.

[e]  Subsection (2A) inserted by the Companies Act 2006 (Consequential Amendments, Transitional
     Provisions and Savings) Order 2009, SI 2009/1941, Sch 1, para 57.

Subsection (1) makes provision for interim reports of investigations. Subsection (1A) requires inspec-    **32.CA85.20**
tors to keep the Secretary of State posted as to ongoing developments in the investigation if so
requested. As stated above there are few instances of court-initiated investigations so subsection (2) is
hardly relevant in practice. Subsection (3) deals with the output of any report resulting from an
investigation. Wide dissemination to all interested parties is the order of the day.

## 438  Power to bring civil proceedings on company's behalf

[Repealed by Companies Act 2006, section 1176]                                                             **32.CA85.21**

The power under subsection (1) had hardly ever been exercised—for a rarity see *Selangor United*    **32.CA85.22**
*Rubber Estates Ltd v Cradock*.[21] The clue for this relative inactivity may have lain in subsection (2),
which involved a potential charge on the public exchequer where a derivative action was brought by the
Secretary of State.

The Company Law Review, *Final Report*[22] (paragraphs 15.26 and 15.27) called for the repeal of this    **32.CA85.23**
provision. See also the White Paper, *Company Law Reform*[23] at paragraph 4.6. The Companies Act
2006 implements this reform.

## 439  Expenses of investigating a company's affairs

  [(1) The expenses of an investigation under any of the powers conferred by this Part shall be defrayed    **32.CA85.24**
       in the first instance by the Secretary of State, but he may recover those expenses from the persons
       liable in accordance with this section.
       There shall be treated as expenses of the investigation, in particular, such reasonable sums as
       the Secretary of State may determine in respect of general staff costs and overheads.][a]
  (2)  A person who is convicted on a prosecution instituted as a result of the investigation, ... may in
       the same proceedings be ordered to pay those expenses to such extent as may be specified in the
       order.[b]
  (3)  [...][c]
  (4)  A body corporate dealt with by [an inspectors' report],[d] where the inspectors were appointed
       otherwise than of the Secretary of State's own motion, is liable except where it was the applicant
       for the investigation, and except so far as the Secretary of State otherwise directs.
  [(5) Where inspectors were appointed—
       (a)  under section 431, or
       (b)  on an application under section 442(3),
       the applicant or applicants for the investigation is or are liable to such extent (if any) as the
       Secretary of State may direct.][e]
  (6)  The report of inspectors appointed otherwise than of the Secretary of State's own motion may, if
       they think fit, and shall if the Secretary of State so directs, include a recommendation as to the
       directions (if any) which they think appropriate, in the light of their investigation, to be given
       under subsection (4) or (5) of this section.
  (7)  [...][f]
  (8)  Any liability to repay the Secretary of State imposed by [subsections (2)][g] above is (subject to
       satisfaction of his right to repayment) a liability also to indemnify all persons against liability under
       subsections (4) and (5); ...[h]
  (9)  A person liable under any one of those subsections is entitled to contribution from any other
       person liable under the same subsection, according to the amount of their respective liabilities
       under it.

---

[21]  [1967] 1 WLR 1168.
[22]  URN 01/942, 2001.
[23]  Cm 6456 (2005).

(10)  Expenses to be defrayed by the Secretary of State under this section shall, so far as not recovered under it, be paid out of money provided by Parliament.

AMENDMENTS AND NOTES

a  Subsection (1) substituted by CA 1989, s 59.

b  Words repealed by CA 2006, s 1176.

c  Subsection (3) repealed by CA 2006, s 1176.

d  Subsection (4) amended by CA 1989, s 59.

e  Subsection (5) substituted by CA 1989, s 59.

f  Subsection (7) repealed by CA 1989, Sch 16.

g  Subsection (8) amended by CA 2006, s 1176.

h  Words repealed by CA 2006, s 1176.

**32.CA85.25**  Subsection (1) specifies who may be liable for the costs of an investigation. Bearing in mind the seniority of inspectors and the protracted nature of investigations this can involve substantial sums of money. If an officer is convicted of an offence arising from matters revealed in the investigation, then he or she may be ordered to meet the expenses of the investigation (subsection (2)). Other possibilities, depending on circumstances are to make the company or applicant(s) liable for investigation costs. Subsections (4) to (5) deal with these possibilities. Subsection (6) permits the inspectors to indicate their views as to liability for expenses.

**32.CA85.26**  Subsections (6) to (10) cover other consequential matters including rights of indemnity and contribution.

### 441  Inspectors' report to be evidence

**32.CA85.27**  (1)  A copy of any report of inspectors appointed under [this Part],a certified by the Secretary of State to be a true copy, is admissible in any legal proceedings as evidence of the opinion of the inspectors in relation to any matter contained in the report [and, in proceedings on an application under [section 8 of the Company Directors Disqualification Act 1986],b [or Article 11 of the Company Directors Disqualification (Northern Ireland) Order 2002]c as evidence of any fact stated therein.]d

(2)  A document purporting to be such a certificate as is mentioned above shall be received in evidence and be deemed to be such a certificate, unless the contrary is proved.

AMENDMENTS AND NOTES

a  Amended by CA 1989, s 61.

b  Amended by the Insolvency Act 1986. For discussion of the admissibility issues in general, see *Aaron v Secretary of State for BERR* [2008] EWCA Civ 1146.

c  Inserted by the Companies Act 2006 (Consequential Amendments, Transitional Provisions and Savings) Order 2009, SI 2009/1941, Sch 1 para 57.

d  Amended by the Insolvency Act 1985.

**32.CA85.28**  This section deals with the evidential status of the inspectors' report in any subsequent legal proceedings (such as director disqualification proceedings under section 8 of theCompany Directors Disqualification Act 1986). See also the Companies Act 2006, section 1039.

### 442  Power to investigate company ownership

**32.CA85.29**  (1)  Where it appears to the Secretary of State that there is good reason to do so, he may appoint one or more competent inspectors to investigate and report on the membership of any company, and otherwise with respect to the company, for the purpose of determining the true persons who are or have been financially interested in the success or failure (real or apparent) of the company or able to control or materially to influence its policy.

(2)  [...]a

(3)  If an application for investigation under this section with respect to particular shares or debentures of a company is made to the Secretary of State by members of the company, and the number of applicants or the amount of shares held by them is not less than that required for an application for the appointment of inspectors under section 431(2)(a) or (b), then, subject to the following provisions, the Secretary of State shall appoint inspectors to conduct the investigation applied for.

[(3A) The Secretary of State shall not appoint inspectors if he is satisfied that the application is vexatious; and where inspectors are appointed their terms of appointment shall exclude any matter in so far as the Secretary of State is satisfied that it is unreasonable for it to be investigated.

(3B)  The Secretary of State may, before appointing inspectors, require the applicant or applicants to give security, to an amount not exceeding £5,000, or such other sum as he may by order specify, for payment of the costs of the investigation.

An order under this subsection shall be made by statutory instrument which shall be subject to annulment in pursuance of a resolution of either House of Parliament.

(3C)  If on an application under subsection (3) it appears to the Secretary of State that the powers conferred by section 444 are sufficient for the purposes of investigating the matters which inspectors would be appointed to investigate, he may instead conduct the investigation under that section.][b]

(4)  Subject to the terms of their appointment, the inspectors' powers extend to the investigation of any circumstances suggesting the existence of an arrangement or understanding which, though not legally binding, is or was observed or likely to be observed in practice and which is relevant to the purposes of the investigation.

AMENDMENTS AND NOTES

[a]  Section 442(2) repealed by CA 2006, s 1035(5) and Sch 16.

[b]  Subsections (3A)–(3C) inserted CA 1989, s 62.

This confers jurisdiction to investigate formally company membership. Such formal investigations are less common these days as public companies themselves can investigate who owns shares by invoking the procedure formerly contained in section 212 of the Companies Act 1985 (now Companies Act 2006, section 793). It is believed that only three section 442 investigations have taken place since 1991.[24] The investigation into Mirror Group Newspapers plc (concluded in 2001) was partly based upon section 442. Informal investigations under section 444 are also a possibility, but these are even rarer birds.  **32.CA85.30**

The 1989 Act amended section 442 of the Companies Act 1985 with regard to investigations into company membership. The Secretary of State is required by section 442(3) to order an investigation if the applicants constitute 200 members or own at least 10 per cent of the voting shares. However, even if that threshold is met, the Secretary of State may dismiss the application as vexatious or limit the scope of the investigation (section 442 (3A)) or order an informal investigation under section 444 instead. Security for costs may be demanded. Subsection (4) would appear to cover investigations into suspected concert parties.  **32.CA85.31**

### 443   Provisions applicable on investigation under section 442

(1)  For purposes of an investigation under section 442, sections 433(1), 434, 436 and 437 apply with the necessary modifications of references to the affairs of the company or to those of any other body corporate, subject however to the following subsections.  **32.CA85.32**

(2)  Those sections apply to—

    (a)  all persons who are or have been, or whom the inspector has reasonable cause to believe to be or have been, financially interested in the success or failure or the apparent success or failure of the company or any other body corporate whose membership is investigated with that of the company, or able to control or materially influence its policy (including persons concerned only on behalf of others), and

    (b)  any other person whom the inspector has reasonable cause to believe possesses information relevant to the investigation,

as they apply in relation to officers and agents of the company or the other body corporate (as the case may be).

(3)  If the Secretary of State is of opinion that there is good reason for not divulging any part of a report made by virtue of section 442 and this section, he may under section 437 disclose the report with the omission of that part; and he may cause to be kept by the registrar of companies a copy of the report with that part omitted or, in the case of any other such report, a copy of the whole report.

(4)  […][a]

AMENDMENTS AND NOTES

[a]  Subsection (4) repealed by CA 1989, s 212 and Sch 24.

This deals with a range of issues consequential upon a section 442 investigation into company membership. Essentially it extends other investigation provisions *mutatis mutandis* to this type of investigation. Subsection (2) indicates the range of persons who may be required to provide information. Subsection (3) permits censored reports under section 442.  **32.CA85.33**

---

[24]  For discussion of the s 442 investigation into House of Fraser shares, see Milman (1984) 5 *Company Law* 188.

**444  Power to obtain information as to those interested in shares, etc.**

**32.CA85.34**

(1)  If it appears to the Secretary of State that there is good reason to investigate the ownership of any shares in or debentures of a company and that it is unnecessary to appoint inspectors for the purpose, he may require any person whom he has reasonable cause to believe to have or to be able to obtain any information as to the present and past interests in those shares or debentures and the names and addresses of the persons interested and of any persons who act or have acted on their behalf in relation to the shares or debentures to give any such information to the Secretary of State.

(2)  For this purpose a person is deemed to have an interest in shares or debentures if he has any right to acquire or dispose of them or of any interest in them, or to vote in respect of them, or if his consent is necessary for the exercise of any of the rights of other persons interested in them, or if other persons interested in them can be required, or are accustomed, to exercise their rights in accordance with his instructions.

(3)  A person who fails to give information required of him under this section, or who in giving such information makes any statement which he knows to be false in a material particular, or recklessly makes any statement which is false in a material particular, commits an offence.[a]

(4)  A person guilty of an offence under this section is liable—
   (a)  on conviction on indictment, to imprisonment for a term not exceeding two years or a fine (or both);
   (b)  on summary conviction—
      (i)  in England and Wales, to imprisonment for a term not exceeding twelve months or to a fine not exceeding the statutory maximum (or both) and, for continued contravention, a daily default fine not exceeding one-fiftieth of the statutory maximum;
      (ii)  in Scotland or Northern Ireland, to imprisonment for a term not exceeding six months, or to a fine not exceeding the statutory maximum (or both) and, for continued contravention, a daily default fine not exceeding one-fiftieth of the statutory maximum.[b]

AMENDMENTS AND NOTES

[a]  Subsection (3) amended by CA 2006, Sch 3.

[b]  Subsection (4) added by CA 2006, Sch 3.

**32.CA85.35**  This offers an informal option for investigating company membership, etc, as an alternative to a formal probe under section 442. Again note the possibility of the company making its own enquiries under the Companies Act 2006, section 793 (formerly Companies Act 1985, section 212).

**32.CA85.36**  For illuminating case law see *Savings and Investment Bank Ltd v Gasco Investments (Netherlands) BV*.[25]

**445  Power to impose restrictions on shares and debentures**

**32.CA85.37**

(1)  If in connection with an investigation under either section 442 or 444 it appears to the Secretary of State that there is difficulty in finding out the relevant facts about any shares (whether issued or to be issued), he may by order direct that the shares shall until further order be subject to the restrictions of Part XV of this Act.

[(1A)If the Secretary of State is satisfied that an order under subsection (1) may unfairly affect the rights of third parties in respect of shares then the Secretary of State, for the purpose of protecting such rights and subject to such terms as he thinks fit, may direct that such acts by such persons or descriptions of persons and for such purposes as may be set out in the order, shall not constitute a breach of the restrictions of Part XV of this Act.][a]

(2)  This section, and Part XV in its application to orders under it, apply in relation to debentures as in relation to shares [save that subsection (1A) shall not so apply.][b]

AMENDMENTS AND NOTES

[a]  Subsection (1A) inserted by the Companies (Disclosure of Interests in Shares) (Orders Imposing Restrictions on Shares) Regulations 1991, SI 1991/1646.

[b]  Subsection (2) amended by the Companies (Disclosure of Interests in Shares) (Orders Imposing Restrictions on Shares) Regulations 1991, SI 1991/1646.

**32.CA85.38**  This confers on the Secretary of State a useful sanction to strengthen the hands of inspectors where an investigation is being carried out either under section 442 or section 444.

**32.CA85.39**  On the possibility of lifting restrictions see *Re Westminster Property Group Ltd*.[26]

---

[25]  [1984] 1 WLR 271.
[26]  [1984] 1 WLR 1117.

## 446  Investigation of share dealings

[Repealed by Schedule 16 of Companies Act 2006]                         **32.CA85.40**

This provided for a different form of investigation concerned with possible breaches of sections 323,    **32.CA85.41**
324, and 328 of the Companies Act 1985. Some of these provisions are repealed by the Companies Act
2006 and indeed section 446 suffered the same fate in that legislation. Section 446 investigations were
rare with only three such investigations having taken place since 1991.

### *Powers of Secretary of State to give directions to inspectors*

### 446A  General powers to give directions[a]

(1) In exercising his functions an inspector shall comply with any direction given to him by the    **32.CA85.42**
    Secretary of State under this section.
(2) The Secretary of State may give an inspector appointed under section 431, 432(2) or 442(1) a
    direction—
    (a) as to the subject matter of his investigation (whether by reference to a specified area of a
        company's operation, a specified transaction, a period of time or otherwise), or
    (b) which requires the inspector to take or not to take a specified step in his investigation.
(3) The Secretary of State may give an inspector appointed under any provision of this Part a direction
    requiring him to secure that a specified report under section 437—
    (a) includes the inspector's views on a specified matter,
    (b) does not include any reference to a specified matter,
    (c) is made in a specified form or manner, or
    (d) is made by a specified date.
(4) A direction under this section—
    (a) may be given on an inspector's appointment,
    (b) may vary or revoke a direction previously given, and
    (c) may be given at the request of an inspector.
(5) In this section—
    (a) a reference to an inspector's investigation includes any investigation he undertakes, or could
        undertake, under section 433(1) (power to investigate affairs of holding company or
        subsidiary);
    (b) 'specified' means specified in a direction under this section.

AMENDMENTS AND NOTES

[a] Section 446A inserted by CA 2006, s 1035(1).

The Government proposed this new statutory power as a form of case management to deal with    **32.CA85.43**
increasingly protracted investigations—see paragraph 6.3 of the 2005 White Paper *Company Law
Reform*.[27] See also the Explanatory Note published with the amended Bill when it entered the
Commons in May 2006 (paragraphs 1207 *et seq*). It must be remembered that investigations are usually
carried out by independent lawyers and accountants of senior status, and there was perceived to be a
need to be more prescriptive as to how investigations should be managed. Protracted investigations
that were going nowhere needed to be terminated to reduce the burden on the public exchequer.
Section 446A enables the Secretary of State to give binding directions to inspectors who are obliged to
comply (section 446A(1)). Section 446A(2) relates to the nature of the directions and is designed to
improve the focus and efficiency of investigations. Report contents also fall under this new prescriptive
regime by virtue of section 446A(3). The timing of these directions is governed by section 446A(4). An
interpretation provision is contained in section 446A(5).

### 446B  Direction to terminate investigation[a]

(1) The Secretary of State may direct an inspector to take no further steps in his investigation.    **32.CA85.44**
(2) The Secretary of State may give a direction under this section to an inspector appointed under
    section 432(1) or 442(3) only on the grounds that it appears to him that—
    (a) matters have come to light in the course of the inspector's investigation which suggest that
        a criminal offence has been committed, and
    (b) those matters have been referred to the appropriate prosecuting authority.
(3) Where the Secretary of State gives a direction under this section, any direction already given to the
    inspector under section 437(1) to produce an interim report, and any direction given to him under
    section 446A(3) in relation to such a report, shall cease to have effect.
(4) Where the Secretary of State gives a direction under this section, the inspector shall not make a
    final report to the Secretary of State unless—

[27] Cm 6456.

    (a)   the direction was made on the grounds mentioned in subsection (2) and the Secretary of State directs the inspector to make a final report to him, or

    (b)   the inspector was appointed under section 432(1) (appointment in pursuance of order of the court).

(5)   An inspector shall comply with any direction given to him under this section.

(6)   In this section, a reference to an inspector's investigation includes any investigation he undertakes, or could undertake, under section 433(1) (power to investigate affairs of holding company or subsidiary).

AMENDMENTS AND NOTES

  ª   Section 446B inserted by CA 2006, s 1035(1).

**32.CA85.45**     This new provision details the power of the Secretary of State in circumstances defined by section 446B(2) to give directions to inspectors to terminate inspections (widely defined by subsection (6)). Such a direction can only be given where criminal matters have come to light and such matters are being dealt with by the prosecuting authority. Again the inspectors are obliged to comply (section 446B(5)). The effect of such a direction is explained by section 446B(3) and (4).

## Resignation, removal and replacement of inspectors

### 446C   Resignation and revocation of appointmentª

**32.CA85.46**     (1)   An inspector may resign by notice in writing to the Secretary of State.

(2)   The Secretary of State may revoke the appointment of an inspector by notice in writing to the inspector.

AMENDMENTS AND NOTES

  ª   Section 446C inserted by CA 2006, s 1036.

**32.CA85.47**     Section 446C deals with the resignation by and revocation of the appointment of an inspector. Where the Secretary of State revokes the appointment there is no explicit requirement for good cause to be shown, though presumably it will be subject to a *Wednesbury*-type unreasonableness test.[28]

### 446D   Appointment of replacement inspectorsª

**32.CA85.48**     (1)   Where—

    (a)   an inspector resigns,

    (b)   an inspector's appointment is revoked, or

    (c)   an inspector dies,

    the Secretary of State may appoint one or more competent inspectors to continue the investigation.

(2)   An appointment under subsection (1) shall be treated for the purposes of this Part (apart from this section) as an appointment under the provision of this Part under which the former inspector was appointed.

(3)   The Secretary of State must exercise his power under subsection (1) so as to secure that at least one inspector continues the investigation.

(4)   Subsection (3) does not apply if—

    (a)   the Secretary of State could give any replacement inspector a direction under section 446B (termination of investigation), and

    (b)   such a direction would (under subsection (4) of that section) result in a final report not being made.

(5)   In this section, references to an investigation include any investigation the former inspector conducted under section 433(1) (power to investigate affairs of holding company or subsidiary).

AMENDMENTS AND NOTES

  ª   Section 446D inserted by CA 2006, s 1036.

**32.CA85.49**     Section 446D deals with the consequence of an inspector resigning, or dying, or being removed by laying down a procedure for the appointment of a replacement inspector to continue the investigation (see section 446D(5)). The Secretary of State cannot let the investigation drop simply because of a vacancy arising—instead, he would have to exercise powers under section 446B of the Companies Act 1985. Note the qualification imposed by section 446D(4).

---

[28]   See *Associated Provincial Picture Houses Ltd v Wednesbury Corporation* [1948] 1 KB 223.

## *Power to obtain information from former inspectors etc*

### 446E  Obtaining information from former inspectors etc.[a]

(1)  This section applies to a person who was appointed as an inspector under this Part—
    (a)  who has resigned, or
    (b)  whose appointment has been revoked.

(2)  This section also applies to an inspector to whom the Secretary of State has given a direction under section 446B (termination of investigation).

(3)  The Secretary of State may direct a person to whom this section applies to produce documents obtained or generated by that person during the course of his investigation to—
    (a)  the Secretary of State, or
    (b)  an inspector appointed under this Part.

(4)  The power under subsection (3) to require production of a document includes power, in the case of a document not in hard copy form, to require the production of a copy of the document—
    (a)  in hard copy form, or
    (b)  in a form from which a hard copy can be readily obtained.

(5)  The Secretary of State may take copies of or extracts from a document produced in pursuance of this section.

(6)  The Secretary of State may direct a person to whom this section applies to inform him of any matters that came to that person's knowledge as a result of his investigation.

(7)  A person shall comply with any direction given to him under this section.

(8)  In this section—
    (a)  references to the investigation of a former inspector or inspector include any investigation he conducted under section 433(1) (power to investigate affairs of holding company or subsidiary), and
    (b)  'document' includes information recorded in any form.

AMENDMENTS AND NOTES

[a]  Section 446E inserted by CA 2006, s 1037(1).

**32.CA85.50**

This new provision enables the Secretary of State to obtain information from a former inspector in hard copy or electronic form (see subsection (4)). It represents a necessary transitional measure and is likely to be of particular importance in cases where an inspector has been removed, a possibility enhanced by the insertion of section 446C. The inspector must comply with directions (see subsection (6)).

**32.CA85.51**

## *Requisition and seizure of books and papers*

### [447  Power to require documents and information

(1)  The Secretary of State may act under subsections (2) and (3) in relation to a company.

(2)  The Secretary of State may give directions to the company requiring it—
    (a)  to produce such documents (or documents of such description) as may be specified in the directions;
    (b)  to provide such information (or information of such description) as may be so specified.

(3)  The Secretary of State may authorise a person (an investigator) to require the company or any other person—
    (a)  to produce such documents (or documents of such description) as the investigator may specify;
    (b)  to provide such information (or information of such description) as the investigator may specify.

(4)  A person on whom a requirement under subsection (3) is imposed may require the investigator to produce evidence of his authority.

(5)  A requirement under subsection (2) or (3) must be complied with at such time and place as may be specified in the directions or by the investigator (as the case may be).

(6)  The production of a document in pursuance of this section does not affect any lien which a person has on the document.

(7)  The Secretary of State or the investigator (as the case may be) may take copies of or extracts from a document produced in pursuance of this section.

(8)  A 'document' includes information recorded in any form.

(9)  The power under this section to require production of a document includes power, in the case of a document not in hard copy form, to require the production of a copy of the document—
    (a)  in hard copy form, or
    (b)  in a form from which a hard copy can be readily obtained.][a], [b]

**32.CA85.52**

AMENDMENTS AND NOTES

[a]  Section 447 substituted by the Companies (Audit, Investigations and Community Enterprise) Act 2004.

[b]  New subs (9) substituted by CA 2006, s 1038(2).

**32.CA85.53** This provision which was remodelled by the 2004 Act represents a lesser form of enquiry in lieu of a full blown enquiry. It enhances the power of investigators to secure access to information. Investigations under section 447 can be conducted by Company Investigation Branch staff rather than requiring the usage of more expensive external inspectors. It enables either the Secretary of State or investigators to demand access to documents etc. Copies can be taken of documents so accessed (subsection (7)). Rights of lien are not prejudiced by these access rights (subsection (6)). The 2004 Act revision has widened the powers of investigators by broadening their power to obtain information without being restricted to seeking answers related to particular documents. Subsection (3) marks a move towards inspectors becoming more like full-fledged investigators. The former requirement that the Secretary of State must have good reason before exercising section 447 powers has been dropped but, in the light of fundamental rights considerations, this is unlikely to dilute the substance of that requirement.

**32.CA85.54** Looking at completed section 447 investigations this genre runs into three figures in most years; in 2004–2005 the figure was 174, representing 100 per cent of all completed investigation activity (source *Companies in 2004–05*, HC 544, Table 2). This figure had fallen to 149 in 2010/11. It takes approximately three months on average to complete a section 447 inquiry as compared to several years for a typical formal investigation. Section 447 investigation reports are not published. Thus section 447 investigations are cost effective and favoured by all parties.

### 447A Information provided: evidence

**32.CA85.55** [(1) A statement made by a person in compliance with a requirement under section 447 may be used in evidence against him.

(2) But in criminal proceedings in which the person is charged with a relevant offence—
  (a) no evidence relating to the statement may be adduced by or on behalf of the prosecution, and
  (b) no question relating to it may be asked by or on behalf of the prosecution,
  unless evidence relating to it is adduced or a question relating to it is asked in the proceedings by or on behalf of that person.

(3) A relevant offence is any offence other than the following—
  (a) an offence under section 451,
  (b) an offence under section 5 of the Perjury Act 1911 (false statement made otherwise than on oath), or
  (c) an offence under section 44(2) of the Criminal Law (Consolidation) (Scotland) Act 1995 (false statement made otherwise than on oath).][a][; or
  (d) an offence under Article 10 of the Perjury (Northern Ireland) Order 1979 (false statements made otherwise than on oath).] [b]

AMENDMENTS AND NOTES

[a] Section 447A inserted by the Companies (Audit, Investigations and Community Enterprise) Act 2004, Sch 2.

[b] Subsection (3)(d) inserted by the Companies Act 2006 (Consequential Amendments, Transitional Provisions and Savings) Order 2009, SI 2009/1941, Sch 1 para 57.

**32.CA85.56** This new provision covers a range of evidential issues. Fundamental rights considerations, in particular the privilege against self incrimination reinforced by the requirements of ECHR, have helped to shape the substance of this section. At the end of the day this provision seeks to maintain a balance between the need for effective investigation procedures and the expectation that an individual's rights will be protected.

### [448 Entry and search of premises

**32.CA85.57** (1) A justice of the peace may issue a warrant under this section if satisfied on information on oath given by or on behalf of the Secretary of State, or by a person appointed or authorised to exercise powers under this Part, that there are reasonable grounds for believing that there are on any premises documents whose production has been required under this Part and which have not been produced in compliance with the requirement.

(2) A justice of the peace may also issue a warrant under this section if satisfied on information on oath given by or on behalf of the Secretary of State, or by a person appointed or authorised to exercise powers under this Part—
  (a) that there are reasonable grounds for believing that an offence has been committed for which the penalty on conviction on indictment is imprisonment for a term of not less than two years and that there are on any premises documents relating to whether the offence has been committed, and
  (b) that the Secretary of State, or the person so appointed or authorised, has power to require the production of the documents under this Part, and

(c)  that there are reasonable grounds for believing that if production was so required the documents would not be produced but would be removed from the premises, hidden, tampered with or destroyed.

(3)  A warrant under this section shall authorise a constable, together with any other person named in it and any other constables—
   (a)  to enter the premises specified in the information, using such force as is reasonably necessary for the purpose;
   (b)  to search the premises and take possession of any documents appearing to be such documents as are mentioned in subsection (1) or (2), as the case may be, or to take, in relation to any such documents, any other steps which may appear to be necessary for preserving them or preventing interference with them;
   (c)  to take copies of any such documents; and
   (d)  to require any person named in the warrant to provide an explanation of them or to state where they may be found.

(4)  If in the case of a warrant under subsection (2) the justice of the peace is satisfied on information on oath that there are reasonable grounds for believing that there are also on the premises other documents relevant to the investigation, the warrant shall also authorise the actions mentioned in subsection (3) to be taken in relation to such documents.

(5)  A warrant under this section shall continue in force until the end of the period of one month beginning with the day on which it is issued.

(6)  Any documents of which possession is taken under this section may be retained—
   (a)  for a period of three months; or
   (b)  if within that period proceedings to which the documents are relevant are commenced against any person for any criminal offence, until the conclusion of those proceedings.

(7)  Any person who intentionally obstructs the exercise of any rights conferred by a warrant issued under this section or fails without reasonable excuse to comply with any requirement imposed in accordance with subsection(3)(d) is guilty of an offence...[a]

(7A)  A person guilty of an offence under this section is liable—
   (a)  on conviction on indictment, to a fine;
   (b)  on summary conviction, to a fine not exceeding the statutory maximum.[b]

(8)  For the purposes of sections 449 and 451A (provision for security of information) documents obtained under this section shall be treated as if they had been obtained under the provision of this Part under which their production was or, as the case may be, could have been required.

(9)  In the application of this section to Scotland for the references to a justice of the peace substitute references to a justice of the peace or a sheriff, and for the references to information on oath substitute references to evidence on oath.

(10) In this section 'document' includes information recorded in any form.][c]

AMENDMENTS AND NOTES

[a]  Words deleted by CA 2006, Sch 16.
[b]  Subsection (7A) added by CA 2006, Sch 3.
[c]  This provision was reconstituted by CA 1989, s 64.

This substitutes a new section 448 in the Companies Act 1985. This is an important ancillary power deemed necessary to facilitate any sort of inquiry. This provision deals with powers of entry/search of premises. Such entry/search will only be permitted if a warrant is first obtained from magistrates or the sheriff in Scotland (section 448(9)) (compare section 448A here). Warrants will only be granted where reasonable suspicion exists. The entry/search must be carried out by a constable together with any other person named in the warrant. Warrants remain in force for a maximum of one month (section 448(5)). It is an offence to obstruct the execution of the warrant (section 448(7)).    **32.CA85.58**

[448A  Protection in relation to certain disclosures: information provided to Secretary of State

(1)  A person who makes a relevant disclosure is not liable by reason only of that disclosure in any proceedings relating to a breach of an obligation of confidence.    **32.CA85.59**

(2)  A relevant disclosure is a disclosure which satisfies each of the following conditions—
   (a)  it is made to the Secretary of State otherwise than in compliance with a requirement under this Part;
   (b)  it is of a kind that the person making the disclosure could be required to make in pursuance of this Part;
   (c)  the person who makes the disclosure does so in good faith and in the reasonable belief that the disclosure is capable of assisting the Secretary of State for the purposes of the exercise of his functions under this Part;

(d)  the information disclosed is not more than is reasonably necessary for the purpose of assisting the Secretary of State for the purposes of the exercise of those functions;

(e)  the disclosure is not one falling within subsection (3) or (4).

(3)  A disclosure falls within this subsection if the disclosure is prohibited by virtue of any enactment [whenever passed or made].[a]

(4)  A disclosure falls within this subsection if—

(a)  it is made by a person carrying on the business of banking or by a lawyer, and

(b)  it involves the disclosure of information in respect of which he owes an obligation of confidence in that capacity.

[(5)  In this section 'enactment' has the meaning given by section 1293 of the Companies Act 2006.][b][c]

AMENDMENTS AND NOTES

[a]  Inserted by the Companies Act 2006 (Consequential Amendments, Transitional Provisions and Savings) Order 2009, SI 2009/1941, Sch 1 para 57.

[b]  Subsection (5) substituted by the Companies Act 2006 (Consequential Amendments, Transitional Provisions and Savings) Order 2009, SI 2009/1941, Sch 1, para 57.

[c]  Section 448A inserted by Companies (Audit, Investigations and Community Enterprise) Act 2004, s 22.

**32.CA85.60**  This provision inserts section 448A into the Companies Act 1985. It excuses parties providing information from any breach of duty of confidentiality in making certain relevant disclosures (as defined by subsections (2) to (5)) to the Secretary of State. The five conditions in subsection (2) must be satisfied for the disclosure to be deemed 'relevant'. In effect, therefore, this is a whistleblowing provision. However according to subsections (3) to (5) the provision does not apply to disclosures made by lawyers or bankers in breach of their duty of confidentiality, nor does it operate if the duty not to disclose is imposed by statute. The disclosure in order to enjoy protection under section 448A must be made in good faith and must be reasonably necessary to enable the Secretary of State to carry out the statutory investigation function. This should facilitate the disclosure of information where such disclosure would otherwise constitute a breach of confidence. Statutory prohibitions on disclosure may also frustrate the investigation.

## [449  Provision for security of information obtained

**32.CA85.61**  (1)  This section applies to information (in whatever form) obtained—

(a)  in pursuance of a requirement imposed under section 447;

(b)  by means of a relevant disclosure within the meaning of section 448A(2);

(c)  by an investigator in consequence of the exercise of his powers under section 453A.

(2)  Such information must not be disclosed unless the disclosure—

(a)  is made to a person specified in Schedule 15C, or

(b)  is of a description specified in Schedule 15D.

(3)  The Secretary of State may by order amend Schedules 15C and 15D.

(4)  An order under subsection (3) must not—

(a)  amend Schedule 15C by specifying a person unless the person exercises functions of a public nature (whether or not he exercises any other function);

(b)  amend Schedule 15D by adding or modifying a description of disclosure unless the purpose for which the disclosure is permitted is likely to facilitate the exercise of a function of a public nature.

(5)  An order under subsection (3) must be made by statutory instrument subject to annulment in pursuance of a resolution of either House of Parliament.

(6)  A person who discloses any information in contravention of this section is guilty of an offence.[a]

(6A) A person guilty of an offence under this section is liable—

(a)  on conviction on indictment, to imprisonment for a term not exceeding two years or a fine (or both);

(b)  on summary conviction—

(i)  in England and Wales, to imprisonment for a term not exceeding twelve months or to a fine not exceeding the statutory maximum (or both);

(ii)  in Scotland or Northern Ireland, to imprisonment for a term not exceeding six months, or to a fine not exceeding the statutory maximum (or both).[b]

(7)  [...][c]

(8)  Any information which may by virtue of this section be disclosed to a person specified in Schedule 15C may be disclosed to any officer or employee of the person.

(9)  This section does not prohibit the disclosure of information if the information is or has been available to the public from any other source.

(10) For the purposes of this section, information obtained by an investigator in consequence of the exercise of his powers under section 453A includes information obtained by a person accompanying the investigator in pursuance of subsection (4) of that section in consequence of that person's accompanying the investigator.

(11) Nothing in this section authorises the making of a disclosure in contravention of the Data Protection Act 1998.]d

AMENDMENTS AND NOTES

a  Subsection (6) amended by CA 2006, Sch 16.

b  Subsection (6A) added by CA 2006, Sch 3.

c  Subsection (7) repealed by CA 2006, Sch 16.

d  Section 449 substituted by the Companies (Audit, Investigations and Community Enterprise) Act 2004, Sch 2.

This represents a significant check and balance by ensuring a degree of confidentiality for information   **32.CA85.62**
gleaned pursuant to an inquiry. However, it must be read in the light of section 451A. Persons to whom
permitted disclosures of information gleaned from investigations are identified in Schedule 15C and
permitted disclosures are listed in Schedule 15D (both inserted by the 2004 Act). These schedules can
by virtue of subsection (3) be amended by statutory instrument—see, for example, The Companies
(Disclosure of Information) (Designated Authorities) Order 2006, SI 2006/1644 which amends Schedule 15D by adding the Gambling Commission to the list.

## 450  Punishment for destroying, mutilating etc. company documents

(1) An officer of a company[a] [...]b who—   **32.CA85.63**
    (a) destroys, mutilates or falsifies, or is privy to the destruction, mutilation or falsification of a
        document affecting, or relating to the company's property or affairs, or
    (b) makes, or is privy to the making of, a false entry in such a document,
is guilty of an offence, unless he proves that he had no intention to conceal the state of affairs of the
company or to defeat the law.
[(1A) Subsection (1) applies to an officer of an authorised insurance company which is not a body
corporate as it applies to an officer of a company.]c
(2) Such a person as above mentioned who fraudulently either parts with, alters or makes an
    omission in any such document or is privy to fraudulent parting with, fraudulent altering or
    fraudulent making of an omission in, any such document, is guilty of an offence.
(3) A person guilty of an offence under this section is liable—
    (a) on conviction on indictment, to imprisonment for a term not exceeding seven years or a fine
        (or both);
    (b) on summary conviction—
        (i) in England and Wales, to imprisonment for a term not exceeding twelve months or to a
           fine not exceeding the statutory maximum (or both);
        (ii) in Scotland or Northern Ireland, to imprisonment for a term not exceeding six months, or
           to a fine not exceeding the statutory maximum (or both).d
(4) [...]e
[(5) In this section 'document' includes information recorded in any form].f

AMENDMENTS AND NOTES

a  Amended by CA 1989, s 66.

b  Repealed by the Financial Services and Markets Act 2000 (Consequential Amendments and Repeals) Order 2001, SI 2001/3649.

c  Subsection (1A) inserted by the Financial Services and Markets Act 2000 (Consequential Amendments and Repeals) Order 2001, SI 2001/3649.

d  New subs (3) substituted by CA 2006, Sch 3.

e  Subsection (4) was repealed by CA 2006, Sch 16.

f  Subsection (5) inserted by CA 1989, s 66.

This provision is necessary to prevent the investigation process being unduly hampered by documents   **32.CA85.64**
(widely construed by subsection (5)) being destroyed or falsified.

## [451  Punishment for furnishing false information

(1) A person commits an offence if in purported compliance with a requirement under section 447 to   **32.CA85.65**
    provide information—
    (a) he provides information which he knows to be false in a material particular;
    (b) he recklessly provides information which is false in a material particular.
(2) A person guilty of an offence under this section is liable—
    (a) on conviction on indictment, to imprisonment for a term not exceeding two years or a fine (or
        both);
    (b) on summary conviction—
        (i) in England and Wales, to imprisonment for a term not exceeding twelve months or to a
           fine not exceeding the statutory maximum (or both);

        (ii)  in Scotland or Northern Ireland, to imprisonment for a term not exceeding six months, or to a fine not exceeding the statutory maximum (or both).[a]

(3)  [...][b, c]

AMENDMENTS AND NOTES

[a]  New subs (2) substituted by CA 2006, Sch 3.

[b]  Subsection (3) repealed by CA 2006, Sch 16.

[c]  Section 451 originally substituted by the Companies (Audit, Investigations and Community Enterprise) Act 2004, Sch 2.

**32.CA85.66**    Again this is a necessary functional measure designed to prevent investigations under section 447 being led astray by the provision of materially false or misleading information. Criminal sanctions are specified for offenders.

### [451A  Disclosure of information by Secretary of State or inspector

**32.CA85.67**    [(1)  This section applies to information obtained—

    (a)  under sections 434 to 446E;

    (b)  by an inspector in consequence of the exercise of his powers under section 453A.][a]

(2)  The Secretary of State may, if he thinks fit—

    (a)  disclose any information to which this section applies to any person to whom, or for any purpose for which, disclosure is permitted under section 449, or

    (b)  authorise or require an inspector appointed under this Part to disclose such information to any such person or for any such purpose.

[(3)  Information to which this section applies may also be disclosed by an inspector appointed under this Part to—

    (a)  another inspector appointed under this Part;

    (b)  a person appointed under—

        (i)  section 167 of the Financial Services and Markets Act 2000 (general investigations),

        (ii)  section 168 of that Act (investigations in particular cases),

        (iii)  section 169(1)(b) of that Act (investigation in support of overseas regulator),

        (iv)  section 284 of that Act (investigations into affairs of certain collective investment schemes), or

        (v)  regulations made as a result of section 262(2)(k) of that Act (investigations into open-ended investment companies),

      to conduct an investigation; or

    (c)  a person authorised to exercise powers under—

        (i)  section 447 of this Act; or

        (ii)  section 84 of the Companies Act 1989 (exercise of powers to assist overseas regulatory authority).][b]

(4)  Any information which may by virtue of subsection (3) be disclosed to any person may be disclosed to any officer or servant of that person.

(5)  The Secretary of State may, if he thinks fit, disclose any information obtained under section 444 to—

    (a)  the company whose ownership was the subject of the investigation,

    (b)  any member of the company,

    (c)  any person whose conduct was investigated in the course of the investigation,

    (d)  the auditors of the company, or

    (e)  any person whose financial interests appear to the Secretary of State to be affected by matters covered by the investigation.

[(6)  For the purposes of this section, information obtained by an inspector in consequence of the exercise of his powers under section 453A includes information obtained by a person accompanying the inspector in pursuance of subsection (4) of that section in consequence of that person's accompanying the inspector.

(7)  The reference to an inspector in subsection (2)(b) above includes a reference to a person accompanying an inspector in pursuance of section 453A(4).]][d]

AMENDMENTS AND NOTES

[a]  Subsection (1) substituted by the Companies (Audit, Investigations and Community Enterprise) Act 2004. Subsection (1) further amended by CA 2006, s 1037(2) to reflect the introduction of ss 446A–E by CA 2006.

[b]  Subsection (3) substituted by the Financial Services and Markets Act 2000 (Consequential Amendments and Repeals) Order 2001, SI 2001/3649.

[c]  Subsections (6) and (7) inserted by the Companies (Audit, Investigations and Community Enterprise) Act 2004.

[d]  Section 451A originally substituted by CA 1989, s 68.

This substituted section 451A of the Companies Act 1985 authorizes the Secretary of State to make   **32.CA85.68**
limited disclosure of information gleaned pursuant to certain inquiries.

It governs disclosure of information gleaned by inspectors or by the Secretary of State. Subsections (2)   **32.CA85.69**
to (5) indicate those parties to whom disclosure is permitted. These range from the specific (such as
other inspectors) to the very general, as indicated by subsection (5)(e).

## 452  Privileged information

[(1) Nothing in sections 431 to 446E compels the disclosure by any person to the Secretary of State or   **32.CA85.70**
        to an inspector appointed by him of information in respect of which in an action in the High Court
        a claim to legal professional privilege, or in an action in the Court of Session a claim to
        confidentiality of communications, could be maintained.]ᵃ

(1A) Nothing in section 434, 443 or 446 requires a person (except as mentioned in subsection (1B)
        below) to disclose information or produce documents in respect of which he owes an obligation
        of confidence by virtue of carrying on the business of banking unless—
   (a)  the person to whom the obligation of confidence is owed is the company or other body
          corporate under investigation,
   (b)  the person to whom the obligation of confidence is owed consents to the disclosure or
          production, or
   (c)  the making of the requirement is authorised by the Secretary of State.

(1B)  Subsection (1A) does not apply where the person owing the obligation of confidence is the
        company or other body corporate under investigation under section 431, 432 or 433.]ᵇ

[(2) Nothing in sections 447 to 451—
   (a)  compels the production by any person of a document or the disclosure by any person of
          information in respect of which in an action in the High Court a claim to legal professional
          privilege, or in an action in the Court of Session a claim to confidentiality of communications,
          could be maintained;
   (b)  authorises the taking of possession of any such document which is in the person's possession.

(3)  The Secretary of State must not under section 447 require, or authorise a person to require—
   (a)  the production by a person carrying on the business of banking of a document relating to the
          affairs of a customer of his, or
   (b)  the disclosure by him of information relating to those affairs,
unless one of the conditions in subsection (4) is met.

(4)  The conditions are—
   (a)  the Secretary of State thinks it is necessary to do so for the purpose of investigating the affairs
          of the person carrying on the business of banking;
   (b)  the customer is a person on whom a requirement has been imposed under section 447;
   (c)  the customer is a person on whom a requirement to produce information or documents has
          been imposed by an investigator appointed by the Secretary of State in pursuance of section
          171 or 173 of the Financial Services and Markets Act 2000 (powers of persons appointed
          under section 167 or as a result of section 168(2) to conduct an investigation).

(5)  Despite subsections (1) and (2) a person who is a lawyer may be compelled to disclose the name
        and address of his client.]ᶜ

AMENDMENTS AND NOTES

ᵃ  Substituted by the Companies (Audit, Investigations and Community Enterprise) Act 2004, Sch 2.
   Subsection (1) further amended by CA 2006, s 1003(3) to reflect the introduction of ss 446A–E by
   CA 2006.

ᵇ  Subsections (1A) and (1B) inserted by CA 1989, s 69.

ᶜ  Subsections (2)–(5) substituted by the Companies (Audit, Investigations and Community Enterprise) Act 2004, Sch 2.

This deals with privileged information. The law seeks to maintain a balance between the need to   **32.CA85.71**
maintain professional privilege and the need to make use of and disclose relevant information.

Subsection (3) (as qualified by subsection (4)) protects banking confidentiality and is consistent with   **32.CA85.72**
the philosophy underpinning *Tournier v National Provincial Bank*.²⁹ However note the qualifications
imposed by paragraphs (a) to (c) in (1A) and by (1B)—in such cases the duty of confidentiality cannot
be used to frustrate the investigation.

Subsection (5) places a limitation upon client confidentiality with respect to lawyers.   **32.CA85.73**

---

²⁹ [1924] 1 KB 461.

### 453 Investigation of [overseas]ᵃ companies

**32.CA85.74**

[(1) The provisions of this Part apply to bodies corporate incorporated outside [the United Kingdom]ᵇ which are carrying on business in [the United Kingdom],ᶜ or have at any time carried on business there, as they apply to companies under this Act; but subject to the following exceptions, adaptations and modifications.

(1A) The following provisions do not apply to such bodies—

   (a)  section 431 (investigation on application of company or its members),

   (b)  [...],ᵈ

   (c)  sections 442 to 445 (investigation of company ownership and power to obtain information as to those interested in shares, etc.), [...]ᵉ

   (d)  [...]ᶠ

(1B) The other provisions of this Part apply to such bodies subject to such adaptations and modifications as may be specified by regulations made by the Secretary of State.]ᵍ

(2)  Regulations under this section shall be made by statutory instrument subject to annulment in pursuance of a resolution of either House of Parliament.

AMENDMENTS AND NOTES

ᵃ Substituted by the Companies Act 2006 (Consequential Amendments, Transitional Provisions and Savings) Order 2009, SI 2009/1941, Sch 1 para 57.

ᵇ Substituted by the Companies Act 2006 (Consequential Amendments, Transitional Provisions and Savings) Order 2009, SI 2009/1941, Sch 1 para 57.

ᶜ Substituted by the Companies Act 2006 (Consequential Amendments, Transitional Provisions and Savings) Order 2009, SI 2009/1941, Sch 1 para 57.

ᵈ Repealed by CA 2006, Sch 6.

ᵉ Repealed by CA 2006, Sch 16.

ᶠ Repealed by CA 2006, Sch 16.

ᵍ Subsections (1)–(1B) amended by CA 1989, s 70 and CA 2006, s 1037(3). Subsection (1A)(b) further amended by CA 2006, s 1176(3) and repealed by Sch 16 to reflect the repeal of s 438 itself.

**32.CA85.75**  This modifies the power (conferred by the Companies Act 1985, section 453) to investigate overseas companies (ie companies incorporated outside the United Kingdom)—this investigation power would encompass companies incorporated in the Isle of Man, and the Channel Islands). The provision formerly applied to companies incorporated outside Great Britain but this limiting factor was changed to companies incorporated outside the United Kingdom by the Companies Act 2006 (Consequential Amendments, Transitional Provisions and Savings) Order 2009 (SI 2009/1941)(Schedule 1 paragraph 57). Note that the investigation jurisdiction for such companies is more limited than for home companies (for example, overseas company membership cannot be investigated). General investigation provisions apply unless modified by the Secretary of State. For the regulation of overseas companies generally see the Companies Act 2006, Part 34.

### [453A  Power to enter and remain on premises

**32.CA85.76**

(1)  An inspector or investigator may act under subsection (2) in relation to a company if—

   (a)  he is authorised to do so by the Secretary of State, and

   (b)  he thinks that to do so will materially assist him in the exercise of his functions under this Part in relation to the company.

(2)  An inspector or investigator may at all reasonable times—

   (a)  require entry to relevant premises, and

   (b)  remain there for such period as he thinks necessary for the purpose mentioned in subsection (1)(b).

(3)  Relevant premises are premises which the inspector or investigator believes are used (wholly or partly) for the purposes of the company's business.

(4)  In exercising his powers under subsection (2), an inspector or investigator may be accompanied by such other persons as he thinks appropriate.

(5)  A person who intentionally obstructs a person lawfully acting under subsection (2) or (4) is guilty of an offence.ᵃ

[(5A) A person guilty of an offence under this section is liable—

   (a)  on conviction on indictment, to a fine;

   (b)  on summary conviction, to a fine not exceeding the statutory maximum].ᵇ

(6)  [...]ᶜ

(7)  An inspector is a person appointed under section 431, 432 or 442.

(8)  An investigator is a person authorised for the purposes of section 447.]ᵈ

AMENDMENTS AND NOTES

ᵃ Subsection (5) amended by CA 2006, Sch 3.

<blockquote>
<sup>b</sup> New subs (5A) inserted by CA 2006, Sch 3.

<sup>c</sup> Subsection (6) omitted by CA 2006, Sch 16.

<sup>d</sup> Section 453A inserted by the Companies (Audit, Investigations and Community Enterprise) Act 2004, s 23.
</blockquote>

Section 453A which was remodelled by the 2004 Act relates to the power of inspectors and investigators    **32.CA85.77**
(both terms defined in subsections (7) and (8)) to enter and remain on premises. Note the requirement
of reasonableness set forth in subsection (2). The premises in question must be wholly or partly used
for business purposes—presumably this might include the family homes of company officers in some
circumstances (eg where a room in the house has been designated as being used for business purposes).
This is important with more and more usage of the home for business activities via exploitation of the
internet etc. Note the offence of obstruction outlined in subsection (5).

## [453B  Power to enter and remain on premises: procedural

(1)  This section applies for the purposes of section 453A.                                          **32.CA85.78**

(2)  The requirements of subsection (3) must be complied with at the time an inspector or investigator
seeks to enter relevant premises under section 453A(2)(a).

(3)  The requirements are—
    (a)  the inspector or investigator must produce evidence of his identity and evidence of his
appointment or authorisation (as the case may be);
    (b)  any person accompanying the inspector or investigator must produce evidence of his identity.

(4)  The inspector or investigator must, as soon as practicable after obtaining entry, give to an
appropriate recipient a written statement containing such information as to—
    (a)  the powers of the investigator or inspector (as the case may be) under section 453A;
    (b)  the rights and obligations of the company, occupier and the persons present on the premises,
as may be prescribed by regulations.

(5)  If during the time the inspector or investigator is on the premises there is no person present who
appears to him to be an appropriate recipient for the purposes of subsection (8), the inspector or
investigator must as soon as reasonably practicable send to the company—
    (a)  a notice of the fact and time that the visit took place, and
    (b)  the statement mentioned in subsection (4).

(6)  As soon as reasonably practicable after exercising his powers under section 453A(2), the inspector
or investigator must prepare a written record of the visit and—
    (a)  if requested to do so by the company he must give it a copy of the record;
    (b)  in a case where the company is not the sole occupier of the premises, if requested to do so
by an occupier he must give the occupier a copy of the record.

(7)  The written record must contain such information as may be prescribed by regulations.

(8)  If the inspector or investigator thinks that the company is the sole occupier of the premises an
appropriate recipient is a person who is present on the premises and who appears to the inspector
or investigator to be—
    (a)  an officer of the company, or
    (b)  a person otherwise engaged in the business of the company if the inspector or investigator
thinks that no officer of the company is present on the premises.

(9)  If the inspector or investigator thinks that the company is not the occupier or sole occupier of the
premises an appropriate recipient is—
    (a)  a person who is an appropriate recipient for the purposes of subsection (8), and (if different)
    (b)  a person who is present on the premises and who appears to the inspector or investigator to
be an occupier of the premises or otherwise in charge of them.

(10) A statutory instrument containing regulations made under this section is subject to annulment in
pursuance of a resolution of either House of Parliament.]<sup>a</sup>

AMENDMENTS AND NOTES

<blockquote>
<sup>a</sup> Section 453B inserted by the Companies (Audit, Investigations and Community Enterprise) Act 2004, s 23.
</blockquote>

Section 453B deals with various procedural aspects of this right of access. Production of identification    **32.CA85.79**
(subsection (3)) is an important safeguard. So is the explanation of the rights of the property owner
(subsection (4)). The production and handing over to appropriate persons of a written record of the
visit (subsections (7) to (9)) also serves to ensure fair play. In compliance with the requirements of
subsections (4), (5), and (6) note the Companies Act 1985 (Power to Enter and Remain on Premises:
Procedural) Regulations 2005, SI 2005/684.

## [453C  Failure to comply with certain requirements

(1)  This section applies if a person fails to comply with a requirement imposed by an inspector, the    **32.CA85.80**
Secretary of State or an investigator in pursuance of either of the following provisions—
    (a)  section 447;

(b)  section 453A.

(2)  The inspector, Secretary of State or investigator (as the case may be) may certify the fact in writing to the court.

(3)  If, after hearing—

(a)  any witnesses who may be produced against or on behalf of the alleged offender;

(b)  any statement which may be offered in defence,

the court is satisfied that the offender failed without reasonable excuse to comply with the requirement, it may deal with him as if he had been guilty of contempt of the court.]<sup>a</sup>

A MENDMENTS AND NOTES

<sup>a</sup>  Section 453C inserted by the Companies (Audit, Investigations and Community Enterprise) Act 2004, s 24.

**32.CA85.81**  This inserted provision seeks to firm up the position of investigators by allowing them to refer instances of non-cooperation to the court which then can use its powers to punish for contempt. Note the defence of 'reasonable excuse' in effect created by subsection (3).

## [453D  Offences by bodies corporate

**32.CA85.82**  Where an offence under any of sections 448, 449 to 451 and 453A is committed by a body corporate, every officer of the body who is in default also commits the offence.

For this purpose—

(a)  any person who purports to act as director, manager or secretary of the body is treated as an officer of the body, and

(b)  if the body is a company, any shadow director is treated as an officer of the company.]<sup>a</sup>

A MENDMENTS AND NOTES

<sup>a</sup>  Section 453D inserted by the Companies Act 2006 (Consequential Amendments etc) Order 2008, SI 2008/948

COMMENCEMENT DATE  6 April 2008

**32.CA85.83**  This new interpretation section was inserted by the Companies Act 2006 (Consequential Amendments etc) Order 2008, SI 2008/948.

# PART XV
## ORDERS IMPOSING RESTRICTIONS ON SHARES
## (SECTIONS 210, 216, 445)

### 454  Consequence of order imposing restrictions

**32.CA85.84**  (1)  So long as any shares are directed to be subject to the restrictions of this Part [then, subject to any directions made in relation to an order pursuant to sections, 445(1A) or 456(1A)—]<sup>a</sup>

(a)  any transfer of those shares or, in the case of unissued shares, any transfer of the right to be issued with them, and any issue of them, is void;

(b)  no voting rights are exercisable in respect of the shares;

(c)  no further shares shall be issued in right of them or in pursuance of any offer made to their holder; and

(d)  except in a liquidation, no payment shall be made of any sums due from the company on the shares, whether in respect of capital or otherwise.

(2)  Where shares are subject to the restrictions of subsection (1)(a), any agreement to transfer the shares or, in the case of unissued shares, the right to be issued with them is void (except [such agreement or right as may be made or exercised under the terms of directions made by the Secretary of State or the court under sections 445(1A), 456(1A) or]<sup>b</sup> an agreement to [transfer]<sup>c</sup> the shares on the making of an order under section 456(3) (b) below).

(3)  Where shares are subject to the restrictions of subsection (1)(c) or (d), an agreement to transfer any right to be issued with other shares in right of those shares, or to receive any payment on them (otherwise than in a liquidation) is void (except [such agreement or right as may be made or exercised under the terms of directions made by the Secretary of State or the court under sections 445(1A), 456(1A) or]<sup>d</sup> an agreement to transfer any such right on the [transfer]<sup>e</sup> of the shares on the making of an order under section 456(3)(b) below).

A MENDMENTS AND NOTES

<sup>a</sup>  Inserted by the Companies (Disclosure of Interests in Shares) (Orders Imposing Restrictions on Shares) Regulations 1991, SI 1991/1646, in turn amended by the Companies Act 2006 (Commencement No 3 and Consequential Amendments, Transitional Provisions and Savings) Order 2007, SI 2007/2194.

ᵇ Inserted by the Companies (Disclosure of Interests in Shares) (Orders Imposing Restrictions on Shares) Regulations 1991, SI 1991/1646, in turn amended by the Companies Act 2006 (Commencement No 3 and Consequential Amendments, Transitional Provisions and Savings) Order 2007, SI 2007/2194.

ᶜ Substituted by CA 1989.

ᵈ Inserted by the Companies (Disclosure of Interests in Shares) (Orders Imposing Restrictions on Shares) Regulations 1991, SI 1991/1646. Further amended by the Companies Act 2006 (Commencement No 3, Consequential Amendments, Transitional Provisions and Savings) Order 2007, SI 2007/2194.

ᵉ Substituted by CA 1989.

This provides for the effect of a share freezing order. This provision has generated litigation.[30] The **32.CA85.85** purpose of share freezing orders is to neutralize the shares in question as an item of valuable property pending the provision of the information sought by the inspector. The court has the power to lift restrictions but will only do so if the information sought has been furnished. Attempts to avoid the restrictions by transferring the shares are blocked by subsections (2) and (3).

**455  Punishment for attempted evasion of restrictions**

(1) [Subject to the terms of any directions made under section 445(1A) or 456]ᵃ a person [commits **32.CA85.86** an offence if he]ᵇ

    (a) exercises or purports to exercise any right to dispose of any shares which, to his knowledge, are for the time being subject to the restrictions of this Part or of any right to be issued with any such shares, or

    (b) votes in respect of any such shares (whether as holder or proxy), or appoints a proxy to vote in respect of them, or

    (c) being the holder of any such shares, fails to notify of their being subject to those restrictions any person whom he does not know to be aware of that fact but does know to be entitled (apart from the restrictions) to vote in respect of those shares whether as holder or as proxy, or

    (d) being the holder of any such shares, or being entitled to any right to be issued with other shares in right of them, or to receive any payment on them (otherwise than in a liquidation), enters into any agreement which is void under section 454 (2) or (3).ᶜ

(2) [Subject to the terms of any directions made under sections 210(5A), 216(1B), 445(1A) or 456 if]ᵈ shares in a company are issued in contravention of the restrictions, an offence is committed by—

    (a) the company, and

    (b) every officer of the company who is in default.ᵉ

(2A) A person guilty of an offence under this section is liable—

    (a) on conviction on indictment, to a fine;

    (b) on summary conviction, to a fine not exceeding the statutory maximum.ᶠ

(3) [...]ᵍ

AMENDMENTS AND NOTES

ᵃ Inserted by the Companies (Disclosure of Interests in Shares) (Orders Imposing Restrictions on Shares) Regulations 1991, SI 1991/1646. Further amended by the Companies Act 2006 (Commencement No 3, Consequential Amendments, Transitional Provisions and Savings) Order 2007, SI 2007/2194.

ᵇ Amended by CA 2006, Sch 3.

ᶜ Subsection (1) amended by CA 2006, Sch 3.

ᵈ Inserted by the Companies (Disclosure of Interests in Shares) (Orders Imposing Restrictions on Shares) Regulations 1991, SI 1991/1646. Further amended by the Companies Act 2006 (Commencement No 3, Consequential Amendments, Transitional Provisions and Savings) Order 2007, SI 2007/2194.

ᵉ Subsection (2) amended by CA 2006, Sch 3.

ᶠ Subsection (2A) also inserted by CA 2006, Sch 3.

ᵍ Repealed by the Companies Act 2006 (Commencement No 3, Consequential Amendments, Transitional Provisions and Savings) Order 2007, SI 2007/2194.

---

[30] For an account of the early jurisprudence on share freezing orders, see Milman and Singh (1992) 13 *Company Law* 51. Since this early boost of case law a relative calm has settled over the law as the working rules have been established by the courts. Hardly any cases on the subject have been reported in the past decade.

**32.CA85.87**   This supports share freezing orders granted under section 454 by attaching criminal sanctions to any attempted breach of the order.

### 456   Relaxation and removal of restrictions

**32.CA85.88**

(1) Where shares in a company are by order made subject to the restrictions of this Part, application may be made to the court for an order directing that the shares be no longer so subject.

[(1A) Where the court is satisfied that an order subjecting the shares to the restrictions of this Part unfairly affects the rights of third parties in respect of shares then the court, for the purpose of protecting such rights and subject to such terms as it thinks fit and in addition to any order it may make under subsection (1), may direct on an application made under that subsection that such acts by such persons or descriptions of persons and for such purposes, as may be set out in the order, shall not constitute a breach of the restrictions of Part XV of this Act. Subsection (3) does not apply to an order made under this subsection.][a]

(2) If the order applying the restrictions was made by the Secretary of State, or he has refused to make an order disapplying them, the application may be made by any person aggrieved; [...][b]

(3) Subject as follows, an order of the court or the Secretary of State directing that shares shall cease to be subject to the restrictions may be made only if—

  (a) the court or (as the case may be) the Secretary of State is satisfied that the relevant facts about the shares have been disclosed to the company and no unfair advantage has accrued to any person as a result of the earlier failure to make that disclosure, or

  (b) the shares are to be [transferred for valuable consideration][c] and the court (in any case) or the Secretary of State (if the order was made under section [...][d] 445) approves the [transfer].[e]

(4) [Without prejudice to the power of the court to give directions under subsection (1A), where][f] shares in a company are subject to the restrictions, the court may on application order the shares to be sold, subject to the court's approval as to the sale, and may also direct that the shares shall cease to be subject to the restrictions. An application to the court under this subsection may be made by the Secretary of State [...][g], or by the company.

(5) Where an order has been made under subsection (4), the court may on application make such further order relating to the sale or transfer of the shares as it thinks fit. An application to the court under this subsection may be made—

  (a) by the Secretary of State [...][h], or

  (b) by the company, or

  (c) by the person appointed by or in pursuance of the order to effect the sale, or

  (d) by any person interested in the shares.

(6) An order (whether of the Secretary of State or the court) directing that shares shall cease to be subject to the restrictions of this Part, if it is—

  (a) expressed to be made with a view to permitting a transfer of the shares, or

  (b) made under subsection (4) of this section,

may continue the restrictions mentioned in paragraphs (c) and (d) of section 454(1), either in whole or in part, so far as they relate to any right acquired or offer made before the transfer.

(7) Subsection (3) does not apply to an order directing that shares shall cease to be subject to any restrictions which have been continued in force in relation to those shares under subsection (6).

AMENDMENTS

[a] Subsection (1A) inserted by the Companies (Disclosure of Interests in Shares) (Orders Imposing Restrictions on Shares) Regulations 1991, SI 1991/1646.

[b] Subsection (2) amended by the Companies Act 2006 (Commencement No 3, Consequential Amendments, Transitional Provisions and Savings) Order 2007, SI 2007/2194.

[c] Substituted by CA 1989.

[d] Repealed by the Companies Act 2006 (Commencement No 3, Consequential Amendments, Transitional Provisions and Savings) Order 2007, SI 2007/2194.

[e] Substituted by CA 1989.

[f] Subsection (4) amended by the Companies (Disclosure of Interests in Shares) (Orders Imposing Restrictions on Shares) Regulations 1991, SI 1991/1646.

[g] Repealed by the Companies Act 2006 (Commencement No 3, Consequential Amendments, Transitional Provisions and Savings) Order 2007, SI 2007/2194.

[h] Repealed by the Companies Act 2006 (Commencement No 3, Consequential Amendments, Transitional Provisions and Savings) Order 2007, SI 2007/2194.

**32.CA85.89**   This deals with the modification/relaxation of share freezing orders by the Secretary of State or by the court. Share freezing orders will not be lifted or relaxed as a matter of course simply because the registered holder agrees to sell the shares—*Re Geers Gross plc*.[31] This is a sensible position for the law to take because the sale might be to a person who is equally reluctant to disclose true beneficial ownership.

On section 456(4) see *Re Ashbourne Investment Ltd*.[32] See also *Re Westminster Property Group Ltd*.[33]    **32.CA85.90**

### 457   Further provisions on sale by court order of restricted shares

(1)  Where shares are sold in pursuance of an order of the court under section 456(4) the proceeds of    **32.CA85.91**
sale, less the costs of the sale, shall be paid into court for the benefit of the persons who are
beneficially interested in the shares; and any such person may apply to the court for the whole or
part of those proceeds to be paid to him.

(2)  On application under subsection (1) the court shall (subject as provided below) order the payment
to the applicant of the whole of the proceeds of sale together with any interest thereon or, if any
other person had a beneficial interest in the shares at the time of their sale, such proportion of
those proceeds and interest as is equal to the proportion which the value of the applicant's interest
in the shares bears to the total value of the shares.

(3)  On granting an application for an order under section 456(4) or (5) the court may order that the
applicant's costs be paid out of the proceeds of sale; and if that order is made, the applicant is
entitled to payment of his costs out of those proceeds before any person interested in the shares
in question.

This deals with a range of consequential matters relating to proceeds of sale where the court has    **32.CA85.92**
permitted the sale of shares subject to a freezing order. Basically the beneficial owners get the proceeds
(plus interest) once sale expenses have been deducted.

---

[31]  [1988] 1 All ER 224.
[32]  [1978] 2 All ER 418.
[33]  [1984] 1 WLR 1117.

# 33

# UK COMPANIES NOT FORMED UNDER THE COMPANIES ACTS

## Companies Act 2006

## PART 33
## UK COMPANIES NOT FORMED UNDER THE COMPANIES ACTS

This Part authorizes the registration of certain companies not formed under the Companies Act 2006. **33.01** The sections in this Part replace Chapter 2 of Part 22 and Schedule 21 of the Companies Act 1985 which re-enacted similar provisions in earlier Companies Acts. The purpose of this Part is, *inter alia*, to enable old companies to which the Act does not apply automatically to obtain registration, with a view to the company's being wound up. This Part also confers a new power (see section 1042 below) on the Secretary of State to make regulations in connection with the registration of a company following an application under section 1040 below, and in the case of unregistered companies, confers a power on the Secretary of State to apply sections of the Companies Acts to certain unregistered companies. The ambit of this part is narrow as companies formed and registered under the earlier Companies Acts are automatically governed by the Companies Act 2006 and do not require re-registration under that Act.[1]

## CHAPTER 1
## COMPANIES NOT FORMED UNDER THE COMPANIES LEGISLATION BUT AUTHORISED TO REGISTER

### 1040 Companies authorised to register under this Act

(1) This section applies to—      **33.1040.01**
    (a) any company that was in existence on 2nd November 1862 (including any company registered under the Joint Stock Companies Acts), and
    (b) any company formed after that date (whether before or after the commencement of this Act)—
        (i) in pursuance of an Act of Parliament other than this Act or any of the former Companies Acts,
        (ii) in pursuance of letters patent, or
        (iii) that is otherwise duly constituted according to law.
(2) Any such company may on making application register under this Act.
(3) Subject to the following provisions, it may register as an unlimited company, as a company limited by shares or as a company limited by guarantee.
(4) A company having the liability of its members limited by Act of Parliament or letters patent—
    (a) may not register under this section unless it is a joint stock company, and
    (b) may not register under this section as an unlimited company or a company limited by guarantee.

---

[1] See s 1 of the Companies Act (CA) 2006.

(5)  A company that is not a joint stock company may not register under this section as a company limited by shares.

(6)  The registration of a company under this section is not invalid by reason that it has taken place with a view to the company's being wound up.

COMMENCEMENT DATE  1 October 2009[2]

**33.1040.02**  This section replaces section 680 of the Companies Act 1985.[3] Subsection (2) provides that companies incorporated within the UK, but not formed under the Companies Acts (or certain earlier companies legislation), may apply to register under the Companies Act 2006.

**33.1040.03**  Subsection (1) lists the types of company that can take advantage of this section. They include companies formed before 2 November 1862; companies formed by private Act of Parliament and companies incorporated by royal charter. In decisions under the previous provision[4] the term 'company' referred to in the expression 'duly constituted according to law' (subsection (1)(b)(iii)) was held to mean a company constituted in some manner analogous to those which the section mentions before, ie by registration under Act of Parliament, or in pursuance of an Act of Parliament, or under letters patent.[5] Similarly, it was held that an association formed solely for the purpose of registration under the previous part of the Companies Act 1985 is not a 'company ... duly constituted according to law'.[6]

**33.1040.04**  Subsection (3) provides that the company may apply to register as a company limited by shares,[7] a company limited by guarantee,[8] or as an unlimited company.[9] Subsections (4) and (5) impose restrictions on this choice. Therefore, a company with limited liability may not register as an unlimited company, and only a company with share capital may register as a company limited by shares. A company may wish to apply to register under the Companies Act 2006 in order to take advantage of legislation applying to companies registered under the Companies Acts. Although Companies House increased their paper registration fees from 6 April 2011, companies registered under this section will not pay an increase in standard paper incorporation/registration fees.[10]

**33.1040.05**  By registration under the Companies Act 2006 a company may acquire powers which it did not have before. Subsection (6) makes it clear that registration shall not be invalid by reason that it has taken place with a view to winding up, and thus a company may register even if it is in order to take advantage of certain sections of the Insolvency Act 1986 not available to unregistered companies.[11] For example, under section 221(4) of the Insolvency Act 1986, unregistered companies may not be wound up under that Act voluntarily.[12] It was held in the past that a company may by registration followed by voluntary liquidation make use of the power of sale given by section 110 of the Insolvency Act 1986.[13]

### 1041  Definition of 'joint stock company'

**33.1041.01**  (1)  For the purposes of section 1040 (companies authorised to register under this Act) 'joint stock company' means a company—

    (a)  having a permanent paid-up or nominal share capital of fixed amount divided into shares, also of fixed amount, or held and transferable as stock, or divided and held partly in one way and partly in the other, and

    (b)  formed on the principle of having for its members the holders of those shares or that stock, and no other persons.

  (2)  Such a company when registered with limited liability under this Act is deemed a company limited by shares.

---

[2]  Companies Act 2006 (Commencement No 8, Transitional Provisions and Savings) Order 2008, SI 2008/2860, art 3(p).

[3]  Section equivalent to s 1040 enabling certain companies not formed under the Companies Acts to register under the Companies Acts was previously made by s 680 of the 1985 Act and before that was made under earlier Companies Acts (such as Part 8 of CA 1948).

[4]  CA 1985, s 680(1).

[5]  *R v Register of Joint Stock Companies ex p Johnston* [1891] 2 QB 598, 612; *Re Cussons Ltd* (1904) 73 LJ Ch 296.

[6]  *R v Register of Joint Stock Companies ex p Johnston* [1891] 2 QB 598.

[7]  For the definition of a company limited by shares see s 3(1) and (2) above.

[8]  For the definition of a company limited by guarantee see s 3(3) (see above). It should be noted that according to ss 1(4) and 680(1) of CA 1985 a company could not register under this part of the Act as a company limited by guarantee and having a share capital.

[9]  For the definition of unlimited company see s 3(4) above.

[10]  See: ⟨http://www.companieshouse.gov.uk/toolsToHelp/april2011FeeChanges.shtml⟩.

[11]  Cf with *Re Hercules Insurance Co* (1871) LR 11 Eq 321, where the court held that registration after the presentation of a winding-up petition must be a mere nullity (this case is of doubtful authority).

[12]  Except in accordance with the EC regulation on insolvency proceedings.

[13]  *Southall v British Mutual Life Assurance Society* (1871) 6 Ch App 614.

COMMENCEMENT DATE 1 October 2009[14]

This section, which is self-explanatory, replaces section 683 of the Companies Act 1985.[15] It explains   **33.1041.02**
what is meant by 'joint stock company'.[16] The definition is the same as that contained in section 683 of
the Companies Act 1985. Section 1040(4)(a) (see above) allows some joint stock companies to register
under the Companies Acts as a company limited by shares. Before registration, joint stock companies
have to produce certain documents to the Registrar.[17]

## 1042   Power to make provision by regulations

(1)   The Secretary of State may make provision by regulations—   **33.1042.01**
    (a)   for and in connection with registration under section 1040 (companies authorised to register
        under this Act), and
    (b)   as to the application to companies so registered of the provisions of the Companies Acts.
(2)   Without prejudice to the generality of that power, regulations under this section may make
    provision corresponding to any provision formerly made by Chapter 2 of Part 22 of the Companies
    Act 1985 (c. 6).
(3)   Regulations under this section are subject to negative resolution procedure.

COMMENCEMENT DATE 1 October 2009[18]

This section is new. It confers a new power on the Secretary of State to make regulations in connection   **33.1042.02**
with the registration of a company following an application under section 1006 (see above). Regulations made under this section replace the law made by sections 681 to 682, 684 to 690, and Schedule 21
of the Companies Act 1985. The regulations will cover the procedural requirements for registration,
the conditions to be satisfied before registration, and the documents to be supplied on an application
for registration. The regulations will also set out the consequences of registration, including the status
of the company following registration and the application of the Companies Acts to such companies
following registration. Subsection (3) makes it clear that the regulations are subject to the negative
resolution procedure.[19]

# CHAPTER 2
## UNREGISTERED COMPANIES

The following section replaces section 718 of the Companies Act 1985. The changes in the law derive   **33.1043.01**
principally from the recommendations in Chapter 11 of the Company Law Review Steering Group's
Final Report (paragraphs 11.34 to 11.37) which noted that the position of unregistered companies is
anomalous, especially for those whose object is the acquisition of gain, which offer shares to the public,
and which are listed on a stock exchange.[20]

## 1043   Unregistered companies

(1)   This section applies to bodies corporate incorporated in and having a principal place of business   **33.1043.02**
    in the United Kingdom, other than—
    (a)   bodies incorporated by, or registered under, a public general Act of Parliament;
    (b)   bodies not formed for the purpose of carrying on a business that has for its object the
        acquisition of gain by the body or its individual members;
    (c)   bodies for the time being exempted from this section by direction of the Secretary of State;

---

[14]   Companies Act 2006 (Commencement No 8, Transitional Provisions and Savings) Order 2008, SI 2008/
2860, art 3(p).
[15]   CA 1985, s 683 was derived from CA 1948, s 382.
[16]   A considerable body of literature has grown up around the subject of the history and evolution of joint stock
companies. See eg WR Scott, *Joint Stock Companies to 1720*; CM Schmitthoff, 'The Origin of the Joint Stock
Company' (1939) 3 Toronto Law Journal 74; A Santuari, 'The Joint Stock Company in 19th Century England and
France' (1993) 14 Journal of Legal History 39.
[17]   The type of documents is covered under the new power to make provision by regulations granted to the
Secretary of State under s 1008 above in connection with the registration of a company following an application
under s 1006.
[18]   Companies Act 2006 (Commencement No 8, Transitional Provisions and Savings) Order 2008, SI 2008/
2860, art 3(p).
[19]   See s 1289 below.
[20]   The Company Law Review Steering Group's Final Report (para 11.37) recommended that those areas of
company law which apply to unregistered companies should continue to apply to those formed for the
acquisition of gain, and that, in addition, the significant omissions (para 11.34) should apply to these companies
as far as practicable.

(d) open-ended investment companies.

(2) The Secretary of State may make provision by regulations applying specified provisions of the Companies Acts to all, or any specified description of, the bodies to which this section applies.

(3) The regulations may provide that the specified provisions of the Companies Acts apply subject to any specified limitations and to such adaptations and modifications (if any) as may be specified.

(4) This section does not—

    (a) repeal or revoke in whole or in part any enactment, royal charter or other instrument constituting or regulating any body in relation to which provisions of the Companies Acts are applied by regulations under this section, or

    (b) restrict the power of Her Majesty to grant a charter in lieu or supplementary to any such charter.

But in relation to any such body the operation of any such enactment, charter or instrument is suspended in so far as it is inconsistent with any of those provisions as they apply for the time being to that body.

(5) In this section 'specified' means specified in the regulations.

(6) Regulations under this section are subject to negative resolution procedure.

COMMENCEMENT DATE 6 April 2007[21]

**33.1043.03** This section replaces section 718 of the Companies Act 1985.[22] The section confers a power on the Secretary of State to apply sections of the Companies Acts to certain unregistered companies. These are companies incorporated in the UK, and having their principal place of business in the UK, but not formed or registered under the Companies Acts or any other public general Act of Parliament. Examples include companies formed by letters patent or by private Act of Parliament.

**33.1043.04** Subsection (1) exempts certain other companies from regulations under this section, including those exempted by direction of the Secretary of State.

**33.1043.05** Subsections (2) and (3) taken together state that regulations under these sections may replace the provisions formerly in Schedule 22 of the Companies Act 1985. The regulations may apply specified sections of the Companies Acts to specified descriptions of unregistered company, and may make limitations, adaptations, and modifications to the application of the Companies Acts to unregistered companies. Subsection (5) makes it clear that the term 'specified' in this section means specified in the regulations. Finally, subsection (6) provides that the regulations are subject to the negative resolution procedure.[23]

**33.1043.06** At first, the Secretary of State used his powers conferred by this section and made the Companies Acts (Unregistered Companies) Regulations 2007, SI 2007/318.[24] These Regulations came into force on 6 April 2007 and were in force until 1 October 2009. They applied Part 28 of that Act (takeovers etc), and certain ancillary provisions, to unregistered companies and in doing so further implemented Council Directive 2004/25/EC of 21 April 2004 on takeover bids. More specifically, the provisions of the Companies Acts listed in the Schedule to these Regulations applied to an unregistered company as to a company within the meaning of section 735(1) of the Companies Act 1985 or article 3(1) of the Companies (Northern Ireland) Order 1986, subject to any limitation, adaptation, or modification specified in the Schedule. There were considered to be no costs and benefits arising from this instrument as it replicated for unregistered companies provisions which were in force under the Takeovers Directive (Interim Implementation) Regulations 2006, SI 2006/1183.[25] Then, on 1 October 2009, the Unregistered Companies Regulations 2009, SI 2009/2436 (hereafter 'the 2009 Regulations')[26]

---

[21] Companies Act 2006 (Commencement No 2, Consequential Amendments, Transitional Provisions and Savings) Order 2007, SI 2007/1093, art 2(1).

[22] Certain provisions of the CA 1985 were made applicable by s 718 of and Sch 22 to the CA 1985 and the Companies (Unregistered Companies) Regulations 1985 (SI 1985/680) to companies not registered under the Act but nevertheless incorporated in and having a place of business in Great Britain, other than companies incorporated by or registered under a public general Act, companies not formed for the purpose of gain, companies exempted by the Department of Trade, and any open-ended investment company within the meaning of the Open-Ended Investment Companies Regulations 2001 (see s 718 (2)(d) and SI 2001/1228).

[23] See s 1289 below.

[24] Available at <http://webarchive.nationalarchives.gov.uk/+/http://www.dti.gov.uk/bbf/co-act-2006/index.html>.

[25] See Explanatory Notes to the Companies Acts (Unregistered Companies) Regulations 2007, available on <http://webarchive.nationalarchives.gov.uk/+/http://www.dti.gov.uk/bbf/co-act-2006/index.html>.

[26] Available at <http://www.opsi.gov.uk/si/si2009/uksi_20092436_en>.

came into force and revoked the Companies Acts (Unregistered Companies) Regulations 2007. The provisions of the Companies Acts specified in Schedule 1 to the 2009 Regulations apply to an unregistered company as to a company within the meaning of section 1 of the Companies Act 2006, subject to any limitation, adaptation, or modification specified in that Schedule. In particular, the following table provides details of the changes as they apply to unregistered companies:

| Subject area | Nature of change | Modifications/details of change |
|---|---|---|
| A company's constitution | 1 Sections 26 and 27 of the Companies Act 2006 (filing obligations in connection with company's articles) apply to unregistered companies, modified so that they read as follows— | **Registrar to be sent copy of company's constitution**<br><br>26.  —<br>(1)  A company must, not later than 15 days after the date of its incorporation, send to the registrar a copy of every instrument constituting or regulating the company.<br>(2)  Where a company amends any instrument constituting or regulating the company, it must, not later than 15 days after the amendment takes effect, send to the registrar a copy of the instrument as amended.<br>(3)  If a company fails to comply with subsection (1) or (2) an offence is committed by—<br>(a)  the company, and<br>(b)  every officer of the company who is in default.<br>(4)  A person guilty of an offence under this section is liable on summary conviction to a fine not exceeding level 3 on the standard scale and, for continued contravention, a daily default fine not exceeding one-tenth of level 3 on the standard scale.<br><br>**Registrar's notice to comply in case of failure with respect to company's constitution**<br><br>27.  —<br>(1)  If it appears to the registrar that a company has failed to comply with—<br>(a)  section 26(1) or (2) (registrar to be sent copy of company's constitution), or<br>(b)  any enactment requiring the company to send to the registrar—<br>(i)  a document making or evidencing an alteration in any instrument constituting or regulating the company, or<br>(ii)  a copy of any such instrument as amended,<br>the registrar may give notice to the company requiring it to comply.<br>(2)  The notice must—<br>(a)  state the date on which it is issued, and<br>(b)  require the company to comply within 28 days from that date.<br>(3)  If the company complies with the notice within the specified time, no criminal proceedings may be brought in respect of the failure mentioned in subsection (1).<br>(4)  If the company does not comply with the notice within the specified time, it is liable to a civil penalty of £200.<br>(5)  This is in addition to any liability to criminal proceedings in respect of the failure mentioned in subsection (1).<br>(6)  The penalty may be recovered by the registrar and is to be paid into the Consolidated Fund.' |

| Subject area | Nature of change | Modifications/details of change |
|---|---|---|
| A company's constitution | 2 Sections 34 and 35 of the Companies Act 2006 (notice to registrar where company's constitution altered) apply to unregistered companies, modified so that they read as follows— | **Notice to registrar where company's constitution altered by enactment**<br><br>34. —<br>(1) This section applies where the constitution of a company is altered by an enactment, other than an enactment amending the general law.<br>(2) The company must give notice of the alteration to the registrar, specifying the enactment, not later than 15 days after the enactment comes into force.<br>(3) In the case of a special enactment the notice must be accompanied by a copy of the enactment.<br>(4) If the enactment amends any instrument constituting or regulating the company, the notice must be accompanied by a copy of the instrument in question, as amended.<br>(5) A 'special enactment' means an enactment that is not a public general enactment, and includes—<br>(a) an Act for confirming a provisional order,<br>(b) any provision of a public general Act in relation to the passing of which any of the standing orders of the House of Lords or the House of Commons relating to Private Business applied, or<br>(c) any enactment to the extent that it is incorporated in or applied for the purposes of a special enactment.<br>(6) If a company fails to comply with this section an offence is committed by—<br>(a) the company, and<br>(b) every officer of the company who is in default.<br>(7) A person guilty of an offence under this section is liable on summary conviction to a fine not exceeding level 3 on the standard scale and, for continued contravention, a daily default fine not exceeding one-tenth of level 3 on the standard scale.<br><br>**Notice to registrar where company's constitution altered by order**<br><br>35. —<br>(1) Where the constitution of a company is altered by an order of a court or other authority, the company must give notice to the registrar of the alteration not later than 15 days after the alteration takes effect.<br>(2) The notice must be accompanied by—<br>(a) a copy of the order, and<br>(b) if the order amends any instrument constituting or regulating the company, a copy of the instrument in question, as amended.<br>(3) If a company fails to comply with this section an offence is committed by—<br>(a) the company, and<br>(b) every officer of the company who is in default.<br>(4) A person guilty of an offence under this section is liable on summary conviction to a fine not exceeding level 3 on the standard scale and, for continued contravention, a daily default fine not exceeding one-tenth of level 3 on the standard scale.<br>(5) This section does not apply where provision is made by another enactment for the delivery to the registrar of a copy of the order in question. |

| Subject area | Nature of change | Modifications/details of change |
|---|---|---|
| A company's capacity and related matters | 3 The following provisions of the Companies Act 2006 apply to unregistered companies— | (a) sections 39 and 40 (a company's capacity and power of directors to bind company); <br> (b) section 41 (constitutional limitations: transactions involving directors or their associates); <br> (c) section 42 (constitutional limitations: companies that are charities); <br> (d) sections 43, 44, 45(1) and 46 (formalities of doing business under the law of England and Wales or Northern Ireland); <br> (e) section 48 (execution of documents under the law of Scotland); <br> (f) section 50 (official seal for share certificates); <br> (g) section 51 (pre-incorporation contracts, deeds, and obligations). |
| Trading disclosures | 4 Sections 82 to 85 of the Companies Act 2006 (trading disclosures) apply to unregistered companies, modified so that they read as follows— | **Requirement to disclose company name and other particulars** <br><br> 82. — <br> (1) Every company must disclose its corporate name on— <br> (a) its business letters, notices and other official publications; <br> (b) its bills of exchange, promissory notes, endorsements and order forms; <br> (c) cheques purporting to be signed by or on behalf of the company; <br> (d) orders for money, goods or services purporting to be signed by or on behalf of the company; <br> (e) its bills of parcels, invoices and other demands for payment, receipts and letters of credit; <br> (f) its applications for licences to carry on a trade or activity; <br> (g) all other forms of its business correspondence and documentation; and <br> (h) its websites. <br> (2) Every company must disclose the further particulars set out in subsection (3) on— <br> (a) its business letters; <br> (b) its order forms; and <br> (c) its websites. <br> (3) The further particulars required are— <br> (a) the part of the United Kingdom in which the company's principal office is situated; <br> (b) the reference number allocated to the company by the registrar; <br> (c) the address of the company's principal office; <br> (d) the manner in which it was incorporated; <br> (e) if it is— <br>    (i) a limited company, or <br>    (ii) an investment company within the meaning of section 833, <br> that fact. <br> (4) If, in the case of a company having a share capital, there is a reference to the amount of share capital on— <br> (a) its business letters, <br> (b) its order forms, or <br> (c) its websites, <br> the reference must be to paid up share capital. <br> (5) In relation to a company, a reference to 'its websites' includes a reference to any part of a website relating to that company which that company has caused or authorised to appear. |

| Subject area | Nature of change | Modifications/details of change |
|---|---|---|

**Civil consequences of failure to make required disclosure**

83.    —

(1)    This section applies to any legal proceedings brought by a company to enforce a right arising out of a contract made in the course of a business in respect of which the company was, at the time the contract was made, in breach of section 82 (requirement to disclose company name and other particulars).

(2)    The proceedings shall be dismissed if the defendant (in Scotland, the defender) to the proceedings shows—

(a)    that he has a claim against the claimant (pursuer) arising out of the contract that he has been unable to pursue by reason of the latter's breach of section 82, or

(b)    that he has suffered some financial loss in connection with the contract by reason of the claimant's (pursuer's) breach of section 82,

unless the court before which the proceedings are brought is satisfied that it is just and equitable to permit the proceedings to continue.

(3)    This section does not affect the right of any person to enforce such rights as he may have against another person in any proceedings brought by that person.

**Criminal consequences of failure to make required disclosure**

84.    —

(1)    Where a company fails, without reasonable excuse, to comply with any requirement of section 82, an offence is committed by—

(a)    the company; and

(b)    every officer of the company who is in default.

(2)    A person guilty of an offence under this section is liable on summary conviction to—

(a)    a fine not exceeding level 3 on the standard scale; and

(b)    for continued contravention, a daily default fine not exceeding one-tenth of level 3 on the standard scale.

(3)    For the purposes of this section a shadow director is to be treated as an officer of the company.

**Minor variations in form of name to be left out of account**

85.    For the purposes of this Chapter, in considering the name of a company no account is to be taken of—

(a)    whether upper or lower case characters (or a combination of the two) are used, or

(b)    whether diacritical marks or punctuation are present or absent, provided there is no real likelihood of names differing only in those respects being taken to be different names.

| Subject area | Nature of change | Modifications/details of change |
|---|---|---|
| A company's principal office in the United Kingdom | 5 Sections 86 and 87 of the Companies Act 2006 (a company's registered office) apply to unregistered companies, modified so that they read as follows— | **A company's principal office**<br><br>86. —<br>(1) Communications and notices may at all times be addressed to a company at its principal office in the United Kingdom.<br>(2) A company must give notice to the registrar, not later than 15 days after the date of the incorporation of the company, of the address of its principal office in the United Kingdom.<br>(3) If a company fails to comply with subsection (2) an offence is committed by—<br>  (a) the company, and<br>  (b) every officer of the company who is in default.<br>(4) A person guilty of an offence under subsection (2) is liable on summary conviction to a fine not exceeding level 3 on the standard scale and, for continued contravention, a daily default fine not exceeding one-tenth of level 3 on the standard scale.<br><br>**Change of principal office**<br><br>87. —<br>(1) Where a company changes its principal office in the United Kingdom, it must send notice of the new address to the registrar not later than 15 days after the change takes effect.<br>(2) If a company fails to comply with subsection (1) an offence is committed by—<br>  (a) the company, and<br>  (b) every officer of the company who is in default.<br>(3) A person guilty of an offence under subsection (1) is liable on summary conviction to a fine not exceeding level 3 on the standard scale and, for continued contravention, a daily default fine not exceeding one-tenth of level 3 on the standard scale.<br>(4) Until the end of the period of 14 days beginning with the date on which the new address is registered a person may validly serve any document on the company at the address previously registered.<br>(5) For the purposes of any duty of a company—<br>  (a) to keep available for inspection at its principal office in the United Kingdom any register or other document, or<br>  (b) to mention the address of that office in any document,<br>a company that changes the address of its principal office in the United Kingdom may make the change as from such date as it may determine, but it is treated as failing to comply with that duty if it does not comply with subsection (1).<br>(6) Where a company unavoidably ceases to perform at its principal office in the United Kingdom any such duty as is mentioned in subsection (5)(a) but—<br>  (a) resumes performance of that duty at other premises as soon as practicable, and<br>  (b) gives notice to the registrar of a change in the address of its principal office in accordance with subsection (1),<br>it is not to be treated as having failed to comply with that duty.' |

| Subject area | Nature of change | Modifications/details of change |
|---|---|---|
| Directors and secretaries | 6(1) Sections 162 to 167 of the Companies Act 2006 (register of directors and register of directors' residential addresses) apply to unregistered companies. | See further below. |
| Directors and secretaries | (2) Section 162 (register of directors) applies with the following modifications— | (a) In subsection (3)(b) (places where register may be kept available for inspection), for 'specified in regulations under section 1136' substitute 'specified in Part 2 of the Companies (Company Records) Regulations 2008 (S.I. 2008/3006)'. (b) In subsection (5)(b) (inspection by non-member on payment), for 'such fee as may be prescribed' substitute 'the fee prescribed by regulation 2(a) of the Companies (Fees for Inspection of Company Records) Regulations 2008 (S.I. 2008/3007)'. |
| Directors and secretaries | 7(1) Sections 240 to 246 of the Companies Act 2006 (directors' residential addresses: protection from disclosure) apply to unregistered companies. | See further below. |
| Directors and secretaries | (2) Section 243 (permitted use or disclosure of protected information by the registrar) applies with the following modifications— | (a) In subsection (2)(a) for 'by regulations made by the Secretary of State' substitute 'in the Companies (Disclosure of Address) Regulations 2009 (S.I. 2009/214)'. (b) For subsection (3) substitute— '(3) The provisions of the Companies (Disclosure of Address) Regulations 2009 (S.I. 2009/214) relating to disclosure of protected information under this section apply. (3A) Those provisions are— (a) Part 2 (disclosure of protected information), (b) Part 4 (matters relating to applications), so far as relating to disclosure under this section, and (c) any other provisions of the Regulations having effect for the purposes of those provisions.'. (c) Omit subsections (4) to (6) and (8). |
| Directors and secretaries | 8(1) Sections 275 to 279 of the Companies Act 2006 (register of secretaries) apply to unregistered companies. | See further below. |
| Directors and secretaries | (2) Section 275 applies with the following modifications— | (a) In subsection (3)(b) (places where register may be kept available for inspection), for 'specified in regulations under section 1136' substitute 'specified in Part 2 of the Companies (Company Records)Regulations 2008 (S.I. 2008/3006)'. (b) In subsection (5)(b) (inspection by non-member on payment), for 'such fee as may be prescribed' substitute 'the fee prescribed by regulation 2(a) of the Companies (Fees for Inspection of Company Records) Regulations 2008 (S.I. 2008/3007)'. |

| Subject area | Nature of change | Modifications/details of change |
|---|---|---|
| Political donations and expenditure | 9  Sections 362 to 379 of the Companies Act 2006 (control of political donations and expenditure) apply to unregistered companies, with the following modifications— | (a)  In section 369(5) (liability of directors to make good unauthorised donations or expenditure: interest), in paragraph (b) for 'such rate as the Secretary of State may prescribe by regulations' substitute, 'the rate specified in the Companies (Interest Rate for Unauthorised Political Donations or Expenditure) Regulations 2007 (S.I. 2007/2242)'.<br>(b)  In section 377 (exemption of certain political expenditure):<br>(i)  in subsection (1) for 'an order of the Secretary of State under this section' substitute 'articles 3 and 4 of the Companies (Political Expenditure Exemption) Order 2007 (S.I. 2007/2081)';<br>(ii)  omit subsection (2);<br>(iii)  in subsection (3) for 'an order under this section' substitute 'the articles mentioned in subsection (1)';<br>(iv)  omit subsection (4). |
| Accounts | 10  Sections 380 to 416, 418 to 469 and 471 to 474 of the Companies Act 2006 (accounts and reports) apply to unregistered companies, with the following modifications— | (a)  In section 383(6)(a) (small companies: determination of net amounts), for 'regulations under section 404' substitute 'Part 1 of Schedule 4 to the Small Companies and Groups (Accounts and Directors' Report) Regulations 2008 (S.I. 2008/409) or Schedule 3 to the Large and Medium-sized Companies and Groups (Accounts and Directors' Reports) Regulations 2008 (S.I. 2008/410)'.<br>(b)  In section 396 (Companies Act individual accounts)—<br>(i)  for subsection (3) (requirements as to form and content of accounts etc) substitute—<br>'(3)  The accounts must comply with the provisions of—<br>(a)  regulation 3 of the Small Companies and Groups (Accounts and Directors' Report) Regulations 2008 (S.I. 2008/409), or<br>(b)  regulations 3 and 4 of the Large and Medium-sized Companies and Groups (Accounts and Directors' Reports) Regulations 2008 (S.I. 2008/410),<br>as to the form and content of the balance sheet and profit and loss account, and additional information to be provided by way of notes to the accounts.';<br>(ii)  in subsection (4) (additional information) after 'regulations' insert 'specified in subsection (3)'.<br>(c)  In section 404 (Companies Act group accounts)—<br>(i)  for subsection (3) (requirements as to form and content of accounts etc) substitute—<br>'(3)  The accounts must comply with the provisions of—<br>(a)  regulation 6 of the Small Companies and Groups (Accounts and Directors' Report) Regulations 2008 (S.I. 2008/409), or<br>(b)  regulation 6 of the Large and Medium-sized Companies and Groups (Accounts and Directors' Reports) Regulations 2008 (S.I. 2008/410),<br>as to the form and content of the consolidated balance sheet and consolidated profit and loss account, and additional information to be provided by way of notes to the accounts.'; |

| Subject area | Nature of change | Modifications/details of change |
|---|---|---|
| | | (ii) in subsection (4) (additional information) after 'regulations' insert 'specified in subsection (3)'. |
| | | (d) In section 409 (information about related undertakings), for subsections (1) to (3) substitute— |
| | | '(1) The notes to the company's annual accounts must contain the information about related undertakings required by— |
| | | (a) regulations 4 and 7 of the Small Companies and Groups (Accounts and Directors' Report) Regulations 2008 (S.I. 2008/409), or |
| | | (b) regulation 5 of the Large and Medium-sized Companies and Groups (Accounts and Directors' Reports) Regulations 2008 (S.I. 2008/410). |
| | | (2) That information need not be disclosed with respect to an undertaking that— |
| | | (a) is established under the law of a country outside the United Kingdom, or |
| | | (b) carries on business outside the United Kingdom, if the following conditions are met.' |
| | | (e) In section 412 (information about directors' benefits: remuneration)— |
| | | (i) for subsections (1) to (3) substitute— |
| | | '(1) The information about directors' remuneration required by— |
| | | (a) the Small Companies and Groups (Accounts and Directors' Report) Regulations 2008 (S.I. 2008/409), or |
| | | (b) the Large and Medium-sized Companies and Groups (Accounts and Directors' Reports) Regulations 2008 (S.I. 2008/410), |
| | | must be given in notes to the company's annual accounts.'; |
| | | (ii) in subsection (4) for 'and regulations made under it' substitute 'and the regulations specified in subsection (1)'; |
| | | (iii) in subsection (5) for 'regulations under this section' substitute 'and the regulations specified in subsection (1)'. |
| | | (f) In section 416 (contents of directors' report: general), for subsection (4) substitute— |
| | | '(4) The directors' report must comply with the provisions of— |
| | | (a) the Small Companies and Groups (Accounts and Directors' Report) Regulations 2008 (S.I. 2008/409), or |
| | | (b) the Large and Medium-sized Companies and Groups (Accounts and Directors' Reports) Regulations 2008 (S.I. 2008/410), |
| | | as to other matters to be included in the report.'. |
| | | (g) In section 421 (contents of directors' remuneration report), for subsections (1) and (2) substitute— |
| | | '(1) The provisions of the Large and Medium-sized Companies and Groups (Accounts and Directors' Reports) Regulations 2008 (S.I. 2008/410) apply as to— |
| | | (a) the information that must be contained in a directors' remuneration report, |
| | | (b) how information is to be set out in the report, and |
| | | (c) what is to be the auditable part of the report.'. |
| | | (h) In section 426 (option to provide summary financial statement)— |

| Subject area | Nature of change | Modifications/details of change |
| --- | --- | --- |
| | | (i)   in subsection (1)(a) for 'regulations made by the Secretary of State' substitute 'the Companies (Summary Financial Statement) Regulations 2008 (S.I. 2008/374)';
(ii)   omit subsections (3) and (6). |
| | (j) | In section 427 (form and contents of summary financial statement: unquoted companies)—
(i)   in subsection (1)(b) for 'regulations made under it' substitute 'the Companies (Summary Financial Statement) Regulations 2008 (S.I. 2008/374)';
(ii)   for subsection (2) substitute—
'(2) The summary financial statement must be in the form and contain such information as is required in the case of an unquoted company by the Companies (Summary Financial Statement) Regulations 2008 (S.I. 2008/374).' |
| | (j) | In section 428 (form and contents of summary financial statement: quoted companies)—
(i)   in subsection (1)(b) for 'regulations made under it' substitute 'the Companies (Summary Financial Statement) Regulations 2008 (S.I. 2008/374)';
(ii)   for subsection (2) substitute—
'(2) The summary financial statement must be in the form and contain such information as is required in the case of a quoted company by the Companies (Summary Financial Statement) Regulations 2008 (S.I. 2008/374).' |
| | (k) | In section 444(3) (filing obligations of companies subject to small companies regime: copies of accounts and reports)—
(i)   in paragraph (a) for 'regulations made by the Secretary of State' substitute 'regulation 5 of the Small Companies and Groups (Accounts and Directors' Report) Regulations 2008 (S.I. 2008/409)';
(ii)   in paragraph (b) for 'the regulations' substitute 'that regulation'. |
| | (l) | In section 445(3) (filing obligations of medium-sized companies: copies of accounts and reports)—
(i)   in paragraph (a) for 'regulations made by the Secretary of State' substitute 'regulation 4 of the Large and Medium-sized Companies and Groups (Accounts and Directors' Reports) Regulations 2008 (S.I. 2008/410)';
(ii)   in paragraph (b) for 'the regulations' substitute 'that regulation'. |
| | (m) | In section 449(2)(b) (special auditor's report where abbreviated accounts delivered: compliance with regulations), for 'regulations under that section' substitute 'regulation 5 of the Small Companies and Groups (Accounts and Directors' Report) Regulations 2008 (S.I. 2008/409) or regulation 4 of the Large and Medium-sized Companies and Groups (Accounts and Directors' Reports) Regulations 2008 (S.I. 2008/410)'. |
| | (n) | In section 450(4) (approval and signing of abbreviated accounts: accounts not complying with requirements), for 'regulations under the relevant section' substitute 'regulation 5 of the Small Companies and Groups (Accounts and Directors' Report) Regulations 2008 (S.I. 2008/409) or regulation 4 of the Large and Medium-sized Companies and Groups (Accounts and Directors' Reports) Regulations 2008 (S.I. 2008/410)'. |
| | (o) | In section 453 (civil penalty for failure to file accounts and reports)— |

| Subject area | Nature of change | Modifications/details of change |
|---|---|---|
| | | (i) in subsection (2) (determination of amount), for 'regulations made by the Secretary of State' substitute 'the relevant provisions of the Companies (Late Filing Penalties) and Limited Liability Partnerships (Filing Periods and Late Filing Penalties) Regulations 2008 (S.I. 2008/497)'; |
| | | (ii) omit subsection (5). |
| | | (p) In section 454 (voluntary revision of accounts), for subsections (3) to (5) substitute— |
| | | '(3) The provisions of the Companies (Revision of Defective Accounts) Regulations 2008 (S.I. 2008/373) apply'. |
| | | (q) In section 457 (other persons authorized to apply to the court)— |
| | | (i) for subsections (1) to (3) substitute— |
| | | '(1) The Companies (Defective Accounts and Directors' Reports) (Authorised Person) and Supervision of Accounts and Reports (Prescribed Body) Order 2008 (S.I. 2008/623) apply as regards— |
| | | (a) the persons authorised by the Secretary of State for the purposes of section 456 (application to court in respect of defective accounts or reports), and |
| | | (b) the requirements and other provisions applying to the exercise of functions as an authorised person.'; |
| | | (ii) omit subsections (5) to (7). |
| | | (r) In section 464 (accounting standards)— |
| | | (i) in subsection (1) for 'such body or bodies as may be prescribed by regulations' substitute 'the body known as the Accounting Standards Board, as prescribed by the Accounting Standards (Prescribed Body) Regulations 2008 (S.I. 2008/651)'; |
| | | (ii) omit subsection (3). |
| Audit | 11(1) Sections 475 to 481 and 484 to 539 of the Companies Act 2006 (audit) apply to unregistered companies, with the following modifications— | (a) Section 494 (disclosure of services provided by auditor or associates and related remuneration) is modified so that it reads as follows— |
| | | **'Disclosure of services provided by auditor or associates and related remuneration** |
| | | 494. The Companies (Disclosure of Auditor Remuneration and Liability Limitation Agreements) Regulations 2008 (S.I. 2008/489) apply as regards the disclosure of— |
| | | (a) the nature of any services provided for a company by the company's auditor (whether in the capacity as auditor or otherwise) or by the auditor's associates; |
| | | (b) the amount of any remuneration received or receivable by the auditor, or the auditor's associates, in respect of any such services'. |
| | | (b) In section 504 (meaning of 'senior statutory auditor'), in subsection (1)(b)(ii) for 'by order of the Secretary of State' substitute 'by the Statutory Auditors (Delegation of Functions etc) Order 2008 (S.I. 2008/496)'. |
| | | (c) Section 538 (disclosure by company of liability limitation agreement) is modified so that it reads as follows— |
| | | 'Disclosure of agreement by company |
| | | 538. A company that has entered into a liability limitation agreement must make the disclosure in connection with the agreement required by the Companies (Disclosure of Auditor Remuneration and Liability Limitation Agreements) Regulations 2008 (S.I. 2008/489)'. |

The Schedule to the Regulations therefore applies the following provisions of the Companies Act 2006   **33.1043.07**
to unregistered companies (subject to the following limitations, adaptations, or modifications):

(i)   In Part 28 (takeovers etc)—
>    Chapter 2 (impediments to takeovers);
>    Chapter 3 ('squeeze-out' and 'sell-out')—the provisions of this Chapter so far as relating
>    to the offeree company apply to an unregistered company only if it has voting shares
>    admitted to trading on a regulated market.

(ii)   In Part 17 (a company's share capital)—
>    section 546 (issued and allotted share capital)—so far as necessary for the purposes of
>    other provisions applied by these Regulations;
>    section 558 (when shares are allotted)—so far as necessary for the purposes of other
>    provisions applied by these Regulations.

(iii)   In Part 36 (offences)—
>    section 1122 (liability of company as officer in default)-so far as relating to offences
>    under provisions applied by these Regulations;
>    section 1132 (production and inspection of documents where offence suspected)— so
>    far as relating to offences under provisions applied by these Regulations.

(iv)   In Part 37 (supplementary provisions)—
>    sections 1134, 1135, and 1138 (company records)—so far as necessary for the purposes
>    of provisions applied by these Regulations;
>    section 1139(1) and (4) (service of documents on company)—so far as necessary for the
>    purposes of provisions applied by these Regulations;
>    section 1140 (service of documents on directors, secretaries and others)—so far as
>    necessary for the purposes of provisions applied by these Regulations.

(v)   In Part 38 (companies: interpretation)—
>    section 1173 (minor definitions: general), the definition of 'Gazette'—so far as necessary
>    for the purposes of provisions applied by these Regulations;
>    Parts 46 and 47 (general supplementary provisions and final provisions)—so far as
>    necessary for the purposes of provisions applied by these Regulations.

**Companies Act 2006**

## PART 34
### OVERSEAS COMPANIES

### *Introductory*

### 1044  Overseas companies

In the Companies Acts an 'overseas company' means a company incorporated outside the United Kingdom.   **34.1044.01**

> COMMENCEMENT DATE 1 October 2009[1]

For the rationale of Part 34, see Explanatory Notes to Act, paragraphs 1326 to 1364. The latest available figures released by BIS for the year 2010–2011 suggest that there are some 10,489 overseas companies registered at the Companies Registry—see Statistical Tables on Companies Registration Activities 2010–11 (Table E1)(Companies House) page 29.   **34.1044.02**

The Companies Acts have for many years contained provisions dealing with foreign incorporated companies engaging in business in the United Kingdom.[2] These rules were originally based on the concept of 'establishing a place of business'—on this criterion see, for example, *Lord Advocate v Huron and Erie Loan and Savings Co*,[3] *South India Shipping Corp Ltd v Export-Import Bank of Korea*,[4] and *Cleveland Museum of Art v Capricorn Art International*.[5] Part XXIII was the base for the old law as supplemented by section 70 of CA 1989. With the implementation of the Eleventh Company Law Directive (EC) 89/666,[6] a parallel set of rules, covering the situation where a 'branch' was set up, was introduced. The result was a hopelessly confusing jumble of cross-referenced sections linked to   **34.1044.03**

---

[1]  Companies Act 2006 (Commencement No 8, Transitional Provisions and Savings) Order 2008, SI 2008/2860, art 3(q).

[2]  For background analysis, see Milman, Ch 5 in *National Corporate Law in a Globalised Market* (Edward Elgar, 2009); Tansinda in (1997) 18 *Company Lawer* 98 and in Chap 12 in Milman (ed), *Regulating Enterprise* (Hart Publishing, 1999).

[3]  1911 SC 612, 616.

[4]  [1985] 2 All ER 219.

[5]  [1990] BCLC 546.

[6]  [1989] OJ L395/36.

Schedule 21A for branches. The regime now outlined in sections 1044 to 1059 of CA 2006 appears to merge both regimes, with the branch concept now being dominant: that is a sensible development that will simplify this increasingly complex area of law. The Company Law Review favoured this rationalization of the regulatory regime—see *Final Report*.[7] Similar proposals were contained in the 2002 White Paper, *Modernising Company Law*,[8] paragraphs 6.16 to 6.17. Like much of the CA 2006, the future shape of the law hinges on secondary rules made by the Secretary of State. Thus, the White Paper of 2005[9] favoured a simplification in the law by making greater use of secondary legislation. Note also Explanatory Notes to the Bill when it entered the Commons in May 2006, paragraphs 1257 *et seq*. Part 34 of CA 2006 therefore frequently replaces substantive provisions with opaque rule-making powers.

**34.1044.04**    Section 1044 defines 'overseas company' in the terms that it is a company incorporated outside the United Kingdom. Under the Companies Act 1985 the limiting factor was Great Britain and not the United Kingdom. Companies incorporated in Scotland and Northern Ireland are therefore not overseas companies under the Companies Act 2006. Companies incorporated in the Isle of Man and the Channel Islands (formerly covered by CA 1985, section 699) are traditionally treated as overseas companies with about 1,000 of such companies appearing on the register in 2003–2004. The Company Law Review[10] at paragraph 11.32 recommended that companies incorporated in the Isle of Man and Channel Islands be treated just like non-EC companies. Under the previous provision the term used was 'oversea' company—we have now moved to the more elegant 'overseas' descriptor.

**34.1044.05**    Part 34 is not the sole source of statutory provision in CA 2006 for overseas companies—see, for example, sections 1066 (registered numbers), 1067 (registered numbers of branches of overseas companies), 1084 (retention by registrar of records), 1120 (application of Part 35), and 1139 (service of documents) of this Act and section 453 of CA 1985 (DBIS investigations). In addition, there is a substantial body of secondary legislation. So, for instance, we have the Overseas Companies Regulations 2009,[11] which deal with registration, accounts, and disclosure requirements for overseas companies, and the Overseas Companies (Execution of Documents and Registration of Charges) Regulations 2009,[12] which, as their designation suggests, deal with particular issues of relevance for overseas companies.

### 1045  Company contracts and execution of documents by companies

**34.1045.01**    (1)  The Secretary of State may make provision by regulations applying sections 43 to 52 (formalities of doing business and other matters) to overseas companies, subject to such exceptions, adaptations or modifications as may be specified in the regulations.

(2)  Regulations under this section are subject to negative resolution procedure.

COMMENCEMENT DATE  1 October 2009[13]

**34.1045.02**    This is a sensible facility. It was necessary for secondary legislation in the form of the Foreign Companies Execution of Documents Regulations 1994,[14] to deal with the issue of whether the standard rules on pre-incorporation contracts applied to contracts made on behalf of foreign companies. However, it would have been more useful for section 1045 to have conferred this power to make dedicated provision without limiting reference to sections 43 to 52. Regulations already exist (see paragraph 34.1044.05 above).

**34.1045.03**    On negative resolutions in subsection (2), see section 1289.

### *Registration of particulars*

### 1046  Duty to register particulars

**34.1046.01**    (1)  The Secretary of State may make provision by regulations requiring an overseas company—

(a)  to deliver to the registrar for registration a return containing specified particulars, and

(b)  to deliver to the registrar with the return specified documents.

(2)  The regulations—

(a)  must, in the case of a company other than a Gibraltar company, require the company to register particulars if the company opens a branch in the United Kingdom, and

---

[7]  URN 01/942 paras 11.21–11.33.

[8]  Cm 5553-I.

[9]  *Company Law Reform* Cm 6456, para 4.13. See generally paras 6.15–6.17 for background.

[10]  See above.

[11]  SI 2009/1801.

[12]  SI 2009/1917.

[13]  Companies Act 2006 (Commencement No 8, Transitional Provisions and Savings) Order 2008, SI 2008/2860, art 3(q).

[14]  SI 1994/950.

(b)  may, in the case of a Gibraltar company, require the company to register particulars if the company opens a branch in the United Kingdom, and

(c)  may, in any case, require the registration of particulars in such other circumstances as may be specified.

(3)  In subsection (2)—

'branch' means a branch within the meaning of the Eleventh Company Law Directive (89/666/EEC);

'Gibraltar company' means a company incorporated in Gibraltar.

(4)  The regulations may provide that where a company has registered particulars under this section and any alteration is made—

(a)  in the specified particulars, or

(b)  in any document delivered with the return,

the company must deliver to the registrar for registration a return containing specified particulars of the alteration.

(5)  The regulations may make provision—

(a)  requiring the return under this section to be delivered for registration to the registrar for a specified part of the United Kingdom, and

(b)  requiring it to be so delivered before the end of a specified period.

(6)  The regulations may make different provision according to—

(a)  the place where the company is incorporated, and

(b)  the activities carried on (or proposed to be carried on) by it.

This is without prejudice to the general power to make different provision for different cases.

(7)  In this section 'specified' means specified in the regulations.

(8)  Regulations under this section are subject to affirmative resolution procedure.

COMMENCEMENT DATE 1 October 2009[15]

Subsection (1) confers power on the Secretary of State to make regulations requiring overseas companies to deliver particulars for registration. Under the former law in CA 1985, section 691 (and Schedule 21A), these details were much more specific. The Overseas Companies Regulations 2009,[16] are used to provide that level of detail in the future.   **34.1046.02**

Subsection (2) states that registration of particulars under the regulations must be required where an overseas company opens a branch. This is a well-established concept of EC law—see *Somafer*.[17] It should be easier to determine this question as opposed to the more opaque test of establishing a place of business which has caused difficulties for the courts—see the commentary to section 1044 above. Note that filing under section 1046 does not make an overseas company a UK-registered company: section 1158.   **34.1046.03**

Subsection (3) indicates that modified particulars will require registration. Subsection (4) deals with the minutiae of the required particulars—but again detail is in the regulations. Separate provision is made for Scotland and Northern Ireland. Under subsection (5) the extent of detail required to be registered can vary according to the place of incorporation. Presumably a two-tier system will be introduced catering for EEA and non-EEA companies—see section 1170 for EEA companies. Different types of business may also justify differential treatment.   **34.1046.04**

Subsection (6) emphasizes that regulations are to be made under this section through the affirmative resolution procedure (as explained by section 1290).   **34.1046.05**

Subsection (7) was a last minute insertion into the Bill.   **34.1046.06**

## 1047   Registered name of overseas company

(1)  Regulations under section 1046 (duty to register particulars) must require an overseas company that is required to register particulars to register its name.   **34.1047.01**

(2)  This may be—

(a)  the company's corporate name (that is, its name under the law of the country or territory in which it is incorporated) or

(b)  an alternative name specified in accordance with section 1048.

(3)  Subject only to subsection (5), an EEA company may always register its corporate name.

(4)  In any other case, the following provisions of Part 5 (a company's name) apply in relation to the registration of the name of an overseas company—

(a)  section 53 (prohibited names);

---

[15]  Companies Act 2006 (Commencement No 8, Transitional Provisions and Savings) Order 2008, SI 2008/2860, art 3(q).

[16]  SI 2009/1801.

[17]  Case 33/78 [1978] ECR 2183.

(b)  sections 54 to 56 (sensitive words and expressions);

(c)  section 65 (inappropriate use of indications of company type or legal form);

(d)  sections 66 to 74 (similarity to other names);

(e)  section 75 (provision of misleading information etc);

(f)  section 76 (misleading indication of activities).

(5)  The provisions of section 57 (permitted characters etc) apply in every case.

(6)  Any reference in the provisions mentioned in subsection (4) or (5) to a change of name shall be read as a reference to registration of a different name under section 1048.

COMMENCEMENT DATE 1 October 2009[18]

**34.1047.02**    Subsections (1) and (2) provide that on registration an overseas company should select a registered name—this can either be its corporate name or an alternative name designated under section 1048. This might be useful if an English translation would aid recognition/goodwill of the firm. For its statutory predecessor see CA 1985, section 693. Under the former CA 1985, section 694, the issue of conflict with a local name was addressed.

**34.1047.03**    Subsection (3) is unclear. On one interpretation, an EEA company (see section 1170 for definition) has no choice—it must register its corporate name. Having said that, the word 'may' is used rather than 'must'.

**34.1047.04**    Subsections (4) and (5) make applicable a number of pertinent provisions in the Act to the registered name (whatever that is). Subsection (6) deals with change of name.

**34.1047.05**    On the registered numbers of overseas companies, see sections 1066(6) and 1120. On registered numbers of branches of overseas companies, note section 1067.

### 1048  Registration under alternative name

**34.1048.01**    (1)  An overseas company that is required to register particulars under section 1046 may at any time deliver to the registrar for registration a statement specifying a name, other than its corporate name, under which it proposes to carry on business in the United Kingdom.

(2)  An overseas company that has registered an alternative name may at any time deliver to the registrar of companies for registration a statement specifying a different name under which it proposes to carry on business in the United Kingdom (which may be its corporate name or a further alternative) in substitution for the name previously registered.

(3)  The alternative name for the time being registered under this section is treated for all purposes of the law applying in the United Kingdom as the company's corporate name.

(4)  This does not—

(a)  affect the references in this section or section 1047 to the company's corporate name,

(b)  affect any rights or obligation of the company, or

(c)  render defective any legal proceedings by or against the company.

(5)  Any legal proceedings that might have been continued or commenced against the company by its corporate name, or any name previously registered under this section, may be continued or commenced against it by its name for the time being so registered.

COMMENCEMENT DATE 1 October 2009[19]

**34.1048.02**    Subsection (1) permits an overseas company to select an alternative name for its registered name. This is consistent with the policy for local companies being permitted to use trading names that are not the same as their registered names—see Part 5 for the rules on company names. For 'registrar', see section 1060.

**34.1048.03**    Subsection (2) indicates that procedures for changing this alternative name will be prescribed.

**34.1048.04**    Subsection (3) states that subject to subsection (4) the registered alternative name is treated as the equivalent of the corporate name for the purposes of UK company law. See CA 1985, section 694(5) for the former provision.

**34.1048.05**    Subsection (5) confirms that a change of name under these provisions does not affect the commencement or continuance of litigation against an overseas company; this reflects the standard position in company law on the impact of change of name.

---

[18] Companies Act 2006 (Commencement No 8, Transitional Provisions and Savings) Order 2008, SI 2008/2860, art 3(q).

[19] Companies Act 2006 (Commencement No 8, Transitional Provisions and Savings) Order 2008, SI 2008/2860, art 3(q).

## *Other requirements*

### 1049   Accounts and reports: general

(1) The Secretary of State may make provision by regulations requiring an overseas company that is required to register particulars under section 1046—

   (a) to prepare the like accounts and directors' report, and

   (b) to cause to be prepared such an auditor's report,

as would be required if the company were formed and registered under this Act.

(2) The regulations may for this purpose apply, with or without modifications, all or any of the provisions of—

   Part 15 (accounts and reports), and

   Part 16 (audit).

(3) The Secretary of State may make provision by regulations requiring an overseas company to deliver to the registrar copies of—

   (a) the accounts and reports prepared in accordance with the regulations, or

   (b) the accounts and reports that it is required to prepare and have audited under the law of the country in which it is incorporated.

(4) Regulations under this section are subject to negative resolution procedure.

COMMENCEMENT DATE 1 October 2009[20]

**34.1049.01**

Subsections (1) and (2) provide that the Secretary of State may make provision governing the preparation of accounts, directors' report, and auditors' report by a registered overseas company. In these regulations standard provisions of UK company law as found in Parts 15 and 16 of the Act may be modified as appropriate (subsection (2)). These regulations (the Overseas Companies Regulations 2009[21] ) replaced sections 699AA to 703 of, and Schedule 21D to, CA 1985.   **34.1049.02**

Subsection (3) indicates that the Secretary of State may make regulations requiring an overseas company to file accounts.   **34.1049.03**

Subsection (4) states that regulations are to be made under this section via the negative resolution procedure (see section 1289).   **34.1049.04**

### 1050   Accounts and reports: credit or financial institutions

(1) This section applies to a credit or financial institution—

   (a) that is incorporated or otherwise formed outside the United Kingdom and Gibraltar,

   (b) whose head office is outside the United Kingdom and Gibraltar, and

   (c) that has a branch in the United Kingdom.

(2) In subsection (1) 'branch' means a place of business that forms a legally dependent part of the institution and conducts directly all or some of the operations inherent in its business.

(3) The Secretary of State may make provision by regulations requiring an institution to which this section applies—

   (a) to prepare the like accounts and directors' report, and

   (b) to cause to be prepared such an auditor's report,

as would be required if the institution were a company formed and registered under this Act.

(4) The regulations may for this purpose apply, with or without modifications, all or any of the provisions of—

   Part 15 (accounts and reports), and

   Part 16 (audit).

(5) The Secretary of State may make provision by regulations requiring an institution to which this section applies to deliver to the registrar copies of—

   (a) accounts and reports prepared in accordance with the regulations, or

   (b) accounts and reports that it is required to prepare and have audited under the law of the country in which the institution has its head office.

(6) Regulations under this section are subject to negative resolution procedure.

COMMENCEMENT DATE 1 October 2009[22]

**34.1050.01**

Subsection (1) (which has as its predecessor CA 1985, section 699A) applies to overseas credit and financial institutions (see section 1173 for definitions) with branches in the United Kingdom. The separate regulation of such bodies is now standard practice and emanates from EC law.   **34.1050.02**

---

[20] Companies Act 2006 (Commencement No 8, Transitional Provisions and Savings) Order 2008, SI 2008/2860, art 3(q).

[21] SI 2009/1801.

[22] Companies Act 2006 (Commencement No 8, Transitional Provisions and Savings) Order 2008, SI 2008/2860, art 3(q).

**34.1050.03** Subsection (2) defines a branch for the purposes of subsection (1). See *Somafer*[23] for further guidance from the ECJ.

**34.1050.04** Subsections (3) and (4) provide that the Secretary of State is empowered to make regulations concerning the preparation of accounts, directors' report, and auditors' report for credit and financial institutions. It is made clear by subsection (4) that the standard provisions of UK company law may be modified as appropriate.

**34.1050.05** Subsection (5) deals with filing requirements. Secondary legislation is crucial here. For 'registrar' see section 1060.

**34.1050.06** Subsection (6) stipulates that the negative resolution procedure (see section 1289) is to be used for regulations made under this section. See the Overseas Companies Regulations 2009.[24]

### 1051 Trading disclosures[a]

**34.1051.01**
(1) The Secretary of State may by regulations make provision requiring overseas companies carrying on business in the United Kingdom—
   (a) to display specified information in specified locations,
   (b) to state specified information in specified descriptions of document or communication, and
   (c) to provide specified information on request to those they deal with in the course of their business.
(2) The regulations—
   (a) shall in every case require a company that has registered particulars under section 1046 to disclose the name registered by it under section 1047, and
   (b) may make provision as to the manner in which any specified information is to be displayed, stated or provided.
(3) The regulations may make provision corresponding to that made by—
      section 83 (civil consequences of failure to make required disclosure), and
      section 84 (criminal consequences of failure to make required disclosure).
(4) In this section 'specified' means specified in the regulations.
(5) Regulations under this section are subject to affirmative resolution procedure.

AMENDMENTS AND NOTES

[a] This section applies with modifications to LLPs by reg 59 of the Limited Liability Partnerships (Application of the Companies Act 2006) Regulations 2009, SI 2009/1804.

COMMENCEMENT DATE 1 October 2009[25]

**34.1051.02** See CA 1985, section 693 for an earlier formulation.

**34.1051.03** Subsection (1) raises the possibility of putative secondary rules dealing with trading disclosure requirements. See Part 41 of this Act) for the general rules on trading disclosures. For specified information, see subsection (4) which was a last-minute insertion into the clause.

**34.1051.04** The proposed regulations must by virtue of subsection (2) require the disclosure of the registered name of the overseas company and may provide for the disclosure of other information.

**34.1051.05** Subsection (3)—sanctions are hereby specified. These should mirror those specified in sections 83 and 84.

**34.1051.06** Subsection (5) states that regulations under this section are to be made using the affirmative resolution procedure (see section 1290). See the Overseas Companies Regulations 2009.[26]

**34.1051.07** As stated above, the issue of trading disclosures for overseas companies is now dealt with by Part 7 of the Overseas Companies Regulations 2009, regulations 58 to 67. Overseas companies carrying on business in the United Kingdom must comply with these Regulations. Under regulation 60 an overseas company must disclose its name and place of incorporation at every business location and service address. Disclosure is also required by virtue of regulation 63 on all business letters, websites etc. EEA companies do not have to disclose place of incorporation. Under regulation 65 persons dealing with an overseas company have the right to demand in writing details of any service address where claims can be lodged, such details to be supplied within five working days. Failure to comply with the requirements in Part 7 can lead to criminal sanctions (regulation 67) and may prejudice civil claims to enforce contracts (regulation 66).

---

[23] Case C33/78 [1978] ECR 2183.
[24] SI 2009/1801.
[25] Companies Act 2006 (Commencement No 8, Transitional Provisions and Savings) Order 2008, SI 2008/ 2860, art 3(q).
[26] SI 2009/1801.

## 1052   Company charges

(1) The Secretary of State may by regulations make provision about the registration of specified charges over property in the United Kingdom of a registered overseas company.                    **34.1052.01**

(2) The power in subsection (1) includes power to make provision about—

   (a) a registered overseas company that—

      (i) has particulars registered in more than one part of the United Kingdom;

      (ii) has property in more than one part of the United Kingdom;

   (b) the circumstances in which property is to be regarded, for the purposes of the regulations, as being, or not being, in the United Kingdom or in a particular part of the United Kingdom;

   (c) the keeping by a registered overseas company of records and registers about specified charges and their inspection;

   (d) the consequences of a failure to register a charge in accordance with the regulations;

   (e) the circumstances in which a registered overseas company ceases to be subject to the regulations.

(3) The regulations may for this purpose apply, with or without modifications, any of the provisions of Part 25 (company charges).

(4) The regulations may modify any reference in an enactment to Part 25, or to a particular provision of that Part, so as to include a reference to the regulations or to a specified provision of the regulations.

(5) Regulations under this section are subject to negative resolution procedure.

(6) In this section—

   'registered overseas company' means an overseas company that has registered particulars under section 1046(1), and

   'specified' means specified in the regulations.

COMMENCEMENT DATE 1 October 2009[27]

This was a late inclusion into the Bill. The problem of applying the company charge registration provisions to overseas companies has caused difficulties both for the courts and for the bureaucrats. See *Slavenburg's Bank NV v Intercontinental Natural Resources*[28] for the classic illustration of the potential for confusion. The basic former provision here was CA 1985, section 409. CA 1989 introduced sections 703A to 703N into the 1985 Act but these provisions were never commenced.                    **34.1052.02**

Subsections (1) to (3) authorize the Secretary of State to customize Part 25 to fit the needs of overseas companies which have charges created over their assets.                    **34.1052.03**

The negative resolution procedure (see section 1289) is to be used for the purposes of making regulations under this section (subsection (5)). See the Overseas Companies (Execution of Documents and Registration of Charges) Regulations 2009.[29]                    **34.1052.04**

Subsection (6) is a local definition provision.                    **34.1052.05**

Under Part 3 of the Overseas Companies (Execution of Documents and Registration of Charges) Regulations 2009,[30] regulations 8 to 28, the position with regard to registration of charges created by overseas companies is fully explained. The obligation to register details of charges only applies to registered overseas companies within the meaning of section 1046 of the Act (regulation 8). This clarifies the law. The Slavenburg register is no more. The obligation to register details only applies to prescribed charges over UK property (regulation 9). Again this is a welcome clarification. Once these points have been resolved, the general rules of domestic charge registration (for the most part) apply. Regulation 28 and the Schedule deal with important transitional matters, particularly with regard to charges created before 1 October 2009 (which is the operative date for the new regime).                    **34.1052.06**

## 1053   Other returns etc

(1) This section applies to overseas companies that are required to register particulars under section 1046.                    **34.1053.01**

(2) The Secretary of State may make provision by regulations requiring the delivery to the registrar of returns—

   (a) by a company to which this section applies that—

      (i) is being wound up, or

---

[27] Companies Act 2006 (Commencement No 8, Transitional Provisions and Savings) Order 2008, SI 2008/2860, art 3(q).

[28] [1980] 1 All ER 955.

[29] SI 2009/1917.

[30] SI 2009/1917.

           (ii)  becomes or ceases to be subject to insolvency proceedings, or an arrangement or composition or any analogous proceedings;

      (b)  by the liquidator of a company to which this section applies.

    (3)  The regulations may specify—

      (a)  the circumstances in which a return is to be made,

      (b)  the particulars to be given in it, and

      (c)  the period within which it is to be made.

    (4)  The Secretary of State may make provision by regulations requiring notice to be given to the registrar of the appointment in relation to a company to which this section applies of a judicial factor (in Scotland).

    (5)  The regulations may include provision corresponding to any provision made by section 1154 of this Act (duty to notify registrar of certain appointments).

    (6)  Regulations under this section are subject to affirmative resolution procedure.

COMMENCEMENT DATE 1 October 2009[31]

**34.1053.02**    This was a late addition to Part 34. For previous provision dealing with these matters, see CA 1985, sections 703O to 703R.

**34.1053.03**    For the affirmative resolution procedure cited in subsection (6) see section 1290.

## *Supplementary*

### 1054  Offences

**34.1054.01**    (1)  Regulations under this Part may specify the person or persons responsible for complying with any specified requirement of the regulations.

    (2)  Regulations under this Part may make provision for offences, including provision as to—

      (a)  the person or persons liable in the case of any specified contravention of the regulations, and

      (b)  circumstances that are, or are not, to be a defence on a charge of such an offence.

    (3)  The regulations must not provide—

      (a)  for imprisonment, or

      (b)  for the imposition on summary conviction of a fine exceeding level 5 on the standard scale and, for continued contravention, a daily default fine not exceeding one-tenth of level 5 on the standard scale.

    (4)  In this section 'specified' means specified in the regulations.

COMMENCEMENT DATE 1 October 2009[32]

**34.1054.02**    Offences are covered by subsection (1). Subsection (2) provides that regulations are to be made to identify liable persons and defences/non-defences.

**34.1054.03**    Subsection (3) emphasizes that any sanctions imposed cannot involve imprisonment nor fines in excess of a specified maximum. For level 5 of the standard scale, see paragraph 1370 of the Explanatory Notes to the Bill when it entered the Commons in May 2006. It is of course difficult to contemplate imprisonment of an offender who will often be non-resident.

**34.1054.04**    Subsection (4) defines the word 'specified' when used in this section. As the core of the future law will be embodied in secondary regulations this is a necessary provision.

### 1055  Disclosure of individual's residential address: protection from disclosure

**34.1055.01**    Where regulations under section 1046 (overseas companies: duty to register particulars) require an overseas company to register particulars of an individual's usual residential address, they must contain provision corresponding to that made by Chapter 8 of Part 10 (directors' residential addresses: protection from disclosure).

COMMENCEMENT DATE 1 October 2009[33]

**34.1055.02**    This deals with particulars of residential address and provides for the confidentiality facility recently introduced into English law (see Criminal Justice and Police Act 2001, section 45, which inserted sections 723B to 723F into CA 1985), to be applied to the overseas company scenario—see now CA 2006, sections 240 to 246 for the general provisions on domestic companies. Elements of this provision can be detected in CA 1985, section 691(5). This is a useful precaution as the activities of terrorists who

---

[31] Companies Act 2006 (Commencement No 8, Transitional Provisions and Savings) Order 2008, SI 2008/2860, art 3(q).

[32] Companies Act 2006 (Commencement No 8, Transitional Provisions and Savings) Order 2008, SI 2008/2860, art 3(q).

[33] Companies Act 2006 (Commencement No 8, Transitional Provisions and Savings) Order 2008, SI 2008/2860, art 3(q).

might wish to threaten directors of companies whose business activities are disapproved of are, with the advent of the internet, no longer territorially limited. Terrorism has gone global.

### 1056  Requirement to identify persons authorised to accept service of documents

Regulations under section 1046 (overseas companies: duty to register particulars) must require an overseas company to register—  **34.1056.01**

(a)  particulars identifying every person resident in the United Kingdom authorised to accept service of documents on behalf of the company, or

(b)  a statement that there is no such person.

COMMENCEMENT DATE  1 October 2009[34]

The Overseas Companies Regulations 2009,[35] regulation 75 identify persons authorized to accept service of documents on behalf of an overseas company or if there is no such person to include a statement to that effect. This is a critical control mechanism designed to facilitate the initiation of legal proceedings against overseas companies. See also section 1139(2). For the statutory predecessor, see CA 1985, section 691(1)(b)(ii).  **34.1056.02**

### 1057  Registrar to whom returns, notices etc to be delivered

(1)  This section applies to an overseas company that is required to register or has registered particulars under section 1046 in more than one part of the United Kingdom.  **34.1057.01**

(2)  The Secretary of State may provide by regulations that, in the case of such a company, anything authorised or required to be delivered to the registrar under this Part is to be delivered—

(a)  to the registrar for each part of the United Kingdom in which the company is required to register or has registered particulars, or

(b)  to the registrar for such part or parts of the United Kingdom as may be specified in or determined in accordance with the regulations.

(3)  Regulations under this section are subject to negative resolution procedure.

COMMENCEMENT DATE  1 October 2009[36]

This was a new provision inserted by Grand Committee in the House of Lords. It covers the scenario where an overseas company has been required to send particulars to more than one registry in the United Kingdom and authorizes the Secretary of State to make regulations (by use of the negative resolution procedure (subsection (3)) to address the situation. 'Registrar' is defined by section 1060. For the negative resolution procedure, see section 1289.  **34.1057.02**

### 1058  Duty to give notice of ceasing to have registrable presence

(1)  The Secretary of State may make provision by regulations requiring an overseas company—  **34.1058.01**

(a)  if it has registered particulars following the opening of a branch, in accordance with regulations under section 1046(2)(a) or (b), to give notice to the registrar if it closes that branch;

(b)  if it has registered particulars in other circumstances, in accordance with regulations under section 1046(2)(c), to give notice to the registrar if the circumstances that gave rise to the obligation to register particulars cease to obtain.

(2)  The regulations must provide for the notice to be given to the registrar for the part of the United Kingdom to which the original return of particulars was delivered.

(3)  The regulations may specify the period within which notice must be given.

(4)  Regulations under this section are subject to negative resolution procedure.

COMMENCEMENT DATE  1 October 2009[37]

Subsection (1) states that the Secretary of State is to make regulation requiring that an overseas company which ceases to have any connection with the UK must notify that fact. The Company Law Review, *Final Report* (paragraph 11.32) recommended that the authorities should be given the power to strike off overseas companies which ceased to operate in the jurisdiction. Maintaining the integrity of the register could be important for statistical purposes. For 'registrar', see section 1060. Any  **34.1058.02**

---

[34]  Companies Act 2006 (Commencement No 8, Transitional Provisions and Savings) Order 2008, SI 2008/2860, art 3(q).

[35]  SI 2009/1801.

[36]  Companies Act 2006 (Commencement No 8, Transitional Provisions and Savings) Order 2008, SI 2008/2860, art 3(q).

[37]  Companies Act 2006 (Commencement No 8, Transitional Provisions and Savings) Order 2008, SI 2008/2860, art 3(q).

regulations made under this provision are to adopt the negative resolution procedure (see section 1289). Note also section 1084. See the Overseas Companies Regulations 2009,[38] regulation 77.

### 1059   Application of provisions in case of relocation of branch

**34.1059.01**    For the purposes of this Part—
> (a) the relocation of a branch from one part of the United Kingdom to another counts as the closing of one branch and the opening of another;
> (b) the relocation of a branch within the same part of the United Kingdom does not.

COMMENCEMENT DATE 1 October 2009[39]

**34.1059.02**    This is provision replaces section 695A(4) of CA 1985. The provision itself reflects the fact that administratively there are three distinct systems of corporate law operating within the United Kingdom so the relocation of a branch from Birmingham to Belfast would be treated as a branch closure. Relocation of a branch within a distinct part of the United Kingdom (eg from Manchester to Lancaster) does not count as a branch closure.

---

[38] SI 2009/1801.
[39] Companies Act 2006 (Commencement No 8, Transitional Provisions and Savings) Order 2008, SI 2008/2860, art 3(q).

# Companies Act 2006

## PART 35
## THE REGISTRAR OF COMPANIES

**35.0.01**   Part 35 sets out the essential functions of the registrar. It replaces the Companies Act 1985, Part XXIV, and also contains a number of new provisions and amendments to reflect the recommendations of the Company Law Review (CLR), together with other changes that were introduced during the course of the Bill's passage through Parliament. Consistently with the approach of the Act as a whole, it makes provision in relation to the whole of the United Kingdom.

### Scheme of this Part

**35.1059A.01**   **1059A   Scheme of this Part**

(1)  The scheme of this Part is as follows.
(2)  The following provisions apply generally (to the registrar, to any functions of the registrar, or to documents delivered to or issued by the registrar under any enactment, as the case may be)—
      sections 1060(1) and (2) and 1061 to 1063 (the registrar),
      sections 1068 to 1071 (delivery of documents to the registrar),
      sections 1072 to 1076 (requirements for proper delivery),
      sections 1080(1), (4) and (5) and 1092 (keeping and production of records),
      section 1083 (preservation of original documents),
      sections 1108 to 1110 (language requirements: transliteration),
      sections 1111 and 1114 to 1119 (supplementary provisions).
(3)  The following provisions apply in relation to companies (to companies or for the purposes of the Companies Acts, as the case may be)—
      section 1060(3) and (4) (references to the registrar in the Companies Acts),
      sections 1064 and 1065 (certificates of incorporation),
      section 1066 (companies' registered numbers),
      sections 1077 to 1079 (public notice of receipt of certain documents),
      sections 1080(2) and (3), 1081, 1082 and 1084 (the register),
      sections 1085 to 1091 (inspection of the register),
      sections 1093 to 1098 (correction or removal of material on the register),
      section 1106 (voluntary filing of translations),
      sections 1112 and 1113 (supplementary provisions).
(4)  The following provisions apply as indicated in the provisions concerned—
      section 1067 (registered numbers of UK establishments of overseas companies),
      sections 1099 to 1101 (the registrar's index of company names),
      sections 1102 to 1105 and 1107 (language requirements: translation).
(5)  Unless the context otherwise requires, the provisions of this Part apply to an overseas company as they apply to a company as defined in section 1.][a]

AMENDMENTS AND NOTES

[a] Inserted by the Companies Act 2006 (Part 35) (Consequential Amendments, Transitional Provisions and Savings) Order 2009, SI 2009/1802.

COMMENCEMENT DATE 1 October 2009[1]

---

[1] Companies Act 2006 (Part 35) (Consequential Amendments, Transitional Provisions and Savings) Order 2009, SI 2009/1802, art 1.

This section was inserted by Article 3 of the Companies Act 2006 (Part 35) (Consequential Amend-   **35.1059A.02**
ments, Transitional Provisions and Savings) Order 2009 using the power in section 1294 of the Act.
Section 1059A sets out how the provisions of Part 35 shall apply. In particular, section 1059A(5) applies
the provisions of Part 35 to overseas companies and thereby preserves the effect of section 1120, which
has been repealed as of 1 October 2009.[2] An overseas company is a company which is incorporated
outside of the UK.[3] An example of a context where Part 35 does not apply to all overseas companies is
section 1066 which requires registered numbers to be allocated only to those overseas companies
whose particulars have been registered under section 1046.[4]

## *The registrar*

### 1060   The registrar

    (1)  There shall continue to be—   **35.1060.01**
        (a)  a registrar of companies for England and Wales,
        (b)  a registrar of companies for Scotland, and
        (c)  a registrar of companies for Northern Ireland.
    (2)  The registrars shall be appointed by the Secretary of State.
    (3)  In the Companies Acts 'the registrar of companies' and 'the registrar' mean the registrar of
        companies for England and Wales, Scotland or Northern Ireland, as the case may require.
    (4)  References in the Companies Acts to registration in a particular part of the United Kingdom are
        to registration by the registrar for that part of the United Kingdom.

COMMENCEMENT DATE 1 October 2009[5]

This section (which derives from the Companies Act 1985, section 704) continues in existence the   **35.1060.02**
registrar of companies. He is appointed by the Secretary of State: section 1060(2). There are broadly
two aspects to his functions. First, he is responsible for the registration and dissolution of companies in
England and Wales, and the recording and keeping of information that companies must deliver to him.
Secondly, he is responsible for making certain information available for public inspection. Part 35 of
the Act brings these functions together in one group.

The office of the registrar is located in Cardiff. His functions are in practice discharged through   **35.1060.03**
Companies House, which is an Executive Agency of the Department for Business, Innovation and
Skills (DBIS) (formerly the Department of Business, Enterprise and Regulatory Reform (BERR)), with
branch offices in a number of different locations. It has Trading Fund status under the Government
Trading Funds Act 1973, which allows it to manage its own finances directly. As a result, provision is
made in section 1118 below, making clear that nothing in the Companies Acts or any other enactment
as to the payment of receipts into the Consolidated Fund (see eg section 1063(6) below) shall be read as
affecting the operation in relation to the registrar of section 3(1) of the 1973 Act (which requires
receipts and payments in respect of the 'funded operations' to be paid into and out of the Trading
Fund).

Section 1060(4) was added by amendment in order to avoid confusion.[6] Now that paper registration is   **35.1060.04**
becoming less and less common, it is potentially confusing to talk about a company registering
information 'in' any particular jurisdiction: for example, a company that is legally registered in
England may be so registered as a result of communications sent electronically from a different
jurisdiction. Accordingly, subsection (4) was added in order to make clear that registration 'in' a
particular jurisdiction means registration with the registrar for that jurisdiction (irrespective of where
the act of registration is performed).

### 1061   The registrar's functions

    (1)  The registrar shall continue—   **35.1061.01**
        [(a)  to perform the functions conferred on the registrar [by or under the Companies Acts or any
           other enactment, and—
            [(i) ...
            (ii) ...]ᵃ

---

  [2] Companies Act 2006 (Part 35) (Consequential Amendments, Transitional Provisions and Savings) Order
2009, SI 2009/1802, art 16.
  [3] See s 1044.
  [4] See s 1066(6).
  [5] Companies Act 2006 (Commencement No 8, Transitional Provisions and Savings) Order 2008, SI 2008/
2860, art 3(r).
  [6] Amendment No A185C to what was then clause 671, 28 March 2006.

(b)  to perform such functions on behalf of the Secretary of State, in relation to the registration
     of companies or other matters, as the Secretary of State may from time to time direct.

[(2) ...

    [a]  ...
    [b]  ...
    [c]  ...
    [d]  ...
    [e]  ...
    [f]   ...
    [g]  ...
    [h]  ...
    [i]   ...
    [j]   ...
    [k]  ...
    [l]   ...
    [m] ...][b]

(3)  References in this Act to the functions of the registrar are to functions within subsection (1)(a) or
     (b).

AMENDMENTS AND NOTES

[a]  Amended by the Companies Act 2006 (Part 35) (Consequential Amendments, Transitional Provi-
     sions and Savings) Order 2009, SI 2009/1802.

[b]  Repealed by the Companies Act 2006 (Part 35) (Consequential Amendments, Transitional Provi-
     sions and Savings) Order 2009, SI 2009/1802.

COMMENCEMENT DATE 1 October 2009[7]

**35.1061.02**  The functions of the registrar are essentially administrative. They are described in outline in the
introduction to this Part of the Act. It is not his responsibility to check or to certify the accuracy of the
information contained in the various documents filed at Companies House. Rather, it is his function to
ensure that documents requiring to be filed are so filed, and that companies comply with their statutory
obligations in that regard.

**35.1061.03**  The volume of work undertaken by Companies House in terms of receiving and storing information is
enormous. There are approximately 2.5 million active companies in England and Wales, and just over
400,000 new companies were incorporated in the year ending March 2011. Approximately 8 million
documents are received annually. In addition, Companies House holds records relating to approximately 3 million companies which have been struck off the Register. Historically, most documents
have been submitted in paper form, but now companies are increasingly taking advantage of electronic
communications: more than 58,000 sets of accounts were e-filed in March 2011 compared with just
over 39,000 in March 2010, and over 93.5 per cent of annual returns and 91.4 per cent of new
incorporations were filed online during the year ending March 2011.

**35.1061.04**  Companies House holds approximately 27 miles of paper files, between 550 and 600 million pages on
microfiche, and (since March 1995) about 160 million pages stored as electronic images. In order to
assist public interrogation of the files, Companies House also collates some of the information it stores,
for example enabling searches to be made of all of a named individual's directorships.

**35.1061.05**  Given the volume of work, it is inevitable that mistakes will occasionally be made by Companies House.
Whether or not the registrar is liable to any person for loss caused by such administrative default will
have to be determined on a case-by-case basis, by reference to general law principles. An opposition
amendment to the Bill was proposed in Committee in the House of Lords[8] which would have had the
effect of creating a statutory indemnity for the benefit of any person who suffers loss or damage or
incurs any expense as a result of a failure by the registrar to perform his functions. However, the
Minister pointed out that although some errors are bound to occur because of the volume of
information handled by Companies House, they are rare and in any event the registrar operates a
system of *ex gratia* payments where loss has been caused through his own default.[9] The proposed
amendment was withdrawn.

---

[7]  Companies Act 2006 (Commencement No 8, Transitional Provisions and Savings) Order 2008, SI 2008/
2860, art 3(r).
[8]  Amendment No A186 to what was then clause 672, 28 March 2006.
[9]  It was said in the Lords that it had only been necessary to make 140 such payments in the preceding
12-month period. In Standing Committee on the 4 July 2006 (debating what was then clause 713), it was said that
only £130,000 in compensation had had to be paid in the previous five years.

## 1062   The registrar's official seal

The registrar shall have an official seal for the authentication of documents in connection with the      **35.1062.01**
performance of the registrar's functions.

COMMENCEMENT DATE 1 October 2009[10]

This section (which derives from the Companies Act 1985, section 704(4)) is a purely administrative   **35.1062.02**
provision. The registrar's seal is used, for example, to authenticate accurate copies of documents filed
with him: see section 1091(5) below.

## 1063   Fees payable to registrar

(1)  The Secretary of State may make provision by regulations requiring the payment to the registrar      **35.1063.01**
     of fees in respect of—
     (a)  the performance of any of the registrar's functions, or
     (b)  the provision by the registrar of services or facilities for purposes incidental to, or otherwise
          connected with, the performance of any of the registrar's functions.
(2)  The matters for which fees may be charged include—
     (a)  the performance of a duty imposed on the registrar or the Secretary of State,
     (b)  the receipt of documents delivered to the registrar, and
     (c)  the inspection, or provision of copies, of documents kept by the registrar.
(3)  The regulations may—
     (a)  provide for the amount of the fees to be fixed by or determined under the regulations;
     (b)  provide for different fees to be payable in respect of the same matter in different circum-
          stances;
     (c)  specify the person by whom any fee payable under the regulations is to be paid;
     (d)  specify when and how fees are to be paid.
(4)  Regulations under this section are subject to negative resolution procedure.
(5)  In respect of the performance of functions or the provision of services or facilities—
     (a)  for which fees are not provided for by regulations, or
     (b)  in circumstances other than those for which fees are provided for by regulations,
     the registrar may determine from time to time what fees (if any) are chargeable.
(6)  Fees received by the registrar are to be paid into the Consolidated Fund.
(7)  The Limited Partnerships Act 1907 (c. 24) is amended as follows—
     (a)  in section 16(1) (inspection of statements registered)—
          (i)   omit the words ', and there shall be paid for such inspection such fees as may be
                appointed by the Board of Trade, not exceeding 5p for each inspection', and
          (ii)  omit the words from 'and there shall be paid for such certificate' to the end;
     (b)  in section 17 (power to make rules)—
          (i)   omit the words '(but as to fees with the concurrence of the Treasury)', and
          (ii)  omit paragraph (a).

COMMENCEMENT DATES 20 January and 6 April 2007[11]

The fees payable to the registrar were originally set out in primary legislation in the Companies Act   **35.1063.02**
1948, section 425 and Schedule 12. However, inflation and the increase in company registrations and
searches meant that this approach became unsustainable, and the Secretary of State was first given power
to make regulations specifying the appropriate level of fees by the Companies Act 1976, section 37.

Immediately before the present Act came into force, the Secretary of State's power was set out in the   **35.1063.03**
Companies Act 1985, section 708(1). However, an element of uncertainty was introduced by the
inclusion in the 1985 Act of section 708(5), which 'declared' (an unusual word for primary legislation)
that the registrar 'may charge a fee for any services provided by him otherwise than in pursuance of an
obligation imposed on him by law'.[12] This raised the question whether the registrar had power by virtue
of section 708(5) not only to charge such a fee, but also to fix the level of any fees charged for services

---

[10]  Companies Act 2006 (Commencement No 8, Transitional Provisions and Savings) Order 2008, SI 2008/
2860, art 3(r).
[11]  Companies Act 2006 (Commencement No 1, Transitional Provisions and Savings) Order 2006, SI 2006/
3428. For transitional provisions, see Sch 5, Part 3, para 6.
[12]  Section 708(5) was introduced by the Companies Act 1976. It seems to have been prompted by a concern
that an express statutory provision allowing fees to be charged for the provision of a service that the Registrar was
legally bound to provide in discharge of his statutory obligations might imply that the Registrar had no power to
charge fees for the provision of services which he was *not* legally obliged to provide: see the comments made by
Lord Winterbottom in the House of Lords on 23 March 1976. Accordingly, s 708(5) served purely to declare that
the position under the general law remained, namely that the Registrar (like any other public authority) is
lawfully entitled to charge a fee for the provision of a service which he is not legally bound to provide: *China
Navigation Company Ltd v Attorney-General* [1932] 2 KB 197, 214, 218, 229–230, 241–243.

not expressly covered by regulations made under section 708(1). The better view is that he probably did, and that is the assumption made in the Explanatory Notes at paragraph 1300. It would seem that section 708(1) allowed the Secretary of State to fix the level of fees which the registrar was entitled to charge in fulfilling any of his statutory obligations, whereas section 708(5) enabled the registrar to fix the level of fees for the provision of services which he was not legally obliged to provide, but which he chose to make available as a public service (such as, for example, the compilation of the Directors' Register).

**35.1063.04**  The uncertainty that existed under section 708 of the 1985 Act has now been removed by the wording of section 1063. Under section 1063(1) to (2), the Secretary of State has power to fix the level of fees in relation to services provided by the registrar in the discharge of his statutory obligations, and also to other incidental and connected services (ie including services which he is not obliged to provide). Similarly, under section 1063(5), the registrar may fix the level of fees to cover circumstances where no provision is made in the Secretary of State's regulations (ie including services which he is obliged to provide).

**35.1063.05**  By virtue of section 1063(3)(a), the fixing of fees can be sub-delegated: they may be 'determined under the regulations'. Under section 1063(3)(b), the Secretary of State can fix different fees at different levels, to reflect the different services provided by Companies House. This would, for example, permit higher fees to be charged for an express service.

**35.1063.06**  The general rule is that fees should be fixed at a level calculated to meet the overall administrative cost of providing the services in question: no more, and no less.[13] Moreover, it would seem not to be lawful for the levels to be deliberately fixed so as to procure that fees charged for one service cross-subsidize the provision of other services.[14] However, exact budgeting is impossible, and it may therefore be lawful for the registrar to recoup a deficit incurred in one year by increasing the level of fees in a subsequent year, even though that will mean that the fees are then set at a level exceeding the amount needed to meet the administrative cost of providing services in relation to that subsequent year.[15]

**35.1063.07**  There is authority for the proposition that a person who pays the registration fees due under statute on the incorporation of a company has no cause of action against it to recover the sums so paid.[16] However, the law on restitution has developed since then,[17] and the point may need to be re-examined.

**35.1063.08**  Regulations made under this section are subject to the negative resolution procedure (section 1063(4)), as to which see section 1289. As to the registrar's rule-making powers generally, see section 1117 below.

## Certificates of incorporation

### 1064  Public notice of issue of certificate of incorporation[a]

**35.1064.01**
(1) The registrar must cause to be published—
   (a)  in the Gazette, or
   (b)  in accordance with section 1116 (alternative means of giving public notice),
   notice of the issue by the registrar of any certificate of incorporation of a company.
(2) The notice must state the name and registered number of the company and the date of issue of the certificate.
(3) This section applies to a certificate of incorporation issued under—
   (a)  section 80 (change of name),
   (b)  section 88 (Welsh companies), or
   (c)  any provision of Part 7 (re-registration),
   as well as to the certificate issued on a company's formation.

AMENDMENTS AND NOTES

[a]  This section applies with modifications to LLPs by reg 61 of the Limited Liability Partnerships(Application of Companies Act 2006) Regulations 2009, SI 2009/1804.

COMMENCEMENT DATE 1 October 2009[18]

---

[13]  See s 1086(2) below. This is required by the First Company Law Directive (Directive (EEC) 68/151 [1968] OJ L65/8, as amended by Directive (EC) 2003/58 and codified by Directive (EC) 2009/101). The same result would in any event have been required by domestic law: see by analogy *R v Manchester CC ex p King* (1991) 89 LGR 696, 709–710, where a licensing fee was quashed on the grounds that it had been fixed by reference to 'what the market would bear'.

[14]  See *R v GLC ex p Rank* (Divisional Court, 18 February 1982) *The Times*, 19 February 1982.

[15]  See by analogy *R v Birmingham CC ex p Quietlynn Ltd* (1985) 83 LGR 461, 516–521.

[16]  *In re National Motor Mail-Coach Company Ltd* [1908] 2 Ch 515, 522–523.

[17]  See eg Goff & Jones on *The Law of Restitution* (8th edn, 2011) para 1-080.

[18]  Companies Act 2006 (Commencement No 8, Transitional Provisions and Savings) Order 2008, SI 2008/2860, art 3(r).

This section sets out the duties of the registrar in relation to the publication of certificates of   **35.1064.02**
incorporation. The registrar has a duty to publish a notice in respect of each certificate of incorporation
which is issued. The rationale of the provision appears similar to its predecessors: Dillon LJ said of the
European Communities Act 1972, section 9 that 'The object of the legislation is that persons dealing
with a company should be officially given an opportunity of finding out important information
concerning the company…'.[19]

Subsection (1) provides for the use by the registrar of means of communication other than the   **35.1064.03**
traditional publication in the Gazette, which have been authorized by the Secretary of State under
section 1116 for the purpose of giving the requisite notice.

The required content of the notice is expanded by subsection (2). Under the Companies Act 1985,   **35.1064.04**
section 711(1)(a) the notice had to include the name of the company, the description of the document
and the date of issue or receipt. As well as the name of the company and the date of the certificate's issue,
the notice must now also include the registered number of the company. The inclusion of this
information will assist in identifying the company to the reader of the notice, particularly if the notice
is in respect of a certificate issued upon a change of name by the company. Notice in this latter situation
is required to be given by subsection (3). Notice is also required upon a change in the stated locale of a
registered office connected with Wales, a change in the company's status (for example between public
and private or limited and unlimited), and of course upon initial incorporation.

## 1065  Right to certificate of incorporation[a]

Any person may require the registrar to provide him with a copy of any certificate of incorporation of   **35.1065.01**
a company, signed by the registrar or authenticated by the registrar's seal.

AMENDMENTS AND NOTES

> [a]  This section applies with modifications to LLPs by reg 61 of the Limited Liability Partnerships
> (Application of Companies Act 2006) Regulations 2009, SI 2009/1804.

COMMENCEMENT DATE 1 October 2009[20]

Since a certificate of incorporation is conclusive evidence that a company is duly registered[21] it is   **35.1065.02**
important that copies should be made available to those wishing to see it. Again, the provision
contemplates that a company may have more than one certificate of incorporation.[22] The entitlement
to a copy extends to all such certificates. The section does not involve a departure of substance from
Companies Act 1985, section 710.

## *Registered numbers*

## 1066  Company's registered numbers[a]

(1)  The registrar shall allocate to every company a number, which shall be known as the company's   **35.1066.01**
registered number.
(2)  Companies' registered numbers shall be in such form, consisting of one or more sequences of
figures or letters, as the registrar may determine.
(3)  The registrar may on adopting a new form of registered number make such changes of existing
registered numbers as appear necessary.
(4)  A change of a company's registered number has effect from the date on which the company is
notified by the registrar of the change.
(5)  For a period of three years beginning with that date any requirement to disclose the company's
registered number imposed by regulations under section 82 or section 1051 (trading disclosures)
is satisfied by the use of either the old number or the new.
(6)  In this section 'company' includes an overseas company whose particulars have been registered
under section 1046, other than a company that appears to the registrar not to be required to
register particulars under that section.

---

[19]  *Official Custodian for Charities v Parway Estates Developments Ltd (In Liquidation)* [1985] 1 Ch 151, 163.
[20]  Companies Act 2006 (Commencement No 8, Transitional Provisions and Savings) Order 2008, SI 2008/
2860, art 3(r).
[21]  See s 15(4).
[22]  For details of charges payable upon requesting copies of certificates of incorporation, see the Registrar of
Companies (Fees) (Companies, Overseas Companies and Limited Liability Partnerships) Regulations 2009, SI
2009/2101.

AMENDMENTS AND NOTES

[a] This section applies with modifications to LLPs by reg 62 of the Limited Liability Partnerships (Application of Companies Act 2006) Regulations 2009, SI 2009/1804 and to unregistered companies by reg 18, Sch 1 of the Unregistered Companies Regulations 2009, SI 2009/2436.

COMMENCEMENT DATE 1 October 2009[23]

**35.1066.02**    The registrar is placed under a duty to allocate a registered number to each company. These registered numbers provide a means of identifying a company notwithstanding any change to its name, operations or styling. The form of registered numbers is an administrative matter in the control of the registrar. As such, it may be changed from time to time by him.

**35.1066.03**    Subsection (3) allows the registrar to take measures in respect of registered numbers allocated prior to any change of format. Presumably, these measures may either be transitional or permanent. Notwithstanding that the Companies Act 1985, section 705 explicitly stated that any such measures may be taken which appear necessary 'to him' (the registrar) the difference in wording seems unlikely to represent a substantive difference.[24]

**35.1066.04**    The only apparent substantive change brought about by this provision is the date of commencement of the three-year period during which requirements to disclose a company's registered number in the course of trading can be satisfied by disclosing the old or new registered number. Subsections (4) and (5) use the same date such that the new number becomes effective (and the three-year grace period begins to run) from the date the company is notified of the change. Previously, (under the Companies Act 1985, section 705(4)), the grace period began running from the potentially earlier point when the registrar sent the notification to the company. The period of three years includes the date on which the company is notified of the change.[25]

**35.1066.05**    By subsection (6), registered numbers must be allocated not only to registered domestic companies but also to those overseas companies which (under any regulations made pursuant to section 1046) must register particulars with the registrar. In the same way as the Companies Act 1985, section 705 was applied to the Societas Europaea by statutory instrument this section is also subject to regulations which apply it, with amendment, to the Societas Europaea.[26]

## 1067 Registered numbers of [UK establishments][a] of overseas company

**35.1067.01**    (1) The registrar shall allocate to every [UK establishment][b] of an overseas company whose particulars are registered under section 1046 a number, which shall be known as the [UK establishment's][c] registered number.

(2) [The registered numbers of UK establishments of overseas companies][d] shall be in such form, consisting of one or more sequences of figures or letters, as the registrar may determine.

(3) The registrar may on adopting a new form of registered number make such changes of existing registered numbers as appear necessary.

(4) A change of [the registered number of a UK establishment][e] has effect from the date on which the company is notified by the registrar of the change.

(5) For a period of three years beginning with that date any requirement to disclose [the UK establishment's registered number][f] imposed by regulations under section 1051 (trading disclosures) is satisfied by the use of either the old number or the new.

[(6) In this Part 'establishment', in relation to an overseas company, means—

(a) a branch within the meaning of the Eleventh Company Law Directive (89/666/EEC), or

(b) a place of business that is not such a branch, and 'UK establishment' means an establishment in the United Kingdom.][g]

AMENDMENTS AND NOTES

[a] Amended by the Companies Act 2006 (Part 35) (Consequential Amendments, Transitional Provisions and Savings) Order 2009, SI 2009/1802.

[b] Amended by the Companies Act 2006 (Part 35) (Consequential Amendments, Transitional Provisions and Savings) Order 2009, SI 2009/1802.

[c] Amended by the Companies Act 2006 (Part 35) (Consequential Amendments, Transitional Provisions and Savings) Order 2009, SI 2009/1802.

---

[23] Companies Act 2006 (Commencement No 8, Transitional Provisions and Savings) Order 2008, SI 2008/2860, art 3(r).

[24] The Explanatory Notes to the Bill state that this section does not intend a change of substance.

[25] *Zoan v Rouamba* [2000] 1 WLR 1509, 1516–1517.

[26] European Public Limited-Liability Company Regulations 2004, SI 2004/2326, reg 1, Sch 2, as amended by reg 38 of the European Public Limited-Liability Company (Amendment) Regulations 2009, SI 2009/2400.

COMMENCEMENT DATE 1 October 2009[27]

The wording of this provision is altered from that originally enacted with effect since 1 October 2009    **35.1067.02**
as a result of the Companies Act 2006 (Part 35) Consequential Amendments, Transitional Provisions
and Savings) Order 2009,[28] article 5. The registrar's duty to allocate a registered number to a UK
establishment only arises upon the registration by an overseas company of particulars under section
1046. If the overseas company has not registered particulars under section 1046, on the wording of
subsection (1), the registrar is not under an obligation to allocate registered numbers to that company's
UK establishments.

The structure in relation to UK establishment registered numbers is very similar to the structure in    **35.1067.03**
relation to company registered numbers. The commentary to section 1066 above should therefore be
read in relation to this section *mutatis mutandis*.

## Delivery of documents to the registrar

### 1068   Registrar's requirements as to form, authentication and manner of delivery

(1)  The registrar may impose requirements as to the form, authentication and manner of delivery of    **35.1068.01**
documents required or authorised to be delivered to the registrar under any enactment.
(2)  As regards the form of the document, the registrar may—
   (a)  require the contents of the document to be in a standard form;
   (b)  impose requirements for the purpose of enabling the document to be scanned or copied.
(3)  As regards authentication, the registrar may—
   (a)  require the document to be authenticated by a particular person or a person of a particular
      description;
   (b)  specify the means of authentication;
   (c)  require the document to contain or be accompanied by the name or registered number [(or
      both)]ᵃ of the company [(or other body)]ᵇ to which it relates.
(4)  As regards the manner of delivery, the registrar may specify requirements as to—
   (a)  the physical form of the document (for example, hard copy or electronic form);
   (b)  the means to be used for delivering the document (for example, by post or electronic means);
   (c)  the address to which the document is to be sent;
   (d)  in the case of a document to be delivered by electronic means, the hardware and software to
      be used, and technical specifications (for example, matters relating to protocol, security,
      antivirus protection or encryption).
(5)  The registrar must secure that as from 1st January 2007 all documents subject to the Directive
disclosure requirements (see section 1078) may be delivered to the registrar by electronic means.
(6)  The power conferred by this section does not authorise the registrar to require documents to be
delivered by electronic means (see section 1069).
(7)  Requirements imposed under this section must not be inconsistent with requirements imposed by
any enactment with respect to the form, authentication or manner of delivery of the document
concerned.

AMENDMENTS AND NOTES

---

[27]  Companies Act 2006 (Commencement No 8, Transitional Provisions and Savings) Order 2008, SI 2008/
2860, art 3(r).
[28]  SI 2009/1802.

<sup>c</sup> This section applies to orders made under reg 19(1) and (2) of the Companies (Cross-Border Mergers) Regulation 2007, SI 2007/2974 by reg 19(4) of those regulations, to LLPs with modifications by reg 60 of the Limited Liability Partnerships (Application of Companies Act 2006) Regulations 2009, SI 2009/1804 and to unregistered companies with modifications by Sch 1, para 17 of the Unregistered Companies Regulations 2009, SI 2009/2436.

COMMENCEMENT DATE 1 January 2007 as to section 1068(5) and (so far as necessary for that purpose) subsections (1) to (4), (6), and (7).[29] As to the balance, it was 15 December 2007, so far as was necessary for the purposes of any regulations made before that date in implementation of Directive (EC) 2005/56 on cross border mergers.[30] Other provisions 1 October 2009.[31]

**35.1068.02**   This section introduced a new regime for the provision of information by companies to the registrar. The section permits the registrar to dictate the form of documents[32] to be delivered to him, as well as the method of authentication and the manner of delivery. The function of prescribing the content of documents to be delivered to the registrar remains with the Secretary of State and is carried out by way of statutory instrument.[33] This reflects the rationale that matters of substance are prescribed by the Secretary of State whereas issues of administration are dictated by the registrar.[34]

**35.1068.03**   The registrar imposed requirements under this section by means of rules, namely the Registrar's Rules 2009.[35] Subsections (2) and (4) set out the scope of the requirements as to the form and manner of delivery,[36] and subsection (3) deals with authentication. In relation to the manner of delivery, the section clearly envisages that the registrar will impose requirements which permit electronic delivery of documents. Indeed, the registrar is obliged by section 1068(5) to ensure that all documents subject to 'Directive disclosure requirements'[37] may be delivered by electronic means. That subsection implements elements of Article 3 of the First Company Law Directive[38] which provides that Member States must by 1 January 2007 permit companies to file all documents and particulars which they are obliged to disclose by Article 2 by electronic means. Section 1168 defines 'electronic means'.[39] It is notable, however, that the registrar cannot require that a document is delivered only by electronic means. That power is conferred solely on the Secretary of State and is contained in section 1069.

**35.1068.04**   Nevertheless, the section gives the registrar wide powers to specify requirements, including whether a document should be submitted in hard copy[40] or electronic form,[41] whether a document should be sent by post or transmitted electronically, the address to which a document should be sent, and, in the case of the submission of a document by electronic means, the specification of hardware and software to be used.

**35.1068.05**   Under subsection (7), any requirements made by the registrar under section 1068 are additional to, and must not be inconsistent with, any requirements imposed under any enactment with respect to the form, authentication or manner of delivery of the document concerned.[42]

---

[29] Companies Act 2006 (Commencement No 1, Transitional Provisions and Savings) Order 2006, SI 2006/3428, art 2(1) and (2).

[30] [2005] OJ L310/1. See art 4 of the Companies Act 2006 (Commencement No 3, Consequential Amendments, Transitional Provisions and Savings) Order, 2007, SI 2007/2194.

[31] Companies Act 2006 (Commencement No 8, Transitional Provisions and Savings) Order 2008, SI 2008/2860, art 3(r). The transitional provisions are set out in the Companies Act 2006 (Commencement No 8, Transitional Provisions and Savings) Order 2008, Sch 2, para 97 as amended by the Companies Act 2006 (Part 35) (Consequential Amendments, Transitional Provisions and Savings) Order 2009, SI 2009/1802, art 18 and the Schedule thereto. These provide that s 1068 applies to documents delivered to the Registrar on or after 1 October 2009 other than those delivered in pursuance of an obligation arising before that date. Where the obligation to deliver a document to the Registrar arose before 1 October 2009, the provisions that would have applied if the document had been delivered before that date continue to apply.

[32] See s 1114(1).

[33] See the definition of 'prescribed' in s 1167, and previously in CA 1985, s 744.

[34] See *Hansard*, HL, Grand Committee, col 346 (28 March 2006).

[35] See eg ss 1071(2) and 1117. The registrar is obliged to publicize the rules in accordance with s 1117. As to the registrar's rule-making powers generally and for the references to the rules, see section 1117 below.

[36] See s 1114(2).

[37] See s 1078.

[38] Directive (EEC) 68/151 [1968] OJ L65/8, as amended by Directive (EC) 2003/58 and codified by Directive (EC) 2009/101.

[39] See also s 1069 which implements Art 3(8) of the First Company Law Directive (Directive (EEC) 68/151 [1968] OJ L65/8, as amended by Directive (EC) 2003/58 and codified by Directive (EC) 2009/101).

[40] See s 1168(2), (6).

[41] See s 1168(3), (5).

[42] See s 1293.

## 1069   Power to require delivery by electronic means

(1) The Secretary of State may make regulations requiring documents that are authorised or required        **35.1069.01**
to be delivered to the registrar to be delivered by electronic means.

(2) Any such requirement to deliver documents by electronic means is effective only if registrar's rules
have been published with respect to the detailed requirements for such delivery.

(3) Regulations under this section are subject to affirmative resolution procedure.

COMMENCEMENT DATE 20 January 2007 (for the purpose of enabling the exercise of powers to make regulations).[43] Otherwise 1 October 2009[44]

AMENDMENTS AND NOTES

[a] This section applies to LLPs with modifications by reg 60 of the Limited Liability Partnerships (Application of Companies Act 2006) Regulations 2009, SI 2009/1804 and to unregistered companies with modifications by Sch 1, para 17 of the Unregistered Companies Regulations 2009, SI 2009/2436.

The term 'electronic means' is defined in section 1168. Under section 1069, only the Secretary of State,      **35.1069.02**
and not the registrar, may make regulations requiring documents[45] that are authorized or required to be delivered to the registrar to be so delivered by electronic means. Under subsection (2), such regulations will only be effective if the registrar has already published rules setting out the detailed requirements for such delivery.[46]

Regulations made by the Secretary of State under this section are subject to the affirmative resolution      **35.1069.03**
procedure (subsection (3)), which is explained in section 1290. At the time of writing, no regulations have been made under this section.

There was some concern expressed when this provision was debated in the House of Lords on the      **35.1069.04**
impact of compulsory electronic filing on small businesses. In response, the Government indicated that it had no intention to make use of this power in the short term.[47]

## 1070   Agreement for delivery by electronic means

(1) The registrar may agree with a company [(or other body)][a] that documents relating to the        **35.1070.01**
company [(or other body)][b] that are required or authorised to be delivered to the registrar—

(a) will be delivered by electronic means, except as provided for in the agreement, and

(b) will conform to such requirements as may be specified in the agreement or specified by the
registrar in accordance with the agreement.

(2) An agreement under this section may relate to all or any description of documents to be delivered
to the registrar.

(3) Documents in relation to which an agreement is in force under this section must be delivered in
accordance with the agreement.

AMENDMENTS AND NOTES

[a] Amended by the Companies Act 2006 (Part 35) (Consequential Amendments, Transitional Provisions and Savings) Order 2009, SI 2009/1802.

[b] Amended by the Companies Act 2006 (Part 35) (Consequential Amendments, Transitional Provisions and Savings) Order 2009, SI 2009/1802.

COMMENCEMENT DATE 1 October 2009[48]

---

[43] Companies Act 2006 (Commencement No 1, Transitional Provisions and Savings) Order 2006, SI 2006/3428, art 3(3).

[44] Companies Act 2006 (Commencement No. 8, Transitional Provisions and Savings) Order 2008, SI 2008/2860, art 3(r). The transitional provisions are set out in the Companies Act 2006 (Commencement No 8, Transitional Provisions and Savings) Order 2008, Sch 2, para 97 as amended by the Companies Act 2006 (Part 35) (Consequential Amendments, Transitional Provisions and Savings) Order 2009, SI 2009/1802, art 18 and the Schedule thereto. These provide that s 1069 applies to documents delivered to the Registrar on or after 1 October 2009 other than those delivered in pursuance of an obligation arising before that date. Where the obligation to deliver a document to the Registrar arose before 1 October 2009, the provisions that would have applied if the document had been delivered before that date continue to apply.

[45] See s 1114(1).

[46] In relation to 'delivery', see s 1114(2).

[47] See *Hansard*, HL, Grand Committee, col 348 (28 March 2006).

[48] Companies Act 2006 (Commencement No 8, Transitional Provisions and Savings) Order 2008, SI 2008/2860, art 3(r). The transitional provisions are set out in the Companies Act 2006 (Commencement No 8, Transitional Provisions and Savings) Order 2008, Sch 2, para 98 as amended by the Companies Act 2006 (Part 35) (Consequential Amendments, Transitional Provisions and Savings) Order 2009, SI 2009/1802, art 18 and the

**35.1070.02**   This section was designed in order to combat fraud and to give companies greater control over the documents filed with the registrar of companies.[49] It allows the registrar to agree with a company that some or all of the documents[50] which are authorized or required to be delivered[51] to the registrar will be delivered by electronic means and will conform to any requirements in the agreement or specified by the registrar.[52] The term 'electronic means' is defined in section 1168. Once an agreement is in force, both the registrar and the company are bound by it.[53] It is evident, however, that the registrar is under no obligation to enter any such agreements.

**35.1070.03**   The system set up by Companies House under this section is called Protected Online Filing (PROOF). To sign up for the scheme, it is necessary to be registered for the Companies House WebFiling Service. Further information is available on the Companies House website.[54]

### 1071   Document not delivered until received

**35.1071.01**   (1)  A document is not delivered to the registrar until it is received by the registrar.

(2)  Provision may be made by registrar's rules as to when a document is to be regarded as received.

AMENDMENTS AND NOTES

[a] This section applies to LLPs with modifications by reg 60 of the Limited Liability Partnerships (Application of Companies Act 2006) Regulations 2009, SI 2009/1804 and to unregistered companies with modifications by Sch 1, para 17 of the Unregistered Companies Regulations 2009, SI 2009/2436.

COMMENCEMENT DATE 1 October 2009[55]

**35.1071.02**   This provision should be read in conjunction with section 1072.[56] A document is not deemed to be delivered to the registrar unless it complies with the requirements of section 1072 and until it is received by him.[57] The registrar can make further provision by means of rules as to when a document is to be regarded as received.[58] The Registrar's Rules 2009 referred to further at s 1117 make such provision. Companies House has issued guidance on the interpretation of the rules.[59]

*Requirements for proper delivery*

### 1072   Requirements for proper delivery

**35.1072.01**   (1)  A document delivered to the registrar is not properly delivered unless all the following requirements are met—

(a)  the requirements of the provision under which the document is to be delivered to the registrar as regards—

(i)   the contents of the document, and

(ii)  form, authentication and manner of delivery;

(b)  any applicable requirements under—

section 1068 (registrar's requirements as to form, authentication and manner of delivery),

section 1069 (power to require delivery by electronic means), or

section 1070 (agreement for delivery by electronic means);

---

Schedule thereto. These provide that s 1070 applies to all documents delivered to the Registrar on or after 1 October 2009.

[49] See *Hansard*, 4 July 2006 Standing Committee D [410] (HC).

[50] See s 1114(1).

[51] In relation to 'delivery', see s 1114(2).

[52] See subs (1).

[53] See s 1070(3).

[54] See ⟨http://www.companieshouse.gov.uk/infoAndGuide/proofWebFiling.shtml⟩.

[55] Companies Act 2006 (Commencement No 8, Transitional Provisions and Savings) Order 2008, SI 2008/2860, art 3(r). The transitional provisions are set out in the Companies Act 2006 (Commencement No 8, Transitional Provisions and Savings) Order 2008, Sch 2, para 99 as amended by the Companies Act 2006 (Part 35) (Consequential Amendments, Transitional Provisions and Savings) Order 2009, SI 2009/1802, art 18 and the Schedule thereto. These provide that s 1071 applies to documents delivered to the Registrar on or after 1 October 2009 other than those delivered in pursuance of an obligation arising before that date. Where the obligation to deliver a document to the Registrar arose before 1 October 2009, the provisions that would have applied if the document had been delivered before that date continue to apply.

[56] For the meaning of 'delivery' see s 1114(2).

[57] See the statement by Vera Baird, Parliamentary Under-Secretary of State for Constitutional Affairs in Hansard, 4 July 2006 Standing Committee D [410] (HC).

[58] See subs (2), ss 1068(4) and 1117.

[59] See the current guidance issued by Companies House; Registrar's rules and powers, May 2012, Chapter 1, question 3 available at ⟨http://www.companieshouse.gov.uk/about/pdf/gp6.pdf⟩.

    (c)  any requirements of this Part as to the language in which the document is drawn up and delivered or as to its being accompanied on delivery by a certified translation into English;

    (d)  in so far as it consists of or includes names and addresses, any requirements of this Part as to permitted characters, letters or symbols or as to its being accompanied on delivery by a certificate as to the transliteration of any element;

    (e)  any applicable requirements under section 1111 (registrar's requirements as to certification or verification);

    (f)  any requirement of regulations under section 1082 (use of unique identifiers);

    (g)  any requirements as regards payment of a fee in respect of its receipt by the registrar.

(2)  A document that is not properly delivered is treated for the purposes of the provision requiring or authorising it to be delivered as not having been delivered, subject to the provisions of section 1073 (power to accept documents not meeting requirements for proper delivery).

AMENDMENTS AND NOTES

[a]  This section applies to LLPs with modifications by reg 60 of the Limited Liability Partnerships (Application of Companies Act 2006) Regulations 2009, SI 2009/1804 and to unregistered companies with modifications by Sch 1, para 17 of the Unregistered Companies Regulations 2009, SI 2009/2436.

COMMENCEMENT DATE 1 October 2009[60]

Subsection (1) lists the criteria which must be satisfied before a document[61] is deemed delivered[62] to the registrar. The criteria include requirements as to the contents, form, authentication, translation, format, certification,[63] verification, and manner of delivery of a document. It is important that all such criteria are satisfied if a document is to be deemed delivered and a failure to comply will lead to the document being treated as not delivered for the purposes of any statutory requirement under this Act. The detail is contained in the Registrar's Rules 2009.[64] and in guidance issued by Companies House.[65]    **35.1072.02**

Under section 1074(4), the registrar may treat an otherwise correctly delivered document which contains unnecessary material as delivered defectively. 'Unnecessary material' is defined in section 1074(2).    **35.1072.03**

This section and the role of the registrar under Part 35 are discussed in *Globespan Airways Ltd (in liquidation), Cartwright v Registrar of Companies*.[66] In that case, the document under consideration was Form 2.34B under the Insolvency Rules 1986, which gives notice of the conversion of an administration into a creditors voluntary liquidation. Briggs J considered that section 1072 had been complied with where the form contained the relevant information, even though the correct box had not been completed: 'The question is not whether the notice set out the addresses of the proposed liquidators on the precise part of the single page document identified in the marginal notes.'[67]    **35.1072.04**

### 1073  Power to accept documents not meeting requirements for proper delivery

(1)  The registrar may accept (and register) a document that does not comply with the requirements for proper delivery.    **35.1073.01**

(2)  A document accepted by the registrar under this section is treated as received by the registrar for the purposes of section 1077 (public notice of receipt of certain documents).

(3)  No objection may be taken to the legal consequences of a document's being accepted (or registered) by the registrar under this section on the ground that the requirements for proper delivery were not met.

---

[60]  Companies Act 2006 (Commencement No 8, Transitional Provisions and Savings) Order 2008, SI 2008/2860, art 3(r). The transitional provisions are set out in the Companies Act 2006 (Commencement No 8, Transitional Provisions and Savings) Order 2008, Sch 2, para 100 as amended by the Companies Act 2006 (Part 35) (Consequential Amendments, Transitional Provisions and Savings) Order 2009, SI 2009/1802, art 18 and the Schedule thereto. These provide that s 1072 applies to documents delivered to the Registrar on or after 1 October 2009 other than those delivered in pursuance of an obligation arising before that date. Where the obligation to deliver a document to the Registrar arose before 1 October 2009, the provisions that would have applied if the document had been delivered before that date (and the registrar's former practice with respect to the requirements for proper delivery and documents containing unnecessary material) continue to apply.

[61]  See s 1114(1).

[62]  In relation to 'delivery', see s 1114(2).

[63]  For 'certified translation', see s 1107(1).

[64]  As to the registrar's rule-making powers generally, see s 1117 below.

[65]  See the current guidance issued by Companies House; Registrar's rules and powers, May 2012, Chapter 1, question 4 available at ⟨http://www.companieshouse.gov.uk/about/pdf/gp6.pdf⟩.

[66]  [2012] EWCA Civ 1159.

[67]  Ibid, at [18].

(4) The acceptance of a document by the registrar under this section does not affect—
    (a)  the continuing obligation to comply with the requirements for proper delivery, or
    (b)  subject as follows, any liability for failure to comply with those requirements.
(5) For the purposes of—
    (a)  section 453 (civil penalty for failure to file accounts and reports), and
    (b)  any enactment imposing a daily default fine for failure to deliver the document,
the period after the document is accepted does not count as a period during which there is default in complying with the requirements for proper delivery.
(6) But if, subsequently—
    (a)  the registrar issues a notice under section 1094(4) in respect of the document (notice of administrative removal from the register), and
    (b)  the requirements for proper delivery are not complied with before the end of the period of 14 days after the issue of that notice,
any subsequent period of default does count for the purposes of those provisions.

AMENDMENTS AND NOTES

[a] This section applies to LLPs with modifications by reg 60 of the Limited Liability Partnerships (Application of Companies Act 2006) Regulations 2009, SI 2009/1804 and to unregistered companies with modifications by Sch 1, para 17 of the Unregistered Companies Regulations 2009, SI 2009/2436.

COMMENCEMENT DATE 1 October 2009[68]

**35.1073.02** This provision was introduced by the Companies Act 2006. Under it, the registrar is entitled to waive strict compliance with section 1072 and choose to register a document[69] which does not comply with the requirements: see subsection (1). However, such registration does not affect the continuing obligation on the person delivering[70] the document to comply with the requirements for proper delivery or any liability that such person may face for failure to comply with his obligations under the Act: see subsection (4).

**35.1073.03** Notably, where the registrar decides to waive strict compliance, no objection may be taken to the legal effect of such action under subsection (3). Given that the registrar's actions in this respect may affect the rights of third parties and that in such circumstances there is a real risk of objection, it is likely that the registrar will only exercise this discretion in relation to minor defects. In relation to the 'daily default fine' referred to in subsection (5), see section 1125.

**35.1073.04** In *Globespan Airways Ltd (in liquidation), Cartwright v Registrar of Companies*,[71] which concerned, inter alia, section 1072, the registrar gave evidence that the policy was to reject incomplete forms without considering whether their perceived omissions could be ignored as a matter of discretion. In that case, Briggs J expressed his surprise at that evidence,[72] and it may be that, in the future, the registrar will be more cautious about rejecting forms without consideration of the particular deficiencies.[73]

## 1074 Documents containing unnecessary material

**35.1074.01** (1) This section applies where a document delivered to the registrar contains unnecessary material.
(2) 'Unnecessary material' means material that—
    (a)  is not necessary in order to comply with an obligation under any enactment, and
    (b)  is not specifically authorised to be delivered to the registrar.
(3) For this purpose an obligation to deliver a document of a particular description, or conforming to certain requirements, is regarded as not extending to anything that is not needed for a document of that description or, as the case may be, conforming to those requirements.

---

[68] Companies Act 2006 (Commencement No 8, Transitional Provisions and Savings) Order 2008, SI 2008/2860, art 3(r). The transitional provisions are set out in the Companies Act 2006 (Commencement No 8, Transitional Provisions and Savings) Order 2008, Sch 2, para 100 as amended by the Companies Act 2006 (Part 35) (Consequential Amendments, Transitional Provisions and Savings) Order 2009, SI 2009/1802, art 18 and the Schedule thereto. These provide that s 1073 applies to documents delivered to the Registrar on or after 1 October 2009 other than those delivered in pursuance of an obligation arising before that date. Where the obligation to deliver a document to the Registrar arose before 1 October 2009, the provisions that would have applied if the document had been delivered before that date (and the registrar's former practice with respect to the requirements for proper delivery and documents containing unnecessary material) continue to apply.

[69] See s 1114(1).
[70] See s 1114(2).
[71] [2012] EWCA Civ 1159.
[72] [2012] EWCA Civ 1159 at [19].
[73] See the current guidance issued by Companies House; Registrar's rules and powers, May 2012, Chapter 1, question 5 available at ⟨http://www.companieshouse.gov.uk/about/pdf/gp6.pdf⟩.

(6) A document that is corrected under this section is treated, for the purposes of any enactment relating to its delivery, as having been delivered when the correction is made.

(7) The power conferred by this section is not exercisable if the document has been registered under section 1073 (power to accept documents not meeting requirements for proper delivery).

AMENDMENTS AND NOTES

ᵃ Amended by the Companies Act 2006 (Part 35) (Consequential Amendments, Transitional Provisions and Savings) Order 2009, SI 2009/1802.

ᵇ Amended by the Companies Act 2006 (Part 35) (Consequential Amendments, Transitional Provisions and Savings) Order 2009, SI 2009/1802.

ᶜ Amended by the Companies Act 2006 (Part 35) (Consequential Amendments, Transitional Provisions and Savings) Order 2009, SI 2009/1802.

ᵈ Amended by the Companies Act 2006 (Part 35) (Consequential Amendments, Transitional Provisions and Savings) Order 2009, SI 2009/1802.

ᵉ Amended by the Companies Act 2006 (Part 35) (Consequential Amendments, Transitional Provisions and Savings) Order 2009, SI 2009/1802.

ᶠ Amended by the Companies Act 2006 (Part 35) (Consequential Amendments, Transitional Provisions and Savings) Order 2009, SI 2009/1802.

COMMENCEMENT DATE 1 October 2009[78]

**35.1075.02** This section introduced a new mechanism for the 'informal' correction of documents[79] delivered[80] to the registrar. It operates as an alternative to the formal mechanism for refiling defective documents under section 1076. Aside from the statutory scheme, the court has no jurisdiction to order the registrar to amend the register.[81] The informal mechanism introduced by this section is invoked if the registrar concludes that a document appears to be incomplete or internally inconsistent: see subsection (1). It is likely to operate in circumstances where there are minor defects in the document, such as where a largely completed document has a missing field or where a document contains an incorrect company number or unnecessary material.[82]

**35.1075.03** In such circumstances, the registrar may make an enquiry of the company or the person who delivered the document to obtain instructions. Whilst the section appears to envisage that the procedure for informal correction is initiated by the registrar (subsection (3)(a)) on identifying some defect in a delivered document, in practice, there appears to be no reason why the section cannot also be invoked when a company identifies an error in a delivered document and contacts the registrar to remedy the defect. In either case, the formal mechanism requires the registrar to make contact with the company and such contact will normally be made by telephone. The registrar may only then correct the document if instructions are received in response to the enquiry and if the company has indicated its desire to avail itself of this section: subsection (2)(a).[83] The instructions must satisfy the criteria set out in subsection (3)—namely, they must be given by an authorized person and they must satisfy the registrar's rules as to form, manner, and authentication.[84]

**35.1075.04** Notably, the section applies to the registration of charges under the Companies Act 2006, Part 25, as well as the delivery of documents to the registrar by the company itself: subsection (5). A corrected document is treated under subsection (6) as having been delivered when the correction is made. As a result, it remains crucial for the person delivering a document subject to a statutory time limit to ensure that it is accurate if he wishes to ensure that he has actually complied with the time limit.

---

[78] Companies Act 2006 (Commencement No 8, Transitional Provisions and Savings) Order 2008, SI 2008/2860, art 3(r). The transitional provisions are set out in the Companies Act 2006 (Commencement No 8, Transitional Provisions and Savings) Order 2008, Sch 2, para 101 as amended by the Companies Act 2006 (Part 35) (Consequential Amendments, Transitional Provisions and Savings) Order 2009, SI 2009/1802, art 18 and the Schedule thereto. These provide that s 1075 applies to documents delivered to the Registrar on or after 1 October 2009 other than those delivered in pursuance of an obligation arising before that date. Where the obligation to deliver a document to the Registrar arose before 1 October 2009, the provisions that would have applied if the document had been delivered before that date (and the registrar's former practice with respect to documents requiring correction) continue to apply.

[79] See s 1114(1).

[80] In relation to 'delivery', see s 1114(2).

[81] *Halifax plc and others v Halifax Repossessions Ltd and others* [2004] EWCA Civ 331.

[82] The latter pursuant to s 1074: see *Hansard*, HL, Standing Committee D, col 412 (4 July 2006).

[83] Subsection (4) provides the way in which a company can opt into the section. For 'electronic form', see s 1168(3), (5).

[84] As to the Registrar's Rules 2009, see s 1117.

(4) If the unnecessary material cannot readily be separated from the rest of the document, the document is treated as not meeting the requirements for proper delivery.

(5) If the unnecessary material can readily be separated from the rest of the document, the registrar may register the document either—

    (a) with the omission of the unnecessary material, or

    (b) as delivered.

AMENDMENTS AND NOTES

[a] This section applies to LLPs with modifications by reg 60 of the Limited Liability Partnerships (Application of Companies Act 2006) Regulations 2009, SI 2009/1804 and to unregistered companies with modifications by Sch 1, para 17 of the Unregistered Companies Regulations 2009, SI 2009/2436.

COMMENCEMENT DATE 1 October 2009[74]

This provision was introduced by the Companies Act 2006. A document[75] which contains unnecessary material is treated, for the purposes of section 1068(4) and section 1071, as failing to comply with the requirements for proper delivery. Unnecessary material is defined as material which meets both requirements of subsection (2) and it is to be a matter for the registrar to decide whether material is unnecessary: see subsection (5).    **35.1074.02**

Where the unnecessary material cannot be readily separated from the rest of the document, the document is treated as not meeting the requirements for proper delivery, pursuant to subsection (4). In circumstances where the unnecessary material can be readily separated from the rest of the document, the registrar may, in his discretion, register the document as delivered and delete the unnecessary material as appropriate.[76]    **35.1074.03**

This section is discussed in guidance issued by Companies House.[77]    **35.1074.04**

## 1075 Informal correction of document

(1) A document delivered to the registrar may be corrected by the registrar if it appears to the registrar to be incomplete or internally inconsistent.    **35.1075.01**

(2) This power is exercisable only—

    (a) on instructions, and

    (b) if the company [(or other body) to which the document relates][a] has given (and has not withdrawn) its consent to instructions being given under this section.

(3) The following requirements must be met as regards the instructions—

    (a) the instructions must be given in response to an enquiry by the registrar;

    (b) the registrar must be satisfied that the person giving the instructions is authorised to do so—

        (i) by the person by whom the document was delivered, or

        (ii) by the company [(or other body)][b] to which the document relates;

    (c) the instructions must meet any requirements of registrar's rules as to—

        (i) the form and manner in which they are given, and

        (ii) authentication.

(4) The consent [of the company (or other body)][c] to instructions being given under this section (and any withdrawal of such consent)—

    (a) may be in hard copy or electronic form, and

    (b) must be notified to the registrar.

(5) This section applies in relation to documents delivered under Part 25 (company charges) by a person other than the company [(or other body)][d] as if the references to the company [(or other body)][e] were to the company [(or other body)][f] or the person by whom the document was delivered.

---

[74] Companies Act 2006 (Commencement No 8, Transitional Provisions and Savings) Order 2008, SI 2008/2860, art 3(r). The transitional provisions are set out in the Companies Act 2006 (Commencement No 8, Transitional Provisions and Savings) Order 2008, Sch 2, para 100 as amended by the Companies Act 2006 (Part 35) (Consequential Amendments, Transitional Provisions and Savings) Order 2009, SI 2009/1802, art 18 and the Schedule thereto. These provide that s 1074 applies to documents delivered to the Registrar on or after 1 October 2009 other than those delivered in pursuance of an obligation arising before that date. Where the obligation to deliver a document to the Registrar arose before 1 October 2009, the provisions that would have applied if the document had been delivered before that date (and the registrar's former practice with respect to the requirements for proper delivery and documents containing unnecessary material) continue to apply.

[75] See s 1114(1).

[76] See subs (5).

[77] See the current guidance issued by Companies House; Registrar's rules and powers, May 2012, Chapter 2, question 1 available at ⟨http://www.companieshouse.gov.uk/about/pdf/gp6.pdf⟩.

and Sch 1, para 19 of the Unregistered Companies Regulations 2009, SI 2009/2436 subject to transitional provisions in Sch 2 of those regulations.

COMMENCEMENT DATE This section came into force on 1 January 2007 save as regards publication by alternative means.[89]

**35.1077.02**  This section and section 1078 replace the Companies Act 1985, section 711.

**35.1077.03**  Article 3(4) of the First Company Law Directive[90] provides for the publication of certain documents in the national gazette of a Member State. The national gazette can be in electronic form and Member States are at liberty to replace publication in their national gazette with an equally effective means using electronic access.

**35.1077.04**  This section implements Article 3(4) and imposes an obligation on the registrar to publish receipt of the relevant documents in the London Gazette as regards companies registered in England or Wales[91] or by some other equally effective means. The relevant documents are set out in section 1078, and alternative publication by equally effective means is dealt with in section 1116.

**35.1077.05**  The information to be published is limited. Article 3(4) provides for the publication of the full or a partial text of the document or a mere reference to the document deposited in the file or entered in the register. This section imposes the least onerous obligation on the registrar and imposes a duty on him merely to publish the name and number of the company, a description of the relevant document and the date of receipt. The document itself will be filed with the registrar and can be inspected in the usual way.

**35.1077.06**  This section and the role of the registrar under Part 35 are discussed in *Globespan Airways Ltd (in liquidation), Cartwright v Registrar of Companies*.[92]

### 1078  Documents subject to Directive disclosure requirements[a]

**35.1078.01**  (1)  The documents subject to the 'Directive disclosure requirements' are as follows.
The requirements referred to are those of Article 3 of the First Company Law Directive (68/151/EEC), as amended, extended and applied.

(2)  In the case of every company—

*Constitutional documents*

1.  The company's memorandum and articles.
2.  Any amendment of the company's articles (including every resolution or agreement required to be embodied in or annexed to copies of the company's articles issued by the company).
3.  After any amendment of the company's articles, the text of the articles as amended.
4.  Any notice of a change of the company's name.

*Directors*

1.  The statement of proposed officers required on formation of the company.
2.  Notification of any change among the company's directors.
3.  Notification of any change in the particulars of directors required to be delivered to the registrar.

*Accounts, reports and returns*

1.  All documents required to be delivered to the registrar under section 441 (annual accounts and reports).
[1A  All documents delivered to the registrar under sections 394A(2)(e), 448A(2)(e), and 479A(2)(e) (qualifying subsidiary companies: conditions for exemptions from the audit, preparation and filing of individual accounts).][b]
2.  The company's annual return.

---

[89]  Companies Act 2006 (Commencement No 1, Transitional Provisions and Savings) Order 2006, SI 2006/3428, art 2(1). For transitional provisions, see Sch 1, para 4(1), revoked by Companies Act 2006 (Commencement No 8, Transitional Provisions and Savings) Order 2008, SI 2008/2860, art 6(1).

[90]  Directive (EEC) 68/151 [1968] OJ65/8, as amended by Directive (EC) 2003/58. Now replaced by Directive (EC) 2009/101.

[91]  See s 1173.

[92]  [2012] EWCA Civ 1159.

This section is discussed in guidance issued by Companies House.[85]     **35.1075.05**

## 1076   Replacement of document not meeting requirements for proper delivery

(1)  The registrar may accept a replacement for a document previously delivered that—     **35.1076.01**
    (a)  did not comply with the requirements for proper delivery, or
    (b)  contained unnecessary material (within the meaning of section 1074).
(2)  A replacement document must not be accepted unless the registrar is satisfied that it is delivered by—
    (a)  the person by whom the original document was delivered, or
    (b)  the company [(or other body)][a] to which the original document relates,
and that it complies with the requirements for proper delivery.
(3)  The power of the registrar to impose requirements as to the form and manner of delivery includes power to impose requirements as to the identification of the original document and the delivery of the replacement in a form and manner enabling it to be associated with the original.
(4)  This section does not apply where the original document was delivered under Part 25 (company charges) (but see sections 873 and 888 (rectification of register of charges)).

AMENDMENTS AND NOTES

[a]  Amended by the Companies Act 2006 (Part 35) (Consequential Amendments, Transitional Provisions and Savings) Order 2009, SI 2009/1802.

COMMENCEMENT DATE 1 October 2009[86]

This section created a new discretionary mechanism for the registrar to accept replacements for     **35.1076.02**
documents[87] which did not comply with the requirements for proper delivery set out in sections 1068(4) and 1071. The section also allows the registrar to make requirements which will enable him to associate the replacement with the original defective document: subsection (3). See the Registrar's Rules 2009. As to the registrar's rule-making powers generally, see section 1117 below.

This section is discussed in guidance issued by Companies House.[88]     **35.1076.03**

### *Public notice of receipt of certain documents*

## 1077   Public notice of receipt of certain documents

(1)  The registrar must cause to be published—     **35.1077.01**
    (a)  in the Gazette, or
    (b)  in accordance with section 1116 (alternative means of giving public notice),
notice of the receipt by the registrar of any document that, on receipt, is subject to the Directive disclosure requirements (see section 1078).
(2)  The notice must state the name and registered number of the company, the description of document and the date of receipt.
(3)  The registrar is not required to cause notice of the receipt of a document to be published before the date of incorporation of the company to which the document relates.

AMENDMENTS AND NOTES

[a]  This section applies to orders delivered to the registrar under reg 19(1) and (2) of the Companies (Cross-Border Mergers) Regulation 2007, SI 2007/2974 by reg 19(4) of those regulations, to LLPs with modifications by reg 63 of the Limited Liability Partnerships (Application of Companies Act 2006) Regulations 2009, SI 2009/1804 and to unregistered companies with modifications by reg 3

---

*Registered office*
> Notification of any change of the company's registered office.

*Winding up*

1. Copy of any winding-up order in respect of the company.
2. Notice of the appointment of liquidators.
3. Order for the dissolution of a company on a winding up.
4. Return by a liquidator of the final meeting of a company on a winding up.

(3) In the case of a public company—

*Share capital*

1. Any statement of capital and initial shareholdings.
2. Any return of allotment and the statement of capital accompanying it.
3. Copy of any resolution under section 570 or 571 (disapplication of pre-emption rights).
4. Copy of any report under section 593 or 599 as to the value of a non-cash asset.
5. Statement of capital accompanying notice given under section 625 (notice by company of redenomination of shares).
6. Statement of capital accompanying notice given under section 627 (notice by company of reduction of capital in connection with redenomination of shares).
7. Notice delivered under section 636 (notice of new name of class of shares) or 637 (notice of variation of rights attached to shares).
8. Statement of capital accompanying order delivered under section 649 (order of court confirming reduction of capital).
9. Notification (under section 689) of the redemption of shares and the statement of capital accompanying it.
10. Statement of capital accompanying return delivered under section 708 (notice of cancellation of shares on purchase of own shares) or 730 (notice of cancellation of shares held as treasury shares).
11. Any statement of compliance delivered under section 762 (statement that company meets conditions for issue of trading certificate).

*Mergers and divisions*

1. Copy of any draft of the terms of a scheme required to be delivered to the registrar under section 906 or 921.
2. Copy of any order under section 899 or 900 in respect of a compromise or arrangement to which Part 27 (mergers and divisions of public companies) applies.

(4) Where a private company re-registers as a public company (see section 96)—
    (a) the last statement of capital relating to the company received by the registrar under any provision of the Companies Acts becomes subject to the Directive disclosure requirements, and
    (b) section 1077 (public notice of receipt of certain documents) applies as if the statement had been received by the registrar when the re-registration takes effect.

(5) In the case of an overseas company, such particulars, returns and other documents required to be delivered under Part 34 as may be specified by the Secretary of State by regulations.

(6) Regulations under subsection (5) are subject to negative resolution procedure.

AMENDMENT AND NOTES

ᵃ This section applies to orders delivered to the registrar under reg 19(1) and (2) of the Companies (Cross-Border Mergers) Regulation 2007, SI 2007/2974 by reg 19(4) of those regulations, to LLPs with modifications by reg 63 of the Limited Liability Partnerships (Application of Companies Act 2006) Regulations 2009, SI 2009/1804 and to unregistered companies with modifications by reg 3 and Sch 1, para 19 of the Unregistered Companies Regulations 2009, SI 2009/2436 subject to transitional provisions in Sch 2 of those regulations.

ᵇ Amended by reg 19 of the Companies and Limited Liabilities Partnerships (Accounts and Audit Exemptions and Change of Accounting Framework) Regulations 2012, SI 2012/2301.

COMMENCEMENT DATE 1 January 2007 as regards certain documents[93]

---

[93] Companies Act 2006 (Commencement No 1, Transitional Provisions and Savings) Order 2006, SI 2006/3428, art 2(1). For transitional provisions, see art 5, and Sch 1, para 5, revoked in part by Companies Act 2006 (Commencement No 5, Transitional Provisions and Savings) Order 2007, SI 2007/3495, art 10(1) and revoked by Companies Act 2006 (Commencement No 8, Transitional Provisions and Savings) Order 2008, SI 2008/2860, art 6(1) subject to transitional provisions and savings in Sch 2, para 103 as amended by the Companies Act 2006 (Part 35)(Consequential Amendments, Transitional Provisions and Savings) Order 2009, SI 2009/1802 art 18 and the schedule thereto.

**35.1078.02**   This section lists the various documents the receipt of which must be published pursuant to section 1077. This list is based on the list in Article 2 of the First Company Law Directive.[94]

**35.1078.03**   Regulations made under subsection (5) are subject to the negative resolution procedure, which is explained in section 1289. Regulation 76 of the Overseas Companies Regulations 2009, SI 2009/1801, specifies the particulars, returns, and other documents of overseas companies which are subject to the Directive disclosure requirements.

**35.1078.04**   This section and the role of the registrar under Part 35 are discussed in Globespan Airways Ltd (in liquidation), Cartwright v Registrar of Companies.[95]

## 1079   Effect of failure to give public notice[a]

**35.1079.01**
(1) A company is not entitled to rely against other persons on the happening of any event to which this section applies unless—
   (a) the event has been officially notified at the material time, or
   (b) the company shows that the person concerned knew of the event at the material time.
(2) The events to which this section applies are—
   (a) an amendment of the company's articles,
   (b) a change among the company's directors,
   (c) (as regards service of any document on the company) a change of the company's registered office,
   (d) the making of a winding-up order in respect of the company, or
   (e) the appointment of a liquidator in a voluntary winding up of the company.
(3) If the material time falls—
   (a) on or before the 15th day after the date of official notification, or
   (b) where the 15th day was not a working day, on or before the next day that was,
   the company is not entitled to rely on the happening of the event as against a person who shows that he was unavoidably prevented from knowing of the event at that time.
(4) 'Official notification' means—
   (a) in relation to an amendment of the company's articles, notification in accordance with section 1077 (public notice of receipt by registrar of certain documents) of the amendment and the amended text of the articles;
   (b) in relation to anything else stated in a document subject to the Directive disclosure requirements, notification of that document in accordance with that section;
   (c) in relation to the appointment of a liquidator in a voluntary winding up, notification of that event in accordance with section 109 of the Insolvency Act 1986 (c. 45) or Article 95 of the Insolvency (Northern Ireland) Order 1989 (S.I.1989/ 2405 (N.I. 19)).

AMENDMENT AND NOTES

a   This section applies to orders delivered to the registrar under reg 19(1) and (2) of the Companies (Cross-Border Mergers) Regulation 2007, SI 2007/2974 by reg 19(4) of those regulations, to LLPs with modifications by reg 63 of the Limited Liability Partnerships (Application of Companies Act 2006) Regulations 2009, SI 2009/1804 and to unregistered companies with modifications by reg 3 and Sch 1, para 19 of the Unregistered Companies Regulations 2009, SI 2009/2436 subject to transitional provisions in Sch 2 of those regulations.

COMMENCEMENT DATE 1 January 2007[96]

**35.1079.02**   This section replaces the Companies Act 1985, section 42.

**35.1079.03**   Article 3(5) of First Company Law Directive[97] provides that certain documents and particulars can be relied upon by the company as against third parties only after they have been disclosed in accordance with Article 3(4), unless the company shows that the third parties already have knowledge thereof. The paragraph further provides that the documents and particulars cannot be relied upon as against third parties who prove that it was impossible for them to have had knowledge of the relevant document or particular as regards transactions taking place before the 16th day following disclosure.

---

94  Directive (EEC) 68/151 [1968] OJ L65/8, as amended by Directive (EC/2003/58). Now replaced by Directive (EC) 2009/101.

95  [2012] EWCA Civ 1159.

96  Companies Act 2006 (Commencement No 1, Transitional Provisions and Savings) Order 2006, SI 2006/3428, art 2(1). For transitional provisions, see Sch 1, para 6, revoked by Companies Act 2006 (Commencement No 8, Transitional Provisions and Savings) Order 2008, SI 2008/2860, art 6(1) subject to transitional provisions and savings in Sch 2, para 104 as amended by the Companies Act 2006 (Part 35) (Consequential Amendments, Transitional Provisions and Savings) Order 2009, SI 2009/1802, art 18 and the Schedule thereto.

97  Directive (EEC) 68/151 [1968] OJ L65/8, as amended by Directive (EC) 2003/58. Now replaced by Directive (EC) 2009/101.

This section complies with Article 3(5) and protects a third party in the limited circumstances **35.1079.04** envisaged by that paragraph. A company is not entitled to rely on an amendment to its articles, a change in directors or registered office (as regards service of documents), a winding-up order, or the appointment of a liquidator in a voluntary liquidation (i) unless the relevant event had been published in accordance with section 1077, or with the Insolvency Act 1986, section 109 as regards the appointment of a liquidator in a voluntary liquidation,[98] or the other person had actual knowledge of the relevant event; or (ii) on or before the 15th day after publication (if not a working day, the next working day) if the other person was unavoidably prevented from knowing of the relevant event. As regards (i), the burden of proving such knowledge lies on the company, but as regards (ii) the burden of proving that the relevant person was unavoidably prevented from knowing of the relevant event falls on that person.

The section is limited in its effect. It merely prevents a company relying on the happening of a relevant **35.1079.05** event in the circumstances specified. Anyone other than the company can rely on the relevant event. Furthermore, publication does not have effect of giving the other person knowledge, constructive or otherwise, of the relevant event.[99]

This section and the role of the registrar under Part 35 are discussed in *Globespan Airways Ltd (in* **35.1079.06** *liquidation), Cartwright v Registrar of Companies.*[100]

## The register

### 1080  The register[a]

(1) The registrar shall continue to keep records of— **35.1080.01**
  (a) the information contained in documents delivered to the registrar under any enactment, [and][b]
  (b) certificates of incorporation issued by the registrar [under any enactment][c]
  (c) [...][d, e]
(2) The records relating to companies are referred to collectively in the Companies Acts as 'the register'.[f]
(3) Information deriving from documents subject to the Directive disclosure requirements (see section 1078) that are delivered to the registrar on or after 1st January 2007 must be kept by the registrar in electronic form.
(4) Subject to that, information contained in documents delivered to the registrar may be recorded and kept in any form the registrar thinks fit, provided it is possible to inspect it and produce a copy of it.
  This is sufficient compliance with any duty of the registrar to keep, file or register the document or to record the information contained in it.[e, f]
(5) The records kept by the registrar must be such that information relating to a company [or other registered body][g] is associated with that [body],[h] in such manner as the registrar may determine, so as to enable all the information relating to the [body][i] to be retrieved.

AMENDMENTS AND NOTES

[a] This section applies to documents delivered to the registrar under reg 12(1) of the Companies (Cross-Border Merger) Regulations 2007, SI 2007/2974 by reg 12(6)(b) of those regulations and to orders delivered to the registrar under reg 19(1) and (2) of the Companies (Cross-Border Mergers) Regulations 2007, SI 2007/2974 by reg 19(4) of those regulations.
[b] Amended by the Companies Act 2006 (Part 35) (Consequential Amendments, Transitional Provisions and Savings) Order 2009, SI 2009/1802.
[c] Amended by the Companies Act 2006 (Part 35) (Consequential Amendments, Transitional Provisions and Savings) Order 2009, SI 2009/1802.
[d] Repealed by the Companies Act 2006 (Part 35) (Consequential Amendments, Transitional Provisions and Savings) Order 2009, SI 2009/1802.
[e] Subsections (1), (4), and (5) apply to LLPs by reg 60 of the Limited Liability Partnerships (Application of Companies Act 2006) Regulations 2009, SI 2009/1804 and to unregistered companies by reg 3 and Sch 1, para 17 of the Unregistered Companies Regulations 2009, SI 2009/2436, subject to transitional provisions in Sch 2 of those regulations.
[f] Subsections (2) and (4) apply to unregistered companies by reg 3 and Sch 1, para 20 of the Unregistered Companies Regulations 2009, SI 2009/2436 subject to transitional provisions in Sch 2 of those regulations.

---

[98] Or art 95 of the Insolvency (Northern Ireland) Order 1989 as regards companies registered in Northern Ireland.
[99] *Official Custodian for Charities v Parway Estates Development Ltd* [1985] Ch 151, [1984] 3 All ER 679.
[100] [2012] EWCA Civ 1159.

<sup>g</sup> Amended by the Companies Act 2006 (Part 35) (Consequential Amendments, Transitional Provisions and Savings) Order 2009, SI 2009/1802.
<sup>h</sup> Amended by the Companies Act 2006 (Part 35) (Consequential Amendments, Transitional Provisions and Savings) Order 2009, SI 2009/1802.
<sup>i</sup> Amended by the Companies Act 2006 (Part 35) (Consequential Amendments, Transitional Provisions and Savings) Order 2009, SI 2009/1802.

COMMENCEMENT DATE 1 January 2007[101]

**35.1080.02**    Article 3(1) of the First Company Law Directive[102] imposes an obligation on a Member State to open a file or register for each of the companies registered in the relevant Member State. Article 3(2) provides for all relevant documents to be kept in the file or entered in the register and Member States must ensure that by 1 January 2007 all documents which are filed as from 1 January 2007 at the latest must be kept in electronic form.

**35.1080.03**    This section complies with Article 3(1) to (2) and imposes an obligation on the registrar of companies to continue to keep records of information delivered to him and certificates of incorporation and certificates of registration of charges issued by him, and to keep all information in certain documents in electronic form. These documents are the documents set out in section 1078 which are delivered to the registrar on or after 1 January 2007. Any other documents[103] can be kept in any form the registrar thinks fit, provided that they can be inspected and copied.

**35.1080.04**    This section and the role of the registrar under Part 35 are discussed in *Globespan Airways Ltd (in liquidation), Cartwright v Registrar of Companies*.[104]

### 1081 Annotation of the register<sup>a</sup>

**35.1081.01**    (1) The registrar must place a note in the register recording—
    (a)  the date on which a document is delivered to the registrar;
    (b)  if a document is corrected under section 1075, the nature and date of the correction;
    (c)  if a document is replaced (whether or not material derived from it is removed), the fact that it has been replaced and the date of delivery of the replacement;
    (d)  if material is removed—
        (i)   what was removed (giving a general description of its contents),
        (ii)  under what power, and
        (iii) the date on which that was done.
    (2) The Secretary of State may make provision by regulations—
    (a)  authorising or requiring the registrar to annotate the register in such other circumstances as may be specified in the regulations, and
    (b)  as to the contents of any such annotation.
    (3) No annotation is required in the case of a document that by virtue of section 1072(2) (documents not meeting requirements for proper delivery) is treated as not having been delivered.
    (4) A note may be removed if it no longer serves any useful purpose.
    (5) Any duty or power of the registrar with respect to annotation of the register is subject to the court's power under section 1097 (powers of court on ordering removal of material from the register) to direct—
    (a)  that a note be removed from the register, or
    (b)  that no note shall be made of the removal of material that is the subject of the court's order.
    (6) Notes placed in the register in accordance with subsection (1), or in pursuance of regulations under subsection (2), are part of the register for all purposes of the Companies Acts.
    (7) Regulations under this section are subject to negative resolution procedure.

AMENDMENTS AND NOTES

<sup>a</sup> This section applies with modifications to LLPs by reg 64 of the Limited Liability Partnerships (Application of Companies Act 2006) Regulations 2009, SI 2009/1804 and to EEIGs and their establishments by reg 18 and Sch 4, para 29 of the European Economic Interest Grouping

---

[101] Companies Act 2006 (Commencement No 1, Transitional Provisions and Savings) Order 2006, SI 2006/3428, art 2(1). For transitional provisions, see Sch 1, para 7, revoked by Companies Act 2006 (Commencement No 8, Transitional Provisions and Savings) Order 2008, SI 2008/2860, art 6(1).
[102] Directive (EEC) 68/151 [1968] OJ L65/8, as amended by Directive (EC) 2003/58. Now replaced by Directive (EC) 2009/101.
[103] i.e. documents not specified in s 1078 and all documents delivered to the registrar before 1 January 2007.
[104] [2012] EWCA Civ 1159.

Regulations 1989, SI 1989/638 as amended by regs 19 and 23(3) of the European Economic Interest Grouping (Amendment) Regulations 2009, SI 2009/2399.

COMMENCEMENT DATE 1 October 2009[105]

This section imposes an obligation on the registrar of companies to annotate the register to show the dates on which documents were delivered, corrected, replaced, or removed, the nature of any correction, the fact of replacement, and details of what was removed and the power under which it was removed. It also gives the registrar power to remove a note if it no longer serves a useful purpose. **35.1081.02**

If the court has ordered any document or part of a document to be removed from the register, it can also direct that no annotation shall be made recording that removal or, if an annotation has already been made, that it should be removed. The registrar's power to annotate the register is subject to any such direction. **35.1081.03**

The Registrar of Companies and Applications for Striking Off Regulations 2009, SI 2009/1803 made under subsection (2) and other sections, amongst other matters, gives the registrar power to make a note on the register if any material on the register is misleading or confusing. **35.1081.04**

The 'negative resolution' procedure is explained in section 1289. **35.1081.05**

This section and the role of the registrar under Part 35 are discussed in *Globespan Airways Ltd (in liquidation), Cartwright v Registrar of Companies*.[106] **35.1081.06**

## 1082 Allocation of unique identifiers[a]

(1) The Secretary of State may make provision for the use, in connection with the register, of reference numbers ('unique identifiers') to identify each person who— **35.1082.01**
   (a) is a director of a company,
   (b) is secretary (or a joint secretary) of a company, or
   (c) in the case of an overseas company whose particulars are registered under section 1046, holds any such position as may be specified for the purposes of this section by regulations under that section.

(2) The regulations may—
   (a) provide that a unique identifier may be in such form, consisting of one or more sequences of letters or numbers, as the registrar may from time to time determine;
   (b) make provision for the allocation of unique identifiers by the registrar;
   (c) require there to be included, in any specified description of documents delivered to the registrar, as well as a statement of the person's name—
      (i) a statement of the person's unique identifier, or
      (ii) a statement that the person has not been allocated a unique identifier;
   (d) enable the registrar to take steps where a person appears to have more than one unique identifier to discontinue the use of all but one of them.

(3) The regulations may contain provision for the application of the scheme in relation to persons appointed, and documents registered, before the commencement of this Act.

(4) The regulations may make different provision for different descriptions of person and different descriptions of document.

(5) Regulations under this section are subject to affirmative resolution procedure.

AMENDMENTS AND NOTES

[a] This section applies with modifications to LLPs by reg 64 of the Limited Liability Partnerships (Application of Companies Act 2006) Regulations 2009, SI 2009/1804, to EEIGs and their establishments by reg 18 and Sch 4, para 30 of the European Economic Interest Grouping Regulations 1989, SI 1989/638 as amended by regs 19 and 23(3) of the European Economic Interest Grouping (Amendment) Regulations 2009, SI 2009/2399 and to the registration or the deletion of registration of SEs and the functions of the registrar in relation to such registration and deletion with modifications by reg 14 and Sch 2, para 2 of the European Public Limited-Liability Company

---

[105] Companies Act 2006 (Commencement No 8, Transitional Provisions and Savings) Order 2008, SI 2008/2860, art 3(r). For transitional provisions, see Sch 2, para 105 as amended by the Companies Act 2006 (Part 35) (Consequential Amendments, Transitional Provisions and Savings) Order 2009, SI 2009/1802, art 18 and the Schedule thereto.

[106] [2012] EWCA Civ 1159.

Regulations 2004, SI 2004/2326 as amended by regs 16 and 38 of the European Public Limited-Liability Company (Amendment) Regulations 2009, SI 2009/2400 subject to transitional provisions in Sch 2 of those regulations.

COMMENCEMENT DATE 1 October 2009[107]

**35.1082.02**     This section allows the Secretary of State to make regulations providing for directors of a company or a secretary of a company or the equivalent in a registered overseas company to be identified by a unique number. This will enable those who inspect the register to distinguish between directors with the same or a similar name, particularly when their home addresses are not disclosed.

**35.1082.03**     The Secretary of State has not yet made any regulations under this section.

**35.1082.04**     The 'affirmative resolution' procedure is explained in section 1290.

**35.1082.05**     This section and the role of the registrar under Part 35 are discussed in *Globespan Airways Ltd (in liquidation), Cartwright v Registrar of Companies*.[108]

### 1083   Preservation of original documents[a]

**35.1083.01**     (1) The originals of documents delivered to the registrar in hard copy form must be kept for three years after they are received by the registrar, after which they may be destroyed provided the information contained in them has been recorded. [...][b]
This is subject to section 1087(3) (extent of obligation to retain material not available for public inspection).

(2) The registrar is under no obligation to keep the originals of documents delivered in electronic form, provided the information contained in them has been recorded [...][c]

(3) This section applies to documents held by the registrar when this section comes into force as well as to documents subsequently received.

AMENDMENTS AND NOTES

[a] This section applies with modifications to LLPs by reg 60 of the Limited Liability Partnerships (Application of Companies Act 2006) Regulations 2009, SI 2009/1804 and to unregistered companies by reg 3 and Sch 1, para 17 of the Unregistered Companies Regulations 2009, SI 2009/2436 subject to transitional provisions in Sch 2 of those regulations.

[b] Amended by the Companies Act 2006 (Part 35) (Consequential Amendments, Transitional Provisions and Savings) Order 2009, SI 2009/1802.

[c] Amended by the Companies Act 2006 (Part 35) (Consequential Amendments, Transitional Provisions and Savings) Order 2009, SI 2009/1802.

COMMENCEMENT DATE 1 October 2009[109]

**35.1083.02**     This section replaces the Companies Act 1985, section 707A(2). It allows the registrar to destroy any documents delivered in hard copy form[110] after three years have expired but not before, provided that the information in those documents has been recorded in the register. Documents which are not made available for public inspection under section 1087 can be destroyed in accordance with that section. The registrar is also given power to destroy the originals of documents delivered in electronic form[111] provided that the information in those documents has been recorded in the register.

### 1084   Records relating to companies that have been dissolved etc[a]

**35.1084.01**     (1) This section applies where—
(a) a company is dissolved,
(b) an overseas company ceases to have any connection with the United Kingdom by virtue of which it is required to register particulars under section 1046, or
(c) a credit or financial institution ceases to be within section 1050 (overseas institutions required to file accounts with the registrar).

(2) At any time after two years from the date on which it appears to the registrar that—
(a) the company has been dissolved,
(b) the overseas company has ceased to have any connection with the United Kingdom by virtue of which it is required to register particulars under section 1046, or

---

[107] Companies Act 2006 (Commencement No 8, Transitional Provisions and Savings) Order 2008, SI 2008/2860, art 3(r).

[108] [2012] EWCA Civ 1159.

[109] Companies Act 2006 (Commencement No 8, Transitional Provisions and Savings) Order 2008, SI 2008/2860, art 3(r).

[110] Defined in s 1168(2).

[111] Defined in s 1168(3).

    (c)   the credit or financial institution has ceased to be within section 1050 (overseas institutions required to file accounts with the registrar),

the registrar may direct that records relating to the company or institution may be removed to the Public Record Office or, as the case may be, the Public Record Office of Northern Ireland.

(3)   Records in respect of which such a direction is given shall be disposed of under the enactments relating to that Office and the rules made under them.

(4)   In subsection (1)(a) 'company' includes a company provisionally or completely registered under the Joint Stock Companies Act 1844 (c. 110).

(5)   This section does not extend to Scotland.

AMENDMENTS AND NOTES

[a]  This section applies with modifications to LLPs by reg 65 of the Limited Liability Partnerships (Application of Companies Act 2006) Regulations 2009, SI 2009/1804, to EEIGs and their establishments by reg 18 and Sch 4, para 31 of the European Economic Interest Grouping Regulations 1989, SI 1989/638 as amended by regs 19 and 23(3) of the European Economic Interest Grouping (Amendment) Regulations 2009, SI 2009/2399 and to the registration or the deletion of registration of SEs and the functions of the registrar in relation to such registration and deletion with modifications by reg 14 and Sch 2, para 3 of the European Public Limited-Liability Company Regulations 2004, SI 2004/2326 as amended by regs 16 and 38 of the European Public Limited-Liability Company (Amendment) Regulations 2009, SI 2009/2400 subject to transitional provisions in Sch 2 of those regulations.

COMMENCEMENT DATE 1 October 2009[112]

This section replaces the Companies Act 1985, section 707A(3) and (4). It gives the registrar power to direct that the records relating to a company which has been dissolved can be removed to the Public Record Office or the Public Records Office for Northern Ireland two years after the company has been dissolved. This section also applies to an overseas company which has ceased to have any connection with the UK, or a credit or financial institution which no longer falls within section 1050 (which applies to credit or financial institutions incorporated or formed and whose head office is outside the UK and Gibraltar but has a branch in the UK). If such a credit or financial institution, for example, ceases to have a branch in the UK, the registrar can exercise the power under this section.  **35.1084.02**

## Inspection etc of the register

### 1085  Inspection of the register[a]

(1)   Any person may inspect the register.  **35.1085.01**

(2)   The right of inspection extends to the originals of documents delivered to the registrar in hard copy form if, and only if, the record kept by the registrar of the contents of the document is illegible or unavailable.

    The period for which such originals are to be kept is limited by section 1083(1).

(3)   This section has effect subject to section 1087 (material not available for public inspection).

AMENDMENTS AND NOTES

[a]  This section applies with modifications to LLPs by reg 66 of the Limited Liability Partnerships (Application of Companies Act 2006) Regulations 2009, SI 2009/1804.

COMMENCEMENT DATE 1 January 2007[113]

Making records available for public inspection is the second aspect of the registrar's functions (the first being to register and dissolve companies, and to receive and store records). The volume of requests for public inspection is enormous. Historically, searches were sought and answered on paper, but inquirers are increasingly making use of electronic communications. Approximately 4 million documents annually are now made available electronically, and about 400,000 annually via an Internet service. However, the largest single means of supplying information is in bulk to customers in the business information industry, who use it in order to compile credit references, company reports, and other specialist products. Approximately 17 million documents annually are made available in bulk for such purposes.  **35.1085.02**

The starting proposition under the Act is that 'any person' may inspect the register: section 1085(1). This reflects the widely held belief that good business ethics demand that the benefits of limited liability  **35.1085.03**

---

[112] Companies Act 2006 (Commencement No 8, Transitional Provisions and Savings) Order 2008, SI 2008/2860, art 3(r).

[113] Companies Act 2006 (Commencement No 1, Transitional Provisions and Savings) Order 2006, SI 2006/3428, art 2(1). For transitional provisions, see Sch 1, para 8, revoked by Companies Act 2006 (Commencement No 8, Transitional Provisions and Savings) Order 2008, SI 2008/2806, art 6(1).

trading should only be enjoyed on conditions of transparency—for example, that the identity of the company's ownership and management, and its up-to-date financial position should be publicly available. An illustration of the enduring nature of this attitude is provided by the statutory provisions requiring the registration of a director's home address. This requirement was originally introduced in 1917 as a wartime measure to ensure that enemy aliens were not able to trade through limited liability companies undetected. When the war ended, the provision immediately lost its original function, but it was nevertheless preserved and came to acquire a new justification in providing useful information on the managerial control of a company, and an address for personal service. It has only now been modified, in the face of considerable opposition from some quarters, in order to meet the recent threat of harm to vulnerable directors (eg from animal rights activists).

**35.1085.04**      Subsection (3) subjects the rights of inspection to certain qualifications set out in section 1087.

**35.1085.05**      Subsection (2) reflects the development of modern technology for data storage and retrieval. Inspection of a paper original is only required if the image maintained by Companies House (eg electronically or on microfiche) is illegible.

### 1086   Right to copy of material on the register[a]

**35.1086.01**      (1) Any person may require a copy of any material on the register.

(2) The fee for any such copy of material derived from a document subject to the Directive disclosure requirements (see section 1078), whether in hard copy or electronic form, must not exceed the administrative cost of providing it.

(3) This section has effect subject to section 1087 (material not available for public inspection).

AMENDMENTS AND NOTES

[a]This section applies with modifications to LLPs by reg 66 of the Limited Liability Partnerships (Application of Companies Act 2006) Regulations 2009, SI 2009/1804.

COMMENCEMENT DATE 1 January 2007[114]

**35.1086.02**      This section provides a right to demand a copy of any material inspected, without which the right of inspection would be valueless. Provision is made in sections 1089 to 1090 as regards the form and manner in which applications may be made and copies provided. Where a copy of material on the register is required under this section and the person expressly requests that the copy be certified as a true copy and the registrar provides the copy in electronic form, the registrar's certificate of the copy must be authenticated by an electronic signature.[115]

**35.1086.03**      Although section 1086(2) expressly provides that the fee for copying a document subject to the First Company Law Directive[116] requirements must not exceed the administrative cost of providing it, the same result is likely also to be achieved by the general law (as to which, see the commentary on section 1063 above) in relation to the fee for any other copies. For the 'Directive disclosure requirements', see section 1078 above.

**35.1086.04**      As with section 1085(3), section 1086(3) makes clear that the right to demand a copy is subject to certain qualifications set out in section 1087.

### 1087   Material not available for public inspection[a]

**35.1087.01**      (1) The following material must not be made available by the registrar for public inspection—

(a) the contents of any document sent to the registrar containing views expressed pursuant to section 56 (comments on proposal by company to use certain words or expressions in company name);

(b) protected information within section 242(1) (directors' residential addresses: restriction on disclosure by registrar) or any corresponding provision of regulations under section 1046 (overseas companies);

[(ba) representations received by the registrar in response to a notice under—

(i) section 245(2) (notice of proposal to put director's usual residential address on the public record), or

(ii) any corresponding provision of regulations under section 1046 (overseas companies);][b]

(c) any application to the registrar under section 1024 (application for administrative restoration to the register) that has not yet been determined or was not successful;

---

[114] Companies Act 2006 (Commencement No 1, Transitional Provisions and Savings) Order 2006, SI 2006/3428, art 2(1).

[115] Companies (Registrar, Languages and Trading Disclosures) Regulations 2006, SI 2006/3429, reg 2.

[116] Directive (EEC) 68/151 [1968] OJ L65/8, as amended by Directive (EC) 2003/58 and codified by Directive (EC) 2009/101.

   (d)  any document received by the registrar in connection with the giving or withdrawal of consent under section 1075 (informal correction of documents);

   (e)  any application or other document delivered to the registrar under section 1088 (application to make address unavailable for public inspection) and any address in respect of which such an application is successful;

   (f)  any application or other document delivered to the registrar under section 1095 (application for rectification of register);

   (g)  any court order under section 1096 (rectification of the register under court order) that the court has directed under section 1097 (powers of court on ordering removal of material from the register) is not to be made available for public inspection;

   (h)  the contents of—

      (i)  any instrument creating or evidencing a charge, [or]$^c$

      (ii)  any certified [or verified]$^d$ copy of an instrument creating or evidencing a charge, delivered to the registrar under [Part 25 (company charges) or regulations under section 1052 (overseas companies);]$^e$

   (i)  any email address, identification code or password deriving from a document delivered for the purpose of authorising or facilitating electronic filing procedures or providing information by telephone;

   (j)  the contents of any documents held by the registrar pending a decision of the Regulator of Community Interest Companies under—

   [(i)  section 36A of the Companies (Audit, Investigations and Community Enterprise) Act 2004 (eligibility for registration as community interest company),

      (ii)  section 38 of that Act (eligibility for conversion to community interest company), or

      (iii)  section 55 of that Act (eligibility for conversion from community interest company to charity),

   and that the registrar is not later required to record;]$^f$

   (k)  any other material excluded from public inspection by or under any other enactment.

  (2)  A restriction applying by reference to material deriving from a particular description of document does not affect the availability for public inspection of the same information contained in material derived from another description of document in relation to which no such restriction applies.

  (3)  Material to which this section applies need not be retained by the registrar for longer than appears to the registrar reasonably necessary for the purposes for which the material was delivered to the registrar.

AMENDMENTS AND NOTES

$^a$  This section applies with modifications to LLPs by reg 66 of the Limited Liability Partnerships (Application of Companies Act 2006) Regulations 2009, SI 2009/1804.

$^b$  Inserted by the Companies Act 2006 (Part 35) (Consequential Amendments, Transitional Provisions and Savings) Order 2009, SI 2009/1802.

$^c$  Amended by the Companies Act 2006 (Part 35) (Consequential Amendments, Transitional Provisions and Savings) Order 2009, SI 2009/1802.

$^d$  Amended by the Companies Act 2006 (Part 35) (Consequential Amendments, Transitional Provisions and Savings) Order 2009, SI 2009/1802.

$^e$  Amended by the Companies Act 2006 (Part 35) (Consequential Amendments, Transitional Provisions and Savings) Order 2009, SI 2009/1802.

$^f$  Amended by the Companies Act 2006 (Consequential Amendments, Transitional Provisions and Savings) Order 2009, SI 2009/1941.

COMMENCEMENT DATE 1 January 2007[117]

This section lists the various provisions which qualify the right to inspect the register, and the right to   **35.1087.02** demand copies. A proposal to withhold members' names and addresses from public inspection was rejected in Standing Committee.[118] The original wording of this section has been amended so as to expand the list of material which the registrar must not make available for public inspection.[119] First, under section 245(5) of the Act the registrar must take into account representations received in response to a notice issued under section 245(3) stating the grounds on which it is proposed to place the usual residential address of a director on the public record. The reference to 'protected information' in section 1087(1)(b) was not wide enough to cover such representations and has, therefore, been extended by section 1087(1)(ba), which provides that the registrar must not make the said

---

  [117] Companies Act 2006 (Commencement No 1, Transitional Provisions and Savings) Order 2006, SI 2006/3428, art 2(1). For transitional provisions, see Sch 1, para 9, revoked by Companies Act 2006 (Commencement No 8, Transitional Provisions and Savings) Order 2008, SI 2008/2806, art 6(1).

  [118] Amendment No 383 to what was then clause 740 of the Bill, 4 July 2006, cols 425–432.

  [119] The Companies Act 2006 (Part 35) (Consequential Amendments, Transitional Provisions and Savings) Order 2009, SI 2009/1802, art 12.

representations available for public inspection. Secondly, section 1087 provides that certain charge instruments must not be made available for public inspection, but the original wording made no reference to copies of other charge instruments delivered to the registrar under Part 25 and regulations with respect to overseas companies. This omission has now been remedied by the amendments to section 1087(1)(h).

**35.1087.03**    Subsection (2) is self-explanatory. Information that is recorded in more than one place on the register may be inspected if a restriction on its inspection applies only to one category of document where it is recorded.

**35.1087.04**    Subsection (3) assists the registrar by enabling him to destroy material to which section 1087 applies as soon as it is no longer reasonably necessary for the purposes for which it was delivered to the registrar.

### 1088 Application to registrar to make address unavailable for public inspection[a]

**35.1088.01**    (1) The Secretary of State may make provision by regulations requiring the registrar, on application, to make an address on the register unavailable for public inspection.
(2) The regulations may make provision as to—
    (a) who may make an application,
    (b) the grounds on which an application may be made,
    (c) the information to be included in and documents to accompany an application,
    (d) the notice to be given of an application and of its outcome, and
    (e) how an application is to be determined.
(3) Provision under subsection (2)(e) may in particular—
    (a) confer a discretion on the registrar;
    (b) provide for a question to be referred to a person other than the registrar for the purposes of determining the application.
(4) An application must specify the address to be removed from the register and indicate where on the register it is.
(5) The regulations may provide—
    (a) that an address is not to be made unavailable for public inspection under this section unless replaced by a service address, and
    (b) that in such a case the application must specify a service address.
(6) Regulations under this section are subject to affirmative resolution procedure.

AMENDMENTS AND NOTES

[a] This section applies with modifications to LLPs by reg 66 of the Limited Liability Partnerships (Application of Companies Act 2006) Regulations 2009, SI 2009/1804.

COMMENCEMENT DATE 1 January 2007[120]

**35.1088.02**    The threat of violence and intimidation, principally by animal rights activists against the directors of certain research companies, prompted the introduction of the Companies Act 1985, sections 723B to 723F.[121] Similar provisions now appear in Chapter 8 (sections 240 to 246). Broadly, they permit a director's usual residential address to be excluded from public inspection. But the critical weakness in those provisions is that they apply only in relation to documents filed with the registrar after the non-disclosure certificate has been issued: see section 242. They do not require the registrar to omit from public inspection any record of the director's usual residential address that may appear on historical records already stored at Companies House. Other than in relation to a first-time director, or a director who has moved house since his usual residential address was last filed with the registrar, it is therefore inevitable that public inspection of the register will be capable of identifying where he lives.

**35.1088.03**    It was considered to be disproportionate to confer on all directors who were granted non-disclosure certificates a right to demand that the historical record should also be amended so as to expunge any reference to their usual residential address. This was partly because of the administrative effort and cost that would be involved, and partly also because the bulk transfer of information to the business data industry means that a director's residential address would still be available from those sources, even if it was expunged from the historical record maintained at Companies House. Nevertheless, it was also recognized that there may be some circumstances in which the continued appearance of a person's address on the public record held by Companies House would be undesirable, and the problem was not confined to directors only, but could include others such as members of the company. Section 1088 was introduced as an amendment to the Bill at the Report stage in the House of Lords[122] in order to deal with these exceptional cases.

---

[120] Companies Act 2006 (Commencement No 1, Transitional Provisions and Savings) Order 2006, SI 2006/3428, art 2(1).

[121] Introduced by the Criminal Justice and Police Act 2001, s 45.

[122] Amendment No 487C, 16 May 2006.

The Act itself simply provides a framework within which the regime will operate. Its detailed scope and operation is determined by the Companies (Disclosure of Address) Regulations 2009.[123]  **35.1088.04**

One significant point is that in practice not only directors, but also former directors and their families might be at risk. The Secretary of State, exercising powers under section 1088(2) has made provision as to who may make an application.[124]  **35.1088.05**

Another important permissive element in the regime is contained in section 1088(3), which allows the Secretary of State to make regulations providing for the registrar to exercise a discretion, and to refer questions (eg risk assessment) to someone else (eg the police). This is embodied in regulations 1(2), 9(5), 10(4), and 11(4) of the Companies (Disclosure of Address) Regulations 2009. This permits a continuation of the arrangements that were put in place to operate the short-lived provisions of the Companies Act 1985, sections 723B to 723F. Under regulation 3 of the Companies (Particulars of Usual Residential Address) (Confidentiality Orders) Regulations 2002[125] the Secretary of State had a similar power to refer matters such as risk assessment to a 'relevant body', and in practice applications for confidentiality orders were determined by reference to a standard form graded risk assessment provided by the police.  **35.1088.06**

The fact that regulations may (by virtue of section 1088(3)(a)), and do, confer a discretion[126] on the registrar appears to undercut the opening words of section 1088(1), which permit the Secretary of State to make regulations 'requiring' the registrar to make an address on the register unavailable for public inspection. If the registrar is only required to withhold an address from public inspection in cases where he, in his discretion, considers it appropriate, then his duty is self-defining. However, since the Act does not define the grounds upon which applications are to be determined, this appears to be unavoidable. The solution for any disappointed applicant is to appeal under the regulations[127] or to bring proceedings for judicial review, challenging any refusal by the registrar to withhold his residential address from public inspection.  **35.1088.07**

The breadth of the rule-making powers conferred on the Secretary of State is reflected by the fact that any regulations made under section 1088 are subject to the affirmative resolution procedure (section 1088(6)) which is explained in section 1290.  **35.1088.08**

## 1089  Form of application for inspection or copy[a]

    (1)  The registrar may specify the form and manner in which application is to be made for—  **35.1089.01**
        (a)  inspection under section 1085, or
        (b)  a copy under section 1086.
    (2)  As from 1st January 2007, applications in respect of documents subject to the Directive disclosure requirements may be submitted to the registrar in hard copy or electronic form, as the applicant chooses.
        This does not affect the registrar's power under subsection (1) above to impose requirements in respect of other matters.

AMENDMENTS AND NOTES

[a]  This section applies with modifications to LLPs by reg 66 of the Limited Liability Partnerships (Application of Companies Act 2006) Regulations 2009, SI 2009/1804.

COMMENCEMENT DATE 1 January 2007[128]

This provision gives the registrar some flexibility in stipulating how applications are made for  **35.1089.02**
inspection and for copies under sections 1085 to 1086. It will be important as technologies continue to

---

[123]  SI 2009/214. The procedure for making an application under s 1088 is set out in Part 3 of the regulations. Under the regulations, the grounds on which an order under s 1088 may be made include circumstances where an individual 'considers that there is a serious risk that he, or a person who lives with him, will be subjected to violence or intimidation as a result of the activities of at least one of the companies' of which he is or was or proposes to be a director (reg 9(2), (3)).

[124]  The regulations (Companies (Disclosure of Address) Regulations 2009, SI 2009/214) provide for applications to be made by a current or former director or secretary or proposed officer (reg 9(1)(a), (b)), or a company (reg 10) or a person who registers a charge (reg 11).

[125]  SI 2002/912.

[126]  The regulations indicate that the registrar has such a discretion: Companies (Disclosure of Address) Regulations 2009, reg 12.

[127]  The regulations contain an appeal procedure to the High Court in England and Wales, or the Court of Session in Scotland: Companies (Disclosure of Address) Regulations 2009, reg 14.

[128]  Companies Act 2006 (Commencement No 1, Transitional Provisions and Savings) Order 2006, SI 2006/3428, art 2(1).

develop, and as Companies House provides new products. As to the registrar's rule-making power generally, see section 1117 below.

**35.1089.03**    Section 1089(2) deals with applications in respect of documents subject to the Directive disclosure requirements, as to which see section 1078 above.

## 1090   Form and manner in which copies to be provided[a]

**35.1090.01**
> (1) The following provisions apply as regards the form and manner in which copies are to be provided under section 1086.
> (2) As from 1st January 2007, copies of documents subject to the Directive disclosure requirements must be provided in hard copy or electronic form, as the applicant chooses.
> This is subject to the following proviso.
> (3) The registrar is not obliged by subsection (2) to provide copies in electronic form of a document that was delivered to the registrar in hard copy form if—
> > (a) the document was delivered to the registrar on or before 31st December 1996, or
> > (b) the document was delivered to the registrar on or before 31st December 2006 and ten years or more elapsed between the date of delivery and the date of receipt of the first application for a copy on or after 1st January 2007.
> (4) Subject to the preceding provisions of this section, the registrar may determine the form and manner in which copies are to be provided.

AMENDMENTS AND NOTES

[a] This section applies with modifications to LLPs by reg 66 of the Limited Liability Partnerships (Application of Companies Act 2006) Regulations 2009, SI 2009/1804.

COMMENCEMENT DATE 1 January 2007[129]

**35.1090.02**    Subject to the specific provisions set out in section 1090(2) to (3), the registrar may determine the form and manner in which copies are to be provided: section 1090(4).

**35.1090.03**    Section 1090(2) deals with documents subject to the Directive disclosure requirements, as to which see section 1078 above. The general rule is that copies must be provided in hard copy or electronic form, as the applicant chooses. However, this is subject to the exception in section 1090(3) which exonerates the registrar from any obligation to provide in electronic form a copy of a document that was delivered to him in hard copy on or before 31 December 1996, or was delivered on or before 31 December 2006 and 10 years or more elapsed between the date of delivery and the date of delivery of the first request for a copy after 1 January 2007.

## 1091   Certification of copies as accurate[a]

**35.1091.01**
> (1) Copies provided under section 1086 in hard copy form must be certified as true copies unless the applicant dispenses with such certification.
> (2) Copies so provided in electronic form must not be certified as true copies unless the applicant expressly requests such certification.
> (3) A copy provided under section 1086, certified by the registrar (whose official position it is unnecessary to prove) to be an accurate record of the contents of the original document, is in all legal proceedings admissible in evidence—
> > (a) as of equal validity with the original document, and
> > (b) as evidence (in Scotland, sufficient evidence) of any fact stated in the original document of which direct oral evidence would be admissible.
> (4) The Secretary of State may make provision by regulations as to the manner in which such a certificate is to be provided in a case where the copy is provided in electronic form.
> (5) Except in the case of documents that are subject to the Directive disclosure requirements (see section 1078), copies provided by the registrar may, instead of being certified in writing to be an accurate record, be sealed with the registrar's official seal.

AMENDMENTS AND NOTES

[a] This section applies with modifications to LLPs by reg 65 of the Limited Liability Partnerships (Application of Companies Act 2006) Regulations 2009, SI 2009/1804.

COMMENCEMENT DATE 1 January 2007.[130]

---

[129] Companies Act 2006 (Commencement No 1, Transitional Provisions and Savings) Order 2006, SI 2006/3428, art 2(1).

[130] Companies Act 2006 (Commencement No 1, Transitional Provisions and Savings) Order 2006, SI 2006/3428, art 2(1).

Certified copies of documents provided by the registrar are admissible in legal proceedings as of equal   **35.1091.02**
validity with the original document (section 1091(3)(a)) and as evidence of any fact stated in the
original document of which direct oral evidence would be admitted (section 1091(3)(b)).

However, the requirement for a copy to be certified depends on the form in which it is provided. If it is   **35.1091.03**
provided in hard copy, it must be certified as authentic, unless the applicant dispenses with certification: section 1091(1). If an electronic copy is provided, it must not be certified, unless the applicant
requests it: section 1091(2).

The manner in which the registrar certifies a copy is dealt with in section 1091(4) to (5). Hard copies   **35.1091.04**
may be certified in writing or by seal (section 1091(5)), except in the case of documents that are subject
to the Directive disclosure requirements (as to which, see section 1078 above).

In relation to electronic copies, the Secretary of State may make provision by regulations as to the   **35.1091.05**
manner in which they are to be certified: section 1091(4). This power has been exercised by making The
Companies (Registrar, Languages and Trading Disclosures) Regulations 2006.[131]

## 1092   Issue of process for production of records kept by the registrar

(1)  No process for compelling the production of a record kept by the registrar shall issue from any    **35.1092.01**
     court except with the permission of the court.
(2)  Any such process shall bear on it a statement that it is issued with the permission of the court.

COMMENCEMENT DATE 1 January 2007[132]

The court's permission must first be obtained before any proceedings are issued seeking an order   **35.1092.02**
compelling the registrar to produce any of the records kept by him: section 1092(1). This provision
reproduces the Companies Act 1985, section 709(5). Any application would have to be made by a
Claim Form under Part 8 of the CPR: see paragraph 5(1) of the Practice Direction in relation to
Applications under the Companies Acts and Other Legislation Relating to Companies.[133]

Where such permission is granted, any proceedings then issued must bear a statement that they are so   **35.1092.03**
issued with the permission of the court: section 1092(2). In practice, this will presumably mean that the
proceedings must identify the judge who gave permission, and the date on which he did so.

## *Correction or removal of material on the register*

## 1093   Registrar's notice to resolve inconsistency on the register[a]

(1)  Where it appears to the registrar that the information contained in a document delivered to the   **35.1093.01**
     registrar is inconsistent with other information on the register, the registrar may give notice to the
     company to which the document relates—
     (a)  stating in what respects the information contained in it appears to be inconsistent with other
          information on the register, and
     (b)  requiring the company to take steps to resolve the inconsistency.
(2)  The notice must—
     (a)  state the date on which it is issued, and
     (b)  require the delivery to the registrar, within 14 days after that date, of such replacement or
          additional documents as may be required to resolve the inconsistency.
(3)  If the necessary documents are not delivered within the period specified, an offence is committed
     by—
     (a)  the company, and
     (b)  every officer of the company who is in default.
(4)  A person guilty of an offence under subsection (3) is liable on summary conviction to a fine not
     exceeding level 5 on the standard scale and, for continued contravention, a daily default fine not
     exceeding one-tenth of level 5 on the standard scale.

AMENDMENTS AND NOTES

ᵃ  This section applies with modifications to LLPs by reg 67 of the Limited Liability Partnerships
   (Application of Companies Act 2006) Regulations 2009, SI 2009/1804 and to the Societas Europaea

[131]  SI 2006/3429, reg 2(2).
[132]  Companies Act 2006 (Commencement No 1, Transitional Provisions and Savings) Order 2006, SI
2006/3428, art 2(1).
[133]  *White Book*, 2011 edn, Vol 2, 746.

by reg 3, Sch 1A of the European Public Limited-Liability Company Regulations 2004, SI 2004/2326, as amended by reg 37 of the European Public Limited-Liability Company (Amendment) Regulations 2009, SI 2009/2400.

COMMENCEMENT DATE 1 October 2009[134]

**35.1093.02**    This section is the first of a number of provisions dealing with the control of information appearing on the register. These sections create various powers to facilitate the correction and removal of information held on the register. This section deals with the consistency of information supplied to the registrar with that already appearing on the register.

**35.1093.03**    Under subsection (1), if the registrar receives a document whose information concerning a company does not fit with existing information on the register, he has the power to require resolution of the inconsistency.[135] This power is exercised by means of a notice sent to the relevant company. The notice must identify how the supplied information is inconsistent with other information held by the registrar. To do so effectively, the registrar may have to specify the information held on the register which is inconsistent with the newly delivered document.

**35.1093.04**    The notice must require the company to take steps to resolve the inconsistency. Pursuant to subsection (2), it must do so by requiring the delivery of additional or replacement documents to the registrar which resolve the inconsistency. The delivery must be made within 14 days of the specified date of the notice's issue. This is a fairly tight timetable since it begins to run from the date of the notice, rather than its receipt by the company, and the relevant documents must actually be delivered to the registrar within the period.

**35.1093.05**    If the company fails to deliver such documents (perhaps because it delivers no documents within the time, or if it delivers documents which do not resolve the inconsistency) an offence is committed. Under subsection (3) the offence is committed by the company and every director of the company in default. The offence is a summary one punishable by a fine (subsection (4)).

**35.1093.06**    The Companies Act 2006 (Commencement No 8, Transitional Provisions and Savings) Order 2008, Schedule 2, paragraph 106 as amended by the Companies Act 2006 (Part 35) (Consequential Amendments, Transitional Provisions and Savings) Order 2009,[136] article 18 sets out which documents delivered to the registrar this section will apply to. For documents which were delivered to the registrar on or after 1 October 2009, the procedure in section 1093 will be applicable save where the delivery is pursuant to an obligation which arose prior to that date.

## 1094  Administrative removal of material from the register[a]

**35.1094.01**    (1)  The registrar may remove from the register anything that there was power, but no duty, to include.

(2)  This power is exercisable, in particular, so as to remove—

    (a)  unnecessary material within the meaning of section 1074, and

    (b)  material derived from a document that has been replaced under—

section 1076 (replacement of document not meeting requirements for proper delivery), or

section 1093 (notice to remedy inconsistency on the register).

(3)  This section does not authorise the removal from the register of—

    (a)  anything whose registration has had legal consequences in relation to the company as regards—

        (i)  its formation,

        (ii)  a change of name,

        (iii)  its re-registration,

        (iv)  its becoming or ceasing to be a community interest company,

        (v)  a reduction of capital,

        (vi)  a change of registered office,

        (vii)  the registration of a charge, or

        (viii) its dissolution;

    (b)  an address that is a person's registered address for the purposes of section 1140 (service of documents on directors, secretaries and others).

---

[134] Companies Act 2006 (Commencement No 8, Transitional Provisions and Savings) Order 2008, SI 2008/2860, art 3(r).

[135] See also reg 3 of the Companies (Registrar of Companies and Applications for Striking Off) Regulations 2009, SI 2009/1803 for the power of the registrar to annotate the register where he believes that any material is misleading or confusing, and s 1081 on the annotation of the Register by the Registrar.

[136] SI 2009/1802.

(4) On or before removing any material under this section (otherwise than at the request of the company) the registrar must give notice—

    (a) to the person by whom the material was delivered (if the identity, and name and address of that person are known), or

    (b) to the company to which the material relates (if notice cannot be given under paragraph (a) and the identity of that company is known).

(5) The notice must—

    (a) state what material the registrar proposes to remove, or has removed, and on what grounds, and

    (b) state the date on which it is issued.

AMENDMENTS AND NOTES

<sup>a</sup> This section applies with modifications to LLPs by reg 67 of the Limited Liability Partnerships (Application of Companies Act 2006) Regulations 2009, SI 2009/1804 and to the Societas Europaea by reg 4, Sch 1A of the European Public Limited-Liability Company Regulations 2004, SI 2004/2326, as amended by reg 37 of the European Public Limited-Liability Company (Amendment) Regulations 2009, SI 2009/2400.

COMMENCEMENT DATE 1 October 2009[137]

The registrar is enabled by this section to remove certain categories of material from the register. The power is aimed at facilitating housekeeping and not at allowing changes to important material on the register which legally must appear there or whose appearance has important consequences. Material may be removed of the registrar's own motion and also following a request from interested parties (subsection (4) contemplates the registrar acting after a request has been made by the company itself). **35.1094.02**

Only materials which have been admitted by the registrar as a matter of discretion may be removed. Under subsection (1), material which the registrar has a duty to include on the register (such as those materials mentioned in section 1080(1)) may not be removed under the powers granted by this section. **35.1094.03**

The material which may be removed under this section is further limited by subsection (3). First, if the registration of the information had certain legal consequences then it may not be the subject of administrative removal. If any legal consequences are not in relation to those important matters listed in subsection (3)(a), then the material may be removed if the other requirements of the section are met. Secondly, the registered address of certain company officers may not be removed by the registrar under this section. Presumably this is to ensure that there remains a public information trail detailing various past addresses in order that anybody wishing to will be able to effect service on those persons. **35.1094.04**

If the material is on the register as a matter of discretion, and not subject to one of these specific exclusions, it may be removed by the registrar if it is unnecessary in the relevant sense of subsection (2). Material may be removed if it is unnecessary within the meaning of section 1074(2) in the sense that its registration is not needed to comply with any statutory requirement and the delivery to the registrar has not been specifically authorized. Secondly, material may also be removed if it is unnecessary in the sense that the document it is contained in has been replaced by another under those provisions listed at subsection (2)(b). Allowing the removal of replaced documents (particularly for reasons of defective delivery and inconsistency) assists the registrar in minimizing the number of formally or substantively unhelpful or confusing entries on the register. **35.1094.05**

Unless the registrar is acting on the request of the company itself, he must give notice before or upon the removal of material under this section. Subsection (4) requires notice to be given in the first place to the person who delivered the information. Presumably this is so that the person who made the filing and presumably the person who ought to know the most about it (perhaps an outside agent of the company dealing with filing and disclosure obligations) will receive the registrar's objections to it and be in a position to respond to them. Only if the identity, name, and address of this person are unknown may the registrar give notice to the company. If the material is such that neither the identity of the person who delivered it nor of the company to which it relates is known then no notice need be given. **35.1094.06**

The notice must specify the material which is planned to be or has been removed and the grounds of such removal. Specification of these grounds will allow the company or the person who delivered the material to respond and, if removal has not already taken place, for the registrar to consider this response in deciding whether to remove the material. Under subsection (5), the notice must also indicate the date of its issue. **35.1094.07**

The Companies Act 2006 (Commencement No 8, Transitional Provisions and Savings) Order 2008, Schedule 2, paragraph 107 as amended by the Companies Act 2006 (Part 35) (Consequential **35.1094.08**

---

[137] Companies Act 2006 (Commencement No 8, Transitional Provisions and Savings) Order 2008, SI 2008/2860, art 3(r).

Amendments, Transitional Provisions and Savings) Order 2009,[138] article 18 sets out which documents delivered to the registrar (and the content thereof and material derived therefrom) this section will apply to. For documents which were delivered to the registrar on or after 1 October 2009, the procedure in section 1094 will be applicable to those documents, their content and material derived therefrom, save where the delivery is pursuant to an obligation which arose prior to that date.

## 1095  Rectification of register on application to registrar[a]

**35.1095.01**
(1)  The Secretary of State may make provision by regulations requiring the registrar, on application, to remove from the register material of a description specified in the regulations that—
    (a)  derives from anything invalid or ineffective or that was done without the authority of the company, or
    (b)  is factually inaccurate, or is derived from something that is factually inaccurate or forged.
(2)  The regulations may make provision as to-
    (a)  who may make an application,
    (b)  the information to be included in and documents to accompany an application,
    (c)  the notice to be given of an application and of its outcome,
    (d)  a period in which objections to an application may be made, and
    (e)  how an application is to be determined.
(3)  An application must—
    (a)  specify what is to be removed from the register and indicate where on the register it is, and
    (b)  be accompanied by a statement that the material specified in the application complies with this section and the regulations.
(4)  If no objections are made to the application, the registrar may accept the statement as sufficient evidence that the material specified in the application should be removed from the register.
(5)  Where anything is removed from the register under this section the registration of which had legal consequences as mentioned in section 1094(3), any person appearing to the court to have a sufficient interest may apply to the court for such consequential orders as appear just with respect to the legal effect (if any) to be accorded to the material by virtue of its having appeared on the register.
(6)  Regulations under this section are subject to affirmative resolution procedure.

AMENDMENTS AND NOTES

[a] This section applies with modifications to LLPs by reg 67 of the Limited Liability Partnerships (Application of Companies Act 2006) Regulations 2009, SI 2009/1804 and to the Societas Europaea by reg 5, Sch 1A of the European Public Limited-Liability Company Regulations 2004, SI 2004/2326, as amended by reg 37 of the European Public Limited-Liability Company (Amendment) Regulations 2009, SI 2009/2400.

COMMENCEMENT DATE The power to make regulations by statutory instrument came into force on 20 January 2007, otherwise 1 October 2009[139]

**35.1095.02**  Section 1095 provides a further means for the removal of material from the register. The route is of intermediate formality between the informal requests or action of the registrar's own initiative under section 1094 and the court procedure under section 1096. Although the section sets out the outline of the power to remove material, the creation and detailed scope of it is more closely defined in the Registrar of Companies and Applications for Striking Off Regulations 2009[140] (referred to in the commentary to this section as 'the Regulations') made pursuant to subsection (1), which makes it clear, however, that the registrar may not act on his own initiative to remove material in the absence of an application.

**35.1095.03**  The section is the product of an amendment introduced in Grand Committee in the House of Lords. The introduction was prompted by the concerns of the Institute of Chartered Accountants in England and Wales that, despite the increase in identity thefts, the Bill as drafted did not allow the registrar to remove fraudulent entries from the register without recourse to the court, which was thought to be 'cumbersome, expensive and time consuming'.[141] In delineating what information may be the subject of any regulations, subsection (1) seeks to address these concerns. The categories are slightly wider

---

[138] SI 2009/1802.
[139] Companies Act 2006 (Commencement No 1, Transitional Provisions and Savings) Order 2006 (SI 2006/3428), art 3(3); Companies Act 2006 (Commencement No 8, Transitional Provisions and Savings) Order 2008, SI 2008/2860, art 3(r).
[140] SI 2009/1803. Draft Regulations were initially published with the government response to consultation on Companies Act 2006 Implementation—The Registrar of Companies Regulations 2008. In the explanatory notes to the draft regulations the policy intention of the section was stated to be 'to maintain an accurate register and to help prevent company hijacking'.
[141] Lord Hodgson of Astley Abbotts, *Hansard*, HL, col GC359 (30 March 2006).

than those which would address only the problem of identity theft. For example, the removal of factually inaccurate information may be provided for by the regulations.[142] However, it is left to the Regulations as to what information may actually be removed under this section.

The Regulations are the source of the detailed procedure for any application to the registrar (as **35.1095.04** envisaged by subsection (2)). They provide that on an application the registrar must remove relevant material which falls within the description at subsection (1) unless there is a valid objection to the application (regulation 4(1) of the Regulations). If a valid objection is made the registrar must reject the application (regulation 5(13) of the Regulations). If no valid objection is made the registrar must notify the applicant accordingly (regulation 5(15) of the Regulations). If a valid objection is made the registrar must acknowledge receipt to the person making the objection and notify the applicant and certain other persons that an objection has been made (regulation 5(14) of the Regulations).

Relevant material for the purpose of the section 1095 procedure means material included in or derived **35.1095.05** from material included in a relevant company form or a relevant overseas company form delivered to the registrar by any person (regulation 4(2) of the Regulations). What these relevant forms are is set out at regulations 4(3) and 4(4) of the Regulations. Save in respect of certain material where an application for removal must be made by the company or overseas company to which the material relates (see regulation 4(5) and (6) of the Regulations), applications can be made to the registrar under section 1095 by the person who delivered the relevant form to the registrar, the company, or overseas company to which the material relates or any other person to whom the material relates (regulation 4(7) of the Regulations).

Subsection (3) requires a minimum content of applications. Each application must specify the **35.1095.06** particular material that is the subject of the application, where it appears on the register, and include a statement that the application complies with the section and the Regulations. If no objections are received in respect of the application, this latter statement may be accepted by the registrar as sufficient evidence that the relevant material should be removed from the register (see subsection (4)). Additionally, regulation 5(1) of the Regulations sets out further requirements for an application such as requiring statements as to who the applicant is, their address, and the reason for the application, namely whether the material in issue derives from anything invalid or ineffective or done without authority, factually inaccurate, or deriving from a forgery. The registrar is obliged to give notice of the application to certain persons depending upon the nature of the application and the material to which it relates.[143]

It was stressed in debates on the Bill that the section should not lead to the registrar becoming **35.1095.07** embroiled in disputes or create a discretion for him which would give rise to inconsistency and uncertainty.[144] The Regulations do not therefore allow the registrar to determine disputed applications. If a valid objection is made the registrar must reject the application (regulation 5(13) of the Regulations). Any person may make an objection to the Registrar (regulation 5(9) of the Regulations). The registrar is not required to make a determination in relation to the validity of an objection: a valid objection is simply an objection made in writing to the registrar which states the name and address of the person making the objection and identifies the application to which the objection relates.[145] For an objection to be valid, persons who received notice of the application from the registrar must object within 28 days of the date of that notice; the registrar must not take into account objections by persons who were not given notice of the application if the objections are received after 28 days from the date on which the registrar issued notice of the application to others.[146] In any event section 1096(1) allows the court to order the removal of the same categories of material provided for by this section, and the court would seem the more appropriate arbiter of disputes in this context.

The court is given a wide power by subsection (5) to make any order as appears just in relation to the **35.1095.08** legal effect of material which did appear on the register but has been removed under this section, upon the application of an interested party. Possible recourse to the court is necessary since, unlike the power of administrative removal under section 1094, material whose registration had a legal effect may be removed by the registrar using this section. The category of persons who may apply under this subsection seems to be very wide. A person may make an application to the court if he has a 'sufficient interest'. The court will therefore need to determine what a 'sufficient interest' is for these purposes.

---

[142]  In debate Lord McKenzie of Luton referred to the narrower category of 'manifestly false information', *Hansard*, HL, col GC360 (30 March 2006).

[143]  The Regulations, reg 5(2)–(8).

[144]  Lord Hodgson of Astley Abbotts and Lord McKenzie of Luton, *Hansard*, HL, col GC360 (30 March 2006).

[145]  The Regulations, reg 4(8) referring to reg 5(10).

[146]  The Regulations, reg 4(8) referring to reg 5(10), (11), and (12).

**35.1095.09**     Regulations passed in respect of this section are subject to the affirmative resolution procedure by virtue of subsection (6), which is explained in section 1290.

**35.1095.10**     The Companies Act 2006 (Commencement No 8, Transitional Provisions and Savings) Order 2008, Schedule 2, paragraph 107 as amended by the Companies Act 2006 (Part 35) Consequential Amendments, Transitional Provisions and Savings) Order 2009,[147] article 18 sets out which documents delivered to the registrar (and the content thereof and material derived therefrom) that the process of rectification set out in this section will apply to. For documents which were delivered to the registrar on or after 1 October 2009, that process will be applicable to those documents, their content and material derived therefrom, save where the delivery is pursuant to an obligation which arose prior to that date.

### 1096 Rectification of the register under court order[a]

**35.1096.01**     (1) The registrar shall remove from the register any material—
        (a) that derives from anything that the court has declared to be invalid or ineffective, or to have been done without the authority of the company, or
        (b) that a court declares to be factually inaccurate, or to be derived from something that is factually inaccurate, or forged,
    and that the court directs should be removed from the register.
    (2) The court order must specify what is to be removed from the register and indicate where on the register it is.
    (3) The court must not make an order for the removal from the register of anything the registration of which had legal consequences as mentioned in section 1094(3) unless satisfied—
        (a) that the presence of the material on the register has caused, or may cause, damage to the company, and
        (b) that the company's interest in removing the material outweighs any interest of other persons in the material continuing to appear on the register.
    (4) Where in such a case the court does make an order for removal, it may make such consequential orders as appear just with respect to the legal effect (if any) to be accorded to the material by virtue of its having appeared on the register.
    (5) A copy of the court's order must be sent to the registrar for registration.
    (6) This section does not apply where the court has other, specific, powers to deal with the matter, for example under—
        (a) the provisions of Part 15 relating to the revision of defective accounts and reports, or
        (b) section 873 or 888 (rectification of the register of charges).

AMENDMENTS AND NOTES

    [a] This section applies with modifications to LLPs by reg 67 of the Limited Liability Partnerships (Application of Companies Act 2006) Regulations 2009, SI 2009/1804 and to the Societas Europaea by reg 6, Sch 1A of the European Public Limited-Liability Company Regulations 2004, SI 2004/2326, as amended by reg 37 of the European Public Limited-Liability Company (Amendment) Regulations 2009, SI 2009/2400.

COMMENCEMENT DATE 1 October 2009[148]

**35.1096.02**     This section creates a residual power for the court to direct the registrar to remove certain material from the register. Subsection (6) provides that the power of the court will not be available where the court has any other specific powers of rectification, for example in relation to defective filed accounts and registered charges. Such a general power did not exist prior to this Act, since the court has no inherent jurisdiction to supervise the registrar beyond requiring compliance with his statutory duties.[149] The court did not have the power to direct the registrar to remove material where a statute did not require its removal[150] in circumstances where there was no applicable statutory provision for rectification.

**35.1096.03**     The material that may be removed by the court under this section is the same as the material that may be removed under section 1095. If the court directs the removal of such material the registrar has a statutory duty to remove it under subsection (1). A copy of the order must be sent to the registrar (subsection (5)). So that he should know which material must be removed from the register, the order must specify the material and its location on the register (subsection (2)).

---

    [147] SI 2009/1802.
    [148] Companies Act 2006 (Commencement No 8, Transitional Provisions and Savings) Order 2008, SI 2008/2860, art 3(r).
    [149] *Re a Company (No 007466 of 2003)* [2004] 1 WLR 1357, [2004] 2 BCLC 434.
    [150] The court does in principle have a jurisdiction to control the way the registrar complies with his statutory duties on public law principles: *Re Calmex Ltd* [1989] BCLC 299, 303, *per* Hoffmann J.

Subsection (3) is important in that it limits the circumstances in which the court can direct the removal    **35.1096.04**
of material which has had legal consequences in relation to those matters detailed at section 1094(3). A
direction for the removal of such material may not be given unless it is established that the company
has sustained or may sustain damage caused by the material's appearance on the register. Secondly,
removal of the material may not be directed unless, after conducting a balancing exercise, the court
concludes that the company's interest in removal outweighs the interest of other persons in the
material's continued appearance on the register. Thus, where the interests of the company and third
parties are equal, the material will remain on the register.

These requirements survived a proposed amendment which would have removed them in respect of    **35.1096.05**
fraudulent filings. It was acknowledged that the court would often take the view that it was unlikely to
be in the public interest that such filings should continue to appear on the register. However, since the
registration of the material under consideration would necessarily have had a legal effect and may have
been relied upon by third parties, the balancing exercise should still take place.[151]

The court has a wide power under subsection (4) to make ancillary orders as to the legal effect of    **35.1096.06**
material it has directed to be removed. The court may make any consequential order in this regard as
appears just.

The Companies Act 2006 (Commencement No 8, Transitional Provisions and Savings) Order 2008,    **35.1096.07**
Schedule 2, paragraph 107 as amended by the Companies Act 2006 (Part 35) Consequential Amendments, Transitional Provisions and Savings) Order 2009,[152] article 18 sets out which documents
delivered to the registrar (and the content thereof and material derived therefrom) that the process of
court-directed rectification set out in this section will apply to. For documents which were delivered to
the registrar on or after 1 October 2009, that process will be applicable to those documents, their
content and material derived therefrom, save where the delivery is pursuant to an obligation which
arose prior to that date.

## 1097  Powers of court on ordering removal of material from the register[a]

   (1)  Where the court makes an order for the removal of anything from the register under section 1096    **35.1097.01**
       (rectification of the register), it may give directions under this section.
   (2)  It may direct that any note on the register that is related to the material that is the subject of the
       court's order shall be removed from the register.
   (3)  It may direct that its order shall not be available for public inspection as part of the register.
   (4)  It may direct—
      (a)  that no note shall be made on the register as a result of its order, or
      (b)  that any such note shall be restricted to such matters as may be specified by the court.
   (5)  The court shall not give any direction under this section unless it is satisfied—
      (a)  that—
         (i)  the presence on the register of the note or, as the case may be, of an unrestricted note,
            or
         (ii)  the availability for public inspection of the court's order,
         may cause damage to the company, and
      (b)  that the company's interest in non-disclosure outweighs any interest of other persons in
        disclosure.

Amendments and Notes

[a]  This section applies with modifications to LLPs by reg 67 of the Limited Liability Partnerships
(Application of Companies Act 2006) Regulations 2009, SI 2009/1804.

Commencement Date 1 October 2009[153]

This section details the power of the court to make ancillary directions after ordering the removal of    **35.1097.02**
material under section 1096. The court may direct that any note relating to the deleted material is
removed (subsection (2)). This measure would seem to enable the court to decide that the register
should appear to the public as if the particular material had never appeared on it by excising both the
material and any note referring to it. Further, the court may direct that any order removing the material
itself should not be made public, and either that no note or only a limited note concerning such order
should appear on the register (subsections (3) and (4)).

[151]  Lord McKenzie of Luton, *Hansard*, HL, col GC362 (30 March 2006).
[152]  SI 2009/1802.
[153]  Companies Act 2006 (Commencement No. 8, Transitional Provisions and Savings) Order 2008, SI
2008/2860, art 3(r).

**35.1097.03**  The court may only make such directions if it is satisfied that publicity of its order, or a note (or an unrestricted note) on the register related to the removed material, may damage the company (subsection (5)). Even if the possibility of damage is accepted, the court must conduct a balancing exercise and may only give a direction under this section if the company's interest in non-disclosure outweighs the interests in favour of disclosure.

**35.1097.04**  As with section 1096 the Court's powers under this section are only applicable to documents delivered to the registrar on or after 1 October 2009, and their content and material derived therefrom, save where the delivery is pursuant to an obligation which arose prior to that date.[154]

### 1098  Public notice of removal of certain material from the register[a]

**35.1098.01**  (1)  The registrar must cause to be published—
   (a)  in the Gazette, or
   (b)  in accordance with section 1116 (alternative means of giving public notice),
   notice of the removal from the register of any document subject to the Directive disclosure requirements (see section 1078) or of any material derived from such a document.
(2)  The notice must state the name and registered number of the company, the description of document and the date of receipt.

AMENDMENTS AND NOTES

[a] This section applies with modifications to LLPs by reg 67 of the Limited Liability Partnerships (Application of Companies Act 2006) Regulations 2009, SI 2009/1804.

COMMENCEMENT DATE 1 October 2009[155]

**35.1098.02**  This section creates an obligation of publicity for the registrar upon the removal of certain material from the register. The obligation corresponds to the registrar's obligation of publicity when such material is filed, which is contained in section 1077. The obligation only relates to the removal of those important documents listed in section 1078 (based on the requirements of the First Company Law Directive[156]) and the removal of material which derived from any such document. The obligation is discharged by a traditional publication in the Gazette, or by such other means as the Secretary of State may provide for in regulations under section 1116. The registrar's notice must at least contain the information specified in subsection (2). The notice requirement under this section only applies to the removal from the register of documents received by the registrar on or after 1 October 2009, save where a document is delivered pursuant to an obligation arising before that date, and to the removal of material deriving from such documents.

### *The registrar's index of company names*

### 1099  The registrar's index of company names[a]

**35.1099.01**  (1)  The registrar of companies must keep an index of the names of the companies and other bodies to which this section applies.
   This is 'the registrar's index of company names'.
(2)  This section applies to—
   (a)  UK-registered companies;
   (b)  any body to which any provision of the Companies Acts applies by virtue of regulations under section 1043 (unregistered companies); and
   (c)  overseas companies that have registered particulars with the registrar under section 1046, other than companies that appear to the registrar not to be required to do so.
(3)  This section also applies to—
   (a)  limited partnerships registered in the United Kingdom;
   (b)  limited liability partnerships incorporated in the United Kingdom;
   (c)  European Economic Interest Groupings registered in the United Kingdom;
   (d)  open-ended investment companies authorised in the United Kingdom;
   (e)  societies registered under the Industrial and Provident Societies Act 1965 (c.12) or the Industrial and Provident Societies Act (Northern Ireland) 1969 (c.24 (N.I.)).

---

[154] Companies Act 2006 (Commencement No. 8, Transitional Provisions and Savings) Order 2008, Sch 2, para 107 as amended by the Companies Act 2006 (part 35) (Consequential Amendments, Transitional Provisions and Savings) Order 2009, SI 2009/1802, art 18.
[155] Companies Act 2006 (Commencement No 8, Transitional Provisions and Savings) Order 2008, SI 2008/2860, art 3(r).
[156] Directive (EEC) 68/151 [1968] OJ L65/8, as amended by Directive (EC) 2003/58, Now replaced by Directive (EC) 2009/101.

(4)  The Secretary of State may by order amend subsection (3)—
    (a)  by the addition of any description of body;
    (b)  by the deletion of any description of body.
(5)  Any such order is subject to negative resolution procedure.

A MENDMENTS AND N OTES

[a]  Applied with modifications by Sch 6(1), para 1 of the Investment Bank Special Administration Regulations 2011, SI 2011/145.

C OMMENCEMENT D ATE 1 October 2009[157]

This section replaces the Companies Act 1985, section 714. It obliges the registrar to retain an index of the names of 'companies' and 'other bodies' to which the section applies. Subsections (2) and (3) respectively list the types of companies and other bodies. The section it replaces previously listed the entities in one grouping.   **35.1099.02**

The Secretary of State has the power to amend subsection (3) by regulations adding or deleting the descriptions of bodies to which the section applies: subsection (4). The fact that this power is exercisable by the Secretary of State as opposed to the registrar is in keeping with the general rationale that matters of substance are for the Secretary of State, whereas the registrar's remit is restricted to matters relating to form and administration.[158]   **35.1099.03**

The Secretary of State's power is expressly restricted to the entities listed in subsection (3) and there is no scope to add to or delete parts of subsection (2) by way of that procedure. Any order made by the Secretary of State in this regard is subject to the negative resolution procedure by virtue of subsection (5), which is explained in section 1289.   **35.1099.04**

## 1100   Right to inspect index[a]

Any person may inspect the registrar's index of company names.   **35.1100.01**

A MENDMENT AND N OTES

[a]  Applied with modifications by Sch 6(1), para 1 of the Investment Bank Special Administration Regulations 2011, SI 2011/145.

C OMMENCEMENT D ATE 1 October 2009[159]

This section retains the important right of the public to inspect the index of company names, which the registrar is required to keep pursuant to section 1099 above. No separate provision was made in the Companies Act 1985 for inspection of the index of company names: the right of inspection was then included as part of the general right to inspect records pursuant to the Companies Act 1985, section 709. Since this new section is of narrower ambit, it does away with the more elaborate provisions of sections 1085 to 1087 above, which relate to the inspection of other records maintained by the registrar.   **35.1100.02**

The index can be searched on the internet at ⟨http://www.companieshouse.gov.uk⟩[160]. The open provision of this information is an important means of access to a public record of all companies incorporated in the UK and it is the database to which all proposed new names of companies are compared in order to prevent public confusion through the duplication of company names or the registering of companies with very similar names to those already on the index.[161]   **35.1100.03**

There is no provision in this section with respect to potential restrictions to open access to the index on the basis of confidentiality or otherwise, given that this specific right to inspect is restricted to the index of company names.[162]   **35.1100.04**

## 1101   Power to amend enactments relating to bodies other than companies[a]

(1)  The Secretary of State may by regulations amend the enactments relating to any description of body for the time being within section 1099(3) (bodies other than companies whose names are to be entered in the registrar's index), so as to—   **35.1101.01**

---

[157]  Companies Act 2006 (Commencement No 8, Transitional Provisions and Savings) Order 2008, SI 2008/2860, art 3(r).
[158]  See *Hansard*, HL, Grand Committee, col 346 (28 March 2006).
[159]  Companies Act 2006 (Commencement No 8, Transitional Provisions and Savings) Order 2008, SI 2008/2860, art 3(r).
[160]  For applicable fees for the provision by the registrar of copies of material on the register, see Registrar of Companies (Fees) (Companies, Overseas Companies and Limited Liability Partnerships) Regulations 2012, SI 2012/1907.
[161]  This point was confirmed in Committee proceedings: *Hansard*, HL, Standing Committee D, col 441 (4 July 2006).
[162]  cf s 1087.

> (a)  require the registrar to be provided with information as to the names of bodies registered, incorporated, authorised or otherwise regulated under those enactments, and
>
> (b)  make provision in relation to such bodies corresponding to that made by—
>
> section 66 (company name not to be the same as another in the index), and
>
> sections 67 and 68 (power to direct change of company name in case of similarity to existing name).
>
> (2)  Regulations under this section are subject to affirmative resolution procedure.

AMENDMENT AND NOTES

ᵃ Applied with modifications by Sch 6(1), para 1 of the Investment Bank Special Administration Regulations 2011, SI 2011/145.

COMMENCEMENT DATE 1 October 2009[163]

**35.1101.02**  This section gives the Secretary of State power to amend the rules in relation to the names that can be adopted by other business entities on the index of company names.[164] The power seeks to remedy a weakness of the previous system in that there was a lack of coordination between the rules relating to the names of the various types of entity entitled to be registered on the index of company names.

**35.1101.03**  Each category of business entity listed in section 1099(3) will have its own applicable rules as to names in order to minimize the risk of public confusion, but they are different from the rules applicable to companies.[165] The system is liable to confuse when these distinct entities are placed onto the single index. This section provides a solution by allowing the Secretary of State to amend the rules applicable to other business entities,[166] the object of which will no doubt be to harmonize the various sets of rules and ensure that the index does not cause confusion, but instead operates consistently across the broad spectrum of companies and other entities listed on it.

**35.1101.04**  Regulations passed in respect of this section are subject to the affirmative resolution procedure by virtue of subsection (2). That procedure is explained in section 1290.

## *Language requirements: translation*

### 1102  Application of language requirementsᵃ

**35.1102.01**
> (1)  The provisions listed below apply to all documents required to be delivered to the registrar under any provision of—
>
> (a)  the Companies Acts, or
>
> (b)  the Insolvency Act 1986 (c.45) or the Insolvency (Northern Ireland) Order 1989 (S.I. 1989/2405 (N.I. 19)).
>
> (2)  The Secretary of State may make provision by regulations applying all or any of the listed provisions, with or without modifications, in relation to documents delivered to the registrar under any enactment.
>
> (3)  The provisions are—
>
> section 1103 (documents to be drawn up and delivered in English),
>
> section 1104 (documents relating to Welsh companies),
>
> section 1105 (documents that may be drawn up and delivered in other languages),
>
> section 1107 (certified translations).
>
> (4)  Regulations under this section are subject to the negative resolution procedure.

AMENDMENT AND NOTES

ᵃ Applied with modifications by Sch 6(1), para 1 of the Investment Bank Special Administration Regulations 2011, SI 2011/145.

COMMENCEMENT DATE 1 January 2007[167]

**35.1102.02**  This section defines the applicability of sections 1103, 1104, 1105, and 1107 of the Act to documents required to be delivered to the registrar pursuant to the Acts listed in subsection (1).

**35.1102.03**  The Secretary of State has power under subsection (2) to extend the applicability of this section to documents required to be delivered under any other enactment in addition to those listed in subsection (1). This is an important provision as it may be appropriate in certain circumstances to apply the language provisions of this section, and related sections, to the requirements of delivering documents

---

[163] Companies Act 2006 (Commencement No 8, Transitional Provisions and Savings) Order 2008, SI 2008/2860, art 3(r).

[164] See s 1099(3).

[165] Eg see ss 66–74.

[166] See Limited Liability Partnerships (Application of Companies Act 2006) Regulations 2009, SI 2009/1804.

[167] Companies Act 2006 (Commencement No 1, Transitional Provisions and Savings) Order 2006, SI 2006/3428.

to the registrar pursuant to other statutory enactments.[168] However, subsection (2) gives the Secretary of State flexibility to apply the language provisions in their entirety or in a modified form as appropriate. The Government has indicated that it is not currently inclined to use the power under subsection (2).[169]

Regulations passed in respect of this section are subject to the negative resolution procedure by virtue of subsection (4). That procedure is explained in section 1289.  **35.1102.04**

### 1103  Documents to be drawn up and delivered in English[a]

(1)  The general rule is that all documents required to be delivered to the registrar must be drawn up and delivered in English.  **35.1103.01**
(2)  This is subject to—
  section 1104 (documents relating to Welsh companies) and
  section 1105 (documents that may be drawn up and delivered in other languages).

AMENDMENTS AND NOTES

[a]  This section applies with modifications to LLPs by reg 68 of the Limited Liability Partnerships (Application of Companies Act 2006) Regulations 2009, SI 2009/1804 to SEs by Pt 2, reg 13A(2)(a) of the European Public Limited-Liability Company (Amendment) Regulations 2009, SI 2009/2400, to special administration orders by Sch 6(1), para 1 of the Investment Bank Special Administration Regulations 2011, SI 2011/245; and to orders delivered to the registrar under reg 19(1) and (2) under the Companies (Cross-Border Mergers) Regulations 2007, SI 2007/2974.

COMMENCEMENT DATE 1 January 2007[170]

Documents delivered to the registrar shall be in English, save for the exceptions listed in subsection (2). Whilst the requirement for documents to be in English was already the general rule applied by the registrar under the Companies Act 1985 the language requirements and any exceptions are now explicitly prescribed in the Act.  **35.1103.02**

The language requirements are separate and distinct from the power of the registrar to impose requirements as to the form of the document, as to which see section 1068.  **35.1103.03**

### 1104  Documents relating to Welsh companies[a]

(1)  Documents relating to a Welsh company may be drawn up and delivered to the registrar in Welsh.  **35.1104.01**
(2)  On delivery to the registrar any such document must be accompanied by a certified translation into English, unless it is—
  (a)  of a description excepted from that requirement by regulations made by the Secretary of State, or
  (b)  in a form prescribed in Welsh (or partly in Welsh and partly in English) by virtue of section 26 of the Welsh Language Act 1993 (c.38).
(3)  Where a document is properly delivered to the registrar in Welsh without a certified translation into English, the registrar must obtain such a translation if the document is to be available for public inspection.
  The translation is treated as if delivered to the registrar in accordance with the same provision as the original.
(4)  A Welsh company may deliver to the registrar a certified translation into Welsh of any document in English that relates to the company and is or has been delivered to the registrar.
(5)  Section 1105 (which requires certified translations into English of documents delivered to the registrar in another language) does not apply to a document relating to a Welsh company that is drawn up and delivered in Welsh.

AMENDMENTS AND NOTES

[a]  This section applies with modifications to LLPs by reg 68 of the Limited Liability Partnerships (Application of Companies Act 2006) Regulations 2009, SI 2009/1804, to orders delivered to the registrar under reg 19(1) and (2) under the Companies (Cross-Border Mergers) Regulations 2007,

---

[168]  See reg 4, Companies (Cross-Border Mergers) Regulations 2007, SI 2007/2974; European Public Limited-Liability Company (Amendment) Regulations 2009, SI 2009/2400.

[169]  See government response to consultation on Companies Act 2006 Implementation—The Registrar of Companies Regulations 2008.

[170]  Companies Act 2006 (Commencement No 1, Transitional Provisions and Savings) Order 2006, SI 2006/3428. For transitional provisions, see Sch 1, para 10.

SI 2007/2974, and to special administration orders by Sch 6(1), para 1 of the Investment Bank Special Administration Regulations 2011, SI 2011/245.

COMMENCEMENT DATE 1 January 2007[171]

**35.1104.02**　This section provides an exception to the general rule that all documents delivered to the registrar must be drawn up in English[172] by allowing documents relating to Welsh companies to be drawn up in Welsh, provided they are accompanied by a certified translation into English on delivery.[173] It replaces, without any substantive change, the Companies Act 1985, section 710B.[174]

**35.1104.03**　Subsection 2(a) gives the Secretary of State power to exempt certain descriptions from the requirement of accompanying a document drawn up in Welsh pursuant to subsection (1) with a certified translation.

**35.1104.04**　Subsection (5) makes clear that section 1105 will not apply to a document drawn up in Welsh relating to a Welsh company, so as not to confuse the ambit of section 1104 with that of section 1105. The latter deals with 'other languages'.

## 1105　Documents that may be drawn up and delivered in other languages[a]

**35.1105.01**
(1) Documents to which this section applies may be drawn up and delivered to the registrar in a language other than English, but when delivered to the registrar they must be accompanied by a certified translation into English.
(2) This section applies to—
　(a) agreements required to be forwarded to the registrar under Chapter 3 of Part 3 (agreements affecting the company's constitution);
　(b) documents required to be delivered under section 400(2)(e) or section 401(2)(f) (company included in accounts of larger group: required to deliver copy of group accounts);
　(c) instruments or copy instruments required to be delivered under Part 25 (company charges);
　(d) documents of any other description specified in regulations made by the Secretary of State.
(3) Regulations under this section are subject to negative resolution procedure.

AMENDMENTS AND NOTES

[a] This section applies with modifications to LLPs by reg 68 of the Limited Liability Partnerships (Application of Companies Act 2006) Regulations 2009, SI 2009/1804, to SEs with modifications by Pt 2, reg 13A of the European Public Limited-Liability Company Regulations 2004, SI 2004/2326 (as amended by regs 16 and 38 of the European Public Limited-Liability Company (Amendment) Regulations 2009, SI 2009/2400 subject to transitional provisions in Sch 2 of those regulations), to special administration orders by Sch 6(1), para 1 of the Investment Bank Special Administration Regulations 2011, SI 2011/245, and to orders delivered to the registrar under reg 19(1) and (2) under the Companies (Cross-Border Mergers) Regulations 2007, SI 2007/2974.

COMMENCEMENT DATE 1 January 2007[175]

**35.1105.02**　This section allows certain documents to be drawn up and delivered to the registrar in languages other than English, provided the document is accompanied with a certified translation at the time of delivery.[176] The section applies only to those documents listed exhaustively in subsection (2), although subsection (2)(d) gives the Secretary of State power to add other categories of documents to the list by way of specific regulations.[177]

---

[171] Companies Act 2006 (Commencement No 1, Transitional Provisions and Savings) Order 2006, SI 2006/3428. For transitional provisions, see Sch 1, para 11.

[172] See s 1103.

[173] See exceptions to the requirement for certified translations at reg 6, Registrar of Companies and Applications for Striking Off Regulations 2009, SI 2009/1803, as amended by reg 21(2) Companies and Limited Liability Partnerships (Accounts and Audit Exemptions and Change of Accounting Framework) Regulations 2012, SI 2012/2301.

[174] CA 1985, s 710B was inserted by the Welsh Language Act 1993, s 30(1), (6).

[175] Companies Act 2006 (Commencement No 1, Transitional Provisions and Savings) Order 2006, SI 2006/3428. For transitional provisions, see Sch 1, para 12.

[176] See s 1107 for the definition of a 'certified translation'.

[177] This power has been exercised in making the Companies (Registrar, Languages and Trading Disclosures) Regulations 2006, SI 2006/3429, art 4, to include contracts required to be delivered to the Registrar pursuant to the CA 1985, s 88(2)(b). See also the Overseas Companies (Execution of Documents and Registration of Charges) Regulations 2009, SI 2009/1917, reg 27, the Overseas Companies Regulations 2009, SI 2009/1801, reg 78, the Registrar of Companies and Applications for Striking Off Regulations 2009, SI 2009/1803, reg 7, and the Companies and Limited Liability Partnerships (Accounts and Audit Exemptions and Change of Accounting Framework) Regulations 2012, SI 2012/2301.

The core documents to which this section relates may well originate in languages other than English. It    **35.1105.03**
may therefore be in the registrar's interest that the originals of such documents are registered along
with a translation in case they ever need to be compared. The ability to file documents in another
language is also advantageous to the individuals concerned who, in many instances, will be able to draw
up the relevant document in a language which will most accurately record their intentions. However,
it should be noted that this section does not seek to prescribe circumstances in which the relevant
documents should be drawn up in a language other than English. That choice is left to the individuals
concerned.

The section has no applicability to documents relating to a Welsh company that are drawn up and    **35.1105.04**
delivered in Welsh: see section 1104(5).

Regulations passed in respect of this section are subject to the negative resolution procedure by virtue    **35.1105.05**
of subsection (3). That procedure is explained in section 1289.

## 1106  Voluntary filing of translations[a]

(1)  A company may deliver to the registrar one or more certified translations of any document    **35.1106.01**
     relating to the company that is or has been delivered to the registrar.
(2)  The Secretary of State may be regulations specify—
     (a)  the languages, and
     (b)  the descriptions of document,
in relation to which this facility is available.
(3)  The regulations must provide that it is available as from 1st January 2007—
     (a)  in relation to all the official languages of the European Union, and
     (b)  in relation to all documents subject to the Directive disclosure requirements (see section
          1078).
(4)  The power of the registrar to impose requirements as to the form and manner of delivery includes
     power to impose requirements as to the identification of the original document and the delivery
     of the translation in a form and manner enabling it to be associated with the original.
(5)  Regulations under this section are subject to negative resolution procedure.
(6)  This section does not apply where the original document was delivered to the registrar before this
     section came into force.

AMENDMENTS AND NOTES

[a]  This section applies with modifications to LLPs by reg 68 of the Limited Liability Partnerships
     (Application of Companies Act 2006) Regulations 2009, SI 2009/1804, to SEs with modifications by
     Pt 2, reg 13A of the European Public Limited-Liability Company Regulations 2004, SI 2004/2326
     (as amended by regs 16 and 38 of the European Public Limited-Liability Company (Amendment)
     Regulations 2009, SI 2009/2400 subject to transitional provisions in Sch 2 of those regulations), to
     special administration orders by Sch 6(1), para 1 of the Investment Bank Special Administration
     Regulations 2011, SI 2011/245, and to orders delivered to the registrar under reg 19(1) and (2)
     under the Companies (Cross-Border Mergers) Regulations 2007, SI 2007/2974.

COMMENCEMENT DATE 1 January 2007[178]

Companies may send the registrar certified translations of any document that is to be held by him    **35.1106.02**
relating to the company. The Secretary of State is given the power under subsection (2) to specify by
way of regulations the languages and documents to which the section applies.[179]

Subsection (3) brings into effect aspects of the First Company Law Directive[180] by providing that the    **35.1106.03**
regulations anticipated by subsection (2) must from 1 January 1997 include provision for all the official
languages of the EU and must apply this section to all the documents subject to the Directive disclosure
requirements.[181] The regulations which may be ordered by the Secretary of State may go beyond the
Directive and specify languages and documents that are not specified in the Directive.

It is noteworthy that under subsection (4) it is the registrar, rather than the Secretary of State, who may    **35.1106.04**
impose requirements in relation to the delivery of documents so as to ensure that the translation can be
correctly associated with its corresponding original.[182] This provision is also derived from the First

---

[178]  Companies Act 2006 (Commencement No 1, Transitional Provisions and Savings) Order 2006, SI
2006/3428.
[179]  That power has been exercised in the Companies (Registrar, Languages and Trading Disclosures) Regulations 2006, SI 2006/3429, reg 5.
[180]  Directive (EEC) 68/151 [1968] OJ L65/8, as amended by Directive (EC) 2003/58. Now replaced by
Directive (EC) 2009/101).
[181]  See s 1078 for list of documents.
[182]  See s 1117 for guidance on how the registrar will impose such rules.

Company Law Directive, which obliges Member States to take necessary measures to avoid discrepancy between an original document and its translation.[183]

**35.1106.05**    Regulations passed in respect of this section are subject to the negative resolution procedure by virtue of subsection (5). That procedure is explained in section 1289.

**35.1106.06**    Subsection (6) limits the applicability of the section to documents delivered after this section comes into force.

### 1107  Certified translations[a]

**35.1107.01**
(1)  In this Part a 'certified translation' means a translation certified to be a correct translation.
(2)  In the case of any discrepancy between the original language version of a document and a certified translation—
  (a)  the company may not rely on the translation as against a third party, but
  (b)  a third party may rely on the translation unless the company shows that the third party had knowledge of the original.
(3)  A 'third party' means a person other than the company or the registrar.

AMENDMENTS AND NOTES

[a]  This section applies with modifications to LLPs by reg 68 of the Limited Liability Partnerships (Application of Companies Act 2006) Regulations 2009, SI 2009/1804, to SEs with modifications by Pt 2, reg 13A of the European Public Limited-Liability Company Regulations 2004, SI 2004/2326 (as amended by regs 16 and 38 of the European Public Limited-Liability Company (Amendment) Regulations 2009, SI 2009/2400 subject to transitional provisions in Sch 2 of those regulations), to special administration orders by Sch 6(1), para 1 of the Investment Bank Special Administration Regulations 2011, SI 2011/245, and to orders delivered to the registrar under reg 19(1) and (2) under the Companies (Cross-Border Mergers) Regulations 2007, SI 2007/2974.

COMMENCEMENT DATE 1 January 2007[184]

**35.1107.02**    This section provides a definition of 'certified translation'. The section was originally drafted as reading 'certified in a manner prescribed by the registrar'. However, the latter wording was taken out during the Bill's passage in Grand Committee.[185] The section does not therefore prescribe what form or standard of certification shall be acceptable, but the registrar does have an express power to impose requirements as to who can give the appropriate certification and verification.[186] Those requirements have been set out in the Registrar's Rules[187]

**35.1107.03**    Subsection (2) implements Article 3a(4) of the First Company Law Directive[188] in providing for a situation where there is a discrepancy between the original document and its certified translation. The section protects third parties by ensuring that the document can be relied upon, notwithstanding any such discrepancy, provided they did not have knowledge of the original. There is no elaboration of what will suffice as 'knowledge' for these purposes and it is as yet unclear whether merely knowing that an original did exist will suffice, or whether the third party must have had access to the original. Where there is an original held by the registrar, questions of the constructive knowledge of the third party may arise in circumstances where no enquiry had been made by them as to the existence of such an original at Companies House.

---

[183]  See Directive (EEC) 68/151 [1968] OJ L65/8, as amended by Directive (EC) 2003/58. Now replaced by Directive (EC) 2009/101).

[184]  Companies Act 2006 (Commencement No 1, Transitional Provisions and Savings) Order 2006, SI 2006/3428.

[185]  See Amendment No A196A, *Hansard*, HL, Grand Committee, col 230 (16 May 2006).

[186]  See s 1111.

[187]  See Registrar's Rules 2009, Part 10 'Translations'. See also form VT01 'Certified voluntary translation of an original document that is or has been delivered to the Registrar of Companies'. For what constitutes a correct certified translation, see also reg 5 of Companies (Welsh Language Forms and Documents) Regulations 1994, SI 1994/117, as amended by Companies Act 2006 (Commencement No 1, Transitional Provisions and Savings) Order 2006, SI 2006/3428.

[188]  Directive (EEC) 68/151 [1968] OJ L65/8, as amended by Directive (EC) 2003/58. Now replaced by Directive (EC) 2009/101.

*Language requirements: transliteration*

### 1108   Transliteration of names and addresses: permitted characters[a]

(1) Names and addresses in a document delivered to the registrar must contain only letters, characters and symbols (including accents and other diacritical marks) that are permitted.

(2) The Secretary of State may make provision by regulations—

    (a) as to the letters, characters and symbols (including accents and other diacritical marks) that are permitted, and

    (b) permitting or requiring the delivery of documents in which names and addresses have not been transliterated into a permitted form.

(3) Regulations under this section are subject to negative resolution procedure.

**35.1108.01**

AMENDMENT AND NOTES

[a] This section applies with modifications to special administration orders by Sch 6(1), para 1 of the Investment Bank Special Administration Regulations 2011, SI 2011/245.

COMMENCEMENT DATE 1 October 2009[189]

This provision had no equivalent in the Companies Act 1985. It deals with the possibility that the names and addresses of overseas companies or their company officers may use a character set which is not derived from Roman characters. The example of Urdu and Japanese characters is used in the Explanatory Notes. The characters that are permitted under this section are set out in The Registrar of Companies and Applications for Striking Off Regulations 2009.[190] Those regulations also provide that the requirement for permitted characters to be used does not apply to the documents listed therein, including memorandums of association and a company's articles.[191]

**35.1108.02**

The section allows the Secretary of State to make provision as to what character sets may be permitted by the registrar. It is notable that subsection (2)(b) clearly envisages the possibility of future regulations permitting the delivery of documents which have not been transliterated into a permitted form as an exception to the general rule, which itself will need to be set down by way of regulations.[192]

**35.1108.03**

There was an indication at Committee stage that, when prescribing regulations pursuant to this provision, consideration would also be given to the question whether the registrar would display a more relaxed attitude than hitherto with respect to companies wishing to use symbols in their names such as '@', '.com' or '4' to denote 'for'. It was thought that such symbols were often an important method by which new company names were created, so as not to duplicate names which already exist on the register.[193]

**35.1108.04**

Regulations passed in respect of this section are subject to the negative resolution procedure by virtue of subsection (3). That procedure is explained in section 1289.

**35.1108.05**

### 1109   Transliterations of names and addresses: voluntary transliteration into Roman characters[a]

(1) Where a name or address is or has been delivered to the registrar in a permitted form using other than Roman characters, the [company (or other body) to which the document relates][b] may deliver to the registrar a transliteration into Roman characters.

(2) The power of the registrar to impose requirements as to the form and manner of delivery includes power to impose requirements as to the identification of the original document and the delivery of the transliteration in a form and manner enabling it to be associated with the original.

**35.1109.01**

---

[189] Companies Act 2006 (Commencement No 8, Transitional Provisions and Savings) Order 2008, SI 2008/2860, art 3(r). This section will apply in relation to all documents delivered to the registrar on or after 1 October 2009 (see para 108 of Sch 2 to the Companies Act 2006 (Commencement No 8, Transitional Provisions and Savings) Order 2008, SI 2008/2860, as amended by Companies Act 2006 (Part 35) (Consequential Amendments, Transitional Provisions and Savings) Order 2009, SI 2009/1802, art 18 and the Schedule thereto.

[190] SI 2009/1803, art 8(3) and the Schedule thereto.

[191] See the Registrar of Companies and Applications for Striking Off Regulations 2009, SI 2009/1803, art 8(2) for the complete list, amended by reg 24 of the European Economic Interest Grouping (Amendment) Regulations 2009, SI 2009/2399, reg 43 of the European Public Limited-Liability Company (Amendment) Regulations 2009, SI 2009/2400, and reg 21(4) of the Companies and Limited Liability Partnerships (Accounts and Audit Exemptions and Change of Accounting Framework) Regulations 2012, SI 2012/2301.

[192] See the Company and Business Names (Miscellaneous Provisions) Regulations 2009, SI 2009/1085, reg 2 and Sch 1, as amended by the Company, Limited Liability Partnership and Business Names (Miscellaneous Provisions) (Amendment) Regulations 2009.

[193] *Hansard*, HL, Standing Committee, col 441 (4 July 2006). See also the Implementation of Companies Act 2006 conservation document, February 2007, Chapter 2, Questions 2.4–2.8.

AMENDMENTS AND NOTES

<sup>a</sup> This section applies with modifications to LLPs by reg 68 of the Limited Liability Partnerships (Application of Companies Act 2006) Regulations 2009, SI 2009/1804, to special administration orders by Sch 6(1), para 1 of the Investment Bank Special Administration Regulations 2011, SI 2011/245, and to unregistered companies by Sch 1 para 17(2)(f) of the Unregistered Companies Regulations 2009, SI 2009/2436.

<sup>b</sup> Amended by the Companies Act 2006 (Part 35) (Consequential Amendments, Transitional Provisions and Savings) Order 2009, SI 2009/1802.

COMMENCEMENT DATE 1 October 2009[194]

**35.1109.02**   This section relates to the power of the Secretary of State to make provision by regulations to permit the delivery of documents in which names and addresses have not been transliterated into Roman characters.[195] In relation to such documents, voluntary transliterations into Roman characters may be delivered to the registrar.

**35.1109.03**   As in the case of voluntary translations,[196] subsection (2) gives the registrar, rather than the Secretary of State, power to impose requirements as to the form and manner of delivery of documents to which this section relates in order to ensure that it can be correctly associated with the original.[197]

### 1110   Transliterations of names and addresses: certification<sup>a</sup>

**35.1110.01**   (1) The Secretary of State may make provision by regulations requiring the certification of transliterations and prescribing the form of certification.
(2) Different provision may be made for compulsory and voluntary transliterations.
(3) Regulations under this section are subject to negative resolution procedure.

AMENDMENTS AND NOTES

<sup>a</sup> This section applies with modifications to LLPs by reg 68 of the Limited Liability Partnerships (Application of Companies Act 2006) Regulations 2009, SI 2009/1804, to special administration orders by Sch 6(1), para 1 of the Investment Bank Special Administration Regulations 2011, SI 2011/245, and to unregistered companies by Sch 1 para 17(2)(f) of the Unregistered Companies Regulations 2009, SI 2009/2436.

COMMENCEMENT DATE 1 October 2009[198]

**35.1110.02**   The Secretary of State has the power under this section to regulate the circumstances in which certification of transliterations shall be required and, if so, what the nature of the certification shall be. Provision is made for the fact that it may be desirable to apply different rules to compulsory and voluntary transliterations: subsection (2).

**35.1110.03**   It is notable that, unlike the sections relating to translations,[199] the delivery of transliterations are not yet subject to the requirement that such transliterations be certified. If and when such certification is required by regulations, those same regulations are also likely to prescribe the form of certification. This is in contrast with the equivalent provision relating to translations which already requires certification, but does not give any indication of what form of certification shall be appropriate other than to provide that the certified translation shall be 'certified to be a correct translation' and that the registrar shall have power to impose relevant requirements.[200]

**35.1110.04**   Regulations passed in respect of this section are subject to the negative resolution procedure by virtue of subsection (3). That procedure is explained in section 1289.

---

[194] Companies Act 2006 (Commencement No 8, Transitional Provisions and Savings) Order 2008, SI 2008/2860, art 3(r). This section will apply in relation to all documents delivered to the registrar on or after 1 October 2009 (see para 108 of Sch 2 to the Companies Act 2006 (Commencement No 8, Transitional Provisions and Savings) Order 2008, SI 2008/2860, as amended by Companies Act 2006 (Part 35) (Consequential Amendments, Transitional Provisions and Savings) Order 2009, SI 2009/1802, art 18 and the Schedule thereto.

[195] See s 1108(2)(b).

[196] See s 1106(4).

[197] See s 1117 for guidance on how the registrar will impose such rules.

[198] Companies Act 2006 (Commencement No 8, Transitional Provisions and Savings) Order 2008, SI 2008/2860, art 3(r). This section will apply in relation to all documents delivered to the registrar on or after 1 October 2009 (see para 108 of Sch 2 to the Companies Act 2006 (Commencement No 8, Transitional Provisions and Savings) Order 2008, SI 2008/2860, as amended by Companies Act 2006 (Part 35) (Consequential Amendments, Transitional Provisions and Savings) Order 2009, SI 2009/1802, art 18 and the Schedule thereto.

[199] See ss 1102–1107.

[200] See ss 1107 and 1111.

## Supplementary provisions

### 1111 Registrar's requirements as to certification or verification

(1) Where a document required or authorised to be delivered to the registrar under any enactment is required— **35.1111.01**

    (a) to be certified as an accurate translation or transliteration, or

    (b) to be certified as a correct copy or verified,

the registrar may impose requirements as to the person, or description of person, by whom the certificate or verification is to be given.

(2) The power conferred by section 1068 (registrar's requirements as to form, authentication and manner of delivery) is exercisable in relation to the certificate or verification as if it were a separate document.

(3) Requirements imposed under this section must not be inconsistent with requirements imposed by any enactment with respect to the certification or verification of the document concerned.

AMENDMENTS AND NOTES

[a] This section applies with modifications to LLPs by reg 68 of the Limited Liability Partnerships (Application of Companies Act 2006) Regulations 2009, SI 2009/1804, to special administration orders by Sch 6(1), para 1 of the Investment Bank Special Administration Regulations 2011, SI 2011/245, and to unregistered companies by Sch 1 para 17(2)(f) of the Unregistered Companies Regulations 2009, SI 2009/2436.

COMMENCEMENT DATE 1 January 2007[201]

Where provisions in the Act require documents to be verified or certified, the registrar is given power to impose requirements as to who must give the appropriate certification or verification.[202] **35.1111.02**

Aside from their substantive purpose in relation to the relevant underlying documents, the certification or verification will in itself be a document required to be delivered to the registrar. Subsection (2) therefore extends the registrar's general power to impose requirements as to the form, authentication, and manner of delivery of documents to the certification or verification as if they were a separate document.[203] For example, if the document containing the certification of a translation does not satisfy requirements as to form and delivery, it is anticipated that this defect will invalidate the delivery of the document containing the translation, notwithstanding that the latter may be otherwise compliant with requirements of form and delivery. **35.1111.03**

### 1112 General false statement offence[a]

(1) It is an offence for a person knowingly or recklessly— **35.1112.01**

    (a) to deliver or cause to be delivered to the registrar, for any purpose of the Companies Acts, a document, or

    (b) to make to the registrar, for any such purpose, a statement,

that is misleading, false or deceptive in a material particular.

(2) A person guilty of an offence under this section is liable—

    (a) on conviction on indictment, to imprisonment for a term not exceeding two years or a fine (or both);

    (b) on summary conviction—

        (i) in England and Wales, to imprisonment for a term not exceeding twelve months[b] or to a fine not exceeding the statutory maximum (or both);

        (ii) in Scotland or Northern Ireland, to imprisonment for a term not exceeding six months, or to a fine not exceeding the statutory maximum (or both).

AMENDMENTS AND NOTES

[a] This section applies with modifications to LLPs by reg 69 of the Limited Liability Partnerships (Application of Companies Act 2006) Regulations 2009, SI 2009/1804 and to EEIGs by Sch 4, para 37 of the European Economic Interest Grouping Regulations 1989, SI 1989/638 as substituted by reg 23(3) of the European Economic Interest Grouping (Amendment) Regulations 2009, SI 2009/2399.

---

[201] Companies Act 2006 (Commencement No 1, Transitional Provisions and Savings) Order 2006, SI 2006/3428.

[202] See para 35.1107.02 above.

[203] See s 1068.

b In relation to any offence committed after the commencement of this section but before the commencement of s 154 of the Criminal Justice Act 2003, the words 'twelve months' in s 1112(2)(b)(i) are replaced with 'six months' (see s 1131).

COMMENCEMENT DATE 1 October 2009[204]

**35.1112.02**    This provision creates a new general offence of knowingly or recklessly delivering[205] any document[206] or making any statement to the registrar which is misleading, false, or deceptive in a material particular. This general offence obviates the need for the Act to have a number of specific false statement offences which were a feature of the Companies Act 1985. Breach is an indictable offence under subsection (2).

### 1113 Enforcement of company's filing obligations[a]

**35.1113.01**    (1)  This section applies where a company has made default in complying with any obligation under the Companies Acts—
    (a)  to deliver a document to the registrar, or
    (b)  to give notice to the registrar of any matter.
(2)  The registrar, or any member or creditor of the company, may give notice to the company requiring it to comply with the obligation.
(3)  If the company fails to make good the default within 14 days after service of the notice, the registrar, or any member or creditor of the company, may apply to the court for an order directing the company, and any specified officer of it, to make good the default within a specified time.
(4)  The court's order may provide that all costs (in Scotland, expenses) of or incidental to the application are to be borne by the company or by any officers of it responsible for the default.
(5)  This section does not affect the operation of any enactment making it an offence, or imposing a civil penalty, for the default.

AMENDMENTS AND NOTES

a This section applies with modifications to LLPs by reg 69 of the Limited Liability Partnerships (Application of Companies Act 2006) Regulations 2009, SI 2009/1804 to SEs with modifications by Sch 2, para 4 of the European Public Limited-Liability Company Regulations 2004, SI 2004/2326 as substituted by reg 38 of the European Public Limited-Liability Company (Amendment) Regulations 2009, SI 2009/2400 subject to transitional provisions in Sch 2 of those regulations.

COMMENCEMENT DATE 1 October 2009[207]

**35.1113.02**    This section is a restatement, in slightly different terms, of the Companies Act 1985, section 713. It enables the registrar or any member or creditor to enforce a company's filing obligations. The enforcing party simply sends a notice to the company requiring compliance within 14 days of service of the notice. If the company fails to make good the default, the registrar, member, or creditor can apply to court for an order directing that the company and any specified officer make good the default within a specified time: subsection (3). A court making an order under this section may require that all costs of and incidental to the application are to be borne by the company or by its officers responsible for the default: subsection (4).

**35.1113.03**    The making of an order under this section can be grounds for making a disqualification order pursuant to the Company Directors Disqualification Act 1986, section 3(3).

### 1114 Application of provisions about documents and delivery

**35.1114.01**    (1)  In this Part—
    (a)  'document' means information recorded in any form, and
    (b)  references to delivering a document include forwarding, lodging, registering, sending, producing or submitting it or (in the case of a notice) giving it.
(2)  Except as otherwise provided, this Part applies in relation to the supply to the registrar of information otherwise than in documentary form as it applies in relation to the delivery of a document.

---

[204] Companies Act 2006 (Commencement No 8, Transitional Provisions and Savings) Order 2008, SI 2008/2860, art 3(r). The transitional provisions are set out in the Companies Act 2006 (Commencement No 8, Transitional Provisions and Savings) Order 2008, Sch 2, para 109 as amended by the Companies Act 2006 (Part 35) Consequential Amendments, Transitional Provisions and Savings) Order 2009 (SI 2009/1802), art 18 and the Schedule thereto. These provide that s 1112 applies to all documents delivered, and statements made, on or after 1 October 2009.

[205] In relation to 'delivery', see s 1114(2).

[206] See s 1114(1).

[207] Companies Act 2006 (Commencement No 8, Transitional Provisions and Savings) Order 2008, SI 2008/2860, art 3(r).

COMMENCEMENT DATE 1 January 2007 so far as necessary for certain provisions[208] coming into force on the same date,[209] but otherwise 1 October 2009[210]

This section includes certain material from the Companies Act 1985, section 715A. Whereas in that section reference to a document 'included' information recorded in any form, document now 'means' such recorded information. Information that is not recorded, such as information sent via a website,[211] would therefore not seem to be a document within the meaning of this section. However, by subsection (2), Part 35 is also applied to such unrecorded information.                 **35.1114.02**

Instances of delivery are also extended beyond sending, forwarding, producing, and the giving of a notice, which were included in the Companies Act 1985, section 715A. Now delivery also extends to lodging, registering and submitting documents. Although the differences between each instance are not all immediately obvious, the aim seems to be to draw the concept of 'delivery' very widely indeed.     **35.1114.03**

## 1115   Supplementary provisions relating to electronic communications

(1)  Registrar's rules may require a company [(or other body)][a] to give any necessary consents to the use of electronic means for communications by the registrar to the company [(or other body)][b] as a condition of making use of any facility to deliver material to the registrar by electronic means.     **35.1115.01**

(2)  A document that is required to be signed by the registrar or authenticated by the registrar's seal shall, if sent by electronic means, be authenticated in such manner as may be specified by registrar's rules.

AMENDMENTS AND NOTES

[a]  Amended by the Companies Act 2006 (Part 35) (Consequential Amendments, Transitional Provisions and Savings) Order 2009, SI 2009/1802.

[b]  Amended by the Companies Act 2006 (Part 35) (Consequential Amendments, Transitional Provisions and Savings) Order 2009, SI 2009/1802.

COMMENCEMENT DATE 1 October 2009[212]

The wording of this provision is extended from that originally enacted to apply to bodies other than companies with effect since 1 October 2009 as a result of the Companies Act 2006 (Part 35) (Consequential Amendments, Transitional Provisions and Savings) Order 2009,[213] article 14. This section replaces the Companies Act 1985, section 710A. Unlike that section, which allowed the registrar to supply documents in any non-legible form that he saw fit (including using electronic media), this section requires a certain reciprocity between the registrar and the relevant company. Only if a company makes use of any facility for delivering documents to the registrar electronically may he require (by rules) that the consent of the company to receive documents electronically be given.     **35.1115.02**

Subsection (2) allows the registrar to provide for methods of authentication when it provides documents using such electronic means.     **35.1115.03**

## 1116   Alternative to publication in the Gazette[a]

(1)  Notices that would otherwise need to be published by the registrar in the Gazette may instead be published by such means as may from time to time be approved by the registrar in accordance with regulations made by the Secretary of State.     **35.1116.01**

(2)  The Secretary of State may make provision by regulations as to what alternative means may be approved.

(3)  The regulations may, in particular—

   (a)  require the use of electronic means;

   (b)  require the same means to be used—

      (i)  for all notices or for all notices of specified descriptions, and

      (ii)  whether the company [(or other body) to which the notice relates][b] is registered in England and Wales, Scotland or Northern Ireland;

   (c)  impose conditions as to the manner in which access to the notices is to be made available.

---

[208]  Companies Act 2006 (Commencement No 1, Transitional Provisions and Savings) Order 2006, SI 2006/3428, art 2(1).

[209]  Companies Act 2006 (Commencement No 1, Transitional Provisions and Savings) Order 2006, SI 2006/3428, art 2(2)(c).

[210]  Companies Act 2006 (Commencement No 8, Transitional Provisions and Savings) Order 2008, SI 2008/2860, art 3(r).

[211]  This is the example given in the Explanatory Notes.

[212]  Companies Act 2006 (Commencement No 8, Transitional Provisions and Savings) Order 2008, SI 2008/2860, art 3(r).

[213]  SI 2009/1802.

(4) Regulations under this section are subject to negative resolution procedure.

(5) Before starting to publish notices by means approved under this section the registrar must publish at least one notice to that effect in the Gazette.

(6) Nothing in this section prevents the registrar from giving public notice both in the Gazette and by means approved under this section.

In that case, the requirement of public notice is met when notice is first given by either means.

AMENDMENTS AND NOTES

ᵃ This section applies to documents delivered to the registrar under reg 12(1) of the Companies (Cross-Border Merger) Regulations 2007, SI 2007/2974 by reg 12(3) of those regulations when regulations under this section have been made, to LLPs with modifications by reg 60 of the Limited Liability Partnerships (Application of Companies Act 2006) Regulations 2009, SI 2009/1804 and to unregistered companies by reg 3 and Sch 1, para 17(2)(g) of the Unregistered Companies Regulations 2009, SI 2009/2436 subject to transitional provisions in Sch 2 of those regulations.

ᵇ Words in square brackets substituted by the Companies Act 2006 (Part 35) (Consequential Amendments, Transitional Provisions and Savings) Order 2009, SI 2009/1802.

COMMENCEMENT DATE 1 October 2009[214]

**35.1116.02**  Under section 1077 the registrar is under an obligation to publish receipt of certain documents in the London Gazette, the Edinburgh Gazette, or the Belfast Gazette, or by some other equally effective means. This section will allow the Secretary of State to make regulations as regards such other equally effective means, in particular electronic means.

**35.1116.03**  Regulations made under this section are subject to the negative resolution procedure (subsection (4)), which is explained in section 1289. As at the time of writing, the Secretary of State has not yet made any regulations under this section.

### 1117 Registrar's rules

**35.1117.01**  (1) Where any provision of this Part enables the registrar to make provision, or impose requirements, as to any matter, the registrar may make such provision or impose such requirements by means of rules under this section.

This is without prejudice to the making of such provision or the imposing of such requirements by other means.

(2) Registrar's rules—

(a) may make different provision for different cases, and

(b) may allow the registrar to disapply or modify any of the rules.

(3) The registrar must—

(a) publicise the rules in a manner appropriate to bring them to the notice of persons affected by them, and

(b) make copies of the rules available to the public (in hard copy or electronic form).

COMMENCEMENT DATE 1 January 2007 so far as necessary for certain provisions[215] coming into force on the same date,[216] 6 April 2008 for subsections (1), (2) and (3) for certain purposes[217] and otherwise on 1 October 2009[218]

**35.1117.02**  This section makes general provision for the exercise of the registrar's various powers under Part 35 to 'make provision' or to 'impose requirements'. Examples of such powers are to be found in section 1063(5) (the fixing of inspection fees) and section 1089(1) (the form and manner of applications for inspection and for copies). Section 1117(1) is permissive, not restrictive: it enables these various powers to be exercised by the registrar by means of rules under section 1117, but it is without prejudice to the making of such provision or the imposing of such requirements by 'other means'. This saving has presumably been included in order to allow the registrar to make rapid changes as circumstances

---

[214] Companies Act 2006 (Commencement No 8, Transitional Provisions and Savings) Order 2008, SI 2008/2860, art 3(r).

[215] Companies Act 2006 (Commencement No 1, Transitional Provisions and Savings) Order 2006, SI 2006/3428, art 2(1).

[216] Companies Act 2006 (Commencement No 1, Transitional Provisions and Savings) Order 2006, SI 2006/3428, art 2(2)(c).

[217] Implemented so far as may be necessary for the purpose of enabling rules to be made under s 1117 before the date on which the section is generally brought into force: Companies Act 2006 (Commencement No 5, Transitional Provisions and Savings) Order 2007, SI 2007/3495, art 3(2).

[218] Companies Act 2006 (Commencement No 8, Transitional Provisions and Savings) Order 2008, SI 2008/2860, art 3(r).

demand eg to the levels of fees charged for different kinds of company search, without being obliged formally to amend any rules made under section 1117.

Under section 1117(3), the registrar is required to publicize any rules that are made, and to make copies available to the public on request. Although some members of the public may continue to ask for hard copies, the obvious and convenient means for publicizing the rules and making copies available will be on the Companies Houses website.                                                                          **35.1117.03**

Rules made under section 1117 are not 'subordinate legislation' for the purposes of the Deregulation   **35.1117.04** and Contracting Out Act 1994, section 71(1)(d), and as a result the registrar's power to make rules can be delegated by him to a contractor: see section 1119(3) below.

The Registrar's Rules were made under section 1117 on 29 September 2009 and came into force on 1   **35.1117.05** October 2009. They are available at ⟨http://www.companieshouse.gov.uk/about/policyDocuments/ registrarsRules.pdf⟩. Volume 1 contains the requirements applicable to documents delivered in electronic form and volume 2 the requirements applicable to documents delivered in paper form.

## 1118  Payments into the Consolidated Fund

Nothing in the Companies Acts or any other enactment as to the payment of receipts into the   **35.1118.01** Consolidated Fund shall be read as affecting the operation in relation to the registrar of section 3(1) of the Government Trading Funds Act 1973 (c. 63).
    COMMENCEMENT DATE 1 October 2009[219]

Companies House has Trading Fund status under the Government Trading Funds Act 1973, which   **35.1118.02** allows it to manage its own finances directly. As a result, provision is made in this section that nothing in the Companies Acts or any other enactment as to the payment of receipts into the Consolidated Fund shall be read as affecting the operation in relation to the registrar of section 3(1) of the 1973 Act (which requires receipts and payments in respect of the 'funded operations' to be paid into and out of the Trading Fund).

## 1119  Contracting out of registrar's functions

(1)  Where by virtue of an order made under section 69 of the Deregulation and Contracting Out Act   **35.1119.01** 1994 (c. 40) a person is authorised by the registrar to accept delivery of any class of documents that are under any enactment to be delivered to the registrar, the registrar may direct that documents of that class shall be delivered to a specified address of the authorised person.
    Any such direction must be printed and made available to the public (with or without payment).

(2)  A document of that class that is delivered to an address other than the specified address is treated as not having been delivered.

(3)  Registrar's rules are not subordinate legislation for the purposes of section 71 of the Deregulation and Contracting Out Act 1994 (functions excluded from contracting out).

    COMMENCEMENT DATE 1 October 2009[220]

This section largely restates provision previously made in the Companies Act 1985, section 704(8) and   **35.1119.02** (9). Under the Deregulation and Contracting Out Act 1994, section 69, statutory functions conferred on a Minister or office-holder may (with certain exceptions) be ordered by the Minister to be discharged by another person—in other words, they may be contracted out. The registrar has previously been given power to contract out a wide range of functions listed in Schedule 1 to the Contracting Out (Functions in Relation to the Registration of Companies) Order 1995.[221]

Where the registrar contracts out functions relating to the receipt of documents required by this Act to   **35.1119.03** be delivered to him, this section makes consequential provision enabling the registrar to specify where the documents are to be delivered (if not at Companies House): section 1119(1). A document so specified that is not delivered to the designated address will be treated as not having been duly delivered (presumably, even if it is in fact delivered to Companies House): section 1119(2).

One of the exceptions to the Deregulation and Contracting Out Act 1994, section 69, is that a 'power to   **35.1119.04** make subordinate legislation' may not be contracted out: section 71(1)(2) of the 1994 Act. However, section 1119(2) above makes clear that rules made under section 1117 are not 'subordinate legislation'

---

[219]  Companies Act 2006 (Commencement No 8, Transitional Provisions and Savings) Order 2008, SI 2008/2860, art 3(r).
[220]  Companies Act 2006 (Commencement No 8, Transitional Provisions and Savings) Order 2008, SI 2008/2860, art 3(r).
[221]  SI 1995/1013.

for these purposes. Accordingly, if the registrar engages a contractor to receive delivery of certain categories of document, he can also delegate to that contractor any associated rule-making power under section 1117.

### 1120  Application of this Part to overseas companies

**35.1120.01**    [...]<sup>a</sup> Amendments and Notes

> <sup>a</sup> Repealed by the Companies Act 2006 (Part 35) (Consequential Amendments, Transitional Provisions and Savings) Order 2009, SI 2009/1802.

**35.1120.02**    This provision was repealed with effect from 1 October 2009 by Companies Act 2006 (Part 35) (Consequential Amendments, Transitional Provisions and Savings) Order 2009,[222] article 16. The application of Part 35 to overseas companies is now dealt with by the new section 1059A(5).

---

[222] SI 2009/1802.

# 36

## OFFENCES UNDER THE COMPANIES ACTS

## Companies Act 2006

### PART 36

### OFFENCES UNDER THE COMPANIES ACTS

#### *Liability of officer in default*

Under the former provisions of the Companies Act 1985 the majority of what were identified by the Company Law Review Steering Group as being 'regulatory offences' attributed criminal liability to the company and 'every officer in default'. The Company Law Review recommended a more targeted approach. As regards the concept of 'officer in default', then contained in section 730(5) of the Companies Act 1985, it was noted that the term was vague and uncertain. The view was expressed that it would be better were criminal liability to be attributed 'to a particular individual or individuals according to the nature of the requirement and who ought to be responsible for ensuring compliance'. In cases where it was appropriate to use the concept of 'officer in default' a more precise definition of 'manager' was proposed as well as a clearer definition of the concept of 'default'.[1] The recommendation regarding 'manager' has not been adopted. The 'default' recommendation has been adopted but with slightly different wording.

**36.0.01**

#### 1121 Liability of officer in default[a]

(1) This section has effect for the purposes of any provision of the Companies Acts to the effect that, in the event of contravention of an enactment in relation to a company, an offence is committed by every officer of the company who is in default.

(2) For this purpose 'officer' includes—

    (a) any director, manager or secretary, and

    (b) any person who is to be treated as an officer of the company for the purposes of the provision in question.

(3) An officer is 'in default' for the purposes of the provision if he authorises or permits, participates in, or fails to take all reasonable steps to prevent, the contravention.

**36.1121.01**

AMENDMENTS AND NOTES

---

[1] See 'Modern Company Law for a Competitive Economy', Final Report (June 2001) Ch 125, esp paras 15.35–15.54.

ᵃ This section applies with modifications to LLPs by reg 49 of the Limited Liability Partnerships (Accounts and Audit) (Application of Companies Act 2006) Regulations 2008, SI 2008/1911. Note also reg 70 of the Limited Liability Partnerships (Application of Companies Act 2006) Regulations 2009, SI 2009/1804.

COMMENCEMENT DATE[2] In each case, for certain purposes: 20 January 2007,[3] 6 April 2007,[4] 1 October 2007,[5] 6 April 2008,[6] 1 October 2008[7]

**36.1121.02** A number of provisions of the Companies Act 2006 attribute criminal liability to an 'officer in default'. These include (and the list is not exhaustive) the following sections dealing with the matters as briefly described:[8]

(i)   Constitutional matters: sections 26 (failure to send registrar copy of amended articles), 30 (failure to send registrar copy of resolution or agreement), 32 (failure to provide constitutional documents to member), 34 (notification to registrar of enactment altering company's constitution), 35 (notification to registrar of order altering company's constitution), 36 (documents not incorporated in or accompanying issued articles of association), 45 (name not legibly inscribed on company seal), 63 (amendment of articles by exempt company in impermissible way), 64 and 67 (failure to change name of exempted company when conditions for exemption no longer apply and directed to do so), 75 (provision of misleading information for the purposes of obtaining registration under a particular name), 76 (provision of misleading indication of activities of company), 84 (failures of disclosure in connection with trading names), 99 (failure to give notice to registrar of application to seek order, or of order, cancelling resolution for re-registration), 108 (failure to deliver statement of capital on re-registration).

(ii)  Register of members: sections 113 (failure to keep and maintain register of members), 114 (failure to notify registrar of location of register of members for inspection purposes), 115 (failures regarding index of members), 118 (register of members, default in inspection or providing copies), 120 (failures re information regarding state of register or index), 123 (entries re single member companies), 130 (failure to give notice to registrar of opening of overseas branch register), 132 (failures re keeping for inspection an overseas branch register or duplicate), 135 (default in giving notice to registrar of discontinuance of overseas branch register).

(iii) Directors: sections 156 (failure to comply with direction of Secretary of State to appoint director), 162 (defaults in connection with register of directors), 165 (default in keeping register of directors' residential addresses), 167 (failure to notify registrar of changes), 228 (default in making available for inspection directors' service contract or terms and in notifying registrar), 229 (default in permitting inspection of service contract or terms), 231 (failures regarding contract with sole member who is director), 237 (failures in connection with qualifying indemnity provision), 246 (failures in connection with director's residential address), 248 (failures regarding minutes of directors' meetings).

(iv)  Company secretaries: sections 272 (failure of plc to comply with Secretary of State's direction to appoint company secretary), 275 (failures in connection with register of secretaries), 276 (failure to notify registrar).

(v)   Meetings: sections 291 and 293 (failures in connection with duty to circulate written resolutions), 315 (failure in connection with duty to circulate members' statement), 325 (failure of notice of meeting to contain information about proxy rights), 326 (failure in connection with company sponsored invitations to appoint proxies), 336 (failure to hold plc AGM), 339 (AGM of plc: failure to circulate members' resolution), 341 (quoted company: failure to make poll result available on website), 343 (polls: failures in connection with appointment of independent assessor), 351 (poll: failures in connection with website publication of report of independent assessor), 355 (failures in

---

² In general this section came into force in relation to each relevant main statutory provision creating an offence as such main statutory provision came force.

³ Companies Act 2006 (Commencement No 1, Transitional Provisions and Savings) Order 2006, SI 2006/3428.

⁴ Companies Act 2006 (Commencement No 2, Consequential Amendments, Transitional Provisions and Savings) Order 2007, SI 2007/1093.

⁵ Companies Act 2006 (Commencement No 3, Consequential Amendments, Transitional Provisions and Savings) Order 2007, SI 2007/2194.

⁶ Companies Act 2006 (Commencement No 5, Transitional Provisions and Savings) Order 2007, SI 2007/3495.

⁷ Companies Act 2006 (Commencement No 5, Transitional Provisions and Savings) Order 2007, SI 2007/3495.

⁸ The Company Law Review Steering Group's hope that 'only a minority of regulatory offences' would be considered appropriate for the 'officer in default' formula, has not proved to the case. For their view in this respect see 'Modern Company Law for a Competitive Economy', Final Report (June 2001), para 15.52.

connection with records of resolutions and meetings), 358 (failures in connection with inspection of records of resolutions and meetings).

(vi) Accounts: sections 387 and 389 (failures in connection with keeping of accounting records), 410 (failure to give information in accounts), 425 (default in sending out copies of accounts and reports), 429 (failures in connection with summary financial statements), 430 (failures regarding quoted companies making information available on the website), 431 and 432 (failure to provide copies of accounts and reports), 433 (failures regarding publication of signatory), 434 and 435 (failures regarding requirements applicable to accounts), 440 (failures in connection with requirement of quoted companies to give notice of resolution to approve directors' remuneration report).

(vii) Auditors: sections 486 and 490 (failure to notify Secretary of State that his power to appoint auditor has become exercisable), 501 (failures of parent company regarding information about overseas subsidiaries), 505 (failures in connection with published auditor's report), 512 (failure to notify registrar of resolution removing auditor), 517 (failure to notify registrar of resignation of auditor), 520 (failure in connection with auditor's statement on ceasing to hold office), 522 and 523 (failure to notify audit authority of auditor ceasing to hold office), 530 (failures in connection with website publication).

(viii) Share capital and members' rights: sections 542 (failures in allotment of shares), 554 (failure to register allotment), 557 (failure to make return of allotments), 590 (contravention of Part 17 Chapter 5: payment for shares), 597 (defaults in connection with valuation of non cash consideration for shares), 602 (failure to deliver resolution to registrar regarding transfer of non cash asset), 607 (breaches of sections 593 and 598), 619 (failure to notify registrar of subdivision or consolidation), 621 (failure to notify registrar of reconversion of stock into shares), 625 (failure to notify registrar of redenomination), 627 (failure to notify registrar of reduction in connection with redenomination), 635 (failure to notify registrar of court order on application regarding variation of class rights), 636 (failure to notify registrar of designation of shares), 637 (failure to notify registrar of variation in class rights), 638 (failure to notify registrar of new class of members), 639 (failure to notify registrar of designation of members), 640 (failure to notify registrar of variation of class rights), 644 (failures in connection with reduction of share capital), 658 (failure to observe requirements regarding company own share purchase), 663 (failure to notify registrar of cancellation of shares), 667 (failure to cancel shares or re-register company), 680 (prohibited financial assistance), 689 (failure to give notice to registrar of redemption), 703 (failures in connection with keeping copies and making available for inspection contract regarding own share purchase), 707 (failures regarding making return to registrar of own share purchase), 708 (failure to notify registrar of cancellation), 720 (failures regarding directors' statement and auditor's report), 722 (failure to notify registrar of court order), 728 (failure to notify registrar of disposal of treasury shares), 729 (failure to notify registrar regarding cancellation of treasury shares), 732 (contravention of Part 18 Chapter 6: Treasury Shares).

(ix) Debentures: sections 741 (failures regarding registration of allotment of debentures), 743 (failure to notify registrar of location of register of debenture holders for inspection purposes), 746 (default in permitting inspection or providing copy of register of debenture holders), 749 (default in providing copy of trust deed).

(x) Business, transfers of shares, issue of certificates, information about shares: sections 767 (doing business etc without trading certificate), 769 (issue of certificates on allotment), 771 and 776 (failures in connection with transfers), 780 failures regarding issue of certificates on surrender of share warrants), 798 (issue of shares in contravention of court order in context of information being sought about shares), 804 (failure to use powers to require information about shares on member's request), 806 (failure to notify registrar of location where reports may be inspected), 807 (failure regarding inspection of reports), 808 to 810, 813, 815, and 819 (failures regarding register of interests and associated index), 858 (failure to deliver annual return).

(xi) Charges: sections 860, 862, 878, 880 (failure to deliver particulars regarding charges), 871 (failures regarding registration of details of enforcement of security), 877 and 892 (failures regarding inspection).

(xii) Arrangements and reconstructions: sections 897 (failures regarding circulation of statement), 900 (failures regarding registration of orders), 901 (failures regarding changes to articles etc effected by order).

(xiii) Takeovers etc: sections 949 (regarding disclosure of information provided to Panel), 970 (failures in communicating opting in or opting out decisions), 984 (failure to give notice).

(xiv) Unfair prejudice: sections 998 (failure to deliver order to registrar), 999 (failure regarding changes to constitution etc. following court order).

(xv) Restoration to the register: section 1033.

(xvi) Registrar of Companies: sections 1093 (failures in connection with registrar's notice to resolve uncertainty in register).

(xvii) Company records etc: sections 1135 (failures in connection with form of books and records), 1138 (failures in connection with prevention of falsification), and 1145 (failures in connection with provision of hard copy versions).

(xviii) Business names: see sections 1193, 1194, 1197, 1198, 1205, 1207.

**36.1121.03**    For these purposes the term 'officer' encompasses any person whom the Companies Act specifically provides is to be treated as being an officer for the purposes of the provision in question[9] and, in addition any director,[10] manager or secretary.[11] The Company Law Review Steering Group recommended that the term 'manager' should be defined as 'a person other than a director or secretary (whether or not employed by the company) who under the immediate authority of a director or secretary, is charged with managerial functions which include the relevant function or (in relation to maintenance, filing or distribution of accounts or records) is responsible for maintaining the accounts or records in question'. This recommendation was not accepted. 'Manager' has not been further defined.

**36.1121.04**    It is thus necessary to refer back to the previous law which the Company Law Reform Steering Group said had the advantages of 'familiarity, the detailed examples from some rather inconsistent case law and the dubious argument that in practice it causes little difficulty because the uncertainty makes action against anyone other than a director or secretary virtually impossible'.[12]

**36.1121.05**    It appears that the definition in subsection (2) may be inclusory rather than exclusory; at least similar words in the 1985 Act were so construed.[13] As regards 'officer', *prima facie*, auditors,[14] bankers,[15] solicitors,[16] and trustees for debenture-holders[17] are not 'officers', but, if appointed to an office under the company and they act as officers they will be officers. An auditor is likely to be an officer of a company, if properly appointed as such and assuming the definition in subsection (2) is inclusory and not exclusionary (see *Re London and General Bank* [1895] 1 Ch 166, *In Re Kingston Cotton Mill Company* [1896] 1 Ch 6). However, someone simply called in to do some audit work will not be an 'officer'.[18] It is unclear whether a liquidator will be an officer.[19] However, administrators have been held to be 'officers'.[20]

**36.1121.06**    The term 'manager' will encompass a person who 'has management of the whole affairs of the company; not an agent who is to do a particular thing, or a servant who is to obey orders, but a person who is entrusted with power to transact the whole of the affairs of the company' and it matters not whether he has been appointed as such or whether he has simply acted as a *de facto* manager, having been permitted to do so by the board (see generally *Gibson v Barton* (1875) 10 LR QB 329). It seems likely that a branch manager will not be a 'manager' for this purpose (see, in the context of the Restrictive Trade Practices Act 1956, *Registrar of Restrictive Trading Agreements v W H Smith & Son* [1968]1 WLR 1541). Apparently a receiver and manager of a company's property will not be a 'manager' of the company (see *In re B Johnson & Co Builders* [1955] Ch 634).

**36.1121.07**    Under the 2006 Act the definition of default has been clarified. Under the Companies Act 1985 an officer in default was a person who 'knowingly and wilfully' authorized or permitted the default, refusal or contravention in question. The requirement of 'knowledge' was met where the defendant knew facts which constituted the offence;[21] there was no need to show that he knew that he was committing an offence or that he was acting with dishonest intention. Nelsonian blindness would suffice.[22] To have

---

[9]  A number of them extend the term to a shadow director.

[10]  See further s 250 of the Companies Act 2006.

[11]  See s 1173 of the Companies Act 2006.

[12]  'Modern Company Law for a Competitive Economy', Final Report (June 2001) para 15.42, n 296.

[13]  Note the section uses the term 'includes' rather than 'means'.

[14]  *Re Western Counties Steam Bakeries and Milling Company* [1897] 1 Ch 617.

[15]  *In re Imperial Land Co of Marseilles* (1870) LR 10 Eq 298; *Re Kingston Cotton Mills Co* [1896] 1 Ch 6, 14.

[16]  *Carter's Case* (1886) 31 Ch D 496. Although if permanently employed at a fixed salary and as a financial manager the position will be different: see *Re Liberator Permanent Benefit Building Society* (1894) 71 LT 406.

[17]  *Re British Guardian Life Assurance Co* [1890] WN 63 (reported, but not on this point, at (1890) 14 Ch D 335. Contrast *Cornell v Hay* (1879) 8 LRCP 328, 335.

[18]  *Re Western Counties Steam Bakeries and Milling Company* [1897] 1 Ch 617.

[19]  Contrast *In Re X Co Ltd* [1907] 2 Ch 92 (where he was assumed to be) and *Re Home and Colonial Insurance Co Ltd* [1930] 1 Ch 102, where it was doubted that a liquidator would be an 'officer' in the context of an article of association providing an indemnity to officers.

[20]  *Re Home Treat Limited* [1991] BCLC 705.

[21]  *Burton v Bevan* [1908] 2 Ch 240, 247 (a case concerning civil proceedings under s 5 of CA 1900).

[22]  *Mallon v Allon* [1964] 1 QB 385, 394 (*per* Lord Parker CJ), a case under the Betting and Gaming Act 1960.

acted 'wilfully' the officer must have acted 'deliberately and intentionally, not by accident or inadvertence, but so that the mind of the person who does the act goes with it'.[23]

Under the current section the test is whether the person in question authorizes or permits, fails to take **36.1121.08** reasonable steps to prevent, or participates in the contravention. Unfortunately the clearer wording suggested by the Company Law Steering Group, which would have identified different gradations of knowledge, has not been adopted.[24] The question therefore is whether a failure to take all reasonable steps to prevent something requires knowledge of the state of affairs concerned or whether a negligent failure to take *all* reasonable steps will encompass the situation where the contravention was reasonably foreseeable and the director had negligently failed to put in place a reasonably adequate system of monitoring and controls to ensure that the contravention did not occur. It is suggested that the latter is the more likely approach that the courts will take. That said, there is limited judicial guidance here and much depends upon the underlying substantive provision that is alleged to have been contravened.

## 1122 Liability of company as officer in default[a]

(1) Where a company is an officer of another company, it does not commit an offence as an officer **36.1122.01** in default unless one of its officers is in default.
(2) Where any such offence is committed by a company the officer in question also commits the offence and is liable to be proceeded against and punished accordingly.
(3) In this section 'officer' and 'in default' have the meanings given by section 1121.

AMENDMENTS AND NOTES

[a] This section applies with modifications to LLPs by reg 49 of the Limited Liability Partnerships (Accounts and Audit) (Application of Companies Act 2006) Regulations 2008, SI 2008/1911. See also reg 70 of the Limited Liability Partnerships (Application of Companies Act 2006) Regulations 2009, SI 2009/1804.

COMMENCEMENT DATE[25] In each case, for certain purposes: 6 April 2007,[26] 1 October 2007,[27] 6 April 2008,[28] 1 October 2008[29]

This section deals with the situation where the officer of a company is itself a company. For these **36.1122.02** purposes 'company' means a company formed and registered under this Act, the Companies Act 1985, or the Companies Northern Ireland Order 1986, or which was an 'existing company' for the purposes of the 1985 Act or the 1986 Order.[30] Section 1123 deals with other bodies corporate.

Where the officer of a company is itself a company, the company which is the officer will not commit **36.1122.03** an offence as an officer in default unless one of its own officers is in default (subsection (1)). If its own officer is in default, both the company and its own officer will bear criminal responsibility (subsection (2)). For these purposes 'officer in default' is defined by section 1121 (subsection (3)).

## 1123 Application to bodies other than companies

(1) Section 1121 (liability of officers in default) applies to a body other than a company as it applies **36.1123.01** to a company.
(2) As it applies in relation to a body corporate other than a company—
   (a) the reference to a director of the company shall be read as referring—
      (i) where the body's affairs are managed by its members, to a member of the body,
      (ii) in any other case, to any corresponding officer of the body, and

---

[23] *R v Senior* [1983] 1 QB 283, 291 (a case under the Prevention of Cruelty to Children Act 1894).
[24] For the meaning which can be attributed to words such as 'cause' or 'permit' and the different states of knowledge which may be relevant see (in the disqualification context) *Re Clean and Colour Limited, Secretary of State for Trade and Industry v Tuck* (unreported) 7 June 2001 and *Re Plazoo Pipes Limited, Kappler v Secretary of State for Trade and Industry* [2006] BCC 845.
[25] In general this section came into force in relation to each relevant main statutory provision creating an offence as such main statutory provision came into force.
[26] Companies Act 2006 (Commencement No 2, Consequential Amendments, Transitional Provisions and Savings) Order 2007, SI 2007/1093 and the Companies Acts (Unregistered Companies) Regulations 2007, SI 2007/318.
[27] Companies Act 2006 (Commencement No 3, Consequential Amendments, Transitional Provisions and Savings) Order 2007 SI 2007/2194.
[28] Companies Act 2006 (Commencement No 5, Transitional Provisions and Savings) Order 2007, SI 2007/3495.
[29] Companies Act 2006 (Commencement No 5, Transitional Provisions and Savings) Order 2007, (SI 2007/3495.
[30] Section 2.

    (b) the reference to a manager or secretary of the company shall be read as referring to any manager, secretary or similar officer of the body.

  (3) As it applies in relation to a partnership—

    (a) the reference to a director of the company shall be read as referring to a member of the partnership, and

    (b) the reference to a manager or secretary of the company shall be read as referring to any manager, secretary or similar officer of the partnership.

  (4) As it applies in relation to an unincorporated body other than a partnership—

    (a) the reference to a director of the company shall be read as referring—

      (i) where the body's affairs are managed by its members, to a member of the body,

      (ii) in any other case, to a member of the governing body, and

    (b) the reference to a manager or secretary of the company shall be read as referring to any manager, secretary or similar officer of the body.

COMMENCEMENT DATE[31] In each case, for certain purposes: 6 April 2007,[32] 1 October 2007,[33] 6 April 2008,[34] 1 October 2008[35]

**36.1123.02** This section applies and adapts the 'officer in default' provision of section 1121 to bodies other than companies, making specific provision in relation to bodies corporate which are not companies, partnerships, and unincorporated bodies, other than partnerships. The statutory predecessor was the Companies Act 1985, sections 733(2) and (3) and 734(6). See also the Companies Act 1989, section 90 which contained some parallel material. These provisions are relevant to certain provisions of the Companies Act 2006 which extend beyond companies (eg Part 41 relating to business names).

**36.1123.03** In each case the references in section 1121 to 'manager' and 'secretary' are to be treated as referring to any manager or secretary or similar officer of the body in question. The references in section 1121 to 'director' are treated as referring, other than in the case of partnerships,[36] to a member of the relevant body (where its affairs are managed by the members) and otherwise to any corresponding officer of the body (in the case of corporate bodies) or any member of its governing body (in the case of unincorporated associations). In the case of partnerships, references in section 1121 to 'director' are treated as referring to any member of the partnership.

## *Offences under the Companies Act 1985*

### 1124  Amendments of the Companies Act 1985

**36.1124.01** Schedule 3 contains amendments of the Companies Act 1985 (c. 6) relating to offences.

COMMENCEMENT DATE 1 October 2007[37]

**36.1124.02** The statutory predecessor was Schedule 24 of the Companies Act 1985. Section 1124 now refers us to Schedule 3. These amendments cover a range of offences relating to investigations by the Secretary of State. See Explanatory Notes to the Bill when it entered the Commons in May 2003, paragraph 1369 *et seq.* As the Bill expanded so what is now Schedule 3 has shrunk. Section 1124 is just one indicator that some provisions of the 1985 Act remain on the statute-book.

## *General provisions*

### 1125  Meaning of 'daily default fine'[a]

**36.1125.01** (1) This section defines what is meant in the Companies Acts where it is provided that a person guilty of an offence is liable on summary conviction to a fine not exceeding a specified amount 'and, for continued contravention, a daily default fine' not exceeding a specified amount.

  (2) This means that the person is liable on a second or subsequent summary conviction of the offence to a fine not exceeding the latter amount for each day on which the contravention is continued (instead of being liable to a fine not exceeding the former amount).

---

[31] In general this section came into force in relation to each relevant main statutory provision creating an offence as such main statutory provision came into force.

[32] Companies Act 2006 (Commencement No 2, Consequential Amendments, Transitional Provisions and Savings) Order 2007, SI 2007/1093.

[33] Companies Act 2006 (Commencement No 3, Consequential Amendments, Transitional Provisions and Savings) Order 2007, SI 2007/2194.

[34] Companies Act 2006 (Commencement No 5, Transitional Provisions and Savings) Order 2007, SI 2007/3495.

[35] Companies Act 2006 (Commencement No 5, Transitional Provisions and Savings) Order 2007, SI 2007/3495.

[36] But excluding for this purpose Limited Liability Partnerships which are bodies corporate and which therefore fall within subs (2).

[37] Companies Act 2006 (Commencement No 3, etc) Order 2007, SI 2007/2194.

AMENDMENTS AND NOTES

a   This section applies with modifications to LLPs by reg 50 of the Limited Liability Partnerships (Accounts and Audit) (Application of Companies Act 2006) Regulations 2008, SI 2008/1911. See also reg 71 of the Limited Liability Partnerships (Application of Companies Act 2006) Regulations 2009, SI 2009/1804.

COMMENCEMENT DATE 1 October 2007,[38] 6 April 2008,[39] 1 October 2008[40]

Subsections (1) and (2) taken together define what is a daily default fine; a concept used in many provisions in Companies Act 2006, eg section 1033(7). See Companies Act 1985, section 730(4) for the former provision.   **36.1125.02**

## 1126  Consents required for certain prosecutions[a]

(1)  This section applies to proceedings for an offence under any of the following provisions—   **36.1126.01**
    section 458, 460 or 949 of this Act (offences of unauthorised disclosure of information);
    section 953 of this Act (failure to comply with rules about takeover bid documents);
    section 448, 449, 450, 451 or 453A of the Companies Act 1985 (c. 6) (offences in connection with company investigations);
    section 798 of this Act or section 455 of the Companies Act 1985 (offence of attempting to evade restrictions on shares).

(2)  No such proceedings are to be brought in England and Wales except by or with the consent of—
    (a)  in the case of an offence under—
        (i)   section 458, 460 or 949 of this Act,
        (ii)  section 953 of this Act, or
        (iii) section 448, 449, 450, 451 or 453A of the Companies Act 1985,
    the Secretary of State or the Director of Public Prosecutions;
    (b)  in the case of an offence under section 798 of this Act or section 455 of the Companies Act 1985, the Secretary of State.

(3)  No such proceedings are to be brought in Northern Ireland except by or with the consent of—
    (a)  in the case of an offence under—
        (i)   section 458, 460 or 949 of this Act,
        (ii)  section 953 of this Act, or
        (iii) section 448, 449, 450, 451 or 453A of the Companies Act 1985,
    the Secretary of State or the Director of Public Prosecutions for Northern Ireland;
    (b)  in the case of an offence under section 798 of this Act or section 455 of the Companies Act 1985, the Secretary of State.

AMENDMENTS AND NOTES

a   This section applies with modifications to LLPs by reg 50 of the Limited Liability Partnerships (Accounts and Audit) (Application of Companies Act 2006) Regulations 2008, SI 2008/1911. See also reg 72 of the Limited Liability Partnerships (Application of Companies Act 2006) Regulations 2009, SI 2009/1804.

COMMENCEMENT DATE 1 October 2007,[41] 6 April 2008[42]

Subsection (1), which draws inspiration from the former Companies Act 1985, section 732, explains the cases where official consent before prosecution is required. This scenario would cover a range of offences, some of which are concerned with the conduct of BIS investigations with others relating to other instances of unauthorized disclosure.   **36.1126.02**

Subsection (2) outlines those officials who can give consent depending upon the relevant offence.   **36.1126.03**

The application of the consent rules in Northern Ireland is hereby mapped out by subsection (3).   **36.1126.04**

## 1127  Summary proceedings: venue[a]

(1)  Summary proceedings for any offence under the Companies Acts may be taken—   **36.1127.01**
    (a)  against a body corporate, at any place at which the body has a place of business, and
    (b)  against any other person, at any place at which he is for the time being.

---

[38]  Companies Act 2006 (Commencement No 3, etc) Order 2007, SI 2007/2194.
[39]  Companies Act 2006 (Commencement No 5, Transitional Provisions and Savings) Order 2007, SI 2007/3495.
[40]  Companies Act 2006 (Commencement No 5, Transitional Provisions and Savings) Order 2007, SI 2007/3495.
[41]  Companies Act 2006 (Commencement No 3, etc) Order 2007, SI 2007/2194.
[42]  Companies Act 2006 (Commencement No 5, Transitional Provisions and Savings) Order 2007, SI 2007/3495.

(2)  This is without prejudice to any jurisdiction exercisable apart from this section.

AMENDMENTS AND NOTES

ᵃ  This section applies with modifications to LLPs by reg 50 of the Limited Liability Partnerships (Accounts and Audit) (Application of Companies Act 20006) Regulations 2008, SI 2008/1911. See also reg 73 of the Limited Liability Partnerships (Application of Companies Act 2006) Regulations 2009, SI 2009/1804.

COMMENCEMENT DATE  1 October 2007,[43] 6 April 2008,[44] 1 October 2008[45]

**36.1127.02**  See Companies Act 1985, section 731(1) for the statutory forerunner.

**36.1127.03**  Subsection (1) prescribes the appropriate venue for summary proceedings. Summary proceedings can be instituted against directors anywhere they may be located. For body corporate see section 1173.

**36.1127.04**  Special jurisdictional rules are hereby preserved by subsection (2).

### 1128  Summary proceedings: time limit for proceedings[a]

**36.1128.01**
(1)  An information relating to an offence under the Companies Acts that is triable by a magistrates' court in England and Wales may be so tried if it is laid—
  (a)  at any time within three years after the commission of the offence, and
  (b)  within twelve months after the date on which evidence sufficient in the opinion of the Director of Public Prosecutions or the Secretary of State (as the case may be) to justify the proceedings comes to his knowledge.
(2)  Summary proceedings in Scotland for an offence under the Companies Acts—
  (a)  must not be commenced after the expiration of three years from the commission of the offence;
  (b)  subject to that, may be commenced at any time—
    (i)  within twelve months after the date on which evidence sufficient in the Lord Advocate's opinion to justify the proceedings came to his knowledge, or
    (ii)  where such evidence was reported to him by the Secretary of State, within twelve months after the date on which it came to the knowledge of the latter.
Section 136(3) of the Criminal Procedure (Scotland) Act 1995 (c. 46) (date when proceedings deemed to be commenced) applies for the purposes of this subsection as for the purposes of that section.
(3)  A magistrates' court in Northern Ireland has jurisdiction to hear and determine a complaint charging the commission of a summary offence under the Companies Acts provided that the complaint is made—
  (a)  within three years from the time when the offence was committed, and
  (b)  within twelve months from the date on which evidence sufficient in the opinion of the Director of Public Prosecutions for Northern Ireland or the Secretary of State (as the case may be) to justify the proceedings comes to his knowledge.
(4)  For the purposes of this section a certificate of the Director of Public Prosecutions, the Lord Advocate, the Director of Public Prosecutions for Northern Ireland or the Secretary of State (as the case may be) as to the date on which such evidence as is referred to above came to his notice is conclusive evidence.

AMENDMENTS AND NOTES

ᵃ  This section applies with modifications to LLPs by reg 50 of the Limited Liability Partnerships (Accounts and Audit) (Application of Companies Act 2006) Regulations 2008, SI 2008/1911. See also reg 73 of the Limited Liability Partnerships (Application of Companies Act 2006) Regulations 2009, SI 2009/1804.

COMMENCEMENT DATE  1 October 2007,[46] 6 April 2008,[47] 1 October 2008[48]

**36.1128.02**  This restates Companies Act 1985, section 731(2) to (4). The effect of subsection (1) is that, although limitation periods normally do not run for criminal offences, this prescribes time limits for summary

---

[43]  Companies Act 2006 (Commencement No 3, etc) Order 2007, SI 2007/2194.
[44]  Companies Act 2006 (Commencement No 5, Transitional Provisions and Savings) Order 2007, SI 2007/3495.
[45]  Companies Act 2006 (Commencement No 5, Transitional Provisions and Savings) Order 2007, SI 2007/3495.
[46]  Companies Act 2006 (Commencement No 3, etc) Order 2007, SI 2007/2194.
[47]  Companies Act 2006 (Commencement No 5, Transitional Provisions and Savings) Order 2007, SI 2007/3495.
[48]  Companies Act 2006 (Commencement No 5, Transitional Provisions and Savings) Order 2007, SI 2007/3495.

proceedings under the Companies Acts. A basic three-year limitation period running from the date of the offence but also subject to the 12-month limitation contained in subsection 1(b) operates.

Subsection (2) regulates the position on time limits in Scotland by providing comparable rules. The    **36.1128.03**
equivalent Northern Irish position is outlined by subsection (3).

Subsection (4) stresses that official certificates as to dates are conclusive, a principle well reflected    **36.1128.04**
elsewhere in this legislation—see Companies Act 2006, section 15(4) (certificate of incorporation).

## 1129  Legal professional privilege[a]

In proceedings against a person for an offence under the Companies Acts, nothing in those Acts is to    **36.1129.01**
be taken to require any person to disclose any information that he is entitled to refuse to disclose on
grounds of legal professional privilege (in Scotland, confidentiality of communications).

> AMENDMENTS AND NOTES
>
> [a]  This section applies with modifications to LLPs by reg 50 of the Limited Liability Partnerships (Accounts
>     and Audit) (Application of Companies Act 2006) Regulations 2008, SI 2008/1911. See also reg 73 of the
>     Limited Liability Partnerships (Application of Companies Act 2006) Regulations 2009, SI 2009/1804.
>
> COMMENCEMENT DATE 1 October 2007,[49] 6 April 2008,[50] 1 October 2008[51]

This provision, which restates Companies Act 1985, section 732(3), reminds us that legal professional    **36.1129.02**
privilege (and its equivalent under Scots law) is to be preserved where alleged offences under the
Companies Act are prosecuted. But such privilege is not absolute; it is subject to erosion by common
law and other legislation. For the former scenario see for example *Barclays Bank v Eustice*.[52]

## 1130  Proceedings against unincorporated bodies[a]

(1)  Proceedings for an offence under the Companies Acts alleged to have been committed by an    **36.1130.01**
     unincorporated body must be brought in the name of the body (and not in that of any of its
     members).

(2)  For the purposes of such proceedings—
     (a)  any rules of court relating to the service of documents have effect as if the body were a body
          corporate, and
     (b)  the following provisions apply as they apply in relation to a body corporate—
          (i)   in England and Wales, section 33 of the Criminal Justice Act 1925 (c. 86) and Schedule
                3 to the Magistrates' Courts Act 1980 (c. 43),
          (ii)  in Scotland, sections 70 and 143 of the Criminal Procedure (Scotland) Act 1995 (c. 46),
          (iii) in Northern Ireland, section 18 of the Criminal Justice Act (Northern Ireland) 1945 (c. 15
                (N.I.)) and Article 166 of and Schedule 4 to the Magistrates' Courts (Northern Ireland)
                Order 1981 (S.I. 1981/1675 (N.I. 26)).

(3)  A fine imposed on an unincorporated body on its conviction of an offence under the Companies
     Acts must be paid out of the funds of the body.

AMENDMENTS AND NOTES

[a]  This section applies with modifications to LLPs by reg 50 of the Limited Liability Partnerships
    (Accounts and Audit) (Application of Companies Act 2006) Regulations 2008, SI 2008/1911. See
    also reg 73 of the Limited Liability Partnerships (Application of Companies Act 2006) Regulations
    2009, SI 2009/1804.

COMMENCEMENT DATE 1 October 2007,[53] 6 April 2008,[54] 1 October 2008[55]

Subsection (1) deals with proceedings under the Companies Acts against unincorporated bodies. The    **36.1130.02**
statutory predecessor was Companies Act 1985, section 734. Such bodies must be prosecuted in their
collective name.

---

[49]  Companies Act 2006 (Commencement No 3, etc) Order 2007, SI 2007/2194.

[50]  Companies Act 2006 (Commencement No 5, Transitional Provisions and Savings) Order 2007, SI 2007/3495.

[51]  Companies Act 2006 (Commencement No 5, Transitional Provisions and Savings) Order 2007, SI 2007/3495.

[52]  [1995] 1 WLR 1238.

[53]  Companies Act 2006 (Commencement No 3, etc) Order 2007, SI 2007/2194.

[54]  Companies Act 2006 (Commencement No 5, Transitional Provisions and Savings) Order 2007, SI 2007/3495.

[55]  Companies Act 2006 (Commencement No 5, Transitional Provisions and Savings) Order 2007, SI 2007/3495.

**36.1130.03**   Subsection (2) makes the necessary procedural modifications (eg as to service of proceedings) where an unincorporated body is prosecuted.

**36.1130.04**   Subsection (3) makes provision for fining unincorporated bodies. What happens if the funds are inadequate is not spelled out but presumably the members would be liable to dip into their own pockets.

### 1131 Imprisonment on summary conviction in England and Wales: transitory provision[a]

**36.1131.01**   (1) This section applies to any provision of the Companies Acts that provides that a person guilty of an offence is liable on summary conviction in England and Wales to imprisonment for a term not exceeding twelve months.

(2) In relation to an offence committed before the commencement of section 154(1) of the Criminal Justice Act 2003 (c. 44), for 'twelve months' substitute 'six months'.

AMENDMENTS AND NOTES

[a] This section applies with modifications to LLPs by reg 50 of the Limited Liability Partnerships (Accounts and Audit) (Application of Companies Act 2006) Regulations 2008, SI 2008/1911. See also reg 73 of the Limited Liability Partnerships (Application of Companies Act 2006) Regulations 2009, SI 2009/1804.

COMMENCEMENT DATE 1 October 2007,[56] 6 April 2008,[57] 1 October 2008[58]

**36.1131.02**   This was a new provision. Subsections (1) and (2) deal with imprisonment on summary conviction—transitory provision is made by reference to section 154 of the Criminal Justice Act 2003, which deals with the general limit on the power of magistrates to impose sentences of imprisonment. That section places a maximum limit of 12 months imprisonment for a single offence. Prior to that the maximum period of imprisonment which magistrates could impose was only six months.

### *Production and inspection of documents*

### 1132 Production and inspection of documents where offence suspected[a]

**36.1132.01**   (1) An application under this section may be made—
(a) in England and Wales, to a judge of the High Court by the Director of Public Prosecutions, the Secretary of State or a chief officer of police;
(b) in Scotland, to one of the Lords Commissioners of Justiciary by the Lord Advocate;
(c) in Northern Ireland, to the High Court by the Director of Public Prosecutions for Northern Ireland, the Department of Enterprise, Trade and Investment or a chief superintendent of the Police Service of Northern Ireland.

(2) If on an application under this section there is shown to be reasonable cause to believe—
(a) that any person has, while an officer of a company, committed an offence in connection with the management of the company's affairs, and
(b) that evidence of the commission of the offence is to be found in any documents in the possession or control of the company, an order under this section may be made.

(3) The order may—
(a) authorise any person named in it to inspect the documents in question, or any of them, for the purpose of investigating and obtaining evidence of the offence, or
(b) require the secretary of the company, or such other officer of it as may be named in the order, to produce the documents (or any of them) to a person named in the order at a place so named.

(4) This section applies also in relation to documents in the possession or control of a person carrying on the business of banking, so far as they relate to the company's affairs, as it applies to documents in the possession or control of the company, except that no such order as is referred to in subsection (3)(b) may be made by virtue of this subsection.

(5) The decision under this section of a judge of the High Court, any of the Lords Commissioners of Justiciary or the High Court is not appealable.

(6) In this section 'document' includes information recorded in any form.

AMENDMENTS AND NOTES

---

[56] Companies Act 2006 (Commencement No 3, etc) Order 2007, SI 2007/2194.
[57] Companies Act 2006 (Commencement No 5, Transitional Provisions and Savings) Order 2007, SI 2007/3495.
[58] Companies Act 2006 (Commencement No 5, Transitional Provisions and Savings) Order 2007, SI 2007/3495.

<sup>a</sup> This section applies with modifications to LLPs by reg 50 of the Limited Liability Partnerships (Acccounts and Audit) (Application of Companies Act 2006) Regulations 2008, SI 2008/1911. See also reg 73 of the Limited Liability Partnerships (Application of Companies Act 2006) Regulations 2009, SI 2009/1804.

COMMENCEMENT DATE  1 October 2007,[59] 6 April 2008,[60] 1 October 2008[61]

This provision was a later insertion into Part 36 having only appeared after the Bill had passed through Standing Committee in the Commons. It establishes procedures appropriate for each part of the UK for the obtaining of court orders for the production and inspection of documents where there is reasonable cause to believe that an offence has been committed under the Companies Act. Note the special provision in subsection (4) relating to banking. For 'officer' see section 1173.          **36.1132.02**

## *Supplementary*

### 1133  Transitional provision<sup>a</sup>

The provisions of this Part except section 1132 do not apply to offences committed before the commencement of the relevant provision.          **36.1133.01**

AMENDMENTS AND NOTES

<sup>a</sup> For application to LLPs, see reg 73 of the Limited Liability Partnerships (Application of Companies Act 2006) Regulations 2009, SI 2009/1804.

COMMENCEMENT DATE  1 October 2007,[62] 6 April 2008,[63] 1 October 2008[64]

This provision, which replicates section 31 of the Companies Consolidation Consequential Provisions Act 1985, indicates that the foregoing provisions on offences (with the exception of section 1132) are not retrospective. Thus, the law here is ECHR-compliant—see in particular the requirements of ECHR, Article 7. This is subject to limitation under Companies Act 2006, section 1028 for summary proceedings.          **36.1133.02**

---

[59] Companies Act 2006 (Commencement No 3, etc) Order 2007, SI 2007/2194.
[60] Companies Act 2006 (Commencement No 5, Transitional Provisions and Savings) Order 2007, SI 2007/3495.
[61] Companies Act 2006 (Commencement No 5, Transitional Provisions and Savings) Order 2007, SI 2007/3495.
[62] Companies Act 2006 (Commencement No 3, etc) Order 2007, SI 2007/2194.
[63] Companies Act 2006 (Commencement No 5, Transitional Provisions and Savings) Order 2007, SI 2007/3495.
[64] Companies Act 2006 (Commencement No 5, Transitional Provisions and Savings) Order 2007, SI 2007/3495.

# 37

## COMPANIES: SUPPLEMENTARY PROVISIONS

## Companies Act 2006

### PART 37
### COMPANIES: SUPPLEMENTARY PROVISIONS

*Company records*

### 1134 Meaning of 'company records'

In this Part 'company records' means—
(a) any register, index, accounting records, agreement, memorandum, minutes or other document required by the Companies Acts to be kept by a company, and
(b) any register kept by a company of its debenture holders various.

COMMENCEMENT DATE Various but unconditionally in force from 1 October 2009[1]

**37.1134.01**

This section is new. Previously there was no definition of 'company records' although the term was used in section 723 of the Companies Act 1985. The main section in relation to record keeping, section 722, covered any register, index, minute book, or accounting records required to be kept. The new definition is wider and covers all documents required to be kept. No commencement date has been set for the provisions in relation to company records in Part 37 of the Act.

**37.1134.02**

---

[1] Sections 1134, 1135 and 1138 commenced when any substantive sections relating to 'company records' were commenced. See art 2(2)(d) of the Companies Act 2006 (Commencement No 2, Consequential Amendments, Transitional Provisions, and Savings) Order 2007, SI 2007/1093, which brought them into force on 6 April 2007 for the purposes of provisions of CA 2006 brought into force on that date by art 2(1) of that Order. The section was brought unconditionally into force from 1 October 2009 by the Companies Act 2008 (Commencement No 8, Transitional Provisions and Savings) Order 2008, SI 2008/2860, art 3(t).

### 1135  Form of company records

**37.1135.01**
(1) Company records—
   (a) may be kept in hard copy or electronic form, and
   (b) may be arranged in such manner as the directors of the company think fit,
   provided the information in question is adequately recorded for future reference.
(2) Where the records are kept in electronic form, they must be capable of being reproduced in hard copy form.
(3) If a company fails to comply with this section, an offence is committed by every officer of the company who is in default.
(4) A person guilty of an offence under this section is liable on summary conviction to a fine not exceeding level 3 on the standard scale and, for continued contravention, a daily default fine not exceeding one-tenth of level 3 on the standard scale.
(5) Any provision of an instrument made by a company before 12th February 1979 that requires a register of holders of the company's debentures to be kept in hard copy form is to be read as requiring it to be kept in hard copy or electronic form.

COMMENCEMENT DATE  Various but unconditionally in force from 1 October 2009[2]

**37.1135.02**    Section 1135 replaces sections 722(1) and 723 of the Companies Act 1985. It reflects a more modern approach to record keeping by emphasizing that the aim of the section is the recording of records in an adequate form for future reference and by using more modern terminology[3] (subsection (1)). Accordingly companies are allowed to keep records in hard copy or electronic form[4] (subsection (1)(a)) and arranged in such manner as the directors think fit (subsection (1)(b)).

**37.1135.03**    Subsection (2) replaces and repeats the requirement of section 723(1) of the Companies Act 1985. Documents held in electronic form must be capable of being reproduced in hard copy form.

**37.1135.04**    Subsections (3) and (4) create an offence committed by any officer of the company who is in default of the provisions of subsections (1) and (2).

**37.1135.05**    Subsection (5) repeats section 723(2) of the Companies Act 1985.[5]

### 1136  Regulations about where certain company records to be kept available for inspection

**37.1136.01**
(1) The Secretary of State may make provision by regulations specifying places other than a company's registered office at which company records required to be kept available for inspection under a relevant provision may be so kept in compliance with that provision.
(2) The 'relevant provisions' are—
   section 114 (register of members);
   section 162 (register of directors);
   section 228 (directors' service contracts);
   section 237 (directors' indemnities);
   section 275 (register of secretaries);
   section 358 (records of resolutions etc);
   section 702 (contracts relating to purchase of own shares);
   section 720 (documents relating to redemption or purchase of own shares out of capital by private company);
   section 743 (register of debenture holders);
   section 805 (report to members of outcome of investigation by public company into interests in its shares);
   section 809 (register of interests in shares disclosed to public company);
   section 877 (instruments creating charges and register of charges: England and Wales);
   section 892 (instruments creating charges and register of charges: Scotland).
(3) The regulations may specify a place by reference to the company's principal place of business, the part of the United Kingdom in which the company is registered, the place at which the company keeps any other records available for inspection or in any other way.
(4) The regulations may provide that a company does not comply with a relevant provision by keeping company records available for inspection at a place specified in the regulations unless conditions specified in the regulations are met.
(5) The regulations—

---

[2]  See n 1 to para 37.1134.01.
[3]  Eg references to 'bound books' (such as in CA 1985, s 722(1)) have been removed.
[4]  The recording of records other than in bound books was allowed under CA 1985, s 723(1).
[5]  The date, 12 Feb 1979, is the date on which the Stock Exchange (Completion of Bargains) Act 1976 came into force.

(a)   need not specify a place in relation to each relevant provision;

(b)   may specify more than one place in relation to a relevant provision.

(6)   A requirement under a relevant provision to keep company records available for inspection is not complied with by keeping them available for inspection at a place specified in the regulations unless all the company's records subject to the requirement are kept there.

(7)   Regulations under this section are subject to negative resolution procedure.

COMMENCEMENT DATE  20 January 2007[6]

Section 1136 is new. It allows the Secretary of State to make regulations specifying places where a company may retain those records identified in subsection (2), which essentially comprise the various registers, records of resolutions, and minutes of meetings, reports, contracts, and instruments which the Act requires are kept available for inspection. Previously a company had no choice but to keep specified records at its registered office. Regulations made under this provision are subject to the negative resolution procedure (subsection (7)).   **37.1136.02**

The discretion to specify places is unfettered (and the Secretary of State may specify more than one place for any category of documents) but subsection (3) identifies a number of particular examples. The regulations may also apply conditions on the ability of a company to retain records at a specified place.   **37.1136.03**

As a result of subsection (6), if a company chooses to keep its records at a specified place it must keep all such records there. Thus, for example, it would not be able to keep some but not all of its directors' service contracts at a specified location. The rationale for this is that a person entitled to inspect particular records should be able to access all of them at one location.   **37.1136.04**

## 1137   Regulations about inspection of records and provision of copies

(1)   The Secretary of State may make provision by regulations as to the obligations of a company that is required by any provision of the Companies Acts—   **37.1137.01**

(a)   to keep available for inspection any company records, or

(b)   to provide copies of any company records.

(2)   A company that fails to comply with the regulations is treated as having refused inspection or, as the case may be, having failed to provide a copy.

(3)   The regulations may—

(a)   make provision as to the time, duration and manner of inspection, including the circumstances in which and extent to which the copying of information is permitted in the course of inspection, and

(b)   define what may be required of the company as regards the nature, extent and manner of extracting or presenting any information for the purposes of inspection or the provision of copies.

(4)   Where there is power to charge a fee, the regulations may make provision as to the amount of the fee and the basis of its calculation.

(5)   Nothing in any provision of this Act or in the regulations shall be read as preventing a company—

(a)   from affording more extensive facilities than are required by the regulations, or

(b)   where a fee may be charged, from charging a lesser fee than that prescribed or none at all.

(6)   Regulations under this section are subject to negative resolution procedure.

COMMENCEMENT DATE  20 January 2007,[7] 30 September 2007,[8] and 1 October 2009[9]

---

[6]  Sections 1136 and 1137 have been in force since 20 January 2007 pursuant to art 3(3) of the Companies Act 2006 (Commencement No 1, Transitional Provisions and Savings) Order 2006, for the purposes of exercising powers to make secondary legislation. Section 1136 is brought unconditionally into force from 1 October 2009 by the Companies Act 2008 (Commencement No 8, Transitional Provisions and Savings) Order 2008, SI 2008/2860, art 3(t). The Commencement No 4 Order, SI 2007/2607, also makes express provision for parts of s 1137 to come into force; as to which, see n 7.

[7]  Sections 1136 and 1137 have been in force since 20 January 2007 pursuant to art 3(3) of the Companies Act 2006 (Commencement No 1, Transitional Provisions and Savings) Order 2006, SI 2006/3428 for the purposes of exercising powers to make secondary legislation. It should be noted, however, that the Commencement No 4 Order, SI 2007/2607 and the Commencement No 8 Order, SI 2008/2860, also make express provision for different parts of s 1137 to come into force; as to which, see nn 8 and 9 below.

[8]  Companies Act 2006 (Commencement No 4, etc) Order 2007, SI 2007/2607 as regards s 1137(1), (4), (5)(b) and (6). As noted in fn 7 above, these sections were already in force pursuant to the No 1 Commencement Order.

[9]  Companies Act 2008 (Commencement No 8, Transitional Provisions and Savings) Order 2008, SI 2008/2860, art 3(t) as regards s 1137(2), (3) and 5(a).

**37.1137.02**  Section 1137 replaces section 723A of the Companies Act 1985 with the substitution of 'company records' for 'register, index or document' and the deletion of section 723A(5).[10] The Secretary of State may make regulations relating to the substantive obligations of a company to make its records available for inspection and to provide copies, such as under section 358 (records of resolutions and meetings). The regulations may cover matters such as the practicalities of inspection, the manner in which copies are to be provided, and any fees to be paid.[11] Regulations made under this provision are subject to the negative resolution procedure (subsection (6)).

**37.1137.03**  Subsections (1) and (2) cover the provisions previously in section 723A(1) of the Companies Act 1985, subsection (3) repeats section 723A(2) and (3), subsection (4) repeats section 723A(4), subsection (5) repeats section 723A(6), and subsection (6) replaces section 723A(7).

### 1138  Duty to take precautions against falsification

**37.1138.01**    (1) Where company records are kept otherwise than in bound books, adequate precautions must be taken—
    (a) to guard against falsification, and
    (b) to facilitate the discovery of falsification.
  (2) If a company fails to comply with this section, an offence is committed by every officer of the company who is in default.
  (3) A person guilty of an offence under this section is liable on summary conviction to a fine not exceeding level 3 on the standard scale and, for continued contravention, a daily default fine not exceeding one-tenth of level 3 on the standard scale.
  (4) This section does not apply to the documents required to be kept under—
    (a) section 228 (copy of director's service contract or memorandum of its terms); or
    (b) section 237 (qualifying indemnity provision).

COMMENCEMENT DATE  Various but unconditionally in force from 1 October 2009[12]

**37.1138.02**  Section 1138 replaces sections 722(2) and (3) of the Companies Act 1985. The obligation to take adequate precautions against falsification and to facilitate its discovery still applies to company records kept other than (a) those kept in bound books (subsection (1)(a)) and (b) copies of directors' service contracts, memoranda of their terms, and qualifying third party indemnity provisions benefiting a director (subsection (4)). It would have been preferable for the obligation to apply to all records but the exceptions are very limited. As before, every officer of a company who is in default commits an offence (subsection (2)).

## *Service addresses*

### 1139  Service of documents on company

**37.1139.01**    (1) A document may be served on a company registered under this Act by leaving it at, or sending it by post to, the company's registered office.
  (2) A document may be served on an overseas company whose particulars are registered under section 1046—
    (a) by leaving it at, or sending it by post to, the registered address of any person resident in the United Kingdom who is authorised to accept service of documents on the company's behalf, or
    (b) if there is no such person, or if any such person refuses service or service cannot for any other reason be effected, by leaving it at or sending by post to any place of business of the company in the United Kingdom.
  (3) For the purposes of this section a person's 'registered address' means any address for the time being shown as a current address in relation to that person in the part of the register available for public inspection.
  (4) Where a company registered in Scotland or Northern Ireland carries on business in England and Wales, the process of any court in England and Wales may be served on the company by leaving

---

[10] The deletion of this subsection, which allowed the regulations to make different provision for different classes of case, should not prevent regulations under the new Act from making such different provisions. The discretion of the Secretary of State to make regulations under s 1137 is broad.

[11] Regulations made so far under s 1137 include the Companies (Fees for Inspection and Copying of Company Records) Regulations 2007, SI 2007/2612; the Companies (Fees for Inspection and Copying of Company Records) (No 2) Regulations 2007, SI 2007/3535; the Companies (Company Records) Regulations 2008, SI 2008/3006; the Companies (Fees for Inspection of Company Records) Regulations 2008, SI 2008/3007.

[12] The section is brought unconditionally into force from 1 October 2009 by the Companies Act 2008 (Commencement No 8, Transitional Provisions and Savings) Order 2008, SI 2008/2860, art 3(t). See also n 1 to s 1134 above.

it at, or sending it by post to, the company's principal place of business in England and Wales, addressed to the manager or other head officer in England and Wales of the company. Where process is served on a company under this subsection, the person issuing out the process must send a copy of it by post to the company's registered office.

(5) Further provision as to service and other matters is made in the company communications provisions (see section 1143).

COMMENCEMENT DATE  Various but unconditionally in force from 1 October 2009[13]

Section 1139 replaces sections 694A, 695 and 725 of the Companies Act 1985. All companies registered in the UK must have a place at which documents can be served.     **37.1139.02**

Subsection (1) replaces section 725(1) of the Companies Act 1985 and provides for service at the registered office of a company registered under the Companies Acts. As before, it is not an exhaustive provision in respect of service on a company and reference must also be had to CPR Part 6.     **37.1139.03**

Subsection (2) replaces sections 694A and 695 of the Companies Act 1985 which applied to companies incorporated outside of the UK and Gibraltar but which had a branch in Great Britain, and to overseas companies respectively. The provisions of subsection (2) apply to all overseas companies whose particulars are registered[14] under section 1046 of the Act[15] and are not limited to the service of documentation relating to the operation of the company in the UK.[16] The provisions of subsection (2) are not an exhaustive provision and service may be effected by any other applicable provision. Previously section 694A was permissive[17] but section 695 was mandatory.[18]     **37.1139.04**

A body of law developed in relation to sections 694A and 695 of the Companies Act 1985 and, notwithstanding the changes to the registration regime, decisions in relation to sections which have largely been repeated are likely to remain of relevance. In particular, as now, sections 694A and 695 had a default provision allowing for service to be made on an established place of business, a phrase which had been considered on several occasions.[19]     **37.1139.05**

Subsection (4) replaces section 725(2) of the Companies Act 1985 in respect of companies registered in Scotland, and extends its operation to companies registered in Northern Ireland. There is still no definition of principal place of business.[20] Sending by post is defined in section 7 of the Interpretation Act 1978 and requires a document to be properly addressed, pre-paid, and posted.     **37.1139.06**

## 1140   Service of documents on directors, secretaries and others

(1) A document may be served on a person to whom this section applies by leaving it at, or sending it by post to, the person's registered address.     **37.1140.01**

(2) This section applies to—
  (a) a director or secretary of a company;
  (b) in the case of an overseas company whose particulars are registered under section 1046, a person holding any such position as may be specified for the purposes of this section by regulations under that section;
  (c) a person appointed in relation to a company as—
    (i) a judicial factor (in Scotland),

---

[13]  Sections 1139–1142 commenced when any substantive sections relating to 'service addresses' were commenced. See Article 2(2)(e) and (f) of the Companies Act 2006 (Commencement No 2, Consequential Amendments, Transitional Provisions and Savings) Order 2007 SI 2007/1093. See also Sch 1, para 5 of that Order for a transitional amendment to s 1139(1). They were brought unconditionally into force from 1 October 2009 by the Companies Act 2008 (Commencement No 8, Transitional Provisions and Savings) Order 2008, SI 2008/2860, art 3(t).

[14]  Where a company no longer carries on business in the UK and has removed its registration under s 1056, service will no longer be possible under this section on a person authorized to accept service. This is the consequence of the use of the present tense in s 1139(2). Compare the previous position as exemplified by *Rome v Punjab National Bank (No 2)* [1990] BCLC 20.

[15]  See s 1046 and the accompanying notes for a more detailed explanation of the registration system.

[16]  The provisions of s 694A applied if the process or notice to be served was in respect of the carrying on of business of the branch registered.

[17]  *Sea Assets Ltd v PT Garuda Indonesia* [2000] 4 All ER 371.

[18]  See *Boocock v Hilton International Co* [1993] 1 WLR 1065.

[19]  The provision also required the place of business to be existing at the time of service: *Deverall v Grant Advertising Inc* [1955] Ch 111. Further, the fact that a company had an agent who received orders and transmitted them to the company abroad did not give it a place of business established by it in Great Britain: *Rakusens Ltd v Baser Ambalaj Plastik Sanayi Ticaret AS* [2002] 1 BCLC 104.

[20]  The term 'principal office' is used in the Companies Clauses Consolidation Act 1845. See also *Palmer v Caledonian Rly Co* [1892] 1 QB 823.

       (ii) a receiver and manager appointed under section 18 of the Charities Act 1993 (c. 10), or

       (iii) a manager appointed under section 47 of the Companies (Audit, Investigations and Community Enterprise) Act 2004 (c. 27).

(3) This section applies whatever the purpose of the document in question.

It is not restricted to service for purposes arising out of or in connection with the appointment or position mentioned in subsection (2) or in connection with the company concerned.

(4) For the purposes of this section a person's 'registered address' means any address for the time being shown as a current address in relation to that person in the part of the register available for public inspection.

(5) If notice of a change of that address is given to the registrar, a person may validly serve a document at the address previously registered until the end of the period of 14 days beginning with the date on which notice of the change is registered.

(6) Service may not be effected by virtue of this section at an address—

       (a) if notice has been registered of the termination of the appointment in relation to which the address was registered and the address is not a registered address of the person concerned in relation to any other appointment;

       (b) in the case of a person holding any such position as is mentioned in subsection (2)(b), if the overseas company has ceased to have any connection with the United Kingdom by virtue of which it is required to register particulars under section 1046.

(7) Further provision as to service and other matters is made in the company communications provisions (see section 1143).

(8) Nothing in this section shall be read as affecting any enactment or rule of law under which permission is required for service out of the jurisdiction.

COMMENCEMENT DATE Various but unconditionally in force from 1 October 2009[21]

**37.1140.02**    Section 1140 is new. It provides for service at a registered address (as defined in subsection (4)), where the person being served is a director or secretary of a company, a person specified under the registration provisions for overseas companies, or the holder of certain other specified positions (subsection (2)). Most notably this provision will provide a method of service even where the document being served does not relate to the carrying out by the person being served of any function in relation to the company (subsection 3)).

**37.1140.03**    This section is linked to the changes to the particulars which must be registered for directors and secretaries. Whereas previously their home addresses had to be recorded on the register available for inspection (unless the limited exceptions for those subject to intimidation applied), the register of directors and secretaries now only has to include a service address which may be the company's registered office.[22]

**37.1140.04**    It should also be noted that (i) this section is not exclusive; (ii) reference must therefore be made to CPR part 6 for other methods of service; and (iii) the section does not allow for service where any enactment or rule of law requires permission for service out of the jurisdiction.[23]

**37.1140.05**    Subsection (6)(b) effectively overrules the position which applied previously under section 695 as a result of the decision in *Rome v Punjab National Bank (No 2)*.[24] Once an overseas company has ceased to have any connection with the UK service will not be possible on a person registered under section 1046 even if the entry remains on the register.

### 1141 Service addresses

**37.1141.01**    (1) In the Companies Acts a 'service address', in relation to a person, means an address at which documents may be effectively served on that person.

(2) The Secretary of State may by regulations specify conditions with which a service address must comply.

(3) Regulations under this section are subject to negative resolution procedure

COMMENCEMENT DATE Various but unconditionally in force from 1 October 2009[25]

---

[21] See n 13 to s 1139 above.

[22] See ss 162–167 (directors) and ss 275–279 (secretaries) of the Act and the accompanying notes for a more detailed explanation of the changes, and s 1141 for the definition of a service address.

[23] See CPR Part 6 for such provisions.

[24] [1990] BCLC 20.

[25] As regards substantive commencement, see n 13 above. As regards the power to make regulations, s 1141 has been in force since 20 January 2007 pursuant to art 3(3) of the Companies Act 2006 (Commencement No 1, Transitional Provisions and Savings) Order 2006, SI 2006/3428.

This section replaces section 723C(7) of the Companies Act 1985. This section (and sections 723B and **37.1141.02**
D–F) which allowed for confidentiality orders to be made in respect of a director's or secretary's home
address have been swept away under the Act. For example, as a result of section 163 there is no longer
any requirement for a home address to appear on the register of directors but rather a service address
must be given, and under sections 241 and 242 a director's usual residential address is 'protected
information' and must not be disclosed by the company or by the Registrar of Companies save in
certain specified circumstances. As a result the confidentiality order regime is no longer required.

As to the regulations, see part 3 of the Companies Act 2006 (Annual Returns and Service Addresses)   **37.1141.03**
Regulations 2008.[26]

## 1142  Requirement to give service address

Any obligation under the Companies Acts to give a person's address is, unless otherwise expressly   **37.1142.01**
provided, to give a service address for that person.

> COMMENCEMENT DATE  Various but unconditionally in force from 1 October 2009[27]

Section 1142 is new. It clarifies those sections of the Act where the type of address required is not made   **37.1142.02**
expressly clear. As referred to under sections 1140 and 1141 above, the new provisions in relation to
registration of particulars of directors and secretaries already use the term 'service address'.

### *Sending or supplying documents or information*

## 1143  The company communications provisions

(1) The provisions of sections 1144 to 1148 and Schedules 4 and 5 ('the company communications   **37.1143.01**
provisions') have effect for the purposes of any provision of the Companies Acts that authorises
or requires documents or information to be sent or supplied by or to a company.
(2) The company communications provisions have effect subject to any requirements imposed, or
contrary provision made, by or under any enactment.
(3) In particular, in their application in relation to documents or information to be sent or supplied to
the registrar, they have effect subject to the provisions of Part 35.
(4) For the purposes of subsection (2), provision is not to be regarded as contrary to the company
communications provisions by reason only of the fact that it expressly authorises a document or
information to be sent or supplied in hard copy form, in electronic form or by means of a website.

> COMMENCEMENT DATE  20 January 2007[28]

Sections 1144 to 1148 and Schedules 4 and 5 of the Act provide a new regime detailing the manner in   **37.1143.02**
which a company may communicate where authorized or required to do so under the Act, and how the
company may be communicated with in such circumstances. These are referred to in the Act as the
'company communications provisions' and were amongst the first provisions in the Act to be brought
into force: they commenced on 20 January 2007,[29] the date on which the EU Transparency Directive
(2004/109/EC), which required certain of the changes in respect of traded companies, came into force.

Whereas previously the Companies Act 1985 (Electronic Communications) Order 2000 (SI 2000/   **37.1143.03**
3373) allowed the use of electronic and web-based communications in certain circumstances,[30] there
was no general provision covering communications from companies as a whole. The new sections
modernize company law in this regard by creating a default position that electronic communications
are permitted if approved by the shareholders. Individual shareholders are, however, allowed to
request paper communication if they wish. The wider use of electronic communication is intended to
bring significant cost savings to business and to improve access to information.

Section 1143 introduces the new provisions by applying them to all provisions requiring documents or   **37.1143.04**
information to be sent or supplied by or to a company (subsection (1)). These provisions are expressly
subject to the requirements of any other enactment (subsection (2)), and, in the case of information to
be provided to the registrar of companies, are subject to Part 35 of the Act (subsection (3)).[31] However,
where a provision under another enactment expressly authorizes a document or information to be

---

[26]  SI 2008/3000.
[27]  See n 13 above.
[28]  Sections 1143–1148 have been in force since 20 January 2007 pursuant to the Companies Act 2006
(Commencement No 1, Transitional Provisions and Savings) Order 2006, SI 2006/3428.
[29]  Companies Act 2006 (Commencement No 1, Transitional Provisions and Savings) Order 2006, SI 2006/
3428.
[30]  This SI operated by adding sections in relation to electronic communications to particular sections of CA
1985 and Table A rather than providing any general provisions.
[31]  See Part 35 and the accompanying notes for the provisions applying to the Registrar of Companies.

provided in a particular form (hard copy, electronic, or by means of a website) that provision is not to be treated as contrary to the company communication provisions. Regulation 79 of the model Plc articles applies the company communication provisions to anything sent or supplied to a public company.

## 1144 Sending or supplying documents or information

**37.1144.01**
(1) Documents or information to be sent or supplied to a company must be sent or supplied in accordance with the provisions of Schedule 4.
(2) Documents or information to be sent or supplied by a company must be sent or supplied in accordance with the provisions of Schedule 5.
(3) The provisions referred to in subsection (2) apply (and those referred to in subsection (1) do not apply) in relation to documents or information that are to be sent or supplied by one company to another

COMMENCEMENT DATE 20 January 2007[32]

**37.1144.02**
Section 1144 introduces Schedules 4 and 5 which provide the detailed provisions relating to the provision of documents/information to a company (Schedule 4) and by a company (Schedule 5). As originally drafted the Act drew a distinction between the provision of documents by a traded company and by any other company. Indeed there were separate draft schedules for the two classes of company. This distinction was not carried through into the final form of the Act. Where a document or information is to be provided by one company to another, the provisions pertaining to the supplying company apply and those relating to the receiving company are disapplied (subsection (3)). The schedules use the terms defined in section 1148.

## 1145 Right to hard copy version

**37.1145.01**
(1) Where a member of a company or a holder of a company's debentures has received a document or information from the company otherwise than in hard copy form, he is entitled to require the company to send him a version of the document or information in hard copy form.
(2) The company must send the document or information in hard copy form within 21 days of receipt of the request from the member or debenture holder.
(3) The company may not make a charge for providing the document or information in that form.
(4) If a company fails to comply with this section, an offence is committed by the company and every officer of it who is in default.
(5) A person guilty of an offence under this section is liable on summary conviction to a fine not exceeding level 3 on the standard scale and, for continued contravention, a daily default fine not exceeding one-tenth of level 3 on the standard scale.

COMMENCEMENT DATE 20 January 2007[33]

**37.1145.02**
Section 1145 allows a member or debenture holder to request a document or information in hard copy form after receipt of a document or information otherwise than in hard copy. The document or information must be sent within 21 days of the receipt by the company of the request (subsection (2)) and must be provided free of charge (subsection (3)). Failure to comply with the provisions of section 1145 is an offence committed by both the company and every officer of it who is in default (subsections (4) and (5)). As originally drafted this section contained an additional subsection which made this right subject to the provisions of any other enactment which provided a different rule. However, this draft section was removed by amendment and therefore the right has no limitations.

## 1146 Requirement of authentication

**37.1146.01**
(1) This section applies in relation to the authentication of a document or information sent or supplied by a person to a company.
(2) A document or information sent or supplied in hard copy form is sufficiently authenticated if it is signed by the person sending or supplying it.
(3) A document or information sent or supplied in electronic form is sufficiently authenticated—
(a) if the identity of the sender is confirmed in a manner specified by the company, or
(b) where no such manner has been specified by the company, if the communication contains or is accompanied by a statement of the identity of the sender and the company has no reason to doubt the truth of that statement.

---

[32] Companies Act 2006 (Commencement No 1, etc) Order 2006, SI 2006/3428.
[33] Companies Act 2006 (Commencement No 1, etc) Order 2006, SI 2006/3428.

(4)  Where a document or information is sent or supplied by one person on behalf of another, nothing in this section affects any provision of the company's articles under which the company may require reasonable evidence of the authority of the former to act on behalf of the latter.

COMMENCEMENT DATE  20 January 2007[34]

Section 1146 sets out how a person can satisfy the requirement to authenticate[35] documents or information sent or supplied to a company. Where authentication is required a person can either sign the document if sent in hard copy (subsection (2)), comply with any requirements specified by the company for electronic communications (subsection (3)(a)), or, if no such requirements are specified, include a statement of his identity in, or send such a statement with, his communication (subsection (3)(b)). This section does not affect any requirements imposed by a company where the documents are sent by one person on behalf of another (subsection (4)). Thus a company can require evidence that the person sending the documents or information is authorized to do so.    **37.1146.02**

## 1147  Deemed delivery of documents and information

(1)  This section applies in relation to documents and information sent or supplied by a company.    **37.1147.01**
(2)  Where—
    (a)  the document or information is sent by post (whether in hard copy or electronic form) to an address in the United Kingdom, and
    (b)  the company is able to show that it was properly addressed, prepaid and posted,
    it is deemed to have been received by the intended recipient 48 hours after it was posted.
(3)  Where—
    (a)  the document or information is sent or supplied by electronic means, and
    (b)  the company is able to show that it was properly addressed,
    it is deemed to have been received by the intended recipient 48 hours after it was sent.
(4)  Where the document or information is sent or supplied by means of a website, it is deemed to have been received by the intended recipient—
    (a)  when the material was first made available on the website, or
    (b)  if later, when the recipient received (or is deemed to have received) notice of the fact that the material was available on the website.
(5)  In calculating a period of hours for the purposes of this section, no account shall be taken of any part of a day that is not a working day.
(6)  This section has effect subject to—
    (a)  in its application to documents or information sent or supplied by a company to its members, any contrary provision of the company's articles;
    (b)  in its application to documents or information sent or supplied by a company to its debentures holders, any contrary provision in the instrument constituting the debentures;
    (c)  in its application to documents or information sent or supplied by a company to a person otherwise than in his capacity as a member or debenture holder, any contrary provision in an agreement between the company and that person.

COMMENCEMENT DATE  20 January 2007[36]

Section 1147 provides the default position in relation to the fact and time of delivery of documents sent by a company. Where documents are sent by post or in electronic form they are deemed to be delivered 48 hours after posting or being sent respectively provided that they are properly addressed and, in the case of posting, prepaid and posted (subsections (2) and (3)). The provision in relation to the use of the post also applies to documents sent by post but which are in electronic form, presumably a reference to telegrams. Under subsection (4) the supply of information by means of a website is deemed to take place on the later of the making available of the information on the website or the receipt (deemed or actual) of notice that the material is available on the website.    **37.1147.02**

The section is subject to any contrary provisions relating to the provision of documentation or information by a company (i) to its members set out in its articles; (ii) to its debenture holders set out in the instrument creating the debenture; and (iii) to any person set out in any agreement between a company and that person (other than in his capacity as a member or debenture holder). The effect of these provisions is that all members or debenture holders must be subject to the same provisions and a company cannot, for example, make particular arrangements with individual members. Further, the deemed delivery provisions appear to apply to information supplied to a company by any person irrespective of any contrary provision as the exception for contrary provisions is limited to the provision of information by a company.    **37.1147.03**

---

[34]  Companies Act 2006 (Commencement No 1, etc) Order 2006, SI 2006/3428.
[35]  Such as in s 314(4) in relation to a request to circulate a members' statement.
[36]  Companies Act 2006 (Commencement No 1, etc) Order 2006, SI 2006/3428.

## 1148 Interpretation of company communications provisions

**37.1148.01**
(1) In the company communications provisions—
'address' includes a number or address used for the purposes of sending or receiving documents or information by electronic means;
'company' includes any body corporate;
'document' includes summons, notice, order or other legal process and registers.
(2) References in the company communications provisions to provisions of the Companies Acts authorising or requiring a document or information to be sent or supplied include all such provisions, whatever expression is used, and references to documents or information being sent or supplied shall be construed accordingly.
(3) References in the company communications provisions to documents or information being sent or supplied by or to a company include references to documents or information being sent or supplied by or to the directors of a company acting on behalf of the company.

COMMENCEMENT DATE 20 January 2007[37]

**37.1148.02**    The most notable features of the definition provisions set out in section 1148 are that the definitions of 'address' and 'document' are not exhaustive and that, pursuant to subsections (2) and (3), the company communication provisions apply to all provisions relating to the sending or supply of documents whether those particular words are used or not.

### *Requirements as to independent valuation*

## 1149 Application of valuation requirements

**37.1149.01**
The provisions of sections 1150 to 1153 apply to the valuation and report required by—
section 93 (re-registration as public company: recent allotment of shares for non-cash consideration);
section 593 (allotment of shares of public company in consideration of non-cash asset);
section 599 (transfer of non-cash asset to public company).

COMMENCEMENT DATE 1 October 2009[38]

**37.1149.02**    Sections 1149 to 1153 set out provisions in relation to the independent valuation and report required by three other sections of the Act: sections 93, 593, and 599.[39] These provisions apply only to public companies (or in the first case a private company seeking to re-register as a public company).

## 1150 Valuation by qualified independent person

**37.1150.01**
(1) The valuation and report must be made by a person ('the valuer') who—
(a) is eligible for appointment as a statutory auditor (see section 1212), and
(b) meets the independence requirement in section 1151.
(2) However, where it appears to the valuer to be reasonable for the valuation of the consideration, or part of it, to be made by (or for him to accept a valuation made by) another person who—
(a) appears to him to have the requisite knowledge and experience to value the consideration or that part of it, and
(b) is not an officer or employee of—
(i) the company, or
(ii) any other body corporate that is that company's subsidiary or holding company or a subsidiary of that company's holding company,
or a partner of or employed by any such officer or employee, he may arrange for or accept such a valuation, together with a report which will enable him to make his own report under this section.
(3) The references in subsection (2)(b) to an officer or employee do not include an auditor.
(4) Where the consideration or part of it is valued by a person other than the valuer himself, the latter's report must state that fact and shall also—
(a) state the former's name and what knowledge and experience he has to carry out the valuation, and
(b) describe so much of the consideration as was valued by the other person, and the method used to value it, and specify the date of that valuation.

---

[37]  Companies Act 2006 (Commencement No 1, etc) Order 2006, SI 2006/3428.
[38]  Companies Act 2008 (Commencement No 8, Transitional Provisions and Savings) Order 2008, SI 2008/2860, art 3(t). The date originally intended (1 October 2008) was put back by a year in late 2007.
[39]  Regard should be had to the notes for these particular sections for detailed commentary on each.

COMMENCEMENT DATE  1 October 2009[40]

Section 1150 replaces section 108(1) to (3) and (5) of the Companies Act 1985 in respect of valuations   **37.1150.02**
required for re-registration as a public company (under section 93 of the Act)[41] and the allotment of
shares in a public company in consideration of non-cash assets (under section 593 of the Act),[42] and
section 109 of the Companies Act 1985 in respect of the transfer of a non-cash asset to a public
company (under section 599 of the Act).[43]

Subsection (1) repeats the provision of section 108(1) of the Companies Act 1985 that the valuer must   **37.1150.03**
be a person eligible for appointment as a statutory auditor. However, it also adds a requirement that the
independence test in section 1151 be satisfied rather than, as with section 108, treating without more a
person qualified to be appointed as auditor of the company as an independent person.

Subsections (2), (3), and (4) repeat in material terms sections 108(2), 108(3), and 108(5) of the   **37.1150.04**
Companies Act 1985. The independent valuer may arrange for the valuation or part of it to be carried
out by another person provided that he appears to the valuer to have the requisite knowledge and
experience to carry out the task and is not disqualified by the provisions of subsection 2(b) (which
apply to officers and employees of the company or companies with a specified connection, and to
partners or employees of any such officer or employee) from so acting. Auditors are not excluded
notwithstanding the reference in subsection 2(b) to officers and employees. The independent valuer's
report must include the details of the third party valuation arranged by him (subsection (4)).

## 1151   The independence requirement

(1)  A person meets the independence requirement for the purposes of section 1150 only if—   **37.1151.01**
    (a)  he is not—
        (i)   an officer or employee of the company, or
        (ii)  a partner or employee of such a person, or a partnership of which such a person is a
            partner;
    (b)  he is not—
        (i)   an officer or employee of an associated undertaking of the company, or
        (ii)  a partner or employee of such a person, or a partnership of which such a person is a
            partner; and
    (c)  there does not exist between—
        (i)   the person or an associate of his, and
        (ii)  the company or an associated undertaking of the company,
      a connection of any such description as may be specified by regulations made by the Secretary
      of State.
(2)  An auditor of the company is not regarded as an officer or employee of the company for this
    purpose.
(3)  In this section—
    'associated undertaking' means—
    (a)  a parent undertaking or subsidiary undertaking of the company, or
    (b)  a subsidiary undertaking of a parent undertaking of the company; and
    'associate' has the meaning given by section 1152.
(4)  Regulations under this section are subject to negative resolution procedure.

COMMENCEMENT DATE  1 October 2009[44]

Section 1151 mirrors the test of independence applied to a statutory auditor by section 1241 of the Act.   **37.1151.02**
The requirements as to independence are wider than are provided in section 1150(2) in respect of other
persons who make valuations at the request of the independent valuer. By way of example a person is
not independent if he is a partner or employee of a partnership in which an officer or employee of the
company is also a partner (subsection (1)(a)(ii)) or if he is an officer or employee of an associated
undertaking[45] (subsection (1)(b)(i)). Further, subsection (1)(c) provides a new power for the Secretary

---

[40]  Companies Act 2008 (Commencement No 8, Transitional Provisions and Savings) Order 2008, SI 2008/
2860, art 3(t).
[41]  Previously s 44 of CA 1985.
[42]  Previously s 103 of CA 1985.
[43]  Previously s 104 of CA 1985.
[44]  Companies Act 2008 (Commencement No 8, Transitional Provisions and Savings) Order 2008, SI 2008/
2860, art 3(t). Note, however, that for the purpose of making regulations, s 1151(1)(c)(ii) was in force from 20
January 2007 pursuant to art 3(3) of the Companies Act 2006 (Commencement No 1, Transitional Provisions and
Savings) Order 2006, SI 2006/3428.
[45]  Defined in s 1151(3) so as to catch other companies in the same group.

of State to make regulations specifying connections between a person or his associate[46] and the company or any associate undertaking which would cause a person to fail to meet the independence requirement. Similar powers are given by sections 344 and 936 of the Act which also refer to an independence requirement.

## 1152 Meaning of 'associate'

**37.1152.01**
(1) This section defines 'associate' for the purposes of section 1151 (valuation: independence requirement).
(2) In relation to an individual, 'associate' means—
    (a) that individual's spouse or civil partner or minor child or step-child,
    (b) any body corporate of which that individual is a director, and
    (c) any employee or partner of that individual.
(3) In relation to a body corporate, 'associate' means—
    (a) any body corporate of which that body is a director,
    (b) any body corporate in the same group as that body, and
    (c) any employee or partner of that body or of any body corporate in the same group.
(4) In relation to a partnership that is a legal person under the law by which it is governed, 'associate' means—
    (a) any body corporate of which that partnership is a director,
    (b) any employee of or partner in that partnership, and
    (c) any person who is an associate of a partner in that partnership.
(5) In relation to a partnership that is not a legal person under the law by which it is governed, 'associate' means any person who is an associate of any of the partners.
(6) In this section, in relation to a limited liability partnership, for 'director' read 'member'.

COMMENCEMENT DATE 1 October 2009[47]

**37.1152.02** Associate is a term which has previously been defined in the Insolvency Act 1986. Section 1152, however, applies a different and simpler definition. By way of example, only spouses, civil partners, and minor children and step-children are caught by the provision whereas the Insolvency Act 1986, section 435 casts its net much wider to include a person's relatives and those of his husband or wife as appropriate. The definition of associate applied in relation to a requirement of independence of a statutory auditor (contained in section 1260 of the Act) is materially the same.

## 1153 Valuer entitled to full disclosure

**37.1153.01**
(1) A person carrying out a valuation or making a report with respect to any consideration proposed to be accepted or given by a company, is entitled to require from the officers of the company such information and explanation as he thinks necessary to enable him to—
    (a) carry out the valuation or make the report, and
    (b) provide any note required by section 596(3) or 600(3) (note required where valuation carried out by another person).
(2) A person who knowingly or recklessly makes a statement to which this subsection applies that is misleading, false or deceptive in a material particular commits an offence.
(3) Subsection (2) applies to a statement—
    (a) made (whether orally or in writing) to a person carrying out a valuation or making a report, and
    (b) conveying or purporting to convey any information or explanation which that person requires, or is entitled to require, under subsection (1).
(4) A person guilty of an offence under subsection (2) is liable—
    (a) on conviction on indictment, to imprisonment for a term not exceeding two years or a fine (or both);
    (b) on summary conviction—
        (i) in England and Wales, to imprisonment for a term not exceeding twelve months or to a fine not exceeding the statutory maximum (or both);
        (ii) in Scotland or Northern Ireland, to imprisonment for a term not exceeding six months, or to a fine not exceeding the statutory maximum (or both).

COMMENCEMENT DATE 1 October 2009[48]

---

[46] Defined in s 1152.
[47] Companies Act 2008 (Commencement No 8, Transitional Provisions and Savings) Order 2008, SI 2008/2860, art 3(t).
[48] Companies Act 2008 (Commencement No 8, Transitional Provisions and Savings) Order 2008, SI 2008/2860, art 3(t).

Section 1153 replaces and repeats in material terms the provisions of section 110 of the Companies Act   **37.1153.02**
1985, save that the maximum sentence for conviction on summary conviction has been doubled to 12
months.[49] The independent valuer is entitled to require the officers of the company to provide such
information and explanation as he thinks necessary to enable him to carry out his tasks under the Act.
An offence is committed by any person who knowingly or recklessly makes a statement which is
misleading, false, or deceptive in a material particular.

## Notice of appointment of certain officers

### 1154   Duty to notify registrar of certain appointments etc

(1) Notice must be given to the registrar of the appointment in relation to a company of—   **37.1154.01**
    (a) a judicial factor (in Scotland),
    (b) a receiver and manager appointed under section 18 of the Charities Act 1993 (c. 10), or
    (c) a manager appointed under section 47 of the Companies (Audit, Investigations and Community Enterprise) Act 2004 (c. 27).
(2) The notice must be given—
    (a) in the case of appointment of a judicial factor, by the judicial factor;
    (b) in the case of appointment of a receiver and manager under section 18 of the Charities Act 1993 (c. 10), by the Charity Commission;
    (c) in the case of appointment of a manager under section 47 of the Companies (Audit, Investigations and Community Enterprise) Act 2004, by the Regulator of Community Interest Companies.
(3) The notice must specify an address at which service of documents (including legal process) may be effected on the person appointed.
    Notice of a change in the address for service may be given to the registrar by the person appointed.
(4) Where notice has been given under this section of the appointment of a person, notice must also be given to the registrar of the termination of the appointment. This notice must be given by the person specified in subsection (2).

Commencement Date   1 October 2009[50]

This section is new. It provides for the registrar of companies to be notified of the appointment of a   **37.1154.02**
judicial factor (in Scotland), a receiver and manager of a charity by the Charities Commission, or a
manager of a community interest company by the regulator of such companies. The latter two
categories of person displace the directors and take over the effective management of the company.
Thus it is obviously relevant that the registrar knows of their appointment so that any relevant matters
can be directed to them rather than the (displaced) directors. The registrar must also be notified of the
termination of such an appointment if notice of the appointment has previously been given.

In addition to the notification requirements imposed by section 1154(1), subsection (3) requires the   **37.1154.03**
persons appointed to provide an address at which they can be served. The notification requirement in
respect of a judicial factor is supplemented by the creation (under section 1155) of a criminal offence
for failure to provide notification pursuant to section 1154.

### 1155   Offence of failure to give notice

(1) If a judicial factor fails to give notice of his appointment in accordance with section 1154 within   **37.1155.01**
the period of 14 days after the appointment he commits an offence.
(2) A person guilty of an offence under this section is liable on summary conviction to a fine not exceeding level 5 on the standard scale and, for continued contravention, a daily default fine not exceeding one-tenth of level 5 on the standard scale.

Commencement Date   1 October 2009[51]

A failure to give the notice required under section 1155 is only an offence if committed by a judicial   **37.1155.02**
factor appointed in Scotland. No offence is committed by a receiver or manager under the Charities Act
1993 or a manager of a Community Interest Company.

---

[49] S 110 and Sch 24 of CA 1985.
[50] Companies Act 2008 (Commencement No 8, Transitional Provisions and Savings) Order 2008, SI 2008/2860, art 3(t).
[51] Companies Act 2008 (Commencement No 8, Transitional Provisions and Savings) Order 2008, SI 2008/2860, art 3(t).

*Courts and legal proceedings*

### 1156   Meaning of 'the court'

**37.1156.01**
(1) Except as otherwise provided, in the Companies Acts 'the court' means—
   (a) in England and Wales, the High Court or (subject to subsection (3)) a county court;
   (b) in Scotland, the Court of Session or the sheriff court;
   (c) in Northern Ireland, the High Court.
(2) The provisions of the Companies Acts conferring jurisdiction on 'the court' as defined above have effect subject to any enactment or rule of law relating to the allocation of jurisdiction or distribution of business between courts in any part of the United Kingdom.
(3) The Lord Chancellor may, with the concurrence of the Lord Chief Justice, by order—
   (a) exclude a county court from having jurisdiction under the Companies Acts, and
   (b) for the purposes of that jurisdiction attach that court's district, or any part of it, to another county court.
(4) The Lord Chief Justice may nominate a judicial office holder (as defined in section 109(4) of the Constitutional Reform Act 2005 (c. 4)) to exercise his functions under subsection (3).

COMMENCEMENT DATE 1 October 2009[52]

**37.1156.02** This was a new provision, though it does embody elements of CA 1985, section 744. Clearly, this provision is relevant for the interpretation of many sections in the Act (such as section 1157 immediately below). Special provision is made for Scotland and Northern Ireland.

**37.1156.03** The critical functional issue is whether in English law a county court enjoys jurisdiction to handle cases involving company law—that matter will to a large extent be determined by allocation of jurisdiction to selected county courts by the Lord Chancellor with the concurrence of the Lord Chief Justice.

### 1157   Power of court to grant relief in certain cases[a]

**37.1157.01**
(1) If in proceedings for negligence, default, breach of duty or breach of trust against—
   (a) an officer of a company, or
   (b) a person employed by a company as auditor (whether he is or is not an officer of the company),
it appears to the court hearing the case that the officer or person is or may be liable but that he acted honestly and reasonably, and that having regard to all the circumstances of the case (including those connected with his appointment) he ought fairly to be excused, the court may relieve him, either wholly or in part, from his liability on such terms as it thinks fit.
(2) If any such officer or person has reason to apprehend that a claim will or might be made against him in respect of negligence, default, breach of duty or breach of trust—
   (a) he may apply to the court for relief, and
   (b) the court has the same power to relieve him as it would have had if it had been a court before which proceedings against him for negligence, default, breach of duty or breach of trust had been brought.
(3) Where a case to which subsection (1) applies is being tried by a judge with a jury, the judge, after hearing the evidence, may, if he is satisfied that the defendant (in Scotland, the defender) ought in pursuance of that subsection to be relieved either in whole or in part from the liability sought to be enforced against him, withdraw the case from the jury and forthwith direct judgment to be entered for the defendant (in Scotland, grant decree of absolvitor) on such terms as to costs (in Scotland, expenses) or otherwise as the judge may think proper.

AMENDMENTS AND NOTES

[a] This section applies with modifications to LLPs by reg 51 of the Limited Liability Partnerships (Accounts and Audit) (Application of Companies Act 2006) Regulations 2008, SI 2008/1911.

COMMENCEMENT DATE 1 October 2008[53]

**37.1157.02** This is a general provision authorizing the court to pardon officers (see section 1173(1)) and auditors for breaches of duty to the company. It replicates CA 1985, section 727 with only cosmetic changes. For consideration by the Company Law Review, see Final Report, paragraphs 6.3 to 6.4. Presumably, the reference to circumstances relating to appointment in subs (1) might permit the court to be more flexible with regard to non-executives.

---

[52] Companies Act 2006 (Commencement No 8, Transitional Provisions and Savings) Order 2008, SI 2008/2860, art 3(t).
[53] Companies Act 2006 (Commencement No 5, etc) Order 2007, SI 2007/3495, art 5.

There is authority that section 1157 relief does not have to be specifically pleaded in advance and that **37.1157.03** it can be granted by the court on being raised late in the day at trial[54] but doubts must exist as to whether this is good practice. There are also doubts whether a director, who has been faced with a misfeasance application brought against him, can, in addition to seeking a pardon under this provision, seek to invoke discretionary relief from the court under section 212(3) of the Insolvency Act 1986.[55]

The provision does not permit a judicial pardon in respect of liability to a third party.[56] Nor can it be **37.1157.04** engaged to mitigate liability for wrongful trading.[57] In reality the utility of this provision remains open to doubt.[58] The main problem is that if an officer can persuade the court that he acted honestly, reasonably and ought fairly to be excused, the chances of him having been found to be in breach of duty in the first place are remote. Most applications under this provision are therefore likely to fail.[59] For a rare success, see *Re D'Jan London Ltd*.[60]

Note the facility of advance clearance mapped out in subsection (2). This provision is rarely utilized. **37.1157.05**

Subsection (3) makes specific provision for Scotland. **37.1157.06**

On indemnity issues, see section 234(3)(b)(iii). **37.1157.07**

---

[54]  *Re Kirby's Coaches Ltd* [1991] BCC 130. It is doubtful, however, if it is appropriate to deal with the question of a pardon on an application for summary relief: *Phillips v McGregor-Paterson* [2010] 1 BCLC 72.
[55]  See the divided opinions of the Court of Appeal on this point in *HMRC v Holland* [2009] EWCA Civ 625. On appeal the Supreme Court (Re Paycheck Services 3 Ltd [2010] UKSC 51, [2011] 1 BCLC 141) did not determine this particular issue because it found by a majority that the individual in question was not a de facto director.
[56]  *Customs and Excise v Hedon Alpha Ltd* [1981] QB 818; *IRC v McEntaggart* [2006] BPIR 750; *First Independent Factors Ltd v Mountford* [2008] BPIR 515.
[57]  *Re Produce Marketing Consortium Ltd (No 1)* (1989) 5 BCC 399.
[58]  For a more positive view, see L Linklater (2002) (3) *Company Law Newsletter* 1.
[59]  See eg *Bairstow v Queens Moat Houses* [2002] BCC 91; *Re Loquitur Ltd* [2003] 2 BCLC 442 (but note here that the court found an alternative way to mitigate liability); *Queensway Systems v Walker* [2007] 2 BCLC 577; *PNC Telecom plc v Thomas (No 2)* [2008] 2 BCLC 95; *Re Oxford Pharmaceuticals Ltd* [2009] 2 BCLC 485, [96] and [104].
[60]  [1993] BCC 646. See also *Re Welfab Engineers Ltd* [1990] BCLC 833 where the court indicated its willingness to grant relief, though that was not required in view of its conclusion that there had been no breach of duty on the facts. In *Re Ortega Associates Ltd* [2008] BCC 256 the court found no breach of duty but would in any case have offered relief.

# 38

## COMPANIES: INTERPRETATION

## Companies Act 2006

### PART 38
### COMPANIES: INTERPRETATION

### *Meaning of 'UK-registered company'*

### 1158 Meaning of 'UK-registered company'

In the Companies Acts 'UK-registered company' means a company registered under this Act.

**38.1158.01**

The expression does not include an overseas company that has registered particulars under section 1046.
COMMENCEMENT DATE 1 October 2007 (for certain purposes),[1] 1 October 2009[2]

This is a self-explanatory definition—for an example of usage, see section 1099(2). Compare the term 'UK' company as defined in section 1183, which is concerned with when a person disqualified outside the UK may be subject to restrictions in the UK. Note the exclusion of overseas companies registered under section 1046 from the definition.

**38.1158.02**

### *Meaning of 'subsidiary' and related expressions*

### 1159 Meaning of 'subsidiary' etc

(1) A company is a 'subsidiary' of another company, its 'holding company', if that other company—

    (a) holds a majority of the voting rights in it, or

    (b) is a member of it and has the right to appoint or remove a majority of its board of directors, or

    (c) is a member of it and controls alone, pursuant to an agreement with other members, a majority of the voting rights in it,

or if it is a subsidiary of a company that is itself a subsidiary of that other company.

**38.1159.01**

---

[1] Companies Act 2006 (Commencement No 3, etc) Order 2007, SI 2007/2194, art 2.
[2] Companies Act 2006 (Commencement No 8, Transitional Provisions and Savings) Order 2008, SI 2008/2860, art 3(u).

(2) A company is a 'wholly-owned subsidiary' of another company if it has no members except that other and that other's wholly-owned subsidiaries or persons acting on behalf of that other or its wholly-owned subsidiaries.

(3) Schedule 6 contains provisions explaining expressions used in this section and otherwise supplementing this section.

(4) In this section and that Schedule 'company' includes any body corporate.

COMMENCEMENT DATE 6 April 2008 (for certain purposes)[3], 1 October 2009[4]

**38.1159.02** This definition was formerly section 736 of the Companies Act 1985. Note the range of permutations specified in subs (1) determining whether a company is a subsidiary. As many modern businesses featuring limited liability companies operate a group structure this provision is of some practical significance, not least because it is not confined to providing a definition for the purposes of the Companies Acts but will also apply to a contract such as a contract for a loan or a shareholders' agreement that uses the terms 'holding company' and 'subsidiary'.[5] For an important example of its application in the Companies Act, see section 678 regarding the provision of financial assistance for an acquisition of shares. Note the broader definition in section 1162 of parent and subsidiary undertakings for the purposes of the provisions on consolidated accounts. The material in Schedule 6 (which is referred to in subs (3)) reproduces details extracted from the former section 736A of the Companies Act 1985. For 'body corporate', see section 1173.

**38.1159.03** For judicial consideration of when a company is a 'subsidiary' in the context of the statutory predecessor, see the Supreme Court ruling in *Farstad Supply A/S v Enviroco*.[6]

### 1160 Meaning of 'subsidiary' etc: power to amend

**38.1160.01** (1) The Secretary of State may by regulations amend the provisions of section 1159 (meaning of 'subsidiary' etc) and Schedule 6 (meaning of 'subsidiary' etc: supplementary provisions) so as to alter the meaning of the expressions 'subsidiary', 'holding company' or 'wholly-owned subsidiary'.

(2) Regulations under this section are subject to negative resolution procedure.

(3) Any amendment made by regulations under this section does not apply for the purposes of enactments outside the Companies Acts unless the regulations so provide.

(4) So much of section 23(3) of the Interpretation Act 1978 (c. 30) as applies section 17(2)(a) of that Act (effect of repeal and re-enactment) to deeds, instruments and documents other than enactments does not apply in relation to any repeal and re-enactment effected by regulations under this section.

COMMENCEMENT DATE 6 April 2008 (for certain purposes)[7], 1 October 2009[8]

**38.1160.02** Section 1160 was derived from section 736B of the Companies Act 1985. It confers on the Secretary of State power to amend section 1159 and Schedule 6. For the negative resolution procedure mentioned in subsection (2), see section 1289. It is made clear by subsection (4) that changing the meaning of subsidiary for the purposes of the Companies Acts does not involve a change of meaning where this term is used in other legislation (eg in the Finance Acts). Subsection (4) deals with transitional matters.

*Meaning of 'undertaking' and related expressions*

### 1161 Meaning of 'undertaking' and related expressions

**38.1161.01** (1) In the Companies Acts 'undertaking' means—

(a) a body corporate or partnership, or

(b) an unincorporated association carrying on a trade or business, with or without a view to profit.

(2) In the Companies Acts references to shares—

(a) in relation to an undertaking with capital but no share capital, are to rights to share in the capital of the undertaking; and

---

[3] Companies Act 2006 (Commencement No 5, Transitional Provisions and Savings) Order 2007, SI 2007/3495, art 3(4).

[4] Companies Act 2006 (Commencement No 8, Transitional Provisions and Savings) Order 2008, SI 2008/2860, art 3(u).

[5] See, for example, *Farstad Supply A/S v Enviroco* [2011] UKSC 16, referred to below.

[6] Above.

[7] Companies Act 2006 (Commencement No 5, Transitional Provisions and Savings) Order 2007, SI 2007/3495, art 3(4).

[8] Companies Act 2006 (Commencement No 8, Transitional Provisions and Savings) Order 2008, SI 2008/2860, art 3(u).

  (b) in relation to an undertaking without capital, are to interests—
    (i) conferring any right to share in the profits or liability to contribute to the losses of the undertaking, or
    (ii) giving rise to an obligation to contribute to the debts or expenses of the undertaking in the event of a winding up.
(3) Other expressions appropriate to companies shall be construed, in relation to an undertaking which is not a company, as references to the corresponding persons, officers, documents or organs, as the case may be, appropriate to undertakings of that description.
This is subject to provision in any specific context providing for the translation of such expressions.
(4) References in the Companies Acts to 'fellow subsidiary undertakings' are to undertakings which are subsidiary undertakings of the same parent undertaking but are not parent undertakings or subsidiary undertakings of each other.
(5) In the Companies Acts 'group undertaking', in relation to an undertaking, means an undertaking which is—
  (a) a parent undertaking or subsidiary undertaking of that undertaking, or
  (b) a subsidiary undertaking of any parent undertaking of that undertaking.

COMMENCEMENT DATE  6 April 2008[9]

This interpretation section was derived from CA 1985, section 259 (as inserted by CA 1989, section 22). **38.1161.02**
It is relevant to the definition of parent and subsidiary undertakings in section 1162 and applies particularly to the provisions of the Act relating to group accounts. Subsection (1) defines 'undertaking' in wide terms, so that it covers not just limited liability companies but any partnership or unincorporated association carrying on a trade or business. The limited liability partnership (LLP) is covered as a body corporate—on the latter phrase, see section 1173 below.

'Shares' are widely defined by subsection (2) so that the definition catches companies having no share **38.1161.03**
capital. For the general definition of shares, see section 540.

Subsections (3), (4), and (5) deal with non-corporate undertakings, fellow subsidiary undertakings, **38.1161.04**
and group undertakings. In respect of these, this definition needs to be read in the light of section 1162 below.

## 1162  Parent and subsidiary undertakings

(1) This section (together with Schedule 7) defines 'parent undertaking' and 'subsidiary undertaking'    **38.1162.01**
for the purposes of the Companies Acts.
(2) An undertaking is a parent undertaking in relation to another undertaking, a subsidiary undertaking, if—
  (a) it holds a majority of the voting rights in the undertaking, or
  (b) it is a member of the undertaking and has the right to appoint or remove a majority of its board of directors, or
  (c) it has the right to exercise a dominant influence over the undertaking—
    (i) by virtue of provisions contained in the undertaking's articles, or
    (ii) by virtue of a control contract, or
  (d) it is a member of the undertaking and controls alone, pursuant to an agreement with other shareholders or members, a majority of the voting rights in the undertaking.
(3) For the purposes of subsection (2) an undertaking shall be treated as a member of another undertaking—
  (a) if any of its subsidiary undertakings is a member of that undertaking, or
  (b) if any shares in that other undertaking are held by a person acting on behalf of the undertaking or any of its subsidiary undertakings.
(4) An undertaking is also a parent undertaking in relation to another undertaking, a subsidiary undertaking, if—
  (a) it has the power to exercise, or actually exercises, dominant influence or control over it, or
  (b) it and the subsidiary undertaking are managed on a unified basis.
(5) A parent undertaking shall be treated as the parent undertaking of undertakings in relation to which any of its subsidiary undertakings are, or are to be treated as, parent undertakings; and references to its subsidiary undertakings shall be construed accordingly.
(6) Schedule 7 contains provisions explaining expressions used in this section and otherwise supplementing this section.
(7) In this section and that Schedule references to shares, in relation to an undertaking, are to allotted shares.

---

[9] Companies Act 2006 (Commencement No 5, Transitional Provisions and Savings) Order 2007, SI 2007/
3495, art 3(o).

COMMENCEMENT DATE 6 April 2008[10]

**38.1162.02**    Subsections (1) and (2) define parent and subsidiary undertaking, as previously covered in CA 1985, section 258 (as inserted by CA 1989, section 22) and the former Schedule 10A. As indicated by subsection (6), schedule 7 to this Act provides important further clarification (see para 48.Sch7.01). The definitions are relevant to the provisions in Part 15 relating to group accounts. The principal difference from the more generally applicable definition of subsidiary in section 1159 is found in subsection (2)(c) and subsection (4).

**38.1162.03**    Subsection (2c) refers to the concept of 'dominant influence' and 'control contract'. If an undertaking has a dominant influence over another undertaking by virtue of provisions in the latter's articles or under a control contract, it will be its parent undertaking regardless of whether or not it a member of the undertaking. Schedule 7 explains further the concept of dominant influence, essentially as meaning the right to give directions with respect to the operating and financial policies of the other undertaking (SU) with which its directors are obliged to comply whether or not they are for the benefit of the other undertaking. It seems that case law has not yet considered this.[11] A control contract is a contract in writing conferring the right to exercise a dominant influence which is of a kind authorized by the articles of the SU and is permitted by the law under which the SU is established.[12]

**38.1162.04**    Subsection (4) also includes the concept of dominant influence, but note that the further explanation of this in schedule 7, para 4 does not apply to the construction of this subsection. It is also not concerned with the right to exercise such influence but whether or not it has the power to do so or actually exercises such influence. Further it also includes the situations where there is the power to exercise or the actual exercise of control over the SU and where the parent and the SU are managed on a unified basis. The latter concept is not further defined.[13]

**38.1162.05**    Subsection (3) explains when an undertaking can be said to be a member of another undertaking.

**38.1162.06**    The effect of subsection (5) is that where there is a chain of companies in a group the ultimate holding company is seen as the parent undertaking vis-à-vis all other group members.

## Other definitions

### 1163 'Non-cash asset'

**38.1163.01**    (1)  In the Companies Acts 'non-cash asset' means any property or interest in property, other than cash.
For this purpose 'cash' includes foreign currency.
(2)  A reference to the transfer or acquisition of a non-cash asset includes—
    (a)  the creation or extinction of an estate or interest in, or a right over, any property, and
    (b)  the discharge of a liability of any person, other than a liability for a liquidated sum.

COMMENCEMENT DATE 1 October 2009[14]

**38.1163.02**    This definition, derived from CA 1985, section 739, is relevant to sections 598 to 604 (the transfer of a non-cash asset to a public company within two years of its receiving its trading certificate etc) and section 845 (distributions in kind).

**38.1163.03**    Subsection (1) contains a very broad definition of what is a non-cash asset so that anything other than cash (whether cash in pounds sterling or a foreign currency) which is property or an interest in property is included. Property will mean anything that the law regards as property, whether that be land or other real property or personal property, tangible or intangible. Interest will mean any recognized legal or equitable interest in property.

**38.1163.04**    Subsection (2) is similarly broad as regards the meaning of the transfer or acquisition of a non-cash asset and it is not necessarily inclusive because of the presence of the word 'includes'. Note that under para (b) the payment of money to discharge a liability, except where that is for a liquidated sum, will amount to a transfer or acquisition.

---

[10]  Companies Act 2006 (Commencement No 5, Transitional Provisions and Savings) Order 2007, SI 2007/3495, art 3(o).

[11]  FRS2—*Accounting for Subsidiary Undertakings*—contains further guidance.

[12]  Sch 7, para 4.

[13]  But FRS2 does contain further guidance.

[14]  Companies Act 2006 (Commencement No 8, Transitional Provisions and Savings) Order 2008, SI 2008/2860, art 3(u).

## 1164   Meaning of 'banking company' and 'banking group'

(1)  This section defines 'banking company' and 'banking group' for the purposes of the Companies Acts.

(2)  'Banking company' means a person who has permission under Part 4 of the Financial Services and Markets Act 2000 (c. 8) to accept deposits, other than—

    (a)  a person who is not a company, and

    (b)  a person who has such permission only for the purpose of carrying on another regulated activity in accordance with permission under that Part.

(3)  The definition in subsection (2) must be read with section 22 of that Act, any relevant order under that section and Schedule 2 to that Act.

(4)  References to a banking group are to a group where the parent company is a banking company or where—

    (a)  the parent company's principal subsidiary undertakings are wholly or mainly credit institutions, and

    (b)  the parent company does not itself carry on any material business apart from the acquisition, management and disposal of interests in subsidiary undertakings.

'Group' here means a parent undertaking and its subsidiary undertakings.

(5)  For the purposes of subsection (4)—

    (a)  a parent company's principal subsidiary undertakings are the subsidiary undertakings of the company whose results or financial position would principally affect the figures shown in the group accounts, and

    (b)  the management of interests in subsidiary undertakings includes the provision of services to such undertakings.

COMMENCEMENT DATE  6 April 2008[15]

**38.1164.01**

This definition, which relates to the special provisions regarding the accounts of banking companies (see especially the Large and Medium-sized Companies and Groups (Accounts and Reports) Regulations 2008[16]) was derived from CA 1985, section 742B. Of necessity it cross-refers to companies that have the appropriate permission under the Financial Services and Markets Act 2000. For credit institutions note section 1173.

**38.1164.02**

## 1165   Meaning of 'insurance company' and related expressions

(1)  This section defines 'insurance company', 'authorised insurance company', 'insurance group' and 'insurance market activity' for the purposes of the Companies Acts.

(2)  An 'authorised insurance company' means a person (whether incorporated or not) who has permission under Part 4 of the Financial Services and Markets Act 2000 (c. 8) to effect or carry out contracts of insurance.

(3)  An 'insurance company' means—

    (a)  an authorised insurance company, or

    (b)  any other person (whether incorporated or not) who—

      (i)  carries on insurance market activity, or

      (ii)  may effect or carry out contracts of insurance under which the benefits provided by that person are exclusively or primarily benefits in kind in the event of accident to or breakdown of a vehicle.

(4)  Neither expression includes a friendly society within the meaning of the Friendly Societies Act 1992 (c. 40).

(5)  References to an insurance group are to a group where the parent company is an insurance company or where—

    (a)  the parent company's principal subsidiary undertakings are wholly or mainly insurance companies, and

    (b)  the parent company does not itself carry on any material business apart from the acquisition, management and disposal of interests in subsidiary undertakings.

'Group' here means a parent undertaking and its subsidiary undertakings.

(6)  For the purposes of subsection (5)—

    (a)  a parent company's principal subsidiary undertakings are the subsidiary undertakings of the company whose results or financial position would principally affect the figures shown in the group accounts, and

    (b)  the management of interests in subsidiary undertakings includes the provision of services to such undertakings.

**38.1165.01**

---

[15]  Companies Act 2006 (Commencement No 5, Transitional Provisions and Savings) Order 2007, SI 2007/ 3495, art 3(p).

[16]  Reproduced in SI.13.

(7) 'Insurance market activity' has the meaning given in section 316(3) of the Financial Services and Markets Act 2000.
(8) References in this section to contracts of insurance and to the effecting or carrying out of such contracts must be read with section 22 of that Act, any relevant order under that section and Schedule 2 to that Act.

COMMENCEMENT DATE 6 April 2008[17]

**38.1165.02** This definition, which relates to the special provisions regarding the accounts of insurance companies (see especially the Large and Medium-sized Companies and Groups (Accounts and Reports) Regulations 2008[18] ) was derived from CA 1985, section 742C. Of necessity it cross-refers to companies that are authorized under the Financial Services and Markets Act 2000. Note that under subsection (4) friendly societies are excluded from the definition of an insurance company.

### 1166 'Employees' share scheme'

**38.1166.01** For the purposes of the Companies Acts an employees' share scheme is a scheme for encouraging or facilitating the holding of shares in or debentures of a company by or for the benefit of—

(a) the bona fide employees or former employees of—
   (i) the company,
   (ii) any subsidiary of the company, or
   (iii) the company's holding company or any subsidiary of the company's holding company, or
(b) the spouses, civil partners, surviving spouses, surviving civil partners, or minor children or step-children of such employees or former employees.

COMMENCEMENT DATE 1 October 2009[19]

**38.1166.02** This interpretation provision, which was derived from CA 1985, section 743, is relevant to a number of provisions in the Act including those dealing with financial assistance—see section 682(2) in particular here, but also note that it is relevant to sections 586(2), 676, and 761. The definition appears self-explanatory and note the extension of the concept of family members to include civil partners. 'Employees' will be construed in accordance with the general meaning of the term, for example for the purposes of employment legislation and will not cover those engaged under a contract for services as opposed to a contract of service. For the meaning of 'subsidiary', see section 1159.

### 1167 Meaning of 'prescribed'

**38.1167.01** In the Companies Acts 'prescribed' means prescribed (by order or by regulations) by the Secretary of State.

COMMENCEMENT DATE 30 September 2007[20]

**38.1167.02** This interpretation provision, previously found in CA 1985, section 744, is self-explanatory. With the extensive use of secondary legislation by CA 2006 it is an important functional measure.

### 1168 Hard copy and electronic form and related expressions

**38.1168.01** (1) The following provisions apply for the purposes of the Companies Acts.
(2) A document or information is sent or supplied in hard copy form if it is sent or supplied in a paper copy or similar form capable of being read.
   References to hard copy have a corresponding meaning.
(3) A document or information is sent or supplied in electronic form if it is sent or supplied—
   (a) by electronic means (for example, by email or fax), or
   (b) by any other means while in an electronic form (for example, sending a disk by post).
   References to electronic copy have a corresponding meaning.
(4) A document or information is sent or supplied by electronic means if it is—
   (a) sent initially and received at its destination by means of electronic equipment for the processing (which expression includes digital compression) or storage of data, and
   (b) entirely transmitted, conveyed and received by wire, by radio, by optical means or by other electromagnetic means.
   References to electronic means have a corresponding meaning.

---

[17] Companies Act 2006 (Commencement No 5, Transitional Provisions and Savings) Order 2007, SI 2007/3495, art 3(p).
[18] Reproduced in SI.13.
[19] Companies Act 2006 (Commencement No 8, Transitional Provisions and Savings) Order 2008, SI 2008/2860, art 3(u).
[20] See the Companies Act 2006 (Commencement No 4 and Commencement No 3 Amendment) Order 2007, SI 2007//2607.

(5) A document or information authorised or required to be sent or supplied in electronic form must be sent or supplied in a form, and by a means, that the sender or supplier reasonably considers will enable the recipient—
   (a) to read it, and
   (b) to retain a copy of it.
(6) For the purposes of this section, a document or information can be read only if—
   (a) it can be read with the naked eye, or
   (b) to the extent that it consists of images (for example photographs, pictures, maps, plans or drawings), it can be seen with the naked eye.
(7) The provisions of this section apply whether the provision of the Companies Acts in question uses the words 'sent' or 'supplied' or uses other words (such as 'deliver', 'provide', 'produce' or, in the case of a notice, 'give') to refer to the sending or supplying of a document or information.

COMMENCEMENT DATE 1 October 2007, 6 April 2008, 1 October 2008, 1 October 2009[21]

This interpretation provision had no statutory predecessor in CA 1985. It deals with changes in technology with regard to information storage and transmission so as to reflect the advent of modern IT processes. At the same time, it offers an explanation of the traditional concept of hard copy.    **38.1168.02**

The section seems self-explanatory and comprehensive in terms of what is meant by electronic form and electronic means. It applies particularly to the company communication provisions in sections 1144 to 1148 together with Schedules 4 and 5. It is particularly important regarding various provisions in Part 13 regarding meetings and resolutions, reflecting one of the key aims of the Act as a whole to facilitate participation by members of companies.    **38.1168.03**

## 1169  Dormant companies[a]

(1) For the purposes of the Companies Acts a company is 'dormant' during any period in which it has no significant accounting transaction.    **38.1169.01**
(2) A 'significant accounting transaction' means a transaction that is required by section 386 to be entered in the company's accounting records.
(3) In determining whether or when a company is dormant, there shall be disregarded—
   (a) any transaction arising from the taking of shares in the company by a subscriber to the memorandum as a result of an undertaking of his in connection with the formation of the company;
   (b) any transaction consisting of the payment of—
      (i) a fee to the registrar on a change of the company's name,
      (ii) a fee to the registrar on the re-registration of the company,
      (iii) a penalty under section 453 (penalty for failure to file accounts), or
      (iv) a fee to the registrar for the registration of an annual return.
(4) Any reference in the Companies Acts to a body corporate other than a company being dormant has a corresponding meaning.

AMENDMENTS AND NOTES

[a] This section applies with modifications to LLPs by reg 6 of the Limited Liability Partnerships (Accounts and Audit) (Application of Companies Act 2006) Regulations 2008, SI 2008/1911.

COMMENCEMENT DATE 6 April 2008[22]

For the statutory predecessor, see CA 1985, section 249AA(4) to (7). A company is regarded as 'dormant' for the purposes of subsection (1) if no significant accounting transaction has taken place in the past financial year. This concept is particularly important for the purposes of accounting concessions.    **38.1169.02**

The concept of a significant accounting transaction is explained in subsection (2). See section 480.    **38.1169.03**

Subsection (3) indicates that certain minor bureaucratic transactions (eg payment of regulatory fees) are not regarded as significant accounting transactions—a company undertaking such transactions can still therefore be regarded as dormant. For 'registrar', see section 1060.    **38.1169.04**

---

[21] Brought into force for the purposes of certain other provisions of the Act by the Companies Act 2006 (Commencement No 3, Consequential Provisions, Transitional Provisions and Savings) Order 2007, SI 2007/2194 and the Companies Act 2006 (Commencement No 5, Transitional Provisions and Savings) Order 2007, SI 20007/3495. For all remaining purposes, Companies Act 2006 (Commencement No 8, Transitional Provisions and Savings) Order 2008, SI 2008/2860, art 3(u).

[22] Companies Act 2006 (Commencement No 5, Transitional Provisions and Savings) Order 2007, SI 2007/3495, art 3(r).

**38.1169.05**    Subsection (4) extends the concept of dormancy (with its accounting concessions) to other corporate bodies which are not companies.

## 1170  Meaning of 'EEA State' and related expressions

**38.1170.01**    In the Companies Acts—

['EEA State' has the meaning given by Schedule 1 to the Interpretation Act 1978;][a]
'EEA company' and 'EEA undertaking' mean a company or undertaking governed by the law of an EEA State.

AMENDMENTS

[a]  Amended by the Companies (EEA State) Regulations 2007, SI 2007/732, reg 3, with effect from 9 March 2007.

COMMENCEMENT DATE  6 April 2007[23]

**38.1170.02**    This section defines an 'EEA State', an 'EEA company', and an 'EEA undertaking'. This definition, which replaces the former section 744 of the CA 1985 definition, is pertinent to a number of sections of the 2006 Act, including sections 164, 400, 401, 948, 964, 970, 971, and 1047. The EEA states are the members of the European Union together with Iceland, Liechtenstein and Norway.

## [1170A  Receiver or manager and certain related references

**38.1170A.01**    (1)  Any reference in the Companies Acts to a receiver or manager of the property of a company, or to a receiver of it, includes a receiver or manager or (as the case may be) a receiver of part only of that property and a receiver only of the income arising from the property or from part of it.
            (2)  Any reference in the Companies Acts to the appointment of a receiver or manager under powers contained in an instrument includes an appointment made under powers that by virtue of an enactment are implied in and have effect as if contained in an instrument.][a]

AMENDMENTS AND NOTES

[a]  Inserted by the Companies Act 2006 (Consequential Amendments, Transitional Provisions and Savings) Order 2009, SI 2009/1941, Sch 1, para 260.

COMMENCEMENT DATE  1 October 2009[24]

## [1170B  Meaning of 'contributory'

**38.1170B.01**    (1)  In the Companies Acts 'contributory' means every person liable to contribute to the assets of a company in the event of its being wound up.
            (2)  For the purposes of all proceedings for determining, and all proceedings prior to the final determination of, the persons who are to be deemed contributories, the expression includes any person alleged to be a contributory.
            (3)  The reference in subsection (1) to persons liable to contribute to the assets does not include a person so liable by virtue of a declaration by the court under—
                (a)  section 213 of the Insolvency Act 1986 or Article 177 of the Insolvency (Northern Ireland) Order 1989 (fraudulent trading), or
                (b)  section 214 of that Act or Article 178 of that Order (wrongful trading).][a]

AMENDMENTS AND NOTES

[a]  Inserted by the Companies Act 2006 (Consequential Amendments, Transitional Provisions and Savings) Order 2009, SI 2009/1941, Sch 1, para 260.

COMMENCEMENT DATE  1 October 2009[25]

## 1171  The former Companies Acts

**38.1171.01**    In the Companies Acts—'the former Companies Acts' means—

                (a)  the Joint Stock Companies Acts, the Companies Act 1862 (c. 89), the Companies (Consolidation) Act 1908 (c. 69), the Companies Act 1929 (c. 23), the Companies Act (Northern Ireland) 1932 (c. 7 (N.I.)), the Companies Acts 1948 to 1983, the Companies Act (Northern Ireland) 1960 (c. 22 (N.I.)), the Companies (Northern Ireland) Order 1986 (S.I. 1986/1032 (N.I. 6)) and the Companies Consolidation (Consequential Provisions) (Northern Ireland) Order 1986 (S.I. 1986/1035 (N.I. 9)), and

---

[23]  Companies Act 2006 (Commencement No 2, etc) Order 2007, SI 2007/1093, art 2.
[24]  Companies Act 2006 (Consequential Amendments, Transitional Provisions and Savings) Order 2009, SI 2009/1941, art 1.
[25]  Companies Act 2006 (Consequential Amendments, Transitional Provisions and Savings) Order 2009, SI 2009/1941, art 1.

    (b)  the provisions of the Companies Act 1985 (c. 6) and the Companies Consolidation (Conse-
        quential Provisions) Act 1985 (c. 9) that are no longer in force;
'the Joint Stock Companies Acts' means the Joint Stock Companies Act 1856 (c. 47), the Joint Stock
Companies Acts 1856, 1857 (20 & 21 Vict. c. 14), the Joint Stock Banking Companies Act 1857 (c. 49),
and the Act to enable Joint Stock Banking Companies to be formed on the principle of limited liability
(1858 c. 91), but does not include the Joint Stock Companies Act 1844 (c. 110).

COMMENCEMENT DATE  1 October 2009[26]

This section defines the phrase 'the former Companies Acts'. This is based upon the precedent in CA   **38.1171.02**
1985, section 735, although, of course, the 1989 Act and 2004 Act are not listed as they are only seen as
amendments to the primary 1985 Act. Unlike section 735, this provision includes Northern Irish
legislation which has been superseded by the 2006 Act—see section 1284. The policy with regard to
Northern Irish legislation was outlined in the Explanatory Notes to the Bill when it entered the
Commons in May 2006 at paragraphs 1616 and 1617. Section 1171 indicates that some sections in CA
1985 continue in force, though the rump in that legislation was pared down during the passage of the
Bill through Parliament to the provisions regarding company investigations and community interest
companies.

By way of comparison, 'the Companies Acts' are defined by section 2.   **38.1171.03**

On continuity in terms of the relationship between the 1985 and 2006 Acts, see section 1297.   **38.1171.04**

## *General*

### 1172  References to requirements of this Act[a]

References in the company law provisions of this Act to the requirements of this Act include the   **38.1172.01**
requirements of regulations and orders made under it.

AMENDMENTS AND NOTES

[a]  This section applies with modifications to LLPs by reg 6 of the Limited Liability Partnerships (Accounts
    and Audit) (Application of Companies Act 2006) Regulations 2008, SI 2008/1911.

COMMENCEMENT DATE  6 April 2008[27]

This interpretation provision anticipates the usage of delegated legislation to introduce supplementary   **38.1172.02**
regulations and orders as well as law reform when that is permitted by particular provisions of the Act.
There has already been a large volume of such legislation.

### 1173  Minor definitions: general[a]

    (1)  In the Companies Acts—   **38.1173.01**
      'body corporate' and 'corporation' include a body incorporated outside the United Kingdom,
      but do not include—
      (a)  a corporation sole, or
      (b)  a partnership that, whether or not a legal person, is not regarded as a body corporate
         under the law by which it is governed;
      'credit institution' means a credit institution as defined in Article 4.1(a) of Directive 2006/
      48/EC of the European Parliament and of the Council relating to the taking up and pursuit of
      the business of credit institutions;
      'financial institution' means a financial institution within the meaning of Article 1.1 of the
      Council Directive on the obligations of branches established in a Member State of credit and
      financial institutions having their head offices outside that Member State regarding the
      publication of annual accounting documents (the Bank Branches Directive, 89/117/EEC);
      'firm' means any entity, whether or not a legal person, that is not an individual and includes
      a body corporate, a corporation sole and a partnership or other unincorporated association;
      'the Gazette' means—
      (a)  as respects companies registered in England and Wales, the London Gazette,
      (b)  as respects companies registered in Scotland, the Edinburgh Gazette, and
      (c)  as respects companies registered in Northern Ireland, the Belfast Gazette;
      'hire-purchase agreement' has the same meaning as in the Consumer Credit Act 1974 (c. 39);
      'officer', in relation to a body corporate, includes a director, manager or secretary;
      'parent company' means a company that is a parent undertaking (see section 1162 and
      Schedule 7);

---

[26]  Companies Act 2006 (Commencement No 8, Transitional Provisions and Savings) Order 2008, SI 2008/
2860, art 3(u).
[27]  Companies Act 2006 (Commencement No 5, Transitional Provisions and Savings) Order 2007, SI 2007/
3495, art 3(s).

'regulated activity' has the meaning given in section 22 of the Financial Services and Markets Act 2000 (c. 8);

'regulated market' has the same meaning as in Directive 2004/39/EC of the European Parliament and of the Council on markets in financial instruments (see Article 4.1 (14));

'working day', in relation to a company, means a day that is not a Saturday or Sunday, Christmas Day, Good Friday or any day that is a bank holiday under the Banking and Financial Dealings Act 1971 (c. 80) in the part of the United Kingdom where the company is registered.

(2) In relation to an EEA State that has not implemented Directive 2004/39/EC of the European Parliament and of the Council on markets in financial instruments, the following definition of 'regulated market' has effect in place of that in subsection (1)— 'regulated market' has the same meaning as it has in Council Directive 93/22/EEC on investment services in the securities field.

AMENDMENTS AND NOTES

[a] This section applies with modifications to LLPs by reg 6 of the Limited Liability Partnerships (Accounts and Audit) (Application of Companies Act 2006) Regulations 2008, SI 2008/1911.

COMMENCEMENT DATE 1 October 2007, 6 April 2008, 1 October 2008, 1 October 2009[28]

**38.1173.02**    This section contains various minor definitions that are self-explanatory. Some have a relatively limited application, but others, including 'body corporate', 'corporation' and 'officer' are important to many of the provisions of the Act.

## 1174 Index of defined expressions

**38.1174.01**    Schedule 8 contains an index of provisions defining or otherwise explaining expressions used in the Companies Acts.

COMMENCEMENT DATE 1 October 2009[29]

**38.1174.02**    This provision refers us to Schedule 8 to the Act, which contains a helpful index of common definition provisions. For example, the ubiquitous 'company' is defined by section 1. Comparable utilitarian provision was to be found in CA 1985, section 735.

---

[28] Brought into force for the purposes of certain other provisions of the Act by the Companies Act 2006 (Commencement No 3, Consequential Amendments, Transitional Provisions and Savings) Order 2007, SI 2007/2194 and the Companies Act 2006 (Commencement No 5, Transitional Provisions and Savings) Order 2007, SI 2007/3495. For all other purposes, Companies Act 2006 (Commencement No 8, Transitional Provisions and Savings) Order 2008, SI 2008/2860, art 3(u).

[29] Companies Act 2006 (Commencement No 8, Transitional Provisions and Savings) Order 2008, SI 2008/2860, art 3(u).

## Companies Act 2006

### PART 39
### COMPANIES: MINOR AMENDMENTS

### 1175 Removal of special provisions about accounts and audit of charitable companies

(1) Part 7 of the Companies Act 1985 (c. 6) and Part 8 of the Companies (Northern Ireland) Order 1986 (accounts and audit) are amended in accordance with Schedule 9 to this Act so as to remove the special provisions about companies that are charities.

**39.1175.01**

(2) In that Schedule—

Part 1 contains repeals and consequential amendments of provisions of the Companies Act 1985;

Part 2 contains repeals and consequential amendments of provisions of the Companies (Northern Ireland) Order 1986.

COMMENCEMENT DATE 1 April 2008[1]

For rationale see Explanatory Notes to Act paragraphs 1492 to 1493. This is a discrete amendment dealing with the accounts and audit of charitable companies. See further Schedule 9.

### 1176 Power of Secretary of State to bring civil proceedings on company's behalf

(1) Section 438 of the Companies Act 1985 (power of Secretary of State to bring civil proceedings on company's behalf) shall cease to have effect.

**39.1176.01**

(2) In section 439 of that Act (expenses of investigating company's affairs)—

(a) in subsection (2) omit, 'or is ordered to pay the whole or any part of the costs of proceedings brought under section 438,';

(b) omit subsections (3) and (7) (which relate to section 438);

(c) in subsection (8)—

(i) for 'subsections (2) and (3)' substitute 'subsection (2)', and

(ii) omit '; and any such liability imposed by subsection (2) is (subject as mentioned above) a liability also to indemnify all persons against liability under subsection (3)'.

(3) In section 453(1A) of that Act (investigation of overseas companies: provisions not applicable), omit paragraph (b) (which relates to section 438).

(4) Nothing in this section affects proceedings brought under section 438 before the commencement of this section.

COMMENCEMENT DATE 6 April 2007[2]

---

[1] Companies Act 2006 (Commencement No 6, Saving and Commencement Nos 3 and 5) (Amendment) Order 2008, SI 2008/674. Commencement in Northern Ireland is not yet determined.

[2] Companies Act 2006 (Commencement No 1, etc) Order 2006, SI 2006/3428, art 4.

**39.1176.02**    Subsection (1) repeals CA 1985, section 438, but not retrospectively (see subsection (4)). As far as is known, the Secretary of State has rarely used the power to institute a derivative action on behalf of a company.[3] The authors are not aware of any live proceedings under CA 1985, section 438. The 2005 White Paper, *Company Law Reform*[4] called for the repeal of section 438.

**39.1176.03**    Subsection (2) amends section 439 of CA 1985. Subsection (3) amends section 453(1A) of CA 1985 to reflect the repeal of section 438 of the 1985 Act.

### 1177   Repeal of certain provisions about company directors

**39.1177.01**    The following provisions of Part 10 of the Companies Act 1985 shall cease to have effect—

> section 311 (prohibition on tax-free payments to directors);
> sections 323 and 327 (prohibition on directors dealing in share options);
> sections 324 to 326 and 328 to 329, and Parts 2 to 4 of Schedule 13 (register of directors' interests);
> sections 343 and 344 (special procedure for disclosure by banks).

> COMMENCEMENT DATE 6 April 2007[5]

**39.1177.02**    This section repeals a number of eclectic provisions in Part X of CA 1985 regulating the conduct of directors. Although these provisions have had limited impact in practice in terms of producing reported litigation, nevertheless the Company Law Review in its *Final Report*[6] (see, for example, paragraph 6.15) recommended such a deregulatory approach, preferring instead that some of these matters be dealt with under the aegis of the FSA's oversight of the financial markets.

### 1178   Repeal of requirement that certain companies publish periodical statement

**39.1178.01**    The following provisions shall cease to have effect—

> section 720 of the Companies Act 1985 (c. 6) (certain companies to publish periodical statement), and
> Schedule 23 to that Act (form of statement under section 720).

> COMMENCEMENT DATE 6 April 2007[7]

**39.1178.02**    Again we have a degree of deregulation in the sense of various repeals affecting specialized disclosure requirements. Section 720 of the 1985 Act (as supplemented by Schedule 23) dealt with the disclosure obligations of insurance and deposit-taking companies. For the rationale, see the Explanatory Notes to the Bill when it entered the Commons in May 2006, paragraph 1430.

### 1179   Repeal of requirement that Secretary of State prepare annual report

**39.1179.01**    Section 729 of the Companies Act 1985 (annual report to Parliament by Secretary of State on matters within the Companies Acts) shall cease to have effect.

> COMMENCEMENT DATE 6 April 2007[8]

**39.1179.02**    This repeals the Companies Act 1985, section 729. Here we have the government lessening the regulatory burden imposed upon its own agencies. Having said that, the DTI annual reports are a very useful source of empirical data for commentators. The government, in response to criticism of the repeal of this facility, argues that such information is available through other publicly accessible sources. Indeed, a perusal of the report for 2005–06 would indicate that such a policy of avoiding duplication of published data has produced a slimmer report for that particular year.

### 1180   Repeal of certain provisions about company charges

**39.1180.01**    Part 4 of the Companies Act 1989 (c. 40) (registration of company charges), which has not been brought into force, is repealed.

> COMMENCEMENT DATE 1 October 2009[9]

---

[3] See A Lidbetter, *DTI Investigations and Public Law* (Hart Publishing, 1999) at 12.1.1.
[4] Cm 4567, para 4.6.
[5] Companies Act 2006 (Commencement No 1, etc) Order 2006, SI 2006/3428, art 4.
[6] URN 01/942.
[7] Companies Act 2006 (Commencement No 1, etc) Order 2006, SI 2006/3428, art 4.
[8] Companies Act 2006 (Commencement No 1, etc) Order 2006, SI 2006/3428, art 4.
[9] Companies Act 2006 (Commencement No 8, Transitional Provisions and Savings) Order 2008, SI 2008/2860, art 3(v).

This repeals Part IV of CA 1989 and thus represents the final act in a sorry saga of company law reform.  **39.1180.02**
Part IV of the 1989 Act was meant to remodel the rules on company charge registration.[10] However,
consultation prior to this enactment was not effective and the enacted provisions were never brought
into force. More recently, the Law Commission, *Company Security Interests*,[11] has proposed its own
way forward for reforming the company charge registration system. We await with interest any action
on such reforms—company law reform orders originally intended to be authorized under this Act may
have been the preferred method of implementing these reforms, but this option has been closed off
with the abandonment of what was originally Part 31 of the Bill after criticism in Parliament. Instead of
making major reforms along the lines proposed by the Law Commission, the 2006 Act has opted for
minor tinkering/restatement (see Part 25), presumably as an interim measure.

In August 2012 a fresh attempt to secure some consensus on reform was launched by the BIS, when it  **39.1180.03**
issued proposed draft regulations for consultation. If implemented, these will make a large number of
changes to Part 25 with a view to unification and modernization of charge registration in the UK. The
new regulations were expected to have been laid before Parliament in Autumn 2012, but this had not
happened at the time of going to press.

## 1181  Access to constitutional documents of RTE and RTM companies

(1) The Secretary of State may by order—  **39.1181.01**
    (a) amend Chapter 1 of Part 1 of the Leasehold Reform, Housing and Urban Development Act
       1993 (c. 28) for the purpose of facilitating access to the provisions of the articles or any other
       constitutional document of RTE companies;
    (b) amend Chapter 1 of Part 2 of the Commonhold and Leasehold Reform Act 2002 (c. 15)
       (leasehold reform) for the purpose of facilitating access to the provisions of the articles or any
       other constitutional document of RTM companies.
(2) References in subsection (1) to provisions of a company's articles or any other constitutional
    document include any provisions included in those documents by virtue of any enactment.
(3) An order under this section is subject to negative resolution procedure.
(4) In this section—
    'RTE companies' has the same meaning as in Chapter 1 of Part 1 of the Leasehold Reform,
    Housing and Urban Development Act 1993;
    'RTM companies' has the same meaning as in Chapter 1 of Part 2 of the Commonhold and
    Leasehold Reform Act 2002.

COMMENCEMENT DATE  1 October 2009[12]

For the rationale, see the Explanatory Notes to the Act, paragraphs 1503 to 1505.  **39.1181.02**

Subsection (1) confers power on the Secretary of State to amend the Leasehold Reform, Housing and  **39.1181.03**
Urban Development Act 1993 and the Commonhold and Leasehold Reform Act 2002, to improve
transparency in the context of specialist companies. This is consistent with the general disclosure
policy—see CA 2006, section 32. For the definition of RTE (right to enfranchise) and RTM (right to
manage) companies, see subsection (4).

Subsections (2) and (4) are interpretation provisions.  **39.1181.04**

Subsection (3) states that the negative resolution procedure (see section 1289) is prescribed for  **39.1181.05**
amendments made in pursuance of this section.

For a detailed explanation of the policy underpinning section 1145, see the Explanatory Notes to the  **39.1181.06**
Bill when it entered the Commons in May 2006, paragraphs 1433 to 1435.

---

  [10] For discussion of its now lapsed provisions, see Ferran and Mayo [1991] JBL 152 and McCormack [1994]
JBL 587.
  [11] LC No 296, 2005. For a full account, see McCormack [2005] (18) *Sweet and Maxwell's Company Law
Newsletter* 1 and, for background, de Lacy [2004] JBL 448. For recent BIS thinking on company charge
registration see [2011] 294 *Sweet and Maxwell's Company Law Newsletter* 1.
  [12] Companies Act 2006 (Commencement No 8, Transitional Provisions and Savings) Order 2008, SI 2008/
2860, art 3(v).

# 40

# COMPANY DIRECTORS: FOREIGN DISQUALIFICATION ETC

## Companies Act 2006

### PART 40

### COMPANY DIRECTORS PROVISIONS: FOREIGN DISQUALIFICATION ETC

Commentary on this section of the CA 2006 has not been included
in this publication.

### *Introductory*

### 1182  Persons subject to foreign restrictions

(1)  This section defines what is meant by references in this Part to a person being subject to foreign restrictions.

(2)  A person is subject to foreign restrictions if under the law of a country or territory outside the United Kingdom—
  (a)  he is, by reason of misconduct or unfitness, disqualified to any extent from acting in connection with the affairs of a company,
  (b)  he is, by reason of misconduct or unfitness, required—
    (i)  to obtain permission from a court or other authority, or
    (ii)  to meet any other condition, before acting in connection with the affairs of a company, or
  (c)  he has, by reason of misconduct or unfitness, given undertakings to a court or other authority of a country or territory outside the United Kingdom—
    (i)  not to act in connection with the affairs of a company, or
    (ii)  restricting the extent to which, or the way in which, he may do so.

(3)  The references in subsection (2) to acting in connection with the affairs of a company are to doing any of the following—
  (a)  being a director of a company,
  (b)  acting as receiver of a company's property, or
  (c)  being concerned or taking part in the promotion, formation or management of a company.

(4)  In this section—
  (a)  'company' means a company incorporated or formed under the law of the country or territory in question, and

40.1182.01

(b) in relation to such a company—
'director' means the holder of an office corresponding to that of director of a UK company; and
'receiver' includes any corresponding officer under the law of that country or territory.

COMMENCEMENT DATE 1 October 2009[1]

### 1183 Meaning of 'the court' and 'UK company'

**40.1183.01**    In this Part—
'the court' means—
(a) in England and Wales, the High Court or a county court;
(b) in Scotland, the Court of Session or the sheriff court;
(c) in Northern Ireland, the High Court;
'UK company' means a company registered under this Act.

COMMENCEMENT DATE 1 October 2009[2]

## *Power to disqualify*

### 1184 Disqualification of persons subject to foreign restrictions

**40.1184.01**    (1) The Secretary of State may make provision by regulations disqualifying a person subject to foreign restrictions from—
(a) being a director of a UK company,
(b) acting as receiver of a UK company's property, or
(c) in any way, whether directly or indirectly, being concerned or taking part in the promotion, formation or management of a UK company.
(2) The regulations may provide that a person subject to foreign restrictions—
(a) is disqualified automatically by virtue of the regulations, or
(b) may be disqualified by order of the court on the application of the Secretary of State.
(3) The regulations may provide that the Secretary of State may accept an undertaking (a 'disqualification undertaking') from a person subject to foreign restrictions that he will not do anything which would be in breach of a disqualification under subsection (1).
(4) In this Part—
(a) a 'person disqualified under this Part' is a person—
(i) disqualified as mentioned in subsection (2)(a) or (b), or
(ii) who has given and is subject to a disqualification undertaking;
(b) references to a breach of a disqualification include a breach of a disqualification undertaking.
(5) The regulations may provide for applications to the court by persons disqualified under this Part for permission to act in a way which would otherwise be in breach of the disqualification.
(6) The regulations must provide that a person ceases to be disqualified under this Part on his ceasing to be subject to foreign restrictions.
(7) Regulations under this section are subject to affirmative resolution procedure.

COMMENCEMENT DATE 1 October 2009[3]

### 1185 Disqualification regulations: supplementary

**40.1185.01**    (1) Regulations under section 1184 may make different provision for different cases and may in particular distinguish between cases by reference to—
(a) the conduct on the basis of which the person became subject to foreign restrictions;
(b) the nature of the foreign restrictions;
(c) the country or territory under whose law the foreign restrictions were imposed.
(2) Regulations under section 1184(2)(b) or (5) (provision for applications to the court)—
(a) must specify the grounds on which an application may be made;
(b) may specify factors to which the court shall have regard in determining an application.
(3) The regulations may, in particular, require the court to have regard to the following factors—
(a) whether the conduct on the basis of which the person became subject to foreign restrictions would, if done in relation to a UK company, have led a court to make a disqualification order

---

[1] Companies Act 2006 (Commencement No 8, Transitional Provisions and Savings) Order 2008, SI 2008/2860, art 3(w).
[2] Companies Act 2006 (Commencement No 8, Transitional Provisions and Savings) Order 2008, SI 2008/2860, art 3(w).
[3] Companies Act 2006 (Commencement No 8, Transitional Provisions and Savings) Order 2008, SI 2008/2860, art 3(w).

on an application under the Company Directors Disqualification Act 1986 (c. 46) or the Company Directors Disqualification (Northern Ireland) Order 2002 (S.I. 2002/3150 (N.I. 4));

(b)  in a case in which the conduct on the basis of which the person became subject to foreign restrictions would not be unlawful if done in relation to a UK company, the fact that the person acted unlawfully under foreign law;

(c)  whether the person's activities in relation to UK companies began after he became subject to foreign restrictions;

(d)  whether the person's activities (or proposed activities) in relation to UK companies are undertaken (or are proposed to be undertaken) outside the United Kingdom.

(4)  Regulations under section 1184(3) (provision as to undertakings given to the Secretary of State) may include provision allowing the Secretary of State, in determining whether to accept an undertaking, to take into account matters other than criminal convictions notwithstanding that the person may be criminally liable in respect of those matters.

(5)  Regulations under section 1184(5) (provision for application to court for permission to act) may include provision—

(a)  entitling the Secretary of State to be represented at the hearing of the application, and

(b)  as to the giving of evidence or the calling of witnesses by the Secretary of State at the hearing of the application.

COMMENCEMENT DATE 1 October 2009[4]

## 1186   Offence of breach of disqualification

(1)  Regulations under section 1184 may provide that a person disqualified under this Part who acts in breach of the disqualification commits an offence.

**40.1186.01**

(2)  The regulations may provide that a person guilty of such an offence is liable—

(a)  on conviction on indictment, to imprisonment for a term not exceeding two years or a fine (or both);

(b)  on summary conviction—

(i)  in England and Wales, to imprisonment for a term not exceeding twelve months or to a fine not exceeding the statutory maximum (or both);

(ii)  in Scotland or Northern Ireland, to imprisonment for a term not exceeding six months, or to a fine not exceeding the statutory maximum (or both).

(3)  In relation to an offence committed before the commencement of section 154(1) of the Criminal Justice Act 2003 (c. 44), for 'twelve months' in subsection (2)(b)(i) substitute 'six months'.

COMMENCEMENT DATE 1 October 2009[5]

## Power to make persons liable for company's debts

## 1187   Personal liability for debts of company

(1)  The Secretary of State may provide by regulations that a person who, at a time when he is subject to foreign restrictions—

**40.1187.01**

(a)  is a director of a UK company, or

(b)  is involved in the management of a UK company, is personally responsible for all debts and other liabilities of the company incurred during that time.

(2)  A person who is personally responsible by virtue of this section for debts and other liabilities of a company is jointly and severally liable in respect of those debts and liabilities with—

(a)  the company, and

(b)  any other person who (whether by virtue of this section or otherwise) is so liable.

COMMENCEMENT DATE 1 October 2009[6]

## Power to require statements to be sent to the registrar of companies

## 1188   Statements from persons subject to foreign restrictions

(1)  The Secretary of State may make provision by regulations requiring a person who—

**40.1188.01**

(a)  is subject to foreign restrictions, and

(b)  is not disqualified under this Part, to send a statement to the registrar if he does anything that, if done by a person disqualified under this Part, would be in breach of the disqualification.

---

[4]  Companies Act 2006 (Commencement No 8, Transitional Provisions and Savings) Order 2008, SI 2008/2860, art 3(w).

[5]  Companies Act 2006 (Commencement No 8, Transitional Provisions and Savings) Order 2008, SI 2008/2860, art 3(w).

[6]  Companies Act 2006 (Commencement No 8, Transitional Provisions and Savings) Order 2008, SI 2008/2860, art 3(w).

(2) The statement must include such information as may be specified in the regulations relating to—
   (a) the person's activities in relation to UK companies, and
   (b) the foreign restrictions to which the person is subject.

(3) The statement must be sent to the registrar within such period as may be specified in the regulations.

(4) The regulations may make different provision for different cases and may in particular distinguish between cases by reference to—
   (a) the conduct on the basis of which the person became subject to foreign restrictions;
   (b) the nature of the foreign restrictions;
   (c) the country or territory under whose law the foreign restrictions were imposed.

(5) Regulations under this section are subject to affirmative resolution procedure.

COMMENCEMENT DATE 1 October 2009[7]

## 1189  Statements from persons disqualified

**40.1189.01**

(1) The Secretary of State may make provision by regulations requiring a statement or notice sent to the registrar of companies under any of the provisions listed below that relates (wholly or partly) to a person who—
   (a) is a person disqualified under this Part, or
   (b) is subject to a disqualification order or disqualification undertaking under the Company Directors Disqualification Act 1986 (c. 46) or the Company Directors Disqualification (Northern Ireland) Order 2002 (S.I. 2002/3150 (N.I. 4)), to be accompanied by an additional statement.

(2) The provisions referred to above are—
   (a) section 12 (statement of a company's proposed officers),
   (b) section 167(2) (notice of person having become director), and
   (c) section 276 (notice of a person having become secretary or one of joint secretaries).

(3) The additional statement is a statement that the person has obtained permission from a court, on an application under section 1184(5) or (as the case may be) for the purposes of section 1(1)(a) of the Company Directors Disqualification Act 1986 (c. 46) or Article 3(1) of the Company Directors Disqualification (Northern Ireland) Order 2002 (S.I. 2002/3150 (N.I. 4)), to act in the capacity in question.

(4) Regulations under this section are subject to affirmative resolution procedure.

COMMENCEMENT DATE 1 October 2009[8]

## 1190  Statements: whether to be made public

**40.1190.01**

(1) Regulations under section 1188 or 1189 (statements required to be sent to registrar) may provide that a statement sent to the registrar of companies under the regulations is to be treated as a record relating to a company for the purposes of section 1080 (the companies register).

(2) The regulations may make provision as to the circumstances in which such a statement is to be, or may be—
   (a) withheld from public inspection, or
   (b) removed from the register.

(3) The regulations may, in particular, provide that a statement is not to be withheld from public inspection or removed from the register unless the person to whom it relates provides such information, and satisfies such other conditions, as may be specified.

(4) The regulations may provide that section 1081 (note of removal of material from the register) does not apply, or applies with such modifications as may be specified, in the case of material removed from the register under the regulations.

(5) In this section 'specified' means specified in the regulations.

COMMENCEMENT DATE 1 October 2009[9]

---

[7] Companies Act 2006 (Commencement No 8, Transitional Provisions and Savings) Order 2008, SI 2008/2860, art 3(w).
[8] Companies Act 2006 (Commencement No 8, Transitional Provisions and Savings) Order 2008, SI 2008/2860, art 3(w).
[9] Companies Act 2006 (Commencement No 8, Transitional Provisions and Savings) Order 2008, SI 2008/2860, art 3(w).

## 1191   Offences

(1)  Regulations under section 1188 or 1189 may provide that it is an offence for a person—                **40.1191.01**

    (a)  to fail to comply with a requirement under the regulations to send a statement to the registrar;

    (b)  knowingly or recklessly to send a statement under the regulations to the registrar that is misleading, false or deceptive in a material particular.

(2)  The regulations may provide that a person guilty of such an offence is liable—

    (a)  on conviction on indictment, to imprisonment for a term not exceeding two years or a fine (or both);

    (b)  on summary conviction—

        (i)   in England and Wales, to imprisonment for a term not exceeding twelve months or to a fine not exceeding the statutory maximum (or both);

        (ii)  in Scotland or Northern Ireland, to imprisonment for a term not exceeding six months, or to a fine not exceeding the statutory maximum (or both).

(3)  In relation to an offence committed before the commencement of section 154(1) of the Criminal Justice Act 2003 (c. 44), for 'twelve months' in subsection (2)(b)(i) substitute 'six months'.

COMMENCEMENT DATE 1 October 2009[10]

---

[10]  Companies Act 2006 (Commencement No 8, Transitional Provisions and Savings) Order 2008, SI 2008/ 2860, art 3(w).

# 41

## BUSINESS NAMES

## Companies Act 2006

### PART 41
### BUSINESS NAMES

Commentary on this section of the CA 2006 has not been included
in this publication.

### CHAPTER 1
### RESTRICTED OR PROHIBITED NAMES

### *Introductory*

### 1192 Application of this Chapter

(1) This Chapter applies to any person carrying on business in the United Kingdom.     **41.1192.01**

(2) The provisions of this Chapter do not prevent—

    (a) an individual carrying on business under a name consisting of his surname without any addition other than a permitted addition, or

    (b) individuals carrying on business in partnership under a name consisting of the surnames of all the partners without any addition other than a permitted addition.

(3) The following are the permitted additions—

    (a) in the case of an individual, his forename or initial;

    (b) in the case of a partnership—

       (i) the forenames of individual partners or the initials of those forenames, or

       (ii) where two or more individual partners have the same surname, the addition of 's' at the end of that surname;

(c) in either case, an addition merely indicating that the business is carried on in succession to a former owner of the business.

COMMENCEMENT DATE 1 October 2009[1]

## Sensitive words or expressions

### 1193   Name suggesting connection with government or public authority

**41.1193.01**

(1) A person must not, without the approval of the Secretary of State, carry on business in the United Kingdom under a name that would be likely to give the impression that the business is connected with—

(a) Her Majesty's Government, any part of the Scottish administration[, the Welsh Assembly Government][a] or Her Majesty's Government in Northern Ireland,

(b) any local authority, or

(c) any public authority specified for the purposes of this section by regulations made by the Secretary of State.

(2) For the purposes of this section— 'local authority' means—

(a) a local authority within the meaning of the Local Government Act 1972 (c. 70), the Common Council of the City of London or the Council of the Isles of Scilly,

(b) a council constituted under section 2 of the Local Government etc. (Scotland) Act 1994 (c. 39), or

(c) a district council in Northern Ireland; 'public authority' includes any person or body having functions of a public nature.

(3) Regulations under this section are subject to affirmative resolution procedure.

(4) A person who contravenes this section commits an offence.

(5) Where an offence under this section is committed by a body corporate, an offence is also committed by every officer of the body who is in default.

(6) A person guilty of an offence under this section is liable on summary conviction to a fine not exceeding level 3 on the standard scale and, for continued contravention, a daily default fine not exceeding one-tenth of level 3 on the standard scale.

AMENDMENTS AND NOTES

[a] Inserted by the Government of Wales Act 2006 (Consequential Modifications, Transitional Provisions and Saving) Order 2009, SI 2009/2958, arts 8, 11.

COMMENCEMENT DATE 1 October 2009[2]

### 1194   Other sensitive words or expressions

**41.1194.01**

(1) A person must not, without the approval of the Secretary of State, carry on business in the United Kingdom under a name that includes a word or expression for the time being specified in regulations made by the Secretary of State under this section.

(2) Regulations under this section are subject to approval after being made.

(3) A person who contravenes this section commits an offence.

(4) Where an offence under this section is committed by a body corporate, an offence is also committed by every officer of the body who is in default.

(5) A person guilty of an offence under this section is liable on summary conviction to a fine not exceeding level 3 on the standard scale and, for continued contravention, a daily default fine not exceeding one-tenth of level 3 on the standard scale.

COMMENCEMENT DATE 1 October 2009[3]

### 1195   Requirement to seek comments of government department or other relevant body

**41.1195.01**

(1) The Secretary of State may by regulations under—

(a) section 1193 (name suggesting connection with government or public authority), or

---

[1] Companies Act 2006 (Commencement No 8, Transitional Provisions and Savings) Order 2008, SI 2008/2860, art 3(x).

[2] Companies Act 2006 (Commencement No 8, Transitional Provisions and Savings) Order 2008, SI 2008/2860, art 3(x).

[3] Companies Act 2006 (Commencement No 8, Transitional Provisions and Savings) Order 2008, SI 2008/2860, art 3(x).

(b)  section 1194 (other sensitive words or expressions), require that, in connection with an application for the approval of the Secretary of State under that section, the applicant must seek the view of a specified Government department or other body.

COMMENCEMENT DATE  1 October 2009[4]

## 1196  Withdrawal of Secretary of State's approval

(1)  This section applies to approval given for the purposes of—                **41.1196.01**
section 1193 (name suggesting connection with government or public authority), or
section 1194 (other sensitive words or expressions).

(2)  If it appears to the Secretary of State that there are overriding considerations of public policy that require such approval to be withdrawn, the approval may be withdrawn by notice in writing given to the person concerned.

(3)  The notice must state the date as from which approval is withdrawn.

COMMENCEMENT DATE  1 October 2009[5]

## *Misleading names*

## 1197  Name containing inappropriate indication of company type or legal form

(1)  The Secretary of State may make provision by regulations prohibiting a person from carrying on    **41.1197.01**
business in the United Kingdom under a name consisting of or containing specified words, expressions or other indications—
  (a)  that are associated with a particular type of company or form of organisation, or
  (b)  that are similar to words, expressions or other indications associated with a particular type of company or form of organisation.

(2)  The regulations may prohibit the use of words, expressions or other indications—
  (a)  in a specified part, or otherwise than in a specified part, of a name;
  (b)  in conjunction with, or otherwise than in conjunction with, such other words, expressions or indications as may be specified.

(3)  In this section 'specified' means specified in the regulations.

(4)  Regulations under this section are subject to negative resolution procedure.

(5)  A person who uses a name in contravention of regulations under this section commits an offence.

(6)  Where an offence under this section is committed by a body corporate, an offence is also committed by every officer of the body who is in default.

(7)  A person guilty of an offence under this section is liable on summary conviction to a fine not exceeding level 3 on the standard scale and, for continued contravention, a daily default fine not exceeding one-tenth of level 3 on the standard scale.

COMMENCEMENT DATE  1 October 2009[6]

## 1198  Name giving misleading indication of activities

(1)  A person must not carry on business in the United Kingdom under a name that gives so    **41.1198.01**
misleading an indication of the nature of the activities of the business as to be likely to cause harm to the public.

(2)  A person who uses a name in contravention of this section commits an offence.

(3)  Where an offence under this section is committed by a body corporate, an offence is also committed by every officer of the body who is in default.

(4)  A person guilty of an offence under this section is liable on summary conviction to a fine not exceeding level 3 on the standard scale and, for continued contravention, a daily default fine not exceeding one-tenth of level 3 on the standard scale.

COMMENCEMENT DATE  1 October 2009[7]

---

[4]  Companies Act 2006 (Commencement No 8, Transitional Provisions and Savings) Order 2008, SI 2008/2860, art 3(x).

[5]  Companies Act 2006 (Commencement No 8, Transitional Provisions and Savings) Order 2008, SI 2008/2860, art 3(x).

[6]  Companies Act 2006 (Commencement No 8, Transitional Provisions and Savings) Order 2008, SI 2008/2860, art 3(x).

[7]  Companies Act 2006 (Commencement No 8, Transitional Provisions and Savings) Order 2008, SI 2008/2860, art 3(x).

*Supplementary*

### 1199 Savings for existing lawful business names

**41.1199.01**
(1) This section has effect in relation to—

sections 1192 to 1196 (sensitive words or expressions), and section 1197 (inappropriate indication of company type or legal form).

(2) Those sections do not apply to the carrying on of a business by a person who—
    (a) carried on the business immediately before the date on which this Chapter came into force, and
    (b) continues to carry it on under the name that immediately before that date was its lawful business name.

(3) Where—
    (a) a business is transferred to a person on or after the date on which this Chapter came into force, and
    (b) that person carries on the business under the name that was its lawful business name immediately before the transfer, those sections do not apply in relation to the carrying on of the business under that name during the period of twelve months beginning with the date of the transfer.

(4) In this section 'lawful business name', in relation to a business, means a name under which the business was carried on without contravening—
    (a) section 2(1) of the Business Names Act 1985 (c. 7) or Article 4(1) of the Business Names (Northern Ireland) Order 1986 (S.I. 1986/1033 N.I. 7)), or
    (b) after this Chapter has come into force, the provisions of this Chapter.

COMMENCEMENT DATE 1 October 2009[8]

# CHAPTER 2
## DISCLOSURE REQUIRED IN CASE OF INDIVIDUAL OR PARTNERSHIP

*Introductory*

### 1200 Application of this Chapter

**41.1200.01**
(1) This Chapter applies to an individual or partnership carrying on business in the United Kingdom under a business name.

References in this Chapter to 'a person to whom this Chapter applies' are to such an individual or partnership.

(2) For the purposes of this Chapter a 'business name' means a name other than—
    (a) in the case of an individual, his surname without any addition other than a permitted addition;
    (b) in the case of a partnership—
      (i) the surnames of all partners who are individuals, and
      (ii) the corporate names of all partners who are bodies corporate, without any addition other than a permitted addition.

(3) The following are the permitted additions—
    (a) in the case of an individual, his forename or initial;
    (b) in the case of a partnership—
      (i) the forenames of individual partners or the initials of those forenames, or
      (ii) where two or more individual partners have the same surname, the addition of 's' at the end of that surname;
    (c) in either case, an addition merely indicating that the business is carried on in succession to a former owner of the business.

COMMENCEMENT DATE 1 October 2009[9]

---

[8] Companies Act 2006 (Commencement No 8, Transitional Provisions and Savings) Order 2008, SI 2008/2860, art 3(x).

[9] Companies Act 2006 (Commencement No 8, Transitional Provisions and Savings) Order 2008, SI 2008/2860, art 3(x).

## [1201 Information required to be disclosed

The 'information required by this Chapter' is—                                               **41.1201.01**

(a)  in the case of an individual, the individual's name;

(b)  in the case of a partnership, the name of each member of the partnership; and in relation to each person so named, an address at which service of any document relating in any way to the business will be effective.

(2)  If the individual or partnership has a place of business in the United Kingdom, the address must be in the United Kingdom.

(3)  If the individual or partnership does not have a place of business in the United Kingdom, the address must be an address at which service of documents can be effected by physical delivery and the delivery of documents is capable of being recorded by the obtaining of an acknowledgement of delivery.][a]

AMENDMENTS AND NOTES

[a] Substituted by the Companies Act 2006 (Substitution of Section 1201) Regulations 2009, SI 2009/3182, reg 2.

COMMENCEMENT DATE  1 October 2009[10]

## *Disclosure requirements*

## 1202  Disclosure required: business documents etc

(1)  A person to whom this Chapter applies must state the information required by this Chapter, in     **41.1202.01** legible characters, on all—

(a)  business letters,

(b)  written orders for goods or services to be supplied to the business,

(c)  invoices and receipts issued in the course of the business, and

(d)  written demands for payment of debts arising in the course of the business.

This subsection has effect subject to section 1203 (exemption for large partnerships if certain conditions met).

(2)  A person to whom this Chapter applies must secure that the information required by this Chapter is immediately given, by written notice, to any person with whom anything is done or discussed in the course of the business and who asks for that information.

(3)  The Secretary of State may by regulations require that such notices be given in a specified form.

(4)  Regulations under this section are subject to negative resolution procedure.

COMMENCEMENT DATE  1 October 2009[11]

## 1203  Exemption for large partnerships if certain conditions met

(1)  Section 1202(1) (disclosure required in business documents) does not apply in relation to a     **41.1203.01** document issued by a partnership of more than 20 persons if the following conditions are met.

(2)  The conditions are that—

(a)  the partnership maintains at its principal place of business a list of the names of all the partners,

(b)  no partner's name appears in the document, except in the text or as a signatory, and

(c)  the document states in legible characters the address of the partnership's principal place of business and that the list of the partners' names is open to inspection there.

(3)  Where a partnership maintains a list of the partners' names for the purposes of this section, any person may inspect the list during office hours.

(4)  Where an inspection required by a person in accordance with this section is refused, an offence is committed by any member of the partnership concerned who without reasonable excuse refused the inspection or permitted it to be refused.

(5)  A person guilty of an offence under subsection (4) is liable on summary conviction to a fine not exceeding level 3 on the standard scale and, for continued contravention, a daily default fine not exceeding one-tenth of level 3 on the standard scale.

COMMENCEMENT DATE  1 October 2009[12]

---

[10] Companies Act 2006 (Commencement No 8, Transitional Provisions and Savings) Order 2008, SI 2008/2860, art 3(x).

[11] Companies Act 2006 (Commencement No 8, Transitional Provisions and Savings) Order 2008, SI 2008/2860, art 3(x).

[12] Companies Act 2006 (Commencement No 8, Transitional Provisions and Savings) Order 2008, SI 2008/2860, art 3(x).

## 1204   Disclosure required: business premises

**41.1204.01**   (1)   A person to whom this Chapter applies must, in any premises—
  (a)   where the business is carried on, and
  (b)   to which customers of the business or suppliers of goods or services to the business have access, display in a prominent position, so that it may easily be read by such customers or suppliers, a notice containing the information required by this Chapter.
  (2)   The Secretary of State may by regulations require that such notices be displayed in a specified form.
  (3)   Regulations under this section are subject to negative resolution procedure.

COMMENCEMENT DATE 1 October 2009[13]

## *Consequences of failure to make required disclosure*

## 1205   Criminal consequences of failure to make required disclosure

**41.1205.01**   (1)   A person who without reasonable excuse fails to comply with the requirements of—
    section 1202 (disclosure required: business documents etc), or
    section 1204 (disclosure required: business premises), commits an offence.
  (2)   Where an offence under this section is committed by a body corporate, an offence is also committed by every officer of the body who is in default.
  (3)   A person guilty of an offence under this section is liable on summary conviction to a fine not exceeding level 3 on the standard scale and, for continued contravention, a daily default fine not exceeding one-tenth of level 3 on the standard scale.
  (4)   References in this section to the requirements of section 1202 or 1204 include the requirements of regulations under that section.

COMMENCEMENT DATE 1 October 2009[14]

## 1206   Civil consequences of failure to make required disclosure

**41.1206.01**   (1)   This section applies to any legal proceedings brought by a person to whom this Chapter applies to enforce a right arising out of a contract made in the course of a business in respect of which he was, at the time the contract was made, in breach of section 1202(1) or (2) (disclosure in business documents etc) or section 1204(1) (disclosure at business premises).
  (2)   The proceedings shall be dismissed if the defendant (in Scotland, the defender) to the proceedings shows—
  (a)   that he has a claim against the claimant (pursuer) arising out of the contract that he has been unable to pursue by reason of the latter's breach of the requirements of this Chapter, or
  (b)   that he has suffered some financial loss in connection with the contract by reason of the claimant's (pursuer's) breach of those requirements, unless the court before which the proceedings are brought is satisfied that it is just and equitable to permit the proceedings to continue.
  (3)   References in this section to the requirements of this Chapter include the requirements of regulations under this Chapter.
  (4)   This section does not affect the right of any person to enforce such rights as he may have against another person in any proceedings brought by that person.

COMMENCEMENT DATE 1 October 2009[15]

---

[13] Companies Act 2006 (Commencement No 8, Transitional Provisions and Savings) Order 2008, SI 2008/2860, art 3(x).
[14] Companies Act 2006 (Commencement No 8, Transitional Provisions and Savings) Order 2008, SI 2008/2860, art 3(x).
[15] Companies Act 2006 (Commencement No 8, Transitional Provisions and Savings) Order 2008, SI 2008/2860, art 3(x).

# CHAPTER 3
## SUPPLEMENTARY

### 1207   Application of general provisions about offences

The provisions of sections 1121 to 1123 (liability of officer in default) and 1125 to 1131 (general provisions about offences) apply in relation to offences under this Part as in relation to offences under the Companies Acts.

**41.1207.01**

COMMENCEMENT DATE 1 October 2009[16]

### 1208   Interpretation

In this Part—

**41.1208.01**

'business' includes a profession;
'initial' includes any recognised abbreviation of a name;
'partnership' means—
   (a)   a partnership within the Partnership Act 1890 (c. 39), or
   (b)   a limited partnership registered under the Limited Partnerships Act 1907 (c. 24), or a firm or entity of a similar character formed under the law of a country or territory outside the United Kingdom;
'surname', in relation to a peer or person usually known by a British title different from his surname, means the title by which he is known.

COMMENCEMENT DATE 1 October 2009[17]

---

[16] Companies Act 2006 (Commencement No 8, Transitional Provisions and Savings) Order 2008, SI 2008/ 2860, art 3(x).
[17] Companies Act 2006 (Commencement No 8, Transitional Provisions and Savings) Order 2008, SI 2008/ 2860, art 3(x).

# 42

## STATUTORY AUDITORS

## Companies Act 2006

# PART 42
## STATUTORY AUDITORS

**42.01** Part 42 of the Companies Act 2006 restates and amends Part II of the Companies Act 1989. In addition, several of the provisions implement the Statutory Audit Directive 2006/43/EC [2006] OJ/157/87 which, amongst others, repealed Council Directive 84/253/EEC [1984] OJ/L126/20 (known as the Eighth Company Law Directive on Audit). Part II of the Companies Act 1989 implemented Council Directive 84/253 [1984] OJ/L126/20. Chapter 3 of Part 42, which deals with Auditors General, implements the recommendations provided by Lord Sharman's report *Holding to Account, The Review of Audit and Accountability for Central Government* (2001).

**42.02** Pursuant to the Statutory Auditors (Amendment of Companies Act 2006 and Delegation of Functions etc) Order 2012, SI 2012/1741[1] , the functions of the Secretary of State under Part 42 of the Act have been transferred to the Financial Reporting Council Limited. Previously these functions were executed by the Professional Oversight Board (POB) which was established under the articles of association of the Professional Oversight Board Limited, a subsidiary of the Financial Reporting Council. Anything relating to the previous activity of the POB remains in force and is now treated as if done by the FRC[2] . The functions of the Secretary of State under the following sections have not been transferred: sections 1210(1)(h), 1214(4), 1231(2)(a) and (3), 1237(3), 1239(1)(b), 1246, 1261(3), and 1263. Certain functions under the following subsections are exercised concurrently by the Secretary of State and the FRC: sections 1224, 1239(8), 1244, 1253A, and 1254. Certain functions transferred to the FRC are only exercisable with the consent of the Secretary of State: sections 1221(1), 1221(7), 1253B(1) and 1253E(7)(a). The function in section 1241(2)(c) remain exercisable concurrently by and with the consent of the Secretary of State only.

---

[1] Art 6 of that SI revokes the Statutory Auditors (Delegation of Functions etc) Order 2008, SI 2008/496 with effect from 2 July 2012.

[2] The Statutory Auditors (Amendment of Companies Act 2006 and Delegation of Functions etc) Order 2012, SI 2012/1741, Art 16.

The Statutory Auditors and Third Party Auditors Regulations 2007, SI 2007/3494, resulted in a   **42.03**
significant number of amendments to the statutory provisions[3] .All these amendments have been
incorporated in the statutory text as set forth below. Many of the amendments implement the Statutory
Audit Directive, amending Council Directives 78/660/EEC and 83/349/EEC, and repealing Council
Directive 84/253. Note that the Statutory Auditors and Third Party Auditors Regulations 2007, SI
2007/3494 have been amended by the Statutory Auditors and Third Country Auditors (Amendment)
Regulations 2011.

# CHAPTER 1
## INTRODUCTORY

### 1209   Main purposes of Part

The main purposes of this Part are—                                             **42.1209.01**

(a)   to secure that only persons who are properly supervised and appropriately qualified are appointed
      as statutory auditors, and
(b)   to secure that audits by persons so appointed are carried out properly, with integrity and with a
      proper degree of independence.

COMMENCEMENT DATE   6 April 2008[4]

The purpose of this Part 42 of the Act is to provide for the regulation of the supervision and   **42.1209.02**
qualifications of statutory auditors, and the regulation of audit practice, auditor integrity, and
independence.

### 1210   Meaning of 'statutory auditor' etc

(1)   In this Part 'statutory auditor' means—                                   **42.1210.01**
      (a)   a person appointed as auditor under Part 16 of this Act,
      (b)   a person appointed as auditor under section 77 of or Schedule 11 to the Building Societies
            Act 1986 (c. 53),
      (c)   a person appointed as auditor of an insurer that is a friendly society under section 72 of or
            Schedule 14 to the Friendly Societies Act 1992 (c. 40),
      (d)   [...][a]
      (e)   a person appointed as auditor for the purposes of regulation 3 of the Insurance Accounts
            Directive (Lloyd's Syndicate and Aggregate Accounts) Regulations 2004 (S.I. 2004/3219) or
            appointed to report on the 'aggregate accounts' within the meaning of those Regulations,
      [(f)   a person appointed as auditor of an insurance undertaking for the purposes of the Insurance
            Accounts Directive (Miscellaneous Insurance Undertakings) Regulations 2008,][b]
      [(g)   a person appointed as auditor of a bank for the purposes of the Bank Accounts Directive
            (Miscellaneous Banks) Regulations 2008,][c]
      (h)   a person appointed as auditor of a prescribed person under a prescribed enactment
            authorizing or requiring the appointment; and the expressions 'statutory audit' and 'statu-
            tory audit work' are to be construed accordingly.
(2)   In this Part 'audited person' means the person in respect of whom a statutory audit is conducted.
(3)   In subsection (1)—
      'bank' means a person who—
      (a)   is a credit institution within the meaning given by Article 4.1(a) of Directive 2006/48/EC of
            the European Parliament and of the Council relating to the taking up and pursuit of the
            business of credit institutions, and
      (b)   is is a company or a firm as defined in Article 54 of the Treaty on the Functioning of the
            European Union[e];
      'friendly society' means a friendly society within the meaning of the Friendly Societies Act
      1992 (c. 40);
      [...][d]
      'industrial and provident society' means—
      (a)   a society registered under the Industrial and Provident Societies Act 1965 (c. 12) or a
            society deemed by virtue of section 4 of that Act to be so registered, or

---

[3]   The Statutory Auditors and Third Party Auditors Regulations 2007 have been amended by the following
amendment regulations: the Statutory Auditors and Third Country Auditors (Amendment) Regulations, SI
2008/499 and the Statutory Auditors and Third Country Auditors (Amendment) (No 2) Regulations, SI
2008/2639 as well as the Statutory Auditors and Third Country Auditors (Amendment) Regulations 2011, SI
2011/1856. References to the Statutory Auditors and Third Party Auditors Regulations 2007 are to the Regulations as amended.
[4]   Companies Act 2006 (Commencement No 5, Transitional Provisions and Savings) Order 2007, SI 2007/
3495, art 3.

(b)  a society registered under the Industrial and Provident Societies Act (Northern Ireland) 1969 or a society deemed by virtue of section 4 of that Act to be so registered;

'insurer' means a person who is an insurance undertaking within the meaning given by Article 2.1 of Council Directive 1991/674/EEC on the annual accounts and consolidated accounts of insurance undertakings;

'prescribed' means prescribed, or of a description prescribed, by order made by the Secretary of State for the purposes of subsection (1)(h).

(4)  An order under this section is subject to negative resolution procedure.

AMENDMENTS AND NOTES

<sup>a</sup> Repealed in relation to insurance undertakings' financial years beginning on or after 6 April 2008 and auditors appointed in respect of those financial years, by the Insurance Accounts Directive (Miscellaneous Insurance Undertakings) Regulations 2008, SI 2008/565, reg 15(1)(b)(i).

<sup>b</sup> Substituted in relation to insurance undertakings' financial years beginning on or after 6 April 2008 and auditors appointed in respect of those financial years, by the Insurance Accounts Directive (Miscellaneous Insurance Undertakings) Regulations 2008, SI 2008/565, reg 15(1)(a).

<sup>c</sup> Substituted in relation to qualifying banks' financial years beginning on or after 6 April 2008 and auditors appointed in respect of those financial years, by the Bank Accounts Directive (Miscellaneous Banks) Regulations 2008, SI 2008/567, reg 14.

<sup>d</sup> Repealed in relation to insurance undertakings' financial years beginning on or after 6 April 2008 and auditors appointed in respect of those financial years, by the Insurance Accounts Directive (Miscellaneous Insurance Undertakings) Regulations 2008, SI 2008/565, reg 1(2).

<sup>e</sup> Amended from 1 August 2012 by the Treaty of Lisbon (Changes in Terminology or Numbering) Order 2012, SI 2012/1809

COMMENCEMENT DATE  6 April 2008[5]

**42.1210.02**   This Part 42 applies to statutory auditors as boardly defined in this section 1210 of the Companies Act 2006. Part 2 of the Companies Act 1989 only regulated company auditors. Accordingly, the broader definition of auditors brings several other auditors in addition to company auditors within the ambit of the statute.

### 1211  Eligibility for appointment as a statutory auditor: overview

**42.1211.01**   A person is eligible for appointment as a statutory auditor only if the person is so eligible—

(a)  by virtue of Chapter 2 (individuals and firms), or

(b)  by virtue of Chapter 3 (Comptroller and Auditor General, etc).

COMMENCEMENT DATE  6 April 2008[6]

**42.1211.02**   This section provides in order to eligible to be a statutory auditor a person must comply with *either* the eligibility requirements for individuals and firms set forth in Chapter 2 of Part 42 *or* the eligibility requirements for comptrollers and Auditors General set forth in Chapter 3 of Part 42.

## CHAPTER 2
## INDIVIDUALS AND FIRMS

### *Eligibility for appointment*

### 1212  Individuals and firms: eligibility for appointment as a statutory auditor

**42.1212.01**   (1)  An individual or firm is eligible for appointment as a statutory auditor if the individual or firm—

(a)  is a member of a recognised supervisory body, and

(b)  is eligible for appointment under the rules of that body.

(2)  In the cases to which section 1222 applies (individuals retaining only 1967 Act authorization) a person's eligibility for appointment as a statutory auditor is restricted as mentioned in that section.

COMMENCEMENT DATE  6 April 2008[7]

---

[5]  Companies Act 2006 (Commencement No 5, Transitional Provisions and Savings) Order 2007, SI 2007/3495, art 3.

[6]  Companies Act 2006 (Commencement No 5, Transitional Provisions and Savings) Order 2007, SI 2007/3495, art 3.

[7]  Companies Act 2006 (Commencement No 5, Transitional Provisions and Savings) Order 2007, SI 2007/3495, art 3. This provision applies to the appointment of auditors for financial years beginning on or after 6 April 2008.

Section 1212 provides for the basic conditions of eligibility, namely, membership of a recognized    **42.1212.02**
supervisory body and eligibility for appointment pursuant to the rules of such body.

## 1213  Effect of ineligibility

(1) No person may act as statutory auditor of an audited person if he is ineligible for appointment as    **42.1213.01**
    a statutory auditor.
(2) If at any time during his term of office a statutory auditor becomes ineligible for appointment as
    a statutory auditor, he must immediately—
    (a)  resign his office (with immediate effect), and
    (b)  give notice in writing to the audited person that he has resigned by reason of his becoming
         ineligible for appointment.
(3) A person is guilty of an offence if—
    (a)  he acts as a statutory auditor in contravention of subsection (1), or
    (b)  he fails to give the notice mentioned in paragraph (b) of subsection (2) in accordance with
         that subsection.
(4) A person guilty of an offence under subsection (3) is liable—
    (a)  on conviction on indictment, to a fine;
    (b)  on summary conviction, to a fine not exceeding the statutory maximum.
(5) A person is guilty of an offence if—
    (a)  he has been convicted of an offence under subsection (3)(a) or this subsection, and
    (b)  he continues to act as a statutory auditor in contravention of subsection (1) after the
         conviction.
(6) A person is guilty of an offence if—
    (a)  he has been convicted of an offence under subsection (3)(b) or this subsection, and
    (b)  he continues, after the conviction, to fail to give the notice mentioned in subsection (2)(b).
(7) A person guilty of an offence under subsection (5) or (6) is liable—
    (a)  on conviction on indictment, to a fine;
    (b)  on summary conviction, to a fine not exceeding one-tenth of the statutory maximum for each
         day on which the act or the failure continues.
(8) In proceedings against a person for an offence under this section it is a defence for him to show
    that he did not know and had no reason to believe that he was, or had become, ineligible for
    appointment as a statutory auditor.

COMMENCEMENT DATE 6 April 2008[8]

Section 1213 provides that an ineligible person may not act as a statutory auditor and if at any time a    **42.1213.02**
statutory auditor becomes ineligible then he must immediately and with immediate effect resign his
office and inform the audited person, for example a company, in writing that he has had to resign
because he is no longer eligible to serve as an auditor.

Section 1213(3) to (7) sets forth the offences and fines applicable to persons who contravene and who    **42.1213.03**
continue to contravene these provisions. Subsection (8) provides a defence where the person in
question 'had no reason to believe' that either he was ineligible or that he had become ineligible for
appointment as statutory auditor.

## *Independence requirement*

## 1214  Independence requirement

(1) A person may not act as statutory auditor of an audited person if one or more of subsections (2),    **42.1214.01**
    (3) and (4) apply to him.
(2) This subsection applies if the person is—
    (a)  an officer or employee of the audited person, or
    (b)  a partner or employee of such a person, or a partnership of which such a person is a partner.
(3) This subsection applies if the person is—
    (a)  an officer or employee of an associated undertaking of the audited person, or
    (b)  a partner or employee of such a person, or a partnership of which such a person is a partner.
(4) This subsection applies if there exists, between—
    (a)  the person or an associate of his, and
    (b)  the audited person or an associated undertaking of the audited person, a connection of any
         such description as may be specified by regulations made by the Secretary of State.
(5) An auditor of an audited person is not to be regarded as an officer or employee of the person for
    the purposes of subsections (2) and (3).

---

[8]  Companies Act 2006 (Commencement No 5, Transitional Provisions and Savings) Order 2007, SI 2007/
3495, art 3. This provision applies to the appointment of auditors for financial years beginning on or after 6 April
2008.

(6) In this section 'associated undertaking', in relation to an audited person, means—
    (a) a parent undertaking or subsidiary undertaking of the audited person, or
    (b) a subsidiary undertaking of a parent undertaking of the audited person.
(7) Regulations under subsection (4) are subject to negative resolution procedure.

COMMENCEMENT DATE 6 April 2008[9]

**42.1214.02**  Although this section's heading refers to 'independence requirement', the section does not use the concept of independence as a precondition to being able to act as a statutory auditor; rather the section sets forth specific auditor–client relationships that would prohibit the auditor from acting. These prohibitions provide that a person cannot act as a statutory auditor if he is an officer or employee of the audited person or of an associated undertaking of the audited person. In addition, neither a partner nor employee of such officer or employee, nor a partnership in which such officer or employee is a partner may act as the statutory auditor. Associated undertaking is defined to include the audited person's parent or subsidiary[10] as well another subsidiary of a common parent (section 1214(6)).

**42.1214.03**  Section 1214(4)(b) enables the Secretary of State to prescribe other types of relationship between the potential auditor and the audited person (or its associated undertaking), or between the auditor's 'associate' and the audited person (or its associated undertaking).This power has been transferred to the Financial Reporting Council (FRC)[11]. 'Associate' is broadly defined for the purposes of this Part of the Act in section 1260.

**42.1214.04**  More comprehensive regulation of the auditor independence requirement is not set forth in the Act. Such regulation is provided by the Auditing Practices Board's[12] *Ethical Standards*, which provide general principled-based independence requirements[13] as well as specific rules to regulate: conflict of interests arising from certain financial, business, employment, and personal relationships;[14] the length of audit partner–client relationships;[15] audit fees, partner remuneration, as well as gifts and hospitality from the audit client;[16] and the provision of non-audit services.[17] These Ethical Standards are given a form of statutory backing by section 1217 as explained at that section.

### 1215   Effect of lack of independence

**42.1215.01**  (1) If at any time during his term of office a statutory auditor becomes prohibited from acting by section 1214(1), he must immediately—
    (a) resign his office (with immediate effect), and
    (b) give notice in writing to the audited person that he has resigned by reason of his lack of independence.
(2) A person is guilty of an offence if—
    (a) he acts as a statutory auditor in contravention of section 1214(1), or
    (b) he fails to give the notice mentioned in paragraph (b) of subsection (1) in accordance with that subsection.
(3) A person guilty of an offence under subsection (2) is liable—
    (a) on conviction on indictment, to a fine;
    (b) on summary conviction, to a fine not exceeding the statutory maximum.
(4) A person is guilty of an offence if—
    (a) he has been convicted of an offence under subsection (2)(a) or this subsection, and
    (b) he continues to act as a statutory auditor in contravention of section 1214(1) after the conviction.
(5) A person is guilty of an offence if—
    (a) he has been convicted of an offence under subsection (2)(b) or this subsection, and
    (b) after the conviction, he continues to fail to give the notice mentioned in subsection (1)(b).
(6) A person guilty of an offence under subsection (4) or (5) is liable—

---

[9] Companies Act 2006 (Commencement No 5, Transitional Provisions and Savings) Order 2007, SI 2007/3495, art 3. This provision applies to the appointment of auditors for financial years beginning on or after 6 April 2008.
[10] Subsidiary is defined in s 1159 of the Companies Act (CA) 2006. This definition includes subsidiaries of subsidiaries.
[11] Statutory Auditors (Amendment of Companies Act 2006 and Delegation of Functions etc) Order 2012, SI 2012/1741, art 2.
[12] The Auditing Practices Board has been replaced, following the reorganization of the Financial Reporting Council (FRC) from July 2012, by the FRC Board. Its literature remains in place, however.
[13] *Ethical Standard 1, Integrity, objectivity and independence.*
[14] *Ethical Standard 2, Financial, business, employment and personal relationships.*
[15] *Ethical Standard 3, Long association with the audit engagement.*
[16] *Ethical Standard 4, Fees, remuneration and evaluation policies, litigation. Gifts and hospitality.*
[17] *Ethical Standard 5, Non-audit services provided to audited entities.*

(a) on conviction on indictment, to a fine;

(b) on summary conviction, to a fine not exceeding one-tenth of the statutory maximum for each day on which the act or the failure continues.

(7) In proceedings against a person for an offence under this section it is a defence for him to show that he did not know and had no reason to believe that he was, or had become, prohibited from acting as statutory auditor of the audited person by section 1214(1).

COMMENCEMENT DATE 6 April 2008[18]

If a statutory auditor becomes ineligible as a result of entering one of the prohibited relationships set **42.1215.02** forth in section 1214 or any regulation made thereunder then he must immediately and with immediate effect resign his office and inform the audited person in writing that he has had to resign because he lacks the required independence to serve as a statutory auditor (section 1215(1)). Subsections (2) to (6) set forth the offences and fines applicable to persons who contravene and who continue to contravene these provisions. Subsection (7) provides a defence where the person in question 'did not know and had no reason to believe' that he did not comply with section 1214(1).

## *Effect of appointment of a partnership*

## 1216 Effect of appointment of a partnership

(1) This section applies where a partnership constituted under the law of— **42.1216.01**

(a) England and Wales,

(b) Northern Ireland, or

(c) any other country or territory in which a partnership is not a legal person,

is by virtue of this Chapter appointed as statutory auditor of an audited person.

(2) Unless a contrary intention appears, the appointment is an appointment of the partnership as such and not of the partners.

(3) Where the partnership ceases, the appointment is to be treated as extending to—

(a) any appropriate partnership which succeeds to the practice of that partnership, or

(b) any other appropriate person who succeeds to that practice having previously carried it on in partnership.

(4) For the purposes of subsection (3)—

(a) a partnership is to be regarded as succeeding to the practice of another partnership only if the members of the successor partnership are substantially the same as those of the former partnership, and

(b) a partnership or other person is to be regarded as succeeding to the practice of a partnership only if it or he succeeds to the whole or substantially the whole of the business of the former partnership.

(5) Where the partnership ceases and the appointment is not treated under subsection (3) as extending to any partnership or other person, the appointment may with the consent of the audited person be treated as extending to an appropriate partnership, or other appropriate person, who succeeds to—

(a) the business of the former partnership, or

(b) such part of it as is agreed by the audited person is to be treated as comprising the appointment.

(6) For the purposes of this section, a partnership or other person is 'appropriate' if it or he—

(a) is eligible for appointment as a statutory auditor by virtue of this Chapter, and

(b) is not prohibited by section 1214(1) from acting as statutory auditor of the audited person.

COMMENCEMENT DATE 6 April 2008[19]

This section provides that when a partnership is appointed statutory auditor it is the partnership and **42.1216.02** not the partners who are appointed. It also addresses the effect of appointing a partnership when the partnership ends and the practice of the partnership is succeeded to by a new partnership. Effectively, the new partnership will be deemed to succeed to the appointment provided it is eligible to become a statutory auditor, does not contravene the independence requirements of section 1214(1), and the new partnership is 'substantially' the same as the old partnership in terms of members and business. Where the successor is eligible to be a statutory auditor but does not comply with either or both of the

---

[18] Companies Act 2006 (Commencement No 5, Transitional Provisions and Savings) Order 2007, SI 2007/3495, art 3. This provision applies to the appointment of auditors for financial years beginning on or after 6 April 2008.

[19] Companies Act 2006 (Commencement No 5, Transitional Provisions and Savings) Order 2007, SI 2007/3495, art 3. This provision applies to the appointment of auditors for financial years beginning on or after 6 April 2008.

membership or business succession requirements, the appointment may be transferred to the successor provided the audited person consents.

**42.1216.03**    Pursuant to regulation 5 of the Companies Act 2006 (Consequential Amendments etc) Order 2008, SI 2008/948, for the purposes of application to other statutory appointments for which eligibility depends on Part 42 eligibility,the reference in subsection 6(b) to being prohibited by virtue of section 1214(1) from acting as statutory auditor 'shall be read as including a reference to being prohibited or disqualified from acting, or ineligible or disqualified for appointment, on the ground of lack of independence (of any description) by virtue of any other enactment applying in relation to the appointment.

## Supervisory bodies

### 1217  Supervisory bodies

**42.1217.01**        (1)  In this Part a 'supervisory body' means a body established in the United Kingdom (whether a body corporate or an unincorporated association) which maintains and enforces rules as to—
        (a)  the eligibility of persons for appointment as a statutory auditor, and
        (b)  the conduct of statutory audit work,
        which are binding on persons seeking appointment or acting as a statutory auditor because they are members of that body [...]ᵃ.
      [(1A)  The rules referred to in paragraphs 9(3)(b) (confidentiality of information) and 10C(3)(a) and (b) (bar on appointment as director or other officer) of Schedule 10 must also be binding on persons who—
        (a)  have sought appointment or acted as a statutory auditor, and
        (b)  have been members of the body at any time after the commencement of this Part.]ᵇ
        (2)  In this Part references to the members of a supervisory body are to the persons who, whether or not members of the body, are subject to its rules in seeking appointment or acting as a statutory auditor.
        (3)  In this Part references to the rules of a supervisory body are to the rules (whether or not laid down by the body itself) which the body has power to enforce and which are relevant for the purposes of this Part.
        This includes rules relating to the admission or expulsion of members of the body, so far as relevant for the purposes of this Part.
        (4)  Schedule 10 has effect with respect to the recognition of supervisory bodies for the purposes of this Part.

AMENDMENTS AND NOTES

ᵃ  Repealed by the Statutory Auditors and Third Country Auditors Regulations 2007, SI 2007/3494, reg 4(1), (2).

ᵇ  Inserted by the Statutory Auditors and Third Country Auditors Regulations 2007, SI 2007/3494, reg 4(1), (3).

COMMENCEMENT DATE  6 April 2008[20]

**42.1217.02**    This section provides for a definition of a supervisory body. In order to be a 'supervisory body' the body must have been established in the UK as a body corporate or an unincorporated association, and must both *maintain* and *enforce* eligibility rules for appointment as a statutory auditor as well as rules relating to the conduct of the audit.[21]

**42.1217.03**    It is worth noting again that in order to be eligible to act as a statutory auditor one has to be a member of a recognized supervisory body (section 1212(1)(a)).

**42.1217.04**    Schedule 10 of the Act sets forth the procedure and regulation of the recognition of a supervisory body by the Secretary of State. These functions have been transferred to the FRC.[22] There are five recognized supervisory bodies: the Institute of Chartered Accountants in England and Wales (ICAEW); the Institute of Chartered Accountants in Scotland (ICAS); the Institute of Chartered Accountants in Ireland (ICAI); the Association of Chartered Certified Accountants (ACCA); and the Association of Authorised Public Accountants (AAPA).

**42.1217.05**    In order to become a recognized supervisory body, the body must have in place a set of rules in the areas set forth in Schedule 10. These include, amongst others, rules on qualifications, integrity and

---

[20]  Companies Act 2006 (Commencement No 5, Transitional Provisions and Savings) Order 2007, SI 2007/3495, art 3. This provision applies to the auditors appointed for financial years beginning on or after 6 April 2008.
[21]

[22]  The Statutory Auditors (Amendment of Companies Act 2006 and Delegation of Functions etc) Order 2012, SI 2012/1741 which revokes Statutory Auditors (Delegation of Functions etc) Order 2008, SI 2008/496.

independence, discipline, and the investigation of complaints and the monitoring of competence (see generally, Part 2 of Schedule 10).

The Schedule 10 requirement for rules on the conduct of audit is the means of giving a form of statutory backing to auditing standards. This arises because the recognized supervisory bodies identify auditing standards issued by the Auditing Practices Board (APB), prior to July 2012, as the technical rules for the conduct of audits. See for example the ICAEW's *Audit regulation and guidance* (June 2012), chapter 3 and chapter 1's definitions. Since July 2012 the Financial Reporting Council, the parent body of the APB, has taken over direct responsibility for setting auditing standards (and the APB no longer exists). It is to be expected that the recognized supervisory bodies will include post-July 2012 FRC auditing standards within the body of technical rules for the conduct of audits. It is assumed that these bodies would not be permitted to continue as recognized supervisory bodies unless this was so. The Schedule 10 requirement for rules on integrity and independence also, in a similar way, leads to some statutory backing for the *APB Ethical standards for auditors*.   **42.1217.06**

The Act delegates to the recognized supervisory bodies certain public law functions and, accordingly, its actions may be subject to judicial review. Applications for judicial review have typically taken place in relation to disciplinary decisions made by the recognized supervisory body. See, for example, *Gorlov v The Institute for Chartered Accountants in England and Wales*[23] and *R v Institute for Chartered Accountants and Others ex p Brindle.*[24]   **42.1217.07**

## 1218   Exemption from liability for damages

(1)  No person within subsection (2) is to be liable in damages for anything done or omitted in the discharge or purported discharge of functions to which this subsection applies.   **42.1218.01**
(2)  The persons within this subsection are—
    (a)  any recognised supervisory body,
    (b)  any officer or employee of a recognised supervisory body, and
    (c)  any member of the governing body of a recognised supervisory body.
(3)  Subsection (1) applies to the functions of a recognised supervisory body so far as relating to, or to matters arising out of, any of the following—
    (a)  rules, practices, powers and arrangements of the body to which the requirements of Part 2 of Schedule 10 apply;
    (b)  the obligations with which paragraph 20 of that Schedule requires the body to comply;
    (c)  any guidance issued by the body;
    (d)  the obligations imposed on the body by or by virtue of this Part.
(4)  The reference in subsection (3)(c) to guidance issued by a recognised supervisory body is a reference to any guidance or recommendation which is—
    (a)  issued or made by it to all or any class of its members or persons seeking to become members, and
    (b)  relevant for the purposes of this Part,
    including any guidance or recommendation relating to the admission or expulsion of members of the body, so far as relevant for the purposes of this Part.
(5)  Subsection (1) does not apply—
    (a)  if the act or omission is shown to have been in bad faith, or
    (b)  so as to prevent an award of damages in respect of the act or omission on the ground that it was unlawful as a result of section 6(1) of the Human Rights Act 1998 (c. 42) (acts of public authorities incompatible with Convention rights).

COMMENCEMENT DATE  6 April 2008[25]

This section provides for an exemption from liability for recognized supervisory bodies, their officers, employees, and members of their governing bodies in the performance of their supervisory functions (set forth in section 1218(3)). These functions include, for example: the matters arising from the rules and standards relating to professional qualifications or the proper conduct of audit work which Part 2 of Schedule 10 (Requirements for Recognition of a Supervisory Body) require the body to have in order to be recognized as a Supervisory Body; any guidance issued by the body, which could include, for example, guidance on audit practice or accounting treatments; and matters arising as a result of the Supervisory Body complying with the obligations imposed on it by Part 42.   **42.1218.02**

Subsection (5) removes the liability exemption where the act or omission was in bad faith or is unlawful pursuant to section 6(1) of the Human Rights Act 1998, which provides that it is unlawful for a public   **42.1218.03**

---

[23]  [2002] EWHC 2202.
[24]  [1994] BCC 297.
[25]  Companies Act 2006 (Commencement No 5, Transitional Provisions and Savings) Order 2007, SI 2007/3495, art 3. This provision applies to the auditors appointed for financial years beginning on or after 6 April 2008.

authority to act in a way that is incompatible with a 'convention right' as defined in section 1 of the Human Rights Act 1998.

## *Professional qualifications*

### 1219  Appropriate qualifications

**42.1219.01**

(1) A person holds an appropriate qualification for the purposes of this Chapter if and only if—

    (a) he holds a recognised professional qualification obtained in the United Kingdom,

    (b) immediately before the commencement of this Chapter, he—

      (i) held an appropriate qualification for the purposes of Part 2 of the Companies Act 1989 (c. 40) (eligibility for appointment as company auditor) by virtue of section 31(1)(a) or (c) of that Act, or

      (ii) was treated as holding an appropriate qualification for those purposes by virtue of section 31(2), (3) or (4) of that Act,

    (c) immediately before the commencement of this Chapter, he—

      (i) held an appropriate qualification for the purposes of Part III of the Companies (Northern Ireland) Order 1990 (S.I. 1990/593 (N.I. 5)) by virtue of Article 34(1)(a) or (c) of that Order, or

      (ii) was treated as holding an appropriate qualification for those purposes by virtue of Article 34(2), (3) or (4) of that Order,

    (d) he is within subsection (2), [or]ᵃ

    (e) […]ᵇ

    (f) subject to any direction under section 1221(5), he is regarded for the purposes of this Chapter as holding an approved [third country]ᶜ qualification.

(2) A person is within this subsection if—

    (a) before 1st January 1990, he began a course of study or practical training leading to a professional qualification in accountancy offered by a body established in the United Kingdom,

    (b) he obtained that qualification on or after 1st January 1990 and before 1st January 1996, and

    (c) the Secretary of State approves his qualification as an appropriate qualification for the purposes of this Chapter.

(3) The Secretary of State may approve a qualification under subsection (2)(c) only if he is satisfied that, at the time the qualification was awarded, the body concerned had adequate arrangements to ensure that the qualification was awarded only to persons educated and trained to a standard equivalent to that required, at that time, in the case of a recognised professional qualification under Part 2 of the Companies Act 1989 (c. 40) (eligibility for appointment as company auditor).

AMENDMENTS AND NOTES

ᵃ Inserted by the Statutory Auditors and Third Country Auditors Regulations 2007, SI 2007/3494, reg 5(a).

ᵇ Repealed by the Statutory Auditors and Third Country Auditors Regulations 2007, SI 2007/3494, reg 5(b).

ᶜ Substituted by the Statutory Auditors and Third Country Auditors Regulations 2007, SI 2007/3494, reg 5(c).

COMMENCEMENT DATE  6 April 2008[26]

**42.1219.02**  This section provides for the meaning of an appropriate qualification. Pursuant to paragraph 6 of Schedule 10 of the Act, in order to be a recognized supervisory body the body must have in place rules providing that a member is not eligible to act as a statutory auditor unless he has an 'appropriate qualification'.

**42.1219.03**  Section 1219 sets forth a list of appropriate qualifications in the UK, in the EU, and overseas. Most importantly for anyone studying in the UK intending to become an accountant, under subsection (1)(a) they must obtain a 'recognized professional qualification' (see section 1220 of the Companies Act 2006, below).

**42.1219.04**  Pursuant to the Statutory Auditors (Amendment of Companies Act 2006 and Delegation of Functions etc) Order 2012, SI 2012/1741, all powers of the Secretary of State under this section have been transferred to the FRC.

---

[26] Companies Act 2006 (Commencement No 5, Transitional Provisions and Savings) Order 2007, SI 2007/3495, art 3. This provision applies to the auditors appointed for financial years beginning on or after 6 April 2008.

## 1220   Qualifying bodies and recognised professional qualifications

(1)  In this Part a 'qualifying body' means a body established in the United Kingdom (whether a body       **42.1220.01**
corporate or an unincorporated association) which offers a professional qualification in accountancy.

(2)  In this Part references to the rules of a qualifying body are to the rules (whether or not laid down
by the body itself) which the body has power to enforce and which are relevant for the purposes
of this Part.

This includes, so far as so relevant, rules relating to—

(a)  admission to or expulsion from a course of study leading to a qualification,

(b)  the award or deprivation of a qualification, or

(c)  the approval of a person for the purposes of giving practical training or the withdrawal of
such approval.

(3)  Schedule 11 has effect with respect to the recognition for the purposes of this Part of a
professional qualification offered by a qualifying body.

COMMENCEMENT DATE  6 April 2008[27]

In order to be eligible to act as a statutory auditor, an auditor must be a member of a recognized       **42.1220.02**
supervisory body (section 1212). In order to be a member of such a body, the auditor must have an
appropriate qualification. One of the appropriate qualifications identified by section 1219(1)(a) is a
'recognised professional qualification obtained in the United Kingdom'. Schedule 11, which is given
effect by section 1220(3), sets out the process for obtaining a grant of recognition of a professional
qualification (Part 1, Schedule 11) as well as the qualification requirements necessary to obtain such
recognition (Part 2, Schedule 11). Such an application may be made by a 'qualifying body' (paragraph
1(1), Schedule 11), which is defined in section 1220(1) as a UK body which offers a professional
accountancy qualification. A 'recognised qualifying body' is a body which provides a 'recognised
professional qualification' (paragraph 1(2), Schedule 11).

The six recognized qualifying bodies are: ICAEW, ICAI, ICAS, ACCA, the Association of International       **42.1220.03**
Accountants, and the Chartered Institute of Public Finance and Accountancy.

Pursuant to the Statutory Auditors ((Amendment of Companies Act 2006 and Delegation of Functions       **42.1220.04**
etc) Order 2012, SI 2012/1741, all powers of the Secretary of State under this section have been
transferred to the FRC.

## 1221   Approval of [third country][a] qualifications

(1)  The Secretary of State may declare that the following are to be regarded for the purposes of this       **42.1221.01**
Chapter as holding an approved [third country][b] qualification—

(a)  persons who are qualified to audit accounts under the law of a specified [third country][c], or

(b)  persons who hold a specified professional qualification in accountancy obtained in a
specified [third country][d].

[(1A)   A declaration under subsection (1)(a) or (b) must be expressed to be subject to the requirement
that any person to whom the declaration relates must pass an aptitude test in accordance with
subsection (7A), unless an aptitude test is not required (see subsection (7B)).][e]

(2)  A declaration under subsection (1)(b) may be expressed to be subject to the satisfaction of any
specified requirement or requirements.

(3)  The Secretary of State may make a declaration under subsection (1) only if he is satisfied that—

(a)  in the case of a declaration under subsection (1)(a), the fact that the persons in question are
qualified to audit accounts under the law of the specified [third country][f], or

(b)  in the case of a declaration under subsection (1)(b), the specified professional qualification
taken with any requirement or requirements to be specified under subsection (2),

affords an assurance of professional competence equivalent to that afforded by a recognised
professional qualification.

(4)  The Secretary of State may make a declaration under subsection (1) only if he is satisfied that the
treatment that the persons who are the subject of the declaration will receive as a result of it is
comparable to the treatment which is, or is likely to be, afforded in the specified [third country][g]
or a part of it to—

(a)  in the case of a declaration under subsection (1)(a), some or all persons who are eligible to be
appointed as a statutory auditor, and

(b)  in the case of a declaration under subsection (1)(b), some or all persons who hold a
corresponding recognised professional qualification.

---

[27]  Companies Act 2006 (Commencement No 5, Transitional Provisions and Savings) Order 2007, SI 2007/
3495, art 3. This provision applies to the auditors appointed for financial years beginning on or after 6 April 2008.

(5) The Secretary of State may direct that persons holding an approved [third country]$^h$ qualification are not to be treated as holding an appropriate qualification for the purposes of this Chapter unless they hold such additional educational qualifications as the Secretary of State may specify for the purpose of ensuring that such persons have an adequate knowledge of the law and practice in the United Kingdom relevant to the audit of accounts.

(6) The Secretary of State may give different directions in relation to different approved [third country]$^i$ qualifications.

(7) The Secretary of State may, if he thinks fit, having regard to the considerations mentioned in subsections (3) and (4), withdraw a declaration under subsection (1) in relation to—

    (a) persons becoming qualified to audit accounts under the law of the specified [third country]$^j$ after such date as he may specify, or

    (b) persons obtaining the specified professional qualification after such date as he may specify.

[(7A) An aptitude test required for the purposes of subsection (1A)—

    (a) must test the person's knowledge of subjects—

        (i) that are covered by a recognised professional qualification,

        (ii) that are not covered by the professional qualification already held by the person, and

        (iii) the knowledge of which is essential for the pursuit of the profession of statutory auditor;

    (b) may test the person's knowledge of rules of professional conduct;

    (c) must not test the person's knowledge of any other matters.

(7B) No aptitude test is required for the purposes of subsection (1A) if the subjects that are covered by a recognized professional qualification and the knowledge of which is essential for the pursuit of the profession of statutory auditor are covered by the professional qualification already held by the person.]$^k$

(8) The Secretary of State may, if he thinks fit, having regard to the considerations mentioned in subsections (3) and (4), vary or revoke a requirement specified under subsection (2) from such date as he may specify.

(9) [...]$^l$

AMENDMENTS AND NOTES

$^a$ Substituted by the Statutory Auditors and Third Country Auditors Regulations 2007, SI 2007/3494, reg 6(1), (2).

$^b$ Substituted by the Statutory Auditors and Third Country Auditors Regulations 2007, SI 2007/3494, reg 6(1), (2).

$^c$ Substituted by the Statutory Auditors and Third Country Auditors Regulations 2007, SI 2007/3494, reg 6(1), (2).

$^d$ Substituted by the Statutory Auditors and Third Country Auditors Regulations 2007, SI 2007/3494, reg 6(1), (3).

$^e$ Inserted by the Statutory Auditors and Third Country Auditors Regulations 2007, SI 2007/3494, reg 6(1), (4).

$^f$ Substituted by the Statutory Auditors and Third Country Auditors Regulations 2007, SI 2007/3494, reg 6(1), (3).

$^g$ Substituted by the Statutory Auditors and Third Country Auditors Regulations 2007, SI 2007/3494, reg 6(1), (3).

$^h$ Substituted by the Statutory Auditors and Third Country Auditors Regulations 2007, SI 2007/3494, reg 6(1), (2).

$^i$ Substituted by the Statutory Auditors and Third Country Auditors Regulations 2007, SI 2007/3494, reg 6(1), (2).

$^j$ Substituted by the Statutory Auditors and Third Country Auditors Regulations 2007, SI 2007/3494, reg 6(1), (3).

$^k$ Inserted by the Statutory Auditors and Third Country Auditors Regulations 2007, SI 2007/3494, reg 6(1), (4).

$^l$ Repealed by the Statutory Auditors and Third Country Auditors Regulations 2007, SI 2007/3494, reg 6(1), (6).

COMMENCEMENT DATE 6 April 2008[28]

**42.1221.02**  This section provides that the Secretary of State may make a declaration that a person qualified or holding qualifications from a specified non-EU country (section 1221(9)) is deemed to hold an 'approved third party qualification' and therefore, subject to any additional educational requirements

---

[28] Companies Act 2006 (Commencement No 5, Transitional Provisions and Savings) Order 2007, SI 2007/3495, art 3. This provision applies to the auditors appointed for financial years beginning on or after 6 April 2008.

specified under section 1221(5),[29] an 'appropriate qualification'.[30] Subsection (4) provides that the Secretary of State may *only* make such a declaration where the third country in question affords reciprocity to UK eligible statutory auditors and persons holding UK recognized professional qualifications.

Pursuant to the Statutory Auditors (Amendment of Companies Act 2006 and Delegation of Functions etc) Order 2012, SI 2012/1741, all powers of the Secretary of State under this section have been transferred to the FRC.                                                                                **42.1221.03**

## 1222   Eligibility of individuals retaining only 1967 Act authorisation

(1) A person whose only appropriate qualification is based on his retention of an authorisation      **42.1222.01**
originally granted by the Board of Trade or the Secretary of State under section 13(1) of the
Companies Act 1967 (c. 81) is eligible only for appointment as auditor of an unquoted company.
(2) A company is 'unquoted' if, at the time of the person's appointment, neither the company, nor
any parent undertaking of which it is a subsidiary undertaking, is a quoted company within the
meaning of section 385(2).
(3) References to a person eligible for appointment as a statutory auditor by virtue of this Part in
enactments relating to eligibility for appointment as auditor of a person other than a company do
not include a person to whom this section applies.

COMMENCEMENT DATE  6 April 2008[31]

This section provides that persons whose appropriate qualification was an authorization granted      **42.1222.02**
under the Companies 1967 may only act as auditor of an unquoted company and no other person. This
restriction applies to quoted companies (as defined in section 358(2)) but also to companies who are
not quoted pursuant to that definition but whose parent undertaking[32] is quoted.

## *Information*

## 1223   Matters to be notified to the Secretary of State

(1) The Secretary of State may require a recognised supervisory body or a recognised qualifying      **42.1223.01**
body—
 (a) to notify him immediately of the occurrence of such events as he may specify in writing and
to give him such information in respect of those events as is so specified;
 (b) to give him, at such times or in respect of such periods as he may specify in writing, such
information as is so specified.
(2) The notices and information required to be given must be such as the Secretary of State may
reasonably require for the exercise of his functions under this Part.
(3) The Secretary of State may require information given under this section to be given in a specified
form or verified in a specified manner.
(4) Any notice or information required to be given under this section must be given in writing unless
the Secretary of State specifies or approves some other manner.

COMMENCEMENT DATE  6 April 2008[33]

This section provides the power to require recognized supervisory bodies and recognized qualifying    **42.1223.02**
bodies to provide immediate notification of and information regarding specified events. Furthermore,
this section provides the power for the Secretary of State to request periodic information from these
bodies. Subsection (2) provides that the powers can only be exercised to the extent that they are
reasonably required to perform the functions delegated to the Secretary of State under Part 42 of the
Companies Act 2006.

Pursuant to the Statutory Auditors (Amendment of Companies Act 2006 and Delegation of Functions     **42.1223.03**
etc) Order 2012, SI 2012/1741, all powers of the Secretary of State under this section have been
transferred to the FRC.

---

[29] No such requirements were specified under the predecessor provision, s 33(4) of the CA 1989.
[30] S 1219(1)(f).
[31] Companies Act 2006 (Commencement No 5, Transitional Provisions and Savings) Order 2007, SI 2007/
3495, art 3. This provision applies to the auditors appointed for financial years beginning on or after 6 April 2008.
[32] See commentary to s 1162.
[33] Companies Act 2006 (Commencement No 5, Transitional Provisions and Savings) Order 2007, SI 2007/
3495, art 3.

**[1223A Notification of matters relevant to other EEA States**

**42.1223A.01**
(1) A recognised supervisory body must notify the Secretary of State of—
   (a) any withdrawal of a notifiable person's eligibility for appointment as a statutory auditor; and
   (b) the reasons for the withdrawal.
(2) A recognised supervisory body must also notify the Secretary of State of any reasonable grounds it has for suspecting that—
   (a) a person has contravened the law of the United Kingdom, or any other EEA State or part of an EEA State, implementing the Audit Directive, and
   (b) the act or omission constituting that contravention took place on the territory of an EEA State other than the United Kingdom.
(3) In this section 'notifiable person' means a member of the recognised supervisory body in question—
   (a) who is also an EEA auditor; and
   (b) in respect of whom the EEA competent authority is not the recognised supervisory body itself.][a]

AMENDMENTS AND NOTES

[a] Inserted by the Statutory Auditors and Third Country Auditors Regulations 2007, SI 2007/3494, reg 7(1).

COMMENCEMENT DATE 6 April 2008[34]

**42.1223A.02**    This provision requires that the recognized supervisory body notify the Secretary of State of any reasonable grounds the body has for suspecting that one of its members has violated the law of a European Economic Area Member State implementing the Audit Directive and where the action in question took place outside the UK but in an EEA state. For this section to apply the statutory auditor in question must be an EEA auditor, as defined in section 1261 of the Companies Act 2006 and the EEA competent authority for that auditor is not the recognized supervisory body which is subject to the notification obligations set forth in this section. However, note that the section only applies to EEA auditors who have been appointed as statutory auditors for the financial years commencing after 6 April 2008.[35]

**42.1223A.03**    Pursuant to the Statutory Auditors (Amendment of Companies Act 2006 and Delegation of Functions etc) Order 2012, SI 2012/1741, all powers of the Secretary of State under this section have been transferred to the FRC.

## 1224 The Secretary of State's power to call for information

**42.1224.01**
(1) The Secretary of State may by notice in writing require a person within subsection (2) to give him such information as he may reasonably require for the exercise of his functions under this Part.
(2) The persons within this subsection are—
   (a) any recognised supervisory body,
   (b) any recognised qualifying body, and
   (c) any person eligible for appointment as a statutory auditor by virtue of this Chapter.
(3) The Secretary of State may require that any information which he requires under this section is to be given within such reasonable time and verified in such manner as he may specify.

COMMENCEMENT DATE 6 April 2008[36]

**42.1224.02**    The section provides that the Secretary of State can require a recognized supervisory body, a recognized qualifying body, or a person eligible to act as a statutory auditor to provide information. Section 1224 extends the remit of these powers to eligible statutory auditors (section 1224(2)(c)). These powers may, however, only be exercised to the extent that they are reasonably required to perform the functions delegated to the Secretary of State under Part 42 of the Companies Act 2006.

**42.1224.03**    Pursuant to the Statutory Auditors (Amendment of Companies Act 2006 and Delegation of Functions etc) Order 2012, SI 2012/1741, all powers of the Secretary of State under this section have been transferred to the FRC.

---

[34] Statutory Auditors and Third Country Auditors Regulations 2007, SI 2007/3494
[35] Statutory Auditors and Third Country Auditors Regulations 2007, SI 2007/3494, reg 7(2).
[36] Companies Act 2006 (Commencement No 5, Transitional Provisions and Savings) Order 2007, SI 2007/3495, art 3.

## [1224A   Restrictions on disclosure

(1)  This section applies to information (in whatever form)—          42.1224A.01
    (a)  relating to the private affairs of an individual, or
    (b)  relating to any particular business,
    that is provided to a body to which this section applies in connection with the exercise of its functions under this Part or sections 522 to 524 (notification to appropriate audit authority of resignation or removal of auditor).

(2)  This section applies to—
    (a)  a recognised supervisory body,
    (b)  a recognised qualifying body,
    (c)  a body performing functions for the purposes of arrangements within paragraph 23(1) (independent monitoring of certain audits), [paragraph 23A(1) (independent monitoring of third country audits)][a] or paragraph 24(1) (independent investigation of public interest cases) of Schedule 10,
    (d)  the Independent Supervisor,
    (e)  the Secretary of State, and
    (f)  a body designated by the Secretary of State under section 1252 (delegation of the Secretary of State's functions).

(3)  No such information may, during the lifetime of the individual or so long as the business continues to be carried on, be disclosed without the consent of that individual or (as the case may be) the person for the time being carrying on that business.

(4)  Subsection (3) does not apply to any disclosure of information that—
    (a)  is made for the purpose of facilitating the carrying out by the body of any of its functions,
    (b)  is made to a person specified in Part 1 of Schedule 11A,
    (c)  is of a description specified in Part 2 of that Schedule, or
    (d)  is made in accordance with Part 3 of that Schedule.

(5)  Subsection (3) does not apply to—
    (a)  the disclosure by an EEA competent authority of information disclosed to it by the body in reliance on subsection (4);
    (b)  the disclosure of such information by anyone who has obtained it directly or indirectly from an EEA competent authority.

(6)  This section does not prohibit the disclosure of information if the information is or has been available to the public from any other source.

(7)  Nothing in this section authorises the making of a disclosure in contravention of the Data Protection Act 1998.][b]

AMENDMENTS AND NOTES

[a]  Inserted by The Statutory Auditors and Third Country Auditors (Amendment) Regulations 2011, SI 2011/1856, reg 3

[b]  Inserted by the Statutory Auditors and Third Country Auditors Regulations 2007, SI 2007/3494, reg 8(1).

COMMENCEMENT DATE  6 April 2008[37]

This section provides for restriction on the disclosure of information[38] relating to a particular business          42.1224A.02
or to the private affairs of an individual by any body exercising functions under Part 42 of the Act or in relation to auditor resignation or removal notifications pursuant to sections 522, 523 and 524 of the 2006 Act. Such information cannot be disclosed without the consent of the individual in question or the person carrying on the business unless such information is already in the public domain or falls within one of the exceptions set forth in subsection (4). Most importantly, these exceptions include a broad general exemption category allowing disclosure where the body in question must disclose in order to carry out its statutory functions. A list of 17 persons to whom disclosure does not result in a violation of section 1224A are set forth in Schedule 11A; these include, for example, the Treasury, the Bank of England and the Financial Services Authority.

## [1224B   Offence of disclosure in contravention of section 1224A

(1)  A person who discloses information in contravention of section 1224A (restrictions on disclosure)          42.1224B.01
is guilty of an offence, unless—
    (a)  he did not know, and had no reason to suspect, that the information had been provided as mentioned in section 1224A(1), or

---

[37]  Statutory Auditors and Third Country Auditors Regulations 2007, SI 2007/3494.
[38]  Pursuant to reg 8(3) of the Statutory Auditors and Third Country Auditors Regulations 2007, SI 2007/3494, this section only applies to information provided on or after 6 April 2008.

(b) he took all reasonable steps and exercised all due diligence to avoid the commission of the offence.

(2) A person guilty of an offence under this section is liable—

    (a) on conviction on indictment, to imprisonment for a term not exceeding two years or a fine (or both);

    (b) on summary conviction—

        (i) in Scotland, to imprisonment for a term not exceeding 12 months or to a fine not exceeding the statutory maximum, or to both;

        (ii) in England and Wales or Northern Ireland, to imprisonment for a term not exceeding three months or to a fine not exceeding the statutory maximum, or to both.][a]

AMENDMENTS AND NOTES

[a] Inserted by the Statutory Auditors and Third Country Auditors Regulations 2007, SI 2007/3494, reg 8(1).

COMMENCEMENT DATE 6 April 2008[39]

**42.1224B.02**   This section sets forth criminal sanctions for any person who fails to comply with the information disclosure restrictions set forth in section 1224A.

## *Enforcement*

### 1225   Enforcement: general

**42.1225.01**

(1) This section applies if at any time it appears to the Secretary of State—

    (a) in the case of a recognised supervisory body, that any requirement of Part 2 or 3 of Schedule 10 is not satisfied,

    (b) in the case of a recognised professional qualification offered by a recognised qualifying body, that any requirement of Part 2 of Schedule 11 is not satisfied, or

    (c) that a recognised supervisory body or a recognised qualifying body has not complied with an obligation imposed on it by or by virtue of this Part (other than an obligation to pay a financial penalty under section 1225D).

(2) The Secretary of State may do any one or more of the following—

    (a) give a direction to the body under section 1225A;

    (b) make an application to the court in respect of the body under section 1225C;

    (c) impose a financial penalty on the body under section 1225D.

(3) Subsection (2) is without prejudice to the powers of the Secretary of State under paragraph 3 of Schedule 10 and paragraph 3 of Schedule 11 (revocation of recognition orders).

AMENDMENTS AND NOTES

Subsection (1) amended by The Statutory Auditors (Amendment of Companies Act 2006 and Delegation of Functions etc) Order 2012, SI 2012/1741, previously read

(1) If at any time it appears to the Secretary of State—

    (a) in the case of a recognised supervisory body, that any requirement of Schedule 10 is not satisfied,

    (b) in the case of a recognised professional qualification, that any requirement of Schedule 11 is not satisfied, or

    (c) that a recognised supervisory body or a recognised qualifying body has failed to comply with an obligation to which it is subject under or by virtue of this Part, he may, instead of revoking the relevant recognition order, make an application to the court under this section.

(2) If on an application under this section the court decides that the requirement in question is not satisfied or, as the case may be, that the body has failed to comply with the obligation in question, it may order the body to take such steps as the court directs for securing that the requirement is satisfied or that the obligation is complied with.

(3) In this section 'the court' means the High Court or, in Scotland, the Court of Session.

COMMENCEMENT DATE 2 July 2012[40]

### 1225A   Direction: general

**42.1225A.01**

(1) A direction under this section is one directing a body to take such steps as the Secretary of State considers will—

    (a) secure that the requirement in question is satisfied or the obligation in question is complied with, or

---

[39] Statutory Auditors and Third Country Auditors Regulations 2007, SI 2007/3494.

[40] The Statutory Auditors (Amendment of Companies Act 2006 and Delegation of Functions etc) Order 2012, SI 2012/1741.

(b) mitigate the effect, or prevent the recurrence, of the failure to satisfy the requirement or comply with the obligation.

(2) A direction under this section—

(a) may only require a body to take steps which it has power to take;

(b) may require a body to refrain from taking a particular course of action.

(3) The power to give a direction under this section is subject to any provision made by or under any other enactment.

(4) The Secretary of State may take such steps as the Secretary of State considers appropriate to monitor the extent to which a direction under this section is being, or has been, complied with.

COMMENCEMENT DATE 2 July 2012[41]

## 1225B  Directions: supplementary

(1) Before giving a direction to a body under section 1225A, the Secretary of State must give the body a notice (a 'notice of proposed direction') accompanied by a copy of the proposed direction.

**42.1225B.01**

(2) A notice of proposed direction must—

(a) state that the Secretary of State proposes to give the body a direction in the form of the accompanying draft,

(b) identify the requirement or obligation in question and state why it appears to the Secretary of State that the requirement is not satisfied or the obligation has not been complied with,

(c) specify a period within which the body may make written representations with respect to the proposal.

(3) The period specified under subsection (2)(c)—

(a) must begin with the date on which the notice of proposed direction is given to the body, and

(b) must not be less than 14 days.

(4) Written representations made by the body within the period specified under subsection (2)(c) must be considered by the Secretary of State.

(5) After considering any such representations or, in their absence, on the expiry of the period specified under subsection (2)(c), the Secretary of State must decide whether to give the body the proposed direction.

(6) The Secretary of State must give notice of the decision (a 'direction decision notice') to the body.

(7) Where the Secretary of State decides to give the proposed direction, the direction decision notice must—

(a) contain the direction,

(b) state the time at which the direction is to take effect, and

(c) specify the Secretary of State's reasons for the decision to give the direction.

(8) Where the Secretary of State decides to give the proposed direction, the Secretary of State must publish the direction decision notice in such manner as the Secretary of State considers appropriate for bringing the direction to the attention of persons likely to be affected.

(9) The Secretary of State may revoke a direction given to a body under section 1225A and, where doing so, must—

(a) give the body notice of the revocation, and

(b) publish the notice in the same manner as the direction decision notice was published.

COMMENCEMENT DATE 2 July 2012[42]

## 1225C  Compliance orders

(1) If on an application under this section in respect of a body, the court decides that a requirement is not satisfied or an obligation has not been complied with, the court may, subject to subsection (2), order the body to take such steps as it considers will secure that the requirement is satisfied or the obligation is complied with.

**42.1225C.01**

(2) Where the obligation is an obligation to comply with a direction under section 1225A, the court may not order compliance with the direction unless it also decides that—

(a) the requirement in respect of which the direction was given is not satisfied, or

(b) the obligation in respect of which the direction was given has not been complied with.

(3) In this section, 'the court' means the High Court or, in Scotland, the Court of Session.

COMMENCEMENT DATE 2 July 2012[43]

---

[41] The Statutory Auditors (Amendment of Companies Act 2006 and Delegation of Functions etc) Order 2012, SI 2012/1741.

[42] The Statutory Auditors (Amendment of Companies Act 2006 and Delegation of Functions etc) Order 2012, SI 2012/1741.

[43] The Statutory Auditors (Amendment of Companies Act 2006 and Delegation of Functions etc) Order 2012, SI 2012/1741.

## 1225D Financial penalties: general

**42.1225D.01**

(1) A financial penalty imposed on a body under this section is a financial penalty of such amount as the Secretary of State considers appropriate, subject to subsection (2).

(2) In deciding what amount is appropriate the Secretary of State—

    (a) must have regard to the nature of the requirement which is not satisfied or the obligation which has not been complied with; and

    (b) must not take into account the Secretary of State's costs in discharging functions under this Part.

(3) A financial penalty under this section is payable to the Secretary of State.

(4) In sections 1225E to 1225G, references to a penalty are to a financial penalty under this section.

COMMENCEMENT DATE 2 July 2012[44]

## 1225E Financial penalties: supplementary

**42.1225E.01**

(1) Before imposing a penalty on a body, the Secretary of State must give the body a notice (a 'notice of proposed penalty')—

    (a) stating that the Secretary of State proposes to impose a penalty and the amount of the penalty proposed,

    (b) identifying the requirement or obligation in question and stating why it appears to the Secretary of State that the requirement is not satisfied or the obligation has not been complied with, and

    (c) specifying a period within which the body may make written representations with respect to the proposed penalty.

(2) The period specified under subsection (1)(c)—

    (a) must begin with the date on which the notice of proposed penalty is given to the body, and

    (b) must not be less than 21 days.

(3) Written representations made by the body before the end of the period specified under subsection (1)(c) must be considered by the Secretary of State.

(4) After considering any such representations or, in their absence, on the expiry of the period specified under subsection (1)(c), the Secretary of State must decide—

    (a) whether to impose a penalty, and

    (b) where the Secretary of State decides to do so, whether to reduce the proposed amount of the penalty.

(5) The Secretary of State must give notice of the decision (a 'penalty decision notice') to the body.

(6) Where the Secretary of State decides to impose a penalty, the penalty decision notice must—

    (a) state that the Secretary of State has imposed a penalty on the body and its amount,

    (b) identify the requirement or obligation in question and state—

        (i) why it appears to the Secretary of State that the requirement is not satisfied or the obligation has not been complied with, or

        (ii) where, by that time, the requirement is satisfied or the obligation has been complied with, why it appeared to the Secretary of State when giving the notice of proposed penalty that the requirement was not satisfied or the obligation had not been complied with, and

    (c) specify a time by which the penalty is required to be paid.

(7) The time specified under subsection (6)(c) must be at least 3 months after the date on which the penalty decision notice is given to the body.

(8) Where the Secretary of State decides to impose a penalty, the Secretary of State must publish the penalty decision notice and must do so in such manner as the Secretary of State considers appropriate for bringing the penalty to the attention of persons likely to be affected.

(9) The Secretary of State may rescind a penalty imposed on a body under section 1225D and, where doing so, must—

    (a) give the body notice of the rescission, and

    (b) publish the notice in the same manner as the penalty decision notice was published.

COMMENCEMENT DATE 2 July 2012[45]

## 1225F Appeals against financial penalties

**42.1225F.01**

(1) A body on which a penalty is imposed may appeal to the court on one or more of the appeal grounds.

(2) The appeal grounds are—

---

[44] The Statutory Auditors (Amendment of Companies Act 2006 and Delegation of Functions etc) Order 2012, SI 2012/1741.

[45] The Statutory Auditors (Amendment of Companies Act 2006 and Delegation of Functions etc) Order 2012, SI 2012/1741.

(a) that, before the giving of the notice under section 1225E(1), the requirement in respect of which the penalty was imposed was satisfied or the obligation in respect of which the penalty was imposed had been complied with;

(b) that, where the penalty was imposed in respect of a failure to comply with a direction under section 1225A, before the giving of the notice under section 1225B(6), the requirement in respect of which the direction was given was satisfied or the obligation in respect of which the direction was given had been complied with;

(c) that any of the requirements of section 1225E have not been complied with in relation to the imposition of the penalty and the interests of the body have been substantially prejudiced by the non-compliance;

(d) that the amount of the penalty is unreasonable;

(e) that it was unreasonable of the Secretary of State to require the penalty imposed to be paid by the time specified in the notice under section 1225E(5).

(3) An appeal under subsection (1) must be made within the period of 3 months beginning with the day on which the notice under section 1225E(5) is given to the body in respect of the penalty.

(4) On any such appeal, where the court considers it appropriate to do so in all the circumstances of the case and is satisfied of one or more of the appeal grounds, the court may—

(a) quash the penalty,

(b) substitute a penalty of such lesser amount as the court considers appropriate, or

(c) in the case of the appeal ground in subsection (2)(e), substitute a later time for the time specified in the notice under section 1225E(5).

(5) Where the court substitutes a penalty of a lesser amount, it may require the payment of interest on the substituted penalty, accruing from the time specified in the notice under section 1225E(5) or such later time as the court considers just and equitable.

(6) Where the court substitutes a later time for the time specified in the notice under section 1225E(5), it may require the payment of interest on the penalty, accruing from the substituted time or such later time as the court considers just and equitable.

(7) Where the court dismisses the appeal, it may require the payment of interest on the penalty, accruing from the time specified in the notice under section 1225E(5).

(8) Where the court requires the payment of interest under this section, the interest is payable at such rate as the court considers just and equitable.

(9) Except as provided by this section, the validity of a penalty is not to be questioned by any legal proceedings whatever.

(10) In this section 'the court' means the High Court or, in Scotland, the Court of Session.

COMMENCEMENT DATE  2 July 2012[46]

## 1225G  Recovery of financial penalties

(1) If the whole or any part of a penalty is not paid by the time by which it is required to be paid, the unpaid balance from time to time carries interest at the rate for the time being specified in section 17 of the Judgments Act 1838 (c 110) (unless a different rate is specified by the court under section 1225F(8)).                                                            **42.1225G.01**

(2) If an appeal is made under section 1225F in relation to a penalty, the penalty is not required to be paid until the appeal has been determined or withdrawn.

(3) Subsection (2) does not prevent the court from specifying that interest is to accrue from an earlier date under section 1225F.

(4) Where a penalty, or any portion of it, has not been paid by the time when it is required to be paid and—

(a) no appeal relating to the penalty has been made under section 1225F during the period within which such an appeal can be made, or

(b) an appeal has been made under that section and has been determined or withdrawn, the Secretary of State may recover from the body, as a debt due to the Secretary of State, any of the penalty and any interest which has not been paid.

COMMENCEMENT DATE  2 July 2012[47]

Sections 1225 to 1225G provide for additional types of action which may be taken against a statutory   **42.1225G.02** auditor's professional body (in connection with securing the body's responsibilities properly to super-vise its statutory auditor members). The Secretary of State may now give a direction to a professional body (eg. directing the body to do specified things) and may now impose a financial penalty upon such a body. This section provides the Secretary of State with an alternative to revocation, where the

---

[46]  The Statutory Auditors (Amendment of Companies Act 2006 and Delegation of Functions etc) Order 2012, SI 2012/1741.

[47]  The Statutory Auditors (Amendment of Companies Act 2006 and Delegation of Functions etc) Order 2012, SI 2012/1741.

requirement of Schedule 10 and/or 11 or any obligations imposed on the recognized bodies by Part 42 of the Companies Act 2006 have not been complied with. The alternative provided by this section is an application to obtain a court order to instruct the relevant body to take a particular course of action (section 1225(2)(b)). Pursuant to paragraph 3 of Schedule 10 of the Companies Act 2006, the Secretary of State has the power to revoke the recognition of a supervisory body for one of the reasons set forth in paragraphs 3(a), (b), or (c) of Schedule 10. Pursuant to paragraph 3 of Schedule 11 the recognition of a professional qualification may also be revoked for one of the reasons set forth in paragraphs 3(a) or 3(b) of Schedule 11.

## CHAPTER 3
### AUDITORS GENERAL

**42.1226.01** Chapter 3 of Part 42 is intended to implement certain of the recommendations of Lord Sharman's report *Holding to Account, The Review of Audit and Accountability for Central Government* (2001)[48] .One of the central recommendations of the report was that 'the Controller and Auditor General be appointed as auditor, on behalf of Parliament, for all [non-departmental public bodies]'.[49] However, in order for the Controller and Auditor General to be able to be appointed as the auditor of non-departmental public bodies that are established as companies a change in the law was required to enable the Controller and Auditor General to be appointed as a statutory auditor. This chapter provides for this change.

*Eligibility for appointment*

### 1226 Auditors General: eligibility for appointment as a statutory auditor

**42.1226.02**
    (1)  In this Part 'Auditor General' means—
        (a)  the Comptroller and Auditor General,
        (b)  the Auditor General for Scotland,
        (c)  the Auditor General for Wales, or
        (d)  the Comptroller and Auditor General for Northern Ireland.
    (2)  An Auditor General is eligible for appointment as a statutory auditor.
    (3)  Subsection (2) is subject to any suspension notice having effect under section 1234 (notices suspending eligibility for appointment as a statutory auditor).
        [new section]

COMMENCEMENT DATE 6 April 2008[50]

**42.1226.03** This section provides that Auditors General, as defined in section 1226(1), are eligible to be appointed as a statutory auditor.

*Conduct of audits*

### 1227 Individuals responsible for audit work on behalf of Auditors General

**42.1227.01** An Auditor General must secure that each individual responsible for statutory audit work on behalf of that Auditor General is eligible for appointment as a statutory auditor by virtue of Chapter 2.

COMMENCEMENT DATE 6 April 2008[51]

**42.1227.02** This section requires, amongst others, that the persons carrying out audit work on behalf of the Auditor General are members of a recognized supervisory body and are eligible for appointment in accordance with such body's rules (section 1212), and that they do not contravene the independence requirements of section 1214 of the Act.

---

[48] http://www.hm-treasury.gov.uk/d/Holding_to_Account.pdf (last checked October 2012).
[49] Lord Sharman's report *Holding to Account, The Review of Audit and Accountability for Central Government* (2001), p 2.
[50] Companies Act 2006 (Commencement No 5, Transitional Provisions and Savings) Order 2007, SI 2007/3495, art 3. This provision applies to the appointment of statutory auditors appointed for financial years beginning on or after 1 April 2008.
[51] Companies Act 2006 (Commencement No 5, Transitional Provisions and Savings) Order 2007, SI 2007/3495, art 3.

### *The Independent Supervisor*

### 1228   Appointment of the Independent Supervisor

(1)   The Secretary of State must appoint a body ('the Independent Supervisor') to discharge the   **42.1228.01**
function mentioned in section 1229(1) ('the supervision function').

(2)   An appointment under this section must be made by order.

(3)   The order has the effect of making the body appointed under subsection (1) designated under
section 5 of the Freedom of Information Act 2000 (c. 36) (further powers to designate public
authorities).

(4)   A body may be appointed under this section only if it is a body corporate or an unincorporated
association which appears to the Secretary of State—
   (a)   to be willing and able to discharge the supervision function, and
   (b)   to have arrangements in place relating to the discharge of that function which are such as to
be likely to ensure that the conditions in subsection (5) are met.

(5)   The conditions are—
   (a)   that the supervision function will be exercised effectively, and
   (b)   where the order is to contain any requirements or other provisions specified under subsection
(6), that that function will be exercised in accordance with any such requirements or
provisions.

(6)   An order under this section may contain such requirements or other provisions relating to the
exercise of the supervision function by the Independent Supervisor as appear to the Secretary of
State to be appropriate.

(7)   An order under this section is subject to negative resolution procedure.

COMMENCEMENT DATE  6 April 2008[52]

Sections 1228 and 1229 provide for the oversight and supervision of an Auditor General's performance   **42.1228.02**
as a statutory auditor. Section 1228 provides for the appointment of an Independent Supervisor. The
FRC has been appointed as the Independent Supervisor[53] . The Independent Supervisor is a public
authority for the purposes of the Freedom of Information Act 2000.

### *Supervision of Auditors General*

### 1229   Supervision of Auditors General by the Independent Supervisor

(1)   The Independent Supervisor must supervise the performance by each Auditor General of his   **42.1229.01**
functions as a statutory auditor.

[(2)   The Independent Supervisor must discharge that duty by—
   (a)   establishing supervision arrangements itself, or
   (b)   entering into supervision arrangements with one or more bodies.

(2A)   If the Independent Supervisor enters into supervision arrangements with one or more bodies, it
must oversee the effective operation of those supervision arrangements.][a]

(3)   For this purpose 'supervision arrangements' are arrangements [established by the Independent
Supervisor or][b] entered into by the Independent Supervisor with a body, for the purposes of this
section, in accordance with which [the Independent Supervisor or][c] the body does [...][d] the
following—
   (a)   determines standards relating to professional integrity and independence which must be
applied by an Auditor General in statutory audit work;
   (b)   determines technical standards which must be applied by an Auditor General in statutory
audit work and the manner in which those standards are to be applied in practice;
   (c)   monitors the performance of statutory audits carried out by an Auditor General;
   (d)   investigates any matter arising from the performance by an Auditor General of a statutory
audit;
   (e)   holds disciplinary hearings in respect of an Auditor General which appear to be desirable
following the conclusion of such investigations;
   (f)   decides whether (and, if so, what) disciplinary action should be taken against an Auditor
General to whom such a hearing related.

[(3A)   The requirements of paragraphs 9 to 10A and 12 to 15 of Schedule 10 (requirements for
recognition of a supervisory body) apply in relation to supervision arrangements as they apply in
relation to the rules, practices and arrangements of supervisory bodies.][e]

(4)   The Independent Supervisor may enter into supervision arrangements with a body despite any
relationship that may exist between the Independent Supervisor and that body.

---

[52]  Companies Act 2006 (Commencement No 5, Transitional Provisions and Savings) Order 2007, SI 2007/
3495, art 3.
[53]  The Statutory Auditors (Amendment of Companies Act 2006 and Delegation of Functions etc) Order 2012,
SI 2012/1741, art 18.

(5)  The Independent Supervisor must notify each Auditor General in writing of any supervision arrangements that it [establishes or]$^f$ enters into under this section.

[(5A)  The Independent Supervisor must, at least once in every calendar year, deliver to the Secretary of State a summary of the results of any inspections conducted for the purposes of subsection (3)(c).]$^g$

(6)  Supervision arrangements within subsection (3)(f) may, in particular, provide for the payment by an Auditor General of a fine to any person.

(7)  Any fine received by the Independent Supervisor under supervision arrangements is to be paid into the Consolidated Fund.

AMENDMENTS AND NOTES

  $^a$  Substituted by the Statutory Auditors and Third Country Auditors Regulations 2007, SI 2007/3494, reg 9(1), (2).

  $^b$  Inserted by the Statutory Auditors and Third Country Auditors Regulations 2007, SI 2007/3494, reg 9(1), (3)(a).

  $^c$  Inserted by the Statutory Auditors and Third Country Auditors Regulations 2007, SI 2007/3494, reg 9(1), (3)(b).

  $^d$  Repealed by the Statutory Auditors and Third Country Auditors Regulations 2007, SI 2007/3494, reg 9(1), (3)(c).

  $^e$  Inserted by the Statutory Auditors and Third Country Auditors Regulations 2007, SI 2007/3494, reg 9(1), (4).

  $^f$  Inserted by the Statutory Auditors and Third Country Auditors Regulations 2007, SI 2007/3494, reg 9(1), (5).

  $^g$  Inserted by the Statutory Auditors and Third Country Auditors Regulations 2007, SI 2007/3494, reg 9(1), (6).

COMMENCEMENT DATE  6 April 2008[54]

**42.1229.02**    This section provides for the supervision of the performance of auditors general as statutory auditors. However, the Independent Supervisor is not required directly to supervise the Auditors General. Rather, pursuant to section 1229(2) the Independent Supervisor is required either to establish its own supervision arrangements or to enter into supervision arrangements with 'one or more bodies' that will carry out the supervision. If it elects for the latter approach it must oversee the supervisory arrangements provided by those bodies. Subsection (3) specifies the nature of the required supervision, which may include a standard-setting role in relation to both technical standards and standards relating to integrity and independence, as well as performance monitoring, and investigation and discipline functions. In the legislative process the Government indicated that existing professional bodies would be likely candidates to perform such supervision functions.

**42.1229.03**    Section 1229(4) provides that the fact that there is an existing relationship between the Independent Supervisor and the body who will carry out the supervision does not prevent the appointment of that body. One example of such a conflict may be where a member of the governing body of the Independent Supervisor is also a member of a candidate professional body.

## 1230  Duties of Auditors General in relation to supervision arrangements

**42.1230.01**    (1)  Each Auditor General must—

(a)  comply with any standards of the kind mentioned in subsection (3)(a) or (b) of section 1229 determined under the supervision arrangements,

(b)  take such steps as may be reasonably required of that Auditor General to enable his performance of statutory audits to be monitored by means of inspections carried out under the supervision arrangements, and

(c)  comply with any decision of the kind mentioned in subsection (3)(f) of that section made under the supervision arrangements.

(2)  Each Auditor General must—

(a)  if the Independent Supervisor has established supervision arrangements, pay to the Independent Supervisor;

(b)  if the Independent Supervisor has entered into supervision arrangements with a body, pay to that body,

such proportion of the costs incurred by the Independent Supervisor or body for the purposes of the arrangements as the Independent Supervisor may notify to him in writing.]$^a$

(3)  Expenditure under subsection (2) is—

---

  [54]  Companies Act 2006 (Commencement No 5, Transitional Provisions and Savings) Order 2007, SI 2007/3495, art 3. This provision applies to statutory auditors appointed for financial years beginning on or after 1 April 2008.

(a)  in the case of expenditure of the Comptroller and Auditor General, to be regarded as expenditure of the National Audit Office for the purposes of section 4(1) of the National Audit Act 1983 (c. 44);

(b)  in the case of expenditure of the Comptroller and Auditor General for Northern Ireland, to be regarded as expenditure of the Northern Ireland Audit Office for the purposes of Article 6(1) of the Audit (Northern Ireland) Order 1987 (S.I. 1987/460 (N.I. 5)).

(4)  In this section 'the supervision arrangements' means the arrangements [established or]$^b$ entered into under section 1229.

AMENDMENTS AND NOTES

$^a$  Substituted by the Statutory Auditors and Third Country Auditors Regulations 2007, SI 2007/3494, reg 10(1), (2).

$^b$  Inserted by the Statutory Auditors and Third Country Auditors Regulations 2007, SI 2007/3494, reg 10(1), (3)

COMMENCEMENT DATE  6 April 2008[55]

This section imposes obligations on each Auditor General to comply with the standards issued in accordance with the supervision arrangements, to co-operate with the performance inspections, and to comply with any disciplinary ruling.   **42.1230.02**

Section 1230(2) provides for a costs contribution to the supervision arrangements from Auditors General. The contribution will be made directly to the bodies with whom the Independent Supervisor enters into supervision arrangements. The Independent Supervisor will make the cost allocation.   **42.1230.03**

## *Reporting requirement*

### 1231   Reports by the Independent Supervisor

(1)  The Independent Supervisor must, at least once in each calendar year, prepare a report on the discharge of its functions.   **42.1231.01**

(2)  The Independent Supervisor must give a copy of each report prepared under subsection (1) to—

(a)  the Secretary of State;

(b)  the First Minister in Scotland;

(c)  the First Minister and the deputy First Minister in Northern Ireland;

(d)  the Assembly First Secretary in Wales.

(3)  The Secretary of State must lay before each House of Parliament a copy of each report received by him under subsection (2)(a).

(4)  In relation to a calendar year during which an appointment of a body as the Independent Supervisor is made or revoked by an order under section 1228, this section applies with such modifications as may be specified in the order.

COMMENCEMENT DATE  6 April 2008[56]

This section imposes an annual report obligation on the Independent Supervisor, which is the Financial Reporting Council[57] , relating to the carrying out of its functions.   **42.1231.02**

## *Information*

### 1232   Matters to be notified to the Independent Supervisor

(1)  The Independent Supervisor may require an Auditor General—   **42.1232.01**

(a)  to notify the Independent Supervisor immediately of the occurrence of such events as it may specify in writing and to give it such information in respect of those events as is so specified;

(b)  to give the Independent Supervisor, at such times or in respect of such periods as it may specify in writing, such information as is so specified.

(2)  The notices and information required to be given must be such as the Independent Supervisor may reasonably require for the exercise of the functions conferred on it by or by virtue of this Part.

(3)  The Independent Supervisor may require information given under this section to be given in a specified form or verified in a specified manner.

---

[55]  Companies Act 2006 (Commencement No 5, Transitional Provisions and Savings) Order 2007, SI 2007/3495, art 3. This provision applies to the statutory auditors appointed for financial years beginning on or after 1 April 2008.

[56]  Companies Act 2006 (Commencement No 5, Transitional Provisions and Savings) Order 2007, SI 2007/3495, art 3.

[57]  The Statutory Auditors (Amendment of Companies Act 2006 and Delegation of Functions etc) Order 2012, SI 2012/1741.

(4)  Any notice or information required to be given under this section must be given in writing unless the Independent Supervisor specifies or approves some other manner.

COMMENCEMENT DATE 6 April 2008[58]

**42.1232.02**   This section provides the Independent Supervisor with the power to require an Auditor General to provide immediate notification of and information regarding specified events. Furthermore, this section provides the power for the Independent Supervisor to request periodic information from an Auditor General. Subsection (2) provides that the powers can only be exercised to the extent that they are reasonably required to perform the functions conferred on the Independent Supervisor.

**42.1232.03**   This section is very similar to section 1223 Section 1223 applies to the recognized supervisory body and the recognized qualifying body. This section, however, applies only to the Auditors General, not the body with whom the Independent Supervisor enters into supervision arrangements.

### 1233   The Independent Supervisor's power to call for information

**42.1233.01**   (1)  The Independent Supervisor may by notice in writing require an Auditor General to give it such information as it may reasonably require for the exercise of the functions conferred on it by or by virtue of this Part.
(2)  The Independent Supervisor may require that any information which it requires under this section is to be given within such reasonable time and verified in such manner as it may specify.

COMMENCEMENT DATE 6 April 2008[59]

**42.1233.02**   This section provides that the Independent Supervisor can require an Auditor General to provide information. These powers may, however, only be exercised to the extent that they are reasonably required to perform the functions conferred on the Independent Supervisor.

**42.1233.03**   This section is very similar to section 1224. Section 1224 applies to the recognized supervisory body and the recognized qualifying body as well as to statutory auditors eligible for appointment under Chapter 2 of Part 42 of the Act. This section, however, only applies to the Auditors General, not the body with whom the Independent Supervisor enters into supervision arrangements.

## *Enforcement*

### 1234   Suspension notices

**42.1234.01**   (1)  The Independent Supervisor may issue—
    (a)  a notice (a 'suspension notice') suspending an Auditor General's eligibility for appointment as a statutory auditor in relation to all persons, or any specified person or persons, indefinitely or until a date specified in the notice;
    (b)  a notice amending or revoking a suspension notice previously issued to an Auditor General.
(2)  In determining whether it is appropriate to issue a notice under subsection (1), the Independent Supervisor must have regard to—
    (a)  the Auditor General's performance of the obligations imposed on him by or by virtue of this Part, and
    (b)  the Auditor General's performance of his functions as a statutory auditor.
(3)  A notice under subsection (1) must—
    (a)  be in writing, and
    (b)  state the date on which it takes effect (which must be after the period of three months beginning with the date on which it is issued).
(4)  Before issuing a notice under subsection (1), the Independent Supervisor must—
    (a)  give written notice of its intention to do so to the Auditor General, and
    (b)  publish the notice mentioned in paragraph (a) in such manner as it thinks appropriate for bringing it to the attention of any other persons who are likely to be affected.
(5)  A notice under subsection (4) must—
    (a)  state the reasons for which the Independent Supervisor proposes to act, and
    (b)  give particulars of the rights conferred by subsection (6).
(6)  A person within subsection (7) may, within the period of three months beginning with the date of service or publication of the notice under subsection (4) or such longer period as the Independent Supervisor may allow, make written representations to the Independent Supervisor and, if desired, oral representations to a person appointed for that purpose by the Independent Supervisor.

[58] Companies Act 2006 (Commencement No 5, Transitional Provisions and Savings) Order 2007, SI 2007/3495, art 3.
[59] Companies Act 2006 (Commencement No 5, Transitional Provisions and Savings) Order 2007, SI 2007/3495, art 3.

(7)  The persons within this subsection are—
   (a)  the Auditor General, and
   (b)  any other person who appears to the Independent Supervisor to be affected.
(8)  The Independent Supervisor must have regard to any representations made in accordance with subsection (6) in determining—
   (a)  whether to issue a notice under subsection (1), and
   (b)  the terms of any such notice.
(9)  If in any case the Independent Supervisor considers it appropriate to do so in the public interest it may issue a notice under subsection (1), without regard to the restriction in subsection (3)(b), even if—
   (a)  no notice has been given or published under subsection (4), or
   (b)  the period of time for making representations in pursuance of such a notice has not expired.
(10)  On issuing a notice under subsection (1), the Independent Supervisor must—
   (a)  give a copy of the notice to the Auditor General, and
   (b)  publish the notice in such manner as it thinks appropriate for bringing it to the attention of persons likely to be affected.
(11)  In this section 'specified' means specified in, or of a description specified in, the suspension notice in question.

COMMENCEMENT DATE  6 April 2008[60]

Subsection (1) empowers the Independent Supervisor to suspend an Auditor General's eligibility to be   **42.1234.02**
appointed as a statutory auditor. Such suspension may be general suspension or relate only to specific persons, and it be may for a specific time period or be an indefinite suspension.

Prior to issuing a suspension notice, the Independent Supervisor must notify the Auditor General   **42.1234.03**
directly, and other affected persons by publishing the notice (section 1234(4)). The Auditor General and the affected persons are then given a minimum three-month period to make written and/or oral representations (section 1234(6)).

Such suspension will normally commence at least three months after the Independent Supervisor   **42.1234.04**
provides written notice to the Auditor General of the suspension (section 1234(3)(b)). However, where the Independent Supervisor deems it to be in the public interest the suspension can come into effect without regard to the three-month notice requirement, and without regard to the pre-suspension notice requirements or the three-month representation period (section 1234(9)).

A copy of the suspension notice must be given to the Auditor General. In addition, the Independent   **42.1234.05**
Supervisor must bring the notice to the attention of other affected persons through an appropriate publication (section 1234(10)).

## 1235   Effect of suspension notices

(1)  An Auditor General must not act as a statutory auditor at any time when a suspension notice   **42.1235.01**
issued to him in respect of the audited person has effect.
(2)  If at any time during an Auditor General's term of office as a statutory auditor a suspension notice issued to him in respect of the audited person takes effect, he must immediately—
   (a)  resign his office (with immediate effect), and
   (b)  give notice in writing to the audited person that he has resigned by reason of his becoming ineligible for appointment.
(3)  A suspension notice does not make an Auditor General ineligible for appointment as a statutory auditor for the purposes of section 1213 (effect of ineligibility: criminal offences).

COMMENCEMENT DATE  6 April 2008[61]

This section provides that an Auditor General must not act as a statutory auditor when a suspension   **42.1235.02**
notice has effect. Subsection (1) could be read as preventing the Auditor General from acting as a statutory auditor in relation to any audited person. However, as section 1234(1) makes clear the suspension order may apply to 'all persons, or any specified persons'. Accordingly, section 1234 contemplates partial suspension which would mean that the Auditor General could continue to act as a statutory auditor in relation to audited persons to whom the suspension notice does not apply. The prohibition in section 1235(1) should be read as restricted to the audited person or persons in relation to whom the suspension notice applies.

---

[60]  Companies Act 2006 (Commencement No 5, Transitional Provisions and Savings) Order 2007, SI 2007/3495, art 3.
[61]  Companies Act 2006 (Commencement No 5, Transitional Provisions and Savings) Order 2007, SI 2007/3495, art 3.

**42.1235.03**    From the time the suspension notice takes effect, which will normally not be sooner than three months after the notice is issued (s.1234(3)(b)), the Auditor General must resign immediately with immediate effect from any audit engagement to which the suspension notice applies (section 1235(2)).

**42.1235.04**    The effect of subsection (3) is to render the offences set forth in section 1213 inapplicable to Auditors General who become unable to act as a statutory auditor by virtue of a suspension notice.

### 1236  Compliance orders

**42.1236.01**
(1)  If at any time it appears to the Independent Supervisor that an Auditor General has failed to comply with an obligation imposed on him by or by virtue of this Part, the Independent Supervisor may make an application to the court under this section.
(2)  If on an application under this section the court decides that the Auditor General has failed to comply with the obligation in question, it may order the Auditor General to take such steps as the court directs for securing that the obligation is complied with.
(3)  In this section 'the court' means the High Court or, in Scotland, the Court of session.

COMMENCEMENT DATE 6 April 2008[62]

**42.1236.02**    This section empowers the Independent Supervisor to apply to court where the Auditor General has failed to comply with any obligation imposed by Part 42 of the Act (not merely Chapter 3) for a court order to direct the Auditor General to comply with any such obligation.

**42.1236.03**    This section is very similar to section 1225. Section 1225 applies to the recognized supervisory body and the recognized qualifying body. This section, however, only applies to the Auditors General not the body with whom the Independent Supervisor enters into supervision arrangements.

## Proceedings

### 1237  Proceedings involving the Independent Supervisor

**42.1237.01**
(1)  If the Independent Supervisor is an unincorporated association, any relevant proceedings may be brought by or against it in the name of any body corporate whose constitution provides for the establishment of the body.
(2)  For this purpose 'relevant proceedings' means proceedings brought in or in connection with the exercise of any function by the body as the Independent supervisor.
(3)  Where an appointment under section 1228 is revoked, the revoking order may make such provision as the Secretary of State thinks fit with respect to pending proceedings.

COMMENCEMENT DATE 6 April 2008[63]

**42.1237.02**    The wording in this section was required as the pre-July 2012 Independent Supervisor, Public Oversight Board for Accounting was an unincorporated association formed pursuant to the articles of association of the Public Oversight Board for Accounting Limited. It allowed proceedings by and against the Public Oversight Board for Accounting (POBA) to be brought by and against the Public Oversight Board for Accounting Limited. The POB has been replaced by the Financial Reporting Council Limited which is an incorporated body.[64]

## Grants

### 1238  Grants to the Independent Supervisor

**42.1238.01**    In section 16 of the Companies (Audit, Investigations and Community Enterprise) Act 2004 (c. 27) (grants to bodies concerned with accounting standards etc), after subsection (2)(k) insert—

'(ka)  exercising functions of the Independent Supervisor appointed under Chapter 3 of Part 42 of the Companies Act 2006;'.

COMMENCEMENT DATE 6 April 2008[65]

**42.1238.02**    This section amends sections 16 of the Companies (Audit, Investigations and Community Enterprise) Act 2004 to enable the Secretary of State to make grants to the Independent Supervisor.

---

[62] Companies Act 2006 (Commencement No 5, Transitional Provisions and Savings) Order 2007, SI 2007/3495, art 3.
[63] Companies Act 2006 (Commencement No 5, Transitional Provisions and Savings) Order 2007, SI 2007/3495, art 3.
[64] The Statutory Auditors (Amendment of Companies Act 2006 and Delegation of Functions etc) Order 2012, SI 2012/1741.
[65] Companies Act 2006 (Commencement No 5, Transitional Provisions and Savings) Order 2007, SI 2007/3495, art 3.

# CHAPTER 4
## THE REGISTER OF AUDITORS ETC

### 1239 The register of auditors

(1) The Secretary of State must make regulations requiring the keeping of a register of—
- (a) the persons eligible for appointment as a statutory auditor, and
- (b) third country auditors (see Chapter 5) who apply to be registered in the specified manner and in relation to whom specified requirements are met.

(2) The regulations must require each person's entry in the register to contain—
- (a) his name and address,
- (b) in the case of an individual eligible for appointment as a statutory auditor, the specified information relating to any firm on whose behalf he is responsible for statutory audit work,
- (c) in the case of a firm eligible for appointment as a statutory auditor, the specified information relating to the individuals responsible for statutory audit work on its behalf,
- (d) in the case of an individual or firm eligible for appointment as a statutory auditor by virtue of Chapter 2, the name of the relevant supervisory body, [...]ᵃ
- (e) in the case of a firm eligible for appointment as a statutory auditor by virtue of Chapter 2 [...]ᵇ or a third country auditor, the information mentioned in subsection (3), [and
- (f) in the case of a third country auditor which is a firm, the name and address of each person who is—
  - (i) an owner or shareholder of the firm, or
  - (ii) a member of the firm's administrative or management body,]ᶜ

and may require each person's entry to contain other specified information.

(3) The information referred to in subsection (2)(e) is—
- (a) in relation to a body corporate, except where paragraph (b) applies, the name and address of each person who is a director of the body or holds any shares in it;
- (b) in relation to a limited liability partnership, the name and address of each member of the partnership;
- (c) in relation to a corporation sole, the name and address of the individual for the time being holding the office by the name of which he is the corporation sole;
- (d) in relation to a partnership, the name and address of each partner.

(4) The regulations may provide that different parts of the register are to be kept by different persons.

(5) The regulations may impose such obligations as the Secretary of State thinks fit on—
- (a) recognised supervisory bodies,
- (b) any body designated by order under section 1252 (delegation of Secretary of State's functions),
- (c) persons eligible for appointment as a statutory auditor,
- (d) third country auditors,
- (e) any person with whom arrangements are made by one or more recognised supervisory bodies, or by any body designated by order under section 1252, with respect to the keeping of the register, or
- (f) the Independent Supervisor appointed under section 1228.

(6) The regulations may include—
- (a) provision requiring that specified entries in the register be open to inspection at times and places specified or determined in accordance with the regulations;
- (b) provision enabling a person to require a certified copy of specified entries in the register;
- (c) provision authorising the charging of fees for inspection, or the provision of copies, of such reasonable amount as may be specified or determined in accordance with the regulations.

(7) The Secretary of State may direct in writing that the requirements imposed by the regulations [...]ᵈ, or such of those requirements as are specified in the direction, are not to apply, in whole or in part, in relation to a particular registered third country auditor or class of registered third country auditors.

(8) The obligations imposed by regulations under this section on such persons as are mentioned in subsection (5)(b) or (e) are enforceable on the application of the Secretary of State by injunction or, in Scotland, by an order under section 45 of the Court of Session Act 1988 (c. 36).

(9) In this section 'specified' means specified by regulations under this section.

(10) Regulations under this section are subject to negative resolution procedure.

AMENDMENTS AND NOTES

ᵃ Repealed by the Statutory Auditors and Third Country Auditors Regulations 2007, SI 2007/3494, reg 30(1), (2).

ᵇ Repealed by the Statutory Auditors and Third Country Auditors Regulations 2007, SI 2007/3494, reg 30(1), (3).

<sup>c</sup> Inserted by the Statutory Auditors and Third Country Auditors Regulations 2007, SI 2007/3494, reg 30(1), (4).

<sup>d</sup> Repealed by the Statutory Auditors and Third Country Auditors Regulations 2007, SI 2007/3494, reg 30(1), (5).

COMMENCEMENT DATE 6 April 2008[66]

**42.1239.02** This section provides that the Secretary of State must make regulations to require the keeping of a register which will contain the names of all persons (both individuals and firms) eligible for appointment as a statutory auditor but also all 'third country auditors' (defined in section 1241) who apply to be registered. Subsections (2) and (3) set forth the information that must be recorded for any registered individual or firm. The powers of the Secretary of State under this section have been transferred to the FRC except in relation to section 1239(1)(b) (third country auditors register).[67]

**42.1239.03** The register of auditors need not be kept by one body. Indeed subsection (4) explicitly provides that different parts of the register may be kept by different persons. Subsection (5) broadens the category of person who could be responsible for fulfilling obligations relating to the register of auditors. These persons include: the recognized supervisory bodies such as the ICAEW or the ICAI; any person with whom the recognized supervisory bodies enter into arrangements for the keeping of a register; persons with delegated authority under this part of the Act, which is currently the FRC; an independent supervisor (see section 1228), which again is the FRC; or eligible statutory or third country auditors.

**42.1239.04** Subsection (6) provides that the regulations may provide for the public availability of certain entries in the register and for reasonable inspection fees.

**42.1239.05** Subsection (7) enables the regulations to disapply certain of the register's information requirements to third country auditors either individually or as a class, for example, third country auditors from the United States. It is expected that such regulations will be made where the third country auditors are subject to equivalent registration requirement in their home jurisdiction.

**42.1239.06** Pursuant to regulation 34 of the Statutory Auditors and Third Country Auditors Regulations 2007, SI 2007/3494 3494 ( as amended by The Statutory Auditors ( Amendment of Companies Act 2006 and Delegation of Functions etc) Order 2012, SI 2012/ 1741), the FRC is the designated body for the purposes of keeping the register. Regulation 34 also details the information to be kept on the Register of Third Country Auditors which includes, for example, the name and registered number of the auditor and the name and address of the body which has authorized the third country auditor to carry out audits. The information on the register is available for electronic inspection. Information on an individual may be excluded by the FRC from the publicly available information if the availability of such information creates 'serious risk that the individual, or any other person, would be subject to violence or intimidation'.[68]

**42.1239.08** Regulations 35 to 38 of the Statutory Auditors and Third Country Auditors Regulations 2007, SI 2007/3494, set forth the procedure for registration as a third country auditor.

## 1240 Information to be made available to public

**42.1240.01**
(1) The Secretary of State may make regulations requiring a person eligible for appointment as a statutory auditor, or a member of a specified class of such persons, to keep and make available to the public specified information, including information regarding—
   (a) the person's ownership and governance,
   (b) the person's internal controls with respect to the quality and independence of its audit work,
   (c) the person's turnover, and
   (d) the audited persons of whom the person has acted as statutory auditor.
(2) Regulations under this section may—
   (a) impose such obligations as the Secretary of State thinks fit on persons eligible for appointment as a statutory auditor;
   (b) require the information to be made available to the public in a specified manner.
(3) In this section 'specified' means specified by regulations under this section.
(4) Regulations under this section are subject to negative resolution procedure.

---

[66] Companies Act 2006 (Commencement No 5, Transitional Provisions and Savings) Order 2007, SI 2007/3495, art 3.

[67] The Statutory Auditors (Amendment of Companies Act 2006 and Delegation of Functions etc) Order 2012, SI 2012/1741.

[68] Statutory Auditors and Third Country Auditors Regulations 2007, SI 2007/3494, reg 34(6) as amended by the Statutory Auditors and Third Country Auditors (Amendment) Regulations 2011, SI 2011/1856, reg 7(5).

COMMENCEMENT DATE  6 April 2008[69]

This section provides the Secretary of State with a discretionary power to make, to the extent he thinks     **42.1240.02**
fit, regulations providing that statutory auditors, whether individuals or firms, must make certain
information publicly available in a specified way. The section refers to a non-exhaustive list of
information including ownership structure and governance arrangements, internal control arrangements, turnover, and client base. The Government in introducing this provision recognized that some
of this information is already provided by some statutory auditors but considered that the provision
was necessary to ensure the integrity of the statutory audit. The powers of the Secretary of State under
this section have been transferred to the FRC.[70]

# CHAPTER 5
# REGISTERED THIRD COUNTRY AUDITORS

## *Introductory*

### 1241  [Meaning of 'third country auditor', and 'UK-traded non-EEA company']ᵃ

(1)  In this Part—                                                                                          **42.1241.01**
    [...]ᵇ
    'registered third country auditor' means a third country auditor who is entered in the register
    kept in accordance with regulations under section 1239(1).
(2)  [In this Part 'UK-traded non-EEA company' means a body corporate—]ᶜ
    (a)  which is incorporated or formed under the law of [a third country]ᵈ
    (b)  whose transferable securities are admitted to trading on a regulated market situated or
        operating in the United Kingdom, and
    (c)  which has not been excluded, or is not of a description of bodies corporate which has been
        excluded, from this definition by an order made by the Secretary of State.
(3)  For this purpose—
    'regulated market' has the meaning given by Article 4.1(14) of Directive 2004/39/EC of the
    European Parliament and of the Council on markets in financial instruments;
    'transferable securities' has the meaning given by Article 4.1(18) of that Directive.
(4)  An order under this section is subject to negative resolution procedure.

AMENDMENTS AND NOTES

ᵃ  Substituted by the Statutory Auditors and Third Country Auditors Regulations 2007, SI 2007/3494,
   reg 31(1), (2).

ᵇ  Repealed by the Statutory Auditors and Third Country Auditors Regulations 2007, SI 2007/3494,
   reg 31(1), (3).

ᶜ  Substituted by the Statutory Auditors and Third Country Auditors Regulations 2007, SI 2007/3494,
   reg 31(1), (4)(a).

ᵈ  Substituted by the Statutory Auditors and Third Country Auditors Regulations 2007, SI 2007/3494,
   reg 31(1), (4)(b).

COMMENCEMENT DATE  6 April 2008[71]

This section provides definitions of both 'registered third country auditor' and 'UK-traded non-EEA     **42.1241.02**
company'. Whether a person is a third country auditor as defined by section 1261 of the Act, is not
dependent on where the auditor is resident or established, rather it is dependent on whether the auditor
is eligible to conduct audits of companies incorporated outside the EEA. A third country auditor who
is registered pursuant to section 1239 is a registered third country auditor.

A UK-traded non-EEA company is a company incorporated outside the EEA but with securities traded     **42.1241.03**
on a regulated market in the UK. Section 1241(2)(c) enables the Secretary of State to exclude companies
from the definition of 'UK-traded non-EEA company'. Regulation 43 of the Statutory Auditors and
Third Country Auditors Regulations 2007, SI 2007/3494, excludes a 'large debt securities issuer' from
the definition of 'UK-traded non-EEA company'. Regulation 43(2) defines a 'large debt securities

---

[69] Companies Act 2006 (Commencement No 5, Transitional Provisions and Savings) Order 2007, SI 2007/
3495, art 3.
[70] The Statutory Auditors (Amendment of Companies Act 2006 and Delegation of Functions etc) Order 2012,
SI 2012/1741.
[71] Companies Act 2006 (Commencement No 5, Transitional Provisions and Savings) Order 2007, SI 2007/
3495, art 3.

issuer' as a body corporate whose only securities traded on a regulated market are debt securities whose denomination per unit is, or is equivalent to, €50,000.

**42.1241.04**    Regulation 35 of the Statutory Auditors and Third Country Auditors Regulations 2007, as amended,[72] provides for the registration procedure to register as a third country auditor with the designated body (the FRC). These procedures require the provision of information by the applicant to the FRC on, amongst others: the independence and auditing standards applicable to the applicant; a description of the applicants' internal quality control system; and information of whether a quality assurance review has been carried out in relation to the applicant and, if so, the outcome of that review.

*Duties*

### 1242    Duties of registered third country auditors

**42.1242.01**    (1)  A registered third country auditor [who audits the accounts of a UK-traded non-EEA company][a] must participate in—
    (a)  arrangements within paragraph 1 of Schedule 12 (arrangements for independent monitoring of audits [...][b]), and
    (b)  arrangements within paragraph 2 of that Schedule (arrangements for independent investigation for disciplinary purposes of public interest cases).
    (2)  A registered third country auditor must—
    (a)  take such steps as may be reasonably required of it to enable its performance of [audits of accounts of UK-traded non-EEA companies][c] to be monitored by means of inspections carried out under the arrangements mentioned in subsection (1)(a), and
    (b)  comply with any decision as to disciplinary action to be taken against it made under the arrangements mentioned in subsection (1)(b).
    (3)  Schedule 12 makes further provision with respect to the arrangements in which registered third country auditors are required to participate.
    (4)  The Secretary of State may direct in writing that subsections (1) to (3) are not to apply, in whole or in part, in relation to
    (a)  a particular registered third country auditor or class of registered third country auditors.
    (b)  [audits of the accounts of a particular UK-traded non-EEA company or class of UK-traded non-EEA companies;
    (c)  audits by a particular registered third country auditor or class of registerd third country auditors of the accounts of a particular UK-traded non- EEA company or class of Uk-traded non-EEA companies.][a]

AMENDMENTS AND NOTES

[a] Inserted by the Statutory Auditors and Third Country Auditors Regulations 2007, SI 2007/3494, reg 32(1), (2)(a).

[b] Repealed by the Statutory Auditors and Third Country Auditors Regulations 2007, SI 2007/3494, reg 32(1), (2)(b).

[c] Substituted by the Statutory Auditors and Third Country Auditors Regulations 2007, SI 2007/3494, reg 32(1), (3).

COMMENCEMENT DATE 29 June 2008[73]

**42.1242.02**    Together with Schedule 12 this section obliges registered third country auditors to participate in any independent monitoring arrangements for the audits of the companies audited by the third country auditors and arrangements for the investigation or disciplinary process arising therefrom. Furthermore, it requires such third country auditors to take reasonable steps to enable performance inspections to be carried out and to comply with any disciplinary decision made against it.

**42.1242.03**    Section 1242(4) empowers the Secretary of State to disapply this section, completely or partially, to a particular registered third country auditor or class of such auditors. Such disapplication must be in writing.

---

[72] Statutory Auditors and Third Country Auditors Regulations 2007 are amended in this regard by the Statutory Auditors and Third Country Auditors (Amendment) (No 2) Regulations 2008, SI 2008/2639, reg 2(3) and the Statutory Auditors and Third Country Auditors (Amendment) Regulations 2011, SI 2011/1856, reg 7(5).

[73] Companies Act 2006 (Commencement No 5, Transitional Provisions and Savings) Order 2007, SI 2007/3495, art 4.

## *Information*

### 1243  Matters to be notified to the Secretary of State

(1)  The Secretary of State may require a registered third country auditor—     **42.1243.01**
   - (a)  to notify him immediately of the occurrence of such events as he may specify in writing and to give him such information in respect of those events as is so specified;
   - (b)  to give him, at such times or in respect of such periods as he may specify in writing, such information as is so specified.

(2)  The notices and information required to be given must be such as the Secretary of State may reasonably require for the exercise of his functions under this Part.

(3)  The Secretary of State may require information given under this section to be given in a specified form or verified in a specified manner.

(4)  Any notice or information required to be given under this section must be given in writing unless the Secretary of State specifies or approves some other manner.

COMMENCEMENT DATE  29 June 2008[74]

This section provides the Secretary of State with the power to require a registered third country auditor    **42.1243.02** to provide immediate notification of and information regarding specified events. Furthermore, this section provides the power for the Secretary of State to request periodic information from a registered third country auditor. Subsection (2) provides that the powers can only be exercised to the extent that they are reasonably required to perform the Secretary of State's functions under this Part 42 of the Act.

### 1244  The Secretary of State's power to call for information

(1)  The Secretary of State may by notice in writing require a registered third country auditor to give    **42.1244.01** him such information as he may reasonably require for the exercise of his functions under this Part.

(2)  The Secretary of State may require that any information which he requires under this section is to be given within such reasonable time and verified in such manner as he may specify.

COMMENCEMENT DATE  29 June 2008[75]

The section provides that the Secretary of State can require a registered third country auditor to    **42.1244.02** provide information. These powers may, however, only be exercised to the extent that they are reasonably required to perform the Secretary of State's functions under this Part 42 of the Act.

## *Enforcement*

### 1245  Compliance orders

(1)  If at any time it appears to the Secretary of State that a registered third country auditor has failed    **42.1245.01** to comply with an obligation imposed on him by or by virtue of this Part, the Secretary of State may make an application to the court under this section.

(2)  If on an application under this section the court decides that the auditor has failed to comply with the obligation in question, it may order the auditor to take such steps as the court directs for securing that the obligation is complied with.

(3)  In this section 'the court' means the High Court or, in Scotland, the Court of Session.

COMMENCEMENT DATE  6 April 2008[76]

This section empowers the Secretary of State to apply to court where the registered third country    **42.1245.02** auditor has failed to comply with any obligation imposed by Part 42 of the Act for a court order to direct the auditor to comply with any such obligation.

### 1246  Removal of third country auditors from the register of auditors

(1)  The Secretary of State may, by regulations, confer on the person keeping the register in    **42.1246.01** accordance with regulations under section 1239(1) power to remove a third country auditor from the register.

---

[74]  Companies Act 2006 (Commencement No 5, Transitional Provisions and Savings) Order 2007, SI 2007/ 3495, art 4.

[75]  Companies Act 2006 (Commencement No 5, Transitional Provisions and Savings) Order 2007, SI 2007/ 3495, art 4.

[76]  Companies Act 2006 (Commencement No 5, Transitional Provisions and Savings) Order 2007, SI 2007/ 3495, art 3.

(2) Regulations under this section must require the person keeping the register, in determining whether to remove a third country auditor from the register, to have regard to the auditor's compliance with obligations imposed on him by or by virtue of this Part.

(3) Where provision is made under section 1239(4) (different parts of the register to be kept by different persons), references in this section to the person keeping the register are to the person keeping that part of the register which relates to third country auditors.

(4) Regulations under this section are subject to negative resolution procedure.

COMMENCEMENT DATE 6 April 2008[77]

**42.1246.02**   This section empowers the Secretary of State to make regulations to enable the person keeping the register of auditors to remove a third country auditor from the register. In this regard, note that it is an offence for a person to describe themselves as a registered third country auditor when his name does not appear on the register of auditors (section 1250(3) of the Companies Act 2006).

**42.1246.03**   Regulation 40 of the Statutory Auditors and Third Country Auditors Regulations 2007, SI 2007/3494,[78] provide that the FRC, as designated body, may remove the third country auditor from the register if the FRC 'considers' that: it has failed to comply with its obligations under sections 1242, 1243 and 1244 of the Act as well as regulation 39 of the Regulations (duty to provide updated information);[79] if it has failed to comply with the auditing and independence standards applicable to it; is unfit to carry out audits of UK traded non-EEA countries; or it appears to the FRC that the third country authority that regulates the third country auditor does not think that the auditor is a fit and proper person or eligible to conduct audits in the third country.

### 1247   Grants to bodies concerned with arrangements under Schedule 12

**42.1247.01**   In section 16 of the Companies (Audit, Investigations and Community Enterprise) Act 2004 (c. 27) (grants to bodies concerned with accounting standards etc), after subsection (2)(ka) (inserted by section 1238) insert— '(kb) establishing, maintaining or carrying out arrangements within paragraph 1 or 2 of Schedule 12 to the Companies Act 2006;'.

COMMENCEMENT DATE 6 April 2008[80]

**42.1247.02**   Section 1247 amends section 16 of the Companies (Audit, Investigations and Community Enterprise) Act 2004 to enable the Secretary of State to make grants to bodies responsible for the monitoring and disciplinary arrangements pursuant to paragraphs 1 and 2 of Schedules 12 to the Act.

## CHAPTER 6
## SUPPLEMENTARY AND GENERAL

*Power to require second company audit*

### 1248   Secretary of State's power to require second audit of a company

**42.1248.01**   (1) This section applies where a person appointed as statutory auditor of a company was not an appropriate person for any part of the period during which the audit was conducted.

(2) The Secretary of State may direct the company concerned to retain an appropriate person—
   (a) to conduct a second audit of the relevant accounts, or
   (b) to review the first audit and to report (giving his reasons) whether a second audit is needed.

(3) For the purposes of subsections (1) and (2) a person is 'appropriate' if he—
   (a) is eligible for appointment as a statutory auditor or, if the person is an Auditor General, for appointment as statutory auditor of the company, and
   (b) is not prohibited by section 1214(1) (independence requirement) from acting as statutory auditor of the company.

(4) The Secretary of State must send a copy of a direction under subsection (2) to the registrar of companies.

---

[77] Companies Act 2006 (Commencement No 5, Transitional Provisions and Savings) Order 2007, SI 2007/ 3495, art 3.

[78] The Statutory Auditors and Third Country Auditors Regulations 2007 are amended in this regard by the Statutory Auditors and Third Country Auditors (Amendment) (No 2) Regulations 2008, SI 2008/2639, reg 2(5) and the Statutory Auditors and Third Country Auditors (Amendment) Regulations 2011, SI 2011/1856, reg 7(6).

[79] As amended by the Statutory Auditors and Third Country Auditors (Amendment) Regulations 2011, SI 2011/ 1856, reg 7(7).

[80] Companies Act 2006 (Commencement No 5, Transitional Provisions and Savings) Order 2007, SI 2007/ 3495, art 3.

(5) The company is guilty of an offence if—
   (a) it fails to comply with a direction under subsection (2) within the period of 21 days beginning with the date on which it is given, or
   (b) it has been convicted of a previous offence under this subsection and the failure to comply with the direction which led to the conviction continues after the conviction.

(6) The company must—
   (a) send a copy of a report under subsection (2)(b) to the registrar of companies, and
   (b) if the report states that a second audit is needed, take such steps as are necessary for the carrying out of that audit.

(7) The company is guilty of an offence if—
   (a) it fails to send a copy of a report under subsection (2)(b) to the registrar within the period of 21 days beginning with the date on which it receives it,
   (b) in a case within subsection (6)(b), it fails to take the steps mentioned immediately it receives the report, or
   (c) it has been convicted of a previous offence under this subsection and the failure to send a copy of the report, or take the steps, which led to the conviction continues after the conviction.

(8) A company guilty of an offence under this section is liable on summary conviction—
   (a) in a case within subsection (5)(a) or (7)(a) or (b), to a fine not exceeding level 5 on the standard scale, and
   (b) in a case within subsection (5)(b) or (7)(c), to a fine not exceeding one tenth of level 5 on the standard scale for each day on which the failure continues.

(9) In this section 'registrar of companies' has the meaning given by section 1060.

COMMENCEMENT DATE  6 April 2008[81]

This section empowers the Secretary of State in certain circumstances either to direct a company to appoint another auditor to conduct a second audit of the company or to direct the company to appoint another auditor to review the existing audit and report on whether a second audit is necessary (section 1212(2)). The Secretary of State is empowered to make such a direction if at any time during the audit period the appointed auditor was ineligible to be appointed as a statutory auditor of the company pursuant to section 1211 or lacked the required independence pursuant to section 1214.  **42.1248.02**

The company commits a criminal offence it fails to comply with a direction within a 21-day period (section 1248(5)) or it fails to send a copy of the second auditor's report to the registrar of companies within 21 days of receipt, or to take immediate steps to carry out a second audit where the report recommends one (section 1248(7)). Such offences are punishable by fine.  **42.1248.03**

Pursuant to the Statutory Auditors (Amendment of Companies Act 2006 and Delegation of Functions etc) Order 2012, SI 2012/1741, all powers of the Secretary of State under section 1248 were delegated to FRC  **42.1248.04**

## 1249  Supplementary provision about second audits

(1) If a person accepts an appointment, or continues to act, as statutory auditor of a company at a time when he knows he is not an appropriate person, the company may recover from him any costs incurred by it in complying with the requirements of section 1248.  **42.1249.01**
For this purpose 'appropriate' is to be construed in accordance with subsection (3) of that section.

(2) Where a second audit is carried out under section 1248, any statutory or other provision applying in relation to the first audit applies also, in so far as practicable, in relation to the second audit.

(3) A direction under section 1248(2) is, on the application of the Secretary of State, enforceable by injunction or, in Scotland, by an order under section 45 of the Court of Session Act 1988 (c. 36).

COMMENCEMENT DATE  6 April 2008[82]

This section provides that the company may recover costs associated with the appointment of the second auditor and possible second audit under section 1248 from the original auditor provided that it can be demonstrated that he knew the original auditor was not eligible to act as a statutory auditor.  **42.1249.02**

Section 1249(2) clarifies that the second auditor is subject to the same statutory and other regulation as the first auditor, to the extent that this is 'practicable'.  **42.1249.03**

---

[81] Companies Act 2006 (Commencement No 5, Transitional Provisions and Savings) Order 2007, SI 2007/3495, art 3.
[82] Companies Act 2006 (Commencement No 5, Transitional Provisions and Savings) Order 2007, SI 2007/3495, art 3.

*False and misleading statements*

### 1250   Misleading, false and deceptive statements

**42.1250.01**   (1) A person is guilty of an offence if—
  (a) for the purposes of or in connection with any application under this Part, or
  (b) in purported compliance with any requirement imposed on him by or by virtue of this Part,
  he knowingly or recklessly furnishes information which is misleading, false or deceptive in a material particular.
  (2) It is an offence for a person whose name does not appear on the register of auditors kept under regulations under section 1239 in an entry made under subsection (1)(a) of that section to describe himself as a registered auditor or so to hold himself out as to indicate, or be reasonably understood to indicate, that he is a registered auditor.
  (3) It is an offence for a person whose name does not appear on the register of auditors kept under regulations under that section in an entry made under subsection (1)(b) of that section to describe himself as a registered third country auditor or so to hold himself out as to indicate, or be reasonably understood to indicate, that he is a registered third country auditor.
  (4) It is an offence for a body which is not a recognised supervisory body or a recognised qualifying body to describe itself as so recognised or so to describe itself or hold itself out as to indicate, or be reasonably understood to indicate, that it is so recognised.
  (5) A person guilty of an offence under subsection (1) is liable—
  (a) on conviction on indictment, to imprisonment for a term not exceeding two years or to a fine (or both);
  (b) on summary conviction—
  (i) in England and Wales, to imprisonment for a term not exceeding twelve months or to a fine not exceeding the statutory maximum (or both),
  (ii) in Scotland or Northern Ireland, to imprisonment for a term not exceeding six months or to a fine not exceeding the statutory maximum (or both).
  In relation to an offence committed before the commencement of section 154(1) of the Criminal Justice Act 2003 (c. 44), for 'twelve months' in paragraph (b)(i) substitute 'six months'.
  (6) Subject to subsection (7), a person guilty of an offence under subsection (2), (3) or (4) is liable on summary conviction—
  (a) in England and Wales, to imprisonment for a term not exceeding 51 weeks or to a fine not exceeding level 5 on the standard scale (or both),
  (b) in Scotland or Northern Ireland, to imprisonment for a term not exceeding six months or to a fine not exceeding level 5 on the standard scale (or both).
  In relation to an offence committed before the commencement of section 281(5) of the Criminal Justice Act 2003, for '51 weeks' in paragraph (a) substitute 'six months'.
  (7) Where a contravention of subsection (2), (3) or (4) involves a public display of the offending description, the maximum fine that may be imposed is an amount equal to level 5 on the standard scale multiplied by the number of days for which the display has continued.
  (8) It is a defence for a person charged with an offence under subsection (2), (3) or (4) to show that he took all reasonable precautions and exercised all due diligence to avoid the commission of the offence.

COMMENCEMENT DATE 6 April 2008[83]

**42.1250.02**   Subsection (1) provides that an offence is committed if a person knowingly or recklessly provides materially misleading, false, or deceptive information either in connection with an application made under Part 42 of the Act or when complying with any requirement imposed under Part 42. The applications to which this section relate include an application to become a recognized supervisory body (in accordance with Schedule 11 to the Act) and an application by a qualifying body for a professional qualification to become a recognized professional qualification (in accordance with Schedule 12 to the Act). This offence is punishable by imprisonment and/or a fine (section 1250(5)).

**42.1250.03**   Subsections (2) and (3) make it an offence for a person to represent himself as a registered auditor or a registered third country auditor, when his name is not on the register of auditors. Subsection (4) makes it an offence for a supervisory body or qualifying body to hold itself out as a recognized body when it has not been recognized. These offences are punishable by fines and/or imprisonment (section 1250(6)). Subsection (8) provides a 'reasonable steps and all due diligence' defence for offences under subsections (2), (3), and (4).

---

[83] Companies Act 2006 (Commencement No 5, Transitional Provisions and Savings) Order 2007, SI 2007/3495, art 3.

*Fees*

## 1251   Fees

(1) An applicant for a recognition order under this Part must pay such fee in respect of his application as the Secretary of State may by regulations prescribe; and no application is to be regarded as duly made unless this subsection is complied with.

(2) The Secretary of State may by regulations prescribe periodical fees to be paid by—
   (a) every recognised supervisory body,
   (b) every recognised qualifying body,
   (c) every Auditor General, and
   (d) every registered third country auditor.

(3) Fees received by the Secretary of State by virtue of this Part are to be paid into the Consolidated Fund.

(4) Regulations under this section are subject to negative resolution procedure.

COMMENCEMENT DATE  6 April 2008[84]

**42.1251.01**

No regulations are extant under this section.                                   **42.1251.02**

## *Duty of Secretary of State to report on inspections*

### 1251A   Duty of the Secretary of State to report on inspections

The Secretary of State must, at least once in every calendar year, publish a report containing a summary of the results of inspections that are delivered to him—           **42.1251A.01**

(a) by the Independent Supervisor under section 1229(5A);
(b) by a recognised supervisory body under paragraph 13(9) of Schedule 10.][a]

AMENDMENTS AND NOTES

[a] Inserted by the Statutory Auditors and Third Country Auditors Regulations 2007, SI 2007/3494, reg 11.

COMMENCEMENT DATE  6 April 2008[85]

The functions of the Secretary of State under section 1251A have been transferred to the FRC.[86]   **42.1251A.02**
Accordingly, section 1251A requires the FRC to publish annually a report summarizing the results of both the inspections carried out in relation to the supervisory arrangements for auditors general put in place in accordance with section 1229 of the Act as well as the inspections carried out as part of the recognized supervisory bodies' audit monitoring function set forth in paragraph 13 of Schedule 10 of the Act.[87]

## *Delegation of Secretary of State's functions*

### 1252   Delegation of the Secretary of State's functions

(1) The Secretary of State may make an order under this section (a 'delegation order') for the purpose of enabling functions of the Secretary of State under this Part to be exercised by a body designated by the order.           **42.1252.01**

(2) The body designated by a delegation order may be either—
   (a) a body corporate which is established by the order, or
   (b) subject to section 1253, a body (whether a body corporate or an unincorporated association) which is already in existence ('an existing body').

(3) A delegation order has the effect of making the body designated by the order designated under section 5 of the Freedom of Information Act 2000 (c. 36) (further powers to designate public authorities).

(4) A delegation order has the effect of transferring to the body designated by it all functions of the Secretary of State under this Part—
   (a) subject to such exceptions and reservations as may be specified in the order, and
   (b) except—
      (i) his functions in relation to the body itself, and
      (ii) his functions under section 1228 (appointment of Independent Supervisor).

---

[84] Companies Act 2006 (Commencement No 5, Transitional Provisions and Savings) Order 2007, SI 2007/3495, art 3.

[85] Statutory Auditors and Third Country Auditors Regulations 2007, SI 2007/3494.

[86] The Statutory Auditors (Amendment of Companies Act 2006 and Delegation of Functions etc) Order 2012, SI 2012/1741.

[87] As amended by the Statutory Auditors and Third Country Auditors Regulations 2007, SI 2007/3494, reg 13.

(5) A delegation order may confer on the body designated by it such other functions supplementary or incidental to those transferred as appear to the Secretary of State to be appropriate.

(6) Any transfer of functions under the following provisions must be subject to the reservation that the functions remain exercisable concurrently by the Secretary of State—

   (a) section 1224 (power to call for information from recognised bodies etc);

   (b) section 1244 (power to call for information from registered third country auditors);

   (c) section 1254 (directions to comply with international obligations).

(7) Any transfer of—

   (a) the function of refusing to make a declaration under section 1221(1) (approval of [third country]ᵃ qualifications) on the grounds referred to in section 1221(4) (lack of comparable treatment), or

   (b) the function of withdrawing such a declaration under section 1221(7) on those grounds, must be subject to the reservation that the function is exercisable only with the consent of the Secretary of State.

(8) A delegation order may be amended or, if it appears to the Secretary of State that it is no longer in the public interest that the order should remain in force, revoked by a further order under this section.

(9) Where functions are transferred or resumed, the Secretary of State may by order confer or, as the case may be, take away such other functions supplementary or incidental to those transferred or resumed as appear to him to be appropriate.

(10) Where a delegation order is made, Schedule 13 has effect with respect to—

   (a) the status of the body designated by the order in exercising functions of the Secretary of State under this Part,

   (b) the constitution and proceedings of the body where it is established by the order,

   (c) the exercise by the body of certain functions transferred to it, and

   (d) other supplementary matters.

(11) An order under this section which has the effect of transferring or resuming any functions is subject to affirmative resolution procedure.

(12) Any other order under this section is subject to negative resolution procedure.

AMENDMENTS AND NOTES

ᵃ Substituted by the Statutory Auditors and Third Country Auditors Regulations 2007, SI 2007/3494, reg 12.

COMMENCEMENT DATE 6 April 2008[88]

**42.1252.02** This section enables the Secretary of State to delegate certain functions under Part 42 of the Act to a separate body. Most of these functions have been delegated to the FRC[89] a public authority for the purposes of the Freedom of Information Act 2000 (section 1252(3)).

**42.1252.03** Subsection (4) excludes from the available scope of the delegation the Secretary of State's function in relation to the delegated body and the appointment of the Independent Supervisor under section 1228. The Secretary of State has, however, appointed the FRC[90] as the Independent Supervisor.

**42.1252.04** The provision provides that certain functions, namely the power to call for information from recognized bodies or registered third country auditors (section 1252(6)), remain exercisable concurrently with the Secretary of State, and that the power to refuse to make or to withdraw a declaration in relation to overseas qualifications because of a lack of reciprocity must be exercised with the consent of the Secretary of State (section 1252(7)).

**42.1252.05** Schedule 13, which applies by virtue of section 1252(10), provides detailed regulations applicable to the delegated body in relation to its governance arrangements, remuneration of members, legislative functions, fees, and reports and accounts. For example: the body does not act on behalf of the crown (paragraph 2); the members of the body and its chairman are appointed by the Secretary of State (paragraph 3); the body must provide an annual report on its activities (paragraph 10).

## 1253 Delegation of functions to an existing body

**42.1253.01** (1) The Secretary of State's power to make a delegation order under section 1252 which designates an existing body is exercisable in accordance with this section.

(2) The Secretary of State may make such a delegation order if it appears to him that—

---

[88] Companies Act 2006 (Commencement No 5, Transitional Provisions and Savings) Order 2007, SI 2007/3495, art 3.

[89] The Statutory Auditors (Amendment of Companies Act 2006 and Delegation of Functions etc) Order 2012, SI 2012/1741.

[90] The Statutory Auditors (Amendment of Companies Act 2006 and Delegation of Functions etc) Order 2012, SI 2012/1741.

      (a)  the body is able and willing to exercise the functions that would be transferred by the order, and

      (b)  the body has arrangements in place relating to the exercise of those functions which are such as to be likely to ensure that the conditions in subsection (3) are met.

  (3)  The conditions are—

      (a)  that the functions in question will be exercised effectively, and

      (b)  where the delegation order is to contain any requirements or other provisions specified under subsection (4), that those functions will be exercised in accordance with any such requirements or provisions.

  (4)  The delegation order may contain such requirements or other provision relating to the exercise of the functions by the designated body as appear to the Secretary of State to be appropriate.

  (5)  An existing body—

      (a)  may be designated by a delegation order under section 1252, and

      (b)  may accordingly exercise functions of the Secretary of State in pursuance of the order,

    despite any involvement of the body in the exercise of any functions under arrangements within [paragraph 21 to 22B, 23(1) or 24(1) of Schedule 10]ª or paragraph 1 or 2 of Schedule 12.

AMENDMENTS AND NOTES

  ª  Substituted by the Statutory Auditors and Third Country Auditors Regulations 2007, SI 2007/3494, reg 13.

COMMENCEMENT DATE  6 April 2008[91]

This section provides that the delegation under section 1252 can be made to an existing body, provided   **42.1253.02** such body complies with the conditions set forth in this section 1253(2) and (3), which require that the body is able, willing, and capable of carrying out the functions in question. Subsection (5) clarifies that the body's involvement in certain arrangements does not exclude it as a candidate for delegation. These arrangements are arrangements for: standard setting relating to professional integrity and independence (Schedule 10, paragraph 21); technical standards (Schedule 10, paragraph 22); independent monitoring of listed company audits (Schedule 10, paragraph 23); public interest investigations and disciplinary proceedings (Schedule 10, paragraph 24); monitoring of traded non-community companies (Schedule 12, paragraph 1); and the investigations and disciplinary proceedings arising from such traded non-community company audits (Schedule 12, paragraph 2).

## *[Cooperation with foreign competent authorities*

### 1253A  Requests to foreign competent authorities

The Secretary of State may request from an EEA competent authority or a third country competent   **42.1253A.01** authority such assistance, information or investigation as he may reasonably require in connection with the exercise of his functions under this Part.]ª

AMENDMENTS AND NOTES

  ª  Inserted by the Statutory Auditors and Third Country Auditors Regulations 2007, SI 2007/3494, reg 14(1).

COMMENCEMENT DATE  6 April 2008[92]

This section provides that the Secretary of State may request assistance, information or an investigation   **42.1253A.02** from a competent authority in the EEA or in any other third country.

The functions of the Secretary of State under section 1253A have been transferred to the FRC and are   **42.1253A.03** exercisable concurrently with the Secretary of State.[93]

### [1253B  Requests from EEA competent authorities

  (1)  The Secretary of State must take all necessary steps to—   **42.1253B.01**

      (a)  ensure that an investigation is carried out, or

      (b)  provide any other assistance or information,

    if requested to do so by an EEA competent authority in accordance with Article 36 of the Audit Directive (cooperation between Member State authorities).

---

  [91]  Companies Act 2006 (Commencement No 5, Transitional Provisions and Savings) Order 2007, SI 2007/3495, art 3.

  [92]  Statutory Auditors and Third Country Auditors Regulations 2007, SI 2007/3494.

  [93]  The Statutory Auditors (Amendment of Companies Act 2006 and Delegation of Functions etc) Order 2012, SI 2012/1741.

(2) Within 28 days following the date on which he receives the request, the Secretary of State must—
    (a) provide the assistance or information required by the EEA competent authority under subsection (1)(b), or
    (b) notify the EEA competent authority which made the request of the reasons why he has not done so.
(3) But the Secretary of State need not take steps to comply with a request under subsection (1) if—
    (a) he considers that complying with the request may prejudice the sovereignty, security or public order of the United Kingdom;
    (b) legal proceedings have been brought in the United Kingdom (whether continuing or not) in relation to the persons and matters to which the request relates; or
    (c) disciplinary action has been taken by a recognised supervisory body in relation to the persons and matters to which the request relates.]ᵃ

AMENDMENTS AND NOTES

ᵃ Inserted by the Statutory Auditors and Third Country Auditors Regulations 2007, SI 2007/3494, reg 14(1).

COMMENCEMENT DATE 6 April 2008[94]

**42.1253B.02** This section provides that in response to a request from an EEA competent authority the Secretary of State must ensure that the requested investigation is carried out or the information and assistance provided. The Secretary of State must provide the information or give reasons why the information has not been provided within a 28-day period following receipt of the request. Subsection (3) provides grounds upon which the Secretary of State can refuse the co-operation. These grounds are based on the grounds set forth in Article 36(4) of the Audit Directive.[95]

**42.1253B.03** The functions of the Secretary of State in this section have been transferred to the FRC.[96]; However, cooperation can only be refused by the FRC with the consent of the Secretary of State.[97]

**42.1253B.04** This section only applies to auditors who are appointed for the financial years commencing on or after 6 April 2008.

## [1253C Notification to competent authorities of other EEA States

**42.1253C.01** (1) The Secretary of State must notify the relevant EEA competent authority if he receives notice from a recognised supervisory body under section 1223A(1) (notification of withdrawal of eligibility for appointment) of the withdrawal of a person's eligibility for appointment as a statutory auditor.
(2) In subsection (1) 'the relevant EEA competent authority' means the EEA competent authority which has approved the person concerned in accordance with the Audit Directive to carry out audits of annual accounts or consolidated accounts required by Community law.
(3) The notification under subsection (1) must include the name of the person concerned and the reasons for the withdrawal of his eligibility for appointment as statutory auditor.
(4) The Secretary of State must notify the relevant EEA competent authority if he has reasonable grounds for suspecting that—
    (a) a person has contravened the law of the United Kingdom, or any other EEA State or part of an EEA State, implementing the Audit Directive, and
    (b) the act or omission constituting that contravention took place on the territory of an EEA State other than the United Kingdom.,
(5) In subsection (4) 'the relevant EEA competent authority' means the EEA competent authority for the EEA State in which the suspected contravention took place.
(6) The notification under subsection (4) must include the name of the person concerned and the grounds for the Secretary of State's suspicion.]ᵃ

AMENDMENTS AND NOTES

ᵃ Inserted by the Statutory Auditors and Third Country Auditors Regulations 2007, SI 2007/3494, reg 14(1).

COMMENCEMENT DATE 6 April 2008[98]

**42.1253C.02** This section provides that if a recognized body notifies the Secretary of State of a person's withdrawal from eligibility to act as a statutory auditor then the Secretary of State must notify the EEA competent

---

[94] Statutory Auditors and Third Country Auditors Regulations 2007, SI 2007/3494.
[95] EU Statutory Audit Directive 2006/43/EC
[96] The Statutory Auditors (Amendment of Companies Act 2006 and Delegation Functions etc) Order 2012, SI 2012/1741.
[97] The Statutory Auditors (Amendment of Companies Act 2006 and Delegation Functions etc) Order 2012, SI 2012/1741, art 7(4)(c).
[98] Statutory Auditors and Third Country Auditors Regulations 2007, SI 2007/3494.

authority who authorized that person the carry out audits. The functions of the Secretary of State under this section have been transferred to the FRC.[99]

## [Transfer of papers to third countries

### 1253D   Restriction on transfer of audit working papers to third countries

  (1)   Audit working papers must not be transferred to a third country competent authority except in accordance with—      **42.1253D.01**

    (a)   section 1253DA (transfer by Secretary of State),

    (b)   section 1253DB (transfer by statutory auditor with approval of Secretary of State), or

    (c)   section 1253DC (transfer by statutory auditor for purposes of investigation of auditor).

  (2)   The following are approved third country competent authorities for the purposes of this Part—

    (a)   the Australian Securities and Investments Commission;

    (b)   the Canadian Public Accountability Board;

    (c)   the Certified Public Accountants and Auditing Oversight Board of Japan;

    (d)   the Financial Services Agency of Japan;

    (e)   the Federal Audit Oversight Authority of Switzerland;

    (f)   the Public Company Accounting Oversight Board of the United States of America;

    (g)   the Securities and Exchange Commission of the United States of America.

  (3)   Nothing in the sections referred to in subsection (1) authorises the making of a disclosure in contravention of the Data Protection Act 1998.[a]

AMENDMENTS AND NOTES

[a]   Inserted by the Statutory Auditors and Third Country Auditors Regulations 2007, SI 2007/3494, reg 15.

### 1253DA   Transfer by Secretary of State

  (1)   The Secretary of State may transfer audit working papers to an approved third country competent authority if the following conditions are met (but see also section 1253DD).

  (2)   The first condition is that the authority has made a request to the Secretary of State for the transfer of the audit working papers.

  (3)   The second condition is that the audit working papers relate to audits of companies that—

    (a)   have issued securities in the third country in which the authority is established, or

    (b)   form part of a group issuing statutory consolidated accounts in that third country.

  (4)   The third condition is that the authority has entered into arrangements with the Secretary of State in accordance with section 1253E.

### 1253DB   Transfer by statutory auditor with approval of Secretary of State

  (1)   A statutory auditor may transfer audit working papers to an approved third country competent authority if the transfer is made—

    (a)   with the prior approval of the Secretary of State, and

    (b)   in accordance with rules of a recognised supervisory body meeting the requirements of paragraph 16AA of Schedule 10.

  (2)   The Secretary of State must not approve a transfer of audit working papers to an approved third country competent authority for the purposes of this section unless the following conditions are met (see also section 1253DD).

  (3)   The first condition is that the authority has made a request to the Secretary of State for the transfer of the audit working papers.

  (4)   The second condition is that the audit working papers relate to audits of companies that—

    (a)   have issued securities in the third country in which the authority is established, or

    (b)   form part of a group issuing statutory consolidated accounts in that third country.

  (5)   The third condition is that the authority has entered into arrangements with the Secretary of State in accordance with section 1253E.

### 1253DC   Transfer by statutory auditor for purposes of investigation of auditor

A statutory auditor may transfer audit working papers to a third country competent authority if the transfer is made—

    (a)   for the purposes of an investigation of an auditor or audit firm, and

    (b)   in accordance with rules of a recognised supervisory body meeting the requirements of paragraph 16AB of Schedule 10.

---

[99]   The Statutory Auditors (Amendment of Companies Act 2006 and Delegation Functions etc) Order 2012, SI 2012/1741.

### 1253DD  Agreement of EEA competent authority

(1) This section applies where—
  (a) an approved third country competent authority makes a request to the Secretary of State for the transfer of audit working papers which relate to the audit of the consolidated accounts of a group, and
  (b) the audit working papers that are the subject of the request—
    (i)   have been created by the auditor of a subsidiary that is located in another EEA State in relation to the audit of that subsidiary, and
    (ii)  are in the possession of a statutory auditor.
(2) In the case of a transfer by the Secretary of State under section 1253DA, the transfer must not take place unless the EEA competent authority responsible for the auditor of the subsidiary has given its express agreement to the transfer.
(3) In the case of a transfer by a statutory auditor under section 1253DB, the Secretary of State must not approve the transfer unless the EEA competent authority responsible for the auditor of the subsidiary has given its express agreement to the transfer.

### 1253DE  Transfer by means of inspection

(1) This section applies in the case of a transfer of audit working papers if—
  (a) it is a transfer to an approved third country competent authority listed in section 1253D(2)(a), (f) or (g),
  (b) it is a transfer under section 1253DA or 1253DB, and
  (c) it is to take place by means of an inspection in the United Kingdom by the authority.
(2) The Secretary of State must participate in the inspection.
(3) The inspection must be under the leadership of the Secretary of State unless the Secretary of State otherwise permits.

(1) 2006 c 46. Section 1253D was inserted by regulation 15 of SI 2007/3.[a]

AMENDMENTS AND NOTES

[a]  Inserted by the Companies Act 2006 (Transfer of Audit Working Papers to Third Countries) Regulations 2010, SI 2010/2537.

COMMENCEMENT DATE 15 November 2010.[100]

**42.1253D.02**  The Companies Act 2006 (Transfer of Audit Working Papers to Third Countries) Regulations 2010 provide that audit working papers must only be transferred to third country competent authorities by a statutory auditor operating in accordance with paragraph 16A of Schedule 10, which is inserted into the Act by the Companies Act 2006 (Transfer of Audit Working Papers to Third Countries) Regulations 2010.[101]

**42.1253D.03**  The functions of the Secretary of State in this section have been transferred to the FRC[102].

### 1253E  Working arrangements for transfer of papers

**42.1253E.01**
(1) The Secretary of State may enter into arrangements with a third country competent authority relating to the transfer of audit working papers—
  (a) from the third country competent authority or a third country auditor regulated by that authority to the Secretary of State, and
  (b) from the Secretary of State or a statutory auditor to the third country competent authority.
(2) The arrangements must provide that a request by the Secretary of State or the third country competent authority for a transfer mentioned in subsection (1) must be accompanied by a statement explaining the reasons for the request.
(3) The arrangements must—
  (a) provide that the Secretary of State may not use audit working papers obtained from the third country competent authority or a third country auditor regulated by that authority except in connection with one or more of the functions mentioned in subsection (4), and
  (b) include comparable provision in relation to audit working papers obtained by the third country competent authority from the Secretary of State or a statutory auditor.
(4) Those functions are—
  (a) quality assurance functions which meet requirements equivalent to those of Article 29 of the Audit Directive (quality assurance);

---

[100]  Statutory Auditors and Third Country Auditors Regulations 2007, SI 2007/3494.
[101]  The Companies Act 2006 (Transfer of Audit Working Papers to Third Countries) Regulations 2010, SI 2010/2537.
[102]  The Statutory Auditors (Amendment of Companies Act 2006 and Delegation Functions etc) Order 2012, SI 2012/1741.

    (b)  investigation or disciplinary functions which meet requirements equivalent to those of Article 30 of the Audit Directive (investigations and penalties);

    (c)  public oversight functions which meet requirements equivalent to those of Article 32 of the Audit Directive (principles of public oversight).

(5)  The arrangements must—

    (a)  provide that the Secretary of State, a person exercising the functions of the Secretary of State and persons employed or formerly employed in discharging those functions must be subject to obligations of confidentiality as to personal data, professional secrets and sensitive commercial information contained in audit working papers transferred to the Secretary of State, and

    (b)  provide that the third country competent authority and persons involved in exercising its functions are subject to comparable obligations in relation to audit working papers transferred to the authority.

(6)  The arrangements must—

    (a)  provide that the Secretary of State may refuse, or direct a statutory auditor to refuse, a request from the third country competent authority for a transfer of audit working papers in a case mentioned in subsection (7)(a) or (b), and

    (b)  provide that the third country competent authority has comparable rights in relation to a request from the Secretary of State.

(7)  Those cases are—

    (a)  where the transfer of the papers would adversely affect the sovereignty, security or public order of the European Union or of the United Kingdom;

    (b)  where legal proceedings have been brought in the United Kingdom (whether continuing or not) in relation to the persons and matters to which the request relates.

(8)  Arrangements with an approved third country competent authority listed in section 1253D(2)(a), (f) or (g) must—

    (a)  provide that any contact between a statutory auditor and the authority relating to a relevant transfer of audit working papers to the authority must take place via the Secretary of State, and

    (b)  include comparable provision in relation to transfers of audit working papers to the Secretary of State.

(9)  'Relevant transfer' means any transfer other than a transfer by a statutory auditor under section 1253DC].[a]

AMENDMENTS AND NOTES

[a]  Inserted by the Companies Act 2006 (Transfer of Audit Working Papers to Third Countries) Regulations 2010, SI 2010/2537.

COMMENCEMENT DATE  15 November 2010[103]

This section sets forth the parameters within which the Secretary of State may enter into arrangements with a third country competent authority for the sharing of audit working papers.    **42.1253E.02**

The functions of the Secretary of State in this section have been transferred to the FRC[104]    **42.1253E.03**

## 1253F  Publication of working arrangements

If the Secretary of State enters into working arrangements in accordance with section 1253E, he must publish on a website without undue delay—    **42.1253F.01**

    (a)  the name of the third country competent authority with which he has entered into such arrangements, and

    (b)  the country or territory in which it is established.][a]

AMENDMENTS AND NOTES

[a]  Inserted by the Statutory Auditors and Third Country Auditors Regulations 2007, SI 2007/3494, reg 15(1).

COMMENCEMENT DATE  6 April 2008[105]

This section provides for the website publication of the country and competent authority details for any 'working arrangements' entered into. The Secretary of State's functions have been transferred to the FRC in relation to these working arrangements it is expected that any details of any such new working arrangements would be published on the FRC website <http:// www. frc. org. uk/>.    **42.1253F.02**

---

[103]  The Companies Act 2006 (Transfer of Audit Working Papers to Third Countries) Regulations 2010.

[104]  The Statutory Auditors (Amendment of Companies Act 2006 and Delegation Functions etc) Order 2012, SI 2012/1741.

[105]  Statutory Auditors and Third Country Auditors Regulations 2007, SI 2007/3494.

*International obligations*

## 1254  Directions to comply with international obligations

**42.1254.01**      (1)  If it appears to the Secretary of State—

(a)  that any action proposed to be taken by a recognised supervisory body or a recognised qualifying body, [the Independent Supervisor]ᵃ or a body designated by order under section 1252, would be incompatible with Community obligations or any other international obligations of the United Kingdom, or

(b)  that any action which that body has power to take is required for the purpose of implementing any such obligations, he may direct the body not to take or, as the case may be, to take the action in question.

(2)  A direction may include such supplementary or incidental requirements as the Secretary of State thinks necessary or expedient.

(3)  A direction under this section given to [the Independent Supervisor or]ᵇ a body designated by order under section 1252 is enforceable on the application of the Secretary of State by injunction or, in Scotland, by an order under section 45 of the Court of Session Act 1988 (c. 36).

AMENDMENTS AND NOTES

ᵃ  Inserted by the Statutory Auditors and Third Country Auditors Regulations 2007, SI 2007/3494, reg 16(1), (2).

ᵇ  Inserted by the Statutory Auditors and Third Country Auditors Regulations 2007, SI 2007/3494, reg 16(1), (3).

COMMENCEMENT DATE 6 April 2008[106]

**42.1254.02**  This section provides the Secretary of State with the power to direct that the Independent Supervisor, recognized bodies or a body to whom powers have been delegated under section 1252 take action or refrain from taking action in order to ensure that European Community and other international obligations are complied with.

**42.1254.03**  Section 40 of the Companies Act 1989 provided that a direction given to the Independent Supervisor, any recognized body or a delegated body could be enforced by injunction.

*General provision relating to offences*

## 1255  Offences by bodies corporate, partnerships and unincorporated associations

**42.1255.01**      (1)  Where an offence under this Part committed by a body corporate is proved to have been committed with the consent or connivance of, or to be attributable to any neglect on the part of, an officer of the body, or a person purporting to act in any such capacity, he as well as the body corporate is guilty of the offence and liable to be proceeded against and punished accordingly.

(2)  Where an offence under this Part committed by a partnership is proved to have been committed with the consent or connivance of, or to be attributable to any neglect on the part of, a partner, he as well as the partnership is guilty of the offence and liable to be proceeded against and punished accordingly.

(3)  Where an offence under this Part committed by an unincorporated association (other than a partnership) is proved to have been committed with the consent or connivance of, or to be attributable to any neglect on the part of, any officer of the association or any member of its governing body, he as well as the association is guilty of the offence and liable to be proceeded against and punished accordingly.

COMMENCEMENT DATE 6 April 2008[107]

**42.1255.02**  This section provides that where an offence has been committed by a body corporate, a partnership, or an unincorporated association and an officer, partner, or member of the governing body/officer of the association, respectively, of the body in question either consented to or connived in the commission of the offence, or the offence resulted from such person's negligence, then not only is the body in question guilty of a criminal offence but so is the officer, partner, or member of the governing body.

---

[106] Companies Act 2006 (Commencement No 5, Transitional Provisions and Savings) Order 2007, SI 2007/3495, art 3.
[107] Companies Act 2006 (Commencement No 5, Transitional Provisions and Savings) Order 2007, SI 2007/3495, art 3.

## 1256  Time limits for prosecution of offences

(1) An information relating to an offence under this Part which is triable by a magistrates' court in England and Wales may be so tried if it is laid at any time within the period of twelve months beginning with the date on which evidence sufficient in the opinion of the Director of Public Prosecutions or the Secretary of State to justify the proceedings comes to his knowledge.  **42.1256.01**

(2) Proceedings in Scotland for an offence under this Part may be commenced at any time within the period of twelve months beginning with the date on which evidence sufficient in the Lord Advocate's opinion to justify proceedings came to his knowledge or, where such evidence was reported to him by the Secretary of State, within the period of twelve months beginning with the date on which it came to the knowledge of the Secretary of State.

(3) For the purposes of subsection (2) proceedings are to be deemed to be commenced on the date on which a warrant to apprehend or cite the accused is granted, if the warrant is executed without undue delay.

(4) A complaint charging an offence under this Part which is triable by a magistrates' court in Northern Ireland may be so tried if it is made at any time within the period of twelve months beginning with the date on which evidence sufficient in the opinion of the Director of Public Prosecutions for Northern Ireland or the Secretary of State to justify the proceedings comes to his knowledge.

(5) This section does not authorise—
  (a) in the case of proceedings in England and Wales, the trial of an information laid,
  (b) in the case of proceedings in Scotland, the commencement of proceedings, or
  (c) in the case of proceedings in Northern Ireland, the trial of a complaint made,
  more than three years after the commission of the offence.

(6) For the purposes of this section a certificate of the Director of Public Prosecutions, the Lord Advocate, the Director of Public Prosecutions for Northern Ireland or the Secretary of State as to the date on which such evidence as is referred to above came to his knowledge is conclusive evidence.

(7) Nothing in this section affects proceedings within the time limits prescribed by section 127(1) of the Magistrates' Courts Act 1980 (c. 43), section 331 of the Criminal Procedure (Scotland) Act 1975 or Article 19 of the Magistrates' Courts (Northern Ireland) Order 1981 (S.I. 1981/1675 (N.I. 26)) (the usual time limits for criminal proceedings).

COMMENCEMENT DATE  6 April 2008[108]

This section sets forth a limitation period for prosecuting any offences under this part which is 12 months from the date that, in the opinion of the relevant prosecution authority in England, Scotland, and Northern Ireland, as the case may be, sufficient evidence comes to his knowledge to justify bringing proceedings.  **42.1256.02**

## 1257  Jurisdiction and procedure in respect of offences

(1) Summary proceedings for an offence under this Part may, without prejudice to any jurisdiction exercisable apart from this section, be taken—  **42.1257.01**
  (a) against a body corporate or unincorporated association at any place at which it has a place of business, and
  (b) against an individual at any place where he is for the time being.

(2) Proceedings for an offence alleged to have been committed under this Part by an unincorporated association must be brought in the name of the association (and not in that of any of its members), and for the purposes of any such proceedings any rules of court relating to the service of documents apply as in relation to a body corporate.

(3) Section 33 of the Criminal Justice Act 1925 (c. 86) and Schedule 3 to the Magistrates' Courts Act 1980 (c. 43) (procedure on charge of offence against a corporation) apply in a case in which an unincorporated association is charged in England and Wales with an offence under this Part as they apply in the case of a corporation.

(4) Section 18 of the Criminal Justice Act (Northern Ireland) 1945 (c. 15 (N.I.)) and Article 166 and Schedule 4 to the Magistrates' Courts (Northern Ireland) Order 1981 (S.I. 1981/1675 (N.I. 26)) (procedure on charge of offence against a corporation) apply in a case in which an unincorporated association is charged in Northern Ireland with an offence under this Part as they apply in the case of a corporation.

(5) In relation to proceedings on indictment in Scotland for an offence alleged to have been committed under this Part by an unincorporated association, section 70 of the Criminal Procedure (Scotland) Act 1995 (proceedings on indictment against bodies corporate) applies as if the association were a body corporate.

---

[108] Companies Act 2006 (Commencement No 5, Transitional Provisions and Savings) Order 2007, SI 2007/3495, art 3.

(6)  A fine imposed on an unincorporated association on its conviction of such an offence must be paid out of the funds of the association.

COMMENCEMENT DATE  6 April 2008[109]

**42.1257.02**   This section provides for certain jurisdictional and procedural matters in relation to proceedings brought in relation to offences under this Part 42.

## *Notices etc*

### 1258   Service of notices

**42.1258.01**
(1)  This section has effect in relation to any notice, direction or other document required or authorised by or by virtue of this Part to be given to or served on any person other than the Secretary of State.

(2)  Any such document may be given to or served on the person in question—
   (a)  by delivering it to him,
   (b)  by leaving it at his proper address, or
   (c)  by sending it by post to him at that address.

(3)  Any such document may—
   (a)  in the case of a body corporate, be given to or served on an officer of that body;
   (b)  in the case of a partnership, be given to or served on any partner;
   (c)  in the case of an unincorporated association other than a partnership, be given to or served on any member of the governing body of that association.

(4)  For the purposes of this section and section 7 of the Interpretation Act 1978 (c. 30) (service of documents by post) in its application to this section, the proper address of any person is his last known address (whether of his residence or of a place where he carries on business or is employed) and also—
   (a)  in the case of a person who is eligible under the rules of a recognised supervisory body for appointment as a statutory auditor and who does not have a place of business in the United Kingdom, the address of that body;
   (b)  in the case of a body corporate or an officer of that body, the address of the registered or principal office of that body in the United Kingdom;
   (c)  in the case of an unincorporated association other than a partnership or a member of its governing body, its principal office in the United Kingdom.

COMMENCEMENT DATE  6 April 2008[110]

**42.1258.02**   This section regulates the service or giving of notices, directions, or other documents pursuant to Part 42. This section does not apply to the Secretary of State.

### 1259   Documents in electronic form

**42.1259.01**
(1)  This section applies where—
   (a)  section 1258 authorises the giving or sending of a notice, direction or other document by its delivery to a particular person ('the recipient'), and
   (b)  the notice, direction or other document is transmitted to the recipient—
     (i)  by means of an electronic communications network, or
     (ii)  by other means but in a form that requires the use of apparatus by the recipient to render it intelligible.

(2)  The transmission has effect for the purposes of this Part as a delivery of the notice, direction or other document to the recipient, but only if the recipient has indicated to the person making the transmission his willingness to receive the notice, direction or other document in the form and manner used.

(3)  An indication to a person for the purposes of subsection (2)—
   (a)  must be given to the person in such manner as he may require,
   (b)  may be a general indication or an indication that is limited to notices, directions or other documents of a particular description,
   (c)  must state the address to be used,
   (d)  must be accompanied by such other information as the person requires for the making of the transmission, and
   (e)  may be modified or withdrawn at any time by a notice given to the person in such manner as he may require.

---

[109] Companies Act 2006 (Commencement No 5, Transitional Provisions and Savings) Order 2007, SI 2007/3495, art 3.
[110] Companies Act 2006 (Commencement No 5, Transitional Provisions and Savings) Order 2007, SI 2007/3495, art 3.

(4)  In this section 'electronic communications network' has the same meaning as in the Communications Act 2003 (c. 21).

COMMENCEMENT DATE  6 April 2008[111]

Section 1259 provides for the effectiveness of service or giving of notices, directions, or other docu- **42.1259.02**
ments by electronic means but only if the recipient of the notice, direction or document has indicated
his willingness to receive it in such form (section 1259(2)). Such indication may be general or restricted
to certain types of notice or document and may be modified or withdrawn by the recipient at any time
(section 1259(3)(e)).

## Interpretation

## 1260  Meaning of 'associate'

(1)  In this Part 'associate', in relation to a person, is to be construed as follows.                    **42.1260.01**
(2)  In relation to an individual, 'associate' means—
   (a)  that individual's spouse, civil partner or minor child or step-child,
   (b)  any body corporate of which that individual is a director, and
   (c)  any employee or partner of that individual.
(3)  In relation to a body corporate, 'associate' means—
   (a)  any body corporate of which that body is a director,
   (b)  any body corporate in the same group as that body, and
   (c)  any employee or partner of that body or of any body corporate in the same group.
(4)  In relation to a partnership constituted under the law of Scotland, or any other country or territory
   in which a partnership is a legal person, 'associate' means—
   (a)  any body corporate of which that partnership is a director,
   (b)  any employee of or partner in that partnership, and
   (c)  any person who is an associate of a partner in that partnership.
(5)  In relation to a partnership constituted under the law of England and Wales or Northern Ireland,
   or the law of any other country or territory in which a partnership is not a legal person, 'associate'
   means any person who is an associate of any of the partners.
(6)  In subsections (2)(b), (3)(a) and (4)(a), in the case of a body corporate which is a limited liability
   partnership, 'director' is to be read as 'member'.

COMMENCEMENT DATE  6 April 2008[112]

This section provides the meaning of associate for the purposes of the independence requirements of **42.1260.02**
section 1214 of the Companies Act 2006. The meaning of associate is separately defined for individuals
(section 1260(2)), for bodies corporate (section 1260(3)), partnerships in Scotland (section 1260(4)),
and partnerships in England and Wales and Northern Ireland (section 1260(5)).

## 1261  Minor definitions

(1)  In this Part, unless a contrary intention appears—                                              **42.1261.01**
   'address' means—
      (a)  in relation to an individual, his usual residential or business address;
      (b)  in relation to a firm, its registered or principal office in the United Kingdom;
   ['the Audit Directive' means Directive 2006/43/EC of the European Parliament and of the Council
   on statutory audits of annual accounts and consolidated accounts, amending Council Directives 78/660/EEC and 83/349/EEC and repealing Council Directive 84/253/EEC, as amended at
   any time before 1st January 2009;][a]
   ['audit working papers' means any documents which—
      (a)  are or have been held by a statutory auditor, an EEA auditor or[aa] a third country auditor,
         and
      (b)  are related to the conduct of an audit conducted by that auditor;][b]
   'company' means any company or other body the accounts of which must be audited in
   accordance with Part 16;
   'director', in relation to a body corporate, includes any person occupying in relation to it the
   position of a director (by whatever name called) and any person in accordance with whose
   directions or instructions (not being advice given in a professional capacity) the directors of the
   body are accustomed to act;

---

[111] Companies Act 2006 (Commencement No 5, Transitional Provisions and Savings) Order 2007, SI
2007/3495, art 3.
[112] Companies Act 2006 (Commencement No 5, Transitional Provisions and Savings) Order 2007, SI
2007/3495, art 3.

['EEA auditor' means an individual or firm approved in accordance with the Audit Directive by an EEA competent authority to carry out audits of annual accounts or consolidated accounts required by European Union law;][c]

['EEA competent authority' means a competent authority within the meaning of Article 2.10 of the Audit Directive of an EEA State other than the United Kingdom;][d]

'firm' means any entity, whether or not a legal person, which is not an individual and includes a body corporate, a corporation sole and a partnership or other unincorporated association;

'group', in relation to a body corporate, means the body corporate, any other body corporate which is its holding company or subsidiary and any other body corporate which is a subsidiary of that holding company;

'holding company' and 'subsidiary' are to be read in accordance with section 1159 and Schedule 6;

'officer', in relation to a body corporate, includes a director, a manager, a secretary or, where the affairs of the body are managed by its members, a member;

'parent undertaking' and 'subsidiary undertaking' are to be read in accordance with section 1162 and Schedule 7.

['third country' means a country or territory that is not an EEA State or part of an EEA State;][e]

['third country auditor' means a person, other than a person eligible for appointment as a statutory auditor, who is eligible to conduct audits of the accounts of bodies corporate incorporated or formed under the law of a third country in accordance with the law of that country;][f]

['third country competent authority' means a body established in a third country exercising functions related to the regulation or oversight of auditors.][g]

['Transfer', in relation to audit working papers, includes physical and electronic transfer and allowing access to such papers][99]

(2) For the purposes of this Part a body is to be regarded as 'established in the United Kingdom' if and only if— [97]

    (a) it is incorporated or formed under the law of the United Kingdom or a part of the United Kingdom, or

    (b) its central management and control are exercised in the United Kingdom; and any reference to a qualification 'obtained in the United Kingdom' is to a qualification obtained from such a body.

[(2A)For the purposes of this Part, Gibraltar shall be treated as if it were an EEA State.][h]

(3) The Secretary of State may by regulations make such modifications of this Part as appear to him to be necessary or appropriate for the purposes of its application in relation to any firm, or description of firm, which is not a body corporate or a partnership.

(4) Regulations under subsection (3) are subject to negative resolution procedure.

AMENDMENTS AND NOTES

[a] Inserted by the Statutory Auditors and Third Country Auditors Regulations 2007, SI 2007/3494, reg 2(1), (2).

[aa] Inserted by the Companies Act 2006 (Transfer of Audit Working Papers to Third Countries) Regulations 2010 reg 6(2).

[b] Inserted by the Statutory Auditors and Third Country Auditors Regulations 2007, SI 2007/3494, reg 2(1), (2).

[c] Inserted by the Companies Act 2006 (Transfer of Audit Working Papers to Third Countries) Regulations 2010 reg 6(3).

[d] Inserted by the Statutory Auditors and Third Country Auditors Regulations 2007, SI 2007/3494, reg 2(1), (2). Article 2(10) of the Audit Directive is as follows: '"competent authorities" means the authorities or bodies designated by law that are in charge of the regulation and/or oversight of statutory auditors and audit firms or of specific aspects thereof; the reference to "competent authority" in a specific article means a reference to the authority or body(ies) responsible for the functions referred to in that Article'.

[e] Inserted by the Statutory Auditors and Third Country Auditors Regulations 2007, SI 2007/3494, reg 2(1), (2).

[f] Inserted by the Statutory Auditors and Third Country Auditors Regulations 2007, SI 2007/3494, reg 2(1), (2).

[g] Inserted by the Statutory Auditors and Third Country Auditors Regulations 2007, SI 2007/3494, reg 2(1), (3).

[99] Inserted by the Companies Act 2006 (Transfer of Audit Working Papers to Third Countries) Regulations 2010 reg 6(2).

COMMENCEMENT DATE 6 April 2008[113]

This section provides in the main a list of minor definitions applicable to Part 42 of the Act. However, in addition, somewhat unusually in a section entitled 'minor definitions', it provides the Secretary of State with a general modification power which is not limited to this section but applies to Part 42 of the Act as a whole (section 1261(3)). This power may be exercised to make modifications which he deems necessary or appropriate in relation to Part 42's application to a firm which is not a body corporate or a partnership. Any such regulation issued under subsection (3) is subject to the negative resolution procedure.   **42.1261.02**

## 1262  Index of defined expressions

The following Table shows provisions defining or otherwise explaining expressions used in this Part   **42.1262.01**
(other than provisions defining or explaining an expression used only in the same section)

| Expression | Provision |
| --- | --- |
| address | section 1261(1) |
| appropriate qualification | section 1219 |
| Approved third country competent authority | section 1253D(2)aa |
| associate | section 1260 |
| [Audit Directive | section 1261(1)]a |
| [audit working papers | section 1261(1)]b |
| audited person | section 1210(2) |
| Auditor General | section 1226(1) |
| company | section 1261(1) |
| delegation order | section 1252(1) |
| director (of a body corporate) | section 1261(1) |
| [EEA auditor | section 1261(1)]c |
| [EEA competent authority | section 1261(1)]d |
| enactment | section 1293 |
| established in the United Kingdom | section 1261(2) |
| firm | section 1261(1) |
| group (in relation to a body corporate) | section 1261(1) |
| holding company | section 1261(1) |
| main purposes of this Part | section 1209 |
| member (of a supervisory body) | section 1217(2) |
| obtained in the United Kingdom | section 1261(2) |
| officer section | section 1261(1) |
| parent undertaking section | section 1261(1) |
| qualifying body section | section 1220(1) |
| recognised, in relation to a professional qualification | section 1220(3) and Schedule 11 |
| recognised, in relation to a qualifying body | paragraph 1(2) of Schedule 11 |
| recognised, in relation to a supervisory body | section 1217(4) and Schedule 10 |
| registered third country auditor | section 1241(1) |
| rules of a qualifying body | section 1220(2) |
| rules of a supervisory body | section 1217(3) |
| statutory auditor, statutory audit and statutory audit work | section 1210(1) |
| subsidiary | section 1261(1) |

| Expression | Provision |
| --- | --- |
| supervisory body | section 1217(1) |
| subsidiary undertaking | section 1261(1) |
| [third country | section 1261(1)]e |
| third country auditor, [...]f | section 1261(1)]g |
| [third country competent authority | section 1261(1)]h |
| [transfer in relation to audit working papers | section 1261(1)hh |
| [UK-traded non-EEA company | section 1261(2)]i |

AMENDMENTS AND NOTES

aa Inserted by the Companies Act 2006 (Transfer of Audit Working Papers to Third Countries) Regulations 2010, SI 2010/2537, reg 6(5).

a Inserted by the Statutory Auditors and Third Country Auditors Regulations 2007, SI 2007/3494, reg 3(1), (2).

b Inserted by the Statutory Auditors and Third Country Auditors Regulations 2007, SI 2007/3494, reg 3(1), (2).

c Inserted by the Statutory Auditors and Third Country Auditors Regulations 2007, SI 2007/3494, reg 3(1), (2).

d Inserted by the Statutory Auditors and Third Country Auditors Regulations 2007, SI 2007/3494, reg 3(1), (2).

e Inserted by the Statutory Auditors and Third Country Auditors Regulations 2007, SI 2007/3494, reg 3(1), (2).

f Repealed by the Statutory Auditors and Third Country Auditors Regulations 2007, SI 2007/3494, reg 3(1), (3).

g Substituted by the Statutory Auditors and Third Country Auditors Regulations 2007, SI 2007/3494, reg 3(1), (3).

h Inserted by the Statutory Auditors and Third Country Auditors Regulations 2007, SI 2007/3494, reg 3(1), (2).

hh Inserted by the Companies Act 2006 (Transfer of Audit Working Papers to Third Countries) Regulations 2010, SI 2010/2537, reg 6(5).

i Inserted by the Statutory Auditors and Third Country Auditors Regulations 2007, SI 2007/3494, reg 3(1), (2).

COMMENCEMENT DATE 6 April 200[114]

## Miscellaneous and general

### 1263  Power to make provision in consequence of changes affecting accountancy bodies

**42.1263.01**

(1) The Secretary of State may by regulations make such amendments of enactments as appear to him to be necessary or expedient in consequence of any change of name, merger or transfer of engagements affecting—
  (a) a recognised supervisory body or recognised qualifying body, or
  (b) a body of accountants referred to in, or approved, authorised or otherwise recognised for the purposes of, any other enactment.
(2) Regulations under this section are subject to negative resolution procedure.

COMMENCEMENT DATE 6 April 2008[115]

**42.1263.02**   This section provides the Secretary of State with the power to make consequential amendments that may be necessary as a result of changes of name or changes arising from mergers or transfers of engagements which affect either recognized supervisory bodies, recognized qualifying bodies, or accounting bodies authorized, approved or recognized pursuant to other enactments.

---

[114] Companies Act 2006 (Commencement No 5, Transitional Provisions and Savings) Order 2007, SI 2007/3495, art 3.

[115] Companies Act 2006 (Commencement No 5, Transitional Provisions and Savings) Order 2007, SI 2007/3495, art 3.

## 1264   Consequential amendments

Schedule 14 contains consequential amendments relating to this Part.                **42.1264.01**

COMMENCEMENT DATE 6 April 2008[116]

Schedule 14 provides for certain consequential amendments to section 16 of the Companies (Audit,   **42.1264.02**
Investigation and Community Enterprise) Act 2004 (grants to bodies concerned with accounting
standards).

---

[116] Companies Act 2006 (Commencement No 5, Transitional Provisions and Savings) Order 2007, SI 2007/
3495, art 3.

# 43

# TRANSPARENCY OBLIGATIONS AND RELATED MATTERS

## Companies Act 2006

## PART 43
## TRANSPARENCY OBLIGATIONS AND
## RELATED MATTERS

Commentary on this section of the CA 2006 has not been included
in this publication.

### Introductory

### 1265 The transparency obligations directive

In Part 6 of the Financial Services and Markets Act 2000 (c. 8) (which makes provision about official **43.1265.01**
listing, prospectus requirements for transferable securities, etc), in section 103(1) (interpretation), at
the appropriate place insert—

'"the transparency obligations directive" means Directive 2004/109/EC of the European Parliament and of
the Council relating to the harmonisation of transparency requirements in relation to information about
issuers whose securities are admitted to trading on a regulated market;'.

COMMENCEMENT DATE 8 November 2006: see s 1300

### Transparency obligations

### 1266 Transparency rules

(1) After section 89 of the Financial Services and Markets Act 2000 insert— **43.1266.01**

*'Transparency obligations*

### 89A Transparency rules

(1) The competent authority may make rules for the purposes of the transparency obligations
   directive.
(2) The rules may include provision for dealing with any matters arising out of or related to any
   provision of the transparency obligations directive.
(3) The competent authority may also make rules—
   (a) for the purpose of ensuring that voteholder information in respect of voting shares traded on
      a UK market other than a regulated market is made public or notified to the competent
      authority;

(b)  providing for persons who hold comparable instruments (see section 89F(1)(c)) in respect of voting shares to be treated, in the circumstances specified in the rules, as holding some or all of the voting rights in respect of those shares.

(4)  Rules under this section may, in particular, make provision—

(a)  specifying how the proportion of—

(i)   the total voting rights in respect of shares in an issuer, or

(ii)  the total voting rights in respect of a particular class of shares in an issuer, held by a person is to be determined;

(b)  specifying the circumstances in which, for the purposes of any determination of the voting rights held by a person ("P") in respect of voting shares in an issuer, any voting rights held, or treated by virtue of subsection (3)(b) as held, by another person in respect of voting shares in the issuer are to be regarded as held by P;

(c)  specifying the nature of the information which must be included in any notification;

(d)  about the form of any notification;

(e)  requiring any notification to be given within a specified period;

(f)  specifying the manner in which any information is to be made public and the period within which it must be made public;

(g)  specifying circumstances in which any of the requirements imposed by rules under this section does not apply.

(5)  Rules under this section are referred to in this Part as "transparency rules".

(6)  Nothing in sections 89B to 89G affects the generality of the power to make rules under this section.

## 89B  Provision of voteholder information

(1)  Transparency rules may make provision for voteholder information in respect of voting shares to be notified, in circumstances specified in the rules—

(a)  to the issuer, or

(b)  to the public, or to both.

(2)  Transparency rules may make provision for voteholder information notified to the issuer to be notified at the same time to the competent authority.

(3)  In this Part "voteholder information" in respect of voting shares means information relating to the proportion of voting rights held by a person in respect of the shares.

(4)  Transparency rules may require notification of voteholder information relating to a person—

(a)  initially, not later than such date as may be specified in the rules for the purposes of the first indent of Article 30.2 of the transparency obligations directive, and

(b)  subsequently, in accordance with the following provisions.

(5)  Transparency rules under subsection (4)(b) may require notification of voteholder information relating to a person only where there is a notifiable change in the proportion of—

(a)  the total voting rights in respect of shares in the issuer, or

(b)  the total voting rights in respect of a particular class of share in the issuer, held by the person.

(6)  For this purpose there is a "notifiable change" in the proportion of voting rights held by a person when the proportion changes—

(a)  from being a proportion less than a designated proportion to a proportion equal to or greater than that designated proportion,

(b)  from being a proportion equal to a designated proportion to a proportion greater or less than that designated proportion, or

(c)  from being a proportion greater than a designated proportion to a proportion equal to or less than that designated proportion.

(7)  In subsection (6) "designated" means designated by the rules.

## 89C  Provision of information by issuers of transferable securities

(1)  Transparency rules may make provision requiring the issuer of transferable securities, in circumstances specified in the rules—

(a)  to make public information to which this section applies, or

(b)  to notify to the competent authority information to which this section applies, or to do both.

(2)  In the case of every issuer, this section applies to—

(a)  information required by Article 4 of the transparency obligations directive;

(b)  information relating to the rights attached to the transferable securities, including information about the terms and conditions of those securities which could indirectly affect those rights; and

(c)  information about new loan issues and about any guarantee or security in connection with any such issue.

(3)  In the case of an issuer of debt securities, this section also applies to information required by Article 5 of the transparency obligations directive.

(4)  In the case of an issuer of shares, this section also applies to—
   (a)  information required by Article 5 of the transparency obligations directive;
   (b)  information required by Article 6 of that directive;
   (c)  voteholder information—
      (i)  notified to the issuer, or
      (ii)  relating to the proportion of voting rights held by the issuer in respect of shares in the issuer;
   (d)  information relating to the issuer's capital; and
   (e)  information relating to the total number of voting rights in respect of shares or shares of a particular class.

## 89D  Notification of voting rights held by issuer

(1)  Transparency rules may require notification of voteholder information relating to the proportion of voting rights held by an issuer in respect of voting shares in the issuer—
   (a)  initially, not later than such date as may be specified in the rules for the purposes of the second indent of Article 30.2 of the transparency obligations directive, and
   (b)  subsequently, in accordance with the following provisions.
(2)  Transparency rules under subsection (1)(b) may require notification of voteholder information relating to the proportion of voting rights held by an issuer in respect of voting shares in the issuer only where there is a notifiable change in the proportion of—
   (a)  the total voting rights in respect of shares in the issuer, or
   (b)  the total voting rights in respect of a particular class of share in the issuer, held by the issuer.
(3)  For this purpose there is a "notifiable change" in the proportion of voting rights held by a person when the proportion changes—
   (a)  from being a proportion less than a designated proportion to a proportion equal to or greater than that designated proportion,
   (b)  from being a proportion equal to a designated proportion to a proportion greater or less than that designated proportion, or
   (c)  from being a proportion greater than a designated proportion to a proportion equal to or less than that designated proportion.
(4)  In subsection (3) "designated" means designated by the rules.

## 89E  Notification of proposed amendment of issuer's constitution

Transparency rules may make provision requiring an issuer of transferable securities that are admitted to trading on a regulated market to notify a proposed amendment to its constitution—
(a)  to the competent authority, and
(b)  to the market on which the issuer's securities are admitted, at times and in circumstances specified in the rules.

## 89F  Transparency rules: interpretation etc

(1)  For the purposes of sections 89A to 89G—
   (a)  the voting rights in respect of any voting shares are the voting rights attached to those shares,
   (b)  a person is to be regarded as holding the voting rights in respect of the shares—
      (i)  if, by virtue of those shares, he is a shareholder within the meaning of Article 2.1(e) of the transparency obligations directive;
      (ii)  if, and to the extent that, he is entitled to acquire, dispose of or exercise those voting rights in one or more of the cases mentioned in Article 10(a) to (h) of the transparency obligations directive;
      (iii)  if he holds, directly or indirectly, a financial instrument which results in an entitlement to acquire the shares and is an Article 13 instrument, and
   (c)  a person holds a "comparable instrument" in respect of voting shares if he holds, directly or indirectly, a financial instrument in relation to the shares which has similar economic effects to an Article 13 instrument (whether or not the financial instrument results in an entitlement to acquire the shares).
(2)  Transparency rules under section 89A(3)(b) may make different provision for different descriptions of comparable instrument.
(3)  For the purposes of sections 89A to 89G two or more persons may, at the same time, each be regarded as holding the same voting rights.
(4)  In those sections—
      "Article 13 instrument" means a financial instrument of a type determined by the European Commission under Article 13.2 of the transparency obligations directive; "UK market" means a market that is situated or operating in the United Kingdom;
      "voting shares" means shares of an issuer to which voting rights are attached.

### 89G  Transparency rules: other supplementary provisions

(1) Transparency rules may impose the same obligations on a person who has applied for the admission of transferable securities to trading on a regulated market without the issuer's consent as they impose on an issuer of transferable securities.

(2) Transparency rules that require a person to make information public may include provision authorising the competent authority to make the information public in the event that the person fails to do so.

(3) The competent authority may make public any information notified to the authority in accordance with transparency rules.

(4) Transparency rules may make provision by reference to any provision of any rules made by the Panel on Takeovers and Mergers under Part 28 of the Companies Act 2006.

(5) Sections 89A to 89F and this section are without prejudice to any other power conferred by this Part to make Part 6 rules.'.

(2) The effectiveness for the purposes of section 155 of the Financial Services and Markets Act 2000 (c. 8) (consultation on proposed rules) of things done by the Financial Services Authority before this section comes into force with a view to making transparency rules (as defined in the provisions to be inserted in that Act by subsection (1) above) is not affected by the fact that those provisions were not then in force.

COMMENCEMENT DATE  8 November 2006: see s 1300

## 1267  Competent authority's power to call for information

**43.1267.01**        In Part 6 of the Financial Services and Markets Act 2000 after the sections inserted by section 1266 above insert—'

### 'Power of competent authority to call for information

### 89H  Competent authority's power to call for information

(1) The competent authority may by notice in writing given to a person to whom this section applies require him—
   (a) to provide specified information or information of a specified description, or
   (b) to produce specified documents or documents of a specified description.

(2) This section applies to—
   (a) an issuer in respect of whom transparency rules have effect;
   (b) a voteholder;
   (c) an auditor of—
     (i) an issuer to whom this section applies, or
     (ii) a voteholder;
   (d) a person who controls a voteholder;
   (e) a person controlled by a voteholder;
   (f) a director or other similar officer of an issuer to whom this section applies;
   (g) a director or other similar officer of a voteholder or, where the affairs of a voteholder are managed by its members, a member of the voteholder.

(3) This section applies only to information and documents reasonably required in connection with the exercise by the competent authority of functions conferred on it by or under sections 89A to 89G (transparency rules).

(4) Information or documents required under this section must be provided or produced—
   (a) before the end of such reasonable period as may be specified, and
   (b) at such place as may be specified.

(5) If a person claims a lien on a document, its production under this section does not affect the lien.

### 89I  Requirements in connection with call for information

(1) The competent authority may require any information provided under section 89H to be provided in such form as it may reasonably require.

(2) The competent authority may require—
   (a) any information provided, whether in a document or otherwise, to be verified in such manner as it may reasonably require;
   (b) any document produced to be authenticated in such manner as it may reasonably require.

(3) If a document is produced in response to a requirement imposed under section 89H, the competent authority may—
   (a) take copies of or extracts from the document; or
   (b) require the person producing the document, or any relevant person, to provide an explanation of the document.

(4) In subsection (3)(b) "relevant person", in relation to a person who is required to produce a document, means a person who—

   (a) has been or is a director or controller of that person;

   (b) has been or is an auditor of that person;

   (c) has been or is an actuary, accountant or lawyer appointed or instructed by that person; or

   (d) has been or is an employee of that person.

(5) If a person who is required under section 89H to produce a document fails to do so, the competent authority may require him to state, to the best of his knowledge and belief, where the document is.

### 89J  Power to call for information: supplementary provisions

(1) The competent authority may require an issuer to make public any information provided to the authority under section 89H.

(2) If the issuer fails to comply with a requirement under subsection (1), the competent authority may, after seeking representations from the issuer, make the information public.

(3) In sections 89H and 89I (power of competent authority to call for information)—

"control" and "controlled" have the meaning given by subsection (4) below;

"specified" means specified in the notice;

"voteholder" means a person who—

   (a) holds voting rights in respect of any voting shares for the purposes of sections 89A to 89G (transparency rules), or

   (b) is treated as holding such rights by virtue of rules under section 89A(3)(b).

(4) For the purposes of those sections a person ("A") controls another person ("B") if—

   (a) A holds a majority of the voting rights in B,

   (b) A is a member of B and has the right to appoint or remove a majority of the members of the board of directors (or, if there is no such board, the equivalent management body) of B,

   (c) A is a member of B and controls alone, pursuant to an agreement with other shareholders or members, a majority of the voting rights in B, or

   (d) A has the right to exercise, or actually exercises, dominant influence or control over B.

(5) For the purposes of subsection (4)(b)—

   (a) any rights of a person controlled by A, and

   (b) any rights of a person acting on behalf of A or a person controlled by A, are treated as held by A.'.

COMMENCEMENT DATE 8 November 2006 see s 1300

## 1268  Powers exercisable in case of infringement of transparency obligation

In Part 6 of the Financial Services and Markets Act 2000 (c. 8), after the sections inserted by section 1267 above insert—          **43.1268.01**

## *'Powers exercisable in case of infringement of transparency obligation*

### 89K  Public censure of issuer

(1) If the competent authority finds that an issuer of securities admitted to trading on a regulated market is failing or has failed to comply with an applicable transparency obligation, it may publish a statement to that effect.

(2) If the competent authority proposes to publish a statement, it must give the issuer a warning notice setting out the terms of the proposed statement.

(3) If, after considering any representations made in response to the warning notice, the competent authority decides to make the proposed 617 statement, it must give the issuer a decision notice setting out the terms of the statement.

(4) A notice under this section must inform the issuer of his right to refer the matter to the Tribunal (see section 89N) and give an indication of the procedure on such a reference.

(5) In this section "transparency obligation" means an obligation under—

   (a) a provision of transparency rules, or

   (b) any other provision made in accordance with the transparency obligations directive.

(6) In relation to an issuer whose home State is a member State other than the United Kingdom, any reference to an applicable transparency obligation must be read subject to section 100A(2).

### 89L  Power to suspend or prohibit trading of securities

(1) This section applies to securities admitted to trading on a regulated market.

(2) If the competent authority has reasonable grounds for suspecting that an applicable transparency obligation has been infringed by an issuer, it may—

   (a) suspend trading in the securities for a period not exceeding 10 days,

   (b) prohibit trading in the securities, or

(c) make a request to the operator of the market on which the issuer's securities are traded—
  (i) to suspend trading in the securities for a period not exceeding 10 days, or
  (ii) to prohibit trading in the securities.
(3) If the competent authority has reasonable grounds for suspecting that a provision required by the transparency obligations directive has been infringed by a voteholder of an issuer, it may—
  (a) prohibit trading in the securities, or
  (b) make a request to the operator of the market on which the issuer's securities are traded to prohibit trading in the securities.
(4) If the competent authority finds that an applicable transparency obligation has been infringed, it may require the market operator to prohibit trading in the securities.
(5) In this section "transparency obligation" means an obligation under—
  (a) a provision contained in transparency rules, or
  (b) any other provision made in accordance with the transparency obligations directive.
(6) In relation to an issuer whose home State is a member State other than the United Kingdom, any reference to an applicable transparency obligation must be read subject to section 100A(2).

## 89M  Procedure under section 89L

(1) A requirement under section 89L takes effect—
  (a) immediately, if the notice under subsection (2) states that that is the case;
  (b) in any other case, on such date as may be specified in the notice.
(2) If the competent authority—
  (a) proposes to exercise the powers in section 89L in relation to a person, or
  (b) exercises any of those powers in relation to a person with immediate effect, it must give that person written notice.
(3) The notice must—
  (a) give details of the competent authority's action or proposed action;
  (b) state the competent authority's reasons for taking the action in question and choosing the date on which it took effect or takes effect;
  (c) inform the recipient that he may make representations to the competent authority within such period as may be specified by the notice (whether or not he had referred the matter to the Tribunal);
  (d) inform him of the date on which the action took effect or takes effect;
  (e) inform him of his right to refer the matter to the Tribunal (see section 89N) and give an indication of the procedure on such a reference.
(4) The competent authority may extend the period within which representations may be made to it.
(5) If, having considered any representations made to it, the competent authority decides to maintain, vary or revoke its earlier decision, it must give written notice to that effect to the person mentioned in subsection (2).

## 89N  Right to refer matters to the Tribunal

A person—
  (a) to whom a decision notice is given under section 89K (public censure), or
  (b) to whom a notice is given under section 89M (procedure in connection with suspension or prohibition of trading), may refer the matter to the Tribunal.'.

COMMENCEMENT DATE  8 November 2006 see s 1300

## *Other matters*

### 1269  Corporate governance rules

**43.1269.01**    In Part 6 of the Financial Services and Markets Act 2000 (c. 8), after the sections inserted by section 1268 above insert—

'Corporate governance

### 89O  Corporate governance rules

(1) The competent authority may make rules ("corporate governance rules")—
  (a) for the purpose of implementing, enabling the implementation of or dealing with matters arising out of or related to, any Community obligation relating to the corporate governance of issuers who have requested or approved admission of their securities to trading on a regulated market;
  (b) about corporate governance in relation to such issuers for the purpose of implementing, or dealing with matters arising out of or related to, any Community obligation.
(2) "Corporate governance", in relation to an issuer, includes—
  (a) the nature, constitution or functions of the organs of the issuer;

  (b) the manner in which organs of the issuer conduct themselves;
  (c) the requirements imposed on organs of the issuer;
  (d) the relationship between the different organs of the issuer;
  (e) the relationship between the organs of the issuer and the members of the issuer or holders of the issuer's securities.
(3) The burdens and restrictions imposed by rules under this section on foreign-traded issuers must not be greater than the burdens and restrictions imposed on UK-traded issuers by—
  (a) rules under this section, and
  (b) listing rules.
(4) For this purpose—
  "foreign-traded issuer" means an issuer who has requested or approved admission of the issuer's securities to trading on a regulated market situated or operating outside the United Kingdom;
  "UK-traded issuer" means an issuer who has requested or approved admission of the issuer's securities to trading on a regulated market situated or operating in the United Kingdom.
(5) This section is without prejudice to any other power conferred by this Part to make Part 6 rules.'.

COMMENCEMENT DATE 8 November 2006: see s 1300

## 1270 Liability for false or misleading statements in certain publications

In Part 6 of the Financial Services and Markets Act 2000 (c. 8), after section 90 insert—[. . .]ᵃ    **43.1270.01**

AMENDMENTS AND NOTES

ᵃ This section inserted a new s 90A into the Financial Services and Markets Act 2000, but that s 90A was replaced with effect from 1 October 2010 by a new s 90A and Sch 10A substituted by the Financial Services and Markets Act 2000 (Liability of Issuers) Regulations 2010, SI 2010/1192.

### 90B Power to make further provision about liability for published information

(1) The Treasury may by regulations make provision about the liability of issuers of securities traded on a regulated market, and other persons, in respect of information published to holders of securities, to the market or to the public generally.
(2) Regulations under this section may amend any primary or subordinate legislation, including any provision of, or made under, this Act'.

## 1271 Exercise of powers where UK is host member State

In Part 6 of the Financial Services and Markets Act 2000 (c. 8), after section 100 insert—    **43.1271.01**

### '100A Exercise of powers where UK is host member state

(1) This section applies to the exercise by the competent authority of any power under this Part exercisable in case of infringement of—
  (a) a provision of prospectus rules or any other provision made in accordance with the prospectus directive, or
  (b) a provision of transparency rules or any other provision made in accordance with the transparency obligations directive, in relation to an issuer whose home State is a member State other than the United Kingdom.
(2) The competent authority may act in such a case only in respect of the infringement of a provision required by the relevant directive. Any reference to an applicable provision or applicable transparency obligation shall be read accordingly.
(3) If the authority finds that there has been such an infringement, it must give a notice to that effect to the competent authority of the person's home State requesting it—
  (a) to take all appropriate measures for the purpose of ensuring that the person remedies the situation that has given rise to the notice, and
  (b) to inform the authority of the measures it proposes to take or has taken or the reasons for not taking such measures.
(4) The authority may not act further unless satisfied—
  (a) that the competent authority of the person's home State has failed or refused to take measures for the purpose mentioned in subsection (3)(a), or
  (b) that the measures taken by that authority have proved inadequate for that purpose. This does not affect exercise of the powers under section 87K(2), 87L(2) or (3) or 89L(2) or (3) (powers to protect market).
(5) If the authority is so satisfied, it must, after informing the competent authority of the person's home State, take all appropriate measures to protect investors.
(6) In such a case the authority must inform the Commission of the measures at the earliest opportunity.'.

COMMENCEMENT DATE 8 November 2006: see s 1300

### 1272  Transparency obligations and related matters: minor and consequential amendments

**43.1272.01**

(1) Schedule 15 to this Act makes minor and consequential amendments in connection with the provision made by this Part.

(2) In that Schedule—

Part 1 contains amendments of the Financial Services and Markets Act 2000 (c. 8);

Part 2 contains amendments of the Companies (Audit, Investigations and Community Enterprise) Act 2004 (c. 27).

### 1273  Corporate governance regulations

**43.1273.01**

(1) The Secretary of State may make regulations—

(a) for the purpose of implementing, enabling the implementation of or dealing with matters arising out of or related to, any Community obligation relating to the corporate governance of issuers who have requested or approved admission of their securities to trading on a regulated market;

(b) about corporate governance in relation to such issuers for the purpose of implementing, or dealing with matters arising out of or related to, any Community obligation.

(2) 'Corporate governance', in relation to an issuer, includes—

(a) the nature, constitution or functions of the organs of the issuer;

(b) the manner in which organs of the issuer conduct themselves;

(c) the requirements imposed on organs of the issuer;

(d) the relationship between different organs of the issuer;

(e) the relationship between the organs of the issuer and the members of the issuer or holders of the issuer's securities.

(3) The regulations may—

(a) make provision by reference to any specified code on corporate governance that may be issued from time to time by a specified body;

(b) create new criminal offences (subject to subsection (4));

(c) make provision excluding liability in damages in respect of things done or omitted for the purposes of, or in connection with, the carrying on, or purported carrying on, of any specified activities.

'Specified' here means specified in the regulations.

(4) The regulations may not create a criminal offence punishable by a greater penalty than—

(a) on indictment, a fine;

(b) on summary conviction, a fine not exceeding the statutory maximum or (if calculated on a daily basis) £100 a day.

(5) Regulations under this section are subject to negative resolution procedure.

(6) In this section 'issuer', 'securities' and 'regulated market' have the same meaning as in Part 6 of the Financial Services and Markets Act 2000 (c. 8).

COMMENCEMENT DATE 8 November 2006: see s 1300

# 44

## MISCELLANEOUS PROVISIONS

## Companies Act 2006

### PART 44

### MISCELLANEOUS PROVISIONS

### *Regulation of actuaries etc*

### 1274 Grants to bodies concerned with actuarial standards etc

(1) Section 16 of the Companies (Audit, Investigations and Community Enterprise) Act 2004 (c. 27) (grants to bodies concerned with accounting standards etc) is amended as follows.    **44.1274.01**

(2) In subsection (2) (matters carried on by bodies eligible for grants) for paragraph (l) substitute—

'(l) issuing standards to be applied in actuarial work;

(m) issuing standards in respect of matters to be contained in reports or other communications required to be produced or made by actuaries or in accordance with standards within paragraph (l);

(n) investigating departures from standards within paragraph (l) or (m);

(o) taking steps to secure compliance with standards within paragraph (l) or (m);

(p) carrying out investigations into public interest cases arising in connection with the performance of actuarial functions by members of professional actuarial bodies;

(q) holding disciplinary hearings relating to members of professional actuarial bodies following the conclusion of investigations within paragraph (p);

(r) deciding whether (and, if so, what) disciplinary action should be taken against members of professional actuarial bodies to whom hearings within paragraph (q) related;

(s) supervising the exercise by professional actuarial bodies of regulatory functions in relation to their members;

(t) overseeing or directing any of the matters mentioned above.'.

(3) In subsection (5) (definitions) at the appropriate places insert—

'"professional actuarial body" means—

(a) the Institute of Actuaries, or

(b) the Faculty of Actuaries in Scotland,

and the "members" of a professional actuarial body include persons who, although not members of the body, are subject to its rules in performing actuarial functions;"

'"regulatory functions", in relation to professional actuarial bodies, means any of the following—

(a) investigatory or disciplinary functions exercised by such bodies in relation to the performance by their members of actuarial functions,

(b) the setting by such bodies of standards in relation to the performance by their members of actuarial functions, and

(c) the determining by such bodies of requirements in relation to the education and training of their members;'.

COMMENCEMENT DATE 8 November 2006[1]

**44.1274.02**  Subsections (1) and (2) make a number of changes to section 16(2) of the Companies (Audit, Investigations and Community Enterprise) Act 2004. Section 16 in turn replaced section 256(3) of the Companies Act 1985. These changes in the 2006 Act relate to the activities of bodies eligible for grants. The full range of regulatory functions carried out by such bodies is clearly extensive. See Explanatory Notes to the Bill when it entered Commons (May 2006) paragraphs 1593 to 1595.

**44.1274.03**  Subsection (3) amends section 16(5) of the aforesaid 2004 Act by inserting further interpretation provision.

### 1275  Levy to pay expenses of bodies concerned with actuarial standards etc

**44.1275.01**
(1) Section 17 of the Companies (Audit, Investigations and Community Enterprise) Act 2004 (c. 27) (levy to pay expenses of bodies concerned with accounting standards etc) is amended in accordance with subsections (2) to (5).

(2) In subsection (3)(a) after 'to which' insert ', or persons within subsection (3A) to whom,'

(3) After subsection (3) insert—

'(3A) The following persons are within this subsection—

(a) the administrators of a public service pension scheme (within the meaning of section 1 of the Pension Schemes Act 1993);

(b) the trustees or managers of an occupational or personal pension scheme (within the meaning of that section).'

(4) After subsection (4)(b) insert—

'(c) make different provision for different cases.'

(5) After subsection (12) insert—

'(13) If a draft of any regulations to which subsection (10) applies would, apart from this subsection, be treated for the purposes of the standing orders of either House of Parliament as a hybrid instrument, it is to proceed in that House as if it were not such an instrument.'

(6) The above amendments have effect in relation to any exercise of the power to make regulations under section 17 of the Companies (Audit, Investigations and Community Enterprise) Act 2004 after this section comes into force, regardless of when the expenses to be met by the levy in respect of which the regulations are made were incurred.

(7) In Schedule 3 to the Pensions Act 2004 (c. 35) (disclosure of information held by the Pensions Regulator), in the entry relating to the Secretary of State, in the second column, for 'or' at the end of paragraph (g) substitute—

'(ga) Section 17 of the Companies (Audit, Investigations and Community Enterprise) Act 2004 (levy to pay expenses of bodies concerned with accounting standards, actuarial standards etc), or'.

COMMENCEMENT DATE 1 October 2009[2]

**44.1275.02**  Subsections (1) to (5) amend section 17 of the Companies (Audit, Investigations and Community Enterprise) Act 2004. They deal with the regulation of the accounting profession and ensure that business and the professions meet part of the upkeep of the main regulatory institutions once government grants have been allowed for. See Explanatory Notes to the Bill when it entered the Commons (May 2006) paragraphs 1596 to 1602.

**44.1275.03**  Subsection (6) is a transitional provision.

**44.1275.04**  Subsection (7) amends Schedule 3 of the Pensions Act 2004.

### 1276  Application of provisions to Scotland and Northern Ireland

**44.1276.01**
(1) Section 16 of the Companies (Audit, Investigations and Community Enterprise) Act 2004 (grants to bodies concerned with accounting standards etc) is amended as follows.

(2) For subsection (6) (application of section to Scotland) substitute—

'(6) In their application to Scotland, subsection (2)(a) to (t) are to be read as referring only to matters provision relating to which would be outside the legislative competence of the Scottish Parliament.'

---

[1] The date of Royal Assent: see s 1300.

[2] The Companies Act 2006 (Commencement No 8, Transitional Provisions and Savings Order 2008, SI 2008/2860, art 3(y)).

(3)  In subsection (2) in paragraph (c), after '1985 (c. 6)' insert 'or the 1986 Order'.
(4)  In subsection (5)—
    (a)  in the definition of 'company' after '1985 (c. 6)' insert 'or the 1986 Order',
    (b)  in the definition of 'subsidiary' after '1985' insert 'or Article 4 of the 1986 Order', and
    (c)  after that definition insert—
'"the 1986 Order" means the Companies (Northern Ireland) Order 1986 (S.I. 1986/1032 (N.I. 6)).'
(5)  In section 66 of that Act (extent), in subsection (2) (provisions extending to Northern Ireland, as well as England and Wales and Scotland) for '17' substitute '16 to 18'.

COMMENCEMENT DATE  8 November 2006[3]

Subsections (1) to (5) make appropriate modifications to sections 16 and 66 of the 2004 Act to deal with   **44.1276.02**
the accountancy regulatory contexts prevailing in Northern Ireland and Scotland.

*Information as to exercise of voting rights by institutional investors*

**1277  Power to require information about exercise of voting rights**

(1)  The Treasury or the Secretary of State may make provision by regulations requiring institutions to   **44.1277.01**
which this section applies to provide information about the exercise of voting rights attached to
shares to which this section applies.
(2)  This power is exercisable in accordance with—
    section 1278 (institutions to which information provisions apply),
    section 1279 (shares to which information provisions apply), and
    section 1280 (obligations with respect to provision of information).
(3)  In this section and the sections mentioned above—
    (a)  references to a person acting on behalf of an institution include—
        (i)  any person to whom authority has been delegated by the institution to take decisions as
           to any matter relevant to the subject matter of the regulations, and
        (ii)  such other persons as may be specified; and
    (b)  'specified' means specified in the regulations.
(4)  The obligation imposed by regulations under this section is enforceable by civil proceedings
brought by—
    (a)  any person to whom the information should have been provided, or
    (b)  a specified regulatory authority.
(5)  Regulations under this section may make different provision for different descriptions of institution, different descriptions of shares and for other different circumstances.
(6)  Regulations under this section are subject to affirmative resolution procedure.

COMMENCEMENT DATE   20 January 2007[4] (for the purpose of enabling the exercise of powers to make
orders or regulations by statutory instrument), 1 October 2008[5] otherwise.

Sections 1277 to 1280 contain new provisions allowing the Secretary of State to make regulations   **44.1277.02**
requiring certain categories of institutional investor to provide information about the exercise of their
voting rights. These provisions follow a recommendation in the CLR Final Report (paragraph 6.39)
that disclosure of voting by institutional shareholders is a desirable objective. In this context certain
institutional investors own and manage assets on behalf of clients and members, and accordingly have
an obligation to manage those assets in their interests. There may be a trustee–beneficiary relationship
between the institution and the client and there will also be contractual and regulatory requirements
which impose duties on the institution in relation to their management of the assets. Although the
voting of shares held in a fund may be a central feature of the ownership of the relevant shares, the
ability of ultimate clients or beneficiaries (such as members of a pension fund) to monitor ways in
which institutional investors exercise voting rights has been limited in practice. There has, however,
been a growing trend internationally to require disclosure. There has also been an increasing trend by
UK fund managers towards voluntary disclosure.

Section 1277 confers a wide power on the Secretary of State and the Treasury to make regulations   **44.1277.03**
regarding certain categories of institutional investor to provide information about the exercise of their
voting rights. This section and the following sections have been drafted intentionally widely so as to
enable any mandatory disclosure regime that is set up to respond to a variety of corporate governance
arrangements and to relate to a range of institutions investing in different markets.

---

    [3]  The date of Royal Assent: see s 1300.
    [4]  Companies Act 2006 (Commencement No. 1, Transitional Provisions and Savings) Order 2006/3428, art
3(3).
    [5]  Companies Act 2006 (Commencement No 5, Transitional Provisions and Savings) Order 2007, SI 2007/
3495, art 5(1)(g) (for savings and transitional provisions, see arts 6, 7, 9, and 12, and Schs 1 and 4).

**44.1277.04**    The institutions to which the information provisions apply, the shares to which they apply, and the obligations with respect to provision of information are described further at sections 1278, 1279, and 1280 respectively.

**44.1277.05**    Exercise of the powers under section 1277 is subject to the affirmative resolution procedure.

**44.1277.06**    Although section 1277(3) expressly explains references 'in this section and in the sections mentioned above' to persons acting on behalf of institutions, it is in fact only section 1280 that contains any relevant reference. The persons referred to include any person to whom authority has been delegated by the institution to take decisions as to any matter relevant to the subject matter of the regulations, and the class of persons can be expanded further by the regulations themselves.

**44.1277.07**    The obligations imposed by the regulations are enforceable in civil proceedings brought by any person to whom the information should, under the regulations, have been provided. In this context, section 1280(4) contains a wide provision enabling regulations to specify the persons to whom information should be provided. The obligations are also enforceable by any regulatory authority specified in the regulations. See section 1277(4).

## 1278  Institutions to which information provisions apply

**44.1278.01**    (1)  The institutions to which section 1277 applies are—
    (a)  unit trust schemes within the meaning of the Financial Services and Markets Act 2000 (c. 8) in respect of which an order is in force under section 243 of that Act;
    (b)  open-ended investment companies incorporated by virtue of regulations under section 262 of that Act;
    (c)  companies approved for the purposes of [Chapter 4 of Part 24 of the Corporation Tax Act 2010][a] (investment trusts);
    (d)  pension schemes as defined in section 1(5) of the Pension Schemes Act 1993 (c. 48) or the Pension Schemes (Northern Ireland) Act 1993 (c. 49);
    (e)  undertakings authorised under the Financial Services and Markets Act 2000 to carry on long-term insurance business (that is, the activity of effecting or carrying out contracts of long-term insurance within the meaning of the Financial Services and Markets (Regulated Activities) Order 2001 (S.I. 2001/544);
    (f)  collective investment schemes that are recognised by virtue of section 270 of that Act (schemes authorised in designated countries or territories).
(2)  Regulations under that section may—
    (a)  provide that the section applies to other descriptions of institution;
    (b)  provide that the section does not apply to a specified description of institution.
(3)  The regulations must specify by whom, in the case of any description of institution, the duty imposed by the regulations is to be fulfilled.

AMENDMENTS

[a]  Substituted by the Corporation Tax Act 2010, with effect from April 1, 2010 (and, pursuant to section 1184 of that Act, has effect, for corporation tax purposes, for accounting periods ending on or after that day, and, for income tax and capital gains tax purposes, for the tax year 2010–11 and subsequent tax years, subject to transitional provisions and savings specified in Schedule 2 of that Act).

COMMENCEMENT DATE 1 October 2008[6]

**44.1278.02**    This section sets out the categories of institution in relation to which the power conferred by section 1277 may be exercised. Subsection (2) enables the Treasury or the Secretary of State to add to or amend the categories of institution, and subsection (3) enables the Treasury or Secretary of State to specify in the case of any institution by whom the duty imposed by the regulations is to be fulfilled.

## 1279  Shares to which information provisions apply

**44.1279.01**    (1)  The shares to which section 1277 applies are shares—
    (a)  of a description traded on a specified market, and
    (b)  in which the institution has, or is taken to have, an interest.
Regulations under that section may provide that the section does not apply to shares of a specified description.
(2)  For this purpose an institution has an interest in shares if the shares, or a depositary certificate in respect of them, are held by it, or on its behalf.
A 'depositary certificate' means an instrument conferring rights (other than options)—
    (a)  in respect of shares held by another person, and

---

[6]  Companies Act 2006 (Commencement No 5, Transitional Provisions and Savings) Order 2007, SI 2007/3495, art 5(1)(g) (for savings and transitional provisions, see arts 6, 7, 9, and 12, and Schs 1 and 4).

    (b) the transfer of which may be effected without the consent of that person.

(3) Where an institution has an interest—

    (a) in a specified description of collective investment scheme (within the meaning of the Financial Services and Markets Act 2000 (c. 8)), or

    (b) in any other specified description of scheme or collective investment vehicle,

it is taken to have an interest in any shares in which that scheme or vehicle has or is taken to have an interest.

(4) For this purpose a scheme or vehicle is taken to have an interest in shares if it would be regarded as having such an interest in accordance with subsection (2) if it was an institution to which section 1277 applied.

COMMENCEMENT DATE 1 October 2008[7]

This section confers the power to specify by regulations the descriptions of shares in relation to which **44.1279.02** the information provisions will apply. As the section makes clear (and subject to the provisions of section 1277(5)), the shares to which the regulations will refer will be traded shares, albeit that the markets are to be specified. Regulations may also exclude the application of the section to shares of a specified description: see section 1279 (1).

Subsection (2) expressly provides for an extended meaning of an 'interest in shares', namely that an **44.1279.03** institution is to be treated as having an interest in shares if the shares or a depositary certificate in respect of them (as defined in the subsection) are held by it or on its behalf.

An institution is also taken to have an interest in any shares (which, as a result of subsection (4) is to be **44.1279.04** taken as having the extended meaning given in subsection (2)) if it has an interest in a specified description of collective investment scheme (within the meaning of the Financial Services and Markets Act 2000) or in any other specified description of scheme or collective investment scheme: see section 1279(3).

## 1280 Obligations with respect to provision of information

(1) Regulations under section 1277 may require the provision of specified information about—     **44.1280.01**

    (a) the exercise or non-exercise of voting rights by the institution or any person acting on its behalf,

    (b) any instructions given by the institution or any person acting on its behalf as to the exercise or non-exercise of voting rights, and

    (c) any delegation by the institution or any person acting on its behalf of any functions in relation to the exercise or non-exercise of voting rights or the giving of such instructions.

(2) The regulations may require information to be provided in respect of specified occasions or specified periods.

(3) Where instructions are given to act on the recommendations or advice of another person, the regulations may require the provision of information about what recommendations or advice were given.

(4) The regulations may require information to be provided—

    (a) in such manner as may be specified, and

    (b) to such persons as may be specified, or to the public, or both.

(5) The regulations may provide—

    (a) that an institution may discharge its obligations under the regulations by referring to information disclosed by a person acting on its behalf, and

    (b) that in such a case it is sufficient, where that other person acts on behalf of more than one institution, that the reference is to information given in aggregated form, that is—

        (i) relating to the exercise or non-exercise by that person of voting rights on behalf of more than one institution, or

        (ii) relating to the instructions given by that person in respect of the exercise or non-exercise of voting rights on behalf of more than one institution, or

        (iii) relating to the delegation by that person of functions in relation to the exercise or non-exercise of voting rights, or the giving of instructions in respect of the exercise or non-exercise of voting rights, on behalf of more than one institution.

(6) References in this section to instructions are to instructions of any description, whether general or specific, whether binding or not and whether or not acted upon.

COMMENCEMENT DATE 1 October 2008[8]

---

  [7] Companies Act 2006 (Commencement No 5, Transitional Provisions and Savings) Order 2007, SI 2007/ 3495, art 5(1)(g) (for savings and transitional provisions, see arts 6, 7, 9, and 12, and Schs 1 and 4).

  [8] Companies Act 2006 (Commencement No 5, Transitional Provisions and Savings) Order 2007, SI 2007/ 3495, art 5(1)(g) (for savings and transitional provisions, see arts 6, 7, 9, and 12, and Schs 1 and 4).

**44.1280.02**    This section specifies the information that can be required following regulations made under section 1277. This covers the exercise or non-exercise of voting rights, instructions given by the institution and any delegation of a function related to the exercise or non-exercise of voting rights. Instructions, in this context, has a wide meaning, as stated by subsection (6), and refers to instructions of any description, whether general or specific, whether or not binding, and whether or not acted upon. Given that institutions may be required to disclose the votes or instructions given by any person acting on the institution's behalf, it will in practice be necessary for institutions to ensure that all their contractual arrangements to which they are party are consistent with this disclosure regime, such that (for example) they permit any relevant disclosure, and (where relevant) persons acting on their behalf may be required to pass information to the institution so as to comply with the information obligations and/or disclose the information on the institution's behalf (as to which, see section 1280(5)).

**44.1280.03**    Subsection (3) extends the categories of information that may be required to information about recommendations or advice given, in cases where the instructions are to act on the recommendations or advice of any person.

**44.1280.04**    So far as concerns how the information is to be provided, both the manner in which the information is to be provided and the persons to whom it is to be provided has been left to be specified in the regulations: section 1280(4). The persons to whom the information may be disclosed may not be limited to, say, clients and members, but may include the public at large.

**44.1280.05**    Under subsection (5) the regulations may provide that an institution can discharge its own obligations to provide information by referring to information disclosed by a person acting on its behalf. That person may, in practice, have authority to act on behalf of a number of institutions, and the subsection accordingly expressly enables the regulations to provide that it may be sufficient for information to be given in aggregated form.

## *Disclosure of information under the Enterprise Act 2002*

### 1281   Disclosure of information under the Enterprise Act 2002

**44.1281.01**    In Part 9 of the Enterprise Act 2002 (c. 40) (information), after section 241 insert—

### '241A Civil proceedings

(1)  A public authority which holds prescribed information to which section 237 applies may disclose that information to any person—
  (a)  for the purposes of, or in connection with, prescribed civil proceedings (including prospective proceedings) in the United Kingdom or elsewhere, or
  (b)  for the purposes of obtaining legal advice in relation to such proceedings, or
  (c)  otherwise for the purposes of establishing, enforcing or defending legal rights that are or may be the subject of such proceedings.
(2)  Subsection (1) does not apply to—
  (a)  information which comes to a public authority in connection with an investigation under Part 4, 5 or 6 of the 1973 Act or under section 11 of the Competition Act 1980;
  (b)  competition information within the meaning of section 351 of the Financial Services and Markets Act 2000;
  (c)  information which comes to a public authority in connection with an investigation under Part 3 or 4 or section 174 of this Act;
  (d)  information which comes to a public authority in connection with an investigation under the Competition Act 1998 (c. 41).
(3)  In subsection (1) 'prescribed' means prescribed by order of the Secretary of State.
(4)  An order under this section—
  (a)  may prescribe information, or civil proceedings, for the purposes of this section by reference to such factors as appear to the Secretary of State to be appropriate;
  (b)  may prescribe for the purposes of this section all information, or civil proceedings, or all information or civil proceedings not falling within one or more specified exceptions;
  (c)  must be made by statutory instrument subject to annulment in pursuance of a resolution of either House of Parliament.
(5)  Information disclosed under this section must not be used by the person to whom it is disclosed for any purpose other than those specified in subsection (1).'.

COMMENCEMENT DATE 6 April 2007[9]

**44.1281.02**    This inserts section 241A into the Enterprise Act 2002 by permitting public authorities to disclose information to parties contemplating or involved in the bringing of prescribed civil proceedings. The Secretary of State will prescribe the information in question (see section 241(A)(3) and (4)), but certain

---

⁹  Companies Act 2006 (Commencement No 1, etc) Order 2006, SI 2006/3428, art 4.

information will not be prescribed (subsection (2)). The Secretary of State also prescribes the proceedings covered by this section. Subsection (5) imposes a limitation on the usage of any such information disclosed. For background see Explanatory Notes to the Bill when it entered the Commons in May 2006, paragraphs 1606 to 1610.

## *Expenses of winding up*

## 1282   Payment of expenses of winding up

(1)   In Chapter 8 of Part 4 of the Insolvency Act 1986 (c. 45) (winding up of companies: provisions of                44.1282.01
general application), before section 176A (under the heading 'Property subject to floating
charge') insert—

### '176ZA Payment of expenses of winding up (England and Wales)

(1)   The expenses of winding up in England and Wales, so far as the assets of the company
available for payment of general creditors are insufficient to meet them, have priority over
any claims to property comprised in or subject to any floating charge created by the company
and shall be paid out of any such property accordingly.

(2)   In subsection (1)—
   (a)   the reference to assets of the company available for payment of general creditors does
         not include any amount made available under section 176A (2)(a);
   (b)   the reference to claims to property comprised in or subject to a floating charge is to the
         claims of—
         (i)    the holders of debentures secured by, or holders of, the floating charge, and
         (ii)   any preferential creditors entitled to be paid out of that property in priority to them.

(3)   Provision may be made by rules restricting the application of subsection (1), in such
circumstances as may be prescribed, to expenses authorised or approved—
   (a)   by the holders of debentures secured by, or holders of, the floating charge and by any
         preferential creditors entitled to be paid in priority to them, or
   (b)   by the court.

(4)   References in this section to the expenses of the winding up are to all expenses properly
incurred in the winding up, including the remuneration of the liquidator.'

(2)   In Chapter 8 of Part 5 of the Insolvency (Northern Ireland) Order 1989 (S.I. 1989/2405 (N.I. 19))
(winding up of companies: provisions of general application), before Article 150A (under the
heading 'Property subject to floating charge') insert—

### '150ZA Payment of expenses of winding up

(1)   The expenses of winding up, so far as the assets of the company available for payment of
general creditors are insufficient to meet them, have priority over any claims to property
comprised in or subject to any floating charge created by the company and shall be paid out
of any such property accordingly.

(2)   In paragraph (1)—
   (a)   the reference to assets of the company available for payment of general creditors does
         not include any amount made available under Article 150A (2)(a);
   (b)   the reference to claims to property comprised in or subject to a floating charge is to the
         claims of—
         (i)    the holders of debentures secured by, or holders of, the floating charge, and
         (ii)   any preferential creditors entitled to be paid out of that property in priority to them.

(3)   Provision may be made by rules restricting the application of paragraph (1), in such
circumstances as may be prescribed, to expenses authorised or approved—
   (a)   by the holders of debentures secured by, or holders of, the floating charge and by any
         preferential creditors entitled to be paid in priority to them, or
   (b)   by the Court.

(4)   References in this Article to the expenses of the winding up are to all expenses properly
incurred in the winding up, including the remuneration of the liquidator.'.

COMMENCEMENT DATE  6 April 2008[10]

Subsection (1) inserts section 176ZA into the Insolvency Act 1986. The effect of this change is to nullify     44.1282.02
the decision of the House of Lords in *Re Leyland DAF Ltd*[11] on liquidation/receivership expenses by
allowing authorized liquidation expenses in the future to be charged against assets subject to a floating
charge. *Leyland DAF* caused concern because it overruled the established Court of Appeal authority of
*Re Barleycorn Enterprises Ltd*[12] which had permitted floating charge assets to be used to reimburse

---

[10]  Companies Act 2006 (Commencement No 5, Transitional Provisions and Savings) Order 2007, SI 2007/
3495.
[11]  [2004] UKHL 9.
[12]  [1970] Ch 465.

liquidation expenses. By limiting the funding available to cover winding-up activities the official policy of encouraging investigations and recovery actions during winding up was seen as being threatened.[13] There was disquiet[14] on the part of the banking community about the retrospective nature of this statutory reform as it originally appeared in the Bill. Questions were likely to have been raised as to whether it infringed Article 1 of the First Protocol of the European Convention on Human Rights. In view of these concerns the Government amended the original clause in the Bill at Grand Committee in the House of Lords to remove any retrospective potential, and is proposing to use secondary legislation to clarify the precise scope of this reform. A consultation exercise on how this secondary legislation might operate in practice with regard to the approval mechanism governing recovery actions by liquidators was conducted by the Insolvency Service over the summer of 2006.

**44.1282.03** Subsection (2) makes a change comparable to subsection (1) for Northern Ireland by inserting Article 150ZA into the Insolvency Order. Section 1282 does not apply in Scotland.

**44.1282.04** These provisions must be read in the light of the Insolvency (Amendment) Rules 2008, SI 2008/737. These rules, which took effect for liquidations commenced after 6 April 2008, provide flesh on the bare bones of s 176ZA of the Insolvency Act 1986 by amending the priority regime for liquidation expenses in Insolvency Rule 4.218 and by adding new Insolvency Rules 4.218A to 4.218E. Under this new regime details of the authorization process under which a liquidator can seek to use floating charge assets to fund recovery proceedings and associated litigation expenses are set forth. If the floating charge holder refuses authorization there is a procedure mapped out in Insolvency Rule 4.218E under which a liquidator can apply to the court for authorization. In effect, therefore, these new rules place pragmatic and procedural restrictions upon the generality of the changes made by s 176ZA.

## Commonhold associations

### 1283 Amendment of memorandum or articles of commonhold association

**44.1283.01** In paragraph 3(1) of Schedule 3 to the Commonhold and Leasehold Reform Act 2002 (c. 15) (alteration of memorandum or articles by commonhold association to be of no effect until altered version registered with Land Registry) for 'An alteration of the memorandum or articles of association' substitute 'Where a commonhold association alters its memorandum or articles at a time when the land specified in its memorandum is commonhold land, the alteration'.

COMMENCEMENT DATE 1 October 2009[15]

**44.1283.02** This section makes a technical linguistic amendment to paragraph 3(1) Schedule 3 of the Commonhold and Leasehold Reform Act 2002. This minor amendment is designed to iron out an unintended anomaly in the law—see Explanatory Notes to the Bill when it entered the Commons in May 2006, paragraphs 1612 to 1615.

---

[13] For critique of *Re Leyland DAF Ltd*, (above), see Mokal (2004) LMCLQ 387 and Mokal, *Corporate Insolvency Law: Theory and Application* (2005, OUP) 311. A more supportive reception was provided by Armour and Walters (2006) 122 LQR 295. See generally RM Goode, *Principles of Corporate Insolvency Law* (4th edn, 2011), Thomson Reuters/Sweet & Maxwell), especially at para 5.01.

[14] See Yeowart (2006) 22 IL&P 3.

[15] Companies Act 2006 (Commencement No 8, Transitional Provisions and Savings) Order 2008, SI 2008/2960, art 3(y).

# 45

# NORTHERN IRELAND

## Companies Act 2006

### PART 45

### NORTHERN IRELAND

Commentary on this section of the CA 2006 has not been included
in this publication.

## 1284 Extension of Companies Acts to Northern Ireland

(1) The Companies Acts as defined by this Act (see section 2) extend to Northern Ireland.

(2) The Companies (Northern Ireland) Order 1986 (S.I. 1986/1032 (N.I. 6)), the Companies Consolidation (Consequential Provisions) (Northern Ireland) Order 1986 (S.I. 1986/1035 (N.I. 9)) and Part 3 of the Companies (Audit, Investigations and Community Enterprise) Order 2005 (S.I. 2005/1967 (N.I. 17)) shall cease to have effect accordingly.

**45.1284.01**

## 1285 Extension of GB enactments relating to SEs

(1) The enactments in force in Great Britain relating to SEs extend to Northern Ireland.

(2) The following enactments shall cease to have effect accordingly—

(a) the European Public Limited-Liability Company Regulations (Northern Ireland) 2004 (SR 2004/417), and

(b) the European Public Limited-Liability Company (Fees) Regulations (Northern Ireland) 2004 (SR 2004/418).

(3) In this section 'SE' means a European Public Limited-Liability Company (or Societas Europaea) within the meaning of Council Regulation 2157/2001/EC of 8 October 2001 on the Statute for a European Company.

**45.1285.01**

## 1286 Extension of GB enactments relating to certain other forms of business organisation

(1) The enactments in force in Great Britain relating to—

(a) limited liability partnerships,

(b) limited partnerships,

(c) open-ended investment companies, and

(d) European Economic Interest Groupings, extend to Northern Ireland.

(2) The following enactments shall cease to have effect accordingly—

(a) the Limited Liability Partnerships Act (Northern Ireland) 2002 (c. 12 (N. I.));

(b) the Limited Partnerships Act 1907 (c. 24) as it formerly had effect in Northern Ireland;

(c) the Open-Ended Investment Companies Act (Northern Ireland) 2002 (c. 13 (N.I.));

(d) the European Economic Interest Groupings Regulations (Northern Ireland) 1989 (SR 1989/216).

**45.1286.01**

## 1287    Extension of enactments relating to business names

45.1287.01    (1)    The provisions of Part 41 of this Act (business names) extend to Northern Ireland.

(2)    The Business Names (Northern Ireland) Order 1986 (S.I. 1986/1033 (N.I. 7)) shall cease to have effect accordingly.

## 1292  Regulations and orders: supplementary

**46.1292.01**

(1) Regulations or orders under this Act may—
   (a) make different provision for different cases or circumstances,
   (b) include supplementary, incidental and consequential provision, and
   (c) make transitional provision and savings.

(2) Any provision that may be made by regulations under this Act may be made by order; and any provision that may be made by order under this Act may be made by regulations.

(3) Any provision that may be made by regulations or order under this Act for which no Parliamentary procedure is prescribed may be made by regulations or order subject to negative or affirmative resolution procedure.

(4) Any provision that may be made by regulations or order under this Act subject to negative resolution procedure may be made by regulations or order subject to affirmative resolution procedure.

COMMENCEMENT DATE 8 November 2006: see s 1300

## *Meaning of 'enactment'*

## 1293  Meaning of 'enactment'

**46.1293.01**

In this Act, unless the context otherwise requires, 'enactment' includes—

(a) an enactment contained in subordinate legislation within the meaning of the Interpretation Act 1978 (c. 30),

(b) an enactment contained in, or in an instrument made under, an Act of the Scottish Parliament, and

(c) an enactment contained in, or in an instrument made under, Northern Ireland legislation within the meaning of the Interpretation Act 1978.

COMMENCEMENT DATE 8 November 2006: see s 1300

## *Consequential and transitional provisions*

## 1294  Power to make consequential amendments etc

**46.1294.01**

(1) The Secretary of State or the Treasury may by order make such provision amending, repealing or revoking any enactment to which this section applies as they consider necessary or expedient in consequence of any provision made by or under this Act.

(2) This section applies to—
   (a) any enactment passed or made before the passing of this Act,
   (b) any enactment contained in this Act or in subordinate legislation made under it, and
   (c) any enactment passed or made before the end of the session after that in which this Act is passed.

(3) Without prejudice to the generality of the power conferred by subsection (1), orders under this section may—
   (a) make provision extending to other forms of organisation any provision made by or under this Act in relation to companies, or
   (b) make provision corresponding to that made by or under this Act in relation to companies, in either case with such adaptations or other modifications as appear to the Secretary of State or the Treasury to be necessary or expedient.

(4) The references in subsection (3) to provision made by this Act include provision conferring power to make provision by regulations, orders or other subordinate legislation.

(5) Amendments and repeals made under this section are additional, and without prejudice, to those made by or under any other provision of this Act.

(6) Orders under this section are subject to affirmative resolution procedure.

## 1295  Repeals

**46.1295.01**

The enactments specified in Schedule 16, which include enactments that are no longer of practical utility, are repealed to the extent specified.

COMMENCEMENT DATE With relevant provisions

## 1296  Power to make transitional provision and savings

**46.1296.01**

(1) The Secretary of State or the Treasury may by order make such transitional provision and savings as they consider necessary or expedient in connection with the commencement of any provision made by or under this Act.

## Companies Act 2006

## PART 46
## GENERAL SUPPLEMENTARY PROVISIONS

Commentary on this section of the CA 2006 has not been included
in this publication.

### *Regulations and orders*

### 1288 Regulations and orders: statutory instrument

Except as otherwise provided, regulations and orders under this Act shall be made by statutory instrument.

**46.1288.01**

COMMENCEMENT DATE 8 November 2006: see s 1300

### 1289 Regulations and orders: negative resolution procedure

Where regulations or orders under this Act are subject to 'negative resolution procedure' the statutory instrument containing the regulations or order shall be subject to annulment in pursuance of a resolution of either House of Parliament.

**46.1289.01**

COMMENCEMENT DATE 8 November 2006: see s 1300

### 1290 Regulations and orders: affirmative resolution procedure

Where regulations or orders under this Act are subject to 'affirmative resolution procedure' the regulations or order must not be made unless a draft of the statutory instrument containing them has been laid before Parliament and approved by a resolution of each House of Parliament.

**46.1290.01**

COMMENCEMENT DATE 8 November 2006: see s 1300

### 1291 Regulations and orders: approval after being made

(1) Regulations or orders under this Act that are subject to 'approval after being made'—
    (a) must be laid before Parliament after being made, and
    (b) cease to have effect at the end of 28 days beginning with the day on which they were made unless during that period they are approved by resolution of each House.
(2) In reckoning the period of 28 days no account shall be taken of any time during which Parliament is dissolved or prorogued or during which both Houses are adjourned for more than four days.
(3) The regulations or order ceasing to have effect does not affect—
    (a) anything previously done under them or it, or
    (b) the making of new regulations or a new order.

**46.1291.01**

COMMENCEMENT DATE 8 November 2006: see s 1300

(2) An order may, in particular, make such adaptations of provisions brought into force as appear to be necessary or expedient in consequence of other provisions of this Act not yet having come into force.

(3) Transitional provision and savings made under this section are additional, and without prejudice, to those made by or under any other provision of this Act.

(4) Orders under this section are subject to negative resolution procedure.

COMMENCEMENT DATE 8 November 2006: see s 1300

## 1297   Continuity of the law

(1) This section applies where any provision of this Act re-enacts (with or without modification) an enactment repealed by this Act.

**46.1297.01**

(2) The repeal and re-enactment does not affect the continuity of the law.

(3) Anything done (including subordinate legislation made), or having effect as if done, under or for the purposes of the repealed provision that could have been done under or for the purposes of the corresponding provision of this Act, if in force or effective immediately before the commencement of that corresponding provision, has effect thereafter as if done under or for the purposes of that corresponding provision.

(4) Any reference (express or implied) in this Act or any other enactment, instrument or document to a provision of this Act shall be construed (so far as the context permits) as including, as respects times, circumstances or purposes in relation to which the corresponding repealed provision had effect, a reference to that corresponding provision.

(5) Any reference (express or implied) in any enactment, instrument or document to a repealed provision shall be construed (so far as the context permits), as respects times, circumstances and purposes in relation to which the corresponding provision of this Act has effect, as being or (according to the context) including a reference to the corresponding provision of this Act.

(6) This section has effect subject to any specific transitional provision or saving contained in this Act.

(7) References in this section to this Act include subordinate legislation made under this Act.

(8) In this section 'subordinate legislation' has the same meaning as in the Interpretation Act 1978 (c. 30).

COMMENCEMENT DATE 8 November 2006: see s 1300

# FINAL PROVISIONS

| | | |
|---|---|---|
| **Companies Act 2006** | 1299  Extent | 47.1299.01 |
| PART 47 FINAL PROVISIONS | 1300  Commencement | 47.1300.01 |
| 1298  Short title | 47.1298.01 | |

## Companies Act 2006

### PART 47
### FINAL PROVISIONS

Commentary on this section of the CA 2006 has not been included in this publication.

### 1298  Short title

The short title of this Act is the Companies Act 2006.

**47.1298.01**

COMMENCEMENT DATE 8 November 2006

### 1299  Extent

Except as otherwise provided (or the context otherwise requires), the provisions of this Act extend to the whole of the United Kingdom.

**47.1299.01**

COMMENCEMENT DATE 8 November 2006

### 1300  Commencement

(1) The following provisions come into force on the day this Act is passed—

**47.1300.01**

    (a) Part 43 (transparency obligations and related matters), except the amendment in paragraph 11(2) of Schedule 15 of the definition of regulated market in Part 6 of the Financial Services and Markets Act 2000 (c. 8),

    (b) in Part 44 (miscellaneous provisions)— section 1274 (grants to bodies concerned with actuarial standards etc), and section 1276 (application of provisions to Scotland and Northern Ireland),

    (c) Part 46 (general supplementary provisions), except section 1295 and Schedule 16 (repeals), and

    (d) this part.

(2) The other provisions of this Act come into force on such day as may be appointed by order of the Secretary of State or the Treasury.

COMMENCEMENT DATE 8 November 2006

# 48

# SCHEDULES

## Companies Act 2006

### SCHEDULE 1      Sections 254 and 255

### CONNECTED PERSONS: REFERENCES TO AN INTEREST IN SHARES OR DEBENTURES

*Introduction*       **48.Sch1.01**

**1**   (1) The provisions of this Schedule have effect for the interpretation of references in sections 254 and 255 (directors connected with or controlling a body corporate) to an interest in shares or debentures.

    (2) The provisions are expressed in relation to shares but apply to debentures as they apply to shares.

*General provisions*

**2**   (1) A reference to an interest in shares includes any interest of any kind whatsoever in shares.

    (2) Any restraints or restrictions to which the exercise of any right attached to the interest is or may be subject shall be disregarded.

    (3) It is immaterial that the shares in which a person has an interest are not identifiable.

    (4) Persons having a joint interest in shares are deemed each of them to have that interest.

*Rights to acquire shares*

**3**   (1) A person is taken to have an interest in shares if he enters into a contract to acquire them.

    (2) A person is taken to have an interest in shares if—

       (a) he has a right to call for delivery of the shares to himself or to his order, or

       (b) he has a right to acquire an interest in shares or is under an obligation to take an interest in shares,
         whether the right or obligation is conditional or absolute.

    (3) Rights or obligations to subscribe for shares are not to be taken for the purposes of sub-paragraph (2) to be rights to acquire or obligations to take an interest in shares.

    (4) A person ceases to have an interest in shares by virtue of this paragraph—

       (a) on the shares being delivered to another person at his order—

         (i) in fulfilment of a contract for their acquisition by him, or

         (ii) in satisfaction of a right of his to call for their delivery;

       (b) on a failure to deliver the shares in accordance with the terms of such a contract or on which such a right falls to be satisfied;

       (c) on the lapse of his right to call for the delivery of shares.

*Right to exercise or control exercise of rights*

**4** (1) A person is taken to have an interest in shares if, not being the registered holder, he is entitled—

    (a) to exercise any right conferred by the holding of the shares, or

    (b) to control the exercise of any such right.

  (2) For this purpose a person is taken to be entitled to exercise or control the exercise of a right conferred by the holding of shares if he—

    (a) has a right (whether subject to conditions or not) the exercise of which would make him so entitled, or

    (b) is under an obligation (whether or not so subject) the fulfilment of which would make him so entitled.

  (3) A person is not by virtue of this paragraph taken to be interested in shares by reason only that—

    (a) he has been appointed a proxy to exercise any of the rights attached to the shares, or

    (b) he has been appointed by a body corporate to act as its representative at any meeting of a company or of any class of its members.

*Bodies corporate*

**5** (1) A person is taken to be interested in shares if a body corporate is interested in them and—

    (a) the body corporate or its directors are accustomed to act in accordance with his directions or instructions, or

    (b) he is entitled to exercise or control the exercise of more than one-half of the voting power at general meetings of the body corporate.

  (2) For the purposes of sub-paragraph (1)(b) where—

    (a) a person is entitled to exercise or control the exercise of more than one-half of the voting power at general meetings of a body corporate, and

    (b) that body corporate is entitled to exercise or control the exercise of any of the voting power at general meetings of another body corporate,

    the voting power mentioned in paragraph (b) above is taken to be exercisable by that person.

*Trusts*

**6** (1) Where an interest in shares is comprised in property held on trust, every beneficiary of the trust is taken to have an interest in shares, subject as follows.

  (2) So long as a person is entitled to receive, during the lifetime of himself or another, income from trust property comprising shares, an interest in the shares in reversion or remainder or (as regards Scotland) in fee shall be disregarded.

  (3) A person is treated as not interested in shares if and so long as he holds them—

    (a) under the law in force in any part of the United Kingdom, as a bare trustee or as a custodian trustee, or

    (b) under the law in force in Scotland, as a simple trustee.

  (4) There shall be disregarded any interest of a person subsisting by virtue of—

    (a) an authorised unit trust scheme (within the meaning of section 237 of the Financial Services and Markets Act 2000 (c. 8));

    (b) a scheme made under section 22 or 22A of the Charities Act 1960 (c. 58), section 25 of the Charities Act (Northern Ireland) 1964 (c. 33 (N.I.)) or section 24 or 25 of the Charities Act 1993 (c. 10), section 11 of the Trustee Investments Act 1961 (c. 62) or section 42 of the Administration of Justice Act 1982 (c. 53); or

    (c) the scheme set out in the Schedule to the Church Funds Investment Measure 1958 (1958 No. 1).

  (5) There shall be disregarded any interest—

    (a) of the Church of Scotland General Trustees or of the Church of Scotland Trust in shares held by them;

    (b) of any other person in shares held by those Trustees or that Trust otherwise than as simple trustees.

    'The Church of Scotland General Trustees' are the body incorporated by the order confirmed by the Church of Scotland (General Trustees) Order Confirmation Act 1921 (1921 c. xxv), and 'the Church of Scotland Trust' is the body incorporated by the order confirmed by the Church of Scotland Trust Order Confirmation Act 1932 (1932 c. xxi).

C<small>OMMENCEMENT</small> D<small>ATE</small> To be appointed.

**48.Sch1.02**  Schedule 1 of the Act relates directly to sections 254 and 255 with regard to connected persons and interests in shares. According to section 254 a 'director is connected with a body corporate if, but only if, he and the persons connected with him together—

(a) are interested in shares comprised in the equity share capital of that body corporate of a nominal value equal to at least 20 per cent of that share capital, or

(b) are entitled to exercise or control the exercise of more than 20 per cent of the voting power at any general meeting of that body.

Similarly section 255 provides that a 'director of a company is taken to control a body corporate if, but     **48.Sch1.03**
only if—

(a)  he or any person connected with him—
   (i)  is interested in any part of the equity share capital of that body, or
   (ii)  is entitled to exercise or control the exercise of any part of the voting power at any general meeting of that body, and
(b)  he, the persons connected with him and the other directors of that company, together—
   (i)  are interested in more than 50% of that share capital, or
   (ii)  are entitled to exercise or control the exercise of more than 50% of that voting power.

In both cases Schedule 1 defines when an interest in shares arises. Thus consistent with the general     **48.Sch1.04**
provisions on interests in shares in sections 820 to 825 Schedule 1 provides a broad general catch all
definition of interests in shares as including 'any interest of any kind whatsoever in shares'[1] but also
specifically deeming a right to acquire shares (Schedule 1(3)), a right to exercise or control the exercise
of rights (Schedule 1(4)), corporate interests (Schedule 1(5)), and trusts (Schedule 1(6)), as potentially
giving rise to an interest in shares.

---

[a,b] [SCHEDULE 2

SPECIFIED PERSONS, DESCRIPTIONS OF DISCLOSURES ETC
FOR THE PURPOSES OF SECTION 948

PART 1
SPECIFIED PERSONS

*(A) United Kingdom*

1   The Secretary of State.     **48.Sch2.01**
2   The Department of Enterprise, Trade and Investment for Northern Ireland.
3   The Treasury.
4   The Bank of England.
5   The Financial Services Authority.[2]
6   The Commissioners for Her Majesty's Revenue and Customs.
7   The Lord Advocate.
8   The Director of Public Prosecutions.
9   The Director of Public Prosecutions for Northern Ireland.
10  A constable.
11  A procurator fiscal.
12  The Scottish Ministers.

*(B) Jersey*

1   The Minister for Economic Development.
2   The Minister for Treasury and Resources.
3   The Jersey Financial Services Commission.
4   The Comptroller of Income Tax.
5   The Agent of the Impôts.
6   Her Majesty's Attorney General for Jersey.
7   The Viscount.
8   A police officer (within the meaning of the Interpretation (Jersey) Law 1954: see Part 1 of the Schedule to that Law).

*(C) Guernsey*

1   The Commerce and Employment Department.
2   The Treasury and Resources Department.

---

[1]  Sch 1(2).
[2]  The Financial Services Act 2012 will substitute references to the Financial Services Authority with references
to 'The Financial Conduct Authority' and The Prudential Regulation Authority' from such day as the Treasury
may by order appoint: Sched 18, para 123.

3    The Guernsey Financial Services Commission.
4    The Director of Income Tax.
5    The Chief Officer of Customs and Excise.
6    Her Majesty's Procureur.
7    A police officer (within the meaning of the Companies (Guernsey) Law 2008: see section 532 of that Law).

*(D)  Isle Of Man*

1    (1) The members and officers of each of the Departments constituted by section 1(1) of the Government Departments Act 1987 (an Act of Tynwald: c. 13).
     (2) In sub-paragraph (1) 'member' has the same meaning as it has by virtue of section 7(1) of that Act.
2    The Treasury of the Isle of Man.
3    The Financial Supervision Commission of the Isle of Man.
4    Her Majesty's Attorney General of the Isle of Man.
5    A constable (within the meaning of the Interpretation Act 1976 (an Act of Tynwald: c. 11): see section 3 of that Act).

PART 2
SPECIFIED DESCRIPTIONS OF DISCLOSURES

*(A)  United Kingdom*

1    A disclosure for the purpose of enabling or assisting a person authorised under section 457 of this Act (revision of defective accounts: persons authorised to apply to court) to exercise their functions.
2    A disclosure for the purpose of enabling or assisting an inspector appointed under Part 14 of the Companies Act 1985 (c. 6) (investigation of companies and their affairs, etc) to exercise their functions.
3    A disclosure for the purpose of enabling or assisting a person authorised under section 447 of the Companies Act 1985 (power to require production of documents) or section 84 of the Companies Act 1989 (c. 40) (exercise of powers by officer etc) to exercise their functions.
4    A disclosure for the purpose of enabling or assisting a person appointed under section 167 of the Financial Services and Markets Act 2000 (c. 8) (general investigations) to conduct an investigation to exercise their functions.
5    A disclosure for the purpose of enabling or assisting a person appointed under section 168 of the Financial Services and Markets Act 2000 (investigations in particular cases) to conduct an investigation to exercise their functions.
6    A disclosure for the purpose of enabling or assisting a person appointed under section 169(1)(b) of the Financial Services and Markets Act 2000 (investigation in support of overseas regulator) to conduct an investigation to exercise their functions.
7    A disclosure for the purpose of enabling or assisting the body corporate responsible for administering the scheme referred to in section 225 of the Financial Services and Markets Act 2000 (the ombudsman scheme) to exercise its functions.
8    A disclosure for the purpose of enabling or assisting a person appointed under paragraph 4 or 5 of Schedule 17 to the Financial Services and Markets Act 2000 (the panel of ombudsmen or the Chief Ombudsman) to exercise their functions.
9    A disclosure for the purpose of enabling or assisting a person appointed under regulations made under section 262(1) and (2)(k) of the Financial Services and Markets Act 2000 (investigations into open-ended investment companies) to conduct an investigation to exercise their functions.
10   A disclosure for the purpose of enabling or assisting a person appointed under section 284 of the Financial Services and Markets Act 2000 (investigations into affairs of certain collective investment schemes) to conduct an investigation to exercise their functions.
11   A disclosure for the purpose of enabling or assisting the investigator appointed under paragraph 7 of Schedule 1 to the Financial Services and Markets Act 2000 (arrangements for investigation of complaints)[3] to exercise their functions.
12   A disclosure for the purpose of enabling or assisting a person appointed by the Treasury to hold an inquiry into matters relating to financial services (including an inquiry under section 15 of the Financial Services and Markets Act 2000[4]) to exercise their functions.

---

[3] The Financial Services Act 2012 will substitute a reference to 'section 84 of the Financial Services Act 2012' from such day as the Treasury may by order appoint Sched 18, para 123.

[4] The Financial Services Act 2012 will substitute a reference to 'section 69 of the Financial Services Act 2012' from such day as the Treasury may by order appoint: ibid. Clause 103(3) Sched 18, para 123.

**13** A disclosure for the purpose of enabling or assisting the Secretary of State or the Treasury to exercise any of their functions under any of the following—

(a) the Companies Acts;

(b) the Insolvency Act 1986 (c. 45);

(c) the Company Directors Disqualification Act 1986 (c. 46);

(d) Part 3 (investigations and powers to obtain information) or 7 (financial markets and insolvency) of the Companies Act 1989 (c. 40);

(e) Part 5 of the Criminal Justice Act 1993 (c. 36) (insider dealing);

(f) the Financial Services and Markets Act 2000;

(g) Part 42 of this Act (statutory auditors).[5]

**14** A disclosure for the purpose of enabling or assisting the Scottish Ministers to exercise their functions under the enactments relating to insolvency.

**15** A disclosure for the purpose of enabling or assisting the Department of Enterprise, Trade and Investment for Northern Ireland to exercise any powers conferred on it by the enactments relating to companies or insolvency.

**16** A disclosure for the purpose of enabling or assisting a person appointed or authorised by the Department of Enterprise, Trade and Investment for Northern Ireland under the enactments relating to companies or insolvency to exercise their functions.

**17** A disclosure for the purpose of enabling or assisting an official receiver (including the Accountant in Bankruptcy in Scotland and the Official Assignee in Northern Ireland) to exercise their functions under the enactments relating to insolvency.

**18** A disclosure for the purpose of enabling or assisting the Insolvency Practitioners Tribunal to exercise its functions under the Insolvency Act 1986 (c. 45).

**19** A disclosure for the purpose of enabling or assisting a body that is for the time being a recognised professional body for the purposes of section 391 of the Insolvency Act 1986 (recognised professional bodies) to exercise its functions as such.

**20** A disclosure for the purpose of enabling or assisting the Pensions Regulator to exercise the functions conferred on it by or by virtue of any of the following—

(a) the Pension Schemes Act 1993 (c. 48);

(b) the Pensions Act 1995 (c. 26);

(c) the Welfare Reform and Pensions Act 1999 (c. 30);

(d) the Pensions Act 2004 (c. 35);

(e) any enactment in force in Northern Ireland corresponding to any of those enactments.

**21** A disclosure for the purpose of enabling or assisting the Board of the Pension Protection Fund to exercise the functions conferred on it by or by virtue of Part 2 of the Pensions Act 2004 or any enactment in force in Northern Ireland corresponding to that Part.

**22** A disclosure for the purpose of enabling or assisting the Bank of England to exercise its functions.

**23** A disclosure for the purpose of enabling or assisting the Commissioners for Her Majesty's Revenue and Customs to exercise their functions.

**24** A disclosure for the purpose of enabling or assisting organs of the Society of Lloyd's (being organs constituted by or under the Lloyd's Act 1982 (c. xiv)) to exercise their functions under or by virtue of the Lloyd's Acts 1871 to 1982.

**25** A disclosure for the purpose of enabling or assisting the Office of Fair Trading to exercise its functions under any of the following—

(a) the Fair Trading Act 1973 (c. 41);

(b) the Consumer Credit Act 1974 (c. 39);

(c) the Estate Agents Act 1979 (c. 38);

(d) the Competition Act 1980 (c. 21);

(e) the Competition Act 1998 (c. 41);

(f) the Financial Services and Markets Act 2000 (c. 8);

(g) the Enterprise Act 2002 (c. 40);

(h) the Unfair Terms in Consumer Contracts Regulations 1999 (S.I. 1999/2083);

(i) the Business Protection from Misleading Marketing Regulations 2008 (S.I. 2008/1276);

(j) the Consumer Protection from Unfair Trading Regulations 2008 (S.I. 2008/1277).[6]

**26** A disclosure for the purpose of enabling or assisting the Competition Commission to exercise its functions under any of the following—

(a) the Fair Trading Act 1973;

(b) the Competition Act 1980;

---

[5] Paragraph 13 is intended to be read so as to include the Investment Bank Special Administration Regulations 2011 SI 2011/245 in the list of enactments in that paragraph: see Reg 27(a), Sch 6, Part 2, para 5(5)(a) with effect from 8 February 2011.

[6] Paragraph 25 is intended to be read so as to include the Banking Act 2009 in the list of enactments in that paragraph: see the Banking Act 2009 (Parts 2 and 3 Consequential Amendments) Order 2009, SI 2009/317, art 6(5)(a), with effect from 21 February 2009. However, see n 3 below on the subsequent amendment of Schedule 2 by SI 2009/1208.

(c)  the Competition Act 1998;

(d)  the Enterprise Act 2002.

**27**  A disclosure with a view to the institution of, or otherwise for the purposes of, proceedings before the Competition Appeal Tribunal.

**28**  A disclosure for the purpose of enabling or assisting an enforcer under Part 8 of the Enterprise Act 2002 (enforcement of consumer legislation) to exercise their functions under that Part.

**29**  A disclosure for the purpose of enabling or assisting the Charity Commission to exercise its functions.

**30**  A disclosure for the purpose of enabling or assisting the Attorney General to exercise their functions in connection with charities.

**31**  A disclosure for the purpose of enabling or assisting the National Lottery Commission to exercise its functions under sections 5 to 10 and 15 of the National Lottery etc. Act 1993 (c. 39) (licensing and power of Secretary of State to require information).

**32**  A disclosure by the National Lottery Commission to the National Audit Office for the purpose of enabling or assisting the Comptroller and Auditor General to carry out an examination under Part 2 of the National Audit Act 1983 (c. 44) into the economy, effectiveness and efficiency with which the National Lottery Commission has used its resources in discharging its functions under sections 5 to 10 of the National Lottery etc. Act 1993.

**33**  A disclosure for the purpose of enabling or assisting a qualifying body under the Unfair Terms in Consumer Contracts Regulations 1999 (S.I. 1999/2083) to exercise its functions under those Regulations.

**34**  A disclosure for the purpose of enabling or assisting an enforcement authority under the Consumer Protection (Distance Selling) Regulations 2000 (S.I. 2000/2334) to exercise its functions under those Regulations.

**35**  A disclosure for the purpose of enabling or assisting an enforcement authority under the Financial Services (Distance Marketing) Regulations 2004 (S.I. 2004/2095) to exercise its functions under those Regulations.

**36**  A disclosure for the purpose of enabling or assisting a local weights and measures authority in England and Wales to exercise its functions under section 230(2) of the Enterprise Act 2002 (c.40) (notice of intention to prosecute, etc).

**37**  A disclosure for the purpose of enabling or assisting the Financial Services Authority[7] to exercise its functions under any of the following—

(a)  the legislation relating to friendly societies or to industrial and provident societies;

(b)  the Building Societies Act 1986 (c. 53);

(c)  Part 7 of the Companies Act 1989 (c. 40) (financial markets and insolvency);

(d)  the Financial Services and Markets Act 2000 (c. 8).[8] [9]

**38**  A disclosure for the purpose of enabling or assisting the competent authority for the purposes of Part 6 of the Financial Services and Markets Act 2000 (official listing) to exercise its functions under that Part.

**39**  A disclosure for the purpose of enabling or assisting a body corporate established in accordance with section 212(1) of the Financial Services and Markets Act 2000 (compensation scheme manager) to exercise its functions.

---

[7]  The Financial Services Act 2012 will substitute a reference to the 'Financial Conduct Authority or the Prudential Regulation Authority' from such day as the Treasury may by order appoint: Sched 18, para 123.

[8]  It appears intended that para 37 is to be read so as to include the Banking Act 2009 in the list of enactments in that paragraph: see the Banking Act 2009 (Parts 2 and 3 Consequential Amendments) Order 2009, SI 2009/317, art 6(5)(b), with effect from 21 February 2009. Article 6(5)(b) refers to para 46 of Sch 2 which, following the substitution of Sch 2 by the Companies Act 2006 (Amendment of Schedule 2) (No 2) Order 2009, SI 2009/1208, art 2, from 1 July 2009, is now para 37. However, it is uncertain if the reference in art 6(5)(b) of SI 2009/317 to para 46 can be transferred to para 37 following amendment of Sch 2. Section 20(2) of the Interpretation Act 1978 states that 'where an Act refers to an enactment, the reference, unless the contrary intention appears, is a reference to that enactment as amended, and includes a reference thereto as extended or applied, by or under any other enactment, including any other provision of that Act'. Section 20(2) applies to subordinate legislation: s 23 of the Interpretation Act 1978. However, in *Willows v Lewis (Inspector of Taxes)* [1982] STC 141, Nourse J held that a provision in similar terms to s 20(2) could not apply to future amendments as it would give it 'a width of application which the wording, at best equivocal, could not bear, especially in a taxing statute'. See also *Megantic Services Limited* (unreported), First Tier Tribunal (Tax), 19 March 2010, Judge Richard Barlow and the discussion on s 20(2) of the Interpretation Act 1978 in FAR Bennion, *Bennion on Statutory Interpretation* (5th edn, LexisNexis, 2008) section 83, 298–299. A further problem is that the numbering of the provisions has changed. To avoid these difficulties SI 2009/1208 should have amended the references in SI 2009/317.

[9]  Paragraph 37 is intended to be read so as to include the Investment Bank Special Administration Regulations 2011 SI 2011/245 in the list of enactments in that paragraph: see Reg 27(a), Sch 6, Part 2, para 5(5)(b) with effect from 8 February 2011.

**40**– (1) A disclosure for the purpose of enabling or assisting a recognised investment exchange or a recognised clearing house to exercise its functions as such.

(2) In sub-paragraph (1) 'recognised investment exchange' and 'recognised clearing house' have the same meaning as in section 285 of the Financial Services and Markets Act 2000.

**41** A disclosure for the purpose of enabling or assisting a person approved under the Uncertificated Securities Regulations 2001 (S.I. 2001/3755) as an operator of a relevant system (within the meaning of those Regulations) to exercise their functions.

**42** A disclosure for the purpose of enabling or assisting a body designated under section 326(1) of the Financial Services and Markets Act 2000 (designated professional bodies) to exercise its functions in its capacity as a body designated under that section.

**43** A disclosure with a view to the institution of, or otherwise for the purposes of, civil proceedings arising under or by virtue of the Financial Services and Markets Act 2000.

**44** A disclosure for the purpose of enabling or assisting a body designated by order under section 1252 of this Act (delegation of functions of Secretary of State) to exercise its functions under Part 42 of this Act (statutory auditors).

**45** A disclosure for the purpose of enabling or assisting a recognised supervisory or qualifying body, within the meaning of Part 42 of this Act, to exercise its functions as such.

**46** A disclosure for the purpose of enabling or assisting the Regulator of Community Interest Companies to exercise functions under the Companies (Audit, Investigations and Community Enterprise) Act 2004 (c. 27).

**47** A disclosure for the purpose of enabling or assisting a person authorised by the Secretary of State under Part 2, 3 or 4 of the Proceeds of Crime Act 2002 (c. 29) to exercise their functions.

**48** A disclosure with a view to the institution of, or otherwise for the purposes of, proceedings on an application under section 6, 7 or 8 of the Company Directors Disqualification Act 1986 (c. 46) (disqualification for unfitness).

**[49** A disclosure with a view to the institution of, or otherwise for the purposes of, proceedings before the Upper Tribunal in respect of—

(a)   a decision of the Financial Services Authority;[10]

(b)   a decision of the Bank of England; or

(c)   a decision of a person relating to the assessment of any compensation or consideration under the Banking (Special Provisions) Act 2008 or the Banking Act 2009.]^c

**50** A disclosure for the purposes of proceedings before [a tribunal in relation to a decision of the Pensions Regulator.[11]]^d

**51** A disclosure for the purpose of enabling or assisting a body appointed under section 14 of the Companies (Audit, Investigations and Community Enterprise) Act 2004 (supervision of periodic accounts and reports of issuers of listed securities) to exercise functions mentioned in subsection (2) of that section.

**52**– (1) A disclosure with a view to the institution of, or otherwise for the purposes of, disciplinary proceedings relating to the performance by a lawyer, auditor, accountant, valuer or actuary of their professional duties.

(2) In sub-paragraph (1) 'lawyer' means—

(a)   a person who for the purposes of the Legal Services Act 2007 (c. 29) is an authorised person in relation to an activity that constitutes a reserved legal activity (within the meaning of that Act),

(b)   a solicitor or barrister in Northern Ireland,

(c)   a solicitor or advocate in Scotland, or

(d)   a person who is a member, and entitled to practise as such, of a legal profession regulated in a jurisdiction outside the United Kingdom.

(3) Until the coming into force of section 18 of the Legal Services Act 2007, the following is substituted for paragraph (a) of sub-paragraph (2) above—

(a)   'a solicitor or barrister in England and Wales,'.

**53**– (1) A disclosure with a view to the institution of, or otherwise for the purposes of, disciplinary proceedings relating to the performance by a public servant of their duties.

---

[10]   The Financial Services Act 2012 will substitute a reference to '(a) a decision of the Financial Conduct Authority; (aa) a decision of the Prudential Regulation Authority' from such day as the Treasury may by order appoint: Sched 18, para 123.

[11]   Paragraph 50 amended by the Transfer of Tribunal Functions Order 2010, SI 2010/22, art 5(1), Sch 2, paras 141, 142(b), with effect from 6 April 2010 and in relation to Northern Ireland by the Pensions Regulator Tribunal (Transfer of Functions) Act (Northern Ireland) 2010 section 3(1) and Sch 1, paras 25–26, with effect from 6 April 2010 (see The Pensions Regulator Tribunal (Transfer of Functions) (2010 Act) (Commencement) Order (Northern Ireland) 2010 SR 2010/101, Art 2). Transitional arrangements are set out in Sch 5 of SI 2010/22 in relation to England, Wales, and Scotland, and Sch 2 of the Pensions Regulator Tribunal (Transfer of Functions) Act (Northern Ireland) 2010 in relation to Northern Ireland.

(2) In sub-paragraph (1) 'public servant' means—
  (a) an officer or employee of the Crown, or
  (b) an officer or employee of any public or other authority for the time being designated for the purposes of this paragraph by the Secretary of State by order subject to negative resolution procedure.

*(B) Jersey*

**1**  A disclosure for the purpose of enabling or assisting an inspector appointed under Part 19 of the Companies (Jersey) Law 1991 to exercise their functions.

**2**  A disclosure for the purpose of enabling or assisting a person appointed under Article 33 of the Financial Services (Jersey) Law 1998 to exercise their functions.

**3**  A disclosure for the purpose of enabling or assisting an inspector appointed under Article 22 of the Collective Investment Funds (Jersey) Law 1988 to exercise their functions.

**4**  A disclosure for the purpose of enabling or assisting the Minister for Economic Development to exercise functions under any of the following—
  (a) the Bankruptcy Désastre (Jersey) Law 1990;
  (b) the Companies (Jersey) Law 1991;
  (c) the Financial Services (Jersey) Law 1998.

**5**  A disclosure for the purpose of enabling or assisting the Comptroller of Income Tax to exercise their functions.

**6**  A disclosure for the purpose of enabling or assisting the Agent of the Impôts to exercise their functions.

**7**  A disclosure for the purpose of enabling or assisting the Jersey Competition Regulatory Authority to exercise its functions.

**8**  A disclosure for the purpose of enabling or assisting Her Majesty's Attorney General for Jersey to exercise their functions in connection with charities.

**9**  A disclosure for the purpose of enabling or assisting Her Majesty's Attorney General for Jersey to exercise their functions under the Distance Selling (Jersey) Law 2007.

**10**  A disclosure for the purpose of enabling or assisting the Viscount to exercise their functions in relation to désastre or in relation to Part 2 of the Proceeds of Crime (Jersey) Law 1999.

**11**  A disclosure with a view to the institution of, or otherwise for the purposes of, proceedings on an application under Article 78 of the Companies (Jersey) Law 1991 (disqualification orders).

**12**– (1) A disclosure with a view to the institution of, or otherwise for the purposes of, disciplinary proceedings relating to the performance by a solicitor, advocate, foreign lawyer, auditor, accountant, valuer or actuary of their professional duties.
  (2) In sub-paragraph (1)—
    (a) 'solicitor' means a person who has been admitted as a solicitor under the Advocates and Solicitors (Jersey) Law 1997;
    (b) 'advocate' means a person who has been admitted to the Bar under that Law; and
    (c) 'foreign lawyer' means a person who has not been admitted as mentioned in paragraph (a) or (b) but is a member, and entitled to practise as such, of a legal profession regulated within a jurisdiction outside Jersey.

**13**  (1) A disclosure with a view to the institution of, or otherwise for the purposes of, disciplinary proceedings relating to the performance by a public servant of their duties.
  (2) In sub-paragraph (1) 'public servant' means—
    (a) an individual who holds office under, or is employed by, the Crown,
    (b) a member, officer or employee of the States of Jersey or an officer or employee in an administration of the States of Jersey,
    (c) a member, officer or employee of the Jersey Financial Services Commission, or
    (d) any person exercising public functions who is declared by Order of the Minister for Economic Development to be a public servant for the purposes of paragraph 25 of the Schedule to the Companies (Takeovers and Mergers Panel) (Jersey) Law 2009.

*(C) Guernsey*

**1**  A disclosure for the purpose of enabling or assisting the Registrar of Companies appointed under the Companies (Guernsey) Law 2008 to exercise their functions under that Law.

**2**  A disclosure for the purpose of enabling or assisting a person appointed under—
  (a) section 27E or 41I of the Protection of Investors (Bailiwick of Guernsey) Law 1987,
  (b) section 27 of the Banking Supervision (Bailiwick of Guernsey) Law 1994,
  (c) section 10 of the Company Securities (Insider Dealing) (Bailiwick of Guernsey) Law 1996,
  (d) section 24 of the Regulation of Fiduciaries, Administration Businesses and Company Directors (Bailiwick of Guernsey) Law 2000,
  (e) section 69 of the Insurance Business (Bailiwick of Guernsey) Law 2002,

(f)   section 46 of the Insurance Managers and Insurance Intermediaries (Bailiwick of Guernsey) Law 2002,

(g)   section 19 of the Registration of Non-Regulated Financial Services Business (Bailiwick of Guernsey) Law 2008, to exercise their functions.

3     A disclosure for the purpose of enabling or assisting Her Majesty's Procureur to exercise their functions in connection with charities.

4     A disclosure for the purpose of enabling or assisting the Guernsey Banking Deposit Compensation Scheme, established under section 46 of the Banking Supervision (Bailiwick of Guernsey) Law 1987 by the Banking Deposit Compensation Scheme (Bailiwick of Guernsey) Ordinance 2008, to exercise its functions.

5     A disclosure for the purpose of enabling or assisting any supervisory body or professional oversight body to exercise its functions under Part XVIA of the Companies (Guernsey) Law 2008 (regulation of auditors).

6     A disclosure with a view to the institution of, or otherwise for the purposes of, proceedings on an application under Part XXV of the Companies (Guernsey) Law 2008 (disqualification orders).

7–    (1)   A disclosure with a view to the institution of, or otherwise for the purposes of, disciplinary proceedings relating to the performance by an Advocate of the Royal Court, foreign lawyer, auditor, accountant, valuer or actuary of their professional duties.

      (2)   In sub-paragraph (1) 'foreign lawyer' means a person who has not been admitted as an Advocate of the Royal Court, but is a member, and entitled to practise as such, of a legal profession regulated within a jurisdiction outside Guernsey.

8–    (1)   A disclosure with a view to the institution of, or otherwise for the purposes of, disciplinary proceedings relating to the performance by a public servant of their duties.

      (2)   In sub-paragraph (1) 'public servant' means—

            (a)   an officer or employee of the Crown,

            (b)   a member, officer or employee of the States of Guernsey,

            (c)   a member, officer or employee of the Guernsey Financial Services Commission, or

            (d)   any person exercising public functions who is declared by regulations of the Commerce and Employment Department to be a public servant for the purposes of paragraph 17 of Schedule 6 to the Companies (Guernsey) Law 2008.

*(D)  Isle of Man*

1     A disclosure for the purpose of enabling or assisting an inspector appointed by the High Court of the Isle of Man under the enactments of the Isle of Man relating to companies to discharge their functions.

2     A disclosure for the purpose of enabling or assisting a person conducting an investigation under—

      (a)   section 16 of the Collective Investment Schemes Act 2008 (an Act of Tynwald: c. 7);

      (b)   Schedule 2 to the Financial Services Act 2008 (an Act of Tynwald: c. 8); or

      (c)   Schedule 5 to the Insurance Act 2008 (an Act of Tynwald: c. 16), to exercise their functions.

3     A disclosure for the purpose of enabling or assisting the Financial Supervision Commission of the Isle of Man to exercise any of its functions.

4     A disclosure for the purpose of enabling or assisting an auditor of a permitted person (within the meaning of the Financial Services Act 2008 (an Act of Tynwald)) to exercise their functions.

5     A disclosure for the purpose of enabling or assisting the Office of Fair Trading of the Isle of Man to exercise its functions under Schedule 4 to the Financial Services Act 2008 (an Act of Tynwald) in relation to a financial services dispute within the meaning of paragraph 1(1) of that Schedule.

6     A disclosure for the purpose of enabling or assisting an adjudicator appointed under paragraph 4 of Schedule 4 to the Financial Services Act 2008 (an Act of Tynwald) to exercise their functions.

7     A disclosure for the purpose of enabling or assisting the body administering a scheme under section 25 of the Financial Services Act 2008 (an Act of Tynwald) (compensation schemes) to exercise its functions under the scheme.

8     A disclosure with a view to the institution of, or otherwise for the purposes of, civil proceedings arising under or by virtue of the Financial Services Act 2008 (an Act of Tynwald).

9     A disclosure for the purpose of enabling or assisting—

      (a)   the Insurance and Pensions Authority of the Isle of Man; or

      (b)   the Retirement Benefits Schemes Supervisor of the Isle of Man,

to exercise its functions under the Retirement Benefits Schemes Act 2000 (an Act of Tynwald: c 14).

10    A disclosure for the purpose of enabling or assisting the Assessor of Income Tax to exercise their functions under enactments of the Isle of Man relating to income tax.

11    A disclosure for the purpose of enabling or assisting the Office of Fair Trading of the Isle of Man to exercise its functions under any of the following—

      (a)   the Unsolicited Goods and Services (Isle of Man) Act 1974 (an Act of Tynwald: c. 5);

      (b)   the Moneylenders Act 1991 (an Act of Tynwald: c. 6);

      (c)   the Consumer Protection Act 1991 (an Act of Tynwald: c. 11);

(d)  the Fair Trading Act 1996 (an Act of Tynwald: c. 15).

12  A disclosure for the purpose of enabling or assisting the Department of Local Government and the Environment of the Isle of Man to exercise its functions under the Estate Agents Act 1975 (an Act of Tynwald: c. 6) or the Estate Agents Act 1999 (an Act of Tynwald: c. 7).

13  A disclosure for the purpose of enabling or assisting Her Majesty's Attorney General of the Isle of Man to exercise their functions in connection with charities.

14  A disclosure for the purpose of enabling or assisting the Treasury of the Isle of Man to exercise its functions under the enactments of the Isle of Man relating to companies, insurance companies or insolvency.

15  A disclosure for the purpose of enabling or assisting an official receiver appointed in the Isle of Man to exercise their functions under the enactments of the Isle of Man relating to insolvency.

16– (1)  A disclosure with a view to the institution of, or otherwise for the purposes of, disciplinary proceedings relating to the performance by an advocate, registered legal practitioner, auditor, accountant, valuer or actuary of their professional duties.

   (2)  In sub-paragraph (1)—
       'advocate' means a person who is qualified to act as an advocate in any court in the Island in accordance with section 7 of the Advocates Act 1976 (an Act of Tynwald: c. 27);
       'registered legal practitioner' means a legal practitioner within the meaning of section 10 of the Legal Practitioners Registration Act 1986 (an Act of Tynwald: c. 15) who is registered within the meaning of that Act.

17– (1)  A disclosure with a view to the institution of, or otherwise for the purposes of, disciplinary proceedings relating to the performance by a public servant of their duties.

   (2)  In sub-paragraph (1) 'public servant' means—
   (a)  an officer or employee of the Crown, or
   (b)  an officer or employee of any public or other authority for the time being designated for the purposes of this paragraph by order made by the Council of Ministers of the Isle of Man.


*(E) General*

1  A disclosure for the purpose of enabling or assisting—
   (a)  the European Central Bank, or
   (b)  the central bank of any country or territory outside the British Islands,
to exercise its functions.

2– (1)  A disclosure for the purpose of enabling or assisting an overseas regulatory authority to exercise its regulatory functions.

   (2)  In sub-paragraph (1) 'overseas regulatory authority' and 'regulatory functions' have the same meaning as in section 82 of the Companies Act 1989 (assistance for overseas regulatory authorities).

3  A disclosure with a view to the institution of, or otherwise for the purposes of, criminal proceedings in the British Islands or elsewhere.

4  A disclosure for the purpose of the provision of a summary or collection of information framed in such a way as not to enable the identity of any person to whom the information relates to be ascertained.

5  A disclosure in pursuance of any [EU]^e obligation.


## PART 3
## OVERSEAS REGULATORY BODIES

1– (1)  A disclosure is made in accordance with this Part of this Schedule if—
       (a)  it is made to a person or body exercising relevant functions under legislation in a country or territory outside the British Islands, and
       (b)  it is made for the purpose of enabling or assisting that person or body to exercise those functions.

   (2)  'Relevant functions' for this purpose are functions of a public nature that appear to the Panel to be similar to its own functions or those of the Financial Services Authority.[12]

2  In determining whether to disclose information to a person or body in accordance with this Part of this Schedule, the Panel must have regard to the following considerations—
   (a)  whether the use that the person or body is likely to make of the information is sufficiently important to justify making the disclosure;

---

[12]  The Financial Services Act 2012 will substitute a reference to the 'Financial Conduct Authority or the Prudential Regulation Authority or similar to the regulatory functions of the Bank of England' from such day as the Treasury may by order appoint: Sched 18, para 123.

    (b)  whether the person or body has adequate arrangements to prevent the information from being used or further disclosed, otherwise than—

        (i)  for the purposes of carrying out the functions mentioned in paragraph 1(1)(a), or

        (ii)  for other purposes substantially similar to those for which information disclosed to the Panel could be used or further disclosed.][d]

AMENDMENTS AND NOTES

[a]  Schedule 2 as substituted by the Companies Act 2006 (Amendment of Schedule 2) (No 2) Order 2009 SI 2009/1208 with effect from 1 July 2009.

[b]  Schedule 2 was extended to the Isle of Man by the Companies Act 2006 (Extension of Takeover Panel Provisions) (Isle of Man) Order 2009 SI 2009/1378, Art 2 with effect from 1 July 2009.

[c]  Para 49 substituted by the Transfer of Tribunal Functions Order 2010, SI 2010/22, art 5(1), Sch 2, paras 141, 142(a), with effect from 6 April 2010. Transitional arrangements are set out in Sch 5 to that order.

[d]  Para 50 amended by the Transfer of Tribunal Functions Order 2010, SI 2010/22, art 5(1), Sch 2, paras 141, 142(b), with effect from 6 April 2010 and in relation to Northern Ireland by the Pensions Regulator Tribunal (Transfer of Functions) Act (Northern Ireland) 2010 section 3(1) and Sch 1, paras 25–26, with effect from 6 April 2010 (see the Pensions Regulator Tribunal (Transfer of Functions) (2010 Act) (Commencement) Order (Northern Ireland) 2010 SR 2010/101, Art 2). Transitional arrangements are set out in Sch 5 of SI 2010/22 in relation to England, Wales and Scotland and Sch 2 of the Pensions Regulator Tribunal (Transfer of Functions) Act (Northern Ireland) 2010 in relation to Northern Ireland.

[e]  Paragraph 5 amended by the Treaty of Lisbon (Changes in Terminology) Order 2011, SI 2011/1043 Article 6(1)(e) with effect from 22 April 2011. The amendment does not apply to a reference that relates only to things done before 1 December 2009 (the date on which the Treaty of Lisbon entered into force) and does not affect any other reference in its application to things done before that date: Ibid. Art 3(3).

COMMENCEMENT DATE: 1 July 2009

**48.Sch2.02**   Section 948(2) imposes a statutory duty of confidentiality on the Panel on Takeovers and Mergers in respect of information relating to the private affairs of an individual or which relates to any particular business. Basically, information is prohibited from being disclosed 'during the lifetime of the individual' if it relates to his private affairs and, in respect of a business, 'so long as the business continues to be carried on'. For further details, see the commentary on section 948 in Chapter 28.

**48.Sch2.03**   Notwithstanding this general protection for confidential information, it may be necessary or expedient for the Panel to disclose information obtained by it. Section 948(3) accordingly permits the disclosures set out in Schedule 2. Section 948(4) enables the Secretary of State to amend the schedule by statutory instrument. The Schedule was amended by the Companies Act 2006 (Amendment of Schedule 2) Order 2009[13] with effect from 1 March 2009 to permit disclosures by the Panel consequent to the extension of Part 28 to the Isle of Man. The Companies Act 2006 (Amendment of Schedule 2) (No 2) Order 2009,[14] replaced Schedule 2 with the text set out above with effect from 1 July 2009. The reason was to permit the Panel to disclose information to persons exercising functions of a public nature in Jersey and Guernsey. The previous amendments in relation to the Isle of Man were re-enacted. The Schedule may also be amended by primary legislation.[15]

**48.Sch2.04**   Schedule 2 does not cover all permitted disclosures and the reader is referred to sections 948(3)(a), 948(6), and 948(8) discussed in the commentary. Section 948(9) should also be noted. This provision prohibits any disclosure if it would contravene the Data Protection Act 1998, and operates to override any right to disclose the information. As the Data Protection Act 1998 applies to personal data it will only be relevant to commercial information where this contains data about identifiable individuals.

**48.Sch2.05**   Part 1 of Schedule 2 permits disclosures to specified persons. The Panel may disclose any information covered by section 948(2) to the persons listed in Part 1. The Act does not impose any further requirements in respect of such disclosure, for example by requiring the disclosure to be necessary or appropriate for the performance of the recipient's public duties. Theoretically, judicial review would be available if the person to whom the information relates was aware of the Panel's intention to disclose the information in advance, and such disclosure was unreasonable, or in bad faith.[16] In practice, it is very unlikely that a person will have advance notice of the Panel's intentions. Disclosure for an improper

---

13  SI 2009/202.

14  SI 2009/1208.

15  The Legal Services Act 2007 amended, prospectively, Sch 2 as originally enacted.

16  The claimant would need to rely on a recognized ground for judicial review.

purpose is not itself civilly actionable unless the disclosure constitutes a nominate tort eg misfeasance in public office.[17] The liability of the Panel is considered in the commentary on section 961.

**48.Sch2.06**    The persons covered by Part 1 are all public officers. The list is divided into persons in (a) the United Kingdom, (b) Jersey, (c) Guernsey, and (d) the Isle of Man.

**48.Sch2.07**    The persons to whom disclosure may be made in the United Kingdom include the Financial Services Authority (and, following its abolition, the Financial Conduct Authority and the Prudential Regulation Authority). The Panel may therefore disclose information it obtains indicating a breach of the Listing Rules, market abuse, or, in the case of an authorized person, contraventions of the FSA's Handbook of Rules and Guidance. The inclusion of a police constable, as well as other law enforcement officials, permits the Panel to disclose suspicions of criminal conduct. This could include offences in connection with a bid (eg a failure to comply with rules about bid documentation), insider dealing, market manipulation, or fraud. Disclosure may also be made to the Secretary of State. An example where this could be relevant is if the circumstances indicate that it may be appropriate to appoint inspectors to investigate the affairs of a company.

**48.Sch2.08**    Section 962 provides that a statement made by a person in response to a requirement under section 947(1), or an order made by the court to secure compliance with such a requirement, may not be used against him in criminal proceedings in which he is charged with an offence. An exception applies to cases of perjury. The effect of section 962 is that such a statement cannot be made the basis for a criminal prosecution (other than for perjury). It follows that if the information is passed on to law enforcement bodies under section 948, then it cannot be used in a prosecution. However, such information may be used in an investigation, and the information may assist the police or other authorities in obtaining admissible evidence of the commission of a crime. Section 962 does not apply to the market abuse regime (which is not treated as criminal under English law) nor to the imposition of regulatory sanctions for contraventions of the FSA's rules including the Principles for Businesses. Whether such a person could rely on the privilege against self-incrimination in such a case is outside the scope of this work.[18]

**48.Sch2.09**    In relation to Jersey the persons to whom disclosure may be made include specified ministers, the Jersey Financial Services Commission, the Attorney General, the Viscount and the police. The list in relation to Guernsey is similar including government departments, the Guernsey Financial Services Commission, the Procureur, and the police. The panel may make disclosures to government departments, the Financial Supervision Commission, the Attorney General, and the police in the Isle of Man.

**48.Sch2.10**    Part 2 lists disclosures that may be made by the Panel. Two requirements must be met in respect of disclosures under Part 2. First, the disclosure must be made to a specified person. Secondly, the disclosure must generally be either:

- 'for the purpose of enabling or assisting' that person in his public function; or
- 'with a view to the institution of, or otherwise for the purposes of' civil, criminal or disciplinary proceedings.

The effect is to restrict the purpose for which disclosures may be made. However, this does not mean that if a disclosure is not made for the specified purpose that the person will have a civil remedy. Judicial review is theoretically available, although for the reasons given in paragraph 48 Sch 2.05 above this is unlikely to provide an effective remedy. Nor are damages available unless the claimant can prove misfeasance in public office or other tortious wrongdoing by the Panel. Such a wrongful disclosure may result in criminal prosecution under section 949, and it seems intended that this is the primary deterrent against improper disclosure.

**48.Sch2.11**    There are separate lists for the United Kingdom, Jersey, Guernsey, and the Isle of Man. In addition, Part 2 includes a number of general disclosures that may be made. These include to enable or assist the ECB or the central bank of any country outside the British Islands to exercise its functions,[19] and a disclosure for the purpose of, enabling or assisting an overseas regulatory authority to exercise its regulatory functions.[20] Disclosures with a view to the institution of, or for the purposes of criminal proceedings anywhere are also permitted.[21]

---

[17]   *Three Rivers District Council v Governor and Company of the Bank of England* [2003] 2 AC 1.
[18]   See eg C Passmore, *Privilege*, 3rd edn (St Albans, 2012) and B Thanki et al, *Law of Privilege*, 2nd edn (Oxford, 2011). Generally privilege does not apply to disciplinary proceedings: *R (on the application of Fleurose) v Securities and Futures Authority Ltd* [2002] IRLR 297.
[19]   Schedule 2, Part 2(E), para 1.
[20]   Schedule 2, Part 2(E), para 2.
[21]   Schedule 2, Part 2(E), para 3.

Finally, Part 3 permits disclosure to overseas regulatory bodies. There are two requirements:  **48.Sch2.12**

- it is made to a person or body exercising relevant functions; and
- it is made for the purpose of enabling or assisting that person or body to exercise those functions.

Part 3 applies to overseas bodies exercising functions of a public nature, under legislation in a country or territory outside of the United Kingdom, that appear to the Panel to be similar to its own functions, or those of the Financial Services Authority (or, following its abolition, the functions of the Financial Conduct Authority or the Prudential Regulation Authority, or similar to the regulatory functions of the bank of England). This is a subjective test as the Panel may make the disclosure if it considers that the relevant overseas body exercises functions similar to its functions or to those of the FSA. There is no requirement that the body does in fact exercise such powers. The disclosure must also be made for the purpose of enabling or assisting the overseas regulator to exercise its functions. Paragraph 2 sets out factors that the Panel must take into account including the use the body will make of the information and whether it has adequate arrangements in place to prevent subsequent disclosure.

Schedule 2 is only concerned with disclosure by the Panel. Section 948(6) permits disclosure by a  **48.Sch2.13** person to whom the Panel has disclosed information, thereby broadening the range of persons to whom information may be disclosed. Section 948(6) applies where a disclosure has been made to the Financial Services Authority, an authority designated as a supervisory authority for the purposes of Article 4.1 of the Takeovers Directive or any other person or body that exercises functions of a public nature in an EEA State other than the UK that are similar to the Panel's functions or to those of the FSA.[22] Section 948(6)(a) permits the further disclosure by such a person. Section 948(6)(b) allows the disclosure of information by anyone who has obtained it directly or indirectly from such a person. Once information has been obtained by the Panel it may subsequently be disseminated to a wide range of persons.

## SCHEDULE 4     Section 1144(1)

### DOCUMENTS AND INFORMATION SENT OR SUPPLIED TO A COMPANY

### PART 1
### INTRODUCTION

*Application of Schedule*  **48.Sch4.01**

1  (1) This Schedule applies to documents or information sent or supplied to a company.
   (2) It does not apply to documents or information sent or supplied by another company (see section 1144(3) and Schedule 5).

### PART 2
### COMMUNICATIONS IN HARD COPY FORM

*Introduction*

2  A document or information is validly sent or supplied to a company if it is sent or supplied in hard copy form in accordance with this Part of this Schedule.

*Method of communication in hard copy form*

3  (1) A document or information in hard copy form may be sent or supplied by hand or by post to an address (in accordance with paragraph 4).
   (2) For the purposes of this Schedule, a person sends a document or information by post if he posts a prepaid envelope containing the document or information.

---

[22] Section 948(7). The Financial Services Act 2012 will substitute a reference to '(a) the Financial Conduct Authority; (aa) the Prudential Regulation Authority; (ab) the Bank of England' from such day as the Treasury may by order appoint: Sched 18, para 123.

*Address for communications in hard copy form*

**4** A document or information in hard copy form may be sent or supplied—
   (a) to an address specified by the company for the purpose;
   (b) to the company's registered office;
   (c) to an address to which any provision of the Companies Acts authorises the document or information to be sent or supplied.

## PART 3
## COMMUNICATIONS IN ELECTRONIC FORM

*Introduction*

**5** A document or information is validly sent or supplied to a company if it is sent or supplied in electronic form in accordance with this Part of this Schedule.

*Conditions for use of communications in electronic form*

**6** A document or information may only be sent or supplied to a company in electronic form if—
   (a) the company has agreed (generally or specifically) that the document or information may be sent or supplied in that form (and has not revoked that agreement), or
   (b) the company is deemed to have so agreed by a provision in the Companies Acts.

*Address for communications in electronic form*

**7** (1) Where the document or information is sent or supplied by electronic means, it may only be sent or supplied to an address—
   (a) specified for the purpose by the company (generally or specifically), or
   (b) deemed by a provision in the Companies Acts to have been so specified.
   (2) Where the document or information is sent or supplied in electronic form by hand or by post, it must be sent or supplied to an address to which it could be validly sent if it were in hard copy form.

## PART 4
## OTHER AGREED FORMS OF COMMUNICATION

**8** A document or information that is sent or supplied to a company otherwise than in hard copy form or electronic form is validly sent or supplied if it is sent or supplied in a form or manner that has been agreed by the company.

COMMENCEMENT DATE 20 January 2007[23]

**48.Sch4.02** Schedule 4 contains the rules concerning the documents or information sent or supplied to a company (other than by another company: para 1(2)). As prefaced in section 1143, the Schedule provides for alternative forms of communication, hard copy and electronic.[24] Each provides a valid method of the supply of information or documentation provided the requirements of the Schedule are satisfied: see para 2 for hard copy form and para 5 for electronic communication. It should be noted, however, that hard copy form will always be acceptable, but electronic communication is only allowed either if the company has agreed that the document or information may be sent to it in that form and has not revoked that agreement (which may be specific or general) or if the company is deemed to have so agreed by reason of some other provision of the Act (para 6).

---

[23] Companies Act 2006 (Commencement No 1 Transitional Provisions and Savings) Order 2006, SI 2006/3428, art 3(1)(e).
[24] These terms are defined in s 1168 of the Act. Hard copy means in a paper copy or similar form capable of being read (s 1168(2)). Electronic form means by electronic means (such as e-mail or fax) (s 1168(3)(a)) or by any other means while in electronic form (such as sending a disk or CD through the post). (s 1168(3)(b)). 'Electronic means' is further defined in s 1168(4) as sent initially and received by means of electronic equipment for the processing or storage of data *and* entirely transmitted, conveyed, and received by wire, radio, optical, or other electromagnetic means. The provisions of s 1168(5) and (6) are repeated in Schs 4 and 5. S 1168(7) makes it clear that the definitions apply to all provisions about the sending or supply of documents or information whatever expression is actually used. In fact the Act already contains a very similar provision in s 1148(2).

Supply in hard copy form involves sending or supplying a document or information by hand or by post **48.Sch4.03**
to an address (para 3(1)). If the postal route is chosen then the envelope containing the document or
information must be prepaid and posted (para 3(2)). The relevant address is either one specified by the
company for the purpose, the company's registered office, or any address to which the supply or
sending of documents or information is authorized by the Act (para 4).

Supply in electronic form also requires the sending or supply of the document or information to an **48.Sch4.04**
address which must be one specified for the purpose by the company (para 7(1)) or one which it is
deemed to have so specified by another provision of the Act (para 7(2)). If the document is supplied in
electronic form by hand or post (such as sending a CD or other data storage device through the post)
the relevant address is that set out in para 4 dealing with hard copy communication.

A company may also agree to some form of communication other than in hard copy or electronic form **48.Sch4.05**
(para 8). The explanatory notes to the Act make it clear that this provision only applies if the Act does
not make some express provision for the method of communication such as in para 291(3)(a).

---

# SCHEDULE 5
## COMMUNICATIONS BY A COMPANY

Section 1144(2)

### PART 1
### INTRODUCTION

*Application of this Schedule*         

**1**    This Schedule applies to documents or information sent or supplied by a company.

### PART 2
### COMMUNICATIONS IN HARD COPY FORM

*Introduction*

**2**    A document or information is validly sent or supplied by a company if it is sent or supplied in hard
copy form in accordance with this Part of this Schedule.

*Method of communication in hard copy form*

**3**    (1) A document or information in hard copy form must be—
       (a) handed to the intended recipient, or
       (b) sent or supplied by hand or by post to an address (in accordance with paragraph 4).
   (2) For the purposes of this Schedule, a person sends a document or information by post if he
posts a prepaid envelope containing the document or information.

*Address for communications in hard copy form*

**4**    (1) A document or information in hard copy form may be sent or supplied by the company—
       (a) to an address specified for the purpose by the intended recipient;
       (b) to a company at its registered office;
       (c) to a person in his capacity as a member of the company at his address as shown in the
          company's register of members;
       (d) to a person in his capacity as a director of the company at his address as shown in the
          company's register of directors;
       (e) to an address to which any provision of the Companies Acts authorises the document or
          information to be sent or supplied.
   (2) Where the company is unable to obtain an address falling within sub-paragraph (1), the
document or information may be sent or supplied to the intended recipient's last address
known to the company.

### PART 3
### COMMUNICATIONS IN ELECTRONIC FORM

*Introduction*

**5**    A document or information is validly sent or supplied by a company if it is sent in electronic form
in accordance with this Part of this Schedule.

*Agreement to communications in electronic form*

**6**    A document or information may only be sent or supplied by a company in electronic form—

(a) to a person who has agreed (generally or specifically) that the document or information may be sent or supplied in that form (and has not revoked that agreement), or

(b) to a company that is deemed to have so agreed by a provision in the Companies Acts.

*Address for communications in electronic form*

**7** (1) Where the document or information is sent or supplied by electronic means, it may only be sent or supplied to an address—

(a) specified for the purpose by the intended recipient (generally or specifically), or

(b) where the intended recipient is a company, deemed by a provision of the Companies Acts to have been so specified.

(2) Where the document or information is sent or supplied in electronic form by hand or by post, it must be—

(a) handed to the intended recipient, or

(b) sent or supplied to an address to which it could be validly sent if it were in hard copy form.

PART 4
COMMUNICATIONS BY MEANS OF A WEBSITE

*Use of website*

**8** A document or information is validly sent or supplied by a company if it is made available on a website in accordance with this Part of this Schedule.

*Agreement to use of website*

**9** A document or information may only be sent or supplied by the company to a person by being made available on a website if the person—

(a) has agreed (generally or specifically) that the document or information may be sent or supplied to him in that manner, or

(b) is taken to have so agreed under—

(i) paragraph 10 (members of the company etc), or

(ii) paragraph 11 (debenture holders),
and has not revoked that agreement.

*Deemed agreement of members of company etc to use of website*

**10** (1) This paragraph applies to a document or information to be sent or supplied to a person—

(a) as a member of the company, or

(b) as a person nominated by a member in accordance with the company's articles to enjoy or exercise all or any specified rights of the member in relation to the company, or

(c) as a person nominated by a member under section 146 to enjoy information rights.

(2) To the extent that—

(a) the members of the company have resolved that the company may send or supply documents or information to members by making them available on a website, or

(b) the company's articles contain provision to that effect,
a person in relation to whom the following conditions are met is taken to have agreed that the company may send or supply documents or information to him in that manner.

(3) The conditions are that—

(a) the person has been asked individually by the company to agree that the company may send or supply documents or information generally, or the documents or information in question, to him by means of a website, and

(b) the company has not received a response within the period of 28 days beginning with the date on which the company's request was sent.

(4) A person is not taken to have so agreed if the company's request—

(a) did not state clearly what the effect of a failure to respond would be, or

(b) was sent less than twelve months after a previous request made to him for the purposes of this paragraph in respect of the same or a similar class of documents or information.

(5) Chapter 3 of Part 3 (resolutions affecting a company's constitution) applies to a resolution under this paragraph.

*Deemed agreement of debenture holders to use of website*

**11** (1) This paragraph applies to a document or information to be sent or supplied to a person as holder of a company's debentures.

(2) To the extent that—

(a) the relevant debenture holders have duly resolved that the company may send or supply documents or information to them by making them available on a website, or

(b) the instrument creating the debenture in question contains provision to that effect,

a debenture holder in relation to whom the following conditions are met is taken to have agreed that the company may send or supply documents or information to him in that manner.

(3) The conditions are that—

(a) the debenture holder has been asked individually by the company to agree that the company may send or supply documents or information generally, or the documents or information in question, to him by means of a website, and

(b) the company has not received a response within the period of 28 days beginning with the date on which the company's request was sent.

(4) A person is not taken to have so agreed if the company's request—

(a) did not state clearly what the effect of a failure to respond would be, or

(b) was sent less than twelve months after a previous request made to him for the purposes of this paragraph in respect of the same or a similar class of documents or information.

(5) For the purposes of this paragraph—

(a) the relevant debenture holders are the holders of debentures of the company ranking pari passu for all purposes with the intended recipient, and

(b) a resolution of the relevant debenture holders is duly passed if they agree in accordance with the provisions of the instruments creating the debentures.

*Availability of document or information*

**12** (1) A document or information authorised or required to be sent or supplied by means of a website must be made available in a form, and by a means, that the company reasonably considers will enable the recipient—

(a) to read it, and

(b) to retain a copy of it.

(2) For this purpose a document or information can be read only if—

(a) it can be read with the naked eye, or

(b) to the extent that it consists of images (for example photographs, pictures, maps, plans or drawings), it can be seen with the naked eye.

*Notification of availability*

**13** (1) The company must notify the intended recipient of—

(a) the presence of the document or information on the website,

(b) the address of the website,

(c) the place on the website where it may be accessed, and

(d) how to access the document or information.

(2) The document or information is taken to be sent—

(a) on the date on which the notification required by this paragraph is sent, or

(b) if later, the date on which the document or information first appears on the website after that notification is sent.

*Period of availability on website*

**14** (1) The company must make the document or information available on the website throughout—

(a) the period specified by any applicable provision of the Companies Acts, or

(b) if no such period is specified, the period of 28 days beginning with the date on which the notification required under paragraph 13 is sent to the person in question.

(2) For the purposes of this paragraph, a failure to make a document or information available on a website throughout the period mentioned in sub-paragraph (1) shall be disregarded if—

(a) it is made available on the website for part of that period, and

(b) the failure to make it available throughout that period is wholly attributable to circumstances that it would not be reasonable to have expected the company to prevent or avoid.

## PART 5
## OTHER AGREED FORMS OF COMMUNICATION

**15** A document or information that is sent or supplied otherwise than in hard copy or electronic form or by means of a website is validly sent or supplied if it is sent or supplied in a form or manner that has been agreed by the intended recipient.

PART 6
SUPPLEMENTARY PROVISIONS

*Joint holders of shares or debentures*

**16** (1) This paragraph applies in relation to documents or information to be sent or supplied to joint holders of shares or debentures of a company.

(2) Anything to be agreed or specified by the holder must be agreed or specified by all the joint holders.

(3) Anything authorised or required to be sent or supplied to the holder may be sent or supplied either—

(a) to each of the joint holders, or

(b) to the holder whose name appears first in the register of members or the relevant register of debenture holders.

(4) This paragraph has effect subject to anything in the company's articles.

*Death or bankruptcy of holder of shares*

**17** (1) This paragraph has effect in the case of the death or bankruptcy of a holder of a company's shares.

(2) Documents or information required or authorised to be sent or supplied to the member may be sent or supplied to the persons claiming to be entitled to the shares in consequence of the death or bankruptcy—

(a) by name, or

(b) by the title of representatives of the deceased, or trustee of the bankrupt, or by any like description,

at the address in the United Kingdom supplied for the purpose by those so claiming.

(3) Until such an address has been so supplied, a document or information may be sent or supplied in any manner in which it might have been sent or supplied if the death or bankruptcy had not occurred.

(4) This paragraph has effect subject to anything in the company's articles.

(5) References in this paragraph to the bankruptcy of a person include—

(a) the sequestration of the estate of a person;

(b) a person's estate being the subject of a protected trust deed (within the meaning of the Bankruptcy (Scotland) Act 1985 (c. 66)).

In such a case the reference in sub-paragraph (2)(b) to the trustee of the bankrupt is to be read as the permanent or interim trustee (within the meaning of that Act) on the sequestrated estate or, as the case may be, the trustee under the protected deed.

COMMENCEMENT DATE 20 January 2007[25]

**48.Sch5.02**  Schedule 5 contains the detailed rules concerning communications by companies. The opening seven sections of Schedule 5 are very similar in form to Schedule 4. First, as with Schedule 4 referred to above, the forms of communication covered are hard copy and electronic. Each provides a valid method of the supply of information or documentation provided the requirements of the Schedule are satisfied: see para 2 for hard copy form and para 5 for electronic communication. It should be noted, however, that hard copy form will always be acceptable but electronic communication is only allowed either if the person supplied has agreed that the document or information may be sent in that form and has not revoked that agreement (which may be specific or general), or (in the case of a corporate recipient) the company is deemed to have so agreed by reason of some other provision of the Act (para 6).

**48.Sch5.03**  Supply in hard copy form involves sending or supplying a document or information by hand or by post to an address (para 3(1)(b)) or the handing of it to the intended recipient (para 3(1)(a)). If the postal route is chosen then the envelope containing the document or information must be prepaid and posted (para 3(2)). The relevant address is either one specified by the recipient for the purpose, or a company's registered office (if the recipient is a company), or, in the case of documents or information sent or supplied to a member or director in his capacity as such, his address in the register of members or directors as appropriate, or any address to which the supply or sending of documents or information is authorized by the Act (para 4(1)). In the absence of an address falling within para 4(1), the documents or information may be sent or supplied to the intended recipient's last known address (para 4(2)).

**48.Sch5.04**  Supply in electronic form also requires the sending or supply of the document or information to an address specified for the purpose by the intended recipient (para 7(1)) or, in the case of a corporate recipient, one which that company is deemed to have so specified by another provision of the Act (para

---

Companies Act 2006 (Commencement No 1 Transitional Provisions and Savings) Order 2006, SI 2006/3428, art 3(1)(e).

7(2)). If the document is supplied in electronic form by hand or post the relevant address is that set out in para 4 dealing with hard copy communication (para 7(2)).

An intended recipient may agree to some form of communication other than in hard copy or electronic form (para 15). **48.Sch5.05**

The differences between Schedules 4 and 5 arise principally in the extended provisions of the latter covering communications by means of a website set out in paras 8 to 14. These provide that, subject to any other requirement of the Act, a document or information is validly sent or supplied if is it made available on a website (para 8). There are several conditions which a company must satisfy in order successfully to take advantage of the website provisions. **48.Sch5.06**

First, a person (which includes a member or holder of a debenture or debt security in the company) must have agreed or be taken to have agreed to the provision of documentation or information by means of a website, and that agreement must not have been revoked (para 9). This agreement will be deemed where three elements are present: (a) the recipient is a member (or a person identified by a member as entitled to exercise all or any specified rights of a member) (para 10(1)) *and* (b) either the company's articles provide that the company may send or supply documents or information by making them available on a website or the members have resolved that it can so supply or send documents or information (para 10(2)) *and* (c) where the company has asked a member or entitled person individually to agree that the company may communicate by means of a website and that person has not responded to the request within 28 days from the date on which the request was sent (para 10(3)). **48.Sch5.07**

A resolution as referred to in para 10(2) must be provided to the Registrar of Companies and incorporated to or annexed in any articles of association issued by the company (para 10(5) and sections 29 to 30 of the Act). **48.Sch5.08**

In order to be effective a request as referred to in para 10(3) must clearly state the effect of a failure to respond and must be made at least 12 months after any previous request (para 10(4)). **48.Sch5.09**

Para 11 provides similar provisions in relation to the deemed agreement of debenture holders to the use of a website. Such agreement is deemed either where the relevant debenture allows such communications (para 11(2)(b)), or where the debenture holders ranking *pari passu* with the intended recipient have resolved that such communication may be used (paras 11(2)(a) and (5)) or where a debenture holder has failed to respond to a request made to him individually to allow such communication (para 11(3)). The latter is subject to the same restrictions as set out in para 10(4) (para 11(4)). **48.Sch5.10**

Secondly, the document or information must be in such a form as the company reasonably considers will allow the recipient to read it and retain a copy of it (para 12(1)). Thus it must be capable of being read or seen by the naked eye (para 12(2)). **48.Sch5.11**

Thirdly, the company must notify the intended recipient of the presence of the document or information on the website, the address of the website, the place on the website where the information or document may be accessed, and how it can be accessed (para 13). Thus even a general agreement to communication by means of a website will require the company to draw the attention of intended recipients to the presence of particular documents or information on the website. It will not be enough for a company simply to say that, for example, all future notices of meetings or resolutions will be on the website. **48.Sch5.12**

Fourthly, the document or information must be available throughout any relevant period specified by the Act or, if there is no such period, 28 days beginning with the date the notification required by para 13 is sent to the intended recipient (para 14(1)). Para 14(2) creates an exception where the document or information is available for part of the relevant period if the period of unavailability is wholly attributable to circumstances that it would not be reasonable to have expected the company to prevent or avoid (para 14(2)). This is clearly an attempt to recognise the fallibility of websites. However, the standard set to take advantage of this exception is a high one as there must be no reason for the unavailability other than the unforeseen and unforeseeable circumstances. The boundaries of this exception will have to be set by the courts in due course but questions are likely to arise in relation to matters such as the failure of a website due to the number of hits being registered on it or the failure of a company to have contingency plans for things such as a server or ISP failure. **48.Sch5.13**

Schedule 5 also sets out how a company should deal with communication with joint holders of shares or debentures (para 16) and where a member dies or is made bankrupt (para 17). **48.Sch5.14**

SCHEDULE 6                                    Section 1159

MEANING OF 'SUBSIDIARY' ETC: SUPPLEMENTARY PROVISIONS

**48.Sch6.01**

*Introduction*

**1**  The provisions of this Part of this Schedule explain expressions used in section 1159 (meaning of 'subsidiary' etc) and otherwise supplement that section.

*Voting rights in a company*

**2**  In section 1159(1)(a) and (c) the references to the voting rights in a company are to the rights conferred on shareholders in respect of their shares or, in the case of a company not having a share capital, on members, to vote at general meetings of the company on all, or substantially all, matters.

*Right to appoint or remove a majority of the directors*

**3**  (1)  In section 1159(1)(b) the reference to the right to appoint or remove a majority of the board of directors is to the right to appoint or remove directors holding a majority of the voting rights at meetings of the board on all, or substantially all, matters.

(2)  A company shall be treated as having the right to appoint to a directorship if—

(a)  a person's appointment to it follows necessarily from his appointment as director of the company, or

(b)  the directorship is held by the company itself.

(3)  A right to appoint or remove which is exercisable only with the consent or concurrence of another person shall be left out of account unless no other person has a right to appoint or, as the case may be, remove in relation to that directorship.

*Rights exercisable only in certain circumstances or temporarily incapable of exercise*

**4**  (1)  Rights which are exercisable only in certain circumstances shall be taken into account only—

(a)  when the circumstances have arisen, and for so long as they continue to obtain, or

(b)  when the circumstances are within the control of the person having the rights.

(2)  Rights which are normally exercisable but are temporarily incapable of exercise shall continue to be taken into account.

*Rights held by one person on behalf of another*

**5**  Rights held by a person in a fiduciary capacity shall be treated as not held by him.

**6**  (1)  Rights held by a person as nominee for another shall be treated as held by the other.

(2)  Rights shall be regarded as held as nominee for another if they are exercisable only on his instructions or with his consent or concurrence.

*Rights attached to shares held by way of security*

**7**  Rights attached to shares held by way of security shall be treated as held by the person providing the security—

(a)  where apart from the right to exercise them for the purpose of preserving the value of the security, or of realising it, the rights are exercisable only in accordance with his instructions, and

(b)  where the shares are held in connection with the granting of loans as part of normal business activities and apart from the right to exercise them for the purpose of preserving the value of the security, or of realising it, the rights are exercisable only in his interests.

*Rights attributed to holding company*

**8**  (1)  Rights shall be treated as held by a holding company if they are held by any of its subsidiary companies.

(2)  Nothing in paragraph 6 or 7 shall be construed as requiring rights held by a holding company to be treated as held by any of its subsidiaries.

(3)  For the purposes of paragraph 7 rights shall be treated as being exercisable in accordance with the instructions or in the interests of a company if they are exercisable in accordance with the instructions of or, as the case may be, in the interests of—

(a)  any subsidiary or holding company of that company, or

(b)  any subsidiary of a holding company of that company.

*Disregard of certain rights*

**9**  The voting rights in a company shall be reduced by any rights held by the company itself.

*Supplementary*

**10**  References in any provision of paragraphs 5 to 9 to rights held by a person include rights falling to be treated as held by him by virtue of any other provision of those paragraphs but not rights which by virtue of any such provision are to be treated as not held by him.

See annotation to section 1159. This amplifies the definition of subsidiary as found in section 1159. It   **48.Sch6.02**
contains material formerly found in the Companies Act 1985 section 736A. On paragraph 6 see
*Michaels v Harley House (Marylebone) Ltd* [1999] BCC 967.

---

S C H E D U L E  7                             Section 1162

P A R E N T  A N D  S U B S I D I A R Y  U N D E R T A K I N G S :  S U P P L E M E N T A R Y

P R O V I S I O N S

*Introduction*                                                                                **48.Sch7.01**

**1**    The provisions of this Schedule explain expressions used in section 1162 (parent and subsidiary
undertakings) and otherwise supplement that section.

*Voting rights in an undertaking*

**2**    (1) In section 1162(2)(a) and (d) the references to the voting rights in an undertaking are to the
rights conferred on shareholders in respect of their shares or, in the case of an undertaking not
having a share capital, on members, to vote at general meetings of the undertaking on all, or
substantially all, matters.

(2) In relation to an undertaking which does not have general meetings at which matters are
decided by the exercise of voting rights the references to holding a majority of the voting rights
in the undertaking shall be construed as references to having the right under the constitution
of the undertaking to direct the overall policy of the undertaking or to alter the terms of its
constitution.

*Right to appoint or remove a majority of the directors*

**3**    (1) In section 1162(2)(b) the reference to the right to appoint or remove a majority of the board
of directors is to the right to appoint or remove directors holding a majority of the voting rights
at meetings of the board on all, or substantially all, matters.

(2) An undertaking shall be treated as having the right to appoint to a directorship if —
   (a) a person's appointment to it follows necessarily from his appointment as director of the
   undertaking, or
   (b) the directorship is held by the undertaking itself.

(3) A right to appoint or remove which is exercisable only with the consent or concurrence of
another person shall be left out of account unless no other person has a right to appoint or,
as the case may be, remove in relation to that directorship.

*Right to exercise dominant influence*

**4**    (1) For the purposes of section 1162(2)(c) an undertaking shall not be regarded as having the right
to exercise a dominant influence over another undertaking unless it has a right to give directions
with respect to the operating and financial policies of that other undertaking which its directors
are obliged to comply with whether or not they are for the benefit of that other undertaking.

(2) A 'control contract' means a contract in writing conferring such a right which—
   (a) is of a kind authorised by the articles of the undertaking in relation to which the right is
   exercisable, and
   (b) is permitted by the law under which that undertaking is established.

(3) This paragraph shall not be read as affecting the construction of section 1162(4)(a).

*Rights exercisable only in certain circumstances or temporarily incapable of exercise*

**5**    (1) Rights which are exercisable only in certain circumstances shall be taken into account only—
   (a) when the circumstances have arisen, and for so long as they continue to obtain, or
   (b) when the circumstances are within the control of the person having the rights.

(2) Rights which are normally exercisable but are temporarily incapable of exercise shall continue
to be taken into account.

*Rights held by one person on behalf of another*

**6**    Rights held by a person in a fiduciary capacity shall be treated as not held by him.

**7**    (1) Rights held by a person as nominee for another shall be treated as held by the other.

(2) Rights shall be regarded as held as nominee for another if they are exercisable only on his
instructions or with his consent or concurrence.

*Rights attached to shares held by way of security*

**8**    Rights attached to shares held by way of security shall be treated as held by the person providing
the security—
   (a) where apart from the right to exercise them for the purpose of preserving the value of the security, or of realising it, the rights are exercisable only in accordance with his instructions, and

    (b) where the shares are held in connection with the granting of loans as part of normal business activities and apart from the right to exercise them for the purpose of preserving the value of the security, or of realising it, the rights are exercisable only in his interests.

*Rights attributed to parent undertaking*

9  (1) Rights shall be treated as held by a parent undertaking if they are held by any of its subsidiary undertakings.

    (2) Nothing in paragraph 7 or 8 shall be construed as requiring rights held by a parent undertaking to be treated as held by any of its subsidiary undertakings.

    (3) For the purposes of paragraph 8 rights shall be treated as being exercisable in accordance with the instructions or in the interests of an undertaking if they are exercisable in accordance with the instructions of or, as the case may be, in the interests of any group undertaking.

*Disregard of certain rights*

10  The voting rights in an undertaking shall be reduced by any rights held by the undertaking itself.

*Supplementary*

11  References in any provision of paragraphs 6 to 10 to rights held by a person include rights falling to be treated as held by him by virtue of any other provision of those paragraphs but not rights which by virtue of any such provision are to be treated as not held by him.

**48.Sch7.02**  See annotation to section 1162. This schedule, which reproduces elements of the former Schedule 10A to the Companies Act 1985, supplements section 1127. On paragraph 6 see *Michaels v Harley House (Marylebone) Ltd.*[26]

---

S C H E D U L E   8            Section 1174

I N D E X   O F   D E F I N E D   E X P R E S S I O N S

**48.Sch8.01**

| | |
|---|---|
| abbreviated accounts (in Part 15) | sections 444(4) and 445(3) |
| accounting reference date and accounting reference period | section 391 |
| accounting standards (in Part 15) | section 464 |
| accounts meeting | section 437(3) |
| acquisition, in relation to a non-cash asset | section 1163(2) |
| address | |
|    —generally in the Companies Acts | section 1142 |
|    —in the company communications provisions | section 1148(1) |
| affirmative resolution procedure, in relation to regulations and orders | section 1290 |
| allotment (time of) | section 558 |
| allotment of equity securities (in Chapter 3 of Part 17) | section 560(2) [and (3)][27] |
| allotted share capital and allotted shares | section 546(1)(b) and (2) |
| annual accounts (in Part 15) | section 471 |
| annual accounts and reports (in Part 15) | section 471 |
| annual general meeting | section 336 |
| annual return | section 854 |
| appropriate audit authority (in sections 522, 523 and 524) | section 525(1) |
| appropriate rate of interest | |
|    —in Chapter 5 of Part 17 | section 592 |
|    —in Chapter 6 of Part 17 | section 609 |
| approval after being made, in relation to regulations and orders | section 1291 |
| arrangement | |
|    —in Part 26 | section 616(1) |
|    —in Chapter 7 of Part 17 | section 895(2) |

---

[26] [1999] BCC 967. Section 1162 and Sch 7 apply with modifications to LLPs by reg 52 of the Limited Liability Partnerships (Accounts and Audit) (Application of Companies Act 2006) Regulations 2008, SI 2008/1911.

[27] Amended by the Companies Act 2006 (Allotment of Shares and Right of Pre-emption) (Amendment) Regulations 2009, SI 2009/2561, reg 2.

| | |
|---|---|
| articles | section 18 |
| associate (in Chapter 3 of Part 28) | section 988 |
| associated bodies corporate and associated company (in Part 10) | section 256 |
| authenticated, in relation to a document or information sent or supplied to a company | section 1146 |
| authorised group, of members of a company (in Part 14) | section 370(3) |
| authorised insurance company | section 1165(2) |
| authorised minimum (in relation to share capital of public company) | section 763 |
| available profits (in Chapter 5 of Part 18) | sections 711 and 712 |
| banking company and banking group | section 1164 |
| body corporate | section 1173(1) |
| called-up share capital | section 547 |
| capital redemption reserve | section 733 |
| capitalisation in relation to a company's profits (in Part 23) | section 853(3) |
| cash (in relation to paying up or allotting shares) | section 583 |
| cause of action, in relation to derivative proceedings (in'Chapter 2 of Part 11) | section 265(7) |
| certified translation (in Part 35) | section 1107 |
| charge (in Chapter 1 of Part 25) | section 861(5) |
| circulation date, in relation to a written resolution (in Part 13) | section 290 |
| class of shares | section 629 |
| the Companies Acts | section 2 |
| Companies Act accounts | sections 395(1)(a) and 403(2)(a) |
| Companies Act group accounts | section 403(2)(a) |
| Companies Act individual accounts | section 395(1)(a) |
| companies involved in the division (in Part 27) | section 919(2) |
| company | |
| —generally in the Companies Acts | section 1 |
| —in Chapter 7 of Part 17 | section 616(1) |
| —in Chapter 1 of Part 25 | section 861(5) |
| —in Chapter 2 of Part 25 | section 879(6) |
| —in Part 26 | section 895(2) |
| —in Chapter 3 of Part 28 | section 991(1) |
| —in the company communications provisions | section 1148(1) |
| the company communications provisions | section 1143 |
| the company law provisions of this Act | section 2(2) |
| company records (in Part 37) | section 1134 |
| connected with, in relation to a director (in Part 10) | sections 252 to 254 |
| constitution, of a company | |
| —generally in the Companies Acts | section 17 |
| —in Part 10 | section 257 |
| [contributory | section 1170B][28] |
| controlling, of a body corporate by a director (in Part 10) | section 255 |
| [corporate governance statement and separate corporate governance statement | |
| —in Part 15] | [section 472A] |
| [—in Part 16] | section 538A[29] |
| corporation | section 1173(1) |
| the court | section 1156 |
| credit institution | section 1173(1) |
| credit transaction (in Chapter 4 of Part 10) | section 202 |
| creditor (in Chapter 1 of Part 31) | section 1011 |
| daily default fine | section 1125 |
| date of the offer (in Chapter 3 of Part 28) | section 991(1) |

[28] Inserted by the Companies Act 2006 (Consequential Amendments, Transitional Provisions and Savings) Order 2009, SI 2009/1941, Sch 1, para 260.
[29] Inserted by the Companies Act 2006 (Accounts, Reports and Audit) Regulations 2009, SI 2009/1581, reg 9.

| | |
|---|---|
| debenture | section 738 |
| derivative claim (in Chapter 1 of Part 11) | section 260 |
| derivative proceedings (in Chapter 2 of Part 11) | section 265 |
| Directive disclosure requirements | section 1078 |
| director | |
|    —generally in the Companies Acts | section 250 |
|    —in Chapter 8 of Part 10 | section 240(3) |
|    —in Chapter 1 of Part 11 | section 260(5) |
|    —in Chapter 2 of Part 11 | section 265(7) |
|    —in Part 14 | section 379(1) |
| directors' remuneration report | section 420 |
| directors' report | section 415 |
| distributable profits | |
|    —in Chapter 2 of Part 18 | section 683(1) |
|    —elsewhere in Part 18 | section 736 |
| distribution | |
|    —in Chapter 2 of Part 18 | section 683(1) |
|    —in Part 23 | section 829 |
| division (in Part 27) | section 919 |
| document | |
|    —in Part 35 | section 1114(1) |
|    —in the company communications provisions | section 1148(1) |
| dormant, in relation to a company or other body corporate | section 1169 |
| EEA State and related expressions | section 1170 |
| electronic form, electronic copy, electronic means | |
|    —generally in the Companies Acts | section 1168(3) and (4) |
|    —in relation to communications to a company | Part 3 of Schedule 4 |
|    —in relation to communications by a company | Part 3 of Schedule 5 |
| eligible members, in relation to a written resolution | section 289 |
| e-money issuer | |
|    —in Part 15 | section 474(1) |
|    —in Part 16 | section 539 |
| employees' share scheme | section 1166 |
| employer and employee (in Chapter 1 of Part 18) | section 676 |
| enactment | section 1293 |
| equity securities (in Chapter 3 of Part 17) | section 560(1) |
| equity share capital | section 548 |
| equity shares (in Chapter 7 of Part 17) | section 616(1) |
| [establishment of an overseas company (in Part 35)] | [section 1067(6)][30] |
| existing company (in Part 27) | section 902(2) |
| fellow subsidiary undertakings | section 1161(4) |
| financial assistance (in Chapter 2 of Part 18) | section 677 |
| financial institution | section 1173(1) |
| financial year, of a company | section 390 |
| firm | section 1173(1) |
| fixed assets (in Part 23) | section 853 |
| the former Companies Acts | section 1171 |
| the Gazette | section 1173(1) |
| group (in Part 15) | section 474(1) |
| group undertaking | section 1161(5) |
| hard copy form and hard copy | |
|    —generally in the Companies Acts | section 1168(2) |
|    —in relation to communications to a company | Part 2 of Schedule 4 |
|    —in relation to communications by a company | Part 2 of Schedule 5 |
| hire-purchase agreement | section 1173(1) |
| holder of shares (in Chapter 3 of Part 17) | section 574 |
| holding company | section 1159 (and see section 1160 and Schedule 6) |

---

[30] Inserted by the Companies Act 2006 (Part 35) (Consequential Amendments, Transitional Provisions and Savings) Order 2009, arts 2, 17.

| | |
|---|---|
| IAS accounts | sections 395(1)(b) and 403(1) and (2)(b) |
| IAS group accounts | section 403(1) and (2)(b) |
| IAS individual accounts | section 395(1)(b) |
| IAS Regulation (in Part 15) | section 474(1) |
| included in the consolidation, in relation to group accounts (in Part 15) | section 474(1) |
| individual accounts | section 394 |
| information rights (in Part 9) | section 146(3) |
| insurance company | section 1165(3) |
| insurance group | section 1165(5) |
| insurance market activity | section 1165(7) |
| interest in shares (for the purposes of Part 22) | sections 820 to 825 |
| international accounting standards (in Part 15) | section 474(1) |
| investment company (in Part 23) | section 833 |
| [...][31] | |
|    —in Part 15 | section 474(1) |
|    —in Part 16 | section 539 |
| issued share capital and issued shares | section 546(1)(a) and (2) |
| the issuing company (in Chapter 7 of Part 17) | section 610(6) |
| the Joint Stock Companies Acts | section 1171 |
| liabilities (in Part 27) | section 941 |
| liability, references to incurring, reducing or discharging (in Chapter 2 of Part 18) | section 683(2) |
| limited by guarantee | section 3(3) |
| limited by shares | section 3(2) |
| limited company | section 3 |
| the main register (of members) (in Chapter 3 of Part 8) | section 131(1) |
| major audit (in sections 522 and 525) | section 525(2) |
| market purchase, by a company of its own shares (in Chapter 4 of Part 18) | section 693(4) |
| member, of a company | |
|    —generally in the Companies Acts | section 112 |
|    —in Chapter 1 of Part 11 | section 260(5) |
|    —in Chapter 2 of Part 11 | section 265(7) |
| memorandum of association | section 8 |
| merger (in Part 27) | section 904 |
| merging companies (in Part 27) | section 904(2) |
| merger by absorption (in Part 27) | section 904(1)(a) |
| merger by formation of a new company (in Part 27) | section 904(1)(b) |
| [MiFID investment firm | |
|    —in Part 15 | section 474(1) |
|    —in Part 16 | section 539][32] |
| negative resolution procedure, in relation to regulations and orders | section 1289 |
| net assets (in Part 7) | section 92 |
| new company (in Part 27) | section 902(2) |
| non-cash asset | section 1163 |
| [non-traded company (in Part 24) | section 855(4)][33] |
| non-voting shares (in Chapter 3 of Part 28) | section 991(1) |
| number, in relation to shares | section 540(4)(b) |
| off-market purchase, by a company of its own shares (in Chapter 4 of Part 18) | section 693(2) |
| offer period (in Chapter 2 of Part 28) | section 971(1) |
| offer to the public (in Chapter 1 of Part 20) | section 756 |
| offeror | |

[31] Repealed by the Markets in Financial Instruments Directive (Consequential Amendments) Regulations 2007, SI 2007/2932, reg 3.

[32] Inserted by the Markets in Financial Instruments Directive (Consequential Amendments) Regulations 2007, SI 2007/2932, reg 3.

[33] Inserted by the Companies Act 2006 (Annual Return and Service Addresses) Regulations 2008, SI 2008/3000, reg 9.

---

[34] Inserted by the Companies Act 2006 (Consequential Amendments, Transitional Provisions and Savings) Order 2009, SI 2009/1941, Sch 1, para 260.

| | |
|---|---|
| —in England and Wales and Northern Ireland | section 869 |
| —in Scotland | section 885 |
| register of directors | section 162 |
| register of directors' residential addresses | section 165 |
| register of members | section 113 |
| register of secretaries | section 275 |
| [...][35] [registered number, of a company (or overseas company)] | [section 1066 (and section 1059A(5))][36] |
| [...][37] [registered number, of a UK establishment of an overseas company] | [section 1067][38] |
| registered office, of a company | section 86 |
| registrar and registrar of companies | section 1060 |
| registrar's index of company names | section 1099 |
| registrar's rules | section 1117 |
| registration in a particular part of the United Kingdom | section 1060(4) |
| regulated activity | |
| —generally in the Companies Acts | section 1173(1) |
| —in Part 15 | section 474(1) |
| regulated market | section 1173(1) |
| relevant accounts (in Part 23) | section 836(2) |
| requirements for proper delivery (in Part 35) | section 1072 (and see section 1073) |
| requirements of this Act | section 1172 |
| [return period] | [section 855(4)][39] |
| securities (and related expressions) | |
| —in Chapter 1 of Part 20 | section 755(5) |
| —in Chapter 2 of Part 21 | section 783 |
| senior statutory auditor | section 504 |
| sent or supplied, in relation to documents or information (in the company communications provisions) | section 1148(2) and (3) |
| service address | section 1141 |
| service contract, of a director (in Part 10) | section 227 |
| shadow director | section 251 |
| share | |
| —generally in the Companies Acts | section 540 (and see section 1161(2)) |
| —in Part 22 | section 792 |
| —in section 1162 and Schedule 7 | section 1162(7) |
| share capital, company having a | section 545 |
| share exchange ratio | |
| —in Chapter 2 of Part 27 | section 905(2) |
| —in Chapter 3 of Part 27 | section 920(2) |
| share premium account | section 610(1) |
| share warrant | section 779(1) |
| [small companies exemption (in relation to directors' report)] | [section 415A][40] |
| small companies regime, for accounts | section 381 |
| solvency statement (in sections 641 to 644) | section 643 |
| special notice, in relation to a resolution | section 312 |
| special resolution | section 283 |
| statutory accounts | section 434(3) |

---

[35] 'Registered number of a branch of an overseas company' repealed by the Companies Act 2006 (Part 35) (Consequential Amendments, Transitional Provisions and Savings) Order 2009 (SI 2009/1802) arts 2, 17.

[36] Inserted by the Companies Act 2006 (Part 35) (Consequential Amendments, Transitional Provisions and Savings) Order 2009, SI 2009/1802, arts 2, 17.

[37] 'Registered number of a company' repealed by the Companies Act 2006 (Part 35) (Consequential Amendments, Transitional Provisions and Savings) Order 2009, SI 2009/1802, arts 2, 17.

[38] Inserted by the Companies Act 2006 (Part 35) (Consequential Amendments, Transitional Provisions and Savings) Order 2009 (SI 2009/1802) arts 2, 17

[39] Inserted by Companies Act 2006 (Annual Return and Service Addresses) Regulations 2008, SI 2008/3000, reg 9.

[40] Inserted by the Companies Act 2006 (Amendment) (Accounts and Reports) Regulations 2008, SI 2008/393, reg 6.

| | |
|---|---|
| subsidiary | section 1159 (and see section 1160 and Schedule 6) |
| subsidiary undertaking | section 1162 (and see Schedule 7) |
| summary financial statement | section 426 |
| takeover bid (in Chapter 2 of Part 28) | section 971(1) |
| takeover offer (in Chapter 3 of Part 28) | section 974 |
| the Takeovers Directive | |
| —in Chapter 1 of Part 28 | section 943(8) |
| —in Chapter 2 of Part 28 | section 971(1) |
| trading certificate | section 761(1) |
| [traded company in Part 13] | [section 360C][41] |
| [traded company (in Part 24)] | [section 855(4)][42] |
| transfer, in relation to a non-cash asset | section 1163(2) |
| treasury shares | section 724(5) |
| turnover | |
| —in Part 15 | section 474(1) |
| —in Part 16 | section 539 |
| UCITS management company | |
| —in Part 15 | section 474(1) |
| —in Part 16 | section 539 |
| [UK-establishment of an overseas company (Part 35)] | [section 1067(6)][43] |
| UK-registered company | section 1158 |
| uncalled share capital | section 547 |
| unconditional, in relation to a contract to acquire shares (in Chapter 3 of Part 28) | section 991(2) |
| undistributable reserves | section 831(4) |
| undertaking | section 1161(1) |
| unique identifier | section 1082 |
| unlimited company | section 3 |
| unquoted company (in Part 15) | section 385 |
| voting rights | |
| —in Chapter 2 of Part 28 | section 971(1) |
| —in Chapter 3 of Part 28 | section 991(1) |
| —in section 1159 and Schedule 6 | paragraph 2 of Schedule 6 |
| —in section 1162 and Schedule 7 | paragraph 2 of Schedule 7 |
| voting shares | |
| —in Chapter 2 of Part 28 | section 971(1) |
| —in Chapter 3 of Part 28 | section 991(1) |
| website, communication by a company by means of | Part 4 of Schedule 5 |
| Welsh company | section 88 |
| wholly-owned subsidiary | section 1159(2) (and see section 1160 and Schedule 6) |
| working day, in relation to a company | section 1173(1) |
| written resolution | section 288 |

**48.Sch8.02**    This is a useful index of common terms. See annotation to section 1174.

---

[41] Inserted by the Companies (Shareholders' Rights) Regulations 2009, SI 2009/1632, reg 21(2).

[42] Inserted by the Companies Act 2006 (Annual Return and Service Addresses) Regulations 2008, SI 2008/3000, reg 9.

[43] Inserted by the Companies Act 2006 (Part 35) (Consequential Amendments, Transitional Provisions and Savings) Order 2009, SI 2009/1802, arts 2, 17.

SCHEDULE **9**        Section 1175

REMOVAL OF SPECIAL PROVISIONS ABOUT ACCOUNTS AND
AUDIT OF CHARITABLE COMPANIES

PART 1
THE COMPANIES ACT 1985 (C. 6)

**1**   In section 240 (requirements in connection with publication of accounts)—        **48.Sch9.01**

     (a) in subsection (1) omit from 'or, as the case may be,' to 'section 249A(2)';

     (b) in subsection (3)(c) omit from 'and, if no such report' to 'any financial year';

     (c) after subsection (3)(c) insert ', and';

     (d) omit subsection (3)(e) and the ', and' preceding it;

     (e) in the closing words of subsection (3) omit from 'or any report' to 'section 249A(2)'.

**2**   In section 245 (voluntary revision of annual accounts or directors' report), in subsection (4)(b) omit 'or reporting accountant'.

**3**   In section 249A (exemptions from audit)—

     (a) omit subsections (2), (3A) and (4);

     (b) in subsection (6) for 'figures for turnover or gross income' substitute 'figure for turnover';

     (c) in subsection (6A) omit 'or (2)';

     (d) in subsection (7) omit the definition of 'gross income' and the', and' preceding it.

**4**   In section 249B (cases where exemptions not available)—

     (a) in the opening words of subsection (1) omit 'or (2)';

     (b) in subsection (1C)(b) omit from 'where the company referred to' to 'is not a charity';

     (c) in subsection (3) omit 'or (2)';

     (d) in subsection (4), in the opening words and in paragraph (a), omit 'or (2)'.

**5**   Omit section 249C (report required for purposes of section 249A(2)).

**6**   Omit section 249D (the reporting accountant).

**7**   In section 249E (effect of exemptions) omit subsection (2).

**8**   In section 262A (index of defined expressions) omit the entry for 'reporting accountant'.

COMMENCEMENT DATE 1 April 2008[44]

PART 2
THE COMPANIES (NORTHERN IRELAND) ORDER 1986 (S.I. 1986/1032 (N.I. 6)

**9**   In Article 248 (requirements in connection with publication of accounts)—

     (a) in paragraph (1) omit from 'or, as the case may be,' to 'Article 257A(2)';

     (b) in paragraph (3)(c) omit from 'and, if no such report' to 'any such financial year';

     (c) after paragraph (3)(c) insert ', and';

     (d) omit paragraph (3)(e) and the word ', and' preceding it;

     (e) in the closing words of paragraph (3) omit from 'or any report' to 'Article 257A(2)'.

**10**   In Article 253 (voluntary revision of annual accounts or directors' report), in paragraph (4)(b) omit 'or reporting accountant'.

**11**   In Article 257A (exemptions from audit)—

     (a) omit paragraphs (2), (3A) and (4);

     (b) in paragraph (6) for 'figures for turnover or gross income' substitute 'figure for turnover';

     (c) in paragraph (6A) omit 'or (2)';

     (d) in paragraph (7) omit the definition of 'gross income' and the ', and' preceding it.

**12**   In Article 257B (cases where exemptions not available)—

     (a) in the opening words of paragraph (1) omit 'or (2)';

     (b) in paragraph (1C)(b) omit from 'where the company referred to' to 'is not a charity';

     (c) in paragraph (3) omit 'or (2)';

     (d) in paragraph (4), in the opening words and in sub-paragraph (a), omit 'or (2)'.

**13**   Omit Article 257C (report required for purposes of Article 257A(2)).

**14**   Omit Article 257D (the reporting accountant).

---

[44] Companies Act 2006 (Commencement No 6, Saving and Commencement Nos 3 and 5 (Amendment)) Order 2008, SI 2008/674, arts (1)(b), (2), (3), 6.

**15** In Article 257E (effect of exemptions) omit paragraph (2).

**16** In Article 270A (index of defined expressions) omit the entry for 'reporting accountant'.

COMMENCEMENT DATE Not available

SCHEDULE **10**                    Section 1217
RECOGNISED SUPERVISORY BODIES

PART 1
GRANT AND REVOCATION OF RECOGNITION OF A SUPERVISORY BODY

**48.Sch10.01**    *Application for recognition of supervisory body*

**1** (1) A supervisory body may apply to the Secretary of State for an order declaring it to be a recognised supervisory body for the purposes of this Part of this Act ('a recognition order').

(2) Any such application must be—

(a) made in such manner as the Secretary of State may direct, and

(b) accompanied by such information as the Secretary of State may reasonably require for the purpose of determining the application.

(3) At any time after receiving an application and before determining it the Secretary of State may require the applicant to furnish additional information.

(4) The directions and requirements given or imposed under sub-paragraphs (2) and (3) may differ as between different applications.

(5) The Secretary of State may require any information to be furnished under this paragraph to be in such form or verified in such manner as he may specify.

(6) Every application must be accompanied by—

(a) a copy of the applicant's rules, and

(b) a copy of any guidance issued by the applicant in writing.

(7) The reference in sub-paragraph (6)(b) to guidance issued by the applicant is a reference to any guidance or recommendation—

(a) issued or made by it to all or any class of its members or persons seeking to become members,

(b) relevant for the purposes of this Part, and

(c) intended to have continuing effect,

including any guidance or recommendation relating to the admission or expulsion of members of the body, so far as relevant for the purposes of this Part.

*Grant and refusal of recognition*

**2** (1) The Secretary of State may, on an application duly made in accordance with paragraph 1 and after being furnished with all such information as he may require under that paragraph, make or refuse to make a recognition order in respect of the applicant.

(2) The Secretary of State may make a recognition order only if it appears to him, from the information furnished by the body and having regard to any other information in his possession, that the requirements of Part 2 of this Schedule are satisfied in the case of that body.

(3) The Secretary of State may refuse to make a recognition order in respect of a body if he considers that its recognition is unnecessary having regard to the existence of one or more other bodies which—

(a) maintain and enforce rules as to the appointment and conduct of statutory auditors, and

(b) have been or are likely to be recognised.

(4) Where the Secretary of State refuses an application for a recognition order he must give the applicant a written notice to that effect—

(a) specifying which requirements, in the opinion of the Secretary of State, are not satisfied, or

(b) stating that the application is refused on the ground mentioned in sub-paragraph (3).

(5) A recognition order must state the date on which it takes effect.

*Revocation of recognition*

**3** (1) A recognition order may be revoked by a further order made by the Secretary of State if at any time it appears to him—

(a) that any requirement of Part 2 of this Schedule is not satisfied in the case of the body to which the recognition order relates ('the recognised body'),

(b) that the body has failed to comply with any obligation imposed on it by or by virtue of this Part of this Act, or

    (c)  that the continued recognition of the body is undesirable having regard to the existence of one or more other bodies which have been or are to be recognised.

(2) An order revoking a recognition order must state the date on which it takes effect, which must be after the period of three months beginning with the date on which the revocation order is made.

(3) Before revoking a recognition order the Secretary of State must—

    (a)  give written notice of his intention to do so to the recognised body,

    (b)  take such steps as he considers reasonably practicable for bringing the notice to the attention of the members of the body, and

    (c)  publish the notice in such manner as he thinks appropriate for bringing it to the attention of any other persons who are in his opinion likely to be affected.

(4) A notice under sub-paragraph (3) must—

    (a)  state the reasons for which the Secretary of State proposes to act, and

    (b)  give particulars of the rights conferred by sub-paragraph (5).

(5) A person within sub-paragraph (6) may, within the period of three months beginning with the date of service or publication of the notice under sub-paragraph (3) or such longer period as the Secretary of State may allow, make written representations to the Secretary of State and, if desired, oral representations to a person appointed for that purpose by the Secretary of State.

(6) The persons within this sub-paragraph are—

    (a)  the recognised body on which a notice is served under sub-paragraph (3),

    (b)  any member of the body, and

    (c)  any other person who appears to the Secretary of State to be affected.

(7) The Secretary of State must have regard to any representations made in accordance with sub-paragraph (5) in determining whether to revoke the recognition order.

(8) If in any case the Secretary of State considers it essential to do so in the public interest he may revoke a recognition order without regard to the restriction imposed by sub-paragraph (2), even if—

    (a)  no notice has been given or published under sub-paragraph (3), or

    (b)  the period of time for making representations in pursuance of such a notice has not expired.

(9) An order revoking a recognition order may contain such transitional provision as the Secretary of State thinks necessary or expedient.

(10) A recognition order may be revoked at the request or with the consent of the recognised body and any such revocation is not subject to—

    (a)  the restrictions imposed by sub-paragraphs (1) and (2), or

    (b)  the requirements of sub-paragraphs (3) to (5) and (7).

(11) On making an order revoking a recognition order in respect of a body the Secretary of State must—

    (a)  give written notice of the making of the order to the body,

    (b)  take such steps as he considers reasonably practicable for bringing the making of the order to the attention of the members of the body, and

    (c)  publish a notice of the making of the order in such manner as he thinks appropriate for bringing it to the attention of any other persons who are in his opinion likely to be affected.

*Transitional provision*

**4**    A recognition order made and not revoked under—

    (a)  paragraph 2(1) of Schedule 11 to the Companies Act 1989 (c. 40), or

    (b)  paragraph 2(1) of Schedule 11 to the Companies (Northern Ireland) Order 1990 (S.I. 1990/593 (N.I. 5)),

    before the commencement of this Chapter of this Part of this Act is to have effect after the commencement of this Chapter as a recognition order made under paragraph 2(1) of this Schedule.

*Orders not statutory instruments*

**5**    Orders under this Part of this Schedule shall not be made by statutory instrument.

COMMENCEMENT DATE 6 April 2008[45]

---

[45] Companies Act 2006 (Commencement No 5, Transitional Provisions and Savings) Order 2007, SI 2007/3495, art 3(1)(u).

PART 2

REQUIREMENTS FOR RECOGNITION OF A SUPERVISORY BODY

*Holding of appropriate qualification*

**6**  (1) The body must have rules to the effect that a person is not eligible for appointment as a statutory auditor unless—

(a)  in the case of an individual [other than an EEA auditor]^a, he holds an appropriate qualification,

[(aa) in the case of an individual who is an EEA auditor—

(i)  he holds an appropriate qualification,

(ii)  he has been authorised on or before 5 April 2008 to practise the profession of company auditor pursuant to the European Communities (Recognition of Professional Qualifications) (First General System) Regulations 2005 (SI 2005/18) and has fulfilled any requirements imposed pursuant to regulation 6 of those Regulations, or

(iii)  he has passed an aptitude test in accordance with sub-paragraph (2), unless an aptitude test is not required (see sub-paragraph (2A)),]^b

(b)  in the case of a firm—

(i)  each individual responsible for statutory audit work on behalf of the firm is eligible for appointment as a statutory auditor, and

(ii)  the firm is controlled by qualified persons (see paragraph 7 below).

[(2) The aptitude test—

(a)  must test the person's knowledge of subjects—

(i)  that are covered by a recognised professional qualification,

(ii)  that are not covered by the professional qualification already held by the person, and

(iii)  the knowledge of which is essential for the pursuit of the profession of statutory auditor;

(b)  may test the person's knowledge of rules of professional conduct;

(c)  must not test the person's knowledge of any other matters.

(2A) No aptitude test is required if the subjects that are covered by a recognised professional qualification and the knowledge of which is essential for the pursuit of the profession of statutory auditor are covered by the professional qualification already held by the person.]^c

(3)  A firm which has ceased to comply with the conditions mentioned in sub-paragraph (1)(b) may be permitted to remain eligible for appointment as a statutory auditor for a period of not more than three months.

**7**  (1) This paragraph explains what is meant in paragraph 6(1)(b) by a firm being 'controlled by qualified persons'.

(2)  In this paragraph references to a person being qualified are—

(a)  in relation to an individual, to his holding—

(i)  an appropriate qualification, or

(ii)  a corresponding qualification to audit accounts under the law of [an EEA State]^d, or part of [an EEA State]^e, other than the United Kingdom;

(b)  in relation to a firm, to its—

(i)  being eligible for appointment as a statutory auditor, or

(ii)  being eligible for a corresponding appointment as an auditor under the law of [an EEA State]^f, or part of [an EEA State]^g, other than the United Kingdom.

(3)  A firm is to be treated as controlled by qualified persons if, and only if—

(a)  a majority of the members of the firm are qualified persons, and

(b)  where the firm's affairs are managed by a board of directors, committee or other management body, a majority of that body are qualified persons or, if the body consists of two persons only, at least one of them is a qualified person.

(4)  A majority of the members of a firm means—

(a)  where under the firm's constitution matters are decided upon by the exercise of voting rights, members holding a majority of the rights to vote on all, or substantially all, matters;

(b)  in any other case, members having such rights under the constitution of the firm as enable them to direct its overall policy or alter its constitution.

(5)  A majority of the members of the management body of a firm means—

(a)  where matters are decided at meetings of the management body by the exercise of voting rights, members holding a majority of the rights to vote on all, or substantially all, matters at such meetings;

(b)  in any other case, members having such rights under the constitution of the firm as enable them to direct its overall policy or alter its constitution.

(6)  Paragraphs 5 to 11 of Schedule 7 to this Act (rights to be taken into account and attribution of rights) apply for the purposes of this paragraph.

AMENDMENTS AND NOTES

^a  Inserted by the Statutory Auditors and Third Country Auditors Regulations 2007, SI 2007/3494, reg 17(1), (2).

^b  Inserted by the Statutory Auditors and Third Country Auditors Regulations 2007, SI 2007/3494, reg 17(1), (3).

<sup>c</sup> Substituted by the Statutory Auditors and Third Country Auditors Regulations 2007, SI 2007/3494, reg 17(1), (4).

<sup>d</sup> Substituted by the Statutory Auditors and Third Country Auditors Regulations 2007, SI 2007/3494, reg 18.

<sup>e</sup> Substituted by the Statutory Auditors and Third Country Auditors Regulations 2007, SI 2007/3494, reg 18.

<sup>f</sup> Substituted by the Statutory Auditors and Third Country Auditors Regulations 2007, SI 2007/3494, reg 18.

<sup>g</sup> Substituted by the Statutory Auditors and Third Country Auditors Regulations 2007, SI 2007/3494, reg 18.

*Auditors to be fit and proper persons*

**8** (1) The body must have adequate rules and practices designed to ensure that the persons eligible under its rules for appointment as a statutory auditor are fit and proper persons to be so appointed.

(2) The matters which the body may take into account for this purpose in relation to a person must include—

(a) any matter relating to any person who is or will be employed by or associated with him for the purposes of or in connection with statutory audit work;

(b) in the case of a body corporate, any matter relating to—
  (i) any director or controller of the body,
  (ii) any other body corporate in the same group, or
  (iii) any director or controller of any such other body; and

(c) in the case of a partnership, any matter relating to—
  (i) any of the partners,
  (ii) any director or controller of any of the partners,
  (iii) any body corporate in the same group as any of the partners, or
  (iv) any director or controller of any such other body.

(3) Where the person is a limited liability partnership, in sub-paragraph (2)(b) 'director' is to be read as 'member'.

(4) In sub-paragraph (2)(b) and (c) 'controller', in relation to a body corporate, means a person who either alone or with an associate or associates is entitled to exercise or control the exercise of 15% or more of the rights to vote on all, or substantially all, matters at general meetings of the body or another body corporate of which it is a subsidiary.

*Professional integrity and independence*

**9** (1) The body must have adequate rules and practices designed to ensure that—

(a) statutory audit work is conducted properly and with integrity, [...]<sup>a</sup>

(b) persons are not appointed as statutory auditors in circumstances in which they have an interest likely to conflict with the proper conduct of the audit.

[(c) persons appointed as statutory auditors take steps to safeguard their independence from any significant threats to it,

(d) persons appointed as statutory auditors record any such threats and the steps taken to safeguard the proper conduct of the audit from them, and

(e) remuneration received or receivable by a statutory auditor in respect of statutory audit work is not—
  (i) influenced or determined by the statutory auditor providing other services to the audited person, or
  (ii) on a contingent fee basis]<sup>b</sup>.

(2) The body must participate in arrangements within paragraph 21, and the rules and practices mentioned in sub-paragraph (1) must include provision requiring compliance with any standards for the time being determined under such arrangements.

[(3) The body must also have adequate rules and practices designed to ensure that—

(a) no firm is eligible under its rules for appointment as a statutory auditor unless the firm has arrangements to prevent any person from being able to exert any influence over the way in which a statutory audit is conducted in circumstances in which that influence would be likely to affect the independence or integrity of the audit;

(b) any rule of law relating to the confidentiality of information received in the course of statutory audit work by persons appointed as statutory auditors is complied with; and

(c) a person ceasing to hold office as a statutory auditor makes available to his successor in that office all relevant information which he holds in relation to that office.

(4) The rules referred to in sub-paragraph (3)(b) (confidentiality of information) must apply to persons who are no longer members of the body as they apply to members and any fine imposed in the enforcement of those rules shall be recoverable by the body as a debt due to it from the person obliged to pay it.]<sup>c</sup>

AMENDMENTS AND NOTES

<sup>a</sup> Repealed by the Statutory Auditors and Third Country Auditors Regulations 2007, SI 2007/3494, reg 19(1), (2).

<sup>b</sup> Inserted by the Statutory Auditors and Third Country Auditors Regulations 2007, SI 2007/3494, reg 19(1), (3).

<sup>c</sup> Substituted by the Statutory Auditors and Third Country Auditors Regulations 2007, SI 2007/3494, reg 19(1), (4).

*Technical standards*

**10** (1) The body must have rules and practices as to—
   (a) the technical standards to be applied in statutory audit work, and
   (b) the manner in which those standards are to be applied in practice.
  (2) The body must participate in arrangements within paragraph 22, and the rules and practices mentioned in sub-paragraph (1) must include provision requiring compliance with any standards for the time being determined under such arrangements.

*[Technical standards for group audits*

**10A** (1) The body must have rules and practices as to technical standards ensuring that group auditors—
   (a) review for the purposes of a group audit the audit work conducted by other persons, and
   (b) record that review.
  (2) The body must participate in arrangements within paragraph 22, and the rules and practices mentioned in sub-paragraph (1) must include provision requiring compliance with any standards for the time being determined under such arrangements.
  (3) The body must also have rules and practices ensuring that group auditors—
   (a) retain copies of any documents necessary for the purposes of the review that they have received from third country auditors who are not covered by working arrangements under section 1253E, or
   (b) agree with those third country auditors proper and unrestricted access to those documents on request.
  (4) The body's rules and practices must ensure that group auditors make those documents available on request to—
   (a) the body;
   (b) any other body with which the body has entered into arrangements for the purposes of paragraph 23 or 24 (independent arrangements for monitoring and investigation);
   (c) the Secretary of State.
  (5) The body may provide that the rules and practices referred to in sub-paragraphs (3) and (4) do not apply if, after taking all reasonable steps, a group auditor is unable to obtain the copies of the documents or the access to the documents necessary for the review.
  (6) If the body does so provide, its rules and practices must ensure that the group auditor records—
   (a) the steps taken to obtain copies of or access to those documents,
   (b) the reasons why the copies or access could not be obtained, and
   (c) any evidence of those steps or those reasons.
  (7) In this paragraph—
   'group auditor' means a person appointed as statutory auditor to conduct an audit of group accounts;
   'group' has the same meaning as in Part 15 of this Act (see section 474).]<sup>a</sup>

AMENDMENTS AND NOTES

<sup>a</sup> Inserted by the Statutory Auditors and Third Country Auditors Regulations 2007, SI 2007/3494, reg 20.

*[Public interest entity reporting requirements*

**10B** (1) The body must have adequate rules and practices designed to ensure that persons appointed as statutory auditors of public interest entities report to the entity's audit committee (if it has one) at least once in each calendar year at any time during which they hold the office of statutory auditor.
  (2) The report must include—
   (a) a statement in writing confirming the person's independence from the public interest entity;
   (b) a description of any services provided by the person to the public interest entity other than in his capacity as statutory auditor;
   (c) a description of any significant threats to the person's independence;
   (d) an explanation of the steps taken by the person to safeguard his independence from those threats;
   (e) a description of any material weaknesses arising from the statutory audit in the public interest entity's internal control in relation to the preparation of accounts; and
   (f) any other significant matters arising from the statutory audit.

(3) The body must participate in arrangements within paragraph 22A (arrangements for setting standards), and the rules and practices mentioned in sub-paragraph (1) must include provision requiring compliance with any standards for the time being determined under such arrangements.

(4) In this paragraph, 'audit committee' means a body which performs the functions referred to in Article 41.2 of the Audit Directive or equivalent functions.

*Public interest entity independence requirements*

**10C** (1) The body must have adequate rules and practices designed to ensure that—

    (a) an individual does not accept an appointment by a public interest entity as statutory auditor if—

        (i) he has been the statutory auditor of the entity for a continuous period of more than seven years, and

        (ii) less than two years have passed since he was last the statutory auditor of the entity;

    (b) where a firm has been appointed by a public interest entity as statutory auditor, an individual may not be a key audit partner if—

        (i) he has been a key audit partner in relation to audits of the entity for a continuous period of more than seven years, and

        (ii) less than two years have passed since he was last the key audit partner in relation to an audit of the entity.

(2) The body must participate in arrangements within paragraph 22B (arrangements for setting standards), and the rules and practices mentioned in sub-paragraph (1) must include provision requiring compliance with any standards for the time being determined under such arrangements.

(3) The body must also have adequate rules and practices designed to ensure that—

    (a) an individual who has been appointed by a public interest entity as statutory auditor may not be appointed as a director or other officer of the entity during a period of two years commencing on the date on which his appointment as statutory auditor ended;

    (b) a key audit partner of a firm which has been appointed by a public interest entity as statutory auditor may not be appointed as a director or other officer of the entity during a period of two years commencing on the date on which his work as key audit partner ended.

(4) The rules referred to in sub-paragraph (3) must apply to persons who are no longer members of the body as they apply to members and any fine imposed in the enforcement of those rules shall be recoverable by the body as a debt due to it from the person obliged to pay it.

(5) An auditor of a public interest entity is not to be regarded as an officer of the entity for the purposes of sub-paragraph (3)(a) and (b).

(6) For the purposes of this paragraph—

    (a) a 'key audit partner' is an individual identified by a firm appointed as statutory auditor as being primarily responsible for the statutory audit; and

    (b) a key audit partner of a firm appointed as statutory auditor of a parent undertaking or a material subsidiary undertaking of a public interest entity is to be treated as if he were a key audit partner of the firm appointed as statutory auditor of the public interest entity.][a]

AMENDMENTS AND NOTES

[a] Inserted by the Statutory Auditors and Third Country Auditors Regulations 2007, SI 2007/3494, reg 21.

*Procedures for maintaining competence*

**11** The body must have rules and practices designed to ensure that persons eligible under its rules for appointment as a statutory auditor continue to maintain an appropriate level of competence in the conduct of statutory audits.

*Monitoring and enforcement*

**12** [(1) The body must—

    (a) have adequate resources for the effective monitoring and enforcement of compliance with its rules, and

    (b) ensure that those resources may not be influenced improperly by the persons monitored.

(1A) The body must—

    (a) have adequate arrangements for the effective monitoring and enforcement of compliance with its rules, and

    (b) ensure that those arrangements operate independently of the persons monitored.][a]

(2) The arrangements for monitoring may make provision for that function to be performed on behalf of the body (and without affecting its responsibility) by any other body or person who is able and willing to perform it.

[(3) The arrangements for enforcement must include provision for—

    (a) sanctions which include—

        (i) the withdrawal of eligibility for appointment as a statutory auditor; and

        (ii) any other disciplinary measures necessary to ensure the effective enforcement of the body's rules; and

(b) the body making available to the public information relating to steps it has taken to ensure the effective enforcement of its rules.]^b

AMENDMENTS AND NOTES

^a  Substituted by the Statutory Auditors and Third Country Auditors Regulations 2007, SI 2007/3494, reg 22(1), (2).

^b  Inserted by the Statutory Auditors and Third Country Auditors Regulations 2007, SI 2007/3494, reg 22(1), (3).

*[Monitoring of audits*

**13** (1) The body must—
  (a) in the case of members of the body who do not perform any statutory audit functions in respect of major audits, have adequate arrangements for enabling the performance by its members of statutory audit functions to be monitored by means of inspections;
  (b) in the case of members of the body who perform any statutory audit functions in respect of major audits, participate in arrangements within paragraph 23(1); and
  (c) have rules designed to ensure that members of the body take such steps as may reasonably be required of them to enable their performance of any statutory audit functions to be monitored by means of inspections.

(2) Any monitoring of members of the body under the arrangements within paragraph 23(1) is to be regarded (so far as their performance of statutory audit functions in respect of major audits is concerned) as monitoring of compliance with the body's rules for the purposes of paragraph 12(1) and (1A).

(3) The arrangements referred to in sub-paragraph (1)(a) must include an inspection which is conducted in relation to each person eligible for appointment as a statutory auditor at least once every six years.

(4) The inspection must be conducted by persons who—
  (a) have an appropriate professional education;
  (b) have experience of—
    (i) statutory audit work, or
    (ii) equivalent work on the audit of accounts under the law of an EEA State, or part of an EEA State, other than the United Kingdom;
  (c) have received adequate training in the conduct of inspections;
  (d) do not have any interests likely to conflict with the proper conduct of the inspection.

(5) The inspection must review one or more statutory audits in which the person to whom the inspection relates has participated.

(6) The inspection must include an assessment of—
  (a) the person's compliance with the body's rules established for the purposes of paragraphs 9 (professional integrity and independence), 10 (technical standards), 10A (technical standards for group audits) and 10C (public interest entity independence requirements);
  (b) the resources allocated by the person to statutory audit work;
  (c) in the case of an inspection in relation to a firm, its internal quality control system;
  (d) the remuneration received by the person in respect of statutory audit work.

(7) An inspection conducted in relation to a firm may be treated as an inspection of all individuals responsible for statutory audit work on behalf of that firm, if the firm has a common quality assurance policy with which each such individual is required to comply.

(8) The main conclusions of the inspection must be recorded in a report which is made available to—
  (a) the person to whom the inspection relates, and
  (b) the body.

(9) The body must, at least once in every calendar year, deliver to the Secretary of State a summary of the results of inspections conducted under this paragraph.

(10) In this paragraph—
  'major audit' means a statutory audit conducted in respect of—
  (a) a public interest entity, or
  (b) any other person in whose financial condition there is a major public interest;
  'statutory audit function' means any function performed as a statutory auditor.]^a

AMENDMENTS AND NOTES

^a  Substituted by the Statutory Auditors and Third Country Auditors Regulations 2007, SI 2007/3494, reg 23.

*Membership, eligibility and discipline*

**14**  The rules and practices of the body relating to—
  (a) the admission and expulsion of members,
  (b) the grant and withdrawal of eligibility for appointment as a statutory auditor, and
  (c) the discipline it exercises over its members,
      must be fair and reasonable and include adequate provision for appeals.

*Investigation of complaints*

**15** (1) The body must have effective arrangements for the investigation of complaints against—

(a) persons who are eligible under its rules for appointment as a statutory auditor, and

(b) the body in respect of matters arising out of its functions as a supervisory body.

(2) The arrangements mentioned in sub-paragraph (1) may make provision for the whole or part of that function to be performed by and to be the responsibility of a body or person independent of the body itself.

*Independent investigation for disciplinary purposes of public interest cases*

**16** (1) The body must—

(a) participate in arrangements within paragraph 24(1), and

(b) have rules and practices designed to ensure that, where the designated persons have decided that any particular disciplinary action should be taken against a member of the body following the conclusion of an investigation under such arrangements, that decision is to be treated as if it were a decision made by the body in disciplinary proceedings against the member.

(2) In sub-paragraph (1) 'the designated persons' means the persons who, under the arrangements, have the function of deciding whether (and if so, what) disciplinary action should be taken against a member of the body in the light of an investigation carried out under the arrangements.

*[Transfer of papers to third countries*

**16A** (1) The body must have adequate rules and practices designed to ensure that persons eligible under its rules for appointment as a statutory auditor deliver audit working papers to a third country competent authority only if—

(a) the authority has entered into arrangements with the Secretary of State in accordance with section 1253E (working arrangements); and

(b) the following four conditions are met.

(2) The first condition is that the competent authority has requested the audit working papers for the purposes of an investigation.

(3) The second condition is that the competent authority has given to the Secretary of State notice of its request.

(4) The third condition is that the papers relate to the audit of a body which—

(a) has issued securities in the country or territory in which the competent authority is established, or

(b) forms part of a group issuing statutory consolidated accounts in that country or territory.

(5) The fourth condition is that no legal proceedings have been brought (whether continuing or not) in relation to the auditor or audit to which the working papers relate.

(6) The body must also have adequate rules and practices designed to ensure that a person eligible under its rules for appointment as a statutory auditor may refuse to deliver audit working papers to a third country competent authority if the Secretary of State certifies that the delivery of the papers would adversely affect the sovereignty, security or public order of the United Kingdom.]ᵃ

AMENDMENTS AND NOTES

ᵃ Inserted by the Statutory Auditors and Third Country Auditors Regulations 2007, SI 2007/3494, reg 24.

*Meeting of claims arising out of audit work*

**17** (1) The body must have adequate rules or arrangements designed to ensure that persons eligible under its rules for appointment as a statutory auditor take such steps as may reasonably be expected of them to secure that they are able to meet claims against them arising out of statutory audit work.

(2) This may be achieved by professional indemnity insurance or other appropriate arrangements.

*Register of auditors and other information to be made available*

**18** The body must have rules requiring persons eligible under its rules for appointment as a statutory auditor to comply with any obligations imposed on them by—

(a) requirements under section 1224 (Secretary of State's power to call for information);

(b) regulations under section 1239 (the register of auditors);

(c) regulations under section 1240 (information to be made available to the public).

*Taking account of costs of compliance*

**19** The body must have satisfactory arrangements for taking account, in framing its rules, of the cost to those to whom the rules would apply of complying with those rules and any other controls to which they are subject.

*Promotion and maintenance of standards*

**20** The body must be able and willing—

  (a) to promote and maintain high standards of integrity in the conduct of statutory audit work, and

  (b) to co-operate, by the sharing of information and otherwise, with the Secretary of State and any other authority, body or person having responsibility in the United Kingdom for the qualification, supervision or regulation of auditors.

*[Interpretation*

  **20A** In this Part of this Schedule—

    'public interest entity' means an issuer—

      (a) whose transferable securities are admitted to trading on a regulated market; and

      (b) the audit of which is a statutory audit (see section 1210(1));

        'issuer' and 'regulated market' have the same meaning as in Part 6 of the Financial Services and Markets Act 2000 (see sections 102A to 103); and

        'transferable securities' means anything which is a transferable security for the purposes of Directive 2004/39/EC of the European Parliament and of the Council on markets in financial instruments.]ᵃ

AMENDMENTS AND NOTES

  ᵃ Inserted by the Statutory Auditors and Third Country Auditors Regulations 2007, SI 2007/3494, reg 25.

COMMENCEMENT DATE 1 April 2008[46]

## PART 3
## ARRANGEMENTS IN WHICH RECOGNISED SUPERVISORY BODIES ARE REQUIRED TO PARTICIPATE

*Arrangements for setting standards relating to professional integrity and independence*

**21** The arrangements referred to in paragraph 9(2) are appropriate arrangements—

  (a) for the determining of standards for the purposes of the rules and practices mentioned in paragraph 9(1), and

  (b) for ensuring that the determination of those standards is done independently of the body.

*Arrangements for setting technical standards*

**22** The arrangements referred to in [paragraphs 10(2) and 10A(2)]ᵃ are appropriate arrangements—

  (a) for the determining of standards for the purposes of the rules and practices mentioned in [paragraphs 10(1) and 10A(1) respectively]ᵇ, and

  (b) for ensuring that the determination of those standards is done independently of the body.

AMENDMENTS AND NOTES

  ᵃ Substituted by the Statutory Auditors and Third Country Auditors Regulations 2007, SI 2007/3494, reg 26(1), (2).

  ᵇ Substituted by the Statutory Auditors and Third Country Auditors Regulations 2007, SI 2007/3494, reg 26(1), (3).

*[Arrangements for setting standards relating to public interest entity reporting requirements*

**22A** The arrangements referred to in paragraph 10B(3) are appropriate arrangements—

  (a) for the determining of standards for the purposes of the rules and practices mentioned in paragraph 10B(1), and

  (b) for ensuring that the determination of those standards is done independently of the body.

*Arrangements for setting standards relating to public interest entity independence requirements*

**22B** The arrangements referred to in paragraph 10C(2) are appropriate arrangements—

  (a) for the determining of standards for the purposes of the rules and practices mentioned in paragraph 10C(1), and

  (b) for ensuring that the determination of those standards is done independently of the body.]ᵃ

AMENDMENTS AND NOTES

  ᵃ Inserted by the Statutory Auditors and Third Country Auditors Regulations 2007, SI 2007/3494, reg 27.

---

[46] Companies Act 2006 (Commencement No 5, Transitional Provisions and Savings) Order 2007, SI 2007/3495, art 3(1)(u).

*Arrangements for independent monitoring of audits of listed companies and other major bodies*

**23** (1) The arrangements referred to in [paragraph 13(1)(b)][a] are appropriate arrangements—

    (a) for enabling the performance by members of the body of statutory audit functions in respect of major audits to be monitored by means of inspections carried out under the arrangements, and

    (b) for ensuring that the carrying out of such monitoring and inspections is done independently of the body.

  [(1A) Subject to sub-paragraph (1C), the arrangements referred to in sub-paragraph (1) must include provision for an inspection conducted in relation to each person eligible for appointment as a statutory auditor at least once every three years.

  (1B)Sub-paragraphs (4) to (9) of paragraph 13 apply in relation to inspections under sub-paragraph (1A) as they apply in relation to inspections under that paragraph.

  (1C)The arrangements referred to in sub-paragraph (1) may provide that the body performing the inspections may decide that all or part of the inspection referred to in sub-paragraph (1A) is not required in the case of a member of a supervisory body who performs statutory audit functions in respect of ten or fewer major audits per year.

  (1D)If—

    (a) the arrangements make the provision referred to in sub-paragraph (1C), and

    (b) the body performing the inspections decides that all of an inspection is not required in relation to a member,

    the supervisory body must ensure that the arrangements referred to in paragraph 13(1)(a) apply in relation to that member, subject to the modification specified in sub-paragraph (1F).

  (1E)If—

    (a) the arrangements make the provision referred to in sub-paragraph (1C), and

    (b) the body performing the inspections decides that part of an inspection is not required in relation to a member,

    the supervisory body must ensure that the arrangements referred to in paragraph 13(1)(a) apply in relation to that part of the inspection of that member, subject to the modification specified in sub-paragraph (1F).

  (1F)For the purposes of sub-paragraphs (1D) and (1E), paragraph 13(3) applies with the substitution of 'three years' for 'six years'.][b]

  (2) In this paragraph 'major audit' and 'statutory audit function' have the same meaning as in paragraph 13.

<small>AMENDMENTS AND NOTES</small>

[a] Substituted by the Statutory Auditors and Third Country Auditors Regulations 2007, SI 2007/3494, reg 28.

[b] Inserted by the Statutory Auditors and Third Country Auditors Regulations 2007, SI 2007/3494, reg 28(1), (3).

*Arrangements for independent investigation for disciplinary purposes of public interest cases*

**24** (1) The arrangements referred to in paragraph 16(1) are appropriate arrangements—

    (a) for the carrying out of investigations into public interest cases arising in connection with the performance of statutory audit functions by members of the body,

    (b) for the holding of disciplinary hearings relating to members of the body which appear to be desirable following the conclusion of such investigations,

    (c) for requiring such hearings to be held in public except where the interests of justice otherwise require,

    (d) for the persons before whom such hearings have taken place to decide whether (and, if so, what) disciplinary action should be taken against the members to whom the hearings related, and

    (e) for ensuring that the carrying out of those investigations, the holding of those hearings and the taking of those decisions are done independently of the body.

  (2) In this paragraph—

  'public interest cases' means matters which raise or appear to raise important issues affecting the public interest;

  'statutory audit function' means any function performed as a statutory auditor.

*Supplementary: arrangements to operate independently of body*

**25** (1) This paragraph applies for the purposes of—

    (a) paragraph 21(b),

    (b) paragraph 22(b),

    (c) paragraph 23(1)(b), or

    (d) paragraph 24(1)(e).

  (2) Arrangements are not to be regarded as appropriate for the purpose of ensuring that a thing is done independently of the body unless they are designed to ensure that the body—

    (a) will have no involvement in the appointment or selection of any of the persons who are to be responsible for doing that thing, and

(b)  will not otherwise be involved in the doing of that thing.

(3)  Sub-paragraph (2) imposes a minimum requirement and does not preclude the possibility that additional criteria may need to be satisfied in order for the arrangements to be regarded as appropriate for the purpose in question.

*Supplementary: funding of arrangements*

**26**  The body must pay any of the costs of maintaining any arrangements within paragraph 21, 22, 23 or 24 which the arrangements provide are to be paid by it.

*Supplementary: scope of arrangement*

**27**  Arrangements may qualify as arrangements within any of paragraphs 21, 22, 23 and 24 even though the matters for which they provide are more extensive in any respect than those mentioned in the applicable paragraph.

Commencement Date  6 April 2008[47]

---

SCHEDULE 11                                              Section 1220

RECOGNISED PROFESSIONAL QUALIFICATIONS

PART 1
GRANT AND REVOCATION OF RECOGNITION OF A PROFESSIONAL
QUALIFICATION

**48.Sch11.01**       *Application for recognition of professional qualification*

**1**   (1)  A qualifying body may apply to the Secretary of State for an order declaring a qualification offered by it to be a recognised professional qualification for the purposes of this Part of this Act ('a recognition order').

(2)  In this Part of this Act 'a recognised qualifying body' means a qualifying body offering a recognised professional qualification.

(3)  Any application must be—

(a)  made in such manner as the Secretary of State may direct, and

(b)  accompanied by such information as the Secretary of State may reasonably require for the purpose of determining the application.

(4)  At any time after receiving an application and before determining it the Secretary of State may require the applicant to furnish additional information.

(5)  The directions and requirements given or imposed under sub-paragraphs (3) and (4) may differ as between different applications.

(6)  The Secretary of State may require any information to be furnished under this paragraph to be in such form or verified in such manner as he may specify.

(7)  In the case of examination standards, the verification required may include independent moderation of the examinations over such a period as the Secretary of State considers necessary.

(8)  Every application must be accompanied by—

(a)  a copy of the applicant's rules, and

(b)  a copy of any guidance issued by the applicant in writing.

(9)  The reference in sub-paragraph (8)(b) to guidance issued by the applicant is a reference to any guidance or recommendation—

(a)  issued or made by it to all or any class of persons holding or seeking to hold a qualification, or approved or seeking to be approved by the body for the purposes of giving practical training,

(b)  relevant for the purposes of this Part of this Act, and

(c)  intended to have continuing effect,
including any guidance or recommendation relating to a matter within sub-paragraph (10).

(10)  The matters within this sub-paragraph are—

(a)  admission to or expulsion from a course of study leading to a qualification,

(b)  the award or deprivation of a qualification, and

---

[47]  Companies Act 2006 (Commencement No 5, Transitional Provisions and Savings) Order 2007, SI 2007/3495, art 3(1)(u).

    (c) the approval of a person for the purposes of giving practical training or the withdrawal of such an approval,
    so far as relevant for the purposes of this Part of this Act.

*Grant and refusal of recognition*

**2** (1) The Secretary of State may, on an application duly made in accordance with paragraph 1 and after being furnished with all such information as he may require under that paragraph, make or refuse to make a recognition order in respect of the qualification in relation to which the application was made.

    (2) The Secretary of State may make a recognition order only if it appears to him, from the information furnished by the applicant and having regard to any other information in his possession, that the requirements of Part 2 of this Schedule are satisfied in relation to the qualification.

    (3) Where the Secretary of State refuses an application for a recognition order he must give the applicant a written notice to that effect specifying which requirements, in his opinion, are not satisfied.

    (4) A recognition order must state the date on which it takes effect.

*Revocation of recognition*

**3** (1) A recognition order may be revoked by a further order made by the Secretary of State if at any time it appears to him—

    (a) that any requirement of Part 2 of this Schedule is not satisfied in relation to the qualification to which the recognition order relates, or

    (b) that the qualifying body has failed to comply with any obligation imposed on it by or by virtue of this Part of this Act.

    (2) An order revoking a recognition order must state the date on which it takes effect, which must be after the period of three months beginning with the date on which the revocation order is made.

    (3) Before revoking a recognition order the Secretary of State must—

    (a) give written notice of his intention to do so to the qualifying body,

    (b) take such steps as he considers reasonably practicable for bringing the notice to the attention of persons holding the qualification or in the course of studying for it, and

    (c) publish the notice in such manner as he thinks appropriate for bringing it to the attention of any other persons who are in his opinion likely to be affected.

    (4) A notice under sub-paragraph (3) must—

    (a) state the reasons for which the Secretary of State proposes to act, and

    (b) give particulars of the rights conferred by sub-paragraph (5).

    (5) A person within sub-paragraph (6) may, within the period of three months beginning with the date of service or publication or such longer period as the Secretary of State may allow, make written representations to the Secretary of State and, if desired, oral representations to a person appointed for that purpose by the Secretary of State.

    (6) The persons within this sub-paragraph are—

    (a) the qualifying body on which a notice is served under sub-paragraph (3),

    (b) any person holding the qualification or in the course of studying for it, and

    (c) any other person who appears to the Secretary of State to be affected.

    (7) The Secretary of State must have regard to any representations made in accordance with sub-paragraph (5) in determining whether to revoke the recognition order.

    (8) If in any case the Secretary of State considers it essential to do so in the public interest he may revoke a recognition order without regard to the restriction imposed by sub-paragraph (2), even if—

    (a) no notice has been given or published under sub-paragraph (3), or

    (b) the period of time for making representations in pursuance of such a notice has not expired.

    (9) An order revoking a recognition order may contain such transitional provision as the Secretary of State thinks necessary or expedient.

    (10) A recognition order may be revoked at the request or with the consent of the qualifying body and any such revocation is not subject to—

    (a) the restrictions imposed by sub-paragraphs (1) and (2), or

    (b) the requirements of sub-paragraphs (3) to (5) and (7).

    (11) On making an order revoking a recognition order the Secretary of State must—

    (a) give written notice of the making of the order to the qualifying body,

    (b) take such steps as he considers reasonably practicable for bringing the making of the order to the attention of persons holding the qualification or in the course of studying for it, and

    (c) publish a notice of the making of the order in such manner as he thinks appropriate for bringing it to the attention of any other persons who are in his opinion likely to be affected.

*Transitional provision*

**4**    A recognition order made and not revoked under—

  (a)  paragraph 2(1) of Schedule 12 to the Companies Act 1989 (c. 40), or

  (b)  paragraph 2(1) of Schedule 12 to the Companies (Northern Ireland) Order 1990 (S.I. 1990/593
       (N.I. 5)),

       before the commencement of this Chapter of this Part of this Act is to have effect after the
       commencement of this Chapter as a recognition order made under paragraph 2(1) of this
       Schedule.

*Orders not statutory instruments*

**5**    Orders under this Part of this Schedule shall not be made by statutory instrument.

COMMENCEMENT DATE 1 April 2008[48]

PART 2

## REQUIREMENTS FOR RECOGNITION OF A PROFESSIONAL QUALIFICATION

*Entry requirements*

**6**    (1)  The qualification must only be open to persons who—

  (a)  have attained university entrance level, or

  (b)  have a sufficient period of professional experience.

   (2)  In relation to a person who has not been admitted to a university or other similar establish-
        ment in the United Kingdom, 'attaining university entrance level' means—

  (a)  being educated to such a standard as would entitle him to be considered for such
       admission on the basis of—

    (i)   academic or professional qualifications obtained in the United Kingdom and recog-
          nised by the Secretary of State to be of an appropriate standard, or

    (ii)  academic or professional qualifications obtained outside the United Kingdom which
          the Secretary of State considers to be of an equivalent standard, or

  (b)  being assessed, on the basis of written tests of a kind appearing to the Secretary of State
       to be adequate for the purpose (with or without oral examination), as of such a standard
       of ability as would entitle him to be considered for such admission.

   (3)  The assessment, tests and oral examination referred to in sub-paragraph (2)(b) may be
        conducted by—

  (a)  the qualifying body, or

  (b)  some other body approved by the Secretary of State.

   (4)  The reference in sub-paragraph (1)(b) to 'a sufficient period of professional experience' is to
        not less than seven years' experience in a professional capacity in the fields of finance, law and
        accountancy.

*Requirement for theoretical instruction or professional experience*

**7**    (1)  The qualification must be restricted to persons who—

  (a)  have completed a course of theoretical instruction in the subjects prescribed for the
       purposes of paragraph 8, or

  (b)  have a sufficient period of professional experience.

   (2)  The reference in sub-paragraph (1)(b) to 'a sufficient period of professional experience' is to
        not less than seven years' experience in a professional capacity in the fields of finance, law and
        accountancy.

*Examination*

**8**    (1)  The qualification must be restricted to persons who have passed an examination (at least part
        of which is in writing) testing—

  (a)  theoretical knowledge of the subjects prescribed for the purposes of this paragraph by
       regulations made by the Secretary of State, and

  (b)  ability to apply that knowledge in practice,
       and requiring a standard of attainment at least equivalent to that required to obtain a
       degree from a university or similar establishment in the United Kingdom.

   (2)  The qualification may be awarded to a person without his theoretical knowledge of a subject
        being tested by examination if he has passed a university or other examination of equivalent
        standard in that subject or holds a university degree or equivalent qualification in it.

   (3)  The qualification may be awarded to a person without his ability to apply his theoretical
        knowledge of a subject in practice being tested by examination if he has received practical
        training in that subject which is attested by an examination or diploma recognised by the
        Secretary of State for the purposes of this paragraph.

   (4)  Regulations under this paragraph are subject to negative resolution procedure.

---

[48] Companies Act 2006 (Commencement No 5, Transitional Provisions and Savings) Order 2007, SI 2007/
3495, art 3(1)(u).

*Practical training*

**9** (1) The qualification must be restricted to persons who have completed at least three years' practical training of which—

(a) part was spent being trained in statutory audit work, and

(b) a substantial part was spent being trained in statutory audit work or other audit work of a description approved by the Secretary of State as being similar to statutory audit work.

(2) For the purpose of sub-paragraph (1) 'statutory audit work' includes the work of a person appointed as the auditor of a person under the law of a country or territory outside the United Kingdom where it appears to the Secretary of State that the law and practice with respect to the audit of accounts is similar to that in the United Kingdom.

(3) The training must be given by persons approved by the body offering the qualification as persons whom the body is satisfied, in the light of undertakings given by them and the supervision to which they are subject (whether by the body itself or some other body or organisation), will provide adequate training.

(4) At least two-thirds of the training must be given by a person—

(a) eligible for appointment as a statutory auditor, or

(b) eligible for a corresponding appointment as an auditor under the law of [an EEA State]ᵃ, or part of [an EEA State]ᵇ, other than the United Kingdom.

AMENDMENTS AND NOTES

ᵃ Substituted by the Statutory Auditors and Third Country Auditors Regulations 2007, SI 2007/3494, reg 44.

ᵇ Substituted by the Statutory Auditors and Third Country Auditors Regulations 2007, SI 2007/3494, reg 44.

*Supplementary provision with respect to a sufficient period of professional experience*

**10** (1) Periods of theoretical instruction in the fields of finance, law and accountancy may be deducted from the required period of professional experience, provided the instruction—

(a) lasted at least one year, and

(b) is attested by an examination recognised by the Secretary of State for the purposes of this paragraph;

but the period of professional experience may not be so reduced by more than four years.

(2) The period of professional experience together with the practical training required in the case of persons satisfying the requirement in paragraph 7 by virtue of having a sufficient period of professional experience must not be shorter than the course of theoretical instruction referred to in that paragraph and the practical training required in the case of persons satisfying the requirement of that paragraph by virtue of having completed such a course.

*The body offering the qualification*

**11** (1) The body offering the qualification must have—

(a) rules and arrangements adequate to ensure compliance with the requirements of paragraphs 6 to 10, and

(b) adequate arrangements for the effective monitoring of its continued compliance with those requirements.

(2) The arrangements must include arrangements for monitoring—

(a) the standard of the body's examinations, and

(b) the adequacy of the practical training given by the persons approved by it for that purpose.

COMMENCEMENT DATE 6 April 2008⁴⁹

---

⁴⁹ Companies Act 2006 (Commencement No 5, Transitional Provisions and Savings) Order 2007, SI 2007/3495, art 3(1)(u).

# [SCHEDULE 11A

## SPECIFIED PERSONS, DESCRIPTIONS, DISCLOSURES ETC FOR THE PURPOSES OF SECTION 1224A

### PART 1
### SPECIFIED PERSONS

**48.Sch11A.01**

1    The Secretary of State.
2    The Department of Enterprise, Trade and Investment for Northern Ireland.
3    The Treasury.
4    The Bank of England.
5    The Financial Services Authority.
6    The Commissioners for Her Majesty's Revenue and Customs.
7    The Lord Advocate.
8    The Director of Public Prosecutions.
9    The Director of Public Prosecutions for Northern Ireland.
10   A constable.
11   A procurator fiscal.
12   The Scottish Ministers.
13   A body designated by the Secretary of State under section 1252 (delegation of the Secretary of State's functions).
14   A recognised supervisory body.
15   A recognised qualifying body.
16   A body with which a recognised supervisory body is participating in arrangements for the purposes of paragraph 23 (independent monitoring of audits) or 24 (independent investigation for disciplinary purposes) of Schedule 10 to this Act.
17   The Independent Supervisor.

COMMENCEMENT DATE 6 April 2008[50]

### PART 2
### SPECIFIED DESCRIPTIONS OF DISCLOSURES

18   A disclosure for the purpose of enabling or assisting a person authorised under section 457 of this Act (persons authorised to apply to court) to exercise his functions.
19   A disclosure for the purpose of enabling or assisting an inspector appointed under Part 14 of the Companies Act 1985 (investigation of companies and their affairs, etc) to exercise his functions.
20   A disclosure for the purpose of enabling or assisting a person authorised under section 447 of the Companies Act 1985 (power to require production of documents) or section 84 of the Companies Act 1989 (c 40) (exercise of powers by officer etc) to exercise his functions.
21   A disclosure for the purpose of enabling or assisting a person appointed under section 167 of the Financial Services and Markets Act 2000 (c 8) (general investigations) to conduct an investigation to exercise his functions.
22   A disclosure for the purpose of enabling or assisting a person appointed under section 168 of the Financial Services and Markets Act 2000 (investigations in particular cases) to conduct an investigation to exercise his functions.
23   A disclosure for the purpose of enabling or assisting a person appointed under section 169(1)(b) of the Financial Services and Markets Act 2000 (investigation in support of overseas regulator) to conduct an investigation to exercise his functions.
24   A disclosure for the purpose of enabling or assisting the body corporate responsible for administering the scheme referred to in section 225 of the Financial Services and Markets Act 2000 (the ombudsman scheme) to exercise its functions.
25   A disclosure for the purpose of enabling or assisting a person appointed under paragraph 4 (the panel of ombudsmen) or 5 (the Chief Ombudsman) of Schedule 17 to the Financial Services and Markets Act 2000 to exercise his functions.
26   A disclosure for the purpose of enabling or assisting a person appointed under regulations made under section 262(1) and (2)(k) of the Financial Services and Markets Act 2000 (investigations into open-ended investment companies) to conduct an investigation to exercise his functions.

---

[50]   Statutory Auditors and Third Country Auditors Regulations 2007, SI 2007/3494, reg 1(2).

27  A disclosure for the purpose of enabling or assisting a person appointed under section 284 of the Financial Services and Markets Act 2000 (investigations into affairs of certain collective investment schemes) to conduct an investigation to exercise his functions.

28  A disclosure for the purpose of enabling or assisting the investigator appointed under paragraph 7 of Schedule 1 to the Financial Services and Markets Act 2000 (arrangements for investigation of complaints) to exercise his functions.

29  A disclosure for the purpose of enabling or assisting a person appointed by the Treasury to hold an inquiry into matters relating to financial services (including an inquiry under section 15 of the Financial Services and Markets Act 2000 (c 8)) to exercise his functions.

30  A disclosure for the purpose of enabling or assisting the Secretary of State or the Treasury to exercise any of their functions under any of the following—

    (a)  the Companies Acts;

    (b)  Part 5 of the Criminal Justice Act 1993 (c 36) (insider dealing);

    (c)  the Insolvency Act 1986 (c 45);

    (d)  the Company Directors Disqualification Act 1986 (c 46);

    (e)  Part 42 of this Act (statutory auditors);

    (f)  Part 3 (investigations and powers to obtain information) or 7 (financial markets and insolvency) of the Companies Act 1989 (c 40);

    (g)  the Financial Services and Markets Act 2000.

31  A disclosure for the purpose of enabling or assisting the Scottish Ministers to exercise their functions under the enactments relating to insolvency.

32  A disclosure for the purpose of enabling or assisting the Department of Enterprise, Trade and Investment for Northern Ireland to exercise any powers conferred on it by the enactments relating to companies or insolvency.

33  A disclosure for the purpose of enabling or assisting a person appointed or authorised by the Department of Enterprise, Trade and Investment for Northern Ireland under the enactments relating to companies or insolvency to exercise his functions.

34  A disclosure for the purpose of enabling or assisting the Pensions Regulator to exercise the functions conferred on it by or by virtue of any of the following—

    (a)  the Pension Schemes Act 1993 (c 48);

    (b)  the Pensions Act 1995 (c 26);

    (c)  the Welfare Reform and Pensions Act 1999 (c 30);

    (d)  the Pensions Act 2004 (c 35);

    (e)  any enactment in force in Northern Ireland corresponding to any of those enactments.

35  A disclosure for the purpose of enabling or assisting the Board of the Pension Protection Fund to exercise the functions conferred on it by or by virtue of Part 2 of the Pensions Act 2004 or any enactment in force in Northern Ireland corresponding to that Part.

36  A disclosure for the purpose of enabling or assisting—

    (a)  the Bank of England,

    (b)  the European Central Bank, or

    (c)  the central bank of any country or territory outside the United Kingdom, to exercise its functions.

37  A disclosure for the purpose of enabling or assisting the Commissioners for Her Majesty's Revenue and Customs to exercise their functions.

38  A disclosure for the purpose of enabling or assisting organs of the Society of Lloyd's (being organs constituted by or under the Act 1982 (c xiv)) to exercise their functions under or by virtue of the Lloyd's Acts 1871 to 1982.

39  A disclosure for the purpose of enabling or assisting the Office of Fair Trading to exercise its functions under any of the following—

    (a)  the Fair Trading Act 1973 (c 41);

    (b)  the Consumer Credit Act 1974 (c 39);

    (c)  the Estate Agents Act 1979 (c 38);

    (d)  the Competition Act 1980 (c 21);

    (e)  the Competition Act 1998 (c 41);

    (f)  the Financial Services and Markets Act 2000 (c 8);

    (g)  the Enterprise Act 2002 (c 40);

    (h)  the Control of Misleading Advertisements Regulations 1988 (SI 1988/915);

    (i)  the Unfair Terms in Consumer Contracts Regulations 1999 (SI 1999/2083).

40  A disclosure for the purpose of enabling or assisting the Competition Commission to exercise its functions under any of the following—

    (a)  the Fair Trading Act 1973;

    (b)  the Competition Act 1980;

(c) the Competition Act 1998;

(d) the Enterprise Act 2002.

**41** A disclosure with a view to the institution of, or otherwise for the purposes of, proceedings before the Competition Appeal Tribunal.

**42** A disclosure for the purpose of enabling or assisting an enforcer under Part 8 of the Enterprise Act 2002 (enforcement of consumer legislation) to exercise its functions under that Part.

**43** A disclosure for the purpose of enabling or assisting the Takeover Panel to perform any of its functions under Part 28 of this Act (takeovers etc).

**44** A disclosure for the purpose of enabling or assisting the Charity Commission to exercise its functions.

**45** A disclosure for the purpose of enabling or assisting the Attorney General to exercise his functions in connection with charities.

**46** A disclosure for the purpose of enabling or assisting the National Lottery Commission to exercise its functions under sections 5 to 10 (licensing) and 15 (power of Secretary of State to require information) of the National Lottery etc Act 1993 (c 39).

**47** A disclosure by the National Lottery Commission to the National Audit Office for the purpose of enabling or assisting the Comptroller and Auditor General to carry out an examination under Part 2 of the National Audit Act 1983 (c 44) into the economy, effectiveness and efficiency with which the National Lottery Commission has used its resources in discharging its functions under sections 5 to 10 of the National Lottery etc Act 1993.

**48** A disclosure for the purpose of enabling or assisting a qualifying body under the Unfair Terms in Consumer Contracts Regulations 1999 (SI 1999/2083) to exercise its functions under those Regulations.

**49** A disclosure for the purpose of enabling or assisting an enforcement authority under the Consumer Protection (Distance Selling) Regulations 2000 (SI 2000/2334) to exercise its functions under those Regulations.

**50** A disclosure for the purpose of enabling or assisting an enforcement authority under the Financial Services (Distance Marketing) Regulations 2004 (SI 2004/2095) to exercise its functions under those Regulations.

**51** A disclosure for the purpose of enabling or assisting a local weights and measures authority in England and Wales to exercise its functions under section 230(2) of the Enterprise Act 2002 (c 40) (notice of intention to prosecute, etc).

**52** A disclosure for the purpose of enabling or assisting the Financial Services Authority to exercise its functions under any of the following—

(a) the legislation relating to friendly societies or to industrial and provident societies;

(b) the Building Societies Act 1986 (c 53);

(c) Part 7 of the Companies Act 1989 (c 40) (financial markets and insolvency);

(d) the Financial Services and Markets Act 2000 (c 8).

**53** A disclosure for the purpose of enabling or assisting the competent authority for the purposes of Part 6 of the Financial Services and Markets Act 2000 (official listing) to exercise its functions under that Part.

**54** A disclosure for the purpose of enabling or assisting a body corporate established in accordance with section 212(1) of the Financial Services and Markets Act 2000 (compensation scheme manager) to exercise its functions.

**55** A disclosure for the purpose of enabling or assisting a recognised investment exchange or a recognised clearing house to exercise its functions as such.

'Recognised investment exchange' and 'recognised clearing house' have the same meaning as in section 285 of the Financial Services and Markets Act 2000.

**56** A disclosure for the purpose of enabling or assisting a person approved under the Uncertificated Securities Regulations 2001 (SI 2001/3755) as an operator of a relevant system (within the meaning of those regulations) to exercise his functions.

**57** A disclosure for the purpose of enabling or assisting a body designated under section 326(1) of the Financial Services and Markets Act 2000 (designated professional bodies) to exercise its functions in its capacity as a body designated under that section.

**58** A disclosure with a view to the institution of, or otherwise for the purposes of, civil proceedings arising under or by virtue of the Financial Services and Markets Act 2000.

**59** A disclosure for the purpose of enabling or assisting a body designated by order under section 1252 of this Act (delegation of functions of Secretary of State) to exercise its functions under Part 42 of this Act (statutory auditors).

**60** A disclosure for the purpose of enabling or assisting a recognised supervisory or qualifying body, within the meaning of Part 42 of this Act, to exercise its functions as such.

**61** A disclosure for the purpose of making available to an audited person information relating to a statutory audit of that person's accounts.

**62** A disclosure for the purpose of making available to the public information relating to monitoring or inspections carried out under arrangements within paragraph 23(1) of Schedule 10 to this Act (arrangements for independent monitoring of audits of listed companies and other major bodies), provided such information does not identify any audited person.

**63** A disclosure for the purpose of enabling or assisting an official receiver (including the Accountant in Bankruptcy in Scotland and the Official Assignee in Northern Ireland) to exercise his functions under the enactments relating to insolvency.

**64** A disclosure for the purpose of enabling or assisting the Insolvency Practitioners Tribunal to exercise its functions under the Insolvency Act 1986 (c 45).

**65** A disclosure for the purpose of enabling or assisting a body that is for the time being a recognised professional body for the purposes of section 391 of the Insolvency Act 1986 (recognised professional bodies) to exercise its functions as such.

**66** A disclosure for the purpose of enabling or assisting an overseas regulatory authority to exercise its regulatory functions.
'Overseas regulatory authority' and 'regulatory functions' have the same meaning as in section 82 of the Companies Act 1989.

**67** A disclosure for the purpose of enabling or assisting the Regulator of Community Interest Companies to exercise functions under the Companies (Audit, Investigations and Community Enterprise) Act 2004 (c 27).

**68** A disclosure with a view to the institution of, or otherwise for the purposes of, criminal proceedings.

**69** A disclosure for the purpose of enabling or assisting a person authorised by the Secretary of State under Part 2, 3 or 4 of the Proceeds of Crime Act 2002 (c 29) to exercise his functions.

**70** A disclosure with a view to the institution of, or otherwise for the purposes of, proceedings on an application under section 6, 7 or 8 of the Company Directors Disqualification Act 1986 (c 46) (disqualification for unfitness).

**[71** A disclosure with a view to the institution of, or otherwise for the purposes of, proceedings before the Upper Tribunal in respect of—
(a) a decision of the Financial Services Authority;
(b) a decision of the Bank of England; or
(c) a decision of a person relating to the assessment of any compensation or consideration under the Banking (Special Provisions) Act 2008 or the Banking Act 2009.][a]

**72** A disclosure for the purposes of proceedings before the Financial Services Tribunal by virtue of the Financial Services and Markets Act 2000 (Transitional Provisions) (Partly Completed Procedures) Order 2001 (SI 2001/3592).

**73** A disclosure for the purposes of proceedings before [a tribunal in relation to a decision of the Pensions Regulator][b].

**74** A disclosure for the purpose of enabling or assisting a body appointed under section 14 of the Companies (Audit, Investigations and Community Enterprise) Act 2004 (supervision of periodic accounts and reports of issuers of listed securities) to exercise functions mentioned in subsection (2) of that section.

**75** A disclosure with a view to the institution of, or otherwise for the purposes of, disciplinary proceedings relating to the performance by a relevant lawyer, foreign lawyer, auditor, accountant, valuer or actuary of his professional duties.
In this paragraph—
'foreign lawyer' means a person (other than a relevant lawyer) who is a foreign lawyer within the meaning of section 89(9) of the Courts and Legal Services Act 1990;
'relevant lawyer' means—
(a) a person who, for the purposes of the Legal Services Act 2007, is an authorised person in relation to an activity which constitutes a reserved legal activity (within the meaning of that Act),
(b) a solicitor or barrister in Northern Ireland, or
(c) a solicitor or advocate in Scotland.

**76** A disclosure with a view to the institution of, or otherwise for the purposes of, disciplinary proceedings relating to the performance by a public servant of his duties.
'Public servant' means an officer or employee of the Crown.

**77** A disclosure for the purpose of the provision of a summary or collection of information framed in such a way as not to enable the identity of any person to whom the information relates to be ascertained.

**78** A disclosure in pursuance of any Community obligation.

AMENDMENTS AND NOTES

[a] Substituted by the Transfer of Tribunal Functions Order 2010, SI 2010/22, Sch 2, para 143.

[b] Substituted by the Transfer of Tribunal Functions Order 2010, SI 2010/22, Sch 2, para 143.

COMMENCEMENT DATE 6 April 2008[51]

PART 3
OVERSEAS REGULATORY BODIES

**79** A disclosure is made in accordance with this Part of this Schedule if it is made to an EEA competent authority in accordance with section 1253B (requests from EEA competent authorities).

**80** A disclosure is made in accordance with this Part of this Schedule if it is—

    (a) a transfer of audit working papers to a third country competent authority in accordance with rules imposed under paragraph 16A of Schedule 10 (transfer of papers to third countries), or

    (b) a disclosure other than a transfer of audit working papers made to a third country competent authority for the purpose of enabling or assisting the authority to exercise its functions.][a]

AMENDMENTS AND NOTES

[a] Inserted by the Statutory Auditors and Third Country Auditors Regulations 2007, SI 2007/3494, reg 8, Schedule.

COMMENCEMENT DATE 6 April 2008[52]

---

SCHEDULE 12                                                    Section 1242
ARRANGEMENTS IN WHICH REGISTERED THIRD COUNTRY
AUDITORS ARE REQUIRED TO PARTICIPATE

**48.Sch12.01**    *Arrangements for independent monitoring of audits of [UK-traded non-EEA companies][a]*

**1** (1) The arrangements referred to in section 1242(1)(a) are appropriate arrangements—

    (a) for enabling the performance by the registered third country auditor of [functions related to the audit of UK-traded non-EEA companies][b] to be monitored by means of inspections carried out under the arrangements, and

    (b) for ensuring that the carrying out of such monitoring and inspections is done independently of the registered third country auditor.

    (2) [...][c]

AMENDMENTS

[a] Substituted by the Statutory Auditors and Third Country Auditors Regulations 2007, SI 2007/3494, reg 33(1), (2).

[b] Substituted by the Statutory Auditors and Third Country Auditors Regulations 2007, SI 2007/3494, reg 33(1), (3)(a).

[c] Repealed by the Statutory Auditors and Third Country Auditors Regulations 2007, SI 2007/3494, reg 33(1), (3)(b).

*Arrangements for independent investigations for disciplinary purposes*

**2** (1) The arrangements referred to in section 1242(1)(b) are appropriate arrangements—

    (a) for the carrying out of investigations into matters arising in connection with the performance of [functions related to the audit of UK-traded non-EEA companies][a] by the registered third country auditor,

    (b) for the holding of disciplinary hearings relating to the registered third country auditor which appear to be desirable following the conclusion of such investigations,

    (c) for requiring such hearings to be held in public except where the interests of justice otherwise require,

    (d) for the persons before whom such hearings have taken place to decide whether (and, if so, what) disciplinary action should be taken against the registered third country auditor, and

    (e) for ensuring that the carrying out of those investigations, the holding of those hearings and the taking of those decisions are done independently of the registered third country auditor.

    (2) In this paragraph—

    'disciplinary action' includes the imposition of a fine; and [...][b]

AMENDMENTS AND NOTES

---

[51] Statutory Auditors and Third Country Auditors Regulations 2007, SI 2007/3494, reg 1(2).
[52] Statutory Auditors and Third Country Auditors Regulations 2007, SI 2007/3494, reg 1(2).

ᵃ Substituted by the Statutory Auditors and Third Country Auditors Regulations 2007, SI 2007/3494, reg 33(1), (4)(a).

ᵇ Repealed by the Statutory Auditors and Third Country Auditors Regulations 2007, SI 2007/3494, reg 33(4)(b).

*Supplementary: arrangements to operate independently of third country auditor*

**3**  (1) This paragraph applies for the purposes of—
    (a)  paragraph 1(1)(b), or
    (b)  paragraph 2(1)(e).
   (2) Arrangements are not to be regarded as appropriate for the purpose of ensuring that a thing is done independently of the registered third country auditor unless they are designed to ensure that the registered third country auditor—
    (a)  will have no involvement in the appointment or selection of any of the persons who are to be responsible for doing that thing, and
    (b)  will not otherwise be involved in the doing of that thing.
   (3) Sub-paragraph (2) imposes a minimum requirement and does not preclude the possibility that additional criteria may need to be satisfied in order for the arrangements to be regarded as appropriate for the purpose in question.

*Supplementary: funding of arrangements*

**4**  (1) The registered third country auditor must pay any of the costs of maintaining any relevant arrangements which the arrangements provide are to be paid by it.
   (2) For this purpose 'relevant arrangements' are arrangements within paragraph 1 or 2 in which the registered third country auditor is obliged to participate.

*Supplementary: scope of arrangements*

**5**  Arrangements may qualify as arrangements within either of paragraphs 1 and 2 even though the matters for which they provide are more extensive in any respect than those mentioned in the applicable paragraph.

*Specification of particular arrangements by the Secretary of State*

**6**  (1) If there exist two or more sets of arrangements within paragraph 1 or within paragraph 2, the obligation of a registered third country auditor under section 1242(1)(a) or (b), as the case may be, is to participate in such set of arrangements as the Secretary of State may by order specify.
   (2) An order under sub-paragraph (1) is subject to negative resolution procedure.

COMMENCEMENT DATE: For the purpose of enabling the exercise of powers to make orders or regulations 20 January 2007.⁵³ Otherwise 6 April 2007⁵⁴

SCHEDULE 13                                    Section 1252

SUPPLEMENTARY PROVISIONS WITH RESPECT TO

DELEGATION ORDER

*Operation of this Schedule*                                              **48.Sch13.01**

**1**  (1) This Schedule has effect in relation to a body designated by a delegation order under section 1252 as follows—
    (a)  paragraphs 2 to 12 have effect in relation to the body where it is established by the order;
    (b)  paragraphs 2 and 6 to 11 have effect in relation to the body where it is an existing body;
    (c)  paragraph 13 has effect in relation to the body where it is an existing body that is an unincorporated association.
   (2) In their operation in accordance with sub-paragraph (1)(b), paragraphs 2 and 6 apply only in relation to—
    (a)  things done by or in relation to the body in or in connection with the exercise of functions transferred to it by the delegation order, and
    (b)  functions of the body which are functions so transferred.
   (3) Any power conferred by this Schedule to make provision by order is a power to make provision by an order under section 1252.

---

⁵³ Companies Act 2006 (Commencement No 1, Transitional Provisions and Savings) Order 2006, SI 2006/3428, art 3(3).
⁵⁴ Companies Act 2006 (Commencement No 5, Transitional Provisions and Savings) Order 2007, SI 2007/3495, art 4.

*Status*

**2**    The body is not to be regarded as acting on behalf of the Crown and its members, officers and employees are not to be regarded as Crown servants.

*Name, members and chairman*

**3**    (1)    The body is to be known by such name as may be specified in the delegation order.

(2)    The body is to consist of such persons (not being less than eight) as the Secretary of State may appoint after such consultation as he thinks appropriate.

(3)    The chairman of the body is to be such person as the Secretary of State may appoint from among its members.

(4)    The Secretary of State may make provision by order as to—

(a)    the terms on which the members of the body are to hold and vacate office;

(b)    the terms on which a person appointed as chairman is to hold and vacate the office of chairman.

*Financial provisions*

**4**    (1)    The body must pay to its chairman and members such remuneration, and such allowances in respect of expenses properly incurred by them in the performance of their duties, as the Secretary of State may determine.

(2)    As regards any chairman or member in whose case the Secretary of State so determines, the body must pay or make provision for the payment of—

(a)    such pension, allowance or gratuity to or in respect of that person on his retirement or death, or

(b)    such contributions or other payment towards the provision of such a pension, allowance or gratuity,
as the Secretary of State may determine.

(3)    Where—

(a)    a person ceases to be a member of the body otherwise than on the expiry of his term of office, and

(b)    it appears to the Secretary of State that there are special circumstances which make it right for that person to receive compensation,
the body must make a payment to him by way of compensation of such amount as the Secretary of State may determine.

*Proceedings*

**5**    (1)    The delegation order may contain such provision as the Secretary of State considers appropriate with respect to the proceedings of the body.

(2)    The delegation order may, in particular—

(a)    authorise the body to discharge any functions by means of committees consisting wholly or partly of members of the body;

(b)    provide that the validity of proceedings of the body, or of any such committee, is not affected by any vacancy among the members or any defect in the appointment of any member.

*Fees*

**6**    (1)    The body may retain fees payable to it.

(2)    The fees must be applied for—

(a)    meeting the expenses of the body in discharging its functions, and

(b)    any purposes incidental to those functions.

(3)    Those expenses include any expenses incurred by the body on such staff, accommodation, services and other facilities as appear to it to be necessary or expedient for the proper performance of its functions.

(4)    In prescribing the amount of fees in the exercise of the functions transferred to it the body must prescribe such fees as appear to it sufficient to defray those expenses, taking one year with another.

(5)    Any exercise by the body of the power to prescribe fees requires the approval of the Secretary of State.

(6)    The Secretary of State may, after consultation with the body, by order vary or revoke any regulations prescribing fees made by the body.

*Legislative functions*

**7**    (1)    Regulations or an order made by the body in the exercise of the functions transferred to it must be made by instrument in writing, but not by statutory instrument.

(2)    The instrument must specify the provision of this Part of this Act under which it is made.

(3)    The Secretary of State may by order impose such requirements as he thinks necessary or expedient as to the circumstances and manner in which the body must consult on any regulations or order it proposes to make.

(4) Nothing in this Part applies to make regulations or an order made by the body subject to negative resolution procedure or affirmative resolution procedure.

8 (1) Immediately after an instrument is made it must be printed and made available to the public with or without payment.

(2) A person is not to be taken to have contravened any regulation or order if he shows that at the time of the alleged contravention the instrument containing the regulation or order had not been made available as required by this paragraph.

9 (1) The production of a printed copy of an instrument purporting to be made by the body on which is endorsed a certificate signed by an officer of the body authorised by it for the purpose and stating—

  (a) that the instrument was made by the body,
  (b) that the copy is a true copy of the instrument, and
  (c) that on a specified date the instrument was made available to the public as required by paragraph 8,
    is evidence (or, in Scotland, sufficient evidence) of the facts stated in the certificate.

(2) A certificate purporting to be signed as mentioned in sub-paragraph (1) is to be deemed to have been duly signed unless the contrary is shown.

(3) Any person wishing in any legal proceedings to cite an instrument made by the body may require the body to cause a copy of it to be endorsed with such a certificate as is mentioned in this paragraph.

*Report and accounts*

10 (1) The body must, at least once in each calendar year for which the delegation order is in force, make a report to the Secretary of State on—

  (a) the discharge of the functions transferred to it, and
  (b) such other matters as the Secretary of State may by order require.

(2) The delegation order may modify sub-paragraph (1) as it has effect in relation to the calendar year in which the order comes into force or is revoked.

(3) The Secretary of State must lay before Parliament copies of each report received by him under this paragraph.

(4) The following provisions of this paragraph apply as follows—

  (a) sub-paragraphs (5) and (6) apply only where the body is established by the order, and
  (b) sub-paragraphs (7) and (8) apply only where the body is an existing body.

(5) The Secretary of State may, with the consent of the Treasury, give directions to the body with respect to its accounts and the audit of its accounts.

(6) A person may only be appointed as auditor of the body if he is eligible for appointment as a statutory auditor.

(7) Unless the body is a company to which section 394 (duty to prepare individual company accounts) applies, the Secretary of State may, with the consent of the Treasury, give directions to the body with respect to its accounts and the audit of its accounts.

(8) Whether or not the body is a company to which section 394 applies, the Secretary of State may direct that any provisions of this Act specified in the directions are to apply to the body, with or without any modifications so specified.

*Other supplementary provisions*

11 (1) The transfer of a function to a body designated by a delegation order does not affect anything previously done in the exercise of the function transferred; and the resumption of a function so transferred does not affect anything previously done in exercise of the function resumed.

(2) The Secretary of State may by order make such transitional and other supplementary provision as he thinks necessary or expedient in relation to the transfer or resumption of a function.

(3) The provision that may be made in connection with the transfer of a function includes, in particular, provision—

  (a) for modifying or excluding any provision of this Part of this Act in its application to the function transferred;
  (b) for applying to the body designated by the delegation order, in connection with the function transferred, any provision applying to the Secretary of State which is contained in or made under any other enactment;
  (c) for the transfer of any property, rights or liabilities from the Secretary of State to that body;
  (d) for the carrying on and completion by that body of anything in the process of being done by the Secretary of State when the order takes effect;
  (e) for the substitution of that body for the Secretary of State in any instrument, contract or legal proceedings.

(4) The provision that may be made in connection with the resumption of a function includes, in particular, provision—

  (a) for the transfer of any property, rights or liabilities from that body to the Secretary of State;
  (b) for the carrying on and completion by the Secretary of State of anything in the process of being done by that body when the order takes effect;

      (c)  for the substitution of the Secretary of State for that body in any instrument, contract or legal proceedings.

**12**  Where a delegation order is revoked, the Secretary of State may by order make provision—

      (a)  for the payment of compensation to persons ceasing to be employed by the body established by the delegation order;

      (b)  as to the winding up and dissolution of the body.

**13**  (1)  This paragraph applies where the body is an unincorporated association.

      (2)  Any relevant proceedings may be brought by or against the body in the name of any body corporate whose constitution provides for the establishment of the body.

      (3)  In sub-paragraph (2) 'relevant proceedings' means proceedings brought in or in connection with the exercise of any transferred function.

      (4)  In relation to proceedings brought as mentioned in sub-paragraph (2), any reference in paragraph 11(3)(e) or (4)(c) to the body replacing or being replaced by the Secretary of State in any legal proceedings is to be read with the appropriate modifications.

COMMENCEMENT DATE: For the purpose of enabling the exercise of powers to make orders or regulations 20 January 2007.[55] Otherwise 6 April 2007[56]

[55] Companies Act 2006 (Commencement No. 1, Transitional Provisions and Savings) Order 2006, SI 2006/3428, art 3(3).

[56] Companies Act 2006 (Commencement No 5, Transitional Provisions and Savings) Order 2007, SI 2007/3495, art 3(1)(u).

# 49

## UNCERTIFICATED SECURITIES REGULATIONS 2001 (SI 2001/3755)

These Regulations, as amended, make provision for dematerialized transfer of securities within a computer-based system. They are drafted so as to allow for the possibility of competing systems. In reality, there is only one system, which is known as CREST. This is now operated by Euroclear UK & Ireland, part of the Euroclear Group which operates securities settlement systems in several European countries. CREST came into operation in April 1997, replacing Talisman, the former settlement system operated by the London Stock Exchange. Euroclear is an approved operator under the Regulations and also a recognized clearing house[1] under the Financial Services and Markets Act 2000.

The CREST system provides settlement facilities for shares and other financial instruments, in particular UK government bonds, money market instruments, covered warrants, UK and Irish unit trusts, and OEICs and exchange traded funds, as well as a wide range of international securities including eurobonds. Ownership and transfer is 'dematerialized' in the sense that CREST operates on an 'uncertificated' basis, with legal title being constituted by entries in the operator register (although it remains possible for an issuer to have certificated shares). While issuers of securities maintain an issuer register that is a mirror image of the (CREST) operator register, it is the latter that is definitive for the purposes of ownership. In order to reduce risk for market participants and credit providers, the system operates on the basis of an advanced form of 'delivery versus payment' in which there is simultaneous and irrevocable transfer of cash and securities for all sterling and euro-denominated transactions.

CREST operates a 'direct' form of settlement in which CREST members own securities directly (although investors who are not CREST members hold their securities indirectly through such members). Securities are transferred within CREST by the operation of an account system that parallels the register maintained by the issuer. CREST maintains such accounts for members showing the same information as the issuer's register. A transfer is made by debiting the CREST account of the seller and crediting the account of the buyer (or the member of CREST acting for a buyer in the case of buyers who are not CREST members). This form of direct transfer of ownership within CREST differs from certificated transfer in that a buyer of certificated securities becomes the legal owner only on entry in the issuer register (and not on delivery of the certificate to the buyer).

In order to reduce risk for market participants and credit providers, the CREST system operates on the basis of an advanced form of 'delivery versus payment' in which there is simultaneous and irrevocable transfer of cash and securities for all sterling and Euro denominated transactions.

## PART 1
### CITATION, COMMENCEMENT, AND INTERPRETATION

**Citation and commencement**                                                    49.USR.03

**1.** These Regulations may be cited as the Uncertificated Securities Regulations 2001 and shall come into force on 26th November 2001.

**Purposes and basic definition**

**2.** (1) These Regulations enable title to units of a security to be evidenced otherwise than by a certificate and transferred otherwise than by a written instrument, and make provision for certain supplementary and incidental matters; and in these Regulations 'relevant system' means a computer-based system, and procedures, which enable title to units of a security to be evidenced and transferred without a written instrument, and which facilitate supplementary and incidental matters.

---

[1] Clearing houses undertake two functions. First, they operate systems that enable settlement of mutual obligations on a net basis. Second, they act as counterparties in transactions, thereby reducing the credit risk that is associated with transactions, especially when the identity of the other party is not known (eg in order-driven markets such as the LSE's SETS).

(2) Where title to a unit of a security is evidenced otherwise than by a certificate by virtue of these Regulations, the transfer of title to such a unit of a security shall be subject to these Regulations.

## Interpretation

**3.** (1) In these Regulations—

['the 1877 Act' means the Treasury Bills Act 1877;

'the 1950 Act' means the Exchequer and Financial Provisions Act (Northern Ireland) 1950;][a]

[…][b]'the 1986 Act' means the Financial Services Act 1986;

'the 2000 Act' means the Financial Services and Markets Act 2000;

['the 2006 Act' means the Companies Act 2006][c]

[…][d][…][e]

['the 1968 Regulations' means the Treasury Bills Regulations 1968;][f]

'the 1974 Regulations' means the Local Authority (Stocks and Bonds) Regulations 1974; and 'local authority' has the same meaning as it has in those Regulations;

'the 1995 Regulations' means the Uncertificated Securities Regulations 1995;

['the 2003 Regulations' means the Uncertificated Securities (Amendment) (Eligible Debt Securities) Regulations 2003;][g]['the 2004 Regulations' means the Government Stock Regulations 2004;][h]

'the Authority' means the Financial Services Authority referred to in section 1 of the 2000 Act;

'certificate' means any certificate, instrument or other document of, or evidencing, title to units of a security;

'company' means a company within the meaning of [section 1(1) of the 2006 Act][i];

'dematerialised instruction' means an instruction sent or received by means of a relevant system;

'designated agency' has the meaning given by regulation 11(1);

['eligible debt security' means—

(a) a security that satisfies the following conditions—

(i) the security is constituted by an order, promise, engagement or acknowledgement to pay on demand, or at a determinable future time, a sum in money to, or to the order of, the holder of one or more units of the security; and

(ii) the current terms of issue of the security provide that its units may only be held in uncertificated form and title to them may only be transferred by means of a relevant system;

(b) an eligible Northern Ireland Treasury Bill; or

(c) an eligible Treasury bill;

'eligible Northern Ireland Treasury Bill' means a security—

(a) constituted by a Northern Ireland Treasury Bill issued in accordance with the 1950 Act as modified by Part 2 of Schedule 1 to the 2003 Regulations; and

(b) whose current terms of issue provide that its units may only be held in uncertificated form and title to them may only be transferred by means of a relevant system;

'eligible Treasury bill' means a security—

(a) constituted by a Treasury bill issued in accordance with the 1877 Act and the 1968 Regulations as modified by Part 1 of Schedule 1 to the 2003 Regulations; and

(b) whose current terms of issue provide that its units may only be held in uncertificated form and title to them may only be transferred by means of a relevant system;][j]

'enactment' includes an enactment comprised in any subordinate legislation within the meaning of the Interpretation Act 1978, and an enactment comprised in, or in an instrument made under, an Act of the Scottish Parliament;

['general local authority security' means a local authority security that is not an eligible debt security;

'general public sector security' means a public sector security that is not an eligible debt security;

'general UK Government security' means a UK Government security that is not an eligible debt security;][k]

'generate', in relation to an Operator-instruction, means to initiate the procedures by which the Operator-instruction comes to be sent;

'guidance', in relation to an Operator, means guidance issued by him which is intended to have continuing effect and is issued in writing or other legible form, which if it were a rule, would come within the definition of a rule;

'instruction' includes any instruction, election, acceptance or any other message of any kind;

'interest in a security' means any legal or equitable interest or right in relation to a security, including—

(a) an absolute or contingent right to acquire a security created, allotted or issued or to be created, allotted or issued; and

(b) the interests or rights of a person for whom a security is held on trust or by a custodian or depositary;

'issue', in relation to a new unit of a security, means to confer title to a new unit on a person;

'issuer-instruction' means a properly authenticated dematerialised instruction attributable to a participating issuer;

'issuer register of members' has the meaning given by regulation 20(1)(a);

'issuer register of securities'—

(a)  in relation to shares, means an issuer register of members; and

[(b) in relation to units of a security other than
    (i)  shares,
    (ii)  securities in respect of which regulation 22(3) applies, or
    (iii)  wholly dematerialised securities,
      means a register of persons holding the units, maintained by or on behalf of the issuer
      or, in the case of public sector securities, by or on behalf of the person specified in
      regulation 21(3)]$^{l}$;

      ['local authority'—

(a)  in relation to a security referred to in paragraph (a)(i) of the definition of 'local authority
    security', has the same meaning as in the 1974 Regulations;

[(b) in relation to a security referred to in paragraph (b) of the definition of 'local authority
    security', has the same meaning as in section 23 of the Local Government Act 2003 ('local
    authority')]$^{m}$;]$^{n}$

      ['local authority security' means a security which is either—

(a)  a security other than an eligible debt security which, when held in certificated form is—
    (i)  transferable in accordance with regulation 7(1) of the 1974 Regulations and title to
       which must be registered in accordance with regulation 5 of those Regulations; or
    (ii)  [...]$^{o}$

(b)  an eligible debt security issued by a local authority;]$^{p}$

      'officer', in relation to an Operator or a participating issuer, includes—

(a)  where the Operator or the participating issuer is a company, such persons as are mentioned
    in [section 1173(1) of the 2006 Act]$^{q}$;

(b)  where the Operator or the participating issuer is a partnership, a partner; or in the event
    that no partner is situated in the United Kingdom, a person in the United Kingdom who is
    acting on behalf of a partner; and

(c)  where the Operator or the participating issuer is neither a company nor a partnership, any
    member of its governing body; or in the event that no member of its governing body is
    situated in the United Kingdom, a person in the United Kingdom who is acting on behalf
    of any member of its governing body;

      'Operator' means a person approved by the Treasury under these Regulations as Operator
      of a relevant system (and in Schedule 1 includes a person who has applied to the
      Treasury under regulation 4 for their approval of him as an Operator);

      'Operator-instruction' means a properly authenticated dematerialised instruction attribut-
      able to an Operator;

      'Operator register of corporate securities' has the meaning given by regulation 22(2)(a)(i);

      ['Operator register of eligible debt securities' has the meaning given by regulation
      22(3A)(a);

      'Operator register of general public sector securities' has the meaning given by regulation
      21(1)(a);]$^{r}$

      'Operator register of members' has the meaning given by regulation 20(1)(b);
      [...]$^{s}$

      'Operator register of securities'—

(a)  in relation to shares, means an Operator register of members;

(b)  in relation to units of a security other than shares, means an Operator register of corporate
    securities, an Operator register of [general public sector securities, an Operator register of
    eligible debt securities or, as the case may be, a register maintained by an Operator in
    accordance with regulation 22(3)(a)]$^{t}$;

      'Operator's conversion rules' means the rules made and practices instituted by the
      Operator in order to comply with paragraph 18 of Schedule 1;

      'Operator-system' means those facilities and procedures which are part of the relevant
      system, which are maintained and operated by or for an Operator, by which he
      generates Operator-instructions and receives dematerialised instructions from system-
      participants and by which persons change the form in which units of a participating
      security are held;

      'participating issuer' means (subject to paragraph (3)) a person who has issued a security
      which is a participating security;

      'participating security' means a security title to units of which is permitted by an Operator
      to be transferred by means of a relevant system;

      'public sector securities' means UK Government securities and local authority securities;

      ['record of uncertificated general public sector securities' has the meaning given by
      regulation 21(2)(a);]$^{u}$

      'record of securities' means any of a record of uncertificated corporate securities, a record
      of uncertificated shares and a record of uncertificated [general public sector securities]$^{v}$;

      'record of uncertificated corporate securities' has the meaning given by regulation
      22(2)(b)(ii);

'record of uncertificated shares' has the meaning given by regulation 20(6)(a); 'register of members' means either or both of an issuer register of members and an Operator register of members;

'register of securities' means either or both of an issuer register of securities and an Operator register of securities;

'relevant system' has the meaning given by regulation 2(1); and 'relevant system' includes an Operator-system;

'rules', in relation to an Operator, means rules made or conditions imposed by him with respect to the provision of the relevant system;

'securities' means shares, stock, debentures, debenture stock, loan stock, bonds, units of a collective investment scheme within the meaning of section 235 of the 2000 Act, rights under a depositary receipt within the meaning of paragraph 4 of Schedule 2 to the Criminal Justice Act 1993, and other securities of any description, and interests in a security;

'settlement', [except in paragraph 28 of Schedule 1,]ᵂ in relation to a transfer of uncertificated units of a security between two system-members by means of a relevant system, means the delivery of those units to the transferee and, where appropriate, the creation of any associated obligation to make payments, in accordance with the rules and practices of the Operator; and 'settle' shall be construed accordingly;

'settlement bank', in relation to a relevant system, means a person who has contracted to make payments in connection with transfers of title to uncertificated units of a security by means of that system;

'share' means share (or stock) in the share capital of a company;

'system-member', in relation to a relevant system, means a person who is permitted by an Operator to transfer by means of that system title to uncertificated units of a security held by him, and shall include, where relevant, two or more persons who are jointly so permitted;

'system-member instruction' means a properly authenticated dematerialised instruction attributable to a system-member;

'system-participant', in relation to a relevant system, means a person who is permitted by an Operator to send and receive properly authenticated dematerialised instructions; and 'sponsoring system-participant' means a system-participant who is permitted by an Operator to send properly authenticated dematerialised instructions attributable to another person and to receive properly authenticated dematerialised instructions on another person's behalf;

'system-user', in relation to a relevant system, means a person who as regards that system is a participating issuer, a system-member, system-participant or settlement bank;

'UK Government security' means a security issued by Her Majesty's Government in the United Kingdom or by a Northern Ireland department;

'uncertificated', in relation to a unit of a security, means (subject to regulation 42(11)(a)) that title to the unit is recorded on the relevant Operator register of securities, and may, by virtue of these Regulations, be transferred by means of a relevant system; and 'certificated', in relation to a unit of a security, means that the unit is not an uncertificated unit;

'unit', in relation to a security, means the smallest possible transferable unit of the security (for example a single share);

'wholly dematerialised security' means—

(a) a strip, in relation to any stock or bond, within the meaning of section 47(1B) of the Finance Act 1942; or

(b) a participating security whose terms of issue (or, in the case of shares, where its terms of issue or the articles of association of the company in question) provide that its units may only be held in uncertificated form and title to them may only be transferred by means of a relevant system;

and other expressions have the meanings given to them by [the Companies Acts (as defined by section 2 of the 2006 Act)]ˣ.

(2) For the purposes of these Regulations—

(a) a dematerialised instruction is properly authenticated if it complies with the specifications referred to in paragraph 5(3) of Schedule 1; or if it was given, and not withdrawn, before these Regulations came into force and was properly authenticated within the meaning of regulation 3(2)(a) of the 1995 Regulations;

(b) a dematerialised instruction is attributable to a person if it is expressed to have been sent by that person, or if it is expressed to have been sent on behalf of that person, in accordance with the rules and specifications referred to in paragraph 5(4) of Schedule 1; and a dematerialised instruction may be attributable to more than one person.

(3) In respect of a participating security which is a [general]ʸ public sector security, references in these Regulations to the participating issuer shall, other than in regulation 41, be taken to be references—

(a) in the case of a local authority security—

        (i)   to the relevant local authority; or

        (ii)  if the local authority has appointed another person to act as registrar for the purpose of the 1974 Regulations in respect of that security, to the person so appointed; and

    (b)  in the case of any other [general]$^z$ public sector security, to [the Registrar of Government Stock]$^{aa}$.

[(4) In respect of a security which is an eligible debt security, references in these regulations to the issuer or the participating issuer of that security (or units of that security) shall be taken to be references to—

    (a)  a person ('P') who undertakes as principal to perform the payment obligation constituted by the security in accordance with its current terms of issue; and

    (b)  any other person who undertakes as principal to perform that obligation in accordance with those terms in the event that P fails to do so.

(5)  For the purposes of paragraph (4)(b), a person who undertakes to perform an obligation under a contract of guarantee or other contract of suretyship is not to be regarded as undertaking to perform it as principal.

(6)  For the purposes of paragraph (a) of the definition of 'eligible debt security' in paragraph (1), a sum of money—

    (a)  is to be regarded as payable at a determinable future time if it is payable—

        (i)   at a future time fixed by or in accordance with the current terms of issue of the security; or

        (ii)  at the expiry of a fixed period after the occurrence of a specified event which is certain to happen, though the time of happening may be uncertain; and

    (b)  is not to be regarded as payable at a determinable future time if it is payable on a contingency.]$^{ab}$

AMENDMENTS AND NOTES

[a]  Inserted by the Uncertificated Securities (Amendment) (Eligible Debt Securities) Regulations 2003, SI 2003/1633, reg 3.

[b]  Revoked by the Companies Act (Consequential Amendments) (Uncertificated Securities) Order 2009, SI 2009/1889, art 2.

[c]  Amended by the Companies Act (Consequential Amendments) (Uncertificated Securities) Order 2009, SI 2009/1889, art 2(2).

[d]  Revoked by the Companies Act (Consequential Amendments) (Uncertificated Securities) Order 2009, SI 2009/1889, art 2.

[e]  Revoked by the Government Stock (Consequential and Transitional Provision) (No 2) Order 2004, SI 2004/1662, Schedule, Pt 3, para 29.

[f]  Inserted by the Uncertificated Securities (Amendment) (Eligible Debt Securities) Regulations 2003, SI 2003/1633, reg 3.

[g]  Inserted by the Uncertificated Securities (Amendment) (Eligible Debt Securities) Regulations 2003, SI 2003/1633, reg 3.

[h]  Inserted by the Government Stock (Consequential and Transitional Provision) (No 2) Order 2004, SI 2004/1662, Schedule, Pt 3, para 29.

[i]  Amended by the Companies Act (Consequential Amendments) (Uncertificated Securities) Order 2009, SI 2009/1889, art 2(2).

[j]  Inserted by the Uncertificated Securities (Amendment) (Eligible Debt Securities) Regulations 2003, SI 2003/1633, reg 3.

[k]  Inserted by the Uncertificated Securities (Amendment) (Eligible Debt Securities) Regulations 2003, SI 2003/1633, reg 3.

[l]  Amended by the Uncertificated Securities (Amendment) (Eligible Debt Securities) Regulations 2003, SI 2003/1633, reg 3.

[m]  Amended by the Local Authorities (Capital Finance) (Further Consequential and Saving Provisions) Order 2004, SI 2004/2044, art 6.

[n]  Inserted by the Uncertificated Securities (Amendment) (Eligible Debt Securities) Regulations 2003, SI 2003/1633, reg 3.

[o]  Revoked by the Local Authorities (Capital Finance) (Further Consequential and Saving Provisions) Order 2004, SI 2004/2044, art 6.

[p]  Amended by the Uncertificated Securities (Amendment) (Eligible Debt Securities) Regulations 2003, SI 2003/1633, reg 3.

[q]  Amended by the Companies Act (Consequential Amendments) (Uncertificated Securities) Order 2009, SI 2009/1889, art 2(2).

[r]  Inserted by the Uncertificated Securities (Amendment) (Eligible Debt Securities) Regulations 2003, SI 2003/1633, reg 3.

[s]  Revoked by the Uncertificated Securities (Amendment) (Eligible Debt Securities) Regulations 2003, SI 2003/1633, reg 3.

[t]  Amended by the Uncertificated Securities (Amendment) (Eligible Debt Securities) Regulations 2003, SI 2003/1633, reg 3.

ᵘ Amended by the Uncertificated Securities (Amendment) (Eligible Debt Securities) Regulations
2003, SI 2003/1633, reg 3.

ᵛ Amended by the Uncertificated Securities (Amendment) (Eligible Debt Securities) Regulations
2003, SI 2003/1633, reg 3.

ʷ Inserted by the Uncertificated Securities (Amendment) Regulations 2007, SI 2007/124, reg 2.

ˣ Amended by the Companies Act (Consequential Amendments) (Uncertificated Securities) Order
2009, SI 2009/1889, art 2(2).

ʸ Inserted by the Uncertificated Securities (Amendment) (Eligible Debt Securities) Regulations 2003,
SI 2003/1633, reg 4.

ᶻ Inserted by the Uncertificated Securities (Amendment) (Eligible Debt Securities) Regulations 2003,
SI 2003/1633, reg 4.

ᵃᵃ Amended by the Government Stock (Consequential and Transitional Provision) (No 2) Order
2004, SI 2004/1662, Schedule, Pt 3, para 29.

ᵃᵇ Inserted by the Uncertificated Securities (Amendment) (Eligible Debt Securities) Regulations
2003, SI 2003/1633, reg 4.

**49.USR.04**    This part of the Regulations mainly sets out definitions that are relevant for the subsequent parts of the
Regulations. The following are of particular significance for the commentary below:

- 'Operator' means a person approved by the Treasury under these Regulations as operator of a
relevant system.
- 'Relevant System' means a computer-based system, and procedures, which enable title to units of a
security to be evidenced and transferred without a written instrument, and which facilitate supplementary and incidental matters.
- 'System Member', in relation to a relevant system, means a person who is permitted by an operator to
transfer by means of that system title to uncertificated units of a security held by him, and shall
include, where relevant, two or more persons who are jointly so permitted.
- 'Participating Issuer' means a person who has issued a security which is a participating security.


# PART 2
## THE OPERATOR
### *Approval and Compliance*

**49.USR.05**    **Applications for approval**

    **4.**  (1)  Any person may apply to the Treasury for their approval of him as Operator of a relevant
system.

        (2)  The application shall be made in such manner as the Treasury may direct and shall be
accompanied by—

            (a)  a copy of the rules and any guidance to be issued by the applicant; and

            (b)  such other information as the Treasury may reasonably require for the purpose of
determining the application.

        (3)  At any time after receiving an application and before determining it, the Treasury may require
the applicant to provide such further information as they reasonably consider necessary to
enable them to determine the application.

        (4)  Information which the Treasury require under this regulation shall, if they so require, be
provided in such form, or verified in such manner, as they may direct.

        (5)  Different directions may be given, or requirements imposed, by the Treasury with respect to
different applications.


**Grant and refusal of approval**

    **5.**  (1)  If, on an application made under regulation 4, it appears to the Treasury that the require-
ments of Schedule 1 (which imposes requirements which must appear to the Treasury to be
satisfied with respect to an Operator, his rules and practices and the relevant system) are
satisfied with respect to the application, they may—

            (a)  subject to the payment of any fee charged by virtue of regulation 6(1); and

            (b)  subject to the provisions of Schedule 2,

          approve the applicant as Operator of a relevant system.

        (2)  In considering an application, the Treasury may have regard to any information which they
consider is relevant to the application.

        (3)  An approval under this regulation shall be by instrument in writing and shall state the date on
which it is to take effect.

        (4)  Schedule 3 shall have effect in relation to a decision to refuse an application made under
regulation 4 as if references to an Operator were to the applicant.

(5) Provided that it had not been withdrawn before these Regulations came into force, an approval granted to a person under regulation 5 of the 1995 Regulations shall be treated as having been granted under this regulation.

## Fees charged by the Treasury

**6.** (1) The Treasury may charge a fee to a person seeking approval as Operator of a relevant system.

(2) The Treasury may charge an Operator a periodical fee.

(3) Any fee chargeable by the Treasury under this regulation shall not exceed an amount which reasonably represents the amount of costs incurred—

(a) in the case of a fee charged to a person seeking approval, in determining whether to grant approval; and

(b) in the case of a periodical fee, in satisfying themselves that the Operator, his rules and practices and the relevant system continue to meet the requirements of Schedule 1 and that the Operator is complying with any obligations imposed on him by or under these Regulations.

(4) For the purposes of paragraph (3), the costs incurred by the Treasury shall be determined on the basis that they include such proportion of the following matters as are properly attributable to the performance of the relevant function—

(a) expenditure on staff, equipment, premises, facilities, research and development;

(b) the allocation, over a period of years, whether before or after the coming into force of these Regulations, of any initial expenditure incurred wholly and exclusively to perform the function or to prepare for its performance;

(c) any notional interest incurred on any capital expended on or in connection with the performance of the function or in preparing for its performance and, in a case in which any function is exercisable by the designated agency, any actual interest payable on any sums borrowed which have been so expended; and

(d) any other matter which, in accordance with generally accepted accounting principles, may properly be taken account of in ascertaining the costs properly attributable to the performance of the function.

(5) For the purposes of paragraph (4)(c)—

(a) 'notional interest' means any interest which that person might reasonably have been expected to have been liable to pay had the sums expended been borrowed at arm's length; and

(b) 'actual interest' means the actual interest paid on sums borrowed in a transaction at arm's length and, where a sum has been borrowed otherwise than in such a transaction, means whichever is the lesser of the interest actually paid and the interest that might reasonably have been expected to be paid had the transaction been at arm's length.

(6) Any fee received by the Treasury under this regulation shall be paid into the Consolidated Fund.

(7) Any fee received by the designated agency under this regulation may be retained by it.

## *Supervision*

## Withdrawal of approval

**7.** (1) The Treasury may withdraw an Operator's approval at the request, or with the consent, of the Operator.

(2) If it appears to the Treasury that—

(a) any requirement of Schedule 1 is not satisfied in relation to an Operator; or

(b) an Operator is failing or has failed to comply with any obligation imposed on him by or under these Regulations,

they may withdraw approval from that Operator by written instrument even though the Operator does not wish his approval to be withdrawn.

(3) Schedule 3 shall have effect as regards the procedure to be followed before withdrawing an Operator's approval under paragraph (2).

(4) An instrument withdrawing an Operator's approval shall state the date on which it is to take effect.

(5) In the case of an instrument withdrawing an Operator's approval under paragraph (2), the date stated shall not be earlier than the end of the period of three months beginning with the day on which the instrument is executed.

(6) An instrument withdrawing an Operator's approval may contain such transitional provisions as the Treasury think necessary or expedient.

## Compliance orders and directions

**8.** (1) This regulation applies if it appears to the Treasury that—

(a) any requirement of Schedule 1 is not satisfied, or is likely not to be satisfied, in relation to an Operator; or

(b) an Operator has failed to comply with any obligation imposed on him by or under these Regulations.

(2) The Treasury may—

(a) make an application to the court; or

(b) subject to paragraph (4), direct the Operator to take specified steps for the purpose of securing—

(i) that the relevant requirement of Schedule 1 is satisfied in relation to the Operator; or

(ii) the Operator's compliance with any obligation of the kind in question.

(3) If on any application by the Treasury under paragraph (2)(a) the court is satisfied that the relevant requirement of Schedule 1 is not satisfied or is likely not to be satisfied, or, as the case may be, that the Operator has failed to comply with the obligation in question, it may order the Operator to take such steps as the court directs for securing that the requirement is satisfied or that the obligation is complied with.

(4) Schedule 3 shall have effect as regards the procedure to be followed before giving a direction under paragraph (2)(b).

(5) A direction under paragraph (2)(b) is enforceable, on the application of the Treasury, by an injunction or, in Scotland, by an order for specific performance under section 45 of the Court of Session Act 1988.

(6) The jurisdiction conferred by paragraph (3) shall be exercisable by the High Court and the Court of Session.

(7) The fact that a rule made or condition imposed by an Operator has been altered in response to a direction given by the Treasury under paragraph (2)(b) or an order of the court under paragraph (3) does not prevent it from being subsequently altered or revoked by the Operator.

## Injunctions and restitution orders

**9.** (1) If on the application of the Treasury the court is satisfied—

(a) that there is a reasonable likelihood that any person will contravene a relevant rule; or

(b) that any person has contravened a relevant rule, and that there is a reasonable likelihood that the contravention will continue or be repeated,

the court may make an order restraining (or in Scotland an interdict prohibiting) the contravention.

(2) If on the application of the Treasury the court is satisfied—

(a) that any person has contravened a relevant rule; and

(b) that there are steps which could be taken for remedying the contravention,

the court may make an order requiring that person and any other person who appears to the court to have been knowingly concerned in the contravention to take such steps as the court may direct to remedy it.

(3) No application shall be made by the Treasury under paragraph (1) or (2) in respect of a relevant rule unless it appears to them that the Operator of the relevant system is unable or unwilling to take appropriate steps to restrain the contravention or to require the person concerned to take such steps as are mentioned in paragraph (2)(b).

(4) If on the application of the Treasury the court is satisfied that any person may have—

(a) contravened a relevant rule; or

(b) been knowingly concerned in the contravention of a relevant rule,

the court may make an order restraining (or in Scotland an interdict prohibiting) him from disposing of, or otherwise dealing with, any assets of his which it is satisfied he is reasonably likely to dispose of or otherwise deal with.

(5) The court may, on the application of the Treasury, make an order under paragraph (6) if it is satisfied that a person has contravened a relevant rule, or been knowingly concerned in the contravention of such a rule, and—

(a) that profits have accrued to him as a result of the contravention; or

(b) that one or more persons have suffered loss or been otherwise adversely affected as a result of the contravention.

(6) The court may order the person concerned to pay to the Treasury such sum as appears to the court to be just having regard—

(a) in a case within subparagraph (a) of paragraph (5), to the profits appearing to the court to have accrued;

(b) in a case within subparagraph (b) of that paragraph, to the extent of the loss or other adverse effect; or

(c) in a case within both of those subparagraphs, to the profits appearing to the court to have accrued and to the extent of the loss or other adverse effect.

(7) Subsections (3) to (5) and (8) of section 382 of the 2000 Act shall apply in relation to an application of the Treasury under paragraph (5) as they have effect in relation to an application of the Authority under subsection (1) of that section; and in those subsections as they so apply—

(a) the references to subsections (1) and (2) shall be taken to be references to paragraphs (5) and (6) respectively;

(b) the references to paragraphs (a) and (b) of subsection (1) shall be taken to be references to subparagraphs (a) and (b) respectively of paragraph (5).

(8) The jurisdiction conferred by this regulation shall be exercisable by the High Court and the Court of Session.

(9) Nothing in this regulation affects the right of any person other than the Treasury to bring proceedings in respect of matters to which this regulation applies.

(10) In this regulation, 'relevant rule' means any provision of the rules of an Operator to which the person in question is subject and which regulate the carrying on by that person of business of any of the following kinds—

(a) dealing in investments as principal;

(b) dealing in investments as agent;

(c) arranging deals in investments;

(d) managing investments;

(e) safeguarding and administering investments;

(f) sending dematerialised instructions;

(g) establishing etc. a collective investment scheme;

(h) advising on investments; or

(i) agreeing to carry on any of the activities mentioned in paragraphs (a) to (h).

(11) In paragraph (2), references to remedying a contravention include references to mitigating its effect.

(12) Paragraph (10) shall be read with—

(a) section 22 of the 2000 Act;

(b) any relevant order under that section; and

(c) Schedule 2 to that Act.

## Provision of information by Operators

**10.** (1) The Treasury may, in writing, require an Operator to give them such information as they may specify.

(2) The Treasury may also, in writing, require an Operator to give them, at such times or in respect of such periods as they may specify, such information relating to that Operator as they may specify.

(3) Any information required to be given under this regulation shall be only such as the Treasury may reasonably require for the exercise of their functions under these Regulations.

(4) The Treasury may require information to be given by a specified time, in a specified form and to be verified in a specified manner.

(5) If an Operator—

(a) alters or revokes any of his rules or guidance; or

(b) makes new rules or issues new guidance,

he shall give written notice to the Treasury without delay.

## Delegation of Treasury functions

**11.** (1) Subject to paragraphs (2) and (5), the Treasury may by instrument in writing delegate all or any of the functions conferred by this Part of these Regulations to the Authority; and references in these Regulations to the 'designated agency' are references to the Authority so far as such functions are so delegated.

(2) The functions conferred on the Treasury by regulation 12 may not be delegated.

(3) The designated agency shall send to the Treasury a copy of any guidance issued by virtue of these Regulations and any requirements imposed by it on an Operator by virtue of regulation 10, and give them written notice of any amendment or revocation of, or addition to, any such guidance or requirements.

(4) The designated agency shall—

(a) send to the Treasury a copy of any guidance issued by it which is intended to have continuing effect and is issued in writing or other legible form; and

(b) give them written notice of any amendment or revocation of, or addition to, guidance issued by it,

but notice need not be given of the revocation of guidance other than is mentioned in subparagraph (a) or of any amendment or addition which does not result in or consist of such guidance as is there mentioned.

(5) The Treasury shall not delegate any function to the Authority unless they are satisfied that—

(a) any guidance issued by it in the exercise of its functions under these Regulations;
(b) any requirements imposed by it on an Operator by virtue of regulation 10;
(c) any guidance proposed to be issued by it in the exercise of its functions under these Regulations; and
(d) any requirements it proposes to impose on an Operator by virtue of regulation 10,

do not have, and are not intended or likely to have, to any significant extent the effect of restricting, distorting or preventing competition, or if they have or are intended or likely to have that effect to any significant extent, that the effect is not greater than is necessary for the protection of investors.

(6) The powers conferred by paragraph (7) shall be exercisable by the Treasury if at any time it appears to them that—
(a) any guidance issued by the designated agency in the exercise of its functions under these Regulations;
(b) any requirements imposed by the designated agency on an Operator by virtue of regulation 10; or
(c) any practices of the designated agency followed in the exercise of its functions under these Regulations,

have, or are intended or likely to have, to any significant extent the effect of restricting, distorting or preventing competition and that the effect is greater than is necessary for the protection of investors.

(7) The powers exercisable under this paragraph are—
(a) to resume all or any of the functions delegated to the designated agency by the written instrument referred to in paragraph (1); or
(b) to direct the designated agency to take specified steps for the purpose of securing that the guidance, requirements or practices in question do not have the effect mentioned in paragraph (6).

(8) The Treasury may by written instrument—
(a) at the request or with the consent of the designated agency; or
(b) if at any time it appears to them that the designated agency is unable or unwilling to discharge all or any of the functions delegated to it,

resume all or any of the functions delegated to the designated agency under paragraph (1).

(9) Neither the designated agency nor any person who is, or is acting as, a member, officer or member of staff of the designated agency shall be liable in damages for anything done or omitted in the discharge or purported discharge of functions delegated under paragraph (1) unless the act or omission is shown to have been in bad faith.

(10) In this regulation—
(a) any reference to guidance issued to an Operator by the designated agency is a reference to any guidance issued or any recommendation made by the designated agency in writing, or other legible form, which is intended to have continuing effect, and is issued or made to an Operator; and
(b) references to the practices of the designated agency are references to the practices of the designated agency in its capacity as such.

(11) If under paragraph (1) the Treasury delegate to the designated agency the Treasury's function of making applications to the court under regulation 9(5), the reference to the Treasury in regulation 9(6) shall, unless the Treasury otherwise provide in the instrument by which that function is delegated, be taken as a reference to the designated agency.

### International obligations

**12.** (1) If it appears to the Treasury that any action proposed to be taken by an Operator or the designated agency would be incompatible with [EU][2] obligations or any other international obligations of the United Kingdom they may direct the Operator or the designated agency, as the case may be, not to take that action.

(2) If it appears to the Treasury that any action which an Operator or the designated agency has power to take is required for the purpose of implementing any such obligations, they may direct the Operator or the designated agency, as the case may be, to take that action.

(3) A direction under this regulation—
(a) may include such supplemental or incidental requirements as the Treasury consider necessary or expedient; and
(b) is enforceable, on an application made by the Treasury, by injunction or, in Scotland, by an order for specific performance under section 45 of the Court of Session Act 1988.

[2] Amended by the Treaty of Lisbon (Changes in Terminology) Order 2011/1043 Pt 2 art. 6(1)(e).

**Prevention of restrictive practices**

    **13.** Schedule 2 (prevention of restrictive practices) shall have effect.

As is made clear in the commentary below, operators are central to the working of a dematerialized   **49.USR.06**
system of transfer of securities. The effect of Part 2 of the Regulations is to require an operator to secure
approval from the Treasury and to subject operators to supervision by the Treasury. Provision is made
for the Treasury's approval and supervision functions to be delegated to the Financial Services
Authority.

In order to secure approval an operator must meet the requirements set out in Schedule 1 to the   **49.USR.07**
Regulations. An operator is required, *inter alia*, to:

(a)  have adequate arrangements and resources for the effective monitoring and enforcement of
     compliance with his rules;

(b)  have adequate financial resources sufficient for the proper performance of his functions as an
     Operator;

(c)  be able and willing to promote and maintain high standards of integrity and fair dealing in the
     operation of the relevant system and to cooperate with the Treasury and other competent
     authorities;

(d)  construct and operate a relevant system in a way that minimizes the possibility of unauthorized
     access;

(e)  ensure that a relevant system enables the Operator to send and respond to properly authenticated
     dematerialized instructions in sufficient volume and speed;

(f)  ensure that a relevant system comprises procedures which provide that it responds only to
     properly authenticated dematerialized instructions which are attributable to a system-user or an
     Operator;

(g)  have rules that bind system members and participating issuers and meet the detailed requirements
     set out in paragraphs 25, 26, and 27 of Schedule 1.

The requirements of Schedule 1 must be met at all times by an approved operator. Failure to comply   **49.USR.08**
with the Schedule 1 requirements or any other obligation imposed by or under the Regulations allows
the Treasury to seek a direction from the court to rectify the failure[3] or to withdraw approval from the
operator.[4]

Schedule 2 provides for the rules and guidance of the operator to be scrutinized by the Director General   **49.USR.09**
of Fair Trading to ensure that they do not distort competition. The Treasury cannot approve a person
as an operator unless they are satisfied that the rules and guidance of the relevant system do not, and are
not intended or likely to have, to any significant extent, the effect of restricting, distorting or preventing
competition. Schedule 3 sets out the procedure to be followed before refusing or withdrawing approval
as an operator, giving a direction to an operator, or exercising certain powers under Schedule 2.

## PART 3
### PARTICIPATING SECURITIES
*Participation by Issuers*

**Participation in respect of shares**                                                                         **49.USR.10**

    **14.** Where—

        (a)  an Operator permits title to shares of a class in relation to which regulation 15 applies, or in
            relation to which a directors' resolution passed in accordance with regulation 16 is effective,
            to be transferred by means of a relevant system; and

        (b)  the company in question permits the holding of shares of that class in uncertificated form and
            the transfer of title to any such shares by means of a relevant system,

        title to shares of that class which are recorded on an Operator register of members may be
        transferred by means of that relevant system.

    **15.** This regulation applies to a class of shares if a company's articles of association are in all respects
        consistent with—

        (a)  the holding of shares of that class in uncertificated form;

        (b)  the transfer of title to shares of that class by means of a relevant system; and

---

[3]  Regulation 8.
[4]  Regulation 7.

(c) these Regulations.

**16.** (1) This regulation applies to a class of shares if a company's articles of association in any respect are inconsistent with—

(a) the holding of shares of that class in uncertificated form;

(b) the transfer of title to shares of that class by means of a relevant system; or

(c) any provision of these Regulations.

(2) A company may resolve, subject to paragraph (6)(a), by resolution of its directors (in this Part referred to as a 'directors' resolution') that title to shares of a class issued or to be issued by it may be transferred by means of a relevant system.

(3) Upon a directors' resolution becoming effective in accordance with its terms, and for as long as it is in force, the articles of association in relation to the class of shares which were the subject of the directors' resolution shall not apply to any uncertificated shares of that class to the extent that they are inconsistent with—

(a) the holding of shares of that class in uncertificated form;

(b) the transfer of title to shares of that class by means of a relevant system; or

(c) any provision of these Regulations.

(4) Unless a company has given notice to every member of the company in accordance with its articles of association of its intention to pass a directors' resolution before the passing of such a resolution, it shall give such notice within 60 days of the passing of the resolution.

(5) Notice given by the company before the coming into force of these Regulations of its intention to pass a directors' resolution which, if it had been given after the coming into force of these Regulations would have satisfied the requirements of paragraph (4), shall be taken to satisfy the requirements of that paragraph.

(6) In respect of a class of shares, the members of a company may by ordinary resolution—

(a) if a directors' resolution has not been passed, resolve that the directors of the company shall not pass a directors' resolution;

(b) if a directors' resolution has been passed but not yet come into effect in accordance with its terms, resolve that it shall not come into effect;

(c) if a directors' resolution has been passed and is effective in accordance with its terms but the class of shares has not yet been permitted by the Operator to be a participating security, resolve that the directors' resolution shall cease to have effect; or

(d) if a directors' resolution has been passed and is effective in accordance with its terms and the class of shares has been permitted by the Operator to be a participating security, resolve that the directors shall take the necessary steps to ensure that title to shares of the class that was the subject of the directors' resolution shall cease to be transferable by means of a relevant system and that the directors' resolution shall cease to have effect,

and the directors shall be bound by the terms of any such ordinary resolution.

[(7) In the event of default in complying with paragraph (4), an offence is committed by every officer of the issuer who is in default.

(7A)A person guilty of such an offence is liable—

(a) on conviction on indictment, to a fine;

(b) on summary conviction, to a fine not exceeding the statutory maximum.]ᵃ

(8) A company shall not permit the holding of shares in such a class as is referred to in paragraph (1) in uncertificated form, or the transfer of title to shares in such a class by means of a relevant system, unless in relation to that class of shares a directors' resolution is effective.

[8(A) Chapter 3 of Part 3 of the 2006 Act (resolutions affecting a company's constitution) applies to—

(a) a directors' resolution passed by virtue of paragraph (2), or

(b) a resolution of a company passed by virtue of paragraph (6) preventing or reversing such a resolution.]ᵇ

(9) This regulation shall not be taken to exclude the right of the members of a company to amend the articles of association of the company, in accordance with the articles, to allow the holding of any class of its shares in uncertificated form and the transfer of title to shares in such a class by means of a relevant system.

**17.** (1) A class of shares in relation to which, immediately before the coming into force of these Regulations—

(a) regulation 15 of the 1995 Regulations applied; or

(b) a directors' resolution passed in accordance with regulation 16 of the 1995 Regulations was effective,

shall be taken to be a class of shares in relation to which regulation 15 of these Regulations applies or, as the case may be, a directors' resolution passed in accordance with regulation 16 is effective.

(2) On the coming into force of these Regulations a company's articles of association in relation to any such class of shares, and the terms of issue of any such class of shares, shall cease to apply to the extent that they are inconsistent with any provision of these Regulations.

AMENDMENTS AND NOTES

ᵃ Amended by the Companies Act 2006 (Commencement No 3, Consequential Amendments, Transitional Provisions and Savings) Order 2007, SI 2007/2194, Sch 4, Pt 3, para 97(2).

b Inserted by the Companies Act 2006 (Commencement No 3, Consequential Amendments, Transitional Provisions and Savings) Order 2007, SI 2007/2194, Sch 4, Pt 3, para 97(3).

## Interpretation of regulations 15, 16 and 17

**18.** For the purposes of regulations 15, 16 and 17 any shares with respect to which share warrants to bearer are issued under [section 779 of the 2006 Act][a] shall be regarded as forming a separate class of shares.

AMENDMENTS AND NOTES

a Amended by the Companies Act (Consequential Amendments) (Uncertificated Securities) Order 2009, SI 2009/1889, art 2(4).

## Participation in respect of securities other than shares

**19.** (1) Subject to paragraph (2), where—

    (a) an Operator permits title to a security other than a share to be transferred by means of a relevant system; and

    (b) the issuer permits the holding of units of that security in uncertificated form and the transfer of title to units of that security by means of a relevant system,

  title to units of that security which are recorded on an Operator register of securities may be transferred by means of that relevant system.

(2) In relation to any security other than a share, if the law under which it is constituted is not the law of England and Wales, Northern Ireland or Scotland, or if the current terms of its issue are in any respect inconsistent with—

    (a) the holding of title to units of that security in uncertificated form;

    (b) the transfer of title to units of that security by means of a relevant system; or

    (c) subject to paragraph (3), these Regulations,

  [an issuer of that security][a] shall not permit the holding of units of that security in uncertificated form, or the transfer of title to units of that security by means of a relevant system.

(3) On the coming into force of these Regulations the current terms of issue of a relevant participating security shall cease to apply to the extent that they are inconsistent with any provision of these Regulations.

(4) For the purposes of this regulation—

    (a) a relevant participating security is a participating security (other than a share) the terms of issue of which, immediately before the coming into force of these Regulations, were in all respects consistent with the 1995 Regulations; and

    (b) the terms of issue of a security shall be taken to include the terms prescribed by the issuer on which units of the security are held and title to them is transferred.

AMENDMENTS AND NOTES

a Amended by the Uncertificated Securities (Amendment) (Eligible Debt Securities) Regulations 2003, SI 2003/1633, reg 5.

## *Keeping of Registers and Records*

## Entries on registers and records in respect of shares

**20.** (1) In respect of every company which is a participating issuer, there shall be—

    (a) a register maintained by the participating issuer, and such a register is referred to in these Regulations as an 'issuer register of members'; and

    (b) a register maintained by the Operator, and such a register is referred to in these Regulations as an 'Operator register of members'.

(2) A participating issuer which is a company shall keep and enter up the issuer register of members in accordance with paragraph 2 of Schedule 4.

(3) In respect of every company which is a participating issuer, the Operator shall keep and enter up the Operator register of members in accordance with paragraph 4 of Schedule 4.

(4) References in any enactment or instrument to a company's register of members shall, unless the context otherwise requires, be construed in relation to a company which is a participating issuer as referring to the company's issuer register of members and Operator register of members.

(5) Paragraph (4) does not apply in relation to a company's issuer register of members to the extent that any of the particulars entered in that register in accordance with paragraph 2(1) of Schedule 4 are inconsistent with the company's Operator register of members.

(6) A participating issuer which is a company shall—

    (a) maintain a record of the entries made in its Operator register of members; and such a record is referred to in these Regulations as a 'record of uncertificated shares'; and

    (b) keep and enter up that record in accordance with paragraph 5 of Schedule 4.

(7) Such sanctions as apply to a company and its officers in the event of a default in complying with [section 113 of the 2006 Act][a] shall apply to—

(a) a company which is a participating issuer and its officers in the event of a default in complying with paragraph (1)(a) or (6)(a), or

(b) an Operator and his officers in the event of a default in complying with paragraph (1)(b).

AMENDMENTS AND NOTES

[a] Amended by the Companies Act (Consequential Amendments) (Uncertificated Securities) Order 2009, SI 2009/1889, art 2(5).

### Entries on registers and records in respect of [general][a] public sector securities

**21.** (1) In respect of every participating security which is a [general][b] public sector security the Operator shall—

(a) maintain a register, and such a register is referred to in these Regulations as an 'Operator register of [general][c] public sector securities'; and

(b) keep and enter up the Operator register of [general][d] public sector securities in accordance with paragraph 12 of Schedule 4.

(2) The person specified in paragraph (3) shall—

(a) maintain a record of the entries made in an Operator register of [general][e] public sector securities; and such a record is referred to in these Regulations as a 'record of uncertificated [general][f] public sector securities'; and

(b) keep and enter up that record in accordance with paragraph 13 of Schedule 4.

(3) The person referred to in paragraph (2) is [the Registrar of Government Stock][g], except where the security to which an Operator register of [general][h] public sector securities relates is a [general][i] local authority security, in which case it is—

(a) the relevant local authority; or

(b) if the local authority has appointed another person to act as registrar for the purpose of the 1974 Regulations in respect of that security, the person so appointed.

(4) Such sanctions as apply to a company and its officers in the event of a default in complying with [section 113 of the 2006 Act][j] shall apply to an Operator and his officers in the event of a default in complying with paragraph (1)(a).

(5) Such sanctions as apply to the registrar, within the meaning of the 1974 Regulations, in the event of a default in complying with regulation 5 of those Regulations shall apply to a participating issuer and his officers in the event of a default in complying with paragraph (2)(a) in respect of a local authority security [falling within paragraph (a)(i) of the definition of 'local authority security' in regulation 3(1)][k].

AMENDMENTS AND NOTES

[a] Inserted by the Uncertificated Securities (Amendment) (Eligible Debt Securities) Regulations 2003, SI 2003/1633, reg 6.

[b] Inserted by the Uncertificated Securities (Amendment) (Eligible Debt Securities) Regulations 2003, SI 2003/1633, reg 6.

[c] Inserted by the Uncertificated Securities (Amendment) (Eligible Debt Securities) Regulations 2003, SI 2003/1633, reg 6.

[d] Inserted by the Uncertificated Securities (Amendment) (Eligible Debt Securities) Regulations 2003, SI 2003/1633, reg 6.

[e] Inserted by the Uncertificated Securities (Amendment) (Eligible Debt Securities) Regulations 2003, SI 2003/1633, reg 6.

[f] Inserted by the Uncertificated Securities (Amendment) (Eligible Debt Securities) Regulations 2003, SI 2003/1633, reg 6.

[g] Amended by the Government Stock (Consequential and Transitional Provision) (No 2) Order 2004, SI 2004/1662, Schedule, Pt 3, para 29.

[h] Inserted by the Uncertificated Securities (Amendment) (Eligible Debt Securities) Regulations 2003, SI 2003/1633, reg 6.

[i] Inserted by the Uncertificated Securities (Amendment) (Eligible Debt Securities) Regulations 2003, SI 2003/1633, reg 8.

[j] Amended by the Companies Act (Consequential Amendments) (Uncertificated Securities) Order 2009, SI 2009/1889, art 2(6).

[k] Inserted by the Uncertificated Securities (Amendment) (Eligible Debt Securities) Regulations 2003, SI 2003/1633, reg 8.

### Entries on registers and records in respect of other securities

**22.** (1) Paragraph (2) applies where a participating issuer is required by or under an enactment or instrument to maintain in the United Kingdom a register of persons holding securities (other than shares[, general public sector securities or eligible debt securities][a]) issued by him.

(2) Where this paragraph applies, then in so far as the register in question relates to any class of security which is a participating security—

    (a) the Operator shall—
       (i) maintain a register, and such a register is referred to in these Regulations as an 'Operator register of corporate securities'; and
       (ii) keep and enter up the Operator register of corporate securities in accordance with paragraph 14 of Schedule 4;
    (b) the participating issuer—
       (i) shall not maintain the register to the extent that it relates to securities held in uncertificated form;
       (ii) shall maintain a record of the entries made in any Operator register of corporate securities, and such a record is referred to in these Regulations as a 'record of uncertificated corporate securities'; and
       (iii) shall keep and enter up that record in accordance with paragraph 15 of Schedule 4.
  (3) Where a participating issuer is not required by or under an enactment or instrument to maintain in the United Kingdom in respect of a participating security [(other than an eligible debt security)]$^b$ issued by him a register of persons holding units of that participating security, the Operator shall—
    (a) maintain a register in respect of that participating security; and
    (b) record in that register—
       (i) the names and addresses of the persons holding units of that security in uncertificated form, and
       (ii) how many units of that security each such person holds in that form.
[(3A) In respect of every participating security which is an eligible debt security, the Operator shall—
    (a) maintain a register, and such a register is referred to in these Regulations as an 'Operator register of eligible debt securities'; and
    (b) record in that register—
       (i) the names and addresses of the persons holding units of that security; and
       (ii) how many units of that security each such person holds.]$^c$
  (4) Such sanctions as apply to a company and its officers in the event of a default in complying with [section 113 of the 2006 Act]$^d$ shall apply to an Operator and his officers in the event of a default in complying with paragraph [(2)(a)(i), (3) or (3A)]$^e$.
  (5) Such sanctions as apply in the event of a default in complying with the requirement to maintain a register imposed by the relevant enactment or instrument referred to in paragraph (1) shall apply to a participating issuer and his officers in the event of a default in complying with paragraph (2)(b)(ii).

AMENDMENTS AND NOTES

$^a$ Amended by the Uncertificated Securities (Amendment) (Eligible Debt Securities) Regulations 2003, SI 2003/1633, reg 6.
$^b$ Inserted by the Uncertificated Securities (Amendment) (Eligible Debt Securities) Regulations 2003, SI 2003/1633, reg 9.
$^c$ Inserted by the Uncertificated Securities (Amendment) (Eligible Debt Securities) Regulations 2003, SI 2003/1633, reg 9.
$^d$ Amended by the Companies Act (Consequential Amendments) (Uncertificated Securities) Order 2009, SI 2009/1889, art 2(7).
$^e$ Amended by the Uncertificated Securities (Amendment) (Eligible Debt Securities) Regulations 2003, SI 2003/1633, reg 9.

## General provisions concerning keeping registers and records

**23.** (1) The obligations of an Operator to maintain and to keep and enter up any register of securities, imposed by these Regulations—
    (a) shall not give rise to any form of duty or liability on the Operator, except such as is expressly provided for in these Regulations or as arises from fraud or other wilful default, or negligence, on the part of the Operator;
    (b) shall not give rise to any form of duty or liability on a participating issuer, other than where the Operator acts on the instructions of that participating issuer, in the absence of fraud or other wilful default, or negligence, on the part of that participating issuer; and
    (c) shall not give rise to any form of duty or liability enforceable by civil proceedings for breach of statutory duty.
  (2) Without prejudice to paragraph (1) or to any lesser period of limitation and to any rule as to the prescription of rights, liability incurred by a participating issuer or by an Operator arising—
    (a) from the making or deletion of an entry in a register of securities or record of securities pursuant to these Regulations; or
    (b) from a failure to make or delete any such entry,
       shall not be enforceable more than [10 years]$^a$ after the date on which the entry was made or deleted or, in the case of a failure, the failure first occurred.
  (3) No notice of any trust, expressed, implied or constructive, shall be entered on an Operator register of securities, or a part of such a register, or be receivable by an Operator.

(4) Schedule 4 (which provides for the keeping of registers and records of participating securities, and which excludes, or applies with appropriate modifications, certain provisions of [the 2006 Act]^b) shall have effect.

[(5) Section 120 of the 2006 Act shall not apply with respect to a company which is a participating issuer.]^c

AMENDMENTS AND NOTES

^a Amended by the Companies Act (Consequential Amendments) (Uncertificated Securities) Order 2009, SI 2009/1889, art 2(8).
^b Amended by the Companies Act (Consequential Amendments) (Uncertificated Securities) Order 2009, SI 2009/1889, art 2(8).
^c Amended by the Companies Act (Consequential Amendments) (Uncertificated Securities) Order 2009, SI 2009/1889, art 2(2).

## Effect of entries on registers

**24.** (1) Subject to regulation 29 and to paragraphs (2) and (3) below, a register of members is prima facie evidence, and in Scotland sufficient evidence unless the contrary is shown, of any matters which are by these Regulations directed or authorised to be inserted in it.

(2) Paragraph (1) does not apply to a company's issuer register of members to the extent that any of the particulars entered in that register in accordance with paragraph 2(1) of Schedule 4 are inconsistent with the company's Operator register of members.

(3) The entry of a person's name and address in a company's issuer register of members shall not be treated as showing that person to be a member of the company unless—
 (a) the issuer register of members also shows him as holding shares in the company in certificated form;
 (b) the Operator register of members shows him as holding shares in the company in uncertificated form; or
 (c) he is deemed to be a member of the company by regulation 32(6)(b).

(4) [Section 127 of the 2006 Act]^a shall not apply with respect to a company which is a participating issuer.

(5) Subject to regulation 29, an Operator register of [general]^b public sector securities is prima facie evidence, and in Scotland sufficient evidence unless the contrary is shown, of any matters which are by these Regulations directed or authorised to be inserted in it.

(6) Subject to regulation 29, an entry on an Operator register of corporate securities which records a person as holding units of a security in uncertificated form shall be evidence of such title to the units as would be evidenced if the entry on that register—
 (a) were an entry on the part maintained by the participating issuer of such register as is mentioned in regulation 22(1); and
 (b) where appropriate, related to units of that security held in certificated form.

(7) Subject to regulation 29, an entry on a register maintained by virtue of regulation 22(3)(a) shall (where the units are capable of being held in certificated form) be prima facie evidence, and in Scotland sufficient evidence unless the contrary is shown, that the person to whom the entry relates has such title to the units of the security which he is recorded as holding in uncertificated form as he would have if he held the units in certificated form.

[(8) Subject to regulation 29, an entry on an Operator register of eligible debt securities shall be prima facie evidence, and in Scotland sufficient evidence unless the contrary is shown, of any matters which are by these Regulations directed or authorised to be inserted in it.]^c

AMENDMENTS AND NOTES

^a Amended by the Companies Act (Consequential Amendments) (Uncertificated Securities) Order 2009, SI 2009/1889, art 2(10).
^b Inserted by the Uncertificated Securities (Amendment) (Eligible Debt Securities) Regulations 2003, SI 2003/1633, reg 6.
^c Inserted by the Uncertificated Securities (Amendment) (Eligible Debt Securities) Regulations 2003, SI 2003/1633, reg 10.

## Rectification of registers of securities

**25.** (1) Unless the circumstances described in paragraph (2) apply, a participating issuer shall not rectify an issuer register of securities if such rectification would also require the rectification of an Operator register of securities.

(2) The circumstances referred to in paragraph (1) are that the rectification of an issuer register of securities is effected—
 (a) with the consent of the Operator; or
 (b) by order of a court in the United Kingdom.

(3) A participating issuer who rectifies an issuer register of securities in order to give effect to an order of a court in the United Kingdom shall immediately give the Operator written

notification of the change to the entry, if any rectification of the Operator register of securities may also be required (unless the change to the issuer register is made in response to an Operator-instruction).

(4) An Operator who rectifies an Operator register of securities shall immediately—

    (a) generate an Operator-instruction to inform the relevant participating issuer of the change to the entry (unless the change is made in response to an issuer-instruction); and

    (b) generate an Operator-instruction to inform the system-members concerned of the change to the entry.

## Closing registers

**26.** Notwithstanding any other enactment, a participating issuer shall not close a register of securities relating to a participating security without the consent of the Operator.

## Registration by an Operator of transfers of securities

**27.** (1) Except where relevant units of a security are transferred by means of a relevant system to a person who is to hold them thereafter in certificated form (and subject to paragraphs (2) and (4))—

    (a) upon settlement of a transfer of uncertificated units of a security in accordance with his rules;

    (b) following receipt of an issuer-instruction notifying him that the circumstances specified in regulation 33(2)(b) have arisen in respect of a transfer of units of a participating security; or

    (c) following receipt of an issuer-instruction given under Regulation 42(8)(b),

an Operator shall register on the relevant Operator register of securities the transfer of title to those units of that security.

(2) An Operator shall refuse to register a transfer of title to units of a participating security in accordance with a system-member instruction or an issuer-instruction (as the case may be) if he has actual notice that the transfer is—

    (a) prohibited by order of a court in the United Kingdom;

    (b) prohibited or avoided by or under an enactment;

    (c) a transfer to a deceased person; or

    (d) where the participating issuer is constituted under the law of Scotland, prohibited by or under an arrestment.

(3) Notwithstanding that an Operator has received, in respect of a transfer of title to units of a participating security, actual notice of the kind referred to in paragraph (2), the Operator may register that transfer of title on the relevant Operator register of securities if at the time that he received the actual notice it was not practicable for him to halt the process of registration.

(4) Without prejudice to his rules, an Operator may refuse to register a transfer of title to units of a participating security in accordance with a system-member instruction or an issuer-instruction (as the case may be) if the instruction requires a transfer of units—

    (a) to an entity which is not a natural or legal person;

    (b) to a minor (which, in relation to a participating issuer constituted under the law of Scotland, shall mean a person under 16 years of age);

    (c) to be held jointly in the names of more persons than is permitted under the terms of the issue of the security; or

    (d) where, in relation to the system-member instruction or the issuer-instruction (as the case may be), the Operator has actual notice of any of the matters specified in regulation 35(5)(a)(i) to (iii).

(5) An Operator shall not register a transfer of title to uncertificated units of a security on an Operator register of securities otherwise than in accordance with paragraph (1) unless he is required to do so by order of a court in the United Kingdom or by or under an enactment.

(6) Paragraph (5) shall not be taken to prevent an Operator from entering on an Operator register of securities a person who is a system-member to whom title to uncertificated units of a security has been transmitted by operation of law.

(7) [Subject to paragraph (7A), immediately upon][a]—

    (a) the registration by an Operator of the transfer of title to units of a participating security in accordance with—

        (i) paragraph (1);

        (ii) an order of a court in the United Kingdom; or

        (iii) a requirement arising by or under an enactment; or

    (b) the making or deletion by an Operator of an entry on an Operator register of securities—

        (i) following the transmission of title to uncertificated units of a security by operation of law; or

        (ii) upon the transfer of uncertificated units of a security to a person who is to hold them thereafter in certificated form, the Operator shall generate an Operator-instruction to inform the relevant participating issuer of the registration, or of the making or deletion of the entry (as the case may be); and where appropriate the participating issuer shall register the transfer or transmission of title to those units on an issuer register of securities in accordance with regulation 28.

[(7A)    Paragraph (7) does not apply in relation to units of an eligible debt security.][b]

(8)    [If an Operator refuses to register a transfer of securities in any of the circumstances specified in paragraphs (2) and (4), the Operator shall, within 2 months of the date on which the relevant system-member instruction or issuer-instruction (as the case may be) was received by the Operator, send an Operator-instruction, or written notification, informing the relevant system-member or participating issuer (as the case may be) of the refusal:][c]

(9)    Such sanctions as apply to a company and its officers in the event of a default in complying with [subsections (1) and (2) of section 771 of the 2006 Act][d] shall apply to an Operator and his officers in the event of a default in complying with that subsection as applied by paragraph (8).

AMENDMENTS AND NOTES

[a]    Amended by the Uncertificated Securities (Amendment) (Eligible Debt Securities) Regulations 2003, SI 2003/1633, reg 11.

[b]    Inserted by the Uncertificated Securities (Amendment) (Eligible Debt Securities) Regulations 2003, SI 2003/1633, reg 11.

[c]    Amended by the Companies Act (Consequential Amendments) (Uncertificated Securities) Order 2009, SI 2009/1889, art 2(12).

[d]    Amended by the Companies Act (Consequential Amendments) (Uncertificated Securities) Order 2009, SI 2009/1889, art 2(12).

## Registration by a participating issuer of transfers of securities upon conversion into certificated form

**28.** (1)    Paragraphs (2) to (5) apply where relevant units of a security are transferred by means of a relevant system to a person who is to hold them thereafter in certificated form.

(2)    Subject to paragraphs (3) and (4), a participating issuer shall (where appropriate) register a transfer of title to relevant units of a security on an issuer register of securities in accordance with an Operator-instruction.

(3)    A participating issuer shall refuse to register a transfer of title to relevant units of a security in accordance with an Operator-instruction if he has actual notice that the transfer is—
(a)    prohibited by order of a court in the United Kingdom;
(b)    prohibited or avoided by or under an enactment;
(c)    a transfer to a deceased person; or
(d)    where the participating issuer is constituted under the law of Scotland, prohibited by or under an arrestment.

(4)    A participating issuer may refuse to register a transfer of title to relevant units of a security in accordance with an Operator-instruction if the instruction requires a transfer of units—
(a)    to an entity which is not a natural or legal person;
(b)    to a minor (which, in relation to a participating issuer constituted under the law of Scotland, shall mean a person under 16 years of age);
(c)    to be held jointly in the names of more persons than is permitted under the terms of the issue of the security; or
(d)    where, in relation to the Operator-instruction. the participating issuer has actual notice from the Operator of any of the matters specified in regulation 35(5)(a)(i) to (iii).

(5)    A participating issuer shall notify the Operator by issuer-instruction whether he has registered a transfer in response to an Operator-instruction to do so.

(6)    A participating issuer shall not register a transfer of title to relevant units of a security on an issuer register of securities unless he is required to do so—
(a)    by an Operator-instruction;
(b)    by an order of a court in the United Kingdom; or
(c)    by or under an enactment.

(7)    A unit of a security is a relevant unit for the purposes of this regulation if, immediately before the transfer in question, it was held by the transferor in uncertificated form.

(8)    [If a participating issuer refuses to register under paragraph (2) a transfer of securities in any of the circumstances specified in paragraphs (3) and (4), the participating issuer shall, within 2 months of the date on which the Operator-instruction was received by the participating issuer, send to the transferee notice of the refusal.][a]

(9)    Such sanctions as apply to a company and its officers in the event of a default in complying with [subsections (1) and (2) of section 771 of the 2006 Act][b] shall apply to a participating issuer and his officers in the event of a default in complying with that subsection as applied by paragraph (8).

AMENDMENTS AND NOTES

a Amended by the Companies Act (Consequential Amendments) (Uncertificated Securities) Order 2009, SI 2009/1889, art 2(13).
b Amended by the Companies Act (Consequential Amendments) (Uncertificated Securities) Order 2009, SI 2009/1889, art 2(13).

## Registration to be in accordance with regulations 27 and 28

**29.** Any purported registration of a transfer of title to an uncertificated unit of a security other than in accordance with regulation 27 or 28 shall be of no effect.

## Registration of linked transfers

**30.** (1) Paragraph (2) applies where an Operator receives two or more system-member instructions requesting him to register two or more transfers of title to uncertificated units of a security, and it appears to the Operator—

(a) either—

   (i) that there are fewer units of the security registered on an Operator register of securities in the name of a person identified in any of the system-member instructions as a transferor than the number of units to be transferred from him under those system-member instructions; or

   (ii) that it has not been established in accordance with paragraph 21(1)(c) of Schedule 1, in relation to any of the transfers taken without regard to the other transfers, that a settlement bank has agreed to make a payment; and

(b) that registration of all of the transfers would result in each of the persons identified in the system-member instructions as a transferor having title to a number of uncertificated units of a security equal to or greater than nil; and

(c) that the combined effect of all the transfers taken together would result in paragraph 21(1)(c) of Schedule 1 being satisfied.

(2) Where this paragraph applies, the Operator may either—

(a) register the combined effect of all the transfers taken together; or

(b) register all the transfers simultaneously,

unless one or more of those transfers may not be registered by virtue of the fact that the Operator has actual notice of any of the circumstances specified in regulation 27(2), or is to be refused registration by virtue of regulation 27(4).

(3) Notwithstanding that an Operator has received, in respect of two or more such system-member instructions as are referred to in paragraph (1), actual notice of the kind referred to in paragraph (2), the Operator may register all the transfers in question or their combined effect if at the time that he received the actual notice it was not practicable for him to halt the process of registration.

## Position of a transferee prior to entry on an issuer register of securities

**31.** (1) Paragraph (2) applies when an Operator deletes an entry on an Operator register of securities in consequence of which—

(a) the Operator must generate an Operator-instruction in accordance with regulation 27(7); and

(b) by virtue of that instruction a participating issuer must register, on an issuer register of securities, a transfer of title to units of a participating security constituted under the law of England and Wales or Northern Ireland.

(2) Where this paragraph applies—

(a) subject to—

   (i) subparagraph (b); and

   (ii) any enactment or rule of law,

   the transferor shall, notwithstanding the deletion of the entry in the Operator register of securities, retain title to the requisite number of units of the relevant participating security until the transferee is entered on the relevant issuer register of securities as the holder thereof; and

(b) the transferee shall acquire an equitable interest in the requisite number of units of that security.

(3) Paragraph (4) applies when an Operator deletes an entry on an Operator register of securities in consequence of which—

(a) the Operator must generate an Operator-instruction in accordance with regulation 27(7); and

(b) by virtue of that instruction a participating issuer must register, on an issuer register of securities, a transfer of title to units of a participating security constituted under the law of Scotland.

(4) Where this paragraph applies—

(a) subject to—

    (i)  subparagraph (b); and

    (ii)  any enactment or rule of law,

    the transferor shall, notwithstanding the deletion of the entry in the Operator register of securities, retain title to the requisite number of units of the relevant participating security until the transferee is entered on the relevant issuer register of securities as the holder thereof; and

(b)  the transferor shall hold the requisite number of units of that security on trust for the benefit of the transferee.

(5)  The requisite number for the purposes of this regulation is the number of units which are to be specified in the Operator-instruction which the Operator must generate in accordance with regulation 27(7).

(6)  This regulation has effect notwithstanding that the units to which the deletion of the entry in the Operator register of securities relates, or in which an interest arises by virtue of paragraph (2)(b) or (4)(b), or any of them, may be unascertained.

(7)  In Scotland—

(a)  this regulation has effect notwithstanding that the requirements relating to the creation of a trust under any enactment or rule of law have not been complied with; and

(b)  as from the time the trust referred to in paragraph (4)(b) arises, any holder, or any holder thereafter, of a floating charge over any part of the property of the transferor shall be deemed to have received notice of the trust's existence and of the property to which it relates.

(8)  Subject to paragraphs (6) and (7), this regulation shall not be construed as conferring a proprietary interest (whether of the kind referred to in paragraph (2)(b) or (4)(b), or of any other kind) in units of a security if the conferring of such an interest at the time specified in these Regulations would otherwise be void by or under any enactment or rule of law.

(9)  In this regulation—

(a)  'the transferee' means the person to be identified in the Operator-instruction as the transferee; and

(b)  'the transferor' means the person to be identified in the Operator-instruction as the transferor.

## Conversions and New Issues

### Conversion of securities into certificated form

**32.** (1)  Except as provided in regulation 42, a unit of a participating security shall not be converted from uncertificated form into certificated form unless an Operator generates an Operator-instruction to notify the relevant participating issuer that a conversion event has occurred; and in this regulation such an Operator-instruction is referred to as a 'rematerialisation notice'.

(2)  A conversion event occurs—

(a)  where such a conversion is permitted by the Operator's conversion rules; or

(b)  following receipt by an Operator of a system-member instruction requiring the conversion into certificated form of uncertificated units of a participating security registered in the name of the system-member; or

(c)  following receipt by an Operator of written notification from a participating issuer which is a company requiring the conversion into certificated form of uncertificated units of a participating security, issued by that participating issuer and registered in the name of a system-member, and which contains a statement that the conversion is required to enable the participating issuer to deal with the units in question in accordance with provisions in that participating issuer's memorandum or articles or in the terms of issue of the units in question.

(3)  An Operator—

(a)  may generate a rematerialisation notice following a conversion event occurring in the circumstances specified in paragraph (2)(a);

(b)  shall generate a rematerialisation notice following a conversion event occurring in the circumstances specified in paragraph (2)(b) unless the participation in the relevant system, by the system-member in whose name the uncertificated units in question are registered, has been suspended pursuant to the Operator's rules; and

(c)  shall generate a rematerialisation notice following a conversion event occurring in the circumstances specified in paragraph (2)(c).

(4)  On the generation of a rematerialisation notice, the Operator shall delete any entry in an Operator register of securities which shows the relevant system-member as the holder of the unit or units specified in the rematerialisation notice.

(5)  On receipt of a rematerialisation notice, the participating issuer to whom the rematerialisation notice is addressed shall, where relevant, enter the name of the system-member on an

issuer register of securities as the holder of the unit or units specified in the rematerialisation notice.

(6) During any period between the deletion of any entry in an Operator register of securities required to be made by paragraph (4) and the making of the entry in an issuer register of securities required to be made by paragraph (5)—

    (a) the relevant system-member shall retain title to the units of the security specified in the rematerialisation notice notwithstanding the deletion of any entry in the Operator register of securities; and

    (b) where those units are shares, the relevant system-member shall be deemed to continue to be a member of the company.

(7) Following—

    (a) the making of an entry in an issuer register of securities in accordance with paragraph (5); or

    (b) registration of a transfer of title to units of a security in accordance with regulation 28,

the relevant participating issuer shall, where the terms of issue of the security in question provide for a certificate to be issued, issue a certificate in respect of the units of the security to the relevant person.

(8) [Subsection (1) of section 776 of the 2006 Act][a] shall apply in relation to the issue of a certificate by a participating issuer pursuant to paragraph (7) as it applies in relation to the completion and having ready for delivery by a company of share certificates, debentures or certificates of debenture stock; and in that subsection as it so applies the reference to the date on which a transfer is lodged with the company shall be a reference to the date on which the participating issuer receives the relevant rematerialisation notice in accordance with this regulation, or the relevant Operator-instruction in accordance with regulation 27(7).

(9) Such sanctions as apply to a company and its officers in the event of a default in complying with [subsections (1) and (2) of section 771 of the 2006 Act][b] shall apply—

    (a) to an Operator and his officers in the event of a default in complying with paragraph (4); and

    (b) to a participating issuer and his officers in the event of a default in complying with paragraph (5).

(10) Such sanctions as apply to a company and its officers in the event of a default in complying with [subsection (1) of section 776 of the 2006 Act][c] shall apply to a participating issuer and his officers in the event of a default in complying with paragraph (7) in accordance with the requirements laid down in paragraph (8).

AMENDMENTS AND NOTES

[a] Amended by the Companies Act (Consequential Amendments) (Uncertificated Securities) Order 2009, SI 2009/1889, art 2(14).

[b] Amended by the Companies Act (Consequential Amendments) (Uncertificated Securities) Order 2009, SI 2009/1889, art 2(14).

[c] Amended by the Companies Act (Consequential Amendments) (Uncertificated Securities) Order 2009, SI 2009/1889, art 2(14).

## Conversion of securities into uncertificated form

**33.** (1) A unit of a participating security shall not be converted from certificated form into uncertificated form unless the participating issuer notifies the Operator by means of an issuer-instruction that any of the circumstances specified in paragraph (2) have arisen; and in this regulation such an issuer-instruction is referred to as a 'dematerialisation notice'.

(2) The circumstances referred to in paragraph (1) are—

    (a) where the unit of the participating security is held by a system-member, that the participating issuer has received—

        (i) a request in writing from the system-member in the form required by the Operator's conversion rules that the unit be converted from certificated form to uncertificated form; and

        (ii) subject to paragraph (4), the certificate relating to that unit; or

    (b) where the unit of the participating security is to be registered on an Operator register of securities in the name of a system-member following a transfer of the unit to him, that the participating issuer—

        (i) subject to paragraph (3), has received (by means of the Operator-system unless the Operator's conversion rules permit otherwise) a proper instrument of transfer in favour of the system-member relating to the unit to be transferred;

        (ii) subject to paragraph (4), has received (by means of the Operator-system unless the Operator's conversion rules permit otherwise) the certificate relating to that unit; and

        (iii) may accept by virtue of the Operator's conversion rules that the system-member to whom the unit is to be transferred wishes to hold it in uncertificated form.

(3) The requirement in paragraph (2)(b)(i) that the participating issuer shall have received an instrument of transfer relating to the unit of the participating security shall not apply in a case where for a transfer of a unit of that security no instrument of transfer is required.

(4) The requirements in paragraphs (2)(a)(ii) and (2)(b)(ii) that the participating issuer shall have received a certificate relating to the unit of the participating security shall not apply in a case where the system-member or transferor (as the case may be) does not have a certificate in respect of the unit to be converted into uncertificated form because no certificate has yet been issued to him or is due to be issued to him in accordance with the terms of issue of the relevant participating security.

(5) Subject to paragraphs (3) and (4), a participating issuer shall not give a dematerialisation notice except in the circumstances specified in paragraph (2).

(6) Upon giving a dematerialisation notice, a participating issuer shall delete any entry in any issuer register of securities which evidences title to the unit or units of the participating security in question.

(7) Following receipt of a dematerialisation notice, an Operator shall enter the name of the relevant system-member on an Operator register of securities as the holder of the relevant unit or units of the participating security in question, provided that this obligation shall be subject to regulation 27 if the notice was given in the circumstances specified in paragraph (2)(b).

(8) When a dematerialisation notice is given, the relevant system-member, or the transferor of the unit or units of the security in question, as the case may be, shall (without prejudice to any equitable interest which the transferee may have acquired in the unit or units in question)—
  (a) retain title to the units of the security specified in the dematerialisation notice notwithstanding the deletion of any entry in any issuer register of securities required to be made by paragraph (6); and
  (b) where those units are shares, be deemed to continue to be a member of the company.

(9) Where a dematerialisation notice is given in the circumstances specified in paragraph (2)(b), such title shall be retained, and (where appropriate) such membership shall be deemed to continue, until the time at which the Operator enters the name of the relevant system-member on an Operator register of securities in accordance with paragraph (7).

(10) Within 2 months of receiving a dematerialisation notice, an Operator shall generate an Operator-instruction informing the participating issuer whether an entry has been made in an Operator register of securities in response to the dematerialisation notice.

(11) Such sanctions as apply to a company and its officers in the event of a default in complying with [subsections (1) and (2) of section 771 of the 2006 Act][a] shall apply—
  (a) to a participating issuer and his officers in the event of a default in complying with paragraph (6); and
  (b) to an Operator and his officers in the event of a default in complying with paragraph (7) or (10).

AMENDMENTS AND NOTES

[a] Amended by the Companies Act (Consequential Amendments) (Uncertificated Securities) Order 2009, SI 2009/1889, art 2(15).

### New issues in uncertificated form

**34.** (1) For the purposes of an issue of units of a participating security, a participating issuer may require the Operator to enter the name of a person in an Operator register of securities as the holder of new units of that security in uncertificated form if, and only if, that person is a system-member; and provided that compliance with any such requirement shall be subject to the rules of the Operator.

(2) For the purposes of calculating the number of new units to which a system-member is entitled a participating issuer may treat a system-member's holdings of certificated and uncertificated units of a security as if they were separate holdings.

(3) A requirement made by a participating issuer under paragraph (1) may be made by means of an issuer-instruction and shall specify the names of the persons to be entered in the Operator register of securities as the holders of new uncertificated units of the security, and the number of such units to be issued to each of those persons.

(4) An Operator who receives a requirement made by a participating issuer under paragraph (1) shall notify the participating issuer, by Operator-instruction or in writing, if he has not entered the name of any one or more of the persons in question in the Operator register of securities as the holder of new units of the security.

**49.USR.11** This part of the Regulations represents the central core of the rules relating to dematerialized holding and transfer of shares. Its scope is broader than the title indicates as it covers: participating issuers and securities; the keeping of registers; the legal effect of entries in the relevant registers; and the mode of transfer of uncertificated securities.

Title to a class of shares may be transferred by means of a relevant system if such transfer is consistent with the company's articles of association.[5] If such transfer is not consistent with the articles, the directors may nevertheless resolve that the relevant class of shares be transferred within a relevant system, in which case the relevant articles will not apply so far as inconsistent with dematerialized transfer.[6] Members are, however, empowered to veto or reverse, by ordinary resolution, a decision of the directors that a class of shares shall be transferred within a relevant system. **49.USR.12**

Securities other than shares can be transferred within a relevant system if the issuer permits the holding of units of that security in uncertificated form and the transfer of title to units of that security by means of a relevant system. However, where such securities are constituted under a legal system outside the UK or if the terms of issue are not consistent with the holding and transfer of the security in dematerialized form, then the issuer cannot permit holding or transfer in such form. **49.USR.13**

It remains possible for the holding and transfer of securities to be managed in the traditional manner using certificates, but transaction costs are higher when securities are held in this form and therefore the vast majority of eligible securities are now held and transferred within the CREST system.[7] When a company has both certificated and uncertificated shares the rules for both are now found in the Regulations. Non-participating issuers (who have no uncertificated shares) are governed by the procedures set out in Chapter 1 of Part 21 of the 2006 Act. Section 786 of the 2006 Act does, however, enable regulations to be made which will (a) enable members of a company or of any designated class of companies to adopt, by ordinary resolution, arrangements under which title to securities is required to be evidenced and transferred in dematerialized form; or (b) require companies, or any designated class of companies, to adopt such arrangements.[8] This clearly envisages movement away from the permissive regime adopted by the current Regulations to a mandatory regime under which certificated holding and transfer of securities is ended. **49.USR.14**

The Regulations require two registers to be maintained.[9] The first is the 'issuer register of members' which is maintained by participating issuers. In this register there is entered: **49.USR.15**

(a)   the names and addresses of the members, with a statement of the certificated shares of each class held and the amount paid on those shares;
(b)   the date on which each person was registered as a member;
(c)   the date at which any person ceased to be a member.

A participating issuer is also required to maintain a 'record of uncertificated shares'. This replicates the information shown in the Operator register of members (see below).

The second register is the 'Operator register of members' which is maintained by the operator. This register must show the names and addresses of members who hold uncertificated shares in the company with a statement of the number of shares (or stock when conversion to stock has occurred) held in each class. **49.USR.16**

These registers are concerned with shares and members and therefore the relevant provisions are not of direct relevance to registers which are maintained in respect of other securities (eg debt) issued by companies. There is no legal obligation comparable to section 113 of the Companies Act 2006 to maintain a register in respect of such securities and this reflects the different manner in which ownership of shares and debt securities is constituted. Ownership of shares is constituted by registration in the relevant register (as above) whereas ownership of debt securities does not require registration: compliance with the formal and substantive requirements of contract law for the creation of a debt obligation is normally sufficient. However, it may be that the instrument creating the debt or a specific legal provision requires the company to maintain a register of the holders. If that is the case, the Regulations make provision for the maintenance of registers to enable holding and transfer in dematerialized form.[10] The main difference is that in the case of 'eligible debt securities'[11] there is no requirement to maintain an issuer register. The rationale is presumably that the main focus of the issuer register of shares is to identify members of the company, and holders of securities other than shares are not members of a company. **49.USR.17**

---

[5]   Regulations 14 and 15.
[6]   Regulations 14 and 16.
[7]   CREST is not limited to listed companies and therefore the securities of other companies (including private companies) can in principle be held and transferred within CREST.
[8]   See s 786 and commentary.
[9]   Regulation 20 and Sch 4 to the Regulations.
[10]   See reg 22.
[11]   These are debt securities whose current terms provide that they can only be held in uncertificated form and title to them may only be transferred by means of a relevant system (reg 3).

**49.USR.18**    The Regulations deal with the status of these registers and the relationship between the registers and the obligation imposed by section 113 of the Companies Act 2006 to maintain a register of members. They also deal with the issue of the evidential value of entries in the registers as regards title to securities and the process by which title is transferred. As will become clear from the discussion below, it is the policy of the Regulations to give priority to the operator register of members in respect of these issues in the event of a conflict between the two registers. The underlying rationale is a policy of minimizing the risks that arise in settlement when transfer of legal title takes place after settlement of a transaction (delivery of evidence of title in exchange for payment). In these circumstances the buyer faces the risk (at least temporarily) of paying and not being the registered owner.[12] This risk is minimized if priority in determining legal title is given to the operator register as the transfer will be recorded first in that register.

**49.USR.19**    As regards the status of the registers, the Regulations provide that in respect of a participating issuer any reference in an enactment or instrument to a company's register of members shall, unless the context requires otherwise, be taken to refer to the two registers.[13] However, in the event of a conflict between the two registers, it is the entry in the operator register of members that prevails.[14] The obligation to maintain a (conventional) register of members under section 113 of the 2006 Act is disapplied in the case of participating issuers but the sanctions for failing to maintain the section 113 register apply equally to failure to maintain the issuer register of members.[15] The rationale for disapplying the obligation to maintain a conventional register under section 113 is presumably that the relevant information is now shown in the new registers.

**49.USR.20**    An entry on either the operator or issuer register of members has the same legal effect in respect of title to dematerialized shares as does a certificate in respect of certificated shares.[16] The entry or certificate is prima facie evidence (in Scotland sufficient evidence unless the contrary is shown) of legal title to shares. However, in the event of a conflict between the two registers, the operator register prevails, but even that entry is not conclusive, as ownership of shares ultimately rests with the person who is entitled to be registered.[17] In the case of securities other than shares, an entry in the operator register alone (there is no equivalent to the issuer register in the case of such securities which are 'eligible debt securities') has the same effect.

**49.USR.21**    Provision is made in the Regulations for rectification of the registers. As an entry provides only prima facie and not conclusive evidence in respect of the matters to which it refers (primarily membership and securities held), it may be that the entries in the register will be disputed. While membership is completed by registration, it also requires agreement[18] and there will be no agreement if the requirements for membership in the articles are not met.[19] The Regulations envisage rectification of the registers by agreement between the issuer and operator or alternatively as a result of a court order made under section 125 of the Companies Act 2006.[20]

**49.USR.22**    Transfer of title to uncertificated shares is effected by the operator who, having verified the relevant electronic settlement instructions that are input by intermediaries following the making of a bargain, effects the transfer by making the appropriate changes in the operator register. The operator than gives an operator-instruction to the issuer to register the transfer (or transmission) in the issuer register of members and the record of uncertificated shares.[21] However, it is clear that transfer of legal title occurs as a result of the entry in the operator register and therefore any delay between the making of that entry and the entry in the Issuer register is of no consequence. A participating issuer is required, unless it is impracticable to do so by virtue of circumstances beyond its control, to ensure that the record of

---

[12]  In a 'real time' delivery-versus-payment settlement system that risk is eliminated as transfer of title occurs at the same time as payment, but in any other system (including those that are described as implementing the principle of delivery-versus-payment but have not implemented a 'real time' version) the risk will be present.

[13]  See eg s 116 of the 2006 Act, providing for the right to inspect the register of members.

[14]  This is the effect of reg 20(5).

[15]  Regulation 20 and Sch 4 (para 5) to the Regulations.

[16]  Regulation 24 and s 768 of the 2006 Act.

[17]  While the Regulations do not in terms modify that principle, the provisions of Pt 4 (below) limit the extent to which a true owner who has been removed from the register can be restored.

[18]  CA 2006, s 112(2).

[19]  Admittedly, this is less likely for listed companies than for other companies as restrictions on transfer are the most obvious source of difficulty and such restrictions are not permitted in the case of listed companies.

[20]  Regulation 25.

[21]  Regulation 27.

uncertificated shares is regularly reconciled with the operator register of members.[22] In the case of 'eligible debt securities', transfer or transmission occurs simply by the making and deletion of entries on the relevant operator register. The Regulations specify circumstances in which the operator must [23] or may[24] refuse to register a transfer, in which case notice of the refusal must be sent to the transferee.

## PART 4
### DEMATERIALISED INSTRUCTIONS ETC.

Properly authenticated dematerialised instructions, etc.                                    49.USR.23

**35.** (1) This regulation has effect for the purpose of determining the rights and obligations of persons to whom properly authenticated dematerialised instructions are attributable and of persons to whom properly authenticated dematerialised instructions are addressed, when such instructions relate to an uncertificated unit of a security, or relate to a right, benefit or privilege attaching to or arising from such a unit, or relate to the details of a holder of such a unit.

(2) Where a properly authenticated dematerialised instruction is expressed to have been sent on behalf of a person by a sponsoring system-participant or the Operator—

    (a) the person on whose behalf the instruction is expressed to have been sent shall not be able to deny to the addressee—

        (i) that the properly authenticated dematerialised instruction was sent with his authority; or

        (ii) that the information contained in the properly authenticated dematerialised instruction is correct; and

    (b) the sponsoring system-participant or the Operator (as the case may be) shall not be able to deny to the addressee—

        (i) that he has authority to send the properly authenticated dematerialised instruction; or

        (ii) that he has sent the properly authenticated dematerialised instruction.

(3) Where a properly authenticated dematerialised instruction is expressed to have been sent by a person, and the properly authenticated dematerialised instruction is not expressed to have been sent on behalf of another person, the person shall not be able to deny to the addressee—

    (a) that the information contained in the properly authenticated dematerialised instruction is correct; or

    (b) that he has sent the properly authenticated dematerialised instruction.

(4) An addressee who receives (whether directly, or by means of the facilities of a sponsoring system-participant acting on his behalf) a properly authenticated dematerialised instruction may, subject to paragraph (5), accept that at the time at which the properly authenticated dematerialised instruction was sent or at any time thereafter—

    (a) the information contained in the instruction was correct;

    (b) the system-participant or the Operator (as the case may be) identified in the instruction as having sent the instruction sent the instruction; and

    (c) the instruction, where relevant, was sent with the authority of the person on whose behalf it is expressed to have been sent.

(5) Subject to paragraph (6), an addressee may not accept any of the matters specified in paragraph (4) if at the time he received the properly authenticated dematerialised instruction or at any time thereafter—

    (a) he was a person other than a participating issuer or a sponsoring system-participant receiving properly authenticated dematerialised instructions on behalf of a participating issuer, and he had actual notice—

        (i) that any information contained in it was incorrect;

        (ii) that the system-participant or the Operator (as the case may be) expressed to have sent the instruction did not send the instruction; or

        (iii) where relevant, that the person on whose behalf it was expressed to have been sent had not given to the Operator or the sponsoring system-participant (as the case may be), identified in the properly authenticated dematerialised instruction as having sent it, his authority to send the properly authenticated dematerialised instruction on his behalf; or

    (b) he was a participating issuer, or a sponsoring system-participant receiving properly authenticated dematerialised instructions on behalf of a participating issuer, and—

        (i) he had actual notice from the Operator of any of the matters specified in subparagraph (a)(i) to (iii); or

---

[22] The standard practice is that at the end of each business day issuers' registrars combine a copy of the record of dematerialized holdings maintained by CREST with their records of certificated holdings to form the full registers.

[23] Regulation 27(2).

[24] Regulation 27(4).

(ii)  if the instruction was an Operator-instruction requiring the registration of a transfer of title, he had actual notice of any of the circumstances specified in regulation 28(3); or

(c)  he was an Operator and the instruction related to a transfer of units of a security which was in excess of any limit imposed by virtue of paragraph 15 of Schedule 1; or

(d)  he was an Operator and he had actual notice of any of the circumstances specified in regulation 27(2) in a case where the instruction was—

(i)  a system-member instruction requesting him to settle a transfer in accordance with his rules; or

(ii)  an issuer-instruction given in the circumstances specified in regulation 33(2)(b) requesting him to register a transfer of title.

(6)  Notwithstanding that an addressee has received, in respect of a properly authenticated dematerialised instruction, actual notice of the kind referred to in paragraph (5), the addressee may accept the matters specified in paragraph (4) if at the time that he received the actual notice it was not practicable for him to halt the processing of the instruction.

(7)  Subject to paragraph (8), this regulation has effect without prejudice to the liability of any person for causing or permitting a dematerialised instruction—

(a)  to be sent without authority; or

(b)  to contain information which is incorrect; or

(c)  to be expressed to have been sent by a person who did not send it.

(8)  Subject to paragraph (9), a person who is permitted by this regulation to accept any matter shall not be liable in damages or otherwise to any person by reason of his having relied on the matter that he was permitted to accept.

(9)  The provisions of paragraph (8) do not affect—

(a)  any liability of the Operator to pay compensation under regulation 36; or

(b)  any liability of a participating issuer under regulation 46 arising by reason of a default in complying with, or contravention of, regulation 28(6).

(10) For the purposes of this regulation—

(a)  a properly authenticated dematerialised instruction is expressed to have been sent by a person or on behalf of a person if it is attributable to that person; and

(b)  an addressee is the person to whom a properly authenticated dematerialised instruction indicates it is addressed in accordance with the rules and specifications referred to in paragraph 5(5) of Schedule 1.

(11) Nothing in this regulation shall be taken, in respect of any authority, to modify or derogate from the protections to a donee or third person given by or under any enactment or to prohibit a donee or third person so protected from accepting any of the matters specified in paragraph (4).

(12) Paragraphs (2) to (4), (5)(a), (6) to (9) and (11) of this regulation shall apply in relation to a written notification given under regulation 25(3) or 32(2)(c) as if—

(a)  each reference to a properly authenticated dematerialised instruction were to such a notification which has been authenticated by the Operator in accordance with rules made and practices instituted by the Operator in order to comply with paragraph 25(g) of Schedule 1;

(b)  each reference to information contained in the properly authenticated dematerialised instruction being correct (or incorrect) included, in the case of written notification given under subparagraph (c) of regulation 32(2), a reference to any statement of the sort referred to in that subparagraph being true (or untrue, as the case may be);

(c)  each reference to an addressee were a reference to the Operator; and

(d)  the reference in paragraph (6) to the processing of the instruction were to acting on the written notification.

### Liability for forged dematerialised instructions, induced amendments to Operator registers of securities, and induced Operator-instructions

**36.** (1)  For the purpose of this regulation—

(a)  a dematerialised instruction is a forged dematerialised instruction if—

(i)  it was not sent from the computers of a system-participant or the computers comprising an Operator-system; or

(ii)  it was not sent from the computers of the system-participant or the computers comprising an Operator-system (as the case may be) from which it is expressed to have been sent;

(b)  an act is a causative act if, not being a dematerialised instruction and not being an act which causes a dematerialised instruction to be sent from the computer of a system-participant, it unlawfully causes the Operator—

(i)  to make, delete or amend an entry on an Operator register of securities; or

(ii)  to send an Operator-instruction to a participating issuer;

(c)  an entry on, deletion from, or amendment to an Operator register of securities is an induced amendment if it is an entry on, deletion from, or amendment to an Operator register of securities which results from a causative act or a forged dematerialised instruction; and

(d) an Operator-instruction is an induced Operator-instruction if it is an Operator-instruction to a participating issuer which results from a causative act or a forged dematerialised instruction.

(2) If, as a result of a forged dematerialised instruction (not being one which results in an induced amendment to an Operator register of securities or an induced Operator-instruction), an induced amendment to an Operator register of securities, or an induced Operator-instruction, any one or more of the following events occurs—

(a) the name of any person remains on, is entered on, or is removed or omitted from, a register of securities;

(b) the number of units of a security in relation to which the name of any person is entered on a register of securities is increased, reduced, or remains unaltered;

(c) the description of any units of a security in relation to which the name of any person is entered on a register of securities is changed or remains unaltered,

and that person suffers loss as a result, he may apply to the court for an order that the Operator compensate him for his loss.

(3) It is immaterial for the purposes of subparagraphs (a) to (c) of paragraph (2) whether the event is permanent or temporary.

(4) The court shall not make an order under paragraph (2)—

(a) if the Operator identifies a person as being responsible (whether alone or with others) for the forged dematerialised instruction (not being one which results in an induced amendment to an Operator register of securities or an induced Operator-instruction) or the causative act or forged dematerialised instruction resulting in the induced amendment to the Operator register of securities or the induced Operator-instruction (as the case may be) notwithstanding that it is impossible (for whatever reason) for the applicant to obtain satisfactory compensation from that person; or

(b) if the Operator shows that a participating issuer would be liable under regulation 46 to compensate the applicant for the loss in respect of which the application is made, by reason of the participating issuer's default in complying with, or contravention of, regulation 28(6).

(5) Subject to paragraphs (6) and (7), the court may award to an applicant compensation for—

(a) each forged dematerialised instruction (not being one which results in an induced amendment to an Operator register of securities or an induced Operator-instruction);

(b) each induced amendment to an Operator register of securities; and

(c) each induced Operator-instruction,

resulting in an event mentioned in subparagraph (a), (b) or (c) of paragraph (2).

(6) The court shall not under paragraph (5) award to an applicant—

(a) more than £50,000 for each such forged dematerialised instruction, induced amendment to an Operator register of securities, or induced Operator-instruction;

(b) compensation for both an induced amendment to an Operator register of securities and an induced Operator-instruction if that induced amendment and that induced Operator-instruction resulted from the same causative act or the same forged dematerialised instruction.

(7) In respect of liability arising under this regulation the court shall—

(a) in awarding compensation only order the Operator to pay such amount of compensation as it appears to it to be just and equitable in all the circumstances having regard to the loss sustained by the applicant as a result of the forged dematerialised instruction, induced amendment to the Operator register of securities, or induced Operator-instruction;

(b) in ascertaining the loss, apply the same rules concerning the duty of a person to mitigate his loss as apply to damages recoverable under the common law of England and Wales, Northern Ireland, or Scotland, (as the case may be); and

(c) where it finds that the loss was to any extent caused or contributed to by any act or omission of the applicant, reduce the amount of the award by such proportion as it thinks just and equitable having regard to that finding.

(8) An application to the court for an order under paragraph (2) shall not prejudice any right of the Operator to recover from a third party any sum that he may be ordered to pay.

(9) An event mentioned in subparagraph (a), (b) or (c) of paragraph (2) shall not give rise to any liability on the Operator other than such as is expressly provided for in this regulation, except such as may arise from fraud or other wilful default, or negligence, on the part of the Operator.

(10) Subject to paragraph (9), this regulation does not affect—

(a) any right which any person may have other than under this regulation (not being a right against the Operator); or

(b) any liability which any person other than the Operator may incur other than under this regulation.

(11) Where an application is made under paragraph (2), and the Operator receives from the applicant a request for information or documents relating to—

      (a)  a forged dematerialised instruction;

      (b)  an induced amendment to an Operator register of securities; or

      (c)  an induced Operator-instruction,

in respect of which the application is made, the Operator shall, in so far as he is able, and in so far as the request is reasonable, within one month give the applicant the information and documents.

(12) The applicant shall, in so far as he is able, within one month give the Operator such information or documents as the Operator reasonably requests in connection with an application under paragraph (2) with respect to—

      (a)  steps taken by the applicant to prevent the giving of any forged dematerialised instruction (whether of the kind referred to in paragraph (2) or of any other kind); and

      (b)  steps taken by the applicant to mitigate the loss suffered by him,

provided that the applicant need not give information or documents pursuant to this paragraph until the Operator has complied with any request made by virtue of paragraph (11).

(13) Neither the Operator nor the applicant shall be required to disclose any information by virtue of, respectively, paragraph (11) or (12) which would be privileged in the course of civil proceedings, or, in Scotland, which they would be entitled to refuse to disclose—

      (a)  on grounds of confidentiality as between client and professional legal adviser in proceedings in the Court of Session; or

      (b)  on grounds of confidentiality of communications made in connection with, or in contemplation of, such proceedings and for the purposes of those proceedings.

(14) The jurisdiction conferred by this regulation shall be exercisable, in the case of a participating security constituted under the law of England and Wales, or Northern Ireland, by the High Court; and in the case of a participating security constituted under the law of Scotland by the Court of Session.

**49.USR.24**   This part deals with the liability of senders and recipients of properly authenticated dematerialized instructions. Subject to limited exceptions, the recipient is entitled to act on the instruction and the person by whom or on behalf of whom it was sent may not deny that it was sent with proper authority and contained accurate information.[25] This appears to have the result that a transfer resulting from an unauthorized or erroneous instruction will stand so long as it appears to emanate from within the system (in which case it will appear to be a 'properly authenticated dematerialized instruction'). That outcome, however, is without prejudice to any liability of any person for causing or permitting a dematerialized instruction to have been sent without authority or to contain information which is incorrect or to be expressed to have been sent by a person who did not send it. Thus, a remedy (eg in damages for negligence) may be available but not rectification of the register as a matter of right.

**49.USR.25**   This part also deals with liability in respect of forged instructions. The Regulations adopt a limited definition of forged instructions in the sense that a forged transfer does not include one that is fabricated by a person operating within the system. Such an instruction would be treated as unauthorized and dealt with as described above. 'Forged instructions' for the purposes of the Regulations are those that emanate from outside the system and or from computers other than those from which it purported to be sent from. The operator may be liable for loss (capped at £50,000 per instruction) resulting from forged instructions that lead to changes on the register but not if the operator identifies a person as being responsible for the relevant instruction. The transferor has no right to rectification of the register in these circumstances. In effect, the rights of the transferee are prioritized and the operator is made liable for security defects in the system (which lead to 'forged instructions') but not for unauthorized use within the system.

# PART 5
## MISCELLANEOUS AND SUPPLEMENTAL
### *Miscellaneous*

**49.USR.26**   Construction of references to transfers etc.

37.   References in any enactment or rule of law to a proper instrument of transfer or to a transfer with respect to securities, or any expression having like meaning, shall be taken to include a reference to an Operator-instruction to a participating issuer to register a transfer of title on the relevant issuer register of securities in accordance with the Operator-instruction.

---

[25]  Regulation 35.

## Certain formalities and requirements not to apply

**38.** (1) Any requirements in an enactment or rule of law which apply in respect of the transfer of securities otherwise than by means of a relevant system shall not prevent—

   (a) an Operator from registering a transfer of title to uncertificated units of a security upon settlement of a transfer of such units in accordance with his rules; or

   (b) an Operator-instruction from requiring a participating issuer to register a transfer of title to uncertificated units of a security.

   (2) Subject to regulation 32(7), notwithstanding any enactment, instrument or rule of law, a participating issuer shall not issue a certificate in relation to any uncertificated units of a participating security.

   (3) A document issued by or on behalf of a participating issuer purportedly evidencing title to an uncertificated unit of a participating security shall not be evidence of title to the unit of the security; and in particular—

   (a) [section 768 of the 2006 Act][a] shall not apply to any document issued with respect to uncertificated shares; and

   (b) [regulation 9(3) of the 2004 Regulations][b] and regulation 6(3) of the 1974 Regulations shall not apply to any document issued with respect to uncertificated units of a public sector security.

   (4) Any requirement in or under any enactment to endorse any statement or information on a certificate evidencing title to a unit of a security—

   (a) shall not prohibit the conversion into, or issue of, units of the security in uncertificated form; and

   (b) in relation to uncertificated units of the security, shall be taken to be a requirement for the relevant participating issuer to provide the holder of the units with the statement or information on request by him.

   (5) Sections 53(1)(c) and 136 of the Law of Property Act 1925 (which impose requirements for certain dispositions and assignments to be in writing) shall not apply (if they would otherwise do so) to—

   (a) any transfer of title to uncertificated units of a security by means of a relevant system; and

   (b) any disposition or assignment of an interest in uncertificated units of a security title to which is held by a relevant nominee.

   (6) In paragraph (5) 'relevant nominee' means a subsidiary undertaking of an Operator designated by him as a relevant nominee in accordance with such rules and practices as are mentioned in paragraph 25(f) of Schedule 1.

   (7) [Section 772 of the 2006 Act][c] shall not apply in relation to the transfer of uncertificated units of a security by means of a relevant system.

AMENDMENTS AND NOTES

[a] Amended by the Companies Act (Consequential Amendments) (Uncertificated Securities) Order 2009, SI 2009/1889, art 2(16).

[b] Amended by the Government Stock (Consequential and Transitional Provision) (No 2) Order 2004, SI 2004/1662, Schedule, Pt 3, para 29.

[c] Amended by the Companies Act (Consequential Amendments) (Uncertificated Securities) Order 2009, SI 2009/1889, art 2(16).

## Fees charged by Operators

**39.** (1) Subject to paragraph (2), nothing in these Regulations prevents an Operator from charging a fee for carrying out any function under Part 3 of these Regulations.

   (2) An Operator may not charge a fee to a participating issuer for maintaining or keeping and entering up an Operator register of securities.

## Trusts, trustees and personal representatives etc.

**40.** (1) Unless expressly prohibited from transferring units of a security by means of any computer-based system, a trustee or personal representative shall not be chargeable with a breach of trust or, as the case may be, with default in administering the estate by reason only of the fact that—

   (a) for the purpose of acquiring units of a security which he has the power to acquire in connection with the trust or estate, he has paid for the units under arrangements which provide for them to be transferred to him from a system-member but not to be so transferred until after the payment of the price;

   (b) for the purpose of disposing of units of a security which he has power to dispose of in connection with the trust or estate, he has transferred the units to a system-member under arrangements which provide that the price is not to be paid to him until after the transfer is made; or

   (c) for the purpose of holding units of a security belonging to the trust or estate in uncertificated form and for transferring title to them by means of a relevant system, he has become a system-member.

(2) Notwithstanding [sections 750 and 751 of the 2006 Act][a], a trustee of a trust deed for securing an issue of debentures shall not be chargeable with a breach of trust by reason only of the fact that he has assented to an amendment of the trust deed only for the purposes of—

(a) allowing the holding of debentures in uncertificated form;

(b) allowing the exercise of rights attaching to the debentures by means of a relevant system; or

(c) allowing the transfer of title to the debentures by means of a relevant system,

provided that he has given or caused to be given notice of the amendment in accordance with the trust deed not less than 30 days prior to its becoming effective to all persons registered as holding the debentures on a date not more than 21 days before the dispatch of the notice.

(3) Without prejudice to regulation 23(3) or [section 126 of the 2006 Act][b], the Operator shall not be bound by or compelled to recognise any express, implied or constructive trust or other interest in respect of uncertificated units of a security, even if he has actual or constructive notice of the said trust or interest.

(4) Paragraph (3) shall not prevent, in the case of a participating issuer constituted under the law of Scotland, an Operator giving notice of a trust to the participating issuer on behalf of a system-member.

AMENDMENTS AND NOTES

[a] Amended by the Companies Act (Consequential Amendments) (Uncertificated Securities) Order 2009, SI 2009/1889, art 2(17).

[b] Amended by the Companies Act (Consequential Amendments) (Uncertificated Securities) Order 2009, SI 2009/1889, art 2(17).

## Notices of meetings etc.

**41.** (1) For the purposes of determining which persons are entitled to attend or vote at a meeting, and how many votes such persons may cast, the participating issuer may specify in the notice of the meeting a time, not more than 48 hours before the time fixed for the meeting, by which a person must be entered on the relevant register of securities in order to have the right to attend or vote at the meeting.

(2) Changes to entries on the relevant register of securities after the time specified by virtue of paragraph (1) shall be disregarded in determining the rights of any person to attend or vote at the meeting, notwithstanding any provisions in any enactment, articles of association or other instrument to the contrary.

(3) For the purposes of—

(a) serving notices of meetings, whether under [section 310(1) of the 2006 Act][a], any other enactment, a provision in the articles of association or any other instrument; or

(b) sending copies of the documents required to be sent to any person by [section 423 (1) of the 2006 Act][b],

a participating issuer may determine that persons entitled to receive such notices, or copies of such documents (as the case may be), are those persons entered on the relevant register of securities at the close of business on a day determined by him.

(4) The day determined by a participating issuer under paragraph (3) may not be more than 21 days before the day that the notices of the meeting, or the copies of the documents as the case may be, are sent.

(5) This regulation is without prejudice to the protection afforded—

(a) by paragraph 5(3) of Schedule 4, to a participating issuer which is a company; and

(b) by paragraph 13(4) or 15(3) of Schedule 4, to a participating issuer.

[(6) In calculating the period mentioned in paragraph (1) above no account shall be taken of any part of a day that is not a working day.][c]

AMENDMENTS AND NOTES

[a] Amended by the Companies Act (Consequential Amendments) (Uncertificated Securities) Order 2009, SI 2009/1889, art 2(18).

[b] Amended by the Companies Act (Consequential Amendments) (Uncertificated Securities) Order 2009, SI 2009/1889, art 2(18).

[c] Amended by the Companies Act (Consequential Amendments) (Uncertificated Securities) Order 2009, SI 2009/1889, art 2(18).

## Notices to minority shareholders

**42.** (1) Paragraphs (2) to (4) shall apply in relation to any uncertificated units of a security (other than a wholly dematerialised security) to which a notice given under [section 979 of the 2006 Act][a] relates, in place of the provisions of [section 981(7)][b] of that Act.

(2) Immediately on receipt of a copy sent under [section 981(6) of the 2006 Act]$^c$ of a notice given under [section 979]$^d$ relating to uncertificated units of a participating security (whether or not it also relates to certificated units of the security), a company which is a participating issuer shall—

    (a) by issuer-instruction—

        (i) inform the Operator that the copy notice has been received, and

        (ii) identify the holding of uncertificated units of the participating security to which the notice relates; and

    (b) enter the name of the relevant system-member on an issuer register of securities as the holder of those uncertificated units.

(3) On receipt of an issuer-instruction under paragraph (2)(a), the Operator shall delete any entry in an Operator register of securities which shows the relevant system-member as the holder of the uncertificated units of the participating security to which the notice relates.

(4) On registration on an issuer register of securities (in accordance with paragraph (2)(b)) of the relevant system-member as the holder of the uncertificated units of the participating security to which the notice relates, the participating issuer—

    (a) shall be under the same obligation to enter the offeror on that register as the holder of those units, in place of the relevant system-member, as it would be if it had received an Operator-instruction under regulation 28(2) requiring it to register a transfer of title to those units in that manner; and regulation 28(9) shall have effect accordingly; and

    (b) where the terms of issue of the security in question provide for a certificate to be issued, shall issue to the offeror a certificate in respect of those units.

(5) [Subsection (1) of section 776 of the 2006 Act]$^e$ shall apply in relation to the issue of a certificate by a participating issuer pursuant to paragraph (4)(b) as it applies in relation to the completion and having ready for delivery by a company of share certificates, debentures or certificates of debenture stock; and in that subsection as it so applies the reference to the date on which a transfer is lodged with the company shall be a reference to the date on which the participating issuer receives the copy notice sent under [section 981(6) of the 2006 Act]$^f$.

(6) Such sanctions as apply to a company and its officers in the event of a default in complying with [subsection (1) of section 776 of the 2006 Act]$^g$ shall apply to a participating issuer and his officers in the event of a default in complying with paragraph (4)(b) in accordance with the requirements laid down in paragraph (5).

(7) Paragraphs (8) to (11) shall apply in relation to any units of a wholly dematerialised security to which a notice given under [section 979 of the 2006 Act]$^h$ relates, in place of the provisions of [section 981(7)]$^i$ of that Act.

(8) Immediately on receipt of a copy sent under [section 981(6)(a) of the 2006 Act]$^j$ of a notice given under [section 979]$^k$ relating to units of a wholly dematerialised security, a company which is a participating issuer shall—

    (a) by issuer-instruction—

        (i) inform the Operator that the copy notice has been received; and

        (ii) identify the holding of units of the wholly dematerialised security to which the notice relates; and

    (b) by a further issuer-instruction, inform the Operator of the name of the transferee.

(9) On receipt of an issuer-instruction under paragraph (8)(a), the Operator shall delete any entry in an Operator register of securities which shows the relevant system-member as the holder of the units to which the notice relates.

(10) On receipt of an issuer-instruction under paragraph (8)(b), the Operator shall enter the transferee on the relevant Operator register of securities as the holder of the units to which the notice relates, in place of the relevant system-member.

(11) Where an Operator deletes an entry in an Operator register of securities pursuant to paragraph (9)—

    (a) the units of the wholly dematerialised security to which the notice relates shall notwithstanding that deletion, continue to be regarded as uncertificated units for the purposes of these Regulations until the Operator enters the transferee on the relevant Operator register of securities as the holder of those units;

    (b) subject to—

        (i) subparagraph (c) or (d), as the case may be; and

        (ii) any enactment or rule of law,

        the relevant system-member shall, notwithstanding that deletion, retain title to the units of the wholly dematerialised security to which the notice relates until the transferee is entered on the relevant Operator register of securities pursuant to paragraph (10);

    (c) in the case of a security constituted under the law of England and Wales or Northern Ireland, the transferee shall acquire an equitable interest in the units of the wholly dematerialised security to which the notice relates;

    (d) in the case of a security constituted under the law of Scotland, the relevant system-member shall hold the units of the wholly dematerialised security to which the notice relates on trust for the benefit of the transferee.

(12) Such sanctions as apply to a company and its officers in the event of a default in complying with [subsections (1) and (2) of section 771 of the 2006 Act][l] shall apply—

    (a) to a participating issuer and his officers in the event of a default in complying with paragraph (2)(b) or (8); and

    (b) to an Operator and his officers in the event of a default in complying with paragraph (3), (9) or (10).

(13) For the purposes of this regulation—

    (a) 'offeror' has the meaning [in section 991(1) of the 2006 Act][m];

    (b) 'relevant system-member' means the system-member identified in the copy notice sent under [section 981(6) of the 2006 Act][n] as the holder of the uncertificated units, or as the case may be the units of the wholly dematerialised security, to which the notice relates; and

    (c) 'transferee' means the offeror or, if the offeror is not a system-member, the system-member in whose name the units of the wholly dematerialised security to which the notice given under [section 979 of the 2006 Act][o] relates are to be registered on the Operator register of securities.

(14) The reference in [section 987(8) of the 2006 Act to section 981(7)][p] shall be taken to include a reference to the provisions of paragraphs (4), (8) and (9).

## AMENDMENTS AND NOTES

[a] Amended by the Companies Act 2006 (Commencement No 2, Consequential Amendments, Transitional Provisions and Savings) Order 2007, SI 2007/1093, Sch 3, para 9(2)(a) (as to the section) and the Companies Act (Consequential Amendments) (Uncertificated Securities) Order 2009, SI 2009/1889, art 2(19) (as to the reference to the 2006 Act).

[b] Amended by the Companies Act 2006 (Commencement No 2, Consequential Amendments, Transitional Provisions and Savings) Order 2007, SI 2007/1093, Sch 3, para 9(2)(b) (as to the section) and the Companies Act (Consequential Amendments) (Uncertificated Securities) Order 2009, SI 2009/1889, art 2(19) (as to the reference to the 2006 Act).

[c] Amended by the Companies Act 2006 (Commencement No 2, Consequential Amendments, Transitional Provisions and Savings) Order 2007, SI 2007/1093, Sch 3, para 9(3)(a) (as to the section) and the Companies Act (Consequential Amendments) (Uncertificated Securities) Order 2009, SI 2009/1889, art 2(19) (as to the reference to the 2006 Act).

[d] Amended by the Companies Act 2006 (Commencement No 2, Consequential Amendments, Transitional Provisions and Savings) Order 2007, SI 2007/1093, Sch 3, para 9(3)(b).

[e] Amended by the Companies Act (Consequential Amendments) (Uncertificated Securities) Order 2009, SI 2009/1889, art 2(19).

[f] Amended by the Companies Act 2006 (Commencement No 2, Consequential Amendments, Transitional Provisions and Savings) Order 2007, SI 2007/1093, Sch 3, para 9(4) (as to the section) and the Companies Act (Consequential Amendments) (Uncertificated Securities) Order 2009, SI 2009/1889, art 2(19) (as to the reference to the 2006 Act).

[g] Amended by the Companies Act (Consequential Amendments) (Uncertificated Securities) Order 2009, SI 2009/1889, art 2(19).

[h] Amended by the Companies Act 2006 (Commencement No 2, Consequential Amendments, Transitional Provisions and Savings) Order 2007, SI 2007/1093, Sch 3, para 9(5) (as to the section) and the Companies Act (Consequential Amendments) (Uncertificated Securities) Order 2009, SI 2009/1889, art 2(19) (as to the reference to the 2006 Act).

[i] Amended by the Companies Act 2006 (Commencement No 2, Consequential Amendments, Transitional Provisions and Savings) Order 2007, SI 2007/1093, Sch 3, para 9(5)

[j] Amended by the Companies Act 2006 (Commencement No 2, Consequential Amendments, Transitional Provisions and Savings) Order 2007, SI 2007/1093, Sch 3, para 9(5) (as to the section) and the Companies Act (Consequential Amendments) (Uncertificated Securities) Order 2009, SI 2009/1889, art 2(19) (as to the reference to the 2006 Act).

[k] Amended by the Companies Act 2006 (Commencement No 2, Consequential Amendments, Transitional Provisions and Savings) Order 2007, SI 2007/1093, Sch 3, para 9(6).

[l] Amended by the Companies Act (Consequential Amendments) (Uncertificated Securities) Order 2009, SI 2009/1889, art 2(19).

[m] Amended by the Companies Act 2006 (Commencement No 2, Consequential Amendments, Transitional Provisions and Savings) Order 2007, SI 2007/1093, Sch 3, para 9(7).

[n] Amended by the Companies Act 2006 (Commencement No 2, Consequential Amendments, Transitional Provisions and Savings) Order 2007, SI 2007/1093, Sch 3, para 9(7) (as to the section) and the Companies Act (Consequential Amendments) (Uncertificated Securities) Order 2009, SI 2009/1889, art 2(19) (as to the reference to the 2006 Act).

° Amended by the Companies Act 2006 (Commencement No 2, Consequential Amendments, Transitional Provisions and Savings) Order 2007, SI 2007/1093, Sch 3, para 9(7) (as to the section) and the Companies Act (Consequential Amendments) (Uncertificated Securities) Order 2009, SI 2009/1889, art 2(19) (as to the reference to the 2006 Act).

ᵖ Amended by the Companies Act 2006 (Commencement No 2, Consequential Amendments, Transitional Provisions and Savings) Order 2007, SI 2007/1093, Sch 3, para 9(8) (as to the section) and the Companies Act (Consequential Amendments) (Uncertificated Securities) Order 2009, SI 2009/1889, art 2(19) (as to the reference to the 2006 Act).

## Irrevocable powers of attorney

**43.** (1) This regulation applies where the terms of an offer for all or any uncertificated units of a participating security provide that a person accepting the offer creates an irrevocable power of attorney in favour of the offeror, or a person nominated by the offeror, in the terms set out in the offer.

(2) An acceptance communicated by properly authenticated dematerialised instruction in respect of uncertificated units of a security shall constitute a grant of an irrevocable power of attorney by the system-member accepting the offer in favour of the offeror, or person nominated by the offeror, in the terms set out in the offer.

(3) Where the contract constituted by such offer and acceptance as are referred to in paragraphs (1) and (2) respectively is governed by the law of England and Wales, section 4 of the Powers of Attorney Act 1971 shall apply to a power of attorney constituted in accordance with this regulation.

(4) A declaration in writing by the offeror stating the terms of a power of attorney and that it has been granted by virtue of this regulation and stating the name and address of the grantor shall be prima facie evidence, and in Scotland sufficient evidence unless the contrary is shown, of the grant; and any requirement in any enactment, rule of law, or instrument to produce a copy of the power of attorney, or such a copy certified in a particular manner, shall be satisfied by the production of the declaration or a copy of the declaration certified in that manner.

(5) In the application of this regulation to an offer, acceptance or contract governed by the law of Scotland, any reference to an irrevocable power of attorney shall mean and include reference to an irrevocable mandate, however expressed.

## Actual notice

**44.** (1) For the purpose of determining under these Regulations whether a person has actual notice of a fact, matter or thing that person shall not under any circumstances be taken to be concerned to establish whether or not it exists or has occurred.

## Participating securities issued in uncertificated form

**45.** Nothing in these Regulations shall require—

(a) a participating issuer or its officers to maintain a register which records how many units of a wholly dematerialised security are held in certificated form; or

(b) an Operator or participating issuer, or their officers, to take any action to change a unit of a wholly dematerialised security from uncertificated form to certificated form or vice versa.

## *Defaults and Contraventions*

## Breaches of statutory duty

**46.** (1) A default in complying with, or a contravention of, regulation 16(8), 19(2), 25(1), 26, 28(5) or (6), 32(5), 33(5), or 42(2) or (8) shall be actionable at the suit of a person who suffers loss as a result of the default or contravention, or who is otherwise adversely affected by it, subject to the defences and other incidents applying to actions for breach of statutory duty.

(2) Paragraph (1) shall not affect the liability which any person may incur, nor affect any right which any person may have, apart from paragraph (1).

## Liability of officers for contraventions

**47.** (1) In regulation 16(7), 20(7), 21(5), 22(5), 28(9), 32(9) or (10), 33(11) or 42(6) or (12) an officer of a participating issuer shall be in default in complying with, or in contravention of, the provision mentioned in that regulation if, and only if, he knowingly and wilfully authorised or permitted the default or contravention.

(2) In regulation 20(7), 21(4), 22(4), 27(9), 32(9), 33(11) or 42(12) an officer of an Operator shall be in default in complying with, or in contravention of, the provision mentioned in that regulation if, and only if, he knowingly and wilfully authorised or permitted the default or contravention.

### Exemption from liability

**48.** Regulations 21(5), 28(9), 32(9) and (10), and 33(11) shall not apply to any of the following or its officers—

  (a) the Crown;

  (b) any person acting on behalf of the Crown;

[(c) the Bank of England;

  (d) the Registrar of Government Stock;

  (e) any previous Registrar of Government Stock; or

  (f) in respect of a security which immediately before it became a participating security was transferable by exempt transfer within the meaning of the Stock Transfer Act 1982, a participating issuer]ᵃ.

AMENDMENTS AND NOTES

ᵃ Amended by the Government Stock (Consequential and Transitional Provision) (No 2) Order 2004, SI 2004/1662, Schedule, Pt 3, para 29.

## Northern Ireland

### Application to Northern Ireland

**49.** (1) In their application to Northern Ireland, these Regulations shall have effect with the following modifications.

  (2) In regulation 38(5)—

    (a) for the reference to section 53(1)(c) of the Law of Property Act 1925 there shall be substituted a reference to section 6 of the Statute of Frauds (Ireland) 1695; and

    (b) for the reference to section 136 of the Law of Property Act 1925 there shall be substituted a reference to section 87 of the Judicature (Northern Ireland) Act 1978.

  (3) In regulation 43(3) for the reference to section 4 of the Powers of Attorney Act 1971 there shall be substituted a reference to section 3 of the Powers of Attorney Act (Northern Ireland) 1971.

  (4) In Schedule 4—ᵃ

    (a) [...]

    (b) [....]

    (c) in paragraph 6(1), for the words from 'in the case of a company registered in England and Wales' to the end there shall be substituted 'elsewhere than in Northern Ireland';

    (d) [...]

    (e) in paragraph 16(2), for subparagraphs (a) and (b) there shall be substituted 'in Northern Ireland'; and

    (f) [...]

  (5) [...]ᵇ

AMENDMENTS

ᵃ Paragraphs 4(a), (b), (d), and (f) deleted by the Companies Act (Consequential Amendments) (Uncertificated Securities) Order 2009, SI 2009/1889, art 2(20).

ᵇ Deleted by the Companies Act (Consequential Amendments) (Uncertificated Securities) Order 2009, SI 2009/1889, art 2(20).

## Transitory Provisions, Amendments, and Revocations

### Transitory provisions

**50.** Schedule 6 (transitory provisions) shall have effect.

### Minor and consequential amendments

**51.** Schedule 7 (minor and consequential amendments) shall have effect.

### Revocations

**52.** (1) The following provisions of the 1965 Regulations are hereby revoked, namely—

    regulation 4(3) and (4);

    regulations 4A and 4B;

regulation 6(5);
regulation 17(7);
regulation 18(5);
regulation 19(2);
regulation 20(2); and
Schedule 1.

(2)  The following provisions of the 1974 Regulations are hereby revoked, namely—
regulation 6(6);
regulation 6A;
regulation 7(1)(b), (4) and (5);
regulation 8(2) and (3);
regulation 9(4);
regulation 10(3);
regulation 16(4);
regulation 21(3); and
Schedule 2.

(3)  The 1995 Regulations are hereby revoked.

(4)  The following provisions of the Open-Ended Investment Companies Regulations 2001 are hereby revoked, namely—
regulation 47(1);
in Schedule 3 —
paragraph 2(2),
paragraph 5(1)(c) and the word 'and' immediately before it, and
paragraph 6(3)(d) and the word 'and' immediately before it;
paragraph 3 of Schedule 4; and
paragraph 12 of Schedule 7.

This part deals with a number of issues in respect of which the Regulations carry implications. **49.USR.27**

The provisions of regulations 40 and 46 to 48 are of particular significance. Regulation 40 exonerates **49.USR.28** trustees and personal representatives from any liability for breach of trust or default in dealing with uncertificated securities unless they are expressly prohibited. It also follows the general principle of company law (section 126 of the Companies Act 2006)[26] in providing that the operator is not bound or compelled to recognize any express, implied or constructive trust or other interest in respect of uncertificated units of a security, even if he has actual or constructive notice of the said trust or interest. Regulation 40 also makes provision for a trustee of a trust deed for securing an issue of debentures to assent to an amendment of the trust deed without liability for breach of trust so as to permit holding and transfer of debentures in uncertificated form.

Regulation 46 sets out a number of contraventions of the regulations which are actionable as breaches **49.USR.29** of statutory duty. Such an action is without prejudice to any other liability which any person may incur. Regulation 47 provides for liability on the part of officers of participating issuers and officers of an Operator for knowingly and wilfully authorizing or permitting certain defaults or contraventions. Regulation 48 provides for exemption from liability in respect of certain Regulations for the Crown and various bodies associated with the Crown.

---

[26]  Note that s 126 does not apply to Scotland and that reg 40 does not prevent an operator giving notice of a trust to a company.

# 50

## CA 1985 PART XVIII COMPANIES FLOATING CHARGES AND RECEIVERS (SCOTLAND)

### Companies Act 1985

## CA 1985 PART XVIII COMPANIES FLOATING CHARGES AND RECEIVERS (SCOTLAND)

### CHAPTER 1
### FLOATING CHARGES

*Introductory note*

The law relating to floating charges and receivers in Scotland falls within the legislative competence of the Scottish Parliament.[1] The Bankruptcy and Diligence etc (Scotland) Act 2007[2] will introduce fundamental changes, implementing the recommendations of the Scottish Law Commission.[3] That Act (referred to in the commentary below as the Scottish Act) provides that the Companies Act provisions be repealed in their entirety and replaced by the new provisions. Commencement of the Scottish Act has been delayed as a result of concerns expressed by certain stakeholders about the impact of commencement.[4] The changes will, in the main, apply only to charges[5] created after the coming into force of the relevant provisions. Thus, subsisting charges will remain subject to the law as it stands before the changes take effect. The most important changes introduced by the Scottish Act are referred to in the commentary below.   **50.CA85.01**

### 462  Power of incorporated company to create floating charge

(1) It is competent under the law of Scotland for an incorporated company (whether a company within the meaning of this Act or not), for the purpose of securing any debt or other obligation (including a cautionary obligation) incurred or to be incurred by, or binding upon, the company or   **50.CA85.02**

---

[1]  The Scotland Act 1998 (s 30 and Sch 5, Pt II, Head C) devolves to the Scottish Parliament power to legislate with respect to floating charges and receivers, excepting the law relating to preferential debts, the regulation of insolvency practitioners, and co-operation among insolvency courts.

[2]  The statute was passed by the Scottish Parliament on the 30 November 2006 and received the Royal assent on 15 January 2007.

[3]  Scottish Law Commission, *Discussion Paper on Registration of Rights in Security by Companies* (No 121, October 2002) and Scottish Law Commission, *Report on Registration of Rights in Security by Companies* (No 197, September 2004).

[4]  See Register of Floating Charges Technical Working Group Report to Scottish Government (August 2011). Concern focuses in particular on the (additional) requirement for registration in the proposed Scottish Register of Floating Charges and the potential for legal uncertainty to arise from the provisions of the Scottish Act, especially for English and overseas companies.

[5]  The term 'charge' is derived from English law, whereas Scots law uses the generic term 'right in security' to describe the (real) right that is held by a secured creditor over and above a personal claim against a debtor. However, since the introduction of the floating charge to Scotland, the term 'charge' has become standard usage in respect of that particular form of security interest.

any other person, to create in favour of the creditor in the debt or obligation a charge, in this Part referred to as a floating charge, over all or any part of the property (including uncalled capital) which may from time to time be comprised in its property and undertaking.

[(2) ...]ᵃ

(4) References in this Part to the instrument by which a floating charge was created are, in the case of a floating charge created by words in a bond or other written acknowledgment, references to the bond or, as the case may be, the other written acknowledgment.

(5) Subject to this Act, a floating charge has effect in accordance with this Part [and Part III of the Insolvency Act 1986]ᵇ in relation to any heritable property in Scotland to which it relates, notwithstanding that the instrument creating it is not recorded in the Register of Sasines or, as appropriate, registered in accordance with the Land Registration (Scotland) Act 1979.

AMENDMENTS AND NOTES

ᵃ Substituted for subss (2) and (3) by CA 1989; repealed by the Law Reform (Miscellaneous Provisions) (Scotland) Act 1990.

ᵇ Substituted by the Insolvency Act 1986.

COMMENCEMENT DATE 1 July 1985[6]

**50.CA85.03** Subsection (1) has the effect that the floating charge is recognized as a valid form of security interest under the law of Scotland. The common law in Scotland did not recognize the floating charge because such a charge represents a non-possessory security over corporeal moveable property. It was only following the introduction of the Companies (Floating Charges) (Scotland) Act 1961 that it became possible for companies incorporated in Scotland to grant such a charge and for floating charges granted by other companies over Scottish property to be enforced.[7] It is clear that the floating charge can secure obligations other then debt, although it is most commonly used in that context.

**50.CA85.04** Heritable property may be subject to a floating charge notwithstanding that the instrument creating it is not recorded in the Register of Sasines or, as appropriate, the Land Register. This sets aside the normal rule that security interests over land must be registered in the Register of Sasines or, as appropriate, the Land Register to be constituted as a real right. The floating charge also modifies the common law rule governing the creation of security interests over moveable property. In the case of corporeal moveables, the floating charge permits the creation of a non-possessory security, which is not recognized in the common law. In the case of incorporeal moveables, the floating charge permits the creation of a security interest without intimation to the account debtor: once again, such a security interest is not recognized by the common law. Floating charges are therefore capable of creating a security interest over any or all of the company's property subject to compliance with the statutory registration requirements. However, the main form of security interest over heritable property, the standard security, remains subject to registration in the Register of Sasines or, as appropriate, the Land Register when granted by a company. In those circumstances there are two sets of registration requirements.[8]

**50.CA85.05** Neither this section nor section 878 of the Companies Act 2006 deals directly with the substance or formalities required for execution of a floating charge. So far as the substance of an instrument creating a floating charge is concerned, the issue of whether a floating charge has been created is determined by the nature of the charge and in particular the chargor's permitted use of the charged assets.[9] Thus, even if the parties intended to create a fixed charge in a form recognized by commercial practice and judicial precedent, it may be that they have in fact created a floating charge if the chargor is given the requisite degree of freedom to deal with the charged assets. The issue of formal validity is regulated primarily by the Requirements of Writing (Sc) Act 1995. While writing is not in principle required to constitute a loan or security interest, the principle adopted by the Companies Act 2006 that a (registrable) security interest granted by a company is valid only if registered, means that there is in effect a requirement for the floating charge to be recorded in written form. If it is intended that the floating charge should benefit from the presumption that it has been executed by the company, it should be signed by:[10]

---

[6] Companies Act 1985, s 746. Repealed by the Bankruptcy and Diligence etc (Scotland) Act 2007, s 46-(1): commencement date to be appointed.

[7] See generally D Cabrelli, 'The Case against the Floating Charge in Scotland' (2005) 9(3) *Edinburgh Law Review* 407.

[8] See the commentary to s 878 of CA 2006.

[9] The House of Lords' decision *In re Spectrum Plus Ltd (in liquidation)* [2005] 2 AC 680 is equally applicable to Scotland in regard to this issue. As noted by Lord Hope (at 702) it is only possible to create a fixed charge over book debts in Scotland by way of an assignation in security followed by intimation to the account debtor. There is no recognition of 'equitable' rights in security in Scotland.

[10] Requirements of Writing (Scotland) Act 1995, s 3(1)–(1C) and Sch 2, para 3(5).

(a)  a director, the company secretary, or a duly authorized person with a witness (stating the name and address of the witness); or

(b)  two directors, a director, and the company secretary or two persons duly authorized (without the need for witnesses in any case).

## 463  Effect of floating charge on winding up

(1)  [Where a company goes into liquidation within the meaning of section 247(2) of the Insolvency Act 1986,]a a floating charge created by the company attaches to the property then comprised in the company's property and undertaking or, as the case may be, in part of that property and undertaking, but does so subject to the rights of any person who—

    (a)  has effectually executed diligence on the property or any part of it; or

    (b)  holds a fixed security over the property or any part of it ranking in priority to the floating charge; or

    (c)  holds over the property or any part of it another floating charge so ranking.

(2)  The provisions of [Part IV of the Insolvency Act (except section 185)]b have effect in relation to a floating charge, subject to subsection (1), as if the charge were a fixed security over the property to which it has attached in respect of the principal of the debt or obligation to which it relates and any interest due or to become due thereon.

[(3)  Nothing in this section derogates from the provisions of sections 53(7) and 54(6) of the Insolvency Act (attachment of floating charge on appointment of receiver), or prejudices the operation of sections 175 and 176 of that Act (payment of preferential debts in winding up).]c

(4)  ... d interest accrues, in respect of a floating charge which after 16th November 1972 attaches to the property of the company, until payment of the sum due under the charge is made.

AMENDMENTS AND NOTES

a  Substituted by CA 1989.

b  Substituted by the Insolvency Act 1986.

c  Substituted by the Insolvency Act 1986.

d  Repealed by the Insolvency Act 1986.

COMMENCEMENT DATE 1 July 1985[11]

**50.CA85.06**

Subsection (1) clarifies the meaning of the 'floating' characteristic of a floating charge. It makes clear that the charge does not attach to specific property until attachment and that attachment occurs when a company goes into liquidation.[12] Prior to attachment, the company remains free to dispose of property subject to the charge or to acquire property which becomes subject to the charge.[13] When attachment (or 'crystallization' as it is often referred to, although the Act does not use the term) occurs, it does so subject to the rights of any person who:

**50.CA85.07**

(a)  has effectually executed diligence on the property or any part of it. Diligence is the legal procedure by which a creditor attaches the property or person of his debtor, with the object of forcing him either (i) to appear in court to answer an action at the creditor's instance, or (ii) to find security for implement of the judgment which may be pronounced against him in such an action, or (iii) to implement a judgment already pronounced;[14]

---

[11]  Companies Act 1985, s 746. Repealed by the Bankruptcy and Diligence etc (Scotland) Act 2007, s 46-(1): commencement date to be appointed

[12]  However, as is clear from subs (3), attachment does not result solely from the company going into liquidation, but also as a result of the appointment of a receiver (Insolvency Act 1986, s 35(7)) or as a result of a notice delivered by an administrator to the registrar of companies under para 115(3) of Sch B1 to the Insolvency Act 1986. There is no clear Scots law authority regarding the validity of clauses in a floating charge providing for automatic attachment but as they contravene the basic principle that publicity is required to constitute real rights in security, it seems unlikely that they would be recognized (in contrast to the position in England—see generally R Goode, *Commercial Law* (3rd edn, 2004, Penguin) 684).

[13]  In the case of a charge covering 'all the property and undertaking' of the company, any new property will become subject to the charge. In other cases, the outcome will depend on the terms of the charge.

[14]  For a brief outline of the law of diligence see ch 52 of Gloag and Henderson, *The Law of Scotland* (11th edn, 2001, Edinburgh, W Green/Sweet & Maxwell).

(b) holds a fixed security over the property or any part of it ranking in priority to the floating charge. In the absence of agreement to the contrary,[15] a fixed security, the right to which has been constituted as a real right[16] before a floating charge has attached, will have priority over a floating charge;[17]

(c) holds over the property or any part of it another floating charge so ranking. In the absence of agreement, floating charges rank with one another according to the time of registration in accordance with Chapter 2 of Part 25 of the Companies Act 2006.

**50.CA85.08**  An important issue is the meaning of the company's 'property' in the context of attachment. It does not include property held by the company on trust[18] or which is subject to a valid reservation of title clause.[19] More problematic is the issue of whether the company's property includes heritable property in respect of which a disposition has been delivered to a buyer but which has not yet been recorded, and which has not therefore been constituted as a real right. In *Sharp v Thomson*,[20] the House of Lords held that, in the context of receivership, such property ceased to form part of the property of the company. However, the later decision of the Inner House in *Burnett's Trustee v Grainger*[21] confirmed that the *ratio* of *Sharp* was properly confined to the statutory provisions dealing with floating charges and receivership. Now that receivership has been largely marginalized as an insolvency procedure,[22] it is more likely that the circumstances which arose in *Sharp* will arise in a liquidation[23] or administration[24] rather than receivership. An important difference in the case of administration by comparison with the receivership scenario in *Sharp* is that the appointment of an administrator does not lead per se to attachment of a floating charge and therefore a creditor has no real right against charged property at that stage. It is only on delivery of the relevant notice to the registrar of companies by the administrator that a floating charge holder will have such a right. It follows that, in administration, the floating charge holder faces the risk, following the *ratio* of *Sharp*, that a purchaser from the company will acquire a beneficial interest before the floating charge has attached and that the relevant property will not therefore be treated as company property.[25]

**50.CA85.09**  The effect of subsection (2) is that a floating charge which has attached is treated as a fixed charge subject to the prior rights of creditors listed in points (a) to (c) of subsection (1). The charge is in respect both of the principal and interest due, which continues to accrue even after winding-up has begun. The principal effect of the charge being a fixed charge is that the debtor's freedom to dispose of the property subject to the charge is brought to an end.

**50.CA85.10**  Subsection (3) confirms that this section does not affect the operation of sections 53(7) or 54(6) of the Insolvency Act. The former provides that attachment occurs on the appointment of a receiver. The latter provides that, following attachment, a floating charge is treated as a fixed charge, with the result that the company is no longer free to dispose of property subject to the charge. From the perspective of ranking under section 464, however, attachment does not affect the nature of a floating charge, which must remain distinct from a charge originally created as a fixed charge. It is also made clear that this

---

[15] In the form of a ranking agreement contained in the instrument creating the floating charge. See the commentary to s 464.

[16] In the case of a standard security, the real right is constituted by registration in the Register of Sasines or, as appropriate, the Land Register.

[17] CA 1985, s 464(4)(a).

[18] *Balfour Beatty v Britannia Life Ltd* 1997 SLT 10; *Style Financial Services v Bank of Scotland (No 2)* 1998 SLT 851.

[19] *Armour v Thyssen Edelstahlwerke AG*, 1990 SLT 891, [1990] 3 All ER 481.

[20] 1997 SLT 636, 1997 SCLR 328.

[21] 2002 SC 580.

[22] As a result of changes introduced by the Enterprise Act 2002: see s 72A(2) of the Insolvency Act 1986, prohibiting the appointment of an 'administrative receiver' (defined in s 251 of the 1986 Act) in respect of 'new' floating charges (those granted on or after 15 September 2003) other than in the case of exceptions falling within ss 72A–72H of the 1986 Act.

[23] Specifically, the issue of what is the company's property is likely to focus on ss 143 and 144 of the Insolvency Act 1986 rather than s 53(7) which was the relevant section in *Sharp*.

[24] In which case the issue of the definition of the company's property is likely to focus on para 115 of Sch B1 to the Insolvency Act 1986. An administrator is empowered by this provision to make a distribution to the holder of a floating charge during the administration. Note also the general power of the administrator to make a distribution to creditors under paras 65 and 67 of Sch B1 of the Insolvency Act 1986.

[25] For an extended discussion see D Cabrelli, 'The Curious Case of the "Unreal" Floating Charge' (2005) 22 SLT 127.

section does not affect the operation of sections 175 and 176 of the Insolvency Act. In particular, section 175 has the effect that preferential debts[26] will be paid in priority to the claims of a holder of a floating charge.[27]

Subsection (4) makes clear that interest accrues on a debt secured by a floating charge until payment of   **50.CA85.11**
the sum due under the charge is made.

## 464  Ranking of floating charges

(1) Subject to subsection (2), the instrument creating a floating charge over all or any part of the   **50.CA85.12**
company's property under section 462 may contain—

    (a) provisions prohibiting or restricting the creation of any fixed security or any other floating charge having priority over, or ranking pari passu with, the floating charge; or

    (b) [with the consent of the holder of any subsisting floating charge or fixed security which would be adversely affected,][a] provisions regulating the order in which the floating charge shall rank with any other subsisting or future floating charges or fixed securities over that property or any part of it.

[(1A)Where an instrument creating a floating charge contains any such provision as is mentioned in subsection (1)(a), that provision shall be effective to confer priority on the floating charge over any fixed security or floating charge created after the date of the instrument.][b]

(2) Where all or any part of the property of a company is subject both to a floating charge and to a fixed security arising by operation of law, the fixed security has priority over the floating charge.

[(3) The order of ranking of the floating charge with any other subsisting or future floating charges or fixed securities over all or any part of the company's property is determined in accordance with the provisions of subsections (4) and (5) except where it is determined in accordance with any provision such as is mentioned in paragraph (a) or (b) of subsection (1).][c]

(4) Subject to the provisions of this section—

    (a) a fixed security, the right to which has been constituted as a real right before a floating charge has attached to all or any part of the property of the company, has priority of ranking over the floating charge;

    (b) floating charges rank with one another according to the time of registration in accordance with Chapter II of Part XII;

    (c) floating charges which have been received by the registrar for registration by the same postal delivery rank with one another equally.

(5) Where the holder of a floating charge over all or any part of the company's property which has been registered in accordance with Chapter II of Part XII has received intimation in writing of the subsequent registration in accordance with that Chapter of another floating charge over the same property or any part thereof, the preference in ranking of the first-mentioned floating charge is restricted to security for—

    (a) the holder's present advances;

    (b) future advances which he may be required to make under the instrument creating the floating charge or under any ancillary document;

    (c) interest due or to become due on all such advances; ...[d]

    (d) any expenses or outlays which may reasonably be incurred by the holder[; and

    (e) (in the case of a floating charge to secure a contingent liability other than a liability arising under any further advances made from time to time) the maximum sum to which that contingent liability is capable of amounting whether or not it is contractually limited.][e]

(6) This section is subject to [Part XII and to][f] [sections 175 and 176 of the Insolvency Act].[g]

AMENDMENTS AND NOTES

[a]  Inserted by CA 1989.

[b]  Inserted by CA 1989.

[c]  Substituted by CA 1989.

[d]  Repealed by CA 1989.

[e]  Inserted by CA 1989.

[f]  Prospectively inserted by CA 1989.

---

[26]  As defined in s 386 of the Insolvency Act 1986.

[27]  As illustrated by the case of *In re Spectrum Plus Ltd (in liquidation)* [2005] AC 680, the categorization of a charge as fixed or floating determines priority against preferential creditors. In that case, attachment of a floating charge over book debts (as a result of liquidation) did not give priority over the preferential creditors. Although the parties had intended to create a fixed charge (which would have given priority) the court concluded that the freedom permitted to the company to deal with bank accounts into which collected debts were paid meant that the charge could only be floating.

9 Substituted by the Insolvency Act 1986.

COMMENCEMENT DATE 1 July 1985[28]

**50.CA85.13**  This section contains both default rules governing the order of ranking of a floating charge with other charges and enabling provisions that allow the order of ranking to be adjusted in most circumstances.

**50.CA85.14**  Subsection (1) contains the enabling provisions. Paragraph (a) refers to what is commonly termed a 'negative pledge' clause, which is intended to confer priority on the floating charge over any subsequent fixed or floating charge. In the absence of such a clause the holder of a floating charge faces the risk that a fixed charge will subsequently be granted by the company and registered before the floating charge attaches, with the result that it ranks ahead of the floating charge.[29] Paragraph (b) refers to what is commonly termed a 'ranking agreement'. As the rights of a creditor cannot be altered without his consent, the holder of any subsisting floating charge or fixed security which would be adversely affected by a ranking agreement is required to give his consent to such an agreement.

**50.CA85.15**  Subsection (1A) gives statutory effect[30] to the decision in *AIB Finance v Bank of Scotland*[31] that a floating charge[32] containing a negative pledge clause operates to give it priority over a fixed security or floating charge created after the date of the instrument. Moreover, the date of creation of a fixed security is taken to be date of registration in the relevant register, whereas the date of creation of a floating charge is the date of its execution by the company.[33] Under the Scottish Act, the date of creation of a floating charge will be the date of registration, subject to the operation of the principle of advance notice.

**50.CA85.16**  Subsection (2) sets out a mandatory rule (which is not subject to alteration) that a fixed security arising by operation of law (such as a lien) has priority over the floating charge.

**50.CA85.17**  Subsection (3) establishes the principle that the default ranking order for a floating charge with any other subsisting or future floating charges or fixed securities is governed by subsections (4) and (5). It makes clear that the order of ranking set out in those subsections can be overridden by either a negative pledge clause or a ranking agreement.

**50.CA85.18**  Subsection (4) sets out the default ranking order of a floating charge with other security interests. A fixed security which has been constituted as a real right (through registration in the appropriate register) before a floating charge has attached has priority over the floating charge. Floating charges rank *inter se* according to time of registration. The Scottish Act alters this default rule so that a floating charge created after the provisions take effect and which has attached will rank with any other floating charge which has attached or any fixed security according to the date of creation.[34] This is a fundamental change from the current regime as the default rule whereby fixed charges take priority over floating charges will end.

**50.CA85.19**  Subsection (5) deals with restriction of the security of a floating charge holder following the grant of a subsequent floating charge by the company over the same property. In principle, restriction operates by the holder of the subsequent floating charge giving notice to the holder of the prior floating charge of the registration of the subsequent floating charge. There are, however, two problems inherent in the statutory provision. First, the reference to 'holder' does not make clear whether the intimation should be to the original holder, an assignee, or both. Second, as the Act does not make express provision for

---

[28] Companies Act 1985, s 746. Repealed by the Bankruptcy and Diligence etc (Scotland) Act 2007, s 46(1): commencement date to be appointed.

[29] This will change following implementation of the Scottish Act: see the commentary to subs (4) below.

[30] It does not apply to a floating charge created before 3 July 1995 nor to any instrument of alteration executed by all the parties before that date: Companies Act 1989 (Commencement No 15 etc) Order 1995, SI 1995/1352. However, *AIB Finance v Bank of Scotland* 1995 SLT 2, 1993 SCLR 851 confirmed that this was already the law.

[31] 1995 SLT 2, 1993 SCLR 851.

[32] The Act does not prohibit negative pledge clauses or ranking agreements being contained in documents other than a floating charge or an instrument of alteration under s 466 (eg a separate agreement) but such documents would not benefit from the statutory priority provided for by subs (1A).

[33] *AIB Finance v Bank of Scotland* 1995 SLT 2, 1993 SCLR 851. Under the Scottish Act, the date of creation of a floating charge will be the date of registration, subject to the operation of the principle of advance notice—see the commentary on s 879 of CA 2006.

[34] In the case of a fixed charge the date of creation will be the date on which it is constituted as a real right and for a floating charge the date of creation will be the date of registration, subject to the operation of the principle of advance notice.

the recording of assignations in either the Register of Charges or the company's internal register, there is no reliable means by which the holder of a subsequent floating charge can discover the identity of an assignee.[35]

The nature of the restriction of the rights of the 'holder' of a prior floating charge is provided for by points (a) to (e) of subsection (5). The restriction appears to apply generally and not only in a question with the holder of the subsequent floating charge. The effect of points (a) to (d) is that the prior floating charge is limited to securing present advances, future advances which the creditor is obliged to make plus interest and expenses. The reference to 'ancillary document' in point (b) is defined by section 486(1) and refers most obviously to a loan agreement or other obligation which the floating charge secures. The effect of point (e) is that when a floating charge secures a contingent liability, the full value of the contingent liability remains secured notwithstanding intimation of a subsequent charge.      **50.CA85.20**

## 465   Continued effect of certain charges validated by Act of 1972

(1)  Any floating charge which—                                                                 **50.CA85.21**
  (a)  purported to subsist as a floating charge on 17th November 1972, and
  (b)  if it had been created on or after that date, would have been validly created by virtue of the Companies (Floating Charges and Receivers) (Scotland) Act 1972,
  is deemed to have subsisted as a valid floating charge as from the date of its creation.
(2)  Any provision which—
  (a)  is contained in an instrument creating a floating charge or in any ancillary document executed prior to, and still subsisting at, the commencement of that Act,
  (b)  relates to the ranking of charges, and
  (c)  if it had been made after the commencement of that Act, would have been a valid provision,
  is deemed to have been a valid provision as from the date of its making.

COMMENCEMENT DATE  1 July 1985[36]

This section retrospectively validates *ab initio* certain charges and provisions in such charges which might otherwise be open to challenge. They are floating charges which might have been invalid because they were not in the form prescribed in the First Schedule to The Companies (Floating Charges) Scotland Act 1961 (subsection (1)) and ranking clauses contained in an instrument of charge or ancillary document (subsection (2)).      **50.CA85.22**

## 466   Alteration of floating charges

(1)  The instrument creating a floating charge under section 462 or any ancillary document may be altered by the execution of an instrument of alteration by the company, the holder of the charge and the holder of any other charge (including a fixed security) which would be adversely affected by the alteration.      **50.CA85.23**
(2)  [Without prejudice to any enactment or rule of law regarding the execution of documents,]^a such an instrument of alteration is validly executed if it is executed—
  (a)  …^b
  (b)  where trustees for debenture-holders are acting under and in accordance with a trust deed, by those trustees; [or]^c
  (c)  where, in the case of a series of secured debentures, no such trustees are acting, by or on behalf of—
    (i)  a majority in nominal value of those present or represented by proxy and voting at a meeting of debenture-holders at which the holders of at least one-third in nominal value of the outstanding debentures of the series are present or so represented; or
    (ii)  where no such meeting is held, the holders of at least one-half in nominal value of the outstanding debentures of the series; …^d
  (d)  …^e
(3)  Section 464 applies to an instrument of alteration under this section as it applies to an instrument creating a floating charge.
(4)  *Subject to the next subsection, section 410(2) and (3) and section 420 apply to an instrument of alteration under this section which—*
  (a)  *prohibits or restricts the creation of any fixed security or any other floating charge having priority over, or ranking pari passu with, the floating charge; or*
  (b)  *varies, or otherwise regulates the order of, the ranking of the floating charge in relation to fixed securities or to other floating charges; or*

---

[35]  It may be prudent to require identification of assignees of prior floating charges as a condition of making a loan (or entering into any other obligation) to be secured by a subsequent floating charge.
[36]  Companies Act 1985, s 746. Repealed by the Bankruptcy and Diligence etc (Scotland) Act 2007, s 46(1): commencement date to be appointed.

    (c) *releases property from the floating charge; or*

    (d) *increases the amount secured by the floating charge.*

  (5) *Section 410(2) and (3) and section 420 apply to an instrument of alteration falling under subsection (4) of this section as if references in the said sections to a charge were references to an alteration to a floating charge, and as if in section 410(2) and (3)—*

    (a) *references to the creation of a charge were references to the execution of such alteration; and*

    (b) *for the words from the beginning of subsection (2) to the word 'applies' there were substituted the words 'Every alteration to a floating charge created by a company'.*[f]

  (6) Any reference (however expressed) in any enactment, including this Act, to a floating charge is, for the purposes of this section and unless the context otherwise requires, to be construed as including a reference to the floating charge as altered by an instrument of alteration *falling under subsection (4) of this section.*[g]

A MENDMENTS AND N OTES

[a] Inserted by CA 1989.

[b] Repealed by CA 1989.

[c] Inserted by CA 1989.

[d] Repealed by CA 1989.

[e] Repealed by CA 1989.

[f] Subsections (4), (5) prospectively repealed by CA 1989.

[g] Words in italics prospectively repealed by CA 1989.

C OMMENCEMENT D ATE 1 July 1985[37]

**50.CA85.24**  Subsection (1) provides that an instrument creating a floating charge under section 462 or any ancillary document may be altered by the execution of an instrument of alteration by the company, the holder of the charge, and the holder of any other charge (including a fixed security) which would be adversely affected by the variation. The procedure for alteration therefore respects the principle that a creditor's rights cannot be adversely adjusted without his agreement: this remains the case under the Scottish Act. However, as discussed below in relation to subsections (4) and (5), the obligation to register alterations to a floating charge[38] is limited in several respects and so too are the sanctions for non-registration.[39] The Scottish Act provides that the terms of a floating charge concerning:

(a) ranking; or

(b) property subject to the charge; or

(c) obligations secured by the charge;

are not amended by an instrument of alteration unless that instrument of alteration has itself been registered.[40]

**50.CA85.25**  Subsection (2) deals with execution of an instrument of alteration in respect of an issue of debentures or a series of debentures. Where trustees act for the debenture-holders, they are entitled to execute the alteration. Where there are no trustees, the majority specified in subsection (2)(c)(i) may approve the alteration at a meeting of debenture-holders or alternatively the alteration may be approved by holders of one-half in nominal value of the outstanding debentures of the series.

**50.CA85.26**  Subsection (3) provides that section 464 (ranking of floating charges) applies to an instrument of alteration as it applies to an instrument creating a floating charge. This means that it is possible to use an instrument of alteration to give effect to a negative pledge clause or ranking agreement following the registration of a charge.

**50.CA85.27**  Subsection (4) deals with the requirement to register an alteration to a floating charge.[41] It lists four types of alteration that require registration. However, there remains some doubt over the consequences

---

[37] Companies Act 1985, s 746. Repealed by the Bankruptcy and Diligence etc (Scotland) Act 2007, s 46(1): commencement date to be appointed.

[38] Although subs (1) refers to the possibility of changes to an ancillary document being registered, there is no obligation to register changes to such a document.

[39] As regards alterations that have the effect of releasing property from the charge, see the commentary on s 887 of CA 2006.

[40] Section 36.

[41] Subsections (4) and (5) would have been repealed by s 140 of CA 1989 had its provisions on floating charges been implemented. They would have been replaced by the registration provisions contained in Part IV of the 1989 Act, which have not been and will not be brought into effect.

of non-registration. While it is stated that section 410(2) (replaced by section 889(1) of the Companies Act 2006) applies to the prescribed variations, the 'void' sanction provided by that subsection in respect of non-registration applies 'so far as any security on the company's property or any part of it is conferred by the charge'. It has been noted that none of the first three forms of alteration (negative pledge, ranking agreement, and release of property from the charge) that require registration confer any security.[42] Following that approach, it can be maintained that there is no 'void' sanction for failure to register an alteration other than one that falls within paragraph (d) (increase in the amount secured by a floating charge). If that is the case, it is surely a drafting error, as it would seem odd that the requirements for registering alterations do not match the requirements for registering particulars under section 885 of the Companies Act 2006.[43]

Subsection (5) applies section 410(2) and (3) (replaced by section 878 of the Companies Act 2006) and   **50.CA85.28**
section 420 (replaced by section 888 of the Companies Act 2006) in adapted form to alterations to a floating charge. It makes clear that, so far as an alteration is concerned, the relevant point in time from which the 21-day registration period runs is the date of the execution of the instrument of alteration. It also raises the question[44] of how section 410(3) (now section 889 of the Companies Act 2006) should be applied to an alteration to a charge. If a charge is expressed as covering all the property and undertaking of a company in respect of a fluctuating advance subject to a ceiling which is altered, the alteration requires to be registered under subsection (4),[45] but the 'money secured' by the alteration is not identifiable and therefore the application of section 410(3) (now section 889 of the Companies Act 2006) is not clear. However, some method of isolating the money secured by the alteration must be found[46] as it was clearly not intended that failure to register an alteration would have the effect of causing acceleration in repayment of the entire amount secured by the floating charge as amended.

## 486  Interpretation for Part XVIII generally

(1) In this Part, unless the context otherwise requires, the following expressions have the following   **50.CA85.29**
meanings respectively assigned to them, that is to say—
'ancillary document' means—
(a) a document which relates to the floating charge and which was executed by the debtor or creditor in the charge before the registration of the charge in accordance with Chapter II of Part XII; or
(b) an instrument of alteration such as is mentioned in section 466 in this Part;
'company', ...[a] means an incorporated company (whether a company within the meaning of this Act or not);
'fixed security', in relation to any property of a company, means any security, other than a floating charge or a charge having the nature of a floating charge, which on the winding up of the company in Scotland would be treated as an effective security over that property, and (without prejudice to that generality) includes a security over that property, being a heritable security within the meaning of section 9(8) of the Conveyancing and Feudal Reform (Scotland) Act 1970; ...[b]
'Register of Sasines' means the appropriate division of the General Register of Sasines.

AMENDMENTS AND NOTES

[a] Repealed by the Insolvency Act 1986.

[b] Repealed by the Insolvency Act 1986.

COMMENCEMENT DATE  1 July 1985[47]

---

[42] See *Palmer's Company Law* (Sweet & Maxwell) para 13.411 (16 January 2000). Note also that s 466 does not apply s 415 (fines for non-registration, replaced by s 878 of CA 2006) to an alteration.
[43] A material difference between initial and subsequent registration requirements serves to reinforce the view (see commentary on s 885 of CA 2006) that the Register of Charges does not provide reliable information (especially for potential creditors).
[44] Noted at para 13.411 of *Palmer's Company Law* (Sweet & Maxwell).
[45] Because the amount secured by the charge has increased.
[46] It may be simplest to assume that the 'money secured' by the alteration is the increase in the ceiling, even though this may have the effect of attaching too severe a sanction to an omission to register a (registrable) alteration: eg an increase in the ceiling from £2m to £3m would be taken to accelerate repayment of £1m even if the actual advance stood at only £1m. Of course, in the case of fixed advances, the 'money secured' by an alteration is more straightforward: eg an advance of £2m secured by a floating charge covering all the property and undertaking of the company is followed by a further advance of £1m, with the result that the 'money secured' by the alteration is £1m and non-registration of the alteration would lead to acceleration in repayment of £1m.
[47] Companies Act 1985, s 746. Repealed by the Bankruptcy and Diligence etc (Scotland) Act 2007, s 46(1): commencement date to be appointed.

**50.CA85.30**    This section sets out definitions of various terms that are referred to in Part XVIII.

### 487 Extent of Part XVIII

**50.CA85.31**    This Part extends to Scotland only.

       COMMENCEMENT DATE 1 July 1985[48]

**50.CA85.32**    This section makes clear that Part XVIII extends to Scotland only.

---

[48] Companies Act 1985, s 746. Repealed by the Bankruptcy and Diligence etc (Scotland) Act 2007, s 46(1): commencement date to be appointed.

# 51

## TABLE A AND MODEL ARTICLES

## TABLE A

*Introductory note*

Below are set out the last two versions of 'Table A'—model articles of association prescribed for companies limited by shares. These are the '1948 version' (contained in Schedule I to the CA 1948) and the '1985 version' (contained in the Schedule to the Companies (Tables A to F) Regulations 1985).[1] Under the power in section 19 of the Companies Act 2006, the Secretary of State has now prescribed *new* model articles of association for three types of company: private companies limited by shares, private companies limited by guarantee and public companies.[2] These new model articles will apply to companies registered under the Companies Act 2006, ie incorporated on or after 1 October 2009.[3] They will apply to such companies 'by default' (that is, to the extent that such companies do not exclude them). The commentary at paragraphs 51.TA.02 to 51.TA.08 below deals only with the 1948 and 1985 versions of Table A.     **51.TA.01**

For companies limited by shares[4] and incorporated prior to 1 October 2009, their articles of association are deemed to incorporate the regulations of the relevant Table A by default.[5] In principle, the 'relevant' Table A is the version in force at the date of the company's registration. Thus, a company limited by shares that was registered under the 1948 Act has (insofar as it did not exclude it) the 1948 version of Table A,[6] whilst one formed under the 1985 Act has the 1985 version.[7] (Similarly, as noted above, for one incorporated on or after 1 October 2009, ie under the Companies Act 2006, the model articles now prescribed under that Act will apply by default.)     **51.TA.02**

The position is, however, rather less clear-cut than the foregoing suggests. The difficulty arises in relation to changes made 'within' each version of Table A. Taking the 1985 version first, its status is addressed by the Companies Act 1985, section 8. Whilst section 8(2) states that the Table applies in default, section 8(3) provides that '[i]f in consequence of regulations under this section Table A is altered, the alteration does not affect a company registered before the alteration takes effect, or repeal as respects that company any portion of the Table'. Some alterations—namely those in the Companies     **51.TA.03**

---

[1] SI 1985/805.

[2] See the Companies (Model Articles) Regulations 2008, SI 2008/3229.

[3] See s 20 of CA 2006.

[4] Under CA 1985, for companies limited by guarantee with a share capital, their articles had to be 'in accordance with' Table C, but that Table did not apply by default. Under CA 2006, the model articles prescribed for guarantee companies do apply by default.

[5] See s 8 of CA 1948; s 8 of CA 1985.

[6] See Sch 2, para 1(1) to the Companies Act 2006 (Commencement No 8, Transitional Provisions and Savings) Order 2008, SI 2008/2860, and art 5 of the Companies Act 2006 (Consequential Amendments and Transitional Provisions) Order SI 2011/265, which together preserve the application of the 1948 Table A to companies registered before the commencement of the 1985 Act.

[7] See s 8(2) of CA 1985, and Sch 1, para 1(1) to the Companies Act 2006 (Commencement No 8, Transitional Provisions and Savings) Order 2008, SI 2008/2860, saving the application of the 1985 Table A to existing companies.

(Tables A to F) (Amendment) Regulations 1985,[8] the Companies (Tables A to F) (Amendment) Regulations 2007[9] and the Companies (Tables A to F) (Amendment) (No 2) Regulations 2007[10] —were indeed made by statutory instrument under section 8, and clearly therefore apply only to companies registered on or after the date those regulations came into force (1 August 1985 for the 1985 Regulations and 1 October 2007 for the others). Another block of alterations, however, was introduced by the Companies Act 1985 (Electronic Communications) Order 2000.[11] This was made not under the Companies Act 1985, section 8, but rather under sections 8 and 9 of the Electronic Communications Act 2000. It is at the very least arguable, then, that for a company with the 1985 version of Table A, that version includes these alterations, regardless of when the company was registered.

**51.TA.04**    Against this, however, several counter-points might be made. The first is that the Companies Act 1985, section 8(2) declares that Table A '(so far as applicable, and as in force at the date of the company's registration) constitutes the company's articles, in the same manner and to the same extent as if articles in the form of that Table had been duly registered'. This, it might be argued, makes clear that the applicable Table A is 'frozen' at the date of registration. However, this looks unconvincing. If this wording (in section 8(2)) is made to bear this meaning, then it renders section 8(3) unnecessary. Since section 8(3) deals specifically with the effect of subsequent alterations by regulation, the wording of section 8(2) must be understood to be aimed at some other purpose. A second counter-point to the argument in paragraph 51.TA.03 might run as follows. The reference in section 8(3) to the alteration of Table A by 'regulations under this section' means, when read in conjunction with section 8(1), merely any regulations made by the Secretary of State that prescribe the content of Table A. Accordingly, even regulations that, in their recitals, refer to their being made under some other statutory provision are still to be considered as regulations prescribing Table A, and thus 'regulations under this section' for the purpose of section 8(3). This also seems unconvincing, however, for section 8(5) spells out, as is usual, the procedure by which regulations 'under this section' are to be made, suggesting that the use of the same wording in section 8(3) means just those regulations made under the power conferred in, and the procedure specified by, this section 8. A third counter-point is that it would be unfortunate if the status of different alterations were to depend upon the mere chance of which statutory instrument (ie which statutory power) happened to be used to achieve the alteration. This is surely true, but nevertheless that unfortunate result may be the one that the wording of section 8 achieves.

**51.TA.05**    The position with regard to alterations made within the 1948 version of Table A is arguably more complex, but thankfully more certain. As noted above, the 1948 version of Table A was prescribed in Schedule 1 to the Companies Act 1948 itself. The alterations that are addressed below were all similarly made by primary legislation. Although the Companies Act 1948, section 454 allows for the alteration of Table A by statutory instrument and provides that 'no alteration … shall affect any company registered before the alteration, or repeal as respects that company any portion of that Table',[12] this clearly does not deal with alterations effected by primary legislation. Moreover, the Companies Act 1948, section 8(2), which deals with the status of the 1948 Table A, omits any reference to Table A 'as in force at the date of the company's registration'. Given all that, it would seem beyond doubt that we must look to what the primary legislation that amends the 1948 Table A says itself about the status of such alterations. And here we must draw a distinction between changes made by the Companies Act 1980 and those made by other primary legislation. Taking the former first, the Companies Act 1980, section 88(4) expressly provides that the alterations and repeals to Table A made by the 1980 Act[13] do not affect any company registered before those changes come into operation.[14] However, other primary legislation that amends the 1948 Table A (eg Companies Act 1967, Companies Act 1976, Companies Act 1981) does not contain a similar limitation on its operation. It would seem, then, that these other statutory amendments to Table A apply to *all* companies whose articles incorporate the 1948 Table A, regardless of when those companies may have been registered.

**51.TA.06**    For some general principles of interpretation applicable to articles of association, and to Table A in particular, the reader is referred back to the commentary on the Companies Act 2006, sections 19 to 20. As to terminology, 'regulation(s)' and 'article(s)' are often used interchangeably. However, insofar as it is possible to discern any consistent pattern in their usage, it seems that 'regulations' is used to refer to the individual provisions in the Tables A, whilst 'articles' is used to refer both to individual provisions drafted by shareholders themselves, and to the collection of such provisions as a whole.

---

8    SI 1985/1052.
9    SI 2007/2541.
10   SI 2007/2826.
11   SI 2000/3373.
12   See s 454(2).
13   These are found in CA 1980, Schs 3 and 4 respectively.
14   See s 88(4) of CA 1980.

VERSION OF TABLE A APPLYING TO COMPANIES LIMITED BY
SHARES REGISTERED FROM 1 JULY 1948 TO 30 JUNE 1985

## Companies Act 1948

(11 & 12 Geo. 6, c 38)

An Act to consolidate the Companies Act 1929, the Companies Act 1947 (other than the provisions thereof relating to the registration of business names, bankruptcy and the prevention of fraud in connection with unit trusts), and certain other enactments amending the first-mentioned Act.

**51.TA.07**

[30 June 1948]

FIRST SCHEDULE[15]
TABLES A, B, C, D AND E

[Schedule introduced by sections 11 and 455]

TABLE A

PART I
REGULATIONS FOR MANAGEMENT OF A COMPANY LIMITED BY SHARES,
NOT BEING A PRIVATE COMPANY[16]

*Interpretation*

1. In these regulations:—
    'the Act' means the Companies Act 1948.
    'the seal' means the common seal of the company.
    'secretary' means any person appointed to perform the duties of the secretary of the company.
    'the United Kingdom' means Great Britain and Northern Ireland.
    Expressions referring to writing shall, unless the contrary intention appears, be construed as including references to printing, lithography, photography, and other modes of representing or reproducing words in a visible form.
    Unless the context otherwise requires, words or expressions contained in these regulations shall bear the same meaning as in the Act or any statutory modification thereof in force at the date at which these regulations become binding on the company.

*Share Capital and Variation of Rights*

2. Without prejudice to any special rights previously conferred on the holders of any existing shares or class of shares, any share in the company may be issued with such preferred, deferred or other special rights or such restrictions, whether in regard to dividend, voting, return of capital or otherwise as the company may from time to time by ordinary resolution determine.
3. Subject to the provisions of *Part III of the Companies Act 1981, any shares*[a] may, with the sanction of an ordinary resolution, be issued on the terms that they are, or at the option of the company are liable, to be redeemed on such terms and in such manner as the company before the issue of the shares may by special resolution determine.
4. If at any time the share capital is divided into different classes of shares,[b] the rights attached to any class (*unless otherwise provided by the terms of issue of the shares of that class*)[c] may, whether or not the company is being wound up, be varied[d] with the consent in writing of the holders of

---

[15] Preserved by Sch 2, para 1(1) to the Companies Act 2006 (Commencement No 8, Transitional Provisions and Savings) Order 2008, SI 2008/2860 together with art 5 of the Companies Act 2006 (Consequential Amendments and Transitional Provisions) Order SI 2011/265.

[16] By a rather convoluted process, the regulations in this Part I (save for regulations 24 and 53) did, in fact, apply to private companies, but indirectly, by virtue of Part II of these regulations (see below). For companies registered on or after 22 December 1980, Part II was repealed and Part I (including regulations 24 and 53) was made to apply directly to private companies (CA 1980, s 88 and Sch 3, para 36(1); Companies Act 1980 (Commencement No 2) Order 1980, SI 1980/1785).

three-fourths of the issued shares of that class, or with the sanction of an extraordinary resolution passed at a separate general meeting of the holders of the shares of the class.[e] *To every such separate general meeting the provisions of these regulations relating to general meetings shall apply, but so that the necessary quorum shall be two persons at least holding or representing by proxy one-third of the issued shares of the class and that any holder of shares of the class present in person or by proxy may demand a poll.*[f]

5.  The rights conferred upon the holders of the shares of any class issued with preferred or other rights shall not, unless otherwise expressly provided by the terms of issue of the shares of that class, be deemed to be varied by the terms of issue of further shares ranking pari passu therewith.

6.  The company may exercise the powers of paying commissions conferred by section 53 of the Act,[g] provided that the rate per cent or the amount of the commission paid or agreed to be paid shall be disclosed in the manner required by the said section and the rate of the commission shall not exceed the rate of 10 per cent of the price at which the shares in respect whereof the same is paid are issued or an amount equal to 10 per cent of such price (as the case may be). Such commission may be satisfied by the payment of cash or the allotment of fully or partly paid shares or partly in one way and partly in the other. The company may also on any issue of shares pay such brokerage as may be lawful.

7.  Except as required by law, no person shall be recognised as holding any share upon any trust, and the company shall not be bound by or be compelled in any way to recognise (even when having notice thereof) any equitable, contingent, future or partial interest in any share or any interest in any fractional part of a share or (except only as by these regulations or by law otherwise provided) any other rights in respect of any share except an absolute right to the entirety thereof in the registered holder.[h]

8.  Every person whose name is entered as a member in the register of members shall be entitled without payment to receive within two months after allotment or lodgment of transfer (or within such other period as the conditions of issue shall provide) one certificate for all his shares or several certificates each for one or more of his shares upon payment of $12\frac{1}{2}p$[i] for every certificate after the first or such less sum as the directors shall from time to time determine. Every certificate shall be under the seal[j] [or under the official seal kept by the company by virtue of section 2 of the Stock Exchange (Completion of Bargains) Act 1976][k] and shall specify the shares to which it relates and the amount paid up thereon. Provided that in respect of a share or shares held jointly by several persons the company shall not be bound to issue more than one certificate, and delivery of a certificate for a share to one of several joint holders shall be sufficient delivery to all such holders.

9.  If a share certificate be defaced, lost or destroyed, it may be renewed on payment of a fee of $12\frac{1}{2}p$[i] or such less sum and on such terms (if any) as to evidence and indemnity and of the payment of out-of-pocket expenses of the company of investigating evidence as the directors think fit.

10. *The company shall not give, whether directly or indirectly, and whether by means of a loan, guarantee, the provision of security or otherwise, any financial assistance for the purpose of or in connection with a purchase or subscription made or to be made by any person of or for any shares in the company or in its holding company nor shall the company make a loan*[m] *for any purpose whatsoever on the security of its shares or those of its holding company, but nothing in this regulation shall prohibit transactions mentioned in the proviso to section 54(1) of the Act.*[n]

AMENDMENTS AND NOTES

[a]  Words in italics introduced by CA 1981, s 119(4) and Sch 3, para 20. (For Part III of CA 1981, see CA 1985, Part V, Chapter VII (ss 159–181) or, from 1 October 2009, see CA 1006, Part 18, Chapter 3 (ss 684–689).)

[b]  As to what constitute classes of shares, see *Cumbrian Newspapers Group v Cumberland and Westmorland Herald Newspapers & Printing Co* [1986] 2 All ER 816.

[c]  In relation to companies registered from 22 December 1980 to 30 June 1985, the words in italics (in both places in this regulation) were repealed by CA 1980, s 88 and Sch 4.

[d]  On the meaning of 'varied', see *Greenhalgh v Arderne Cinemas Ltd (No 1)* [1946] 1 All ER 512.

[e]  On the rights of the holders of not less in the aggregate than 15 per cent of the issued shares of the class in question to apply to the court to have the variation cancelled, see CA 1985, s 127.

[f]  Note 1 above.

[g]  By virtue of the Interpretation Act 1978, ss 17(2)(a) and 23(3), this is to be construed as a reference to CA 1985, s 97 or, from 1 October 2009, to CA 2006, s 553.

[h]  This regulation goes beyond the provision, found in CA 2006, s 126, that no notice of any trust is to be entered on the register. In order for a lawful trust of shares to be created, there is no requirement of any board minute approving or recording the declaration of such a trust: *Singh v Anand* [2007] EWHC 3346.

[i]  Sum in italics substituted for sum of '2s.6d.' by the Decimal Currency Act 1969, as from 15 February 1971.

<sup>j</sup> Although regulation 8 refers to share certificates being sealed by the company, by virtue of CA 2006, s 46(4) a document signed by two 'authorised signatories' of the company, or by one director in the presence of a witness who attests the signature, has the same effect as if executed under the common seal of the company (as noted in *Jordan v Roberts* [2009] EWHC 2313).

<sup>k</sup> Wording in parenthesis introduced by the Stock Exchange (Completion of Bargains) Act 1976 from 12 February 1979. (By virtue of the Interpretation Act 1978, ss 17(2)(a) and 23(3), the reference to the 1976 Act, s 2 is to be construed as a reference to CA 1985, s 40 or, from 1 October 2009, to CA 2006, s 50.)

<sup>l</sup> Sum in italics substituted for sum of '2s.6d.' by the Decimal Currency Act 1969, as from 15 February 1971.

<sup>m</sup> For a (somewhat narrow) definition of 'loan' for the purposes of regulation 10, see *Champagne Perrier-Jouet SA v HH Finch Ltd* [1982] 3 All ER 713.

<sup>n</sup> This regulation repealed by CA 1981, s 119(5) and Sch 4.

### Lien

**11.** The company shall have a first and paramount lien on every share (not being a fully paid share) for all moneys (whether presently payable or not) called or payable at a fixed time in respect of that share, *and the company shall also have a first and paramount lien on all shares (other than fully paid shares) standing registered in the name of a single person for all moneys presently payable by him or his estate to the company;*[a] but the directors may at any time declare any share to be wholly or in part exempt from the provisions of this regulation. The company's lien, if any, on a share shall extend to all dividends payable thereon.[b]

**12.** The company may sell, in such manner as the directors think fit, any shares on which the company has a lien, but no sale shall be made unless a sum in respect of which the lien exists is presently payable, nor until the expiration of 14 days after a notice in writing, stating and demanding payment of such part of the amount in respect of which the lien exists as is presently payable, has been given to the registered holder for the time being of the share, or the person entitled thereto by reason of his death or bankruptcy.

**13.** To give effect to any such sale the directors may authorise some person to transfer the shares sold to the purchaser thereof. The purchaser shall be registered as the holder of the share comprised in any such transfer, and he shall not be bound to see to the application of the purchase money, nor shall his title to the shares be affected by any irregularity or invalidity in the proceedings in reference to the sale.

**14.** The proceeds of the sale shall be received by the company and applied in payment of such part of the amount in respect of which the lien exists as is presently payable, and the residue, if any, shall (subject to a like lien for sums not presently payable as existed upon the shares before the sale) be paid to the person entitled to the shares at the date of the sale.

AMENDMENTS AND NOTES

<sup>a</sup> In relation to companies registered from 22 December 1980 to 30 June 1985, the words in italics were repealed by CA 1980, s 88(2) and Sch 4.

<sup>b</sup> Some potential problems in the timing of the lien created by this regulation, and thus in the priority it might afford over other equitable interests in the shares (even before the regulation's amendment in CA 1980), are illustrated by *Champagne Perrier-Jouet SA v HH Finch Ltd* [1982] 3 All ER 713.

### Calls on Shares

**15.** The directors may from time to time make calls upon the members in respect of moneys unpaid on their shares (whether on account of the nominal value of the shares or by way of premium) and not by the conditions of allotment thereof made payable at fixed times, provided that no call shall exceed one-fourth of the nominal value of the share or be payable at less than one month from the date fixed for the payment of the last preceding call,[a] and each member shall (subject to receiving at least 14 days' notice specifying the time or times and place of payment) pay to the company at the time or times and place so specified the amount called on his shares. A call may be revoked or postponed as the directors may determine.[b]

**16.** A call shall be deemed to have been made at the time when the resolution of the directors authorising the call was passed and may be required to be paid by instalments.

**17.** The joint holders of a share shall be jointly and severally liable to pay all calls in respect thereof.

**18.** If a sum called in respect of a share is not paid before or on the day appointed for payment thereof, the person from whom the sum is due shall pay interest on the sum from the day appointed for payment thereof to the time of actual payment at such rate not exceeding 5 per cent per annum as the directors may determine, but the directors shall be at liberty to waive payment of such interest wholly or in part.

**19.** Any sum which by the terms of issue of a share becomes payable on allotment or at any fixed date, whether on account of the nominal value of the share or by way of premium, shall for the purposes of these regulations be deemed to be a call duly made and payable on the date on which by the terms of issue the same becomes payable, and in case of non-payment all the relevant provisions of these regulations as to payment of interest and expenses, forfeiture or otherwise shall apply as if such sum had become payable by virtue of a call duly made and notified.

20. The directors may, on the issue of shares, differentiate between the holders as to the amount of calls to be paid and the times of payment.

21. The directors may, if they think fit, receive from any member willing to advance the same, all or any part of the moneys uncalled and unpaid upon any shares held by him, and upon all or any of the moneys so advanced may (until the same would, but for such advance, become payable) pay interest at such rate not exceeding (unless the company in general meeting shall otherwise direct) 5 per cent per annum, as may be agreed upon between the directors and the member paying such sum in advance.

AMENDMENTS AND NOTES

a Provided that the dates for *payment* of successive calls satisfy this requirement, the calls themselves may be issued on the same day: *The Universal Corporation Ltd v Hughes* [1909] SC 1434.

b In exercising their power to make calls, directors must act in good faith. On directors differentiating amongst shareholders in the making of calls, see *Galloway v Hallé Concerts Society* [1915] 2 Ch 233.

*Transfer of Shares*

22. The instrument of transfer of any share shall be executed by or on behalf of the transferor and transferee, and, *except as provided by sub-paragraph (4) of paragraph 2 of the Seventh Schedule to the Act,*[a] the transferor shall be deemed to remain a holder of the share until the name of the transferee is entered in the register of members in respect thereof.

23. Subject to such restrictions of these regulations as may be applicable, any member may transfer all or any of his shares by instrument in writing in any usual or common form or any other form which the directors may approve.

24. The directors may decline to register the transfer of a share (not being a fully paid share) to a person of whom they shall not approve, and they may also decline to register the transfer of a share on which the company has a lien.[b]

25. The directors may also decline to recognise any instrument of transfer unless:—
    (a) a fee of *12½p*[c] or such lesser sum as the directors may from time to time require is paid to the company in respect thereof;
    (b) the instrument of transfer is accompanied by the certificate of the shares to which it relates, and such other evidence as the directors may reasonably require to show the right of the transferor to make the transfer; and
    (c) the instrument of transfer is in respect of only one class of share.

26. If the directors refuse to register a transfer they shall within two months after the date on which the transfer was lodged with the company send to the transferee notice of the refusal.

27. The registration of transfers may be suspended at such times and for such periods as the directors may from time to time determine, provided always that such registration shall not be suspended for more than 30 days in any year.

28. The company shall be entitled to charge a fee not exceeding *12½p*[d] on the registration of every probate, letters of administration, certificate of death or marriage, power of attorney, notice in lieu of distringas, or other instrument.

AMENDMENTS AND NOTES

a Words in italics repealed by CA 1967, s 130(4)(c) and Sch 8, with effect from 28 January 1968. The Seventh Schedule to CA 1948 dealt with the 'exempt private company', a type abolished by CA 1967.

b Compare regulation 3 of Part II of this Table A, applicable to *private* companies. For private companies registered from 22 December 1980 to 30 June 1985, Part II was repealed and Part I (including this regulation) then became applicable to such companies.

c Sum in italics substituted for the sum of '2s.6d.' by the Decimal Currency Act 1969, as from 15 February 1971.

d Sum in italics substituted for sum of '2s.6d.' by the Decimal Currency Act 1969, as from 15 February 1971.

*Transmission of Shares*

29. In case of the death of a member the survivor or survivors where the deceased was a joint holder, and the legal personal representatives of the deceased where he was a sole holder, shall be the only persons recognised by the company as having any title to his interest in the shares; but nothing herein contained shall release the estate of a deceased joint holder from any liability in respect of any share which had been jointly held by him with other persons.

30. Any person becoming entitled to a share in consequence of the death or bankruptcy of a member may, upon such evidence being produced as may from time to time properly be required by the directors and subject as hereinafter provided, elect either to be registered himself as holder of the share or to have some person nominated by him registered as the transferee thereof, but the

directors shall, in either case, have the same right to decline or suspend registration as they would have had in the case of a transfer of the share by that member before his death or bankruptcy, as the case may be.[a]

**31.** If the person so becoming entitled shall elect to be registered himself, he shall deliver or send to the company a notice in writing signed by him stating that he so elects. If he shall elect to have another person registered he shall testify his election by executing to that person a transfer of the share. All the limitations, restrictions and provisions of these regulations relating to the right to transfer and the registration of transfers of shares shall be applicable to any such notice or transfer as aforesaid as if the death or bankruptcy of the member had not occurred and the notice or transfer were a transfer signed by that member.[b]

**32.** A person becoming entitled to a share by reason of the death or bankruptcy of the holder shall be entitled to the same dividends and other advantages to which he would be entitled if he were the registered holder of the share, except that he shall not, before being registered as a member in respect of the share, be entitled in respect of it to exercise any right conferred by membership in relation to meetings of the company:

Provided always that the directors may at any time give notice requiring any such person to elect either to be registered himself or to transfer the share, and if the notice is not complied with within 90 days the directors may thereafter withhold payment of all dividends, bonuses or other moneys payable in respect of the share until the requirements of the notice have been complied with.

AMENDMENTS AND NOTES

[a] In *Stothers v William Steward (Holdings) Ltd* [1994] 2 BCLC 266, Peter Gibson LJ held that the words of regulations 30 and 31 required one to imagine that the deceased member were making the transfer of shares and, on that assumption, then to ask what restrictions, if any, would have existed under the company's articles had the deceased member been making the transfer.

[b] See the note to regulation 31, above.

*Forfeiture of Shares*

**33.** If a member fails to pay any call or instalment of a call on the day appointed for payment thereof, the directors may, at any time thereafter during such time as any part of the call or instalment remains unpaid, serve a notice on him requiring payment of so much of the call or instalment as is unpaid, together with any interest which may have accrued.

**34.** The notice shall name a further day (not earlier than the expiration of 14 days from the date of service of the notice) on or before which the payment required by the notice is to be made, and shall state that in the event of non-payment at or before the time appointed the shares in respect of which the call was made will be liable to be forfeited.

**35.** If the requirements of any such notice as aforesaid are not complied with, any share in respect of which the notice has been given may at any time thereafter, before the payment required by the notice has been made, be forfeited by a resolution of the directors to that effect.

**36.** A forfeited share may be sold or otherwise disposed of on such terms and in such manner as the directors think fit, and at any time before a sale or disposition the forfeiture may be cancelled on such terms as the directors think fit.

**37.** A person whose shares have been forfeited shall cease to be a member in respect of the forfeited shares, but shall, notwithstanding, remain liable to pay to the company all moneys which, at the date of forfeiture, were payable by him to the company in respect of the shares, but his liability shall cease if and when the company shall have received payment in full of all such moneys in respect of the shares.

**38.** A statutory declaration in writing that the declarant is a director or the secretary of the company, and that a share in the company has been duly forfeited on a date stated in the declaration, shall be conclusive evidence of the facts therein stated as against all persons claiming to be entitled to the share. The company may receive the consideration, if any, given for the share on any sale or disposition thereof and may execute a transfer of the share in favour of the person to whom the share is sold or disposed of and he shall thereupon be registered as the holder of the share, and shall not be bound to see to the application of the purchase money, if any, nor shall his title to the share be affected by any irregularity or invalidity in the proceedings in reference to the forfeiture, sale or disposal of the share.

**39.** The provisions of these regulations as to forfeiture shall apply in the case of non-payment of any sum which, by the terms of issue of a share, becomes payable at a fixed time, whether on account of the nominal value of the share or by way of premium, as if the same had been payable by virtue of a call duly made and notified.

*Conversion of Shares into Stock*

**40.** The company may by ordinary resolution convert any paid-up shares into stock, and reconvert any stock into paid-up shares of any denomination.

**41.** The holders of stock may transfer the same, or any part thereof, in the same manner, and subject to the same regulations, as and subject to which the shares from which the stock arose might previously to conversion have been transferred, or as near thereto as circumstances admit; and the directors may from time to time fix the minimum amount of stock transferable but so that such minimum shall not exceed the nominal amount of the shares from which the stock arose.

**42.** The holders of stock shall, according to the amount of stock held by them, have the same rights, privileges and advantages as regards dividends, voting at meetings of the company and other matters as if they held the shares from which the stock arose, but no such privilege or advantage (except participation in the dividends and profits of the company and in the assets on winding up) shall be conferred by an amount of stock which would not, if existing in shares, have conferred that privilege or advantage.

**43.** Such of the regulations of the company as are applicable to paid-up shares shall apply to stock, and the words 'share' and 'shareholder' therein shall include 'stock' and 'stockholder'.

### Alteration of Capital

**44.** The company may from time to time by ordinary resolution increase the share capital by such sum, to be divided into shares of such amount, as the resolution shall prescribe.

**45.** The company may by ordinary resolution
  (a) consolidate and divide all or any of its share capital into shares of larger amount than its existing shares;
  (b) subdivide its existing shares, or any of them, into shares of smaller amount than is fixed by the memorandum of association subject, nevertheless, to the provisions of section 61(1)(d) of the Act;[a]
  (c) cancel any shares which, at the date of the passing of the resolution, have not been taken or agreed to be taken by any person.

**46.** The company may by special resolution reduce its share capital, any capital redemption reserve fund or any share premium account in any manner and with, and subject to, any incident authorised, and consent required, by law.

AMENDMENTS AND NOTES

[a]  By virtue of the Interpretation Act 1978, ss 17(2)(a) and 23(3), this is to be construed as a reference to CA 1985, s 121(2)(d) and (3) or, from 1 October 2009, to CA 2006, ss 618–619.

### General Meetings

**47.** The company shall in each year hold a general meeting as its annual general meeting in addition to any other meetings in that year, and shall specify the meeting as such in the notices calling it; and not more than 15 months shall elapse between the date of one annual general meeting of the company and that of the next. Provided that so long as the company holds its first annual general meeting within 18 months of its incorporation, it need not hold it in the year of its incorporation or in the following year. The annual general meeting shall be held at such time and place as the directors shall appoint.

**48.** All general meetings other than annual general meetings shall be called extraordinary general meetings.

**49.** The directors may, whenever they think fit, convene an extraordinary general meeting, and extraordinary general meetings shall also be convened on such requisition, or, in default, may be convened by such requisitionists, as provided by section 132 of the Act.[a] If at any time there are not within the United Kingdom sufficient directors capable of acting to form a quorum, any director or any two members of the company may convene an extraordinary general meeting in the same manner as nearly as possible as that in which meetings may be convened by the directors.

AMENDMENTS AND NOTES

[a]  By virtue of the Interpretation Act 1978, ss 17(2)(a) and 23(3), this is to be construed as a reference to CA 1985, s 368 or, from 1 October 2009, to CA 2006, ss 303–305.

### Notice of General Meetings

**50.** An annual general meeting and a meeting called for the passing of a special resolution shall be called by 21 days' notice in writing at the least, and a meeting of the company other than an annual general meeting or a meeting for the passing of a special resolution shall be called by 14 days' notice in writing at the least. The notice shall be exclusive of the day on which it is served or deemed to be served and of the day for which it is given, and shall specify the place, the day and the hour of meeting and, in case of special business, the general nature of that business, and shall be given, in manner hereinafter mentioned or in such other manner, if any, as may be prescribed by the company in general meeting, to such persons as are, under the regulations of the company, entitled to receive such notices from the company:

Provided that a meeting of the company shall, notwithstanding that it is called by shorter notice than that specified in this regulation, be deemed to have been duly called if it is so agreed

(a) in the case of a meeting called as the annual general meeting, by all the members entitled to attend and vote thereat; and

(b) in the case of any other meeting, by a majority in number of the members having a right to attend and vote at the meeting, being a majority together holding not less than 95 per cent in nominal value of the share giving that right.

**51.** The accidental omission to give notice of a meeting to, or the non-receipt of notice of a meeting by, any person entitled to receive notice shall not invalidate the proceedings of that meeting.[a]

AMENDMENTS AND NOTES

[a] It has been held that regulation 51 also operates to validate the proceedings of a meeting called to pass a special (as well as an ordinary) resolution: *In re West Canadian Collieries Ltd* [1962] Ch 370. On the meaning of 'accidental omission to give notice', see *Re P&O Steam Navigation Co* [2006] EWHC 389 and *In the Matter of Halcrow Holdings Ltd* [2011] EWHC 3662 (Ch).

*Proceedings at General Meetings*

**52.** All business shall be deemed special that is transacted at an extraordinary general meeting, and also all that is transacted at an annual general meeting, with the exception of declaring a dividend, the consideration of the accounts, balance sheets, and the reports of the directors and auditors, the election of directors in the place of those retiring and the appointment of, and the fixing of the remuneration of, the auditors.

**53.** No business shall be transacted at any general meeting unless a quorum of members is present at the time when the meeting proceeds to business; save as herein otherwise provided, *three members present in person shall be a quorum.*[a]

**54.** If within half an hour from the time appointed for the meeting a quorum is not present, the meeting if convened upon the requisition of members shall be dissolved; in any other case it shall stand adjourned to the same day in the next week, at the same time and place or to such other day and at such other time and place as the directors may determine, *and if at the adjourned meeting a quorum is not present within half an hour from the time appointed for the meeting, the members present shall be a quorum.*[b]

**55.** The chairman, if any, of the board of directors shall preside as chairman at every general meeting of the company, or if there is no such chairman, or if he shall not be present within 15 minutes after the time appointed for the holding of the meeting or is unwilling to act the directors present shall elect one of their number to be chairman of the meeting.

**56.** If at any meeting no director is willing to act as chairman or if no director is present within 15 minutes after the time appointed for holding the meeting, the members present shall choose one of their number to be chairman of the meeting.

**57.** The chairman may, with the consent of any meeting at which a quorum is present (and shall if so directed by the meeting), adjourn the meeting from time to time and from place to place, but no business shall be transacted at any adjourned meeting other than the business left unfinished at the meeting from which the adjournment took place. When a meeting is adjourned for 30 days or more, notice of the adjourned meeting shall be given as in the case of an original meeting. Save as aforesaid it shall not be necessary to give any notice of an adjournment or of the business to be transacted at an adjourned meeting.

**58.** At any general meeting a resolution put to the vote of the meeting shall be decided on a show of hands unless a poll is (before or on the declaration of the result of the show of hands) demanded

(a) by the chairman; or

(b) by at least *three*[c] members present in person or by proxy; or

(c) by any member or members present in person or by proxy and representing not less than one-tenth of the total voting rights of all the members having the right to vote at the meeting; or

(d) by a member or members holding shares in the company conferring a right to vote at the meeting being shares on which an aggregate sum has been paid up equal to not less than one-tenth of the total sum paid up on all the shares conferring that right.

Unless a poll be so demanded a declaration by the chairman that a resolution has on a show of hands been carried or carried unanimously, or by a particular majority, or lost and an entry to that effect in the book containing the minutes of the proceedings of the company shall be conclusive evidence of the fact without proof of the number or proportion of the votes recorded in favour of or against such resolution.

The demand for a poll may be withdrawn.

**59.** Except as provided in regulation 61, if a poll is duly demanded it shall be taken in such manner as the chairman directs, and the result of the poll shall be deemed to be the resolution of the meeting at which the poll was demanded.

60. In the case of an equality of votes, whether on a show of hands or on a poll, the chairman of the meeting at which the show of hands takes place or at which the poll is demanded, shall be entitled to a second or casting vote.

61. A poll demanded on the election of a chairman or on a question of adjournment shall be taken forthwith. A poll demanded on any other question shall be taken at such time as the chairman of the meeting directs, and any business other than that upon which a poll has been demanded may be proceeded with pending the taking of the poll.

A MENDMENTS AND N OTES

<sup>a</sup> In relation to companies registered from 22 December 1980 to 30 June 1985, words in italics substituted by words 'two members present in person or by proxy shall be a quorum' by CA 1980, s 88(1) and Sch 3. See also the commentary to CA 2006, s 306 on the principles to be applied by the court in determining whether to order a meeting to be held at which one member alone shall constitute a quorum.

<sup>b</sup> For companies registered from 22 December 1980 to 30 June 1985, words in italics repealed by CA 1980, s 88(2) and Sch 4.

<sup>c</sup> For companies registered from 22 December 1980 to 30 June 1985, word in italics substituted by word 'two' by CA 1980, s 88(1) and Sch 3.

*Votes of Members*

62. Subject to any rights or restrictions for the time being attached to any class or classes of shares, on a show of hands every member present in person shall have one vote, and on a poll every member shall have one vote for each share of which he is the holder.

63. In the case of joint holders the vote of the senior who tenders a vote, whether in person or by proxy, shall be accepted to the exclusion of the votes of the other joint holders; and for this purpose seniority shall be determined by the order in which the names stand in the register of members.

64. A member of unsound mind, or in respect of whom an order has been made by any court having jurisdiction in lunacy, may vote, whether on a show of hands or on a poll, by his committee, receiver, curator bonis, or other person in the nature of a committee, receiver or curator bonis appointed by that court, and any such committee, receiver, curator bonis or other person may, on a poll, vote by proxy.

65. No member shall be entitled to vote at any general meeting unless all calls or other sums presently payable by him in respect of shares in the company have been paid.[a]

66. No objection shall be raised to the qualification of any voter except at the meeting or adjourned meeting at which the vote objected to is given or tendered, and every vote not disallowed at such meeting shall be valid for all purposes. Any such objection made in due time shall be referred to the chairman of the meeting, whose decision shall be final and conclusive.

67. On a poll votes may be given either personally or by proxy.

68. The instrument appointing a proxy shall be in writing under the hand of the appointer or of his attorney duly authorised in writing, or, if the appointer is a corporation, either under seal, or under the hand of an officer or attorney duly authorised. A proxy need not be a member of the company.

69. The instrument appointing a proxy and the power of attorney or other authority, if any, under which it is signed or a notarially certified copy of that power or authority shall be deposited at the registered office of the company or at such other place within the United Kingdom as is specified for that purpose in the notice convening the meeting, not less than 48 hours before the time for holding the meeting or adjourned meeting, at which the person named in the instrument proposes to vote, or, in the case of a poll, not less than 24 hours before the time appointed for the taking of the poll, and in default the instrument of proxy shall not be treated as valid.

70. An instrument appointing a proxy shall be in the following form or a form as near thereto as circumstances admit '........................... Limited

I/We, ..........................., of ..........................., in the county of ..........................., being a member/members of the above-named company, hereby appoint ........................... of ..........................., or failing him, ........................... of ..........................., as my/our proxy to vote for me/us on my/our behalf at the [annual or extraordinary, as the case may be] general meeting of the company to be held on the ........................... day of ........................... 19....., and at any adjournment thereof.

Signed this ........................... day of ........................... 19....'

71. Where it is desired to afford members an opportunity of voting for or against a resolution the instrument appointing a proxy shall be in the following form or a form as near thereto as circumstances admit '........................... Limited

I/We, ..........................., of ........................... in the county of ..........................., being a member/members of the above-named company, hereby appoint ........................... of ..........................., or failing him ........................... of ..........................., as my/our proxy to vote for me/us on my/our behalf at the [annual or extraordinary, as the case may be] general

meeting of the company, to be held on the ............................ day of ........................... 19....,
and at any adjournment thereof.

Signed this .......................... day of ........................... 19....'

This form is to be used *in favour of/against the resolution. Unless otherwise instructed, the proxy will vote as he thinks fit.

       \*Strike out whichever is not desired.'

**72.** The instrument appointing a proxy shall be deemed to confer authority to demand or join in demanding a poll.

**73.** A vote given in accordance with the terms of an instrument of proxy shall be valid notwithstanding the previous death or insanity of the principal or revocation of the proxy or of the authority under which the proxy was executed, or the transfer of the share in respect of which the proxy was given, provided that no intimation in writing of such death, insanity, revocation or transfer as aforesaid shall have been received by the company at the office before the commencement of the meeting or adjourned meeting at which the proxy is used.

**[73A.[b]** Subject to the provisions of the Companies Acts 1948 to 1981,[c] a resolution in writing signed by all the members for the time being entitled to receive notice of and to attend and vote at general meetings (or being corporations by their duly authorised representatives) shall be as valid and effective as if the same had been passed at a general meeting of the company duly convened and held.]

AMENDMENTS AND NOTES

[a] In *Re Bradford Investments Ltd* [1991] BCLC 224, Hoffmann J (as he then was) held that a provision in a company's articles that was in relevant respects identical to regulation 65 was to be understood as providing that 'a member cannot vote if there is money owing in respect of any of the shares for which he is registered'. The equivalent regulation in the 1985 Table A (regulation 57) now makes clear that a member is only prevented from voting in respect of the particular shares on which moneys are due.

[b] For companies registered from 22 December 1980 to 30 June 1985, regulation 73A inserted by Companies Act 1980, s 88(1) and Sch 3.

[c] Year in italics introduced by CA 1981, s 119(4) and Sch 3 (replacing '1980'). (For the Companies Acts 1948 to 1981, see now CA 2006.)

*Corporations Acting by Representatives at Meetings*

**74.** Any corporation which is a member of the company may by resolution of its directors or other governing body authorise such person as it thinks fit to act as its representative at any meeting of the company or of any class of members of the company, and the person so authorised shall be entitled to exercise the same powers on behalf of the corporation which he represents as that corporation could exercise if it were an individual member of the company.

*Directors*

**75.** The number of the directors and the names of the first directors shall be determined in writing by the subscribers of the memorandum of association or a majority of them.

**76.** The remuneration of the directors shall from time to time be determined by the company in general meeting. Such remuneration shall be deemed to accrue from day to day. The directors may also be paid all travelling, hotel and other expenses properly incurred by them in attending and returning from meetings of the directors or any committee of the directors or general meetings of the company or in connection with the business of the company.[a]

**77.** The shareholding qualification for directors may be fixed by the company in general meeting, and unless and until so fixed no qualification shall be required.

**78.** A director of the company may be or become a director or other officer of, or otherwise interested in, any company promoted by the company or in which the company may be interested as shareholder or otherwise, and no such director shall be accountable to the company for any remuneration or other benefits received by him as a director or officer of, or from his interest in, such other company unless the company otherwise direct.

AMENDMENTS AND NOTES

[a] In *re Duomatic Ltd* [1969] 2 Ch 365, the failure of the company in general meeting to determine the directors' remuneration was 'cured' by the unanimous assent, of all those shareholders entitled to attend and vote at the general meeting, to the remuneration paid to the directors. As was noted in *Irvine v Irvine* [2007] 1 BCLC 349, for directors who hold an executive office, the board has the authority under reg 84(3) to settle that director's remuneration. See also the commentary to regulation 108 below.

*Borrowing Powers*

**79.** The directors may exercise all the powers of the company to borrow money, and to mortgage or charge its undertaking, property and uncalled capital, or any part thereof, and, *subject to section 14 of the Companies Act 1980*,[a] to issue debentures, debenture stock, and other securities whether outright or as security for any debt, liability or obligation of the company or of any third party:

Provided that the amount for the time being remaining undischarged of moneys borrowed or secured by the directors as aforesaid (apart from temporary loans obtained from the company's bankers in the ordinary course of business) shall not at any time, without the previous sanction of the company in general meeting, exceed the nominal amount of the share capital of the company for the time being issued, but nevertheless no lender or other person dealing with the company shall be concerned to see or inquire whether this limit is observed, No debt incurred or security given in excess of such limit shall be invalid or ineffectual except in the case of express notice to the lender or the recipient of the security at the time when the debt was incurred or security given that the limit hereby imposed had been or was thereby exceeded.

AMENDMENTS AND NOTES

[a] In relation to companies registered from 22 December 1980 to 30 June 1985, words in italicsinserted by CA 1980, s 88(1) and Sch 3. (By virtue of the Interpretation Act 1978, ss 17(2)(a) and 23(3), CA 1980, s 14 is to be construed as a reference to CA 1985, s 80 or, from 1 October 2009, to CA 2006, s 549.)

*Powers and Duties of Directors*

**80.** The business of the company shall be managed by the directors, who may pay all expenses incurred in promoting and registering the company, and may exercise all such powers of the company as are not, by the *Companies Acts 1948 to 1981*[a] or by these regulations, required to be exercised by the company in general meeting, subject, nevertheless, to any of these regulations, to the provisions of the *Companies Acts 1948 to 1981*[b] and to such regulations, being not inconsistent with the aforesaid regulations or provisions, as may be prescribed by the company in general meeting; but no regulation made by the company in general meeting shall invalidate any prior act of the directors which would have been valid if that regulation had not been made.[c]

**81.** The directors may from time to time and at any time by power of attorney appoint any company, firm or person or body of persons, whether nominated directly or indirectly by the directors, to be the attorney or attorneys of the company for such purposes and with such powers, authorities and discretions (not exceeding those vested in or exercisable by the directors under these regulations) and for such period and subject to such conditions as they may think fit, and any such powers of attorney may contain such provisions for the protection and convenience of persons dealing with any such attorney as the directors may think fit and may also authorise any such attorney to delegate all or any of the powers, authorities and discretions vested in him.

**82.** The company may exercise the powers conferred by section 35 of the Act[d] with regard to having an official seal for use abroad, and such powers shall be vested in the directors.

**83.** The company may exercise the powers conferred by sections 119 to 123 (both inclusive) of the Act[e] with regard to the keeping of a dominion register, and the directors may (subject to the provisions of those sections) make and vary such regulations as they may think fit respecting the keeping of any such register.

**84.** (1) A director who is in any way, whether directly or indirectly, interested in a contract or proposed contract with the company shall declare the nature of his interest at a meeting of the directors in accordance with section 199 of the Act.[f]

(2) A director shall not vote in respect of any contract or arrangement in which he is interested, and if he shall do so his vote shall not be counted, nor shall he be counted in the quorum present at the meeting,[g] but neither of these prohibitions shall apply to

(a) any arrangement for giving any director any security or indemnity in respect of money lent by him to or obligations undertaken by him for the benefit of the company; or

(b) to any arrangement for the giving by the company of any security to a third party in respect of a debt or obligation of the company for which the director himself has assumed responsibility in whole or in part under a guarantee or indemnity or by the deposit of a security; or

(c) any contract by a director to subscribe for or underwrite shares or debentures of the company; or

(d) any contract or arrangement with any other company in which he is interested only as an officer of the company or as holder of shares or other securities;

and these prohibitions may at any time be suspended or relaxed to any extent, and either generally or in respect of any particular contract, arrangement or transaction, by the company in general meeting.

(3) A director may hold any other office or place of profit under the company (other than the office of auditor) in conjunction with his office of director for such period and on such terms

(as to remuneration and otherwise) as the directors may determine and no director or intending director shall be disqualified by his office from contracting with the company either with regard to his tenure of any such other office or place of profit or as vendor, purchaser or otherwise, nor shall any such contract, or any contract or arrangement entered into by or on behalf of the company in which any director is in any way interested, be liable to be avoided, nor shall any director so contracting or being so interested be liable to account to the company for any profit realised by any such contract or arrangement by reason of such director holding that office or of the fiduciary relation thereby established.[h]

(4) A director, notwithstanding his interest, may be counted in the quorum present at any meeting whereat he or any other director is appointed to hold any such office or place of profit under the company or whereat the terms of any such appointment are arranged, and he may vote on any such appointment or arrangement other than his own appointment or the arrangement of the terms thereof.

(5) Any director may act by himself or his firm in a professional capacity for the company, and he or his firm shall be entitled to remuneration for professional services as if he were not a director; provided that nothing herein contained shall authorise a director or his firm to act as auditor to the company.

**85.** All cheques, promissory notes, drafts, bills of exchange and other negotiable instruments, and all receipts for moneys paid to the company, shall be signed, drawn, accepted, endorsed, or otherwise executed, as the case may be, in such manner as the directors shall from time to time by resolution determine.

**86.** The directors shall cause minutes to be made in books provided for the purpose
(a) of all appointments of officers made by the directors;
(b) of the names of the directors present at each meeting of the directors and of any committee of the directors;
(c) of all resolutions and proceedings at all meetings of the company,
and of the directors, and of committees of directors; and every director present at any meeting of directors or committee of directors shall sign his name in a book to be kept for that purpose.

**87.** The directors on behalf of the company may pay a gratuity or pension or allowance on retirement to any director who has held any other salaried office or place of profit with the company or to his widow or dependants and may make contributions to any fund and pay premiums for the purchase or provision of any such gratuity, pension or allowance.

AMENDMENTS AND NOTES

[a] Words in italics in both places introduced by CA 1980, s 88(1) and Sch 3, as amended by CA 1981, s 119(4) and Sch 3. (For the Companies Acts 1948 to 1981 see now CA 2006.)

[b] Words in italics in both places introduced by CA 1980, s 88(1) and Sch 3, as amended by CA 1981, s 119(4) and Sch 3. (For the Companies Acts 1948 to 1981 see now CA 2006.).

[c] It is now well-settled that an article in the form of regulation 80 gives the directors an exclusive right to manage the company. Members cannot, by ordinary resolution, interfere with that right: see eg *Automatic Self-Cleansing Filter Syndicate Co Ltd v Cuninghame* [1906] 2 Ch 34; *Quin & Axtens v Salmon* [1909] AC 442; *Shaw & Sons (Salford) Ltd v Shaw* [1935] 2 KB 113. This is so notwithstanding regulation 80's stipulation that the power of the directors is subject to 'regulations … prescribed by the company in general meeting'. The equivalent provision of the 1985 Table A (regulation 70) makes clear that the power of the directors is subject to directions given by *special* resolution. In *Breckland Group Holdings Ltd v London and Suffolk Properties Ltd* [1989] BCLC 100, it was held that regulation 80 precludes a majority of shareholders from adopting an action that had been brought in the name of the company but without the authority of the board.

[d] By virtue of the Interpretation Act 1978, ss 17(2)(a) and 23(3), this is to be construed as a reference to CA 1985, s 39 or, from 1 October 2009, to CA 2006, s 49.

[e] By virtue of the Interpretation Act 1978, ss 17(2)(a) and 23(3), this is to be construed as a reference to CA 1985, s 362 and Sch 14 or, from 1 October 2009, to CA 2006, ss 129–135.

[f] By virtue of the Interpretation Act 1978, ss 17(2)(a) and 23(3), this is to be construed as a reference to CA 2006, ss 182–187. See the commentary to regulation 85 of the 1985 Table A regarding the nature of the disclosure required under the equivalent provision in that Table.

[g] In *Eastford Limited v Thomas Graham Gillespie, Airdrie North Limited* [2009] CSOH 119, Lord Hodge held that the authorities relevant in interpreting the statutory prohibition on conflicts of interest (in CA 2006, s 175(1)) were also relevant in interpreting regulation 94 of the 1985 Table A. Although the latter regulation differs somewhat in its wording from this regulation 84 (of the 1948 Table A), it seems likely that the same approach would be followed in interpreting this regulation 84.

<sup>h</sup> Regulation 84(3) provides a constitutional 'waiver' of the no-conflict rule. An article similar to regulation 84 (but which in fact gave interested directors a greater freedom to vote on contracts in which directors were interested) was upheld as valid, notwithstanding (what is now) CA 2006, s 232, in *Movitex Ltd v Bulfield* [1988] BCLC 104.

### Disqualification of Directors

**88.** The office of director shall be vacated if the director
  (a) ceases to be a director by virtue of section 182 or 185 of the Act;<sup>a</sup> or
  (b) becomes bankrupt or makes any arrangement or composition with his creditors generally;<sup>b</sup> or
  (c) becomes prohibited from being a director by reason of any order made under section 188 of the Act<sup>c</sup> [...];<sup>d</sup> or
  (d) becomes of unsound mind; or
  (e) resigns his office by notice in writing to the company; or
  (f) shall for more than six months have been absent without permission of the directors from meetings of the directors held during that period.

AMENDMENTS AND NOTES

<sup>a</sup> These provisions repealed by CA 2006.

<sup>b</sup> On the unlikelihood of a director being able to plead an 'estoppel by convention' to prevent the company relying upon this regulation against the director, see *Re Siteburn Ltd* [2006] BPIR 1009. In *Witherdale Ltd v Registrar of Companies* [2008] 1 BCLC 174, the court held that a person who was a director at the time of a dissolution of the company, and *subsequently* became bankrupt, lost the authority to apply to have the company restored to the register.

<sup>c</sup> By virtue of the Interpretation Act 1978, ss 17(2)(a) and 23(3), this is to be construed as a reference to the Company Directors Disqualification Act 1986.

<sup>d</sup> Words [or under section 28 of the Companies Act 1976] introduced by CA 1976, s 42(1) and Sch 2, and repealed by CA 1981, s 119(5) and Sch 4.

### Rotation of Directors

**89.** At the first annual general meeting of the company all the directors shall retire from office, and at the annual general meeting in every subsequent year one-third of the directors for the time being, or, if their number is not three or a multiple of three, then the number nearest one-third, shall retire from office.

**90.** The directors to retire in every year shall be those who have been longest in office since their last election, but as between persons who became directors on the same day those to retire shall (unless they otherwise agree among themselves) be determined by lot.

**91.** A retiring director shall be eligible for re-election.

**92.** The company at the meeting at which a director retires in manner aforesaid may fill the vacated office by electing a person thereto, and in default the retiring director shall if offering himself for re-election be deemed to have been re-elected, unless at such meeting it is expressly resolved not to fill such vacated office or unless a resolution for the re-election of such director shall have been put to the meeting and lost.

**93.** No person other than a director retiring at the meeting shall unless recommended by the directors be eligible for election to the office of director at any general meeting unless not less than three nor more than 21 days before the date appointed for the meeting there shall have been left at the registered office of the company notice in writing, signed by a member duly qualified to attend and vote at the meeting for which such notice is given, of his intention to propose such person for election, and also notice in writing signed by that person of his willingness to be elected.

**94.** The company may from time to time by ordinary resolution increase or reduce the number of directors, and may also determine in what rotation the increased or reduced number is to go out of office.

**95.** The directors shall have power at any time, and from time to time, to appoint any person to be a director, either to fill a casual vacancy or as an addition to the existing directors, but so that the total number of directors shall not at any time exceed the number fixed in accordance with these regulations. Any director so appointed shall hold office only until the next following annual general meeting, and shall then be eligible for re-election but shall not be taken into account in determining the directors who are to retire by rotation at such meeting.

**96.** The company may by ordinary resolution, of which special notice has been given in accordance with section 142 of the Act,<sup>a</sup> remove any director before the expiration of his period of office notwithstanding anything in these regulations or in any agreement between the company and such director. Such removal shall be without prejudice to any claim such director may have for damages for breach of any contract of service between him and the company.

**97.** The company may by ordinary resolution appoint another person in place of a director removed from office under the immediately preceding regulation, and without prejudice to the powers of the directors under regulation 95 the company in general meeting may appoint any person to be a director either to fill a casual vacancy or as an additional director. A person appointed in place of a director so removed or to fill such a vacancy shall be subject to retirement at the same time as if he had become a director on the day on which the director in whose place he is appointed was last elected a director.

AMENDMENTS AND NOTES

[a] By virtue of the Interpretation Act 1978, ss 17(2)(a) and 23(3), this is to be construed as a reference to CA 2006, s 312.

### Proceedings of Directors

**98.** The directors may meet together for the dispatch of business, adjourn, and otherwise regulate their meetings, as they think fit. Questions arising at any meeting shall be decided by a majority of votes. In case of an equality of votes, the chairman shall have a second or casting vote. A director may, and the secretary on the requisition of a director shall, at any time summon a meeting of the directors. It shall not be necessary to give notice of a meeting of directors to any director for the time being absent from the United Kingdom.

**99.** The quorum necessary for the transaction of the business of the directors may be fixed by the directors, and unless so fixed shall be two.[a]

**100.** The continuing directors may act notwithstanding any vacancy in their body, but, if and so long as their number is reduced below the number fixed by or pursuant to the regulations of the company as the necessary quorum of directors, the continuing directors or director may act for the purpose of increasing the number of directors to that number, or of summoning a general meeting of the company, but for no other purpose.

**101.** The directors may elect a chairman of their meetings and determine the period for which he is to hold office; but if no such chairman is elected, or if at any meeting the chairman is not present within five minutes after the time appointed for holding the same, the directors present may choose one of their number to be chairman of the meeting.

**102.** The directors may delegate any of their powers to committees consisting of such member or members of their body as they think fit; any committee so formed shall in the exercise of the powers so delegated conform to any regulations that may be imposed on it by the directors.[17]

**103.** A committee may elect a chairman of its meetings; if no such chairman is elected, or if at any meeting the chairman is not present within five minutes after the time appointed for holding the same, the members present may choose one of their number to be chairman of the meeting.

**104.** A committee may meet and adjourn as it thinks proper. Questions arising at any meeting shall be determined by a majority of votes of the members present, and in the case of an equality of votes the chairman shall have a second or casting vote.

**105.** All acts done by any meeting of the directors or of a committee of directors or by any person acting as a director shall, notwithstanding that it be afterwards discovered that there was some defect in the appointment of any such director or person acting as aforesaid, or that they or any of them were disqualified, be as valid as if every such person had been duly appointed and was qualified to be a director.

**106.** A resolution in writing, signed by all the directors for the time being entitled to receive notice of a meeting of the directors, shall be as valid and effectual as if it had been passed at a meeting of the directors duly convened and held.[b]

AMENDMENTS AND NOTES

[a] On whether a director who acts in breach of her fiduciary duty at a board meeting can be counted towards the quorum, and on the relationship between the quorum requirement and s 35A of CA 1985 (now s 39 of CA 2006), see the commentary to regulation 89 of the 1985 Table A. Note that regulation 99 does not say (in contrast to regulation 89 of the 1985 Table A) that an alternate director counts towards the quorum.

[b] It was held in *Hood Sailmakers Ltd v Axford* [1996] 4 All ER 830 that this regulation does not change the company's quorum (as say provided for in regulation 99). Thus, where a company's quorum was two directors, but one director was absent from the UK and thus not entitled to notice (by virtue of Art 98), a resolution signed by the only other director was invalid.

### Managing Director

**107.** The directors may from time to time appoint one or more of their body to the office of managing director for such period and on such terms as they think fit, and, subject to the terms of any agreement entered into in any particular case, may revoke such appointment. A director so appointed shall not, whilst holding that office, be subject to retirement by rotation or be taken into account in determining the rotation of retirement of directors, but his appointment shall be automatically determined if he cease from any cause to be a director.[a]

---

[17] See the commentary to regulation 72 of the 1985 Table A.

108.  A managing director shall receive such remuneration (whether by way of salary, commission or participation in profits, or partly in one way and partly in another) as the directors may determine.[b]

109.  The directors may entrust to and confer upon a managing director any of the powers exercisable by them upon such terms and conditions and with such restrictions as they may think fit, and either collaterally with or to the exclusion of their own powers and may from time to time revoke, withdraw, alter or vary all or any of such powers.

AMENDMENTS AND NOTES

[a]  On the operation of the 'automatic termination' aspect of this regulation, see the commentary to regulation 84 of the 1985 Table A.

[b]  It was held in *Re Richmond Gate Property Co Ltd* [1964] 3 All ER 936 that a managing director who was also a member of the company had a contract with the company based upon the articles, and this contract precluded any claim in *quantum meruit* for work undertaken. (Since the directors had failed to determine that any remuneration was payable under the article, there was also no contractual sum for which the managing director could sue.) This case sits somewhat uneasily, however, with those cases suggesting that a member can only enforce the contract based upon the articles in her capacity as a member.

### Secretary

110.  *Subject to section 21(5) of the Companies Act 1976*[a] the secretary shall be appointed by the directors for such term, at such remuneration and upon such conditions as they may think fit; and any secretary so appointed may be removed by them.

111.  No person shall be appointed or hold office as secretary who is
      (a)  the sole director of the company; or
      (b)  a corporation the sole director of which is the sole director of the company; or
      (c)  the sole director of a corporation which is the sole director of the company.

112.  A provision of the Act[b] or these regulations requiring or authorising a thing to be done by or to a director and the secretary shall not be satisfied by its being done by or to the same person acting both as director and as, or in place of, the secretary.

AMENDMENTS AND NOTES

[a]  Words in italics introduced by CA 1976, s 42(1) and Sch 2. (By virtue of the Interpretation Act 1978, ss 17(2)(a) and 23(3), the reference to CA 1976, s 21(5) is to be construed as a reference to CA 1985, s 13(5) or, from 1 October 2009, to CA 2006, s 16(6).)

[b]  See now CA 2006.

### The Seal

113.  The directors shall provide for the safe custody of the seal, which shall only be used by the authority of the directors or of a committee of the directors authorised by the directors in that behalf, and every instrument to which the seal shall be affixed shall be signed by a director and shall be countersigned by the secretary or by a second director or by some other person appointed by the directors for the purpose.

### Dividends and Reserve

114.  The company in general meeting may declare dividends, but no dividend shall exceed the amount recommended by the directors.

115.  The directors may from time to time pay to the members such interim dividends as appear to the directors to be justified by the profits of the company.

116.  *No dividend shall be paid otherwise than out of profits.*[a]

117.  The directors may, before recommending any dividend, set aside out of the profits of the company such sums as they think proper as a reserve or reserves which shall, at the discretion of the directors, be applicable for any purpose to which the profits of the company may be properly applied, and pending such application may, at the like discretion, either be employed in the business of the company or be invested in such investments (other than shares of the company) as the directors may from time to time think fit. The directors may also without placing the same to reserve carry forward any profits which they may think prudent not to divide.

118.  Subject to the rights of persons, if any, entitled to shares with special rights as to dividend, all dividends shall be declared and paid according to the amounts paid or credited as paid on the shares in respect whereof the dividend is paid, but no amount paid or credited as paid on a share in advance of calls shall be treated for the purposes of this regulation as paid on the share. All dividends shall be apportioned and paid proportionately to the amounts paid or credited as paid on the shares during any portion or portions of the period in respect of which the dividend is paid; but if any share is issued on terms providing that it shall rank for dividend as from a particular date such share shall rank for dividend accordingly.

119.   The directors may deduct from any dividend payable to any member all sums of money (if any) presently payable by him to the company on account of calls or otherwise in relation to the shares of the company.

120.   Any general meeting declaring a dividend or bonus may direct payment of such dividend or bonus wholly or partly by the distribution of specific assets and in particular of paid-up shares, debentures or debenture stock of any other company or in any one or more of such ways, and the directors shall give effect to such resolution, and where any difficulty arises in regard to such distribution, the directors may settle the same as they think expedient, and in particular may issue fractional certificates and fix the value for distribution of such specific assets or any part thereof and may determine that cash payments shall be made to any members upon the footing of the value so fixed in order to adjust the rights of all parties, and may vest any such specific assets in trustees as may seem expedient to the directors.

121.   Any dividend, interest or other moneys payable in cash in respect of shares may be paid by cheque or warrant sent through the post directed to the registered address of the holder or, in the case of joint holders, to the registered address of that one of the joint holders who is first named on the register of members or to such person and to such address as the holder or joint holders may in writing direct. Every such cheque or warrant shall be made payable to the order of the person to whom it is sent. Any one of two or more joint holders may give effectual receipts for any dividends, bonuses or other moneys payable in respect of the shares held by them as joint holders.

122.   No dividend shall bear interest against the company.

AMENDMENTS AND NOTES

[a]   In relation to companies registered from 22 December 1980 to 30 June 1985, the text in italics substituted (by CA 1980, s 88(1) and Sch 3) by the following:

'116. No dividend or interim dividend shall be paid otherwise than in accordance with the provisions of Part III of the Companies Act 1980 which apply to the company.' (By virtue of the Interpretation Act 1978, ss 17(2)(a) and 23(3), the reference to CA 1980, Part III is to be construed as a reference to CA 2006, Part 23 (ss 829–853).)

*Accounts*

123.   *The directors shall cause accounting records to be kept in accordance with section 12 of the Companies Act 1976.*[a]

124.   *The accounting records shall be kept at the registered office of the company or, subject to section 12(6) and (7) of the Companies Act 1976, at such other place or places as the directors think fit, and shall always be open to the inspection of the officers of the company.*[b]

125.   The directors shall from time to time determine whether and to what extent and at what times and places and under what conditions or regulations the accounts and books of the company or any of them shall be open to the inspection of members not being directors, and no member (not being a director) shall have any right of inspecting any account or book or document of the company except as conferred by statute or authorised by the directors or by the company in general meeting.

126.   The directors shall from time to time, in accordance with *sections 150 and 157 of the Act and sections 1, 6 and 7 of the Companies Act 1976*[c] cause to be prepared and to be laid before the company in general meeting such profit and loss accounts, balance sheets, group accounts (if any) and reports as are referred to in those sections.

127.   A copy of every balance sheet (including every document required by law to be annexed thereto) which is to be laid before the company in general meeting, together with a copy of the auditors' report *and directors' report,*[d] shall not less than 21 days before the date of the meeting be sent to every member of, and every holder of debentures of, the company and to every person registered under regulation 31. Provided that this regulation shall not require a copy of those documents to be sent to any person of whose address the company is not aware or to more than one of the joint holders of any shares or debentures.

AMENDMENTS AND NOTES

[a]   Words in italics introduced by CA 1976, s 42(1) and Sch 2. (By virtue of the Interpretation Act 1978, ss 17(2)(a) and 23(3), the reference to CA 1976, s 12 is to be construed as a reference to CA 2006, ss 386–389.) The italicized words replaced the words:

'123. The directors shall cause proper books of account to be kept with respect to:—

   (a)   all sums of money received and expended by the company and the matters in respect of which the receipt and expenditure takes place;
   (b)   all sales and purchases of goods by the company; and
   (c)   the assets and liabilities of the company.

Proper books shall not be deemed to be kept if there are not kept such books of account as are necessary to give a true and fair view of the state of the company's affairs and to explain its transactions.'

ᵇ Words in italics introduced by CA 1976, s 42(1) and Sch 2. (By virtue of the Interpretation Act 1978, ss 17(2)(a) and 23(3), the reference to CA 1976, s 12(6) and (7) is to be construed as a reference to CA 2006, s 388–389.) The italicized words replaced the words:

'124. The books of account shall be kept at the registered office of the company, or, subject to section 147(3) of the Act, at such other place or places as the directors think fit, and shall always be open to the inspection of the directors.' (By virtue of the Interpretation Act 1978, ss 17(2)(a) and 23(3), the reference to section 147(3) of the Companies Act 1948 was to be construed as a reference to CA 2006, s 388–389.) In *Oxford Legal Group Ltd v Sibbasbridge Services plc* [2008] EWCA Civ 387, it was said that the right of a director to inspect the books of the company was intended to enable the director to fulfil her duties to the company, and that accordingly that right would be lost if the director were using the right of inspection for an improper purpose.

ᶜ Words in italics introduced by CA 1976, s 42(1) and Sch 2. (By virtue of the Interpretation Act 1978, ss 17(2)(a) and 23(3), the reference to ss 150, 157 of the Act, and to CA 1976, ss 1, 6, 7 are to be construed as a reference to CA 2006, ss 394, 395, 399, 403, 415, 418, 419, 437, 438, 441, 442, 444–447, 451 and 452.) The italicized words replaced the words 'sections 148, 150 and 157 of the Act'. (By virtue of the Interpretation Act 1978, ss 17(2)(a) and 23(3), the references to the Act, ss 148, 150, 157 are to be construed as a reference to CA 2006, 394, 395, 399, 403, 415, 418, 419, 437, 438, and 442.)

ᵈ Words in italics added by CA 1976, s 42(1) and Sch 2.

### Capitalisation of Profits

128.  The company in general meeting may upon the recommendation of the directors resolve that it is desirable to capitalise any part of the amount for the time being standing to the credit of any of the company's reserve accounts or to the credit of the profit and loss account or otherwise available for distribution, and accordingly that such sum be set free for distribution amongst the members who would have been entitled thereto if distributed by way of dividend and in the same proportions on condition that the same be not paid in cash but be applied either in or towards paying up any amounts for the time being unpaid on any shares held by such members respectively or paying up in full unissued shares or debentures of the company to be allotted and distributed credited as fully paid up to and amongst such members in the proportion aforesaid, or partly in the one way and partly in the other, and the directors shall give effect to such resolution:
Provided that a share premium account and a capital redemption reserve fund may, for the purposes of this regulation, only be applied in the paying up of unissued shares to be issuedᵃ to members of the company as fully paid bonus shares.ᵇ

[128A. The company in general meeting may on the recommendation of the directors resolve that it is desirable to capitalise any part of the amount for the time being standing to the credit of any of the company's reserve accounts or to the credit of the profit and loss account which is not available for distribution by applying such sum in paying up in full unissued shares to be allotted as fully paid bonus shares to those members of the company who would have been entitled to that sum if it were distributed by way of dividend (and in the same proportions), and the directors shall give effect to such resolution.]ᶜ

129.  *Whenever such a resolution as aforesaid shall have been passed*ᵈ the directors shall make all appropriations and applications of the undivided profits resolved to be capitalised thereby, and all allotments and issues of fully paid shares or debentures, if any, and generally shall do all acts and things required to give effect thereto, with full power to the directors to make such provision by the issue of fractional certificates or by payment in cash or otherwise as they think fit for the case of shares or debentures becoming distributable in fractions, and also to authorise any person to enter on behalf of all the members entitled thereto into an agreement with the company providing for the allotment to them respectively, credited as fully paid up, of any further shares or debentures to which they may be entitled upon such capitalisation, or (as the case may require) for the payment up by the company on their behalf, by the application thereto of their respective proportions of the profits resolved to be capitalised, of the amounts or any part of the amounts remaining unpaid on their existing shares, and any agreement made under such authority shall be effective and binding on all such members.

AMENDMENTS AND NOTES

ᵃ For companies registered from 22 December 1980 to 30 June 1985, word in italics substituted by word 'allotted' by CA 1980, s 88(1) and Sch 3.

ᵇ In a case involving the equivalent regulation (110) of the 1985 Table A, the Court of Appeal held that a shareholder receiving a bonus issue was not 'a person dealing with the company' for the purposes of CA 1985, s 35A(1). See *EIC Services Ltd v Phipps* [2005] 1 All ER 338.

ᶜ Inserted by CA 1980, s 88(1) and Sch 3 for companies registered from 22 December 1980 to 30 June 1985.

<sup>d</sup> For companies registered from 22 December 1980 to 30 June 1985, words in italics substituted by words 'Whenever a resolution is passed in pursuance of regulation 128 or 128A above', by CA 1980, s 88(1) and Sch 3.

### Audit

**130.** Auditors shall be appointed and their duties regulated in accordance with *sections 159 to 162 of the Act*[a]

AMENDMENTS AND NOTES

[a] Words in italics substituted by words 'sections 159 to 161 of the Act and section 14 of the Companies Act 1967' by CA 1967. Words in italics substituted by words 'section 161 of the Act, section 14 of the Companies Act 1967 and sections 13 to 18 of the Companies Act 1976' by CA 1976. Words in italics substituted by words 'section 161 of the Act, sections 14 and 23A of the Companies Act 1967 and sections 13 to 18 of the Companies Act 1976 and sections 7 and 12 of the Companies Act 1981' by CA 1981. (For all these sections, see now CA 2006, ss 444, 445, 449, 475, 480, 481, 495–497, 1169, and Part 42.)

### Notices

**131.** Any notice may be given by the company to any member either personally or by sending it by post to him or to his registered address, or (if he has no registered address within the United Kingdom) to the address, if any, within the United Kingdom supplied by him to the company for the giving of notice to him. Where a notice is sent by post, service of the notice shall be deemed to be effected by properly addressing, prepaying, and posting a letter containing the notice, and to have been effected in the case of a notice of a meeting at the expiration of 24 hours after the letter containing the same is posted, and in any other case at the time at which the letter would be delivered in the ordinary course of post.[a]

**132.** A notice may be given by the company to the joint holders of a share by giving the notice to the joint holder first named in the register of members in respect of the share.

**133.** A notice may be given by the company to the persons entitled to a share in consequence of the death or bankruptcy of a member by sending it through the post in a prepaid letter addressed to them by name, or by the title of representatives of the deceased, or trustee of the bankrupt, or by any like description, at the address, if any, within the United Kingdom supplied for the purpose by the persons claiming to be so entitled, or (until such an address has been so supplied) by giving the notice in any manner in which the same might have been given if the death or bankruptcy had not occurred.

**134.** Notice of every general meeting shall be given in any manner hereinbefore authorised to
    (a) every member except those members who (having no registered address within the United Kingdom) have not supplied to the company an address within the United Kingdom for the giving of notice to them;
    (b) every person upon whom the ownership of a share devolves by reason of his being a legal representative or a trustee in bankruptcy of a member where the member but for his death or bankruptcy would be entitled to receive notice of the meeting; and
    (c) the auditor for the time being of the company. No other person shall be entitled to receive notices of general meetings.

AMENDMENTS AND NOTES

[a] In *Parkstone Ltd v Gulf Guarantee Bank plc* [1990] BCLC 850, Warner J held that the first sentence of this regulation 'affords the company a choice of methods by which it may give a notice to a member'. Thus, where a corporate member, with a registered office outside of the UK, had supplied the company with an address in the UK for the giving of notice, the company might still choose to send the notice to the member's (non-UK) registered address. See also the commentary to regulations 112 and 115 of the 1985 Table A.

### Winding Up

**135.** If the company shall be wound up, the liquidator may, with the sanction of an extraordinary resolution of the company and any other sanction required by the Act,[a] divide amongst the members in specie or kind the whole or any part of the assets of the company (whether they shall consist of property of the same kind or not) and may, for such purpose, set such value as he deems fair upon any property to be divided as aforesaid and may determine how such division shall be carried out as between the members or different classes of members. The liquidator may, with the like sanction, vest the whole or any part of the assets in trustees upon such trusts for the benefit of the contributories as the liquidator, with the like sanction, shall think fit, but so that no member shall be compelled to accept any shares or other securities whereon there is any liability.

AMENDMENTS AND NOTES

[a] See now the Insolvency Act 1986.

*Indemnity*

**136.** Every director, managing director, agent, auditor, secretary and other officer for the time being of the company shall be indemnified out of the assets of the company against any liability incurred by him in defending any proceedings, whether civil or criminal, in which judgment is given in his favour or in which he is acquitted or in connection with any application under section 448 of the Act[a] in which relief is granted to him by the court.[b]

AMENDMENTS AND NOTES

[a] By virtue of the Interpretation Act 1978, ss 17(2)(a) and 23(3), this is to be construed as a reference to CA 2006, s 1157.

[b] Regulation 136 also applies to proceedings brought by *the company* as well as those brought by a third party (*John v Price Waterhouse* [2002] 1 WLR 953). However, a director, auditor, or other officer seeking to rely upon this regulation must show that it has been incorporated into an 'extrinsic' contract between herself and the company. The statutory contract based upon the articles (CA 1985, s 14, CA 2006, s 33) operates only between the members and the company, or the members *inter se*. In *Re New British Iron Company ex parte Beckwith* [1898] 1 Ch 324, the court was prepared to find that an article (in that case concerning the remuneration of a director) had been incorporated into an extrinsic contract with a director where the director was employed by the company 'on the footing of the article' and where the director had accepted office on those terms. In *Re City Equitable Fire Assurance Co Ltd.* [1925] Ch 407, 521, however, Warrington LJ declared that, where the terms of employment 'are expressed in a separate document, then that document must be taken to define the conditions of [the auditors'] engagement, and it would not be proper to assume any implied terms either from the provisions of the articles or elsewhere'.

## PART II
### REGULATIONS FOR MANAGEMENT OF A PRIVATE COMPANY LIMITED BY SHARES[a]

**1.** The regulations contained in Part I of Table A (with the exception of regulations 24 and 53) shall apply.

**2.** The company is a private company and accordingly
   (a) *the right to transfer shares is restricted in manner hereinafter prescribed;*
   (b) *the number of members of the company (exclusive of persons who are in the employment of the company and of persons who having been formerly in the employment of the company were while in such employment and have continued after the determination of such employment to be members of the company) is limited to 50. Provided that where two or more persons hold one or more shares in the company jointly they shall for the purpose of this regulation be treated as a single member;*
   (c) *any invitation to the public to subscribe for any shares or debentures of the company is prohibited;*
   (d) *the company shall not have power to issue share warrants to bearer.*

**3.** [b]*The directors may, in their absolute discretion and without assigning any reason therefore, decline to register any transfer of any share, whether or not is a fully paid share.*

**4.** [c]*No business shall be transacted at any general meeting unless a quorum of members is present at the time when the meeting proceeds to business; save as herein otherwise provided two members present in person or by proxy shall be a quorum.*

**5.** *Subject to the provisions of the Act,[d] a resolution in writing signed by all the members for the time being entitled to receive notice of and to attend and vote at general meetings (or being corporations by their duly authorised representatives) shall be as valid and effective as if the same had been passed at a general meeting of the company duly convened and held.*

**6.** [e] *The directors may at any time require any person whose name is entered in the register of members of the company to furnish them with any information, supported (if the directors so require) by a statutory declaration, which they may consider necessary for the purpose of determining whether or not the company is an exempt private company within the meaning of subsection (4) of section 129 of the Act.[f]*

AMENDMENTS AND NOTES

[a] Part II repealed by CA 1980, s 88(2) and Sch 4, for companies registered on or after 22 December 1980 (but for such companies the regulations contained in Part I of this Table become directly applicable).

[b] Regulation 3 is an alternative to regulation 24 of Part I.

[c] Regulation 4 is an alternative to regulation 53 of Part I.

[d] See now CA 2006.

[e] Regulation 6 repealed by CA 1967 with effect from 28 January 1968.

[f] CA 1948, s 129 repealed by CA 1967.

VERSION OF TABLE A APPLYING TO COMPANIES LIMITED BY
SHARES REGISTERED BETWEEN 1 JULY 1985 AND 30
SEPTEMBER 2009[a]

## Companies Act 1985 Table A

(SI 1985/805, Schedule)

AMENDMENTS AND NOTES

[a] See CA 1985, s 8(2) and the discussion at para 51.TA.02 above. Perhaps more accurately, we should note that this version of Table A applies by default to a company where the application to register it is received by the registrar of companies, and the requirements as to registration are met, before 1 October 2009, even if registration is effected after that date: see Sch 2, para 3(1) to the Companies Act 2006 (Commencement No 8, Transitional Provisions and Savings) Order 2008, SI 2008/2860. By way of saving provision, Sch 2, para 1(1)(b) provides that nothing in CA 2006 affects the application in relation to an existing company of the Companies (Tables A to F) Regulations 1985.

Table A
Regulations for Management of a Company Limited by Shares

1. In these regulations—                                                                    **51.TA.08**
    ['the Act' means the Companies Act 1985 including any statutory modification or re-enactment thereof for the time being in force.][a]
    'the articles' means the articles of the company.
    'clear days' in relation to the period of a notice means that period excluding the day when the notice is given or deemed to be given and the day for which it is given or on which it is to take effect.
    ['communication' means the same as in the Electronic Communications Act 2000.][b]
    ['electronic communication' means the same as in the Electronic Communications Act 2000.][c]
    'executed' includes any mode of execution.
    'office' means the registered office of the company.
    'the holder' in relation to shares means the member whose name is entered in the register of members as the holder of the shares.
    'the seal' means the common seal of the company.
    'secretary' means the secretary of the company or any other person appointed to perform the duties of the secretary of the company, including a joint, assistant or deputy secretary.
    'the United Kingdom' means Great Britain and Northern Ireland.
    Unless the context otherwise requires, words or expressions contained in these regulations bear the same meaning as in the Act but excluding any statutory modification thereof not in force when these regulations become binding on the company.

AMENDMENTS AND NOTES

[a] For companies registered on or after 1 October 2007, words in square brackets replaced with the following words by the Companies (Tables A to F) (Amendment) Regulations 2007, SI 2007/2541: '"the Act" means the Companies Act 1985 (including any statutory modification or re-enactment thereof for the time being in force and any provisions of the Companies Act 2006 for the time being in force;'.

[b] Words in square brackets inserted by the Companies Act 1985 (Electronic Communications) Order, SI 2000/3373. That Order came into force on 22 December 2000. As to whether these changes apply only to companies registered on or after that date, see the discussion at paragraph 51.TA.03 above.

[c] Words in square brackets inserted by the Companies Act 1985 (Electronic Communications) Order, SI 2000/3373. That Order came into force on 22 December 2000. As to whether these changes apply only to companies registered on or after that date, see the discussion at para 51.TA.03 above.

*Share Capital*

2. Subject to the provisions of the Act and without prejudice to any rights attached to any existing shares, any share may be issued with such rights or restrictions as the company may by ordinary resolution determine.
3. Subject to the provisions of the Act, shares may be issued which are to be redeemed or are to be liable to be redeemed at the option of the company or the holder on such terms and in such manner as may be provided by the articles.

4.  The company may exercise the powers of paying commissions conferred by the Act. Subject to the [provision][a] of the Act, any such commission may be satisfied by the payment of cash or by the allotment of fully or partly paid shares or partly in one way and partly in the other.

5.  Except as required by law, no person shall be recognised by the company as holding any share upon any trust and (except as otherwise provided by the articles or by law) the company shall not be bound by or recognise any interest in any share except an absolute right to the entirety thereof in the holder.[b]

AMENDMENTS AND NOTES

[a]  For companies registered on or after 1 August 1985, the word in square brackets replaced with 'provisions' by the Companies (Tables A to F) (Amendment) Regulations 1985, SI 1985/1052.

[b]  In order for a lawful trust of shares to be created, there is no requirement of any board minute approving or recording the declaration of such a trust: *Singh v Anand* [2007] EWHC 3346.

*Share Certificates*

6.  Every member, upon becoming the holder of any shares, shall be entitled without payment to one certificate for all the shares of each class held by him (and, upon transferring a part of his holding of shares of any class, to a certificate for the balance of such holding) or several certificates each for one or more of his shares upon payment for every certificate after the first of such reasonable sum as the directors may determine. Every certificate shall be sealed with the seal[a] and shall specify the number, class and distinguishing numbers (if any) of the shares to which it relates and the amount or respective amounts paid up thereon. The company shall not be bound to issue more than one certificate for shares held jointly by several persons and delivery of a certificate to one joint holder shall be a sufficient delivery to all of them.

7.  If a share certificate is defaced, worn-out, lost or destroyed, it may be renewed on such terms (if any) as to evidence and indemnity and payment of the expenses reasonably incurred by the company in investigating evidence as the directors may determine but otherwise free of charge, and (in the case of defacement or wearing-out) on delivery up of the old certificate.

*Lien*

8.  The company shall have a first and paramount lien on every share (not being a fully paid share) for all moneys (whether presently payable or not) payable at a fixed time or called in respect of that share. The directors may at any time declare any share to be wholly or in part exempt from the provisions of this regulation. The company's lien on a share shall extend to any amount payable in respect of it.[b]

9.  The company may sell in such manner as the directors determine any shares on which the company has a lien if a sum in respect of which the lien exists is presently payable and is not paid within fourteen clear days after notice has been given to the holder of the share or to the person entitled to it in consequence of the death or bankruptcy of the holder, demanding payment and stating that if the notice is not complied with the shares may be sold.

10.  To give effect to a sale the directors may authorise some person to execute an instrument of transfer of the shares sold to, or in accordance with the directions of, the purchaser. The title of the transferee to the shares shall not be affected by any irregularity in or invalidity of the proceedings in reference to the sale.

11.  The net proceeds of the sale, after payment of the costs, shall be applied in payment of so much of the sum for which the lien exists as is presently payable, and any residue shall (upon surrender to the company for cancellation of the certificate for the shares sold and subject to a like lien for any moneys not presently payable as existed upon the shares before the sale) be paid to the person entitled to the shares at the date of the sale.

AMENDMENTS AND NOTES

[a]  See the commentary to regulation 8 of Table A 1948.

[b]  For some potential problems in the timing of the lien (and thus in the priority it might afford over other equitable interests in the shares) created by a regulation drafted in these terms, see *Champagne Perrier-Jouet SA v HH Finch Ltd* [1982] 3 All ER 713.

*Calls on Shares and Forfeiture*

12.  Subject to the terms of allotment, the directors may make calls upon the members in respect of any moneys unpaid on their shares (whether in respect of nominal value or premium) and each member shall (subject to receiving at least fourteen clear days' notice specifying when and where payment is to be made) pay to the company as required by the notice the amount called on his shares. A call may be required to be paid by instalments. A call may, before receipt by the company of any sum due thereunder, be revoked in whole or part and payment of a call may be postponed in whole or part. A person upon whom a call is made shall remain liable for calls made upon him notwithstanding the subsequent transfer of the shares in respect whereof the call was made.[a]

**13.** A call shall be deemed to have been made at the time when the resolution of the directors authorising the call was passed.

**14.** The joint holders of a share shall be jointly and severally liable to pay all calls in respect thereof.

**15.** If a call remains unpaid after it has become due and payable the person from whom it is due and payable shall pay interest on the amount unpaid from the day it became due and payable until it is paid at the rate fixed by the terms of allotment of the share or in the notice of the call or, if no rate is fixed, at the appropriate rate (as defined by the Act) but the directors may waive payment of the interest wholly or in part.

**16.** An amount payable in respect of a share on allotment or at any fixed date, whether in respect of nominal value or premium or as an instalment of a call, shall be deemed to be a call and if it is not paid the provisions of the articles shall apply as if that amount had become due and payable by virtue of a call.

**17.** Subject to the terms of allotment, the directors may make arrangements on the issue of shares for a difference between the holders in the amounts and times of payment of calls on their shares.

**18.** If a call remains unpaid after it has become due and payable the directors may give to the person from whom it is due not less than fourteen clear days' notice requiring payment of the amount unpaid together with any interest which may have accrued. The notice shall name the place where payment is to be made and shall state that if the notice is not complied with the shares in respect of which the call was made will be liable to be forfeited.

**19.** If the notice is not complied with any share in respect of which it was given may, before the payment required by the notice has been made, be forfeited by a resolution of the directors and the forfeiture shall include all dividends or other moneys payable in respect of the forfeited shares and not paid before the forfeiture.

**20.** Subject to the provisions of the Act, a forfeited share may be sold, re-allotted or otherwise disposed of on such terms and in such manner as the directors determine either to the person who was before the forfeiture the holder or to any other person and at any time before sale, re-allotment or other disposition, the forfeiture may be cancelled on such terms as the directors think fit. Where for the purposes of its disposal a forfeited share is to be transferred to any person the directors may authorise some person to execute an instrument of transfer of the share to that person.

**21.** A person any of whose shares have been forfeited shall cease to be a member in respect of them and shall surrender to the company for cancellation the certificate for the shares forfeited but shall remain liable to the company for all moneys which at the date of forfeiture were presently payable by him to the company in respect of those shares with interest at the rate at which interest was payable on those moneys before the forfeiture or, if no interest was so payable, at the appropriate rate (as defined in the Act) from the date of forfeiture until payment but the directors may waive payment wholly or in part or enforce payment without any allowance for the value of the shares at the time of forfeiture or for any consideration received on their disposal.

**22.** A statutory declaration by a director or the secretary that a share has been forfeited on a specified date shall be conclusive evidence of the facts stated in it as against all persons claiming to be entitled to the share and the declaration shall (subject to the execution of an instrument of transfer if necessary) constitute a good title to the share and the person to whom the share is disposed of shall not be bound to see to the application of the consideration, if any, nor shall his title to the share be affected by any irregularity in or invalidity of the proceedings in reference to the forfeiture or disposal of the share.

AMENDMENTS AND NOTES

[a] In exercising their power to make calls, directors must act in good faith. On directors differentiating amongst shareholders in the making of calls, see *Galloway v Hallé Concerts Society* [1915] 2 Ch 233.

*Transfer of Shares*

**23.** The instrument of transfer of a share may be in any usual form or in any other form which the directors may approve and shall be executed by or on behalf of the transferor and, unless the share is fully paid, by or on behalf of the transferee.

**24.** The directors may refuse to register the transfer of a share which is not fully paid to a person of whom they do not approve and they may refuse to register the transfer of a share on which the company has a lien. They may also refuse to register a transfer unless—

    (a) it is lodged at the office or at such other place as the directors may appoint and is accompanied by the certificate for the shares to which it relates and such other evidence as the directors may reasonably require to show the right of the transferor to make the transfer;

    (b) it is in respect of only one class of shares; and

    (c) it is in favour of not more than four transferees.

**25.** If the directors refuse to register a transfer of a share, they shall within two months after the date on which the transfer was lodged with the company send to the transferee notice of the refusal.

**26.** The registration of transfers of shares or of transfers of any class of shares may be suspended at such times and for such periods (not exceeding thirty days in any year) as the directors may determine.

**27.** No fee shall be charged for the registration of any instrument of transfer or other document relating to or affecting the title to any share.

**28.** The company shall be entitled to retain any instrument of transfer which is registered, but any instrument of transfer which the directors refuse to register shall be returned to the person lodging it when notice of the refusal is given.

### Transmission of Shares

**29.** If a member dies the survivor or survivors where he was a joint holder, and his personal representatives where he was a sole holder or the only survivor of joint holders, shall be the only persons recognised by the company as having any title to his interest; but nothing herein contained shall release the estate of a deceased member from any liability in respect of any share which had been jointly held by him.

**30.** A person becoming entitled to a share in consequence of the death or bankruptcy of a member may, upon such evidence being produced as the directors may properly require, elect either to become the holder of the share or to have some person nominated by him registered as the transferee. If he elects to become the holder he shall give notice to the company to that effect. If he elects to have another person registered he shall execute an instrument of transfer of the share to that person. All the articles relating to the transfer of shares shall apply to the notice or instrument of transfer as if it were an instrument of transfer executed by the member and the death or bankruptcy of the member had not occurred.[a]

**31.** A person becoming entitled to a share in consequence of the death or bankruptcy of a member shall have the rights to which he would be entitled if he were the holder of the share, except that he shall not, before being registered as the holder of the share, be entitled in respect of it to attend or vote at any meeting of the company or at any separate meeting of the holders of any class of shares in the company.

AMENDMENTS AND NOTES

[a] See the commentary to regulations 30 and 31 of Table A 1948, whose wording is similar to that of regulations 30 and 31 of this Table.

### Alteration of Share Capital

**32.** The company may by ordinary resolution—
- (a) increase its share capital by new shares of such amount as the resolution prescribes;
- (b) consolidate and divide all or any of its share capital into shares of larger amount than its existing shares;
- (c) subject to the provisions of the Act, sub-divide its shares, or any of them, into shares of smaller amount and the resolution may determine that, as between the shares resulting from the sub-division, any of them may have any preference or advantage as compared with the others; and
- (d) cancel shares which, at the date of the passing of the resolution, have not been taken or agreed to be taken by any person and diminish the amount of its share capital by the amount of the shares so cancelled.

**33.** Whenever as a result of a consolidation of shares any members would become entitled to fractions of a share, the directors may, on behalf of those members, sell the shares representing the fractions for the best price reasonably obtainable to any person (including, subject to the provisions of the Act, the company) and distribute the net proceeds of sale in due proportion among those members, and the directors may authorise some person to execute an instrument of transfer of the shares to, or in accordance with the directions of, the purchaser. The transferee shall not be bound to see to the application of the purchase money nor shall his title to the shares be affected by any irregularity in or invalidity of the proceedings in reference to the sale.

**34.** Subject to the provisions of the Act, the company may by special resolution reduce its share capital, any capital redemption reserve and any share premium account in any way.

### Purchase of Own Shares

**35.** Subject to the provisions of the Act, the company may purchase its own shares (including any redeemable shares) and, if it is a private company, make a payment in respect of the redemption or purchase of its own shares otherwise than out of distributable profits of the company or the proceeds of a fresh issue of shares.

### General Meetings

**36.** All general meetings other than annual general meetings shall be called extraordinary general meetings.[a]

**37.** The directors may call general meetings and, on the requisition of members pursuant to the provisions of the Act, shall forthwith proceed to convene [an extraordinary][b] general meeting [for a date not later than eight weeks after receipt of the requisition]<sup>c</sup>. If there are not within the United Kingdom sufficient directors to call a general meeting, any director or any member of the company may call a general meeting.

AMENDMENTS AND NOTES

<sup>a</sup> For companies registered on or after 1 October 2007, regulation 36 ceases to have effect by virtue of the Companies (Tables A to F) (Amendment) Regulations 2007, SI 2007/2541.

<sup>b</sup> For companies registered on or after 1 October 2007, words in square brackets replaced with 'a' by the Companies (Tables A to F) (Amendment) Regulations 2007, SI 2007/2541.

<sup>c</sup> For companies registered on or after 1 October 2007, words in square brackets replaced with 'in accordance with the provisions of the Act' by the Companies (Tables A to F) (Amendment) Regulations 2007, SI 2007/2541.

### Notice of General Meetings

**38.** [An annual general meeting and an *extraordinary general meeting called for the passing of a special resolution or a resolution appointing a person as a director* shall be called by at least twenty-one clear days' notice. All other *extraordinary*]<sup>a</sup> general meetings shall be called by at least fourteen clear days' notice but a general meeting may be called by shorter notice if it is so agreed—
  (a) in the case of an annual general meeting, by all the members entitled to attend and vote thereat; and<sup>b</sup>
  (b) [in the case of any other meeting] by a majority in number of the members having a right to attend and vote being a majority together holding not less than ninety[-five]<sup>c</sup> per cent in nominal value of the shares giving that right.
The notice shall specify the time and place of the meeting and the general nature of the business to be transacted [and, in the case of an annual general meeting, shall specify the meeting as such]<sup>d</sup>.
Subject to the provisions of the articles and to any restrictions imposed on any shares, the notice shall be given to all the members, to all persons entitled to a share in consequence of the death or bankruptcy of a member and to the directors and auditors.

**39.** The accidental omission to give notice of a meeting to, or the non-receipt of notice of a meeting by, any person entitled to receive notice shall not invalidate the proceedings at that meeting.<sup>e</sup>

AMENDMENTS AND NOTES

<sup>a</sup> Words in square brackets omitted for *private* companies registered on or after 1 October 2007 by the Companies (Tables A to F) (Amendment) Regulations 2007, SI 2007/2541. For *public* companies registered on or after 1 October 2007, the words in italics are omitted by the Companies (Tables A to F) (Amendment) Regulations 2007 SI 2007/2541.

<sup>b</sup> Paragraph (a) omitted for *private* companies registered on or after 1 October 2007 by the Companies (Tables A to F) (Amendment) Regulations 2007, SI 2007/2541.

<sup>c</sup> Words in square brackets at both places in para (b) omitted for *private* companies registered on or after 1 October 2007 by the Companies (Tables A to F) (Amendment) Regulations 2007, SI 2007/2541.

<sup>d</sup> Words in square brackets omitted for *private* companies registered on or after 1 October 2007 by the Companies (Tables A to F) (Amendment) Regulations 2007, SI 2007/2541.

<sup>e</sup> Regulation 39 also operates to validate the proceedings of a meeting called to pass a special (as well as an ordinary) resolution: *In re West Canadian Collieries Ltd* [1962] Ch 370. On the meaning of 'accidental omission to give notice', see *Re P&O Steam Navigation Co* [2006] EWHC 389.

### Proceedings at General Meetings

**40.** No business shall be transacted at any meeting unless a quorum is present. [Save in the case of a company with a single member]<sup>a</sup> Two persons entitled to vote upon the business to be transacted, each being a member or a proxy for a member or a duly authorised representative of a corporation, shall be a quorum.<sup>b</sup>

**41.** If such a quorum is not present within half an hour from the time appointed for the meeting, or if during a meeting such a quorum ceases to be present, the meeting shall stand adjourned to the same day in the next week at the same time and place or [to]<sup>c</sup> such time and place as the directors may determine.

**42.** The chairman, if any, of the board of directors or in his absence some other director nominated by the directors shall preside as chairman of the meeting, but if neither the chairman nor such other director (if any) be present within fifteen minutes after the time appointed for holding the meeting and willing to act, the directors present shall elect one of their number to be chairman and, if there is only one director present and willing to act, he shall be chairman.

**43.** If no director is willing to act as chairman, or if no director is present within fifteen minutes after the time appointed for holding the meeting, the members present and entitled to vote shall choose one of their number to be chairman.

**44.** A director shall, notwithstanding that he is not a member, be entitled to attend and speak at any general meeting and at any separate meeting of the holders of any class of shares in the company.

**45.** The chairman may, with the consent of a meeting at which a quorum is present (and shall if so directed by the meeting), adjourn the meeting from time to time and from place to place, but no business shall be transacted at an adjourned meeting other than business which might properly have been transacted at the meeting had the adjournment not taken place. When a meeting is adjourned for fourteen days or more, at least seven clear days' notice shall be given specifying the time and place of the adjourned meeting and the general nature of the business to be transacted. Otherwise it shall not be necessary to give any such notice.

**46.** A resolution put to the vote of a meeting shall be decided on a show of hands unless before, or on the declaration of the result of, the show of hands a poll is duly demanded. Subject to the provisions of the Act, a poll may be demanded—
   (a) by the chairman; or
   (b) by at least two members having the right to vote at the meeting; or
   (c) by a member or members representing not less than one-tenth of the total voting rights of all the members having the right to vote at the meeting; or
   (d) by a member or members holding shares conferring a right to vote at the meeting being shares on which an aggregate sum has been paid up equal to not less than one-tenth of the total sum paid up on all the shares conferring that right;
   and a demand by a person as proxy for a member shall be the same as a demand by the member.

**47.** Unless a poll is duly demanded a declaration by the chairman that a resolution has been carried or carried unanimously, or by a particular majority, or lost, or not carried by a particular majority and an entry to that effect in the minutes of the meeting shall be conclusive evidence of the fact without proof of the number or proportion of the votes recorded in favour of or against the resolution.

**48.** The demand for a poll may, before the poll is taken, be withdrawn but only with the consent of the chairman and a demand so withdrawn shall not be taken to have invalidated the result of a show of hands declared before the demand was made.

**49.** A poll shall be taken as the chairman directs and he may appoint scrutineers (who need not be members) and fix a time and place for declaring the result of the poll. The result of the poll shall be deemed to be the resolution of the meeting at which the poll was demanded.

**50.** In the case of an equality of votes, whether on a show of hands or on a poll, the chairman shall be entitled to a casting vote in addition to any other vote he may have.[d]

**51.** A poll demanded on the election of a chairman or on a question of adjournment shall be taken forthwith. A poll demanded on any other question shall be taken either forthwith or at such time and place as the chairman directs not being more than thirty days after the poll is demanded. The demand for a poll shall not prevent the continuance of a meeting for the transaction of any business other than the question on which the poll was demanded. If a poll is demanded before the declaration of the result of a show of hands and the demand is duly withdrawn, the meeting shall continue as if the demand had not been made.

**52.** No notice need be given of a poll not taken forthwith if the time and place at which it is to be taken are announced at the meeting at which it is demanded. In any other case at least seven clear days' notice shall be given specifying the time and place at which the poll is to be taken.

**53.** A resolution in writing executed by or on behalf of each member who would have been entitled to vote upon it if it had been proposed at a general meeting at which he was present shall be as effectual as if it had been passed at a general meeting duly convened and held and may consist of several instruments in the like form each executed by or on behalf of one or more members.[e]

Amendments and Notes

[a] Words in square brackets inserted for *private* companies registered on or after 1 October 2007 by the Companies (Tables A to F) (Amendment) Regulations 2007, SI 2007/2541.

[b] See also the commentary to CA 2006, s 306 on the principles to be applied by the court in determining whether to order a meeting to be held at which one member alone shall constitute a quorum.

[c] For companies registered on or after 1 August 1985, word in square brackets inserted by the Companies (Tables A to F) (Amendment) Regulations 1985, SI 1985/1052.

[d] For companies registered on or after 1 October 2007, regulation 50 ceases to have effect by virtue of the Companies (Tables A to F) (Amendment) (No 2) Regulations 2007, SI 2007/2826.

[e] For companies registered on or after 1 October 2007, regulation 53 ceases to have effect by virtue of the Companies (Tables A to F) (Amendment) Regulations 2007, SI 2007/2541.

*Votes of Members*

**54.** Subject to any rights or restrictions attached to any shares, on a show of hands every member who (being an individual) is present in person [or by proxy] or (being a corporation) is present by a duly authorised representative [or by proxy], *not being* [unless the proxy (in either case) or the representative is] himself a member entitled to vote, shall have one vote and on a poll every member shall have one vote for every share of which he is the holder.[a]

**55.** In the case of joint holders the vote of the senior who tenders a vote, whether in person or by proxy, shall be accepted to the exclusion of the votes of the other joint holders; and seniority shall be determined by the order in which the names of the holders stand in the register of members.

**56.** A member in respect of whom an order has been made by any court having jurisdiction (whether in the United Kingdom or elsewhere) in matters concerning mental disorder may vote, whether on a show of hands or on a poll, by his receiver, curator bonis or other person authorised in that behalf appointed by that court, and any such receiver, curator bonis or other person may, on a poll, vote by proxy. Evidence to the satisfaction of the directors of the authority of the person claiming to exercise the right to vote shall be deposited at the office, or at such other place as is specified in accordance with the articles for the deposit of instruments of proxy, not less than 48 hours before the time appointed for holding the meeting or adjourned meeting at which the right to vote is to be exercised and in default the right to vote shall not be exercisable.

**57.** No member shall vote at any general meeting or at any separate meeting of the holders of any class of shares in the company, either in person or by proxy, in respect of any share held by him unless all moneys presently payable by him in respect of that share have been paid.[b]

**58.** No objection shall be raised to the qualification of any voter except at the meeting or adjourned meeting at which the vote objected to is tendered, and every vote not disallowed at the meeting shall be valid. Any objection made in due time shall be referred to the chairman whose decision shall be final and conclusive.

**59.** On a poll votes may be given either personally or by proxy. A member may appoint more than one proxy to attend on the same occasion.

**60.** [The appointment of][c] a proxy shall be....,[d] executed by or on behalf of the appointor and shall be in the following form (or in a form as near thereto as circumstances allow or in any other form which is usual or which the directors may approve)—

'..............................................................................PLC/Limited

I/We, ................................., of..........................................................., being a................................. member/members of the above-named company, hereby ap-point............................. of..............................., or failing him,........................................................................................................................... of................................., as my/our proxy to vote in my/our name[s] and on my/our behalf at the [annual/*extraordinary*][e] general meeting of the company to be held on......................... 19............, and at any adjournment thereof.

Signed on.................................19....................'

**61.** Where it is desired to afford members an opportunity of instructing the proxy how he shall act the [appointment of][f] a proxy shall be in the following form (or in a form as near thereto as circumstances allow or in any other form which is usual or which the directors may approve)—

'...............................................PLC/Limited

I/We,................................., of..........................................................., being a................................. member/members of the above-named company, hereby ap-point.............................of.........................................................,or failing him, .............................................................. of................................., as my/our proxy to vote in my/our name[s] and on my/our behalf at the [annual/*extraordinary*][g] general meeting of the company, to be held on......................... 19......,...................., and at any adjournment thereof.

This form is to be used in respect of the resolutions mentioned below as follows:

Resolution No 1 *for *against

Resolution No 2 *for *against.

*Strike out whichever is not desired.

Unless otherwise instructed, the proxy may vote as he thinks fit or abstain from voting.

Signed this...................day of.........................19.........................'

**62.** [The appointment of][h] a proxy and any authority under which it is executed or a copy of such authority certified notarially or in some other way approved by the directors may—

    (a) [in the case of an instrument in writing][i] be deposited at the office or at such other place within the United Kingdom as is specified[j] in the notice convening the meeting or in any instrument of proxy sent out by the company in relation to the meeting not less than 48 hours before the time for holding the meeting or adjourned meeting at which the person named in the instrument proposes to vote; or

    [(aa) in the case of an appointment contained in an electronic communication, where an address has been specified for the purpose of receiving electronic communications—

        (i) in the notice convening the meeting, or

        (ii) in any instrument of proxy sent out by the company in relation to the meeting, or

(iii) in any invitation contained in an electronic communication to appoint a proxy issued by the company in relation to the meeting,

be received at such address not less than 48 hours before the time for holding the meeting or adjourned meeting at which the person named in the appointment proposes to vote;]$^k$

(b) in the case of a poll taken more than 48 hours after it is demanded, be deposited [or received]$^l$ as aforesaid after the poll has been demanded and not less than 24 hours before the time appointed for the taking of the poll; or

(c) where the poll is not taken forthwith but is taken not more than 48 hours after it was demanded, be delivered at the meeting at which the poll was demanded to the chairman or to the secretary or to any director;

[and an appointment of proxy which is not deposited, delivered or received]$^m$ in a manner so permitted shall be invalid.

[In this regulation and the next, 'address', in relation to electronic communications, includes any number or address used for the purposes of such communications.]$^n$

**63.** A vote given or poll demanded by proxy or by the duly authorised representative of a corporation shall be valid notwithstanding the previous determination of the authority of the person voting or demanding a poll unless notice of the determination was received by the company at the office or at such other place at which the instrument of proxy was duly deposited [or, where the appointment of the proxy was contained in an electronic communication, at the address at which such appointment was duly received]$^o$ before the commencement of the meeting or adjourned meeting at which the vote is given or the poll demanded or (in the case of a poll taken otherwise than on the same day as the meeting or adjourned meeting) the time appointed for taking the poll.

AMENDMENTS AND NOTES

$^a$ Words in square brackets inserted, and words in italics omitted, for companies registered on or after 1 October 2007, by the Companies (Tables A to F) (Amendment) (No 2) Regulations 2007, SI 2007/2826.

$^b$ Unlike the comparable provision (regulation 47) of the 1948 Table A, this regulation makes clear that a member loses the right to vote only in respect of the particular shares on which money is outstanding (and not all shares that are held by the member).

$^c$ Words in square brackets substituted by the Companies Act 1985 (Electronic Communications) Order 2000, SI 2000/3373. See the commentary to regulation 1 above.

$^d$ Revoked by the Companies Act 1985 (Electronic Communications) Order 2000, SI 2000/3373. See the commentary to regulation 1 above.

$^e$ Words in square brackets omitted for *private* companies registered on or after 1 October 2007 by the Companies (Tables A to F) (Amendment) Regulations 2007, SI 2007/2541. For *public* companies registered on or after 1 October 2007, the word 'extraordinary' is replaced by the words 'any other' by the Companies (Tables A to F) (Amendment) Regulations 2007, SI 2007/2541.

$^f$ Words in square brackets substituted by the Companies Act 1985 (Electronic Communications) Order 2000, SI 2000/3373. See the commentary to regulation 1 above.

$^g$ Words in square brackets omitted for *private* companies registered on or after 1 October 2007 by the Companies (Tables A to F) (Amendment) Regulations 2007, SI 2007/2541. For *public* companies registered on or after 1 October 2007, the word 'extraordinary' is replaced by the words 'any other' by the Companies (Tables A to F) (Amendment) Regulations 2007, SI 2007/2541.

$^h$ Words in square brackets substituted by the Companies Act 1985 (Electronic Communications) Order 2000, SI 2000/3373. See the commentary to regulation 1 above.

$^i$ Words in square brackets inserted by the Companies Act 1985 (Electronic Communications) Order 2000, SI 2000/3373. See the commentary to regulation 1 above.

$^j$ In *Branch v Bagley* [2004] EWHC 426, a complaint that the notice was defective, on the ground that it failed to state that the proxy form had to be deposited not less than 48 hours before the meeting, was rejected (although the judge seemed influenced by the fact that the proxy form had in any case not been returned *at all*).

$^k$ Paragraph (aa) inserted by the Companies Act 1985 (Electronic Communications) Order 2000, SI 2000/3373. See the commentary to regulation 1 above.

$^l$ Words in square brackets inserted by the Companies Act 1985 (Electronic Communications) Order 2000, SI 2000/3373. See the commentary to regulation 1 above.

$^m$ Words in square brackets substituted by the Companies Act 1985 (Electronic Communications) Order 2000, SI 2000/3373. See the commentary to regulation 1 above.

$^n$ Words in square brackets inserted by the Companies Act 1985 (Electronic Communications) Order 2000, SI 2000/3373. See the commentary to regulation 1 above.

$^o$ Words in square brackets inserted by the Companies Act 1985 (Electronic Communications) Order 2000, SI 2000/3373. See the commentary to regulation 1 above.

### Number of Directors

**64.** Unless otherwise determined by ordinary resolution, the number of directors (other than alternate directors) shall not be subject to any maximum but shall be not less than two.

### Alternate Directors

**65.** Any director (other than an alternate director) may appoint any other director, or any other person approved by resolution of the directors and willing to act, to be an alternate director and may remove from office an alternate director so appointed by him.

**66.** An alternate director shall be entitled to receive notice of all meetings of directors and of all meetings of committees of directors of which his appointor is a member, to attend and vote at any such meeting at which the director appointing him is not personally present, and generally to perform all the functions of his appointor as a director in his absence but shall not be entitled to receive any remuneration from the company for his services as an alternate director. But it shall not be necessary to give notice of such a meeting to an alternate director who is absent from the United Kingdom.

**67.** An alternate director shall cease to be an alternate director if his appointor ceases to be a director; but, if a director retires by rotation or otherwise but is reappointed or deemed to have been reappointed at the meeting at which he retires, any appointment of an alternate director made by him which was in force immediately prior to his retirement shall continue after his reappointment.

**68.** Any appointment or removal of an alternate director shall be by notice to the company signed by the director making or revoking the appointment or in any other manner approved by the directors.

**69.** Save as otherwise provided in the articles, an alternate director shall be deemed for all purposes to be a director and shall alone be responsible for his own acts and defaults and he shall not be deemed to be the agent of the director appointing him.

### Powers of Directors

**70.** Subject to the provisions of the Act, the memorandum and the articles and to any directions given by special resolution, the business of the company shall be managed by the directors who may exercise all the powers of the company. No alteration of the memorandum or articles and no such direction shall invalidate any prior act of the directors which would have been valid if that alteration had not been made or that direction had not been given. The powers given by this regulation shall not be limited by any special power given to the directors by the articles and a meeting of directors at which a quorum is present may exercise all powers exercisable by the directors.[a]

**71.** The directors may, by power of attorney or otherwise, appoint any person to be the agent of the company for such purposes and on such conditions as they determine, including authority for the agent to delegate all or any of his powers.

AMENDMENTS AND NOTES

[a] This regulation confers on directors an exclusive power to manage the business of the company, subject to the three stated limitations. These limitations are, first, provisions in the CA 1985 (see eg CA 1985, ss 80, 303 etc); second, provisions in the articles (see eg regulation 78); and third, directions given by *special* resolution. It is thus now clear that shareholders cannot, by an ordinary resolution, instruct the directors how to act. This reflects the position ultimately adopted by the courts in their interpretation of the (more ambiguous) regulation 80 of the 1948 Table A. On the inability of a simple majority of shareholders to adopt an action that had been brought in the name of the company but without the authority of the board, see *Breckland Group Holdings Ltd v London and Suffolk Properties Ltd* [1989] BCLC 100 (decided under regulation 80 of the 1948 Table A). Regulation 70 confers on the board as a whole the authority to commence proceedings on behalf of the company; an individual director does not, under regulation 70, have such power (*Mitchell & Hobbs (UK) Ltd v Mill* [1996] 2 BCLC 102).

### Delegation of Directors' Powers

**72.** The directors may delegate any of their powers to any committee consisting of one or more directors. They may also delegate to any managing director or any director holding any other executive office such of their powers as they consider desirable to be exercised by him. Any such delegation may be made subject to any conditions the directors may impose, and either collaterally with or to the exclusion of their own powers and may be revoked or altered. Subject to any such conditions, the proceedings of a committee with two or more members shall be governed by the articles regulating the proceedings of directors so far as they are capable of applying.[18]

### *Appointment and Retirement of Directors*

**73.** At the first annual general meeting all the directors shall retire from office, and at every subsequent annual general meeting one-third of the directors who are subject to retirement by rotation or, if their number is not three or a multiple of three, the number nearest to one-third shall retire from office; but, if there is only one director who is subject to retirement by rotation, he shall retire.[a]

**74.** Subject to the provisions of the Act, the directors to retire by rotation shall be those who have been longest in office since their last appointment or reappointment, but as between persons who became or were last reappointed directors on the same day those to retire shall (unless they otherwise agree among themselves) be determined by lot.[b]

**75.** If the company, at the meeting at which a director retires by rotation, does not fill the vacancy the retiring director shall, if willing to act, be deemed to have been reappointed unless at the meeting it is resolved not to fill the vacancy or unless a resolution for the reappointment of the director is put to the meeting and lost.[c]

**76.** No person [other than a director retiring by rotation][d] shall be appointed or reappointed a director at any general meeting unless—
(a)  he is recommended by the directors; or
(b)  not less than fourteen nor more than thirty-five clear days before the date appointed for the meeting, notice executed by a member qualified to vote at the meeting has been given to the company of the intention to propose that person for appointment or reappointment stating the particulars which would, if he were so appointed or reappointed, be required to be included in the company's register of directors together with notice executed by that person of his willingness to be appointed or reappointed.[e]

**77.** Not less than seven nor more than twenty-eight clear days before the date appointed for holding a general meeting notice shall be given to all who are entitled to receive notice of the meeting of any person [(other than a director retiring by rotation at the meeting)][f] who is recommended by the directors for appointment or reappointment as a director at the meeting or in respect of whom notice has been duly given to the company of the intention to propose him at the meeting for appointment or reappointment as a director. The notice shall give the particulars of that person which would, if he were so appointed or reappointed, be required to be included in the company's register of directors.[g]

**78.** [Subject as aforesaid][h], the company may by ordinary resolution appoint a person who is willing to act to be a director either to fill a vacancy or as an additional director and may also determine the rotation in which any additional directors are to retire.

**79.** The directors may appoint a person who is willing to act to be a director, either to fill a vacancy or as an additional director, provided that the appointment does not cause the number of directors to exceed any number fixed by or in accordance with the articles as the maximum number of directors. [A director so appointed shall hold office only until the next following annual general meeting and shall not be taken into account in determining the directors who are to retire by rotation at the meeting. If not reappointed at such annual general meeting, he shall vacate office at the conclusion thereof.][i]

**80.** Subject as aforesaid, a director who retires at an annual general meeting may, if willing to act, be reappointed. If he is not reappointed, he shall retain office until the meeting appoints someone in his place, or if it does not do so, until the end of the meeting.[j]

AMENDMENTS AND NOTES

[a]  For *private* companies registered on or after 1 October 2007, regulation 73 ceases to have effect by virtue of the Companies (Tables A to F) (Amendment) Regulations 2007, SI 2007/2541.

[b]  For *private* companies registered on or after 1 October 2007, regulation 74 ceases to have effect by virtue of the Companies (Tables A to F) (Amendment) Regulations 2007, SI 2007/2541.

[c]  For *private* companies registered on or after 1 October 2007, regulation 75 ceases to have effect by virtue of the Companies (Tables A to F) (Amendment) Regulations 2007, SI 2007/2541.

[d]  Words in square brackets omitted for *private* companies registered on or after 1 October 2007 by the Companies (Tables A to F) (Amendment) Regulations 2007, SI 2007/2541.

---

[18]  Regulation 72 permits the board to delegate powers to one or more directors, but the regulation does not itself effect such a delegation of powers; see Mitchell & Hobbs (UK) Ltd v Mill [1996] 2 BCLC 102 and Smith v Butler [2012] EWHC Civ 314.

e  In *Branch v Bagley* [2004] EWHC 426 it was declared that regulations 76 and 77 do not require the company to include, in the notice calling an EGM at which person(s) are to be proposed for appointment or reappointment as directors, the *name(s)* of those persons. Rather, their name(s) need only be given under regulation 77 by notice of not less than seven clear days before the meeting.

f  Words in square brackets omitted for *private* companies registered on or after 1 October 2007 by the Companies (Tables A to F) (Amendment) Regulations 2007, SI 2007/2541.

g  See discussion of *Branch v Bagley* [2004] EWHC 426 in relation to regulation 76 above.

h  Words in square brackets omitted for *private* companies registered on or after 1 October 2007 by the Companies (Tables A to F) (Amendment) Regulations 2007, SI 2007/2541.

i  Words in square brackets omitted for *private* companies registered on or after 1 October 2007 by the Companies (Tables A to F) (Amendment) Regulations 2007, SI 2007/2541.

j  For *private* companies registered on or after 1 October 2007, regulation 80 ceases to have effect by virtue of the Companies (Tables A to F) (Amendment) Regulations 2007, SI 2007/2541.

### *Disqualification and Removal of Directors*

**81.**  The office of a director shall be vacated if—

    (a)  he ceases to be a director by virtue of any provision of the Act or he becomes prohibited by law from being a director; or

    (b)  he becomes bankrupt or makes any arrangement or composition with his creditors general-ly;[a] or

    (c)  he is, or may be, suffering from mental disorder and either—

        (i)  he is admitted to hospital in pursuance of an application for admission for treatment under the Mental Health Act 1983 or, in Scotland, an application for admission under the Mental Health (Scotland) Act 1960, or

        (ii)  an order is made by a court having jurisdiction (whether in the United Kingdom or elsewhere) in matters concerning mental disorder for his detention or for the appoint-ment of a receiver, curator bonis or other person to exercise powers with respect to his property or affairs; or

    (d)  he resigns his office by notice to the company; or

    (e)  he shall for more than six consecutive months have been absent without permission of the directors from meetings of directors held during that period and the directors resolve that his office be vacated.

AMENDMENTS AND NOTES

a  On the unlikelihood of a director being able to plead an 'estoppel by convention' to prevent the company relying upon this regulation against the director, see *Re Siteburn Ltd* [2006] BPIR 1009. In *Witherdale Ltd v Registrar of Companies* [2008] 1 BCLC 174, the court held that a person who was a director at the time of a dissolution of the company, and subsequently became bankrupt, lost the authority to apply to have the company restored to the register.

### *Remuneration of Directors*

**82.**  The directors shall be entitled to such remuneration as the company may by ordinary resolution determine and, unless the resolution provides otherwise, the remuneration shall be deemed to accrue from day to day.[a]

AMENDMENTS AND NOTES

a  It was held in *Re Richmond Gate Property Co Ltd* [1964] 3 All ER 936 that a managing director who was also a member of the company had a contract with the company based upon the articles, and this contract precluded any claim in *quantum meruit* for work undertaken. Since the company had failed to determine that any remuneration was payable under the article, there was also no contractual sum for which the managing director could sue.) This case sits somewhat uneasily, however, with those cases suggesting that a member can only enforce the contract based upon the articles in her capacity as a member. In *Tayplan Ltd (In Admin) v Smith* [2012] BCC 523, however, the court ruled that a claim for a *quantum merit* would not be available in any event, for a director, as a fiduciary, cannot make a profit from his position, except as the articles otherwise permit. In *re Duomatic Ltd* [1969] 2 Ch 365, the failure of the company in general meeting to determine the directors' remuneration was 'cured' by the unanimous assent, of all those shareholders entitled to attend and vote at the general meeting, to the remuneration paid to the directors. And, as was noted in *Irvine v Irvine* [2007] 1 BCLC 349 (a case dealing with the comparable provisions in the 1948 Table A), for directors who hold an executive office, the board has the authority under regulation 84 to settle that director's remuneration.

*Directors' Expenses*

**83.** The directors may be paid all travelling, hotel, and other expenses properly incurred by them in connection with their attendance at meetings of directors or committees of directors or general meetings or separate meetings of the holders of any class of shares or of debentures of the company or otherwise in connection with the discharge of their duties.

*Directors' Appointments and Interests*

**84.** Subject to the provisions of the Act, the directors may appoint one or more of their number to the office of managing director or to any other executive office under the company and may enter into an agreement or arrangement with any director for his employment by the company or for the provision by him of any services outside the scope of the ordinary duties of a director. Any such appointment, agreement or arrangement may be made upon such terms as the directors determine and they may remunerate any such director for his services as they think fit. Any appointment of a director to an executive office shall terminate if he ceases to be a director but without prejudice to any claim to damages for breach of the contract of service between the director and the company. A managing director and a director holding any other executive office shall not be subject to retirement by rotation.[a]

**85.** Subject to the provisions of the Act, and provided that he has disclosed to the directors the nature and extent of any material interest of his, a director notwithstanding his office—
   (a)  may be a party to, or otherwise interested in, any transaction or arrangement with the company or in which the company is otherwise interested;
   (b)  may be a director or other officer of, or employed by, or a party to any transaction or arrangement with, or otherwise interested in, any body corporate promoted by the company or in which the company is otherwise interested; and
   (c)  shall not, by reason of his office, be accountable to the company for any benefit which he derives from any such office or employment or from any such transaction or arrangement or from any interest in any such body corporate and no such transaction or arrangement shall be liable to be avoided on the ground of any such interest or benefit.[b]

**86.** For the purposes of regulation 85—
   (a)  a general notice given to the directors that a director is to be regarded as having an interest of the nature and extent specified in the notice in any transaction or arrangement in which a specified person or class of persons is interested shall be deemed to be a disclosure that the director has an interest in any such transaction of the nature and extent so specified; and
   (b)  an interest of which a director has no knowledge and of which it is unreasonable to expect him to have knowledge shall not be treated as an interest of his.

AMENDMENTS AND NOTES

[a]  In *Mountain Spring Water Company Ltd v Colesby* (unreported) the EAT drew a distinction in the operation of the 'automatic termination' element of regulation 84. Where a director was appointed to an executive directorship, and was given an employment contract as such, then that contract would terminate automatically upon the director's removal from the board. However (although strictly *obiter*), the tribunal noted that some (non-executive) directors might enter into agreements with the company for the 'provision of services outside the scope of the ordinary duties of a director', such as where a non-executive director also acted as the legal adviser to the company. In such a case, removing the director from the board would not trigger the automatic termination of the agreement for the director's provision of (legal) services.

[b]  In *Lee Panavision Ltd v Lee Lighting Ltd* [1992] BCC 620 Harman J held that the disclosure required of a director under regulation 85 is to be imported from the disclosure regime under CA 1985, s 317, and is thus to be 'to the board at a meeting and at the meeting when the relevant contract first comes to be considered' (at 627). The Court of Appeal declined to offer its view on the construction and effect of regulation 85, having already decided to uphold Harman J's decision on other grounds. The law governing conflicts of interest has itself been codified, and in the process somewhat amended, by CA 2006. Reference should be made to the commentary accompanying ss 175–177 of that Act. For further discussion of the disclosure requirement in regulation 85, see also *Kleanthous v Paphitis* [2011] EWHC 2287 (Ch) at para 50. In *Movitex Ltd v Bulfield* [1988] BCLC 104, an article similar to regulation 85 (but which in fact gave interested directors a greater freedom to vote on contracts in which directors were interested) was upheld as valid, notwithstanding (what is now) CA 2006, s 232.

*Directors' Gratuities and Pensions*

**87.** The directors may provide benefits, whether by the payment of gratuities or pensions or by insurance or otherwise, for any director who has held but no longer holds any executive office or employment with the company or with any body corporate which is or has been a subsidiary of the company or a predecessor in business of the company or of any such subsidiary, and for any member of his family (including a spouse and a former spouse) or any person who is or was dependent on him, and may (as well before as after he ceases to hold such office or employment) contribute to any fund and pay premiums for the purchase or provision of any such benefit.

### Proceedings of Directors

**88.** Subject to the provisions of the articles, the directors may regulate their proceedings as they think fit. A director may, and the secretary at the request of a director shall, call a meeting of the directors. It shall not be necessary to give notice of a meeting to a director who is absent from the United Kingdom. Questions arising at a meeting shall be decided by a majority of votes. In the case of an equality of votes, the chairman shall have a second or casting vote. A director who is also an alternate director shall be entitled in the absence of his appointor to a separate vote on behalf of his appointor in addition to his own vote.[19]

**89.** The quorum for the transaction of the business of the directors may be fixed by the directors and unless so fixed at any other number shall be two. A person who holds office only as an alternate director shall, if his appointor is not present, be counted in the quorum.[a]

**90.** The continuing directors or a sole continuing director may act notwithstanding any vacancies in their number, but, if the number of directors is less than the number fixed as the quorum, the continuing directors or director may act only for the purpose of filling vacancies or of calling a general meeting.

**91.** The directors may appoint one of their number to be the chairman of the board of directors and may at any time remove him from that office. Unless he is unwilling to do so, the director so appointed shall preside at every meeting of directors at which he is present. But if there is no director holding that office, or if the director holding it is unwilling to preside or is not present within five minutes after the time appointed for the meeting, the directors present may appoint one of their number to be chairman of the meeting.

**92.** All acts done by a meeting of directors, or of a committee of directors, or by a person acting as a director shall, notwithstanding that it be afterwards discovered that there was a defect in the appointment of any director or that any of them were disqualified from holding office, or had vacated office, or were not entitled to vote, be as valid as if every such person had been duly appointed and was qualified and had continued to be a director and had been entitled to vote.

**93.** A resolution in writing signed by all the directors entitled to receive notice of a meeting of directors or of a committee of directors shall be as valid and effectual as it if had been passed at a meeting of directors or (as the case may be) a committee of directors duly convened and held and may consist of several documents in the like form each signed by one or more directors; but a resolution signed by an alternate director need not also be signed by his appointor and, if it is signed by a director who has appointed an alternate director, it need not be signed by the alternate director in that capacity.[b]

**94.** Save as otherwise provided by the articles, a director shall not vote at a meeting of directors or of a committee of directors on any resolution concerning a matter in which he has, directly or indirectly, an interest or duty which is material and which conflicts or may conflict with the interests of the company[c] unless his interest or duty arises only because the case falls within one or more of the following paragraphs—

   (a) the resolution relates to the giving to him of a guarantee, security, or indemnity in respect of money lent to, or an obligation incurred by him for the benefit of, the company or any of its subsidiaries;

   (b) the resolution relates to the giving to a third party of a guarantee, security, or indemnity in respect of an obligation of the company or any of its subsidiaries for which the director has assumed responsibility in whole or part and whether alone or jointly with others under a guarantee or indemnity or by the giving of security;

   (c) his interest arises by virtue of his subscribing or agreeing to subscribe for any shares, debentures or other securities of the company or any of its subsidiaries, or by virtue of his being, or intending to become, a participant in the underwriting or sub-underwriting of an offer of any such shares, debentures, or other securities by the company or any of its subsidiaries for subscription, purchase or exchange;

   (d) the resolution relates in any way to a retirement benefits scheme which has been approved, or is conditional upon approval, by the Board of Inland Revenue for taxation purposes.

For the purposes of this regulation, an interest of a person who is, for any purpose of the Act (excluding any statutory modification thereof not in force when this regulation becomes binding on the company), connected with a director shall be treated as an interest of the director and, in relation to an alternate director, an interest of his appointor shall be treated as an interest of the alternate director without prejudice to any interest which the alternate director has otherwise.

---

[19] It was held in Sneddon v MacCallum [2011] CSOH 59 that whilst, in accordance with regulations 88 and 111, it was required that notice of a directors' meeting be given to each director, this was not the same as saying that notice had to be received by each director to make the meeting valid.

95. A director shall not be counted in the quorum present at a meeting in relation to a resolution on which he is not entitled to vote.

96. The company may by ordinary resolution suspend or relax to any extent, either generally or in respect of any particular matter, any provision of the articles prohibiting a director from voting at a meeting of directors or of a committee of directors.

97. Where proposals are under consideration concerning the appointment of two or more directors to offices or employments with the company or any body corporate in which the company is interested the proposals may be divided and considered in relation to each director separately and (provided he is not for another reason precluded from voting) each of the directors concerned shall be entitled to vote and be counted in the quorum in respect of each resolution except that concerning his own appointment.

98. If a question arises at a meeting of directors or of a committee of directors as to the right of a director to vote, the question may, before the conclusion of the meeting, be referred to the chairman of the meeting and his ruling in relation to any director other than himself shall be final and conclusive.

AMENDMENTS AND NOTES

[a] A director who acts in breach of his fiduciary duty by the manner in which he votes upon a resolution should not be counted in the quorum of the meeting *Colin Gwyer & Associates Ltd v London Wharf (Limehouse) Ltd* [2003] 2 BCLC 153. Under CA 1985, s 35A (CA 2006, s 39) in favour of a person dealing with a company in good faith, the power of the board to bind the company is deemed to be free of any limitation under the company's constitution. It seems that such a person cannot rely on that section to overcome the failure of a company to meet a quorum requirement for board meetings in the company's constitution: see *Smith v Henniker-Major & Co* [2002] 2 BCLC 655. On the other hand, it may be possible for such a person to rely on the 'rule in *Turquand's* case' (1855) 5 E & B 248.

[b] On the invalidity of a written resolution signed by all directors entitled to receive notice, but nevertheless by fewer than would be required to make up a quorum for a board meeting, see *Hood Sailmakers Ltd v Axford* [1996] 4 All ER 830 (which was decided on regulation 106 of the 1948 Table A but whose wording is, so far as is relevant here, the same as that in regulation 93).

[c] In *Eastford Limited v Thomas Graham Gillespie, Airdrie North Limited* [2010] CSOH 132, Lord Hodge opined that the authorities relevant to interpreting the statutory prohibition on conflicts of interest (in CA 2006, s 175(1)) were also relevant in interpreting regulation 94; see the commentary to that section.

### Secretary

99. Subject to the provisions of the Act, the secretary shall be appointed by the directors for such term, at such remuneration and upon such conditions as they may think fit; and any secretary so appointed may be removed by them.

### Minutes

100. The directors shall cause minutes to be made in books kept for the purpose—
    (a) of all appointments of officers made by the directors; and
    (b) of all proceedings at meetings of the company, of the holders of any class of shares in the company, and of the directors, and of committees of directors, including the names of the directors present at each such meeting.

### The Seal

101. The seal shall only be used by the authority of the directors or of a committee of directors authorised by the directors. The directors may determine who shall sign any instrument to which the seal is affixed and unless otherwise so determined it shall be signed by a director and by the secretary or by a second director.

### Dividends

102. Subject to the provisions of the Act, the company may by ordinary resolution declare dividends in accordance with the respective rights of the members, but no dividend shall exceed the amount recommended by the directors.

103. Subject to the provisions of the Act, the directors may pay interim dividends if it appears to them that they are justified by the profits of the company available for distribution. If the share capital is divided into different classes, the directors may pay interim dividends on shares which confer deferred or non-preferred rights with regard to dividend as well as on shares which confer preferential rights with regard to dividend, but no interim dividend shall be paid on shares carrying deferred or non-preferred rights if, at the time of payment, any preferential

dividend is in arrear. The directors may also pay at intervals settled by them any dividend payable at a fixed rate if it appears to them that the profits available for distribution justify the payment. Provided the directors act in good faith they shall not incur any liability to the holders of shares conferring preferred rights for any loss they may suffer by the lawful payment of an interim dividend on any shares having deferred or non-preferred rights.

**104.** Except as otherwise provided by the rights attached to shares, all dividends shall be declared and paid according to the amounts paid up on the shares on which the dividend is paid. All dividends shall be apportioned and paid proportionately to the amounts paid up on the shares during any portion or portions of the period in respect of which the dividend is paid; but, if any share is issued on terms providing that it shall rank for dividend as from a particular date, that share shall rank for dividend accordingly.

**105.** A general meeting declaring a dividend may, upon the recommendation of the directors, direct that it shall be satisfied wholly or partly by the distribution of assets and, where any difficulty arises in regard to the distribution, the directors may settle the same and in particular may issue fractional certificates and fix the value for distribution of any assets and may determine that cash shall be paid to any member upon the footing of the value so fixed in order to adjust the rights of members and may vest any assets in trustees.

**106.** Any dividend or other moneys payable in respect of a share may be paid by cheque sent by post to the registered address of the person entitled or, if two or more persons are the holders of the share or are jointly entitled to it by reason of the death or bankruptcy of the holder, to the registered address of that one of those persons who is first named in the register of members or to such person and to such address as the person or persons entitled may in writing direct. Every cheque shall be made payable to the order of the person or persons entitled or to such other person as the person or persons entitled may in writing direct and payment of the cheque shall be a good discharge to the company. Any joint holder or other person jointly entitled to a share as aforesaid may give receipts for any dividend or other moneys payable in respect of the share.

**107.** No dividend or other moneys payable in respect of a share shall bear interest against the company unless otherwise provided by the rights attached to the share.

**108.** Any dividend which has remained unclaimed for twelve years from the date when it became due for payment shall, if the directors so resolve, be forfeited and cease to remain owing by the company.

### Accounts

**109.** No member shall (as such) have any right of inspecting any accounting records or other book or document of the company except as conferred by statute or authorised by the directors or by ordinary resolution of the company.

### Capitalisation of Profits

**110.** The directors may with the authority of an ordinary resolution of the company—

(a) subject as hereinafter provided, resolve to capitalise any undivided profits of the company not required for paying any preferential dividend (whether or not they are available for distribution) or any sum standing to the credit of the company's share premium account or capital redemption reserve;

(b) appropriate the sum resolved to be capitalised to the members who would have been entitled to it if it were distributed by way of dividend and in the same proportions and apply such sum on their behalf either in or towards paying up the amounts, if any, for the time being unpaid on any shares held by them respectively, or in paying up in full unissued shares or debentures of the company of a nominal amount equal to that sum, and allot the shares or debentures credited as fully paid to those members, or as they may direct, in those proportions, or partly in one way and partly in the other: but the share premium account, the capital redemption reserve, and any profits which are not available for distribution may, for the purposes of this regulation, only be applied in paying up unissued shares to be allotted to members credited as fully paid;

(c) make such provision by the issue of fractional certificates or by payment in cash or otherwise as they determine in the case of shares or debentures becoming distributable under this regulation in fractions; and

(d) authorise any person to enter on behalf of all the members concerned into an agreement with the company providing for the allotment to them respectively, credited as fully paid, of any shares or debentures to which they are entitled upon such capitalisation, any agreement made under such authority being binding on all such members.[a]

AMENDMENTS AND NOTES

<sup>a</sup> Note that this regulation requires an ordinary resolution to authorize the directors to undertake the various actions listed in paras (a)–(d). In *EIC Services Ltd v Phipps* [2005] 1 All ER 338, in which the directors failed to obtain such a resolution, the Court of Appeal held that a shareholder receiving a bonus issue was not 'a person dealing with the company' for the purposes of CA 1985, s 35A(1), and was thus unable to rely on s 35A to cure that failure. Given that holding, the court did not need to decide whether the requirement of an ordinary resolution amounted to a limitation on the power of the board of directors within the meaning of that section.

### Notices

**[111.**  Any notice to be given to or by any person pursuant to the articles (other than a notice calling a meeting of the directors) shall be in writing or shall be given using electronic communications to an address for the time being notified for that purpose to the person giving the notice. In this regulation, 'address', in relation to electronic communications, includes any number or address used for the purposes of such communications.]<sup>a</sup>

**112.**  The company may<sup>b</sup> give any notice to a member either personally or by sending it by post in a prepaid envelope addressed to the member at his registered address or by leaving it at that address [or by giving it using electronic communications to an address for the time being notified to the company by the member].<sup>c</sup> In the case of joint holders of a share, all notices shall be given to the joint holder whose name stands first in the register of members in respect of the joint holding and notice so given shall be sufficient notice to all the joint holders. A member whose registered address is not within the United Kingdom and who gives to the company an address within the United Kingdom at which notices may be given to him, [or an address to which notices may be sent using electronic communications,]<sup>d</sup> shall be entitled to have notices given to him at that address, but otherwise no such member shall be entitled to receive any notice from the company.
[In this regulation and the next, 'address', in relation to electronic communications, includes any number or address used for the purposes of such communications.]<sup>e</sup>

**113.**  A member present, either in person or by proxy, at any meeting of the company or of the holders of any class of shares in the company shall be deemed to have received notice of the meeting and, where requisite, of the purposes for which it was called.

**114.**  Every person who becomes entitled to a share shall be bound by any notice in respect of that share which, before his name is entered in the register of members, has been duly given to a person from whom he derives his title.

**115.**  Proof that an envelope containing a notice was properly addressed, prepaid and posted shall be conclusive evidence that that the notice was given.<sup>f</sup> [Proof that a notice contained in an electronic communication was sent in accordance with guidance issued by the Institute of Chartered Secretaries and Administrators shall be conclusive evidence that the notice was given.]<sup>g</sup> A notice shall, *unless the contrary is proved*<sup>h</sup> be deemed to be given at the expiration of 48 hours after the envelope containing it was posted [or, in the case of a notice contained in an electronic communication, at the expiration of 48 hours after the time it was sent].<sup>i</sup>

**116.**  A notice may be given by the company to the persons entitled to a share in consequence of the death or bankruptcy of a member by sending or delivering it, in any manner authorised by the articles for the giving of notice to a member, addressed to them by name, or by the title of representatives of the deceased, or trustee of the bankrupt or by any like description at the address, if any, within the United Kingdom supplied for that purpose by the persons claiming to be so entitled. Until such an address has been supplied, a notice may be given in any manner in which it might have been given if the death or bankruptcy had not occurred.

AMENDMENTS AND NOTES

<sup>a</sup> Regulation 111 substituted by the Companies Act 1985 (Electronic Communications) Order 2000, SI 2000/3373. See the commentary to regulation 1 above.

<sup>b</sup> Regulation 112 has been held not to be mandatory, but rather merely offers one means by which a notice might be sent (with, say, regulation 115 providing an alternative means): see *Hunter v Senate Support Services Ltd* [2005] 1 BCLC 175.

<sup>c</sup> Words in square brackets inserted by the Companies Act 1985 (Electronic Communications) Order 2000, SI 2000/3373. See the commentary to regulation 1 above.

<sup>d</sup> Words in square brackets inserted by the Companies Act 1985 (Electronic Communications) Order 2000, SI 2000/3373. See the commentary to regulation 1 above.

<sup>e</sup> Words in square brackets inserted by the Companies Act 1985 (Electronic Communications) Order 2000, SI 2000/3373. See the commentary to regulation 1 above.

<sup>f</sup> An envelope would be 'properly addressed' if it were 'accurately addressed': see *Hunter v Senate Support Services Ltd* [2005] 1 BCLC 175.

<sup>g</sup> Words in square brackets inserted by the Companies Act 1985 (Electronic Communications) Order 2000, SI 2000/3373. See the commentary to regulation 1 above.

<sup>h</sup> For companies registered on or after 1 August 1985 words in italics deleted by the Companies (Tables A to F) (Amendment) Regulations 1985, SI 1985/1052.

<sup>i</sup> Words in square brackets inserted by the Companies Act 1985 (Electronic Communications) Order 2000, SI 2000/3373. See the commentary to regulation 1 above.

*Winding Up*

**117.** If the company is wound up, the liquidator may, with the sanction of [an extraordinary]<sup>a</sup> resolution of the company and any other sanction required by the Act, divide among the members in specie the whole or any part of the assets of the company and may, for that purpose, value any assets and determine how the division shall be carried out as between the members or different classes of members. The liquidator may, with the like sanction, vest the whole or any part of the assets in trustees upon such trusts for the benefit of the members as he with the like sanction determines, but no member shall be compelled to accept any assets upon which there is a liability.

AMENDMENTS AND NOTES

<sup>a</sup> For companies registered on or after 1 October 2007, the words in square brackets replaced with the words 'a special' by the Companies (Tables A to F) (Amendment) Regulations 2007, SI 2007/2541.

*Indemnity*

**118.** Subject to the provisions of the Act but without prejudice to any indemnity to which a director may otherwise be entitled, every director or other officer or auditor of the company shall be indemnified out of the assets of the company against any liability incurred by him in defending any proceedings, whether civil or criminal, in which judgment is given in his favour or in which he is acquitted or in connection with any application in which relief is granted to him by the court from liability for negligence, default, breach of duty or breach of trust in relation to the affairs of the company.<sup>a</sup>

AMENDMENTS AND NOTES

<sup>a</sup> See the commentary to regulation 136 of the 1948 Table A.

# THE MODEL ARTICLES

*Default application of model articles*

The Companies Act 2006 ('the 2006 Act') has retained and expanded the principle of the default application of model articles which existed under the Companies Act 1985 in Table A[20] and which has existed under previous Companies Acts since 1856. **51.MA.01**

Explanatory Note 71 to the 2006 Act confirms the standard rationale for the default operation of model articles and states that such articles are intended to operate as a safety net to allow the company to operate effectively, in circumstances where a company has failed to provide for a particular eventuality in its articles. **51.MA.02**

The Companies (Model Articles) Regulations 2008 ('the Regulations') were made on 16 December 2008, under the authority conferred by section 19(1) of the 2006 Act (as to which see paragraph 51.MA.07 below). They came into force on 1 October 2009. The Regulations prescribe forms of model articles for three different types of company: (i) private companies limited by shares; (ii) private companies limited by guarantee; and (iii) public companies. The Regulations apply by default to companies of the corresponding type incorporated under the 2006 Act on or after 1 October 2009, save to the extent that the Regulations are excluded or modified, whether explicitly or implicitly, by separate articles of association devised by the company. **51.MA.03**

Table A[21] continues to apply by default to companies limited by shares that were incorporated under the Companies Act 1985. Moreover, companies incorporated under the 2006 Act can still choose to adopt certain of the provisions of Table A, if they first exclude the application of the relevant form of model articles under the Regulations. **51.MA.04**

---

[20] Companies (Tables A to F) Regulations 1985, SI 1985/805; see paras 51.TA.01–51.TA.08.
[21] Companies (Tables A to F) Regulations 1985, SI 1985/805; see paras 51.TA.01–51.TA.08.

*Statutory framework*

**51.MA.05**   The sections of the 2006 Act that relate to a company's constitution are set out in Part 3 of the Act. Chapter 2 of Part 3 sets out the provisions relating to a company's articles of association (sections 18 to 28).

**51.MA.06**   Section 18(1) provides that a company must have articles of association to prescribe the basis on which the company and its members should regulate themselves. Section 18(2) provides that a company must register articles of its own devising, save in circumstances where model articles apply by default to the company. Section 18(3) provides that any articles of association registered by a company must be contained in a single document and be divided into paragraphs that are numbered consecutively (as to which see paragraph 51.MA.17).

**51.MA.07**   Section 19(1) of the 2006 Act confers on the Secretary of State the power to make regulations to prescribe model articles of association for companies. Section 19(2) provides that different forms of model articles may be prescribed for different descriptions of company. The 2006 Act does not stipulate how the Secretary of State should exercise this discretion when deciding for which descriptions of company model articles should be prescribed.

**51.MA.08**   Section 20 sets out the framework for the default application of model articles. Section 20(1) confirms that the default application applies to limited companies. This is broader than the scope of the corresponding provision in the Companies Act 1985 (section 8(2)), which provided that the default application would only operate in respect of companies limited by shares. (Whilst proposed forms of articles of association did exist for certain other types of company under the Companies Act 1985 (for example, Table C, Table D, and Table F), those forms of articles did not operate by default.)

**51.MA.09**   Section 20(1)(a) and (b) confirm that the relevant model articles will apply to a limited company either: (i) if it has not registered articles of association of its own devising; or (ii) to the extent that the articles of association it has registered do not exclude or modify the relevant model articles. This corresponds to the previous position under section 8(2) of the Companies Act 1985. Section 20(2) defines what is meant by the relevant model articles in section 20(1) and stipulates that it means the 'model articles prescribed for a company of that description'.

**51.MA.10**   Section 20(2) confirms that the model articles that apply to a company will be the model articles which have been prescribed for a company of the corresponding description and which are in force at the date on which the company is registered. This provision should be read in conjunction with section 19(4), which provides that any amendments made to the model articles by regulations made by the Secretary of State under section 19 will not affect a company that has been registered before the amendment takes effect. This is consistent with the approach taken in the Companies Act 1985. However, it does leave the question open, as raised in paragraph 51.TA.03, as to the effect of any amendment made to the Regulations other than by means of further secondary legislation made under section 19(1) of the 2006 Act.

*Consultation process*

**51.MA.11**   Several drafts of each of the forms of model articles contained in the Regulations were issued for consultation.[22] As part of this process, and to accompany successive drafts of the Regulations, DBERR (now DBIS)[23] issued commentaries on the consultation process in which it set out its policy intentions and rationale for taking the drafting approach that has been adopted. Reference is made in this section to certain of the policy approaches taken by DBERR (now DBIS) as a result of this consultation process.

---

[22]   The original draft form of model articles for private companies was first published in March 2005, as part of the White Paper on Company Law Reform. A consultation draft of the form of model articles for public companies was first published by the DTI in June 2006. Revised drafts of each of these sets of regulations, together with a form of model articles for private companies limited by guarantee, were then published in February 2007 as part of the DTI publication *Implementation of Companies Act 2006*, which also included general and specific commentary on the approach to the model articles (Chap 3). Successive drafts of the three sets of articles were published in August 2007 (URN 07/1227/GR) and April 2008 (URN 08/706/GR and URN 08/707/GR), as a result of the Government's ongoing consultation process, together with explanatory notes commenting on respondents' comments and the rationale for the changes that had been made.

[23]   The Department for Business, Innovation and Skills (formerly the Department of Trade and Industry and the Department for Business, Enterprise and Regulatory Reform).

## Companies (Model Articles) Regulations 2008[24]

The Government's approach to the Regulations was driven by its recognition that the drafting of the provisions of Table A was 'user-unfriendly, poorly laid out and often unintelligible to non-specialists'.[25] It was noted that in addition to the drafting shortcomings, there were also many substantive areas addressed by Table A that were of minimal or no relevance to the vast majority of small, owner-managed private companies. Accordingly, the policy decision underlying the reform of Table A was to introduce: (i) a shorter, more simplified set of model articles for private companies limited by shares, in plainer English and covering those areas that were previously addressed in Table A that are also of relevance to smaller, owner-managed private companies; (ii) a longer set of model articles for public companies, to cover the same substantive areas that were covered in Table A, in plainer English and with clearer drafting; and (iii) a set of model articles for private companies limited by guarantee. In broad terms, the Regulations reflect the stated policy objective.

**51.MA.12**

This policy approach highlights two key differences of note between the approach taken under the 2006 Act and the corresponding framework and regulations under the Companies Act 1985.[26]

**51.MA.13**

Firstly, whereas the provisions of Table A applied by default to both private companies limited by shares and to public companies, separate forms of model articles have been prescribed for each of these types of company.

**51.MA.14**

Second, there is now a form of model articles for private companies limited by guarantee. The form of model articles prescribed by the Regulations for private companies limited by guarantee applies by default (to the extent that the articles are not excluded or modified, expressly or by virtue of the inclusion of inconsistent provisions) to all companies of that type. Previously, forms of articles were prescribed for private companies limited by guarantee and not having a share capital in Table C, and for private companies limited by guarantee and having a share capital in Table D.[27] However, those forms of articles of association did not operate by default to companies of the corresponding type: section 8(4)(c) of the Companies Act 1985 prescribed that a company of this type should submit articles in the form of Table C or Table D, as appropriate, or 'in a form as near that form as circumstances admit'. It should be noted that the form of model articles prescribed by the Regulations for private companies limited by guarantee does not contain any provisions relating to share capital.

**51.MA.15**

In the explanatory memorandum published by DBERR (now DBIS) that accompanied the publication of the Regulations, DBERR acknowledged that it only intended to prescribe model articles for the three most commonly used types of company.[28] It also acknowledged that forms of model articles of association could be prescribed for other types of company, but noted that such types of company either did not differ sufficiently from the types of company for which model articles have been prescribed to merit their own statutory set of model articles or that their requirements were such that they would typically require bespoke articles of association.[29]

**51.MA.16**

DBIS published its final guidance on the Regulations in September 2009 as part of its general guidance on constitutional matters under the 2006 Act.[30] Part 3 of this guidance is dedicated to the model articles, with the prime focus being on the model articles for private companies. The approach taken in the guidance as regards the model articles affirms the approach taken through the consultation process (as to which see paragraphs 51.MA.11 to 51.MA.16 above). The guidance also confirms that for the purposes of compliance with section 18(3) of the 2006 Act, it is sufficient when filing articles of association with the registrar for such articles to contain cross-references to any model articles that are being applied and, if relevant, to set out details of where any of the model articles are being modified (whether by the omission, amendment, and/or replacement of particular articles). This is consistent with the approach that was taken in relation to Table A under the Companies Act 1985.[31]

**51.MA.17**

---

[24] SI 2008/3229.

[25] White Paper on Company Law Reform, Chap 4, para 4.3.

[26] Companies (Tables A to F) Regulations 1985, SI 1985/805.

[27] Companies (Tables A to F) Regulations 1985, SI 1985/805.

[28] Explanatory Memorandum to the Companies (Model Articles) Regulations 2008, SI 2008/3229, para 7.2.

[29] Explanatory Memorandum to the Companies (Model Articles) Regulations 2008, SI 2008/3229, para 7.3.

[30] Department for Business, Innovation and Skills, *Companies Act 2006 final implementation—changes to constitutional documents, including model articles: a summary of what the new approach means* (September 2009).

[31] Department for Business, Innovation and Skills, *Companies Act 2006 final implementation—changes to constitutional documents, including model articles: a summary of what the new approach means* (September 2009), Part 1, para 1.36.

### Model articles of association for private companies limited by shares

**51.MA.18** The form of model articles for private companies limited by shares is a simplified and shortened form of Table A. In keeping with the Government's stated policy objective of 'thinking small first', these Regulations are predicated on the assumption that the majority of small private companies, whose generic needs the default articles are seeking to address, will have a simple capital structure, will only issue shares on a fully paid basis in certificated form and will not require provision for alternate directors.[32] Accordingly, provisions corresponding to those provisions in Table A that addressed these areas are not included in the default model articles for private companies limited by shares. The assumption is that where a company has more complex, bespoke needs it will devise its own articles to deal with these specific requirements. It is acknowledged that this may well be the case for more complex private companies.

### Model articles of association for private companies limited by guarantee

**51.MA.19** The model articles for private companies limited by guarantee are in substantially the same form as the form of model articles for private companies limited by shares, save that they include provisions relating to the guarantee given by members and the transfer of membership interests and do not include any of the provisions relating to the company's share capital. The approach is similarly predicated on the assumption that most private companies limited by guarantee only have comparatively simple requirements. It was noted that where a private company limited by guarantee might have more complex requirements, this would generally be a result of its specific circumstances which would be too individual to be addressed in a generic form of model articles of association.

### Model articles of association for public companies

**51.MA.20** The form of model articles for public companies is intended to cover all of the areas that were previously dealt with in Table A, save to the extent that matters, which were previously provided for in Table A are now dealt with in the 2006 Act (for example, Part 13 of the 2006 Act, which relates to resolutions and meetings). In its February 2007 consultation document, the DTI[33] reported, by way of clarification on the point, that the Government was not seeking to produce a set of model articles for public companies that would satisfy listing requirements or best practice requirements for companies admitted to trading on the main market of the London Stock Exchange or that would comply with rules or best practice requirements for companies traded on AIM and/or with the requirements of relevant institutional shareholder bodies and certain guidelines of the Institutional Shareholders' Committee. The assumption is that when a public company is to seek a listing of its shares it will obtain appropriate advice and put in place appropriate bespoke articles of association at that point. In paragraph 3.32 of its consultative document, DBERR (now DBIS) stated that it envisaged that the model articles for public companies would be used as a drafting resource for particular types of provision, rather than as a complete template for any company's articles. The report also notes that the Government anticipated that the model articles for public companies (or certain of the provisions contained in that form of model articles) would be of use to more complex private companies.

### Companies Act 2006

**51.MA.21** It should be noted that the model articles are not intended to duplicate provisions in relation to matters that are already addressed in the 2006 Act. This is most notably the case in relation to the provisions in Part 13 of the 2006 Act. Many of these provisions (or aspects of these provisions) were previously addressed in Table A but now fall within the scope of the 2006 Act itself.

**51.MA.22** The second point to note is that where the 2006 Act provides that a company's articles of association may vary or supplement a particular provision in the 2006 Act, as a general principle, the Regulations do not adopt the approach of providing any such variation, although in certain instances, they supplement the provisions of the 2006 Act.

---

[32] Department of Trade and Industry, *Implementation of Companies Act 2006* (February 2007), Ch 3, para 3.26.

[33] The Department of Trade and Industry, now the Department for Business, Innovation and Skills.

*Commentary on the Regulations*

The majority of the provisions in all three Schedules to the Regulations correspond to some degree to    **51.MA.23**
provisions in Table A. As a general principle, the intention has not been to restate the commentary on
the corresponding provision of Table A. Reference is, however, made to the corresponding provision
of Table A, if any. Save where the context indicates otherwise, references to Table A are to Table A of
the Companies Act 1985.[34]

As referred to at paragraph 51.MA.20 above, the form of model articles for public companies does not    **51.MA.24**
seek to address the approaches advocated by the Institutional Shareholders' Committee or various
institutional shareholder bodies for listed public companies. In keeping with this approach, the
commentary does not seek to indicate where the form of model articles would need to be varied or
supplemented in order to bring it in line with these requirements and constraints.

---

[34] Companies (Tables A to F) Regulations 1985, SI 1985/805.

MODEL ARTICLES APPLYING TO PRIVATE COMPANIES
LIMITED BY SHARES

## The Companies (Model Articles) Regulations 2008

SCHEDULE 1                                              Regulation 2

Model Articles for Private Companies Limited by Shares[a], [b], [c], [d]

PART 1
INTERPRETATION AND LIMITATION OF LIABILITY

**Defined terms**

51.MA.25     **1.**   In the articles, unless the context requires otherwise—

'articles' means the company's articles of association;[e]

'bankruptcy' includes individual insolvency proceedings in a jurisdiction other than England and Wales or Northern Ireland which have an effect similar to that of bankruptcy;

'chairman' has the meaning given in article 12;

'chairman of the meeting' has the meaning given in article 39;

'Companies Acts' means the Companies Acts (as defined in section 2 of the Companies Act 2006), in so far as they apply to the company;

'director' means a director of the company, and includes any person occupying the position of director, by whatever name called;[f]

'distribution recipient' has the meaning given in article 31;

'document' includes, unless otherwise specified, any document sent or supplied in electronic form;[g]

'electronic form' has the meaning given in section 1168 of the Companies Act 2006;

'fully paid' in relation to a share, means that the nominal value and any premium to be paid to the company in respect of that share have been paid to the company;[h]

'hard copy form' has the meaning given in section 1168 of the Companies Act 2006;

'holder' in relation to shares means the person whose name is entered in the register of members as the holder of the shares;

'instrument' means a document in hard copy form;

'ordinary resolution' has the meaning given in section 282 of the Companies Act 2006;

'paid' means paid or credited as paid;

'participate', in relation to a directors' meeting, has the meaning given in article 10;

'proxy notice' has the meaning given in article 45;

'shareholder' means a person who is the holder of a share;[i]

'shares' means shares in the company;

'special resolution' has the meaning given in section 283 of the Companies Act 2006;

'subsidiary' has the meaning given in section 1159 of the Companies Act 2006;

'transmittee' means a person entitled to a share by reason of the death or bankruptcy of a shareholder or otherwise by operation of law; and

'writing' means the representation or reproduction of words, symbols or other information in a visible form by any method or combination of methods, whether sent or supplied in electronic form or otherwise.[j]

Unless the context otherwise requires, other words or expressions contained in these articles bear the same meaning as in the Companies Act 2006 as in force on the date when these articles become binding on the company.

AMENDMENTS AND NOTES

[a]  This form of model articles applies by default to private companies limited by shares registered on or after 1 October 2009 (as to which see s 20 of the Companies Act 2006 (see Chapter 3)).

[b]  The form of model articles for private companies limited by shares adopts a different order to Table A. The order adopted is intended to reflect the relative order of importance that directors will attribute to those areas that the provisions cover (as to which see para 3.36 of Ch 3 of the *Implementation of Companies Act 2006* (Department of Trade and Industry (DTI)) (February 2007)). See also the form of model articles for public companies, which is predicated on the same approach but which inverts the order of Part 3 ('Shares and distributions') and Part 4 ('Decision making by shareholders').

[c]  See s 4(1) of the Companies Act 2006 for the definition of a 'private company' and s 3(1) and (2) of the Companies Act 2006 for the definitions of 'limited company' and 'limited by shares' (as to both sections, see Chapter 1).

ᵈ Per s 20(2) of the Companies Act 2006 (see Chapter 3), the form of model articles for private companies limited by shares applies by default to companies which are of that description at the point at which they are incorporated (save to the extent that the provisions of the model articles are modified or excluded), notwithstanding that they may subsequently be re-registered as a public or unlimited company.

ᵉ The change from 'regulations' in Table A to 'articles' in the Regulations is consistent with the change in approach in ss 19 and 20 of the Companies Act 2006 (see Chapter 3). Reference should also be made to para 76 of the Explanatory Notes that accompany the Companies Act 2006.

ᶠ The definition of the term 'director' is consistent with the definition given to that term in s 250 (see Chapter 10) of the Companies Act 2006. The term 'secretary' is not defined in the form of model articles for private companies: s 270 of the Companies Act 2006 (see Chapter 12) provides that a private company is not required to have a secretary.

ᵍ This definition expressly includes documents in electronic form within the meaning of s 1168 of the Companies Act 2006, which includes documents or information sent by electronic means (s 1168(3)(a)) but also extends to documents and information sent by any other means whilst in an electronic form (such as sending a disk by post) (see s 1168(3)(b)). See also article 48 of the form of model articles for private companies limited by shares.

ʰ The form of model articles for private companies limited by shares anticipates that all shares issued by such companies will be issued on a fully paid basis: this is in keeping with the Government's policy approach—as to which see para 51.MA.18. To the extent that the articles are to be tailored for a private company wanting the flexibility to be able to issue shares on a partly paid basis, the relevant provisions would need to be imported from the form of model articles for public companies.

ⁱ The form of model articles for public companies in Sch 3 also includes a definition of 'member' that is not included in the form of model articles for private companies limited by shares: this is consistent with the simplified drafting approach that has been taken in relation to the form of model articles for private companies limited by shares which avoids the duplication of definitions (as to the general principle, see para 51.MA.18). See also s 112 of the Companies Act 2006 (see Chapter 8), which defines a member as someone who agrees to become a member of the company and whose name is entered in the register of members. In this form of model articles a shareholder is defined as the person whose name is entered in the register of members as the holder of the relevant shares.

ʲ The scope of this definition includes not just physical hand or type written script, but also extends to other representations or reproductions of words that are evidenced on electronic media, so long as they satisfy the requirement to be in a visible form. The non-specific nature of this definition will allow it to keep pace with future technological developments: this reflects the general approach of ensuring that the form of the Regulations should be flexible and adaptable.

### Liability of members[a]

**2.** The liability of the members is limited to the amount, if any, unpaid on the shares held by them.  **51.MA.26**

AMENDMENTS AND NOTES

ᵃ Under the Companies Act 1985 a statement as to the limit of the liability of the members of that company was required to be included in a company's memorandum of association. This will ceased to be the case with effect from 1 October 2009, when the provisions of s 3 of the Companies Act 2006 came into force. This section requires a liability limitation statement to be included in the articles of association of any limited liability company (see also s 17 of the Companies Act 2006, which is considered in Chapter 3).

# PART 2
## DIRECTORS

### *Directors' Powers and Responsibilities*[a]

### Directors' general authority[b]

**51.MA.27**    **3.**   Subject to the articles, the directors are responsible for the management of the company's business, for which purpose they may exercise all the powers of the company.

AMENDMENTS AND NOTES

[a]  Whilst the Companies Act 2006 has codified a number of the directors' duties and responsibilities towards the company and its shareholders (ss 170–177 of the Companies Act 2006 (as to which, see Chapter 10)), it remains within the scope of the articles to stipulate what the directors can do. This article is broadly in line with the provisions of Table A reg 70. Reference should also be made to the provisions of s 171(a) and (b), which stipulate that a director must act in accordance with the company's constitution and only exercise the powers for the purposes for which they are conferred. See DTI, *Implementation of Companies Act 2006*, paras 3.44–3.47.

[b]  This article contemplates that the directors of a company will be able to exercise all of the powers of such company. Accordingly, the scope and extent of these delegated powers will be a function of the scope and extent of the objects of the company. For companies incorporated on or after 1 October 2009 (other than transitional companies within the meaning of s 2—see the Companies Act 2006 (Commencement No 8, Transitional Provisions and Savings) Order 2008, SI 2008/2860), s 31(1) of the Companies Act 2006 provides that a company will be deemed to have unrestricted objects, save where specific restrictions are contained in its articles of association.

### Shareholders' reserve power[a]

**51.MA.28**    **4.**   (1)  The shareholders may, by special resolution, direct the directors to take, or refrain from taking, specified action.
              (2)  No such special resolution invalidates anything which the directors have done before the passing of the resolution.

AMENDMENTS AND NOTES

[a]  This is a simplified re-statement of the outstanding part of Table A reg 70 that is not addressed in article 3. It is consistent with the principle that the members of a company may choose to exercise, or control the use of, the management function that has been delegated to the board (see DTI, *Implementation of Companies Act 2006*, para 3.48).

### Directors may delegate[a]

**51.MA.29**    **5.**   (1)  Subject to the articles, the directors may delegate any of the powers[b] which are conferred on them under the articles—
                  (a)  to such person or committee;
                  (b)  by such means (including by power of attorney);
                  (c)  to such an extent;
                  (d)  in relation to such matters or territories; and
                  (e)  on such terms and conditions;
                  as they think fit.
              (2)  If the directors so specify,[c] any such delegation may authorise further delegation of the directors' powers by any person to whom they are delegated.
              (3)  The directors may revoke any delegation in whole or part, or alter its terms and conditions.

AMENDMENTS AND NOTES

[a]  Article 5 articulates the possible scope and extent of what might be delegated and the manner of any such delegation in greater detail than was the case in the corresponding provision of Table A (regs 71 and 72).

[b]  This article contemplates delegation by the board of directors. The common law position remains that an individual director may not delegate his responsibility as a director (as to which, see the discussion at para 20 of the *Government response to consultation on the Companies Act 2006: model articles for companies incorporated on or after 1 October 2008* (Department for Business Enterprise and Regulatory Reform (DBERR)) (July 2007) (URN 07/1227/GR)).

[c]  The scope of the power to delegate is expressly limited in article 5(2): further delegation by a delegatee is only permitted to the extent that the directors have specifically authorised any such further delegation in their initial delegation. This provision was considered at length during the consultation process: it was considered appropriate to expressly impose this limitation upon the power to delegate (see DTI, *Implementation of Companies Act 2006*, paras 3.54–3.56).

### Committees[a]

**6.** (1) Committees to which the directors delegate any of their powers must follow procedures which are based as far as they are applicable on those provisions of the articles which govern the taking of decisions by directors.

    (2) The directors may make rules of procedure for all or any[b] committees, which prevail over rules derived from the articles if they are not consistent with them.

**51.MA.30**

AMENDMENTS AND NOTES

[a] In line with the approach in Table A, the term 'committee' is not defined in these articles. An early draft introduced a definition, but this was subsequently removed. The Government took the policy decision that there was no need to change the approach that was previously taken in Table A (see URN 07/1227/GR, para 14). This article is consistent with the approach of Table A reg 72, which sets out the basis for regulating committees. However, this article can be distinguished from the approach in reg 72 in one key respect: there is no longer an obligation to ensure that at least one of the members of the committee is a director of the company. This constraint was removed as a result of responses received during the consultation process. It is also worth noting in this regard that a committee may consist of just one person.

[b] The use of the words 'all or any' here is intended to make it clear that the board may make different rules for different committees (see URN 07/1227/GR, para 21).

## *Decision-Making by Directors*

### Directors to take decisions[a] collectively[b]

**7.** (1) The general rule about decision-making by directors is that any decision of the directors must be either a majority decision at a meeting or a decision taken in accordance with article 8.

    (2) If—

      (a) the company only has one director, and

      (b) no provision of the articles requires it to have more than one director,

    the general rule does not apply, and the director may take decisions without regard to any of the provisions of the articles relating to directors' decision-making.

**51.MA.31**

AMENDMENTS AND NOTES

[a] The provisions update the corresponding provisions in Table A: namely, regs 88 and 93.

[b] The form of model articles for private companies limited by shares provides that directors of private companies limited by shares may make decisions in one of two ways: (i) by means of a unanimous decision (evidence of which can be provided by a broad range of media); or (ii) by means of a majority decision taken by the directors at a duly convened board meeting. As to the case law on directors' unanimous decisions, see the commentary to Table A, reg 88.

### Unanimous decisions

**8.** (1) A decision of the directors is taken in accordance with this article when all eligible directors indicate to each other by any means[a] that they share a common view on a matter.

    (2) Such a decision may take the form of a resolution in writing,[b] copies of which have been signed by each eligible[c] director or to which each director has otherwise indicated agreement in writing.

    (3) References in this article to eligible directors are to director who would have been entitled to vote on the matter had it been proposed as a resolution at a directors' meeting.

    (4) A decision may not be taken in accordance with this article if the eligible directors would not have formed a quorum at the meeting.

**51.MA.32**

AMENDMENTS AND NOTES

[a] The policy decision underlying this article was the desire to reflect the fact that for small private companies, the decision process may not be taken formally at a meeting or by means of a formal written resolution. This article was intended to relax the more structured framework of Table A in this regard, and to facilitate the commercial reality that directors of small private companies may want to take decisions on a more ad hoc basis by means of a sequence of text messages, emails or phone calls (see DTI, *Implementation of Companies Act 2006*, paras 3.60 and 3.61). Whilst it does seem appropriate to modernize the approach taken in Table A, a practical consequence may be that there will be scope for dispute in certain circumstances as to whether a given sequence of text messages or emails do, in fact, demonstrate that the eligible directors have clearly indicated to each other that they share a 'common view' within the meaning of this article. See also article 15, which imposes an obligation on the directors to keep a record of all unanimous decisions made by the board of directors.

[b] The model articles for private companies limited by shares attribute greater weight to the written resolution regime than was the case under Table A reg 93 (see DTI, *Implementation of Companies Act 2006*, paras 3.77–3.82).

[c] Only eligible directors within the meaning of article 8(3) need participate in the unanimous decision procedure. See article 14(6) which, when read in conjunction with article 8(3), has the effect of conferring upon the chairman the right to determine whether or not a particular director is eligible in relation to a particular resolution.

### Calling a directors' meeting[a]

**51.MA.33**

**9.** (1) Any director may call a directors' meeting by giving notice of the meeting to the directors or by authorising the company secretary (if any) to give such notice.

(2) Notice of any directors' meeting must indicate—[b]

    (a) its proposed date and time;

    (b) where it is to take place; and

    (c) if it is anticipated that directors participating in the meeting will not be in the same place, how it is proposed that they should communicate with each other during the meeting.

(3) Notice of a directors' meeting must be given to each director, but need not be in writing.[c]

(4) Notice of a directors' meeting need not be given to directors who waive their entitlement to notice of that meeting, by giving notice to that effect to the company not more than 7 days after the date on which the meeting is held. Where such notice is given after the meeting has been held, that does not affect the validity of the meeting, or of any business conducted at it.[d]

AMENDMENTS AND NOTES

[a] The corresponding provision of Table A (reg 88) includes only very limited provisions regulating the calling of directors' meetings. Most notably, reg 88 provided that there was no obligation to give notice of a meeting to a director who was absent from the United Kingdom at the point at which notice of the meeting was given. This caveat has been removed from all three forms of model articles, in recognition of the fact that this is no longer a relevant distinction to make in light of modern communications technology (see DTI, *Implementation of the Companies Act 2006*, para 3.63). However, it is worth noting that there is persuasive authority to the effect that even in circumstances where the relevant section of reg 88 had been included in a company's articles of association, the extent to which directors were able to rely on this practice was more limited in circumstances where it would have been possible to give notice to an absentee director, notwithstanding that he was overseas.

[b] Article 9(2) prescribes the basic elements that need to be addressed in a notice of a board meeting. It does not impose an obligation to observe a particular notice period, nor does it impose an obligation to provide details of the matters to be considered at the meeting. In the absence of a specific notice period being prescribed under the articles of association of a company, the common law has determined that the notice period should be reasonable; the company's past practice will be relevant in determining whether or not a particular notice period meets this standard. A company may amend this as appropriate.

[c] This reflects the common law position that a notice of a meeting need not be in writing.

[d] An earlier draft of the model articles included a provision that would have enabled directors to give a blanket waiver of their right to receive notice of board meetings. Reliance on such a waiver by directors would have been likely to result in them being in breach of their statutory duties towards the company (see URN 07/1227/GR, para 25). The resulting provision is narrower and allows a director who is likely to be absent for a holiday, or otherwise absent, to give such a waiver prior to his departure or, indeed, up to seven days after the particular meeting has occurred.

### Participation in directors' meetings[a]

**51.MA.34**

**10.** (1) Subject to the articles, directors participate in a directors' meeting, or part of a directors' meeting, when—

    (a) the meeting has been called and takes place in accordance with the articles, and

    (b) they can each communicate to the others any information or opinions they have on any particular item of the business of the meeting.

(2) In determining whether directors are participating in a directors' meeting, it is irrelevant where any director is or how they communicate with each other.[b]

(3) If all the directors participating in a meeting are not in the same place, they may decide that the meeting is to be treated as taking place wherever any of them is[c].

AMENDMENTS AND NOTES

[a] There is no corresponding provision in Table A.

[b] This provision enables board meetings to be convened other than by means of a physical meeting where all are present: it permits meetings to be held by conference call or by video conference, or by any other means that would satisfy the requirement that the directors be able to communicate with each other (see DTI, *Implementation of the Companies Act 2006*, para 3.65). There is no definition of 'communication' for these purposes. This article is an expansion of Table A reg 88. Whilst reg 88

permits directors to regulate their proceedings as they see fit, it has never been beyond doubt that this would extend to convening telephone board meetings or convening meetings by video conference. The safe approach to the point has always been to include a specific, permissive article to sanction meetings being held remotely. Article 10 adopts this broader approach explicitly. See also the provisions of article 16.

<sup>c</sup> There is no corresponding provision in Table A. A common approach for companies that have adopted their own bespoke provisions on this point has been to provide that the meeting takes place where the majority of directors are present or where the chairman of the meeting is present.

### Quorum for directors' meetings[a], [b]

**11.** (1) At a directors' meeting, unless a quorum is participating, no proposal is to be voted on, except a proposal to call another meeting.

    (2) The quorum for directors' meetings may be fixed from time to time by a decision of the directors,[c] but it must never be less than two,[d] and unless otherwise fixed it is two.

    (3) If the total number of directors for the time being is less than the quorum required, the directors must not take any decision other than a decision—

        (a) to appoint further directors, or

        (b) to call a general meeting so as to enable the shareholders to appoint further directors.[e]

51.MA.35

AMENDMENTS AND NOTES

<sup>a</sup> This article corresponds to the provisions of Table A regs 89 and 90. See also article 7(2).

<sup>b</sup> The model articles for private companies limited by shares do not include provisions for the appointment of alternate directors. It should be noted that the ability to appoint an alternate is a matter to be addressed in the constitution of a particular company, as opposed to being a matter of statute. Consequently, in the absence of a specific provision on the point in a company's articles of association, a company incorporated with the model articles for private companies limited by shares will need to amend its articles in order to enable its directors to be able to appoint alternate directors. It was noted in the consultation process that there may be a requirement for directors of larger private companies to be able to appoint alternate directors. In these circumstances, it was contemplated that the relevant provisions of the form of model articles for public companies (namely articles 25–27) could be incorporated to this end.

<sup>c</sup> The members of the company may also amend the quorum requirements for board meetings by means of passing a special resolution to amend the articles of association of a company. However, during the course of the various rounds of the consultation process, it was determined that, in the first instance, it would be appropriate to leave this as a matter for the directors to regulate, as is the case under the corresponding provision of Table A (reg 89) (as to which, see DTI, *Implementation of Companies Act 2006*, para 3.68).

<sup>d</sup> However, see the provisions of s 154(1) of the Companies Act 2006 in this regard (see Chapter 10). The quorum requirement under the model articles for private companies limited by shares operates as an overlay to the statutory requirement to have just one director of a private company.

<sup>e</sup> This corresponds to Table A reg 90. However, the reference to vacancies in the number of directors that appeared in reg 90 has now been omitted. Until 1985, previous forms of Table A had provided that the number of directors a company was to have should be determined by the subscribers to its memorandum of association. On that basis, the number of directors was entrenched, thereby giving rise to the concept that vacancies or a vacancy arose as and when the number of directors of the company fell below this stipulated level. Private companies are now required to have one director; this provision is contained in s 154(1) of the Companies Act 2006 (as to which, see note 4 to para 51.MA.35).

### Chairing of directors' meetings

**12.** (1) The directors may[a] appoint a director to chair their meetings.

    (2) The person so appointed for the time being is known as the chairman.

    (3) The directors may terminate the chairman's appointment at any time.

    (4) If the chairman is not participating in a directors' meeting within ten[b] minutes of the time at which it was to start, the participating directors must appoint one of themselves to chair it.

51.MA.36

AMENDMENTS AND NOTES

<sup>a</sup> This is consistent with the approach in Table A reg 91, which permits the appointment of a chairman but does not make it mandatory.

<sup>b</sup> This is an expansion of the five-minute period referred to in the corresponding provision of Table A reg 91.

### Casting vote[a]

**51.MA.37**

**13.** (1) If the numbers of votes for and against a proposal are equal, the chairman or other director chairing the meeting has a casting vote.

(2) But this does not apply if, in accordance with the articles, the chairman or other director is not to be counted as participating in the decision-making process for quorum or voting purposes.

AMENDMENTS AND NOTES

[a] This corresponds to one of the provisions contained in Table A reg 88. As part of the consultation process, some concern was expressed as to whether this provision might be open to abuse. However, the view taken by the Government is that this is the only practical way of ensuring that proceedings may be unblocked in the event of a deadlock at board level. There may be certain types of company where commercially it is inappropriate to include this provision.

### Conflicts of interest[a], [b]

**51.MA.38**

**14.** (1) If a proposed decision of the directors is concerned with an actual or proposed transaction or arrangement[c] with the company in which a director is interested, that director is not to be counted as participating in the decision-making process for quorum or voting purposes.[d]

(2) But if paragraph (3) applies, a director who is interested in an actual or proposed transaction or arrangement with the company is to be counted as participating in the decision-making process for quorum and voting purposes

(3) This paragraph applies when—

(a) the company by ordinary resolution disapplies the provision of the articles which would otherwise prevent a director from being counted as participating in the decision-making process;

(b) the director's interest cannot reasonably be regarded as likely to give rise to a conflict of interest;[e] or

(c) the director's conflict of interest arises from a permitted cause.

(4) For the purposes of this article, the following are permitted causes—[f]

(a) a guarantee given, or to be given, by or to a director in respect of an obligation incurred by or on behalf of the company or any of its subsidiaries;

(b) subscription, or an agreement to subscribe, for shares or other securities of the company or any of its subsidiaries, or to underwrite, sub-underwrite, or guarantee subscription for any such shares or securities; and

(c) arrangements[g] pursuant to which benefits are made available to employees and directors or former employees and directors of the company or any of its subsidiaries which do not provide special benefits for directors or former directors.

(5) For the purposes of this article, references to proposed decisions and decision-making processes include any directors' meeting or part of a directors' meeting.

(6) Subject to paragraph (7), if a question arises at a meeting of directors or of a committee of directors as to the right of a director to participate in the meeting (or part of the meeting) for voting or quorum purposes, the question may, before the conclusion of the meeting, be referred to the chairman whose ruling in relation to any director other than the chairman is to be final and conclusive.[h]

(7) If any question as to the right to participate in the meeting (or part of the meeting) should arise in respect of the chairman, the question is to be decided by a decision of the directors at that meeting, for which purpose the chairman is not to be counted as participating in the meeting (or that part of the meeting) for voting or quorum purposes.

AMENDMENTS AND NOTES

[a] This provision deals with transactional conflicts of interest (namely those conflicts of interests contemplated in s 177 of the Companies Act 2006) and not with situational conflicts of interest (as contemplated in s 175 of the Companies Act 2006). It should be noted that the equitable rule that directors may not have interests in transactions with the company unless the interest has been authorised by the members has been replaced by the disclosure duty set out in s 177 (in this regard, see the effect of s 170(3) and the related Explanatory Note 347 to the Companies Act 2006). Table A reg 85 was historically included to provide the requisite shareholder authorization of directors' conflicts of interest. In view of the effect of s 170(3) and the broadened scope of s 177, this provision is no longer required in relation to transactional conflicts of interest. However, companies may continue to include additional provisions requiring explicit shareholder authorisation of transactional conflicts in their articles.

[b] For private companies incorporated on or after 1 October 2008, to the extent that there is nothing to the contrary included in their articles of association, the non-interested directors on the board of that company may rely on s 175(4)(b) of the Companies Act 2006 to authorise any situational conflict of interest that another director may have within the scope of s 175(1) of the Companies Act 2006.

c  This article reflects the language of ss 177 and 182 of the Companies Act 2006 with respect to transactional conflicts.

d  Article 14 in part restates and partly updates regs 94 and 95 of Table A, but is expressly limited to transactional conflicts. It is also worth noting that the scope of s. 177 is arguably broader than the scope of Article 14(1) inasmuch as it refers to a director being in any way, directly or indirectly, interested in a proposed transaction or arrangement with the company.

e  Conflicts of interest for the purpose of article 14(3)(b) appears to be confined to transactional conflicts within the meaning of ss 177 and 182 of the Companies Act 2006.

f  These provisions address substantially the same key carve-outs as were included in Table A reg 94(a)–(d) (see, however, note g to para 51.MA.38).

g  This provision was specifically broadened during the consultation process to enable it to extend to share incentive schemes which are not necessarily contracts.

h  This restates the provisions of Table A reg 98, but introduces a clarificatory carve-out in sub-para (7) of this article.

### Records of decisions to be kept[a]

**15.** The directors must ensure that the company keeps a record, in writing, for at least 10 years from the date of the decision recorded, of every unanimous or majority decision taken by the directors.

**51.MA.39**

AMENDMENTS AND NOTES

a  Section 248 of the Companies Act 2006 (see Chapter 10) requires companies to keep records of proceedings at directors' meetings. The effect of this article is that a company is under the same obligation in respect of any unanimous decisions that it reaches under article 8, which have not been reached at a directors' meeting. (In effect, this is an expansion of the corresponding provision of Table A (reg 100)).

### Directors' discretion to make further rules[a]

**16.** Subject to the articles, the directors may make any rule which they think fit about how they take decisions, and about how such rules are to be recorded or communicated to directors.

**51.MA.40**

AMENDMENTS AND NOTES

a  This is an expansion of the first sentence of Table A reg 88. Historically, one approach to the scope and extent of reg 88 has been that it is confined to the fixing of the timing of periodic meetings, the circulation of agendas and other administrative matters (see DTI, *Implementation of Companies Act 2006*, paras 3.84 and 3.85). This provision states explicitly that directors have the scope to 'fill in' any gaps (again, see para 3.85) with respect to any further rules that need to be made in relation to the manner in which they regulate their proceedings, subject always to the proviso that such additional rules do not contradict any other provisions of the articles.

## *Appointment of Directors*[a, b]

### Methods of appointing directors[c]

**17.** (1) Any person who is willing to act as a director, and is permitted by law to do so, may be appointed to be a director—

(a) by ordinary resolution, or

(b) by a decision of the directors.[d]

**51.MA.41**

(2) In any case where, as a result of death, the company has no shareholders and no directors, the personal representatives of the last shareholder to have died have the right, by notice in writing, to appoint a person to be a director.

(3) For the purposes of paragraph (2), where 2 or more shareholders die in circumstances rendering it uncertain who was the last to die, a younger shareholder is deemed to have survived an older shareholder.

AMENDMENTS AND NOTES

a  The model articles for private companies limited by shares do not provide for retirement by rotation.

b  Section 154(1) of the Companies Act 2006 (see Chapter 10) requires all private companies to have at least one director. Accordingly, there is no requirement to include a provision corresponding to Table A reg 64.

c  This provision restates Table A regs 78 and 79. See note e to paragraph 51.MA.35 above for the discussion on references to vacancies in the number of directors in a company. The position is now regulated by s 154(1) of the Companies Act 2006, which prescribes that a private company must have at least one director. However, the form of model articles for private companies assumes that the quorum for transacting business shall be two directors.

<sup>d</sup> For private companies, there is no requirement to have an appointment effected under article 17(1)(b) approved at a subsequent general meeting of the company (see para 16 of the *Government response to July 2007 consultation on the draft Companies Act 2006 model articles for companies incorporated on or after 1 October 2009* (DBERR) (March 2008) (URN 08/707/GR)). This contrasts with the position for public companies limited by shares, as to which, see article 51(3) below.

### Termination of director's appointment<sup>a</sup>

**51.MA.42**    **18.** A person ceases to be a director as soon as—

  (a)  that person ceases to be a director by virtue of any provision of the Companies Act 2006 or is prohibited from being a director by law;<sup>b</sup>

  (b)  a bankruptcy order is made against that person;

  (c)  a composition is made with that person's creditors generally in satisfaction of that person's debts;<sup>c</sup>

  (d)  a registered medical practitioner who is treating that person gives a written opinion to the company stating that that person has become physically or mentally incapable of acting as a director and may remain so for more than three months;

  (e)  by reason of that person's mental health, a court makes an order which wholly or partly prevents that person from personally exercising any powers or rights which that person would otherwise have;<sup>d</sup>

  (f)  notification is received by the company from the director that the director is resigning from office, and such resignation has taken effect in accordance with its terms.<sup>e</sup>

AMENDMENTS AND NOTES

<sup>a</sup> This is an updated restatement of the corresponding provision of Table A reg 81. In keeping with the approach taken in that regulation, this provision stipulates that a director will cease to hold office following the occurrence of certain trigger events. In addition, it is worth noting that a company may also remove a director by ordinary resolution pursuant to the provisions of s.168 of the Companies Act 2006.

<sup>b</sup> It is possible that such termination may be triggered in various circumstances, including by way of example, in the context of proceedings commenced under the Company Directors Disqualification Act 1986.

<sup>c</sup> This has been included to deal, in generic terms, with any other creditor arrangement (such as, but not limited to, an individual voluntary arrangement) that may be entered into by a director.

<sup>d</sup> The Government's intention with the drafting of sub-paras (d) and (e) was to remove references to the provisions of specific legislation that may be superseded; such references were previously included in sub-para (c)(i) of reg 81 of Table A (see DTI, *Implementation of Companies Act 2006*, para 3.99). Sub-paragraphs (d) and (e) of article 18 seek to capture circumstances in which a director has been judged (either by a court or by a doctor) to be suffering from physical or mental illness. The provision has been drafted so as to ensure that it does not capture people at the stage at which they are submitted for assessment, but who, ultimately, are not judged to be suffering from mental illness, as might have been the case under reg 81(c)(i) or (ii) of Table A.

<sup>e</sup> As part of the consultation process, an additional provision was rejected: this contemplated that a director could be removed from office in circumstances where the other directors were of a consensus that he should be removed. See URN 07/1227/GR, para 34 and URN 08/707/GR, para 18.

### Directors' remuneration<sup>a</sup>

**51.MA.43**    **19.** (1)  Directors may undertake any services for the company that the directors decide.

  (2)  Directors are entitled to such remuneration as the directors determine—

    (a)  for their services to the company as directors, and

    (b)  for any other service which they undertake for the company.

  (3)  Subject to the articles, a director's remuneration may—

    (a)  take any form, and

    (b)  include any arrangements in connection with the payment of a pension, allowance or gratuity, or any death, sickness or disability benefits, to or in respect of that director.

  (4)  Unless the directors decide otherwise, directors' remuneration accrues from day to day.

  (5)  Unless the directors decide otherwise, directors are not accountable to the company for any remuneration which they receive as directors or other officers or employees of the company's subsidiaries or of any other body corporate in which the company is interested.

AMENDMENTS AND NOTES

<sup>a</sup> Article 19 reflects the matters previously addressed in Table A regs 82 and 84, and addresses both types of remuneration that were contemplated in those regulations: (i) remuneration for services rendered to the company as a statutory director; and (ii) remuneration for services rendered to the company in some other executive function. However, whilst article 19 recognises both categories of service, there is no requirement to seek shareholder approval of remuneration for services rendered as a statutory director. In both cases, directors' remuneration is a matter to be determined by the board.

### Directors' expenses[a]

**20.** The company may[b] pay any reasonable expenses which the directors properly incur in connection with their attendance at—       **51.MA.44**

(a) meetings of directors or committees of directors,

(b) general meetings, or

(c) separate meetings of the holders of any class of shares or of debentures of the company,

or otherwise in connection with the exercise of their powers and the discharge of their responsibilities in relation to the company.

AMENDMENTS AND NOTES

<sup>a</sup> This is an expansion of Table A reg 83. The three sub-paragraphs referred to in this article 20 correspond to the three heads of expenditure contemplated in Table A reg 83. However, the last provision of this article broadens the scope to cover expenses that directors have properly incurred in circumstances other than those set out in sub-paras (a)–(c) of article 20. The default provisions have been broadened to take account of the fact that many directors now have responsibilities that extend beyond attendance at board meetings.

<sup>b</sup> As part of the consultation, the payment of expenses was reduced from a mandatory provision to a permissive provision (see URN 07/1227/GR, para 36).

Part 3

SHARES AND DISTRIBUTIONS

*Shares*<sup>a</sup>

### All shares to be fully paid up[b]

**21.** (1) No share is to be issued for less than the aggregate of its nominal value and any premium to be paid to the company in consideration for its issue.       **51.MA.45**

(2) This does not apply to shares taken on the formation of the company by the subscribers to the company's memorandum.

AMENDMENTS AND NOTES

<sup>a</sup> As a consequence of the fact that the articles do not contemplate that shares may be issued on a partly paid basis (with the one exception of the subscriber shares, as to which, see the provisions of article 21(2)), there is no need to provide in these articles for liens over partly paid shares and for forfeiture or surrender of such shares.

<sup>b</sup> The Government's stated assumption is that private companies that wish to have a more elaborate share structure are likely to draft specific provisions to deal with this. The default setting for these articles is aimed at companies with a relatively simple share structure (see para 51.MA.18). As referred to at para 51.MA.18, the approach in the form of model articles for private companies limited by shares is predicated on the assumption that all shares will be issued on a fully paid-up basis. In addition, there are no provisions for dematerialized shares or for share warrants (as to which, see articles 50 and 51 of the model articles for public companies). There is no corresponding provision in Table A.

### Powers to issue different classes of share[a]

**22.** (1) Subject to the articles, but without prejudice to the rights attached to any existing share, the company may issue shares[b] with such rights or restrictions as may be determined by ordinary resolution.       **51.MA.46**

(2) The company may issue shares which are to be redeemed, or are liable to be redeemed at the option of the company or the holder, and the directors may determine the terms, conditions and manner of redemption of any such shares.[c]

AMENDMENTS AND NOTES

<sup>a</sup> This corresponds to the provisions of Table A regs 2 and 3.

<sup>b</sup> Section 545 of the Companies Act 2006 (see Chapter 17) defines companies having a share capital for the purposes of the Act as being companies that have a power under their constitution to issue shares.

<sup>c</sup> Section 684(1) of the Companies Act 2006 (see Chapter 18), which comes into force on 1 October 2009, provides that private companies limited by shares may issue redeemable shares. Section 684(2) provides that such an issue may be specifically excluded or restricted in the articles. In the absence of such a provision, the default setting under the Companies Act is that a private company may make such an issue: consequently, there is no requirement to include the first part of article 22(2) in order for such a company to be able to make such an issue. However, the second part of article 22(2) confers the power on directors contemplated under s 685(1)(a) of the Companies Act 2006, which does need to be specifically included if it is to apply.

### Company not bound by less than absolute interests[a]

**51.MA.47**

**23.** Except as required by law, no person is to be recognised by the company as holding any share upon any trust, and except as otherwise required by law or the articles, the company is not in any way to be bound by or recognise any interest in a share other than the holder's absolute ownership of it and all the rights attaching to it.

AMENDMENTS AND NOTES

<sup>a</sup> This restates the provisions of Table A reg 5. See also s 126 of the Companies Act 2006 (see Chapter 8). The provisions of this article do permit, and are not inconsistent with, the provisions of the nomination arrangements contemplated in s 145 of the Companies Act 2006 (see Chapter 9). These provisions operate as an additional statutory overlay where the shareholders have expressly approved the adoption of arrangements in their articles which will enable a shareholder to nominate another person or persons as entitled to enjoy or exercise all or any specified rights of the member in relation to the company. Consistent with the more simplified drafting approach taken in the form of model articles for private companies limited by shares, these articles do not include provisions within the meaning of s 145. As part of the consultation process relating to the form of model articles for public companies, the Government indicated that it did not think that it was appropriate to enable the s 145 regime as a default approach; but thought that it would be more appropriate to leave individual companies to enable this regime, if they elected to do so (see URN 07/1227/GR, paras 60 and 61).

### Share certificates[a], [b]

**51.MA.48**

**24.** (1) The company must issue each shareholder, free of charge, with one or more certificates in respect of the shares which that shareholder holds.
  (2) Every certificate must specify—
    (a) in respect of how many shares, of what class, it is issued;
    (b) the nominal value of those shares;
    (c) that the shares are fully paid;<sup>c</sup> and
    (d) any distinguishing numbers assigned to them.<sup>d</sup>
  (3) No certificate may be issued in respect of shares of more than one class.
  (4) If more than one person holds a share, only one certificate may be issued in respect of it.
  (5) Certificates must—
    (a) have affixed to them the company's common seal, or
    (b) be otherwise executed in accordance with the Companies Acts.<sup>e</sup>

AMENDMENTS AND NOTES

<sup>a</sup> Sections 769 and 776 of the Companies Act 2006 (see Chapter 21) provide that a company must issue a share certificate following an allotment or transfer of shares. This article is consistent with those provisions. This article does not, however, restate the provisions of s 769(1) or 776(1) (see Chapter 21), which provide that a share certificate must be issued within two months of an allotment of shares or of the date of transfer of shares; this requirement will apply in any event as a matter of law.

<sup>b</sup> The provisions correspond to Table A reg 6.

<sup>c</sup> This provision is consistent with the general approach taken in the model articles for private companies limited by shares that shares in such companies may only be issued on a fully paid basis.

<sup>d</sup> Section 543 of the Companies Act 2006 (see Chapter 17) provides that distinguishing numbers need not be assigned to shares if (i) all of the issued shares in a company are fully paid up and rank pari passu for all purposes, or (ii) all of the issued shares of a particular class in a company are fully paid up and rank pari passu for all purposes. In view of the fact that the form of model articles for private companies limited by shares assumes that all shares will be issued on a fully paid basis, it is not clear when this provision would be of relevance, save with respect to the effect that the issue of the subscriber shares on a partly paid basis may have.

<sup>e</sup> This provides for share certificates to be executed in accordance with the provisions of ss 44–50 of the Companies Act 2006 (see Chapter 4). This includes the mode of execution introduced by s 44(2)(a), which permits one director to execute a deed with an attestation clause.

### Replacement share certificates[a]

**25.** (1)  If a certificate issued in respect of a shareholder's shares is—

    (a)  damaged or defaced, or

    (b)  said to be lost, stolen or destroyed,

    that shareholder is entitled to be issued with a replacement certificate in respect of the same shares.

    (2)  A shareholder exercising the right to be issued with such a replacement certificate—

      (a)  may at the same time exercise the right to be issued with a single certificate or separate certificates;

      (b)  must return the certificate which is to be replaced to the company if it is damaged or defaced; and

      (c)  must comply with such conditions as to evidence, indemnity and the payment of a reasonable fee as the directors decide.

**51.MA.49**

AMENDMENTS AND NOTES

[a]  This provision corresponds to the provisions of Table A reg 7.

### Share transfers[a]

**26.** (1)  Shares may be transferred by means of an instrument of transfer in any usual form or any other form approved by the directors, which is executed by or on behalf of the transferor.

    (2)  No fee may be charged for registering any instrument of transfer or other document relating to or affecting the title to any share.

    (3)  The company may retain any instrument of transfer which is registered.

    (4)  The transferor remains the holder of a share until the transferee's name is entered in the register of members as holder of it.

    (5)  The directors may refuse to register the transfer of a share,[b] and if they do so, the instrument of transfer must be returned to the transferee with the notice of refusal unless they suspect that the proposed transfer may be fraudulent.

**51.MA.50**

AMENDMENTS AND NOTES

[a]  This provision corresponds to the provisions of Table A regs 23 and 25–28. See also s 770 of the Companies Act 2006.

[b]  Sections 771(1)(b) and (2) of the Companies Act 2006 (see Chapter 21) provide that a company must give reasons for refusing to register a transfer of shares.

### Transmission of shares[a]

**27.** (1)  If title to a share passes to a transmittee, the company may only recognise the transmittee as having any title to that share.

    (2)  A transmittee who produces such evidence of entitlement to shares as the directors may properly require—

      (a)  may, subject to the articles, choose either to become the holder of those shares or to have them transferred to another person, and

      (b)  subject to the articles, and pending any transfer of the shares to another person, has the same rights as the holder had.

    (3)  But transmittees do not have the right to attend or vote at a general meeting, or agree to a proposed written resolution, in respect of shares to which they are entitled, by reason of the holder's death or bankruptcy or otherwise, unless they become the holders of those shares.

**51.MA.51**

AMENDMENTS AND NOTES

[a]  These provisions are confined to matters of company law procedure which are incidental to the transmission of shares. The Government stated that it did not want to include in any form of the model articles any 'substantive propositions of general law about property rights in the event of death, bankruptcy' or other operation of law provisions, as was the case with the corresponding provisions in Table A (regs 29–31) (see DTI, *Implementation of Companies Act 2006*, para 3.134).

### Exercise of transmittees' rights

**28.** (1)  Transmittees who wish to become the holders of shares to which they have become entitled must notify the company in writing of that wish.

    (2)  If the transmittee wishes to have a share transferred to another person, the transmittee must execute an instrument of transfer in respect of it.

    (3)  Any transfer made or executed under this article is to be treated as if it were made or executed by the person from whom the transmittee has derived rights in respect of the share, and as if the event which gave rise to the transmission had not occurred.

**51.MA.52**

**Transmittees bound by prior notices**

**51.MA.53**     **29.** If a notice is given to a shareholder in respect of shares and a transmittee is entitled to those shares, the transmittee is bound by the notice if it was given to the shareholder before the transmittee's name has been entered in the register of members.

## Dividends and Other Distributions[a]

**Procedure for declaring dividends[b]**

**51.MA.54**     **30.** (1) The company may by ordinary resolution declare dividends, and the directors may decide to pay interim dividends.[c]

 (2) A dividend must not be declared unless the directors have made a recommendation as to its amount. Such a dividend must not exceed the amount recommended by the directors.

 (3) No dividend may be declared or paid unless it is in accordance with shareholders' respective rights.

 (4) Unless the shareholders' resolution to declare or directors' decision to pay a dividend, or the terms on which shares are issued, specify otherwise, it must be paid by reference to each shareholder's holding of shares on the date of the resolution or decision to declare or pay it.[d]

 (5) If the company's share capital is divided into different classes, no interim dividend may be paid on shares carrying deferred or non-preferred rights if, at the time of payment, any preferential dividend is in arrear.[e]

 (6) The directors may pay at intervals any dividend payable at a fixed rate if it appears to them that the profits available for distribution justify the payment.

 (7) If the directors act in good faith,[f] they do not incur any liability to the holders of shares conferring preferred rights for any loss they may suffer by the lawful payment of an interim dividend on shares with deferred or non-preferred rights.

AMENDMENTS AND NOTES

[a]  These provisions correspond to regs 102–108 of Table A, with only minor modifications.

[b]  This provision corresponds to Table A regs 102–104.

[c]  Table A reg 102 included a requirement that directors were only entitled to declare and pay interim dividends if they were of the view that such dividends were justified by reference to the profits of the company available for distribution. This provision is now omitted. However, directors are obliged to comply with this requirement in any event, by virtue of the provisions of s 830(1) (and also ss 836 and 838, as the case may be) of the Companies Act 2006 (see Chapter 23).

[d]  This contrasts with the position under Table A reg 104, which provides that dividends shall be declared and paid according to the amounts paid up on the shares in respect of which the dividend is to be paid. The approach taken in this sub-paragraph is consistent with the general approach in the model articles for private companies limited by shares that shares may only be issued on a fully paid basis.

[e]  This corresponds to the same provision in Table A reg 103.

[f]  The reference to acting in good faith follows the approach taken in Table A reg 103. It is aimed at protecting directors from liability for negligence when paying interim dividends, provided that they act in good faith (see URN 08/707/GR, para 22).

**Payment of dividends and other distributions[a]**

**51.MA.55**     **31.** (1) Where a dividend or other sum which is a distribution is payable in respect of a share, it must be paid by one or more of the following means—

 (a) transfer to a bank or building society account specified by the distribution recipient either in writing or as the directors may otherwise decide;

 (b) sending a cheque made payable to the distribution recipient by post to the distribution recipient at the distribution recipient's registered address (if the distribution recipient is a holder of the share), or (in any other case) to an address specified by the distribution recipient either in writing or as the directors may otherwise decide;

 (c) sending a cheque made payable to such person by post to such person at such address as the distribution recipient has specified either in writing or as the directors may otherwise decide; or

 (d) any other means of payment as the directors agree with the distribution recipient either in writing or by such other means as the directors decide.

 (2) In the articles, 'the distribution recipient' means, in respect of a share in respect of which a dividend or other sum is payable—

 (a) the holder of the share; or

 (b) if the share has two or more joint holders, whichever of them is named first in the register of members; or

(c) if the holder is no longer entitled to the share by reason of death or bankruptcy, or otherwise by operation of law, the transmittee.

AMENDMENTS AND NOTES

[a] Sub-paragraphs (1)(a) and (d) of article 31 contemplate that more up-to-date payment practices may be used for payment of dividends than was the case under Table A reg 106, which only contemplated payment of dividends by means of a cheque.

### No interest on distributions

**32.** The company may not pay interest on any dividend or other sum payable in respect of a share unless otherwise provided by—
    (a) the terms on which the share was issued, or
    (b) the provisions of another agreement between the holder of that share and the company.[a]

**51.MA.56**

AMENDMENTS AND NOTES

[a] This provision corresponds to Table A reg 107. A dividend that is declared and which has become due and payable creates a debt for the amount that is due and payable as between the company and the relevant shareholder. However, the principle is that in the absence of a specific agreement to the contrary (whether in the articles or some other collateral agreement) this debt will not bear interest. Sub-paragraph (1)(b) of article 33 amplifies and clarifies the reference to 'rights attached to shares' that was previously included in Table A reg 107.

### Unclaimed distributions

**33.** (1) All dividends or other sums which are—
    (a) payable in respect of shares, and
    (b) unclaimed after having been declared or become payable,
    may be invested or otherwise made use of by the directors for the benefit of the company until claimed.[a]
  (2) The payment of any such dividend or other sum into a separate account does not make the company a trustee in respect of it.
  (3) If—
    (a) twelve years have passed from the date on which a dividend or other sum became due for payment, and
    (b) the distribution recipient has not claimed it,
    the distribution recipient is no longer entitled to that dividend or other sum and it ceases to remain owing by the company.

**51.MA.57**

AMENDMENTS AND NOTES

[a] Sub-paragraphs (1) and (2) of article 34 were not contained in the corresponding provision in Table A (reg 108). These sub-paragraphs permit a company to apply unclaimed dividend monies for its own purposes pending such monies being claimed by the distribution recipient. Sub-paragraph (3) restates Table A (reg 108).

### Non-cash distributions[a]

**34.** (1) Subject to the terms of issue of the share in question, the company may, by ordinary resolution on the recommendation of the directors, decide to pay all or part of a dividend or other distribution payable in respect of a share by transferring non-cash assets of equivalent value (including, without limitation, shares or other securities in any company).
  (2) For the purposes of paying a non-cash distribution, the directors may make whatever arrangements they think fit, including, where any difficulty arises regarding the distribution—
    (a) fixing the value of any assets;
    (b) paying cash to any distribution recipient on the basis of that value in order to adjust the rights of recipients; and
    (c) vesting any assets in trustees.

**51.MA.58**

AMENDMENTS AND NOTES

[a] This article corresponds to the provisions of Table A reg 105, with the one exception that there is no express ability under this article to issue certificates for fractional entitlements.

### Waiver of distributions[a]

**35.** Distribution recipients may waive their entitlement to a dividend or other distribution payable in respect of a share by giving the company notice in writing to that effect, but if—
    (a) the share has more than one holder, or
    (b) more than one person is entitled to the share, whether by reason of the death or bankruptcy of one or more joint holders, or otherwise,

**51.MA.59**

the notice is not effective unless it is expressed to be given, and signed, by all the holders or persons otherwise entitled to the share.

AMENDMENTS AND NOTES

[a] There is no corresponding provision in Table A.

## Capitalisation of Profits

### Authority to capitalise and appropriation of capitalised sums

**51.MA.60**

**36.** (1) Subject to the articles, the directors may, if they are so authorised by an ordinary resolution—

    (a) decide to capitalise any profits of the company (whether or not they are available for distribution) which are not required for paying a preferential dividend, or any sum standing to the credit of the company's share premium account or capital redemption reserve; and

    (b) appropriate any sum which they so decide to capitalise (a 'capitalised sum') to the persons who would have been entitled to it if it were distributed by way of dividend (the 'persons entitled') and in the same proportions.

  (2) Capitalised sums must be applied—

    (a) on behalf of the persons entitled, and

    (b) in the same proportions as a dividend would have been distributed to them.

  (3) Any capitalised sum may be applied in paying up new shares of a nominal amount equal to the capitalised sum which are then allotted credited as fully paid to the persons entitled or as they may direct.[a]

  (4) A capitalised sum which was appropriated from profits available for distribution may be applied in paying up new debentures of the company which are then allotted credited as fully paid to the persons entitled or as they may direct.

  (5) Subject to the articles the directors may—

    (a) apply capitalised sums in accordance with paragraphs (3) and (4) partly in one way and partly in another;

    (b) make such arrangements as they think fit to deal with shares or debentures becoming distributable in fractions under this article (including the issuing of fractional certificates or the making of cash payments); and

    (c) authorise any person to enter into an agreement with the company on behalf of all the persons entitled which is binding on them in respect of the allotment of shares and debentures to them under this article.

AMENDMENTS AND NOTES

[a] This article does not need to permit the application of any capitalized amounts to pay up unpaid share capital, since there is no concept of partly paid shares in this form of model articles. This contrasts to the position in Table A reg 110 and article 78(4)(a) of the model articles for public companies.

## Part 4
## DECISION-MAKING BY SHAREHOLDERS

### Organisation of General Meetings[a]

### Attendance and speaking at general meetings[b]

**51.MA.61**

**37.** (1) A person is able to exercise the right to speak at a general meeting when that person is in a position to communicate to all those attending the meeting, during the meeting, any information or opinions which that person has on the business of the meeting.

  (2) A person is able to exercise the right to vote at a general meeting when—

    (a) that person is able to vote, during the meeting, on resolutions put to the vote at the meeting, and

    (b) that person's vote can be taken into account in determining whether or not such resolutions are passed at the same time as the votes of all the other persons attending the meeting.

  (3) The directors may make whatever arrangements they consider appropriate to enable those attending a general meeting to exercise their rights to speak or vote at it.

  (4) In determining attendance at a general meeting, it is immaterial whether any two or more members attending it are in the same place as each other.

  (5) Two or more persons who are not in the same place as each other attend a general meeting if their circumstances are such that if they have (or were to have) rights to speak and vote at that meeting, they are (or would be) able to exercise them.

AMENDMENTS AND NOTES

a   Under the Companies Act 1985, most of the detailed provisions regulating general meetings were included in Table A. The Companies Act 2006 has modified this approach. As referred to at para 51.MA.21, Part 13 of the Companies Act 2006 addresses many of the substantive areas that were previously addressed in Table A (regs 36–39). Whilst the provisions of Part 13 do contemplate that individual companies may vary the statutory approach, as a general rule it has not been the Government's intention that any such modifications should be incorporated as part of the model articles. It is left to individual companies to tailor these articles of association as they think appropriate.

b   Article 37 contemplates either physical or virtual attendance at general meetings. Under sub-para (3), the directors are given a broad discretion to enable those who are in attendance to exercise their rights to speak or vote. The ability to speak for these purposes is satisfied when a person is able to communicate to all others who are in attendance, irrespective of whether this would be by means of actual speech or some other medium. There is no corresponding provision in Table A.

### Quorum for general meetings[a]

**38.** No business other than the appointment of the chairman of the meeting is to be transacted at a general meeting if the persons attending it do not constitute a quorum.     **51.MA.62**

AMENDMENTS AND NOTES

a   Table A reg 40 prescribed the quorum for general meetings. The quorum for general meetings is prescribed by s 318 of the Companies Act 2006 (see Chapter 13). This section provides that in the case of a company limited by shares that has only one member, a meeting will be quorate with one qualifying member present. Conversely, if the company has more than one member, then a meeting will be quorate, if at least two qualifying members are present, save if the articles of association of the company provide otherwise. A qualifying person is defined in s 318(3) of the Companies Act 2006.

### Chairing general meetings[a]

**39.** (1) If the directors have appointed a chairman, the chairman shall chair general meetings if present and willing to do so.     **51.MA.63**

    (2) If the directors have not appointed a chairman, or if the chairman is unwilling to chair the meeting or is not present within ten[b] minutes of the time at which a meeting was due to start—

      (a) the directors present, or

      (b) (if no directors are present), the meeting,

    must appoint a director or shareholder to chair the meeting, and the appointment of the chairman of the meeting must be the first business of the meeting.

    (3) The person chairing a meeting in accordance with this article is referred to as 'the chairman of the meeting'.

AMENDMENTS AND NOTES

a   Section 319(1) of the Companies Act 2006 (see Chapter 13) provides that the shareholders of a company may appoint one of their number to be the chairman of a general meeting, by means of an ordinary resolution. This provision is expressed to be subject to any provision in the articles which states who shall be chairman. Article 39(1) is a restatement of Table A reg 42 and provides that in circumstances where the directors have appointed a chairman (as to which, see article 12), the chairman of the board shall also be the chairman of any general meeting.

b   This is a modification of the position in Table A (reg 43), which contemplates a waiting period of 15 minutes.

### Attendance and speaking by directors and non-shareholders[a]

**40.** (1) Directors may attend and speak at general meetings, whether or not they are shareholders.     **51.MA.64**

    (2) The chairman of the meeting may permit other persons who are not—

      (a) shareholders of the company, or

      (b) otherwise entitled to exercise the rights of shareholders in relation to general meetings,

    to attend and speak at a general meeting.

AMENDMENTS AND NOTES

a   This corresponds to the provisions of Table A reg 44, save that the provision has been expanded to include the ability to permit other persons (not being shareholders or persons who are entitled to exercise shareholders' rights at general meetings) to attend general meetings. This confers a fairly broad discretion upon the chairman. In practice, the shareholders may wish to expand this provision to stipulate how this discretion may be exercised.

**Adjournment**[a]

**51.MA.65**  **41.** (1) If the persons attending a general meeting within half an hour of the time at which the meeting was due to start do not constitute a quorum, or if during a meeting a quorum ceases to be present, the chairman of the meeting must adjourn it.[b]

(2) The chairman of the meeting may adjourn a general meeting at which a quorum is present if—[c]

    (a) the meeting consents to an adjournment, or

    (b) it appears to the chairman of the meeting that an adjournment is necessary to protect the safety of any person attending the meeting or ensure that the business of the meeting is conducted in an orderly manner.

(3) The chairman of the meeting must adjourn a general meeting if directed to do so by the meeting.[d]

(4) When adjourning a general meeting, the chairman of the meeting must—

    (a) either specify the time and place to which it is adjourned or state that it is to continue at a time and place to be fixed by the directors,[e] and

    (b) have regard to any directions as to the time and place of any adjournment which have been given by the meeting.

(5) If the continuation of an adjourned meeting is to take place more than 14 days after it was adjourned, the company must give at least 7 clear days' notice of it (that is, excluding the day of the adjourned meeting and the day on which the notice is given)—

    (a) to the same persons to whom notice of the company's general meetings is required to be given, and

    (b) containing the same information which such notice is required to contain.

(6) No business may be transacted at an adjourned general meeting which could not properly have been transacted at the meeting if the adjournment had not taken place.

AMENDMENTS AND NOTES

[a] This article expands the provisions of Table A reg 45 (as to which, see notes b–e to para 51.MA.65).

[b] This article includes some minor modifications not included in the corresponding provision of Table A (reg 41). This article makes it clear that the power to adjourn the meeting in these circumstances is conferred upon the chairman. The provision previously contained in Table A reg 41, which automatically adjourned the meeting to the same time and place in the next week in such circumstances, has been removed.

[c] The provisions of article 41(2)(a) correspond to certain provisions of Table A reg 45. Article 41(2)(b) confers a power on the chairman not previously expressly included in Table A.

[d] There was no corresponding provision in Table A. The manner in which the meeting should direct the chairman that the meeting has been adjourned is not specified.

[e] Article 41(4)(a) provides for two possibilities, the latter of which would, in theory, permit the directors the possibility of an indefinite adjournment (see DTI, *Implementation of Companies Act 2006*, para 3.117). There is no corresponding provision in Table A.

## Voting at General Meetings[a]

**Voting: general**

**51.MA.66**  **42.** A resolution put to the vote of a general meeting must be decided on a show of hands unless a poll is duly demanded in accordance with the articles.[b]

AMENDMENTS AND NOTES

[a] With effect from 1 October 2007, private companies ceased to be under a statutory obligation to convene an annual general meeting. Also with effect from 1 October 2007, the provisions relating to extraordinary general meetings were repealed, with the effect that all meetings of the shareholders of a private company are now referred to as general meetings.

[b] The corresponding provision of Table A (reg 46) was amended to reflect the position in ss 281 and 282 of the Companies Act 2006 (see Chapter 13), which came into force on 1 October 2007 and which no longer permit a chairman to have a casting vote in respect of matters tabled at a general meeting of the company. For companies incorporated prior to 1 October 2007, paragraph 23A of Schedule 3 to the Companies Act 2006 (Commencement No. 3, Consequential Amendments, Transitional Provisions and Savings) Order 2007 includes a saving provision which allows companies that had a provision in their articles prior to 1 October 2007 giving the chairman a casting vote in the event of an equality of votes on an ordinary resolution (whether on a poll or a show of hands) to retain that provision, or, if it was removed after 1 October 2007, to reinstate it.

**Errors and disputes**

**43.** (1)  No objection may be raised to the qualification of any person voting at a general meeting          **51.MA.67**
except at the meeting or adjourned meeting at which the vote objected to is tendered, and
every vote not disallowed at the meeting is valid.

(2)  Any such objection must be referred to the chairman of the meeting, whose decision is final.[a]

AMENDMENTS AND NOTES

[a]  Whilst one of the respondents to the consultation process noted that the discretion conferred upon
the chairman in this situation was open to abuse, in line with the approach in Table A reg 58, the
Government decided to retain this provision in the interests of certainty of procedure.

**Poll votes**

**44.** (1)  A poll on a resolution may be demanded—          **51.MA.68**
   (a)  in advance of the general meeting where it is to be put to the vote,[a] or
   (b)  at a general meeting, either before a show of hands on that resolution or immediately
        after the result of a show of hands on that resolution is declared.

(2)  A poll may be demanded by—[b]
   (a)  the chairman of the meeting;
   (b)  the directors;[c]
   (c)  two or more persons having the right to vote on the resolution;[d] or
   (d)  a person[e] or persons representing not less than one tenth of the total voting rights of all
        the shareholders having the right to vote on the resolution.[f]

(3)  A demand for a poll may be withdrawn if—
   (a)  the poll has not yet been taken, and
   (b)  the chairman of the meeting consents to the withdrawal.

(4)  Polls must be taken immediately and in such manner as the chairman of the meeting directs.[g]

AMENDMENTS AND NOTES

[a]  There was no corresponding provision under the provisions of Table A which explicitly permitted
a shareholder with the requisite shareholding to call for a poll in advance of a meeting. In practice,
it may be that this provision is more suited for use by institutional shareholders in public
companies.

[b]  The provisions of article 45(2) are consistent with the requirements of s 321(2) of the Companies
Act 2006 (see Chapter 13).

[c]  Under the corresponding provisions of Table A (regs 46, 48, 49 and 51), the directors of a company
did not have the right to call for a poll vote. The drafting of the article does not state whether a
majority of the directors present could call for a poll vote in these circumstances or whether it would
require unanimity on their part.

[d]  This provision is consistent with the corresponding provision in Table A (reg 46). However, the
right to demand a vote on a poll is now triggered by an entitlement to vote on the resolution in
respect of which the poll vote is being sought, as opposed to the previous formulation, where the
right to demand a vote on a poll was triggered by a right to vote at the meeting in question. See also
s 321(2) of the Companies Act 2006 on this point. Certain respondents to the consultation process
indicated that two shareholders was too low a threshold in this regard, in the absence of an
additional aggregate shareholding requirement (see URN 07/1227/GR, para 46 and DTI, *Implementation of Companies Act 2006*, para 3.119). However, the Government thought that it was
appropriate to preserve the approach previously taken under Table A.

[e]  The model articles now refer to 'person' or 'persons', whereas the corresponding provision in Table
A (reg 46) referred to 'member' or 'members'. This permits the provisions to operate as regards any
person nominated to exercise rights under s 145 of the Companies Act 2006 (albeit that no enabling
provisions to this effect are included in the form of model articles for private companies limited by
shares). See note a to para 51.MA.47. The drafting of this article also contemplated that the right to
call for a poll may be exercised by a person nominated by an underlying shareholder, who would
otherwise have the right to call for such a poll. Similarly, the reference to person would also capture
corporate representatives who have been appointed under s 323 of the Companies Act 2006 (see
Chapter 13). It should also be noted that the effect of article 44 is consistent with the provisions of
s 329 of the Companies Act 2006 (see Chapter 13), which provides that the demand for a poll by a
proxy is the same as the demand for a poll by a member.

[f]  The provision contained in Table A reg 46(d) has been removed: this section permitted a shareholder or shareholders who held voting shares representing no less than one-tenth of the total
amount of paid up voting share capital to call for a vote on a poll.

[g]  There are no provisions in the Companies Act 2006 which regulate the timing of taking a vote on a
poll. Therefore, it is open to the shareholders of a company to modify these provisions of their articles
of association, if required. However, the provisions of s 327(2) should also be noted in this regard.

### Content of proxy notices[a]

**51.MA.69**

**45.** (1) Proxies may only validly be appointed by a notice in writing (a 'proxy notice') which—

(a) states the name and address of the shareholder appointing the proxy;

(b) identifies the person appointed to be that shareholder's proxy and the general meeting in relation to which that person is appointed;

(c) is signed by or on behalf of the shareholder appointing the proxy, or is authenticated in such manner as the directors may determine;[b] and

(d) is delivered to the company in accordance with the articles and any instructions contained in the notice of the general meeting to which they relate.

(2) The company may require proxy notices to be delivered in a particular form, and may specify different forms for different purposes.

(3) Proxy notices may specify how the proxy appointed under them is to vote (or that the proxy is to abstain from voting) on one or more resolutions.

(4) Unless a proxy notice indicates otherwise, it must be treated as—

(a) allowing the person appointed under it as a proxy discretion as to how to vote on any ancillary or procedural resolutions put to the meeting, and

(b) appointing that person as a proxy in relation to any adjournment of the general meeting to which it relates as well as the meeting itself.

AMENDMENTS AND NOTES

[a] This contrasts with the approach in the corresponding provision of Table A (reg 60), which prescribed the format of a proxy notice.

[b] See note b to para 51.MA.154, with respect to authentication of forms of proxy submitted in relation to dematerialized shares (see also URN 07/1227/GR, para 44).

### Delivery of proxy notices

**51.MA.70**

**46.** (1) A person who is entitled to attend, speak or vote (either on a show of hands or on a poll) at a general meeting remains so entitled in respect of that meeting or any adjournment of it, even though a valid proxy notice has been delivered to the company by or on behalf of that person.

(2) An appointment under a proxy notice may be revoked by delivering to the company a notice given by or on behalf of the person by whom or on whose behalf the proxy notice was given.

(3) A notice revoking a proxy appointment only takes effect if it is delivered before the start of the meeting or adjourned meeting to which it relates.

(4) If a proxy notice is not executed by the person appointing the proxy, it must be accompanied by written evidence of the authority of the person who executed it to execute it on the appointor's behalf.

### Amendments to resolutions

**51.MA.71**

**47.** (1) An ordinary resolution to be proposed at a general meeting may be amended by ordinary resolution[a] if—

(a) notice of the proposed amendment is given to the company in writing by a person entitled to vote at the general meeting at which it is to be proposed not less than 48 hours[b] before the meeting is to take place (or such later time as the chairman of the meeting may determine), and

(b) the proposed amendment does not, in the reasonable opinion of the chairman of the meeting, materially alter the scope of the resolution.

(2) A special resolution to be proposed at a general meeting may be amended by ordinary resolution,[c] if—

(a) the chairman of the meeting proposes the amendment at the general meeting at which the resolution is to be proposed, and

(b) the amendment does not go beyond what is necessary to correct a grammatical or other non-substantive[d] error in the resolution.

(3) If the chairman of the meeting, acting in good faith, wrongly decides that an amendment to a resolution is out of order, the chairman's error does not invalidate the vote on that resolution.

AMENDMENTS AND NOTES

[a] Article 47(1) is intended to state the common law position as regards the ability to amend an ordinary resolution by means of a further ordinary resolution. There was no corresponding provision in Table A. The 48-hour rule restricts the ability to submit late proposed changes to a meeting; it is not clear that this restriction applied under the pre-existing common law.

[b] This timeline is intended to reduce the risk of matters being raised by shareholders immediately prior to or at the meeting.

<sup>c</sup> Articles 47(2) is intended to state the common law position as regards the ability to amend a special resolution.

<sup>d</sup> There may be circumstances in which a manifest clerical error does not amount to either a grammatical or other non-substantive error, and where this language may have a limiting effect.

## Part 5
## ADMINISTRATIVE ARRANGEMENTS

### Means of communication to be used<sup>a</sup>

**48.** (1) Subject to the articles, anything sent or supplied by or to the company under the articles may be sent or supplied in any way in which the Companies Act 2006 provides for documents or information which are authorised or required by any provision of that Act to be sent or supplied by or to the company.

    (2) Subject to the articles, any notice or document to be sent or supplied to a director in connection with the taking of decisions by directors may also be sent or supplied by the means by which that director has asked to be sent or supplied with such notices or documents for the time being.<sup>b</sup>

    (3) A director may agree with the company that notices or documents sent to that director in a particular way are to be deemed to have been received within a specified time of their being sent, and for the specified time to be less than 48 hours.

**51.MA.72**

AMENDMENTS AND NOTES

<sup>a</sup> Whilst the language in this section is conformed to the language used in the provisions relating to electronic communications in the Companies Act 2006 and contemplates that documents may be supplied in any format contemplated by these provisions, the form of model articles for private companies limited by shares does not include the additional optional language required to facilitate shareholder approval of communication by means of a website or consent to the use of a specified email address provided by a shareholder, as contemplated in Part 3 ('Communications in electronic form') and Part 4 ('Communications by means of a website') of Sch 5 ('Communications by a company') of the Companies Act 2006. The Government decided not to include these provisions as a default setting in the model articles for private companies limited by shares, on the basis that, this is a matter that the shareholders of a given company can choose to consider and approve separately as a matter of individual choice for the company concerned. See note b at para 51.MA.195 and URN 07/1227/GR, para 62.

<sup>b</sup> The language in both of articles 49(1) and (2) has been conformed with the language in s 1143(1) of the Companies Act 2006.

### Company seals

**49.** (1) Any common seal may only be used by the authority of the directors.

    (2) The directors may decide by what means and in what form any common seal is to be used.

    (3) Unless otherwise decided by the directors, if the company has a common seal and it is affixed to a document, the document must also be signed by at least one authorised person in the presence of a witness who attests the signature.

    (4) For the purposes of this article, an authorised person is—

        (a) any director of the company;

        (b) the company secretary (if any); or

        (c) any person authorised by the directors for the purpose of signing documents to which the common seal is applied.

**51.MA.73**

### No right to inspect accounts and other records<sup>a</sup>

**50.** Except as provided by law or authorised by the directors or an ordinary resolution of the company, no person is entitled to inspect any of the company's accounting or other records or documents merely by virtue of being a shareholder.

**51.MA.74**

AMENDMENTS AND NOTES

<sup>a</sup> The Companies Act 2006 does not confer any rights on shareholders to inspect the company's accounting records or to inspect the minutes of board meetings. Shareholders are entitled to inspect records of resolutions and meetings upon request (s 358(3)) and may request copies of such documentation upon payment of a prescribed fee (s 358(4)). There are various other rights of inspection conferred as a matter of statute.

**Provision for employees on cessation of business[a]**

**51.MA.75**

**51.** The directors may decide to make provision for the benefit of persons employed or formerly employed by the company or any of its subsidiaries (other than a director or former director or shadow director) in connection with the cessation or transfer to any person of the whole or part of the undertaking of the company or that subsidiary.

AMENDMENTS AND NOTES

[a] There was no equivalent provision in Table A. Section 247 of the Companies Act 2006 (see Chapter 10) stipulates that the powers of the directors of a company extend to the power to make provision for the benefit of persons employed or formerly employed by the company, or any of its subsidiaries, in connection with the cessation or the transfer to any person of the whole or part of the undertaking of the company or that subsidiary. Section 247(4) provides that this power may only be exercised if it has been sanctioned either by a resolution of the company or a resolution of the directors. Article 51 provides the requisite authorisation in the articles of the directors' resolution, as contemplated in s 247(5)(a) of the Companies Act 2006.

## *Directors' Indemnity and Insurance*[a]

**Indemnity**

**51.MA.76**

**52.** (1) Subject to paragraph (2), a relevant director of the company or an associated company may be indemnified out of the company's assets against—

(a) any liability incurred by that director in connection with any negligence, default, breach of duty or breach of trust in relation to the company or an associated company,

(b) any liability incurred by that director in connection with the activities of the company or an associated company in its capacity as a trustee of an occupational pension scheme (as defined in section 235(6) of the Companies Act 2006),

(c) any other liability incurred by that director as an officer of the company or an associated company.

(2) This article does not authorise any indemnity which would be prohibited or rendered void by any provision of the Companies Acts or by any other provision of law.

(3) In this article—

(a) companies are associated if one is a subsidiary of the other or both are subsidiaries of the same body corporate, and

(b) a 'relevant director' means any director or former director of the company or an associated company.

AMENDMENTS AND NOTES

[a] During the course of the consultation process, the Government considered both: (i) the inclusion of elaborate indemnity and insurance provisions; and (ii) the complete omission of any such provisions. The final position has been to include short permissive articles which allow the requisite protection to be given to directors, subject always to the provisions of the Companies Act 2006 (see URN 08/707/GR, para 27). The provisions of the indemnity are restricted to cover directors and former directors of the company and any associated companies. This contrasts with the provisions of Table A reg 118, which contemplated other officers and auditors being indemnified. As part of the consultation process, the reference in earlier drafts to other officers was specifically excluded. Separate provisions in the Companies Act 2006 now regulate auditors' liability (see ss 532–538, which address auditors' liability limitation agreements (see Chapter 16)).

**Insurance**

**51.MA.77**

**53.** (1) The directors may decide to purchase and maintain insurance, at the expense of the company, for the benefit of any relevant director in respect of any relevant loss.

(2) In this article—

(a) a 'relevant director' means any director or former director of the company or an associated company

(b) a 'relevant loss' means any loss or liability which has been or may be incurred by a relevant director in connection with that relevant director's duties or powers in relation to the company, any associated company or any pension fund or employees' share scheme of the company or associated company, and

(c) companies are associated if one is a subsidiary of the other or both are subsidiaries of the same body corporate.

MODEL ARTICLES APPLYING TO PRIVATE COMPANIES
LIMITED BY GUARANTEE

## The Companies (Model Articles) Regulations 2008

SCHEDULE 2                                Regulation 3

Model Articles for Private Companies Limited by Gurantee[a, b, c, d]

PART 1
INTERPRETATION AND LIMITATION OF LIABILITY

**Defined terms**

1.   In the articles, unless the context requires otherwise—                **51.MA.78**
     'articles' means the company's articles of association;[e]
     'bankruptcy' includes individual insolvency proceedings in a jurisdiction other than England
         and Wales or Northern Ireland which have an effect similar to that of bankruptcy;
     'chairman' has the meaning given in article 12;
     'chairman of the meeting' has the meaning given in article 25;
     'Companies Acts' means the Companies Acts (as defined in section 2 of the Companies Act
         2006), in so far as they apply to the company;
     'director' means a director of the company, and includes any person occupying the position of
         director, by whatever name called;[f]
     'document' includes, unless otherwise specified, any document sent or supplied in electronic
         form;[g]
     'electronic form' has the meaning given in section 1168 of the Companies Act 2006;
     'member' has the meaning given in section 112 of the Companies Act 2006;[h]
     'ordinary resolution' has the meaning given in section 282 of the Companies Act 2006;
     'participate', in relation to a directors' meeting, has the meaning given in article 10;
     'proxy notice' has the meaning given in article 31;
     'special resolution' has the meaning given in section 283 of the Companies Act 2006;
     'subsidiary' has the meaning given in section 1159 of the Companies Act 2006; and
     'writing' means the representation or reproduction of words, symbols or other information in
         a visible form by any method or combination of methods, whether sent or supplied in
         electronic form or otherwise.[i]
     Unless the context otherwise requires, other words or expressions contained in these articles bear
     the same meaning as in the Companies Act 2006 as in force on the date when these articles
     become binding on the company.

AMENDMENTS AND NOTES

[a]  This form of model articles applies by default to private companies limited by guarantee registered
     on or after 1 October 2009 (as to which, see note b of the Companies Act 2006). ).

[b]  The form of model articles for private companies limited by guarantee follows a different order to
     Table A. The order is intended to reflect the relative order of importance that directors will attribute
     to the areas the provisions cover. See also note b to para 51.MA.25.

[c]  See s 4(1) of the Companies Act 2006 for the definition of private company.

[d]  Per s 20(2) of the Companies Act 2006, the form of model articles for private companies limited by
     guarantee applies by default to companies that are of that description at the point at which they are
     incorporated (save to the extent that the provisions of the regulations are modified or excluded),
     notwithstanding that they may subsequently be re-registered as a public or unlimited company.

[e]  See note e to para 51.MA.25.

[f]  See note f to para 51.MA.25.

[g]  See note g to para 51.MA.25.

[h]  There is no definition of 'shareholder' in these articles.

[i]  See note j to para 51.MA.25.

**Liability of members[a]**

2.   The liability of each member is limited to £1, being the amount that each member undertakes to     **51.MA.79**
     contribute to the assets of the company in the event of its being wound up while he is a member
     or within one year after he ceases to be a member, for
     (a)  payment of the company's debts and liabilities contracted before he ceases to be a member,
     (b)  payment of the costs, charges and expenses of winding, and
     (c)  adjustment of the rights of the contributories among themselves.

AMENDMENTS AND NOTES

<sup>a</sup> The form of articles for private companies limited by guarantee now includes a full statement of the guarantee. This corresponds to the provisions that previously applied in Table C. See also s 11 of the Companies Act 2006.

# Part 2
## DIRECTORS

### *Directors' Powers and Responsibilities*<sup>a</sup>

#### Directors' general authority<sup>b</sup>

**51.MA.80**     **3.**   Subject to the articles, the directors are responsible for the management of the company's business, for which purpose they may exercise all the powers of the company.

AMENDMENTS AND NOTES

<sup>a</sup> See note a to para 51.MA.27.

<sup>b</sup> See note b to para 51.MA.27.

#### Members' reserve power<sup>a</sup>

**51.MA.81**     **4.**   (1)  The members may, by special resolution, direct the directors to take, or refrain from taking, specified action.

(2)  No such special resolution invalidates anything which the directors have done before the passing of the resolution.

AMENDMENTS AND NOTES

<sup>a</sup> See note a to para 51.MA.28.

#### Directors may delegate<sup>a</sup>

**51.MA.82**     **5.**   (1)  Subject to the articles, the directors may delegate any of the powers<sup>b</sup> which are conferred on them under the articles—

(a)  to such person or committee;

(b)  by such means (including by power of attorney);

(c)  to such an extent;

(d)  in relation to such matters or territories; and

(e)  on such terms and conditions;

as they think fit.

(2)  If the directors so specify,<sup>c</sup> any such delegation may authorise further delegation of the directors' powers by any person to whom they are delegated.

(3)  The directors may revoke any delegation in whole or part, or alter its terms and conditions.

AMENDMENTS AND NOTES

<sup>a</sup> See note a to para 51.MA.29.

<sup>b</sup> See note b to para 51.MA.29.

<sup>c</sup> See note c to para 51.MA.29.

#### Committees<sup>a</sup>

**51.MA.83**     **6.**   (1)  Committees to which the directors delegate any of their powers must follow procedures which are based as far as they are applicable on those provisions of the articles which govern the taking of decisions by directors.

(2)  The directors may make rules of procedure for all or any committees, which prevail over rules derived from the articles if they are not consistent with them.

AMENDMENTS AND NOTES

<sup>a</sup> See note a to para 51.MA.30.

### *Decision-Making by Directors*

#### Directors to take decisions<sup>a</sup> collectively<sup>b</sup>

**51.MA.84**     **7.**   (1)  The general rule about decision-making by directors is that any decision of the directors must be either a majority decision at a meeting or a decision taken in accordance with article 8.

(2)  If—

(a)  the company only has one director, and

(b)  no provision of the articles requires it to have more than one director,

the general rule does not apply, and the director may take decisions without regard to any of the provisions of the articles relating to directors' decision-making.

AMENDMENTS AND NOTES

### Unanimous decisions

**8.**  (1)  A decision of the directors is taken in accordance with this article when all eligible directors     **51.MA.85**
indicate to each other by any means[a] that they share a common view on a matter.

    (2)  Such a decision may take the form of a resolution in writing,[b] copies of which have been signed by each eligible[c] director or to which each eligible director has otherwise indicated agreement in writing.

    (3)  References in this article to eligible directors are to directors who would have been entitled to vote on the matter had it been proposed as a resolution at a directors' meeting.

    (4)  A decision may not be taken in accordance with this article if the eligible directors would not have formed a quorum at such a meeting.

AMENDMENTS AND NOTES

<sup>a</sup> See note a to para 51.MA.32.

<sup>b</sup> See note b to para 51.MA.32.

<sup>c</sup> See note c to para 51.MA.32.

### Calling a directors' meeting[a]

**9.**  (1)  Any director may call a directors' meeting by giving notice of the meeting to the directors or     **51.MA.86**
by authorising the company secretary (if any) to give such notice.

    (2)  Notice of any directors' meeting must indicate—[b]

       (a)  its proposed date and time;

       (b)  where it is to take place; and

       (c)  if it is anticipated that directors participating in the meeting will not be in the same place, how it is proposed that they should communicate with each other during the meeting.

    (3)  Notice of a directors' meeting must be given to each director, but need not be in writing.

    (4)  Notice of a directors' meeting need not be given to directors who waive their entitlement to notice of that meeting, by giving notice to that effect to the company not more than 7 days after the date on which the meeting is held. Where such notice is given after the meeting has been held, that does not affect the validity of the meeting, or of any business conducted at it.[c]

AMENDMENTS AND NOTES

<sup>a</sup> See note a to para 51.MA.33.

<sup>b</sup> See note b to para 51.MA.33.

<sup>c</sup> See note d to para 51.MA.33.

### Participation in directors' meetings[a]

**10.** (1)  Subject to the articles, directors participate in a directors' meeting, or part of a directors'     **51.MA.87**
meeting, when—

       (a)  the meeting has been called and takes place in accordance with the articles, and

       (b)  they can each communicate to the others any information or opinions they have on any particular item of the business of the meeting.

    (2)  In determining whether directors are participating in a directors' meeting, it is irrelevant where any director is or how they communicate with each other.[b]

    (3)  If all the directors participating in a meeting are not in the same place, they may decide that the meeting is to be treated as taking place wherever any of them is.

AMENDMENTS AND NOTES

<sup>a</sup> See note a to para 51.MA.34.

<sup>b</sup> See note b to para 51.MA.34.

### Quorum for directors' meetings[a, b]

**11.** (1)  At a directors' meeting, unless a quorum is participating, no proposal is to be voted on,     **51.MA.88**
except a proposal to call another meeting.

    (2)  The quorum for directors' meetings may be fixed from time to time by a decision of the directors,[c] but it must never be less than two,[d] and unless otherwise fixed it is two.

    (3)  If the total number of directors for the time being is less than the quorum required, the directors must not take any decision other than a decision—

       (a)  to appoint further directors, or

       (b)  to call a general meeting so as to enable the members to appoint further directors.[e]

AMENDMENTS AND NOTES

<sup>a</sup> See note a to para 51.MA.35.

<sup>b</sup> See note b to para 51.MA.35.

^c See note c to para 51.MA.35.

^d See note d to para 51.MA.35.

^e See note e to para 51.MA.35.

### Chairing of directors' meetings

**51.MA.89**     **12.** (1)  The directors may^a appoint a director to chair their meetings.

(2)  The person so appointed for the time being is known as the chairman.

(3)  The directors may terminate the chairman's appointment at any time.

(4)  If the chairman is not participating in a directors' meeting within ten^b minutes of the time at which it was to start, the participating directors must appoint one of themselves to chair it.

AMENDMENTS AND NOTES

^a See note a to para 51.MA.36.

^b See note b to para 51.MA.36.

### Casting vote^a

**51.MA.90**     **13.** (1)  If the numbers of votes for and against a proposal are equal, the chairman or other director chairing the meeting has a casting vote.

(2)  But this does not apply if, in accordance with the articles, the chairman or other director is not to be counted as participating in the decision-making process for quorum or voting.

AMENDMENTS AND NOTES

^a See note a to para 51.MA.37.

### Conflicts of interest^a, b

**51.MA.91**     **14.** (1)  If a proposed decision of the directors is concerned with an actual or proposed transaction or arrangement^c with the company in which a director is interested, that director is not to be counted as participating in the decision-making process for quorum or voting purposes.^d

(2)  But if paragraph (3) applies, a director who is interested in an actual or proposed transaction or arrangement with the company is to be counted as participating in the decision-making process for quorum and voting purposes.

(3)  This paragraph applies when—

(a)  the company by ordinary resolution disapplies the provision of the articles which would otherwise prevent a director from being counted as participating in the decision-making process;

(b)  the director's interest cannot reasonably be regarded as likely to give rise to a conflict of interest;^e or

(c)  the director's conflict of interest arises from a permitted cause.

(4)  For the purposes of this article, the following are permitted causes—^f

(a)  a guarantee given, or to be given, by or to a director in respect of an obligation incurred by or on behalf of the company or any of its subsidiaries;

(b)  subscription, or an agreement to subscribe, for securities of the company or any of its subsidiaries, or to underwrite, sub-underwrite, or guarantee subscription for any such securities; and

(c)  arrangements^g pursuant to which benefits are made available to employees and directors or former employees and directors of the company or any of its subsidiaries which do not provide special benefits for directors or former directors.

(5)  For the purposes of this article, references to proposed decisions and decision-making processes include any directors' meeting or part of a directors' meeting.

(6)  Subject to paragraph (7), if a question arises at a meeting of directors or of a committee of directors as to the right of a director to participate in the meeting (or part of the meeting) for voting or quorum purposes, the question may, before the conclusion of the meeting, be referred to the chairman whose ruling in relation to any director other than the chairman is to be final and conclusive.^h

(7)  If any question as to the right to participate in the meeting (or part of the meeting) should arise in respect of the chairman, the question is to be decided by a decision of the directors at that meeting, for which purpose the chairman is not to be counted as participating in the meeting (or that part of the meeting) for voting or quorum purposes.

AMENDMENTS AND NOTES

^a See note a to para 51.MA.38.

^b See note b to para 51.MA.38.

^c See note c to para 51.MA.38.

^d See note d to para 51.MA.38.

^e See note e to para 51.MA.38.

f  See note f to para 51.MA.38.

g  See note g to para 51.MA.38.

h  See note h to para 51.MA.38.

### Records of decisions to be kept[a]

**15.** The directors must ensure that the company keeps a record, in writing, for at least 10 years from the date of the decision recorded, of every unanimous or majority decision taken by the directors.     **51.MA.92**

AMENDMENTS AND NOTES

a  See note a to para 51.MA.39.

### Directors' discretion to make further rules[a]

**16.** Subject to the articles, the directors may make any rule which they think fit about how they take decisions, and about how such rules are to be recorded or communicated to directors.     **51.MA.93**

AMENDMENTS AND NOTES

a  See note a to para 51.MA.40.

## *Appointment of Directors*[a, b]

### Methods of appointing directors[c]

**17.** (1) Any person who is willing to act as a director, and is permitted by law to do so, may be appointed to be a director—     **51.MA.94**
    (a) by ordinary resolution, or
    (b) by a decision of the directors.[d]
  (2) In any case where, as a result of death, the company has no members and no directors, the personal representatives of the last member to have died have the right, by notice in writing, to appoint a person to be a director.
  (3) For the purposes of paragraph (2), where 2 or more members die in circumstances rendering it uncertain who was the last to die, a younger member is deemed to have survived an older member.

AMENDMENTS AND NOTES

a  See note a to para 51.MA.41.

b  See note b to para 51.MA.41.

c  See note c to para 51.MA.41.

d  See note d to para 51.MA.41.

### Termination of director's appointment[a]

**18.** A person ceases to be a director as soon as—     **51.MA.95**
    (a) that person ceases to be a director by virtue of any provision of the Companies Act 2006 or is prohibited from being a director by law;[b]
    (b) a bankruptcy order is made against that person;
    (c) a composition is made with that person's creditors generally in satisfaction of that person's debts;[c]
    (d) a registered medical practitioner who is treating that person gives a written opinion to the company stating that that person has become physically or mentally incapable of acting as a director and may remain so for more than three months;
    (e) by reason of that person's mental health, a court makes an order which wholly or partly prevents that person from personally exercising any powers or rights which that person would otherwise have;[d]
    (f) notification is received by the company from the director that the director is resigning from office, and such resignation has taken effect in accordance with its terms.[e]

AMENDMENTS AND NOTES

a  See note a to para 51.MA.42.

b  See note b to para 51.MA.42.

c  See note c to para 51.MA.42.

d  See note d to para 51.MA.42.

e  See note e to para 51.MA.42.

### Directors' remuneration[a]

**19.** (1) Directors may undertake any services for the company that the directors decide.     **51.MA.96**
  (2) Directors are entitled to such remuneration as the directors determine—
    (a) for their services to the company as directors, and
    (b) for any other service which they undertake for the company.

(3) Subject to the articles, a director's remuneration may—
  (a) take any form, and
  (b) include any arrangements in connection with the payment of a pension, allowance or gratuity, or any death, sickness or disability benefits, to or in respect of that director.
(4) Unless the directors decide otherwise, directors' remuneration accrues from day to day.
(5) Unless the directors decide otherwise, directors are not accountable to the company for any remuneration which they receive as directors or other officers or employees of the company's subsidiaries or of any other body corporate in which the company is interested.

AMENDMENTS AND NOTES

[a] See note a to para 51.MA.43.

### Directors' expenses[a]

**51.MA.97**    **20.** The company may pay any reasonable expenses which the directors properly incur in connection with their attendance at—
  (a) meetings of directors or committees of directors,
  (b) general meetings, or
  (c) separate meetings of the holders of debentures of the company,
or otherwise in connection with the exercise of their powers and the discharge of their responsibilities in relation to the company.

AMENDMENTS AND NOTES

[a] See note a to para 51.MA.44.

## Part 3
## MEMBERS

### *Becoming and Ceasing to be a Member*

### Applications for membership[a]

**51.MA.98**    **21.** No person shall become a member of the company unless—
  (a) that person has completed an application for membership in a form approved by the directors, and
  (b) the directors have approved the application.

AMENDMENTS AND NOTES

[a] This provision corresponds to the provisions of Table C reg 3.

### Termination of membership[a]

**51.MA.99**    **22.** (1) A member may withdraw from membership of the company by giving 7 days' notice to the company in writing.
  (2) Membership is not transferable.
  (3) A person's membership terminates when that person dies or ceases to exist.

AMENDMENTS AND NOTES

[a] This provision corresponds to the provisions of Table C reg 4.

### *Organisation of General Meetings*[a]

### Attendance and speaking at general meetings[b]

**51.MA.100**    **23.** (1) A person is able to exercise the right to speak at a general meeting when that person is in a position to communicate to all those attending the meeting, during the meeting, any information or opinions which that person has on the business of the meeting.
  (2) A person is able to exercise the right to vote at a general meeting when—
  (a) that person is able to vote, during the meeting, on resolutions put to the vote at the meeting, and
  (b) that person's vote can be taken into account in determining whether or not such resolutions are passed at the same time as the votes of all the other persons attending the meeting.
  (3) The directors may make whatever arrangements they consider appropriate to enable those attending a general meeting to exercise their rights to speak or vote at it.
  (4) In determining attendance at a general meeting, it is immaterial whether any two or more members attending it are in the same place as each other.
  (5) Two or more persons who are not in the same place as each other attend a general meeting if their circumstances are such that if they have (or were to have) rights to speak and vote at that meeting, they are (or would be) able to exercise them.

AMENDMENTS AND NOTES

[a] See note a to para 51.MA.61.

[b] See note b to para 51.MA.61.

### Quorum for general meetings[a]

**24.** No business other than the appointment of the chairman of the meeting is to be transacted at a general meeting if the persons attending it do not constitute a quorum.

    **51.MA.101**

AMENDMENTS AND NOTES

[a] See note a to para 51.MA.62.

### Chairing general meetings[a]

**25.** (1) If the directors have appointed a chairman, the chairman shall chair general meetings if present and willing to do so.

    **51.MA.102**

    (2) If the directors have not appointed a chairman, or if the chairman is unwilling to chair the meeting or is not present within ten[b] minutes of the time at which a meeting was due to start—

        (a) the directors present, or

        (b) (if no directors are present), the meeting,

        must appoint a director or member to chair the meeting, and the appointment of the chairman of the meeting must be the first business of the meeting.

    (3) The person chairing a meeting in accordance with this article is referred to as 'the chairman of the meeting'.

AMENDMENTS AND NOTES

[a] See note a to para 51.MA.63.

[b] See note b to para 51.MA.63.

### Attendance and speaking by directors and non-members[a]

**26.** (1) Directors may attend and speak at general meetings, whether or not they are members.

    **51.MA.103**

    (2) The chairman of the meeting may permit other persons who are not members of the company to attend and speak at a general meeting.

AMENDMENTS AND NOTES

[a] See note a to para 51.MA.64.

### Adjournment[a]

**27.** (1) If the persons attending a general meeting within half an hour of the time at which the meeting was due to start do not constitute a quorum, or if during a meeting a quorum ceases to be present, the chairman of the meeting must adjourn it.[b]

    **51.MA.104**

    (2) The chairman of the meeting may adjourn a general meeting at which a quorum is present if—[c]

        (a) the meeting consents to an adjournment, or

        (b) it appears to the chairman of the meeting that an adjournment is necessary to protect the safety of any person attending the meeting or ensure that the business of the meeting is conducted in an orderly manner.

    (3) The chairman of the meeting must adjourn a general meeting if directed to do so by the meeting.[d]

    (4) When adjourning a general meeting, the chairman of the meeting must—

        (a) either specify the time and place to which it is adjourned or state that it is to continue at a time and place to be fixed by the directors,[e] and

        (b) have regard to any directions as to the time and place of any adjournment which have been given by the meeting.

    (5) If the continuation of an adjourned meeting is to take place more than 14 days after it was adjourned, the company must give at least 7 clear days' notice of it (that is, excluding the day of the adjourned meeting and the day on which the notice is given)—

        (a) to the same persons to whom notice of the company's general meetings is required to be given, and

        (b) containing the same information which such notice is required to contain.

    (6) No business may be transacted at an adjourned general meeting which could not properly have been transacted at the meeting if the adjournment had not taken place.

AMENDMENTS AND NOTES

[a] See note a to para 51.MA.65.

[b] See note b to para 51.MA.65.

[c] See note c to para 51.MA.65.

[d] See note d to para 51.MA.65.

[e] See note e to para 51.MA.65.

*Voting at General Meetings*[a]

**Voting: general**

51.MA.105    **28.** A resolution put to the vote of a general meeting must be decided on a show of hands unless a poll is duly demanded in accordance with the articles.[b]

AMENDMENTS AND NOTES

[a] See note a to para 51.MA.66.

[b] See note b to para 51.MA.66.

**Errors and disputes**

51.MA.106    **29.** (1) No objection may be raised to the qualification of any person voting at a general meeting except at the meeting or adjourned meeting at which the vote objected to is tendered, and every vote not disallowed at the meeting is valid.

(2) Any such objection must be referred to the chairman of the meeting whose decision is final.[a]

AMENDMENTS AND NOTES

[a] See note a to para 51.MA.67.

**Poll votes**

51.MA.107    **30.** (1) A poll on a resolution may be demanded—

(a) in advance of the general meeting where it is to be put to the vote,[a] or

(b) at a general meeting, either before a show of hands on that resolution or immediately after the result of a show of hands on that resolution is declared.

(2) A poll may be demanded by,[b]

(a) the chairman of the meeting;

(b) the directors;[c]

(c) two or more persons having the right to vote on the resolution;[d] or

(d) a person[e] or persons representing not less than one tenth of the total voting rights of all the members having the right to vote on the resolution.[f]

(3) A demand for a poll may be withdrawn if—

(a) the poll has not yet been taken, and

(b) the chairman of the meeting consents to the withdrawal.

(4) Polls must be taken immediately and in such manner as the chairman of the meeting directs.

AMENDMENTS AND NOTES

[a] See note a to para 51.MA.68.

[b] See note b to para 51.MA.68.

[c] See note c to para 51.MA.68.

[d] See note d to para 51.MA.68.

[e] See note e to para 51.MA.68.

[f] See note f to para 51.MA.68.

**Content of proxy notices**[a]

51.MA.108    **31.** (1) Proxies may only validly be appointed by a notice in writing (a 'proxy notice') which—

(a) states the name and address of the member appointing the proxy;

(b) identifies the person appointed to be that member's proxy and the general meeting in relation to which that person is appointed;

(c) is signed by or on behalf of the member appointing the proxy, or is authenticated in such manner as the directors may determine;[b] and

(d) is delivered to the company in accordance with the articles and any instructions contained in the notice of the general meeting to which they relate.

(2) The company may require proxy notices to be delivered in a particular form, and may specify different forms for different purposes.

(3) Proxy notices may specify how the proxy appointed under them is to vote (or that the proxy is to abstain from voting) on one or more resolutions.

(4) Unless a proxy notice indicates otherwise, it must be treated as—

(a) allowing the person appointed under it as a proxy discretion as to how to vote on any ancillary or procedural resolutions put to the meeting, and

(b) appointing that person as a proxy in relation to any adjournment of the general meeting to which it relates as well as the meeting itself.

AMENDMENTS AND NOTES

[a] See note a to para 51.MA.69.

[b] See note b to para 51.MA.69.

**Delivery of proxy notices**

**32.** (1) A person who is entitled to attend, speak or vote (either on a show of hands or on a poll) at    **51.MA.109**
a general meeting remains so entitled in respect of that meeting or any adjournment of it,
even though a valid proxy notice has been delivered to the company by or on behalf of that
person.

    (2) An appointment under a proxy notice may be revoked by delivering to the company a notice
given by or on behalf of the person by whom or on whose behalf the proxy notice was given.

    (3) A notice revoking a proxy appointment only takes effect if it is delivered before the start of the
meeting or adjourned meeting to which it relates.

    (4) If a proxy notice is not executed by the person appointing the proxy, it must be accompanied
by written evidence of the authority of the person who executed it to execute it on the
appointor's behalf.

**Amendments to resolutions**

**33.** (1) An ordinary resolution to be proposed at a general meeting may be amended by ordinary    **51.MA.110**
resolution[a] if—

    (a) notice of the proposed amendment is given to the company in writing by a person
entitled to vote at the general meeting at which it is to be proposed not less than 48
hours[b] before the meeting is to take place (or such later time as the chairman of the
meeting may determine), and

    (b) the proposed amendment does not, in the reasonable opinion of the chairman of the
meeting, materially alter the scope of the resolution.

    (2) A special resolution to be proposed at a general meeting may be amended by ordinary
resolution,[c] if—

    (a) the chairman of the meeting proposes the amendment at the general meeting at which
the resolution is to be proposed, and

    (b) the amendment does not go beyond what is necessary to correct a grammatical or other
non-substantive error in the resolution.

    (3) If the chairman of the meeting, acting in good faith, wrongly decides that an amendment to
a resolution is out of order, the chairman's error does not invalidate the vote on that
resolution.

AMENDMENTS AND NOTES

[a] See note a to para 51.MA.71.

[b] See note b to para 51.MA.71.

[c] See note c to para 51.MA.71.

Part 4
## ADMINISTRATIVE ARRANGEMENTS

**Means of communication to be used[a]**

**34.** (1) Subject to the articles, anything sent or supplied by or to the company under the articles may    **51.MA.111**
be sent or supplied in any way in which the Companies Act 2006 provides for documents or
information which are authorised or required by any provision of that Act to be sent or
supplied by or to the company.

    (2) Subject to the articles, any notice or document to be sent or supplied to a director in
connection with the taking of decisions by directors may also be sent or supplied by the
means by which that director has asked to be sent or supplied with such notices or
documents for the time being.[b]

    (3) A director may agree with the company that notices or documents sent to that director in a
particular way are to be deemed to have been received within a specified time of their being
sent, and for the specified time to be less than 48 hours.

AMENDMENTS AND NOTES

[a] See note a to para 51.MA.72.

[b] See note b to para 51.MA.72.

**Company seals**

**35.** (1) Any common seal may only be used by the authority of the directors.    **51.MA.112**

    (2) The directors may decide by what means and in what form any common seal is to be used.

    (3) Unless otherwise decided by the directors, if the company has a common seal and it is affixed
to a document, the document must also be signed by at least one authorised person in the
presence of a witness who attests the signature.

    (4) For the purposes of this article, an authorised person is—

    (a) any director of the company;

(b) the company secretary (if any); or

(c) any person authorised by the directors for the purpose of signing documents to which the common seal is applied.

### No right to inspect accounts and other records[a]

**51.MA.113**

**36.** Except as provided by law or authorised by the directors or an ordinary resolution of the company, no person is entitled to inspect any of the company's accounting or other records or documents merely by virtue of being a member.

AMENDMENTS AND NOTES

[a] See note a to para 51.MA.74.

### Provision for employees on cessation of business[a]

**51.MA.114**

**37.** The directors may decide to make provision for the benefit of persons employed or formerly employed by the company or any of its subsidiaries (other than a director or former director or shadow director) in connection with the cessation or transfer to any person of the whole or part of the undertaking of the company or that subsidiary.

AMENDMENTS AND NOTES

[a] See note a to para 51.MA.75.

## *Directors' Indemnity and Insurance*[a]

### Indemnity

**51.MA.115**

**38.** (1) Subject to paragraph (2), a relevant director of the company or an associated company may be indemnified out of the company's assets against—

(a) any liability incurred by that director in connection with any negligence, default, breach of duty or breach of trust in relation to the company or an associated company,

(b) any liability incurred by that director in connection with the activities of the company or an associated company in its capacity as a trustee of an occupational pension scheme (as defined in section 235(6) of the Companies Act 2006),

(c) any other liability incurred by that director as an officer of the company or an associated company.

(2) This article does not authorise any indemnity which would be prohibited or rendered void by any provision of the Companies Acts or by any other provision of law.

(3) In this article—

(a) companies are associated if one is a subsidiary of the other or both are subsidiaries of the same body corporate, and

(b) a 'relevant director' means any director or former director of the company or an associated company.

AMENDMENTS AND NOTES

[a] See note a to para 51.MA.76.

### Insurance

**51.MA.116**

**39.** (1) The directors may decide to purchase and maintain insurance, at the expense of the company, for the benefit of any relevant director in respect of any relevant loss.

(2) In this article—

(a) a 'relevant director' means any director or former director of the company or an associated company

(b) a 'relevant loss' means any loss or liability which has been or may be incurred by a relevant director in connection with that relevant director's duties or powers in relation to the company, any associated company or any pension fund or employees' share scheme of the company or associated company, and

(c) companies are associated if one is a subsidiary of the other or both are subsidiaries of the same body corporate.

MODEL ARTICLES APPLYING TO PUBLIC COMPANIES

## The Companies (Model Articles) Regulations 2008

SCHEDULE 3                                               Regulation 4


Model Articles for Public Companies[a, b]

### PART 1
#### INTERPRETATION AND LIMITATION OF LIABILITY

**Defined terms**

1.  In the articles,[c] unless the context requires otherwise—                    **51.MA.117**

'alternate' or 'alternate director' has the meaning given in article 25;

'appointor' has the meaning given in article 25;

'articles' means the company's articles of association;

'bankruptcy' includes individual insolvency proceedings in a jurisdiction other than England and Wales or Northern Ireland which have an effect similar to that of bankruptcy;

'call' has the meaning given in article 54;

'call notice' has the meaning given in article 54;

'certificate' means a paper certificate (other than a share warrant) evidencing a person's title to specified shares or other securities;

'certificated' in relation to a share, means that it is not an uncertificated share or a share in respect of which a share warrant has been issued and is current;

'chairman' has the meaning given in article 12;

'chairman of the meeting' has the meaning given in article 31;

'Companies Acts' means the Companies Acts (as defined in section 2 of the Companies Act 2006), in so far as they apply to the company;

'company's lien' has the meaning given in article 52;

'director' means a director of the company, and includes any person occupying the position of director, by whatever name called;[d]

'distribution recipient' has the meaning given in article 72;

'document' includes, unless otherwise specified, any document sent or supplied in electronic form;[e]

'electronic form' has the meaning given in section 1168 of the Companies Act 2006;

'fully paid' in relation to a share, means that the nominal value and any premium to be paid to the company in respect of that share have been paid to the company;

'hard copy form' has the meaning given in section 1168 of the Companies Act 2006;

'holder' in relation to shares means the person whose name is entered in the register of members as the holder of the shares, or, in the case of a share in respect of which a share warrant has been issued (and not cancelled), the person in possession of that warrant;

'instrument' means a document in hard copy form;

'lien enforcement notice' has the meaning given in article 53;

'member' has the meaning given in section 112 of the Companies Act 2006;[f]

'ordinary resolution' has the meaning given in section 282 of the Companies Act 2006;

'paid' means paid or credited as paid;

'participate', in relation to a directors' meeting has the meaning given in article 9;

'partly paid' in relation to a share means that part of that share's nominal value or any premium at which it was issued has not been paid to the company;

'proxy notice' has the meaning given in article 38;

'securities seal' has the meaning given in article 47;

'shares' means shares in the company;

'special resolution' has the meaning given in section 283 of the Companies Act 2006;

'subsidiary' has the meaning given in section 1159 of the Companies Act 2006;

'transmittee' means a person entitled to a share by reason of the death or bankruptcy of a shareholder or otherwise by operation of law;

'uncertificated' in relation to a share means that, by virtue of legislation (other than section 778 of the Companies Act 2006) permitting title to shares to be evidenced and transferred without a certificate, title to that share is evidenced and may be transferred without a certificate; and

'writing' means the representation or reproduction of words, symbols or other information in a visible form by any method or combination of methods, whether sent or supplied in electronic form or otherwise.

Unless the context otherwise requires, other words or expressions contained in these articles bear the same meaning as in the Companies Act 2006 as in force on the date when these articles become binding on the company.

AMENDMENTS AND NOTES

[a] See s 4(2) of the Companies Act 2006 (see Chapter 1) for the definition of public company.

[b] Per s 20(2) of the Companies Act 2006 (see Chapter 3), the form of model articles for public companies applies by default to a company of the relevant description, namely a company which is incorporated as a public company and not to a company which has been re-registered as a public company. As referred to at paras 51.MA.20 and 51.MA.24 above, the Government was not seeking to produce a set of model articles for public companies that would satisfy the listing requirements or best practice requirements for companies that were admitted to trading on the main market of the London Stock Exchange or that will comply will the rules or best practice requirement for companies traded on AIM and/or with the requirements of relevant institutional shareholder bodies and certain guidelines of the Institutional Shareholders' Committee. The assumption is that when a public company is to seek a listing of its shares it will obtain appropriate advice and put in place appropriate bespoke articles of association at that point.

[c] See note e to para 51.MA.25.

[d] See note f to para 51.MA.25. A public company is required to have a company secretary pursuant to s 271 of the Companies Act 2006 (see Chapter 12). Nonetheless, there is no definition of secretary for the purposes of these articles.

[e] See note g to para 51.MA.25.

[f] As part of the consultation process (see URN 07/1227/GR, para 15), the Government considered whether the appropriate term of reference for the purposes of the form of model articles for public companies should be to 'nominated member' as opposed to 'member', in order to ensure that the articles operated effectively for the purposes of any persons who had nominated rights pursuant to s 145 of the Companies Act 2006 (see Chapter 9) or, in the case of traded companies, for the purposes of ss 146–151 of the Companies Act 2006. The Government concluded that there was no need to extend the definition to include such persons, since the provisions of the Companies Act would deal adequately with such persons.

### Liability of members[a]

**51.MA.118**     2.   The liability of the members is limited to the amount, if any, unpaid on the shares held by them.

AMENDMENTS AND NOTES

[a] See note a to para 51.MA.26.

## Part 2
## DIRECTORS

### *Directors' Powers And Responsibilities*

### Directors' general authority[a]

**51.MA.119**     3.   Subject to the articles, the directors are responsible for the management of the company's business, for which purpose they may exercise all the powers of the company.

AMENDMENTS AND NOTES

[a] See note b to para 51.MA.27.

### Members' reserve power[a]

**51.MA.120**     4.   (1)   The members may, by special resolution, direct the directors to take, or refrain from taking, specified action.

(2)   No such special resolution invalidates anything which the directors have done before the passing of the resolution.

AMENDMENTS AND NOTES

[a] See note a to para 51.MA.28.

### Directors may delegate[a]

**51.MA.121**     5.   (1)   Subject to the articles, the directors may delegate any of the powers which are conferred on them under the articles—

(a)   to such person or committee;

(b)   by such means (including by power of attorney);

(c)   to such an extent;

(d)   in relation to such matters or territories; and

(e)   on such terms and conditions;

as they think fit.

(2) If the directors so specify,[b] any such delegation may authorise further delegation of the directors' powers by any person to whom they are delegated.

(3) The directors may revoke any delegation in whole or part, or alter its terms and conditions.

AMENDMENTS AND NOTES

[a] See note a to para 51.MA.29.

[b] See note c to para 51.MA.29.

### Committees[a]

**6.** (1) Committees to which the directors delegate any of their powers must follow procedures     **51.MA.122** which are based as far as they are applicable on those provisions of the articles which govern the taking of decisions by directors.

(2) The directors may make rules of procedure for all or any[b] committees, which prevail over rules derived from the articles if they are not consistent with them.

AMENDMENTS AND NOTES

[a] See note a to para 51.MA.30.

[b] See note b to para 51.MA.30.

## *Decision-Making by Directors*[a]

### Directors to take decisions collectively

**7.** Decisions of the directors may be taken—     **51.MA.123**

(a) at a directors' meeting, or

(b) in the form of a directors' written resolution.

AMENDMENTS AND NOTES

[a] Where directors are to take decisions as a board (as opposed to where their decision-making powers have been delegated to a committee), they are required to take decisions collectively either (i) in a formal directors meeting, or (ii) by means of a directors' written resolution. See the corresponding provisions for private companies limited by shares at articles 7 and 8 of the model articles for private companies limited by shares.

### Calling a directors' meeting[a]

**8.** (1) Any director may call a directors' meeting.     **51.MA.124**

(2) The company secretary[b] must call a directors' meeting if a director so requests.

(3) A directors' meeting is called by giving notice of the meeting to the directors.

(4) Notice of any directors' meeting must indicate—[c]

(a) its proposed date and time;

(b) where it is to take place; and

(c) if it is anticipated that directors participating in the meeting will not be in the same place, how it is proposed that they should communicate with each other during the meeting.

(5) Notice of a directors' meeting must be given to each director, but need not be in writing.[d]

(6) Notice of a directors' meeting need not be given to directors who waive their entitlement to notice of that meeting, by giving notice to that effect to the company not more than 7 days after the date on which the meeting is held. Where such notice is given after the meeting has been held, that does not affect the validity of the meeting, or of any business conducted at it.[e]

AMENDMENTS AND NOTES

[a] See note a to para 51.MA.33.

[b] Under s 271 of the Companies Act 2006 (see Chapter 12), a public company is required to have a secretary. This requirement does not apply to private companies (see s 270 of the Companies Act 2006), therefore this provision is not included in the model articles for private companies limited by shares.

[c] See note b to para 51.MA.33.

[d] See note c to para 51.MA.33.

[e] See note d to para 51.MA.33.

### Participation in directors' meetings[a]

**9.** (1) Subject to the articles, directors participate in a directors' meeting, or part of a directors'     **51.MA.125** meeting, when—

(a) the meeting has been called and takes place in accordance with the articles, and

(b) they can each communicate to the others any information or opinions they have on any particular item of the business of the meeting.

(2) In determining whether directors are participating in a directors' meeting, it is irrelevant

where any director is or how they communicate with each other.[b]

    (3) If all the directors participating in a meeting are not in the same place, they may decide that the meeting is to be treated as taking place wherever any of them is.[c]

AMENDMENTS AND NOTES

[a] See note a to para 51.MA.34.

[b] See note b to para 51.MA.34.

[c] See note c to para 51.MA.34.

### Quorum for directors' meetings[a]

**51.MA.126**

**10.** (1) At a directors' meeting, unless a quorum is participating, no proposal is to be voted on, except a proposal to call another meeting.

    (2) The quorum for directors' meetings may be fixed from time to time by a decision of the directors, but it must never be less than two,[b] and unless otherwise fixed it is two.

AMENDMENTS AND NOTES

[a] See notes a and b to para 51.MA.35.

[b] For public companies, the quorum requirement corresponds to the minimum number of directors a public company is required to have under s 154(2) of the Companies Act 2006 (see Chapter 10), namely two directors.

### Meetings where total number of directors less than quorum[a]

**51.MA.127**

**11.** (1) This article applies where the total number of directors for the time being is less than the quorum for directors' meetings.

    (2) If there is only one director, that director may appoint sufficient directors to make up a quorum or call a general meeting to do so.

    (3) If there is more than one director—

        (a) a directors' meeting may take place, if it is called in accordance with the articles and at least two directors participate in it, with a view to appointing sufficient directors to make up a quorum or calling a general meeting to do so, and

        (b) if a directors' meeting is called but only one director attends at the appointed date and time to participate in it, that director may appoint sufficient directors to make up a quorum or call a general meeting to do so.[b]

AMENDMENTS AND NOTES

[a] The provisions in this article are a slightly more elaborate formulation of the corresponding provisions contemplated for private companies limited by shares (as to which, see note e to para 51.MA.35).

[b] Article 11(3) allows a director to appoint other directors in circumstances where non-attendance by other directors is obstructing the board's ability to conduct the company's affairs. This power goes significantly beyond the corresponding provision in Table A (reg 90). There is no corresponding provision in the model articles for private companies limited by shares.

### Chairing directors' meetings[a]

**51.MA.128**

**12.** (1) The directors may[b] appoint a director to chair their meetings.

    (2) The person so appointed for the time being is known as the chairman.

    (3) The directors may appoint other directors as deputy or assistant chairmen to chair directors' meetings in the chairman's absence.[c]

    (4) The directors may terminate the appointment of the chairman, deputy or assistant chairman at any time.

    (5) If neither the chairman nor any director appointed generally to chair directors' meetings in the chairman's absence is participating in a meeting within ten[d] minutes of the time at which it was to start, the participating directors must appoint one of themselves to chair it.

AMENDMENTS AND NOTES

[a] This corresponds to the provisions of Table A reg 91.

[b] See note a to para 51.MA.36. There is no statutory obligation on a public company to have a chairman of its board.

[c] This provision is broader than the corresponding provision in the model articles for private companies limited by shares, which does not make provision for deputy or assistant chairmen.

[d] See note b to para 51.MA.36.

### Voting at directors' meetings: general rules[a]

**51.MA.129**

**13.** (1) Subject to the articles, a decision is taken at a directors' meeting by a majority of the votes of the participating directors.[b]

    (2) Subject to the articles, each director participating in a directors' meeting has one vote.

(3) Subject to the articles,[c] if a director has an interest in an actual or proposed transaction or arrangement with the company—

    (a) that director and that director's alternate may not vote on any proposal relating to it, but

    (b) this does not preclude the alternate from voting in relation to that transaction or arrangement on behalf of another appointor who does not have such an interest.

AMENDMENTS AND NOTES

[a] This corresponds to the provisions of Table A regs 88 and 94.

[b] Conversely, a decision taken as a written resolution will need to be signed by all of the directors of the company who would be entitled to vote at a meeting: as to which, see article 18. This is consistent with the approach taken in the form of the model articles for private companies limited by shares.

[c] Reference should be made to article 16 (conflicts of interest) in construing this article.

### Chairman's casting vote at directors' meetings[a]

**14.** (1) If the numbers of votes for and against a proposal are equal, the chairman or other director chairing the meeting has a casting vote.

    (2) But this does not apply if, in accordance with the articles, the chairman or other director is not to be counted as participating in the decision-making process for quorum or voting purposes.

**51.MA.130**

AMENDMENTS AND NOTES

[a] See note a to para 51.MA.37.

### Alternates voting at directors' meetings[a]

**15.** A director who is also an alternate director has an additional vote on behalf of each appointor who is—

    (a) not participating in a directors' meeting, and

    (b) would have been entitled to vote if they were participating in it.

**51.MA.131**

AMENDMENTS AND NOTES

[a] This provision corresponds broadly with the corresponding provision within Table A reg 88. See articles 25–27 in relation to the ability to appoint alternate directors.

### Conflicts of interest[a, b]

**16.** (1) If a directors' meeting, or part of a directors' meeting, is concerned with an actual or proposed transaction or arrangement[c] with the company in which a director is interested, that director is not to be counted as participating in that meeting, or part of a meeting, for quorum or voting purposes.

    (2) But if paragraph (3) applies, a director who is interested in an actual or proposed transaction or arrangement with the company is to be counted as participating in a decision at a directors' meeting, or part of a directors' meeting, relating to it for quorum and voting purposes.

    (3) This paragraph applies when—

        (a) the company by ordinary resolution disapplies the provision of the articles which would otherwise prevent a director from being counted as participating in, or voting at, a directors' meeting;

        (b) the director's interest cannot reasonably be regarded as likely to give rise to a conflict of interest; or

        (c) the director's conflict of interest arises from a permitted cause.

    (4) For the purposes of this article, the following are permitted causes—

        (a) a guarantee given, or to be given, by or to a director in respect of an obligation incurred by or on behalf of the company or any of its subsidiaries;

        (b) subscription, or an agreement to subscribe, for shares or other securities of the company or any of its subsidiaries, or to underwrite, sub-underwrite, or guarantee subscription for any such shares or securities; and

        (c) arrangements[d] pursuant to which benefits are made available to employees and directors or former employees and directors of the company or any of its subsidiaries which do not provide special benefits for directors or former directors.

    (5) Subject to paragraph (6), if a question arises at a meeting of directors or of a committee of directors as to the right of a director to participate in the meeting (or part of the meeting) for voting or quorum purposes, the question may, before the conclusion of the meeting, be referred to the chairman whose ruling in relation to any director other than the chairman is to be final and conclusive.

    (6) If any question as to the right to participate in the meeting (or part of the meeting) should arise in respect of the chairman, the question is to be decided by a decision of the directors at that meeting, for which purpose the chairman is not to be counted as participating in the meeting (or that part of the meeting) for voting or quorum purposes.

**51.MA.132**

AMENDMENTS AND NOTES

[a] The provisions of article 16 address directors' transactional conflicts of interest. See notes a and b to para 51.MA.38. This article corresponds to the provisions of Table A regs 94–96 and reg 98.

[b] Pursuant to the provisions of s 175(5)(b) of the Companies Act 2006 (see Chapter 10), a public company will need to include a specific provision in its articles of association in order to enable the board to approve directors' situational conflicts. The form of model articles for public companies does not include, as a default setting, any language to enable the board approval regime for situational conflicts. In the consultation documentation, the Government indicated that it did not think that it would be appropriate to include this permissive provision as a default setting in the model articles for public companies, and that it would be more appropriate for this to be a matter of individual decision for the companies concerned as to whether they want to confer this power on the directors in question (as to which, see DTI, *Implementation of Companies Act 2006*, para 3.76). This is inconsistent with the approach taken for private companies (as to which, see note a to para 51.MA.38), where, in the absence of a contrary provision in that form of model articles, the board approval regime is automatically enabled for private companies incorporated on or after 1 October 2008. It appears to be increasingly common practice for public companies to amend their articles of association so as to include an article that permits the board to approve situational conflicts.

[c] See note c to para 51.MA.38.

[d] See note g to para 51.MA.38.

### Proposing directors' written resolutions[a]

**51.MA.133**

**17.** (1) Any director may propose a directors' written resolution.

(2) The company secretary must propose a directors' written resolution if a director so requests.

(3) A directors' written resolution is proposed by giving notice of the proposed resolution to the directors.[b]

(4) Notice of a proposed directors' written resolution must indicate—

    (a) the proposed resolution, and

    (b) the time by which it is proposed that the directors should adopt it.[c]

(5) Notice of a proposed directors' written resolution must be given in writing to each director.

(6) Any decision which a person giving notice of a proposed directors' written resolution takes regarding the process of adopting that resolution must be taken reasonably in good faith.

AMENDMENTS AND NOTES

[a] The provisions of articles 17 and 18 provide a greater level of detail as to how the director's written resolution should operate than was the case with the corresponding provision of Table A (reg 93). Regulation 93 was not intended to function as a general substitute for the holding of directors' meetings in the manner contemplated under the model articles for public companies (see DTI, *Implementation of Companies Act 2006*, paras 3.77–3.82).

[b] A director's written resolution for a public company must be signed by all of the directors of that company who would have been entitled to vote on that resolution at a meeting of the board of directors. See also article 16(5) as regards the power conferred on the chairman of the board to determine whether a director's conflict of interest precludes that director from voting in relation to a particular resolution.

[c] The obligation to include a long-stop date is mandatory under article 17(4)(b). However, reference should also be made to article 18(2), which stipulates that signature of a written resolution after the nominated long-stop date will not affect the validity of the resolution.

### Adoption of directors' written resolutions[a]

**51.MA.134**

**18.** (1) A proposed directors' written resolution is adopted when all the directors who would have been entitled to vote on the resolution at a directors' meeting have signed one or more copies of it, provided that those directors would have formed a quorum at such a meeting.

(2) It is immaterial whether any director signs the resolution before or after the time by which the notice proposed that it should be adopted.

(3) Once a directors' written resolution has been adopted, it must be treated as if it had been a decision taken at a directors' meeting in accordance with the articles.

(4) The company secretary must ensure that the company keeps a record, in writing, of all directors' written resolutions for at least ten years from the date of their adoption.[b]

AMENDMENTS AND NOTES

[a] This article corresponds to Table A regs 93 and 100.

[b] See note a to para 51.MA.39.

### Directors' discretion to make further rules[a]

**19.** Subject to the articles, the directors may make any rule which they think fit about how they take decisions, and about how such rules are to be recorded or communicated to directors.

**51.MA.135**

AMENDMENTS AND NOTES

[a] See note a to para 51.MA.40.

## Appointment of Directors

### Methods of appointing directors[a]

**20.** Any person who is willing to act as a director, and is permitted by law to do so, may be appointed to be a director—

(a) by ordinary resolution, or

(b) by a decision of the directors.

**51.MA.136**

AMENDMENTS AND NOTES

[a] This article corresponds to the provisions of Table A regs 78 and 79.

### Retirement of directors by rotation[a]

**21.** (1) At the first annual general meeting all the directors must retire from office.

(2) At every subsequent annual general meeting any directors—

(a) who have been appointed by the directors since the last annual general meeting, or

(b) who were not appointed or reappointed at one of the preceding two annual general meetings,

must retire from office and may offer themselves for reappointment by the members.[b]

**51.MA.137**

AMENDMENTS AND NOTES

[a] Article 21 provides that the directors will be subject to periodic re-election. (This is consistent with the approach in Table A reg 73.) The approach adopted for the purposes of the model articles for public companies is in line with the approach advocated by paragraph B.7.1 of the UK Corporate Governance Code, which provides that directors of companies other than FTSE 350 companies should be subject to re-election after the first year of their appointment, after which the periodic retirement of directors should occur at intervals of no more than three years. For FTSE 350 companies, the UK Corporate Governance Code provides that all directors should be subject to annual re-election by shareholders. This retirement obligation operates individually for each director, as opposed to collectively (as was previously the case, when the retirement obligation operated in respect of one-third of the board under reg 73 of Table A). This article also provides for retirement and reappointment if a director has been appointed by the directors since the last annual general meeting. This is consistent with the approach in Table A reg 73. However, see note d to para 51.MA.41 for the position in relation to private companies limited by shares. (See DTI, *Implementation of the Companies Act*, paras 3.91–3.94)

[b] The model articles for public companies do not provide a mechanism by which members may propose a candidate for appointment to the board in place of an existing director who is retiring by rotation. Part 13 of the Companies Act 2006 permits members of the company to do this (by virtue of the operation of the provisions of ss 292, 303, 338 and 340).

### Termination of director's appointment[a]

**22.** A person ceases to be a director as soon as—

(a) that person ceases to be a director by virtue of any provision of the Companies Act 2006 or is prohibited from being a director by law;[b]

(b) a bankruptcy order is made against that person;

(c) a composition is made with that person's creditors generally in satisfaction of that person's debts;[c]

(d) a registered medical practitioner who is treating that person gives a written opinion to the company stating that that person has become physically or mentally incapable of acting as a director and may remain so for more than three months;

(e) by reason of that person's mental health, a court makes an order which wholly or partly prevents that person from personally exercising any powers or rights which that person would otherwise have;[d]

(f) notification is received by the company from the director that the director is resigning from office as director, and such resignation has taken effect in accordance with its terms.[e]

**51.MA.138**

AMENDMENTS AND NOTES

[a] See note a to para 51.MA.42.

[b] See note b to para 51.MA.42.

[c] See note c to para 51.MA.42.

<sup>d</sup> See note d to para 51.MA.42.

<sup>e</sup> See note e to para 51.MA.42. This is commonly included in bespoke public company articles of association.

**Directors' remuneration<sup>a</sup>**

**51.MA.139**   **23.** (1) Directors may undertake any services for the company that the directors decide.
   (2) Directors are entitled to such remuneration as the directors determine—
       (a) for their services to the company as directors, and
       (b) for any other service which they undertake for the company.
   (3) Subject to the articles, a director's remuneration may—
       (a) take any form, and
       (b) include any arrangements in connection with the payment of a pension, allowance or gratuity, or any death, sickness or disability benefits, to or in respect of that director.
   (4) Unless the directors decide otherwise, directors' remuneration accrues from day to day.
   (5) Unless the directors decide otherwise, directors are not accountable to the company for any remuneration which they receive as directors or other officers or employees of the company's subsidiaries or of any other body corporate in which the company is interested.

AMENDMENTS AND NOTES

<sup>a</sup> Table A draws a distinction between the remuneration that directors receive as holders of an executive position with the company and the remuneration they receive by virtue of their appointment as statutory director. In Table A (reg 81), non-executive remuneration is approved by an ordinary resolution, whereas executive remuneration is approved at board level. The model articles for public companies preserve the distinction between the two forms of remuneration, but no longer seek to make a distinction between the types of approval required. In any event, it has been common practice among public companies with a significant institutional shareholder base to have both executive and non-executive remuneration determined at board level. No distinction is made between these separate elements of remuneration in the statutory provisions that relate to the reporting of directors' remuneration or the approval of directors' remuneration reports by the members of quoted companies. In circumstances where members disapprove of the level at which board remuneration has been set, they may choose to vote against the resolution proposed at the annual general meeting to approve the report and accounts. See also note a to para 51.MA.43.

**Directors' expenses<sup>a</sup>**

**51.MA.140**   **24.** The company may pay any reasonable expenses which the directors properly incur in connection with their attendance at—
   (a) meetings of directors or committees of directors,
   (b) general meetings, or
   (c) separate meetings of the holders of any class of shares or of debentures of the company,
or otherwise in connection with the exercise of their powers and the discharge of their responsibilities in relation to the company.

AMENDMENTS AND NOTES

<sup>a</sup> See note a to para 51.MA.44.

## *Alternate Directors*

**Appointment and removal of alternates<sup>a, b</sup>**

**51.MA.141**   **25.** (1) Any director (the 'appointor') may appoint as an alternate any other director, or any other person approved by resolution of the directors, to—
       (a) exercise that director's powers, and
       (b) carry out that director's responsibilities,
       in relation to the taking of decisions by the directors in the absence of the alternate's appointor.<sup>c, d</sup>
   (2) Any appointment or removal of an alternate must be effected by notice in writing to the company signed by the appointor, or in any other manner approved by the directors.
   (3) The notice must—
       (a) identify the proposed alternate, and
       (b) in the case of a notice of appointment, contain a statement signed by the proposed alternate that the proposed alternate is willing to act as the alternate of the director giving the notice.<sup>e</sup>

AMENDMENTS AND NOTES

<sup>a</sup> This article corresponds to the provisions of Table A regs 65 and 68.

<sup>b</sup> The Government considered two possible policy approaches as regards the scope and extent of the role of an alternate director: (i) a narrow approach, which contemplates that an alternate may only act in relation to formal decision-making function of his appointor; or (ii) a broader approach, which contemplates that an alternate may exercise all of the same rights and responsibilities that his appointor has as a director (see DTI, *Implementation of Companies Act 2006*, paras 3.107 and 3.109). The Government has chosen to follow the narrower approach: this assumes that alternates are more likely to be of use in relation to the formal decision-making process where a specific number of directors is likely to be required in order to ensure that a quorum is present. However, see also URN 07/1227/GR, para 37, which indicates that a broader approach has been taken, albeit that this is not entirely supported by the provisions of articles 25(1) and 26(1), which contemplate that an alternate shall have the same powers as his appointor as regards the decision-making function.

<sup>c</sup> The scope and extent of an alternate's powers set out in article 25(1) should be read in conjunction with the provisions of article 26(1). See also note b to para 51.MA.141. In keeping with the underlying policy approach, it does not appear that an alternate's powers would extend to executing documentation for and on behalf of the company.

<sup>d</sup> This is consistent with the approach taken in Table A, but is a more specific formulation of the corresponding provision of Table A (reg 66).

<sup>e</sup> Table A did not include an explicit obligation to secure a written confirmation from the proposed alternate director that he was willing to act in this capacity. Table A reg 65 simply made reference to the fact that an alternate had to be willing to act as such.

### Rights and responsibilities of alternate directors<sup>a</sup>

**26.** (1) An alternate director has the same rights, in relation to any directors' meeting or directors' written resolution, as the alternate's appointor.<sup>b</sup>

(2) Except as the articles specify otherwise, alternate directors—
    (a) are deemed for all purposes to be directors;
    (b) are liable for their own acts and omissions;
    (c) are subject to the same restrictions as their appointors; and
    (d) are not deemed to be agents of or for their appointors.

(3) A person who is an alternate director but not a director—
    (a) may be counted as participating for the purposes of determining whether a quorum is participating (but only if that person's appointor is not participating), and
    (b) may sign a written resolution (but only if it is not signed or to be signed by that person's appointor).
No alternate may be counted as more than one director for such purposes.

(4) An alternate director is not entitled to receive any remuneration from the company for serving as an alternate director except such part of the alternate's appointor's remuneration as the appointor may direct by notice in writing made to the company.<sup>c</sup>

51.MA.142

AMENDMENTS AND NOTES

<sup>a</sup> This articles corresponds to Table A regs 66 and 69.

<sup>b</sup> See note a to para 51.MA.140.

<sup>c</sup> Article 26(4) elaborates on the corresponding provision in Table A (reg 66).

### Termination of alternate directorship<sup>a</sup>

**27.** An alternate director's appointment as an alternate terminates—

(a) when the alternate's appointor revokes the appointment by notice to the company in writing specifying when it is to terminate;

(b) on the occurrence in relation to the alternate of any event which, if it occurred in relation to the alternate's appointor, would result in the termination of the appointor's appointment as a director;

(c) on the death of the alternate's appointor;<sup>b</sup> or

(d) when the alternate's appointor's appointment as a director terminates, except that an alternate's appointment as an alternate does not terminate when the appointor retires by rotation at a general meeting and is then re-appointed as a director at the same general meeting.

51.MA.143

AMENDMENTS AND NOTES

<sup>a</sup> This article corresponds to the provisions of Table A regs 65, 67 and 68.

<sup>b</sup> Article 27(b) and (c) were not included in the corresponding provision of Table A (reg 67).

Part 3
## DECISION-MAKING BY MEMBERS

*Organisation of General Meetings*[a]

**Members can call general meeting if not enough directors**[b]

**51.MA.144**    **28.** If—

(a) the company has fewer than two directors, and

(b) the director (if any) is unable or unwilling to appoint sufficient directors to make up a quorum or to call a general meeting to do so,

then two or more members may call a general meeting[c] (or instruct the company secretary to do so) for the purpose of appointing one or more directors.

AMENDMENTS AND NOTES

[a]  See note a to para 51.MA.61.

[b]  The directors of a company will convene a general meeting either on their own initiative or as a result of a requisition received from the members of the company (ss 302–304 of the Companies Act 2006 (see Chapter 13)). This article enables members to call a meeting in circumstances where the company only has one director and where this remaining director is unwilling to take the necessary steps to appoint another director. There is no directly corresponding provision in Table A: this provision goes further than Table A reg 37.

[c]  This has the effect of relaxing the requisite percentages stipulated in s 303(2) of the Companies Act 2006 (see Chapter 13) in relation to requisitioning a general meeting (namely members who represent at least 5 per cent. of the voting rights of all the members having a right to vote at general meetings) in the specific set of circumstances contemplated in article 28.

**Attendance and speaking at general meetings**[a, b]

**51.MA.145**    **29.** (1) A person is able to exercise the right to speak at a general meeting when that person is in a position to communicate to all those attending the meeting, during the meeting, any information or opinions which that person has on the business of the meeting.

(2) A person is able to exercise the right to vote at a general meeting when—

(a) that person is able to vote, during the meeting, on resolutions put to the vote at the meeting, and

(b) that person's vote can be taken into account in determining whether or not such resolutions are passed at the same time as the votes of all the other persons attending the meeting.

(3) The directors may make whatever arrangements they consider appropriate to enable those attending a general meeting to exercise their rights to speak or vote at it.

(4) In determining attendance at a general meeting, it is immaterial whether any two or more members attending it are in the same place as each other.

(5) Two or more persons who are not in the same place as each other attend a general meeting if their circumstances are such that if they have (or were to have) rights to speak and vote at that meeting, they are (or would be) able to exercise them.

AMENDMENTS AND NOTES

[a]  Neither the Companies Act 2006 nor the model articles for public companies provides a definition of 'record date' for the purposes of determining entitlement to attend and vote at a general meeting.

[b]  See note b to para 51.MA.61.

**Quorum for general meetings**[a]

**51.MA.146**    **30.** No business other than the appointment of the chairman of the meeting is to be transacted at a general meeting if the persons attending it do not constitute a quorum.

AMENDMENTS AND NOTES

[a]  See note a to para 51.MA.62. See the provisions of s 318(2) of the Companies Act 2006 (see Chapter 13) as regards how the appointment of more than one proxy or corporate representative by a single shareholder will not amount to a quorum for these purposes.

**Chairing general meetings**[a]

**51.MA.147**    **31.** (1) If the directors have appointed a chairman, the chairman shall chair general meetings if present and willing to do so.

(2) If the directors have not appointed a chairman, or if the chairman is unwilling to chair the meeting or is not present within ten[b] minutes of the time at which a meeting was due to start—

(a) the directors present, or

(b) (if no directors are present), the meeting,

must appoint a director or member to chair the meeting, and the appointment of the chairman of the meeting must be the first business of the meeting.

(3) The person chairing a meeting in accordance with this article is referred to as 'the chairman of the meeting'.

AMENDMENTS AND NOTES

[a] This article corresponds to Table A reg 42. See note a to para 51.MA.63.

[b] See note b to para 51.MA.63.

### Attendance and speaking by directors and non-members[a]

**32.** (1) Directors may attend and speak at general meetings, whether or not they are members.

(2) The chairman of the meeting may permit other persons who are not—

(a) members of the company, or

(b) otherwise entitled to exercise the rights of members in relation to general meetings,

to attend and speak at a general meeting.

51.MA.148

AMENDMENTS AND NOTES

[a] See note a to para 51.MA.64.

### Adjournment[a]

**33.** (1) If the persons attending a general meeting within half an hour of the time at which the meeting was due to start do not constitute a quorum, or if during a meeting a quorum ceases to be present, the chairman of the meeting must adjourn it.[b]

(2) The chairman of the meeting may adjourn a general meeting at which a quorum is present if—[c]

(a) the meeting consents to an adjournment, or

(b) it appears to the chairman of the meeting that an adjournment is necessary to protect the safety of any person attending the meeting or ensure that the business of the meeting is conducted in an orderly manner.

(3) The chairman of the meeting must adjourn a general meeting if directed to do so by the meeting.[d]

(4) When adjourning a general meeting, the chairman of the meeting must—

(a) either specify the time and place to which it is adjourned or state that it is to continue at a time and place to be fixed by the directors,[e] and

(b) have regard to any directions as to the time and place of any adjournment which have been given by the meeting.

(5) If the continuation of an adjourned meeting is to take place more than 14 days[f] after it was adjourned, the company must give at least 7 clear days' notice of it (that is, excluding the day of the adjourned meeting and the day on which the notice is given)—

(a) to the same persons to whom notice of the company's general meetings is required to be given, and

(b) containing the same information which such notice is required to contain.

(6) No business may be transacted at an adjourned general meeting which could not properly have been transacted at the meeting if the adjournment had not taken place.

51.MA.149

AMENDMENTS AND NOTES

[a] See note a to para 51.MA.65.

[b] See note b to para 51.MA.65.

[c] See note c to para 51.MA.65.

[d] See note d to para 51.MA.65.

[e] See note e to para 51.MA.65.

[f] This period of time reflects the period contemplated in Table A reg 45.

## Voting at General Meetings

### Voting: general[a]

**34.** A resolution put to the vote of a general meeting must be decided on a show of hands unless a poll is duly demanded in accordance with the articles.

51.MA.150

AMENDMENTS AND NOTES

[a] See note b to para 51.MA.66.

### Errors and disputes

**35.** (1) No objection may be raised to the qualification of any person voting at a general meeting except at the meeting or adjourned meeting at which the vote objected to is tendered, and every vote not disallowed at the meeting is valid.

51.MA.151

(2)  Any such objection must be referred to the chairman of the meeting whose decision is final.[a]

AMENDMENTS AND NOTES

[a]  Article 35 corresponds to reg 58 of Table A. See note a to para 51.MA.67.

### Demanding a poll[a]

**51.MA.152**    **36.** (1)  A poll on a resolution may be demanded—
        (a)  in advance[b] of the general meeting where it is to be put to the vote, or
        (b)  at a general meeting, either before a show of hands on that resolution or immediately
            after the result of a show of hands on that resolution is declared.
    (2)  A poll may be demanded[c] by—
        (a)  the chairman of the meeting;
        (b)  the directors;[d]
        (c)  two or more persons having the right to vote on the resolution;[e] or
        (d)  a person or persons[f] representing not less than one tenth of the total voting rights of all
            the members having the right to vote on the resolution.
    (3)  A demand for a poll may be withdrawn if—[g]
        (a)  the poll has not yet been taken, and
        (b)  the chairman of the meeting consents to the withdrawal.

AMENDMENTS AND NOTES

[a]  This article corresponds to Table A regs 46 and 48.

[b]  See note a to para 51.MA.68: this provision was not previously included in Table A. This provision
    will permit public companies to bypass what might otherwise be an unrepresentative vote on a
    show of hands.

[c]  See note b to para 51.MA.68.

[d]  See note c to para 51.MA.68.

[e]  See note d to para 51.MA.68.

[f]  See note e to para 51.MA.68.

[g]  None of the forms of model articles includes a provision which corresponds to Table A reg 48. This
    regulation confirmed the effectiveness of the result of a vote taken on a show of hands, in
    circumstances where a vote on a poll is subsequently demanded and then withdrawn. This is now
    addressed as part of s 320(3) of the Companies Act 2006 (see Chapter 13).

### Procedure on a poll[a]

**51.MA.153**    **37.** (1)  Subject to the articles, polls at general meetings must be taken as and when, where and in
        such manner as the chairman of the meeting directs.
    (2)  The chairman of the meeting may appoint scrutineers[b] (who need not be members) and
        decide how and when the result of the poll is to be declared.
    (3)  The result of a poll shall be the decision of the meeting in respect of the resolution on which
        the poll was demanded.
    (4)  A poll on—
        (a)  the election of the chairman of the meeting, or
        (b)  a question of adjournment,
        must be taken immediately.[c]
    (5)  Other polls must be taken within 30 days of their being demanded.[d]
    (6)  A demand for a poll does not prevent a general meeting from continuing, except as regards
        the question on which the poll was demanded.[e]
    (7)  No notice need be given of a poll not taken immediately if the time and place at which it is
        to be taken are announced at the meeting at which it is demanded.[f]
    (8)  In any other case, at least 7 days' notice must be given specifying the time and place at which
        the poll is to be taken.[g]

AMENDMENTS AND NOTES

[a]  These provisions are more elaborate than the corresponding provisions in the model articles for
    private companies limited by shares. This article corresponds to Table A regs 49 and 51.

[b]  This corresponds broadly to the provisions of Table A reg 49.

[c]  This corresponds broadly to the provisions of Table A reg 51. See also s 321 of the Companies Act
    2006.

[d]  This is consistent with Table A reg 51.

[e]  This corresponds to the provisions of Table A reg 51.

[f]  This corresponds to the provisions of Table A reg 52.

[g]  This corresponds to the provisions of Table A reg 52.

### Content of proxy notices[a]

**38.** (1) Proxies may only validly be appointed by a notice in writing (a 'proxy notice') which—

    (a) states the name and address of the member appointing the proxy;

    (b) identifies the person appointed to be that member's proxy and the general meeting in relation to which that person is appointed;

    (c) is signed by or on behalf of the member appointing the proxy, or is authenticated in such manner as the directors may determine;[b] and

    (d) is delivered to the company in accordance with the articles and any instructions contained in the notice of the general meeting to which they relate.

(2) The company may require proxy notices to be delivered in a particular form, and may specify different forms for different purposes.

(3) Proxy notices may specify how the proxy appointed under them is to vote (or that the proxy is to abstain from voting) on one or more resolutions.

(4) Unless a proxy notice indicates otherwise, it must be treated as—

    (a) allowing the person appointed under it as a proxy discretion as to how to vote on any ancillary or procedural resolutions put to the meeting, and

    (b) appointing that person as a proxy in relation to any adjournment of the general meeting to which it relates as well as the meeting itself.

51.MA.154

AMENDMENTS AND NOTES

[a] See note a to para 51.MA.69 above. This article corresponds to Table A regs 52, 60 and 61.

[b] This contemplates the use of electronic forms of shareholder identification: for example the forms of identification used in connection with forms of proxy that are submitted by means of the CREST system.

### Delivery of proxy notices

**39.** (1) Any notice of a general meeting must specify the address or addresses ('proxy notification address')[a] at which the company or its agents will receive proxy notices relating to that meeting, or any adjournment of it, delivered in hard copy or electronic form.[b]

(2) A person who is entitled to attend, speak or vote (either on a show of hands or on a poll) at a general meeting remains so entitled in respect of that meeting or any adjournment of it, even though a valid proxy notice has been delivered to the company by or on behalf of that person.[c]

(3) Subject to paragraphs (4) and (5), a proxy notice must be delivered to a proxy notification address not less than 48 hours before the general meeting or adjourned meeting to which it relates.[d]

(4) In the case of a poll taken more than 48 hours after it is demanded, the notice must be delivered to a proxy notification address not less than 24 hours before the time appointed for the taking of the poll.

(5) In the case of a poll not taken during the meeting but taken not more than 48 hours after it was demanded, the proxy notice must be delivered:[e]

    (a) in accordance with paragraph (3), or

    (b) at the meeting at which the poll was demanded to the chairman, secretary or any director.

(6) An appointment under a proxy notice may be revoked by delivering a notice given by or on behalf of the person by whom or on whose behalf the proxy notice was given to a proxy notification address.

(7) A notice revoking a proxy appointment only takes effect if it is delivered before—

    (a) the start of the meeting or adjourned meeting to which it relates, or

    (b) (in the case of a poll not taken on the same day as the meeting or adjourned meeting) the time appointed for taking the poll to which it relates.[f]

(8) If a proxy notice is not signed by the person appointing the proxy, it must be accompanied by written evidence of the authority of the person who executed it to execute it on the appointor's behalf.[g]

51.MA.155

AMENDMENTS AND NOTES

[a] For most public companies, the notice of general meeting will stipulate that proxy documentation should be returned to the company's registrar, as opposed to the company's registered office. This provision preserves flexibility in this regard. Article 39(1) is not included in the model articles for private companies.

[b] This imports the provisions of s 1168 of the Companies Act 2006. This article will also permit forms of proxy to be submitted by means of the CREST system.

[c] See also s 330 of the Companies Act 2006 as regards the provisions regulating notice of termination of a proxy's authority (see Chapter 13).

<sup>d</sup> This provision corresponds to Table A reg 62. See also s 327(2)(a) of the Companies Act 2006 (see Chapter 13). However, note that s 327(3) specifically provides that in calculating the time periods for the purposes of s 327, no account shall be taken of any part of a day that is not a working day. This constraint has not been imported into the provisions of the model articles.

<sup>e</sup> This corresponds to the provisions of Table A reg 62.

<sup>f</sup> See also s 330(3) of the Companies Act 2006 in relation to notice being required of termination of a proxy's authority.

<sup>g</sup> This corresponds to the provisions of Table A reg 62.

### Amendments to resolutions

**51.MA.156**

**40.** (1) An ordinary resolution to be proposed at a general meeting may be amended by ordinary resolution<sup>a</sup> if—

   (a) notice of the proposed amendment is given to the company secretary in writing by a person entitled to vote at the general meeting at which it is to be proposed not less than 48 hours before the meeting is to take place (or such later time as the chairman of the meeting may determine), and

   (b) the proposed amendment does not, in the reasonable opinion of the chairman of the meeting, materially alter the scope of the resolution.

  (2) A special resolution to be proposed at a general meeting may be amended by ordinary resolution,<sup>b</sup> if—

   (a) the chairman of the meeting proposes the amendment at the general meeting at which the resolution is to be proposed, and

   (b) the amendment does not go beyond what is necessary to correct a grammatical or other non-substantive error in the resolution.

  (3) If the chairman of the meeting, acting in good faith, wrongly decides that an amendment to a resolution is out of order, the chairman's error does not invalidate the vote on that resolution.

AMENDMENTS AND NOTES

<sup>a</sup> See note a to para 51.MA.71.

<sup>b</sup> See note b to para 51.MA.71.

## Restrictions on Members' Rights

### No voting of shares on which money owed to company

**51.MA.157**

**41.** No voting rights attached to a share may be exercised at any general meeting, at any adjournment of it, or on any poll called at or in relation to it, unless all amounts payable to the company in respect of that share have been paid.<sup>a</sup>

AMENDMENTS AND NOTES

<sup>a</sup> This corresponds to the provisions of Table A reg 57.

## Application of Rules to Class Meetings

### Class meetings<sup>a</sup>

**51.MA.158**

**42.** The provisions of the articles relating to general meetings apply, with any necessary modifications, to meetings of the holders of any class of shares.

AMENDMENTS AND NOTES

<sup>a</sup> The model articles for public companies do not include any provisions governing the variation of class rights. Accordingly, the provisions of s 630 of the Companies Act 2006 (see Chapter 17) would apply to any proposed variation of rights attached to any class of shares in a company to which this form of articles of association applies.

## Part 4
## SHARES AND DISTRIBUTIONS
### Issue of Shares

### Powers to issue different classes of share

**51.MA.159**

**43.** (1) Subject to the articles, but without prejudice to the rights attached to any existing share, the company may issue shares with such rights or restrictions as may be determined by ordinary resolution.<sup>a</sup>

  (2) The company may issue shares which are to be redeemed, or are liable to be redeemed at the option of the company or the holder, and the directors may determine the terms, conditions and manner of redemption of any such shares.<sup>b</sup>

AMENDMENTS AND NOTES

<sup>a</sup> See note b to para 51.MA.46.

<sup>b</sup> Section 684(3) of the Companies Act 2006 (see Chapter 18) provides that a public company may only issue redeemable shares if it is specifically authorised to do so by its articles. Section 685(1)(a) provides that the directors of a limited company may only determine the terms, conditions, and manner of redemption of shares if they are authorised to do so by the company's articles or by a resolution of the company.

### Payment of commissions on subscription for shares[a]

**44.** (1) The company may pay any person a commission in consideration for that person—

    (a) subscribing, or agreeing to subscribe, for shares, or

    (b) procuring, or agreeing to procure, subscriptions for shares.

(2) Any such commission may be paid—

    (a) in cash, or in fully paid or partly paid shares or other securities, or partly in one way and partly in the other, and

    (b) in respect of a conditional or an absolute subscription.

**51.MA.160**

AMENDMENTS AND NOTES

<sup>a</sup> This is broadly consistent with the approach taken in Table A reg 4. Permitted commissions are regulated by s 553(1) and (2) of the Companies Act 2006 (see Chapter 17).

## Interests in Shares

### Company not bound by less than absolute interests[a]

**45.** Except as required by law, no person is to be recognised by the company as holding any share upon any trust, and except as otherwise required by law or the articles, the company is not in any way to be bound by or recognise any interest in a share other than the holder's absolute ownership of it and all the rights attaching to it.

**51.MA.161**

AMENDMENTS AND NOTES

<sup>a</sup> See note a to para 51.MA.47.

## Share Certificates[a]

### Certificates to be issued except in certain cases

**46.** (1) The company must issue each member with one or more certificates in respect of the shares which that member holds.

(2) This article does not apply to—

    (a) uncertificated shares;<sup>b</sup>

    (b) shares in respect of which a share warrant has been issued; or

    (c) shares in respect of which the Companies Acts permit the company not to issue a certificate.

(3) Except as otherwise specified in the articles, all certificates must be issued free of charge.

(4) No certificate may be issued in respect of shares of more than one class.

(5) If more than one person holds a share, only one certificate may be issued in respect of it.

**51.MA.162**

AMENDMENTS AND NOTES

<sup>a</sup> See notes a and b to para 51.MA.48.

<sup>b</sup> The model articles for public companies contemplate that a company may issue shares in uncertificated form, as to which see article 50 and related commentary.

### Contents and execution of share certificates

**47.** (1) Every certificate must specify—

    (a) in respect of how many shares, of what class, it is issued;

    (b) the nominal value of those shares;

    (c) the amount paid up on them; and

    (d) any distinguishing numbers assigned to them.

(2) Certificates must—

    (a) have affixed to them the company's common seal or an official seal which is a facsimile of the company's common seal with the addition on its face of the word 'Securities' (a 'securities seal'),<sup>a</sup> or

    (b) be otherwise executed in accordance with the Companies Acts<sup>b</sup>.

**51.MA.163**

AMENDMENTS AND NOTES

<sup>a</sup> See article 81 as regards the authority to affix seals.

<sup>b</sup> See note e to para 51.MA.48.

**Consolidated share certificates**

**51.MA.164**

**48.** (1) When a member's holding of shares of a particular class increases, the company may issue that member with—

(a) a single, consolidated certificate in respect of all the shares of a particular class which that member holds, or

(b) a separate certificate in respect of only those shares by which that member's holding has increased.

(2) When a member's holding of shares of a particular class is reduced, the company must ensure that the member is issued with one or more certificates in respect of the number of shares held by the member after that reduction. But the company need not (in the absence of a request from the member) issue any new certificate if—

(a) all the shares which the member no longer holds as a result of the reduction, and

(b) none of the shares which the member retains following the reduction,

were, immediately before the reduction, represented by the same certificate.

(3) A member may request the company, in writing, to replace—

(a) the member's separate certificates with a consolidated certificate, or

(b) the member's consolidated certificate with two or more separate certificates representing such proportion of the shares as the member may specify.

(4) When the company complies with such a request it may charge such reasonable fee as the directors may decide for doing so.

(5) A consolidated certificate must not be issued unless any certificates which it is to replace have first been returned to the company for cancellation.[b]

AMENDMENTS AND NOTES

[a] This article simplifies and clarifies the corresponding provision of Table A (reg 6).

[b] This is consistent with the provisions of Table A reg 7.

**Replacement share certificates**[a]

**51.MA.165**

**49.** (1) If a certificate issued in respect of a member's shares is—

(a) damaged or defaced, or

(b) said to be lost, stolen or destroyed,

that member is entitled to be issued with a replacement certificate in respect of the same shares.

(2) A member exercising the right to be issued with such a replacement certificate—

(a) may at the same time exercise the right to be issued with a single certificate or separate certificates;

(b) must return the certificate which is to be replaced to the company if it is damaged or defaced; and

(c) must comply with such conditions as to evidence, indemnity and the payment of a reasonable fee as the directors decide.

AMENDMENTS AND NOTES

[a] See note a to para 51.MA.49.

## Shares Not Held in Certificated Form[a]

**Uncertificated shares**

**51.MA.166**

**50.** (1) In this article, 'the relevant rules' means—

(a) any applicable provision of the Companies Acts about the holding, evidencing of title to, or transfer of shares other than in certificated form, and

(b) any applicable legislation, rules or other arrangements made under or by virtue of such provision.[b]

(2) The provisions of this article have effect subject to the relevant rules.

(3) Any provision of the articles which is inconsistent with the relevant rules must be disregarded, to the extent that it is inconsistent, whenever the relevant rules apply.

(4) Any share or class of shares of the company may be issued or held on such terms, or in a such a way, that—

(a) title to it or them is not, or must not be, evidenced by a certificate, or

(b) it or they may or must be transferred wholly or partly without a certificate.

(5) The directors have power to take such steps as they think fit in relation to—

(a) the evidencing of and transfer of title to uncertificated shares (including in connection with the issue of such shares);

(b) any records relating to the holding of uncertificated shares;

(c) the conversion of certificated shares into uncertificated shares; or

(d) the conversion of uncertificated shares into certificated shares.

(6) The company may by notice to the holder of a share require that share—

(a) if it is uncertificated, to be converted into certificated form, and

(b) if it is certificated, to be converted into uncertificated form,
to enable it to be dealt with in accordance with the articles.
(7) If—
(a) the articles give the directors power to take action, or require other persons to take action, in order to sell, transfer or otherwise dispose of shares, and
(b) uncertificated shares are subject to that power, but the power is expressed in terms which assume the use of a certificate or other written instrument,
the directors may take such action as is necessary or expedient to achieve the same results when exercising that power in relation to uncertificated shares.
(8) In particular, the directors may take such action as they consider appropriate to achieve the sale, transfer, disposal, forfeiture, re-allotment or surrender of an uncertificated share or otherwise to enforce a lien in respect of it.
(9) Unless the directors otherwise determine, shares which a member holds in uncertificated form must be treated as separate holdings from any shares which that member holds in certificated form.
(10) A class of shares must not be treated as two classes simply because some shares of that class are held in certificated form and others are held in uncertificated form.

AMENDMENTS AND NOTES

[a] There were no provisions specifically relating to dematerialized shares in Table A. The provisions of article 50 are relatively comprehensive. However, the effect of article 50(2) is to give primacy to any other conflicting rules in the Companies Act 2006 or in any other applicable legislation enacted under the Companies Act 2006 that address dematerialized shares. See the commentary in relation to s 785(1) of the Companies Act at note b to para 51.MA.166.

[b] Section 785(1) of the Companies Act 2006 (see Chapter 21) makes provision for secondary legislation to enable title to securities to be evidenced and transferred without a written instrument. Section 785 restates s 207 of the Companies Act 1989. No such secondary legislation has yet been proposed or made under the authority of s 785; the previous regulations remain in force, see Chapter 49. The Institute of Chartered Secretaries and Administrators previously consulted as part of an industry dematerialization working group, which considered a proposal to remove the requirement for paper share certificates and stock transfer forms.

### Share warrants[a]

**51.** (1) The directors may issue a share warrant in respect of any fully paid share. **51.MA.167**
(2) Share warrants must be—
(a) issued in such form, and
(b) executed in such manner,
as the directors decide.
(3) A share represented by a share warrant may be transferred by delivery of the warrant representing it.
(4) The directors may make provision for the payment of dividends in respect of any share represented by a share warrant.
(5) Subject to the articles, the directors may decide the conditions on which any share warrant is issued. In particular, they may—
(a) decide the conditions on which new warrants are to be issued in place of warrants which are damaged or defaced, or said to have been lost, stolen or destroyed;
(b) decide the conditions on which bearers of warrants are entitled to attend and vote at general meetings;
(c) decide the conditions subject to which bearers of warrants may surrender their warrant so as to hold their shares in certificated or uncertificated form instead;[b] and
(d) vary the conditions of issue of any warrant from time to time,
and the bearer of a warrant is subject to the conditions and procedures in force in relation to it, whether or not they were decided or specified before the warrant was issued.
(6) Subject to the conditions on which the warrants are issued from time to time, bearers of share warrants have the same rights and privileges as they would if their names had been included in the register as holders of the shares represented by their warrants.[c]
(7) The company must not in any way be bound by or recognise any interest in a share represented by a share warrant other than the absolute right of the bearer of that warrant to that warrant.

AMENDMENTS AND NOTES

[a] Table A does not contain provisions relating to share warrants. See s 122 of the Companies Act 2006, and which indicates that share warrants may be issued directly following the initial allotment of the shares represented by the share warrants (see s 122(1)(b) and s 769(2)(c)).

<sup>b</sup> Section 780 of the Companies Act 2006 (see Chapter 21) provides that when a share warrant is surrendered for cancellation, a company has a period of two months to complete, and have ready for issue, a share certificate for the shares specified in the share warrant, unless that company has a contrary provision in its articles of association. There is no contrary provision in the model articles for public companies. (See also s 769(2)(c) of the Companies Act 2006 as regards the relaxation of the duty of a company to issue a share certificate following an allotment of shares (s 769(1)), in circumstances where, following the allotment, a share warrant is issued in respect of such shares.)

<sup>c</sup> See s 122(3) of the Companies Act 2006 (see Chapter 8) in this regard: this section provides that if the articles of a company so provide, the bearer of a share warrant will be deemed to be a member of the company within the meaning of the Companies Act 2006 either to the full extent or for any purposes defined in the articles.

## *Partly Paid Shares*<sup>a</sup>

### Company's lien over partly paid shares<sup>b</sup>

**51.MA.168**

**52.** (1) The company has a lien ('the company's lien') over every share which is partly paid for any part of—

    (a) that share's nominal value, and

    (b) any premium at which it was issued,

    which has not been paid to the company, and which is payable immediately or at some time in the future, whether or not a call notice has been sent in respect of it.

  (2) The company's lien over a share—

    (a) takes priority over any third party's interest in that share, and

    (b) extends to any dividend or other money payable by the company in respect of that share and (if the lien is enforced and the share is sold by the company) the proceeds of sale of that share.

  (3) The directors may at any time decide that a share which is or would otherwise be subject to the company's lien shall not be subject to it, either wholly or in part.

AMENDMENTS AND NOTES

<sup>a</sup> The model articles make provision for the company's lien over partly paid shares, for calls on shares and for forfeiture and surrender of shares: the provisions as to liens and forfeiture are substantially in keeping with the provisions of the current Table A. These provisions are only relevant if a company wishes to make provision for the issue of partly paid shares. (See notes a and b to para 51.MA.45). These provisions are not included in the model articles for private companies limited by shares. The Government does contemplate, however, that more complex private companies may choose to issue (or wish to preserve the ability to issue) shares on a partly paid basis and, accordingly, that such companies may want to incorporate these provisions into their articles of association (see para 51.MA.18).

<sup>b</sup> This corresponds broadly to the provisions of Table A reg 8 (as to which, see the commentary on the priority afforded to the lien created at note b to reg 8 of the Table A CA 1985 annotated commentary). The extension of the lien in article 52(2)(b) was not expressly addressed in Table A. See commentary to the corresponding regulations of Table A, for a detailed discussion of the case law relating to liens, call notices and forfeiture.

### Enforcement of the company's lien

**51.MA.169**

**53.** (1) <sup>a</sup> Subject to the provisions of this article, if—

    (a) a lien enforcement notice has been given in respect of a share, and

    (b) the person to whom the notice was given has failed to comply with it,

    the company may sell that share in such manner as the directors decide.

  (2) A lien enforcement notice—

    (a) may only be given in respect of a share which is subject to the company's lien, in respect of which a sum is payable and the due date for payment of that sum has passed;

    (b) must specify the share concerned;

    (c) must require payment of the sum payable within 14 days of the notice;

    (d) must be addressed either to the holder of the share or to a person entitled to it by reason of the holder's death or bankruptcy or otherwise; and

    (e) must state the company's intention to sell the share if the notice is not complied with.

  (3) <sup>b</sup> Where shares are sold under this article—

    (a) the directors may authorise any person to execute an instrument of transfer of the shares to the purchaser or a person nominated by the purchaser, and

    (b) the transferee is not bound to see to the application of the consideration, and the transferee's title is not affected by any irregularity in or invalidity of the process leading to the sale.

  (4) <sup>c</sup> The net proceeds of any such sale (after payment of the costs of sale and any other costs of enforcing the lien) must be applied—

(a) first, in payment of so much of the sum for which the lien exists as was payable at the date of the lien enforcement notice,

(b) second, to the person entitled to the shares at the date of the sale, but only after the certificate for the shares sold has been surrendered to the company for cancellation or a suitable indemnity has been given for any lost certificates, and subject to a lien equivalent to the company's lien over the shares before the sale for any money payable in respect of the shares after the date of the lien enforcement notice.

(5) [d] A statutory declaration by a director or the company secretary that the declarant is a director or the company secretary and that a share has been sold to satisfy the company's lien on a specified date—

    (a) is conclusive evidence of the facts stated in it as against all persons claiming to be entitled to the share, and

    (b) subject to compliance with any other formalities of transfer required by the articles or by law, constitutes a good title to the share.

AMENDMENTS AND NOTES

[a] The provisions of article 53(1) and (2) are substantially in line with the provisions of Table A reg 9.

[b] The provisions of article 53(3) are substantially in line with certain of the provisions of Table A reg 10.

[c] The provisions of article 53(4) are substantially in line with the provisions of Table A reg 11.

[d] The provisions of article 55(5) restate certain of the provisions of Table A reg 10.

### Call notices

**54.** (1) Subject to the articles and the terms on which shares are allotted, the directors may send a notice (a 'call notice') to a member requiring the member to pay the company a specified sum of money (a 'call') which is payable in respect of shares which that member holds at the date when the directors decide to send the call notice.     **51.MA.170**

(2) A call notice—

    (a) may not require a member to pay a call which exceeds the total sum unpaid on that member's shares (whether as to the share's nominal value or any amount payable to the company by way of premium);

    (b) must state when and how any call to which it relates it is to be paid; and

    (c) may permit or require the call to be paid by instalments.

(3) A member must comply with the requirements of a call notice, but no member is obliged to pay any call before 14 days have passed since the notice was sent.

(4) [a] Before the company has received any call due under a call notice the directors may—

    (a) revoke it wholly or in part, or

    (b) specify a later time for payment than is specified in the notice,

by a further notice in writing to the member in respect of whose shares the call is made.

AMENDMENTS AND NOTES

[a] This corresponds broadly to certain of the provisions of Table A reg 12.

### Liability to pay calls

**55.** (1) [a] Liability to pay a call is not extinguished or transferred by transferring the shares in respect of which it is required to be paid.     **51.MA.171**

(2) Joint holders of a share are jointly and severally liable to pay all calls in respect of that share.

(3) [b] Subject to the terms on which shares are allotted, the directors may, when issuing shares, provide that call notices sent to the holders of those shares may require them—

    (a) to pay calls which are not the same, or

    (b) to pay calls at different times.

AMENDMENTS AND NOTES

[a] The provisions of article 55(1) and 55(2) correspond broadly to the provisions of Table A reg 12.

[b] The provisions of article 55(3) correspond broadly to the provisions of Table A reg 17.

### When call notice need not be issued

**56.** (1) [a] A call notice need not be issued in respect of sums which are specified, in the terms on which a share is issued, as being payable to the company in respect of that share (whether in respect of nominal value or premium)—     **51.MA.172**

    (a) on allotment;

    (b) on the occurrence of a particular event; or

    (c) on a date fixed by or in accordance with the terms of issue.

(2) But if the due date for payment of such a sum has passed and it has not been paid, the holder of the share concerned is treated in all respects as having failed to comply with a call notice in respect of that sum, and is liable to the same consequences as regards the payment of interest and forfeiture.

AMENDMENTS AND NOTES

ᵃ The provisions of article 56(1) correspond broadly to the provisions of Table A reg 16.

### Failure to comply with call notice: automatic consequences

**51.MA.173**  **57.** (1) ᵃ If a person is liable to pay a call and fails to do so by the call payment date—

(a) the directors may issue a notice of intended forfeiture to that person, and

(b) until the call is paid, that person must pay the company interest on the call from the call payment date at the relevant rate.

(2) ᵇ For the purposes of this article—

(a) the 'call payment date' is the time when the call notice states that a call is payable, unless the directors give a notice specifying a later date, in which case the 'call payment date' is that later date;

(b) the 'relevant rate' is—

(i) the rate fixed by the terms on which the share in respect of which the call is due was allotted;

(ii) such other rate as was fixed in the call notice which required payment of the call, or has otherwise been determined by the directors; or

(iii) if no rate is fixed in either of these ways, 5 per cent per annum.

(3) The relevant rate must not exceed by more than 5 percentage points the base lending rate most recently set by the Monetary Policy Committee of the Bank of England in connection with its responsibilities under Part 2 of the Bank of England Act 1998.ᶜ

(4) The directors may waive any obligation to pay interest on a call wholly or in part.

AMENDMENTS AND NOTES

ᵃ This corresponds to the provisions of Table A reg 15.

ᵇ This is more detailed than the corresponding provision of Table A reg 15.

ᶜ 1998 C. 11.

### Notice of intended forfeiture

**51.MA.174**  **58.** ᵃ A notice of intended forfeiture—

(a) may be sent in respect of any share in respect of which a call has not been paid as required by a call notice;

(b) must be sent to the holder of that share or to a person entitled to it by reason of the holder's death, bankruptcy or otherwise;

(c) must require payment of the call and any accrued interest by a date which is not less than 14 days after the date of the notice;

(d) must state how the payment is to be made; and

(e) must state that if the notice is not complied with, the shares in respect of which the call is payable will be liable to be forfeited.

AMENDMENTS AND NOTES

ᵃ This corresponds to the provisions of Table A reg 18.

### Directors' power to forfeit shares

**51.MA.175**  **59.** If a notice of intended forfeiture is not complied with before the date by which payment of the call is required in the notice of intended forfeiture, the directors may decide that any share in respect of which it was given is forfeited, and the forfeiture is to include all dividends or other moneys payable in respect of the forfeited shares and not paid before the forfeiture.

### Effect of forfeiture

**51.MA.176**  **60.** (1) Subject to the articles, the forfeiture of a share extinguishes—

(a) all interests in that share, and all claims and demands against the company in respect of it, and

(b) all other rights and liabilities incidental to the share as between the person whose share it was prior to the forfeiture and the company.

(2) Any share which is forfeited in accordance with the articles—

(a) is deemed to have been forfeited when the directors decide that it is forfeited;

(b) is deemed to be the property of the company; and

(c) may be sold, re-allotted or otherwise disposed of as the directors think fit.

(3) If a person's shares have been forfeited—

(a) the company must send that person notice that forfeiture has occurred and record it in the register of members;

(b) that person ceases to be a member in respect of those shares;

(c) that person must surrender the certificate for the shares forfeited to the company for cancellation;

(d) that person remains liable to the company for all sums payable by that person under the articles at the date of forfeiture in respect of those shares, including any interest (whether accrued before or after the date of forfeiture); and

(e) the directors may waive payment of such sums wholly or in part or enforce payment without any allowance for the value of the shares at the time of forfeiture or for any consideration received on their disposal.

(4) At any time before the company disposes of a forfeited share, the directors may decide to cancel the forfeiture on payment of all calls and interest due in respect of it and on such other terms as they think fit.

### Procedure following forfeiture

**61.** (1) If a forfeited share is to be disposed of by being transferred, the company may receive the consideration for the transfer and the directors may authorise any person to execute the instrument of transfer.      **51.MA.177**

(2) A statutory declaration by a director or the company secretary that the declarant is a director or the company secretary and that a share has been forfeited on a specified date—
  (a) is conclusive evidence of the facts stated in it as against all persons claiming to be entitled to the share, and
  (b) subject to compliance with any other formalities of transfer required by the articles or by law, constitutes a good title to the share.

(3) A person to whom a forfeited share is transferred is not bound to see to the application of the consideration (if any) nor is that person's title to the share affected by any irregularity in or invalidity of the process leading to the forfeiture or transfer of the share.

(4) If the company sells a forfeited share, the person who held it prior to its forfeiture is entitled to receive from the company the proceeds of such sale, net of any commission, and excluding any amount which—
  (a) was, or would have become, payable, and
  (b) had not, when that share was forfeited, been paid by that person in respect of that share, but no interest is payable to such a person in respect of such proceeds and the company is not required to account for any money earned on them.

### Surrender of shares[a]

**62.** (1) A member may surrender any share—      **51.MA.178**
  (a) in respect of which the directors may issue a notice of intended forfeiture;
  (b) which the directors may forfeit; or
  (c) which has been forfeited.

(2) The directors may accept the surrender of any such share.

(3) The effect of surrender on a share is the same as the effect of forfeiture on that share.

(4) A share which has been surrendered may be dealt with in the same way as a share which has been forfeited.

AMENDMENTS AND NOTES

[a] There is no corresponding provision in Table A.

## Transfer and Transmission of Shares

### Transfers of certificated shares[a]

**63.** (1) Certificated shares may be transferred by means of an instrument of transfer in any usual form or any other form approved by the directors, which is executed by or on behalf of—      **51.MA.179**
  (a) the transferor, and
  (b) (if any of the shares is partly paid) the transferee.

(2) No fee may be charged for registering any instrument of transfer or other document relating to or affecting the title to any share.

(3) The company may retain any instrument of transfer which is registered.

(4) The transferor remains the holder of a certificated share until the transferee's name is entered in the register of members as holder of it.

(5) The directors may refuse to register the transfer of a certificated share if—
  (a) the share is not fully paid;[b]
  (b) the transfer is not lodged at the company's registered office or such other place as the directors have appointed;
  (c) the transfer is not accompanied by the certificate for the shares to which it relates, or such other evidence as the directors may reasonably require to show the transferor's right to make the transfer, or evidence of the right of someone other than the transferor to

make the transfer on the transferor's behalf;

   (d) the transfer is in respect of more than one class of share; or

   (e) the transfer is in favour of more than four transferees.

(6) If the directors refuse to register the transfer of a share,[c] the instrument of transfer must be returned to the transferee with the notice of refusal unless they suspect that the proposed transfer may be fraudulent.

AMENDMENTS AND NOTES

[a] This corresponds to the provisions of Table A regs 23, 24, 27 and 28.

[b] There is no requirement to provide, as an additional limb to this provision, that it is not possible to transfer a share that is subject to a lien: this will be the consequence, in any event, of providing that a share may not be transferred if it is not fully paid.

[c] See note b to para 51.MA.50.

### Transfer of uncertificated shares

**51.MA.180**    **64.** A transfer of an uncertificated share must not be registered if it is in favour of more than four transferees.

### Transmission of shares[a]

**51.MA.181**    **65.** (1) If title to a share passes to a transmittee, the company may only recognise the transmittee as having any title to that share.

    (2) Nothing in these articles releases the estate of a deceased member from any liability in respect of a share solely or jointly held by that member.

AMENDMENTS AND NOTES

[a] See note a to para 51.MA.51.

### Transmittees' rights

**51.MA.182**    **66.** (1) A transmittee who produces such evidence of entitlement to shares as the directors may properly require—

    (a) may, subject to the articles, choose either to become the holder of those shares or to have them transferred to another person, and

    (b) subject to the articles, and pending any transfer of the shares to another person, has the same rights as the holder had.

    (2) But transmittees do not have the right to attend or vote at a general meeting in respect of shares to which they are entitled, by reason of the holder's death or bankruptcy, unless they become the holders of those shares.

### Exercise of transmittees' rights

**51.MA.183**    **67.** (1) Transmittees who wish to become the holders of shares to which they have become entitled must notify the company in writing of that wish.

    (2) If the share is a certificated share and a transmittee wishes to have it transferred to another person, the transmittee must execute an instrument of transfer in respect of it.

    (3) If the share is an uncertificated share and the transmittee wishes to have it transferred to another person, the transmittee must—

    (a) procure that all appropriate instructions are given to effect the transfer, or

    (b) procure that the uncertificated share is changed into certificated form and then execute an instrument of transfer in respect of it.

    (4) Any transfer made or executed under this article is to be treated as if it were made or executed by the person from whom the transmittee has derived rights in respect of the share, and as if the event which gave rise to the transmission had not occurred.

### Transmittees bound by prior notices

**51.MA.184**    **68.** If a notice is given to a member in respect of shares and a transmittee is entitled to those shares, the transmittee is bound by the notice if it was given to the member before the transmittee's name has been entered in the register of members.

## Consolidation of Shares[a]

### Procedure for disposing of fractions of shares

**51.MA.185**    **69.** (1) This article applies where—

    (a) there has been a consolidation or division of shares, and

        (b)  as a result, members are entitled to fractions of shares.
    (2)  The directors may—
        (a)  sell the shares representing the fractions to any person including the company for the best price reasonably obtainable;
        (b)  in the case of a certificated share, authorise any person to execute an instrument of transfer of the shares to the purchaser or a person nominated by the purchaser; and
        (c)  distribute the net proceeds of sale in due proportion among the holders of the shares.
    (3)  Where any holder's entitlement to a portion of the proceeds of sale amounts to less than a minimum figure determined by the directors, that member's portion may be distributed to an organisation which is a charity for the purposes of the law of England and Wales, Scotland or Northern Ireland.
    (4)  The person to whom the shares are transferred is not obliged to ensure that any purchase money is received by the person entitled to the relevant fractions.
    (5)  The transferee's title to the shares is not affected by any irregularity in or invalidity of the process leading to their sale.

AMENDMENTS AND NOTES

ᵃ  This provision restates and expands Table A reg 33. See also s 618 of the Companies Act 2006 (see Chapter 17).

## Distributionsᵃ

### Procedure for declaring dividendsᵇ

**70.** (1)  The company may by ordinary resolution declare dividends, and the directors may decide to pay interim dividends.ᶜ                                                    **51.MA.186**
    (2)  A dividend must not be declared unless the directors have made a recommendation as to its amount. Such a dividend must not exceed the amount recommended by the directors.
    (3)  No dividend may be declared or paid unless it is in accordance with members' respective rights.
    (4)  Unless the members' resolution to declare or directors' decision to pay a dividend, or the terms on which shares are issued, specify otherwise, it must be paid by reference to each member's holding of shares on the date of the resolution or decision to declare or pay it.ᵈ
    (5)  If the company's share capital is divided into different classes, no interim dividend may be paid on shares carrying deferred or non-preferred rights if, at the time of payment, any preferential dividend is in arrear.ᵉ
    (6)  The directors may pay at intervals any dividend payable at a fixed rate if it appears to them that the profits available for distribution justify the payment.
    (7)  If the directors act in good faith,ᶠ they do not incur any liability to the holders of shares conferring preferred rights for any loss they may suffer by the lawful payment of an interim dividend on shares with deferred or non-preferred rights.

AMENDMENTS AND NOTES

ᵃ  The substantive rules relating to when dividends are to be paid are contained in Part 23 of the Companies Act 2006.
ᵇ  See note b to para 51.MA.54. This article corresponds to the provisions of Table A regs 102 and 103.
ᶜ  See note c to para 51.MA.54.
ᵈ  See note d to para 51.MA.54. See also article 71(1).
ᵉ  See note e to para 51.MA.54.
ᶠ  See note f to para 51.MA.54.

### Calculation of dividendsᵃ

**71.** (1)  Except as otherwise provided by the articles or the rights attached to shares, all dividends must be—                                                                 **51.MA.187**
        (a)  declared and paid according to the amounts paid up on the shares on which the dividend is paid, and
        (b)  apportioned and paid proportionately to the amounts paid up on the shares during any portion or portions of the period in respect of which the dividend is paid.
    (2)  If any share is issued on terms providing that it ranks for dividend as from a particular date, that share ranks for dividend accordingly.
    (3)  For the purposes of calculating dividends, no account is to be taken of any amount which has been paid up on a share in advance of the due date for payment of that amount.

AMENDMENTS AND NOTES

ᵃ  This corresponds to the provisions of Table A reg 104. There are no corresponding provisions in the articles for private companies limited by shares and by guarantee.

**Payment of dividends and other distributions**[a]

**51.MA.188**   **72.** (1)  Where a dividend or other sum which is a distribution is payable in respect of a share, it must be paid by one or more of the following means—

(a)  transfer to a bank or building society account specified by the distribution recipient either in writing or as the directors may otherwise decide;

(b)  sending a cheque made payable to the distribution recipient by post to the distribution recipient at the distribution recipient's registered address (if the distribution recipient is a holder of the share), or (in any other case) to an address specified by the distribution recipient either in writing or as the directors may otherwise decide;

(c)  sending a cheque made payable to such person by post to such person at such address as the distribution recipient has specified either in writing or as the directors may otherwise decide; or

(d)  any other means of payment as the directors agree with the distribution recipient either in writing or by such other means as the directors decide.

(2)  In the articles, 'the distribution recipient' means, in respect of a share in respect of which a dividend or other sum is payable—

(a)  the holder of the share; or

(b)  if the share has two or more joint holders, whichever of them is named first in the register of members (the 'senior holder'); or

(c)  if the holder is no longer entitled to the share by reason of death or bankruptcy, or otherwise by operation of law, the transmittee.

AMENDMENTS AND NOTES

[a]  See note a to para 51.MA.55. This corresponds to the provisions of Table A reg 106.

**Deductions from distributions in respect of sums owed to the company**[a]

**51.MA.189**   **73.** (1)  If—

(a)  a share is subject to the company's lien, and

(b)  the directors are entitled to issue a lien enforcement notice in respect of it,

they may, instead of issuing a lien enforcement notice, deduct from any dividend or other sum payable in respect of the share any sum of money which is payable to the company in respect of that share to the extent that they are entitled to require payment under a lien enforcement notice.

(2)  Money so deducted must be used to pay any of the sums payable in respect of that share.

(3)  The company must notify the distribution recipient in writing of—

(a)  the fact and amount of any such deduction;

(b)  any non-payment of a dividend or other sum payable in respect of a share resulting from any such deduction; and

(c)  how the money deducted has been applied.

AMENDMENTS AND NOTES

[a]  There is no corresponding provision in Table A.

**No interest on distributions**[a]

**51.MA.190**   **74.** The company may not pay interest on any dividend or other sum payable in respect of a share unless otherwise provided by—

(a)  the terms on which the share was issued, or

(b)  the provisions of another agreement between the holder of that share and the company.

AMENDMENTS AND NOTES

[a]  This corresponds to the provisions of Table A reg 107. See note a to para 51.MA.56.

**Unclaimed distributions**[a]

**51.MA.191**   **75.** (1)  All dividends or other sums which are—

(a)  payable in respect of shares, and

(b)  unclaimed after having been declared or become payable,

may be invested or otherwise made use of by the directors for the benefit of the company until claimed.

(2)  The payment of any such dividend or other sum into a separate account does not make the company a trustee in respect of it.

(3)  If—

(a)  twelve years have passed from the date on which a dividend or other sum became due for payment, and

(b)  the distribution recipient has not claimed it,

the distribution recipient is no longer entitled to that dividend or other sum and it ceases to remain owing by the company.

AMENDMENTS AND NOTES

[a] This is a restatement and expansion of Table A reg 108. Article 75(3) now makes it explicit that the company may apply dividend sums pending the distribution recipient claiming such sums; the corresponding provision of Table A was silent on this point. See note a to para 51.MA.57.

### Non-cash distributions[a]

**76.** (1) Subject to the terms of issue of the share in question, the company may, by ordinary resolution on the recommendation of the directors, decide to pay all or part of a dividend or other distribution payable in respect of a share by transferring non-cash assets of equivalent value (including, without limitation, shares or other securities in any company).

    (2) If the shares in respect of which such a non-cash distribution is paid are uncertificated, any shares in the company which are issued as a non-cash distribution in respect of them must be uncertificated.

    (3) For the purposes of paying a non-cash distribution, the directors may make whatever arrangements they think fit,[b] including, where any difficulty arises regarding the distribution—

        (a) fixing the value of any assets;

        (b) paying cash to any distribution recipient on the basis of that value in order to adjust the rights of recipients; and

        (c) vesting any assets in trustees.

**51.MA.192**

AMENDMENTS AND NOTES

[a] See note a to para 51.MA.58. This corresponds to the provisions of Table A reg 105.

[b] As per the corresponding provision of Table A (reg 105), the directors may only exercise this discretion in circumstances where difficulty arises regarding the distribution.

### Waiver of distributions[a]

**77.** Distribution recipients may waive their entitlement to a dividend or other distribution payable in respect of a share by giving the company notice in writing to that effect, but if—

    (a) the share has more than one holder, or

    (b) more than one person is entitled to the share, whether by reason of the death or bankruptcy of one or more joint holders, or otherwise,

the notice is not effective unless it is expressed to be given, and signed, by all the holders or persons otherwise entitled to the share.

**51.MA.193**

AMENDMENTS AND NOTES

[a] See note a to para 51.MA.59. There is no corresponding provision in Table A.

## *Capitalisation of Profits*[a]

### Authority to capitalise and appropriation of capitalised sums

**78.** (1) Subject to the articles, the directors may, if they are so authorised by an ordinary resolution—

        (a) decide to capitalise any profits of the company (whether or not they are available for distribution) which are not required for paying a preferential dividend, or any sum standing to the credit of the company's share premium account or capital redemption reserve; and

        (b) appropriate any sum which they so decide to capitalise (a 'capitalised sum') to the persons who would have been entitled to it if it were distributed by way of dividend (the 'persons entitled') and in the same proportions.

    (2) Capitalised sums must be applied—

        (a) on behalf of the persons entitled, and

        (b) in the same proportions as a dividend would have been distributed to them.

    (3) Any capitalised sum may be applied in paying up new shares of a nominal amount equal to the capitalised sum which are then allotted credited as fully paid to the persons entitled or as they may direct.

    (4) A capitalised sum which was appropriated from profits available for distribution may be applied—

        (a) in or towards paying up any amounts unpaid on existing shares held by the persons entitled, or

        (b) in paying up new debentures of the company which are then allotted credited as fully paid to the persons entitled or as they may direct.

    (5) Subject to the articles the directors may—

        (a) apply capitalised sums in accordance with paragraphs (3) and (4) partly in one way and partly in another;

        (b) make such arrangements as they think fit to deal with shares or debentures becoming distributable in fractions under this article (including the issuing of fractional certificates or the making of cash payments); and

**51.MA.194**

(c)  authorise any person to enter into an agreement with the company on behalf of all the persons entitled which is binding on them in respect of the allotment of shares and debentures to them under this article.

AMENDMENTS AND NOTES

[a]  See note a to para 51.MA.60. This corresponds to the provisions of Table A reg 110.

## Part 5
## MISCELLANEOUS PROVISIONS[a]

### *Communications*[b]

**Means of communication to be used**

**51.MA.195**   **79.** (1)  Subject to the articles, anything sent or supplied by or to the company under the articles may be sent or supplied in any way in which the Companies Act 2006 provides for documents or information which are authorised or required by any provision of that Act to be sent or supplied by or to the company.[c]

(2)  Subject to the articles, any notice or document to be sent or supplied to a director in connection with the taking of decisions by directors may also be sent or supplied by the means by which that director has asked to be sent or supplied with such notices or documents for the time being.[d]

(3)  A director may agree with the company that notices or documents sent to that director in a particular way are to be deemed to have been received within a specified time of their being sent, and for the specified time to be less than 48 hours.

AMENDMENTS AND NOTES

[a]  There are no provisions in any of the forms of model articles dealing with the exercise of members' rights under s 145 of the Companies Act 2006 (see Chapter 9). The Government was of the view that this was a matter that companies should consider on a case-by-case basis. Whilst an earlier draft of the model articles for public companies included some proposed provisions, these were ultimately removed as part of the consultation process. See note a to para 51.MA.47 and URN 07/1227/GR, paras 60 and 61 for the discussions in relation to these points during the consultation process. The provisions of s 145 should be distinguished from the provisions of ss 146–151 of the Companies Act 2006, which are conferred on members of companies admitted to trading on a regulated market. A regulated market for these purposes is defined in the Financial Services and Markets Act 2000 (Markets in Financial Instruments) Regulations, SI 2007/126. These rights are conferred directly by the relevant sections of the Companies Act 2006. See DTI, *Implementation of Companies Act 2006*, para 3.140.

[b]  It should be noted that the model articles do not contain the optional article that is required in order to enable the 28-day notice period for individual members' agreement to website communications. Again, this will need to be a matter of individual consideration for a given company as to whether or not it wants to enable this. The Government has chosen not to enable this regime as a default setting. (See URN 07/1227/GR.) In addition, the language in these articles will not be sufficient in itself to permit communication by means of email. This would also require individual members to provide a contact email address for this purpose, in accordance with the provisions of Sch 5 to the Companies Act 2006. See also note a to para 51.MA.72.

[c]  This tracks the language and scope of s 1143(1) of the Companies Act 2006.

[d]  See note b to para 51.MA.72.

**Failure to notify contact details**

**51.MA.196**   **80.** (1)  If—

(a)  the company sends two consecutive documents to a member over a period of at least 12 months, and

(b)  each of those documents is returned undelivered, or the company receives notification that it has not been delivered,

that member ceases to be entitled to receive notices from the company.

(2)  A member who has ceased to be entitled to receive notices from the company becomes entitled to receive such notices again by sending the company—

(a)  a new address to be recorded in the register of members, or

(b)  if the member has agreed that the company should use a means of communication other than sending things to such an address, the information that the company needs to use that means of communication effectively.

# *Administrative Arrangements*

## Company seals[a]

**81.** (1) Any common seal may only be used by the authority of the directors.     **51.MA.197**

    (2) The directors may decide by what means and in what form any common seal or securities seal is to be used.

    (3) Unless otherwise decided by the directors, if the company has a common seal and it is affixed to a document, the document must also be signed by at least one authorised person in the presence of a witness who attests the signature.

    (4) For the purposes of this article, an authorised person is—

       (a) any director of the company;

       (b) the company secretary; or

       (c) any person authorised by the directors for the purpose of signing documents to which the common seal is applied.

    (5) If the company has an official seal for use abroad, it may only be affixed to a document if its use on that document, or documents of a class to which it belongs, has been authorised by a decision of the directors.

    (6) If the company has a securities seal, it may only be affixed to securities by the company secretary or a person authorised to apply it to securities by the company secretary.

    (7) For the purposes of the articles, references to the securities seal being affixed to any document include the reproduction of the image of that seal on or in a document by any mechanical or electronic means which has been approved by the directors in relation to that document or documents of a class to which it belongs.

AMENDMENTS AND NOTES

[a] This corresponds to the provisions of Table A reg 101.

## Destruction of documents[a]

**82.** (1) The company is entitled to destroy—     **51.MA.198**

       (a) all instruments of transfer of shares which have been registered, and all other documents on the basis of which any entries are made in the register of members, from six years after the date of registration;

       (b) all dividend mandates, variations or cancellations of dividend mandates, and notifications of change of address, from two years after they have been recorded;

       (c) all share certificates which have been cancelled from one year after the date of the cancellation;

       (d) all paid dividend warrants and cheques from one year after the date of actual payment; and

       (e) all proxy notices from one year after the end of the meeting to which the proxy notices relates.

    (2) If the company destroys a document in good faith, in accordance with the articles, and without notice of any claim to which that document may be relevant, it is conclusively presumed in favour of the company that—

       (a) entries in the register purporting to have been made on the basis of an instrument of transfer or other document so destroyed were duly and properly made;

       (b) any instrument of transfer so destroyed was a valid and effective instrument duly and properly registered;

       (c) any share certificate so destroyed was a valid and effective certificate duly and properly cancelled; and

       (d) any other document so destroyed was a valid and effective document in accordance with its recorded particulars in the books or records of the company.

    (3) This article does not impose on the company any liability which it would not otherwise have if it destroys any document before the time at which this article permits it to do so.

    (4) In this article, references to the destruction of any document include a reference to its being disposed of in any manner.

AMENDMENTS AND NOTES

[a] There is no corresponding provision in Table A.

## No right to inspect accounts and other records[a]

**83.** Except as provided by law or authorised by the directors or an ordinary resolution of the company, no person is entitled to inspect any of the company's accounting or other records or documents merely by virtue of being a member.     **51.MA.199**

AMENDMENTS AND NOTES

[a] See note a to para 51.MA.74.

**Provision for employees on cessation of business**[a]

**51.MA.200**

84. The directors may decide to make provision for the benefit of persons employed or formerly employed by the company or any of its subsidiaries(other than a director orformer director or shadow director) in connection with the cessation or transfer to any person of the whole or part of the undertaking of the company or that subsidiary.

AMENDMENTS AND NOTES

[a] There is no corresponding provision in Table A.

## Directors' Indemnity and Insurance[a]

**Indemnity**

**51.MA.201**

85. (1) Subject to paragraph (2), a relevant director of the company or an associated company may be indemnified out of the company's assets against—

(a) any liability incurred by that director in connection with any negligence, default, breach of duty or breach of trust in relation to the company or an associated company,

(b) any liability incurred by that director in connection with the activities of the company or an associated company in its capacity as a trustee of an occupational pension scheme (as defined in section 235(6) of the Companies Act 2006),

(c) any other liability incurred by that director as an officer of the company or an associated company.

(2) This article does not authorise any indemnity which would be prohibited or rendered void by any provision of the Companies Acts or by any other provision of law.

(3) In this article—

(a) companies are associated if one is a subsidiary of the other or both are subsidiaries of the same body corporate, and

(b) a 'relevant director' means any director or former director of the company or an associated company.

AMENDMENTS AND NOTES

[a] See note b to para 51.MA.76.

**Insurance**[a]

**51.MA.202**

86. (1) The directors may decide to purchase and maintain insurance, at the expense of the company, for the benefit of any relevant director in respect of any relevant loss.

(2) In this article—

(a) a 'relevant director' means any director or former director of the company or an associated company,

(b) a 'relevant loss' means any loss or liability which has been or may be incurred by a relevant director in connection with that director's duties or powers in relation to the company, any associated company (within the meaning of article 85(4)(a)) or any pension fund or employees' share scheme of the company or associated company and

(c) companies are associated if one is a subsidiary of the other or both are subsidiaries of the same body corporate.

AMENDMENTS AND NOTES

[a] There is no corresponding provision in Table A.

# 52

## STATUTORY INSTRUMENTS

THE COMPANIES (REGISTRAR, LANGUAGES AND TRADING
DISCLOSURES) REGULATIONS 2006
(SI 2006/3429)

COMMENCEMENT DATE 1 July 2005

**SI.01**    **Citation, commencement and interpretation**

**1.** (1) These Regulations may be cited as the Companies (Registrar, Languages and Trading
Disclosures) Regulations 2006 and shall come into force on 1st January 2007.

(2) In these Regulations—

'the 1985 Act' means the Companies Act 1985,[1]

'the 1986 Order' means the Companies (Northern Ireland) Order 1986,[2] and

'the 2006 Act' means the Companies Act 2006.

**Certification of electronic copies by registrar**

**2.** (1) Where—

(a) a person requires a copy of material on the register under section 1086 of the 2006 Act,

(b) that person expressly requests that the copy be certified as a true copy, and

(c) the registrar provides the copy in electronic form,

the registrar's certificate that the copy is an accurate record of the contents of the original
document must be provided in accordance with the following provisions.

(2) The certificate must be authenticated by means of an electronic signature that—

(a) is uniquely linked to the registrar,

(b) indicates that the registrar has caused it to be applied,

(c) is created using means that the registrar can maintain under his sole control, and

(d) is linked—

(i) to the certificate, and

(ii) to the copy provided under section 1086 of the 2006 Act

in such a manner that any subsequent change of the data comprised in either is
detectable.

(3) For the purposes of this regulation, an 'electronic signature' means data in electronic form
which are attached to or logically associated with other electronic data and which serve as a
method of authentication.

**Provisions requiring office copies to be delivered to the registrar**

**3.** (1) In the following provisions (which require an office copy of certain orders to be delivered to
the registrar) for 'an office copy' substitute 'a copy'—

(a) section 54(7) of the 1985 Act and article 64(7) of the 1986 Order (order on litigated
objection to resolution that public company be re-registered as private),

(b) section 425(3) of the 1985 Act[3] and article 418(3) of the 1986 Order[4] (order sanctioning
compromise or arrangement),

(c) section 427(5) of the 1985 Act[5] and article 420(5) of the 1986 Order[6] (order sanctioning
compromise or arrangement),

(d) section 201(4) of the Insolvency Act 1986[7] and article 166(4) of the Insolvency (Northern
Ireland) Order 1989[8] (order deferring date at which dissolution of company after winding
up is to take effect).

(2) In—

(a) Form 139, in Schedule 3 to the Companies (Forms) Regulations 1985[9] and

(b) Form 149, in Schedule 3 to the Companies (Forms) Regulations (Northern Ireland) 1986[10],

---

[1]  1985 c.6.

[2]  SI 1986/1032 (NI 6).

[3]  Section 425(3) is applied to limited liability partnerships by the Limited Liability Partnerships Regulations
2001 (SI 2001/1090), regulation 4 and Schedule 2, Part 1.

[4]  Art 418(3) is applied to limited liability partnerships by the Limited Liability Partnerships Regulations
(Northern Ireland) 2004 (SR (NI) 2004 No 307), regulation 4 and Schedule 2, Part 1.

[5]  Section 427(5) is applied to limited liability partnerships by the Limited Liability Partnerships Regulations
2001 (SI 2001/1090), regulation 4 and Schedule 2, Part 1.

[6]  Art 420(5) is applied to limited liability partnerships by the Limited Liability Partnerships Regulations
(Northern Ireland) 2004 (SR (NI) 2004 No 307), regulation 4 and Schedule 2, Part 1.

[7]  1986 c. 45; section 201(4) is applied to limited liability partnerships by the Limited Liability Partnerships
Regulations 2001 (SI 2001/1090), regulation 5.

[8]  SI 1989/2405 (NI 19); article 166(4) is applied to limited liability partnerships by the Limited Liability
Partnerships Regulations (Northern Ireland) 2004 (SR (NI) 2004 No 307), regulation 5.

[9]  SI 1985/854.

[10]  SR (NI) 1986 No 287.

for 'Office copy' substitute 'Copy'.

(3) For the purposes of their application to limited liability partnerships by the Limited Liability Partnerships Regulations 2001[11] or the Limited Liability Partnerships Regulations (Northern Ireland) 2004[12], the provisions specified in paragraph (1)(b), (c) and (d) have effect as if not amended by this regulation.

### Language requirements: contracts relating to allotments of shares

**4.** Section 1105 of the 2006 Act (documents that may be drawn up and delivered in languages other than English) applies to contracts required to be delivered to the registrar under section 88(2)(b)(i) of the 1985 Act or article 98(2)(b)(i) of the 1986 Order.

### Voluntary filing of translations

**5.** The facility described in section 1106 of the 2006 Act (voluntary filing of translations) is available in relation to—
(a) all the official languages of the European Union, and
(b) all documents subject to the Directive disclosure requirements.

### Trading disclosures: amendment of companies legislation

**6.** [...][a]

AMENDMENTS AND NOTES

[a] Revoked by the Companies (Trading Disclosures) Regulations 2008, S.I. 2008/495, reg 11.

### Trading disclosures: statement that company is being wound up

**7.** (1) For section 188(1)[13] of the Insolvency Act 1986 substitute—

'(1) When a company is being wound up, whether by the court or voluntarily—
(a) every invoice, order for goods, business letter or order form (whether in hard copy, electronic or any other form) issued by or on behalf of the company, or a liquidator of the company or a receiver or manager of the company's property, being a document on or in which the name of the company appears, and
(b) all the company's websites,
must contain a statement that the company is being wound up.'

(2) For article 159(1)[14] of the Insolvency (Northern Ireland) Order 1989 substitute—

'(1) When a company is being wound up, whether by the High Court or voluntarily—
(a) every invoice, order for goods, business letter or order form (whether in hard copy, electronic or any other form) issued by or on behalf of the company, or a liquidator of the company or a receiver or manager of the company's property, being a document on or in which the name of the company appears, and
(b) all the company's websites,
must contain a statement that the company is being wound up.'.

SCHEDULE 1                                    Regulation 6
TRADING DISCLOSURES: AMENDMENT OF 1985 ACT

[. . .][a]AMENDMENTS AND NOTES

[a] Revoked by the Companies (Trading Disclosures) Regulations 2008, S.I. 2008/495, reg 11.

SCHEDULE 2                                    Regulation 6
TRADING DISCLOSURES: AMENDMENT OF 1986 ORDER

[. . .][a]AMENDMENTS AND NOTES

[a] Revoked by the Companies (Trading Disclosures) Regulations 2008, S.I. 2008/495, reg 11.

[11] SI 2001/1090.
[12] SR (NI) 2004 No 307.
[13] Section 188 is applied to limited liability partnerships by the Limited Liability Partnerships Regulations 2001 (SI 2001/1090), regulation 5 and the Limited Liability Partnerships (Scotland) Regulations 2001 (SI 2001/128), regulation 3 and Schedule 1.
[14] Article 159 is applied to limited liability partnerships by the Limited Liability Partnerships Regulations (Northern Ireland) 2004 (SR (NI) 2004 No 307), regulation 5.

# THE COMPANIES ACTS (UNREGISTERED COMPANIES) REGULATIONS 2007
### (SI 2007/318)

**SI.02**    [. . .]ᵃ

AMENDMENTS AND NOTES

ᵃ Revoked by SI 2009/2436, reg 8(c), as from 1 October 2009.

---

# THE COMPANIES (POLITICAL EXPENDITURE EXEMPTION) ORDER 2007
### (SI 2007/2081)

COMMENCEMENT DATE In accordance with article 1(1)

**SI.03**    **Citation, commencement and interpretation**

**1.** (1) This Order may be cited as the Companies (Political Expenditure Exemption) Order 2007 and shall come into force—

(a) for the purposes of its application to Great Britain, on 1st October 2007;

(b) for the purposes of its application to Northern Ireland, on 1st November 2007.

(2) In this Order, 'news material' means material relating to—

(a) news,

(b) public and political affairs,

(c) public and political events, or

(d) views, opinion or comment on such news, affairs or events.

**Exemption from authorisation**

**2.** Political expenditure is exempt from the need for authorisation under Part 14 of the Companies Act 2006 if it is—

(a) political expenditure to which article 3 applies, and

(b) incurred by a company to which article 4 applies.

**Description of political expenditure**

**3.** (1) This article applies to political expenditure incurred in respect of the preparation, publication or dissemination of news material, where that material contains matter which would render that preparation, publication or dissemination on the part of the company an activity on the part of the company that is capable of being reasonably regarded as intended—

(a) to affect public support for a political party or other political organisation, or an independent election candidate, or

(b) to influence voters in relation to any national or regional referendum held under the law of a member State.

(2) Until 1st October 2008, paragraph (1)(a) has effect as if the words 'or an independent election candidate' were omitted.

**Description of company**

**4.** (1) This article applies to any company whose ordinary course of business includes, or is proposed to include, the publication or dissemination to the public, or any part of the public, of news material, or the preparation of such material for publication or dissemination to the public, or any part of the public.

(2) For the purposes of paragraph (1), it is to be irrelevant—

(a) by which means or modes the news material is to be prepared, published or disseminated; or

(b) where the public, or any part of the public, to which such material is published or disseminated is located or the identity or description of the public or any part of it.

## THE COMPANIES (FEES FOR INSPECTION AND COPYING OF COMPANY RECORDS) REGULATIONS 2007
### (SI 2007/2612)

COMMENCEMENT DATE 1 October 2007

**Citation, commencement and interpretation**                                              SI.04

**1.** (1) These Regulations may be cited as the Companies (Fees for Inspection and Copying of Company Records) Regulations 2007 and shall come into force on 1st October 2007.

(2) In these Regulations—

'the Act' means the Companies Act 2006; and

'the Commencement Order' means the Companies Act 2006 (Commencement No. 3, Consequential Amendments, Transitional Provisions and Savings) Order 2007[15].

**Fee for inspection of registers**

**2.** For the purpose of section 116(1)(b) of the Act (inspection of register and index of members' names) the fee prescribed is £3.50 for each hour or part thereof during which the right of inspection is exercised.

**Fee for copy of registers**

**3.** (1) For the purposes of the following sections of the Act—

(a) section 116(2) (copy of company's register of members); and

(b) section 811(2) (copy of entries in register of interests in shares disclosed), the fee prescribed is—

(i) the amount per number of entries copied by the company as set out in paragraph (2); and

(ii) the reasonable costs incurred by the company in delivering the copy of the entries to the person entitled to be provided with that copy.

(2) The amounts per number of entries copied are—

(a) £1 for each of the first 5 entries;

(b) £30 for the next 95 entries or part thereof;

(c) £30 for the next 900 entries or part thereof;

(d) £30 for the next 99,000 entries or part thereof; and

(e) £30 for the remainder of the entries in the register or part thereof.

**Fee for copy of company records**

**4.** For the purposes of the following sections of the Act—

(a) section 229(2) (copy of director's service contract or memorandum setting out the terms of that contract);

(b) section 238(2) (copy of director's qualifying indemnity provision);

(c) section 358(4) (copy of records of resolutions and meetings); and

(d) section 807(2) (copy of report under section 805 of the Act), the fee prescribed is —

(i) 10 pence per 500 words or part thereof copied; and

(ii) the reasonable costs incurred by the company in delivering the copy of the company record to the person entitled to be provided with that copy.

**Revocation and savings: Great Britain**

**5.** (1) In the Companies (Inspection and Copying of Registers, Indices and Documents) Regulations 1991[16] ('the 1991 Regulations') the following paragraphs of Schedule 2 are revoked, subject to paragraphs (2) and (3) of this regulation—

(a) paragraph 1(d);

(b) paragraph 2(b);

(c) paragraph 2(d); and

(d) paragraph 3(b).

(2) The fees prescribed in the following paragraphs of Schedule 2 to the 1991 Regulations—

(a) paragraph 1(d) (fee for inspection of register of members and index); and

(b) paragraph 2(d) (fee for copies of entries in the register of members),

shall continue to apply in respect of requests relating to the register of members or the index of members' names of a company which are subject to section 356 of the Companies Act 1985[17] by virtue of paragraph 2(2) of Schedule 3 to the Commencement Order.

---

[15]  SI 2007/2194 (C. 84).

[16]  SI 1991/1998.

[17]  1985 c. 6.

(3) The fee prescribed in paragraph 3(b) of Schedule 2 to the 1991 Regulations shall continue to apply in respect of requests relating to minutes of general meetings which are subject to section 383 of the Companies Act 1985 by virtue of paragraph 40(2) of Schedule 3 to the Commencement Order.

**Revocation and savings: Northern Ireland**

**6.** (1) In the Companies (Inspection and Copying of Registers, Indices and Documents) Regulations (Northern Ireland) 1993[18] ('the 1993 Regulations') the following paragraphs of Schedule 2 are revoked, subject to paragraphs (2) and (3) of this regulation—

(a) paragraph 1(d);

(b) paragraph 2(b);

(c) paragraph 2(d); and

(d) paragraph 3(b).

(2) The fees prescribed in the following paragraphs of Schedule 2 to the 1993 Regulations—

(a) paragraph 1(d) (fee for inspection of register of members and index); and

(b) paragraph 2(d) (fee for copies of entries in the register of members),

shall continue to apply in respect of requests relating to the register of members or the index of members' names of a company which are subject to Article 364 of the Companies (Northern Ireland) Order 1986[19] by virtue of paragraph 2(2) of Schedule 3 to the Commencement Order.

(3) The fee prescribed in paragraph 3(b) of Schedule 2 to the 1993 Regulations shall continue to apply in respect of requests relating to minutes of general meetings which are subject to Article 391 of the Companies (Northern Ireland) Order 1986 by virtue of paragraph 40(2) of Schedule 3 to the Commencement Order.

---

# The Company and Business Names (Amendment) (No. 2) Regulations 2007
## (SI 2007/3152)

**SI.05** [...]ᵃ

AMENDMENTS AND NOTES

ᵃ Revoked by SI 2009/2615, reg 7(e), as from 1 October 2009.

---

# The Independent Supervisor Appointment Order 2007
## (SI 2007/3534)

COMMENCEMENT DATE 6 April 2008

**SI.06** **Citation and commencement**

**1.** This Order may be cited as the Independent Supervisor Appointment Order 2007 and comes into force on 6th April 2008.

**Interpretation**

**2.** In this Order 'the Act' means the Companies Act 2006.

**Appointment of Independent Supervisor**

**3.** The body known as the Professional Oversight Board, established under the articles of association of The Financial Reporting Council Limited[20], is appointed for the purposes of section 1228 of the Act (appointment of the Independent Supervisor) to discharge the supervision function.

---

[18] SR (NI) 1993 No. 66.
[19] SI 1986/1032 (NI 6).
[20] Registered number 0248.

**Requirements and provisions concerning the exercise of the supervision function**

**4.** The report which is required under section 1231 of the Act (reports by the Independent Supervisor) must include—

   (a) an account of how the Independent Supervisor has discharged the supervision function, including why it considers that this function has been discharged effectively;

   (b) an account of the extent to which each Auditor General has complied with its duties under the Act;

   (c) an account of any matters notified to the Independent Supervisor under section 1232 of the Act (matters to be notified to the Independent Supervisor);

   (d) an account of the Independent Supervisor's enforcement activity, including the issue of any suspension notices and any applications for compliance orders; and

   (e) an account of the activities carried out by the Independent Supervisor as a consequence of its status as a public authority for the purpose of the Freedom of Information Act 2000[21].

**5.** (1) The Independent Supervisor must, at least once in each calendar year, prepare and publish in such manner as it sees fit financial statements of its expenditure.

   (2) The financial statements shall be audited by a person other than an Auditor General who is eligible for appointment as a statutory auditor.

**6.** (1) The Independent Supervisor must consult with the Auditors General and such other persons as seem to it to be appropriate before establishing or entering into a supervision arrangement for the purposes of section 1229 of the Act (supervision of Auditors General by the Independent Supervisor).

   (2) Any consultation carried out for this purpose before the date on which this Order comes into force, including by the Public Oversight Board established under the articles of association of The Public Oversight Board Limited[22], shall be treated as if it had been carried out under this article.

**7.** The Independent Supervisor shall have satisfactory arrangements for recording decisions made in the exercise of the supervision function and for the safekeeping of those records which ought to be preserved.

---

## THE COMPANIES (FEES FOR INSPECTION AND COPYING OF COMPANY RECORDS) (NO.2) REGULATIONS 2007
### (SI 2007/3535)

COMMENCEMENT DATE 6 April 2008

**Citation, commencement and interpretation** SI.07

**1.** (1) These Regulations may be cited as the Companies (Fees for Inspection and Copying of Company Records) (No. 2) Regulations 2007 and come into force on 6th April 2008.

   (2) In these Regulations—

     (a) 'the Act' means the Companies Act 2006; and

     (b) 'the Commencement Order' means the Companies Act 2006 (Commencement No. 5, Transitional Provisions and Savings) Order 2007[23].

**Fee for inspection of register of debenture holders**

**2.** For the purpose of section 744(1)(b) of the Act (inspection of register of debenture holders) the fee prescribed is £3.50 for each hour or part thereof during which the right of inspection is exercised.

**Fee for copy of register of debenture holders**

**3.** (1) The fee prescribed for the purpose of section 744(2) of the Act (copy of entries in register of debenture holders) is—

     (a) the amount per number of entries copied by the company as set out in paragraph (2); and

     (b) the reasonable costs incurred by the company in delivering the copy of the entries to the person entitled to be provided with that copy.

   (2) The amounts per number of entries copied are—

     (a) £1 for each of the first 5 entries;

---

[21] 2000 c.36; under section 1228(3) of the Companies Act 2006. This Order has the effect of making the Independent Supervisor designated under section 5 of the Freedom of Information Act 2000.

[22] Registered number 05081885.

[23] SI 2007/3495 (C. 150).

(b) £30 for the next 95 entries or part thereof;

(c) £30 for the next 900 entries or part thereof;

(d) £30 for the next 99,000 entries or part thereof; and

(e) £30 for the remainder of the entries in the register or part thereof.

### Fee for copy of debenture trust deed

**4.** The fee prescribed for the purpose of section 749(1) of the Act (right of debenture holder to copy of debenture trust deed) is—

(a) 10 pence per 500 words or part thereof copied; and

(b) the reasonable costs incurred by the company in delivering the copy of the debenture trust deed or part thereof to the person entitled to be provided with it.

### Revocation and savings: Great Britain

**5.** (1) In the Companies (Inspection and Copying of Registers, Indices and Documents) Regulations 1991[24] ('the 1991 Regulations') the following paragraphs of Schedule 2 are revoked, subject to paragraph (2) of this regulation—

(a) paragraph 1(a) (fee for inspection of register of debenture holders);

(b) paragraph 2(a) (fee for copies of entries in the register of debenture holders); and

(c) paragraph 3(a) (fees for copies of trust deeds).

(2) The fees prescribed in paragraphs 1(a), 2(a) and 3(a) of Schedule 2 to the 1991 Regulations shall continue to apply in respect of requests relating to the register of debenture holders or a debenture trust deed of a company which are subject to section 191(1) to (6) of the Companies Act 1985[25] by virtue of paragraph 22(2) of Schedule 4 to the Commencement Order.

### Revocation and savings: Northern Ireland

**6.** (1) In the Companies (Inspection and Copying of Registers, Indices and Documents) Regulations 1993 (Northern Ireland)[26] ('the 1993 Regulations') the following paragraphs of Schedule 2 are revoked, subject to paragraph (2) of this regulation —

(a) paragraph 1(a) (fee for inspection of register of debenture holders);

(b) paragraph 2(a) (fee for copies of entries in the register of debenture holders); and

(c) paragraph 3(a) (fees for copies of trust deeds).

(2) The fees prescribed in paragraphs 1(a), 2(a) and 3(a) of Schedule 2 to the 1993 Regulations shall continue to apply in respect of requests relating to the register of debenture holders or a debenture trust deed of a company which are subject to Article 200(1) to (6) of the Companies (Northern Ireland) Order 1986[27] by virtue of paragraph 22(2) of Schedule 4 to the Commencement Order.

# THE STATUTORY AUDITORS AND THIRD COUNTRY AUDITORS REGULATIONS 2007
## (SI 2007/3494)

COMMENCEMENT DATE In accordance with regulation 1(2) and (3)

## PART 1
## CITATION, COMMENCEMENT AND INTERPRETATION

**SI.08**    ### Citation and commencement

**1.** (1) These Regulations may be cited as the Statutory Auditors and Third Country Auditors Regulations 2007.

(2) These Regulations, except for the provisions referred to in paragraph (3), come into force on 6th April 2008.

[(3) Regulations 32, 33 and 40(2)(b) to (d) come into force on 29th June 2008.][a]

AMENDMENTS AND NOTES

[a] Substituted by the Statutory Auditors and Third Country Auditors (Amendment) Regulations 2008, SI 2008/499, reg 2.

---

[24] SI 1991/1998.

[25] 1985 c.6.

[26] SR (NI) 1993 No. 66.

[27] SI 1986/1032 (NI 6).

### Minor definitions

**2.** (1) Section 1261 of the Companies Act 2006 (minor definitions) is amended as follows.

(2) At the appropriate places in subsection (1), insert the following definitions—

"the Audit Directive' means Directive 2006/43/EC of the European Parliament and of the Council on statutory audits of annual accounts and consolidated accounts, amending Council Directives 78/660/EEC and 83/349/EEC and repealing Council Directive 84/253/EEC, as amended at any time before 1st January 2009;';

'audit working papers' means any documents which—

(a) are or have been held by a statutory auditor or a third country auditor, and

(b) are related to the conduct of an audit conducted by that auditor;';

'EEA auditor' means an individual who is approved in accordance with the Audit Directive by an EEA competent authority to carry out audits of annual accounts or consolidated accounts required by Community law;';

'EEA competent authority' means a competent authority within the meaning of Article 2.10 of the Audit Directive of an EEA State other than the United Kingdom;';

'third country' means a country or territory that is not an EEA State or part of an EEA State;';

'third country auditor' means a person, other than a person eligible for appointment as a statutory auditor, who is eligible to conduct audits of the accounts of bodies corporate incorporated or formed under the law of a third country in accordance with the law of that country;';

'third country competent authority' means a body established in a third country exercising functions related to the regulation or oversight of auditors;'.

(3) After subsection (2) insert—

'(2A) For the purposes of this Part, Gibraltar shall be treated as if it were an EEA State.'.

### Index of defined expressions

**3.** (1) Section 1262 of the Companies Act 2006 (index of defined expressions) is amended as follows.

(2) At the appropriate places, insert the following entries in the Table—

(3) In the entry for 'third country auditor'—

(a) in the left-hand column, omit 'third country audit and third country audit work';

(b) in the right-hand column, for 'section 1241(1)' substitute 'section 1261(1)'.

| | |
|---|---|
| 'Audit Directive | section 1261(1)'; |
| 'audit working papers | section 1261(1)'; |
| 'EEA auditor | section 1261(1)'; |
| 'EEA competent authority | section 1261(1)'; |
| 'third country | section 1261(1)'; |
| 'third country competent authority | section 1261(1)'; |
| 'UK-traded non-EEA company | section 1241(2)'. |

PART 2

## STATUTORY AUDITORS

### Supervisory bodies

**4.** (1) Section 1217 of the Companies Act 2006 (supervisory bodies) is amended as follows.

(2) In subsection (1) omit the word 'either' and the words from 'or because' to the end.

(3) After subsection (1) insert—

'(1A) The rules referred to in paragraphs 9(3)(b) (confidentiality of information) and 10C(3)(a) and (b) (bar on appointment as director or other officer) of Schedule 10 must also be binding on persons who—

(a) have sought appointment or acted as a statutory auditor, and

(b) have been members of the body at any time after the commencement of this Part.'.

### Appropriate qualifications

**5.** In section 1219(1) of the Companies Act 2006 (appropriate qualifications)—

(a) after paragraph (d) insert 'or';

(b) omit paragraph (e);

(c) in paragraph (f), for 'overseas' substitute 'third country'.

### Approval of third country qualifications

**6.** (1) Section 1221 of the Companies Act 2006 (approval of overseas qualifications) is amended as follows.

(2)  In subsections (1), (5) and (6) and the section heading, for 'overseas' substitute 'third country'.

(3)  In subsections (1)(a) and (b), (3)(a), (4) and (7)(a), for 'foreign country' substitute 'third country'.

(4)  After subsection (1) insert—

'(1A) A declaration under subsection (1)(a) or (b) must be expressed to be subject to the requirement that any person to whom the declaration relates must pass an aptitude test in accordance with subsection (7A), unless an aptitude test is not required (see subsection (7B)).'.

(5)  After subsection (7) insert—

'(7A) An aptitude test required for the purposes of subsection (1A)—
    (a)  must test the person's knowledge of subjects—
        (i)   that are covered by a recognised professional qualification,
        (ii)  that are not covered by the professional qualification already held by the person, and
        (iii) the knowledge of which is essential for the pursuit of the profession of statutory auditor;
    (b)  may test the person's knowledge of rules of professional conduct;
    (c)  must not test the person's knowledge of any other matters.
(7B) No aptitude test is required for the purposes of subsection (1A) if the subjects that are covered by a recognised professional qualification and the knowledge of which is essential for the pursuit of the profession of statutory auditor are covered by the professional qualification already held by the person.'.

(6)  Omit subsection (9).

## PART 3
## COMPETENT AUTHORITIES

### Notification of matters relevant to other EEA States

**7.**—(1) After section 1223 of the Companies Act 2006[a] (matters to be notified to the Secretary of State) insert—

### 'Notification of matters relevant to other EEA States

**1223A.** (1) A recognised supervisory body must notify the Secretary of State of —
    (a)  any withdrawal of a notifiable person's eligibility for appointment as a statutory auditor; and
    (b)  the reasons for the withdrawal.
(2)  A recognised supervisory body must also notify the Secretary of State of any reasonable grounds it has for suspecting that—
    (a)  a person has contravened the law of the United Kingdom, or any other EEA State or part of an EEA State, implementing the Audit Directive, and
    (b)  the act or omission constituting that contravention took place on the territory of an EEA State other than the United Kingdom.
(3)  In this section 'notifiable person' means a member of the recognised supervisory body in question—
    (a)  who is also an EEA auditor; and
    (b)  in respect of whom the EEA competent authority is not the recognised supervisory body itself.'.

(2)  [...][b]

AMENDMENTS AND NOTES

[a]  2006 c.46.

[b]  Revoked by the Statutory Auditors and Third Country Auditors (Amendment) Regulations 2008, SI 2008/499, reg 2.

### Restrictions on disclosure

**8.** (1)  After section 1224 of the Companies Act 2006 (Secretary of State's power to call for information) insert—

### 'Restrictions on disclosure

**1224A.** (1)  This section applies to information (in whatever form)—
    (a)  relating to the private affairs of an individual, or
    (b)  relating to any particular business,
        that is provided to a body to which this section applies in connection with the exercise of its functions under this Part or sections 522 to 524 (notification to appropriate audit authority of resignation or removal of auditor).

(2) This section applies to—
    (a) a recognised supervisory body,
    (b) a recognised qualifying body,
    (c) a body performing functions for the purposes of arrangements within paragraph 23(1) (independent monitoring of certain audits) or paragraph 24(1) (independent investigation of public interest cases) of Schedule 10,
    (d) the Independent Supervisor,
    (e) the Secretary of State, and
    (f) a body designated by the Secretary of State under section 1252 (delegation of the Secretary of State's functions).

(3) No such information may, during the lifetime of the individual or so long as the business continues to be carried on, be disclosed without the consent of that individual or (as the case may be) the person for the time being carrying on that business.

(4) Subsection (3) does not apply to any disclosure of information that —
    (a) is made for the purpose of facilitating the carrying out by the body of any of its functions,
    (b) is made to a person specified in Part 1 of Schedule 11A,
    (c) is of a description specified in Part 2 of that Schedule, or
    (d) is made in accordance with Part 3 of that Schedule.

(5) Subsection (3) does not apply to—
    (a) the disclosure by an EEA competent authority of information disclosed to it by the body in reliance on subsection (4);
    (b) the disclosure of such information by anyone who has obtained it directly or indirectly from an EEA competent authority.

(6) This section does not prohibit the disclosure of information if the information is or has been available to the public from any other source.

(7) Nothing in this section authorises the making of a disclosure in contravention of the Data Protection Act 1998.

### Offence of disclosure in contravention of section 1224A

**1224B.** (1) A person who discloses information in contravention of section 1224A (restrictions on disclosure) is guilty of an offence, unless—
    (a) he did not know, and had no reason to suspect, that the information had been provided as mentioned in section 1224A(1), or
    (b) he took all reasonable steps and exercised all due diligence to avoid the commission of the offence.

(2) A person guilty of an offence under this section is liable—
    (a) on conviction on indictment, to imprisonment for a term not exceeding two years or a fine (or both);
    (b) on summary conviction—
        (i) in Scotland, to imprisonment for a term not exceeding 12 months or to a fine not exceeding the statutory maximum, or to both;
        (ii) in England and Wales or Northern Ireland, to imprisonment for a term not exceeding three months or to a fine not exceeding the statutory maximum, or to both.'.

(2) After Schedule 11 to the Companies Act 2006 insert the Schedule 11A set out in the Schedule to these Regulations.

(3) Section 1224A of the Companies Act 2006 only applies to information that is provided to a body on or after 6th April 2008.

### Supervision of Auditors General by the Independent Supervisor

**9.** (1) Section 1229 of the Companies Act 2006 (supervision of Auditors General by the Independent Supervisor) is amended as follows.

(2) For subsection (2) substitute—

'(2) The Independent Supervisor must discharge that duty by—
    (a) establishing supervision arrangements itself, or
    (b) entering into supervision arrangements with one or more bodies.
(2A) If the Independent Supervisor enters into supervision arrangements with one or more bodies, it must oversee the effective operation of those supervision arrangements.'.

(3) In the opening words of subsection (3)—
    (a) after 'are arrangements' insert 'established by the Independent Supervisor or';
    (b) after 'in accordance with which' insert 'the Independent Supervisor or';
    (c) omit 'one or more of'.

(4) After subsection (3) insert—
'(3A) The requirements of paragraphs 9 to 10A and 12 to 15 of Schedule 10 (requirements for recognition of a supervisory body) apply in relation to supervision arrangements as they apply in relation to the rules, practices and arrangements of supervisory bodies.'.

(5) In subsection (5) after 'arrangements that it' insert 'establishes or'.

(6) After subsection (5) insert—

'(5A) The Independent Supervisor must, at least once in every calendar year, deliver to the Secretary of State a summary of the results of any inspections conducted for the purposes of subsection (3)(c).'.

### Duties of Auditors General in relation to supervision arrangements

**10.** (1) Section 1230 of the Companies Act 2006 (duties of Auditors General in relation to supervision arrangements) is amended as follows.

(2) For subsection (2) substitute—

'(2) Each Auditor General must—
(a) if the Independent Supervisor has established supervision arrangements, pay to the Independent Supervisor;
(b) if the Independent Supervisor has entered into supervision arrangements with a body, pay to that body,
such proportion of the costs incurred by the Independent Supervisor or body for the purposes of the arrangements as the Independent Supervisor may notify to him in writing.'.

(3) In subsection (4) after 'the arrangements' insert 'established or'.

### Reports of the Secretary of State

**11.** After section 1251 of the Companies Act 2006 (fees) insert—

#### 'Duty of Secretary of State to report on inspections

#### Duty of the Secretary of State to report on inspections

**1251A.** The Secretary of State must, at least once in every calendar year, publish a report containing a summary of the results of inspections that are delivered to him—
(a) by the Independent Supervisor under section 1229(5A);
(b) by a recognised supervisory body under paragraph 13(9) of Schedule 10.'.

### Delegation of Secretary of State's functions

**12.** In section 1252(7)(a) of the Companies Act 2006 (consent of Secretary of State for delegation of certain functions), for 'overseas' substitute 'third country'.

### Delegation of functions to an existing body

**13.** In section 1253(5) of the Companies Act 2006 (delegation of functions to an existing body) for 'paragraph 21, 22, 23(1) or 24(1) of Schedule 10' substitute 'paragraph 21 to 22B, 23(1) or 24(1) of Schedule 10'.

### Cooperation with foreign competent authorities

**14.** (1) After section 1253 of the Companies Act 2006 (delegation of functions to an existing body) insert—

#### 'Cooperation with foreign competent authorities

#### Requests to foreign competent authorities

**1253A.** The Secretary of State may request from an EEA competent authority or a third country competent authority such assistance, information or investigation as he may reasonably require in connection with the exercise of his functions under this Part.

#### Requests from EEA competent authorities

**1253B**(1) The Secretary of State must take all necessary steps to—
(a) ensure that an investigation is carried out, or
(b) provide any other assistance or information,
if requested to do so by an EEA competent authority in accordance with Article 36 of the Audit Directive (cooperation between Member State authorities).

(2) Within 28 days following the date on which he receives the request, the Secretary of State must—
(a) provide the assistance or information required by the EEA competent authority under subsection (1)(b), or
(b) notify the EEA competent authority which made the request of the reasons why he has not done so.

(3) But the Secretary of State need not take steps to comply with a request under subsection (1) if—
(a) he considers that complying with the request may prejudice the sovereignty, security or public order of the United Kingdom;
(b) legal proceedings have been brought in the United Kingdom (whether continuing or not) in relation to the persons and matters to which the request relates; or
(c) disciplinary action has been taken by a recognised supervisory body in relation to the persons and matters to which the request relates.

### Notification to competent authorities of other EEA States

**1253C.** (1) The Secretary of State must notify the relevant EEA competent authority if he receives notice from a recognised supervisory body under section 1223A(1) (notification of withdrawal of eligibility for appointment) of the withdrawal of a person's eligibility for appointment as a statutory auditor.

   (2) In subsection (1) 'the relevant EEA competent authority' means the EEA competent authority which has approved the person concerned in accordance with the Audit Directive to carry out audits of annual accounts or consolidated accounts required by Community law.

   (3) The notification under subsection (1) must include the name of the person concerned and the reasons for the withdrawal of his eligibility for appointment as statutory auditor.

   (4) The Secretary of State must notify the relevant EEA competent authority if he has reasonable grounds for suspecting that—

      (a) a person has contravened the law of the United Kingdom, or any other EEA State or part of an EEA State, implementing the Audit Directive, and

      (b) the act or omission constituting that contravention took place on the territory of an EEA State other than the United Kingdom.,

   (5) In subsection (4) 'the relevant EEA competent authority' means the EEA competent authority for the EEA State in which the suspected contravention took place.

   (6) The notification under subsection (4) must include the name of the person concerned and the grounds for the Secretary of State's suspicion.'

  (2) Section 1253B of the Companies Act 2006 (requests from EEA competent authorities) applies only to investigations, assistance or information relating to auditors appointed for financial years beginning on or after 6th April 2008.

### Transfer of papers to third countries

**15.** (1) After section 1253C of the Companies Act 2006[1] (inserted by regulation 14 above), insert—

#### 'Transfer of papers to third countries

### Restriction on transfer of audit working papers to third countries

**1253D.** Audit working papers must not be transferred to a third country competent authority by any person other than a statutory auditor acting in accordance with rules imposed under paragraph 16A of Schedule 10 (transfer of papers to third countries).

### Working arrangements for transfer of papers

**1253E.** (1) The Secretary of State may enter into arrangements with a third country competent authority relating to the transfer of audit working papers—

      (a) from the third country competent authority or third country auditors regulated by that authority to the Secretary of State; and

      (b) from statutory auditors to the third country competent authority.

   (2) The arrangements must provide that—

      (a) the Secretary of State has the rights and duties referred to in subsections (3) to (5) in relation to papers he requests from the third country competent authority or third country auditors, and

      (b) the third country competent authority has comparable rights and duties in relation to papers it requests from statutory auditors.

   (3) Any request by the Secretary of State for audit working papers from the third country competent authority or a third country auditor must be accompanied by a statement explaining the reasons for the request.

   (4) The Secretary of State may use the audit working papers he receives in response to a request only in connection with—

      (a) quality assurance functions which meet requirements equivalent to those of Article 29 of the Audit Directive (quality assurance),

      (b) investigation or disciplinary functions which meet requirements equivalent to those of Article 30 of the Audit Directive (investigations and penalties), or

      (c) public oversight functions which meet requirements equivalent to those of Article 32 of the Audit Directive (principles of public oversight).

   (5) The Secretary of State, a person exercising the functions of the Secretary of State and persons employed in discharging those functions must be subject to obligations of professional secrecy in relation to audit papers supplied to the Secretary of State by a third country competent authority or a third country auditor.

### Publication of working arrangements

**1253F.** If the Secretary of State enters into working arrangements in accordance with section 1253E, he must publish on a website without undue delay—

      (a) the name of the third country competent authority with which he has entered into such arrangements, and

      (b) the country or territory in which it is established.'.

  [(2) ...][a]

AMENDMENTS AND NOTES

ᵃ Reg 15(2) substituted by the Statutory Auditors and Third Country Auditors (Amendment) Regulations 2008, SI 2008/499, reg 2; reg 15(2) revoked by the Statutory Auditors and Third Country Auditors (Amendment) Regulations 2009, SI 2009/2798, reg 2.

### Directions to comply with international obligations

**16.** (1) Section 1254 of the Companies Act 2006 (directions to comply with international obligations) is amended as follows.

(2) In subsection (1)(a) after 'recognised qualifying body,' insert 'the Independent Supervisor'.

(3) In subsection (3) after 'given to' insert 'the Independent Supervisor or'.

## PART 4
## RECOGNISED SUPERVISORY BODIES

### EEA auditors

**17.** (1) Paragraph 6 of Schedule 10 to the Companies Act 2006 (holding of appropriate qualification) is amended as follows.

(2) In sub-paragraph (1)(a), after 'individual' insert 'other than an EEA auditor'.

(3) After sub-paragraph (1)(a), insert—

'(aa) in the case of an individual who is an EEA auditor—
    (i) he holds an appropriate qualification,
    (ii) he has been authorised on or before 5 April 2008 to practise the profession of company auditor pursuant to the European Communities (Recognition of Professional Qualifications) (First General System) Regulations 2005 (S.I. 2005/18) and has fulfilled any requirements imposed pursuant to regulation 6 of those Regulations, or
    (iii) he has passed an aptitude test in accordance with sub-paragraph (2), unless an aptitude test is not required (see sub-paragraph (2A))'.

(4) For sub-paragraph (2) substitute—

'(2) The aptitude test—
    (a) must test the person's knowledge of subjects—
        (i) that are covered by a recognised professional qualification,
        (ii) that are not covered by the professional qualification already held by the person, and
        (iii) the knowledge of which is essential for the pursuit of the profession of statutory auditor;
    (b) may test the person's knowledge of rules of professional conduct;
    (c) must not test the person's knowledge of any other matters.
(2A) No aptitude test is required if the subjects that are covered by a recognised professional qualification and the knowledge of which is essential for the pursuit of the profession of statutory auditor are covered by the professional qualification already held by the person.'.

### Meaning of 'controlled by qualified persons'

**18.** (1) Paragraph 7 of Schedule 10 to the Companies Act 2006 (meaning of 'controlled by qualified persons') is amended as follows.

(2) In sub-paragraph (2), in paragraphs (a)(ii) and (b)(ii), for 'a member State', in each place where it occurs, substitute 'an EEA State'.

### Professional integrity and independence

**19.** (1) Paragraph 9 of Schedule 10 to the Companies Act 2006 (professional integrity and independence) is amended as follows.

(2) In sub-paragraph (1)(a), after 'integrity' omit 'and'.

(3) After sub-paragraph (1)(b) insert—

'(c) persons appointed as statutory auditors take steps to safeguard their independence from any significant threats to it,
(d) persons appointed as statutory auditors record any such threats and the steps taken to safeguard the proper conduct of the audit from them, and
(e) remuneration received or receivable by a statutory auditor in respect of statutory audit work is not—
    (i) influenced or determined by the statutory auditor providing other services to the audited person, or
    (ii) on a contingent fee basis.'.

(4) For sub-paragraph (3) substitute—

'(3) The body must also have adequate rules and practices designed to ensure that—

(a) no firm is eligible under its rules for appointment as a statutory auditor unless the firm has arrangements to prevent any person from being able to exert any influence over the way in which a statutory audit is conducted in circumstances in which that influence would be likely to affect the independence or integrity of the audit;

(b) any rule of law relating to the confidentiality of information received in the course of statutory audit work by persons appointed as statutory auditors is complied with; and

(c) a person ceasing to hold office as a statutory auditor makes available to his successor in that office all relevant information which he holds in relation to that office.'.

(5) For sub-paragraph (4) substitute—

'(4) The rules referred to in sub-paragraph (3)(b) (confidentiality of information) must apply to persons who are no longer members of the body as they apply to members and any fine imposed in the enforcement of those rules shall be recoverable by the body as a debt due to it from the person obliged to pay it.'.

### Technical standards for group audits

**20.** (1) After paragraph 10 of Schedule 10 to the Companies Act 2006[28] (technical standards) insert—

### 'Technical standards for group audits

**10A.** (1) The body must have rules and practices as to technical standards ensuring that group auditors—

(a) review for the purposes of a group audit the audit work conducted by other persons, and

(b) record that review.

(2) The body must participate in arrangements within paragraph 22, and the rules and practices mentioned in sub-paragraph (1) must include provision requiring compliance with any standards for the time being determined under such arrangements.

(3) The body must also have rules and practices ensuring that group auditors—

(a) retain copies of any documents necessary for the purposes of the review that they have received from third country auditors who are not covered by working arrangements under section 1253E, or

(b) agree with those third country auditors proper and unrestricted access to those documents on request.

(4) The body's rules and practices must ensure that group auditors make those documents available on request to—

(a) the body;

(b) any other body with which the body has entered into arrangements for the purposes of paragraph 23 or 24 (independent arrangements for monitoring and investigation);

(c) the Secretary of State.

(5) The body may provide that the rules and practices referred to in sub-paragraphs (3) and (4) do not apply if, after taking all reasonable steps, a group auditor is unable to obtain the copies of the documents or the access to the documents necessary for the review.

(6) If the body does so provide, its rules and practices must ensure that the group auditor records—

(a) the steps taken to obtain copies of or access to those documents,

(b) the reasons why the copies or access could not be obtained, and

(c) any evidence of those steps or those reasons.

(7) In this paragraph—

'group auditor' means a person appointed as statutory auditor to conduct an audit of group accounts;

'group' has the same meaning as in Part 15 of this Act (see section 474).'.

### Public interest entity reporting and independence requirements

**21.** After paragraph 10A of Schedule 10 to the Companies Act 2006 (inserted by regulation 20 above) insert—

### 'Public interest entity reporting requirements

**10B.** (1) The body must have adequate rules and practices designed to ensure that persons appointed as statutory auditors of public interest entities report to the entity's audit committee (if it has one) at least once in each calendar year at any time during which they hold the office of statutory auditor.

(2) The report must include—

(a) a statement in writing confirming the person's independence from the public interest entity;

---

[28] 2006 c.46.

(b)  a description of any services provided by the person to the public interest entity other than in his capacity as statutory auditor;

(c)  a description of any significant threats to the person's independence;

(d)  an explanation of the steps taken by the person to safeguard his independence from those threats;

(e)  a description of any material weaknesses arising from the statutory audit in the public interest entity's internal control in relation to the preparation of accounts; and

(f)  any other significant matters arising from the statutory audit.

(3)  The body must participate in arrangements within paragraph 22A (arrangements for setting standards), and the rules and practices mentioned in sub-paragraph (1) must include provision requiring compliance with any standards for the time being determined under such arrangements.

(4)  In this paragraph, 'audit committee' means a body which performs the functions referred to in Article 41.2 of the Audit Directive or equivalent functions.

### Public interest entity independence requirements

**10C.** (1)  The body must have adequate rules and practices designed to ensure that—

(a)  an individual does not accept an appointment by a public interest entity as statutory auditor if—

(i)  he has been the statutory auditor of the entity for a continuous period of more than seven years, and

(ii)  less than two years have passed since he was last the statutory auditor of the entity;

(b)  where a firm has been appointed by a public interest entity as statutory auditor, an individual may not be a key audit partner if—

(i)  he has been a key audit partner in relation to audits of the entity for a continuous period of more than seven years, and

(ii)  less than two years have passed since he was last the key audit partner in relation to an audit of the entity.

(2)  The body must participate in arrangements within paragraph 22B (arrangements for setting standards), and the rules and practices mentioned in sub-paragraph (1) must include provision requiring compliance with any standards for the time being determined under such arrangements.

(3)  The body must also have adequate rules and practices designed to ensure that—

(a)  an individual who has been appointed by a public interest entity as statutory auditor may not be appointed as a director or other officer of the entity during a period of two years commencing on the date on which his appointment as statutory auditor ended;

(b)  a key audit partner of a firm which has been appointed by a public interest entity as statutory auditor may not be appointed as a director or other officer of the entity during a period of two years commencing on the date on which his work as key audit partner ended.

(4)  The rules referred to in sub-paragraph (3) must apply to persons who are no longer members of the body as they apply to members and any fine imposed in the enforcement of those rules shall be recoverable by the body as a debt due to it from the person obliged to pay it.

(5)  An auditor of a public interest entity is not to be regarded as an officer of the entity for the purposes of sub-paragraph (3)(a) and (b).

(6)  For the purposes of this paragraph—

(a)  a 'key audit partner' is an individual identified by a firm appointed as statutory auditor as being primarily responsible for the statutory audit; and

(b)  a key audit partner of a firm appointed as statutory auditor of a parent undertaking or a material subsidiary undertaking of a public interest entity is to be treated as if he were a key audit partner of the firm appointed as statutory auditor of the public interest entity.'.

### Monitoring and enforcement

**22.** (1)  Paragraph 12 of Schedule 10 to the Companies Act 2006 (monitoring and enforcement) is amended as follows.

(2)  For sub-paragraph (1) substitute—

'(1)  The body must—

(a)  have adequate resources for the effective monitoring and enforcement of compliance with its rules, and

(b)  ensure that those resources may not be influenced improperly by the persons monitored.

(1A)  The body must—

(a)  have adequate arrangements for the effective monitoring and enforcement of compliance with its rules, and

(b)  ensure that those arrangements operate independently of the persons monitored.'.

(3)  After sub-paragraph (2) insert—

'(3)  The arrangements for enforcement must include provision for—

(a) sanctions which include—
(i) the withdrawal of eligibility for appointment as a statutory auditor; and
(ii) any other disciplinary measures necessary to ensure the effective enforcement of the body's rules; and
(b) the body making available to the public information relating to steps it has taken to ensure the effective enforcement of its rules.'.

## Monitoring of audits

**23.** For paragraph 13 of Schedule 10 to the Companies Act 2006[29] (independent monitoring of audits of listed companies and other major bodies) substitute—

### 'Monitoring of audits

**13.** (1) The body must—
(a) in the case of members of the body who do not perform any statutory audit functions in respect of major audits, have adequate arrangements for enabling the performance by its members of statutory audit functions to be monitored by means of inspections;
(b) in the case of members of the body who perform any statutory audit functions in respect of major audits, participate in arrangements within paragraph 23(1); and
(c) have rules designed to ensure that members of the body take such steps as may reasonably be required of them to enable their performance of any statutory audit functions to be monitored by means of inspections.
(2) Any monitoring of members of the body under the arrangements within paragraph 23(1) is to be regarded (so far as their performance of statutory audit functions in respect of major audits is concerned) as monitoring of compliance with the body's rules for the purposes of paragraph 12(1) and (1A).
(3) The arrangements referred to in sub-paragraph (1)(a) must include an inspection which is conducted in relation to each person eligible for appointment as a statutory auditor at least once every six years.
(4) The inspection must be conducted by persons who—
(a) have an appropriate professional education;
(b) have experience of—
(i) statutory audit work, or
(ii) equivalent work on the audit of accounts under the law of an EEA State, or part of an EEA State, other than the United Kingdom;
(c) have received adequate training in the conduct of inspections;
(d) do not have any interests likely to conflict with the proper conduct of the inspection.
(5) The inspection must review one or more statutory audits in which the person to whom the inspection relates has participated.
(6) The inspection must include an assessment of—
(a) the person's compliance with the body's rules established for the purposes of paragraphs 9 (professional integrity and independence), 10 (technical standards), 10A (technical standards for group audits) and 10C (public interest entity independence requirements);
(b) the resources allocated by the person to statutory audit work;
(c) in the case of an inspection in relation to a firm, its internal quality control system;
(d) the remuneration received by the person in respect of statutory audit work.
(7) An inspection conducted in relation to a firm may be treated as an inspection of all individuals responsible for statutory audit work on behalf of that firm, if the firm has a common quality assurance policy with which each such individual is required to comply.
(8) The main conclusions of the inspection must be recorded in a report which is made available to—
(a) the person to whom the inspection relates, and
(b) the body.
(9) The body must, at least once in every calendar year, deliver to the Secretary of State a summary of the results of inspections conducted under this paragraph.
(10) In this paragraph—
'major audit' means a statutory audit conducted in respect of—
(a) a public interest entity, or
(b) any other person in whose financial condition there is a major public interest;
'statutory audit function' means any function performed as a statutory auditor.'.

## Transfer of papers to third countries

**24.** After paragraph 16 of Schedule 10 to the Companies Act 2006 (independent investigation for disciplinary purposes of public interest cases) insert—

---

[29] 2006 c.46.

### 'Transfer of papers to third countries

**16A.** (1) The body must have adequate rules and practices designed to ensure that persons eligible under its rules for appointment as a statutory auditor deliver audit working papers to a third country competent authority only if—

(a) the authority has entered into arrangements with the Secretary of State in accordance with section 1253E (working arrangements); and

(b) the following four conditions are met.

(2) The first condition is that the competent authority has requested the audit working papers for the purposes of an investigation.

(3) The second condition is that the competent authority has given to the Secretary of State notice of its request.

(4) The third condition is that the papers relate to the audit of a body which—

(a) has issued securities in the country or territory in which the competent authority is established, or

(b) forms part of a group issuing statutory consolidated accounts in that country or territory.

(5) The fourth condition is that no legal proceedings have been brought (whether continuing or not) in relation to the auditor or audit to which the working papers relate.

(6) The body must also have adequate rules and practices designed to ensure that a person eligible under its rules for appointment as a statutory auditor may refuse to deliver audit working papers to a third country competent authority if the Secretary of State certifies that the delivery of the papers would adversely affect the sovereignty, security or public order of the United Kingdom.'.

#### Interpretation

**25.** After paragraph 20 of Schedule 10 to the Companies Act 2006 (promotion and maintenance of standards), insert—

### 'Interpretation

**20A.** In this Part of this Schedule—

'public interest entity' means an issuer—

(a) whose transferable securities are admitted to trading on a regulated market; and

(b) the audit of which is a statutory audit (see section 1210(1));

'issuer' and 'regulated market' have the same meaning as in Part 6 of the Financial Services and Markets Act 2000 (see sections 102A to 103); and

'transferable securities' means anything which is a transferable security for the purposes of Directive 2004/39/EC of the European Parliament and of the Council on markets in financial instruments.'.

#### Arrangements for setting technical standards

**26.** (1) Paragraph 22 of Schedule 10 to the Companies Act 2006 (arrangements for setting technical standards) is amended as follows.

(2) For 'paragraph 10(2)' substitute 'paragraphs 10(2) and 10A(2)'.

(3) In paragraph (a) for 'paragraph 10(1)' substitute 'paragraphs 10(1) and 10A(1) respectively'.

#### Arrangements for setting standards relating to public interest entity reporting and independence requirements

**27.** After paragraph 22 of Schedule 10 to the Companies Act 2006 (arrangements for setting technical standards), insert—

### 'Arrangements for setting standards relating to public interest entity reporting requirements

**22A.** The arrangements referred to in paragraph 10B(3) are appropriate arrangements—

(a) for the determining of standards for the purposes of the rules and practices mentioned in paragraph 10B(1), and

(b) for ensuring that the determination of those standards is done independently of the body.

### 'Arrangements for setting standards relating to public interest entity independence requirements

**22B.** The arrangements referred to in paragraph 10C(2) are appropriate arrangements—

(a) for the determining of standards for the purposes of the rules and practices mentioned in paragraph 10C(1), and

(b) for ensuring that the determination of those standards is done independently of the body.'.

**Arrangements for independent monitoring of audits of listed companies
and other major bodies**

**28.** (1)  Paragraph 23 of Schedule 10 to the Companies Act 2006 (arrangements for independent monitoring of audits of listed companies and other major bodies) is amended as follows.

(2)  In sub-paragraph (1) for 'paragraph 13(1)' substitute 'paragraph 13(1)(b)'.

(3)  After sub-paragraph (1) insert—

'(1A)  Subject to sub-paragraph (1C), the arrangements referred to in sub-paragraph (1) must include provision for an inspection conducted in relation to each person eligible for appointment as a statutory auditor at least once every three years.

(1B)  Sub-paragraphs (4) to (9) of paragraph 13 apply in relation to inspections under sub-paragraph (1A) as they apply in relation to inspections under that paragraph.

(1C)  The arrangements referred to in sub-paragraph (1) may provide that the body performing the inspections may decide that all or part of the inspection referred to in sub-paragraph (1A) is not required in the case of a member of a supervisory body who performs statutory audit functions in respect of ten or fewer major audits per year.

(1D)  If—

(a)  the arrangements make the provision referred to in sub-paragraph (1C), and

(b)  the body performing the inspections decides that all of an inspection is not required in relation to a member, the supervisory body must ensure that the arrangements referred to in paragraph 13(1)(a) apply in relation to that member, subject to the modification specified in sub-paragraph (1F).

(1E)  If—

(a)  the arrangements make the provision referred to in sub-paragraph (1C), and

(b)  the body performing the inspections decides that part of an inspection is not required in relation to a member,

the supervisory body must ensure that the arrangements referred to in paragraph 13(1)(a) apply in relation to that part of the inspection of that member, subject to the modification specified in sub-paragraph (1F).

(1F)  For the purposes of sub-paragraphs (1D) and (1E), paragraph 13(3) applies with the substitution of 'three years' for 'six years'.'.

PART 5

REGISTRATION OF THIRD COUNTRY AUDITORS

**[Interpretation**

**29.** In this Part of these Regulations—

'the Commission Decision' means Commission Decision 2008/627/EC of 29 July 2008 concerning a transitional period for audit activities of certain third country auditors and audit entities;

'the designated body' means the body known as the Professional Oversight Board established under the articles of association of The Financial Reporting Council Limited;[a]

'exempt third country auditor means a third country auditor—

(a)  who is—

(i)  overseen or regulated by a third country competent authority established in a specified third country, and

(ii)  eligible to conduct audits of the accounts of bodies corporate incorporated or formed under the law of that specified third country; and

(b)  in relation to whom the designated body has, for the purposes of the Commission Decision, directed under section 1239(7) of the Companies Act 2006 that requirements imposed by this Part specified in the direction are not to apply;

specified third country means any of the Channel Islands, the Isle of Man and the following countries and territories—

Argentina, Australia, The Bahamas, Bermuda, Brazil, Canada, Cayman Islands, Chile, China, Croatia, Hong Kong, India, Indonesia, Israel, Japan, Kazakhstan, Malaysia, Mauritius, Mexico, Morocco, New Zealand, Pakistan, Russia, Singapore, South Africa, South Korea, Switzerland, Taiwan, Thailand, Turkey, Ukraine, United Arab Emirates, United States of America.][b]

AMENDMENTS AND NOTES

[a]  Registered number 02486368.

[b]  Substituted by the Statutory Auditors and Third Country Auditors (Amendment) (No 2) Regulations 2008, SI 2008/2639, reg 2.

**The register of auditors**

**30.** (1)  Section 1239 of the Companies Act 2006 (register of auditors) is amended as follows.

(2)  At the end of subsection (2)(d) omit 'and'.

(3)  In subsection (2)(e) omit the words 'or a third country auditor'.

(4)  After subsection (2)(e) insert—

'and

(f) in the case of a third country auditor which is a firm, the name and address of each person who is—

    (i)   an owner or shareholder of the firm, or

    (ii)  a member of the firm's administrative or management body.'.

(5) In subsection (7) omit the words 'in accordance with subsections (2)(e) and (3)'.

### Meaning of 'registered third country auditor' and 'UK-traded non-EEA company'

**31.** (1) Section 1241 of the Companies Act 2006 (meaning of 'third country auditor' etc) is amended as follows.

(2) For the heading, substitute 'Meaning of 'registered third country auditor' and 'UK-traded non-EEA company'.

(3) In subsection (1) omit the definition of 'third country auditor'.

(4) In subsection (2)—

    (a) for the opening words substitute 'In this Part 'UK-traded non-EEA company' means a body corporate—';

    (b) in paragraph (a), for 'a country or territory which is not a member State or part of a member State' substitute 'a third country'.

### Duties of registered third country auditors

**32.** (1) Section 1242 of the Companies Act 2006 (duties of registered third country auditors) is amended as follows.

(2) In subsection (1)—

    (a) after 'third country auditor' insert 'who audits the accounts of a UK-traded non-EEA company';

    (b) in paragraph (a), omit 'of traded non-Community companies'.

(3) In subsection (2)(a), for 'third country audits' substitute 'audits of accounts of UK-traded non-EEA companies'.

### Arrangements for registered third country auditors: consequential amendments

**33.** (1) Schedule 12 to the Companies Act 2006 (arrangements in which registered third country auditors are required to participate) is amended as follows.

(2) In the italic cross-heading above paragraph 1, for 'traded non-Community companies' substitute 'UK-traded non-EEA companies'.

(3) In paragraph 1—

    (a) in sub-paragraph (1)(a) for 'third country audit functions' substitute 'functions related to the audit of UK-traded non-EEA companies';

    (b) omit sub-paragraph (2).

(4) In paragraph 2—

    (a) in sub-paragraph (1)(a) for 'third country audit functions' substitute 'functions related to the audit of UK-traded non-EEA companies';

    (b) in sub-paragraph (2), omit the definition of 'third country audit function'.

### Register of third country auditors

**34.** (1) The designated body must keep the register of third country auditors (see section 1239 of the Companies Act 2006).

(2) The register must contain the following information [in relation to each registered third country auditor][a] who is an individual—

    (a) his name and address;

    (b) his registered number;

    (c) an indication that he is a third country auditor;

    (d) if he is responsible for audit work on behalf of a third country auditor which is a firm, the firm's name, address, registered number and, if it has a website, its address;

    (e) in the case of a third country auditor who has registered with an EEA competent authority—

        (i)   the name and address of that authority, and

        (ii)  the registration number which that authority has allocated to it;

    (f) the name and address of any body which has authorised the third country auditor to conduct audits in accordance with the law of a third country; and

    (g) if he has entered into arrangements with a body for the purposes of section 1242(1) of the Companies Act 2006 (duties of registered third country auditors), the name and address of that body.

(3) The register must contain the following information [in relation to each registered third country auditor][b] which is a firm—

    (a) its name and address;

    (b) the address of each of its offices in which it carries out third country audit work;

    (c) its registered number;

    (d) an indication that it is a third country auditor;

    (e) its contact information and, if it has a website, its address;

    (f) its legal form;

    (g) the name and address of each person who is—

        (i) an owner or shareholder of the firm, or

        (ii) a member of the firm's administrative or management body;

    (h) the name, address and registered number of each individual who performs third country audits on behalf of the firm;

    (i) in the case of a third country auditor which is a member of a network—

        (i) a list of the names and addresses of the other members of that network, or

        (ii) an indication of where that information is available to the public;

    (j) in the case of a third country auditor which has registered with an EEA competent authority—

        (i) the name and address of that authority, and

        (ii) the registration number which that authority has allocated to it;

    (k) the name and address of any body which has authorised the third country auditor to conduct audits in accordance with the law of a third country; and

    (l) if it has entered into arrangements with a body for the purposes of section 1242(1) of the Companies Act 2006 (duties of registered third country auditors), the name and address of that body.

(4) The register of third country auditors must be kept in electronic form.

(5) The information on the register must be kept available for inspection by any person by electronic means, unless it is excluded in accordance with paragraph (6).

(6) Information on the register relating to an individual may be excluded from being made available for inspection if making the information so available would create or be likely to create a serious risk that the individual, or any other person, would be subject to violence or intimidation.

(7) In this regulation 'network' means an association of persons cooperating in audit work by way of—

    (a) profit sharing,

    (b) cost sharing,

    (c) common ownership, control or management,

    (d) common quality control policies and procedures,

    (e) common business strategy, or

    (f) use of a common brand name.

(8) For the purposes of this regulation—

    (a) a network is not a firm, and

    (b) an association of individuals which is a firm is not a network.

AMENDMENTS AND NOTES

[a] Substituted by the Statutory Auditors and Third Country Auditors (Amendment) Regulations 2008, SI 2008/499, reg 2.

[b] Substituted by the Statutory Auditors and Third Country Auditors (Amendment) Regulations 2008, SI 2008/499, reg 2.

### Application for registration of third country auditor

**35.** (1) A third country auditor may apply to the designated body for registration in accordance with this regulation.

(2) An application for registration must be in writing.

(3) An application for registration of a third country auditor must include—

    (a) the information required for his entry in the register (see regulation 34), other than

        (i) his registered number, and

        (ii) the name and address of any body with which he has entered into arrangements for the purposes of section 1242(1) of the Companies Act 2006 (duties of registered third country auditors);

    (b) the statement required by regulation 36 (application statement); and

    (c) evidence demonstrating that the matters included in the statement required by regulation 36 (application statement) are correct.

[(3A) An application for registration of an exempt third country auditor must include —

    (a) a statement of the auditing standards and independence requirements applied to the audit or audits in respect of which the application is made,

    (b) a description of the auditor's internal quality control system,

    (c) a statement of whether and (if so) when a quality assurance review has been carried out in respect of the auditor,

    (d) information required by the designated body about the outcome of a quality assurance review.][a]

(4) For the purposes of paragraph (3)(c) a statement by the third country competent authority which oversees or regulates the third country auditor to the effect that the third country

auditor is a fit and proper person to conduct audits in that third country may be treated as evidence demonstrating that the statement required by regulation 36(c) is correct.

(5) An application for registration must—

    (a) in the case of a third country auditor who is an individual, be signed by the third country auditor;

    (b) in the case of a third country auditor which is a firm, be signed by a person authorised by the firm to sign on its behalf.

(6) An application may be delivered to the designated body by electronic means, if the designated body so agrees.

AMENDMENTS AND NOTES

[a] Inserted by the Statutory Auditors and Third Country Auditors (Amendment) (No 2) Regulations 2008, SI 2008/2639, reg 2.

### Application statement

**36.** (1) A third country auditor must make a statement for the purposes of his [application under regulation 35][a] (application for registration of third country auditor) to the effect that—

    (a) in the case of a third country auditor who is an individual, he holds a qualification which meets requirements equivalent to those which apply to an appropriate qualification for the purposes of section 1219 of the Companies Act 2006;

    (b) in the case of a third country auditor which is a firm—

        (i) a majority of the members of the firm's administrative or management body hold qualifications which meet requirements equivalent to those which apply to an appropriate qualification for the purposes of that section, and

        (ii) each individual who conducts audits of UK-traded non-EEA companies (within the meaning of Part 42 of the Companies Act 2006) on behalf of that firm holds a qualification which meets requirements equivalent to those which apply to an appropriate qualification for the purposes of that section;

    (c) he is a fit and proper person to conduct audits of UK-traded non-EEA companies;

    (d) he conducts such audits in accordance with standards equivalent to those required by Articles 22, 24 and 25 of the Audit Directive (independence, objectivity and audit fees);

    (e) he conducts such audits in accordance with standards equivalent to those determined under arrangements within paragraph 22 of Schedule 10 to the Companies Act 2006 (independent determination of technical standards); and

    (f) he publishes on a website an annual transparency report equivalent to that required for auditors of public interest entities by Article 40 of the Audit Directive (transparency report).

AMENDMENTS AND NOTES

[a] Substituted by the Statutory Auditors and Third Country Auditors (Amendment) Regulations 2008, SI 2008/499, reg 2.

### Acceptance and refusal of application for registration

**37.** (1) The designated body may register a third country auditor if he has made an application in accordance with regulation 35 (application for registration of third country auditor).

(2) The designated body may not register a third country auditor if it considers that the statement required by regulation 36 (application statement) made by him is not correct.

(3) If the designated body refuses to register a third country auditor, it must give him written notice to that effect stating the reason for the refusal.

### Allocation of registered number

**38.** The designated body must allocate a number to each third country auditor which it registers, which shall be known as the third country auditor's registered number.

### Duty to provide updated information

**39.** (1) A registered third country auditor must take all reasonable steps to notify the designated body without undue delay of—

    (a) the name and address of any body he has entered into arrangements with for the purposes of section 1242(1) of the Companies Act 2006 (arrangements for monitoring of audits of UK-traded non-EEA companies);

    (b) any information or event which may lead the designated body to consider that the statement required by regulation 36 (application statement) made by the third country auditor is not correct;

    (c) any information necessary to ensure that the information in the register relating to him is correct.

[(2) An exempt third country auditor who for the purpose of registration has provided to the designated body information falling within subparagraphs (a) to (d) and the first sentence of subparagraph (e) of Article 1.1 of the Commission Decision must take all reasonable steps to notify the designated body without undue delay of any change or addition to that information.][a]

AMENDMENTS AND NOTES

[a] Inserted by the Statutory Auditors and Third Country Auditors (Amendment) (No 2) Regulations 2008, SI 2008/2639, reg 2.

### Removal of third country auditor from the register

**40.** (1) If the designated body considers that the statement required by regulation 36 (application statement) made by the third country auditor is no longer correct, it must—

(a) notify the third country auditor of the steps he must take to ensure that the statement is correct, and

(b) if the third country auditor has not taken those steps on or before the date three months after the notification, remove him from the register.

(2) The designated body may remove a third country auditor from the register if it considers that the third country auditor has failed to comply with his obligations under—

(a) [regulation 39(1)][a] (duty to provide updated information),

(b) section 1242 of the Companies Act 2006[b] (duties of registered third country auditors),

(c) section 1243 of that Act (matters to be notified to the Secretary of State), or

(d) section 1244 of that Act (Secretary of State's power to call for information).

[(3) The designated body may remove an exempt third country auditor from the register if—

(a) it considers that the auditor—

(i) has failed—

(aa) to comply with the obligations of the auditor under regulation 39(2) (duty of exempt third country auditor to provide updated information), or

(bb) to apply the auditing standards and independence requirements set out in the statement provided for in regulation 35(3A)(a), or

(ii) is not a fit and proper person to conduct audits of the accounts of UK-traded non-EEA companies, or

(b) it appears to the designated body that a third country competent authority which oversees or regulates the auditor considers that the auditor is not—

(i) a fit and proper person to conduct audits in the specified third country in which the authority is established, or

(ii) eligible to conduct audits of the accounts of bodies corporate incorporated or formed under the law of that country.][c]

AMENDMENTS AND NOTES

[a] Substituted by the Statutory Auditors and Third Country Auditors (Amendment) (No 2) Regulations 2008, SI 2008/2639, reg 2.

[b] 2006 c.46.

[c] Inserted by the Statutory Auditors and Third Country Auditors (Amendment) (No 2) Regulations 2008, SI 2008/2639, reg 2.

## PART 6
## OTHER AMENDMENTS AND REVOCATIONS

### Meaning of 'appropriate audit authority' and 'major audit'

**41.** (1) Section 525(1) of the Companies Act 2006 (meaning of 'appropriate audit authority') is amended as follows.

(2) In paragraph (a) after 'major audit' insert '(other than one conducted by an Auditor General)'.

(3) In paragraph (b) after 'an audit' insert '(other than one conducted by an Auditor General)'.

(4) After paragraph (b) insert—

'(c) in the case of an audit conducted by an Auditor General, the Independent Supervisor.'.

(5) In the closing words—

(a) for 'Supervisory body' has the same meaning' substitute 'Supervisory body' and 'Independent Supervisor' have the same meaning';

(b) for 'section 1217' substitute 'sections 1217 and 1228'.

### Grounds for petition by company member

**42.** (1) In section 994 of the Companies Act 2006 (protection of members against unfair prejudice: petition by company member), after subsection (1) insert—

'(1A) For the purposes of subsection (1)(a), a removal of the company's auditor from office—

(a) on grounds of divergence of opinions on accounting treatments or audit procedures, or

(b) on any other improper grounds,

shall be treated as being unfairly prejudicial to the interests of some part of the company's members.'.

(2) This amendment does not apply in relation to auditors appointed for financial years beginning before 6th April 2008.

**Exclusion of large debt securities issuer from definition of 'UK-traded non-EEA company'**

**43.** (1)  A large debt securities issuer is excluded from the definition of 'UK-traded non-EEA company' for the purposes of Part 42 of the Companies Act 2006 (see section 1241(2)).

(2)  In paragraph (1) 'large debt securities issuer' means a body corporate whose only issued transferable securities admitted to trading on a regulated market are debt securities, the denomination per unit of which is not less than—

(a)  50,000 euros, or

(b)  in the case of debt securities denominated in a currency other than euros, a sum equivalent at the date of issue to 50,000 euros.

(3)  In paragraph (2)—

'debt securities' has the same meaning as in Article 2.1(b) of Directive 2004/109/EC of the European Parliament and of the Council on the harmonisation of transparency requirements in relation to information about issuers whose securities are admitted to trading on a regulated market and amending Directive 2001/34/EC[30];

'transferable securities' and 'regulated market' have the same meaning as in section 1241(3) of the Companies Act 2006.

**Practical training**

**44.** In paragraph 9(4)(b) of Schedule 11 to the Companies Act 2006[31] (practical training) for 'a member State' in both places where it occurs substitute 'an EEA State'.

**Revocations and savings**

**45.** (1)  The Company Auditors (Examinations) Regulations 1990[32] are revoked.

(2)  The Company Auditors (Examinations) Regulations (Northern Ireland) 1990[33] are revoked.

(3)  The Companies Act 1989 (Register of Auditors and Information About Audit Firms) Regulations 1991[34] are revoked.

(4)  The Companies (1990 Order) (Register of Auditors and Information About Audit Firms) Regulations (Northern Ireland) 1991[35] are revoked.

(5)  The European Communities (Recognition of Professional Qualifications) (First General System) Regulations 2005[36] are revoked for the purposes of their application to the profession of company auditor, except for the purposes of their application in relation to auditors appointed for financial years beginning before 6th April 2008.

SCHEDULE                                                    Regulation 10(2)
SCHEDULE 11 TO THE COMPANIES ACT 2006

SCHEDULE 11A
SPECIFIED PERSONS, DESCRIPTIONS, DISCLOSURES ETC FOR
THE PURPOSES OF SECTION 1224A

PART 1
SPECIFIED PERSONS

**1.** The Secretary of State.

**2.** The Department of Enterprise, Trade and Investment for Northern Ireland.

**3.** The Treasury.

**4.** The Bank of England.

**5.** The Financial Services Authority.

**6.** The Commissioners for Her Majesty's Revenue and Customs.

**7.** The Lord Advocate.

**8.** The Director of Public Prosecutions.

**9.** The Director of Public Prosecutions for Northern Ireland.

**10.** A constable.

---

[30]  OJ L 390, 31.12.2004, p 38.
[31]  2006 c.46.
[32]  SI 1990/1146.
[33]  SR 1990/309.
[34]  SI 1991/1566.
[35]  SR 1991/500.
[36]  SI 2005/18. The 2005 Regulations were revoked for all other purposes by regulation 39 of, and Schedule 6 to, the European Communities (Recognition of Professional Qualifications) Regulations 2007 (SI 2007/2781).

**11.** A procurator fiscal.

**12.** The Scottish Ministers.

**13.** A body designated by the Secretary of State under section 1252 (delegation of the Secretary of State's functions).

**14.** A recognised supervisory body.

**15.** A recognised qualifying body.

**16.** A body with which a recognised supervisory body is participating in arrangements for the purposes of paragraph 23 (independent monitoring of audits) or 24 (independent investigation for disciplinary purposes) of Schedule 10 to this Act.

**17.** The Independent Supervisor.

## PART 2
## SPECIFIED DESCRIPTIONS OF DISCLOSURES

**18.** A disclosure for the purpose of enabling or assisting a person authorised under section 457 of this Act (persons authorised to apply to court) to exercise his functions.

**19.** A disclosure for the purpose of enabling or assisting an inspector appointed under Part 14 of the Companies Act 1985 (investigation of companies and their affairs, etc) to exercise his functions.

**20.** A disclosure for the purpose of enabling or assisting a person authorised under section 447 of the Companies Act 1985 (power to require production of documents) or section 84 of the Companies Act 1989 (c.40) (exercise of powers by officer etc) to exercise his functions.

**21.** A disclosure for the purpose of enabling or assisting a person appointed under section 167 of the Financial Services and Markets Act 2000 (c.8) (general investigations) to conduct an investigation to exercise his functions.

**22.** A disclosure for the purpose of enabling or assisting a person appointed under section 168 of the Financial Services and Markets Act 2000 (investigations in particular cases) to conduct an investigation to exercise his functions.

**23.** A disclosure for the purpose of enabling or assisting a person appointed under section 169(1)(b) of the Financial Services and Markets Act 2000 (investigation in support of overseas regulator) to conduct an investigation to exercise his functions.

**24.** A disclosure for the purpose of enabling or assisting the body corporate responsible for administering the scheme referred to in section 225 of the Financial Services and Markets Act 2000 (the ombudsman scheme) to exercise its functions.

**25.** A disclosure for the purpose of enabling or assisting a person appointed under paragraph 4 (the panel of ombudsmen) or 5 (the Chief Ombudsman) of Schedule 17 to the Financial Services and Markets Act 2000 to exercise his functions.

**26.** A disclosure for the purpose of enabling or assisting a person appointed under regulations made under section 262(1) and (2)(k) of the Financial Services and Markets Act 2000 (investigations into open-ended investment companies) to conduct an investigation to exercise his functions.

**27.** A disclosure for the purpose of enabling or assisting a person appointed under section 284 of the Financial Services and Markets Act 2000 (investigations into affairs of certain collective investment schemes) to conduct an investigation to exercise his functions.

**28.** A disclosure for the purpose of enabling or assisting the investigator appointed under paragraph 7 of Schedule 1 to the Financial Services and Markets Act 2000 (arrangements for investigation of complaints) to exercise his functions.

**29.** A disclosure for the purpose of enabling or assisting a person appointed by the Treasury to hold an inquiry into matters relating to financial services (including an inquiry under section 15 of the Financial Services and Markets Act 2000 (c.8)) to exercise his functions.

**30.** A disclosure for the purpose of enabling or assisting the Secretary of State or the Treasury to exercise any of their functions under any of the following—
   (a) the Companies Acts;
   (b) Part 5 of the Criminal Justice Act 1993 (c.36) (insider dealing);
   (c) the Insolvency Act 1986 (c.45);
   (d) the Company Directors Disqualification Act 1986 (c.46);
   (e) Part 42 of this Act (statutory auditors)
   (f) Part 3 (investigations and powers to obtain information) or 7 (financial markets and insolvency) of the Companies Act 1989 (c.40);
   (g) the Financial Services and Markets Act 2000.

**31.** A disclosure for the purpose of enabling or assisting the Scottish Ministers to exercise their functions under the enactments relating to insolvency.

**32.** A disclosure for the purpose of enabling or assisting the Department of Enterprise, Trade and Investment for Northern Ireland to exercise any powers conferred on it by the enactments relating to companies or insolvency.

**33.** A disclosure for the purpose of enabling or assisting a person appointed or authorised by the Department of Enterprise, Trade and Investment for Northern Ireland under the enactments relating to companies or insolvency to exercise his functions.

**34.** A disclosure for the purpose of enabling or assisting the Pensions Regulator to exercise the functions conferred on it by or by virtue of any of the following—
  (a) the Pension Schemes Act 1993 (c.48);
  (b) the Pensions Act 1995 (c.26);
  (c) the Welfare Reform and Pensions Act 1999 (c.30);
  (d) the Pensions Act 2004 (c.35);
  (e) any enactment in force in Northern Ireland corresponding to any of those enactments.

**35.** A disclosure for the purpose of enabling or assisting the Board of the Pension Protection Fund to exercise the functions conferred on it by or by virtue of Part 2 of the Pensions Act 2004 or any enactment in force in Northern Ireland corresponding to that Part.

**36.** A disclosure for the purpose of enabling or assisting—
  (a) the Bank of England,
  (b) the European Central Bank, or
  (c) the central bank of any country or territory outside the United Kingdom, to exercise its functions.

**37.** A disclosure for the purpose of enabling or assisting the Commissioners for Her Majesty's Revenue and Customs to exercise their functions.

**38.** A disclosure for the purpose of enabling or assisting organs of the Society of Lloyd's (being organs constituted by or under the Lloyd's Act 1982 (c.xiv)) to exercise their functions under or by virtue of the Lloyd's Acts 1871 to 1982.

**39.** A disclosure for the purpose of enabling or assisting the Office of Fair Trading to exercise its functions under any of the following—
  (a) the Fair Trading Act 1973 (c.41);
  (b) the Consumer Credit Act 1974 (c.39);
  (c) the Estate Agents Act 1979 (c.38);
  (d) the Competition Act 1980 (c.21);
  (e) the Competition Act 1998 (c.41);
  (f) the Financial Services and Markets Act 2000 (c.8);
  (g) the Enterprise Act 2002 (c.40);
  (h) the Control of Misleading Advertisements Regulations 1988 (S.I. 1988/915);
  (i) the Unfair Terms in Consumer Contracts Regulations 1999 (S.I. 1999/2083).

**40.** A disclosure for the purpose of enabling or assisting the Competition Commission to exercise its functions under any of the following—
  (a) the Fair Trading Act 1973;
  (b) the Competition Act 1980;
  (c) the Competition Act 1998;
  (d) the Enterprise Act 2002.

**41.** A disclosure with a view to the institution of, or otherwise for the purposes of, proceedings before the Competition Appeal Tribunal.

**42.** A disclosure for the purpose of enabling or assisting an enforcer under Part 8 of the Enterprise Act 2002 (enforcement of consumer legislation) to exercise its functions under that Part.

**43.** A disclosure for the purpose of enabling or assisting the Takeover Panel to perform any of its functions under Part 28 of this Act (takeovers etc).

**44.** A disclosure for the purpose of enabling or assisting the Charity Commission to exercise its functions.

**45.** A disclosure for the purpose of enabling or assisting the Attorney General to exercise his functions in connection with charities.

**46.** A disclosure for the purpose of enabling or assisting the National Lottery Commission to exercise its functions under sections 5 to 10 (licensing) and 15 (power of Secretary of State to require information) of the National Lottery etc. Act 1993 (c.39).

**47.** A disclosure by the National Lottery Commission to the National Audit Office for the purpose of enabling or assisting the Comptroller and Auditor General to carry out an examination under Part 2 of the National Audit Act 1983 (c.44) into the economy, effectiveness and efficiency with which the National Lottery Commission has used its resources in discharging its functions under sections 5 to 10 of the National Lottery etc. Act 1993.

**48.** A disclosure for the purpose of enabling or assisting a qualifying body under the Unfair Terms in Consumer Contracts Regulations 1999 (S.I. 1999/2083) to exercise its functions under those Regulations.

**49.** A disclosure for the purpose of enabling or assisting an enforcement authority under the Consumer Protection (Distance Selling) Regulations 2000 (S.I. 2000/2334) to exercise its functions under those Regulations.

**50.** A disclosure for the purpose of enabling or assisting an enforcement authority under the Financial Services (Distance Marketing) Regulations 2004 (S.I. 2004/2095) to exercise its functions under those Regulations.

**51.** A disclosure for the purpose of enabling or assisting a local weights and measures authority in England and Wales to exercise its functions under section 230(2) of the Enterprise Act 2002 (c.40) (notice of intention to prosecute, etc).

**52.** A disclosure for the purpose of enabling or assisting the Financial Services Authority to exercise its functions under any of the following—
   (a) the legislation relating to friendly societies or to industrial and provident societies;
   (b) the Building Societies Act 1986 (c.53);
   (c) Part 7 of the Companies Act 1989 (c.40) (financial markets and insolvency);
   (d) the Financial Services and Markets Act 2000 (c.8).

**53.** A disclosure for the purpose of enabling or assisting the competent authority for the purposes of Part 6 of the Financial Services and Markets Act 2000 (official listing) to exercise its functions under that Part.

**54.** A disclosure for the purpose of enabling or assisting a body corporate established in accordance with section 212(1) of the Financial Services and Markets Act 2000 (compensation scheme manager) to exercise its functions.

**55.** A disclosure for the purpose of enabling or assisting a recognised investment exchange or a recognised clearing house to exercise its functions as such.
   'Recognised investment exchange' and 'recognised clearing house' have the same meaning as in section 285 of the Financial Services and Markets Act 2000.

**56.** A disclosure for the purpose of enabling or assisting a person approved under the Uncertificated Securities Regulations 2001 (S.I. 2001/3755) as an operator of a relevant system (within the meaning of those regulations) to exercise his functions.

**57.** A disclosure for the purpose of enabling or assisting a body designated under section 326(1) of the Financial Services and Markets Act 2000 (designated professional bodies) to exercise its functions in its capacity as a body designated under that section.

**58.** A disclosure with a view to the institution of, or otherwise for the purposes of, civil proceedings arising under or by virtue of the Financial Services and Markets Act 2000.

**59.** A disclosure for the purpose of enabling or assisting a body designated by order under section 1252 of this Act (delegation of functions of Secretary of State) to exercise its functions under Part 42 of this Act (statutory auditors).

**60.** A disclosure for the purpose of enabling or assisting a recognised supervisory or qualifying body, within the meaning of Part 42 of this Act, to exercise its functions as such.

**61.** A disclosure for the purpose of making available to an audited person information relating to a statutory audit of that person's accounts.

**62.** A disclosure for the purpose of making available to the public information relating to monitoring or inspections carried out under arrangements within paragraph 23(1) of Schedule 10 to this Act (arrangements for independent monitoring of audits of listed companies and other major bodies), provided such information does not identify any audited person.

**63.** A disclosure for the purpose of enabling or assisting an official receiver (including the Accountant in Bankruptcy in Scotland and the Official Assignee in Northern Ireland) to exercise his functions under the enactments relating to insolvency.

**64.** A disclosure for the purpose of enabling or assisting the Insolvency Practitioners Tribunal to exercise its functions under the Insolvency Act 1986 (c.45).

**65.** A disclosure for the purpose of enabling or assisting a body that is for the time being a recognised professional body for the purposes of section 391 of the Insolvency Act 1986 (recognised professional bodies) to exercise its functions as such.

**66.** A disclosure for the purpose of enabling or assisting an overseas regulatory authority to exercise its regulatory functions.
   'Overseas regulatory authority' and 'regulatory functions' have the same meaning as in section 82 of the Companies Act 1989.

**67.** A disclosure for the purpose of enabling or assisting the Regulator of Community Interest Companies to exercise functions under the Companies (Audit, Investigations and Community Enterprise) Act 2004 (c.27).

**68.** A disclosure with a view to the institution of, or otherwise for the purposes of, criminal proceedings.

**69.** A disclosure for the purpose of enabling or assisting a person authorised by the Secretary of State under Part 2, 3 or 4 of the Proceeds of Crime Act 2002 (c.29) to exercise his functions.

**70.** A disclosure with a view to the institution of, or otherwise for the purposes of, proceedings on an application under section 6, 7 or 8 of the Company Directors Disqualification Act 1986 (c.46) (disqualification for unfitness).

**71.** A disclosure with a view to the institution of, or otherwise for the purposes of, proceedings before the Financial Services and Markets Tribunal.

**72.** A disclosure for the purposes of proceedings before the Financial Services Tribunal by virtue of the Financial Services and Markets Act 2000 (Transitional Provisions) (Partly Completed Procedures) Order 2001 (S.I. 2001/3592).

**73.** A disclosure for the purposes of proceedings before the Pensions Regulator Tribunal.

**74.** A disclosure for the purpose of enabling or assisting a body appointed under section 14 of the Companies (Audit, Investigations and Community Enterprise) Act 2004 (supervision of periodic accounts and reports of issuers of listed securities) to exercise functions mentioned in subsection (2) of that section.

**75.** A disclosure with a view to the institution of, or otherwise for the purposes of, disciplinary proceedings relating to the performance by a relevant lawyer, foreign lawyer, auditor, accountant, valuer or actuary of his professional duties.

In this paragraph—

'foreign lawyer' means a person (other than a relevant lawyer) who is a foreign lawyer within the meaning of section 89(9) of the Courts and Legal Services Act 1990;

'relevant lawyer' means—

(a) a person who, for the purposes of the Legal Services Act 2007, is an authorised person in relation to an activity which constitutes a reserved legal activity (within the meaning of that Act),

(b) a solicitor or barrister in Northern Ireland, or

(c) a solicitor or advocate in Scotland.

**76.** A disclosure with a view to the institution of, or otherwise for the purposes of, disciplinary proceedings relating to the performance by a public servant of his duties.

'Public servant' means an officer or employee of the Crown.

**77.** A disclosure for the purpose of the provision of a summary or collection of information framed in such a way as not to enable the identity of any person to whom the information relates to be ascertained.

**78.** A disclosure in pursuance of any Community obligation.

## PART 3
### OVERSEAS REGULATORY BODIES

**79.** A disclosure is made in accordance with this Part of this Schedule if it is made to an EEA competent authority in accordance with section 1253B (requests from EEA competent authorities).

**80.** A disclosure is made in accordance with this Part of this Schedule if it is—

(a) a transfer of audit working papers to a third country competent authority in accordance with rules imposed under paragraph 16A of Schedule 10 (transfer of papers to third countries), or

(b) a disclosure other than a transfer of audit working papers made to a third country competent authority for the purpose of enabling or assisting the authority to exercise its functions.'

---

# THE COMPANIES (REVISION OF DEFECTIVE ACCOUNTS AND REPORTS) REGULATIONS 2008
## (SI 2008/373)

COMMENCEMENT DATE 6 April 2008

## PART 1
### INTRODUCTION

**SI.09**

**Citation, commencement and application**

**1.** (1) These Regulations may be cited as the Companies (Revision of Defective Accounts and Reports) Regulations 2008.

(2) These Regulations come into force on 6th April 2008 and apply in relation to companies' financial years beginning on or after that date.

**Interpretation**

**2.** (1) In these Regulations—

'the 2006 Act' means the Companies Act 2006;

'date of the original annual accounts' means the date on which the original annual accounts were approved by the board of directors under section 414 of the 2006 Act (approval and signing of accounts);

'date of the original directors' remuneration report' means the date on which the original directors' remuneration report was approved by the board of directors under section 422 of the 2006 Act (approval and signing of directors' remuneration report);

'date of the original directors' report' means the date on which the original directors' report was approved by the board of directors under section 419 of the 2006 Act (approval and signing of directors' report);

'date of revision' means the date on which revised accounts are approved by the board of directors under regulation 4 or (as the case may be) a revised directors' report or directors' remuneration report is approved by them under regulation 5 or 6;

'original', in relation to annual accounts, or a directors' report or directors' remuneration report, means the annual accounts or (as the case may be) directors' report or directors' remuneration report which are the subject of revision by, respectively, revised accounts or a revised report and, in relation to abbreviated accounts or a summary financial statement, means abbreviated accounts or a summary financial statement based on the original annual accounts or directors' report or directors' remuneration report;

'revised accounts' mean revised annual accounts of a company prepared by the directors under section 454 of the 2006 Act (voluntary revision of accounts etc), either through revision by replacement or revision by supplementary note; in the latter case the revised accounts comprise the original annual accounts together with the supplementary note;

'revised report' means a revised directors' report or directors' remuneration report prepared by the directors under section 454 of the 2006 Act, either through revision by replacement or revision by supplementary note; in the latter case the revised report comprises the original directors' report or directors' remuneration report together with the supplementary note;

'revision by replacement' means revision by the preparation of a replacement set of accounts, directors' report or directors' remuneration report, in substitution for the original annual accounts, directors' report or directors' remuneration report; and

'revision by supplementary note' means revision by the preparation of a note indicating corrections to be made to the original annual accounts, directors' report or directors' remuneration report.

(2) References in these Regulations to a member or members of a company include a reference to a person nominated to enjoy information rights under section 146 of the 2006 Act (traded companies: nomination of persons to enjoy information rights).

(3) References in these Regulations to provisions or requirements of the 2006 Act as to matters to be included in annual accounts and reports include relevant provisions of the Small Companies and Groups (Accounts and Directors' Report) Regulations 2008[37] and the Large and Medium-sized Companies and Groups (Accounts and Reports) Regulations 2008[38].

## PART 2
## REVISED ACCOUNTS AND REPORTS

**Content of revised accounts or revised report**

**3.** (1) Subject to regulation 19(1), the provisions of the 2006 Act and, where applicable, Article 4 of the IAS Regulation as to the matters to be included in the annual accounts of acompany apply to revised accounts as if the revised accounts were prepared and approved by the directors as at the date of the original annual accounts.

(2) In particular—

    (a) in the case of Companies Act accounts—

        (i) section 393 of the 2006 Act (accounts to give true and fair view),

        (ii) section 396(2) of that Act (Companies Act individual accounts: true and fair view), and

        (iii) section 404(2) of that Act (Companies Act group accounts: true and fair view), and

    (b) in the case of IAS accounts, section 393 of the 2006 Act and international accounting standards,

apply so as to require a true and fair view to be shown in the revised accounts of the matters referred to in those accounts, viewed as at the date of the original annual accounts.

(3) In the case of Companies Act accounts, paragraph 13(b) of Schedule 1 to the Small Companies and Groups (Accounts and Directors' Report) Regulations 2008 or (where applicable) paragraph 13(b) of Schedule 1 to the Large and Medium-sized Companies and Groups (Accounts and Reports) Regulations 2008 apply to revised accounts as if the reference in those paragraphs to the date on which the accounts were signed was to the date of the original annual accounts.

(4) The provisions of the 2006 Act as to the matters to be included in a directors' report or directors' remuneration report apply to a revised report as if the revised report was prepared and approved by the directors of the company as at the date of the original directors' report or directors' remuneration report.

---

[37] SI 2008/409.
[38] SI 2008/410.

**Approval and signature of revised accounts**

**4.** (1) Section 414 of the 2006 Act applies to revised accounts, save that in the case of revision by supplementary note, it applies as if it required a signature on the supplementary note instead of on the company's balance sheet.

(2) Where copies of the original annual accounts have been sent out to members under section 423(1) of the 2006 Act (duty to circulate copies of annual accounts and reports), laid before the company in general meeting under section 437(1) of that Act (public companies: laying of accounts and reports before general meeting) in the case of a public company, or delivered to the registrar under section 441(1) of that Act (duty to file accounts and reports with the registrar), the directors must before approving the revised accounts under section 414, cause statements as to the following matters to be made in a prominent position in the revised accounts (in the case of a revision by supplementary note, in that note)—

(a) in the case of a revision by replacement—

(i) that the revised accounts replace the original annual accounts for the financial year (specifying it),

(ii) that they are now the statutory accounts of the company for that financial year,

(iii) that they have been prepared as at the date of the original annual accounts and not as at the date of revision and accordingly do not deal with events between those dates,

(iv) the respects in which the original annual accounts did not comply with the requirements of the 2006 Act, and

(v) any significant amendments made consequential upon the remedying of those defects,

(b) in the case of a revision by supplementary note—

(i) that the note revises in certain respects the original annual accounts of the company and is to be treated as forming part of those accounts, and

(ii) that the annual accounts have been revised as at the date of the original annual accounts and not as at the date of revision and accordingly do not deal with events between those dates

and must, when approving the revised accounts, cause the date on which the approval is given to be stated in them (in the case of revision by supplementary note, in that note); section 414(4) and (5) apply with respect to a failure to comply with this paragraph as if the requirements of this paragraph were requirements of Part 15 of that Act.

**Approval and signature of revised directors' report**

**5.** (1) Section 419 of the 2006 Act applies to a revised directors' report, save that in the case of revision by supplementary note, it applies as if it required the signature to be on the supplementary note.

(2) Where copies of the original directors' report have been sent out to members under section 423(1) of the 2006 Act, laid before the company in general meeting under section 437(1) of that Act in the case of a public company, or delivered to the registrar under section 441(1), the directors must, before approving the revised report under section 419, cause statements as to the following matters to be made in a prominent position in the revised report (in the case of a revision by supplementary note, in that note)—

(a) in the case of a revision by replacement—

(i) that the revised report replaces the original report for the financial year (specifying it),

(ii) that it has been prepared as at the date of the original directors' report and not as at the date of revision and accordingly does not deal with any events between those dates,

(iii) the respects in which the original directors' report did not comply with the requirements of the 2006 Act, and

(iv) any significant amendments made consequential upon the remedying of those defects,

(b) in the case of a revision by supplementary note—

(i) that the note revises in certain respects the original directors' report of the company and is to be treated as forming part of that report, and

(ii) that the directors' report has been revised as at the date of the original directors' report and not as at the date of the revision and accordingly does not deal with events between those dates,

and must, when approving the revised report, cause the date on which the approval is given to be stated in them (in the case of a revision by supplementary note, in that note); section 419(3) and (4) of the 2006 Act apply with respect to a failure to comply with this paragraph as if the requirements of this paragraph were requirements of Part 15 of that Act.

**Approval and signature of revised directors' remuneration report**

**6.** (1) Section 422 of the 2006 Act applies to a revised directors' remuneration report, save that in the case of revision by supplementary note, it applies as if it required the signature to be on the supplementary note.

(2) Where copies of the original directors' remuneration report have been sent out to members under section 423(1) of the 2006 Act, laid before the company in general meeting under section 437(1) of that Act in the case of a public company, or delivered to the registrar under section 441(1) of that Act, the directors must, before approving the revised report under section 422, cause statements as to the following matters to be made in a prominent position in the revised report (in the case of a revision by supplementary note, in that note)—

(a) in the case of a revision by replacement—

    (i) that the revised report replaces the original report for the financial year (specifying it),

    (ii) that it has been prepared as at the date of the original directors' remuneration report and not as at the date of revision and accordingly does not deal with any events between those dates,

    (iii) the respects in which the original directors' remuneration report did not comply with the requirements of the 2006 Act, and

    (iv) any significant amendments made consequential upon the remedying of those defects,

(b) in the case of a revision by supplementary note—

    (i) that the note revises in certain respects the original directors' remuneration report of the company and is to be treated as forming part of that report, and

    (ii) that the directors' remuneration report has been revised as at the date of the original directors' remuneration report and not as at the date of the revision and accordingly does not deal with events between those dates,

and must, when approving the revised report, cause the date on which the approval is given to be stated in it (in the case of a revision by supplementary note, in that note); section 422(2) and (3) of the 2006 Act apply with respect to a failure to comply with this paragraph as if the requirements of this paragraph were requirements of Part 15 of that Act.

## PART 3
## AUDITOR'S REPORTS

### Auditor's report on revised accounts and revised report

**7.** (1) Subject to paragraph (2), a company's current auditor shall make a report or (as the case may be) further report under section 495 of the 2006 Act (auditor's report on company's annual accounts), to the company's members under this regulation on any revised accounts prepared under section 454 of that Act and—

(a) section 498 of that Act (duties of auditor) applies with any necessary modifications, and

(b) section 495(1) does not apply with respect to the revised accounts.

(2) Where the auditor's report on the original annual accounts was not made by the company's current auditor, the directors of the company may resolve that the report required by paragraph (1) is to be made by the person or persons who made that report, provided that that person or those persons agree to do so and would be qualified for appointment as auditor of the company.

(3) Subject to regulation 19(1), an auditor's report under this regulation must state whether in the auditor's opinion the revised accounts have been properly prepared in accordance with the provisions of the 2006 Act and, where applicable, Article 4 of the IAS Regulation as they have effect under these Regulations, and in particular whether a true and fair view, seen as at the date the original annual accounts were approved, is given by the revised accounts with respect to the matters set out in section 495(3)(a) to (c) of that Act.

The report must also state whether in the auditor's opinion the original annual accounts failed to comply with the requirements of the 2006 Act and, where applicable, Article 4 of the IAS Regulation in the respects identified by the directors (in the case of a revision by replacement) in the statement required by regulation 4(2)(a)(iv) or (in the case of a revision by supplementary note) in the supplementary note.

(4) The auditor must also state whether the information contained in the directors' report for the financial year for which the annual accounts are prepared (which is, if the report has been revised under these Regulations, that revised report) is consistent with those accounts.

(5) Sections 503 to 506 of the 2006 Act (signature of auditor's report) apply to an auditor's report under this regulation as they apply to an auditor's report under section 495(1) of that Act, with any necessary modifications.

(6) An auditor's report under this regulation shall, upon being signed under section 503 of the 2006 Act as so applied, be, as from the date of signature, the auditor's report on the annual accounts of the company in place of the report on the original annual accounts.

### Auditor's report where company ceases to be exempt from audit

**8.** (1) Where as a result of the revisions to the accounts, the company is no longer entitled to exemption from audit under Chapter 1 of Part 16 of the 2006 Act, the company shall cause an auditor's report on the revised accounts to be prepared.

(2)  The auditor's report must be delivered to the registrar within 28 days after the date of revision of the accounts.

(3)  Sections 451 (default in filing accounts and reports: offences) and 452 (default in filing accounts: court order) of the 2006 Act apply with respect to a failure to comply with the requirements of this regulation as they apply with respect to a failure to comply with the requirements of section 441 of that Act but as if—

    (a)  the references in section 451(1) and in section 452(1)(a) to 'the period for filing those accounts and reports' were references to the period of 28 days referred to in paragraph (2); the reference in section 451(1) and (2) to 'that period' are to be construed accordingly, and

    (b)  the references in section 451(3) to 'the documents in question' and 'this Part' were, respectively, a reference to the auditor's report referred to in paragraph (2) and the provisions of Part 16 of the 2006 Act as applied by these Regulations.

### Auditor's report on revised report alone

**9.**  (1)  Subject to paragraph (2), a company's current auditor shall make a report or (as the case may be) further report under section 496 or 497 of the 2006 Act (as the case may be) to the company's members under this regulation on any revised report prepared under section 454 of that Act if the relevant annual accounts have not been revised at the same time.

(2)  Where the auditor's report on the annual accounts for the financial year covered by the revised report was not made by the company's current auditor, the directors of the company may resolve that the report required by paragraph (1) is to be made by the person or persons who made that report, provided that that person or those persons agree to do so and would be qualified for appointment as auditor of the company.

(3)  Where a revised directors' report is prepared under section 454 of the 2006 Act, the auditor's report must state whether in his opinion the information given in that revised report is consistent with the annual accounts for the relevant year (specifying it).

(4)  Where a revised directors' remuneration report is prepared under section 454 of the 2006 Act, the auditor's report must state whether in his opinion any auditable part of that revised report has been properly prepared ('auditable part' being a part containing information required by Part 3 of Schedule 8 to the Large and Medium-sized Companies and Groups (Accounts and Reports) Regulations 2008).

(5)  Sections 503 to 506 of the 2006 Act apply to an auditor's report under this regulation as they apply to an auditor's report under section 495 of that Act, with any necessary modifications.

## PART 4
## EFFECT OF REVISION

### Effect of revision of accounts

**10.**  (1)  Upon the directors approving revised accounts under regulation 4, the provisions of the 2006 Act have effect as if the revised accounts were, as from the date of their approval, the annual accounts of the company in place of the original annual accounts.

(2)  In particular, the revised accounts shall as from that date be the company's annual accounts for the relevant financial year for the purposes of the following provisions of the 2006 Act—

    (a)  section 431 (right of member or debenture holder to copies of accounts and reports: unquoted companies),

    (b)  section 432 (right of member or debenture holder to copies of accounts and reports: quoted companies),

    (c)  section 434(3) (requirements in connection with publication of statutory accounts), and

    (d)  sections 423 (duty to circulate copies of annual accounts and reports), 437 (public companies; laying of accounts and reports before general meeting) and 441 (duty to file accounts and reports with the registrar), if the requirements of those sections have not been complied with prior to the date of revision.

### Effect of revision of report

**11.**  (1)  Subject to the following provisions of these Regulations, upon the directors approving a revised report under regulation 5 or 6 the provisions of the 2006 Act have effect as if the revised report was, as from the date of its approval, the directors' report or the directors' remuneration report (as the case may be) in place of the original directors' report or directors' remuneration report (as the case may be).

(2)  In particular, the revised report shall as from that date be the directors' report or the directors' remuneration report for the relevant financial year for the purposes of—

    (a)  sections 431 and 432 of the 2006 Act, and

    (b)  sections 423, 437 and 441 of that Act if the requirements of those sections have not been complied with prior to the date of revision.

## PART 5
## PUBLICATION, LAYING AND DELIVERY OF REVISED ACCOUNTS ETC

### Publication of revised accounts and reports

**12.** (1) This regulation has effect where the directors have prepared revised accounts or a revised report under section 454 of the 2006 Act and copies of the original annual accounts or report have been sent to any person under section 423 or 146 of that Act.

(2) The directors must send to any such person—

    (a) in the case of a revision by replacement, a copy of the revised accounts, or (as the case may be) the revised report, together with a copy of the auditor's report on those accounts, or (as the case may be) on that report, or

    (b) in the case of a revision by supplementary note, a copy of that note together with a copy of the auditor's report on the revised accounts, or (as the case may be) on the revised report, not more than 28 days after the date of revision.

(3) The directors must also, not more than 28 days after the revision, send a copy of the revised accounts or (as the case may be) revised report, together with a copy of the auditor's report on those accounts or (as the case may be) on that report, to any person who is not a person entitled to receive a copy under paragraph (2) but who is, as at the date of revision—

    (a) a member of the company,

    (b) a holder of the company's debentures, or

    (c) a person who is entitled to receive notice of general meetings,

    unless the company would be entitled at that date to send to that person a summary financial statement under section 426 of the 2006 Act (option to provide summary financial statement). Section 423(2) to (4) of that Act apply to this paragraph as they apply to section 423(1).

(4) Section 425 of the 2006 Act (default in sending out copies of accounts and reports: offences) applies to a default in complying with this regulation as if the provisions of this regulation were provisions of section 423 and as if the references in that section to 'the company' and 'every officer of the company who is in default' were a reference to each of the directors who approved the revised accounts under regulation 4 or revised report under regulation 5 or 6.

(5) Where, prior to the date of revision of the original annual accounts, the company had completed sending out copies of those accounts under section 423 of the 2006 Act, references in that Act to the day on which accounts are sent out under section 423 are to be construed as referring to the day on which the original accounts were sent out (applying section 423(5) as necessary) notwithstanding that those accounts have been revised; where the company had not completed, prior to the date of revision, the sending out of copies of those accounts under that section, such references are to the day, or the last day, on which the revised accounts are sent out.

### Laying of revised accounts or a revised report

**13.** (1) This regulation has effect where the directors of a public company have prepared revised accounts or a revised report under section 454 of the 2006 Act and copies of the original annual accounts or report have been laid before a general meeting under section 437 of that Act.

(2) A copy of the revised accounts or (as the case may be) the revised report, together with a copy of the auditor's report on those accounts, or (as the case may be) on that report, must be laid before the next general meeting of the company held after the date of revision at which any annual accounts for a financial year are laid, unless the revised accounts, or (as the case may be) the revised report, have already been laid before an earlier general meeting.

(3) Section 438 of the 2006 Act (public companies: offence of failure to lay accounts and reports) applies with respect to a failure to comply with the requirements of this regulation as it has effect with respect to a failure to comply with the requirements of section 437 of that Act but as if—

    (a) the reference in section 438(1) to 'the period allowed' was a reference to the period between the date of revision of the revised accounts or (as the case may be) the revised report and the date of the next general meeting of the company held after the date of revision at which any annual accounts for a financial year are laid; references in section 438(1) and (2) to 'that period' are to be construed accordingly; and

    (b) the references in section 438(3) to 'the documents in question' and 'this Part' were, respectively, a reference to the documents referred to in paragraph (2) and the provisions of Part 15 of the 2006 Act as applied by these Regulations.

### Delivery of revised accounts or a revised report

**14.** (1) This regulation has effect where the directors have prepared revised accounts or a revised report under section 454 of the 2006 Act and a copy of the original annual accounts or report has been delivered to the registrar under section 441(1) of that Act.

(2) The directors of the company must, within 28 days of the date of revision, deliver to the registrar—

    (a) in the case of a revision by replacement, a copy of the revised accounts or (as the case may be) the revised report, together with a copy of the auditor's report on those accounts or (as the case may be) on that report, or

    (b) in the case of a revision by supplementary note, a copy of that note, together with a copy of the auditor's report on the revised accounts or (as the case may be) on the revised report.

(3) Sections 451 (default in filing accounts and reports: offences) and 452 (default in filing accounts: court order) of the 2006 Act apply with respect to a failure to comply with the requirements of this regulation as they apply with respect to a failure to comply with the requirements of section 441 of that Act but as if—

    (a) the references in section 451(1) and in section 452(1)(a) to 'the period for filing those accounts and reports' were references to the period of 28 days referred to in paragraph (2); the references in section 451(1) and (2) to 'that period' are to be construed accordingly, and

    (b) the references in section 451(3) to 'the documents in question' and 'this Part' were, respectively, a reference to the documents referred to in paragraph (2) and the provisions of Part 15 of the 2006 Act as applied by these Regulations.

<h1 style="text-align:center">PART 6</h1>
<h2 style="text-align:center">ABBREVIATED ACCOUNTS AND SUMMARY<br/>FINANCIAL STATEMENTS</h2>

**Small and medium sized companies**

**15.** (1) This regulation has effect (subject to regulation 19(2)) where the directors have prepared revised accounts under section 454 of the 2006 Act and the company has, prior to the date of revision, delivered to the registrar accounts which are abbreviated accounts within the meaning of section 444(3) and (4) (filing obligations of companies subject to small companies regime) or 445(3) and (4) (filing obligations of medium-sized companies) of that Act.

(2) Where the abbreviated accounts so delivered to the registrar would, if they had been prepared by reference to the revised accounts, not comply with the provisions of the 2006 Act (whether because the company would not have qualified as a small or (as the case may be) medium-sized company in the light of the revised accounts or because the accounts have been revised in a manner which affects the content of the abbreviated accounts), the directors of the company shall cause the company either—

    (a) to deliver to the registrar a copy of the revised accounts, together with a copy of the directors' report and the auditor's report on the revised accounts, or

    (b) (if on the basis of the revised accounts they would be entitled under the 2006 Act to do so) to prepare further abbreviated accounts drawn up in accordance with the provisions of that Act and deliver them to the registrar together with a statement as to the effect of the revisions made.

(3) Where the abbreviated accounts would, if they had been prepared by reference to the revised accounts, comply with the requirements of the 2006 Act, the directors of the company shall cause the company to deliver to the registrar—

    (a) a note stating that the annual accounts of the company for the relevant financial year (specifying it) have been revised in a respect which has no bearing on the abbreviated accounts delivered for that year, together with

    (b) a copy of any auditor's report on the revised accounts.

(4) Revised abbreviated accounts or a note under this regulation must be delivered to the registrar within 28 days after the date of revision of the revised accounts.

(5) Sections 451 (default in filing accounts and reports: offences) and 452 (default in filing accounts: court order) of the 2006 Act apply with respect to a failure to comply with the requirements of this regulation as they apply with respect to a failure to comply with the requirements of section 441 of that Act but as if—

    (a) the references in section 451(1) and in section 452(1)(a) to 'the period for filing those accounts and reports' were references to the period of 28 days referred to in paragraph (4); the references in section 451(1) and (2) to 'that period' are to be construed accordingly, and

    (b) the references in section 451(3) to 'the documents in question' and 'this Part' were, respectively, a reference to the documents referred to in paragraph (4) and the provisions of Part 15 of the 2006 Act as applied by these Regulations.

**16.** (1) This regulation has effect (subject to regulation 19(2)) where the directors have delivered to the registrar abbreviated accounts which do not comply with the provisions of the 2006 Act for reasons other than those specified in regulation 15 (2).

(2) The directors of the company shall cause the company—

       (a) to prepare further abbreviated accounts in accordance with the provisions of section 444(3) and (4) or 445(3) and (4) of the 2006 Act (as the case may be), and

       (b) to deliver those accounts to the registrar within 28 days after the date of revision together with a statement as to the effect of the revisions made.

  (3) Sections 451 and 452 of the 2006 Act apply with respect to a failure to comply with the requirements of this regulation as they apply with respect to a failure to comply with the requirements of section 441 of that Act but as if—

       (a) the references in section 451(1) and in section 452(1)(a) to 'the period for filing those accounts and reports' were references to the period of 28 days referred to in paragraph (2); the references in section 451(1) and (2) to 'that period' are to be construed accordingly, and

       (b) the references in section 451(3) to 'the documents in question' and 'this Part' were, respectively, a reference to the documents referred to in paragraph (2) and the provisions of Part 15 of the 2006 Act as applied by these Regulations.

### Summary financial statements

**17.** (1) This regulation has effect subject to regulation 19(3) where a summary financial statement has been sent to any person specified in regulation 3 of the Companies (Summary Financial Statement) Regulations 2008[39].

  (2) Where the summary financial statement does not comply with the requirements of section 426 of the 2006 Act or the Companies (Summary Financial Statement) Regulations 2008, or if it had been prepared by reference to revised accounts or a revised report would not have complied with those requirements, the directors of the company shall, subject to paragraphs (4) and (5), cause the company to prepare a further summary financial statement under section 426 of that Act and to send that statement to—

       (a) any person who received a copy of the original summary financial statement, and

       (b) any person to whom the company would be entitled, as at the date the revised summary financial statement is prepared, to send a summary financial statement for the current financial year,

       and sections 426(1) to (4), 434(6) and 435(7) of that Act (requirements in connection with the publication of statutory accounts and of non-statutory accounts) respectively apply with necessary modifications to a summary financial statement under this regulation.

  (3) A summary financial statement prepared under paragraph (2) must contain a short statement of the revisions made and their effect.

  (4) The directors of the company may, instead of causing the company to prepare a further summary financial statement under paragraph (2), cause the company to prepare and send to the persons mentioned in that paragraph a supplementary note indicating the corrections to the original summary financial statement, and sections 426(1) and (2), 434(6) and 435(7) of the 2006 Act apply with necessary modifications to such a supplementary note.

  (5) A supplementary note prepared under the last paragraph must contain a statement that it revises the original summary financial statement in certain respects and is to be treated as forming part of that statement.

  (6) Where the summary financial statement would, if it had been prepared by reference to the revised accounts or revised report, comply with the requirements of section 426 of the 2006 Act and the Companies (Summary Financial Statement) Regulations 2008, the directors of the company shall cause the company to send to the persons referred to in paragraph (2) a note stating that the annual accounts of the company for the relevant financial year (specifying it) or (as the case may be) the directors' report or directors' remuneration report for that year have or has been revised in a respect which has no bearing on the summary financial statement for that year.

      If the auditor's report under regulation 7, 8 or 9 on the revised accounts or revised report is qualified, a copy of that report must be attached to the note sent out under this paragraph.

  (7) A summary financial statement revised, or a note prepared, under this regulation must be sent to the persons referred to in paragraph (2) within 28 days after the date of revision of the revised accounts or revised report.

  (8) Section 429 of the 2006 Act (summary financial statements: offences) applies with respect to a failure to comply with the requirements of this regulation as if the provisions of this regulation were provisions of that section and as if the reference in that section to 'the company', and 'every officer of the company who is in default' were references to each of the directors of the company who approved the revised accounts under regulation 4, the revised directors' report under regulation 5 or the revised directors' remuneration report under regulation 6.

---

[39] SI 2008/374.

PART 7

COMPANIES EXEMPT FROM AUDIT

### Companies exempt from audit under section 477 or 480

**18.** Where, in respect of any financial year, a company is exempt under section 477 (small companies: conditions for exemption from audit) or 480 (dormant companies: conditions for exemption from audit) of the 2006 Act from the requirements of that Act relating to the audit of accounts, these Regulations apply as if they omitted any reference to an auditor's report, or to the making of such a report.

PART 8

FINAL PROVISIONS

### Modifications of the 2006 Act

**19.** (1) Where the provisions of the 2006 Act as to the matters to be included in the annual accounts of a company or (as the case may be) in a directors' report or directors' remuneration report have been amended after the date of the original annual accounts or (as the case may be) directors' report or directors' remuneration report but prior to the date of revision, references in regulations 3 and 7(3) to the provisions of that Act are to be construed as references to the provisions of that Act as in force at the date of the original annual accounts or (as the case may be) directors' report or directors' remuneration report.

(2) Where the provisions of sections 444(3) and (4) and 445(3) and (4) of the 2006 Act as to the matters to be included in abbreviated accounts have been amended after the date of delivery of the original abbreviated accounts but prior to the date of revision of the revised accounts or report, references in regulations 15 and 16 to the provisions of the 2006 Act or to any particular provisions of that Act are to be construed as references to the provisions of that Act, or to the particular provision, as in force at the date of the delivery of the original abbreviated accounts.

(3) Where the provisions of section 426 of the 2006 Act or of the Companies (Summary Financial Statement) Regulations 2008 as to the matters to be included in a summary financial statement have been amended after the date of the sending out of the original summary financial statement but prior to the date of revision of the revised accounts or report, references in regulation 17 to section 426 or to those Regulations are to be construed as references to that section or those Regulations as in force at the date of the sending out of the original summary financial statements.

### Revocations etc.

**20.** (1) The Companies (Revision of Defective Accounts and Report) Regulations 1990[40] and the Companies (Revision of Defective Accounts and Report) Regulations (Northern Ireland) 1991[41] are revoked.

(2) Notwithstanding the revocation of the regulations specified in paragraph (1), the provisions of those regulations continue to apply in relation to financial years of a company beginning before 6th April 2008.

---

# THE COMPANIES (SUMMARY FINANCIAL STATEMENT) REGULATIONS 2008

(SI 2008/374)

COMMENCEMENT DATE 6 April 2008

PART 1

INTRODUCTION

### Citation, commencement and application

**1.** (1) These Regulations may be cited as the Companies (Summary Financial Statement) Regulations 2008.

(2) These Regulations come into force on 6th April 2008 and apply in relation to companies' financial years beginning on or after that date.

---

[40] SI 1990/2570 as amended by SIs 1994/1935, 1995/2092, 1996/315, 2005/2282 and 2005/3442.

[41] SR 1991/268, as amended by regulation 10 of SR 1993/267, regulation 5 of, and Schedule 2 to, SR 1995/128, regulation 12 of SR 1996/179, SR 1997/423 and SR 2006/139.

### Interpretation

**2.** In these Regulations, unless otherwise stated—

'the 2006 Act' means the Companies Act 2006;

'the Large and Medium-sized Companies Accounts Regulations' means the Large and Medium-sized Companies and Groups (Accounts and Reports) Regulations 2008[42];

'the Small Companies Accounts Regulations' means the Small Companies (Accounts and Directors' Report) Regulations 2008[43];

'full accounts and reports' means, in relation to a company, the annual accounts and reports, copies of which the company is required to send to the persons specified in section 423(l) of the 2006 Act, and 'full' in relation to any balance sheet, profit and loss account, group accounts, directors' report or directors' remuneration report means any such document contained in the full accounts and reports.

### Persons to whom a company may send a summary financial statement

**3.** Subject to these Regulations, a company may send a summary financial statement instead of a copy of its full accounts and reports to—

(a) a person specified in section 423(l) of the 2006 Act (duty to circulate copies of annual accounts and reports); and

(b) a person nominated to enjoy information rights under section 146 of the 2006 Act (traded companies: nomination of persons to enjoy information rights).

PART 2

CONDITIONS FOR SENDING OUT SUMMARY
FINANCIAL STATEMENT

### Cases in which sending of summary financial statement prohibited

**4.** (1) In the following cases a company may not send a summary financial statement to a person specified in regulation 3—

(a) in the case of any such person, where it is prohibited from doing so by any relevant provision of its constitution, and

(b) in the case of any such person who is the holder of a debenture, where it is prohibited from doing so by a relevant provision in any instrument constituting or otherwise governing any of the company's debentures of which that person is a holder.

(2) In the following cases a company may not send a summary financial statement to any person specified in regulation 3 in relation to any financial year—

(a) where, in relation to that year, no auditor's report has been made in respect of the annual accounts of the company, or the directors' report, or the auditable part of the directors' remuneration report, where relevant, under sections 495 (auditor's report on company's annual accounts), 496 (auditor's report on directors' report) and 497 (auditor's report on auditable part of directors' remuneration report) of the 2006 Act respectively;

(b) where the period for filing accounts and reports for that year under section 442 of the 2006 Act (period for filing accounts) has expired;

(c) where the summary financial statement in respect of that financial year has not been approved by the board of directors and the original statement has not been signed on behalf of the board by a director of the company.

(3) For the purposes of paragraph (l) any provision (however expressed) which requires copies of the full accounts and reports to be sent to a person specified in regulation 3, or which forbids the sending of summary financial statements under section 426 of the 2006 Act (option to provide summary financial statement), is a relevant provision.

### Ascertainment of the wishes of a person specified in regulation 3

**5.** (1) A company may not send a summary financial statement to a person specified in regulation 3 unless the company has ascertained that the person does not wish to receive copies of its full accounts and reports, and paragraphs (2) and (3) apply for the ascertainment of whether or not such a person wishes to receive copies of the full accounts and reports for a financial year.

(2) Where a person specified in regulation 3 has expressly notified the company either that he wishes to receive copies of the full accounts and reports or that he wishes, instead of copies of those documents, to receive summary financial statements, the company must send copies of the full accounts and reports or summary financial statement, as appropriate, to that person in respect of the financial years to which the notification applies.

---

[42] SI 2008/410.
[43] SI 2008/409.

(3) Where there has been no such express notification to the company by such a person, that person may be taken to have elected to receive summary financial statements if he fails to respond to an opportunity to elect to receive copies of the full accounts and reports given to him either—

(a) by a consultation notice under regulation 6, or

(b) as part of a relevant consultation of his wishes by the company under regulation 7.

(4) For the purposes of paragraph (2) a notification has effect in relation to a financial year if it relates to that year (whether or not it has been given at the invitation of the company) and if it has been received by the company not later than 28 days before the first date on which copies of the full accounts and reports for that year are sent to the persons specified in regulation 3 in accordance with section 423 of the 2006 Act.

### Consultation by notice

**6.** (1) A consultation notice under this regulation is notice given by a company to a person specified in regulation 3 which—

(a) states that for the future, so long as he is a person so specified, he will be sent a summary financial statement for each financial year instead of a copy of the company's full accounts and reports, unless he notifies the company that he wishes to receive full accounts and reports,

(b) states that the summary financial statement for a financial year will contain a summary of the company's or group's profit and loss account, balance sheet and, in the case of a quoted company, directors' remuneration report for that year, and may contain additional information derived from the directors' report,

(c) states that the card or form accompanying the notice in accordance with regulation 8(3) must be returned by a date specified in the notice, being a date at least 21 days after service of the notice and not less than 28 days before the first date on which copies of the full accounts and reports for the next financial year for which that person is entitled to receive them are sent out to persons specified in regulation 3 in accordance with section 423 of the 2006 Act,

(d) includes a statement in a prominent position to the effect that a summary financial statement will not contain sufficient information to allow as full an understanding of the results and state of affairs of the company or group as would be provided by the full annual accounts and reports and that persons specified in regulation 3 requiring more detailed information have the right to obtain, free of charge, a copy of the company's last full accounts and reports.

(2) In the case of an unquoted company the notice must also state that the summary financial statement will—

(a) contain a statement by the company's auditor of his opinion as to whether the summary financial statement—

(i) is consistent with the company's annual accounts and, where information derived from the directors' report is included in the statement, with that report, and

(ii) complies with the requirements of section 427 of the 2006 Act (form and contents of summary financial statement: unquoted companies) and of these Regulations;

(b) state whether the auditor's report on the annual accounts was unqualified or qualified.

(3) In the case of a quoted company the notice must also state that the summary financial statement will—

(a) contain a statement by the company's auditor of his opinion as to whether the summary financial statement—

(i) is consistent with the company's annual accounts and the directors' remuneration report and, where information derived from the directors' report is included in the statement, with that report, and

(ii) complies with the requirements of section 428 of the 2006 Act (form and contents of summary financial statement: quoted companies) and of these Regulations;

(b) state whether the auditor's report on the annual accounts was unqualified or qualified.

### Relevant consultation

**7.** (1) A company may conduct a relevant consultation to ascertain the wishes of a person specified in regulation 3.

(2) For the purposes of this regulation, a relevant consultation of the wishes of such a person is a notice given to that person which—

(a) states that for the future, so long as he is a person specified in regulation 3, he will be sent a summary financial statement instead of the full accounts and reports of the company, unless he notifies the company that he wishes to continue to receive full accounts and reports;

(b) accompanies a copy of the full accounts and reports; and

(c) accompanies a copy of a summary financial statement, prepared in accordance with section 426 of the 2006 Act, and sections 427 and 428 of that Act, as appropriate, and these Regulations, with respect to the financial year covered by those full accounts and reports and which is identified in the notice as an example of the document which that person will receive for the future, so long as he is a person specified in regulation 3, unless he notifies the company to the contrary.

**Supplementary provisions for Part 2**

**8.** (1) Subject to any requirement or contrary provision of this Part the company communications provisions of the 2006 Act apply to any notice or other communication required or authorised to be sent to or by the company by any provision in this Part.

(2) This regulation and regulations 5, 6 and 7 apply to a person who is entitled, whether conditionally or unconditionally, to become a person specified in section 423(l) of the 2006 Act in relation to the company, but who has not yet become such a person, as they apply to a person specified in regulation 3.

(3) Subject to paragraph (4), a notice given under regulation 6 or 7 must be accompanied by a card or form—

(a) in respect of which, in the case of a card or form sent by post, any postage necessary for its return to the company has been, or will be, paid by the company, and

(b) which is so worded as to enable a person specified in regulation 3, by marking a box and returning the card or form, to notify the company that he wishes to receive full accounts and reports for the next financial year for which he is entitled to receive them as such a person and for all future financial years after that.

(4) The company need not pay the postage in respect of the return of the card or form in the following circumstances—

(a) if the address of a member to which notices are sent in accordance with the company's constitution is not within an EEA State,

(b) if the address of a debenture holder to which notices are sent in accordance with the terms of any instrument constituting or otherwise governing the debentures of which he is a holder is not within an EEA State, or

(c) if the address of a person to whom paragraph (2) applies to which notices are sent, in accordance with the contractual provisions under which he has a right (conditionally or unconditionally) to become a person specified in section 423(l) of the 2006 Act, is not within an EEA State.

PART 3

FORM AND CONTENT OF SUMMARY FINANCIAL STATEMENT

**Provisions applying to all companies and groups**

**9.** (1) Every summary financial statement issued by a company in place of the full accounts and reports must comply with this regulation.

(2) The summary financial statement must state the name of the person who signed it on behalf of the board.

(3) The summary financial statement of a company the directors of which do not prepare group accounts under Part 15 of the 2006 Act must include a statement in a prominent position to the effect that the summary financial statement does not contain sufficient information to allow as full an understanding of the results and state of affairs of the company, and of its policies and arrangements concerning directors' remuneration (where appropriate) as would be provided by the full annual accounts and reports, and that persons specified in regulation 3 requiring more detailed information have the right to obtain, free of charge, a copy of the company's last full accounts and reports.

(4) The summary financial statement of a company the directors of which prepare group accounts under Part 15 of the 2006 Act must include a statement in a prominent position to the effect that the summary financial statement does not contain sufficient information to allow as full an understanding of the results of the group and state of affairs of the company or of the group, and of their policies and arrangements concerning directors' remuneration (where appropriate) as would be provided by the full annual accounts and reports, and that persons specified in regulation 3 requiring more detailed information have the right to obtain, free of charge, a copy of the company's last full accounts and reports.

(5) The summary financial statement must contain a clear, conspicuous statement—

(a) of how persons specified in regulation 3 can obtain, free of charge, a copy of the company's last full accounts and reports, and

(b) of how such persons may elect to receive full accounts and reports in place of summary financial statements for all future financial years.

(6) The summary financial statement must contain the whole of, or a summary of, that portion of the notes to the accounts for the financial year in question which sets out the information required by paragraph l of Schedule 3 to the Small Companies Accounts Regulations or paragraph 1 of Schedule 5 to the Large and Medium-sized Companies Accounts Regulations, as the case may be (total amount of directors' remuneration etc.).

(7) The summary financial statement must contain the information prescribed in relation to the company by the provisions of this Part of the Regulations which apply to the company in such order, and under such headings, as the directors consider appropriate.

(8) The summary financial statement must contain any other information necessary to ensure that the statement is consistent with the full accounts and reports for the financial year in question.

### Provisions applying only to certain types of company

**10.** (1) The summary financial statement of a company having certain securities publicly traded as specified in paragraph 13 of Schedule 7 to the Large and Medium-sized Companies Accounts Regulations (disclosure required by certain publicly-traded companies) must—

(a) include in the statement the explanatory material required to be included in the directors' report by paragraph 14 of that Schedule, or

(b) send that material to the person receiving the summary financial statement at the same time as it sends the statement.

(2) The summary financial statement of a quoted company must contain the whole of, or a summary of, those portions of the directors' remuneration report for the financial year in question which set out the matters required by paragraphs 3 (statement of company's policy on directors' remuneration) and 5 (performance graph) of Schedule 8 to the Large and Medium-sized Companies Accounts Regulations.

### Contents of summary financial statements

**11.** (1) Subject to regulations 9 and 10, the summary financial statement of a company must be in such form, and contain such information, as is prescribed in relation to that company in the following paragraphs of this regulation so far as applicable to that company.

(2) The summary financial statement of a company (other than a banking or insurance company) the directors of which—

(a) do not prepare group accounts under Part 15 of the 2006 Act, and

(b) prepare Companies Act individual accounts under section 396 of the 2006 Act, must comply with Schedule 1 to these Regulations.

(3) The summary financial statement of a banking company the directors of which —

(a) do not prepare group accounts under Part 15 of the 2006 Act, and

(b) prepare Companies Act individual accounts under section 396 of the 2006 Act, must comply with Schedule 2 to these Regulations.

(4) The summary financial statement of an insurance company the directors of which—

(a) do not prepare group accounts under Part 15 of the 2006 Act, and

(b) prepare Companies Act individual accounts under section 396 of the 2006 Act, must comply with Schedule 3 to these Regulations.

(5) The summary financial statement of a parent company (other than the parent company of a banking or insurance group) the directors of which prepare Companies Act group accounts under section 403 of the 2006 Act (group accounts: applicable accounting framework), must comply with Schedule 4 to these Regulations.

(6) The summary financial statement of the parent company of a banking group the directors of which prepare Companies Act group accounts under section 403 of the 2006 Act, must comply with Schedule 5 to these Regulations.

(7) The summary financial statement of the parent company of an insurance group the directors of which prepare Companies Act group accounts under section 403 of the 2006 Act, must comply with Schedule 6 to these Regulations.

(8) Where the directors of a company do not prepare group accounts but prepare IAS individual accounts, the provisions of Schedule 7 to these Regulations apply to the company's summary financial statement.

(9) Where the directors of a company prepare IAS group accounts the provisions of Schedule 8 to these Regulations apply to the company's summary financial statement.

PART 4

SUPPLEMENTARY PROVISIONS

### Revocation, transitionals and saving

**12.** (1) Subject to paragraph (2), the Companies (Summary Financial Statement) Regulations 1995[44] and the Companies (Summary Financial Statement) Regulations (Northern Ireland) 1996[45] are revoked.

---

[44] SI 1995/2092, as amended by SIs 2000/3373, 2002/1780 and 2005/2281.

[45] SR 1996/179, as amended by Article 29 of, and Schedule 2 to, SR 2003/3, SR 2005/57 and SR 2006/138.

(2) The Companies (Summary Financial Statement) Regulations 1995 and the Companies (Summary Financial Statement) Regulations (Northern Ireland) 1996 continue to apply in relation to financial years beginning before 6th April 2008.

(3) Paragraph (4) has effect in relation to the ascertainment of the wishes of any person for the purposes of section 426 of the 2006 Act and these Regulations.

(4) So far as anything done under or for the purposes of any provision of either the Companies (Summary Financial Statement) Regulations 1995 or the Companies (Summary Financial Statement) Regulations (Northern Ireland) 1996 could have been done under or for the purposes of the corresponding provision of these Regulations, it is not invalidated by the revocation of that provision but has effect as if done under or for the purposes of the corresponding provision.

SCHEDULE 1            Regulation 11(2)

FORM AND CONTENT OF SUMMARY FINANCIAL STATEMENT
OF COMPANY PREPARING COMPANIES ACT INDIVIDUAL
ACCOUNTS (OTHER THAN A BANKING OR
INSURANCE COMPANY)

**Summary profit and loss account**

1. (1) The summary financial statement must contain a summary profit and loss account showing, in so far as they may be derived from the full profit and loss account, the items, or combinations of items, listed in sub-paragraph (3), in the order set out in that sub-paragraph.

(2) The items or combinations of items listed in sub-paragraph (3) may appear under such headings as the directors consider appropriate.

(3) The items, or combinations of items, referred to in sub-paragraph (1) are—

(a) turnover—
  (i) format 1, item 1
  (ii) format 2, item 1
  (iii) format 3, item B1
  (iv) format 4, item B1;

(b) income from shares in group undertakings and participating interests; the combination of the following two items—
  (i) format 1, items 7 and 8
  (ii) format 2, items 9 and 10
  (iii) format 3, items B3 and B4
  (iv) format 4, items B5 and B6;

(c) other interest receivable and similar income and interest payable and similar charges; the net figure resulting from the combination of the following two items—
  (i) format 1, items 10 and 12
  (ii) format 2, items 12 and 14
  (iii) format 3, items B6 and A5
  (iv) format 4, items B8 and A7;

(d) the profit or loss on ordinary activities before taxation;

(e) tax on profit or loss on ordinary activities—
  (i) format 1, item 13
  (ii) format 2, item 15
  (iii) format 3, item A6
  (iv) format 4, item A8;

(f) profit or loss on ordinary activities after taxation—
  (i) format 1, item 14
  (ii) format 2, item 16
  (iii) format 3, item A7 or B7
  (iv) format 4, item A9 or B9;

(g) extraordinary income and charges after tax; the net figure resulting from the combination of the following items—
  (i) format 1, items 17 and 18
  (ii) format 2, items 19 and 20
  (iii) format 3, items A8, A9 and B8
  (iv) format 4, items A10, A11 and B10; and

(h) profit or loss for the financial year—
  (i) format 1, item 20
  (ii) format 2, item 22
  (iii) format 3, item A11 or B9
  (iv) format 4, item A13 or B11.

**Dividends**

**2.** The summary financial statement must also contain the information concerning recognized and proposed dividends included in the full accounts and reports.

**Summary balance sheet**

**3.** (1) The summary financial statement must contain a summary balance sheet.

(2) Subject to sub-paragraphs (3) and (4), the summary balance sheet must show, in so far as it can be derived from the full balance sheet and under such heading as the directors consider appropriate, a single amount for each of the headings to which letters are assigned in the balance sheet format which has been used for the full balance sheet (where necessary by the combination of the items to which Roman and Arabic numbers are assigned under those headings) in the order set out in the full balance sheet.

(3) Where an alternative position is permitted for any item in the balance sheet format used, the summary balance sheet must use the position used by the full balance sheet.

(4) Where the full balance sheet used is format 2 in Schedule 1 to the Small Companies Accounts Regulations or format 2 in Schedule 1 to the Large and Medium-sized Companies Accounts Regulations, then in the case of heading C under 'Liabilities' two figures must be shown, one figure for amounts falling due within one year and one for amounts falling due after one year.

**Corresponding amounts**

**4.** (1) In respect of every item shown in the summary profit and loss account, or in the summary balance sheet, the corresponding amount must be shown for the immediately preceding financial year.

(2) For the purposes of sub-paragraph (1), 'the corresponding amount' is the amount shown in the summary financial statement for that year or which would have been so shown had such a statement been prepared for that year, taking account of any adjustments to corresponding amounts made in the full accounts and reports.

SCHEDULE 2                                          Regulation 11(3)

FORM AND CONTENT OF SUMMARY FINANCIAL STATEMENT OF BANKING
COMPANY PREPARING COMPANIES ACT INDIVIDUAL ACCOUNTS

**Summary profit and loss account**

**1.** (1) The summary financial statement must contain a summary profit and loss account showing, in so far as they may be derived from the full profit and loss account, the items, or combinations of items, listed in sub-paragraph (3), in the order set out in that sub-paragraph.

(2) The items or combinations of items listed in sub-paragraph (3) may appear under such headings as the directors consider appropriate.

(3) The items, or combinations of items, referred to in sub-paragraph (1) are—

(a) interest receivable and payable; the net figure resulting from the combination of the following two items—
  (i) format 1, items 1 and 2
  (ii) format 2, items A1 and B1;

(b) dividend income, fees and commissions receivable and payable, dealing profits or losses and other operating income; the net figure resulting from the combination of the following items—
  (i) format 1, items 3, 4, 5, 6 and 7
  (ii) format 2, items A2, A3, B2, B3, B4 and B7;

(c) administrative expenses, depreciation and amortisation, other operating charges, amounts written off, and adjustments to amounts written off, fixed asset investments; the net figure resulting from the combination of the following items—
  (i) format 1, items 8, 9, 10, 13 and 14
  (ii) format 2, items A4, A5, A6, A8 and B6;

(d) provisions and adjustments to provisions; the net figure resulting from the combination of the following two items—
  (i) format 1, items 11 and 12
  (ii) format 2, items A7 and B5;

(e) profit or loss on ordinary activities before tax—
  (i) format 1, item 15
  (ii) format 2, item A9 or B8;

(f) tax on profit or loss on ordinary activities—
  (i) format 1, item 16
  (ii) format 2, item A10;

(g) profit or loss on ordinary activities after tax—

    (i)   format 1, item 17
    (ii)  format 2, item A11 or B9;
  (h)  extraordinary profit or loss after tax—
    (i)   format 1, item 22
    (ii)  the net figure resulting from the combination of format 2, items A14 and B11;
  (i)   other taxes not shown under the preceding items—
    (i)   format 1, item 23
    (ii)  format 2, item A15; and
  (j)   profit or loss for the financial year—
    (i)   format 1, item 24
    (ii)  format 2, item A16 or B12.

### Dividends

**2.** The summary financial statement must also contain the information concerning recognised and proposed dividends included in the full accounts and reports.

### Summary balance sheet

**3.** (1) The summary financial statement must contain a summary balance sheet which must show, in so far as they may be derived from the full balance sheet, the items, or combinations of items, set out in sub-paragraph (2), in the order set out in that sub-paragraph and under such headings as the directors consider appropriate.

  (2) The items, or combinations of items, referred to in sub-paragraph (1) are as follows—

    (a)  cash and balances at central [or post office] banks, treasury bills and other eligible bills—
        the aggregate of items 1 and 2 under the heading 'ASSETS';
    (b)  loans and advances to banks—
        item 3 under the heading 'ASSETS';
    (c)  loans and advances to customers—
        item 4 under the heading 'ASSETS';
    (d)  debt securities [and other fixed income securities], equity shares [and other variable-yield securities], participating interests and shares in group undertakings—
        the aggregate of items 5, 6, 7 and 8 under the heading 'ASSETS';
    (e)  intangible and tangible fixed assets—
        the aggregate of items 9 and 10 under the heading 'ASSETS';
    (f)  called up capital not paid, own shares, other assets, prepayments and accrued income—
        the aggregate of items 11 (or 14), 12, 13 and 15 under the heading 'ASSETS';
    (g)  total assets under the heading 'ASSETS';
    (h)  deposits by banks—
        item 1 under the heading 'LIABILITIES';
    (i)  customer accounts—
        item 2 under the heading 'LIABILITIES';
    (j)  debt securities in issue—
        item 3 under the heading 'LIABILITIES';
    (k)  other liabilities, accruals and deferred income and provisions for liabilities and charges—
        the aggregate of items 4, 5 and 6 under the heading 'LIABILITIES';
    (l)  subordinated liabilities—
        item 7 under the heading 'LIABILITIES';
    (m)  called up share capital, share premium account, reserves, revaluation reserve and profit and loss account—
        the aggregate of items 8, 9, 10, 11 and 12 under the heading 'LIABILITIES';
    (n)  total liabilities under the heading 'LIABILITIES';
    (o)  contingent liabilities—
        item 1 under the heading 'MEMORANDUM ITEMS', and
    (p)  commitments—
        item 2 under the heading 'MEMORANDUM ITEMS'.

### Corresponding amounts

**4.** (1) In respect of every item shown in the summary profit and loss account, or in the summary balance sheet, the corresponding amount must be shown for the immediately preceding financial year.

  (2) For the purposes of sub-paragraph (1), 'the corresponding amount' is the amount shown in the summary financial statement for that year or which would have been so shown had such a statement been prepared for that year, taking account of any adjustments to corresponding amounts made in the full account and reports.

SCHEDULE 3　　　　　　　　Regulation 11(4)

## FORM AND CONTENT OF SUMMARY FINANCIAL STATEMENT OF INSURANCE COMPANY PREPARING COMPANIES ACT INDIVIDUAL ACCOUNTS

**Summary profit and loss account**

**1.** (1) The summary financial statement must contain a summary profit and loss account showing, in so far as they may be derived from the full profit and loss account, the items, or combinations of items, listed in sub-paragraph (3), in the order set out in that sub-paragraph.

(2) The items or combinations of items listed in sub-paragraph (3) may appear under such headings as the directors consider appropriate.

(3) The items, or combinations of items referred to in sub-paragraph (1) are—

(a) gross premiums written-general business—
item I 1(a);

(b) gross premiums written-long term business—
item II 1(a);

(c) balance on the technical account for general business—
item I 10;

(d) balance on the technical account for long term business—
item II 13;

(e) other income and charges; the net figure resulting from the combination of the following items—

(i)　item III 3

(ii)　item III 3a

(iii)　item III 4

(iv)　item III 5

(v)　item III 5a

(vi)　item III 6

(vii)　item III 7

(viii)　item III 8;

(f) the profit or loss on ordinary activities before tax—
item III 8a;

(g) tax on profit or loss on ordinary activities—
item III 9;

(h) profit or loss on ordinary activities after tax—
item III 10;

(i) extraordinary profit or loss after tax—
the net figure resulting from the combination of items III 13 and 14;

(j) other taxes—
item III 15; and

(k) profit or loss for the financial year—
item III 16.

**Dividends**

**2.** The summary financial statement must also contain the information concerning recognized and proposed dividends included in the full accounts and reports.

**Summary balance sheet**

**3.** (1) The summary financial statement must contain a summary balance sheet which must show, in so far as they may be derived from the full balance sheet, the items, or combinations of items, set out in sub-paragraph (2) in the order of that sub-paragraph and under such headings as the directors consider appropriate.

(2) The items, or combinations of items, referred to in sub-paragraph (1) are—

(a) investments—
the aggregate of items C and D under the heading 'ASSETS';

(b) reinsurers' share of technical provisions—
item Da under the heading 'ASSETS';

(c) other assets—
the aggregate of items A or E(IV), B, E(I) to (III), F and G under the heading 'ASSETS';

(d) total assets under the heading 'ASSETS';

(e) capital and reserves—
item A under the heading 'LIABILITIES';

(f) subordinated liabilities—
item B under the heading 'LIABILITIES';

(g) fund for future appropriations—
item Ba under the heading 'LIABILITIES';

(h) gross technical provisions—

the aggregate of items C.1(a), C.2(a), C.3(a), C.4(a), C.5, C.6(a) and D(a) under the heading 'LIABILITIES';
(i) technical provisions-reinsurance amounts—
the aggregate of items C.1(b), C.2(b), C.3(b), C.4(b), C.6(b) and D(b) under the heading 'LIABILITIES';
(j) other liabilities—
the aggregate of items E, F, G and H under the heading 'LIABILITIES'; and
(k) total liabilities under the heading 'LIABILITIES'.

### Corresponding amounts

**4.** (1) In respect of every item shown in the summary profit and loss account, or in the summary balance sheet, the corresponding amount must be shown for the immediately preceding financial year.

(2) For the purposes of sub-paragraph (1), 'the corresponding amount' is the amount shown in the summary financial statement for that year or which would have been so shown had such a statement been prepared for that year, taking account of any adjustments to corresponding amounts made in the full accounts and reports.

SCHEDULE 4            Regulation 11(5)

FORM AND CONTENT OF SUMMARY FINANCIAL STATEMENT OF PARENT
COMPANY PREPARING COMPANIES ACT GROUP ACCOUNTS (OTHER THAN
BANKING OR INSURANCE GROUP ACCOUNTS)

### Summary profit and loss account

**1.** (1) The summary financial statement must contain a summary consolidated profit and loss account showing the items or combinations of items required by paragraph 1 of Schedule 1 to these Regulations in the order required by that paragraph and under such headings as the directors consider appropriate, but with the modifications specified in sub-paragraph (3).

(2) The summary financial statement must also contain the information required by paragraph 2 of Schedule 1 to these Regulations.

(3) The modifications referred to in sub-paragraph (1) are as follows—
(a) in place of the information required by paragraph 1(3)(b) of Schedule 1 to these Regulations, there must be shown, under such heading as the directors consider appropriate, the item 'Income from interests in associated undertakings' required to be shown—
(i) in the profit and loss account formats in Part 1 of Schedule 1 to the Small Companies Accounts Regulations by paragraph 1(3) of Schedule 6 to those Regulations (Companies Act: group accounts), or
(ii) in the profit and loss account formats in Part 1 of Schedule 1 to the Large and Medium-sized Companies Accounts Regulations, by paragraph 20(3) of Schedule 6 to those Regulations (Companies Act: group accounts);
(b) between the information required by paragraph 1(3)(f) and that required by paragraph 1(3)(g) of Schedule 1 to these Regulations there must in addition be shown, under such heading as the directors consider appropriate, the item required to be shown—
(i) in the profit and loss account formats in Part 1 of Schedule 1 to the Small Companies Accounts Regulations by paragraph 17(3)(a) of Schedule 6 to those Regulations (minority interests), or
(ii) in the profit and loss account formats in Part 1 of Schedule 1 to the Large and Medium-sized Companies Accounts Regulations, by paragraph 17(3)(a) of Schedule 6 to those Regulations (minority interests); and
(c) the figure required by paragraph 1(3)(g) of Schedule 1 to these Regulations must be shown after the deduction or the addition (as the case may be) of the item required to be shown—
(i) in the profit and loss account formats in Part 1 of Schedule 1 to the Small Companies Accounts Regulations by paragraph 17(3)(b) of Schedule 6 to those Regulations (minority interests), or
(ii) in the profit and loss account formats in Part 1 of Schedule 1 to the Large and Medium-sized Companies Accounts Regulations, by paragraph 17(3)(b) of Schedule 6 to those Regulations (minority interests).

**Summary balance sheet**

**2.** The summary financial statement must contain a summary consolidated balance sheet showing the items required by paragraph 3 of Schedule 1 to these Regulations in the order required by that paragraph and under such headings as the directors consider appropriate, but with the addition of the item required to be inserted—

(a) by paragraph 17(2) of Schedule 6 to the Small Companies Accounts Regulations (minority interests), or

(b) by paragraph 17(2) of Schedule 6 to the Large and Medium-sized Companies Accounts Regulations (minority interests).

**Corresponding amounts**

**3.** (1) In respect of every item shown in the summary consolidated profit and loss account, or in the summary consolidated balance sheet, the corresponding amount must be shown for the immediately preceding financial year.

(2) For the purposes of sub-paragraph (1), 'the corresponding amount' is the amount shown in the summary financial statement for that year or which would have been so shown had such a statement been prepared for that year, taking account of any adjustments to corresponding amounts made in the full accounts and reports.

SCHEDULE 5                                                    Regulation 11(6)

FORM AND CONTENT OF SUMMARY FINANCIAL STATEMENT OF PARENT
COMPANY OF BANKING GROUP PREPARING COMPANIES ACT
GROUP ACCOUNTS

**Summary profit and loss account**

**1.** (1) The summary financial statement must contain a summary consolidated profit and loss account showing the items, or combinations of items, required by paragraph 1 of Schedule 2 to these Regulations, in the order required by that paragraph and under such headings as the directors consider appropriate, but with the modifications specified in sub-paragraph (3).

(2) The summary financial statement must also contain the information required by paragraph 2 of Schedule 2 to these Regulations.

(3) The modifications referred to in sub-paragraph (1) are as follows—

(a) between the information required by paragraph 1(3)(d) and that required by paragraph 1(3)(e) of Schedule 2 to these Regulations there must in addition be shown, under such heading as the directors consider appropriate, the item 'Income from associated undertakings' required to be shown in the profit and loss account formats in Schedule 2 to the Large and Medium-sized Companies Accounts Regulations (banking companies: Companies Act individual accounts) by paragraph 25(4)(ii) of Schedule 6 to those Regulations;

(b) between the information required by paragraph 1(3)(g) and that required by paragraph 1(3)(h) of Schedule 2 to these Regulations there must in addition be shown, under such heading as the directors consider appropriate, the item required to be shown in the formats in Schedule 2 to the Large and Medium-sized Companies Accounts Regulations by paragraph 17(3)(a) of Schedule 6 to those Regulations (minority interests) as applied by paragraph 25 of Schedule 6 to those Regulations; and

(c) the figures required by paragraph 1(3)(h) and (i) of Schedule 2 to these Regulations must each be shown after the deduction or the addition (as the case may be) of the item required to be shown in the formats in Schedule 2 to the Large and Medium-sized Companies Accounts Regulations by paragraph 17(3)(b) of Schedule 6 to those Regulations (minority interests) as applied by paragraph 25 of Schedule 6 to those Regulations.

**Summary balance sheet**

**2.** (1) The summary financial statement must contain a summary consolidated balance sheet showing the items required by paragraph 3 of Schedule 2 to these Regulations, in the order required by that paragraph and under such headings as the directors consider appropriate, but with the addition specified in sub-paragraph (2).

(2) Between the items required by paragraph 3(2)(1) and (m) or after the item required by paragraph 3(2)(m) (whichever is the position adopted for the full accounts), there must in addition be shown under an appropriate heading the item required to be shown in the balance sheet format in Schedule 2 to the Large and Medium-sized Companies Accounts Regulations by paragraph 17(2) of Schedule 6 to those Regulations (minority interests) as applied by paragraph 25 in Part 2 of Schedule 6 to those Regulations.

**Corresponding amounts**

3. (1) In respect of every item shown in the summary consolidated profit and loss account, or in the summary consolidated balance sheet, the corresponding amount must be shown for the immediately preceding financial year.

(2) For the purposes of sub-paragraph (1), 'the corresponding amount' is the amount shown in the summary financial statement for that year or which would have been so shown had such a statement been prepared for that year, taking account of any adjustments to corresponding accounts made in the full accounts and reports.

SCHEDULE 6            Regulation 11(7)

FORM AND CONTENT OF SUMMARY FINANCIAL STATEMENT OF
PARENT COMPANY OF INSURANCE GROUP PREPARING COMPANIES
ACT GROUP ACCOUNTS

**Summary profit and loss account**

1. (1) The summary financial statement must contain a summary consolidated profit and loss account showing the items, or combinations of items, required by paragraph 1 of Schedule 3 to these Regulations, in the order required by that paragraph and under such headings as the directors consider appropriate, but with the modifications specified in sub-paragraph (3).

(2) The summary financial statement must also contain the information required by paragraph 2 of that Schedule.

(3) The modifications referred to in sub-paragraph (1) are as follows—

(a) between the information required by paragraph 1(3)(e) and that required by paragraph 1(3)(f) of Schedule 3 to these Regulations there must in addition be shown, under such heading as the directors consider appropriate, the item 'Income from associated undertakings' required to be shown in the profit and loss account formats in Schedule 3 to the Large and Medium-sized Companies Accounts Regulations (insurance companies: Companies Act individual accounts) by paragraph 20(3)(b) of Schedule 6 to those Regulations as substituted by paragraph 37 of Schedule 6 to those Regulations;

(b) between the information required by paragraph 1(3)(h) and that required by paragraph 1(3)(i) of Schedule 3 to these Regulations there must in addition be shown, under such heading as the directors consider appropriate, the item required to be shown in the profit and loss account formats in Schedule 3 to the Large and Medium-sized Companies Accounts Regulations by paragraph 17(3)(a) of Schedule 6 to those Regulations (minority interests) as applied by paragraph 36 of Schedule 6 to those Regulations; and

(c) the figures required by paragraph 1(3)(i) and (j) of Schedule 3 to these Regulations must each be shown after the deduction or the addition (as the case may be) of the item required to be shown in the profit and loss account formats in Schedule 3 to the Large and Medium-sized Companies Accounts Regulations by paragraph 17(3)(b) of Schedule 6 to those Regulations (minority interests) as applied by paragraph 36 of Schedule 6 to those Regulations.

**Summary balance sheet**

2. (1) The summary financial statement must contain a summary consolidated balance sheet showing the items required by paragraph 3 of Schedule 3 to these Regulations, in the order required by that paragraph and under such headings as the directors consider appropriate, but with the addition of the item specified in sub-paragraph (2).

(2) Between the items required by paragraph 3(2)(d) and (e) of Schedule 3 to these Regulations, there must in addition be shown under an appropriate heading the item required to be shown in the balance sheet format in Schedule 3 to the Large and Medium-sized Companies Accounts Regulations by paragraph 17(2) of Schedule 6 to those Regulations (minority interests), as applied by paragraph 36 of Schedule 6 to those Regulations.

**Corresponding amounts**

3. (1) In respect of every item shown in the summary consolidated profit and loss account, or in the summary consolidated balance sheet, the corresponding amount must be shown for the immediately preceding financial year.

(2) For the purposes of sub-paragraph (1), 'the corresponding amount' is the amount shown in the summary financial statement for that year or which would have been so shown had such a statement been prepared for that year, taking account of any adjustments to corresponding amounts made in the full accounts and reports.

SCHEDULE 7 Regulation 11(8)

## FORM AND CONTENT OF SUMMARY FINANCIAL STATEMENT OF COMPANY PREPARING IAS INDIVIDUAL ACCOUNTS

**Summary profit and loss account**

**1.** (1) The summary financial statement must contain a summary profit and loss account showing either—

(a) each of the headings and sub-totals included in the full profit and loss account in accordance with international accounting standards, or

(b) where the directors consider it appropriate, a combination of such headings and sub-totals where they are of a similar nature.

(2) The summary financial statement must also contain the information concerning recognised and proposed dividends included in the full accounts and reports.

(3) In this paragraph and in paragraph 2, the expressions 'headings' and 'subtotals' have the same meaning as in international accounting standard 1 on the presentation of financial statements[46].

**Summary balance sheet**

**2.** The summary financial statement must contain a summary balance sheet showing either—

(a) each of the headings and sub-totals included in the full balance sheet in accordance with international accounting standards, or

(b) where the directors consider it appropriate, a combination of such headings and sub-totals where they are of a similar nature.

**Corresponding amounts**

**3.** (1) In respect of every item shown in the summary profit and loss account, or in the summary balance sheet, the corresponding amount must be shown for the immediately preceding financial year.

(2) For the purposes of sub-paragraph (1), 'the corresponding amount' is the amount shown in the summary financial statement for that year or which would have been so shown had such a statement been prepared for that year, taking account of any adjustments to corresponding amounts made in the full accounts and reports.

SCHEDULE 8 Regulation 11(9)

## FORM AND CONTENT OF SUMMARY FINANCIAL STATEMENT OF COMPANY PREPARING IAS GROUP ACCOUNTS

**Summary profit and loss account**

**1.** (1) The summary financial statement must contain a summary consolidated profit and loss account showing either—

(a) each of the headings and sub-totals included in the full consolidated profit and loss account in accordance with international accounting standards, or

(b) where the directors consider it appropriate, a combination of such headings and sub-totals where they are of a similar nature.

(2) The summary financial statement must also contain the information concerning recognised and proposed dividends included in the full accounts and reports.

(3) In this paragraph and in paragraph 2, the expressions 'headings' and 'subtotals' have the same meaning as in international accounting standard 1 on the presentation of financial statements.

**Summary balance sheet**

**2.** The summary financial statement must contain a summary consolidated balance sheet showing either—

(a) each of the headings and sub-totals included in the full consolidated balance sheet in accordance with international accounting standards, or

(b) where the directors consider it appropriate, a combination of such headings and sub-totals where they are of a similar nature.

---

[46] IAS 1 was adopted by EC Commission Regulation (EC) No. 1725/2003 of 29th September 2003 adopting certain international accounting standards in accordance with Regulation (EC) No. 1606/2002 of the European Parliament and the Council (OJ L261 of 13.10.2003, pages 1–420).

**Corresponding amounts**

**3.** (1) In respect of every item shown in the summary consolidated profit and loss account, or in the summary consolidated balance sheet, the corresponding amount must be shown for the immediately preceding financial year.

(2) For the purposes of sub-paragraph (1), 'the corresponding amount' is the amount shown in the summary financial statement for that year or which would have been so shown had such a statement been prepared for that year, taking account of any adjustments to corresponding amounts made in the full accounts and reports.

---

# THE COMPANIES ACT 2006 (AMENDMENT) (ACCOUNTS AND REPORTS) REGULATIONS 2008
## (SI 2008/393)

COMMENCEMENT DATE 6 April 2008

## PART 1
## INTRODUCTION

**Citation and interpretation** SI.11

**1.** (1) These Regulations may be cited as the Companies Act 2006 (Amendment) (Accounts and Reports) Regulations 2008.

(2) In these Regulations 'the 2006 Act' means the Companies Act 2006.

**Commencement and application**

**2.** (1) These Regulations come into force on 6th April 2008.

(2) They apply in relation to financial years beginning on or after 6th April 2008.

(3) In determining whether a company or group qualifies as small or medium-sized under section 382(2), 383(3), 465(2) or 466(3) of the 2006 Act (qualification in relation to subsequent financial year by reference to circumstances in preceding financial years) in relation to a financial year ending on or after 6th April 2008, the company or group shall be treated as having qualified as small or medium-sized (as the case may be) in any previous financial year in which it would have so qualified if amendments to the same effect as those made by these Regulations had been in force.

## PART 2
## SMALL AND MEDIUM-SIZED COMPANIES AND GROUPS

**Conditions for company or group to qualify as small**

**3.** (1) In the table in section 382(3) of the 2006 Act (conditions to be met by company to qualify as small)—

(a) in item 1 (turnover) for 'Not more than £5.6 million' substitute 'Not more than £6.5 million', and

(b) in item 2 (balance sheet total) for 'Not more than £2.8 million' substitute 'Not more than £3.26 million'.

(2) In the table in section 383(4) of the 2006 Act (conditions to be met by group for parent company to qualify as small)—

(a) in item 1 (aggregate turnover) for 'Not more than £5.6 million net (or £6.72 million gross)' substitute 'Not more than £6.5 million net (or £7.8 million gross)', and

(b) in item 2 (aggregate balance sheet total) for 'Not more than £2.8 million net (or £3.36 million gross)' substitute 'Not more than £3.26 million net (or £3.9 million gross)'.

**Conditions for company or group to qualify as medium-sized**

**4.** (1) In the table in section 465(3) of the 2006 Act (conditions to be met by company to qualify as medium-sized)—

(a) in item 1 (turnover) for 'Not more than £22.8 million' substitute 'Not more than £25.9 million', and

(b) in item 2 (balance sheet total) for 'Not more than £11.4 million' substitute 'Not more than £12.9 million'.

(2) In the table in section 466(4) of the 2006 Act (conditions to be met by group for parent company to qualify as medium-sized)—

(a) in item 1 (aggregate turnover) for 'Not more than £22.8 million net (or £27.36 million gross)' substitute 'Not more than £25.9 million net (or £31.1 million gross)', and

(b) in item 2 (aggregate balance sheet total) for 'Not more than £11.4 million net (or £13.68 million gross)' substitute 'Not more than £12.9 million net (or £15.5 million gross)'.

### Conditions for small companies exemption from audit

**5.** (1) In section 477(2) of the 2006 Act (conditions to be met by company to be exempt from audit)—

    (a) in paragraph (b) (turnover), for 'not more than £5.6 million' substitute 'not more than £6.5 million', and

    (b) in paragraph (c) (balance sheet total), for 'not more than £2.8 million' substitute 'not more than £3.26 million'.

  (2) In section 479(2) of the 2006 Act (conditions to be met by group for group company to be exempt from audit)—

    (a) in paragraph (b) (aggregate turnover), for 'not more than £5.6 million net (or £6.72 million gross)' substitute 'not more than £6.5 million net (or £7.8 million gross)', and

    (b) in paragraph (c) (aggregate balance sheet total), for 'not more than £2.8 million net (or £3.36 million gross)' substitute 'not more than £3.26 million net (or £3.9 million gross)'.

### Small companies exemption in relation to directors' report

**6.** (1) In section 381 of the 2006 Act (companies subject to the small companies regime), omit 'for accounts and reports'.

  (2) After section 415 of that Act insert—

#### 'Directors' report: small companies exemption

**415A.** (1) A company is entitled to small companies exemption in relation to the directors' report for a financial year if—

    (a) it is entitled to prepare accounts for the year in accordance with the small companies regime, or

    (b) it would be so entitled but for being or having been a member of an ineligible group.

  (2) The exemption is relevant to—

section 416(3) (contents of report: statement of amount recommended by way of dividend),

section 417 (contents of report: business review), and

sections 444 to 446 (filing obligations of different descriptions of company).'.

  (3) In section 416(3) of that Act (contents of report: statement of amount recommended by way of dividend), for 'subject to the small companies regime' substitute 'entitled to the small companies exemption'.

  (4) In section 417(1) of that Act (contents of report: business review), for 'subject to the small companies regime' substitute 'entitled to the small companies exemption'.

  (5) In section 419(2) of that Act (statement to be contained in report) for the words from 'If the report' to 'regime,' substitute 'If in preparing the report advantage is taken of the small companies exemption,'.

  (6) In section 441(1) of that Act (duty to file accounts and reports with the registrar), at the appropriate place insert—

'section 444A (filing obligations of companies entitled to small companies exemption in relation to directors' report),'.

  (7) After section 444 of that Act insert—

#### 'Filing obligations of companies entitled to small companies exemption in relation to directors' report

**444A.** (1) The directors of a company that is entitled to small companies exemption in relation to the directors' report for a financial year—

    (a) must deliver to the registrar a copy of the company's annual accounts for that year, and

    (b) may also deliver to the registrar a copy of the directors' report.

  (2) The directors must also deliver to the registrar a copy of the auditor's report on the accounts (and any directors' report) that it delivers.

This does not apply if the company is exempt from audit and the directors have taken advantage of that exception.

  (3) The copies of the balance sheet and directors' report delivered to the registrar under this section must state the name of the person who signed it on behalf of the board.

  (4) The copy of the auditor's report delivered to the registrar under this section must —

    (a) state the name of the auditor and (where the auditor is a firm) the name of the person who signed it as senior statutory auditor, and

    (b) be signed by the auditor or (where the auditor is a firm) in the name of the firm by a person authorised to sign on its behalf,

or, if the conditions in section 506 (circumstances in which names may be omitted) are met, state that a resolution has been passed and notified to the Secretary of State in accordance with that section.

(5) This section does not apply to companies within section 444 (filing obligations of companies subject to the small companies regime).'.

(8) In section 445 of that Act (filing obligations of medium-sized companies), for subsection (7) substitute—

'(7) This section does not apply to companies within—

(a) section 444 (filing obligations of companies subject to the small companies regime), or

(b) section 444A (filing obligations of companies entitled to small companies exemption in relation to directors' report).'.

(9) In section 446(5) of that Act (filing obligations of unquoted companies: disapplication of section in relation to companies subject to other provisions), omit the 'or' at the end of paragraph (a) and after that paragraph insert—

'(aa) section 444A (filing obligations of companies entitled to small companies exemption in relation to directors' report), or'.

(10) In section 498 of that Act (duties of auditor) for subsection (5) substitute—

'(5) If the directors of the company—

(a) have prepared accounts in accordance with the small companies regime, or

(b) have taken advantage of small companies exemption in preparing the directors' report,

and in the auditor's opinion they were not entitled to do so, the auditor shall state that fact in his report.'.

(11) In Schedule 8 to that Act (index of defined expressions), in the entry relating to 'small companies regime' for ', for accounts and reports' substitute '(for accounts)'.

(12) In that Schedule, at the appropriate place insert—

"small companies exemption (in relation to directors' report) section 415A.

### Companies entitled to take advantage of provisions applying to medium-sized companies

**7.** In section 467 of the 2006 Act (companies excluded from being treated as medium-sized)[47] after subsection (3) insert—

'(4) This section does not prevent a company from taking advantage of section 417(7) (business review: non-financial information) by reason only of its having been a member of an ineligible group at any time within the financial year in question.'.

## PART 3
## OFF-BALANCE SHEET ARRANGEMENTS

### Information about off-balance sheet arrangements

**8.** After section 410 of the 2006 Act insert—

**'410A.** (1) In the case of a company that is not subject to the small companies regime, if in any financial year—

(a) the company is or has been party to arrangements that are not reflected in its balance sheet, and

(b) at the balance sheet date the risks or benefits arising from those arrangements are material,

the information required by this section must be given in notes to the company's annual accounts.

(2) The information required is—

(a) the nature and business purpose of the arrangements, and

(b) the financial impact of the arrangements on the company.

(3) The information need only be given to the extent necessary for enabling the financial position of the company to be assessed.

(4) If the company qualifies as medium-sized in relation to the financial year (see sections 465 to 467) it need not comply with subsection (2)(b).

(5) This section applies in relation to group accounts as if the undertakings included in the consolidation were a single company.'

## PART 4
## MINOR AMENDMENTS

### Individual accounts: applicable accounting framework

**9.** In section 395(4) of the 2006 Act (circumstances in which company which has opted to prepare IAS individual accounts may prepare Companies Act individual accounts), after paragraph (a) insert—

'(aa) the company ceases to be a subsidiary undertaking,'.

---

[47] Section 467 was amended by regulation 3(3) of SI2007/2932.

**Individual profit and loss account where group accounts prepared**

**10.** In section 408(2) of the 2006 Act (no obligation for profit and loss account to include information about employee numbers and costs where group accounts prepared) for 'The profit and loss account' substitute 'The company's individual profit and loss account'.

**Information about employee numbers and costs: group accounts**

**11.** For section 411(7) of the 2006 Act (information about employee numbers and costs: group accounts) substitute—

'(7)   This section applies in relation to group accounts as if the undertakings included in the consolidation were a single company.'.

**Requirement to deliver auditor's report on accounts and reports**

**12.** In section 444(2) of the 2006 Act (filing obligations of company subject to small companies regime: duty to deliver auditor's report), for 'those accounts (and on the directors' report)' substitute 'the accounts (and any directors' report) that it delivers'.

**Unlimited companies exemption from obligation to file accounts**

**13.** In section 448(3) of the 2006 Act (unlimited companies exemption from obligation to file accounts: companies to which the exemption does not apply)—

(a)  for paragraph (b) substitute—

'(b)  each of the members of the company is—
(i)    a limited company,
(ii)   another unlimited company each of whose members is a limited company, or
(iii)  a Scottish partnership each of whose members is a limited company.';

(b)  after that paragraph insert—

'The references in paragraph (b) to a limited company, another unlimited company or a Scottish partnership include a comparable undertaking incorporated in or formed under the law of a country or territory outside the United Kingdom.'.

---

# THE SMALL COMPANIES AND GROUPS (ACCOUNTS AND DIRECTORS' REPORT) REGULATIONS 2008
### (SI 2008/409)

COMMENCEMENT DATE 6 April 2008

## PART 1
## INTRODUCTION

**SI.12**

**Citation and interpretation**

**1.**  (1)  These Regulations may be cited as the Small Companies and Groups (Accounts and Directors' Report) Regulations 2008.

(2)  In these Regulations 'the 2006 Act' means the Companies Act 2006.

**Commencement and application**

**2.**  (1)  These Regulations come into force on 6th April 2008.

(2)  They apply in relation to financial years beginning on or after 6th April 2008.

(3)  They apply to companies which are subject to the small companies regime under Part 15 of the 2006 Act (see section 381 of that Act[48]).

## PART 2
## FORM AND CONTENT OF INDIVIDUAL ACCOUNTS

**Companies Act individual accounts**

**3.**  (1)  Companies Act individual accounts under section 396 of the 2006 Act (Companies Act: individual accounts) must comply with the provisions of Schedule 1 to these Regulations as to the form and content of the balance sheet and profit and loss account, and additional information to be provided by way of notes to the accounts.

---

[48] Section 381 is amended by regulation 6(1) of SI 2008/393.

(2) The profit and loss account of a company that falls within section 408 of the 2006 Act (individual profit and loss account where group accounts prepared)[49] need not contain the information specified in paragraphs 59 to 61 of Schedule 1 to these Regulations (information supplementing the profit and loss account).

(3) Accounts are treated as having complied with any provision of Schedule 1 to these Regulations if they comply instead with the corresponding provision of Schedule 1 to the Large and Medium-Sized Companies and Groups (Accounts and Reports) Regulations 2008[50].

### Information about related undertakings (Companies Act or IAS individual accounts)

**4.** (1) Companies Act or IAS individual accounts must comply with the provisions of Schedule 2 to these Regulations as to information about related undertakings to be given in notes to the company's accounts.

(2) Information otherwise required to be given by Schedule 2 to these Regulations need not be disclosed with respect to an undertaking that—

(a) is established under the law of a country outside the United Kingdom, or

(b) carries on business outside the United Kingdom, if the conditions specified in section 409(4) of the 2006 Act are met (see section 409(5) of the 2006 Act for disclosure required where advantage taken of this exemption).

This paragraph does not apply in relation to the information required by paragraphs 4 and 8 of Schedule 2 to these Regulations.

### Information about directors' benefits: remuneration (Companies Act or IAS individual accounts)

**5.** Companies Act or IAS individual accounts must comply with the provisions of Schedule 3 to these Regulations as to information about directors' remuneration to be given in notes to the company's accounts.

### Accounts for delivery to registrar of companies (Companies Act individual accounts)

**6.** (1) The directors of a company for which they are preparing Companies Act individual accounts may deliver to the registrar of companies under section 444 of the 2006 Act (filing obligations of companies subject to small companies regime) a copy of a balance sheet which complies with Schedule 4 to these Regulations rather than Schedule 1.

(2) Companies Act individual accounts delivered to the registrar need not give the information required by—

(a) paragraph 4 of Schedule 2 to these Regulations (shares of company held by subsidiary undertakings), or

(b) Schedule 3 to these Regulations (directors' benefits).

PART 3
DIRECTORS' REPORT

### Directors' report

**7.** The report which the directors of a company are required to prepare under section 415 of the 2006 Act (duty to prepare directors' report) must disclose the matters specified in Schedule 5 to these Regulations.

PART 4
FORM AND CONTENT OF GROUP ACCOUNTS

### Companies Act group accounts

**8.** (1) Where the directors of a parent company which—

(a) is subject to the small companies regime, and

(b) has prepared Companies Act individual accounts in accordance with regulation 3, prepare Companies Act group accounts under section 398 of the 2006 Act (option to prepare group accounts), those accounts must comply with the provisions of Part 1 of Schedule 6 to these Regulations as to the form and content of the consolidated balance sheet and consolidated profit and loss account, and additional information to be provided by way of notes to the accounts.

(2) Accounts are treated as having complied with any provision of Part 1 of Schedule 6 if they comply instead with the corresponding provision of Schedule 6 to the Large and Medium-Sized Companies and Groups (Accounts and Reports) Regulations 2008.

---

[49] Section 408 is amended by regulation 10 of SI 2008/393.
[50] SI 2008/410.

#### Information about directors' benefits: remuneration (Companies Act or IAS group accounts)

**9.** Companies Act or IAS group accounts must comply with the provisions of Schedule 3 to these Regulations as to information about directors' remuneration to be given in notes to the company's accounts.

#### Information about related undertakings (Companies Act or IAS group accounts)

**10.** (1) Companies Act or IAS group accounts must comply with the provisions of Part 2 of Schedule 6 to these Regulations as to information about related undertakings to be given in notes to the company's accounts.

(2) Information otherwise required to be given by Part 2 of Schedule 6 need not be disclosed with respect to an undertaking that—

(a) is established under the law of a country outside the United Kingdom, or

(b) carries on business outside the United Kingdom,

if the conditions specified in section 409(4) of the 2006 Act are met (see section 409(5) of the 2006 Act for disclosure required where advantage taken of this exemption).

This paragraph does not apply in relation to the information required by paragraphs 26 and 35 of Schedule 6 to these Regulations.

#### Accounts for delivery to registrar of companies (Companies Act group accounts)

**11.** Companies Act group accounts delivered to the registrar of companies under section 444 of the 2006 Act need not give the information required by—

(a) Schedule 3 to these Regulations (directors' benefits), or

(b) paragraph 25 of Schedule 6 to these Regulations (shares of company held by subsidiary undertakings).

### PART 5
### INTERPRETATION

#### Definition of 'provisions'

**12.** Schedule 7 to these Regulations defines 'provisions' for the purpose of these Regulations and for the purposes of—

(a) section 677(3)(a) (Companies Act accounts: relevant provisions for purposes of financial assistance) in Part 18 of the 2006 Act,

(b) section 712(2)(b)(i) (Companies Act accounts: relevant provisions to determine available profits for redemption or purchase by private company out of capital) in that Part, [...]ª

(c) section 836(1)(b)(i) (Companies Act accounts: relevant provisions for distribution purposes) in Part 23 of that Act. [, and

(d) section 841(2)(a) (Companies Act accounts: provisions to be treated as realised losses) in that Part]ᵇ.

AMENDMENTS AND NOTES

ª Revoked by the Companies Act 2006 (Accounts, Reports and Audit) Regulations 2009, SI 2009/1581, reg 11(2)(a), in relation to financial years beginning on or after 6 April 2008 which have not ended before 27 June 2009.

ᵇ Inserted by the Companies Act 2006 (Accounts, Reports and Audit) Regulations 2009, SI 2009/1581, reg 11(2)(b), in relation to financial years beginning on or after 6 April 2008 which have not ended before 27 June 2009.

#### General interpretation

**13.** Schedule 8 to these Regulations contains general definitions for the purposes of these Regulations.

### SCHEDULE 1                                    Regulation 3(1)
### COMPANIES ACT INDIVIDUAL ACCOUNTS
### PART 1
### GENERAL RULES AND FORMATS

### SECTION A
### GENERAL RULES

**1.** (1) Subject to the following provisions of this Schedule—

(a) every balance sheet of a company must show the items listed in either of the balance sheet formats in Section B of this Part, and

      (b) every profit and loss account must show the items listed in any one of the profit and loss account formats in Section B.

  (2) References in this Schedule to the items listed in any of the formats in Section B are to those items read together with any of the notes following the formats which apply to those items.

  (3) The items must be shown in the order and under the headings and sub-headings given in the particular format used, but—

      (a) the notes to the formats may permit alternative positions for any particular items, and

      (b) the heading or sub-heading for any item does not have to be distinguished by any letter or number assigned to that item in the format used.

**2.** (1) Where in accordance with paragraph 1 a company's balance sheet or profit and loss account for any financial year has been prepared by reference to one of the formats in Section B, the company's directors must use the same format in preparing Companies Act individual accounts for subsequent financial years, unless in their opinion there are special reasons for a change.

  (2) Particulars of any such change must be given in a note to the accounts in which the new format is first used, and the reasons for the change must be explained.

**3.** (1) Any item required to be shown in a company's balance sheet or profit and loss account may be shown in greater detail than required by the particular format used.

  (2) The balance sheet or profit and loss account may include an item representing or covering the amount of any asset or liability, income or expenditure not otherwise covered by any of the items listed in the format used, save that none of the following may be treated as assets in any balance sheet—

      (a) preliminary expenses,

      (b) expenses of, and commission on, any issue of shares or debentures,

      (c) costs of research.

**4.** (1) Where the special nature of the company's business requires it, the company's directors must adapt the arrangement, headings and sub-headings otherwise required in respect of items given an Arabic number in the balance sheet or profit and loss account format used.

  (2) The directors may combine items to which Arabic numbers are given in any of the formats set out in Section B if—

      (a) their individual amounts are not material to assessing the state of affairs or profit or loss of the company for the financial year in question, or

      (b) the combination facilitates that assessment.

  (3) Where sub-paragraph (2)(b) applies, the individual amounts of any items which have been combined must be disclosed in a note to the accounts.

**5.** (1) Subject to sub-paragraph (2), the directors must not include a heading or sub-heading corresponding to an item in the balance sheet or profit and loss account format used if there is no amount to be shown for that item for the financial year to which the balance sheet or profit and loss account relates.

  (2) Where an amount can be shown for the item in question for the immediately preceding financial year that amount must be shown under the heading or sub-heading required by the format for that item.

**6.** Every profit and loss account must show the amount of a company's profit or loss on ordinary activities before taxation.

**7.** (1) For every item shown in the balance sheet or profit and loss account the corresponding amount for the immediately preceding financial year must also be shown.

  (2) Where that corresponding amount is not comparable with the amount to be shown for the item in question in respect of the financial year to which the balance sheet or profit and loss account relates, the former amount may be adjusted, and particulars of the non-comparability and of any adjustment must be disclosed in a note to the accounts.

**8.** Amounts in respect of items representing assets or income may not be set off against amounts in respect of items representing liabilities or expenditure (as the case may be), or vice versa.

**9.** The company's directors must, in determining how amounts are presented within items in the profit and loss account and balance sheet, have regard to the substance of the reported transaction or arrangement, in accordance with generally accepted accounting principles or practice.

## SECTION B
## THE REQUIRED FORMATS FOR ACCOUNTS[51]

### BALANCE SHEET FORMATS

*Format 1*

A.   Called up share capital not paid *(1)*
B.   Fixed assets
    I.   Intangible assets
        1.   Goodwill *(2)*
        2.   Other intangible assets *(3)*
    II.   Tangible assets
        1.   Land and buildings
        2.   Plant and machinery etc.
    III.   Investments
        1.   Shares in group undertakings and participating interests
        2.   Loans to group undertakings and undertakings in which the company has a participating
            interest
        3.   Other investments other than loans
        4.   Other investments *(4)*
C.   Current assets
    I.   Stocks
        1.   Stocks
        2.   Payments on account
    II.   Debtors *(5)*
        1.   Trade debtors
        2.   Amounts owed by group undertakings and undertakings in which the company has a
            participating interest
        3.   Other debtors *(1)*
    III.   Investments
        1.   Shares in group undertakings
        2.   Other investments *(4)*
    IV.   Cash at bank and in hand
D.   Prepayments and accrued income *(6)*
E.   Creditors: amounts falling due within one year
    1.   Bank loans and overdrafts
    2.   Trade creditors
    3.   Amounts owed to group undertakings and undertakings in which the company has a
        participating interest
    4.   Other creditors *(7)*
F.   Net current assets (liabilities) *(8)*
G.   Total assets less current liabilities
H.   Creditors: amounts falling due after more than one year
    1.   Bank loans and overdrafts
    2.   Trade creditors
    3.   Amounts owed to group undertakings and undertakings in which the company has a
        participating interest
    4.   Other creditors *(7)*
I.   Provisions for liabilities
J.   Accruals and deferred income *(7)*
K.   Capital and reserves
    I.   Called up share capital *(9)*
    II.   Share premium account
    III.   Revaluation reserve
    IV.   Other reserves
    V.   Profit and loss account

---

[51]  A number in brackets following any item is a reference to the note of that number in the notes following the formats.

# BALANCE SHEET FORMATS

*Format 2*

ASSETS

A.   Called up share capital not paid *(1)*
B.   Fixed assets
    I.    Intangible assets
        1.   Goodwill *(2)*
        2.   Other intangible assets *(3)*
    II.   Tangible assets
        1.   Land and buildings
        2.   Plant and machinery etc.
    III.  Investments
        1.   Shares in group undertakings and participating interests
        2.   Loans to group undertakings and undertakings in which the company has a participating interest
        3.   Other investments other than loans
        4.   Other investments *(4)*
C.   Current assets
    I.    Stocks
        1.   Stocks
        2.   Payments on account
    II.   Debtors *(5)*
        1.   Trade debtors
        2.   Amounts owed by group undertakings and undertakings in which the company has a participating interest
        3.   Other debtors *(1)*
    III.  Investments
        1.   Shares in group undertakings
        2.   Other investments *(4)*
    IV.   Cash at bank and in hand
D.   Prepayments and accrued income *(6)*

LIABILITIES

A.   Capital and reserves
    I.    Called up share capital *(9)*
    II.   Share premium account
    III.  Revaluation reserve
    IV.   Other reserves
    V.    Profit and loss account
B.   Provisions for liabilities
C.   Creditors *(10)*
        1.   Bank loans and overdrafts
        2.   Trade creditors
        3.   Amounts owed to group undertakings and undertakings in which the company has a participating interest
        4.   Other creditors *(7)*
D.   Accruals and deferred income *(7)*

# NOTES ON THE BALANCE SHEET FORMATS

*(1)* *Called up share capital not paid*
(Formats 1 and 2, items A and C.II.3.)
This item may either be shown at item A or included under item C.II.3 in Format 1 or 2.

*(2)* *Goodwill*
(Formats 1 and 2, item B.I.1.)
Amounts representing goodwill must only be included to the extent that the goodwill was acquired for valuable consideration.

*(3)* *Other intangible assets*
(Formats 1 and 2, item B.I.2.)
Amounts in respect of concessions, patents, licences, trade marks and similar rights and assets must only be included in a company's balance sheet under this item if either—
   (a)   the assets were acquired for valuable consideration and are not required to be shown under goodwill, or

(b) the assets in question were created by the company itself.

(4) *Others: Other investments*
(Formats 1 and 2, items B.III.4 and C.III.2.)
Where amounts in respect of own shares held are included under either of these items, the nominal value of such shares must be shown separately.

(5) *Debtors*
(Formats 1 and 2, items C.II.1 to 3.)
The amount falling due after more than one year must be shown separately for each item included under debtors unless the aggregate amount of debtors falling due after more than one year is disclosed in the notes to the accounts.

(6) *Prepayments and accrued income*
(Formats 1 and 2, item D.)
This item may alternatively be included under item C.II.3 in Format 1 or 2.

(7) *Other creditors*
(Format 1, items E.4, H.4 and J and Format 2, items C.4 and D.) There must be shown separately—
(a) the amount of any convertible loans, and
(b) the amount for creditors in respect of taxation and social security.
Payments received on account of orders must be included in so far as they are not shown as deductions from stocks.
In Format 1, accruals and deferred income may be shown under item J or included under item E.4 or H.4, or both (as the case may require). In Format 2, accruals and deferred income may be shown under item D or within item C.4 under Liabilities.

(8) *Net current assets (liabilities)*
(Format 1, item F.)
In determining the amount to be shown under this item any prepayments and accrued income must be taken into account wherever shown.

(9) *Called up share capital*
(Format 1, item K.I and Format 2, Liabilities item A.I.)
The amount of allotted share capital and the amount of called up share capital which has been paid up must be shown separately.

(10) *Creditors*
(Format 2, Liabilities items C.1 to 4.)
Amounts falling due within one year and after one year must be shown separately for each of these items and for the aggregate of all of these items unless the aggregate amount of creditors falling due within one year and the aggregate amount of creditors falling due after more than one year is disclosed in the notes to the accounts.

## PROFIT AND LOSS ACCOUNT FORMATS

*Format 1*

(see note (14) below)

1. Turnover
2. Cost of sales *(11)*
3. Gross profit or loss
4. Distribution costs *(11)*
5. Administrative expenses *(11)*
6. Other operating income
7. Income from shares in group undertakings
8. Income from participating interests
9. Income from other fixed asset investments *(12)*
10. Other interest receivable and similar income *(12)*
11. Amounts written off investments
12. Interest payable and similar charges *(13)*
13. Tax on profit or loss on ordinary activities
14. Profit or loss on ordinary activities after taxation
15. Extraordinary income
16. Extraordinary charges
17. Extraordinary profit or loss
18. Tax on extraordinary profit or loss
19. Other taxes not shown under the above items
20. Profit or loss for the financial year

## PROFIT AND LOSS ACCOUNT FORMATS

*Format 2*

1. Turnover
2. Change in stocks of finished goods and in work in progress
3. Own work capitalised
4. Other operating income
5. (a) Raw materials and consumables
   (b) Other external charges
6. Staff costs
   (a) wages and salaries
   (b) social security costs
   (c) other pension costs
7. (a) Depreciation and other amounts written off tangible and intangible fixed assets
   (b) Exceptional amounts written off current assets
8. Other operating charges
9. Income from shares in group undertakings
10. Income from participating interests
11. Income from other fixed asset investments *(12)*
12. Other interest receivable and similar income *(12)*
13. Amounts written off investments
14. Interest payable and similar charges *(13)*
15. Tax on profit or loss on ordinary activities
16. Profit or loss on ordinary activities after taxation
17. Extraordinary income
18. Extraordinary charges
19. Extraordinary profit or loss
20. Tax on extraordinary profit or loss
21. Other taxes not shown under the above items
22. Profit or loss for the financial year

## PROFIT AND LOSS ACCOUNT FORMATS

*Format 3*

### (see note (14) below)

A. Charges
   1. Cost of sales *(11)*
   2. Distribution costs *(11)*
   3. Administrative expenses *(11)*
   4. Amounts written off investments
   5. Interest payable and similar charges *(13)*
   6. Tax on profit or loss on ordinary activities
   7. Profit or loss on ordinary activities after taxation
   8. Extraordinary charges
   9. Tax on extraordinary profit or loss
   10. Other taxes not shown under the above items
   11. Profit or loss for the financial year
B. Income
   1. Turnover
   2. Other operating income
   3. Income from shares in group undertakings
   4. Income from participating interests
   5. Income from other fixed asset investments *(12)*
   6. Other interest receivable and similar income *(12)*
   7. Profit or loss on ordinary activities after taxation
   8. Extraordinary income
   9. Profit or loss for the financial year

# PROFIT AND LOSS ACCOUNT FORMATS

*Format 4*

A. Charges
    1. Reduction in stocks of finished goods and in work in progress
    2. (a) Raw materials and consumables
       (b) Other external charges
    3. Staff costs
       (a) wages and salaries
       (b) social security costs
       (c) other pension costs
    4. (a) Depreciation and other amounts written off tangible and intangible fixed assets
       (b) Exceptional amounts written off current assets
    5. Other operating charges
    6. Amounts written off investments
    7. Interest payable and similar charges *(13)*
    8. Tax on profit or loss on ordinary activities
    9. Profit or loss on ordinary activities after taxation
    10. Extraordinary charges
    11. Tax on extraordinary profit or loss
    12. Other taxes not shown under the above items
    13. Profit or loss for the financial year

B. Income
    1. Turnover
    2. Increase in stocks of finished goods and in work in progress
    3. Own work capitalised
    4. Other operating income
    5. Income from shares in group undertakings
    6. Income from participating interests
    7. Income from other fixed asset investments *(12)*
    8. Other interest receivable and similar income *(12)*
    9. Profit or loss on ordinary activities after taxation
    10. Extraordinary income
    11. Profit or loss for the financial year

# NOTES ON THE PROFIT AND LOSS ACCOUNT FORMATS

*(11)Cost of sales: distribution costs: administrative expenses*
(Format 1, items 2, 4 and 5 and Format 3, items A.1, 2 and 3.)
These items must be stated after taking into account any necessary provisions for depreciation or diminution in value of assets.

*(12)Income from other fixed asset investments: other interest receivable and similar income*
(Format 1, items 9 and 10; Format 2, items 11 and 12; Format 3, items B.5 and 6 and Format 4, items B.7 and 8.)
Income and interest derived from group undertakings must be shown separately from income and interest derived from other sources.

*(13)Interest payable and similar charges*
(Format 1, item 12; Format 2, item 14; Format 3, item A.5 and Format 4, item A.7.) The amount payable to group undertakings must be shown separately.

*(14)Formats 1 and 3*
The amount of any provisions for depreciation and diminution in value of tangible and intangible fixed assets falling to be shown under items 7(a) and A.4(a) respectively in Formats 2 and 4 must be disclosed in a note to the accounts in any case where the profit and loss account is prepared using Format 1 or Format 3.

PART 2

ACCOUNTING PRINCIPLES AND RULES

SECTION A

## Accounting Principles

**Preliminary**

**10.** (1) The amounts to be included in respect of all items shown in a company's accounts must be determined in accordance with the principles set out in this Section.

(2) But if it appears to the company's directors that there are special reasons for departing from any of those principles in preparing the company's accounts in respect of any financial year they may do so, in which case particulars of the departure, the reasons for it and its effect must be given in a note to the accounts.

**Accounting principles**

**11.** The company is presumed to be carrying on business as a going concern.

**12.** Accounting policies must be applied consistently within the same accounts and from one financial year to the next.

**13.** The amount of any item must be determined on a prudent basis, and in particular—

(a) only profits realised at the balance sheet date must be included in the profit and loss account, and

(b) all liabilities which have arisen in respect of the financial year to which the accounts relate or a previous financial year must be taken into account, including those which only become apparent between the balance sheet date and the date on which it is signed on behalf of the board of directors in accordance with section 414 of the 2006 Act (approval and signing of accounts).

**14.** All income and charges relating to the financial year to which the accounts relate must be taken into account, without regard to the date of receipt or payment.

**15.** In determining the aggregate amount of any item, the amount of each individual asset or liability that falls to be taken into account must be determined separately.

SECTION B

HISTORICAL COST ACCOUNTING RULES

**Preliminary**

**16.** Subject to Sections C and D of this Part of this Schedule, the amounts to be included in respect of all items shown in a company's accounts must be determined in accordance with the rules set out in this Section.

*Fixed assets*

**General rules**

**17.** (1) The amount to be included in respect of any fixed asset must be its purchase price or production cost.

(2) This is subject to any provision for depreciation or diminution in value made in accordance with paragraphs 18 to 20.

**Rules for depreciation and diminution in value**

**18.** In the case of any fixed asset which has a limited useful economic life, the amount of?—

(a) its purchase price or production cost, or

(b) where it is estimated that any such asset will have a residual value at the end of the period of its useful economic life, its purchase price or production cost less that estimated residual value, must be reduced by provisions for depreciation

calculated to write off that amount systematically over the period of the asset's useful economic life.

**19.** (1) Where a fixed asset investment of a description falling to be included under item B.III of either of the balance sheet formats set out in Part 1 of this Schedule has diminished in value, provisions for diminution in value may be made in respect of it and the amount to be included in respect of it may be reduced accordingly.

(2) Provisions for diminution in value must be made in respect of any fixed asset which has diminished in value if the reduction in its value is expected to be permanent (whether its

useful economic life is limited or not), and the amount to be included in respect of it must be reduced accordingly.

(3) Any provisions made under sub-paragraph (1) or (2) which are not shown in the profit and loss account must be disclosed (either separately or in aggregate) in a note to the accounts.

**20.** (1) Where the reasons for which any provision was made in accordance with paragraph 19 have ceased to apply to any extent, that provision must be written back to the extent that it is no longer necessary.

(2) Any amounts written back in accordance with sub-paragraph (1) which are not shown in the profit and loss account must be disclosed (either separately or in aggregate) in a note to the accounts.

### Development costs

**21.** (1) Notwithstanding that an item in respect of 'development costs' is included under 'fixed assets' in the balance sheet formats set out in Part 1 of this Schedule, an amount may only be included in a company's balance sheet in respect of development costs in special circumstances.

(2) If any amount is included in a company's balance sheet in respect of development costs the following information must be given in a note to the accounts—

(a) the period over which the amount of those costs originally capitalised is being or is to be written off, and

(b) the reasons for capitalising the development costs in question.

### Goodwill

**22.** (1) The application of paragraphs 17 to 20 in relation to goodwill (in any case where goodwill is treated as an asset) is subject to the following.

(2) Subject to sub-paragraph (3), the amount of the consideration for any goodwill acquired by a company must be reduced by provisions for depreciation calculated to write off that amount systematically over a period chosen by the directors of the company.

(3) The period chosen must not exceed the useful economic life of the goodwill in question.

(4) In any case where any goodwill acquired by a company is shown or included as an asset in the company's balance sheet there must be disclosed in a note to the accounts—

(a) the period chosen for writing off the consideration for that goodwill, and

(b) the reasons for choosing that period.

### Current assets

**23.** Subject to paragraph 24, the amount to be included in respect of any current asset must be its purchase price or production cost.

**24.** (1) If the net realisable value of any current asset is lower than its purchase price or production cost, the amount to be included in respect of that asset must be the net realisable value.

(2) Where the reasons for which any provision for diminution in value was made in accordance with sub-paragraph (1) have ceased to apply to any extent, that provision must be written back to the extent that it is no longer necessary.

*Miscellaneous and supplementary provisions*

### Excess of money owed over value received as an asset item

**25.** (1) Where the amount repayable on any debt owed by a company is greater than the value of the consideration received in the transaction giving rise to the debt, the amount of the difference may be treated as an asset.

(2) Where any such amount is so treated—

(a) it must be written off by reasonable amounts each year and must be completely written off before repayment of the debt, and

(b) if the current amount is not shown as a separate item in the company's balance sheet, it must be disclosed in a note to the accounts.

### Assets included at a fixed amount

**26.** (1) Subject to sub-paragraph (2), assets which fall to be included—

(a) amongst the fixed assets of a company under the item 'tangible assets', or

(b) amongst the current assets of a company under the item 'raw materials and consumables',may be included at a fixed quantity and value.

(2) Sub-paragraph (1) applies to assets of a kind which are constantly being replaced where—

(a) their overall value is not material to assessing the company's state of affairs, and

(b) their quantity, value and composition are not subject to material variation.

**Determination of purchase price or production cost**

**27.** (1) The purchase price of an asset is to be determined by adding to the actual price paid any expenses incidental to its acquisition.

(2) The production cost of an asset is to be determined by adding to the purchase price of the raw materials and consumables used the amount of the costs incurred by the company which are directly attributable to the production of that asset.

(3) In addition, there may be included in the production cost of an asset—

(a) a reasonable proportion of the costs incurred by the company which are only indirectly attributable to the production of that asset, but only to the extent that they relate to the period of production, and

(b) interest on capital borrowed to finance the production of that asset, to the extent that it accrues in respect of the period of production, provided, however, in a case within paragraph (b), that the inclusion of the interest in determining the cost of that asset and the amount of the interest so included is disclosed in a note to the accounts.

(4) In the case of current assets distribution costs may not be included in production costs.

**28.** (1) The purchase price or production cost of—

(a) any assets which fall to be included under any item shown in a company's balance sheet under the general item 'stocks', and

(b) any assets which are fungible assets (including investments), may be determined by the application of any of the methods mentioned in sub-paragraph (2) in relation to any such assets of the same class, provided that the method chosen is one which appears to the directors to be appropriate in the circumstances of the company.

(2) Those methods are—

(a) the method known as 'first in, first out' (FIFO),

(b) the method known as 'last in, first out' (LIFO),

(c) a weighted average price, and

(d) any other method similar to any of the methods mentioned above.

(3) For the purposes of this paragraph, assets of any description must be regarded as fungible if assets of that description are substantially indistinguishable one from another.

**Substitution of original stated amount where price or cost unknown**

**29.** (1) This paragraph applies where—

(a) there is no record of the purchase price or production cost of any asset of a company or of any price, expenses or costs relevant for determining its purchase price or production cost in accordance with paragraph 27, or

(b) any such record cannot be obtained without unreasonable expense or delay.

(2) In such a case, the purchase price or production cost of the asset must be taken, for the purposes of paragraphs 17 to 24, to be the value ascribed to it in the earliest available record of its value made on or after its acquisition or production by the company.

SECTION C
ALTERNATIVE ACCOUNTING RULES

**Preliminary**

**30.** (1) The rules set out in Section B are referred to below in this Schedule as the historical cost accounting rules.

(2) Those rules, with the omission of paragraphs 16, 22 and 26 to 29, are referred to below in this Part of this Schedule as the depreciation rules; and references below in this Schedule to the historical cost accounting rules do not include the depreciation rules as they apply by virtue of paragraph 33.

**31.** Subject to paragraphs 33 to 35, the amounts to be included in respect of assets of any description mentioned in paragraph 32 may be determined on any basis so mentioned.

**Alternative accounting rules**

**32.** (1) Intangible fixed assets, other than goodwill, may be included at their current cost.

(2) Tangible fixed assets may be included at a market value determined as at the date of their last valuation or at their current cost.

(3) Investments of any description falling to be included under item B III of either of the balance sheet formats set out Part 1 of this Schedule may be included either—

(a) at a market value determined as at the date of their last valuation, or

(b) at a value determined on any basis which appears to the directors to be appropriate in the circumstances of the company. But in the latter case particulars of the method of valuation adopted and of the reasons for adopting it must be disclosed in a note to the accounts.

(4) Investments of any description falling to be included under item C III of either of the balance sheet formats set out in Part 1 of this Schedule may be included at their current cost.

(5) Stocks may be included at their current cost.

### Application of the depreciation rules

**33.** (1) Where the value of any asset of a company is determined on any basis mentioned in paragraph 32, that value must be, or (as the case may require) be the starting point for determining, the amount to be included in respect of that asset in the company's accounts, instead of its purchase price or production cost or any value previously so determined for that asset.The depreciation rules apply accordingly in relation to any such asset with the substitution for any reference to its purchase price or production cost of a reference to the value most recently determined for that asset on any basis mentioned in paragraph 32.

(2) The amount of any provision for depreciation required in the case of any fixed asset by paragraphs 18 to 20 as they apply by virtue of sub-paragraph (1) is referred to below in this paragraph as the adjusted amount, and the amount of any provision which would be required by any of those paragraphs in the case of that asset according to the historical cost accounting rules is referred to as the historical cost amount.

(3) Where sub-paragraph (1) applies in the case of any fixed asset the amount of any provision for depreciation in respect of that asset—

(a) included in any item shown in the profit and loss account in respect of amounts written off assets of the description in question, or

(b) taken into account in stating any item so shown which is required by note (11) of the notes on the profit and loss account formats set out in Part 1 of this Schedule to be stated after taking into account any necessary provision for depreciation or diminution in value of assets included under it, may be the historical cost amount instead of the adjusted amount, provided that the amount of any difference between the two is shown separately in the profit and loss account or in a note to the accounts.

### Additional information to be provided in case of departure from historical cost accounting rules

**34.** (1) This paragraph applies where the amounts to be included in respect of assets covered by any items shown in a company's accounts have been determined on any basis mentioned in paragraph 32.

(2) The items affected and the basis of valuation adopted in determining the amounts of the assets in question in the case of each such item must be disclosed in a note to the accounts.

(3) In the case of each balance sheet item affected (except stocks) either—

(a) the comparable amounts determined according to the historical cost accounting rules, or

(b) the differences between those amounts and the corresponding amounts actually shown in the balance sheet in respect of that item, must be shown separately in the balance sheet or in a note to the accounts.

(4) In sub-paragraph (3), references in relation to any item to the comparable amounts determined as there mentioned are references to—

(a) the aggregate amount which would be required to be shown in respect of that item if the amounts to be included in respect of all the assets covered by that item were determined according to the historical cost accounting rules, and

(b) the aggregate amount of the cumulative provisions for depreciation or diminution in value which would be permitted or required in determining those amounts according to those rules.

### Revaluation reserve

**35.** (1) With respect to any determination of the value of an asset of a company on any basis mentioned in paragraph 32, the amount of any profit or loss arising from that determination (after allowing, where appropriate, for any provisions for depreciation or diminution in value made otherwise than by reference to the value so determined and any adjustments of any such provisions made in the light of that determination) must be credited or (as the case may be) debited to a separate reserve ('the revaluation reserve').

(2) The amount of the revaluation reserve must be shown in the company's balance sheet under a separate sub-heading in the position given for the item 'revaluation reserve' in Format 1 or 2 of the balance sheet formats set out in Part 1 of this Schedule, but need not be shown under that name.

(3) An amount may be transferred—

(a) from the revaluation reserve—

(i) to the profit and loss account, if the amount was previously charged to that account or represents realised profit, or

        (ii) on capitalisation,

    (b) to or from the revaluation reserve in respect of the taxation relating to any profit or loss credited or debited to the reserve.

The revaluation reserve must be reduced to the extent that the amounts transferred to it are no longer necessary for the purposes of the valuation method used.

  (4) In sub-paragraph (3)(a)(ii) 'capitalisation', in relation to an amount standing to the credit of the revaluation reserve, means applying it in wholly or partly paying up unissued shares in the company to be allotted to members of the company as fully or partly paid shares.

  (5) The revaluation reserve must not be reduced except as mentioned in this paragraph.

  (6) The treatment for taxation purposes of amounts credited or debited to the revaluation reserve must be disclosed in a note to the accounts.

## SECTION D
## FAIR VALUE ACCOUNTING

### Inclusion of financial instruments at fair value

**36.** (1) Subject to sub-paragraphs (2) to (5), financial instruments (including derivatives) may be included at fair value.

  (2) Sub-paragraph (1) does not apply to financial instruments that constitute liabilities unless—

    (a) they are held as part of a trading portfolio,

    (b) they are derivatives, or

    (c) they are financial instruments falling within sub-paragraph (4).

  (3) Unless they are financial instruments falling within sub-paragraph (4), sub-paragraph (1) does not apply to—

    (a) financial instruments (other than derivatives) held to maturity,

    (b) loans and receivables originated by the company and not held for trading purposes,

    (c) interests in subsidiary undertakings, associated undertakings and joint ventures,

    (d) equity instruments issued by the company,

    (e) contracts for contingent consideration in a business combination, or

    (f) other financial instruments with such special characteristics that the instruments, according to generally accepted accounting principles or practice, should be accounted for differently from other financial instruments.

  (4) Financial instruments that, under international accounting standards adopted by the European Commission on or before 5th September 2006 in accordance with the IAS Regulation, may be included in accounts at fair value, may be so included, provided that the disclosures required by such accounting standards are made.

  (5) If the fair value of a financial instrument cannot be determined reliably in accordance with paragraph 37, sub-paragraph (1) does not apply to that financial instrument.

  (6) In this paragraph—

'associated undertaking' has the meaning given by paragraph 19 of Schedule 6 to these Regulations;

'joint venture' has the meaning given by paragraph 18 of that Schedule.

### Determination of fair value

**37.** (1) The fair value of a financial instrument is its value determined in accordance with this paragraph.

  (2) If a reliable market can readily be identified for the financial instrument, its fair value is to be determined by reference to its market value.

  (3) If a reliable market cannot readily be identified for the financial instrument but can be identified for its components or for a similar instrument, its fair value is determined by reference to the market value of its components or of the similar instrument.

  (4) If neither sub-paragraph (2) nor (3) applies, the fair value of the financial instrument is a value resulting from generally accepted valuation models and techniques.

  (5) Any valuation models and techniques used for the purposes of sub-paragraph (4) must ensure a reasonable approximation of the market value.

### Hedged items

**38.** A company may include any assets and liabilities, or identified portions of such assets or liabilities, that qualify as hedged items under a fair value hedge accounting system at the amount required under that system.

**Other assets that may be included at fair value**

**39.** (1)  This paragraph applies to—
   (a)  investment property, and
   (b)  living animals and plants,
      that, under international accounting standards, may be included in accounts at fair value.

   (2)  Such investment property and such living animals and plants may be included at fair value, provided that all such investment property or, as the case may be, all such living animals and plants are so included where their fair value can reliably be determined.

   (3)  In this paragraph, 'fair value' means fair value determined in accordance with relevant international accounting standards.

**Accounting for changes in value**

**40.** (1)  This paragraph applies where a financial instrument is valued in accordance with paragraph 36 or 38 or an asset is valued in accordance with paragraph 39.

   (2)  Notwithstanding paragraph 13 in this Part of this Schedule, and subject to sub-paragraphs (3) and (4), a change in the value of the financial instrument or of the investment property or living animal or plant must be included in the profit and loss account.

   (3)  Where—
   (a)  the financial instrument accounted for is a hedging instrument under a hedge account-ing system that allows some or all of the change in value not to be shown in the profit and loss account, or
   (b)  the change in value relates to an exchange difference arising on a monetary item that forms part of a company's net investment in a foreign entity,
      the amount of the change in value must be credited to or (as the case may be) debited from a separate reserve ('the fair value reserve').

   (4)  Where the instrument accounted for—
   (a)  is an available for sale financial asset, and
   (b)  is not a derivative,
      the change in value may be credited to or (as the case may be) debited from the fair value reserve.

**The fair value reserve**

**41.** (1)  The fair value reserve must be adjusted to the extent that the amounts shown in it are no longer necessary for the purposes of paragraph 40(3) or (4).

   (2)  The treatment for taxation purposes of amounts credited or debited to the fair value reserve must be disclosed in a note to the accounts.

PART 3

NOTES TO THE ACCOUNTS

**Preliminary**

**42.**  Any information required in the case of any company by the following provisions of this Part of this Schedule must (if not given in the company's accounts) be given by way of a note to those accounts.

**Reserves and dividends**

**43.**  There must be stated—
   (a)  any amount set aside or proposed to be set aside to, or withdrawn or proposed to be withdrawn from, reserves,
   (b)  the aggregate amount of dividends paid in the financial year (other than those for which a liability existed at the immediately preceding balance sheet date),
   (c)  the aggregate amount of dividends that the company is liable to pay at the balance sheet date, and
   (d)  the aggregate amount of dividends that are proposed before the date of approval of the accounts, and not otherwise disclosed under paragraph (b) or (c).

**Disclosure of accounting policies**

**44.**  The accounting policies adopted by the company in determining the amounts to be included in respect of items shown in the balance sheet and in determining the profit or loss of the company must be stated (including such policies with respect to the depreciation and diminution in value of assets).

*Information supplementing the balance sheet*

**45.** Paragraphs 46 to 58 require information which either supplements the information given with respect to any particular items shown in the balance sheet or is otherwise relevant to assessing the company's state of affairs in the light of the information so given.

## Share capital

**46.** (1) Where shares of more than one class have been allotted, the number and aggregate nominal value of shares of each class allotted must be given.

(2) In the case of any part of the allotted share capital that consists of redeemable shares, the following information must be given—

   (a) the earliest and latest dates on which the company has power to redeem those shares,

   (b) whether those shares must be redeemed in any event or are liable to be redeemed at the option of the company or of the shareholder, and

   (c) whether any (and, if so, what) premium is payable on redemption.

**47.** If the company has allotted any shares during the financial year, the following information must be given—

(a) the classes of shares allotted, and

(b) as respects each class of shares, the number allotted, their aggregate nominal value, and the consideration received by the company for the allotment.

## Fixed assets

**48.** (1) In respect of each item which is or would but for paragraph 4(2)(b) be shown under the general item 'fixed assets' in the company's balance sheet the following information must be given—

   (a) the appropriate amounts in respect of that item as at the date of the beginning of the financial year and as at the balance sheet date respectively,

   (b) the effect on any amount shown in the balance sheet in respect of that item of—

      (i)   any revision of the amount in respect of any assets included under that item made during that year on any basis mentioned in paragraph 32,

      (ii)  acquisitions during that year of any assets,

      (iii) disposals during that year of any assets, and

      (iv)  any transfers of assets of the company to and from that item during that year.

(2) The reference in sub-paragraph (1)(a) to the appropriate amounts in respect of any item as at any date there mentioned is a reference to amounts representing the aggregate amounts determined, as at that date, in respect of assets falling to be included under that item on either of the following bases, that is to say—

   (a) on the basis of purchase price or production cost (determined in accordance with paragraphs 27 and 28), or

   (b) on any basis mentioned in paragraph 32, (leaving out of account in either case any provisions for depreciation or diminution in value).

(3) In respect of each item within sub-paragraph (1) there must also be stated—

   (a) the cumulative amount of provisions for depreciation or diminution in value of assets included under that item as at each date mentioned in sub-paragraph(1)(a),

   (b) the amount of any such provisions made in respect of the financial year,

   (c) the amount of any adjustments made in respect of any such provisions during that year in consequence of the disposal of any assets, and

   (d) the amount of any other adjustments made in respect of any such provisions during that year.

**49.** Where any fixed assets of the company (other than listed investments) are included under any item shown in the company's balance sheet at an amount determined on any basis mentioned in paragraph 32, the following information must be given—

(a) the years (so far as they are known to the directors) in which the assets were severally valued and the several values, and

(b) in the case of assets that have been valued during the financial year, the names of the persons who valued them or particulars of their qualifications for doing so and (whichever is stated) the bases of valuation used by them.

## Investments

**50.** (1) In respect of the amount of each item which is or would but for paragraph 4(2)(b) be shown in the company's balance sheet under the general item 'investments' (whether as fixed assets or as current assets) there must be stated how much of that amount is ascribable to listed investments.

(2) Where the amount of any listed investments is stated for any item in accordance with sub-paragraph (1), the following amounts must also be stated—

   (a) the aggregate market value of those investments where it differs from the amount so stated, and

    (b) both the market value and the stock exchange value of any investments of which the former value is, for the purposes of the accounts, taken as being higher than the latter.

### Information about fair value of assets and liabilities

**51.** (1) This paragraph applies where financial instruments have been valued in accordance with paragraph 36 or 38.

    (2) There must be stated—

        (a) the significant assumptions underlying the valuation models and techniques used where the fair value of the instruments has been determined in accordance with paragraph 37(4),

        (b) for each category of financial instrument, the fair value of the instruments in that category and the changes in value—

           (i) included in the profit and loss account, or

           (ii) credited to or (as the case may be) debited from the fair value reserve, in respect of those instruments, and

        (c) for each class of derivatives, the extent and nature of the instruments, including significant terms and conditions that may affect the amount, timing and certainty of future cash flows.

    (3) Where any amount is transferred to or from the fair value reserve during the financial year, there must be stated in tabular form—

        (a) the amount of the reserve as at the date of the beginning of the financial year and as at the balance sheet date respectively,

        (b) the amount transferred to or from the reserve during that year, and

        (c) the source and application respectively of the amounts so transferred.

**52.** (1) This paragraph applies if—

        (a) the company has financial fixed assets that could be included at fair value by virtue of paragraph 36,

        (b) the amount at which those items are included under any item in the company's accounts is in excess of their fair value, and

        (c) the company has not made provision for diminution in value of those assets in accordance with paragraph 19(1) of this Schedule.

    (2) There must be stated—

        (a) the amount at which either the individual assets or appropriate groupings of those individual assets are included in the company's accounts,

        (b) the fair value of those assets or groupings, and

        (c) the reasons for not making a provision for diminution in value of those assets, including the nature of the evidence that provides the basis for the belief that the amount at which they are stated in the accounts will be recovered.

### Information where investment property and living animals and plants included at fair value

**53.** (1) This paragraph applies where the amounts to be included in a company's accounts in respect of investment property or living animals and plants have been determined in accordance with paragraph 39.

    (2) The balance sheet items affected and the basis of valuation adopted in determining the amounts of the assets in question in the case of each such item must be disclosed in a note to the accounts.

    (3) In the case of investment property, for each balance sheet item affected there must be shown, either separately in the balance sheet or in a note to the accounts—

        (a) the comparable amounts determined according to the historical cost accounting rules, or

        (b) the differences between those amounts and the corresponding amounts actually shown in the balance sheet in respect of that item.

    (4) In sub-paragraph (3), references in relation to any item to the comparable amounts determined in accordance with that sub-paragraph are to—

        (a) the aggregate amount which would be required to be shown in respect of that item if the amounts to be included in respect of all the assets covered by that item were determined according to the historical cost accounting rules, and

        (b) the aggregate amount of the cumulative provisions for depreciation or diminution in value which would be permitted or required in determining those amounts according to those rules.

### Reserves and provisions

**54.** (1) This paragraph applies where any amount is transferred—

        (a) to or from any reserves, or

        (b) to any provisions for liabilities, or

        (c) from any provision for liabilities otherwise than for the purpose for which the provision was established, and the reserves or provisions are or would but for paragraph 4(2)(b) be shown as separate items in the company's balance sheet.

(2) The following information must be given in respect of the aggregate of reserves or provisions included in the same item—

(a) the amount of the reserves or provisions as at the date of the beginning of the financial year and as at the balance sheet date respectively,

(b) any amounts transferred to or from the reserves or provisions during that year, and

(c) the source and application respectively of any amounts so transferred.

(3) Particulars must be given of each provision included in the item 'other provisions' in the company's balance sheet in any case where the amount of that provision is material.

**Details of indebtedness**

**55.** (1) For the aggregate of all items shown under 'creditors' in the company's balance sheet there must be stated the aggregate of the following amounts—

(a) the amount of any debts included under 'creditors' which are payable or repayable otherwise than by instalments and fall due for payment or repayment after the end of the period of five years beginning with the day next following the end of the financial year, and

(b) in the case of any debts so included which are payable or repayable by instalments, the amount of any instalments which fall due for payment after the end of that period.

(2) In respect of each item shown under 'creditors' in the company's balance sheet there must be stated the aggregate amount of any debts included under that item in respect of which any security has been given by the company.

(3) References above in this paragraph to an item shown under 'creditors' in the company's balance sheet include references, where amounts falling due to creditors within one year and after more than one year are distinguished in the balance sheet—

(a) in a case within sub-paragraph (1), to an item shown under the latter of those categories,

(b) in a case within sub-paragraph (2), to an item shown under either of those categories. References to items shown under 'creditors' include references to items which would but for paragraph 4(2)(b) be shown under that heading.

**56.** If any fixed cumulative dividends on the company's shares are in arrear, there must be stated—

(a) the amount of the arrears, and

(b) the period for which the dividends or, if there is more than one class, each class of them are in arrear.

**Guarantees and other financial commitments**

**57.** (1) Particulars must be given of any charge on the assets of the company to secure the liabilities of any other person, including, where practicable, the amount secured.

(2) The following information must be given with respect to any other contingent liability not provided for—

(a) the amount or estimated amount of that liability,

(b) its legal nature, and

(c) whether any valuable security has been provided by the company in connection with that liability and if so, what.

(3) There must be stated, where practicable, the aggregate amount or estimated amount of contracts for capital expenditure, so far as not provided for.

(4) Particulars must be given of—

(a) any pension commitments included under any provision shown in the company's balance sheet, and

(b) any such commitments for which no provision has been made, and where any such commitment relates wholly or partly to pensions payable to past directors of the company separate particulars must be given of that commitment so far as it relates to such pensions.

(5) Particulars must also be given of any other financial commitments that—

(a) have not been provided for, and

(b) are relevant to assessing the company's state of affairs.

(6) Commitments within any of sub-paragraphs (1) to (5) which are undertaken on behalf of or for the benefit of—

(a) any parent undertaking or fellow subsidiary undertaking, or

(b) any subsidiary undertaking of the company, must be stated separately from the other commitments within that sub-paragraph, and commitments within paragraph (a) must also be stated separately from those within paragraph (b).

**Miscellaneous matters**

**58.** Particulars must be given of any case where the purchase price or production cost of any asset is for the first time determined under paragraph 29.

### Information supplementing the profit and loss account

**59.** Paragraphs 60 and 61 require information which either supplements the information given with respect to any particular items shown in the profit and loss account or otherwise provides particulars of income or expenditure of the company or of circumstances affecting the items shown in the profit and loss account (see regulation 3(2) for exemption for companies falling within section 408 of the 2006 Act).

### Particulars of turnover

**60.** (1) If the company has supplied geographical markets outside the United Kingdom during the financial year in question, there must be stated the percentage of its turnover that, in the opinion of the directors, is attributable to those markets.

(2) In analysing for the purposes of this paragraph the source of turnover, the directors of the company must have regard to the manner in which the company's activities are organised.

### Miscellaneous matters

**61.** (1) Where any amount relating to any preceding financial year is included in any item in the profit and loss account, the effect must be stated.

(2) Particulars must be given of any extraordinary income or charges arising in the financial year.

(3) The effect must be stated of any transactions that are exceptional by virtue of size or incidence though they fall within the ordinary activities of the company.

### Sums denominated in foreign currencies

**62.** Where sums originally denominated in foreign currencies have been brought into account under any items shown in the balance sheet or profit and loss account, the basis on which those sums have been translated into sterling (or the currency in which the accounts are drawn up) must be stated.

### Dormant companies acting as agents

**63.** Where the directors of a company take advantage of the exemption conferred by section 480 of the 2006 Act (dormant companies: exemption from audit), and the company has during the financial year in question acted as an agent for any person, the fact that it has so acted must be stated.

SCHEDULE 2                                                   Regulation 4

INFORMATION ABOUT RELATED UNDERTAKINGS WHERE COMPANY
NOT PREPARING GROUP ACCOUNTS (COMPANIES ACT OR IAS
INDIVIDUAL ACCOUNTS)

PART 1
REQUIRED DISCLOSURES

### Subsidiary undertakings

**1.** (1) The following information must be given where at the end of the financial year the company has subsidiary undertakings.

(2) The name of each subsidiary undertaking must be stated.

(3) There must be stated with respect to each subsidiary undertaking—

(a) if it is incorporated outside the United Kingdom, the country in which it is incorporated,

(b) if it is unincorporated, the address of its principal place of business.

### Holdings in subsidiary undertakings

**2.** (1) There must be stated in relation to shares of each class held by the company in a subsidiary undertaking—

(a) the identity of the class, and

(b) the proportion of the nominal value of the shares of that class represented by those shares.

(2) The shares held by or on behalf of the company itself must be distinguished from those attributed to the company which are held by or on behalf of a subsidiary undertaking.

#### Financial information about subsidiary undertakings

**3.** (1) There must be disclosed with respect to each subsidiary undertaking—

(a) the aggregate amount of its capital and reserves as at the end of its relevant financial year, and

(b) its profit or loss for that year.

(2) That information need not be given if the company would (if it were not subject to the small companies regime) be exempt by virtue of section 400 or 401 of the 2006 Act (parent company included in accounts of larger group) from the requirement to prepare group accounts.

(3) That information need not be given if the company's investment in the subsidiary undertaking is included in the company's accounts by way of the equity method of valuation.

(4) That information need not be given if—

(a) the subsidiary undertaking is not required by any provision of the 2006 Act to deliver a copy of its balance sheet for its relevant financial year and does not otherwise publish that balance sheet in the United Kingdom or elsewhere, and

(b) the company's holding is less than 50% of the nominal value of the shares in the undertaking.

(5) Information otherwise required by this paragraph need not be given if it is not material.

(6) For the purposes of this paragraph the 'relevant financial year' of a subsidiary undertaking is—

(a) if its financial year ends with that of the company, that year, and

(b) if not, its financial year ending last before the end of the company's financial year.

#### Shares of company held by subsidiary undertakings

**4.** (1) The number, description and amount of the shares in the company held by or on behalf of its subsidiary undertakings must be disclosed.

(2) Sub-paragraph (1) does not apply in relation to shares in the case of which the subsidiary undertaking is concerned as personal representative or, subject as follows, as trustee.

(3) The exception for shares in relation to which the subsidiary undertaking is concerned as trustee does not apply if the company, or any subsidiary undertaking of the company, is beneficially interested under the trust, otherwise than by way of security only for the purposes of a transaction entered into by it in the ordinary course of a business which includes the lending of money.

(4) Part 2 of this Schedule has effect for the interpretation of the reference in sub-paragraph (3) to a beneficial interest under a trust.

#### Significant holdings in undertakings other than subsidiary undertakings

**5.** (1) The information required by paragraphs 6 and 7 must be given where at the end of the financial year the company has a significant holding in an undertaking which is not a subsidiary undertaking of the company.

(2) A holding is significant for this purpose if—

(a) it amounts to 20% or more of the nominal value of any class of shares in the undertaking, or

(b) the amount of the holding (as stated or included in the company's accounts) exceeds 20% of the amount (as so stated) of the company's assets.

#### Membership of certain undertakings

**6.** (1) The name of the undertaking must be stated.

(2) There must be stated—

(a) if the undertaking is incorporated outside the United Kingdom, the country in which it is incorporated,

(b) if it is unincorporated, the address of its principal place of business.

(3) There must also be stated—

(a) the identity of each class of shares in the undertaking held by the company, and

(b) the proportion of the nominal value of the shares of that class represented by those shares.

**7.** (1) There must also be stated—

(a) the aggregate amount of the capital and reserves of the undertaking as at the end of its relevant financial year, and

(b) its profit or loss for that year.

(2) That information need not be given if—

(a) the company would (if it were not subject to the small companies regime) be exempt by virtue of section 400 or 401 of the 2006 Act (parent company included in accounts of larger group) from the requirement to prepare group accounts, and

(b) the investment of the company in all undertakings in which it has such a holding as is mentioned in sub-paragraph (1) is shown, in aggregate, in the notes to the accounts by way of the equity method of valuation.

(3) That information need not be given in respect of an undertaking if—

    (a) the undertaking is not required by any provision of the 2006 Act to deliver to the registrar a copy of its balance sheet for its relevant financial year and does not otherwise publish that balance sheet in the United Kingdom or elsewhere, and

    (b) the company's holding is less than 50% of the nominal value of the shares in the undertaking.

(4) Information otherwise required by this paragraph need not be given if it is not material.

(5) For the purposes of this paragraph the 'relevant financial year' of an undertaking is—

    (a) if its financial year ends with that of the company, that year, and

    (b) if not, its financial year ending last before the end of the company's financial year.

### Membership of certain undertakings

**8.** (1) The information required by this paragraph must be given where at the end of the financial year the company is a member of a qualifying undertaking.

(2) There must be stated—

    (a) the name and legal form of the undertaking, and

    (b) the address of the undertaking's registered office (whether in or outside the United Kingdom) or, if it does not have such an office, its head office (whether in or outside the United Kingdom).

(3) Where the undertaking is a qualifying partnership there must also be stated either—

    (a) that a copy of the latest accounts of the undertaking has been or is to be appended to the copy of the company's accounts sent to the registrar under section 444 of the 2006 Act, or

    (b) the name of at least one body corporate (which may be the company) in whose group accounts the undertaking has been or is to be dealt with on a consolidated basis.

(4) Information otherwise required by sub-paragraph (2) need not be given if it is not material.

(5) Information otherwise required by sub-paragraph (3)(b) need not be given if the notes to the company's accounts disclose that advantage has been taken of the exemption conferred by regulation 7 of the [Partnerships (Accounts) Regulations 2008][a].

(6) In this paragraph—

'dealt with on a consolidated basis', 'member' and 'qualifying partnership' have the same meanings as in the [Partnerships (Accounts) Regulations 2008][b];

'qualifying undertaking' means—

    (a) a qualifying partnership, or

    (b) an unlimited company each of whose members is—

        (i) a limited company,

        (ii) another unlimited company each of whose members is a limited company, or

        (iii) a Scottish partnership each of whose members is a limited company,

        and references in this paragraph to a limited company, another unlimited company or a Scottish partnership include a comparable undertaking incorporated in or formed under the law of a country or territory outside the United Kingdom.

AMENDMENTS AND NOTES

[a] Substituted by the Partnerships (Accounts) Regulations 2008, SI 2008/569, reg 17.

### Parent undertaking drawing up accounts for larger group

**9.** (1) Where the company is a subsidiary undertaking, the following information must be given with respect to the parent undertaking of—

    (a) the largest group of undertakings for which group accounts are drawn up and of which the company is a member, and

    (b) the smallest such group of undertakings.

(2) The name of the parent undertaking must be stated.

(3) There must be stated—

    (a) if the undertaking is incorporated outside the United Kingdom, the country in which it is incorporated,

    (b) if it is unincorporated, the address of its principal place of business.

(4) If copies of the group accounts referred to in sub-paragraph (1) are available to the public, there must also be stated the addresses from which copies of the accounts can be obtained.

### Identification of ultimate parent company

**10.** (1) Where the company is a subsidiary undertaking, the following information must be given with respect to the company (if any) regarded by the directors as being the company's ultimate parent company.

(2) The name of that company must be stated.

(3) If that company is incorporated outside the United Kingdom, the country in which it is incorporated must be stated (if known to the directors).

(4) In this paragraph 'company' includes any body corporate.

### Construction of references to shares held by company

**11.** (1) References in this Part of this Schedule to shares held by a company are to be construed as follows.

(2) For the purposes of paragraphs 2 and 3 (information about subsidiary undertakings)—

   (a) there must be attributed to the company any shares held by a subsidiary undertaking, or by a person acting on behalf of the company or a subsidiary undertaking; but

   (b) there must be treated as not held by the company any shares held on behalf of a person other than the company or a subsidiary undertaking.

(3) For the purposes of paragraphs 5 to 7 (information about undertakings other than subsidiary undertakings)—

   (a) there must be attributed to the company shares held on its behalf by any person; but

   (b) there must be treated as not held by a company shares held on behalf of a person other than the company.

(4) For the purposes of any of those provisions, shares held by way of security must be treated as held by the person providing the security—

   (a) where apart from the right to exercise them for the purpose of preserving the value of the security, or of realising it, the rights attached to the shares are exercisable only in accordance with his instructions, and

   (b) where the shares are held in connection with the granting of loans as part of normal business activities and apart from the right to exercise them for the purpose of preserving the value of the security, or of realising it, the rights attached to the shares are exercisable only in his interests.

## PART 2
## INTERPRETATION OF REFERENCES TO 'BENEFICIAL INTEREST'

### Introduction

**12.** (1) References in this Schedule to a beneficial interest are to be interpreted in accordance with the following provisions.

(2) This Part of this Schedule applies in relation to debentures as it applies in relation to shares.

### Residual interests under pension and employees' share schemes

**13.** (1) Where shares in an undertaking are held on trust for the purposes of a pension scheme or an employees' share scheme, there must be disregarded any residual interest of the undertaking or any of its subsidiary undertakings (the 'residual beneficiary') that has not vested in possession.

(2) A 'residual interest' means a right to receive any of the trust property in the event of—

   (a) all the liabilities arising under the scheme having been satisfied or provided for, or

   (b) the residual beneficiary ceasing to participate in the scheme, or

   (c) the trust property at any time exceeding what is necessary for satisfying the liabilities arising or expected to arise under the scheme.

(3) In sub-paragraph (2)—

   (a) references to a right include a right dependent on the exercise of a discretion vested by the scheme in the trustee or any other person, and

   (b) references to liabilities arising under a scheme include liabilities that have resulted or may result from the exercise of any such discretion.

(4) For the purposes of this paragraph a residual interest vests in possession—

   (a) in a case within sub-paragraph (2)(a), on the occurrence of the event there mentioned, whether or not the amount of the property receivable pursuant to the right mentioned in that sub-paragraph is then ascertained,

   (b) in a case within sub-paragraph (2)(b) or (c), when the residual beneficiary becomes entitled to require the trustee to transfer to it any of the property receivable pursuant to that right.

### Employer's charges and other rights of recovery

**14.** (1) Where shares in an undertaking are held on trust there must be disregarded—

   (a) if the trust is for the purposes of a pension scheme, any such rights as are mentioned in sub-paragraph (2),

   (b) if the trust is for the purposes of an employees' share scheme, any such rights as are mentioned in paragraph (a) of that sub-paragraph, being rights of the undertaking or any of its subsidiary undertakings.

(2) The rights referred to are—

   (a) any charge or lien on, or set-off against, any benefit or other right or interest under the scheme for the purpose of enabling the employer or former employer of a member of the scheme to obtain the discharge of a monetary obligation due to him from the member,

(b) any right to receive from the trustee of the scheme, or as trustee of the scheme to retain, an amount that can be recovered or retained under section 61 of the Pension Schemes Act 1993[52] or section 57 of the Pension Schemes (Northern Ireland) Act 1993[53] (deduction of contributions equivalent premium from refund of scheme contributions) or otherwise, as reimbursement or partial reimbursement for any contributions equivalent premium paid in connection with the scheme under Chapter 3 of Part 3 of that Act.

### Trustee's right to expenses, remuneration, indemnity etc.

**15.** (1) Where an undertaking is a trustee, there must be disregarded any rights which the undertaking has in its capacity as trustee.

(2) This includes in particular—

(a) any right to recover its expenses or be remunerated out of the trust property, and

(b) any right to be indemnified out of that property for any liability incurred by reason of any act or omission of the undertaking in the performance of its duties as trustee.

### Meaning of 'pension scheme'

**16.** (1) In this Part of this Schedule 'pension scheme' means any scheme for the provision of benefits consisting of or including relevant benefits for or in respect of employees or former employees.

(2) For this purpose 'relevant benefits' means any pension, lump sum, gratuity or other like benefit given or to be given on retirement or on death or in anticipation of retirement or, in connection with past service, after retirement or death.

### Application of provisions to directors

**17.** In paragraphs 14(2) and 16, 'employee' and 'employer' are to be read as if a director of an undertaking were employed by it.

### SCHEDULE 3 Regulations 5 and 9
## INFORMATION ABOUT DIRECTORS' BENEFITS: REMUNERATION
## (COMPANIES ACT OR IAS ACCOUNTS)

### PART 1
### INFORMATION REQUIRED TO BE DISCLOSED

### Total amount of directors' remuneration etc.

**1.** (1) There must be shown the overall total of the following amounts—

(a) the amount of remuneration paid to or receivable by directors in respect of qualifying services;

(b) the amount of money paid to or receivable by directors, and the net value of assets (other than money, share options or shares) received or receivable by directors, under long term incentive schemes in respect of qualifying services; and

(c) the value of any company contributions—

(i) paid, or treated as paid, to a pension scheme in respect of directors' qualifying services, and

(ii) by reference to which the rate or amount of any money purchase benefits that may become payable will be calculated.

(2) There must be shown the number of directors (if any) to whom retirement benefits are accruing in respect of qualifying services—

(a) under money purchase schemes, and

(b) under defined benefit schemes.

### Compensation to directors for loss of office

**2.** (1) There must be shown the aggregate amount of any payments made to directors or past directors for loss of office.

(2) 'Payment for loss of office' has the same meaning as in section 215 of the 2006 Act.

---

[52] 1993 c.48.
[53] 1993 c.49.

**Sums paid to third parties in respect of directors' services**

**3.** (1) There must be shown the aggregate amount of any consideration paid to or receivable by third parties for making available the services of any person—

(a) as a director of the company, or

(b) while director of the company—

(i) as director of any of its subsidiary undertakings, or

(ii) otherwise in connection with the management of the affairs of the company or any of its subsidiary undertakings.

(2) In sub-paragraph (1)—

(a) the reference to consideration includes benefits otherwise than in cash, and

(b) in relation to such consideration the reference to its amount is to the estimated money value of the benefit. The nature of any such consideration must be disclosed.

(3) For the purposes of this paragraph a 'third party' means a person other than—

(a) the director himself or a person connected with him or body corporate controlled by him, or

(b) the company or any of its subsidiary undertakings.

# PART 2
## SUPPLEMENTARY PROVISIONS

**General nature of obligations**

**4.** (1) This Schedule requires information to be given only so far as it is contained in the company's books and papers or the company has the right to obtain it from the persons concerned.

(2) For the purposes of this Schedule any information is treated as shown if it is capable of being readily ascertained from other information which is shown.

**Provisions as to amounts to be shown**

**5.** (1) The following provisions apply with respect to the amounts to be shown under this Schedule.

(2) The amount in each case includes all relevant sums, whether paid by or receivable from the company, any of the company's subsidiary undertakings or any other person.

(3) References to amounts paid to or receivable by a person include amounts paid to or receivable by a person connected with him or a body corporate controlled by him (but not so as to require an amount to be counted twice).

(4) Except as otherwise provided, the amounts to be shown for any financial year are—

(a) the sums receivable in respect of that year (whenever paid) or,

(b) in the case of sums not receivable in respect of a period, the sums paid during that year.

(5) Sums paid by way of expenses allowance that are charged to United Kingdom income tax after the end of the relevant financial year must be shown in a note to the first accounts in which it is practicable to show them and must be distinguished from the amounts to be shown apart from this provision.

(6) Where it is necessary to do so for the purpose of making any distinction required in complying with this Schedule, the directors may apportion payments between the matters in respect of which they have been paid or are receivable in such manner as they think appropriate.

**Exclusion of sums liable to be accounted for to company etc.**

**6.** (1) The amounts to be shown under this Schedule do not include any sums that are to be accounted for—

(a) to the company or any of its subsidiary undertakings, or

(b) by virtue of sections 219 and 222(3) of the 2006 Act (payments in connection with share transfers: duty to account), to persons who sold their shares as a result of the offer made.

(2) Where—

(a) any such sums are not shown in a note to the accounts for the relevant financial year on the ground that the person receiving them is liable to account for them, and

(b) the liability is afterwards wholly or partly released or is not enforced within a period of two years,

those sums, to the extent to which the liability is released or not enforced, must be shown in a note to the first accounts in which it is practicable to show them and must be distinguished from the amounts to be shown apart from this provision.

**Meaning of 'remuneration'**

**7.** (1) In this Schedule 'remuneration' of a director includes—

    (a) salary, fees and bonuses, sums paid by way of expenses allowance (so far as they are chargeable to United Kingdom income tax), and

    (b) subject to sub-paragraph (2), the estimated money value of any other benefits received by him otherwise than in cash.

  (2) The expression does not include—

    (a) the value of any share options granted to a director or the amount of any gains made on the exercise of any such options,

    (b) any company contributions paid, or treated as paid, in respect of him under any pension scheme or any benefits to which he is entitled under any such scheme, or

    (c) any money or other assets paid to or received or receivable by him under any long term incentive scheme.

**Meaning of 'long term incentive scheme'**

**8.** (1) In this Schedule 'long term incentive scheme' means an agreement or arrangement—

    (a) under which money or other assets may become receivable by a director, and

    (b) which includes one or more qualifying conditions with respect to service or performance which cannot be fulfilled within a single financial year.

  (2) For this purpose the following must be disregarded—

    (a) bonuses the amount of which falls to be determined by reference to service or performance within a single financial year;

    (b) compensation for loss of office, payments for breach of contract and other termination payments; and

    (c) retirement benefits.

**Meaning of 'shares' and 'share option' and related expressions**

**9.** In this Schedule—

    (a) 'shares' means shares (whether allotted or not) in the company, or any undertaking which is a group undertaking in relation to the company, and includes a share warrant as defined by section 779(1) of the 2006 Act; and

    (b) 'share option' means a right to acquire shares.

**Meaning of 'pension scheme' and related expressions**

**10.** (1) In this Schedule—

'pension scheme' means a retirement benefits scheme as defined by section 611 of the Income and Corporation Taxes Act 1988[54]; and 'retirement benefits' has the meaning given by section 612(1) of that Act.

  (2) In this Schedule, 'company contributions', in relation to a pension scheme and a director, means any payments (including insurance premiums) made, or treated as made, to the scheme in respect of the director by a person other than the director.

  (3) In this Schedule, in relation to a director—

'defined benefits' means retirement benefits payable under a pension scheme that are not money purchase benefits; 'defined benefit scheme' means a pension scheme that is not a money purchase scheme; 'money purchase benefits' means retirement benefits payable under a pension scheme the rate or amount of which is calculated by reference to payments made, or treated as made, by the director or by any other person in respect of the director and which are not average salary benefits; and 'money purchase scheme' means a pension scheme under which all of the benefits that may become payable to or in respect of the director are money purchase benefits.

  (4) Where a pension scheme provides for any benefits that may become payable to or in respect of any director to be whichever are the greater of—

    (a) money purchase benefits as determined by or under the scheme; and

    (b) defined benefits as so determined, the company may assume for the purposes of this paragraph that those benefits will be money purchase benefits, or defined benefits, according to whichever appears more likely at the end of the financial year.

  (5) For the purpose of determining whether a pension scheme is a money purchase or defined benefit scheme, any death in service benefits provided for by the scheme are to be disregarded.

**References to subsidiary undertakings**

**11.** (1) Any reference in this Schedule to a subsidiary undertaking of the company, in relation to a person who is or was, while a director of the company, a director also, by virtue of the

---

[54] 1988 c.1.

company's nomination (direct or indirect) of any other undertaking, includes that undertaking, whether or not it is or was in fact a subsidiary undertaking of the company.

(2) Any reference to a subsidiary undertaking of the company—

    (a) for the purposes of paragraph 1 (remuneration etc.) is to an undertaking which is a subsidiary undertaking at the time the services were rendered, and

    (b) for the purposes of paragraph 2 (compensation for loss of office) is to a subsidiary undertaking immediately before the loss of office as director.

### Other minor definitions

**12.** (1) In this Schedule—

'net value', in relation to any assets received or receivable by a director, means value after deducting any money paid or other value given by the director in respect of those assets;

'qualifying services', in relation to any person, means his services as a director of the company, and his services while director of the company—

    (a) as director of any of its subsidiary undertakings; or

    (b) otherwise in connection with the management of the affairs of the company or any of its subsidiary undertakings.

(2) For the purposes of this Schedule, remuneration paid or receivable or share options granted in respect of a person's accepting office as a director are treated as emoluments paid or receivable or share options granted in respect of his services as a director.

SCHEDULE 4         Regulation 6(1)

COMPANIES ACT ABBREVIATED ACCOUNTS FOR DELIVERY
TO REGISTRAR OF COMPANIES

PART 1

THE REQUIRED BALANCE SHEET FORMATS

**1.** (1) A company may deliver to the registrar a copy of the balance sheet showing the items listed in either of the balance sheet formats set out below, in the order and under the headings and sub-headings given in the format adopted, but in other respects corresponding to the full balance sheet.

(2) The copy balance sheet must contain in a prominent position a statement that it has been prepared in accordance with the provisions applicable to companies subject to the small companies regime.

**BALANCE SHEET FORMATS**

*Format 1*

A. Called up share capital not paid
B. Fixed assets
    I. Intangible assets
    II. Tangible assets
    III. Investments
C. Current assets
    I. Stocks
    II. Debtors *(1)*
    III. Investments
    IV. Cash at bank and in hand
D. Prepayments and accrued income
E. Creditors: amounts falling due within one year
F. Net current assets (liabilities)
G. Total assets less current liabilities
H. Creditors: amounts falling due after more than one year
I. Provisions for liabilities
J. Accruals and deferred income
K. Capital and reserves
    I. Called up share capital
    II. Share premium account
    III. Revaluation reserve
    IV. Other reserves
    V. Profit and loss account

# BALANCE SHEET FORMATS

*Format 2*

ASSETS

A.  Called up share capital not paid
B.  Fixed assets
    I.    Intangible assets
    II.   Tangible assets
    III.  Investments
C.  Current assets
    I.    Stocks
    II.   Debtors *(1)*
    III.  Investments
    IV.  Cash at bank and in hand
D.  Prepayments and accrued income


LIABILITIES

A.  Capital and reserves
    I.    Called up share capital
    II.   Share premium account
    III.  Revaluation reserve
    IV.  Other reserves
    V.   Profit and loss account
B.  Provisions for liabilities
C.  Creditors *(2)*
D.  Accruals and deferred income


# NOTES ON THE BALANCE SHEET FORMATS

*(1)* **Debtors**
(Formats 1 and 2, items C.II.)
The aggregate amount of debtors falling due after more than one year must be shown separately, unless it is disclosed in the notes to the accounts.

*(2)* **Creditors**
(Format 2, Liabilities item C.)
The aggregate amount of creditors falling due within one year and of creditors falling due after more than one year must be shown separately, unless it is disclosed in the notes to the accounts.


# PART 2
# NOTES TO THE ACCOUNTS

**Preliminary**

  **2.**  Any information required in the case of any company by the following provisions of this Part of this Schedule must (if not given in the company's accounts) be given by way of a note to those accounts.

**Disclosure of accounting policies**

  **3.**  The accounting policies adopted by the company in determining the amounts to be included in respect of items shown in the balance sheet and in determining the profit or loss of the company must be stated (including such policies with respect to the depreciation and diminution in value of assets).

*Information supplementing the balance sheet*

**Share capital and debentures**

  **4.**  (1)  Where shares of more than one class have been allotted, the number and aggregate nominal value of shares of each class allotted must be given.
       (2)  In the case of any part of the allotted share capital that consists of redeemable shares, the following information must be given—

(a) the earliest and latest dates on which the company has power to redeem those shares,

(b) whether those shares must be redeemed in any event or are liable to be redeemed at the option of the company or of the shareholder, and

(c) whether any (and, if so, what) premium is payable on redemption.

**5.** If the company has allotted any shares during the financial year, the following information must be given—

(a) the classes of shares allotted, and

(b) as respects each class of shares, the number allotted, their aggregate nominal value, and the consideration received by the company for the allotment.

## Fixed assets

**6.** (1) In respect of each item to which a letter or Roman number is assigned under the general item 'fixed assets' in the company's balance sheet the following information must be given—

(a) the appropriate amounts in respect of that item as at the date of the beginning of the financial year and as at the balance sheet date respectively,

(b) the effect on any amount shown in the balance sheet in respect of that item of—

(i) any revision of the amount in respect of any assets included under that item made during that year on any basis mentioned in paragraph 32 of Schedule 1 to these Regulations,

(ii) acquisitions during that year of any assets,

(iii) disposals during that year of any assets, and

(iv) any transfers of assets of the company to and from that item during that year.

(2) The reference in sub-paragraph (1)(a) to the appropriate amounts in respect of any item as at any date there mentioned is a reference to amounts representing the aggregate amounts determined, as at that date, in respect of assets falling to be included under that item on either of the following bases, that is to say—

(a) on the basis of purchase price or production cost (determined in accordance with paragraphs 27 and 28 of Schedule 1 to these Regulations), or

(b) on any basis mentioned in paragraph 32 of that Schedule, (leaving out of account in either case any provisions for depreciation or diminution in value).

(3) In respect of each item within sub-paragraph (1) there must also be stated—

(a) the cumulative amount of provisions for depreciation or diminution in value of assets included under that item as at each date mentioned in sub-paragraph (1)(a),

(b) the amount of any such provisions made in respect of the financial year,

(c) the amount of any adjustments made in respect of any such provisions during that year in consequence of the disposal of any assets, and

(d) the amount of any other adjustments made in respect of any such provisions during that year.

## Financial fixed assets

**7.** (1) This paragraph applies if—

(a) the company has financial fixed assets that could be included at fair value by virtue of paragraph 36 of Schedule 1 to these Regulations,

(b) the amount at which those items are included under any item in the company's accounts is in excess of their fair value, and

(c) the company has not made provision for diminution in value of those assets in accordance with paragraph 19(1) of that Schedule.

(2) There must be stated—

(a) the amount at which either the individual assets or appropriate groupings of those individual assets are included in the company's accounts,

(b) the fair value of those assets or groupings, and

(c) the reasons for not making a provision for diminution in value of those assets, including the nature of the evidence that provides the basis for the belief that the amount at which they are stated in the accounts will be recovered.

## Details of indebtedness

**8.** (1) For the aggregate of all items shown under 'creditors' in the company's balance sheet there must be stated the aggregate of the following amounts—

(a) the amount of any debts included under 'creditors' which are payable or repayable otherwise than by instalments and fall due for payment or repayment after the end of the period of five years beginning with the day next following the end of the financial year, and

(b) in the case of any debts so included which are payable or repayable by instalments, the amount of any instalments which fall due for payment after the end of that period.

(2) In respect of each item shown under 'creditors' in the company's balance sheet there must be stated the aggregate amount of any debts included under that item in respect of which any security has been given by the company.

**Sums denominated in foreign currencies**

**9.** Where sums originally denominated in foreign currencies have been brought into account under any items shown in the balance sheet or profit and loss account, the basis on which those sums have been translated into sterling (or the currency in which the accounts are drawn up) must be stated.

**Dormant companies acting as agents**

**10.** Where the directors of a company take advantage of the exemption conferred by section 480 of the 2006 Act (dormant companies: exemption from audit), and the company has during the financial year in question acted as an agent for any person, the fact that it has so acted must be stated.

SCHEDULE 5                                                    Regulation 7

MATTERS TO BE DEALT WITH IN DIRECTORS' REPORT

**Introduction**

**1.** In addition to the information required by section 416 of the 2006 Act, the directors' report must contain the following information.

**Political donations and expenditure**

**2.** (1) If—
  (a) the company (not being the wholly-owned subsidiary of a company incorporated in the United Kingdom) has in the financial year—
     (i)  made any political donation to any political party or other political organisation,
     (ii)  made any political donation to any independent election candidate, or
     (iii)  incurred any political expenditure, and
  (b) the amount of the donation or expenditure, or (as the case may be) the aggregate amount of all donations and expenditure falling within paragraph (a), exceeded £2000, the directors' report for the year must contain the following particulars.

  (2) Those particulars are—
  (a) as respects donations falling within sub-paragraph (1)(a)(i) or (ii)—
     (i)  the name of each political party, other political organisation or independent election candidate to whom any such donation has been made, and
     (ii)  the total amount given to that party, organisation or candidate by way of such donations in the financial year; and
  (b) as respects expenditure falling within sub-paragraph (1)(a)(iii), the total amount incurred by way of such expenditure in the financial year.

  (3) If—
  (a) at the end of the financial year the company has subsidiaries which have, in that year, made any donations or incurred any such expenditure as is mentioned in sub-paragraph (1)(a), and
  (b) it is not itself the wholly-owned subsidiary of a company incorporated in the United Kingdom, the directors' report for the year is not, by virtue of sub-paragraph (1), required to contain the particulars specified in sub-paragraph (2). But, if the total amount of any such donations or expenditure (or both) made or incurred in that year by the company and the subsidiaries between them exceeds £2000, the directors' report for the year must contain those particulars in relation to each body by whom any such donation or expenditure has been made or incurred.

  (4) Any expression used in this paragraph which is also used in Part 14 of the 2006 Act (control of political donations and expenditure) has the same meaning as in that Part.

**3.** (1) If the company (not being the wholly-owned subsidiary of a company incorporated in the United Kingdom) has in the financial year made any contribution to a non-EU political party, the directors' report for the year must contain—
  (a) a statement of the amount of the contribution, or
  (b) (if it has made two or more such contributions in the year) a statement of the total amount of the contributions.

  (2) If—
  (a) at the end of the financial year the company has subsidiaries which have, in that year, made any such contributions as are mentioned in sub-paragraph (1), and
  (b) it is not itself the wholly-owned subsidiary of a company incorporated in the United Kingdom, the directors' report for the year is not, by virtue of sub-paragraph (1), required to contain any such statement as is there mentioned, but it must instead contain a statement of the total amount of the contributions made in the year by the company and the subsidiaries between them.

(3) In this paragraph, 'contribution', in relation to an organisation, means—

   (a) any gift of money to the organisation (whether made directly or indirectly);

   (b) any subscription or other fee paid for affiliation to, or membership of, the organisation; or

   (c) any money spent (otherwise than by the organisation or a person acting on its behalf) in paying any expenses incurred directly or indirectly by the organisation.

(4) In this paragraph, 'non-EU political party' means any political party which carries on, or proposes to carry on, its activities wholly outside the member States.

### Charitable donations

**4.** (1) If—

   (a) the company (not being the wholly-owned subsidiary of a company incorporated in the United Kingdom) has in the financial year given money for charitable purposes, and

   (b) the money given exceeded £2000 in amount, the directors' report for the year must contain, in the case of each of the purposes for which money has been given, a statement of the amount of money given for that purpose.

(2) If—

   (a) at the end of the financial year the company has subsidiaries which have, in that year, given money for charitable purposes, and

   (b) it is not itself the wholly owned subsidiary of a company incorporated in the United Kingdom, sub-paragraph (1) does not apply to the company.But, if the amount given in that year for charitable purposes by the company and the subsidiaries between them exceeds £2000, the directors' report for the year must contain, in the case of each of the purposes for which money has been given by the company and the subsidiaries between them, a statement of the amount of money given for that purpose.

(3) Money given for charitable purposes to a person who, when it was given, was ordinarily resident outside the United Kingdom is to be left out of account for the purposes of this paragraph.

(4) For the purposes of this paragraph, 'charitable purposes' means purposes which are exclusively charitable, and as respects Scotland a purpose is charitable if it is listed in section 7(2) of the Charities and Trustee Investment (Scotland) Act 2005[55].

### Disclosure concerning employment etc. of disabled persons

**5.** (1) This paragraph applies to the directors' report where the average number of persons employed by the company in each week during the financial year exceeded 250.

(2) That average number is the quotient derived by dividing, by the number of weeks in the financial year, the number derived by ascertaining, in relation to each of those weeks, the number of persons who, under contracts of service, were employed in the week (whether throughout it or not) by the company, and adding up the numbers ascertained.

(3) The directors' report must in that case contain a statement describing such policy as the company has applied during the financial year—

   (a) for giving full and fair consideration to applications for employment by the company made by disabled persons, having regard to their particular aptitudes and abilities,

   (b) for continuing the employment of, and for arranging appropriate training for, employees of the company who have become disabled persons during the period when they were employed by the company, and

   (c) otherwise for the training, career development and promotion of disabled persons employed by the company.

(4) In this paragraph—

   (a) 'employment' means employment other than employment to work wholly or mainly outside the United Kingdom, and 'employed' and 'employee' are to be construed accordingly; and

   (b) 'disabled person' means the same as in the Disability Discrimination Act 1995[56].

### Disclosure required by company acquiring its own shares etc.

**6.** (1) This paragraph applies where shares in a company—

   (a) are purchased by the company or are acquired by it by forfeiture or surrender in lieu of forfeiture, or in pursuance of any of the following provisions (acquisition of own shares by company limited by shares)—

      (i) section 143(3) of the Companies Act 1985,[57]

      (ii) Article 153(3) of the Companies (Northern Ireland) Order 1986[58], or

---

[55] 2005 asp 10.

[56] 1995 c.50.

[57] Section 143 is prospectively repealed by the 2006 Act.

[58] Article 153 is prospectively repealed by the 2006 Act.

   (iii) section 659 of the 2006 Act, or
  (b) are acquired by another person in circumstances where paragraph (c) or (d) of any of the following provisions applies (acquisition by company's nominee, or by another with company financial assistance, the company having a beneficial interest)—
   (i) section 146(1) of the Companies Act 1985[59],
   (ii) Article 156(1) of the Companies (Northern Ireland) Order 1986[60], or
   (iii) section 662(1) of the 2006 Act, or
  (c) are made subject to a lien or other charge taken (whether expressly or otherwise) by the company and permitted by any of the following provisions (exceptions from general rule against a company having a lien or charge on its own shares)—
   (i) section 150(2) or (4) of the Companies Act 1985[61],
   (ii) Article 160(2) or (4) of the Companies (Northern Ireland) Order 1986[62], or
   (iii) section 670(2) or (4) of the 2006 Act.
 (2) The directors' report for a financial year must state—
  (a) the number and nominal value of the shares so purchased, the aggregate amount of the consideration paid by the company for such shares and the reasons for their purchase;
  (b) the number and nominal value of the shares so acquired by the company, acquired by another person in such circumstances and so charged respectively during the financial year;
  (c) the maximum number and nominal value of shares which, having been so acquired by the company, acquired by another person in such circumstances or so charged (whether or not during that year) are held at any time by the company or that other person during that year;
  (d) the number and nominal value of the shares so acquired by the company, acquired by another person in such circumstances or so charged (whether or not during that year) which are disposed of by the company or that other person or cancelled by the company during that year;
  (e) where the number and nominal value of the shares of any particular description are stated in pursuance of any of the preceding sub-paragraphs, the percentage of the called-up share capital which shares of that description represent;
  (f) where any of the shares have been so charged the amount of the charge in each case; and
  (g) where any of the shares have been disposed of by the company or the person who acquired them in such circumstances for money or money's worth the amount or value of the consideration in each case.

SCHEDULE 6    Regulations 8(1) and 10

GROUP ACCOUNTS

PART 1

FORM AND CONTENT OF COMPANIES ACT GROUP ACCOUNTS

**General rules**

**1.** (1) Subject to sub-paragraphs (1) and (2), group accounts must comply so far as practicable with the provisions of Schedule 1 to these Regulations (Companies Act individual accounts) as if the undertakings included in the consolidation ('the group') were a single company.
 (2) For item B.III in each balance sheet format set out in that Schedule substitute—

'B. III. Investments
1. Shares in group undertakings
2. Interests in associated undertakings
3. Other participating interests
4. Loans to group undertakings and undertakings in which a participating interest is held
5. Other investments other than loans
6. Others'.

 (3) In the profit and loss account formats replace the items headed 'Income from participating interests', that is—

---

[59] Section 146(1)(aa) was inserted by section 102C(5) of 1986 c.53, as inserted by section 1(1) of 1997 c.41. Section 146 is prospectively repealed by the 2006 Act.
[60] Article 156(1)(aa) was inserted by section 102C(6) of 1986 c.53, as inserted by section 1(1) of 1997 c.41. Article 156 is prospectively repealed by the 2006 Act.
[61] Section 150 is prospectively repealed by the 2006 Act.
[62] Article 160 is prospectively repealed by the 2006 Act.

(a) in Format 1, item 8,

(b) in Format 2, item 10,

(c) in Format 3, item B.4, and

(d) in Format 4, item B.6,by two items: 'Income from interests in associated undertakings' and 'Income from other participating interests'.

**2.** (1) The consolidated balance sheet and profit and loss account must incorporate in full the information contained in the individual accounts of the undertakings included in the consolidation, subject to the adjustments authorised or required by the following provisions of this Schedule and to such other adjustments (if any) as may be appropriate in accordance with generally accepted accounting principles or practice.

(2) If the financial year of a subsidiary undertaking included in the consolidation does not end with that of the parent company, the group accounts must be made up—

(a) from the accounts of the subsidiary undertaking for its financial year last ending before the end of the parent company's financial year, provided that year ended no more than three months before that of the parent company, or

(b) from interim accounts prepared by the subsidiary undertaking as at the end of the parent company's financial year.

**3.** (1) Where assets and liabilities to be included in the group accounts have been valued or otherwise determined by undertakings according to accounting rules differing from those used for the group accounts, the values or amounts must be adjusted so as to accord with the rules used for the group accounts.

(2) If it appears to the directors of the parent company that there are special reasons for departing from sub-paragraph (1) they may do so, but particulars of any such departure, the reasons for it and its effect must be given in a note to the accounts.

(3) The adjustments referred to in this paragraph need not be made if they are not material for the purpose of giving a true and fair view.

**4.** Any differences of accounting rules as between a parent company's individual accounts for a financial year and its group accounts must be disclosed in a note to the latter accounts and the reasons for the difference given.

**5.** Amounts that in the particular context of any provision of this Schedule are not material may be disregarded for the purposes of that provision.

### Elimination of group transactions

**6.** (1) Debts and claims between undertakings included in the consolidation, and income and expenditure relating to transactions between such undertakings, must be eliminated in preparing the group accounts.

(2) Where profits and losses resulting from transactions between undertakings included in the consolidation are included in the book value of assets, they must be eliminated in preparing the group accounts.

(3) The elimination required by sub-paragraph (2) may be effected in proportion to the group's interest in the shares of the undertakings.

(4) Sub-paragraphs (1) and (2) need not be complied with if the amounts concerned are not material for the purpose of giving a true and fair view.

### Acquisition and merger accounting

**7.** (1) The following provisions apply where an undertaking becomes a subsidiary undertaking of the parent company.

(2) That event is referred to in those provisions as an 'acquisition', and references to the 'undertaking acquired' are to be construed accordingly.

**8.** An acquisition must be accounted for by the acquisition method of accounting unless the conditions for accounting for it as a merger are met and the merger method of accounting is adopted.

**9.** (1) The acquisition method of accounting is as follows.

(2) The identifiable assets and liabilities of the undertaking acquired must be included in the consolidated balance sheet at their fair values as at the date of acquisition.

(3) The income and expenditure of the undertaking acquired must be brought into the group accounts only as from the date of the acquisition.

(4) There must be set off against the acquisition cost of the interest in the shares of the undertaking held by the parent company and its subsidiary undertakings the interest of the parent company and its subsidiary undertakings in the adjusted capital and reserves of the undertaking acquired.

(5) The resulting amount if positive must be treated as goodwill, and if negative as a negative consolidation difference.

**10.** (1) The conditions for accounting for an acquisition as a merger are—

(a) that at least 90% of the nominal value of the relevant shares in the undertaking acquired (excluding any shares in the undertaking held as treasury shares) is held by or on behalf of the parent company and its subsidiary undertakings,

    (b)  that the proportion referred to in paragraph (a) was attained pursuant to an arrangement providing for the issue of equity shares by the parent company or one or more of its subsidiary undertakings,

    (c)  that the fair value of any consideration other than the issue of equity shares given pursuant to the arrangement by the parent company and its subsidiary undertakings did not exceed 10% of the nominal value of the equity shares issued, and

    (d)  that adoption of the merger method of accounting accords with generally accepted accounting principles or practice.

(2)  The reference in sub-paragraph (1)(a) to the 'relevant shares' in an undertaking acquired is to those carrying unrestricted rights to participate both in distributions and in the assets of the undertaking upon liquidation.

**11.** (1)  The merger method of accounting is as follows.

(2)  The assets and liabilities of the undertaking acquired must be brought into the group accounts at the figures at which they stand in the undertaking's accounts, subject to any adjustment authorised or required by this Schedule.

(3)  The income and expenditure of the undertaking acquired must be included in the group accounts for the entire financial year, including the period before the acquisition.

(4)  The group accounts must show corresponding amounts relating to the previous financial year as if the undertaking acquired had been included in the consolidation throughout that year.

(5)  There must be set off against the aggregate of—

    (a)  the appropriate amount in respect of qualifying shares issued by the parent company or its subsidiary undertakings in consideration for the acquisition of shares in the undertaking acquired, and

    (b)  the fair value of any other consideration for the acquisition of shares in the undertaking acquired, determined as at the date when those shares were acquired, the nominal value of the issued share capital of the undertaking acquired held by the parent company and its subsidiary undertakings.

(6)  The resulting amount must be shown as an adjustment to the consolidated reserves.

(7)  In sub-paragraph (5)(a) 'qualifying shares' means—

    (a)  shares in relation to which any of the following provisions applies (merger relief), and in respect of which the appropriate amount is the nominal value—

        (i)  section 131 of the Companies Act 1985[63],

       (ii)  Article 141 of the Companies (Northern Ireland) Order 1986[64], or

      (iii)  section 612 of the 2006 Act, or

    (b)  shares in relation to which any of the following provisions applies (group reconstruction relief), and in respect of which the appropriate amount is the nominal value together with any minimum premium value within the meaning of that section—

        (i)  section 132 of the Companies Act 1985[65],

       (ii)  Article 142 of the Companies (Northern Ireland) Order 1986[66], or

      (iii)  section 611 of the 2006 Act.

**12.** (1)  Where a group is acquired, paragraphs 9 to 11 apply with the following adaptations.

(2)  References to shares of the undertaking acquired are to be construed as references to shares of the parent undertaking of the group.

(3)  Other references to the undertaking acquired are to be construed as references to the group; and references to the assets and liabilities, income and expenditure and capital and reserves of the undertaking acquired must be construed as references to the assets and liabilities, income and expenditure and capital and reserves of the group after making the set-offs and other adjustments required by this Schedule in the case of group accounts.

**13.** (1)  The following information with respect to acquisitions taking place in the financial year must be given in a note to the accounts.

(2)  There must be stated—

    (a)  the name of the undertaking acquired or, where a group was acquired, the name of the parent undertaking of that group, and

    (b)  whether the acquisition has been accounted for by the acquisition or the merger method of accounting; and in relation to an acquisition which significantly affects the figures shown in the group accounts, the following further information must be given.

(3)  The composition and fair value of the consideration for the acquisition given by the parent company and its subsidiary undertakings must be stated.

(4)  Where the acquisition method of accounting has been adopted, the book values immediately prior to the acquisition, and the fair values at the date of acquisition, of each class of assets and liabilities of the undertaking or group acquired must be stated in tabular form, including

---

[63]  Section 131 is prospectively repealed by the 2006 Act.

[64]  Article 141 is prospectively repealed by the 2006 Act.

[65]  Section 132 is prospectively repealed by the 2006 Act.

[66]  Article 142 is prospectively repealed by the 2006 Act.

a statement of the amount of any goodwill or negative consolidation difference arising on the acquisition, together with an explanation of any significant adjustments made.

(5) In ascertaining for the purposes of sub-paragraph (4) the profit or loss of a group, the book values and fair values of assets and liabilities of a group or the amount of the assets and liabilities of a group, the set-offs and other adjustments required by this Schedule in the case of group accounts must be made.

**14.** (1) There must also be stated in a note to the accounts the cumulative amount of goodwill resulting from acquisitions in that and earlier financial years which has been written off otherwise than in the consolidated profit and loss account for that or any earlier financial year.

(2) That figure must be shown net of any goodwill attributable to subsidiary undertakings or businesses disposed of prior to the balance sheet date.

**15.** Where during the financial year there has been a disposal of an undertaking or group which significantly affects the figure shown in the group accounts, there must be stated in a note to the accounts—

(a) the name of that undertaking or, as the case may be, of the parent undertaking of that group, and

(b) the extent to which the profit or loss shown in the group accounts is attributable to profit or loss of that undertaking or group.

**16.** The information required by paragraph 13, 14 or 15 need not be disclosed with respect to an undertaking which—

(a) is established under the law of a country outside the United Kingdom, or

(b) carries on business outside the United Kingdom, if in the opinion of the directors of the parent company the disclosure would be seriously prejudicial to the business of that undertaking or to the business of the parent company or any of its subsidiary undertakings and the Secretary of State agrees that the information should not be disclosed.

### Minority interests

**17.** (1) The formats set out in Schedule 1 to these Regulations have effect in relation to group accounts with the following additions.

(2) In the Balance Sheet Formats there must be shown, as a separate item and under an appropriate heading, the amount of capital and reserves attributable to shares in subsidiary undertakings included in the consolidation held by or on behalf of persons other than the parent company and its subsidiary undertakings.

(3) In the Profit and Loss Account Formats there must be shown, as a separate item and under an appropriate heading—

(a) the amount of any profit or loss on ordinary activities, and

(b) the amount of any profit or loss on extraordinary activities, attributable to shares in subsidiary undertakings included in the consolidation held by or on behalf of persons other than the parent company and its subsidiary undertakings.

(4) For the purposes of paragraph 4 of Schedule 1 (power to adapt or combine items)—

(a) the additional item required by sub-paragraph (2) is treated as one to which a letter is assigned, and

(b) the additional items required by sub-paragraph (3)(a) and (b) are treated as ones to which an Arabic number is assigned.

### Joint ventures

**18.** (1) Where an undertaking included in the consolidation manages another undertaking jointly with one or more undertakings not included in the consolidation, that other undertaking ('the joint venture') may, if it is not—

(a) a body corporate, or

(b) a subsidiary undertaking of the parent company, be dealt with in the group accounts by the method of proportional consolidation.

(2) The provisions of this Schedule relating to the preparation of consolidated accounts apply, with any necessary modifications, to proportional consolidation under this paragraph.

### Associated undertakings

**19.** (1) An 'associated undertaking' means an undertaking in which an undertaking included in the consolidation has a participating interest and over whose operating and financial policy it exercises a significant influence, and which is not—

(a) a subsidiary undertaking of the parent company, or

(b) a joint venture dealt with in accordance with paragraph 18.

(2) Where an undertaking holds 20% or more of the voting rights in another undertaking, it is presumed to exercise such an influence over it unless the contrary is shown.

(3) The voting rights in an undertaking means the rights conferred on shareholders in respect of their shares or, in the case of an undertaking not having a share capital, on members, to vote at general meetings of the undertaking on all, or substantially all, matters.

(4) The provisions of paragraphs 5 to 11 of Schedule 7 to the 2006 Act (parent and subsidiary undertakings: rights to be taken into account and attribution of rights) apply in determining for the purposes of this paragraph whether an undertaking holds 20% or more of the voting rights in another undertaking.

**20.** (1) The interest of an undertaking in an associated undertaking, and the amount of profit or loss attributable to such an interest, must be shown by the equity method of accounting (including dealing with any goodwill arising in accordance with paragraphs 17 to 20 and 22 of Schedule 1 to these Regulations).

(2) Where the associated undertaking is itself a parent undertaking, the net assets and profits or losses to be taken into account are those of the parent and its subsidiary undertakings (after making any consolidation adjustments).

(3) The equity method of accounting need not be applied if the amounts in question are not material for the purpose of giving a true and fair view.

## PART 2
## INFORMATION ABOUT RELATED UNDERTAKINGS WHERE COMPANY PREPARING GROUP ACCOUNTS (COMPANIES ACT OR IAS GROUP ACCOUNTS)

### Introduction and interpretation

**21.** In this Part of this Schedule 'the group' means the group consisting of the parent company and its subsidiary undertakings.

### Subsidiary undertakings

**22.** (1) The following information must be given with respect to the undertakings that are subsidiary undertakings of the parent company at the end of the financial year.

(2) The name of each undertaking must be stated.

(3) There must be stated—
   (a) if the undertaking is incorporated outside the United Kingdom, the country in which it is incorporated,
   (b) if it is unincorporated, the address of its principal place of business.

(4) It must also be stated whether the subsidiary undertaking is included in the consolidation and, if it is not, the reasons for excluding it from consolidation must be given.

(5) It must be stated with respect to each subsidiary undertaking by virtue of which of the conditions specified in section 1162(2) or (4) of the 2006 Act it is a subsidiary undertaking of its immediate parent undertaking. That information need not be given if the relevant condition is that specified in subsection (2)(a) of that section (holding of a majority of the voting rights) and the immediate parent undertaking holds the same proportion of the shares in the undertaking as it holds voting rights.

### Holdings in subsidiary undertakings

**23.** (1) The following information must be given with respect to the shares of a subsidiary undertaking held—
   (a) by the parent company, and
   (b) by the group, and the information under paragraphs (a) and (b) must (if different) be shown separately.

(2) There must be stated—
   (a) the identity of each class of shares held, and
   (b) the proportion of the nominal value of the shares of that class represented by those shares.

### Financial information about subsidiary undertakings not included in the consolidation

**24.** (1) There must be shown with respect to each subsidiary undertaking not included in the consolidation—
   (a) the aggregate amount of its capital and reserves as at the end of its relevant financial year, and
   (b) its profit or loss for that year.

(2) That information need not be given if the group's investment in the undertaking is included in the accounts by way of the equity method of valuation or if—
   (a) the undertaking is not required by any provision of the 2006 Act to deliver a copy of its balance sheet for its relevant financial year and does not otherwise publish that balance sheet in the United Kingdom or elsewhere, and

(b) the holding of the group is less than 50% of the nominal value of the shares in the undertaking.

(3) Information otherwise required by this paragraph need not be given if it is not material.

(4) For the purposes of this paragraph the 'relevant financial year' of a subsidiary undertaking is—

    (a) if its financial year ends with that of the company, that year, and

    (b) if not, its financial year ending last before the end of the company's financial year.

## Shares of company held by subsidiary undertakings

**25.** (1) The number, description and amount of the shares in the company held by or on behalf of its subsidiary undertakings must be disclosed.

(2) Sub-paragraph (1) does not apply in relation to shares in the case of which the subsidiary undertaking is concerned as personal representative or, subject as follows, as trustee.

(3) The exception for shares in relation to which the subsidiary undertaking is concerned as trustee does not apply if the company or any of its subsidiary undertakings is beneficially interested under the trust, otherwise than by way of security only for the purposes of a transaction entered into by it in the ordinary course of a business which includes the lending of money.

(4) Part 2 of Schedule 2 to these Regulations has effect for the interpretation of the reference in sub-paragraph (3) to a beneficial interest under a trust.

## Joint ventures

**26.** (1) The following information must be given where an undertaking is dealt with in the consolidated accounts by the method of proportional consolidation in accordance with paragraph 18 of this Schedule (joint ventures)—

    (a) the name of the undertaking,

    (b) the address of the principal place of business of the undertaking,

    (c) the factors on which joint management of the undertaking is based, and

    (d) the proportion of the capital of the undertaking held by undertakings included in the consolidation.

(2) Where the financial year of the undertaking did not end with that of the company, there must be stated the date on which a financial year of the undertaking last ended before that date.

## Associated undertakings

**27.** (1) The following information must be given where an undertaking included in the consolidation has an interest in an associated undertaking.

(2) The name of the associated undertaking must be stated.

(3) There must be stated—

    (a) if the undertaking is incorporated outside the United Kingdom, the country in which it is incorporated,

    (b) if it is unincorporated, the address of its principal place of business.

(4) The following information must be given with respect to the shares of the undertaking held—

    (a) by the parent company, and

    (b) by the group, and the information under paragraphs (a) and (b) must be shown separately.

(5) There must be stated—

    (a) the identity of each class of shares held, and

    (b) the proportion of the nominal value of the shares of that class represented by those shares.

(6) In this paragraph 'associated undertaking' has the meaning given by paragraph 19 of this Schedule; and the information required by this paragraph must be given notwithstanding that paragraph 20(3) of this Schedule (materiality) applies in relation to the accounts themselves.

## Other significant holdings of parent company or group

**28.** (1) The information required by paragraphs 29 and 30 must be given where at the end of the financial year the parent company has a significant holding in an undertaking which is not one of its subsidiary undertakings and does not fall within paragraph 26 (joint ventures) or paragraph 27 (associated undertakings).

(2) A holding is significant for this purpose if—

    (a) it amounts to 20% or more of the nominal value of any class of shares in the undertaking, or

    (b) the amount of the holding (as stated or included in the company's individual accounts) exceeds 20% of the amount of its assets (as so stated).

**29.** (1) The name of the undertaking must be stated.

(2) There must be stated—

    (a) if the undertaking is incorporated outside the United Kingdom, the country in which it is incorporated,

    (b) if it is unincorporated, the address of its principal place of business.

(3) The following information must be given with respect to the shares of the undertaking held by the parent company.

(4) There must be stated—

    (a) the identity of each class of shares held, and

    (b) the proportion of the nominal value of the shares of that class represented by those shares.

**30.** (1) There must also be stated—

    (a) the aggregate amount of the capital and reserves of the undertaking as at the end of its relevant financial year, and

    (b) its profit or loss for that year.

(2) That information need not be given in respect of an undertaking if—

    (a) the undertaking is not required by any provision of the 2006 Act to deliver a copy of its balance sheet for its relevant financial year and does not otherwise publish that balance sheet in the United Kingdom or elsewhere, and

    (b) the company's holding is less than 50% of the nominal value of the shares in the undertaking.

(3) Information otherwise required by this paragraph need not be given if it is not material.

(4) For the purposes of this paragraph the 'relevant financial year' of an undertaking is—

    (a) if its financial year ends with that of the company, that year, and

    (b) if not, its financial year ending last before the end of the company's financial year.

**31.** (1) The information required by paragraphs 32 and 33 must be given where at the end of the financial year the group has a significant holding in an undertaking which is not a subsidiary undertaking of the parent company and does not fall within paragraph 26 (joint ventures) or paragraph 27 (associated undertakings).

(2) A holding is significant for this purpose if—

    (a) it amounts to 20% or more of the nominal value of any class of shares in the undertaking, or

    (b) the amount of the holding (as stated or included in the group accounts) exceeds 20% of the amount of the group's assets (as so stated).

**32.** (1) The name of the undertaking must be stated.

(2) There must be stated—

    (a) if the undertaking is incorporated outside the United Kingdom, the country in which it is incorporated,

    (b) if it is unincorporated, the address of its principal place of business.

(3) The following information must be given with respect to the shares of the undertaking held by the group.

(4) There must be stated—

    (a) the identity of each class of shares held, and

    (b) the proportion of the nominal value of the shares of that class represented by those shares.

**33.** (1) There must also be stated—

    (a) the aggregate amount of the capital and reserves of the undertaking as at the end of its relevant financial year, and

    (b) its profit or loss for that year.

(2) That information need not be given if—

    (a) the undertaking is not required by any provision of the 2006 Act to deliver a copy of its balance sheet for its relevant financial year and does not otherwise publish that balance sheet in the United Kingdom or elsewhere, and

    (b) the holding of the group is less than 50% of the nominal value of the shares in the undertaking.

(3) Information otherwise required by this paragraph need not be given if it is not material.

(4) For the purposes of this paragraph the 'relevant financial year' of an outside undertaking is—

    (a) if its financial year ends with that of the parent company, that year, and

    (b) if not, its financial year ending last before the end of the parent company's financial year.

### Parent company's or group's membership of certain undertakings

**34.** (1) The information required by this paragraph must be given where at the end of the financial year the parent company or group is a member of a qualifying undertaking.

(2) There must be stated—

    (a) the name and legal form of the undertaking, and

    (b) the address of the undertaking's registered office (whether in or outside the United Kingdom) or, if it does not have such an office, its head office (whether in or outside the United Kingdom).

   (3) Where the undertaking is a qualifying partnership there must also be stated either—
      (a) that a copy of the latest accounts of the undertaking has been or is to be appended to the copy of the company's accounts sent to the registrar under section 444 of the 2006 Act, or
      (b) the name of at least one body corporate (which may be the company) in whose group accounts the undertaking has been or is to be dealt with on a consolidated basis.
   (4) Information otherwise required by sub-paragraph (2) need not be given if it is not material.
   (5) Information otherwise required by sub-paragraph (3)(b) need not be given if the notes to the company's accounts disclose that advantage has been taken of the exemption conferred by regulation 7 of the [Partnerships (Accounts) Regulations 2008][a].
   (6) In this paragraph—'dealt with on a consolidated basis', 'member' and 'qualifying partnership' have the same meanings as in the [Partnerships (Accounts) Regulations 2008][b]; 'qualifying undertaking' means—
      (a) a qualifying partnership, or
      (b) an unlimited company each of whose members is—
         (i) a limited company,
         (ii) another unlimited company each of whose members is a limited company, or
         (iii) a Scottish partnership each of whose members is a limited company, and references in this paragraph to a limited company, another unlimited company or a Scottish partnership include a comparable undertaking incorporated in or formed under the law of a country or territory outside the United Kingdom.

Amendments

[a] Substituted by the Partnerships (Accounts) Regulations 2008, SI 2008/569, reg 17.

[b] Substituted by the Partnerships (Accounts) Regulations 2008, SI 2008/569, reg 17.

### Parent undertaking drawing up accounts for larger group

**35.** (1) Where the parent company is itself a subsidiary undertaking, the following information must be given with respect to that parent undertaking of the company which heads—
      (a) the largest group of undertakings for which group accounts are drawn up and of which that company is a member, and
      (b) the smallest such group of undertakings.
   (2) The name of the parent undertaking must be stated.
   (3) There must be stated—
      (a) if the undertaking is incorporated outside the United Kingdom, the country in which it is incorporated,
      (b) if it is unincorporated, the address of its principal place of business.
   (4) If copies of the group accounts referred to in sub-paragraph (1) are available to the public, there must also be stated the addresses from which copies of the accounts can be obtained.

### Identification of ultimate parent company

**36.** (1) Where the parent company is itself a subsidiary undertaking, the following information must be given with respect to the company (if any) regarded by the directors as being that company's ultimate parent company.
   (2) The name of that company must be stated.
   (3) If that company is incorporated outside the United Kingdom, the country in which it is incorporated must be stated (if known to the directors).
   (4) In this paragraph 'company' includes any body corporate.

### Construction of references to shares held by parent company or group

**37.** (1) References in this Part of this Schedule to shares held by the parent company or the group are to be construed as follows.
   (2) For the purposes of paragraphs 23, 27(4) and (5) and 28 to 30 (information about holdings in subsidiary and other undertakings)—
      (a) there must be attributed to the parent company shares held on its behalf by any person; but
      (b) there must be treated as not held by the parent company shares held on behalf of a person other than the company.
   (3) References to shares held by the group are to any shares held by or on behalf of the parent company or any of its subsidiary undertakings; but any shares held on behalf of a person other than the parent company or any of its subsidiary undertakings are not to be treated as held by the group.
   (4) Shares held by way of security must be treated as held by the person providing the security—
      (a) where apart from the right to exercise them for the purpose of preserving the value of the security, or of realising it, the rights attached to the shares are exercisable only in accordance with his instructions, and
      (b) where the shares are held in connection with the granting of loans as part of normal

business activities and apart from the right to exercise them for the purpose of preserving the value of the security, or of realising it, the rights attached to the shares are exercisable only in his interests.

## SCHEDULE 7

Regulation 12

INTERPRETATION OF TERM 'PROVISIONS'

## PART 1

MEANING FOR PURPOSES OF THESE REGULATIONS

**Definition of 'Provisions'**

1. (1) In these Regulations, references to provisions for depreciation or diminution in value of assets are to any amount written off by way of providing for depreciation or diminution in value of assets.
   (2) Any reference in the profit and loss account formats set out in Part 1 of Schedule 1 to these Regulations to the depreciation of, or amounts written off, assets of any description is to any provision for depreciation or diminution in value of assets of that description.
2. References in these Regulations to provisions for liabilities are to any amount retained as reasonably necessary for the purpose of providing for any liability the nature of which is clearly defined and which is either likely to be incurred, or certain to be incurred but uncertain as to amount or as to the date on which it will arise.

## PART 2

MEANING FOR PURPOSES OF PARTS 18 AND 23 OF THE 2006 ACT

**Financial assistance for purchase of own shares**

3. The specified provisions for the purposes of section 677(3)(a) of the 2006 Act (Companies Act accounts: relevant provisions for purposes of financial assistance) are provisions for liabilities within paragraph 2 of this Schedule.

**Redemption or purchase by private company out of capital**

4. The specified provisions for the purposes of section 712(2)(b)(i) of the 2006 Act (Companies Act accounts: relevant provisions to determine available profits for redemption or purchase out of capital) are provisions of any of the kinds mentioned in paragraphs 1 and 2 of this Schedule.

**Justification of distribution by references to accounts**

5. The specified provisions for the purposes of section 836(1)(b)(i) of the 2006 Act (Companies Act accounts: relevant provisions for distribution purposes) are provisions of any of the kinds mentioned in paragraphs 1 and 2 of this Schedule.

**[Realised losses**

6. The specified provisions for the purposes of section 841(2)(a) of the 2006 Act (Companies Act accounts: treatment of provisions as realised losses) are provisions of any of the kinds mentioned in paragraphs 1 and 2 of this Schedule.]ᵃ

AMENDMENTS AND NOTES

ᵃ Inserted by the Companies Act 2006 (Accounts, Reports and Audit) Regulations 2009, SI 2009/1581, reg 11(3), in relation to financial years beginning on or after 6 April 2008 which have not ended before 27 June 2009.

## SCHEDULE 8

Regulation 13

GENERAL INTERPRETATION

**Financial instruments**

1. References to 'derivatives' include commodity-based contracts that give either contracting party the right to settle in cash or in some other financial instrument, except where such contracts—
   (a) were entered into for the purpose of, and continue to meet, the company's expected purchase, sale or usage requirements,
   (b) were designated for such purpose at their inception, and
   (c) are expected to be settled by delivery of the commodity.

**2.** (1) The expressions listed in sub-paragraph (2) have the same meaning as they have in Council Directive 78/660/EEC on the annual accounts of certain types of companies[67].

   (2) Those expressions are 'available for sale financial asset', 'business combination', 'commodity-based contracts', 'derivative', 'equity instrument', 'exchange difference', 'fair value hedge accounting system', 'financial fixed asset', 'financial instrument', 'foreign entity', 'hedge accounting', 'hedge accounting system', 'hedged items', 'hedging instrument', 'held for trading purposes', 'held to maturity', 'monetary item', 'receivables', 'reliable market' and 'trading portfolio'.

### Fixed and current assets

**3.** 'Fixed assets' means assets of a company which are intended for use on a continuing basis in the company's activities, and 'current assets' means assets not intended for such use.

### Historical cost accounting rules

**4.** References to the historical cost accounting rules are to be read in accordance with paragraph 30 of Schedule 1 to these Regulations.

### Listed investments

**5.** (1) 'Listed investment' means an investment as respects which there has been granted a listing on—

   (a) a recognised investment exchange other than an overseas investment exchange, or
   (b) a stock exchange of repute outside the United Kingdom.

   (2) 'Recognised investment exchange' and 'overseas investment exchange' have the meaning given in Part 18 of the Financial Services and Markets Act 2000[68].

### Loans

**6.** A loan is treated as falling due for repayment, and an instalment of a loan is treated as falling due for payment, on the earliest date on which the lender could require repayment or (as the case may be) payment, if he exercised all options and rights available to him.

### Materiality

**7.** Amounts which in the particular context of any provision of Schedule 1 to these Regulations are not material may be disregarded for the purposes of that provision.

### Participating interests

**8.** (1) A 'participating interest' means an interest held by an undertaking in the shares of another undertaking which it holds on a long-term basis for the purpose of securing a contribution to its activities by the exercise of control or influence arising from or related to that interest.

   (2) A holding of 20% or more of the shares of the undertaking is to be presumed to be a participating interest unless the contrary is shown.

   (3) The reference in sub-paragraph (1) to an interest in shares includes—

   (a) an interest which is convertible into an interest in shares, and
   (b) an option to acquire shares or any such interest, and an interest or option falls within paragraph (a) or (b) notwithstanding that the shares to which it relates are, until the conversion or the exercise of the option, unissued.

   (4) For the purposes of this paragraph an interest held on behalf of an undertaking is to be treated as held by it.

   (5) In the balance sheet and profit and loss formats set out in Part 1 of Schedule 1 and Part 1 of Schedule 4 to these Regulations, 'participating interest' does not include an interest in a group undertaking.

   (6) For the purpose of this paragraph as it applies in relation to the expression 'participating interest'—

   (a) in those formats as they apply in relation to group accounts, and
   (b) in paragraph 19 of Schedule 6 (group accounts: undertakings to be accounted for as associated undertakings), the references in sub-paragraphs (1) to (4) to the interest held by, and the purposes and activities of, the undertaking concerned are to be construed as references to the interest held by, and the purposes and activities of, the group (within the meaning of paragraph 1 of that Schedule).

---

[67] OJ L222 of 14.8.1978, page 11, as amended in particular by Directives 2001/65/EEC, 2003/51/EEC and 2006/46/EEC of the European Parliament and of the Council (OJ L238 of 27.12.2001, page 28, OJ L178 of 17.7.2003, page 16 and OJ L224 of 16.8.2006, page 1).

[68] 2000 c.8.

**Purchase price**

**9.** 'Purchase price', in relation to an asset of a company or any raw materials or consumables used in the production of such an asset, includes any consideration (whether in cash or otherwise) given by the company in respect of that asset or those materials or consumables, as the case may be.

**Realised profits and losses**

**10.** 'Realised profits' and 'realised losses' have the same meaning as in section 853(4) and (5) of the 2006 Act.

**Staff costs**

**11.** (1) 'Social security costs' means any contributions by the company to any state social security or pension scheme, fund or arrangement.

(2) 'Pension costs' includes—

(a) any costs incurred by the company in respect of any pension scheme established for the purpose of providing pensions for persons currently or formerly employed by the company,

(b) any sums set aside for the future payment of pensions directly by the company to current or former employees, and

(c) any pensions paid directly to such persons without having first been set aside.

(3) Any amount stated in respect of the item 'social security costs' or in respect of the item 'wages and salaries' in the company's profit and loss account must be determined by reference to payments made or costs incurred in respect of all persons employed by the company during the financial year under contracts of service.

# THE LARGE AND MEDIUM-SIZED COMPANIES AND GROUPS (ACCOUNTS AND REPORTS) REGULATIONS 2008

### (SI 2008/410)

COMMENCEMENT DATE 6 April 2008

## PART 1
## INTRODUCTION

**Citation and interpretation**

**1.** (1) These Regulations may be cited as the Large and Medium-sized Companies and Groups (Accounts and Reports) Regulations 2008.

(2) In these Regulations 'the 2006 Act' means the Companies Act 2006.

**Commencement and application**

**2.** (1) These Regulations come into force on 6th April 2008.

(2) Subject to paragraph (3), they apply in relation to financial years beginning on or after 6th April 2008.

(3) The requirement for disclosure in paragraph 4 of Schedule 8 to these Regulations (directors' remuneration report: disclosure relating to consideration of conditions in company and group) applies in relation to financial years beginning on or after 6th April 2009.

(4) These Regulations apply to companies other than those which are subject to the small companies regime under Part 15 of the 2006 Act.

## PART 2
## FORM AND CONTENT OF ACCOUNTS

**Companies Act individual accounts (companies other than banking and insurance companies)**

**3.** (1) Subject to regulation 4, the directors of a company—

(a) for which they are preparing Companies Act individual accounts under section 396 of the 2006 Act (Companies Act: individual accounts), and

(b) which is not a banking company or an insurance company, must comply with the provisions of Schedule 1 to these Regulations as to the form and content of the balance sheet and profit and loss account, and additional information to be provided by way of notes to the accounts.

(2) The profit and loss account of a company that falls within section 408 of the 2006 Act (individual profit and loss account where group accounts prepared) need not contain the information specified in paragraphs 65 to 69 of Schedule 1 to these Regulations (information supplementing the profit and loss account).

### Medium-sized companies: exemptions for Companies Act individual accounts

**4.** (1) This regulation applies to a company—

(a) which qualifies as medium-sized in relation to a financial year under section 465 of the 2006 Act[69], and

(b) the directors of which are preparing Companies Act individual accounts under section 396 of that Act for that year.

(2) The individual accounts for the year need not comply with the following provisions of Schedule 1 to these Regulations—

(a) paragraph 45 (disclosure with respect to compliance with accounting standards), and

(b) paragraph 72 (related party transactions).

(3) The directors of the company may deliver to the registrar of companies a copy of the accounts for the year—

(a) which includes a profit and loss account in which the following items listed in the profit and loss account formats set out in Schedule 1 are combined as one item—

items 2, 3 and 6 in format 1;

items 2 to 5 in format 2;

items A.1 and B.2 in format 3;

items A.1, A.2 and B.2 to B.4 in format 4;

(b) which does not contain the information required by paragraph 68 of Schedule 1 (particulars of turnover).

### Companies Act individual accounts: banking companies

**5.** (1) The directors of a company—

(a) for which they are preparing Companies Act individual accounts under section 396 of the 2006 Act, and

(b) which is a banking company, must comply with the provisions of Schedule 2 to these Regulations as to the form and content of the balance sheet and profit and loss account, and additional information to be provided by way of notes to the accounts.

(2) The profit and loss account of a banking company that falls within section 408 of the 2006 Act (individual profit and loss account where group accounts prepared) need not contain the information specified in paragraphs 85 to 91 of Schedule 2 to these Regulations (information supplementing the profit and loss account).

(3) Accounts prepared in accordance with this regulation must contain a statement that they are prepared in accordance with the provisions of these Regulations relating to banking companies.

### Companies Act individual accounts: insurance companies

**6.** (1) The directors of a company—

(a) for which they are preparing Companies Act individual accounts under section 396 of the 2006 Act, and

(b) which is an insurance company, must comply with the provisions of Schedule 3 to these Regulations as to the form and content of the balance sheet and profit and loss account, and additional information to be provided by way of notes to the accounts.

(2) The profit and loss account of a company that falls within section 408 of the 2006 Act (individual profit and loss account where group accounts prepared)[70] need not contain the information specified in paragraphs 83 to 89 of Schedule 3 to these Regulations (information supplementing the profit and loss account).

(3) Accounts prepared in accordance with this regulation must contain a statement that they are prepared in accordance with the provisions of these Regulations relating to insurance companies.

### Information about related undertakings (Companies Act or IAS individual or group accounts)

**7.** (1) Companies Act or IAS individual or group accounts must comply with the provisions of Schedule 4 to these Regulations as to information about related undertakings to be given in notes to the company's accounts.

(2) In Schedule 4—

Part 1 contains provisions applying to all companies

---

[69] Section 465 is amended by regulation 4(1) of SI 2008/393.

[70] Section 408 is amended by regulation 9 of SI 2008/393.

Part 2 contains provisions applying only to companies not required to prepare group accounts

Part 3 contains provisions applying only to companies required to prepare group accounts

Part 4 contains additional disclosures for banking companies and groups

Part 5 contains interpretative provisions.

(3) Information otherwise required to be given by Schedule 4 need not be disclosed with respect to an undertaking that—

(a) is established under the law of a country outside the United Kingdom, or

(b) carries on business outside the United Kingdom, if the conditions specified in section 409(4) of the 2006 Act are met (see section 409(5) of the 2006 Act for disclosure required where advantage taken of this exemption). This paragraph does not apply in relation to the information otherwise required by paragraph 3, 7 or 21 of Schedule 4.

### Information about directors' benefits: remuneration (Companies Act or IAS individual or group accounts: quoted and unquoted companies)

**8.** (1) Companies Act or IAS individual or group accounts must comply with the provisions of Schedule 5 to these Regulations as to information about directors' remuneration to be given in notes to the company's accounts.

(2) In Schedule 5—

Part 1 contains provisions applying to quoted and unquoted companies, Part 2 contains provisions applying only to unquoted companies, and Part 3 contains supplementary provisions.

### Companies Act group accounts

**9.** (1) Subject to paragraphs (2) and (3), where the directors of a parent company prepare Companies Act group accounts under section 403 of the 2006 Act (group accounts: applicable accounting framework), those accounts must comply with the provisions of Part 1 of Schedule 6 to these Regulations as to the form and content of the consolidated balance sheet and consolidated profit and loss account, and additional information to be provided by way of notes to the accounts.

(2) The directors of the parent company of a banking group preparing Companies Act group accounts must do so in accordance with the provisions of Part 1 of Schedule 6 as modified by Part 2 of that Schedule.

(3) The directors of the parent company of an insurance group preparing Companies Act group accounts must do so in accordance with the provisions of Part 1 of Schedule 6 as modified by Part 3 of that Schedule.

(4) Accounts prepared in accordance with paragraph (2) or (3) must contain a statement that they are prepared in accordance with the provisions of these Regulations relating to banking groups or to insurance groups, as the case may be.

## PART 3
## DIRECTORS' REPORT

### Directors' report

**10.** (1) The report which the directors of a company are required to prepare under section 415 of the 2006 Act (duty to prepare directors' report) must disclose the matters specified in Schedule 7 to these Regulations.

(2) In Schedule 7—

Part 1 relates to matters of a general nature, including changes in asset values and contributions for political and charitable purposes,

Part 2 relates to the acquisition by a company of its own shares or a charge on them,

Part 3 relates to the employment, training and advancement of disabled persons,

Part 4 relates to the involvement of employees in the affairs, policy and performance of the company, and

Part 5 relates to the company's policy and practice on the payment of creditors.

## PART 4
## DIRECTORS' REMUNERATION REPORT

### Directors' remuneration report (quoted companies)

**11.** (1) The remuneration report which the directors of a quoted company are required to prepare under section 420 of the 2006 Act (duty to prepare directors' remuneration report) must contain the information specified in Schedule 8 to these Regulations, and must comply with any requirement of that Schedule as to how information is to be set out in the report.

(2) In Schedule 8—

Part 1 is introductory,

Part 2 relates to information about remuneration committees, performance related remuneration, consideration of conditions elsewhere in company and group and liabilities in respect of directors' contracts,

Part 3 relates to detailed information about directors' remuneration (information included under Part 3 is required to be reported on by the auditor (see subsection (3)), and

Part 4 contains interpretative and supplementary provisions.

(3) For the purposes of section 497 in Part 16 of the 2006 Act (auditor's report on auditable part of directors' remuneration report), 'the auditable part' of a directors' remuneration report is the part containing the information required by Part 3 of Schedule 8 to these Regulations.

## PART 5
## INTERPRETATION

### Definition of 'provisions'

**12.** Schedule 9 to these Regulations defines 'provisions' for the purposes of these Regulations and for the purposes of—

(a) section 677(3)(a) (Companies Act accounts: relevant provisions for purposes of financial assistance) in Part 18 of the 2006 Act,

(b) section 712(2)(b)(i) (Companies Act accounts: relevant provisions to determine available profits for redemption or purchase by private company out of capital) in that Part, [...][a]

(c) sections 831(3)(a) (Companies Act accounts: net asset restriction on public company distributions), 832(4)(a) (Companies Act accounts: investment companies distributions) and 836(1)(b)(i) (Companies Act accounts: relevant provisions for distribution purposes) in Part 23 of that Act [, and

(d) section 841(2)(a) (Companies Act accounts: provisions to be treated as realised losses) in that Part][b].

AMENDMENTS AND NOTES

[a] Revoked by the Companies Act 2006 (Accounts, Reports and Audit) Regulations 2009, S.I. 2009/1581, reg 12(2)(a), in relation to financial years beginning on or after 6 April 2008 which have not ended before 27 June 2009.

[b] Inserted by the Companies Act 2006 (Accounts, Reports and Audit) Regulations 2009, S.I. 2009/1581, reg 12(2)(b), in relation to financial years beginning on or after 6 April 2008 which have not ended before 27 June 2009.

### General interpretation

**13.** Schedule 10 to these Regulations contains general definitions for the purposes of these Regulations.

## SCHEDULE 1            Regulation 3(1)
## COMPANIES ACT INDIVIDUAL ACCOUNTS: COMPANIES WHICH ARE NOT BANKING OR INSURANCE COMPANIES

## PART 1
## GENERAL RULES AND FORMATS

## SECTION A
## GENERAL RULES

**1.** (1) Subject to the following provisions of this Schedule—

(a) every balance sheet of a company must show the items listed in either of the balance sheet formats in Section B of this Part, and

(b) every profit and loss account must show the items listed in any one of the profit and loss account formats in Section B.

(2) References in this Schedule to the items listed in any of the formats in Section B are to those items read together with any of the notes following the formats which apply to those items.

(3) The items must be shown in the order and under the headings and sub-headings given in the particular format used, but—

      (a)  the notes to the formats may permit alternative positions for any particular items, and

      (b)  the heading or sub-heading for any item does not have to be distinguished by any letter or number assigned to that item in the format used.

**2.**  (1)  Where in accordance with paragraph 1 a company's balance sheet or profit and loss account for any financial year has been prepared by reference to one of the formats in Section B, the company's directors must use the same format in preparing Companies Act individual accounts for subsequent financial years, unless in their opinion there are special reasons for a change.

     (2)  Particulars of any such change must be given in a note to the accounts in which the new format is first used, and the reasons for the change must be explained.

**3.**  (1)  Any item required to be shown in a company's balance sheet or profit and loss account may be shown in greater detail than required by the particular format used.

     (2)  The balance sheet or profit and loss account may include an item representing or covering the amount of any asset or liability, income or expenditure not otherwise covered by any of the items listed in the format used, save that none of the following may be treated as assets in any balance sheet—

      (a)  preliminary expenses,

      (b)  expenses of, and commission on, any issue of shares or debentures, and

      (c)  costs of research.

**4.**  (1)  Where the special nature of the company's business requires it, the company's directors must adapt the arrangement, headings and sub-headings otherwise required in respect of items given an Arabic number in the balance sheet or profit and loss account format used.

     (2)  The directors may combine items to which Arabic numbers are given in any of the formats in Section B if—

      (a)  their individual amounts are not material to assessing the state of affairs or profit or loss of the company for the financial year in question, or

      (b)  the combination facilitates that assessment.

     (3)  Where sub-paragraph (2)(b) applies, the individual amounts of any items which have been combined must be disclosed in a note to the accounts.

**5.**  (1)  Subject to sub-paragraph (2), the directors must not include a heading or sub-heading corresponding to an item in the balance sheet or profit and loss account format used if there is no amount to be shown for that item for the financial year to which the balance sheet or profit and loss account relates.

     (2)  Where an amount can be shown for the item in question for the immediately preceding financial year that amount must be shown under the heading or sub-heading required by the format for that item.

**6.**  Every profit and loss account must show the amount of a company's profit or loss on ordinary activities before taxation.

**7.**  (1)  For every item shown in the balance sheet or profit and loss account the corresponding amount for the immediately preceding financial year must also be shown.

     (2)  Where that corresponding amount is not comparable with the amount to be shown for the item in question in respect of the financial year to which the balance sheet or profit and loss account relates, the former amount may be adjusted, and particulars of the non-comparability and of any adjustment must be disclosed in a note to the accounts.

**8.**  Amounts in respect of items representing assets or income may not be set off against amounts in respect of items representing liabilities or expenditure (as the case may be), or vice versa.

**9.**  The company's directors must, in determining how amounts are presented within items in the profit and loss account and balance sheet, have regard to the substance of the reported transaction or arrangement, in accordance with generally accepted accounting principles or practice.

SECTION B

THE REQUIRED FORMATS FOR ACCOUNTS[71]

**BALANCE SHEET FORMATS**

*Format 1*

A.   Called up share capital not paid *(1)*

B.   Fixed assets

    I.   Intangible assets

       1.  Development costs

---

[71]  A number in brackets following any item is a reference to the note of that number in the notes following the formats.

      2. Concessions, patents, licences, trade marks and similar rights and assets *(2)*
      3. Goodwill *(3)*
      4. Payments on account
   II. Tangible assets
      1. Land and buildings
      2. Plant and machinery
      3. Fixtures, fittings, tools and equipment
      4. Payments on account and assets in course of construction
   III. Investments
      1. Shares in group undertakings
      2. Loans to group undertakings
      3. Participating interests
      4. Loans to undertakings in which the company has a participating interest
      5. Other investments other than loans
      6. Other loans
      7. Own shares *(4)*
C. Current assets
   I. Stocks
      1. Raw materials and consumables
      2. Work in progress
      3. Finished goods and goods for resale
      4. Payments on account
   II. Debtors *(5)*
      1. Trade debtors
      2. Amounts owed by group undertakings
      3. Amounts owed by undertakings in which the company has a participating interest
      4. Other debtors
      5. Called up share capital not paid *(1)*
      6. Prepayments and accrued income *(6)*
   III. Investments
      1. Shares in group undertakings
      2. Own shares *(4)*
      3. Other investments
   IV. Cash at bank and in hand
D. Prepayments and accrued income *(6)*
E. Creditors: amounts falling due within one year
      1. Debenture loans *(7)*
      2. Bank loans and overdrafts
      3. Payments received on account *(8)*
      4. Trade creditors
      5. Bills of exchange payable
      6. Amounts owed to group undertakings
      7. Amounts owed to undertakings in which the company has a participating interest
      8. Other creditors including taxation and social security *(9)*
      9. Accruals and deferred income *(10)*
F. Net current assets (liabilities) *(11)*
G. Total assets less current liabilities
H. Creditors: amounts falling due after more than one year
      1. Debenture loans *(7)*
      2. Bank loans and overdrafts
      3. Payments received on account *(8)*
      4. Trade creditors
      5. Bills of exchange payable
      6. Amounts owed to group undertakings
      7. Amounts owed to undertakings in which the company has a participating interest
      8. Other creditors including taxation and social security *(9)*
      9. Accruals and deferred income *(10)*
I. Provisions for liabilities
      1. Pensions and similar obligations
      2. Taxation, including deferred taxation
      3. Other provisions
J. Accruals and deferred income *(10)*
K. Capital and reserves
   I. Called up share capital *(12)*
   II. Share premium account
   III. Revaluation reserve
   IV. Other reserves

        1.  Capital redemption reserve
        2.  Reserve for own shares
        3.  Reserves provided for by the articles of association
        4.  Other reserves
    V.  Profit and loss account

# BALANCE SHEET FORMATS

*Format 2*

ASSETS

A.  Called up share capital not paid *(1)*

B.  Fixed assets
    I.   Intangible assets
        1.  Development costs
        2.  Concessions, patents, licences, trade marks and similar rights and assets *(2)*
        3.  Goodwill *(3)*
        4.  Payments on account
    II.  Tangible assets
        1.  Land and buildings
        2.  Plant and machinery
        3.  Fixtures, fittings, tools and equipment
        4.  Payments on account and assets in course of construction
    III.  Investments
        1.  Shares in group undertakings
        2.  Loans to group undertakings
        3.  Participating interests
        4.  Loans to undertakings in which the company has a participating interest
        5.  Other investments other than loans
        6.  Other loans
        7.  Own shares *(4)*

C.  Current assets
    I.   Stocks
        1.  Raw materials and consumables
        2.  Work in progress
        3.  Finished goods and goods for resale
        4.  Payments on account
    II.  Debtors *(5)*
        1.  Trade debtors
        2.  Amounts owed by group undertakings
        3.  Amounts owed by undertakings in which the company has a participating interest
        4.  Other debtors
        5.  Called up share capital not paid *(1)*
        6.  Prepayments and accrued income *(6)*
    III.  Investments
        1.  Shares in group undertakings
        2.  Own shares *(4)*
        3.  Other investments
    IV.  Cash at bank and in hand

D.  Prepayments and accrued income *(6)*

LIABILITIES

A.  Capital and reserves
    I.   Called up share capital *(12)*
    II.  Share premium account
    III.  Revaluation reserve
    IV.  Other reserves
        1.  Capital redemption reserve
        2.  Reserve for own shares
        3.  Reserves provided for by the articles of association
        4.  Other reserves
    V.  Profit and loss account

B.  Provisions for liabilities
    1.  Pensions and similar obligations
    2.  Taxation, including deferred taxation

      3.   Other provisions

C.  Creditors *(13)*

      1.   Debenture loans *(7)*

      2.   Bank loans and overdrafts

      3.   Payments received on account *(8)*

      4.   Trade creditors

      5.   Bills of exchange payable

      6.   Amounts owed to group undertakings

      7.   Amounts owed to undertakings in which the company has a participating interest

      8.   Other creditors including taxation and social security *(9)*

      9.   Accruals and deferred income *(10)*

D.  Accruals and deferred income *(10)*

## NOTES ON THE BALANCE SHEET FORMATS

*(1) Called up share capital not paid*

(Formats 1 and 2, items A and C.II.5.)

This item may be shown in either of the two positions given in formats 1 and 2.

*(2) Concessions, patents, licences, trade marks and similar rights and assets*

(Formats 1 and 2, item B.I.2.)

Amounts in respect of assets are only to be included in a company's balance sheet under this item if either—

(a)  the assets were acquired for valuable consideration and are not required to be shown under goodwill, or

(b)  the assets in question were created by the company itself.

*(3) Goodwill*

(Formats 1 and 2, item B.I.3.)

Amounts representing goodwill are only to be included to the extent that the goodwill was acquired for valuable consideration.

*(4) Own shares*

(Formats 1 and 2, items B.III.7 and C.III.2.)

The nominal value of the shares held must be shown separately.

*(5) Debtors*

(Formats 1 and 2, items C.II.1 to 6.)

The amount falling due after more than one year must be shown separately for each item included under debtors.

*(6) Prepayments and accrued income*

(Formats 1 and 2, items C.II.6 and D.)

This item may be shown in either of the two positions given in formats 1 and 2.

*(7) Debenture loans*

(Format 1, items E.1 and H.1 and format 2, item C.1.)

The amount of any convertible loans must be shown separately.

*(8) Payments received on account*

(Format 1, items E.3 and H.3 and format 2, item C.3.)

Payments received on account of orders must be shown for each of these items in so far as they are not shown as deductions from stocks.

*(9) Other creditors including taxation and social security*

(Format 1, items E.8 and H.8 and format 2, item C.8.)

The amount for creditors in respect of taxation and social security must be shown separately from the amount for other creditors.

*(10) Accruals and deferred income*

(Format 1, items E.9, H.9 and J and format 2, items C.9 and D.)

The two positions given for this item in format 1 at E.9 and H.9 are an alternative to the position at J, but if the item is not shown in a position corresponding to that at J it may be shown in either or both of the other two positions (as the case may require).

The two positions given for this item in format 2 are alternatives.

*(11) Net current assets (liabilities)*

(Format 1, item F.)

In determining the amount to be shown for this item any amounts shown under 'prepayments and accrued income' must be taken into account wherever shown.

*(12) Called up share capital*

(Format 1, item K.I and format 2, item A.I.)

The amount of allotted share capital and the amount of called up share capital which has been paid up must be shown separately.

*(13) Creditors*

(Format 2, items C.1 to 9.)

Amounts falling due within one year and after one year must be shown separately for each of these items and for the aggregate of all of these items.

## PROFIT AND LOSS ACCOUNT FORMATS[72]

*Format 1*

(see note (17) below)

1. Turnover
2. Cost of sales *(14)*
3. Gross profit or loss
4. Distribution costs *(14)*
5. Administrative expenses *(14)*
6. Other operating income
7. Income from shares in group undertakings
8. Income from participating interests
9. Income from other fixed asset investments *(15)*
10. Other interest receivable and similar income *(15)*
11. Amounts written off investments
12. Interest payable and similar charges *(16)*
13. Tax on profit or loss on ordinary activities
14. Profit or loss on ordinary activities after taxation
15. Extraordinary income
16. Extraordinary charges
17. Extraordinary profit or loss
18. Tax on extraordinary profit or loss
19. Other taxes not shown under the above items
20. Profit or loss for the financial year

## PROFIT AND LOSS ACCOUNT FORMATS[73]

*Format 2*

1. Turnover
2. Change in stocks of finished goods and in work in progress
3. Own work capitalised
4. Other operating income
5. (a) Raw materials and consumables
   (b) Other external charges
6. Staff costs
   (a) wages and salaries
   (b) social security costs
   (c) other pension costs
7. (a) Depreciation and other amounts written off tangible and intangible fixed assets
   (b) Exceptional amounts written off current assets
8. Other operating charges
9. Income from shares in group undertakings
10. Income from participating interests
11. Income from other fixed asset investments *(15)*
12. Other interest receivable and similar income *(15)*
13. Amounts written off investments
14. Interest payable and similar charges *(16)*
15. Tax on profit or loss on ordinary activities
16. Profit or loss on ordinary activities after taxation
17. Extraordinary income

---

[72] See regulation 4(3)(a) for exemption for medium-sized companies in accounts delivered to registrar of companies.

[73] See regulation 4(3)(a) for exemption for medium-sized companies in accounts delivered to registrar of companies.

18. Extraordinary charges
19. Extraordinary profit or loss
20. Tax on extraordinary profit or loss
21. Other taxes not shown under the above items
22. Profit or loss for the financial year

## PROFIT AND LOSS ACCOUNT FORMATS[74]

*Format 3*

### (see note (17) below)

A. Charges
1. Cost of sales *(14)*
2. Distribution costs *(14)*
3. Administrative expenses *(14)*
4. Amounts written off investments
5. Interest payable and similar charges *(16)*
6. Tax on profit or loss on ordinary activities
7. Profit or loss on ordinary activities after taxation
8. Extraordinary charges
9. Tax on extraordinary profit or loss
10. Other taxes not shown under the above items
11. Profit or loss for the financial year
B. Income
1. Turnover
2. Other operating income
3. Income from shares in group undertakings
4. Income from participating interests
5. Income from other fixed asset investments *(15)*
6. Other interest receivable and similar income *(15)*
7. Profit or loss on ordinary activities after taxation
8. Extraordinary income
9. Profit or loss for the financial year

## PROFIT AND LOSS ACCOUNT FORMATS[75]

*Format 4*

A. Charges
　1. Reduction in stocks of finished goods and in work in progress
　2. (a) Raw materials and consumables
　　 (b) Other external charges
　3. Staff costs
　　 (a) wages and salaries
　　 (b) social security costs
　　 (c) other pension costs
　4.
　　 (a) Depreciation and other amounts written off tangible and intangible fixed assets
　　 (b) Exceptional amounts written off current assets
　5. Other operating charges
　6. Amounts written off investments
　7. Interest payable and similar charges *(16)*
　8. Tax on profit or loss on ordinary activities
　9. Profit or loss on ordinary activities after taxation
　10. Extraordinary charges
　11. Tax on extraordinary profit or loss
　12. Other taxes not shown under the above items
　13. Profit or loss for the financial year
B. Income

---

[74] See regulation 4(3)(a) for exemption for medium-sized companies in accounts delivered to registrar of companies.

[75] See regulation 4(3)(a) for exemption for medium-sized companies in accounts delivered to registrar of companies.

1. Turnover
2. Increase in stocks of finished goods and in work in progress
3. Own work capitalised
4. Other operating income
5. Income from shares in group undertakings
6. Income from participating interests
7. Income from other fixed asset investments *(15)*
8. Other interest receivable and similar income *(15)*
9. Profit or loss on ordinary activities after taxation
10. Extraordinary income
11. Profit or loss for the financial year

## NOTES ON THE PROFIT AND LOSS ACCOUNT FORMATS

*(14)Cost of sales: distribution costs: administrative expenses*
(Format 1, items 2, 4 and 5 and format 3, items A.1, 2 and 3.)
These items must be stated after taking into account any necessary provisions for depreciation or diminution in value of assets.

*(15)Income from other fixed asset investments: other interest receivable and similar income*
(Format 1, items 9 and 10; format 2, items 11 and 12; format 3, items B.5 and 6 and format 4, items B.7 and 8.)
Income and interest derived from group undertakings must be shown separately from income and interest derived from other sources.

*(16)Interest payable and similar charges*
(Format 1, item 12; format 2, item 14; format 3, item A.5 and format 4, item A.7.)
The amount payable to group undertakings must be shown separately.

*(17)Formats 1 and 3*
The amount of any provisions for depreciation and diminution in value of tangible and intangible fixed assets falling to be shown under items 7(a) and A.4(a) respectively in formats 2 and 4 must be disclosed in a note to the accounts in any case where the profit and loss account is prepared using format 1 or format 3.

PART 2
ACCOUNTING PRINCIPLES AND RULES

SECTION A
ACCOUNTING PRINCIPLES

**Preliminary**
**10.** (1) The amounts to be included in respect of all items shown in a company's accounts must be determined in accordance with the principles set out in this Section.
(2) But if it appears to the company's directors that there are special reasons for departing from any of those principles in preparing the company's accounts in respect of any financial year they may do so, in which case particulars of the departure, the reasons for it and its effect must be given in a note to the accounts.

**Accounting principles**
**11.** The company is presumed to be carrying on business as a going concern.
**12.** Accounting policies must be applied consistently within the same accounts and from one financial year to the next.
**13.** The amount of any item must be determined on a prudent basis, and in particular—
(a) only profits realised at the balance sheet date are to be included in the profit and loss account, and
(b) all liabilities which have arisen in respect of the financial year to which the accounts relate or a previous financial year must be taken into account, including those which only become apparent between the balance sheet date and the date on which it is signed on behalf of the board of directors in accordance with section 414 of the 2006 Act (approval and signing of accounts).
**14.** All income and charges relating to the financial year to which the accounts relate must be taken into account, without regard to the date of receipt or payment.
**15.** In determining the aggregate amount of any item, the amount of each individual asset or liability that falls to be taken into account must be determined separately.

## SECTION B
## HISTORICAL COST ACCOUNTING RULES

### Preliminary

**16.** Subject to Sections C and D of this Part of this Schedule, the amounts to be included in respect of all items shown in a company's accounts must be determined in accordance with the rules set out in this Section.

*Fixed assets*

### General rules

**17.** (1) The amount to be included in respect of any fixed asset must be its purchase price or production cost.

(2) This is subject to any provision for depreciation or diminution in value made in accordance with paragraphs 18 to 20.

### Rules for depreciation and diminution in value

**18.** In the case of any fixed asset which has a limited useful economic life, the amount of?—

(a) its purchase price or production cost, or

(b) where it is estimated that any such asset will have a residual value at the end of the period of its useful economic life, its purchase price or production cost less that estimated residual value,

must be reduced by provisions for depreciation calculated to write off that amount systematically over the period of the asset's useful economic life.

**19.** (1) Where a fixed asset investment falling to be included under item B.III of either of the balance sheet formats set out in Part 1 of this Schedule has diminished in value, provisions for diminution in value may be made in respect of it and the amount to be included in respect of it may be reduced accordingly.

(2) Provisions for diminution in value must be made in respect of any fixed asset which has diminished in value if the reduction in its value is expected to be permanent (whether its useful economic life is limited or not), and the amount to be included in respect of it must be reduced accordingly.

(3) Any provisions made under sub-paragraph (1) or (2) which are not shown in the profit and loss account must be disclosed (either separately or in aggregate) in a note to the accounts.

**20.** (1) Where the reasons for which any provision was made in accordance with paragraph 19 have ceased to apply to any extent, that provision must be written back to the extent that it is no longer necessary.

(2) Any amounts written back in accordance with sub-paragraph (1) which are not shown in the profit and loss account must be disclosed (either separately or in aggregate) in a note to the accounts.

### Development costs

**21.** (1) Notwithstanding that an item in respect of 'development costs' is included under 'fixed assets' in the balance sheet formats set out in Part 1 of this Schedule, an amount may only be included in a company's balance sheet in respect of development costs in special circumstances.

(2) If any amount is included in a company's balance sheet in respect of development costs the following information must be given in a note to the accounts—

(a) the period over which the amount of those costs originally capitalised is being or is to be written off, and

(b) the reasons for capitalising the development costs in question.

### Goodwill

**22.** (1) The application of paragraphs 17 to 20 in relation to goodwill (in any case where goodwill is treated as an asset) is subject to the following.

(2) Subject to sub-paragraph (3), the amount of the consideration for any goodwill acquired by a company must be reduced by provisions for depreciation calculated to write off that amount systematically over a period chosen by the directors of the company.

(3) The period chosen must not exceed the useful economic life of the goodwill in question.

(4) In any case where any goodwill acquired by a company is shown or included as an asset in the company's balance sheet there must be disclosed in a note to the accounts—

(a) the period chosen for writing off the consideration for that goodwill, and

(b) the reasons for choosing that period.

**Current assets**

**23.** Subject to paragraph 24, the amount to be included in respect of any current asset must be its purchase price or production cost.

**24.** (1) If the net realisable value of any current asset is lower than its purchase price or production cost, the amount to be included in respect of that asset must be the net realisable value.

(2) Where the reasons for which any provision for diminution in value was made in accordance with sub-paragraph (1) have ceased to apply to any extent, that provision must be written back to the extent that it is no longer necessary.

*Miscellaneous and supplementary provisions*

**Excess of money owed over value received as an asset item**

**25.** (1) Where the amount repayable on any debt owed by a company is greater than the value of the consideration received in the transaction giving rise to the debt, the amount of the difference may be treated as an asset.

(2) Where any such amount is so treated—

(a) it must be written off by reasonable amounts each year and must be completely written off before repayment of the debt, and

(b) if the current amount is not shown as a separate item in the company's balance sheet, it must be disclosed in a note to the accounts.

**Assets included at a fixed amount**

**26.** (1) Subject to sub-paragraph (2), assets which fall to be included—

(a) amongst the fixed assets of a company under the item 'tangible assets', or

(b) amongst the current assets of a company under the item 'raw materials and consumables',

may be included at a fixed quantity and value.

(2) Sub-paragraph (1) applies to assets of a kind which are constantly being replaced where—

(a) their overall value is not material to assessing the company's state of affairs, and

(b) their quantity, value and composition are not subject to material variation.

**Determination of purchase price or production cost**

**27.** (1) The purchase price of an asset is to be determined by adding to the actual price paid any expenses incidental to its acquisition.

(2) The production cost of an asset is to be determined by adding to the purchase price of the raw materials and consumables used the amount of the costs incurred by the company which are directly attributable to the production of that asset.

(3) In addition, there may be included in the production cost of an asset—

(a) a reasonable proportion of the costs incurred by the company which are only indirectly attributable to the production of that asset, but only to the extent that they relate to the period of production, and

(b) interest on capital borrowed to finance the production of that asset, to the extent that it accrues in respect of the period of production,

provided, however, in a case within paragraph (b), that the inclusion of the interest in determining the cost of that asset and the amount of the interest so included is disclosed in a note to the accounts.

(4) In the case of current assets distribution costs may not be included in production costs.

**28.** (1) The purchase price or production cost of—

(a) any assets which fall to be included under any item shown in a company's balance sheet under the general item 'stocks', and

(b) any assets which are fungible assets (including investments), may be determined by the application of any of the methods mentioned in sub-paragraph (2) in relation to any such assets of the same class, provided that the method chosen is one which appears to the directors to be appropriate in the circumstances of the company.

(2) Those methods are—

(a) the method known as 'first in, first out' (FIFO),

(b) the method known as 'last in, first out' (LIFO),

(c) a weighted average price, and

(d) any other method similar to any of the methods mentioned above.

(3) Where in the case of any company—

(a) the purchase price or production cost of assets falling to be included under any item shown in the company's balance sheet has been determined by the application of any method permitted by this paragraph, and

(b) the amount shown in respect of that item differs materially from the relevant alternative amount given below in this paragraph,

the amount of that difference must be disclosed in a note to the accounts.

(4) Subject to sub-paragraph (5), for the purposes of sub-paragraph (3)(b), the relevant alternative amount, in relation to any item shown in a company's balance sheet, is the amount which would have been shown in respect of that item if assets of any class included under that item at an amount determined by any method permitted by this paragraph had instead been included at their replacement cost as at the balance sheet date.

(5) The relevant alternative amount may be determined by reference to the most recent actual purchase price or production cost before the balance sheet date of assets of any class included under the item in question instead of by reference to their replacement cost as at that date, but only if the former appears to the directors of the company to constitute the more appropriate standard of comparison in the case of assets of that class.

### Substitution of original stated amount where price or cost unknown

**29.** (1) This paragraph applies where—
    (a) there is no record of the purchase price or production cost of any asset of a company or of any price, expenses or costs relevant for determining its purchase price or production cost in accordance with paragraph 27, or
    (b) any such record cannot be obtained without unreasonable expense or delay.

(2) In such a case, the purchase price or production cost of the asset must be taken, for the purposes of paragraphs 17 to 24, to be the value ascribed to it in the earliest available record of its value made on or after its acquisition or production by the company.

## SECTION C
## ALTERNATIVE ACCOUNTING RULES

### Preliminary

**30.** (1) The rules set out in Section B are referred to below in this Schedule as the historical cost accounting rules.

(2) Those rules, with the omission of paragraphs 16, 22 and 26 to 29, are referred to below in this Part of this Schedule as the depreciation rules; and references below in this Schedule to the historical cost accounting rules do not include the depreciation rules as they apply by virtue of paragraph 33.

**31.** Subject to paragraphs 33 to 35, the amounts to be included in respect of assets of any description mentioned in paragraph 32 may be determined on any basis so mentioned.

### Alternative accounting rules

**32.** (1) Intangible fixed assets, other than goodwill, may be included at their current cost.

(2) Tangible fixed assets may be included at a market value determined as at the date of their last valuation or at their current cost.

(3) Investments of any description falling to be included under item B III of either of the balance sheet formats set out in Part 1 of this Schedule may be included either—
    (a) at a market value determined as at the date of their last valuation, or
    (b) at a value determined on any basis which appears to the directors to be appropriate in the circumstances of the company.
    But in the latter case particulars of the method of valuation adopted and of the reasons for adopting it must be disclosed in a note to the accounts.

(4) Investments of any description falling to be included under item C III of either of the balance sheet formats set out in Part 1 of this Schedule may be included at their current cost.

(5) Stocks may be included at their current cost.

### Application of the depreciation rules

**33.** (1) Where the value of any asset of a company is determined on any basis mentioned in paragraph 32, that value must be, or (as the case may require) be the starting point for determining, the amount to be included in respect of that asset in the company's accounts, instead of its purchase price or production cost or any value previously so determined for that asset.
    The depreciation rules apply accordingly in relation to any such asset with the substitution for any reference to its purchase price or production cost of a reference to the value most recently determined for that asset on any basis mentioned in paragraph 32.

(2) The amount of any provision for depreciation required in the case of any fixed asset by paragraphs 18 to 20 as they apply by virtue of sub-paragraph (1) is referred to below in this paragraph as the adjusted amount, and the amount of any provision which would be required by any of those paragraphs in the case of that asset according to the historical cost accounting rules is referred to as the historical cost amount.

(3) Where sub-paragraph (1) applies in the case of any fixed asset the amount of any provision for depreciation in respect of that asset—

(a) included in any item shown in the profit and loss account in respect of amounts written off assets of the description in question, or

(b) taken into account in stating any item so shown which is required by note (14) of the notes on the profit and loss account formats set out in Part 1 of this Schedule to be stated after taking into account any necessary provision for depreciation or diminution in value of assets included under it,

may be the historical cost amount instead of the adjusted amount, provided that the amount of any difference between the two is shown separately in the profit and loss account or in a note to the accounts.

### Additional information to be provided in case of departure from historical cost accounting rules

**34.** (1) This paragraph applies where the amounts to be included in respect of assets covered by any items shown in a company's accounts have been determined on any basis mentioned in paragraph 32.

(2) The items affected and the basis of valuation adopted in determining the amounts of the assets in question in the case of each such item must be disclosed in a note to the accounts.

(3) In the case of each balance sheet item affected (except stocks) either—

(a) the comparable amounts determined according to the historical cost accounting rules, or

(b) the differences between those amounts and the corresponding amounts actually shown in the balance sheet in respect of that item, must be shown separately in the balance sheet or in a note to the accounts.

(4) In sub-paragraph (3), references in relation to any item to the comparable amounts determined as there mentioned are references to—

(a) the aggregate amount which would be required to be shown in respect of that item if the amounts to be included in respect of all the assets covered by that item were determined according to the historical cost accounting rules, and

(b) the aggregate amount of the cumulative provisions for depreciation or diminution in value which would be permitted or required in determining those amounts according to those rules.

### Revaluation reserve

**35.** (1) With respect to any determination of the value of an asset of a company on any basis mentioned in paragraph 32, the amount of any profit or loss arising from that determination (after allowing, where appropriate, for any provisions for depreciation or diminution in value made otherwise than by reference to the value so determined and any adjustments of any such provisions made in the light of that determination) must be credited or (as the case may be) debited to a separate reserve ('the revaluation reserve').

(2) The amount of the revaluation reserve must be shown in the company's balance sheet under a separate sub-heading in the position given for the item 'revaluation reserve' in format 1 or 2 of the balance sheet formats set out in Part 1 of this Schedule, but need not be shown under that name.

(3) An amount may be transferred—

(a) from the revaluation reserve—

(i)   to the profit and loss account, if the amount was previously charged to that account or represents realised profit, or

(ii)  on capitalisation,

(b) to or from the revaluation reserve in respect of the taxation relating to any profit or loss credited or debited to the reserve. The revaluation reserve must be reduced to the extent that the amounts transferred to it are no longer necessary for the purposes of the valuation method used.

(4) In sub-paragraph (3)(a)(ii) 'capitalisation', in relation to an amount standing to the credit of the revaluation reserve, means applying it in wholly or partly paying up unissued shares in the company to be allotted to members of the company as fully or partly paid shares.

(5) The revaluation reserve must not be reduced except as mentioned in this paragraph.

(6) The treatment for taxation purposes of amounts credited or debited to the revaluation reserve must be disclosed in a note to the accounts.

## SECTION D
## FAIR VALUE ACCOUNTING

### Inclusion of financial instruments at fair value

**36.** (1) Subject to sub-paragraphs (2) to (5), financial instruments (including derivatives) may be included at fair value.

(2) Sub-paragraph (1) does not apply to financial instruments that constitute liabilities unless—
   (a) they are held as part of a trading portfolio,
   (b) they are derivatives, or
   (c) they are financial instruments falling within sub-paragraph (4).

(3) Unless they are financial instruments falling within sub-paragraph (4), sub-paragraph (1) does not apply to—
   (a) financial instruments (other than derivatives) held to maturity,
   (b) loans and receivables originated by the company and not held for trading purposes,
   (c) interests in subsidiary undertakings, associated undertakings and joint ventures,
   (d) equity instruments issued by the company,
   (e) contracts for contingent consideration in a business combination, or
   (f) other financial instruments with such special characteristics that the instruments, according to generally accepted accounting principles or practice, should be accounted for differently from other financial instruments.

(4) Financial instruments that, under international accounting standards adopted by the European Commission on or before 5th September 2006 in accordance with the IAS Regulation, may be included in accounts at fair value, may be so included, provided that the disclosures required by such accounting standards are made.

(5) If the fair value of a financial instrument cannot be determined reliably in accordance with paragraph 37, sub-paragraph (1) does not apply to that financial instrument.

(6) In this paragraph—
   'associated undertaking' has the meaning given by paragraph 19 of Schedule 6 to these Regulations;
   'joint venture' has the meaning given by paragraph 18 of that Schedule.

### Determination of fair value

**37.** (1) The fair value of a financial instrument is its value determined in accordance with this paragraph.

(2) If a reliable market can readily be identified for the financial instrument, its fair value is determined by reference to its market value.

(3) If a reliable market cannot readily be identified for the financial instrument but can be identified for its components or for a similar instrument, its fair value is determined by reference to the market value of its components or of the similar instrument.

(4) If neither sub-paragraph (2) nor (3) applies, the fair value of the financial instrument is a value resulting from generally accepted valuation models and techniques.

(5) Any valuation models and techniques used for the purposes of sub-paragraph (4) must ensure a reasonable approximation of the market value.

### Hedged items

**38.** A company may include any assets and liabilities, or identified portions of such assets or liabilities, that qualify as hedged items under a fair value hedge accounting system at the amount required under that system.

### Other assets that may be included at fair value

**39.** (1) This paragraph applies to—
   (a) investment property, and
   (b) living animals and plants,
      that, under international accounting standards, may be included in accounts at fair value.

(2) Such investment property and such living animals and plants may be included at fair value, provided that all such investment property or, as the case may be, all such living animals and plants are so included where their fair value can reliably be determined.

(3) In this paragraph, 'fair value' means fair value determined in accordance with relevant international accounting standards.

### Accounting for changes in value

**40.** (1) This paragraph applies where a financial instrument is valued in accordance with paragraph 36 or 38 or an asset is valued in accordance with paragraph 39.

(2) Notwithstanding paragraph 13 in this Part of this Schedule, and subject to sub-paragraphs (3) and (4), a change in the value of the financial instrument or of the investment property or living animal or plant must be included in the profit and loss account.

(3) Where—
   (a) the financial instrument accounted for is a hedging instrument under a hedge account-
       ing system that allows some or all of the change in value not to be shown in the profit and
       loss account, or
   (b) the change in value relates to an exchange difference arising on a monetary item that
       forms part of a company's net investment in a foreign entity,
       the amount of the change in value must be credited to or (as the case may be) debited
       from a separate reserve ('the fair value reserve').
(4) Where the instrument accounted for—
   (a) is an available for sale financial asset, and
   (b) is not a derivative,
       the change in value may be credited to or (as the case may be) debited from the fair value
       reserve.

### The fair value reserve

**41.** (1) The fair value reserve must be adjusted to the extent that the amounts shown in it are no
           longer necessary for the purposes of paragraph 40(3) or (4).
      (2) The treatment for taxation purposes of amounts credited or debited to the fair value reserve
           must be disclosed in a note to the accounts.

## PART 3
## NOTES TO THE ACCOUNTS

### Preliminary

**42.** Any information required in the case of any company by the following provisions of this Part of
       this Schedule must (if not given in the company's accounts) be given by way of a note to the
       accounts.

*General*

### Reserves and dividends

**43.** There must be stated—
   (a) any amount set aside or proposed to be set aside to, or withdrawn or proposed to be
       withdrawn from, reserves,
   (b) the aggregate amount of dividends paid in the financial year (other than those for which a
       liability existed at the immediately preceding balance sheet date),
   (c) the aggregate amount of dividends that the company is liable to pay at the balance sheet
       date, and
   (d) the aggregate amount of dividends that are proposed before the date of approval of the
       accounts, and not otherwise disclosed under sub-paragraph (b) or (c).

### Disclosure of accounting policies

**44.** The accounting policies adopted by the company in determining the amounts to be included in
       respect of items shown in the balance sheet and in determining the profit or loss of the company
       must be stated (including such policies with respect to the depreciation and diminution in value
       of assets).

**45.** It must be stated whether the accounts have been prepared in accordance with applicable
       accounting standards and particulars of any material departure from those standards and the
       reasons for it must be given (see regulation 4(2) for exemption for medium-sized companies).

### Information supplementing the balance sheet

**46.** Paragraphs 47 to 64 require information which either supplements the information given with
       respect to any particular items shown in the balance sheet or is otherwise relevant to assessing the
       company's state of affairs in the light of the information so given.

### Share capital and debentures

**47.** (1) The following information must be given with respect to the company's share capital—
      (a) where shares of more than one class have been allotted, the number and aggregate
          nominal value of shares of each class allotted, and
      (b) where shares are held as treasury shares, the number and aggregate nominal value of the
          treasury shares and, where shares of more than one class have been allotted, the number
          and aggregate nominal value of the shares of each class held as treasury shares.
      (2) In the case of any part of the allotted share capital that consists of redeemable shares, the
          following information must be given—
      (a) the earliest and latest dates on which the company has power to redeem those shares,

    (b) whether those shares must be redeemed in any event or are liable to be redeemed at the option of the company or of the shareholder, and

    (c) whether any (and, if so, what) premium is payable on redemption.

**48.** If the company has allotted any shares during the financial year, the following information must be given—

    (a) the classes of shares allotted, and

    (b) as respects each class of shares, the number allotted, their aggregate nominal value, and the consideration received by the company for the allotment.

**49.** (1) With respect to any contingent right to the allotment of shares in the company the following particulars must be given—

    (a) the number, description and amount of the shares in relation to which the right is exercisable,

    (b) the period during which it is exercisable, and

    (c) the price to be paid for the shares allotted.

  (2) In sub-paragraph (1) 'contingent right to the allotment of shares' means any option to subscribe for shares and any other right to require the allotment of shares to any person whether arising on the conversion into shares of securities of any other description or otherwise.

**50.** (1) If the company has issued any debentures during the financial year to which the accounts relate, the following information must be given—

    (a) the classes of debentures issued, and

    (b) as respects each class of debentures, the amount issued and the consideration received by the company for the issue.

  (2) Where any of the company's debentures are held by a nominee of or trustee for the company, the nominal amount of the debentures and the amount at which they are stated in the accounting records kept by the company in accordance with section 386 of the 2006 Act (duty to keep accounting records) must be stated.

**Fixed assets**

**51.** (1) In respect of each item which is or would but for paragraph 4(2)(b) be shown under the general item 'fixed assets' in the company's balance sheet the following information must be given—

    (a) the appropriate amounts in respect of that item as at the date of the beginning of the financial year and as at the balance sheet date respectively,

    (b) the effect on any amount shown in the balance sheet in respect of that item of—

      (i) any revision of the amount in respect of any assets included under that item made during that year on any basis mentioned in paragraph 32,

      (ii) acquisitions during that year of any assets,

      (iii) disposals during that year of any assets, and

      (iv) any transfers of assets of the company to and from that item during that year.

  (2) The reference in sub-paragraph (1)(a) to the appropriate amounts in respect of any item as at any date there mentioned is a reference to amounts representing the aggregate amounts determined, as at that date, in respect of assets falling to be included under that item on either of the following bases, that is to say—

    (a) on the basis of purchase price or production cost (determined in accordance with paragraphs 27 and 28), or

    (b) on any basis mentioned in paragraph 32, (leaving out of account in either case any provisions for depreciation or diminution in value).

  (3) In respect of each item within sub-paragraph (1) there must also be stated—

    (a) the cumulative amount of provisions for depreciation or diminution in value of assets included under that item as at each date mentioned in sub-paragraph (1)(a),

    (b) the amount of any such provisions made in respect of the financial year,

    (c) the amount of any adjustments made in respect of any such provisions during that year in consequence of the disposal of any assets, and

    (d) the amount of any other adjustments made in respect of any such provisions during that year.

**52.** Where any fixed assets of the company (other than listed investments) are included under any item shown in the company's balance sheet at an amount determined on any basis mentioned in paragraph 32, the following information must be given—

    (a) the years (so far as they are known to the directors) in which the assets were severally valued and the several values, and

    (b) in the case of assets that have been valued during the financial year, the names of the persons who valued them or particulars of their qualifications for doing so and (whichever is stated) the bases of valuation used by them.

**53.** In relation to any amount which is or would but for paragraph 4(2)(b) be shown in respect of the item 'land and buildings' in the company's balance sheet there must be stated—

(a) how much of that amount is ascribable to land of freehold tenure and how much to land of leasehold tenure, and

(b) how much of the amount ascribable to land of leasehold tenure is ascribable to land held on long lease and how much to land held on short lease.

## Investments

**54.** (1) In respect of the amount of each item which is or would but for paragraph 4(2)(b) be shown in the company's balance sheet under the general item 'investments' (whether as fixed assets or as current assets) there must be stated how much of that amount is ascribable to listed investments.

(2) Where the amount of any listed investments is stated for any item in accordance with sub-paragraph (1), the following amounts must also be stated—

(a) the aggregate market value of those investments where it differs from the amount so stated, and

(b) both the market value and the stock exchange value of any investments of which the former value is, for the purposes of the accounts, taken as being higher than the latter.

## Information about fair value of assets and liabilities

**55.** (1) This paragraph applies where financial instruments have been valued in accordance with paragraph 36 or 38.

(2) There must be stated—

(a) the significant assumptions underlying the valuation models and techniques used where the fair value of the instruments has been determined in accordance with paragraph 37(4),

(b) for each category of financial instrument, the fair value of the instruments in that category and the changes in value—

(i) included in the profit and loss account, or

(ii) credited to or (as the case may be) debited from the fair value reserve, in respect of those instruments, and

(c) for each class of derivatives, the extent and nature of the instruments, including significant terms and conditions that may affect the amount, timing and certainty of future cash flows.

(3) Where any amount is transferred to or from the fair value reserve during the financial year, there must be stated in tabular form—

(a) the amount of the reserve as at the date of the beginning of the financial year and as at the balance sheet date respectively,

(b) the amount transferred to or from the reserve during that year, and

(c) the source and application respectively of the amounts so transferred.

**56.** Where the company has derivatives that it has not included at fair value, there must be stated for each class of such derivatives—

(a) the fair value of the derivatives in that class, if such a value can be determined in accordance with paragraph 37, and

(b) the extent and nature of the derivatives.

**57.** (1) This paragraph applies if—

(a) the company has financial fixed assets that could be included at fair value by virtue of paragraph 36,

(b) the amount at which those items are included under any item in the company's accounts is in excess of their fair value, and

(c) the company has not made provision for diminution in value of those assets in accordance with paragraph 19(1) of this Schedule.

(2) There must be stated—

(a) the amount at which either the individual assets or appropriate groupings of those individual assets are included in the company's accounts,

(b) the fair value of those assets or groupings, and

(c) the reasons for not making a provision for diminution in value of those assets, including the nature of the evidence that provides the basis for the belief that the amount at which they are stated in the accounts will be recovered.

## Information where investment property and living animals and plants included at fair value

**58.** (1) This paragraph applies where the amounts to be included in a company's accounts in respect of investment property or living animals and plants have been determined in accordance with paragraph 39.

(2) The balance sheet items affected and the basis of valuation adopted in determining the amounts of the assets in question in the case of each such item must be disclosed in a note to the accounts.

(3) In the case of investment property, for each balance sheet item affected there must be shown, either separately in the balance sheet or in a note to the accounts—

    (a) the comparable amounts determined according to the historical cost accounting rules, or

    (b) the differences between those amounts and the corresponding amounts actually shown in the balance sheet in respect of that item.

(4) In sub-paragraph (3), references in relation to any item to the comparable amounts determined in accordance with that sub-paragraph are to—

    (a) the aggregate amount which would be required to be shown in respect of that item if the amounts to be included in respect of all the assets covered by that item were determined according to the historical cost accounting rules, and

    (b) the aggregate amount of the cumulative provisions for depreciation or diminution in value which would be permitted or required in determining those amounts according to those rules.

## Reserves and provisions

**59.** (1) This paragraph applies where any amount is transferred—

    (a) to or from any reserves, or

    (b) to any provision for liabilities, or

    (c) from any provision for liabilities otherwise than for the purpose for which the provision was established, and the reserves or provisions are or would but for paragraph 4(2)(b) be shown as separate items in the company's balance sheet.

(2) The following information must be given in respect of the aggregate of reserves or provisions included in the same item—

    (a) the amount of the reserves or provisions as at the date of the beginning of the financial year and as at the balance sheet date respectively,

    (b) any amounts transferred to or from the reserves or provisions during that year, and

    (c) the source and application respectively of any amounts so transferred.

(3) Particulars must be given of each provision included in the item 'other provisions' in the company's balance sheet in any case where the amount of that provision is material.

## Provision for taxation

**60.** The amount of any provision for deferred taxation must be stated separately from the amount of any provision for other taxation.

## Details of indebtedness

**61.** (1) For the aggregate of all items shown under 'creditors' in the company's balance sheet there must be stated the aggregate of the following amounts—

    (a) the amount of any debts included under 'creditors' which are payable or repayable otherwise than by instalments and fall due for payment or repayment after the end of the period of five years beginning with the day next following the end of the financial year, and

    (b) in the case of any debts so included which are payable or repayable by instalments, the amount of any instalments which fall due for payment after the end of that period.

(2) Subject to sub-paragraph (3), in relation to each debt falling to be taken into account under sub-paragraph (1), the terms of payment or repayment and the rate of any interest payable on the debt must be stated.

(3) If the number of debts is such that, in the opinion of the directors, compliance with sub-paragraph (2) would result in a statement of excessive length, it is sufficient to give a general indication of the terms of payment or repayment and the rates of any interest payable on the debts.

(4) In respect of each item shown under 'creditors' in the company's balance sheet there must be stated—

    (a) the aggregate amount of any debts included under that item in respect of which any security has been given by the company, and

    (b) an indication of the nature of the securities so given.

(5) References above in this paragraph to an item shown under 'creditors' in the company's balance sheet include references, where amounts falling due to creditors within one year and after more than one year are distinguished in the balance sheet—

    (a) in a case within sub-paragraph (1), to an item shown under the latter of those categories, and

    (b) in a case within sub-paragraph (4), to an item shown under either of those categories. References to items shown under 'creditors' include references to items which would but for paragraph 4(2)(b) be shown under that heading.

**62.** If any fixed cumulative dividends on the company's shares are in arrear, there must be stated—

    (a) the amount of the arrears, and

    (b) the period for which the dividends or, if there is more than one class, each class of them are in arrear.

**Guarantees and other financial commitments**

**63.** (1) Particulars must be given of any charge on the assets of the company to secure the liabilities of any other person, including, where practicable, the amount secured.

(2) The following information must be given with respect to any other contingent liability not provided for—
   (a) the amount or estimated amount of that liability,
   (b) its legal nature, and
   (c) whether any valuable security has been provided by the company in connection with that liability and if so, what.

(3) There must be stated, where practicable, the aggregate amount or estimated amount of contracts for capital expenditure, so far as not provided for.

(4) Particulars must be given of—
   (a) any pension commitments included under any provision shown in the company's balance sheet, and
   (b) any such commitments for which no provision has been made, and where any such commitment relates wholly or partly to pensions payable to past directors of the company separate particulars must be given of that commitment so far as it relates to such pensions.

(5) Particulars must also be given of any other financial commitments that—
   (a) have not been provided for, and
   (b) are relevant to assessing the company's state of affairs.

**Miscellaneous matters**

**64.** (1) Particulars must be given of any case where the purchase price or production cost of any asset is for the first time determined under paragraph 29.

(2) Where any outstanding loans made under the authority of section 682(2)(b), (c) or (d) of the 2006 Act (various cases of financial assistance by a company for purchase of its own shares) are included under any item shown in the company's balance sheet, the aggregate amount of those loans must be disclosed for each item in question.

**Information supplementing the profit and loss account**

**65.** Paragraphs 66 to 69 require information which either supplements the information given with respect to any particular items shown in the profit and loss account or otherwise provides particulars of income or expenditure of the company or of circumstances affecting the items shown in the profit and loss account (see regulation 3(2) for exemption for companies falling within section 408 of the 2006 Act (individual profit and loss account where group accounts prepared)).

**Separate statement of certain items of income and expenditure**

**66.** (1) Subject to sub-paragraph (2), there must be stated the amount of the interest on or any similar charges in respect of bank loans and overdrafts, and loans of any other kind made to the company.

(2) Sub-paragraph (1) does not apply to interest or charges on loans to the company from group undertakings, but, with that exception, it applies to interest or charges on all loans, whether made on the security of debentures or not.

**Particulars of tax**

**67.** (1) Particulars must be given of any special circumstances which affect liability in respect of taxation of profits, income or capital gains for the financial year or liability in respect of taxation of profits, income or capital gains for succeeding financial years.

(2) The following amounts must be stated—
   (a) the amount of the charge for United Kingdom corporation tax,
   (b) if that amount would have been greater but for relief from double taxation, the amount which it would have been but for such relief,
   (c) the amount of the charge for United Kingdom income tax, and
   (d) the amount of the charge for taxation imposed outside the United Kingdom of profits, income and (so far as charged to revenue) capital gains.
   These amounts must be stated separately in respect of each of the amounts which is or would but for paragraph 4(2)(b) be shown under the items 'tax on profit or loss on ordinary activities' and 'tax on extraordinary profit or loss' in the profit and loss account.

**Particulars of turnover**

**68.** (1) If in the course of the financial year the company has carried on business of two or more classes that, in the opinion of the directors, differ substantially from each other, the amount of the turnover attributable to each class must be stated and the class described (see regulation 4(3)(b) for exemption for medium-sized companies in accounts delivered to registrar).

(2) If in the course of the financial year the company has supplied markets that, in the opinion of the directors, differ substantially from each other, the amount of the turnover attributable to each such market must also be stated.

In this paragraph 'market' means a market delimited by geographical bounds.

(3) In analysing for the purposes of this paragraph the source (in terms of business or in terms of market) of turnover, the directors of the company must have regard to the manner in which the company's activities are organised.

(4) For the purposes of this paragraph—

(a) classes of business which, in the opinion of the directors, do not differ substantially from each other must be treated as one class, and

(b) markets which, in the opinion of the directors, do not differ substantially from each other must be treated as one market, and any amounts properly attributable to one class of business or (as the case may be) to one market which are not material may be included in the amount stated in respect of another.

(5) Where in the opinion of the directors the disclosure of any information required by this paragraph would be seriously prejudicial to the interests of the company, that information need not be disclosed, but the fact that any such information has not been disclosed must be stated.

## Miscellaneous matters

**69.** (1) Where any amount relating to any preceding financial year is included in any item in the profit and loss account, the effect must be stated.

(2) Particulars must be given of any extraordinary income or charges arising in the financial year.

(3) The effect must be stated of any transactions that are exceptional by virtue of size or incidence though they fall within the ordinary activities of the company.

## Sums denominated in foreign currencies

**70.** Where any sums originally denominated in foreign currencies have been brought into account under any items shown in the balance sheet format or profit and loss account formats, the basis on which those sums have been translated into sterling (or the currency in which the accounts are drawn up) must be stated.

## Dormant companies acting as agents

**71.** Where the directors of a company take advantage of the exemption conferred by section 480 of the 2006 Act (dormant companies: exemption from audit), and the company has during the financial year in question acted as an agent for any person, the fact that it has so acted must be stated.

## Related party transactions

**72.** (1) Particulars may be given of transactions which the company has entered into with related parties, and must be given if such transactions are material and have not been concluded under normal market conditions (see regulation 4(2) for exemption for medium-sized companies).

(2) The particulars of transactions required to be disclosed by sub-paragraph (1) must include—

(a) the amount of such transactions,

(b) the nature of the related party relationship, and

(c) other information about the transactions necessary for an understanding of the financial position of the company.

(3) Information about individual transactions may be aggregated according to their nature, except where separate information is necessary for an understanding of the effects of related party transactions on the financial position of the company.

(4) Particulars need not be given of transactions entered into between two or more members of a group, provided that any subsidiary undertaking which is a party to the transaction is wholly-owned by such a member.

(5) In this paragraph, 'related party' has the same meaning as in international accounting standards.

PART 4

SPECIAL PROVISION WHERE COMPANY IS A PARENT COMPANY OR
SUBSIDIARY UNDERTAKING

**Company's own accounts: guarantees and other financial commitments
in favour of group undertakings**

**73.** Commitments within any of sub-paragraphs (1) to (5) of paragraph 63 (guarantees and other
financial commitments) which are undertaken on behalf of or for the benefit of—
(a) any parent undertaking or fellow subsidiary undertaking, or
(b) any subsidiary undertaking of the company,
must be stated separately from the other commitments within that paragraph, and commitments within paragraph (a) must also be stated separately from those within paragraph (b).


PART 5

SPECIAL PROVISIONS WHERE THE COMPANY
IS AN INVESTMENT COMPANY

**74.** (1) Paragraph 35 does not apply to the amount of any profit or loss arising from a determination
of the value of any investments of an investment company on any basis mentioned in
paragraph 32(3).
(2) Any provisions made by virtue of paragraph 19(1) or (2) in the case of an investment company
in respect of any fixed asset investments need not be charged to the company's profit and loss
account provided they are either—
(a) charged against any reserve account to which any amount excluded by sub-paragraph
(1) from the requirements of paragraph 35 has been credited, or
(b) shown as a separate item in the company's balance sheet under the sub-heading 'other
reserves'.
(3) For the purposes of this paragraph, as it applies in relation to any company, 'fixed asset
investment' means any asset falling to be included under any item shown in the company's
balance sheet under the subdivision 'investments' under the general item 'fixed assets'.
**75.** (1) Any distribution made by an investment company which reduces the amount of its net assets
to less than the aggregate of its called-up share capital and undistributable reserves shall be
disclosed in a note to the company's accounts.
(2) For purposes of this paragraph, a company's net assets are the aggregate of its assets less the
aggregate of its liabilities (including any provision for liabilities within paragraph 2 of
Schedule 9 to these Regulations that is made in Companies Act accounts and any provision
that is made in IAS accounts); and 'undistributable reserves' has the meaning given by section
831(4) of the 2006 Act.
(3) A company shall be treated as an investment company for the purposes of this Part of this
Schedule in relation to any financial year of the company if—
(a) during the whole of that year it was an investment company as defined by section 833
of the 2006 Act, and
(b) it was not at any time during that year prohibited from making a distribution by virtue of
section 832 of the 2006 Act due to either or both of the conditions specified in section
832(5)(a) or (b) (no distribution where capital profits have been distributed etc) not being
met.


SCHEDULE 2                                                    Regulation 5(1)

BANKING COMPANIES: COMPANIES ACT INDIVIDUAL ACCOUNTS

PART 1

GENERAL RULES AND FORMATS

SECTION A

GENERAL RULES

**1.** Subject to the following provisions of this Part of this Schedule—
(a) every balance sheet of a company must show the items listed in the balance sheet format set
out in Section B of this Part, and

   (b)  every profit and loss account must show the items listed in either of the profit and loss account formats in Section B.

**2.**  (1)  References in this Part of this Schedule to the items listed in any of the formats set out in Section B, are to those items read together with any of the notes following the formats which apply to those items.

   (2)  The items must be shown in the order and under the headings and sub-headings given in the particular format used, but—

     (a)  the notes to the formats may permit alternative positions for any particular items,

     (b)  the heading or sub-heading for any item does not have to be distinguished by any letter or number assigned to that item in the format used, and

     (c)  where the heading of an item in the format used contains any wording in square brackets, that wording may be omitted if not applicable to the company.

**3.**  (1)  Where in accordance with paragraph 1 a company's profit and loss account for any financial year has been prepared by reference to one of the formats in Section B, the company's directors must use the same format in preparing the profit and loss account for subsequent financial years, unless in their opinion there are special reasons for a change.

   (2)  Particulars of any change must be given in a note to the accounts in which the new format is first used, and the reasons for the change must be explained.

**4.**  (1)  Any item required to be shown in a company's balance sheet or profit and loss account may be shown in greater detail than required by the particular format used.

   (2)  The balance sheet or profit and loss account may include an item representing or covering the amount of any asset or liability, income or expenditure not specifically covered by any of the items listed in the format used, save that none of the following may be treated as assets in any balance sheet—

     (a)  preliminary expenses,

     (b)  expenses of, and commission on, any issue of shares or debentures, and

     (c)  costs of research.

**5.**  (1)  Items to which lower case letters are assigned in any of the formats in Section B may be combined in a company's accounts for any financial year if—

     (a)  their individual amounts are not material for the purpose of giving a true and fair view, or

     (b)  the combination facilitates the assessment of the state of affairs or profit or loss of the company for that year.

   (2)  Where sub-paragraph (1)(b) applies, the individual amounts of any items so combined must be disclosed in a note to the accounts and any notes required by this Schedule to the items so combined must, notwithstanding the combination, be given.

**6.**  (1)  Subject to sub-paragraph (2), the directors must not include a heading or sub-heading corresponding to an item in the balance sheet or profit and loss account format used if there is no amount to be shown for that item for the financial year to which the balance sheet or profit and loss account relates.

   (2)  Where an amount can be shown for the item in question for the immediately preceding financial year, that amount must be shown under the heading or sub-heading required by the format for that item.

**7.**  (1)  For every item shown in the balance sheet or profit and loss account the corresponding amount for the immediately preceding financial year must also be shown.

   (2)  Where that corresponding amount is not comparable with the amount to be shown for the item in question in respect of the financial year to which the balance sheet or profit and loss account relates, the former amount may be adjusted, and particulars of the non-comparability and of any adjustment must be disclosed in a note to the accounts.

**8.**  (1)  Subject to the following provisions of this paragraph and without prejudice to note (6) to the balance sheet format, amounts in respect of items representing assets or income may not be set off against amounts in respect of items representing liabilities or expenditure (as the case may be), or vice versa.

   (2)  Charges required to be included in profit and loss account format 1, items 11(a) and 11(b) or format 2, items A7(a) and A7(b) may be set off against income required to be included in format 1, items 12(a) and 12(b) or format 2, items B5(a) and B5(b) and the resulting figure shown as a single item (in format 2 at position A7 if negative and at position B5 if positive).

   (3)  Charges required to be included in profit and loss account format 1, item 13 or format 2, item A8 may also be set off against income required to be included in format 1, item 14 or format 2, item B6 and the resulting figure shown as a single item (in format 2 at position A8 if negative and at position B6 if positive).

**9.**  (1)  Assets must be shown under the relevant balance sheet headings even where the company has pledged them as security for its own liabilities or for those of third parties or has otherwise assigned them as security to third parties.

   (2)  A company may not include in its balance sheet assets pledged or otherwise assigned to it as security unless such assets are in the form of cash in the hands of the company.

(3) Assets acquired in the name of and on behalf of third parties must not be shown in the balance sheet.

**10.** The company's directors must, in determining how amounts are presented within items in the profit and loss account and balance sheet, have regard to the substance of the reported transaction or arrangement, in accordance with generally accepted accounting principles or practice.

## SECTION B
## THE REQUIRED FORMATS[76]

### Balance sheet format

ASSETS

1. Cash and balances at central [or post office] banks *(1)*
2. Treasury bills and other eligible bills *(20)*
   (a) Treasury bills and similar securities *(2)*
   (b) Other eligible bills *(3)*
3. Loans and advances to banks *(4)*, *(20)*
   (a) Repayable on demand
   (b) Other loans and advances
4. Loans and advances to customers *(5)*, *(20)*
5. Debt securities [and other fixed-income securities] *(6)*, *(20)*
   (a) Issued by public bodies
   (b) Issued by other issuers
6. Equity shares [and other variable-yield securities]
7. Participating interests
8. Shares in group undertakings
9. Intangible fixed assets *(7)*
10. Tangible fixed assets *(8)*
11. Called up capital not paid *(9)*
12. Own shares *(10)*
13. Other assets
14. Called up capital not paid *(9)*
15. Prepayments and accrued income

Total assets

LIABILITIES

1. Deposits by banks *(11)*, *(20)*
   (a) Repayable on demand
   (b) With agreed maturity dates or periods of notice
2. Customer accounts *(12)*, *(20)*
   (a) Repayable on demand
   (b) With agreed maturity dates or periods of notice
3. Debt securities in issue *(13)*, *(20)*
   (a) Bonds and medium term notes
   (b) Others
4. Other liabilities
5. Accruals and deferred income
6. Provisions for liabilities
   (a) Provisions for pensions and similar obligations
   (b) Provisions for tax
   (c) Other provisions
7. Subordinated liabilities *(14)*, *(20)*
8. Called up share capital *(15)*
9. Share premium account
10. Reserves
    (a) Capital redemption reserve
    (b) Reserve for own shares

---

[76] A number in brackets following any item is a reference to the note of that number in the notes following the formats.

    (c) Reserves provided for by the articles of association
    (d) Other reserves
11. Revaluation reserve
12. Profit and loss account

Total liabilities
MEMORANDUM ITEMS

1. Contingent liabilities *(16)*
    (1) Acceptances and endorsements
    (2) Guarantees and assets pledged as collateral security *(17)*
    (3) Other contingent liabilities
2. Commitments *(18)*
    (1) Commitments arising out of sale and option to resell transactions *(19)*
    (2) Other commitments

## NOTES ON THE BALANCE SHEET FORMAT AND MEMORANDUM ITEMS

*(1) Cash and balances at central [or post office] banks*
(Assets item 1.)
Cash is to comprise all currency including foreign notes and coins.
Only those balances which may be withdrawn without notice and which are deposited with central or post office banks of the country or countries in which the company is established may be included in this item. All other claims on central or post office banks must be shown under assets items 3 or 4.

*(2) Treasury bills and other eligible bills: Treasury bills and similar securities*
(Assets item 2.(a).)
Treasury bills and similar securities are to comprise treasury bills and similar debt instruments issued by public bodies which are eligible for refinancing with central banks of the country or countries in which the company is established. Any treasury bills or similar debt instruments not so eligible must be included under assets item 5(a).

*(3) Treasury bills and other eligible bills: Other eligible bills*
(Assets item 2.(b).)
Other eligible bills are to comprise all bills purchased to the extent that they are eligible, under national law, for refinancing with the central banks of the country or countries in which the company is established.

*(4) Loans and advances to banks*
(Assets item 3.)
Loans and advances to banks are to comprise all loans and advances to domestic or foreign credit institutions made by the company arising out of banking transactions. However loans and advances to credit institutions represented by debt securities or other fixed-income securities must be included under assets item 5 and not this item.

*(5) Loans and advances to customers*
(Assets item 4.)
Loans and advances to customers are to comprise all types of assets in the form of claims on domestic and foreign customers other than credit institutions. However loans and advances represented by debt securities or other fixed-income securities must be included under assets item 5 and not this item.

*(6) Debt securities [and other fixed-income securities]*
(Assets item 5.)
This item is to comprise transferable debt securities and any other transferable fixed-income securities issued by credit institutions, other undertakings or public bodies. Debt securities and other fixed-income securities issued by public bodies are, however, only to be included in this item if they may not be shown under assets item 2.
Where a company holds its own debt securities these must not be included under this item but must be deducted from liabilities item 3.(a) or (b), as appropriate.
Securities bearing interest rates that vary in accordance with specific factors, for example the interest rate on the inter-bank market or on the Euromarket, are also to be regarded as fixed-income securities to be included under this item.

*(7) Intangible fixed assets*

(Assets item 9.)

This item is to comprise—

(a) development costs,

(b) concessions, patents, licences, trade marks and similar rights and assets,

(c) goodwill, and

(d) payments on account.

Amounts are, however, to be included in respect of (b) only if the assets were acquired for valuable consideration or the assets in question were created by the company itself.

Amounts representing goodwill are only to be included to the extent that the goodwill was acquired for valuable consideration. The amount of any goodwill included in this item must be disclosed in a note to the accounts.

(8) *Tangible fixed assets*

(Assets item 10.)

This item is to comprise—

(a) land and buildings,

(b) plant and machinery,

(c) fixtures and fittings, tools and equipment, and

(d) payments on account and assets in the course of construction.

The amount included in this item with respect to land and buildings occupied by the company for its own activities must be disclosed in a note to the accounts.

(9) *Called up capital not paid*

(Assets items 11 and 14.)

The two positions shown for this item are alternatives.

(10) *Own shares*

(Assets item 12.)

The nominal value of the shares held must be shown separately under this item.

(11) *Deposits by banks*

(Liabilities item 1.)

Deposits by banks are to comprise all amounts arising out of banking transactions owed to other domestic or foreign credit institutions by the company. However liabilities in the form of debt securities and any liabilities for which transferable certificates have been issued must be included under liabilities item 3 and not this item.

(12) *Customer accounts*

(Liabilities item 2.)

This item is to comprise all amounts owed to creditors that are not credit institutions. However liabilities in the form of debt securities and any liabilities for which transferable certificates have been issued must be shown under liabilities item 3 and not this item.

(13) *Debt securities in issue*

(Liabilities item 3.)

This item is to include both debt securities and debts for which transferable certificates have been issued, including liabilities arising out of own acceptances and promissory notes. (Only acceptances which a company has issued for its own refinancing and in respect of which it is the first party liable are to be treated as own acceptances.)

(14) *Subordinated liabilities*

(Liabilities item 7.)

This item is to comprise all liabilities in respect of which there is a contractual obligation that, in the event of winding up or bankruptcy, they are to be repaid only after the claims of other creditors have been met.

This item must include all subordinated liabilities, whether or not a ranking has been agreed between the subordinated creditors concerned.

(15) *Called up share capital*

(Liabilities item 8.)

The amount of allotted share capital and the amount of called up share capital which has been paid up must be shown separately.

(16) *Contingent liabilities*

(Memorandum item 1.)

This item is to include all transactions whereby the company has underwritten the obligations of a third party.

Liabilities arising out of the endorsement of rediscounted bills must be included in this item. Acceptances other than own acceptances must also be included.

(17) *Contingent liabilities: Guarantees and assets pledged as collateral security*

(Memorandum item 1(2).)

This item is to include all guarantee obligations incurred and assets pledged as collateral security on behalf of third parties, particularly in respect of sureties and irrevocable letters of credit.

(18) *Commitments*

(Memorandum item 2.)

This item is to include every irrevocable commitment which could give rise to a credit risk.

(19) *Commitments: Commitments arising out of sale and option to resell transactions*

(Memorandum item 2(1).)

This item is to comprise commitments entered into by the company in the context of sale and option to resell transactions.

(20) *Claims on, and liabilities to, undertakings in which a participating interest is held or group undertakings*

(Assets items 2 to 5, liabilities items 1 to 3 and 7.)

The following information must be given either by way of subdivision of the relevant items or by way of notes to the accounts.

The amount of the following must be shown for each of assets items 2 to 5—

(a) claims on group undertakings included therein, and

(b) claims on undertakings in which the company has a participating interest included therein.

The amount of the following must be shown for each of liabilities items 1, 2, 3 and 7?—

(i) liabilities to group undertakings included therein, and

(ii) liabilities to undertakings in which the company has a participating interest included therein.

*Special rules*

**Subordinated assets**

**11.** (1) The amount of any assets that are subordinated must be shown either as a subdivision of any relevant asset item or in the notes to the accounts; in the latter case disclosure must be by reference to the relevant asset item or items in which the assets are included.

(2) In the case of assets items 2 to 5 in the balance sheet format, the amounts required to be shown by note (20) to the format as sub-items of those items must be further subdivided so as to show the amount of any claims included therein that are subordinated.

(3) For this purpose, assets are subordinated if there is a contractual obligation to the effect that, in the event of winding up or bankruptcy, they are to be repaid only after the claims of other creditors have been met, whether or not a ranking has been agreed between the subordinated creditors concerned.

**Syndicated loans**

**12.** (1) Where a company is a party to a syndicated loan transaction the company must include only that part of the total loan which it itself has funded.

(2) Where a company is a party to a syndicated loan transaction and has agreed to reimburse (in whole or in part) any other party to the syndicate any funds advanced by that party or any interest thereon upon the occurrence of any event, including the default of the borrower, any additional liability by reason of such a guarantee must be included as a contingent liability in Memorandum item 1(2).

**Sale and repurchase transactions**

**13.** (1) The following rules apply where a company is a party to a sale and repurchase transaction.

(2) Where the company is the transferor of the assets under the transaction—

(a) the assets transferred must, notwithstanding the transfer, be included in its balance sheet,

(b) the purchase price received by it must be included in its balance sheet as an amount owed to the transferee, and

(c) the value of the assets transferred must be disclosed in a note to its accounts.

(3) Where the company is the transferee of the assets under the transaction, it must not include the assets transferred in its balance sheet but the purchase price paid by it to the transferor must be so included as an amount owed by the transferor.

**Sale and option to resell transactions**

**14.** (1) The following rules apply where a company is a party to a sale and option to resell transaction.

(2) Where the company is the transferor of the assets under the transaction, it must not include in its balance sheet the assets transferred but it must enter under Memorandum item 2 an amount equal to the price agreed in the event of repurchase.

(3) Where the company is the transferee of the assets under the transaction it must include those assets in its balance sheet.

### Managed funds

**15.** (1) For the purposes of this paragraph, 'managed funds' are funds which the company administers in its own name but on behalf of others and to which it has legal title.

(2) The company must, in any case where claims and obligations arising in respect of managed funds fall to be treated as claims and obligations of the company, adopt the following accounting treatment.

(3) Claims and obligations representing managed funds are to be included in the company's balance sheet, with the notes to the accounts disclosing the total amount included with respect to such assets and liabilities in the balance sheet and showing the amount included under each relevant balance sheet item in respect of such assets or (as the case may be) liabilities.

## PROFIT AND LOSS ACCOUNT FORMATS

*Format 1*

Vertical layout

1. Interest receivable *(1)*
    (1) Interest receivable and similar income arising from debt securities [and other fixed-income securities]
    (2) Other interest receivable and similar income
2. Interest payable *(2)*
3. Dividend income
    (a) Income from equity shares [and other variable-yield securities]
    (b) Income from participating interests
    (c) Income from shares in group undertakings
4. Fees and commissions receivable *(3)*
5. Fees and commissions payable *(4)*
6. Dealing [profits] [losses] *(5)*
7. Other operating income
8. Administrative expenses
    (a) Staff costs
        (i) Wages and salaries
        (ii) Social security costs
        (iii) Other pension costs
    (b) Other administrative expenses
9. Depreciation and amortisation *(6)*
10. Other operating charges
11. Provisions
    (a) Provisions for bad and doubtful debts *(7)*
    (b) Provisions for contingent liabilities and commitments *(8)*
12. Adjustments to provisions
    (a) Adjustments to provisions for bad and doubtful debts *(9)*
    (b) Adjustments to provisions for contingent liabilities and commitments *(10)*
13. Amounts written off fixed asset investments *(11)*
14. Adjustments to amounts written off fixed asset investments *(12)*
15. [Profit] [loss] on ordinary activities before tax
16. Tax on [profit] [loss] on ordinary activities
17. [Profit] [loss] on ordinary activities after tax
18. Extraordinary income
19. Extraordinary charges
20. Extraordinary [profit] [loss]
21. Tax on extraordinary [profit] [loss]
22. Extraordinary [profit] [loss] after tax
23. Other taxes not shown under the preceding items
24. [Profit] [loss] for the financial year

# PROFIT AND LOSS ACCOUNT FORMATS

*Format 2*

Horizontal layout

A. Charges
1. Interest payable *(2)*
2. Fees and commissions payable *(4)*
3. Dealing losses *(5)*
4. Administrative expenses
   (a) Staff costs
       (i) Wages and salaries
       (ii) Social security costs
       (iii) Other pension costs
   (b) Other administrative expenses
5. Depreciation and amortisation *(6)*
6. Other operating charges
7. Provisions
   (a) Provisions for bad and doubtful debts *(7)*
   (b) Provisions for contingent liabilities and commitments *(8)*
8. Amounts written off fixed asset investments *(11)*
9. Profit on ordinary activities before tax
10. Tax on [profit] [loss] on ordinary activities
11. Profit on ordinary activities after tax
12. Extraordinary charges
13. Tax on extraordinary [profit] [loss]
14. Extraordinary loss after tax
15. Other taxes not shown under the preceding items
16. Profit for the financial year

B. Income
1. Interest receivable *(1)*
   (1) Interest receivable and similar income arising from debt securities [and other fixed-income securities]
   (2) Other interest receivable and similar income
2. Dividend income
   (a) Income from equity shares [and other variable-yield securities]
   (b) Income from participating interests
   (c) Income from shares in group undertakings
3. Fees and commissions receivable *(3)*
4. Dealing profits *(5)*
5. Adjustments to provisions
   (a) Adjustments to provisions for bad and doubtful debts *(9)*
   (b) Adjustments to provisions for contingent liabilities and commitments *(10)*
6. Adjustments to amounts written off fixed asset investments *(12)*
7. Other operating income
8. Loss on ordinary activities before tax
9. Loss on ordinary activities after tax
10. Extraordinary income
11. Extraordinary profit after tax
12. Loss for the financial year

## NOTES ON THE PROFIT AND LOSS ACCOUNT FORMATS

*(1) Interest receivable*
(Format 1, item 1; format 2, item B1.)
This item is to include all income arising out of banking activities, including—
(a) income from assets included in assets items 1 to 5 in the balance sheet format, however calculated,
(b) income resulting from covered forward contracts spread over the actual duration of the contract and similar in nature to interest, and
(c) fees and commissions receivable similar in nature to interest and calculated on a time basis or by reference to the amount of the claim (but not other fees and commissions receivable).

*(2) Interest payable*
(Format 1, item 2; format 2, item A1.)
This item is to include all expenditure arising out of banking activities, including—
(a) charges arising out of liabilities included in liabilities items 1, 2, 3 and 7 in the balance sheet format, however calculated,

(b) charges resulting from covered forward contracts, spread over the actual duration of the contract and similar in nature to interest, and

(c) fees and commissions payable similar in nature to interest and calculated on a time basis or by reference to the amount of the liability (but not other fees and commissions payable).

**(3)** *Fees and commissions receivable*

(Format 1, item 4; format 2, item B3.)

Fees and commissions receivable are to comprise income in respect of all services supplied by the company to third parties, but not fees or commissions required to be included under interest receivable (format 1, item 1; format 2, item B1).

In particular the following fees and commissions receivable must be included (unless required to be included under interest receivable)—

(a) fees and commissions for guarantees, loan administration on behalf of other lenders and securities transactions,

(b) fees, commissions and other income in respect of payment transactions, account administration charges and commissions for the safe custody and administration of securities,

(c) fees and commissions for foreign currency transactions and for the sale and purchase of coin and precious metals, and

(d) fees and commissions charged for brokerage services in connection with savings and insurance contracts and loans.

**(4)** *Fees and commissions payable*

(Format 1, item 5; format 2, item A2.)

Fees and commissions payable are to comprise charges for all services rendered to the company by third parties but not fees or commissions required to be included under interest payable (format 1, item 2; format 2, item A1).

In particular the following fees and commissions payable must be included (unless required to be included under interest payable)—

(a) fees and commissions for guarantees, loan administration and securities transactions;

(b) fees, commissions and other charges in respect of payment transactions, account administration charges and commissions for the safe custody and administration of securities;

(c) fees and commissions for foreign currency transactions and for the sale and purchase of coin and precious metals; and

(d) fees and commissions for brokerage services in connection with savings and insurance contracts and loans.

**(5)** *Dealing [profits] [losses]*

(Format 1, item 6; format 2, items B4 and A3.) This item is to comprise—

(a) the net profit or net loss on transactions in securities which are not held as financial fixed assets together with amounts written off or written back with respect to such securities, including amounts written off or written back as a result of the application of paragraph 33(1),

(b) the net profit or loss on exchange activities, save in so far as the profit or loss is included in interest receivable or interest payable (format 1, items 1 or 2; format 2, items B1 or A1), and

(c) the net profits and losses on other dealing operations involving financial instruments, including precious metals.

**(6)** *Depreciation and amortisation*

(Format 1, item 9; format 2, item A5.)

This item is to comprise depreciation and other amounts written off in respect of balance sheet assets items 9 and 10.

**(7)** *Provisions: Provisions for bad and doubtful debts*

(Format 1, item 11(a); format 2, item A7(a).)

Provisions for bad and doubtful debts are to comprise charges for amounts written off and for provisions made in respect of loans and advances shown under balance sheet assets items 3 and 4.

**(8)** *Provisions: Provisions for contingent liabilities and commitments*

(Format 1, item 11(b); format 2, item A7(b).)

This item is to comprise charges for provisions for contingent liabilities and commitments of a type which would, if not provided for, be shown under Memorandum items 1 and 2.

**(9)** *Adjustments to provisions: Adjustments to provisions for bad and doubtful debts*

(Format 1, item 12(a); format 2, item B5(a).)

This item is to include credits from the recovery of loans that have been written off, from other advances written back following earlier write offs and from the reduction of provisions previously made with respect to loans and advances.

*(10)Adjustments to provisions: Adjustments to provisions for contingent liabilities and commitments*
(Format 1, item 12(b); format 2, item B5(b).)
This item comprises credits from the reduction of provisions previously made with respect to contingent liabilities and commitments.

*(11)Amounts written off fixed asset investments*
(Format 1, item 13; format 2, item A8.)
Amounts written off fixed asset investments are to comprise amounts written off in respect of assets which are transferable securities held as financial fixed assets, participating interests and shares in group undertakings and which are included in assets items 5 to 8 in the balance sheet format.

*(12)Adjustments to amounts written off fixed asset investments*
(Format 1, item 14; format 2, item B6.)
Adjustments to amounts written off fixed asset investments are to include amounts written back following earlier write offs and provisions in respect of assets which are transferable securities held as financial fixed assets, participating interests and group undertakings and which are included in assets items 5 to 8 in the balance sheet format.

PART 2

ACCOUNTING PRINCIPLES AND RULES

SECTION A

ACCOUNTING PRINCIPLES

**Preliminary**

**16.** (1) The amounts to be included in respect of all items shown in a company's accounts must be determined in accordance with the principles set out in this Section.
  (2) But if it appears to the company's directors that there are special reasons for departing from any of those principles in preparing the company's accounts in respect of any financial year they may do so, in which case particulars of the departure, the reasons for it and its effect must be given in a note to the accounts.

**Accounting principles**

**17.** The company is presumed to be carrying on business as a going concern.

**18.** Accounting policies must be applied consistently within the same accounts and from one financial year to the next.

**19.** The amount of any item must be determined on a prudent basis, and in particular—
  (a) only profits realised at the balance sheet date are to be included in the profit and loss account, and
  (b) all liabilities which have arisen in respect of the financial year to which the accounts relate or a previous financial year must be taken into account, including those which only become apparent between the balance sheet date and the date on which it is signed on behalf of the board of directors in accordance with section 414 of the 2006 Act (approval and signing of accounts).

**20.** All income and charges relating to the financial year to which the accounts relate must be taken into account, without regard to the date of receipt or payment.

**21.** In determining the aggregate amount of any item, the amount of each individual asset or liability that falls to be taken into account must be determined separately.

SECTION B

HISTORICAL COST ACCOUNTING RULES

**Preliminary**

**22.** Subject to Sections C and D of this Part of this Schedule, the amounts to be included in respect of all items shown in a company's accounts must be determined in accordance with the rules set out in this Section.

*Fixed assets*

### General rules

**23.** (1) The amount to be included in respect of any fixed asset is its cost.

(2) This is subject to any provision for depreciation or diminution in value made in accordance with paragraphs 24 to 26.

### Rules for depreciation and diminution in value

**24.** In the case of any fixed asset which has a limited useful economic life, the amount of—

(a) its cost, or

(b) where it is estimated that any such asset will have a residual value at the end of the period of its useful economic life, its cost less that estimated residual value, must be reduced by provisions for depreciation calculated to write off that amount systematically over the period of the asset's useful economic life.

**25.** (1) Where a fixed asset investment to which sub-paragraph (2) applies has diminished in value, provisions for diminution in value may be made in respect of it and the amount to be included in respect of it may be reduced accordingly.

(2) This sub-paragraph applies to fixed asset investments of a description falling to be included under assets item 7 (participating interests) or 8 (shares in group undertakings) in the balance sheet format, or any other holding of securities held as a financial fixed asset.

(3) Provisions for diminution in value must be made in respect of any fixed asset which has diminished in value if the reduction in its value is expected to be permanent (whether its useful economic life is limited or not), and the amount to be included in respect of it must be reduced accordingly.

(4) Any provisions made under this paragraph which are not shown in the profit and loss account must be disclosed (either separately or in aggregate) in a note to the accounts.

**26.** (1) Where the reasons for which any provision was made in accordance with paragraph 25 have ceased to apply to any extent, that provision must be written back to the extent that it is no longer necessary.

(2) Any amounts written back in accordance with sub-paragraph (1) which are not shown in the profit and loss account must be disclosed (either separately or in aggregate) in a note to the accounts.

### Development costs

**27.** (1) Notwithstanding that amounts representing 'development costs' may be included under assets item 9 in the balance sheet format, an amount may only be included in a company's balance sheet in respect of development costs in special circumstances.

(2) If any amount is included in a company's balance sheet in respect of development costs the following information must be given in a note to the accounts—

(a) the period over which the amount of those costs originally capitalised is being or is to be written off, and

(b) the reasons for capitalising the development costs in question.

### Goodwill

**28.** (1) The application of paragraphs 23 to 26 in relation to goodwill (in any case where goodwill is treated as an asset) is subject to the following.

(2) Subject to sub-paragraph (3), the amount of the consideration for any goodwill acquired by a company must be reduced by provisions for depreciation calculated to write off that amount systematically over a period chosen by the directors of the company.

(3) The period chosen must not exceed the useful economic life of the goodwill in question.

(4) In any case where any goodwill acquired by a company is included as an asset in the company's balance sheet there must be disclosed in a note to the accounts—

(a) the period chosen for writing off the consideration for that goodwill, and

(b) the reasons for choosing that period.

### Treatment of fixed assets

**29.** (1) Assets included in assets items 9 (intangible fixed assets) and 10 (tangible fixed assets) in the balance sheet format must be valued as fixed assets.

(2) Other assets falling to be included in the balance sheet must be valued as fixed assets where they are intended for use on a continuing basis in the company's activities.

### Financial fixed assets

**30.** (1) Debt securities, including fixed-income securities, held as financial fixed assets must be included in the balance sheet at an amount equal to their maturity value plus any premium, or less any discount, on their purchase, subject to the following provisions of this paragraph.

(2) The amount included in the balance sheet with respect to such securities purchased at a premium must be reduced each financial year on a systematic basis so as to write the premium off over the period to the maturity date of the security and the amounts so written off must be charged to the profit and loss account for the relevant financial years.

(3) The amount included in the balance sheet with respect to such securities purchased at a discount must be increased each financial year on a systematic basis so as to extinguish the discount over the period to the maturity date of the security and the amounts by which the amount is increased must be credited to the profit and loss account for the relevant years.

(4) The notes to the accounts must disclose the amount of any unamortized premium or discount not extinguished which is included in the balance sheet by virtue of sub-paragraph (1).

(5) For the purposes of this paragraph 'premium' means any excess of the amount paid for a security over its maturity value and 'discount' means any deficit of the amount paid for a security over its maturity value.

## Current assets

**31.** The amount to be included in respect of loans and advances, debt or other fixed-income securities and equity shares or other variable yield securities not held as financial fixed assets must be their cost, subject to paragraphs 32 and 33.

**32.** (1) If the net realisable value of any asset referred to in paragraph 31 is lower than its cost, the amount to be included in respect of that asset is the net realisable value.

(2) Where the reasons for which any provision for diminution in value was made in accordance with sub-paragraph (1) have ceased to apply to any extent, that provision must be written back to the extent that it is no longer necessary.

**33.** (1) Subject to paragraph 32, the amount to be included in the balance sheet in respect of transferable securities not held as financial fixed assets may be the higher of their cost or their market value at the balance sheet date.

(2) The difference between the cost of any securities included in the balance sheet at a valuation under sub-paragraph (1) and their market value must be shown (in aggregate) in the notes to the accounts.

*Miscellaneous and supplementary provisions*

## Excess of money owed over value received as an asset item

**34.** (1) Where the amount repayable on any debt owed by a company is greater than the value of the consideration received in the transaction giving rise to the debt, the amount of the difference may be treated as an asset.

(2) Where any such amount is so treated—

(a) it must be written off by reasonable amounts each year and must be completely written off before repayment of the debt, and

(b) if the current amount is not shown as a separate item in the company's balance sheet, it must be disclosed in a note to the accounts.

## Determination of cost

**35.** (1) The cost of an asset that has been acquired by the company is to be determined by adding to the actual price paid any expenses incidental to its acquisition.

(2) The cost of an asset constructed by the company is to be determined by adding to the purchase price of the raw materials and consumables used the amount of the costs incurred by the company which are directly attributable to the construction of that asset.

(3) In addition, there may be included in the cost of an asset constructed by the company—

(a) a reasonable proportion of the costs incurred by the company which are only indirectly attributable to the construction of that asset, but only to the extent that they relate to the period of construction, and

(b) interest on capital borrowed to finance the construction of that asset, to the extent that it accrues in respect of the period of construction, provided, however, in a case within paragraph (b), that the inclusion of the interest in determining the cost of that asset and the amount of the interest so included is disclosed in a note to the accounts.

**36.** (1) The cost of any assets which are fungible assets (including investments), may be determined by the application of any of the methods mentioned in sub-paragraph (2) in relation to any such assets of the same class, provided that the method chosen is one which appears to the directors to be appropriate in the circumstances of the company.

(2) Those methods are—

(a) the method known as 'first in, first out' (FIFO),

(b) the method known as 'last in, first out' (LIFO),

(c) a weighted average price, and

(d) any other method similar to any of the methods mentioned above.

(3) Where in the case of any company—

(a) the cost of assets falling to be included under any item shown in the company's balance sheet has been determined by the application of any method permitted by this paragraph, and

(b) the amount shown in respect of that item differs materially from the relevant alternative amount given below in this paragraph, the amount of that difference must be disclosed in a note to the accounts.

(4) Subject to sub-paragraph (5), for the purposes of sub-paragraph (3)(b), the relevant alternative amount, in relation to any item shown in a company's balance sheet, is the amount which would have been shown in respect of that item if assets of any class included under that item at an amount determined by any method permitted by this paragraph had instead been included at their replacement cost as at the balance sheet date.

(5) The relevant alternative amount may be determined by reference to the most recent actual purchase price before the balance sheet date of assets of any class included under the item in question instead of by reference to their replacement cost as at that date, but only if the former appears to the directors of the company to constitute the more appropriate standard of comparison in the case of assets of that class.

### Substitution of original stated amount where price or cost unknown

**37.** (1) This paragraph applies where—

(a) there is no record of the purchase price of any asset acquired by a company or of any price, expenses or costs relevant for determining its cost in accordance with paragraph 35, or

(b) any such record cannot be obtained without unreasonable expense or delay.

(2) In such a case, its cost is to be taken, for the purposes of paragraphs 23 to 33, to be the value ascribed to it in the earliest available record of its value made on or after its acquisition by the company.

## SECTION C
## ALTERNATIVE ACCOUNTING RULES

### Preliminary

**38.** (1) The rules set out in Section B are referred to below in this Schedule as the historical cost accounting rules.

(2) Paragraphs 23 to 26 and 30 to 34 are referred to below in this Section as the depreciation rules; and references below in this Schedule to the historical cost accounting rules do not 2include the depreciation rules as they apply by virtue of paragraph 41.

**39.** Subject to paragraphs 41 to 43, the amounts to be included in respect of assets of any description mentioned in paragraph 40 may be determined on any basis so mentioned.

### Alternative accounting rules

**40.** (1) Intangible fixed assets, other than goodwill, may be included at their current cost.

(2) Tangible fixed assets may be included at a market value determined as at the date of their last valuation or at their current cost.

(3) Investments of any description falling to be included under assets items 7 (participating interests) or 8 (shares in group undertakings) of the balance sheet format and any other securities held as financial fixed assets may be included either—

(a) at a market value determined as at the date of their last valuation, or

(b) at a value determined on any basis which appears to the directors to be appropriate in the circumstances of the company.

But in the latter case particulars of the method of valuation adopted and of the reasons for adopting it must be disclosed in a note to the accounts.

(4) Securities of any description not held as financial fixed assets (if not valued in accordance with paragraph 33) may be included at their current cost.

### Application of the depreciation rules

**41.** (1) Where the value of any asset of a company is determined in accordance with paragraph 40, that value must be, or (as the case may require) be the starting point for determining, the amount to be included in respect of that asset in the company's accounts, instead of its cost or any value previously so determined for that asset. The depreciation rules apply accordingly in relation to any such asset with the substitution for any reference to its cost of a reference to the value most recently determined for that asset in accordance with paragraph 40.

(2) The amount of any provision for depreciation required in the case of any fixed asset by

paragraphs 24 to 26 as they apply by virtue of sub-paragraph (1) is referred to below in this paragraph as the adjusted amount, and the amount of any provision which would be required by any of those paragraphs in the case of that asset according to the historical cost accounting rules is referred to as the historical cost amount.

(3) Where sub-paragraph (1) applies in the case of any fixed asset the amount of any provision for depreciation in respect of that asset included in any item shown in the profit and loss account in respect of amounts written off assets of the description in question may be the historical cost amount instead of the adjusted amount, provided that the amount of any difference between the two is shown separately in the profit and loss account or in a note to the accounts.

### Additional information to be provided in case of departure from historical cost accounting rules

**42.** (1) This paragraph applies where the amounts to be included in respect of assets covered by any items shown in a company's accounts have been determined in accordance with paragraph 40.

(2) The items affected and the basis of valuation adopted in determining the amounts of the assets in question in the case of each such item must be disclosed in a note to the accounts.

(3) In the case of each balance sheet item affected either—

    (a) the comparable amounts determined according to the historical cost accounting rules, or

    (b) the differences between those amounts and the corresponding amounts actually shown in the balance sheet in respect of that item, must be shown separately in the balance sheet or in a note to the accounts.

(4) In sub-paragraph (3), references in relation to any item to the comparable amounts determined as there mentioned are references to—

    (a) the aggregate amount which would be required to be shown in respect of that item if the amounts to be included in respect of all the assets covered by that item were determined according to the historical cost accounting rules, and

    (b) the aggregate amount of the cumulative provisions for depreciation or diminution in value which would be permitted or required in determining those amounts according to those rules.

### Revaluation reserve

**43.** (1) With respect to any determination of the value of an asset of a company in accordance with paragraph 40, the amount of any profit or loss arising from that determination (after allowing, where appropriate, for any provisions for depreciation or diminution in value made otherwise than by reference to the value so determined and any adjustments of any such provisions made in the light of that determination) must be credited or (as the case may be) debited to a separate reserve ('the revaluation reserve').

(2) The amount of the revaluation reserve must be shown in the company's balance sheet under liabilities item 11 in the balance sheet format, but need not be shown under that name.

(3) An amount may be transferred—

    (a) from the revaluation reserve—

        (i) to the profit and loss account, if the amount was previously charged to that account or represents realised profit, or

        (ii) on capitalisation,

    (b) to or from the revaluation reserve in respect of the taxation relating to any profit or loss credited or debited to the reserve. The revaluation reserve must be reduced to the extent that the amounts transferred to it are no longer necessary for the purposes of the valuation method used.

(4) In sub-paragraph (3)(a)(ii) 'capitalisation', in relation to an amount standing to the credit of the revaluation reserve, means applying it in wholly or partly paying up unissued shares in the company to be allotted to members of the company as fully or partly paid shares.

(5) The revaluation reserve must not be reduced except as mentioned in this paragraph.

(6) The treatment for taxation purposes of amounts credited or debited to the revaluation reserve must be disclosed in a note to the accounts.

## SECTION D
## FAIR VALUE ACCOUNTING

### Inclusion of financial instruments at fair value

**44.** (1) Subject to sub-paragraphs (2) to (5), financial instruments (including derivatives) may be included at fair value.

(2) Sub-paragraph (1) does not apply to financial instruments that constitute liabilities unless—

    (a) they are held as part of a trading portfolio,

(b)  they are derivatives, or

(c)  they are financial instruments falling within sub-paragraph (4).

(3)  Unless they are financial instruments falling within sub-paragraph (4), sub-paragraph (1) does not apply to—

(a)  financial instruments (other than derivatives) held to maturity,

(b)  loans and receivables originated by the company and not held for trading purposes,

(c)  interests in subsidiary undertakings, associated undertakings and joint ventures,

(d)  equity instruments issued by the company,

(e)  contracts for contingent consideration in a business combination, or

(f)  other financial instruments with such special characteristics that the instruments, according to generally accepted accounting principles or practice, should be accounted for differently from other financial instruments.

(4)  Financial instruments that, under international accounting standards adopted by the European Commission on or before 5th September 2006 in accordance with the IAS Regulation, may be included in accounts at fair value, may be so included, provided that the disclosures required by such accounting standards are made.

(5)  If the fair value of a financial instrument cannot be determined reliably in accordance with paragraph 45, sub-paragraph (1) does not apply to that financial instrument.

(6)  In this paragraph—

'associated undertaking' has the meaning given by paragraph 19 of Schedule 6 to these Regulations;

'joint venture' has the meaning given by paragraph 18 of that Schedule.

### Determination of fair value

**45.** (1)  The fair value of a financial instrument is its value determined in accordance with this paragraph.

(2)  If a reliable market can readily be identified for the financial instrument, its fair value is determined by reference to its market value.

(3)  If a reliable market cannot readily be identified for the financial instrument but can be identified for its components or for a similar instrument, its fair value is determined by reference to the market value of its components or of the similar instrument.

(4)  If neither sub-paragraph (2) nor (3) applies, the fair value of the financial instrument is a value resulting from generally accepted valuation models and techniques.

(5)  Any valuation models and techniques used for the purposes of sub-paragraph (4) must ensure a reasonable approximation of the market value.

### Hedged items

**46.** A company may include any assets and liabilities, or identified portions of such assets or liabilities, that qualify as hedged items under a fair value hedge accounting system at the amount required under that system.

### Other assets that may be included at fair value

**47.** (1)  This paragraph applies to—

(a)  investment property, and

(b)  living animals and plants,

that, under international accounting standards, may be included in accounts at fair value.

(2)  Such investment property and such living animals and plants may be included at fair value, provided that all such investment property or, as the case may be, all such living animals and plants are so included where their fair value can reliably be determined.

(3)  In this paragraph, 'fair value' means fair value determined in accordance with relevant international accounting standards.

### Accounting for changes in value

**48.** (1)  This paragraph applies where a financial instrument is valued in accordance with paragraph 44 or 46 or an asset is valued in accordance with paragraph 47.

(2)  Notwithstanding paragraph 19 in this Part of this Schedule, and subject to sub-paragraphs (3) and (4), a change in the value of the financial instrument or of the investment property or living animal or plant must be included in the profit and loss account.

(3)  Where—

(a)  the financial instrument accounted for is a hedging instrument under a hedge accounting system that allows some or all of the change in value not to be shown in the profit and loss account, or

(b)  the change in value relates to an exchange difference arising on a monetary item that forms part of a company's net investment in a foreign entity,

the amount of the change in value must be credited to or (as the case may be) debited from a separate reserve ('the fair value reserve').

(4)  Where the instrument accounted for—

(a) is an available for sale financial asset, and

(b) is not a derivative,

   the change in value may be credited to or (as the case may be) debited from the fair value reserve.

### The fair value reserve

**49.** (1) The fair value reserve must be adjusted to the extent that the amounts shown in it are no longer necessary for the purposes of paragraph 48(3) or (4).

   (2) The treatment for taxation purposes of amounts credited or debited to the fair value reserve must be disclosed in a note to the accounts.

### Assets and liabilities denominated in foreign currencies

**50.** (1) Subject to the following sub-paragraphs, amounts to be included in respect of assets and liabilities denominated in foreign currencies must be in sterling (or the currency in which the accounts are drawn up) after translation at an appropriate spot rate of exchange prevailing at the balance sheet date.

   (2) An appropriate rate of exchange prevailing on the date of purchase may however be used for assets held as financial fixed assets and assets to be included under assets items 9 (intangible fixed assets) and 10 (tangible fixed assets) in the balance sheet format, if they are not covered or not specifically covered in either the spot or forward currency markets.

   (3) An appropriate spot rate of exchange prevailing at the balance sheet date must be used for translating uncompleted spot exchange transactions.

   (4) An appropriate forward rate of exchange prevailing at the balance sheet date must be used for translating uncompleted forward exchange transactions.

   (5) This paragraph does not apply to any assets or liabilities held, or any transactions entered into, for hedging purposes or to any assets or liabilities which are themselves hedged.

**51.** (1) Subject to sub-paragraph (2), any difference between the amount to be included in respect of an asset or liability under paragraph 50 and the book value, after translation into sterling (or the currency in which the accounts are drawn up) at an appropriate rate, of that asset or liability must be credited or, as the case may be, debited to the profit and loss account.

   (2) In the case, however, of assets held as financial fixed assets, of assets to be included under assets items 9 (intangible fixed assets) and 10 (tangible fixed assets) in the balance sheet format and of transactions undertaken to cover such assets, any such difference may be deducted from or credited to any non-distributable reserve available for the purpose.

## PART 3
## NOTES TO THE ACCOUNTS

### Preliminary

**52.** Any information required in the case of any company by the following provisions of this Part of this Schedule must (if not given in the company's accounts) be given by way of a note to the accounts.

*General*

### Disclosure of accounting policies

**53.** The accounting policies adopted by the company in determining the amounts to be included in respect of items shown in the balance sheet and in determining the profit or loss of the company must be stated (including such policies with respect to the depreciation and diminution in value of assets).

**54.** It must be stated whether the accounts have been prepared in accordance with applicable accounting standards and particulars of any material departure from those standards and the reasons for it must be given.

### Sums denominated in foreign currencies

**55.** Where any sums originally denominated in foreign currencies have been brought into account under any items shown in the balance sheet format or profit and loss account formats, the basis on which those sums have been translated into sterling (or the currency in which the accounts are drawn up) must be stated.

**Reserves and dividends**

**56.** There must be stated—
> (a) any amount set aside or proposed to be set aside to, or withdrawn or proposed to be withdrawn from, reserves,
> (b) the aggregate amount of dividends paid in the financial year (other than those for which a liability existed at the immediately preceding balance sheet date),
> (c) the aggregate amount of dividends that the company is liable to pay at the balance sheet date, and
> (d) the aggregate amount of dividends that are proposed before the date of approval of the accounts, and not otherwise disclosed under sub-paragraph (b) or (c).

**Information supplementing the balance sheet**

**57.** Paragraphs 58 to 84 require information which either supplements the information given with respect to any particular items shown in the balance sheet or is otherwise relevant to assessing the company's state of affairs in the light of the information so given.

**Share capital and debentures**

**58.** (1) Where shares of more than one class have been allotted, the number and aggregate nominal value of shares of each class allotted must be given.
> (2) In the case of any part of the allotted share capital that consists of redeemable shares, the following information must be given—
> > (a) the earliest and latest dates on which the company has power to redeem those shares,
> > (b) whether those shares must be redeemed in any event or are liable to be redeemed at the option of the company or of the shareholder, and
> > (c) whether any (and, if so, what) premium is payable on redemption.

**59.** If the company has allotted any shares during the financial year, the following information must be given—
> (a) the classes of shares allotted, and
> (b) as respects each class of shares, the number allotted, their aggregate nominal value and the consideration received by the company for the allotment.

**60.** (1) With respect to any contingent right to the allotment of shares in the company the following particulars must be given—
> > (a) the number, description and amount of the shares in relation to which the right is exercisable,
> > (b) the period during which it is exercisable, and
> > (c) the price to be paid for the shares allotted.
> (2) In sub-paragraph (1) 'contingent right to the allotment of shares' means any option to subscribe for shares and any other right to require the allotment of shares to any person-whether arising on the conversion into shares of securities of any other description or otherwise.

**61.** (1) If the company has issued any debentures during the financial year to which the accounts relate, the following information must be given—
> > (a) the classes of debentures issued, and
> > (b) as respects each class of debentures, the amount issued and the consideration received by the company for the issue.
> (2) Where any of the company's debentures are held by a nominee of or trustee for the company, the nominal amount of the debentures and the amount at which they are stated in the accounting records kept by the company in accordance with section 386 of the 2006 Act (duty to keep accounting records) must be stated.

Fixed assets

**62.** (1) In respect of any fixed assets of the company included in any assets item in the company's balance sheet the following information must be given by reference to each such item—
> > (a) the appropriate amounts in respect of those assets included in the item as at the date of the beginning of the financial year and as at the balance sheet date respectively,
> > (b) the effect on any amount shown included in the item in respect of those assets of—
> > > (i) any determination during that year of the value to be ascribed to any of those assets in accordance with paragraph 40,
> > > (ii) acquisitions during that year of any fixed assets,
> > > (iii) disposals during that year of any fixed assets, and
> > > (iv) any transfers of fixed assets of the company to and from that item during that year.
> (2) The reference in sub-paragraph (1)(a) to the appropriate amounts in respect of any fixed assets (included in an assets item) as at any date there mentioned is a reference to amounts representing the aggregate amounts determined, as at that date, in respect of fixed assets falling to be included under the item on either of the following bases—
> > (a) on the basis of cost (determined in accordance with paragraphs 35 and 36), or

    (b) on any basis permitted by paragraph 40,

        (leaving out of account in either case any provisions for depreciation or diminution in value).

(3) In addition, in respect of any fixed assets of the company included in any assets item in the company's balance sheet, there must be stated (by reference to each such item)—

    (a) the cumulative amount of provisions for depreciation or diminution in value of those assets included under that item as at each date mentioned in sub-paragraph (1)(a),

    (b) the amount of any such provisions made in respect of the financial year,

    (c) the amount of any adjustments made in respect of any such provisions during that year in consequence of the disposal of any of those assets, and

    (d) the amount of any other adjustments made in respect of any such provisions during that year.

(4) The requirements of this paragraph need not be complied with to the extent that a company takes advantage of the option of setting off charges and income afforded by paragraph 8(3) in Part 1 of this Schedule.

**63.** Where any fixed assets of the company (other than listed investments) are included under any item shown in the company's balance sheet at an amount determined in accordance with paragraph 40, the following information must be given—

    (a) the years (so far as they are known to the directors) in which the assets were severally valued and the several values, and

    (b) in the case of assets that have been valued during the financial year, the names of the persons who valued them or particulars of their qualifications for doing so and (whichever is stated) the bases of valuation used by them.

**64.** In relation to any amount which is included under assets item 10 in the balance sheet format (tangible fixed assets) with respect to land and buildings there must be stated—

    (a) how much of that amount is ascribable to land of freehold tenure and how much to land of leasehold tenure, and

    (b) how much of the amount ascribable to land of leasehold tenure is ascribable to land held on long lease and how much to land held on short lease.

**65.** There must be disclosed separately the amount of—

    (a) any participating interests, and

    (b) any shares in group undertakings that are held in credit institutions.

## Information about fair value of assets and liabilities

**66.** (1) This paragraph applies where financial instruments have been valued in accordance with paragraph 44 or 46.

(2) There must be stated—

    (a) the significant assumptions underlying the valuation models and techniques used where the fair value of the instruments has been determined in accordance with paragraph 45(4),

    (b) for each category of financial instrument, the fair value of the instruments in that category and the changes in value—

        (i) included in the profit and loss account, or

        (ii) credited to or (as the case may be) debited from the fair value reserve, in respect of those instruments, and

    (c) for each class of derivatives, the extent and nature of the instruments, including significant terms and conditions that may affect the amount, timing and certainty of future cash flows.

(3) Where any amount is transferred to or from the fair value reserve during the financial year, there must be stated in tabular form—

    (a) the amount of the reserve as at the date of the beginning of the financial year and as at the balance sheet date respectively,

    (b) the amount transferred to or from the reserve during that year, and

    (c) the source and application respectively of the amounts so transferred.

**67.** Where the company has derivatives that it has not included at fair value, there must be stated for each class of such derivatives—

    (a) the fair value of the derivatives in that class, if such a value can be determined in accordance with paragraph 45, and

    (b) the extent and nature of the derivatives.

**68.** (1) This paragraph applies if—

    (a) the company has financial fixed assets that could be included at fair value by virtue of paragraph 44,

    (b) the amount at which those items are included under any item in the company's accounts is in excess of their fair value, and

    (c) the company has not made provision for diminution in value of those assets in accordance with paragraph 25(1) in Part 2 of this Schedule.

(2) There must be stated—

(a) the amount at which either the individual assets or appropriate groupings of those individual assets are included in the company's accounts,

(b) the fair value of those assets or groupings, and

(c) the reasons for not making a provision for diminution in value of those assets, including the nature of the evidence that provides the basis for the belief that the amount at which they are stated in the accounts will be recovered.

### Information where investment property and living animals and plants included at fair value

**69.** (1) This paragraph applies where the amounts to be included in a company's accounts in respect of investment property or living animals and plants have been determined in accordance with paragraph 47.

(2) The balance sheet items affected and the basis of valuation adopted in determining the amounts of the assets in question in the case of each such item must be disclosed in a note to the accounts.

(3) In the case of investment property, for each balance sheet item affected there must be shown, either separately in the balance sheet or in a note to the accounts—

(a) the comparable amounts determined according to the historical cost accounting rules, or

(b) the differences between those amounts and the corresponding amounts actually shown in the balance sheet in respect of that item.

(4) In sub-paragraph (3), references in relation to any item to the comparable amounts determined in accordance with that sub-paragraph are to—

(a) the aggregate amount which would be required to be shown in respect of that item if the amounts to be included in respect of all the assets covered by that item were determined according to the historical cost accounting rules, and

(b) the aggregate amount of the cumulative provisions for depreciation or diminution in value which would be permitted or required in determining those amounts according to those rules.

### Reserves and provisions

**70.** (1) This paragraph applies where any amount is transferred—

(a) to or from any reserves, or

(b) to any provision for liabilities, or

(c) from any provision for liabilities otherwise than for the purpose for which the provision was established, and the reserves or provisions are or would but for paragraph 5(1) in Part 1 of this Schedule be shown as separate items in the company's balance sheet.

(2) The following information must be given in respect of the aggregate of reserves or provisions included in the same item—

(a) the amount of the reserves or provisions as at the date of the beginning of the financial year and as at the balance sheet date respectively,

(b) any amounts transferred to or from the reserves or provisions during that year, and

(c) the source and application respectively of any amounts so transferred.

(3) Particulars must be given of each provision included in liabilities item 6.(c) (other provisions) in the company's balance sheet in any case where the amount of that provision is material.

### Provision for taxation

**71.** The amount of any provision for deferred taxation must be stated separately from the amount of any provision for other taxation.

### Maturity analysis

**72.** (1) A company must disclose separately for each of assets items 3.(b) and 4 and liabilities items 1.(b), 2.(b) and 3.(b) the aggregate amount of the loans and advances and liabilities included in those items broken down into the following categories—

(a) those repayable in not more than three months,

(b) those repayable in more than three months but not more than one year,

(c) those repayable in more than one year but not more than five years,

(d) those repayable in more than five years,

from the balance sheet date.

(2) A company must also disclose the aggregate amounts of all loans and advances falling within assets item 4 (loans and advances to customers) which are—

(a) repayable on demand, or

(b) are for an indeterminate period, being repayable upon short notice.

(3) For the purposes of sub-paragraph (1), where a loan or advance or liability is repayable by instalments, each such instalment is to be treated as a separate loan or advance or liability.

### Debt and other fixed-income securities

**73.** A company must disclose the amount of debt and fixed-income securities included in assets item 5 (debt securities [and other fixed-income securities]) and the amount of such securities included in liabilities item 3.(a) (bonds and medium term notes) that (in each case) will become due within one year of the balance sheet date.

### Subordinated liabilities

**74.** (1) The following information must be disclosed in relation to any borrowing included in liabilities item 7 (subordinated liabilities) that exceeds 10 % of the total for that item—
    (a) its amount,
    (b) the currency in which it is denominated,
    (c) the rate of interest and the maturity date (or the fact that it is perpetual),
    (d) the circumstances in which early repayment may be demanded,
    (e) the terms of the subordination, and
    (f) the existence of any provisions whereby it may be converted into capital or some other form of liability and the terms of any such provisions.
  (2) The general terms of any other borrowings included in liabilities item 7 must also be stated.

### Fixed cumulative dividends

**75.** If any fixed cumulative dividends on the company's shares are in arrear, there must be stated—
    (a) the amount of the arrears, and
    (b) the period for which the dividends or, if there is more than one class, each class of them are in arrear.

### Details of assets charged

**76.** (1) There must be disclosed, in relation to each liabilities and memorandum item of the balance sheet format—
    (a) the aggregate amount of any assets of the company which have been charged to secure any liability or potential liability included under that item,
    (b) the aggregate amount of the liabilities or potential liabilities so secured, and
    (c) an indication of the nature of the security given.
  (2) Particulars must also be given of any other charge on the assets of the company to secure the liabilities of any other person, including, where practicable, the amount secured.

### Guarantees and other financial commitments

**77.** (1) There must be stated, where practicable, the aggregate amount or estimated amount of contracts for capital expenditure, so far as not provided for.
  (2) Particulars must be given of—
    (a) any pension commitments included under any provision shown in the company's balance sheet, and
    (b) any such commitments for which no provision has been made,
    and where any such commitment relates wholly or partly to pensions payable to past directors of the company separate particulars must be given of that commitment so far as it relates to such pensions.
  (3) Particulars must also be given of any other financial commitments, including any contingent liabilities, that—
    (a) have not been provided for,
    (b) have not been included in the memorandum items in the balance sheet format, and
    (c) are relevant to assessing the company's state of affairs.
  (4) Commitments within any of the preceding sub-paragraphs undertaken on behalf of or for the benefit of—
    (a) any parent company or fellow subsidiary undertaking of the company, or
    (b) any subsidiary undertaking of the company,
    must be stated separately from the other commitments within that sub-paragraph (and commitments within paragraph (a) must be stated separately from those within paragraph (b)).
  (5) There must be disclosed the nature and amount of any contingent liabilities and commitments included in Memorandum items 1 and 2 which are material in relation to the company's activities.

### Memorandum items: Group undertakings

**78.** (1) With respect to contingent liabilities required to be included under Memorandum item 1 in the balance sheet format, there must be stated in a note to the accounts the amount of such contingent liabilities incurred on behalf of or for the benefit of—
    (a) any parent undertaking or fellow subsidiary undertaking, or
    (b) any subsidiary undertaking,

of the company; in addition the amount incurred in respect of the undertakings referred to in paragraph (a) must be stated separately from the amount incurred in respect in respect of the undertakings referred to in paragraph (b).

(2) With respect to commitments required to be included under Memorandum item 2 in the balance sheet format, there must be stated in a note to the accounts the amount of such commitments undertaken on behalf of or for the benefit of—

(a) any parent undertaking or fellow subsidiary undertaking, or

(b) any subsidiary undertaking,

of the company; in addition the amount incurred in respect of the undertakings referred to in paragraph (a) must be stated separately from the amount incurred in respect of the undertakings referred to in paragraph (b).

## Transferable securities

**79.** (1) There must be disclosed for each of assets items 5 to 8 in the balance sheet format the amount of transferable securities included under those items that are listed and the amount of those that are unlisted.

(2) In the case of each amount shown in respect of listed securities under sub-paragraph (1), there must also be disclosed the aggregate market value of those securities, if different from the amount shown.

(3) There must also be disclosed for each of assets items 5 and 6 the amount of transferable securities included under those items that are held as financial fixed assets and the amount of those that are not so held, together with the criterion used by the directors to distinguish those held as financial fixed assets.

## Leasing transactions

**80.** The aggregate amount of all property (other than land) leased by the company to other persons must be disclosed, broken down so as to show the aggregate amount included in each relevant balance sheet item.

## Assets and liabilities denominated in a currency other than sterling (or the currency in which the accounts are drawn up)

**81.** (1) The aggregate amount, in sterling (or the currency in which the accounts are drawn up), of all assets denominated in a currency other than sterling (or the currency used) together with the aggregate amount, in sterling (or the currency used), of all liabilities so denominated, is to be disclosed.

(2) For the purposes of this paragraph an appropriate rate of exchange prevailing at the balance sheet date must be used to determine the amounts concerned.

## Sundry assets and liabilities

**82.** Where any amount shown under either of the following items is material, particulars must be given of each type of asset or liability included in that item, including an explanation of the nature of the asset or liability and the amount included with respect to assets or liabilities of that type—

(a) assets item 13 (other assets),

(b) liabilities item 4 (other liabilities).

## Unmatured forward transactions

**83.** (1) The following must be disclosed with respect to unmatured forward transactions outstanding at the balance sheet date—

(a) the categories of such transactions, by reference to an appropriate system of classification,

(b) whether, in the case of each such category, they have been made, to any material extent, for the purpose of hedging the effects of fluctuations in interest rates, exchange rates and market prices or whether they have been made, to any material extent, for dealing purposes.

(2) Transactions falling within sub-paragraph (1) must include all those in relation to which income or expenditure is to be included in—

(a) format 1, item 6 or format 2, items B4 or A3 (dealing [profits][losses]),

(b) format 1, items 1 or 2, or format 2, items B1 or A1, by virtue of notes (1)(b) and (2)(b) to the profit and loss account formats (forward contracts, spread over the actual duration of the contract and similar in nature to interest).

## Miscellaneous matters

**84.** (1) Particulars must be given of any case where the cost of any asset is for the first time determined under paragraph 37 in Part 2 of this Schedule.

(2) Where any outstanding loans made under the authority of section 682(2)(b), (c) or (d) of the 2006 Act (various cases of financial assistance by a company for purchase of its own shares) are included under any item shown in the company's balance sheet, the aggregate amount of those loans must be disclosed for each item in question.

### Information supplementing the profit and loss account

**85.** Paragraphs 86 to 91 require information which either supplements the information given with respect to any particular items shown in the profit and loss account or otherwise provides particulars of income or expenditure of the company or of circumstances affecting the items shown in the profit and loss account (see regulation 5(2) for exemption for companies falling within section 408 of the 2006 Act (individual profit and loss account where group accounts prepared)).

### Particulars of tax

**86.** (1) Particulars must be given of any special circumstances which affect liability in respect of taxation of profits, income or capital gains for the financial year or liability in respect of taxation of profits, income or capital gains for succeeding financial years.

(2) The following amounts must be stated—
  (a) the amount of the charge for United Kingdom corporation tax,
  (b) if that amount would have been greater but for relief from double taxation, the amount which it would have been but for such relief,
  (c) the amount of the charge for United Kingdom income tax, and
  (d) the amount of the charge for taxation imposed outside the United Kingdom of profits, income and (so far as charged to revenue) capital gains.
  These amounts must be stated separately in respect of each of the amounts which is shown under the following items in the profit and loss account, that is to say format 1 item 16, format 2 item A10 (tax on [profit][loss] on ordinary activities) and format 1 item 21, format 2 item A13 (tax on extraordinary [profit][loss]).

### Particulars of income

**87.** (1) A company must disclose, with respect to income included in the following items in the profit and loss account formats, the amount of that income attributable to each of the geographical markets in which the company has operated during the financial year—
  (a) format 1 item 1, format 2 item B1 (interest receivable),
  (b) format 1 item 3, format 2 item B2 (dividend income),
  (c) format 1 item 4, format 2 item B3 (fees and commissions receivable),
  (d) format 1 item 6, format 2 item B4 (dealing profits), and
  (e) format 1 item 7, format 2 item B7 (other operating income).

(2) In analysing for the purposes of this paragraph the source of any income, the directors must have regard to the manner in which the company's activities are organised.

(3) For the purposes of this paragraph, markets which do not differ substantially from each other shall be treated as one market.

(4) Where in the opinion of the directors the disclosure of any information required by this paragraph would be seriously prejudicial to the interests of the company, that information need not be disclosed, but the fact that any such information has not been disclosed must be stated.

### Management and agency services

**88.** A company providing any management and agency services to customers must disclose that fact, if the scale of such services provided is material in the context of its business as a whole.

### Subordinated liabilities

**89.** Any amounts charged to the profit and loss account representing charges incurred during the year with respect to subordinated liabilities must be disclosed.

### Sundry income and charges

**90.** Where any amount to be included in any of the following items is material, particulars must be given of each individual component of the figure, including an explanation of their nature and amount—
  (a) in format 1—
    (i)   items 7 and 10 (other operating income and charges),
    (ii)  items 18 and 19 (extraordinary income and charges);
  (b) in format 2—
    (i)   items A6 and B7 (other operating charges and income),
    (ii)  items A12 and B10 (extraordinary charges and income).

### Miscellaneous matters

**91.** (1) Where any amount relating to any preceding financial year is included in any item in the profit and loss account, the effect must be stated.

(2) The effect must be stated of any transactions that are exceptional by virtue of size or incidence though they fall within the ordinary activities of the company.

**Related party transactions**

**92.** (1) Particulars may be given of transactions which the company has entered into with related parties, and must be given if such transactions are material and have not been concluded under normal market conditions.

(2) The particulars of transactions required to be disclosed by sub-paragraph (1) must include—

(a) the amount of such transactions,

(b) the nature of the related party relationship, and

(c) other information about the transactions necessary for an understanding of the financial position of the company.

(3) Information about individual transactions may be aggregated according to their nature, except where separate information is necessary for an understanding of the effects of related party transactions on the financial position of the company.

(4) Particulars need not be given of transactions entered into between two or more members of a group, provided that any subsidiary undertaking which is a party to the transaction is wholly-owned by such a member.

(5) In this paragraph, 'related party' has the same meaning as in international accounting standards.

# PART 4
## INTERPRETATION OF THIS SCHEDULE

**Definitions for this Schedule**

**93.** The following definitions apply for the purposes of this Schedule.

**Financial fixed assets**

**94.** 'Financial fixed assets' means loans and advances and securities held as fixed assets; participating interests and shareholdings in group undertakings are to be regarded as financial fixed assets.

**Financial instruments**

**95.** For the purposes of this Schedule, references to 'derivatives' include commodity-based contracts that give either contracting party the right to settle in cash or in some other financial instrument, except when such contracts—

(a) were entered into for the purpose of, and continue to meet, the company's expected purchase, sale or usage requirements,

(b) were designated for such purpose at their inception, and

(c) are expected to be settled by delivery of the commodity.

**96.** (1) The expressions listed in sub-paragraph (2) have the same meaning in paragraphs 44 to 49, 66 to 68 and 95 of this Schedule as they have in Council Directives 78/660/EEC on the annual accounts of certain types of companies[77] and 86/635/EEC on the annual accounts and consolidated accounts of banks and other financial institutions[78].

(2) Those expressions are 'available for sale financial asset', 'business combination', 'commodity-based contracts', 'derivative', 'equity instrument', 'exchange difference', 'fair value hedge accounting system', 'financial fixed asset', 'financial instrument', 'foreign entity', 'hedge accounting', 'hedge accounting system', 'hedged items', 'hedging instrument', 'held for trading purposes', 'held to maturity', 'monetary item', 'receivables', 'reliable market' and 'trading portfolio'.

**Repayable on demand**

**97.** 'Repayable on demand', in connection with deposits, loans or advances, means that they can at any time be withdrawn or demanded without notice or that a maturity or period of notice of not more than 24 hours or one working day has been agreed for them.

**Sale and repurchase transaction**

**98.** (1) 'Sale and repurchase transaction' means a transaction which involves the transfer by a credit institution or customer ('the transferor') to another credit institution or customer ('the transferee') of assets subject to an agreement that the same assets, or (in the case of fungible

---

[77] OJ L222 of 14.8.1978, page 11, as amended in particular by Directives 2001/65/EEC, 2003/51/EEC and 2006/46/EEC of the European Parliament and of the Council (OJ L238 of 27.12.2001, page 28, OJ L178 of 17.7.2003, page 16 and OJ L224 of 16.8.2006, page 1).

[78] OJ No. L372 of 31st December 1986, page 1, as amended in particular by Directives 2001/65/EEC, 2003/51/EEC and 2006/46/EEC of the European Parliament and of the Council (OJ L238 of 27.12.2001, page 28, OJ L178 of 17.7.2003, page 16 and OJ L224 of 16.8.2006, page 1).

assets) equivalent assets, will subsequently be transferred back to the transferor at a specified price on a date specified or to be specified by the transferor.

(2) The following are not to be regarded as sale and repurchase transactions for the purposes of sub-paragraph (1)—

(a) forward exchange transactions,

(b) options,

(c) transactions involving the issue of debt securities with a commitment to repurchase all or part of the issue before maturity, or

(d) any similar transactions.

### Sale and option to resell transaction

**99.** 'Sale and option to resell transaction' means a transaction which involves the transfer by a credit institution or customer ('the transferor') to another credit institution or customer ('the transferee') of assets subject to an agreement that the transferee is entitled to require the subsequent transfer of the same assets, or (in the case of fungible assets) equivalent assets, back to the transferor at the purchase price or another price agreed in advance on a date specified or to be specified.

SCHEDULE 3                                   Regulation 6(1)

INSURANCE COMPANIES: COMPANIES ACT INDIVIDUAL ACCOUNTS

PART 1

GENERAL RULES AND FORMATS

SECTION A

GENERAL RULES

**1.** (1) Subject to the following provisions of this Schedule—

(a) every balance sheet of a company must show the items listed in the balance sheet format in Section B of this Part, and

(b) every profit and loss account must show the items listed in the profit and loss account format in Section B.

(2) References in this Schedule to the items listed in any of the formats in Section B are to those items read together with any of the notes following the formats which apply to those items.

(3) The items must be shown in the order and under the headings and sub-headings given in the particular format, but—

(a) the notes to the formats may permit alternative positions for any particular items, and

(b) the heading or sub-heading for any item does not have to be distinguished by any letter or number assigned to that item in the format used.

**2.** (1) Any item required to be shown in a company's balance sheet or profit and loss account may be shown in greater detail than required by the particular format.

(2) The balance sheet or profit and loss account may include an item representing or covering the amount of any asset or liability, income or expenditure not specifically covered by any of the items listed in the formats set out in Section B, save that none of the following may be treated as assets in any balance sheet—

(a) preliminary expenses,

(b) expenses of, and commission on, any issue of shares or debentures, and

(c) costs of research.

**3.** (1) The directors may combine items to which Arabic numbers are given in the balance sheet format set out in Section B (except for items concerning technical provisions and the reinsurers' share of technical provisions), and items to which lower case letters in parentheses are given in the profit and loss account format so set out (except for items within items I.1 and 4 and II.1, 5 and 6) if—

(a) their individual amounts are not material for the purpose of giving a true and fair view, or

(b) the combination facilitates the assessment of the state of affairs or profit or loss of the company for the financial year in question.

(2) Where sub-paragraph (1)(b) applies—

(a) the individual amounts of any items which have been combined must be disclosed in a note to the accounts, and

(b) any notes required by this Schedule to the items so combined must, notwithstanding the combination, be given.

**4.** (1) Subject to sub-paragraph (2), the directors must not include a heading or sub-heading corresponding to an item in the balance sheet or profit and loss account format used if there is no amount to be shown for that item for the financial year to which the balance sheet or profit and loss account relates.

(2) Where an amount can be shown for the item in question for the immediately preceding financial year that amount must be shown under the heading or sub-heading required by the format for that item.

5. (1) For every item shown in the balance sheet or profit and loss account the corresponding amount for the immediately preceding financial year must also be shown.

(2) Where that corresponding amount is not comparable with the amount to be shown for the item in question in respect of the financial year to which the balance sheet or profit and loss account relates, the former amount may be adjusted, and particulars of the non-comparability and of any adjustment must be disclosed in a note to the accounts.

6. Subject to the provisions of this Schedule, amounts in respect of items representing assets or income may not be set off against amounts in respect of items representing liabilities or expenditure (as the case may be), or vice versa.

7. (1) The provisions of this Schedule which relate to long-term business apply, with necessary modifications, to business which consists of effecting or carrying out relevant contracts of general insurance which—

(a) is transacted exclusively or principally according to the technical principles of long-term business, and

(b) is a significant amount of the business of the company.

(2) For the purposes of paragraph (1), a contract of general insurance is a relevant contract if the risk insured against relates to—

(a) accident, or

(b) sickness.

(3) Sub-paragraph (2) must be read with—

(a) section 22 of the Financial Services and Markets Act 2000[79],

(b) the Financial Services and Markets Act 2000 (Regulated Activities) Order 2001[80], and

(c) Schedule 2 to that Act.

8. The company's directors must, in determining how amounts are presented within items in the profit and loss account and balance sheet, have regard to the substance of the reported transaction or arrangement, in accordance with generally accepted accounting principles or practice.

## SECTION B
## THE REQUIRED FORMATS[81]

### PRELIMINARY

9. (1) Where in respect of any item to which an Arabic number is assigned in the balance sheet or profit and loss account format, the gross amount and reinsurance amount or reinsurers' share are required to be shown, a sub-total of those amounts must also be given.

(2) Where in respect of any item to which an Arabic number is assigned in the profit and loss account format, separate items are required to be shown, then a separate sub-total of those items must also be given in addition to any sub-total required by sub-paragraph (1).

10. (1) In the profit and loss account format set out below—

(a) the heading 'Technical account — General business' is for business which consists of effecting or carrying out contracts of general business; and

(b) the heading 'Technical account — Long-term business' is for business which consists of effecting or carrying out contracts of long-term insurance.

(2) In sub-paragraph (1), references to—

(a) contracts of general or long-term insurance, and

(b) the effecting or carrying out of such contracts,

must be read with section 22 of the Financial Services and Markets Act 2000, the Financial Services and Markets Act 2000 (Regulated Activities) Order 2001, and Schedule 2 to that Act.

---

[79] 2000 c.8.

[80] SI 2001/544, as amended by SI 2001/3544, SI 2002/682, SI 2002/1310, SI 2002/1776, SI 2002/1777, SI 2003/1475, SI 2003/1476, SI 2003/2822, SI 2004/1610, SI 2004/2737, SI 2004/3379, SI 2005/593, SI 2005/1518, SI 2005/2114 and SI 2006/1969.

[81] A number in brackets following any item is a reference to the note of that number in the notes following the formats.

# BALANCE SHEET FORMAT

## ASSETS

A. Called up share capital not paid *(1)*
B. Intangible assets
    1. Development costs
    2. Concessions, patents, licences, trade marks and similar rights and assets *(2)*
    3. Goodwill *(3)*
    4. Payments on account
C. Investments
    I. Land and buildings *(4)*
    II. Investments in group undertakings and participating interests
        1. Shares in group undertakings
        2. Debt securities issued by, and loans to, group undertakings
        3. Participating interests
        4. Debt securities issued by, and loans to, undertakings in which the company has a participating interest
    III. Other financial investments
        1. Shares and other variable-yield securities and units in unit trusts
        2. Debt securities and other fixed-income securities *(5)*
        3. Participation in investment pools *(6)*
        4. Loans secured by mortgages *(7)*
        5. Other loans *(7)*
        6. Deposits with credit institutions *(8)*
        7. Other *(9)*
    IV. Deposits with ceding undertakings *(10)*
D. Assets held to cover linked liabilities *(11)*
Da. Reinsurers' share of technical provisions *(12)*
        1. Provision for unearned premiums
        2. Long-term business provision
        3. Claims outstanding
        4. Provisions for bonuses and rebates
        5. Other technical provisions
        6. Technical provisions for unit-linked liabilities
E. Debtors *(13)*
    I. Debtors arising out of direct insurance operations
        1. Policyholders
        2. Intermediaries
    II. Debtors arising out of reinsurance operations
    III. Other debtors
    IV. Called up share capital not paid *(1)*
F. Other assets
    I. Tangible assets
        1. Plant and machinery
        2. Fixtures, fittings, tools and equipment
        3. Payments on account (other than deposits paid on land and buildings) and assets (other than buildings) in course of construction
    II. Stocks
        1. Raw materials and consumables
        2. Work in progress
        3. Finished goods and goods for resale
        4. Payments on account
    III. Cash at bank and in hand
    IV. Own shares *(14)*
    V. Other *(15)*
G. Prepayments and accrued income
    I. Accrued interest and rent *(16)*
    II. Deferred acquisition costs *(17)*
    III. Other prepayments and accrued income

## LIABILITIES

A. Capital and reserves
    I. Called up share capital or equivalent funds
    II. Share premium account

      III.  Revaluation reserve
      IV.  Reserves
          1.  Capital redemption reserve
          2.  Reserve for own shares
          3.  Reserves provided for by the articles of association
          4.  Other reserves
      V.  Profit and loss account

B.  Subordinated liabilities *(18)*
Ba. Fund for future appropriations *(19)*
C.  Technical provisions
      1.  Provision for unearned premiums *(20)*
          (a)  gross amount
          (b)  reinsurance amount *(12)*
      2.  Long-term business provision *(20) (21) (26)*
          (a)  gross amount
          (b)  reinsurance amount *(12)*
      3.  Claims outstanding *(22)*
          (a)  gross amount
          (b)  reinsurance amount *(12)*
      4.  Provision for bonuses and rebates *(23)*
          (a)  gross amount
          (b)  reinsurance amount *(12)*
      5.  Equalisation provision *(24)*
      6.  Other technical provisions *(25)*
          (a)  gross amount
          (b)  reinsurance amount *(12)*
D.  Technical provisions for linked liabilities *(26)*
          (a)  gross amount
          (b)  reinsurance amount *(12)*
E.  Provisions for other risks
      1.  Provisions for pensions and similar obligations
      2.  Provisions for taxation
      3.  Other provisions
F.  Deposits received from reinsurers *(27)*
G.  Creditors *(28)*
      I.   Creditors arising out of direct insurance operations
      II.  Creditors arising out of reinsurance operations
      III. Debenture loans *(29)*
      IV. Amounts owed to credit institutions
      V.  Other creditors including taxation and social security
H.  Accruals and deferred income

## NOTES ON THE BALANCE SHEET FORMAT

*(1) Called up share capital not paid*
(Assets items A and E.IV.)
This item may be shown in either of the positions given in the format.

*(2) Concessions, patents, licences, trade marks and similar rights and assets*
(Assets item B.2.)
Amounts in respect of assets are only to be included in a company's balance sheet under this item if either—

(a)  the assets were acquired for valuable consideration and are not required to be shown under goodwill, or

(b)  the assets in question were created by the company itself.

*(3) Goodwill*
(Assets item B.3.)
Amounts representing goodwill are only to be included to the extent that the goodwill was acquired for valuable consideration.

*(4) Land and buildings*
(Assets item C.I.)
The amount of any land and buildings occupied by the company for its own activities must be shown separately in the notes to the accounts.

*(5) Debt securities and other fixed-income securities*
(Assets item C.III.2.)

This item is to comprise transferable debt securities and any other transferable fixed-income securities issued by credit institutions, other undertakings or public bodies, in so far as they are not covered by assets item C.II.2 or C.II.4.

Securities bearing interest rates that vary in accordance with specific factors, for example the interest rate on the inter-bank market or on the Euromarket, are also to be regarded as debt securities and other fixed-income securities and so be included under this item.

(6) *Participation in investment pools*
(Assets item C.III.3.)
This item is to comprise shares held by the company in joint investments constituted by several undertakings or pension funds, the management of which has been entrusted to one of those undertakings or to one of those pension funds.

(7) *Loans secured by mortgages and other loans*
(Assets items C.III.4 and C.III.5.)
Loans to policyholders for which the policy is the main security are to be included under 'Other loans' and their amount must be disclosed in the notes to the accounts. Loans secured by mortgage are to be shown as such even where they are also secured by insurance policies. Where the amount of 'Other loans' not secured by policies is material, an appropriate breakdown must be given in the notes to the accounts.

(8) *Deposits with credit institutions*
(Assets item C.III.6.)
This item is to comprise sums the withdrawal of which is subject to a time restriction. Sums deposited with no such restriction must be shown under assets item F.III even if they bear interest.

(9) *Other*
(Assets item C.III.7.)
This item is to comprise those investments which are not covered by assets items C.III.1 to 6. Where the amount of such investments is significant, they must be disclosed in the notes to the accounts.

(10) *Deposits with ceding undertakings*
(Assets item C.IV.)
Where the company accepts reinsurance this item is to comprise amounts, owed by the ceding undertakings and corresponding to guarantees, which are deposited with those ceding undertakings or with third parties or which are retained by those undertakings. These amounts may not be combined with other amounts owed by the ceding insurer to the reinsurer or set off against amounts owed by the reinsurer to the ceding insurer.
Securities deposited with ceding undertakings or third parties which remain the property of the company must be entered in the company's accounts as an investment, under the appropriate item.

(11) *Assets held to cover linked liabilities*
(Assets item D.)
In respect of long-term business, this item is to comprise investments made pursuant to long-term policies under which the benefits payable to the policyholder are wholly or partly to be determined by reference to the value of, or the income from, property of any description (whether or not specified in the contract) or by reference to fluctuations in, or in an index of, the value of property of any description (whether or not so specified). This item is also to comprise investments which are held on behalf of the members of a tontine and are intended for distribution among them.

(12) *Reinsurance amounts*
(Assets item Da: liabilities items C.1.(b), 2.(b), 3.(b), 4.(b) and 6.(b) and D.(b).)
The reinsurance amounts may be shown either under assets item Da or under liabilities items C.1.(b), 2.(b), 3.(b), 4.(b) and 6.(b) and D.(b).
The reinsurance amounts are to comprise the actual or estimated amounts which, under contractual reinsurance arrangements, are deducted from the gross amounts of technical provisions.
As regards the provision for unearned premiums, the reinsurance amounts must be calculated according to the methods referred to in paragraph 50 below or in accordance with the terms of the reinsurance policy.

(13) *Debtors*
(Assets item E.)

Amounts owed by group undertakings and undertakings in which the company has a participating interest must be shown separately as sub-items of assets items E.I, II and III.

(14) *Own shares*

(Assets item F.IV.)

The nominal value of the shares must be shown separately under this item.

(15) *Other*

(Assets item F.V.)

This item is to comprise those assets which are not covered by assets items F.I to IV. Where such assets are material they must be disclosed in the notes to the accounts.

(16) *Accrued interest and rent*

(Assets item G.I.)

This item is to comprise those items that represent interest and rent that have been earned up to the balance-sheet date but have not yet become receivable.

(17) *Deferred acquisition costs*

(Assets item G.II.)

This item is to comprise the costs of acquiring insurance policies which are incurred during a financial year but relate to a subsequent financial year ('deferred acquisition costs'), except in so far as—

(a) allowance has been made in the computation of the long-term business provision made under paragraph 52 below and shown under liabilities item C2 or D in the balance sheet, for—

(i) the explicit recognition of such costs, or

(ii) the implicit recognition of such costs by virtue of the anticipation of future income from which such costs may prudently be expected to be recovered, or

(b) allowance has been made for such costs in respect of general business policies by a deduction from the provision for unearned premiums made under paragraph 50 below and shown under liabilities item C.I in the balance sheet.

Deferred acquisition costs arising in general business must be distinguished from those arising in long-term business.

In the case of general business, the amount of any deferred acquisition costs must be established on a basis compatible with that used for unearned premiums. There must be disclosed in the notes to the accounts—

(c) how the deferral of acquisition costs has been treated (unless otherwise expressly stated in the accounts), and

(d) where such costs are included as a deduction from the provisions at liabilities item C.I, the amount of such deduction, or

(e) where the actuarial method used in the calculation of the provisions at liabilities item C.2 or D has made allowance for the explicit recognition of such costs, the amount of the costs so recognised.

(18) *Subordinated liabilities*

(Liabilities item B.)

This item is to comprise all liabilities in respect of which there is a contractual obligation that, in the event of winding up or of bankruptcy, they are to be repaid only after the claims of all other creditors have been met (whether or not they are represented by certificates).

(19) *Fund for future appropriations*

(Liabilities item Ba.)

This item is to comprise all funds the allocation of which either to policyholders or to shareholders has not been determined by the end of the financial year.

Transfers to and from this item must be shown in item II.12a in the profit and loss account.

(20) *Provision for unearned premiums*

(Liabilities item C.1.)

In the case of long-term business the provision for unearned premiums may be included in liabilities item C.2 rather than in this item.

The provision for unearned premiums is to comprise the amount representing that part of gross premiums written which is estimated to be earned in the following financial year or to subsequent financial years.

(21) *Long-term business provision*

(Liabilities item C.2.)

This item is to comprise the actuarially estimated value of the company's liabilities (excluding technical provisions included in liabilities item D), including bonuses already declared and after deducting the actuarial value of future premiums.

This item is also to comprise claims incurred but not reported, plus the estimated costs of settling such claims.

(*22*) *Claims outstanding*

(Liabilities item C.3.)

This item is to comprise the total estimated ultimate cost to the company of settling all claims arising from events which have occurred up to the end of the financial year (including, in the case of general business, claims incurred but not reported) less amounts already paid in respect of such claims.

(*23*) *Provision for bonuses and rebates*

(Liabilities item C.4.)

This item is to comprise amounts intended for policyholders or contract beneficiaries by way of bonuses and rebates as defined in Note *(5)* on the profit and loss account format to the extent that such amounts have not been credited to policyholders or contract beneficiaries or included in liabilities item Ba or in liabilities item C.2.

(*24*) *Equalisation provision*

(Liabilities item C.5.)

This item is to comprise the amount of any equalisation reserve maintained in respect of general business by the company, in accordance with the rules in section 1.4 of the Prudential Sourcebook for Insurers[82] made by the Financial Services Authority under Part 10 of the Financial Services and Markets Act 2000.

This item is also to comprise any amounts which, in accordance with Council Directive 87/343/EEC of 22nd June 1987[83], are required to be set aside by a company to equalise fluctuations in loss ratios in future years or to provide for special risks.

A company which otherwise constitutes reserves to equalise fluctuations in loss ratios in future years or to provide for special risks must disclose that fact in the notes to the accounts.

(*25*) *Other technical provisions*

(Liabilities item C.6.)

This item is to comprise, inter alia, the provision for unexpired risks as defined in paragraph 91 below. Where the amount of the provision for unexpired risks is significant, it must be disclosed separately either in the balance sheet or in the notes to the accounts.

(*26*) *Technical provisions for linked liabilities*

(Liabilities item D.)

This item is to comprise technical provisions constituted to cover liabilities relating to investment in the context of long-term policies under which the benefits payable to policyholders are wholly or partly to be determined by reference to the value of, or the income from, property of any description (whether or not specified in the contract) or by reference to fluctuations in, or in an index of, the value of property of any description (whether or not so specified).

Any additional technical provisions constituted to cover death risks, operating expenses or other risks (such as benefits payable at the maturity date or guaranteed surrender values) must be included under liabilities item C.2.

This item must also comprise technical provisions representing the obligations of a tontine's organiser in relation to its members.

(*27*) *Deposits received from reinsurers*

(Liabilities item F.)

Where the company cedes reinsurance, this item is to comprise amounts deposited by or withheld from other insurance undertakings under reinsurance contracts. These amounts may not be merged with other amounts owed to or by those other undertakings.

Where the company cedes reinsurance and has received as a deposit securities which have been transferred to its ownership, this item is to comprise the amount owed by the company by virtue of the deposit.

---

[82] FSA 2006/42.

[83] OJ No. L185 of 4th July 1987, p 72.

(28) *Creditors*
> (Liabilities item G.)
> Amounts owed to group undertakings and undertakings in which the company has a participating interest must be shown separately as sub-items.

(29) *Debenture loans*
> (Liabilities item G.III.)
> The amount of any convertible loans must be shown separately.

## SPECIAL RULES FOR BALANCE SHEET FORMAT

### Additional items

**11.** (1) Every balance sheet of a company which carries on long-term business must show separately as an additional item the aggregate of any amounts included in liabilities item A (capital and reserves) which are required not to be treated as realised profits under section 843 of the 2006 Act.

(2) A company which carries on long-term business must show separately, in the balance sheet or in the notes to the accounts, the total amount of assets representing the long-term fund valued in accordance with the provisions of this Schedule.

### Managed funds

**12.** (1) For the purposes of this paragraph 'managed funds' are funds of a group pension fund—

(a) the management of which constitutes long-term insurance business, and

(b) which the company administers in its own name but on behalf of others, and

(c) to which it has legal title.

(2) The company must, in any case where assets and liabilities arising in respect of managed funds fall to be treated as assets and liabilities of the company, adopt the following accounting treatment: assets and liabilities representing managed funds are to be included in the company's balance sheet, with the notes to the accounts disclosing the total amount included with respect to such assets and liabilities in the balance sheet and showing the amount included under each relevant balance sheet item in respect of such assets or (as the case may be) liabilities.

### Deferred acquisition costs

**13.** The costs of acquiring insurance policies which are incurred during a financial year but which relate to a subsequent financial year must be deferred in a manner specified in Note *(17)* on the balance sheet format.

## PROFIT AND LOSS ACCOUNT FORMAT

I. Technical account — General business
1. Earned premiums, net of reinsurance
   (a) gross premiums written *(1)*
   (b) outward reinsurance premiums *(2)*
   (c) change in the gross provision for unearned premiums
   (d) change in the provision for unearned premiums, reinsurers' share
2. Allocated investment return transferred from the non-technical account (item III.6) *(10)*
2a. Investment income *(8) (10)*
   (a) income from participating interests, with a separate indication of that derived from group undertakings
   (b) income from other investments, with a separate indication of that derived from group undertakings
       (aa) income from land and buildings
       (bb) income from other investments
   (c) value re-adjustments on investments
   (d) gains on the realisation of investments
3. Other technical income, net of reinsurance
4. Claims incurred, net of reinsurance *(4)*
   (a) claims paid
       (aa) gross amount
       (bb) reinsurers' share
   (b) change in the provision for claims
       (aa) gross amount
       (bb) reinsurers' share
5. Changes in other technical provisions, net of reinsurance, not shown under other headings

6. Bonuses and rebates, net of reinsurance *(5)*
7. Net operating expenses
    (a) acquisition costs *(6)*
    (b) change in deferred acquisition costs
    (c) administrative expenses *(7)*
    (d) reinsurance commissions and profit participation
8. Other technical charges, net of reinsurance
8a. Investment expenses and charges *(8)*
    (a) investment management expenses, including interest
    (b) value adjustments on investments
    (c) losses on the realisation of investments
9. Change in the equalisation provision
10. Sub-total (balance on the technical account for general business) (item III.1)
II. Technical account — Long-term business
1. Earned premiums, net of reinsurance
    (a) gross premiums written *(1)*
    (b) outward reinsurance premiums *(2)*
    (c) change in the provision for unearned premiums, net of reinsurance *(3)*
2. Investment income *(8) (10)*
    (a) income from participating interests, with a separate indication of that derived from group undertakings
    (b) income from other investments, with a separate indication of that derived from group undertakings
        (aa) income from land and buildings
        (bb) income from other investments
    (c) value re-adjustments on investments
    (d) gains on the realisation of investments
3. Unrealised gains on investments *(9)*
4. Other technical income, net of reinsurance
5. Claims incurred, net of reinsurance *(4)*
    (a) claims paid
        (aa) gross amount
        (bb) reinsurers' share
    (b) change in the provision for claims
        (aa) gross amount
        (bb) reinsurers' share
6. Change in other technical provisions, net of reinsurance, not shown under other headings
    (a) Long-term business provision, net of reinsurance *(3)*
        (aa) gross amount
        (bb) reinsurers' share
    (b) other technical provisions, net of reinsurance
7. Bonuses and rebates, net of reinsurance *(5)*
8. Net operating expenses
    (a) acquisition costs *(6)*
    (b) change in deferred acquisition costs
    (c) administrative expenses *(7)*
    (d) reinsurance commissions and profit participation
9. Investment expenses and charges *(8)*
    (a) investment management expenses, including interest
    (b) value adjustments on investments
    (c) losses on the realisation of investments
10. Unrealised losses on investments *(9)*
11. Other technical charges, net of reinsurance
11a.Tax attributable to the long-term business
12. Allocated investment return transferred to the non-technical account (item III.4)
12a.Transfers to or from the fund for future appropriations
13. Sub-total (balance on the technical account — long-term business) (item III.2)
III. Non-technical account
1. Balance on the general business technical account (item I.10)
2. Balance on the long-term business technical account (item II.13)
2a. Tax credit attributable to balance on the long-term business technical account
3. Investment income *(8)*
    (a) income from participating interests, with a separate indication of that derived from group undertakings
    (b) income from other investments, with a separate indication of that derived from group undertakings
        (aa) income from land and buildings

          (bb) income from other investments
          (c)  value re-adjustments on investments
          (d)  gains on the realisation of investments

3a. Unrealised gains on investments *(9)*

4. Allocated investment return transferred from the long-term business technical account (item II.12) *(10)*

5. Investment expenses and charges *(8)*
    (a)  investment management expenses, including interest
    (b)  value adjustments on investments
    (c)  losses on the realisation of investments

5a. Unrealised losses on investments *(9)*

6. Allocated investment return transferred to the general business technical account (item I.2) *(10)*

7. Other income

8. Other charges, including value adjustments

8a. Profit or loss on ordinary activities before tax

9. Tax on profit or loss on ordinary activities

10. Profit or loss on ordinary activities after tax

11. Extraordinary income

12. Extraordinary charges

13. Extraordinary profit or loss

14. Tax on extraordinary profit or loss

15. Other taxes not shown under the preceding items

16. Profit or loss for the financial year

## NOTES ON THE PROFIT AND LOSS ACCOUNT FORMAT

(1) *Gross premiums written*
(General business technical account: item I.1.(a). Long-term business technical account: item II.1.(a).)
This item is to comprise all amounts due during the financial year in respect of insurance contracts entered into regardless of the fact that such amounts may relate in whole or in part to a later financial year, and must include inter alia—
  (i)   premiums yet to be determined, where the premium calculation can be done only at the end of the year;
  (ii)  single premiums, including annuity premiums, and, in long-term business, single premiums resulting from bonus and rebate provisions in so far as they must be considered as premiums under the terms of the contract;
  (iii) additional premiums in the case of half-yearly, quarterly or monthly payments and additional payments from policyholders for expenses borne by the company;
  (iv) in the case of co-insurance, the company's portion of total premiums;
  (v)  reinsurance premiums due from ceding and retroceding insurance undertakings, including portfolio entries,
after deduction of cancellations and portfolio withdrawals credited to ceding and retroceding insurance undertakings.
The above amounts must not include the amounts of taxes or duties levied with premiums.

(2) *Outward reinsurance premiums*
(General business technical account: item I.1.(b). Long-term business technical account: item II.1.(b).)
This item is to comprise all premiums paid or payable in respect of outward reinsurance contracts entered into by the company. Portfolio entries payable on the conclusion or amendment of outward reinsurance contracts must be added; portfolio withdrawals receivable must be deducted.

(3) *Change in the provision for unearned premiums, net of reinsurance*
(Long-term business technical account: items II.1.(c) and II.6.(a).)
In the case of long-term business, the change in unearned premiums may be included either in item II.1.(c) or in item II.6.(a) of the long-term business technical account.

(4) *Claims incurred, net of reinsurance*
(General business technical account: item I.4. Long-term business technical account: item II.5.)
This item is to comprise all payments made in respect of the financial year with the addition of the provision for claims (but after deducting the provision for claims for the preceding financial year).

These amounts must include annuities, surrenders, entries and withdrawals of loss provisions to and from ceding insurance undertakings and reinsurers and external and internal claims management costs and charges for claims incurred but not reported such as are referred to in paragraphs 53(2) and 55 below.

Sums recoverable on the basis of subrogation and salvage (within the meaning of paragraph 53 below) must be deducted.

Where the difference between—

(a) the loss provision made at the beginning of the year for outstanding claims incurred in previous years, and

(b) the payments made during the year on account of claims incurred in previous years and the loss provision shown at the end of the year for such outstanding claims,

is material, it must be shown in the notes to the accounts, broken down by category and amount.

(5) *Bonuses and rebates, net of reinsurance*

(General business technical account: item I.6. Long-term business technical account: item II.7.)

Bonuses are to comprise all amounts chargeable for the financial year which are paid or payable to policyholders and other insured parties or provided for their benefit, including amounts used to increase technical provisions or applied to the reduction of future premiums, to the extent that such amounts represent an allocation of surplus or profit arising on business as a whole or a section of business, after deduction of amounts provided in previous years which are no longer required.

Rebates are to comprise such amounts to the extent that they represent a partial refund of premiums resulting from the experience of individual contracts.

Where material, the amount charged for bonuses and that charged for rebates must be disclosed separately in the notes to the accounts.

(6) *Acquisition costs*

(General business technical account: item I.7.(a).

Long-term business technical account: item II.8.(a).)

This item is to comprise the costs arising from the conclusion of insurance contracts. They must cover both direct costs, such as acquisition commissions or the cost of drawing up the insurance document or including the insurance contract in the portfolio, and indirect costs, such as advertising costs or the administrative expenses connected with the processing of proposals and the issuing of policies.

In the case of long-term business, policy renewal commissions must be included under item II.8.(c) in the long-term business technical account.

(7) *Administrative expenses*

(General business technical account: item I.7.(c).

Long-term business technical account: item II.8.(c).)

This item must include the costs arising from premium collection, portfolio administration, handling of bonuses and rebates, and inward and outward reinsurance. They must in particular include staff costs and depreciation provisions in respect of office furniture and equipment in so far as these need not be shown under acquisition costs, claims incurred or investment charges.

Item II.8.(c) must also include policy renewal commissions.

(8) *Investment income, expenses and charges*

(General business technical account: items I.2a and 8a. Long-term business technical account: items II.2 and 9. Non-technical account: items III.3 and 5.)

Investment income, expenses and charges must, to the extent that they arise in the long-term fund, be disclosed in the long-term business technical account. Other investment income, expenses and charges must either be disclosed in the non-technical account or attributed between the appropriate technical and non-technical accounts. Where the company makes such an attribution it must disclose the basis for it in the notes to the accounts.

(9) *Unrealised gains and losses on investments*

(Long-term business technical account: items II.3 and 10. Non-technical account: items III.3a and 5a.)

In the case of investments attributed to the long-term fund, the difference between the valuation of the investments and their purchase price or, if they have previously been valued, their valuation as at the last balance sheet date, may be disclosed (in whole or in part) in item II.3 or II.10 (as the case may be) of the long-term business technical account, and in the case of investments shown as assets under assets item D (assets held to cover linked liabilities) must be so disclosed.

In the case of other investments, the difference between the valuation of the investments and their purchase price or, if they have previously been valued, their valuation as
at the last balance sheet date, may be disclosed (in whole or in part) in item III.3a or III.5a
(as the case may require) of the non-technical account.

(10) *Allocated investment return*

(General business technical account: item I.2. Long-term business technical account: item II.2.
Non-technical account: items III.4 and 6.)

The allocated return may be transferred from one part of the profit and loss account to
another.

Where part of the investment return is transferred to the general business technical
account, the transfer from the non-technical account must be deducted from item III.6
and added to item I.2.

Where part of the investment return disclosed in the long-term business technical account is
transferred to the non-technical account, the transfer to the non-technical account shall be
deducted from item II.12 and added to item III.4.

The reasons for such transfers (which may consist of a reference to any relevant statutory
requirement) and the bases on which they are made must be disclosed in the notes to the
accounts.

PART 2

ACCOUNTING PRINCIPLES AND RULES

SECTION A

ACCOUNTING PRINCIPLES

**Preliminary**

**14.** The amounts to be included in respect of all items shown in a company's accounts must be
determined in accordance with the principles set out in this Section.

**15.** But if it appears to the company's directors that there are special reasons for departing from any
of those principles in preparing the company's accounts in respect of any financial year they may
do so, in which case particulars of the departure, the reasons for it and its effect must be given in
a note to the accounts.

**Accounting principles**

**16.** The company is presumed to be carrying on business as a going concern.

**17.** Accounting policies must be applied consistently within the same accounts and from one financial
year to the next.

**18.** The amount of any item must be determined on a prudent basis, and in particular—

(a) subject to note (9) on the profit and loss account format, only profits realised at the balance
sheet date are to be included in the profit and loss account, and

(b) all liabilities which have arisen in respect of the financial year to which the accounts relate or
a previous financial year must be taken into account, including those which only become
apparent between the balance sheet date and the date on which it is signed on behalf of the
board of directors in accordance with section 414 of the 2006 Act (approval and signing of
accounts).

**19.** All income and charges relating to the financial year to which the accounts relate are to be taken
into account, without regard to the date of receipt or payment.

**20.** In determining the aggregate amount of any item, the amount of each individual asset or liability
that falls to be taken into account must be determined separately.

**Valuation**

**21.** (1) The amounts to be included in respect of assets of any description mentioned in paragraph
22 (valuation of assets: general) must be determined either—

(a) in accordance with that paragraph and paragraph 24 (but subject to paragraphs 27 to
29), or

(b) so far as applicable to an asset of that description, in accordance with Section C
(valuation at fair value).

(2) The amounts to be included in respect of assets of any description mentioned in paragraph
24 (alternative valuation of fixed-income securities) may be determined—

(a) in accordance with that paragraph (but subject to paragraphs 27 to 29), or

(b) so far as applicable to an asset of that description, in accordance with Section C.

(3) The amounts to be included in respect of assets which—

(a) are not assets of a description mentioned in paragraph 22 or 23, but

      (b)  are assets of a description to which Section C is applicable, may be determined in accordance with that Section.

  (4)  Subject to sub-paragraphs (1) to (3), the amounts to be included in respect of all items shown in a company's accounts are determined in accordance with Section C.

## SECTION B
## CURRENT VALUE ACCOUNTING RULES

**Valuation of assets: general**

**22.** (1)  Subject to paragraph 24, investments falling to be included under assets item C (investments) must be included at their current value calculated in accordance with paragraphs 25 and 26.

  (2)  Investments falling to be included under assets item D (assets held to cover linked liabilities) must be shown at their current value calculated in accordance with paragraphs 25 and 26.

**23.** (1)  Intangible assets other than goodwill may be shown at their current cost.

  (2)  Assets falling to be included under assets items F.I (tangible assets) and F.IV (own shares) in the balance sheet format may be shown at their current value calculated in accordance with paragraphs 25 and 26 or at their current cost.

  (3)  Assets falling to be included under assets item F.II (stocks) may be shown at current cost.

**Alternative valuation of fixed-income securities**

**24.** (1)  This paragraph applies to debt securities and other fixed-income securities shown as assets under assets items C.II (investments in group undertakings and participating interests) and C.III (other financial investments).

  (2)  Securities to which this paragraph applies may either be valued in accordance with paragraph 22 or their amortised value may be shown in the balance sheet, in which case the provisions of this paragraph apply.

  (3)  Subject to sub-paragraph (4), where the purchase price of securities to which this paragraph applies exceeds the amount repayable at maturity, the amount of the difference—

      (a)  must be charged to the profit and loss account, and

      (b)  must be shown separately in the balance sheet or in the notes to the accounts.

  (4)  The amount of the difference referred to in sub-paragraph (3) may be written off in instalments so that it is completely written off when the securities are repaid, in which case there must be shown separately in the balance sheet or in the notes to the accounts the difference between the purchase price (less the aggregate amount written off) and the amount repayable at maturity.

  (5)  Where the purchase price of securities to which this paragraph applies is less than the amount repayable at maturity, the amount of the difference must be released to income in instalments over the period remaining until repayment, in which case there must be shown separately in the balance sheet or in the notes to the accounts the difference between the purchase price (plus the aggregate amount released to income) and the amount repayable at maturity.

  (6)  Both the purchase price and the current value of securities valued in accordance with this paragraph must be disclosed in the notes to the accounts.

  (7)  Where securities to which this paragraph applies which are not valued in accordance with paragraph 22 are sold before maturity, and the proceeds are used to purchase other securities to which this paragraph applies, the difference between the proceeds of sale and their book value may be spread uniformly over the period remaining until the maturity of the original investment.

**Meaning of 'current value'**

**25.** (1)  Subject to sub-paragraph (5), in the case of investments other than land and buildings, current value means market value determined in accordance with this paragraph.

  (2)  In the case of listed investments, market value means the value on the balance sheet date or, when the balance sheet date is not a stock exchange trading day, on the last stock exchange trading day before that date.

  (3)  Where a market exists for unlisted investments, market value means the average price at which such investments were traded on the balance sheet date or, when the balance sheet date is not a trading day, on the last trading day before that date.

  (4)  Where, on the date on which the accounts are drawn up, listed or unlisted investments have been sold or are to be sold within the short term, the market value must be reduced by the actual or estimated realisation costs.

  (5)  Except where the equity method of accounting is applied, all investments other than those referred to in sub-paragraphs (2) and (3) must be valued on a basis which has prudent regard to the likely realisable value.

**26.** (1)  In the case of land and buildings, current value means the market value on the date of valuation, where relevant reduced as provided in sub-paragraphs (4) and (5).

(2)  Market value means the price at which land and buildings could be sold under private contract between a willing seller and an arm's length buyer on the date of valuation, it being assumed that the property is publicly exposed to the market, that market conditions permit orderly disposal and that a normal period, having regard to the nature of the property, is available for the negotiation of the sale.

(3)  The market value must be determined through the separate valuation of each land and buildings item, carried out at least every five years in accordance with generally recognised methods of valuation.

(4)  Where the value of any land and buildings item has diminished since the preceding valuation under sub-paragraph (3), an appropriate value adjustment must be made.

(5)  The lower value arrived at under sub-paragraph (4) must not be increased in subsequent balance sheets unless such increase results from a new determination of market value arrived at in accordance with sub-paragraphs (2) and (3).

(6)  Where, on the date on which the accounts are drawn up, land and buildings have been sold or are to be sold within the short term, the value arrived at in accordance with sub-paragraphs (2) and (4) must be reduced by the actual or estimated realisation costs.

(7)  Where it is impossible to determine the market value of a land and buildings item, the value arrived at on the basis of the principle of purchase price or production cost is deemed to be its current value.

### Application of the depreciation rules

**27.** (1)  Where—

(a)  the value of any asset of a company is determined in accordance with paragraph 22 or 23, and

(b)  in the case of a determination under paragraph 22, the asset falls to be included under assets item C.I, that value must be, or (as the case may require) must be the starting point for determining, the amount to be included in respect of that asset in the company's accounts, instead of its cost or any value previously so determined for that asset. Paragraphs 36 to 41 and 43 apply accordingly in relation to any such asset with the substitution for any reference to its cost of a reference to the value most recently determined for that asset in accordance with paragraph 22 or 23 (as the case may be).

(2)  The amount of any provision for depreciation required in the case of any asset by paragraph 37 or 38 as it applies by virtue of sub-paragraph (1) is referred to below in this paragraph as the adjusted amount, and the amount of any provision which would be required by that paragraph in the case of that asset according to the historical cost accounting rules is referred to as the historical cost amount.

(3)  Where sub-paragraph (1) applies in the case of any asset the amount of any provision for depreciation in respect of that asset included in any item shown in the profit and loss account in respect of amounts written off assets of the description in question may be the historical cost amount instead of the adjusted amount, provided that the amount of any difference between the two is shown separately in the profit and loss account or in a note to the accounts.

### Additional information to be provided

**28.** (1)  This paragraph applies where the amounts to be included in respect of assets covered by any items shown in a company's accounts have been determined in accordance with paragraph 22 or 23.

(2)  The items affected and the basis of valuation adopted in determining the amounts of the assets in question in the case of each such item must be disclosed in a note to the accounts.

(3)  The purchase price of investments valued in accordance with paragraph 22 must be disclosed in the notes to the accounts.

(4)  In the case of each balance sheet item valued in accordance with paragraph 23 either—

(a)  the comparable amounts determined according to the historical cost accounting rules (without any provision for depreciation or diminution in value), or

(b)  the differences between those amounts and the corresponding amounts actually shown in the balance sheet in respect of that item, must be shown separately in the balance sheet or in a note to the accounts.

(5)  In sub-paragraph (4), references in relation to any item to the comparable amounts determined as there mentioned are references to—

(a)  the aggregate amount which would be required to be shown in respect of that item if the amounts to be included in respect of all the assets covered by that item were determined according to the historical cost accounting rules, and

(b)  the aggregate amount of the cumulative provisions for depreciation or diminution in value which would be permitted or required in determining those amounts according to those rules.

**Revaluation reserve**

**29.** (1) Subject to sub-paragraph (7), with respect to any determination of the value of an asset of a company in accordance with paragraph 22 or 23, the amount of any profit or loss arising from that determination (after allowing, where appropriate, for any provisions for depreciation or diminution in value made otherwise than by reference to the value so determined and any adjustments of any such provisions made in the light of that determination) must be credited or (as the case may be) debited to a separate reserve ('the revaluation reserve').

(2) The amount of the revaluation reserve must be shown in the company's balance sheet under liabilities item A.III, but need not be shown under the name 'revaluation reserve'.

(3) An amount may be transferred—

   (a) from the revaluation reserve—

      (i) to the profit and loss account, if the amount was previously charged to that account or represents realised profit, or

      (ii) on capitalisation,

   (b) to or from the revaluation reserve in respect of the taxation relating to any profit or loss credited or debited to the reserve.

   The revaluation reserve must be reduced to the extent that the amounts transferred to it are no longer necessary for the purposes of the valuation method used.

(4) In sub-paragraph (3)(a)(ii) 'capitalisation', in relation to an amount standing to the credit of the revaluation reserve, means applying it in wholly or partly paying up unissued shares in the company to be allotted to members of the company as fully or partly paid shares.

(5) The revaluation reserve must not be reduced except as mentioned in this paragraph.

(6) The treatment for taxation purposes of amounts credited or debited to the revaluation reserve must be disclosed in a note to the accounts.

(7) This paragraph does not apply to the difference between the valuation of investments and their purchase price or previous valuation shown in the long-term business technical account or the non-technical account in accordance with note (9) on the profit and loss account format.

## SECTION C
## VALUATION AT FAIR VALUE

**Inclusion of financial instruments at fair value**

**30.** (1) Subject to sub-paragraphs (2) to (5), financial instruments (including derivatives) may be included at fair value.

(2) Sub-paragraph (1) does not apply to financial instruments that constitute liabilities unless—

   (a) they are held as part of a trading portfolio,

   (b) they are derivatives, or

   (c) they are financial instruments falling within paragraph (4).

(3) Except where they fall within paragraph (4), or fall to be included under assets item D (assets held to cover linked liabilities), sub-paragraph (1) does not apply to?—

   (a) financial instruments (other than derivatives) held to maturity,

   (b) loans and receivables originated by the company and not held for trading purposes,

   (c) interests in subsidiary undertakings, associated undertakings and joint ventures,

   (d) equity instruments issued by the company,

   (e) contracts for contingent consideration in a business combination, or

   (f) other financial instruments with such special characteristics that the instruments, according to generally accepted accounting principles or practice, should be accounted for differently from other financial instruments.

(4) Financial instruments that, under international accounting standards adopted by the European Commission on or before 5th September 2006 in accordance with the IAS Regulation, may be included in accounts at fair value, may be so included, provided that the disclosures required by such accounting standards are made.

(5) If the fair value of a financial instrument cannot be determined reliably in accordance with paragraph 31, sub-paragraph (1) does not apply to that financial instrument.

(6) In this paragraph—

   'associated undertaking' has the meaning given by paragraph 19 of Schedule 6 to these Regulations; and

   'joint venture' has the meaning given by paragraph 18 of that Schedule.

**Determination of fair value**

**31.** (1) The fair value of a financial instrument is its value determined in accordance with this paragraph.

(2) If a reliable market can readily be identified for the financial instrument, its fair value is determined by reference to its market value.

(3) If a reliable market cannot readily be identified for the financial instrument but can be identified for its components or for a similar instrument, its fair value is determined by reference to the market value of its components or of the similar instrument.

(4) If neither sub-paragraph (2) nor (3) applies, the fair value of the financial instrument is a value resulting from generally accepted valuation models and techniques.

(5) Any valuation models and techniques used for the purposes of sub-paragraph (4) must ensure a reasonable approximation of the market value.

### Hedged items

**32.** A company may include any assets and liabilities, or identified portions of such assets or liabilities, that qualify as hedged items under a fair value hedge accounting system at the amount required under that system.

### Other assets that may be included at fair value

**33.** (1) This paragraph applies to—
  (a) investment property, and
  (b) living animals and plants, that, under international accounting standards, may be included in accounts at fair value.

(2) Such investment property and such living animals and plants may be included at fair value, provided that all such investment property or, as the case may be, all such living animals and plants are so included where their fair value can reliably be determined.

(3) In this paragraph, 'fair value' means fair value determined in accordance with relevant international accounting standards.

### Accounting for changes in value

**34.** (1) This paragraph applies where a financial instrument is valued in accordance with paragraph 30 or 32 or an asset is valued in accordance with paragraph 33.

(2) Notwithstanding paragraph 18 in this Part of this Schedule, and subject to sub-paragraphs (3) and (4), a change in the value of the financial instrument or of the investment property or living animal or plant must be included in the profit and loss account.

(3) Where—
  (a) the financial instrument accounted for is a hedging instrument under a hedge accounting system that allows some or all of the change in value not to be shown in the profit and loss account, or
  (b) the change in value relates to an exchange difference arising on a monetary item that forms part of a company's net investment in a foreign entity,
  the amount of the change in value must be credited to or (as the case may be) debited from a separate reserve ('the fair value reserve').

(4) Where the instrument accounted for—
  (a) is an available for sale financial asset, and
  (b) is not a derivative, the change in value may be credited to or (as the case may be) debited from the fair value reserve.

### The fair value reserve

**35.** (1) The fair value reserve must be adjusted to the extent that the amounts shown in it are no longer necessary for the purposes of paragraph 34(3) or (4).

(2) The treatment for taxation purposes of amounts credited or debited to the fair value reserve must be disclosed in a note to the accounts.

## SECTION D
## HISTORICAL COST ACCOUNTING RULES

*Valuation of assets*

### General rules

**36.** (1) The rules in this Section are 'the historical cost accounting rules'.

(2) Subject to any provision for depreciation or diminution in value made in accordance with paragraph 37 or 38, the amount to be included in respect of any asset in the balance sheet format is its cost.

**37.** In the case of any asset included under assets item B (intangible assets), C.I (land and buildings), F.I (tangible assets) or F.II (stocks) which has a limited useful economic life, the amount of—
  (a) its cost, or
  (b) where it is estimated that any such asset will have a residual value at the end of the period of its useful economic life, its cost less that estimated residual value, must be reduced by provisions for depreciation calculated to write off that amount systematically over the period of the asset's useful economic life.

**38.** (1) This paragraph applies to any asset included under assets item B (intangible assets), C (investments), F.I (tangible assets) or F.IV (own shares).

(2) Where an asset to which this paragraph applies has diminished in value, provisions for diminution in value may be made in respect of it and the amount to be included in respect of it may be reduced accordingly.

(3) Provisions for diminution in value must be made in respect of any asset to which this paragraph applies if the reduction in its value is expected to be permanent (whether its useful economic life is limited or not), and the amount to be included in respect of it must be reduced accordingly.

(4) Any provisions made under sub-paragraph (2) or (3) which are not shown in the profit and loss account must be disclosed (either separately or in aggregate) in a note to the accounts.

**39.** (1) Where the reasons for which any provision was made in accordance with paragraph 38 have ceased to apply to any extent, that provision must be written back to the extent that it is no longer necessary.

(2) Any amounts written back in accordance with sub-paragraph (1) which are not shown in the profit and loss account must be disclosed (either separately or in aggregate) in a note to the accounts.

**40.** (1) This paragraph applies to assets included under assets items E.I, II and III (debtors) and F.III (cash at bank and in hand) in the balance sheet.

(2) If the net realisable value of an asset to which this paragraph applies is lower than its cost the amount to be included in respect of that asset is the net realisable value.

(3) Where the reasons for which any provision for diminution in value was made in accordance with sub-paragraph (2) have ceased to apply to any extent, that provision must be written back to the extent that it is no longer necessary.

### Development costs

**41.** (1) Notwithstanding that amounts representing 'development costs' may be included under assets item B (intangible assets) in the balance sheet format, an amount may only be included in a company's balance sheet in respect of development costs in special circumstances.

(2) If any amount is included in a company's balance sheet in respect of development costs the following information must be given in a note to the accounts—

(a) the period over which the amount of those costs originally capitalised is being or is to be written off, and

(b) the reasons for capitalising the development costs in question.

### Goodwill

**42.** (1) The application of paragraphs 36 to 39 in relation to goodwill (in any case where goodwill is treated as an asset) is subject to the following.

(2) Subject to sub-paragraph (3), the amount of the consideration for any goodwill acquired by a company must be reduced by provisions for depreciation calculated to write off that amount systematically over a period chosen by the directors of the company.

(3) The period chosen must not exceed the useful economic life of the goodwill in question.

(4) In any case where any goodwill acquired by a company is included as an asset in the company's balance sheet, there must be disclosed in a note to the accounts—

(a) the period chosen for writing off the consideration for that goodwill, and

(b) the reasons for choosing that period.

*Miscellaneous and supplementary provisions*

### Excess of money owed over value received as an asset item

**43.** (1) Where the amount repayable on any debt owed by a company is greater than the value of the consideration received in the transaction giving rise to the debt, the amount of the difference may be treated as an asset.

(2) Where any such amount is so treated—

(a) it must be written off by reasonable amounts each year and must be completely written off before repayment of the debt, and

(b) if the current amount is not shown as a separate item in the company's balance sheet, it must be disclosed in a note to the accounts.

### Assets included at a fixed amount

**44.** (1) Subject to sub-paragraph (2), assets which fall to be included under assets item F.I (tangible assets) in the balance sheet format may be included at a fixed quantity and value.

(2) Sub-paragraph (1) applies to assets of a kind which are constantly being replaced where—

(a) their overall value is not material to assessing the company's state of affairs, and

(b) their quantity, value and composition are not subject to material variation.

### Determination of cost

**45.** (1) The cost of an asset that has been acquired by the company is to be determined by adding to the actual price paid any expenses incidental to its acquisition.

(2) The cost of an asset constructed by the company is to be determined by adding to the purchase price of the raw materials and consumables used the amount of the costs incurred by the company which are directly attributable to the construction of that asset.

(3) In addition, there may be included in the cost of an asset constructed by the company—

(a) a reasonable proportion of the costs incurred by the company which are only indirectly attributable to the construction of that asset, but only to the extent that they relate to the period of construction, and

(b) interest on capital borrowed to finance the construction of that asset, to the extent that it accrues in respect of the period of construction, provided, however, in a case within paragraph (b), that the inclusion of the interest in determining the cost of that asset and the amount of the interest so included is disclosed in a note to the accounts.

**46.** (1) The cost of any assets which are fungible assets may be determined by the application of any of the methods mentioned in sub-paragraph (2) in relation to any such assets of the same class, provided that the method chosen is one which appears to the directors to be appropriate in the circumstances of the company.

(2) Those methods are—

(a) the method known as 'first in, first out' (FIFO),

(b) the method known as 'last in, first out' (LIFO),

(c) a weighted average price, and

(d) any other method similar to any of the methods mentioned above.

(3) Where in the case of any company—

(a) the cost of assets falling to be included under any item shown in the company's balance sheet has been determined by the application of any method permitted by this paragraph, and

(b) the amount shown in respect of that item differs materially from the relevant alternative amount given below in this paragraph, the amount of that difference must be disclosed in a note to the accounts.

(4) Subject to sub-paragraph (5), for the purposes of sub-paragraph (3)(b), the relevant alternative amount, in relation to any item shown in a company's balance sheet, is the amount which would have been shown in respect of that item if assets of any class included under that item at an amount determined by any method permitted by this paragraph had instead been included at their replacement cost as at the balance sheet date.

(5) The relevant alternative amount may be determined by reference to the most recent actual purchase price before the balance sheet date of assets of any class included under the item in question instead of by reference to their replacement cost as at that date, but only if the former appears to the directors of the company to constitute the more appropriate standard of comparison in the case of assets of that class.

### Substitution of original amount where price or cost unknown

**47.** (1) This paragraph applies where—

(a) there is no record of the purchase price of any asset acquired by a company or of any price, expenses or costs relevant for determining its cost in accordance with paragraph 45, or

(b) any such record cannot be obtained without unreasonable expense or delay.

(2) In such a case, the cost of the asset must be taken, for the purposes of paragraphs 36 to 42, to be the value ascribed to it in the earliest available record of its value made on or after its acquisition by the company.

## SECTION E
## RULES FOR DETERMINING PROVISIONS

### Preliminary

**48.** Provisions which are to be shown in a company's accounts are to be determined in accordance with this Section.

### Technical provisions

**49.** The amount of technical provisions must at all times be sufficient to cover any liabilities arising out of insurance contracts as far as can reasonably be foreseen.

### Provision for unearned premiums

**50.** (1) The provision for unearned premiums must in principle be computed separately for each insurance contract, save that statistical methods (and in particular proportional and flat rate methods) may be used where they may be expected to give approximately the same results as individual calculations.

(2) Where the pattern of risk varies over the life of a contract, this must be taken into account in the calculation methods.

## Provision for unexpired risks

**51.** The provision for unexpired risks (as defined in paragraph 91) must be computed on the basis of claims and administrative expenses likely to arise after the end of the financial year from contracts concluded before that date, in so far as their estimated value exceeds the provision for unearned premiums and any premiums receivable under those contracts.

## Long-term business provision

**52.** (1) The long-term business provision must in principle be computed separately for each long-term contract, save that statistical or mathematical methods may be used where they may be expected to give approximately the same results as individual calculations.

(2) A summary of the principal assumptions in making the provision under sub-paragraph (1) must be given in the notes to the accounts.

(3) The computation must be made annually by a Fellow of the Institute or Faculty of Actuaries on the basis of recognised actuarial methods, with due regard to the actuarial principles laid down in Directive 2002/83/EC of the European Parliament and of the Council of 5th November 2002 concerning life assurance[84].

*Provisions for claims outstanding*

## General business

**53.** (1) A provision must in principle be computed separately for each claim on the basis of the costs still expected to arise, save that statistical methods may be used if they result in an adequate provision having regard to the nature of the risks.

(2) This provision must also allow for claims incurred but not reported by the balance sheet date, the amount of the allowance being determined having regard to past experience as to the number and magnitude of claims reported after previous balance sheet dates.

(3) All claims settlement costs (whether direct or indirect) must be included in the calculation of the provision.

(4) Recoverable amounts arising out of subrogation or salvage must be estimated on a prudent basis and either deducted from the provision for claims outstanding (in which case if the amounts are material they must be shown in the notes to the accounts) or shown as assets.

(5) In sub-paragraph (4), 'subrogation' means the acquisition of the rights of policy holders with respect to third parties, and 'salvage' means the acquisition of the legal ownership of insured property.

(6) Where benefits resulting from a claim must be paid in the form of annuity, the amounts to be set aside for that purpose must be calculated by recognised actuarial methods, and paragraph 54 does not apply to such calculations.

(7) Implicit discounting or deductions, whether resulting from the placing of a current value on a provision for an outstanding claim which is expected to be settled later at a higher figure or otherwise effected, is prohibited.

**54.** (1) Explicit discounting or deductions to take account of investment income is permitted, subject to the following conditions—

(a) the expected average interval between the date for the settlement of claims being discounted and the accounting date must be at least four years;

(b) the discounting or deductions must be effected on a recognised prudential basis;

(c) when calculating the total cost of settling claims, the company must take account of all factors that could cause increases in that cost;

(d) the company must have adequate data at its disposal to construct a reliable model of the rate of claims settlements;

(e) the rate of interest used for the calculation of present values must not exceed a rate prudently estimated to be earned by assets of the company which are appropriate in magnitude and nature to cover the provisions for claims being discounted during the period necessary for the payment of such claims, and must not exceed either—

(i) a rate justified by the performance of such assets over the preceding five years, or

(ii) a rate justified by the performance of such assets during the year preceding the balance sheet date.

---

[84] OJ L345 of 19th December 2002, p 1.

(2) When discounting or effecting deductions, the company must, in the notes to the accounts, disclose—

(a) the total amount of provisions before discounting or deductions,

(b) the categories of claims which are discounted or from which deductions have been made,

(c) for each category of claims, the methods used, in particular the rates used for the estimates referred to in sub-paragraph (1)(d) and (e), and the criteria adopted for estimating the period that will elapse before the claims are settled.

**Long-term business**

**55.** The amount of the provision for claims must be equal to the sums due to beneficiaries, plus the costs of settling claims.

**Equalisation reserves**

**56.** The amount of any equalisation reserve maintained in respect of general business by the company, in accordance with the rules in section 1.4 of the Prudential Sourcebook for Insurers made by the Financial Services Authority under Part 10 of the Financial Services and Markets Act 2000[85], must be determined in accordance with such rules.

**Accounting on a non-annual basis**

**57.** (1) Either of the methods described in paragraphs 58 and 59 may be applied where, because of the nature of the class or type of insurance in question, information about premiums receivable or claims payable (or both) for the underwriting years is insufficient when the accounts are drawn up for reliable estimates to be made.

(2) The use of either of the methods referred to in sub-paragraph (1) must be disclosed in the notes to the accounts together with the reasons for adopting it.

(3) Where one of the methods referred to in sub-paragraph (1) is adopted, it must be applied systematically in successive years unless circumstances justify a change.

(4) In the event of a change in the method applied, the effect on the assets, liabilities, financial position and profit or loss must be stated in the notes to the accounts.

(5) For the purposes of this paragraph and paragraph 58, 'underwriting year' means the financial year in which the insurance contracts in the class or type of insurance in question commenced.

**58.** (1) The excess of the premiums written over the claims and expenses paid in respect of contracts commencing in the underwriting year shall form a technical provision included in the technical provision for claims outstanding shown in the balance sheet under liabilities item C.3.

(2) The provision may also be computed on the basis of a given percentage of the premiums written where such a method is appropriate for the type of risk insured.

(3) If necessary, the amount of this technical provision must be increased to make it sufficient to meet present and future obligations.

(4) The technical provision constituted under this paragraph must be replaced by a provision for claims outstanding estimated in accordance with paragraph 53 as soon as sufficient information has been gathered and not later than the end of the third year following the underwriting year.

(5) The length of time that elapses before a provision for claims outstanding is constituted in accordance with sub-paragraph (4) must be disclosed in the notes to the accounts.

**59.** (1) The figures shown in the technical account or in certain items within it must relate to a year which wholly or partly precedes the financial year (but by no more than 12 months).

(2) The amounts of the technical provisions shown in the accounts must if necessary be increased to make them sufficient to meet present and future obligations.

(3) The length of time by which the earlier year to which the figures relate precedes the financial year and the magnitude of the transactions concerned must be disclosed in the notes to the accounts.

---

[85] FSA 2006/42.

## PART 3

## NOTES TO THE ACCOUNTS

### Preliminary

**60.** Any information required in the case of any company by the following provisions of this Part of this Schedule must (if not given in the company's accounts) be given by way of a note to the accounts.

*General*

### Disclosure of accounting policies

**61.** The accounting policies adopted by the company in determining the amounts to be included in respect of items shown in the balance sheet and in determining the profit or loss of the company must be stated (including such policies with respect to the depreciation and diminution in value of assets).

**62.** It must be stated whether the accounts have been prepared in accordance with applicable accounting standards and particulars of any material departure from those standards and the reasons for it must be given.

### Sums denominated in foreign currencies

**63.** Where any sums originally denominated in foreign currencies have been brought into account under any items shown in the balance sheet or profit and loss account format, the basis on which those sums have been translated into sterling (or the currency in which the accounts are drawn up) must be stated.

### Reserves and dividends

**64.** There must be stated—
   (a)  any amount set aside or proposed to be set aside to, or withdrawn or proposed to be withdrawn from, reserves,
   (b)  the aggregate amount of dividends paid in the financial year (other than those for which a liability existed at the immediately preceding balance sheet date),
   (c)  the aggregate amount of dividends that the company is liable to pay at the balance sheet date, and
   (d)  the aggregate amount of dividends that are proposed before the date of approval of the accounts, and not otherwise disclosed under sub-paragraph (b) or (c).

*Information supplementing the balance sheet*

### Share capital and debentures

**65.** (1)  Where shares of more than one class have been allotted, the number and aggregate nominal value of shares of each class allotted must be given.
   (2)  In the case of any part of the allotted share capital that consists of redeemable shares, the following information must be given—
      (a)  the earliest and latest dates on which the company has power to redeem those shares,
      (b)  whether those shares must be redeemed in any event or are liable to be redeemed at the option of the company or of the shareholder, and
      (c)  whether any (and, if so, what) premium is payable on redemption.

**66.** If the company has allotted any shares during the financial year, the following information must be given—
   (a)  the classes of shares allotted, and
   (b)  as respects each class of shares, the number allotted, their aggregate nominal value and the consideration received by the company for the allotment.

**67.** (1)  With respect to any contingent right to the allotment of shares in the company the following particulars must be given—
      (a)  the number, description and amount of the shares in relation to which the right is exercisable,
      (b)  the period during which it is exercisable, and
      (c)  the price to be paid for the shares allotted.
   (2)  In sub-paragraph (1) 'contingent right to the allotment of shares' means any option to subscribe for shares and any other right to require the allotment of shares to any person

whether arising on the conversion into shares of securities of any other description or otherwise.

**68.** (1) If the company has issued any debentures during the financial year to which the accounts relate, the following information must be given—

(a) the classes of debentures issued, and

(b) as respects each class of debentures, the amount issued and the consideration received by the company for the issue.

(2) Where any of the company's debentures are held by a nominee of or trustee for the company, the nominal amount of the debentures and the amount at which they are stated in the accounting records kept by the company in accordance with section 386 of the 2006 Act (duty to keep accounting records) must be stated.

### Assets

**69.** (1) In respect of any assets of the company included in assets items B (intangible assets), C.I (land and buildings) and C.II (investments in group undertakings and participating interests) in the company's balance sheet the following information must be given by reference to each such item—

(a) the appropriate amounts in respect of those assets included in the item as at the date of the beginning of the financial year and as at the balance sheet date respectively,

(b) the effect on any amount included in assets item B in respect of those assets of—

(i) any determination during that year of the value to be ascribed to any of those assets in accordance with paragraph 23,

(ii) acquisitions during that year of any assets,

(iii) disposals during that year of any assets, and

(iv) any transfers of assets of the company to and from the item during that year.

(2) The reference in sub-paragraph (1)(a) to the appropriate amounts in respect of any assets (included in an assets item) as at any date there mentioned is a reference to amounts representing the aggregate amounts determined, as at that date, in respect of assets falling to be included under the item on either of the following bases—

(a) on the basis of cost (determined in accordance with paragraphs 45 and 46), or

(b) on any basis permitted by paragraph 22 or 23, (leaving out of account in either case any provisions for depreciation or diminution in value).

(3) In addition, in respect of any assets of the company included in any assets item in the company's balance sheet, there must be stated (by reference to each such item)—

(a) the cumulative amount of provisions for depreciation or diminution in value of those assets included under the item as at each date mentioned in sub-paragraph (1)(a),

(b) the amount of any such provisions made in respect of the financial year,

(c) the amount of any adjustments made in respect of any such provisions during that year in consequence of the disposal of any of those assets, and

(d) the amount of any other adjustments made in respect of any such provisions during that year.

**70.** Where any assets of the company (other than listed investments) are included under any item shown in the company's balance sheet at an amount determined on any basis mentioned in paragraph 22 or 23, the following information must be given—

(a) the years (so far as they are known to the directors) in which the assets were severally valued and the several values, and

(b) in the case of assets that have been valued during the financial year, the names of the persons who valued them or particulars of their qualifications for doing so and (whichever is stated) the bases of valuation used by them.

**71.** In relation to any amount which is included under assets item C.I (land and buildings) there must be stated—

(a) how much of that amount is ascribable to land of freehold tenure and how much to land of leasehold tenure, and

(b) how much of the amount ascribable to land of leasehold tenure is ascribable to land held on long lease and how much to land held on short lease.

### Investments

**72.** In respect of the amount of each item which is shown in the company's balance sheet under assets item C (investments) there must be stated how much of that amount is ascribable to listed investments.

### Information about fair value of assets and liabilities

**73.** (1) This paragraph applies where financial instruments have been valued in accordance with paragraph 30 or 32.

(2) The items affected and the basis of valuation adopted in determining the amounts of the financial instruments must be disclosed.

(3) The purchase price of the financial instruments must be disclosed.

(4) There must be stated—

    (a) the significant assumptions underlying the valuation models and techniques used, where the fair value of the instruments has been determined in accordance with paragraph 31(4),

    (b) for each category of financial instrument, the fair value of the instruments in that category and the changes in value—

        (i) included in the profit and loss account, or

        (ii) credited to or (as the case may be) debited from the fair value reserve, in respect of those instruments, and

    (c) for each class of derivatives, the extent and nature of the instruments, including significant terms and conditions that may affect the amount, timing and certainty of future cash flows.

(5) Where any amount is transferred to or from the fair value reserve during the financial year, there must be stated in tabular form—

    (a) the amount of the reserve as at the date of the beginning of the financial year and as at the balance sheet date respectively,

    (b) the amount transferred to or from the reserve during that year, and

    (c) the source and application respectively of the amounts so transferred.

**74.** Where the company has derivatives that it has not included at fair value, there must be stated for each class of such derivatives—

  (a) the fair value of the derivatives in that class, if such a value can be determined in accordance with paragraph 31, and

  (b) the extent and nature of the derivatives.

**75.** (1) This paragraph applies if—

    (a) the company has financial fixed assets that could be included at fair value by virtue of paragraph 30,

    (b) the amount at which those assets are included under any item in the company's accounts is in excess of their fair value, and

    (c) the company has not made provision for diminution in value of those assets in accordance with paragraph 38(2) of this Schedule.

(2) There must be stated—

    (a) the amount at which either the individual assets or appropriate groupings of those individual assets are included in the company's accounts,

    (b) the fair value of those assets or groupings, and

    (c) the reasons for not making a provision for diminution in value of those assets, including the nature of the evidence that provides the basis for the belief that the amount at which they are stated in the accounts will be recovered.

## Information where investment property and living animals and plants included at fair value

**76.** (1) This paragraph applies where the amounts to be included in a company's accounts in respect of investment property or living animals and plants have been determined in accordance with paragraph 33.

(2) The balance sheet items affected and the basis of valuation adopted in determining the amounts of the assets in question in the case of each such item must be disclosed in a note to the accounts.

(3) In the case of investment property, for each balance sheet item affected there must be shown, either separately in the balance sheet or in a note to the accounts—

    (a) the comparable amounts determined according to the historical cost accounting rules, or

    (b) the differences between those amounts and the corresponding amounts actually shown in the balance sheet in respect of that item.

(4) In sub-paragraph (3), references in relation to any item to the comparable amounts determined in accordance with that sub-paragraph are to—

    (a) the aggregate amount which would be required to be shown in respect of that item if the amounts to be included in respect of all the assets covered by that item were determined according to the historical cost accounting rules, and

    (b) the aggregate amount of the cumulative provisions for depreciation or diminution in value which would be permitted or required in determining those amounts according to those rules.

## Reserves and provisions

**77.** (1) This paragraph applies where any amount is transferred—

    (a) to or from any reserves,

    (b) to any provisions for other risks, or

    (c) from any provisions for other risks otherwise than for the purpose for which the provision was established, and the reserves or provisions are or would but for paragraph 3(1) be shown as separate items in the company's balance sheet.

(2) The following information must be given in respect of the aggregate of reserves or provisions included in the same item—
  (a) the amount of the reserves or provisions as at the date of the beginning of the financial year and as at the balance sheet date respectively,
  (b) any amounts transferred to or from the reserves or provisions during that year, and
  (c) the source and application respectively of any amounts so transferred.

(3) Particulars must be given of each provision included in liabilities item E.3 (other provisions) in the company's balance sheet in any case where the amount of that provision is material.

### Provision for taxation

**78.** The amount of any provision for deferred taxation must be stated separately from the amount of any provision for other taxation.

### Details of indebtedness

**79.** (1) In respect of each item shown under 'creditors' in the company's balance sheet there must be stated the aggregate of the following amounts—
  (a) the amount of any debts included under that item which are payable or repayable otherwise than by instalments and fall due for payment or repayment after the end of the period of five years beginning with the day next following the end of the financial year, and
  (b) in the case of any debts so included which are payable or repayable by instalments, the amount of any instalments which fall due for payment after the end of that period.

(2) Subject to sub-paragraph (3), in relation to each debt falling to be taken into account under sub-paragraph (1), the terms of payment or repayment and the rate of any interest payable on the debt must be stated.

(3) If the number of debts is such that, in the opinion of the directors, compliance with sub-paragraph (2) would result in a statement of excessive length, it is sufficient to give a general indication of the terms of payment or repayment and the rates of any interest payable on the debts.

(4) In respect of each item shown under 'creditors' in the company's balance sheet there must be stated—
  (a) the aggregate amount of any debts included under that item in respect of which any security has been given by the company, and
  (b) an indication of the nature of the securities so given.

(5) References above in this paragraph to an item shown under 'creditors' in the company's balance sheet include references, where amounts falling due to creditors within one year and after more than one year are distinguished in the balance sheet—
  (a) in a case within sub-paragraph (1), to an item shown under the latter of those categories, and
  (b) in a case within sub-paragraph (4), to an item shown under either of those categories. References to items shown under 'creditors' include references to items which would but for paragraph 3(1)(b) be shown under that heading.

**80.** If any fixed cumulative dividends on the company's shares are in arrear, there must be stated—
  (a) the amount of the arrears, and
  (b) the period for which the dividends or, if there is more than one class, each class of them are in arrear.

### Guarantees and other financial commitments

**81.** (1) Particulars must be given of any charge on the assets of the company to secure the liabilities of any other person, including, where practicable, the amount secured.

(2) The following information must be given with respect to any other contingent liability not provided for (other than a contingent liability arising out of an insurance contract)—
  (a) the amount or estimated amount of that liability,
  (b) its legal nature, and
  (c) whether any valuable security has been provided by the company in connection with that liability and if so, what.

(3) There must be stated, where practicable, the aggregate amount or estimated amount of contracts for capital expenditure, so far as not provided for.

(4) Particulars must be given of—
  (a) any pension commitments included under any provision shown in the company's balance sheet, and
  (b) any such commitments for which no provision has been made,
    and where any such commitment relates wholly or partly to pensions payable to past directors of the company separate particulars must be given of that commitment so far as it relates to such pensions.

(5) Particulars must also be given of any other financial commitments, other than commitments arising out of insurance contracts, that—

    (a) have not been provided for, and

    (b) are relevant to assessing the company's state of affairs.

  (6) Commitments within any of the preceding sub-paragraphs undertaken on behalf of or for the benefit of—

    (a) any parent undertaking or fellow subsidiary undertaking, or

    (b) any subsidiary undertaking of the company,

      must be stated separately from the other commitments within that sub-paragraph, and commitments within paragraph (a) must also be stated separately from those within paragraph (b).

### Miscellaneous matters

**82.** (1) Particulars must be given of any case where the cost of any asset is for the first time determined under paragraph 47.

  (2) Where any outstanding loans made under the authority of section 682(2)(b), (c) or (d) of the 2006 Act (various cases of financial assistance by a company for purchase of its own shares) are included under any item shown in the company's balance sheet, the aggregate amount of those loans must be disclosed for each item in question.

*Information supplementing the profit and loss account*[86]

### Separate statement of certain items of income and expenditure

**83.** (1) Subject to sub-paragraph (2), there must be stated the amount of the interest on or any similar charges in respect of—

    (a) bank loans and overdrafts, and

    (b) loans of any other kind made to the company.

  (2) Sub-paragraph (1) does not apply to interest or charges on loans to the company from group undertakings, but, with that exception, it applies to interest or charges on all loans, whether made on the security of debentures or not.

### Particulars of tax

**84.** (1) Particulars must be given of any special circumstances which affect liability in respect of taxation of profits, income or capital gains for the financial year or liability in respect of taxation of profits, income or capital gains for succeeding financial years.

  (2) The following amounts must be stated—

    (a) the amount of the charge for United Kingdom corporation tax,

    (b) if that amount would have been greater but for relief from double taxation, the amount which it would have been but for such relief,

    (c) the amount of the charge for United Kingdom income tax, and

    (d) the amount of the charge for taxation imposed outside the United Kingdom of profits, income and (so far as charged to revenue) capital gains.

      Those amounts must be stated separately in respect of each of the amounts which is shown under the following items in the profit and loss account, that is to say item III.9 (tax on profit or loss on ordinary activities) and item III.14 (tax on extraordinary profit or loss).

### Particulars of business

**85.** (1) As regards general business a company must disclose—

    (a) gross premiums written,

    (b) gross premiums earned,

    (c) gross claims incurred,

    (d) gross operating expenses, and

    (e) the reinsurance balance.

  (2) The amounts required to be disclosed by sub-paragraph (1) must be broken down between direct insurance and reinsurance acceptances, if reinsurance acceptances amount to 10 per cent or more of gross premiums written.

  (3) Subject to sub-paragraph (4), the amounts required to be disclosed by sub-paragraphs (1) and (2) with respect to direct insurance must be further broken down into the following groups of classes—

    (a) accident and health,

    (b) motor (third party liability),

    (c) motor (other classes),

    (d) marine, aviation and transport,

    (e) fire and other damage to property,

---

[86] See regulation 6(2) for exemption for companies falling within section 408 of the 2006 Act (individual profit and loss account where group accounts prepared).

(f)  third-party liability,

(g)  credit and suretyship,

(h)  legal expenses,

(i)  assistance, and

(j)  miscellaneous,

where the amount of the gross premiums written in direct insurance for each such group exceeds 10 million Euros.

(4)  The company must in any event disclose the amounts relating to the three largest groups of classes in its business.

**86.** (1)  As regards long-term business, the company must disclose—

(a)  gross premiums written, and

(b)  the reinsurance balance.

(2)  Subject to sub-paragraph (3)—

(a)  gross premiums written must be broken down between those written by way of direct insurance and those written by way of reinsurance, and

(b)  gross premiums written by way of direct insurance must be broken down—

(i)  between individual premiums and premiums under group contracts,

(ii)  between periodic premiums and single premiums, and

(iii)  between premiums from non-participating contracts, premiums from participating contracts and premiums from contracts where the investment risk is borne by policyholders.

(3)  Disclosure of any amount referred to in sub-paragraph (2)(a) or (2)(b)(i), (ii) or (iii) is not required if it does not exceed 10 per cent of the gross premiums written or (as the case may be) of the gross premiums written by way of direct insurance.

**87.** (1)  Subject to sub-paragraph (2), there must be disclosed as regards both general and long-term business the total gross direct insurance premiums resulting from contracts concluded by the company—

(a)  in the member State of its head office,

(b)  in the other member States, and

(c)  in other countries.

(2)  Disclosure of any amount referred to in sub-paragraph (1) is not required if it does not exceed 5 per cent of total gross premiums.

## Commissions

**88.** There must be disclosed the total amount of commissions for direct insurance business accounted for in the financial year, including acquisition, renewal, collection and portfolio management commissions.

## Miscellaneous matters

**89.** (1)  Where any amount relating to any preceding financial year is included in any item in the profit and loss account, the effect must be stated.

(2)  Particulars must be given of any extraordinary income or charges arising in the financial year.

(3)  The effect must be stated of any transactions that are exceptional by virtue of size or incidence though they fall within the ordinary activities of the company.

## Related party transactions

**90.** (1)  Particulars may be given of transactions which the company has entered into with related parties, and must be given if such transactions are material and have not been concluded under normal market conditions.

(2)  The particulars of transactions required to be disclosed by sub-paragraph (1) must include—

(a)  the amount of such transactions,

(b)  the nature of the related party relationship, and

(c)  other information about the transactions necessary for an understanding of the financial position of the company.

(3)  Information about individual transactions may be aggregated according to their nature, except where separate information is necessary for an understanding of the effects of related party transactions on the financial position of the company.

(4)  Particulars need not be given of transactions entered into between two or more members of a group, provided that any subsidiary undertaking which is a party to the transaction is wholly-owned by such a member.

(5)  In this paragraph, 'related party' has the same meaning as in international accounting standards.

## PART 4
## INTERPRETATION OF THIS SCHEDULE

### Definitions for this Schedule

**91.** The following definitions apply for the purposes of this Schedule and its interpretation—

'general business' means business which consists of effecting or carrying out contracts of general insurance;

'long-term business' means business which consists of effecting or carrying out contracts of long-term insurance;

'long-term fund' means the fund or funds maintained by a company in respect of its long-term business in accordance with rule 1.5.22 in the Prudential Sourcebook for Insurers made by the Financial Services Authority under Part 10 of the Financial Services and Markets Act 2000[87];

'policyholder' has the meaning given by article 3 of the Financial Services and Markets Act 2000 (Meaning of 'Policy' and 'Policyholder') Order 2001[88];

'provision for unexpired risks' means the amount set aside in addition to unearned premiums in respect of risks to be borne by the company after the end of the financial year, in order to provide for all claims and expenses in connection with insurance contracts in force in excess of the related unearned premiums and any premiums receivable on those contracts.

## SCHEDULE 4 Regulation 7
## INFORMATION ON RELATED UNDERTAKINGS REQUIRED WHETHER PREPARING COMPANIES ACT OR IAS ACCOUNTS

## PART 1
## PROVISIONS APPLYING TO ALL COMPANIES

### Subsidiary undertakings

**1.** (1) The following information must be given where at the end of the financial year the company has subsidiary undertakings.

(2) The name of each subsidiary undertaking must be stated.

(3) There must be stated with respect to each subsidiary undertaking—

(a) if it is incorporated outside the United Kingdom, the country in which it is incorporated,

(b) if it is unincorporated, the address of its principal place of business.

### Financial information about subsidiary undertakings

**2.** (1) There must be disclosed with respect to each subsidiary undertaking not included in consolidated accounts by the company—

(a) the aggregate amount of its capital and reserves as at the end of its relevant financial year, and

(b) its profit or loss for that year.

(2) That information need not be given if the company is exempt by virtue of section 400 or 401 of the 2006 Act from the requirement to prepare group accounts (parent company included in accounts of larger group).

(3) That information need not be given if the company's investment in the subsidiary undertaking is included in the company's accounts by way of the equity method of valuation.

(4) That information need not be given if—

(a) the subsidiary undertaking is not required by any provision of the 2006 Act to deliver a copy of its balance sheet for its relevant financial year and does not otherwise publish that balance sheet in the United Kingdom or elsewhere, and

(b) the company's holding is less than 50% of the nominal value of the shares in the undertaking.

(5) Information otherwise required by this paragraph need not be given if it is not material.

(6) For the purposes of this paragraph the 'relevant financial year' of a subsidiary undertaking is—

(a) if its financial year ends with that of the company, that year, and

(b) if not, its financial year ending last before the end of the company's financial year.

---

[87] FSA 2006/42.
[88] SI 2001/2361.

**Shares and debentures of company held by subsidiary undertakings**

**3.** (1) The number, description and amount of the shares in the company held by or on behalf of its subsidiary undertakings must be disclosed.

(2) Sub-paragraph (1) does not apply in relation to shares in the case of which the subsidiary undertaking is concerned as personal representative or, subject as follows, as trustee.

(3) The exception for shares in relation to which the subsidiary undertaking is concerned as trustee does not apply if the company, or any of its subsidiary undertakings, is beneficially interested under the trust, otherwise than by way of security only for the purposes of a transaction entered into by it in the ordinary course of a business which includes the lending of money.

(4) Part 5 of this Schedule has effect for the interpretation of the reference in sub-paragraph (3) to a beneficial interest under a trust.

**Significant holdings in undertakings other than subsidiary undertakings**

**4.** (1) The information required by paragraphs 5 and 6 must be given where at the end of the financial year the company has a significant holding in an undertaking which is not a subsidiary undertaking of the company, and which does not fall within paragraph 18 (joint ventures) or 19 (associated undertakings).

(2) A holding is significant for this purpose if—

(a) it amounts to 20% or more of the nominal value of any class of shares in the undertaking, or

(b) the amount of the holding (as stated or included in the company's individual accounts) exceeds one-fifth of the amount (as so stated) of the company's assets.

**5.** (1) The name of the undertaking must be stated.

(2) There must be stated—

(a) if the undertaking is incorporated outside the United Kingdom, the country in which it is incorporated,

(b) if it is unincorporated, the address of its principal place of business.

(3) There must also be stated—

(a) the identity of each class of shares in the undertaking held by the company, and

(b) the proportion of the nominal value of the shares of that class represented by those shares.

**6.** (1) Subject to paragraph 14, there must also be stated—

(a) the aggregate amount of the capital and reserves of the undertaking as at the end of its relevant financial year, and

(b) its profit or loss for that year.

(2) That information need not be given in respect of an undertaking if—

(a) the undertaking is not required by any provision of the 2006 Act to deliver a copy of its balance sheet for its relevant financial year and does not otherwise publish that balance sheet in the United Kingdom or elsewhere, and

(b) the company's holding is less than 50% of the nominal value of the shares in the undertaking.

(3) Information otherwise required by this paragraph need not be given if it is not material.

(4) For the purposes of this paragraph the 'relevant financial year' of an undertaking is—

(a) if its financial year ends with that of the company, that year, and

(b) if not, its financial year ending last before the end of the company's financial year.

**Membership of certain undertakings**

**7.** (1) The information required by this paragraph must be given where at the end of the financial year the company is a member of a qualifying undertaking.

(2) There must be stated—

(a) the name and legal form of the undertaking, and

(b) the address of the undertaking's registered office (whether in or outside the United Kingdom) or, if it does not have such an office, its head office (whether in or outside the United Kingdom).

(3) Where the undertaking is a qualifying partnership there must also be stated either—

(a) that a copy of the latest accounts of the undertaking has been or is to be appended to the copy of the company's accounts sent to the registrar under section 444 of the 2006 Act, or

(b) the name of at least one body corporate (which may be the company) in whose group accounts the undertaking has been or is to be dealt with on a consolidated basis.

(4) Information otherwise required by sub-paragraph (2) need not be given if it is not material.

(5) Information otherwise required by sub-paragraph (3)(b) need not be given if the notes to the company's accounts disclose that advantage has been taken of the exemption conferred by regulation 7 of the [Partnerships (Accounts) Regulations 2008[a].

(6) In this paragraph—

'dealt with on a consolidated basis', 'member' and 'qualifying partnership' have the same meanings as in the [Partnerships (Accounts) Regulations 2008][b];
'qualifying undertaking' means—
(a) a qualifying partnership, or
(b) an unlimited company each of whose members is—
 (i) a limited company,
 (ii) another unlimited company each of whose members is a limited company, or
 (iii) a Scottish partnership each of whose members is a limited company, and references in this paragraph to a limited company,
 another unlimited company or a Scottish partnership include a comparable undertaking incorporated in or formed under the law of a country or territory outside the United Kingdom.

AMENDMENTS AND NOTES

[a] Substituted by the Partnerships (Accounts) Regulations 2008, SI 2008/569, reg 17.

[b] Substituted by the Partnerships (Accounts) Regulations 2008, SI 2008/569, reg 17.

### Parent undertaking drawing up accounts for larger group

**8.** (1) Where the company is a subsidiary undertaking, the following information must be given with respect to the parent undertaking of—
 (a) the largest group of undertakings for which group accounts are drawn up and of which the company is a member, and
 (b) the smallest such group of undertakings.
(2) The name of the parent undertaking must be stated.
(3) There must be stated—
 (a) if the undertaking is incorporated outside the United Kingdom, the country in which it is incorporated,
 (b) if it is unincorporated, the address of its principal place of business.
(4) If copies of the group accounts referred to in sub-paragraph (1) are available to the public, there must also be stated the addresses from which copies of the accounts can be obtained.

### Identification of ultimate parent company

**9.** (1) Where the company is a subsidiary undertaking, the following information must be given with respect to the company (if any) regarded by the directors as being the company's ultimate parent company.
(2) The name of that company must be stated.
(3) If that company is incorporated outside the United Kingdom, the country in which it is incorporated must be stated (if known to the directors).
(4) In this paragraph 'company' includes any body corporate.

## PART 2
## COMPANIES NOT REQUIRED TO PREPARE GROUP ACCOUNTS

### Reason for not preparing group accounts

**10.** (1) The reason why the company is not required to prepare group accounts must be stated.
(2) If the reason is that all the subsidiary undertakings of the company fall within the exclusions provided for in section 405 of the 2006 Act (Companies Act group accounts: subsidiary undertakings included in the consolidation), it must be stated with respect to each subsidiary undertaking which of those exclusions applies.

### Holdings in subsidiary undertakings

**11.** (1) There must be stated in relation to shares of each class held by the company in a subsidiary undertaking—
 (a) the identity of the class, and
 (b) the proportion of the nominal value of the shares of that class represented by those shares.
(2) The shares held by or on behalf of the company itself must be distinguished from those attributed to the company which are held by or on behalf of a subsidiary undertaking.

### Financial years of subsidiary undertakings

**12.** Where—
 (a) disclosure is made under paragraph 2(1) with respect to a subsidiary undertaking, and
 (b) that undertaking's financial year does not end with that of the company, there must be stated in relation to that undertaking the date on which its last financial year ended (last before the end of the company's financial year).

**Exemption from giving information about significant holdings in non-subsidiary undertakings**

**13.** (1) The information otherwise required by paragraph 6 (significant holdings in undertakings other than subsidiary undertaking) need not be given if—

(a) the company is exempt by virtue of section 400 or 401 of the 2006 Act from the requirement to prepare group accounts (parent company included in accounts of larger group), and

(b) the investment of the company in all undertakings in which it has such a holding as is mentioned in sub-paragraph (1) is shown, in aggregate, in the notes to the accounts by way of the equity method of valuation.

**Construction of references to shares held by company**

**14.** (1) References in Parts 1 and 2 of this Schedule to shares held by a company are to be construed as follows.

(2) For the purposes of paragraphs 2, 11 and 12 (information about subsidiary undertakings)—

(a) there must be attributed to the company any shares held by a subsidiary undertaking, or by a person acting on behalf of the company or a subsidiary undertaking; but

(b) there must be treated as not held by the company any shares held on behalf of a person other than the company or a subsidiary undertaking.

(3) For the purposes of paragraphs 4 to 6 (information about undertakings other than subsidiary undertakings)—

(a) there must be attributed to the company shares held on its behalf by any person; but

(b) there must be treated as not held by a company shares held on behalf of a person other than the company.

(4) For the purposes of any of those provisions, shares held by way of security must be treated as held by the person providing the security—

(a) where apart from the right to exercise them for the purpose of preserving the value of the security, or of realising it, the rights attached to the shares are exercisable only in accordance with that person's instructions, and

(b) where the shares are held in connection with the granting of loans as part of normal business activities and apart from the right to exercise them for the purpose of preserving the value of the security, or of realising it, the rights attached to the shares are exercisable only in that person's interests.

PART 3

COMPANIES REQUIRED TO PREPARE GROUP ACCOUNTS

**Introductory**

**15.** In this Part of this Schedule 'the group' means the group consisting of the parent company and its subsidiary undertakings.

**Subsidiary undertakings**

**16.** (1) In addition to the information required by paragraph 2, the following information must also be given with respect to the undertakings which are subsidiary undertakings of the parent company at the end of the financial year.

(2) It must be stated whether the subsidiary undertaking is included in the consolidation and, if it is not, the reasons for excluding it from consolidation must be given.

(3) It must be stated with respect to each subsidiary undertaking by virtue of which of the conditions specified in section 1162(2) or (4) of the 2006 Act it is a subsidiary undertaking of its immediate parent undertaking.

That information need not be given if the relevant condition is that specified in subsection (2)(a) of that section (holding of a majority of the voting rights) and the immediate parent undertaking holds the same proportion of the shares in the undertaking as it holds voting rights.

**Holdings in subsidiary undertakings**

**17.** (1) The following information must be given with respect to the shares of a subsidiary undertaking held—

(a) by the parent company, and

(b) by the group,

and the information under paragraphs (a) and (b) must (if different) be shown separately.

(2) There must be stated—

(a) the identity of each class of shares held, and

(b) the proportion of the nominal value of the shares of that class represented by those shares.

### Joint ventures

**18.** (1) The following information must be given where an undertaking is dealt with in the consolidated accounts by the method of proportional consolidation in accordance with paragraph 18 of Schedule 6 to these Regulations (joint ventures)—

(a) the name of the undertaking,

(b) the address of the principal place of business of the undertaking,

(c) the factors on which joint management of the undertaking is based, and

(d) the proportion of the capital of the undertaking held by undertakings included in the consolidation.

(2) Where the financial year of the undertaking did not end with that of the company, there must be stated the date on which a financial year of the undertaking last ended before that date.

### Associated undertakings

**19.** (1) The following information must be given where an undertaking included in the consolidation has an interest in an associated undertaking.

(2) The name of the associated undertaking must be stated.

(3) There must be stated—

(a) if the undertaking is incorporated outside the United Kingdom, the country in which it is incorporated,

(b) if it is unincorporated, the address of its principal place of business.

(4) The following information must be given with respect to the shares of the undertaking held—

(a) by the parent company, and

(b) by the group, and the information under paragraphs (a) and (b) must be shown separately.

(5) There must be stated—

(a) the identity of each class of shares held, and

(b) the proportion of the nominal value of the shares of that class represented by those shares.

(6) In this paragraph 'associated undertaking' has the meaning given by paragraph 19 of Schedule 6 to these Regulations; and the information required by this paragraph must be given notwithstanding that paragraph 21(3) of that Schedule (materiality) applies in relation to the accounts themselves.

### Requirement to give information about other significant holdings of parent company or group

**20.** (1) The information required by paragraphs 5 and 6 must also be given where at the end of the financial year the group has a significant holding in an undertaking which is not a subsidiary undertaking of the parent company and does not fall within paragraph 18 (joint ventures) or 19 (associated undertakings), as though the references to the company in those paragraphs were a reference to the group.

(2) A holding is significant for this purpose if—

(a) it amounts to 20% or more of the nominal value of any class of shares in the undertaking, or

(b) the amount of the holding (as stated or included in the group accounts) exceeds one-fifth of the amount of the group's assets (as so stated).

(3) For the purposes of those paragraphs as applied to a group the 'relevant financial year' of an outside undertaking is—

(a) if its financial year ends with that of the parent company, that year, and

(b) if not, its financial year ending last before the end of the parent company's financial year.

### Group's membership of certain undertakings

**21.** The information required by paragraph 7 must also be given where at the end of the financial year the group is a member of a qualifying undertaking.

### Construction of references to shares held by parent company or group

**22.** (1) References in Parts 1 and 3 of this Schedule to shares held by that parent company or group are to be construed as follows.

(2) For the purposes of paragraphs 4 to 6, 17, 19(4) and (5) and 12 (information about holdings in subsidiary and other undertakings)—

(a) there must be attributed to the parent company shares held on its behalf by any person; but

(b) there must be treated as not held by the parent company shares held on behalf of a person other than the company.

(3) References to shares held by the group are to any shares held by or on behalf of the parent company or any of its subsidiary undertakings; but any shares held on behalf of a person other than the parent company or any of its subsidiary undertakings are not to be treated as held by the group.

(4) Shares held by way of security must be treated as held by the person providing the security—

    (a) where apart from the right to exercise them for the purpose of preserving the value of the security, or of realising it, the rights attached to the shares are exercisable only in accordance with his instructions, and

    (b) where the shares are held in connection with the granting of loans as part of normal business activities and apart from the right to exercise them for the purpose of preserving the value of the security, or of realising it, the rights attached to the shares are exercisable only in his interests.

## PART 4

## ADDITIONAL DISCLOSURES FOR BANKING COMPANIES AND GROUPS

**23.** (1) This paragraph applies where accounts are prepared in accordance with the special provisions of Schedules 2 and 6 relating to banking companies or groups.

(2) The information required by paragraph 5 of this Schedule, modified where applicable by paragraph 20 (information about significant holdings of the company or group in undertakings other than subsidiary undertakings) need only be given in respect of undertakings (otherwise falling within the class of undertakings in respect of which disclosure is required) in which the company or group has a significant holding amounting to 20 % or more of the nominal value of the shares in the undertaking. In addition any information required by those paragraphs may be omitted if it is not material.

(3) Paragraphs 14(3) and (4) and 22(3) and (4) of this Schedule apply with necessary modifications for the purposes of this paragraph.

## PART 5

## INTERPRETATION OF REFERENCES TO 'BENEFICIAL INTEREST'

### Residual interests under pension and employees' share schemes

**24.** (1) Where shares in an undertaking are held on trust for the purposes of a pension scheme or an employees' share scheme, there must be disregarded any residual interest which has not vested in possession, being an interest of the undertaking or any of its subsidiary undertakings.

(2) In this paragraph a 'residual interest' means a right of the undertaking in question (the 'residual beneficiary') to receive any of the trust property in the event of—

    (a) all the liabilities arising under the scheme having been satisfied or provided for, or

    (b) the residual beneficiary ceasing to participate in the scheme, or

    (c) the trust property at any time exceeding what is necessary for satisfying the liabilities arising or expected to arise under the scheme.

(3) In sub-paragraph (2) references to a right include a right dependent on the exercise of a discretion vested by the scheme in the trustee or any other person; and references to liabilities arising under a scheme include liabilities that have resulted or may result from the exercise of any such discretion.

(4) For the purposes of this paragraph a residual interest vests in possession—

    (a) in a case within sub-paragraph (2)(a), on the occurrence of the event there mentioned, whether or not the amount of the property receivable pursuant to the right mentioned in that sub-paragraph is then ascertained,

    (b) in a case within sub-paragraph (2)(b) or (c), when the residual beneficiary becomes entitled to require the trustee to transfer to that beneficiary any of the property receivable pursuant to that right.

### Employer's charges and other rights of recovery

**25.** (1) Where shares in an undertaking are held on trust there must be disregarded—

    (a) if the trust is for the purposes of a pension scheme, any such rights as are mentioned in sub-paragraph (2),

    (b) if the trust is for the purposes of an employees' share scheme, any such rights as are mentioned in paragraph (a) of that sub-paragraph, being rights of the undertaking or any of its subsidiary undertakings.

(2) The rights referred to are—

    (a) any charge or lien on, or set-off against, any benefit or other right or interest under the scheme for the purpose of enabling the employer or former employer of a member of the scheme to obtain the discharge of a monetary obligation due to him from the member, and

    (b) any right to receive from the trustee of the scheme, or as trustee of the scheme to retain, an amount that can be recovered or retained under section 61 of the Pension Schemes Act 1993[89] or section 57 of the Pension Schemes (Northern Ireland) Act 1993[90] (deduction of contributions equivalent premium from refund of scheme contributions) or otherwise as reimbursement or partial reimbursement for any contributions equivalent premium paid in connection with the scheme under Chapter 3 of Part 3 of that Act.

### Trustee's right to expenses, remuneration, indemnity etc.

**26.** Where an undertaking is a trustee, there must be disregarded any rights which the undertaking has in its capacity as trustee including, in particular, any right to recover its expenses or be remunerated out of the trust property and any right to be indemnified out of that property for any liability incurred by reason of any act or omission of the undertaking in the performance of its duties as trustee.

### Supplementary

**27.** (1) This Schedule applies in relation to debentures as it applies in relation to shares.

    (2) 'Pension scheme' means any scheme for the provision of benefits consisting of or including relevant benefits for or in respect of employees or former employees; and 'relevant benefits' means any pension, lump sum, gratuity or other like benefit given or to be given on retirement or on death or in anticipation of retirement or, in connection with past service, after retirement or death.

    (3) In sub-paragraph (2) of this paragraph and in paragraph 25(2) 'employee' and 'employer' are to be read as if a director of an undertaking were employed by it.

SCHEDULE 5            Regulation 8

INFORMATION ABOUT BENEFITS OF DIRECTORS

PART 1

PROVISIONS APPLYING TO QUOTED AND UNQUOTED COMPANIES

### Total amount of directors' remuneration etc.

**1.** (1) There must be shown—

    (a) the aggregate amount of remuneration paid to or receivable by directors in respect of qualifying services;

    (b) the aggregate of the amount of gains made by directors on the exercise of share options;

    (c) the aggregate of the amount of money paid to or receivable by directors, and the net value of assets (other than money and share options) received or receivable by directors, under long term incentive schemes in respect of qualifying services; and

    (d) the aggregate value of any company contributions—

        (i) paid, or treated as paid, to a pension scheme in respect of directors' qualifying services, and

        (ii) by reference to which the rate or amount of any money purchase benefits that may become payable will be calculated.

    (2) There must be shown the number of directors (if any) to whom retirement benefits are accruing in respect of qualifying services—

    (a) under money purchase schemes, and

    (b) under defined benefit schemes.

    (3) In the case of a company which is not a quoted company and whose equity share capital is not listed on the market known as AIM—

    (a) sub-paragraph (1) has effect as if paragraph (b) were omitted and, in paragraph (c), 'assets' did not include shares; and

    (b) the number of each of the following (if any) must be shown, namely—

        (i) the directors who exercised share options, and

        (ii) the directors in respect of whose qualifying services shares were received or receivable under long term incentive schemes.

---

[89] 1993 c.48.
[90] 1993 c.49.

PART 2

PROVISIONS APPLYING ONLY TO UNQUOTED COMPANIES

**Details of highest paid director's emoluments etc.**

**2.** (1) Where the aggregates shown under paragraph 1(1)(a), (b) and (c) total £200,000 or more, there must be shown—
   (a) so much of the total of those aggregates as is attributable to the highest paid director, and
   (b) so much of the aggregate mentioned in paragraph 1(1)(d) as is so attributable.

   (2) Where sub-paragraph (1) applies and the highest paid director has performed qualifying services during the financial year by reference to which the rate or amount of any defined benefits that may become payable will be calculated, there must also be shown—
   (a) the amount at the end of the year of his accrued pension, and
   (b) where applicable, the amount at the end of the year of his accrued lump sum.

   (3) Subject to sub-paragraph (4), where sub-paragraph (1) applies in the case of a company which is not a listed company, there must also be shown—
   (a) whether the highest paid director exercised any share options, and
   (b) whether any shares were received or receivable by that director in respect of qualifying services under a long term incentive scheme.

   (4) Where the highest paid director has not been involved in any of the transactions specified in sub-paragraph (3), that fact need not be stated.

**Excess retirement benefits of directors and past directors**

**3.** (1) Subject to sub-paragraph (2), there must be shown the aggregate amount of—
   (a) so much of retirement benefits paid to or receivable by directors under pension schemes, and
   (b) so much of retirement benefits paid to or receivable by past directors under such schemes, as (in each case) is in excess of the retirement benefits to which they were respectively entitled on the date on which the benefits first became payable or 31st March 1997, whichever is the later.

   (2) Amounts paid or receivable under a pension scheme need not be included in the aggregate amount if—
   (a) the funding of the scheme was such that the amounts were or, as the case may be, could have been paid without recourse to additional contributions, and
   (b) amounts were paid to or receivable by all pensioner members of the scheme on the same basis.

   (3) In sub-paragraph (2), 'pensioner member', in relation to a pension scheme, means any person who is entitled to the present payment of retirement benefits under the scheme.

   (4) In this paragraph—
   (a) references to retirement benefits include benefits otherwise than in cash, and
   (b) in relation to so much of retirement benefits as consists of a benefit otherwise than in cash, references to their amount are to the estimated money value of the benefit, and the nature of any such benefit must also be disclosed.

**Compensation to directors for loss of office**

**4.** (1) There must be shown the aggregate amount of any compensation to directors or past directors in respect of loss of office.

   (2) This includes compensation received or receivable by a director or past director—
   (a) for loss of office as director of the company, or
   (b) for loss, while director of the company or on or in connection with his ceasing to be a director of it, of—
       (i) any other office in connection with the management of the company's affairs, or
       (ii) any office as director or otherwise in connection with the management of the affairs of any subsidiary undertaking of the company.

   (3) In this paragraph references to compensation for loss of office include—
   (a) compensation in consideration for, or in connection with, a person's retirement from office, and
   (b) where such a retirement is occasioned by a breach of the person's contract with the company or with a subsidiary undertaking of the company—
       (i) payments made by way of damages for the breach, or
       (ii) payments made by way of settlement or compromise of any claim in respect of the breach.

   (4) In this paragraph—
   (a) references to compensation include benefits otherwise than in cash, and
   (b) in relation to such compensation references to its amount are to the estimated money value of the benefit. The nature of any such compensation must be disclosed.

### Sums paid to third parties in respect of directors' services

**5.** (1) There must be shown the aggregate amount of any consideration paid to or receivable by third parties for making available the services of any person—

    (a) as a director of the company, or

    (b) while director of the company—

        (i) as director of any of its subsidiary undertakings, or

        (ii) otherwise in connection with the management of the affairs of the company or any of its subsidiary undertakings.

  (2) In sub-paragraph (1)—

    (a) the reference to consideration includes benefits otherwise than in cash, and

    (b) in relation to such consideration the reference to its amount is to the estimated money value of the benefit.

    The nature of any such consideration must be disclosed.

  (3) For the purposes of this paragraph a 'third party' means a person other than—

    (a) the director himself or a person connected with him or a body corporate controlled by him, or

    (b) the company or any of its subsidiary undertakings.

## PART 3
## SUPPLEMENTARY PROVISIONS

### General nature of obligations

**6.** (1) This Schedule requires information to be given only so far as it is contained in the company's books and papers or the company has the right to obtain it from the persons concerned.

  (2) For the purposes of this Schedule any information is treated as shown if it is capable of being readily ascertained from other information which is shown.

### Provisions as to amounts to be shown

**7.** (1) The following provisions apply with respect to the amounts to be shown under this Schedule.

  (2) The amount in each case includes all relevant sums, whether paid by or receivable from the company, any of the company's subsidiary undertakings or any other person.

  (3) References to amounts paid to or receivable by a person include amounts paid to or receivable by a person connected with him or a body corporate controlled by him (but not so as to require an amount to be counted twice).

  (4) Except as otherwise provided, the amounts to be shown for any financial year are—

    (a) the sums receivable in respect of that year (whenever paid), or

    (b) in the case of sums not receivable in respect of a period, the sums paid during that year.

  (5) Sums paid by way of expenses allowance that are charged to United Kingdom income tax after the end of the relevant financial year must be shown in a note to the first accounts in which it is practicable to show them and must be distinguished from the amounts to be shown apart from this provision.

  (6) Where it is necessary to do so for the purpose of making any distinction required in complying with this Schedule, the directors may apportion payments between the matters in respect of which they have been paid or are receivable in such manner as they think appropriate.

### Exclusion of sums liable to be accounted for to company etc.

**8.** (1) The amounts to be shown under this Schedule do not include any sums that are to be accounted for—

    (a) to the company or any of its subsidiary undertakings, or

    (b) by virtue of sections 219 and 222(3) of the 2006 Act (payments in connection with share transfers: duty to account) to persons who sold their shares as a result of the offer made.

  (2) Where—

    (a) any such sums are not shown in a note to the accounts for the relevant financial year on the ground that the person receiving them is liable to account for them, and

    (b) the liability is afterwards wholly or partly released or is not enforced within a period of two years, those sums, to the extent to which the liability is released or not enforced, must be shown in a note to the first accounts in which it is practicable to show them and must be distinguished from the amounts to be shown apart from this provision.

### Meaning of 'remuneration'

**9.** (1) In this Schedule 'remuneration' of a director includes—

    (a) salary, fees and bonuses, sums paid by way of expenses allowance (so far as they are chargeable to United Kingdom income tax), and

    (b) subject to sub-paragraph (2), the estimated money value of any other benefits received by the director otherwise than in cash.

  (2) The expression does not include—

    (a)  the value of any share options granted to the director or the amount of any gains made on the exercise of any such options,

    (b)  any company contributions paid, or treated as paid, under any pension scheme or any benefits to which the director is entitled under any such scheme, or

    (c)  any money or other assets paid to or received or receivable by the director under any long term incentive scheme.

### Meaning of 'highest paid director'

**10.** In this Schedule, 'the highest paid director' means the director to whom is attributable the greatest part of the total of the aggregates shown under paragraph 1(1)(a), (b) and (c).

### Meaning of 'long term incentive scheme'

**11.** (1)  In this Schedule 'long term incentive scheme' means an agreement or arrangement—

    (a)  under which money or other assets may become receivable by a director, and

    (b)  which includes one or more qualifying conditions with respect to service or performance which cannot be fulfilled within a single financial year.

  (2)  For this purpose the following must be disregarded—

    (a)  bonuses the amount of which falls to be determined by reference to service or performance within a single financial year;

    (b)  compensation for loss of office, payments for breach of contract and other termination payments; and

    (c)  retirement benefits.

### Meaning of 'shares' and 'share option' and related expressions

**12.** In this Schedule—

    (a)  'shares' means shares (whether allotted or not) in the company, or any undertaking which is a group undertaking in relation to the company, and includes a share warrant as defined by section 779(1) of the 2006 Act; and

    (b)  'share option' means a right to acquire shares.

### Meaning of 'pension scheme' and related expressions

**13.** (1)  In this Schedule—

'pension scheme' means a retirement benefits scheme as defined by section 611 of the Income and Corporation Taxes Act 1988[91]; and

'retirement benefits' has the meaning given by section 612(1) of that Act.

  (2)  In this Schedule 'accrued pension' and 'accrued lump sum', in relation to any pension scheme and any director, mean respectively the amount of the annual pension, and the amount of the lump sum, which would be payable under the scheme on his attaining normal pension age if—

    (a)  he had left the company's service at the end of the financial year,

    (b)  there was no increase in the general level of prices in the United Kingdom during the period beginning with the end of that year and ending with his attaining that age,

    (c)  no question arose of any commutation of the pension or inverse commutation of the lump sum, and

    (d)  any amounts attributable to voluntary contributions paid by the director to the scheme, and any money purchase benefits which would be payable under the scheme, were disregarded.

  (3)  In this Schedule, 'company contributions', in relation to a pension scheme and a director, means any payments (including insurance premiums) made, or treated as made, to the scheme in respect of the director by a person other than the director.

  (4)  In this Schedule, in relation to a director—

'defined benefits' means retirement benefits payable under a pension scheme that are not money purchase benefits;

'defined benefit scheme' means a pension scheme that is not a money purchase scheme;

'money purchase benefits' means retirement benefits payable under a pension scheme the rate or amount of which is calculated by reference to payments made, or treated as made, by the director or by any other person in respect of the director and which are not average salary benefits; and

'money purchase scheme' means a pension scheme under which all of the benefits that may become payable to or in respect of the director are money purchase benefits.

  (5)  In this Schedule, 'normal pension age', in relation to any pension scheme and any director, means the age at which the director will first become entitled to receive a full pension on retirement of an amount determined without reduction to take account of its payment

---

[91]  1988 c.1.

before a later age (but disregarding any entitlement to pension upon retirement in the event of illness, incapacity or redundancy).

(6) Where a pension scheme provides for any benefits that may become payable to or in respect of any director to be whichever are the greater of—

    (a) money purchase benefits as determined by or under the scheme; and

    (b) defined benefits as so determined, the company may assume for the purposes of this paragraph that those benefits will be money purchase benefits, or defined benefits, according to whichever appears more likely at the end of the financial year.

(7) For the purpose of determining whether a pension scheme is a money purchase or defined benefit scheme, any death in service benefits provided for by the scheme are to be disregarded.

### References to subsidiary undertakings

**14.** (1) Any reference in this Schedule to a subsidiary undertaking of the company, in relation to a person who is or was, while a director of the company, a director also, by virtue of the company's nomination (direct or indirect) of any other undertaking, includes that undertaking, whether or not it is or was in fact a subsidiary undertaking of the company.

(2) Any reference to a subsidiary undertaking of the company—

    (a) for the purposes of paragraph 1 (remuneration etc.) is to an undertaking which is a subsidiary undertaking at the time the services were rendered, and

    (b) for the purposes of paragraph 4 (compensation for loss of office) is to a subsidiary undertaking immediately before the loss of office as director.

### Other minor definitions

**15.** (1) In this Schedule—

'net value', in relation to any assets received or receivable by a director, means value after deducting any money paid or other value given by the director in respect of those assets;

'qualifying services', in relation to any person, means his services as a director of the company, and his services while director of the company—

    (a) as director of any of its subsidiary undertakings; or

    (b) otherwise in connection with the management of the affairs of the company or any of its subsidiary undertakings.

(2) References in this Schedule to a person being 'connected' with a director, and to a director 'controlling' a body corporate, are to be construed in accordance with sections 252 to 255 of the 2006 Act.

(3) For the purposes of this Schedule, remuneration paid or receivable or share options granted in respect of a person's accepting office as a director are treated as emoluments paid or receivable or share options granted in respect of his services as a director.

SCHEDULE 6                   Regulation 9

COMPANIES ACT GROUP ACCOUNTS

PART 1

GENERAL RULES

### General rules

**1.** (1) Group accounts must comply so far as practicable with the provisions of Schedule 1 to these Regulations as if the undertakings included in the consolidation ('the group') were a single company (see Parts 2 and 3 of this Schedule for modifications for banking and insurance groups).

(2) Where the parent company is treated as an investment company for the purposes of Part 5 of Schedule 1 (special provisions for investment companies) the group must be similarly treated.

**2.** (1) The consolidated balance sheet and profit and loss account must incorporate in full the information contained in the individual accounts of the undertakings included in the consolidation, subject to the adjustments authorised or required by the following provisions of this Schedule and to such other adjustments (if any) as may be appropriate in accordance with generally accepted accounting principles or practice.

(2) If the financial year of a subsidiary undertaking included in the consolidation does not end with that of the parent company, the group accounts must be made up—

    (a) from the accounts of the subsidiary undertaking for its financial year last ending before the end of the parent company's financial year, provided that year ended no more than three months before that of the parent company, or

    (b) from interim accounts prepared by the subsidiary undertaking as at the end of the parent company's financial year.

3. (1) Where assets and liabilities to be included in the group accounts have been valued or otherwise determined by undertakings according to accounting rules differing from those used for the group accounts, the values or amounts must be adjusted so as to accord with the rules used for the group accounts.

(2) If it appears to the directors of the parent company that there are special reasons for departing from sub-paragraph (1) they may do so, but particulars of any such departure, the reasons for it and its effect must be given in a note to the accounts.

(3) The adjustments referred to in this paragraph need not be made if they are not material for the purpose of giving a true and fair view.

4. Any differences of accounting rules as between a parent company's individual accounts for a financial year and its group accounts must be disclosed in a note to the latter accounts and the reasons for the difference given.

5. Amounts that in the particular context of any provision of this Schedule are not material may be disregarded for the purposes of that provision.

### Elimination of group transactions

6. (1) Debts and claims between undertakings included in the consolidation, and income and expenditure relating to transactions between such undertakings, must be eliminated in preparing the group accounts.

(2) Where profits and losses resulting from transactions between undertakings included in the consolidation are included in the book value of assets, they must be eliminated in preparing the group accounts.

(3) The elimination required by sub-paragraph (2) may be effected in proportion to the group's interest in the shares of the undertakings.

(4) Sub-paragraphs (1) and (2) need not be complied with if the amounts concerned are not material for the purpose of giving a true and fair view.

### Acquisition and merger accounting

7. (1) The following provisions apply where an undertaking becomes a subsidiary undertaking of the parent company.

(2) That event is referred to in those provisions as an 'acquisition', and references to the 'undertaking acquired' are to be construed accordingly.

8. An acquisition must be accounted for by the acquisition method of accounting unless the conditions for accounting for it as a merger are met and the merger method of accounting is adopted.

9. (1) The acquisition method of accounting is as follows.

(2) The identifiable assets and liabilities of the undertaking acquired must be included in the consolidated balance sheet at their fair values as at the date of acquisition.

(3) The income and expenditure of the undertaking acquired must be brought into the group accounts only as from the date of the acquisition.

(4) There must be set off against the acquisition cost of the interest in the shares of the undertaking held by the parent company and its subsidiary undertakings the interest of the parent company and its subsidiary undertakings in the adjusted capital and reserves of the undertaking acquired.

(5) The resulting amount if positive must be treated as goodwill, and if negative as a negative consolidation difference.

10. (1) The conditions for accounting for an acquisition as a merger are—

(a) that at least 90% of the nominal value of the relevant shares in the undertaking acquired (excluding any shares in the undertaking held as treasury shares) is held by or on behalf of the parent company and its subsidiary undertakings,

(b) that the proportion referred to in paragraph (a) was attained pursuant to an arrangement providing for the issue of equity shares by the parent company or one or more of its subsidiary undertakings,

(c) that the fair value of any consideration other than the issue of equity shares given pursuant to the arrangement by the parent company and its subsidiary undertakings did not exceed 10% of the nominal value of the equity shares issued, and

(d) that adoption of the merger method of accounting accords with generally accepted accounting principles or practice.

(2) The reference in sub-paragraph (1)(a) to the 'relevant shares' in an undertaking acquired is to those carrying unrestricted rights to participate both in distributions and in the assets of the undertaking upon liquidation.

11. (1) The merger method of accounting is as follows.

(2) The assets and liabilities of the undertaking acquired must be brought into the group accounts at the figures at which they stand in the undertaking's accounts, subject to any adjustment authorised or required by this Schedule.

(3) The income and expenditure of the undertaking acquired must be included in the group accounts for the entire financial year, including the period before the acquisition.

    (4) The group accounts must show corresponding amounts relating to the previous financial year as if the undertaking acquired had been included in the consolidation throughout that year.

    (5) There must be set off against the aggregate of—

      (a) the appropriate amount in respect of qualifying shares issued by the parent company or its subsidiary undertakings in consideration for the acquisition of shares in the undertaking acquired, and

      (b) the fair value of any other consideration for the acquisition of shares in the undertaking acquired,

      determined as at the date when those shares were acquired, the nominal value of the issued share capital of the undertaking acquired held by the parent company and its subsidiary undertakings.

    (6) The resulting amount must be shown as an adjustment to the consolidated reserves.

    (7) In sub-paragraph (5)(a) 'qualifying shares' means—

      (a) shares in relation to which any of the following provisions applies (merger relief), and in respect of which the appropriate amount is the nominal value—

        (i) section 131 of the Companies Act 1985[92],

        (ii) Article 141 of the Companies (Northern Ireland) Order 1986[93], or

        (iii) section 612 of the 2006 Act, or

      (b) shares in relation to which any of the following provisions applies (group reconstruction relief), and in respect of which the appropriate amount is the nominal value together with any minimum premium value within the meaning of that section—

        (i) section 132 of the Companies Act 1985[94],

        (ii) Article 142 of the Companies (Northern Ireland) Order 1986[95], or

        (iii) section 611 of the 2006 Act.

**12.** (1) Where a group is acquired, paragraphs 9 to 11 apply with the following adaptations.

    (2) References to shares of the undertaking acquired are to be construed as references to shares of the parent undertaking of the group.

    (3) Other references to the undertaking acquired are to be construed as references to the group; and references to the assets and liabilities, income and expenditure and capital and reserves of the undertaking acquired must be construed as references to the assets and liabilities, income and expenditure and capital and reserves of the group after making the set-offs and other adjustments required by this Schedule in the case of group accounts.

**13.** (1) The following information with respect to acquisitions taking place in the financial year must be given in a note to the accounts.

    (2) There must be stated—

      (a) the name of the undertaking acquired or, where a group was acquired, the name of the parent undertaking of that group, and

      (b) whether the acquisition has been accounted for by the acquisition or the merger method of accounting;

      and in relation to an acquisition which significantly affects the figures shown in the group accounts, the following further information must be given.

    (3) The composition and fair value of the consideration for the acquisition given by the parent company and its subsidiary undertakings must be stated.

    (4) Where the acquisition method of accounting has been adopted, the book values immediately prior to the acquisition, and the fair values at the date of acquisition, of each class of assets and liabilities of the undertaking or group acquired must be stated in tabular form, including a statement of the amount of any goodwill or negative consolidation difference arising on the acquisition, together with an explanation of any significant adjustments made.

    (5) In ascertaining for the purposes of sub-paragraph (4) the profit or loss of a group, the book values and fair values of assets and liabilities of a group or the amount of the assets and liabilities of a group, the set-offs and other adjustments required by this Schedule in the case of group accounts must be made.

**14.** (1) There must also be stated in a note to the accounts the cumulative amount of goodwill resulting from acquisitions in that and earlier financial years which has been written off otherwise than in the consolidated profit and loss account for that or any earlier financial year.

    (2) That figure must be shown net of any goodwill attributable to subsidiary undertakings or businesses disposed of prior to the balance sheet date.

**15.** Where during the financial year there has been a disposal of an undertaking or group which significantly affects the figure shown in the group accounts, there must be stated in a note to the accounts—

---

92 Section 131 is prospectively repealed by the 2006 Act.
93 Article 141 is prospectively repealed by the 2006 Act.
94 Section 132 is prospectively repealed by the 2006 Act.
95 Article 142 is prospectively repealed by the 2006 Act.

         (a)  the name of that undertaking or, as the case may be, of the parent undertaking of that group, and

         (b)  the extent to which the profit or loss shown in the group accounts is attributable to profit or loss of that undertaking or group.

**16.** The information required by paragraph 13, 14 or 15 need not be disclosed with respect to an undertaking which—

         (a)  is established under the law of a country outside the United Kingdom, or

         (b)  carries on business outside the United Kingdom,

            if in the opinion of the directors of the parent company the disclosure would be seriously prejudicial to the business of that undertaking or to the business of the parent company or any of its subsidiary undertakings and the Secretary of State agrees that the information should not be disclosed.

### Minority interests

**17.** (1) The formats set out in Schedule 1 to these Regulations have effect in relation to group accounts with the following additions.

    (2)  In the balance sheet formats there must be shown, as a separate item and under an appropriate heading, the amount of capital and reserves attributable to shares in subsidiary undertakings included in the consolidation held by or on behalf of persons other than the parent company and its subsidiary undertakings.

    (3)  In the profit and loss account formats there must be shown, as a separate item and under an appropriate heading—

         (a)  the amount of any profit or loss on ordinary activities, and

         (b)  the amount of any profit or loss on extraordinary activities,

            attributable to shares in subsidiary undertakings included in the consolidation held by or on behalf of persons other than the parent company and its subsidiary undertakings.

    (4)  For the purposes of paragraph 4(1) and (2) of Schedule 1 (power to adapt or combine items)—

         (a)  the additional item required by sub-paragraph (2) above is treated as one to which a letter is assigned, and

         (b)  the additional items required by sub-paragraph (3)(a) and (b) above are treated as ones to which an Arabic number is assigned.

### Joint ventures

**18.** (1) Where an undertaking included in the consolidation manages another undertaking jointly with one or more undertakings not included in the consolidation, that other undertaking ('the joint venture') may, if it is not—

         (a)  a body corporate, or

         (b)  a subsidiary undertaking of the parent company, be dealt with in the group accounts by the method of proportional consolidation.

    (2)  The provisions of this Schedule relating to the preparation of consolidated accounts apply, with any necessary modifications, to proportional consolidation under this paragraph.

### Associated undertakings

**19.** (1) An 'associated undertaking' means an undertaking in which an undertaking included in the consolidation has a participating interest and over whose operating and financial policy it exercises a significant influence, and which is not—

         (a)  a subsidiary undertaking of the parent company, or

         (b)  a joint venture dealt with in accordance with paragraph 18.

    (2)  Where an undertaking holds 20% or more of the voting rights in another undertaking, it is presumed to exercise such an influence over it unless the contrary is shown.

    (3)  The voting rights in an undertaking means the rights conferred on shareholders in respect of their shares or, in the case of an undertaking not having a share capital, on members, to vote at general meetings of the undertaking on all, or substantially all, matters.

    (4)  The provisions of paragraphs 5 to 11 of Schedule 7 to the 2006 Act (parent and subsidiary undertakings: rights to be taken into account and attribution of rights) apply in determining for the purposes of this paragraph whether an undertaking holds 20% or more of the voting rights in another undertaking.

**20.** (1) The formats set out in Schedule 1 to these Regulations have effect in relation to group accounts with the following modifications.

    (2)  In the balance sheet formats replace the items headed 'Participating interests', that is—

         (a)  in format 1, item B.III.3, and

         (b)  in format 2, item B.III.3 under the heading 'ASSETS',

             by two items: 'Interests in associated undertakings' and 'Other participating interests'.

    (3)  In the profit and loss account formats replace the items headed 'Income from participating interests', that is—

         (a)  in format 1, item 8,

      (b)  in format 2, item 10,

      (c)  in format 3, item B.4, and

      (d)  in format 4, item B.6, by two items: 'Income from interests in associated undertakings' and 'Income from other participating interests'.

**21.** (1)  The interest of an undertaking in an associated undertaking, and the amount of profit or loss attributable to such an interest, must be shown by the equity method of accounting (including dealing with any goodwill arising in accordance with paragraphs 17 to 20 and 22 of Schedule 1 to these Regulations).

    (2)  Where the associated undertaking is itself a parent undertaking, the net assets and profits or losses to be taken into account are those of the parent and its subsidiary undertakings (after making any consolidation adjustments).

    (3)  The equity method of accounting need not be applied if the amounts in question are not material for the purpose of giving a true and fair view.

### Related party transactions

**22.** Paragraph 72 of Schedule 1 to these Regulations applies to transactions which the parent company, or other undertakings included in the consolidation, have entered into with related parties, unless they are intra group transactions.

## PART 2

## MODIFICATIONS FOR BANKING GROUPS

### General application of provisions applicable to individual accounts

**23.** In its application to banking groups, Part 1 of this Schedule has effect with the following modifications.

**24.** In paragraph 1 of this Schedule—

      (a)  the reference in sub-paragraph (1) to the provisions of Schedule 1 to these Regulations is to be construed as a reference to the provisions of Schedule 2 to these Regulations, and

      (b)  sub-paragraph (2) is to be omitted.

### Minority interests and associated undertakings

**25.** (1)  This paragraph adapts paragraphs 17 and 20 (which require items in respect of 'Minority interests' and associated undertakings to be added to the formats set out in Schedule 1 to these Regulations) to the formats prescribed by Schedule 2 to these Regulations.

    (2)  In paragraph 17—

      (a)  in sub-paragraph (1), for the reference to Schedule 1 to these Regulations, substitute a reference to Schedule 2, and

      (b)  paragraph 17(4) is not to apply, but for the purposes of paragraph 5(1) of Part I of Schedule 2 to these Regulations (power to combine items) the additional items required by the foregoing provisions of this paragraph are to be treated as items to which a letter is assigned.

    (3)  Paragraph 20(2) is to apply with respect to a balance sheet prepared under Schedule 2 to these Regulations as if it required assets item 7 (participating interests) in the balance sheet format to be replaced by the two replacement items referred to in that paragraph.

    (4)  Paragraph 20(3) is not to apply, but the following items in the profit and loss account formats—

      (a)  format 1 item 3(b) (income from participating interests),

      (b)  format 2 item B2(b) (income from participating interests), are replaced by the following—

          (i)   'Income from participating interests other than associated undertakings', to be shown at position 3(b) in format 1 and position B2(b) in format 2, and

         (ii)  'Income from associated undertakings', to be shown at an appropriate position.

**26.** In paragraph 21(1) of this Schedule, for the references to paragraphs 17 to 20 and 22 of Schedule 1 to these Regulations substitute references to paragraphs 23 to 26 and 28 of Schedule 2 to these Regulations.

### Related party transactions

**27.** In paragraph 22 of this Schedule, for the reference to paragraph 72 of Schedule 1 to these Regulations substitute a reference to paragraph 92 of Schedule 2 to these Regulations.

### Foreign currency translation

**28.** Any difference between—

      (a)  the amount included in the consolidated accounts for the previous financial year with respect to any undertaking included in the consolidation or the group's interest in any associated undertaking, together with the amount of any transactions undertaken to cover any such interest, and

(b) the opening amount for the financial year in respect of those undertakings and in respect of any such transactions, arising as a result of the application of paragraph 50 of Schedule 2 to these Regulations may be credited to (where (a) is less than (b)), or deducted from (where (a) is greater than (b)), (as the case may be) consolidated reserves.

**29.** Any income and expenditure of undertakings included in the consolidation and associated undertakings in a foreign currency may be translated for the purposes of the consolidated accounts at the average rates of exchange prevailing during the financial year.

### Information as to undertaking in which shares held as a result of financial assistance operation

**30.** (1) The following provisions apply where the parent company of a banking group has a subsidiary undertaking which—

(a) is a credit institution of which shares are held as a result of a financial assistance operation with a view to its reorganisation or rescue, and

(b) is excluded from consolidation under section 405(3)(c) of the 2006 Act (interest held with a view to resale).

(2) Information as to the nature and terms of the operations must be given in a note to the group accounts, and there must be appended to the copy of the group accounts delivered to the registrar in accordance with section 441 of the 2006 Act a copy of the undertaking's latest individual accounts and, if it is a parent undertaking, its latest group accounts. If the accounts appended are required by law to be audited, a copy of the auditor's report must also be appended.

(3) Any requirement of Part 35 of the 2006 Act as to the delivery to the registrar of a certified translation into English must be met in relation to any document required to be appended by sub-paragraph (2).

(4) The above requirements are subject to the following qualifications—

(a) an undertaking is not required to prepare for the purposes of this paragraph accounts which would not otherwise be prepared, and if no accounts satisfying the above requirements are prepared none need be appended;

(b) the accounts of an undertaking need not be appended if they would not otherwise be required to be published, or made available for public inspection, anywhere in the world, but in that case the reason for not appending the accounts must be stated in a note to the consolidated accounts.

(5) Where a copy of an undertaking's accounts is required to be appended to the copy of the group accounts delivered to the registrar, that fact must be stated in a note to the group accounts.

### PART 3
### MODIFICATIONS FOR INSURANCE GROUPS

### General application of provisions applicable to individual accounts

**31.** In its application to insurance groups, Part 1 of this Schedule has effect with the following modifications.

**32.** In paragraph 1 of this Schedule—

(a) the reference in sub-paragraph (1) to the provisions of Schedule 1 to these Regulations is to be construed as a reference to the provisions of Schedule 3 to these Regulations, and

(b) sub-paragraph (2) is to be omitted.

### Financial years of subsidiary undertakings

**33.** In paragraph 2(2)(a), for 'three months' substitute 'six months'.

### Assets and liabilities to be included in group accounts

**34.** In paragraph 3, after sub-paragraph (1) insert—

'(1A) Sub-paragraph (1) is not to apply to those liabilities items the valuation of which by the undertakings included in a consolidation is based on the application of provisions applying only to insurance undertakings, nor to those assets items changes in the values of which also affect or establish policyholders' rights.

(1B) Where sub-paragraph (1A) applies, that fact must be disclosed in the notes to the consolidated accounts.'.

### Elimination of group transactions

**35.** For sub-paragraph (4) of paragraph 6 substitute—

'(4) Sub-paragraphs (1) and (2) need not be complied with—

(a) where a transaction has been concluded according to normal market conditions and a policyholder has rights in respect of the transaction, or

(b) if the amounts concerned are not material for the purpose of giving a true and fair view.

(5) Where advantage is taken of sub-paragraph (4)(a) that fact must be disclosed in the notes to the accounts, and where the transaction in question has a material effect on the assets, liabilities, financial position and profit or loss of all the undertakings included in the consolidation that fact must also be so disclosed.'.

### Minority interests

**36.** In paragraph 17—

(a) in sub-paragraph (1), for the reference to Schedule 1 to these Regulations, substitute a reference to Schedule 3, and

(b) for sub-paragraph (4) substitute—

'(4) Paragraph 3(1) of Schedule 3 to these Regulations (power to combine items) does not apply in relation to the additional items required by the above provisions of this paragraph.'.

### Associated undertakings

**37.** In paragraph 20—

(a) in sub-paragraph (1), for the reference to Schedule 1 to these Regulations substitute a reference to Schedule 3 to these Regulations, and

(b) for sub-paragraphs (2) and (3) substitute—

'(2) In the balance sheet format, replace asset item C.II.3 (participating interests) with two items, 'Interests in associated undertakings' and 'Other participating interests'.

(3) In the profit and loss account format, replace items II.2.(a) and III.3.(a) (income from participating interests, with a separate indication of that derived from group undertakings) with—

(a) 'Income from participating interests other than associated undertakings, with a separate indication of that derived from group undertakings', to be shown as items II.2.(a) and III.3.(a), and

(b) 'Income from associated undertakings', to be shown as items II.2.(aa) and III.3.(aa).'.

**38.** In paragraph 21(1) of this Schedule, for the references to paragraphs 17 to 20 and 22 of Schedule 1 to these Regulations, substitute references to paragraphs 36 to 39 and 42 of Schedule 3 to these Regulations.

### Related party transactions

**39.** In paragraph 22 of this Schedule, for the reference to paragraph 72 of Schedule 1 to these Regulations substitute a reference to paragraph 90 of Schedule 3 to these Regulations.

### Modifications of Schedule 3 to these Regulations for purposes of paragraph 31

**40.** (1) For the purposes of paragraph 31 of this Schedule, Schedule 3 to these Regulations is to be modified as follows.

(2) The information required by paragraph 11 (additional items) need not be given.

(3) In the case of general business, investment income, expenses and charges may be disclosed in the non-technical account rather than in the technical account.

(4) In the case of subsidiary undertakings which are not authorised to carry on long-term business in the United Kingdom, notes (8) and (9) to the profit and loss account format have effect as if references to investment income, expenses and charges arising in the long-term fund or to investments attributed to the long-term fund were references to investment income, expenses and charges or (as the case may be) investments relating to long-term business.

(5) In the case of subsidiary undertakings which do not have a head office in the United Kingdom, the computation required by paragraph 52 must be made annually by an actuary or other specialist in the field on the basis of recognised actuarial methods.

(6) The information required by paragraphs 85 to 88 need not be shown.

SCHEDULE 7            Regulation 10

MATTERS TO BE DEALT WITH IN DIRECTORS' REPORT

PART 1

MATTERS OF A GENERAL NATURE

### Introduction

**1.** In addition to the information required by section 416 of the 2006 Act, the directors' report must contain the following information.

### Asset values

**2.** (1) If, in the case of such of the fixed assets of the company as consist in interests in land, their market value (as at the end of the financial year) differs substantially from the amount at which they are included in the balance sheet, and the difference is, in the directors' opinion, of such significance as to require that the attention of members of the company or of holders of its debentures should be drawn to it, the report must indicate the difference with such degree of precision as is practicable.

(2) In relation to a group directors' report sub-paragraph (1) has effect as if the reference to the fixed assets of the company was a reference to the fixed assets of the company and of its subsidiary undertakings included in the consolidation.

### Political donations and expenditure

**3.** (1) If—

(a) the company (not being the wholly-owned subsidiary of a company incorporated in the United Kingdom) has in the financial year—

(i) made any political donation to any political party or other political organisation,

(ii) made any political donation to any independent election candidate, or

(iii) incurred any political expenditure, and

(b) the amount of the donation or expenditure, or (as the case may be) the aggregate amount of all donations and expenditure falling within paragraph (a), exceeded £2000, the directors' report for the year must contain the following particulars.

(2) Those particulars are—

(a) as respects donations falling within sub-paragraph (1)(a)(i) or (ii)—

(i) the name of each political party, other political organisation or independent election candidate to whom any such donation has been made, and

(ii) the total amount given to that party, organisation or candidate by way of such donations in the financial year; and

(b) as respects expenditure falling within sub-paragraph (1)(a)(iii), the total amount incurred by way of such expenditure in the financial year.

(3) If—

(a) at the end of the financial year the company has subsidiaries which have, in that year, made any donations or incurred any such expenditure as is mentioned in sub-paragraph (1)(a), and

(b) it is not itself the wholly-owned subsidiary of a company incorporated in the United Kingdom,

the directors' report for the year is not, by virtue of sub-paragraph (1), required to contain the particulars specified in sub-paragraph (2). But, if the total amount of any such donations or expenditure (or both) made or incurred in that year by the company and the subsidiaries between them exceeds £2000, the directors' report for the year must contain those particulars in relation to each body by whom any such donation or expenditure has been made or incurred.

(4) Any expression used in this paragraph which is also used in Part 14 of the 2006 Act (control of political donations and expenditure) has the same meaning as in that Part.

**4.** (1) If the company (not being the wholly-owned subsidiary of a company incorporated in the United Kingdom) has in the financial year made any contribution to a non-EU political party, the directors' report for the year must contain—

(a) a statement of the amount of the contribution, or

(b) (if it has made two or more such contributions in the year) a statement of the total amount of the contributions.

(2) If—

(a) at the end of the financial year the company has subsidiaries which have, in that year, made any such contributions as are mentioned in sub-paragraph (1), and

(b) it is not itself the wholly-owned subsidiary of a company incorporated in the United Kingdom, the directors' report for the year is not, by virtue of sub-paragraph (1), required to contain any such statement as is there mentioned, but it must instead contain a statement of the total amount of the contributions made in the year by the company and the subsidiaries between them.

(3) In this paragraph, 'contribution', in relation to an organisation, means—

(a) any gift of money to the organisation (whether made directly or indirectly);

(b) any subscription or other fee paid for affiliation to, or membership of, the organisation; or

(c) any money spent (otherwise than by the organisation or a person acting on its behalf) in paying any expenses incurred directly or indirectly by the organisation.

(4) In this paragraph, 'non-EU political party' means any political party which carries on, or proposes to carry on, its activities wholly outside the member States.

### Charitable donations

**5.** (1) If—

    (a) the company (not being the wholly-owned subsidiary of a company incorporated in the United Kingdom) has in the financial year given money for charitable purposes, and

    (b) the money given exceeded £2000 in amount,

        the directors' report for the year must contain, in the case of each of the purposes for which money has been given, a statement of the amount of money given for that purpose.

(2) If—

    (a) at the end of the financial year the company has subsidiaries which have, in that year, given money for charitable purposes, and

    (b) it is not itself the wholly owned subsidiary of a company incorporated in the United Kingdom,

        sub-paragraph (1) does not apply to the company.

But, if the amount given in that year for charitable purposes by the company and the subsidiaries between them exceeds £2000, the directors' report for the year must contain, in the case of each of the purposes for which money has been given by the company and the subsidiaries between them, a statement of the amount of money given for that purpose.

(3) Money given for charitable purposes to a person who, when it was given, was ordinarily resident outside the United Kingdom is to be left out of account for the purposes of this paragraph.

(4) For the purposes of this paragraph, 'charitable purposes' means purposes which are exclusively charitable, and as respects Scotland a purpose is charitable if it is listed in section 7(2) of the Charities and Trustee Investment (Scotland) Act 2005[96].

### Financial instruments

**6.** (1) In relation to the use of financial instruments by a company, the directors' report must contain an indication of—

    (a) the financial risk management objectives and policies of the company, including the policy for hedging each major type of forecasted transaction for which hedge accounting is used, and

    (b) the exposure of the company to price risk, credit risk, liquidity risk and cash flow risk, unless such information is not material for the assessment of the assets, liabilities, financial position and profit or loss of the company.

(2) In relation to a group directors' report sub-paragraph (1) has effect as if the references to the company were references to the company and its subsidiary undertakings included in the consolidation.

(3) In sub-paragraph (1) the expressions 'hedge accounting', 'price risk', 'credit risk', 'liquidity risk' and 'cash flow risk' have the same meaning as they have in Council Directive 78/660/EEC on the annual accounts of certain types of companies, and in Council Directive 83/349/EEC on consolidated accounts[97].

### Miscellaneous

**7.** (1) The directors' report must contain—

    (a) particulars of any important events affecting the company which have occurred since the end of the financial year,

    (b) an indication of likely future developments in the business of the company,

    (c) an indication of the activities (if any) of the company in the field of research and development, and

    (d) (unless the company is an unlimited company) an indication of the existence of branches (as defined in section 1046(3) of the 2006 Act) of the company outside the United Kingdom.

(2) In relation to a group directors' report paragraphs (a), (b) and (c) of sub-paragraph (1) have effect as if the references to the company were references to the company and its subsidiary undertakings included in the consolidation.

---

[96] 2005 asp 10.

[97] OJL222 of 14.8.1978, page 11, and OJ L193 of 18.7.1983, page 1, as amended in particular by Directives 2001/65/EEC and 2003/51/EEC of the European Parliament and of the Council (OJ L238 of 27.12.2001, page 28, and OJ L178 of 17.7.2003, page 16).

## PART 2

## DISCLOSURE REQUIRED BY COMPANY ACQUIRING ITS OWN SHARES ETC.

**8.** This Part of this Schedule applies where shares in a company—

(a) are purchased by the company or are acquired by it by forfeiture or surrender in lieu of forfeiture, or in pursuance of any of the following provisions (acquisition of own shares by company limited by shares)—

   (i) section 143(3) of the Companies Act 1985[98],

   (ii) Article 153(3) of the Companies (Northern Ireland) Order 1986[99], or

   (iii) section 659 of the 2006 Act, or

(b) are acquired by another person in circumstances where paragraph (c) or (d) of any of the following provisions applies (acquisition by company's nominee, or by another with company financial assistance, the company having a beneficial interest)—

   (i) section 146(1) of the Companies Act 1985[100],

   (ii) Article 156(1) of the Companies (Northern Ireland) Order 1986[101], or

   (iii) section 662(1) of the 2006 Act applies, or

(c) are made subject to a lien or other charge taken (whether expressly or otherwise) by the company and permitted by any of the following provisions (exceptions from general rule against a company having a lien or charge on its own shares)—

   (i) section 150(2) or (4) of the Companies Act 1985[102],

   (ii) Article 160(2) or (4) of the Companies (Northern Ireland) Order 1986[103], or

   (iii) section 670(2) or (4) of the 2006 Act.

**9.** The directors' report for a financial year must state—

(a) the number and nominal value of the shares so purchased, the aggregate amount of the consideration paid by the company for such shares and the reasons for their purchase;

(b) the number and nominal value of the shares so acquired by the company, acquired by another person in such circumstances and so charged respectively during the financial year;

(c) the maximum number and nominal value of shares which, having been so acquired by the company, acquired by another person in such circumstances or so charged (whether or not during that year) are held at any time by the company or that other person during that year;

(d) the number and nominal value of the shares so acquired by the company, acquired by another person in such circumstances or so charged (whether or not during that year) which are disposed of by the company or that other person or cancelled by the company during that year;

(e) where the number and nominal value of the shares of any particular description are stated in pursuance of any of the preceding sub-paragraphs, the percentage of the called-up share capital which shares of that description represent;

(f) where any of the shares have been so charged the amount of the charge in each case; and

(g) where any of the shares have been disposed of by the company or the person who acquired them in such circumstances for money or money's worth the amount or value of the consideration in each case.

## PART 3

## DISCLOSURE CONCERNING EMPLOYMENT ETC. OF DISABLED PERSONS

**10.** (1) This Part of this Schedule applies to the directors' report where the average number of persons employed by the company in each week during the financial year exceeded 250.

(2) That average number is the quotient derived by dividing, by the number of weeks in the financial year, the number derived by ascertaining, in relation to each of those weeks, the number of persons who, under contracts of service, were employed in the week (whether throughout it or not) by the company, and adding up the numbers ascertained.

(3) The directors' report must in that case contain a statement describing such policy as the company has applied during the financial year—

(a) for giving full and fair consideration to applications for employment by the company made by disabled persons, having regard to their particular aptitudes and abilities,

(b) for continuing the employment of, and for arranging appropriate training for, employees

---

[98] Section 143 is prospectively repealed by the 2006 Act.

[99] Article 153 is prospectively repealed by the 2006 Act.

[100] Section 146(1)(aa) was inserted by section 102C(5) of 1986 c.53, as inserted by section 1(1) of 1997 c.41. Section 146 is prospectively repealed by the 2006 Act.

[101] Article 156(1)(aa) was inserted by section 102C(6) of 1986 c.53, as inserted by section 1(1) of 1997 c.41. Article 156 is prospectively repealed by the 2006 Act.

[102] Section 150 is prospectively repealed by the 2006 Act.

[103] Article 160 is prospectively repealed by the 2006 Act.

of the company who have become disabled persons during the period when they were
employed by the company, and

(c) otherwise for the training, career development and promotion of disabled persons
employed by the company.

(4) In this Part—

(a) 'employment' means employment other than employment to work wholly or mainly
outside the United Kingdom, and 'employed' and 'employee' are to be construed
accordingly; and

(b) 'disabled person' means the same as in the Disability Discrimination Act 1995[104].

## PART 4
## EMPLOYEE INVOLVEMENT

**11.** (1) This Part of this Schedule applies to the directors' report where the average number of
persons employed by the company in each week during the financial year exceeded 250.

(2) That average number is the quotient derived by dividing, by the number of weeks in the
financial year, the number derived by ascertaining, in relation to each of those weeks, the
number of persons who, under contracts of service, were employed in the week (whether
throughout it or not) by the company, and adding up the numbers ascertained.

(3) The directors' report must in that case contain a statement describing the action that has
been taken during the financial year to introduce, maintain or develop arrangements aimed
at—

(a) providing employees systematically with information on matters of concern to them as
employees,

(b) consulting employees or their representatives on a regular basis so that the views of
employees can be taken into account in making decisions which are likely to affect their
interests,

(c) encouraging the involvement of employees in the company's performance through an
employees' share scheme or by some other means,

(d) achieving a common awareness on the part of all employees of the financial and
economic factors affecting the performance of the company.

(4) In sub-paragraph (3) 'employee' does not include a person employed to work wholly or
mainly outside the United Kingdom; and for the purposes of sub-paragraph (2) no regard is
to be had to such a person.

## PART 5
## POLICY AND PRACTICE ON PAYMENT OF CREDITORS

**12.** (1) This Part of this Schedule applies to the directors' report for a financial year if—

(a) the company was at any time within the year a public company, or

(b) the company did not qualify as small or medium-sized in relation to the year by virtue of
section 382 or 465 of the 2006 Act and was at any time within the year a member of a
group of which the parent company was a public company.

(2) The report must state, with respect to the next following financial year—

(a) whether in respect of some or all of its suppliers it is the company's policy to follow any
code or standard on payment practice and, if so, the name of the code or standard and
the place where information about, and copies of, the code or standard can be obtained,

(b) whether in respect of some or all of its suppliers it is the company's policy—

(i) to settle the terms of payment with those suppliers when agreeing the terms of each
transaction,

(ii) to ensure that those suppliers are made aware of the terms of payment, and

(iii) to abide by the terms of payment,

(c) where the company's policy is not as mentioned in paragraph (a) or (b) in respect of some
or all of its suppliers, what its policy is with respect to the payment of those suppliers;
and if the company's policy is different for different suppliers or classes of suppliers,
the report must identify the suppliers to which the different policies apply. In this
sub-paragraph references to the company's suppliers are references to persons who
are or may become its suppliers.

(3) The report must also state the number of days which bears to the number of days in the
financial year the same proportion as X bears to Y where—

---

[104] 1995 c.50.

X = the aggregate of the amounts which were owed to trade creditors at the end of the year; and

Y = the aggregate of the amounts in which the company was invoiced by suppliers during the year.

(4) For the purposes of sub-paragraphs (2) and (3) a person is a supplier of the company at any time if—

    (a) at that time, he is owed an amount in respect of goods or services supplied, and

    (b) that amount would be included under the heading corresponding to item E.4 (trade creditors) in format 1 if—

        (i) the company's accounts fell to be prepared as at that time,

        (ii) those accounts were prepared in accordance with Schedule 1 to these Regulations, and

        (iii) that format were adopted.

(5) For the purpose of sub-paragraph (3), the aggregate of the amounts which at the end of the financial year were owed to trade creditors is taken to be—

    (a) where in the company's accounts format 1 of the balance sheet formats set out in Part 1 of Schedule 1 to these Regulations is adopted, the amount shown under the heading corresponding to item E.4 (trade creditors) in that format,

    (b) where format 2 is adopted, the amount which, under the heading corresponding to item C.4 (trade creditors) in that format, is shown as falling due within one year, and

    (c) where the company's accounts are prepared in accordance with Schedule 2 or 3 to these Regulations or the company's accounts are IAS accounts, the amount which would be shown under the heading corresponding to item E.4 (trade creditors) in format 1 if the company's accounts were prepared in accordance with Schedule 1 and that format were adopted.

# PART 6
## DISCLOSURE REQUIRED BY CERTAIN PUBLICLY-TRADED COMPANIES

**13.** (1) This Part of this Schedule applies to the directors' report for a financial year if the company had securities carrying voting rights admitted to trading on a regulated market at the end of that year.

(2) The report must contain detailed information, by reference to the end of that year, on the following matters—

    (a) the structure of the company's capital, including in particular—

        (i) the rights and obligations attaching to the shares or, as the case may be, to each class of shares in the company, and

        (ii) where there are two or more such classes, the percentage of the total share capital represented by each class;

    (b) any restrictions on the transfer of securities in the company, including in particular—

        (i) limitations on the holding of securities, and

        (ii) requirements to obtain the approval of the company, or of other holders of securities in the company, for a transfer of securities;

    (c) in the case of each person with a significant direct or indirect holding of securities in the company, such details as are known to the company of—

        (i) the identity of the person,

        (ii) the size of the holding, and

        (iii) the nature of the holding;

    (d) in the case of each person who holds securities carrying special rights with regard to control of the company—

        (i) the identity of the person, and

        (ii) the nature of the rights;

    (e) where—

        (i) the company has an employees' share scheme, and

        (ii) shares to which the scheme relates have rights with regard to control of the company that are not exercisable directly by the employees, how those rights are exercisable;

    (f) any restrictions on voting rights, including in particular—

        (i) limitations on voting rights of holders of a given percentage or number of votes,

        (ii) deadlines for exercising voting rights, and

        (iii) arrangements by which, with the company's co-operation, financial rights carried by securities are held by a person other than the holder of the securities;

    (g) any agreements between holders of securities that are known to the company and may result in restrictions on the transfer of securities or on voting rights;

    (h) any rules that the company has about—

        (i) appointment and replacement of directors, or

        (ii) amendment of the company's articles of association;

    (i) the powers of the company's directors, including in particular any powers in relation to the issuing or buying back by the company of its shares;

    (j)  any significant agreements to which the company is a party that take effect, alter or terminate upon a change of control of the company following a takeover bid, and the effects of any such agreements;

    (k)  any agreements between the company and its directors or employees providing for compensation for loss of office or employment (whether through resignation, purported redundancy or otherwise) that occurs because of a takeover bid.

(3) For the purposes of sub-paragraph (2)(a) a company's capital includes any securities in the company that are not admitted to trading on a regulated market.

(4) For the purposes of sub-paragraph (2)(c) a person has an indirect holding of securities if—

    (a)  they are held on his behalf, or

    (b)  he is able to secure that rights carried by the securities are exercised in accordance with his wishes.

(5) Sub-paragraph (2)(j) does not apply to an agreement if—

    (a)  disclosure of the agreement would be seriously prejudicial to the company, and

    (b)  the company is not under any other obligation to disclose it.

(6) In this paragraph—

'securities' means shares or debentures;

'takeover bid' has the same meaning as in the Takeovers Directive;

'the Takeovers Directive' means Directive 2004/25/EC of the European Parliament and of the Council[105];

'voting rights' means rights to vote at general meetings of the company in question, including rights that arise only in certain circumstances.

**14.** The directors' report must also contain any necessary explanatory material with regard to information that is required to be included in the report by this Part.


SCHEDULE 8            Regulation 11

QUOTED COMPANIES: DIRECTORS' REMUNERATION REPORT

PART 1

INTRODUCTORY

**1.** (1) In the directors' remuneration report for a financial year ('the relevant financial year') there must be shown the information specified in Parts 2 and 3.

  (2) Information required to be shown in the report for or in respect of a particular person must be shown in the report in a manner that links the information to that person identified by name.


PART 2

INFORMATION NOT SUBJECT TO AUDIT

**Consideration by the directors of matters relating to directors' remuneration**

**2.** (1) If a committee of the company's directors has considered matters relating to the directors' remuneration for the relevant financial year, the directors' remuneration report must—

    (a)  name each director who was a member of the committee at any time when the committee was considering any such matter;

    (b)  name any person who provided to the committee advice, or services, that materially assisted the committee in their consideration of any such matter;

    (c)  in the case of any person named under paragraph (b), who is not a director of the company, state—

       (i)  the nature of any other services that that person has provided to the company during the relevant financial year; and

      (ii)  whether that person was appointed by the committee.

  (2) In sub-paragraph (1)(b) 'person' includes (in particular) any director of the company who does not fall within sub-paragraph (1)(a).

**Statement of company's policy on directors' remuneration**

**3.** (1) The directors' remuneration report must contain a statement of the company's policy on directors' remuneration for the following financial year and for financial years subsequent to that.

  (2) The policy statement must include—

---

[105] OJ No. L142, 30.4.2004, p12.

(a) for each director, a detailed summary of any performance conditions to which any entitlement of the director—
  (i) to share options, or
  (ii) under a long term incentive scheme, is subject;
(b) an explanation as to why any such performance conditions were chosen;
(c) a summary of the methods to be used in assessing whether any such performance conditions are met and an explanation as to why those methods were chosen;
(d) if any such performance condition involves any comparison with factors external to the company—
  (i) a summary of the factors to be used in making each such comparison, and
  (ii) if any of the factors relates to the performance of another company, of two or more other companies or of an index on which the securities of a company or companies are listed, the identity of that company, of each of those companies or of the index;
(e) a description of, and an explanation for, any significant amendment proposed to be made to the terms and conditions of any entitlement of a director to share options or under a long term incentive scheme; and
(f) if any entitlement of a director to share options, or under a long term incentive scheme, is not subject to performance conditions, an explanation as to why that is the case.
(3) The policy statement must, in respect of each director's terms and conditions relating to remuneration, explain the relative importance of those elements which are, and those which are not, related to performance.
(4) The policy statement must summarise, and explain, the company's policy on—
(a) the duration of contracts with directors, and
(b) notice periods, and termination payments, under such contracts.
(5) In sub-paragraphs (2) and (3), references to a director are to any person who serves as a director of the company at any time in the period beginning with the end of the relevant financial year and ending with the date on which the directors' remuneration report is laid before the company in general meeting.

**Statement of consideration of conditions elsewhere in company and group**

**4.** The directors' remuneration report must contain a statement of how pay and employment conditions of employees of the company and of other undertakings within the same group as the company were taken into account when determining directors' remuneration for the relevant financial year.

**Performance graph**

**5.** (1) The directors' remuneration report must—
(a) contain a line graph that shows for each of—
  (i) a holding of shares of that class of the company's equity share capital whose listing, or admission to dealing, has resulted in the company falling within the definition of 'quoted company', and
  (ii) a hypothetical holding of shares made up of shares of the same kinds and number as those by reference to which a broad equity market index is calculated,
  a line drawn by joining up points plotted to represent, for each of the financial years in the relevant period, the total shareholder return on that holding; and
(b) state the name of the index selected for the purposes of the graph and set out the reasons for selecting that index.
(2) For the purposes of sub-paragraphs (1) and (4), 'relevant period' means the five financial years of which the last is the relevant financial year.
(3) Where the relevant financial year—
(a) is the company's second, third or fourth financial year, sub-paragraph (2) has effect with the substitution of 'two', 'three' or 'four' (as the case may be) for 'five'; and
(b) is the company's first financial year, 'relevant period', for the purposes of sub-paragraphs (1) and (4), means the relevant financial year.
(4) For the purposes of sub-paragraph (1), the 'total shareholder return' for a relevant period on a holding of shares must be calculated using a fair method that—
(a) takes as its starting point the percentage change over the period in the market price of the holding;
(b) involves making—
  (i) the assumptions specified in sub-paragraph (5) as to reinvestment of income, and
  (ii) the assumption specified in sub-paragraph (7) as to the funding of liabilities, and
(c) makes provision for any replacement of shares in the holding by shares of a different description;
  and the same method must be used for each of the holdings mentioned in sub-paragraph (1).
(5) The assumptions as to reinvestment of income are—
(a) that any benefit in the form of shares of the same kind as those in the holding is added to the holding at the time the benefit becomes receivable; and

(b) that any benefit in cash, and an amount equal to the value of any benefit not in cash and not falling within paragraph (a), is applied at the time the benefit becomes receivable in the purchase at their market price of shares of the same kind as those in the holding and that the shares purchased are added to the holding at that time.

(6) In sub-paragraph (5) 'benefit' means any benefit (including, in particular, any dividend) receivable in respect of any shares in the holding by the holder from the company of whose share capital the shares form part.

(7) The assumption as to the funding of liabilities is that, where the holder has a liability to the company of whose capital the shares in the holding form part, shares are sold from the holding—

(a) immediately before the time by which the liability is due to be satisfied, and

(b) in such numbers that, at the time of the sale, the market price of the shares sold equals the amount of the liability in respect of the shares in the holding that are not being sold.

(8) In sub-paragraph (7) 'liability' means a liability arising in respect of any shares in the holding or from the exercise of a right attached to any of those shares.

### Service contracts

**6.** (1) The directors' remuneration report must contain, in respect of the contract of service or contract for services of each person who has served as a director of the company at any time during the relevant financial year, the following information—

(a) the date of the contract, the unexpired term and the details of any notice periods;

(b) any provision for compensation payable upon early termination of the contract; and

(c) such details of other provisions in the contract as are necessary to enable members of the company to estimate the liability of the company in the event of early termination of the contract.

(2) The directors' remuneration report must contain an explanation for any significant award made to a person in the circumstances described in paragraph 15.

## PART 3

## INFORMATION SUBJECT TO AUDIT

### Amount of each director's emoluments and compensation in the relevant financial year

**7.** (1) The directors' remuneration report must for the relevant financial year show, for each person who has served as a director of the company at any time during that year, each of the following—

(a) the total amount of salary and fees paid to or receivable by the person in respect of qualifying services;

(b) the total amount of bonuses so paid or receivable;

(c) the total amount of sums paid by way of expenses allowance that are—

(i) chargeable to United Kingdom income tax (or would be if the person were an individual), and

(ii) paid to or receivable by the person in respect of qualifying services;

(d) the total amount of—

(i) any compensation for loss of office paid to or receivable by the person, and

(ii) any other payments paid to or receivable by the person in connection with the termination of qualifying services;

(e) the total estimated value of any benefits received by the person otherwise than in cash that—

(i) do not fall within any of paragraphs (a) to (d) or paragraphs 8 to 12,

(ii) are emoluments of the person, and

(iii) are received by the person in respect of qualifying services; and

(f) the amount that is the total of the sums mentioned in paragraphs (a) to (e).

(2) The directors' remuneration report must show, for each person who has served as a director of the company at any time during the relevant financial year, the amount that for the financial year preceding the relevant financial year is the total of the sums mentioned in paragraphs (a) to (e) of sub-paragraph (1).

(3) The directors' remuneration report must also state the nature of any element of a remuneration package which is not cash.

(4) The information required by sub-paragraphs (1) and (2) must be presented in tabular form.

### Share options

**8.** (1) The directors' remuneration report must contain, in respect of each person who has served as a director of the company at any time in the relevant financial year, the information specified in paragraph 9.

(2) Sub-paragraph (1) is subject to paragraph 10 (aggregation of information to avoid excessively lengthy reports).

(3) The information specified in sub-paragraphs (a) to (c) of paragraph 9 must be presented in tabular form in the report.

(4) In paragraph 9 'share option', in relation to a person, means a share option granted in respect of qualifying services of the person.

9. The information required by sub-paragraph (1) of paragraph 8 in respect of such a person as is mentioned in that sub-paragraph is—

    (a) the number of shares that are subject to a share option—

        (i) at the beginning of the relevant financial year or, if later, on the date of the appointment of the person as a director of the company, and

        (ii) at the end of the relevant financial year or, if earlier, on the cessation of the person's appointment as a director of the company,

        in each case differentiating between share options having different terms and conditions;

    (b) information identifying those share options that have been awarded in the relevant financial year, those that have been exercised in that year, those that in that year have expired unexercised and those whose terms and conditions have been varied in that year;

    (c) for each share option that is unexpired at any time in the relevant financial year—

        (i) the price paid, if any, for its award,

        (ii) the exercise price,

        (iii) the date from which the option may be exercised, and

        (iv) the date on which the option expires;

    (d) a description of any variation made in the relevant financial year in the terms and conditions of a share option;

    (e) a summary of any performance criteria upon which the award or exercise of a share option is conditional, including a description of any variation made in such performance criteria during the relevant financial year;

    (f) for each share option that has been exercised during the relevant financial year, the market price of the shares, in relation to which it is exercised, at the time of exercise; and

    (g) for each share option that is unexpired at the end of the relevant financial year—

        (i) the market price at the end of that year, and

        (ii) the highest and lowest market prices during that year,

        of each share that is subject to the option.

10. (1) If, in the opinion of the directors of the company, disclosure in accordance with paragraphs 8 and 9 would result in a disclosure of excessive length then, (subject to sub-paragraphs (2) and (3))—

    (a) information disclosed for a person under paragraph 9(a) need not differentiate between share options having different terms and conditions;

    (b) for the purposes of disclosure in respect of a person under paragraph 9(c)(i) and (ii) and (g), share options may be aggregated and (instead of disclosing prices for each share option) disclosure may be made of weighted average prices of aggregations of share options;

    (c) for the purposes of disclosure in respect of a person under paragraph 9(c)(iii) and (iv), share options may be aggregated and (instead of disclosing dates for each share option) disclosure may be made of ranges of dates for aggregation of share options.

(2) Sub-paragraph (1)(b) and (c) does not permit the aggregation of—

    (a) share options in respect of shares whose market price at the end of the relevant financial year is below the option exercise price, with

    (b) share options in respect of shares whose market price at the end of the relevant financial year is equal to, or exceeds, the option exercise price.

(3) Sub-paragraph (1) does not apply (and accordingly, full disclosure must be made in accordance with paragraphs 8 and 9) in respect of share options that during the relevant financial year have been awarded or exercised or had their terms and conditions varied.

### Long term incentive schemes

11. (1) The directors' remuneration report must contain, in respect of each person who has served as a director of the company at any time in the relevant financial year, the information specified in paragraph 12.

(2) Sub-paragraph (1) does not require the report to contain share option details that are contained in the report in compliance with paragraphs 8 to 10.

(3) The information specified in paragraph 12 must be presented in tabular form in the report.

(4) For the purposes of paragraph 12—

    (a) 'scheme interest', in relation to a person, means an interest under a long term incentive scheme that is an interest in respect of which assets may become receivable under the scheme in respect of qualifying services of the person; and

    (b) such an interest 'vests' at the earliest time when—

        (i) it has been ascertained that the qualifying conditions have been fulfilled, and

    (ii)  the nature and quantity of the assets receivable under the scheme in respect of the interest have been ascertained.

(5) In this Schedule 'long term incentive scheme' means any agreement or arrangement under which money or other assets may become receivable by a person and which includes one or more qualifying conditions with respect to service or performance that cannot be fulfilled within a single financial year, and for this purpose the following must be disregarded, namely—

  (a)  any bonus the amount of which falls to be determined by reference to service or performance within a single financial year;

  (b)  compensation in respect of loss of office, payments for breach of contract and other termination payments; and

  (c)  retirement benefits.

**12.** (1) The information required by sub-paragraph (1) of paragraph 11 in respect of such a person as is mentioned in that sub-paragraph is—

  (a)  details of the scheme interests that the person has at the beginning of the relevant financial year or if later on the date of the appointment of the person as a director of the company;

  (b)  details of the scheme interests awarded to the person during the relevant financial year;

  (c)  details of the scheme interests that the person has at the end of the relevant financial year or if earlier on the cessation of the person's appointment as a director of the company;

  (d)  for each scheme interest within paragraphs (a) to (c)—

    (i)  the end of the period over which the qualifying conditions for that interest have to be fulfilled (or if there are different periods for different conditions, the end of whichever of those periods ends last); and

    (ii)  a description of any variation made in the terms and conditions of the scheme interests during the relevant financial year; and

  (e)  for each scheme interest that has vested in the relevant financial year—

    (i)  the relevant details (see sub-paragraph (3)) of any shares,

    (ii)  the amount of any money, and

    (iii)  the value of any other assets, that have become receivable in respect of the interest.

(2) The details that sub-paragraph (1)(b) requires of a scheme interest awarded during the relevant financial year include, if shares may become receivable in respect of the interest, the following—

  (a)  the number of those shares;

  (b)  the market price of each of those shares when the scheme interest was awarded; and

  (c)  details of qualifying conditions that are conditions with respect to performance.

(3) In sub-paragraph (1)(e)(i) 'the relevant details', in relation to any shares that have become receivable in respect of a scheme interest, means—

  (a)  the number of those shares;

  (b)  the date on which the scheme interest was awarded;

  (c)  the market price of each of those shares when the scheme interest was awarded;

  (d)  the market price of each of those shares when the scheme interest vested; and

  (e)  details of qualifying conditions that were conditions with respect to performance.

**Pensions**

**13.** (1) The directors' remuneration report must, for each person who has served as a director of the company at any time during the relevant financial year, contain the information in respect of pensions that is specified in sub-paragraphs (2) and (3).

(2) Where the person has rights under a pension scheme that is a defined benefit scheme in relation to the person and any of those rights are rights to which he has become entitled in respect of qualifying services of his—

  (a)  details—

    (i)  of any changes during the relevant financial year in the person's accrued benefits under the scheme, and

    (ii)  of the person's accrued benefits under the scheme as at the end of that year;

  [(b)  the transfer value, calculated in accordance with regulations 7 to 7E of the Occupational Pension Schemes (Transfer Values) Regulations 1996, of the person's accrued benefits under the scheme at the end of the relevant financial year;]ª

  (c)  the transfer value of the person's accrued benefits under the scheme that in compliance with paragraph (b) was contained in the directors' remuneration report for the previous financial year or, if there was no such report or no such value was contained in that report, the transfer value, calculated in such a manner as is mentioned in paragraph (b), of the person's accrued benefits under the scheme at the beginning of the relevant financial year;

  (d)  the amount obtained by subtracting—

(i)   the transfer value of the person's accrued benefits under the scheme that is required to be contained in the report by paragraph (c), from

(ii)  the transfer value of those benefits that is required to be contained in the report by paragraph (b),

and then subtracting from the result of that calculation the amount of any contributions made to the scheme by the person in the relevant financial year.

(3) Where—

(a)  the person has rights under a pension scheme that is a money purchase scheme in relation to the person, and

(b)  any of those rights are rights to which he has become entitled in respect of qualifying services of his,

details of any contribution to the scheme in respect of the person that is paid or payable by the company for the relevant financial year or paid by the company in that year for another financial year.

AMENDMENTS AND NOTES

[a]  Amended by the Companies Act 2006 (Accounts, Reports and Audit) Regulations 2009, SI 2009/1581, reg 12(3), in relation to financial years beginning on or after 6 April 2008 which have not ended before 27 June 2009.

### Excess retirement benefits of directors and past directors

**14.** (1)  Subject to sub-paragraph (3), the directors' remuneration report must show in respect of each person who has served as a director of the company—

(a)  at any time during the relevant financial year, or

(b)  at any time before the beginning of that year, the amount of so much of retirement benefits paid to or receivable by the person under pension schemes as is in excess of the retirement benefits to which he was entitled on the date on which the benefits first became payable or 31st March 1997, whichever is the later.

(2)  In subsection (1) 'retirement benefits' means retirement benefits to which the person became entitled in respect of qualifying services of his.

(3)  Amounts paid or receivable under a pension scheme need not be included in an amount required to be shown under sub-paragraph (1) if—

(a)  the funding of the scheme was such that the amounts were or, as the case may be, could have been paid without recourse to additional contributions; and

(b)  amounts were paid to or receivable by all pensioner members of the scheme on the same basis;

and in this sub-paragraph 'pensioner member', in relation to a pension scheme, means any person who is entitled to the present payment of retirement benefits under the scheme.

(4)  In this paragraph—

(a)  references to retirement benefits include benefits otherwise than in cash; and

(b)  in relation to so much of retirement benefits as consists of a benefit otherwise than in cash, references to their amount are to the estimated money value of the benefit,

and the nature of any such benefit must also be shown in the report.

### Compensation for past directors

**15.** The directors' remuneration report must contain details of any significant award made in the relevant financial year to any person who was not a director of the company at the time the award was made but had previously been a director of the company, including (in particular) compensation in respect of loss of office and pensions but excluding any sums which have already been shown in the report under paragraph 7(1)(d).

### Sums paid to third parties in respect of a director's services

**16.** (1)  The directors' remuneration report must show, in respect of each person who served as a director of the company at any time during the relevant financial year, the aggregate amount of any consideration paid to or receivable by third parties for making available the services of the person—

(a)  as a director of the company, or

(b)  while director of the company—

(i)   as director of any of its subsidiary undertakings, or

(ii)  as director of any other undertaking of which he was (while director of the company) a director by virtue of the company's nomination (direct or indirect), or

(iii) otherwise in connection with the management of the affairs of the company or any such other undertaking.

(2)  The reference to consideration includes benefits otherwise than in cash; and in relation to such consideration the reference to its amount is to the estimated money value of the benefit. The nature of any such consideration must be shown in the report.

(3) The reference to third parties is to persons other than—

    (a) the person himself or a person connected with him or a body corporate controlled by him, and

    (b) the company or any such other undertaking as is mentioned in sub-paragraph (1)(b)(ii).

## PART 4
## INTERPRETATION AND SUPPLEMENTARY

**17.** (1) In this Schedule—

'amount', in relation to a gain made on the exercise of a share option, means the difference between—

    (a) the market price of the shares on the day on which the option was exercised; and

    (b) the price actually paid for the shares;

'company contributions', in relation to a pension scheme and a person, means any payments (including insurance premiums) made, or treated as made, to the scheme in respect of the person by anyone other than the person;

'defined benefit scheme', in relation to a person, means a pension scheme which is not a money purchase scheme in relation to the person;

'emoluments' of a person—

    (a) includes salary, fees and bonuses, sums paid by way of expenses allowance (so far as they are chargeable to United Kingdom income tax or would be if the person were an individual), but

    (b) does not include any of the following, namely—

        (i) the value of any share options granted to him or the amount of any gains made on the exercise of any such options;

        (ii) any company contributions paid, or treated as paid, in respect of him under any pension scheme or any benefits to which he is entitled under any such scheme; or

        (iii) any money or other assets paid to or received or receivable by him under any long term incentive scheme;

'long term incentive scheme' has the meaning given by paragraph 11(5);

'money purchase benefits', in relation to a person, means retirement benefits the rate or amount of which is calculated by reference to payments made, or treated as made, by the person or by any other person in respect of that person and which are not average salary benefits;

'money purchase scheme', in relation to a person, means a pension scheme under which all of the benefits that may become payable to or in respect of the person are money purchase benefits in relation to the person;

'pension scheme' means a retirement benefits scheme within the meaning given by section 611 of the Income and Corporation Taxes Act 1988;

'qualifying services', in relation to any person, means his services as a director of the company, and his services at any time while he is a director of the company—

    (a) as a director of an undertaking that is a subsidiary undertaking of the company at that time;

    (b) as a director of any other undertaking of which he is a director by virtue of the company's nomination (direct or indirect); or

    (c) otherwise in connection with the management of the affairs of the company or any such subsidiary undertaking or any such other undertaking;

'retirement benefits' means relevant benefits within the meaning given by section 612(1) of the Income and Corporation Taxes Act 1988;

'shares' means shares (whether allotted or not) in the company, or any undertaking which is a group undertaking in relation to the company, and includes a share warrant as defined by section 779(1) of the 2006 Act;

'share option' means a right to acquire shares;

'value', in relation to shares received or receivable on any day by a person who is or has been a director of the company, means the market price of the shares on that day.

(2) In this Schedule 'compensation in respect of loss of office' includes compensation received or receivable by a person for—

    (a) loss of office as director of the company, or

    (b) loss, while director of the company or on or in connection with his ceasing to be a director of it, of—

        (i) any other office in connection with the management of the company's affairs, or

        (ii) any office as director or otherwise in connection with the management of the affairs of any undertaking that, immediately before the loss, is a subsidiary undertaking of the company or an undertaking of which he is a director by virtue of the company's nomination (direct or indirect);

    (c) compensation in consideration for, or in connection with, a person's retirement from office; and

(d) where such a retirement is occasioned by a breach of the person's contract with the company or with an undertaking that, immediately before the breach, is a subsidiary undertaking of the company or an undertaking of which he is a director by virtue of the company's nomination (direct or indirect)—
(i) payments made by way of damages for the breach; or
(ii) payments made by way of settlement or compromise of any claim in respect of the breach.

(3) References in this Schedule to compensation include benefits otherwise than in cash; and in relation to such compensation references in this Schedule to its amounts are to the estimated money value of the benefit.

(4) References in this Schedule to a person being 'connected' with a director, and to a director 'controlling' a body corporate, are to be construed in accordance with sections 252 to 255 of the 2006 Act.

**18.** (1) For the purposes of this Schedule emoluments paid or receivable or share options granted in respect of a person's accepting office as a director are to be treated as emoluments paid or receivable or share options granted in respect of his services as a director.

(2) Where a pension scheme provides for any benefits that may become payable to or in respect of a person to be whichever are the greater of—
(a) such benefits determined by or under the scheme as are money purchase benefits in relation to the person; and
(b) such retirement benefits determined by or under the scheme to be payable to or in respect of the person as are not money purchase benefits in relation to the person, the company may assume for the purposes of this Schedule that those benefits will be money purchase benefits in relation to the person, or not, according to whichever appears more likely at the end of the relevant financial year.

(3) In determining for the purposes of this Schedule whether a pension scheme is a money purchase scheme in relation to a person or a defined benefit scheme in relation to a person, any death in service benefits provided for by the scheme are to be disregarded.

**19.** (1) The following applies with respect to the amounts to be shown under this Schedule.

(2) The amount in each case includes all relevant sums paid by or receivable from—
(a) the company; and
(b) the company's subsidiary undertakings; and
(c) any other person, except sums to be accounted for to the company or any of its subsidiary undertakings or any other undertaking of which any person has been a director while director of the company, by virtue of section 219 of the 2006 Act (payment in connection with share transfer: requirement of members' approval), to past or present members of the company or any of its subsidiaries or any class of those members.

(3) Reference to amounts paid to or receivable by a person include amounts paid to or receivable by a person connected with him or a body corporate controlled by him (but not so as to require an amount to be counted twice).

**20.** (1) The amounts to be shown for any financial year under Part 3 of this Schedule are the sums receivable in respect of that year (whenever paid) or, in the case of sums not receivable in respect of a period, the sums paid during that year.

(2) But where—
(a) any sums are not shown in the directors' remuneration report for the relevant financial year on the ground that the person receiving them is liable to account for them as mentioned in paragraph 19(2), but the liability is thereafter wholly or partly released or is not enforced within a period of 2 years; or
(b) any sums paid by way of expenses allowance are charged to United Kingdom income tax after the end of the relevant financial year or, in the case of any such sums paid otherwise than to an individual, it does not become clear until the end of the relevant financial year that those sums would be charged to such tax were the person an individual,
those sums must, to the extent to which the liability is released or not enforced or they are charged as mentioned above (as the case may be), be shown in the first directors' remuneration report in which it is practicable to show them and must be distinguished from the amounts to be shown apart from this provision.

**21.** Where it is necessary to do so for the purpose of making any distinction required by the preceding paragraphs in an amount to be shown in compliance with this Part of this Schedule, the directors may apportion any payments between the matters in respect of which these have been paid or are receivable in such manner as they think appropriate.

**22.** The Schedule requires information to be given only so far as it is contained in the company's books and papers, available to members of the public or the company has the right to obtain it.

SCHEDULE 9              Regulation 12

INTERPRETATION OF TERM 'PROVISIONS'

PART 1

MEANING FOR PURPOSES OF THESE REGULATIONS

### Definition of 'Provisions'

**1.** (1) In these Regulations, references to provisions for depreciation or diminution in value of assets are to any amount written off by way of providing for depreciation or diminution in value of assets.

(2) Any reference in the profit and loss account formats or the notes to them set out in Schedule 1, 2 or 3 to these Regulations to the depreciation of, or amounts written off, assets of any description is to any provision for depreciation or diminution in value of assets of that description.

**2.** References in these Regulations to provisions for liabilities or, in the case of insurance companies, to provisions for other risks are to any amount retained as reasonably necessary for the purpose of providing for any liability the nature of which is clearly defined and which is either likely to be incurred, or certain to be incurred but uncertain as to amount or as to the date on which it will arise.

PART 2

MEANING FOR PURPOSES OF PARTS 18 AND 23 OF THE 2006 ACT

### Financial assistance for purchase of own shares

**3.** The specified provisions for the purposes of section 677(3)(a) of the 2006 Act (Companies Act accounts: relevant provisions for purposes of financial assistance) are provisions within paragraph 2 of this Schedule.

### Redemption or purchase by private company out of capital

**4.** The specified provisions for the purposes of section 712(2)(b)(i) of the 2006 Act (Companies Act accounts: relevant provisions to determine available profits for redemption or purchase out of capital) are provisions of any of the kinds mentioned in paragraphs 1 and 2 of this Schedule.

### Net asset restriction on public companies distributions

**5.** The specified provisions for the purposes of section 831(3)(a) of the 2006 Act (Companies Act accounts: net asset restriction on public company distributions) are?—

(a) provisions within paragraph 2 of this Schedule, and

(b) in the case of an insurance company, any amount included under liabilities items Ba (fund for future appropriations), C (technical provisions) and D (technical provisions for linked liabilities) in a balance sheet drawn up in accordance with Schedule 3 to these Regulations.

### Distributions by investment companies

**6.** The specified provisions for the purposes of section 832(4)(a) of the 2006 Act (Companies Act accounts: investment companies distributions) are provisions within paragraph 2 of this Schedule.

### Justification of distribution by references to accounts

**7.** The specified provisions for the purposes of section 836(1)(b)(i) of the 2006 Act (Companies Act accounts: relevant provisions for distribution purposes)—

(a) are provisions of any of the kinds mentioned in paragraphs 1 and 2 of this Schedule, and

(b) in the case of an insurance company, any amount included under liabilities items Ba (fund for future appropriations), C (technical provisions) and D (technical provisions for linked liabilities) in a balance sheet drawn up in accordance with Schedule 3 to these Regulations.

### [Realised losses

**8.** The specified provisions for the purposes of section 841(2)(a) of the 2006 Act (Companies Act accounts: treatment of provisions as realised losses) are provisions of any of the kinds mentioned in paragraphs 1 and 2 of this Schedule.][a]

AMENDMENTS

[a] Inserted by the Companies Act 2006 (Accounts, Reports and Audit) Regulations 2009, SI 2009/1581, reg 12(4), in relation to financial years beginning on or after 6 April 2008 which have not ended before 27 June 2009.

SCHEDULE 10                                     Regulation 13
GENERAL INTERPRETATION

**Capitalisation**

**1.** 'Capitalisation', in relation to work or costs, means treating that work or those costs as a fixed asset.

**Financial instruments**

**2.** Save in Schedule 2 to these Regulations, references to 'derivatives' include commodity-based contracts that give either contracting party the right to settle in cash or in some other financial instrument, except where such contracts—

   (a) were entered into for the purpose of, and continue to meet, the company's expected purchase, sale or usage requirements,

   (b) were designated for such purpose at their inception, and

   (c) are expected to be settled by delivery of the commodity (for banking companies, see the definition in paragraph 94 of Schedule 2 to these Regulations).

**3.** (1) Save in Schedule 2 to these Regulations, the expressions listed in sub-paragraph (2) have the same meaning as they have in Council Directive 78/660/EEC on the annual accounts of certain types of companies[106] and 91/674/EEC on the annual accounts and consolidated accounts of insurance undertakings[107] (for banking companies, see the definition in paragraph 96 of Schedule 2 to these Regulations).

   (2) Those expressions are 'available for sale financial asset', 'business combination', 'commodity-based contracts', 'derivative', 'equity instrument', 'exchange difference', 'fair value hedge accounting system', 'financial fixed asset', 'financial instrument', 'foreign entity', 'hedge accounting', 'hedge accounting system', 'hedged items', 'hedging instrument', 'held for trading purposes', 'held to maturity', 'monetary item', 'receivables', 'reliable market' and 'trading portfolio'.

**Fixed and current assets**

**4.** 'Fixed assets' means assets of a company which are intended for use on a continuing basis in the company's activities, and 'current assets' means assets not intended for such use.

**Fungible assets**

**5.** 'Fungible assets' means assets of any description which are substantially indistinguishable one from another.

**Historical cost accounting rules**

**6.** References to the historical cost accounting rules are to be read in accordance with paragraph 30 of Schedule 1, paragraph 38 of Schedule 2 and paragraph 36(1) of Schedule 3 to these Regulations.

**Leases**

**7.** (1) 'Long lease' means a lease in the case of which the portion of the term for which it was granted remaining unexpired at the end of the financial year is not less than 50 years.

   (2) 'Short lease' means a lease which is not a long lease.

   (3) 'Lease' includes an agreement for a lease.

**Listed investments**

**8.** (1) 'Listed investment' means an investment as respects which there has been granted a listing on—

   (a) a recognised investment exchange other than an overseas investment exchange, or

   (b) a stock exchange of repute outside the United Kingdom.

   (2) 'Recognised investment exchange' and 'overseas investment exchange' have the meaning given in Part 18 of the Financial Services and Markets Act 2000[108].

---

[106] OJ L222 of 14.8.1978, page 11, as amended in particular by Directives 2001/65/EEC, 2003/51/EEC and 2006/46/EEC of the European Parliament and of the Council (OJ L238 of 27.12.2001, page 28, OJ L178 of 17.7.2003, page 16 and OJ L224 of 16.8.2006, page 1).

[107] O.J L374 of 31.12.1991, page 7, as amended in particular by Directives 2001/65/EEC, 2003/51/EEC and 2006/46/EEC of the European Parliament and of the Council (OJ L238 of 27.12.2001, page 28, OJ L178 of 17.7.2003, page 16 and OJ L224 of 16.8.2006, page 1).

[108] 2000 c.8.

### Loans

**9.** A loan or advance (including a liability comprising a loan or advance) is treated as falling due for repayment, and an instalment of a loan or advance is treated as falling due for payment, on the earliest date on which the lender could require repayment or (as the case may be) payment, if he exercised all options and rights available to him.

### Materiality

**10.** Amounts which in the particular context of any provision of Schedules 1, 2 or 3 to these Regulations are not material may be disregarded for the purposes of that provision.

### Participating interests

**11.** (1) A 'participating interest' means an interest held by an undertaking in the shares of another undertaking which it holds on a long-term basis for the purpose of securing a contribution to its activities by the exercise of control or influence arising from or related to that interest.

(2) A holding of 20% or more of the shares of the undertaking is to be presumed to be a participating interest unless the contrary is shown.

(3) The reference in sub-paragraph (1) to an interest in shares includes—

(a) an interest which is convertible into an interest in shares, and

(b) an option to acquire shares or any such interest, and an interest or option falls within paragraph (a) or (b) notwithstanding that the shares to which it relates are, until the conversion or the exercise of the option, unissued.

(4) For the purposes of this regulation an interest held on behalf of an undertaking is to be treated as held by it.

(5) In the balance sheet and profit and loss formats set out in Schedules 1, 2 and 3 to these Regulations, 'participating interest' does not include an interest in a group undertaking.

(6) For the purpose of this regulation as it applies in relation to the expression 'participating interest'—

(a) in those formats as they apply in relation to group accounts, and

(b) in paragraph 19 of Schedule 6 (group accounts: undertakings to be accounted for as associated undertakings),

the references in sub-paragraphs (1) to (4) to the interest held by, and the purposes and activities of, the undertaking concerned are to be construed as references to the interest held by, and the purposes and activities of, the group (within the meaning of paragraph 1 of that Schedule).

### Purchase price

**12.** 'Purchase price', in relation to an asset of a company or any raw materials or consumables used in the production of such an asset, includes any consideration (whether in cash or otherwise) given by the company in respect of that asset or those materials or consumables, as the case may be.

### Realised profits and realised losses

**13.** 'Realised profits' and 'realised losses' have the same meaning as in section 853(4) and (5) of the 2006 Act.

### Staff costs

**14.** (1) 'Social security costs' means any contributions by the company to any state social security or pension scheme, fund or arrangement.

(2) 'Pension costs' includes—

(a) any costs incurred by the company in respect of any pension scheme established for the purpose of providing pensions for persons currently or formerly employed by the company,

(b) any sums set aside for the future payment of pensions directly by the company to current or former employees, and

(c) any pensions paid directly to such persons without having first been set aside.

(3) Any amount stated in respect of the item 'social security costs' or in respect of the item 'wages and salaries' in the company's profit and loss account must be determined by reference to payments made or costs incurred in respect of all persons employed by the company during the financial year under contracts of service.

### Scots land tenure

**15.** In the application of these Regulations to Scotland, 'land of freehold tenure' means land in respect of which the company is the owner; 'land of leasehold tenure' means land of which the company is the tenant under a lease.tpdel

THE COMPANIES (DISCLOSURE OF AUDITOR REMUNERATION AND
LIABILITY LIMITATION AGREEMENTS) REGULATIONS 2008
(SI 2008/489)

COMMENCEMENT DATE 6 April 2008

PART 1

INTRODUCTION

**SI.14    Citation and commencement**
   **1.** These Regulations may be cited as the Companies (Disclosure of Auditor Remuneration and
   Liability Limitation Agreements) Regulations 2008 and come into force on 6th April 2008.

**Application and revocation**
   **2.** (1) Regulations 3 to 7 do not apply to the accounts of a company for any financial year beginning
       before 6th April 2008.
   (2) The Companies (Disclosure of Auditor Remuneration) Regulations 2005[109] continue to apply
       to the accounts of a company for any financial year beginning before 6th April 2008.
   (3) Subject to paragraph (2), the Companies (Disclosure of Auditor Remuneration) Regulations
       2005 are revoked.

**Interpretation**
   **3.** (1) In these Regulations—
       'the Act' means the Companies Act 2006;
       'associated pension scheme' means, in relation to a company, a scheme for the provision of
       benefits for or in respect of directors or employees (or former directors or employees) of the
       company or any subsidiary of the company where—
       (a) the benefits consist of or include any pension, lump sum, gratuity or other like benefit
           given or to be given on retirement or on death or in anticipation of retirement or, in
           connection with past service, after retirement or death; and
       (b) either—
           (i)  a majority of the trustees are appointed by, or by a person acting on behalf of, the
                company or a subsidiary of the company; or
           (ii) the company, or a subsidiary of the company, exercises a dominant influence over the
                appointment of the auditor (if any) of the scheme;
           'parent' means a parent undertaking (as defined in section 1162 of the Act) which is
           a body corporate, and 'parent company' is a parent which is a company;
           'principal terms' has the meaning in section 536(4) of the Act;
           'remuneration' includes payments in respect of expenses and benefits in kind;
           'subsidiary' means a subsidiary undertaking (as defined in section 1162 of the Act)
           which is a body corporate, and 'subsidiary company' is a subsidiary which is a company.
   (2) For the purposes of these Regulations—
       (a) a company is small in relation to a financial year if the small companies regime as defined
           in section 381 of the Act applies to it for that year;
       (b) a company is medium-sized in relation to a financial year if—
           (i)  it qualifies as medium-sized in relation to that year under section 465 of the Act; and
           (ii) it is not excluded from being medium-sized under section 467(1) of the Act;
       (c) references to an associate of a company are references to—
           (i)  any subsidiary of that company, other than a subsidiary in respect of which severe
                long-term restrictions substantially hinder the exercise of the rights of the company
                over the assets or management of that subsidiary; and
           (ii) any scheme which is an associated pension scheme in relation to that company; and
       (d) a person is an associate, or a distant associate, of a company's auditor if that person is
           specified as such by Schedule 1 to these Regulations.

---

[109]  SI 2005/2417.

# PART 2

## DISCLOSURE OF REMUNERATION

**Disclosure of remuneration: small and medium-sized companies**

**4.** (1) A note to the annual accounts of a small or medium-sized company must disclose the amount of any remuneration receivable by the company's auditor for the auditing of those accounts.

(2) Where the remuneration includes benefits in kind, the nature and estimated money-value of those benefits must also be disclosed in a note.

(3) Where more than one person has been appointed as a company's auditor in respect of the period to which the accounts relate, separate disclosure is required in respect of the remuneration of each such person.

(4) For the purposes of section 1224 of the Act, the functions of the Secretary of State under Part 42 of the Act include (without prejudice to the generality of that section) consideration of the total remuneration receivable by the auditor of a medium-sized company for the supply by the auditor to the company of each of the following types of service where that remuneration is not disclosed in a note to the company's annual accounts—

(a) assurance services other than the auditing of the company's accounts;

(b) tax advisory services;

(c) other services.

**Disclosure of remuneration: other companies**

**5.** (1) A note to the annual accounts of a company which is not a small or medium-sized company must disclose the amount of—

(a) any remuneration receivable by the company's auditor for the auditing of those accounts; and

(b) subject to paragraph (6) and regulation 6(2), any remuneration receivable in respect of the period to which the accounts relate by—

(i) the company's auditor; or

(ii) any person who was, at any time during the period to which the accounts relate, an associate of the company's auditor,

for the supply of other services to the company or any associate of the company.

(2) Where the remuneration includes benefits in kind, the nature and estimated money-value of those benefits must also be disclosed in a note.

(3) Separate disclosure is required in respect of the auditing of the accounts in question and of each type of service specified in Schedule 2, but not in respect of each service falling within a type of service.

(4) Separate disclosure is required in respect of services supplied to the company and its subsidiaries on the one hand and to associated pension schemes on the other.

(5) Where more than one person has been appointed as a company's auditor in respect of the period to which the accounts relate, separate disclosure is required in respect of the remuneration of each such person and his associates.

(6) Disclosure is not required of remuneration receivable for the supply of services falling within paragraph 10 of Schedule 2 supplied by a distant associate of the company's auditor where the total remuneration receivable for all of those services supplied by that associate does not exceed either—

(a) £10,000, or

(b) 1% of the total audit remuneration received by the company's auditor in the most recent financial year of the auditor which ended no later than the end of the financial year of the company to which the accounts relate.

(7) In paragraph (6)(b)—

(a) 'financial year of the auditor' means—

(i) the period of not more than 18 months in respect of which the auditor's profit and loss account is required to be made up (whether by law or by or in accordance with the auditor's constitution (if any)), or

(ii) failing any such requirement, the period of 12 months beginning with 1st April;

(b) 'total audit remuneration received' means the total remuneration received for the auditing pursuant to legislation (including that of countries and territories outside the United Kingdom) of any accounts of any person.

**Group Accounts**

**6.** (1) Group accounts must comply with regulation 5(1)(b) as if the undertakings included in the consolidation were a single company except where the group—

(a) qualifies as small or medium-sized under section 383 or 466 of the Act; and

(b) is not an ineligible group under section 384(2) or 467(2) of the Act.

(2) A note to the individual accounts of—

    (a) a parent company which is required to prepare and does prepare group accounts in accordance with the Act; and

    (b) a subsidiary company where its parent is required to prepare and does prepare group accounts in accordance with the Act and the company is included in the consolidation; does not have to disclose the information required by regulation 5(1)(b) if the conditions in paragraph (3) are satisfied.

(3) Those conditions are that—

    (a) the group accounts are required to comply with paragraph (1); and

    (b) the individual accounts state that the group accounts are so required.

### Duty of auditor to supply information

**7.** The auditor of a company must supply the directors of the company with such information as is necessary to enable the disclosure required by regulation 5(1)(b) or 6(1) to be made.

# PART 3

## LIABILITY LIMITATION AGREEMENTS

### Disclosure of liability limitation agreements

**8.** (1) A company which has entered into a liability limitation agreement must disclose—

    (a) its principal terms; and

    (b) the date of the resolution approving the agreement or the agreement's principal terms or, in the case of a private company, the date of the resolution waiving the need for such approval,

    in a note to the company's annual accounts.

(2) The annual accounts in which the disclosure required by paragraph (1) must be made shall be those for the financial year to which the agreement relates unless the agreement was entered into too late for it to be reasonably practicable for the disclosure to be made in those accounts.

(3) If the agreement was entered into too late for it to be reasonably practicable for the disclosure required by paragraph (1) to be made in the accounts for the financial year to which the agreement relates, the disclosure shall be made in a note to the company's next following annual accounts.

## SCHEDULE 1                                              Regulation 3(2)(d)

## ASSOCIATES OF A COMPANY'S AUDITOR

**1.** (1) Each of the following shall be regarded as an associate of a company's auditor—

    (a) any person controlled by the company's auditor or by any associate of the company's auditor (whether alone or through two or more persons acting together to secure or exercise control), but only if that control does not arise solely by virtue of the company's auditor or any associate of the company's auditor acting—

        (i) as an insolvency practitioner in relation to any person;

        (ii) in the capacity of a receiver, or a receiver or manager, of the property of a company or other body corporate; or

        (iii) as a judicial factor on the estate of any person;

    (b) any person who, or group of persons acting together which, has control of the company's auditor;

    (c) any person using a trading name which is the same as or similar to a trading name used by the company's auditor, but only if the company's auditor uses that trading name with the intention of creating the impression of a connection between the auditor and that other person;

    (d) any person who is a party to an arrangement with the company's auditor, with or without any other person, under which costs, profits, quality control, business strategy or significant professional resources are shared.

**2.** Where a company's auditor is a partnership, each of the following shall also be regarded as an associate of the auditor—

    (a) any other partnership which has a partner in common with the company's auditor;

    (b) any partner in the company's auditor;

    (c) any body corporate which is in the same group as a body corporate which is a partner in the company's auditor;

    (d) any body corporate which is in the same group as a body corporate which is a partner in a partnership which has a partner in common with the company's auditor;

(e) any body corporate of which a partner in the company's auditor is a director.

**3.** Where a company's auditor is a body corporate (other than one which is also a partnership as defined in paragraph 5(c)), each of the following shall also be regarded as an associate of the auditor—

(a) any other body corporate which has a director in common with the company's auditor;

(b) any director of the company's auditor;

(c) any body corporate which is in the same group as a body corporate which is a director of the company's auditor;

(d) any body corporate which is in the same group as a body corporate which has a director in common with the company's auditor;

(e) any partnership in which a director of the company's auditor is a partner;

(f) any body corporate which is in the same group as the company's auditor;

(g) any partnership in which any body corporate which is in the same group as the company's auditor is a partner.

**4.** A distant associate of a company's auditor is a person who is an associate of that auditor by reason only that that person is an associate within one or more of—

(a) paragraph 1(a) where the person in question is controlled by a distant associate of the company's auditor but not by the auditor or by an associate who is not a distant associate;

(b) paragraph 2(a), (d) or (e);

(c) paragraph 3(a), (d) or (e).

**5.** In this Schedule—

(a) 'acting as an insolvency practitioner' shall be construed in accordance with section 388 of the Insolvency Act 1986[110] or Article 3 of the Insolvency (Northern Ireland) Order 1989[111];

(b) 'partner' includes a member of a limited liability partnership;

(c) 'partnership' includes a limited liability partnership and a partnership constituted under the law of a country or a territory outside the United Kingdom;

(d) a reference to 'a receiver, or a receiver or manager, of the property of a company or other body corporate' includes a receiver, or (as the case may be) a receiver or manager, of part only of that property;

(e) a person able, directly or indirectly to control or materially to influence the operating and financial policy of another person shall be treated as having control of that other person; and

(f) a body corporate is in the same group as another body corporate if it is a parent or subsidiary of that body corporate, or a subsidiary of a parent of that body corporate.

SCHEDULE 2                Regulation 5(3)

**Type of service in respect of which disclosure is to be made**

**1.** The auditing of accounts of associates of the company pursuant to legislation (including that of countries and territories outside the United Kingdom).

**2.** Other services supplied pursuant to such legislation.

**3.** Other services relating to taxation.

**4.** Services relating to information technology.

**5.** Internal audit services.

**6.** Valuation and actuarial services.

**7.** Services relating to litigation.

**8.** Services relating to recruitment and remuneration.

**9.** Services relating to corporate finance transactions entered into or proposed to be entered into on behalf of the company or any of its associates.

**10.** All other services.

# The Companies (Trading Disclosures) Regulations 2008

## (SI 2008/495)

COMMENCEMENT DATE 1 October 2008

---

[110] 1986 c.45; section 388 has been amended by section 4(2)(a) to (c) of the Insolvency Act 2000 (c.39), by section 11(1) of the Bankruptcy (Scotland) Act 1993 (c.6) and by SI 1994/2421, 2002/1240 and 2002/2708.

[111] SI 1989/2405 (NI 19); Article 3 has been amended by Article 6(1)(a) to (c) of the Insolvency (Northern Ireland) Order 2002 (SI 2002/3152 (NI 6); and by SR 1995/225, 2002/334 and 2003/550.

### Citation, commencement and interpretation

**1.** (1) These Regulations may be cited as the Companies (Trading Disclosures) Regulations 2008 and come into force on 1st October 2008.

(2) In these Regulations—

(a) 'the Act' means the Companies Act 2006;

(b) 'company record' means—

(i) any register, index, accounting records, agreement, memorandum, minutes or other document required by the Companies Acts to be kept by a company; and

(ii) any register kept by a company of its debenture holders[112];

(c) 'inspection place' means any location, other than a company's registered office, at which a company keeps available for inspection any company record which it is required under the Companies Acts to keep available for inspection;

(d) a reference to any type of document is a reference to a document of that type in hard copy, electronic or any other form; and

(e) in relation to a company, a reference to 'its websites' includes a reference to any part of a website relating to that company which that company has caused or authorised to appear.

### Legibility of displays and disclosures

**2.** Any display or disclosure of information required by these Regulations must be in characters that can be read with the naked eye.

### Requirement to display registered name at registered office and inspection place

**3.** (1) A company shall display its registered name at—

(a) its registered office; and

(b) any inspection place.

(2) But paragraph (1) does not apply to any company which has at all times since its incorporation been dormant.

[(3) Paragraph (1) shall also not apply to the registered office or an inspection place of a company where—

(a) in respect of that company, a liquidator, administrator or administrative receiver has been appointed; and

(b) the registered office or inspection place is also a place of business of that liquidator, administrator or administrative receiver.][a]

AMENDMENTS AND NOTES

[a] Inserted by the Companies (Trading Disclosures) (Amendment) Regulations 2009 (S.I. 2009/218, reg 2).

### Requirement to display registered name at other business locations

**4.** (1) This regulation applies to a location other than a company's registered office or any inspection place.

(2) A company shall display its registered name at any such location at which it carries on business.

(3) But paragraph (2) shall not apply to a location which is primarily used for living accommodation.

[(4) Paragraph (2) shall also not apply to any location at which business is carried on by a company where—

(a) in respect of that company, a liquidator, administrator or administrative receiver has been appointed; and

(b) the location is also a place of business of that liquidator, administrator or administrative receiver.

(5) Paragraph (2) shall also not apply to any location at which business is carried on by a company of which every director who is an individual is a relevant director.

(6) In this regulation—

(a) 'administrative receiver' has the meaning given—

(i) in England and Wales or Scotland, by section 251 of the Insolvency Act 1986, and

(ii) in Northern Ireland, by Article 5 of the Insolvency (Northern Ireland) Order 1989;

(b) 'credit reference agency' has the meaning given in section 243(7) of the Act;

(c) 'protected information' has the meaning given in section 240 of the Act; and

---

[112] This is the definition of 'company records' used in Part 37 of the Act. The definition of 'the Companies Acts' is contained in section 2 of the Act but is subject to a transitional adaptation contained in paragraph 1 of Schedule 1 to the Companies Act 2006 (Commencement No. 2, Consequential Amendments, Transitional Provisions and Savings) Order 2007 (SI 2007/1093 (C. 49)).

(d) 'relevant director' means an individual in respect of whom the registrar is required by regulations made pursuant to section 243(4) of the Act to refrain from disclosing protected information to a credit reference agency.][a]

AMENDMENTS AND NOTES

[a] Inserted by the Companies (Trading Disclosures) (Amendment) Regulations 2009 (S.I. 2009/218, reg 3).

### Manner of display of registered name

**5.** (1) This regulation applies where a company is required to display its registered name at any office, place or location.

(2) The registered name shall be so positioned that it may be easily seen by any visitor to that office, place or location.

(3) The registered name shall be displayed continuously but where any such office, place or location is shared by six or more companies, each such company is only required to display its registered name for at least fifteen continuous seconds at least once in every three minutes.

### Registered name to appear in communications

**6.** (1) Every company shall disclose its registered name on—

(a) its business letters, notices and other official publications;

(b) its bills of exchange, promissory notes, endorsements and order forms;

(c) cheques purporting to be signed by or on behalf of the company;

(d) orders for money, goods or services purporting to be signed by or on behalf of the company;

(e) its bills of parcels, invoices and other demands for payment, receipts and letters of credit;

(f) its applications for licences to carry on a trade or activity; and

(g) all other forms of its business correspondence and documentation.

(2) Every company shall disclose its registered name on its websites.

### Further particulars to appear in business letters, order forms and websites

**7.** (1) Every company shall disclose the particulars set out in paragraph (2) on—

(a) its business letters;

(b) its order forms; and

(c) its websites.

(2) The particulars are—

(a) the part of the United Kingdom in which the company is registered;

(b) the company's registered number;

(c) the address of the company's registered office;

(d) in the case of a limited company exempt from the obligation to use the word 'limited' as part of its registered name under [section 60 of the Act][a], the fact that it is a limited company;

(e) in the case of a community interest company which is not a public company, the fact that it is a limited company; and

(f) in the case of an investment company within the meaning of section 833 of the Act, the fact that it is such a company.

(3) If, in the case of a company having a share capital, there is a disclosure as to the amount of share capital on—

(a) its business letters;

(b) its order forms; or

(c) its websites, that disclosure must be to paid up share capital.

AMENDMENTS AND NOTES

[a] Amended by the Companies (Trading Disclosures) (Amendment) Regulations 2009 (S.I. 2009/218, reg 4).

### Disclosure of names of directors

**8.** (1) Where a company's business letter includes the name of any director of that company, other than in the text or as a signatory, the letter must disclose the name of every director of that company.

(2) In paragraph (1), 'name' has the following meanings—

(a) in the case of a director who is an individual, 'name' has the meaning given in section 163(2) of the Act; and

(b) in the case of a director who is a body corporate or a firm that is a legal person under the law by which it is governed, 'name' means corporate name or firm name.

**Disclosures relating to registered office and inspection place**

**9.** (1) A company shall disclose—
   (a) the address of its registered office;
   (b) any inspection place; and
   (c) the type of company records which are kept at that office or place, to any person it deals with in the course of business who makes a written request to the company for that information.

(2) The company shall send a written response to that person within five working days of the receipt of that request.

**Offence**

**10.** (1) Where a company fails, without reasonable excuse, to comply with any requirement in regulations 2 to 9, an offence is committed by—
   (a) the company; and
   (b) every officer of the company who is in default.

(2) A person guilty of an offence under paragraph (1) is liable on summary conviction to—
   (a) a fine not exceeding level 3 on the standard scale; and
   (b) for continued contravention, a daily default fine not exceeding one-tenth of level 3 on the standard scale.

(3) For the purposes of this regulation a shadow director is to be treated as an officer of the company.

**Revocation**

**11.** (1) The Companies (Registrar, Languages and Trading Disclosures) Regulations 2006[113] are amended as follows.

(2) Revoke regulation 6 and Schedules 1 and 2.


# The Statutory Auditors (Delegation of Functions etc) Order 2008

## (SI 2008/496)

Commencement Date In accordance with article 1

**Citation and commencement**

**1.** (1) This Order may be cited as the Statutory Auditors (Delegation of Functions etc) Order 2008.
(2) This article and article 2 come into force on 1st March 2008.
(3) Articles 3, 6 and 8 come into force on 1st March 2008 for the purposes of functions in relation to appointments of auditors for financial years beginning on or after 6th April 2008.
(4) Subject to paragraph (6), articles 4, 5, 7 and 9 to 11 come into force on 6th April 2008 for the purposes of functions in relation to appointments of auditors for financial years beginning on or after 6th April 2008.
(5) Article 12 comes into force on 6th April 2008.
(6) Articles 4 and 9 come into force on 29th June 2008 for the purpose of transferring the functions under sections 1242, 1243 and 1244 of, and Schedule 12 to, the Act (registered third country auditors) in relation to appointments of registered third country auditors for financial years beginning on or after 29th June 2008.

**Interpretation**

**2.** In this Order—
   'the Act' means the Companies Act 2006;
   'the first designated body' means the body known as the Professional Oversight Board established under the articles of association of The Professional Oversight Board Limited;
   'the second designated body' means the body known as the Professional Oversight Board established under the articles of association of The Financial Reporting Council Limited.

**Transfer of certain functions conferring a power to make regulations**

**3.** (1) The functions of the Secretary of State conferring a power to make regulations under—
   (a) section 1239 of the Act (register of auditors) except for the function under subsection (1)(b) of that section,
   (b) section 1240 of the Act (information to be made available to public), and

---

[113] SI 2006/3429.

    (c)  paragraph 8(1)(a) of Schedule 11 to the Act (prescription of examination subjects),

are transferred to the first designated body, subject to the reservation specified in paragraph (2).

(2)  The transfer of the functions conferring a power to make regulations referred to in paragraph (1) is subject to the reservations that such regulations—

    (a)  must not come into force before 6th April 2008; and

    (b)  must not apply in relation to appointments of auditors for financial years beginning before 6th April 2008.

(3)  The transfer of the functions referred to in paragraph (1) ceases to have effect on 6th April 2008.

## Transfer of functions

**4.** (1)  All the functions of the Secretary of State under Part 42 of the Act (statutory auditors) are transferred to the second designated body, subject to—

    (a)  the exceptions specified in section 1252(4)(b) of the Act (functions not transferred by the Order);

    (b)  the exceptions specified in paragraph (2); and

    (c)  the reservations specified in paragraphs (3) and (4).

(2)  The functions of the Secretary of State under—

    (a)  section 1210 of the Act (meaning of 'statutory auditor'),

    (b)  section 1214 of the Act (power to specify connection between persons for purposes of independence requirement),

    (c)  section 1231 of the Act (laying report by independent supervisor of auditors general before each House of Parliament),

    (d)  section 1237(3) of the Act (provision for pending proceedings in order revoking appointment of independent supervisor),

    (e)  section 1239(1)(b) of the Act (making regulations for register of third country auditors),

    (f)  section 1241(2)(c) of the Act (exclusion of bodies corporate from definition of 'traded non-Community company'),

    (g)  section 1246 of the Act (removal of third country auditors from the register of auditors),

    (h)  section 1261(3) of the Act (power to modify Part 42 of the Act (statutory auditors) for purposes of application to certain bodies), and

    (i)  section 1263 of the Act (power to amend enactments in consequence of changes affecting accountancy bodies),

are not transferred by this Order.

(3)  The transfer of the functions of the Secretary of State under—

    (a)  section 1224 of the Act (power to call for information from recognised bodies etc),

    (b)  section 1239(8) of the Act (obligations relating to register enforceable by injunction etc),

    (c)  section 1244 of the Act (power to call for information from registered third country auditors),

    (d)  section 1253A of the Act[114] (requests to EEA competent authorities), and

    (e)  section 1254 of the Act (directions to comply with international obligations),

is subject to the reservation that the functions remain exercisable concurrently by the Secretary of State.

(4)  The transfer of the functions of the Secretary of State of—

    (a)  refusing to make a declaration under section 1221(1) of the Act (approval of overseas qualification) on the grounds referred to in section 1221(4) (lack of comparable treatment),

    (b)  withdrawing such a declaration under section 1221(7) of the Act on those grounds,

    (c)  refusing to comply with a request under section 1253B(1) of the Act (requests from EEA competent authorities) on the grounds referred to in section 1253B(3)(a) (prejudice to sovereignty, security or public order), and

    (d)  certifying under paragraph 16A(6) of Schedule 10[115] (transfer of papers to third countries) that the delivery of audit working papers to a third country competent authority would adversely affect the sovereignty, security or public order of the United Kingdom,

is subject to the reservation that the functions are exercisable only with the consent of the Secretary of State.

---

[114] Sections 1253A and 1253B were inserted by regulation 14 of the Statutory Auditors and Third Country Auditors Regulations 2007 (SI 2007/3494).

[115] Paragraph 16A was inserted by regulation 24 of the Statutory Auditors and Third Country Auditors Regulations 2007 (SI 2007/3494).

### Appropriate audit authority

**5.** The functions of the second designated body include the receipt of notices under sections 522 and 523 of the Act (notice of auditor ceasing to hold office) (and accordingly the second designated body is the appropriate authority under section 525(1)(a)(ii) of the Act (notices concerning auditors ceasing to hold office)).

### Consultation requirement

**6.** (1) Before the first designated body or the second designated body makes any regulations in exercise of the functions transferred to it by this Order, it must, unless paragraph (2) applies—

    (a) publish the proposed regulations in such manner as appears to the body to be best calculated to bring them to the attention of persons who may be affected by the proposed regulations;

    (b) publish at the same time a statement that representations in respect of the proposals may be made to the body within a specified period which must not be less than 12 weeks following the date of publication of the proposed regulations; and

    (c) have regard to any representations duly made in accordance with the statement before making the regulations.

    (2) Paragraph (1) does not apply in any case in which the body considers that the delay involved in complying with that paragraph would be prejudicial to the public interest.

    (3) Documents published by the first designated body or the second designated body before the date on which this article comes into force shall be treated as meeting the requirements of paragraph (1)(a) and (b) if documents published in the same way after that date would have met those requirements.

    (4) For the purposes of this article, on or after 6th April 2008 any document published by the first designated body before that date shall be treated as if it had been published by the second designated body.

### Annual work programme

**7.** The second designated body must publish a work programme at least once in every calendar year.

### Requirements for recording decisions

**8.** The first designated body and the second designated body must have satisfactory arrangements for—

    (a) recording decisions made in the exercise of the functions transferred by this Order; and

    (b) the safekeeping of those records.

### Matters notified to the designated body

**9.** (1) If the second designated body requires a notification or the provision of information for the purposes of section 1223(1) or 1243(1), it must notify the Secretary of State of the requirement without undue delay.

    (2) If the Secretary of State so requests, the second designated body must send to him a copy of any such notification or information received pursuant to the requirement.

### Time limits for prosecution of offences

**10.** Section 1256(1), (2), (4) and (6) of the Act (time limits for prosecution of offences) has effect as if the references to the Secretary of State were references to the Secretary of State or the second designated body.

### Appointment of body to issue guidance on senior statutory auditors

**11.** The body known as the Auditing Practices Board established under the articles of association of The Financial Reporting Council Limited[116] is appointed for the purposes of section 504(1)(b)(ii) of the Act (body to issue guidance on meaning of senior statutory auditor).

### Companies Act 1989 (Delegation) Order 2005

**12.** (1) For article 2(2) of the Companies Act 1989 (Delegation) Order 2005[117] substitute—

    '(2) 'designated body' means the body known as the Professional Oversight Board established under the articles of association of The Financial Reporting Council Limited; and'.

    (2) The Companies Act 1989 (Delegation) Order 2005 continues to apply in relation to functions relating to appointments of company auditors for any financial year beginning before 6th April 2008.

    (3) Subject to paragraph (2), the Companies Act 1989 (Delegation) Order 2005 is revoked.

---

[116] Registered number 02486368.
[117] SI 2005/2337.

# The Companies (Late Filing Penalties) and Limited Liability Partnerships (Filing Periods and Late Filing Penalties) Regulations 2008
## (SI 2008/497)

Commencement Date 6 April 2008

### Citation, commencement and interpretation

1. (1) These Regulations may be cited as the Companies (Late Filing Penalties) and Limited Liability Partnerships (Filing Periods and Late Filing Penalties) Regulations 2008.
   (2) These Regulations come into force on 6th April 2008.
   (3) References in these Regulations to late filing, or to a failure to comply with filing requirements, are to a failure to comply with the requirements of section 441 of the Companies Act 2006 (which apply in relation to financial years beginning on or after 6th April 2008) in relation to a company's accounts and reports before the end of the period for filing those accounts and reports.
   (4) For the purposes of regulations 2 and 4, whether a company is a public company or a private company depends upon its status at the end of the financial year in question.

### Late filing penalties under the Companies Act 2006 as from 6th April 2008

2. (1) This regulation applies where the requirements of section 441 of the Companies Act 2006 are complied with before 1st February 2009.
   (2) The amount of the civil penalty to which a company is liable under section 453 of the Companies Act 2006 in a case of late filing is that shown in the following table:

| Length of period | Public company | Private company |
|---|---|---|
| Not more than 3 months. | £500 | £100 |
| More than 3 months but not more than 6 months. | £1,000 | £250 |
| More than 6 months. | £2,000 | £500 |

   (3) The first column of the table ('length of period') refers to the length of the period between the end of the period for filing the accounts and reports in question and the day on which the requirements of section 441 are complied with.

### Late filing penalties under the Companies Act 1985 as from 6th April 2008

3. (1) This regulation applies where the requirements of section 242(1) of the Companies Act 1985 are complied with on or after 6th April 2008.
   (2) In section 242A of that Act[118], after subsection (2) insert—
   '(2A) For the purposes of subsection (2), whether a company is a public company or a private company depends upon its status at the end of the financial year in question.'.

### Late filing penalties under the Companies Act 2006 as from 1st February 2009

4. (1) This regulation applies where the requirements of section 441 of the Companies Act 2006 are complied with on or after 1st February 2009.
   (2) The amount of the civil penalty to which a company is liable under section 453 of the Companies Act 2006 in a case of late filing is that shown in the following table or, if there was a failure to comply with filing requirements in relation to the previous financial year of the company and that previous financial year had begun on or after 6th April 2008, double that shown in the table:

| Length of period | Public company | Private company |
|---|---|---|
| Not more than 1 month. | £750 | £150 |
| More than 1 month but not more than 3 months. | £1,500 | £375 |
| More than 3 months but not more than 6 months. | £3,000 | £750 |
| More than 6 months. | £7,500 | £1,500 |

---

[118] Section 242A was inserted by the Companies Act 1989, section 11.

(3) The first column of the table ('length of period') refers to the length of the period between the end of the period for filing the accounts and reports in question and the day on which the requirements of section 441 are complied with.

### Late filing penalties under the Companies Act 1985 as from 1st February 2009

**5.** (1) This regulation applies where the requirements of section 242(1) of the Companies Act 1985 (which continue to apply in relation to financial years beginning before 6th April 2008 and, in the case of limited liability partnerships, in relation to financial years beginning on or after that date as well)[119] are complied with on or after 1st February 2009.

(2) For the table in section 242A(2) of the Companies Act 1985[120] substitute the following table:

| Length of period | Public company | Private company |
|---|---|---|
| Not more than 1 month. | £750 | £150 |
| More than 1 month but not more than 3 months. | £1,500 | £375 |
| More than 3 months but not more than 6 months. | £3,000 | £750 |
| More than 6 months. | £7,500 | £1,500 |

### Limited liability partnerships: filing periods and late filing penalties

**6.** (1) Section 443 of the Companies Act 2006 (calculation of period allowed for filing accounts and reports) applies to limited liability partnerships with the modification in Part 1 of the Schedule to these Regulations.

(2) Schedule 1 to the Limited Liability Partnership Regulations 2001[a] is amended as provided in Part 2 of the Schedule to these Regulations.

(3) This regulation applies to accounts and auditors' reports for financial years beginning on or after 6th April 2008[, but paragraph (1) does not apply to accounts or reports for financial years beginning on or after 1st October 2008][b].

AMENDMENTS

[a] S.I. 2001/1090, to which there are amendments not relevant to these Regulations.

[b] Amended by the Limited Liability Partnerships (Accounts and Audit) (Application of Companies Act 2006) Regulations 2008, S.I. 2008/1911, reg 22(2).

## SCHEDULE
Regulation 6

### PART 1
## MODIFICATION OF SECTION 443 OF THE COMPANIES ACT 2006 IN ITS APPLICATION TO LIMITED LIABILITY PARTNERSHIPS

In subsection (1), for the words 'the period for filing a company's reports and accounts' substitute 'the period allowed for delivering the accounts and the auditor's report'.

### PART 2
## AMENDMENTS TO SCHEDULE 1 TO THE LIMITED LIABILITY PARTNERSHIPS REGULATIONS 2001

**1.** At the end of the entry relating to section 242A, add in the first column 'subsection (2A)' and in the second column 'Omit subsection (2A)'[121].

**2.** In the second column, opposite the entry relating to section 244(1), for '10 months' substitute '9 months'.

**3.** In the second column, for the words opposite the entry relating to section 244(2) substitute, 'In paragraph (a), for the words '10 months or 7 months, as the case may be' substitute '9 months'.'.

---

[119] Section 242(1) is applied, with modifications, to limited liability partnerships by SI 2001/1090, regulation 3 and Schedule 1.

[120] The table is applied, with modifications, to limited liability partnerships by SI 2001/1090, regulation 3 and Schedule 1.

[121] Subsection (2A) is inserted by regulation 3(2) of these Regulations.

# THE STATUTORY AUDITORS AND THIRD COUNTRY AUDITORS (AMENDMENT) REGULATIONS 2008
### (SI 2008/499)

COMMENCEMENT DATE 5 April 2008

**1.** (1) These Regulations may be cited as the Statutory Auditors and Third Country Auditors (Amendment) Regulations 2008 and come into force on 5th April 2008.

**SI.18**

**2.** (1) The Statutory Auditors and Third Country Auditors Regulations 2007[122] are amended as follows.

(2) For regulation 1(3) substitute—

'(3) Regulations 32, 33 and 40(2)(b) to (d) come into force on 29th June 2008.'.

(3) Omit regulation 7(2).

(4) For regulation 15(2) substitute—

'(2) Sections 1253D and 1253E of the Companies Act 2006 only apply to working papers for audits conducted by auditors appointed for financial years beginning on or after 6th April 2008.'.

(5) In regulation 34, for 'in relation to each third country auditor' in each of paragraphs (2) and (3) substitute 'in relation to each registered third country auditor'.

(6) In regulation 36[123], for 'application under regulation 33' substitute 'application under regulation 35'.

# THE INSURANCE ACCOUNTS DIRECTIVE (MISCELLANEOUS INSURANCE UNDERTAKINGS) REGULATIONS 2008
### (SI 2008/565)

COMMENCEMENT DATE 6 April 2008

## PART 1
## INTRODUCTION

### Citation, commencement and application

**SI.19**

**1.** (1) These Regulations may be cited as the Insurance Accounts Directive (Miscellaneous Insurance Undertakings) Regulations 2008.

(2) These Regulations come into force on 6th April 2008 and apply in relation to—

(a) insurance undertakings' financial years beginning on or after that date, and

(b) auditors appointed in respect of those financial years.

### Interpretation

**2.** (1) In these Regulations—

'the Companies Accounts Regulations' means the Large and Medium-sized Companies and Groups (Accounts and Reports) Regulations 2008[124];

'the appropriate audit authority' means—

(a) the Secretary of State, or

(b) if the Secretary of State has delegated functions under section 1252 of the Companies Act 2006[125] to a body whose functions include receiving the equivalent notice under section 522 or 523 of that Act, that body;

'the Authority' means the Financial Services Authority[126];

'director' includes, in the case of an undertaking which is not a company, any corresponding officer of that body;

'enactment' includes—

---

[122] SI 2007/3494.

[123] Regulation 36 consists of only one paragraph but is incorrectly designated '36(1)'.

[124] SI 2008/410.

[125] 2006 c.46.

[126] See the Financial Services and Markets Act 2000 (c.8), section 1.

(a) an enactment contained in subordinate legislation, other than these Regulations,

(b) an enactment contained in, or in an instrument made under, an Act of the Scottish Parliament,

(c) an enactment contained in, or in an instrument made under, Northern Ireland legislation, and

(d) an enactment contained in, or in an instrument made under, a Measure or Act of the National Assembly for Wales;

'friendly society' has the same meaning as in the Financial Services and Markets Act 2000[127];

'industrial and provident society' means a registered society within the meaning of either section 74 of the Industrial and Provident Societies Act 1965[128] or section 101 of the Industrial and Provident Societies Act (Northern Ireland) 1969[129];

'insurance undertaking' shall be construed in accordance with paragraphs (2) and (3).

(2) Subject to paragraph (3), a body incorporated in or formed under the law of any part of the United Kingdom is an insurance undertaking for the purposes of these Regulations if it—

(a) is incorporated by or registered under any public general Act of Parliament,

(b) requires permission under Part 4 of the Financial Services and Markets Act 2000 to effect or carry out contracts of insurance without contravening the prohibition imposed by section 19 of that Act, and

(c) is not required by any enactment to prepare accounts under Part 15 of the Companies Act 2006 (accounts and reports).

(3) Paragraph (2)(b) must be read with—

(a) section 22 of the Financial Services and Markets Act 2000,

(b) the Financial Services and Markets Act 2000 (Regulated Activities) Order 2001[130],

(c) Schedule 2 to that Act.

(4) A body is not an insurance undertaking for the purposes of these Regulations if it—

(a) is excluded from the scope of Council Directive 73/239/EEC[131] by Article 3 of that Directive,

(b) is referred to in Article 3(2) to (6) of Directive 2002/83/EC of the European Parliament and of the Council of 5th November 2002 concerning life assurance[132] or

(c) is a friendly society.

(5) Any reference in these Regulations to the accounts required by or prepared under regulation 3 are references to the annual accounts, the directors' report and the auditor's report required by or prepared under paragraph (1) of that regulation.

(6) Any reference in these Regulations to 'financial year' in relation to an insurance undertaking means—

(a) any period in respect of which a profit and loss account, or in the case of an industrial and provident society, an annual return, of that undertaking is required to be made up by or in accordance with its constitution or by any enactment (whether that period is a year or not), or

(b) failing any such requirement, each period of 12 months beginning with 1st April.

(7) Except as otherwise provided in these Regulations, words and expressions used in the Companies Act 2006 have the same meaning in these Regulations as they have in that Act.

# PART 2

## ACCOUNTS

**Preparation of accounts by insurance undertakings**

**3.** (1) The directors of an insurance undertaking must in respect of each financial year of the undertaking—

(a) prepare the like annual accounts and directors' report, and

(b) cause to be prepared such an auditor's report,

as would be required under the provisions mentioned in paragraph (3) if the undertaking were a company which is an insurance company or the parent company of an insurance group.

(2) The accounts required by this regulation must—

---

[127]  2000 c.8.

[128]  1965 c.12.

[129]  1969 c.24 (NI).

[130]  SI 2001/544 as amended by SI 2001/3544, SI 2002/682, SI 2002/1310, SI 2002/1776, SI 2002/1777, SI 2003/1475, SI 2003/1476, SI 2003/2822, SI 2004/1610, SI 2004/2737, SI 2004/3379, SI 2005/593, SI 2005/1518, SI 2005/2114 and SI 2006/1969.

[131]  OJ L228, 16.8.1973, p3.

[132]  OJ L345, 19.12.2002, p1.

    (a) be prepared within the period of 6 months beginning immediately after the end of the undertaking's financial year,

    (b) state that they are prepared under this regulation, and

    (c) comply with such of the requirements of the provisions mentioned in paragraph (3) as relate to the contents of accounts or reports subject, where the insurance undertaking is unincorporated, to any necessary modifications to take account of that fact.

(3) The provisions referred to in paragraphs (1) and (2) are the following provisions of the Companies Act 2006 and the Companies Accounts Regulations—

    (a) Chapters 4 and 5 of Part 15 of the Companies Act 2006 (accounts and reports),

    (b) sections 433 (name of signatory to be stated in published copies of accounts and reports) and 436 (meaning of 'publication' in relation to accounts and reports) of that Act as far as the latter section has effect for the purposes of section 433,

    (c) section 469 of that Act (preparation and filing of accounts in euros),

    (d) sections 475(1) (requirement for audited accounts), 495 (auditor's report on annual accounts), 496 (auditor's report on directors' report), 498 (duties of auditor), 503 (signature of auditor's report) and 505 (names to be stated in published copies of auditor's report) of that Act,

    (e) where Companies Act individual accounts are prepared, Schedule 3 to the Companies Accounts Regulations (insurance companies: Companies Act individual accounts) other than paragraphs 11, 62, 68, 70, 71, 72, 82(2), 83 and 84 and, in paragraph 2(2), the words from 'save that none of the following' to the end,

    (f) Schedule 4 to those Regulations (information on related undertakings required whether preparing Companies Act or IAS accounts) other than paragraphs 9 and 12,

    (g) Schedule 5 to those Regulations (information about benefits of directors) other than paragraphs 2, 4 and 5,

    (h) where Companies Act group accounts are prepared, Part 1 of Schedule 6 to the Companies Accounts Regulations (Companies Act group accounts: general rules) (as modified by Part 3 of that Schedule (modifications for insurance groups)) other than paragraphs 13(3) and (4), 14 and 15,

    (i) paragraphs 6 and 7 of Schedule 7 to those Regulations (directors' report).

(4) For the purposes of those provisions as applied to accounts prepared under this regulation, these Regulations are to be regarded as part of the requirements of the Companies Act 2006 and the Companies Accounts Regulations.

(5) Regulations 5 and 6 of the Companies (Disclosure of Auditor Remuneration and Liability Limitation Agreements) Regulations 2008[133] apply in relation to the accounts required by this regulation as they apply in relation to the annual accounts of a company or group which is not a small or medium-sized company or group.

## Publication of accounts

**4.** (1) An insurance undertaking must—

    (a) make available the latest accounts and reports prepared under regulation 3 for inspection by any person, without charge and during business hours, at the undertaking's head office in the United Kingdom, and

    (b) supply to any person upon request a copy of those accounts (or such part of those accounts as may be requested) at a price not exceeding the administrative cost of making the copy.

(2) In the case of industrial and provident societies which are insurance undertakings, the obligation in paragraph (1) (b) is subject to the provisions of section 39(5) of the Industrial and Provident Societies Act 1965 or section 48(6) of the Industrial and Provident Societies Act (Northern Ireland) 1969, as the case may be.

## Penalties for non-compliance (accounts)

**5.** (1) If the directors of an insurance undertaking fail to comply with paragraph (1) of regulation 3 within the period referred to in paragraph (2) of that regulation, an offence is committed by every person who, immediately before the end of that period, was a director of the undertaking.

(2) If accounts and reports which are made available for inspection under regulation 4(1) do not comply with the requirements of regulation 3, an offence is committed by every person who, at the time when the accounts and reports were or the account was first made available for inspection, was a director of the insurance undertaking.

(3) If an insurance undertaking fails to comply with regulation 4(1) an offence is committed by—

    (a) the insurance undertaking, and

    (b) every director of the insurance undertaking who is in default.

---

[133] SI 2008/489.

(4) Where the affairs of an insurance undertaking are managed by its members, any reference in this regulation to a director of the insurance undertaking shall be read as referring to a member of the undertaking.

(5) In proceedings for an offence under this section it is a defence for the person charged to show that he took all reasonable steps and exercised all due diligence to avoid the commission of the offence.

(6) A person guilty of an offence under this regulation is liable on summary conviction to a fine not exceeding level 5 on the standard scale.

(7) Section 1130 of the Companies Act 2006 (proceedings against unincorporated bodies) applies to an offence under paragraph (3) as it does to an offence under section 519 of that Act (statement by auditor to be deposited with company).

PART 3

AUDITORS

### Appointment of auditors

**6.** (1) Sections 485 (appointment of auditors of private company: general), 486 (appointment of auditors of private company: default power of Secretary of State), 487 (term of office of auditors of private company) and 488 (prevention by members of deemed re-appointment of auditor) of the Companies Act 2006 apply in relation to the appointment of auditors of an insurance undertaking subject—

(a) where the undertaking concerned is unincorporated, to any necessary modifications to take account of that fact,

(b) to the modifications made by paragraph (2), and

(c) to paragraph (3).

(2) The modifications are—

(a) in section 485(2)(a), the reference to 'the time allowed for sending out copies of the company's annual accounts and reports' is to be construed as a reference to the time allowed under regulation 3(2)(a) of these Regulations for preparing the accounts required by regulation 3;

(b) in section 485(2)(b), the reference to 'the day on which copies of the company's annual accounts and reports for the previous financial year are sent out under section 423' is to be construed as a reference to the day on which the accounts required by regulation 3 are prepared;

(c) in section 487(3), the reference to 'the provisions of this Part as to removal and resignation of auditors' is to be construed as a reference to provisions in these Regulations, and to any public general Act governing an insurance undertaking, as to removal and resignation of auditors;

(d) in section 488(3)(c), the reference to 'the accounting reference period' is to be construed as a reference to the financial year.

(3) Sections 1121 (liability of officer in default), 1122 (liability of company as officer in default), 1123 (application to bodies other than companies) and 1130 (proceedings against unincorporated bodies) of the Companies Act 2006 apply in relation to an offence committed under section 486(3) of that Act as applied by this regulation.

(4) This regulation does not apply in relation to industrial and provident societies which prepare accounts under the provisions of these Regulations.

### Functions of auditor

**7.** (1) The following provisions of the Companies Act 2006 apply to the auditor of an insurance undertaking as they apply to an auditor of a company—

(a) section 495 (auditor's report on company's annual accounts);

(b) section 498 (duties of auditor);

(c) section 499 (auditor's general right to information).

(2) The auditor of an insurance undertaking must supply the directors of that undertaking with such information as is necessary to enable the disclosure required by regulation 3(5) to be made.

(3) This regulation does not apply in relation to industrial and provident societies which prepare accounts under the provisions of these Regulations.

### Signature of auditor's report

**8.** (1) Sections 503 to 506 of the Companies Act 2006 (signature of auditor's report) apply in relation to the auditor's report required by regulation 3(1)(b), subject to—

(a) any necessary modifications to take account of the fact that the insurance undertaking is unincorporated, and

(b) the modifications made by paragraph (2).

(2) The modifications are—

(a) in section 505(1)(b) and section 506(2)(b), the references to the Secretary of State are to be construed as references to the Authority, and

(b) in section 506(1)(b), the reference to the copy of the report delivered to the registrar under Chapter 10 of Part 15 (filing of accounts and reports) is to be construed as a reference to any copy of the report made available for inspection by, or supplied to, the Authority.

(3) The reference to section 505 of the Companies Act 2006 in regulation 3(3)(d) is to be construed in accordance with this regulation.

### Removal of auditors on improper grounds

**9.** (1) Where the auditor of an insurance undertaking is removed from office an application may be made to the High Court under this regulation.

(2) The persons who may make such an application are—

(a) any member of the insurance undertaking who was also a member at the time of the removal, and

(b) the Authority.

(3) If the court is satisfied that the removal was—

(a) on grounds of divergence of opinion on accounting treatments or audit procedures, or

(b) on any other improper grounds,

it may make such order as it thinks fit for giving relief in respect of the removal.

(4) The court may, in particular—

(a) declare that any resolution of the insurance undertaking removing an auditor, or appointing a new auditor in his place, is void;

(b) require the directors of the insurance undertaking to re-appoint the dismissed auditor until the next general meeting of the insurance undertaking;

(c) give directions as to the conduct of the insurance undertaking's affairs in the future.

(5) In the application of this regulation to an insurance undertaking whose principal place of business is in Scotland or Northern Ireland, references to the High Court are to be read as references to the Court of Session or, as the case may be, the High Court in Northern Ireland.

### Duty of auditor to notify appropriate audit authority

**10.** (1) Where an auditor of an insurance undertaking ceases for any reason to hold office, he must notify the appropriate audit authority.

(2) The notice must—

(a) inform the appropriate audit authority that he has ceased to hold office, and

(b) if the auditor resigns, be accompanied by a copy of any notice of resignation and a statement of the reasons for his resignation.

(3) The auditor must comply with this regulation—

(a) if he resigns, at the same time as he deposits his notice of resignation at the head office of the insurance undertaking or otherwise informs it of his resignation;

(b) in any other case, not later than the end of the period of 14 days beginning with the date on which he ceases to hold office.

### Duty of insurance undertaking to notify appropriate audit authority

**11.** (1) Where an auditor of an insurance undertaking ceases to hold office before the end of his term of office, the undertaking must notify the appropriate audit authority.

(2) The notice must—

(a) inform the appropriate audit authority that the auditor has ceased to hold office, and

(b) be accompanied by—

(i) a statement by the undertaking of the reasons for his ceasing to hold office, or

(ii) if the auditor has resigned and he has given the insurance undertaking a statement of the reasons for his resignation, a copy of that statement.

(3) The insurance undertaking must give notice under this paragraph—

(a) if the auditor resigns, not later than the end of the period of 14 days beginning with the date on which the auditor first informs the insurance undertaking of his resignation (whether by notice deposited at its head office or otherwise);

(b) in any other case, not later than the end of the period of 14 days beginning with the date on which the auditor ceases to hold office.

### Penalties for non-compliance (notification of appropriate audit authority)

**12.** (1) If an auditor fails to comply with regulation 10, an offence is committed by—

(a) the auditor, and

(b) if the auditor is a firm, every officer of the firm who is in default.

(2) If an insurance undertaking fails to comply with regulation 11, an offence is committed by—

(a) the insurance undertaking, and

(b) every director of the insurance undertaking who is in default.

(3) Where the affairs of an insurance undertaking are managed by its members, any reference in

this regulation to a director of the insurance undertaking shall be read as referring to a member of the undertaking.

(4) In proceedings for an offence under this section it is a defence for the person charged to show that he took all reasonable steps and exercised all due diligence to avoid the commission of the offence.

(5) A person guilty of an offence under this regulation is liable—
 (a) on conviction on indictment, to a fine, and
 (b) on summary conviction, to a fine not exceeding the statutory maximum.

(6) Sections 1121 (liability of officer in default), 1122 (liability of company as officer in default), 1123 (application to bodies other than companies) and 1130 (proceedings against unincorporated bodies) of the Companies Act 2006 apply to an offence under paragraphs (1) and (2) as they apply to an offence under section 519 of that Act (statement by auditor to be deposited with company).

## PART 4
## FINAL PROVISIONS

### Summary proceedings: venue and time limit

**13.** Sections 1127 (summary proceedings: venue) and 1128 (summary proceedings: time limit for proceedings) of the Companies Act 2006 apply in relation to summary proceedings for any offence under these Regulations as they apply in relation to such proceedings for any offence under that Act.

### Industrial and provident societies

**14.** (1) Schedule 1 to these Regulations makes provision for the modification of the Friendly and Industrial and Provident Societies Act 1968[134] in its application to industrial and provident societies that are insurance undertakings for the purposes of these Regulations.

(2) Schedule 2 makes provision for the modification of the Industrial and Provident Societies (Northern Ireland) Act 1969 in its application to industrial and provident societies that are insurance undertakings for the purposes of these Regulations.

(3) The Industrial and Provident Societies (Group Accounts) Regulations 1969[135] and the Industrial and Provident Societies Act (Group Accounts) Regulations (Northern Ireland) 1969[136] do not apply to industrial and provident societies that are insurance undertakings for the purposes of these Regulations.

(4) Notwithstanding anything in the rules of the society, the committee of an industrial and provident society that is an insurance undertaking for the purposes of these Regulations may by resolution passed before 1st April 2009 make such amendments of the rules of the society as may be consequential on the provisions of these Regulations.

(5) The Authority is not required to register any amendment of the rules of such a society unless such consequential amendments of the rules of the society as are mentioned in paragraph (4) either have been made before the application for registration of that amendment or are to be effected by that amendment.

### Consequential amendments

**15.** (1) In section 1210 of the Companies Act 2006[137] (meaning of 'statutory auditor' etc)—
 (a) for subsection (1)(f) substitute—
 '(f) a person appointed as auditor of an insurance undertaking for the purposes of the Insurance Accounts Directive (Miscellaneous Insurance Undertakings) Regulations 2008,'; and
 (b) omit—
 (i) subsection (1)(d), and
 (ii) in subsection (3), omit the definition of 'industrial and provident society'.

(2) In section 4A(3) of the Friendly and Industrial and Provident Societies Act 1968 (power to disapply obligation to appoint auditor: excluded cases)[138], omit paragraph (d) (but not the word 'or' following it).

(3) In section 38A of the Industrial and Provident Societies (Northern Ireland) Act 1969 (power to disapply obligation to appoint auditor: excluded cases)[139], omit paragraph (c) (but not the word 'or' following it).

---

[134] 1968 c.55.
[135] SI 1969/1037.
[136] SR 1969/359.
[137] 2006 c.46.
[138] Section 4A was inserted by article 8(1) of SI 1996/1738.
[139] 1969 c.24 (NI). Section 38A was inserted by paragraph 6 of Schedule 2 to SI 1997/2984 (NI 22).

**Revocation**

**16.** (1) The Insurance Accounts Directive (Miscellaneous Insurance Undertakings) Regulations 1993[140] and the Insurance Accounts Directive (Miscellaneous Insurance Undertakings) Regulations (Northern Ireland) 1994[141] are revoked.

(2) The regulations specified in paragraph (1) continue to apply to any financial year of an insurance undertaking beginning before 6th April 2008.

SCHEDULE 1           Regulation 14(1)

MODIFICATION OF THE FRIENDLY AND INDUSTRIAL AND
PROVIDENT SOCIETIES ACT 1968

**1.** In its application to industrial and provident societies that are insurance undertakings for the purposes of these Regulations, the Friendly and Industrial and Provident Societies Act 1968 has effect subject to the following modifications.

**2.** Section 3 (general provisions as to accounts and balance sheets of societies) does not apply.

**3.** In section 3A (publication of accounts and balance sheets of societies)[142], for subsections (2) to (12), substitute—

'(2) If a society publishes any of its statutory accounts, they must be accompanied by the relevant auditors' report under the Insurance Accounts Directive (Miscellaneous Insurance Undertakings) Regulations 2008.

(3) A society which is required to prepare group accounts for a financial year shall not publish its statutory individual accounts for that year without also publishing with them its statutory group accounts.

(4) If a society publishes non-statutory accounts, it shall publish with them a statement indicating—

(a) that they are not the society's statutory accounts,

(b) whether statutory accounts dealing with any financial year with which the non-statutory accounts purport to deal have been delivered to the Authority,

(c) whether the society's auditors have made a report under the Insurance Accounts Directive (Miscellaneous Insurance Undertakings) Regulations 2008,

(d) whether any such auditors' report—

(i) was qualified or unqualified, or included a reference to any matters to which the auditors drew attention by way of emphasis without qualifying the report, or

(ii) contained a statement under section 498(2) or (3) of the Companies Act 2006 as applied to industrial and provident societies by the Insurance Accounts Directive (Miscellaneous Insurance Undertakings) Regulations 2008 (accounting records or returns inadequate, accounts not agreeing with records and returns or failure to obtain necessary information and explanations),

and it shall not publish with the non-statutory accounts any auditors' report under the Insurance Accounts Directive (Miscellaneous Insurance Undertakings) Regulations 2008.

(5) For the purposes of this section a society shall be regarded as publishing a document if it publishes, issues or circulates it or otherwise generally makes it available for public inspection in a manner calculated to invite members of the public generally, or any class of members of the public, to read it.

(6) References in this section to a society's statutory accounts are to its individual or group accounts for a financial year as required to be prepared by the Insurance Accounts Directive (Miscellaneous Insurance Undertakings) Regulations 2008; and references to the publication by a society of 'non-statutory accounts' are to the publication of—

(a) any balance sheet or profit and loss account relating to, or purporting to deal with, a financial year of the society, or

(b) an account in any form purporting to be a balance sheet or profit and loss account for the group consisting of the society and its subsidiary undertakings relating to, or purporting to deal with, a financial year of the society,

otherwise than as part of the society's statutory accounts.'.

**4.** Sections 4 and 4A (appointment of auditors) do not apply.

**5.** In section 5 (re-appointment and removal of auditors)[143]—

(a) in subsection (1), at the end of paragraph (d) insert—

---

[140] SI 1993/3245, as amended by article 450 of SI 2001/3649, by regulation 8 of SI 2004/3379, by regulation 18 of SI 2004/3219 and by regulations 2 to 4 of SI 2005/1985.

[141] SR 1994/429, as amended by SR 2006/353.

[142] Section 3A was inserted by SI 1996/1738, article 9(4).

[143] Section 5 was amended by SI 1996/1738, article 9(6).

', or

(e)  he was appointed by the committee, or

(f)  the society's rules require actual re-appointment, or

(g)  the re-appointment is prevented by the members under section 5A'.

(b)  after subsection (2) insert—

'(3) A person who is not automatically re-appointed as auditor by virtue of subsection (1)(e) of this subsection may be re-appointed by the committee for the current year of account and for any subsequent year of account commencing before the next general meeting of the society. However, he may only be re-appointed for any year of account commencing on or after the date of that general meeting by a resolution of the society at that meeting.'.

**6.** After section 5, insert—

### 'Prevention by members of automatic re-appointment of auditor

5A.    (1)  An auditor of a society is not automatically re-appointed under section 5 of this Act if the society has received notices under this section from members representing at least the requisite percentage of the total voting rights of all members who would be entitled to vote on a resolution that the auditor should not be re-appointed.

(2)  The 'requisite percentage' is 5%, or such lower percentage as is specified for this purpose in the society's rules.

(3)  A notice under this section—

(a)  may be in hard copy or electronic form,

(b)  must be authenticated by the person or persons giving it, and

(c)  must be received by the society before the end of the year of account immediately preceding the year of account for which the automatic re-appointment would have effect.'.

**7.** For section 7 (qualified auditors) substitute—

### 'Qualified auditors

7. References in this Act to a qualified auditor, in relation to a society, are to a person who—

(a)  is eligible for appointment as a statutory auditor under Part 42 of the Companies Act 2006, and

(b)  is not prohibited from acting as statutory auditor of the society by virtue of section 1214 of that Act (independence requirement).'.

**8.** Section 8 (restrictions on appointment of auditors) does not apply.

**9.** In section 9 (auditors' report and rights), only subsection (5) (auditors' rights of access to books and to require information and explanations) applies.

**10.** Sections 9A to 9C (reporting accountant procedure) do not apply.

**11.** In section 10 (remuneration of auditors)[144], the following do not apply—

(a)  in subsection (1), the words from 'or for the making of a report' to the end;

(b)  in subsection (2), the words 'or reporting accountant';

(c)  subsection (3).

**12.** In section 11 (annual returns)[145]—

(a)  in subsection (2)(a), for 'the revenue account or accounts of the society prepared in accordance with section 3(2) of this Act' substitute 'the profit and loss account required to be prepared by section 396 of the Companies Act 2006 as applied by regulation 3 of the Insurance Accounts Directive (Miscellaneous Insurance Undertakings) Regulations 2008';

(b)  for subsection (2)(b) substitute—

'(b) shall not contain any other accounts.';

(c)  subsection (5A) does not apply.

**13.** In section 13 (group accounts)[146]—

(a)  subsections (1) to (5) do not apply;

(b)  in subsection (6) for 'under the last preceding subsection' substitute 'on those accounts'.

**14.** Section 14 (exemption from requirements in respect of group accounts) does not apply.

**15.** Section 15 (meaning of 'subsidiary') does not apply.

**16.** In section 18 (offences), the words from 'or any direction' to 'section 9C(1) of this Act' do not apply.

**17.** In section 19(2) (regulations), the words 'section 4 or' do not apply.

---

[144]  Section 10(1) was amended by SI 1996/1738, article 9(7). Section 10(2) was amended by SI 2001/2617, Schedule 3, paragraph 252.

[145]  Section 11 was amended by the Friendly Societies Act 1974 (c.46), section 116 and Schedule 11. Section 11(1) was also amended by SI 2001/2617, Schedule 3, paragraphs 246 and 253. Section 11(2) was also amended by SI 1996/1738, article 9(10).

[146]  Section 13(6) was amended by SI 2001/2617, Schedule 3, paragraphs 246 and 255(c).

**18.** In section 21(1) (interpretation)[147]—

(a) insert at the appropriate place—

' "accounts" means the profit and loss account required to be prepared by section 396 of the Companies Act 2006 as applied by regulation 3 of the Insurance Accounts Directive (Miscellaneous Insurance Undertakings) Regulations 2008;';

(b) for the definition of "group accounts" substitute—

' "group accounts" means the accounts required to be prepared by section 404 of the Companies Act 2006 as applied by regulation 3 of the Insurance Accounts Directive (Miscellaneous Insurance Undertakings) Regulations 2008;';

(c) the definition of 'subsidiary' does not apply.


SCHEDULE 2                                          Regulation 14(2)

MODIFICATION OF THE INDUSTRIAL AND PROVIDENT SOCIETIES ACT
(NORTHERN IRELAND) 1969


**1.** In its application to industrial and provident societies that are insurance undertakings for the purposes of these Regulations the Industrial and Provident Societies Act (Northern Ireland) 1969 shall have effect subject to the following modifications.

**2.** Section 37 (general provisions as to accounts and balance sheets of societies) does not apply.

**3.** In section 37A (publication of accounts and balance sheets of registered societies)[148], for subsections (2) to (12) substitute—

'(2) If a society publishes any of its statutory accounts, they must be accompanied by the relevant auditors' report under the Insurance Accounts Directive (Miscellaneous Insurance Undertakings) Regulations 2008.

(3) A society which is required to prepare group accounts for a financial year shall not publish its statutory individual accounts for that year without also publishing with them its statutory group accounts.

(4) If a society publishes non-statutory accounts, it shall publish with them a statement indicating—

(a) that they are not the society's statutory accounts,

(b) whether statutory accounts dealing with any financial year with which the non-statutory accounts purport to deal have been delivered to the registrar,

(c) whether the society's auditors have made a report under the Insurance Accounts Directive (Miscellaneous Insurance Undertakings) Regulations 2008,

(d) whether any such auditors' report—

(i) was qualified or unqualified, or included a reference to any matters to which the auditors drew attention by way of emphasis without qualifying the report, or

(ii) contained a statement under section 498(2) or (3) of the Companies Act 2006 as applied to industrial and provident societies by the Insurance Accounts Directive (Miscellaneous Insurance Undertakings) Regulations 2008 (accounting records or returns inadequate, accounts not agreeing with records and returns or failure to obtain necessary information and explanations), and it shall not publish with the non-statutory accounts any auditors' report under the Insurance Accounts Directive (Miscellaneous Insurance Undertakings) Regulations 2008.

(5) For the purposes of this section a society shall be regarded as publishing a document if it publishes, issues or circulates it or otherwise generally makes it available for public inspection in a manner calculated to invite members of the public generally, or any class of members of the public, to read it.

(6) References in this section to a society's statutory accounts are to its individual or group accounts for a financial year as required to be prepared by the Insurance Accounts Directive (Miscellaneous Insurance Undertakings) Regulations 2008; and references to the publication by a society of 'non-statutory accounts' are to the publication of—

(a) any balance sheet or profit and loss account relating to, or purporting to deal with, a financial year of the society, or

(b) an account in any form purporting to be a balance sheet or profit and loss account for the group consisting of the society and its subsidiary undertakings relating to, or purporting to deal with, a financial year of the society,

otherwise than as part of the society's statutory accounts.'.

**4.** Sections 38 and 38A (appointment of auditors) do not apply.

---

[147] Section 21(1) was amended by the Friendly Societies Act 1974, section 116(4), and Schedule 11; by SI 2001/3649, article 185; and by S.I 2001/2617, schedule 3, paragraphs 246, 260.

[148] Section 37A was inserted by SI 1997/2984 (NI 22), Schedule 2, paragraph 5.

5.  In section 39 (re-appointment and removal of auditors)[149]—
    (a)  in subsection (1), at the end of paragraph (d) insert—

    ', or
    (e) he was appointed by the committee, or
    (f) the society's rules require actual re-appointment, or
    (g) the re-appointment is prevented by the members under section 39A'.
    (b)  after subsection (2) insert—

    '(3) A person who is not automatically re-appointed as auditor by virtue of subsection (1)(e) of this subsection may be re-appointed by the committee for the current year of account and for any subsequent year of account commencing before the next general meeting of the society.
    However, he may only be re-appointed for any year of account commencing on or after the date of that general meeting by a resolution of the society at that meeting.'.
6.  After section 39, insert—

### 'Prevention by members of automatic re-appointment of auditor

**39A.**   (1)  An auditor of a society is not automatically re-appointed under section 39 of this Act if the society has received notices under this section from members representing at least the requisite percentage of the total voting rights of all members who would be entitled to vote on a resolution that the auditor should not be re-appointed.
    (2)  The 'requisite percentage' is 5%, or such lower percentage as is specified for this purpose in the society's rules.
    (3)  A notice under this section—
        (a)  may be in hard copy or electronic form,
        (b)  must be authenticated by the person or persons giving it, and
        (c)  must be received by the society before the end of the year of account immediately preceding the year of account for which the automatic re-appointment would have effect.'.
7.  For section 41 (qualified auditors) substitute—

### 'Qualified auditors

**41.**  References in this Act to a qualified auditor, in relation to a society, are to a person who—
        (a)  is eligible for appointment as a statutory auditor under Part 42 of the Companies Act 2006, and
        (b)  is not prohibited from acting as statutory auditor of the society by virtue of section 1214 of that Act (independence requirement).'.

8.  Section 42 (restrictions on appointment of auditors) does not apply.
9.  In section 43 (auditors' report and rights), only subsection (5) (auditors' rights of access to books and to require information and explanations) applies.
10.  Sections 43A to 43C (reporting accountant procedure) do not apply.
11.  In section 44 (remuneration of auditors)[150], the following do not apply—
    (a)  in subsection (1), the words from 'or for the making of a report' to the end;
    (b)  in subsection (2), the words 'or reporting accountant';
    (c)  subsection (3).
12.  In section 45 (group accounts)—
    (a)  subsections (1) to (5) do not apply;
    (b)  in subsection (6) for 'under subsection (5)' substitute 'on those accounts'.
13.  Section 46 (exemption from requirements in respect of group accounts) does not apply.
14.  Section 47 (meaning of 'subsidiary') does not apply.
15.  In section 48 (annual returns)[151]—
    (a)  in subsection (1), for paragraphs (a) and (b) substitute 'the documents mentioned in subsection (1B)';
    (b)  subsection (1A) does not apply;
    (c)  in subsection (2) (a), for 'the revenue account or accounts of the society prepared in accordance with section 37(2)' substitute 'the profit and loss account required to be prepared by section 396 of the Companies Act 2006 as applied by regulation 3 of the Insurance Accounts Directive (Miscellaneous Insurance Undertakings) Regulations 2008'; and
    (d)  for subsection (2)(b) substitute—

    '(b) shall not contain any other accounts.';

    (e)  subsection (6A) does not apply.

---

[149]  Section 39 was amended by SI 1997/2984 (NI 22), Schedule 2, paragraph 7.
[150]  Section 44 was amended by SI 1997/2984 (NI 22), Schedule 2, paragraph 9.
[151]  Section 48 was amended by SI 1997/2984 (NI 22), Schedule 2, paragraph 11.

**16.** In section 101 (interpretation)—

    (a) insert at the appropriate place—

        '"accounts" means the profit and loss account required to be prepared by section 396 of the Companies Act 2006 as applied by regulation 3 of the Insurance Accounts Directive (Miscellaneous Insurance Undertakings) Regulations 2008;';

    (b) for the definition of 'group accounts' substitute—

        '"group accounts" means the accounts required to be prepared by section 404 of the Companies Act 2006 as applied by regulation 3 of the Insurance Accounts Directive (Miscellaneous Insurance Undertakings) Regulations 2008;';

    (c) the definition of 'subsidiary' does not apply.

# THE BANK ACCOUNTS DIRECTIVE (MISCELLANEOUS BANKS) REGULATIONS 2008

## (SI 2008/567)

COMMENCEMENT DATE 6 April 2008

## PART 1

## INTRODUCTION

**Citation, commencement and application**         SI.20

**1.** (1) These Regulations may be cited as the Bank Accounts Directive (Miscellaneous Banks) Regulations 2008.

    (2) These Regulations come into force on 6th April 2008 and apply in relation to—

        (a) qualifying banks' financial years beginning on or after that date, and

        (b) auditors appointed in respect of those financial years.

**Interpretation**

**2.** (1) In these Regulations—

    'the Companies Accounts Regulations' means the Large and Medium-sized Companies and Groups (Accounts and Reports) Regulations 2008[152];

    'accounts' means the annual accounts, the directors' report and the auditor's report required by regulation 4(1);

    'the appropriate audit authority' means—

        (a) the Secretary of State, or

        (b) if the Secretary of State has delegated functions under section 1252 of the Companies Act 2006[153] to a body whose functions include receiving the equivalent notice under section 522 or 523 of that Act, that body;

    'the Authority' means the Financial Services Authority[154];

    'director' includes, in the case of a body which is not a company, any corresponding officer of that body;

    'enactment' includes—

        (a) an enactment contained in subordinate legislation, other than these Regulations,

        (b) an enactment contained in, or in an instrument made under, an Act of the Scottish Parliament,

        (c) an enactment contained in, or in an instrument made under, Northern Ireland legislation, and

        (d) an enactment contained in, or in an instrument made under, a Measure or Act of the National Assembly for Wales;

    'financial year', in relation to a qualifying bank, means any period in respect of which a profit and loss account of that bank is required to be made up by or in accordance with its constitution or by any enactment (whether that period is a year or not) or, failing any such requirement, each period of 12 months beginning with 1st April,

    'qualifying bank' shall be construed in accordance with regulation 3.

    (2) Except as otherwise provided in these Regulations, words and expressions used in the Companies Act 2006 have the same meaning in these Regulations as they have in that Act.

---

[152] SI 2008/410.

[153] 2006 c.46.

[154] See the Financial Services and Markets Act 2000 (c.8), section 1.

**Meaning of 'qualifying bank'**

**3.** (1)  Any body of persons, whether incorporated or unincorporated, which—

(a)  is incorporated or formed by or established under any public general Act of Parliament passed before the year 1837,

(b)  has a principal place of business within the United Kingdom,

(c)  is an authorised deposit taker, and

(d)  is not required by any enactment to prepare accounts under Part 15 of the Companies Act 2006,

is a qualifying bank for the purposes of these Regulations.

(2)  In paragraph (1), 'authorised deposit taker' means a person with permission under Part 4 of the Financial Services and Markets Act 2000 to accept deposits, but excludes—

(a)  a building society, within the meaning of section 119 of the Building Societies Act 1986[155],

(b)  a credit union, within the meaning of the Credit Unions Act 1979[156] or the Credit Unions (Northern Ireland) Order 1985[157],

(c)  a specially authorised friendly society, within the meaning of section 7(1)(f) of the Friendly Societies Act 1974[158], and

(d)  a person who has permission to accept deposits only in the course of effecting or carrying out contracts of insurance in accordance with that permission.

(3)  References in paragraph (2) to—

(a)  accepting deposits, and

(b)  effecting and carrying out contracts of insurance,

must be read with section 22 of the Financial Services and Markets Act 2000, the Financial Services and Markets Act 2000 (Regulated Activities) Order 2001[159], and Schedule 2 to that Act.

PART 2

ACCOUNTS

**Preparation of accounts**

**4.** (1)  The directors of a qualifying bank must in respect of each financial year of the bank—

(a)  prepare such annual accounts and directors' report, and

(b)  cause to be prepared such auditor's report, as would be required under Part 15 (accounts and reports) and Chapter 1 of Part 16 (requirement for audited accounts) of the Companies Act 2006, and under the Companies Accounts Regulations if the bank were a company which is a banking company or the parent company of a banking group, subject to the provisions of the Schedule to these Regulations.

(2)  Regulations 5 and 6 of the Companies (Disclosure of Auditor Remuneration and Liability Limitation Agreements) Regulations 2008[160] apply in relation to the accounts required by this regulation as they apply in relation to the annual accounts of a company or group which is not a small or medium-sized company or group.

(3)  The accounts required by paragraph (1) must be prepared within a period of 6 months beginning immediately after the end of the qualifying bank's financial year.

**Publication of accounts**

**5.** (1)  A qualifying bank must make available the latest accounts prepared under regulation 4 for inspection by any person, without charge and during business hours, at the bank's principal place of business within the United Kingdom.

(2)  The bank must supply to any person upon request a copy of those accounts (or such part of those accounts as may be requested) at a price not exceeding the administrative cost of making the copy.

(3)  Paragraph (2) applies whether the request for a copy is made orally during inspection under paragraph (1), by post or otherwise.

---

[155]  1986 c.53.

[156]  1979 c.34.

[157]  SI 1985/1285 (NI 12).

[158]  1974 c.46.

[159]  SI 2001/544, as amended by SI 2001/3544, SI 2002/682, SI 2002/1310, SI 2002/1776, SI 2002/1777, SI 2003/1475, SI 2003/1476, SI 2003/2822, SI 2004/1610, SI 2004/2737, SI 2004/3379, SI 2005/593, SI 2005/1518, SI 2005/2114 and SI 2006/1969.

[160]  SI 2008/ 489.

**Penalties for non-compliance (accounts)**

**6.** (1) If the directors of a qualifying bank fail to prepare, or (in the case of the auditor's report) fail to cause to be prepared, the accounts required by regulation 4(1) within the period referred to in regulation 4(3), an offence is committed by every person who, immediately before the end of that period, was a director of the bank.

(2) If any annual accounts or directors' report are made available for inspection under regulation 5 which do not comply with the requirements of regulation 4(1) as to the matters to be included in them, an offence is committed by every person who, at the time the annual accounts or report were first made available for inspection, was a director of the bank.

(3) If a qualifying bank fails to comply with regulation 5 an offence is committed by—
 (a) the qualifying bank, and
 (b) every director of the qualifying bank who is in default.

(4) Where the affairs of a qualifying bank are managed by its members, any reference in this regulation to a director of the qualifying bank shall be read as referring to a member of the bank.

(5) In proceedings for an offence under this section it is a defence for the person charged to show that he took all reasonable steps and exercised all due diligence to avoid the commission of the offence.

(6) A person guilty of an offence under this regulation is liable on summary conviction to a fine not exceeding level 5 on the standard scale.

(7) Sections 1127 and 1128 (summary proceedings: venue and time limit for proceedings) and 1130 of the Companies Act 2006 (proceedings against unincorporated bodies) apply to an offence under this regulation.

PART 3

AUDITORS

**Appointment of auditor**

**7.** (1) Sections 485 (appointment of auditors of private company: general), 486 (appointment of auditors of private company: default power of Secretary of State), 487 (term of office of auditors of private company) and 488 (prevention by members of deemed re-appointment of auditor) of the Companies Act 2006 apply in relation to the appointment of auditors of a qualifying bank subject—
 (a) where the bank concerned is unincorporated, to any necessary modifications to take account of that fact, and
 (b) to the provisions of the Schedule to these Regulations.

(2) Sections 1121 (liability of officer in default), 1123 (application to bodies other than companies) and 1130 (proceedings against unincorporated bodies) of the Companies Act 2006 apply in relation to an offence committed under section 486(3) of that Act as applied by this regulation.

**Functions of auditor**

**8** (1) The following provisions of the Companies Act 2006 apply to the auditor of a qualifying bank as they apply to an auditor of a company—
 (a) section 495 (auditor's report on company's annual accounts);
 (b) section 498 (duties of auditor);
 (c) section 499 (auditor's general right to information).

(2) The auditor of a qualifying bank must supply the directors of that bank with such information as is necessary to enable the disclosure required by regulation 4(2) to be made.

**Signature of auditor's report**

**9.** Sections 503 to 506 of the Companies Act 2006 (signature of auditor's report) apply in relation to the auditor's report required by regulation 4(1)(b), subject to—
 (a) any necessary modifications to take account of the fact that the qualifying bank is unincorporated, and
 (b) the provisions of the Schedule to these Regulations.

**Removal of auditor on improper grounds**

**10.** (1) Where the auditor of a qualifying bank is removed from office an application may be made to the High Court under this regulation.

(2) The persons who may make such an application are—

(a) any member of the qualifying bank who was also a member at the time of the removal, and

(b) the Authority.

(3) If the court is satisfied that the removal was—

(a) on grounds of divergence of opinion on accounting treatments or audit procedures, or

(b) on any other improper grounds, it may make such order as it thinks fit for giving relief in respect of the removal.

(4) The court may, in particular—

(a) declare that any resolution of the qualifying bank removing an auditor, or appointing a new auditor in his place, is void;

(b) require the directors of the qualifying bank to re-appoint the dismissed auditor until the next general meeting of the qualifying bank;

(c) give directions as to the conduct of the qualifying bank's affairs in the future.

(5) In the application of this regulation to a qualifying bank whose principal place of business is in Scotland or Northern Ireland, references to the High Court are to be read as references to the Court of Session or, as the case may be, the High Court in Northern Ireland.

### Duty of auditor to notify appropriate audit authority

**11.** (1) Where an auditor of a qualifying bank ceases for any reason to hold office, he must notify the appropriate audit authority.

(2) The notice must—

(a) inform the appropriate audit authority that he has ceased to hold office, and

(b) if the auditor resigns, be accompanied by a copy of any notice of resignation and a statement of the reasons for his resignation.

(3) The auditor must comply with this regulation—

(a) if he resigns, at the same time as he deposits his notice of resignation at the principal office of the qualifying bank or otherwise informs it of his resignation;

(b) in any other case, not later than the end of the period of 14 days beginning with the date on which he ceases to hold office.

### Duty of qualifying bank to notify appropriate audit authority

**12.** (1) Where an auditor of a qualifying bank ceases to hold office before the end of his term of office, the bank must notify the appropriate audit authority.

(2) The notice must—

(a) inform the appropriate audit authority that the auditor has ceased to hold office, and

(b) be accompanied by—

(i) a statement by the bank of the reasons for his ceasing to hold office, or

(ii) if the auditor has resigned and he has given the qualifying bank a statement of the reasons for his resignation, a copy of that statement.

(3) The qualifying bank must give notice under this regulation—

(a) if the auditor resigns, not later than the end of the period of 14 days beginning with the date on which the auditor first informs the qualifying bank of his resignation (whether by notice deposited at its principal office or otherwise);

(b) in any other case, not later than the end of the period of 14 days beginning with the date on which the auditor ceases to hold office.

### Penalties for non-compliance (notification of appropriate audit authority)

**13.** (1) If an auditor fails to comply with regulation 11, an offence is committed by—

(a) the auditor, and

(b) if the auditor is a firm, every officer of the firm who is in default.

(2) If a qualifying bank fails to comply with regulation 12, an offence is committed by—

(a) the qualifying bank, and

(b) every director of the qualifying bank who is in default.

(3) Where the affairs of a qualifying bank are managed by its members, any reference in this regulation to a director of the qualifying bank shall be read as referring to a member of the bank.

(4) In proceedings for an offence under this section it is a defence for the person charged to show that he took all reasonable steps and exercised all due diligence to avoid the commission of the offence.

(5) A person guilty of an offence under this regulation is liable—

(a) on conviction on indictment, to a fine, and

(b) on summary conviction, to a fine not exceeding the statutory maximum.

(6) Sections 1127 and 1128 (summary proceedings: venue and time limit for proceedings) and 1130 of the Companies Act 2006 (proceedings against unincorporated bodies) shall apply to an offence under paragraph (3) as it does to an offence under section 519 of that Act (statement by auditor to be deposited with company).

## PART 4

## FINAL PROVISIONS

**Consequential amendment**

**14.** In section 1210 of the Companies Act 2006 (meaning of 'statutory auditor' etc), for subsection (1)(g) substitute—

> '(g) a person appointed as auditor of a bank for the purposes of the Bank Accounts Directive (Miscellaneous Banks) Regulations 2008,'.

**Revocation and transitional provision**

**15.** (1) The Bank Accounts Directive (Miscellaneous Banks) Regulations 1991[161] are revoked.

(2) The regulations specified in paragraph (1) continue to apply to any financial year of a qualifying bank beginning before 6th April 2008.

---

SCHEDULE Regulation 4

## MODIFICATIONS AND ADAPTATIONS OF THE COMPANIES ACT 2006 AND THE COMPANIES ACCOUNTS REGULATIONS

**1.** (1) Where a qualifying bank is unincorporated, the accounts shall comply with—

(a) the requirements of Part 15 (accounts and reports) and Chapter 1 of Part 16 (requirement for audited accounts) of the Companies Act 2006[162]

(b) the provisions of the Companies Act 2006 applied by regulations 7 to 9 of these regulations, and

(c) the Companies Accounts Regulations, subject to any necessary modifications to take account of that fact.

(2) In particular, the accounts shall comply with those provisions subject to the provisions of section 1161(2) and (3) of the Companies Act 2006 (meaning of references to shares and other expressions appropriate to companies).

**2.** Accounts prepared under these Regulations shall state they are so prepared.

**3.** Sections 390 to 392 of the Companies Act 2006 (a company's financial year) shall not apply.

**4.** Accounts prepared under section 396 of the Companies Act 2006 (Companies Act individual accounts) as applied by these Regulations shall comply with the provisions of Part 1 of Schedule 2 to the Companies Accounts Regulations subject to the following modifications—

(a) in Section B of Chapter I of that Part, the profit and loss account formats there prescribed shall apply as if item 15 of format 1 and Charges item 9 and Income item 8 of format 2 were omitted; and

(b) in Part 3 of that Schedule, paragraphs 54, 61, 63, 64, 79(2), 84(2) and 86 shall not apply.

**5.** Accounts prepared under these Regulations shall comply with the provisions of Schedule 4 to the Companies Accounts Regulations (information on related undertakings) (as modified by Part 4 of that Schedule) as if paragraph 12 was omitted.

**6.** Accounts prepared under these Regulations shall comply with the provisions of Schedule 5 to the Companies Accounts Regulations (information about benefits of directors) as if paragraphs 2, 4 and 5 were omitted.

**7.** Accounts prepared under section 404 of the Companies Act 2006 (Companies Act group accounts) as applied by these Regulations shall comply with the provisions of Schedule 6 to the Companies Accounts Regulations (as modified by Part 2 of that Schedule) as if paragraphs 13(3) and (4), 14 and 15 were omitted.

**8.** (1) Accounts prepared under these Regulations shall comply with paragraphs 6 and 7 of Schedule 7 to the Companies Accounts Regulations (disclosures in directors' report relating to financial instruments and miscellaneous matters), but otherwise that Schedule shall not apply.

(2) Where a qualifying bank has a share capital and may lawfully acquire its own shares, the directors' report of that bank shall, in addition to the matters referred to in sub-paragraph (1), state—

(a) the reasons for any acquisition of such shares during the financial year,

(b) the number and nominal value of any such shares acquired during the financial year and the number and nominal value of any such shares disposed of during the financial year, together, in each case, with the percentage of the total issued share capital of the bank that they represent,

(c) the value and nature of any consideration given for the acquisition of such shares and the

---

[161] SI 1991/2704, as amended by article 417 of SI 2001/3649 and SI 2005/1984.
[162] 2006 c.46.

value and nature of any consideration received for the disposal of such shares during the financial year, and

(d) the number and nominal value of all such shares held by the bank at the end of the financial year, together with the percentage they represent of the total issued share capital of the bank.

9. Sections 485 to 488 of the Companies Act 2006 apply with the following modifications—

    (a) in section 485(2)(a), the reference to 'the time allowed for sending out copies of the company's annual accounts and reports' shall be construed as a reference to the time allowed under regulation 4(3) of these Regulations for preparing the accounts;

    (b) in section 485(2)(b), the reference to 'the day on which copies of the company's annual accounts and reports for the previous financial year are sent out under section 423' shall be construed as a reference to the day on which the accounts are prepared;

    (c) in section 487(3), the reference to 'the provisions of this Part as to removal and resignation of auditors' shall be construed as a reference to provisions in these Regulations, and to any public general Act governing a qualifying bank, as to removal and resignation of auditors;

    (d) in section 488(3)(c), the reference to 'the accounting reference period' shall be construed as a reference to the financial year.

10. Sections 505 and 506 of the Companies Act 2006 apply with the following modifications—

    (a) in section 505(1)(b) and section 506(2)(b), the references to the Secretary of State shall be construed as references to the Authority, and

    (b) in section 506(1)(b), the reference to the copy of the report delivered to the registrar under Chapter 10 of Part 15 (filing of accounts and reports) shall be construed as a reference to any copy of the report made available for inspection by, or supplied to, the Authority.

11. For the purposes of the relevant provisions of the Companies Act 2006 and the Companies Accounts Regulations as applied by these Regulations, these Regulations shall be regarded as part of the requirements of that Act and those Regulations.

12. Paragraphs 4 to 7 of this Schedule shall not be construed as affecting the requirement to give a true and fair view under sections 393, 396 and 404 of the Companies Act 2006, as applied by these Regulations.

---

# THE PARTNERSHIPS (ACCOUNTS) REGULATIONS 2008
## (SI 2008/569)

COMMENCEMENT DATE 6 April 2008

## PART 1
## INTRODUCTION

**Citation, commencement and application**

1. (1) These Regulations may be cited as the Partnerships (Accounts) Regulations 2008.

    (2) These Regulations come into force on 6th April 2008 and apply in relation to—

        (a) qualifying partnerships' financial years beginning on or after that date, and

        (b) auditors appointed in respect of those financial years.

**Interpretation**

2. (1) In these Regulations—

    'the accounts', in relation to a qualifying partnership, means the annual accounts, the directors'    report and the auditor's report required by regulation 4,

    'dealt with on a consolidated basis' means dealt with by the method of full consolidation, the method of proportional consolidation or the equity method of accounting,

    'financial year', in relation to a qualifying partnership, means any period of not more than 18 months in respect of which a profit and loss account of the partnership is required to be made up by or in accordance with its constitution or, failing any such requirement, each period of 12 months beginning with 1st April, 'the Fourth Directive' means the Fourth Council Directive (78/660/EEC) of 25th July 1978 on the    annual accounts of certain types of companies[163],

'general partner' has the same meaning as in the Limited Partnerships Act 1907[164],

'the Large and Medium-sized Companies Accounts Regulations' means the Large and Medium-    sized Companies and Groups (Accounts and Reports) Regulations 2008[165],

'limited company' means a company limited by shares or limited by guarantee,

'limited partnership' means a partnership formed in accordance with the Limited Partnerships Act    1907,

'qualifying partnership' has the meaning given by regulation 3,

'the Seventh Directive' means the Seventh Council Directive (83/349/EEC) of 13th June 1983 on    consolidated accounts[166],

'the Small Companies Accounts Regulations' means the Small Companies and Groups (Accounts    and Directors' Report) Regulations 2008[167],

and except as otherwise provided in these Regulations, words and expressions used in the Companies Act 2006 have the same meaning in these Regulations as they have in that Act.

(2) Any reference in these Regulations to the members of a qualifying partnership is to be construed, in relation to a limited partnership, as a reference to its general partner or partners.

## Qualifying partnerships

3. (1) A partnership which is formed under the law of any part of the United Kingdom is a qualifying partnership for the purposes of these Regulations if each of its members is—

(a) a limited company, or

(b) an unlimited company, or a Scottish partnership, each of whose members is a limited company.

(2) Where the members of a qualifying partnership include—

(a) an unlimited company, or a Scottish partnership, each of whose members is a limited company, or

(b) a member of another partnership each of whose members is—

(i) a limited company, or

(ii) an unlimited company, or a Scottish partnership, each of whose members is a limited company,

any reference in these Regulations to the members of the qualifying partnership includes a reference to the members of that company or other partnership.

(3) The requirements of these Regulations apply without regard to any change in the members of a qualifying partnership which does not result in it ceasing to be such a partnership.

(4) Any reference in paragraph (1) or (2) to a limited company, an unlimited company or a partnership includes a reference to any comparable undertaking incorporated in or formed under the law of any country or territory outside the United Kingdom.

# PART 2

# PARTNERSHIP ACCOUNTS

## Preparation of accounts of qualifying partnerships

4. (1) Subject to regulation 7, the persons who are members of a qualifying partnership at the end of any financial year of the partnership must, in respect of that year—

(a) prepare the like annual accounts and directors' report, and

---

[163] OJ L222, 14.8.1978, p 11. Relevant amendments to the Fourth Directive have been made by (i) the Seventh Council Directive (83/349/EEC) of 13th June 1983 on consolidated accounts (OJ L193, 18.7.1983, p 1); (ii) Council Directive (90/604/EEC) of 8th November 1990 on small and medium-sized companies (OJ L317, 16.11.1990, p 57), (iii) Directive 2001/65/EC on fair value accounting (OJ L283, 27.10.2001, p 28), (iv) Directive 2003/51/EC on accounts modernisation (OJ L178, 17.7.2003, p 16) and (v) Directive 2006/46/EC on company reporting (OJ L224, 16.8.2006, p 1).

[164] 1907 c.24.

[165] SI 2008/410.

[166] OJ L193, 18.7.1983, p 1. Relevant amendments to the Seventh Directive have been made by Council Directive (90/604/EEC) of 8th November 1990 on small and medium-sized companies (OJ L317, 16.11.1990, p 57), (iii) Directive 2001/65/EC on fair value accounting (OJ L283, 27.10.2001, p 28), (iv) Directive 2003/51/EC on accounts modernisation (OJ L178, 17.7.2003, p 16) and (v) Directive 2006/46/EC on company reporting (OJ L224, 16.8.2006, p 1).

[167] SI 2008/409.

(b) cause to be prepared such an auditor's report,

as would be required, if the partnership were a company, under Part 15 (accounts and reports) and Chapter 1 of Part 16 (requirement for audited accounts) of the Companies Act 2006, and under the Small Companies Accounts Regulations or the Large and Medium-sized Companies Accounts Regulations (as the case may be).

(2) Regulations 4 to 6 of the Companies (Disclosure of Auditor Remuneration and Liability Limitation Agreements) Regulations 2008[168] apply in relation to the accounts required by this regulation as they apply in relation to the annual accounts of a company or group.

(3) The accounts required by this regulation must—

(a) be prepared within the period of 9 months beginning immediately after the end of the partnership's financial year, and

(b) state that they are prepared under this regulation.

(4) Part 1 of the Schedule to these Regulations sets out certain modifications and adaptations for the purposes of this regulation.

### Delivery of accounts of qualifying partnerships to registrar etc.

**5.** (1) Subject to regulation 7, each limited company which is a member of a qualifying partnership at the end of any financial year of the partnership must append to the copy of its accounts and reports which is next delivered to the registrar in accordance with section 441(1) of the Companies Act 2006 (duty to file accounts and reports with the registrar) a copy of the accounts of the partnership prepared for that year under regulation 4.

(2) Subject to regulation 7, a limited company which is a member of a qualifying partnership must supply to any person upon request—

(a) the name of each member of the partnership which is to deliver, or has delivered, a copy of the latest accounts of the partnership to the registrar under paragraph (1), and

(b) the name of each member of the partnership incorporated in a member State other than the United Kingdom which is to publish, or has published, the latest accounts for the partnership in accordance with the provisions of the Fourth or Seventh Directive.

### Publication of accounts of qualifying partnerships at head office

**6.** (1) Subject to paragraph (2) and regulation 7, this regulation applies where a qualifying partnership's head office is in the United Kingdom and each of its members is—

(a) an undertaking comparable to a limited company which is incorporated in a country or territory outside the United Kingdom, or

(b) an undertaking comparable to an unlimited company or partnership—

(i) which is incorporated in or formed under the law of such a country or territory, and

(ii) each of whose members is such an undertaking as is mentioned in sub-paragraph (a).

(2) This regulation does not apply where any member of a qualifying partnership is—

(a) an undertaking comparable to a limited company which is incorporated in a member State other than the United Kingdom, or

(b) an undertaking comparable to an unlimited company or partnership—

(i) which is incorporated in or formed under the law of such a State, and

(ii) each of whose members is such an undertaking as is mentioned in sub-paragraph (a), and (in either case) the latest accounts of the qualifying partnership have been or are to be appended to the accounts of any member of the partnership and published under the law of that State and in accordance with the provisions of the Fourth or Seventh Directive.

(3) The members of the qualifying partnership—

(a) must make the latest accounts of the partnership available for inspection by any person, without charge and during business hours, at the head office of the partnership, and

(b) if any document comprised in those accounts is in a language other than English, must annex to that document a translation of it into English, certified as an accurate translation—

(i) if the translation was made in the United Kingdom, by—

(aa) a notary public in any part of the United Kingdom;

(bb) a solicitor (if the translation was made in Scotland), a solicitor of the Supreme Court of Judicature of England and Wales (if it was made in England or Wales), or a solicitor of the Supreme Court of Judicature of Northern Ireland (if it was made in Northern Ireland); or

(cc) a person certified by a person mentioned above to be known to be competent to translate the document into English; or

(ii) if the translation was made outside the United Kingdom, by—

(aa) a notary public;

(bb) a person authorised in the place where the translation was made to administer an oath;

---

[168] SI 2008/489.

> (cc) any of the British officials mentioned in section 6 of the Commissioners for Oaths Act 1889[169];
> (dd) a person certified by a person mentioned above to be known to be competent to translate the document into English.

(4) A member of the qualifying partnership must supply to any person upon request—

> (a) a copy of the accounts required by paragraph (3)(a) to be made available for inspection, and
> (b) a copy of any translation required by paragraph (3)(b) to be annexed to any document comprised in those accounts,
>
> at a price not exceeding the administrative cost of making the copy.

### Exemption from regulations 4 to 6 where accounts consolidated

**7.** (1) The members of a qualifying partnership are exempt from the requirements of regulations 4 to 6 if the partnership is dealt with on a consolidated basis in group accounts prepared by—

> (a) a member of the partnership which is established under the law of a member State, or
> (b) a parent undertaking of such a member which parent undertaking is so established,
>
> and (in either case) the conditions mentioned in paragraph (2) are complied with.

(2) The conditions are—

> (a) that the group accounts are prepared and audited under the law of the member State concerned in accordance with the provisions of the Seventh Directive or of international accounting standards, and
> (b) the notes to those accounts disclose that advantage has been taken of the exemption conferred by this regulation.

(3) Where advantage is taken of the exemption conferred by this regulation, any member of the qualifying partnership which is a limited company must disclose on request the name of at least one member or parent undertaking in whose group accounts the partnership has been or is to be dealt with on a consolidated basis.

## PART 3

## AUDITORS

### Appointment of auditor

**8.** An auditor may be appointed for the purposes of regulation 4(1)(b) only by the members of a qualifying partnership.

### Functions of auditor

**9.** (1) The following provisions of the Companies Act 2006 apply to the auditor of a qualifying partnership as they apply to an auditor of a company—

> (a) section 495 (auditor's report on company's annual accounts);
> (b) section 498 (duties of auditor);
> (c) section 499 (auditor's general right to information).

(2) The auditor of a qualifying partnership must supply the members of the qualifying partnership with such information as is necessary to enable any disclosure required by regulation 4(2) to be made.

### Signature of auditor's report

**10.** Sections 503 to 506 of the Companies Act 2006 (signature of auditor's report) apply in relation to the auditor's report required by regulation 4(1)(b), subject to—

> (a) any necessary modifications to take account of the fact that the qualifying partnership is unincorporated, and
> (b) the modification set out in Part 2 of the Schedule to these Regulations.

### Removal of auditors on improper grounds

**11.** (1) Where the auditor of a qualifying partnership is removed from office an application may be made to the High Court under this regulation.

(2) The persons who may make such an application are—

> (a) any member of the qualifying partnership who was also a member at the time of the removal, and
> (b) the Secretary of State.

(3) If the court is satisfied that the removal was—

> (a) on grounds of divergence of opinion on accounting treatments or audit procedures, or

---

[169] 1889 c.10.

(b)  on any other improper grounds,
it may make such order as it thinks fit for giving relief in respect of the removal.

(4)  The court may, in particular—

(a)  declare that any decision of the qualifying partnership removing an auditor, or appointing a new auditor in his place, is void;

(b)  require the members of the qualifying partnership to re-appoint the dismissed auditor;

(c)  give directions as to the conduct of the qualifying partnership's affairs in the future.

(5)  In the application of this regulation to a qualifying partnership formed under the law of Scotland or Northern Ireland, references to the High Court are to be read as references to the Court of Session or, as the case may be, the High Court in Northern Ireland.

### Duty of auditor to notify supervisory body

**12.** (1)  Where an auditor of a qualifying partnership ceases to hold office before the end of his term of office, he must notify the supervisory body of which he is a member.

(2)  The notice must—

(a)  inform the supervisory body that he has ceased to hold office, and

(b)  be accompanied by a statement of any circumstances connected with his ceasing to hold office.

(3)  The auditor must notify the supervisory body not more than 14 days after the date on which he ceases to hold office.

(4)  In this regulation and regulation 13, 'supervisory body' has the same meaning as in Part 42 of the Companies Act 2006 (statutory auditors) (see section 1217).

### Duty of members of qualifying partnership to notify supervisory body

**13.** (1)  Where an auditor of a qualifying partnership ceases to hold office before the end of his term of office, the members of the partnership must notify the supervisory body of which the auditor is a member.

(2)  The notice must—

(a)  inform the supervisory body that the auditor has ceased to hold office, and

(b)  be accompanied by a statement by the body of the reasons for his ceasing to hold office.

(3)  The members of the qualifying partnership must notify the supervisory body not more than 14 days after the date on which the auditor ceases to hold office.

### Statutory auditors

**14.**  For the purposes of section 1210(1)(h) of the Companies Act 2006 (meaning of 'statutory auditor')—

(a)  a qualifying partnership is a prescribed person, and

(b)  regulation 4(1)(b) is a prescribed enactment,
and accordingly a person appointed as auditor of a qualifying partnership for the purposes of regulation 4(1)(b) is a statutory auditor.

## PART 4

## OFFENCES

### Penalties for non-compliance by members of qualifying partnership

**15.** (1)  If, in respect of a financial year of a qualifying partnership, the requirements of paragraph (1) of regulation 4 are not complied with within the period referred to in paragraph (3) of that regulation, every person who was a member of the partnership or a director of such a member at the end of that year is liable on summary conviction to a fine not exceeding level 5 on the standard scale.

(2)  If the accounts of a qualifying partnership—

(a)  a copy of which is delivered to the registrar under regulation 5, or

(b)  which are made available for inspection under regulation 6,
do not comply with the requirements of regulation 4(1), every person who, at the time when the copy was so delivered or (as the case may be) the accounts were first made available for inspection, was a member of the partnership or a director of such a member is liable on summary conviction to a fine not exceeding level 5 on the standard scale.

(3)  If a member of a qualifying partnership fails to comply with regulation 5, 6, 7(3) or 13, that member and any director of that member is liable on summary conviction to a fine not exceeding level 5 on the standard scale.

(4)  In proceedings for an offence under this section it is a defence for the person charged to show that he took all reasonable steps and exercised all due diligence to avoid the commission of the offence.

(5)  The following provisions of the Companies Act 2006, namely—

(a) sections 1127 and 1128 (summary proceedings: venue and time limit for proceedings), and

(b) section 1130 (proceedings against unincorporated bodies),

apply to an offence under this regulation.

### Penalties for non-compliance by auditors of qualifying partnerships

**16.** (1) If a person ceasing to hold office as auditor fails to comply with regulation 12, an offence is committed by—

(a) that person, and

(b) if that person is a firm, every officer of the firm who is in default.

(2) In proceedings for an offence under this section it is a defence for the person charged to show that he took all reasonable steps and exercised all due diligence to avoid the commission of the offence.

(3) A person guilty of an offence under this regulation is liable—

(a) on conviction on indictment, to a fine, and

(b) on summary conviction, to a fine not exceeding the statutory maximum.

(4) The following provisions of the Companies Act 2006, namely—

(a) sections 1121 to 1123 (liability of officer in default),

(b) sections 1127 and 1128 (summary proceedings: venue and time limit for proceedings), and

(c) section 1130 (proceedings against unincorporated bodies),

apply to an offence under this regulation.

## PART 5

## FINAL PROVISIONS

### Consequential amendments

**17.** (1) In the following provisions of the Small Companies Accounts Regulations, for 'Partnerships and Unlimited Companies (Accounts) Regulations 1993' substitute 'Partnerships (Accounts) Regulations 2008'—

(a) paragraph 8(5) and (6) in Part 1 of Schedule 2, and

(b) paragraph 34(5) and (6) in Part 2 of Schedule 6.

(2) In paragraph 7(5) and (6) in Part 1 of Schedule 4 to the Large and Medium-sized Companies Accounts Regulations for 'Partnerships and Unlimited Companies (Accounts) Regulations 1993' substitute 'Partnerships (Accounts) Regulations 2008'.

### Revocation and transitional provisions etc.

**18** (1) The Partnerships and Unlimited Companies (Accounts) Regulations 1993[170] and the Partnerships and Unlimited Companies (Accounts) Regulations (Northern Ireland) 1994[171] are revoked.

(2) The regulations specified in paragraph (1) continue to apply to any financial year of a qualifying partnership beginning before 6th April 2008.

## SCHEDULE

Regulation 4(4) and 10(b)

## MODIFICATIONS AND ADAPTATIONS FOR PURPOSES OF REGULATION 4

**1.** (1) Accounts prepared under regulation 4 of these Regulations must comply with the requirements of Part 15 and Chapter 1 of Part 16 of the Companies Act 2006, and with the Small Companies Accounts Regulations or the Large and Medium-sized Companies Accounts Regulations (as the case may be) subject to—

(a) the provisions of section 1161(2) and (3) of that Act (how to construe 'shares' and other expressions appropriate to companies),

(b) the omission of the provisions of the Small Companies Accounts Regulations mentioned in paragraph 2(1) below,

(c) the omission of the provisions of the Large and Medium-sized Companies Accounts Regulations mentioned in paragraph 2(2) below, and

(d) any necessary modifications to take account of the fact that partnerships are unincorporated.

(2) For the purposes of the provisions of Part 15 and Chapter 1 of Part 16 of the Companies Act

---

[170] SI 1993/1820.

[171] SR 1994/133, as amended by SR 2006/354.

2006 and of the Small Companies Accounts Regulations and the Large and Medium-sized Companies Accounts Regulations as applied to the accounts and report so prepared, these Regulations are to be regarded as part of the requirements of that Act and those regulations.

**2.** (1) The provisions of the Small Companies Accounts Regulations referred to in paragraph 1(1)(b) are—

    (a) in Part 1 of Schedule 1—

        (i) in paragraph 3(2), the words from 'used' to the end, and

        (ii) paragraph 6,

    (b) in Part 2 of Schedule 1, paragraph 21,

    (c) in Part 3 of Schedule 1, paragraphs 49 and 50,

    (d) in Part 1 of Schedule 2, paragraph 10,

    (e) in Part 1 of Schedule 3, paragraph 3,

    (f) Schedule 5, and

    (g) in Part 1 of Schedule 6, paragraphs 13(3) and (4), 14 and 15, and in Part 2 of that Schedule, paragraph 36.

(2) The provisions of the Large and Medium-sized Companies Accounts Regulations referred to in paragraph 1(1)(c) are—

    (a) in Part 1 of Schedule 1—

        (i) in paragraph 3(2), the words from 'used' to the end, and

        (ii) paragraph 6,

    (b) in Part 2 of Schedule 1, paragraph 21,

    (c) in Part 3 of Schedule 1, paragraphs 45, 50, 52, 53, 54, 64(2), 66 and 67,

    (d) in Part 1 of Schedule 4, paragraph 9, and in Part 2 paragraph 12,

    (e) in Schedule 5, paragraphs 2, 4 and 5,

    (f) in Part 1 of Schedule 6 to those Regulations, paragraphs 13(3) and (4), 14 and 15, and

    (g) Schedule 7 to those Regulations except paragraph 7.

(3) Sub-paragraphs (1) and (2) are not to be construed as affecting the requirement to give a true and fair view under sections 393, 396 and 404 of the Companies Act 2006.

## PART 2

### MODIFICATION FOR PURPOSES OF REGULATION 10

**3.** In section 506(1)(b) of the Companies Act 2006 the reference to the copy of the report delivered to the registrar under Chapter 10 of Part 15 (filing of accounts and reports) is treated as a reference to the copy of the accounts required to be delivered to the registrar under regulation 5(1).

---

# THE COMPANIES (AUTHORISED MINIMUM) REGULATIONS 2008

## (SI 2008/729)

COMMENCEMENT DATE 1 October 2008

**Citation, commencement and interpretation**

**1.** (1) These Regulations may be cited as the Companies (Authorised Minimum) Regulations 2008 and shall come into force on 6th April 2008.

(2) In these Regulations—

    'the 1985 Act' means the Companies Act 1985[172];

    'the 1986 Order' means the Companies (Northern Ireland) Order 1986[173];

    'the 2006 Act' means the Companies Act 2006;

    'the appropriate spot rate of exchange' is to be interpreted in accordance with regulation 4(1);

    'the certified spot rate' has the meaning given in regulation 4(3);

    'published spot rate' has the meaning given in regulation 4(2);

    'reference date' is to be interpreted in accordance with regulation 4(7) and (8);

    'relevant day' is to be interpreted in accordance with regulation 4(5) and (6); and

---

[172] 1985 c.6.
[173] SI 1986/1032 (NI 6).

'working day' means a day which is not a Saturday or Sunday, Christmas Day, Good Friday or any    day that is a bank holiday under the Banking and Financial Dealings Act 1971[174] in England and Wales.

## Authorised minimum in euros

**2.** [...]ᵃ

AMENDMENTS

ᵃ Revoked by the Companies (Authorised Minimum) Regulations 2009, S.I. 2009/2425, reg 8.

## Application of the authorised minimum where a public company has shares denominated in more than one currency

**3.** (1) This regulation applies for either of the purposes in paragraphs (2) and (3).

(2) The first purpose is to determine whether, for the purposes of section 139 of the 1985 Act or Article 149 of the 1986 Order, a court order under section 137 of the 1985 Act or Article 147 of the 1986 Order has the effect of bringing the nominal value of a public company's allotted share capital below the authorised minimum.

(3) The second purpose is to determine whether, for the purposes of section 146(2)(b) of the 1985 Act or Article 156(2)(b) of the 1986 Order, the cancellation of a public company's shares under that section or that Article will have the effect of bringing the nominal value of the company's allotted share capital below the authorised minimum.

(4) This regulation applies only where the company has or will have allotted share capital denominated in more than one currency, taking account (where the purpose is that in paragraph (2)) of the effect of the court order or (where the purpose is that in paragraph (3)) of the cancellation of the shares.

(5) The nominal value of a public company's allotted share capital is to be treated as being below the authorised minimum if—

(a) the sterling value is less than £50,000; and

(b) the euro value is less than £65,600.

(6) The 'sterling value' is the sum in sterling of—

(a) the nominal value of the company's allotted share capital denominated in sterling;

(b) the nominal value of the company's allotted share capital denominated in euros if it were to be converted into sterling at the appropriate spot rate of exchange; and

(c) the nominal value of the company's allotted share capital denominated in a currency other than sterling or euros if it were to be converted into sterling at the appropriate spot rate of exchange.

(7) The 'euro value' is the sum in euros of—

(a) the nominal value of the company's allotted share capital denominated in euros;

(b) the nominal value of the company's allotted share capital denominated in sterling if it were to be converted into euros at the appropriate spot rate of exchange; and

(c) the nominal value of the company's allotted share capital denominated in a currency other than sterling or euros if it were to be converted into euros at the appropriate spot rate of exchange.

(8) Regulation 4 applies to determine the appropriate spot rate of exchange.

## The appropriate spot rate of exchange

**4.** (1) The appropriate spot rate of exchange for a currency conversion referred to in regulation 3(6) and (7) is the published spot rate relevant to the currency conversion in question or, where the circumstances in paragraph (4) exist, the certified spot rate relevant to that currency conversion.

(2) The published spot rate is the middle spot exchange rate prevailing on the foreign exchange market at 4pm on the relevant day as published in respect of that day by the Financial Times.

(3) The certified spot rate is the middle spot exchange rate prevailing on the foreign exchange market at 4pm on the relevant day and stated in a certificate obtained by the company from—

(a) a person, nominated by the company, who under Part 4 of the Financial Services and Markets Act 2000[175] has permission to accept deposits; or

(b) a firm, nominated by the company, which has permission to carry on the activity of accepting deposits in the United Kingdom by virtue of Schedule 3 to that Act.

(4) The circumstances in this paragraph exist where—

(a) the Financial Times has not, on or before the reference date, published an exchange rate referred to in paragraph (2) relevant to the currency conversion in question; or

(b) the Financial Times has, on or before the reference date, published what appears to be

---

[174] 1971 c.80.
[175] 2000 c.8.

an exchange rate referred to in paragraph (2) relevant to the currency conversion in question but the company can show that there was a publication error; or

(c) there is no evidence of what (if any) was the rate referred to in paragraph (2) relevant to the currency conversion in question as published on or before the reference date by the Financial Times.

(5) Where the currency conversion is relevant to the calculation of the sterling value or the euro value for the purpose in regulation 3(2), the 'relevant day' is the working day which immediately preceded the working day immediately preceding the date of the court order under section 137 of the 1985 Act or Article 147 of the 1986 Order.

(6) Where the currency conversion is relevant to the calculation of the sterling value or the euro value for the purpose in regulation 3(3), the 'relevant day' is—

(a) in a case within section 146(1)(a) or (aa)[176] of the 1985 Act or Article 156(1)(a) or (aa)[177] of the 1986 Order, the working day immediately preceding the date of the forfeiture or surrender; and

(b) in a case within section 146(1)(b), (c) or (d) of the 1985 Act or Article 156(1)(b), (c) or (d) of the 1986 Order, the working day immediately preceding the date of the acquisition.

(7) Where the currency calculation is relevant to the calculation of the sterling value or the euro value for the purpose in regulation 3(2), the 'reference date' is the date of the court order under section 137 of the 1985 Act or Article 147 of the 1986 Order.

(8) Where the currency conversion is relevant to the calculation of the sterling value or the euro value for the purpose in regulation 3(3), the 'reference date' is—

(a) in the case within section 146(1)(a) or (aa) of the 1985 Act or Article 156(1)(a) or (aa) of the 1986 Order, the fifth working day following the date of the forfeiture or surrender; and

(b) in the case within section 146(1)(b), (c) or (d) of the 1985 Act or Article 156(1)(b), (c) or (d) of the 1986 Order, the fifth working day following the date of the acquisition.

**Registration of a court order confirming a capital reduction and applications by public companies for re-registration: assumptions which may be made by the registrar**

5. (1) This regulation applies where—

(a) a public company delivers to the registrar under section 138 of the 1985 Act or Article 148 of the 1986 Order a copy of an order of the court confirming a reduction of its share capital and the court has not directed the order to be registered; or

(b) an application is made to the registrar under section 147(3) of the 1985 Act or Article 157(3) of the 1986 Order for re-registration of a public company as a private company.

(2) Where the circumstances in paragraph (3), (4) or (5) exist, the registrar may make (in a case within paragraph (1)(a)) the assumption in paragraph (6) or (in a case within paragraph (1)(b)) the assumption in paragraph (7).

(3) The circumstances in this paragraph are that—

(a) the company has or will have (taking account, where the case is within paragraph (1)(a), of the effect of the court order or, where the case is within paragraph (1)(b), of the effect of the cancellation of shares under section 146(2)(a) of the 1985 Act or Article 156(2)(a) of the 1986 Order) allotted share capital denominated in more than one currency;

(b) either the Financial Times did not publish, on or before the reference date, an exchange rate referred to in regulation 4(2) relevant to converting into sterling a currency in which the company's allotted share capital is denominated or it did not publish, on or before that date, such a rate relevant to converting such a currency into euros; and

(c) the company has not delivered to the registrar, in respect of every such currency for which the Financial Times did not publish such an exchange rate on or before the reference date, a copy of a certificate referred to in regulation 4(3).

(4) The circumstances in this paragraph are that—

(a) the company has or will have (taking account, where the case is within paragraph (1)(a), of the effect of the court order or, where the case is within paragraph (1)(b), of the effect of the cancellation of shares under section 146(2)(a) of the 1985 Act or Article 156(2)(a) of the 1986 Order) allotted share capital denominated in more than one currency;

(b) the Financial Times published, on or before the reference date, what appears to be an exchange rate referred to in regulation 4(2) relevant to converting into sterling or euros a currency in which the company's allotted share capital is denominated but the company can show that there was a publication error; and

(c) the company has not delivered to the registrar, for every currency in respect of which the

---

[176] Section 146(1)(aa) was inserted by the Building Societies Act 1986, section 102C(5). Section 102C(5) of that Act was inserted by the Building Societies (Distributions) Act 1997, section 1(1).

[177] Article 156(1)(aa) was inserted by the Building Societies Act 1986, section 102C(6). Section 102C(6) of that Act was inserted by the Building Societies (Distributions) Act 1997, section 1(1).

company can show such a publication error, a copy of a certificate referred to in regulation 4(3).

(5) The circumstances in this paragraph are that—

  (a) the company has or will have (taking account, where the case is within paragraph (1)(a), of the effect of the court order or, where the case is within paragraph (1)(b), of the effect of the cancellation of shares under section 146(2)(a) of the 1985 Act or Article 156(2)(a) of the 1986 Order) allotted share capital denominated in more than one currency;

  (b) in respect of one or more of the exchange rates referred to in regulation 4(2) relevant to converting into sterling or euros the currencies in which the company's allotted share capital is denominated there is no evidence of what (if any) was the rate published on or before the reference date by the Financial Times; and

  (c) the company has not delivered to the registrar, for every such currency in respect of which there is no such evidence, a copy of a certificate referred to in regulation 4(3).

(6) The registrar may (but is not required to) assume for the purposes of sections 138(1) and 139(2) of the 1985 Act or Articles 148(1) and 149(2) of the 1986 Order that the court order has the effect of bringing the nominal value of the company's allotted share capital below the authorised minimum.

(7) The registrar may (but is not required to) assume for the purposes of section 147(4) of the 1985 Act or Article 157(4) of the 1986 Order that the effect of the cancellation of shares under section 146(2)(a) of the 1985 Act or Article 156(2)(a) of the 1986 Order is or will be that the nominal value of the company's allotted share capital is brought below the authorised minimum.

### Determination of exchange rates by the court in certain proceedings

**6.** (1) This regulation applies to—

  (a) proceedings against a public company or any officer of a public company for an offence under section 149(2) of the 1985 Act or Article 159(2) of the 1986 Order; and

  (b) proceedings under section 757 or 758 or Part 30 of the 2006 Act.

(2) Where the circumstances in paragraph (3) exist, the court may make a determination referred to in paragraph (4) in the proceedings.

(3) The circumstances are that—

  (a) in proceedings referred to in paragraph (1)(a) it is alleged that, or in proceedings referred to in paragraph (1)(b) the question arises whether, the effect of a cancellation of the company's shares under section 146(2)(a) of the 1985 Act or Article 156(2)(a) of the 1986 Order was or will be that the nominal value of the company's allotted share capital was or is brought below the authorised minimum; and

  (b) as a result of that cancellation the company had (or continued to have) allotted share capital denominated in more than one currency.

(4) The court may make such determination as it thinks fit as to the exchange rate to be applied to a currency conversion referred to in regulation 3(6) and (7) where—

  (a) the Financial Times did not publish, on or before the reference date, an exchange rate referred to in regulation 4(2) relevant to that currency conversion; or

  (b) the Financial Times published, on or before the reference date, what appears to be an exchange rate referred to in regulation 4(2) relevant to that currency conversion but the company or officer of the company (as the case may be) can show that there was a publication error; or

  (c) there is no evidence of what (if any) was the exchange rate referred to in regulation 4(2) as published on or before the reference date by the Financial Times relevant to that currency conversion,

    and there has not been produced to the court in the proceedings a copy of a certificate referred to in regulation 4(3) in respect of that currency conversion.

(5) In this regulation, 'the court' in relation to proceedings referred to in paragraph (1)(a) means the court of criminal jurisdiction in which the proceedings are brought.

### Exclusion of liability in respect of publication of spot rate

**7.** No person shall be liable to any other person as a result of—

  (a) that or any other person having placed reliance for the purposes of these Regulations upon a rate published by the Financial Times; or

  (b) any error in a rate published by the Financial Times which is relied upon for the purposes of these Regulations; or

  (c) any act or omission as a result of which the Financial Times did not publish a rate capable of being relied upon for the purposes of these Regulations.

# The Companies Act 1985 (Annual Return) and Companies (Principal Business Activities) (Amendment) Regulations 2008

## (SI 2008/1659)

Commencement Date 1 October 2008

**SI.23**

### Citation, commencement

**1.** (1) These Regulations may be cited as the Companies Act 1985 (Annual Return) and Companies (Principal Business Activities) (Amendment) Regulations 2008.

(2) These Regulations come into force on 1st October 2008 and apply in relation to annual returns made up to that date or a later date.

### Information about whether shares admitted to trading on regulated market

**2.** (1) In section 364 of the Companies Act 1985 (contents of annual return: general), in subsection (1), after paragraph (i), insert—

'(j) whether the company was a traded company at any time during the return period.'.

### Information about shareholders

**3.** In section 364A of the Companies Act 1985 (contents of annual return: particulars of share capital and shareholders)—

(a) in the heading omit 'and shareholders';

(b) in subsection (1) omit 'and members'; and

(c) omit subsections (4) to (7).

**4.** After that section insert—

### 'Contents of annual return: information about shareholders: non-traded companies

**364B.** The annual return of a company that was a non-traded company throughout the return period must also contain the following information.

(2) The return must contain a list of the names of every person who was a member of the company at any time during the return period. If the names are not arranged in alphabetical order the return must have annexed to it an index sufficient to enable the name of any person in the list to be easily found.

(3) The return must also state—

(a) the number of shares of each class held at the end of the date to which the return is made up by each person who was a member of the company at that time,

(b) the number of shares of each class transferred during the return period by or to each person who was a member of the company at any time during that period, and

(c) the dates of registration of those transfers.

(4) If either of the two immediately preceding returns has given the full particulars required by subsections (2) and (3), the return need only give such particulars as relate—

(a) to persons who became, or ceased to be, members during the return period, and

(b) to shares transferred during that period.

(5) Subsections (2) and (3) do not require the inclusion of particulars entered in an overseas branch register if copies of those entries have not been received at the company's registered office by the date to which the return is made up. Those particulars must be included in the company's next annual return after they are received.

### Contents of annual return: information about shareholders: traded companies

**364C.** The annual return of a company that was a traded company at any time during the return period must also contain the following information.

(2) The return must contain a list of the names and addresses of every person who held at least 5% of the issued shares of any class of the company at any time during the return period. If the names are not arranged in alphabetical order the return must have annexed to it an index sufficient to enable the name of any person in the list to be easily found.

(3) The return must also state—

(a) the number of shares of each class held at the end of the date to which the return is made up by each person who held at least 5% of the issued shares of any class of the company at that time,

(b) the number of shares of each class transferred during the return period by or to each person who held at least 5% of the issued shares of any class of the company at any time during the return period, and

(c) the dates of registration of those transfers.

(4) If either of the two immediately preceding returns has given the full particulars required by subsections (2) and (3), the return need only give such particulars as relate—

(a) to persons who came to hold, or ceased to hold, at least 5% of the issued shares of any class of the company during the return period, and

(b) to shares transferred during that period.

(5) Subsections (2) and (3) do not require the inclusion of particulars entered in an overseas branch register if copies of those entries have not been received at the company's registered office by the date to which the return is made up. Those particulars must be included in the company's next annual return after they are received.

## Contents of annual return: information about shareholders: supplementary

**364D.** In sections 364, 364B and 364C—

'non-traded company' means a company none of whose shares are shares admitted to trading on a regulated market (so that 'traded company' means a company any of whose shares are shares admitted to trading on a regulated market);

'regulated market' means a market which appears on the list drawn up by an EEA State pursuant to Article 47 of Directive 2004/39/EC of the European Parliament and of the Council of 21 April 2004 on markets in financial instruments[178]; and

'return period', in relation to an annual return, means the period beginning immediately after the date to which the last return was made up (or, in the case of the first return, with the incorporation of the company) and ending with the date to which the return is made up.

(2) Where a company has converted any of its shares into stock, the return must give information in relation to that stock corresponding to that required by section 364B or 364C (as the case may be) in relation to shares of the company, stating the amount of stock instead of the number of shares.'.

### Amendments relating to principal business activities

**5.** (1) The Companies (Forms Amendment No. 2 and Company's Type and Principal Business Activities) Regulations 1990[179] are amended as follows.

(2) In Part II of Schedule 3 to those Regulations—

(a) before '9800 RESIDENTS' PROPERTY MANAGEMENT COMPANY' insert '7499 NON-TRADING COMPANY'; and

(b) after '9800 RESIDENTS' PROPERTY MANAGEMENT COMPANY' insert '9999 DORMANT COMPANY'.

---

# THE COMPANY NAMES ADJUDICATOR RULES 2008

## (SI 2008/1738)

COMMENCEMENT DATE 1 October 2008

## INTRODUCTION

### Citation, commencement and interpretation                                SI.24

**1.** (1) These Rules may be cited as the Company Names Adjudicator Rules 2008 and come into force on 1st October 2008.

(2) In these Rules—

'the Act' means the Companies Act 2006 and references to a 'section' are to a section of the Act;

'the appropriate form' means the form determined by the Chief Adjudicator in relation to a particular matter; and

'the Office' means the office of the company names adjudicator at the Intellectual Property Office, Concept House, Cardiff Road, Newport, South Wales, NP10 8QQ.

(3) In these Rules references to the filing of any application or other document are to be construed as references to its being delivered to the adjudicator at the Office.

---

[178] OJ No. L145, 30.4.2004, p 1
[179] 1990/1766, amended by SI 1996/1105, 2002/3081.

**Forms and fees**

**2.** (1) The Chief Adjudicator shall have the power to determine the form and content of any form required to be used by these Rules.

(2) Where a form is required to be used by these Rules that form shall be accompanied by the fee, if any, specified in the Schedule in respect of that matter.

**Proceedings before the adjudicator**

Procedure for objecting to a company's registered name

**3.** (1) An application under section 69(2) shall—

(a) be made on the appropriate form;

(b) include a concise statement of the grounds on which the application is made;

(c) include an address for service in the United Kingdom; and

(d) be filed at the Office.

(2) The adjudicator shall send a copy of the appropriate form to the primary respondent.

(3) The adjudicator shall specify a period within which the primary respondent must file its defence.

(4) The primary respondent, before the end of that period, shall file a counter-statement on the appropriate form, otherwise the adjudicator may treat it as not opposing the application and may make an order under section 73(1).

(5) In its counter-statement the primary respondent shall—

(a) include an address for service in the United Kingdom;

(b) include a concise statement of the grounds on which it relies;

(c) state which of the allegations in the statement of grounds of the applicant it admits and which it denies; and

(d) state which of the allegations it is unable to admit or deny, but which it requires the applicant to prove.

(6) Any member or director of the primary respondent who is joined as a respondent to the application must be joined before the end of a period specified by the adjudicator.

(7) The adjudicator shall send a copy of the appropriate form referred to in paragraph (4) to the applicant.

**Evidence rounds**

**4.** (1) When the period specified under rule 3(3) has expired, the adjudicator shall specify the periods within which evidence may be filed by the parties.

(2) All evidence must be—

(a) accompanied by the appropriate form, and

(b) copied to all other parties in the proceedings.

**Decision of adjudicator and hearings**

**5.** (1) Where the applicant files no evidence in support of its application the adjudicator may treat it as having withdrawn its application.

(2) The adjudicator may strike out the application or any defence in whole or in part if it is vexatious, has no reasonable prospect of success or is otherwise misconceived.

(3) Any party may, by filing the appropriate form, request to be heard in person before a decision is made by the adjudicator under the Act or these Rules.

(4) Following a request under rule 5(3) the adjudicator shall decide whether a decision can be made without an oral hearing in circumstances where—

(a) the primary respondent files no evidence; or

(b) the applicant files no evidence in reply to the respondent's evidence; or

(c) the decision will not terminate the proceedings.

(5) Where the adjudicator decides that a decision can be made without an oral hearing the adjudicator will specify a period for the parties to submit written submissions before making a decision.

(6) Where the adjudicator decides that a hearing is necessary he shall require the parties or their legal representatives to attend a hearing and shall give the parties at least 14 days' notice of the hearing.

(7) When the adjudicator has made a decision on the application under section 69(2) he shall send to the parties written notice of it, stating the reasons for his decision.

(8) The date on which the decision was sent to the parties shall be taken to be the date of the decision for the purposes of any appeal.

**General powers of adjudicator in relation to proceedings before him**

**6.** (1) At any stage of proceedings before him, the adjudicator may direct that the parties to the proceedings attend a case management conference or pre-hearing review.

(2) The adjudicator may give such directions as to the management of the proceedings as he thinks fit, and in particular he may—

(a) direct a document to be filed or to be copied to a party to proceedings within a specified period;

(b) allow for the electronic filing and sending of documents;

(c) direct how documents filed or sent electronically are to be authenticated;

(d) direct that a document shall not be available for public inspection;

(e) require a translation of any document;

(f) direct that a witness be cross-examined;

(g) consolidate proceedings;

(h) direct that proceedings are to be heard by more than one adjudicator;

(i) direct that part of any proceedings be dealt with as separate proceedings; or

(j) suspend or stay proceedings.

(3) The adjudicator may control the evidence by giving directions as to—

(a) the issues on which he requires evidence;

(b) the nature of the evidence which he requires to decide those issues; and

(c) the way in which the evidence is to be placed before him, and the adjudicator may use his power under this paragraph to exclude evidence which would otherwise be admissible.

### Requests for extensions of time

**7.** (1) The adjudicator may extend (or further extend) any period which has been specified under any provision of these Rules even if the period has expired.

(2) Any party can request an extension of any time period specified under any provision of these Rules.

(3) Any request for a retrospective extension must be filed before the end of the period of 2 months beginning with the date the time period in question expired.

(4) Any request made under paragraph (2) shall be made on the appropriate form and shall include reasons why the extra time is required. A request for a retrospective extension shall also include reasons why the request is being made out of time.

### Public proceedings

**8.** (1) Subject to paragraphs (3) and (4), any hearing before the adjudicator of proceedings relating to an application under section 69(2) shall be held in public.

(2) Any party to the proceedings may apply to the adjudicator for the hearing to be held in private.

(3) The adjudicator shall only grant an application under paragraph (2) where—

(a) it is in the interests of justice for the hearing to be in held in private; and

(b) all the parties to the proceedings have had an opportunity to be heard on the matter, and where the application is granted the hearing shall be held in private.

(4) Any hearing of an application under paragraph (2) shall be held in private.

(5) In this rule a reference to a hearing includes any part of a hearing.

(6) Nothing in this rule shall prevent a member of the Administrative Justice and Tribunals Council or of its Scottish Committee from attending a hearing.

(7) All documents connected to proceedings shall be available for public inspection unless the adjudicator directs otherwise.

### Evidence in proceedings before the adjudicator

**9.** (1) Subject to rule 6(3), evidence filed under these Rules may be given—

(a) by witness statement, affidavit or statutory declaration; or

(b) in any other form which would be admissible as evidence in proceedings before the court, and a witness statement may only be given in evidence if it includes a statement of truth.

(2) For the purposes of these Rules, a statement of truth—

(a) means a statement that the person making the statement believes that the facts stated in a particular document are true; and

(b) shall be dated and signed by the maker of the statement.

(3) In these Rules, a witness statement is a written statement signed by a person that contains the evidence which that person would be allowed to give orally.

### Correction of irregularities of procedure

**10.** (1) Any irregularity in procedure may be rectified on such terms as the adjudicator may direct.

(2) Where rectification includes the amendment of a document by the adjudicator the parties will be given notice of this amendment.

*Costs or expenses*

### Costs or expenses of proceedings

**11.** The adjudicator may, at any stage in any proceedings before him under the Act, award to any party by order such costs (in Scotland, expenses) as he considers reasonable, and direct how and by what parties they are to be paid.

### Security for costs or expenses

**12.** An application for security for costs (in Scotland, caution for expenses) shall be made on the appropriate form. The adjudicator may require a person to give security for costs (in Scotland, caution for expenses) if he is satisfied, having regard to all the circumstances of the case, that it is just to require such security or caution.

*Address for service*

### Address for service

**13.** (1) Where a person has provided an address for service in the United Kingdom under rule 3 he may substitute a new address for service in the United Kingdom by notifying the adjudicator on the appropriate form.

(2) Where the primary respondent has a registered office in the United Kingdom the adjudicator may treat this as the address for service in the United Kingdom unless and until an alternative address is provided.

*Miscellaneous*

### Hours of business

**14.** (1) For the transaction of relevant business by the public under the Act the Office shall be open—
  (a) on Monday to Friday between 9.00 am and midnight; and
  (b) on Saturday between 9.00 am and 1.00 pm, unless the day is an excluded day (see rule 15).

(2) For the transaction of all other business by the public under the Act the Office shall be open on Monday to Friday between 9.00 am and 5.00 pm unless the day is an excluded day (see rule 15).

(3) In this rule and in rule 15 'relevant business' means the filing of any application or other document.

### Excluded days

**15.** (1) The following shall be excluded days for the transaction of any business by the public under the Act—
  (a) a Sunday;
  (b) Good Friday;
  (c) Christmas Day;
  (d) a day which is specified or proclaimed to be a bank holiday by or under section 1 of the Banking and Financial Dealings Act 1971[180]; or
  (e) a Saturday where the previous Friday and the following Monday are both excluded days.

(2) Any application or document received on an excluded day shall be treated as having been filed on the next day on which the Office is open for relevant business.

(3) Where any period for filing any document ends on an excluded day that period shall be extended to the next day on which the Office is open for relevant business.

## SCHEDULE
### FEES

| Form | Fee (£) |
| --- | --- |
| Form required by rule 3(1) | 400 |
| Form required by rule 3(4) | 150 |
| Form required by rule 4(2) | 150 |
| Form required by rule 5(3) | 100 |
| Form required by rule 7(4) | 100 |
| Form required by rule 12 | 150 |

[180] 1971 c.80.

# THE COMPANIES (REDUCTION OF SHARE CAPITAL) ORDER 2008
## (SI 2008/1915)

COMMENCEMENT DATE 1 October 2008

**1.** (1) This Order may be cited as the Companies (Reduction of Share Capital) Order 2008 and    **SI.25**
comes into force on 1st October 2008.

(2) In this Order, 'the Act' means the Companies Act 2006.

**2.** A solvency statement under section 643 of the Act must—

    (a) be in writing,

    (b) indicate that it is a solvency statement for the purposes of section 642 of the Act, and

    (c) be signed by each of the directors.

**3.** (1) If an unlimited company reduces its share capital—

    (a) the prohibition in section 654(1) of the Act does not apply, and

    (b) a reserve arising from the reduction is to be treated for the purposes of Part 23 of the Act
    as a realised profit.

(2) If a private company limited by shares reduces its share capital and the reduction is supported
by a solvency statement but has not been the subject of an application to the court for an
order confirming it—

    (a) the prohibition in section 654(1) of the Act does not apply, and

    (b) a reserve arising from the reduction is to be treated for the purposes of Part 23 of the Act
    as a realised profit.

(3) If a limited company having a share capital reduces its share capital and the reduction is
confirmed by order of the court—

    (a) the prohibition in section 654(1) of the Act does not apply, and

    (b) a reserve arising from the reduction is to be treated for the purposes of Part 23 of the Act
    as a realised profit unless the court orders otherwise under section 648(1) of the Act.

(4) This article is without prejudice to any contrary provision of—

    (a) an order of, or undertaking given to, the court,

    (b) the resolution for, or any other resolution relevant to, the reduction of share capital, or

    (c) the company's memorandum or articles of association.

# THE STATUTORY AUDITORS AND THIRD COUNTRY AUDITORS
## (AMENDMENT) (NO. 2) REGULATIONS 2008
### (SI 2008/2639)

COMMENCEMENT DATE 31 October 2008[181]

**1.** These Regulations may be cited as the Statutory Auditors and Third Country Auditors (Amend-    **SI.26**
ment) (No. 2) Regulations 2008 and come into force on 31st October 2008.

**2.** (1) The Statutory Auditors and Third Country Auditors Regulations 2007[182] are amended as
follows.

(2) For regulation 29 (interpretation) substitute—

'**29.** In this Part of these Regulations—

"the Commission Decision" means Commission Decision 2008/627/EC of 29 July 2008
concerning a transitional period for audit activities of certain third country auditors
and audit entities[183];

"the designated body" means the body known as the Professional Oversight Board
established under the articles of association of The Financial Reporting Council
Limited[184];

"exempt third country auditor" means a third country auditor—

    (a) who is—

---

[181] 2006 c. 46.

[182] SI 2007/3494, amended by SI 2008/499.

[183] OJ L202, 31.7.2008, p 70.

[184] Registered number 02486368.

           (i)   overseen or regulated by a third country competent authority established in a specified third country, and

           (ii)  eligible to conduct audits of the accounts of bodies corporate incorporated or formed under the law of that specified third country; and

    (b)  in relation to whom the designated body has, for the purposes of the Commission Decision, directed under section 1239(7) of the Companies Act 2006[185] that requirements imposed by this Part specified in the direction are not to apply;

"specified third country" means any of the Channel Islands, the Isle of Man and the following countries and territories—

Argentina, Australia, The Bahamas, Bermuda, Brazil, Canada, Cayman Islands, Chile, China, Croatia, Hong Kong, India, Indonesia, Israel, Japan, Kazakhstan, Malaysia, Mauritius, Mexico, Morocco, New Zealand, Pakistan, Russia, Singapore, South Africa, South Korea, Switzerland, Taiwan, Thailand, Turkey, Ukraine, United Arab Emirates, United States of America.'.

(3)  In regulation 35 (application for registration of third country auditor), after paragraph (3) insert—

    '(3A) An application for registration of an exempt third country auditor must include—

        (a)   a statement of the auditing standards and independence requirements applied to the audit or audits in respect of which the application is made,

        (b)  a description of the auditor's internal quality control system,

        (c)  a statement of whether and (if so) when a quality assurance review has been carried out in respect of the auditor,

        (d)  information required by the designated body about the outcome of a quality assurance review.'.

(4)  At the end of regulation 39 (duty to provide updated information) add—

    '(2) An exempt third country auditor who for the purpose of registration has provided to the designated body information falling within subparagraphs (a) to (d) and the first sentence of subparagraph (e) of Article 1.1 of the Commission Decision[186] must take all reasonable steps to notify the designated body without undue delay of any change or addition to that information.'.

(5)  In regulation 40 (removal of third country auditor from the register)—

    (a)  in paragraph (2)(a), for 'regulation 39' substitute 'regulation 39(1)', and

    (b)  after paragraph (2) insert—

    '(3) The designated body may remove an exempt third country auditor from the register if—

        (a)  it considers that the auditor—

           (i)  has failed—

              (aa) to comply with the obligations of the auditor under regulation 39(2) (duty of exempt third country auditor to provide updated information), or

              (bb) to apply the auditing standards and independence requirements set out in the statement provided for in regulation 35(3A)(a), or

           (ii)  is not a fit and proper person to conduct audits of the accounts of UK-traded non-EEA companies, or

        (b)  it appears to the designated body that a third country competent authority which oversees or regulates the auditor considers that the auditor is not—

           (i)  a fit and proper person to conduct audits in the specified third country in which the authority is established, or

           (ii)  eligible to conduct audits of the accounts of bodies corporate incorporated or formed under the law of that country.'.

**3.**  If—

    (a)  before 31st October 2008 an exempt third country auditor, with a view to being registered in accordance with Article 1.2 of Commission Decision 2008/627/EC of 29 July 2008 concerning a transitional period for audit activities of certain third country auditors and audit entities, has provided to the designated body information falling within subparagraphs (a) to (d) and the first sentence of subparagraph (e) of Article 1.1 of that Decision, and

    (b)  that information satisfies the requirements of regulation 35 of the Statutory Auditors and Third Country Auditors Regulations 2007 as it applies to that auditor,

the designated body may register the auditor under regulation 37 of those Regulations as if the auditor had made an application in accordance with regulation 35.

---

[185] Section 1239(7) was amended by SI 2007/3494, regulation 30(5). The function of the Secretary of State under that section was delegated to the designated body (defined in regulation 29 of SI 2007/3494) by SI 2008/496.

[186] Those subparagraphs are set out in the Explanatory Note to these Regulations.

# THE COMPANIES (PARTICULARS OF COMPANY CHARGES) REGULATIONS 2008
## (SI 2008/2996)

COMMENCEMENT DATE 1 October 2009[187]

**Citation, commencement and interpretation**                                                    SI.27

1. (1) These Regulations may be cited as the Companies (Particulars of Company Charges) Regulations 2008 and come into force on 1st October 2009.
   (2) In these Regulations 'the Act' means the Companies Act 2006.

**Prescribed particulars of charges created by a company**

2. The prescribed particulars for the purposes of section 860(1) of the Act are—
   (a) the date of the creation of the charge;
   (b) a description of the instrument (if any) creating or evidencing the charge;
   (c) the amount secured by the charge;
   (d) the name and address of the person entitled to the charge; and
   (e) short particulars of the property charged.
3. The prescribed particulars for the purposes of section 878(1) of the Act are—
   (a) the particulars prescribed by regulation 2; and
   (b) in the case of a floating charge, a statement as to any provisions of the charge and of any instrument relating to it which prohibit or restrict or regulate the power of the company to grant further securities ranking in priority to, or pari passu with, the floating charge, or which vary or otherwise regulate the order of ranking of the floating charge in relation to subsisting securities.

**Prescribed particulars of charges existing on property acquired**

4. The prescribed particulars for the purposes of sections 862(2) and 880(2) of the Act are—
   (a) the particulars prescribed by regulation 2; and
   (b) the date of the acquisition of the property which is subject to the charge.

# THE COMPANIES ACT 2006 (ANNUAL RETURN AND SERVICE ADDRESSES) REGULATIONS 2008
## (SI 2008/3000)

COMMENCEMENT DATE 1 October 2009[188]

## PART 1
### INTRODUCTION

**Citation, commencement and application**                                                        SI.28

1. (1) These Regulations may be cited as the Companies Act 2006 (Annual Return and Service Addresses) Regulations 2008 and come into force on 1st October 2009.
   (2) Part 2 applies in relation to annual returns made up to 1st October 2009 or a later date.

## PART 2
### ANNUAL RETURNS

**Required particulars of directors and secretaries**

2. (1) In section 855(1)(c) of the Companies Act 2006 (contents of annual return: particulars of directors and secretaries), for 'the prescribed particulars' substitute 'the required particulars (see section 855A)'.

---

[187] 2006 c. 46.
[188] 2006 c.46.

(2) After that section insert—

### 'Required particulars of directors and secretaries

**855A.**(1) For the purposes of section 855(1)(c) the required particulars of a director are—
  (a) where the director is an individual, the particulars required by section 163 to be entered in the register of directors (subject to subsection (2) below); and
  (b) where the director is a body corporate or a firm that is a legal person under the law by which it is governed, the particulars required by section 164 to be entered in the register of directors.
(2) The former name of a director who is an individual is a required particular in relation to an annual return only if the director was known by the name for business purposes during the return period.
(3) For the purposes of section 855(1)(c)(ii) the required particulars of a secretary are—
  (a) where a secretary is an individual, the particulars required by section 277 to be entered in the register of secretaries (subject to subsection (4) below); and
  (b) where a secretary is a body corporate or a firm that is a legal person under the law by which it is governed, the particulars required by section 278(1) to be entered in the register of secretaries.
(4) The former name of a secretary who is an individual is a required particular in relation to an annual return only if the secretary was known by the name for business purposes during the return period.
(5) Where all the partners in a firm are joint secretaries, the required particulars are the particulars that would be required to be entered in the register of secretaries if the firm were a legal person and the firm had been appointed secretary.'.

### Information about where company records are kept

**3.** In section 855(1) of the Companies Act 2006 (contents of annual return: general), for paragraphs (d) and (e) (information about place where register of members or register of debenture holders is kept) substitute—
  '(d) if any company records are (in accordance with regulations under section 1136) kept at a place other than the company's registered office, the address of that place and the records that are kept there;'.

### Information whether shares admitted to trading on regulated market

**4.** (1) In section 855(1) of the Companies Act 2006 (contents of annual return: general), after paragraph (d) (substituted by regulation 3 above) insert—
  '(f) whether the company was a traded company at any time during the return period.'.
(2) In that section, after subsection (3) insert—
  '(4) In this Part—
    "return period", in relation to an annual return, means the period beginning immediately after the date to which the last return was made up (or, in the case of the first return, with the incorporation of the company) and ending with the date to which the return is made up; and
    "traded company" means a company any of whose shares are shares admitted to trading on a regulated market (so that "non-traded company" means a company none of whose shares are shares admitted to trading on a regulated market).'.

### Classification scheme for company type

**5.** (1) The classification scheme set out in the table in Schedule 1 is prescribed for the purposes of section 855(2) of the Companies Act 2006.
(2) The annual return must indicate the type of company to which the return relates as set out in column 1 of that table by reference to the code opposite that type in column 2.

### Classification system for company's principal business activities

**6.** (1) The Standard Industrial Classification 2003 is prescribed for the purposes of section 855(3) of the Companies Act 2006, with the addition of the codes and designations in the table in Schedule 2, where the code set out in column 1 of the table represents the designation opposite it in column 2 of the table.
(2) In paragraph (1), 'Standard Industrial Classification 2003' means the UK Standard Industrial Classification of Economic Activities 2003, prepared by the Office for National Statistics and published by The Stationery Office with ISBN number 0116216417.

### Information about shareholders

**7.** (1) In section 856 of the Companies Act 2006 (contents of annual return: information about share capital and shareholders)—
  (a) in the heading omit 'and shareholders';
  (b) in subsection (1) for paragraphs (a) and (b) substitute 'a statement of capital';
  (c) in subsection (2)(c)(i) for 'prescribed particulars of the rights' substitute 'the voting rights';

    (d) omit—
       (i) subsections (3) to (5), and
       (ii) subsection (6) (which is unnecessary).
(2) After that section insert—

**'Contents of annual return: information about shareholders: non-traded companies**

**856A.** (1) The annual return of a company that was a non-traded company throughout the return period must also contain the following information.

    (2) The return must contain the name (as it appears in the company's register of members) of every person who was a member of the company at any time during the return period.

The return must conform to the following requirements for the purpose of enabling the entries relating to any given person to be easily found—
    (a) the entries must be listed in alphabetical order by name; or
    (b) the return must have annexed to it an index that is sufficient to enable the name of the person in question to be easily found.

    (3) The return must also state—
    (a) the number of shares of each class held at the end of the date to which the return is made up by each person who was a member of the company at that time,
    (b) the number of shares of each class transferred during the return period by or to each person who was a member of the company at any time during that period, and
    (c) the dates of registration of those transfers.

    (4) If either of the two immediately preceding returns has given the full particulars required by subsections (2) and (3), the return need only give such particulars as relate—
    (a) to persons who became, or ceased to be, members during the return period, and
    (b) to shares transferred during that period.

**Contents of annual return: information about shareholders: traded companies**

**856B.** (1) The annual return of a company that was a traded company at any time during the return period must also contain the following information.

    (2) The return must contain the name and address (as they appear in the company's register of members) of every person who held at least 5% of the issued shares of any class of the company at any time during the return period.

The return must conform to the following requirements for the purpose of enabling the entries relating to any given person to be easily found—
    (a) the entries must be listed in alphabetical order by name; or
    (b) the return must have annexed to it an index that is sufficient to enable the name of the person in question to be easily found.

    (3) The return must also state—
    (a) the number of shares of each class held at the end of the date to which the return is made up by each person who held at least 5% of the issued shares of any class of the company at that time,
    (b) the number of shares of each class transferred during the return period by or to each person who held at least 5% of the issued shares of any class of the company at any time during that period, and
    (c) the dates of registration of those transfers.

    (4) If either of the two immediately preceding returns has given the full particulars required by subsections (2) and (3), the return need only give such particulars as relate—
    (a) to persons who came to hold, or ceased to hold, at least 5% of the issued shares of any class of the company during the return period, and
    (b) to shares transferred during that period.'.

**Shadow directors**

**8.** (1) In section 858(1) of the Companies Act 2006 (liability of directors and others for failure to deliver annual return), after paragraph (c) insert—

'For this purpose a shadow director is treated as a director.'.

(2) Omit section 859 of the Companies Act 2006 (application of Part to shadow directors).

**Index of defined expressions**

**9.** In Schedule 8 to the Companies Act 2006 (index of defined expressions), at the appropriate places insert—

| | |
|---|---|
| '"non-traded company" (in Part 24) | section 855(4)'; |
| '"return period" (in Part 24) | section 855(4)'; |
| '"traded company" (in Part 24) | section 855(4)'. |

## PART 3
## SERVICE ADDRESSES

**Service addresses**

**10.** For the purposes of section 1141 of the Companies Act 2006 (conditions with which a service address must comply) the conditions are that the service address must be a place where—

(a) the service of documents can be effected by physical delivery; and

(b) the delivery of documents is capable of being recorded by the obtaining of an acknowledge-ment of delivery.

## SCHEDULE 1
Regulation 5
## CLASSIFICATION SCHEME FOR TYPE OF COMPANY

| Column 1 | Column 2 |
| --- | --- |
| Type of company | Code |
| Public limited company | T1 |
| Private company limited by shares | T2 |
| Private company limited by guarantee | T3 |
| Private company limited by shares exempt under section 60 of the Companies Act 2006 | T4 |
| Private company limited by guarantee exempt under section 60 of the Companies Act 2006 | T5 |
| Private unlimited company with share capital | T6 |
| Private unlimited company without share capital | T7 |

## SCHEDULE 2
Regulation 6
## ADDITIONAL CODES AND DESIGNATIONS

| Column 1 | Column 2 |
| --- | --- |
| Codes | Designations |
| 7499 | Non-trading company |
| 9800 | Residents' property management company |
| 9999 | Dormant company |

# THE COMPANIES (COMPANY RECORDS) REGULATIONS 2008
## (SI 2008/3006)

COMMENCEMENT DATE 1 October 2009[189]

## PART 1
## INTRODUCTORY

**SI.29**

**Citation, commencement, application and interpretation**

**1.** (1) These Regulations may be cited as the Companies (Company Records) Regulations 2008 and come into force on 1st October 2009.

(2) Part 4 applies to any request made on or after 1st October 2009 to be provided with a copy of a company record.

(3) In these Regulations 'the Act' means the Companies Act 2006.

---

[189] 2006 c.46.

**Revocations and saving**

**2.** (1) The following Regulations are revoked subject to paragraph (2)—
   (a) the Companies (Inspection and Copying of Registers, Indices and Documents) Regulations 1991[190] ('the 1991 Regulations'); and
   (b) the Companies (Inspection and Copying of Registers, Indices and Documents) Regulations (Northern Ireland) 1993[191] ('the 1993 Regulations').
   (2) The 1991 Regulations and the 1993 Regulations continue to apply to any request made before 1st October 2009 to be provided with a copy of a company record.

## PART 2
## ALTERNATIVE INSPECTION LOCATION

**Single alternative inspection location**

**3.** The specified place in respect of the relevant provisions listed in section 1136(2) of the Act—
   (a) is a place that is situated in the part of the United Kingdom in which the company is registered;
   (b) must be the same place for all the relevant provisions; and
   (c) must have been notified to the registrar as being the company's alternative inspection location.

## PART 3
## INSPECTION OF COMPANY RECORDS

**Inspection: private company**

**4.** (1) A private company shall make its company records available for inspection by a person on a day which has been specified by that person ('the specified day') provided that—
   (a) the specified day is a working day; and
   (b) that person gives the company the required notice of the specified day.
   (2) The required notice is at least 2 working days' notice of the specified day if the notice is given—
   (a) during the period of notice for a general meeting or a class meeting; or
   (b) where the company circulates a written resolution, during the period provided for in section 297(1) of the Act,
      provided that the notice given both begins and ends during the period referred to in sub-paragraph (a) or (b) (as the case may be).
   (3) In all other cases the required notice is at least 10 working days' notice of the specified day.
   (4) When the person gives notice of the specified day he shall also give notice of the time on that day at which he wishes to start the inspection (which shall be any time between 9 am and 3 pm) and the company shall make its company records available for inspection by that person for a period of at least 2 hours beginning with that time.

**Inspection: public company**

**5.** A public company shall make its company records available for inspection for at least 2 hours between 9 am and 5 pm on each working day.

**Inspection: general**

**6.** (1) A company is not required for the purposes of inspection of a company record to present information in that record in a different order, structure or form from that set out in that record.
   (2) A company shall permit a person to make a copy of the whole or any part of a company record in the course of inspection at—
   (a) the location at which the record is made available for inspection; and

---

[190] SI 1991/1998.
[191] SR (NI) 1993 No 66.

(b)  any time during which the record is made available for inspection,

but a company is not required to assist that person in making his copy of that record.

## PART 4
## PROVISION OF COPIES OF COMPANY RECORDS

### Right to hard copy

**7.** Where a company is requested to provide a copy of a company record in hard copy form, the company shall provide that copy in hard copy form.

### Copy in electronic form

**8.** (1)  Where a person requests a company to provide a copy of a company record in electronic form, the company shall provide that copy in such electronic form as the company shall decide.

(2)  But where a company keeps a company record in hard copy form only, it is not required to provide a copy of that record in electronic form.

(3)  Where a company provides a copy of a company record in electronic form to a member of the company or to a holder of the company's debentures, the company is not required to provide a hard copy of that record in accordance with section 1145 of the Act.

### Re-ordering of information in copy of record

**9.** A company is not required to present information in a copy of a company record that it provides in a different order, structure or form from that set out in the record.

## THE COMPANIES (FEES FOR INSPECTION OF COMPANY RECORDS) REGULATIONS 2008
### (SI 2008/3007)

COMMENCEMENT DATE 1 October 2009[192]

### Citation, commencement and application

**1.** (1)  These Regulations may be cited as the Companies (Fees for Inspection of Company Records) Regulations 2008 and come into force on 1st October 2009.

(2)  These Regulations apply where a person inspects a register or instrument referred to in regulation 2 on or after 1st October 2009 regardless of the date on which the request to inspect that register or instrument was made.

### Fee for inspection of company records

**2.** For the purposes of the following provisions of the Companies Act 2006—

(a)  section 162(5)(b) (register of directors);

(b)  section 275(5)(b) (register of secretaries);

(c)  section 877(4)(b) (instruments creating charges and register of charges: England and Wales and Northern Ireland); and

(d)  section 892(4)(b) (instruments creating charges and register of charges: Scotland), the fee prescribed is £3.50 for each hour or part thereof during which the right of inspection is exercised.

---

[192]  2006 c. 46.

# The Companies (Registration) Regulations 2008
## (SI 2008/3014)

## Companies

Commencement Date 1 October 2009[193]

### Citation, commencement and interpretation

SI.31

**1.** (1) These Regulations may be cited as the Companies (Registration) Regulations 2008 and come into force on 1st October 2009.

(2) In these Regulations 'the Act' means the Companies Act 2006.

### Memorandum of association

**2.** For the purposes of section 8 of the Act—

(a) the memorandum of association of a company having a share capital shall be in the form set out in Schedule 1; and

(b) the memorandum of association of a company not having a share capital shall be in the form set out in Schedule 2.

### Statement of capital and initial shareholdings

**3.** For the purposes of section 10(3) of the Act, the statement of capital and initial shareholdings shall contain the name and address of each subscriber to the memorandum of association.

### Statement of guarantee

**4.** For the purposes of section 11(2) of the Act, the statement of guarantee shall contain the name and address of each subscriber to the memorandum of association.

### Form of assent for re-registration of private limited company as unlimited

**5.** The form set out in Schedule 3 is the form prescribed for the purposes of section 103(2)(a) of the Act.

### Form of assent for re-registration of public company as private and unlimited

**6.** The form set out in Schedule 4 is the form prescribed for the purposes of section 110(2)(a) of the Act.

---

[193] 2006 c.46.

SCHEDULE 1           Regulation 2(a)

COMPANY HAVING A SHARE CAPITAL

**Memorandum of association of** [*insert name of company*]

**Each subscriber to this memorandum of association wishes to form a company under the Companies Act 2006 and agrees to become a member of the company and to take at least one share.**

| *Name of each subscriber* | *Authentication by each subscriber* |
|---|---|
| | |

**Dated**

SCHEDULE 2           Regulation 2(b)

COMPANY NOT HAVING A SHARE CAPITAL

**Memorandum of association of** [*insert name of company*]

**Each subscriber to this memorandum of association wishes to form a company under the Companies Act 2006 and agrees to become a member of the company.**

| *Name of each subscriber* | *Authentication by each subscriber* |
|---|---|
| | |

**Dated**

SCHEDULE 3    Regulation 5

FORM OF ASSENT FOR RE-REGISTRATION OF PRIVATE
LIMITED COMPANY AS UNLIMITED

Assent by each member to public re-registered as private
and unlimited

**In accordance
with section
110(2)(a) of the
Companies Act
2006**

Company number

Company name

Each member or the company assents to the company
being re-registered as unlimited

Member's name in full

Authentication of member
(or person lawfully authorised
to authenticate on the member's behalf)    Date

Member's name in full

Authentication of member
(or person lawfully authorised
to authenticate on the member's behalf)    Date

Member's name in full

Authentication of member
(or person lawfully authorised
to authenticate on the member's behalf)    Date

Member's name in full

Authentication of member
(or person lawfully authorised
to authenticate on the member's behalf)    Date

Please enter in the box opposite the number of continuation sheets attached (if any)

SCHEDULE 4                                    Regulation 6

FORM OF ASSENT FOR RE-REGISTRATION OF PUBLIC COMPANY AS PRIVATE AND
UNLIMITED

Assent to private limited company being re-registered as unlimited

**In accordance
with section
103(2)(a) of the
Companies Act
2006**

Company number

Company name

Each member or the company assents to the company
being re-registered as unlimited

Member's name in full

Authentication of member
(or person lawfully authorised
to authenticate on the member's behalf)                Date

Member's name in full

Authentication of member
(or person lawfully authorised
to authenticate on the member's behalf)                Date

Member's name in full

Authentication of member
(or person lawfully authorised
to authenticate on the member's behalf)                Date

Member's name in full

Authentication of member
(or person lawfully authorised
to authenticate on the member's behalf)                Date

Please enter in the box opposite the number of continuation sheets attached (if any)

# THE COMPANIES (DISCLOSURE OF ADDRESS) REGULATIONS 2009

## (SI 2009/214)

COMMENCEMENT DATE 1 October 2009[194]

## PART 1

**Citation, commencement and interpretation**                                              SI.32

**1.** (1) These Regulations may be cited as the Companies (Disclosure of Address) Regulations 2009 and come into force on 1st October 2009.

(2) In these Regulations—

'the Act' means the Companies Act 2006 and, unless the context otherwise requires, any reference to a numbered section is to a section so numbered in that Act;

'the 1985 Act' means the Companies Act 1985[195];

'the 1986 Order' means the Companies (Northern Ireland) Order 1986[196];

'confidentiality order' means an order under section 723B of the 1985 Act[197] (confidentiality orders);

'former name' means a name by which an individual was formerly known and which has been notified to the registrar under section 10 (documents to be sent to the registrar) or section 288 (register of directors and secretaries) of the 1985 Act, or Article 21 or 296 of the 1986 Order, [or regulation 80C of the SEs Regulations, or regulation 79 of the old SEs Regulations, or regulation 77 of the Northern Ireland SEs Regulations,][198] or section 12 (statement of proposed officers) or section 167 (duty to notify registrar of changes) of the Act;

'limited liability partnership' means a limited liability partnership incorporated under the Limited Liability Partnerships Act 2000[199] or Limited Liability Partnerships Act (Northern Ireland) 2002[200];

'name' means a person's Christian name (or other forename) and surname, except that in the case of—

(a) a peer; or

(b) an individual usually known by a title,

the title may be stated instead of his Christian name (or other forename) and surname or in addition to either or both of them;

['the Northern Ireland SEs Regulations' means the European Public Limited-Liability Company Regulations (Northern Ireland) 2004;][201]

['the old SEs Regulations' means the SEs Regulations, disregarding the amendments made by the European Public Limited-Liability Company (Amendment) Regulations 2009;][202]

'permanent representative' means an individual who was a permanent representative for the purposes of sections 723B and 723C (effect of confidentiality orders) of the 1985 Act[203];

'police force' means a police force within the meaning of section 101(1) of the Police Act 1996[204] (interpretation), section 50 of the Police (Scotland) Act 1967[205] (meaning of police area, etc) or section 1 of the Police (Northern Ireland) Act 2000[206] (name of the police in Northern Ireland);

---

[194] 2006 c.46. Section 1292(4) of the Companies Act 2006 provides that any provision which may be made by regulations under that Act subject to negative resolution procedure may be made by regulations subject to affirmative resolution procedure.

[195] 1985 c.6.

[196] SI 1986/1032 (NI 6).

[197] Section 723B was inserted by section 45 of the Criminal Justice and Police Act 2001 (c.16).

[198] Amended by the European Public Limited-Liability Company (Amendment) Regulations 2009 (SI 2009/2400, reg 42(2)(b)).

[199] 2000 c.12.

[200] 2002 c.12 (NI).

[201] Inserted by the European Public Limited-Liability Company (Amendment) Regulations 2009 (SI 2009/2400, reg 42(2)(a)).

[202] Inserted by the European Public Limited-Liability Company (Amendment) Regulations 2009 (SI 2009/2400, reg 42(2)(a)).

[203] Sections 723B and 723C were inserted by section 45 of the Criminal Justice and Police Act 2001.

[204] 1996 c.16.

[205] 1967 c.77.

[206] 2000 c.32.

'relevant body' means any police force and any other person whom the registrar considers may be able to assist in answering a question referred to that person by the registrar under these Regulations;

'relevant organisation' means the Government Communications Headquarters, the Secret Intelligence Service, the Security Service or a police force;

'section 243 applicant' means an individual by whom or in respect of whom a section 243 application has been made but in respect of which application the registrar either has not made a determination, or has made a determination, not being a section 243 decision, and any appeal to the court in respect of that application under regulation 14 has not been determined by the court;

'section 243 application' means an application under section 243(4) (permitted use or disclosure by the registrar) for the purpose of requiring the registrar to refrain from disclosing protected information relating to a director to a credit reference agency;

'section 243 beneficiary' means—

(a) an individual who has made a section 243 application in respect of which a section 243 decision has been made; or

(b) an individual on whose behalf a company or a subscriber to a memorandum of association has made a section 243 application in respect of which a section 243 decision has been made; or

(c) an individual in relation to whom a confidentiality order was in force immediately before 1st October 2009 and who, by paragraph 37 of Schedule 2 to the Companies Act 2006 (Commencement No. 8, Transitional Provisions and Savings) Order 2008[207] is treated as having made a section 243 application in respect of which a section 243 decision has been made;

'section 243 decision' means a determination by the registrar on a section 243 application in favour of the applicant;

'section 1088 application' means an application under section 1088 (application to registrar to make address unavailable for public inspection) for the purpose of requiring the registrar to make an address on the register unavailable for public inspection;

'section 1088 beneficiary' means a person who has made a section 1088 application in respect of which a section 1088 decision has been made;

'section 1088 decision' means a determination by the registrar on a section 1088 application in favour of the applicant;

['the SEs Regulations' means the European Public Limited-Liability Company Regulations 2004;][208]

'specified public authority' means any public authority specified in Schedule 1 to these Regulations; and

'working day' means a day that is not a Saturday or Sunday, Christmas Day, Good Friday or any day that is a bank holiday under the Banking and Financial Dealings Act 1971[209] in England and Wales.

## PART 2

### DISCLOSURE OF PROTECTED INFORMATION

**Permitted disclosure by the registrar to specified public authorities**

2. (1) The registrar may disclose protected information to a specified public authority where the conditions specified in paragraphs 2 and 3 of Schedule 2 are satisfied.

(2) A specified public authority shall deliver to the registrar such information or evidence as he may direct for the purpose of enabling him to determine in accordance with these Regulations whether to disclose protected information.

(3) The registrar may require such information or evidence to be verified in such manner as he may direct.

(4) The specified public authority must inform the registrar immediately of any change in respect of any statement delivered to the registrar pursuant to Schedule 2 or information or evidence provided for the purpose of enabling the registrar to determine whether to disclose protected information.

(5) The public authorities specified for the purposes of section 243(2) are set out in Schedule 1 to these Regulations.

---

[207] SI 2008//2860 (C. 126).

[208] Inserted by the European Public Limited-Liability Company (Amendment) Regulations 2009 (SI 2009/2400, reg 42(2)(a)).

[209] 1971 c.80.

### Permitted disclosure by the registrar to credit reference agencies

**3.** (1) Subject to regulation 4, the registrar may disclose protected information to a credit reference agency where the conditions specified in paragraphs 6 to 10 of Schedule 2 are satisfied.

(2) The registrar may rely on a statement delivered to him by a credit reference agency under paragraph 10 of Schedule 2 as sufficient evidence of the matters stated in it.

(3) Notwithstanding paragraph (2), a credit reference agency shall deliver to the registrar such information or evidence in addition to the statement required by paragraph 10 of Schedule 2 as he may direct for the purpose of enabling him to determine in accordance with these Regulations whether to disclose protected information.

(4) The registrar may require such information or evidence to be verified in such manner as he may direct.

(5) The credit reference agency must inform the registrar immediately of any change in respect of any statement delivered to the registrar pursuant to Schedule 2 or information or evidence provided for the purpose of enabling the registrar to determine whether to disclose protected information.

### Registrar to refrain from disclosure of protected information

**4.** The registrar shall refrain from disclosing protected information to a credit reference agency if such information relates to a section 243 beneficiary or a section 243 applicant.

### Application under section 243 by an individual

**5.** (1) A section 243 application may be made to the registrar by an individual who is, or proposes to become, a director.

(2) The grounds on which an application under paragraph (1) may be made are that the individual making the application—

    (a) considers that there is a serious risk that he, or a person who lives with him, will be subjected to violence or intimidation as a result of the activities of at least one of—

        (i) the companies of which he is, or proposes to become, a director;

        (ii) the companies of which he was a director;

        (iii) the overseas companies of which he is or has been a director, secretary or permanent representative; or,

        (iv) the limited liability partnerships of which he is or has been a member; or

    (b) is or has been employed by a relevant organisation.

(3) The application shall—

    (a) contain—

        (i) a statement of the grounds on which the application is made;

        (ii) the name and any former name of the applicant;

        (iii) the date of birth of the applicant;

        (iv) the usual residential address of the applicant;

        (v) where the registrar has allocated a unique identifier to the applicant, that unique identifier;

        (vi) the name and registered number of each company of which the applicant is, or proposes to become, a director;

        (vii) where the grounds of the application are those described in paragraph (2)(a)(ii), (iii) or (iv), the name and registered number of the company, overseas company or limited liability partnership; and

    (b) be accompanied by evidence which—

        (i) where the grounds of the application are those described in paragraph (2)(a) supports the applicant's statement of the grounds of the application; or,

        (ii) where the grounds of the application are those described in paragraph (2)(b), establishes that the applicant is or has been employed by a relevant organisation.

(4) The registrar may refer to a relevant body any question relating to an assessment of—

    (a) where the grounds of the application are those described in paragraph (2)(a), the nature and extent of any risk of violence or intimidation considered by the applicant to arise in relation to himself, or to a person who lives with him; or

    (b) where the grounds of the application are those described in paragraph (2)(b), whether the applicant is or has been employed by a relevant organisation.

(5) The registrar shall determine the application and send the applicant to his usual residential address, as stated in his application, notice of his determination on the section 243 application within five working days of that determination being made.

### Application under section 243 by a company

**6.** (1) A section 243 application may be made to the registrar by a company on behalf of any of its directors who are individuals.

(2) The grounds on which an application under paragraph (1) may be made are that the company making the application considers that there is a serious risk that the director on behalf of whom the application is made, or a person who lives with that director, will be

subjected to violence or intimidation as a result of the activities of the company making the application.

(3) The application shall—

    (a) contain—

        (i)   a statement of the grounds on which the application is made;

        (ii)  the name and registered number of the applicant;

        (iii) the name and any former name of each director on behalf of whom the application is made;

        (iv) the date of birth of each such director;

        (v)  the usual residential address of each such director;

        (vi) where the registrar has allocated a unique identifier to any such director, that unique identifier;

        (vii) the name and registered number of each company of which each such director is a director; and

    (b) be accompanied by evidence which supports the applicant's statement of the grounds of the application.

(4) The registrar may refer to a relevant body any question relating to an assessment of the nature and extent of any risk of violence or intimidation considered by the applicant toarise in relation to its directors on behalf of whom the application is made or to persons who live with those directors as a result of any of its activities.

(5) The registrar shall determine the application and send—

    (a) the applicant, to its registered office; and

    (b) each director on behalf of whom the application was made, to his usual residential address as stated in the application,

    notice of his determination on the section 243 application within five working days of that determination being made.

### Application under section 243 by a subscriber to a memorandum of association

**7.** (1) A section 243 application may be made to the registrar by a subscriber to a memorandum of association on behalf of any of the proposed directors of a proposed company who are individuals.

(2) The grounds on which an application under paragraph (1) may be made are that the subscriber making the application considers that there is a serious risk that the proposed directors of the proposed company on behalf of whom the application is made, or persons who live with them, will be subjected to violence or intimidation as a result of the proposed activities of that proposed company.

(3) The application shall—

    (a) contain—

        (i)   a statement of the grounds on which the application is made;

        (ii)  the name of the applicant;

        (iii) the address of the applicant;

        (iv) the name of the proposed company;

        (v)  the name and any former name of each of the proposed directors on behalf of whom the application is made;

        (vi) the date of birth of each such proposed director;

        (vii) the usual residential address of each such proposed director;

        (viii) the name and registered number of each company of which each such proposed director is a director; and

    (b) be accompanied by evidence which supports the applicant's statement of the grounds of the application.

(4) The registrar may refer to a relevant body any question relating to an assessment of the nature and extent of any risk of violence or intimidation considered by the applicant to arise in relation to its proposed directors on behalf of whom the application is made or to persons who live with those proposed directors as a result of any of the proposed activities of the proposed company.

(5) The registrar shall determine the application and send—

    (a) the applicant, to the address stated in the application, and

    (b) each of the proposed directors on behalf of whom the application was made, to their usual residential address as stated in the application,

    notice of his determination on the section 243 application within five working days of that determination being made.

### Matters relating to a section 243 application

**8.** (1) For the purpose of regulations 5, 6 and 7 the registrar may direct that additional information or evidence should be delivered to him, what such information or evidence should be and how it should be verified.

(2) The registrar shall not make available for public inspection—

    (a) any section 243 application; or

(b) any documents provided in support of that application.

(3) For the purpose of determining any section 243 application the registrar may accept any answer to a question referred in accordance with regulation 5(4), 6(4) or 7(4) as providing sufficient evidence of—

    (a) the nature and extent of any risk relevant to—

        (i) where the grounds of the application are those described in regulation 5(2)(a), the applicant;

        (ii) where the grounds of the application are those described in regulation 6(2), the directors on behalf of whom the application is made;

        (iii) where the grounds of the application are those described in regulation 7(2), the proposed directors on behalf of whom the application is made,

        or to persons who live with any of the above individuals, or

    (b) whether an applicant is or has been employed by a relevant organisation.

## PART 3

## APPLICATION TO MAKE AN ADDRESS UNAVAILABLE FOR PUBLIC INSPECTION UNDER SECTION 1088

**Application under section 1088 to make an address unavailable for public inspection by an individual**

**9.** (1) A section 1088 application may be made to the registrar by an individual whose usual residential address was placed on the register either—

    (a) under section 10 (documents to be sent to registrar)[a], 288 (register of directors and secretaries)[b], 363 (duty to deliver annual returns)[c], 691 (documents to be delivered to registrar)[d] or 692 (registration of altered particulars)[e] of or paragraph 2 of Schedule 21A[f] to the 1985 Act;

    (b) under Article 21, 296, 371, 641 or 642 of the 1986 Order[g]; [...][h]

    [(ba)as a service address under regulation 80C of the SEs Regulations (duty to notify registrar of changes of particulars of members of an SE's supervisory organ),

    [(bb)under regulation 79 of the old SEs Regulations or regulation 77 of the Northern Ireland SEs Regulations, or][i]

    (c) as a service address under section 12 (statement of proposed officers), 167 (duty to notify registrar of changes of director's particulars) or 855 (contents of annual return) of the Act,

in respect of that usual residential address where it was placed on the register on or after 1st January 2003.

(2) The grounds on which an application under paragraph (1) may be made are that the individual making the application—

    (a) considers that there is a serious risk that he, or a person who lives with him, will be subjected to violence or intimidation as a result of the activities of at least one of the companies of which—

        (i) he is, or proposes to become, a director; or

        (ii) he is not a director but of which he has been at any time a director, secretary or permanent representative;

    (b) he is or has been employed by a relevant organisation;

    (c) is a section 243 beneficiary.

(3) The application shall—

    (a) contain—

        (i) a statement of the grounds on which the application is made;

        (ii) the name and any former name of the applicant;

        (iii) the usual residential address of the applicant that is to be made unavailable for public inspection;

        (iv) an address for correspondence in respect of the application;

        (v) the name and registered number of each company of which the applicant is or has been at any time since 1st January 2003 a director, secretary or permanent representative;

        (vi) the service address which is to replace that usual residential address on the register;

        (vii) subject to paragraph (4)—

            (aa) the date of birth of the applicant;

            (bb) the name of each company of which the applicant proposes to become a director; and

            (cc) where the registrar has allotted a unique identifier to the applicant, that unique identifier; and

    (b) be accompanied by evidence which—

        (i) where the grounds of the application are those described in paragraph (2)(a), supports the applicant's assertion that his application falls within the grounds stated in his application;

(ii) where the grounds of the application are those described in paragraph (2)(b), establishes that the applicant is or has been employed by a relevant organisation;

(iii) where the grounds of the application are those described in paragraph (2)(c), establishes that he is a section 243 beneficiary.

(4) The application need not contain the information described at paragraph (3)(a)(vii) where the application is delivered to the registrar on the same day as the applicant delivers a section 243 application.

(5) The registrar may refer to a relevant body any question relating to an assessment of—

(a) the nature and extent of any risk of violence or intimidation considered by the applicant to arise in relation to himself, or a person who lives with him, as a result of the activities of any company of which he is or proposes to become a director or has been at any time a director, secretary or permanent representative; or

(b) whether the applicant is or has been employed by a relevant organisation.

(6) The registrar shall determine the application and send the applicant to the address for correspondence stated in his application, notice of his determination on the section 1088 application within five working days of that determination being made.

AMENDMENTS

a Section 10 was amended by the Companies (Particulars of Usual Residential Address) (Confidentiality Orders) Regulations 2002 (S.I. 2002/912).

b Section 288 was amended by the Companies (Particulars of Usual Residential Address) (Confidentiality Orders) Regulations 2002 (S.I. 2002/912).

c Section 363 was substituted by section 139(1) of the Companies Act 1989 (c.40).

d Section 691 was amended by the Companies (Particulars of Usual Residential Address) (Confidentiality Orders) Regulations 2002 (S.I. 2002/912). Section 691(2), (3) and (4) was substituted by section 145 of the Companies Act 1989.

e Section 692 was amended by the Companies (Particulars of Usual Residential Address) (Confidentiality Orders) Regulations 2002 (S.I. 2002/912).

f Schedule 21A was inserted by the Overseas Companies and Credit and Financial Institutions (Branch Disclosure) Regulations 1992 (S.I. 1992/3179) and amended by S.I. 2002/912.

g Article 371 was substituted by Article 74 of, and Article 641 was amended by Article 78 of and paragraph 6 of Schedule 5 to, the Companies (No. 2) (Northern Ireland) Order 1990 (SI 1990/1504 (N.I. 10)).

h Revoked by the European Public Limited-Liability Company (Amendment) Regulations 2009 (S.I. 2009/2400, reg 42(3)).

i Inserted by the European Public Limited-Liability Company (Amendment) Regulations 2009 (S.I. 2009/2400, reg 42(3)).

**Application under section 1088 to make an address unavailable for public inspection by a company**

**10.** (1) A section 1088 application may be made to the registrar by a company in respect of the addresses of—

(a) all of its members and former members whose addresses were contained in—

(i) an annual return; or

(ii) a return of allotment of shares,

delivered to the registrar on or after 1st January 2003; or

(b) the subscribers to its memorandum of association where that memorandum was delivered to the registrar on or after 1st January 2003.

(2) The grounds on which an application under paragraph (1) may be made are that the company making the application considers that, as a result of its activities, the availability to members of the public of the addresses described in paragraph (1) creates a serious risk that its members or former members or subscribers, or persons who live at those addresses, will be subjected to violence or intimidation.

(3) The application shall—

(a) contain—

(i) the name of the applicant and its registered number; and

(ii) a statement of the grounds on which the application is made; and

(b) be accompanied by evidence—

(i) which supports the applicant's assertion that its application falls within the grounds stated in its application; or

(ii) where the court has made an order under section 117(3) (register of members: response to request for inspection or copy) directing the applicant not to comply with a request under section 116 (rights to inspect and require copies), a copy of that order.

(4) The registrar may refer to a relevant body any question relating to the assessment of the nature and extent of any risk of violence or intimidation considered by the applicant to arise in relation to any of its members or former members or subscribers, or persons who live at the addresses described in paragraph (1), as a result of its activities by virtue of the availability to members of the public of particulars of the addresses of such members or former members or subscribers.

(5) The registrar shall determine the application and send the applicant to its registered office notice of his determination on the section 1088 application within five working days of that determination being made.

### Application under section 1088 to make an address unavailable for public inspection by a person who registers a charge

**11.** (1) A section 1088 application may be made to the registrar by a person who—

(a) (i) on or after 1st January 2003, registered a charge under Part 12 of the 1985 Act (registration of charges) or Part 13 of the 1986 Order; or

(ii) has registered a charge under Part 25 of the Act (company charges); and

(b) is not the company which created the charge or acquired the property subject to a charge,in respect of his address delivered to the registrar for the purposes of that registration.

(2) The grounds on which an application under paragraph (1) may be made are that the person making the application considers that there is a serious risk that he, or if applicable his employees, or persons who live with him or his employees, will be subjected to violence or intimidation as a result of the activities of the company which is, or was, subject to the charge.

(3) The application shall—

(a) contain—

(i) a statement of the grounds on which the application is made;

(ii) the name of the applicant, and where the applicant is a company, its registered number;

(iii) the address of the applicant that is to be made unavailable for public inspection;

(iv) the name and registered number of the company which is or was subject to the charge;

(v) an address for correspondence with the registrar in respect of the application;

(vi) where the applicant is the chargee, the service address which is to replace the address of the applicant on the register; and

(b) be accompanied by evidence which supports the applicant's assertion that there is a serious risk that he or, if applicable, his employees, or persons who live with him or his employees, will be subjected to violence or intimidation as a result of the activities of the company which is or was subject to the charge.

(4) The registrar may refer to a relevant body any question relating to the assessment of the nature and extent of any risk of violence or intimidation considered by the applicant to arise in relation to himself or, if applicable, his employees, or persons who live with him or his employees, as a result of the activities of the company which is or was subject to the charge.

(5) The registrar shall determine the application and send the applicant to the address stated in the application in accordance with paragraph (3)(a)(v) notice of his determination on the section 1088 application within five working days of that determination being made.

### Matters relevant to section 1088 applications

**12.** (1) For the purpose of regulations 9, 10 and 11 the registrar may direct that additional information or evidence should be delivered to him, what such information or evidence should be and how it should be verified.

(2) For the purpose of determining any section 1088 application the registrar may accept any answer to a question referred in accordance with regulation 9(5), 10(4) or 11(4) as providing sufficient evidence of—

(a) the nature and extent of any risk relevant to—

(i) where the grounds of the application are those described in regulation 9(2)(a), the applicant;

(ii) where the grounds of the application are those described in regulation 10(2), the subscribers or members or former members of an applicant; or

(iii) where the grounds of the application are those described in regulation 11(2), where the applicant is an individual, the applicant, or any employees of an applicant, or to persons who live with any of the above individuals or, in the case of members, former members or subscribers, to persons who live at their addresses, or

(b) whether an applicant is or has been employed by a relevant organisation.

**Effect of a successful section 1088 application**

**13.** (1) Where a section 1088 application has been determined in favour of the applicant the registrar shall—

(a) in the case of an application made under regulation 9(1) or 11(1) make the specified address unavailable for public inspection;

(b) in the case of an application under regulation 10(1) make all of the members', former members' or subscribers' addresses unavailable for public inspection;

(c) in the case of a person to whom paragraph 36 of Schedule 2 to the Companies Act 2006 (Commencement No. 8, Transitional Provisions and Savings) Order 2008 applies, make unavailable for public inspection the address referred to in sub-paragraph (1)(a) of that paragraph.

(2) In this regulation 'specified address' means the address specified in the application as being the one to be made unavailable for public inspection.

## PART 4

### MATTERS RELATING TO APPLICATIONS UNDER SECTION 243 AND UNDER SECTION 1088

**Appeals**

**14.** (1) An applicant who has received notice under regulation 5(5), 6(5), 7(5), 9(6), 10(5) or 11(5) that his application has been unsuccessful may appeal to the High Court or, in Scotland, the Court of Session on the grounds that the decision—

(a) is unlawful;

(b) is irrational or unreasonable;

(c) has been made on the basis of a procedural impropriety or otherwise contravenes the rules of natural justice.

(2) No appeal under this regulation may be brought unless the leave of the court has been obtained.

(3) An applicant must bring an appeal within 21 days of the date of the notice or, with the court's permission, after the end of such period, but only if the court is satisfied—

(a) where permission is sought before the end of that period, that there is good reason for the applicant being unable to bring the appeal in time; or

(b) where permission is sought after that time, that there was a good reason for the applicant's failure to bring the appeal in time and for any delay in applying for permission.

(4) The court determining an appeal may—

(a) dismiss the appeal; or

(b) quash the decision,

and where the court quashes a decision it may refer the matter to the registrar with a direction to reconsider it and make a determination in accordance with the findings of the court.

**Duration of a section 243 decision or a section 1088 decision**

**15.** (1) A section 243 decision shall continue to have effect until—

(a) either—

(i) the section 243 beneficiary, or

(ii) his personal representative,

has notified the registrar in writing that he wishes the section 243 decision to cease to apply; or

(b) the registrar has made a revocation decision in relation to that beneficiary, whichever first occurs.

(2) A section 1088 decision shall continue to have effect until the registrar has made a revocation decision in relation to the section 1088 beneficiary.

(3) In this regulation—

'personal representative' means the executor, original or by representation, or administrator for the time being of a deceased person; and

'revocation decision' in relation to a section 243 decision or a section 1088 decision means a determination by the registrar to revoke that decision in accordance with regulation 16.

**Revocation of a section 243 decision or a section 1088 decision**

**16.** (1) The registrar may revoke a section 243 decision or a section 1088 decision at any time if he is satisfied that the section 243 beneficiary or section 1088 beneficiary, as the case may be, or any other person, in purported compliance with any provision of these Regulations, is found guilty of an offence under section 1112 (general false statement offence) ('a revocation decision').

(2) If the registrar proposes to make a revocation decision he shall send the beneficiary notice of his intention.

(3) The notice must—

    (a) inform the beneficiary that he may, within the period of 28 days beginning with the date of the notice, deliver representations in writing to the registrar; and

    (b) state that if representations are not received by the registrar within that period, the revocation decision will be made at the expiry of that period.

(4) If within the period specified in paragraph (3) the beneficiary delivers representations as to why the revocation decision should not be made, the registrar shall have regard to the representations in determining whether to make the revocation decision, and shall, within five working days of making his decision, send notice of it to the beneficiary.

(5) Any communication by the registrar in respect of a revocation decision or proposed revocation decision shall be sent to the beneficiary—

    (a) in the case of an individual, to his usual residential address;

    (b) in the case of a company, to its registered office; or

    (c) in the case of a partnership, to the address specified in its section 1088 application.

(6) In this regulation—

'partnership' includes a limited liability partnership;

'section 243 beneficiary' includes where the section 243 decision was made following an application under regulation 6 or 7, the applicant.

SCHEDULE 1             Regulation 2

SPECIFIED PUBLIC AUTHORITIES

The Secretary of State;

any Northern Ireland Department;

the Scottish Ministers;

the Welsh Ministers;

the Treasury;

the Commissioners for Her Majesty's Revenue and Customs;

the Bank of England;

the Director of Public Prosecutions;

the Director of Public Prosecutions for Northern Ireland;

the Serious Fraud Office;

the Secret Intelligence Service;

the Security Service;

the Government Communications Headquarters;

the Financial Services Authority;

the Competition Commission;

the Pensions Regulator;

the Panel on Takeovers and Mergers;

the Regulator of Community Interest Companies;

the Registrar of Credit Unions for Northern Ireland;

the Office of Fair Trading;

the Office of the Information Commissioner;

the Charity Commission;

the Charity Commission for Northern Ireland;

the Office of the Scottish Charity Regulator;

the Postal Services Commission;

the Gas and Electricity Markets Authority;

the Northern Ireland Authority for Utility Regulation;

the Gambling Commission;

the Serious Organised Crime Agency;

the Health and Safety Executive;

the Health and Safety Executive for Northern Ireland;

the Food Standards Agency;

the Gangmasters Licensing Authority;

the Security Industry Authority;

a local authority within the meaning of section 54(2) of the Act;

an official receiver appointed under section 399 of the Insolvency Act 1986[210] (appointment, etc, of official receivers);

the Official Receiver for Northern Ireland;

the Crown Office and Procurator Fiscal Services;

a person acting as an insolvency practitioner within the meaning of section 388 of the Insolvency Act 1986[211] (meaning of 'act as an insolvency practitioner') or Article 3 of the Insolvency (Northern Ireland) Order 1989[212] ('act as an insolvency practitioner');

an inspector appointed under Part 14 of the 1985 Act (investigation of companies and their affairs: requisition of documents) or Part 15 of the 1986 Order or a person appointed under regulation 30 of the Open-Ended Investment Companies Regulations 2001[213] (power to investigate) or regulation 22 of the Open-Ended Investment Companies Regulations (Northern Ireland) 2004[214];

any person authorised to exercise powers under section 447 of the 1985 Act[215] (power to require documents and information), or section 84 of the Companies Act 1989[216] (exercise of powers by officers, etc) or Article 440 of the 1986 Order;

any person exercising functions conferred by Part 6 of the Financial Services and Markets Act 2000[217]

(official listing) or the competent authority under that Part;

a person appointed to make a report under section 166 (reports by skilled persons) of the Financial Services and Markets Act 2000;

a person appointed to conduct an investigation under section 167 (appointment of persons to carry out general investigations) or 168(3) or (5) (appointment of persons to carry out investigations in particular cases) of the Financial Services and Markets Act 2000[218];

an inspector appointed under section 284 (power to investigate) of the Financial Services and Markets Act 2000;

an overseas regulatory authority within the meaning of section 82 of the Companies Act 1989[219] (request for assistance by overseas regulatory authority);

a police force.

SCHEDULE 2                                              Regulations 2 and 3

CONDITIONS FOR PERMITTED DISCLOSURE

PART 1

DISCLOSURE TO SPECIFIED PUBLIC AUTHORITIES

1. Paragraphs 2 and 3 set out the conditions specified for the disclosure of protected information by the registrar to a specified public authority.
2. The specified public authority has delivered to the registrar a statement that it intends to use the protected information only for the purpose of facilitating the carrying out by that specified public authority of a public function ('the permitted purpose').
3. Subject to paragraph 4, the specified public authority ('the authority') has delivered to the registrar a statement that it will, where it supplies a copy of the protected information to a processor for the purpose of processing the information for use in respect of the permitted purpose—
   (a) ensure that the processor is one who carries on business in the European Economic Area;

---

[210]  1986 c.45. Section 399 was amended by section 269 of the Enterprise Act 2002 (c.40).

[211]  Section 388 was amended by section 4 of the Insolvency Act 2000 (c.39) and the Insolvency Act (Amendment) (No. 2) Regulations 2002 (SI 2002/1240).

[212]  SI 1989/2405 (NI 9).

[213]  SI 2001/1228.

[214]  SR (NI) 2004 No 335.

[215]  Section 447 was substituted by section 21 of the Companies (Audit, Investigations and Community Enterprise) Act 2004 (c.27).

[216]  1989 c.40.

[217]  2000 c.8.

[218]  Sections 167 and 168 were amended by the Financial Services and Markets Act 2000 (Markets in Financial Instruments) Regulations 2007 (SI 2007/176).

[219]  Section 82 was amended by section 79 of the Criminal Justice Act 1993 (c.36), the Financial Services and Markets Act 2000 (Consequential Amendments and Repeals) Order 2001 (SI 2001/3649) and the Prospectus Regulations 2005 (SI 2005/1433).

(b) require that the information is not transmitted outside the European Economic Area by the processor; and

(c) require that the processor does not disclose the information except to the authority or an employee of the authority.

**4.** Paragraph 3 does not apply where the specified public authority is the Secret Intelligence Service, Security Service or Government Communications Headquarters.

## PART 2
## DISCLOSURE TO A CREDIT REFERENCE AGENCY

**5.** Paragraphs 6 to 10 set out the conditions specified for the disclosure of protected information by the registrar to a credit reference agency.

**6.** The credit reference agency—

(a) is carrying on in the United Kingdom or in another EEA State a business comprising the furnishing of information relevant to the financial standing of individuals, being information collected by the agency for that purpose;

(b) maintains appropriate procedures—

(i) to ensure that an independent person can investigate and audit the measures maintained by the agency for the purposes of ensuring the security of any protected information disclosed to that agency; and

(ii) for the purposes of ensuring that it complies with its obligations under the Data Protection Act 1998[220], or, where the agency carries on business in a EEA State other than the United Kingdom, with its obligations under legislation implementing Directive 95/46/EC of the European Parliament and of the Council of 24 October 1995 on the protection of individuals with regard to the processing of personal data and on the free movement of such data[221];

(c) has not been found guilty of an offence under—

(i) section 1112 (general false statement offence) of the Act or section 2 of the Fraud Act 2006[222] (fraud by false representation); or

(ii) section 47 (failure to comply with enforcement notice) of the Data Protection Act 1998 in circumstances where it has used the protected information for purposes other than those described in sub-paragraphs (a) to (e) of paragraph 7 below.

**7.** The credit reference agency has delivered to the registrar a statement that it intends to use the protected information only for the purposes of—

(a) providing an assessment of the financial standing of a person;

(b) meeting any obligations contained in the Money Laundering Regulations 2007[223] or any rules made pursuant to section 146 of the Financial Services and Markets Act 2000[224] (money laundering rules), or in any legislation of another EEA State implementing Directive 2005/60/EC of the European Parliament and of the Council of 26 October 2005 on the prevention of the use of the financial system for the purpose of money laundering and terrorist financing[225];

(c) conducting conflict of interest checks required or made necessary by any enactment;

(d) the provision of protected information to—

(i) a public authority specified in Schedule 1 which has satisfied the requirements of paragraphs 2 and 3 of this Schedule; or

(ii) a credit reference agency which has satisfied the requirements of this Part of this Schedule; or

(e) conducting checks for the prevention and detection of crime and fraud.

**8.** The credit reference agency has delivered to the registrar a statement that it intends to take delivery of and to use the protected information only in the United Kingdom or in another EEA State.

**9.** The credit reference agency has delivered to the registrar a statement that it will, where it supplies a copy of the protected information to a processor for the purpose of processing the information for use in respect of the purposes referred to in paragraph 7—

(a) ensure that the processor is one who carries on business in the European Economic Area;

---

[220] 1998 c.29.

[221] OJ L 81, 23.11.1995, p 31.

[222] 2006 c.35.

[223] SI 2007/2157.

[224] Section 146 enables the making of rules by the Financial Services Authority in relation to the prevention and detection of money laundering in connection with the carrying on of regulated activities by authorised persons.

[225] OJ L 309, 25.11.2005, p 15.

    (b)  require that the information is not transmitted outside the European Economic Area by the processor; and

    (c)  require that the processor does not disclose the information except to the credit reference agency or an employee of the credit reference agency.

**10.** The credit reference agency has delivered to the registrar a statement that it meets the conditions in paragraph 6 above.

PART 3

INTERPRETATION OF THIS SCHEDULE

**11.** (1) In this Schedule—

'processor' means any person who provides a service which consists of putting information into data form or processing information in data form and any reference to a processor includes a reference to his employees; and

'public function' includes—

    (a)  any function conferred by or in accordance with any provision contained in any enactment;

    (b)  any function conferred by or in accordance with any provision contained in the Community Treaties or any Community instrument;

    (c)  any similar function conferred on persons by or under provisions having effect as part of the law of a country or territory outside the United Kingdom; and

    (d)  any function exercisable in relation to the investigation of any criminal offence or for the purpose of any criminal proceedings.

(2) In this Schedule any reference to—

    (a)  an employee of any person who has access to protected information shall be deemed to include any person working or providing services for the purposes of that person or employed by or on behalf of, or working for, any person who is so working or who is supplying such a service; and

    (b)  the disclosure for the purpose of facilitating the carrying out of a public function includes disclosure in relation to, and for the purpose of, any proceedings whether civil, criminal or disciplinary in which the specified public authority engages while carrying out its public functions.

# THE COMPANIES (TRADING DISCLOSURES) (AMENDMENT) REGULATIONS 2009

## (SI 2009/218)

COMMENCEMENT DATE 1 October 2009[226]

**SI.33**

### Citation, commencement and interpretation

**1.** (1) These Regulations may be cited as the Companies (Trading Disclosures) (Amendment) Regulations 2009 and come into force on 1st October 2009.

(2) In these Regulations 'the Regulations' means the Companies (Trading Disclosures) Regulations 2008[227].

### Requirement to display registered name at registered office and inspection place

**2.** (1) Regulation 3 of the Regulations is amended as follows.

(2) After regulation 3(2) insert—

'(3) Paragraph (1) shall also not apply to the registered office or an inspection place of a company where—

    (a)  in respect of that company, a liquidator, administrator or administrative receiver has been appointed; and

    (b)  the registered office or inspection place is also a place of business of that liquidator, administrator or administrative receiver.'.

---

[226] 2006 c.46.

[227] SI 2008/495.

**Requirement to display registered name at other business locations**

**3.** (1) Regulation 4 of the Regulations is amended as follows.

(2) After regulation 4(3) insert—

'(4) Paragraph (2) shall also not apply to any location at which business is carried on by a company where—

(a) in respect of that company, a liquidator, administrator or administrative receiver has been appointed; and

(b) the location is also a place of business of that liquidator, administrator or administrative receiver.

(5) Paragraph (2) shall also not apply to any location at which business is carried on by a company of which every director who is an individual is a relevant director.

(6) In this regulation—

(a) 'administrative receiver' has the meaning given—

(i) in England and Wales or Scotland, by section 251 of the Insolvency Act 1986[228], and

(ii) in Northern Ireland, by Article 5 of the Insolvency (Northern Ireland) Order 1989[229];

(b) 'credit reference agency' has the meaning given in section 243(7) of the Act;

(c) 'protected information' has the meaning given in section 240 of the Act; and

(d) 'relevant director' means an individual in respect of whom the registrar is required by regulations made pursuant to section 243(4) of the Act to refrain from disclosing protected information to a credit reference agency.'.

**Minor amendment to regulation 7 of the Regulations**

**4.** In regulation 7(2)(d) of the Regulations omit from 'section 30' to 'Order 1986' and substitute 'section 60 of the Act'.

---

# The Companies (Shares and Share Capital) Order 2009

## (SI 2009/388)

COMMENCEMENT DATE 1 October 2009[230]

**Citation, commencement and interpretation**                                SI.34

**1.** (1) This Order may be cited as the Companies (Shares and Share Capital) Order 2009 and shall come into force on 1st October 2009.

(2) In this Order, a reference to a section is a reference to a section of the Companies Act 2006.

**Statements of capital, and returns of allotment by unlimited companies: prescribed particulars of the rights attached to shares**

**2.** (1) The particulars in paragraph (3) are prescribed for the purposes of the provisions in paragraph (2).

(2) The provisions are—

(a) section 10(2)(c)(i);

(b) section 32(2)(c)(i);

(c) section 108(3)(c)(i);

(d) section 555(4)(c)(i);

(e) section 556(3);

(f) section 619(3)(c)(i);

(g) section 621(3)(c)(i);

(h) section 625(3)(c)(i);

(i) section 627(3)(c)(i);

(j) section 644(2)(c)(i);

(k) section 649(2)(c)(i);

(l) section 663(3)(c)(i);

(m) section 689(3)(c)(i);

(n) section 708(3)(c)(i); and

---

[228] 1986 c.45.

[229] SI 1989/2405 (NI 19).

[230] 2006 c.46.

(o) section 730(5)(c)(i).

(3) The particulars are—

(a) particulars of any voting rights attached to the shares, including rights that arise only in certain circumstances;

(b) particulars of any rights attached to the shares, as respects dividends, to participate in a distribution;

(c) particulars of any rights attached to the shares, as respects capital, to participate in a distribution (including on winding up); and

(d) whether the shares are to be redeemed or are liable to be redeemed at the option of the company or the shareholder.

### Prescribed information for a return of an allotment by a limited company

**3.** (1) The information in paragraph (2) is prescribed for the purposes of section 555(3)(a) (information to be contained in a return of an allotment by a limited company).

(2) The information is—

(a) the number of shares allotted;

(b) the amount paid up and the amount (if any) unpaid on each allotted share (whether on account of the nominal value of the share or by way of premium); and

(c) where the shares are allotted as fully or partly paid up (as to their nominal value or any premium on them) otherwise than in cash, the consideration for the allotment.

### Shares deemed paid up in or allotted for cash, and sale of treasury shares for a cash consideration: meaning of cash consideration

**4.** (1) The creation of an obligation on the part of a settlement bank to make a relevant payment in respect of the allotment of a share to a system-member by means of a relevant system is to be regarded as a means of payment falling within section 583(3)(e).

(2) The creation of an obligation on the part of a settlement bank to make a relevant payment in respect of the payment up of a share by a system-member by means of a relevant system is to be regarded as a means of payment falling within section 583(3)(e).

(3) The creation of an obligation on the part of a settlement bank to make a relevant payment in respect of the transfer by a company to a system-member, by means of a relevant system, of a share held by the company as a treasury share is to be regarded as a means of payment falling within section 727(2)(e).

(4) In this article—

(a) the expressions 'Operator', 'relevant system', 'rules', 'settlement bank', 'system-member' and 'uncertificated' have the meanings given in the Uncertificated Securities Regulations 2001[231]; and

(b) 'relevant payment' means a payment in accordance with the rules and practices of an Operator of a relevant system.

### Redemption or purchase of own shares out of capital by a private company: prescribed form of, and information with respect to the nature of the company's business to be contained in, a directors' statement

**5.** (1) The directors' statement required by section 714 (directors' statement to be made where a private company makes a payment out of capital for the redemption or purchase of its own shares) must—

(a) be in writing;

(b) indicate that it is a directors' statement made under that section; and

(c) be signed by each of the company's directors.

(2) The statement must state—

(a) whether the company's business includes that of a banking company; and

(b) whether its business includes that of an insurance company.

THE COMPANY AND BUSINESS NAMES (MISCELLANEOUS PROVISIONS) REGULATIONS 2009

(SI 2009/1085)

COMMENCEMENT DATE 1 October 2009[232]

---

[231] SI 2001/3755; relevant amending instruments are SI 2003/1633, 2007/124.
[232] 2006 c.46.

# PART 1

## INTRODUCTORY

### Citation, commencement and interpretation                                        SI.35

**1.** (1) These Regulations may be cited as the Company and Business Names (Miscellaneous Provisions) Regulations 2009 and come into force on 1st October 2009.

(2) In these Regulations—

'the Act' means the Companies Act 2006;

'expression or abbreviation specified as similar' has the meaning given in paragraph 4 of Schedule 2 and 'abbreviation specified as similar' has the meaning that would be given to it in that paragraph if that paragraph made no reference to 'expressions';

'permitted characters' has the meaning given in regulation 2(1);

'word or abbreviation specified as similar' has the meaning given in paragraph 2 of Schedule 2; and

'word specified as similar' has the meaning given in paragraph 2 of Schedule 2.

(3) For the purposes of computing the number of permitted characters in regulation 2(4) and paragraph 7 of Schedule 3 (but not in regulation 2(3)), any blank space between one permitted character and another in the name shall be counted as though it was a permitted character.

# PART 2

## COMPANY NAMES

### Permitted characters

**2.** (1) This regulation sets out the characters, signs, symbols and punctuation that may be used in the name of a company registered under the Act ('the permitted characters').

(2) The following permitted characters may be used in any part of the name—

(a) any character, sign or symbol set out in table 1 in Schedule 1;

(b) 0, 1, 2, 3, 4, 5, 6, 7, 8 or 9;

(c) full stop, comma, colon, semi-colon or hyphen; and

(d) any other punctuation referred to in column 1 of table 2 in Schedule 1 but only in one of the forms set out opposite that punctuation in column 2 of that table.

(3) The signs and symbols set out in table 3 in Schedule 1 are permitted characters that may be used but not as one of the first three permitted characters of the name.

(4) The name must not consist of more than 160 permitted characters.

### Exemption from requirement as to use of 'limited'

**3.** (1) A private company limited by guarantee is exempt from the requirement of section 59 of the Act (requirement to have name ending with 'limited' or permitted alternative) so long as it meets the following two conditions.

(2) The first condition is that the objects of that company are the promotion or regulation of commerce, art, science, education, religion, charity or any profession, and anything incidental or conducive to any of those objects.

(3) The second condition is that the company's articles—

(a) require its income to be applied in promoting its objects;

(b) prohibit the payment of dividends, or any return of capital, to its members; and

(c) require all the assets that would otherwise be available to its members generally to be transferred on its winding up either—

(i) to another body with objects similar to its own; or

(ii) to another body the objects of which are the promotion of charity and anything incidental or conducive thereto,

(whether or not the body is a member of the company).

### Inappropriate indication of company type or legal form: generally applicable provisions

**4.** (1) A company must not be registered under the Act by a name that includes, otherwise than at the end of the name, an expression or abbreviation specified in inverted commas in paragraph 3(a) to (f) of Schedule 2 (or any expression or abbreviation specified as similar).

(2) A company must not be registered under the Act by a name that includes in any part of the name an expression or abbreviation specified in inverted commas in paragraph 3(g) or (h) of Schedule 2 (or any expression or abbreviation specified as similar) unless that company is a RTE company within the meaning of section 4A of the Leasehold Reform, Housing and Urban Development Act 1993[233].

---

[233] 1993 c.28; section 4A was inserted by section 122 of the Commonhold and Leasehold Reform Act 2002 (c.15) but section 122 is not yet in force.

(3) A company must not be registered under the Act by a name that includes in any part of the name an expression or abbreviation specified in inverted commas in paragraph 3(i) or (j) of Schedule 2 (or any expression or abbreviation specified as similar) unless that company is a RTM company within the meaning of section 73 of the Commonhold and Leasehold Reform Act 2002[234].

(4) A company must not be registered under the Act by a name that includes in any part of the name an expression or abbreviation specified in inverted commas in paragraph 3(k) to (u) of Schedule 2 (or any expression or abbreviation specified as similar).

(5) A company must not be registered under the Act by a name that includes immediately before an expression or abbreviation specified in inverted commas in paragraph 3(a) to (j) of Schedule 2 an abbreviation specified in inverted commas in paragraph 3(v) of that Schedule (or any abbreviation specified as similar).

(6) Paragraph (1) is subject to regulations 5(b) and 6(b).

### Inappropriate indication of company type or legal form: company exempt from requirement to have name ending in 'limited'

**5.** A company which is exempt from the requirement of section 59 of the Act (requirement to have name ending with 'limited' or permitted alternative) under section 60 of the Act must not be registered under the Act by a name that concludes with—

(a) a word specified in inverted commas in paragraph 1(c) or (d) of Schedule 2 (or any word specified as similar); or

(b) an expression or abbreviation specified in inverted commas in paragraph 3(a) to (f) or (v) of Schedule 2 (or any expression or abbreviation specified as similar).

### Inappropriate indication of company type or legal form: unlimited company

**6.** An unlimited company must not be registered under the Act by a name that concludes with—

(a) a word or abbreviation specified in inverted commas in paragraph 1(a) or (b) of Schedule 2 (or any word or abbreviation specified as similar); or

(b) an expression or abbreviation specified in inverted commas in paragraph 3(a) to (f) or (v) of Schedule 2 (or any expression or abbreviation specified as similar).

### Name not to be the same as another in the registrar's index of company names

**7.** For the purposes of section 66 of the Act (determining whether a name to be registered under the Act is the same as another name appearing in the registrar's index of company names) Schedule 3 has effect for setting out—

(a) the matters that are to be disregarded; and

(b) the words, expressions, signs and symbols that are to be regarded as the same.

### Consent to registration of a name which is the same as another in the registrar's index of company names

**8.** (1) A company may be registered under the Act by a proposed same name if the conditions in paragraph (2) are met.

(2) The conditions are—

(a) the company or other body whose name already appears in the registrar's index of company names ('Body X') consents to the proposed same name being the name of a company ('Company Y');

(b) Company Y forms, or is to form, part of the same group as Body X; and

(c) Company Y provides to the registrar a copy of a statement made by Body X indicating—

(i) the consent of Body X as referred to in sub-paragraph (a); and

(ii) that Company Y forms, or is to form, part of the same group as Body X.

(3) If the proposed same name is to be taken by a company which has not yet been incorporated, the copy of such statement must be provided to the registrar instead by the person who delivers to the registrar the application for registration of the company (and the reference in paragraph (1) to the conditions in paragraph (2) shall be read accordingly).

(4) The registrar may accept the statement referred to in paragraph (2)(c) as sufficient evidence that the conditions referred to in paragraph (2)(a) and (b) have been met.

(5) If the consent referred to in paragraph (2)(a) is given by Body X, a subsequent withdrawal of that consent does not affect the registration of Company Y by that proposed same name.

(6) In this regulation—

(a) 'group' has the meaning given in section 474(1) of the Act; and

(b) 'proposed same name' means a name which is, due to the application of regulation 7 and Schedule 3, considered the same as a name appearing in the registrar's index of company names and differs from that name appearing in the index only by one of the matters set out in inverted commas in paragraph 4 of Schedule 3.

---

[234] 2002 c.15.

## PART 3

## OVERSEAS COMPANY NAMES

### Interpretation and permitted characters

**9.** Regulations 1(2) and (3) and 2 apply to the name of an overseas company which is registered by that company under Part 34 of the Act (overseas companies) as they apply to the name of a company formed and registered under the Act.

### Inappropriate indication of company type or legal form

**10.** (1) An overseas company must not be registered under the Act by a name that concludes with a word or abbreviation specified in inverted commas in paragraph 1(a) or (b) of Schedule 2 (or any word or abbreviation specified as similar) unless the liability of the members of the company is limited by its constitution.

(2) An overseas company must not be registered under the Act by a name that concludes with a word specified in inverted commas in paragraph 1(c) or (d) of Schedule 2 (or any word specified as similar) unless the liability of the members of the company is not limited by its constitution.

(3) An overseas company must not be registered under the Act by a name that includes in any part of the name an expression or abbreviation specified in inverted commas in paragraph 3 of Schedule 2 (or any expression or abbreviation specified as similar).

### Name not to be the same as another in the registrar's index of company names

**11.** Regulation 7 applies to the name of an overseas company which is registered by that company under Part 34 of the Act as it applies to the name of a company formed and registered under the Act.

### Consent to registration of a name which is the same as another in the registrar's index of company names

**12.** (1) Regulation 8 applies to the proposed same name of an overseas company as it applies to the proposed same name of a company formed and registered under the Act.

(2) In this regulation 'proposed same name' has the same meaning as in regulation 8.

## PART 4

## BUSINESS NAMES

### 'Limited' and permitted alternatives

**13.** (1) A person must not carry on business in the United Kingdom under a name that concludes with any word or abbreviation set out in inverted commas in paragraph 1(a) or (b) of Schedule 2 unless that person is—

(a) a company or an overseas company registered in the United Kingdom by that name;

(b) an overseas company incorporated with that name; [...][a]

(c) a society registered under the Industrial and Provident Societies Act 1965[b] or the Industrial and Provident Societies Act (Northern Ireland) 1969[c] by that name;

[(d) an incorporated friendly society (as defined in section 116 of the Friendly Societies Act 1992) which has that name; or

(e) a company to which section 1040 of the Companies Act 2006 (companies authorised to register under the Companies Act 2006) applies which has that name][d].

(2) A person must not carry on business in the United Kingdom under a name that concludes with any word or abbreviation specified as similar to any word or abbreviation set out in inverted commas in paragraph 1(a) or (b) of Schedule 2.

AMENDMENTS AND NOTES

[a] Revoked by the Company, Limited Liability Partnership and Business Names (Miscellaneous Provisions) (Amendment) Regulations 2009 (S.I. 2009/2404, reg 2(2)(a)).

[b] 1965 c.12.

[c] 1969 c.24 (N.I.).

[d] Inserted by the Company, Limited Liability Partnership and Business Names (Miscellaneous Provisions) (Amendment) Regulations 2009 (S.I. 2009/2404, reg 2(2)(b)).

### Other indications of legal form

**14.** (1) A person must not carry on business in the United Kingdom under a name that includes any expression or abbreviation set out in inverted commas in paragraph 3 of Schedule 2 unless that person is such a company, partnership, grouping or organisation as is indicated in that expression or abbreviation.

(2) A person must not carry on business in the United Kingdom under a name that includes any expression or abbreviation specified as similar to any expression or abbreviation set out in inverted commas in paragraph 3 of Schedule 2.

**Transitional provisions**

**15.** (1) Regulation 14 does not apply to the carrying on of a business under a name by a person who—

(a) carried on that business under that name immediately before these Regulations came into force; and

(b) continues to carry it on under that name,

if it was lawful for the business to be carried on under that name immediately before these Regulations came into force.

(2) Regulation 14 does not apply to the carrying on of a business under a name by a person to whom the business is transferred on or after the date on which these Regulations came into force—

(a) where that person continues to carry on the business under that name; and

(b) where it was lawful for the business to be carried on under that name immediately before the transfer,

during the period of 12 months beginning with the date of the transfer.

SCHEDULE 1      Regulation 2

CHARACTERS, SIGNS, SYMBOLS AND PUNCTUATION

TABLE 1

| Characters, signs and symbols | | | | |
|---|---|---|---|---|
| A | B | C | D | E |
| F | G | H | I | J |
| K | L | M | N | O |
| P | Q | R | S | T |
| U | V | W | X | Y |
| Z | & | @ | £ | $ |
| ¤ | ¥ | | | |

TABLE 2

| Type of punctuation | Punctuation mark |
|---|---|
| Apostrophe | ‘ ’ ’ |
| Bracket | ( ) [ ] { } < > |
| Exclamation mark | ! |
| Guillemet | « » |
| Inverted comma | “ ” " |
| Question mark | ? |
| Solidus | \ / |

Table 1

| *Signs and symbols* |
|---|
| * |
| = |
| # |
| % |
| + |

SCHEDULE 2        Regulations 1, 4 to 6, 10, 13 and 14

SPECIFIED WORDS, EXPRESSIONS AND ABBREVIATIONS

**1.** The words and abbreviations specified are—
  (a) 'LIMITED' or (with or without full stops) the abbreviation 'LTD';
  (b) 'CYFYNGEDIG' or (with or without full stops) the abbreviation 'CYF';
  (c) 'UNLIMITED'; and
  (d) 'ANGHYFYNGEDIG'.
**2.** The words and abbreviations specified as similar to the words and abbreviations set out in inverted commas in paragraph 1(a) and (b) and the words specified as similar to the words set out in inverted commas in paragraph 1(c) and (d) are any in which—
  (a) one or more characters has been omitted;
  (b) one or more characters, signs, symbols or punctuation has been added; or
  (c) each of one or more characters has been substituted by one or more other characters, signs, symbols or punctuation,
  in such a way as to be likely to mislead the public as to the legal form of a company or business if included in the registered name of the company or in a business name.
**3.** The expressions and abbreviations specified are—
  (a) 'PUBLIC LIMITED COMPANY' or (with or without full stops) the abbreviation 'PLC';
  (b) 'CWMNI CYFYNGEDIG CYHOEDDUS' or (with or without full stops) the abbreviation 'CCC';
  (c) 'COMMUNITY INTEREST COMPANY' or (with or without full stops) the abbreviation 'CIC';
  (d) 'CWMNI BUDDIANT CYMUNEDOL' or (with or without full stops) the abbreviation 'CBC';
  (e) 'COMMUNITY INTEREST PUBLIC LIMITED COMPANY' or (with or without full stops) the abbreviation 'COMMUNITY INTEREST PLC';
  (f) 'CWMNI BUDDIANT CYMUNEDOL CYHOEDDUS CYFYNGEDIG' or (with or without full stops) the abbreviation ['CWMNI BUDDIANT CYMUNEDOL CCC'][a];
  (g) 'RIGHT TO ENFRANCHISEMENT' or (with or without full stops) the abbreviation 'RTE';
  (h) 'HAWL I RYDDFREINIAD';
  (i) 'RIGHT TO MANAGE' or (with or without full stops) the abbreviation 'RTM';
  (j) 'CWMNI RTM CYFYNGEDIG';
  (k) 'EUROPEAN ECONOMIC INTEREST GROUPING' or (with or without full stops) the abbreviation 'EEIG';
  (l) 'INVESTMENT COMPANY WITH VARIABLE CAPITAL';
  (m) 'CWMNI BUDDSODDI A CHYFALAF NEWIDIOL';
  (n) 'LIMITED PARTNERSHIP';
  (o) 'PARTNERIAETH CYFYNGEDIG';
  (p) 'LIMITED LIABILITY PARTNERSHIP';
  (q) 'PARTNERIAETH ATEBOLRWYDD CYFYNGEDIG';
  (r) 'OPEN-ENDED INVESTMENT COMPANY';
  (s) 'CWMNI BUDDSODDIANT PENAGORED';
  (t) 'CHARITABLE INCORPORATED ORGANISATION';
  (u) 'SEFDYDLIAD ELUSENNOL CORFFOREDIG'; [...][b]
  [(ua) 'INDUSTRIAL AND PROVIDENT SOCIETY'; and][c]
  (v) the following abbreviations (with or without full stops) of the expressions specified in sub-paragraphs (n), (o), (p), (q), (t) and (u) respectively, namely 'LP', 'PC', 'LLP', 'PAC', 'CIO' and 'SEC'.
**4.** The expressions and abbreviations specified as similar to the expressions and abbreviations set out in inverted commas in paragraph 3 are any in which—
  (a) one or more characters has been omitted;
  (b) one or more characters, signs, symbols or punctuation has been added; or
  (c) each of one or more characters has been substituted by one or more other characters, signs, symbols or punctuation,
  in such a way as to be likely to mislead the public as to the legal form of a company or business if included in the registered name of the company or in a business name.

AMENDMENTS AND NOTES

<sup>a</sup> Amended by the Company, Limited Liability Partnership and Business Names (Miscellaneous Provisions) (Amendment) Regulations 2009 (S.I. 2009/2404, reg 2(3)(a)).

<sup>b</sup> Revoked by the Company, Limited Liability Partnership and Business Names (Miscellaneous Provisions) (Amendment) Regulations 2009 (S.I. 2009/2404, reg 2(3)(b)).

<sup>c</sup> Inserted by the Company, Limited Liability Partnership and Business Names (Miscellaneous Provisions) (Amendment) Regulations 2009 (S.I. 2009/2404, reg 2(3)(c)).

## SCHEDULE 3    Regulations 7 and 8

### NAME SAME AS ANOTHER IN THE REGISTRAR'S INDEX OF COMPANY NAMES

1. In determining whether a name is the same as another name appearing in the registrar's index of company names the provisions in this Schedule are to be applied in the order set out in the Schedule.

2. Disregard any word, expression or abbreviation set out in inverted commas in Schedule 2 where it appears at the end of the name.

3. (1) Taking the name remaining after the application of paragraph 2, regard each of the words, expressions, signs and symbols set out in inverted commas in any of the paragraphs of sub-paragraph (2) ('relevant matters') as the same as the other relevant matters set out in that paragraph where each relevant matter—

   (a) is preceded by and followed by a blank space; or
   (b) where the relevant matter is at the beginning of the name, where it is followed by a blank space.

   (2) The words, expressions, signs and symbols are—

   (a) 'AND' and '&';
   (b) 'PLUS' and '+';
   (c) '0', 'ZERO' and 'O';
   (d) '1' and 'ONE';
   (e) '2', 'TWO', 'TO' and 'TOO';
   (f) '3' and 'THREE';
   (g) '4', 'FOUR' and 'FOR';
   (h) '5' and 'FIVE';
   (i) '6' and 'SIX';
   (j) '7' and 'SEVEN';
   (k) '8' and 'EIGHT';
   (l) '9' and 'NINE';
   (m) '£' and 'POUND';
   (n) '€' and 'EURO';
   (o) '$' and 'DOLLAR';
   (p) '¥' and 'YEN';
   (q) '%', 'PER CENT', 'PERCENT', 'PER CENTUM' and 'PERCENTUM'; and
   (r) '@' and 'AT'.

4. (1) Taking the name remaining after the application of paragraphs 2 and 3, disregard at the end of the name the matters set out in inverted commas in sub-paragraph (2) (or any combination of such matters) where the matter (or combination) is preceded by the following punctuation or symbol in inverted commas—

   (a) a blank space;
   (b) a full stop; or
   (c) '@'.

   (2) The matters are—

   (a) 'BIZ';
   (b) 'CO';
   (c) 'CO UK';
   (d) 'CO.UK';
   (e) 'COM';
   (f) 'COMPANY';
   (g) 'EU';
   (h) 'EXPORTS';

    (i)  'GB';
    (j)  'GREAT BRITAIN';
    (k)  'GROUP';
    (l)  'HOLDINGS';
    (m) 'IMPORTS';
    (n)  'INTERNATIONAL';
    (o)  'NET';
    (p)  'NI';
    (q)  'NORTHERN IRELAND';
    (r)  'ORG';
    (s)  'ORG UK';
    (t)  'ORG.UK';
    (u)  'SERVICES';
    (v)  'UK';
    (w)  'UNITED KINGDOM';
    (x)  'WALES';
    (y)  'ALLFORION';
    (z)  'CWMNI';
    (aa) 'CYM';
    (bb) 'CYMRU';
    (cc) 'CYNHEILIAID';
    (dd) 'CYRDDAU';
    (ee) 'DALIADAU';
    (ff) 'DU';
    (gg) 'GRWP';
    (hh) 'GWASANAETHAU';
    (ii) 'MEWNFORION';
    (jj) 'PF';
    (kk) 'PRYDAIN FAWR';
    (ll) 'RHYNGWLADOL';
    (mm)'RYNGWLADOL'; and
    (nn) 'Y DEYRNAS UNEDIG'.

**5.** Taking the name remaining after the application of paragraphs 2 to 4, disregard the following matters in any part of the name—
    (a)  any punctuation set out in regulation 2(2)(c) or in column 2 of table 2 in Schedule 1; and
    (b)  the following symbols set out in inverted commas—
        (i)   '*';
        (ii)  '='; and
        (iii) '#'.

**6.** Taking the name remaining after the application of paragraphs 2 to 5, disregard the letter 'S' at the end of the name.

**7.** Taking the name remaining after the application of paragraphs 2 to 6, disregard any permitted character after the first 60 permitted characters of the name.

**8.** Taking the name remaining after the application of paragraphs 2 to 7, disregard the following matters or any combination of the following matters set out in inverted commas where they appear at the beginning of the name—
    (a)  '@';
    (b)  'THE' (but only where followed by a blank space); and
    (c)  'WWW'.

**9.** Taking the name remaining after the application of paragraphs 2 to 8, disregard blank spaces between permitted characters.

# THE COMPANIES (SHAREHOLDERS' RIGHTS) REGULATIONS 2009
## (SI 2009/1632)

COMMENCEMENT DATE 3 August 2009[235]

## PART 1
### INTRODUCTORY

SI.36

**Citation and commencement**

**1.** (1) These Regulations may be cited as the Companies (Shareholders' Rights) Regulations 2009.
(2) They come into force on 3rd August 2009 and apply in relation to meetings of which notice is given, or first given, on or after that date.

## PART 2
### AMENDMENTS OF GENERAL APPLICATION

**Voting on show of hands**

**2.** (1) In section 282(3) of the Companies Act 2006[236] (ordinary resolutions: majority required on show of hands), for the words from 'a simple majority of' to the end substitute 'a simple majority of the votes cast by those entitled to vote'.

(2) In section 283(4) of that Act (special resolutions: majority required on show of hands), for the words from 'not less than 75% of' to the end substitute 'not less than 75% of the votes cast by those entitled to vote'.

(3) In section 284 of that Act (votes: general rules), for subsection (2) substitute—

'(2) On a vote on a resolution on a show of hands at a meeting, each member present in person has one vote.'.

(4) After subsection (4) of that section add—

'(5) Nothing in this section is to be read as restricting the effect of—
section 152 (exercise of rights by nominees),
section 285 (voting by proxy),
section 322 (exercise of voting rights on poll),
section 322A (voting on a poll: votes cast in advance), or
section 323 (representation of corporations at meetings).'.

**Voting by proxy**

**3.** For section 285 of the Companies Act 2006 (voting: specific requirements) substitute—

**'Voting by proxy**

**285.** (1) On a vote on a resolution on a show of hands at a meeting, every proxy present who has been duly appointed by one or more members entitled to vote on the resolution has one vote.
This is subject to subsection (2).

(2) On a vote on a resolution on a show of hands at a meeting, a proxy has one vote for and one vote against the resolution if—
(a) the proxy has been duly appointed by more than one member entitled to vote on the resolution, and
(b) the proxy has been instructed by one or more of those members to vote for the resolution and by one or more other of those members to vote against it.

(3) On a poll taken at a meeting of a company all or any of the voting rights of a member may be exercised by one or more duly appointed proxies.

(4) Where a member appoints more than one proxy, subsection (3) does not authorise the exercise by the proxies taken together of more extensive voting rights than could be exercised by the member in person.

(5) Subsections (1) and (2) have effect subject to any provision of the company's articles.

---

[235]  SI 2007/193.
[236]  2006 c.46.

#### Voting rights on poll or written resolution

**285A.** In relation to a resolution required or authorised by an enactment, if a private company's articles provide that a member has a different number of votes in relation to a resolution when it is passed as a written resolution and when it is passed on a poll taken at a meeting—

    (a) the provision about how many votes a member has in relation to the resolution passed on a poll is void, and

    (b) a member has the same number of votes in relation to the resolution when it is passed on a poll as the member has when it is passed as a written resolution.'.

#### Members' power to require directors to call general meetings

**4.** (1) Section 303 of the Companies Act 2006 (members' power to require directors to call general meeting) is amended as follows.

(2) In subsection (2)(a) and (b), for 'the required percentage' substitute '5%'.

(3) Omit subsection (3).

#### Advance voting on a poll

**5.** (1) After section 322 of the Companies Act 2006 insert—

##### 'Voting on a poll: votes cast in advance

**322A.** (1) A company's articles may contain provision to the effect that on a vote on a resolution on a poll taken at a meeting, the votes may include votes cast in advance.

    (2) In the case of a traded company any such provision in relation to voting at a general meeting may be made subject only to such requirements and restrictions as are—

        (a) necessary to ensure the identification of the person voting, and

        (b) proportionate to the achievement of that objective.

        Nothing in this subsection affects any power of a company to require reasonable evidence of the entitlement of any person who is not a member to vote.

    (3) Any provision of a company's articles is void in so far as it would have the effect of requiring any document casting a vote in advance to be received by the company or another person earlier than the following time—

        (a) in the case of a poll taken more than 48 hours after it was demanded, 24 hours before the time appointed for the taking of the poll;

        (b) in the case of any other poll, 48 hours before the time for holding the meeting or adjourned meeting.

    (4) In calculating the periods mentioned in subsection (3), no account is to be taken of any part of a day that is not a working day.'.

(2) In section 282(4) and section 283(5) of that Act (passing of ordinary or special resolution on a poll), for 'in person or by proxy' substitute 'in person, by proxy or in advance (see section 322A)'.

#### Representation of corporations at meetings

**6.** In section 323 of the Companies Act 2006 (representation of corporations at meetings), for subsections (2) to (4) substitute—

'(2) A person authorised by a corporation is entitled to exercise (on behalf of the corporation) the same powers as the corporation could exercise if it were an individual member of the company.

    Where a corporation authorises more than one person, this subsection is subject to subsections (3) and (4).

(3) On a vote on a resolution on a show of hands at a meeting of the company, each authorised person has the same voting rights as the corporation would be entitled to.

(4) Where subsection (3) does not apply and more than one authorised person purport to exercise a power under subsection (2) in respect of the same shares—

    (a) if they purport to exercise the power in the same way as each other, the power is treated as exercised in that way;

    (b) if they do not purport to exercise the power in the same way as each other, the power is treated as not exercised.'.

#### Obligations of proxies

**7.** After section 324 of the Companies Act 2006 insert—

##### 'Obligation of proxy to vote in accordance with instructions

**324A.** A proxy must vote in accordance with any instructions given by the member by whom the proxy is appointed.'.

**Electronic meetings and voting**

**8.** After section 360 of the Companies Act 2006 insert—

**'Electronic meetings and voting**

   **360A.** —(1) Nothing in this Part is to be taken to preclude the holding and conducting of a meeting in such a way that persons who are not present together at the same place may by electronic means attend and speak and vote at it.

   (2) In the case of a traded company the use of electronic means for the purpose of enabling members to participate in a general meeting may be made subject only to such requirements and restrictions as are—

      (a) necessary to ensure the identification of those taking part and the security of the electronic communication, and

      (b) proportionate to the achievement of those objectives.

   (3) Nothing in subsection (2) affects any power of a company to require reasonable evidence of the entitlement of any person who is not a member to participate in the meeting.'.

PART 3

AMENDMENTS RELATING TO TRADED COMPANIES

**Traded companies: notice of general meetings**

**9.** (1) In section 307 of the Companies Act 2006 (notice required of a general meeting), before subsection (1) insert—

   '(A1) This section applies to—

      (a) a general meeting of a company that is not a traded company; and

      (b) a general meeting of a traded company that is an opted-in company (as defined by section 971(1)), where—

         (i) the meeting is held to decide whether to take any action that might result in the frustration of a takeover bid for the company; or

         (ii) the meeting is held by virtue of section 969 (power of offeror to require general meeting to be held).

   (A2) For corresponding provision in relation to general meetings of traded companies (other than meetings within subsection (A1)(b)), see section 307A.'.

   (2) After that section insert—

**'Notice required of general meeting: certain meetings of traded companies**

   **307A.**(1) A general meeting of a traded company must be called by notice of—

      (a) in a case where conditions A to C (set out below) are met, at least 14 days;

      (b) in any other case, at least 21 days.

   (2) Condition A is that the general meeting is not an annual general meeting.

   (3) Condition B is that the company offers the facility for members to vote by electronic means accessible to all members who hold shares that carry rights to vote at general meetings.

   This condition is met if there is a facility, offered by the company and accessible to all such members, to appoint a proxy by means of a website.

   (4) Condition C is that a special resolution reducing the period of notice to not less than 14 days has been passed—

      (a) at the immediately preceding annual general meeting, or

      (b) at a general meeting held since that annual general meeting.

   (5) In the case of a company which has not yet held an annual general meeting, condition C is that a special resolution reducing the period of notice to not less than 14 days has been passed at a general meeting.

   (6) The company's articles may require a longer period of notice than that specified in subsection (1).

   (7) Where a general meeting is adjourned, the adjourned meeting may be called by shorter notice than required by subsection (1).

   But in the case of an adjournment for lack of a quorum this subsection applies only if—

      (a) no business is to be dealt with at the adjourned meeting the general nature of which was not stated in the notice of the original meeting, and

      (b) the adjourned meeting is to be held at least 10 days after the original meeting.

   (8) Nothing in this section applies in relation to a general meeting of a kind mentioned in section 307(A1)(b) (certain meetings regarding takeover of opted-in company).'.

   (3) In section 360(1) of the Companies Act 2006 (computation of periods of notice etc: clear day rule), after the entry relating to section 307(1) and (2) of that Act, insert—

'section 307A(1), (4), (5) and (7)(b) (notice required of general meeting of traded company),'.

### Traded companies: contents of notice of meeting

**10.** (1) Section 311 of the Companies Act 2006 (contents of notices of meetings) is amended as follows.

(2) In subsection (2) (notice to state general nature of business to be dealt with), for the second sentence substitute 'In relation to a company other than a traded company, this subsection has effect subject to any provision of the company's articles.'.

(3) After that subsection insert—

'(3) Notice of a general meeting of a traded company must also include—

(a) a statement giving the address of the website on which the information required by section 311A (traded companies: publication of information in advance of general meeting) is published;

(b) a statement—

   (i) that the right to vote at the meeting is determined by reference to the register of members, and

   (ii) of the time when that right will be determined in accordance with section 360B(2) (traded companies: share dealings before general meetings);

(c) a statement of the procedures with which members must comply in order to be able to attend and vote at the meeting (including the date by which they must comply);

(d) a statement giving details of any forms to be used for the appointment of a proxy;

(e) where the company offers the facility for members to vote in advance (see section 322A) or by electronic means (see section 360A), a statement of the procedure for doing so (including the date by which it must be done, and details of any forms to be used); and

(f) a statement of the right of members to ask questions in accordance with section 319A (traded companies: questions at meetings).'.

### Traded companies: publication of information in advance of general meeting

**11.** After section 311 of the Companies Act 2006 insert—

#### 'Traded companies: publication of information in advance of general meeting

**311A.** (1) A traded company must ensure that the following information relating to a general meeting of the company is made available on a website—

(a) the matters set out in the notice of the meeting;

(b) the total numbers of—

   (i) shares in the company, and

   (ii) shares of each class,

   in respect of which members are entitled to exercise voting rights at the meeting;

(c) the totals of the voting rights that members are entitled to exercise at the meeting in respect of the shares of each class;

(d) members' statements, members' resolutions and members' matters of business received by the company after the first date on which notice of the meeting is given.

(2) The information must be made available on a website that—

(a) is maintained by or on behalf of the company, and

(b) identifies the company.

(3) Access to the information on the website, and the ability to obtain a hard copy of the information from the website, must not be conditional on payment of a fee or otherwise restricted.

(4) The information—

(a) must be made available—

   (i) in the case of information required by subsection (1)(a) to (c), on or before the first date on which notice of the meeting is given, and

   (ii) in the case of information required by subsection (1)(d), as soon as reasonably practicable, and

(b) must be kept available throughout the period of two years beginning with the date on which it is first made available on a website in accordance with this section.

(5) A failure to make information available throughout the period specified in subsection (4)(b) is disregarded if—

(a) the information is made available on the website for part of that period, and

(b) the failure is wholly attributable to circumstances that it would not be reasonable to have expected the company to prevent or avoid.

(6) The amounts mentioned in subsection (1)(b) and (c) must be ascertained at the latest practicable time before the first date on which notice of the meeting is given.

(7) Failure to comply with this section does not affect the validity of the meeting or of anything done at the meeting.

(8) If this section is not complied with as respects any meeting, an offence is committed by every officer of the company who is in default.

(9) A person guilty of an offence under this section is liable on summary conviction to a fine not exceeding level 3 on the standard scale.'.

### Traded companies: questions at meetings

**12.** (1) After section 319 of the Companies Act 2006 insert—

#### 'Traded companies: questions at meetings

**319A.**(1) At a general meeting of a traded company, the company must cause to be answered any question relating to the business being dealt with at the meeting put by a member attending the meeting.

(2) No such answer need be given—

    (a) if to do so would—

        (i) interfere unduly with the preparation for the meeting, or

        (ii) involve the disclosure of confidential information;

    (b) if the answer has already been given on a website in the form of an answer to a question; or

    (c) if it is undesirable in the interests of the company or the good order of the meeting that the question be answered.'.

(2) In section 145(3) of the Companies Act 2006 (effect of provision of articles as to enjoyment or exercise of members' rights), after paragraph (e) insert—

'(ea) section 319A (right to ask question at meeting of traded company);'.

### Traded companies: appointment of proxy and termination of proxy's authority

**13.** (1) In section 327 of the Companies Act 2006 (notice required of appointment of proxy etc), before subsection (1) insert

'(A1) In the case of a traded company

    (a) the appointment of a person as proxy for a member must be notified to the company in writing;

    (b) where such an appointment is made, the company may require reasonable evidence of—

        (i) the identity of the member and of the proxy,

        (ii) the member's instructions (if any) as to how the proxy is to vote, and

        (iii) where the proxy is appointed by a person acting on behalf of the member, authority of that person to make the appointment;

        but may not require to be provided with anything else relating to the appointment. '.

(2) In subsection (1) of that section, for 'This section applies to' substitute 'The following provisions apply in the case of traded companies and other companies as regards'.

(3) In section 330 of that Act (notice required of termination of proxy's authority) —

    (a) before subsection (1) insert—

    '(A1) In the case of a traded company the termination of the authority of a person to act as proxy must be notified to the company in writing.';

    (b) in subsection (1) for 'This section applies to' substitute 'The following provisions apply in the case of traded companies and other companies as regards'.

(4) After section 333 of that Act insert—

#### 'Traded company: duty to provide electronic address for receipt of proxies etc

**333A.** (1) A traded company must provide an electronic address for the receipt of any document or information relating to proxies for a general meeting.

(2) The company must provide the address either—

    (a) by giving it when sending out an instrument of proxy for the purposes of the meeting or issuing an invitation to appoint a proxy for those purposes; or

    (b) by ensuring that it is made available, throughout the period beginning with the first date on which notice of the meeting is given and ending with the conclusion of the meeting, on the website on which the information required by section 311A(1) is made available.

(3) The company is deemed to have agreed that any document or information relating to proxies for the meeting may be sent by electronic means to the address provided (subject to any limitations specified by the company when providing the address).

(4) In this section—

    (a) documents relating to proxies include—

        (i) the appointment of a proxy for a meeting,

        (ii) any document necessary to show the validity of, or otherwise relating to, the appointment of a proxy, and

        (iii) notice of the termination of the authority of a proxy;

    (b) 'electronic address' has the meaning given by section 333(4).'.

**Traded companies: class meetings**

**14.** (1) Section 334 of the Companies Act 2006 (application of provisions as to resolutions at general meetings in relation to class meetings) is amended as follows.

(2) In subsection (1), for '(2) and (3)' substitute '(2) to (3)'.

(3) In subsection (2)—

(a) omit the 'and' at the end of paragraph (a);

(b) after paragraph (b) insert—

', and

(c) sections 311(3), 311A, 319A, 327(A1), 330(A1) and 333A (additional requirements relating to traded companies).'.

(4) After subsection (2) insert—

'(2A) Section 307(1) to (6) apply in relation to a meeting of holders of a class of shares in a traded company as they apply in relation to a meeting of holders of a class of shares in a company other than a traded company (and, accordingly, section 307A does not apply in relation to such a meeting).'.

**Traded companies: duty to hold AGM**

**15.** (1) Section 336 of the Companies Act 2006 (public companies: annual general meeting) is amended as follows.

(2) After subsection (1) insert—

'(1A) Every private company that is a traded company must hold a general meeting as its annual general meeting in each period of 9 months beginning with the day following its accounting reference date (in addition to any other meetings held during that period).'.

(3) In subsections (2) and (3), after 'subsection (1)' in each place in which it occurs insert 'or (1A)'.

(4) In the section heading, after 'Public companies' insert 'and traded companies'.

(5) In the heading to Chapter 4 of Part 13 of the Companies Act 2006 (public companies: additional requirements for AGMs), after 'PUBLIC COMPANIES' insert 'AND TRADED COMPANIES'.

**Traded companies: notice of AGM**

**16.** (1) Section 337 of the Companies Act 2006 (public companies: notice of AGM) is amended as follows.

(2) In subsection (1) (notice to state that meeting is AGM), after 'public company' insert 'or a private company that is a traded company'.

(3) In subsection (2), after 'annual general meeting' insert 'of a public company that is not a traded company'.

(4) After that subsection insert—

'(3) Where a notice calling an annual general meeting of a traded company is given more than 6 weeks before the meeting, the notice must include—

(a) if the company is a public company, a statement of the right under section 338 to require the company to give notice of a resolution to be moved at the meeting, and

(b) whether or not the company is a public company, a statement of the right under section 338A to require the company to include a matter in the business to be dealt with at the meeting.'.

(5) In the section heading, after 'Public companies' insert 'and traded companies'.

(6) In section 360 of the Companies Act 2006 (computation of periods of notice etc: clear day rule), after the entry relating to section 316(2)(b), insert—

'section 337(3) (contents of notice of AGM of traded company),'.

**Traded companies: members' power to include other matters in business dealt with at AGM**

**17.** (1) After section 338 of the Companies Act 2006 insert—

**'Traded companies: members' power to include other matters in business dealt with at AGM**

**338A.** (1) The members of a traded company may request the company to include in the business to be dealt with at an annual general meeting any matter (other than a proposed resolution) which may properly be included in the business.

(2) A matter may properly be included in the business at an annual general meeting unless—

(a) it is defamatory of any person, or

(b) it is frivolous or vexatious.

(3) A company is required to include such a matter once it has received requests that it do so from—

(a) members representing at least 5% of the total voting rights of all the members who have a right to vote at the meeting, or

> > > > (b) at least 100 members who have a right to vote at the meeting and hold shares in the company on which there has been paid up an average sum, per member, of at least £100.
> > >
> > > See also section 153 (exercise of rights where shares held on behalf of others).
> > >
> > > (4) A request—
> > > > (a) may be in hard copy form or in electronic form,
> > > > (b) must identify the matter to be included in the business,
> > > > (c) must be accompanied by a statement setting out the grounds for the request, and
> > > > (d) must be authenticated by the person or persons making it.
> > >
> > > (5) A request must be received by the company not later than—
> > > > (a) 6 weeks before the meeting, or
> > > > (b) if later, the time at which notice is given of the meeting.'.

> (2) In section 145(3) of the Companies Act 2006 (effect of provision of articles as to enjoyment or exercise of members' rights), after paragraph (g) insert—
>
> '(ga) section 338A (traded companies: members' power to include matters in business dealt with at AGM);'.
>
> (3) In section 153(1) of the Companies Act 2006 (exercise of rights where shares held on behalf of others: members' requests), after paragraph (b) insert—
>
> '(ba) section 338A (traded companies: members' power to include matters in business dealt with at AGM),'.
>
> (4) In section 360(1) of the Companies Act 2006 (computation of periods of notice etc: clear day rule), after the entry relating to section 338(4)(d)(i) insert—
>
> 'section 338A(5) (request to include matter in the business to be dealt with at AGM of traded company),'.

### Traded companies: company's duty to circulate members' matters for AGM

**18.** (1) After section 340 of the Companies Act 2006 insert—

#### 'Traded companies: duty to circulate members' matters for AGM

**340A.**(1) A company that is required under section 338A to include any matter in the business to be dealt with at an annual general meeting must—
> (a) give notice of it to each member of the company entitled to receive notice of the annual general meeting—
> > (i) in the same manner as notice of the meeting, and
> > (ii) at the same time as, or as soon as reasonably practicable after, it gives notice of the meeting, and
>
> (b) publish it on the same website as that on which the company published the information required by section 311A.

(2) Subsection (1) has effect subject to section 340B(2) (deposit or tender of sum in respect of expenses of circulation).

(3) In the event of default in complying with this section, an offence is committed by every officer of the company who is in default.

(4) A person guilty of an offence under this section is liable—
> (a) on conviction on indictment, to a fine;
> (b) on summary conviction, to a fine not exceeding the statutory maximum.

#### Traded companies: expenses of circulating members' matters to be dealt with at AGM

**340B.**(1) The expenses of the company in complying with section 340A need not be paid by the members who requested the inclusion of the matter in the business to be dealt with at the annual general meeting if requests sufficient to require the company to include the matter are received before the end of the financial year preceding the meeting.

(2) Otherwise—
> (a) the expenses of the company in complying with that section must be paid by the members who requested the inclusion of the matter unless the company resolves otherwise, and
> (b) unless the company has previously so resolved, it is not bound to comply with that section unless there is deposited with or tendered to it, not later than—
> > (i) six weeks before the annual general meeting to which the requests relate, or
> > (ii) if later, the time at which notice is given of that meeting,
> >
> > a sum reasonably sufficient to meet its expenses in complying with that section.'.

(2) In section 360(1) of the Companies Act 2006 (computation of periods of notice etc: clear day rule), omit the 'and' before the entry relating to section 340(2)(b)(i) and after that entry insert—

', and

section 340B(2)(b) (traded companies: duty to circulate members' matters for AGM).'.

**Traded companies: website publication of poll results**

**19.** (1) Section 341 of the Companies Act 2006 (quoted companies: results of polls to be made available on website) is amended as follows.

(2) In subsection (1), after 'quoted company' insert 'that is not a traded company'.

(3) After subsection (1) insert—

'(1A)Where a poll is taken at a general meeting of a traded company, the company must ensure that the following information is made available on a website—

(a) the date of the meeting,

(b) the text of the resolution or, as the case may be, a description of the subject matter of the poll,

(c) the number of votes validly cast,

(d) the proportion of the company's issued share capital (determined at the time at which the right to vote is determined under section 360B(2)) represented by those votes,

(e) the number of votes cast in favour,

(f) the number of votes cast against, and

(g) the number of abstentions (if counted).

(1B) A traded company must comply with subsection (1A) by—

(a) the end of 16 days beginning with the day of the meeting, or

(b) if later, the end of the first working day after the day on which the result of the poll is declared.'.

(4) In section 352 of that Act (application of provisions to class meetings), for subsection (1) substitute—

'(1) The provisions of section 341 (results of poll to be made available on website) apply (with any necessary modifications) in relation to a meeting of holders of a class of shares of a quoted company or traded company in connection with the variation of the rights attached to such shares as they apply in relation to a general meeting of the company.

(1A) The provisions of section 342 to 351 (independent report on poll) apply (with any necessary modifications) in relation to a meeting of holders of a class of shares of a quoted company in connection with the variation of the rights attached to such shares as they apply in relation to a general meeting of the company.'.

(5) In the heading for Chapter 5 of Part 13, after 'QUOTED COMPANIES' insert 'AND TRADED COMPANIES'.

**Traded companies: share dealings before general meetings**

**20.** After section 360A of the Companies Act 2006 insert—

**'Traded companies: requirements for participating in and voting at general meetings**

**360B.** (1) Any provision of a traded company's articles is void in so far as it would have the effect of—

(a) imposing a restriction on a right of a member to participate in and vote at a general meeting of the company unless the member's shares have (after having been acquired by the member and before the meeting) been deposited with, or transferred to, or registered in the name of another person, or

(b) imposing a restriction on the right of a member to transfer shares in the company during the period of 48 hours before the time for the holding of a general meeting of the company if that right would not otherwise be subject to that restriction.

(2) A traded company must determine the right to vote at a general meeting of the company by reference to the register of members as at a time (determined by the company) that is not more than 48 hours before the time for the holding of the meeting.

(3) In calculating the period mentioned in subsection (1)(b) or (2), no account is to be taken of any part of a day that is not a working day.

(4) Nothing in this section affects—

(a) the operation of—

(i) Part 22 of this Act (information about interests in a company's shares),

(ii) Part 15 of the Companies Act 1985[237] (orders imposing restrictions on shares), or

(iii) any provision in a company's articles relating to the application of any provision of either of those Parts; or

(b) the validity of articles prescribed, or to the same effect as articles prescribed, under section 19 of this Act (power of Secretary of State to prescribe model articles).'.

---

[237] 1985 c. 6.

### Meaning of 'traded company'

**21.** (1) After section 360B of the Companies Act 2006 insert—

**'Meaning of 'traded company'**

**360C.** In this Part, 'traded company' means a company any shares of which—
  (a) carry rights to vote at general meetings, and
  (b) are admitted to trading on a regulated market in an EEA State by or with the consent of the company.'.

(2) In Schedule 8 to the Companies Act 2006 (index of defined expressions), at the appropriate place, insert—

'traded company (in Part 13) section 360C'.

### Traded companies: disapplication of saving for casting votes

**22.** In paragraph 23A of Schedule 3 to the Companies Act 2006 (Commencement No. 3, Consequential Amendments, Transitional Provisions and Savings) Order 2007[238] (saving for provisions of a company's articles giving the chairman a second or casting vote in the event of an equality of votes on an ordinary resolution), at the end insert—

'(4) Nothing in this paragraph applies in relation to a traded company (as defined by section 360C of the Companies Act 2006).'.

### Transitional provisions

**23.** In section 307A(4) and (5) of the Companies Act 2006, references to annual general meetings and general meetings include ones held before 3 August 2009.

---

## THE REGISTRAR OF COMPANIES AND APPLICATIONS FOR STRIKING OFF REGULATIONS 2009

### (SI 2009/1803)

COMMENCEMENT DATE 1st October 2009[239]

**SI.37**   ### Citation, commencement and interpretation

**1.** (1) These Regulations may be cited as the Registrar of Companies and Applications for Striking Off Regulations 2009 and come into force on 1st October 2009.
  (2) In these Regulations—
    (a) 'relevant company form' has the meaning given in regulation 4(3);
    (b) 'relevant material' has the meaning given in regulation 4(2);
    (c) 'relevant overseas company form' has the meaning given in regulation 4(4); and
    (d) 'valid objection' has the meaning given in regulation 4(8).

### Voluntary striking off: contents of an application

**2.** (1) An application under section 1003 of the Companies Act 2006 (application for voluntary striking off) must contain a declaration that neither section 1004 nor section 1005[240] of that Act prevents the application from being made.
  (2) The declaration must be made by the directors who are making the application on behalf of the company.

### Annotation of the register

**3.** Where it appears to the registrar that material on the register is misleading or confusing, the registrar may place a note in the register containing such information as appears to the registrar to be necessary to remedy, as far as possible, the misleading or confusing nature of the material.

### Rectification of the register on application

**4.** (1) On application under this regulation (but not if there is a valid objection to the application) the registrar must remove from the register any relevant material that—

---

[238] SI 2007/2194 (C. 84); paragraph 23A of Schedule 3 was inserted by SI 2007/3495 (C. 150), Schedule 5, paragraph 2(5).

[239] 2006 c.46.

[240] Section 1005 was modified by article 3 of SI 2009/317.

(a) derives from anything invalid or ineffective or that was done without the authority of the company or overseas company to which the material relates, or

(b) is factually inaccurate, or is derived from something that is factually inaccurate or forged.

(2) 'Relevant material' means material on the register that was included in, or is derived from material that was included in, a relevant company form or a relevant overseas company form delivered to the registrar by any person.

(3) A 'relevant company form' is—

    (a) a standard form required for giving notice under section 87 (change of address of registered office), section 167 (changes relating to directors) or section 276 (changes relating to secretaries) of the Companies Act 2006; or

    (b) so much of a standard form required for delivering an application under section 9 of that Act (application for registration of a company) as is required for the statement of a company's proposed officers referred to in section 9(4)(c).

(4) A 'relevant overseas company form' is—

    (a) so much of a standard form required for delivering a return under regulation 4 of the Overseas Companies Regulations 2009[241] as is required for—

      (i) the list referred to in regulation 6(1)(d) of those Regulations (list of directors and secretary of an overseas company);

      (ii) the names and service addresses referred to in regulation 7(1)(e) of those Regulations (names and service addresses of persons authorised to accept service of documents on behalf of an overseas company in respect of a UK establishment); or

      (iii) the list referred to in regulation 7(1)(f) of those Regulations (list of permanent representatives of an overseas company in respect of a UK establishment); or

    (b) so much of a standard form required for delivering a return under regulation 13 of those Regulations as is required for details of the alteration of particulars delivered under—

      (i) regulation 6(1)(d) of those Regulations (directors and secretary);

      (ii) regulation 7(1)(a) of those Regulations (address of UK establishment);

      (iii) regulation 7(1)(e) of those Regulations (names and service addresses of persons authorised to accept service); or

      (iv) regulation 7(1)(f) of those Regulations (list of permanent representatives).

(5) An application to the registrar for the removal from the register (on the grounds in paragraph (1)) of material that was included in a standard form required for giving notice under section 87 of the Companies Act 2006 (change of address of registered office), or of material that is derived from material that was included in such a form, may be made by (and only by) the company to which the material relates.

(6) An application to the registrar for the removal from the register (on the grounds in paragraph (1)) of material that was included in, or is derived from material that was included in, so much of a standard form required for delivering a return under regulation 13 of the Overseas Companies Regulations 2009 as is required for details of the alteration of particulars delivered under regulation 7(1)(a) of those Regulations (address of UK establishment) may be made by (and only by) the overseas company to which the material relates.

(7) An application to the registrar for the removal from the register on the grounds in paragraph (1) of relevant material other than material referred to in paragraph (5) or (6) may be made by (and only by)—

    (a) the person by whom the relevant company form or relevant overseas company form (as the case may be) was delivered to the registrar;

    (b) the company or overseas company to which the material relates; or

    (c) any other person to whom the material relates.

(8) A 'valid objection' is—

    (a) an objection made in accordance with regulation 5(10) and (11) by a person to whom notice of the application was given under regulation 5(2), (3), (4) or (5), or

    (b) an objection made in accordance with regulation 5(10) by any other person which is not an objection that the registrar is prevented from taking into account under regulation 5(12).

(9) In this regulation 'required' means required by rules made by the registrar under section 1117 of the Companies Act 2006.

### Applications to rectify: further requirements, objections and notices to be issued by the registrar

**5.** (1) An application to the registrar under regulation 4 must, in addition to satisfying the requirements of section 1095(3) of the Companies Act 2006—

    (a) state the applicant's name and address;

    (b) where the application is an application referred to in regulation 4(5) or (6), confirm that the applicant is the company or (as the case may be) the overseas company to which the relevant material which is the subject of the application relates;

---

[241] SI 2009/1801.

    (c)  in any other case, state whether the applicant is a person mentioned in regulation 4(7)(a), a person mentioned in regulation 4(7)(b) or a person mentioned in regulation 4(7)(c); and

    (d)  state whether the relevant material which is the subject of the application—

        (i)   derives from anything invalid or ineffective;

        (ii)  derives from anything that was done without the authority of the company or overseas company to which the material relates;

        (iii) is factually inaccurate or is derived from something that is factually inaccurate; or

        (iv) is derived from something that is forged.

(2)  Where the application is an application referred to in regulation 4(5), the registrar must give notice of the application to—

    (a)  the person who delivered the standard form mentioned in that regulation to the registrar (but only if the registrar knows the identity and name and address of that person);

    (b)  every person who (to the registrar's knowledge) was a director or secretary of the company at the time when the application was delivered to the registrar; and

    (c)  the company at the address of its registered office.

(3)  Where the material which is the subject of the application relates to a company (rather than an overseas company), but the application is not an application referred to in regulation 4(5), the registrar must give notice of the application to—

    (a)  every person mentioned in regulation 4(7) whose identity and name and address the registrar knows (other than the applicant); and

    (b)  every person who (to the registrar's knowledge) was a director or secretary of the company at the time when the application was delivered to the registrar.

(4)  Where the application is an application referred to in regulation 4(6), the registrar must give notice of the application to—

    (a)  the person who delivered the standard form mentioned in that regulation to the registrar (but only if the registrar knows the identity and name and address of that person);

    (b)  every person registered under regulation 4 or 13 of the Overseas Companies Regulations 2009, at the time when the application was delivered to the registrar, as a director or secretary of the overseas company;

    (c)  the persons mentioned in paragraph (6); and

    (d)  the overseas company.

(5)  Where the material which is the subject of the application relates to an overseas company, but the application is not an application referred to in regulation 4(6), the registrar must give notice of the application to—

    (a)  every person mentioned in regulation 4(7) whose identity and name and address the registrar knows (other than the applicant);

    (b)  every person registered under regulation 4 or 13 of the Overseas Companies Regulations 2009, at the time when the application was delivered to the registrar, as a director or secretary of the overseas company; and

    (c)  the persons mentioned in paragraph (6).

(6)  The persons are—

    (a)  every person registered under regulation 4 or 13 of the Overseas Companies Regulations 2009, at the time when the application was delivered to the registrar, as a person authorised to accept service of documents on behalf of the overseas company in respect of a UK establishment of the company; and

    (b)  every person registered under regulation 4 or 13 of those Regulations, at the time when the application was delivered to the registrar, as a permanent representative of the overseas company in respect of a UK establishment of the company.

(7)  Where the material which is the subject of the application is material that was included in, or is derived from material that was included in, a relevant overseas company form described in regulation 4(4)(a)(ii) or (iii) or regulation 4(4)(b)(ii), (iii) or (iv), the notice which the registrar is required by paragraph (4) or (5) to give to the overseas company must be given to the company at the address which was, at the time when the application was delivered to the registrar, registered under regulation 4 or 13 of the Overseas Companies Regulations 2009 as the address of the company's UK establishment to which the material relates (and notice need not be given to the company at any other address).

(8)  The notice given by the registrar under paragraph (2), (3), (4) or (5) must—

    (a)  where the material which is the subject of the application relates to a company (rather than an overseas company), state the name and registered number of the company to which the material relates;

    (b)  where the material which is the subject of the application relates to an overseas company, state the overseas company's name registered under regulation 4 or 13 of the Overseas Companies Regulations 2009 or section 1048 of the Companies Act 2006 and its registered number allocated under section 1066 of that Act;

    (c)  where the material which is the subject of the application is material that was included in, or is derived from material that was included in, a relevant overseas company form described in regulation 4(4)(a)(ii) or (iii) or regulation 4(4)(b)(ii), (iii) or (iv), state the registered number allocated under section 1067[242] of the Companies Act 2006 to the UK establishment to which the material relates;

    (d) specify what is to be removed from the register and indicate where on the register it is;

    (e) state the information provided to the registrar under paragraph (1)(d);

    (f) state the date on which the notice is issued;

    (g) give particulars of the recipient's right to object to the application and the requirements applying to that right under paragraphs (10) and (11);

    (h) explain the effect of paragraph (13); and

    (i) explain the effect of regulation 4(1) and of section 1095(4) of the Companies Act 2006.

(9) An objection to an application under regulation 4 may be made to the registrar by any person.

(10) An objection must be made by giving notice in writing to the registrar, and the notice must state the name and address of the person making the objection and identify the application to which the objection relates.

(11) A person to whom notice of an application was given under paragraph (2), (3), (4) or (5) and who wishes to object to the application must do so before the end of the period of 28 days beginning with the date on which that notice was issued (as stated in the notice).

(12) The registrar must not take account of an objection made by any other person after the end of the period of 28 days beginning with the date on which the notices under paragraph (2), (3), (4) or (5) were issued.

(13) If a valid objection is made to the application, the registrar must reject the application.

(14) When a valid objection is made, the registrar must also—

    (a) send an acknowledgment of receipt to the person who made the objection;

    (b) notify the applicant of the fact that an objection has been made; and

    (c) notify every other person to whom the registrar gave notice under paragraph (2), (3), (4) or (5) (but not the person who made the objection or any other person who has made an objection).

(15) If no valid objection is made, the registrar must notify the applicant of that fact.

(16) In this regulation 'UK establishment' has the meaning given in section 1067(6) of the Companies Act 2006.[243]

### Documents relating to Welsh companies: exceptions to the requirement for a certified translation, and revocation of previous exceptions

**6.** (1) The documents in paragraph (2) are excepted from the requirement in section 1104(2) of the Companies Act 2006 that a document relating to a Welsh company must, on delivery to the registrar in Welsh, be accompanied by a certified translation into English.

(2) The documents are—

    (a) a non-traded company's memorandum of association;

    (b) a non-traded company's articles;

    (c) a community interest company report prepared for a non-traded company under section 34 of the Companies (Audit, Investigations and Community Enterprise) Act 2004;[244]

    (d) a resolution or agreement which was agreed to by members of a non-traded company and to which Chapter 3 of Part 3 of the Companies Act 2006 applies, except for a resolution or agreement listed in paragraph (3);

    (e) annual accounts and reports of a non-traded company required to be delivered to the registrar under Part 15[245] of the Companies Act 2006;

    (f) a declaration referred to in regulation 11(1)(b) or regulation 12(1)(b) or (c) of the Community Interest Company Regulations 2005[246] which relates to a non-traded company;

    (g) revised accounts and any revised report of a non-traded company, and any auditor's report on such revised accounts and reports, required to be delivered to the registrar by the Companies (Revision of Defective Accounts and Reports) Regulations 2008;[247]

    (h) a document required to be appended to the group accounts of a non-traded company by paragraph 30(2) of Schedule 6 to the Large and Medium-sized Companies and Groups (Accounts and Reports) Regulations 2008[248] (banking groups: information as to undertaking in which shares held as a result of financial assistance operation).

(3) The following is the list of resolutions and agreements referred to in paragraph (2)(d)—

---

[242] Section 1067 was amended by article 5 of SI 2009/1802.

[243] Section 1067(6) was inserted by article 5 of SI 2009/1802.

[244] 2004 c.27; section 34 was amended by SI 2007/1093, 2007/2194, 2008/948.

[245] Part 15 was amended by SI 2007/2932, 2008/393, 2008/948.

[246] SI 2005/1788, amended by SI 2007/1093; there are other amending instruments but none is relevant.

[247] SI 2008/373.

[248] SI 2008/410.

    (a) a special resolution that—

        (i) a private company should be re-registered as a public company;

        (ii) a public company should be re-registered as a private limited company;

        (iii) a private limited company should be re-registered as an unlimited company; or

        (iv) an unlimited company should be re-registered as a limited company;

    (b) a special resolution agreeing to the change of a company's name;

    (c) a special resolution required by section 37[249] of the Companies (Audit, Investigations and Community Enterprise) Act 2004 (requirements for an existing company to become a community interest company);

    (d) a resolution or agreement as altered by an enactment other than an enactment amending the general law, required to be delivered to the registrar under section 34 of the Companies Act 2006;

    (e) a resolution or agreement as altered by an order of a court or other authority, required to be delivered to the registrar under section 35 or 999 of that Act;

    (f) a special resolution under section 88(2) of that Act requiring the register to be amended so that it states that a company's registered office is to be situated in Wales;

    (g) a special resolution under section 626 of that Act (reduction of capital in connection with redenomination);

    (h) a special resolution under section 641(1)(a) of that Act (resolution for reducing the share capital of a private limited company supported by solvency statement);

    (i) a resolution under section 664(1) of that Act that a public company should be re-registered as a private company to comply with section 662.

(4) For the purposes of paragraph (2)(g), 'revised accounts' and 'revised report' have the meanings given in regulation 2 of the Companies (Revision of Defective Accounts and Reports) Regulations 2008.

(5) Regulation 4 of the Companies (Welsh Language Forms and Documents) Regulations 1994[250] is revoked.

### Documents that may be delivered under the Companies Acts in a language other than English

**7.** (1) The documents listed in paragraph (2) are specified for the purposes of section 1105(2)(d) of the Companies Act 2006 as documents which may be drawn up and delivered to the registrar under the Companies Acts in a language other than English but which must, when delivered to the registrar, be accompanied by a certified translation into English.

(2) The documents are—

    (a) a memorandum of association;

    (b) a company's articles;

    (c) a valuation report required to be delivered to the registrar under section 94(2)(d) of the Companies Act 2006;

    (d) any order made by a competent court in the United Kingdom or elsewhere.

### Permitted characters and symbols for names and addresses in documents delivered to the registrar

**8.** (1) The characters and symbols specified in paragraph (3) are permitted for the purposes of section 1108(1) of the Companies Act 2006 (and names and addresses in documents delivered to the registrar must therefore contain only those characters and symbols).

(2) But the requirement in section 1108(1) does not apply to the following documents—

    (a) a memorandum of association;

    (b) a company's articles;

    (c) an order made by a competent court in the United Kingdom or elsewhere;

    (d) an agreement required to be forwarded to the registrar under Chapter 3 of Part 3 of the Companies Act 2006 (agreements affecting a company's constitution);

    (e) a valuation report required to be delivered to the registrar under section 94(2)(d) of that Act;

    (f) a document required to be delivered to the registrar under section 400(2)(e) or section 401(2)(f) of that Act (company included in accounts of larger group: required to deliver copy of group accounts);[251]

---

[249] Section 37 was amended by paragraph 7 of Schedule 4 to S.I 2007/1093 and by paragraph 105 of Schedule 4 to SI 2007/2194.

[250] SI 1994/117; relevant amending instruments are SI 1994/727, 1994/734. By virtue of SI 2006/3428, regulation 4 has effect with adaptations as if made under section 1104(2) of the Companies Act 2006.

[251] Sections 400 and 401 were applied to limited liability partnerships by regulation 10 of SI 2008/1911.

(g) an instrument or copy instrument required to be delivered to the registrar under Part 25 of that Act (company charges);[252]

(h) a certified copy of the constitution of an overseas company required to be delivered to the registrar under regulation 8, 14 or 15 of the Overseas Companies Regulations 2009;

(i) a copy of accounting documents of an overseas company required to be delivered to the registrar under regulation 9, 32, 45 or 46 of those Regulations;

(j) a copy of the annual accounts of an overseas company, or of a credit or financial institution to which Chapter 2 of Part 6 of the Overseas Companies Regulations 2009 applies, required to be delivered to the registrar under section 441 of the Companies Act 2006;[253]

(3) The characters and symbols specified in this paragraph are—

(a) those in the Schedule;

(b) full stops, commas, colons, semi-colons and hyphens;

(c) the numerals 0, 1, 2, 3, 4, 5, 6, 7, 8 and 9.

(4) In this regulation the expressions 'accounting documents', 'certified copy' and 'constitution' have the meanings given in the Overseas Companies Regulations 2009.

SCHEDULE                                   Regulation 8(3)
PERMITTED CHARACTERS AND SYMBOLS

| *Characters and symbols referred to in regulation 8(3) (a)* | | | | |
|---|---|---|---|---|
| A | a | B | b | C |
| c | D | d | E | e |
| F | f | G | g | H |
| h | I | i | J | j |
| K | k | L | l | M |
| m | N | n | O | o |
| P | p | Q | q | R |
| r | S | s | T | t |
| U | u | V | v | W |
| w | X | x | Y | y |
| Z | z | & | @ | £ |
| $ | € | ¥ | * | = |
| # | % | + | ' | ' |
| ' | ( | ) | [ | ] |
| { | } | < | > | ! |
| « | » | ? | " | " |
| " | \ | / | | |

## THE COMPANIES (SHARE CAPITAL AND ACQUISITION BY COMPANY OF ITS OWN SHARES) REGULATIONS 2009
### (SI 2009/2022)

COMMENCEMENT DATE 1st October 2009[254]

---

[252] Sections 860 to 892 in Part 25 were applied to limited liability partnerships by regulations 32 to 44 of SI 2009/1804.

[253] Section 441 was applied with modifications to overseas companies and to certain credit and financial institutions by, respectively, regulation 40 and regulation 55 of SI 2009/1801.

[254] 2006 c.46.

SI.38

**Citation and commencement**

**1.** (1) These Regulations may be cited as the Companies (Share Capital and Acquisition by Company of its Own Shares) Regulations 2009.

(2) They come into force on 1st October 2009.

**Rights issues**

**2.** In section 562(5) of the Companies Act 2006 (communication of pre-emption offers to shareholders: minimum period during which offer may be accepted) for '21 days' substitute '14 days'.

**Reduction of capital: creditor protection**

**3.** In section 646(1) of the Companies Act 2006 (application to court for order confirming reduction of share capital: creditors entitled to object)—

(a) after 'who' insert '— (a)', and

(b) after 'admissible in proof against the company' insert—

'', and

(b) can show that there is a real likelihood that the reduction would result in the company being unable to discharge his debt or claim when it fell due,'.

**Acquisition by company of its own shares**

**4.** (1) In each of sections 694(5), 697(4) and 700(4) of the Companies Act 2006 (authority for off-market purchase, variation of contract for off-market purchase and release of off-market purchase rights: public companies) for '18 months' substitute 'five years'.

(2) In section 701(5) of the Companies Act 2006 (authority for market purchase) for '18 months' substitute 'five years'.

**Treasury shares**

**5.** (1) Section 725 of the Companies Act 2006 (treasury shares: maximum holdings) is repealed.

(2) Any outstanding obligation to dispose of or cancel excess shares arising under section 725(3) of that Act (duty to dispose of excess shares) shall cease to exist on 1st October 2009, whether or not the period mentioned in that provision has expired, but this is subject to paragraph (3).

(3) This amendment does not affect any liability under section 732 of that Act (treasury shares: offences) in respect of a failure

to comply with section 725(3) where the period mentioned in that provision expired before 1st October 2009.

---

# THE COMPANY, LIMITED LIABILITY PARTNERSHIP AND BUSINESS NAMES (MISCELLANEOUS PROVISIONS) (AMENDMENT) REGULATIONS 2009

## (SI 2009/2404)

COMMENCEMENT DATE 1st October 2009[255, 256]

SI.39

**Citation and commencement**

**1.** These Regulations may be cited as the Company, Limited Liability Partnership and Business Names (Miscellaneous Provisions) (Amendment) Regulations 2009 and come into force on 1st October 2009.

**Amendments**

**2.** (1) The Company and Business Names (Miscellaneous Provisions) Regulations 2009[257] are amended as follows.

(2) In regulation 13(1)—

(a) omit the 'or' at the end of sub-paragraph (b); and

---

[255] 2000 c.12; section 17 has been amended by SI 2009/1804, Schedule 3, paragraph 7.

[256] 2006 c.46.

[257] SI 2009/1085.

(b) after sub-paragraph (c) insert—

'(d) an incorporated friendly society (as defined in section 116 of the Friendly Societies Act 1992[258]) which has that name; or

(e) a company to which section 1040 of the Companies Act 2006 (companies authorised to register under the Companies Act 2006) applies which has that name.'.

(3) In Schedule 2, including that Schedule as applied to limited liability partnerships[259]—

(a) in paragraph 3(f) for 'CWMNI BUDDIANT CCC' substitute 'CWMNI BUDDIANT CYMUNEDOL CCC';

(b) omit the 'and' at the end of paragraph 3(u); and

(c) after paragraph 3(u) insert—

'(ua) 'INDUSTRIAL AND PROVIDENT SOCIETY'; and'.

---

# THE COMPANIES (AUTHORISED MINIMUM) REGULATIONS 2009
## (SI 2009/2425)

COMMENCEMENT DATE 1st October 2009[260]

### Citation, commencement and interpretation

SI.40

**1.** (1) These Regulations may be cited as the Companies (Authorised Minimum) Regulations 2009 and come into force on 1st October 2009.

(2) In these Regulations—

'the appropriate spot rate of exchange' is to be interpreted in accordance with regulation 4(1);

'the certified spot rate' has the meaning given in regulation 4(3);

'published spot rate' has the meaning given in regulation 4(2);

'reference date' is to be interpreted in accordance with regulation 4(7) and (8);

'relevant day' is to be interpreted in accordance with regulation 4(5) and (6); and

'working day' means a day which is not a Saturday or Sunday, Christmas Day, Good Friday or any day that is a bank holiday under the Banking and Financial Dealings Act 1971[261] in England and Wales.

(3) In these Regulations a reference to any Part or section is, unless otherwise stated, a reference to a Part or section of the Companies Act 2006.

### Authorised minimum in euros

**2.** For the purposes of the definition of 'the authorised minimum' in section 763(1), but subject to regulation 9, the amount in euros that is to be treated as equivalent to the sterling amount[262] is €57,100.

### Application of the authorised minimum requirement for certain purposes

**3.** (1) This regulation applies for either of the purposes in paragraphs (2) and (3), and is subject to regulation 9.

(2) The first purpose is to determine, for the purposes of section 650, whether a reduction of a public company's share capital confirmed by a court order under section 648 has the effect of bringing the nominal value of the company's allotted share capital below the authorised minimum.

(3) The second purpose is to determine, for the purposes of section 662(2)(b), whether the cancellation of a public company's shares and the diminution of the amount of its share capital under section 662(2)(a) have the effect of bringing the nominal value of the company's allotted share capital below the authorised minimum.

(4) This regulation only applies where the company has allotted share capital denominated in more than one currency, taking account of the effect of the reduction of the company's share capital or (as the case may be) the effect of the cancellation of the company's shares and the diminution of the amount of its allotted share capital.

---

[258] 1992 c.40.
[259] See SI 2009/1804, regulation 10.
[260] 2006 c.46.
[261] 1971 c.80.
[262] The sterling amount specified in section 763(1) of the Companies Act 2006 is £50,000.

(5) The nominal value of a public company's allotted share capital is to be treated as being below the authorised minimum if—
  (a) the sterling value is less than £50,000; and
  (b) the euro value is less than €57,100.
(6) The 'sterling value' is the sum in sterling of—
  (a) the nominal value of the company's allotted share capital denominated in sterling;
  (b) the nominal value of the company's allotted share capital denominated in euros if it were to be converted into sterling at the appropriate spot rate of exchange; and
  (c) the nominal value of the company's allotted share capital denominated in a currency other than sterling or euros if it were to be converted into sterling at the appropriate spot rate of exchange.
(7) The 'euro value' is the sum in euros of—
  (a) the nominal value of the company's allotted share capital denominated in euros;
  (b) the nominal value of the company's allotted share capital denominated in sterling if it were to be converted into euros at the appropriate spot rate of exchange; and
  (c) the nominal value of the company's allotted share capital denominated in a currency other than sterling or euros if it were to be converted into euros at the appropriate spot rate of exchange.

### The appropriate spot rate of exchange

**4.** (1) The appropriate spot rate of exchange for a currency conversion referred to in regulation 3(6) and (7) is the published spot rate relevant to the currency conversion in question or, where the circumstances in paragraph (4) exist, the certified spot rate relevant to that currency conversion.
(2) The published spot rate is the middle spot exchange rate prevailing on the foreign exchange market at 4pm on the relevant day as published in respect of that day by the Financial Times.
(3) The certified spot rate is the middle spot exchange rate prevailing on the foreign exchange market at 4pm on the relevant day and stated in a certificate obtained by the company from—
  (a) a person, nominated by the company, who under Part 4 of the Financial Services and Markets Act 2000[263] has permission to accept deposits; or
  (b) a firm, nominated by the company, which has permission to carry on the activity of accepting deposits in the United Kingdom by virtue of Schedule 3 to that Act.
(4) The circumstances in this paragraph exist where—
  (a) the Financial Times has not, on or before the reference date, published an exchange rate referred to in paragraph (2) relevant to the currency conversion in question; or
  (b) the Financial Times has, on or before the reference date, published what appears to be an exchange rate referred to in paragraph (2) relevant to the currency conversion in question but the company can show that there was a publication error; or
  (c) there is no evidence of what (if any) was the rate referred to in paragraph (2) relevant to the currency conversion in question as published on or before the reference date by the Financial Times.
(5) Where the currency conversion is relevant to the calculation of the sterling value or the euro value for the purpose in regulation 3(2), the 'relevant day' is the working day which immediately preceded the working day immediately preceding the date of the court order.
(6) Where the currency conversion is relevant to the calculation of the sterling value or the euro value for the purpose in regulation 3(3), the 'relevant day' is—
  (a) in a case within section 662(1)(a) or (b), the working day immediately preceding the date of the forfeiture or surrender; and
  (b) in a case within section 662(1)(c), (d) or (e), the working day immediately preceding the date of the acquisition.
(7) Where the currency calculation is relevant to the calculation of the sterling value or the euro value for the purpose in regulation 3(2), the 'reference date' is the date of the court order.
(8) Where the currency conversion is relevant to the calculation of the sterling value or the euro value for the purpose in regulation 3(3), the 'reference date' is—
  (a) in a case within section 662(1)(a) or (b), the fifth working day following the date of the forfeiture or surrender; and
  (b) in a case within section 662(1)(c), (d) or (e), the fifth working day following the date of the acquisition.

---

[263] 2000 c.8.

**Registration of a court order confirming a capital reduction: assumptions which may be made by the registrar**

5. (1) This regulation applies where a public company delivers to the registrar under section 649 a copy of an order of the court confirming a reduction of its share capital and the court has not directed the order to be registered.

(2) Where the circumstances in paragraph (3), (4) or (5) exist, the registrar may make the assumption in paragraph (6).

(3) The circumstances in this paragraph are that—

(a) taking account of the effect of the reduction of its capital, the company has allotted share capital denominated in more than one currency;

(b) either the Financial Times did not publish, on or before the reference date, an exchange rate referred to in regulation 4(2) relevant to converting into sterling a currency in which the company's allotted share capital is denominated or it did not publish, on or before that date, such a rate relevant to converting such a currency into euros; and

(c) the company has not delivered to the registrar, in respect of every such currency for which the Financial Times did not publish such an exchange rate on or before the reference date, a copy of a certificate referred to in regulation 4(3).

(4) The circumstances in this paragraph are that—

(a) taking account of the effect of the reduction of its share capital, the company has allotted share capital denominated in more than one currency;

(b) the Financial Times published, on or before the reference date, what appears to be an exchange rate referred to in regulation 4(2) relevant to converting into sterling or euros a currency in which the company's allotted share capital is denominated but the company can show that there was a publication error; and

(c) the company has not delivered to the registrar, for every currency in respect of which the company can show such a publication error, a copy of a certificate referred to in regulation 4(3).

(5) The circumstances in this paragraph are that—

(a) taking account of the effect of the reduction of its share capital, the company has allotted share capital denominated in more than one currency;

(b) in respect of one or more of the exchange rates referred to in regulation 4(2) relevant to converting into sterling or euros the currencies in which the company's allotted share capital is denominated there is no evidence of what (if any) was the rate published on or before the reference date by the Financial Times; and

(c) the company has not delivered to the registrar, for every such currency in respect of which there is no such evidence, a copy of a certificate referred to in regulation 4(3).

(6) The registrar may (but is not required to) assume for the purposes of sections 649(1) and 650(1) and (2) that the reduction of the company's share capital has the effect of bringing the nominal value of the company's allotted share capital below the authorised minimum.

**Determination of exchange rates by the court in certain proceedings**

6. (1) This regulation applies to—

(a) proceedings against a public company or any officer of a public company for an offence under section 667; and

(b) proceedings under section 757 or 758 or Part 30.

(2) Where the circumstances in paragraph (3) exist, the court may make a determination referred to in paragraph (4) in the proceedings.

(3) The circumstances are that—

(a) in proceedings under section 667 it is alleged that, or in proceedings referred to in paragraph (1)(b) the question arises whether, the effect of a cancellation of the company's shares and diminution of the amount of the company's share capital under section 662(2)(a) was that the nominal value of the company's allotted share capital was brought below the authorised minimum; and

(b) as a result of that cancellation and diminution the company had (or continued to have) allotted share capital denominated in more than one currency.

(4) The court may make such determination as it thinks fit as to the exchange rate to be applied to a currency conversion referred to in regulation 3(6) and (7) where—

(a) the Financial Times did not publish, on or before the reference date, an exchange rate referred to in regulation 4(2) relevant to that currency conversion; or

(b) the Financial Times published, on or before the reference date, what appears to be an exchange rate referred to in regulation 4(2) relevant to that currency conversion but the company or officer of the company (as the case may be) can show that there was a publication error; or

(c) there is no evidence of what (if any) was the exchange rate referred to in regulation 4(2) as published on or before the reference date by the Financial Times relevant to that currency conversion, and there has not been produced to the court in the proceedings a copy of a certificate referred to in regulation 4(3) in respect of that currency conversion.

(5) In this regulation, 'the court' in relation to proceedings referred to in paragraph (1)(a) means the court of criminal jurisdiction in which the proceedings are brought.

### Exclusion of liability in respect of the publication or non-publication of a spot rate

**7.** No person shall be liable to any other person as a result of—

(a) that or any other person having placed reliance for the purposes of these Regulations upon a rate published by the Financial Times; or

(b) any error in a rate published by the Financial Times which is relied upon for the purposes of these Regulations; or

(c) any act or omission as a result of which the Financial Times did not publish a rate capable of being relied upon for the purposes of these Regulations.

### Revocation

**8.** Regulation 2 of the Companies (Authorised Minimum) Regulations 2008[264] is revoked.

### Transitional provisions and savings

**9.** (1) The figure of €57,100 in regulation 2 is to be read as €65,600 where that regulation applies for any of the purposes in paragraph (2).

(2) The purposes are—

(a) to determine whether the nominal value of a public company's allotted share capital is less than the authorised minimum for the purposes of an application for a trading certificate under section 761 where the application was received by the registrar before 1st October 2009;

(b) to determine for the purposes of section 91(1)(a) whether the nominal value of a private company's allotted share capital is less than the authorised minimum in a case where the special resolution that the company should be re-registered as a public company was passed before 1st October 2009;[265]

(c) to determine whether, for the purposes of section 139 of the Companies Act 1985 or Article 149 of the Companies (Northern Ireland) Order 1986,[266] the effect of a reduction of share capital is to bring the nominal value of a company's allotted share capital below the authorised minimum;

(d) to determine for the purposes of section 650 whether the effect of a reduction of capital is to bring the nominal value of a company's allotted share capital below the authorised minimum in a case where the special resolution for reducing the company's share capital was passed before 1st October 2009;[267]

(e) to determine for the purposes of section 662(2)(b) whether the effect of cancelling shares and diminishing a company's share capital under section 662(2)(a) is to bring the nominal value of the company's allotted share capital below the authorised minimum in a case where the period for complying with the obligations under section 662(2) began before 1st October 2009.[268]

(3) The figure of €57,100 in regulation 3(5)(b) is to be read as €65,600 where that regulation applies for either of the purposes in paragraph (4).

(4) The purposes are—

(a) to determine for the purposes of section 650 whether the effect of a reduction of capital is to bring the nominal value of a company's allotted share capital below the authorised minimum in a case where the special resolution for reducing the company's share capital was passed before 1st October 2009;[269]

(b) to determine for the purposes of section 662(2)(b) whether the effect of cancelling shares and diminishing a company's share capital under section 662(2)(a) is to bring the nominal value of the company's allotted share capital below the authorised minimum in a case where the period for complying with the obligations under section 662(2) began before 1st October 2009.[270]

---

[264] SI 2008/729.

[265] See SI 2008/2860 (C. 126), Schedule 2, paragraph 22(1) and (5).

[266] See SI 2008/2860 (C. 126), Schedule 2, paragraph 68.

[267] See SI 2008/2860 (C. 126), Schedule 2, paragraph 68(1) and (2).

[268] See SI 2008/2860 (C. 126), Schedule 2, paragraph 70(2).

[269] See SI 2008/2860 (C. 126), Schedule 2, paragraph 68(1) and (2).

[270] See SI 2008/2860 (C. 126), Schedule 2, paragraph 70(2).

# THE UNREGISTERED COMPANIES REGULATIONS 2009
## (SI 2009/2436)

COMMENCEMENT DATE 1st October 2009[271]

### Citation and commencement

**1.** (1) These Regulations may be cited as the Unregistered Companies Regulations 2009.

(2) These Regulations come into force on 1st October 2009.

### Interpretation

**2.** In these Regulations—

(a) 'unregistered company' means a body corporate incorporated in, and having a principal place of business in, the United Kingdom, other than—

(i) a body incorporated by, or registered under, a public general enactment,

(ii) a body not formed for the purpose of carrying on a business that has for its object the acquisition of gain by the body or its individual members,

(iii) a body for the time being exempted from section 1043 of the Companies Act 2006 by a direction of the Secretary of State under subsection (1)(c) of that section, or

(iv) an open-ended investment company;

(b) 'instrument constituting or regulating the company', in relation to an unregistered company, means any enactment, royal charter, letters patent, deed of settlement, contract of partnership, or other instrument constituting or regulating the company.

### Application of provisions of the Companies Acts

**3.** The provisions of the Companies Acts specified in Schedule 1 to these Regulations apply to an unregistered company as to a company within the meaning of section 1 of the Companies Act 2006, subject to any limitation, adaptation or modification specified in that Schedule.

### References to registered office and registration

**4.** For the purposes of the application to an unregistered company of the provisions of the Companies Acts applying to it by virtue of these Regulations—

(a) any reference to the company's registered office shall be read as a reference to the company's principal office in the United Kingdom;

(b) any reference to the part of the United Kingdom in which the company is registered shall be read as a reference to the part of the United Kingdom in which the company's principal office is situated (and references to the registrar of companies shall be read accordingly);

(c) any reference to the company's registered number shall be read as a reference to the reference number allocated to the company by the registrar.

### Other general adaptations

**5.** (1) In the application of any provision of the Companies Acts by virtue of these Regulations—

(a) any reference to a public company shall be read, in relation to an unregistered company, as referring to a company that has power under its constitution to offer its shares or debentures to the public;

(b) any reference to a private company shall be read, in relation to an unregistered company, as referring to a company that does not have power to offer its shares or debentures to the public;

(c) any reference to the company's constitution, or to its articles of association, shall be read, in relation to an unregistered company, as referring to any instrument constituting or regulating the company;

(d) any reference to the common seal of the company shall be read, in relation to an unregistered company, as referring to the common or authorised seal of the company.

(2) In the application of any provision of the Companies Acts to an unregistered company by virtue of these Regulations an expression defined, or otherwise having a particular meaning or effect, in relation to a company within the meaning of section 1 of the Companies Act 2006, has effect with any adaptations necessary to ensure a corresponding meaning or effect in relation to an unregistered company.

(3) Paragraphs (1) and (2) are subject to any specific adaptation or modification provided for in these Regulations.

---

[271] 2006 c. 46.

**Application of provisions relating to statutory auditors**

**6.** For the purposes of section 1210(1)(h) of the Companies Act 2006 (meaning of 'statutory auditor')—

(a) an unregistered company is a prescribed person, and

(b) Part 16 of that Act (audit) as applied to unregistered companies by these Regulations is a prescribed enactment.

(and accordingly a person appointed as auditor of an unregistered company under Part 16 of that Act as so applied is a statutory auditor).

**Saving**

**7.** Nothing in these Regulations affects the application of any provision to an unregistered company otherwise than by virtue of these Regulations.

**Revocations**

**8.** The following Regulations are revoked—

(a) the Companies (Unregistered Companies) Regulations 1985,[272]

(b) the Companies (Unregistered Companies) Regulations (Northern Ireland) 1986,[273] and

(c) the Companies Acts (Unregistered Companies) Regulations 2007.[274]

**Transitional provisions and savings**

**9.** Schedule 2 contains transitional provisions and savings.

## SCHEDULE 1

Regulation 3

## PROVISIONS OF THE COMPANIES ACTS APPLYING TO UNREGISTERED COMPANIES

**A company's constitution**

**1.** Sections 26 and 27 of the Companies Act 2006 (filing obligations in connection with company's articles) apply to unregistered companies, modified so that they read as follows—

### 'Registrar to be sent copy of company's constitution

**26.** (1) A company must, not later than 15 days after the date of its incorporation, send to the registrar a copy of every instrument constituting or regulating the company.

(2) Where a company amends any instrument constituting or regulating the company, it must, not later than 15 days after the amendment takes effect, send to the registrar a copy of the instrument as amended.

(3) If a company fails to comply with subsection (1) or (2) an offence is committed by—

(a) the company, and

(b) every officer of the company who is in default.

(4) A person guilty of an offence under this section is liable on summary conviction to a fine not exceeding level 3 on the standard scale and, for continued contravention, a daily default fine not exceeding one-tenth of level 3 on the standard scale.

### Registrar's notice to comply in case of failure with respect to company's constitution

**27.** (1) If it appears to the registrar that a company has failed to comply with—

(a) section 26(1) or (2) (registrar to be sent copy of company's constitution), or

(b) any enactment requiring the company to send to the registrar—

(i) a document making or evidencing an alteration in any instrument constituting or regulating the company, or

(ii) a copy of any such instrument as amended,

the registrar may give notice to the company requiring it to comply.

(2) The notice must—

(a) state the date on which it is issued, and

(b) require the company to comply within 28 days from that date.

(3) If the company complies with the notice within the specified time, no criminal proceedings may be brought in respect of the failure mentioned in subsection (1).

(4) If the company does not comply with the notice within the specified time, it is liable to a civil penalty of £200.

(5) This is in addition to any liability to criminal proceedings in respect of the failure mentioned in subsection (1).

---

272 SI 1985/680, as amended.

273 SR (NI) 1986 No 305, as amended.

274 SI 2007/318.

(6) The penalty may be recovered by the registrar and is to be paid into the Consolidated Fund.'.

**2.** Sections 34 and 35 of the Companies Act 2006 (notice to registrar where company's constitution altered) apply to unregistered companies, modified so that they read as follows—

### 'Notice to registrar where company's constitution altered by enactment

**34.** (1) This section applies where the constitution of a company is altered by an enactment, other than an enactment amending the general law.

(2) The company must give notice of the alteration to the registrar, specifying the enactment, not later than 15 days after the enactment comes into force.

(3) In the case of a special enactment the notice must be accompanied by a copy of the enactment.

(4) If the enactment amends any instrument constituting or regulating the company, the notice must be accompanied by a copy of the instrument in question, as amended.

(5) A 'special enactment' means an enactment that is not a public general enactment, and includes—

    (a) an Act for confirming a provisional order,

    (b) any provision of a public general Act in relation to the passing of which any of the standing orders of the House of Lords or the House of Commons relating to Private Business applied, or

    (c) any enactment to the extent that it is incorporated in or applied for the purposes of a special enactment.

(6) If a company fails to comply with this section an offence is committed by—

    (a) the company, and

    (b) every officer of the company who is in default.

(7) A person guilty of an offence under this section is liable on summary conviction to a fine not exceeding level 3 on the standard scale and, for continued contravention, a daily default fine not exceeding one-tenth of level 3 on the standard scale.

### Notice to registrar where company's constitution altered by order

**35.** (1) Where the constitution of a company is altered by an order of a court or other authority, the company must give notice to the registrar of the alteration not later than 15 days after the alteration takes effect.

(2) The notice must be accompanied by—

    (a) a copy of the order, and

    (b) if the order amends any instrument constituting or regulating the company, a copy of the instrument in question, as amended.

(3) If a company fails to comply with this section an offence is committed by—

    (a) the company, and

    (b) every officer of the company who is in default.

(4) A person guilty of an offence under this section is liable on summary conviction to a fine not exceeding level 3 on the standard scale and, for continued contravention, a daily default fine not exceeding one-tenth of level 3 on the standard scale.

(5) This section does not apply where provision is made by another enactment for the delivery to the registrar of a copy of the order in question.'.

### A company's capacity and related matters

**3.** The following provisions of the Companies Act 2006 apply to unregistered companies—

    (a) sections 39 and 40 (a company's capacity and power of directors to bind company);

    (b) section 41 (constitutional limitations: transactions involving directors or their associates);

    (c) section 42 (constitutional limitations: companies that are charities);

    (d) sections 43, 44, 45(1) and 46 (formalities of doing business under the law of England and Wales or Northern Ireland);

    (e) section 48 (execution of documents under the law of Scotland);

    (f) section 50 (official seal for share certificates);

    (g) section 51 (pre-incorporation contracts, deeds and obligations).

### Trading disclosures

**4.** Sections 82 to 85 of the Companies Act 2006 (trading disclosures) apply to unregistered companies, modified so that they read as follows—

### 'Requirement to disclose company name and other particulars

**82.** (1) Every company must disclose its corporate name on—

    (a) its business letters, notices and other official publications;

    (b) its bills of exchange, promissory notes, endorsements and order forms;

    (c) cheques purporting to be signed by or on behalf of the company;

    (d) orders for money, goods or services purporting to be signed by or on behalf of the company;

    (e)  its bills of parcels, invoices and other demands for payment, receipts and letters of credit;

    (f)  its applications for licences to carry on a trade or activity;

    (g)  all other forms of its business correspondence and documentation; and

    (h)  its websites.

(2)  Every company must disclose the further particulars set out in subsection (3) on—

    (a)  its business letters;

    (b)  its order forms; and

    (c)  its websites.

(3)  The further particulars required are—

    (a)  the part of the United Kingdom in which the company's principal office is situated;

    (b)  the reference number allocated to the company by the registrar;

    (c)  the address of the company's principal office;

    (d)  the manner in which it was incorporated;

    (e)  if it is—

    (i)  a limited company, or

    (ii)  an investment company within the meaning of section 833,

      that fact.

(4)  If, in the case of a company having a share capital, there is a reference to the amount of share capital on—

    (a)  its business letters,

    (b)  its order forms, or

    (c)  its websites,

      the reference must be to paid up share capital.

(5)  In relation to a company, a reference to 'its websites' includes a reference to any part of a website relating to that company which that company has caused or authorised to appear.

### Civil consequences of failure to make required disclosure

**83.** (1)  This section applies to any legal proceedings brought by a company to enforce a right arising out of a contract made in the course of a business in respect of which the company was, at the time the contract was made, in breach of section 82 (requirement to disclose company name and other particulars).

(2)  The proceedings shall be dismissed if the defendant (in Scotland, the defender) to the proceedings shows—

    (a)  that he has a claim against the claimant (pursuer) arising out of the contract that he has been unable to pursue by reason of the latter's breach of section 82, or

    (b)  that he has suffered some financial loss in connection with the contract by reason of the claimant's (pursuer's) breach of section 82,

      unless the court before which the proceedings are brought is satisfied that it is just and equitable to permit the proceedings to continue.

(3)  This section does not affect the right of any person to enforce such rights as he may have against another person in any proceedings brought by that person.

### Criminal consequences of failure to make required disclosure

**84.** (1)  Where a company fails, without reasonable excuse, to comply with any requirement of section 82, an offence is committed by—

    (a)  the company; and

    (b)  every officer of the company who is in default.

(2)  A person guilty of an offence under this section is liable on summary conviction to—

    (a)  a fine not exceeding level 3 on the standard scale; and

    (b)  for continued contravention, a daily default fine not exceeding one-tenth of level 3 on the standard scale.

(3)  For the purposes of this section a shadow director is to be treated as an officer of the company.

### Minor variations in form of name to be left out of account

**85.** For the purposes of this Chapter, in considering the name of a company no account is to be taken of—

    (a)  whether upper or lower case characters (or a combination of the two) are used, or

    (b)  whether diacritical marks or punctuation are present or absent,

      provided there is no real likelihood of names differing only in those respects being taken to be different names.'.

#### A company's principal office in the United Kingdom

**5.** Sections 86 and 87 of the Companies Act 2006 (a company's registered office) apply to unregistered companies, modified so that they read as follows—

## 'A company's principal office

**86.** (1) Communications and notices may at all times be addressed to a company at its principal office in the United Kingdom.

(2) A company must give notice to the registrar, not later than 15 days after the date of the incorporation of the company, of the address of its principal office in the United Kingdom.

(3) If a company fails to comply with subsection (2) an offence is committed by—

    (a) the company, and

    (b) every officer of the company who is in default.

(4) A person guilty of an offence under subsection (2) is liable on summary conviction to a fine not exceeding level 3 on the standard scale and, for continued contravention, a daily default fine not exceeding one-tenth of level 3 on the standard scale.

## Change of principal office

**87.** (1) Where a company changes its principal office in the United Kingdom, it must send notice of the new address to the registrar not later than 15 days after the change takes effect.

(2) If a company fails to comply with subsection (1) an offence is committed by—

    (a) the company, and

    (b) every officer of the company who is in default.

(3) A person guilty of an offence under subsection (1) is liable on summary conviction to a fine not exceeding level 3 on the standard scale and, for continued contravention, a daily default fine not exceeding one-tenth of level 3 on the standard scale.

(4) Until the end of the period of 14 days beginning with the date on which the new address is registered a person may validly serve any document on the company at the address previously registered.

(5) For the purposes of any duty of a company—

    (a) to keep available for inspection at its principal office in the United Kingdom any register or other document, or

    (b) to mention the address of that office in any document,

    a company that changes the address of its principal office in the United Kingdom may make the change as from such date as it may determine, but it is treated as failing to comply with that duty if it does not comply with subsection (1).

(6) Where a company unavoidably ceases to perform at its principal office in the United Kingdom any such duty as is mentioned in subsection (5)(a) but—

    (a) resumes performance of that duty at other premises as soon as practicable, and

    (b) gives notice to the registrar of a change in the address of its principal office in accordance with subsection (1),

    it is not to be treated as having failed to comply with that duty.'.

### Directors and secretaries

**6.** (1) Sections 162 to 167 of the Companies Act 2006 (register of directors and register of directors' residential addresses) apply to unregistered companies.

(2) Section 162 (register of directors) applies with the following modifications—

    (a) in subsection (3)(b) (places where register may be kept available for inspection), for 'specified in regulations under section 1136' substitute 'specified in Part 2 of the Companies (Company Records) Regulations 2008 (S.I. 2008/3006)';

    (b) in subsection (5)(b) (inspection by non-member on payment), for 'such fee as may be prescribed' substitute 'the fee prescribed by regulation 2(a) of the Companies (Fees for Inspection of Company Records) Regulations 2008 (S.I. 2008/3007)'.

**7.** (1) Sections 240 to 246 of the Companies Act 2006 (directors' residential addresses: protection from disclosure) apply to unregistered companies.

(2) Section 243 (permitted use or disclosure of protected information by the registrar) applies with the following modifications—

    (a) in subsection (2)(a) for 'by regulations made by the Secretary of State' substitute 'in the Companies (Disclosure of Address) Regulations 2009 (S.I. 2009/214)';

    (b) for subsection (3) substitute—

      '(3) The provisions of the Companies (Disclosure of Address) Regulations 2009 (S.I. 2009/214) relating to disclosure of protected information under this section apply.

      (3A) Those provisions are—

        (a) Part 2 (disclosure of protected information),

        (b) Part 4 (matters relating to applications), so far as relating to disclosure under this section, and

        (c) any other provisions of the Regulations having effect for the purposes of those provisions.';

    (c) omit subsections (4) to (6) and (8).

**8.** (1) Sections 275 to 279 of the Companies Act 2006 (register of secretaries) apply to unregistered companies.

(2) Section 275 applies with the following modifications—

    (a) in subsection (3)(b) (places where register may be kept available for inspection), for 'specified in regulations under section 1136' substitute 'specified in Part 2 of the Companies (Company Records) Regulations 2008 (S.I. 2008/3006)';

    (b) in subsection (5)(b) (inspection by non-member on payment), for 'such fee as may be prescribed' substitute 'the fee prescribed by regulation 2(a) of the Companies (Fees for Inspection of Company Records) Regulations 2008 (S.I. 2008/3007)'.

### Political donations and expenditure

**9.** (1) Sections 362 to 379 of the Companies Act 2006 (control of political donations and expenditure) apply to unregistered companies, with the following modifications.

(2) In section 369(5) (liability of directors to make good unauthorised donations or expenditure: interest), in paragraph (b) for 'such rate as the Secretary of State may prescribe by regulations' substitute, 'the rate specified in the Companies (Interest Rate for Unauthorised Political Donations or Expenditure) Regulations 2007 (S.I. 2007/2242)'.

(3) In section 377 (exemption of certain political expenditure)—

    (a) in subsection (1) for 'an order of the Secretary of State under this section' substitute 'articles 3 and 4 of the Companies (Political Expenditure Exemption) Order 2007 (S.I. 2007/2081)';

    (b) omit subsection (2);

    (c) in subsection (3) for 'an order under this section' substitute 'the articles mentioned in subsection (1)';

    (d) omit subsection (4).

### Accounts

**10.** (1) Sections 380 to 416, 418 to 469 and 471 to 474 of the Companies Act 2006 (accounts and reports) apply to unregistered companies, with the following modifications.

(2) In section 383(6)(a) (small companies: determination of net amounts), for 'regulations under section 404' substitute 'Part 1 of Schedule 4 to the Small Companies and Groups (Accounts and Directors' Report) Regulations 2008 (S.I. 2008/409) or Schedule 3 to the Large and Medium-sized Companies and Groups (Accounts and Directors' Reports) Regulations 2008 (SI 2008/410)'.

(3) In section 396 (Companies Act individual accounts)—

    (a) for subsection (3) (requirements as to form and content of accounts etc) substitute—

      '(3) The accounts must comply with the provisions of—

        (a) regulation 3 of the Small Companies and Groups (Accounts and Directors' Report) Regulations 2008 (S.I. 2008/409), or

        (b) regulations 3 and 4 of the Large and Medium-sized Companies and Groups (Accounts and Directors' Reports) Regulations 2008 (S.I. 2008/410),

        as to the form and content of the balance sheet and profit and loss account, and additional information to be provided by way of notes to the accounts.';

    (b) in subsection (4) (additional information) after 'regulations' insert 'specified in subsection (3)'.

(4) In section 404 (Companies Act group accounts)—

    (a) for subsection (3) (requirements as to form and content of accounts etc) substitute—

      '(3) The accounts must comply with the provisions of—

        (a) regulation 6 of the Small Companies and Groups (Accounts and Directors' Report) Regulations 2008 (S.I. 2008/409), or

        (b) regulation 6 of the Large and Medium-sized Companies and Groups (Accounts and Directors' Reports) Regulations 2008 (S.I. 2008/410),

        as to the form and content of the consolidated balance sheet and consolidated profit and loss account, and additional information to be provided by way of notes to the accounts.';

    (b) in subsection (4) (additional information) after 'regulations' insert 'specified in subsection (3)'.

(5) In section 409 (information about related undertakings), for subsections (1) to (3) substitute—

    '(1) The notes to the company's annual accounts must contain the information about related undertakings required by—

      (a) regulations 4 and 7 of the Small Companies and Groups (Accounts and Directors' Report) Regulations 2008 (S.I. 2008/409), or

      (b) regulation 5 of the Large and Medium-sized Companies and Groups (Accounts and Directors' Reports) Regulations 2008 (S.I. 2008/410).

    (2) That information need not be disclosed with respect to an undertaking that—

      (a) is established under the law of a country outside the United Kingdom, or

      (b) carries on business outside the United Kingdom,

    if the following conditions are met.'.

(6) In section 412 (information about directors' benefits: remuneration)—

    (a) for subsections (1) to (3) substitute—

        '(1) The information about directors' remuneration required by—

            (a) the Small Companies and Groups (Accounts and Directors' Report) Regulations 2008 (S.I. 2008/409), or

            (b) the Large and Medium-sized Companies and Groups (Accounts and Directors' Reports) Regulations 2008 (S.I. 2008/410),

            must be given in notes to the company's annual accounts.';

    (b) in subsection (4) for 'and regulations made under it' substitute 'and the regulations specified in subsection (1)';

    (c) in subsection (5) for 'regulations under this section' substitute 'and the regulations specified in subsection (1)'.

(7) In section 416 (contents of directors' report: general), for subsection (4) substitute—

    '(4) The directors' report must comply with the provisions of—

        (a) the Small Companies and Groups (Accounts and Directors' Report) Regulations 2008 (S.I. 2008/409), or

        (b) the Large and Medium-sized Companies and Groups (Accounts and Directors' Reports) Regulations 2008 (S.I. 2008/410),

    as to other matters to be included in the report.'.

(8) In section 421 (contents of directors' remuneration report), for subsections (1) and (2) substitute—

    '(1) The provisions of the Large and Medium-sized Companies and Groups (Accounts and Directors' Reports) Regulations 2008 (S.I. 2008/410) apply as to—

        (a) the information that must be contained in a directors' remuneration report,

        (b) how information is to be set out in the report, and

        (c) what is to be the auditable part of the report.'.

(9) In section 426 (option to provide summary financial statement)—

    (a) in subsection (1)(a) for 'regulations made by the Secretary of State' substitute 'the Companies (Summary Financial Statement) Regulations 2008 (S.I. 2008/374)';

    (b) omit subsections (3) and (6).

(10) In section 427 (form and contents of summary financial statement: unquoted companies)—

    (a) in subsection (1)(b) for 'regulations made under it' substitute 'the Companies (Summary Financial Statement) Regulations 2008 (S.I. 2008/374)';

    (b) for subsection (2) substitute—

        '(2) The summary financial statement must be in the form and contain such information as is required in the case of an unquoted company by the Companies (Summary Financial Statement) Regulations 2008 (S.I. 2008/374).'.

(11) In section 428 (form and contents of summary financial statement: quoted companies)—

    (a) in subsection (1)(b) for 'regulations made under it' substitute 'the Companies (Summary Financial Statement) Regulations 2008 (S.I. 2008/374)';

    (b) for subsection (2) substitute—

        '(2) The summary financial statement must be in the form and contain such information as is required in the case of a quoted company by the Companies (Summary Financial Statement) Regulations 2008 (S.I. 2008/374).'.

(12) In section 444(3) (filing obligations of companies subject to small companies regime: copies of accounts and reports)—

    (a) in paragraph (a) for 'regulations made by the Secretary of State' substitute 'regulation 5 of the Small Companies and Groups (Accounts and Directors' Report) Regulations 2008 (S.I. 2008/409)';

    (b) in paragraph (b) for 'the regulations' substitute 'that regulation'.

(13) In section 445(3) (filing obligations of medium-sized companies: copies of accounts and reports)—

    (a) in paragraph (a) for 'regulations made by the Secretary of State' substitute 'regulation 4 of the Large and Medium-sized Companies and Groups (Accounts and Directors' Reports) Regulations 2008 (S.I. 2008/410)';

    (b) in paragraph (b) for 'the regulations' substitute 'that regulation'.

(14) In section 449(2)(b) (special auditor's report where abbreviated accounts delivered: compliance with regulations), for 'regulations under that section' substitute 'regulation 5 of the Small Companies and Groups (Accounts and Directors' Report) Regulations 2008 (S.I. 2008/409) or regulation 4 of the Large and Medium-sized Companies and Groups (Accounts and Directors' Reports) Regulations 2008 (S.I. 2008/410)'.

(15) In section 450(4) (approval and signing of abbreviated accounts: accounts not complying with requirements), for 'regulations under the relevant section' substitute 'regulation 5 of the Small Companies and Groups (Accounts and Directors' Report) Regulations 2008 (S.I. 2008/409) or regulation 4 of the Large and Medium-sized Companies and Groups (Accounts and Directors' Reports) Regulations 2008 (S.I. 2008/410)'.

(16) In section 453 (civil penalty for failure to file accounts and reports)—
  (a) in subsection (2) (determination of amount), for 'regulations made by the Secretary of State' substitute 'the relevant provisions of the Companies (Late Filing Penalties) and Limited Liability Partnerships (Filing Periods and Late Filing Penalties) Regulations 2008 (S.I. 2008/497)';
  (b) omit subsection (5).

(17) In section 454 (voluntary revision of accounts), for subsections (3) to (5) substitute—
  '(3) The provisions of the Companies (Revision of Defective Accounts) Regulations 2008 (S.I. 2008/373) apply.'.

(18) In section 457 (other persons authorised to apply to the court)—
  (a) for subsections (1) to (3) substitute—
    '(1) The Companies (Defective Accounts and Directors' Reports) (Authorised Person) and Supervision of Accounts and Reports (Prescribed Body) Order 2008 (S.I. 2008/623) apply as regards—
      (a) the persons authorised by the Secretary of State for the purposes of section 456 (application to court in respect of defective accounts or reports), and
      (b) the requirements and other provisions applying to the exercise of functions as an authorised person.';
  (b) omit subsections (5) to (7).

(19) In section 464 (accounting standards)—
  (a) in subsection (1) for 'such body or bodies as may be prescribed by regulations' substitute 'the body known as the Accounting Standards Board, as prescribed by the Accounting Standards (Prescribed Body) Regulations 2008 (S.I. 2008/651)';
  (b) omit subsection (3).

### Audit

**11.** (1) Sections 475 to 481 and 484 to 539 of the Companies Act 2006 (audit) apply to unregistered companies, with the following modifications.

(2) Section 494 (disclosure of services provided by auditor or associates and related remuneration) is modified so that it reads as follows—

### Disclosure of services provided by auditor or associates and related remuneration

**494.** The Companies (Disclosure of Auditor Remuneration and Liability Limitation Agreements) Regulations 2008 (S.I. 2008/489) apply as regards the disclosure of—
  (a) the nature of any services provided for a company by the company's auditor (whether in the capacity as auditor or otherwise) or by the auditor's associates;
  (b) the amount of any remuneration received or receivable by the auditor, or the auditor's associates, in respect of any such services.'.

(3) In section 504 (meaning of 'senior statutory auditor'), in subsection (1)(b)(ii) for 'by order of the Secretary of State' substitute 'by the Statutory Auditors (Delegation of Functions etc) Order 2008 (S.I. 2008/496)'.

(4) Section 538 (disclosure by company of liability limitation agreement) is modified so that it reads as follows—

### Disclosure of agreement by company

**538.** A company that has entered into a liability limitation agreement must make the disclosure in connection with the agreement required by the Companies (Disclosure of Auditor Remuneration and Liability Limitation Agreements) Regulations 2008 (S.I. 2008/489).'.

### Share certificates

**12.** (1) The following provisions of the Companies Act 2006 apply to unregistered companies—
  (a) section 768 (share certificate to be evidence of title);
  (b) section 778 (issue of certificates etc: allotment or transfer to financial institution).

(2) In section 778 as it applies to unregistered companies, for 'section 769(1) or 776(1) (duty of company as to issue of certificates etc)' substitute 'any provision of any instrument constituting or regulating the company'.

### Annual return

**13.** (1) Sections 854 to 859 of the Companies Act 2006 (a company's annual return) apply to unregistered companies.

(2) Section 855 (contents of annual return: general) applies with the following modifications—
  (a) in subsection (1)(d) (place where company records kept), omit '(in accordance with regulations under section 1136)';
  (b) in subsection (2) (classification of company type), for 'prescribed for the purposes of this section' insert 'prescribed by regulation 5 of and Schedule 1 to the Companies Act 2006 (Annual Return and Service Addresses) Regulations 2008 (S.I. 2008/3000)';
  (c) in subsection (3) (classification of business activities), for 'any prescribed system of classifying business activities' substitute 'the system of classifying business activities

prescribed by regulation 6 of and Schedule 2 to the Companies Act 2006 (Annual Return and Service Addresses) Regulations 2008 (S.I. 2008/3000)'.

### Takeovers

**14.** (1) Sections 966 to 973 of the Companies Act 2006 (impediments to takeovers) apply to unregistered companies.

(2) Sections 974 to 991 of that Act ('squeeze-out' and 'sell-out') apply to unregistered companies, but so far as relating to the offeree company only if the unregistered company has voting shares admitted to trading on a regulated market.

### Fraudulent trading

**15.** Section 993 of the Companies Act 2006 (fraudulent trading) applies to an unregistered company.

### Company Investigations

**16.** Parts 14 and 15 of the Companies Act 1985[275] (company investigations etc) apply to unregistered companies.

### The registrar of companies

**17.** (1) The application to unregistered companies by the following paragraphs of certain provisions of Part 35 of the Companies Act 2006 is without prejudice to the application in relation to unregistered companies of the provisions of that Part that are of general application.

(2) Those provisions are—
   (a) sections 1060(1) and (2) and 1061 to 1063 (the registrar),
   (b) sections 1068 to 1071 (delivery of documents to the registrar),
   (c) sections 1072 to 1076 (requirements for proper delivery),
   (d) sections 1080(1), (4) and (5) and 1092 (keeping and production of records),
   (e) section 1083 (preservation of original documents),
   (f) sections 1108 to 1110 (language requirements: transliteration),
   (g) sections 1111 and 1114 to 1119 (supplementary provisions).

**18.** Section 1066 of the Companies Act 2006 (registered numbers) applies to unregistered companies, modified so that it reads as follows—

## Companies' reference numbers

**1066.** (1) The registrar shall allocate to every company a number, which shall be known as the company's reference number.

(2) Companies' reference numbers shall be in such form, consisting of one or more sequences of figures or letters, as the registrar may determine.

(3) The registrar may on adopting a new form of reference number make such changes of existing reference numbers as appear necessary.

(4) A change of a company's reference number has effect from the date on which the company is notified by the registrar of the change.

(5) For a period of three years beginning with that date any requirement to disclose the company's reference number imposed by section 82 (trading disclosures) is satisfied by the use of either the old number or the new.'.

**19.** Sections 1077 to 1079 of the Companies Act 2006 (public notice of receipt of certain documents) apply to unregistered companies, modified so that they read as follows—

## Public notice of receipt of certain documents

**1077.** (1) The registrar must cause to be published—
   (a) in the Gazette, or
   (b) in accordance with section 1116 (alternative means of giving public notice),
      notice of the receipt by the registrar of any document specified in section 1078.

(2) The notice must state the name and reference number of the company, the description of document and the date of receipt.

(3) The registrar is not required to cause notice of the receipt of a document to be published before the date of incorporation of the company to which the document relates.

## The section 1077 documents

**1078.** The following documents are specified for the purposes of section 1077—

---

[275] 1985 c. 6.

### Constitutional documents

1. Any instrument constituting or regulating the company.
2. After any alteration of such an instrument, any copy of the instrument as amended.
3. Any notice of the change of the company's name.

### Accounts and returns

1. All documents required to be delivered to the registrar under section 441 (annual accounts).
2. The company's annual return.

### Principal office

Notification of any change of the company's principal office in the United Kingdom.

### Winding up

1. Copy of any winding-up order in respect of the company.
2. Notice of the appointment of liquidators.
3. Order for the dissolution of the company on a winding up.
4. Return by a liquidator of the final meeting of the company on a winding up.

### Effect of failure to give public notice

**1079.** (1) A company is not entitled to rely against other persons on the happening of any event to which this section applies unless—

    (a) the event has been officially notified at the material time, or

    (b) the company shows that the person concerned knew of the event at the material time.

(2) The events to which this section applies are—

    (a) (as regards service of any document on the company) a change of the company's principal office in the United Kingdom,

    (b) the making of a winding-up order in respect of the company, or

    (c) the appointment of a liquidator in a voluntary winding up of the company.

(3) If the material time falls—

    (a) on or before the 15th day after the date of official notification, or

    (b) where the 15th day was not a working day, on or before the next day that was, the company is not entitled to rely on the happening of the event as against a person who shows that he was unavoidably prevented from knowing of the event at that time.

(4) 'Official notification' means—

    (a) in relation to anything stated in a document specified in section 1078, notification of that document in accordance with section 1077;

    (b) in relation to the appointment of a liquidator in a voluntary winding up, notification of that event in accordance with section 109 of the Insolvency Act 1986 (c. 45) or Article 95 of the Insolvency (Northern Ireland) Order 1989 (S.I. 1989/2405 (N.I. 19)).'.

**20.** (1) The following provisions of the Companies Act 2006 apply to unregistered companies—

    (a) section 1080(2) and (4) (meaning of 'register' and form in which documents to be recorded and kept);

    (b) sections 1085 and 1086 (inspection of the register and right to take copies on the register);

    (c) sections 1087 and 1088 (material not available for public inspection and application to registrar to make address unavailable for public inspection);

    (d) sections 1089 and 1090 (form and manner of application for inspection or copy);

    (e) section 1091 (certification of copies as accurate).

(2) In section 1087 (material not available for public inspection) as it applies to unregistered companies, in subsection (1)—

    (a) omit paragraph (a);

    (b) in paragraph (b) omit 'or any corresponding provision of regulations under section 1046 (overseas companies)';

    (c) in paragraph (ba), omit sub-paragraph (ii);

    (d) omit paragraphs (c) to (h) and (j).

(3) For section 1088 as it applies to unregistered companies substitute—

### Application to registrar to make address unavailable for public inspection

**1088.** (1) The relevant provisions of the Companies (Disclosure of Address) Regulations 2009 (S.I. 2009/214) apply with respect to applications to the registrar to make an address on the register unavailable for public inspection.

(2) Those provisions are—

    (a) Part 3 (applications to make address unavailable for public inspection), and

    (b) Part 4 (matters relating to application), so far as relating to such applications, and

(c) any other provisions of the Regulations having effect for the purposes of those provisions.'.

(4) In section 1091 (certification of copies as accurate) as it applies to unregistered companies, for subsection (4) substitute—

'(4) Regulation 2 of the Companies (Registrar, Languages and Trading Disclosures) Regulations 2006 (S.I. 2006/3429) (certification of electronic copies by registrar) applies where the copy is provided in electronic form.'.

### Supplementary provisions

**21.** The provisions of the Companies Acts relating to offences, interpretation and other supplementary matters have effect in relation to unregistered companies so far as necessary for the purposes of the application and enforcement of the provisions applied to unregistered companies by these Regulations.

SCHEDULE 2          Regulation 9

TRANSITIONAL PROVISIONS AND SAVINGS

### Introduction

**1.** (1) In this Schedule—

(a) 'the 1985 Act' means the Companies Act 1985 and 'the 1985 Regulations' means the Companies (Unregistered Companies) Regulations 1985;

(b) 'the 1986 Order' means the Companies (Northern Ireland) Order 1986[276] and 'the 1986 Regulations' means the Companies (Unregistered Companies) Regulations (Northern Ireland) 1986;

(c) 'existing company' means an unregistered company that was incorporated before 1st October 2009.

(2) References in this Schedule to provisions of the 1985 Act or 1986 Order, or to provisions of the Companies Act 2006, are to those provisions as applied to unregistered companies.

### A company's constitution

**2.** (1) Section 26(1) of the Companies Act 2006 (registrar to be sent copy of instruments constituting or regulating company) applies where the company is incorporated on or after 1st October 2009.

(2) Section 18 of the 1985 Act as modified by regulation 6(b)(ii) of the 1985 Regulations or Article 29 of the 1986 Order as modified by regulation 6(b)(ii) of the 1986 Regulations continues to apply where the company was incorporated before that date.

**3.** (1) Section 26(2) of the Companies Act 2006 (registrar to be sent copy of amended instrument constituting or regulating company) applies where the amendment takes effect on or after 1st October 2009.

(2) Section 18(2) and (3) of the 1985 Act or Article 29(2) and (3) of the 1986 Order continue to apply in relation to amendments taking effect before that date.

**4.** (1) Section 34 of the Companies Act 2006 (notice to registrar where company's constitution altered by enactment) applies where the enactment in question comes into force on or after 1st October 2009.

(2) Section 18(1) and (3) of the 1985 Act or Article 29(1) and (3) of the 1986 Order continue to apply in relation to alterations made by statutory provisions coming into force before that date.

**5.** Section 35 of the Companies Act 2006 (notice to registrar where company's constitution altered by order) applies in relation to orders made on or after 1st October 2009.

### A company's capacity and related matters

**6.** (1) Section 39 of the Companies Act 2006 (a company's capacity) applies to acts of a company done on or after 1st October 2009.

(2) Section 35 of the 1985 Act or Article 45 of the 1986 Order continues to apply to acts of a company done before that date.

**7.** (1) Section 44 of the Companies Act 2006 (execution of documents) applies in relation to the execution of documents on or after 1st October 2009.

(2) Section 36A of the 1985 Act or Article 46A of the 1986 Order continues to apply in relation to documents executed before that date.

(3) For the purposes of this paragraph a document signed by one authorised signatory before 1st

---

[276] SI 1986/1032 (NI 6).

October 2009 and by another on or after that date is treated as executed on or after 1st October 2009.

### A company's principal office in the United Kingdom

**8.** Section 86(2) of the Companies Act 2006 (registrar to be notified of address of company's principal office in the United Kingdom) applies where the company is incorporated on or after 1st October 2009.

### Directors and secretaries

**9.** On and after 1st October 2009 the register of directors and secretaries kept by a company under section 288(1) of the 1985 Act or Article 296(1) of the 1986 Order shall be treated as two separate registers—

    (a) a register of directors kept under and for the purposes of section 162 of the Companies Act 2006, and

    (b) a register of secretaries kept under and for the purposes of section 275 of that Act.

**10.** (1) Subject to the following provisions, an existing company need not comply with any provision of the Companies Act 2006 requiring the company's register of directors or secretaries to contain particulars additional to those required by the 1985 Act or the 1986 Order until the earlier of—

    (a) the date to which the company makes up its first annual return made up to a date on or after 1st October 2009, and

    (b) the last date to which the company should have made up that return.

  (2) Sub-paragraph (1) does not apply in relation to a director or secretary of whom particulars are first registered on or after 1st October 2009 (whether the director or secretary was appointed before, on or after that date).

  (3) Sub-paragraph (1) ceases to apply in relation to a director or secretary whose registered particulars fall to be altered on or after 1st October 2009 because they have changed (whether the change occurred before, on or after that date).

  (4) This paragraph does not affect the particulars required to be included in the company's annual return.

**11.** (1) In the case of an existing company—

    (a) the relevant existing address of a director or secretary is deemed, on and after 1st October 2009, to be a service address, and

    (b) any entry in the company's register of directors or secretaries stating that address is treated, on and after that date, as complying with the obligation in section 163(1)(b) or 277(1)(b) of the Companies Act 2006 to state a service address.

  (2) The relevant existing address is—

    (a) the address that immediately before 1st October 2009 appeared in the company's register of directors and secretaries as having been notified to the company under section 289(1A) or 290(1A) of the 1985 Act (service address notified by individual applying for confidentiality order in respect of usual residential address), or

    (b) if no such address appeared, the address that immediately before that date appeared in the company's register of directors and secretaries as the director's or secretary's usual residential address.

  (3) Any notification of a change of a relevant existing address occurring before 1st October 2009 that is received by the company on or after that date is treated as being or, as the case may be, including notification of a change of service address.

  (4) The operation of this paragraph does not give rise to any duty to notify the registrar under section 167 or 276 of the Companies Act 2006 (duty to notify registrar of changes in particulars contained in register).

**12.** (1) An existing company must remove from its register of directors on 1st October 2009 any entry relating to a shadow director.

  (2) Section 167 of the Companies Act 2006 (duty to notify registrar of changes) applies as if the shadow director had ceased to be a director on that date.

**13.** The removal by an existing company from its register of directors or secretaries on or after 1st October 2009 of particulars required by the 1985 Act or the 1986 Order but not required by the Companies Act 2006 does not give rise to any duty to notify the registrar under section 167 or 276 of the Companies Act 2006 (duty to notify registrar of changes in particulars contained in register).

**14.** (1) The duty of a company to keep a register of directors' residential addresses has effect on and after 1st October 2009.

  (2) The entry on that register of information that immediately before that date was contained in the company's register of directors and secretaries does not give rise to any duty to notify the registrar under section 167 of the Companies Act 2006 (duty to notify registrar of changes in particulars contained in register).

**15.** (1) Sections 167 and 276 of the Companies Act 2006 (duty to notify registrar of changes) apply in relation to—

(a) a change among a company's directors or in its secretaries, or

(b) a change in the particulars contained in the register,

    occurring on or after 1st October 2009.

(2) Sections 288(2), (4) and (6), 289 and 290 of the 1985 Act or Articles 296(2), (4) and (6), 297 and 298 of the 1986 Order (notification to registrar of changes) continue to apply in relation to a change occurring before that date.

**16.** (1) The registrar may make such entries in the register as appear to be appropriate having regard to paragraphs 10 to 14 and the information appearing on the register immediately before 1st October 2009 or notified to the registrar in accordance with paragraph 15(2).

(2) In particular, the registrar may record as a service address a relevant existing address (within the meaning of paragraph 11).

(3) Any notification of a change of a relevant existing address occurring before 1st October 2009 that is received by the registrar on or after that date is treated as being or, as the case may be, including notification of a change of service address.

**17.** Where a director's usual residential address appears as a service address—

(a) in the company's register of directors by virtue of paragraph 11, or

(b) in the register of companies by virtue of paragraph 16,

that address is not protected information for the purposes of Chapter 8 of Part 10 of the Companies Act 2006.

**18.** (1) Section 242(1) of the Companies Act 2006 (duty of registrar to omit protected information from material available for inspection) does not apply—

(a) to material delivered to the registrar before 1st October 2009, or

(b) to material delivered to the registrar on or after 1st October 2009 by virtue of paragraph 15(2) (notification of change occurring before that date).

(2) In section 242(2)(b) of the Companies Act 2006 (exclusion of material registered before commencement) the reference to things registered before Chapter 8 of Part 10 of that Act comes into force is treated as including anything registered as a result of a notification in accordance with paragraph 15(2) (notification on or after 1st October 2009 of change occurring before that date).

**19.** In determining under section 245(1) of the Companies Act 2006 whether to put a director's usual residential address on the public record, the registrar may take into account only—

(a) communications sent by the registrar on or after 1st October 2009, and

(b) evidence as to the effectiveness of service coming to the registrar's attention on or after that date.

### Political donations and expenditure

**20.** (1) Sections 362 to 379 of the Companies Act 2006 (political donations and expenditure) apply to donations made or expenditure incurred on or after 1st October 2007.

(2) Section 379(2) of that Act applies as to the time when a donation is regarded as made or expenditure as incurred, including where it is made or incurred in pursuance of a contract entered into before that date.

(3) Part 10A of the 1985 Act continues to apply to donations or expenditure in relation to which the relevant time, as defined in section 347A(10) of that Act, is before that date.

(4) The repeal of that Part does not affect paragraph 3(4) of Schedule 7 to the 1985 Act (matters to be dealt with in directors' report: expressions to have same meaning as in Part 10A).

### Accounts

**21.** (1) Sections 380 to 416, 418 to 469 and 471 to 474 of the Companies Act 2006 (accounts and reports) apply to accounts and reports for financial years beginning on or after 1st October 2009.

(2) The corresponding provisions of the 1985 Act or 1986 Order continue to apply to accounts and reports for financial years beginning before that date.

**22.** Any question whether—

(a) for the purposes of section 382, 383, 384(3) or 467(3) of the Companies Act 2006, a company or group qualified as small in a financial year beginning before 1st October 2009, or

(b) for the purposes of section 465 or 466 of that Act a company or group qualified as medium-sized in any such financial year,

is to be determined by reference to the corresponding provisions of the 1985 Act or 1986 Order.

### Audit

**23.** (1) In Chapter 1 of Part 16 of the Companies Act 2006 (requirement for audited accounts)—

(a) sections 475 to 481 (general provisions) apply to accounts for financial years beginning on or after 1st October 2009; and

(b) section 484 (general power of amendment by regulations) applies accordingly.

(2) Sections 235(1), 249A(1), (3) and (6) to (7), 249AA and 249B of the 1985 Act or Articles 243(1), 257A(1), (3) and (6) to (7), 257AA and 257B of the 1986 Order continue to apply to accounts for financial years beginning before that date.

**24.** (1) Sections 485 to 488 of the Companies Act 2006 (appointment of auditors of private companies) apply in relation to appointments for financial years beginning on or after 1st October 2009.

(2) Sections 384 to 388A of the 1985 Act or Articles 392 to 396A of the 1986 Order continue to apply in relation to appointments for financial years beginning before that date.

(3) Where—

(a) a private company has elected under section 386 of the 1985 Act or Article 394 of the 1986 Order to dispense with the annual appointment of auditors, and

(b) the election is in force immediately before 1st October 2009.

section 487(2)(a) of the Companies Act 2006 (no deemed reappointment of auditors appointed by directors) does not prevent the deemed reappointment under that subsection of auditors first appointed before 1st October 2009.

**25.** (1) This paragraph applies where immediately before 1st October 2009 a resolution of a private company under section 390A of the 1985 Act or Article 398A of the 1986 Order (remuneration of auditors) was in force and was expressed (in whatever terms) to continue to have effect so long as a resolution under section 386 of that Act or Article 394 of that Order (election to dispense with annual appointment of auditors) continued in force.

(2) The repeal of section 386 of the 1985 Act or Article 394 of the 1986 Order does not affect the continued operation of the resolution, which shall continue to have effect until—

(a) it is revoked or superseded by a further resolution,

(b) the auditors to which it applies cease to hold office, or

(c) it otherwise ceases to have effect in accordance with its terms.

**26.** (1) In Chapter 2 of Part 16 of the Companies Act 2006 (appointment of auditors)—

(a) sections 489 and 490 (appointment of auditors by public companies) apply to appointments for financial years beginning on or after 1st October 2009;

(b) section 491 (term of office of auditors of public company) applies to auditors appointed for financial years beginning on or after that date.

(2) Sections 384, 385, 387 and 388(1), (3) and (4) of the 1985 Act or Articles 392, 393, 395 and 396(1), (3) and (4) of the 1986 Order continue to apply to appointments by public companies for financial years beginning before that date.

**27.** (1) The following provisions apply to auditors appointed for financial years beginning on or after 1st October 2009—

(a) section 492 (fixing of auditor's remuneration),

(b) section 493 (disclosure of terms of audit appointment), and

(c) section 494 (disclosure of services provided by auditor or associated and related remuneration).

(2) Sections 390A and 390B of the 1985 Act or Articles 398A and 398B of the 1986 Order continue to apply to auditors appointed for financial years beginning before that date.

(3) The repeal of section 390A of the 1985 Act and Article 398A of the 1986 Order (remuneration of auditors) does not affect the operation of any such resolution as is mentioned in paragraph 25 above.

**28.** (1) In Chapter 3 of Part 16 of the Companies Act 2006 (functions of auditor)—

(a) sections 495 to 498 (auditor's report and duties of auditor) apply to auditors' reports on accounts or reports for financial years beginning on or after 1st October 2009;

(b) sections 499 to 501 (rights of auditors) apply to auditors appointed for financial years beginning on or after that date;

(c) sections 503 to 509 (signature of auditor's report and offences in connection with auditor's report) apply to auditors' reports on accounts or reports for financial years beginning on or after that date.

(2) Sections 235 to 237, 389A and 389B of the 1985 Act or Articles 243 to 245, 397A and 397B of the 1986 Order continue to apply as regards financial years beginning before that date.

**29.** (1) Section 502 of the Companies Act 2006 (auditor's rights in relation to resolutions and meetings) applies to auditors appointed on or after 1st October 2009.

(2) Section 390 of the 1985 Act or Article 398 of the 1986 Order continues to apply to auditors appointed before that date.

**30.** (1) In Chapter 4 of Part 16 of that Act (removal, resignation, etc of auditors), sections 510 to 513 (removal of auditor) apply where notice of the intended resolution is given to the company on or after 1st October 2009.

(2) Sections 391 and 391A of the 1985 Act or Articles 399 and 399A of the 1986 Order continue to apply where notice of the intended resolution is given to the company before that date.

(3) In section 513 (rights of auditor removed from office) as it applies in relation to an auditor appointed before 1st October 2009, the reference to rights under section 502(2) shall be read as a reference to rights under section 390(1) of the 1985 Act or Article 398(1) of the 1986 Order.

**31.** (1) Sections 514 and 515 of the Companies Act 2006 (failure to re-appoint auditor) apply to appointments for financial years beginning on or after 1st October 2009.

(2) Section 391A of the 1985 Act or Article 399A of the 1986 Order continues to apply to appointments for financial years beginning before that date.

**32.** (1) Sections 516 to 518 of the Companies Act 2006 (resignation of auditor) apply to resignations occurring on or after 1st October 2009.

(2) Sections 392 and 392A of the 1985 Act or Articles 400 and 400A of the 1986 Order continue to apply to resignations occurring before that date.

(3) In section 518 (rights of resigning auditor) as it applies in relation to an auditor appointed before 1st October 2009, the reference to rights under section 502(2) shall be read as a reference to rights under section 390(1) of the 1985 Act or Article 398(1) of the 1986 Order.

**33.** (1) Sections 519 to 525 of the Companies Act 2006 (statement by auditor ceasing to hold office) apply where the auditor ceases to hold office on or after 1st October 2009.

(2) Sections 394 and 394A of the 1985 Act or Articles 401A and 401B of the 1986 Order continue to apply where the auditor ceases to hold office before that date.

**34.** (1) Section 526 of the Companies Act 2006 (effect of casual vacancies) applies where the vacancy occurs on or after 1st October 2009.

(2) Section 388(2) of the 1985 Act or Article 396(2) of the 1986 Order continues to apply where the vacancy occurred before that date.

**35.** In section 527 of the Companies Act 2006—

(a) subsection (1)(a) (matters relating to audit of company's accounts) applies to accounts for financial years beginning on or after 1st October 2009, and

(b) subsection (1)(b) (matters relating to circumstances connected with an auditor of the company) applies to auditors appointed for financial years beginning on or after that date.

**36.** A resolution passed before 1st October 2009 authorising a liability limitation agreement is effective for the purposes of section 536 of the Companies Act 2006 (authorisation of agreement by members of company) if it complies with the requirements of that section.

## Annual return

**37.** (1) Sections 854 to 859 of the Companies Act 2006 (a company's annual return) apply to annual returns made up to a date on or after 1st October 2009.

(2) Sections 363 to 365 of the 1985 Act or Articles 371 to 373 of the 1986 Order continue to apply to annual returns made up to a date before 1st October 2009.

(3) Any reference in the Companies Act 2006 to a company's last return, or to a return delivered in accordance with Part 24 of that Act, shall be read as including (so far as necessary to ensure the continuity of the law) a return made up to a date before 1st October 2009 or delivered in accordance with the 1985 Act or the 1986 Order.

## Fraudulent trading

**38.** (1) Section 458 of the 1985 Act or Article 451 of the 1986 Order (offences of fraudulent trading) continues to apply to offences completed before 1st October 2009.

(2) Where, in the case of an offence—

(a) a relevant event occurs before 1st October 2009, and

(b) another relevant event occurs on or after 1st October 2009,

the offence must be charged under section 993 of the Companies Act 2006 (and not under section 458 of the 1985 Act or Article 451 of the 1986 Order).

(3) If in the case of any such offence a relevant event occurred before 15th January 2007, section 993(3)(a) applies with the substitution of 'seven years' for 'ten years'.

(4) 'Relevant event' means an act, omission or other event (including any result of one or more acts or omissions) proof of which is required for conviction of the offence.

## Company investigations

**39.** (1) The extension to Northern Ireland by section 1284 of the Companies Act 2006 of Parts 14 and 15 of the 1985 Act (company investigations) has effect to enable the exercise of the powers conferred by those Parts in relation to unregistered companies having their principal office in Northern Ireland, and otherwise in relation to Northern Ireland, on and after 1st October 2009.

(2) Parts 15 and 16 of the 1986 Order, and any other provision of that Order having effect for the purposes of Part 15, continue to apply (subject to sub-paragraph (3) below)—

(a) in relation to inspectors appointed under Part 15 before 1st October 2009 and matters arising in connection with or in consequence of any such appointment or any report of inspectors so appointed;

(b) in relation to any exercise before 1st October 2009 of any power of the Department of Enterprise, Trade and Investment in Northern Ireland not within paragraph (a), and matters arising in connection with or in consequence of any such exercise.

(3) A direction in force immediately before 1st October 2009 under Article 438(1A) or 449(1A) of the 1986 Order (direction limiting or relaxing restrictions on shares) shall continue in force and have effect on and after that date as if made under the corresponding provision of Part 14 of the 1985 Act, and the provisions of Part 15 of that Act shall apply accordingly.

**Saving for provisions as to form or manner in which documents to be delivered**

**40.** (1) Any saving in this Schedule for the effect of a provision of the 1985 Act or 1986 Order requiring use of a prescribed form extends to the form and the power under which it is prescribed.

(2) Any saving in this Schedule for the effect of a provision of the 1985 Act or 1986 Order requiring a document to be delivered to the registrar extends to section 707B of the 1985 Act or Article 656B of the 1986 Order (delivery to the registrar using electronic communications) so far as relating to the provision in question and the delivery of documents under it.

**Savings for provisions relating to offences**

**41.** (1) The repeal of any provision of the 1985 Act or 1986 Order creating an offence does not affect the continued operation of that provision in relation to an offence committed before 1st October 2009.

(2) Any saving in this Schedule for the effect of a provision of the 1985 Act or 1986 Order that creates an offence extends to the entry relating to that provision in Schedule 24 to that Act or Schedule 23 to that Order (punishment of offences).

(3) References in this paragraph to provisions of the 1985 Act or 1986 Order include provisions of regulations or orders made under that Act or Order.

---

# The Company, Limited Liability Partnership and Business Names (Sensitive Words and Expressions) Regulations 2009

## (SI 2009/2615)

Commencement Date 1st October 2009

SI.42    The Secretary of State makes the following Regulations in exercise of the powers conferred by sections 55(1), 56(1)(b), 1194(1), 1195(1)(b) and 1292(1) of the Companies Act 2006[277] and sections 55(1), 56(1)(b) and 1292(1) of the Companies Act 2006 as applied to limited liability partnerships by regulations 8 and 81 of the Limited Liability Partnerships (Application of Companies Act 2006) Regulations 2009.[278]

**Citation and commencement**

**1.** These Regulations may be cited as the Company, Limited Liability Partnership and Business Names (Sensitive Words and Expressions) Regulations 2009 and come into force on 1st October 2009.

**Interpretation**

**2.** (1) In these Regulations 'the 2006 Act' means the Companies Act 2006.

(2) Any reference in these Regulations to section 55 or 88 of the 2006 Act includes a reference to that section as applied by regulation 8 or 17 of the Limited Liability Partnerships (Application of Companies Act 2006) Regulations 2009.

**Specified words and expressions applicable to sections 55 and 1194 of the 2006 Act**

**3.** (1) The following words and expressions are specified for the purposes of sections 55(1) and 1194(1) of the 2006 Act—

(a) the words and expressions set out in Part 1 of Schedule 1;

(b) the plural and possessive forms of those words and expressions, and, where relevant, the feminine form; and

(c) in the case of the words and expressions set out in Part 1 of Schedule 1 which are marked with an asterisk, the grammatically mutated forms of those words and expressions.

(2) For the purposes of section 55(1) of the 2006 Act any word or expression specified in Part 1 of Schedule 1 which contains an accent or other diacritical mark is to be read as though that accent or other diacritical mark were omitted.

**Specified words and expressions applicable to section 55 of the 2006 Act**

**4.** The following words and expressions are specified for the purposes of section 55(1) of the 2006 Act—

(a) the words and expressions set out in Part 2 of Schedule 1;

---

[277]  2006 c.46.
[278]  SI 2009/1804.

(b) the plural and possessive forms of those words and expressions, and, where relevant, the feminine form; and

(c) in the case of the words and expressions set out in Part 2 of Schedule 1 which are marked with an asterisk, the grammatically mutated forms of those words and expressions.

### Applications where situation of registered office or principal place of business is irrelevant

**5.** In connection with an application for the approval of the Secretary of State under section 55 or 1194 of the 2006 Act in relation to a name that includes a word or expression specified in column (1) of Part 1 of Schedule 2 the applicant must seek the view of the Government department or other body set out opposite that word or expression in column (2) of Part 1 of Schedule 2.

### Applications where situation of registered office or principal place of business is relevant

**6.** In connection with an application for the approval of the Secretary of State under section 55 or 1194 of the 2006 Act in relation to a name that includes a word or expression specified in column (1) of Part 2 of Schedule 2 the applicant must seek the view of a Government department or other body as follows—

(a) in the case of—

    (i) a company or limited liability partnership that has already been registered, whose registered office is situated in England and Wales;

    (ii) a proposed company or limited liability partnership that has not yet been registered under the 2006 Act, whose registered office is to be situated in England and Wales;

    (iii) a business, whose principal place of business is or is to be situated in England; and

    (iv) an overseas company (see section 1044 of the 2006 Act),

    the Government department or other body set out in column (2) of Part 2 of Schedule 2 opposite that word or expression;

(b) in the case of—

    (i) a company or limited liability partnership that has already been registered, that is a Welsh company or Welsh LLP (see section 88 of the 2006 Act);

    (ii) a proposed company or limited liability partnership that has not yet been registered, that is to be a Welsh company or Welsh LLP; and

    (iii) a business, whose principal place of business is or is to be situated in Wales,

    the Government department or other body set out in column (3) of Part 2 of Schedule 2 opposite that word or expression;

(c) in the case of—

    (i) a company or limited liability partnership that has already been registered, whose registered office is situated in Scotland;

    (ii) a proposed company or limited liability partnership that has not yet been registered, whose registered office is to be situated in Scotland; and

    (iii) a business, whose principal place of business is or is to be situated in Scotland,

    the Government department or other body set out in column (4) of Part 2 of Schedule 2 opposite that word or expression; and

(d) in the case of—

    (i) a company or limited liability partnership that has already been registered, whose registered office is situated in Northern Ireland;

    (ii) a proposed company or limited liability partnership that has not yet been registered, whose registered office is to be situated in Northern Ireland; and

    (iii) a business, whose principal place of business is or is to be situated in Northern Ireland,

    the Government department or other body set out in column (5) of Part 2 of Schedule 2 opposite that word or expression.

**7.** The following Regulations are revoked—

(a) the Company and Business Names Regulations 1981,[279]

(b) the Company and Business Names (Amendment) Regulations 1982,[280]

(c) the Company and Business Names (Amendment) Regulations 1992,[281]

(d) the Company and Business Names (Amendment) Regulations 1995,[282]

(e) the Company and Business Names (Amendment) Regulations 2001,[283] and

(f) the Company and Business Names (Amendment) (No.2) Regulations 2007.[284]

---

[279] SI 1981/1685.
[280] SI 1982/1653.
[281] SI 1992/1196.
[282] SI 1995/3022.
[283] SI 2001/259.
[284] SI 2007/3152.

## SCHEDULE 1
### SPECIFIED WORDS AND EXPRESSIONS

### PART 1
#### SPECIFIED WORDS AND EXPRESSIONS APPLICABLE TO SECTIONS 55(1) AND 1194(1) OF THE 2006 ACT

| | | |
|---|---|---|
| Abortion | European | Pregnancy termination |
| Accredit | Federation | *Prifysgol |
| Accreditation | Friendly Society | Prince |
| Accredited | Foundation | *Prionnsa |
| Accrediting | Fund | *Prydain |
| Adjudicator | Giro | *Prydeinig |
| Association | Government Group | Queen |
| Assurance | *Gwasanaeth iechyd | Reassurance |
| Assurer | *Gwladol | Reassurer |
| Audit office | Health centre | Register |
| Auditor General | Health service | Registered |
| Authority | Health visitor | Registrar |
| *Banc | His Majesty | Registration |
| Bank | Holding | Registry |
| Banking | HPSS | Regulation |
| Banknote | HSC | Regulator |
| Benevolent | Human rights | Reinsurance |
| Board | Inspectorate | Reinsurer |
| *Breatannach | Institute | *Riaghaltas |
| *Breatainn | Institution | *Rìgh |
| *Brenhinol | Insurance | Rìoghachd Aonaichte |
| *Brenin | Insurer | Rìoghail |
| *Brenhiniaeth | International | Rìoghalachd |
| Britain | Judicial appointment | Royal |
| British | King | Royalty |
| *Cenedlaethol | Licensing | Rule committee |
| Chamber of | *Llywodraeth | Scotland |
| Charitable | Medical centre | Scottish |
| Charity | Midwife | Senedd |
| Charter | Midwifery | Sheffield |
| Chartered | *Mòrachd | Siambr |
| Child maintenance | Mutual | Social service |
| Child support | National | Society |
| *Coimisean | NHS | Special school |
| *Comhairle | Northern Ireland | Standards |
| *Comisiwn | Northern Irish | Stock exchange |
| Commission | Nurse | Swyddfa archwilio |
| Co-operative | Nursing | *Teyrnas Gyfunol |
| Council | Oifis sgrùdaidh | *Teyrnas Unedig |
| *Cyngor | *Oilthigh | Trade union |
| Data protection | Ombudsman | Tribunal |
| Dental | *Ombwdsmon | Trust |
| Dentistry | Oversight | *Tywysog |
| Disciplinary | *Parlamaid | Underwrite |
| Discipline | Parliament | Underwriting |
| *Diùc | Parliamentarian | United Kingdom |
| *Dug | Parliamentary | University |
| Duke | Patent | Wales |
| Ei Fawrhydi | Patentee | Watchdog |
| England | Police | Welsh |
| English | Polytechnic | Windsor |
| | Post office | |

PART 2

SPECIFIED WORDS AND EXPRESSIONS APPLICABLE TO
SECTION 55(1) OF THE 2006 ACT

Alba

Albannach

Na h-Alba

*Cymru

*Cymraeg

*Cymreig

SCHEDULE 2             Regulations 5 and 6

LIST OF GOVERNMENT DEPARTMENTS AND OTHER BODIES WHOSE VIEWS
MUST BE SOUGHT

PART 1

APPLICATIONS WHERE SITUATION OF REGISTERED OFFICE OR PRINCIPAL PLACE OF
BUSINESS IS RELEVANT

| Column (1)<br>Word or expression specified under<br>regulation 3 | Column (2)<br>Specified Government department or other body<br>whose view must be sought |
| --- | --- |
| Abortion | Department of Health |
| Accredit | Department for Business, Innovation & Skills |
| Accreditation | Department for Business, Innovation & Skills |
| Accredited | Department for Business, Innovation & Skills |
| Accrediting | Department for Business, Innovation & Skills |
| Assurance | Financial Services Authority |
| Assurer | Financial Services Authority |
| Banc | Financial Services Authority |
| Bank | Financial Services Authority |
| Banking | Financial Services Authority |
| Banknote | The Governor and Company of the Bank of England |
| Brenhinol | The Welsh Assembly Government |
| Brenin | The Welsh Assembly Government |
| Brenhiniaeth | The Welsh Assembly Government |
| Child maintenance | Child Maintenance and Enforcement Commission |
| Child support | Child Maintenance and Enforcement Commission |
| Data protection | Information Commissioner's Office |
| Dental | General Dental Council |
| Dentistry | General Dental Council |
| Diùc | The Scottish Executive |
| Dug | The Welsh Assembly Government |
| Ei Fawrhydi | The Welsh Assembly Government |
| Friendly Society | Financial Services Authority |
| Fund | Financial Services Authority |
| Gwasanaeth iechyd | The Welsh Assembly Government |

| Column (1) | Column (2) |
|---|---|
| Word or expression specified under regulation 3 | Specified Government department or other body whose view must be sought |
| Health visitor | Nursing & Midwifery Council |
| HPSS | Department of Health, Social Services and Public Safety |
| HSC | Department of Health, Social Services and Public Safety |
| Insurance | Financial Services Authority |
| Insurer | Financial Services Authority |
| Judicial appointment | Ministry of Justice |
|  | The Welsh Assembly Government |
| Llywodraeth |  |
| Medical centre | Department of Health, Social Services and Public Safety |
| Midwife | Nursing & Midwifery Council |
| Midwifery | Nursing & Midwifery Council |
| Mòrachd | The Scottish Executive |
| Mutual | Financial Services Authority |
| NHS | Department of Health |
| Nurse | Nursing & Midwifery Council |
| Nursing | Nursing & Midwifery Council |
| Oifis sgrùdaidh | Audit Scotland |
| Oilthigh | The Scottish Executive |
| Parlamaid | The Scottish Parliamentary Corporate Body |
|  | The Corporate Officer of the House of Lords and |
| Parliament | The Corporate Officer of the House of Commons |
|  | The Corporate Officer of the House of Lords and |
| Parliamentarian | The Corporate Officer of the House of Commons |
|  | The Corporate Officer of the House of Lords and |
| Parliamentary | The Corporate Officer of the House of Commons |
| Patent | The Patent Office |
| Patentee | The Patent Office |
| Polytechnic | Department for Business, Innovation & Skills |
| Pregnancy termination | Department of Health |
| Prifysgol | The Welsh Assembly Government |
| Prionnsa | The Scottish Executive |
| Reassurance | Financial Services Authority |
| Reassurer | Financial Services Authority |
| Reinsurance | Financial Services Authority |
| Reinsurer | Financial Services Authority |
| Riaghaltas | The Scottish Executive |
| Rìgh | The Scottish Executive |
| Rìoghail | The Scottish Executive |
| Rìoghalachd | The Scottish Executive |
| Rule committee | Ministry of Justice |
| Senedd | The National Assembly for Wales |
| Sheffield | The Company of Cutlers in Hallamshire |
| Swyddfa archwilio | Auditor General for Wales |
| Tywysog | The Welsh Assembly Government |
| Underwrite | Financial Services Authority |
| Underwriting | Financial Services Authority |

PART 2

APPLICATIONS WHERE SITUATION OF REGISTERED OFFICE OR
PRINCIPAL PLACE OF BUSINESS IS IRRELEVANT

| Column (1) | Column (2) | Column (3) | Column (4) | Column (5) |
|---|---|---|---|---|
| | *Specified Government department or other body whose view must be sought* | | | |
| *Word or expression specified under regulation 3* | *under regulation 6(a)* | *under regulation 6(b)* | *under regulation 6(c)* | *under regulation 6(d)* |
| Audit office | Comptroller & Auditor General | Auditor General for Wales | Audit Scotland | Northern Ireland Audit Office |
| Charitable Charity | The Charity Commission | The Charity Commission | Office of the Scottish Charity Regulator | The Charity Commission |
| Duke His Majesty King Prince Queen Royal Royalty Windsor | Ministry of Justice | The Welsh Assembly Government | The Scottish Executive | Ministry of Justice |
| Health centre Health service | Department of Health | The Welsh Assembly Government | The Scottish Executive | Department of Health, Social Services and Public Safety |
| Police | The Home Office | The Home Office | The Scottish Executive | Northern Ireland Office |
| Special school | Department for Children, Schools and Families | The Welsh Assembly Government | The Scottish Executive | Department of Education |
| University | Department for Business, Innovation & Skills | The Welsh Assembly Government | The Scottish Executive | Department for Employment and Learning |

# 53

## INTRODUCTORY NOTE

### Financial Service and Markets Act 2000

Part 6 of the Financial Services and Markets Act 2000 (the "Act"), as amended by the Financial   **53.0.01**
Services Act 2012, provides the legal basis for the regulation of the listing, offering and trading of securities in the UK. Part 6 empowers the Financial Conduct Authority (the "FCA") – to regulate these
activities by making and enforcing "Part 6 rules". The Part 6 rules comprise the listing rules, prospectus
rules and disclosure rules, all of which are contained in the FCA Handbook.

The scope of Part 6 is now much greater than that of its predecessor, Part 4 of the Financial Services Act   **53.0.02**
1986. This expansion has been driven by the enactment of a significant amount of European legislation
in this area, particularly the Prospectus Directive (2003/71/EC), Market Abuse Directive (2003/6/EC)
and Transparency Directive (2004/109/EC).

In this chapter, we include the text of all the current sections in Part 6, but provide commentary only on   **53.0.03**
those sections which relate directly to, or have an important bearing on, the UK's prospectus regime. As
the Act only provides a framework for the regulation of prospectuses, and on account of the heavy
influence of European legislation, the commentary includes numerous references to the prospectus
rules and various sources of European law.

## PART VI
## OFFICIAL LISTING

72 [...][1]                                                                                                 **53.72.01**

73 [...][2]                                                                                                 **53.73.01**

### [Rules][3]

[73A  Part 6 Rules                                                                                          **53.73A.01**

    (1) The FCA may make rules ("Part 6 rules") for the purposes of this Part.

    (2) Provisions of Part 6 rules expressed to relate to the official list are referred to in this Part as "listing rules".

    (3) Provisions of Part 6 rules expressed to relate to disclosure of information in respect of financial instruments which have been admitted to trading on a regulated market or for which a request for admission to trading on such a market has been made, are referred to in this Part as "disclosure rules".

    [(4) Provisions of Part 6 rules expressed to relate to transferable securities are referred to in this Part as "prospectus rules".

    (5) In relation to prospectus rules, the purposes of this Part include the purposes of the prospectus directive. ][4]

    [(6) Transparency rules and corporate governance rules are not listing rules, disclosure rules or prospectus rules, but are Part 6 rules. ][5] ][6]

---

  [1]  Repealed by Financial Services Act 2012 c.21 s.16(14)(a) (24 January 2013; 1 April 2013)
  [2]  Repealed by Financial Services Act 2012 c.21 s.16(14)(b) (24 January 2013; 1 April 2013)
  [3]  Inserted by Financial Services Act 2012 c.21 s. 16(4) (24 January 2013; 1 April 2013)
  [4]  Added by Prospectus Regulations 2005/1433 Sch.1 para. 1 (1 July 2005)
  [5]  Added by Companies Act 2006 c.46 Sch.15(1) para.3 (8 November 2006)
  [6]  Added by Financial Services and Markets Act 2000 (Market Abuse) Regulations 2005/381 Sch.1 para. 2 (17
March 2005)

**53.73A.02**   Part 6 of the Act has been amended by the Financial Services Act 2012, although the changes have not altered the operation of the prospectus regime significantly. Sections 72 and 73 have been repealed; consequently, section 73A is now the opening provision of Part 6.

**53.73A.03**   Before the Financial Services Act 2012 came into force, the Act did not refer to the Financial Services Authority ("FSA") by name, but rather as the "competent authority". Accordingly, it was not always clear whether the Act was referring to the UK's competent authority, or the competent authority of another Member State. The Financial Services Act 2012 has removed any potential confusion by replacing references to the UK's competent authority with explicit references to the FSA's successor for conduct of business regulation, the FCA.[7]

**53.73A.04**   The first such reference appears at section 73A(1), which empowers the FCA to make rules for the purposes of Part 6.

**53.73A.05**   Sections 73A(2), (3) and (4) introduce shorthand definitions for three of the sets of rules which are established by Part 6: "listing rules", "disclosure rules" and "prospectus rules". These definitions are restated in the interpretation section at the end of Part 6: section 103.

**53.73A.06**   Section 73A(5) notes that the purposes of Part 6 include the purposes of the Prospectus Directive. The purposes of the Prospectus Directive are set out in its first article and, specifically, in Article 1(1): "to harmonise requirements for the drawing up, approval and distribution of the prospectus to be published when securities are offered to the public or admitted to trading on a regulated market situated or operating within a Member State."

## The official list

**53.74.01**   **74  The official list.**

   (1)  The FCA must maintain the official list.
   (2)  The FCA may admit to the official list such securities and other things as it considers appropriate.
   (3)  But–
       (a)  nothing may be admitted to the official list except in accordance with this Part; and
       (b)  the Treasury may by order provide that anything which falls within a description or category specified in the order may not be admitted to the official list.
   (4)  [...][8]
   (5)  In the following provisions of this Part–
       [...][9]
       "listing" means being included in the official list in accordance with this Part.

## Listing

**53.75.01**   **75  Applications for listing.**

   (1)  Admission to the official list may be granted only on an application made to the FCA in such manner as may be required by listing rules.
   (2)  No application for listing may be entertained by the FCA unless it is made by, or with the consent of, the issuer of the securities concerned.
   (3)  No application for listing may be entertained by the FCA in respect of securities which are to be issued by a body of a prescribed kind.
   (4)  The FCA may not grant an application for listing unless it is satisfied that–
       (a)  the requirements of listing rules (so far as they apply to the application), and
       (b)  any other requirements imposed by the FCA in relation to the application,
       are complied with.
   (5)  An application for listing may be refused if, for a reason relating to the issuer, the FCA considers that granting it would be detrimental to the interests of investors.
   (6)  An application for listing securities which are already officially listed in another EEA State may be refused if the issuer has failed to comply with any obligations to which he is subject as a result of that listing.

---

[7]  Financial Services Act 2012 c.21 ss.2, 3, 6-13 (24 January 2013; 1 April 2013)
[8]  Repealed by Financial Services and Markets Act 2000 (Market Abuse) Regulations 2005/381 Sch.1 para.3 (17 March 2005)
[9]  Repealed by Prospectus Regulations 2005/1433 Sch.1 para.2 (1 July 2005)

## 76 Decision on application.

    (1) The FCA must notify the applicant of its decision on an application for listing–

        (a) before the end of the period of six months beginning with the date on which the application is received; or

        (b) if within that period the FCA has required the applicant to provide further information in connection with the application, before the end of the period of six months beginning with the date on which that information is provided.

    (2) If the FCA fails to comply with subsection (1), it is to be taken to have decided to refuse the application.

    (3) If the FCA decides to grant an application for listing, it must give the applicant written notice.

    (4) If the FCA proposes to refuse an application for listing, it must give the applicant a warning notice.

    (5) If the FCA decides to refuse an application for listing, it must give the applicant a decision notice.

    (6) If the FCA decides to refuse an application for listing, the applicant may refer the matter to the Tribunal.

    (7) If securities are admitted to the official list, their admission may not be called in question on the ground that any requirement or condition for their admission has not been complied with.

## 77 Discontinuance and suspension of listing.

    (1) The FCA may, in accordance with listing rules, discontinue the listing of any securities if satisfied that there are special circumstances which preclude normal regular dealings in them.

    (2) The FCA may, in accordance with listing rules, suspend the listing of any securities.

    [(2A) The FCA may discontinue under subsection (1) or suspend under subsection (2) the listing of any securities on its own initiative or on the application of the issuer of those securities.][10]

    (3) If securities are suspended under subsection (2) they are to be treated, for the purposes of [section 96 and paragraph 23(6) of Schedule 1ZA][11], as still being listed.

    (4) this section applies to securities whenever they were admitted to the official list.

    (5) If the FCA discontinues or suspends the listing of any securities, [on its own initiative, ][12] the issuer may refer the matter to the Tribunal.

## 78 Discontinuance or suspension: procedure.

    (1) A discontinuance or suspension [by the FCA on its own initiative ][13] takes effect–

        (a) immediately, if the notice under subsection (2) states that that is the case;

        (b) in any other case, on such date as may be specified in that notice.

    (2) If [on its own initiative ][14] the FCA–

        (a) proposes to discontinue or suspend the listing of securities, or

        (b) discontinues or suspends the listing of securities with immediate effect,

    it must give the issuer of the securities written notice.

    (3) The notice must–

        (a) give details of the discontinuance or suspension;

        (b) state the FCA's reasons for the discontinuance or suspension and for choosing the date on which it took effect or takes effect;

        (c) inform the issuer of the securities that he may make representations to the FCA within such period as may be specified in the notice (whether or not he has referred the matter to the Tribunal);

        (d) inform him of the date on which the discontinuance or suspension took effect or will take effect; and

        (e) inform him of his right to refer the matter to the Tribunal.

    (4) The FCA may extend the period within which representations may be made to it.

    (5) If, having considered any representations made by the issuer of the securities, the FCA decides–

        (a) to discontinue or suspend the listing of the securities, or

        (b) if the discontinuance or suspension has taken effect, not to cancel it,

    the FCA must give the issuer of the securities written notice.

---

[10] Added by Regulatory Reform (Financial Services and Markets Act 2000) Order 2007/1973 art.5(a) (12 July 2007)

[11] Substituted by Financial Services Act 2012 c.21 s.16(5) (24 January 2013; 1 April 2013)

[12] Inserted by Regulatory Reform (Financial Services and Markets Act 2000) Order 2007/1973 art.5(b) (12 July 2007)

[13] Inserted by Regulatory Reform (Financial Services and Markets Act 2000) Order 2007/1973 art.6(a) (12 July 2007)

[14] Inserted by Regulatory Reform (Financial Services and Markets Act 2000) Order 2007/1973 art.6(b) (12 July 2007)

(6) A notice given under subsection (5) must inform the issuer of the securities of his right to refer the matter to the Tribunal.

(7) If a notice informs a person of his right to refer a matter to the Tribunal, it must give an indication of the procedure on such a reference.

(8) If the FCA decides–
   (a) not to discontinue or suspend the listing of the securities, or
   (b) if the discontinuance or suspension has taken effect, to cancel it,
   the FCA must give the issuer of the securities written notice.

(9) The effect of cancelling a discontinuance is that the securities concerned are to be readmitted, without more, to the official list.

(10) If the FCA has suspended the listing of securities [on its own initiative]$^{15}$ and proposes to refuse an application by the issuer of the securities for the cancellation of the suspension, it must give him a warning notice.

(11) The FCA must, having considered any representations made in response to the warning notice–
   (a) if it decides to refuse the application, give the issuer of the securities a decision notice;
   (b) if it grants the application, give him written notice of its decision.

(12) If the FCA decides to refuse an application for the cancellation of the suspension of listed securities, the applicant may refer the matter to the Tribunal.

(13) "Discontinuance" means a discontinuance of listing under section 77(1).

(14) "Suspension" means a suspension of listing under section 77(2).

**53.78A.01    [78A.  Discontinuance or suspension at the request of the issuer: procedure**

(1) A discontinuance or suspension by the FCA on the application of the issuer of the securities takes effect—
   [(a) immediately, if the notification under subsection (2) so provides;
   (b) in any other case, on such date as may be provided for in that notification.]$^{16}$

(2) If the FCA discontinues or suspends the listing of securities on the application of the issuer of the securities it must [notify the issuer (whether in writing or otherwise)].$^{17}$

[(3) The notification must—
   (a) notify the issuer of the date on which the discontinuance or suspension took effect or will take effect, and
   (b) notify the issuer of such other matters (if any) as are specified in the listing rules.]$^{18}$

(4) If the FCA proposes to refuse an application by the issuer of the securities for the discontinuance or suspension of the listing of the securities, it must give him a warning notice.

(5) The FCA must, having considered any representations made in response to the warning notice, if it decides to refuse the application, give the issuer of the securities a decision notice.

(6) If the FCA decides to refuse an application by the issuer of the securities for the discontinuance or suspension of the listing of the securities, the issuer may refer the matter to the Tribunal.

(7) If the FCA has suspended the listing of securities on the application of the issuer of the securities and proposes to refuse an application by the issuer for the cancellation of the suspension, it must give him a warning notice.

(8) The FCA must, having considered any representations made in response to the warning notice—
   (a) if it decides to refuse the application for the cancellation of the suspension, give the issuer of the securities a decision notice;
   (b) if it grants the application, give him written notice of its decision.

(9) If the FCA decides to refuse an application for the cancellation of the suspension of listed securities, the applicant may refer the matter to the Tribunal.

(10) "Discontinuance" means a discontinuance of listing under section 77(1).

(11) "Suspension" means a suspension of listing under section 77(2).]$^{19}$

---

$^{15}$  Inserted by Regulatory Reform (Financial Services and Markets Act 2000) Order 2007/1973 art.6(c) (12 July 2007)

$^{16}$  Substituted by the Financial Services Act 2012 c.21 s.17(2)(a) (24 January 2013; 1 April 2013)

$^{17}$  Substituted by the Financial Services Act 2012 c.21 s.17(2)(b) (24 January 2013; 1 April 2013)

$^{18}$  Substituted by the Financial Services Act 2012 c.21 s.17(2)(c) (24 January 2013; 1 April 2013)

$^{19}$  Added by Regulatory Reform (Financial Services and Markets Act 2000) Order 2007/1973 art.7 (12 July 2007)

*Listing particulars*

## 79  Listing particulars and other documents.                                          **53.79.01**

   (1)  Listing rules may provide that securities [...][20] of a kind specified in the rules may not be admitted
       to the official list unless–
      (a)  listing particulars have been submitted to, and approved by, the FCA and published; or
      (b)  in such cases as may be specified by listing rules, such document (other than listing particulars
          or a prospectus of a kind required by listing rules) as may be so specified has been published.
   (2)  "Listing particulars" means a document in such form and containing such information as may be
       specified in listing rules.
   (3)  For the purposes of this Part, the persons responsible for listing particulars are to be determined
       in accordance with regulations made by the Treasury.
  [(3A) Listing rules made under subsection (1) may not specify securities of a kind for which an
       approved prospectus is required as a result of section 85.][21]
   (4)  Nothing in this section affects the FCA's general power to make listing rules.

Sections 79-82 set out the listing particulars regime. Before the implementation of the Prospectus **53.79.02**
Directive in the UK on 1 July 2005, listing particulars were the most common form of offer document.
Since that date, a prospectus has been the standard offer document and listing particulars have
become a comparative rarity. Therefore, the placement of the provisions relating to listing particulars
ahead of those relating to prospectuses is somewhat misleading.

Under section 79(1), the obligation to produce listing particulars is triggered by an application for **53.79.03**
admission of securities (of a kind specified in the listing rules) to the Official List. The securities
specified in the listing rules are those contained in Schedule 11A of the Act (excluding paragraphs 2,
4 and 9) and any other "specialist securities" for which a prospectus is not required under the
Prospectus Directive.[22] The relevant securities from Schedule 11A include units in an open-ended
collective investment scheme and certain kinds of deposit-related security. In the FCA Handbook,
specialist securities are defined as "securities which, because of their nature, are normally bought and
traded by a limited number of investors who are particularly knowledgeable in investment matters." In
practice, all types of bonds are considered specialist securities.

Section 79(3A) clarifies that the listing rules cannot specify securities for which an approved prospec- **53.79.04**
tus is required under section 85. Consequently, an offer or application for admission to trading cannot
be subject to both the listing particulars and prospectus regimes.

The listing particulars which are submitted to the FCA for approval tend to relate to issues of specialist **53.79.05**
debt securities or depositary receipts on the Professional Securities Market (the "PSM"). In order for
securities to be traded on the PSM they must be admitted to the Official List; however, as the PSM is
an unregulated market for the purposes of the Act, there is no requirement to produce a prospectus
(assuming that there is no offer to the public).

Section 79(2) indicates that the listing particulars regime is only sketched out in the Act; the detailed **53.79.06**
provisions, which govern matters such as form and content, are found in Listing Rule ("LR") 4.

The Treasury regulations referred to in section 79(3) are the Financial Services and Markets Act 2000 **53.79.07**
(Official Listing of Securities) Regulations 2001. These regulations must be read in conjunction with
LR 4.2.12G and LR 4.2.13R. In the case of specialist securities, the issuer must state in the listing
particulars that it accepts responsibility for those particulars. It is open to the directors and other
persons to make a similar statement. If other persons accept responsibility, the statements of the issuer
and any directors may be modified accordingly.[23] In all other cases, the issuer, each director and each
person who has authorised the contents of the particulars are automatically responsible. Each
consenting person who is named as a director, or as having agreed to become a director, is also
responsible. As before, other persons may also make statements of responsibility.[24]

---

  [20]  Repealed by Prospectus Regulations 2005/1433 Sch.1 para.3(2) (1 July 2005)
  [21]  Added by Prospectus Regulations 2005/1433 Sch.1 para.3(3) (1 July 2005)
  [22]  Listing Rule ("LR") 4.1.1R
  [23]  Regulation 9, Financial Services and Markets Act 2000 (Official Listing of Securities) Regulations 2001; LR
4.2.13R
  [24]  Regulation 6, Financial Services and Markets Act 2000 (Official Listing of Securities) Regulations 2001

**53.80.01**    **80  General duty of disclosure in listing particulars.**

(1)  Listing particulars submitted to the FCA under section 79 must contain all such information as investors and their professional advisers would reasonably require, and reasonably expect to find there, for the purpose of making an informed assessment of–

(a)  the assets and liabilities, financial position, profits and losses, and prospects of the issuer of the securities; and

(b)  the rights attaching to the securities.

(2)  That information is required in addition to any information required by–

(a)  listing rules, or

(b)  the FCA,

as a condition of the admission of the securities to the official list.

(3)  Subsection (1) applies only to information–

(a)  within the knowledge of any person responsible for the listing particulars; or

(b)  which it would be reasonable for him to obtain by making enquiries.

(4)  In determining what information subsection (1) requires to be included in listing particulars, regard must be had (in particular) to–

(a)  the nature of the securities and their issuer;

(b)  the nature of the persons likely to consider acquiring them;

(c)  the fact that certain matters may reasonably be expected to be within the knowledge of professional advisers of a kind which persons likely to acquire the securities may reasonably be expected to consult; and

(d)  any information available to investors or their professional advisers as a result of requirements imposed on the issuer of the securities by a recognised investment exchange, by listing rules or by or under any other enactment.

**53.80.02**    Pursuant to section 80(2), listing particulars must contain any information required by the listing rules or the FCA as a condition of the admission of the securities to the official list. This duty of disclosure is specific to listing particulars; the information which must be included in prospectuses is described at section 87A.

**53.80.03**    LR 4.2.5G states that, in order to determine the minimum information to be included in listing particulars, issuers should follow the most appropriate schedules and building blocks contained in the Prospectus Directive Regulation (No 2004/809/EC) (the "PD Regulation"). As listing particulars are only required in relation to a small class of specialised securities, the minimum information requirements in the relevant schedules and building blocks will be among the least onerous. Therefore, listing particulars will tend to disclose less information than a prospectus.

**53.80.04**    LR 3.2.6G empowers the FCA to carry out enquiries and request further information when considering an application for admission to listing. If the FCA exercises this power, then any such further information will need to be added the listing particulars.

**53.80.05**    In addition to the requirements of section 80(2), section 80(1) sets out an "informed assessment" test, which may necessitate the disclosure of information not specified by either the listing rules or the FCA. The persons responsible for the listing particulars must decide whether or not the information required to be disclosed pursuant to section 80(2) enables investors and their professional advisers to make an informed assessment of the assets and liabilities, financial position, profits and losses, and prospects of the issuer and the rights attaching to the securities.

**53.80.06**    The "informed assessment" test is qualified by sections 80(3) and (4). Sections 80(4)(c) and (d) invite the assumption that prospective investors have taken suitable professional advice and are aware of certain publicly available information about the issuer. Pursuant to section 80(3), the test should only draw in information that is either within the knowledge of the responsible persons or which it would be reasonable for them to obtain through enquiries. These provisions lessen the amount of additional disclosure that is likely to be required under the test.

**53.80.07**    These qualifications distinguish the section 80 test from the test found at section 87A, which applies to prospectuses. In each case, the subject of the informed assessment (i.e. the assets and liabilities of the issuer, etc.) is similar; however, in section 87A, the qualifications noted in the previous paragraph are absent. Consequently, the section 87A test is broader as there is no suggestion that the prospective investors can be taken to be advised. This differentiation is appropriate as it ensures that retail investors are afforded a high level of protection while reducing the administrative burden on issuers whose securities are only available to professionals.

**53.80.08**    Section 146 of the Financial Services Act 1986, which was the predecessor to section 80, has been considered in several cases. In *Eagle Trust plc v SBC Securities Ltd*, Arden J suggested that "any consensus in the market place as to the disclosure requirements" would be expected to inform a financial adviser's decision about whether or not a specific matter should be disclosed.[25] In *The Secretary of State for Business Enterprise and Regulatory Reform v Anthony Frederick Sullman, Colin David Poole*, counsel for the first defendant, in reliance on *Eagle Trust*, submitted that certain extracts from a prospectus could not be weighed in evidence as the Secretary of State had not adduced any expert evidence as to market practice. The point was not taken by Mr Justice Norris, but he did state separately that the words of section 146 should be construed generously.[26]

### 81 Supplementary listing particulars.        53.81.01

    (1) If at any time after the preparation of listing particulars which have been submitted to the FCA under section 79 and before the commencement of dealings in the securities concerned following their admission to the official list–

      (a) there is a significant change affecting any matter contained in those particulars the inclusion of which was required by–

        (i) section 80,

        (ii) listing rules, or

        (iii) the FCA, or

      (b) a significant new matter arises, the inclusion of information in respect of which would have been so required if it had arisen when the particulars were prepared,

      the issuer must, in accordance with listing rules, submit supplementary listing particulars of the change or new matter to the FCA, for its approval and, if they are approved, publish them.

    (2) "Significant" means significant for the purpose of making an informed assessment of the kind mentioned in section 80(1).

    (3) If the issuer of the securities is not aware of the change or new matter in question, he is not under a duty to comply with subsection (1) unless he is notified of the change or new matter by a person responsible for the listing particulars.

    (4) But it is the duty of any person responsible for those particulars who is aware of such a change or new matter to give notice of it to the issuer.

    (5) Subsection (1) applies also as respects matters contained in any supplementary listing particulars previously published under this section in respect of the securities in question.

Under section 81, an issuer may be required to produce supplementary listing particulars after listed particulars have been submitted to the FCA. This section is equivalent to the supplementary prospectus provisions, which are found in section 87G.   **53.81.02**

An issuer may be required to produce supplementary listing particulars between the submission of listing particulars to the FCA and the commencement of dealing in the securities concerned. The requirement may be triggered by a significant change affecting any matter that was required to be included in the particulars by section 80, the listing rules or the FCA. Presumably, if there is a significant change affecting a matter which was, instead, disclosed voluntarily, supplementary particulars will not be necessary. The requirement may also be triggered by a significant new matter, which would have been required to be included had it arisen prior to the submission of the listing particulars.   **53.81.03**

The listing rules offer little additional guidance on this topic. LR 4.4.1G copies out section 81 of the Act. LR 4.4.2R reminds the issuer of its obligation to file and publish any approved supplementary particulars in accordance with the requirements set out in Prospectus Rule ("PR") 3.2 and the PD Regulation.   **53.81.04**

Section 81(3) attaches a knowledge qualifier to the issuer's duty to comply with subsection (1); however, section 81(4) places a duty on each person responsible for the listing particulars to notify the issuer of any changes or new matters which come to his attention. In effect, these back-to-back duties impute the knowledge of the responsible persons to the issuer.   **53.81.05**

Notably, the publication of supplementary listing particulars does not give a person who has agreed to buy or subscribe for the relevant securities the right to withdraw. By way of comparison, under section 87Q, if an issuer publishes a supplementary prospectus, a similarly situated person has two working days to withdraw their acceptance.   **53.81.06**

Under section 90(4), a breach of section 81 will result in civil liability to any person who acquires the securities in question and suffers a loss as a result of the failure to publish supplementary particulars.   **53.81.07**

---

[25] [1995] B.C.C. 231

[26] [2008] EWHC (Ch) 3179

**53.82.01** **82 Exemptions from disclosure.**

(1) The FCA may authorise the omission from listing particulars of any information, the inclusion of which would otherwise be required by section 80 or 81, on the ground–
  (a) that its disclosure would be contrary to the public interest;
  (b) that its disclosure would be seriously detrimental to the issuer; or
  (c) in the case of securities of a kind specified in listing rules, that its disclosure is unnecessary for persons of the kind who may be expected normally to buy or deal in securities of that kind.

(2) But–
  (a) no authority may be granted under subsection (1)(b) in respect of essential information; and
  (b) no authority granted under subsection (1)(b) extends to any such information.

(3) The Secretary of State or the Treasury may issue a certificate to the effect that the disclosure of any information (including information that would otherwise have to be included in listing particulars for which they are themselves responsible) would be contrary to the public interest.

(4) The FCA is entitled to act on any such certificate in exercising its powers under subsection (1)(a).

(5) This section does not affect any powers of the FCA under listing rules made as a result of section 101(2).

(6) "Essential information" means information which a person considering acquiring securities of the kind in question would be likely to need in order not to be misled about any facts which it is essential for him to know in order to make an informed assessment.

(7) "Listing particulars" includes supplementary listing particulars.

**53.82.02** It will be unusual for the FCA to authorise omissions from listing particulars under section 82(1)(a), as such omissions will rarely be in the public interest. The most likely application of this subsection is to issuers in the defence sector or whose business is otherwise connected to national security. An application for authorisation under subsection (1)(a) will usually be supported by a certificate from the Secretary of State or the Treasury, pursuant to subsection (3). Under subsection (4), the FCA is entitled to accept such a certificate as evidence of the disclosure being contrary to the public interest.

**53.82.03** Section 82(1)(b) is of limited application as the omission of information seriously detrimental to issuer is likely to defeat the object of investor protection. Furthermore, subsection (2) clarifies that "essential information" – defined in subsection (6) – cannot be omitted under subsection (1)(b).

**53.82.04** The securities referred to in section 82(1)(c) are "specialist securities", as defined in the FCA Handbook. In practice, a specialist security can be any kind of bond. Consequently, this subsection allows the FCA to authorise the omission of basic information, which will be familiar to professional investors.

**53.82.05** The procedure for making a request to omit information from listing particulars is set out at LR 4.2.10R. The request must be made by the issuer in writing, specify the information and reasons for its omission and state why one or more of the section 82 grounds applies.

**53.83.01** **83 [...]**[27]

*[Transferable securities: public offers and admission to trading]*[28]

**53.84.01** **84 [Matters which may be dealt with by prospectus rules**

(1) Prospectus rules may make provision as to—
  (a) the required form and content of a prospectus (including a summary);
  (b) the cases in which a summary need not be included in a prospectus;
  (c) the languages which may be used in a prospectus (including a summary);
  (d) the determination of the persons responsible for a prospectus;
  (e) the manner in which applications to the FCA for the approval of a prospectus are to be made.

(2) Prospectus rules may also make provision as to—
  (a) the period of validity of a prospectus;
  (b) the disclosure of the maximum price or of the criteria or conditions according to which the final offer price is to be determined, if that information is not contained in a prospectus;
  (c) the disclosure of the amount of the transferable securities which are to be offered to the public or of the criteria or conditions according to which that amount is to be determined, if that information is not contained in a prospectus;
  (d) the required form and content of other summary documents (including the languages which may be used in such a document);
  (e) the ways in which a prospectus that has been approved by the FCA may be made available to the public;

---

[27] Repealed by Prospectus Regulations 2005/1433 Sch.1 para.4 (1 July 2005)
[28] Ss.84-87R substituted for ss.84-87 by Prospectus Regulations 2005/1433 Sch.1 para.5 (1 July 2005)

    (f) the disclosure, publication or other communication of such information as the FCA may reasonably stipulate;

    (g) the principles to be observed in relation to advertisements in connection with an offer of transferable securities to the public or admission of transferable securities to trading on a regulated market and the enforcement of those principles;

    (h) the suspension of trading in transferable securities where continued trading would be detrimental to the interests of investors;

    (i) elections under section 87 or under Article 2.1(m)(iii) of the prospectus directive as applied for the purposes of this Part by section 102C.

(3) [...][29]

(4) Prospectus rules may make provision for the purpose of dealing with matters arising out of or related to any provision of the prospectus directive.

(5) In relation to cases where the home State in relation to an issuer of transferable securities is an EEA State other than the United Kingdom, prospectus rules may make provision for the recognition of elections made in relation to such securities under the law of that State in accordance with Article 1.3 or 2.1(m)(iii) of the prospectus directive.

(6) In relation to a document relating to transferable securities issued by an issuer incorporated in a non-EEA State and drawn up in accordance with the law of that State, prospectus rules may make provision as to the approval of that document as a prospectus.

(7) Nothing in this section affects the FCA's general power to make prospectus rules.][30]

Subsections (1) and (2) identify a number of provisions from the Prospectus Directive that are **53.84.02** addressed in the prospectus rules. Subsection (4) clarifies that the FCA may make rules dealing with any matter arising out of or related to any provision of the Prospectus Directive. Section 84 demonstrates that the implementation of the Prospectus Directive was largely delegated to the FSA with only its key provisions being enacted through primary legislation.

## 85 [Prohibition of dealing etc. in transferable securities without approved prospectus   **53.85.01**

(1) It is unlawful for transferable securities to which this subsection applies to be offered to the public in the United Kingdom unless an approved prospectus has been made available to the public before the offer is made.

(2) It is unlawful to request the admission of transferable securities to which this subsection applies to trading on a regulated market situated or operating in the United Kingdom unless an approved prospectus has been made available to the public before the request is made.

(3) A person who contravenes subsection (1) or (2) is guilty of an offence and liable—

    (a) on summary conviction, to imprisonment for a term not exceeding 3 months or a fine not exceeding the statutory maximum or both;

    (b) on conviction on indictment, to imprisonment for a term not exceeding 2 years or a fine or both.

(4) A contravention of subsection (1) or (2) is actionable, at the suit of a person who suffers loss as a result of the contravention, subject to the defences and other incidents applying to actions for breach of statutory duty.

(5) Subsection (1) applies to all transferable securities other than—

    (a) those listed in Schedule 11A;

    (b) such other transferable securities as may be specified in prospectus rules.

(6) Subsection (2) applies to all transferable securities other than—

    (a) those listed in Part 1 of Schedule 11A;

    (b) such other transferable securities as may be specified in prospectus rules.

(7) "Approved prospectus" means, in relation to transferable securities to which this section applies, a prospectus approved by the competent authority of the home State in relation to the issuer of the securities.][31]

Section 85(1) addresses offers of transferable securities to the public in the UK. It is unlawful to make **53.85.02** such an offer unless an approved prospectus has been made available to the public beforehand. Subsection (5) establishes the class of securities which may be offered to the public without an accompanying prospectus: those listed in Schedule 11A of the Act and those listed in PR 1.2.2R.

Section 102B reproduces the pan-European definition of an "offer of securities to the public", which **53.85.03** appears in Article 2(1)(d) of the Prospectus Directive. Before the implementation of the Prospectus Directive, each Member State had been allowed to retain its own definition of a public offer. This

---

[29] Repealed by Prospectus Regulations 2012/1538 reg.3(1) (1 July 2012)

[30] Ss.84-87R substituted for ss.84-87 by Prospectus Regulations 2005/1433 Sch.1 para.5 (1 July 2005)

[31] Ss.84-87R substituted for ss.84-87 by Prospectus Regulations 2005/1433 Sch.1 para.5 (1 July 2005)

discouraged capital raising on a European scale as the same operation could be regarded as a private placement in one Member State and a public offer requiring a prospectus in another. A very broad definition was adopted in order to accommodate each Member State's conception of a public offer. Neither the Prospectus Directive nor Part 6 provides a definition of "public"; however, the intended scope of an "offer to the public" becomes clearer when the definition is read alongside the exemptions in section 86.

**53.85.04**   In its consultation paper on the implementation of the Prospectus Directive, the Treasury expressed concern that the definition could capture trading in the secondary market.[32] This concern is addressed at subsection (5), which expressly excludes market trading from the definition.

**53.85.05**   Section 85(2) addresses requests for the admission of transferable securities to trading on a regulated market in the UK. It is unlawful to make such a request unless an approved prospectus has been made available to the public beforehand. In addition to an approved prospectus, securities cannot be admitted to trading without being admitted to the Official List. In practice, these applications will take place simultaneously. Subsection (6) establishes the class of securities which can be admitted to trading without an accompanying prospectus: those listed in Part 1 of Schedule 11A of the Act and those listed in PR 1.2.3R.

**53.85.06**   Under Article 47 of the Markets in Financial Instruments Directive (2004/39/EC) (the "MiFID"), the UK is required to produce a list of regulated markets for which it is Home Member State. This list is published on the FCA website. At the time of writing, the regulated markets in the UK were: ICE Futures Europe, London Stock Exchange – Regulated Market (1), NYSE EURONEXT LONDON, PLUS-listed market, The London International Financial Futures and Options Exchange and the London Metal Exchange.

**53.85.07**   Contravention of either section 85(1) or section 85(2) triggers criminal liability. The penalties, which are the same in each case, are set out in subsection (3). Furthermore, under subsection (4), any person who suffers loss as a result of a contravention can bring a civil action for breach of statutory duty.

**53.86.01**   **86 [Exempt offers to the public**

(1)  A person does not contravene section 85(1) if—
   (a)  the offer is made to or directed at qualified investors only;
   (b)  the offer is made to or directed at fewer than [ 150 persons][33], other than qualified investors, per EEA State;
   (c)  the minimum consideration which may be paid by any person for transferable securities acquired by him pursuant to the offer is at least [100,000 euros ][34] (or an equivalent amount);
   (d)  the transferable securities being offered are denominated in amounts of at least [100,000 euros][35] (or equivalent amounts); [...][36]
   (e)  the total consideration for the transferable securities being offered [in the EEA States ][37] cannot exceed 100,000 euros (or an equivalent amount) [;or ][38]
   [(f)  the offer falls within subsection (1A).][39]

[(1A)  An offer ("the current offer") falls within this subsection if the transferable securities are being sold or placed through a financial intermediary where—
   (a)  the transferable securities have previously been the subject of one or more offers to the public;
   (b)  in respect of one or more of those previous offers any of paragraphs (a) to (e) of subsection (1) applied;
   (c)  a prospectus is available for the securities which has been approved by the FCA no earlier than 12 months before the date the current offer is made; and
   (d)  the issuer or other person who was responsible for drawing up the prospectus has given written consent to the use of the prospectus for the purpose of the current offer.][40]

---

[32]  pp.21-22, UK Implementation of the Prospectus Directive 2003/71/EC – A consultation document, October 2004 (http://webarchive.nationalarchives.gov.uk/+/http://www.hm-treasury.gov.uk/media/DFE/27/DFE27339-BCDC-D4B3-16FD311B308ABF54.pdf)
[33]  Substituted by Prospectus Regulations 2011/1668 reg.2(2) (31 July 2011)
[34]  Substituted by Prospectus Regulations 2012/1538 reg.2(1)(a) (1 July 2012)
[35]  Substituted by Prospectus Regulations 2012/1538 reg.2(1)(a) (1 July 2012)
[36]  Repealed by Prospectus Regulations 2012/1538 reg.2(1)(b) (1 July 2012)
[37]  Inserted by Prospectus Regulations 2012/1538 reg.2(1)(c) (1 July 2012)
[38]  Added by Prospectus Regulations 2012/1538 reg.2(1)(d) (1 July 2012)
[39]  Added by Prospectus Regulations 2012/1538 reg.2(1)(d) (1 July 2012)
[40]  Added by Prospectus Regulations 2012/1538 reg.2(2) (1 July 2012)

(2) Where—

    (a) a person who is not a qualified investor ("the client") has engaged a qualified investor falling within [point (1) of Section I of Annex II to the markets in financial instruments directive][41] to act as his agent, and

    (b) the terms on which the qualified investor is engaged enable him to make decisions concerning the acceptance of offers of transferable securities on the client's behalf without reference to the client,

an offer made to or directed at the qualified investor is not to be regarded for the purposes of subsection (1) as also having been made to or directed at the client.

(3) For the purposes of subsection (1)(b), the making of an offer of transferable securities to—

    (a) trustees of a trust,

    (b) members of a partnership in their capacity as such, or

    (c) two or more persons jointly,

is to be treated as the making of an offer to a single person.

(4) In determining whether subsection (1)(e) is satisfied in relation to an offer ("offer A"), offer A is to be taken together with any other offer of transferable securities of the same class made by the same person which—

    (a) was open at any time within the period of 12 months ending with the date on which offer A is first made; and

    (b) had previously satisfied subsection (1)(e).

(5) For the purposes of this section, an amount (in relation to an amount denominated in euros) is an "equivalent amount" if it is an amount of equal value denominated wholly or partly in another currency or unit of account.

(6) The equivalent is to be calculated at the latest practicable date before (but in any event not more than 3 working days before) the date on which the offer is first made.

[(7) "Qualified investor", in relation to an offer of transferable securities, means—

    (a) a person described in points (1) to (4) of Section I of Annex II to the markets in financial instruments directive, other than a person who, before the making of the offer, has agreed in writing with the relevant firm (or each of the relevant firms) to be treated as a non-professional client in accordance with the final paragraph of Section I of Annex II to that directive;

    (b) a person who has made a request to one or more relevant firms to be treated as a professional client in accordance with Section II of Annex II to that directive and has not subsequently, but before the making of the offer, agreed in writing with that relevant firm (or each of those relevant firms) to be treated as a nonprofessional client in accordance with the final paragraph of Section I of Annex II to that directive;

    (c) a person who is an eligible counterparty in accordance with Article 24 of that directive and has not, before the making of the offer, agreed in writing with the relevant firm (or each of the relevant firms) to be treated as a non-professional client in accordance with the final paragraph of Section I of Annex II to that directive; or

    (d) a person whom any relevant firm is authorised to continue to treat as a professional client in accordance with Article 71(6) of that directive.][42]

[(8) In subsection (7) "relevant firm" means an investment firm or credit institution acting in connection with the offer.

(9) Investment firms and credit institutions which are authorised persons must communicate their classification of their clients as being or not being qualified investors on request to an issuer subject to complying with the Data Protection Act 1998 or any directly applicable EU legislation relating to data protection.

(10) In subsections (8) and (9), "credit institution" means—

    (a) a credit institution authorised under the banking consolidation directive; or

    (b) an institution which would satisfy the requirements for authorisation as a credit institution under that directive if it had its registered office (or if it does not have one, its head office) in an EEA State.][43] ][44]

Section 86 sets out a series of exemptions to the prohibition on offering transferable securities to the **53.86.02** public. Issuers who do not wish to produce a prospectus will try to bring their offer within one or more of these exemptions. It should be noted that, even if an issuer takes advantage of a section 86 exemption, it may still need to produce a prospectus in order to comply with section 85(2) in connection with admission to trading.

---

[41] Substituted by Prospectus Regulations 2012/1538 reg.3(2)(a) (1 July 2012)
[42] Substituted by Prospectus Regulations 2012/1538 reg.3(2)(b) (1 July 2012)
[43] Added by Prospectus Regulations 2012/1538 reg.3(2)(c) (1 July 2012)
[44] Ss.84-87R substituted for ss.84-87 by Prospectus Regulations 2005/1433 Sch.1 para.5 (1 July 2005)

53.86.03 Under section 86(1)(a), an offer is exempt if it is made to qualified investors only. "Qualified investor" is defined in subsection (7). This definition was inserted by the Prospectus Regulations 2012/1538 (the "2012 Regulations") in order to harmonise the qualified investors exemption, which was established by the Prospectus Regulations 2005/1433 (the "2005 Regulations"), with the client classification categories under the MiFID.

53.86.04 Under subsection (9), financial intermediaries are obliged to disclose to an issuer whether or not a client is a qualified investor, subject to data protection legislation.

53.86.05 The 2012 Regulations also repealed section 87R, which obliged the FSA to establish and maintain a register of qualified investors. These changes should make it more straightforward for issuers to utilise the qualified investors exemption while simultaneously reducing the administrative burden on financial intermediaries.

53.86.06 Section 86(2) was inserted by the 2005 Regulations to confirm that an offer made to a discretionary private client broker, acting as his client's agent, would fall within the qualified investor exemption. This preserved the position under the Public Offers of Securities Regulations 1995 (the "POS Regulations") where such offers fell within the "professionals only" exemption.

53.86.07 Under section 86(1)(b), an offer is exempt if it is made to fewer than 150 persons per EEA state. The threshold was increased from 100 to 150 persons by Directive 2010/73/EU (the "Amending Directive"). This was one of the provisions of the Amending Directive that was implemented ahead of schedule by the Prospectus Regulations 2011/1668 (the "2011 Regulations"). The Treasury considered that the amendment was particularly beneficial for smaller companies as it would enable them to offer securities to a wider set of investors, thereby raising capital more cost-efficiently. In its consultation paper, the Treasury proposed to "gold-plate" this provision by aggregating the number of offerees over a 12 month period. The proposal was ultimately rejected, however, the FCA is responsible for ensuring that the exemption is not abused, e.g. by an issuer making successive offers to groups of 99 investors.[45]

53.86.08 Under section 86(1)(c), an offer is exempt if the minimum consideration is €100,000 (or an equivalent amount). Under section 86(1)(d), an offer is exempt if the denomination of the securities is at least €100,000 (or an equivalent amount). These thresholds were increased from €50,000 to €100,000 by the Amending Directive on the basis that a €50,000 threshold no longer reflected the distinction between retail and professional investors in terms of investor capacity.[46]

53.86.09 Section 86(1)(e) provides a narrow exemption for very small offers of €100,000 or less. To prevent abuse of this exemption, section 86(4) provides that €100,000 is in effect an annual cap and the exemption is only open to the extent it has not been utilised in the 12 months preceding an offer.

53.86.10 Section 86(1)(f) is a new exemption, which was added by the 2012 Regulations.

53.86.11 When an offering has a retail component, securities do not pass directly from an issuer to the retail investors; instead, they are sold to such investors by retail distributors. Retail distributors acquire securities from the initial subscribers, which are typically investment banks. This chain of transactions is known as the "retail cascade".

53.86.12 Under the pre-Prospectus Directive regime, these sales and re-sales were unproblematic as they were covered by the approved listing particulars published by the issuer. However, after the implementation of the Prospectus Directive, it was arguable that each sale in the chain breached the prohibition on offers to the public in section 85(1).

53.86.13 Despite these concerns, market practice in the UK did not change significantly. Nonetheless, the Amending Directive sought to clarify the status of the re-sale of securities via financial intermediaries by way of a new exemption. Under subsection 1(f), a sale or placing of securities through a financial intermediary will be an exempt offer provided that, amongst other things, a prospectus approved by the FCA in the last 12 months is available and the issuer (or other person responsible for drawing up that prospectus) consents to its use for the purposes of the offer.

53.86.14 The manner in which an issuer (or other person responsible) consents to the use of a prospectus by financial intermediaries was one of the matters in relation to which the Commission sought advice from the European Securities and Markets Authority ("ESMA"). ESMA's technical advice on this

---

[45] pp,4-5, Feedback Statement to Prospectus Directive Consultation Document (http://webarchive
.nationalarchives.gov.uk/+/http://www.hm-treasury.gov.uk/media/E/D/
prospectus_directive_Feedback_statement_to_PD_condoc2.pdf)

[46] p.21, Final report from ECON Committee of European Parliament on the EC's proposed PD Amending Directive, 26 March 2010 (http://www.europarl.europa.eu/sides/getDoc.do?pubRef=-//EP//NONSGML+REPORT+A7-2010-0102+0+DOC+PDF+V0//EN)

matter was implemented by Commission Delegated Regulation (EU) No 862/2012, which amended the PD Regulation. As regulations are directly applicable, the changes immediately became law in the Member States. Under article 20a of the amended PD Regulation, in order for a prospectus to qualify for the section 86(1)(f) exemption, it must contain the additional information set out in new Annex XXX. Amongst other things, the issuer (or other person responsible) must accept responsibility for the content of the prospectus for a specified period and indicate the Member States in which financial intermediaries may use it. The consent can be extended to all financial intermediaries or confined to those named in the prospectus. At the time of writing, an industry standard form of consent was being prepared by the International Capital Market Association.

Before the implementation of the Prospectus Directive, major shareholders who wished to sell their   **53.86.15**
shares after a flotation could take advantage of the approved listing particulars published by the issuer. Since 1 July 2005, such sales have had to be made by way of exempt offer. It should be noted that the new exemption does not alter the position of such shareholders. They still will need to rely on one of the other section 86(1) exemptions in order to avoid breaching the prohibition in section 85(1).

## 87  [Election to have prospectus                                                          53.87.01

(1)  A person who proposes—
    (a)  to issue transferable securities to which this section applies,
    (b)  to offer to the public transferable securities to which this section applies, or
    (c)  to request the admission to a regulated market of transferable securities to which this section applies,
    may elect, in accordance with prospectus rules, to have a prospectus in relation to the securities.
(2)  If a person makes such an election, the provisions of this Part and of prospectus rules apply in relation to those transferable securities as if, in relation to an offer of the securities to the public or the admission of the securities to trading on a regulated market, they were transferable securities for which an approved prospectus would be required as a result of section 85.
(3)  Listing rules made under section 79 do not apply to securities which are the subject of an election.
(4)  The transferable securities to which this section applies are those which fall within any of the following paragraphs of Schedule 11A—
    (a)  paragraph 2,
    (b)  paragraph 4,
    (c)  paragraph 8, or
    (d)  paragraph 9,
    where the United Kingdom is the home State in relation to the issuer of the securities.][47]

This section allows a person to elect to comply with Part 6 and the prospectus rules when the securities   **53.87.02**
concerned would otherwise be exempt.

The majority of types of security fall within the prospectus regime. However, those listed in Schedule   **53.87.03**
11A are exempt from either one or both of the prohibitions in section 85. Most of these securities are covered instead by the listing particulars regime. However, the following three types of security are exempt from both: non-equity securities issued by the government of an EEA State, a local or regional authority of an EEA State, a public international body of which an EEA state is a member, the European Central Bank or the central bank of an EEA State; securities guaranteed by the government, or a local or regional authority, of an EEA State; and securities included in an offer with a total consideration of less than €5,000,000.

In certain cases, an issuer of securities which are exempt from one or both regimes may wish to   **53.87.04**
produce a prospectus voluntarily. For example, the issuer may want to take advantage of investors' familiarity with the format, or demonstrate that the highest possible standard of disclosure has been provided.

Section 87 applies to deposit-related securities of the kind described in paragraph 8 of Schedule 11A   **53.87.05**
and the three types of securities that are exempt from both regimes, provided that the UK is the home state of the issuer of the securities in question.

If a person makes an election under section 87(1), the provisions of Part 6 and the prospectus rules   **53.87.06**
(including disclosure requirements) will apply to the securities concerned. In effect, section 85(5) and/or section 85(6) will be ignored and the public offering or admission to trading of the securities will contravene section 85(1) and/or section 85(2) unless an approved prospectus is published before the offer, or request for admission is made.

---

[47]  Ss.84-87R substituted for ss.84-87 by Prospectus Regulations 2005/1433 Sch.1 para.5 (1 July 2005)

**53.87.07** Subsection (3) was presumably included to ensure that deposit-related securities of the kind described in paragraph 8 of Schedule 11A, which are not exempt from the listing particulars regime, do not become subject to both regimes simultaneously if an election is made under section 87 in respect of them.

*[Approval of prospectus ]* [48]

**53.87A.01** **[87A Criteria for approval of prospectus by FCA**

(1) The FCA may not approve a prospectus unless it is satisfied that—
  (a) the United Kingdom is the home State in relation to the issuer of the transferable securities to which it relates,
  (b) the prospectus contains the necessary information, and
  (c) all of the other requirements imposed by or in accordance with this Part or the prospectus directive have been complied with (so far as those requirements apply to a prospectus for the transferable securities in question).

(2) The necessary information is the information necessary to enable investors to make an informed assessment of—
  (a) the assets and liabilities, financial position, profits and losses, and prospects of the issuer of the transferable securities and of any guarantor; and
  (b) the rights attaching to the transferable securities.

[(2A) If, in the case of transferable securities to which section 87 applies, the prospectus states that the guarantor is a specified EEA State, the prospectus is not required to include other information about the guarantor. ] [49]

(3) The necessary information must be presented in a form which is comprehensible and easy to analyse.

(4) The necessary information must be prepared having regard to the particular nature of the transferable securities and their issuer.

(5) The prospectus must include a summary (unless the transferable securities in question are ones in relation to which prospectus rules provide that a summary is not required).

[(6) The summary must convey concisely, in non-technical language and in an appropriate structure, the key information relevant to the securities which are the subject of the prospectus and, when read with the rest of the prospectus, must be an aid to investors considering whether to invest in the securities.] [50]

(7) Where the prospectus for which approval is sought does not include the final offer price or the amount of transferable securities to be offered to the public, [the applicant must, as soon as that element is finalised— ] [51]
  [(a) inform, in writing, the FCA and any competent authority of any EEA State which the applicant has requested be supplied with a certificate of approval under section 87I; and
  (b) make that information available, in writing, to prospective investors. ] [52]

[(7A) The document containing the final offer price or the amount of transferable securities to be offered to the public may only contain information that relates to the securities note and must not be used to supplement the prospectus. ] [53]

(8) "Prospectus" (except in subsection (5)) includes a supplementary prospectus.

[(9) "the key information" means the information which is essential to enable investors to understand the transferable securities to which the prospectus relates and to decide whether to consider the offer further.

(10) The key information must include —
  (a) the essential characteristics of, and risks associated with, the issuer and any guarantor, including their assets, liabilities and financial positions;
  (b) the essential characteristics of, and risks associated with, investment in the transferable securities, including any rights attaching to the securities;
  (c) the general terms of the offer, including an estimate of the expenses charged to an investor by the issuer and the person offering the securities to the public, if not the issuer;
  (d) details of the admission to trading; and
  (e) the reasons for the offer and proposed use of the proceeds.] [54] ] [55]

[48] Ss.84-87R substituted for ss.84-87 by Prospectus Regulations 2005/1433 Sch.1 para.5 (1 July 2005)
[49] Added by Prospectus Regulations 2012/1538 reg.2(3) (1 July 2012)
[50] Substituted by Prospectus Regulations 2012/1538 reg.4(a) (1 July 2012)
[51] Substituted by Prospectus Regulations 2012/1538 reg.4(b) (1 July 2012)
[52] Substituted by Prospectus Regulations 2012/1538 reg.4(b) (1 July 2012)
[53] Added by Prospectus Regulations 2012/1538 reg.4(c) (1 July 2012)
[54] Added by Prospectus Regulations 2012/1538 reg.4(d) (1 July 2012)
[55] Ss.84-87R substituted for ss.84-87 by Prospectus Regulations 2005/1433 Sch.1 para.5 (1 July 2005)

The FCA cannot approve a prospectus unless it contains the information necessary for investors to make an "informed assessment". This concept is familiar from the listing particulars regime, however, a higher standard of disclosure is plainly required under section 87A. First, the information must be sufficient for investors to make an informed assessment unaided by professional advisers. Secondly, disclosure is not qualified by the knowledge of the persons responsible for the prospectus. Thirdly, investors must be able to make an informed assessment of any guarantor as well as the issuer.    **53.87A.02**

The "informed assessment" requirement is cumulative to the contents requirements set out in the prospectus rules. Section 84(1)(a) states that the prospectus rules may make provision as to the required form and content of a prospectus. PR 2.3 states that Articles 3 to 23 of the PD Regulation provide for the minimum information to be included in a prospectus. Those articles refer to various schedules and building blocks, which are annexed to the PD Regulation. The schedules are specific to different types of issuer and security; building blocks may be required if the issue is guaranteed or the securities are exotic. An issuer must select the relevant schedules and building blocks (if any) and draft the prospectus on the basis of the minimum information requirements therein.    **53.87A.03**

PR 2.4 permits a prospectus to incorporate information by reference, which was not permissible under English law prior to the implementation of the Prospectus Directive. A prospectus (excluding the prospectus summary) may incorporate information by reference to documents that have been approved by the competent authority of the relevant home state. Documents that have been filed with or notified to that competent authority in accordance with the Prospectus Directive are also acceptable. Article 28 of the PD Regulation provides examples of information that may be incorporated by reference, including annual and interim financial information and articles of association.    **53.87A.04**

A prospectus is not required in relation to securities guaranteed by a Member State. However, in accordance with subsection (2), if an issuer of such securities elects to have a prospectus under section 87, it will not have to provide information about that Member State on the basis that there is already abundant information about the finances of the Member States in the public domain.[56]    **53.87A.05**

Article 5.2 of the Prospectus Directive (as amended by the Amending Directive) states that a prospectus summary should provide "key information" and be drawn up in a common format to facilitate comparability of the summaries of similar securities. The key information requirement was inserted by the 2012 Regulations at section 87A(6). Key information is defined in subsection (9) and divided into five sub-categories in subsection (10).    **53.87A.06**

The specific form of the key information to be included in the summary was one of the matters in relation to which the Commission sought advice from ESMA. ESMA's technical advice on this matter was implemented by Commission Delegated Regulation (EU) No 486/2012, which amended the PD Regulation. On account of the direct applicability of regulations, the changes immediately became law in the Member States. Under article 24 of the amended PD Regulation, a prospectus summary must contain the key information items set out in Annex XXII. The Annex is comprised of five sections – introduction and warnings, issuer and any guarantor, securities, risks and offer – each of which is divided into a series of elements. A prospectus summary must adhere to the tabular format of the Annex, addressing each section and element in turn.    **53.87A.07**

PR 2.1.3R provides a narrow exemption to the section 87A(5) summary requirement in the case of a prospectus relating to the admission to trading of non-equity transferable securities with a denomination of at least €100,000 (or equivalent amount).    **53.87A.08**

The Amending Directive has tightened up the provisions that allow a base prospectus to be published without certain "final terms" such as the size of the issue and final offer price. Issuers' obligations under subsection (7) have been extended. Previously, an issuer was only obliged to inform the FCA of the final terms. Now, in addition to the FCA, the applicant must inform the prospective investors and the competent authority of any EEA state into which the prospectus has been passported. A new subsection – (7A) – addresses the perceived mischief of issuers using final terms to, in effect, supplement a base prospectus. Accordingly, the content of final terms should be restricted to information such as ISIN, issue price, maturity, coupon, exercise date, exercise price and redemption price.[57] Material information relating to the issuer or the securities that has emerged since the publication of the base prospectus should normally be included in a supplementary prospectus, published in accordance with section 87G.    **53.87A.09**

---

[56]  p.8, EU Council general approach to the EC's proposed PD Amending Directive, 4 February 2010 (http:// register.consilium.europa.eu/pdf/en/09/st17/st17451-re01.en09.pdf)
[57]  p.8, EU Council general approach to the EC's proposed PD Amending Directive, 4 February 2010 (http:// register.consilium.europa.eu/pdf/en/09/st17/st17451-re01.en09.pdf)

**53.87B.01** **[87B Exemptions from disclosure**

(1) The FCA may authorise the omission from a prospectus of any information, the inclusion of which would otherwise be required, on the ground—

  (a) that its disclosure would be contrary to the public interest;

  (b) that its disclosure would be seriously detrimental to the issuer, provided that the omission would be unlikely to mislead the public with regard to any facts or circumstances which are essential for an informed assessment of the kind mentioned in section 87A(2); or

  (c) that the information is only of minor importance for a specific offer to the public or admission to trading on a regulated market and unlikely to influence an informed assessment of the kind mentioned in section 87A(2).

(2) The Secretary of State or the Treasury may issue a certificate to the effect that the disclosure of any information would be contrary to the public interest.

(3) The FCA is entitled to act on any such certificate in exercising its powers under subsection (1)(a).

(4) This section does not affect any powers of the FCA under prospectus rules.

(5) "Prospectus" includes a supplementary prospectus.][58]

**53.87B.02** The FCA may authorise the omission of information from a prospectus under section 87B(1)(a) if its disclosure would be contrary to the public interest. The most likely application of this subsection is to issuers in the defence sector or whose business is otherwise connected to national security. An application for authorisation under subsection (1)(a) will usually be supported by a certificate from the Secretary of State or the Treasury, pursuant to subsection (2). Under subsection (3), the FCA is entitled to accept such a certificate as evidence of the disclosure being contrary to the public interest.

**53.87B.03** The FCA may authorise the omission of information under Section 87B(1)(b) if the disclosure would be seriously detrimental to issuer, provided that the information concerned is not essential to an informed assessment of the issuer, any guarantor and the securities. It is unlikely that this section will be of wide application as the very existence of information which would be seriously detrimental to the issuer is likely to be essential to an investor's assessment.

**53.87B.04** Under section 87B(1)(c) the FCA may authorise the omission of information deemed to be of minor importance and unlikely to influence an informed assessment of the issuer, any guarantor and the securities. This provision gives the FCA the flexibility to derogate from the prospectus rules where a prescribed disclosure would be inappropriate or disproportionate in the context of a particular prospectus.

**53.87B.05** The procedure for making a request to omit information from a prospectus is set out at PR 2.5.3R. The request must be made by the issuer in writing, specify the information and reasons for its omission and state why one or more of the section 87B grounds applies.

**53.87C.01** **[87C Consideration of application for approval**

(1) The FCA must notify the applicant of its decision on an application for approval of a prospectus before the end of the period for consideration.

(2) The period for consideration—

  (a) begins with the first working day after the date on which the application is received; but

  (b) if the FCA gives a notice under subsection (4), is to be treated as beginning with the first working day after the date on which the notice is complied with.

(3) The period for consideration is—

  (a) except in the case of a new issuer, 10 working days; or

  (b) in that case, 20 working days.

(4) The FCA may by notice in writing require a person who has applied for approval of a prospectus to provide—

  (a) specified documents or documents of a specified description, or

  (b) specified information or information of a specified description.

(5) No notice under subsection (4) may be given after the end of the period, beginning with the first working day after the date on which the application is received, of—

  (a) except in the case of a new issuer, 10 working days; or

  (b) in that case, 20 working days.

(6) Subsection (4) applies only to information and documents reasonably required in connection with the exercise by the FCA of its functions in relation to the application.

(7) The FCA may require any information provided under this section to be provided in such form as it may reasonably require.

---

[58] Ss.84-87R substituted for ss.84-87 by Prospectus Regulations 2005/1433 Sch.1 para.5 (1 July 2005)

(8)  The FCA may require—
  (a)  any information provided, whether in a document or otherwise, to be verified in such manner, or
  (b)  any document produced to be authenticated in such manner, as it may reasonably require.
(9)  The FCA must notify the applicant of its decision on an application for approval of a supplementary prospectus before the end of the period of 7 working days beginning with the date on which the application is received; and subsections (4) and (6) to (8) apply to such an application as they apply to an application for approval of a prospectus.
(10) The FCA's failure to comply with subsection (1) or (9) does not constitute approval of the application in question.
(11) "New issuer" means an issuer of transferable securities which—
  (a)  does not have transferable securities admitted to trading on any regulated market; and
  (b)  has not previously offered transferable securities to the public.][59]

Section 87C establishes a timetable for the approval of a prospectus or supplementary prospectus by the FCA. The FCA has either 10 or 20 working days, beginning with the first working day after an application is submitted, to consider a prospectus. The longer time limit will only apply in the case of an issuer without securities admitted to trading on a regulated market who has not previously offered securities to the public. The time limit for a supplementary prospectus is always 7 working days, beginning with the date on which the application is received.  **53.87C.02**

During the relevant period for consideration, the FCA may request that the applicant to provides such additional documents and information as it reasonably requires to make its decision. If the FCA makes such a request, the initial period for consideration is disregarded and a new period runs from the day after the date on which the applicant complies with the request. Importantly, subsection (10) notes that any failure by the FCA to comply with section 87C does not constitute an approval of the application under consideration.  **53.87C.03**

The timetable in section 87C does not reflect the reality in practice, as it does not acknowledge the preliminary steps that must be taken. Most significantly, the FCA will comment on a series of drafts before a formal application is made. Further details of the approval procedure are set out in PR 3.1, including the requirements for draft documents (PR 3.1.4R and 3.1.5R).  **53.87C.04**

It should be noted that, by virtue of LR 4.3.3G, the same time limits apply to an application for approval of listing particulars.  **53.87C.05**

### [87D  Procedure for decision on application for approval    53.87D.01

(1)  If the FCA approves a prospectus, it must give the applicant written notice.
(2)  If the FCA proposes to refuse to approve a prospectus, it must give the applicant written notice.
(3)  The notice must state the FCA's reasons for the proposed refusal.
(4)  If the FCA decides to refuse to approve a prospectus, it must give the applicant written notice.
(5)  The notice must—
  (a)  give the FCA's reasons for refusing the application; and
  (b)  inform the applicant of his right to refer the matter to the Tribunal.
(6)  If the FCA refuses to approve a prospectus, the applicant may refer the matter to the Tribunal.
(7)  In this section "prospectus" includes a supplementary prospectus.][60]

Under section 87D, an applicant will receive written notice from the FCA upon the approval, proposed refusal or refusal of an application for approval of a prospectus. In the case of a proposed refusal or a refusal, the FCA must provide reasons. If the FCA refuses to approve a prospectus, the applicant may refer the matter to the Tribunal.  **53.87D.02**

In practice, if the FCA has any concerns about a prospectus, it will raise them during the exchange of drafts and comments which precedes the formal application, rather than employing the public rejection process.  **53.87D.03**

### *[Transfer of application for approval of a prospectus ]*[61]

### [87E  Transfer by FCA of application for approval    53.87E.01

(1)  The FCA may transfer an application for the approval of a prospectus or a supplementary prospectus to the competent authority of another EEA State ("the transferee authority").

---

[59]  Ss.84–87R substituted for ss.84–87 by Prospectus Regulations 2005/1433 Sch.1 para.5 (1 July 2005)
[60]  Ss.84–87R substituted for ss.84–87 by Prospectus Regulations 2005/1433 Sch.1 para.5 (1 July 2005)
[61]  Ss.84–87R substituted for ss.84–87 by Prospectus Regulations 2005/1433 Sch.1 para.5 (1 July 2005)

(2) Before doing so, the FCA must obtain the agreement of the transferee authority [and notify ESMA.][62]

(3) The FCA must inform the applicant of the transfer within 3 working days beginning with the first working day after the date of the transfer.

(4) On making a transfer under subsection (1), the FCA ceases to have functions under this Part in relation to the application transferred.][63]

**53.87E.02**    This section permits the FCA to transfer an application for approval of a prospectus (or supplementary prospectus) to the competent authority of another EEA State. Before making a transfer, the FCA must obtain the agreement of the transferee authority and notify ESMA. Once a transfer has been made and the applicant informed, the FCA will have no functions under Part 6 in relation to the transferred application.

**53.87E.03**    Article 13(1) of the Prospectus Directive states that no prospectus shall be published until it has been approved by the competent authority of the home Member State. Under Article 2(1)(m)(i), an EEA issuer's home Member State will be the Member State in which the issuer has its registered office. Under Article 2(1)(m)(ii), issuers of non-equity securities with a denomination of at least €1,000 as well as issuers of convertibles and Global Depositary Receipts (subject to certain conditions) may choose their home Member State. Recital 8 of the Amending Directive proposes that the Commission consider the extending this freedom of choice to issuers of lower denomination non-equity securities.

**53.87E.04**    In practice, transfers to another competent authority will be made at the request of the applicant. Under PR 3.1.12R, requests must be made in writing at least 10 working days before the date the transfer is sought. A request should state the name of the proposed alternative competent authority and the reasons for the proposed transfer. A (substantially complete) copy of the draft prospectus should be attached. The FCA will look favourably on applications where the issuer does not have securities listed in the UK, is not making an offer in the UK and has most of its shareholders outside of the UK. However, where the FCA has a "clear regulatory interest", a transfer request is unlikely to be granted.[64]

**53.87E.05**    Sections 87E and 87F are of obvious application to groups of companies which operate in multiple Member States. In particular, the ability to transfer applications has allowed issuers of non-equity securities to use a single issuance programme for several issuers within a pan-European group.

**53.87F.01**    [87F  Transfer to FCA of application for approval

(1) Where the FCA agrees to the transfer to it of an application for the approval of a prospectus made to the competent authority of another EEA State—

(a) the United Kingdom is to be treated for the purposes of this Part as the home State in relation to the issuer of the transferable securities to which the prospectus relates, and

(b) this Part applies to the application as if it had been made to the FCA but with the modification in subsection (2).

(2) Section 87C applies as if the date of the transfer were the date on which the application was received by the FCA.][65]

**53.87F.02**    Section 87F provides for the receipt of an application for approval of a prospectus (or supplementary prospectus) from the competent authority of another Member State. Any such application will be processed by the FCA in accordance with Part 6, as if the UK were the home State of the issuer in question. "Home State" is defined in section 102C as an issuer's home Member State for the purposes of the Prospectus Directive.

**53.87F.03**    Subsection (2) clarifies that the section 87C timetable will run from the date on which the application was received by the FCA.

*[Supplementary prospectus ]*[66]

**53.87G.01**    [87G  Supplementary prospectus

(1) Subsection (2) applies if, during the relevant period, there arises or is noted a significant new factor, material mistake or inaccuracy relating to the information included in a prospectus approved by the FCA.

---

[62]  Inserted by Financial Services (Omnibus 1 Directive) Regulations 2012/916 reg.2(3) (16 April 2012)

[63]  Ss.84-87R substituted for ss.84-87 by Prospectus Regulations 2005/1433 Sch.1 para.5 (1 July 2005)

[64]  pp.12-13, UKLA Publications, List!, Issue No. 18 March 2008.

[65]  Ss.84-87R substituted for ss.84-87 by Prospectus Regulations 2005/1433 Sch.1 para.5 (1 July 2005)

[66]  Ss.84-87R substituted for ss.84-87 by Prospectus Regulations 2005/1433 Sch.1 para.5 (1 July 2005)

(2) The person on whose application the prospectus was approved must, in accordance with prospectus rules, submit a supplementary prospectus containing details of the new factor, mistake or inaccuracy to the FCA for its approval.

(3) The relevant period begins when the prospectus is approved and ends—
  (a) with the closure of the offer of the transferable securities to which the prospectus relates; or
  (b) when trading in those securities on a regulated market begins.

[(3A) But where the prospectus relates both to an offer of transferable securities to the public and the admission of those securities to trading on a regulated market, subsection (3) does not apply and the relevant period begins when the prospectus is approved and ends with the later of—
  (a) the closure of the offer to the public to which the prospectus relates, or
  (b) the time when trading in those securities on a regulated markets begins.][67]

(4) "Significant" means significant for the purposes of making an informed assessment of the kind mentioned in section 87A(2).

(5) Any person responsible for the prospectus who is aware of any new factor, mistake or inaccuracy which may require the submission of a supplementary prospectus in accordance with subsection (2) must give notice of it to—
  (a) the issuer of the transferable securities to which the prospectus relates, and
  (b) the person on whose application the prospectus was approved.

(6) A supplementary prospectus must provide sufficient information to correct any mistake or inaccuracy which gave rise to the need for it.

(7) Subsection (1) applies also to information contained in any supplementary prospectus published under this section.][68]

An applicant will need to submit a supplementary prospectus to the FCA if a significant new factor **53.87G.02** arises, or a material mistake or inaccuracy is noted, in connection with information included in an approved prospectus during the "relevant period". Under subsection (6), a supplementary prospectus must provide sufficient information to correct the mistake or inaccuracy which necessitated it. Importantly, the publication of a supplementary prospectus may give investors who have agreed to buy or subscribe for securities the right to withdraw in accordance with section 87Q.

Under subsection (3), the relevant period begins with the approval of the prospectus and ends with **53.87G.03** either the closing of the public offer or the beginning of trading on a regulated market. Subsection (3A), inserted by the 2012 Regulations, provides that, where a prospectus relates to securities that are being offered to the public and admitted to trading on a regulated market, the relevant period does not end until both events have taken place.

A supplementary prospectus must be submitted to the FCA in accordance with PR 3.4. Pursuant to PR **53.87G.04** 3.4.3R, the submission must be made as soon as practicable. PR 3.4.2R states that a supplementary prospectus must also, if necessary, include an amendment or supplement to the prospectus summary. If the prospectus has been passported, the amended summary may require translation.

Under subsection (5), any person responsible for the prospectus (in accordance with PR 5.5) who is **53.87G.05** aware of any new factor, mistake or inaccuracy must notify both the issuer of the securities and, where applicable, the original applicant.

Section 87G also applies to information contained in a supplementary prospectus. **53.87G.06**

Under section 90(4), a breach of section 87G will result in civil liability to any person who acquires the **53.87G.07** securities in question and suffers a loss as a result of the failure to publish a supplementary prospectus.

## *[Passporting ]*[69]

## [87H  Prospectus approved in another EEA State **53.87H.01**

(1) A prospectus approved by the competent authority of an EEA State other than the United Kingdom is not an approved prospectus for the purposes of section 85 unless that authority has [notified ESMA and ][70] provided the FCA with—
  (a) a certificate of approval;
  (b) a copy of the prospectus as approved; and
  (c) if requested by the FCA, a translation of the summary of the prospectus.

(2) A document is not a certificate of approval unless it states that the prospectus—
  (a) has been drawn up in accordance with the prospectus directive; and

---

[67]  Added by Prospectus Regulations 2012/1538 reg.5(1) (1 July 2012)
[68]  Ss.84-87R substituted for ss.84-87 by Prospectus Regulations 2005/1433 Sch.1 para.5 (1 July 2005)
[69]  Ss.84-87R substituted for ss.84-87 by Prospectus Regulations 2005/1433 Sch.1 para.5 (1 July 2005)
[70]  Inserted by Financial Services (Omnibus 1 Directive) Regulations 2012/916 reg.2(4)(a) (16 April 2012)

        (b)  has been approved, in accordance with that directive, by the competent authority providing the certificate.

    (3)  A document is not a certificate of approval unless it states whether (and, if so, why) the competent authority providing it authorised, in accordance with the prospectus directive, the omission from the prospectus of information which would otherwise have been required to be included.

    [(3A)  The FCA must publish on its website a list of certificates of approval provided to it in accordance with this section.

    (3B)  The list referred to in subsection (3A) must—

        (a)  be kept up-to-date,

        (b)  retain items on it for a period of at least 12 months, and

        (c)  include hyperlinks to any certificate of approval and prospectus published on the website of—

            (i)  the competent authority of the EEA State which provided the certificate,

            (ii)  the issuer, or

            (iii)  the regulated market where admission to trading is sought.][71]

    (4)  "Prospectus" includes a supplementary prospectus.][72]

**53.87H.02** This section facilitates the "passporting" of prospectuses that have been approved by the competent authority of another Member State into the UK. The term is derived from the idea that an approved prospectus, regardless of the competent authority to which it was submitted, should act as a "passport" for a public offer or admission to trading in any other EEA country. The efficient passporting of prospectuses was one of the principal objectives of the Prospectus Directive.[73] Although passporting was permitted under the previous regime, the competent authority of a target Member State could require both the disclosure of additional information and the translation of the entire document. The procedure was complex, costly and time-consuming and consequently few issuers were prepared to undertake pan-European offerings.

**53.87H.03** A prospectus approved by another competent authority will become an approved prospectus for the purposes of section 85 if that authority fulfils the requirements of section 87H(1). In each case, the authority must notify ESMA that the prospectus is being passported and provide the FCA with a certificate of approval and a copy of the prospectus. The FCA may request a translation of the prospectus summary, however, it cannot require the translation of the entire document or impose any other conditions. PR 4.1.6R indicates that, if an offer is being made in the UK, the FCA will always require that a foreign language prospectus summary be translated into English.

**53.87H.04** It is noted that the securities to which a passported prospectus relates will need to be admitted to the Official List before they can be admitted to trading on a market in the UK. As the listing and prospectus regimes are separate, compliance with the Prospective Directive does not guarantee that the issuer or the securities will meet the eligibility requirements contained in the Listing Rules. Consequently, the UK Listing Authority invites applicants who intend to seek admission to the Official List to submit an eligibility letter and a draft of the proposed prospectus before a formal application for approval is made in the applicant's home Member State.[74]

**53.87H.05** Subsections (2) and (3) set out the requirements for a certificate of approval. A certificate of approval must state that the prospectus has been drawn up and approved by the competent authority in accordance with the Prospectus Directive. It must also record whether the authority authorised the omission of any information.

**53.87H.06** New subsections (3A) and (3B) were added by the Financial Services (Omnibus 1 Directive) Regulations 2012/916. These subsections oblige the FCA to publish on its websites an up-to-date list of the certificates of approval it has received in the last 12 months. Where a copy of a certificate of approval and/or the associated prospectus is available online, a hyperlink should be provided.

**53.87I.01** [87I  **Provision of information to host Member State**

    (1)  The FCA must, if requested to do so, supply the competent authority of a specified EEA State with—

        (a)  a certificate of approval;

        (b)  a copy of the specified prospectus (as approved by the FCA); and

---

[71]  Added by Financial Services (Omnibus 1 Directive) Regulations 2012/916 reg.2(4)(b) (16 April 2012)

[72]  Ss.84-87R substituted for ss.84-87 by Prospectus Regulations 2005/1433 Sch.1 para.5 (1 July 2005)

[73]  Recital 1, Prospectus Directive (2003/71/EC)

[74]  pp.1-2, UKLA Procedural Note (Eligibility Process) – consultation, July 2012 (http://www.fsa.gov.uk/pubs/ukla/ukla_eligibility_review_process.pdf)

    (c)  a translation of the summary of the specified prospectus (if the request states that one has been requested by the [ … ]⁷⁵ competent authority).

[(1A)  If the FCA supplies a certificate of approval to the competent authority of the specified EEA State, it must also supply a copy of that certificate [ to— ]⁷⁶

    [(a)  the person who made the request under this section; and

    (b)  ESMA. ]⁷⁷ ]⁷⁸

(2)  Only the following may make a request under this section—

    (a)  the issuer of the transferable securities to which the specified prospectus relates;

    (b)  a person who wishes to offer the transferable securities to which the specified prospectus relates to the public in an EEA State other than (or as well as) the United Kingdom;

    (c)  a person requesting the admission of the transferable securities to which the specified prospectus relates to a regulated market situated or operating in an EEA State other than (or as well as) the United Kingdom.

(3)  A certificate of approval must state that the prospectus—

    (a)  has been drawn up in accordance with this Part and the prospectus directive; and

    (b)  has been approved, in accordance with those provisions, by the FCA.

(4)  A certificate of approval must state whether (and, if so, why) the FCA authorised, in accordance with section 87B, the omission from the prospectus of information which would otherwise have been required to be included.

(5)  The FCA must comply with a request under this section—

    (a)  if the prospectus has been approved before the request is made, within 3 working days beginning with [ the date the request is received ]⁷⁹ ; or

    (b)  if the request is submitted with an application for the approval of the prospectus, on the first working day after the date on which it approves the prospectus.

(6)  "Prospectus" includes a supplementary prospectus.

(7)  "Specified" means specified in a request made for the purposes of this section.] ⁸⁰

Section 87I set outs the procedure for passporting a prospectus that has been approved by the FCA.   **53.87I.02**
Under subsection (2), a prospectus can only be passported at the request of the issuer of the securities, a person who wishes to offer the securities in another EEA state or a person requesting the admission of the securities to a regulated market in another EEA state.

If the FCA is asked to passport a prospectus, it must furnish the specified competent authority with a   **53.87I.03**
certificate of approval and send copies to the applicant and to ESMA. It must also supply the specified authority with a copy of the prospectus and, on request, a translation of the prospectus summary. In the case of a pre-approved prospectus, the FCA must comply with the request within three working days of receiving it. If a request for passporting is submitted with an application for approval of a prospectus, the FCA must comply by the first working day after the date of approval.

Subsections (3) and (4) set out the requirements for a certificate of approval. A certificate of approval   **53.87I.04**
must state that the prospectus has been drawn up and approved by the competent authority in accordance with Part 6 and the Prospectus Directive. It must also record whether the authority authorised the omission of any information under section 87B.

*[Transferable securities: powers of FCA]*⁸¹

### [87J  Requirements imposed as condition of approval                              53.87J.01

(1)  As a condition of approving a prospectus, the FCA may by notice in writing—

    (a)  require the inclusion in the prospectus of such supplementary information necessary for investor protection as the FCA may specify;

    (b)  require a person controlling, or controlled by, the applicant to provide specified information or documents;

    (c)  require an auditor or manager of the applicant to provide specified information or documents;

    (d)  require a financial intermediary commissioned to assist either in carrying out the offer to the public of the transferable securities to which the prospectus relates or in requesting their admission to trading on a regulated market, to provide specified information or documents.

---

⁷⁵  Repealed by Financial Services Act 2012 c.21 s.16(10)(a)(iii) (24 January 2013; 1 April 2013)
⁷⁶  Substituted by Prospectus Regulations 2012/1538 reg.6(a) (1 July 2012)
⁷⁷  Substituted by Prospectus Regulations 2012/1538 reg.6(a) (1 July 2012)
⁷⁸  Added by Financial Services (Omnibus 1 Directive) Regulations 2012/916 reg.2(5) (16 April 2012)
⁷⁹  Substituted by Prospectus Regulations 2012/1538 reg.6(b) (1 July 2012)
⁸⁰  Ss.84-87R substituted for ss.84-87 by Prospectus Regulations 2005/1433 Sch.1 para.5 (1 July 2005)
⁸¹  Ss.84-87R substituted for ss.84-87 by Prospectus Regulations 2005/1433 Sch.1 para.5 (1 July 2005)

(2) "Specified" means specified in the notice.
(3) "Prospectus" includes a supplementary prospectus.][82]

**53.87J.02** Section 87J sets out the conditions that the FCA may impose on the approval of a prospectus. Under subsection (1)(a), if information that the FCA deems necessary for investor protection has been omitted from the prospectus, the applicant may be required to include it. Under subsections (1)(b), (1)(c) and (1)(d), the FCA may require "a person controlling, or controlled by, the applicant", "an auditor or manager of the applicant" or a financial intermediary commissioned by the applicant to provide specified information or documents. Any requirements imposed by the FCA under section 87J must be set out in a written notice.

**53.87J.03** In practice, if the FCA requires supplementary information to be included in a prospectus, it will alert the applicant during the exchange of drafts and comments. Consequently, if information is required from a third party, this can be obtained by the applicant before the prospectus is submitted to FCA and without the need for formal notices.

**53.87K.01** [87K **Power to suspend or prohibit offer to the public**

(1) This section applies where a person ("the offeror") has made an offer of transferable securities to the public in the United Kingdom ("the offer").
(2) If the FCA has reasonable grounds for suspecting that an applicable provision has been infringed, it may—
   (a) require the offeror to suspend the offer for a period not exceeding 10 working days;
   (b) require a person not to advertise the offer, or to take such steps as the FCA may specify to suspend any existing advertisement of the offer, for a period not exceeding 10 working days.
(3) If the FCA has reasonable grounds for suspecting that it is likely that an applicable provision will be infringed, it may require the offeror to withdraw the offer.
(4) If the FCA finds that an applicable provision has been infringed, it may require the offeror to withdraw the offer.
(5) "An applicable provision" means—
   (a) a provision of this Part,
   (b) a provision contained in prospectus rules,
   (c) any other provision made in accordance with the prospectus directive,
applicable in relation to the offer.][83]

**53.87K.02** Section 87K gives the FCA the power to suspend or prohibit a public offer (or an advertisement) if it finds, or suspects, that an "applicable provision" has been infringed. Under subsection (5), an "applicable provision" is a provision of Part 6, a provision of the prospectus rules or any other provision made in accordance with the Prospectus Directive (such as a provision of the Prospectus Regulation) that is applicable in relation to the offer to the public.

**53.87K.03** Under subsection (4), if the FCA finds that an applicable provision has been infringed, it may require the offeror to withdraw the offer. Under subsection (3), the FCA may do the same if it has reasonable grounds for suspecting that it is likely that an applicable provision will be infringed.

**53.87K.04** Under subsection (2), if the FCA has reasonable grounds for suspecting an infringement has occurred, it may require the offeror to suspend the offer for up to 10 working days. The FCA may also prevent the advertisement of the offer for 10 working days. The FCA can use such period to determine whether an infringement has in fact taken place and, if so, consider whether to use its powers under subsection (4).

**53.87K.05** PR 5.6.3G states that the FCA will use its powers under sections 87K and 87L in order to protect investors and ensure the smooth operation of the market.

**53.87L.01** [87L **Power to suspend or prohibit admission to trading on a regulated market**

(1) This section applies where a person has requested the admission of transferable securities to trading on a regulated market situated or operating in the United Kingdom.
(2) If the FCA has reasonable grounds for suspecting that an applicable provision has been infringed and the securities have not yet been admitted to trading on the regulated market in question, it may—
   (a) require the person requesting admission to suspend the request for a period not exceeding 10 working days;

---

[82] Ss.84–87R substituted for ss.84–87 by Prospectus Regulations 2005/1433 Sch.1 para.5 (1 July 2005)
[83] Ss.84–87R substituted for ss.84–87 by Prospectus Regulations 2005/1433 Sch.1 para.5 (1 July 2005)

    (b)   require a person not to advertise the securities to which it relates, or to take such steps as the FCA may specify to suspend any existing advertisement in connection with those securities, for a period not exceeding 10 working days.

(3)  If the FCA has reasonable grounds for suspecting that an applicable provision has been infringed and the securities have been admitted to trading on the regulated market in question, it may—

    (a)   require the market operator to suspend trading in the securities for a period not exceeding 10 working days;

    (b)   require a person not to advertise the securities, or to take such steps as the FCA may specify to suspend any existing advertisement in connection with those securities, for a period not exceeding 10 working days.

(4)  If the FCA finds that an applicable provision has been infringed, it may require the market operator to prohibit trading in the securities on the regulated market in question.

(5)  "An applicable provision" means—

    (a)   a provision of this Part,

    (b)   a provision contained in prospectus rules,

    (c)   any other provision made in accordance with the prospectus directive,

applicable in relation to the admission of the transferable securities to trading on the regulated market in question.][84]

---

Section 87L gives the FCA the power to suspend or prohibit admission to trading on a regulated market (or an advertisement) if it finds, or suspects, that an "applicable provision" has been infringed. Under subsection (5), an "applicable provision" is a provision of Part 6, a provision of the prospectus rules or any other provision made in accordance with the Prospectus Directive that is applicable in relation to the admission of securities to trading on the regulated market in question. In effect, section 87L is to section 87K what section 85(2) is to section 85(1).   **53.87L.02**

If the FCA finds that an applicable provision has been infringed, it may require the relevant market operator to prohibit trading of the securities concerned under subsection (4).   **53.87L.03**

If the FCA only has reasonable grounds for suspecting an infringement, its powers are determined by whether the securities are admitted to trading at the relevant time. Under subsection (2), which applies if the securities are yet to be admitted, the FCA may require the applicant to suspend its request for admission for up to 10 working days. Under subsection (3), which is engaged if the securities are already admitted to trading, the FCA may require the market operator to suspend trading for the same period. In each case, the FCA may also prevent the advertisement of the securities for 10 working days.   **53.87L.04**

It is notable that sections 87K and 87L strike slightly different balances between investor protection and the interests of offerors and applicants. Section 87L does not contain an equivalent provision to section 87K(3); consequently, even if the FCA has reasonable grounds to suspect that an applicable provision is likely to be infringed in the future, it is unable to exercise its powers under section 87L.   **53.87L.05**

## [87M  Public censure of issuer                                                   53.87M.01

(1)  If the FCA finds that—

    (a)   an issuer of transferable securities,

    (b)   a person offering transferable securities to the public, or

    (c)   a person requesting the admission of transferable securities to trading on a regulated market,

is failing or has failed to comply with his obligations under an applicable provision, it may publish a statement to that effect.

(2)  If the FCA proposes to publish a statement, it must give the person a warning notice setting out the terms of the proposed statement.

(3)  If, after considering any representations made in response to the warning notice, the FCA decides to make the proposed statement, it must give the person a decision notice setting out the terms of the statement.

(4)  "An applicable provision" means—

    (a)   a provision of this Part,

    (b)   a provision contained in prospectus rules,

    (c)   any other provision made in accordance with the prospectus directive,

applicable to a prospectus in relation to the transferable securities in question.

(5)  "Prospectus" includes a supplementary prospectus.][85]

---

This section provides that the FCA may publish a statement of censure if an issuer, offeror or applicant for admission of securities to trading is failing or has failed to comply with its obligations under an   **53.87M.02**

---

[84]  Ss.84-87R substituted for ss.84-87 by Prospectus Regulations 2005/1433 Sch.1 para.5 (1 July 2005)
[85]  Ss.84-87R substituted for ss.84-87 by Prospectus Regulations 2005/1433 Sch.1 para.5 (1 July 2005)

applicable provision. Under subsection (4), an "applicable provision" is a provision of Part 6, a provision of the prospectus rules or any other provision made in accordance with the Prospectus Directive that is applicable to a prospectus in relation to the securities in question.

**53.87M.03**  Before publishing a statement of censure, the FCA must provide the wrongdoer with a warning notice and, having considered any representations made in response, a decision notice. The warning notice and decision notice should set out the terms of the proposed statement and final statement respectively.

**53.87M.04**  The FCA publishes decision notices on its website. The absence of decision notices relating to section 87M suggests that the power of censure has rarely been used, or that warning notices have dealt with any non-compliance effectively.

**53.87N.01**  [87N  Right to refer matters to the Tribunal

    (1)  A person to whom a decision notice is given under section 87M may refer the matter to the Tribunal.

    (2)  A person to whom a notice is given under section 87O may refer the matter to the Tribunal.][86]

**53.87N.02**  Subsection (1) permits a person to make a reference to the Tribunal on receipt of a decision notice setting out the terms of a statement of censure under section 87M(3) (but not a warning notice setting out proposed terms under 87M(2)).

**53.87N.03**  Subsection (2) permits a person to make a reference to the Tribunal on receipt of any notice given under section 87O. The FCA is required to give notice under section 87O whenever it proposes to, or exercises with immediate effect, its powers under sections 87K and 87L, or decides to maintain, vary or revoke an earlier decision.

**53.87N.04**  It should be noted that this section will not apply when the FCA is exercising its powers under sections 87K and 87L pursuant to a request from another competent authority.

**53.87N.05**  References under this section are made directly to the Tax and Chancery Chamber of the Upper Tribunal.

**53.87O.01**  [87O  Procedure under sections 87K and 87L

    (1)  A requirement under section 87K or 87L takes effect—

        (a)  immediately, if the notice under subsection (2) states that that is the case;

        (b)  in any other case, on such date as may be specified in that notice.

    (2)  If the FCA—

        (a)  proposes to exercise the powers in section 87K or 87L in relation to a person, or

        (b)  exercises any of those powers in relation to a person with immediate effect,

        it must give that person written notice.

    (3)  The notice must—

        (a)  give details of the FCA's action or proposed action;

        (b)  state the FCA's reasons for taking the action in question and choosing the date on which it took effect or takes effect;

        (c)  inform the recipient that he may make representations to the FCA within such period as may be specified by the notice (whether or not he has referred the matter to the Tribunal);

        (d)  inform him of the date on which the action took effect or takes effect; and

        (e)  inform him of his right to refer the matter to the Tribunal.

    (4)  The FCA may extend the period within which representations may be made to it.

    (5)  If, having considered any representations made to it, the FCA decides to maintain, vary or revoke its earlier decision, it must give written notice to that effect to the person mentioned in subsection (2).

    (6)  A notice given under subsection (5) must inform that person, where relevant, of his right to refer the matter to the Tribunal.

    (7)  If a notice informs a person of his right to refer a matter to the Tribunal, it must give an indication of the procedure on such a reference.

    (8)  If a notice under this section relates to the exercise of the power conferred by section 87L(3), the notice must also be given to the person at whose request the transferable securities were admitted to trading on the regulated market.][87]

---

[86]  Ss.84-87R substituted for ss.84-87 by Prospectus Regulations 2005/1433 Sch.1 para.5 (1 July 2005)
[87]  Ss.84-87R substituted for ss.84-87 by Prospectus Regulations 2005/1433 Sch.1 para.5 (1 July 2005)

This section obliges the FCA to give written notice to any person in relation to whom it exercises, or proposes to exercise, the powers under section 87K or 87L.  **53.87O.02**

Under section 87K or 87L, a requirement can take effect either immediately or on a future date, as specified in the notice. The detailed requirements for the notice are set out in subsection (3). As well as the effective date, the notice must contain details of the FCA's action (or proposed action) and give reasons for taking it and choosing the effective date. It must also inform the recipient of his rights to make representations to the FCA within a specified period and to refer the matter to the Tribunal. These rights are not mutually exclusive.  **53.87O.03**

If the FCA receives representations from the recipient of a notice given under this section, it must render a second written notice stating whether it has maintained, varied or revoked its earlier decision. Where relevant, the second notice should reiterate the recipient's right to refer the matter to the Tribunal.  **53.87O.04**

Subsection (8) provides that, if the FCA requires a market operator to suspend trading in certain securities under section 87L(3), it must also give a copy of the notice required by section 87O(2) to the original applicant.  **53.87O.05**

[87P  **Exercise of powers at request of competent authority of another EEA State**  53.87P.01

    (1)  This section applies if—
        (a)  the competent authority of an EEA State other than the United Kingdom has approved a prospectus,
        (b)  the transferable securities to which the prospectus relates have been offered to the public in the United Kingdom or their admission to trading on a regulated market has been requested, and
        (c)  that competent authority makes a request that the FCA assist it in the performance of its functions under the law of that State in connection with the prospectus directive.
    (2)  For the purpose of complying with the request mentioned in subsection (1)(c), the powers conferred by sections 87K and 87L may be exercised as if the prospectus were one which had been approved by the FCA.
    (3)  Section 87N does not apply to an exercise of those powers as a result of this section.
    (4)  Section 87O does apply to such an exercise of those powers but with the omission of subsections (3)(e), (6) and (7).][88]

Section 87P deals with the situation where a prospectus approved by the competent authority of another EEA State has been passported into the UK and the securities to which it relates have been offered to the public or admitted to trading on a regulated market.  **53.87P.02**

In the ordinary course, the FCA would be unable to exercise its powers under sections 87K and 87L in respect of such securities. However, section 87P permits the FCA to exercise these powers if it is acting in compliance with a request made by the competent authority that approved the prospectus. In accordance with subsections (3) and (4), when the FCA exercises its section 87K and 87L powers pursuant to such a request, the offeror or person requesting admission may not refer the matter to the Tribunal. Accordingly, the FCA is not required to set out the referral process in notices delivered pursuant to section 87O.  **53.87P.03**

*[Rights of investors]*[89]

[87Q  **Right of investor to withdraw**  53.87Q.01

    (1)  Where a person agrees to buy or subscribe for transferable securities in circumstances where the final offer price or the amount of transferable securities to be offered to the public is not included in the prospectus, he may withdraw his acceptance before the end of the withdrawal period.
    (2)  The withdrawal period—
        (a)  begins with the investor's acceptance; and
        (b)  ends at the end of the second working day after the date on which the FCA is informed of the information in accordance with section 87A(7).
    (3)  Subsection (1) does not apply if the prospectus contains—
        (a)  in the case of the amount of transferable securities to be offered to the public, the criteria or conditions (or both) according to which that element will be determined, or
        (b)  in the case of price, the criteria or conditions (or both) according to which that element will be determined or the maximum price.

---

[88]  Ss.84-87R substituted for ss.84-87 by Prospectus Regulations 2005/1433 Sch.1 para.5 (1 July 2005)
[89]  Ss.84-87R substituted for ss.84-87 by Prospectus Regulations 2005/1433 Sch.1 para.5 (1 July 2005)

[(4) A person ("P") may withdraw P's acceptance of an offer of transferable securities to the public before the specified time where the conditions in subsection (5) are satisfied.][90]

[(5) The conditions are that—

    (a) a prospectus which relates to an offer of transferable securities to the public has been published;

    (b) a supplementary prospectus has been published;

    (c) prior to the publication of the supplementary prospectus, P agreed to buy or subscribe for transferable securities to which the offer relates; and

    (d) the significant new factor, material mistake or inaccuracy referred to in section 87G(1) which caused the supplementary prospectus to be published arose before delivery of the securities.

(6) The specified time is—

    (a) the end of the second working day after the day on which the supplementary prospectus was published; or

    (b) such later time as may be specified in the supplementary prospectus.][91] ][92]

**53.87Q.02** The Prospectus Directive grants investors withdrawal rights in two distinct situations. First, when the final offer price and amount of securities to be offered are not included in the prospectus.[93] Secondly, when an issuer or offeror is required to publish a supplementary prospectus.[94] Both provisions were implemented through section 87R.

**53.87Q.03** Under subsections (1) and (2), if an issuer or offeror publishes a base prospectus that omits either the final offer price or the amount of securities to be offered, investors who agree to buy or subscribe for the securities will be able to withdraw their acceptance until the end of the second working day after the FCA is advised of the missing information in accordance with section 87A(7)(a). The risk of investors withdrawing after the publication of the final terms is one that few issuers or offerors will be prepared to take. Therefore a compromise position is set out at subsection (3). The withdrawal rights under subsection (1) will not apply providing that the base prospectus contains the criteria or conditions according to which the piece or pieces of missing information will be determined. Instead of providing the criteria and conditions which will determine the final offer price, the issuer or offeror can opt to fix a maximum price.

**53.87Q.04** The Amending Directive has made changes to an investor's right to withdraw on publication of a supplementary prospectus. These changes are reflected by the new subsections (4), (5) and (6), which were inserted by the 2012 Regulations. Subsection (5)(a) provides that an investor may only withdraw if the original prospectus related to a public offer. Under the previous regime, withdrawal rights were triggered by a supplementary prospectus irrespective of whether there had been an offer to the public. Moreover, withdrawal rights were previously triggered by a supplement published prior to admission to trading, even if the offer had closed and the securities been delivered. This position was presumably deemed too generous to investors, so subsection 5(d) confirms that withdrawal rights will only be available before the delivery of securities.

**53.87Q.05** The Amending Directive also sought to harmonise the timeframe in which an investor could exercise its right to withdraw. The Prospectus Directive originally gave Member States discretion over the time limit for withdrawal, provided that it was not shorter than two days. Consequently, the timeframe varied from State to State. The Amending Directive fixes a time limit of two working days after the publication of the supplement, but allows the issuer or offeror to prescribe a longer period. This provision is implemented by subsection (6).

**53.87Q.06** Article 16(2) of the Prospectus Directive (as amended by the Amending Directive) provides that the final date of the right of withdrawal should be stated in a supplementary prospectus. This provision is not reflected in either the Act or the prospectus rules, however, issuers should arguably include the final date as a matter of best practice.

---

[90] Substituted by Prospectus Regulations 2012/1538 reg.5(2)(a) (1 July 2012)

[91] Added by Prospectus Regulations 2012/1538 reg.5(2)(b) (1 July 2012)

[92] Ss.84-87R substituted for ss.84-87 by Prospectus Regulations 2005/1433 Sch.1 para.5 (1 July 2005)

[93] Article 8, Prospectus Directive (2003/71/EC)

[94] Article 16, Prospectus Directive (2003/71/EC)

*[Registered investors]*[95]

[87R [...][96]                                                                                    53.87R.01

## Sponsors

**88 Sponsors.**                                                                           53.88.01

(1) Listing rules may require a person to make arrangements with a sponsor for the performance by the sponsor of such services in relation to him as may be specified in the rules.

(2) "Sponsor" means a person approved by the FCA for the purposes of the rules.

(3) Listing rules made by virtue of subsection (1) may–

(a) provide for the FCA to maintain a list of sponsors;

(b) specify services which must be performed by a sponsor;

(c) impose requirements on a sponsor in relation to the provision of services or specified services;

(d) specify the circumstances in which a person is qualified for being approved as a sponsor;

[(e) provide for limitations or other restrictions to be imposed on the services to which an approval relates (whether or not the approval has already been granted);

(f) provide for the approval of a sponsor to be suspended on the application of the sponsor.][97]

(4) If the FCA proposes–

(a) to refuse a person's application [under sponsor rules][98],

[(aa) to impose limitations or other restrictions on the services to which a person's approval relates, ][99] or

(b) to cancel a person's approval as a sponsor [ otherwise than at his request ][100],

it must give him a warning notice.

(5) If, after considering any representations made in response to the warning notice, the FCA decides–

(a) to grant the application [under sponsor rules][101],

[(aa) not to impose limitations or other restrictions on the services to which a person's approval relates, or][102]

(b) not to cancel the approval,

it must give the person concerned, and any person to whom a copy of the warning notice was given, written notice of its decision.

(6) If, after considering any representations made in response to the warning notice, the FCA decides–

(a) to refuse to grant the application [under sponsor rules][103],

[(aa) to impose limitations or other restrictions on the services to which a person's approval relates, or][104]

(b) to cancel the approval,

it must give the person concerned a decision notice.

(7) A person to whom a decision notice is given under this section may refer the matter to the Tribunal.

[(8) In this section any reference to an application under sponsor rules means –

(a) an application for approval as a sponsor,

(b) an application for the suspension of an approval as a sponsor,

(c) an application for the withdrawal of the suspension of an approval as a sponsor, or

(d) an application for the withdrawal or variation of a limitation or other restriction on the services to which a sponsor's approval relates.][105]

---

[95] Ss.84-87R substituted for ss.84-87 by Prospectus Regulations 2005/1433 Sch.1 para.5 (1 July 2005)

[96] Repealed by Prospectus Regulations 2012/1538 reg.3(3) (1 July 2012)

[97] Inserted by Financial Services Act 2012 c.21 s.18(2)(a) (24 January 2013; 1 April 2013)

[98] Substituted by Financial Services Act 2012 c.21 s.18(2)(b) (24 January 2013; 1 April 2013)

[99] Inserted by Financial Services Act 2012 c.21 s.18(2)(c) (24 January 2013; 1 April 2013)

[100] Inserted by Regulatory Reform (Financial Services and Markets Act 2000) Order 2007/1973 art.9 (12 July 2007)

[101] Substituted by Financial Services Act 2012 c.21 s.18(2)(d) (24 January 2013; 1 April 2013)

[102] Inserted by Financial Services Act 2012 c.21 s.18(2)(e) (24 January 2013; 1 April 2013)

[103] Substituted by Financial Services Act 2012 c.21 s.18(2)(f) (24 January 2013; 1 April 2013)

[104] Inserted by Financial Services Act 2012 c.21 s.18(2)(g) (24 January 2013; 1 April 2013)

[105] Inserted by Financial Services Act 2012 c.21 s.18(2)(h) (24 January 2013; 1 April 2013)

**53.88A.01**    **[88A  Disciplinary powers: contravention of s.88(3)(c) or (e)**

    (1)  The FCA may take action against a sponsor under this section if it considers that the sponsor has contravened a requirement or restriction imposed on the sponsor by rules made as a result of section 88(3)(c) or (e).

    (2)  If the FCA is entitled to take action under this section against a sponsor, it may do one or more of the following—

        (a)  impose a penalty on the sponsor of such amount as it considers appropriate;

        (b)  suspend, for such period as it considers appropriate, the sponsor's approval;

        (c)  impose, for such period as it considers appropriate, such limitations or other restrictions in relation to the performance of services to which the sponsor's approval relates as it considers appropriate;

        (d)  publish a statement to the effect that the sponsor has contravened a requirement or restriction imposed on the sponsor by rules made as a result of section 88(3)(c) or (e).

    (3)  The period for which a suspension or restriction is to have effect may not exceed 12 months.

    (4)  A suspension may relate only to the performance in specified circumstances of a service to which the approval relates.

    (5)  A restriction may, in particular, be imposed so as to require the sponsor to take, or refrain from taking, specified action.

    (6)  The FCA may—

        (a)  withdraw a suspension or restriction; or

        (b)  vary a suspension or restriction so as to reduce the period for which it has effect or otherwise to limit its effect.

    (7)  The FCA may not take action against a sponsor under this section after the end of the limitation period unless, before the end of that period, it has given a warning notice to the sponsor under section 88B(1).

    (8)  "The limitation period" means the period of 3 years beginning with the first day on which the FCA knew that the sponsor had contravened the requirement or restriction.

    (9)  For this purpose the FCA is to be treated as knowing that a sponsor has contravened a requirement or restriction if it has information from which that can reasonably be inferred.][106]

**53.88B.01**    **[88B  Action under s.88A: procedure and right to refer to Tribunal**

    (1)  If the FCA proposes to take action against a sponsor under section 88A, it must give the sponsor a warning notice.

    (2)  A warning notice about a proposal to impose a penalty must state the amount of the penalty.

    (3)  A warning notice about a proposal—

        (a)  to suspend an approval, or

        (b)  to impose a restriction in relation to the performance of a service,

        must state the period for which the suspension or restriction is to have effect.

    (4)  A warning notice about a proposal to publish a statement must set out the terms of the statement.

    (5)  If the FCA decides to take action against a sponsor under section 88A, it must give the sponsor a decision notice.

    (6)  A decision notice about the imposition of a penalty must state the amount of the penalty.

    (7)  A decision notice about—

        (a)  the suspension of an approval, or

        (b)  the imposition of a restriction in relation to the performance of a service,

        must state the period for which the suspension or restriction is to have effect.

    (8)  A decision notice about the publication of a statement must set out the terms of the statement.

    (9)  If the FCA decides to take action against a sponsor under section 88A, the sponsor may refer the matter to the Tribunal.][107]

**53.88C.01**    **[88C  Action under s.88A: statement of policy**

    (1)  The FCA must prepare and issue a statement of its policy with respect to—

        (a)  the imposition of penalties, suspensions or restrictions under section 88A,

        (b)  the amount of penalties under that section, and

        (c)  the period for which suspensions or restrictions under that section are to have effect.

---

[106]  Ss. 88A – 88F substituted for s. 89 by Financial Services Act 2012 c.21 s.18(4) (24 January 2013; 1 April 2013)

[107]  Ss. 88A – 88F substituted for s. 89 by Financial Services Act 2012 c.21 s.18(4) (24 January 2013; 1 April 2013)

(2) The FCA's policy in determining what the amount of a penalty should be, or what the period for which a suspension or restriction is to have effect should be, must include having regard to—
  (a) the seriousness of the contravention in question in relation to the nature of the requirement concerned,
  (b) the extent to which that contravention was deliberate or reckless, and
  (c) whether the sponsor concerned is an individual.
(3) The FCA may at any time alter or replace a statement issued under this section.
(4) If a statement issued under this section is altered or replaced, the FCA must issue the altered or replacement statement.
(5) In exercising, or deciding whether to exercise, its power under section 88A in the case of any particular contravention, the FCA must have regard to any statement of policy published under this section and in force at a time when the contravention in question occurred.
(6) A statement issued under this section must be published by the FCA in the way appearing to the FCA to be best calculated to bring it to the attention of the public.
(7) The FCA may charge a reasonable fee for providing a person with a copy of the statement.
(8) The FCA must, without delay, give the Treasury a copy of any statement which it publishes under this section.][108]

## [88D  Statement of policy under s.88C: procedure                    53.88D.01

(1) Before issuing a statement under section 88C, the FCA must publish a draft of the proposed statement in the way appearing to the FCA to be best calculated to bring it to the attention of the public.
(2) The draft must be accompanied by notice that representations about the proposal may be made to the FCA within a specified time.
(3) Before issuing the proposed statement, the FCA must have regard to any representations made to it in accordance with subsection (2).
(4) If the FCA issues the proposed statement it must publish an account, in general terms, of—
  (a) the representations made to it in accordance with subsection (2); and
  (b) its response to them.
(5) If the statement differs from the draft published under subsection (1) in a way which is, in the opinion of the FCA, significant, the FCA must (in addition to complying with subsection (4)) publish details of the difference.
(6) The FCA may charge a reasonable fee for providing a person with a copy of a draft published under subsection (1).
(7) This section also applies to a proposal to alter or replace a statement.][109]

## [88E  Powers exercisable to advance operational objectives           53.88E.01

(1) The FCA may take action against a sponsor under this section if it considers that it is desirable to do so in order to advance one or more of its operational objectives.
(2) If the FCA is entitled to take action under this section against a sponsor, it may—
  (a) suspend, for such period as it considers appropriate, the sponsor's approval, or
  (b) impose, for such period as it considers appropriate, such limitations or other restrictions in relation to the performance of services to which the sponsor's approval relates as it considers appropriate.
(3) A suspension may relate only to the performance in specified circumstances of a service to which the approval relates.
(4) A restriction may, in particular, be imposed so as to require the sponsor to take, or refrain from taking, specified action.
(5) The FCA may—
  (a) withdraw a suspension or restriction, or
  (b) vary a suspension or restriction so as to reduce the period for which it has effect or otherwise to limit its effect.
(6) A person against whom the FCA takes action under this section may refer the matter to the Tribunal.][110]

---

[108] Ss. 88A – 88F substituted for s. 89 by Financial Services Act 2012 c.21 s.18(4) (24 January 2013; 1 April 2013)

[109] Ss. 88A – 88F substituted for s. 89 by Financial Services Act 2012 c.21 s.18(4) (24 January 2013; 1 April 2013)

[110] Ss. 88A – 88F substituted for s. 89 by Financial Services Act 2012 c.21 s.18(4) (24 January 2013; 1 April 2013)

53.88F.01 **[88F Action under s.88E: procedure**

(1) Action against a sponsor under section 88E takes effect—
  (a) immediately, if the notice given under subsection (3) so provides, or
  (b) on such later date as may be specified in the notice.
(2) If the FCA—
  (a) proposes to take action against a sponsor under that section, or
  (b) takes action against a sponsor under that section with immediate effect,
  it must given the sponsor written notice.
(3) The notice must—
  (a) give details of the action,
  (b) state the FCA's reasons for taking the action and for its determination as to when the action takes effect,
  (c) inform the sponsor that the sponsor may make representations to the FCA within such period as may be specified in the notice (whether or not the matter has been referred to the Tribunal),
  (d) inform the sponsor of when the action takes effect,
  (e) inform the sponsor of the right to refer the matter to the Tribunal, and
  (f) give an indication of the procedure on such a reference.
(4) The FCA may extend the period allowed under the notice for making representations.
(5) If the FCA decides—
  (a) to take the action in the way proposed, or
  (b) if the action has taken effect, not to rescind it,
  the FCA must give the sponsor written notice.
(6) If the FCA decides—
  (a) not to take the action in the way proposed,
  (b) to take action under section 88E that differs from the action originally proposed, or
  (c) to rescind action which has taken effect,
the FCA must give the sponsor written notice.
(7) A notice under subsection (5) must—
  (a) inform the sponsor of the right to refer the matter to the Tribunal, and
  (b) give an indication of the procedure on such a reference.
(8) A notice under subsection (6)(b) must comply with subsection (3).][111]

53.89.01 **89 [...][112]**

*[Transparency obligations ][113]*

53.89A.01 **[89A Transparency rules**

(1) The FCA may make rules for the purposes of the transparency obligations directive.
(2) The rules may include provision for dealing with any matters arising out of or related to any provision of the transparency obligations directive.
(3) The FCA may also make rules–
  (a) for the purpose of ensuring that voteholder information in respect of voting shares traded on a UK market other than a regulated market is made public or notified to the FCA;
  (b) providing for persons who hold comparable instruments (see section 89F(1)(c)) in respect of voting shares to be treated, in the circumstances specified in the rules, as holding some or all of the voting rights in respect of those shares.
(4) Rules under this section may, in particular, make provision–
  (a) specifying how the proportion of–
    (i) the total voting rights in respect of shares in an issuer, or
    (ii) the total voting rights in respect of a particular class of shares in an issuer,
    held by a person is to be determined;
  (b) specifying the circumstances in which, for the purposes of any determination of the voting rights held by a person ("P") in respect of voting shares in an issuer, any voting rights held, or treated by virtue of subsection (3)(b) as held, by another person in respect of voting shares in the issuer are to be regarded as held by P;
  (c) specifying the nature of the information which must be included in any notification;
  (d) about the form of any notification;

---

[111] Ss. 88A – 88F substituted for s. 89 by Financial Services Act 2012 c.21 s.18(4) (24 January 2013; 1 April 2013)
[112] Ss. 88A – 88F substituted for s. 89 by Financial Services Act 2012 c.21 s.18(4) (24 January 2013; 1 April 2013)
[113] Added by Companies Act 2006 c. 46 Pt 43 s.1266(1) (8 November 2006)

(e)  requiring any notification to be given within a specified period;

(f)  specifying the manner in which any information is to be made public and the period within which it must be made public;

(g)  specifying circumstances in which any of the requirements imposed by rules under this section does not apply.

(5)  Rules under this section are referred to in this Part as "transparency rules".

(6)  Nothing in sections 89B to 89G affects the generality of the power to make rules under this section.]<sup>114</sup>

## [89B  Provision of voteholder information

53.89B.01

(1)  Transparency rules may make provision for voteholder information in respect of voting shares to be notified, in circumstances specified in the rules–

(a)  to the issuer, or

(b)  to the public,

or to both.

(2)  Transparency rules may make provision for voteholder information notified to the issuer to be notified at the same time to the FCA.

(3)  In this Part "voteholder information" in respect of voting shares means information relating to the proportion of voting rights held by a person in respect of the shares.

(4)  Transparency rules may require notification of voteholder information relating to a person–

(a)  initially, not later than such date as may be specified in the rules for the purposes of the first indent of Article 30.2 of the transparency obligations directive, and

(b)  subsequently, in accordance with the following provisions.

(5)  Transparency rules under subsection (4)(b) may require notification of voteholder information relating to a person only where there is a notifiable change in the proportion of–

(a)  the total voting rights in respect of shares in the issuer, or

(b)  the total voting rights in respect of a particular class of share in the issuer,

held by the person.

(6)  For this purpose there is a "notifiable change" in the proportion of voting rights held by a person when the proportion changes–

(a)  from being a proportion less than a designated proportion to a proportion equal to or greater than that designated proportion,

(b)  from being a proportion equal to a designated proportion to a proportion greater or less than that designated proportion, or

(c)  from being a proportion greater than a designated proportion to a proportion equal to or less than that designated proportion.

(7)  In subsection (6) "designated" means designated by the rules.]<sup>115</sup>

## [89C  Provision of information by issuers of transferable securities

53.89C.01

(1)  Transparency rules may make provision requiring the issuer of transferable securities, in circumstances specified in the rules–

(a)  to make public information to which this section applies, or

(b)  to notify to the FCA information to which this section applies,

or to do both.

(2)  In the case of every issuer, this section applies to–

(a)  information required by Article 4 of the transparency obligations directive;

(b)  information relating to the rights attached to the transferable securities, including information about the terms and conditions of those securities which could indirectly affect those rights; and

(c)  information about new loan issues and about any guarantee or security in connection with any such issue.

(3)  In the case of an issuer of debt securities, this section also applies to information required by Article 5 of the transparency obligations directive.

(4)  In the case of an issuer of shares, this section also applies to–

(a)  information required by Article 5 of the transparency obligations directive;

(b)  information required by Article 6 of that directive;

(c)  voteholder information–

(i)  notified to the issuer, or

(ii)  relating to the proportion of voting rights held by the issuer in respect of shares in the issuer;

---

<sup>114</sup>  Added by Companies Act 2006 c. 46 Pt 43 s.1266(1) (8 November 2006)

<sup>115</sup>  Added by Companies Act 2006 c. 46 Pt 43 s.1266(1) (8 November 2006)

(d) information relating to the issuer's capital; and

(e) information relating to the total number of voting rights in respect of shares or shares of a particular class.][116]

**53.89D.01**  **[89D  Notification of voting rights held by issuer**

(1) Transparency rules may require notification of voteholder information relating to the proportion of voting rights held by an issuer in respect of voting shares in the issuer–

(a) initially, not later than such date as may be specified in the rules for the purposes of the second indent of Article 30.2 of the transparency obligations directive, and

(b) subsequently, in accordance with the following provisions.

(2) Transparency rules under subsection (1)(b) may require notification of voteholder information relating to the proportion of voting rights held by an issuer in respect of voting shares in the issuer only where there is a notifiable change in the proportion of–

(a) the total voting rights in respect of shares in the issuer, or

(b) the total voting rights in respect of a particular class of share in the issuer,

held by the issuer.

(3) For this purpose there is a "notifiable change" in the proportion of voting rights held by a person when the proportion changes–

(a) from being a proportion less than a designated proportion to a proportion equal to or greater than that designated proportion,

(b) from being a proportion equal to a designated proportion to a proportion greater or less than that designated proportion, or

(c) from being a proportion greater than a designated proportion to a proportion equal to or less than that designated proportion.

(4) In subsection (3) "designated" means designated by the rules.][117]

**53.89E.01**  **[89E  Notification of proposed amendment of issuer's constitution**

Transparency rules may make provision requiring an issuer of transferable securities that are admitted to trading on a regulated market to notify a proposed amendment to its constitution–

(a) to the FCA, and

(b) to the market on which the issuer's securities are admitted,

at times and in circumstances specified in the rules.][118]

**53.89F.01**  **[89F  Transparency rules: interpretation etc**

(1) For the purposes of sections 89A to 89G–

(a) the voting rights in respect of any voting shares are the voting rights attached to those shares,

(b) a person is to be regarded as holding the voting rights in respect of the shares–

(i) if, by virtue of those shares, he is a shareholder within the meaning of Article 2.1(e) of the transparency obligations directive;

(ii) if, and to the extent that, he is entitled to acquire, dispose of or exercise those voting rights in one or more of the cases mentioned in Article 10(a) to (h) of the transparency obligations directive;

(iii) if he holds, directly or indirectly, a financial instrument which results in an entitlement to acquire the shares and is an Article 13 instrument, and

(c) a person holds a "comparable instrument" in respect of voting shares if he holds, directly or indirectly, a financial instrument in relation to the shares which has similar economic effects to an Article 13 instrument (whether or not the financial instrument results in an entitlement to acquire the shares).

(2) Transparency rules under section 89A(3)(b) may make different provision for different descriptions of comparable instrument.

(3) For the purposes of sections 89A to 89G two or more persons may, at the same time, each be regarded as holding the same voting rights.

(4) In those sections–

"Article 13 instrument" means a financial instrument of a type determined by the European Commission under Article 13.2 of the transparency obligations directive;

[116] Added by Companies Act 2006 c. 46 Pt 43 s.1266(1) (8 November 2006)

[117] Added by Companies Act 2006 c. 46 Pt 43 s.1266(1) (8 November 2006)

[118] Added by Companies Act 2006 c. 46 Pt 43 s.1266(1) (8 November 2006)

[ "financial instrument" has the meaning given in Article 4.1(17) of Directive 2004/39/EC on markets in financial instruments; ][119]

"UK market" means a market that is situated or operating in the United Kingdom;

"voting shares" means shares of an issuer to which voting rights are attached.][120]

## [89G  Transparency rules: other supplementary provisions

53.89G.01

(1) Transparency rules may impose the same obligations on a person who has applied for the admission of transferable securities to trading on a regulated market without the issuer's consent as they impose on an issuer of transferable securities.

(2) Transparency rules that require a person to make information public may include provision authorising the FCA to make the information public in the event that the person fails to do so.

(3) The FCA may make public any information notified to the FCA in accordance with transparency rules.

(4) Transparency rules may make provision by reference to any provision of any rules made by the Panel on Takeovers and Mergers under Part 28 of the Companies Act 2006.

(5) Sections 89A to 89F and this section are without prejudice to any other power conferred by this Part to make Part 6 rules.][121]

## *[Power of FCA to call for information ]*[122]

## [89H  FCA's power to call for information

53.89H.01

(1) The FCA may by notice in writing given to a person to whom this section applies require him–
   (a)  to provide specified information or information of a specified description, or
   (b)  to produce specified documents or documents of a specified description.

(2) This section applies to–
   (a)  an issuer in respect of whom transparency rules have effect;
   (b)  a voteholder;
   (c)  an auditor of–
      (i)  an issuer to whom this section applies, or
      (ii)  a voteholder;
   (d)  a person who controls a voteholder;
   (e)  a person controlled by a voteholder;
   (f)  a director or other similar officer of an issuer to whom this section applies;
   (g)  a director or other similar officer of a voteholder or, where the affairs of a voteholder are managed by its members, a member of the voteholder.

(3) This section applies only to information and documents reasonably required in connection with the exercise by the FCA of functions conferred on it by or under sections 89A to 89G (transparency rules).

(4) Information or documents required under this section must be provided or produced–
   (a)  before the end of such reasonable period as may be specified, and
   (b)  at such place as may be specified.

(5) If a person claims a lien on a document, its production under this section does not affect the lien.][123]

## [89I  Requirements in connection with call for information

53.89I.01

(1) The FCA may require any information provided under section 89H to be provided in such form as it may reasonably require.

(2) The FCA may require–
   (a)  any information provided, whether in a document or otherwise, to be verified in such manner as it may reasonably require;
   (b)  any document produced to be authenticated in such manner as it may reasonably require.

(3) If a document is produced in response to a requirement imposed under section 89H, the FCA may–
   (a)  take copies of or extracts from the document; or

---

[119]  Inserted by Definition of Financial Instrument Order 2008/3053 art.2(2) (31 January 2009)
[120]  Added by Companies Act 2006 c. 46 Pt 43 s.1266(1) (8 November 2006)
[121]  Added by Companies Act 2006 c. 46 Pt 43 s.1266(1) (8 November 2006)
[122]  Added by Companies Act 2006 c. 46 Pt 43 s.1267 (8 November 2006)
[123]  Added by Companies Act 2006 c. 46 Pt 43 s.1267 (8 November 2006)

(b)  require the person producing the document, or any relevant person, to provide an explanation of the document.

(4)  In subsection (3)(b) "relevant person", in relation to a person who is required to produce a document, means a person who–
    (a)  has been or is a director or controller of that person;
    (b)  has been or is an auditor of that person;
    (c)  has been or is an actuary, accountant or lawyer appointed or instructed by that person; or
    (d)  has been or is an employee of that person.

(5)  If a person who is required under section 89H to produce a document fails to do so, the FCA may require him to state, to the best of his knowledge and belief, where the document is.][124]

**53.89J.01**    **[89J  Power to call for information: supplementary provisions**

(1)  The FCA may require an issuer to make public any information provided to the FCA under section 89H.

(2)  If the issuer fails to comply with a requirement under subsection (1), the FCA may, after seeking representations from the issuer, make the information public.

(3)  In sections 89H and 89I (power of FCA to call for information)–
"control" and "controlled" have the meaning given by subsection (4) below;
"specified" means specified in the notice;
"voteholder" means a person who–
    (a)  holds voting rights in respect of any voting shares for the purposes of sections 89A to 89G (transparency rules), or
    (b)  is treated as holding such rights by virtue of rules under section 89A(3)(b).

(4)  For the purposes of those sections a person ("A") controls another person ("B") if–
    (a)  A holds a majority of the voting rights in B,
    (b)  A is a member of B and has the right to appoint or remove a majority of the members of the board of directors (or, if there is no such board, the equivalent management body) of B,
    (c)  A is a member of B and controls alone, pursuant to an agreement with other shareholders or members, a majority of the voting rights in B, or
    (d)  A has the right to exercise, or actually exercises, dominant influence or control over B.

(5)  For the purposes of subsection (4)(b)–
    (a)  any rights of a person controlled by A, and
    (b)  any rights of a person acting on behalf of A or a person controlled by A,
are treated as held by A.][125]

*[Powers exercisable in case of infringement of transparency obligation ][126]*

**53.89K.01**    **[89K  Public censure of issuer**

(1)  If the FCA finds that an issuer of securities admitted to trading on a regulated market is failing or has failed to comply with an applicable transparency obligation, it may publish a statement to that effect.

(2)  If the FCA proposes to publish a statement, it must give the issuer a warning notice setting out the terms of the proposed statement.

(3)  If, after considering any representations made in response to the warning notice, the FCA decides to make the proposed statement, it must give the issuer a decision notice setting out the terms of the statement.

(4)  A notice under this section must inform the issuer of his right to refer the matter to the Tribunal (see section 89N) and give an indication of the procedure on such a reference.

(5)  In this section "transparency obligation" means an obligation under–
    (a)  a provision of transparency rules, or
    (b)  any other provision made in accordance with the transparency obligations directive.

(6)  In relation to an issuer whose home State is a member State other than the United Kingdom, any reference to an applicable transparency obligation must be read subject to section 100A(2).][127]

---

[124]  Added by Companies Act 2006 c. 46 Pt 43 s.1267 (8 November 2006)
[125]  Added by Companies Act 2006 c. 46 Pt 43 s.1267 (8 November 2006)
[126]  Added by Companies Act 2006 c. 46 Pt 43 s.1268 (8 November 2006)
[127]  Added by Companies Act 2006 c. 46 Pt 43 s.1268 (8 November 2006)

## [89L  Power to suspend or prohibit trading of securities                    53.89L.01

(1)  This section applies to securities admitted to trading on a regulated market.

(2)  If the FCA has reasonable grounds for suspecting that an applicable transparency obligation has been infringed by an issuer, it may–
  (a)  suspend trading in the securities for a period not exceeding 10 days,
  (b)  prohibit trading in the securities, or
  (c)  make a request to the operator of the market on which the issuer's securities are traded–
    (i)  to suspend trading in the securities for a period not exceeding 10 days, or
    (ii)  to prohibit trading in the securities.

(3)  If the FCA has reasonable grounds for suspecting that a provision required by the transparency obligations directive has been infringed by a voteholder of an issuer, it may–
  (a)  prohibit trading in the securities, or
  (b)  make a request to the operator of the market on which the issuer's securities are traded to prohibit trading in the securities.

(4)  If the FCA finds that an applicable transparency obligation has been infringed, it may require the market operator to prohibit trading in the securities.

(5)  In this section "transparency obligation" means an obligation under–
  (a)  a provision contained in transparency rules, or
  (b)  any other provision made in accordance with the transparency obligations directive.

(6)  In relation to an issuer whose home State is a member State other than the United Kingdom, any reference to an applicable transparency obligation must be read subject to section 100A(2).][128]

## [89M  Procedure under section 89L                    53.89M.01

(1)  A requirement under section 89L takes effect–
  (a)  immediately, if the notice under subsection (2) states that that is the case;
  (b)  in any other case, on such date as may be specified in the notice.

(2)  If the FCA–
  (a)  proposes to exercise the powers in section 89L in relation to a person, or
  (b)  exercises any of those powers in relation to a person with immediate effect,
  it must give that person written notice.

(3)  The notice must–
  (a)  give details of the FCA's action or proposed action;
  (b)  state the FCA's reasons for taking the action in question and choosing the date on which it took effect or takes effect;
  (c)  inform the recipient that he may make representations to the FCA within such period as may be specified by the notice (whether or not he had referred the matter to the Tribunal);
  (d)  inform him of the date on which the action took effect or takes effect;
  (e)  inform him of his right to refer the matter to the Tribunal (see section 89N) and give an indication of the procedure on such a reference.

(4)  The FCA may extend the period within which representations may be made to it.

(5)  If, having considered any representations made to it, the FCA decides to maintain, vary or revoke its earlier decision, it must give written notice to that effect to the person mentioned in subsection (2).][129]

## [89N  Right to refer matters to the Tribunal                    53.89N.01

A person–

(a)  to whom a decision notice is given under section 89K (public censure), or
(b)  to whom a notice is given under section 89M (procedure in connection with suspension or prohibition of trading),

may refer the matter to the Tribunal.][130]

---

[128]  Added by Companies Act 2006 c. 46 Pt 43 s.1268 (8 November 2006)
[129]  Added by Companies Act 2006 c. 46 Pt 43 s.1268 (8 November 2006)
[130]  Added by Companies Act 2006 c. 46 Pt 43 s.1268 (8 November 2006)

*[Corporate governance ]*[131]

**53.89O.01    [89O  Corporate governance rules**

(1)  The FCA may make rules ("corporate governance rules")–
    (a)  for the purpose of implementing, enabling the implementation of or dealing with matters arising out of or related to, any [ EU ][132] obligation relating to the corporate governance of issuers who have requested or approved admission of their securities to trading on a regulated market;
    (b)  about corporate governance in relation to such issuers for the purpose of implementing, or dealing with matters arising out of or related to, any [ EU ][133] obligation.
(2)  "Corporate governance", in relation to an issuer, includes–
    (a)  the nature, constitution or functions of the organs of the issuer;
    (b)  the manner in which organs of the issuer conduct themselves;
    (c)  the requirements imposed on organs of the issuer;
    (d)  the relationship between the different organs of the issuer;
    (e)  the relationship between the organs of the issuer and the members of the issuer or holders of the issuer's securities.
(3)  The burdens and restrictions imposed by rules under this section on foreign-traded issuers must not be greater than the burdens and restrictions imposed on UK-traded issuers by–
    (a)  rules under this section, and
    (b)  listing rules.
(4)  For this purpose–
    "foreign-traded issuer" means an issuer who has requested or approved admission of the issuer's securities to trading on a regulated market situated or operating outside the United Kingdom;
    "UK-traded issuer" means an issuer who has requested or approved admission of the issuer's securities to trading on a regulated market situated or operating in the United Kingdom.
(5)  This section is without prejudice to any other power conferred by this Part to make Part 6 rules.][134]


*[Primary information providers]*[135]

**53.89P.01    [89P  Primary information providers**

(1)  Part 6 rules may require issuers of financial instruments to use primary information providers for the purpose of giving information of a specified description to a market of a specified description.
(2)  "Primary information provider" means a person approved by the FCA for the purposes of this section.
(3)  "Specified" means specified in the Part 6 rules.
(4)  Part 6 rules made by virtue of subsection (1) may—
    (a)  provide for the FCA to maintain a list of providers;
    (b)  impose requirements on a provider in relation to the giving of information or of information of a specified description;
    (c)  specify the circumstances in which a person is qualified for being approved as a provider;
    (d)  provide for limitations or other restrictions to be imposed on the giving of information to which an approval relates (whether or not the approval has already been granted);
    (e)  provide for the approval of a provider to be suspended on the application of the provider.
(5)  If the FCA proposes—
    (a)  to refuse a person's application under information provider rules,
    (b)  to impose limitations or other restrictions on the giving of information to which a person's approval relates, or
    (c)  to cancel a person's approval as a provider otherwise than at the person's request,
    it must give the person a warning notice.
(6)  If the FCA decides—
    (a)  to grant the application under information provider rules,

---

[131]  Added by Companies Act 2006 c. 46 Pt 43 s.1269 (8 November 2006)
[132]  Substituted by Treaty of Lisbon (Changes in Terminology) Order 2011/1043 Pt 2 art.6(1)(e) (22 April 2011)
[133]  Substituted by Treaty of Lisbon (Changes in Terminology) Order 2011/1043 Pt 2 art.6(1)(e) (22 April 2011)
[134]  Added by Companies Act 2006 c. 46 Pt 43 s.1269 (8 November 2006)
[135]  Inserted by Financial Services Act 2012 c.21 s.19(1) (24 January 2013; 1 April 2013)

    (b)  not to impose limitations or other restrictions on the giving of information to which a person's approval relates, or

    (c)  not to cancel the approval,

it must give the person concerned written notice of its decision.

(7)  If the FCA decides—

    (a)  to refuse to grant the application under information provider rules,

    (b)  to impose limitations or other restrictions on the giving of information to which a person's approval relates, or

    (c)  to cancel the approval,

it must give the person concerned a decision notice.

(8)  A person to whom a decision notice is given under this section may refer the matter to the Tribunal.

(9)  In this section any reference to an application under information provider rules means —

    (a)  an application for approval as a provider,

    (b)  an application for the suspension of an approval as a provider,

    (c)  an application for the withdrawal of the suspension of an approval as a provider, or

    (d)  an application for the withdrawal or variation of a limitation or other restriction on the giving of information to which a provider's approval relates.][136]

## [89Q  Disciplinary powers: contravention of s.89P(4)(b) or (d)          53.89Q.01

(1)  The FCA may take action against a provider under this section if it considers that the provider has contravened a requirement or restriction imposed on the provider by rules made as a result of section 89P(4)(b) or (d).

(2)  If the FCA is entitled to take action under this section against a provider, it may do one or more of the following—

    (a)  impose a penalty on the provider of such amount as it considers appropriate;

    (b)  suspend, for such period as it considers appropriate, the provider's approval;

    (c)  impose, for such period as it considers appropriate, such limitations or other restrictions in relation to the giving by the provider of information as it considers appropriate;

    (d)  publish a statement to the effect that the provider has contravened a requirement or restriction imposed on the provider by rules made as a result of section 89P(4)(b) or (d).

(3)  The period for which a suspension or restriction is to have effect may not exceed 12 months.

(4)  A suspension may relate only to the giving of information in specified circumstances.

(5)  A restriction may, in particular, be imposed so as to require the provider to take, or refrain from taking, specified action.

(6)  The FCA may—

    (a)  withdraw a suspension or restriction; or

    (b)  vary a suspension or restriction so as to reduce the period for which it has effect or otherwise to limit its effect.

(7)  The FCA may not take action against a provider under this section after the end of the limitation period unless, before the end of that period, it has given a warning notice to the provider under section 89R(1).

(8)  "The limitation period" means the period of 3 years beginning with the first day on which the FCA knew that the provider had contravened the requirement or restriction.

(9)  For this purpose the FCA is to be treated as knowing that a provider has contravened a requirement or restriction if it has information from which that can reasonably be inferred.][137]

## [89R  Action under s.89Q: procedure and right to refer to Tribunal          53.89R.01

(1)  If the FCA proposes to take action against a provider under section 89Q, it must give the provider a warning notice.

(2)  A warning notice about a proposal to impose a penalty must state the amount of the penalty.

(3)  A warning notice about a proposal—

    (a)  to suspend an approval, or

    (b)  to impose a restriction in relation to the giving of information, must state the period for which the suspension or restriction is to have effect.

(4)  A warning notice about a proposal to publish a statement must set out the terms of the statement.

(5)  If the FCA decides to take action against a provider under section 89Q, it must give the provider a decision notice.

(6)  A decision notice about the imposition of a penalty must state the amount of the penalty.

---

[136]  Added by Financial Services Act 2012 c.21 s.19(1) (24 January 2013; 1 April 2013)

[137]  Added by Financial Services Act 2012 c.21 s.19(1) (24 January 2013; 1 April 2013)

(7) A decision notice about—
   (a) the suspension of an approval, or
   (b) the imposition of a restriction in relation to the giving of information,
   must state the period for which the suspension or restriction is to have effect.

(8) A decision notice about the publication of a statement must set out the terms of the statement.

(9) If the FCA decides to take action against a provider under section 89Q, the provider may refer the matter to the Tribunal.][138]

**53.89S.01**    **[89S  Action under s.89Q: statement of policy**

(1) The FCA must prepare and issue a statement of its policy with respect to—
   (a) the imposition of penalties, suspensions or restrictions under section 89Q,
   (b) the amount of penalties under that section;
   (c) the period for which suspensions or restrictions under that section are to have effect, and
   (d) the matters in relation to which suspensions or restrictions under that section are to have effect.

(2) The FCA's policy in determining what the amount of a penalty should be, or what the period for which a suspension or restriction is to have effect should be, must include having regard to—
   (a) the seriousness of the contravention in question in relation to the nature of the requirement concerned,
   (b) the extent to which that contravention was deliberate or reckless, and
   (c) whether the provider concerned is an individual.

(3) The FCA may at any time alter or replace a statement issued under this section.

(4) If a statement issued under this section is altered or replaced, the FCA must issue the altered or replacement statement.

(5) In exercising, or deciding whether to exercise, its power under section 89Q in the case of any particular contravention, the FCA must have regard to any statement of policy published under this section and in force at a time when the contravention in question occurred.

(6) A statement issued under this section must be published by the FCA in the way appearing to the FCA to be best calculated to bring it to the attention of the public.

(7) The FCA may charge a reasonable fee for providing a person with a copy of the statement.

(8) The FCA must, without delay, give the Treasury a copy of any statement which it publishes under this section.][139]

**53.89T.01**    **[89T  Statement of policy under s.89S: procedure**

(1) Before issuing a statement under section 89S, the FCA must publish a draft of the proposed statement in the way appearing to the FCA to be best calculated to bring it to the attention of the public.

(2) The draft must be accompanied by notice that representations about the proposal may be made to the FCA within a specified time.

(3) Before issuing the proposed statement, the FCA must have regard to any representations made to it in accordance with subsection (2).

(4) If the FCA issues the proposed statement it must publish an account, in general terms, of—
   (a) the representations made to it in accordance with subsection (2); and
   (b) its response to them.

(5) If the statement differs from the draft published under subsection (1) in a way which is, in the opinion of the FCA, significant, the FCA must (in addition to complying with subsection (4)) publish details of the difference.

(6) The FCA may charge a reasonable fee for providing a person with a copy of a draft published under subsection (1).

(7) This section also applies to a proposal to alter or replace a statement.][140]

**53.89U.01**    **[89U  Powers exercisable to advance operational objectives**

(1) The FCA may take action against a provider under this section if it considers that it is desirable to do so in order to advance one or more of its operational objectives.

(2) If the FCA is entitled to take action under this section against a provider, it may—
   (a) suspend, for such period as it considers appropriate, the provider's approval, or

---

[138] Added by Financial Services Act 2012 c.21 s.19(1) (24 January 2013; 1 April 2013)
[139] Added by Financial Services Act 2012 c.21 s.19(1) (24 January 2013; 1 April 2013)
[140] Added by Financial Services Act 2012 c.21 s.19(1) (24 January 2013; 1 April 2013)

(b)  impose, for such period as it considers appropriate, such limitations or other restrictions in relation to the giving by the provider of information as it considers appropriate.

(3)  A suspension may relate only to the giving of information in specified circumstances.

(4)  A restriction may, in particular, be imposed so as to require the provider to take, or refrain from taking, specified action.

(5)  The FCA may—

(a)  withdraw a suspension or restriction, or

(b)  vary a suspension or restriction so as to reduce the period for which it has effect or otherwise to limit its effect.

(6)  A person against whom the FCA takes action under this section may refer the matter to the Tribunal.][141]

## [89V  Action under s.89U: procedure                                                53.89V.01

(1)  Action against a provider under section 89U takes effect—

(a)  immediately, if the notice given under subsection (2) so provides, or

(b)  on such later date as may be specified in the notice.

(2)  If the FCA—

(a)  proposes to take action against a provider under that section, or

(b)  takes action against a provider under that section with immediate effect,

it must give the provider written notice.

(3)  The notice must—

(a)  give details of the action,

(b)  state the FCA's reasons for taking the action and for its determination as to when the action takes effect;

(c)  inform the provider that the provider may make representations to the FCA within such period as may be specified in the notice (whether or not the matter has been referred to the Tribunal);

(d)  inform the provider of when the action takes effect;

(e)  inform the provider of the right to refer the matter to the Tribunal; and

(f)  give an indication of the procedure on such a reference.

(4)  The FCA may extend the period allowed under the notice for making representations.

(5)  If the FCA decides—

(a)  to take the action in the way proposed, or

(b)  if the action has taken effect, not to rescind it,

the FCA must give the provider written notice.

(6)  If the FCA decides—

(a)  not to take the action in the way proposed,

(b)  to take action under section 89U that differs from the action originally proposed, or

(c)  to rescind action which has taken effect,

the FCA must give the provider written notice.

(7)  A notice under subsection (5) must—

(a)  inform the provider of the right to refer the matter to the Tribunal; and

(b)  give an indication of the procedure on such a reference.

(8)  A notice under subsection (6)(b) must comply with subsection (3).][142]

## *[Compensation for false or misleading statements etc ]*[143]

## 90  [Compensation for statements in listing particulars or prospectus ][144]          53.90.01

(1)  Any person responsible for listing particulars is liable to pay compensation to a person who has–

(a)  acquired securities to which the particulars apply; and

(b)  suffered loss in respect of them as a result of–

(i)  any untrue or misleading statement in the particulars; or

(ii)  the omission from the particulars of any matter required to be included by section 80 or 81.

(2)  Subsection (1) is subject to exemptions provided by Schedule 10.

(3)  If listing particulars are required to include information about the absence of a particular matter, the omission from the particulars of that information is to be treated as a statement in the listing particulars that there is no such matter.

---

[141]  Added by Financial Services Act 2012 c.21 s.19(1) (24 January 2013; 1 April 2013)

[142]  Added by Financial Services Act 2012 c.21 s.19(1) (24 January 2013; 1 April 2013)

[143]  Substituted by Companies Act 2006 c. 46 Sch.15(1) para.4 (8 November 2006)

[144]  Substituted by Companies Act 2006 c. 46 Sch.15(1) para.5 (8 November 2006)

(4) Any person who fails to comply with section 81 is liable to pay compensation to any person who has–
    (a) acquired securities of the kind in question; and
    (b) suffered loss in respect of them as a result of the failure.
(5) Subsection (4) is subject to exemptions provided by Schedule 10.
(6) This section does not affect any liability which may be incurred apart from this section.
(7) References in this section to the acquisition by a person of securities include references to his contracting to acquire them or any interest in them.
(8) No person shall, by reason of being a promoter of a company or otherwise, incur any liability for failing to disclose information which he would not be required to disclose in listing particulars in respect of a company's securities–
    (a) if he were responsible for those particulars; or
    (b) if he is responsible for them, which he is entitled to omit by virtue of section 82.
(9) The reference in subsection (8) to a person incurring liability includes a reference to any other person being entitled as against that person to be granted any civil remedy or to rescind or repudiate an agreement.
(10) "Listing particulars", in subsection (1) and Schedule 10, includes supplementary listing particulars.
[(11) This section applies in relation to a prospectus as it applies to listing particulars, with the following modifications—
    (a) references in this section or in Schedule 10 to listing particulars, supplementary listing particulars or sections 80, 81 or 82 are to be read, respectively, as references to a prospectus, supplementary prospectus and sections 87A, 87G and 87B;
    (b) references in Schedule 10 to admission to the official list are to be read as references to admission to trading on a regulated market;
    (c) in relation to a prospectus, "securities" means "transferable securities".
[(12) A person is not to be subject to civil liability solely on the basis of a summary in a prospectus unless the summary, when read with the rest of the prospectus—
    (a) is misleading, inaccurate or inconsistent; or
    (b) does not provide key information (as defined in section 87A(9) and (10)),
and in this subsection a summary includes any translation of it.][145] ][146]

**53.90.02**    The evolution of statutory liability for misstatements in prospectuses – from the Directors' Liability Act 1890 to the Financial Services Act 1986 – was helpfully traced by Lightman J in his judgment in the case of *Possfund Custodian Trustee Ltd* v *Diamond*.[147] Since *Possfund*, the Financial Services Act 1986 has been superseded by the Act and liability for such misstatements is now governed by section 90. The Act came into force before the Prospectus Directive and, accordingly, the original section 90 applied only to listing particulars. By virtue of subsection (11), which was added by the 2005 Regulations, the section 90 framework now applies to both listing particulars and prospectuses. This commentary considers section 90 as it applies to prospectuses.

**53.90.03**    Under subsection (1), any person responsible for a prospectus is liable to compensate a person who acquired the relevant securities and suffered loss in respect of them, if the loss was a result of an untrue or misleading statement ("misstatement") in, or an omission from, the prospectus.

**53.90.04**    Under subsection (4), any person who fails to comply with the requirement to produce a supplementary prospectus is liable to compensate a person who acquired the relevant securities and suffered a loss in respect of them as a result of that failure.

**53.90.05**    An investor does not need to have actually purchased securities in order to make a claim under section 90. In accordance with subsection (7), a contract to acquire securities – such as an option – will be sufficient.

**53.90.06**    There will be a wide range of potential defendants to a claim made under this section. The persons responsible for a prospectus are determined by PR 5.5. The following persons will be responsible for a prospectus relating to non-equity securities: the issuer, each person named as accepting responsibility for it and anyone else who has authorised its contents. In the context of an offer or request for admission to trading, where the offeror or person requesting admission is not the issuer, that entity will also be responsible.

**53.90.07**    If a prospectus relates to equity securities, liability is extended to the directors of the issuer and, where relevant, the directors of the offeror or person requesting admission to trading. The imposition of

[145] Substituted by Prospectus Regulations 2012/1538 reg.7 (1 July 2012)
[146] Added by Prospectus Regulations 2005/1433 Sch.1 para.6(2) (1 July 2005)
[147] [1996] 2 BCLC 665

personal liability gives the directors of companies issuing or offering equity securities a strong incentive to eliminate misstatements from any prospectus they publish.

It should be noted that if an issue of non-equity securities is guaranteed, the guarantor will be responsible for information relating to the guarantor and the guarantee. A guarantor will not be liable for a prospectus in relation to equity securities.[148]  **53.90.08**

The persons responsible for a prospectus have a number of defences (or "exemptions") to a claim under Section 90, which are set out in Schedule 10. Under paragraph 1, a person will not be liable if he reasonably believed that a statement was true and not misleading (or a matter properly omitted). Under paragraph 2, a reasonable belief that a statement had been made by a competent and consenting expert (such as a professional adviser) will have the same effect. In either case, if the responsible person realised his mistake before the securities in question were acquired, it will normally be necessary for him to have endeavoured to bring a correction to the attention of prospective investors in order to rely on the exemption.  **53.90.09**

Under paragraph 3, a responsible person may avoid liability if he can satisfy the court that a statement had been corrected, or it was reasonable for him to think that it had been, before the securities were acquired. Paragraph 4 provides that there can be no liability for statements made by an official person, or taken from a public official document, which are reproduced in a prospectus. Under paragraph 5, there is no liability if the investor knew that the statement in question was false or misleading, or that a matter had been improperly omitted, before acquiring the securities.  **53.90.10**

Despite the exemptions, a claim made under section 90 will have significant advantages over one made at common law or under the Misrepresentation Act 1967 (the "Misrepresentation Act").  **53.90.11**

To bring a claim in tort or under the Misrepresentation Act, the claimant will have to show that he relied on the particular misstatement or omission. This is likely to be difficult given the scale and complexity of modern prospectuses. Under section 90, liability for a misstatement or omission arises regardless of whether the claimant relied on it. It may not even be necessary for the claimant to have read the prospectus, provided that the loss suffered is a result of the misstatement or omission.  **53.90.12**

To bring a claim in tort, the claimant must show that the issuer or offeror owed him a duty of care. This may not be an obstacle for an initial subscriber, however, there is no precedent for a duty of care being owed to aftermarket purchasers. Likewise, a claim under the Misrepresentation Act 1967 will only be available to initial subscribers on the basis that an aftermarket purchaser does not have a contract with the representor – the issuer or offeror. Under section 90, anyone who has "acquired securities" can make a claim, i.e. both subscribers and aftermarket purchasers. It should be noted that aftermarket purchasers will still have to prove that their loss arose "as a result of" the misstatement or omission. Clearly, the longer the period between the publication of the prospectus and the acquisition of the securities, the easier it will be for a defendant to argue that the chain of causation has been broken by intervening factors.  **53.90.13**

Despite these advantages, a limited number of claims under section 90 have gone through the Courts. The only reference to section 90 in a reported case was in *Hall v Cable and Wireless plc*[149] , where Teare J confirmed that the section only gives investors an action in respect of statements made in the prospectus (and any supplementary prospectus) and not statements made after listing.  **53.90.14**

Section 90 does not specify a measure of damages for successful claims and, in the absence of a decided case, this remains uncertain. It is generally accepted that a tortious, rather than a contractual, measure of damages would be applied. However, it is not clear whether a court would restrict an award to the amount of the acquisition price that was attributable to the misstatement or omission, or allow an investor to recover all the losses which flowed directly from the transaction.  **53.90.15**

Prior to the implementation of the Amending Directive, civil liability only attached to a prospectus summary (including any translation of it) if it was is misleading, inaccurate or inconsistent when read with the rest of the prospectus. The 2012 Regulations extended subsection (12) so a person may also be liable if the summary does not provide "key information", as defined in section 87A(9), when read with the rest of the prospectus.  **53.90.16**

As part of his 2007 review of issuer liability, Paul Davies QC considered whether the prospectus standard for civil liability (i.e. negligence) should be imposed on periodic disclosures to the market as  **53.90.17**

---

[148]  Prospectus Rule ("PR") 5.5.4(2)(e)
[149]  [2009] EWHC 1793 (Comm)

required by the Transparency Directive, or if fraud be maintained as the standard of liability under section 90A. The review concluded that the extension of the prospectus standard would be costly for issuers and could lead to bland and defensive disclosures. However, the Financial Services and Markets Act 2000 (Liability of Issuers) Regulations 2010 did extend the periodic disclosure regime to cover all recognised information service announcements and made issuers liable to a wider class of persons.[150]

**53.90ZA.01**    **[90ZA.— Liability for key investor information**

(1)  A person is not to be subject to civil liability solely on the basis of the key investor information produced in relation to a collective investment scheme or a sub-fund of such a scheme in accordance with rules or other provisions implementing Chapter IX of the UCITS directive, or of any translation of that information, unless the key investor information is misleading, inaccurate or inconsistent with the relevant parts of the prospectus published for that collective investment scheme or sub-fund in accordance with rules made by the FCA under section 248 of this Act.

(2)  In this section, a reference to a sub-fund of a collective investment scheme is a reference to a part of the property of the collective investment scheme which forms a separate pool where—

   (a)  the collective investment scheme provides arrangements for separate pooling of the contributions of the participants and the profits and income out of which payments are made to them; and

   (b)  the participants are entitled to exchange rights in one pool for rights in another.][151]

**53.90A.01**    **[90A  Liability of issuers in connection with published information**

Schedule 10A makes provision about the liability of issuers of securities to pay compensation to persons who have suffered loss as a result of—

(a)  a misleading statement or dishonest omission in certain published information relating to the securities, or

(b)  a dishonest delay in publishing such information.][152]

**53.90B.01**    **[90B  Power to make further provision about liability for published information**

(1)  The Treasury may by regulations make provision about the liability of issuers of securities traded on a regulated market, and other persons, in respect of information published to holders of securities, to the market or to the public generally.

(2)  Regulations under this section may amend any primary or subordinate legislation, including any provision of, or made under, this Act.][153]

*Penalties*

**53.91.01**    **91  [Penalties for breach of Part 6 rules ]**[154]

[[(1) If the FCA considers that–

   (a)  an issuer of listed securities, or

   (b)  an applicant for listing, has contravened any provision of listing rules,

   it may impose on him a penalty of such amount as it considers appropriate.

(1ZA)  If the FCA considers that–

   (a)  an issuer who has requested or approved the admission of a financial instrument to trading on a regulated market,

   (b)  a person discharging managerial responsibilities within such an issuer, or

   (c)  a person connected with such a person discharging managerial responsibilities,

   has contravened any provision of disclosure rules, it may impose on him a penalty of such amount as it considers appropriate.][155]

[(1A)  If the FCA considers that—

   (a)  an issuer of transferable securities,

---

[150]  Davies Review of Issuer Liability: Final Report (June 2007) (http://www.hm-treasury.gov.uk/d/davies_review_finalreport_040607.pdf)

[151]  Added by Undertakings for Collective Investment in Transferable Securities Regulations 2011/1613 Pt 2 reg.2(3) (1 July 2011)

[152]  Substituted by Financial Services and Markets Act 2000 (Liability of Issuers) Regulations 2010/1192 reg.2(2) (1 October 2010)

[153]  Added by Companies Act 2006 c. 46 Pt 43 s.1270 (8 November 2006)

[154]  Substituted by Prospectus Regulations 2005/1433 Sch.1 para.7(4) (1 July 2005)

[155]  S.91(1)-(1ZA) substituted for s.91(1) by Companies Act 2006 c. 46 Sch.15(1) para.6(2) (8 November 2006)

    (b)  a person offering transferable securities to the public or requesting their admission to trading on a regulated market,

    (c)  an applicant for the approval of a prospectus in relation to transferable securities,

    (d)  a person on whom a requirement has been imposed under section 87K or 87L, or

    (e)  any other person to whom a provision of the prospectus directive applies, has contravened a provision of this Part or of prospectus rules, or a provision otherwise made in accordance with the prospectus directive or a requirement imposed on him under such a provision,

it may impose on him a penalty of such amount as it considers appropriate.][156]

[(1B)  If the FCA considers–

    (a)  that a person has contravened–

        (i)  a provision of transparency rules or a provision otherwise made in accordance with the transparency obligations directive, or

        (ii)  a provision of corporate governance rules, or

    (b)  that a person on whom a requirement has been imposed under section 89L (power to suspend or prohibit trading of securities in case of infringement of applicable transparency obligation), has contravened that requirement, it may impose on the person a penalty of such amount as it considers appropriate.][157]

(2)  If, in the case of a contravention [ by a person ][158] referred to in subsection [ (1), (1ZA)(a), (1A) or (1B) ][159] [ ("P") ][160] , the FCA considers that [ another person ][161] who was at the material time a director of [P][162] was knowingly concerned in the contravention, it may impose upon him a penalty of such amount as it considers appropriate. ][163]

(3)  If the FCA is entitled to impose a penalty on a person under this section in respect of a particular matter it may, instead of imposing a penalty on him in respect of that matter, publish a statement censuring him.

(4)  Nothing in this section prevents the FCA from taking any other steps which it has power to take under this Part.

(5)  A penalty under this section is payable to the FCA.

(6)  The FCA may not take action against a person under this section after the end of the period of [3 years][164] beginning with the first day on which it knew of the contravention unless proceedings against that person, in respect of the contravention, were begun before the end of that period.

(7)  For the purposes of subsection (6)–

    (a)  the FCA is to be treated as knowing of a contravention if it has information from which the contravention can reasonably be inferred; and

    (b)  proceedings against a person in respect of a contravention are to be treated as begun when a warning notice is given to him under section 92.

## 92 Procedure.

                                                        53.92.01

(1)  If the FCA proposes to take action against a person under section 91, it must give him a warning notice.

(2)  A warning notice about a proposal to impose a penalty must state the amount of the proposed penalty.

(3)  A warning notice about a proposal to publish a statement must set out the terms of the proposed statement.

(4)  If the FCA decides to take action against a person under section 91, it must give him a decision notice.

(5)  A decision notice about the imposition of a penalty must state the amount of the penalty.

(6)  A decision notice about the publication of a statement must set out the terms of the statement.

(7)  If the FCA decides to take action against a person under section 91, he may refer the matter to the Tribunal.

---

[156]  Added by Prospectus Regulations 2005/1433 Sch.1 para.7(2) (1 July 2005)

[157]  Added by Companies Act 2006 c. 46 Sch.15(1) para.6(3) (8 November 2006)

[158]  Substituted by Prospectus Regulations 2005/1433 Sch.1 para.7(3)(a) (1 July 2005)

[159]  Substituted by Companies Act 2006 c. 46 Sch.15(1) para.6(4) (8 November 2006)

[160]  Substituted by Prospectus Regulations 2005/1433 Sch.1 para.7(3)(b) (1 July 2005)

[161]  Substituted by Prospectus Regulations 2005/1433 Sch.1 para.7(3)(c) (1 July 2005)

[162]  Substituted by Prospectus Regulations 2005/1433 Sch.1 para.7(3)(d) (1 July 2005)

[163]  Substituted by Financial Services and Markets Act 2000 (Market Abuse) Regulations 2005/381 Sch.1 para.4 (1 July 2005)

[164]  Substituted by the Financial Services Act 2012 c.21 s.20 (24 January 2013; 1 April 2013)

**53.93.01**   93  **Statement of policy.**

   (1)  The FCA must prepare and issue a statement ("its policy statement") of its policy with respect to–
        (a)  the imposition of penalties under section 91; and
        (b)  the amount of penalties under that section.
   (2)  The FCA's policy in determining what the amount of a penalty should be must include having regard to–
        (a)  the seriousness of the contravention in question in relation to the nature of the requirement contravened;
        (b)  the extent to which that contravention was deliberate or reckless; and
        (c)  whether the person on whom the penalty is to be imposed is an individual.
   (3)  The FCA may at any time alter or replace its policy statement.
   (4)  If its policy statement is altered or replaced, the FCA must issue the altered or replacement statement.
   (5)  In exercising, or deciding whether to exercise, its power under section 91 in the case of any particular contravention, the FCA must have regard to any policy statement published under this section and in force at the time when the contravention in question occurred.
   (6)  The FCA must publish a statement issued under this section in the way appearing to the FCA to be best calculated to bring it to the attention of the public.
   (7)  The FCA may charge a reasonable fee for providing a person with a copy of the statement.
   (8)  The FCA must, without delay, give the Treasury a copy of any policy statement which it publishes under this section.

**53.94.01**   94  **Statements of policy: procedure.**

   (1)  Before issuing a statement under section 93, the FCA must publish a draft of the proposed statement in the way appearing to the FCA to be best calculated to bring it to the attention of the public.
   (2)  The draft must be accompanied by notice that representations about the proposal may be made to the FCA within a specified time.
   (3)  Before issuing the proposed statement, the FCA must have regard to any representations made to it in accordance with subsection (2).
   (4)  If the FCA issues the proposed statement it must publish an account, in general terms, of–
        (a)  the representations made to it in accordance with subsection (2); and
        (b)  its response to them.
   (5)  If the statement differs from the draft published under subsection (1) in a way which is, in the opinion of the FCA, significant, the FCA must (in addition to complying with subsection (4)) publish details of the difference.
   (6)  The FCA may charge a reasonable fee for providing a person with a copy of a draft published under subsection (1).
   (7)  This section also applies to a proposal to alter or replace a statement.

*Competition*

**53.95.01**   95  [...][165]

*Miscellaneous*

**53.96.01**   96  **Obligations of issuers of listed securities.**

   (1)  Listing rules may–
        (a)  specify requirements to be complied with by issuers of listed securities; and
        (b)  make provision with respect to the action that may be taken by the FCA in the event of non-compliance.
   (2)  If the rules require an issuer to publish information, they may include provision authorising the FCA to publish it in the event of his failure to do so.
   (3)  This section applies whenever the listed securities were admitted to the official list.

**53.96A.01**   [96A  **Disclosure of information requirements**

   (1)  Disclosure rules must include provision specifying the disclosure of information requirements to be complied with by—

---

[165]  Repealed by Financial Services Act 2012 c.21 s.21 (24 January 2013; 1 April 2013)

      (a)  issuers who have requested or approved admission of their financial instruments to trading on a regulated market in the United Kingdom;

      (b)  persons acting on behalf of or for the account of such issuers;

      (c)  persons discharging managerial responsibilities within an issuer—

         (i)  who is registered in the United Kingdom and who has requested or approved admission of its shares to trading on a regulated market; or

         (ii)  who is not registered in the United Kingdom or any other EEA State but who has requested or approved admission of its shares to trading on a regulated market and [ whose home State is the United Kingdom ][166] ;

      (d)  persons connected to such persons discharging managerial responsibilities.

  (2)  The rules must in particular—

      (a)  require an issuer to publish specified inside information;

      (b)  require an issuer to publish any significant change concerning information it has already published in accordance with paragraph (a);

      (c)  allow an issuer to delay the publication of inside information in specified circumstances;

      (d)  require an issuer (or a person acting on his behalf or for his account) who discloses inside information to a third party to publish that information without delay in specified circumstances;

      (e)  require an issuer (or person acting on his behalf or for his account) to draw up a list of those persons working for him who have access to inside information relating directly or indirectly to that issuer; and

      (f)  require persons discharging managerial responsibilities within an issuer falling within subsection (1)(c)(i) or (ii), and persons connected to such persons discharging managerial responsibilities, to disclose transactions conducted on their own account in shares of the issuer, or derivatives or any other financial instrument relating to those shares.

  (3)  Disclosure rules may make provision with respect to the action that may be taken by the FCA in respect of non-compliance.][167]


## [96B  [Disclosure rules: persons responsible for compliance ][168]     53.96B.01

  (1)  [For the purposes of the provisions of this Part relating to disclosure rules ][169], a "person discharging managerial responsibilities within an issuer" means—

      (a)  a director of an issuer falling within section 96A(1)(c)(i) or (ii); or

      (b)  a senior executive of such an issuer who—

         (i)  has regular access to inside information relating, directly or indirectly, to the issuer, and

         (ii)  has power to make managerial decisions affecting the future development and business prospects of the issuer.

  [(2)  Schedule 11B (connected persons) has effect for the purposes of the provisions of this Part relating to disclosure rules.][170] ][171]


## [96C  Suspension of trading     53.96C.01

  (1)  The FCA may, in accordance with disclosure rules, suspend trading in a financial instrument.

  (2)  If the FCA does so, the issuer of that financial instrument may refer the matter to the Tribunal.

  (3)  The provisions relating to suspension of listing of securities in section 78 apply to the suspension of trading in a financial instrument and the references to listing and securities are to be read as references to trading and financial instruments respectively for the purposes of this section.][172]

---

[166]  Substituted by Prospectus Regulations 2012/1538 reg.8 (1 July 2012)

[167]  Added by Financial Services and Markets Act 2000 (Market Abuse) Regulations 2005/381 Sch.1 para.6 (17 March 2005)

[168]  Substituted by Companies Act 2006 c. 46 Sch.15(1) para.7(a) (8 November 2006)

[169]  Substituted by Companies Act 2006 c. 46 Sch.15(1) para.7(b) (8 November 2006)

[170]  Substituted by Financial Services and Markets Act 2000 (Amendment) Regulations 2009/2461 reg.2(1) (1 October 2009)

[171]  Added by Financial Services and Markets Act 2000 (Market Abuse) Regulations 2005/381 Sch.1 para.6 (17 March 2005)

[172]  Added by Financial Services and Markets Act 2000 (Market Abuse) Regulations 2005/381 Sch.1 para.6 (17 March 2005)

**53.97.01**    **97   Appointment by FCA of persons to carry out investigations.**

    (1)   Subsection (2) applies if it appears to the FCA that there are circumstances suggesting that–

         [(a)   there may have been a contravention of–

              (i)   a provision of this Part or of Part 6 rules, or

              (ii)   a provision otherwise made in accordance with the prospectus directive or the transparency obligations directive;

         (b)   a person who was at the material time a director of a person mentioned in section 91(1),

    (1ZA)   (a), (1A) or (1B) has been knowingly concerned in a contravention by that person of–

              (i)   a provision of this Part or of Part 6 rules, or

              (ii)   a provision otherwise made in accordance with the prospectus directive or the transparency obligations directive;][173]

         (c)   [...][174]

         (d)   there may have been a contravention of [ 85 or 87G ][175] .

    (2)   The FCA may appoint one or more competent persons to conduct an investigation on its behalf.

    (3)   Part XI applies to an investigation under subsection (2) as if–

         (a)   the investigator were appointed under section 167(1);

         (b)   references to the investigating authority in relation to him were to the FCA;

         (c)   references to the offences mentioned in section 168 were to those mentioned in subsection (1)(d);

         (d)   references to an authorised person were references to the person under investigation.

**53.98.01**    **98   [...][176]**

**53.99.01**    **99   [...][177]**

**53.100.01**    **100   [...][178]**

**53.100A.01**    **[100A   Exercise of powers where UK is host member state**

    (1)   This section applies to the exercise by the FCA of any power under this Part exercisable in case of infringement of–

         (a)   a provision of prospectus rules or any other provision made in accordance with the prospectus directive, or

         (b)   a provision of transparency rules or any other provision made in accordance with the transparency obligations directive,

         in relation to an issuer whose home State is a member State other than the United Kingdom.

    (2)   The FCA may act in such a case only in respect of the infringement of a provision required by the relevant directive. Any reference to an applicable provision or applicable transparency obligation shall be read accordingly.

    [(3)   If the FCA finds that there has been such an infringement, it must—

         (a)   give a notice to that effect to the competent authority of the person's home State requesting it—

              (i)   to take all appropriate measures for the purpose of ensuring that the person remedies the situation that has given rise to the notice, and

              (ii)   to inform the FCA of the measures it proposes to take or has taken or the reasons for not taking such measures, and

         (b)   notify ESMA.][179]

    (4)   The FCA may not act further unless satisfied–

         (a)   that the competent authority of the person's home State has failed or refused to take measures for the purpose mentioned in subsection (3)(a), or

         (b)   that the measures taken by that authority have proved inadequate for that purpose. This does not affect exercise of the powers under section 87K(2), 87L(2) or (3) or 89L(2) or (3) (powers to protect market).

    (5)   If the FCA is so satisfied, it must, after informing the competent authority of the person's home State [ and ESMA ][180] , take all appropriate measures to protect investors.

---

[173]   Substituted by Companies Act 2006 c. 46 Sch.15(1) para.8 (8 November 2006)

[174]   Repealed by Financial Services and Markets Act 2000 (Market Abuse) Regulations 2005/381 Sch.1 para.7(c) (1 July 2005)

[175]   Inserted by Financial Services Act 2012 c.21 Sch.18(1) para.7 (24 January 2013; 1 April 2013)

[176]   Repealed by Prospectus Regulations 2005/1433 Sch.1 para.9 (1 July 2005)

[177]   Repealed by Financial Services Act 2012 c.21 s.16(14)(c) (24 January 2013; 1 April 2013)

[178]   Repealed by Financial Services Act 2012 c.21 s.16(14)(d) (24 January 2013; 1 April 2013)

[179]   Substituted by Financial Services (Omnibus 1 Directive) Regulations 2012/916 reg.2(6)(a) (16 April 2012)

[180]   Inserted by Financial Services (Omnibus 1 Directive) Regulations 2012/916 reg.2(6)(b) (16 April 2012)

(6) In such a case the FCA must inform the Commission [ and ESMA ]$^{181}$ of the measures at the earliest opportunity.]$^{182}$

## 101 Listing rules: general provisions

53.101.01

(1) [...]$^{183}$
(2) [ Part 6 rules ]$^{184}$ may authorise the FCA to dispense with or modify the applications of the rules in particular cases and by reference to any circumstances.
(3) [...]
(4) [...]
(5) [...]
(6) [...]
(7) [...]
(8) [...]$^{185}$

## 102 [...]$^{186}$

53.102.01

### *[Interpretative provisions ]$^{187}$*

## [102A Meaning of "securities" etc.

53.102A.01

(1) This section applies for the purposes of this Part.
(2) "Securities" means (except in section 74(2) and the expression "transferable securities") anything which has been, or may be, admitted to the official list.
(3) "Transferable securities" means anything which is a transferable security for the purposes of [Directive 2004/39/EC of the European Parliament and of the Council on markets in financial instruments ]$^{188}$, other than money-market instruments for the purposes of that directive which have a maturity of less than 12 months.
[(3A) "Debt securities" has the meaning given in Article 2.1(b) of the transparency obligations directive. ]$^{189}$
(4) "Financial instrument" has [ (except in section 89F) ]$^{190}$ the meaning given in Article 1.3 of Directive 2003/6/EC of the European Parliament and of the Council of 28 January 2003 on insider dealing and market manipulation [ (as modified by Article 69 of Directive 2004/39/EC on markets in financial instruments) ]$^{191}$.
(5) "Non-equity transferable securities" means all transferable securities that are not equity securities; and for this purpose "equity securities" has the meaning given in Article 2.1(b) of the prospectus directive.
(6) "Issuer"—
  (a) in relation to an offer of transferable securities to the public or admission of transferable securities to trading on a regulated market for which an approved prospectus is required as a result of section 85, means a legal person who issues or proposes to issue the transferable securities in question,
  [(aa)  in relation to transparency rules, means a legal person whose securities are admitted to trading on a regulated market or whose voting shares are admitted to trading on a UK market other than a regulated market, and in the case of depository receipts representing securities, the issuer is the issuer of the securities represented; ]$^{192}$
  (b) in relation to anything else which is or may be admitted to the official list, has such meaning as may be prescribed by the Treasury, and
  (c) in any other case, means a person who issues financial instruments.]$^{193}$

---

$^{181}$  Inserted by Financial Services (Omnibus 1 Directive) Regulations 2012/916 reg.2(6)(c) (16 April 2012)
$^{182}$  Added by Companies Act 2006 c. 46 Pt 43 s.1271 (8 November 2006)
$^{183}$  Repealed by Financial Services Act 2012 c.21 s.16(14)(e) (24 January 2013; 1 April 2013)
$^{184}$  Substituted by Financial Services and Markets Act 2000 (Market Abuse) Regulations 2005/381 Sch.1 para.10 (1 July 2005)
$^{185}$  Repealed by Financial Services Act 2012 s.16(14)(e) (24 January 2013; 1 April 2013)
$^{186}$  Repealed by Financial Services Act 2012 s.16(14)(f) (24 January 2013; 1 April 2013)
$^{187}$  Ss.102A-103 substituted for s.103 by Prospectus Regulations 2005/1433 Sch.1 para.11 (1 July 2005)
$^{188}$  Substituted by Companies Act 2006 c. 46 Sch.15(1) para.10(3) (8 November 2006)
$^{189}$  Added by Companies Act 2006 c. 46 Sch.15(1) para.10(2) (8 November 2006)
$^{190}$  Inserted by Definition of Financial Instrument Order 2008/3053 art.3(2)(a) (31 January 2009)
$^{191}$  Inserted by Definition of Financial Instrument Order 2008/3053 art.3(2)(b) (31 January 2009)
$^{192}$  Added by Companies Act 2006 c. 46 Sch.15(1) para.10(4) (8 November 2006)
$^{193}$  Ss.102A-103 substituted for s.103 by Prospectus Regulations 2005/1433 Sch.1 para.11 (1 July 2005)

**53.102B.01**    [102B  Meaning of "offer of transferable securities to the public" etc.

    (1)  For the purposes of this Part there is an offer of transferable securities to the public if there is a communication to any person which presents sufficient information on—

      (a)  the transferable securities to be offered, and

      (b)  the terms on which they are offered,

    to enable an investor to decide to buy or subscribe for the securities in question.

    (2)  For the purposes of this Part, to the extent that an offer of transferable securities is made to a person in the United Kingdom it is an offer of transferable securities to the public in the United Kingdom.

    (3)  The communication may be made—

      (a)  in any form;

      (b)  by any means.

    (4)  Subsection (1) includes the placing of securities through a financial intermediary.

    (5)  Subsection (1) does not include a communication in connection with trading on—

      (a)  a regulated market;

      (b)  a multilateral trading facility; or

      (c)  a market prescribed by an order under section 130A(3).

    (6)  "Multilateral trading facility" means a multilateral system, operated by an investment firm [...][194] or a market operator, which brings together multiple third-party buying and selling interests in financial instruments in accordance with non-discretionary rules so as to result in a contract.][195]

**53.102C.01**    [102C  Meaning of "home State" in relation to transferable securities

In this Part, in relation to an issuer of transferable securities, the "home-State" is the EEA State which is the "home Member State" for the purposes of the prospectus directive (which is to be determined in accordance with Article 2.1(m) of that directive). ][196]

**53.103.01**    103  [Interpretation of this Part

    (1)  In this Part, save where the context otherwise requires—

"disclosure rules" has the meaning given in section 73A;

"inside information" has the meaning given in section 118C;

"listed securities" means anything which has been admitted to the official list;

"listing" has the meaning given in section 74(5);

"listing particulars" has the meaning given in section 79(2);

"listing rules" has the meaning given in section 73A;

"market operator" means a person who manages or operates the business of a regulated market;

"offer of transferable securities to the public" has the meaning given in section 102B;

"the official list" means the list maintained by the FCA as that list has effect for the time being;

"Part 6 rules" has the meaning given in section 73A;

"the prospectus directive" means Directive 2003/71/EC of the European Parliament and of the Council of 4 November 2003 on the prospectus to be published when securities are offered to the public or admitted to trading [ as amended by Directive 2010/73/EU of the European Parliament and of the Council of 24 November 2010 and by Directive 2010/78/EU of the European Parliament and of the Council of 24 November 2010 ][197];

"prospectus rules" has the meaning given in section 73A;

"regulated market" has the meaning given in [ Article 4.1(14) of Directive 2004/39/EC of the European Parliament and of the Council on markets in financial instruments ][198];

"supplementary prospectus" has the meaning given in section 87G;

["the transparency obligations directive" means Directive 2004/ 109/EC of the European Parliament and of the Council relating to the harmonisation of transparency requirements in relation to information about issuers whose securities are admitted to trading on a regulated market [ as amended by Directive 2010/73/EU of the European Parliament and of the Council of 24 November 2010 and by Directive 2010/78/EU of the European Parliament and of the Council of 24 November 2010 ][199]; ][200]

---

[194]  Repealed by Financial Services and Markets Act 2000 (Markets in Financial Instruments) Regulations 2007/126 Sch.5 para.6 (1 November 2007)

[195]  Ss.102A-103 substituted for s.103 by Prospectus Regulations 2005/1433 Sch.1 para.11 (1 July 2005)

[196]  Ss.102A-103 substituted for s.103 by Prospectus Regulations 2005/1433 Sch.1 para.11 (1 July 2005)

[197]  Inserted by Prospectus Regulations 2012/1538 reg.9(a) (1 July 2012)

[198]  Substituted by Companies Act 2006 c. 46 Sch.15(1) para.11(2) (1 October 2008)

[199]  Inserted by Prospectus Regulations 2012/1538 reg.9(b) (1 July 2012)

[200]  Inserted by Companies Act 2006 c. 46 Pt 43 s.1265 (8 November 2006)

["transparency rules" has the meaning given by section 89A(5);
"voteholder information" has the meaning given by section 89B(3); ]²⁰¹
"working day" means any day other that a Saturday, a Sunday, Christmas Day, Good Friday or a day which is a bank holiday under the Banking and Financial Dealings Act 1971 (c. 80) in any part of the United Kingdom.

(2)  […]²⁰²
(3)  […]²⁰³ ]²⁰⁴

²⁰¹  Inserted by Companies Act 2006 c. 46 Sch.15(1) para.11(3) (8 November 2006)
²⁰²  Repealed by Financial Services Act 2012 c.21 s.16(14)(g) (24 January 2013; 1 April 2013)
²⁰³  Repealed by Financial Services Act 2012 c.21 s.16(14)(g) (24 January 2013; 1 April 2013)
²⁰⁴  Ss.102A-103 substituted for s.103 by Prospectus Regulations 2005/1433 Sch.1 para.11 (1 July 2005)

# INDEX

References are to chapter and paragraph number, e.g. 15.444.06 is chapter 15, paragraph 444.06, and to separate commentaries on the Uncertificated Securities Regulations and the Schedules.

*Abbreviations:* Sch Schedule; USR Uncertificated Securities Regulations